THE GARGANTUAN GUIDE TO
HARRY POTTER

THE GARGANTUAN GUIDE TO
HARRY POTTER

WAKING LION PRESS

ISBN 978-1-4341-0317-8

The source for the text of this book is accessible online at Wikibooks under the title of *The Muggles' Guide to Harry Potter*:

http://en.wikibooks.org/wiki/Muggles%27_Guide_to_Harry_Potter

There you will also find information about the sources consulted and the people who have contributed.

This book and its online source are available under the Creative Commons Attribution-ShareAlike License:

http://creativecommons.org/licenses/by-sa/3.0/

The text of this book has been slightly edited in some places and then reformatted to make it suitable for distribution in printed form.

The views expressed in this book are the responsibility of the contributors and do not necessarily represent the position of the publisher. The reader alone is responsible for the use of any ideas or information provided by this book.

This book discusses works of fiction. The characters, places, and incidents discussed are the products of the imagination or are represented fictitiously. Any resemblance of characters or events to actual persons or events is coincidental.

Published by Waking Lion Press, an imprint of The Editorium, which has no affiliation with Wikibooks or with the author or publisher of the Harry Potter books and makes no claim on their copyrights or trademarks. This book is an unauthorized, independent commentary published for educational purposes.

Waking Lion Press™, the Waking Lion Press logo, and The Editorium™ are trademarks of The Editorium, LLC

The Editorium, LLC
West Valley City, UT 84128-3917
wakinglionpress.com
wakinglion@editorium.com

CONTENTS

Introduction	xxvii
Philosopher's Stone	1
Chapter 1: The Boy Who Lived	1
Chapter 2: The Vanishing Glass	3
Chapter 3: The Letters From No One	3
Chapter 4: The Keeper of the Keys	4
Chapter 5: Diagon Alley	5
Chapter 6: The Journey from Platform Nine and Three-Quarters	6
Chapter 7: The Sorting Hat	7
Chapter 8: The Potions Master	8
Chapter 9: The Midnight Duel	9
Chapter 10: Halloween	10
Chapter 11: Quidditch	10
Chapter 12: The Mirror of Erised	11
Chapter 13: Nicholas Flamel	12
Chapter 14: Norbert the Norwegian Ridgeback	13
Chapter 15: The Forbidden Forest	14
Chapter 16: Through the Trapdoor	15
Chapter 17: The Man with Two Faces	16
Chamber of Secrets	18
Chapter 1: The Worst Birthday	18
Chapter 2: Dobby's Warning	19
Chapter 3: The Burrow	20
Chapter 4: At Flourish and Blotts	21
Chapter 5: The Whomping Willow	22
Chapter 6: Gilderoy Lockhart	23
Chapter 7: Mudbloods and Murmurs	24
Chapter 8: The Deathday Party	25
Chapter 9: The Writing on the Wall	26
Chapter 10: The Rogue Bludger	28
Chapter 11: The Dueling Club	29

    Chapter 12: The Polyjuice Potion 30
    Chapter 13: The Very Secret Diary 32
    Chapter 14: Cornelius Fudge 33
    Chapter 15: Aragog 35
    Chapter 16: The Chamber of Secrets 36
    Chapter 17: The Heir of Slytherin 37
    Chapter 18: Dobby's Reward 39

Prisoner of Azkaban   42

    Chapter 1: Owl Post 42
    Chapter 2: Aunt Marge's Big Mistake 43
    Chapter 3: The Knight Bus 44
    Chapter 4: The Leaky Cauldron 45
    Chapter 5: The Dementor 47
    Chapter 6: Talons and Tea Leaves 48
    Chapter 7: The Boggart in the Wardrobe 50
    Chapter 8: Flight of the Fat Lady 51
    Chapter 9: Grim Defeat 53
    Chapter 10: The Marauder's Map 54
    Chapter 11: The Firebolt 56
    Chapter 12: The Patronus 58
    Chapter 13: Gryffindor Versus Ravenclaw 60
    Chapter 14: Snape's Grudge 61
    Chapter 15: The Quidditch Final 63
    Chapter 16: Professor Trelawney's Prediction 64
    Chapter 17: Cat, Rat and Dog 66
    Chapter 18: Moony, Wormtail, Padfoot, and Prongs 67
    Chapter 19: The Servant of Lord Voldemort 68
    Chapter 20: The Dementor's Kiss 70
    Chapter 21: Hermione's Secret 71
    Chapter 22: Owl Post Again 72

Goblet of Fire   75

    Chapter 1: The Riddle House 75
    Chapter 2: The Scar 76
    Chapter 3: The Invitation 77
    Chapter 4: Back to the Burrow 78
    Chapter 5: Weasley's Wizard Wheezes 79
    Chapter 6: The Portkey 80
    Chapter 7: Bagman and Crouch 81
    Chapter 8: The Quidditch World Cup 83

- Chapter 9: The Dark Mark 85
- Chapter 10: Mayhem at the Ministry 87
- Chapter 11: Aboard the Hogwart's Express 88
- Chapter 12: The Triwizard Tournament 90
- Chapter 13: Mad-Eye Moody 91
- Chapter 14: The Unforgivable Curses 92
- Chapter 15: Beauxbatons and Durmstrang 94
- Chapter 16: The Goblet of Fire 96
- Chapter 17: The Four Champions 98
- Chapter 18: The Weighing of the Wands 100
- Chapter 19: The Hungarian Horntail 102
- Chapter 20: The First Task 103
- Chapter 21: The House-Elf Liberation Front 105
- Chapter 22: The Unexpected Task 106
- Chapter 23: The Yule Ball 108
- Chapter 24: Rita Skeeter's Scoop 111
- Chapter 25: The Egg and the Eye 112
- Chapter 26: The Second Task 114
- Chapter 27: Padfoot Returns 117
- Chapter 28: The Madness of Mr. Crouch 119
- Chapter 29: The Dream 122
- Chapter 30: The Pensieve 123
- Chapter 31: The Third Task 126
- Chapter 32: Flesh, Blood, and Bone 128
- Chapter 33: The Death Eaters 129
- Chapter 34: Priori Incantatem 131
- Chapter 35: Veritaserum 132
- Chapter 36: The Parting of the Ways 134
- Chapter 37: The Beginning 137

Order of the Phoenix   140

- Chapter 1: Dudley Demented 140
- Chapter 2: A Peck of Owls 142
- Chapter 3: The Advance Guard 143
- Chapter 4: Number Twelve, Grimmauld Place 144
- Chapter 5: The Order of the Phoenix 145
- Chapter 6: The Noble and Most Ancient House of Black 147
- Chapter 7: The Ministry of Magic 148
- Chapter 8: The Hearing 149
- Chapter 9: The Woes of Mrs. Weasley 150

Chapter 10: Luna Lovegood 152

Chapter 11: The Sorting Hat's New Song 153

Chapter 12: Professor Umbridge 155

Chapter 13: Detention with Dolores 156

Chapter 14: Percy and Padfoot 158

Chapter 15: The Hogwarts High Inquisitor 159

Chapter 16: In the Hog's Head 161

Chapter 17: Educational Decree Number Twenty-Four 162

Chapter 18: Dumbledore's Army 164

Chapter 19: The Lion and the Serpent 166

Chapter 20: Hagrid's Tale 167

Chapter 21: The Eye of the Snake 168

Chapter 22: St.Mungo's Hospital for Magical Maladies and Injuries 170

Chapter 23: Christmas on the Closed Ward 172

Chapter 24: Occlumency 173

Chapter 25: The Beetle at Bay 175

Chapter 26: Seen and Unforeseen 177

Chapter 27: The Centaur and the Sneak 179

Chapter 28: Snape's Worst Memory 180

Chapter 29: Careers Advice 182

Chapter 30: Grawp 184

Chapter 31: O.W.L.s 186

Chapter 32: Out of the Fire 187

Chapter 33: Fight and Flight 188

Chapter 34: The Department of Mysteries 190

Chapter 35: Beyond the Veil 191

Chapter 36: The Only One He Ever Feared 193

Chapter 37: The Lost Prophecy 193

Chapter 38: The Second War Begins 195

Half-Blood Prince   197

Chapter 1: The Other Minister 197

Chapter 2: Spinner's End 199

Chapter 3: Will and Won't 201

Chapter 4: Horace Slughorn 202

Chapter 5: An Excess of Phlegm 203

Chapter 6: Draco's Detour 204

Chapter 7: The Slug Club 206

Chapter 8: Snape Victorious 207

Chapter 9: The Half-Blood Prince 208

- Chapter 10: The House of Gaunt ... 210
- Chapter 11: Hermione's Helping Hand ... 211
- Chapter 12: Silver and Opals ... 213
- Chapter 13: The Secret Riddle ... 214
- Chapter 14: Felix Felicis ... 215
- Chapter 15: The Unbreakable Vow ... 217
- Chapter 16: A Very Frosty Christmas ... 218
- Chapter 17: A Sluggish Memory ... 219
- Chapter 18: Birthday Surprises ... 220
- Chapter 19: Elf Tails ... 221
- Chapter 20: Lord Voldemort's Request ... 223
- Chapter 21: The Unknowable Room ... 224
- Chapter 22: After the Burial ... 225
- Chapter 23: Horcruxes ... 226
- Chapter 24: Sectumsempra ... 228
- Chapter 25: The Seer Overheard ... 229
- Chapter 26: The Cave ... 230
- Chapter 27: The Lightning-Struck Tower ... 231
- Chapter 28: Flight of the Prince ... 232
- Chapter 29: The Phoenix Lament ... 234
- Chapter 30: The White Tomb ... 235

Deathly Hallows 237

- Chapter 1: The Dark Lord Ascending ... 237
- Chapter 2: In Memoriam ... 238
- Chapter 3: The Dursleys Departing ... 240
- Chapter 4: The Seven Potters ... 240
- Chapter 5: Fallen Warrior ... 241
- Chapter 6: The Ghoul in Pyjamas ... 243
- Chapter 7: The Will of Albus Dumbledore ... 245
- Chapter 8: The Wedding ... 247
- Chapter 9: A Place to Hide ... 249
- Chapter 10: Kreacher's Tale ... 251
- Chapter 11: The Bribe ... 253
- Chapter 12: Magic is Might ... 254
- Chapter 13: The Muggle-Born Registration Commission ... 256
- Chapter 14: The Thief ... 259
- Chapter 15: The Goblin's Revenge ... 261
- Chapter 16: Godric's Hollow ... 263
- Chapter 17: Bathilda's Secret ... 264

Chapter 18: The Life and Lies of Albus Dumbledore 266

Chapter 19: The Silver Doe 269

Chapter 20: Xenophilius Lovegood 271

Chapter 21: The Tale of the Three Brothers 272

Chapter 22: The Deathly Hallows 274

Chapter 23: Malfoy Manor 275

Chapter 24: The Wandmaker 277

Chapter 25: Shell Cottage 280

Chapter 26: Gringotts 281

Chapter 27: The Final Hiding Place 283

Chapter 28: The Missing Mirror 284

Chapter 29: The Lost Diadem 286

Chapter 30: The Sacking of Severus Snape 288

Chapter 31: The Battle of Hogwarts 289

Chapter 32: The Elder Wand 292

Chapter 33: The Prince's Tale 293

Chapter 34: The Forest Again 296

Chapter 35: King's Cross 297

Chapter 36: The Flaw in the Plan 300

Epilogue: Nineteen Years Later 302

Extended Analysis 304

Overall Analysis 304

Possible Points of Confusion 305

Character Development 306

Major Themes 307

Real-World Connections 309

Characters 310

Aberforth Dumbledore 314

Adrian Pucey 315

Alastor Moody 316

Albert Runcorn 317

Albus Dumbledore 318

Alecto Carrow 338

Alice Longbottom 338

Alicia Spinnet 339

Ambrosius Flume 340

Amelia Bones 340

Amycus Carrow 340

Amos Diggory 341

Contents

Andrew Kirke	341
Andromeda Tonks	341
Angelina Johnson	342
Anthony Goldstein	343
Antonin Dolohov	344
Arabella Figg	344
Aragog	345
Argus Filch	346
Ariana Dumbledore	349
Armando Dippet	350
Arthur Weasley	351
Augusta Longbottom	354
Augustus Rookwood	355
Auntie Muriel	355
Avery	356
Bane	356
Bartemius Crouch Sr.	357
Barty Crouch Jr.	358
Bathilda Bagshot	359
Bellatrix Lestrange	360
Benjy Fenwick	362
Bertha Jorkins	362
Bill Weasley	363
Black Family	364
Blaise Zabini	365
Bob Ogden	366
Bogrod	366
Bole	367
Borgin	367
Broderick Bode	367
Buckbeak	368
Cadwallader	368
Caractacus Burke	368
Caradoc Dearborn	368
Cedric Diggory	369
Charlie Weasley	369
Cho Chang	370
Colin Creevey	372
Cormac McLaggen	373

Cornelius Fudge	374
Crabbe, Sr.	376
Crookshanks	376
Dawlish	377
Dean Thomas	378
Dedalus Diggle	379
Demelza Robins	380
Dennis Creevey	380
Derrick	381
Dexter Fortescue	381
Dilys Derwent	381
Dirk Cresswell	381
Dobby	382
Dolores Umbridge	384
Dorcas Meadowes	385
Draco Malfoy	386
Dudley Dursley	390
Dumbledore's Army	394
Edgar Bones	396
Eleanor Branstone	397
Eloise Midgeon	397
Elphias Doge	397
Emmeline Vance	397
Eric Munch	398
Ernie Macmillan	398
Ernie Prang	399
Errol	399
Evan Rosier	399
Everard	400
Fabian Prewett	400
Fawcett	400
Fawkes	401
Fenrir Greyback	402
Filius Flitwick	402
Firenze	404
Fleur Delacour	405
Florean Fortescue	406
Frank Bryce	407
Frank Longbottom	407

- *Fred and George Weasley* 407
- *Gabrielle Delacour* 412
- *Gawain Robards* 412
- *Gellert Grindelwald* 412
- *Gibbon* 414
- *Gideon Prewett* 414
- *Gilderoy Lockhart* 414
- *Ginny Weasley* 417
- *Godric Gryffindor* 422
- *Goyle, Sr.* 423
- *Graham Pritchard* 423
- *Grawp* 423
- *Gregorovitch* 424
- *Gregory Goyle* 424
- *Griphook* 426
- *Hannah Abbott* 427
- *Harper* 427
- *Harry Potter* 427
- *Hedwig* 432
- *Helga Hufflepuff* 434
- *Hepzibah Smith* 434
- *Hermes* 434
- *Hermione Granger* 435
- *Hestia Jones* 441
- *Hokey* 441
- *Horace Slughorn* 442
- *House of Gaunt* 444
- *Igor Karkaroff* 445
- *Irma Pince* 445
- *Jack Sloper* 446
- *James Potter* 446
- *Jimmy Peakes* 448
- *Jugson* 448
- *Justin Finch-Fletchley* 448
- *Katie Bell* 449
- *Kendra Dumbledore* 450
- *Kevin Whitby* 450
- *Kingsley Shacklebolt* 450
- *Kreacher* 451

Laura Madley	453
Lavender Brown	453
Lee Jordan	455
Lily Potter	456
Lisa Turpin	457
Lord Voldemort	458
Lucius Malfoy	470
Ludovic Bagman	472
Luna Lovegood	474
Madam Rosmerta	477
Mafalda Hopkirk	477
Magorian	478
Malcolm Baddock	478
Mandy Brocklehurst	478
Marauders	478
Marcus Belby	479
Marcus Flint	479
Marge Dursley	479
Marietta Edgecombe	480
Marlene McKinnon	481
Marvolo Gaunt	481
Mary Macdonald	481
Merope Gaunt	482
Michael Corner	482
Miles Bletchley	483
Millicent Bullstrode	483
Minerva McGonagall	483
Miriam Strout	488
Moaning Myrtle	489
Molly Weasley	490
Montague	499
Morfin Gaunt	499
Mulciber	500
Mundungus Fletcher	500
Nagini	502
Narcissa Malfoy	503
Natalie McDonald	504
Nearly Headless Nick	504
Neville Longbottom	505

Contents

- *Norbert* 512
- *Nott* 512
- *Nymphadora Tonks* 513
- *Oliver Wood* 515
- *Ollivander* 516
- *Olympe Maxime* 516
- *Orion Black* 518
- *Orla Quirke* 518
- *Owen Cauldwell* 518
- *Padma Patil* 519
- *Pansy Parkinson* 519
- *Parvati Patil* 520
- *Peeves* 522
- *Penelope Clearwater* 524
- *Percy Weasley* 525
- *Percival Dumbledore* 527
- *Peter Pettigrew* 527
- *Petunia Dursley* 530
- *Phineas Nigellus Black* 533
- *Piers Polkiss* 534
- *Pigwidgeon* 534
- *Pius Thicknesse* 535
- *Pomona Sprout* 536
- *Poppy Pomfrey* 537
- *Professor Binns* 539
- *Professor Quirrell* 540
- *Professor Sinistra* 542
- *Professor Vector* 542
- *Rabastan Lestrange* 542
- *Regulus Black* 543
- *Remus Lupin* 544
- *Rita Skeeter* 547
- *Ritchie Coote* 549
- *Rodolphus Lestrange* 549
- *Roger Davies* 549
- *Rolanda Hooch* 549
- *Romilda Vane* 550
- *Ron Weasley* 550
- *Ronan* 560

- *Rose Zeller* 561
- *Rowena Ravenclaw* 561
- *Rubeus Hagrid* 561
- *Rufus Scrimgeour* 567
- *Salazar Slytherin* 568
- *Scabbers* 569
- *Seamus Finnigan* 570
- *Selwyn* 571
- *Septima Vector* 571
- *Severus Snape* 572
- *Sibyll Trelawney* 585
- *Sir Cadogan* 587
- *Sirius Black* 588
- *Sorting Hat* 593
- *Stan Shunpike* 595
- *Stewart Ackerley* 595
- *Sturgis Podmore* 596
- *Summerby* 596
- *Summers* 596
- *Susan Bones* 596
- *Terence Higgs* 597
- *Terry Boot* 597
- *The Bloody Baron* 597
- *The Fat Friar* 598
- *The Fat Lady* 598
- *The Grey Lady* 599
- *Theodore Nott* 599
- *Thorfinn Rowle* 599
- *Tom Marvolo Riddle* 600
- *Travers* 602
- *Trevor* 602
- *Urquhart* 603
- *Vaisey* 603
- *Vernon Dursley* 603
- *Viktor Krum* 607
- *Vincent Crabbe* 609
- *Walburga Black* 610
- *Walden Macnair* 611
- *Warrington* 611

Weasley Family	611
Wilhelmina Grubbly-Plank	613
Wilkes	613
Wilkie Twycross	614
Willy Widdershins	614
Winky	614
Witherwings	615
Xenophilius Lovegood	615
Yaxley	615
Zacharias Smith	616

Places — 617

Azkaban	617
Beauxbatons Academy of Magic	618
Borgin and Burkes	619
Chamber of Secrets	619
Diagon Alley	620
Durmstrang Institute	621
Forbidden Forest	622
Godric's Hollow	622
Gringotts	623
Grimmauld Place	624
Gryffindor House	626
Headmaster's Office, Hogwarts	626
Hog's Head Inn	627
Hogsmeade	628
Hogwarts School of Witchcraft and Wizardry	628
Honeyduke's Sweetshop	631
House of Gaunt	631
Hufflepuff House	631
Knockturn Alley	632
Little Hangleton	632
Malfoy Manor	633
Ministry of Magic	633
Platform 9 and Three Quarters	635
Privet Drive	636
Ravenclaw House	636
Riddle Manor	637
Room of Requirement	638
Shell Cottage	638

Shrieking Shack 639
Slytherin House 639
Spinner's End 640
St.Mungo's Hospital for Magical Maladies and Injuries 640
The Burrow 641
The Three Broomsticks 641
The Leaky Cauldron 642
Weasleys' Wizard Wheezes 642

Major Events — 644

Battle at the Department of Mysteries 644
Battle of Hogwarts 646
Breakin at Gringotts 649
Cedric's Death 650
Duel in the Cemetery 651
Duel in the Chamber of Secrets 653
Cho Chang relationships 655
Death Eaters 657
Dobby's Death 659
Dumbledore's Army 660
Dumbledore's Death 663
Escape from Privet Drive 664
Events in the Shrieking Shack 666
First Task 667
Fred Weasley's Death 668
Ginny Weasley relationships 669
Harry Voldemort Shared Thoughts 671
Harry Potter relationships 679
Head Boy 682
Hermione Granger relationships 683
House Cup 686
Infiltration of the Ministry of Magic 686
Inquisitorial Squad 689
Mad-Eye Moody's Death 689
N.E.W.T. exams 690
Nymphadora's Death 691
Order of the Phoenix 692
O.W.L. exams 694
Pettigrew's Death 695
Prefects 696

Contents

xix

    Quidditch 697

    Quidditch captain 699

    Quidditch World Cup 699

    Remus' Death 701

    Ron Weasley relationships 702

    Second Task 704

    Sirius' Death 705

    Snape's Death 707

    S.P.E.W. 708

    Third Task 710

    Tower Battle (Hogwarts) 711

    Triwizard Tournament 713

    Viktor Krum relationships 715

    Voldemort's Death 715

    Yearend exams 716

    Yule Ball 717

Magic   **720**

    Accio 723

    Acromantula 723

    Aguamenti 724

    Alohomora 724

    Amortentia 724

    Anapneo 725

    Ancient Runes 725

    Animagus 725

    Aparecium 726

    Apparation 726

    Arithmancy 727

    Ashwinder 727

    Astronomy 728

    Augurey 728

    Auror 728

    Avada Kedavra 728

    Avis 729

    Banishing Charm 729

    Basilisk 730

    Bat Bogey Hex 730

    Bezoar 731

    Billywig 731

Blood Blisterpod	731
Blood-Sucking Bugbear	731
Boggart	732
Books and Textbooks	733
Boomslang	734
Bowtruckle	735
Brooms	735
Bubble-Head Charm	736
Bubotuber	736
Bundimun	737
Canary Cream	737
Care of Magical Creatures	737
Centaur	737
Charms	738
Chimaera	738
Chizpurfle	738
Clabbert	738
Cockatrice	738
Colloportus	739
Confringo	739
Confundus	739
Conjunctivitus	739
Crucio	739
Crumple Horned Snorkack	740
Crup	740
Dark Mark	740
Darkness Powder	741
Deathly Hallows	741
Decoy Detonator	743
Decree for the Reasonable Restriction of Underage Sorcery	744
Defence Against the Dark Arts	745
Defodio	745
Deletrius	745
Deluminator	746
Dementor	746
Demiguise	747
Densaugeo	747
Deprimo	748
Descendo	748

- *Devil's Snare* 748
- *Diffindo* 748
- *Diricawl* 749
- *Disappearing Cabinets* 749
- *Disillusionment* 749
- *Dissendium* 750
- *Dittany* 750
- *Divination* 750
- *Doxy* 751
- *Dragon* 751
- *Draught of Living Death* 752
- *Dreamless Sleep Potion* 752
- *Dugbog* 752
- *Duro* 753
- *Enervate* 753
- *Engorgio* 753
- *Episkey* 753
- *Erkling* 753
- *Erumpent* 754
- *Evanesco* 754
- *Expecto Patronum* 754
- *Expelliarmus* 755
- *Expulso* 755
- *Extendable Ear* 756
- *Fairy* 756
- *Felix Felicis* 756
- *Ferula* 757
- *Fidelius* 757
- *Fiendfyre* 758
- *Finite* 758
- *Finite Incantatem* 758
- *Firecall* 759
- *Fire Crab* 759
- *Flagrante* 759
- *Flagrate* 759
- *Flobberworm* 759
- *Floo Network* 760
- *Floo Powder* 760
- *Flutterby bush* 761

Flying	761
Foe Glass	761
Ford Anglia	762
Furnunculus	762
Fwooper	762
Geminio	762
Gemino	763
Ghost	763
Ghoul	764
Giant	764
Gillyweed	765
Glisseo	765
Glumbumble	765
Gnome	766
Goblet of Fire	766
Gobbledegook	766
Goblin	766
Graphorn	767
Griffin	767
Grim	767
Grindylow	767
Gurdyroot	768
Halfblood	768
Hand of Glory	768
Herbology	768
Hinkypunk	769
Hippocampus	769
Hippogriff	769
History of Magic	769
Homenum Revelio	769
Horcrux	770
Horcruxes	771
Horklump	773
House Elf	773
Howler	774
Imp	775
Impedimenta	775
Imperio	775
Imperturbable Charm	776

Contents

Impervius 776

Incarcerous 776

Incendio 777

Inferius 777

Invisibility Cloak 777

Jarvey 778

Jobberknoll 778

Kappa 778

Kelpie 778

Knarl 778

Kneazle 778

Knight Bus 779

Langlock 779

Legilimency 779

Legilimens 780

Leprechaun 780

Lethifold 780

Levicorpus 781

Liberacorpus 781

Lobalug 781

Locomotor 781

Locomotor Mortis 781

Love Potion 782

Lumos 782

Mackled Malaclaw 782

Mandrake 782

Manticore 783

Marauder's Map 783

Mermish 784

Merpeople 784

Metamorphmagus 784

Mimbulus Mimbletonia 785

Mirror of Erised 785

Mobiliarbus 786

Mobilicorpus 787

Moke 787

Money 787

Mooncalf 788

Morsmordre 788

Mudblood	789
Muffliato	789
Muggle	789
Muggleborn	789
Muggle Studies	790
Murtlap	790
Niffler	790
Nogtail	790
Nox	790
Nudu	791
Obliviate	791
Occamy	791
Occlumency	791
Omnioculars	792
Oppugno	792
Orchideous	792
Paintings	792
Parselmouth	793
Parseltongue	793
Patronus	794
Pensieve	794
Pepper-Up Potion	795
Permanent Sticking Charm	795
Peskipiksi Pesternomi	795
Petrificus Totalus	796
Philosopher's Stone	796
Phoenix	797
Photograph	797
Pixie	797
Plimpy	798
Pogrebin	798
Point Me	798
Polyjuice Potion	798
Porlock	799
Portkey	799
Portus	800
Potions	800
Prior Incantato	801
Priori Incantatem	801

Probity Probe	801
Prophecy	801
Protean Charm	802
Protego	802
Puffskein	802
Pureblood	803
Pygmy Puff	803
Quick-Quotes Quill	803
Quietus	803
Quintaped	804
Ramora	804
Re'em	804
Red Cap	804
Reducio	804
Reducto	804
Relashio	805
Remembrall	805
Rennervate	805
Reparo	805
Rictusempra	805
Riddikulus	806
Runespoor	806
Salamander	806
Scourgify	806
Sea Serpent	806
Secrecy Sensor	806
Sectumsempra	806
Serpensortia	807
Shrake	807
Silencio	807
Skiving Snackbox	807
Skrewt	807
Snargaluff	808
Sneakoscope	808
Snidget	809
Sonorus	809
Specialis Revelio	809
Sphinx	809
Squib	810

Streeler 810

Stupefy 810

Sword of Gryffindor 810

Tarantallegra 811

Tebo 811

Tergeo 811

The Daily Prophet 811

The Quibbler 812

Thestral 812

Time-Turner 813

Ton-Tongue Toffee 814

Tonguetying Curse 814

Transfiguration 814

Transfiguration Today 815

Troll 815

Unbreakable Vow 815

Undetectable Extension Charm 815

Unforgivable Curses 816

Unicorn 816

Vampire 817

Veela 817

Venomous Tentacula 818

Veritaserum 818

Waddiwasi 818

Wand 818

Werewolf 820

Whomping Willow 820

Wingardium Leviosa 820

Winged horse 821

Witch Weekly 821

Wizengamot 821

Wolfsbane Potion 822

Yeti 822

Timeline   **824**

INTRODUCTION

Welcome to *The Gargantuan Guide to Harry Potter*, the source of which is the online *Muggles' Guide to Harry Potter*, a collaborative effort towards providing an extensive guidebook to the Harry Potter series. This book is under development at Wikibooks (www.wikibooks.org), a site providing a collection of open-content textbooks. Anyone can edit this book at Wikibooks, and all who are interested in helping out the project are encouraged to be bold and dive right in to make it one of the most useful books on Harry Potter anywhere.

This book is a study guide meant to accompany the reading of the Harry Potter series in a course or classroom context (although individual readers may also find it a useful reference); it is not, of course, meant to replace the Harry Potter books, nor does it contain the text of those books (except brief quotations for purposes of illustration, commentary, or analysis); to include the text would be a violation of copyright. We strongly recommend that if you do not already own a copy of the Harry Potter series, a very good place to start, even before looking any further at this Guide, is to obtain copies of the seven books in the series.

What This Book Will Cover

This book wishes to provide in-depth analysis and specific detailing of all things in the Harry Potter series. Readers should be able to learn more about the characters, places, events, and magic than what is merely present in the books. Critical commentary on each chapter, character, place, and event is provided in an effort to help the reader better understand detailed content and realize possible underlying connections to a greater storyline. This book is meant to cover only the actual series, the seven books that make up the actual story. There are a number of additional publications that are only indirectly related to the main story; some of these are:

• A number of issues of *The Daily Prophet* were issued to fans, containing short "news stories" about happenings in the Wizarding world. Apparently copyright by J. K. Rowling, the events these newspapers cover are outside the events of the main story and thus are not covered here.

• "Chocolate Frog" candy was produced for a while, containing Famous Wizard cards; additionally, a Famous Wizards trading card game was produced at one point. These cards were written by the author of the series. In at least a few instances, the text from these cards has enhanced understanding of the series, and thus has been referenced in this work.

In addition, three books were published to raise money for charity.

• *Fantastic Beasts and Where to Find Them,* by "Newt Scamander," which has details of magical creatures that improve our understanding of the role they play in the main books, is included in this study.

• *Quidditch Through the Ages* has little to tell us that we cannot learn through the primary seven books, and so is largely excluded. Some information from this book appears in the article on Quidditch.

• *The Tales of Beedle the Bard* includes some information that sheds light on some characters and some magic in the main story arc. This information is included in this study.

The author's web site[1] also contains rather a lot of authoritative information about the overlooked corners of the wizarding world. While much of its content is irrelevant to our study, those areas that cast some illumination on the books and on the creative process are referenced herein.

Various interviews with the author have appeared, both during production of the books and afterwards. Transcripts of these interviews have appeared on some fan sites. Where these interviews have improved understanding of the books, they have been referenced, though it is not always possible to provide links. This book will explicitly not cover the Harry Potter films, video games, fan fiction, or other authorized or unauthorized works in the same fiction universe.

Where To Start

This book is designed to handle several different levels of readers of the Harry Potter series. Therefore, the book has several parts that detail suggested reading guides for specific levels of reading:

• Beginner—Readers who are new to the Harry Potter series in general. These are readers who have read only a small amount of the Harry Potter books or are just interested in a general overview of the storyline and biographical information.

• Intermediate—Readers who have read most of the Harry Potter series and are clued in to many of the principal characters and places. They will be interested in analysis of characters, places, and events and detailed summaries of the books.

---

1. http://www.jkrowling.com

- Advanced — Readers who have read all of the series and are looking to develop detailed knowledge of much of the books' content and realize the greater picture. A slight step up from the intermediate level, almost every topic in the books is covered, providing a comprehensive view of the series.

Spoilers

For those who want to avoid spoilers (details that could ruin the enjoyment and surprise for parts of the story you haven't read yet), we add this caution: Particularly on the Character pages, and to a lesser extent the Magic pages, there are sections where analysis requires that we cover things that the reader may not yet have seen. In particular, several characters are suddenly seen in a new light in the last two books. Inasmuch as it is possible, we mark sections where they appear with the name of the book or chapter to which they apply. In a character Analysis section, therefore, there might be a heading "Deathly Hallows"; this is an indication that the following section *should be avoided* until you have read *Harry Potter and the Deathly Hallows,* to avoid spoilers.

Beginner

Included Content   The Beginner reader is not expected to have fully explored the Harry Potter storyline. A Beginner reader is assumed to have read perhaps one or two of the books (maybe even none at all). Content for Beginners includes some short synopses of the book plots, brief introductions to some of the key characters in the series, and overviews of several important locations where many important events happen in the series.

Excluded Content   Much of the Harry Potter series has yet to be explored. A great majority of the character list as well as all of the chapter summaries are beyond the Beginner level.

What's Next   Once the reader has completed more of the Harry Potter series, the next step is the Intermediate level. The Intermediate level covers much more of the storyline and is suited for a reader who has nearly completed reading the series.

Intermediate

Included Content   The Intermediate reader is expected to be rather well-versed in the Harry Potter storyline. Much of the plot is known to the reader and he/she wishes to expand on that with analysis and commentary. Most of the character pages and sections will be of interest to the Intermediate reader. In addition, Intermediate readers may want to read the chapter summaries for referencing specific details.

Excluded Content   Not much is kept from the Intermediate reader. Most major content is covered and filling in the gaps is all that is left. An Intermediate reader should feel knowledgeable about the topics covered in the books, but perhaps not quite grasping the full importance of scenes and character actions, referred to as the *Greater Picture*, which the Intermediate reader may want to exclude until the reading of the series can be finished.

What's Next   Once the reader has completed the entire Harry Potter series, the next step is the Advanced level. The Advanced level details the entire storyline. Advanced readers will benefit from the *Greater Picture* section seen on many pages that connects all the pieces together.

Advanced

Included Content   The Advanced reader should be knowledgeable in all areas of the Harry Potter series. No topic has been left unaddressed and all commentary/analysis is understood. Every page and section is of interest, including *Greater Picture,* to make sure that all aspects of the plot have been covered and understood in order to realize the full magnitude of scenes and relationships in the storyline.

Excluded Content   Nothing is kept from the Advanced reader. The Advanced reader has free reign over all content in the Guide.

What's Next   There is no step past the Advanced level. Advanced readers are asked to review analysis and questions to make sure content is understood.

Books

Detailed Plot Summaries   A full overview of the books and the content contained within them.

- *Harry Potter and the Philosopher's Stone*
- *Harry Potter and the Chamber of Secrets*
- *Harry Potter and the Prisoner of Azkaban*
- *Harry Potter and the Goblet of Fire*
- *Harry Potter and the Order of the Phoenix*
- *Harry Potter and the Half-Blood Prince*
- *Harry Potter and the Deathly Hallows*

Extended Analysis

Supplementary material regarding the end of the series.

PHILOSOPHER'S STONE

CHAPTERS

    Chapter 1: The Boy Who Lived
    Chapter 2: The Vanishing Glass
    Chapter 3: The Letters From No One
    Chapter 4: The Keeper of the Keys
    Chapter 5: Diagon Alley
    Chapter 6: The Journey from Platform Nine and Three-Quarters
    Chapter 7: The Sorting Hat
    Chapter 8: The Potions Master
    Chapter 9: The Midnight Duel
    Chapter 10: Hallowe'en
    Chapter 11: Quidditch
    Chapter 12: The Mirror of Erised
    Chapter 13: Nicholas Flamel
    Chapter 14: Norbert the Norwegian Ridgeback
    Chapter 15: The Forbidden Forest
    Chapter 16: Through the Trapdoor
    Chapter 17: The Man with Two Faces

OVERVIEW

The first book in the Harry Potter series, *Harry Potter and the Philosopher's Stone* (or *Harry Potter and the Sorcerer's Stone* in the US) is written from the point of view of the 11-year-old Harry Potter. While its prime audience is children aged 8 to about 11, the story has enough depth to make it a satisfying, if short, read for even adult readers, and the characters show realistic development over the course of the book.

This book came out with different titles in the UK and in the US. In the UK, and in most other English editions, it was named *Harry Potter and the Philosopher's Stone*. Apparently the US publisher felt that his audience would not have sufficient background into classical mythology to know what the Philosopher's Stone was, and so titled the book *Harry Potter and the Sorcerer's Stone*. While many fan sites, mostly in the US, have chosen the latter title, and the film and video games have done likewise, this book uses the UK title as being somewhat closer to the author's intent.

BOOK HIGHLIGHTS

- New places visited: Privet Drive, Diagon Alley, Hogwarts, Forbidden Forest
  - *Defence Against the Dark Arts* teacher: Quirrell
  - Title refers to: the Philosopher's Stone

Chapter 1: The Boy Who Lived

SYNOPSIS

Mr Dursley notices strange events on his way to work: a cat on Privet Drive happens to be reading a map, and people dressed in colourful robes are walking in the streets. Mr Dursley attempts to disregard these oddities. During his lunch break, he sees another group of curiously robed people, and hears mention of the Potters and their son, Harry. He is reminded of the Dursleys' shameful secret, and the reason why they pretend the Potters don't exist. When Mr Dursley arrives home, he hears reports of unforeseen shooting stars and flocks of owls flying during the daytime. Previously unwilling to discuss the Potters with Mrs Dursley, he finally verifies with her that their nephew's name *is* Harry. Mr Dursley sleeps uneasily.

Later that night, a mysterious man by the name of Albus Dumbledore appears in Privet Drive. He removes from his robes a Put-Outer with which he extinguishes the street lights. Dumbledore addresses the cat which seemed to be reading a map earlier as Professor McGonagall, prompting the cat to transform into a robed woman. The couple talk about how recent celebrations have left "Muggles" inquisitive. Dumbledore confirms with McGonagall that James and Lily Potter are dead, and their infant son Harry was apparently involved in the defeat of their assailant, an entity named "You-Know-Who" or Voldemort. Harry, according to Dumbledore, is due to arrive at Privet Drive soon by means of someone named Hagrid.

Hagrid arrives transporting himself and Harry on a flying motorbike. Dumbledore leaves the baby on the doorstep of number four with a letter. McGonagall despairs at the fact that Harry, a definite celebrity, will spend his childhood with such people. Hagrid re-mounts his motorcycle, McGonagall once again becomes a cat, Dumbledore re-illuminates the streetlights, and they all depart.

ANALYSIS

This is one of five chapters in the series that is not written from Harry's point of view. The other chapters are chapter 1 of *Harry Potter and the Goblet of Fire*, chapter 1 and chapter 2 of *Harry Potter and the Half Blood Prince*, and chapter 1 of *Harry Potter and the Deathly Hallows*.

Evidence in the series indicates that Harry is born on 31 July 1980, and orphaned on 31 October 1981—Hallowe'en night—when he is one year and three months old. Critics point out a lack of "trick-or-treating" and similar festivities on Privet Drive that night, but it should be mentioned that we don't actually see Privet Drive on the 31st; it is the 1st of November when Vernon Dursley drives off to work, and the night of the 1st when Dumbledore and Hagrid arrive.

Evidence also suggests that there is a day between the death of Harry's parents and his arrival at Privet Drive; Harry is orphaned on 31 October, 1981, and the story opens with Vernon Dursley leaving for work on the morning of 1 November. This has sparked speculation amongst readers; is there an accident of dates, or is the "missing day" a purposeful addition by the author? It was believed by many readers that the occurrences during that day would be important, possibly even pivotal, to events in the seventh book.

There is also a contradiction: 1 November 1981 was, in reality, a Sunday, and the book states that that day is a Tuesday. Much of the series has minor internal conflicts of this sort. These errors or oversights do not detract from the sweep of the story, so while they may be mentioned, they are provided more as a curiosity than as something for the readers to concern themselves with.

Questions

Review   1. What caused the Dursleys' embarrassment of the Potters? Why is it a secret to the Dursleys that they are related?
2. What exactly is the cat on Privet Drive?
3. Who are the robed people Mr Dursley sees in the streets?
4. Who is "You-Know-Who"?

Further Study   1. While many people seem to be celebrating the defeat of this Voldemort, Dumbledore seems to think the celebrations premature. What would make him think this?

Greater Picture

This chapter provides the framework for the contrast that will be echoed throughout the series between the magical and the mundane.

The events that immediately result in Harry's being orphaned are not discussed in this chapter, but are gradually revealed throughout the series. They are included here by way of reference.

Harry Potter is orphaned when the Dark Lord Voldemort murders his wizarding parents, Lily and James Potter. Voldemort breaks into the Potters' house in the village of Godric's Hollow and duels with James. Voldemort kills James and attempts to do the same to Lily and Harry. He is successful in killing Lily, ignoring her pleas to spare their lives, but his attempt to kill Harry backfires and Voldemort is apparently killed instead. When Harry is older and, during his first year at Hogwarts, meets with Voldemort, Voldemort states that Harry's mother need not have died. Lily's sacrificial attempt to save Harry, however, causes the curse, which Voldemort consequently attempts on Harry, to backfire. This forms a connection between attacker and victim, during which, parts of Voldemort's powers are transferred to the infant, and give Harry a lightning-bolt shaped scar on his forehead. The protection that Lily gives her son—which Albus Dumbledore later explains as her "love" for Harry—destroys Voldemort's physical body and would have killed him completely had it not been for the Dark magic he had been using to split his soul, called Horcruxes. The downfall of Voldemort renders Harry an extremely popular figure in the wizarding world.

It is entirely possible that, because of the Fidelius charm that was meant to protect the Potters from Voldemort still being active, Hagrid would have been unable to find the place until one of the parties to the secret was there. We can safely assume that Sirius, as one of James' closest friends, would have been aware of the Potters' location; in fact, he does say, in *Harry Potter and the Prisoner of Azkaban*, that he had seen "the bodies and the destruction" of the house, so he must have known the secret, either before the Fidelius charm was performed, or by Peter Pettigrew (who we will not meet until the third book) informing him of it afterwards. It has been conjectured that Hagrid was unable to enter the remains of the house to recover Harry until Sirius appeared on the scene, and it could have been Sirius who actually removed Harry from the wreckage and passed him to Hagrid to carry back to Little Whinging. Hagrid does say, however, in chapter 4, that he took Harry from the wreckage himself, so we have to assume either that Hagrid was in on the secret, or else that the Fidelius charm ends automatically when the secret it is designed to protect (in this case, the whereabouts of James and Lily) is no longer operative. We could speculate as to which it is, but given that the house is apparently visible to all wizards by the time of the seventh book, it is most likely that the charm had simply ended with Lily's death.

The fact that Sirius had seen "the wreckage" was also thought to be significant; the Killing Curse does not affect things, only people, and so does not leave wreckage. So the house would have been intact when Voldemort died, giving us a standing house, three dead bodies, and Harry. Add to this the fact that in *Harry Potter and the Goblet of Fire*, Voldemort had his wand back, and we are drawn inescapably to the conclusion that someone, most likely Peter Pettigrew, was there with Voldemort, was aware of his downfall, recovered his wand (and perhaps concealed his body), and destroyed the house, either in revenge or in frustration, while leaving Harry untouched, likely out of fear that whatever had felled Voldemort would kill anyone who tried to attack Harry. We have found out since that the destruction in the house was restricted to the room in which Lily was killed and Harry was sleeping; it is possible that Pettigrew blasted his way out of the house carrying Voldemort's body rather than trying to carry it back down the stairs. The fact that Voldemort, in his memory of that night as viewed in the seventh book, does not recall Peter accompanying him is inconclusive; Voldemort does not seem to pay much attention to his Death Eaters, unless they are directly in his way.

Chapter 2: The Vanishing Glass

Synopsis

Ten years have passed since baby Harry was left with the Dursleys. The living room is full of pictures of Dudley, but none of Harry.

Harry, who sleeps in a spidery cupboard, is awakened by his aunt Petunia, who is telling him to cook breakfast. It is Dudley's birthday and the kitchen table is covered with presents. We are told that Dudley enjoys punching Harry but doesn't usually catch him. Harry is described in detail. Dudley comes into the kitchen and almost throws a tantrum because he has fewer presents than the year before.

The Dursleys find out that Mrs. Figg, the cat-obsessed lady nearby who usually watches Harry while the Dursleys take Dudley on his birthday trip, has broken her leg. They discuss what to do with Harry, and Dudley wails that he doesn't want him to come. Dudley's friend, Piers Polkiss, arrives and because they don't know what else to do with him, Harry gets to come along to the zoo. Uncle Vernon warns Harry that if anything strange happens, Harry will be in major trouble. (Strange things seem to happen around Harry, and the Dursleys don't believe him when he says he didn't cause them.)

On the way to the zoo, Uncle Vernon becomes angry when Harry mentions he dreamed about a flying motorcycle. The zoo goes well at first, and Harry even gets some ice cream. When they get to the reptile house, Harry has a conversation with a large boa constrictor. When Dudley pushes Harry out of the way so he can see the snake's strange behavior, the glass enclosing the snake vanishes. The snake slides out, saying that it will go to his natural environment in Brazil and thanking Harry.

In the car, Dudley and Piers greatly exaggerate their encounter with the snake, and when they are home and Piers is gone, Harry is sent to his cupboard by a furious Uncle Vernon.

Later, Harry is lying in his cupboard, thinking. The only thing he remembers about his past is a flash of green light and a pain in his forehead. He also remembers how sometimes, when he's out with the Dursleys, strange-looking people seem to recognize him.

Analysis

This is the first chapter in which we see how the Dursleys are treating Harry. They treat him as if he was a slave, and they show him no respect at all. Importantly, however, Harry has been made neither timid nor bitter by this treatment, an early sign of the admirable qualities which are so vital to his destiny.

This is also the chapter in which we see Harry's magical talents being shown, such as being able to talk to snakes (this will be explained more fully in this book's successor, *Harry Potter and the Chamber of Secrets*). Rowling has said that this uncontrolled magical ability is normal for wizarding children who haven't yet learned to control their magical powers. Strangely, Harry does not seem frightened by these bizarre incidents, and only casually questions them. This suggests an innate acceptance of magic, and perhaps an unconscious awareness of his true magical nature.

Questions

Review   1. Why did Dudley pretend to cry?
2. Why did Dudley stop his fake crying when his friend came?
3. What kinds of strange things happen around Harry?

Further Study   1. What do these strange things that happen around Harry teach us about his character?

Greater Picture

The scene with the snake could be construed as a hint of what is to come in the next two chapters. Harry and the snake are in almost the same position, as both are prisoners and are cut off from the world in which they belong: Harry, stuck with the Dursleys, is being prevented from joining the Wizarding world, just as the snake, captive in the zoo, cannot enter the world of the Amazon jungle. Also, both were raised away from their home, and so have no knowledge of their native worlds. And finally, each in turn is released from their prison, and head for an unknown future, somehow believing that it must be better then what they are leaving behind.

In this chapter we learn of Harry's ability to speak to snakes, a fact that will be extremely important in future books. While it seems that these early signs of magic could be the trigger which sent the active phase of Albus Dumbledore's great plan into action, we must recall that Harry is about to turn 11, and it is in the September after they reach the age of 11 that magical children are invited to attend school. The author has stated that Hogwarts is the only Wizarding school in the UK, thus every magical child will receive the opportunity to attend when he or she reaches 11. Not all children do attend; some, like Marvolo Gaunt, who we will meet later, likely would not trust the established school system with their children.

Under the pretext of telling us why the Dursleys are afraid to leave Harry home alone, we learn how Harry used his powers before he knew he was a Wizard, basically in self-defense. This story is contrasted in *Harry Potter and the Half-Blood Prince* with the story of how the boy Tom Riddle (later known as Lord Voldemort) used his powers to terrorize others before he knew he was a wizard. This comparison adds another layer to the good vs. evil theme.

Chapter 3: The Letters From No One

Synopsis

Harry is finally let out of the cupboard after being punished for the boa constrictor episode. The summer holidays have started and Dudley and his friends harass Harry daily, enjoying their favorite sport, "Harry Hunting." Dudley finds he has been accepted to Uncle Vernon's old public school (US: private school), Smeltings, whereas Harry will be going to a local comprehensive (US:public school), Stonewall High.

In July, Petunia takes Dudley shopping for his school clothes. The next morning Harry finds her dyeing some of Dudley's old clothes grey, to make him a "school uniform." As everyone sits down for breakfast the mail arrives. Harry has a short fight with Dudley over who has to retrieve the mail. Harry loses. Picking up the mail, Harry sees there is a letter addressed to him:

> Mr. H. Potter
> The Cupboard under the Stairs
> 4 Privet Drive
> Little Whinging
> Surrey

Harry had never received mail before and wasn't sure who this could be from. The envelope was a thick, heavy, yellow parchment with a strange wax seal on the back. Back in the kitchen, Uncle Vernon snatches the letter from Harry as he tries to read it. Uncle Vernon is shocked at the contents of the letter and immediately sends Dudley and Harry out of the kitchen so he and Petunia can discuss it. Dudley and Harry listen to the conversation through the keyhole and the gap under the door, and overhear them decide to ignore the letter and not respond. Uncle Vernon moves Harry up into Dudley's second room. Day after day more letters show up for Harry, but they are now addressed to him in "The Smallest Bedroom," despite Vernon's attempts to prevent their entering the house. Vernon does manage to prevent Harry from getting any of the letters. On Sunday, when Uncle Vernon is sure no post is coming, the letters come streaming out of the fireplace. Vernon decides enough is enough, packs everyone into the car and drives all day to a run-down hotel on the outskirts of some city. The next day "about a hundred letters" show up at the hotel for Harry. Next, Uncle Vernon finds a rickety old shack out on a rocky island off the coast, accessible only by boat. As they settle in for the night Harry stares at Dudley's watch, counting down the minutes to midnight and his eleventh birthday. A storm is raging outside but Harry thinks he hears something else outside the shack. Just as he counts the final second down to his birthday a huge *boom* shakes the shack. Someone is knocking on the door.

Analysis

Uncle Vernon's attempts to shut out, and then run away from, the letters can be seen as an analogy with people's tendency to try to ignore facts. The tendency to try to avoid unpleasant truth is a common human weakness. The idea that if you refuse to admit something to yourself, then it can't be true, may be very comforting sometimes. The problem is that, just like the letters that burst out of the fireplace, the truth has a tendency to come back and strike you in the face. Unfortunately, this is a lesson that Vernon Dursley never seems to learn, as determined denial and brutish ignorance are the key qualities of his character. This chapter has an enjoyably tense atmosphere, as it almost as if Harry's true identity and destiny is rushing toward him, and no matter how hard the Dursleys try to outrun it, with a *"boom!"* on the door it catches up, and nothing will ever be the same again.

As mentioned in chapter 1, there are a few places in the stories where days and dates don't line up. We have already seen that this book covers events largely in 1991 and 1992. The Dursleys leave Privet Drive for the hotel on Sunday, leave the hotel and drive to the island on Monday (Dudley complains because he is missing The Great Umberto on TV), and so Harry's birthday falls on Tuesday. However, July 31, 1991 is a Wednesday. This trivial error does not truly affect the story in any way, and is included here more as a curiosity than as something for the scholar to concern himself with.

Questions

Review 1. Why does Uncle Dursley decide to move Harry out of the cupboard? What does Dudley think of this change?

Further Study 1. How could the writer of the letters know where Harry's room/place was at any given moment?
  2. Who is the person that is sending these letters?
  3. Who is the person that comes to get Harry?
  4. Does Harry get to read his letter? And when?

Greater Picture

This chapter shows the great lengths that the Dursleys are willing to go to in order to appear normal to neighbors and not to draw attention to themselves. Their need to appear normal in front of others is the reason they hide Harry in his room and is also the reason they keep him at their home after the dramatic events at the beginning of Harry's fifth year.

Chapter 4: The Keeper of the Keys

Synopsis

Boom! The knockings continue outside the door. Vernon comes running in with a rifle as the door is smashed in. A huge man with a bearded face enters. He twists Uncle Vernon's gun like a pretzel, sits down and wishes Harry happy birthday, and gives him a squished cake. The giant man makes himself at home, starts a fire and makes tea and sausages. He introduces himself as Rubeus Hagrid, Keeper of Keys and Grounds at Hogwarts. Hagrid is dismayed to find the Dursleys have told Harry nothing of his past or of his parents, and furious that they told Harry that his parents died in a car crash. Hagrid explains that Harry is a wizard, a very famous wizard. He gives Harry his letter, now addressed to him at the shack. The letter explains that Harry has been accepted to Hogwarts School of Witchcraft and Wizardry.

Hagrid sends an owl to Professor Dumbledore saying he found Harry and will be taking him to get his school supplies. Petunia begins ranting and Harry learns that she and Uncle Vernon have lied to him about his past. Hagrid tells Harry about a very dark wizard, by the name of Voldemort (though Hagrid seems to have enormous difficulty saying the name, apparently out of fear), who ten years ago (when Harry was only one year old) tracked down and killed Harry's parents,

James and Lily Potter. He tried to kill Harry too, but failed, and that is how Harry got the scar on his forehead. Harry asks Hagrid what happened to Voldemort and Hagrid tells him that no one is sure, but something happened to him (on the Hallowe'en night he tried to kill Harry) that drove him into hiding. Harry questions whether he is really a wizard, but Hagrid asks whether he had ever made things happen when he was angry or scared. Harry remembers things he had done, most recently the boa constrictor, and smiles. Uncle Vernon cuts in and says Harry isn't going to a magic school. He then insults Albus Dumbledore, calling him a crackpot. This sends Hagrid into a fit of rage and he causes a pig's tail to grow out of Dudley's back side. The Dursleys scramble into the other room, terribly afraid of Hagrid. Hagrid asks Harry not to mention the magic he performed to anyone at Hogwarts, as he isn't supposed to do magic anymore. Harry asks why not, and Hagrid explains that he had been expelled from Hogwarts during his third year. Harry questions him further, but Hagrid changes the subject saying it's late and they have lots of things to do the next day. At that they go to sleep, Hagrid on the couch, Harry under Hagrid's huge coat on the floor.

Analysis

In this chapter, we learn a bit more of what happened the night Lord Voldemort came to Godric's Hollow. We also get a feeling for the dread that most wizards have for Voldemort, or even his name.

The Dursley's behaviour here is a classic example of the human tendency for ignorance and fear to go hand in hand. In a vicious circle, their ignorance about magic makes them afraid of it, and their fear prevents them from developing a better understanding. In contrast, Harry's willingness to accept his magical nature when the evidence is shown to him, clearly indicates his open-minded intelligence.

One of the central themes to these books is the danger of prejudice and divisiveness, and this chapter, particularly Petunia's tirade, gives a picture of the prejudiced view from the Muggle side of the Muggle/Magic divide.

Questions

Review 1. What does this chapter tell us about Aunt Petunia's character?

2. Why do Aunt Petunia and Uncle Vernon hide Harry's secret?

3. Do they tell him what his secret is? Why or why not?

Further Study 1. Can you think of a reason, aside from ignorance and fear, for Petunia's apparent hatred of her sister Lily?

Greater Picture

This chapter briefly mentions Hagrid's expulsion from Hogwarts, which will be important to the plot of the next book, *Harry Potter and the Chamber of Secrets*.

Hagrid's fear of saying Voldemort's name will be echoed through almost all of the series, with people referring to Voldemort as "you-know-who" and variants on that theme. This dread, though constant, will be greatly reinforced in the seventh book, where we will learn that Voldemort has, in fact, placed a taboo on his name, such that anyone who speaks it will be immediately detected and subject to reprisals. We will find that the taboo is specifically aimed at those who would fight him, as they are the only ones who dare speak his name. While this is never mentioned, it is entirely likely that a similar taboo was in place in Voldemort's initial time in power, and it would be this taboo which had engendered a fear of speaking the name among the Wizarding populace.

In this chapter, by learning his true nature, Harry has taken the first step on the path of his eventual destiny. He will continue on this path throughout the entire series, with occasional setbacks.

Chapter 5: Diagon Alley

Synopsis

Harry wakes up to find an owl attacking Hagrid's coat. Hagrid tells him to give the owl five Knuts, which turn out to be odd-looking coins, and they set off for London. Walking down the street, Harry notices Muggles (non-magical folk) are looking at them strangely and are scrambling to let Hagrid pass.

After climbing broken down escalators to the London Underground and getting Hagrid stuck at the ticket barrier (and after complaints from Hagrid that the seats were too small and trains too slow), they finally reach Central London.

Soon, they reach a place called the Leaky Cauldron. Harry notices the Muggles' gaze traveling from the record shop on one side to the bookstore on the other side, not noticing the pub in-between. He has a feeling that of those present, only Hagrid and himself can see it.

On entering the pub, Harry is greeted enthusiastically by many excited people, including one Quirrell, who Hagrid says will be teaching Harry about Defence Against the Dark Arts. Leaving the Leaky Cauldron, Harry and Hagrid find themselves in a small courtyard behind the pub. While Harry thinks over the responses of the people, Hagrid starts counting the bricks on top of the bin with his umbrella. He then taps a brick three times and a hole appears, getting bigger and bigger, and turns into an archway. They enter Diagon Alley.

Harry and Hagrid walk past the wizard shops to the end of the street, where Gringotts, the wizard bank, stands. At Gringotts, Hagrid provides the key to Harry's parents' vault, and a note authorizing him to enter another vault on behalf of Dumbledore. After a high-speed cart ride with Griphook the goblin (which makes Hagrid queasy), they reach Harry's vault, which is full of wizard money (galleons, sickles and knuts). Hagrid helps Harry draw enough for school supplies and a year at school, and educates him on the wizard monetary system. After another cart ride, Hagrid removes the only contents of vault seven hundred thirteen, a small grubby parcel, without explaining what it is.

Back on the surface, Harry, with Hagrid's assistance, buys school supplies. He meets another first-year Hogwarts student who seems quite full of himself; but before introductions can be completed, Harry's robes are finished and he moves on to buy other supplies: books, a cauldron, a telescope, and potion supplies. For his birthday, Hagrid buys him an owl, Hedwig. Finally, at Ollivander's, Harry buys a wand, which turns out, according to Mr. Ollivander, to be twin to the one sold to Voldemort, each being made with one of the only two tail-feathers ever given by one particular phoenix.

ANALYSIS

Harry is amazed that he is so respected by these people. Without realizing it, he is famous, a hero to an entire people. In this chapter, we see Harry's reaction to fame; mostly, he is a bit embarrassed, because he feels he has done nothing to deserve the adulation that is being cast his way. We will be contrasting this with the behaviour of someone who lives for fame in the next book, *Harry Potter and the Chamber of Secrets*.

We are also here, for the first time, exposed to the parallel Wizarding economy, and to the magical creatures that exist in the Wizarding world. We meet goblins, and hear about phoenixes, dragons, unicorns, hags, and vampires; this is our first intimation that these creatures out of mythology may have a real, parallel existence. Harry finds that having a wand related to Voldemort's makes him uneasy; while Ollivander sees it as an indication that Harry will be a great wizard, Harry finds it disturbing that he could have even that small a similarity to a wizard who is universally seen as evil, further evidence of his admirable character. The provenance of the magical core of Harry's wand will become important in *Harry Potter and the Goblet of Fire* and in *Harry Potter and the Deathly Hallows*.

QUESTIONS

Review 1. Hagrid says that the Wizarding monetary system is simple. Is it?

Further Study 1. We see that Harry and Hagrid get off the island by using the same boat that Harry and the Dursleys used to get there. If Harry and Hagrid take the only boat on the whole island, how did the Dursleys get home?

2. When asked how he had gotten to the island, Hagrid reported that he had flown there. Apparently, wizards cannot fly without equipment such as a broom, a flying car or motorcycle, or a flying carpet. How could Hagrid fly there?

GREATER PICTURE

The "small, grubby parcel" that Hagrid removes from the vault will turn out to be the titular Philosopher's Stone (US: Sorcerer's Stone), which will be the effective center of this book's plot. Harry, with his limited classical education, does not understand why this stone should be so prized, but its function will be explained to him by a classmate, Hermione Granger.

Mention is made of Harry's humility, above. While this character trait will serve him well, it will for a long time be masked by his unique position as "the Boy Who Lived." Harry will defeat Voldemort repeatedly, and in the process will begin to believe that he is the only one who can perform certain activities. Close examination will reveal that while he accepts, to some extent, the description of himself as a hero, he does not use this as a way of increasing status; rather, he sees it as increasing his obligations. Late in the series, he becomes known as The Chosen One, as the Ministry tries to use him as a means of showing that they are doing something; despite being thrust into the limelight in this manner, Harry does not use his fame as a way of improving his lot, instead shunning it so that he can continue the mission he has been given.

It is mentioned in the description of Ollivander's that the window display consists of a single wand on a cushion. We will find out in later books, notably *Harry Potter and the Half-Blood Prince*, that Voldemort has been hunting artifacts of the Founders in order to make them into Horcruxes. It was suggested that the wand in Ollivander's window is Rowena Ravenclaw's; this might have had something to do with Ollivander's disappearance in *Harry Potter and the Half-Blood Prince* as well. It turns out, however, that the artifact of Ravenclaw's that Voldemort was after had been found by him many years before; he had located her lost diadem, and had turned it into a Horcrux before he met Harry.

The idea that "The wand chooses the wizard" will also become a key point in the larger story. It will become particularly important in *Harry Potter and the Deathly Hallows*.

Chapter 6: The Journey from Platform Nine and Three-Quarters

SYNOPSIS

Back at the Dursleys,' Harry now has to wait out the month before he can go to Hogwarts. Uncle Vernon agrees to take him to London only because he has to take Dudley to a surgeon to get his pig's tail removed. The Dursleys then leave him standing in the station, unable to find Platform 9–3/4 where his train is supposed to leave. Harry then spots another apparent wizarding family, and tags along with them to get to the Hogwarts Express. This family, who recognize him for who he is, turn out to be the Weasleys, and Harry is introduced to three of the four Weasley children who are currently attending Hogwarts: Fred, George, and Ron, who ends up sharing a compartment with him. (Percy Weasley is also attending, but he is a Prefect and so rides in the special Prefects compartment at the head of the train.) Ron tells him about the treat, Chocolate Frogs, and the enclosed Famous Wizard cards; Harry gets Albus Dumbledore's card, among others. Ron also happens to mention that there had been a break-in at Gringotts Wizarding Bank in Diagon Alley; Harry is interested in this because of his own recent trip there.

During the trip to school, various other students introduce themselves to him. Neville stops by looking for his toad, Trevor; Hermione Granger stops by shortly afterwards trying to help Neville find Trevor. Draco Malfoy, flanked by Crabbe and Goyle, tries to coerce Harry into an alliance, and when that fails, in part because of Malfoy's bad-mouthing the Weasley family, the three try to steal some of Harry's snacks; in this, they are stopped by Scabbers, Ron's pet rat, who attacks Goyle. Finally, Hermione returns, to let them know that they are about to arrive and should get into uniform.

At Hogsmeade Station, Hagrid reappears to shepherd the first-years down to a fleet of small boats that carry the students across the lake to Hogwarts castle.

Analysis

Hermione, here in her first appearance of the series, is portrayed as a true grind—a girl whose "know-it-all" attitude is immediately off-putting. Both Harry and Ron dislike her at once . . . though not in the same way that they dislike the anti-trio, Malfoy, Crabbe, and Goyle, whom they immediately despise. It is interesting how Hermione mellows during the course of the series; this ongoing maturation of the characters, especially Hermione and, to a slightly lesser extent, Harry, is a significant part of what makes the overall story so compelling.

Draco's attitude to Ron gives us our first glimpse of the lineage-related prejudice which plagues the wizard world, and is the obsession of Voldemort and most of his followers.

Albus Dumbledore's "Famous Wizards" card is the key that provides a major clue to the riddle that needs to be solved in the course of this book.

Greater Picture

While much of what Harry reads on Dumbledore's Chocolate Frog card will prove important to the story of this book, it will turn out that it will be somewhat important up until the very end of the series. In part of what will be an almost stunning amount of interconnection between the first of the series and the last, we will find that Grindelwald, mentioned on Dumbledore's Chocolate Frog card, was in fact an influence on the young Dumbledore, and has a large, though not central, role in the final book of the series.

Chapter 7: The Sorting Hat

Synopsis

Upon reaching the school, Hagrid hands the new students over to a teacher, Professor McGonagall. She leads the students to an anteroom, where they wait to be sorted into Houses. They are understandably nervous about this process, and are further unnerved by a small crowd of ghosts who pass through the anteroom on their way to the Great Hall. Shortly, Professor McGonagall returns, leads them into the Great Hall, and places them, one by one, under the Sorting Hat, which calls out the house to which they are assigned. There are four houses in Hogwarts, each with very specific characteristics. Slytherin is filled with ambitious, cunning witches and wizards. Ravenclaw is home to the most intelligent witches and wizards. Gryffindor houses only the brave, and Hufflepuff is where the most fair and honest go. The Sorting Hat suggests quietly that Harry might fit well in Slytherin, but when Harry balks at this, it places him instead in Gryffindor House.

Ron and Hermione also are Sorted into Gryffindor, along with several others. Professor Dumbledore then makes a few eccentric prefatory remarks, and the feast begins. In the course of the feast, we are introduced to Sir Nicholas de Mimsy-Porpington, the Gryffindor house ghost, who is nicknamed Nearly Headless Nick; and to some of the other students in Harry's year: Neville, who had almost lost his toad on the train; Seamus; and Dean, who is mentioned in the US editions of the book as being a "tall, black boy," but is not described in the British editions of the book. Harry also has an episode of pain in his scar when he is scrutinized by Professor Snape, the Potions teacher.

After the meal, there are a few start-of-term announcements, including one that catches Harry's ear: *"this year, the third floor corridor on the right-hand side is out of bounds to everyone who does not wish to die a very painful death."* Harry asks Percy if Dumbledore is serious, and Percy replies that he must be.

Now that the meal is finished, it is time to sing the school song: *"everyone pick their favorite tune,"* said Dumbledore, *"and off we go!"* Afterwards, they leave for their dormitories. Percy leads the first-year Griffindors through a very convoluted path, though all paths through Hogwarts seem convoluted; Harry is bemused by the paintings on the walls, whose occupants are aware of the passing students and comment on them. They are briefly harassed by Peeves, but eventually reach the entrance to the Gryffindor common room, which is guarded by a portrait of a fat lady. Percy gives the password (*"Caput Draconis"*), and everyone goes up to their dormitories and to bed. During the night, Harry has a dream, involving Quirrell's turban and Malfoy turning into Snape. Harry wakes up sweating, and goes back to sleep, and when he wakes up the next morning he doesn't even remember the dream.

Analysis

The purpose of this chapter seems to be to introduce us to the houses in Hogwarts; to give us our first taste of the character of the Headmaster, Albus Dumbledore, and to introduce us also to the idea that Harry's scar can be a barometer, if you will, of the passing scene. We are also given another indication of Harry's fame in the Wizarding world, through the response made by the rest of the school when his name is called out for Sorting. We are also given some ideas about how the Wizarding world differs from the Muggle world that Harry has been trapped in so far. The understanding of the operation of the Wizarding world here is not only appropriate to Harry's age level (11), but also is at about the level of detail that would be comprehended by someone of that age who was suddenly introduced to the magical world. For instance, the food of the banquet fades in on the plates; Harry doesn't stop to wonder who prepared it or how it got placed on the plates.

That curiosity and the resultant understanding doesn't come about for another three years.

Harry's dream is, of course, foreshadowing of the main plot line of this book. At this point, the reader does not know enough to interpret this dream, but may understand that there is some connection between the pain Harry is feeling in his scar, and Quirrell's turban.

QUESTIONS

Further Study 1. Do you think Dumbledore is really as "barmy" as seems to be popularly believed? If not, is his behaviour an affectation, or does he have wisdom that other wizards don't understand and thus dismiss as eccentricity?

GREATER PICTURE

In this book, we see half of a timeline contradiction. At Nearly Headless Nick's deathday party, commemorating the five-hundredth anniversary of his death, in *Harry Potter and the Chamber of Secrets,* his death is stated to have been on 1492-10-31. However, in this chapter, Nearly Headless Nick states that he has been dead for nearly 400 years. It is assumed that this is an error on the part of the author, and in fact the author has corrected this, by making Nick say that he has been dead for nearly 500 years, in later editions of this book.

As mentioned in the Greater Picture section for that Deathday Party chapter, the date of Nearly Headless Nick's death can be used to determine a timeline for the entire series, leading us to all the specific dates of the book. However, this timeline is not critical to the plot or events of the books, as it only affects the interactions between the events in the books and the Muggle world, and those interactions are very few.

The byplay between Harry and the Sorting Hat becomes more germane in the course of the second book, *Harry Potter and the Chamber of Secrets,* and later in illustrating the difference between Harry and Voldemort. While the Hat recognizes qualities in Harry bestowed on him by the connection between him and Voldemort, it is ultimately Harry's exercising of choice and free will that leads to his assignment to Gryffindor.

Harry's dream may actually be a foreshadowing of events in the entire series, rather than in just this book. It may be that his dream is actually an unconscious attempt by Voldemort to influence Harry's actions by means of Legilimency, as he will do again in *Harry Potter and the Order of the Phoenix.* While this is neither confirmed nor refuted by later events, it is unlikely that it is a conscious use of Legilimency by Voldemort; Voldemort did not start deliberately using Legilimency on Harry in that book until he became aware of the existing connection at about Christmas.

We are meant to believe that the explosion of pain in Harry's scar is because Snape is looking at him. It is true that Snape is not pleased to see him; at that distance, Snape can only see the similarity between Harry and his father James. We will find out that James and Snape were in the same year at Hogwarts, and that they did not get along. In actual fact, the pain in Harry's scar is because Voldemort, then riding Quirrell, is either looking at Harry through Quirrell's turban, or is using Legilimency to observe the room, and has just detected Harry.

Harry's scar did not hurt when he first met Quirrell in the Leaky Cauldron, and Quirrell's skin did not burn when they shook hands there (see The Man with Two Faces), because he wasn't wearing the turban at the time, and hence Voldemort was not possessing him from the back of his head. Quoting from the text, at the welcoming feast, "Harry spotted Quirrell, too, the nervous young man from from the Leaky Cauldron. *He was looking very peculiar in a large purple turban."* (Emphasis ours.) This implies that this is the first time Harry has seen him wearing the turban.

Chapter 8: The Potions Master

SYNOPSIS

Harry finds his first few days at Hogwarts very trying indeed. The other students keep looking at him as though he is some kind of celebrity, which makes him nervous. The castle itself is very convoluted and he and Ron repeatedly get lost on their way to class and are late, or are caught accidentally trying to enter forbidden areas, which puts them (on the very first day at Hogwarts) on the wrong side of the caretaker, Argus Filch. And the lessons themselves are difficult.

Harry meets his teachers for the first time: Professor Sprout for Herbology, Professor Binns for History of Magic, and Professor Flitwick for Charms. He also has Professor McGonagall for Transfiguration, and Professor Quirrell for Defence Against the Dark Arts, though of course he has met them before. At breakfast on Friday, Harry receives his first message by owl post, from Hagrid, inviting him to tea after class; he then attends his first Potions class with Professor Snape, a double length class shared with Slytherin first-years. This class does not go at all well, with Snape singling Harry out, and ridiculing him for his lack of magical knowledge. Snape, who apparently disapproves of Harry's celebrity status, continues to be harder on Harry than even the other Gryffindors in the class. In particular, when Neville melts the cauldron he shares with Seamus, Snape unjustly holds Harry partly responsible and penalizes Gryffindor House one point because of it. When Harry (and Ron) get to Hagrid's hut for tea, Harry finds a clipping from the *Daily Prophet,* which mentions the robbery from Gringotts Wizarding Bank. Hagrid refuses to talk about it, and Harry ends up coming to the conclusion that the vault that was burglarized was in fact the one that Hagrid himself had emptied during their trip to Diagon Alley.

ANALYSIS

In this chapter we meet most of the Hogwarts teachers, at least most of the ones who will be major characters in this and later books. We discover that while most of the teachers are delighted to have Harry in their classes, Snape is less than impressed. As we progress through the books, Snape's singling out of Harry becomes a regular occurrence. Later we find out precisely why Snape hates Harry so much; for now, we are led to believe that it is Harry's celebrity that Snape dislikes.

Chapter 9: The Midnight Duel

This will be reinforced in the next book, where we will see Snape's reaction to a celebrity teacher.

In the conversation with Hagrid at the end of this chapter, we see Harry's urge to understand and investigate, a quality which equips him to solve (with help) the many mysteries which will be put before him throughout his seven-year story.

QUESTIONS

Further Study 1. Why didn't Snape call on Hermione when she raised her hand?

2. Why does Snape hate Harry so much?

GREATER PICTURE

Snape's great dislike for Harry becomes a main feature in many of the later books.

This first ever Potions class will actually foreshadow a lot of the events in the books. Snape says, in his introduction, that he can teach the students to "brew fame, bottle fortune, and even stopper death." The sheer number of connections of this scene, as described below, to later parts of the series, had led many fans to speculate, following the events at the end of the sixth book, that Dumbledore and Snape had conspired to fake Dumbledore's death. In fact, the potion mentioned had been used in that book, although we do not find out about that until late in the final book; Snape had, in fact, prevented or reversed Dumbledore's death from his touching a cursed ring. The discussion of aconite or monkshood, and the associated Draught of Living Death, reappear in the sixth book, first when Professor Slughorn has Harry's class brew this potion, and possibly (in the US edition only) on the top of the Astronomy tower, when Dumbledore is trying to convince Draco to switch sides, and tells him that can make Draco and all his family appear to be dead. The bezoar that Snape asks Harry to describe will play a small role in the fourth book, and a much larger one in the sixth book.

The fact that Harry and Ron constantly get lost shows the magical qualities and enormity of the castle. Hogwarts has many secrets, many of which will become very important later in the series.

Chapter 9: The Midnight Duel

SYNOPSIS

Harry is dismayed to find out, in his second week of school, that flying lessons are also going to be shared with Slytherin house, and because he has no idea about how to fly, he will be subject to ridicule from Draco Malfoy, who has become as well-loved by Harry as cousin Dudley.

Neville receives a Remembrall from his grandmother, which Draco attempts to steal, but is prevented from doing so by the arrival of Professor McGonagall.

At the flying lesson, Neville falls off his broom and injures himself. The instructor, Madam Hooch, takes him off to the hospital wing, ordering the rest of the class to stay on the ground. Draco spots Neville's Remembrall on the ground, and takes off to place it in a tree for Neville to fetch later. Harry flies off after him, and finds that flying on a broomstick is something he is naturally good at. Draco changes his mind and throws the Remembrall away in the air, but Harry dives after it and catches it mid-air, just inches above the ground. He is immediately accosted by Professor McGonagall, who has been watching from her office. Professor McGonagall drags him away from the lesson, apparently in disgrace, but then introduces him to the captain of the Gryffindor Quidditch team, Oliver Wood, and tells him Harry's the new Seeker.

Surprised to find Harry at dinner that evening, Draco challenges Harry to a Wizard's Duel in the trophy room at midnight. Ron volunteers to be Harry's second. As Harry and Ron leave the common room later that night, circumstance adds Neville and Hermione to the party. As they reach the trophy room, they hear Filch looking for them. Evidently Draco had no intention of showing up, but simply sent Filch after Harry to get him in trouble. Making a run for it because Peeves yelled that he found students out of bed, Harry's group end up in the forbidden third-floor corridor, looking for a place to hide. Though they do avoid Filch, they are dismayed to find that their hiding place is occupied also by a huge three-headed dog. Managing to escape, they return to the common room, where Hermione points out that the dog was standing on a trap door and apparently guarding something. Harry leaps to the conclusion that the dog was guarding the package that Hagrid had taken from the vault at Gringotts.

ANALYSIS

This is one of the happiest chapters, at least initially, of Harry's early school career. We've seen how he felt initially out of place — apart from the natural dislocation of being in a new school, Harry has had to deal with sudden celebrity, and the associated ongoing feeling that he's a bit of a fraud. This is compounded by the fact that he doesn't seem to be able to do magic with the natural fluidity of some of his peers, such as Hermione (it seems that she knows anything that can be learned from a book, while Harry has to muddle along). Harry is also concerned that his years of living among Muggles, particularly *those* Muggles, may have crippled his magical abilities — all the other students will have had magical upbringings and will bring an understanding to the school that he does not have. In this situation, imagine his joy to discover that flying on a broomstick is something magical that he can do, not only naturally and well, but better than anyone else in the class. Compound this with the discovery that his father also flew well, that he will not have to attend further flying classes with the Slytherins, that the school will be providing him with a top-quality broom for use in Quidditch matches . . . and you can see that by dinner time, Harry could likely fly from sheer joy, without needing a broom.

The Wizards' duel, which may appear somewhat arbitrary, is a natural progression; Draco has been humiliated, and he must have his revenge. And for Draco, betraying Harry (and, peripherally, Ron) to Filch would be every bit as satisfying as beating him, if he could, personally, at a duel, and carries much less risk of further humiliation — what if Harry met him at the duel and actually beat him? This is also a glimpse of the lack of courage to act for himself which will later land Draco in more trouble than he can imagine.

It is also necessary for Harry to find clues to the location of Hagrid's grubby little package. It will seem that many different people are all seeking that one small thing ... and Harry of course will have to know where it is if he is to do his part in keeping it safe.

GREATER PICTURE

The trap door under the three-headed dog Fluffy is one of the many Hogwarts secrets foreshadowed in the previous chapter. The trap door also provides a huge question to be answered in this series: "What is under the trap door?" If the dog is guarding Hagrid's parcel, then one must question what else could lie beneath the floors of the castle. Hogwarts holds many secrets that will be discovered in later books.

Chapter 10: Halloween

SYNOPSIS

The next morning, Harry receives a long, thin package in the morning post. The attached note warns him not to open it at the table, that it is a broom, and is signed "Professor M. McGonagall." Malfoy is already dismayed that Harry and Ron apparently escaped his plan to have them thrown out, and so arranges to find out what is in the package. Discovering that it is a broomstick, he informs Professor Flitwick of his discovery, and is then further dismayed that not only does the staff know about this breach of the rule that first-years are not allowed to have broomsticks, but they also approve of it.

That evening, as directed, Harry goes down to the Quidditch pitch, where he meets Oliver Wood. Oliver explains the rules of the game, and does some basic practice with Harry. After this, Oliver has the team practicing three evenings a week; Harry of course is practicing as well.

A month and a half passes; and it is Hallowe'en. Professor Flitwick decides that the class is ready to actually use the spell to make things float that they have been learning (Wingardium Leviosa). Hermione corrects Ron's pronunciation of the incantation and is the first to succeed. Later Ron says to Harry that Hermione is unbearable and that is why she has no friends. Hermione overhears them and runs crying into the girls' bathroom. During the Hallowe'en feast that evening, Professor Quirrell bursts into the Great Hall, hysterical, announcing the appearance of a mountain troll in the dungeons. As they are being shepherded back to their common room, Harry and Ron remember that Hermione is still in the bathroom, and head off to inform her of the troll. On the way, they see Professor Snape apparently headed for the forbidden third floor corridor. They then find the troll, which attacks Harry, Ron and Hermione in the bathroom. Frightened, Ron calls out the first spell that comes to his head, Wingardium Leviosa, which causes the troll's club to float into the air and later crash down on its head, leaving it unconscious. Upon the arrival of the teachers, Hermione lies to Professor McGonagall and says that it was her idea to try to defeat the troll, and that Harry and Ron had arrived just in time to save her. Professor McGonagall chides Hermione and takes away five points from Gryffindor for her action, but awards Harry and Ron five points apiece for defeating the troll. From then on, Hermione becomes friends with Harry and Ron.

ANALYSIS

In the early part of the chapter, we see Harry once again receiving great joy from his flying ability. The fact that he has been presented with a world-class racing broom, and that he is able to put it so lightly through its paces, is very heartening for him. Flying and Quidditch are quickly becoming his centering point; he can retreat to the air or the pitch when things become too confusing to bear.

JK Rowling has said: "When we were editing 'Philosopher's Stone' my editor wanted me to cut the scene in which Harry, Ron and Hermione fight the troll. Although I had accepted most of the smaller cuts he wanted me to make I argued hard for this one. Hermione, bless her, is so very annoying in the early part of 'Philosopher's Stone' that I really felt it needed something (literally) huge to bring her together with Harry and Ron."[1] This is the beginning of the change in Hermione. At this point, we are starting the process of having her turn into a sympathetic character; previously, she had been the two-dimensional goody-two-shoes grind, and now we very suddenly see that there is some hope for her. This is also the first example of the "trio" working together, and their success when their skills are combined indicates how powerful and vital this friendship will be in the greater story.

GREATER PICTURE

Harry receives his broom, which he becomes very attached to in the later books, as flying is the one thing he is best at in his year. One of the most devastating moments in the coming books will be when this broom is destroyed; and throughout the series, he will be periodically deprived of flight and will suffer because of this. Hermione suddenly appears in a more sympathetic light by lying to save Harry and Ron, a key hint towards how her caring and thoughtfulness will be essential to the Trio's success across later years. The bond between the Trio, first formed here, is arguably the most important relationship in the whole story.

Chapter 11: Quidditch

SYNOPSIS

Quidditch season starts in November, and Harry is lucky to have Hermione as his friend, because the extra practices are taking away his homework time, and it is only Hermione's help that allows him to get through

---

1. http://www.jkrowling.com/textonly/en/extrastuff_view.cfm?id=8

it all. Also, she has become a bit more relaxed about breaking rules, so when she, Harry, and Ron are out in the courtyard one day, she creates a small wizard fire to keep them warm. Professor Snape, seeing them there, confiscates the book Harry was reading, *Quidditch Through the Ages*, on a pretext. Harry and Ron notice that he is limping.

That evening, Harry decides to ask Snape to return the book. Hoping to catch him with other teachers so as to defuse his anger, he looks into the staff room. There he finds Snape with a very bad wound on his leg tended by Filch, and talking about something with three heads that apparently injured him. Snape notices Harry and, enraged, orders him out of the staff room. Harry, Ron, and Hermione jointly decide that his injury is likely caused by the three-headed dog in the forbidden third floor corridor.

The following morning is the day of Harry's first Quidditch match, which would be against Slytherin. The match proceeds well, until Harry's broom starts acting strangely. Hermione notices that Professor Snape is staring fixedly at Harry and muttering, and comes to the conclusion that he is jinxing it. To stop this, she runs across the stands, knocking Professor Quirrell over in the process, and sets Snape's robes on fire, thus breaking his concentration. Regaining control of the broom, Harry dives for the pitch, in the process nearly swallowing the Snitch and thus winning the match.

After the match, Harry, Ron, and Hermione are discussing events in Hagrid's hut. Hagrid voices disbelief that Snape could have been jinxing Harry's broom. Harry mentions that Snape had apparently run afoul of the three-headed dog, which Hagrid accidentally identifies as "Fluffy." Hagrid later mentions that whatever he's guarding, "that's between Professor Dumbledore an' Nicholas Flamel—" thus accidentally providing another clue to the nature of the object being guarded.

ANALYSIS

Hermione's intelligence and generosity are already proving useful, if only in the small (comparative to what comes later) matter of homework.

It is also quite clear now that someone has malicious intentions against Harry. It certainly seems obvious that it is Snape, from the events in this chapter. We also have seen that Snape seems to have a particular interest in the forbidden Third Floor corridor, the trap door, and perhaps what is underneath it.

QUESTIONS

Further Study 1. Why would Snape treat his own leg wound, or get assistance from Filch, instead of visiting Madam Pomfrey in the Hospital Wing?

GREATER PICTURE

There is one timing issue in this chapter, which perhaps adds to the suspicion on Snape (as opposed to Quirrell). As Hermione is rushing along the teacher's row to reach Professor Snape, she knocks Professor Quirrell over; but then "It took perhaps thirty seconds for Snape to realize that he was on fire." Thirty seconds is a long time, when you're trying to counter a jinx or doing something that requires that level of concentration; so for thirty seconds Snape is trying to stop a jinx that is no longer going on, because Quirrell has been knocked over and has had his concentration broken. It is possible that the author meant something closer to five seconds, which would be more reasonable all around.

As can be seen here, if the Trio have a weakness it is a tendency to become stubbornly fixed on a single idea; their determined belief that Snape has malevolent intentions could have had nasty consequences at the Quidditch match had luck not favoured them.

In what has been hailed as one of the better displays of the interconnectedness of the series, the fact that Harry catches the Snitch in his mouth will become a plot point in the seventh book.

Chapter 12: The Mirror of Erised

SYNOPSIS

Now that they have the name "Nicholas Flamel," Hermione, Ron, and Harry are spending all their spare time in the library, trying to find out who he is, a pastime that annoys Hagrid, when he finds out about it. Despite searching for a fortnight, however, they have not found him by Christmas break, when Hermione returns home for the holidays. Ron is staying at Hogwarts because his parents are going off to visit their son Charlie in Romania and Harry is staying because Hogwarts is more of a home to him than Privet Drive ever could be. Hermione reminds them to keep looking for information on Flamel.

On Christmas Day, both Harry and Ron receive gifts. Among Harry's are a sweater from Mrs. Weasley, and an Invisibility Cloak from an anonymous sender. The note with the cloak says that it had been Harry's father's, and advises him to use it well.

Christmas Dinner is very merry, including various magical accessories and truly amazing amounts of food. Following dinner, Harry remembers the Invisibility Cloak, and decides to explore the Restricted section of the library in the hopes of finding Flamel's name. The first book he selects, however, screams when opened, causing Harry to break his lamp, and attracts Filch. On the run from Filch, he ends up in a room containing a magic mirror, which shows him standing amidst a crowd of people. On inspection, this crowd turns out to be his parents and relations—not the Dursleys, but his magical relatives.

Harry wakes Ron up and brings him down also to see this mirror, so that Ron can see Harry's parents, but Ron instead sees himself with a Head Boy's badge, and holding the Quidditch Cup.

Harry repeats his visit to the mirror a few times, eventually being surprised in the act by Professor Dumbledore. Dumbledore identifies the mirror as the Mirror of Erised, and that it shows "only the deepest desire of our hearts." When asked what he sees when he looks into the mirror, Dumbledore replies that he sees himself holding a pair of socks, which Harry suspects is a lie. Dumbledore then says that he is going to hide the mirror, and asks Harry to not seek it out again.

Analysis

Family has recently become very important to Harry: raised by the Dursleys, who barely mask their contempt for him, Harry was largely unaware of his lack. Recently, though, exposure to Ron Weasley and his family has allowed Harry to begin to understand what it feels like to be part of a family, and to have people who are concerned about him. He is touched when Mrs. Weasley, knowing that he wouldn't be receiving many gifts from other people, sends him Christmas presents.

By looking in the Mirror of Erised, Harry gets his first glimpse of his real family. He is transfixed by the sight of his parents and relatives he never knew, and so continues to come back to look in the mirror at his parents. Dumbledore explains the way the mirror works, and it is apparent at this point in his life, Harry wishes more than anything to have a normal life with his family restored to him.

Questions

Further Study   1. When Harry asks Dumbledore what he sees when he looks into the Mirror, Dumbledore replies that he sees himself holding a pair of socks. Is that really what Dumbledore sees?

Greater Picture

Harry's desire to have an ordinary, peaceful life with a family around him is a feeling which will follow him throughout his story. It will also serve as an incentive that will drive him to do what he needs to do. After asking what Dumbledore sees in the mirror, Harry thinks to himself that he has just asked a very impertinent question, and much later in the series comes to the conclusion that Dumbledore had not been entirely truthful. It is revealed much later, in *Harry Potter and the Deathly Hallows*, that Dumbledore's heart's desire is the same as Harry's—to be reunited with his departed family, especially his mother Kendra and sister Ariana. At this stage in the books, we do not know who had returned the Invisibility Cloak to Harry. At the end of this book, it will be revealed that, in fact, Dumbledore was the sender. However, that raises a very large question. When Harry is caught at the Mirror of Erised, Dumbledore mentions that he does not need a cloak to be invisible. We will learn later that invisibility can be provided by a spell, the Disillusionment charm, and we can guess that Dumbledore is very good at it. Why, then, would Dumbledore want James Potter's Invisibility Cloak? He has no need for it, after all. This last point is particularly of interest, as the author mentions that it is a peculiarly never-asked question.[1] It will be a key issue in the final book in the series, as it turns out that the Cloak is one of the Deathly Hallows of the title. It should be noted that there is technique involved in concealing the fact that this is even a question. The previous ownership of the Invisibility Cloak is separated in the text from Dumbledore's statement that he doesn't need one, by several exciting events, even though the two do fall in the same chapter, and the admission that it was Dumbledore who had been keeping the Cloak for the intervening decade is several chapters ahead. This separation of the three parts of the paradox removes the immediacy that makes it a question that the reader thinks about. Dumbledore's interest in this Cloak will be echoed again in the seventh book.

Chapter 13: Nicholas Flamel

Synopsis

Quidditch practice is picking up again as Harry and the rest of the team prepare for an upcoming match against Hufflepuff. Harry is horrified to be told that Professor Snape will be refereeing this match, as are Ron and Hermione when he tells them.

Harry gives a Chocolate Frog to Neville, who gives him back the card; Harry sees that it is the card of Albus Dumbledore, and suddenly recalls that it was on that card that he had seen Nicholas Flamel's name: *Professor Dumbledore is particularly famous for his defeat of the dark wizard Grindelwald in 1945, for the discovery of the twelve uses of dragon's blood, and his work on alchemy with his partner Nicholas Flamel*. The mention of Alchemy reminds Hermione of a book she had taken out of the library which mentions Flamel as being now 665 years old. Further research leads Harry, Ron, an Hermione to the conclusion that the mysterious package Hagrid had brought to the school was in fact the only known instance of the Philosopher's Stone. Eternal life and all the gold you could want. No wonder Snape wants it, they think . . .

Harry decides to play Quidditch even with Snape refereeing. In the course of the game, a fight breaks out in the stands between some of the Gryffindors (notably Ron and Neville) and some of the Slytherins (led by Draco Malfoy). The match lasts only about five minutes as Harry spots and catches the Snitch before Snape has been able to do more than award one penalty to Hufflepuff.

After the match, Harry sees Snape enter the Forbidden Forest. Using his broom, he is able to get close enough to eavesdrop on a conversation between Snape and Professor Quirrell. The conversation confirms Harry, Ron, and Hermione's belief that the package is the Philosopher's Stone, and leads them to conclude that Quirrell is the only thing standing between Snape and the Stone.

Analysis

Much of this chapter actually serves as reinforcement.

• Harry gives Neville the Chocolate Frog because Neville has been jinxed by Draco Malfoy. This serves to reinforce both Draco's disdain for rules and for Gryffindors, and Neville's relative incompetence.
• Snape's refereeing of the match allows some further reinforcement of his dislike of Gryffindor House in general, and Harry in particular.
• Harry's overhearing Snape and Quirrell serves to reinforce Harry's belief, and thus also Ron's and

---

1. http://www.jkrowling.com/textonly/en/extrastuff_view.cfm?id=23

Hermione's, that Snape is trying to get the Philosopher's Stone, and poor, weak Quirrell is trying to stop him.

The only major plot advance at this point is the discovery that it is, in fact, the Philosopher's Stone that is being guarded on the one hand, and sought on the other. We are given some clue as well to its usefulness by being told the length of time that Flamel has been alive. Clearly, some of the Stone's function has to do with prolonging life. We will find out a bit more than this shortly.

GREATER PICTURE

At one point in this chapter, Harry notices that he seems to be running into Snape far more frequently than usual. He wonders if Snape knows that he, Ron, and Hermione have found out about the Philosopher's Stone, and he has the horrible feeling that Snape can read minds. Harry has felt this to a greater or lesser degree a number of times, but this is the first time he has expressed the thought this clearly, even to himself. This will be a recurring concern for Harry, and will come to full fruition in the fifth book in the series.

Once again, Harry's single-minded view of Snape's character twists his perspective on the things he witnesses, so that he can only see one possible interpretation. This persistent prejudice towards Snape will come back to haunt Harry as the larger story reaches its climax.

We do not yet have any idea that Voldemort is still around, apart from Hagrid's earlier comment that he thinks Voldemort was "too evil to die." We will, however, receive a large hint in that direction shortly, when a Centaur speaks with Harry about the uses of Unicorn blood.

Chapter 14: Norbert the Norwegian Ridgeback

Synopsis

Professor Quirrell, though, seems to prove stronger than expected, as Fluffy remains alert and growling behind the door. But with only 10 weeks left until end of the year exams, Hermione starts laying out timetables for studying and insisting that Harry and Ron do likewise. So it is when they are studying in the library that they find Hagrid taking a book out of the dragon section. Asked directly about Nicholas Flamel and the Philosopher's Stone, he promises to tell them something about it, but not in the library; students aren't supposed to know about it.

At Hagrid's hut, they find out that the Stone is protected by Fluffy, and enchantments by Professors Sprout, Flitwick, McGonagall, Quirrell, Dumbledore, and . . . Professor Snape. This is alarming as of course Snape is the one who is trying to get the Stone, but to add to the confusion, it turns out Hagrid has won a dragon's egg from someone down in the village, and is planning to hatch it despite living in a wooden house.

In due course, the egg hatches. Hagrid invites Harry, Ron and Hermione down to witness it. Draco Malfoy unfortunately overhears and sees the dragon hatch as well, through Hagrid's window. Of course, this means that they will have to get rid of it somehow, before Malfoy tells Professor Dumbledore. Harry has an idea: Ron's brother Charlie is working with dragons in Romania, maybe he can find Norbert (as Hagrid has named the dragon) a home. Hagrid is not happy about this, but finally agrees, and Charlie also agrees.

Malfoy manages to find out about Charlie's schedule, and is waiting when Harry and Hermione (Ron being incapacitated by a dragon bite) carry a crated Norbert towards the tower where Charlie's friends will take him away. Harry and Hermione see him being caught by Professor McGonagall, who penalizes him twenty House points, and gives him detention. Harry and Hermione, safe beneath the Invisibility Cloak, make it to the top of the tower and see Norbert off, but then are caught by Filch on their way back to the dormitory—in their excitement, they have forgotten the Cloak on the top of the tower.

Analysis

At first glance, this chapter seems to have little purpose in the book—Norbert is introduced and sent away all in one chapter and never re-appears in the series, except occasionally Hagrid gets to missing him, and there is a mention in passing in the seventh book. The purpose of the chapter seems to be largely preparatory.

Part of the purpose is making the need to get to the stone more urgent. The Trio at this point quite firmly believe, and with reason, that it is Professor Snape who is seeking the Stone. Knowing that Snape was involved in setting up the guardians for it, they are sure that he also now knows enough about the guardian spells to start making his way through them.

Another part of the purpose is setting up the scene in the Forbidden Forest, in the next chapter. Without detention, there would be no need for Harry to go into the Forest, and no way for him to witness the events that occur there. A third part of the purpose is actually setting up the final scene in the book. As we have not reached that scene yet, we will not discuss it here, except to say that a victory is sweeter if it follows, and reverses, a defeat.

And finally, this chapter shines a light on part of the character of Draco Malfoy. Having found that he has an advantage over Hagrid and the Trio, in that he knows Hagrid is doing something horribly illegal and the Trio is helping him do it, he does not report this to the authorities. Instead, he holds this knowledge tight, using it to torment Ron in the hospital wing, and trying to get additional advantage out of the situation. This is classic Slytherin deviousness and ambition.

Questions

Further Study 1. How did Charlie's friends fly to the school to get Norbert if there are numerous enchantments protecting the school?

GREATER PICTURE

As mentioned in the Analysis section, this chapter also is a significant part of the set-up for the final scenes in the book. Having been instrumental in losing a huge number of House Points for Gryffindor, as Harry will be in the opening pages of the next chapter, how much sweeter is it that he is also instrumental in winning them all back, and more?

Norbert does reappear in passing in the seventh book. Hagrid and Charlie happen to be together at the Weasley home, and Hagrid inquires about Norbert. Charlie says that they are calling her Norberta now. Hagrid asks how they know she is female, and Charlie says that the females are more fierce.

In this chapter we also see Harry's willingness to break rules if he has a good reason. This ability to think independently will be useful in later years as more and more daunting tasks are put before him.

Chapter 15: The Forbidden Forest

SYNOPSIS

When Filch hauls Hermione and Harry up before their head of house, Professor McGonagall, she already has Neville in front of her for being out and wandering the halls so late. Neville says he was on his way to warn Harry, which leads Professor McGonagall to believe that Harry and Hermione had made up this story about the dragon specifically to lure Draco out into the halls at midnight, in the hopes of getting him detention. She assigns detention for all three of them, and penalizes each of them fifty House points. (She had earlier penalized Malfoy twenty points and given him detention.) In one night, Harry has been involved in an action that bumped Gryffindor to the bottom of the standings in House points. He resolves not to get involved in anything else except schoolwork, and to avoid anything that might cost more House points.

Detention takes place about a week before exams. Filch meets Harry, Hermione, Neville, and Draco in the Entrance Hall, and takes them down to Hagrid's hut. Hagrid tells them that something in the Forbidden Forest has been killing unicorns, and tells them that they are going to separate into two parties, and follow the trails of unicorn blood from a wounded unicorn in hopes of finding what it is, and if necessary put the unicorn out of its misery. Hagrid, Harry, and Hermione will be one party, Draco and Neville, with Fang (Hagrid's boarhound), will be the other. They separate. Hagrid hears something unexpected, a sort of slithery sound, but can't find what caused it. Hagrid's party then meets with Ronan the centaur. Ronan makes a few remarks about astronomy, and the party is then joined by Bane, another centaur, who also comments on astronomy. Hagrid leaves the centaurs, then Hermione sees red wand sparks, and Hagrid runs off to investigate, leaving Harry and Hermione standing on the path.

It turns out Draco had frightened Neville, and he had panicked and sent up the sparks. Hagrid, figuring Harry would be harder to scare, re-groups Harry with Draco and Fang, taking Hermione and Neville. After about an hour, Harry and Draco find the unicorn, dead. Then they hear the slithery noise again, and a hooded figure appears and starts drinking the unicorn's blood. Malfoy and Fang run away. The hooded figure starts advancing on Harry, whose scar starts searing with pain.

A centaur appears and chases away the hooded figure. He introduces himself as Firenze, tells Harry that the forest is not a safe place for him, and offers him a ride back to Hagrid. Ronan and Bane gallop alongside, angry at Firenze for allowing a human to ride him "as if he were a common mule," and also for interfering with the portents of the heavens. Firenze departs with Harry, saying that he will fight the evil, even alongside humans if he must. As they head back to Hagrid, Firenze explains that unicorn blood will keep you alive, "even if you are only an inch from death," but it will be a cursed sort of half-life. Harry wonders why that would be better than death. Firenze says maybe the hooded figure is waiting for something stronger, that will restore him to full life. Harry realizes that this means the Elixir of Life, a product of the Philosopher's Stone, and comes to the conclusion that the hooded creature is Voldemort, who is probably only somewhat alive, as Hagrid had said back in July. They reach Hagrid at this point, who lets the students return to the castle. Harry then tells Ron and Hermione what has been happening overnight, and they conclude that Voldemort is now just waiting for Professor Snape to get the Stone, and then will reappear to kill Harry.

There is one last surprise in the night: when Harry reaches his bed as dawn nears, he finds his Invisibility Cloak, neatly folded, with a note: *"Just in case."*

ANALYSIS

In this chapter we have learned that it is quite likely that Voldemort is still alive, even if only just, and that he is taking measures to return to life. We are also introduced to the Centaurs who inhabit the forest, and get a taste of their feelings about humanity and Wizard-kind. In particular, we can see, even after exposure to only three centaurs, that there are clearly factions among them, those like Ronan and Bane who would have nothing to do with Humans, and those like Firenze who are willing to put aside their feelings about "inferior races" for the good of all involved. This is also our first introduction to the Forbidden Forest and the creatures that live in it. We can guess at this point that the Forbidden Forest will play at least some role in the remainder of the story.

There is one other, small point of interest. Harry's Invisibility Cloak is returned to him by apparently the same person who had originally given it to him for Christmas. We recall that Harry and Hermione had left the Cloak on the top of the Astronomy Tower. The Astronomy Tower will be in fairly frequent use, as Astronomy students do their practical work there; it would be a reasonable assumption, in fact, that there would be a class up there every clear night. Wizards being subject to the same foibles as any other humans, we can safely guess that it is unlikely that the Cloak would have been returned to Harry if a student had found it. So whoever had found it must be an adult, one who is either commonly up on the Astronomy Tower during daylight, or else is singularly aware of everything passing in the school. The person in question must be a teacher, as no student would have been able to borrow the Cloak from Harry's father, but we cannot yet be certain which. We can, however, rule out Professor McGonagall, as Harry recognizes the handwriting as having been the same as on the initial note, and does not recognize it as hers, though a note from her accompanied his broom in September. While we, as readers, are beginning to suspect that the "oddly spiky" handwriting might be Professor Dumbledore's, Harry does not feel himself to be important enough to merit that level of attention from the school's Headmaster, and so dismisses the possibility.

QUESTIONS

Further Study   1. Ronan and Bane both comment that Mars is shining brightly. Mars is the Roman god of war. Are these comments meant to foreshadow upcoming events in the wizarding world?

GREATER PICTURE

We will shortly find out that the unidentified figure who is killing the unicorn is, in fact, Quirrell. The actions of Quirrell, who we will later find out is entirely under the control of Voldemort, show that Voldemort will stop at nothing to regain his power. He shows no remorse for killing the unicorn, and indeed, shows no remorse for any of his actions that lead to others' deaths. Given that his soul has been split into pieces and stored in horcruxes, Voldemort is not quite human. While his physical appearance in a later book would seem to bear out his lack of humanity, we should bear in mind that Voldemort's physical appearance is likely something that he chose himself: as the self-proclaimed heir of Slytherin, and thus with great affinity for snakes, Voldemort very likely has chosen to model himself physically on a snake. We will find out that he didn't always look like a snake, even after he had started creating Horcruxes.

Chapter 16: Through the Trapdoor

SYNOPSIS

End of term exam time comes, with both written and practical tests. Harry can't figure out how he was able to take exams while worrying that Voldemort was about to burst through the door and kill him. With the end of exams, Ron and Hermione are relaxed, but Harry is not; his scar is hurting more than ever, which indicates danger is coming.

It suddenly dawns on Harry that he has to check something with Hagrid—he needs more detail about where the dragon's egg had come from. They're not exactly the sort of thing one carries around idly after all. Hagrid, confronted, says he doesn't know what the man he won the egg from looked like, because he kept his cloak on. Hagrid also mentions that he had told this stranger that Fluffy the three-headed dog would calm right down if he was played a bit of music.

Harry, Ron, and Hermione now know that someone knows how to get past the three-headed dog, and they run off to tell Professor Dumbledore, but Professor McGonagall informs them that he is not at Hogwarts, he has been called away to London. They try to trail Professor Snape, but fail in doing so. Harry resolves to go down the trap door as soon as the Gryffindor common room clears; Hermione and Ron immediately elect to go with him. As they prepare to leave, Neville notices them and attempts to stop them from leaving, he can't stand to let them lose any more House points for Gryffindor. Hermione is forced to put him in a full body bind so they can leave the common room. Under the Invisibility Cloak, they make their way to the third-floor corridor, finding the door already open. Using the flute that Hagrid had given Harry for Christmas, Harry plays Fluffy to sleep and then they jump down through the trap door, right into a crop of Devil's Snare. Hermione recognizes it, and manages to neutralize it. From there, they end up in a chamber that they can escape only by catching a flying key with the aid of a broomstick. Naturally, Harry manages this. The next trap is a Wizard chess set. Ron navigates them across this by winning the game, but in the process is incapacitated. After checking that he is still alive, Harry and Hermione pass through a chamber in which there is a troll, luckily already knocked out, and move on to the next challenge, a logic puzzle, which Hermione solves. However, only one can proceed forward. Harry chooses to go on, sending Hermione back to help Ron, and to send an owl to summon Dumbledore. Harry then proceeds into the last chamber. And there is someone there, but it isn't Snape, and it isn't Voldemort.

ANALYSIS

In this chapter we start to see the Trio working together, and the strength they have as a group. Each of the three has a vital role to play in helping Harry reach the Philosopher's Stone. No one of them, nor even two of them, could have succeeded in reaching the Stone. Hermione's knowledge was required to free them from the Devil's Snare and to defeat the logic puzzle; Harry's flying ability was required to catch the key; and Ron's chess-playing ability was required on the Wizard Chess board. Notably, however, they were not simply taking turns. Ron had to remind Hermione about making a light to evade the Devil's Snare, and Harry needed Ron's and Hermione's help on brooms to corner the key.

It was mentioned earlier that a number of teachers had provided protection for the Stone. In order, that would be Hagrid (Fluffy), Professor Sprout (Devil's Snare), Professor Flitwick (charmed keys), Professor McGonagall (wizard chess set), Professor Quirrell (troll), and Professor Snape (potions for the logic puzzle). While we have been told that Professor Dumbledore has also provided protection, we have not yet seen the form his magic will take. The logic puzzle Hermione solves is interesting, in that we see the question, and the solution, but not the initial setup. The solution, as determined by Hermione, is that the smallest bottle will take you forwards, and the one at the right end of the line will take you back. Clearly, from the arrangement of the bottles and the associated clues, it is possible for Hermione to determine which potion is which. Is it possible, from the clues and Hermione's solution, to work backwards and determine what the arrangement must have been? In fact, it does not, as the third clue is based on the sizes of the bottles, which we are not told; however, it does refine it to one of two possible setups, either of which is uniquely solvable from the clues provided. A discussion of this puzzle, and the possible solutions, appears on the Discussion page for this chapter.

Questions

Further Study 1. If someone had previously passed through the room, why then were all the potions in the logic puzzle still present? Would that person not have had to drink the "onwards" potion at least? And if it was some form of magically refilling bottle, why would only Harry to be able to proceed?

Greater Picture

This chapter is almost pure action; there is very little here that is carried forwards to further books. However, the following points should be mentioned.

Neville standing up to the Trio is the first occasion where we have seen him evince any sort of bravery. Until now, he has seemed to be ineffectual, very weak magically, and at the mercy of the passing scene. Here, for the first time, we see him standing up against opposition; futilely, to be sure, but he is standing up for what he believes. This marks the start of a trend of maturation and increasing strength that will result, by the seventh book, in Neville being leader of an underground resistance to a Dark organization.

Hermione here shows some concern for Ron; it is impossible to judge, at this early stage, whether this is the start of the relationship that develops in books six and seven, but one could say that a seed has been sown here. It is perhaps interesting that Ron's words here to Hermione, "*Are you a witch, or what?*" are echoed precisely by Hermione, speaking to Ron near the end of *Harry Potter and the Deathly Hallows*. While this was certainly a conscious choice by the author, one must wonder whether it was meant to be a conscious choice by Hermione.

Chapter 17: The Man with Two Faces

Synopsis

Note: This chapter ties up a large number of plot threads in a relatively small space. In order to catch the necessary high points, the synopsis must be relatively long.

The man in the final chamber is Quirrell. But a changed Quirrell, no longer twitching and stuttering, no longer unsure of himself. Quirrell is quick to point out that being seen as ineffective, particularly alongside Snape, is a very effective disguise. Snape was suspected of all the mischief that Quirrell had done, such as enchanting Harry's broom in the Quidditch match against Slytherin — apparently Snape was working a countercharm, and it was Hermione knocking Quirrell off his feet that stopped the enchantment. Quirrell also admits to having let the troll into the dungeons at Halloween, so that he could look at what was guarding the Stone, in which he was also thwarted by Snape.

Now all that stands before him is the final guardian of the Stone, which Harry recognizes as the Mirror of Erised. While examining the Mirror, Quirrell mentions that Snape was at school with Harry's father, and that they hated each other. He also says that "his Master," which apparently means Lord Voldemort, is with him wherever he goes. When Quirrell is unable to decode the secret of the Mirror, he asks for help, and a voice tells him to "use the boy." Quirrel stands Harry in front of the mirror. Harry sees himself taking the Stone out of his pocket and finds that it is, in fact, in his pocket. He tells Quirrell that he sees himself winning the Quidditch cup, but the mysterious voice says he's lying and demands to speak to Harry face to face. Quirrell demurs, but eventually removes his turban to reveal a second face on the back of his head, that of Lord Voldemort. Voldemort orders Quirrell to seize Harry, but Quirrell cannot — his skin burns and blisters when he tries. Quirrell prepares to curse Harry to death but Harry grabs his opponent's face, and Quirrell is in too much pain to utter the jinx. But by now, the pain in Harry's head, from his scar, is enough to drive him out of consciousness.

Harry wakes up in the hospital wing, with Professor Dumbledore in attendance. Dumbledore tells him that Quirrell did not get the stone, that Dumbledore arrived just in time to save Harry from Quirrell, and that the Stone has been destroyed. Yes, that means Nicholas Flamel and his wife Perenelle will die, but they have enough time to get their affairs in order, and "after all, to the well-organized mind, death is but the next great adventure." Dumbledore agrees with Harry that Voldemort is still out there, possibly looking for another body to inhabit, possibly looking for some other way to return but refuses, for the moment, to explain to Harry why Voldemort wants to kill him. Quirrell could not touch Harry, according to Dumbledore, because Harry's mother died to save him, and a love that strong provides protection against some forms of magic. Dumbledore also admits to having been the source of the Invisibility Cloak which Harry has been using — Harry's father had left it in Dumbledore's care. Dumbledore also mentions that the reason Snape seems to hate Harry so much is because Harry's father saved Snape's life, leaving Snape in his debt, something that has continued to bother Snape. Dumbledore then mentions that Harry got the Stone out of the Mirror because the enchantment on the mirror was such that if someone wanted to use the Stone, they would only see themselves using it, but someone who wanted to find it but not use it, would find it.

After Dumbledore's departure, Ron and Hermione are allowed to visit. Harry lets them know what had happened in the last chamber and what Dumbledore had told him. They come to the conclusion that Dumbledore had allowed Harry to fight Voldemort, if he chose, rather than trying to protect him from Voldemort. Next day, Harry has another visitor: Hagrid. Hagrid is in tears, because he was the one who had given

Chapter 17: The Man with Two Faces

Quirrell the final piece of information he needed in order to figure out how to reach the Stone. Harry manages to calm him, and Hagrid remembers that he has a gift for Harry. The gift is a photo album, containing wizarding pictures of Harry's parents.

Late in the day, Madam Pomfrey, the nurse, relents and lets Harry go to the end-of-term feast. There, after much good food, Professor Dumbledore rises to award the House Cup. Slytherin is in the lead, in part because without Harry in the final match, Ravenclaw defeated Gryffindor rather badly at Quidditch, and in part because of all the points Harry lost in the Norbert debacle. "However, recent events must be taken into account—I have some last-minute points to dish out." Harry, Ron, Hermione, and—surprisingly—Neville have earned between them enough house points to regain the lead and win the House cup for Gryffindor.

Exam results appear and while Hermione, as expected, is top of her class, both Ron and Harry have managed decent passes, and even Neville has managed to scrape through. And finally it's time for the Hogwarts Express to take everybody back home. Ron and Hermione promise to write, and Ron promises to invite them both to stay with him. And although they have all received notes telling them they are not allowed to do magic outside of school, Harry knows that the Dursleys have no idea about that. "I'm going to have a lot of fun with Dudley this summer . . ."

ANALYSIS

Clearly the big surprise here is that it is not Snape, but Quirrell, who is behind the ongoing attack on Harry. We already know of Snape's dislike of Harry, and Harry of course is equally aware of it. It is because of this dislike that Harry has evidently decided Snape is the main mover behind the attacks. It does not occur to Harry that there might be other reasons behind Snape's dislike of him, as it does not occur to him that such obvious dislike would make Snape the main suspect in any attack against Harry. Snape's dislike of Harry is widely known, even among the staff, though Dumbledore seems to discount it somewhat; it is almost certain that Snape will have been interrogated following the attacks on Harry and will have been cleared. Harry apparently assumes that as he has not heard of such questioning, it has not happened. It does not seem to occur to him that teachers might not feel a need to discuss disciplinary details with an 11-year-old student.

Many fan sites have pointed out a discrepancy in this chapter. Hermione says that she found Dumbledore in the Entrance Hall as she was on her way to send an owl to him. Yet the trap door is in the third-floor hallway, and the Owlery, we will find later, is high in the castle, on the seventh floor. Why would Hermione head down to the main floor on her way from the third to the seventh floor? One possible answer to this can actually be found in the Harry Potter films, in which we see a large central stairwell in the castle. Combine that with Percy's earlier warning that the stairways like to move, and it is entirely possible that Hermione, emerging from the third floor corridor, would have found herself on the side of the central stairwell away from the Owlery with no staircases leading upwards at that moment. On her way downwards to find a staircase that would bridge the gap, she might either have been forced all the way to the Entry Hall, or else happened to see Dumbledore, below her, as he returned to the castle. The speculation provided above is intended to quiet one of the few small issues that can hamper the enjoyment of the story; it is unsupported by anything in the books.

QUESTIONS

Further Study 1. Why did Dumbledore have Harry's father's invisibility cloak at the time of his death, given that Dumbledore could make himself invisible without a cloak?

GREATER PICTURE

In this chapter, Harry survives his second encounter with Lord Voldemort, and that which protected him the first time, his mother's love, protects him again, and apparently will continue to protect him. We will later learn that part of this protection is based on his having a home where someone of his mother's blood (in this case, her sister, Harry's Aunt Petunia) lives. This is why Harry must return to Privet Drive each summer, as much as he hates it. This is also the first place where the seeming hatred between James Potter and Severus Snape is mentioned. This is featured prominently in the later books, especially the fifth. As this apparent hatred is one of the axes on which the series plot turns, we will see it repeatedly over the entire story arc, and will eventually learn the full reasons for it.

One of the key questions driving the series is asked here for the first time, as well, and is not answered. Harry asks why Voldemort is trying to kill him, and Dumbledore says that he must refuse to answer that. We will learn later that there is a prophecy that says that either Harry or Voldemort must die, as "neither can live while the other survives." Dumbledore feels that as a child of 11 years, Harry is still too young to learn this, arguably extremely harsh, fact. The prophecy will be revealed to Harry in four years, along with Dumbledore's reasons for withholding it. In this chapter, also, Dumbledore voices one of the philosophies that centers the series: "after all, to the well-organized mind, death is but the next great adventure." This does not, at first glance, seem to be a particularly useful philosophy, but it will turn out that this is the key difference between Voldemort and those who would defeat him. Much of the series revolves around death and the attitudes towards it. Voldemort, we will find, fears death, to the point of killing other people in cold blood in order to preserve his own life. Dumbledore, and to a large extent Harry, are prepared to die, if necessary, to destroy the great evil that Voldemort represents. It is the one who is prepared to meet death, on his own terms, who fully masters it; running away from death will not allow one to avoid it. It is because of this that Harry, we are told, is the stronger wizard when he meets Voldemort and duels him near the end of book 4.

CHAMBER OF SECRETS

CHAPTERS

   Chapter 1: The Worst Birthday
   Chapter 2: Dobby's Warning
   Chapter 3: The Burrow
   Chapter 4: At Flourish and Blotts
   Chapter 5: The Whomping Willow
   Chapter 6: Gilderoy Lockhart
   Chapter 7: Mudbloods and Murmurs
   Chapter 8: The Deathday Party
   Chapter 9: The Writing on the Wall
   Chapter 10: The Rogue Bludger
   Chapter 11: The Dueling Club
   Chapter 12: The Polyjuice Potion
   Chapter 13: The Very Secret Diary
   Chapter 14: Cornelius Fudge
   Chapter 15: Aragog
   Chapter 16: The Chamber of Secrets
   Chapter 17: The Heir of Slytherin
   Chapter 18: Dobby's Reward

OVERVIEW

The second book in the Harry Potter series, *Harry Potter and the Chamber of Secrets* is written from the point of view of the now-12-year-old Harry Potter. The book's title refers to a chamber which was, according to legend, created in Hogwarts castle by one of the founders, Salazar Slytherin, at the time of his departure from Hogwarts; and much of the action of the book revolves around that chamber, and what may be in it, if in fact it exists.

BOOK HIGHLIGHTS

• New places visited: Whomping Willow, The Burrow, Knockturn Alley, Slytherin common room, Chamber of Secrets
• New characters met: Dobby, Mr. Weasley, Gilderoy Lockhart, Moaning Myrtle, Colin Creevey, Lucius Malfoy
• *Defence Against the Dark Arts* teacher: Gilderoy Lockhart
• Title refers to: the Chamber of Secrets.

Chapter 1: The Worst Birthday

SYNOPSIS

Harry has returned to stay with the Durlseys for the summer holidays, and things are not running smoothly. On Harry's birthday, Harry and Uncle Vernon have an argument over breakfast, triggered by Dudley commanding Harry to pass him the bacon, and Harry informing him that he forgot the magic word. The mere mention of magic or anything like it is enough to send Uncle Vernon into a towering rage.

Uncle Vernon then launches into his plans for the evening, entertaining a prospective client, who was called Mr. Mason. Harry's part in these plans is very simple, reiterated many times: he will remain in his room, making no noise, pretending not to be there.

When Harry is sitting in the yard later that day, Dudley nastily reminds him that it is Harry's birthday and asks why all his "weird friends" have not even bothered to send him any cards or presents. Harry tells him he is trying to set the garden hedge on fire with magic; although he is only teasing, as he is not allowed to practice magic outside Hogwarts. But Dudley tells his aunt, and as a punishment for mentioning magic Harry has to work all day at cleaning the house.

That evening, as Mr. and Mrs. Mason arrive, Harry is sent to his room. However, when Harry enters the room, he is shocked to see there is someone sitting on his bed.

ANALYSIS

As is usual, this first chapter reinforces the framework for the contrast that will be echoed throughout the series between the magical and the mundane. In this chapter and the one following, we will see the spiritual poverty and deprivation of Harry's non-magical life.

QUESTIONS

Further Study   1. Harry notices something with very large, green eyes apparently looking at him from within the hedge. What or who could this be? Is magic sneaking into the staunchly Muggle environs of Privet Drive?

GREATER PICTURE

We will find out shortly that the green eyes in the hedge belong to Dobby, a House-elf. Dobby will prove to be an important character throughout the remainder of the series.

What we see, mostly, in this chapter, is the characters of the Dursleys, the family that Harry has been living with. We see how they remain stolidly pinned to the fabric of the everyday, and how they live by the impression they make on their neighbours and associates. As the series progresses, we will see some character growth and change on the part of Dudley; he will eventually come to realize that there may be some good in magic. Vernon and Petunia will remain stubbornly convinced that magic is wrong. Petunia's reasons for this belief will eventually become clear to us; Vernon, likely, was simply the least magical person that Petunia could think of to marry.

Chapter 2: Dobby's Warning

SYNOPSIS

The strange creature on Harry's bed introduces himself as Dobby, the house-elf. Dobby is unable to reveal the wizarding family he works for, as he starts hitting himself uncontrollably each time he tries. He also needs to punish himself for speaking badly of his masters and for leaving his home without consent, yet he did this in order to deliver Harry a dire warning: He must not return to Hogwarts for terrible events will happen at the school. Dobby is once again unable to provide more details. When Harry refuses to stay home from Hogwarts, Dobby taunts him about how his friends have not written to him all summer. When Harry asks how Dobby had known about that, he admits having intercepted Harry's letters hoping that if Harry felt his friends did not care about him, he would not want to go back to school.

Furious, Harry chases Dobby downstairs, where the Dursleys are having dinner with the Masons. Dobby then uses his powers to levitate Aunt Petunia's cake and threatens to let it fall unless Harry promises not to return to Hogwarts. Harry refuses, so Dobby drops the cake, filling the Dursley's spotless kitchen with cream before vanishing magically. The noise attracts the attention of the Dursleys, who blame Harry. At first it seems Uncle Vernon manages to gloss things over, explaining to the Masons that his nephew is slightly disturbed, but then an owl arrives with a message for Harry, scaring Mrs. Mason and dashing Uncle Vernon's hopes for a huge business opportunity. The letter is an official warning from Mafalda Hopkirk at the Ministry of Magic. Apparently, Harry has violated the Decree for the Reasonable Restriction of Underage Sorcery by performing a Hover Charm, and the letter states that further use of magic on Harry's part away from school could lead to his expulsion from Hogwarts. Uncle Vernon tells Harry to read the letter aloud, and decides to lock Harry into his bedroom and bar the window, now knowing that he can not use magic to break out.

Three days later, Harry is awoken by rattling at the bars across his window, and finds Ron peering in at him in the moonlight.

ANALYSIS

Harry, it turns out, is once again being manipulated by forces beyond his control. In this case, a house-elf has apparently decided to try and keep him away from Hogwarts, nominally for his own protection. Harry, believing in his own strength, seems not to consider that there could be any danger to him at Hogwarts, at least not one serious enough to prevent him returning to the place he feels most at home.

The letter from the Ministry is clearly a surprise to Harry. While he had been cautioned about use of magic at home, he had not been aware that he was being monitored by the Ministry. Harry's obvious fear in the kitchen earlier, as far as we know, was occasioned purely by the concern that Vernon would hear him, and would be enraged at Harry's having violated the instructions he was given. Harry knows that Vernon still has significant power over him and can make his time most uncomfortable. Harry may also fear that Vernon may be able to prevent his returning to Hogwarts, a fear that seems manifest when Harry's bedroom is turned into a virtual jail cell.

Throughout the course of this chapter, the tension gradually mounts as the chances of Harry's returning to the place he loves seem to grow ever more remote. With the appearance of Ron at the window, there is an immediate sense of relief, but associated with this comes a question: Ron, equally, is underage. Though he is now aware of the situation, what can he do to help Harry escape it?

QUESTIONS

Further Study 1. How could Dobby, as a servant in another wizard household, be able to stop Harry's mail for all that time without his masters' noticing his absence?

2. Why was Dobby's magic noticed, and not the magic that Hagrid used in the first book?

GREATER PICTURE

Though we don't yet know this, as Dobby cannot tell Harry, it will turn out that Dobby is the house-elf of the Malfoy family. Perhaps not surprisingly, the poor condition of Dobby shows how the Malfoys treat their inferiors. We have already seen this attitude toward those the Malfoys deem less than themselves, as Draco has displayed it towards both Harry and Ron, and we will see that it continues almost throughout the series. It is the similarity of this shabby treatment of Dobby by his family, with the treatment of Ron, Hermione, and Harry by Draco, that leads the reader to guess, possibly even before Harry does, that Dobby is the Malfoy house-elf.

Dobby, while never a major character, will yet prove extremely useful to Harry during the course of the series. We can see here that Dobby is violating orders to speak to Harry; we gather that it is because Dobby is aware of how the lot of House-Elves have improved since the fall of the Dark Lord, and, aware that the Malfoys are somehow planning mischief at Hogwarts, has taken it upon himself to warn Harry. Dobby's freely-given loyalty to Harry will continue throughout the series, and will only be enhanced by Harry's treating Dobby with the respect due an equal. The contrast between Dobby's response to Harry's needs, and his responses to the Malfoys, provides something of an object lesson in the value of loyalty freely given against that which is demanded.

It should perhaps be noted here that Dobby's low expectations for treatment from humans seem to be common across all House Elves; we will see it again in Winky and Kreacher. Later, we will see that Ron also treats House Elves as menials, though both Harry and Hermione do not; Hermione is even moved to create a student organization, S.P.E.W., to try and get some rights for them. Perhaps Harry's being raised in a non-magical household, which has prevented him learning of the existence of house-elves, has also isolated him from the prevailing beliefs that house-elves should be treated as an under-class.

The specific thing that the Malfoys have planned is the return of Tom Riddle's diary to the school. It is always uncertain whether Lucius Malfoy is entirely aware of exactly what the result of this will be; the diary, we will later learn, had likely been given to him with information that would lead him to believe it was an anti-Mudblood weapon, though not precisely how it would act. If he had known that the weapon was only barely controlled and somewhat indiscriminate, it is likely Lucius would have balked at putting it in proximity to his son Draco. It is mentioned elsewhere that stories about magic have a very real danger: by making anything possible and largely effortless, it becomes far too easy for the hero to succeed, and the story becomes uninteresting. The Decree for the Reasonable Restriction of Underage Sorcery is one of the more intriguing ways that the author has developed to provide limits on the magic. Harry certainly could make his life easier by judicious use of magic during his summer vacations, but that would remove one of the points of interest in the story. The Dursleys, annoying as they are, will remain a useful contrast to Harry's life in Hogwarts, and his means of dealing with them without the use of magic will be a way of measuring his own increasing strength of character and maturity. The Decree will also provide a significant point of interest in the story in later books.

Chapter 3: The Burrow

Synopsis

Ron Weasley and his brothers Fred and George are outside Harry's window in a flying Ford Anglia. Ron says they have come to rescue him. They yank the bars off the window, freeing Harry. Fred and George gather Harry's Hogwarts belongings that are locked in the cupboard under the stairs.

As they are leaving, Hedwig screeches, reminding Harry that he has forgotten her. The screeching awakens Uncle Vernon, and he barges into Harry's room as Harry is half way out the window. He grabs Harry's ankle and attempts to pull him back in, but Harry manages to escape, and he, Ron, Fred, and George are off to the Weasleys' home, The Burrow.

On the ride there, Harry tells Ron, Fred, and George about Dobby, and they speculate about who owns him, eventually deciding that he could be the Malfoys.' Harry also learns that Draco Malfoy's father, Lucius Malfoy, once supported Lord Voldemort.

They arrive at The Burrow, only to find Mrs. Weasley waiting for them. She is furious over them "borrowing" the car. After yelling at Fred, George, and Ron, she greets Harry warmly. While eating breakfast, Harry meets, or rather gets a fleeting glimpse of, Ron's sister, Ginny.

As punishment for taking the car, Mrs. Weasley sets the twins and Ron the task of ridding the garden of gnomes, using a technique from *Gilderoy Lockhart's Guide to Household Pests.* Harry assists, even though Mrs. Weasley says he does not need to.

After degnoming the garden, Harry meets Arthur Weasley, and learns that he works for the Ministry of Magic. He is a fan of Muggle technology and gadgets.

Harry is overjoyed to get away from the Dursleys, and looks forward to spending the remaining summer with Ron.

Analysis

We mentioned, at the end of the last chapter, the question: what can Ron do? Ron is underage, and so are Fred and George, capable though they may be, so they cannot use magic to release Harry from his prison. However, apart from the flying car, which apparently does not trigger the prohibition against magic, Fred and George don't attempt to use magic to free Harry. The bars are pulled off his window by the car, and Fred and George pick the lock of his bedroom door and the lock on the cupboard under the stairs with a Muggle implement, a hairpin. Either Harry or Ron, it is not exactly made clear, then uses the same hairpin to pick the lock on Hedwig's cage, to allow Hedwig the first bit of freedom she has had all summer. It is never made clear in the series why casting a spell or presumably making a potion would trigger the prohibition against magic, but using a charmed object like the flying car would not; for some speculation on this matter, please see the article on The Decree for the Reasonable Restriction of Underage Sorcery.

Gilderoy Lockhart, who will play a large role in the book, is introduced in this chapter, although he is only mentioned by name. He is handsome ("'Mum fancies him,' said Fred in a very audible whisper"), and his solutions for problems look good, but only seem to work temporarily. By sunset, Harry, looking out Ron's window, can see the gnomes sneaking one-by-one back through the Weasley's hedge.

Ginny Weasley is reintroduced to the series, although she still only glances at Harry from afar; every time she sees him (twice in this chapter), she squeaks and runs away. Says Ron, "You don't know how weird it is for her to be this shy, she never shuts up normally..." This is a classic schoolgirl crush; she has built Harry up in her mind as some heroic figure, and now that he is actually physically in her presence, she is afraid to speak.

Greater Picture

Ginny's reaction to Harry makes it seem likely that their relationship is doomed. So many times, a schoolgirl crush simply fades over time, and Ginny's feelings to seem to have the superficiality of that sort of hero-worshiping relationship. Ginny, however, will be the center of several events that will bring her a great deal of maturity in a very short time, and her feelings for Harry will deepen as she comes to understand more about who he really is. Starting even before this chapter, Ginny will reward a more in-depth study, as we can see that the author writes a very realistic maturation for her, ending with a true romantic relationship with Harry.

Harry, even after only a day at The Burrow, has learned what a functional family is and how it interacts with itself. He thinks to himself, at the end of the day, how much he feels at home there. This is what he has been missing, what he has wanted all these years, and what he will continue to want throughout the series. Hogwarts, we have already seen, provides a sort of surrogate home, a place where he knows everyone and everyone knows him, where his abilities are not feared and hated but welcomed. However, good as it is, there is no real family there; the teachers must remain, to a large extent, professionally remote in order to do their jobs. Here, in The Burrow, there are people who like him, who make him feel at home, and he knows that this is what he has been missing. Several other small points might be mentioned as well. We have already mentioned that Gilderoy Lockhart will re-appear in this book, and will be true to the image we already have of him: extremely attractive physically, plausible in his descriptions and instructions, but ultimately unreliable. The flying Ford Anglia will also have a few more appearances in this book. Arthur Weasley mentions one Mundungus Fletcher, who tried to jinx him when his back was turned; he, too, will reappear, and will be as shady as this brief mention leads us to expect, in the fourth book and each book after that. And Mr. Weasley's job with the Ministry will also prove important in later books, not only because it will give him the power to investigate other characters for Dark magic, but because his lack of ambition, his joy in what he actually does rather than the seeking of status apparently common among other Ministry employees, is unusual and apparently attracts attention from the likes of Lucius Malfoy.

Chapter 4: At Flourish and Blotts

SYNOPSIS

Life for Harry has never been this good, far better than Privet Drive. Finally, he has found a family that accepts him, and that treats him as one of their own, rather than as an inferior. True, he still cannot do magic, but magic is all around him, and is an accepted part of life.

The letters from Hogwarts, including Harry's, arrive at the same time. As always, the letters start with the reminder that the term starts September 1st, and provide the list of schoolbooks.

Second year students will require:
- *"The Standard Book of Spells, Grade 2,"* by Miranda Goshawk
  - *"Break With A Banshee,"* by Gilderoy Lockhart
  - *"Gadding with Ghouls,"* by Gilderoy Lockhart
  - *"Holidays with Hags,"* by Gilderoy Lockhart
  - *"Travels with Trolls,"* by Gilderoy Lockhart
  - *"Voyages with Vampires,"* by Gilderoy Lockhart
  - *"Wandering with Werewolves,"* by Gilderoy Lockhart
  - *"Year with the Yeti,"* by Gilderoy Lockhart

Based on the list's content, Fred surmises that the new Defence Against the Dark Arts teacher is a witch and a fan of Lockhart. George has a more practical thought: "This lot won't come cheap." Mrs. Weasley says they will manage, although she seems worried.

An owl arrives from Hermione suggesting they all meet in Diagon Alley. Mrs. Weasley agrees that that makes sense, and the boys then go off to practice Quidditch. On the way, they mention that their brother, Percy has been acting oddly and often remains shut up in his room.

On the appointed day, the Weasleys head to Diagon Alley using Floo powder, something Harry has never done before. Unfortunately, he mispronounces the destination and goes one grate too far, landing in what appears to be a Dark Magic shop. While there, he sees Draco Malfoy and his father, and overhears a conversation between Mr. Malfoy and the proprietor, Borgin, in which it appears Mr. Malfoy is offering to sell some magical equipment back to Borgin.

Harry exits the shop undetected, only to discover he was in Borgin and Burkes in Knockturn Alley, an unsafe area frequented by dark wizards and other unsavory characters. Fortunately, Harry is soon found by Hagrid, who steers him back to Diagon Alley. Harry finds the Weasleys and Hermione, and they proceed to Gringotts Bank. Harry is embarrassed by the wealth in his vault, particularly after seeing the small sum the Weasleys have to draw on.

The group separates to do their shopping, agreeing to meet later at Flourish & Blotts for school books. They arrive there during a book-signing event. The popular author, Gilderoy Lockhart, is signing copies of his autobiography, *Magical Me*, and the long line has to be held in check by a "harassed little wizard." Spotting Harry, Lockhart drags him to the front and presents him with a complete set of his autographed books while posing for photos. Lockhart then announces that he is the new Defence Against the Dark Arts teacher for Hogwarts.

Staggering away from the limelight, Harry dumps the Lockhart books into Ginny's cauldron; Draco Malfoy observes this byplay and taunts Harry. Mr. Malfoy suddenly appears, and examining one of Ginny's second-hand books, makes rude comments before returning it to her cauldron. Mr. Weasley comes over and begins arguing with Mr. Malfoy. The argument becomes physical; Hagrid reappears and drags the Weasleys away from the battle while the Malfoys stalk off. The Weasleys, Hermione, and Harry, return to the Leaky Cauldron and then back home.

ANALYSIS

This is our first exposure to Gilderoy Lockhart in person; he is handsome, charismatic, and has a legion of fans, comprised largely of middle-aged witches like Mrs. Weasley. He is also vain, opportunistic, and a fame-seeker who exploits Harry to get his photo onto the front page of the *Daily Prophet*. Lockhart's celebrity was achieved by writing about his many exciting adventures, and he seems to believe that everyone, most notably Harry, is as driven for fame as he. When the fight erupts between Lucius Malfoy and Arthur Weasley, Lockhart is heard planning to spin it to promote himself in the paper.

This chapter also marks our first real exposure to Ginny Weasley's true character. When Draco insults Harry for the attention he gets in Flourish and Blotts with Gilderoy Lockhart, Ginny tells him to leave Harry alone, and that he didn't want the attention. This shows us that, despite Ginny's schoolgirl crush on Harry, she is very aware that he does not like the fame he gets from his history with Voldemort. It is possible that she is unable to speak to him in part out of fear that he will think her attention is rooted in his fame, rather than in himself. It is characteristic of a schoolgirl crush, however, that the person with the crush is afraid to talk to the person she has the crush on. Another Malfoy family member is introduced: Lucius Malfoy. Proud, rich, and arrogant, he is a strict and demanding parent who holds a tight rein on Draco. In the bookstore, he is insulting and bullying towards Ginny Weasley, although just why his attention falls on her is as yet uncertain. It is learned that the Malfoys and the Weasleys, both old pure-blood wizarding families, have very different ideas of what "disgraces Wizardkind."

The argument between Lucius Malfoy and Arthur Weasley points up one of the great divisions among the characters in our story. Lucius is clearly scornful of Arthur's endless lobbying on behalf of the Muggles, where Arthur is affronted at Malfoy's apparent belief in his own superiority in ancestry. What is highlighted here is that one group of wizards feels themselves superior to others because of their breeding, and the fact that there are no non-Magical people in their bloodlines. This group has come to feel that those who cannot do magic are somehow subhuman, and that those wizards who choose to work with them or protect them are somehow traitors to the idea of blood purity. While the Weasley family is as old and pure a bloodline as any other, to the "pure-blood" wizards, their ongoing commerce with Muggles is seen as somehow demeaning them

Greater Picture

Three items shown in Borgin and Burkes come back in a later book. Draco uses the Hand of Glory in *Harry Potter and the Half-Blood Prince* while he is departing the Room of Requirement. The opal necklace with the note warning that it was cursed is used in an attempt to kill Dumbledore, also in *Harry Potter and the The Half-Blood Prince*. And it turns out that the cabinet in which Harry is hiding will also make an appearance in that book.

Lucius Malfoy's looking at one of the books that Ginny is holding is an excuse to put Tom Riddle's diary inside it. As we later find out, Voldemort had left the diary with Lucius, with the intent that it would be used at some point against Hogwarts. Lucius, not knowing exactly what the diary was, had apparently decided that, given his son's discouraging marks (as mentioned to Borgin), it was time to cause some problems for the school. While we have not seen this explicitly yet, we can already begin to guess that it is among the pure-blood families that Voldemort had found his allies. We see that Lucius is returning some Dark magic items to Borgin and Burkes, and hear him saying that it is getting dangerous for him to have them around. We also see Lucius' disdain for those of less pure-blood breeding than himself, and his annoyance that Draco, pureblood though he is, is not able to beat Hermione's grades. In the previous chapter we learned that Lucius had been believed to be one of Voldemort's supporters; his possession of Dark magical objects seems to lend weight to this, as we have been told that Voldemort was a Dark wizard. This suggests quite strongly that Voldemort may have been playing on the pure-blood belief in their own superiority to fuel his initial rise to power.

Chapter 5: The Whomping Willow

Synopsis

Summer is quickly over, and it is soon time to return to Hogwarts. After several false starts, everything is loaded into Mr. Weasley's car, the flying Ford Anglia. The car is magically larger inside than out, so they all fit in quite easily, and head to King's Cross Station. It is nearly time for the Hogwarts Express to depart; everyone is on the platform, except Harry and Ron, who cannot get through the barrier. The clock strikes 11:00 a.m and the train leaves, stranding Harry and Ron at the station and without any Muggle money.

Harry suggests waiting back by the car; Ron, worried that his parents may be unable to get back out through the barrier (except in the US edition, where Ron states that his parents can apparate) and in a panic about getting to school, suggests flying to Hogwarts in the car. They take off, flying above the clouds except to occasionally see where the Hogwarts Express is. The flight is uneventful until they reach the school. On the final approach, the car loses power and crashes into the Whomping Willow, breaking Ron's wand. The massive tree pounds the car. The battered Ford extricates itself and lands on the ground, then ejects Harry, Ron, and their luggage before wildly driving off into the Forbidden Forest.

Harry and Ron peer into Great Hall through a window, seeing that the Sorting ceremony has started. Unable to locate Professor Snape at the staff table, they speculate on why he is absent, only to find him standing behind them. He takes them into his office, demanding they explain themselves and wanting to know what they have done with the car—the *Evening Prophet* has reported that a flying car was sighted by several Muggles. Snape fetches Professor McGonagall, who requires that Ron and Harry repeat their story. She asks why they did not send an owl, since they actually have one. Ron admits that he did not think of that.

Professor Dumbledore enters and hears the story. He says he will be writing to their parents, although they will not be expelled. Their punishment will be decided by Professor McGonagall, their House Head. After Snape and Dumbledore return to the Feast, Professor McGonagall says each will serve detention but, possibly because Ron points out that school hadn't actually started yet, does not deduct any House points. They have missed the Sorting ceremony but McGonagall says that Ginny was placed into Gryffindor House. She provides them sandwiches, telling them to eat in Snape's office and then go directly to their dormitory.

Hermione meets them outside the The Fat Lady's portrait and gives them the password ("*wattlebird*"). She is definitely unhappy about what they did, as are Harry and Ron, but the other Gryffindors in the Common room applaud their audacity for driving a flying car into the Whomping Willow.

Analysis

We have already seen that it takes some effort to select a wand, and a reasonably large amount of money to buy one. We can guess that Ron, already in trouble for taking and wrecking the car, will not be likely to report to his parents that his wand has broken; however, we don't yet know what the effect of the wand's breaking will be. We do know that Hagrid's wand was broken when he was expelled, but that it still seems to work somewhat; we don't know how that compares to the damage that Ron's wand has taken. In any event, Ron is almost certainly going to try to make some sort of temporary repair and carry on as best he can with a damaged wand.

We can see in this chapter that Snape dearly wants to get rid of Harry, and is hoping that McGonagall or Dumbledore will see fit to expel him, along with Ron. Snape is quite clearly disappointed that Dumbledore requires that Snape accompany him to the Great Hall, leaving Harry and Ron with McGonagall—we can see that he wants to witness the punishment that Harry will receive. We also see that McGonagall, though never losing her sternness, is still trying to be fair. She likely knows that Ron will be disciplined by his mother, and chooses to lighten her own punishment accordingly, even though this will mean that Harry gets off relatively lightly.

Questions

Review   1. What kind of tree do Harry and Ron crash into, and with what?

Greater Picture

Ron's broken wand will prove to be a useful plot element throughout this book, as it will produce humorous effects at several places in the book, and will finally backfire at an ideal time, rendering harmless a major threat to Ron and Harry. It will be replaced when Ron's family wins a contest at the beginning of the next book.

The flying Ford Anglia will also prove useful in this book, saving Ron and Harry from a colony of Acromantulae. It will not be seen after that time, however.

The Whomping Willow proves to be an important element in the next book. The tree was planted over an entrance to a tunnel that leads from the school grounds to the Shrieking Shack, where, as a student, Lupin went every month during the full moon. We will see that this tunnel, which proved useful some thirty years before the series began, and will be an important plot item in the third book, will also be useful in the final book. It is perhaps of interest that Snape seems to believe that Harry and Ron deliberately chose to arrive at Hogwarts by flying car, in order to gain some fame for themselves. We will see shortly that Gilderoy Lockhart shares this misunderstanding of Harry's motives. With Lockhart this is understandable, as his main motivation is fame, but it is not clear why Snape has this belief; in almost every other respect, Snape seems to oppose Lockhart to the best of his abilities.

Chapter 6: Gilderoy Lockhart

Synopsis

The next day begins less appealingly. Ron receives a Howler during breakfast in the Great Hall. Mrs. Weasley's voice loudly scolds him for taking the car. Ron is utterly humiliated in front of his classmates. Professor McGonagall hands out timetables; first class is double Herbology with the Hufflepuffs. Professor Sprout arrives late; she has been bandaging the Whomping Willow, "assisted" by Professor Lockhart who gave "valuable pointers." A disgruntled Professor Sprout directs the class to Greenhouse Three, which contains more interesting and dangerous plants like the Venomous Tentacula.

Professor Lockhart draws Harry aside and says he understands why he and Ron took the flying car—for fame and recognition. Lockhart blames himself for giving Harry a taste of fame at Flourish & Blotts and ignores Harry's protest that he and Ron only did it to get to school.

As Harry returns to the greenhouse, he finds that the class is preparing to transplant Mandrakes. The trio is joined by Justin Finch-Fletchley, a Hufflepuff, who casually mentions that he is Muggle-born and was headed for Eton before he got his Hogwarts letter.

Next class is Transfiguration with Professor McGonagall. Harry seems to have forgotten all he learned last year and is unable to Transfigure his beetle into a coat button. Ron is having problems with his wand. Although he repaired it with magical tape, it is producing grey smokey clouds and unexpected noises.

After lunch, Harry is cornered by little Colin Creevey, who wants to take Harry's picture to show his parents that he has actually met "Harry Potter." Overhearing this, Draco begin badgering Harry about signing photos. Lockhart comes over and forces Harry to pose for a photo, then hauls him away for some "fatherly advice" on handling fame. They enter Defence Against the Dark Arts class together, although Harry hides in the back. Lockhart sets a test to see how much the students knows about him. Predictably, Hermione, who apparently thinks Lockhart is wonderful, gets a perfect score. Next, Lockhart releases Cornish Pixies into the classroom, but he is unable to control them. At the bell, he flees, leaving it to Harry, Ron, and Hermione to get the remaining pixies back into their cage. Ron and Harry are now suspicious about how truthful Lockhart's books really are, though Hermione still seems to have a bad case of hero worship.

Analysis

In this chapter, we see one of Harry's great dislikes reinforced. As in Flourish and Blotts, Harry finds himself very uncomfortable with his fame, particularly as expressed by Colin, who is quite a rabid fan. Colin Creevey, in his enthusiasm at meeting Harry, easily forgets that Harry may not wish to be photographed and that he could, perhaps, not desire fame. Of course, other people take it out of context: Draco Malfoy starts to noise it about, in his usual way, that Harry is signing autographs, while Lockhart, quite plainly still believing that Harry is as motivated by fame as he is himself, lectures Harry on going too fast with his career as a famous person. In Lockhart's self-centeredness, he cannot see that anyone would deliberately shun the limelight, and so disregards Harry's attempts to say that he didn't want to be photographed.

Also, it seems that Ron and Harry are starting to have doubts about their Defence Against the Dark Arts teacher. If Gilderoy Lockhart has done so many wonderful things, why wasn't he able to stop the Cornish pixies? Hermione, who seems to have a crush on him, dismisses the possibility that Lockhart didn't have an idea about the pixies, saying that he has done many things, although Ron subtly remarks that he can't offer any real proof that he has done them apart from his word. One must wonder why Hermione is so blind to what Lockhart's abilities actually are, even at this early stage.

Questions

Review 1. What is the spell Professor Lockhart uses to control the pixies? Does it work? Is there anything strange about it?

Further Study 1. Is Gilderoy Lockhart's teaching likely to be useful to Harry, Ron and Hermione? If not, why?

Greater Picture

Hermione's trust in Lockhart's abilities will continue throughout much of the book, despite significant evidence that he is a sham. He will never again try to demonstrate Defence Against the Dark Arts, the Dueling Club he starts up will prove to be a travesty, and his attempt to heal Harry's broken arm will result in Harry's arm being de-boned, among other less-than-stellar accomplishments. Faced with all of this, why will Hermione persist in believing in his abilities? The author does not provide many clues, but Ron, in later years, will indicate that he believes that it was Lockhart's good looks that kept Hermione in thrall, and that certainly seems to be what's happening at this stage. Possibly, also, Hermione has a subconscious trust in books, and a belief that if it is in a book, it must be true. In this chapter, she does say "Look at all the things he's done!" Ron, more skeptical, does not seem to agree with her trust that what's in the books actually happened. We will see this blind faith in published works again as late as *Harry Potter and the Half-Blood Prince*, where Hermione sticks to the published text in her copy of *Advanced Potion-Making*, despite the fact that the marginal notes in Harry's copy seem to produce much better results.

Chapter 7: Mudbloods and Murmurs

Synopsis

During the first week of classes, Harry has avoided Professor Lockhart with some success and Colin Creevey with less, only to be awakened far too early Saturday morning by Oliver Wood who wants to start Quidditch practice before the other House teams. First he gives the team a long lecture on tactics. When they finally get to the pitch, and after doing some basic warm-ups, they find they have been pre-empted: the Slytherin team is there. A note from Professor Snape gives them permission to use the Pitch to train their new seeker: Draco Malfoy. It also seems that Draco's father has presented the entire Slytherin team with new Nimbus 2001 brooms that are even faster than Harry's Nimbus 2000.

Ron and Hermione have appeared to watch the practice. Hermione comments that nobody on the Gryffindor team had to buy their way in. Malfoy, angered by the aspersion, calls Hermione a "mudblood." To retaliate, an angry Ron attempts to jinx Malfoy, but his broken wand backfires and he jinxes himself instead. Hermione and Harry carry him, belching slugs, to Hagrid's hut, where they narrowly miss Professor Lockhart, who is just leaving. Hagrid uncharacteristically criticizes Professor Lockhart, suggesting that his books may not be entirely truthful. He also mentions that Lockhart was the only applicant for the Defence Against the Dark Arts job. Apparently word is out that the position may be jinxed.

Ron tells Hagrid he tried to curse Malfoy because he called Hermione a mudblood. Hagrid is shocked. This is evidently the most insulting term used to denigrate a Muggleborn's ancestry.

Hagrid then pokes a bit of fun at Harry for giving out signed photos. He says Lockhart was displeased to hear his opinion that Harry was more famous than Lockhart would ever be. He then takes them out to his pumpkin patch to see what he has been growing. Apparently, despite being prohibited from performing magic, he has managed an Engorgement charm. The pumpkins, with a month to go before Hallowe'en, are the size of small boulders. At lunchtime, they return to the Castle. Professor McGonagall meets them in the entrance hall and tells them their detentions. Ron will be polishing silver with Mr. Filch; Harry will be helping Professor Lockhart answer his fan mail.

That evening, Harry goes to Professor Lockhart's office to serve his detention. Lockhart's office is decorated with pictures of himself, some even signed. As midnight nears, Harry, worn out with stuffing envelopes and ignoring Lockhart pontificating about fame, hears a low voice muttering violently. Harry jerks to attention to try and follow what it is being said. Lockhart says he cannot hear it, but notices that it is nearly midnight and dismisses Harry. Ron arrives at the dormitory half an hour later. He has had a rough time, having one final slug attack on a Special Award for Services to the School which required massive amounts of work to clean up. When told about the voice, Ron comments that it is odd Lockhart could not hear it, particularly since the door remained closed. Even if someone was invisible, they would have had to open the door to get in.

ANALYSIS

There are several main points that are brought up in this chapter. The first of these is, of course, Draco's addition to the Slytherin Quidditch team, and the appearance of the team's new brooms, which are very probably related. We have been told that members of Slytherin house will use any advantage they can to achieve their goals, and it is quite likely that Draco, having decided that he must oppose Harry directly in Quidditch, had convinced his father to buy brooms for the team on condition that he was selected as Seeker. Likely his plan was to try and humiliate Harry by outflying him. We don't yet know how well this will work.

Draco's animosity towards those he perceives as less well-bred than himself is also now brought into sharp focus. We see him here insulting Hermione on the basis of her parentage, using terms that quite shock both Ron and Hagrid, even though Hermione does not understand the depth of the insult that has been thrown at her. Another point brought out is Ron's wand. We have already seen that it has become unpredictable, producing clouds of grey smoke and odd noises, but we now see that it no longer necessarily casts spells in the desired direction, even when it does work.

We are led to believe that there is a certain amount of solidarity among the teachers, that one teacher will generally not criticize another. This will be stated explicitly in a later book, but so far has been only implied. Given that Hagrid does state that Lockhart's books might not be entirely truthful, one gathers that there is a lot of suspicion in the staff room that Lockhart is not anywhere near as good a wizard as he pretends.

We are exposed to an extremely large dose of Lockhart's personality as Harry serves his detention. Lockhart here clearly believes that Harry is as driven by celebrity as he is, and is in need of tips as to how to handle fame. We see that Lockhart deeply enjoys being famous, to the extent that he does not even seem to mind having to send out tons of autographed pictures every week. Possibly, Lockhart's self-image is fueled by the belief that, being so widely known, he is universally loved, and he cannot conceive of anyone not being similarly in need of affirmation by the masses.

This also is the first appearance of the mysterious voice within the walls. Something seems to be murderously angry in the castle, and Harry already is concerned that he will need to find out what it is, despite being worried that he seems to be the only one who can hear it.

GREATER PICTURE

The Award for Special Services to the School is specifically singled out in later chapters, because it was the one given to Tom Riddle. Tom will play a large part in the end of this book, and it will turn out that he will play a significant part in the series as a whole.

As we will see later in the book, the voice Harry heard in Lockhart's office was actually the Basilisk, the monster in the Chamber, which had been released and is now starting to roam through the school. Harry is the only one that can hear the voice because he is a Parselmouth; to everyone else, the sound is a low and undefined hissing noise. It is interesting that Harry perceives Parseltongue as English; this will prove to be a plot point much later in the series.

Hermione learns that Harry can understand snakes, and from the effects of the Monster, and Harry's description of how it seems to be moving through the castle, she eventually determines that it is a Basilisk. Harry does manage to get this information from her even after she is Petrified herself.

It is also important to note how Ron's wand backfired and hit him instead of Malfoy. This plays a big part later in the book when Harry, Ron, and Professor Lockhart delve into the Chamber of Secrets to rescue Ginny.

Chapter 8: The Deathday Party

SYNOPSIS

October is marked by continuous rainstorms; the lake rises, the flowerbeds turn into muddy streams, and Hagrid's pumpkins swell to the size of garden sheds. Oliver Wood, however, does not see any reason to let up on Quidditch practice, so it is no surprise that Harry is soaked and dripping mud one Saturday morning as he walks back to Gryffindor Tower after practice. On the way he meets Nearly Headless Nick, and they discuss their respective troubles: Nick is upset because his application to join the Headless Hunt has been rejected again, it seems that being nearly headless is not enough to qualify. Harry, meanwhile, is not looking forward to meeting Slytherin at Quidditch with the entire team mounted on new Nimbus 2001 brooms. As Harry is speaking, he is interrupted by Mrs. Norris, Filch's cat. Nick mentions that Filch is in a bad mood. Harry tries to make a quick escape but is thwarted by Filch's sudden appearance through a tapestry. Incensed at the water and mud dripping off Harry's Quidditch robes, Filch orders him to his office where he fills out a form recommending punishment for "befouling the castle." A loud noise interrupts him, and Filch charges off after Peeves in the hopes that he has finally done something unforgivable that will permanently ban him from Hogwarts.

During Filch's absence, Harry notices an envelope on his desk. It is for a correspondence course called "Kwikspell," intended to improve a person's magical abilities. When Filch returns, he notices the envelope has been moved and, becoming embarrassed, lets Harry go without being punished.

On exiting Filch's office, Harry meets Nearly Headless Nick again. Nick tells him that he arranged for Peeves to tip over a black and gold cabinet to distract Filch. Nick is relieved it worked and invites Harry to his Deathday Party to celebrate the five hundredth anniversary of his death, which occurred 31 October, 1492. He also invites Ron and Hermione, who are both keen to go.

On Hallowe'en, they descend to the Dungeons where they are met by Nick and a panoply of ghosts, including Moaning Myrtle and Peeves. The gathering is rather uncomfortable for living people, and when Peeves insults Moaning Myrtle sending her off in tears, Harry,

Ron, and Hermione decide it is a good time to exit. As they depart the Dungeon, Harry hears the same voice he heard in Professor Lockhart's office. He follows it upwards, with Hermione and Ron following, through the Entry Hall to the first floor. Sloshing through a puddle of water on the floor, he sees writing on the wall: "The Chamber Of Secrets Has Been Opened. Enemies Of the Heir, Beware." Mrs. Norris is hanging from a torch bracket, apparently dead. Before the Trio can react, students leaving the Hallowe'en Feast surround them. Malfoy's voice rings out: "Enemies of the Heir, beware! You'll be next, Mudbloods!"

Analysis

One of the main things that the author excels at is called "the set-up and the pay-off," the ability to write something that begs a question, followed by, at some later point, the answer which illuminates much more than the question was asking. This chapter contains a relatively minor instance of this: we see that Filch has, on his desk, an envelope from a course that seems designed to teach basic magic, and we see that Filch is horribly embarrassed by this. Why? This is the first place that we get a concrete date for when the series is taking place within the books themselves. Unfortunately, this date conflicts with many of the days of the week reported in the story; specifically, for instance, in *Harry Potter and the Philosopher's Stone*, we learn that Harry was orphaned on October 31. If his second year at Hogwarts starts in September 1992, as here implied by the date given for Nearly Headless Nick's Deathday, then he must have turned 11 on 31 July 1991. As his birth date then would be 31 July 1980, he would have been orphaned on October 31, 1981. The book explicitly states that the next day was a Tuesday; but November 1, 1981 was a Sunday. Similarly, days of the week are given for Hallowe'en and for all three tasks in *Harry Potter and the Goblet of Fire*, but do not line up with the days of the week in 1994 and 1995.

These failures of correspondence between the series calendar and our physical calendar are unimportant to the sweep of the story, so while they may be mentioned, they are provided more as a curiosity than as something for the scholar to concern himself with.

Greater Picture

Moaning Myrtle's departure from the party proves somewhat critical for reasons that are fully explained later in the story. Because Peeves had so upset her, Myrtle floods the hallway outside her bathroom. While we don't go into the bathroom this time to see this, in a later instance, when someone "throws a book through Myrtle's head," Harry and Ron will enter the bathroom and find all of the taps turned on and water all over the floor and the hall outside. As an aside, one of the popular slang terms for someone starting to cry is "turning on the waterworks;" it seems that Myrtle takes the expression literally. We will find out in the next chapter that Mrs. Norris is Petrified; if the hallway had not been flooded, the basilisk's glance would have killed Mrs. Norris. Because Mrs. Norris saw the Basilisk's reflection from the water, instead of looking at it directly, she was spared. Mrs. Norris will be the first to avoid direct sight of the Basilisk, and through luck or design all the other victims of the Basilisk this time will equally avoid direct eye contact, but we will also learn that earlier, the same had not been true.

Harry has inadvertently discovered a secret about Filch: he is a squib. Squibs are born into wizarding families but have no magical abilities themselves. Filch is apparently attempting to overcome this "accident-of-birth" by taking a correspondence magic course. Harry's understanding, though, is incomplete at this point. While Harry now knows that Filch is trying to learn magic, he does not yet understand the import of this fact. Harry will learn the details in the next chapter.

It is worth noting that although the cabinet that Peeves knocks over to distract Filch is insignificant to the overall storyline of this book, it reappears in *Harry Potter and the Order of the Phoenix*, and in *Harry Potter and the Half-Blood Prince* it is a major plot device. In both of these appearances, it is an important fact that it is broken.

Chapter 9: The Writing on the Wall

Synopsis

Filch appears and immediately accuses Harry of killing his cat. The situation is defused by the arrival of Professor Dumbledore and several other teachers. Dumbledore indicates that he needs a place to examine Mrs. Norris, and Professor Lockhart volunteers his office. Professor Dumbledore asks Filch, Harry, Ron, and Hermione to accompany him. Professors Lockhart, McGonagall, and Snape tag along. While Lockhart babbles about deaths he has prevented, Dumbledore examines Mrs. Norris, concluding she is not dead, merely Petrified, and that Harry could not have done it. Filch still believes that Harry was somehow involved because he knows Filch is a Squib. Harry states he does not even know what a Squib is. Snape suggests that while Harry, Ron, and Hermione were possibly just in the wrong place at the wrong time, it is suspicious that they were absent from the Hallowe'en feast. They explain that they were at the Deathday party but do not say why they did not go to the Feast afterwards. Harry does not want to reveal that he heard voices, but the excuse he does offer is rather flimsy. Snape suggests punishment for dishonesty, but is overruled by McGonagall and Dumbledore, to Filch's great displeasure. Harry, Ron, and Hermione are dismissed, and Ron explains to Harry that a Squib is a non-magical person born to wizard parents.

The possible opening of the Chamber causes a change in some students: Justin Finch-Fletchley avoids Harry in the halls, and Hermione is spending all her time in the library, among other things. Harry goes to speak with Ron in the library and finds that Hermione is upset because she cannot find any copies of *Hogwarts: A History*. In their next class, History of Magic with Professor Binns, she manages to persuade the old ghost to recount the legend of the Chamber of Secrets.

Binns says that over a thousand years ago there was a falling out amongst the school's four founders, Godric Gryffindor, Salazar Slytherin, Rowena Ravenclaw, and

Chapter 9: The Writing on the Wall

Helga Hufflepuff. They argued over whether Muggle-borns and Muggles' descendants (half-bloods) should be admitted to Hogwarts. Slytherin alone believed only pure-bloods should be admitted, and he left the school when the others rejected his beliefs. The legend says he created a secret Chamber and hid a monster within it. Only Slytherin's true Heir can control the monster or open the Chamber. Although the Chamber has never been found, Binns is unsuccessful in convincing the class it does not exist.

While passing between classes, little Colin Creevey mentions that someone said Harry could be the Heir; Harry realizes this could explain why Justin avoided him earlier.

While walking in the hall, Harry, Ron, and Hermione realize they have reached the spot where Mrs. Norris was Petrified. They see a clutch of spiders running away from something. Ron is terrified of spiders, and, to change the subject, Harry mentions the water that is all over the floor. It is coming from the girls' bathroom that Moaning Myrtle inhabits. This bathroom is now in disrepair; it is also very wet, evidently because a moping Myrtle causes floods. She is less than communicative with them. Percy catches the three leaving the bathroom and docks five House points from Gryffindor.

During a later discussion, Ron suggests that Malfoy would be the logical choice to be the Heir. Hermione says there is a way to find out. They could use Polyjuice Potion to impersonate someone else. However, she needs a copy of *Moste Potente Potions* from the library's restricted section to learn how to make it. For that, she needs a teacher's signature. "But what teacher," says Ron, "would be so thick?"

Analysis

In this chapter we see the pay-off of the set-up that was made by the discovery of Argus Filch's Kwikspell course in the previous chapter. Filch admits that he is a Squib; Ron explains what a Squib is. In these two passages, we have learned why Filch feels the need to buy a beginner's magic course, and why he was not educated in the normal manner for Wizards. However, much more than this: we can now see why he is so very bitter. Year after year, he sees children that could have come from his family enter, get trained in the ways of magic that he can never know, and leave to careers he possibly once dreamed of, while he remains behind. Being a Squib is a horrible sort of half life, aware of the world of magic, but despite being surrounded by it, not being a part of it.

We are also granted a bit more insight into the nature of Gilderoy Lockhart. As we step into his office, all of the pictures of him whisk themselves out of their frames and into hiding; some of them, overcome by curiosity, reappear later, and Harry notes that some of them are wearing hairnets. Lockhart himself, instead of helping with the investigation, babbles on about deaths he has supposedly prevented. When Mrs. Norris is found to be merely petrified, Lockhart suggests that he could whip up a restorative potion in short order, irritating Snape, who of course, as Potions master, would expect that job to be his.

This last point also highlights the dislike that Snape has for Lockhart. By this stage, most of the teachers have dismissed Lockhart as a fraud, and no doubt Snape shares that opinion. We suspect that Professor Dumbledore is aware of this as well, and has only hired him as Lockhart was the only applicant for the post (according to Hagrid). We should note that Snape was apparently irritated in particular by Harry's fame in the previous book; it was the fact that Harry was famous that Snape had dwelt on in Harry's first Potions lesson. Harry does not actively seek the spotlight, but Lockhart does, to the point that almost everything he does is aimed at getting himself more attention. This can only serve to increase Snape's dislike of Lockhart, a dislike that is heightened still more by Lockhart's self-serving attempt to take over some of Snape's duties.

The core of the plot line of this story is here revealed. While Binns states that there can be no Chamber of Secrets, that multiple headmasters have looked for it for years and never found even a broom-closet of secrets, still it is evident to the reader, as it is to the students, that the Chamber does exist and does have some monster in it. There is no other possible explanation for the petrification of Mrs. Norris.

Questions

Further Study 1. Since Mrs. Norris is just a cat (not an Animagus), why would she have been selected as the first victim?

Greater Picture

While Harry, Hermione and Ron are examining the area where Mrs. Norris's body was found, they notice some strangely-behaving spiders. Ron admits that he has a fear of spiders, which is confirmed later in this book, and also in the next two books: by his Boggart in *Harry Potter and the Prisoner of Azkaban*, and his behavior during Mad-Eye Moody's Unforgivable Curse demonstration in *Harry Potter and the Goblet of Fire*. The peculiar behavior of the spiders in this scene sets the stage for events later on by giving a clue about the monster Slytherin concealed within the Chamber.

One must wonder about Professor Binns' vehement denial of the existence of the Chamber of Secrets. We will find out that the Chamber had been opened before, some fifty years previously, and the headmaster of the day, Professor Dippet, had considered closing the school as a result of that. While it is possible that occurrence had been before Professor Binns joined the school, that seems unlikely; Binns' apparent refusal to teach anything later than about the nineteenth century argues for his having been a teacher for many more years than a mere fifty. It is noted in this chapter that Percy penalizes Harry and Ron house points; this could be a plot hole since prefects, as we find out in later books, are not given this power. It is possible, however, that Percy has taken on an over-inflated sense of his own importance, and when that importance is questioned, as Ron does here, Percy reacts by saying he's docking House points, when in fact he can do no such thing. The author said in an interview that she believes Percy is more likely to be right than Ron, who said in *Harry Potter and the Order of the Phoenix* that prefects could not dock House points; she later reinforced this statement on her official web site.[1] Against this, however, we must mention that Draco Malfoy, then a prefect, agreed that Prefects could not dock House points. One can be sure that if Draco were able to dock House points from Gryffindors, he would, and in fact as a member of the Inquisitorial Squad he was allowed to, and did. In this particular case, it makes more sense in the story as a whole to have Percy be overstepping his boundaries through over-officiousness, a very Percy-like thing to do, than to have Draco later refrain from abusing a power he has been given.

Chapter 10: The Rogue Bludger

Synopsis

After the rather disastrous episode with the Pixies, Professor Lockhart has changed the Defense Against the Dark Arts course; now it is mostly Lockhart re-enacting scenes from his books with the unwilling assistance of Harry. Today Harry is being a werewolf, playing along because he wants to stay on Lockhart's good side. At the end of class, Hermione asks him to sign a note for a book that will help her understand something in one of his works; he signs it without bothering to see what the book is, then offers to provide Harry advice on being a Quidditch Seeker. At the school library, Madam Pince accepts the note, though with some misgivings, and gets a copy of *Moste Potente Potions* for Hermione.

Shortly thereafter, Hermione, Harry, and Ron are in Moaning Myrtle's bathroom; this is one place they are unlikely to be disturbed. Looking over the ingredients and methods for the Polyjuice Potion, they find that they need ingredients (Boomslang skin and Bicorn horn) not stocked in the student supplies cupboard. The potion will take about a month to make. Hermione, surprisingly, convinces Harry and Ron that they have to take some chances in order to do this.

Next day is Quidditch against Slytherin. As soon as they get into the air, a Bludger targets Harry. Despite Fred and George's best efforts, the Bludger seems determined to knock Harry off his broom; as the rest of the team is getting slaughtered by the remaining Bludger and the Slytherin Beaters, Harry tells Fred and George to let him deal with the Bludger on his own. Eventually, Harry spots the Snitch, hovering over Malfoy's head, but while lining it up to grab it, he is hit by the Bludger. It breaks his arm, but he manages to catch the Snitch with the other hand and land on the ground intact. Regaining consciousness, he is dismayed to see Lockhart standing over him. Lockhart promptly uses a spell to "mend" Harry's broken arm but it instead removes all the bones from his arm and hand. In the hospital wing, Madam Pomfrey is furious—she can easily fix broken bones, but regrowing them will be an overnight job, and a painful one at that. Ron helps Harry into pyjamas. The Gryffindor team arrives to celebrate the win over Slytherin but are promptly thrown out by Madam Pomfrey.

Later that night, Harry is awakened by Dobby sponging his forehead. Dobby admits that he closed the barrier at Kings Cross station to prevent Harry from returning to school and that he enchanted the Bludger in hopes it would injure Harry enough to send him home where he would be safe. He tells Harry that a House-elf can only be freed if his Master gives him clothing, which is why he wears an old pillowcase. He also mentions that the Chamber of Secrets has been opened once before. Realizing he was not meant to mention that, he punishes himself by smashing Harry's water jug over his own head. Hearing a noise, he vanishes. Professor Dumbledore and Professor McGonagall bring in a Petrified Colin Creevey, who was apparently on his way to visit Harry, carrying his camera and a bunch of grapes. Colin's camera is completely melted inside; Dumbledore says that this proves that the Chamber is open again, but the main question is not *who*, but *how*?

Analysis

Lockhart's apparent ineptness with magic is shown in significantly more detail. Now, instead of teaching charms for self-defence, Lockhart has chosen to re-enact scenes from his books, seemingly in order to avoid something like the Cornish Pixies incident. And, despite his claim that he is an expert in healing magic, his attempt to heal Harry only results in a worse injury. One must wonder why Hermione, normally so logical, again rejects the possibility of Lockhart being incompetent despite this proof. It is perhaps telling that at the close of the previous chapter, Ron asks, he thinks rhetorically, which teacher would be so thick as to give second-year students permission to take a book out of the Restricted section of the library, and at the beginning of this chapter, we see that Hermione is assisting in getting a signature from Lockhart. Could she be starting to see, despite her infatuation, that he is perhaps not quite as brilliant as he claims?

Dobby is clearly still trying to convince Harry to leave Hogwarts; he quite clearly knows that the Chamber has been opened in relatively recent memory and that something happened then that could indicate that Harry's life is in peril. His attempts to chase Harry away, or prevent his traveling to Hogwarts, are almost laughable. We have seen four attempts so far. Dobby first tried intercepting all of Harry's mail to try and convince him that none of his Hogwarts friends cared about him, so that he would choose to stay home instead. When that failed, he threatened to wreck a dessert in the Dursley kitchen unless Harry promised to stay away from Hogwarts. Harry's refusal to promise resulted in the dessert being wrecked. Dobby could not have predicted the side effects of that; the owl from the Ministry of Magic, and Uncle Vernon's decision to lock Harry into his room were not things that Dobby would have expected to happen. Dobby's next attempt, blocking the barrier to the platform, failed when Harry and Ron used the flying car to get to Hogwarts, and this last attempt, to injure Harry badly enough to send

---

1. http://www.jkrowling.com/textonly/en/faq_view.cfm?id=40

him home, seems extremely poorly thought out. Does Dobby actually believe that Muggle medical care is better than what Harry can receive at Hogwarts? Or does he believe that Uncle Vernon and Aunt Petunia would allow magical healing to happen in their house? Dobby seems to be blind to the idea that Harry's house is not a home for him, and that even with the threat that Dobby is unable to enunciate, Hogwarts is a more welcoming place than Privet Drive.

GREATER PICTURE

After stating that the Chamber of Secrets has been reopened, Dumbledore comments that the question should not be *who* opened it, but *how* it was opened. This implies that Dumbledore does not follow the commonly-held belief that Hagrid opened it before, and Tom Riddle had caught him in the act and stopped it. If Dumbledore suspects that Riddle had opened the Chamber fifty years ago and believes that he has reopened it now, Dumbledore may have already formulated theories about horcruxes. Until the revelation of the diary, however, any such theory would be extremely tentative; Dumbledore no doubt also remembers the year before when the shade of Voldemort was riding Professor Quirrell, and may be wondering if Voldemort might have found another mount, despite rumours placing him in Albania.

It seems that Dobby is more aware of the nature of the weapon that Lucius has brought into the school than Lucius himself is. We will find out in a later book that Hogwarts employs several hundred House Elves, and it is extremely likely that the House Elf society communicates amongst themselves. So it is quite likely that Dobby knows, if not the true nature of what the Chamber of Secrets conceals, at the very least that Lucius has provided the means to reopen the Chamber, and the fact that the chamber had been opened fifty years previous and that a student had then died. It is almost certainly fear for Harry's life that is causing Dobby to carry out these ineffective, almost childlike attempts to get Harry to return "home" to Privet Drive.

Having revealed that he is, in fact, trying to get Harry back home, and having been so fiercely rebuffed, Dobby will not attempt again. Dobby likely is now aware that, if anything occurs which appears to be trying to send Harry home, Harry will believe that it is Dobby up to his old tricks, and so further attempts would be ineffective.

Chapter 11: The Dueling Club

SYNOPSIS

By morning, Harry's arm is better and he is discharged from the hospital wing after breakfast. He finds Ron and Hermione in Moaning Myrtle's washroom, already making the Polyjuice Potion. Harry tells them about Dobby's visit; Ron observes that if Dobby does not stop trying to help Harry, he is likely to kill him. The news about Colin Creevey's Petrification has spread, and Ginny, who is in Colin's class, is distraught; also, there is a brisk business in Talismans and other supposedly magical protective objects. Neville buys a lot before being reminded that he is a Pureblood, but he says "they went for Filch first," and believes he may be a target due to his weak magical ability.

Harry, Ron, and Hermione sign up to stay at the school over Christmas after hearing that Malfoy is doing the same. But the Polyjuice potion is nowhere near ready, and they will need to raid Professor Snape's private stores for some ingredients. Surprisingly, Hermione volunteers to steal the ingredients if Harry or Ron can create a diversion. During the next Potions class, Harry tosses a firecracker into Goyle's Swelling Solution. The resulting splashed potion requires Snape to administer Deflating Draughts to everyone. While he is occupied, Hermione sneaks into Snape's office and retrieves Boomslang skin and Bicorn horn. After class has ended, Hermione adds the new ingredients to the potion, saying it will be ready in a fortnight.

A week later, Harry, Ron, and Hermione see a notice about a Dueling Club being started. Harry reckons it will be useful, so at 8:00 P.M. all three are in the Great Hall, only to find out that it is being taught by none other than Professor Lockhart, with Professor Snape as his assistant. In the first demonstration, Professor Snape throws Professor Lockhart across the room with an Expelliarmus jinx. Rather than try a second time, Lockhart breaks the students into pairs with Snape's assistance; Harry is paired with Malfoy, Ron with Seamus, and Hermione with Miss Bullstrode. Lockhart counts down and mayhem ensues: Malfoy jinxes Harry before the start signal, but Harry retaliates; Ron's wand misfires, doing something horrible to Seamus. Hermione and Millicent Bullstrode have dropped their wands and are wrestling—Millicent has Hermione in a headlock, and Harry has to break her out of it, a tough job considering Millicent is bigger than he is. Lockhart suggests they have one pair of students on stage to demonstrate, and suggests Neville and Justin Finch-Fletchley; Snape overrules him and suggests Harry and Malfoy. At the count, Malfoy conjures a snake that slides down the stage towards Harry. Lockhart attempts to eliminate it, but merely sends it flying ten feet into the air. When it lands, it seems to be preparing to attack Justin; Harry yells at the snake to leave Justin alone. Surprisingly the snake obeys. Justin makes a comment to Harry and leaves the Great Hall at a near run as Snape destroys the snake. Ron drags Harry out of the room exclaiming, "I didn't know you were a Parselmouth!" Harry does not know what that is, and Ron explains it is someone who can talk to snakes. Hermione adds that it is a very rare ability, and it is what Salazar Slytherin was famous for. Now Harry has to wonder—could he be the Heir of Slytherin?

Harry wants to explain to Justin exactly what happened, but next day's Herbology class is canceled due to snow. At Hermione's urging, Harry goes to the library to find Justin and overhears Hufflepuffs talking about why he has gone into hiding. Justin fears Harry is the Heir of Slytherin and would Petrify him next because he is a Muggle-born. Harry tries to explain what happened, but Ernie, the group's apparent leader, says that all he saw was Harry speaking Parseltongue and chasing the snake towards Justin. Furious, Harry stalks out and runs straight into Hagrid, who is on his way to see the Headmaster about something that is killing his roosters. Leaving Hagrid, Harry trips over a Petrified Justin Finch-Fletchley and finds himself staring at Nearly Headless Nick, now black and smoky rather than his usual transparent white, and also apparently Petrified. Harry also notices spiders running away from the bodies.

While Harry is trying to figure out what to do, Peeves discovers him and determines that the most fun thing to do is summon everyone. Professor McGonagall arrives and sends everyone back to class. She assigns Ernie Macmillan to take Nick to the Hospital Wing while Professor Flitwick and Professor Sinistra take Justin. Professor McGonagall then leads Harry through a door guarded by a gargoyle (password: Sherbet Lemon), up a revolving spiral stone staircase and to an oaken door. Harry knows he has been brought to see Professor Dumbledore.

Analysis

Hermione's ongoing unbending is shown here in her willingness to raid Snape's stores for the ingredients they need for the Polyjuice potion. Her willingness to break the rules should not be much of a surprise to the reader, who has been watching her get steadily less stiff through this and the previous book; however, it is quite a shock to Ron, who will continue to believe that Hermione is rule-bound, despite evidence to the contrary, well into *Harry Potter and the Goblet of Fire*.

The Dueling Club shows us Gilderoy Lockhart's continuing ineptness, as he is unable to block a simple spell from Snape, stop the student duels, or eliminate the snake that Draco had produced. By now, we should be starting to wonder whether Gilderoy is a wizard at all, or merely a very good self-promoter. It is curious that Hermione is still so apparently taken with him. Snape, of course, sees through Lockhart; Ron observes that if Snape had looked at him like he was looking at Lockhart, Ron would have run for cover.

In the dueling club, we also learn that Harry can talk to snakes, and that this is a very rare achievement, linked only to Salazar Slytherin and his descendants. Given that the school is now fearing the ongoing depredations of "the Heir of Slytherin," this is a major concern, of course; proof of the connection between Salazar Slytherin and Harry could not be any plainer, and Harry, who is unsure of his ancestry, cannot disprove even to himself that he could be the Heir. The only mitigating factor that we, as readers, have is the knowledge that Harry himself was not present when the petrifications happened. Harry knows this as well, but cannot prove it in the two cases preceding the Dueling Club, or the one following. (The final one, as we will see, largely proves his innocence; but that does not occur for several months yet.)

This whole episode throws Harry into a great deal of confusion. The Sorting Hat wanted to put him into Slytherin house; he remembers quite plainly that the only reason it didn't was that he didn't want to be there. Obviously, the Hat had recognized the link to Slytherin that is now made manifest by Harry's Parseltongue ability. Yet Harry has come to enjoy being a Gryffindor; is he there under false pretenses? This uncertainty, to a greater or lesser extent, preys on Harry for the remainder of the book.

Greater Picture

Colin Creevey is the first Petrification of a student. The fact that he is in Ginny's class is apparently sufficient to cause her concern; in fact, her concern is caused by the slowly-dawning realization that she may be the one responsible for it, as it happened during a time that she cannot remember what she was doing.

The wrestling match between Hermione and Millicent Bullstrode is useful to our plot, as it is here that Hermione collects a hair that will later be used as part of Hermione's dose of Polyjuice Potion. This will, however, turn out to be something of a disaster as the hair in question does not come from Millicent herself.

We will learn in *Harry Potter and the Deathly Hallows* that Harry's ability with Parseltongue is in fact due to a link with Slytherin; it will be a sideways link, though, as it is related to the piece of Voldemort's soul that adhered to Harry and remains with him. The author has confirmed in a later interview that Harry's parseltongue ability vanished with that soul shard, and he has not missed it since.

Dumbledore later quiets Harry's doubts by showing him that he has received the Sword of Gryffindor from the Sorting Hat. "Only a true Gryffindor could have pulled that out of the Hat, Harry." While Dumbledore likely already knows about the soul shard, it is not something that he believes Harry is ready to hear about yet. It is only at the end of Harry's fifth year that Dumbledore finally tells Harry of the prophecy, which says either he or Voldemort must die. Dumbledore already understands that Harry will have to die in order to destroy the soul shard he carries; he believes, probably correctly, at the age of twelve Harry is too young to carry that weight of destiny.

Chapter 12: The Polyjuice Potion

Synopsis

Leaving Harry in the office, Professor McGonagall departs. Looking around, Harry sees intricate small mechanisms on the many tables, portraits of sleeping past Headmasters and Headmistresses on the walls, and the Sorting Hat on a shelf behind a desk. Seeing nobody around, Harry tries on the Hat, asking it if it still believes he should be in Slytherin. The Hat says Harry would have been great there. Replacing it on the shelf, Harry tells it that it is wrong. A slight noise attracts Harry's attention, and he sees an ill-looking bird sitting on a perch burst into flames. As it crumbles into ashes, Professor Dumbledore enters. He seem unperturbed about the bird catching fire. He explains, "Fawkes is a Phoenix, Harry. Phoenixes burst into flames when it is time for them to die and are reborn from the ashes." Lifting a chick from the ashes and placing it back on the perch, Dumbledore tells Harry that Phoenixes are extremely beautiful, except on a burning day. Also, "they can carry extremely heavy loads, their tears have healing powers, and they make *extremely* faithful pets."

Chapter 12: The Polyjuice Potion

Dumbledore is about to ask Harry something when he is interrupted by Hagrid, who bursts into the office, loudly proclaiming Harry's innocence. Dumbledore assures Hagrid that he does not suspect Harry of anything. Abashed, Hagrid leaves the office.

Dumbledore asks Harry if there is anything he would like to tell him. Harry silently recalls Ron's comment that hearing voices no one else can, even in the Wizarding world, is a bad thing, so he decides to say nothing to Dumbledore about it. Dumbledore dismisses him, and he returns to his dorm.

Nearly everyone in the school is now convinced that Harry is the Heir; Fred and George, however, joke about it, which Harry appreciates, as it makes it clear they do not believe it. Ginny, however, seems quite distraught. The term ends, and there are a few stayovers for Christmas, including Draco Malfoy, and his cronies Crabbe and Goyle. On Christmas day, Hermione barges into the boys' dormitory, waking them up and letting them know the Polyjuice Potion is ready. Harry receives Christmas presents from the Weasleys, while the Dursleys have sent him a toothpick. After Christmas dinner, Hermione gives Harry and Ron a pair of small cakes loaded with Sleeping Potion. They place them where they know Crabbe and Goyle will find them after stuffing themselves at dinner and leaving the Great Hall. Spying the cakes, Crabbe and Goyle promptly eat them; Ron and Harry drag the unconscious pair into a closet, gather a few hairs, and take their shoes. They head off to Moaning Myrtle's washroom where Hermione awaits with the potion.

Hermione has a hair from Millicent Bullstrode's robes, acquired during the Dueling Club debacle. After each adds a hair to their potion and drinks it, Ron and Harry painfully transform into Crabbe and Goyle's likenesses. Hermione, as did Ron, quickly retreated to a cubicle as the potion took effect. A few moments later Hermione tells Harry and Ron to go without her—something seems amiss, but she does not elaborate.

After much searching, Ron and Harry finally find the Slytherin Common room, although they run into Percy, who threatens detention for being in the halls after hours. They are rescued by Malfoy, who demands to know where they have been and leads them into the Common room. He begins discussing the Chamber of Secrets and says the Chamber was opened once before. A girl died then, killed by the Monster, and that the person who released it is likely still in Azkaban. Although he does not know who the Heir is, he wishes it was himself. He says his father has told him not to become involved in the matter, however.

As the potion starts wearing off, Harry and Ron rush back to Moaning Myrtle's washroom, politely leaving Crabbe and Goyle's shoes outside the closet they are still stashed in. They find Moaning Myrtle is happier than they have ever seen her, laughing wildly at Hermione. Apparently, the hair Hermione plucked off Millicent Bullstrode's robes was not Millicent's at all, but her cat's. Hermione now has a furry face, pointed ears, yellow eyes with slit pupils, and a bushy tail. As Polyjuice Potion is not intended for species transformations, it will not wear off on its own.

Analysis

Our introduction to Dumbledore's office here gives us additional insight into the nature of the Headmaster. At this point, we should be able to see that the Put-Outer, which we saw in the first chapter of the first book, is the same sort of magical / mechanical device which fills Dumbledore's office. We will gather that Dumbledore actually creates these things, rather than simply collecting and using them.

Once again, the Sorting Hat states that Harry would be great in Slytherin House. Harry, by this time, has started seeing indications that there is a link between him and Slytherin, notably Harry's ability to speak Parseltongue. This has left him unsure of whether he is, in fact, the Heir of Slytherin, as he has no way to trace his ancestry at this point. Despite his vehement denial of the Hat's belief, Harry, already troubled at the possibility, must be even more upset at the Hat's insistence on this link.

The emphasis that Dumbledore places on the abilities of the Phoenix seems a little more than we would expect; it is likely that this is a bit of foreshadowing. We are told of extreme loyalty, ability to lift heavy weights, and that its tears have healing powers; how could these abilities be of assistance to Harry?

Questions

Further Study 1. Should Harry have told Dumbledore about hearing voices? What would Dumbledore have done?

Greater Picture

It is in this chapter that Harry first meets Fawkes, Professor Dumbledore's phoenix. Fawkes plays an important part later in the year, saving Harry from dying twice (once by blinding the Basilisk, the other one by curing him from the Basilisk venom). Additionally, his other abilities are necessary in the end of this book, because it is his loyalty that will summon him to Harry's defence, and his ability to lift heavy weights will be what brings Harry and his co-adventurers back to the surface after the battle is complete. Fawkes will prove helpful both to Harry and to Dumbledore throughout the series.

In *Harry Potter and the Goblet of Fire*, Harry learns that the phoenix feather core of his holly wand comes from Fawkes, as does the core of Voldemort's yew wand.

Draco's admission that he does not know who the Heir of Slytherin is, and that his father hasn't told him anything except to stay out of it, is somewhat telling. Knowing what the Diary actually is, we can see that the Heir of Slytherin is, as Dumbledore has suggested, the same person as it was last time, Tom Riddle. However, the fact that Lucius has given Draco no instructions except to stay clear, again indicates that Lucius does not have a clear idea of what he has unleashed.

Ginny's being distraught at the Twins' fooling around is worthy of mention. We believe that Ginny has a crush on Harry, and we presume that this alone is enough to leave Ginny upset; the twins seem to be making fun of Harry, and we believe that Ginny is upset at this, despite Harry's appreciation of the fact that at least two people find the association of him with Slytherin to be laughable. In fact, though, a large part of Ginny's dismay is likely due to her beginning to wonder if she is acting as the Heir. Clearly, by this time, she has determined that the times when these things happen are times that she cannot remember what she has been doing, and, as the horcrux of Tom Riddle tells us later, is beginning to fear that she is losing her mind.

The portraits of the sleeping headmasters and headmistresses will play a part starting from *Harry Potter and the Order of the Phoenix.* The reader must be a bit curious, actually, as to why all these portraits are so sleepy when the portraits in the school proper are talkative and interact with the students. It will turn out that their apparent sleepiness is a form of concealment.

Chapter 13: The Very Secret Diary

Synopsis

Returning to Gryffindor tower after visiting Hermione in the Hospital Wing, Harry and Ron hear an outburst from Filch and cautiously investigate. A large puddle of water has covered the floor near Filch's usual post, the hallway where Mrs. Norris was petrified. The water is coming from Moaning Myrtle's washroom. When Harry and Ron enter the washroom, they find she is even more distraught than usual. Someone threw a book at her while she was in her favorite U-bend pipe. In her watery reaction, she washed the book from the cubicle and onto the floor. Harry finds it is a diary, dated fifty years previously, belonging to one T. M. Riddle, but the pages are blank. From his detention, Ron remembers that a T. M. Riddle received an award for Special Services to the School fifty years ago. He especially remembers having to polish it about fifty times because of slug slime.

In early February, Hermione, now fur-free and tailless, leaves the Hospital Wing. Harry tells her about Riddle's diary. She notices a correlation between the diary and the Chamber of Secrets: the Chamber was last opened fifty years ago. Thinking the diary may contain information about the Chamber, she attempts several revealing spells on it, but it remains stubbornly blank. Harry visits the Trophy Room to find some information about Riddle, but apart from his award, and his name on the list of Head Boys, there is no mention of what he did or who he is. Harry keeps the diary, hoping to learn about Riddle.

The mood at school is lighter; the attacks have ceased for now and spring is coming. The only cloud on the horizon is Professor Lockhart claiming credit for halting the attacks. Lockhart proposes a little "morale-booster" for Valentine's Day, which turns out to be a squad of dwarves dressed as Cupids running around the school delivering live Valentines. One corners Harry to deliver a Valentine (most likely from Ginny). In the resulting fracas, Harry's bag is ripped, and ink from a broken bottle spills over everything. Malfoy is there, grabs the diary, and starts waving it around. Ginny seems terrified, and Harry reclaims the diary using the disarming jinx. Harry notices that the diary does not have any ink stains. He tries to point this out to Ron, but Ron is occupied with his recalcitrant wand and ignores him.

That night, Harry discovers that if he writes in the diary, it responds with Tom Riddle's written words. When Harry asks about the Chamber of Secrets, the diary shows him the events of 13 June, fifty years back. Tom Riddle asks then-headmaster, Professor Dippet, if he can remain at Hogwarts for the summer, rather than return to his orphanage "home." Professor Dippet says because the Chamber of Secrets has been opened, that is impossible, and the school may have to close permanently. Riddle is then seen in the dungeons, secretly watching another student sneak in to care for an unknown large creature. It is Hagrid, then a third-year student. Tom confronts Hagrid and accuses him of releasing the Monster from the Chamber. As the creature scuttles away, Harry is suddenly ejected from the memory. He then tells Ron what he saw and that it was Hagrid who supposedly opened the Chamber of Secrets fifty years ago.

Analysis

It is mentioned here that Filch's usual post is a chair under the writing on the wall where Mrs. Norris was found. Thus, Mrs. Norris was found very close to Moaning Myrtle's washroom. While Harry and Ron never consciously make this connection, it may help Harry solve the riddle of the entrance to the Chamber later in the story. This also, incidentally, explains where the water came from that was on the floor of the hallway when Mrs. Norris was found. We had already seen that Peeves' insults had chased Myrtle back to her washroom; her distraught turning on of all the water in the washroom on that occasion, and the resulting flood in the hall, will likely prove important to the story.

The "mood lightener" at the school shows exactly how little understanding Lockhart has of how real people think. It does allow us to see how the other teachers feel about Lockhart. Additionally, it causes Harry to ask a question about the diary (why didn't it get ink-stained?), and as a result he learns how to communicate with it. The episode with the diary will reconfirm that the Chamber had been opened fifty years before, and a girl had died at that time. Draco Malfoy had told us this earlier, and that he did not know who had been responsible then. Evidence later in the series will indicate that Lucius Malfoy, Draco's father had attended Hogwarts some twenty years before Harry, so he could not have been there when the Chamber had been opened previously; it is possible that Lucius does not actually know who the Heir is, as he told Draco, though by now he may be having some suspicions.

This will be the first, but by no means the last, of Harry's experiences in other people's memories. Note that Harry is initially confused that Dippet does not react to him; this is the key indicator that he is in someone else's memories, which are of course unchanging. One possibly confusing issue is that if we are in Tom's memory, as stated, how can we see what Dippet is doing before Tom arrives? This is never completely explained. The author has said that when you are in someone else's memory, what you see is what happened, not what they perceived. It is possible that there is a range of effectiveness of the charm that retrieves the memory, such that anything happening within 30 feet (10M) or so of the owner of the memory can be retrieved.

GREATER PICTURE

For several reasons, this is a pivotal chapter in the book.

An important part of the whole plot of the Harry Potter series is shown here: this is Harry's first contact with Tom Riddle's diary, which we learn in *Harry Potter and the Half-Blood Prince* was the first Horcrux found of six believed made by Voldemort (whose original name was Tom Marvolo Riddle). We will learn that it is this soul shard of Tom's that is opening the Chamber, and he is doing it by controlling Ginny. It is because Ginny has finally connected the diary with the strangeness that is going on that she attempts to get rid of it by flushing it down the toilet in Moaning Myrtle's washroom, thus arousing Myrtle's ire and attracting Harry and Ron's attention. The episode with Draco Malfoy, where he is waving the diary around, particularly disturbs Ginny because she recognizes the diary and thought she had gotten rid of it, and now was deathly afraid that Harry might learn how to communicate with it, and through it learn the secrets that she had entrusted to it. We are led to believe, however, that her mortification is because she is the originator of the Valentine greeting being delivered to Harry. It is because Ginny no longer has the diary, and thus is no longer being controlled by it, that the attacks cease. Ginny will eventually retrieve the diary, and the attacks will immediately start up again, though nobody will make the connection between the two events.

This is also where Harry learns a fundamental piece of the story, although it is incomplete: apparently, Hagrid had something to do with the opening of the Chamber of Secrets fifty years ago. However, we will shortly learn that the pet Tom Riddle saw him with was an Acromantula, a large spider which is capable of speech. While Hagrid and the Acromantula will prove to be totally unconnected with the Chamber, it will be this Acromantula, Aragog, who will give Harry a clue he needs to find the entrance to the Chamber of Secrets.

While the memory that Tom shows Harry is accurate, it is incomplete and is slanted to imply Tom is innocent and Hagrid is the one who opened the Chamber. Harry, like the school of Tom Riddle's day, is taken in by this. Of course, it was Tom, who was the only remaining heir of Slytherin at that time, and who had been exploring the school extensively, who had found and opened the Chamber, and who was controlling the Monster within it. It is because of Tom's exposure of Hagrid, and his carefully not releasing the Monster again after Hagrid's expulsion, that the Headmaster of the day, Dippet, and the rest of the school (with the possible exception of Professor Dumbledore), believed he had correctly identified the one who was opening the Chamber. It is for this that Tom was given the Special Services award.

As a side note, we should mention that memories of this nature can be edited; we will see an instance of that in *Harry Potter and the Half-Blood Prince* that Professor Slughorn has edited his memories before giving them to Professor Dumbledore. The editing in that case was done rather clumsily. Unlike Slughorn, Riddle does not try to replace segments of memory which he wants to keep hidden; instead he simply jumps over them. It is actually in this book, looking back on it from the end of the series, that we first see the habit of Dumbledore to hold his cards extremely close to his vest. Dumbledore, we are told, had his suspicions about Riddle from the beginning, suspicions that were held by none of the other staff. Dumbledore seems to have suspected that Riddle had not been entirely truthful in his exposure of Hagrid as the one who was opening the Chamber. Dumbledore has clearly retained this suspicion through the intervening fifty years, and believes that it is Riddle who is again opening the Chamber, but as seen in an earlier chapter, only wonders how he is doing it.

Chapter 14: Cornelius Fudge

SYNOPSIS

Harry, Ron, and Hermione discuss this revelation endlessly—none want to believe that Hagrid would have anything to do with a monster. And yet, they know he was expelled from Hogwarts and likes large and scary creatures, like "Fluffy," the giant three-headed dog that guarded the Philosopher's Stone the previous year. The attacks must have stopped after Tom Riddle turned in Hagrid. Otherwise, Tom would not have received the Special Services award. They decided to do nothing unless there are more attacks. The school seems to be returning to normal, and the Mandrake plants are maturing and almost ready be used to treat those who have been Petrified. Starting in their third year, Hogwarts students can attend elective courses, so over Easter Break, the second-years are to select their third-year classes. Everyone wants advice on what to take, except Hermione, who eventually decides to take everything. Harry asks Percy, who pompously tells him to stay with his strengths. Feeling he has no strengths except Quidditch, Harry decides to take the same courses as Ron so they can work together. Oliver Wood is mercilessly practicing the Quidditch team. The game against Hufflepuff House is coming up, and they have the best chance in years to win the trophy. Returning from practice, Harry discovers his dorm has been ransacked, apparently by someone searching for something. While reorganizing his things, Harry discovers Riddle's diary is gone. Harry surmises that a Gryffindor must have taken it; nobody else knows the password to the tower. The next day, as Harry heads to the Quidditch pitch for the match against Hufflepuff, he hears the voice again. Ron and Hermione, who are with him, hear nothing, but something suddenly occurs to Hermione. With her usual cryptic comments, she heads to the library. Ron and Harry go to the Pitch, but just before the game starts, Professor McGonagall announces it has been canceled and orders everyone to their House Common rooms. She singles out Harry and Ron and has them follow her to the infirmary. There has been a double attack: a Ravenclaw girl and Hermione have been petrified. Both were found near the library, and Hermione was clutching a small mirror. Professor McGonagall announces new restrictions, including a 6:00 P.M. curfew. A teacher must escort students between classes, and there is a ban on all evening activities, including Quidditch practice. She also says the school may close permanently.

The attacked Ravenclaw girl is a Prefect, Penelope Clearwater. Percy is in shock, apparently having believed Prefects were immune from attacks. Harry and Ron decide it is time to ask Hagrid what he knows about the Chamber of Secrets. Using Harry's Invisibility Cloak, they go to his hut, but before they can ask him anything, they are interrupted by a knock at the door. Harry and Ron hide under the Cloak as Professor Dumbledore and Minister of Magic Cornelius Fudge enter. Fudge apparently believes, like Harry and Ron, that it was Hagrid who opened the Chamber fifty years earlier. Over Dumbledore's protests, Fudge is sending Hagrid to Azkaban as a precaution. Ron whispers to Harry that Azkaban is the Wizard prison. Lucius Malfoy arrives with an Order signed by the Governors of Hogwarts calling for Dumbledore's removal as Headmaster, although Fudge objects. As he is leaving, Dumbledore says, "I will only *truly* have left the school when none here are loyal to me. You will also find that help will be given at Hogwarts to those who ask for it." As he speaks, he looks directly at Harry and Ron huddled under the Cloak. Malfoy and Dumbledore then leave. Hagrid says that if anyone wants to find some answers, they should just follow the spiders, and he leaves as well, escorted by Fudge.

ANALYSIS

The revelation that Hagrid may be involved with the opening of the Chamber is clearly a hard one for Harry to deal with. The proof seems incontrovertible, Harry has actually seen the events of the day Hagrid was discovered. Harry's trust in Hagrid has been shaken, but still remains in place for the moment; it is only after the attacks start again that Harry feels he has to approach Hagrid to find out about the events that resulted in his expulsion. In the meanwhile, the diary has been stolen; Harry seems to believe that it was a targeted theft, as nothing else of his has been taken. Harry and Ron have also concluded that it was someone in Gryffindor. Both of these facts could turn out to be significant. One thing that is certain at this point is that Harry will not be able to learn anything more about the night Hagrid was expelled from Hogwarts by this route.

If Harry had braced Hagrid about those events, almost certainly he would also have had to explain how he had seen them, and the early revelation of the role of the diary would have significantly weakened the story. Thus, Hagrid's arrest at this point, or some other way of rendering Hagrid unavailable for the remainder of the year, is necessary to the story line. Having Hagrid arrested at this point also introduces us to Azkaban Prison and the fear wizards have of the place. From the title of the next book, *Harry Potter and the Prisoner of Azkaban*, we can figure that Azkaban will figure largely in it; and as it has been at least mentioned now in both this and the previous book, we can guess that Azkaban will reappear a number of times in future books as well.

From what we have seen of him already, we can gather that Lucius Malfoy is seldom, if ever, straightforward in his motives. In this case, he tells us that the Board of Hogwarts has seen fit to suspend Dumbledore for not preventing the attacks on the students. Readers are, by this time, well aware that his motives are seldom what they seem, and his machinations are extensive. It is a safe assumption that he has coerced the board into suspending Dumbledore; his evident air of satisfaction when delivering the document speaks to that. However, we are left wondering exactly what he hopes to gain by this action. Is his hatred of Dumbledore sufficient for this level of action against him? Or is there something more that we have not yet discovered?

Hagrid is careful to tell Harry and Ron about the spiders; we don't yet know why. We have seen the spiders acting oddly already, near Moaning Myrtle's bathroom.

QUESTIONS

Further Study 1. Before he leaves, Dumbledore seems to look directly at Harry and Ron, though they are under the Invisibility Cloak. Can Dumbledore really see them?

GREATER PICTURE

It should be noted that a new attack occurs immediately after the theft of the diary. It is certain that the diary was deliberately disposed of; carrying something into a disused bathroom and flushing it down the toilet is not something that would happen accidentally. Almost immediately after the diary is stolen from Harry, there is another attack. If in fact the diary is somehow connected to the attacks, which seems likely, then equally it seems likely that the original owner has stolen it back for some reason. Additionally, we are told that the thief is almost certainly a Gryffindor student. We will find out that the diary is, in fact, associated with the attacks and with a Gryffindor student in the final chapters of this book.

We are led to believe, by what the Twins say, that Percy is distressed only because a Prefect has been attacked. Percy had quite plainly believed that Prefects would be invulnerable. Even so, his reaction appears to be extreme, until we learn in the end of this book that Ginny had caught him kissing Penelope Clearwater. Revelation of this romantic entanglement makes Percy's shock understandable at last.

The fact that Hermione runs to the library after Harry hears "the voice" again is perhaps the thing that will help Harry the most in his task of saving the day again: she is able to connect the fact that Harry is the only one that can hear a voice inside the walls with some details her own intelligence provides. She comes to the conclusion at this point that the monster is a Basilisk, which Harry can hear because of his Parseltongue ability, which allows him to speak to snakes. A Basilisk kills with its gaze if someone looks directly into his eyes. However, no one in this book has yet died, because they have seen the monster in an indirect fashion: Mrs. Norris reflected in the puddle of water outside

Myrtle's bathroom, Colin through his camera, Justin through Nearly-Headless Nick (who sees it directly, but since he is already dead, it can't kill him again), and Hermione and Penelope reflected in a mirror Hermione was carrying. Hermione also guesses why the voice that Harry hears seems to pass easily through floors, and does not appear to have a source: the Basilisk uses the pipes to go through the walls of the school unmolested. Lucius' motives in getting Dumbledore suspended are never entirely cleared up, but some clarification comes from the understanding that Lucius engineered the attacks, even though he apparently remains not entirely certain of the mechanism involved. Knowing that Lucius provided the weapon, we can see that his arranging for Dumbledore's suspension is an attempt to give the weapon free reign. Of all of the teachers at Hogwarts, only three seem to be willing to accept the idea that there might be a Chamber of Secrets that could contain a monster: Dumbledore, who had been at Hogwarts at the time, McGonagall, who accepts Dumbledore's word on it implicitly, and Lockhart, who is utterly ineffectual. By removing Dumbledore, Lucius is effectively halving the strength of the forces countering the monster.

Chapter 15: Aragog

Synopsis

Security is tighter than ever. Harry and Ron are unable to visit Hermione in the infirmary. Teachers shepherd students around in little groups. Most students are upset and frightened, although Malfoy is seemingly pleased over having played some role in Dumbledore's removal.

About a fortnight later in Herbology, Ernie Macmillan, the Hufflepuff who had earlier accused Harry of being the Heir of Slytherin, apologizes and asks Harry if he believes Malfoy could be the Heir. Harry points out some spiders to Ron, the first they have seen since Hagrid's arrest, and comments that they appear to be headed for the Forbidden Forest. Ron is not cheerful over this news. As they are escorted to their next class, Defence Against the Dark Arts, Harry says that in order to follow the spiders, they will need his Invisibility Cloak, and they should take Fang. Professor Lockhart bounds into the classroom, gaily saying that with Hagrid arrested, the danger has passed. Ron wants to dispute that, but Harry reminds him that they were not actually there. Harry decides they should follow the spiders that night.

Waiting until past midnight for the Common room to clear, Harry and Ron make their way through the halls, crowded with teachers and ghosts looking for signs of the Monster. They get Fang from Hagrid's hut and, making their way into the Forest, follow the spiders by wand light. Hearing something large moving, they investigate. It is Mr. Weasley's flying car, wandering the Forest. As they look to see how it is doing, they are caught by giant spiders and dragged to a hollow among the trees. There they meet Aragog, the patriarch of a huge giant spider colony. Aragog, cranky at having his sleep disturbed, tells his children to kill Harry and Ron. Harry forestalls this by saying they are Hagrid's friends, and he is in trouble, arrested again for apparently opening the Chamber. Aragog admits he was believed to be the Monster, but he was not. The Monster is another creature, one that is an enemy to spiders, and such that he cannot even name it. Aragog was blamed for killing a girl, but he says the girl died in a bathroom, a part of the Castle he was never in. Hagrid kept him in a cupboard in the dungeon. As Aragog is unable to help them further, Harry says they will just go. Aragog says no, his children will not harm Hagrid on his command, but he does not have enough control over them to keep Hagrid's friends safe. As the spiders start their attack, Mr. Weasley's car screeches onto the scene. Harry and Ron bundle themselves and Fang into it, and it carries them back to Hagrid's hut, leaves them, and returns to the Forest.

Back in the Gryffindor dorm, Harry has a sudden thought: was the girl killed in the bathroom Moaning Myrtle?

Analysis

Hermione's being Petrified, as alarming as it is, is not without some good effects. Until now, Harry had been suspected of being the Heir of Slytherin, because of his being able to talk to snakes. Now, though, even the most suspicious of Harry's fellow students agree that Harry cannot be the instigator of the attacks, as he would not have injured Hermione. Ernie, in particular, announces his belief that it is not Harry but Malfoy who is the Heir; Ron's evident amusement at the idea is probably due to Harry and Ron having come up with the same idea several months previously.

We see here the truth to Hagrid's utterance that if people wanted to learn some stuff, they should follow the spiders. Whenever we have seen the spiders in the past, Harry has thought that it looked like they were trying to run away from something. It now seems that they were trying to run towards something. We find that they are apparently headed for a spider colony in the Forbidden Forest led by Aragog, perhaps feeling that the Acromantula colony will afford them some protection. It is from Aragog that Harry and Ron learn at least some of the truth about events at Hagrid's expulsion from Hogwarts. And Aragog also gives Harry a clue to where the entrance to the Chamber is. It is, for a while, uncertain as to whether Harry will be able to use this knowledge, as they seem to be surrounded by masses of inimical and hungry spiders. The flying car being present and willing to help them seems fortuitous, but is an indication of the author's deftness at preparing situations to pay off in future chapters (and future books). We were led to believe that, having delivered Harry and Ron to Hogwarts and gone off to sulk in the Forest, the role of the flying car was done; we are pleased to see that in fact there is still something that the aging and ailing car can do for Harry. While it certainly seems odd, at first glance, to assign personality to a machine, we see that the car in this chapter does show personality, and that personality is consistent from the arrival at Hogwarts through this chapter.

Questions

Further Study   1. The monster, now, has petrified Mrs. Norris, Colin Creevey, Justin Finch-Fletchley, Hermione, and Penelope Clearwater. Is it targeting those who are not pure-blooded? Or is this random?

2. The flying car has come to Harry's rescue; will it do so again, in a later book?

Greater Picture

There is very little in this chapter that will carry forward to later books. We will learn that Harry's guess, that the girl who died is Moaning Myrtle, is correct, and we will learn how she died. We see further illumination of Lockhart's character in this chapter. We learn of the existence of Aragog. However, rather than laying groundwork for future books, this chapter is almost entirely involved with the business of moving this book's story forward to its close. Aragog's fate is revisited in *Harry Potter and the Half-Blood Prince*, when he dies from old age and brings Hagrid, Professor Slughorn, and Harry together to mourn his death. Hagrid at that point will be surprised to find that Aragog's offspring do not grant him free passage, but rather actually try to attack him. Given their experiences in this chapter, neither Harry nor Ron is at all surprised by their behaviour.

Aragog's children will appear again in the closing chapters of the last book, *Harry Potter and the Deathly Hallows*, and Hagrid will again assume that they are less dangerous than they are.

We will not see the flying car again, and while Moaning Myrtle will appear in future books, the circumstances of her death will not prove important after this book.

Chapter 16: The Chamber of Secrets

Synopsis

With increased security, getting into Moaning Myrtle's bathroom will be difficult, but Harry and Ron will need to talk to Myrtle to find out if their guess is correct.

Professor McGonagall reminds them that exams will be starting in only a week's time. Apparently this catches everyone by surprise. With the school in the state it is in, it seemed unlikely that exams would continue. Three days later, Professor McGonagall announces at breakfast that the Mandrakes are ready, and the Petrified victims will be revived that night. Ginny sits down beside Harry and Ron. It seems she has something important to say to them, but when Percy arrives after a night's patrolling, she runs away. Percy says he knows what she was going to talk to them about, and that it had nothing to do with the Chamber; but he deflects questions about what it was.

While it is possible that the mystery will be solved with Hermione's revival, Harry still wants to see if Moaning Myrtle can help them. An opportunity appears that morning: as Professor Lockhart escorts students to History of Magic class, Harry and Ron suggest that he doesn't really need to guard them with Hagrid arrested and the threat gone, and he agrees and goes off to take a nap. Harry and Ron manage to leave the group and head for Myrtle's bathroom, but are found by Professor McGonagall, who demands to know what they are doing. Harry says they want to visit Hermione in the hospital wing. Touched by their concern, McGonagall allows them to go, and now they are forced to actually go to the infirmary. While visiting Hermione, they find paper caught in her hand. Removing it with some difficulty, they see it is a page from a book describing Basilisks. "Pipes" is handwritten in the margin. Harry realizes that a Basilisk kills with its gaze, but because no one was looking directly at it, nobody died. Mrs. Norris saw a reflection in the water on the floor. Colin Creevey was looking through his camera lens. Justin saw it through Nearly Headless Nick, and, of course, Hermione had her mirror. This explains both the spiders fleeing it and the roosters being killed—a rooster's crow is fatal to it. Harry can hear the voice because he is a Parselmouth—the Basilisk is a snake. It travels through the walls and ceilings using the plumbing. It occurs to Ron that, if Myrtle was the Basilisk's victim last time, the Chamber's entrance may be in Moaning Myrtle's washroom. Harry and Ron go to the staff room to report their findings to Professor McGonagall; nobody is there, so they decide to wait. There is an announcement ordering all students to their Houses. Harry and Ron hide so they can find out what has happened. Professor McGonagall and the staff arrive, and McGonagall says a student has been taken into the Chamber. It is Ginny Weasley. Lockhart arrives, belatedly, and is told what has happened. Several teachers call him on his boasts over the past few weeks and he is appointed to open the Chamber and defeat the Monster. He excuses himself to go to his office and "prepare." Having gotten rid of him, the remaining instructors plan how they will inform the students and the future of the school.

Harry and Ron rush to Lockhart's office to tell him what they know. There they find him hastily packing his belongings. He admits that he never actually did the feats in his books. Rather, he took credit for other wizards accomplishments and used a charm to erase their memories. He threatens Harry and Ron with a memory charm, but Harry disarms him, and Ron throws his wand out the window. They force Lockhart to go with them to Moaning Myrtle's washroom. Myrtle says that when she was a student, she went into the washroom to have a bit of a cry. Hearing a boy's voice, she looked out of the cubicle and saw big yellow eyes—then she died. She points out one particular basin. Harry addresses it in Parseltongue, and it opens to reveal a vertical shaft. Ron and Harry push Lockhart down the shaft first, then follow.

Finding themselves in a tunnel, they investigate. A giant snake skin is lying on the ground. Lockhart pretends to faint, but as Ron approaches him, he grabs Ron's wand. He says he will tell everyone that he defeated the monster, and use a piece of the snake skin as proof, but that Harry and Ron were unfortunately rendered insane after seeing Ginny's dead body. He casts a memory charm, but Ron's broken wand backfires and explodes, causing Lockhart to erase his own memory and the ceiling to collapse. Harry and Ron are unhurt, but the fallen rubble separates them. Harry leaves Ron to clear the rock fall while he explores the tunnel further ahead. He finds a door, which also opens when he speaks Parseltongue.

Analysis

It is here that the truth about Lockhart's abilities is revealed: all the things he said he did in his books were actually done by other people, and having learned their stories, he alters their memory so that he can claim the credit for the others' doings, without fear of their contradicting his claims. As we have seen, he is magically quite weak, with the apparent exception of his Memory charms, and here is defeated by Harry's disarmament charm, as he was by Professor Snape in the Dueling Club. We can suppose that he is somewhat transparent to other wizards as well; he is certainly not held in particular esteem by any of the instructors at Hogwarts, so it is entirely possible that he is given misinformation by those whose stories he is stealing. This would, in fact, explain his confidence in the ineffectual Pixie-banishing charm he had used in the first Defence Against the Dark Arts class. Of course, he had never used it himself, merely borrowing it from a more accomplished wizard. It is likely that the wizard he borrowed it from, out of disgust at Lockhart's general pandering to the audience, gave him an ineffectual charm in hopes that it would bring Lockhart down a few notches when he did try to use it.

It is worthwhile examining the technique used by the Weasley children for de-gnoming the garden earlier in the light of this revelation. While we are never explicitly told that the technique was from Lockhart's book, the reference to *Gilderoy Lockhart's Guide to Household Pests* does tend to indicate that as the source. The fact that the technique is, ultimately, ineffectual would also tend to suggest Lockhart as the original source. This is a particularly telling comment on the nature of celebrity and those who seek it. Lockhart, who the author has said was modeled on a real person,[1] is clearly willing to sacrifice anyone and anything in order to keep his own star bright. Harry, who Hagrid had earlier said was more famous than Lockhart would ever be, clearly is not interested in the fame he has fallen into; we see throughout this book that he is trying, in some cases futilely, to stay out of the limelight. In contrast to Harry, who remains a solid, sympathetic character despite his renown, Lockhart has made himself into a glossy, empty shell, and the reader cannot help but be pleased to see him hoist by his own petard.

When they are approaching the Chamber, Ron's broken wand finally does something well: when Lockhart steals it and, ignoring the possibility that Ginny may still be alive, attempts to erase Harry and Ron's memories, it backfires and Obliviates him, as well as causing a small explosion. This backfire ends Lockhart's plan to claim to have found the Chamber and destroyed the Monster, at the cost of three student lives; it also causes a rock fall that separates Harry and Ron. Now, Harry will have to search for Ginny alone, without his friends' help.

Greater Picture

We will later find out that the effects of the memory charm backfire on Lockhart are quite long-lasting, and Lockhart is not yet recovered when we meet him some three years later. This is to be expected, in a way; Lockhart had been intending the charm he placed on Ron to be permanent, so when it backfired on him, it is only to be expected that it act permanently.

Even as early as this, we start to see some signs of the future romantic entanglements of the main characters in the series. Ginny, having something important that she needs to tell people, approaches Harry first, rather than one of her own brothers. Of course, earlier in the book, we had seen that Ginny was showing all the signs of the classic schoolgirl crush on Harry, but it should be noted that a person with such a crush is almost always too much in awe of the subject of the crush to ever approach him. This would be an indication that Ginny's feelings have matured and deepened, possibly beyond the crush level. Despite several side roads on both Harry's and Ginny's part, this relationship will persist, off and on, throughout the entire series.

We also see the first of several progressively-larger hints that the author drops about the relationship between Ron and Hermione. While Ron is upset at the depredations of the Monster, we can see that he is much more upset at Hermione's Petrification than at the fate of anyone else, except Ginny, his sister. True to his character, though, Ron will not recognize his concern for what it is for several years yet.

The fact that Harry is unable to tell whether he is speaking English or Parseltongue should be unsurprising, as he cannot tell the difference between the two languages when hearing them. It is in this chapter that this is pointed up; nobody else can hear the Basilisk, because to them its speech is a low, undifferentiated hissing, but to Harry it sounds like plain speech. This will prove a plot point in the final book of the series.

Chapter 17: The Heir of Slytherin

Synopsis

Harry finds himself at one end of a long chamber; at the other is a giant statue, probably Salazar Slytherin. The statue has an ancient, monkey-like face with a long thin beard, and is wearing sweeping robes. Lying on the floor is Ginny. His efforts to revive Ginny are interrupted by a tall, black-haired boy who identifies himself as Tom Riddle. Riddle, who is holding Harry's dropped wand, explains he is a memory, preserved in his diary for fifty years. He opened the Chamber of Secrets fifty years ago, intending to purge Muggle-borns and half-bloods from the school. However, when the school was to close due to the attacks and because Dumbledore (then the Transfiguration teacher) was keeping such a close watch on him, he halted the attacks and framed Hagrid. Not wanting to waste the years spent searching

---
[1] http://www.jkrowling.com/textonly/en/extrastuff_view.cfm?id=9

for the Chamber, he left behind a diary containing the memory of his sixteen-year-old self in hopes it would, one day, fall into the hands of an unsuspecting victim who would help finish his work.

Ginny had been writing in the diary all year. Riddle wrote back sympathetically, and Ginny confessed her fears, hopes, and feelings to him. She essentially poured some of her soul into him, which was exactly what he wanted. He gradually grew more powerful and eventually poured some of his soul back into her, possessing her and using her body to strangle the school roosters, write on the walls, and open the Chamber of Secrets. He tells Harry how Ginny told him Harry's entire history and how happy he was when Harry picked up the diary after Ginny became fearful and threw it away. He says he was disappointed when Ginny reclaimed it. Having seen Harry with the diary on Valentine's day, she was afraid it would reveal her secrets, and so she ransacked Harry's room to retrieve it. Tom forced Ginny into the Chamber for two purposes: first, to sap her remaining life force and come fully to life; and second, to lure Harry Potter there so he could meet him directly.

Tom wants to know how Harry, an ordinary baby wizard, could have defeated Lord Voldemort, the most powerful wizard of the age. Harry wonders why Tom cares. Riddle reveals he is, in fact, a half-blood. His mother named him Tom after his Muggle father and Marvolo after his wizard grandfather, a descendant of Salazar Slytherin. He scrambled his name to create a new one—Lord Voldemort, a name he knew people would fear when he became the most powerful wizard in the world. It was also a way to eliminate his Muggle father's name. Harry states Voldemort was not the most powerful wizard, Albus Dumbledore is. He says Dumbledore probably saw right through Tom when he was at school and is still stronger than Voldemort. When Tom says Dumbledore was driven from the school by Tom's memory, Harry retorts that Dumbledore may be closer than Tom realizes. Fawkes, Dumbledore's Phoenix, suddenly appears in a burst of fire and drops the Sorting Hat at Harry's feet. It then perches on his shoulder. Tom is openly contemptuous: a songbird and an old hat. This is what Dumbledore sends to his allies? Tom again demands to know how Harry defeated Voldemort. Harry notices that Riddle's form is becoming more solid while Ginny's life force fades. Harry must act quickly if he is to defeat Riddle. Harry tells Riddle that by sacrificing her life for her son, his mother saved him from Voldemort and reduced him to an ineffectual remnant.

Mastering his rage, Tom agrees that indeed would be a powerful protection. He then summons the Monster—it is the Basilisk. Harry avoids its deadly gaze, as Fawkes leaves his shoulder. Harry is smashed against the wall by the snake's coil but is not bitten. He sees that Fawkes has blinded the Basilisk. Tom is still ordering the serpent to kill Harry, telling it to smell him. The thrashing snake has swept the Sorting Hat into Harry's arms. He puts it on, thinking "Help me!" The Hat constricts sharply and something hits him in the head. Taking it off, Harry finds a sword inside. As the Basilisk strikes, Harry impales it through the roof of its mouth and into its brain, killing it. But a single venomous fang pierces his arm.

Harry removes the fang, but it is too late. As the venom spreads, Harry dimly sees Fawkes land beside him. Riddle tells Harry he will soon be dead, even Dumbledore's bird knows; he is weeping. But both have forgotten that Phoenix tears heal wounds. Tom suddenly realizes this and attempts a killing curse. Before he can strike, Fawkes drops the diary into Harry's lap, and Harry stabs the diary with the fang. Tom Riddle is destroyed.

As Riddle vanishes, Ginny awakens. She gives a great gasp, begins crying, and says she wanted to tell Harry at breakfast that it was her that who was helping Riddle, that the diary was controlling her, but she could not speak in front of Percy. Now she is afraid of being expelled. Harry comforts her and takes her to where Ron has been clearing rocks. Ron wants to know where the sword and the bird came from, but Harry wants to explain later when Ginny is not around. Harry asks where Lockhart is. Ron points to the end of the tunnel. Lockhart has forgotten everything, even his own name.

Fawkes hovers near Harry, and Harry remembers that Phoenixes can lift amazingly heavy loads. Everyone holds on to each other and, with Harry holding Fawkes' tail, are flown from the Chamber to Moaning Myrtle's washroom. Myrtle seems mildly upset that Harry is still alive. She was going to offer him space in her toilet if he died. Fawkes flies to Professor McGonagall's office. Harry knocks on the door and opens it.

Analysis

This chapter is largely concerned with first, providing the hidden story behind the events that have occurred, and second, the action involved in defeating the adversary (here, Voldemort, as in the first book) and the Monster, and saving Ginny. As such, in the context of the book, there is not much analysis that can be done. The first part of the chapter is largely exposition, with Riddle explaining the back story; then, there is the brief battle with the Basilisk, and the return to the end of the tunnel where Ron waits. This leaves very little to analyze. However, it is perhaps useful to note that "a memory of Tom Riddle" can act independently and can take over another person's life force to return itself to life. This may prove unusual enough a characteristic to warrant special attention.

Questions

Review 1. How does Harry see the Basilisk without dying?

Further Study 1. Fawkes must see the the Basilisk's eyes, in order to puncture them. How does he do so without dying?

2. How does Tom Riddle manage to see the Basilisk? He, too, will be vulnerable to its eyes. Or can the Basilisk switch that function on and off at will?

GREATER PICTURE

Riddle repeatedly says that the diary contains a memory of Tom. What Harry is seeing and talking to is only a memory. However, in *Harry Potter and the Half-Blood Prince*, Professor Dumbledore points out that Riddle's diary does far more than a memory should be able to—it can think and respond on its own, it can take over another person and make them do its bidding, and it can sap the life force from another person to create a body for itself. This strongly indicates that the diary is actually a Horcrux. Or rather, *was* a Horcrux; Harry has destroyed it. In *Harry Potter and the Deathly Hallows*, it will be revealed that Harry has lucked into one of the very few techniques that will destroy a Horcrux: Basilisk venom. In that book, it is revealed that a Horcrux will act to keep its physical container intact, to the full extent of ordinary magic; in order to destroy a Horcrux, its physical container must be damaged beyond the ability of ordinary magic. Also in that chapter, it will be revealed that the only known cure for Basilisk venom is Phoenix tears, which, due to the extreme rarity of Phoenixes, are certainly outside the realm of ordinary magic.

This of course leads to an apparent problem: there is actually a phoenix in close proximity shortly before Harry stabs the diary. Could not the diary, making use of more ordinary magic similar to the Accio charm, summon some of Fawkes' tears to itself? Possibly it could, but the author has stated, in an interview given after the publication of *Harry Potter and the Deathly Hallows*, that she had very carefully distanced the phoenix before the death blow. And looking at the sequence of events, we see that Riddle had, in fact, attempted to Curse Fawkes, driving him away and presumably out of range, before Harry stabbed the diary.

There are a few other useful items that are mentioned in passing in this chapter. Thinking Harry will shortly be dead, Riddle mentions his grandfather's name, Marvolo, something that we will learn much later Voldemort had been taking some pains to conceal. This will not be useful to Harry, though Dumbledore, who also knows it, uses it to unearth one of the Horcruxes: given the approximate age, and the name Marvolo which evidently is not common in the Wizarding world, plus the name Riddle associated with a Wizard-caused death in Tom's youth, Dumbledore is able to locate Tom's mother's home and retrieve a Horcrux hidden there. Tom also mentions what has likely become his greatest shame in the intervening fifty years: that despite being the last heir of Slytherin, Tom is descended from a Muggle, and so is one of the very half-bloods that he despises. Harry is able to cause some dissension in the ranks of a group of Death Eaters that he is facing in *Harry Potter and the Order of the Phoenix*, before the Battle in the Ministry, by mentioning that to them.

Chapter 18: Dobby's Reward

SYNOPSIS

In Professor McGonagall's office, Harry finds Mrs. Weasley and Mr. Weasley, who immediately sweep Ginny into a hug. Also present are Professor Dumbledore and, of course, Professor McGonagall. McGonagall demands to know what happened, so Harry tells them, omitting Ginny's role and the diary as much as possible. Professor Dumbledore wonders how Lord Voldemort enchanted Ginny, as he is currently hiding in Albania. Harry is relieved, as this means Dumbledore is aware Ginny was under the influence of someone else. He says it was Riddle's diary, which he has brought with him, along with the sword and the Sorting Hat. Dumbledore confirms that Riddle and Voldemort are one and the same. Mr. Weasley chastises Ginny: "Never trust anything that can think for itself if you can't see where it keeps its brain!" Dumbledore sends her to the hospital wing, saying that there will be no punishment, as it is not her fault. "Older and wiser wizards than she have been hoodwinked by Lord Voldemort." He also says she should have bed rest and perhaps a large mug of hot chocolate, one of his favorite things to do when he is distraught. He says that Madam Pomfrey will still be awake, giving out Mandrake juice. Ron is heartened to discover that Hermione will have suffered no permanent damage. Mr. and Mrs. Weasley leave with Ginny. Dumbledore dispatches Professor McGonagall to alert the kitchens that a feast is called for.

Professor Dumbledore awards Ron and Harry Special Awards for Services to the School plus two hundred House points each; then asks Professor Lockhart why he is so quiet about his part in the adventure. Lockhart gazes vaguely around to see who Dumbledore is talking about, as Ron explains about his wand backfire. Dumbledore has Ron take Lockhart to the hospital wing. Professor Dumbledore and Harry are now alone.

Harry admits to Dumbledore that Riddle alarmed him by noting their similarities: they are both orphans, dark-haired, and speak Parseltongue. Dumbledore believes Voldemort transferred some of his powers, including the ability to speak Parseltongue, when his curse on the one-year-old Harry failed. Harry says the Sorting Hat saw Slytherin's power in him and wanted to put him in Slytherin. Dumbledore said it put him in Gryffindor instead. Harry says it was only because he asked it to. Dumbledore says, "It is our choices, Harry, that show what we truly are, far more than our abilities." He then shows Harry the sword. Engraved on the blade is, Godric Gryffindor. "Only a true Gryffindor could have pulled *that* out of the Hat, Harry."

The door bursts open and Lucius Malfoy stalks in, accompanied by, to Harry's amazement, Dobby. Lucius is furious that Dumbledore has returned after being suspended. Dumbledore replies that when the news of the attack on Mr. Weasley's daughter had gotten out, he was asked to return by the other eleven Governors, some of whom had been under the impression that if they had not voted for his suspension, Malfoy would have cursed them and their families. Lucius demands to know if the culprit has been found. Dumbledore says it was the same as last time, via the diary, and most ingeniously. If the plot succeeded, Ginny Weasley would been blamed, reflecting badly on Arthur Weasley and his Muggle Protection Act. Behind Mr. Malfoy's back, Dobby is performing a charade, which Harry suddenly understands: it was Malfoy who gave the diary to

Ginny at Flourish and Blotts. Lucius demands that they prove this accusation. Dumbledore says that is impossible with the diary destroyed, but if other such artifacts are passed to anyone, Arthur Weasley will be sure to link them back to Lucius Malfoy. Lucius stomps off, kicking Dobby along the way. Harry takes Riddle's diary, wraps it in one of his socks, and runs out to return it to Lucius. Lucius angrily strips the sock off and tosses it aside. Dobby catches it. He is free at last. He protects Harry against Mr. Malfoy's rage. Lucius leaves Hogwarts, defeated on all fronts. Dobby asks how he can repay Harry, and Harry says all he has to do is never try to save his life again.

The feast is an odd one, even for Hogwarts, with everyone in pyjamas, lasting all night, and enlivened by the return of the Petrified students and Hagrid. Everyone is further cheered by the announcement that exams are canceled; all except Hermione.

The remaining year is peaceful. The only grim face is Draco Malfoy's. His father has been fired from the Board of Directors. On the train back home, Harry asks Ginny what she knew about that Percy had not wanted her to tell anyone about. Ginny reveals that Percy has a girlfriend, the same Penelope Clearwater who was Petrified with Hermione. She saw them kissing. Fred and George plan to have some fun with Percy about this over the summer. Harry does not expect to have any fun at all, and asks Hermione and Ron to call him on the telephone so they can arrange to meet. And then the train pulls into Platform Nine and Three Quarters.

Analysis

Having used the time-honoured technique of having the villain explain to the hero exactly what had happened in the previous chapter, the author here completes the story by laying out the parts the other players had in the events. We learn here that the diary originated with Lucius Malfoy, and that Dobby, as we suspected, was his house-elf. We learn also that Dumbledore was perhaps more aware of what had been going on than we suspected, but was constrained, probably by forces with which we are not yet aware, from taking a more active role in things. Finally, we also see, with almost breakneck speed, the closing days of the school year, with the recovery of the victims of the Basilisk, the return of Hagrid, and the eventual return to London on the Hogwarts Express.

It is interesting to note that Tom Riddle, Ron, and Harry all received Special Awards for Services to the School for closing the Chamber of Secrets. Fifty years on, other students may be wondering what Ronald Weasley did to merit this award. It is unlikely that Harry's role will be questioned: after all, he is the *famous* Harry Potter. One of the guiding principles of the series is here voiced, by Dumbledore, of course: "It is our choices, Harry, that show what we truly are, far more than our abilities." Although in the mouth of another character, such as Percy Weasley, this would seem overly sententious, Dumbledore is able to say this without pontificating, perhaps in part due to his reputation as an eccentric. It is perhaps worthwhile at this point to look back and see where Harry had been given a choice, and which choices he has taken. Already we can see that Harry has seldom taken the easy choice, often choosing the hardest course because he thought it was right. It will probably be instructive to see if Harry maintains this course.

This particular instance is of interest in another direction as well. Throughout this book, we have seen Harry's increasing doubt that he is, in fact, meant to be in Gryffindor house where he has been placed by the Sorting Hat. In his meeting with Tom Riddle, we see this doubt again, though interestingly it does not seem to affect his course of action. It is Dumbledore's pronouncement, as mentioned above, coupled with the discovery that the sword in the hat was Gryffindor's, that finally removes Harry's doubt about the Sorting Hat's decision. We can safely guess that Harry will not be troubled about this matter again.

Questions

Further Study 1. How did they administer a restorative potion to Nearly Headless Nick? He is a ghost, and ghosts can't even taste ordinary food. How could a potion have any effect on him?

Greater Picture

Curiously, the fact that Voldemort is currently believed to be hiding in Albania will prove germane to the overall story arc. Voldemort had found an artifact that he had changed into one of his Horcruxes there, and had apparently returned there as a disembodied spirit after his initial encounter with Harry. It was there, apparently, that Professor Quirrell had encountered him, and it was there that Peter Pettigrew will rejoin him between books three and four. One wonders what attraction Voldemort had to Albania, or what the author intended him to find there.

It is in the sixth book that we will discover that this "memory of Tom Riddle" is, in fact, a Horcrux, and that Dumbledore had been very concerned when he discovered this fact, though we will not see that here: Dumbledore, throughout the relation of this story, seems as imperturbable as ever. Later, however, Dumbledore will tell Harry that the discovery of this Horcrux had worried him. As long as the Horcrux remains intact, the wizard who created it cannot die, his soul remaining tied to the earth by the Horcrux; thus, the primary purpose of a Horcrux is immortality, and wizards who do create them invariably protect them as they would their own lives. Yet this one was apparently crafted to be used as a weapon, and placed in the hands of a schoolgirl. Dumbledore concludes that there must be others, that this is not Voldemort's only Horcrux, and attempts to determine how many others there might be. Harry manages to secure a memory which suggests that Tom Riddle saw seven as the most magical number, and so Dumbledore concludes, correctly, that Voldemort had intended to have seven pieces of his soul: one remaining within himself, and six in Horcruxes.

We can see immediately that Harry's arranging Dobby's release from servitude, and Dobby's gratitude for that act, will have some effect on Harry's future, but it is not exactly clear yet what that effect will be. Dobby does not rejoin the story until the fourth book, and at that time he will help Harry solve one of the three major problems he is set. True to Harry's request, Dobby will not again try to save Harry's life, until directed to do so late in the seventh book; but in the mean while, Dobby will assist Harry in his work with Dumbledore's Army in *Harry Potter and the Order of the Phoenix,* and his attempts to determine Draco's mission in *Harry Potter and the Half-Blood Prince.*

PRISONER OF AZKABAN

CHAPTERS

Chapter 1: Owl Post
Chapter 2: Aunt Marge's Big Mistake
Chapter 3: The Knight Bus
Chapter 4: The Leaky Cauldron
Chapter 5: The Dementor
Chapter 6: Talons and Tea Leaves
Chapter 7: The Boggart in the Wardrobe
Chapter 8: Flight of the Fat Lady
Chapter 9: Grim Defeat
Chapter 10: The Marauder's Map
Chapter 11: The Firebolt
Chapter 12: The Patronus
Chapter 13: Gryffindor Versus Ravenclaw
Chapter 14: Snape's Grudge
Chapter 15: The Quidditch Final
Chapter 16: Professor Trelawney's Prediction
Chapter 17: Cat, Rat and Dog
Chapter 18: Moony, Wormtail, Padfoot, and Prongs
Chapter 19: The Servant of Lord Voldemort
Chapter 20: The Dementor's Kiss
Chapter 21: Hermione's Secret
Chapter 22: Owl Post Again

OVERVIEW

The third installment in the Harry Potter series, *Harry Potter and the Prisoner of Azkaban* is written from the point-of-view of 13 year-old Harry Potter. The title refers to convicted criminal, Sirius Black, who has escaped Azkaban, a wizard prison. Black's life previously intersected with Harry's history and continues to do so in the present.

BOOK HIGHLIGHTS
- New places visited: Hogsmeade, Shrieking Shack
- *Defence Against the Dark Arts* teacher: Remus Lupin
- Title refers to: Sirius Black, Azkaban Prison

Chapter 1: Owl Post

SYNOPSIS

It is near midnight, and Harry crouches under his bed covers at the Dursleys, reading *The History of Magic* and writing a summer homework essay on witch burning. Harry has much homework to do over the holiday and had to steal his books, quill, parchment, and ink from his chest after Uncle Vernon locked them away in the cupboard. As usual, Harry celebrates his birthday alone. With the exception of a botched telephone call from Ron, which had ended when Uncle Vernon hung up on him, Harry has not heard from his Hogwarts friends all summer. As Harry is preparing to go to sleep, though, Hedwig and Errol (the Weasley's owl) arrive with presents for Harry. Ron sends him a Pocket Sneakoscope and a Daily Prophet article about Ron's father winning a contest. The Weasleys use the prize money for a trip to Egypt; the article's photo shows the entire Weasley family, including Ron's rat and Percy wearing his new Head Boy badge. Hermione sends Harry a Broomstick Servicing Kit while she is on vacation in France with her parents. Hagrid sends him a strange book titled, *The Monster Book of Monsters*. It almost seems alive, nipping at Harry and nearly waking the Dursleys as it scrambles around the room before Harry subdues it.

There is also the usual Hogwarts' letter with instructions about classes, textbooks, and supplies. Professor McGonagall has also sent a letter with an enclosed permission slip that needs to be signed by a parent or guardian, giving students permission to visit Hogsmeade (a wizarding village), during the school year. Harry is unsure how he can persuade the Dursleys to sign it, but for now, he is happy that it is his birthday.

ANALYSIS

Once again, Harry must endure another unhappy summer with the Dursleys. His confinement there only reinforces what little connection Harry feels left to the Muggle world and how he longs to return to the Wizard realm, the only place he believes he truly belongs. He has not been totally shut off however; reading *A History of Magic* is one means by which he remains connected during his enforced absence. Also, Ron, Hermione, and Hagrid have not forgotten him and sent birthday gifts and letters. Ron's present, the Sneakoscope, will soon appear to be defective, but it will play a significant role in the plot, as does the photograph of the Weasley family on holiday in Egypt. Hagrid's gift is also notable, as it indicates there may be a change at Hogwarts that Harry is as yet unaware, leaving him confused as to why he was given such a "ferocious" book. The "Monster" book, as well as Hermione's present, may foreshadow upcoming plot elements.

Readers might notice what may be a minor mistake. The textbook that Harry is reading, *A History of Magic*, is said to be by Adalbert Waffling. In *Harry Potter and the Philosopher's Stone* and *Harry Potter and the Deathly Hallows*, we are told that *A History of Magic* is by Bathilda Bagshot. Adalbert Waffling is the author of *Magical Theory*, according to Book 1. This mistake is pointed up by Bathilda's becoming a more important character in book 7. However, as in the Muggle world, it is possible that these are two separate books by different authors that just happen to have identical titles and that *Magical Theory* is another book by Waffling.

QUESTIONS

Review 1. What is unusual about the book Hagrid sends to Harry?

2. What is the permission slip for? Why is Harry concerned?

3. What does Ron send Harry for his birthday? What is it for?

GREATER PICTURE

The photo of the Weasleys in Egypt, though seemingly innocuous, is what spurs on the majority of the book's action. If Sirius Black had not seen the picture in the Daily Prophet, he never would have recognized Ron's rat as being something other than a pet, and would not have escaped from Azkaban prison and gone to Hogwarts. Ron mentions that the Sneakoscope is cheap and probably not reliable. However, the two times he mentions it going off are both times that it should have gone off, leaving us wondering whether Ron is correct in his analysis. We will see it go off twice more, and both times it will be disregarded, though in fact it will be telling us, quite correctly, that there is someone untrustworthy around. Ron's inability to see that the Sneakoscope going off when he is tying it to Errol's leg for transport is it functioning exactly as intended, may be a sign of Ron's immaturity. Unawareness of consequences, like Ron's choice to use Errol for a forbidden extended trip, is typical of his lack of maturity. Hermione's gift, the broomstick servicing kit, may be intended to point up the significance of brooms to Harry. As such, while it does not play any direct role in events, it is perhaps foreshadowing the loss of Harry's broom, its replacement, confiscation of the replacement, and its eventual return.

We will find out that Hagrid has become the new Care of Magical Creatures teacher. *The Monster Book of Monsters* is his chosen "set book" (textbook), and he has selected in part because he sees it as a bit of a joke. The book will not open until you stroke it, whereupon it purrs and relaxes. Not one of the students that we see has been able to figure this out.

Chapter 2: Aunt Marge's Big Mistake

SYNOPSIS

At breakfast the next morning, Harry is hardly surprised when nobody wishes him a Happy Birthday. Everyone is watching the new kitchen TV, which had been installed because Dudley was complaining about the long walk from the living room TV to the fridge. The TV newscaster is reporting on an escaped prisoner, Sirius Black, saying he is armed and dangerous; Aunt Petunia immediately goes to the window to see if he might be outside. Uncle Vernon prepares to leave for the train station to collect Aunt Marge, Vernon's sister and Harry's least favorite relative. Harry has unhappy memories of Marge's past visits when she tortured him, and he is unhappy that she is staying for a whole week. Uncle Vernon warns Harry to keep a civil tongue and that there will not be any funny stuff (presumably meaning magic). He reminds Harry that Marge believes he attends St. Brutus's Secure Center for Incurably Criminal Boys. As Uncle Vernon is leaving, Harry corners him with a counter proposal: if he behaves during Marge's visit, Uncle Vernon will sign his Hogsmeade permission slip. Uncle Vernon, reminded about how easy it would be for Harry to slip up and say something about his magical connections, and how little he has to lose by doing so, angrily agrees, and slams off to the station as Harry, resigned to acting like a Muggle for the week, sadly puts away all his magical stuff and sends Hedwig and Errol to Ron for the week. The visit begins poorly, with Marge giving Dudley a big hug and a kiss and £20, while treating Harry as a porter. Throughout the week, Marge repeatedly insults Harry, at one point commenting about how problems in the parents usually appear in the offspring. When her wine glass suddenly shatters, she passes it off as her having such strong hands, unsuspecting that it could have been Harry who caused it to break—Harry is angry enough to have done it, but is unsure whether he did. On her last day, Aunt Marge goes into a diatribe about Harry's "good-for-nothing parents." Harry's anger causes her to start swelling, eventually inflating like a balloon and bobbing around on the ceiling. Harry knows he is probably in trouble for twice violating the Decree for the Reasonable Restriction of Under-Age Sorcery, an action that could result in having his wand snapped in two and/or being expelled from Hogwarts. Harry hurriedly packs his belongings, and dragging his trunk behind him, runs into the night.

ANALYSIS

It would have seemed that no one could be more unpleasant to Harry than Uncle Vernon, but Aunt Marge is equally hateful toward him. Her derogatory comment, "If there is something wrong with the bitch, there'll be something wrong with the pup," is meant as an aspersion at Harry by targeting his mother's character, but it might also be a thinly disguised insult against Aunt Petunia, who Marge may consider inferior and tainted by her blood relationship to Harry. This animosity does not extend to Dudley, despite his blood connection to Harry and Petunia. Marge dotes on her young nephew.

Harry's interactions, both with Vernon and with Marge, show how he has matured and grown in self-confidence. He is here able to bargain, almost as an equal, with Vernon; he is aware of the strength he holds, and is not afraid to use it to get what he wants. With Marge, he is able to restrain himself for almost the full week, only losing control of himself when she starts insulting his parents. It is perhaps worthy of note that we see Vernon attempting to defuse the situation. Vernon surely knows that Harry is being pushed to his limits, and is afraid of what might happen if Harry is pushed beyond those limits. This does illustrate the changing dynamic of their relationship; even one year earlier, Vernon would not have worried about Harry in a similar situation.

Harry shows how he has become more sophisticated and adept at manipulating and interacting with people. Knowing that Vernon fears Aunt Marge might learn he is a wizard, Harry barters with his uncle, offering good behavior and agreeing to act like a Muggle in exchange for having his Hogsmeade permission slip signed. However, when Harry is unable to control his anger with the obnoxious Aunt Marge, he loses this opportunity. Although his uncontrolled reaction lost him his chance to visit Hogsmeade, it also shows just how powerful Harry's magical abilities have become. Without realizing it, Harry has twice or three times demonstrated "wandless magic," a nearly impossible feat for most wizards. While Harry himself is unsure whether he caused Aunt Marge's wine glass to shatter, it is certain that both his blowing up of Aunt Marge, and the lock of the cupboard opening when he retrieves his trunk, are magic, and as Harry's wand is locked in the cupboard at that point, Harry is doing this magic without its assistance.

Despite the changed relationship between Harry and Uncle Vernon, Harry is still a child, and his reactions are still quite childish. Having gotten into trouble in Vernon's house, and presuming himself in trouble with the law, Harry's impulse is to run away. He has no clear idea of where he will go, or what he will do when he gets there; he simply decides that he must become a fugitive, believing that he can gather his money from Gringotts and go into hiding. For one as famous as Harry, this is clearly wishful thinking at its worst; there is no way that Harry would be able to remain hidden. This actually is an interesting contract to Harry's behaviour in his first year, where, knowing that he was headed into possibly mortal danger, Harry pressed ahead anyway. It likely would prove interesting to examine this event, and Harry's earlier excursion *Through the Trap Door*, to see how Harry's character is motivated in each case.

Questions

Review 1. Why does Harry run away?

2. How does Harry plan to have Uncle Vernon sign his Hogsmeade permission slip? What does this say about Harry's character?

Further Study 1. How is Harry able to unintentionally and without his wand perform magic?

Greater Picture

We do not realize until the next chapter that Sirius Black is actually a wizard fugitive, but dangerous enough for the Muggles to know about him. The method by which Muggles are alerted about the Wizarding world is shown in *Harry Potter and the Half-Blood Prince*. Though, for the most part, the Wizarding world is kept secret and separate from Muggles, in some situations it becomes necessary to break the silence.

Chapter 3: The Knight Bus

Synopsis

Harry finds himself, with his possessions but no Muggle money, on a dark deserted street. Fearing Ministry officials are searching for him and will expel him from the Wizarding community, Harry figures that using more magic could not worsen his situation. He intends to magically lighten his trunk, and, hidden under his Invisibility cloak, fly to London on his broom to retrieve his Wizarding fortune from Gringotts. While rummaging through his trunk, he has an uneasy feeling eyes are upon him. Flashing his wand-light at a dark corner, he sees a huge dog; recoiling, he trips over his trunk and falls into the street. He is almost run over by a purple triple-decker bus that suddenly appears from nowhere.

A conductor in an equally purple outfit hops out and introduces himself as Stan Shunpike, conductor for the Knight Bus. Only after he partially gets through his spiel does Stan realize that the person who "flagged" the bus is lying on the ground. Helping him up, Stan asks Harry his name. Figuring he is by now a wanted fugitive, Harry identifies himself as his Hogwarts' classmate, Neville Longbottom. Stan tells him the Knight Bus will take him to London for eleven sickles; for thirteen, he gets hot chocolate, and for fifteen, a hot water bottle and a toothbrush. Harry climbs on board, while Ernie, the driver, manhandles his trunk into the bus. Inside, the bus is furnished with four-poster beds rather than chairs.

The ride is very bumpy, and Harry is unable to sleep. Stan is reading *The Daily Prophet*. On the front page, Harry sees a picture of Sirius Black, the same fugitive that was on Muggle TV. The story says Black killed thirteen people with a single curse, and it is believed he was a strong supporter of Voldemort.

The Knight Bus arrives at The Leaky Cauldron the next morning—Minister of Magic Cornelius Fudge greets Harry. Stan Shunpike is astounded that Fudge wants to talk to his passenger and that he addresses him as "Harry." Stan is in awe of "The Boy Who Lived." Fudge escorts Harry to a private parlor in the Leaky Cauldron and informs him that his Aunt Marge has been punctured and her memory altered. He also says that his Uncle Vernon and Aunt Petunia are willing to take him back next summer if he stays at Hogwarts for Christmas and Easter. And, most puzzling, given what happened when Dobby the house elf used magic at his home last year, Harry learns there will be no consequences for having performed under-age wizardry.

Harry is to stay at the Leaky Cauldron until school starts, and Fudge requests that he confine his travels to within Diagon Alley and to not venture into Muggle London. Harry asks Fudge if he will sign his Hogsmeade permission slip, but Fudge seems very disconcerted by this and refuses. Harry finds Hedwig inside his room, where he promptly falls asleep.

Chapter 4: The Leaky Cauldron

ANALYSIS

Harry, thrown into a panic, is thinking and acting irrationally, and, in what becomes a typical behavioral pattern, packs his trunk and runs away. Although his reaction is childish, he also knows from his own past experience the harsh penalty for using underage magic; he expects only the worst: expulsion from Hogwarts and having his wand snapped in two. His brief foray into the nighttime Muggle world is frightening, and however unhappy he was at the Dursleys, he was at least safe and comforted by knowing he would always return to Hogwarts. Now everything he holds dear seems to have vanished, and Harry is too used to unfair treatment to expect the incident to be resolved favorably. He is unsure what to do next, but decides his only option is to become an outcast living clandestinely on the wizarding world's fringe. Fortunately, his faulty plan is derailed by a scary large dog and the Knight Bus' timely arrival. Stan Shunpike, a rather comical and ineffectual character, represents Harry's lifeline back into the Wizarding world, although the return trip is bumpy, both literally and figuratively. Along the way, Harry learns about the escaped fugitive, Sirius Black, though he only briefly takes notice. It seems that Harry's concern and panicked reaction over the episode with Aunt Marge was unnecessary—Fudge, surprisingly, brushes off the entire incident and arranges for Harry to stay in Diagon Alley until school starts.

As a minor aside, there is a small numerical discrepancy here. Harry's birthday, and the start of Aunt Marge's visit, fall on the 31st of July; Aunt Marge's visit is only one week long, and Harry leaves on her last night there, which should be August 6. The next day, Fudge twice remarks that Harry will be staying in the Leaky Cauldron for the last two weeks of his vacation; but if school starts on 1 September, Harry's stay in the Leaky Cauldron should be closer to three and a half weeks rather than two.

QUESTIONS

Review 1. What does Harry see when he is on the dark street?
2. What is the Knight Bus and how did it know where to find Harry?

Further Study 1. Why does Fudge brush off the incident involving Harry's aunt? 2. Why would Fudge refuse to sign Harry's permission slip?

GREATER PICTURE

Throughout the year, Harry repeatedly sees the same black dog that he observed moments before accidentally hailing the Knight Bus. At first, he believes it is the Grim, a magical creature believed to be an omen of death. The first few times Harry sees it, he finds himself in a possible mortal situation. However, before one Quidditch match, he sees Crookshanks and the dog together, which reassures him that the canine cannot be supernatural. Ironically, although Harry initially considered it a death omen, the dog's first appearance actually aids Harry by causing him to stumble backwards and raising his wand arm, thus hailing the Knight Bus that carries him to safety. Harry finally learns that the dog is actually Sirius Black, who is an Animagus (a wizard that can transform himself into an animal), and the reason they have continually encountered each other is because Sirius wants to see Harry, who is his godson.

At this point in the story, Harry is still a hero: "The Boy Who Lived," who is widely believed to have been the reason for the downfall of Voldemort some twelve years earlier. As such, the fact that Fudge wants to be perceived as being "on Harry's side" is unsurprising. Add to that the belief in the Wizarding community at large that Sirius Black is (or was) Voldemort's right-hand man, and that he is trying to kill Harry, and we can quickly see that it would be political suicide for Fudge to be identified as the head of a government that had stripped the hero, Harry, of his only defences against Black. Mystifying as it may be for Harry, this forgiveness of his magical misbehaviour is the only course that the politically-driven Fudge can possibly follow.

By the same token, of course, Fudge can neither allow Harry out into London proper, or into Hogsmeade village, both places where he would be relatively unprotected from attacks by Black. It is a little surprising that Fudge waffles at the prospect of signing Harry's permission form; one would expect that he would have an excuse at the ready.

Stan Shunpike reappears throughout the series, although he remains a minor character. While he occasionally engages in petty mischief, Shunpike will represent how easily innocents can become the hapless pawns and scapegoats of a corrupt institution.

Chapter 4: The Leaky Cauldron

SYNOPSIS

Harry's time in Diagon Alley is his own; he browses the many shops, and in the afternoon works on his homework, with free sundaes, at Florean Fortescue's Ice Cream Parlour. Harry sees the new Firebolt broom at Quality Quidditch Supplies. Harry has to buy his school supplies and is surprised to see the book Hagrid gave him for his birthday, *The Monster Book of Monsters*, displayed in Flourish & Blotts. Checking his booklist, he sees it is required for his Care of Magical Creatures class, which comes as a relief to Harry who was worried that Hagrid wanted help with some new "pet." It is also a relief to the Flourish & Blotts clerk, as it is difficult to extract the aggressive tomes from their cage. While looking for his Divination text, Harry sees *Death Omens: What To Do When You Know The Worst Is Coming*. On the cover is something similar to the large black dog he saw when the Knight Bus stopped for him. He tries convincing himself that it is not a death omen.

Although many Hogwarts students are appearing in Diagon Alley, including Dean Thomas, Seamus Finnigan, and the *real* Neville Longbottom, Ron and Hermione do not show until the day before school starts. Ron has a new wand, while Hermione has three bags of books. She also wants to buy an owl. Ron wants to have the sickly Scabbers looked at, so they troop into the nearby Magical Menagerie pet store. When a large cat named Crookshanks tries to attack Scabbers,

Hermione buys it, and also the rat tonic recommended by the clerk for Scabbers.

At the Leaky Cauldron they meet Mr. Weasley. He mentions that Sirius Black is still at large, and the Ministry is putting all its efforts into capturing him. The other Weasleys sweep in: Mrs. Weasley, Percy, who is now Hogwarts Head Boy and as pompous as a Lord Mayor, the twins, Fred and George, who try to take Percy down a notch by imitating his mannerisms, and Ginny. The Weasleys, Harry, and Hermione dine in a private salon at the Leaky Cauldron. Mr. Weasley says the Ministry is providing cars to the train station. Ron has misplaced Scabbers' Rat Tonic, and Harry volunteers to look for it in the salon while Ron helps Percy look for his Head Boy badge. On the way, Harry overhears Mr. and Mrs. Weasley arguing. The Ministry believes Sirius Black escaped Azkaban expressly to find and kill Harry as revenge for him having defeated the Dark Lord. Dementors, guards from Azkaban, have been placed around Hogwarts to protect Harry.

Surprisingly, Harry is unconcerned and believes Black will not be any harder to deal with than Voldemort. The Dementors are more worrisome, however, as it appears he will have to somehow slip past them to get into Hogsmeade village.

Harry stops by Ron and Percy's room, and finds that Fred and George have changed Percy's *Head Boy* badge to read *Bighead Boy*.

Analysis

For the first time, Harry is on his own, although he is likely being remotely monitored. He uses his time to explore and observe the hidden Wizarding realm, comparing and contrasting it to the parallel Muggle world he grew up in, unencumbered by any adult limitations or interpretations. When Harry is finally reunited with Ron and Hermione, he happily rejoins the Weasley family chaos as the children prepare to return to Hogwarts. Mr. and Mrs. Weasley warmly greet him, as do Ron and Ginny. Fred and George, meanwhile, seem even more irreverent, and, propelled by Fred's more dominant personality, are likely planning new mischief for Hogwarts. Percy, now Hogwarts Head Boy, is more pompous and insufferable than ever, somewhat distancing himself from his younger siblings, and making him an irresistible target for the twins' pranks. All these familial interactions provide Harry with rare doses of the happy, cozy family life he so sorely craves.

Three important plot elements unfold in this chapter. Most significant is that Sirius Black's escape from Azkaban prison is somehow tied to Harry. Only now does Harry understand why Fudge so quickly dismissed the incident involving his aunt and realizes that he was probably being closely watched by wizards while in Diagon Alley. Secondly, and in Harry's mind most important, is Harry's intent to somehow attend the Hogsmeade school outings, despite lacking custodial permission. Finally, there is the ongoing battle between Crookshanks and Scabbers, a situation that likely will continue to escalate, straining Ron and Hermione's friendship, possibly permanently estranging them. We have seen already that Crookshanks will attack Scabbers, ignoring the nearby caged rats, so it is likely this specific antipathy will continue.

Harry is beginning to realize that the frequent canine images he has encountered may be more than coincidence and actually may have some significant hidden meaning. Harry also learns about Dementors, the guards of Azkaban Prison, although he is unaware of exactly what they are. Surprisingly, and considering how worried he is about the possible death omens he repeatedly sees, he seems unperturbed that Sirius Black may be hunting him.

Questions

Review 1. Why is Harry seemingly unconcerned when he learns that Sirius Black is looking for him?
2. Why does Harry believe he is seeing Death Omens? What are they, and where specifically has he seen them?

Further Study 1. Fred and George have bewitched Percy's prefect badge. Is their replacement caption valid or is this a just mean-spirited prank on their part? How long before Percy is likely to notice?
2. What might account for Percy's growing estrangement from his family?
3. Why would Hermione decide to buy a cat instead of an owl, especially one that tries to attack Ron's pet rat?
4. As Harry spends time alone in Diagon Alley, what comparisons and contrasts might he make between the Muggle and Wizarding realms?

Greater Picture

In a later book, as Voldemort openly returns to power, we will be told that Florean Fortescue has apparently been captured. One has to wonder exactly why the Death Eaters would attack someone as harmless as an ice cream merchant.

As we surmise, the conflict between Scabbers and Crookshanks will come to a head with Scabbers' apparent death in about April. This will result in an extended estrangement between Ron and Hermione. When Scabbers reappears in June, we will find out that Crookshanks' distrust of him is wholly justified, to the point that before accepting a new pet, Ron asks for, and receives, Crookshanks' approval. It is perhaps useful to comment at this point that Crookshanks is not simply a cat, but a cat / Kneazle cross-breed, and thus much more intelligent than the average feline.

Near the end of the story, we also learn that the widely held belief, that Sirius is trying to kill Harry, is incorrect; it is true that Sirius is trying to kill someone at Hogwarts, but it isn't Harry. However, this mistaken belief, and the associated beliefs concerning the reason that Sirius was incarcerated initially, will drive a lot of the story. The Firebolt broom that we see in Diagon Alley will prove to be a plot point, starting at about Christmas. It will result in an estrangement between Hermione and the other two, when Hermione suspects the origins of the broom.

Chapter 5: The Dementor

Synopsis

Surprisingly, the Weasleys, Hermione, and Harry are all ready on time the next morning. Ministry cars spirit them away to catch the Hogwarts Express at King's Cross Station. At Platform Nine and Three Quarters, Mr. Weasley takes Harry aside to discuss Sirius Black. Harry admits that he overheard him and Mrs. Weasley. Mr. Weasley asks him to promise that, no matter what he hears, he will not go looking for Sirius Black. Harry is puzzled, but the departing Hogwarts Express prevents him from making that promise. Wanting to talk privately to Ron and Hermione, they chase away Ron's sister Ginny. The only available compartment is occupied by someone named R. J. Lupin, although he is apparently fast asleep. Despite his presence, Harry relates everything he knows about Black, including what Mr. Weasley said. The pocket Sneakoscope Ron gave Harry starts whistling. Ron says it is cheap and likely defective, so Harry bundles it back up in his trunk to deaden the noise.

The conversation turns to Hogsmeade, and Ron and Hermione are appalled that Harry will be unable to join them, as neither Uncle Vernon nor Fudge would sign his permission slip. Later, Draco and his two sidekicks, Crabbe and Goyle, show up intending to cause mayhem, but Lupin's presence deters them.

The train lurches to an unexpected stop. Ginny and Neville Longbottom make their way through darkness to Harry's compartment, and amidst the confusion, Lupin wakes up and provides some illumination. As he is about to go and find out what is happening, the compartment door slides open and a black-robed figure, as tall as the doorway, glides in, briefly displaying a hideous, dead-looking hand. Harry hears someone screaming and passes out. When he regains consciousness, the creature is gone and the train is moving again. Lupin says it was a Dementor, an Azkaban prison guard searching for Sirius Black. To counteract the Dementor's effect, he gives each student chocolate, then leaves to speak with the driver. In his absence, Harry asks if anyone else fainted, but they tell him no, nor did they hear a woman screaming. Hermione tells Harry that Lupin repelled the Dementor by casting a silvery object from his wand.

They arrive at Hogwarts in a driving rain. As Hagrid rounds up the first-years for the boat ride across the lake, the trio find horseless carriages waiting for them. Upon hearing from Neville that Harry fainted, Malfoy maliciously attempts to taunt him, but Lupin arrives on the scene, defusing the incident. As they head to the Great Hall, Professor McGonagall asks to see Harry and Hermione in her office; she reassures Ron that his two friends are not in any trouble. Hearing about Harry's encounter with the Dementor, she has summoned him to be checked over by Madam Pomfrey, who approves Lupin giving the students chocolate. Professor McGonagall suggests keeping Harry in the infirmary overnight. Not wishing to give Malfoy further ammunition to humiliate him with, Harry insists he is fine and asks to attend the Welcoming Feast. Professor McGonagall grants permission, and then asks for a private word with Hermione about her class schedule. Afterwards, they go to the feast together.

Although they have missed the Sorting ceremony, the Feast is just beginning; Professor Dumbledore warns students that the school grounds are being guarded by Dementors and any attempt to slip past them by subterfuge will fail as they do not rely on sight to hunt their prey. He also welcomes two new teachers: Rubeus Hagrid, who will be teaching Care of Magical Creatures and Professor Lupin, the new Defence Against the Dark Arts teacher. Harry notes that Lupin receives a loathing look from Professor Snape. Harry, Ron, and Hermione congratulate Hagrid on his appointment and then head for Gryffindor Tower.

Analysis

The Ministry providing cars to transport Harry, Hermione, and the Weasleys to King's Cross Station is highly unusual, and it indicates that there is deep concern for Harry's safety that is probably tied to Sirius Black's escape. Mr. Weasley's warning to Harry to not go looking for Black is revealing, although Harry nonchalantly dismisses its significance, more concerned with finding a way to attend the Hogsmeade weekends with his friends than with avoiding an escaped murderer.

This chapter shows a possible hint of Harry's and Ginny's relationship in the future. As Percy goes to meet his girlfriend Penelope, Harry and Ginny look at each other and silently laugh. Although this does not mean that Harry is interested in Ginny, it does show that they have a similar sense of humor, and therefore have common ground on which to build a relationship.

While Harry is thinking foolishly by brushing off concerns about Sirius Black, he soon becomes fixated on Dementors. Although the eerie creatures have been assigned to protect him and hunt Black, they strongly affect anyone near them, feeding on unhappy emotions and memories, while leaving behind darkness, coldness, and despair. The Dementor that entered Harry's compartment may have deliberately targeted Harry, though its purpose is unknown. This, compounded with what Harry believes is a recurring death omen and Sirius Black's escape, likely foreshadows a difficult and dangerous year ahead at Hogwarts. Professor Lupin, however, unexpectedly demonstrates an ability to repel Dementors with an unknown spell, suggesting that it is possible to protect one's self from them.

Also, a valuable story clue may appear here, but Harry quickly bundles it up and stows it away. There is some question as to whether the Sneakoscope actually works; Ron, in the note he included when he sent it to Harry, claimed it was just a cheap device. Apparently, it is more effective than anyone realizes, even though it seems to be giving off false alarms; when Ron used it before sending it to Harry, it was responding correctly.

Questions

Review 1. Why would the Ministry of Magic provide cars to transport Harry, Hermione, and the Weasley family to the train station?

2. Why does Lupin give the students chocolate after their encounter with the Dementor?

3. Why is Harry the only one who faints in the Dementor's presense?

Further Study 1. Who might Harry have heard screaming as he fainted? Why did no one else hear it?

2. Why would Snape give Professor Lupin such a loathing look during the Welcoming Feast? Is it because Lupin got the job that Snape has long wanted or is it something else?

3. Why does Harry's Sneakoscope sound an alarm? Is it faulty as Ron claims, or could something be amiss?

4. Why would Mr. Weasley ask Harry to promise not to go looking for Sirius Black?

GREATER PICTURE

Harry's reaction to the Dementors is by far the most severe of anyone he is aware of. Nobody else heard screaming, nobody else fainted. Harry is afraid that this is caused by some weakness in himself. Lupin will reassure him later that this is not so; Dementors feed on happy memories, leaving only despair in the minds of their victims, and Harry, having had so many bad experiences in his life, is much more deeply affected by them. The memory that the Dementors seem to be fixating on in Harry is the time of his mother's death; as Harry encounters Dementors through this story, the memory will be repeatedly brought forward and strengthened until he is able to recall not only his mother's words but Voldemort's.

Harry will learn much later that the "horseless" carriages are actually pulled by creatures that are invisible to most people.

We have seen no evidence whatsoever so far that the pocket Sneakoscope is giving false warnings. Assuming that it is working, we can guess that one of the people in the compartment is not trustworthy. Apart from the Trio, the only other human in the compartment is Lupin, who being asleep is certainly not untrustworthy, leaving only Crookshanks, Hedwig, and Scabbers as potentially untrustworthy. We have already had our attention pointed at Scabbers, as he has apparently lived a good deal longer than any rat ought to have. Still, when the truth about Scabbers is revealed late in this book, it will be a surprise to us.

Lupin's shabby appearance has also been quite strongly pointed out to us. This would be an indication that he is having a hard time finding work, which would also be possible explanation for his taking the Defence Against the Dark Arts post, one that is now widely believed to be jinxed. We will discover later that Lupin is a werewolf, and over the next few books we will discover that there is a significant anti-werewolf prejudice in the Wizarding world. It is this prejudice, merited or not, that presumably has prevented Lupin from finding work.

Chapter 6: Talons and Tea Leaves

SYNOPSIS

The next morning, Malfoy entertains the Slytherin table by imitating Harry's reaction to the Dementors. The Weasley twins remark that Draco was less brave when the Dementors were near *his* compartment. Ron notices that Hermione's class schedule lists Arithmancy, Muggle Studies, and Divination, all at nine o'clock. When Ron teasingly asks if she is going to be in all three classes at the same time, Hermione says only that it is all worked out with Professor McGonagall.

Harry and Ron have trouble finding the Divination classroom at the top of the North Tower. Sir Cadogan, an inept Knight in a portrait, clatters through several paintings, leading them to a room with a trapdoor in the ceiling. A nameplate reads "Sibyll Trelawney, Divination Teacher." The trap door opens, and a silvery ladder descends. Harry clambers up followed by the others. With great drama and fortuneteller's tricks, Professor Trelawney tells them Divination is a difficult subject, one that cannot be learned from books. Hermione seems skeptical. Today's lesson is reading tea leaves, and Trelawney sees a dog shape in Harry's cup that she identifies as the Grim, an omen of death. She predicts someone will die, leaving Harry a bit worried; it is the third time a dog shape has appeared to him recently.

Harry and the entire class are so disturbed by Trelawney's prediction that during their next class, Transfiguration, they seem unimpressed when Professor McGonagall transfigures herself into a cat to demonstrate how Animagi change shape. Somewhat nettled, Professor McGonagall, who appears to have little respect for Divination or its teacher's abilities, explains that it is an imprecise branch of magical study. Every year Professor Trelawney predicts some student's imminent demise and none have ever died. McGonagall carefully stops short of denigrating Professor Trelawney.

At lunch, Hermione comments that she is quite unimpressed by Divination, proclaiming it a woolly and almost useless subject, particularly compared with her Arithmancy class. Ron is amazed, as she has been with them all morning and wonders how she could also have Arithmancy.

Harry, Ron, and Hermione head to Hagrid's Care of Magical Creatures class. Hagrid is dismayed that no one has been able to open their textbook—the secret is to stroke it, whereupon it becomes quiescent. In a paddock in the Forbidden Forest are Hippogriffs, magical creatures with a horse's hindquarters, and the wings, talons, and head of a bird. Harry is volunteered to be the first to approach them. He steps up to Buckbeak and, acting as Hagrid instructed, is accepted. Hagrid convinces him to climb onto Buckbeak, whereupon Buckbeak takes him for a quick flight around the Forest and back to the paddock. The students lose their fear and address the Hippogriffs properly; Malfoy, however, insults Buckbeak, and the angry Hippogriff slashes his arm with its talons. Hagrid carries Malfoy to the hospital wing as the class disperses in disarray.

Chapter 6: Talons and Tea Leaves

When Hagrid is not at dinner, the Trio decide to visit him later. Hagrid has been drinking, convinced he will be sacked. Harry, Ron, and Hermione insist that Professor Dumbledore would not do that and that they are witnesses that Malfoy behaved improperly. Hermione tells Hagrid he has had enough to drink. He soaks his head in the rain barrel and, suddenly realizing Harry is outside the castle after dark, soundly berates them.

Analysis

Once again, Harry sees a dog image. Professor Trelawney identifies a shape in the tea leaves as a Grim; this is the first time that it is actually named and specifically identified as a death omen. This, along with Ron's description of the Grim that his uncle had seen shortly before he died, further supports Harry's growing suspicion that he is seeing a true death symbol. Coupled with the ever-present Dementors, this is making Harry extremely anxious and fearful for his own safety.

Readers no doubt will be appalled at the level of fakery in the Divination course as taught by Professor Trelawney. The cultivation of the mystical, misty atmosphere in her classroom, and the careful impreciseness of her "predictions," clearly reflects the fortune-telling methods used by Muggle "mediums." It is particularly curious that Trelawney's classroom seems less designed to teach the methods of fortune-telling, than to be a place where Trelawney's fortune-telling abilities can be showcased. It seems that Trelawney is held in less than great esteem by the other teachers at the school. Although she very carefully avoids speaking ill of another teacher, McGonagall clearly does not feel that the brand of Divination taught by Trelawney is of any use. We can see that Professor Dumbledore, despite his eccentricities, is very level-headed and aware of what is transpiring in the school, and he almost certainly shares McGonagall's lack of faith in the validity of Trelawney's teachings. Given this, one must wonder exactly why she is kept on.

Readers should also pay close attention to Professor McGonagall's class lecture and demonstration. Hermione is in all of Harry and Ron's classes, but it would appear from her timetable that she is taking many other subjects they are not, including ones that are taught at the same time. She remains cryptic and evasive when Harry and Ron ask just how she can be taking so many courses, saying only that she has arranged it with Professor McGonagall. There is as yet no explanation as to how Hermione is managing this, although there is probably some magical means behind it.

Hagrid, who was recently exonerated after being falsely accused of releasing the monster from the Chamber of Secrets, based on suspicion that he was repeating actions falsely attributed to him some fifty years before, soon finds his new-found confidence and self-esteem severely shaken after the incident involving Draco Malfoy and Buckbeak. Malfoy's character is further illuminated when he uses the Dementor incident to mock Harry, as the Twins tell Harry that Draco is also terrified by them. Although he is a bully, he is a cowardly one who only acts when he is accompanied by his ever-present minions. False accusations and incorrect assumptions will likely continue to be a recurring theme throughout the novel.

Questions

Review 1. Why is this chapter called "Talons and Tea Leaves"? What does that represent?

2. What is seen in Harry's tea leaves and what does it signify? Has Harry seen it before?

3. What does Trelawney predict and how do the students react to it?

4. What does McGonagall have to say about Trelawney's prediction?

5. What is Hermione's opinion about Divination? Explain.

6. Why does Buckbeak attack Draco Malfoy?

Further Study 1. How does Hagrid react after the Malfoy/Buckbeak incident? Is his behavior justified or not?

2. Why might Hermione be so evasive about her class schedule? How can she be taking classes that are scheduled at the same time? What effect might this eventually have on her?

Greater Picture

It is at the end of this book that we will learn part of the reason for Trelawney's tenure. During Harry's Divination exam, Trelawney will lapse into a trance and make an actual prophecy. Told of this later, Professor Dumbledore will remark that this is her second real prophecy. We will later learn that her first prophecy had concerned Harry and Voldemort, and that Dumbledore had witnessed it just after deciding not to hire Trelawney as Divination teacher. He later also refuses to allow her to leave the school, apparently fearing for her welfare should Voldemort learn that she was the source of the first prophecy, which Voldemort badly wanted. We will also learn that Divination is an examined subject, as an O.W.L. exam is offered in that course. Though, given what Trelawney is teaching, one must wonder exactly what is being examined.

In Professor McGonagall's class, we learn about the Animagus transformation. We are told by Hermione that there are only seven registered Animagi, but of course we do not learn yet about unregistered Animagi. Most readers, unlike Hermione, will understand that it is possible to be outside the law in small ways, and after learning about registration of Animagi, will wonder if the registered ones are all there are. It will turn out that there are several unregistered Animagi, one of whom is Sirius Black.

As noted, Hermione seems somehow to be taking more classes than humanly possible. We will learn that what she has arranged with Professor McGonagall is a technique for moving back in time, using a device called a time-turner. However, Hermione soon realizes she may have taken on a heavier load than she can comfortably handle and is beginning to discover her own limitations. Through the course of the book, Hermione will get steadily more stressed by the work she has to do, to the point that she actually slaps Malfoy. At the end of the book, she will drop a class, leaving her with a humanly-possible workload, and will return the time-turner to McGonagall. The time-turner will be destroyed accidentally in the fifth book, along with all other known examples of that artifact. Despite his size and strength, and his bravery in facing various monsters, Hagrid is curiously insecure in himself. It will take a long time for him to recover from the incident with Draco and Buckbeak, and he will struggle throughout most of the book to prove Buckbeak's innocence. Meanwhile, Malfoy, who deliberately insulted Buckbeak, shows no remorse over how he damages the lives of those he considers inferior to himself, nor will he hesitate to allow an innocent being to be condemned.

Chapter 7: The Boggart in the Wardrobe

Synopsis

Draco Malfoy reappears on Thursday, midway through Professor Snape's Double Potions class, claiming his injury is still painful. He sits himself at Harry and Ron's bench, and Snape orders them to prepare Malfoy's ingredients for him. Malfoy taunts them with threats of Hagrid's imminent dismissal thanks to his father, Lucius, who apparently still has influence with the Ministry. Malfoy also contends that if he was Harry, he would want revenge on Sirius Black. Harry later asks Ron why he would want revenge against Black; Ron cannot answer. Meanwhile, Hermione helps Neville make his potion correctly, against Snape's orders; Snape penalizes Gryffindor five House points, because he assumes (correctly) that Hermione helped him. As the Trio leave the dungeon, Hermione suddenly seems to disappear. Looking around, Ron sees her catching up while tucking something down her robe. Her bag splits, and Ron asks why she is carrying so many books, as there is nothing that afternoon except Defence Against the Dark Arts. She does not answer.

In Defence Against the Dark Arts, Professor Lupin tells the class to put their books away and bring out their wands. This will be a practical class. He leads them to the staff room, wherethey find Snape. When Snape, as he departs, snidely comments about Neville's undisciplined magic, Lupin replies that he hoped Neville would lead off the demonstration. Lupin explains that there is a Boggart in the wardrobe. No one knows what a Boggart looks like because it styles itself after a person's deepest fear. To repel it, it must be forced to change into a humorous shape by casting the *Riddikulus* charm. Neville's greatest fear is Snape. Lupin tells Neville to imagine the scary professor wearing his grandmother's clothing. Each student similarly comes up with their own fear and then pictures it as a funny image. Harry first thinks of Voldemort, but on further thought decides that his greatest fear is a Dementor; he wonders how can he make that funny. The wardrobe is opened and "Snape" emerges. Neville casts the spell that dresses Snape as his grandmother. Following Neville's success, each student takes a shot at the Boggart. As Harry goes to take his turn, Lupin steps in before the Boggart takes shape. It rapidly turns into a floating white orb, and Lupin forces it back to Neville, who spells it one last time, whereupon it vanishes. Class is dismissed. Harry wonders why he was prevented from repelling the Boggart, while Parvati is curious as to why Lupin fears crystal balls. Ron wants to know what Hermione's worst fear is, but she also did not have a chance at the Boggart.

Analysis

Professor Lupin's character is becoming more defined here. Understanding that students require respect, he shows that to them. Despite Snape's aspersions against Neville, Lupin has him lead off against the Boggart, and coaches him to where he has the confidence to perform the spell twice. This proves to be an important milestone in Neville Longbottom's development. To date, Neville has always felt that he was in the wrong place. He once remarked that his family believed he was, "almost a squib," in *Harry Potter and the Chamber of Secrets*, and he himself fears he has no real magical abilities. Indeed, it does appear that he has little, if any, skill in Potions, and he is apparently just as lost in Divination as Harry and Ron. Lupin, by having him lead off the class against the Boggart and later having him finish the lesson, boosts his confidence. Additionally, the astute reader may note that Lupin uses the students' Christian names rather than their surnames, as is the British custom. While this could be seen as excessive familiarity, particularly in schools run on the English public-school model, in this context, it seems to change Lupin from a professor into a teacher.

The Boggart represents how everyone's fears are different. Curiously, it is not Voldemort that Harry fears most, but Dementors. It may be that Harry fears Dementors more because he has difficulty comprehending what the eerie creatures are and does not know how to react to them. Voldemort, although an evil and powerful enemy, is a human being (albeit a still disembodied one), and Harry can better understand his more predictable human traits. Dementors, in contrast, are dark, hideous creatures that are not entirely understood by wizards, are unpredictable, and apparently are difficult to keep under control; they also seem to show a particular interest in Harry, whose encounter with them left a deep emotional wound.

Note that Peeves is especially disrespectful towards Lupin when they meet in the hall. Peeves may know something about Lupin's earlier school years, and the song he sings ("Loony, loopy Lupin") may refer to Lupin's "furry little problem." Lupin's Boggart, a silvery orb, may provide a clue as to just what this problem is. However, Lupin demonstrates that he is able to hold his own against Peeves and, in the process, reinforces his students' admiration. We also receive a few more insights into Snape's character, but we learn little that is new; he is wholly biased towards his own house, Slytherin, and seems to purposely belittle Gryffindors, especially Neville.

Questions

Review 1. What is a Boggart, and what form do they assume?

2. Why does Lupin step in when it is Harry's turn to face the Boggart?

3. Why does Lupin ask Neville Longbottom to be the first to confront the Boggart in class?

Further Study 1. What could the shape of Lupin's Boggart mean?

2. What might Draco mean when he says Harry should want revenge against Sirius Black?

3. What could account for Hermione seeming to suddenly vanish and reappear as the Trio is leaving class?

4. Why does Harry fear Dementors more than Voldemort?

5. What shape might Hermione's Boggart assume?

Greater Picture

We will find out the reason for Draco's taunt at Christmas time. It is then that we will discover that Sirius Black is widely believed to be the one who betrayed Harry's parents to Voldemort. While this belief will later be disproved, it has a certain consistency about it, and Harry will be driven by this belief for much of the rest of the book. Hermione disappearing and reappearing is, of course, the work of the time-turner. Hermione is using it to attend more classes than would be physically possible. Hermione's bag splitting open is a nice distraction from the question of where Hermione was and how she had vanished and reappeared. Several times during this book, Hermione will similarly appear in places where she had not been mere moments before, and always there will be some distraction that will prevent us from wondering overmuch what had caused her appearance.

The confidence that Lupin instills in Neville sustains him through his next two years at Hogwarts, and Harry later builds upon it in Dumbledore's Army. It also allows Neville to join Harry in the Battle at the Department of Mysteries in *Harry Potter and the Order of the Phoenix*. Without this initial success, Neville likely would have remained ineffectual, depressed, and useless, never discovering his strengths in Herbology, Charms, and Defence Against the Dark Arts.

Harry, as mentioned, is upset because Lupin did not allow him a chance at the Boggart. In the next chapter, Lupin explains that he had stepped in because he did not think that the class was prepared to face a simulacrum of Lord Voldemort. When Harry admits that he had thought of Voldemort first, but had quickly decided that it was Dementors of which he was more afraid, Lupin admits that he is impressed by Harry being more afraid of fear rather than an actual being. When fear is intangible and incomprehensible, it often becomes more terrifying. Although Hermione also never had a chance at the Boggart in Lupin's class, it will be revealed later that her greatest fear is Professor McGonagall telling her that she failed all her classes.

It will be revealed later that the "silvery orb" that Lupin fears is not a crystal ball, but the full moon, which of course is connected to his being a werewolf. Parvati's mistake in believing it to be a crystal ball is wholly in character and a nice bit of misdirection on the part of the author; we will see later that Parvati has a significant aptitude for Divination, so likely is already predisposed to seeing things related to Divination.

Chapter 8: Flight of the Fat Lady

Synopsis

Defence Against the Dark Arts is now the most interesting and popular class. Although Slytherins complain about Professor Lupin's patched robes, everyone else enjoys the lessons and actually finds them practical. Unfortunately, this is their only fun class. Potions is dreadful, particularly since Professor Snape heard about Neville turning the Boggart into a simulacrum of him dressed in an old woman's clothing. Snape now bullies Neville mercilessly in class. Divination is almost as bad, with Professor Trelawney constantly predicting Harry's death and looking at him tearfully. Care of Magical Creatures is also just as bad now that Hagrid has lost confidence and only teaches about Flobberworms.

On a brighter note, Quidditch is starting up, and Oliver Wood has had the team practicing since early October. Wood, now a seventh-year, sees this as his last chance to win the Quidditch cup for Gryffindor. He feels that it should have been theirs for the past two years, but Harry was out of commission at the critical match in his first year, and his second year, the Quidditch Cup had been canceled.

A notice is posted for the first Hogsmeade weekend. Ron suggests that Harry, who lacks his guardian's permission, should ask Professor McGonagall. As they are discussing this, Hermione's cat, Crookshanks, attacks Scabbers, Ron's pet rat. Ron is still upset the next day, and barely speaks to Hermione. Harry asks Professor McGonagall for permission to visit Hogsmeade with the other students, but she refuses to bend the rules that far. Harry must resign himself to staying behind. Percy only makes things worse with his over-pompous attempts to console Harry.

Wandering aimlessly around the castle on Saturday, Harry runs into Professor Lupin. He invites Harry into his office for tea and to see the Grindylow that he has just received for their next class. When Harry asks why he was prevented from facing the Boggart, Lupin explains he was concerned it would turn into Lord Voldemort and terrify the class. Harry, mildly surprised that Lupin uses Voldemort's name, is somewhat mollified by this explanation. He says his first thought was Voldemort, but then realized he was more frightened by Dementors. Lupin is impressed that Harry is more afraid of fear than the actual creature. They are interrupted by Professor Snape who delivers a steaming goblet to Lupin. After Snape leaves, Harry, worried about the possible contents of the goblet, warns Lupin that many believe Snape would do anything to get Lupin's job, but he drinks the potion nevertheless.

Ron and Hermione return with many stories about Hogsmeade. They are also amazed that Lupin would dare to drink anything prepared by Snape. It is time for the Halloween Feast. Lupin attends the festivities, but Harry notices he looks unhappy. He observes Snape watching Lupin rather more intently than usual. Students head back to Gryffindor Tower, but there is a jam at the entrance; the Fat Lady is missing, her portrait slashed. Professor Dumbledore is summoned, and he questions Peeves, who says Sirius Black shredded the painting.

ANALYSIS

While it is not mentioned in the chapter summary, possible reasons can be seen for Hermione's disdain for Divination. It is mentioned in chapter 6, *Talons and Tea Leaves*, that Professor Trelawney used fortune-teller's tricks; one of these was deliberately-vague "prediction" given to Lavender Brown, "That thing you are dreading. It is going to happen on Friday the sixteenth of October." On October 16th, Lavender receives word that her pet bunny, Binky, was killed by a fox. Hermione questions how this actually fits with the prediction by recalling exactly what it said. Was the bunny's death even a surprise or was Lavender expecting it? Did it happen on the 16th, or is it only on the 16th that she had heard about it? Hermione surmises that Lavender has rationalized her experience to match the prediction. Lavender and Parvati Patil, however, now seem to almost worship Professor Trelawney. Throughout the remainder of the book, these two spend much spare time in the Divination classroom. Also, the battle between Crookshanks and Scabbers escalates, putting more strain on Ron and Hermione's relationship. We also see, although Hermione evidently does not, that Crookshanks is deliberately targeting Scabbers, although it is unknown why. Even though cats attack small animals, Crookshanks has shown no interest in other pets such as Trevor, Neville's toad. Why has he become so fixated only on Scabbers? Considering Draco's comments in the previous chapter that Harry should want revenge against Sirius Black, a correlation can be made as to why authority figures such as Fudge (in chapter 3) and McGonagall (here) refused Harry permission to visit Hogsmeade, and why Mr. Weasley attempted to get a promise from Harry that he would not set out after Sirius. As yet, however, Harry is unaware what Sirius has done and is unable to make that correlation.

From the discussion with Professor Lupin, we see his concern for Harry's emotional well being and for the entire class. Lupin perhaps is more concerned about the students than any other teacher, with the possible exception of Professor Dumbledore. The Slytherins, meanwhile, are acting as normal, making rude comments about Lupin's patched robes, obviously more impressed by someone's superficial outer appearance than with their inner character and abilities.

At the chapter's end, it is learned that Sirius Black has breached the castle's supposedly impenetrable security as well as bypassing the vicious Dementors. It is now believed that Black may have broken into Hogwarts in the same manner in which he escaped from Azkaban, although just what that is has not been revealed.

QUESTIONS

Review   1. Why does McGonagall refuse to give Harry permission to visit Hogsmeade?
2. What is Lupin's explanation to Harry about why he prevented Harry from facing the Boggart? Is he telling the truth?
3. Why would Snape give Lupin a potion? Why does Harry warn him against drinking it, and what is Lupin's response?

Further Study   1. Why would Crookshanks only attack Scabbers and not other pets?
2. Hogwarts' security is supposed to be impenetrable. How could Sirius Black have bypassed the safeguards?
3. The Dementors work for the Ministry of Magic and are stationed at Hogwarts to protect Harry while searching for Sirius Black. Why would Harry fear them more than Voldemort or even Sirius Black? Based on what has been seen, is Harry's fear justified?

GREATER PICTURE

It is mentioned that Lavender and Parvati spend much of this book with Professor Trelawney. Their near-obsession with Divination extends beyond this one book; they apparently pass their Divination O.W.L. exams, because in their first year of N.E.W.T.-level studies, in *Harry Potter and the Half-Blood Prince*, both of them do go off to Divination.

It is uncertain how Sirius had gotten into Hogwarts, though it is clear that he has managed somehow to get onto the castle grounds. We will find out later that there are two secret passages into the school, one that starts at the Shrieking Shack and ends at the Whomping Willow, and one that goes to the interior of the school from the basement of Honeyduke's Sweetshop. It is possible that Sirius either broke into the Shrieking Shack and used the tunnel from there, or else sneaked into the basement of Honeyduke's. It is also possible that he simply walked in. The protective spells around Hogwarts must be specific to people, as owls, for instance, can pass freely in and out of the school grounds. However, we cannot know whether these spells see the transformed Sirius as a person or a dog. Crookshanks, we will learn later, is definitely aware of the difference; his attacks on Scabbers seem to be almost entirely because of what Scabbers is: an Animagus. Sirius will tell us later that it had taken a long time for him to earn Crookshanks' trust. Crookshanks will make no attempt either on Trevor, as mentioned, or on Pigwidgeon, both of whom are the sorts of creatures that Crookshanks would normally hunt.

It will be some months yet before Harry learns that Sirius is widely believed to have betrayed his parents to Voldemort, and some months after that before he learns the truth of what actually happened. Until he hears the generally-accepted story, he, and we, will be unable to determine why there is such reluctance on the part of authority to allow him to visit Hogsmeade. We do already know that Sirius is apparently trying to murder Harry, though Harry doesn't see this as any more of a threat than what he has already faced three times from Voldemort. With the Dementors prowling Hogsmeade and protecting the school, likely the authority figures would feel Harry was safe from Sirius, but are uncertain whether Harry is in possession of the commonly-believed story about Sirius betraying Harry's parents. Likely they believe that if Harry knew that Sirius had betrayed his parents, Harry would chase after Sirius, thus taking him out of the protection nominally afforded by the Dementors. It is perhaps significant that the authorities, with the possible exception of Dumbledore, have not thought that if Sirius was able to pass the Dementors once on Azkaban in order to escape, he certainly could do so again in order to reach Harry. Also, with the possible exception of Lupin, nobody has noticed that the Dementors have a strange attraction to Harry and may be more dangerous to him than even Sirius.

Chapter 9: Grim Defeat

Synopsis

Following Sirius Black's break-in into the castle, Professor Dumbledore orders all students to spend the night in the Great Hall. Prefects stand guard while the teachers search the castle. Harry, Ron, and Hermione are still awake when Professor Dumbledore receives the all clear from Professor Snape. Snape reminds Dumbledore that he had expressed concerns over an appointment Dumbledore made. Dumbledore interrupts, saying he is certain that nobody in the castle would have helped Black.

Sir Cadogan becomes the new Gryffindor guard, the only portrait brave enough to take the job. There is wild speculation throughout the school as to how Black broke in. It becomes apparent that the school knows Black's objective: Harry notices that a teacher is always walking alongside him, and the pompous Percy Weasley trails behind, reinforcing Harry's belief that he is Black's target. Additionally, Professor McGonagall tells him about Black, but is taken aback when he admits he already knows. When McGonagall suggests that Quidditch practice might be an unnecessary risk, Harry protests; it is only a week until the match with Slytherin. Professor McGonagall relents and suggests that Madam Hooch can watch him during practice.

In the final practice session before the Slytherin match, team Captain, Oliver Wood, announces a schedule change: they are playing Hufflepuff rather than Slytherin. This means that their practice to counter Slytherin's moves is wasted. Hufflepuff has a completely different playing style, due in part to their new Captain and Seeker, Cedric Diggory.

Oliver keeps cornering Harry between classes with strategy pointers, making Harry ten minutes late for Defence Against the Dark Arts. Unfortunately, Snape is substituting for an absent Professor Lupin. After doling out House point penalties, Snape lectures about werewolves, although this topic is scheduled for later in the term. He assigns a homework essay on recognizing and means to defeat werewolves.

The Quidditch match is played in a fierce storm, and Harry is unable to see. During a time-out, Hermione spells Harry's glasses to repel water. Harry is now able to play properly, although his lighter body weight causes the wind to push him around more than Cedric. Momentarily distracted by a large black dog, possibly a Grim, in the stands, Harry nearly misses seeing the Snitch that Cedric has already started after. As he chases it, Dementors appear, and hearing screaming inside his head, Harry loses consciousness and falls off his broom. Harry awakens in the Hospital Wing to find his teammates, still in their muddy uniforms, surrounding his bed. Gryffindor lost, but Harry learns that Diggory had demanded a rematch after what happened, even though Wood admitted Gryffindor had been beaten. Harry is depressed that this is the first Quidditch match he has ever lost. Madam Pomfrey ousts everyone except Ron and Hermione. They say that Professor Dumbledore stopped Harry's fall and has banished the Dementors. Unfortunately, Harry's Nimbus 2000 was blown into the Whomping Willow and destroyed.

Analysis

Although Snape clearly despises Lupin, why he does is unknown. When he substitutes for Lupin in Defence Against the Dark Arts class, there seems to be a particular reason that he has the class study werewolves before it is scheduled. Snape is also being required by Professor Dumbledore (presumably) to do things he is clearly unhappy about. One, as seen in the previous chapter, is having to prepare a potion for Lupin. Although Harry suspects Snape may have poisoned it in an attempt to get rid of Lupin so he can have his job, Lupin apparently trusts Snape enough to drink it.

After Black breaks into the castle, Snape's comments to Dumbledore about a misguided appointment also seems pointed at Lupin, although his name is never mentioned. Doubtless Snape previously expressed his opinion that Dumbledore erred in appointing Lupin as the Defence Against the Dark Arts teacher. Snape appears to believe that Lupin assisted Black to get into Hogwarts, an implication Dumbledore clearly disputes. It is unclear why Snape believes Lupin is helping Black, but it indicates that Snape may know about some prior connection between the two. The Dementors entering the castle grounds against strict orders to remain outside is disturbing, even more so when they blatantly approach Harry during the Quidditch match. These strange creatures are unpredictable, and this is the second time they have singled out Harry, who they are supposedly guarding. Their actions are highly suspect. Harry, meanwhile, is at a low point. He has not only lost his first Quidditch match, but also his prized Nimbus 2000. Further complicating matters is his unusually sensitive reaction to the Dementors, and he struggles to understand why he is more affected by them than others, and for the reason he hears someone screaming every time they approach. That Hufflepuff won the match against Gryffindor is significant. Traditionally, they have always been the weakest team. Hufflepuff House rarely attains much glory in anything and is perhaps considered by many as being the repository for those students who failed to be sorted into the more specialized Gryffindor, Ravenclaw, and Slytherin Houses. There have been notable Hufflepuff students, of course, and Cedric Diggory appears to be one, although it almost seems that the Sorting Hat placed him in the wrong House. This becomes even more evident in the next book. However, Cedric's character also demonstrates fairness, loyalty, and a strong work ethic, which are Hufflepuff traits. Cedric's superb athletic skills and leadership abilities have helped Hufflepuff gain some long-awaited recognition.

QUESTIONS

Review   1. What happens when Harry is approached by a Dementor during the Quidditch match? 2. Other than the Dementors, what unusual thing does Harry see during the game?

Further Study   1. What does Snape mean when he says he expressed concerns over an appointment Dumbledore made? What is Dumbledore's response?

2. Why would Snape, who is substituting for an absent Lupin, suddenly assign homework on werewolves, a subject that was scheduled to be covered later in the term?

3. Why would the Dementors continually single out and approach Harry in such a menacing manner?

GREATER PICTURE

Snape is, apparently, questioning Dumbledore about Lupin's appointment as the Dark Arts Professor. This ironically mirrors the same suspicions others will express about Snape in the future. Despite the obvious things that Snape does at Dumbledore's behest, such as making the Wolfsbane Potion for Lupin and giving Harry Occlumency lessons in *Harry Potter and the Order of the Phoenix,* Snape's Death Eater history cannot be easily forgotten. Snape, on the other hand, has either fully accepted the Ministry story about Sirius, or is using it to suit his own ends, and will express the belief that Lupin, who was fast friends with Sirius, the late James Potter, and the supposedly late Peter Pettigrew, is helping his old friend enter the castle undetected. However, Dumbledore trusts both Snape and Lupin and does not publicly entertain doubts regarding either man's loyalty.

Snape, of course, has been aware that Lupin was a werewolf since his own school days. We will find out that, as students, Pettigrew and Sirius had almost managed to get Snape into the Shrieking Shack with the transformed Lupin, something that would have proven fatal to him; he was only saved through James' intervention. While he likely has agreed to not reveal that Lupin is a werewolf, his teaching Harry's class about werewolves is an attempt to get around that restriction. Snape is hoping that someone in the class will recognize were characteristics in Lupin and release that information. Lupin is lucky in that the only person who actually does the assignment is Hermione. While Hermione does, as we will shortly see, recognize that Lupin is a werewolf, she also chooses not to reveal that fact to anyone, not even Harry and Ron.

The large black dog that Harry sees will turn out to be Sirius, coming to watch his godson playing Quidditch. Harry is unaware of this, and fears it is a Grim. Shortly after this, he is nearly injured when the Dementors appear on the pitch. The juxtaposition of the dog and Harry's nearly falling to his death will reinforce Harry's belief that he is seeing a Grim, rather than simply a dog. Harry will continue to fret about this until one night when he sees the dog in company with Crookshanks. Once he has this proof that the dog is physical rather than spectral, his fear of it will pass. Sirius will later be apologetic that he had so scared Harry.

Chapter 10: The Marauder's Map

SYNOPSIS

Harry is deeply disappointed over his first-ever Quidditch loss and losing his broom. He is also worried that he has seen the Grim three times; twice he was nearly killed, once by the Knight Bus, and then by falling off his broom during a Quidditch game. He says nothing, however, to Hermione, who would scoff, or Ron, who would panic. The Dementors also trouble him, and Harry is beginning to realize it is his mother's screams as she was being murdered that he hears when they approach him.

Returning to classes on Monday is a relief, even with Draco's taunts. Professor Lupin also returns and cancels the Werewolf essay Professor Snape assigned. After class, he tells Harry he is sorry that the Whomping Willow destroyed his broomstick. The willow was planted during his first year at Hogwarts. Lupin says that Harry's reaction to the Dementors is not weakness. Dementors drain peoples' happiness and good memories, leaving only the bad. Harry's dreadful memories make him particularly vulnerable. Harry says that when the Dementors are near, he can hear Voldemort murdering his mother, a revelation that leaves Lupin visibly shaken. Harry asks Lupin to teach him how to defend himself against the Dementors the way Lupin did on the Hogwarts Express. Lupin promises he will after the Christmas holidays.

With that promise, and Ravenclaw flattening Hufflepuff in Quidditch, Harry's outlook brightens. Also, Ron and Hermione are staying at Hogwarts over Christmas, further bolstering his morale. Even the prospect of missing yet another Hogsmeade weekend does not bother him too much. Borrowing *Which Broomstick* from Oliver Wood, Harry intends to spend the Hogsmeade weekend reading up on a replacement for his destroyed broomstick. Fred and George, however, have other ideas. Claiming Harry's needs are greater than their own, they bequeath him their Marauder's Map, a magical parchment they stole from Filch their first year. The map, apparently created by Messrs "Moony," "Wormtail," "Padfoot," and "Prongs," shows seven secret passageways in and out of Hogwarts, as well as every person's location within the castle. Fred and George say Filch apparently only knows about four tunnels. One of the remaining three has caved in, and one starts under the Whomping Willow, making it too dangerous. The passage at the One-Eyed Witch statue goes directly to Honeyduke's Sweet Shop in Hogsmeade village. To activate the map, the user must say, "I solemnly swear that I am up to no good," and "Mischief managed" to make it blank again.

Harry opens the One-Eyed Witch's hump with a spell ("Dissendium!") provided by the map and heads down the passageway. He emerges in Honeyduke's basement. Upstairs, Harry sneaks up behind Ron and Hermione. Ron believes he Apparated, but Harry tells him about the Map. Ron is upset that Fred and George did not give him the map. Hermione demands Harry turn it in to Professor McGonagall, but Harry refuses, believing Sirius cannot be using the two usable passageways because Hogsmeade is swarming with Dementors. They set off for the Three Broomsticks. Ron, who seems to have a slight crush on Madam Rosmerta, the pub's owner, gets a round of Butterbeer.

Professor McGonagall, Professor Flitwick, Hagrid, and Cornelius Fudge, the Minister for Magic, enter. Ron and Hermione quickly hide Harry under the table. The four, plus Madam Rosmerta, sit down at an adjacent table. When Rosmerta complains the Dementors are affecting her business, Fudge explains they are necessary because Black is so dangerous. Rosmerta mentions that Sirius and James Potter were great friends once, always in the Three Broomsticks together. This surprises Harry. Fudge says that not only was Sirius James' best friend, but also best man at his wedding and Harry's godfather. James and Lily knew Voldemort was hunting them and went into hiding. They used the Fidelius charm to conceal themselves and appointed Sirius their Secret-Keeper. Dumbledore, aware someone close to them was leaking secrets, offered to be their Secret-Keeper, but they declined. Barely a week later, Voldemort killed James and Lily, although he met his own demise in baby Harry. Obviously Black, tired of playing double agent, had thrown his lot in with Voldemort but, after his defeat, fled for his life. Peter Pettigrew, another Potter friend, caught up to Black the next day and accused him of betraying James and Lily. Black killed him and twelve Muggle bystanders with a single curse. Only Pettigrew's bloodstained robes and a severed finger remained. Black was sentenced to Azkaban. It is believed he is trying to reunite with Voldemort, perhaps after killing Harry to prove his loyalty. The teachers depart; Harry, Ron, and Hermione are too stunned to speak.

Analysis

Professor Lupin seems particularly upset about the Whomping Willow destroying Harry's broomstick. Curiously, the Marauder's Map shows a secret passageway starting from the Whomping Willow, although it is unknown why a tunnel would be next to such a dangerous tree or where it leads to. Lupin tells Harry that the Willow was planted the year he started Hogwarts. This is obviously no ordinary tree, and its massive size would indicate it is much older. It is probable that magic was used to accelerate its growth in addition to making it "whomping," although for what purpose is unknown.

The Marauder's Map is an extraordinary magical creation. Whoever Padfoot, Moony, Wormtail, and Prongs may be, they were obviously exceptionally talented wizards. Since the map is of Hogwarts, it can be presumed they were students there, although it is unknown when. The twin's gift gives Harry newfound freedom and power over his own actions, and he feels no hesitation in using the map to break school rules, although Hermione, as usual, objects, while Ron urges him on. However, when Harry secretly slips into Hogsmeade to join his friends, his excursion will ultimately bring unwelcome news and additional distress. While in the Three Broomsticks, the supposed back story behind Black's imprisonment is revealed, along with why he is attempting to break into the castle. Harry, thrown into a turmoil after learning that Black betrayed his parents, now understands the reason there is so much concern over his safety and why Black is supposedly trying to kill him. That this person is also his godfather, someone who is supposed to love and protect him, only adds to Harry's despair. Harry realizes that when Malfoy was talking to Harry about wanting revenge, Malfoy knew that the Potters were betrayed by Black, as did Mr. Weasley when he spoke to Harry at the train station, although neither told him this.

In this chapter, we begin to see Fudge's remaining fear of the previous Wizarding war, as he states here that he still has nightmares of the events of the day that Sirius Black was captured. With the escape of Sirius following Fudge's last meeting with him, Fudge seems to see the prospect of a revival of Voldemort's previous reign of terror, and does everything he can conceive of, with his limited imagination, to protect the Wizarding world from the possibility of that recurrence.

As was mentioned in the last chapter, when Snape substituted for Lupin's Defence Against the Dark Arts class, he assigned a paper on werewolves; while there is not yet enough information to understand why Snape chose this particular subject, Hermione may have some idea.

Questions

Review 1. What is the Marauder's Map and how does it work?

2. How did Fred and George come into possession of the Marauder's Map, and why do they give it to Harry?

3. What was Sirius Black's relationship with James and Lily Potter?

4. Why is it believed that Sirius Black betrayed Lily and James Potter and Peter Pettigrew?

Further Study 1. Why would a dangerous tree like the Whomping Willow have been planted on school grounds during Lupin's first year at Hogwarts? Why would it be planted over a tunnel and where might the tunnel lead to?

2. If the huge Whomping Willow had only been planted the year Lupin started at Hogwarts, it is likely magic was used to accelerate its growth. Why?

3. Why would Lupin be so shaken when Harry tells him that the screams he hears are his mother's when she is being murdered?

4. Who might Moony, Padfoot, Prongs, and Wormtail be? What could their relationship to the Marauder's Map be?

5. The Marauder's Map only responds to precise instructions. How could Fred and George have figured out how to use it?

6. What might the names "Moony," "Padfoot," "Prongs," and "Wormtail" actually mean? Do they fit any characters that have been seen so far?

7. Does Sirius Black's betrayal of James and Lily Potter seem logical? Is there another explanation, given what is known about the personalities involved?

GREATER PICTURE

Harry receives another relic of his father's: the Marauder's Map, which James Potter, along with Sirius Black, Remus Lupin and Peter Pettigrew, created in their sixth year using their combined knowledge about Charms and Hogwarts' grounds. This map aids Harry in many ways during the series, usually by helping him avoid detection during his night-time sojourns around Hogwarts, to guard against and spy on Malfoy in *Harry Potter and the Half-Blood Prince,* and to gaze at Ginny's name in *Harry Potter and the Deathly Hallows.* It also plays a role in Barty Crouch Jr.'s plan to murder his own father during Harry's next year because the map shows when Crouch Sr. arrives at Hogwarts.

Lupin may feel partially responsible for Harry's broom being destroyed by the Whomping Willow because it was on his behalf that the dangerous tree was planted when he first arrived at Hogwarts as a student. We will find out that the tree was planted expressly to protect the entrance to the secret passage, and that the passage leads to the Shrieking Shack, where Lupin penned himself up at the full moon, so that he could transform safely. With the exception of one teacher (Lupin), the Hogwarts faculty are unaware that the One-eyed Witch tunnel exists. It will be revealed later, however, that Dumbledore, and several other faculty, know about the tunnel leading from the Whomping Willow. Also, Snape is aware that Sirius Black knows it exists. Regardless, it appears that this passageway, which will be used by the Trio later in the story, was never monitored or sealed off after Black's escape. It is unclear why Dumbledore failed to consider this a necessary precaution, especially after Black by-passed the castle's security. Perhaps the fact that the tunnel starts outside the castle proper and ends inside a boarded-up house leads to something of a false sense of security.

According to Minister Fudge, Sirius Black was the Potter's Secret Keeper in an attempt to hide them from Lord Voldemort, but Sirius betrayed them and later killed Peter Pettigrew, leaving only Pettigrew's finger behind. This ties in to another fact: Scabbers, Ron's pet rat, lacks a toe on one paw. It will be discovered that Scabbers is actually Peter Pettigrew, who, like Sirius and James, was an Animagus, his rat form prompting the nickname, "Wormtail." Pettigrew severed his own finger to make his escape appear more convincing. Sirius, seeing the picture in the *Prophet* of the Weasley family in Egypt, has recognized Pettigrew in his rat shape, and by the lack of a finger has realized what Pettigrew had done; it is actually because of Pettigrew that he has come to Hogwarts. In the next book, Pettigrew will again be forced to sever a body part.

It is extremely interesting to note that in this chapter, Fudge seems to believe in the possibility of a re-animated Voldemort; when Madam Rosmerta suggests that as a horrible possibility, Fudge admits that they believe that is Sirius' plan. Yet, in the next book, when Dumbledore asserts that Voldemort *has* returned, Fudge refuses to accept this. One must wonder what has happened in the meanwhile to cause Fudge's beliefs to change so wildly.

Chapter 11: The Firebolt

SYNOPSIS

Harry is in emotional turmoil, so distraught that he cannot even remember how he got from the Three Broomsticks and through the secret passage back into Hogwarts. Why had no one told him the truth about Sirius Black? Unfortunately, there is no opportunity to talk to Ron and Hermione that night, and Harry does not fall asleep until almost 5:00 A.M. He awakes at around noon to an empty Common room. The Christmas holiday has begun, and nearly everyone has left Hogwarts.

Harry is filled with rage and black thoughts of revenge; Ron and Hermione are unable to reason with him. Harry remembers Draco saying that if it was him, he would hunt Black down, but Ron tells Harry he would be better advised to listen to his friends rather than his enemies. To change the subject, Ron suggests visiting Hagrid, but this backfires when Harry seizes on it as an opportunity to ask Hagrid why he never mentioned Black. Ron is now reluctant to go, but Harry is adamant. They find Hagrid sobbing uncontrollably. Although Hagrid has been exonerated in Buckbeak's attack on Draco, his father's complaint has been upheld. Buckbeak must appear before the Committee for the Disposal of Dangerous Creatures. A distraught Hagrid is certain Buckbeak will be condemned, being that the committee members are all in Lucius Malfoy's pocket. Harry, Ron, and Hermione promise to find precedents that will save Buckbeak. Hagrid considers setting Buckbeak free, but how does one explain to a Hippogriff that it has to go into hiding? And, after his unfortunate sojourn in Azkaban, Hagrid is terrified of breaking the law. This all helps distract Harry, and he, Ron, and Hermione search the library for cases of dangerous creatures avoiding execution. Unfortunately, they find little information.

With Christmas comes presents; Harry gets the usual hand-knit jumper (US: sweater) from Mrs. Weasley, bright red with the Gryffindor lion woven into it, plus various treats. There is also a long thin package containing a broom. Not just any broom—a Firebolt. Harry and Ron are stunned. It is the finest and fastest broom there is. Harry has no idea who sent it. Hermione is immediately suspicious, and says no one should ride it yet. Ron demands to know why but is interrupted by Crookshanks attacking Scabbers. In the commotion, Harry's pocket Sneakoscope starts whistling shrilly. Hermione and Crookshanks leave, and Harry tucks away the Sneakoscope in his trunk. Harry and Ron tend to Scabbers, who is looking poorly.

They head to the Great Hall where one table is set for twelve. In addition to themselves, only Professor

Chapter 11: The Firebolt

Dumbledore, the four House Heads, Filch, and three other students are having Christmas dinner. Professor Trelawney joins them, and suddenly realizes there are thirteen at the table. She melodramatically declares that the first to rise will be the first to die, although Professor McGonagall is skeptical. Professor Lupin, who is apparently sick again, will not be joining them. Trelawney predicts his imminent "departure," but Dumbledore mildly says he does not think he is in any immediate danger, then checks with Professor Snape that Lupin has received a potion. As Harry and Ron rise from the table two hours later, Trelawney demands to know who got up first. Because they rose together, they are unable to answer. Hermione stays behind to speak to Professor McGonagall. Minutes later, Professor McGonagall arrives in the Common room and confiscates Harry's Firebolt. Because it is unknown who sent it, Madam Hooch and Professor Flitwick will test it for any Dark Magic that may be embedded in it. If it is jinx-free, Harry will get it back. It should only take a few weeks. Both Harry and Ron are furious with Hermione, but she says that she and McGonagall believe the broom was sent by Sirius Black.

Analysis

Ron shows his budding maturity here; rather than supporting Harry's desire for revenge as might be expected, Ron instead reasons with him, wisely advising Harry to heed his friends' advice rather than listen to enemies like Draco Malfoy. Ron's attempts to diffuse Harry's rage by redirecting his focus backfires when Harry finds a new target (Hagrid) to vent his frustration at. Hagrid's being in need of help himself is a good bit of timing; it allows us to perceive the depth of Harry's dismay at his discovery of Sirius' story, but prevents Harry from dwelling on it, as we can see he is likely to do. In this way, while we see Harry's concern and the depth of it, we do not become bored by his continuing reactions.

Trelawney's prediction that Lupin will soon depart Hogwarts actually has a high probability of coming true. However, she has probably (subconsciously) based this on historical fact rather than on any divination ability, although she no doubt believes she has truly foreseen the unknown future. No Defense Against the Dark Arts teacher has ever lasted more than one year at Hogwarts, and it remains to be seen if Lupin can break this pattern. It is true that Trelawney is hinting that Lupin will die, but we have come to expect this; Trelawney is over-dramatizing, an age-old fortune-teller's trick. Trelawney's prediction that the first to rise from the table will be the first to die is a similar over-dramatization, which will prove false. Once again, we are exposed to the massive amount of fakery that passes for a magical discipline in this exposure to Divination.

The confiscation of the Firebolt is likely to create a rift between Hermione and the other two. Hermione clearly sees the risk associated with this very expensive and anonymous gift, as does McGonagall; Harry and Ron are blinded to the risk by the glamour of the broom itself. One does wonder whether, rather than leaving it to Flitwick and Madam Hooch to analyze, the broom ought to be returned to the factory for a check out. Perhaps McGonagall feels that the factory would be best able to check out its motive spells, but less able to decipher Dark magic added to it than the school wizards.

Questions

Review 1. What is Harry's reaction when he learns that Black was responsible for betraying his parents to Voldemort, as well as murdering Pettigrew and twelve Muggles?

2. Why does McGonagall confiscate Harry's Firebolt? Who told her about it?

3. Who do McGonagall and Hermione believe sent Harry the Firebolt?

4. Although Hagrid was exonerated in the incident involving Draco Malfoy and Buckbeak, why is he still upset? What have the Trio offered to do to help?

Further Study 1. Why would Trelawney predict Lupin's "imminent departure?" Is there a more logical explanation than Divination?

2. Why was the truth about the his parents' murders and his relationship to Sirius Black kept from Harry?

3. Why are Harry and Ron so angry at Hermione? Was she justified in what she did?

4. What does Ron mean when he says Harry should listen to his friends rather than his enemies?

5. Why does Professor McGonagall choose to have the broom examined by Madam Hooch and Professor Flitwick? Would it not be more sensible to have the Firebolt factory technicians examine it?

Greater Picture

Once again, the pocket Sneakoscope is providing a clue: someone untrustworthy is nearby. But the only people present are the Trio, plus Crookshanks and Scabbers. We have learned about Animagi, but Hermione has categorically ruled out that there is another registered Animagus around. It is likely that Hermione's perhaps excessive concern about rules leads her to the unconscious belief that other people also will be generally rule-abiding; the possibility that there may be unregistered Animagi does not seem to have occurred to her. We will find out later that the untrustworthy person is, in fact, Scabbers, who is an unregistered Animagus. McGonagall confiscating the Firebolt starts another rift within the Trio. Harry and Ron both feel that Hermione is unfairly depriving Harry of his new broom. While Hermione is correct, that it could be jinxed and it would be unsafe to fly on, Harry and Ron are acting childishly, and they can only see the Firebolt's loss, rather than the legitimate reasons behind the confiscation and the real danger such an expensive and anonymous gift could realistically pose. As a result, neither speaks to Hermione for almost four months, until the Firebolt is returned in mid-April. It is interesting, and also unnoticed by Harry and Ron, that although Hermione turns in Harry's new broom to McGonagall, she never reveals to any Hogwarts teacher what she knows about the Marauder's Map or the secret tunnels listed on it, despite knowing that Sirius Black could possibly use one to enter Hogwarts undetected. Hermione's loyalty to her friends, as well as fearing their reprisals, has always overruled her need to adhere to school rules. However, this time the Firebolt posed too great a danger for her to ignore.

It is also probable that the reason for not sending the Firebolt back to the factory for analysis is involved here. Likely, analysis at the factory, by wizards familiar with the workings of the Firebolt's charms, would take only about a week; by leaving it with Flitwick and Madam Hooch, the analysis process takes several months, which allows the rift between Hermione and the other two time to widen and solidify, and also allows time for Harry to brood about its loss.

Chapter 12: The Patronus

Synopsis

Harry and Ron remain furious at Hermione for the confiscation of Harry's new Firebolt. Because of this, Hermione tends to avoid the Common room. Holidays end, and the night before classes start, Oliver Wood corners Harry and asks if he has his Dementor problem sorted out. Harry says that Professor Lupin has promised to help with that. Oliver asks about a new broom, and Ron tells him about the Firebolt. Oliver thinks it is unlikely it was sent by Black, a fugitive on the run. He promises to make Professor McGonagall see sense. Classes start but are no fun. Hagrid, however, has cheered up, and for his first lesson has a large bonfire full of flame-loving salamanders for them. Professor Trelawney has moved the Divination class on to palmistry and wastes no time in pronouncing that Harry has the shortest life lines she has ever seen. Harry is eager for Defence Against the Dark Arts class and Professor Lupin's promised anti-Dementor lessons. Ron mentions that Lupin looks sick and wonders what is wrong with him. Hermione overhears them and says it is obvious, but does not elaborate.

Harry meets with Lupin, who is carrying a Boggart in a case, that evening. Lupin says it will turn into a Dementor against which Harry can practice. Lupin teaches Harry the Patronus charm. Harry, concentrating on a happy memory, causes white vapour to come out from his wand. He says he is ready for a test. The Boggart is released and appears as a Dementor. Harry tries to cast a Patronus, but hearing his mother screams, passes out. Lupin brings him around and gives him a Chocolate Frog. Harry wants to try again and selects a new memory. When he tries again he hears the screaming and also his father, then faints. When he revives, Harry says this time he heard his father; Lupin, looking shaken, admits that he knew James and says they should call it a night. But Harry wants to continue and selects another memory, the day he learned he was a wizard and would be leaving the Dursleys. The Boggart is released. Harry tries to conjure a Patronus, and again, he hears screaming, but fainter. Something huge and white bursts from his wand, and the false Dementor is halted. Lupin quickly steps in and uses the Riddikulus charm to return it to the case. Lupin tells Harry that he has done enough and says they will try again next week. Harry asks if he knew Sirius Black, and Lupin admits that he and Black went to Hogwarts at the same time.

Ravenclaw plays Slytherin and loses by a slim margin. This cheers Oliver Wood because if Gryffindor can beat Ravenclaw, they will be in second place. Wood increases practice to five times a week, which combined with weekly anti-Dementor lessons leaves Harry only one night a week to do homework. Hermione seems to have it worse, although she is somehow is getting to all her classes, even those which seemed to be at the same time. Oliver tells Harry that Professor McGonagall will not be returning the Firebolt immediately. Oliver felt that having Harry flying a jinxed broom would not be a problem if he won the match before it threw him off, although McGonagall, for some reason he is unable to fathom, felt this was rather insensitive. He suggests Harry order a Nimbus 2001, but Harry declines.

The anti-Dementor lessons are not going well either. Despite his earlier success, Harry can now only produce a thin, silvery mist. After one long session, Professor Lupin brings out Butterbeer from the Three Broomsticks. Harry nearly lets it slip that he has been there. They discuss Dementors, and Harry states that Black deserves the Dementor's Kiss (sucking out a person's soul), although Lupin expresses some skepticism.

Professor McGonagall returns the Firebolt to Harry, declaring it jinx free. He heads to the Common room with his broom, finding Ron on the way. Outside Sir Cadogan's portrait, Neville is in tears. He had written down the passwords for the week—Sir Cadogan changes them several times a day—but he has lost the list. Harry gives the password, and they enter. Nearly everyone wants to see the Firebolt, and there is renewed hope of winning the Cup. Harry and Ron finally reconcile with Hermione. Ron offers to take the Firebolt up to the dorm room, it being time for Scabbers' rat tonic. Harry is again wondering how Hermione can be taking so many courses; she seems as exhausted as Professor Lupin. Ron suddenly reappears, howling that Scabbers is gone, and carrying a bloody sheet covered with cat hairs that look like Crookshanks.'

Analysis

While Harry is dejected over his destroyed Nimbus 2000 and angry about the confiscated Firebolt, these are losses he could afford to replace with the considerable fortune his parents left him. However, he refuses to do so and remains upset over his lost brooms. Rather than finding a workable solution, his anger, stubbornness, and emotional immaturity cause him to do nothing, and he slips into a temporary, self-pitying state-of-mind. Underlying all this is Harry's strong emotional attachment to these two objects that he believes cannot be replaced merely by buying substitutes. The Firebolt, in particular, is meaningful because he convinces himself that it must have been sent by someone who secretly cares for his well being, rather than by an enemy wanting to murder him, although he has no proof for either possibility. However, Harry will overcome this emotional state when the Firebolt is returned jinx free, further bolstering his belief that someone may be watching over him.

Chapter 12: The Patronus

Although the Firebolt's return patches the rift between Hermione and the boys, a new one erupts over Scabbers's apparent killing by Crookshanks. While the evidence is only circumstantial, it does seem that Crookshanks is guilty. This rift is perhaps even harder on Hermione, who is already massively overburdened by her schoolwork. This time, however, only Ron is upset with her.

There is yet another of the series' endemic date and schedule contradictions here. The anti-Dementor lesson that Harry is leaving when he runs into McGonagall on her way to return his Firebolt to him is said to be his fifth—he has been unable to produce more than a faint mist in the four lessons since the first successful one; and the first lesson was in the first week of classes, "soon after the New Year." As these lessons are supposed to be every week, by that count, it can be no later than early February. However, it is only two days later that they have the match with Ravenclaw. Less than a week later, Harry and Ron visit Hagrid and find that they are only a day away from the hearing at the Committee for the Disposal of Dangerous Creatures, which is April 20th. By that count, Scabbers should have vanished about 12 April, and Harry should have had about 12 lessons rather than 4; with perhaps three of them interrupted by Professor Lupin's "illness," there should still have been at least nine anti-Dementor lessons. While it's certainly true that as a teacher, Lupin will have had other things to deal with and would likely not have been able to fit twelve lessons in, still we are left with the impression that these lessons are meant to be every week, rather than every three weeks. In this case, the schedule confusion does cause a small problem in the story, as the compression at this point leads us to believe that the end-of-term exams are happening in about March.

QUESTIONS

Review 1. Why does Oliver Wood think McGonagall's comment about his being "insensitive" regarding Harry is unwarranted?

2. Why is it difficult for Harry to recall a strong "happy" memory?

3. Why is Neville having (more than usual) difficulty remembering the password to the Gryffindor Common room? What does he do to help him remember and what happens after he does?

Further Study 1. Why is it "obvious," at least according to Hermione, what is wrong with Lupin? What might his problem be and how did Hermione figure it out? Why does she refuse to elaborate?

2. Is Ron justified in assuming that Crookshanks killed Scabbers? How does this affect his relationship with Hermione?

3. Lupin tells Harry that Sirius Black was a student at Hogwarts the same time he was. Is it possible he knows Black better than he is letting on? Why might he disagree with Harry about Black deserving the "Dementor's Kiss"?

4. Harry has inherited a large fortune, and could easily order a new broom. Why does he resist?

GREATER PICTURE

At this point, Hermione is clearly aware of Lupin's "furry little problem," as it will later be referred to, presumably as a result of applying what she had learned while writing the werewolf report demanded by Snape. We have gathered that she was the only student to write that report, so it is not surprising that neither Harry nor Ron knows why Lupin looks ill. Hermione's estrangement from Harry and Ron is important at this point, as it is this estrangement that prevents Hermione from explaining to Harry and Ron.

Knowing that Lupin is a werewolf, and finding the effect the Boggart has on Harry, leaves us with something of a contradiction. Clearly the Boggart, in Dementor form, is having the same magical effect on Harry that a real Dementor would, leaving Harry despairing and bringing horrible, buried memories to the front of Harry's mind. And yet, when the Boggart takes the form of the full moon, Lupin's greatest fear, it does not affect him. One can only surmise that this is due to something similar to the "placebo effect": if you believe something will have an effect on you, it quite often does. To this end, the Boggart-as-Dementor is believable, as being something that could be present in the classroom, and so has an effect on Harry because he believes it will; the Boggart-as-full-moon is not believable, as a full moon cannot exist inside a classroom, and being unbelievable, has no effect on Lupin. Neville losing the list of passwords will turn out to not be his fault. Crookshanks had stolen that list at the request of Sirius Black, who will use it two nights hence to enter Gryffindor tower. That event will cause some confusion, as Black will apparently be found attacking Ron, rather than Harry who he is supposed to be trying to kill; it will, however, turn out to be the departed Scabbers that Black is looking for. It is worth noting, however, that the selection of Neville to lose this list was very well-made; Neville has been characterized from the beginning of the series as having memory problems, particularly with passwords, so his losing the list that he has made is of a piece with his character.

We learn that Lupin had gone to school with Harry's father and Sirius Black. We know also by now that "little Peter Pettigrew" was one of their friends, and we may also recall that Snape had been in school at the same time—Professor Dumbledore had mentioned that James saved Snape's life. While it is still not possible for us to recognize James, Sirius, Pettigrew, and Lupin together as a group, we should be aware at this point that they knew each other. It is a little curious that Harry is more interested at the moment in talking with Lupin about Sirius than about his father, but it is true that Sirius is someone who seems to be more immediate for him. Repeatedly, through this book, we see a pattern recur: someone wonders how Hermione can be taking so many classes, and promptly there is an interruption of some sort that prevents us from wondering further. It is a tribute to the author's skill that the interruptions do not seem contrived, but are simply normal occurrences, or as normal as they can be in this situation. This chapter shows one of these interruptions: the apparent death of Scabbers interrupts Harry's musing on this topic. While the event itself is extraordinary, it is not entirely unexpected. Like Ron and, to a lesser extent, Harry, we can see that Crookshanks has been targeting Scabbers since he was introduced to the story. Thus Scabbers' apparent demise, seemingly at Crookshanks' claws, while something of a surprise, is still a natural progression, and the interruption seems quite natural.

Chapter 13: Gryffindor Versus Ravenclaw

SYNOPSIS

Scabbers' apparent demise at the claws of Crookshanks appears to have ended Ron and Hermione's friendship. Ron feels that Hermione is unsympathetic; she apparently believes that attacking rats is normal cat behavior and that there is no real evidence that Crookshanks attacked Scabbers. Harry, however, thinks there is, given the physical evidence and Crookshanks' history of attacking Scabbers. Hermione, feeling Harry always sides with Ron, storms off. Ron is taking the loss hard, and not even the twins' reminding him that he thought Scabbers was useless (mere days before) seems to have any effect. Finally, Harry invites him to Quidditch practice, offering him a chance to ride his Firebolt, which cheers him up a bit.

Arriving at the Quidditch pitch, Harry meets the team and Madam Hooch, who has been delegated to guard Harry during practice. She is entranced by the Firebolt, as the Gryffindor common room had been, and soliloquizes about it until Oliver reminds her they have to practice. And it is a magnificent practice. Inspired by the Firebolt, everyone works so well that Oliver does not have a single criticism—a first for him. Oliver asks Harry about his Dementor problem, and Harry replies, a bit untruthfully, that he has mastered the spell. As practice breaks up, Ron flies the Firebolt into the darkening sky. Madam Hooch awakens, reprimands Harry and Ron for letting her fall asleep, and sends them to the castle. On the way back, Harry thinks he sees a pair of eyes watching him. Ron uses the Lumos charm to reveal Crookshanks. Harry does not want to admit that he thought it might be a Grim. The Quidditch match is the next morning. The Gryffindors form an honor guard and carry the Firebolt down to breakfast. Students from the other Houses, including Ravenclaw, come over to check it out, including Draco Malfoy who, as expected, makes a wisecrack. The team head for the Quidditch pitch where Ravenclaw are already waiting. Oliver mentions Ravenclaw's new Seeker, Cho Chang, saying she is good, but is riding a slower broom, a Comet Two-Sixty. Harry notices she is pretty. Madam Hooch blows her whistle, and the match is on. Lee Jordan is commentating, but repeatedly lapses into descriptions of the Firebolt instead of the game, for which he gets a stern warning. Harry spots and loses the Snitch several times, finally seeing it by the Gryffindor goalposts, when he accelerates for it. So does Cho, but she gasps and points downwards. Harry, seeing three Dementors on the field, pulls his wand and summons a Patronus, sending it at the Dementors. Then he blasts ahead of Cho to grab the Snitch, winning the game.

In the ensuing celebrations on the field, Professor Lupin comments that Harry produced quite the Patronus. Harry says the Dementors had not affected him, but Lupin says they were not Dementors. It was actually Draco Malfoy, Crabbe, Goyle, and Marcus Flint disguised in Dementor-like robes (with Draco and Goyle having shared a robe, to appear larger). Professor McGonagall berates them soundly and deducts House points. There is a celebration in the Gryffindor Common room. Fred and George hand out treats from Honeyduke's and The Three Broomsticks. Hermione does not join the party, saying she has 422 pages of Muggle Studies to read before Monday. Ron comments loudly that Scabbers would have liked to be there, and Hermione departs crying. Harry asks Ron to cut her some slack, but Ron says not until she starts acting a little sorry about Scabbers. The party goes on until one in the morning, when Professor McGonagall appears and sends everyone to bed. Harry is awakened by Ron screaming. Sirius Black has slashed Ron's bed curtains and was standing over him with a knife. Harry sprints down to the Common room. The noise has brought most Gryffindors from their dormitories, and Percy orders everyone back to bed. Ron tells him Black was there. Professor McGonagall arrives and asks Sir Cadogan how Black got in. Sir Cadogan states proudly that he allowed a man in because he had the passwords—a whole list of them. Livid, McGonagall demands to know who was stupid enough to write down all the passwords and then lose the list. A shamed-faced Neville raises his hand.

ANALYSIS

Madam Hooch's rhapsodizing about the Firebolt actually feels quite out of place. Readers may not understand why it feels wrong, but will be somewhat disturbed by it all the same. If we look back through this book, we will find that two chapters earlier, when Professor McGonagall had confiscated the broom, she had said that she was going to have Madam Hooch and Professor Flitwick examine it for hidden jinxes. Thus, Madam Hooch has been working with the broom for almost four months, from late December to mid-April, which is certainly enough time for the (non-magical) charm to wear off.

Harry produces a Patronus, but concentrating on the Snitch, he is unable to see what form it takes. Lupin, however, appears shaken by what he sees, although he later congratulates Harry on it. If Harry managed to produce a corporeal Patronus, then nearly everyone in the Quidditch pitch now knows he can produce one and what form it takes. However, only Lupin seems to understand the shape's significance.

Unable to remember the numerous passwords, Neville made a list and then apparently lost it, allowing Black to find the list and use it to enter the castle. The repercussions for Neville are severe: he is humiliated in front of his classmates and punished by McGonagall. We will learn later just how this list fell into Sirius' hands. Ron was terrified by his experience with Sirius Black, but Black's behavior in Gryffindor Tower seems at odds with his mass murderer record. Though he slashes Ron's curtains with a knife, he does not harm either Ron or Harry. They wonder why, when Ron yelled, Sirius ran away. Presuming, as everyone does, that Sirius was targeting Harry, it would have been simple enough for such a vicious killer to permanently silence Ron and quickly move on to the next bed to find his real target.

Meanwhile, there is a widening rift between Ron and Hermione. Hermione's refusal to express any sympathy or take responsibility for Scabbers' apparent demise could indicate that something is preventing her from behaving appropriately. Being that she has just patched things up with Ron and Harry after a long and difficult estrangement, she may be unwilling to admit that there is another problem that could threaten their friendship. She is also increasingly tired and shrill and clearly under much stress from her studies. Considering she has always easily been at the top of her class, this is difficult to understand.

Harry has his first encounter with Ravenclaw's Seeker, Cho Chang, the first girl he is strongly attracted to. Harry *"felt a slight jolt in the region of his stomach that he didn't think had anything to do with nerves."* Cho is pretty and also a very good flier, who, at least once, thwarts Harry for the Snitch despite having a slower broom. This may make her even more attractive to Harry.

This is also the first and only time that Harry plays a game against Ravenclaw. In all of the other books something in Harry's adventures causes him to miss playing against them.

Questions

Review   1. How was Sirius Black able to get into the Gryffindor Common room?

Further Study   1. Is Hermione acting insensitively towards Ron after Scabbers disappears? Is she taking responsibility for what Crookshanks might have done?
2. Was Crookshanks actually responsible for Scabbers' disappearance? Explain.
3. Although Sirius Black enters Harry's dorm, he does nothing to harm him and instead slashes Ron's bed curtains? Why?
4. Remus Lupin congratulates Harry on the strong Patronus he conjures during the Quidditch game, but its form surprises Lupin (although its shape remains unknown to readers). What form might it have taken and why was Lupin so affected by it?

Greater Picture

Harry's Patronus will later be revealed to be a stag. At this point, only three people know the significance of this; Black, Lupin, and Pettigrew, James' friends, would recognize the stag as James' Animagus form. Of the three, Lupin is the only one here present.

The fact that Harry can produce a corporeal Patronus in his third year at Hogwarts is a sign that, if properly motivated, he can do magic at quite an advanced level. The Patronus charm is normally taught to sixth or seventh year students. It is because of this that, in Harry's fifth year, many students seem awed by Harry's ability to perform this charm. One might wonder why they are surprised, having quite possibly seen the Patronus on the Quidditch pitch in this chapter. It is, of course, possible that the students who are most surprised by Harry's ability either were looking at something else at the time and didn't notice the white and misty stag, or if they did see it, did not understand what it was.

Later explanation will reveal that Sirius was actually after Scabbers, who is now missing and presumed killed by Crookshanks. Sirius may have learned from Crookshanks that Scabbers is Ron's pet, and which bed Ron sleeps in. This would explain why Sirius targeted Ron. It is likely that, with Scabbers' apparent demise being so recent, Sirius was unaware of it.

This also is an explanation for Scabbers' disappearance. While Ron seems to believe that Scabbers' haggard appearance is due to the actions of Crookshanks, we should recall that he was already looking poorly when Ron and Hermione met up with Harry in Diagon Alley. Ron was buying rat tonic at the time as he felt that Scabbers needed it; and it was in that same visit that Crookshanks first attacked Scabbers, and Hermione bought him. Scabbers' bedraggled appearance actually dates back to the Weasley household's discovery of Black's escape; Scabbers will have heard it being discussed and will know that Black is on his way to Hogwarts. As Black got ever closer to the Gryffindor common room, Scabbers will have decided that it was time to disappear, and will have faked his own death, as we will find out he had done before, before he departed to another location where he could still stay in touch with the Wizarding world.

It will be found later that Black, in his Animagus form, had managed to win Crookshanks' confidence. Crookshanks had stolen the list of passwords from Neville and had passed them to Black. It is uncertain why Crookshanks was unable to inform Black of Scabbers' departure.

The rift between Ron and Hermione will be mended only by an outside event: Hagrid writing to say that Buckbeak had lost his final appeal. The Trio will reunite to visit Hagrid, against his instructions, to try and comfort him.

Chapter 14: Snape's Grudge

Synopsis

A sleepless night in Gryffindor Tower ensues. At dawn, Professor McGonagall reports that Sirius Black has escaped. Sir Cadogan is sacked and the the Fat Lady returns as the guard to the Common room, although she demands extra protection in the form of a squad of security trolls. Every opening into the castle, even ones as small as a mouse hole, are boarded over except, Harry notices, the One-eyed Witch tunnel. Harry and Ron believe that the Dementors in Hogsmeade will prevent Sirius from entering the tunnel in Honeyduke's, and they decide not to report it.

Ron basks in the attention he receives over Black's break-in. But he wonders, when Sirius realized he was not Harry, why did he not permanently silence Ron and go to the next bed? Why did he run? Harry cannot answer. Neville suffers the worst from the fallout. He is banned from future Hogsmeade visits, given detention, and forbidden to have any passwords. He also receives a Howler from his grandmother.

Hagrid invites Harry and Ron to tea. When they see Hagrid's best suit hanging out, they suddenly remember that Buckbeak's hearing is that Friday, and they are dismayed that they forgot their promise to help with his defense. Hagrid tells them that Hermione is very upset that no one is talking to her, and he tells them that friends are more important than pet rats or new brooms. Chastised, they return to the castle at around 9:00 P.M. A Hogsmeade visit is scheduled for that weekend, and Harry plans to sneak in wearing his Invisibility Cloak. Neville and Professor Snape nearly prevent him from getting to the One-eyed Witch passage, but he evades them and meets Ron in Hogsmeade. They visit the Post Office and Zonko's Joke Shop, then head to the Shrieking Shack. While he and Ron are discussing the Shack's reputation as the most haunted building in Britain, Ron is approached by Draco, Crabbe, and Goyle. They start insulting Ron, but Harry attacks them. In the fracas, Harry's Invisibility Cloak slips down, revealing his head. Draco panics and runs off, and Harry rushes back to Hogwarts through the secret passage, discarding the Cloak in the tunnel just below the statue of the witch. He exits at the Hogwarts end and closes the passage, but is immediately apprehended by Snape and taken to his office. Snape says Draco reported seeing Harry's head in Hogsmeade, and demands to know what Harry was doing there. Snape reveals that although Harry's father James, once saved his (Snape's) life, it was because he and his friends had played a potentially fatal trick on him. He claims James got cold feet and warned him at the last minute only to protect *himself*. When Snape orders Harry to turn out his pockets, he finds the Marauder's Map. He demands it reveal its contents, but the Map's four authors, Moony, Prongs, Padfoot, and Wormtail, each respond with an insult. Snape summons Professor Lupin and asks if the map contains Dark Magic. Although Lupin seems taken aback when he sees the map, he responds that it looks like a common joke scroll. Ron bursts in, claiming he bought it at Zonko's ages ago. Lupin says that settles it, and, collecting Ron, Harry, and the map, departs. Lupin sternly tells Harry he knows it is a map, he knew the creators, and that he cannot return it—not after what happened when someone else left information lying about. He also says the creators would have wanted to lure Harry from the castle, and that risking his life is a poor way to repay his parents for their sacrifice.

As Harry and Ron approach the Gryffindor Common room, they meet Hermione who is almost in tears. She tells them Buckbeak is to be executed.

Analysis

Hermione reappears after being absent for several chapters, and readers can see how deeply affected she is by the rift with Ron and Harry. Her feelings are relayed to them through Hagrid, who attempts to patch things up; his efforts to seem to result in some small change. However, immediately after Harry and Ron visit Hagrid, Hermione dares to suggest that Harry going to Hogsmeade is irresponsible and could land him into trouble, and Ron savages her. Ron's belief that Sirius cannot be getting into Hogwarts through Honeyduke's is likely incorrect. Harry and Ron are both aware that Sirius must have evaded the Dementors earlier to escape Azkaban. Both Ron and Harry have lulled themselves into a false sense of security, believing only they (and Hermione and the Twins) know about the tunnel's existence. They are obviously more concerned with keeping the tunnel secret, so Harry can continue to sneak into Hogsmeade, than protecting him from Black.

When Snape shows Lupin the Marauder's Map, Lupin barely hides his reaction to seeing it, indicating he knows something about it. Although he tells Snape it is only a joke shop item, not only does he know it is a map and how to utilize it, but also that it could be used by Sirius Black to lead him to Harry.

While Harry could possibly have avoided being caught by Snape by judiciously using the Map and the Cloak when exiting the secret passage, he was panicked and in a rush to get back to his dormitory before Draco could report his appearance in Hogsmeade. Given what we have learned about Harry, this is a consistent reaction for him.

Questions

Review 1. What finally ends Ron and Hermione's feud?

2. What happens when Snape attempts to use the Marauder's Map?

3. How could the Marauder's Map be dangerous to Harry?

Further Study 1. How could Lupin know so much about the Marauder's Map and how to use it? Why did he cover for Harry?

2. Why does Snape often seem to know what Harry has been up to?

3. Snape admits James Potter once saved his life. Why is he still resentful towards him and, by extension, Harry?

Greater Picture

Snape calls Lupin into his office by throwing a handful of glittering powder into the fire. The powder is probably similar to Floo powder, though it does not show quite the same effects (Snape's fire does not burn green, for instance, and Snape does not have to stick his head in the fireplace to talk to Lupin, he merely has to speak) and shows another way of communication within the wizarding world. We will see Floo powder used for communication by Amos Diggory and Sirius Black in *Harry Potter and the Goblet of Fire,* and by Sirius and Harry in *Harry Potter and the Order of the Phoenix.*

Snape's explanation of why he owes James Potter (and, by proxy, Harry) a life debt is biased towards his own feelings: Snape believes that the joke Sirius had planned (which we learn later was to send him to the Shrieking Shack while Lupin, who is a werewolf, is transforming) was planned by all four of the Marauders. However, James was unaware until a few moments before the moonrise, and he intercepted Snape, saving him from a certain death.

Chapter 15: The Quidditch Final

While in Snape's study, Harry suspects that Snape is reading his thoughts; this is the second time he has felt this sensation, and this has actually bothered Harry since his first year at Hogwarts. In *Harry Potter and the Philosopher's Stone*, Harry wonders whether Snape has this ability. Although Snape's close inspection of the One-eyed Witch statue hints that Snape might have glimpsed the secret tunnel in Harry's mind, Harry did not sense it then. This does tie in with Snape's legilimency, which we will learn about in a later book. We will find out later that Lupin is, in fact, one of the Marauders of the Marauders' Map, the others being James Potter, Sirius Black, and Peter Pettigrew. It is a little surprising that Snape is not aware of this, although he seems to have some suspicion that there might be a connection between "Moony" and Lupin.

Chapter 15: The Quidditch Final

SYNOPSIS

Harry, Ron, and Hermione are dismayed when Hagrid tells them Buckbeak is to be executed. Ron promises that he and Harry will work on the appeal with Hermione, who finally apologizes to Ron for what Crookshanks did to Scabbers. Apparently, all is patched up between them.

With the tight security measures, the only time they can talk to Hagrid is during Care of Magical Creatures class. Hagrid says losing the case was his fault; facing the black-robed committee flustered him, and Lucius Malfoy's presentation was so smooth they simply ruled in his favor. Hagrid starts crying and runs off, causing Draco Malfoy to makes a snide comment. Hermione punches him in the nose. Draco, with his sidekicks in tow, retreats in confusion. As a result, Harry and Ron arrive late for Charms class, and Professor Flitwick reprimands them. As they prepare to learn Cheering Charms, Ron notices that Hermione, who was just behind them, has disappeared. She is not at lunch either, and Harry worries that Draco has done something to her. They find her asleep in the Gryffindor Common room. She wakes up and says Malfoy got her so worked up that she forgot to go to Charms and runs off to apologize to Professor Flitwick. Harry and Ron wonder how she could forget when she was walking behind them as they headed to class.

In Divination, Professor Trelawney is starting crystal ball gazing. She says she has been vouchsafed the information that the crystal ball will be on the exams. Hermione mutters that it is no great prediction considering Trelawney sets the exam. When Trelawney claims to see the Grim in Harry's crystal ball, Hermione protests. When Trelawney suggests that Hermione is insensitive to the Inner Eye, Hermione packs up and leaves, saying she is dropping the course. Parvati and Lavender see this as fulfillment of Trelawney's earlier prediction that at around Easter, "one of our number will leave us forever."

Easter Holidays start, but few are relaxed. The third-years have more homework than ever, and Neville looks like he might break under the load. Hermione has more work than anyone and is first into the library in the morning and last into bed at night. Ron has been working on Buckbeak's appeal in between his homework. Harry is trying to fit homework in between Quidditch practice. They are playing Slytherin, who are leading by 200 points, the Saturday after Easter break. Gryffindor House is obsessed with the match, it being the first time they are in the running for the Cup since Ron's brother Charlie was Seeker. For Harry, it is a personal conflict between himself and Draco, while Oliver sees it as his last chance to win the Quidditch cup. Tensions are also high in the Slytherin camp. Slytherins try to trip Harry in the hallways and Crabbe and Goyle constantly appear wherever he is, slouching away disappointed when they find him safely amidst chattering Gryffindors.

Waking from a bad dream, Harry looks out his window and sees what looks like Crookshanks and a large black dog. He realizes that if Crookshanks can see the dog, then it must be a real animal and not a Grim. Before he can wake Ron, they have moved out of his view.

The next day is the final Quidditch game against Slytherin. Harry blushes when Cho Chang wishes him luck. The match starts, and it is a dirty game, with Slytherin committing multiple fouls against Gryffindor. Harry cannot catch the Snitch until Gryffindor is more than fifty points up or else Slytherin will win the series. He is trying to pay attention to the game and the Snitch. Gryffindor is up by sixty points (largely through penalties). Harry sees the Snitch, but is thwarted by Draco, who holds on to Harry's broom, preventing him from reaching it. Gryffindor lose the advantage because everyone on the team is getting angry at Slytherin's antics. Harry helps Gryffindor regain their lead by blocking the entire Slytherin team, then manages to catch the Snitch, edging out Draco by inches. Gryffindor wins the match and the Cup.

ANALYSIS

Hermione's evolving character is showing its many facets. Although stubborn by nature and never doubting she is right, she finally admits that Crookshanks was the likely culprit in Scabbers' disappearance, and she apologizes to Ron. However, Ron and Harry have been far too harsh with her, reacting as they did when she turned in Harry's broom; Harry, ecstatic over his new prize, refused to consider the real possibility that it could contain Dark magic that could harm or kill him. Harry and Ron also forgot that even though Hermione has often strongly objected to their many rule-breaking activities, she has never reported them, including Harry using the Marauder's Map, an object that could potentially lead Black to Harry. She has even helped them break the rules on occasion, usually against her better judgment. Obviously under a tremendous burden from her heavy workload, it takes little to provoke her, as seen by her reaction to Trelawney and what she considers a bogus subject, and also to Malfoy, who she uncharacteristically punches in the nose for his rude behavior. Surprisingly, Malfoy does not retaliate, although Harry initially worries that he has when he and Ron are briefly unable locate Hermione. Her overall behavior has become odd, however, such as claiming she "forgot" to go to Charms class when she was clearly walking to the classroom with Ron and Harry before suddenly vanishing. Harry and Ron suspect something unusual is going on that she is withholding.

Gryffindor's win over Slytherin is a true victory, considering they won it fairly and through their superb Quidditch skills while Slytherin blatantly broke rules and played a dirty match. This appears to be how many Slytherins operate in general life, succeeding by using whatever methods they can, and taking pride only in what they obtain, not the means by which they achieved it. Draco Malfoy particularly embodies these traits, and the expensive brooms that Lucius Malfoy bought the Slytherin Quidditch team (in *Harry Potter and the Chamber of Secrets*) to ensure Draco's recruitment is a typical example.

QUESTIONS

Review   1. Why does Hermione drop her Divination class?

2. After Hermione drops Divination, Lavender Brown and Parvati Patil claim Trelawney's earlier prediction that one of their number would leave them forever around Easter has come true. Was the prediction accurate or only a coincidence? Why?

3. What does Harry think when he sees Crookshanks and the dog together?

4. Why did Hermione punch Draco in the nose? Was it deserved?

5. What makes Harry blush? Why?

Further Study   1. Why would Crookshanks, a rather unusual cat, be in the company of a large dog?

2. Why does Hermione miss Charms class? What is her explanation, and is it believable? What else might this indicate about her?

3. What does Slytherin's playing style in the Quidditch match reflect about their character in general?

GREATER PICTURE

We had seen earlier that Hermione, given a choice of subjects to take, had chosen to take all of them. Of course, we never see her in any courses except the ones that Harry and Ron also take, but we are led to believe that she is taking multiple additional courses with conflicting schedules. At lunch on the first day of the school year, Hermione had remarked, for instance, that she much preferred Arithmancy to Divination, despite there having been no time when she could have taken it. We will learn that she is making use of a Time-Turner, a device which allows her to go backwards in time. Using this, she is able to attend one class, then step back an hour and attend a different class at the same time, subject only to the constraint that she must never be seen to be in two places at the same time. As a result, she is able initially to take twelve subjects, double the normal work load. As the year has worn on, though, she has suffered from the strain; her days must be inordinately long, and she is likely shorting herself on sleep. We see this here, where she very uncharacteristically punches Draco, and where she forgets to go to a class. Additionally, there is little opportunity for her to use the time-turner to get extra study time during the Easter break; as she is seen to enter the library early in the day, and leave late at night, the only place she can be is in the library. Thus she cannot use the time-turner to grant herself extra study time, and so she has less time than she thinks she needs to study the eleven subjects she is still taking.

We will soon learn that the large dog which has been appearing to Harry is, in fact, real, if not exactly a dog. It will turn out that this is Sirius Black in his Animagus form.

We have already seen that the Patronus charm requires a happy memory to drive it. Harry's victory in this Quidditch match will give him an extremely strong happy memory that he will use as the foundation for Patronus charms in the future.

Chapter 16: Professor Trelawney's Prediction

SYNOPSIS

It is late May, and exams are looming. Harry and Ron see that Hermione has two exams scheduled for Monday morning and two for Monday afternoon. When Harry asks if there is any chance of an explanation as to how Hermione expects to sit two exams at once, Hermione cheerfully says, "No," then looks for her Ancient Runes book. Hedwig delivers a note from Hagrid: Buckbeak's appeal is 6 June, and it will be at the school. A Committee wizard and an executioner will attend, making it appear to Harry that the Committee's decision is already made. Ron is dismayed over the wasted work he has done on the appeal. Draco, who lost some of his usual swagger after Slytherin's Quidditch defeat, appears to be getting it back. Worse, the tight security has made it impossible to visit Hagrid, and Harry has not yet dared to retrieve the Invisibility Cloak from the One-Eyed Witch tunnel.

Exams begin, and they are as rough as expected. In Transfiguration, students had to transfigure a teapot into a tortoise, which was a problem for most. In Charms, they were tested on Cheering Charms, the one class Hermione missed. Tuesday's Care of Magical Creatures was a simple exam; they only had to keep Flobberworms alive for one hour. Harry, Ron, and Hermione use this time to exchange a few words with Hagrid, who says Buckbeak is tired of being penned up. It will be several days before they know the appeal's outcome. The Potions exam does not go well. Snape gives Harry a zero. Astronomy is Tuesday at midnight, History of Magic Wednesday morning, and Herbology is Wednesday afternoon. Thursday morning is Defence Against the Dark Arts, and Professor Lupin has set them a practical test: students have to wade across a deep pool containing a Grindylow, cross a series of potholes containing Red Caps, cross a stretch of marshland while avoiding being distracted by a Hinkypunk, then climb into an armoire to battle a Boggart. Harry gets a perfect score, but Ron is distracted and led astray by the Hinkypunk. Hermione is unable to defeat the Boggart who has taken the form of Professor McGonagall telling her she has failed every subject.

Heading back, they run into the Minister for Magic on the castle steps. Fudge says he is there for a very sad duty—witnessing the execution of a dangerous animal.

Chapter 16: Professor Trelawney's Prediction

Ron protests that the hippogriff might be exonerated, but before Fudge can answer, he is joined by a testy old wizard and a tall, strapping man carrying a large axe. Convinced the appeal is a mockery, Ron starts say something, but Hermione drags him away to protect Mr. Weasley's job.

After lunch, Harry and Ron have their Divination exam, while Hermione has Muggle Studies. Professor Trelawney examines students individually. Harry, examined last, pretends to see a hippogriff in the crystal ball and claims it is flying away. As Trelawney dismisses him, she suddenly enters into a trance and speaks in a strange voice: "*It will happen tonight. The Dark Lord lies alone and friendless, abandoned by his followers. His servant has been chained these twelve years. Tonight, before midnight, the servant will break free and set out to rejoin his master. The Dark Lord will rise again with his servant's aid, greater and more terrible than ever before. Tonight ... before midnight ... the servant ... will set out ... to rejoin ... his master ...*" Suddenly awakening, Trelawney is unaware of what she has just said, and chastises Harry for repeating it to her.

Uncertain if Trelawney was merely adding melodrama to the exam or experiencing a real prediction, Harry heads back to the Common room. Before he can share what Trelawney said, Ron and Hermione tell him Hagrid sent a note that Buckbeak lost the appeal and will be executed at sunset. He orders them to stay away. Harry bemoans that his Invisibility Cloak is still in the One-eyed Witch tunnel, otherwise they could visit Hagrid. However, if Snape catches Harry anywhere near there, he will be expelled. Hermione dashes off, returning shortly with the Cloak. Donning the Invisibility Cloak, the three head to Hagrid's hut. A distraught Hagrid says Macnair, the executioner, is Lucius Malfoy's friend, but at least the end will be quick and clean. Professor Dumbledore is also coming to support Hagrid. Says Hagrid, "Great man, Dumbledore." Fetching a pitcher, Hermione discovers Scabbers hiding inside. Scabbers seems frantic to remain hidden, trying to climb back into the milk jug even as Ron grabs him. Hagrid spots the execution committee coming and shoos Harry, Ron, and Hermione out the back door. As they head to the castle under the Invisibility Cloak, Scabbers makes another bid for freedom. As Ron tries to contain him, they hear the swish and thud of the executioner's falling axe.

Analysis

Trelawney's prediction leaves Harry stunned and confused, unsure if what he has just heard was mere melodrama or a true prophecy. It should be remembered, however, that Trelawney has a poor record for making accurate predictions. There is also no indication as to who Voldemort's servant may be. Harry can only wait and let events unfold; the prediction, if it is real, is that events will happen before midnight, far too short a time for Harry to consult with other wizards to try and find a meaning.

Questions

Review 1. What happens during Trelawney's Divination final exam? What might it mean?
2. Who retrieves Harry's Invisibility Cloak and why?
3. What makes Harry believe that Buckbeak's appeal has been decided even before the committee convenes?

Further Study 1. Scabbers vanished in April, and it is now early June. Why did he remain hidden in Hagrid's hut all this time, rather than leave Hogwarts?
2. What might Trelawney's prediction mean?
3. Who is Voldemort's servant mentioned in the prediction?

Greater Picture

Although Harry's made-up prediction that Buckbeak flies safely away is wishful thinking, it foreshadows events in the book's conclusion. It is perhaps lucky that Harry is aware that he is making this up; if he had been a little less sure of himself, he might have somehow come to the conclusion that he had a touch of the Talent. Trelawney's strange pronouncement is, in fact, a true Prophecy, and Dumbledore later tells us that it is her second while in Hogwarts' employ. We will later find out that the first concerned Harry and Voldemort, and had occurred on the occasion of her initial hiring by Dumbledore. It is apparently on the strength of these two prophecies that Dumbledore keeps her on staff; otherwise, it would seem that he shares the general opinion of the staff that the subject, Divination, is purest flummery and does not deserve a place at Hogwarts.

The reader may believe that this is a true prophecy; it is certainly delivered in a convincing manner. If so, the reader will be misled by the belief that Sirius is the Dark Lord's servant. It is true that Sirius, imprisoned in Azkaban, could be said to be chained "these past twelve years," except that he has by now been free for almost a year. Despite the various bits of foreshadowing—the Sneakoscope, the revelation of the Animagus transform, Sirius' attack on Ron, and Crookshanks' repeated attacks on Scabbers—we are somehow unable to predict that Scabbers will turn out to be the Animagus form of Peter Pettigrew.

The Invisibility Cloak has lain, undiscovered, in the secret passage leading from Hogwarts to Hogsmeade after Harry was forced to abandon it there in mid-April. It was still there in early June, when Hermione went to retrieve it. We know that Sirius was in the school on the night after the match against Ravenclaw, before the Cloak is left in the passage, and Harry sees him in his Animagus form the night before the Slytherin match, after it had been left. Did Sirius enter the school via that passage? If so, did he pass by the Cloak, and, recognizing it as once belonging to James Potter, leave it aside? Or did he use another means to get into Hogwarts? The author never clears this point up, but it is quite possible that Sirius has opened one of the boarded-up windows of the Shrieking Shack, and is using the tunnel under the Whomping Willow to enter the school grounds.

Chapter 17: Cat, Rat and Dog

Synopsis

Still hiding under the Invisibility Cloak, Harry, Ron, and Hermione debate whether to return to comfort Hagrid, eventually deciding to proceed to the castle. Scabbers bites Ron, who is struggling to hold on to him. Harry spots Crookshanks approaching, apparently homing in on Scabbers' squeaks. Scabbers escapes and runs off, with Crookshanks in hot pursuit. Ron takes off after Scabbers. Harry and Hermione fling off the cloak and chase after him. Ron catches Scabbers, but before they can get under the cloak again, a black dog appears, knocking Harry aside and grabbing Ron. Something strikes Harry's face as the dog drags Ron under the Whomping Willow, breaking Ron's leg as he is dragged through a hole.

Crookshanks dives under the branches and presses his paws against a knot in the tree trunk. The flailing branches fall still; following Ron and the black dog, Harry and Hermione enter a tunnel that leads to the Shrieking Shack. Upstairs, Ron is lying beside a decrepit four-poster bed. He warns them it is a trap; the dog is Sirius Black, an Animagus. Black disarms Harry and Hermione with Ron's wand.

Sirius remarks he is glad Harry acted like his father, coming to save his friend rather than running for a teacher; that will make things easier. Ron says that if Black is going to kill Harry, he will have to kill them all, but Black tells him to lie down so he does not injure his leg further. There will only be one murder tonight. Harry demands to know if killing twelve Muggles plus Peter Pettigrew were not enough and lunges at the visibly weakened Black, grabbing his wand wrist. Black chokes Harry with his free hand. Hermione kicks Black while Ron grabs his wand hand. Harry breaks away and as he grabs his wand, Crookshanks claws his hand. Defenseless, Black asks if Harry is going to kill him. Harry tells Black he knows that he betrayed his parents to Voldemort. Black admits he was responsible but says there is more to the story. While Harry decides whether or not to hear him out, Crookshanks deliberately sits on Black's chest, resisting Black's efforts to shift him off.

Professor Lupin suddenly bursts in and disarms Harry, Ron and Hermione. He asks Black, "Where is he?" and Black points at Ron. Lupin asks, "Why hasn't he shown himself? Unless . . . you switched . . . and didn't tell me?" Black nods. Lupin pulls Black to his feet, embracing him. Hermione, sounding betrayed, tells Lupin that she trusted him and protected his secret that he is is a werewolf. Lupin admits that he is, but that he has not been helping Black, nor does he want Harry dead. The Hogwarts staff knows he is a werewolf; Professor Dumbledore convinced them he was trustworthy. Professor Snape set the werewolf assignment with the expectation that a student would detect Lupin and give away his secret.

When challenged by Harry that he was helping Black, Lupin denies it, and returns the Trio's wands, placing his own wand in his belt. He then asks the Trio to listen, as they now hold the advantage. Lupin explains he saw Black on the Marauder's Map, a map he helped create when he was a student. He is "Moony." When he saw the three returning from Hagrid's on the map, he saw someone else—Sirius Black. He also one other. He asks Ron's to hand over Scabbers, who Lupin and Black claim is actually a wizard Animagus named Peter Pettigrew. Harry is shocked by Lupin's apparent betrayal, and, overwhelmed by extreme emotions, is thinking and reacting illogically. He initially wants to execute Black, who even admits he was responsible for the Potters' deaths, although Black's demeanor and concern over Ron's injury belies his supposedly murderous intent. However, nothing is as it seems, and Lupin's timely and surprising arrival prevents Harry from inflicting any serious harm to Sirius, although it is doubtful whether Harry would intentionally kill him. His underlying humanity ultimately prohibits him from committing violence. Only after Harry has been forced to calm down is he willing to hear out Lupin, although his explanation that Scabbers is actually an Animagus wizard seems incredible.

Hermione is also feeling betrayed by Lupin, having trusted him and protected his secret. If Lupin is lying and was actually aiding Black, by remaining silent, Hermione may have unwittingly doomed Harry. Lupin, of course, has denied this, but given what we have been told about Sirius to date, we are having as hard a time believing this as Hermione, Harry, and Ron are.

Now that we know that Sirius' Animagus form is a large black dog, we may also wonder if he was the dog that Harry had seen in Privet Drive and in the Quidditch match against Hufflepuff, that he took for a Grim. If he was, and the author's economical writing style would seem to imply that, what was Sirius interested in if he was not in fact planning to murder Harry?

Questions

Review 1. What does Black mean when he says he is glad Harry acted like his father?

2. Why did Hermione never reveal Lupin's secret? How did she figure it out?

3. What did Lupin, Pettigrew, and Black keep secret about themselves? Why?

4. Lupin knew Black and Pettigrew were in the Shrieking Shack by using the Marauder's Map. How could he know how to use it?

Further Study 1. Why would Crookshanks attack Harry when he reaches for his wand?

2. How does Crookshanks know how to still the Whomping Willow?

3. What might Lupin mean when he asks if Black "switched?"

Greater Picture

As is usual in the Potter books, the end of the book contains a series of revelations that explain much of what has gone before, but leave questions open for the future. In this book, we are faced with a significant number of revelations, so we cannot get everything wrapped up in a single chapter. The story-closing revelations thus span three chapters, and the resulting activities on the part of the principals take three more. The necessary revelations appear so densely that these final six chapters, about one third of the 22-chapter book, actually cover only about four hours of the school year.

In this chapter, we have learned that Sirius does not intend to murder Harry, as we had been led to believe, although we still doubt this; that Lupin does not believe Sirius has evil intent towards Harry; that Lupin is a werewolf and that Hermione knew this; and that Peter Pettigrew, who we had thought long dead, is actually still alive in the form of Scabbers. We also learn that Lupin, under his nickname Moony, was one of the Marauders, leading us to believe that possibly Sirius, Harry's father, and Pettigrew were the other three. At this point, we can see that things are not as we had been led to believe, but we are not yet sure what the truth is. Over the next two chapters, we will be given corroboration, not only by Sirius and Lupin, but also inadvertently by Snape, that Sirius is, in fact, blameless of the crime for which he was imprisoned, and that Sirius feels responsible for Harry's parents' deaths, though he did not betray them. We will also receive proof, in the form of Pettigrew being forced to take his human shape, that Sirius' murder of Pettigrew had not happened.

We learned, back at Christmas, that Sirius was Harry's godfather. Sirius has retained affection for Harry, and has been trying to see how Harry had grown up while he was imprisoned. Sirius will tell us later that he had visited Privet Drive to see Harry, and had been present at the Quidditch match to see how well he could fly.

Chapter 18: Moony, Wormtail, Padfoot, and Prongs

SYNOPSIS

Harry, Ron, and Hermione insist Lupin and Black must be crazy, Scabbers could not be Peter Pettigrew; Sirius Black murdered him twelve years ago. Black says he did try to kill him, but, unknown to him, Peter escaped. Black lunges at Scabbers. Ron, still holding Scabbers, yells in pain when his leg is jostled. Lupin tells Black that Harry must understand everything before Pettigrew dies. Black acquiesces, but demands Lupin be quick, he wants to commit the murder for which he was imprisoned. When Ron reminds Black there were witnesses, Black contends they were fooled. Hermione points out that Pettigrew is not listed among the seven registered Animagi. Lupin claims there were three unregistered Animagi running around Hogwarts.

Ron, noting a door apparently opening by itself, says the Shrieking Shack is haunted, but Lupin says it is not. The howls the villagers believed were ghosts were actually his. Before there was a potion to allow a werewolf to retain his mind, the Shrieking Shack was built specifically to confine Lupin during his transformations. The Whomping Willow was planted to guard the tunnel leading to the shack. Terrible as the transformations were, he did have three great friends: Sirius Black, Peter Pettigrew, and James Potter. They discovered he was a werewolf, but rather than shunning him, they secretly became Animagi to support him. It took them three years to learn how, perfecting it in their fifth year. James and Sirius learned on their own, but Peter needed their help. When transformed, they could safely run with Lupin in the Forbidden Forest. Sirius and James were large enough to keep a werewolf in check, although there were near misses. That was how they chose their nicknames; Sirius was Padfoot, James was Prongs. Pettigrew, the rat, was Wormtail.

Harry asks what animal his father was, but Hermione interrupts, saying it was dangerous to allow a werewolf to run free. Lupin admits it was, but they were young and uncaring. Lupin regrets never telling Dumbledore that Sirius is an Animagus, but says he was ashamed to admit to him that he betrayed his trust by once roaming the village as a werewolf. Lupin says he believed Black was in league with Voldemort and convinced himself that Black used Dark Magic to enter the castle, rather than his Animagus form. He confesses that Snape was partially right, that he was aiding Black. Sirius demands to know how Snape is involved, and Lupin explains that Snape is now a Hogwarts teacher. Lupin goes on to explain that Black once played a trick on Snape, who became curious about where Lupin disappeared to each month. Black told him about the tunnel and how to get past the Whomping Willow. It was only James' last-minute intervention that saved Snape from being trapped in the Shack with a deadly werewolf. Dumbledore had, of course, forbidden Snape from telling anyone, but Snape now knew what Lupin was. Says Harry, "So that's why Snape hates you." Behind Lupin, pulling off the Invisibility Cloak, Snape replies, "That's right."

Many questions are answered, but Harry is barely able to digest what is happening. Nothing is what it seemed, and Harry had become so entrenched in his belief that Sirius Black was guilty that he is barely able to consider any other explanation. Te revelations concerning Lupin's and Pettigrew's roles only add further confusion. Regardless, Harry learns much about his father and his comrades that he never knew before, and gains some insight into Snape's animosity towards him and James Potter.

There have been few Animagi; presumably, mastering the ability is too difficult a feat for most wizards, and it is mentioned elsewhere that Pettigrew nearly failed in the process and had to be coached by James and Sirius. Being an Animagus is certainly a useful ability, although it is a skill that can also be used for illegal or unethical purposes. That is why all Animagus wizards must be registered with the Ministry of Magic, and failing to do so is a serious crime. That obviously never deterred James Potter, Sirius Black, and Peter Pettigrew, whose solidarity for their friend, Remus Lupin, outweighed any legal concerns. Of the four Marauders, Pettigrew was the weakest member, physically, intellectually, and magically lagging behind the others in ability. They befriended him because he was able to ingratiate himself into their inner circle, but his weak, cowardly character eventually resulted in him defecting to Voldemort and betraying his friends. The Sorting Hat having placed Pettigrew into Gryffindor is a mysterious decision and is never explained. However, that

Pettigrew was able to become an Animagus at all may indicate that he has some noteworthy magical ability.

An Animagus does not choose his animal form; rather, it reflects that person's inner character. The rat form seems appropriate here for Pettigrew (Wormtail), representing that animal's less desirable traits, while Sirius' (Padfoot) dog shape emphasizes amity and fidelity. It should be noted that in the Western world, the rat is usually associated with mostly unsavory characteristics such as cowardice, treachery, deceit, and filth. However, in other cultures it can represent admirable qualities, and in the Chinese Zodiac the rat symbolizes intelligence, adaptability, and industriousness. Rowling is using the Western characterization here, although some Eastern characteristics could also apply to Pettigrew including: edginess, shrewdness, and opportunism. It is unknown yet what James Potter's Animagus form was, although the nickname "Prongs" should provide some clue.

The opening of the door, apparently by itself, that prompts Ron to say that the Shrieking Shack is haunted, should be noted. It is reasonably clear that this is the point where Snape, under the Invisibility Cloak, has entered the room, though it is entirely possible that he had been listening from outside for some time before that. Thus, he will certainly have heard that the Marauders were Animagi, but may not have heard that Pettigrew was Scabbers.

Questions

Review 1. Why did Sirius Black, James Potter, and Peter Pettigrew become unregistered Animagi? How did they achieve this?

2. What do Lupin and Black reveal about "Scabbers"?
3. Why does Black want to kill Pettigrew?
4. Why was the Shrieking Shack built? Is it haunted?
5. What is Severus Snape's past connection to Black, Lupin, Pettigrew, and James Potter?

Further Study 1. What might James Potter's nickname (Prongs) indicate about his Animagus animal shape?

2. Why have there been so few Animagi in Wizarding history?
3. Why do all wizard Animagi have to be registered with the Ministry of Magic?
4. Although Lupin had always believed that Black was guilty, why did he never reveal Black's secret Animagus ability?

Greater Picture

We will find shortly that Prongs is a reference to James Potter's Animagus shape, a stag. Interestingly, this is the same shape that Harry's Patronus takes, when it is fully formed. It is because of this that Lupin is so shaken after the Quidditch match with Ravenclaw in a previous chapter; he recognizes the shape that James had taken. With the possible exception of Black, who had been present at an earlier match, nobody else present at the match understands the significance of that shape; and Harry, busy catching the Snitch, does not see it himself, and so does not receive that clue to what James' nickname might have referred to.

A large part of Ron's reluctance to accept that Scabbers may actually be Pettigrew is likely denial. If Scabbers is Pettigrew, Ron has been sharing his bed, unknowingly, with a grown man for the past three years at least. This prospect, horrifying for Ron to contemplate, is something that he cannot help resisting.

Harry's reluctance to accept what is being revealed stems from his sharing the common belief that Sirius had betrayed his parents. He is, however, being convinced by the extremely precise recounting of events by Lupin and Black, helped by his personal trust of Lupin. Snape's appearance will actually bolster the solidity of Black's account as Snape will clearly reject everything that Lupin and Black have said, even those things that are immediately provable. Harry's distrust of Snape, combined with Snape's attempted refutation, will leave Harry more certain of Black's good intentions than almost anything else could.

As mentioned, based on what has been said since he entered the room under the Invisibility Cloak, Snape will have heard that the Marauders were Animagi, but not heard Black's and Lupin's claim that Pettigrew was still alive, and in fact was Scabbers. However, this does not seem to be particularly germane to Snape. We will see in the next chapter that Snape has formed his own ideas of what happened, and will act on those ideas, literally stifling anyone who would dissent.

Chapter 19: The Servant of Lord Voldemort

Synopsis

Snape found Harry's Invisibility Cloak by the Whomping Willow. He was bringing Lupin his Wolfsbane potion when he noticed a very interesting map on Lupin's desk. As he suspected, the map showed that Lupin was helping Black. Snape magically binds Lupin before he can explain, and tells everyone they are returning to the castle to have a word with the Dementors. Harry blocks the door and demands Snape listen. Snape orders him out of the way, but Harry disarms him, helped by Ron and, surprisingly, Hermione. Their triple-force spell throws Snape against the wall and knocks him out.

Harry does not yet fully believe Lupin's story. Lupin asks Ron to hand over Scabbers, and he will provide proof. Ron protests. Even if Peter Pettigrew is an Animagus in the form of a rat, why should it be Scabbers? Sirius explains that he saw Scabbers in the photograph of Ron's family on vacation in Egypt. He had gotten the paper from Fudge when the Minister visited him at Azkaban. He recognized Pettigrew, having seen him transform many times, and he noticed that Scabbers was missing a toe. Pettigrew severed his own finger before killing the Muggles. Shouting that it was Sirius who killed James and Lily for bystanders to hear, Pettigrew blew up the street, and transforming, disappeared into the sewer. He left his severed finger behind as evidence he was dead. Ron insists this is impossible, but Lupin reminds him that Scabbers has been in the Weasley family for twelve years, whereas a common rat

Chapter 19: The Servant of Lord Voldemort

lives only three or four. Lupin observes that Scabbers is not looking too good at the moment, although Ron claims it is strain caused by "that mad cat" going after him all the time. Harry figures differently: Scabbers was already looking stressed in Diagon Alley, just after returning from Egypt, presumably because he had heard about Black's escape in the meanwhile.

Sirius says Crookshanks recognized Pettigrew for what he was. He had also spotted Sirius and initially distrusted him, but helped him once he understood what Sirius was after. Unable to bring Scabbers to Sirius, Crookshanks stole Neville's password list and later told Sirius that Scabbers had vanished, leaving blood on Ron's sheets. After all, appearing dead had worked once before.

Sirius is about to kill Pettigrew, but Harry says he should have let Snape take Sirius to the Dementors. It was Sirius who was his parents' Secret-Keeper and betrayed them. Sirius says he was not the Secret Keeper. He was responsible for their deaths, but only because he persuaded James and Lily to use Pettigrew as their Secret-Keeper rather than himself, believing no one would suspect a weak wizard like Pettigrew. When Black checked on Pettigrew's hiding place, he found him absent with no signs of a struggle, he feared the worst. He then went to Godric's Hollow, and finding James and Lily's bodies amid their destroyed house, realized what had happened—Pettigrew had betrayed the Potters to Voldemort.

Lupin calls a halt, and he and Sirius cast a spell to transform Scabbers into a human: a short man with vaguely rat-like features, colorless hair, and a large bald spot—it is Peter Pettigrew. Lupin demands that Pettigrew explain about the night James and Lily died. Pettigrew says he knew Sirius was going to escape and come after him, because he has powers that "He Who Must Not Be Named" taught him. Black says that Voldemort's followers are unhappy with Pettigrew, that Voldemort went to the Potters' on Peter's information and died there. The Death Eaters in Azkaban think Pettigrew double-crossed Voldemort, and many are still at large. Lupin asks why an innocent man would stay hidden for twelve years. Peter claims he was scared because he put Voldemort's top lieutenant, Sirius Black, in Azkaban. Sirius angrily reminds Pettigrew that he (Pettigrew) was the Potter's Secret-Keeper. Black says Pettigrew never harmed Harry because he would not risk acting on Voldemort's behalf unless Voldemort could protect him. Sirius also explains that he remained sane in Azkaban by changing into a dog when things became unbearable. A dog's simpler thoughts are not as affected by the Dementors as a human's. Because Dementors cannot see, they were unable to detect him transforming. Instead, they feel and navigate towards emotions. When Black recognized Pettigrew's animal form in the photograph, he realized the traitor had to be exposed. As a dog, he was able to evade the Dementors during his escape. He journeyed north to Hogwarts and lived in the Forbidden Forest, emerging to watch the Quidditch matches.

Finally, Harry believes Sirius is innocent. Pettigrew's pleas for mercy are ignored. He admits to working for the Dark Lord, but claims he would have been killed if he resisted. Black says he should have died for his friends, as they would have done so for him. Lupin and Black prepare to execute Peter, but Harry intervenes, not wanting his father's two best friends to become murderers; they will turn Pettigrew over to the Dementors. Black and Lupin relent, and Lupin binds Peter and splints Ron's leg. Black warns Pettigrew that if he transforms, he will kill him. Lupin charms the unconscious Snape to float along with them. Black suggests that two people should be chained to Peter to prevent his escape, Lupin and Ron volunteer, and Black, using Snape's wand, conjures manacles. With Crookshanks leading, they return to the tunnel.

Analysis

Harry's actions are often ruled by his emotions and carried out without considering all facts. He was single-mindedly determined to kill Sirius to avenge the Potters, disregarding any consequences. However, Harry's already admirable character takes a great leap forward here. When he learns that it was actually Pettigrew who betrayed his parents, he acts to prevent Black and Lupin from executing him. After the initial shock and confusion, Harry quickly regains his composure and by logically analyzing the situation realizes the probable outcome: if Lupin and Black kill Pettigrew, even if it was to avenge the Potters, they would be convicted of murder. Harry acts to save them and protect the truth, and he will allow justice to deal with Pettigrew in the proper manner. For once, it is the student guiding the teacher.

In chapter 13, it was believed that Neville lost the password list, and that Sirius Black had found it. In fact, as we discover here, Crookshanks stole them from Neville at Sirius' request. Granted, losing the list is the sort of thing Neville would likely do, but it appears, in this case, that he was punished for something that was only partially his fault.

Snape here has quite clearly decided what is going on, and not accepting explanations that might destroy his "understanding," has bound and gagged both Sirius and Lupin. While Harry does not yet fully believe Sirius' story, he is certain of Lupin's trustworthiness, and rebels against Snape's refusal to even listen to what Lupin has to say. While it is expected that Ron would join this rebellion, it is surprising to everyone, including herself, that Hermione also joins in.

Questions

Review 1. Crookshanks is a cat / kneazle cross, which makes him very intelligent for a cat, but how could he have "told" Sirius that Scabbers had vanished?

2. How did Black learn that Pettigrew was still alive?

3. Why did Black and Pettigrew switch places as the Potters' "Secret Keeper"?

4. Why do Harry, Ron, and Hermione knock out Snape in the Shrieking Shack?

5. How did Black escape from Azkaban prison? Why were the Dementors unable to detect him?

6. Why does Harry prevent Lupin and Black from killing Pettigrew?

7. Why did Pettigrew, who had close access to Harry, never try to kill him?

8. Although Sirius is innocent, why does he, by his own admission, claim he is responsible for the Potters' deaths?

Further Study 1. Why didn't the Weasley family ever notice or question Scabbers' unusually long life?

Greater Picture

It has become obvious over the past few chapters that Crookshanks is not an ordinary cat. According to the author,[1] he is actually part Kneazle, a cat-like creature that often associates with wizards. Intelligent, they are able to communicate with other animals, which is how Sirius, in his dog form, was able to receive and relay information. Harry's decision to prevent Lupin and Black from executing Pettigrew has large repercussions. Pettigrew will escape, as we will discover shortly, and will, as predicted, return to Voldemort. He will also manage to trap one Bertha Jorkins, an employee of the Ministry of Magic, and it will be with her unwilling assistance, and Pettigrew's help, that Voldemort will be able to capture Harry and re-embody himself.

It should be noted here that Lupin's having failed to take the final dose of Wolfsbane Potion will have serious consequences. It is the night of the full moon, and Lupin will transform, thus putting all of his companions at risk. If Lupin had remembered to take the final dose, he would retain his mind after the transformation and Pettigrew would, in consequence, have been unable to escape. Without that final dose, however, Lupin will become a mindless animal, and Sirius will have to transform to dog shape to protect Harry and Ron. With both fully grown wizards occupied, Pettigrew will be able to transform himself and escape.

Chapter 20: The Dementor's Kiss

Synopsis

Proceeding down the tunnel, Sirius realizes he will be a free man once Pettigrew is turned over to the authorities. He mentions to Harry that he is his godfather and also his guardian. Sirius hesitantly offers to let Harry live with him. Harry's enthusiastic, "Yes!" catches him rather by surprise, and his smile makes him look ten years younger.

As they exit the tunnel, a shifting cloud bathes them in full moonlight. Lupin, who has forgotten his potion, transforms into a werewolf. Sirius yells at Harry to run, but he cannot—Ron is still chained to Pettigrew. Sirius transforms into a dog to defend the others. Lupin, now a werewolf, is no longer shackled to Pettigrew, who grabs Lupin's dropped wand and stuns Ron and Crookshanks. Harry disarms Pettigrew, but he transforms into a rat and vanishes into the grass. Lupin, prevented by Sirius from attacking Harry, Hermione, and the Stunned Ron, bounds off into the Forbidden Forest chased by a wounded Black.

Harry and Hermione run to Ron's aid, but they are unable to undo Pettigrew's jinx. Hearing a whining yelp, Harry and Hermione run to the lake and find the human Sirius cowering on the shore. About a hundred Dementors are approaching from all directions. Harry and Hermione leap to Sirius' defense, but there are too many Dementors, and Harry's Patronus charm is too weak to repel them. Both Harry and Hermione are overwhelmed by the creatures' presence. Harry falls and feels himself being lifted by one to administer the "Kiss."

As consciousness fades, Harry sees a bright light. He somehow senses the brightness is running around him, scattering the Dementors. As they disperse, he sees a large animal in the light's midst. On the opposite lake shore, he sees something impossible before losing consciousness.

Analysis

When the truth is finally revealed and Pettigrew is exposed, Harry and Sirius form an instant familial bond. It appears that Harry will not only be freed from his unhappy life with the Dursleys, but has finally found a loving home and a real father figure, who will finally be exonerated for a crime he did not commit. Unfortunately, Harry and Sirius' new-found happiness is short-lived and circumstances quickly change when Pettigrew, and the truth, escape, leaving Sirius a hunted fugitive once again.

Questions

Review 1. What is the light Harry sees before losing consciousness?

Further Study 1. Lupin does not transform into a werewolf when the moon rises, but rather once he is directly exposed to moonlight. Why, then, was the Shrieking Shack necessary when he was a student? Why not simply confine him in a windowless room?

2. Why would the Dementors try to administer the "Kiss" to Harry?

3. What might Harry have seen on the lake shore?

Greater Picture

This is the third time Dementors have attacked Harry, and it seems obvious that each incident is deliberate. Why the Dementors have continually targeted Harry is unknown, but it raises suspicions that they may have ties to Voldemort and his Death Eaters. This is not borne out by anything in the story so far. It is true that the Dementors defect to Voldemort quite quickly after his return, but until his return to power there is no center of Dark wizardry for them to return to; the Death Eaters are disorganized, and remain so until the end of the fourth book. Lupin has told us earlier that Harry is more deeply affected by the Dementors because he has suffered so greatly. It is entirely possible that the Dementors focus on Harry because he has such a rich fund of horrible memories to feast on, possibly more

---

1. http://www.jkrowling.com/textonly/en/extrastuff_view.cfm?id=10

than nearly any other wizard at Hogwarts, and because he is unable to properly defend himself.

Chapter 21: Hermione's Secret

SYNOPSIS

Harry awakens in the infirmary and hears Minister for Magic Cornelius Fudge and Professor Snape discussing the night's events. Snape says that the cut on his head was Harry, Ron, and Hermione's work but that they were probably under a Confundus charm by Black. When he regained consciousness, the Dementors were returning to their posts, and he found Harry, Hermione, and Black unconscious beside the lake. He conjured stretchers and brought them to the Hospital Wing. Fudge says this will probably put him in line for the Order of Merlin, Third Class. Harry opens his eyes and sees Hermione in the next bed, wide awake and looking frightened. Nearby, Madam Pomfrey is attending to Ron. Hermione tells Harry that Black has been captured, and the Dementors will shortly administer the *Kiss*. Harry leaps up, shouting that Sirius is innocent and Peter Pettigrew is alive and is an Animagus. Snape says he is obviously Confunded, and Madam Pomfrey forces him back into bed. When Professor Dumbledore arrives, Harry also tells him. Dumbledore says he has spoken with Black and needs to speak to Harry and Hermione alone. Madam Pomfrey and Fudge depart, but Snape protests that Black has shown that he was capable of killing someone when he was 16. Dumbledore responds that he is aware, and Snape leaves stiffly.

Harry and Hermione try to explain what happened, but Dumbledore says their unsupported word will not save Sirius. Neither can Lupin, even if he were not currently roaming the Forbidden Forest. Apart from being Sirius' old friend, a werewolf's word counts for little. Snape's version will bear the most credibility, and while Dumbledore believes Harry and Hermione, he cannot force other people to see the truth. "What we need," Dumbledore comments, "is more *time*." Hermione apparently understands. He mentions Black is in Professor Flitwick's office. He cryptically says it is five minutes before midnight, that they must not be seen, and that more than one innocent life can be saved. He tells Hermione that "three turns" should do it, then leaves, locking them in the infirmary. Harry is mystified, but Hermione produces a tiny sparkling hourglass from her robes. She loops the chain around herself and Harry, and turns the hourglass over three times. The world becomes a spinning blur; when it settles, they are standing in the deserted Entrance Hall, and the sun is shining. Pushing them into a broom closet, Hermione tells Harry that they are now three hours in the past. Slow footsteps are heard going past, and Hermione says that it is themselves under the Invisibility Cloak; Harry is trying to comprehend being in two places at the same time, in the closet with Hermione as well as under the Cloak with Ron and Hermione heading for Hagrid's hut. Hermione explains that the hourglass is a Time-Turner; she has been using it all year to get to all her classes. Professor McGonagall instructed her to tell no one about it.

Now that they have gone back three hours, Hermione is unsure what Dumbledore expects them to do. Harry guesses that he intends for them to save Buckbeak and Sirius, who is locked in Flitwick's office. Buckbeak can fly them to Flitwick's window to save Sirius. They head for the Forbidden Forest, edging around it until they reach Hagrid's pumpkin patch. There they watch themselves going in the hut. Harry wants to grab Buckbeak, but Hermione says the Committee must see him first, otherwise they will think Hagrid freed him. They hear Hagrid breaking the milk jug and the other Hermione finding Scabbers. Harry wants to dash in and grab Pettigrew, but Hermione asks what would he think if he suddenly saw himself bursting in that way. There is a reason Dumbledore said they must not be seen.

The Committee, including Professor Dumbledore and Cornelius Fudge, approach. Harry and Hermione watch Harry, Ron, and Hermione vanish under the Invisibility Cloak and exit at the back while the Committee enter the front. The executioner, Macnair, spots Buckbeak. Deciding it is time to act, Harry bows to Buckbeak and starts leading him into the forest, but Buckbeak resists. As the Committee starts to exit the hut, Dumbledore calls them back, saying that the decree needs another signature. Just as Harry gets Buckbeak into the woods, the Committee emerges to find Buckbeak gone. Macnair buries his axe in the fence in anger.

Harry and Hermione, with Buckbeak, move closer to the Whomping Willow and watch as the black dog drags Ron into the tunnel. Shortly, Crookshanks stills the branches and their other selves go into the tunnel. Almost immediately, Dumbledore, Macnair, Fudge, and the old Committee member walk past on their way back to the castle. Now they see Professor Lupin running to the Whomping Willow and diving into the passage. Harry wonders if he could dash out and collect his Invisibility Cloak, but Hermione dissuades him. Two minutes later, Snape arrives, and, putting on the Invisibility Cloak, goes into the tunnel.

Now they must wait while the events inside the Shrieking Shack unfold. Hermione wonders how they were saved from all those Dementors. Harry says it must have been a powerful Patronus; he believes the caster is his late father.

An hour later, everyone exits the tunnel and Lupin transforms into a werewolf. Realizing they are standing where Lupin is about to run, Harry and Hermione rapidly retreat to Hagrid's empty hut. Despite a werewolf roaming loose, Harry wants to see who cast the Patronus and takes off for where the spell-caster was standing. No one is there. Harry suddenly understands: it was not his father he saw, it was himself. As the Dementors attack Sirius and the earlier Harry and Hermione, he casts the Patronus. A large animal bursts from his wand, and charging the Dementors, scatters them. When they disperse, the Patronus, in the form of a large silver stag, canters back across the lake to Harry, who now realizes his father's Animagus form was a stag, hence the nickname, "Prongs." Hermione appears, furious that Harry has been up to something. He explains that his earlier self had seen his later self casting the spell, and he was only performing the events that already happened. They watch as Snape conjures stretchers and transports everyone to the castle. They mount Buckbeak and fly to the West Tower. Hermione opens the window, and Sirius climbs out onto Buckbeak. Harry and Hermione dismount on the tower top, and Harry urges Sirius to leave quickly. Sirius first asks about Ron, then escapes with Buckbeak into the night.

Analysis

Many small mysteries in the book are cleared up with the revelation of the Time-Turner. The Time-Turner explains why Hermione is able to take three exams on the same morning, why she is continually appearing and disappearing, and how she could "forget" Flitwick's class when she had been headed to it with Harry and Ron immediately after hitting Draco in an earlier chapter. It also explains a lot of Hermione's stress: she is artificially lengthening her days, and likely is not getting enough sleep.

Dumbledore already knows that Buckbeak will be saved at the start of this chapter, although he may not yet know how; he was in the party that was present for the earlier execution. One rather wonders if he has not planned this rescue; it was Dumbledore who called Macnair back into the hut for his signature on the form, giving Harry the few extra seconds he needed to get Buckbeak under cover. It is certain that Dumbledore was aware that Buckbeak had vanished between their arrival at Hagrid's and several minutes later. If he had not been planning Buckbeak's rescue, he was certainly able to connect the fact of the rescue with Hermione's Time-turner, and provide the clues that Hermione and Harry needed to rescue both Buckbeak and Sirius. It is possible that Dumbledore had seen, through Hagrid's window, that Harry was pulling Buckbeak into the forest.

This chapter seems to show how far Fudge will go in order to keep the Wizarding world from falling into chaos. Though he hears from both Harry and Hermione that Sirius is innocent, he convinces himself that Snape is telling the truth. He further accepts Snape's theory that the Trio are under some sort of spell, and brushes off their claims. Fudge is so overjoyed that Sirius is in custody, and that the threat he sees to the Wizarding world is contained, that he gives the Dementors permission to administer the *"kiss"* to Sirius.

It appears that Dumbledore was unaware that Sirius, James, and Peter Pettigrew were Animagi until his talk with Sirius.

Before escaping, Sirius asks Harry how Ron is before he flies off on Buckbeak. This is apparently meant to illuminate something about Sirius' character; like Lupin, he is concerned about how his actions affect others. In this case, he knows Ron was injured, and inquires about his condition before saving himself.

In the film version of this chapter, there is significant interaction between Harry and Hermione, and their earlier selves. When the Committee is coming down the hill, Hermione (later) gets Harry (earlier)'s attention by tossing snails at him. When Lupin changes to a werewolf, Hermione (later) attracts his attention away from Harry and Hermione (earlier) by howling like a werewolf herself. This, of course, goes against Dumbledore's repeated injunction, *"You must not be seen!"* In the book, Hermione is deathly afraid of being seen, and for good reason; as she explains to Harry, many wizards have died because they allowed their earlier selves to see them, and the earlier self thought that the later self was a Dark attack. It is this fear that makes Hermione so shocked when she learns that Harry actually produced the Patronus that saved them. Hermione here is facing a conflict: doing something against the rules has saved their lives, is it possible that rules are not always there to be followed?

Questions

Review 1. How was Hermione getting to her many classes during the year?

2. What does Dumbledore mean when he tells Harry and Hermione they need more "time"?

3. Harry initially believed it was his father he saw on the lake shore who cast the Patronus. Who did he actually see?

4. How does Sirius escape? Who goes with him and why?

Further Study 1. Why would the Ministry of Magic consider Harry, Ron, Hermione, and also Lupin, as unreliable witnesses regarding Sirius' innocence?

2. Why is Hermione so concerned that she and Harry not be seen when they use the Time Turner? What might have happened if they were seen?

3. Why is Harry so convinced that it was his late father who cast the Patronus?

Greater Picture

We will learn more of Fudge's personality in later books. We can already see that he seems quite pleased with himself at Sirius' capture, perhaps inordinately so, particularly given his apparent belief, expressed at Christmas, that Voldemort is still out there, seeking allies to help him return to power. It will turn out, unsurprisingly, that Fudge's main motivation is to keep himself in power. This will explain his readiness to accept Snape's story over Harry's and Hermione's; if Sirius is the threat that Fudge believes him to be, then his capture and execution, while Fudge is in charge, can only enhance Fudge's reputation and consolidate his grip on power. Snape's story, of course, supports this view. Accepting Harry's story would be political suicide: the placement of Dementors in Hogsmeade has proven extremely unpopular, and the revelation that the Ministry could be so easily hoodwinked as to put an innocent man in Azkaban for twelve years would seriously affect the population's trust in the Ministry.

Chapter 22: Owl Post Again

Synopsis

Hermione tugs at Harry's sleeve, saying they have only ten minutes before Dumbledore locks the Hospital Wing. They dash off, hiding as Snape and Fudge walk past on their way to watch the Dementors administer the *Kiss* to Sirius Black, and again as Peeves drifts past. They reach the Hospital Wing just as Dumbledore is coming out. Harry and Hermione tell him Sirius is

Chapter 22: Owl Post Again

safely away on Buckbeak. Dumbledore lets them into the Hospital Wing, empty except for the still unconscious Ron, and locks the door.

Madam Pomfrey, nettled, returns but is interrupted by a roar of rage from above. Shortly, they hear Snape outside, shouting that Black could not have Disapparated because it is impossible inside the castle. Someone must have freed him, and as he slams the doors to the infirmary open, he says that Potter must somehow be involved. Dumbledore says Harry has been locked in the infirmary, and Madam Pomfrey verifies that no one has left. Snape, snarling imprecations, leaves. Fudge suggests he may be unbalanced, but Dumbledore says that he has simply suffered a great disappointment. Fudge says The Daily Prophet will have a field day if they find out Black was in custody and escaped again. When Dumbledore suggests removing the Dementors from Hogwarts, Fudge complies—if they tried to administer the *Kiss* to an innocent boy, then they are certainly unsafe. Dumbledore and Fudge leave, and Madam Pomfrey relocks the door and returns to her office. When Ron wakes up, he asks what had happened; Harry tells Hermione to explain.

The castle is nearly deserted when Harry, Ron, and Hermione are released from the Hospital Wing the next day. It is another Hogsmeade weekend, but Ron and Hermione decide to stay at Hogwarts with Harry. Relaxing by the lake, they are met by Hagrid, who says Buckbeak escaped. They pretend to act surprised. Hagrid also says that Snape told the Slytherins at breakfast that Professor Lupin was a werewolf, and Lupin has resigned. Harry finds him in his office, where nearly everything is packed. Lupin says he cannot stay—too many parents would object to a werewolf teaching their children. He then asks about the previous night's events, including Harry's Patronus. He says that Harry is correct, that James transformed into a stag, hence his nickname "Prongs." Lupin returns the Invisibility Cloak and the Marauder's Map to Harry, saying James would have been disappointed if Harry had not found any of the secret passages.

Dumbledore arrives to tell Lupin his carriage is ready. After Lupin leaves, an upset Harry tells Dumbledore that what he did made no difference: Pettigrew still got away. Dumbledore replies that his actions saved two innocent lives. Harry remembers Professor Trelawney's prediction during his exam, and tells Dumbledore. Dumbledore is quite pleased, saying that brings Trelawney's true predictions up to two. Harry is dismayed that even forewarned, he was unable to prevent Pettigrew's return to Voldemort. Dumbledore points out that Pettigrew now owes Harry a life debt. Voldemort will be displeased at having a servant who owes so much to his worst enemy. Harry tells Dumbledore about his Patronus' form, and that he thought it was his father casting it. Dumbledore says "You think the dead that we have loved, ever truly leave us?" He said that it was the memory of James that allowed him to produce that particular Patronus. Harry realizes Dumbledore must now know about James' Animagus ability. Dumbledore says Sirius told him about it.

Meanwhile, Malfoy is furious that Buckbeak escaped and is convinced Hagrid is responsible, and nearly everyone is upset over Lupin's departure.

Marks come out at the end of the term, and Harry is amazed he has passed everything, even Potions. Ron and Hermione also pass everything. Percy has his top-grade N.E.W.T.s, while the twins have each managed to scrape a handful of O.W.L.s. Gryffindor wins the House Cup for the third straight year, largely from winning the Quidditch Cup.

As they head home on the Hogwarts Express, Hermione tells Ron and Harry that she has dropped Muggle Studies. With that and Divination off her schedule, she will not need the Time-turner and so has returned it to Professor McGonagall. Ron suggests Harry might like to come to the Quidditch World Cup. His dad is usually able to get tickets. Hermione spots something flying outside the widow. Harry reaches out and grabs a tiny Scops owl carrying a message far too big for it. It is from Sirius, who writes that he is safe. He says that it was he who sent Harry the Firebolt for Christmas. He got Crookshanks to carry the message to the Owl Office for him. Enclosed is a Hogsmeade permission form for Harry. Because he was instrumental in losing Ron's rat, Sirius gives him the little owl. Holding the owl up to Crookshanks, Ron asks if he thinks it is real. Crookshanks purrs, so Ron claims him.

As he meets his uncle at King's Cross Station, Harry tells him that he has met his godfather, Sirius, who is a wizard and a convicted murderer on the run. Since Sirius is very interested in Harry's well-being, Harry can now expect that he will have at least a bit more fun with the Dursleys than in previous years.

Analysis

The book concludes as usual with Harry returning to the Dursleys' at school's end. Unlike the previous two summers, Harry has a much happier outlook about the time he must spend there. He is comforted by knowing that he now has a caring godfather that he may eventually be able to live with. Harry also knows that Sirius being a wanted fugitive has provide him with some leverage with the Dursleys, who will likely be intimidated by this new information into treating Harry better. Ron also throws out hope that Harry's stay there will be shorter than usual, further uplifting Harry's spirits. Harry is probably relieved that Hermione will be returning to a normal class schedule, making her company in the coming school year far more agreeable.

There is one small inconsistency in this chapter. Fred and George apparently receive their O.W.L. results at the end of term, and Percy receives his N.E.W.T. results at the same time. While Harry, Ron, and Hermione sit their O.W.L.s at the end of *Harry Potter and the Order of the Phoenix*, they don't get their results until the summer. As the description of Harry receiving his O.W.L. results is quite detailed, where the description in this chapter of Percy and the twins getting their results is one throw-away sentence, this is almost certainly a slight mistake by the author. It is much more likely that the twins wouldn't have actually gotten their results until summer, because decisions depending on O.W.L. results aren't necessarily made until the following September. However, as employment starts right after graduation, and would be expected to depend upon N.E.W.T. results, it is likely that these results would have come back sooner for Percy, quite possibly before end of term. This is, of course, assuming that Wizard bureaucracy is no more inefficient than Muggle civil servants.

QUESTIONS

Review 1. Why does Lupin resign?

2. What does Dumbledore tell Harry about his Patronus?

3. What does Black give Harry? What does he give to Ron and why?

4. Why does Harry tell Uncle Vernon about his newfound godfather?

Further Study 1. Dumbledore tells Snape that Harry could not have set Sirius free, saying, "Unless you are suggesting that Harry and Hermione can be in two places at the same time." Is Dumbledore deliberately giving Snape a hint as to what has happened? If so, why? Wouldn't Snape likely already know about Hermione using the Time Turner all year?

2. What does Pettigrew now owe Harry? How will this affect Pettigrew's relationship with Voldemort?

GREATER PICTURE

When Dumbledore mentions that this would be Trelawney's second *real* prediction it is easy to brush it off as unimportant, but this is actually a major plot detail for the fifth installment, *Harry Potter and the Order of the Phoenix*. In that book, Voldemort's energies will be bent towards procuring the record of that first prophecy, which will eventually result in Voldemort tricking Harry into retrieving the record for him. Voldemort's attempt will, however, fail in the end.

We can already guess that, despite our seeing him wing off into the sunset, we have not seen the last of Sirius Black. He will appear again in the next two books, and again in the seventh. Lupin also will reappear; he will be mentioned in the fourth book, and will appear in person in the fifth, sixth, and seventh books. Despite Sirius being Harry's godfather, we see that Lupin's ideas and personality, resonating more closely with Harry's, will have something of a greater effect on Harry's maturation than Sirius will.

Pettigrew's owing a life debt to Harry will not have any immediate effect on the relationship between Voldemort and Pettigrew. Voldemort understands what Pettigrew is, a weak, largely ineffectual menial, almost a classic toady, who is hitching himself to Voldemort's star as a way to gain rewards for himself. We have already seen that in his nature in the Shrieking Shack, and cannot be surprised that Voldemort, a keen judge of character, sees it in him as well. As a result, Voldemort will use Pettigrew as a means of returning from near-dead, will at least initially depend on him for survival, but will understand that Pettigrew's loyalty is to the main chance, and so will never entirely trust him. In the end, this life-debt will save Harry's life at the cost of Pettigrew's; Harry, at a critical point, will remind Pettigrew of the debt, and Pettigrew will hesitate. The weapon he is wielding, which was given to him by Voldemort, will sense this hesitation and fatally turn on Pettigrew.

GOBLET OF FIRE

CHAPTERS

Chapter 1: The Riddle House
Chapter 2: The Scar
Chapter 3: The Invitation
Chapter 4: Back to the Burrow
Chapter 5: Weasley's Wizard Wheezes
Chapter 6: The Portkey
Chapter 7: Bagman and Crouch
Chapter 8: The Quidditch World Cup
Chapter 9: The Dark Mark
Chapter 10: Mayhem at the Ministry
Chapter 11: Aboard the Hogwart's Express
Chapter 12: The Triwizard Tournament
Chapter 13: Mad-Eye Moody
Chapter 14: The Unforgivable Curses
Chapter 15: Beauxbatons and Durmstrang
Chapter 16: The Goblet of Fire
Chapter 17: The Four Champions
Chapter 18: The Weighing of the Wands
Chapter 19: The Hungarian Horntail
Chapter 20: The First Task
Chapter 21: The House-Elf Liberation Front
Chapter 22: The Unexpected Task
Chapter 23: The Yule Ball
Chapter 24: Rita Skeeter's Scoop
Chapter 25: The Egg and the Eye
Chapter 26: The Second Task
Chapter 27: Padfoot Returns
Chapter 28: The Madness of Mr. Crouch
Chapter 29: The Dream
Chapter 30: The Pensieve
Chapter 31: The Third Task
Chapter 32: Flesh, Blood, and Bone
Chapter 33: The Death Eaters
Chapter 34: Priori Incantatem
Chapter 35: Veritaserum
Chapter 36: The Parting of the Ways
Chapter 37: The Beginning

OVERVIEW

The fourth book in the Harry Potter series, *Harry Potter and the Goblet of Fire* is told from the viewpoint of the now fourteen-year-old Harry. Apart from the usual magic, events at Hogwarts School, and frustration of the Dursleys, it includes a visit to the Quidditch World Cup, and an ancient tournament that, after a hiatus of over a century, is being restarted at Hogwarts School. Darker and more mature than the preceding entries in the series, this book again shows us Harry maturing and gaining strength in preparation to fight the gathering darkness. While this book is rather daunting in appearance at 636 pages (Bloomsbury / Raincoast edition), it is set in larger type than the previous three volumes. If set in the same type as *Harry Potter and the Philosopher's Stone*, it would be 487 pages (approximately) to 223 for *Harry Potter and the Philosopher's Stone*.

BOOK HIGHLIGHTS

• New places visited: Quidditch World Cup Stadium, Little Hangleton, Hogwarts's kitchen, Prefects' bathroom
• *Defence Against the Dark Arts* teacher: Alastor "Mad-Eye" Moody
• Title refers to: The Goblet of Fire

Chapter 1: The Riddle House

SYNOPSIS

The story opens in the small village of Little Hangleton at "The Riddle House." Many villagers still call it that, even though many years have passed since the Riddle family actually lived there. Atop a hill overlooking the village, the former manor was the largest building in the area.

The house has a creepy reputation. Half a century ago, the Riddle family, including the son, then about thirty years old, and his parents, were found dead in the living room. Frank Bryce, the Riddles' gardener, was arrested on suspicion of homicide but was released when it was determined the victims were not murdered; they simply died. But the villagers remain suspicious.

Bryce now lives alone on the Riddle property, caring for the house and grounds for its absent owners as best he can despite his advancing age. Late one night, Bryce investigates a light in one of the house's windows. Inside, he overhears Lord Voldemort and Wormtail (Peter Pettigrew) planning to take action after the Quidditch World Cup, although Bryce has no idea what that is. Lord Voldemort apparently distrusts Wormtail to act alone, and talks about his *"faithful* servant." It appears they have already killed someone named Bertha Jorkins. Bryce is discovered by Nagini, Voldemort's huge snake, and Wormtail forces him into the room. Bryce threatens them with the police; Voldemort, calling him a Muggle, completely disdains Bryce's threat and slays him with a killing curse.

Two hundred miles away, Harry Potter suddenly awakens with a sharp pain in his scar.

Analysis

This marks the second time in the series that a book has opened somewhere other than with Harry Potter at the Dursleys. The first was *Harry Potter and the Philosopher's Stone*. Readers are also witness to a murder first-hand, whereas before, anyone who has been killed was mentioned after the fact. Arguably, Harry is viewing the events in a dream, although given the detail he sees and his strong reaction to it, it is likely to be much more than that. Also, the story starts with the villagers' view of events that occurred in the old Riddle house some 50 years ago, and then shifts to Frank Bryce's current point-of-view. Harry's recollection seems to be as a detached third (or fifth) party, as he recalls, upon awakening, both seeing Frank fall, and the armchair swivel from Frank's viewpoint. It should be mentioned that Voldemort, discussing his *"faithful* servant," is clearly talking about someone other than Wormtail. This third person's identity is left unclear. Wormtail is quite frightened, however, as the implication is that Voldemort does not consider Wormtail to be entirely loyal, and therefore subject to punishment and perhaps death. This again illuminates Voldemort's character: he rules his associates through fear and pain, rather than commanding their respect or fidelity.

This also marks Voldemort's pet snake, Nagini's, first appearance. Wormtail is apparently milking Nagini for some substance, possibly venom, to keep Lord Voldemort alive. If this is truly Voldemort, and not a dream, then even in his weakened state, his power is already strong and likely growing.

Questions

Review 1. Why does the Riddle manor have a "creepy" reputation?

2. Why was Frank Bryce accused and later exonerated of the Riddle family's murders?

Further Study 1. Who is the "rich" owner of the Riddle house?

2. Why does Harry awaken in pain, 200 miles away, just as Frank Bryce is murdered?

Greater Picture

Later in this book, and also in a subsequent book, Harry will have "*dreams*" that appear to reflect actual occurrences happening in Voldemort's mind; internal evidence in the book leads credence that events in this chapter may well be such a "dream." Professor Dumbledore surmises that this link is, partially, the residual effects from Voldemort's curse when he attempted to kill baby Harry. This act may have resulted in Voldemort's soul shard being transferred to Harry, thus unintentionally making Harry one of Voldemort's seven Horcruxes. Much later, Dumbledore speculates that this perhaps constitutes a true link between their minds. Voldemort initially seems unaware that this connection exists, but he later exploits it in an attempt to entrap Harry; this happens throughout the fifth book.

Nagini seems more biddable and intelligent than a snake ought to be. Finding a Muggle standing in the hall, as Nagini does, a normal snake would attack, hide, or otherwise react; Nagini glides past unconcernedly and promptly reports his presence to her master. Nagini, we will find later, is also a Horcrux, and perhaps some human-like intelligence was passed to the snake in the process of moving Voldemort's soul shard to her.

While the *"faithful* servant" who will be returning to bring Voldemort's plans against Harry to fruition is unknown, we are clearly meant to guess, given Harry's distrust of his potions master, that Voldemort is referring to Professor Snape. However, upon closer inspection of Wormtail and Snape's careers, we can see that each reacted similarly at Voldemort's downfall; Wormtail went into hiding, and Snape continued working for Dumbledore. Neither, during Voldemort's absence, professed loyalty to his ideals; each, in his own way, repudiated Voldemort's scheme for Wizardkind. In fact, as Snape seemed to have been hindering Voldemort's attempts to regain the Philosopher's Stone in the first book of the series, it is likely that Voldemort believes Snape has entirely turned to the good side, an assumption which may be echoed in a later chapter of this book, and which is not repudiated in detail until the sixth book. While it is never made entirely clear exactly who Voldemort's *faithful* servant is, it is likely that Voldemort is referring to Barty Crouch Jr., whose existence he had discovered by questioning Bertha Jorkins. The "one more curse" that Voldemort refers to is likely the Imperius curse which Wormtail will cast on Bartemius Crouch.

Chapter 2: The Scar

Synopsis

Harry awakes with a start, his scar burning painfully. He goes over the dream he just had and remembers seeing Wormtail and Voldemort in a dark room, killing an old man. Concentrating, he recalls that they were also plotting to kill someone else—him. Focusing on his current whereabouts, Privet Drive, Harry deliberates over what to do about this—his burning scar usually has something to do with Voldemort. Should he tell his friends? Hermione comes to mind, and he imagines her advice; he should just tell Dumbledore. Ron would want to ask his Dad about the usual behaviour of scars made by Curses.

He decides to write to his godfather, Sirius Black, and tell him what has been happening with the Dursleys and his scar. He finishes the letter and waits for his owl, Hedwig, to return from hunting.

Analysis

Much in this chapter revisits familiar ground—reintroducing Harry, his friends, his school, and the Wizarding world in general. This is a common pattern in the series, and the author may feel it is necessary to reestablish ground rules and bring new readers up to speed on the plot, or at least the characters and situation.

Ron and Hermione are reintroduced by Harry's imagined reactions to him telling them his latest news. The Dursley family is also mentioned in this way, as is Professor Dumbledore, by way of Harry's thoughts about what the consequences might be if he were to reveal what has happened. Harry's relationship with Sirius Black is also revisited, and it is Sirius who Harry believes is the one person he can confide in about his dream without any concern over how he will react. This may indicate that Harry now considers Sirius as his real family.

We are led to believe that the dream Harry has experienced is a real event by the narration of the previous chapter. That chapter travels seamlessly from past events which Harry could not have known about, through current events as seen by Frank Bryce, and brings us back into the story with his fatal encounter with Voldemort and Wormtail. In this chapter, we see Harry doubting its reality and wondering if he had seen a real event. We don't have any proof at the moment, but we accept that somehow, by means of his scar, Harry has perceived something that is occurring in Voldemort's life.

QUESTIONS

Review 1. When was the last time Harry's scar was burning?

2. In the dream, Wormtail attempts to discourage Voldemort from using Harry in Voldemort's scheme. Why would Wormtail do this?

3. Why does Harry choose to write to his godfather rather than Ron or Hermione about his scar hurting?

Further Study 1. Why doesn't Voldemort experience the same mental connection with Harry that Harry has with him?

GREATER PICTURE

Harry's scar has taken on a significant new role. While it has always been a focal point in the story, until now it has mostly served as a visible symbol of Harry's near-fatal encounter with Voldemort, while also acting as a warning beacon, alerting Harry to Voldemort's presence by causing pain. Now it seems to provide a mental connection between Harry and Voldemort, allowing Harry glimpses into Voldemort's thoughts. Voldemort is as yet apparently unaware that this connection exists, but it may well prove to be both dangerous and useful to Harry under certain conditions. And while Harry remembers few details about his dream, which was not a dream at all, we at least have learned that Wormtail (Pettigrew) seemed unwilling to involve Harry in whatever scheme Voldemort is planning. This may be tied to the life debt that Wormtail now owes Harry. Voldemort is probably still unaware that his servant has such an extreme obligation to his greatest enemy, and will likely be extremely displeased when he learns of it. It is important to the story line, actually, that Harry perceive Voldemort's mind only when he is asleep. Voldemort reveals things to us that Harry is likely to want to pursue if he recalls them. In particular, the name Bertha Jorkins is mentioned in the "dream," and will be mentioned again repeatedly in the next months. If Harry was able to recall that name from the dream sequence just past, likely he would mention the occurrence to someone, most likely Arthur Weasley or Professor Dumbledore, and our story probably would have developed differently.

No real reason is ever given as to why Harry can sense Voldemort's thoughts, but Voldemort cannot sense Harry's, at least not until a year later. We can, of course, speculate: Harry is able to perceive Voldemort's thoughts only when Voldemort is feeling very strong emotions. During this sequence, for instance, Voldemort is first planning the demise of his most hated enemy, and is likely inflamed with rage against Harry for daring to exist; and then, he is murdering Frank Bryce, a spell which requires deep hatred of the target. In this book, and the subsequent one, Harry only senses Voldemort's thoughts when he is asleep or nearly so. One can assume that the reverse transmission of thoughts can only happen when Harry is feeling strong emotions, and when Voldemort is in a similarly relaxed state. It is likely simply an accident of timing, that Voldemort is never in a receptive frame of mind when Harry is experiencing his strongest emotions.

There is a small inconsistency regarding when Harry actually learns Sirius is his godfather. It says here that: "he had only found out that Sirius was his godfather two months ago." In fact, it was around the previous Christmas when he overheard a conversation in the Three Broomsticks that Sirius was James Potter's best friend and Harry's godfather. However, at that time, he still believed Sirius was a mass murderer and responsible for his parents' deaths, so he could have disavowed the connection. It may have only been after the revelations in the Shrieking Shack, which happened just two months before, that Harry finally accepted that Sirius was truly his godfather.

Chapter 3: The Invitation

SYNOPSIS

Harry enters the kitchen. Dudley is being given a grapefruit quarter by Aunt Petunia, who has put Dudley on a diet after his school wrote a letter saying they did not have any knickerbockers large enough to fit him. The entire family is put on a diet to make it easier for Dudley. A hungry Harry had requested help by owl post and has received snacks from Hagrid, Hermione, and Ron that he stashed under the floorboard upstairs. They and Sirius Black had also each sent him cakes for his birthday, now two weeks past, and he still has two left. A letter arrives from Molly Weasley, which was surprisingly sent through Muggle mail rather than by owl post. To Uncle Vernon's dismay, the envelope is nearly completely covered in stamps, and the postman has rung because this is unusual. Mrs. Weasley invites Harry to attend the The Quidditch World Cup with the Weasley family and suggests he stay with them until school starts. This creates a quandary for Uncle Vernon: if he lets Harry go, it will be something fun for him, which he always tries to prevent; however, it also means Harry would be gone a good two weeks earlier than Vernon and Petunia could have hoped for.

After a long discussion, Uncle Vernon is about to forbid Harry to go the Weasleys when Harry deliberately mentions that he has to finish his letter to Sirius Black. He says his godfather has not heard from him in a while and might be getting worried. Suddenly afraid, Uncle Vernon allows Harry to go. When Harry returns to his room, he finds owls waiting. Ron sent a letter via his tiny owl, saying that they will come and get him whether the Dursleys like it or not. Harry replies that he has permission. Hedwig, his own owl, has returned from hunting, so Harry finishes his message to Sirius, explaining where he is going, and gives it to Hedwig.

ANALYSIS

While this chapter advances the story somewhat, it is the characters of cousin Dudley and Uncle Vernon that are highlighted here. In addition to his increasingly abusive and bullying personality, Dudley, who rarely exhibits restraint in anything, has grown so fat that he is unable to fit into his school clothing. Mortified, Petunia not only puts Dudley on a diet, but the entire family as well, feeling that Dudley should not have to suffer alone. Additionally, there are some visible changes in Uncle Vernon's behavior; as Harry grows older, Vernon begins showing fear, if not necessarily respect, towards Harry. His underlying motivation continues is to make Harry's life as miserable as possible, but now he does so with more passive—aggressive behavior. Aware that his status in the household has increased, Harry is not averse to using his new-found power judiciously to get what he wants, although he is never malicious.

QUESTIONS

Review 1. Why does Aunt Petunia insist on putting the entire family on a diet when it is Dudley who is overweight?

2. Why is Uncle Vernon conflicted over giving Harry permission to visit the Weasleys?

3. Why does Harry mention that he is writing to his godfather? What is Uncle Vernon's reaction?

Further Study 1. How and why has the relationship between Harry and Uncle Vernon changed?

2. Why did Molly Weasley send the Dursleys a letter using Muggle mail service rather than Owl Post? Does it make a difference?

GREATER PICTURE

There is surprisingly little in this chapter that has any bearing on what will happen in the future of this book or of the series. It is true that Harry's letter, when it reaches Sirius, will cause Sirius to try to return to England to confer directly with Harry; and similarly, and as we now expect, Harry will attend the Quidditch World Cup. Apart from that, the only change that might be signaled by events in this chapter is in Dudley: over the next year, his diet will prove effective in causing him to lose weight, but instead he will take up wrestling and become an urban tough.

Chapter 4: Back to the Burrow

SYNOPSIS

Harry finishes packing his belongings by noon the next day and eagerly awaits the Weasleys's arrival. Uncle Vernon is, of course, worried about the neighbors noticing anything strange happening and starts asking how the Weasleys will be dressed—will it be those odd Wizard's robes or "normal" peoples' clothes? Uncle Vernon also wonders by what means they will be traveling there.

The hour comes and passes. The Weasleys finally arrive. They travelled by the Floo Network, which they arranged to be connected to the Dursleys' fireplace. However, their hearth has been blocked up, and Mr. Weasley has to blast his way through. After this rocky start, Mr. Weasley has no luck in engaging the Dursleys in a conversation, while Fred and George fetch Harry's trunk. Harry and the other Weasleys depart for the Burrow, one by one entering the chimney, and using the Floo powder, exclaim, "The Burrow!" Fred, however, drops a bag of toffees. He collects all but one before he, George, and Ron exit. Harry and Mr. Weasley are still there when cousin Dudley finds and eats the toffee. It promptly expands his tongue to a length of several feet. Uncle Vernon starts attacking Mr. Weasley, who he blames for this outrage. Harry exits for the Burrow as Uncle Vernon starts throwing china figurines at Mr. Weasley.

ANALYSIS

Although the Dursleys meeting with the Weasley clan is humorously depicted, Vernon and Petunia's steadfast refusal to acknowledge Arthur and the others' presence symbolizes the deep division that exists between the Wizarding and Muggle realms; it likely represents how most Muggles would react if they knew such a world existed. Vernon and Petunia are particularly resistant to any interaction with magic, and, fearing and loathing what they are unable to understand, they simply choose to ignore its existence as much as possible. Being forced to raise a young wizard in their home only exacerbates their intolerance to anything or anyone different from themselves, which is why Harry is forbidden to acknowledge his own magical abilities while under their roof. The Twins, employing their usual mischief, only make matters worse, although they are generally unconcerned whether it is Wizard or Muggle who falls prey to their unique pranks. For Harry, any opportunity to escape from this restrictive and unhappy household is a welcome respite, and he is grateful to the Weasleys for arranging his early departure, regardless of how much it angers or offends his aunt and uncle.

This is the second time that Floo powder has been used since *Harry Potter and the Chamber of Secrets* (where it was introduced). Professor Snape may have used Floo powder or something similar to summon Professor Lupin to his study in *Harry Potter and the Prisoner of Azkaban*.

QUESTIONS

Review 1. Why do the Dursleys refuse to talk with Arthur Weasley, despite his friendly attempts to make conversation? 2. Why is Uncle Vernon so concerned about how the Weasleys will be dressed and how they will arrive?

Further Study 1. There is definitely magic happening here—the Floo powder, the wall being blown apart, figurines being destroyed, and Ton-Tongue Toffees, at the very least. The Ministry chastised Harry two years ago because of a simple Hover Charm performed by Dobby the House-elf. Why are there no such missives this time?

GREATER PICTURE

This is the first time Fred and George Weasley have been seen deliberately tormenting other people; granted, Dudley may have deserved it and the damage inflicted was only temporary. While their pranks will largely remain harmless, there will be occasional episodes of what might well be described as viciousness in this book, and in *Harry Potter and the Order of the Phoenix*, though in every case seemingly directed at a deserving victim.

Eventually, the Twins' magical abilities are such that the joke products they invent will evolve into defensive weapons that are used by the Ministry in the fight against Voldemort and his Death Eaters. Although Uncle Vernon despises anything different from what he knows or is unable to understand, we have already seen, in *Harry Potter and the Philosopher's Stone*, that Aunt Petunia's hatred of the Magical world seems to be rooted in jealousy of her sister Lily, Harry's mother. It is only in the final book in the series that we learn the deepest roots of that jealousy.

We learn, in this chapter, a few more details about the Floo Network. It is in this chapter that we learn that not all fireplaces are automatically on the Network, that there is a department of the Ministry of Magic that is in control of that. In the next book, we will learn that the Ministry has the ability to monitor, as well as control, the use of fireplaces on the Network. This will play a role in the fifth book, as Harry must find an unmonitored fireplace for his communication, and in the seventh, as Harry is unable to leave Privet Drive via the Floo Network because of that monitoring.

Chapter 5: Weasley's Wizard Wheezes

SYNOPSIS

Harry arrives at the Weasleys' home and is introduced to Bill and Charlie, the two oldest Weasley brothers. Charlie works with dragons in Romania, while Bill, a one-time Head Boy at Hogwarts who now works for Gringotts Wizarding Bank in Egypt, is a surprise: he sports a pony tail, an earring (with what looks like a fang), and dragon-hide boots.

Fred and George are having a row with their father over them dropping a Ton-Tongue Toffee, apparently deliberately, and causing Harry's cousin Dudley's tongue to grow several feet long. Mrs. Weasley enters the argument, demanding to know if it had anything to do with their Weasleys' Wizard Wheezes. Hermione and Ginny enter the room behind Mrs. Weasley; Hermione, to avoid the family argument, suggests they show Harry where he is sleeping.

On the way to Ron's bedroom, Ron and Hermione explain to Harry about "Weasleys' Wizard Wheezes," which are magical tricks and jokes the Twins have invented. What they just escaped was an ongoing battle: Mrs. Weasley wants the Twins to work for the Ministry of Magic, but they want to open their own joke shop. Ron's room is much the same as it was two years ago, except for his new owl, given to him by Sirius Black, which is bouncing excitedly in its cage. Ginny named it Pigwidgeon, which Ron often shortens to "Pig." When the fight between Mrs. Weasley and the Twins has apparently ended, Harry, Ron, Hermione, and Ginny return to the kitchen, where they catch a small rant about Fred and George from Mrs. Weasley while she prepares dinner. Outside, Charlie and Bill are jousting with the picnic tables and Crookshanks is chasing Gnomes. As evening falls, the Weasleys, Harry, and Hermione enjoy a lovely dinner in the garden, with some home-made strawberry ice cream for dessert. Conversation at the table ranges widely, covering the upcoming Quidditch World Cup, Bill's personal appearance, Sirius Black's whereabouts, a missing Ministry witch named Bertha Jorkins, and a top secret event that Percy mentions in hopes that someone will ask him about it.

ANALYSIS

The story is only advanced slightly in this chapter. Much time is devoted to reintroducing the Burrow's atmosphere, the Weasley family home, and contrasting its somewhat grubby friendliness with the Dursley household's overly antiseptic aloofness. This is also the first time the entire Weasley clan has been seen together, and the differences between the seven siblings is evident. The more Bohemian and unconventional Bill and Charlie, as well as the rowdy Twins, are a stark contrast to the sedate Percy, whose starchy and bossy personality irritates his siblings. Ron is neither rowdy nor sedate and usually feels overwhelmed and intimidated by his talented older brothers. Ginny, being the youngest and the only girl, is able to develop her own magical abilities and strong-willed persona apart from her doting and protective family, although she may feel a bit isolated being the only female child. Bill and Charlie, both powerful wizards, display an irreverent sense of humor similar to the Twins when they are seen dueling each other with the picnic tables.

Weasleys' Wizard Wheezes is introduced. The Twins are planning to open their own joke shop after leaving Hogwarts, although Mrs. Weasley, who constantly chastises them for wasting time with their incessant pranks, strongly disapproves. Failing to recognize their unique talents and entrepreneurial abilities, she instead wants them to pursue more conventional and secure occupations. For American and international readers, it should be noted that a "wheeze" in England can be a joke; the idea is that you laugh so hard it leaves you wheezing.

There is independent confirmation regarding some events in Harry's "dream" from chapter 1 as well. Specifically, that Bertha Jorkins, a witch who works for the Ministry of Magic, has been missing for some time while in Albania. Bertha appeared in Harry's dream, even if Harry is unable to remember it. This is an indication that Voldemort is alive as a separate entity, and that Wormtail has returned to his service.

Questions

Review 1. What can be learned about Charlie and Bill's personalities based on their appearances and behavior seen here? How do they differ from Percy?

2. How does Ron's character contrast to his older brothers? What accounts for this?

3. Why does Ron feel overwhelmed by his brothers, while Ginny apparently does not?

Further Study 1. It is only two days since Harry's "dream," and Bertha Jorkins' name, mentioned in that dream, has just come up in a conversation that she was in Albania and is now missing. Thinking back to the end of *Harry Potter and the Chamber of Secrets*, Professor Dumbledore says that his information is that Voldemort is hiding in Albania. Why might Harry not have recalled his "dream," with so much prompting?

2. Why is Mrs. Weasley so strongly opposed to the Twins opening their own joke shop? Would working for the Ministry of Magic, as she wants them to, be a good career option for them? Explain.

Greater Picture

It is perhaps intriguing to note how much of the dinner table conversation is actually foreshadowing events in this book, and to a certain extent later books.

We will see that Mrs. Weasley's battle with Bill over the length of his hair is an ongoing one. Mrs. Weasley does not manage to win this battle until Bill's wedding; Harry suspects, though, that as soon as he is safely out of range, Bill's hair will be long again.

We can see that Percy is "hiding" a secret of some sort. The author has managed to show that Percy is hoping someone will ask him what he's talking about, so that he can boost his own status by refusing to tell. We will later find out that several others there at the table already know the secret; specifically, Mrs. Weasley, Charlie, and Bill all do, and we can safely assume that the information came from Mr. Weasley. It is interesting to contrast Percy's handling of this secret, with the way the rest of the family does. We will shortly discover that the secret in question is the re-starting of the Triwizard Tournament, a competition that will quite unexpectedly snare Harry and form the axis on which the entire book turns.

The discussion of Bertha Jorkins, as mentioned, somewhat confirms the belief that Harry's dream actually reflected real events. We will later find that Bertha had been brought to Albania by Pettigrew, and there she had been killed by Voldemort. Before she died, though, she revealed the existence of the Tournament to Voldemort, and had at the same time revealed that Barty Crouch Jr., one of the more faithful Death Eaters, was not only free, but was in hiding, believed dead, and so was available to carry out the plan Voldemort had devised to capture Harry. Sirius is quite some distance away; as mentioned, his last few messages have been brought by tropical birds. Harry has sent him a message about his scar hurting, and as soon as he receives it, Sirius will return to England, much against Harry's wishes. Sirius' actual location, though, remains unknown.

The twins' joke shop will be in full operation by Harry's sixth year. It has been mentioned that each of them get only a handful of O.W.L.s, but over the course of this book and the next, we will see that the Twins are extremely deft practical wizards, creating and selling magical materials of amazing quality. In fact, some of their magical wares are so good that the Ministry buys them for protection of their less-able wizards. Harry, Ron, and Hermione will also make significant use of their wares over the rest of the series.

Chapter 6: The Portkey

Synopsis

It is far too early the next morning when Harry is awakened by Mrs. Weasley. He, Ron, Ginny, Hermione, and the twins are travelling with Mr. Weasley, while Percy, Bill, and Charlie will go on their own. Fred and George want to know why they cannot Apparate like the older boys, but Mr. Weasley says they do not have their licenses yet, and without training, they would probably get *splinched*—leaving parts of themselves behind. Ginny and Hermione complain about getting up so early, but Mr. Weasley explains that they have a bit of a walk ahead. Harry asks if they are walking to the Quidditch World Cup. Mr. Weasley starts to explain, but is interrupted by Mrs. Weasley, who discovers Ton-Tongue Toffees hidden in George's pockets, which she angrily confiscates using the "Accio" charm.

Mrs. Weasley, who is staying behind, remains in a bad humour as they leave. As the group walks in the chilly morning, Mr. Weasley explains that there was a huge logistical problem in locating a place where the approximately one hundred thousand wizards could gather. The Ministry of Magic had to create a stadium in the backwoods and charm it to look unappealing to Muggles. There was also the problem of transporting people, and arrivals have to be carefully timed and planned so they will attract little attention. Additionally, two hundred Portkeys have been located around Britain. They are going to Stoatshead Hill to use the Portkey that has been placed there. When they arrive at Stoatshead Hill, they meet Cedric Diggory, and his father, Amos. Mr. Diggory makes a big fuss over his son being the Seeker in the only Quidditch match in which Harry's team was beaten the previous year, although Cedric is more modest. Mr. Weasley asks if there are any others coming. Mr. Diggory says the Lovegoods have already left, and the Fawcetts were unable to get tickets, and that is everyone in the vicinity. Mr. Weasley checks his watch and has everyone hold onto an old boot that Mr. Diggory has found. As the countdown reaches zero, Harry feels himself being yanked rapidly through the air and lands hard on the ground. A voice says "Seven past five from Stoatshead Hill."

Analysis

While the Quidditch World Cup may seem more like an interesting and fun diversion to open the story, its importance in introducing a critical theme, mutual cooperation, cannot be overemphasized. The World Cup is far more than a mere sporting event; it is a means to unite wizards from many countries. Organizing such a huge international event is a massive venture, requiring extensive planning, collaboration, and coordination among the world's magical populations. It is probably the most difficult wizard undertaking to be kept hidden from Muggles, although, as will be seen, there are occasional security leaks. And while there are the usual rivalries among the teams and fans, it is the commonly shared passion for the sport that bonds the magical community together in a peaceful setting that helps build lasting global recognition, understanding, and harmony. Although Harry relishes this experience, he still fails to realize that if Voldemort is to be defeated, it must be accomplished through a similarly united effort, and not by one person alone.

It is Rowling's attention to detail that helps make the Harry Potter series such an intriguing adventure. One hundred thousand wizards are expected to attend the World Cup. Exactly how do so many people travel to such an event without alarming Muggles or revealing the Wizarding world's existence? Harry's introduction to the Portkey demonstrates one way wizards are transported, although, as readers have seen, there are other methods, although each has limitations. The author's explanation as to how this particular logistical puzzle is managed, while not critical to the storyline here, shows an awareness of her characters' needs and makes the story more complex, textured, and believable. Readers, however, should make a mental note regarding how Portkeys work.

The Lovegood family is mentioned for the first time, although none are actually seen. The author often introduces characters, objects, or places by name prior to their actual appearance, often several books before. Sirius Black was first mentioned in *Harry Potter and the Philosopher's Stone* but did not appear until *Harry Potter and the Prisoner of Azkaban* where he played a crucial role. Rowling may want readers to have a early indication that some seemingly insignificant characters may become important later in the storyline.

QUESTIONS

Review 1. Why is Mrs. Weasley angry at finding a toffee in George's pocket?

2. How does the Ministry keep the arrival of over one hundred thousand wizards secret from Muggles?

3. Why does Mr. Diggory make such a big fuss about Cedric?

Further Study 1. Why would Mrs. Weasley stay behind?

2. Considering the logistical difficulties, why does the Wizarding community choose to undertake such a huge international event?

GREATER PICTURE

We are given a better introduction to Cedric Diggory, who will have a significant role in this book. Cedric strongly believes in playing fair, to the extent that he offered to replay the Quidditch match against Gryffindor (in the previous book); he felt Hufflepuff's win was invalid because the Dementors interfered. His strong ethical sense will play a strong role in the upcoming Triwizard competition. We can already see differences between Cedric and his father, Amos, and it may be interesting to compare their personalities throughout the book. It is possible that Cedric and Amos are intended as a contrast to Harry's feelings about his own father, James. Cedric and Amos are quite different people; though both are competitive, Cedric steadfastly believes that honesty and fair competition is paramount, while Amos shades more towards the Slytherin view that advantages should be taken. Although Harry should be able to see from this that fathers and sons can be quite different from one another, he is apparently unable to apply this lesson to himself.

We are also shown the Accio spell, which is used for summoning items. Harry will use Accio in the Triwizard Tournament, and it will be used repeatedly throughout the rest of the series.

The Portkey, which wizards use to travel from one location to another, becomes a device that will unexpectedly transport Harry and Cedric Diggory into a deadly situation. Creating Portkeys is apparently regulated by the Ministry. Perhaps this is why Portkeys are only used seven times in the entire series: four times in this book (to the World Cup and back, and to the cemetery and back), twice in *Harry Potter and the Order of the Phoenix* (from Dumbledore's office to Headquarters, and from the Ministry to Dumbledore's office), and once in *Harry Potter and the Deathly Hallows* (from the Tonks' house to The Burrow). The Floo Network and Disapparating seem to be more common transportation methods, though, as Mr. Weasley points out, many wizards avoid Disapparating because Splinching is an inherent risk.

Luna Lovegood, the Trio's rather odd schoolmate and future fellow Dumbledore's Army member, will be introduced in *Harry Potter and the Order of the Phoenix*. The family also includes Luna's widowed father, Xenophillius, who appears in the last book. The Lovegoods will be invited to Bill Weasley and Fleur Delacour's wedding, which will play a significant part in *Harry Potter and the Deathly Hallows*. Both characters play important roles in that book.

Chapter 7: Bagman and Crouch

SYNOPSIS

Harry, Ron, Ginny, Hermione, the twins, Mr. Weasley, Cedric Diggory, and Amos Diggory arrive in what looks like a deserted misty moor. Two tired and grumpy looking wizards are there. Mr. Weasley greets one as "Basil," and hands him the Portkey, which is tossed into a large box with other Portkeys. Basil tells them where their campsite is; the Diggorys are at a different camp site. The campsite owner, a Muggle named Roberts, mentions that the people renting the spaces seem odd. As he expounds on this, a harassed-looking wizard pops in and modifies his memory. Roberts dreamily gives Mr. Weasley his change and a map of the campsite. The wizard comments that Mr. Roberts needs to be charmed ten times a day, and that Ludo Bagman is not helping by bouncing around and talking about Bludgers and Quaffles.

The Weasleys, Harry, and Hermione head for their campsite. On the way, Ginny comments that if Bagman is head of Magical Games and Sports, he should certainly know better than to talk about magical things near Muggles. Mr. Weasley agrees, Bagman has always been rather lax about security. It seems to be a common failing, though, as on their way through the campground, they pass numerous tents far more spectacular than anything sold in Muggle stores. Mr. Weasley remarks that when large group of wizards are together, they cannot resist showing off a little. They find their campsite, and Mr. Weasley asks Harry's advice on how to proceed. Harry, of course, has never been camping, but manages to figure things out, eventually setting up a pair of shabby two-man tents. Harry wonders how they will all fit, but when he enters one, the tent opens into a large, three-room apartment complete with a kitchen, and furnished like Mrs. Figg's house, right down to the cat smell.

Mr. Weasley sends Ron, Harry, and Hermione for water. On the way they meet some fellow students. Oliver Wood drags them off to meet his parents and tells them he has just been signed to the Puddlemere United Quidditch team. They also see Ernie Macmillan and Cho Chang. Harry notices some strange teenagers and asks where they are from. Ron says they must be from some other Wizarding school. There are several in Europe, and Charlie has been corresponding with someone in Brazil. Back at the campsite, Mr. Weasley finally manages to light the fire. They have just started cooking breakfast when Percy, Charlie, and Bill walk in from the woods where they just Apparated.

Arthur Weasley greets Ministry people as they walk by. Ludo Bagman, a blond, fat wizard wearing brightly colored (and over-tight) Quidditch robes, appears, and Arthur flags him down. Bagman is overjoyed at the game's prospects, and offers a little wager on the outcome. Arthur puts a Galleon on Ireland. Fred and George bet all their savings (thirty-seven Galleons, fifteen Sickles, and three Knuts) on Ireland to win, but Viktor Krum (the Seeker for Bulgaria) will get the Snitch. Over Arthur's protests, Bagman accepts the bet. Mr. Weasley asks Ludo whether there has been any word of Bertha Jorkins yet. Ludo says no, but expects she will appear in October. Mr. Crouch shows up, looking for Ludo. He accepts a cup of tea from Percy but cannot remember his name. Shortly, Crouch and Bagman depart to respond to a crisis. Before they leave, Bagman mentions that something will be happening at Hogwarts. Fred asks what, but Mr. Weasley and Percy only say that they will find out when the time is right. The evening brings the souvenir sellers, and Harry, Ron, and Hermione go out to buy stuff. Harry purchases Omnioculars for himself, Ron, and Hermione, at ten Galleons each. Ron, upset because Harry has money and he is always poor, protests, but when Harry says it will be his Christmas present for the next ten years, Ron accepts. Finally, as dusk falls, a deep, booming gong sounds in the nearby wood; it is time to enter the stadium.

ANALYSIS

To date, Harry's interaction with the Wizarding community has been rather limited, mostly confined to Hogwarts, Hogsmeade, and short trips to Diagon Alley. Now Harry meets foreign wizards in an international setting for the first time, although it seems he has given little consideration to magical realms outside Britain. Indeed, Harry seems surprised to encounter teen-aged wizards unknown to him, or that other wizarding schools even exist. Although the Quidditch World Cup is a global competition among rival teams, it is meant to serve another function: to help build solidarity and cooperation among the world's wizards. This same opportunity will soon be brought to Hogwarts on a smaller scale, although Harry and most other students are as yet unaware.

This chapter highlights the rather flamboyant Ludo Bagman and the bureaucratic Barty Crouch, Sr. Their personalities, personal interactions, and mannerisms could not be more different, although both work for the Ministry of Magic and are heavily involved in running the Quidditch World Cup. Bagman is not averse to what the English call "having a little flutter," and he is apparently engaging in a sideline (and probably illegal) gambling racket. Readers may know that a "bagman" is a dishonest official, someone who collects racketeering money. It is also a traveling salesman who makes calls to his customers. The name certainly fits. From his reaction when the Twins place their bet, it can be seen that Ludo is perhaps not making as good odds as he expected and may even have doubts regarding his own abilities. It is possible that this will get him into trouble shortly. And where Bagman is open and friendly, although it is mostly a façade for his clients' benefit, Crouch remains tense, aloof, and guarded, always interacting with others in a professional but brusque manner. Crouch is so lacking in interpersonal skills that he continually fails to recognize his own employee, Percy Weasley. Crouch appears to be concealing much about his personal self, while Bagman seems to hide little, although perhaps he should. Even Ginny Weasley notices that Bagman freely dispenses too much information to too many people.

In the interaction between Arthur Weasley and the campground owner, we see plainly that despite the adjuration from the Ministry for Wizards to act like Muggles, much magic is leaking through the seams. The Ministry's need to frequently modify the poor man's memory, even in the match's early stages, might lead one to wonder as to just how he will remember this episode. Also, Mr. Weasley's difficulty using Muggle camping gear is played largely for entertainment value; however, it also contrasts the differences between Ron's purely magical family and Harry's entirely Muggle home. Interestingly, when Mr. Weasley has a question about how to do Muggle things, he asks Harry, rather than Hermione. Perhaps he does not realize that Harry's home life could possibly be as constricted as the Dursleys have made it. On the other hand, there is a common Muggle bias that girls are less interested or capable in recreational activities like camping. If this same belief is present in the Wizarding world, this may explain why Mr. Weasley assumes Harry to be the outdoors expert, rather than Hermione, who may have camping experience. Meanwhile, Ron's reaction to Harry buying the Omnioculars seems minor, but it is actually revealing. Even though Harry is his closest friend, Ron struggles with occasional jealousy and resentment towards him. The constant attention and celebrity surrounding Harry often pushes Ron into the shadows, although Harry has never relished or sought the spotlight, and his fame has also caused Harry anguish. The Weasleys' financial difficulties also take a toll on Ron's psyche, causing him to feel menial and an object of scorn among some wizarding families, particularly the Malfoys. He resents his brothers' hand-me-downs, having to buy everything second-hand, or going without altogether—Harry's wealth only reinforces his sense of deprivation and social inferiority.

Bertha Jorkins' continued absence reinforces the suggestion that Harry's "dream" in chapter 1 was actually a true vision. It also establishes her association with the Department of Magical Games and Sports and that this might be a way that Voldemort could be aware of upcoming events throughout the book.

As an interesting side note, among the magical citizens attending the World Cup are American wizards from Salem, Massachusetts, the site of the infamous 1692 witch trials in which nineteen men and women were condemned and hanged for witchcraft.

QUESTIONS

Review 1. Why might the tent smell like Mrs. Figg's house?

2. Why does Mr. Weasley ask Harry for advice about Muggle camping, but not Hermione?

3. Why can't Mr. Crouch ever remember Percy's name?

4. Why does Mr. Weasley permit the Twins to bet all their savings on the World Cup, even though he disapproves of what they're doing?

5. Why does Ron object to Harry buying him the Omnioculars as a gift?

Further Study 1. Harry heard Bertha Jorkins' name before—she was mentioned by Voldemort in what Harry thought was a dream as someone who had been killed, and again in a conversation at the Weasley's house as being missing. Ludo Bagman also mentions that Bertha Jorkins is still missing. Why didn't Harry draw an obvious connection?

2. Ludo Bagman mentions something that might be happening at Hogwarts. What might that be?

3. Why does Ludo Bagman openly talk about Wizarding matters when Muggles can overhear, especially when he knows he should not? What results from his carelessness?

4. Why is Harry so surprised to learn that there are students from other Wizarding schools?

5. Compare and contrast Mr. Crouch and Ludo Bagman's personalities and how they each handle their World Cup duties.

GREATER PICTURE

Though Mrs. Figg will play a significant, and unexpected, role later in the series, Harry noticing that the tent's interior looks and smells much like her house may or may not be incidental. There is a certain odour that seems common to older peoples' homes, particularly those owning cats, and, despite the similarity, it is unlikely that the author is trying to tell us that Mrs. Figg was the tent's former owner. We are told that it previously belonged to a Ministry wizard who gave up camping due to his lumbago. Among other things, it is also doubtful that a wizard would marry a Squib, although they are known to wed Muggles. Dumbledore once mentioned that wizards probably would have died out if they had not inter-married with non-magical humans. On the other hand, though Mrs. Figg is a Squib, she was raised among wizards and knows their ways; she likely uses goods, merchandise, and decorations in her home that are similar to those in wizarding households. Harry had previously noticed the peculiar smell in Mrs. Figg's residence, and the familiar odour in the tent may be a subtle clue to readers that Mrs. Figg is tied to the magical community. Readers should take note, although Harry will not, when Dumbledore later mentions someone named Arabella Figg.

Mr. Crouch's continual failure to recognize Percy Weasley, his own employee, may have some magical reason. However, the author never fully answers this. We will find out later that Mr. Crouch is labouring under the effects of a spell that could cause this effect. However, this chapter of the book precedes that spell being invoked. Given that, it is more likely that it is simple absent-mindedness coupled with a total lack of regard for subordinates; Crouch simply fails to notice his underlings, in this case "Weatherby."

Ludo's "little flutter" will, indeed, turn out to be ill-advised. Ludo will end up owing more than he has, and will later try to recoup his losses by making more bets with the Goblins who are his major creditors. That bet will be on Harry to win the Triwizard Tournament, and throughout the book Ludo, a Tournament judge, will unethically be trying to better his chances of winning by secretly offering Harry hints. Harry, believing that accepting assistance from a Tournament judge is cheating, steadfastly refuses Ludo's proffered advice, though he does accept help from others. Mr. Weasley's asking Harry, rather than Hermione, for help with the camping gear will be even less well-advised than we had previously expected. In *Harry Potter and the Deathly Hallows*, Hermione mentions that the places she takes the Trio to are actually camping sites she has visited with her family; of course, Harry has never been camping, as the Dursleys would dislike the untidiness of an unmanicured outdoors, nor would Harry likely have been fully included even if they did engage in such activities.

Chapter 8: The Quidditch World Cup

SYNOPSIS

Harry, Ron, Ginny, Hermione, the Twins, Percy, Charlie, Bill, and Mr. Weasley make their way through the woods. After a twenty-minute walk, they reach the stadium. It is large enough to hold one hundred thousand spectators. Taking a full year to construct, every inch is charmed to be Muggle-repelling. Their tickets are for the Top Box, as high as they can go. They are the first there, except for a single house-elf. Harry thinks it is Dobby, but the elf identifies itself as Winky, belonging to the Crouch family. Winky knows Dobby, and says he is having a hard time because he wants to be paid for his work. "House-elves are not for paying, sir." Winky says she is holding a seat for Mr. Crouch, although she is afraid of heights.

People are filing into the Top Box: the Bulgarian dignitaries, the Minister for Magic, and finally Lucius Malfoy, with his wife Narcissa and son Draco. Mr. Malfoy has just made a large donation to St. Mungo's Hospital for Magical Maladies and Injuries and is there as Cornelius Fudge's guest.

The team mascots perform before the game starts. First up are the Bulgarians. Beautiful Veela, infinitely alluring women, dance on the pitch. Every male is seized by a temptation to do something to show off. Harry decides that a swan dive from the Top Box to the field would be a reasonable way to ensure them noticing him. Luckily, Hermione and Mr. Weasley (who has seen them before), manage to restrain him and Ron, who apparently has the same urge. Next, the Irish mascots perform. Leprechauns fly in showering the stands with gold coins and forming green Irish symbols in the sky. Ron gathers up a fistful of fallen Galleons and gives them to Harry to pay for the Omnioculars.

With the mascots arrayed on the sidelines, the Bulgarian team enters to applause and dancing. Viktor Krum, the Bulgarian Seeker and one of Ron's heroes, receives special note. The Irish team enters, and the game is on. The action is so fast that Ludo Bagman, who is announcing, can barely name the player holding the Quaffle before it is passed or stolen. Even Harry, with his Omnioculars set on Slow, is having trouble following the action. It is a very instructional game for Harry, watching every move the Seekers make and watching the Chasers as they work like three parts of a single machine. In the end, an injured Krum beats the Irish Seeker to grab the Snitch, making the final score Ireland 170, Bulgaria 160. After the presentation of the Cup and the victory laps (spectators give Krum the loudest applause of all), the Twins brace Ludo Bagman for their winnings.

ANALYSIS

Harry and Ron's budding sexuality is hinted at here when both become deeply affected by the beautiful and alluring Veela women. Their initial interest in the opposite sex continually develops throughout the series, as does that of their peers at school, with both humorous and poignant outcomes. Harry and Ron have not yet learned the difference between true love and mere infatuation, or how jealousy and sexual politics further complicates relationships. Also, although Harry, Ron, and virtually every other male in the stands are deeply affected by the seductive Veela, Harry is shocked when he later sees that their true physical form is actually unattractive, sporting angular bird-like facial features and scaly wings. Harry is gradually learning that outer beauty is not only superficial, but it can also mask an uglier reality.

Ron's insistence on paying Harry for the Omnioculars, even though Harry gave them as a gift, is a matter of deep pride to Ron, whose family can barely afford minimal necessities. Ron must often do without even the smallest luxuries or extras that most take for granted. Now he feels somewhat vindicated that, for once, he is able to pay his own way with the gold the Leprechauns tossed into the stands. But even though Ron is often resentful that he must often go without, it has actually shaped his character in a positive way. As Ron matures, he will never feel that life owes him anything; he will accept that if he wants anything, he must earn it himself. This is a stark contrast to many Slytherins who believe they are entitled to whatever they want based solely on what they consider is their superior lineage, social rank, and wealth, rather than through talent, ability, and hard work. Readers will recall that Draco Malfoy became the Slytherin Seeker (in *Harry Potter and the Chamber of Secrets*) after his father, Lucius Malfoy, bought the team new broomsticks, and apparently not because Draco earned the position on his abilities.

QUESTIONS

Review   1. Why does Ron insist on paying Harry for the Omnioculars, even though Harry gave them as a gift?

2. How did Harry's freeing Dobby from the Malfoys' service (in *Chamber of Secrets*) change Dobby's life, and is he better or worse off than before?

3. Why are Harry, Ron, and many other males so affected by the Veela women?

4. What is Harry's reaction when he sees the Veelas' true appearance?

Further Study   1. How are Fred and George able to correctly (and so precisely) predict the World Cup's final outcome?

2. Being that Mr. Crouch is a Ministry official who is helping present the World Cup, why does his saved seat in the grandstand remain empty?

GREATER PICTURE

The gold Ron gives Harry to pay for the Omnioculars is actually Leprechaun gold, which, unknown to either Ron and Harry, soon vanishes. In chapter 28, Ron is upset when he learns it disappeared, and angry that Harry never even noticed that it was gone, showing, from Ron's perspective at least, how few concerns Harry has regarding money while Ron has many. The Weasley family's strained financial situation is an ongoing embarrassment to Ron, especially compared to Harry's wealth, although Harry spends relatively little on himself and collects few material possessions. Ron's comparisons are rather faulty, however. While Harry has money, which he cares little about, he lacks the loving, supportive family life Ron takes for granted, and which Harry would probably gladly give up his wealth in exchange for.

Quidditch champion Viktor Krum, is introduced here, and although Krum is Ron's "hero," Ron will soon feel quite differently about him in upcoming chapters.

Winky will have a large role to play in the next few chapters. Mr. Crouch has been hiding a secret, with Winky's active help, for many years at this point, and that secret has nearly escaped. That near-escape will be why Winky is dismissed from service. Winky's dismissal will actually prove instrumental in that secret's final and complete escape. Much of the book's remainder involves that escape's aftermath.

The episodes with the Veela in this and the following chapters highlight Harry and Ron's budding sexuality, as noted above. Ron will, in the next chapter, be more susceptible to the Veela's charms than Harry; this will also result in his being infatuated with Fleur Delacour, a character who is later revealed to be one-quarter Veela. The series' strong writing is reflected in the realistic romantic entanglements our heroes experience. Ron, clearly less emotionally mature than either Harry or Hermione, has difficulty distinguishing love from infatuation, even after the effects of Fleur's close proximity are shaken off. Harry shows equal immaturity after a crush that ignites in this book blossoms into romance in the next; he becomes infatuated with Cho Chang, a relationship that will ultimately be doomed by Harry's youthful inexperience and his inability to comprehend Cho's fragile emotional state. Every reader has either undergone similar toils, or knows someone who has. In a book that emphasizes adventure and conflict, it is easy to expect that romance and the characters' similar maturation will be secondary to the plot and are only hinted at rather than written about. To the author's great credit, she realizes just how central romance is to a young man's life, whether Wizard or Muggle. By showing Harry's romantic life, along with Ron's and Hermione's, the author brings the characters properly alive, causing us to care even more about them.

Ludo Bagman's wagers have gone disastrously wrong, although like any good bookmaker he puts on a good face to keep his clients happy. He comments that the game's outcome was totally unexpected and one that will be talked about for years (although that outcome seems to have been less surprising to the Twins). Finding himself deeply in the red, Ludo uses extreme measures to pay off bettors. It is revealed in chapter 37 that he pays off the Twins with Leprechaun gold, which, as noted above, soon vanishes. He also owes a large sum to high-ranking Goblins. In chapter 9, as Harry wanders through the forest, he passes Goblins who are counting their gold and chuckling; this is presumably winnings from Bagman. It turns out, however, that at least part of what Bagman owed to the Goblins was also paid off in Leprechaun gold. Throughout the book, Bagman can often be seen negotiating with Goblins about this debt and also avoiding Fred and George, who are attempting to recoup their winnings.

Chapter 9: The Dark Mark

SYNOPSIS

Money in hand, the Twins return to the campsite with Harry, Ron, Ginny, Hermione, Percy, Charlie, Bill, and Mr. Weasley (who, upon reflection, prefers not knowing why the Twins want the money). Everyone discusses Quidditch until Ginny falls asleep at the table. Mr. Weasley sends them to bed, and they fall asleep to the ongoing magical celebration noise. Soon after, Harry is shaken awake by Mr. Weasley; Harry immediately realizes something is wrong, the banging noises are louder and the singing has been replaced by screams and running feet. Outside, hooded wizards are shouting, blasting random tents, and suspending four Muggles, including Mr. Roberts, the campground owner, high in the air. Mr. Weasley orders Fred, George, Harry, Ron, Hermione, and Ginny to hide in the woods; he, Bill, Charlie, and Percy help the Ministry wizards break up the mob.

In the woods, Draco Malfoy is casually learning against a tree, unperturbed by the ensuing chaos. He implies that the mob is Death Eaters hunting Muggles and that they would also attack a Mudblood. Ron takes umbrage, but Hermione pulls them away, heading further into the forest, although Ginny and the Twins become separated from them. They run into a clutch of teenagers in pyjamas, arguing in French; Hermione identifies them as students from Beauxbatons Academy, another Wizarding school. As they pass, Ron illuminates his wand; Harry reaches for his wand, only to discover it missing. As they search for it, Winky the House-elf darts across their path in an odd manner, looking as if something invisible is holding her back. Harry surmises it is because no one gave her permission to run away. Hermione becomes indignant over House-elves' status, complaining they are basically slaves. Ron claims they are happiest that way; they say so themselves.

Finding a quiet place, they settle down and wait. A worried-looking Ludo Bagman appears from behind a tree, seemingly unaware a riot is underway, but immediately Disapparates upon being told. Hermione suggests he is not quite on top of matters. When the campsite has quieted, the Trio thinks the riot may be over, but they hear someone in the bushes behind them. A deep voice calls out, "Morsmordre!." A large green skull with a snake protruding from the mouth appears in the sky as screams sound. Hermione recognizes it as Voldemort's Dark Mark, but before they can get away, about twenty Ministry wizards Apparate around them. Harry, Hermione, and Ron hit the ground as stun spells criss-cross over them. Mr. Weasley halts the spell casting, and Bartemius Crouch demands to know who conjured the Dark Mark. Hermione points to where the shout was heard. Amos Diggory says that the conjurer may not have Disapparated before he was Stunned. A few wizards investigate and return carrying an unconscious Winky, shocking Crouch, who leaves to investigate. Diggory notes that Winky had a wand. Ludo Bagman Apparates in, shocked to see the Dark Mark and a stunned Winky. Crouch returns empty-handed; wanting to interrogate Winky, Diggory revives her. Winky denies conjuring the mark, she does not know how. When Harry recognizes the wand as his own, Diggory accuses him of conjuring the Mark, but Mr. Weasley reminds him who he is speaking to. Diggory accuses Winky, but Hermione reports hearing a much deeper and definitely human voice. Ron and Harry concur. Using the Prior Incatato spell, it is determined that Harry's wand conjured the Dark Mark. Claiming Winky disobeyed him, Crouch tells her, "This means clothes!" (Giving clothes to House-elves releases them from servitude.) Nobody else believes this as a dismissal-level offence, but Crouch is adamant; Winky is being discharged.

Mr. Weasley and the Trio head back to their tent where Fred, George, and Ginny have safely returned. Asking about the "skull thing," Harry and Ron are told that Voldemort's mark was usually left floating over a house where Death Eaters had killed all within. Its reappearance after thirteen years is nearly as frightening as Voldemort himself. Bill suggests that the rioters were likely Death Eaters who evaded capture. Ron wonders why Death Eaters would Disapparate when the Mark appeared. Bill says it is because they avoided Azkaban by disavowing any connection to Voldemort. If he is around, they would be in the Dark Lord's bad graces for having denied him. Mr. Weasley tells everyone to get some sleep before catching an early-morning Portkey back to the Burrow. But it is a long time before Harry can doze off. Three days ago his scar was acting up, and tonight, the Dark Mark. Is there a connection?

ANALYSIS

While most wizards believe that Voldemort is long-dead, the havoc and mayhem caused by his surviving Death Eaters shows how deeply his evil remains embedded within the Wizarding world, and how quickly and easily it can incite terror and panic. And though it appears the hooded rampagers randomly attacked anyone in the campground, Draco's pointed comment indicates that they may have been targeting Muggle-borns like Hermione. As a reminder, Voldemort's earlier ascendancy to power was built upon "pure-blood" wizards' belief that they were somehow, by birth, superior to Muggles and Muggles' magical offspring. Draco Malfoy's smug amusement over Muggles and Muggle-borns being attacked suggests he has some insider knowledge about the riot and that his father, Lucius, is probably involved. The elitist Malfoys and their many contemporaries have a long connection to the Dark Arts and support a pure-blood ethos advocating bigotry and violence to suppress (and even eliminate) those considered inferior; Draco's dispassionate reaction not only reflect his personal feelings but also represents his social class' belief that Muggle-borns pose a threat by competing for important and influential positions within the magical community for which only they should be entitled to by birth.

Mr. Crouch's accusation that one of the Trio conjured the Dark Mark is not only a rush to judgment, but suspicious, and he immediately spotlights Harry as the prime suspect, despite flimsy circumstantial evidence. A "mob mentality" quickly overtakes the group, and when Harry's stolen wand is determined to have cast the Dark Mark, Amos Diggory immediately accuses Harry, then Winky, who is obviously innocent of conjuring it. Only Mr. Weasley's timely intervention restores reason among the nearly irrational Ministry officials. Crouch firing his House-elf, Winky for a seemingly minor offense, may indicate that he knows something about the attacks and is attempting to deflect suspicion. Ludo Bagman's behaviour is peculiar as well, and he clearly has been somewhere he should not, most likely tending to his gambling clients.

Winky's unjust firing so outrages Hermione that she resolves to champion House-elves rights, although few, including House-elves, will initially support her cause. Once the seed is sown, however, Hermione remains passionately committed to fighting oppression and bigotry, a recurring theme throughout the series. And while many creatures suffer from disdain to outright racial hatred and discrimination, House-elves are perhaps the most mistreated and maligned among all magical folk, being virtual slaves without rights, representation, or purpose other than serving the Wizard families they are indentured to. Ironically, House-elves are magically powerful creatures, as seen when Dobby protected Harry by threatening Lucius Malfoy in *Harry Potter and the Chamber of Secrets*. Dobby's threat alone was enough for Malfoy to immediately reconsider his actions. It is therefore curious as to just how House-elves became enslaved by wizards, although suppressing an intelligent and potentially magically superior race may have partially been their motivation. While this is never explained, it is possible elves were subjected to centuries-long and magically-induced behavioral conditioning (brainwashing), resulting in them willingly accepting slavery and deriving their status and identity from the Wizard Houses they happily and loyally serve, even those who are mistreated. Hermione must overcome this huge obstacle if she is ever to realize her goal to liberate such a contented group.

QUESTIONS

Review 1. How are House-elves fired?
2. Why does Mr. Crouch fire his House-elf, Winky? Was this justified, or does Crouch have some other reason for dismissing Winky?
3. Who were the hooded figures, and why were they rioting?
4. What was left floating in the night sky? Who is responsible for it and what does it represent?
5. What do the Trio hear someone in the bushes shouting? What happens immediately after? Who recognizes it?
6. How is Mr. Weasley able to convince the others that Harry is innocent?

Further Study 1. If most wizards believe Lord Voldemort is long-dead, why does seeing his Dark Mark cause such terror?
2. Why is Draco Malfoy so calm and unconcerned during the riot? What does he tell the Trio?
3. Why was Harry so immediately suspected of casting the Dark Mark? What evidence, other than his stolen wand, would support this?
4. How was Mr. Weasley able to convince the Ministry officials that Harry is innocent? Was he believed?

5. Why would Ludo Bagman, a Ministry official, be unaware that an attack was underway? Where might he have been and why was he there?

6. Was Ludo Bagman's worried look about the riot, or something else? What might that be?

Greater Picture

When Amos Diggory retrieves the Stunned Winky from the woods behind the clearing, Bartemius Crouch immediately recognizes her as his own House-elf. When he goes into the same woods afterwards, he is looking for someone who Winky had been charged with guarding. Winky is unable to explain what happened or tell anyone who cast the Dark Mark because she is magically bound to conceal anything she knows about the family she serves. Winky's offence was not that she was in the woods without permission, or even in possession of a wand, but for failing to protect a family secret. This is a far more serious offence and the real reason she is sacked, although readers should consider why Crouch would dismiss such a valuable servant or why he had been so quick to accuse Harry.

There are several clues that Winky is guarding a person in this chapter. Harry's wand vanishes, later turning up in Winky's possession. This could only have happened if Winky, or the man she was guarding, had either picked up the wand in the forest if Harry had dropped it, or had lifted it from his pocket in the Top Box while Harry was watching the Quidditch match. When Winky runs across the forest path, she is apparently talking to herself and acting as if she is being restrained. In fact, someone is restraining her, but he is hidden under an Invisibility Cloak, unseen to Harry. It is this man who casts the Morsmordre spell, and though he is Stunned by Ministry wizards, he falls under the cloak and remains hidden from Amos Diggory. Crouch, though, knowing what he is looking for, finds and sends him home.

It is to the author's credit that, despite giving strong clues in this single chapter, we are unable to conclude that Winky was guarding someone until later in the story when that person, Barty Crouch Jr., explains what had happened during the riot.

It is perhaps ironic that Crouch dismissing Winky is very likely what leads to the secret's final revelation, as Winky is Crouch's most powerful assistant in keeping that secret.

Ludo Bagman's worries, we will learn, are likely because his "little flutter" has gone rather badly wrong, and it seems that he now owes more money than he has. Bagman was likely aware that the Leprechaun gold was transient when he used it to pay off the goblins. Though it has bought him some time, he is probably now worried over how to deal with the inevitable fallout when that gold vanishes.

Chapter 10: Mayhem at the Ministry

Synopsis

The Twins, Harry, Ron, Ginny, Hermione, Percy, Charlie, Bill, and Mr. Weasley catch an early rubber tyre back to Stoatshead Hill, after quick negotiation with Basil, the keeper of the Portkeys. As they reach The Burrow, Mrs. Weasley charges out, overjoyed to see them safe. After reading about the riot in the *Daily Prophet*, she did not want her cross parting words to Twins to have been the last thing she said to them. The *Daily Prophet*'s main story is slanted to put the Ministry in the worst possible light; it is written by Rita Skeeter, a scribe who, Percy says, has it in for the Ministry. Mr. Weasley finds that although he has been quoted accurately, his words have been deliberately slanted. Because he was the one quoted and it has made things worse, he must now patch things up. Percy offers to go with him, Mr. Crouch will need all hands on deck. Harry corrals Ron and Hermione and tells them that his scar hurt three days ago and about the dream he had. He says he is expecting Hedwig to bring a response from Sirius about what he should do.

Over the next two weeks, Percy and Mr. Weasley are busy dealing with fallout from the riot. Just before the students are to leave for Hogwarts, Percy is lamenting the many Howlers that have arrived at his office, saying they have scorched his desk. All have to do with security at the Quidditch World Cup and demanding compensation for losses. One Mundungus Fletcher, for instance, is demanding compensation for a twelve-bedroom tent with an ensuite Jacuzzi, although Percy knows he was sleeping under a cloak stretched over sticks. Fred and George are hunched over a piece of parchment. Mrs. Weasley asks if they are making a new order form for Weasleys' Wizard Wheezes, but Fred dodges the question. Mr. Weasley arrives home and says that Rita Skeeter has discovered that Bertha Jorkins is missing and nobody has been looking for her. Mr. Weasley points out that Mr. Crouch's House-elf being found with the wand that cast the Dark Mark would be headlines for a week. This sets Hermione off; she says that House-elves are basically slaves, but before she can get properly started on her rant, Mrs. Weasley sends everyone off to check if they are packed.

Sorting through the parcels Mrs. Weasley has gotten him, Ron finds an ancient dress robe, frayed and edged with lace. Mrs. Weasley says he will need dress robes this year for formal occasions and that she also got some for Harry. With some trepidation, Harry opens his to find that they are not embarrassing at all, looking like his school robes only bottle-green. Ron demands to know why he could not have robes like that, but Mrs. Weasley says they can only afford second-hand. After she leaves, Ron laments, "Why is everything I own rubbish?"

Analysis

The Weasley family is spotlighted here, including Ron, who is continually embarrassed and anguished over being poor and having to buy used textbooks and other lower-quality chattels. This time, he is humiliated when Mrs. Weasley buys him hideous, ancient dress robes for formal school occasions; Mrs. Weasley's well-meaning, but misguided, attempt to provide for her youngest son's material requirements goes awry when she utterly fails to comprehend Ron's emotional needs, and that teen-agers, even wizard ones, desperately desire to fit in with their peers, not be different from them.

She has unintentionally made Ron a more tempting target to his detractors. Ron is even more upset when he sees that Mrs. Weasley selected presentable dress robes for Harry because he can afford them. This contrast between Ron's relative poverty and Harry's inherited wealth appears several times throughout the book, and it will continually strain their friendship. Though Ron is sometimes jealous over Harry's affluence, he has yet to realize that Harry lacks and desperately wants what Ron takes for granted: a loving, supportive, and stable family. And while Ron will always have an opportunity to improve his lot in life if he so chooses, Harry can never hope to regain his parents.

Meanwhile, Mr. Weasley finds himself in a difficult position at work after his quotes were deliberately skewed by Rita Skeeter in her slanted article; now he must protect his job by attempting to repair damage inflicted on the Ministry of Magic. Percy's growing pompousness only makes matters worse. Even though his boss, Mr. Crouch, continually forgets his name, Percy convinces himself that he is needed at work to help handle the fallout following the World Cup riot. Adding to the Ministry's woes is Skeeter's discovery that Bertha Jorkins is missing, although, incredibly, Ministry officials have taken no action regarding this.

As with other characters, Rowling introduces Daily Prophet journalist, Rita Skeeter, only by name, hinting that Skeeter will later play an important role. An unethical and ruthless reporter, Skeeter employs any means to uncover a story that she then pads with juicy lies, exaggerated facts, and fabricated sensationalism to enthrall her readers and boost her paper's circulation. Skeeter's slanted articles have inflamed the already wide-spread fallout following the Death Eater attacks at the World Cup, although it remains unclear if she actually is biased against the Ministry of Magic, as Percy claims, or merely seeking notoriety. Regardless, she shows little interest in reporting the truth, and even less consideration for those victimized by her falsehoods. And while Skeeter freely abuses veracity, her character also represents just how prevalently the truth is skewered and manipulated by other characters in the series, often to malign Harry and Dumbledore and/or to benefit and protect themselves.

QUESTIONS

Review 1. Why does Harry only choose to tell Ron and Hermione about his dream now?

2. How are the Twins able to manipulate Mrs. Weasley's relief over their safety to their own advantage?

3. Why does Mrs. Weasley fail to understand why Ron is upset over the dress robes she bought him? Why does this further strain Ron's friendship with Harry?

Further Study 1. Why has no one been searching for the missing Bertha Jorkins?

2. Is Percy's claim that the Daily Prophet and Rita Skeeter have it in for the Ministry correct? If so, why, and what evidence supports this?

GREATER PICTURE

The Twins manipulate Mrs. Weasley's relief that they are safely home to help defuse further questions about Weasley's Wizard Wheezes. The letter the Twins are writing is likely to Ludo Bagman, informing him that his payment (in Leprechaun gold) has vanished. Even though they were not working on another Weasley's Wizard Wheezes order form as Mrs. Weasley suspected, it would have been equally precarious for the Twins to admit to their mother what it actually was. Not only was it connected with the Wheezes enterprise, it also involved gambling, which the Twins are forbidden to do. By invoking her earlier relief for their safety, Fred is able to deflect Mrs. Weasley's inquiry about the parchment, without admitting what it is.

Mr. Crouch continually forgetting Percy's name and his other odd behavior, as described here in passing, may stem from something other than him being an eccentric and inattentive boss. It will turn out that Mr. Crouch is being controlled by Peter Pettigrew, using the Imperius curse, in order to assist Barty Crouch Jr. in his attempts to force the Triwizard Tournament's outcome in Voldemort's chosen direction. However, it is unclear exactly when this curse is applied. It is believed it is before the start of the school year, as we are later shown that Crouch was under control before Moody was subdued, and it must have happened after Harry's dream as Pettigrew and Voldemort were then in Little Hangleton, while Crouch was still in London; so while it is safe to assume that Crouch was taken over sometime during this fortnight, we are unable to see exactly when his behaviour changed. The journalist Rita Skeeter, introduced in this chapter, will have a large role in this book, writing embarrassing stories about Harry and Hermione in particular. She will ultimately be nullified by Hermione, though she will again play a role in *Harry Potter and the Order of the Phoenix*, and will be brought back indirectly, through interviews and her own writing, in *Harry Potter and the Deathly Hallows*. In the series' final book, Skeeter's acid pen poses questions that Harry will need to answer, primarily about Dumbledore.

Chapter 11: Aboard the Hogwart's Express

SYNOPSIS

The next morning, Harry and Ron put on Muggle clothing to avoid attracting attention at the train station. Mrs. Weasley tells Arthur that there is an urgent message from the Ministry. Mr. Weasley talks to Amos Diggory's head, which is floating in the fireplace. They are discussing someone named "Mad-Eye" who thought he heard someone creeping around his house. Mad Eye booby-trapped his garbage bins to attack intruders. Apparently Mr. Weasley and Diggory want to minimize the charges against Mad Eye, so it will not be reported in the news. Harry learns that this person is apparently rather famous, is starting a new job, and the Ministry wants to keep his reputation relatively clean. Bill, Fred, and George evidently recognize Mad Eye's name, as does Charlie, who tells Harry that Mad-Eye Moody was a great Auror but is now retired. He still has many enemies, mostly families of those he put into Azkaban, and he has apparently become paranoid in his old age. Mrs. Weasley braved the telephone in the village post office and so there are three Muggle taxis waiting to take them to London. Bill and Charlie are going with them, but Percy decides that he is needed at the Ministry. They arrive at King's Cross Station and head to Platform Nine and Three Quarters. Harry, Ron, and Hermione find a compartment on the train, then hop off again to say goodbye. Bill and Charlie hint that something interesting will be happening at Hogwarts this year, but Ron, Harry, Fred, and George are unable to get any additional information from them or Mrs. Weasley, who apparently knows the secret.

As the train departs London, Draco Malfoy is overheard in the next compartment saying that he almost went to Durmstrang, another wizarding school. Hermione comments that it probably would have suited him, there is more emphasis on the Dark Arts there. No one knows Durmstrang's location, both it and the Beauxbatons Academy conceal themselves, much as Hogwarts does. This is news to Ron, who was unaware that Hogwarts is concealed. He asks, "How can you conceal a bloody great castle?" Hermione explains the various ways, including that the castle cannot be mapped and no one can Apparate or Disapparate within it. The Trio greet old friends like Dean Thomas, Seamus Finnigan, and Neville Longbottom, and the conversation turns to the Quidditch World Cup until Draco enters the compartment. Spotting Ron's embarrassing dress robes draped over Pigwidgeon's cage to quiet him, Draco mocks Ron, then asks if he is entering. When it becomes apparent that Ron has no idea what Draco is talking about, Draco sneers that maybe Ron's father and brother are not high enough employees within the Ministry to know what is going on and leaves without further explanation.

They arrive at Hogsmeade station in a thundering downpour, and quickly head to the horseless carriages that carry students to the castle. Hermione does not envy the first-years their trip across the lake.

Analysis

Two main plot lines are advanced or initiated. Early on, the character, Alastor Moody, a former Auror, is introduced when the Ministry is forced to cover up actions resulting from his paranoia. Moody sets booby-traps to safeguard his property, and he is likely to attack anyone he considers a threat, although it is unclear why or by whom he would be attacked. The Ministry being so concerned that the public might learn about the incident at Moody's home indicates that his new job is probably a high-profile and closely scrutinized position. Although it is unknown yet just what Moody has been hired for, readers may be able to surmise what it is based on his previous career. Hints are being dropped that something mysterious and exciting may be happening at Hogwarts. Mr. and Mrs. Weasley, Bill, and Charlie know about it, and likely that is what Percy was actually begging questions about at the family dinner before the World Cup. On the Hogwarts Express,

Draco, as obnoxious as ever, indicates that the Malfoy family knows the secret and seizes this as an opportunity to further undermine Ron and his family. The astute reader may be wondering if this is what Ludo Bagman was alluding to in an earlier chapter. Readers should also pay attention to Draco's comment about almost attending Durmstrang, as there seems to be a particular reason it is mentioned here.

In chapter 9, it was learned that there are other Wizarding schools in Europe, including Beauxbatons, which is apparently in France. Durmstrang, which has a slightly less than savory reputation, is mentioned in this chapter. Durmstrang is likely in the cold northern regions of East Europe, because its uniform includes fur-lined capes, although its actual location is secret.

Questions

Review 1. Why would Mrs. Weasley use Muggle taxis to transport the children to King's Cross Station?

2. Why doesn't Ron know that Hogwarts Castle is magically hidden, and what does that say about his character in general?

3. What might Malfoy mean when he asks Ron if he is "entering"? What other hints have been dropped that something special is happening at Hogwarts this year?

Further Study 1. Based on his former occupation, what new job might Alastor "Mad Eye" Moody be starting?

2. Why is it so important that Mr. Weasley and Mr. Diggory get the charges against Moody minimized?

3. What might the nickname, "Mad Eye" refer to?

4. Would Draco Malfoy's character be different if he had attended Durmstrang instead of Hogwarts? If so, how? What are some possible reasons why he did not attend that school?

Greater Picture

It will be learned later that the incident with Moody and his trash cans is actually when Wormtail and Barty Crouch Jr. overpower and kidnap him. It is Barty who animates the garbage bins so there will be something to report as having caused the commotion when Ministry wizards arrive. Evidently Moody's paranoia was well-founded. It is not known if there actually were traps on Moody's property; it is only important that Wizarding officials believe there were, and given Amos Diggory's and Arthur Weasley's reactions to the story given by Moody's impostor, they believe this.

It will shortly be revealed that the Bulgarian Quidditch team's Seeker, Viktor Krum, is a student at Durmstrang. This could indicate the school is located in Bulgaria, or at least draws some of its students from there as well as other near-by countries, although that is only speculation. Krum will have a larger role to play in this book, as he is a potential Champion for Durmstrang in the upcoming Triwizard Tournament. Another Wizard school, Beauxbatons, has also been mentioned, and will provide the third Champion in that tournament. The tournament, in fact, is the pending event at Hogwarts which Bill, Charlie, Percy, Mrs. Weasley, and Draco Malfoy have all alluded to.

Krum will also become romantically interested in Hermione, which affects Ron, who becomes jealous. Krum is sporadically seen throughout the rest of the series, triggering attacks of jealousy and insecurity in Ron at each appearance. Hermione, knowing her own heart better than Ron knows his, will retain Krum as a friend, but never seriously reciprocates his romantic interest.

Chapter 12: The Triwizard Tournament

Synopsis

Harry, Ron, and Hermione are greeted at the Entrance Hall with water balloons courtesy of Peeves. Professor McGonagall shoos him away, and the Trio enter the Great Hall where Colin Creevey excitedly tells Harry that his brother Dennis is starting his first year at Hogwarts. Harry asks if brothers and sisters are always sorted into the same House, like the Weasleys, but Hermione points out that Parvati Patil is a Gryffindor, but her twin sister, Padma, was sorted into Ravenclaw.

Scanning the head table, Harry notices many empty chairs, but he does not think about who is missing until Hermione wonders who is teaching Defence Against the Dark Arts. Harry realizes that there does not seem to be a teacher for that subject, but, almost immediately, the first-year students enter and the Sorting ceremony commences. Once the Sorting has ended, the feast begins. Nearly Headless Nick informs Harry and Ron that there nearly was not a feast because Peeves, upset he was uninvited, was wreaking havoc in the kitchens, disrupting the House-elves. Hermione, distraught to discover that there are over one hundred House-elves at Hogwarts providing for the residents' needs, refuses to eat any more, claiming slave labour produced the feast.

After the feast, Professor Dumbledore rises to make several announcements. First, the inter-house Quidditch championship is canceled, but before he can explain further, a man with a prosthetic leg, a magical false eye, and a badly damaged face enters the Hall. He speaks with Professor Dumbledore, who introduces him as Professor Moody, the new Defence Against the Dark Arts teacher. Harry asks Ron if this is the same Moody that his father had bailed out that morning, and Ron believes it is. They watch as Moody eats and notices that he only drinks from a hip flask. Dumbledore continues, and announces that Hogwarts is hosting the inter-school Triwizard Tournament. A one thousand Galleon prize will be awarded to the winner. Only students 17 years and older can enter, causing Fred and George to protest; they do not turn 17 until April and want to compete. Dumbledore says that representatives from the competing Beauxbatons and Durmstrang schools are arriving shortly and will stay at Hogwarts during the Tournament.

Heading to their dormitory, Fred and George are already plotting ways to bypass the age rule and enter the competition, assuming the judges will not notice if they take an Aging Potion. Harry, dreaming about the Tournament, imagines himself as the champion, admired by Cho Chang.

Analysis

Ever since entering the wizarding world, Harry has learned to expect the unexpected. However, when he was prematurely extricated from the unpleasant Dursley household, he anticipated an enjoyable time with the Weasleys and Hermione at the Quidditch World Cup before returning to Hogwarts' familiar and comfortable routine. Since departing Privet Drive, however, life has been anything but peaceful, starting with the upheaval at the World Cup. Even returning to Hogwarts will be different what with the Triwizard Tournament and foreign students spending the academic year at the school. The Tournament is creating much excitement and anticipation, however, and it is an opportunity for one student to win glory and a substantial prize. And though Harry is underage and usually prefers to avoid putting additional attention on himself (nor does he need the prize money), he is, nonetheless, intrigued by the prospect of competing in such a difficult challenge and being proclaimed a hero. Even though Harry is already famous and considered a "hero" in the wizarding world, he may feel that this title was bestowed by fate, rather than by his own deliberate action or design; Harry was a mere infant when Voldemort met his demise, and Harry remembers little about that night's events. And though he has since confronted Voldemort, the general wizarding community is either unaware or simply refuses to believe that the Dark Lord has returned. The Tournament would provide an opportunity to achieve glory and renown on his own terms, and there would be no lingering doubts or unanswered questions after its conclusion. Harry also considers the Tournament as a missed opportunity to impress Cho Chang, his first major crush. Adding to the quandary, not only is Harry barred from entering the Tournament, he must also cope with the cancellation of Quidditch, an activity he dearly loves and one that provides him a means to reduce stress and excess energy, as well as earning him recognition; it is also an interest he shares with Cho Chang, the Ravenclaw Seeker.

Dumbledore was probably instrumental in reviving the long-suspended (and very dangerous) Triwizard Tournament with a specific purpose in mind. With Voldemort apparently regaining strength and reorganizing his Death Eaters, Dumbledore knows it is imperative that the differing Wizarding populations unite in order to fight the Dark Lord. Like the Quidditch World Cup, bringing students together in a long-term competition is an opportunity to create lasting ties and friendships, as well as build strong international cooperation.

Hermione's determination to free House-elves shows little sign of abating, although refusing to eat meals prepared at Hogwarts seems a childish and ineffective way to achieve her objective. Hermione will need a more concrete and organized method to promote her cause.

Harry and Hermione's conversation regarding how siblings are sorted into their Houses, while unimportant to the overall plot, is interesting. The Patil sisters are identical twins, but the Sorting Hat obviously detected enough differences to sort them into different Houses. The same could be said about Fred and George who, despite their closeness, have many contrasts to their personalities. Fred is more aggressive and outgoing than George, who tends to be quieter and more cerebral, making him a possible candidate for Ravenclaw (if he were able to discipline himself academically). However, the Sorting Hat takes many factors into consideration when sorting new students, including an individual's own preference. It was Harry's strong desire to be in Gryffindor that prompted the Sorting Hat to place him there, rather than Slytherin. This could also be why Fred and George were both put in Gryffindor and the Patil twins were not. And while it would seem that, given her intellect, Hermione should have been placed in Ravenclaw, she is better suited to Gryffindor in many other ways.

QUESTIONS

Review   1. Why might the Triwizard Tournament have been revived after so many years? Why was it disbanded, and has it changed?

Further Study   1. Can Hermione boycotting food prepared by Hogwarts House-elves help free them? If not, why? What might be an alternative solution?

2. Why might Harry, already considered a "hero" in the wizarding world, want to compete in the Triwizard Tournament? What reasons might he not want to enter, other than being underaged?

3. Why might the Sorting Hat have placed the identical Patil twins into separate Houses, while Fred and George were both sorted into Gryffindor?

4. What might Mad Eye Moody be drinking from his hip flask? Why does no one investigate or seem suspicious?

GREATER PICTURE

Despite the Weasleys being traditionally sorted into Gryffindor, Ron, and also Neville Longbottom, seem ill-suited to a House known for bravery. Initially, it appears that they would likely do better in Hufflepuff House. Both boys seem to lack courage and have not demonstrated any outstanding magical ability; Neville, in fact, is nearly incompetent in magic. Why then were they placed in Gryffindor? It is likely the Sorting Hat can detect deeply hidden and untapped qualities within students, even if they are not yet visible to the individual or others. By the series end, each boy will prove they are true Gryffindors and show that bravery comes in many forms. They overcome their fears and inabilities to help battle Voldemort, and both, mostly under Harry's guidance, develop into strong, capable wizards.

One reason Harry wants to compete in the Triwizard Tournament is, if victorious, he will be proclaimed a hero as a result of his own efforts, without anyone doubting the outcome. Harry will get his wish to compete, but his "triumph" will be disputed and create even more doubts and unanswered questions regarding Voldemort and Harry's unproven claims that the Dark Lord has returned.

Winky's mistreatment at the World Cup has so stirred Hermione's outrage over the injustice meted out to House-elves that she will forever champion rights and ethical treatment for non-human magical creatures. It also becomes the foundation for S.P.E.W., the organization she will start.

Chapter 13: Mad-Eye Moody

SYNOPSIS

At breakfast, Fred, George, and Lee Jordan are plotting ways to bypass the Tournament age limit. Hermione decides to eat breakfast, saying there are better ways to promote elf rights. Harry looks for, but does not receive, a message from Sirius Black in the morning post. In their first class, Herbology, with the Hufflepuffs, they are squeezing pus from bubotubers. Their second class is Care of Magical Creatures, with the Slytherins. Hagrid is teaching them to care for Blast-Ended Skrewts. The Skrewts scare the entire class, and Dean Thomas is burned by one, while Lavender Brown discovers some have stingers.

During lunch, Hermione bolts down her meal, then heads for the library, while Harry and Ron wait for the bell and proceed to Divination. Professor Trelawney, with her by-now familiar mystical air, predicts her usual doom for Harry and then announces they will be studying the stars. Trelawney states that Harry's appearance clearly indicates that he was born in midwinter, under the influence of Saturn; Harry replies that he was born in July. Professor Trelawney assigns massive astrology homework.

While queuing for dinner, Draco Malfoy reads aloud from the *Daily Prophet*. Ron's father is mentioned in an extremely scurrilous article by Rita Skeeter. The article criticizes the Ministry and, in particular, Arthur Weasley, although Skeeter gets his name wrong. An exchange of insults ensues. When Draco attempts to curse Harry behind his back, Professor Moody Transfigures Draco into a white ferret and bounces him off the floor. Professor McGonagall arrives and sternly warns Moody that students are never transfigured as punishment, then transforms Draco back into himself. Moody tells Draco to warn his father that he will be keeping an eye on his son, and comments that they are "old acquaintances." He escorts Draco to his House's Head, Professor Snape, another "old friend." As Ron eats dinner and savors the vision of "Draco Malfoy, the bouncing white ferret," Fred and George and Lee Jordan tell Ron and Harry that, even apart from the Malfoy episode, Moody is quite cool, and his Defence Against the Dark Arts classes are incredible. Mad Eye has actually fought Dark wizards. Ron laments that he must wait until Thursday for Moody's class.

ANALYSIS

Professor Moody is proving to be an eccentric and unconventional teacher, even more than others that students have seen at Hogwarts. His gruff, rebellious nature is a bit frightening, although he demonstrates a strong sense of fair play when he transfigured Malfoy into a ferret for attempting to curse Harry behind his back. His apparent willingness to flout Ministry rules and teach practical (although dangerous) defensive magic makes his class an instant favorite with students. The Twins' enthusiasm only increases Ron and Harry's eagerness to attend their first session. Readers should perhaps take notice of Moody's hip flask.

It is unlikely that Hermione has abandoned her mission to liberate House-elves, despite deciding against boycotting Hogwarts' meals. Based on her behavior here, she probably realizes she needs a more practical approach for promoting her cause and has dashed off to the library to research a more effective way. For Hermione, an idea that was born in a fit of childish emotion is gradually giving way to a more logical, methodical, and mature reasoning process to achieve her goals. This may be why Hermione was sorted into Gryffindor House rather than Ravenclaw—she actively applies her great intellect to achieve specific goals, combining her intelligence with bravery, initiative, persistence, and occasional rule-breaking, even when others strongly disapprove, are indifferent, or mock her. This is unlike the cerebral Ravenclaws, who, although they are known for their high intelligence, tend to be more introspective and less proactive. If Hermione had been sorted into Ravenclaw, frequent conflicts with her housemates would likely have occurred.

Fred and George's attempts to by-pass the Tournament's age limit are likely futile, but their continual attempts to experiment with and create new magic shows, despite their poor academic record, just how talented, powerful, and resourceful these clever young wizards actually are; they have already invented many new and innovative spells, charms, and jinxes, and they are well on their way to opening their own unique joke shop, if they can secure the financing. The Twins are a stark contrast to Harry and Ron, who, to date, have tended only to study the required O.W.L.-level curriculum and have not yet shown the initiative or ability to create new magic. This does not mean they are incapable or lack talent, however. Harry, being a latecomer to the wizarding world, still has much general knowledge to learn that most wizard children have been exposed to since birth. He has also had to cope with many calamities in his life, particularly since he started at Hogwarts. However, his natural ability in Defensive Arts is already apparent and will likely inspire him to experiment once he becomes more proficient in general magic; he has already learned more defensive spells than most students know when they leave Hogwarts. Hermione, a latecomer like Harry, also shows little inclination to experiment; instead, she concentrates on mastering traditional spells that are within prescribed academic boundaries while nurturing her inquisitive mind with books, although this will likely change as she matures. Ron, meanwhile, still feels too intimidated and overshadowed by his magically accomplished family, even Ginny, who is already developing into a powerful witch.

QUESTIONS

Review 1. Why does Trelawney say Harry was born in mid-winter when it was she who once made a prophecy (that is revealed to Harry in *Order of the Phoenix*) that he would, "be born as the seventh month dies"?
2. Why does Rita Skeeter particularly criticize Arthur Weasley in her articles about the World Cup riots?
3. Why does Hagrid's Care of Magical Creatures class often feature animals that are mildly dangerous and that frighten (and occasionally injure) students?
4. What does Moody mean when he refers to Snape and Lucius Malfoy as "old acquaintances"?

Further Study 1. Why does Hermione decide against boycotting meals prepared by House-elves? Is she giving up on her plan to liberate House-elves or might she be planning something else and what might that be?
2. Despite knowing how difficult Dobby's life was after Harry liberated him, why has Hermione given such little thought to how House-elves would fare if they were freed? What obstacles would they face?

GREATER PICTURE

We again see Rita Skeeter's poisonous brand of writing in this chapter. As mentioned previously, Rita and her journalistic style will play a role in this and future books in the series.

Hermione's concerns for the wellbeing of the House-Elves will shortly result in her creating an organization, the Society for the Promotion of Elfish Welfare, which will prove a relatively minor plot point in this book. Hermione's investigations into the status of house-elves at Hogwarts will lead her to Dobby and Winky, both of whom are working in the Hogwarts kitchens as Free Elves. While it will play little role in future books, the welfare of non-human magical races will remain a concern of Hermione's throughout the rest of the series.

Chapter 14: The Unforgivable Curses

SYNOPSIS

Professor Snape, as usual, is in a bad mood, and the confrontation with Professor Moody must have been galling. Additionally, it is common belief that Snape wanted the Defence Against The Dark Arts position. Snape also seems to fear Moody and, as he cannot act against him, retaliates against students. On Thursday, the students eagerly queue outside Professor Moody's classroom early, except for Hermione, who arrives from the library just in time. Moody tells the class that Professor Lupin told him they have tackled a variety of Dark creatures, but they are deficient in handling curses. He says Ministry guidelines state they should only be taught *counter*-curses, and not be shown the actual curses until sixth year. But Professor Dumbledore feels that even fourth years need a better understanding of what they may be up against. Professor Moody asks the class if they can identify the three Unforgivable curses, according to the Ministry. Ron says his father has mentioned the Imperius curse. Moody casts it on a spider, forcing it to dance. Moody says the curse makes it difficult to tell who is truly Dark and who is being controlled by magic.

Chapter 14: The Unforgivable Curses

Moody asks for another curse; Neville shakily mentions the Cruciatus curse. Moody enlarges another spider and casts Crucio on it. Even though it is only a spider, it is obviously in extreme pain. Neville becomes distressed while watching this. Relenting, Moody reduces the spider and lets it go. Moody asks for the third illegal curse; Hermione mentions the Killing Curse. Moody fetches another spider and curses it; in a jet of green light, it simply dies. Moody says only one person is known to have survived that particular curse: Harry Potter. This curse is a small revelation to Harry, as he has memories of the green light and the rushing noise it makes. As they leave the classroom, Hermione notices Neville is extremely shaken. Professor Moody approaches and takes Neville aside. He also asks if Harry is all right, and says that Harry has to know (the implication being that he should know about the curse that killed his parents). Moody then takes Neville to his office for a cup of tea, while Hermione and Ron wonder what that is about. When they return to the Common room after dinner, Neville is reading a book Professor Moody gave him titled, *Magical Mediterranean Water-Plants and Their Properties*, and says that Moody was told by Professor Sprout that he is adept at Herbology.

Harry and Ron start their Divination homework, but as usual, it is too confusing, and they revert to inventing their own predictions. Harry notices Fred and George working on a parchment and sees George scratch out a line and say, "No, that sounds like we're accusing him. Got to be careful." But Harry's homework is more important, so he returns to his fabrication. As they finish, Hermione returns from the library with the beginnings of an organization she calls S.P.E.W.: the Society for the Promotion of Elfish Welfare. She lays out how the society will work. She coerces Harry and Ron into being officers, but is interrupted by Hedwig appearing at the window with a message from Sirius Black. Sirius writes that Harry's painful scar, coupled with other things he has heard, concerns him, and he is returning to England. Harry frets, convinced he has summoned Sirius into danger. If Sirius is captured, Harry could never forgive himself. A peeved Harry shoos away the hungry Hedwig, who angrily flies off to the Owlery to find something to eat.

Analysis

The plot advances in various ways. First, Professor Moody further demonstrates his idiosyncratic teaching style and a willingness to flout Ministry regulations, as well as an awareness and sensitivity towards students. His decision to teach the three "Unforgivable Curses" has a particularly profound effect on two students: Harry and Neville. Realizing that the Cruciatus Curse demonstration has visibly upset Neville, Moody takes him aside after class and calms him down. Moody also checks on Harry, whose parents he knows were killed with the Avada Kedavra curse that nearly took Harry's life and left him with his scar, although Harry is less shaken than Neville. Readers will note that Moody describes the Avada Kedavra curse as killing its victim without leaving any mark. However, Harry's scar was caused by the deadly curse. This is most likely the after effect of his mother's protective charm when the curse rebounded off Harry's forehead and back to Voldemort, killing him.

Also, Neville, who is rarely, if ever, singled out for being good at anything, is extremely flattered and grateful when Moody gives him the Herbology book after being told by Professor Sprout that Neville has an aptitude for this subject. Harry thinks that Moody's gesture is similar to what Professor Lupin would have done. Hermione championing rights for House-elves (that they actually do not want) formally begins in this chapter. Although S.P.E.W. becomes a smaller subplot in later books, Hermione continues to believe, quite correctly, that House-elves are a slave caste and should be freed.

Snape's behavior here is revealing. Rather than the disdain and disrespect he usually heaps on whoever is the current Defensive Arts teacher, a position Snape has long coveted but is repeatedly denied, he appears to show cautious fear and maintains a respectful distance from the crusty, former Auror. Moody's earlier sarcastic remark regarding Snape being an "old friend" hints at an unresolved history between them, most likely relating to Snape's Death Eater past. Typically, Snape vents his frustration on his students.

Finally, Sirius, concerned about Harry's safety, is returning to England with Buckbeak, although Harry rightly fears he may have endangered Sirius by writing to him about his dreams and his scar hurting. And though Sirius' concern and devotion for his godson is commendable and shows how much he loves Harry, his decision seems rather reckless; just how Sirius can help Harry while he remains a hunted fugitive is uncertain. This all causes Harry even more stress and turmoil and could even put him at risk.

Questions

Review 1. Why were Unforgivable Curses made illegal?

2. Why was Neville so affected by Moody demonstrating the Cruciatus curse? Does Moody know the reason? If so, how would he know?

3. Why is the Avada Kedavra curse of such interest to Harry?

4. Why is Harry upset that Sirius is returning to England?

Further Study 1. Why does Moody demonstrate the Unforgivable Curses to the class, despite Ministry policy against teaching them?

2. Why would the Ministry want to prevent students from learning the Unforgivable Curses?

3. Why was Harry less affected by Moody's in-class demonstration than Neville?

4. How does Snape treat Moody differently than other former Defensive Arts teachers? Why?

5. Who might the Twins be writing to and why would they be contacting this person?

6. Why does George tell Fred they have to be "careful"?

7. Why would Moody give Neville a Herbology book about water plants?

Greater Picture

Harry and the other students are, at this point, unaware that Neville Longbottom's parents, Frank and Alice, are permanently committed to St. Mungo's Hospital. When we and Harry learn this later, it is also revealed that Moody was present at the Death Eaters' trial, and thus knows that they tortured the Longbottoms into insanity using the Cruciatus curse. This sheds some light on these occurrences, as it is meant to; we suddenly understand why Neville became so upset while watching the curse demonstration and why Moody apparently took such pains to comfort him. In the final chapter, however, it is revealed that Alastor Moody is actually Barty Crouch, Jr. in disguise. He is one of four Death Eaters sentenced to Azkaban for torturing the Longbottoms to insanity using the Cruciatus Curse. It is particularly interesting that Crouch (as Moody) can show such compassion to one whose parents he drove insane, although that is keeping in character with what the real Moody probably would have done under the same circumstances. And while Crouch giving Neville the Herbology book seems like yet another magnanimous gesture to help boost Neville's low self-esteem, it is actually because the book contains information that Crouch wants passed on to Harry that can help him win the Tournament, thus leading Harry into Voldemort's trap. Crouch may well have been banking on the Cruciatus demonstration to badly upset the sensitive Neville, solely to give Crouch an opportunity to present Neville with the book without his motives appearing suspicious. This extreme deviousness illustrates, upon reflection, something unsavory about Crouch's character in particular, and perhaps Death Eaters in general. Also, Barty's comment that Snape and Karkaroff are "old acquaintances," may not only be truthful, implying that he knew them as fellow Death Eaters, but it also demonstrates a rather perverse sense of humor. Considering that Snape and Karkaroff betrayed Voldemort, Barty's sarcastic comment could have the same double-entendre implication as what the real Alastor Moody would mean had he said it.

It will turn out that the Twins are writing to Ludo Bagman. This is part of a subplot that will run the entire duration of the year, as Ludo refuses to pay off his gambling debt to them. Ludo is clearly more afraid of his other debtors, who are Goblins, and who can seriously injure him if they are not paid; when Ludo's debts finally go completely sour at the end of the book, he will go into hiding, leaving the Twins and the Goblins unpaid. In her attempts to free the House-elves, Hermione fails to consider that freedom comes with a price and must be carefully orchestrated if elves are to survive and thrive without discrimination or retribution within the wizarding world. Simply turning loose what most wizards consider an inferior race (even more so than other non-human magical folk) would create great hardship, just as it will for Winky, who has few, if any, prospects as a free elf. It would take a huge effort to realign both the general wizarding population's attitude and the House-elves' thinking to accept House-elves as equal and free agents. It would be advisable for Hermione to study how emancipated slaves fared following the American Civil War in the mid-1860s. Although former slaves were now free U.S. citizens, they struggled against severe discrimination, hatred, violence, and poverty while attempting to assimilate themselves into a white, patriarchal-dominated society, all while lacking (and being denied) adequate education, jobs, and other opportunities needed to fend for themselves. As in the Wizard world, more than one race was discriminated against: Irish, Asians, Hispanics, Italians, etc. were routinely denied equal opportunities based solely on their ethnicity. However, much like some non-human magical folk in Wizard society, these particular ethnic groups were never enslaved and they had functioned within their own home countries as free citizens and most had at least some education. Also, immigrants were often able to establish their own small, protective communities while gradually integrating themselves into American culture, whereas freed slaves created a sudden and rather chaotic influx into a new social order in which there was little management or oversight (and extensive corruption) resulting in abuse and exploitation. Over a century later, these struggles are still existent and are likely similar to what House-elves would experience.

Chapter 15: Beauxbatons and Durmstrang

Synopsis

Early in the morning, Harry writes to Sirius telling him that he is perfectly alright and not to worry about him. He goes to the Owlery and persuades a still-aloof Hedwig to carry the message to Sirius. Harry is certain Sirius' reply will make things better. Hermione remonstrates with him later, saying that what he wrote to Sirius is a lie. Harry says he does not care; he will not do anything that risks Sirius going to Azkaban again. Classes are harder than ever, particularly Defence Against the Dark Arts. Professor Moody is going to use the Imperius curse on each student to teach them how to resist it. Hermione objects, saying it is illegal. Moody responds that Dumbledore wants them to know what it feels like and offers to excuse her from class. She decides to stay, and Moody puts each student under the curse. Harry feels euphoric while he is cursed. When a little voice breaks in telling him to jump on Moody's desk, Harry thinks, "But why?" As the command gets more forceful, Harry both jumps and tries to prevent himself from jumping and smashes into Moody's desk. Moody is overjoyed and repeats the process four times, until Harry is able to cast off the curse perfectly.

As they leave class, Ron comments that Moody seems to believe everyone is on the verge of being attacked and mentions a few events that would make the Ministry glad not to have Moody around to worry about. Harry and Ron wonder how to cope with the extra homework on resisting the Imperius curse in addition to all the other homework teachers are piling on. Professor McGonagall explains in Transfiguration that it is to prepare students for their Fifth-year O.W.L.s.

Luckily, Professor Trelawney approves their Divination homework, even reading sections to the class. Harry and Ron are amused, but less so when she asks

Chapter 15: Beauxbatons and Durmstrang

them to repeat this the month after next; they are running out of catastrophes to predict. Meanwhile, Professor Binns is having students write weekly essays on the Goblin Rebellions. Professor Snape has them researching antidotes, and Professor Flitwick assigns three books in preparation for Summoning Charms. Even Hagrid gives extra work. The Blast-Ended Skrewts are growing apace, even though nobody knows what they eat. Hagrid has the class record their behaviour on alternate evenings. Returning to the Castle one evening after Care of Magical Creatures, the Trio see a notice that delegations from Durmstrang and Beauxbatons will arrive the following Friday. Ernie Macmillan runs off to tell Cedric Diggory. Ron expresses dismay that Cedric could be the Hogwarts' champion, but Hermione says he is a good student and a Hufflepuff Prefect. Ron accuses her of liking him because he is handsome.

The next week, much of the Castle is cleaned, and teachers are tense that the visitors might discover that some Hogwarts students are not quite up to standard. On the 30th, the day the representatives are to arrive, the Great Hall is decorated with silk banners representing the four Houses. At breakfast, Ron and Harry interrupt the twins who are discussing what to do about someone who does not answer them. Hermione mentions that the champions will be judged on how well they perform the set tasks and that three House Heads, among others, will be the judges. She then notes indignantly that *A History of Hogwarts* fails to mention that the school enslaves over a hundred House-elves. Her diatribe is interrupted by arriving post owls, including Hedwig bearing Sirius' reply. Sirius says he is back in the country and well hidden. He does not believe Harry's most recent letter that everything is fine now ("Nice try, Harry!") and advises Harry to use different owls for future messages. Hermione points out that Hedwig, a snowy owl, is too easily noticed.

Classes end a half hour early, and the students are marshaled outside the Entrance Hall. At dusk, the Beauxbatons representative arrives in a giant flying carriage pulled by enormous winged horses. Emerging from the carriage, the headmistress, Madam Maxime is revealed to be large as Hagrid. After Professor Dumbledore greets her, she takes her students inside Hogwarts where it is warm. Dumbledore assures her Hagrid is quite capable of tending to the horses, although Madame Maxime expresses some concern.

Durmstrang arrives in an apparently derelict sailing ship, surfacing from beneath the lake. Headmaster Igor Karkaroff warmly greets Dumbledore and asks if they can proceed immediately into the Castle. Viktor, he says, has a slight cold. As they pass, Ron recognizes that "Viktor" is the Bulgarian Quidditch Seeker, Victor Krum.

ANALYSIS

Harry has a a rather juvenile belief that writing to Sirius will always solve his problems; it does not, but finally having someone he can reach out to for help provides the comfort and security as well as family that has been lacking from his life. Harry realizes that any communication with Sirius, who is a hunted fugitive, is risky. Hermione chastising Harry for "lying" in his letter, even though Harry is only trying to protect Sirius, shows that she is persisting in rather two-dimensional, child-like thinking. Hermione strictly follows rules without questioning them, and it hardly occurs to her that telling the truth could actually be harmful. To her thinking, rules provide a safe, predictable outcome—breaking them leads to disorder and consequences. However, Hermione has broken rules and bent the truth in the past when she strongly believed it served a greater purpose, indicating that she is developing a more independent and analytical personality. This also creates a conflict within herself regarding her need for conformity and acceptance, although her growing maturity is gradually overcoming this, and it is why she has taken the first steps to challenge the entire wizarding world defending House-elves. Ron, meanwhile, is unknowingly developing a romantic interest in Hermione, and appears to become jealous when he suspects she is attracted to the handsome Cedric Diggory.

Sirius returning to England shows how devoted he is to his godson, although Harry is now terrified that he has endangered his godfather. But Sirius willingly risks his own freedom to ensure that Harry is safe. And though Sirius will sometimes be an imperfect role model to Harry, his actions show that he is a protective and loving guardian who willingly and responsibly assumed his parenting responsibilities.

Hogwarts is in an uproar as preparations are underway for the Durmstrang and Beauxbatons arrivals. The three schools could not be more different from one another, with Durmstrang representing a darker masculine personality, while the Beauxbatons have a more serene, feminine persona (although there are male students); Hogwarts embodies all these traits. Whether their interactions can build harmony or instead create discord will be tested. And although Dumbledore revived the Triwizard Tournament to unify the three schools, it also places him under immense pressure to present Hogwarts, and its teachers and students, in the best possible fashion. Being the host institution is a disadvantage, however. The Beauxbatons and Durmstrang schools remain unseen, and they can showcase only their brightest and most accomplished pupils, while Hogwarts and all its staff and students are on full display, even those less adept than others. Enhancing Durmstrang's image is Viktor Krum, the famed Seeker for the Bulgarian team that played in the Quidditch World Cup Final, although Harry is equally famous. Krum, an international sports star, is an unexpected surprise, particularly to many excited female students vying for his attention, and to Ron, who idolizes him as a hero. We may suspect, from the preferential treatment he seems to be receiving, that Krum is the favored candidate to become the Durmstrang Triwizard Champion.

It should be noted that the action in the book apparently takes place in 1994 and 1995; but the other schools' arrival date, October 30, 1994, is not a Friday but a Sunday. This does not affect the story in any way;

the discrepancy is noted only as a curiosity rather than as something the scholar should be concerned with. It may be worth mentioning, however, that the book is internally consistent; every date for which a day of the week is mentioned is off by two days.

QUESTIONS

Review 1. Is Hermione correct that Harry is lying to Sirius in his letter? What does Harry say?

2. Why does Hermione object to Professor Moody teaching the Unforgivable Curses, even though Dumbledore gave his approval to do so? What is Moody's response?

3. Why do the teachers fear that some Hogwarts students will fail to impress the Durmstrang and Beauxbatons visitors? Do Durmstrang and Beauxbatons have an advantage over Hogwarts in this regard? If so, how?

4. Why does Ron consider Hufflepuff student, Cedric Diggory, an unsuitable competitor for the Triwizard Tournament? Is he correct?

5. What does Hermione have to say regarding Ron's objection to Cedric as a Champion, and why does Ron disagree with her opinion?

Further Study 1. How can Sirius, a hunted fugitive, help Harry by returning to England? Is his decision to return wise or reckless, or even both?

2. Why does Hermione choose to remain in class, even though Moody gives her permission to be excused during the Unforgivable Curses demonstration?

3. Why does Professor Trelawney continually praise Ron and Harry for their increasingly outlandish predictions, even though none come true? What does this say about Trelawney's abilities as the Divination teacher?

4. Why did no one know that the World Cup Quidditch champion, Viktor Krum, is still a student?

GREATER PICTURE

While this has not been stated anywhere in the books so far, we have an informal belief that there is something odd about Hagrid; he is too large and hairy to be believed to be fully human, and his size seems, so far, unique in the Wizarding world. It is a partial relief to discover, with Madam Maxime's arrival, that he is not the only one so oversized. It is hardly surprising that Hagrid, upon seeing Madam Maxime for the first time, is instantly smitten, and it seems appropriate that they eventually start spending time together. This will cause some difficulty, however; while Hagrid admits, privately, to Madame Maxime that he is half-Giant, she denies that part of her heritage, and is insulted when Hagrid suggests that she has some Giant in her background. This also causes further difficulty as Hagrid is overheard by Rita Skeeter, who publishes his confession in the *Daily Prophet*. As Giants are still large, fierce, and destructive, this creates a certain backlash against Hagrid's employment and causes Hagrid to tender his resignation as Care of Magical Creatures teacher. Dumbledore, of course, refuses to accept Hagrid's resignation, and many other students and staff come to his support.

Readers should probably note that Snape is emphasizing antidotes in his Potions class this year. While they only play a small part in this book, some of what Harry learns here may be useful in *Harry Potter and the Half-Blood Prince*, when Ron is accidentally poisoned. It is true that Harry fears being deliberately poisoned by Snape, as Snape proposes to use that technique to test the students' antidotes, but he escapes that possibility due to the Weighing of the Wands ceremony.

The Skrewts will remain puzzling to Harry; in the end, there are only two left, and in the final Task maze, Harry will encounter and disable one. It is never determined what they eat, and it is suggested that these are a new hybrid of two existing species. Apart from the ongoing travails regarding their care, however, they play a minor role in the story. Interestingly, Draco challenges Hagrid over how he handles the Skrewts, which causes Hagrid to stand up to him. Harry seems to think Hagrid is showing an uncharacteristic amount of backbone in this instance.

Chapter 16: The Goblet of Fire

SYNOPSIS

Ron is stunned that the greatest Quidditch Seeker in the world, Victor Krum, is still in school. The students struggle to get into the Great Hall to get his autograph. The Beauxbatons representatives are seated at the Ravenclaw table. Despite Ron's efforts, the Durmstrang students sit with Slytherin. Harry wonders why Filch is setting out four extra chairs, as only two Headmasters have arrived, but the Headmasters enter the hall, interrupting his thoughts. Professor Dumbledore welcomes each guest and the feast begins.

The House-elves have produced a larger variety of dishes than usual, including some French ones which Hermione recognizes and recommends. Ron refuses to try any, preferring English cooking instead. A Beauxbatons girl with long blonde hair asks if they are finished with the bouillabaise. Ron is unable to answer, but Harry says she can go ahead. As she leaves, Ron remarks that she must be part Veela. Hermione disagrees, but many Hogwarts boys seem affected by her the way Ron is. Hermione notices that the two extra chairs at head table are now occupied by Ludo Bagman and Bartemius Crouch.

When dinner is over, Professor Dumbledore rises to explain the Triwizard Tournament rules. He then introduces Bagman and Crouch as the judges. Filch brings in an ornate wooden chest containing the Goblet of Fire, a large, roughly-hewn wooden cup that is "full to the brim with dancing, blue-white flames." Dumbledore says that anyone wishing to enter the competition should submit their name to the Goblet within twenty-four hours. At the Hallowe'en Feast, the three champions will be selected. He also says there will be an Age Line surrounding the Goblet preventing anyone under 17-years-old from entering. As they leave the Great Hall, Professor Karkaroff spots Harry and stops and stares in amazement. While he and the Durmstrang students stare at Harry, Professor Moody comes up behind Karkaroff, telling him he is blocking the doorway.

Karkaroff is shocked and apparently frightened at seeing Moody and hurries back to the Durmstrang ship.

In the morning, Harry and Ron go early to the Entrance Hall to see the Goblet. A third-year girl says the Durmstrang students have already entered their names but no one from Hogwarts has yet. Fred, George, and Lee Jordan arrive and try to fool the age line, but fail, Fred and George growing white beards in the process. According to Professor Dumbledore, others have similarly tried and been unsuccessful. Many students place their names in the Goblet throughout the day, including Angelina Johnson, all the Beauxbatons students, and Cedric Diggory. Harry, Ron, and Hermione go to visit Hagrid. Hermione wants to ask Hagrid to join S.P.E.W., so she gathers up her box of badges, and trailing the Beauxbatons students who have just placed their names into the Goblet, they head to Hagrid's hut. Along the way, they discover that the Beauxbatons students are lodging in their giant carriage. Hagrid is quite the sight. He has apparently attempted to tame his wild hair with massive quantities of what looks like axle grease, and he is wearing his best suit. Stunned by Hagrid's finery, Hermione, at a loss for words, asks about the Skrewts. They have begun killing each other, but Hagrid has saved about twenty and is keeping them in separate boxes. They discuss the Tournament. Hagrid knows something about the tasks but can say nothing. He gently declines Hermione's offer to join S.P.E.W., explaining that it is House-elves' nature to serve wizards, and they are happy as they are; it would be a disservice to free them. For the Hallowe'en feast, Hagrid has put on some eau de cologne, but he has rather overdone it. While washing it off in the rain barrel outside, he glimpses Madame Maxime and her students heading to the castle. He hurries off to join her, leaving Harry, Ron, and Hermione alone in his hut to speculate that he must be sweet on Madame Maxime.

Following the feast, the Goblet of Fire selects the three Triwizard Champions. The Goblet has chosen Viktor Krum for Durmstrang. The Beauxbatons champion is Fleur Delacour, the girl Ron suspects is part Veela. The Hogwarts' champion is Cedric Diggory, a Hufflepuff. And then, only a few moments later, the Goblet unexpectedly ejects a fourth name ... Harry Potter.

Analysis

Dumbledore's intention to integrate Beauxbatons and Durmstrang with Hogwarts students to foster lasting friendships and alliances may not be going exactly as planned; divisions are already forming as Durmstrang, which has an affinity for the Dark Arts, mostly fraternizes with Slytherins, while the rather snobbish Beauxbatons align themselves with the intellectual (and presumably more cultured and aloof) Ravenclaws. The visitors appear to take little interest in either the Hufflepuff or Gryffindor Houses, despite Ron's incessant overtures to Durmstrang to join their table and the famous Harry Potter being a Gryffindor. Considering that Voldemort supporters are mostly former Slytherins and Karkaroff may have Death Eater ties, Durmstrang's affiliation with Slytherin House seems inevitable and could potentially benefit Voldemort by recruiting new followers rather than opponents. With this possible connection, it is curious why Durmstrang was invited to compete in the Triwizard competition, although it may not entirely have been Dumbledore's decision, and the Ministry still believes Voldemort is dead and therefore poses no threat. Regardless, Dumbledore must also have a particularly strong faith that Karkaroff has fully renounced any Death Eater ties he may have had. However, it may take some effort on Dumbledore's part to persuade the students to step outside their familiar "comfort zones" and interact with others different from themselves. Although most everyone is surprised that Viktor Krum is a Durmstrang student, Karkaroff seems just as amazed that Harry attends Hogwarts. While this has never been kept secret, it may not be general knowledge outside Great Britain. Durmstrang, however, is far more clandestine. Karkaroff is equally stunned to discover "Mad Eye" Moody at Hogwarts, and, judging from his fearful reaction, it can be assumed that Moody, a former Auror, may be an old nemesis and that Karkaroff, like Snape, has a Death Eater past.

It appears that love, or at least infatuation, is running rampant at Hogwarts. Although little is known about the Hogwarts teachers' personal lives, and all have apparently remained unattached, it seems that the lonely Hagrid may have found love when he becomes smitten with Madame Maxime. And though Madame Maxime is similarly sized to Hagrid, her refined elegance may be at odds with Hagrid's rather uncouth nature, although he is attempting to make a good impression. We are also seeing budding romantic feelings in Harry, Ron, and Hermione, among others. Hagrid's refusal to join S.P.E.W. is interesting for two reasons. First, Hagrid shows that many wizards believe House-elves are treated well and generally are happy with their station in life. And secondly, Hagrid says that it is in House-elves nature to serve wizards. This could imply that House-elves may have freely entered into servitude, but at some point in history, wizards could have gained an advantage that allowed them to turn elves into slaves. This may have been achieved through selective breeding and magical mind manipulation. It is also possible Elves became domesticated naturally over time. Despite how this relationship evolved, we will see in later chapters that House-elves seem genuinely happiest when they have masters to serve, which apparently confirms what Hagrid is saying here. It is debatable then as to how well House-elves could, or would, adapt to sudden and unexpected new-found freedom.

Questions

Review 1. What might account for Ron's attraction to Fleur Delacour? 2. Why has Hagrid suddenly changed his appearance?

Further Study 1. Why does Karkaroff have such a strong reaction to seeing "Mad Eye" Moody at Hogwarts?

2. It is no secret that Harry is a Hogwarts student. Why is Karkaroff so surprised to see him there?

3. How could Harry's name have been placed into the Goblet of Fire? Why would someone want to enter him?

4. Why does Hagrid decline Hermione's request to join S.P.E.W.?

5. Why do Beauxbaton students prefer to sit at Ravenclaw's table while Durmstrang seats themselves with Slytherin in the Great Hall? What does this say about the foreign students and also about the Gryffindor and Hufflepuff Houses?

6. Why does Ron invite Durmstrang students to sit with Gryffindor but ignores Beauxbatons?

7. Why does Ron feel it is permissible for him to be attracted to Fleur, but becomes upset when he suspects Hermione notices someone?

Greater Picture

While initially it may seem that Harry and Krum, who are equally famous in the Wizarding world, would consider each other rivals, for Harry, having someone as well-known as himself at Hogwarts actually helps lessen the unwanted spotlight that constantly shines on him. And though Krum may relish fame while Harry shuns it, Krum is secure enough as a person, as well as being a gracious guest, that he never attempts to undermine Harry. Although Harry and Krum generally ignore one another, at least initially, there appears to be no animosity or resentment between them, and they will eventually establish a friendly relationship. It should be noted that Harry and Krum's celebrity is quite different and almost opposite from one another. Destiny forced fame upon Harry as an infant, and ever since, his life has been dictated by that fate rather than from his own deliberate actions or desires. He has, however, learned to make choices from within that predetermined scenario. In contrast, Krum, a gifted athlete, consciously chose his own path and made calculated decisions that led to his becoming an idolized world-class Quidditch player. He also did so from an age when he better understood the realities and consequences of achieving his goals. It is perhaps these differences that allow Harry and Krum to become friendly competitors rather than bitter opponents.

Students are struggling with romantic dilemmas, many for the first time, and their initial awkward attempts at romance are both amusing and painful. Harry, naive about girls in general, experiences his first crush when he is attracted to Cho Chang, who seems to reciprocate his interest but is actually dating someone else. Ginny Weasley, still harboring unrequited feelings for Harry, has apparently accepted that Harry will probably never be interested in her and is moving on. Much to Hermione's irritation, Ron is attracted to Fleur Delacour, who he suspects is part Veela and which may account for his interest in her. And though Ron apparently feels entitled to notice other girls, he becomes resentful and sullen when he suspects Hermione is interested in Cedric Diggory or any other boy, although it is unlikely that he interprets his feelings as jealousy. Unknown to Hermione, someone other than Cedric has cast his amorous eye upon her.

We should note how Dumbledore worded his instructions when the Goblet is initially presented. While he says here that placing one's name in the Goblet constitutes a binding contract, in the next chapter, Crouch will claim that having one's name ejected from the Goblet constitutes a contract. Though Crouch is present at Dumbledore's speech, he does not contradict him. There will be additional commentary on this wording in the next chapter's analysis.

Chapter 17: The Four Champions

Synopsis

The first three Champions' announcements were received with applause, but Harry's name is met with stunned silence. To Professor Dumbledore's repeated summons, Harry silently makes his way to the head table, then joins the other champions, Viktor Krum, Fleur Delacour, and Cedric Diggory in the other room. Ludo Bagman bursts in and introduces Harry as the fourth Triwizard champion. Krum is angry, while Cedric seems nonplussed. Fleur Delacour claims it must be a joke, he is too young, but Bagman replies that the age restriction was never in the previous rules and because his name was selected by the Goblet, he is required to compete. Professor Dumbledore, Mr. Crouch, Madame Maxime, Professor Karkaroff, Professor McGonagall, and Professor Snape enter. Madame Maxime and Professor Karkaroff immediately tax Professor Dumbledore as to how this could have happened. Snape insists Harry must have cheated and that he has broken school rules ever since he arrived at Hogwarts. Dumbledore cuts Snape off, and he asks Harry if he entered his own name or had an older student put it into the Goblet. Harry says he did not. Madame Maxime, convinced he is lying, suggests Dumbledore made a mistake with the age line, although McGonagall disputes this. Karkaroff appeals to the "impartial" judges, Crouch and Bagman. Crouch says the rules are specific, anyone whose name comes from the Goblet is magically bound to compete. Karkaroff demands that they resubmit names into the Goblet until each school has two Champions, but Bagman points out that the Goblet is now extinguished, and it will not reignite until the next Tournament. Karkaroff is threatening to withdraw when Professor Moody enters and reminds Karkaroff that the Durmstrang Champion is bound to compete by the same rules that prevent Harry from quitting. He suggests Harry's name may have been entered in hopes he would die in the Tournament and says someone must have used powerful magic to hoodwink the Goblet into believing Harry was the sole competitor from a fourth school. Karkaroff accuses Moody of looking for plots where none exist

Dumbledore interrupts the heated debate, saying their path is clear; all four Champions must compete. Madame Maxime protests, but when Dumbledore asks for alternatives, she has none. Dumbledore asks Mr. Crouch to brief the Champions on the first task. Looking rather wearied, Mr. Crouch says the first task will test their daring, but they will not be told what it is. It takes place the 24th of November, they are not allowed to ask for or accept help from their teachers, and will be armed with only their wands. Champions will be excused from end-of-year exams, as the Tasks are so difficult.

Seeming concerned by Crouch's appearance, Dumbledore invites Mr. Crouch to spend the night at the

Chapter 17: The Four Champions

castle, but he declines. Dumbledore offers the same invitation to Karkaroff and Madame Maxime, but they are already departing with their respective Champions. Dumbledore suggests Harry and Cedric head to their Houses so they can join the parties that are probably in progress.

On his way to Gryffindor tower, Harry thinks about Moody's words; someone entered him into the Tournament to put him into harm's way. The obvious candidate is Voldemort, and Harry remembers from his dream that Voldemort is apparently plotting to somehow kill him—but how? His musings are cut short when he reaches the Common room. There he immediately becomes the center of a grand celebration, into which his repeated protestations that he did not enter the Tournament are ignored. As quickly as he can, he retreats to his dormitory where he finds Ron. Ron asks the same question, wondering if it was the Cloak that got him across the age line. When Harry repeats that he never put his name into the Goblet, Ron is affronted that Harry refuses to tell him the "truth." Harry is left facing the closed curtains of one of the few people he thought would believe him.

Analysis

Harry is stunned, but also fearful, when his name is mysteriously selected by the Goblet of Fire, and he once again finds himself mired in unwanted attention and suspicious activities. The Goblet has determined that Harry must compete in the Tournament, disregarding his wishes and overriding the careful precautions and strict rules implemented by the Ministry of Magic, showing how little control they occasionally have over magical matters. Nearly everyone suspects Harry cheated to enter, although reactions are mixed. At this chapter's end, it seems Dumbledore is the only Tournament official who outwardly believes that someone other than Harry entered him, though Moody, who suspects there is a dark plot to murder Harry, and possibly McGonagall, seem to share his opinion. Karkaroff and Madame Maxime, the foreign outsiders, are certain that Dumbledore and the Ministry rigged the Tournament in Hogwarts' favor, while Mr. Crouch only seems concerned about following the rules. Ludo Bagman apparently views the upheaval as vastly amusing. Harry may have other concerns; although he is a talented young wizard, he is several years younger than the other champions and lacks the experience and advanced training they have. He will have to work hard to master new spells they likely already know. Meanwhile, Ron, who continues to fawn over Viktor Krum, grows increasingly resentful over Harry's celebrity, although Ron is perhaps bothered more by his own perceived inability to stand out in any significant way. Ron believes Harry somehow bypassed the age restriction line and, unconcerned whether or not Harry cheated, feels betrayed because he thinks Harry did not confide in him. Despite Harry's unfaltering friendship and confidence in him, Ron convinces himself that Harry is only concerned with seeking more fame and attention, further straining their friendship.

Bartemius Crouch's odd behavior should be noted. He appears to be acting woodenly and unable to display even the minimal fluidity that he normally has. In particular:

- Mr. Crouch states that if someone's name is ejected from the Goblet, they are required to compete in the Tournament. The rule-book wording almost certainly states that any person entering their name into the Goblet must compete if they are selected. The previous evening, Professor Dumbledore had mentioned to the students that, "The placing of your name in the Goblet constitutes a binding magical contract"; however, Mr. Crouch neglects to mention this.

- Mr. Crouch avoids firelight, possibly to prevent people from seeing him acting differently than usual, and he says almost nothing; when he does step into the light, he looks old and tired, possibly ill, to the point where Dumbledore is concerned.

- Mr. Crouch declines a drink, making a thin excuse to leave Hogwarts.

- Professor Moody appears in the room very quickly, in theory to keep a closer eye on Karkaroff, but quite possibly to keep a better handle on the situation unfolding with Mr. Crouch.

It should also be mentioned that Karkaroff is, at least in Moody's eyes, a suspicious character. Though Harry has not yet had this confirmed, he is beginning to suspect that Karkaroff was, or still is, a Death Eater. In the previous chapter, Karkaroff was stunned to see Harry at Hogwarts; Moody seems to think that there might be buried hatred, or perhaps not buried so deeply.

Questions

Review   1. Why are some Tournament officials (Snape, Karkaroff, Madame Maxine, etc.) convinced Harry cheated or refuse to consider that he might be an innocent victim?

2. Why does Ron believe that Harry really entered his own name in the Goblet? Has Harry ever lied to Ron before?

3. Why aren't the Champions told what the first task will be?

Further Study   1. Professor Dumbledore is very careful in his questions: he asks if Harry put his own name into the Goblet, or had an older student do it for him. Why did he not ask him if a non-student did this?

2. Why did Dumbledore not comment when Mr. Crouch gave a different interpretation of the rules than Dumbledore had the previous evening?

3. Why is Mr. Crouch only concerned with following the rules, rather than investigating that the Tournament may have been tampered with or there could be a plot against Harry?

4. Why does Ludo Bagman seem unconcerned about Harry being mysteriously entered into the Tournament?

GREATER PICTURE

We will find, early in the next chapter, that it is not only Dumbledore and Moody who believe Harry was entered into this contest against his will. Hagrid and Hermione also are convinced that Harry was railroaded into it. It is interesting to note the reason for this conclusion: Harry's expression revealed that it was an unwelcome and utter surprise when his name was called. Ron, watching Harry at the same time, failed to perceive what Hermione did; this is another indication, if one is needed, of Ron's jealousy and resentment adding to his already ongoing lack of emotional sensitivity. There is, of course, a very good reason why Moody believes Harry from the very beginning. Ludo Bagman has no involvement in the plot to enter Harry into the Triwizard Tournament, but he immediately uses the upset as an opportunity to make money by betting heavily on Harry to win. It is probable that Ludo hopes to win enough to pay off his gambling debts from the Quidditch World Cup. And though Ludo will continually offer Harry advice to help win each challenge, Harry always refuses. Unknown to Harry, however, others are secretly working to ensure his victory.

It is also interesting how easily "Moody" stays in character. Barty probably had little time to study the real Moody before overpowering him and assuming his identity; yet he always acts in an extremely convincing manner and knows things that only Moody would. Additionally, he is, to a certain extent, controlling the real Moody while in character. It is possible, although unlikely, that there is some Legilimency going on here; at the book's conclusion, Barty is easily captured, and, arguably, if he were a Legilimens, he would have been reading Harry's mind, and seen what Harry saw in the foe-glass. It is much more likely that, apart from having the real Moody under the Imperius curse, he is periodically dosing the real Moody with Veritaserum and quizzing him on what he knows. Not only does Barty remain in character as Moody so well, he continually shows a rather twisted sense of humor while doing it. As Moody, he theorizes that there is a "dark plot" against Harry, all while knowing that anything he says is the actual truth, and that everyone will either write him off as being over-reactive and paranoid or unable to prove anything. It is a large clue that it is Moody who suggests how the Goblet was hoodwinked, since, as it turns out, that is what happened, and it was he who had done it.

It should be noted that both Moody and Barty would suspect Karkaroff, Moody because Karkaroff was once a Death Eater, and Barty because, once captured, Karkaroff had named other Death Eaters to save his own skin. Thus Moody distrusting Karkaroff is an easy part for Barty to play.

Chapter 18: The Weighing of the Wands

SYNOPSIS

Harry wakes up feeling miserable and wanting to talk with Ron, but his bed is empty. He gets dressed and heads to breakfast. Everyone in the Gryffindor Common room cheers as Harry enters, so he heads out the portrait hole. Hermione arrives bearing toast and asks him to take a walk with her. Wanting to avoid the crowd in the Great Hall, Harry accepts. As they stroll around the lake, Hermione says she knew Harry did not enter, from his shocked look when his name was announced. Ron, however, is unconvinced; he is jealous over Harry's fame. Hermione suggests Harry write Sirius about what has happened, though Harry worries that it could risk getting Sirius arrested. Hermione says he will learn about it anyway, and Harry's being in the Tournament may already be in the Daily Prophet. When Harry finishes the letter, Hedwig flies down to deliver it. Sirius had earlier warned Harry that Hedwig is too recognizable, so Harry instead uses a school owl; Hedwig, offended, turns her back on Harry.

During lessons, Harry is unable to avoid other students, and Herbology with the Hufflepuffs is particularly tense. Their House seldom receives any glory, and they feel Harry is stealing what little they had. In Care of Magical Creatures with the Slytherins, Draco Malfoy is his usual insulting self, but he is interrupted by Hagrid telling the students that the Skrewts need exercising. Each student is given a Skrewt on a leash. The Skrewts are now so large that they drag the students around the lawn. Hagrid takes Harry aside to ask if he knows who entered his name. Harry, relieved Hagrid believes him, admits he does not.

Draco's taunts are becoming extremely pointed, and his attacks peak when he starts distributing lapel buttons that alternately display slogans reading, "Support Cedric Diggory—the Real Hogwarts Champion" or "Potter Stinks." When a duel erupts between Harry and Draco, their spells collide in mid-air, hitting two by-standers: Hermione and Goyle. Ron is aghast at Hermione's injury. Professor Snape appears, demanding to know what is going on. He sends Goyle to the Hospital Wing, but claims to see nothing wrong with Hermione, who leaves in tears. Harry and Ron both shout at Snape over his indifferent treatment towards Hermione. When the echoes die away, Snape penalizes Gryffindor House fifty points and Harry and Ron each receive a detention.

In Potions, Snape begins lecturing about antidotes, saying that they will be testing one in class. Colin Creevey enters, saying that Harry has been summoned by Ludo Bagman. The Champions are to have their pictures taken. With ill grace, Snape releases Harry, who follows Colin to a small classroom where Ludo Bagman, a photographer, a witch Harry has never seen before, and the other champions are waiting. Bagman tells Harry this is the Wand Weighing ceremony, to verify that their wands are in good working order. Bagman introduces the witch as Rita Skeeter, a reporter writing a story for the *Daily Prophet*. Rita takes Harry aside into a broom closet and, producing a Quick-Quotes Quill, starts interviewing him. Harry answers as best he can, but notices that the Quill records his comments inaccurately. Before he can do anything about it, the closet door opens and Professor Dumbledore asks Rita to allow Harry to return, as the wand weighing is about to start.

Back in the classroom with the five judges—Bagman, Mr. Crouch, Igor Karkaroff, Madame Maxime, and Professor Dumbledore, the Champions are introduced to

Chapter 18: The Weighing of the Wands

Mr. Ollivander. Ollivander examines the four Champions' wands. First up is Fleur, whose wand is rosewood and contains a Veela hair in its core, which Fleur says is her grandmother's. Ollivander goes on to test Cedric's wand (ash and unicorn's tail hair), Krum's (hornbeam and dragon heartstring), and Harry's (holly and phoenix feather). Ollivander declares them all in perfect working order. The Daily Prophet photographer makes a big fuss over taking the Champions' pictures with the judges. Afterwards, Harry goes to dinner, and returning to his dormitory, finds Ron, who tells him he has received an owl. He also says that their detentions are set for tomorrow night in Snape's dungeon. When he leaves, Harry wants to chase after him, but Sirius' letter is a greater lure. Sirius writes that he has more to say than is safe by owl post, and he asks Harry to be alone by the Gryffindor fireplace at 1:00 a.m on 22 November. He adds that Harry's participation in the Tournament is risky, but he should be safe as long as Dumbledore and Moody are there. However, Sirius believes someone wants to harm Harry.

Analysis

Harry has become a near outcast among many students, especially Hufflepuff, who seldom excel in anything and now feel that Harry has deliberately undermined their Champion, Cedric Diggory, thus lessening their House's chances for acclaim. The only student who believes someone else entered him in the Tournament is Hermione. Harry feels alienated, just as he did during his second year when many believed he was the Heir of Slytherin and responsible for the attacks on Muggle-borns. At least Ron was on his side then, but without his support now, his peers' disdain is almost unbearable. Ironically, even though most Gryffindor students believe Harry cheated to enter the Tournament, they are ecstatic that a Champion represents their House, contentedly basking in Harry's reflected glory and unperturbed with how or why he was entered. They also seem unconcerned or oblivious that Harry could be in mortal danger. And though Harry is uncomfortable at having more unwanted attention heaped on him and upset over being called a cheater, especially by Ron, he is nonetheless excited about competing in the Tournament; it is an opportunity to impress Cho Chang.

Hagrid and Hermione also believe that Harry has been railroaded into the Tournament. It is interesting to note Hermione's reason for her conclusion: she could see from Harry's shocked expression when his name was announced that it was an unwelcomed and utter surprise. Ron was also watching Harry, but he failed to perceive what Hermione did; this is another indication, if one is needed, of Ron's immaturity and ongoing lack of emotional sensitivity. The widening rift with Ron actually brings Harry closer to Hermione. Although Harry has always considered her a close friend, he has never felt quite the same about Hermione as he does Ron. This is hardly surprising, as Harry would naturally feel more at ease among his own gender. Now, however, Hermione not only fills a void, but assumes a new role, demonstrating her unwavering loyalty, trust, and support while never doubting Harry's word as others often do, including Ron. Despite Hermione's somewhat overbearing and bossy nature, she is always concerned over Harry and Ron's well-being; she offers solid, logical, if overly cautious, advice, although Harry and Ron have tended to be dismissive, especially if it interfered with their (sometimes prohibited) activities. Without Ron's presence, however, Harry is more receptive to her input. And though Harry has yet to consider Hermione fully equal to Ron, her trust and loyalty never falter throughout the entire series. Hermione and Harry also share much in common: both were raised as Muggles, learning about their magical abilities late in childhood and having to adapt to a strange, new world. Also, each being an only-child creates a stronger bond between them, and they gradually, and perhaps unknowingly, become as brother and sister, whereas Ron, who has many siblings, mostly considers Harry a "best friend."

Harry has his first encounter with Rita Skeeter, a reporter he already knows by her less-than-stellar reputation. She immediately isolates Harry for an interview, rendering him virtually powerless as she pumps him for information and purposely misquotes him, despite his protests; even before interviewing Harry, she has apparently pre-fabricated just how he will be portrayed in her embarrassingly inaccurate article in which she mentions nothing about the other Champions, causing Harry further despair. Skeeter not only shows here how a single individual can abuse the truth, causing immense personal damage, but she also represents how easily a powerful entity like the news media can insidiously manipulate the general public's opinions and perceptions with calculated lies and manufactured misconceptions on a much grander scale.

The analysis of Fleur's wand confirms Ron's suspicions that she is part Veela. The hair forming its core belonged to her grandmother, making her one-quarter Veela.

Questions

Review 1. Why does Hermione encourage Harry to write to his godfather, despite the risk to Sirius?

2. Why is Hufflepuff House particularly upset that Harry is a Triwizard Champion?

3. Why are the wands weighed and inspected?

4. Why does Sirius think it is safe for Harry to compete in the Tournament, even though he believes someone wants to harm him?

Further Study 1. Why are Gryffindor students so ecstatic that Harry is a Champion, even though they believe he cheated to enter the Tournament? Why do most other Hogwarts students treat him as an outcast?

2. Considering her reputation, why is Rita Skeeter allowed to interview the Champions?

3. Why does Snape send Goyle to the Hospital Wing, but not Hermione? Why is she so upset?

GREATER PICTURE

The author once again draws the reader's attention to Snape teaching about antidotes. And though Harry dislikes Potions, mostly because Snape makes it so miserable for him, his knowledge about this subject will prove crucial in the sixth book, *Harry Potter and the Half-Blood Prince*.

It should be noted that though a rift developed between Harry and Hermione following Harry's Firebolt being confiscated, it was entirely Harry's decision to avoid her; Hermione has stayed a true friend to Harry throughout, and will continue to do so until the series' end. In this chapter Ron has allowed jealousy to create a rift between him and Harry, and it continues until Ron realizes Harry's life really is at risk. During their secret mission in *Harry Potter and the Deathly Hallows*, Ron will desert Harry and Hermione, on what might be considered petty matters, keeping Trio separated for some months. It is reasonable to assume that Ron's behavior is intended to reflect his character and immaturity relative to Harry and Hermione.

Chapter 19: The Hungarian Horntail

SYNOPSIS

When the shock of being a Champion wears off, Harry starts worrying about the first task. It is comforting that he will soon talk with Sirius, and he and Hermione figure out ways to clear the common room before 1:00 A.M. But things become more difficult for him after Rita Skeeter's story about the Tournament is published. Unfortunately, it mostly contains embarrassing and false information about Harry, including that he and Hermione are in love. Harry hopes he and Ron will reconcile during detention with Professor Snape, but it is the same day that the article comes out, fueling Ron's belief that Harry only seeks more publicity. About the only high point is when Cho Chang stops by to wish him luck. But even then, he gets off on the wrong foot, snapping at her because he mistakenly thinks she is also poking fun at him.

Harry is still having difficulty mastering the Summoning charm, and he practices it with Hermione in the library. Curiously, and to Hermione's annoyance, Victor Krum seems to frequently be in there, along with a clutch of girls following him about, hoping to get his autograph.

The Saturday before the first task is a Hogsmeade weekend. Hermione suggests they go, and, when pressed, admits she is hoping to meet up with Ron in the Three Broomsticks. Harry vetoes that part of the idea, and says he will go but only under his Invisibility Cloak. Hermione protests but agrees, and once he is in Hogsmeade, Harry is delighted he can travel without people hurling snide remarks at him. Hermione says he should remove the cloak because there is nobody there who will bother him, but Harry points out that Rita Skeeter and her photographer just left the Three Broomsticks. It appears she is staying in the village. Harry suggests she is there to watch the First Task.

Hermione steers them into The Three Broomsticks, telling Harry he does not have to talk to Ron, who is sitting with Fred, George and Lee Jordan. Hermione brings Harry a Butterbeer, then spreads out her notes about S.P.E.W. to avoid looking silly sitting by herself. They suddenly notice Hagrid. As big as he is, they had overlooked him earlier because he was crouched, talking to Professor Moody. He stands, preparing to leave. Harry waves, then realizes that Hagrid cannot see him, but Moody pokes Hagrid in the back, and they both come over and say hello to Hermione. In an undertone, Moody says "Nice cloak, Potter." Harry realizes that Moody's magical eye can penetrate Invisibility Cloaks. Before leaving, Hagrid asks Harry to be at his hut at midnight with his cloak.

Harry is meeting Sirius by the Gryffindor fireplace that night but decides he can quickly visit Hagrid and be back by 1:00 A.M. At midnight, he slips down to Hagrid's, who takes the cloaked Harry to the Beauxbatons carriage. There he meets Madame Maxime. Harry, very confused, trails behind Hagrid and Madame Maxime around the Forbidden Forest's edge, finally coming to a large corral containing four full-grown dragons. Wizards have to Stun the dragons to calm them. Charlie Weasley, Ron's older brother, comes over to talk to Hagrid. He is concerned about allowing Madame Maxime to see the dragons, but Hagrid says he just thought she would be interested. Harry heads back to the castle, bumping into Professor Karkaroff, who is checking out the tumult. Evidently, assuming Madame Maxime and Professor Karkaroff will talk to their respective Champions, Cedric is the only Champion unaware of the dragons.

Returning to an empty common room, Harry finds Sirius' head floating in the fireplace flames. Harry relates everything that has happened, but Sirius says there are other concerns. Karkaroff, for one, was a Death Eater, but was released from Azkaban, possibly because he provided names to the Ministry. He suggests that could be why Moody is at Hogwarts; it was Moody who arrested Karkaroff. While Skeeter's story implied the attack on Moody the night before he left for Hogwarts was a false alarm, Sirius thinks it was meant to scare Moody from taking the job. And Bertha Jorkins, the Ministry official who vanished in Albania, which is also where Voldemort was last believed to be, would have known about the Tournament and could have somehow tipped off Voldemort. Sirius also says that Stunning spells are ineffective against dragons, but before he can say what would work, Harry hears someone coming down the stairs and warns Sirius to vanish. Ron appears, and he and Harry quarrel, causing Harry to storm off to bed.

ANALYSIS

In his conversation with Sirius, Harry learns that Karkaroff was a Death Eater; he revealed other Death Eaters' names to avoid Azkaban. Moody believes he never really recanted and abandoned Dark magic only because he feared severe punishment. He suspects Karkaroff secretly remains devoted to the Dark Lord and would willingly rejoin Voldemort given the opportunity. When Moody first suggested that someone may have entered Harry into the Tournament in order to kill him, the ensuing silence is possibly because there is an unspoken accusation against Karkaroff. However, Karkaroff had seemed genuinely surprised that Harry was even a student at Hogwarts, indicating he is unlikely involved in a pre-planned plot.

Cedric Diggory being the only Champion who is unaware that the first task involves dragons not only reveals much about his character, but also Hufflepuff House. This House, while seldom receiving much glory or producing many notable students, is known for valuing hard work, honesty, and fairness. It appears, however, that these virtues have put Diggory at a disadvantage here, as the other Champions, including Harry, have uncovered valuable information that make them more competitive. Although the Champions are supposed to perform the tasks without any outside assistance and cheating is strictly prohibited, there seems to be an unspoken tradition and expectation that some underhandedness occurs. Harry, despite being a talented wizard, knows he needs help and freely uses what Hagrid shows him, listens to the (interrupted) advice from Sirius, will take a "hint" from Moody, and is coached by Hermione, all to help him develop a strategy, although it could be argued that this is not technically cheating. Cedric, meanwhile, apparently does little or nothing as he patiently awaits the first event, completely clueless regarding what it entails. Even though Hufflepuff's traits are admirable, their integrity can also breed complacency and naivete, as well as shows a certain lack of ingenuity and initiative, thus allowing their more resourceful (and somewhat devious) opponents to seize the advantage. This may be why Cedric, despite having many outstanding abilities, was sorted into this House.

As Sirius mentions, the supposed attack on Moody at his home, which the Ministry wrote off as a false alarm, actually did occur the night before his departure for Hogwarts and, knowing his paranoid nature, was probably meant to scare him away from there. There is now evidence that Bertha Jorkin's disappearance could be tied to Voldemort, and that he could have somehow extracted information from her (either willingly or unwillingly on her part) about the Triwizard Tournament being held at Hogwarts. Ministry officials, meanwhile, have still not taken any action regarding poor Bertha's whereabouts, continuing to pass it off to her simply "forgetting" to return from her holiday.

QUESTIONS

Review 1. Why is Cedric Diggory the only Champion who is unaware that the first event involves dragons? What does this say about his character and also about Hufflepuff House in general?

2. Why did Harry think Cho Chang was teasing him? Was she?

3. Why does the Ministry believe that the attack at Moody's home was only a "false alarm," while Sirius thinks it was not?

4. Could there be a link between Bertha Jorkins' disappearance and Voldemort's last known whereabouts? Explain.

5. Why does Sirius think Moody was hired as the Defensive Arts teacher?

Further Study 1. Why does Viktor Krum spend so much time at the library? Who does it annoy and why?

2. Why is Harry having so much troubling learning a simple spell like the Summoning charm?

3. Why, after such a long absence, does the Ministry continue to believe that Bertha Jorkins simply "forgot" to come back to work?

4. Could Bertha Jorkins' disappearance be tied to Harry and the Triwizard Tournament, or is the author purposely misleading the reader with false clues? Explain.

GREATER PICTURE

Although Sirius correctly speculates that the incident at Moody's house is somehow tied to Voldemort, he failed to realize that rather than it being an attempt to scare Moody away from Hogwarts, it was actually a kidnapping plot to replace the real Moody with the impostor, Barty Crouch, Jr. If Barty (as Moody) is correct that Karkaroff is still a Death Eater and loyal to Voldemort, he may see him as a potential ally at Hogwarts. However, Voldemort rarely, if ever, forgives those who have betrayed him or his followers, and Barty may well be targeting Karkaroff to avenge his fellow Death Eaters. Curiously, Barty never shares his opinion about Snape.

Early on, Cedric Diggory, a decent and honest young wizard, seems to lack initiative and inventiveness, although this changes as he competes in the Triwizard Tournament. Harry tips off Cedric about the dragons for this first Task, but their situations are reversed in the second challenge when Harry needs another helpful push. A magical Egg, captured by each Champion during the first event, holds a vital clue to completing the next task. However, Harry, who often procrastinates until he is prodded, does little to decipher its hidden meaning while Cedric quickly solves the riddle. In gratitude for Harry's previous help, Cedric gives him a valuable hint. In this case, Cedric's honesty and fairness are not a disadvantage and shows that Hufflepuff's attributes can be used effectively. It is likely that, given time, Cedric's talents would have far exceeded Hufflepuff's usual standards. Unfortunately, this opportunity will tragically be cut short.

Chapter 20: The First Task

SYNOPSIS

The next morning, Harry drags Hermione off for another walk around the lake, during which he relates what he learned from Hagrid and what Sirius told him. They return to the library, looking for a simple spell that will defeat a dragon, but their search is fruitless. Krum's arrival in the library annoys Hermione, and she and Harry return to the Gryffindor Common room.

On Monday, Harry realizes that only Cedric is unaware that the First Task involves dragons. Sending Hermione on ahead, he trails Diggory through the halls. To get him alone, Harry charms Cedric's bag so that it falls apart. When Cedric stops to pick up his belongings, Harry runs up and tells him about the dragons. Cedric asks why Harry is telling him, and he says that both Fleur and Krum know. Professor Moody appears and sends Cedric to class. He takes Harry to his office and commends him for his fairness. He says cheating is also a Tournament tradition. Moody does not tell Harry how to get past the dragon, but tells him he needs to play to his strengths. Harry believes he has none, apart from Quidditch, but Moody says Harry is a darned good flyer. He suggests using a simple spell to *get what he needs*. Harry understands, and he tells Hermione he has to learn how to do a proper Summoning charm before the First Task next afternoon. Hermione is adamant about not missing classes, so they practice through lunch and after dinner. Finally, in the Gryffindor Common room at two in the morning, Harry seems to have the spell working properly.

The concentration needed to learn the spell has eased his nerves, but they come back in full force the next day. Professor McGonagall escorts him onto the grounds for the First Task. Harry sees the dragon enclosure and a tent in front of it. The other champions are already inside, along with Ludo Bagman. Ludo has them draw tokens from a bag. Each token represents the item they will face, and their task is to retrieve a golden Egg. Fleur draws a Welsh Green dragon, number 2; Krum, a Chinese Fireball, number 3; Cedric, a Swedish Short-snout, number 1; and Harry, the Hungarian Horntail, number 4. Harry notices from their reactions that the other champions knew what they were facing. Ludo explains that the numbers are the order in which they will compete. He requests a private word with Harry and asks if he is OK or if there is anything he can get for him. Harry says he is fine, he has a plan. The first whistle sounds for Cedric's Task, and Ludo bolts—he is supposed to be commentating.

The waiting is tortuous. Harry can hear the roaring crowd, and the commentating only tantalizes, but it does not tell him what is happening. Finally, it is his turn. He walks into the enclosure and sees the Hungarian Horntail and the golden egg. He casts the Summoning spell, and, to his surprise, his broom arrives. He flies over the dragon's head, baiting it. When it lunges, he swoops down and grabs the Egg. He is not unscathed; the Horntail's tail tagged him, and he is bleeding. As he is attended to in the first aid tent, Hermione and Ron come in. Ron is finally convinced that Harry never cheated to enter the Tournament. Harry acts aloof, but they eventually reconcile. The judges post Harry's scores: 8, 9, 9, 10 (from Ludo), and 4 (from Karkaroff), tying Harry for first place with Krum. Charlie Weasley runs in to congratulate Harry. He says he has to send an owl to Mrs. Weasley to let her know what happened and mentions that Mr. Bagman wants to see all the Champions back in the tent.

When the champions reassemble, Ludo says the next task will take place at half past nine in the morning of February 24th, and that there is a clue in the golden egg that they have just retrieved. He dismisses them, and Harry and Ron head back to the castle. On the way, they run into Rita Skeeter, who asks Harry for a few words; Harry refuses to comment.

ANALYSIS

Harry attempts to research ways to defeat a dragon, but, in what will become a familiar pattern, he becomes so terrified that he briefly considers running away to the Dursleys, although he quickly abandons this idea. Instead, he accepts help from others, and in this, and nearly all future endeavors, Harry will learn to rely on and trust his friends. This shows that, despite his many talents, he is, in essence, the sum of many parts. And while Harry wants to win the Tournament, he wants to do so without any inequitable advantages. Cedric's ignorance about the Dragons while the other Champions are using ill-gotten information to prepare their strategies represents an uneven playing field to Harry. It would never be a true victory if another Champion was at an unfair disadvantage. Moody commends Harry for his honesty and fairness, which Moody has already shown are traits he values in himself, as well as others. Cedric is also grateful, and it is probably something he himself would have done if their situations had been reversed. A few additional noteworthy points:

First, Moody seems to be handing the First Task to Harry. While it does take Harry some time to realize what Moody is hinting at, Moody has provided Harry a tool that will serve him better than any other Champion. Whether Moody has any special reason for wanting Harry to win is unknown, although it could be motivated by his concern over how and why Harry was entered into the Tournament.

Second, Ludo makes a clumsy attempt to assist Harry with the challenge, then assigns him a perfect score, which Harry feels is unwarranted. It seems Bagman also wants him to win, but why is unclear.

Finally, Rita Skeeter continually appears from nowhere, even though it is learned later that she has been banned from the school.

It should be noted that the action in the book apparently takes place in 1994 and 1995; but the date of the first task, November 24th 1994, is not a Tuesday but a Thursday, which is consistent with the day of the week mentioned in chapter 15. This does not affect the story in any way; the fact that there is this conflict is provided more as a curiosity than as something for the scholar to concern himself with.

QUESTIONS

Review   1. Why does Harry tell Cedric Diggory about the dragons?

2. Why does Moody give Harry advice about the first task? Is Moody breaking the rules?

3. Why does Harry ignore Ludo Bagman's advice and feel that the high score Ludo gives him is unwarranted?

Further Study   1. Why does Ludo Bagman give Harry unsolicited advice and a perfect score?

2. Harry usually masters basic spells quickly. Why then is the Summoning charm so difficult for him to learn?

3. What clue might be hidden in the Golden Egg?

Chapter 21: The House-Elf Liberation Front

Greater Picture

Of note, Harry stops reading the dragon book just before the passage containing the spell he needs. The passage he does read aloud from *Men Who Love Dragons Too Much* goes: "*Dragons are extremely difficult to slay, owing to the ancient magic that imbues their thick hides, which none but the most powerful spells can penetrate.*" The next passage would probably discuss their one weak point, which Sirius later identifies as their eyes. In a later message from Sirius, we learn that if their conversation had not been interrupted, Sirius would have suggested using the Conjunctivitus curse to blind the dragon. This is what Krum did; but the blinded dragon, flailing about, broke some of its own eggs, losing Krum points. Curiously, although Harry observed first-hand how Charlie Weasley and the other handlers subdued and controlled the caged dragons with Stunning spells, he fails to consider how he might use this in his strategy.

We will later learn that Ludo is trying to recoup his losses on the Quidditch World Cup by betting on Harry to win the Tournament. His clumsy attempts to assist Harry, which will be uniformly rejected, are an unethical attempt to influence the Tournament's outcome, made worse because he is a Tournament judge. Moody also intends for Harry to win the Tournament; offering Harry a strategy to complete the First Task is his most overt attempt in his role as a trusted mentor to ensure Harry's victory. Moody's other assistance will be less obvious to Harry, revealed only when Moody explains it after the Third Task.

It is only Harry's inherent honesty and belief in fairness that prompts him to share information about the dragons with Cedric, and also to reject Ludo's proffered assistance. In a future chapter, Cedric rewards Harry for his fairness towards him: when Cedric solves the Egg's riddle, he will pass on an important hint to Harry.

Chapter 21: The House-Elf Liberation Front

Synopsis

Harry, Ron, and Hermione head to the Owlery to send Sirius a letter reporting Harry's progress in the Tournament. On the way, Harry tells Ron what Sirius told him. Ron, like Hermione, is surprised that Karkaroff was a Death Eater. They adjourn to the victory party in the Gryffindor Common room. Harry, prompted by the other Gryffindors, unlatches the Golden Egg. The inside is hollow, but it emits a loud screeching noise, which frightens Neville: he thinks someone is being tortured. Hermione asks Fred if the party food came from the kitchens. He says it did, imitating a House-elf to demonstrate how easy it was to get it. Hermione asks for directions to the kitchen. Fred tells her, and George asks if she is going to lead a House-elves rebellion. Hermione refrains from answering.

The weather is turning cold and miserable. The Beauxbatons horses are getting their preferred drink, single-malt whisky, but the fumes surrounding Hagrid's hut and the Care of Magical Creatures classes is making the class light-headed. They need their wits about them while tending to the Skrewts. Arriving at Hagrid's hut one day, the students find that Hagrid has prepared nesting boxes for the ten remaining to see if they want to hibernate. They do not, preferring to destroy the boxes and rampage around Hagrid's pumpkin patch. As the Trio and Hagrid round up the last one, the remainder of the class having retreated into Hagrid's hut in fear, Rita Skeeter appears and evinces great interest in the Skrewts; she arranges for an interview with Hagrid later in the week.

Harry and Ron, now reconciled, quietly chortle their way through double Divination, annoying Professor Trelawney. Searching for Hermione later, they check the library, finding Krum. They are just about to enter the Common room when Hermione comes running up, talking about a great discovery she has made. She drags Harry and Ron to a ground-floor corridor; Ron asks if this is *spew* business, but Hermione says no, and it is not "spew" anyway. Ron sarcastically asks if it is called the House Elf Liberation Front now? Hermione says it has nothing to do with that, and drags them into the kitchen where Harry is greeted by Dobby. Dobby says that Dumbledore has hired him and Winky to work in the Hogwarts household staff. Dobby has only been there a week. It is hard for a House-elf to get paid work, and since he and Winky decided to look together, they thought Hogwarts was likely the only place that would hire them both. Winky feels disgraced, however, and all the other House-elves in the kitchen have distanced themselves from Dobby: House-elves feel it is demeaning to accept payment. In this conversation, Winky, who is crying, says she believes her master, Mr. Crouch, is a good wizard, but she does not understand how he is getting along without her. She also says Ludo Bagman is a bad wizard, but she will not divulge why, saying she always keeps her masters' secrets, despite Dobby reminding her that he is no longer her master.

Hermione is pleased that Dobby is there. She thinks that if the other Elves see how happy a free Elf is, they may eventually adopt the idea. Harry thinks Winky might prove to be a counter-example, but Hermione says, uncertainly, that she will cheer up as she adapts.

Analysis

Harry's victory in the first task has helped to lighten his mood considerably, despite the ongoing fears he suffers over his safety and Sirius' freedom. He thoroughly enjoys himself at the Gryffindor celebration, momentarily forgetting his worries while being swept up in his classmates' jubilation. But it is his and Ron's reconciliation that is most meaningful to him. Without Ron's friendship and support, facing the ongoing adversity and uncertainty in his life was nearly unbearable. Unfortunately, it took Harry nearly being killed in the first task for Ron to realize that Harry never cheated or lied, prompting Ron to reconcile with him. This may be a small turning point in Ron's maturation, being able to admit he was wrong and accepting that his abilities and strengths, if he strives to recognize and develop them, will always be different from Harry's.

Neville's terrified reaction to the screeching Egg (believing someone is being tortured) is similar to how he behaved when Professor Moody demonstrated the Cruciatus curse in class; readers learned it is an illegal torturing method. There may may be a connection between these two incidents.

Rita Skeeter constantly appearing as if from nowhere is highly suspicious, not only considering Hogwarts' tight security during the Tournament, but also because it is impossible to Disapparate in or out of the castle and its grounds. Upon seeing her, Ron wonders how she was able to enter despite being banned from Hogwarts, although readers should consider how several other characters have been able to access or exit secure areas undetected. However, preventing Skeeter from interviewing Hagrid quickly becomes a more pressing concern. This is the first time Hogwarts' kitchen has been seen; like many places in the castle, it is hidden. Not even Dumbledore knows all Hogwarts' secrets, and it is to the Twins' credit that they uncovered its location. However, visiting the kitchen provides Hermione a reality check when she witnesses first-hand just how truly satisfied House-elves are with their indentured lives, at least those at Hogwarts. They are quite literally "happy slaves" who believe their only purpose in life is to freely serve wizards, and they are resistant to change. The only exceptions are Dobby and Winky, who the other House-elves disdain for being paid workers. While Dobby is proud to be a free agent, Winky is ashamed and despondent that she no longer has a wizard family to call her own; as a result, she has become a sad, pathetic alcoholic, still pining for her former master, Mr. Crouch, who cruelly and unjustly dismissed her. Hermione has seen how freedom created immense hardship for Dobby and Winky, and knows how few opportunities there are available for masterless House-elves. Dobby, by his own report, spent a year-and-a-half seeking work; and while the clever Dobby is resourceful and adaptable, Winky likely would never have sought other employment on her own, and, without Dobby's help, probably would have suffered a miserable demise. Only Dumbledore's kindness has saved them both. Regardless, Hermione remains passionately, though rather naively, committed to liberating House-elves, though she gives little thought to just how they can be integrated into the general wizarding population.

QUESTIONS

Review 1. Why does Hermione want directions to the kitchen?

2. Why did Dumbledore hire Dobby and Winky?

3. Why do the other House-elves shun Dobby and Winky?

4. Why would Rita Skeeter want to interview Hagrid about Skrewts?

5. Why does Winky remain so loyal to the Crouch family, despite being wrongly fired by Mr. Crouch?

Further Study 1. Why would Neville think someone is being tortured when he hears the screeching Egg?

2. How can an unintelligible screeching sound be a clue? What might it mean?

3. Why would the kitchen's location be kept secret? How might the Twins have found it?

4. Why might Winky believe that Ludo Bagman is a bad wizard?

GREATER PICTURE

Given Neville's extreme reaction during Moody's Cruciatus Curse demonstration in Defence Against the Dark Arts class, it is hardly surprising that he believes someone is being tortured when he hears the screeching Egg. In a later chapter, Harry accidentally learns that when Neville was a small child, Death Eaters (including Barty Crouch, Jr.) tortured Neville's parents, Frank and Alice Longbottom, into insanity with the Cruciatus Curse. Their condition is irreversible, and they are permanently committed to St. Mungo's Hospital, where Neville regularly visits them. Neville has never revealed this to anyone, and it is why he lives with his grandmother. Harry will keep Neville's secret to himself, until it is accidentally revealed to Ron, Hermione, and Ginny; this revelation will help create a stronger bond between the two boys.

While Winky's role in the story at this point is somewhat slim, when Barty Crouch Jr. reappears, she will be able to confirm his true identity. Though she does not actually corroborate his story regarding his actions, her presence and her reactions to his account lend truth to his revelations. However, Winky's main purpose here is to highlight Hermione's uphill battle in getting better treatment for House-elves.

Winky's belief that Bagman is a bad wizard will have come from her previous master, Mr. Crouch. Sirius will shortly tell us that Bagman was tried for passing information to Voldemort but was acquitted; Harry, later, will see Bagman's acquittal in Dumbledore's Pensieve. In Dumbledore's memory, Harry will note that Crouch seems disgruntled that Bagman goes unconvicted; he seems to think that Bagman's fame and charisma saves him from Azkaban. Likely he carried that opinion home with him, and Winky adopted it.

Readers may have noticed that Rita Skeeter has somehow reappeared on the school grounds, despite being banned. We will eventually discover that Skeeter is an unregistered Animagus, and likely is entering Hogwarts in her beetle form.

Chapter 22: The Unexpected Task

SYNOPSIS

In Transfiguration class, Professor McGonagall announces that there is a Yule Ball; afterward, she takes Harry aside, and tells him that the Champions and their partners traditionally open the first dance. Ignoring his protests, McGonagall sternly tells Harry that as a Champion he represents Hogwarts, and he is expected to find a date, learn to dance, and be prepared to lead the schools into the Ball on 25 December.

The Ball is now only one month away. Harry wants to invite Cho Chang, but unable to ever find her alone, he wonders why girls always travel in packs. Ron is also having difficulty finding a date, but he fails to understand why Harry is having trouble—he is a Champion after all. Soon, girls start inviting Harry, including a fifth-year who is significantly taller than him. Life in general seems a bit easier; there are less *Support Cedric Diggory* buttons visible now and fewer people are laughing at Draco's repetitive slurs. Harry suspects Cedric told his supporters to lay off him.

Rita Skeeter's story about Hagrid has not yet appeared. During Care of Magical Creatures class, Hermione asks Hagrid how the interview with Skeeter went. Hagrid says that she mostly asked about Harry, wanting to know negative things about him. Ron speculates that she is looking for a new angle to her Harry stories. Ron asks if Hagrid is coming to the Ball, and he responds that he intends to drop by for at least a short while. The week before the Yule Ball is rather tumultuous; many teachers, including Professor Flitwick, have stopped teaching classes, although Professor Binns continues to plough through the Goblin Rebellions, and Professor Snape schedules a test on antidotes for the last day of class. Hermione scolds Harry for neglecting the Egg riddle, but Harry lazily brushes her off, insisting there is still plenty of time. Hermione warns that it could take weeks to figure it out, and he will look foolish if the other Champions have solved it and he has not. When Ron defends Harry, Hermione makes a mocking comment about his hideous dress robes. As they bemoan Snape's lack of Christmas spirit, the Weasley twins appear and ask Ron if they can borrow Pigwidgeon. Ron asks Fred who he is taking to the Ball, who responds he is going with Angelina Johnson. Fred and George then take off to get a school owl.

On the last day of term, Harry and Ron still lack Yule Ball dates. They decide to just grit their teeth and do it. Harry's concentration is shot, and he misses a crucial ingredient in his antidote potion—a bezoar—and receives bottom marks. Running off, he finds Cho coming from class and asks her for a private word. Nervous, awkward, and barely coherent, he invites her to the Ball. Embarrassed, she says she is sorry, but that she is already going with Cedric Diggory.

Utterly defeated, Harry skips dinner and returns to the Gryffindor common room. There he finds Ron looking as bad as he feels. Ginny informs Harry that Ron had just asked Fleur Delacour, who was talking to Cedric Diggory and did not even bother to respond. Harry tells Ron she was probably trying to get Cedric to invite her, but Cedric is going with Cho. Ron says that Neville asked Hermione and was turned down. Ron suggests that if he and Harry are unable to find any girls other than "trolls," then they can always ask Hermione and Ginny to go. Hermione angrily responds that she is unavailable and leaves. Ginny says she is unable to be Harry's date because she is going with Neville, although she looks miserable as she leaves for dinner. Harry sees Parvati Patil and Lavender Brown come in. Harry, now somewhat desperate, invites Parvati. She accepts. He also asks Lavender if she will go with Ron, but she is already going with Seamus. Parvati says her sister, Padma, has not been asked yet, and might be willing. Harry feels that this whole Ball thing is far more work than it is worth.

Analysis

The Twins are corresponding with someone again; one suspects that they are having little success. When they ask to borrow Pigwidgeon, he is unavailable, having not yet returned from delivering a letter to Sirius. Interestingly, Pigwidgeon takes three weeks for the round trip, even though Sirius is in England.

For Harry, finding Yule Ball dates for him and Ron could be considered "the fourth Triwizard Task," as well as the most daunting. Like most adolescents entering their teen dating years, Hogwarts students are discovering that male-female social relationships are not only complicated, but filled with awkward and embarrassing moments, as well as painful rejections. Although girls are vying to go with him, Harry's inability to adeptly navigate most social situations leaves him either oblivious or disinterested, and he somewhat rudely rebuffs their attention. When he asks Lavender to go with Ron, she giggles—a trait Harry finds annoying and feels should be outlawed. While it is too early for any inference to be made, this may foreshadow Ron and Lavender possibly being paired later. Ron, who is even more socially immature than Harry, is content to let Harry find him a partner after his own miserable attempts failed. When Harry reveals Fleur's Veela ancestry to Ron, he shows little interest, probably because he is still distraught over humiliating himself with her. Ron also invoked Hermione's ire after insultingly suggesting that she and Ginny could go to the Ball as his and Harry's dates only so they can avoid going with "trolls." Ron is stunned that someone has invited Hermione, although she refuses to reveal who, further incensing Ron. A relationship may be blossoming between Harry and Cho Chang, and, despite his nervous and clumsy invitation, it appears that she was hoping he would ask her to the Ball. Cho genuinely seemed embarrassed and disappointed that she had already accepted Cedric Diggory's invitation. Harry, also disappointed, now feels some rivalry and resentment towards Cedric, emotions previously absent and that actually could help increase Harry's competitiveness.

Harry's faults are also on display here: Although he is disappointed when Cho turns down him down, his reluctance and procrastination in asking her may have been partially responsible, resulting in her accepting Cedric Diggory's invitation. Harry also shows laziness by ignoring the Egg riddle, continually telling others he nearly has it worked out when he has not even begun to work on it. When Hermione chastises him for avoiding it, he defends himself, saying there is still time, never considering that even if he solves it before the next task, there may be additional steps he must prepare for.

Ginny, in this chapter, shows she has matured significantly from the shy, timid, quiet girl we knew in the second book. When Ron starts poking fun at Neville for asking Hermione to the Ball, and indirectly mocks Hermione, apparently to make himself feel a bit better, Ginny has the courage to tell him to stop. Later, when Hermione arrives, Ginny tells her out loud that Harry and Ron were unable to get dates for the Ball. This shows increasing confidence in herself, and significantly less fear of speaking in Harry's presence. Unlike Hermione, however, Ginny appears quite miserable at having to forgo Ron's suggestion that she be Harry's date, even if it is as a "last resort." She may feel that by having accepted Neville's invitation she has missed her chance to be more to Harry than just "Ron's kid sister." Regardless, a more mature, more forward Ginny is firmly established in this scene, and her increased popularity among the series' fans seems to have started here. This new-found assertiveness shows that she is a true Gryffindor.

Although the Trio seems unconcerned about Rita Skeeter's interview with Hagrid, they should perhaps have paid more attention to the "red flags" that are raised by her particular questions.

Also, a bezoar stone has been seen before and will be mentioned again. Rowling could be focusing readers' attention on it for a reason, although it may not be significant in this book. Seemingly insignificant people or mundane objects that are spotlighted early on, often become important later in the series.

QUESTIONS

Review 1. Why is it so difficult for Harry to find a Yule Ball date despite so many girls wanting to go with him?
2. Why did Harry wait so long to invite Cho Chang?
3. Why does Harry finally decide to invite Parvati to the Ball?
4. Why does Ron tease Neville for having invited Hermione to the Ball?

Further Study 1. Why does Ginny look miserable after telling Ron she is going to the Ball with Neville?
2. How might things have turned out differently if Ginny was not Neville's date?
3. Why does Ginny stand up to Ron? What accounts for her new-found confidence?
4. Why doesn't Hermione tell anyone who her date for the Ball is? Who might her date be?
5. Why didn't Ron invite Hermione as his date early on? Did Ron expect anyone (other than Neville) to ask her? Would she have accepted Ron's invitation?

GREATER PICTURE

The Twin's correspondent is probably Ludo Bagman, who has avoided paying them their winnings with real money. He originally paid them off in Leprechaun gold, and they will end up writing it off as a bad job when Ludo, having lost another bet to the Goblins, runs; but for the moment, they still hope to collect. Ron will spend nearly the entire Yule Ball either glowering at Hermione or refusing to dance with Padma. This may further ruin any chance he had with either, particularly Hermione, although Ron still fails to recognize that their frequent spats are mostly fueled with romantic tension.

Ginny's new-found confidence is partially due to Hermione's influence. Ginny had confided her feelings about Harry to Hermione, who encouraged Ginny to just be herself around him. Ginny is beginning to put Hermione's advice into action in this chapter, but it will take some time for her to overcome her shyness and the tension she feels around Harry. At the Yule Ball, for instance, which she is attending with Neville, she will meet, and agree to date, Michael Corner. Her relationship with Michael allows her to give up hope that Harry will ever reciprocate her feelings. Only then does she feel relaxed enough to show her true self around him, allowing Harry to know the girl she really is. Paradoxically, then, it will be Ginny's giving up hope of winning Harry that will allow her, finally, to win him.

The bezoar, which made its first appearance in *Harry Potter and the Philosopher's Stone*, and Harry's knowledge about it, plays a significant role in *Harry Potter and the Half-Blood Prince*.

Chapter 23: The Yule Ball

SYNOPSIS

Although it is the end of term, almost no one has left school, and despite his homework load, Harry enjoys himself in the week between the term's end and Christmas. Ron is still trying to learn who Hermione's Yule Ball date is, but she says nothing. Ron also notices that her teeth are different; Hermione explains that after Draco's misfired spell made her teeth bigger, she had Madam Pomfrey shrink them to smaller than their original large size. While she is explaining this, Pigwidgeon returns with Sirius' letter. A group of thirteen-year-old girls see Pigwidgeon and think he's cute, which leads Ron to call him a "stupid, feathery git." In the message, Sirius congratulates Harry and says that he would have suggested a Conjunctivitus spell to blind the dragon. He warns Harry to watch himself around Karkaroff. Hermione suggests this is a good time to try and figure out the Egg's secret, but Harry says he would not be able to hear it over the ruckus in the common room.

On Christmas day, Harry is awakened by Dobby bringing him presents. To reciprocate, Harry gives Dobby the horrible mustard-colored socks that he had wrapped his Sneakoscope in to muffle it. Dobby is ecstatic, socks are his favorite clothing. Ron also gives him some mauve socks and the sweater he received. Dobby is overwhelmed by Ron's generosity. Dobby also gives Harry handmade socks, one red with broomsticks, and one green, with Snitches. Dobby returns to the kitchen where preparations for the Ball are underway.

At about 5:00 P.M., after watching the big snowball fight that started after lunch, Hermione rises to get ready for the Ball. Ron asks if she really needs three hours and wants to know who she is going with, but she says nothing. They break off their battle and head upstairs. Ron is highly embarrassed by his robes, which look more like a dress, although he has removed the tatty lace. Harry meets Parvati, dressed in bright pink robes, in the Common room, and they and the other Gryffindors proceed to the Entry Hall. Clad in turquoise robes, Padma is rather aghast at Ron's appearance; Ron just wants to hide from Fleur Delacour, who is going with Roger Davies. The Slytherins arrive, and neither Crabbe or Goyle have a date. The Durmstrang students enter from outside; Viktor Krum is accompanied by a pretty girl Harry does not recognize. Professor McGonagall summons the Champions, telling them they will enter in procession after the others are seated. Harry looks over at the other Champions

Chapter 23: The Yule Ball

and suddenly recognizes Krum's date: it is Hermione. She has straightened her hair, and her posture is different. Harry is not the only one astonished by her changed appearance; Parvati is astonished, and Ron walks past without looking at her. Krum's female fan club glare at Hermione with deep loathing.

The long tables in the Great Hall have been replaced by smaller ones, each having space for a dozen people. The four Champions and their partners are to be seated at the head table, along with Professor Dumbledore, Madame Maxime, Professor Karkaroff, Ludo Bagman, and—surprisingly—Percy Weasley, who is substituting for Mr. Crouch. Percy, wearing navy blue robes, pulls out a chair for Harry and excitedly tells him he has been promoted to Mr. Crouch's personal assistant. He says the Tournament preparations has left Mr. Crouch stressed and tired and that he has somewhat lost his domestic comforts after dismissing his House-elf—Blinky, "or whatever her name is"—and is having a restful Christmas at home, sending his instructions to the office by owl. Dumbledore, surveying the menu, says "Pork chops!" to his plate, whereupon they appear; everyone else follows his example.

Hermione is deep in conversation with Krum who tells her that Durmstrang castle is not as comfortable or big as Hogwarts, having only four floors. Karkaroff warns him about sharing too much information or else Durmstrang's location could be revealed. Professor Dumbledore suggests that perhaps there is too much concern about secrecy. Karkaroff asks if he is not happier that only he, Dumbledore, knows Hogwarts' secrets. Dumbledore responds that he would never presume to believe that he knows all the school's secrets. Only recently did he stumble upon a room filled with chamber pots that he had never seen before. He has been unable to find that room since. When dinner is over, Dumbledore asks everyone to stand and sweeps the tables to the side with his wand. A stage rises against one wall, and the band starts playing. Parvati drags Harry to his feet, saying that they are supposed to dance. Their dancing is not too bad, as Parvati is leading. Soon the floor fills with other couples, many worse than Harry. Neville frequently steps on Ginny's feet. Professor Moody compliments Harry on his socks, causing Parvati to comment that his magical eye is rather creepy.

After the first song ends, Harry sits with Ron and Padma. Both Parvati and Padma are disgruntled that they do not get to dance again. Parvati finally leaves to dance with a Beauxbatons boy. An elated Hermione floats over, but Ron attacks her for "fraternizing with the enemy." Heated words are exchanged, and Hermione angrily disappears into the crowd. Padma also leaves, joining Parvati. Viktor appears looking for Hermione, and he is also dismissed by Ron. Percy comes over, talking about how the Tournament is meant to foster international co-operation, and it is great that Ron is making friends with Viktor. When Ludo crosses the dance floor on his way to the head table, he is intercepted by the Weasley twins. He shakes them off and goes over to talk to Harry. He claims the Twins were asking him for marketing assistance on their trick wands. Harry is certain Percy will report this to Mrs. Weasley. Harry and Ron escape as Percy talks shop with Ludo.

Outside in the rose garden, Karkaroff talking with Professor Snape about something that is becoming more distinct. Snape suggests that Karkaroff can run for it if he is that worried. Harry and Ron wonder how the two of them got on a first-name basis. Harry and Ron become unwilling eavesdroppers on a conversation between Madame Maxime and Hagrid. Hagrid reveals he is half-giant and suggests that Madame Maxime is the same. She indignantly insists she is just big-boned and stalks off. Ron asks Harry if he knew Hagrid was half-giant. Harry says no, but so what? Ron mentions that wizards generally fear giants because they are mindlessly vicious. Ron thinks this fear may carry over to Hagrid, at least among those who do not know him.

Back in the Hall, Harry and Ron continue discussing Giants. There are apparently very few left in England. They were already dying out but many were killed by Aurors. Those left are somewhere in the European mountains. Ron says he does not know who Madame Maxime thinks she is kidding; there is no way she could be just big-boned. The Ball ends at midnight. Hermione heads to Gryffindor tower, shooting Ron a cold look as she passes. Cedric calls Harry aside and says that because Harry helped him with the dragon, it is only fair that he should return the favor for the second task. He suggests Harry take a bath with his Egg and tells him how to get into the Prefect's bathroom. Harry, apart from his resentment over Cedric being Cho Chang's date, is uncertain how to react to this, but he says nothing. Cedric leaves to say goodnight to Cho.

Reaching the Gryffindor common room, Harry finds Ron and Hermione in a shouting match. Hermione tells Ron that if he does not like it then, "The next time there's a Ball, ask me before someone else does, and not as a last resort!" Hermione storms off to her dormitory. Ron, stunned, tells Harry that Hermione is quite clearly missing the point. Harry privately thinks Hermione has a much clearer idea about what Ron is feeling than Ron does.

Analysis

Although the Yule Ball is a disappointment for Harry and Ron, not to mention their hapless dates, their later stroll through the rose garden reveals much character information. Karkaroff knows that he is in poor standing with surviving Death Eaters. As revealed by Sirius, he named names to avoid being sent to Azkaban. Something may lead Karkaroff to believe that the Dark Lord may be returning to power. Because of this, Karkaroff could be considering disappearing to save himself, either from Death Eaters or Voldemort. Snape, however, seems unconcerned for his own safety, indicating that he may retain the Dark Lord's favor.

Harry and Ron also learn that Hagrid is half-giant, a fact he has apparently kept secret, although it has been rather obvious to most everyone else, including Hermione. An insulted Madame Maxime, however, vehemently denies any such ancestry, although this seems a foregone conclusion. Harry also seems oblivious that many wizards have deep-seated fear and prejudice towards giants, as well as many other magical folk, which explains why Hagrid and Madame Maxime would conceal their mutual heritage. In this particular case, wizards' fear may be partially justified—giants are prone to unprovoked violence, though Hagrid and Madame Maxime have gentle natures. Prejudice and discrimination are continual themes throughout the series, most notably through Hermione's efforts to liberate House-elves.

One noteworthy fact is the order in which these revelations are made. Clearly, that both Karkaroff and Snape may be, or have been, Death Eaters, is worth further discussion. Why then do Harry and Ron fail to discuss this further, and perhaps reach the conclusion that Snape is or was a Death Eater, despite what Sirius previously told them? Because Hagrid's confession to Madame Maxime takes precedence, casting it from their minds. This bit of literary legerdemain allows the author to foreshadow revelations later in the book and in the series, while managing to mask that revelation's weight by having the characters effectively dismiss it.

And though Hermione's efforts to liberate House-elves are seemingly frustrated, she may be having a positive effect in another way as seen when Ron gives Dobby some cast-off clothing. This act is something he probably never would have considered if not for both Hermione's and Harry's influence—Harry treats Dobby as a friend, and Hermione believes House-elves deserve equal rights. This may be a small milestone in Ron's maturation, and for once, he is thoughtful about someone other than himself, a close friend, or a family member. Without this example, it is unlikely Ron would ever consider House-elves as anything more than what they already are, even a liberated one like Dobby. Hermione has perhaps unknowingly sown a seed in Ron's consciousness, and, if she is to accomplish her goal, she must change both House-elves and the general wizarding community's thinking—a rather daunting, although not impossible, challenge.

The Yule Ball has yielded several other unexpected outcomes: Ron and Hermione's long simmering and deeply buried feelings for one another are brought closer to the surface, although they can only express themselves with mutual jealousy, anger, and immature bickering. In addition to seeing Hermione with Krum, Hermione's growing attractiveness also seems to have had a strong effect on Ron, forcing him to see her differently, although it is apparently still unclear to him exactly what the difference is. Harry, meanwhile, is no closer to solving the Egg riddle, and does little to figure it out, despite Hermione's constant prodding. Unexpectedly, he receives assistance from an unlikely source. In appreciation for Harry tipping him off about the dragon task, Cedric helps Harry with the Egg. However, rather than outright telling Harry what he needs know as Harry did with the dragons, Cedric instead only gives him a hint so he can solve it himself. But Harry's stubbornness and resentment over Cedric dating Cho Chang may prevent him from utilizing this valuable information.

Also, Mr. Crouch's health is apparently deteriorating. In the meeting with the Champions at Hallowe'en, he seemed unwell enough that Dumbledore actually suggested that he might want to spend the night at Hogwarts. In what seems a logical progression, he is now so ill that he is unable to attend the Triwizard ceremonies and Percy has been deputed to fill in for him.

Attention should be paid to Professor Dumbledore mentioning the room with the chamber pots, as well as the beetle crawling on the stone reindeer during Hagrid's conversation with Madame Maxime.

Questions

Review 1. Why doesn't Harry recognize Krum's date? What is Ron's reaction?
2. Why is Madame Maxime insulted that Hagrid suggested she is half-giant?
3. Why is Harry conflicted about accepting Cedric's help with the Egg?
4. What are Ron and Hermione arguing about? Who is right?

Further Study 1. Why won't Hermione reveal who her Yule Ball date is?
2. Why would the long tables in the Great Hall be replaced by smaller ones?
3. Why does Cedric only offer Harry a hint about the Egg, rather than telling him outright how to solve it?
4. What might be the real reason that Harry rebuffs Hermione's suggestion that he work on solving the Egg's clue?

Greater Picture

We will discover that Mr. Crouch's deteriorating health is subterfuge; Mr. Crouch is actually the Dark Lord's servant, being controlled by Peter Pettigrew (Wormtail). Wormtail's control over him has always been rather shaky; rather than risk his increasing eccentricity being discovered, Voldemort confines Mr. Crouch to his house, where he and Wormtail are hiding. Voldemort restricts communication to an easier-to-fake method. Percy will be reprimanded later by his superiors for failing to detect Mr. Crouch's odd behavior, although they may be using Percy as a scapegoat to deflect blame away from themselves.

At the Yule Ball, Karkaroff says that something is becoming more distinct. This is likely the "Dark Mark" on his forearm—the Death Eaters' sign. It becoming more visible is an indication that Voldemort is gaining strength, perhaps is close to returning. Having informed on Death Eaters, Karkaroff knows that he will likely be killed if Voldemort returns to power, and clearly is planning to bolt in that eventuality.

Later, we learn that the beetle, mentioned above, is actually Rita Skeeter, in her unregistered Animagus form. She will write a story about Hagrid's half-Giant ancestry which will prove devastating to him; this is where she learns of it, though she clearly does some research after hearing the bare fact from Hagrid.

The chamber-pot filled room Dumbledore mentions seems to be the Room of Requirement, which he apparently never knew existed, and will play a large role in each succeeding book. When Hermione is reluctant to use the room for their secret student meetings (in *Harry Potter and the Order of the Phoenix*), Harry allays her fears by saying Dumbledore had told him about it. Readers will also learn that the room only appears when someone needs it, and it comes equipped with whatever is necessary to fulfill that need. It is curious, then, why Dumbledore (or anyone) would require a room filled with so many chamber pots.

The final scene is crucial to Ron and Hermione's evolving relationship. In about a year's time, Hermione will comment that Ron has "the emotional depth of a teaspoon"; it is apparent at this point that he is having serious feelings for Hermione although he is unable to understand just what they are or how to react to them, and when Hermione makes her comment, he will be very little closer to recognizing them.

While we are as yet unaware, a turning point in Snape's life occurs in this chapter. In *Harry Potter and the Deathly Hallows*, one of the memories that Snape passes on to Harry is of himself and Dumbledore watching students return to their common rooms after the Ball. Snape tells Dumbledore that his Dark Mark is growing more distinct, Karkaroff's also; we will also view that scene in Dumbledore's memories in the Pensieve later in this book. When Snape goes on to say that Karkaroff may run, Dumbledore asks if Snape would be following; Snape responds that his place is at Dumbledore's side, always. Following this remark, Dumbledore muses that perhaps students are Sorted too soon. Snape, who was Sorted into Slytherin House and away from his beloved Lily Evans, who was a Gryffindor, is stunned at the thought.

Chapter 24: Rita Skeeter's Scoop

Synopsis

Hermione and Ron seem willing to overlook their fight, although Harry notices they are oddly formal with each other. Harry and Ron tell Hermione what they had overheard about Hagrid being half-giant. Hermione seems unsurprised, saying he is too large to be human, but that Giants typically are twenty feet tall, and he is not that big. And there must be decent Giants, just as there are decent werewolves.

Christmas is over, and it is time to work on the neglected homework. Harry is worried, however. February 24th looks much closer from this side of Christmas, and he must still solve the Egg's riddle. While remembering Cedric's hint, he is feeling somewhat unfriendly towards him and disinclined to heed his advice. It is still snowy and cold when classes resume. Nobody is looking forward to Care of Magical Creatures, but when they arrive at Hagrid's hut, they are met by Professor Grubbly-Plank. Ignoring Harry's questions about where Hagrid is, she leads them to the edge of the Forbidden Forest where a Unicorn is tethered. She waves the boys back, saying that unicorns interact better with girls. This leaves Harry close to Malfoy, who comments that Hagrid is too ashamed to show his face and produces the *Daily Prophet*. In it is a scurrilous article by Rita Skeeter about Hagrid. It claims the Blast-Ended Skrewts are not only dangerous, but illegal, and some students have been injured. Crabbe is quoted as saying he was bitten by a Flobberworm. The article also mentions Hagrid's mixed Giant-human ancestry. Harry is incensed, pointing out that Flobberworms do not even have teeth. Malfoy says parents will be scared that Hagrid will eat their children and that the article will end Hagrid's teaching career. Professor Grubbly-Plank continues the lesson, but Harry is so angry he is barely able to concentrate. At the end, Parvati declares it was better than any lesson Hagrid has ever given, and she hopes Professor Grubbly-Plank will be there for a long time. Harry, Ron, and Hermione go to Hagrid's hut after Divination, but to no avail. Their repeated knocks go unanswered. Hagrid remains absent the next week, and Professor Grubbly-Plank continues teaching his classes. Hagrid is not even seen performing his grounds-keeping duties.

A Hogsmeade weekend is scheduled for mid-January, and Harry plans to go, much to Hermione's surprise and displeasure; she was expecting him to work on solving the Egg riddle. Harry lies and says he pretty well has it figured out. There are still five weeks left, after all. Heading to Hogsmeade, they spot Viktor Krum diving into the lake, apparently unaffected by the cold. Ron is almost hoping the giant squid will get him.

In Hogsmeade, they stop in at the Three Broomsticks. Harry looks for Hagrid, but does not see him. They spot Ludo Bagman, however, deep in conversation with Goblins. When Ludo notices Harry, he charges over and asks for a private word. When Harry asks what Bagman is talking to the Goblins about, he says they want to contact Barty Crouch, but nobody knows where he is. Percy, apparently, says he is still home sick and sends instructions by owl post. If Rita Skeeter finds out, she will probably report that he is missing, just like Bertha Jorkins. When Harry asks if Bertha has shown up, Ludo admits she has not. He offers to help Harry with the Egg, but Harry refuses, claiming it is nearly solved. Fred and George suddenly appear and offer to buy Ludo a drink, but he declines, insisting he must go. He leaves with the Goblins trailing after him. As Harry, Ron, and Hermione discuss what Ludo disclosed, Rita Skeeter enters, telling her photographer that someone (probably Ludo) refused to talk to her. Harry accuses her of intentionally ruining other peoples' lives. She responds that the public has the right to know the truth, and asks Harry for his side of the story. Before leaving, Hermione tells her she is an evil woman, but looking back, Harry sees Rita's quill racing across parchment. Ron suspects Hermione may be next in line for her axe. Back at Hogwarts, Hermione beats on Hagrid's door, demanding to be let in. The door opens, and Professor Dumbledore greets them. Abashed, Hermione insists on seeing Hagrid, and Dumbledore invites them in. Harry tells Hagrid he should just disregard Skeeter. According to Dumbledore, many letters have arrived supporting Hagrid and demanding that he stay at Hogwarts. Hagrid protests that he is half-giant, but Harry points out that he is himself related to the Dursleys, and Dumbledore mentions his brother Aberforth, who was prosecuted for practicing inappropriate charms on a goat. Hermione asks Hagrid to return, and Dumbledore, as he leaves, says Hagrid is expected back on the job Monday, no excuses. Hagrid shows the Trio a picture of him and his father, who died during Hagrid's second year. Hagrid says he would be disappointed with Hagrid's behavior. Hagrid then asks how Harry is doing with the Egg, and Harry responds that he nearly has it solved. When Hagrid says how proud of him he is, Harry is ashamed he lied. Back inside the castle, Harry finally concedes that it is time to swallow his pride and give Cedric's hint a try.

Analysis

That Hagrid immediately went into hiding after Rita Skeeter's article was published shows his rather childlike nature. Rather than confronting an issue and standing up for himself, he instead retreats into seclusion, to the extent that even his friends and supporters are unable to convince him to do otherwise. Hagrid symbolizes how innocent individuals are easily victimized by powerful entities like the media. Rita Skeeter represents the bigotry that permeates the series and how fear and suspicion can be deliberately manipulated to inflame peoples' hatred, perpetuating racial stereotypes. And while Skeeter's article is bias driven, it may be less about her personal beliefs than deliberately skewing the facts to incite readers' terror about giants purely to sell more newspapers. Despite Hagrid's gentleness and devoted service to Hogwarts, Skeeter falsely casts him as a dangerous and irresponsible individual. Surprisingly, the backlash results in supporters rallying to Hagrid's defense rather than condemning him; many are probably former Hogwarts students who know Hagrid. And while Skeeter represents many characters' bigoted views and racial oppression, Dumbledore and Hermione become its antithesis, championing equal rights and opportunities for all magical denizens who may be at even greater risk as Voldemort's power continues to rise. Of the many characters Harry has a close relationship with, it is clearly seen here that Hagrid is one of the most important and influential people in his life, and whose good opinion Harry cultivates and values. Although Harry never means to disappoint others, his laziness results in him lying to everyone (and probably to himself) about solving the Egg riddle, and he remains unaffected by Hermione's criticism over his procrastination. However, he is completely shamed and humbled by Hagrid's total and unconditional faith in him, a faith Harry has failed to meet. Possibly only Sirius, Lupin, and Dumbledore could have close to same effect on him that Hagrid has. Harry guiltily realizes his actions have hardly represented how a Triwizard Champion is expected to behave, letting down those who have supported and believed in him. Harry resolves to work hard on solving the Egg riddle. Just how much Ron is lacking in emotional sensitivity is shown here as well. Immediately after Dumbledore orders Hagrid back to work, the room is still emotionally wrought, Ron asks if he can have a cake; however, he probably unintentionally helped break the tension somewhat.

Questions

Review 1. Why has Harry been so reluctant to work on solving the Egg's riddle, even despite Hermione's prodding and Cedric's hint?

2. Why does Harry feel ashamed when he lies to Hagrid about the Egg, but not to others?

3. Why does Harry finally decide to use Cedric's hint?

4. Why has Hagrid gone into hiding? Why does he agree to come back?

Further Study 1. What motivated Rita Skeeter to write such a scathing story?

2. Why does Ron think that Hermione will be Rita Skeeter's next "victim"? What does he mean by this? Is he right?

Greater Picture

Ludo's conversation with the Goblins in the Three Broomsticks appears to be going badly, and he seems to have lost much of his bounce. Ludo is in trouble with the Goblins over his gambling debts, and this is yet another episode where he attempts to settle matters with them. His abrupt retreat indicates he was unsuccessful, although Fred and George's sudden arrival may also have scared him off; he is avoiding the Twins because he also has refused to pay their winnings.

We see, in that encounter, another clumsy attempt by Ludo to help Harry with the Tournament. Almost certainly, the Goblins that Ludo is speaking with are the same group with which he is betting on Harry's victory. One might wonder why the Goblins allow him to talk to Harry so blatantly, as Ludo has already demonstrated that he is not particularly trustworthy. The Goblins must suspect that Ludo would try to influence things in his own favour, despite being a judge of the tournament.

Rita's story about Hagrid points up the prejudice and discrimination that the Wizarding world retains towards the other magical races; we will see this brought out again, in the person of Dolores Umbridge, in *Harry Potter and the Order of the Phoenix*. Umbridge will exhibit this prejudice to an extreme, displaying an irrational hatred for "half-breeds" like Hagrid and, illogically, the entire Centaur race. Voldemort will use this prejudice to win himself allies among those races that have been subjected to discrimination, notably the few remaining Giants and the Dementors.

Readers have probably noticed that many characters are first introduced by name before they actually appear in the story. Here, Dumbledore mentions his somewhat wayward brother, Aberforth, who will play a significant role in *Harry Potter and the Deathly Hallows*.

Chapter 25: The Egg and the Eye

Synopsis

On Thursday night, Harry sneaks out of Gryffindor Tower with his Egg and heads for the Prefects' Bathroom, armed with his Invisibility Cloak and the Marauder's Map to avoid being caught again by Filch for breaking curfew. The bathroom is luxuriously decorated in white marble and contains stacks of fluffy towels and a pool-sized tub with hundreds of jeweled taps

Chapter 25: The Egg and the Eye

that spew many-colored bubbles. On the wall is a painting of a beautiful mermaid. Harry slips into the water and plays with the taps a bit before opening the Egg. It wails horribly. He slams it shut and is startled by Moaning Myrtle, who suddenly appears, sitting on the tub's edge. She suggests putting the Egg in the water. Once submerged, a faint singing is heard. Dunking his head, Harry hears the Egg singing about something he will sorely miss that will be at the bottom of the lake. He will have only one hour to find it. Harry guesses that there are Merpeople in the lake, which Myrtle confirms. She is upset when Harry ponders how he will be able to breathe underwater, saying that nobody remembers that she can't breathe any more. Harry gathers the Egg and his other belongings and, covered by his cloak, prepares to head back to Gryffindor tower. First he checks the Map, confirming no one is in the halls except Peeves. Someone is in Professor Snape's office: Bartemius Crouch. Harry wonders why Mr. Crouch is at Hogwarts so late, particularly as he is apparently ill and was unable to attend the Yule Ball. Harry decides to investigate, but as he is concentrating on the map, his foot becomes trapped in a trick step, causing him to drop the Egg and the Marauder's Map. The Egg rolls down the staircase and starts wailing, summoning Filch who in turn yells at Peeves, assuming the Poltergeist had stolen a Champion's Egg. Snape arrives and dismisses Filch's accusations about Peeves, and claims someone broke into his office. It had to be a wizard; Snape seals his office with a Charm to prevent Peeves from entering. Professor Moody appears and is concerned that someone was in Snape's office. Moody's magical eye spots Harry under his Cloak, but he pretends Harry is not there and offers to go with Snape and investigate the break-in. Snape demurs, saying he believes it was a student stealing potion ingredients. Moody wonders if Snape could be hiding something else, to which Snape retorts that Moody has already searched his office. Moody says that it is an Auror's privilege. Although Dumbledore may have faith in Snape's loyalty, Moody is not the trusting sort. Moody dismisses Snape, causing Snape to bridle. Spying the Marauder's Map on the floor, Moody asks if Snape or Filch dropped something. Snape immediately recognizes it. Harry, under his Invisibility Cloak, gesticulates madly to let Moody know that it is his. Moody summons the map, and it slips through Snape's fingers over to him. Snape, furious, probes the air looking for Harry hiding under his cloak. Moody says nobody is there, although he thinks it curious how quickly Snape's thoughts turned to Harry. Detecting a threat, Snape departs. Filch, after protesting that the Egg is evidence, reluctantly hands it over to Moody and leaves.

The map fascinates Moody, who is seemingly unable to keep either eye off it. He helps Harry from the trap step and asks if the map showed who was in Snape's office. Harry replies it was Mr. Crouch. Moody is amazed, and explains that Crouch is obsessed with catching Dark wizards, far more than Moody himself. Moody asks to borrow the map. Harry, deeply relieved he does not have to explain where he got it (and thereby implicate Fred and George), agrees. As he goes into his office, Moody suggests that Harry consider becoming an Auror. When Moody asks if Harry was just taking his Egg for a stroll, Harry says he was working out the clue. Later, Harry thinks he would like to see how badly scarred other Aurors are before choosing that career path.

Analysis

Several important things should be noted: one, Bartemius Crouch, who was too ill to attend the Yule Ball and sent Percy Weasley in his place, is apparently well enough to travel to Hogwarts and root through Snape's office. Another is the Egg and its song; solving the Egg's riddle only leads to yet another problem for Harry—how to breathe underwater for one hour. The Tournament is now only a few weeks away, and Harry's procrastination in solving the riddle has wasted much valuable time; he will need help and have to work especially hard if he is to solve this next crucial step in time.

Additionally, there is Professor Moody's odd behavior when he spots the Marauder's Map. He is intensely interested in it, staring fixedly at the parchment when he realizes what it is, and then borrowing it from Harry. Just as Processor Lupin had in *Harry Potter and the Prisoner of Azkaban*, Moody's timely intervention here prevents Snape from punishing Harry. Here Moody shows his unconventional personality, and, as he has previously demonstrated, he is far less concerned about rule breaking than either Filch or Snape. This trait has helped make him a popular teacher, although his actions here may have as much to do with his ongoing enmity with Snape as it does with protecting Harry. Also like Lupin, Moody prevented Snape from confiscating the Marauder's Map, scooping it from his grasp with the Summoning spell. Some readers may wonder why Harry did not do the same; he had his wand, attempting to blank the map with it when Filch appeared. It seems likely that Harry, with the Egg screaming and Filch rapidly approaching, may simply have panicked. One can imagine the words "Why didn't I remember that?" flashing across Harry's mind when Moody used the Summoning charm. This particular charm had proved especially difficult for Harry to learn, however, and he may still be having some trouble casting it. Harry's gratitude to Moody is such that he readily agrees to loan him the map, although Harry is probably wondering just why and how Moody intends to use it.

Questions

Review 1. Why does Moaning Myrtle help Harry with the Egg?

2. Why is Myrtle upset about Harry's next Triwizard task? How will Harry overcome this obstacle?

3. Why did Snape suspect that Harry was involved in the ruckus in the hallway? Even though Harry was there, were Snape's suspicions justified or was it his usual rush to judgment where Harry is concerned?

Further Study 1. Why would Mr. Crouch be in Snape's office so late at night?

2. Why would Moody have previously searched Snape's office?

3. Why does Moody hide Harry's presence from the others in the hall?

4. Why does Moody want to borrow the Marauder's Map? Why does Harry agree to let him use it?

5. Why does Moody suggest that Harry become an Auror? Explain why you agree or disagree? What is Harry's reaction?

Greater Picture

The Marauder's Map's power once again strips away disguises; in *Harry Potter and the Prisoner of Azkaban*, it correctly spotted Peter Pettigrew when, in his Animagus form, he was disguised as Scabbers. In this case, it showed "Bartemius Crouch" in Snape's office. Of course, it was the false Moody collecting ingredients to brew more Polyjuice Potion. While the Marauder's Map correctly gave his name, it is apparently unable to differentiate between Bartemius Crouch Sr., and Bartemius Crouch Jr., who is using the Polyjuice Potion to impersonate Moody. However, this is a clear indication that the Map is not fooled by Polyjuice potion, any more than it is deceived by Animagi.

This explains Moody's interest in the map, and why he is so keen to borrow it; apart from it being a useful tool that shows everyone's whereabouts at the school, it can expose him as an impostor. He must act to get the map away from Harry to conceal his true identity. There may have been a more immediate need for Moody getting the map into his possession: Harry could have noticed that the map showed that it was Barty Crouch who was standing directly opposite him rather than the real Mad Eye Moody. Moody's suggestion that Harry become an Auror may be intended as flattery to deflect questions by Harry as to exactly why Moody wants the map. However, Harry is indeed well-suited to becoming an Auror, Defense Against the Dark Arts being his best subject, something Barty may realize he needs to be cautious about. Also, it does seem that if Harry had been a little more observant, he would have noticed on the map that the real "Mad Eye" Moody never appears to leave the Defensive Arts instructor's living quarters (where he is being imprisoned) or that Barty Crouch is often in places and at times when only Mad Eye Moody should be there.

In a later chapter, Sirius claims Snape was never accused of being a Death Eater; this is actually incorrect, Snape was accused, but Dumbledore vouched for him. It was Moody who arrested Snape, and who is probably still suspicious that he is a Death Eater; the false Moody will display this same belief in order to be true to his model, and to avoid making Dumbledore suspicious. Karkaroff is a known Death Eater, Sirius mentioned that just before the first task. If Snape was or still is a Death Eater, as Ron, Harry, and to a lesser extent Hermione suspect, that would explain why he and Karkaroff were on a first-name basis at the Yule Ball.

Finally, it is unknown whether Barty Crouch, Jr. actually knows if Snape was a Death Eater. It is learned at the end of this book that Snape bears the Dark Mark, which not only brands Death Eaters, but also acts as a summons from the Dark Lord. In the second chapter of *Harry Potter and the Half-Blood Prince*, we learn that Snape was not only a Death Eater, but was in Voldemort's inner council. Considering how young Barty was when he was imprisoned, it is possible that he was never directly connected with Voldemort, but only associated with the Dark Lord's supporters after Voldemort himself was gone. If so, he might have learned that Snape was in Voldemort's inner council from Bellatrix Lestrange or her associates, or possibly, more recently, from the true Alastor Moody. Barty is likely unaware that Dumbledore vouched for Snape's allegiance, but he would immediately see that Dumbledore had complete trust in him despite his earlier Dark association.

Chapter 26: The Second Task

Synopsis

In Charms class, Harry, Ron, and Hermione are learning Banishing charms, the opposite of Summoning. Fortunately, the class noise and confusion muffles their private conversation. Harry reveals what he has learned about the second task. He must find a way to breathe underwater for one hour and recover whatever the Merpeople have taken from him. He also says Mr. Crouch was in Snape's office that same night. Hermione is curious as to why Mr. Crouch would be there. Harry remembers Moody saying that Professor Dumbledore believes in second chances, and he wonders just what Snape did to warrant one.

As requested, Harry sends an owl letter to Sirius recapping everything that happened. Over the next several weeks, he, Hermione, and Ron scour the library searching for ways to breathe underwater, but to no avail. The only joyful spot is an owl letter from Sirius that arrives the day before the second task, though Sirius only wants to know when the Hogsmeade weekend is. Harry responds, and glumly goes to Care of Magical Creatures class. Hagrid appears to have given up on the Blast-Ended Skrewts, as only two are left. He seems to be trying to prove that he can teach as well as Professor Grubbly-Plank by continuing the lesson about unicorns, and it seems he actually knows many useful things about them. Today, he has captured a pair of foals, and Parvati and Lavender are absolutely delighted by them. While telling everyone to gather round, Hagrid takes Harry aside to let him know that he is sure Harry will be able to beat the second challenge. Harry is too nervous to answer. As evening approaches, Harry, Hermione, and Ron are racing through spellbooks looking for a way that Harry can survive underwater. As the sun sets, Fred and George appear and tell Ron and Hermione that Professor McGonagall wants to see them. Saying they will see Harry in the common room after, Ron and Hermione leave. When the library closes, Harry takes as many books as he can carry back to the Gryffindor common room. As he frantically scours through them, the common room gradually empties. He has searched all the books, and Ron and Hermione have still not returned. Harry gets his

Chapter 26: The Second Task

Invisibility Cloak and returns to the library where he finally falls asleep reading spell-books by wand light.

Dobby wakes him mere minutes before the second task. Harry says it is too late to compete, but Dobby says he must because he has to retrieve his "Wheezy." Harry finally understands that "Wheezy" is Ron. Dobby says he knows that Harry did not find the right spell, so he did. He overheard Professor McGonagall and Professor Moody talking about the second task and realized that Gillyweed would allow Harry to recover "his Wheezy." He presents Harry a handful and returns to the kitchens. Harry arrives at the lake shore just in time. Percy Weasley, again filling in for Mr. Crouch, is upset when Ludo Bagman insists Harry be given a moment to catch his breath. As he positions the Champions at the shore, Ludo asks if Harry is okay and has a plan. Replying more confidently than he actually feels, Harry responds that he does.

The challenge starts. Harry wades into the lake chewing the Gillyweed but nothing happens. Suddenly, gills sprout on his neck, and, unable to breathe, he dives underwater. Discovering he also has webbed toes, Harry sets off. Grindylows attack and he jinxes them off. Moaning Myrtle appears and indicates which way Harry should travel, complaining she dislikes it there because the Grindylows always chase her. Harry finds a sizable, if crude, Mermish village. Tied to a large statue in the "village square" are four figures: Ron, Hermione, Cho Chang, and a young girl, about eight years old, who, from her fanning white-blonde hair, Harry guesses is probably Fleur's sister.

The Mermish guards do not interfere, but they refuse Harry's attempt to borrow a spear to cut Ron free. Harry finds a sharp stone and cuts Ron free. Worried that the other Champions have not appeared, he also tries to free Hermione, but is stopped by the Mermish guards. Harry is still trying to save Hermione when Cedric arrives with a large air bubble around his head. He tells Harry to get going, Fleur and Krum are almost there. Cutting Cho free, he heads for the surface. Krum appears with his head transformed into a shark; he is unable to bite through Hermione's ropes, so Harry hands him his sharp rock, which Krum uses to cut her free and heads to the surface.

When Fleur does not appear, Harry attempts to cut the last hostage free but is again prevented by the mermen. This time he threatens them with his wand and they back away nervously. Harry frees the girl and Ron and heads to the surface, accompanied by the mermen, making Harry nervous. Harry's watch has stopped, and he worries that they might be pulled back down when the hour is up. As the surface appears, the Gillyweed wears off. Harry barely makes it to the top. Wild, green-haired faces surround him, but they are all smiling. Ron and the girl wake up and are looking around. A great cheer erupts from the stands, and Harry gets Ron to help with the girl. On the shore, Madam Pomfrey is treating Cedric, Cho, Krum, and Hermione. Fleur is restrained by Madame Maxime from throwing herself into the lake to get to her sister. Ludo Bagman and Dumbledore are beaming, and Percy, looking somehow younger, runs into the lake to help Ron.

Once they are all ashore, Fleur runs to hug her sister, Gabrielle, saying she was stopped by the Grindylows. Madam Pomfrey wraps Harry tightly in a blanket and administers a pepper-up potion that causes steam to come out his ears. Hermione compliments Harry on figuring out the task on his own. Seeing that Krum is listening, Harry decides to tell her later that Dobby helped him. Krum, possibly to regain Hermione's attention, points out that she has a water beetle in her hair. Hermione brushes it away and asks Harry if it had taken long to find them. Harry is now feeling rather silly and embarrassed. First Ron, and now Hermione, have pointed out that Dumbledore would never have allowed them to die, so his staying to make sure all the hostages were rescued was pointless.

Meanwhile, Dumbledore is in conference with the Mermen Chief, Merchieftainess Murcus. He then asks to confer with the judges before the final marks are given. Madam Pomfrey has rescued Ron from Percy's clutches and administers a pepper-up potion to him as well. Fleur, still bedraggled, has numerous cuts on her face and arms, and her robe is torn, but she refuses Madam Pomfrey's help, demanding she treat Gabrielle first. She approaches Harry, saying that he saved her sister when he did not have to, and kisses him twice on each cheek. Harry can almost feel steam coming out his ears again. Fleur says that Ron also helped and swoops to kiss him as well. Hermione looks furious, but before she can say anything, the judges break their huddle. Ludo announces the standings. Fleur, although using the Bubble-Head Charm, failed to rescue her hostage and only gets 25 points; Cedric Diggory, also using the Bubble-Head Charm, brought his hostage to the surface one minute outside the allotted hour, getting 47 points; Viktor Krum, using a partial Transfiguration, returned second with his hostage for 40 points. Harry Potter returned last, but according to the Merchieftainess' report, arrived at the hostages first, and was delayed by his determination to free all the hostages, not only his own. Most of the judges feel this shows moral fiber and deserves full marks. Harry is awarded 45 points, tying him for first place with Cedric.

Ludo announces the next task is scheduled for the 24th of June; the Champions will be briefed about the task's nature exactly one month prior. Harry is immensely relieved that the second task is over, and there is nothing to worry about until 24 June. He resolves that next Hogsmeade trip, he will buy Dobby a year's supply of socks.

Analysis

Harry's performance during the second task reflects how he behaves in most situations. As the first Champion to reach the tethered hostages (with help from Moaning Myrtle), he then feels obligated to ensure the other three "victims" are rescued. And though Harry behaved admirably during the first task by tipping off Cedric about the dragons, here his reasoning is flawed. It never occurs to him that every possible safety precaution has been implemented and the volunteers' lives were never endangered. Rather than heading for the surface, guaranteeing a win, he instead waits for the other Champions to arrive and retrieve their hostages, then insists on "rescuing" Gabrielle when Fleur fails to show. Only later does Harry realize how foolishly he behaved when Ron and Hermione insist they were always safe and that Dumbledore would never jeopardize any student's safety. It actually would have been more logical for Harry to search for the missing Fleur, as the Triwizard Champions lack the same protection as the volunteers. Destined since birth as the "chosen one," Harry's ongoing conflict with Voldemort has skewed his overall thinking somewhat, and, in his mind, the battle has become his burden alone to carry, his mission to accomplish by himself. As a result, Harry feels compelled to rush in and be the hero whenever he feels others are threatened, even those able to fight their own battles. Though Harry feels he must face most obstacles alone, he is only able to compete in the Tournament because others such as Hermione, Moody, Dobby, Cedric, and Hagrid have guided him, and will continue to do so. While Harry is gradually learning to rely on others, he is still generally reluctant to accept outside help, especially when it is suspicious characters like Ludo Bagman, who Harry now suspects has some ulterior motive. Even though Harry's heroism was misguided, it is still rewarded when Dumbledore persuades the judges to assign Harry extra points for "moral fiber."

Harry foolishly protecting the hostages from a nonexistent danger does have a very real and useful value in the story. This light on Harry's character suggests quite strongly that under real dangerous circumstances, he would never abandon others in peril, even to save himself.

Harry is also learning that things are sometimes other than what they initially appear to be. As with the Veela, the Merpeople are first introduced to readers as beautiful ethereal creatures, as represented by the stylized painting in the Prefects' bathroom. Harry is rather shocked to discover that their true appearance is far different. The author shows here that beauty, or the lack of it, does not accurately reflect any person's inner character, although assumptions are often based on superficial physical traits. And while appearance may legitimately represent someone's character to a limited degree, it is mostly one's actions that determine who and what an individual or group truly are. While Merpeople have a rather hideous and scary appearance, they are benign beings loyal to Dumbledore and Hogwarts. Harry, forgetting this was only a competition, got a little carried away with his "rescue mission" and rushed to judgment when faced with something unknown; he adopted a defensive and threatening posture against the Mermen that was based more on appearances than actions, even though these were obviously Tournament officials.

Curiously, Harry seems to pay little attention to Cho Chang immediately after the event. He notices Madame Pomfrey tending to her injuries, but following that, he only focuses on Hermione, Ron, and the judges. This may indicate that his infatuation, if that is what it is, with Cho may be waning, or was less than he thought it was. It is interesting that Hermione is apparently angry when Fleur kisses Ron, even though it is quite innocent and Viktor Krum is also attempting to attract Hermione's attention. Although Harry is in no state to notice Hermione's furious expression when she witnesses this, we are presumably meant to see it, as it hints that Hermione may have serious feelings for Ron.

This is the second time the Grindylows have been seen, the first being in Professor Lupin's office in *Harry Potter and the Prisoner of Azkaban*. At that time, it was noted that the Grindylow's fingers are extraordinarily long and relatively easy to break, but Harry does not use this information when he is attacked.

One must wonder why Fleur is portrayed as having so much trouble getting past the Grindylows. She must be among the best that Beauxbatons has to offer, or Madame Maxime would not have brought her to the Tournament, and yet her magic seems, comparatively, rather weak. We are not presented with any reason for this portrayal. The "water-beetle" in Hermione's hair should be noted.

QUESTIONS

Review 1. Why does Harry stay and help the other Champions with the task, allowing them to reach the surface before he does?

2. Was Gabrielle in any danger? What prompted Harry to rescue her?

3. What do Ron and Hermione tell Harry after the second task, and why does that embarrasses him?

4. Were the judges justified in awarding Harry extra points for "moral fiber"? Just what did Harry do to earn that?

Further Study 1. The other Champions were prepared for the second task. Why were Harry, Ron, and Hermione unable to find a spell for breathing underwater?

2. Why does Hermione look so furious just after the task? Why did Krum try to distract her?

3. Why might Sirius want to know when the next Hogsmeade weekend is?

GREATER PICTURE

The water-beetle, of course, will turn out to be Rita Skeeter, who is an unregistered Animagus. Overhearing the private conversation between Hermione and Viktor, she will use that as the basis of a scurrilous story that will appear in Witch Weekly at the beginning of the next chapter. That story will create a rift between Hermione and Mrs. Weasley that will remain unresolved until the book's end.

Harry's need to be the "hero" will play a crucial, and ultimately tragic, role in Book Five, *Harry Potter and the The Order of the Phoenix*. Hermione later admonishes Harry for always wanting to rush to the rescue, even when there is no real danger, and citing the underwater "hostages" as an example. Despite her warning, when Harry receives a vision that Voldemort is torturing Sirius, he immediately goes to save him without verifying first if the vision is genuine or considering whether or not his predictable behavior is being used to lure him into a trap. We are here also seemingly laying the groundwork for the creation of an alliance between Hogwarts (in the person of Hermione) and Durmstrang (represented by Krum). By the time this is actually useful, Krum will have graduated—as he did not grow a beard when crossing the Age Line, he must have been at least 17-years-old, making him either a sixth or seventh year student—but he may well have some influence in that part of the world. In fact, while Krum will reappear in *Harry Potter and the Deathly Hallows*, his contribution will be more personal; the alliance will be with Hermione rather than with Hogwarts, and will simply allow Harry to remember a specific fact that will be useful in the remainder of his quest.

Chapter 27: Padfoot Returns

SYNOPSIS

After the Second Task, everyone wants to hear what happened in the lake, which makes Ron much in demand. His stories become more embellished with each retelling until Hermione acidly suggests that the only way he could have battled Merpeople would have been to snore at them. After that, Ron reverts to the original enchanted-sleep version.

The March weather is extremely windy, causing delays in the owl post. The Friday before the Hogsmeade weekend, the owl Harry sent to Sirius returns with its feathers ruffled the wrong way. It immediately takes off once Harry retrieves the letter, as if afraid it will be sent out again. Sirius asks Harry to be at the stile beyond Dervish and Banges at two o'clock Saturday and to bring food. Ron is amazed that Sirius could be back in Hogsmeade. Harry wonders how he dares to, but Ron points out it is no longer swarming with Dementors.

When they arrive at Potions class, the Slytherins are huddled around something and sniggering. Pansy Parkinson tosses Hermione a copy of *Witch Weekly*. Hermione riffles through it, finding an article, *Harry Potter's Secret Heartache*, by Rita Skeeter. The article suggests that Hermione is Harry's girlfriend and is abandoning him for Viktor Krum, who has invited her to visit him during the summer. Hermione is unimpressed, even by Pansy Parkinson's quote that insinuates Hermione might be using love potions. She wonders how Skeeter knew about Krum's invitation. Ron is interested in hearing how she answered, but she ignores this. Professor Snape approaches from behind and penalizes Gryffindor ten points for Hermione's talking and ten more for having *Witch Weekly* in class. He reads Rita Skeeter's article aloud to gales of laughter from the Slytherins. Snape now separates the three, placing Hermione with Pansy, leaving Ron where he is, and placing Harry at the table immediately facing his desk. In a soft undertone, Snape accuses Harry of stealing Boomslang skin and Gillyweed from his stores. Harry remembers that Hermione stole Boomslang skin during their second year to make the Polyjuice potion and that Dobby swiped the Gillyweed, but he lies and claims he has no idea what Snape is talking about. Snape produces a vial containing Veritaserum. Just three drops in Harry's pumpkin juice, Snape threatens, and Harry would babble his innermost secrets. Igor Karkaroff enters the dungeon wanting to speak to Snape, who says they can talk after class. Karkaroff claims Snape has been avoiding him and stays until the class ends. Harry knocks over his armadillo bile, and, crouching behind his cauldron, sees Karkaroff show Snape his left forearm. He says, "It has never been that clear, not since . . ." Snape orders him to put it away, they can discuss it later. Spotting Harry, he demands to know what he is doing there. Harry replies innocently that he is cleaning up his armadillo bile. Karkaroff leaves, and Harry decides it would be a good idea to do likewise.

On Saturday, the Hogsmeade weekend, Harry, Ron, and Hermione grab extra food from lunch and set off for the village. They buy socks for Dobby at Gladrags Wizard Wear, and then head past Dervish and Banges, finding a stile and a familiar-looking black dog. The dog leads them to a cave in the surrounding mountainside. Inside is a tethered Buckbeak. The dog transforms into Sirius. Famished from living mostly on rats, he tears into the chicken. Harry's letters, he says between bites, have made events sound increasingly suspicious, especially when combined with what Sirius reads in scrounged *Daily Prophets*. Sirius claims that Crouch being sick is unusual; Harry mentions that he had looked bad when the Goblet selected the Triwizard Champions. When Hermione says he is getting his just desserts for firing his House-elf, Winky, Harry explains about the Quidditch World Cup and his wand being stolen. Sirius asks if Harry checked his pockets before leaving the top box, but Harry says he did not check until he was in the woods. Sirius suggests someone could have lifted Harry's wand; Ron suspects Lucius Malfoy, although Hermione reminds them Ludo Bagman was also there. Sirius wonders why Bagman keeps offering to help Harry win the Tournament. According to Sirius, Crouch taking days off is uncharacteristic. It was Crouch who sent him to Azkaban without a trial. Pressed for more explanation, Sirius explains how desperate times resulted in desperate measures, including using deadly force against suspected Death Eaters. Crouch, who headed the Aurors, championed these measures, achieving some results. He was tapped as the next Minister for Magic until his son, Barty Crouch, Jr., was found with Death Eaters who were attempting to return Voldemort to power. Crouch presided over his own son's trial and sentenced him to Azkaban. Sirius says Crouch and his wife made a deathbed visit to their son, and he later saw Dementors burying him. Crouch lost his son, his wife (who died shortly after), and his shot at the Ministry, eventually getting shunted aside to the Department of International Magical Cooperation. Sirius suspects Crouch wants to capture one last Dark Wizard to revive his career, although it is unlikely Crouch would make a special trip to Hogwarts to search Snape's office. He had ample excuse to do that when he was there for the Triwizard judging. Ron and Hermione start squabbling over whether or not Snape is a Dark Wizard. Sirius says Snape certainly associated with Slytherins who became Death Eaters: Rosier and Wilkes; Bellatrix Lestrange and her husband; Avery, but Snape was never accused. Harry mentions that Snape and Karkaroff know each other and tells how Karkaroff showed Snape something on his arm, although Sirius does not know what that could be. When Ron mentions that his brother is Mr. Crouch's personal assistant, Sirius asks him to learn what he can from Percy about Mr. Crouch's illness and also about Bertha Jorkins' disappearance. Bagman was quoted in an article as saying that Bertha's memory is very bad, but Sirius claims that is untrue. Bertha had an excellent memory while at school, at least for gossip. At 3:30 P.M., Sirius sends the Trio back to Hogwarts. He wants to be updated on any new information and reminds them to address letters to him as "Snuffles." In his dog form, he leaves with them to scrounge for another newspaper in the village. Ron wonders if Percy knew about Mr. Crouch, but concludes that he would probably approve Crouch's refusal to bend the rules for his own son; Percy loves rules after all.

ANALYSIS

Although Hermione deflates Ron's exaggerated boasts about his participation in the second task, he nonetheless remains rather pleased with himself, basking in some unfamiliar but welcomed attention that is, for once, separate from Harry's celebrity. Meanwhile, Harry must defend himself for something he did not do—stealing from Snape's stores. Snape certainly has some legitimate reason to suspect Harry. During Harry's second year, as mentioned above, Hermione stole Boomslang skin and Bicorn horn from Snape's office to make Polyjuice Potion. No doubt Harry remembers this, but he is unsure whether Snape is talking about that occasion, or something more recent. The Gillyweed that Snape mentions most certainly is more recent than that; Harry knows that Dobby had stolen it, so that Harry could get his "Wheezy" back. Though Harry can rightfully protest that he was not involved in either theft, he does believe that he knows who was responsible in both cases.

Readers, along with the boys in the school, have watched as Hermione has blossomed from a smart, but rather plain girl into an intelligent, attractive young woman. Despite new-found male attention, she avoids developing an inflated ego as other girls might, or relying on feminine wiles to get what she wants. Instead, she remains grounded and unaffected as she matures in more significant ways, never feeling too intimidated to use her abilities and intellect. Unfazed by Pansy Parkinson's and Snape's feeble attempts to embarrass her in class, Hermione merely shrugs it off, and, ignoring Ron's inquiries about Krum, instead focuses her attention on figuring out just how Rita Skeeter learned about Viktor Krum's invitation. Considering her usual determination, she likely will not stop until she has found an answer. And though Hermione now has a potential (if currently one-sided) romantic relationship with Viktor, her loyalty is only to Hogwarts and her friends, and she is committed to helping Harry succeed in each task, help for which she rarely seeks any credit.

Having returned to England, and now with his meeting Harry in Hogsmeade, Sirius shows his devotion and concern for his godson, even though Sirius is taking a huge risk that he could be caught and, as a fugitive, there is actually little he can do to help Harry. Sirius thrives on risk taking, however, and his long confinement in Azkaban and being on the run may have impaired his judgment somewhat. Regardless, the Trio are delighted to see him, and having his godfather close by, giving him the love and security he sorely craves but rarely feels, revitalizes Harry. Sirius also provides the Trio some valuable information, including much about Mr. Crouch, a man who was apparently so coldheartedly dedicated to his job that he would convict and sentence his own son to life imprisonment in Azkaban for having been found with Death Eaters, although it was never proved if Barty was actually one himself. Whether or not Crouch Jr. deserved such a severe punishment, most fathers in that situation would have recused themselves to allow another judge to preside over the case. Crouch's motive appears to have been to protect his own reputation by showing he would unhesitatingly mete out justice to his own son. But the scandal forever tainted his career, and he was consequently demoted to a relatively menial position. Sirius is also particularly curious as to why Mr. Crouch's saved seat at the World Cup remained empty, questioning why someone so involved in the Tournament is apparently off doing something else.

Bagman stated for the *Daily Prophet* that Bertha Jorkins had a bad memory. While that claim was apparently untrue when Sirius knew her in school, the implication is that her memory had deteriorated or been magically altered before she vanished.

Harry wonders why Ludo Bagman always wants to help him with the Tournament. While it is possible that Bagman is a Death Eater and may have been attempting to put Harry in harm's way, this is unlikely as Bagman actually seems to be trying to help Harry, although just why is unknown. However, we have already seen that Bagman is a gambler, and while there is still little evidence regarding this, he may be trying to influence the Tournament's outcome because he is wagering on Harry to win. Sirius seems to re-enforce Harry's suspicions when he also wonders what Bagman's motive might be in helping Harry.

QUESTIONS

Review 1. What does Karkaroff show Snape on his arm? Why does he accuse Snape of avoiding him? Is he right?

2. How does Ron's version about his underwater experience compare to Hermione's? What accounts for this difference?

3. Has Boomslang skin been seen before? If so, where, and what was it used for?

4. Why is Sirius suspicious about Mr. Crouch's illness?

Further Study 1. Why doesn't Harry repair his water-damaged wristwatch with a Reparo spell?

2. How did Rita Skeeter know that Viktor Krum invited Hermione to visit him? Why is Ron interested in knowing how Hermione responded?

3. Why does Snape suspect that it was Harry who broke into his office? Are Snape's suspicions justified?

4. Who might be stealing the Boomslang skin and Gillyweed? Why?

5. Why would Mr. Crouch have presided over his own son's trial and sentence him to Azkaban prison rather than allow another judge to oversee the case?

6. If Bertha Jorkins had as excellent a memory in school as Sirius claims, why would she have had problems with it now?

7. Why would Ludo Bagman want to help Harry win the Tournament?

8. Why does Sirius think Mr. Crouch's seat remaining empty at the Quidditch World Cup is significant?

GREATER PICTURE

While Harry seems to believe that the Boomslang skin theft is from two years back, we will discover that it is a more recent occurrence. Shortly after Harry sees Bartemius Crouch in Snape's office on the Marauder's Map, Snape discovers Boomslang skin is again missing. It is reasonable to assume that Snape would connect the missing Boomslang skin to his office being broken into, which happened the same night. It is further reasonable that Snape, believing Harry to be out after hours when the Egg and the Marauder's Map are found, suspects that Harry may be involved in making some unauthorized potion again. Harry, of course, has no idea that anyone is using Polyjuice Potion, so he can only make a connection to Hermione's earlier theft. Interestingly, Snape does not seem to suspect that Hermione may be involved, even though she is apparently far more adept at Potions than Harry, and it was she who brewed the Polyjuice Potion two years before.

Although Harry has yet to figured this out, it was actually Barty Crouch, Jr. who was in Snape's office the night Harry was nearly caught by Snape and Filch. Barty Jr. is, as we later discover, using Polyjuice Potion to disguise himself as Moody; when Harry saw who he believed was Crouch Sr. on the Marauder's Map, it was actually Barty Jr. getting the necessary potion ingredients for his next batch.

Readers learn that Bartemius Crouch, Sr. sentenced Barty, Jr. to Azkaban, demonstrating how he mercilessly convicted any Death Eater, even his own son. However, it will be revealed later that it was Crouch Sr., along with his dying wife, who planned and executed the successful scheme to free Barty, Jr. from Azkaban. While Barty confesses that Bartemius had arranged Barty's escape at his mother's (Bartemius' wife's) request, Bartemius' actions were probably motivated by something more than a father rescuing his son from a miserable fate—a fate that he personally dealt him. Bartemius was an ambitious, dedicated, and rather ruthless Ministry official who was on track to become Minister for Magic. By convicting Barty, Bartemius may have been attempting to protect his own career by displaying no partiality. However, the embarrassing scandal and the ensuing fallout caused the Ministry of Magic to shunt Bartemius aside into a relatively unimportant and low-profile job, forever derailing his lofty goals. Freeing Barty may partly have been a vengeful act against the Ministry for their callous ill-treatment. Indeed, there appears to have been little love between father and son that would have compelled Bartemius to free him, and he had openly disowned Barty; and if Mrs. Crouch's plan was to save Barty from lifelong incarceration, leaving him locked up in the Crouch home was little improvement over his previous situation and certainly not what she would have wished. Bartemius had little choice but to keep his son confined, however, rightly suspecting that Barty would bolt and return to Voldemort's service. The parent-child relationship is complicated, ever-changing, and has many facets, and though Bartemius may have sought retaliation against the Ministry, he may also have been unable to live with what he had doomed his son to, as well as wanting to honor his wife's dying wish.

Sirius says he has no idea if Barty, Jr. was a Death Eater, only that he was found in the company of known Death Eaters, including Bellatrix Lestrange, Sirius' cousin. It will be revealed that Barty is indeed a loyal Death Eater who participated in torturing into insanity the Aurors Frank and Alice Longbottom to extract information about what had happened to Voldemort. Neville has never revealed to his classmates what happened to his parents, but Harry learns about this in a later chapter; at Dumbledore's request, Harry keeps Neville's secret to himself. When speaking about Bartemius Crouch, Sirius tells Harry, "If you want to know what a man's like, take a good look at how he treats his inferiors, not his equals." We will see later with Kreacher that Sirius, at least in this respect, does not treat his subordinate well. However, Kreacher is half-mad and fanatically loyal to the late Mrs. Black, who disowned her son, and he despises Sirius. This may account for Sirius' unkind treatment. Sirius also mentions that Snape was never accused of being a Death Eater. This is not quite true: we find out later that he had been accused, but Dumbledore vouched for his having become a double agent before Voldemort fell. By this book's end, we will learn the story behind Bertha Jorkins. Bertha, who has been missing and is eventually found to be dead, worked for Bartemius Crouch Sr. She happened to visit his home when Bartemius was gone and accidentally discovered that Barty, recently escaped from Azkaban, was alive and being hidden there. Either Bartemius or Winky, the Crouch's House-elf, used a memory charm on her to protect their secret. This charm, as it had to mask out large areas of her memory, apparently affected her overall memory. Soon after, she was transferred to Ludo Bagman's department. Ludo, who had never met her before the memory charm had been applied, only knew her when she was having spell-induced memory problems, prompting his comment in the *Daily Prophet* about her poor memory.

Chapter 28: The Madness of Mr. Crouch

SYNOPSIS

The next day, as Sirius requested, Ron sends a message to Percy asking for any additional information about Mr. Crouch. Then he, Harry, and Hermione, visit the kitchens to give Dobby his socks. Dobby is ecstatic, and Ron takes advantage of his evident joy to ask for any leftover eclairs. Hermione is amazed, as he has just eaten breakfast, but it reminds Harry that Sirius asked for some extra food. Ron also requests some. Hermione asks about Winky, and Dobby points her out sitting by the fire. She is filthy, quite evidently not caring for herself, and apparently drunk. Dobby confides that she is drinking six bottles of Butterbeer a day, pining for her old master, Mr. Crouch. Harry asks Winky if she knows what is wrong with Mr. Crouch, and Winky says Mr. Crouch needs her. Not only did she care for him and his house, Mr. Crouch entrusted her with his greatest secrets. She then passes out on the hearth, and other Elves apologetically cover her up. Hermione is unhappy that the House-elves try cheering her up, but the head kitchen Elf says, "House-elves has no right to be unhappy when there is work to be done and Masters to be served." Hermione embarrasses Dobby when she cites him as an example of how they can be independent. The House-elves, also seemingly embarrassed, push Ron, Harry, and Hermione from the kitchens, along with the extra food they gave them. Ron is convinced the House-elves will never allow them in the kitchens again, while Hermione is upset Ron did nothing to promote House-elf liberation. Harry, tired of their squabbling, takes the extra food to the Owlery by himself and sends it to Sirius. He then relishes the peace, watching Hagrid digging by his hut until night falls.

The next day, Hermione, looking for her new subscription to the *Daily Prophet* in the post, is surprised to receive many owl letters. It is hate mail, inspired by Rita Skeeter's article about the Harry-Hermione-Viktor "love triangle" in *Witch Weekly*. One letter contains raw Bubotuber pus, which sends Hermione to the hospital wing with boils on her hands. As Ron and Harry head to Care of Magical Creatures class, they notice Hagrid has numerous open boxes. Ron dreads it might be another Skrewt hatching, but the boxes contain Nifflers. Hagrid has buried some gold, which the Nifflers are attracted to. Each student takes a Niffler, which dive in and out of the freshly turned dirt. Hagrid says that the student whose Niffler returns the most gold at the end of the hour wins a prize. He cautions Goyle not to steal any; it is Leprechaun gold, and it will quickly vanish. Ron's Niffler finds the most gold, winning Ron a slab of Honeyduke's chocolate. As Ron, Harry, and also Hermione, who has returned from the infirmary, head for the castle, Ron suddenly remembers that the gold he gave Harry at the Quidditch World Cup to pay for the omnioculars that summer was Leprechaun gold. Embarrassed that his debt remains unpaid, he asks why Harry never told him it had vanished. When Harry replies he simply never noticed, Ron, quite upset, wishes he could be so rich that he, too, would not notice that a ruddy great lot of gold had simply disappeared. The hate mail continues. Hermione dares not open it now, but some are Howlers that explode at the table, screaming insults at her. Hermione again wonders how Rita knew about Viktor Krum's invitation, or that Hagrid had told Madame Maxime he was half-Giant. Hermione checks with Professor Moody, who says Skeeter is not using an Invisibility Cloak. Harry suggests Rita may have them electronically bugged, but Hermione says that is impossible. Muggle devices are ineffective at Hogwarts because there is too much magic. She leaves to try and figure it out.

Percy's response to Ron's inquiry about Mr. Crouch does not arrive until the end of Easter break. It is uninformative, reiterating only what was reported in *The Daily Prophet*. Easter eggs also arrive from Ron's mother, who has sent huge chocolate eggs filled with toffee for Ron and Harry, and only a tiny egg for Hermione. Ron confirms that his mother reads *Witch Weekly*.

One evening in late May, Professor McGonagall sends Harry to the Quidditch pitch for the meeting about the third Triwizard task. Along the way, Harry meets up with Cedric. Reaching the pitch, Harry is dismayed that it has been transformed into a massive hedge maze. In the center is Ludo Bagman, along with the other Champions, Fleur Delacour and Viktor Krum. Bagman says the Triwizard Cup will be at the center, and there are spells and creatures (provided by Hagrid) they must overcome. The first Champion to reach and touch the Cup receives full marks. Harry is a little concerned, knowing the creatures Hagrid will likely provide. As they exit the maze, Bagman asks for a word with Harry; Viktor Krum also wants to speak to Harry. Guessing what Ludo wants to talk about, Harry chooses to speak with Viktor. Near the Forbidden Forest, Krum asks if Hermione is Harry's girlfriend. Taken aback, Harry assures Viktor they are only friends. As Harry is about to leave, something moves in the Forest behind Krum. Harry draws his wand, but is surprised to see Mr. Crouch, who has apparently gone insane. He is talking to a tree he believes is Percy Weasley. He demands to see Professor Dumbledore. Leaving Krum to guard Mr. Crouch, Harry runs to the castle for help.

Finding the entrance to Dumbledore's office, Harry uses the password, but it no longer works. The entrance suddenly opens to reveal Professor Snape, who says that Dumbledore is too busy for any nonsense. While Harry struggles to get past Snape, the doorway opens again and Dumbledore appears. When Harry reports that Mr. Crouch is on the grounds, Dumbledore asks him to show the way. As they head for the Forbidden Forest, Harry recounts what he saw. With each revelation, Dumbledore moves faster, until they are running. As they arrive, Harry and Dumbledore find that Krum has been Stunned, and Mr. Crouch is gone. Dumbledore sends a message to summon Hagrid, then revives Krum. Viktor says Crouch attacked him from behind. When Hagrid arrives, Dumbledore instructs him to bring Karkaroff and Professor Moody. Moody appears before Hagrid leaves, saying Snape told him where Dumbledore had gone. Dumbledore says it is imperative they find Crouch. Moody pulls out his wand and leaves while Hagrid fetches Karkaroff. When they return, Karkaroff begins ranting that a Triwizard judge attacked his Champion. He claims it is obvious treachery and accuses Dumbledore of complicity. Hagrid loses his temper and, picking up Karkaroff, threatens him. Dumbledore calms Hagrid enough that he sets down Karkaroff. Dumbledore has Hagrid escort Harry to Gryffindor Tower and orders Harry to stay there until morning. Any messages he wants to send can wait until then. Harry wonders how Dumbledore knew he was planning to write to Sirius. As he enters the Tower, he immediately updates Ron and Hermione about what happened.

Analysis

Prior to this chapter, Dumbledore suspected that there could be a dark plot against Harry, while others simply believed he cheated to enter the Tournament. Now more sinister events are unfolding that seemingly support Dumbledore and that could be threatening Harry and the other Champions, although this may or may not sway the doubters' opinions. Mr. Crouch's behavior, although erratic, indicates he probably knows something so dire that he had to somehow get himself to Hogwarts to warn Dumbledore. His disappearance and the attack on Krum only fuels this speculation. However, it is unclear just who stunned Krum or why or where Mr. Crouch has disappeared. Snape's behavior also seems suspicious here. His attempt to block Harry from reaching Dumbledore's office may indicate he knows something about what has just happened and wants to prevent Dumbledore from immediately finding out, although this may just be his usual dismissiveness regarding anything to do with Harry. Meanwhile, Hermione's mission to liberate House-elves is stymied again, this time by the Elves who continually resist change, insisting they are happy only when there is work to be done. Scorning Dobby, they believe freedom is shameful, and the pathetic Winky only proves how miserable their lives would become without masters to serve. It is doubtful if Hermione can ever overcome this obstacle. Hermione is also experiencing the full brunt of Rita Skeeter's vicious story about her. Although Hermione had previously brushed it off, she probably never anticipated the hateful backlash that so many strangers are now heaping on her. Skeeter represents how powerful the media is and the way in which it can easily victimize someone by swaying readers opinions, either with the truth, lies, or both. Curiously, Skeeter's equally slanderous article about Hagrid being a dangerous giant had the opposite effect, with readers rushing to his defense. While many may personally know Hagrid, prompting their support, it seems that Hermione is being unfairly judged by a different standard here, with the public reacting as if she is an "unfaithful hussy" who is two-timing Harry and Viktor, two well-known and admired young wizards. Surprisingly, even Mrs. Weasley believes Skeeter, becoming hostile towards Hermione, despite knowing both her and Harry so well. Krum's asking Harry if there is anything between him and Hermione is a clear indication that Krum is romantically pursuing her. Krum, like many series fans, mistakenly believes Hermione and Harry are "an item," because Hermione often talks about Harry and (presumably) his exploits. Readers should notice Ron's jealousy over their developing relationship, through this book and the next, and how little the relationship seems to discomfit Harry. It is also interesting how little Ron understands his true feelings for Hermione, even explicitly disclaiming them after the Yule Ball.

Ron struggles with other issues, and the Nifflers episode is a mechanism for him to discover that the Leprechaun gold he paid Harry for the omnioculars had vanished. Harry claiming that he was unaware that it was gone only further upsets Ron, who feels Harry has so much money that he does not even notice when it disappears. The author has stated[1] that this is meant to contrast Harry's relative wealth with the Weasley's ongoing poverty, a situation that Ron abhors and is continually embarrassed about. It also causes him to occasionally resent Harry, although Ron fails to understand that his family's financial woes are unrelated to Harry, nor does Harry ever flaunt his affluence. One thing to note here also is how Dumbledore summons Hagrid. Dumbledore actually casts and sends a Patronus with a message for Hagrid; this method of dispatching messages was apparently developed by Dumbledore.

Questions

Review   1. Why would Ludo Bagman want to speak to Harry?

2. How does Hermione embarrass Dobby? Was it intentional? What is Dobby's reaction?

3. Why is Harry worried about what creatures Hagrid may put in the maze? Is he right to be concerned?

4. Why would Mrs. Weasley, who knows Hermione, be angry at her? Is it justified?

5. Why would Karkaroff believe that a Triwizard judge and Dumbledore are involved in the attack on Krum? Is there any proof for that?

6. Why does Percy Weasley send Ron so little information about Mr. Crouch?

Further Study   1. Why does Harry feel it is safe to meet privately with Krum? They are both Champions; eliminating Harry would improve Krum's chances significantly.

2. Why was Viktor Krum Stunned? Who might have done this?

3. Why would Mr. Crouch suddenly appear at Hogwarts to see Dumbledore? What might be causing his strange behavior?

4. Why would Snape want to prevent Harry from seeing Dumbledore, especially during an emergency?

5. What secrets might Mr. Crouch have entrusted to Winky? If these secrets were vital, why would he have discharged her from his house?

6. Why is public reaction to Skeeter's story about Hermione so different from what it was about her story on Hagrid? Is Hermione being held to a different standard than Hagrid? If so, explain why and what that standard might be.

7. Why is Ron often upset with Harry for having money? Are Ron's feeling justified? What is Harry's reaction?

---

1. http://www.jkrowling.com/textonly/en/faq_view.cfm?id=69

GREATER PICTURE

The many hidden events in this chapter are explained in chapter 35. Barty Crouch was alerted to Mr. Crouch's escape by Voldemort, and using the Marauder's Map, saw Crouch enter the grounds. Concealed under an Invisibility Cloak, Barty Jr. tracked his father to where Harry and Krum found him. After Harry went for help, Barty stunned Krum, killed his father and hid his remains under the Cloak. He then returned as Moody to where he had stunned Krum, claiming Snape told him something was amiss; presumably, he had seen Snape and Harry's altercation on the Map. Later, he buried his father's remains in the same ground the Nifflers had been digging in. Hermione will discover Rita Skeeter's secret before the end of the book.

The Imperius curse's effects, as shown in this chapter, are apparently inconsistent with what Harry experiences when Professor Moody casts it on him in class, although Moody may have been using a milder version for the in-class demonstration. In chapter 35, Barty Crouch Jr. states that his father was controlled by Voldemort using the Imperius curse. Both Bartemius Crouch and Voldemort are powerful wizards, and Bartemius was attempting to break the Imperius curse for the past several months. It is now late May, and Voldemort and Wormtail attacked and placed Bartemius under this curse in late August, nine months previously. It is possible that resisting Voldemort for that long damaged Bartemius' mind to the point that he was able to escape Voldemort's control over him. This tallies with Bartemius' disorientation when Harry finds him in the Forbidden Forest. In the next chapter, Voldemort blames Wormtail for Crouch's escape, punishing him severely for his failure. In *Harry Potter and the Half-Blood Prince*, Tonks casts a Patronus and sends it off carrying a message, using the same technique that Dumbledore uses to summon Hagrid in this chapter. The author has stated[1] that this method was invented by Dumbledore, and has only been revealed to members of the Order of the Phoenix; it is used to carry messages between Order members. We will see it used thrice more in *Harry Potter and the Deathly Hallows*; once by Kingsley Shacklebolt announcing the fall of the Ministry, and twice by Mr. Weasley, to announce the arrival of the Minister Of Magic at the Burrow, and to reassure the gone-to-ground Ron that the rest of the family is all right.

Chapter 29: The Dream

SYNOPSIS

Harry, Ron, and Hermione discuss the evening's event far into the night but are unable to determine who Stunned Krum or what happened to Mr. Crouch. They are still trying to figure it out in the morning when they go to the Owlery to send Sirius a message letting him know what is happening. Fred and George suddenly arrive. Thinking they were alone, they had been discussing whether what they are doing looked like blackmail, but upon seeing the Trio, they halt their conversation and parry questions as they send off their letter. After their departure, Ron says they are serious about starting a joke shop, and not just to annoy their mother. They are trying to raise the money, which might cause them to avoid talking to Dumbledore, even if they know something about Mr. Crouch, if it might interfere with their funding.

After History of Magic class, they stop by Professor Moody's classroom, to learn what happened overnight; Moody says that even with Harry's map, he was unable to find Mr. Crouch. Ron thinks he Disapparated, but Hermione reminds him that is impossible on Hogwarts grounds and suggests there are other ways he could have departed the Forest. Moody suggests she consider becoming an Auror; her mind works the right way. Sirius' letter arrives the next morning. Surprisingly, he lectures Harry over how risky it was to stray out-of-bounds with Viktor Krum and demands he stay put. Harry thinks this is rather rich coming from Sirius, but Hermione says Sirius and Moody are right: someone put Harry's name in the Goblet for a reason, and it is safer to stay inside the school and practice for the Third Task.

For the next few days, Harry is stuck indoors practicing jinxes. Hermione thinks Harry has mastered the Stunning spell, using a somewhat battered Ron as a target, and suggests practicing the Impediment jinx. However, it is time for Divination class. Professor Trelawney lectures about planetary divination. The room is hot and the topic so boring that, lulled by an insect buzzing behind him, Harry falls asleep. He dreams he is flying on an eagle owl that goes into an old house, landing on a large armchair. Harry sees Wormtail writhing in pain on a hearthrug, as well as a large snake. A voice from the armchair says that Wormtail is in luck; his blunder has not ruined everything, the man is dead and that Harry Potter may also soon be dead. The voice then says that Wormtail needs another reminder not to blunder again and curses him again.

Harry wakes up screaming on the classroom floor, his scar burning. Brushing off Professor Trelawney's attempts to have him share his experience so she can interpret it, Harry leaves, ostensibly for the infirmary. Instead, he goes to see Dumbledore. Harry gives the gargoyle guarding Dumbledore's office the password, "sherbet lemon," but it fails to open. Other candy flavours also do not work. When he jokingly tries "cockroach cluster," the gargoyle leaps aside. Outside Dumbledore's office, Harry hears a conversation within. The Minister for Magic, Cornelius Fudge is attempting to put a positive spin on Bertha Jorkins' disappearance, saying there is no indication that there is foul play and also suggests that Crouch might have just wandered off. When Dumbledore says he would have had to wander rather quickly, Fudge implies that Madame Maxime could be involved with his disappearance, given her ancestry. Moody interrupts to say that Potter is outside, hearing everything.

---

1. http://www.jkrowling.com/textonly/en/faq_view.cfm?id=99

Analysis

As in chapter 1, Harry once again "dreams" about Voldemort, although he is unaware that he may actually be viewing events as they are occurring. His burning scar implies that there could be a telepathic connection between Harry and Voldemort, one that neither apparently is aware exists. It is interesting that in the dream, an eagle owl carries the message to Voldemort. Only twice before have eagle owls been seen; one flew towards the school, looped the Owlery, and flew away while Harry was lying under a tree by the lake. It is also mentioned in *Harry Potter and the Philosopher's Stone* that Malfoy's eagle owl was always bringing him treats from home. Also, the house in the dream is described as being atop a hill, and the owl flies through a broken window in it. It is unclear if we are meant to draw a connection by these incidents, but the author may be dropping a subtle hint that the Malfoy family is tied to Voldemort, although there is no indication that they know Voldemort's whereabouts. The house could be the old Riddle manor near Little Hangleton, and it may be Voldemort's secret headquarters. Also, Wormtail's "blunder" that results in him being severely punished and the dead man Voldemort mentions are likely related to Mr. Crouch's mysterious disappearance, although just how and why remains unknown.

Despite Mr. Crouch's disappearance and the attack on Krum, Harry is a bit confused and annoyed with Sirius for ordering him to remain inside Hogwarts. Knowing that his godfather can often be daring and reckless himself, Harry feels Sirius is employing an unfair double standard here. But Sirius is being a responsible guardian who is acting in Harry's best interest, and he sternly orders Harry to stay put to prevent him from engaging in any unnecessary risky behavior. Sirius also believes there could be a plot against Harry's life, and knowing his godson as he does, he realizes Harry will likely be unconcerned about his own safety.

It is also a little curious that Harry hears an insect buzzing in the Divination classroom. Being that the room is located atop a tower, there should be fewer insects up there than there are closer to the ground. Granted, on at least one occasion Harry found an insect in the Divination classroom; he was practicing Summoning spells on it. Could there be any particular significance to Harry hearing an insect?

Questions

Review   1. Is Ron correct that if the Twins knew about Mr. Crouch's disappearance they would say nothing about it to Dumbledore? Why wouldn't they?

2. Why is Harry so surprised by what Sirius says in his letter? Given what we know at this point, is Sirius right?

3. Even though Moody has a magical eye, how does he know that Harry is listening outside Dumbledore's door?

Further Study   1. Just what might the Twins be doing that could be considered blackmail? Why do they refuse to explain what this is?

2. Why would Harry see an eagle owl in his dream?

3. How did an insect get so far up in the Tower?

4. Where might Mr. Crouch be? Why was Moody unable to find him on Harry's Marauders' Map?

5. Just how might Wormtail have blundered so badly that Voldemort punishes him for it? Could it be related to anything happening at Hogwarts? If so, what?

6. Why does Fudge continue to claim that nothing bad has happened to Bertha Jorkins? Is he right, and what is he basing his opinion on?

Greater Picture

The eagle owl is a slight misdirection; at this point, the only Death Eaters who know that Voldemort is still alive are Barty Crouch and Wormtail. This remains true until after Voldemort summons his Death Eaters, about a month from now in our story. In his present state, Voldemort is relatively weak, and he wants to avoid revealing his presence by alerting the Death Eaters.

We will also learn later that Voldemort had been hiding in London, in Bartemius Crouch's house, while Mr. Crouch was under Wormtail's control with the Imperius Curse. Once Crouch escaped, however, that house was no longer safe, because when Crouch was found it would lead his finders back to the Crouch residence. At that point, Voldemort and Wormtail would have had to shift to new quarters, and Riddle Manor was likely the most opportune. With Frank Bryce gone, it is unlikely anyone would dare enter the grounds anyway; and if they did, Wormtail would easily be able to dissuade them.

In some possible foreshadowing, George, as he is sending off his owl, tells Ron that he is starting to sound like their older brother, Percy, and warns him that if he continues, he will be made Prefect. Ron, to his and everyone's great surprise, is made a Gryffindor Prefect in the next book.

The buzzing insect in the Divination classroom is Rita Skeeter in her unregistered Animagus form, spying on Harry. Considering that Harry had previously practiced spells on an insect in the Divination classroom, it is lucky for Skeeter that he did not do so this time, although this could have proved particularly entertaining for the readers.

Chapter 30: The Pensieve

Synopsis

Professor Moody opens the door and invites Harry in. Cornelius Fudge asks if it was he who found Mr. Crouch. Knowing it is useless to pretend he did not overhear their conversation, Harry admits he did, but says that Madame Maxime was not there, adding, "And she'd have a job hiding, wouldn't she?" Fudge suggests he return to class, but Harry wants to see Professor Dumbledore. Dumbledore suggests he wait there while he, Professor Moody, and Fudge survey the spot where Mr. Crouch was found.

Alone in Dumbledore's office, Harry is intrigued by a shimmering light on the wall. Hunting its source, he finds a partially opened cupboard containing a stone bowl. It is filled with an odd, glittering, substance, halfway between a liquid and a gas. Inside it he sees a torch-lit stone room, filled with tiny witches and wizards. He moves closer for a better view, poking it with his wand, but when his nose tip touches the surface, he is catapulted into the scene. Nobody notices him, not even Professor Dumbledore next to him. Harry recalls when he similarly observed Tom Riddle's memories, and settles down to watch.

Harry has tumbled into a courtroom, an empty chair with chains on its arms sits in the middle. A trial is underway, and spectators are watching a door, which soon opens and two Dementors enter, dragging Igor Karkaroff between them. Karkaroff is placed in the chair; the Dementors exit, and the chains glow golden and enwrap Karkaroff's arms and legs. The proceedings are headed by a younger Bartemius Crouch; Alastor Moody is also present, talking to Dumbledore. Karkaroff, bargaining for his freedom, offers to identify Death Eaters. He names Antonin Dolohov, but Crouch responds he is already in custody. Increasingly desperate, Karkaroff mentions Evan Rosier, Travers, and Mulciber, only to hear that each has been captured or killed. He finally mentions Augustus Rookwood, who works in the Department of Mysteries and was passing information to Voldemort. Crouch admits they did not know about Rookwood, but then says Karkaroff will be returned to Azkaban while they deliberate. In desperation, Karkaroff says that Severus Snape was a Death Eater. Dumbledore rises to say that while Severus had been a Death Eater, he had turned double agent before Voldemort's downfall and is now no more a Death Eater than Dumbledore himself.

The memory fades and returns. It is the same room, but the atmosphere is lighter. This time, it is a younger Ludo Bagman who walks into the room and takes a seat. To his evident relief, the chair does not chain him. Mr. Crouch says he stands accused of aiding Death Eaters. Bagman claims he was a bit idiotic, being unaware that Rookwood was working for Death Eaters. He believed he was collecting information for "our side." The Wizengamot votes to free him, although Moody and Crouch are annoyed at this outcome.

Again the memory fades. When the room returns, it is grimmer. As a witch sobs in the center, a door opens to admit six Dementors escorting four people. Over the woman's piteous cries, a gaunter-looking Mr. Crouch says they stand accused of using the Cruciatus Curse on the Auror Frank Longbottom in an attempt to discover Voldemort's whereabouts. That failing, they then used it on his wife, Alice Longbottom. He calls for the Wizengamot to vote; the assembled witches and wizards unanimously sentence them to life in Azkaban. The lone woman defiantly cries out that the Dark Lord will return. The crying boy is Barty Crouch, Jr., who pleads with his father not to send him back to Azkaban, but Crouch, stony-faced, states he is not his son; he has no son. From the audience, a weeping Mrs. Crouch watches as Barty is condemned.

A second Dumbledore says it is time to go, and, taking Harry's elbow, they rise and return to Hogwarts. Harry starts apologizing but Dumbledore assures Harry that he quite understands. He explains that the bowl is Pensieve. When too many thoughts and memories are crammed into his mind, it is a relief to siphon some off and store them there. It is possible to see patterns inside the Pensieve that are not immediately apparent. Using his wand, Dumbledore extracts a thought and places it in the Pensieve. Harry is surprised to see his own face, only to watch it smoothly turning into Snape's who says, "It's coming back, Karkaroff's too . . ." Dumbledore muses that it is a connection he would have been able to make without help. Harry again apologizes, but Dumbledore responds that curiosity is not a sin, but it requires caution. A teenaged girl's image then rises from the Pensieve. She is explaining that a boy jinxed her because she said she had seen him kissing Florence behind the greenhouses. Dumbledore asks why she followed him behind the greenhouses in the first place. Dumbledore says that this is Bertha Jorkins as she was when he knew her at Hogwarts.

Dumbledore reminds Harry he that he came to see him about something, and Harry recounts his dream. Dumbledore asks if there was any other time, other than the end of the summer, when his scar hurt. Harry says no, but then stops—how did Dumbledore know about his scar hurting? Dumbledore says that Harry is not Sirius' only correspondent. Dumbledore seems to be analyzing this dream, pacing, and periodically removing thoughts from his mind and placing them in the Pensieve. Dumbledore tells Harry he believes his scar hurts whenever Voldemort is nearby and feeling particularly strong emotions. Dumbledore tells Harry that it, "was no ordinary dream." Harry says that he did not see Voldemort in it, only an armchair from behind, but there would be nothing to see: Voldemort still lacks a body. Asked if Voldemort is getting stronger, Dumbledore replies that his earlier accession to power was marked by unexplained disappearances. There have been three unexplained disappearances recently: Bertha Jorkins, Bartemius Crouch, Sr., and a Muggle, Frank Bryce, who vanished from Tom Riddle Sr.'s home village. Dumbledore believes they are linked, although the Ministry does not.

Harry inquires if it was Neville's parents who were mentioned in the memory. Dumbledore asks if Harry had ever wondered why Neville lived with his grandmother, and then goes on to say that yes, that was Neville's parents. They were tortured to insanity and now permanently reside in St. Mungo's Hospital for Magical Maladies and Injuries. They no longer recognize Neville. Dumbledore also tells Harry that Ludo Bagman has been uninvolved in anything Dark since his trial. Neither has Severus Snape. Dumbledore assures Harry that he trusts Snape, but why is between Snape and himself. Dumbledore requests that Harry say nothing about Neville's parents, not even to Ron or Hermione. That is Neville's story to tell. Finally, he wishes Harry luck in the third task.

Analysis

Readers have watched the story unfold mostly through Harry's point-of-view or as told to him by other characters; gradually, the author has added additional mechanisms for Harry (and readers) to gain information about Voldemort and his Death Eaters. In *Harry Potter and the Chamber of Secrets,* Harry viewed Tom Riddle's memories that were stored in his diary. Now Dumbledore's Pensieve provides yet another means for Harry to observe historical events first-hand. The Pensieve is also introducing new characters who are from the past that readers may be seeing again in the future. It also sheds light on some current characters, such as Ludo Bagman, who was interrogated but never convicted as a Voldemort follower, although his actual involvement is still suspect. And though Harry learns much by watching both Voldemort's and Dumbledore's memories, these are still memories, and they may be imperfect and affected by personal viewpoints and biases.

It is also becoming apparent to us, gradually, that Harry has also been occasionally watching events in real time through a mental connection that exists between him and Voldemort. As these mostly play out at times when Harry is asleep, Harry still believes he is just having bad dreams. Harry's mental connection to Voldemort may become his most valuable information avenue, as he is viewing things that are currently happening although he has not, as yet, completely utilized this, being previously unsure if what he had been seeing was actually real; also, the information he does receive is sporadic and incomplete, making it difficult to analyze. There is also a danger that Voldemort can learn as much through Harry if he also discovers this link; it is probably only a matter of time before he does. Also, Dumbledore has presumably been depositing his abundant thoughts into the Pensieve for many decades, including ones unrelated to Harry or Voldemort. How then does Harry happen to see only those memories directly related to current events and that are the most helpful to him? Is it possible that Dumbledore intended for Harry to view these particular recollections? It may be that Dumbledore is legally or ethically prevented from sharing such confidential information, and by making his memories available, he is able to pass this on to Harry without reprisal. The opened cupboard door almost seemed like an invitation for Harry to peer inside. This is, of course, only speculation and unfortunately, it remains unanswered. The Pensieve also reveals much about Neville Longbottom through what happened to his parents. The trauma Neville has suffered over his mother and father's sad fate may explain, at least partially, why his memory and magical abilities have been impaired. For whatever reason, Neville has chosen to keep his parents' condition secret, but Harry's knowledge about this will bring the two boys closer together, Harry realizing that Neville lost his parents to Voldemort, just as Harry lost his.

As a side note, it is interesting that even though the courtroom scenes are from Dumbledore's viewpoint, he is seen as a bystander. This matches what had happened in Tom Riddle's memories; though it was Tom's memories, Harry was always standing beside Tom, rather than seeing directly through Tom's eyes.

Questions

Review 1. Why has Neville never told anyone about what happened to his parents? How might this knowledge change Harry's relationship with Neville?

2. Why is Harry so surprised that Dumbledore has been communicating with Sirius? Why has Sirius never mentioned this to Harry?

3. Why did Harry wait so long to tell Dumbledore about his dreams?

4. Why is Dumbledore convinced that Harry's visions are something other than dreams?

Further Study 1. Why does Dumbledore refuse to tell Harry the reason he trusts Snape? Is Dumbledore's trust warranted?

2. Why does the Ministry maintain that Bertha Jorkins,' Mr. Crouch's, and Frank Bryce's disappearances are unrelated? Are they? Explain.

3. Did Dumbledore intend for Harry to view his memories in the Pensieve? What evidence is there for this? If he did intend for Harry to see them, why didn't he just tell Harry all this instead?

Greater Picture

Knowing now that Harry has had at least two "dreams" which were apparent mirrors of Voldemort's thoughts, Dumbledore is now beginning to understand the nature of the link between Harry's mind and Voldemort's. This will cause Harry great concern in the next book, as Dumbledore will be taking great pains to conceal the nature of the relationship between himself and Harry from any potential eavesdropping by Voldemort through that link. Dumbledore feels, correctly as it turns out, that if Voldemort is aware of any feelings between Harry and himself more than student to headmaster, he will make use of those feelings as a weapon against Harry, Dumbledore, or both. In order to conceal his affection for Harry, Dumbledore will studiously avoid even making eye contact with Harry. As a result, Harry will feel that Dumbledore has abandoned him, and will, at several points in the book, refuse to pass information to Dumbledore that might have proved useful. Voldemort will become aware of the link near Christmas time, when Harry becomes aware of an attack being made on Mr. Weasley by means of the link, and throughout much of the remainder of that book, Voldemort will be attempting to use that link to use Harry to steal a Prophecy for him.

The Pensieve will be used by Harry again, providing him answers not only about Voldemort, but also his father and mother, Aunt Petunia, and also Snape. Perhaps interestingly, the function of the Pensieve will not be to store and look for connections between existing memories, as is implied here. The function of the Pensieve, as it will be used, is the way Harry uses it first: to replay memories placed in it. In the next book, we will use it to show an episode in Snape's life. In *Harry Potter and the Half-Blood Prince,* we will be examining the memories of those who have some knowledge of Voldemort in his younger days, when he was still known as Tom Riddle. And in *Harry Potter and the Deathly Hallows,* we will be using it to replay memories of Snape's youth and adult life, thereby learning no small amount about Harry's parents.

Chapter 31: The Third Task

Synopsis

Harry immediately tells Ron and Hermione what transpired in Professor Dumbledore's office and in the Pensieve. He also informs Sirius by owl post. Of course, they already knew Karkaroff was a Death Eater, but this is the first confirmation that Professor Snape was one or that Ludo Bagman was involved. Hermione wonders if this is what Rita Skeeter meant by saying that Bagman had an evil past. Hermione suddenly remembers that they are supposed to practice jinxes with Harry, but it is late, and she sends Harry and Ron to bed. Harry finds it hard to sleep, thinking about the four Death Eaters who tortured Neville's parents and Mr. Crouch's son, who died in Azkaban a year later.

Rather than studying for the exams that are scheduled the week before the third task, Ron and Hermione instead coach Harry on jinxes. When Ron, tired of being Stunned, suggests Hermione take a turn, she quickly decides that Harry knows the spells well enough. Ron sees Draco Malfoy outside, with his cronies, Crabbe and Goyle standing guard, apparently talking to something in his hand. Harry thinks he may be using a walkie-talkie, but Hermione dismisses that, saying electronic devices do not work around Hogwarts.

Sirius, concerned about Harry finishing the third task, sends owls almost daily with tips and pointers, plus adjurations to ignore what is happening outside Hogwarts. He feels that Harry will be safe at Hogwarts under Dumbledore's protection. Navigating the maze safely is the first priority. Once the third task is over, they can consider other problems.

On the day of the third task, a new story about Harry appears in the *Daily Prophet*. Rita Skeeter claims that Harry has mental problems, has collapsed, and complains about pain in his scar. Draco Malfoy is quoted as saying Harry is a Parselmouth. Harry takes the article lightly, unlike Ron and Hermione, who were almost afraid to show it to him. Harry wonders, however, how Skeeter knew that he fainted in Divination. He remembers an open window during class, but Hermione points out that the North Tower classroom is too far above ground level for them to be overheard. When Harry reminds Hermione that she is supposed to be researching magical bugging methods, something suddenly occurs to her. As usual, she says nothing, but runs to the library for some last-minute research. As Ron heads for his History of Magic exam, Professor McGonagall tells Harry that the Champions and their families are congregating in the chamber off the Great Hall. Not having any relatives present, Harry watches as the other Champions head into the chamber. As he is about to leave, Cedric calls out, "They're waiting for you!" Inside are Mrs. Weasley and Bill. Harry's pleasure at seeing them overrides Cedric's father suggesting that Harry, "isn't so full of himself," now that Cedric is tied with him. However, Amos Diggory appears upset that Rita Skeeter's first story only mentioned Harry as the Hogwarts Champion. Not even Mrs. Weasley reminding him that Rita delights in making mischief calms him down.

Harry, Mrs. Weasley, and Bill enjoy a lovely morning touring the Hogwarts grounds, with Mrs. Weasley reminiscing about her time there. Mrs. Weasley says the Ministry has become suspicious that Mr. Crouch's instructions may not be genuine, and Percy has been called in for questioning. As a result, Cornelius Fudge is taking Percy's place as a judge. Returning to the castle for lunch, they meet Ron and Hermione. Mrs. Weasley is rather cold towards Hermione until Harry, remembering Skeeter's article in *Witch Weekly*, tells her that Hermione is not his girlfriend. Because Mrs. Weasley is present, Hermione is unable to tell Harry and Ron something. Harry, Bill, and Mrs. Weasley return to the Great Hall for dinner. The judges have arrived and are sitting at the head table. Harry notices that Madame Maxime's eyes seem red, and Hagrid keeps glancing at her.

An afternoon of touring the grounds with Bill and Mrs. Weasley rounds out Harry's day. As the sky darkens, Professor Dumbledore sends the Champions to the maze. Ludo Bagman checks if Harry is feeling confident, then announces the four patrollers: Professor McGonagall, Professor Moody, Professor Flitwick, and Hagrid, who will patrol the maze from outside. If a Champion gets into trouble, red wand sparks can be sent up, and he will be extracted from the maze. After Ludo sends the patrollers off, Harry and Cedric enter the maze. At the first intersection, they separate. Harry hears the whistle sending Krum into the maze, and five minutes later, the one for Fleur. Using the Four Points charm, Harry navigates towards the maze's center. Already unnerved by its apparent emptiness, Harry hears a noise behind him. It is Cedric, still smoking after a run-in with a Blast-Ended Skrewt. Shortly after, Harry successfully defends himself against a Boggart disguised as a Dementor. As he negotiates an antigravity spell, he hears Fleur screaming. Once through the spell, he is unable to locate her and continues towards the center, running into a Skrewt. Temporarily stopping the Skrewt, Harry looks for another route and hears Krum using the Cruciatus curse on Cedric. Burning a hole through a hedge, Harry Stuns Krum, and sends up red sparks. He and Cedric separate and again head for the center.

Nearing the center, Harry encounters a Sphinx and correctly answers its question. Seeing the Cup, he starts running for it, only to have Cedric appear from a side passage ahead. He sees a giant spider. He warns Cedric and attempts to tackle the spider. Together, they defeat it, but Harry's leg is injured. Harry tells Cedric to take the Cup, but Cedric demurs, saying Harry earned it. Because they have continually helped each other throughout the Tournament, Harry suggests they grasp it simultaneously. Cedric agrees, and helps Harry to it; each grabs a handle. The Cup is a Portkey, and a great howling wind whirls them from the maze.

Chapter 31: The Third Task

Analysis

The author may have chosen a maze for the third task not only because it makes for a difficult and interesting obstacle for the Champions to maneuver, but also for its mythic symbolism. In mythology, a labyrinth, or maze, represents a difficult challenge or quest that the hero must overcome by navigating a convoluted and dangerous path leading to its center where whatever is being sought awaits. Magic and battling strange creatures often play a significant role in these epic myths, just as it does in our story. In this task, each Champion must enter the maze alone, away from the cheering crowd, and with almost no advance information regarding what they will encounter; this challenge is less about competing against one's opponents than it is about overcoming personal frailties. That the third task begins at dusk adds an additional eerie twist, as what lies inside becomes more intangible and less definable when cloaked in nightfall. And while darkness can represent evil and oppression, it also symbolizes fear and uncertainty, which often seem magnified at night and less daunting by day. It can also represent the unknown, transition, and also life—darkness preceding birth. The maze could also be interpreted as a metaphor for Harry's life. His late induction into the wizarding world was much like entering the maze at twilight—he was faced with murky, unknown paths, difficult obstacles, and occasional dead ends that had to be retraced and alternate routes found. Harry also navigates a tangled emotional labyrinth, searching for a center containing answers about his parents, Voldemort, and himself.

The Triwizard Champions were chosen because they are the best students in their respective schools. Cedric and Harry each represent their Houses' finest traits: Harry is a brave and resourceful Gryffindor, while Cedric embodies Hufflepuff virtues of hard work, honesty, and fair play. However, throughout the Tournament, they have both shown characteristics that each House values. Harry shows integrity and fairness, first by tipping Cedric off about the Dragons, and now by insisting that he equally share the victory. Cedric has demonstrated increasing cleverness and ingenuity by quickly figuring out the Egg riddle and developing a successful strategy for the second task; he also shows great courage, both inside the maze and with the dragon. Each Champion has continually helped the other throughout the Tournament, and as they reach the Cup, each feels the other deserves to win; therefore, it is fitting that they agree to grab the Triwizard Cup together, although the outcome is unexpected.

Draco speaking to his hand seems as peculiar as Mr. Crouch talking with a tree. It is unlikely Draco is suffering from any mental malady like Crouch, however, and he is probably engaged in some activity he should not. We will learn shortly what this is, but for now, it is sufficient to know that he is holding something in his hand, and there is a reason he is conversing with it.

It seems a little odd that Sirius should be telling Harry not to worry about things outside the school; that sort of insularity in a school environment happens normally anyway. However, Sirius' belief ought to be right; Dumbledore should be able to keep Harry safe.

Questions

Review 1. Just what might Hermione know that she wants to tell Harry about?

2. Why are Madame Maxime's eyes red? Why is Hagrid looking at her?

3. Why might the author have chosen to use a maze for the third task, and what could it represent?

4. Why does Harry insist that he and Cedric grab the Triwizard Cup at the same time? What does Cedric think?

Further Study 1. Why is Draco talking to his hand? Is he going mad like Mr. Crouch?

2. Why is Sirius confident that Harry is safe at Hogwarts, even though he suspects someone wants to kill him? Is Harry really safe?

3. Mrs. Weasley tells Amos Diggory that Rita Skeeter likes to create trouble by printing lies about Harry. Why then does she continue to believe Skeeter's story about Hermione?

4. Why would Krum attack Fleur and Cedric? Does he also intend to harm Harry?

5. Why would the Triwizard Cup be a Portkey? Where might it be transporting Harry and Cedric to?

6. Even though Harry and Cedric were sorted into different Houses, they both have many qualities that reflect the other's House. Compare and contrast these qualities.

Greater Picture

Note that Mr. Crouch's son having died while imprisoned in Azkaban is being mentioned here again. However, we will learn shortly that it was someone other than Barty who actually died in Azkaban. The reiteration of this mistaken belief is almost certainly meant to heighten our surprise at the discovery of what Barty has been doing since his supposed death.

Sirius here admits that he believes someone at the school may be trying to kill Harry; likely Dumbledore does also, but neither suspects it is Barty Crouch, believing he is dead and unaware that the real Alastor "Mad Eye" Moody has been kidnapped. Given this belief, though, it is odd that Sirius is ordering Harry to stay at the school and play out the Tournament. It would seem that if someone has entered Harry in the Tournament in order to get him killed, it would be to Harry's advantage to deliberately fail on the three Tasks in such a way as to avoid any risk. Harry, however, seems to be unable to give any mission less than his full effort.

Draco is talking to his hand because he is holding Rita Skeeter, who is in her beetle Animagus form. Draco has been passing information to her about Harry and others that she then uses in her articles. She was in her beetle form when Harry had his nightmare in the Divination tower, and she saw that event directly. Hermione, because of the repetition of the word "bugged," has come to the conclusion that Rita can transform into an insect, and presumably goes to the library to research whether that transformation is even possible. Though she has confirmed her conclusion by the time we see her at lunch, the author has managed to arrange things so that Hermione cannot discuss her discovery with either Harry or Ron then, and presumably Hermione is too concerned with the Third Task after her final exam of the day to discuss Rita with Ron.

Harry thinks to himself that the Maze is easier to pass through than he had expected. Barty Crouch will admit later that he had deliberately eased Harry's path through the maze, and had controlled Krum to try and eliminate Harry's competition. Barty, like Ludo, had intended Harry to win the Triwizard specifically so that he would be the first to reach and touch the Cup, and so that the Cup would then carry Harry away to an as-yet unknown destination.

Chapter 32: Flesh, Blood, and Bone

Synopsis

The Triwizard Cup is a Portkey and deposits Harry and Cedric in a graveyard (which readers may suspect is in Little Hangleton). As they look around and wonder where they are, a figure approaches them, apparently carrying a baby. Harry's scar begins burning; the intense pain causes him to drop his wand and fall to the ground. A high voice orders, "Kill the spare." Cedric is instantly murdered by the approaching man. Harry, through his pain, dimly realizes he is being tied to a grave marker with the name Tom Riddle inscribed on it. He recognizes his assailant—Wormtail (Peter Pettigrew).

Wormtail checks Harry's bonds and gags him roughly, then departs. Looking at the bundle next to the graveside, Harry is appalled by the half-infant, half-snake creature. His scar burns again as the thing glares back through red, slitted eyes. Wormtail returns with a huge stone cauldron containing a clear potion, placing it beside the bundle and lighting a fire beneath. Wormtail picks up the creature and drops it into the cauldron; Harry hopes it drowns. Wormtail causes the grave under Harry's feet to disgorge something that looks like dust; he chants, "Bone of the father unknowingly given. You will renew your son!" Wormtail sends it into the cauldron. Slicing off his right hand and dropping it into the cauldron, he continues haltingly, "Flesh—of the servant—w-willingly given—you will revive—your master." In pain and weeping, he slits Harry's arm with the knife and collects blood in a vial. As it drips into the cauldron, he chants, "B-blood of the enemy... forcibly taken... you will... resurrect your foe." The cauldron emits huge vaporous clouds from which a tall, skeletal man ascends and alights on the ground. He orders Wormtail to robe him. Lord Voldemort has arisen.

Analysis

Just as Cedric dies, Voldemort is reborn. Cedric's death is a tragedy, but it is all the more so because he is killed only because he was an unexpected impediment to Voldemort's evil plan. After his hard-fought and well-deserved victory, Cedric's life was flicked away in an instant as if he was nothing more than an annoying insect. Not only does Harry see Cedric die, but he also witnesses Voldemort's horrific resurrection, which Harry is forced to participate in, his blood being added to the monstrous recipe helps restore the Dark Lord's body. In addition to being tied by their brother wands and Harry's scar, through which Harry imbibed some of Voldemort's powers, they are now bound even closer by their blood; just how this bond will affect future events is unknown. When Harry comes face-to-face with the completely restored and now powerful Voldemort, he sees him for the first time as a fully formed human. Previously, he was only a grotesque face attached to Professor Quirrell's head (in *Harry Potter and the Philosopher's Stone*) and as the young Tom Riddle's memory in the diary (in *Harry Potter and the Chamber of Secrets*). Now he is a flesh and blood being, poised to kill Harry before inflicting more evil on the unsuspecting Wizarding world that he intends to conquer.

Questions

Review 1. Why was Cedric Diggory killed?
2. Was Harry transported to this particular cemetery for a reason? If so, why?
3. Why does Voldemort use Harry's blood in the ritual?

Further Study 1. Why would Wormtail sacrifice his hand? Could his blood being used in the ritual change his relationship with either Harry or Voldemort? Explain.
2. For the first time, Harry sees Voldemort as a fully restored human. How does this change Harry's perspective about Voldemort, and how will this affect their ongoing conflict?

Greater Picture

Voldemort, by using Harry's blood for his resurrection, has unintentionally strengthened the existing connection between them. This connection was forged by Voldemort's attempt to kill the one-year-old Harry. Professor Dumbledore, upon hearing that Voldemort used Harry's blood, displays a "gleam of something like triumph." In Book Seven, *Deathly Hallows*, when Voldemort casts the killing curse on Harry, this blood tie between Harry and Voldemort is all that tethers Harry to life, enabling him to survive the Avada Kedavra curse a second and third time, and it ultimately causes Voldemort's downfall.

Curiously, Wormtail's blood and flesh are also used in the ritual, although it is never revealed if this also gives him any significant tie to either Harry or Voldemort. Wormtail already owes Harry a life debt. Could their intermingled blood strengthen that obligation? While interesting to consider, this is only speculation.

Witnessing Cedric's murder will adversely affect Harry, giving him nightmares through the coming summer. It will also alter his relationship with Cho Chang, who first looks to Harry for information about Cedric's death, then clings to him for consolation that he is unable give, and finally leaves him when she is unable to cope with her loss. It will also enable Harry to see creatures that are visible only to those who have seen death first-hand. These creatures, called Thestrals, will play a role in *Harry Potter and the Order of the Phoenix*.

Though Dumbledore accepts them immediately, Harry's claims that Voldemort has returned will be disputed by the Ministry of Magic, who will continue to deny this "inconvenient truth" while subjecting both Harry and Dumbledore to public damnation and ridicule, painting Harry as a delusional, attention-seeking liar. Adding insult, the Ministry will also claim that Cedric died from injuries resulting from his own carelessness during the Tournament. This refusal of the Ministry to accept Voldemort's return will cause a year-long conflict between Dumbledore and the Ministry, with the students at Hogwarts, especially Harry, becoming victims trapped between the two forces.

Chapter 33: The Death Eaters

SYNOPSIS

Ignoring the weeping Wormtail, the newly-risen Lord Voldemort examines himself closely. Producing his wand from a robe pocket, he slams Wormtail into the tombstone Harry is bound to. He laughingly demands that Wormtail extend his arm. When Wormtail proffers his severed limb, Voldemort demands his other arm, and ignoring Wormtail's continued sobs, pushes back the sleeve to expose the vivid red Dark Mark. Musing that, "They will all have noticed it," Voldemort touches it with a finger. Harry's scar burns fiercely again while Wormtail howls. When Voldemort removes his finger from the mark, it is black. Voldemort appears to be waiting for something, impatiently pacing back and forth. He tells Harry he is standing on Riddle, Sr.'s grave, and the house on the hillside above them was his father's home. His father, a Muggle and a fool, abandoned his mother before he was born, leaving Voldemort to be raised in an orphanage after his mother died in childbirth. Voldemort vowed revenge upon Tom Riddle, Sr. "But look, Harry! My *true* family returns." Hooded figures begin appearing. They approach Voldemort, kiss his robe hem, and retreat to form a circle around the Dark Lord, Harry, the sobbing Wormtail, and Tom Riddle's grave. Voldemort chastises them for believing him defeated and asks if they now owe their allegiance to Albus Dumbledore. One Death Eater, Avery, falls at Voldemort's feet again, pleading for forgiveness. Voldemort curses him. Ordering him to get up, Voldemort says that he does not forgive, he does not forget, and that he will want thirteen years repayment from all his Death Eaters. Wormtail has already done some repayment, and will be rewarded for his service in bringing him back to life. Voldemort then creates a magical silver hand that attaches itself to Wormtail's wrist. Wormtail stops sobbing immediately, kisses Voldemort's robe, and scurries to take his place in the circle.

Voldemort strolls around the Death Eaters, speaking first to Lucius Malfoy, who claims he was waiting for a sign from Voldemort. He would have appeared instantly if he had known his master was still alive, but Voldemort cuts him off. He accuses Lucius of running from the Dark Mark at the Quidditch World Cup. Voldemort pauses at another empty space, saying it should be occupied by the Lestranges, who were sentenced to Azkaban for supporting Voldemort's cause. They will be rewarded when Azkaban is broken and the Dementors are recruited to the Dark side. Voldemort also says he will recall the banished giants, he will have all his allies at his side. Continuing around the circle, Voldemort says a few words to the Death Eaters: Macnair, Crabbe, Goyle, Nott. He pauses at the largest gap, where he says six Death Eaters should be standing. Three dead in his service, one too cowardly to return, one may never return and needs to be killed. His most faithful servant, who is at Hogwarts, had already re-entered his service and by whose efforts Harry Potter has now joined them for Voldemort's rebirthing. Lucius Malfoy submissively asks Voldemort how he returned. Voldemort says it is an interesting story that both starts and ends with Harry Potter. On the night he went to kill Harry, Lily Potter died attempting to save her son. Her death gave Harry an unforeseen protection: Voldemort was unable to touch him. Voldemort says that has been overcome and demonstrates by touching Harry's face. Lily's sacrifice, Voldemort continues, caused his killing curse to rebound upon him, ripping his soul from his body. Even Voldemort, who has "gone further than anyone along the path leading to immortality," did not understand what he had become. He was pure spirit, less even than a ghost, but still alive. In this less-than-ghostly state, he traveled to a far land, waiting for his trusted Death Eaters to find him, but none did. Without a body, without a wand, there was no magic he could do to save himself, except possess other bodies. He did this, taking over animals, but none suited his needs, and none lived long. Four years previous, though, a young, gullible wizard wandered across his path. This wizard, a teacher at Dumbledore's school, was nearly ideal for his needs. After traveling with him to England, Voldemort took over his body to complete his plan to steal the Philosopher's Stone, but failed, thwarted by Harry Potter. The servant died when Voldemort fled his body, and, weak as before, returned to his forest haunts.

Wormtail, driven from hiding by those he thought his friends, came looking for Voldemort, helped by his ability to communicate with rats. Stopping at an inn, he ran into Bertha Jorkins, a Ministry employee. Bertha might have been an end to Voldemort's hopes at that point, but Wormtail managed to overpower her. He brought Bertha to Voldemort, who learned about the Triwizard Tournament from her and discovered that a faithful Death Eater was willing to help. When she was of no further use, Voldemort murdered her. Wormtail managed to fashion a rudimentary body, and using Nagini's venom as a potion ingredient, kept him alive. Voldemort knew that old Dark magic could restore his body. One vital ingredient, the flesh of the servant, was readily available. The "bone of the father" meant the ritual had to be performed in Little Hangleton, where Tom Riddle was buried. The "blood of the foe" is Harry's blood. This would remove the protection afforded by Lily's sacrifice, and Voldemort would be able to touch Harry without damage to himself. But how to get Harry? By turning the Cup into a Portkey and ensuring that Harry won the Triwizard Tournament, Harry could be removed from Dumbledore's protection. With help from Voldemort's faithful servant, it was done. Now Harry is here and defenceless. And to prove this, Voldemort performs the Cruciatus curse on him; Harry suddenly experiences more pain than he has ever felt before. Just as suddenly, it ends. Voldemort says it was foolish to think this boy could cause his end; but he offers him a chance. He will be allowed to fight, and the Death Eaters will see who is stronger. He orders Wormtail to untie Harry and return his wand.

Analysis

By updating his Death Eaters about his exile, Voldemort confirms much that was surmised about him earlier in the series. He considers himself superior to everyone, even believing that fate favors him more—he has overcome death itself. Voldemort also believes that Harry's repeated survival is nothing more than chance or luck, rather than any special talent. This belief, and thus underestimation of Harry's abilities, is one of Voldemort's greater flaws, and it is one reason Harry survives. Voldemort's maniacal personality is also on full display here as he lords over his cowering Death Eaters. Voldemort rules by fear and intimidation, punishing followers for any perceived mistake or disloyalty, often lashing out randomly in uncontrollable rage. And though Voldemort does reward loyalty, he does so sparingly and at a high cost; he also simultaneously punishes followers, as shown by his cruel indifference to Wormtail's suffering, even though he was instrumental in bringing about Voldemort's resurrection. Voldemort replaces his severed hand only after a prolonged agonizing period, knowing that Wormtail serves him only to protect himself, not because he is a loyal servant. It will be a long time, if ever, before Wormtail's debt to Voldemort is settled.

Voldemort also believes his supreme abilities will be proved beyond doubt by defeating Harry in a duel. It is questionable how Voldemort rationalizes to himself that defeating a young, unqualified wizard that Voldemort proclaims has no special talent will prove this, although Voldemort will likely claim otherwise after Harry's death. For the moment, Voldemort savors any opportunity to grandstand before his cowering Death Eater audience, and he intends to herald his return by slaying the famous Harry Potter, shocking the Wizarding world and undermining resistance to his takeover.

Just how Voldemort survived his first encounter with Harry thirteen years before is also hinted at here, although the full story is still unknown. Voldemort believes Harry survived the Avada Kedavra curse because old magic that was combined with Lily Potter's love for her child protected Harry. Readers have seen how new magic is constantly being invented (the Weasley Twins are a prime example), with many spells, charms, and hexes constantly falling in and out of fashion. Voldemort places great importance on it being ancient magic that protected Harry, indicating that it may grow stronger as it survives through the centuries, forgotten by many perhaps, but a powerful tool for those few wizards who know its existence. The ancient magic that saved Harry is also what ripped Voldemort's soul from his body when his Killing curse rebounded off baby Harry, striking him. Harry is privy to this explanation only because Voldemort chooses to share it, perceiving Harry as being nearly powerless, and delighting in showing off his "superior" knowledge before killing him. But if Harry can escape the cemetery, he will carry this valuable information back to Hogwarts and to Dumbledore.

Voldemort's "servant" who died after Voldemort failed to steal the Philosopher's Stone is obviously Professor Quirrell; this is our first complete confirmation that he died after Voldemort fled his body.

Questions

Review   1. Which servant that died when Voldemort fled is he referring to?

2. Why does Voldemort tell Harry what happened to him (Voldemort) after he was disembodied, why Harry survived the Avada Kedavra curse, how Lily's love protected her son, and so on?

Further Study   1. Voldemort had a body—an infantile one—when he is first seen. Where might it have come from?

2. Why would Voldemort challenge Harry to a duel, rather than kill him outright?

3. Why does Voldemort place such importance on it being "old magic" that protected Harry?

4. Why does Voldemort consider the Death Eaters his "true family"? Are they? Explain.

5. Voldemort says his Death Eaters knew he was still alive. How did he know this? Why wouldn't they have searched for him if they suspected he still lived?

6. Why does Voldemort wait so long to replace Wormtail's hand and relieve his suffering? What does this say about how he treats his followers?

7. Who might Voldemort's faithful servant at Hogwarts be? Snape, or someone else?

Greater Picture

As Voldemort struts around his Death Eaters, commenting on the gaps in the circle, he comes to *the largest gap of all . . ."And here we have six missing Death Eaters . . . three dead in my service. One, too cowardly to return . . . he will pay. One, who I believe has left me for ever . . . he will be killed, of course . . . and one, who remains my most faithful servant, and who has already re-entered my service. . . . He is at Hogwarts, that faithful servant, and it was through his efforts that our young friend arrived tonight . . ."* By withholding these Death Eaters' names, and by not completing the circle, the author leaves in doubt as to who is being referred to here. We are led to believe, correctly, that it is Karkaroff who has run, but it is unclear whether he is the cowardly one, or the one who has left Voldemort's service forever. Being unaware of Barty Crouch at this point, we are misled into believing that the faithful servant who has already re-entered Voldemort's service is Severus Snape. And despite the revelation of Barty's role in the events preceding this chapter, the casual reader may well retain this mistaken belief even after that revelation, and may see this particular scene as confirming Snape's continuing loyalty to the Dark Lord. In fact, the faithful servant is Barty, Karkaroff is the cowardly one, and it is Snape who Voldemort feels has left. Snape has been working at Dumbledore's side for the thirteen years since Voldemort vanished, and he did prevent Voldemort from retrieving the Philosopher's Stone in the first book. Snape does explain, later, that he was unaware that it was Voldemort seeking the stone, believing instead that Quirrell wanted the Stone for his own benefit alone, and says that Voldemort had accepted this explanation and also his reason for not immediately responding to Voldemort's summons.

By sparing Wormtail's life (in *Harry Potter and the Prisoner of Azkaban*), Harry can claim a "life debt" from him. Wormtail repays this debt in the final book, *Harry Potter and the Deathly Hallows*, when he momentarily hesitates to kill Harry on Voldemort's command. Wormtail's actions result in his being fatally strangled by the silver hand Voldemort has just given him; Voldemort, who may have known that Wormtail owes Harry this debt, and certainly knew the weakness of Wormtail's character, must have charmed the hand to kill Wormtail should he exhibit any disloyalty or fail to carry out any order.

Voldemort here tells his gathered followers that he "has gone further than anyone along the path leading to immortality." Dumbledore has also theorized this about Voldemort, although he has yet to reveal his suspicions. Dumbledore has come to the correct conclusion by this point that the "path to immortality" of which Voldemort speaks here involves the creation and concealment of Horcruxes, soul shards that anchor the soul of a dead person to the earth, and has recognized that Tom Riddle's diary, which we saw in *Harry Potter and the Chamber of Secrets*, is one such. In two years, he will tell Harry that he was worried, however, because ordinarily Horcruxes are considered extremely valuable and are carefully concealed; yet the diary was crafted to be a weapon and was used as one. This is not how one deals with one's only shot at immortality. Thus, Dumbledore suspects the existence of at least one more Horcrux, and this is largely confirmed by Voldemort's statement. Much of *Harry Potter and the Half-Blood Prince* is involved with determining the number of Horcruxes, and trying to determine where they might be found.

Chapter 34: Priori Incantatem

SYNOPSIS

As ordered, Wormtail removes Harry's gag, and with a single slash of his new hand, cuts the bonds. Harry considers running, but his injured leg is still weak, and Death Eaters are closing in, filling the gaps where some are missing. Wormtail retrieves Harry's wand from near Cedric's body, and roughly thrusts it at Harry. Voldemort asks if Harry knows how to duel, telling him the first step is to bow to each other. When Harry stands mute, Voldemort raises his wand, forcing Harry to bend forward. "And then, we duel," says Voldemort; and Harry is again in unbelievable pain as Voldemort uses the Cruciatus curse. When the pain stops, Harry recovers his feet. Shaking, he falls into the wall of Death Eaters who push him back into the circle's center. Voldemort asks if that hurt and would he like a bit more. Harry remains mute, knowing it does not matter; Voldemort is going to kill him. Voldemort casts the Imperius curse to force a response and is impressed when Harry resists it. As Voldemort raises his wand again, Harry ducks behind Tom Riddle's gravestone, hearing it crack as the curse hits it. Saying they are not playing "hide and seek," Voldemort asks if Harry wants to end it quickly. Harry, not wanting to die while crouched subserviently, stands up and casts the Disarmament jinx, as Voldemort hurls the killing curse. The wands' streams meet in mid-air, fusing into a single, golden beam. Harry and Voldemort are lifted into the air and set down some distance away from Riddle's headstone. They are surrounded by a dome of golden light. Voldemort, taken aback by what has happened, orders the Death Eaters to do nothing. Harry hears a familiar sound: a Phoenix song. It speaks of Dumbledore and says: *Don't break the connection.* Beads of golden light appear on the wands' connection. As one approaches Harry, he feels his wand heat up and fears it will explode. Concentrating, he forces the bead away, and it begins moving towards Voldemort. As a bead reaches Voldemort's wand, screams are heard, and a smoky replica of Wormtail's silvery hand appears. More screams, and the ghostly head, torso, and finally legs of Cedric Diggory emerge from Voldemort's wand.

Harry grips his wand tightly as, amidst more screams, Cedric is joined by an old man that Harry saw in a dream, and Bertha Jorkins. Harry's father and mother appear next; Voldemort becomes fearful as his victims prowl around him. Lily Potter quietly tells Harry that when the wands' connection is broken their spirit echoes can only remain a few moments to protect him as he escapes to the Portkey. Cedric asks Harry to take his body to his parents. At his father's command, Harry breaks the connection. The golden dome disappears, and the spirits converge on Voldemort. Dodging curses, Harry sprints to Cedric's body. Reaching it, Harry Summons the Triwizard Cup. As it touches his hand, he is pulled from the graveyard, hearing Voldemort's furious screams as he is whisked to Hogwarts.

ANALYSIS

The themes of life, death, and rebirth are seen throughout the series as Harry is confronted by, and struggles with, not only loss and grief, but a tantalizing hope that magic can restore dead loved ones to him, just as it has resurrected Voldemort, although it was powerful Dark magic that revived him. This hope to be reunited with his parents is reborn by Harry's encounter with their spirit echoes that are released from Voldemort's wand. For the first time, Harry is able to communicate directly with James and Lily, and they, in turn, are able to protect their son. Even though their powers may be limited, the shades are unafraid—Voldemort can no longer harm them, though he apparently fears them. He also now fears Harry who, apparently the stronger wizard, forced the interlocking magical streams backwards into Voldemort's wand, a feat Voldemort never anticipated. The Potters and the other spirits disgorged from Voldemort's wand were, collectively, able to protect Harry long enough for him to escape as they perpetrated their retribution upon Voldemort for having stolen their lives.

Throughout the series, ghosts have mostly been seen as benign but ineffectual spirits floating through Hogwarts, seemingly limited to observing the living world, occasionally providing important information, but unable to actively participate in human affairs. Here it is shown that spirits actually can play a more significant role by directly influencing events from beyond the grave. Harry may also have been aided by a living person—Dumbledore is mentioned in the Phoenix song. If Dumbledore is somehow communicating with Harry, then it is logical to conclude that it was Fawkes' song that Harry heard. Could Fawkes have detected Harry's danger, just as he did in *Harry Potter and the Chamber of Secrets*? This may be what occurred here, although there could be an additional reason why it was Fawkes' song that was heard, one that may be tied to something that both Harry and Voldemort possess. It is unclear yet if these spirit echoes are actually ghosts or something else. Also, the order in which Voldemort's victims appear from the wand is slightly wrong. Harry's father died first, and therefore should have emerged last from Voldemort's wand. The author has stated[1] that she had originally written it that way, but her American editor, who was almost always right about such details, had questioned it at the end of a marathon editing session, and short on sleep, she had agreed to change it.

This is the first time that Harry and Voldemort actually duel. Before this, the disembodied Voldemort had ordered others to fight for him.

Questions

Review   1. Why does Voldemort fear the spirits? Does he also fear Harry? If so, why? 2. Why are Harry and Voldemort's wands considered "brothers"?

Further Study   1. Why does Harry hear the Phoenix song? Why is Harry reminded of Dumbledore?

2. What causes the streams from Harry and Voldemort's wands to interconnect? Who and what are the images that spill out from Voldemort's wand?

Greater Picture

Why does Harry hear the Phoenix song? Recall what lies within his wand's core: one of only two tail feathers from a particular Phoenix. The other feather is within Voldemort's wand, making them "brothers." The Phoenix who gave the feathers, as revealed shortly, is Fawkes. We will learn at the same time that the effect that Harry experienced, the so-called "priori incantatem" effect, is triggered by two wands, having the same origin for their cores and thus being "brothers," dueling. The effect is similar to that caused by the Prior Incantato charm. The images that appear during the Priori Incantatem are not actually ghosts, but the "spirit echoes" or shades of victims killed with Voldemort's wand, although each person's essence is retained somewhat. A wand records the former spells that it has performed, and under certain circumstances, those spells can be shown in the reverse order they were cast. In this case, the spell being retrieved from the wand is the killing curse, which separates soul from body, so the spell's echo represents the separated soul.

Mention is made above that Harry was able to force the beads of light back into Voldemort's wand because he was the stronger wizard. Much later, Dumbledore will tell Harry that Voldemort was weaker in that instance because he feared death, while Harry was prepared for it. He will also tell Harry that at this encounter, Harry's wand had taken some of the power inherent in Voldemort's wand. The exact effect that this would have, however, was unsure; it is the deepest sort of wand lore, something that was nearly impossible to study or predict.

It is also mentioned that this is the first time Harry duels Voldemort directly. It is not the last; he will duel Voldemort again in the next book, and three times in the final book.

Chapter 35: Veritaserum

Synopsis

Reappearing at the maze's edge, Harry finds himself overwhelmed by noise, but still clutching the Triwizard cup and Cedric's body. Amidst the confusion and shouts that Diggory is dead, the Minister for Magic claims that Cedric is only injured, while Professor Dumbledore tells Harry to stay put. Dazed, someone lifts Harry and walks him to the Castle. As they enter the school, Harry realizes Professor Moody is guiding him to his office. Once inside, Moody begins asking about Voldemort's return. Harry remembers that he must tell Dumbledore that there is a Death Eater at Hogwarts who put Harry's name in the Goblet of Fire. Harry guesses it is Karkaroff, but he ran off when the Dark Mark on his arm flared up. Incredibly, Moody tells Harry that it was he who placed Harry's name in the Goblet. Moody wants to know if Voldemort has forgiven those Death Eaters who failed to search for him, but Harry, still stunned by this revelation, is unable to answer. Harry, disbelieving, listens as Moody recounts how he entered Harry's name in the Goblet, nudged Hagrid into showing Harry the dragons, and gave Harry the hint on how to beat them. Moody gave Neville the Herbology book containing information Harry needed for the Second Task, and when that failed, had made sure Dobby passed it on. And in the Third Task, Moody Stunned Fleur Delacour and put Krum under the Imperius curse to eliminate Cedric. Harry sees three approaching figures in Moody's Foe-Glass, although Moody, focused on Harry, fails to notice; he says he will be the Dark Lord's most trusted servant after killing Harry Potter, who the Dark Lord has wanted dead for so long. As he raises his wand to cast the fatal spell, the door behind Harry explodes inwards. Moody is Stunned and falls to the floor. Professor Dumbledore, Professor McGonagall, and Professor Snape rush in. Dumbledore overrules McGonagall, who wants Harry to go the hospital wing, saying Harry

---

1. http://www.jkrowling.com/textonly/en/faq_view.cfm?id=19

needs to know that this Alastor Moody is an impostor. Snape is sent to fetch truth serum and Winky from the kitchen, while McGonagall is dispatched to take the large black dog in Hagrid's pumpkin patch to Dumbledore's office. Moody's trunk is opened, revealing multiple compartments within. The true Alastor Moody is trapped inside the last one. Stunned and under the Imperius curse, he is weak but still alive. Examining the impostor's hip flask reveals it contains Polyjuice Potion. The false Moody begins transforming into his true identity—Barty Crouch Jr. Snape arrives with the serum and Winky, and McGonagall returns immediately after. Winky, certain Barty is dead, is hardly reassured when Dumbledore says he is only stunned. Dumbledore pours the Veritaserum, the same potion Snape threatened Harry with earlier, into Barty's mouth and resuscitates him. Crouch confesses his part in the past year's events. It was Bartemius Crouch, Sr. and his wife who instigated Barty Jr.'s escape from Azkaban. Mrs. Crouch was terminally ill, and as her dying wish, asked Bartemius to free Barty from prison. While visiting their son in prison, she and Barty Jr. switched identities using Polyjuice potion. Mrs. Crouch died soon after (that is who Sirius saw the Dementors burying). Although Barty Jr. was freed, his father kept him at his home concealed under an Invisibility Cloak and controlled by the Imperius curse to prevent him returning to Voldemort. Winky, the Crouch's House-elf, helped care for him. When Bertha Jorkins, who worked for Bartemius, unexpectedly visited the Crouch home while Bartemius was gone, she discovered Barty Jr. was being hidden there. Bartemius cast a memory charm on Jorkins to erase what she knew. She was soon transferred to Ludo Bagman's department, but the charm caused continuing memory problems.

Winky prevailed upon Bartemius Crouch Sr. to allow Barty to go to the Quidditch World Cup, hidden under an Invisibility Cloak. However, he managed to escape both Bartemius' and Winky's control, stole a wand (Harry's), and cast the Dark Mark. Bartemius, as a result, dismissed Winky and recaptured Barty, returning him to the Crouch home and restraining him more forcefully. Bertha, meanwhile, had gone to Albania on vacation and run into Wormtail, who brought her to Voldemort. Voldemort unlocked the memory charm and discovered that Barty Jr. had escaped Azkaban and was captive in his father's home. He also learned about the Triwizard Tournament and devised the plot to capture Harry. After murdering Jorkins, Wormtail and Voldemort traveled to London. They freed Barty Jr. and placed Bartemius under an Imperius spell, forcing him to continue his work as if nothing was wrong. Barty Jr. and Wormtail then captured the real Mad-Eye Moody and placed him under the Imperius spell; Barty Jr. used Polyjuice Potion to assume Moody's identity, while Moody was kept alive to supply his hair for more potion and provide Barty with information. Barty procured potion ingredients from Snape's office, claiming he (as Moody) was under orders to search it. When Voldemort judged it was no longer safe to allow people to see Bartemius Crouch, he imprisoned Crouch Sr. in his own home. The Ministry of Magic, meanwhile, believed Crouch Sr. was home sick and sending instructions by owl post to his assistant, Percy Weasley. But Wormtail "neglected his duty." When Crouch Sr. was able to break Wormtail's Imperius spell and escape to Hogwarts to warn Dumbledore, Barty Jr. tracked his father using Harry's previously borrowed Marauder's Map, murdered him, and hid the body.

Finally, Barty admits that, while he was placing the Triwizard Cup inside the maze, he had charmed it into a Portkey that transported Harry to the Dark Lord; Voldemort will now honor him above all other wizards.

ANALYSIS

The Veritaserum has revealed many truths. And while this chapter solves many mysteries regarding Harry and Voldemort, it also reveals just how vulnerable Harry actually is. The comforting notion throughout the series that Harry is protected as long as he is within Hogwarts's secure walls has been forever dispelled by Barty Crouch's clever deception that allowed him direct access to Harry. From here on, Harry will have difficulty finding a completely safe haven. Now that Voldemort has fully regained his body, he will likely execute another attack on Harry as soon as possible. Voldemort's power will begin spreading as well, quietly and methodically seeping into nearly all wizarding areas, taking hold in key institutions until he has gained control.

Also, Harry's earlier wish to compete as a Triwizard Champion came to fruition, but the experience was far from what he could have imagined. Now Harry must cope with the tragic aftermath, forever haunted by knowing that rather than being the celebrated hero, he was instead duped and manipulated into a false victory that cost Cedric Diggory his life. Harry had also placed his trust and admiration in (the fake) Alastor Moody, but having been so horribly deceived, he may never again ever fully trust anyone to be who or what they seem. Harry's relationship with Dumbledore may also be affected. Dumbledore has always seemed invincible, but his failure to detect Barty Crouch and to fully protect Harry exposes a chink in his otherwise infallible power. As the newly reborn Voldemort gains strength, is Dumbledore growing weaker with age? It is unclear if that is what is happening here, but Dumbledore failing to anticipate someone being able to breach Hogwarts' tight security is surprising, especially considering how both Sirius Black (on multiple occasions in *Harry Potter and the Prisoner of Azkaban*) and, more recently, Rita Skeeter so easily slipped into the castle undetected. In fact, Harry has never truly been completely safe at Hogwarts, only safer.

Cornelius Fudge, meanwhile, ineptly attempts to implement damage control, claiming Cedric is not dead, merely injured. While he may be attempting to shield the Diggorys, feeling it would be inappropriate to inform them their son is dead when such a large audience is present, he is also protecting his and the Ministry's public image. This attempt to either spin or minimize bad news reappears in the next chapter.

It is also interesting that Barty Jr., as Professor Moody, taught students how to repel an Imperius curse, which he presumably mastered while detained in his father's house. As reprehensible and evil as Crouch Jr. was, he was apparently a good Defence Against the Dark Arts teacher, although almost certainly some of his Defence information was forced from the real Alastor Moody, who was kept captive in his office.

One thing that has troubled some readers is that this seems an extremely convoluted plan, with multiple points of failure, to achieve one objective: the arrival of Harry Potter, alone, in the graveyard at Little Hangleton at a specific time. Having managed to win Dumbledore's trust, the false Moody could have, at any time, given Harry an object that was a Portkey. Clearly, this would have caused some problem for the author, as the series quite plainly is designed to cover the seven years of Harry's education, with a climax coming at or near the end of each school year. The author must have determined some reason that Voldemort would have chosen so involved a plan for such a simple outcome, in order to make her story timing work. While her reasons are never revealed, we can make a guess. Voldemort seems to be a particularly vindictive sort of person; we have seen him torturing his own followers because of real or imagined slights. It seems entirely likely that Voldemort would be amused by bringing Harry to defeat and death immediately after he had won a major competition, particularly if Harry was made aware that his winning the competition had been engineered, and that he had not won it by his own efforts at all. In this light, the only thing that is surprising is that it was not Voldemort who told Harry this, but Moody / Barty.

Questions

Review 1. Why did Crouch, Sr. keep Barty Jr. hidden and forcibly restrained in his home? How was the situation later reversed?

2. Why does Moody immediately take Harry to his office?

3. Is Barty Crouch's confession truthful? Explain.

4. Why was Sirius (in his Animagus dog form) in Hagrid's pumpkin patch?

Further Study 1. What prompts Fudge to claim that Cedric Diggory is only injured and not, in fact, dead?

2. How did Professor Dumbledore know that Moody was an impostor and that Harry was in danger?

3. Why did Bartemius Crouch, Sr., a powerful and trustworthy Ministry official who disowned his son, Barty, Jr. for being a Death Eater and sentenced him to life in Azkaban, later help him escape from prison? Who else was involved and why?

4. Why did Winky want Mr. Crouch to take Barty Jr. to the Quidditch World Cup? Why would he have agreed to such a risky venture?

Greater Picture

As a side note, it is interesting that Jorkin's memory problems seem somewhat similar to Neville Longbottom's. Is it possible that he could have been likewise charmed as a small child? If he was, why or by whom is unknown. One possibility is that his grandmother Augusta could have charmed him to prevent what happened to his parents from haunting him. If that is the case, it is also worth noting that Professor McGonagall mentions that Augusta failed her Charms O.W.L. test. Considering Neville's increasingly important role in the later books, it is also possible he may unknowingly hold important information that someone wants to remain concealed, although this is only speculation. It may be that his memory and magical abilities were affected by the extreme trauma in his life, resulting in his development in these areas being stunted. Regardless, Neville constantly struggles to break through an ever-present fog that clouds his memory and affects his magical powers. If his memory has been tampered with, it may be nearly impossible to break the charm without causing permanent damage, as was the case with Bertha Jorkins. Neville's memory problems will plague him throughout the series, although, with Harry's help, he gradually outgrows this handicap, as well as his magical impairment, to develop into a capable wizard. However, the source of his memory problems is never actually explained, and whether it was from early childhood trauma, a dark spell, or some other cause remains unknown, and it does not play a significant role in the story's eventual outcome. In considering Fudge's motives for minimizing Cedric's condition, it should be remembered that Fudge is the consummate politician, interested in retaining power for power's sake only. It is only natural that he would "spin" any situation into something less negative to protect his chances for retaining his office. When Harry first returns with Cedric's body, Fudge maintained that Cedric was only injured, not to protect Cedric's parents, but partly to prevent mass panic by the crowd, and mostly to protect his own interests. Fudge desperately wants to avoid the Triwizard Tournament, for which he was instrumental in reviving, being remembered as an event resulting in a student's death. Like many politicians, Fudge has lost the long view, forgetting that no matter what he says here, Cedric's death will be always be remembered.

Fudge will later dispute Harry's claims that Voldemort has returned. Again, Fudge is unable to face being known as the Minister who was in power when Voldemort returned, so he must deny, first, that Voldemort has returned, second, that Voldemort killed Cedric, and finally, that Voldemort was involved in Mr. Crouch's mysterious illness. This refusal to believe, and then to act, will prove important in the next book, resulting in repercussions against Harry, Professor Dumbledore, and Hogwarts. The Ministry's continued inactivity combined with Voldemort's hidden presence, will also make it easier for the Dark Lord to regroup his Death Eaters' core members.

Chapter 36: The Parting of the Ways

Synopsis

After hearing Barty Crouch's confession, Professor Dumbledore binds him tightly, then asks Professor McGonagall to stand guard while he takes Harry upstairs. Dumbledore asks Professor Snape to arrange for

Chapter 36: The Parting of the Ways

the real Alastor Moody to be taken to the Hospital wing and to bring Cornelius Fudge so he can interrogate Barty. Dumbledore and Harry then go to Dumbledore's office where Sirius is waiting. Looking as haggard as when he escaped from Azkaban, Sirius demands to know what has happened. Dumbledore relates Barty's confession. Harry, exhausted, lets the words wash over him as Fawkes perches on his knee. Dumbledore asks Harry to tell what, exactly, happened after he touched the Triwizard Cup. Sirius protests, saying Harry is too exhausted. Dumbledore says that if he thought it would help, he would put Harry into a dreamless sleep, but delaying will only make matters more difficult. Harry has shown extreme bravery, and he must demonstrate that courage again. Fawkes sings a single note, and Harry, taking strength from the phoenix song, begins.

Dumbledore and Sirius seem shocked when Harry relates how Wormtail took his blood for the charm; Dumbledore inspects the wound. Voldemort told Harry that his blood gave him the same protection Harry has, and he can now touch him. For a moment, Harry sees what looks like a triumphant gleam in Dumbledore's eyes, but Dumbledore only comments that Voldemort has overcome that particular barrier.

Harry continues, but finds it difficult to explain how his wand and Voldemort's connected. Dumbledore says that this is a Priori Incantatem effect: when wands sharing a single source for their magical cores are forced to duel, one will be forced to disgorge the spells it had last cast. Dumbledore tells Sirius and Harry that Harry's wand and Voldemort's share a magical core: tail feathers from a single phoenix—Fawkes. Therefore, Voldemort's wand was forced to disgorge its most recent spells. Dumbledore asks if Cedric appeared, and Harry says he did and spoke to him. He says he also saw an old man, Bertha Jorkins, and his father and mother. Dumbledore explains that these figures are not ghosts, but only the spirit echoes or shadows that were created by Voldemort's victims when they were killed by his wand.

When Harry is unable to continue talking, Fawkes flutters to the floor. His tears fall on Harry's leg, healing his wound. Dumbledore says Harry has shown exceptional bravery, equal to wizards who faced Voldemort at the height of their powers. He recommends the Hospital Wing and a sleeping potion. Sirius changes to his dog form and walks with Harry and Dumbledore to the Infirmary. There, Mrs. Weasley, Bill Weasley, Ron, and Hermione are grilling Madam Pomfrey about Harry. Dumbledore forestalls Mrs. Weasley's questions by saying Harry needs sleep; questions can wait until morning. Dumbledore tells Madam Pomfrey the dog will be staying with Harry. When Harry spots Alastor Moody in another bed, Madam Pomfrey says he will recover. She gives Harry a purple potion, but Harry falls asleep before drinking it all.

Harry is awakened by loud voices. The doors burst open and Cornelius Fudge, Professor McGonagall, and Professor Snape enter. McGonagall angrily berates Fudge as he demands to speak to Dumbledore. Dumbledore enters, wanting to know what has happened. He expresses surprise at McGonagall, who was left guarding Barty Crouch Jr. McGonagall shouts that nobody needs to guard Crouch any more. The Dementor that Fudge brought for protection sensed Barty and administered the "Kiss," sucking out his soul. Fudge is unconcerned by the fuss, claiming Crouch was no loss. Dumbledore points out he is now unable to testify, to which Fudge claims that would have been pointless, as it appears that he was only following You-Know-Who's instructions. Dumbledore says that he *was* following Voldemort's instructions for his resurrection, and the plan was successful—Voldemort is back. A blustering Fudge now attempts to deny that Voldemort has returned. Dumbledore tells him Crouch's confession and what happened to Harry. Fudge asks if Dumbledore is prepared to base his belief on Harry's evidence, saying that Harry has been a less than reliable witness. Harry suggests Fudge has been reading Rita Skeeter's stories. Fudge more or less admits that, but suggests Harry may be suffering hallucinations. Harry states he was there, he saw it, and he can name Death Eaters. Fudge discounts this, saying the names are public record. Fudge reiterates that this is a scare story, and they cannot claim that Voldemort has returned, it would destroy everything they have been working towards for the past thirteen years.

Dumbledore calmly avers that Voldemort has returned. If Fudge accepts that truth and acts now, they may be able to save the situation. The first step is to remove the Dementors from Azkaban. Fudge resists, saying that half the Wizarding population only feel safe at night because Dementors are guarding Azkaban; Dumbledore says that the other half will lose sleep, knowing the Dementors will defect to Voldemort because he can offer them far more than being a prison guard. Next, continues Dumbledore, envoys need to be sent to the giants. Fudge interrupts, saying he cannot do that, he would be voted out immediately. Dumbledore says his love of the office has blinded him to what must be done. If their interests have diverged so greatly, then they have reached an impasse and must part ways. Fudge must do as he sees fit, as will he.

Fudge accuses Dumbledore of working against him, but Dumbledore replies he is only working against Voldemort. If Fudge is against Voldemort, they are still on the same side. Fudge plaintively says, "He can't be back, Dumbledore, he just can't be. . . ." Snape pulls back his left sleeve, exposing his forearm. He tells Fudge the Dark Mark is the Death Eater sign. It has been growing more distinct all year and tonight it burned black. Death Eaters must respond when Voldemort summons them. Karkaroff was also summoned; that is why he bolted. Fudge claims he does not know what Dumbledore is playing at, but he must return to the Ministry. He places a large bag on Harry's bedside table. "Your winnings," he explains, saying that there would normally be a ceremony, but under the circumstances . . . his voice then trails off.

After Fudge leaves, Dumbledore begins assigning missions. Asking Mrs. Weasley if he can count on her and Arthur, he warns them to avoid getting anyone at the Ministry in trouble. Bill Weasley volunteers to tell his father and leaves. Dumbledore dispatches Professor McGonagall to fetch Hagrid and Madame Maxime to meet with him in his office as soon as possible. He sends Madam Pomfrey to tend to Winky, who is still with Crouch. Dumbledore then asks Sirius to show himself. Mrs. Weasley is alarmed when the dog transforms into Sirius, but Dumbledore and Ron calm her. Dumbledore tells Sirius and Snape that he understands they can never be friends, but they must cooperate with each other; they briefly shake hands, still showing their mutual deep loathing. Dumbledore sends Sirius to alert the "old crowd": Mundungus Fletcher, Remus Lupin, Arabella Figg, and to then lay low at Lupin's until he contacts him. When he asks Snape if he is ready for the mission they have discussed, Snape replies he is. Dumbledore sends him off without further instructions.

Dumbledore tells Harry to drink the potion, he needs sleep, and departs. Harry, fretting about the Tournament prize, says he does not want it. He blames himself for Cedric's death, and his family should at least have the Galleons. Mrs. Weasley tells him not to worry about it, but she is interrupted by a loud slamming. Next to the window, Hermione apologizes for the noise. Harry drinks the remaining sleeping potion and finally falls asleep.

ANALYSIS

Although many questions have been answered, new ones arise, and the characters must now deal with the dire aftermath that Voldemort's return has created. To prepare for the impending war he knows is coming and cannot be stopped, Dumbledore's only recourse, given the total lack of cooperation he can expect from the Ministry, is to quickly regroup his former allies. Reiterating the book's theme that Voldemort can only be defeated through mutual cooperation, Dumbledore requests that Snape and Sirius set aside their mutual hatred and work together to fight Voldemort. They grudgingly agree, but whether they can maintain a truce or if Snape truly is loyal to Dumbledore remains to be seen.

At this cooperative spectrum's other end, Dumbledore's efforts to defeat Voldemort are stymied by absolutely no cooperation from Cornelius Fudge and the Ministry of Magic. We can see that Fudge is preparing to vehemently deny publicly that the Dark Lord has returned, an action that will only aid Voldemort's rise to power. Fudge allowing (or perhaps ordering) the Dementor to administer the *Kiss* to Barty Crouch is not only shocking and likely illegal, but it suggests he could be a Voldemort accomplice or that he is in such extreme denial about unfolding events that he will use any means to protect himself and the Ministry, including using a Dementor to suck out Crouch's soul so he is unable to corroborate Harry's claims, as well as hurling accusations that Harry hallucinated everything that happened to him. Even if Harry is administered Veritaserum, the Ministry can then argue that Harry actually believes his hallucinations are the truth. Fudge's action, we can already see, will result in an acrimonious and irreparable split between him and Dumbledore, and also between Dumbledore and the Ministry of Magic.

The "gleam of triumph" in Dumbledore's eyes as Harry tells about Voldemort using his blood in his re-animation has been endlessly discussed by fans. Of course, this blood tie creates yet an additional connection between Harry and Voldemort, and it can be assumed from Dumbledore's reaction that it may actually somehow weaken the Dark Lord. However, this is still speculation, and it is yet unknown just how it will affect the story's outcome. All that is known is Voldemort claiming that his greatest enemy's blood will make him stronger; it is debatable, however, as to just who his greatest enemy actually is: Harry or Dumbledore.

Fawkes is relatively central to the scene in Dumbledore's office. In addition to learning that this is the Phoenix who donated the tail feathers that lie within Harry and Voldemort's wands, it is Fawkes who gives Harry the strength to retell his story and provides the tears to heal his injured leg.

It is unknown just what Hermione was doing by the hospital window at this chapter's conclusion, but it will prove to be meaningful later.

Also, although Harry feels responsible for Cedric's death, it is probable that he would have been killed anyway. Cedric would have reached the Triwizard Cup first, but, grateful for Harry's help, wanted Harry to take it. Harry instead insisted they grab it together because they helped each other equally throughout the Tournament. If Cedric alone had grasped it, he would have been transported to the cemetery rather than Harry, and, being useless to Voldemort's rebirth, likely would have been instantly murdered on Voldemort's command.

QUESTIONS

Review 1. Why would Fudge allow a Dementor to administer the *Kiss* to Barty Crouch? Were his actions legal?

2. What is the significance of the mark on Snape's forearm?

3. Why does Harry feel he is responsible for Cedric's death? Is he justified in believing so?

4. Cedric would have reached the Triwizard Cup first. What would have happened if he alone had grabbed it?

5. Why does Fawkes only sing a single note to Harry when he is in Dumbledore's office? How does it affect Harry? What else does Fawkes do that helps Harry?

6. Why is Harry given a potion for "dreamless" sleep?

Further Study 1. Who and what might the "old crowd" be that Dumbledore is referring to?

2. Harry shows no reaction when Dumbledore mentions someone named Arabella Figg. Should he?

3. What missions might Dumbledore assign to Hagrid and Olympe Maxime and also to Snape?

4. Why might Hermione be making such a commotion next to the hospital window? Why does she say nothing about it?

5. Snape and Sirius loathe each other. Is it possible that they can suppress their mutual hatred and work together as Dumbledore has requested?

6. Why does Dumbledore have a "gleam of triumph" in his eyes after Harry tells him Voldemort used some of Harry's blood for his reanimation?

GREATER PICTURE

After Fudge's departure, Dumbledore begins dispatching various people on separate missions. The missions, only hinted at here, are fully explained in later books. Bill Weasley updates his father, Arthur Weasley, as to what has happened. Arthur, along with Molly, will be working within the Ministry of Magic. Hagrid and Olympe Maxime will seek out and contact the giants, to attempt to win them to Dumbledore's side, or at least keep them neutral. In Voldemort's previous time in power, Dumbledore had headed a group called the Order of the Phoenix, who worked against Voldemort outside of the Ministry; Sirius has been sent to alert former Order of the Phoenix members, including Remus Lupin, Mundungus Fletcher, and Arabella Figg to reactivate that group. Lupin is later sent to infiltrate and spy on a werewolf pack headed by the particularly vicious Fenrir Greyback, who has formed an alliance with Voldemort. And Snape is apparently sent to re-establish contact with Voldemort, although this will not be revealed to us until two books later.

It is also interesting, but hardly surprising, that Harry fails to recognize Arabella Figg's name; neither he, nor most readers, have yet to connect her with batty, old Mrs. Figg with all her cats back in Privet Drive. She is later revealed to be a Squib, and she has been guarding Harry since he first arrived at the Dursleys.

In the next chapter, we will learn that Hermione has discovered how Rita Skeeter is able to "bug" so many private conversations; she is, in fact, an unregistered Animagus, taking the form of a beetle. The commotion Hermione was making at the infirmary window was her trapping Skeeter in a jar.

It is learned in the final book that the "triumphant gleam" in Dumbledore's eyes is when he realizes that Harry's blood that is now within Voldemort's body will actually protect Harry from Voldemort, a fact unknown to the Dark Lord when he reanimated himself. Dumbledore explains that when Voldemort used Harry's blood, he also transferred the protection that had been conferred on Harry by Lily's sacrifice; thus, Harry now cannot die, at least not at Voldemort's wand, as long as this embodiment of Voldemort is alive.

Chapter 37: The Beginning

SYNOPSIS

Over the next few days, Harry's worst memory is of Cedric Diggory's parents. They never seemed angry, and instead thanked Harry for returning Cedric's body. They expressed relief that he did not suffer and died only after winning the Tournament. Harry offered them the Tournament winnings, saying Cedric would have reached the Cup first, but they had refused.

Harry returns to Gryffindor Tower after Professor Dumbledore addresses the school. Ron and Hermione tell him that Dumbledore has instructed everyone to refrain asking Harry about what happened in the maze. Harry, Ron, and Hermione reach their own tacit agreement to avoid discussing it. Mrs. Weasley has asked Dumbledore if Harry could stay with them for the summer, but Dumbledore says Harry must first spend time at Privet Drive. When Harry wonders why, Ron says that his mother assumes Dumbledore has his reasons.

The only person Harry can confide in is Hagrid. With no Defence Against the Dark Arts teacher, that time is free, and the Trio heads to Hagrid's hut. He is pleased to see Harry and invites them all in. When Harry notices a second bucket-sized teacup on the table, Hagrid admits he was having tea with Madame Maxime. Hagrid startles Harry by saying that he knew Voldemort would return, it was only a matter of time. Hagrid says that Harry did as much as his father would have, and there is no higher praise than that. Harry smiles for the first time in days. When asked, Hagrid is unable to tell Harry what mission Dumbledore is sending Hagrid and Madame Maxime on; Hagrid almost has Madame Maxime convinced to go with him. He jokingly invites them to visit the last Skrewt. The Leaving Feast is a sad affair; the Great Hall is draped in black. Professor Karkaroff is still missing, and Harry wonders whether he has been caught yet. The real Alastor Moody is there, looking jumpy. Snape has returned from his mission, still looking sour; Harry remembers from the Pensieve that Dumbledore told the Wizengamot that Snape became a spy at great personal risk before Voldemort's fall. Dumbledore rises to address the school, starting with a tribute to Cedric Diggory. Cedric, he says, exemplified the attributes of Hufflepuff House, he was a good and loyal friend, and a hard worker. It is only fair to reveal how he died: he was murdered by Lord Voldemort. The Ministry, he continues, "does not want me to tell you this, and some of your parents will be horrified, but truth is generally preferable to lies, and saying Cedric died from an accident is an insult to his memory." Dumbledore says he must also mention Harry Potter. Harry faced Lord Voldemort, escaped, and risked his life to return Cedric's body. He toasts Harry, as do most in the Great Hall; but through a gap in the standing figures, Harry sees that Draco and his cronies do not.

Finally, Dumbledore singles out the Beauxbatons and Durmstrang students, and says that in light of Voldemort's return, anyone now in the Hall is welcome to return to Hogwarts any time. Discord is Voldemort's main weapon, and Dumbledore asks that when given a choice between what is right, and what is easy, that they remember Cedric, who died because he strayed across Voldemort's path.

As Harry, Ron, and Hermione prepare to leave Hogwarts the next day, Fleur runs up to say goodbye to Harry; she is hoping to get a job in England to improve her English. When Ron says that it is very good already, Hermione scowls. As Fleur leaves, Ron wonders aloud how the Durmstrang students will get back without Karkaroff. Krum says that Karkaroff did not steer the ship, the students did. He asks Hermione for a private word. After they return, Krum says that he liked Cedric, and shakes Harry's hand, and then Ron's.

On the Hogwarts Express, Harry, Ron, and Hermione have a compartment to themselves, and

Harry finally feels free to share what happened. They talk uninterrupted, until the lunch trolley arrives. Returning from the trolley, Hermione drops a copy of the *Daily Prophet,* saying there are not any Harry stories in it other than news about him winning the Tournament. She thinks Fudge is putting pressure on them. When Ron suggests that Rita Skeeter would never miss a story like that, Hermione admits that she discovered how Rita was getting her stories. Harry gave her a clue talking about electronic bugging. She then produces a jar containing a large beetle. It is Rita Skeeter, an unregistered Animagus. Hermione spotted her in the Hospital Wing the night Cedric died and trapped her in the jar. Ron and Harry recall that with every story Rita wrote, a large beetle had been nearby during their private conversations. Hermione will release her when they reach London, but if she writes any stories for one year, Rita will be reported to the Ministry of Magic.

Draco barges in, saying how clever Hermione is trapping a journalist. He tells Harry he has picked the wrong side; Voldemort is back, and Cedric is only the first to die. Wand-flashes suddenly fill the compartment, and Draco, Crabbe and Goyle are suddenly lying, unconscious and disfigured, on the floor. Harry, Ron, and Hermione each used a different hex on them, in addition to ones fired by Fred and George. After dumping Malfoy, Crabbe, and Goyle in the corridor, Fred and George join the Trio for the trip's remainder.

Harry asks who Fred and George were blackmailing. Fred responds it was Ludo Bagman, but they have given up. Ludo paid their winnings with vanishing Leprechaun gold. When they demanded real money, he became virtuous, telling them boys their age should not be gambling anyway. Apparently, he also cheated Lee Jordan's father. Ludo also wagered on the Quidditch World Cup with the Goblins and lost heavily. He was betting on Harry to win the Triwizard Tournament, which is why he was always trying to help Harry. When Harry and Cedric touched the cup simultaneously, the Goblins claimed it was a draw, and Ludo had run.

Reaching King's Cross Station, Hermione and Ron maneuver their trunks past the still-stunned Draco and his cronies. Harry privately calls George and Fred aside and gives them his Triwizard prize. George exclaims that he must be mental, but Harry insists he does not want or need it. He wants the Twins to finance their own joke shop with it, but there is one condition: they must buy Ron new dress robes. After bidding goodbye to Hermione and Ron, and receiving Fred and George's fervent thanks, Harry leaves with Uncle Vernon, awaiting whatever may happen next.

Analysis

As the book ends, the final chapter's title ("The Beginning") indicates that Lord Voldemort's second rise to power has begun. Knowing that far worse times are fast approaching, Dumbledore realizes that Voldemort's evil plan will likely include conquering Wizarding realms outside Britain. During his tribute, Dumbledore appeals to all Hogwarts, Beauxbatons, and Durmstrang students to not only remember Cedric Diggory, but to embrace the international ties they have built and to unite as allies against the Dark Lord, offering an open door to Hogwarts to anyone needing help. He warns that Voldemort uses discord to create divisions and disharmony, allowing him to build strength by gaining footholds within the many Wizarding realms and recruiting the discontented within to his side. Harry's refusal to keep the Tournament prize money and instead offer it to the Diggorys (who also refuse) shows Harry's honesty and integrity. He will not accept anything unless he earned or won it fairly, which could be considered a Hufflepuff characteristic. Instead, he uses it to finance Fred and George's joke shop enterprise, believing in their magical abilities, trusting them to spend the money responsibly, and knowing they will honour his condition to buy new dress robes for Ron, who would refuse this from Harry. Harry also insists that they keep their arrangement secret, not wanting any credit for helping them.

Questions

Review 1. How did Hermione discover that Rita Skeeter is an unregistered Animagus? How did Harry unintentionally give her a hint?

2. Why were Fred and George blackmailing Ludo Bagman, and what was the outcome?

3. How and why does Harry help the Twins out of their situation, and why does he want it kept secret? Why does he place a condition on this help, and what is that condition?

4. Why does Dumbledore tell the Beauxbatons and Durmstrang students that they are now always welcome at Hogwarts?

Further Study 1. What does Dumbledore mean when he says Voldemort uses discord as a weapon? Give examples of that.

2. Why does Harry wait to tell Ron and Hermione what happened in the maze and immediately after?

3. Why is Harry able to talk to Hagrid about what happened, but not to anyone else?

4. Why did the Diggorys refuse the prize money, even though Cedric (technically) won the Tournament?

5. Can Rita Skeeter be trusted to keep her word that she will not write any stories about Harry for one year, despite Hermione's threat? How might Skeeter overcome this?

6. What does Dumbledore mean when he says it is only right to tell students how Cedric actually died?

7. Why might Dumbledore insist that Harry spend time at the Dursleys before staying with the Weasleys for the summer?

Greater Picture

Dumbledore's refusal to allow anyone to talk to Harry about the events in the graveyard, and the limited amount of information he provides at the Leaving Feast, seems to be adequate to the reader, who of course has been present for the entire sequence. For Harry, and for Dumbledore, the information Dumbledore provides should be enough to go on with. For the student body, however, there is not enough information available to be certain whether Harry or Dumbledore are telling the truth. The large number of unanswered

Chapter 37: The Beginning

questions will lead a significant part of the student body to doubt Harry's story. Harry will have to fight this disbelief, which will be aided by the Ministry's attack on their credibility, through a large part of the next book.

Dumbledore and Harry are not only battling Voldemort, but also the Ministry of Magic, who will refuse to admit that Voldemort has returned, and will mount their own attack against Harry and Dumbledore, publicly renouncing their claims and undermining their credibility. We have already seen the start of this campaign, as Fudge, denying all evidence he is presented, says that if Dumbledore persists in this story that Voldemort has returned, the Ministry will fight him. This is, presumably, why Dumbledore states that the Ministry does not want him to tell the students that Voldemort has returned. We will see, in the next book, that the Ministry carries this policy of denial to almost incredible lengths, abandoning it finally only when Voldemort is seen by Fudge and other witnesses in the Ministry atrium.

Harry recalls from the Pensieve that when Dumbledore vouched for Snape's loyalty, saying he become a Ministry spy at "great personal risk," he did so while in Karkaroff's presence. Karkaroff, who has gone into hiding, is a weak and cowardly character, as shown when he divulged Death Eaters' names in exchange for his release from Azkaban. If a Death Eater finds him, he may again attempt to barter information for his life, and Snape turning informant is a huge bargaining chip. It will be revealed that Karkaroff is killed about a year after going into hiding, found in a hut with the Dark Mark floating overhead. Assuming the Ministry left his memory intact, could Karkaroff have revealed Snape's defection to his murderer? If so, and the Death Eater passed on this information, would an arrogant Voldemort believe it rather that his own Legilimency that Snape is loyal? As it turns out, Snape's loyalty to Voldemort is restored by the mission that he has just completed, and is apparently not cast into doubt by anything Karkaroff might have managed to say, as by the beginning of the final book, Snape is Voldemort's right-hand man.

It will be mentioned in the next book that Harry's protection, which he received when his mother died to save him, will remain in force only as long as he has a place that he can call home, where his mother's blood (Aunt Petunia) remains. It is because of this that Dumbledore is taking pains to ensure that the house at Privet Drive will remain a home for Harry, despite Harry's patent dislike for the place.

ORDER OF THE PHOENIX

CHAPTERS

Chapter 1: Dudley Demented
Chapter 2: A Peck of Owls
Chapter 3: The Advance Guard
Chapter 4: Number Twelve, Grimmauld Place
Chapter 5: The Order of the Phoenix
Chapter 6: The Noble and Most Ancient House of Black
Chapter 7: The Ministry of Magic
Chapter 8: The Hearing
Chapter 9: The Woes of Mrs. Weasley
Chapter 10: Luna Lovegood
Chapter 11: The Sorting Hat's New Song
Chapter 12: Professor Umbridge
Chapter 13: Detention with Dolores
Chapter 14: Percy and Padfoot
Chapter 15: The Hogwarts High Inquisitor
Chapter 16: In the Hog's Head
Chapter 17: Educational Decree Number Twenty-Four
Chapter 18: Dumbledore's Army
Chapter 19: The Lion and the Serpent
Chapter 20: Hagrid's Tale
Chapter 21: The Eye of the Snake
Chapter 22: St. Mungo's Hospital for Magical Maladies and Injuries
Chapter 23: Christmas on the Closed Ward
Chapter 24: Occlumency
Chapter 25: The Beetle at Bay
Chapter 26: Seen and Unforeseen
Chapter 27: The Centaur and the Sneak
Chapter 28: Snape's Worst Memory
Chapter 29: Careers Advice
Chapter 30: Grawp
Chapter 31: O.W.L.s
Chapter 32: Out of the Fire
Chapter 33: Fight and Flight
Chapter 34: The Department of Mysteries
Chapter 35: Beyond the Veil
Chapter 36: The Only One He Ever Feared
Chapter 37: The Lost Prophecy
Chapter 38: The Second War Begins

OVERVIEW

The fifth book in the Harry Potter series, *Harry Potter and the Order of the Phoenix* is told from the viewpoint of the now fifteen-year-old Harry.

This is possibly the darkest book in the Harry Potter series, even darker then the final book, *Harry Potter and the Deathly Hallows*. Surprisingly, perhaps, it is not the return of Voldemort and his Death Eaters that give this book its power, for in fact they do very little during this year. Its grimness is the multiplicity of enemies facing Harry, as the Ministry of Magic, headed by Cornelius Fudge, has also set itself against Harry and Dumbledore. Additionally, Harry must deal with a new nemesis and possibly the series' most hated character, Dolores Umbridge, a petty Ministry bureaucrat.

Apart from the usual magic, events at Hogwarts School, and the frustrating Dursleys, this book includes the resurrection of the Order of the Phoenix, a group dedicated to Lord Voldemort's downfall, and Voldemort openly returning. Darker and more mature than the preceding entries in the series, this book shows Harry coping with loss and dealing with adversity, while growing in maturity and ability.

While the book appears daunting at 766 pages (Bloomsbury / Raincoast edition), it is set in somewhat larger type than the first three volumes. If set in the same type as *Harry Potter and the Philosopher's Stone*, it would be 655 pages (approximately) to 223 for *Harry Potter and the Philosopher's Stone*. At this, though, it is still the largest of the seven volumes.

BOOK HIGHLIGHTS

• New places visited: Grimmauld Place, the Ministry of Magic, St. Mungo's Hospital for Magical Maladies and Injuries, The Room of Requirement
• *Defence Against the Dark Arts* teacher: Dolores Umbridge
• Title refers to: The Order of the Phoenix

Chapter 1: Dudley Demented

SYNOPSIS

Harry spends another dreadful summer with Aunt Petunia and Uncle Vernon. He is angry and frustrated that he has had little communication with either Ron or Hermione, and feeling isolated and cut off, is desperate for any information about Voldemort and the Wizarding world. One day, he hides in the Dursleys' flower bed under the living room window so he can overhear the Muggle news on TV. He is listening for any reports of unexplained events that, as a wizard, he would recognize as being caused by Dark magic. Hearing a cracking noise that he recognizes as someone Disapparating, Harry jumps up, wand at the ready, but bumps his head on the window frame, giving away his presence. An argument ensues with Uncle Vernon, but Harry leaves to investigate the noise. He encounters Dudley with his

Chapter 1: Dudley Demented

motley friends in the park. Harry, knowing that Dudley fears his magical powers, restrains himself from taunting him. After Dudley's companions leave, he and Harry head back to Privet Drive. As they reach an alley, it suddenly becomes dark and cold, and they are attacked by Dementors. Harry repels the Dementors with a Patronus Charm. However, Dudley is chilled to the bone and later becomes nauseous. Mrs. Figg (Harry's neighbour) appears on the scene, and amazingly, she is not at all surprised to see Harry's magic wand, ordering him not to put it away.

Analysis

Readers can see how lonely Harry is at his erstwhile relatives' home and how unhappy he has always been there. He is trapped inside a world in which he no longer belongs, nor wants to be part of, but Professor Dumbledore has apparently decreed that he must endure living there each summer. We don't, as yet, know why, but at the end of the previous book, Ron had said that Dumbledore had vetoed Mrs. Weasley's invitation to have Harry spend the entire summer at the Burrow. Once again, the Dursleys show how little they care for their nephew's needs. However, they do treat him better than they used to, and, like Dudley, have come to fear Harry's magical powers. While Harry and the Dursleys' relationship remains unchanged, there has been a gradual shift in power within the household, seen as far back as the first book, when Harry was given Dudley's "extra" bedroom and no longer had to sleep in the cupboard under the stairs. While Harry would never use magic against his relatives, he knows they fear his increasing magical abilities, and this has progressively granted him some bargaining leverage. Harry is hungry for information about the Wizarding world that he has been cut off from. In the previous book, he witnessed Voldemort's resurrection, and he knows, perhaps as no other excepting Dumbledore, how much evil has returned. However, it seems that Harry is deliberately being denied information, making him angry and frustrated. While Hagrid was sent on a mission at the end of the last book and is likely unable to write, it seems that Ron and Hermione are deliberately withholding important details from their letters, leaving Harry feeling abandoned. Harry has been carefully watching for any signs that Voldemort's activity restarted, not only in the Wizarding realm but in the Muggle world, which is why he eagerly listens for any news. Harry is aware that Voldemort considers Muggles unworthy of preservation. The Dementor attack is a sign that Voldemort is becoming active, and it actually helps relieve Harry's anger and frustration by reestablishing his ties to the magical world. Discovering that batty old Mrs. Figg possesses knowledge about Wizards delivers Harry a powerful shock, given the vacuum he has been forced to stay in. There have been clues that Mrs. Figg is connected to the Wizarding world since the first book, such as the strange odors emanating from her kitchen and her unusual cats, although Harry was too young and inexperienced a wizard to have recognized them for what they were.

The attack also brings another character into focus: Dudley. Being a Muggle, he should have been unaware and largely unaffected by the Dementors' presence; however, he was obviously affected by them, just as they were able to detect him. This could indicate that Dudley possibly has some latent magical ability.

Questions

Review   1. How is Dudley affected by the Dementors?
2. Why is Harry so intent on listening to the Muggle news?
3. How has Harry's relationship with the Dursleys changed? What accounts for this?
4. Why would Harry expect to hear news about the Wizarding world reported on Muggle TV?

Further Study   1. How does Mrs. Figg know about the Wizarding world?
2. Why do letters from Harry's friends contain so little information about the Wizard world?
3. Why would Dudley, a Muggle who should be unaware of a Dementor's presence, be so affected by them? Why would a Dementor attack him along with Harry?
4. Who could have sent the Dementors to Privet Drive and why?

Greater Picture

Mrs. Figg's connection to the Wizarding world was mentioned at the end of the previous book, though it is very carefully formed so as to not attract attention. We never know Mrs. Figg's first name, even the Dursleys call her "old Mrs. Figg," and the complexity of her first name (Arabella) seems to be carefully selected so as to overshadow her last name when Dumbledore mentions it. We will find out that Mrs. Figg is an associate of Dumbledore's and a member of the Order of the Phoenix from Voldemort's first rise to power, and has been charged with watching over Harry since he was first left at Privet Drive.

Slightly connected to this is Dumbledore's insistence that Harry spend time at Privet Drive each summer. Dumbledore has set protective spells on Harry and the house, based on the protection given Harry when his mother died to save him. That protection will only hold so long as Harry is sheltered by his mother's blood, which is to say as long as his home is the place where one of his mothers' close blood relatives lives. If he stops being able to call Privet Drive home, or reaches the age of majority, that protection will cease. Harry's returning each summer is sufficient to keep Privet Drive his home. While this is Harry's strongest protection, Dumbledore never has only one string to his bow, and has arranged for Harry to be watched and guarded by other means, including Mrs. Figg. Harry is correct in his assumption that Ron and Hermione are deliberately telling him little in their letters. This is at Dumbledore's orders, though why Dumbledore has said that Harry is to remain unknowing is never fully revealed. It is possible that, even at this early stage, Dumbledore worries that Voldemort might be aware of the linkage between Harry's mind and his own, and be trying to minimize the possible damage should Voldemort snoop in Harry's mind. Dumbledore is aware that, even before Voldemort re-embodied himself, there were two episodes where Harry apparently received clear images from Voldemort's mind.

While we never do find out quite why the Dementors were there, we do learn that they were sent by Dolores Umbridge, who we will meet a little later in this book. The only reason Umbridge gives for sending the Dementors is that *"something* had to be done," though she remains mute on why something had to be done, and why Dementors were the reasonable choice for that something.

Dudley should have been unaffected by the Dementors. In the first chapter of *Harry Potter and the Half-Blood Prince*, it is stated that Muggles are unable to perceive Dementors, and the author has said[1] that Squibs are also unable to see them. According to Rowling, in an interview given before publication of the third book, a character, previously believed to be a Muggle[2] would develop magical abilities unexpectedly late in life ("late" meaning after age 11 or so), and that it would not be Aunt Petunia.[3] Although this was expected to happen in *Harry Potter and the Deathly Hallows*, Rowling later decided to omit this from the storyline. However, if Dudley is able to perceive Dementors, it is possible he has other latent magical abilities, and he may be the character Rowling was referring to.

Chapter 2: A Peck of Owls

Synopsis

As Harry struggles to comprehend the Dementor attack and Arabella Figg's enigmatic announcement, Mrs. Figg assumes control of the situation. She reveals that she is a Squib and that she has long been in contact with Albus Dumbledore. In her frustration with the situation, she tells Harry that he has been followed all summer; Mundungus Fletcher was supposed to be on duty but left early. As the two struggle to move Dudley to the house, Mundungus reappears. Mrs. Figg berates him, hitting him with her shopping bag, and sends him off to inform Dumbledore about what has happened. Mrs. Figg and Harry reach Harry's front door. Mrs. Figg now leaves to await Dumbledore's orders, leaving Harry to face the Dursleys alone.

While Vernon and Petunia Dursley confront him about their now-ill son, Harry receives a letter from the Ministry of Magic expelling him from Hogwarts and saying his wand will shortly be destroyed. Harry decides that his only option is to become a fugitive, but before he can get past Uncle Vernon, another owl letter arrives from Arthur Weasley saying to stay in his uncle's house, not let Ministry representatives break his wand, and not to use magic again; Dumbledore is straightening things out. Harry sits at the kitchen table, trying to explain what happened and insisting that it was Dementors who use magic against Dudley. When Uncle Vernon asks what Dementors are, Aunt Petunia responds, "they are the guards of the Wizard prison, Azkaban."

Petunia's shocking revelation stuns everyone, including Petunia, who belatedly covers her mouth, as if realizing she had uttered something horribly obscene. As Harry sits in Aunt Petunia's antiseptic kitchen answering questions about the Wizarding world, another owl arrives from Mr. Weasley, and one from Sirius, briefly telling Harry that the situation is being sorted out. Finally, a second owl from the Ministry of Magic arrives revoking his expulsion and wand destruction. Harry's fate now rests on a hearing scheduled for "9 A.M. on August 12th."

When Harry says Lord Voldemort has returned, Uncle Vernon, recognizing the danger while they house Harry, demands he leave. However, this is interrupted by one final owl carrying a Howler—surprisingly, for Petunia Dursley. A menacing voice reverberates throughout the kitchen: *"Remember my last, Petunia!"* Petunia quickly overrides her husband, insisting that Harry remain at their house, but sending him to bed immediately.

Analysis

Even the unsophisticated reader, reading the series for entertainment, will be left with questions after this chapter. The two largest, unanswered questions are: How did Petunia learn about Dementors, and given that she knows that much, what else does she know about the Wizarding world that she hasn't told us? And the Howler was sent by someone who not only had a reasonable idea of what was happening in the house, probably based on knowledge of Petunia and Vernon's likely reactions, but also holds some sort of power over Petunia, seeing how quickly she changed her mind when the Howler uttered its four words; who could that be? While we can speculate on those questions, the true answers will not be given to us until later in the series.

Petunia's explanation about Dementors and Azkaban not only shocks her family, but shows she knows far more about the wizarding world than she has ever admitted. Based largely on this, Harry leaps to the conclusion that Dumbledore sent her the Howler; this is fueled largely by wishful thinking, as Harry has been hoping for a communication from Dumbledore all summer without receiving anything. However, if the Howler is from Dumbledore, it implies that Petunia has had more contact with him than has yet been revealed; although Harry may be unaware, this is hardly surprising as Petunia, being Harry's legal guardian, would need to be informed regarding any event affecting her nephew, regardless what her personal feelings are toward him.

That Harry would be expelled from school and have his wand broken, without an official inquiry and for such a minor offense, indicates the Ministry of Magic probably has some ulterior motive in moving so quickly against him. Obviously, others (apparently including

---

1. http://www.jkrowling.com/textonly/en/extrastuff_view.cfm?id=19
2. http://www.accio-quote.org/articles/1999/0399-barnesandnoble.html#magic
3. http://www.jkrowling.com/textonly/en/rumours_view.cfm?id=37

Dumbledore) have intervened on his behalf to prevent this, and a hearing has been scheduled to allow Harry to present his side. As Harry often does, his first response to a difficult situation is to run away or isolate himself, rather than attempt to find a solution or seek help from others. Luckily, in this case, he is overridden by instructions from Arthur Weasley.

Although Harry has been protected from Voldemort since infancy by spells Dumbledore cast that reinforce the protection created by his mother's death, Dumbledore has taken additional precautions to ensure Harry's safety. Arabella Figg, a squib, has apparently been keeping a close eye on Harry since he came to live with the Dursleys. She explains that she has been rather mean to him because she knows if his aunt and uncle thinks he has a friend, they would not have allowed her to occasionally watch him. No doubt there are others who have also been watching Harry when he stays with the Dursleys.

QUESTIONS

Review 1. Who or what are 'Squibs'?

2. How does Petunia know about Dementors and Azkaban prison?

3. Why does Uncle Vernon order Harry to leave the house? Who overrules him and why?

Further Study 1. Why would the Ministry of Magic want to break Harry's wand and expel him from Hogwarts without an official inquiry?

2. Who sent Petunia the Howler? What does its message say and what might it mean?

3. Why does Petunia react so strongly to the Howler?

GREATER PICTURE

Dumbledore mentions later in the book that the Howler was, as Harry surmised, from him. This, in association with comments Dumbledore makes in *Harry Potter and the Half-Blood Prince*, would indicate he has kept a closer eye on the Dursley household than we have, to date, realized. Mrs. Figg's revelation that the house is being watched, at Dumbledore's instructions, would account for some of the knowledge he has of the Dursleys, but the sort of observation that Mrs. Figg would be capable of likely would not include sufficient detail to allow Dumbledore to understand the need for a Howler at that specific time.

It is perhaps interesting that Dumbledore's Howler says "Remember my last" instead of "Remember my letter." The implication here is that there have been more letters than the single one which we have seen, left with Harry on the doorstep at the beginning of the series. It is not until the final book of the series that we learn that Dumbledore had written a letter to Petunia earlier, refusing her entry into Hogwarts. We learn at the same time that much of Petunia's understanding of the Wizarding world actually comes, not from Harry's father, as we would expect given her apparent dislike of "that dreadful boy," but Severus Snape, who at the time was telling Lily Evans, Petunia's sister and later Harry's mother, what to expect in the Wizarding world.

Chapter 3: The Advance Guard

SYNOPSIS

Harry immediately writes letters to Sirius, Hermione, and Ron. He instructs Hedwig to get detailed replies from each. Frustration overwhelms him: he has no idea what is happening in the wizarding world and, cut off, feels he is being treated like a "naughty child" by Arthur Weasley, Dumbledore, and Sirius, who sent instructions. An annoyed Harry remains locked in his room for the next three days.

On the third day, Uncle Vernon, Petunia, and Dudley leave to attend an award ceremony for the best kept lawn in England. Harry is ordered to stay in his room and not steal food or touch their possessions. Uncle Vernon leaves, locking the door behind him. Later, as Harry ponders his lack of feeling about all this, he hears a crash in the kitchen. Grabbing his wand, he is startled when the door clicks open. He cautiously advances to the stairs where nine witches and wizards, including the real Mad-Eye Moody and Remus Lupin greet him.

Harry is being taken from the Dursleys,' and he returns upstairs with Nymphadora Tonks to pack. Tonks curiously changes her appearance, explaining that she is a Metamorphmagus and (impressing Harry) an Auror. Lupin leaves a note for the Dursleys, then the entire group heads outside. Because Harry cannot yet apparate, they mount broomsticks and begin a long, cold flight. They finally descend in what appears to be a lower-class neighborhood. Moody shows Harry a scrap of paper which reads: "The headquarters of the Order of the Phoenix may be found at Number Twelve, Grimmauld Place, London."

ANALYSIS

Harry has become increasingly upset and frustrated at being isolated, both physically and mentally, from his friends and the wizarding world. Clearly, someone is preventing him receiving detailed information, which leaves Harry feeling that he is being treated like a small, untrustworthy child. This is especially galling to him as, having fought Lord Voldemort twice successfully, and certainly being capable of understanding the overall situation, he feels as though he should be treated as an adult. However, even though Harry is on the verge of adulthood, we have seen that he sometimes acts immaturely and impulsively, often reacting in anger and frustration rather than logically evaluating what the actual circumstances may be and taking appropriate action. In particular, we note from the previous chapter that, on being informed that he was in trouble with the Ministry for underage use of magic, his impulse again was to run away.

The arrival of the Advance Guard tells us several things. First, there is the fact that the number of wizards that have come to collect Harry is so large. This is another indication of Harry's fame in the Wizarding world; Harry is surprised by the number because he has not internalized his own celebrity status. We are introduced for the first time to the true Mad-Eye Moody, and are exposed to the level of paranoia that he works under; we also find that even the other Aurors find his planned precautions to be excessive. Finally, their appearance is a clear indicator that Harry has not been forgotten, is not being ignored, but has simply been "put on ice," kept in his safe-house until there was another place to keep him safe. We as yet have no grounds to speculate why Harry was not told of these plans for his removal from Uncle Vernon's house, or for that matter, why he has been kept in the dark on all matters occurring in the Magical world, since he left Hogwarts. One thing we can see quite clearly is Harry's relief and excitement at being able to rejoin the Magical world, even if, as Moody seems to expect, it puts him in more danger.

QUESTIONS

Review   1. Why is Harry so frustrated?
2. What is a Metamorphmagus?
3. Why did so many people come to get Harry?

Further Study   1. Why has Harry been denied information about Voldemort and what is happening in the Wizard world?

GREATER PICTURE

We will find out shortly that it is at Dumbledore's bidding that Harry has been kept uninformed. Part of this is due to Dumbledore's awareness of the link between Harry and Voldemort, and his understanding of what exactly it is. In *Harry Potter and the Chamber of Secrets*, Dumbledore learned that Voldemort had made at least one Horcrux, and was alarmed to find that the Horcrux had been designed as a weapon, and used as one, rather than being kept safely hidden. From this, Dumbledore suspected that Voldemort had created multiple Horcruxes, a suspicion that was confirmed by Voldemort's saying that he had "gone further along the road to immortality than any other wizard." Eventually, Dumbledore will guess that the link between Harry and Voldemort is actually a soul fragment that had been torn away from Voldemort and had adhered to Harry's soul; whether he already has guessed this, or is simply aware of the existence of the link at this point is uncertain. In any event, Dumbledore's reasoning for keeping Harry uninformed is largely to decrease the chance that Voldemort would learn of the plans against him through that link. Additionally, the adult Wizards, notably Dumbledore and, to a lesser extent, Mrs. Weasley, have withheld information from Harry because they believe it could put him, and also his peers, in jeopardy by making them easy targets for Death Eaters. The less Harry knows for now, the safer he is.

Chapter 4: Number Twelve, Grimmauld Place

SYNOPSIS

Mad-Eye Moody instructs Harry to focus on the paper he has just been shown. When he does, a dilapidated-looking house materializes, and the Advance Guard ushers him in. The dark interior is as rundown and shabby as the outside. They are welcomed by Molly Weasley, who sends Harry upstairs to where Ron and Hermione are while the adults conduct a meeting. Harry's friends warmly greet him, though he is still upset that they withheld information; seeing Hedwig's peck marks on their hands pacifies him somewhat. Ron and Hermione insist Dumbledore swore them to secrecy, but that does not stop Harry from shouting his frustration at them. When he finally calms down, he begins asking questions.

Ron and Hermione identify the house as the headquarters for the Order of the Phoenix, a secret society founded by Dumbledore to combat Lord Voldemort. As they have been barred from any meetings, Ron and Hermione have little more information to offer. Instead, they have been busy cleaning the house. George, Fred, and Ginny Weasley enter the room. During the conversation, they reveal that Percy Weasley has become estranged from the family. He was promoted to a prestigious position in the Ministry of Magic, which is surprising considering his involvement in the events concerning his former boss, Mr. Crouch (in *Harry Potter and the Goblet of Fire*). When Arthur Weasley suggested he was promoted so he could spy on the Weasley family, a fight erupted, ending with Percy moving to London. Also, *The Daily Prophet* has been using Harry as a "standing joke" to discredit his claims that Lord Voldemort has returned.

Finally, the meeting ends, and Mrs. Weasley announces dinner. As Harry passes two tall, moth-eaten curtains in the hallway, Tonks knocks over an umbrella stand. Apparently in response to the noise, the curtains to fly open. Behind them is a portrait of an old woman horribly screaming: "Half-breeds, mutants, freaks, begone from this place! How dare you befoul the house of my fathers . . ." Mrs. Weasley and Tonks try ineffectually to close the curtains. Sirius Black enters and wrenches them shut. Greeting Harry, he comments that Harry has just met his mother.

ANALYSIS

Harry is relieved to return to the wizarding world and be reunited with Sirius, but, still angry, he lashes out at Ron and Hermione for withholding information, despite them having been under strict orders to divulge nothing in their letters to him. Although Harry takes a slightly perverse pleasure that Hedwig painfully pecked their hands on his behalf, Ron and Hermione actually had little to share; despite staying at Grimmauld Place, they have been nearly as cut off from the Order's business as Harry, they being too young to participate more than superficially in these very dangerous and adult matters. This hardly mollifies Harry, who continues to feel frustrated and angry at being denied knowledge regarding events in which he plays an integral part. Now, however, he has others to vent his anger on, however undeserved. Harry's frustration and emotional outbursts are mostly affected by puberty, and he suffers from the usual teenage angst that is exacerbated by his isolation and post-traumatic stress regarding Cedric Diggory's recent death and Voldemort's return. Harry could learn much from Fred and George's example, however. Despite being legal age, they are still students and are also excluded from the

Order's affairs. But rather than ranting and raving like Harry, they instead use their ingenuity to devise unique magical methods for gathering information, which they then share with Harry and the group.

The boundary between adults and youths has been clearly defined here, and although Harry and the others have continually proved their worth in fighting Voldemort, and Harry has personally faced the Dark Lord three times, they are still underaged and unqualified wizards; entrusting youths with the Order's secrets would only make them more tempting targets for Death Eaters to capture and torture for that information. Harry and the others fail to consider that, or that Harry just barely escaped Voldemort's trap, and Cedric lost his life. The less they all know, the safer they are, at least for now, although they will continue to do whatever they can to learn the Order's business. The rift with Percy Weasley causes Ron and his family additional stress and anguish. Although Percy has always been rather pompous and self-serving, his ambition has blinded him to what is truly happening within the Ministry of Magic and the wizarding world at large. He also discounts the belief that Voldemort has returned. Regarding his sudden promotion, two factors make it logical. First, as the other Weasleys suggest, the Ministry recruited him to spy upon his own family, who are known supporters of Harry and Dumbledore. Second, the Ministry was covering up Percy's severe blunder. Percy, as his family is aware, seriously erred by failing to recognize that Mr. Crouch had fallen under Voldemort's and Wormtail's control. The official Ministry of Magic stance continues to be that Voldemort is still dead and Wormtail was murdered by Sirius Black thirteen years ago; therefore, they must deny Harry's explanation regarding Mr. Crouch, no matter how well it explains what has been happening. Percy's only official misstep was that he never realized how "sick" Crouch was, for which he can be forgiven because Crouch apparently hid the depths of his illness, and his promotion is simply part of the fiction that the Ministry must create to explain what happened to Crouch. Percy, having whole-heartedly bought into the Ministry mindset, never questions his promotion, apparently believing that it is purely in recognition of his abilities.

QUESTIONS

Review 1. Why is Harry so angry with Ron and Hermione? How else could he have expressed his frustration?

2. What is the Order of the Phoenix and why was it established? Who founded it?

3. What has caused Percy's estrangement from the Weasley family? Did he react appropriately?

4. Why does the *Daily Prophet* continually ridicule Harry? Who might be responsible for projecting this image?

Further Study 1. Why does Number Twelve, Grimmauld Place resemble a Dark wizard's residence? What is its current purpose? 2. Why was so much information withheld from Harry until now? Was this wise?

GREATER PICTURE

Percy will continue, oblivious to the changes in the Ministry, until very near the end of our story. Finally recognizing that the Ministry has changed, fundamentally, into an instrument of evil, Percy will return to his family as the battle at Hogwarts begins. Until he reaches that realization, though, there will be friction between himself and his father, as they both continue to work at the Ministry.

Fred and George, in order to determine what is happening in the Order meetings, have invented Extendable Ears, which they try to use to listen in on the meetings in the kitchen. These devices, with their ability to eavesdrop on other wizards, will prove useful in this and all future books.

The appearance of the house will give the reader some concern, as with its snake-head door handle, display of preserved House Elf heads, and screaming portraits, it is clearly the house of Wizards who feel some kinship to Slytherin and espouse Voldemort's views on Wizarding racial purity. We will find, in the next few chapters, that the male line of the Black family has almost completely died out, leaving Sirius as the sole living Black, and that he is trying to eliminate the Dark magic of his house as part of the process of rejecting his family's values, which he feels are repugnant to him. It is presumed that Harry will continue this cleaning up of the house, which he inherits on Sirius' death, once the more pressing matters of his education and Voldemort's defeat are dealt with.

Chapter 5: The Order of the Phoenix

SYNOPSIS

Sirius Black explains to a bewildered Harry that the portrait is his mother, the late Mrs. Black. Number 12, Grimmauld Place, the Blacks' ancestral home, was inherited by Sirius upon his mother's death, though he was in Azkaban at the time. He adds gloomily that providing the house as the headquarters for the Order of the Phoenix is one of the few useful contributions he has been able to make.

In the kitchen, the Weasleys and several Order members are busy preparing dinner. Bill Weasley is also there, and he and Mr. Weasley are studying numerous parchment rolls at the kitchen table, apparently Order of the Phoenix business. Bill quickly gathers everything up when Harry enters. Fred and George attempt to magically serve the meal, sending a chopping board and knife, a pitcher of Butterbeer, and a pot of stew careening through the air and onto the table. The results are less than stellar, with the stew barely staying on the table's edge, half the Butterbeer spilled, and the knife's point landing in the table right where Sirius' hand had been moments before. Mrs. Weasley scolds them: just because they are allowed to do magic does not mean that they have to.

During dinner, Harry catches snippets of conversation around the room: Tonks taking requests for different-shaped noses, Bill discussing the Goblins' stance on Lord Voldemort and how it was affected by their dealings with Ludo Bagman the previous year, and the thief Mundungus Fletcher's comical business dealings. Following dinner, Sirius breaks the comfortable ambiance by suggesting that Harry ask questions about Voldemort. There is a brief argument between Mrs. Weasley and Sirius over how much Harry should know. Sirius thinks Harry should have more information, but Mrs. Weasley feels he is too young and accuses Sirius of treating Harry more like a substitute for James Potter, rather than as his godson. Lupin and Mr. Weasley side with Sirius, however. There is a somewhat longer disagreement between Mrs. Weasley and the others as to which of the younger set should be allowed to listen in, and finally, Mrs. Weasley drags a fiercely-protesting Ginny off to bed. Harry begins asking questions while Fred, George, Ron, and Hermione listen. Sirius, Lupin, and Mr. Weasley answer Harry's questions. No murders have been committed because Voldemort wants to keep a low profile. The Ministry of Magic fervently denies Voldemort has returned, and Albus Dumbledore has been demoted from the Chairmanship of the International Confederation of Wizards and from Chief Warlock of the Wizengamot after publicly announcing that Lord Voldemort was active again. The Order is recruiting new members, including foreign ones, and is also concentrating on the Auror department in the Ministry. Members who work for the Ministry must tread carefully, however, as the Minister has threatened to fire anyone friendly with Dumbledore. The Minister is paranoid that Dumbledore is plotting to take over the Ministry of Magic. Sirius also lets slip that there is a weapon the Order is trying to guard, at which point Molly Weasley interrupts. Lupin agrees that enough information has been given, and everyone is sent to bed.

There is some discussion after lights out amongst Harry, Ron, and the twins, who had previously heard everything that was discussed that evening via the Extendable Ears. The only revelation to them is that a weapon has been mentioned. Their conversation is cut short by Mrs. Weasley's return, and Harry falls asleep, only to have nightmares.

Analysis

The main point of this chapter is to bring Harry, and thus the reader, up to speed on what has been happening in the Wizarding world over the past month and a bit. Now that Voldemort has returned, Harry is aware that the Wizarding world has changed significantly, and we have seen his growing perplexity that the expected evil has not yet materialized. In this meeting, we learn why nothing seems to be happening, and what Dumbledore, the only authority who seems to believe Harry, is doing about it. We are also able to find out more about what has happened to some important adult characters, notably Sirius and Lupin, and are offered some more insight into the relationship between Mr. and Mrs. Weasley.

Although Sirius is free after spending twelve years in Azkaban Prison for a crime he never committed, he is as much a prisoner as ever. As a still-wanted fugitive, he must remain in hiding, effectively being incarcerated in the dreary Black home that has always been an unhappy place for him. And although he is an Order of the Phoenix member, he is unable to actively participate in the fight against Voldemort. As a result, he is becoming increasingly depressed, irritable, and reckless, as well as mentally unstable. This, coupled with his rather underdeveloped maturity that was effectively suppressed during his long imprisonment, will affect his relationship with Harry. As Molly Weasley points out, Sirius tends to view Harry more as a replacement for James Potter, rather than as his godson. That is not to say Sirius does not love Harry or have his best interest in mind, but he is not as good an adult role model as he should be.

Molly's character is also becoming more defined here. While she is a strong-willed, powerful witch and a valuable Order of the Phoenix member, her maternal instincts often take precedence over all other matters. By wanting to withhold all information from the youngsters, she not only is trying to protect her children for as long as possible, but also Harry, who she has come to love like a son. She cannot, however, continue to keep him and the younger Weasley children sequestered in childhood innocence. Providing too little information can be as dangerous as giving them too much.

Questions

Review 1. Why was Dumbledore demoted from important Wizarding posts, and by whom?

2. Why is Mrs. Weasley angry with Fred and George? Should she be?

3. What are some of the tasks the Order of the Phoenix is trying to accomplish?

4. What does Sirius mean when he says offering the Black family house to the Order of the Phoenix is one of the few useful things he can do?

Further Study 1. What could the weapon be that Sirius mentions? Where is it?

2. Why might the Order have to be kept secret?

3. Why is there an argument over how much information Harry should be allowed to hear? What should he know?

4. Why does Molly Weasley accuse Sirius of treating Harry more like a friend than a godson? Is she right? If so, why do Lupin and the others side with Sirius?

Greater Picture

We will find out, later in the book, that the weapon is not, in fact, a weapon as such, but rather a prophecy having to do with Harry and Voldemort. However, the idea of a supremely powerful weapon will fill Harry's, Hermione's, and Ron's thoughts to the point that when they need to lure Professor Umbridge away from the school, the idea that Hermione hits upon is a secret weapon that Dumbledore had supposedly left for them to finish. It has been mentioned earlier that Ron had overheard Order members talking about guard duty; Harry at the time had sourly suggested that what they were guarding was himself. Now, though, we learn that there is this object that the Order is guarding. We will find that at least two Order members, Mr. Weasley and Sturgis Podmore, get into trouble while on guard duty.

The prophecy, which we will not actually hear until the penultimate chapter of this book, could only be considered a weapon in that it tells what power Harry has that will be Voldemort's undoing, and that it will be the Dark Lord's marking him as an equal which will give him power over Voldemort. Voldemort has already heard the first part of the prophecy, which predicts Harry's birth and parentage, and that he will have power the Dark Lord knows not; Voldemort will spend the largest part of this book trying to recapture that prophecy in the hopes that it will also describe how he might defeat Harry. Like so many prophecies, if Voldemort actually had managed to retrieve the prophecy, its most important part for him would have already been foregone. The part of the prophecy that Voldemort has not heard is that the Dark Lord will "mark him as an equal." In fact, that mark, the scar on Harry's forehead that resulted from Voldemort's attempt to murder Harry, is the visible indicator of Voldemort's soul shard that remains within Harry, and which gives him insight into Voldemort's plans throughout the series' final book. The final part, about "the power that the Dark Lord knows not," is by this time an open secret, though Voldemort still discounts it. By the time he returns, he knew that it was Lily's sacrifice that protected Harry, and thus that the magic set to oppose him was based on love; not knowing love himself, Voldemort could not truly understand its power.

However, a more conventional weapon does exist, and it plays an important part later in the series. In the final book, *Harry Potter and the Deathly Hallows*, as Voldemort's wand has been proven ineffective against Harry's, he will seek the legendary Elder Wand. It is supposedly the most powerful wand ever crafted, and Voldemort hopes it will help defeat Harry.

Chapter 6: The Noble and Most Ancient House of Black

Synopsis

Harry, Hermione and the Weasleys spend the next morning ridding the parlour of doxies. Harry catches Fred pocketing a paralyzed doxy; Fred explains that he and George can experiment with its venom for new products (Skiving Snackboxes) for their joke shop. Mundungus Fletcher arrives, bringing stolen cauldrons to store at the house, sending Mrs. Weasley into a rage. While she furiously prepares lunch, a wizened House-elf wanders into the drawing room, muttering obscenities about "mudbloods," evidently meaning Hermione. The elf, Kreacher, who is apparently still extremely devoted to Mrs. Black, has been taking orders from her portrait for the past ten years. Hermione's attempts to be kind to him are thwarted by the twins and Sirius, who has just entered the room.

When Harry notices an old tapestry, Sirius explains sarcastically that it is the "Noble and Most Ancient House of Black" family tree. Mrs. Black has blasted off various members for "sins" against the family—namely, associating with, marrying, or sympathizing with Half-bloods and Muggles. Sirius points out that pure-blood wizarding families like the Blacks are almost all interrelated. Notable Black family connections include the Malfoys, the Lestranges, the Weasleys, the Prewetts, the Tonks, and former Hogwarts Headmaster Phineas Nigellus. In addition, his brother, Regulus, was once a Death Eater. According to Sirius, "He got in so far, then panicked about what he was being asked to do and tried to back out." This led to his death.

The next few days are filled with more cleaning tasks, often interrupted by Kreacher creeping around rescuing family heirlooms and Dark objects that are being tossed out, and with visits from Order members. Finally, Mrs. Weasley reminds Harry that his Ministry of Magic hearing is the next day, causing him apprehension. Mr. Weasley is to escort him, as requested by Professor Dumbledore when he visited Grimmauld Place the night before. Harry, worried as he is about the hearing, now also feels vexed with Dumbledore for not wanting to see Harry while he was there. Harry now feels that Dumbledore has avoided him all summer.

Analysis

Despite Voldemort, the upcoming hearing, Sirius' increasing depression, and Harry's frustration, Grimmauld Place offers rare snippets of domestic bliss that Harry and his godfather enjoy with the Weasleys. Neither Sirius nor Harry has ever experienced a happy family life, and Harry relishes these brief interludes. Harry and Sirius actually share much in common, growing up isolated and miserable in loveless households: Grimmauld Place and Privet Drive. And while Harry only has to endure his unhappy home for the summer, Sirius is now trapped inside a house containing many unpleasant (and magically permanent) reminders of his difficult youth—his mad mother's screaming portrait, a sullen house-elf, and the family-tree tapestry bearing scorch marks where he and his other "blood traitor" relatives were blasted away by Mrs. Black. But a house can only reflect the people living in it, and Harry and Sirius have taken the first steps in creating their own happy family there. The pleasant time they share together will be short-lived, however. Hogwarts starts soon, and Sirius and Harry must part company; Sirius will likely be more lonely and miserable than ever.

Harry also learns more about Sirius' ancestry and how interrelated wizard families are. It is quite possible that Harry and Sirius are distant blood relatives as well as godfather and godson. Harry may even be related to the Weasleys. Hermione looking out the drawing room window and down at the front steps may be somewhat confusing for US readers. The house at Grimmauld Place is built to the London pattern, very much vertical, and apparently has four stories above the ground floor. The drawing room or parlour is apparently located one floor above ground level, on what U.S. readers would call the second floor, and European readers call the first floor. More information is available here.

Questions

Review 1. Why does Kreacher continually retrieve discarded items? 2. What was Sirius' relationship with his family?

Further Study 1. Why doesn't Sirius directly answer Harry when he asks if he can live at Grimmauld Place if he is expelled? 2. Why would Dumbledore ignore Harry while he was at 12 Grimmauld Place?

GREATER PICTURE

This chapter marks the first mention of Sirius' brother Regulus. In *Harry Potter and the Half-Blood Prince,* a note is found that is signed only with the initials R.A.B.; this R.A.B. is Regulus Arcturus Black, as confirmed by Kreacher in *Harry Potter and the Deathly Hallows.*

Also in this chapter, amongst the miscellaneous stuff being tossed out, is mention of "a heavy locket that none of them could open." We will later find that a locket, which can be traced back to Salazar Slytherin, plays a major part in the story. Dumbledore believes that Voldemort used this locket to create a Horcrux, and in *Harry Potter and the Half-Blood Prince,* they go to retrieve it, only to find that it has been replaced with a fake locket and the above-mentioned note. It is ironic that this locket had been at Headquarters all this time. As a Slytherin relic, this would likely be among the items Kreacher would squirrel away for safe-keeping, along with pictures of members of the Black family, such as Bellatrix Lestrange. We will have the history of the locket explained to us by Kreacher and Mundungus Fletcher in *Harry Potter and the Deathly Hallows,* and we will see its eventual destruction in that book as well.

Chapter 7: The Ministry of Magic

SYNOPSIS

Harry wakes early in the morning, too nervous to eat breakfast. He and Arthur Weasley depart for the Ministry of Magic, commuting in a "thoroughly nonmagical fashion" to make a better impression. Upon arriving, Mr. Weasley and Harry cram into a broken telephone booth and are transported underground. They enter a huge, brightly lit atrium with a large fountain at its center (a wizard and witch surrounded by various magical creatures wearing servile expressions).

Harry passes through the security screening, then follows Mr. Weasley into a lift (elevator). Wizards and witches continually enter and exit, as do hovering paper airplanes. Mr. Weasley identifies these as interdepartmental memos, saying they had earlier tried owls, which had created an unbelievable mess. Harry notices that underground windows in the hallway have sunlight streaming through them. Mr. Weasley explains that they are controlled by Magical Maintenance, who, among other maintenance tasks at the Ministry, determine the apparent weather. They pass the Auror offices, which are covered with pictures of family, Quidditch, and Sirius Black. Kingsley Shacklebolt approaches, acting as though he and Mr. Weasley are on poor terms. He slips them a magazine in amongst some files, quietly saying that Sirius might be interested in it. Mr. Weasley equally quietly invites him to dinner, then he and Harry move on.

Mr. Weasley, whose office is noticeably tiny, mentions his work investigating exploding toilets caused by anti-Muggle pranksters. A co-worker, Perkins, runs in announcing that the hearing's time and location has been changed, making Harry late. The new location is in old Courtroom 10 in the building's basement. Because the lift does not descend that far, Harry and Mr. Weasley race down the stairs. Just outside the courtroom, Mr. Weasley stops; Harry must face the hearing alone.

ANALYSIS

This is Harry's first time to the Ministry of Magic. Until now, he has had relatively little exposure to the adult Wizarding society, having only been to Diagon Alley, Hogwarts, and Hogsmeade village. The Ministry is the hub of the Wizarding community in the U.K., and it governs nearly all its activities. Unfortunately, Harry's first visit here is an unpleasant one.

We should take particular note of the Fountain of Magical Brethren in the Ministry atrium, as it represents how the power of the Ministry is wielded only by wizards, with all other magical creatures under their domain. Harry notes that the expressions of syrupy subservience seem out of place on all the sculpted magical races except the House Elf.

The sudden change in the hearing's time and location is an obvious ploy by certain Ministry officials to prevent Harry from testifying on his own behalf and to convict him in absentia. They likely know that he is innocent, but to prevent his making further claims that Voldemort has returned, they will use any means to censure and exile him from the Wizarding world. Whether Voldemort's Death Eaters are behind this, or it is merely corrupt Ministry officials who refuse to believe that Voldemort has returned or who do not wish the general population to know what is really happening, is still unclear. What is apparent is that this is a technique used by the author to reinforce what we have been told. Hermione has told Harry that the *Daily Prophet* is making Harry, and Dumbledore with him, into something of a laughing stock so as to "spin" their message of Voldemort's return into oblivion. This does not have much of an impact on the reader, because it does not happen directly to the viewpoint character (Harry). With the sudden rescheduling of the hearing, we are actually shown that there may be some ill-feeling against Harry, and some machinations within the Ministry may be going on to try and get Harry finally out of the Ministry's way.

QUESTIONS

Review 1. Why would the time and location for Harry's hearing have been changed so suddenly? 2. Why might Mr. Weasley be prevented from attending the hearing?

Further Study 1. How might the Fountain of Magical Brethren represent an inaccurate picture of the wizarding world? 2. What is the significance of holding a hearing for using underage magic in Courtroom 10?

GREATER PICTURE

The question of whether the Ministry's ongoing denigration of Harry and Dumbledore is being driven by Voldemort, or simply by the Ministry following Fudge's plan to attempt to retain power, is never completely resolved. Fudge's need to retain power, though, would seem to be enough to explain the ongoing discrediting of Harry and Dumbledore.

Harry will feel a need to re-enter the Ministry at the end of this book. It is in this chapter that he learns where the Visitor's Entrance to the Ministry is located, and how one uses it to access the Ministry. This information, plus what Harry learns about the layout of the Ministry in the course of this visit, will be vital to his later visit and attempt to rescue Sirius.

The Fountain of Magical Brethren depicts, with almost uncanny realism, the way that the Ministry expects other Magical races to treat Wizards; though never stated, Ministry policy has always been to treat non-Human Magical races as second-class citizens. This fountain will be destroyed at the end of this book; Harry will not see a need to re-enter the Ministry until the final book, at which time we shall see the replacement. That replacement status, showing a Wizarding family seated on thrones made of tormented Muggles, will again echo the stated policy of the Ministry.

Chapter 8: The Hearing

SYNOPSIS

Upon entering the courtroom, Harry realizes this is where the Death Eaters were tried—the place he had entered in Dumbledore's Pensieve during his previous year at Hogwarts. Cornelius Fudge is acting as the head of the Wizengamot (wizard high court), and Harry is surprised to see Percy Weasley as the scribe. Dumbledore sweeps in, to the evident discomfiture of several members of the court, and announces himself as witness for the defence. Fudge begins the questioning, giving Harry little time to answer completely. Frustrated, Harry exclaims, "I did it because of the Dementors!" This seems to stun the Wizengamot. Amelia Bones questions him further about the Dementors' presence. Dumbledore steps in, noting that they have a witness, Arabella Figg. Summoned, she seems particularly batty and frightened and begins her testimony as though she has memorized it. There is doubt as to whether Squibs can see Dementors, but Mrs. Figg describes them accurately. After Mrs. Figg leaves, Fudge struggles to regain the courtroom's flow, insisting Harry's actions have little to do with the Dementors presence. A few court members aid Fudge, notably Dolores Umbridge, who obviously remains convinced Harry is guilty. Dumbledore quickly asserts that Harry has broken no laws if he was protecting himself and Dudley from a life-threatening danger, as is noted in the Decree for the Reasonable Restriction of Underage Sorcery. Fudge quickly brings up other instances where Harry has broken the Decree, but Dumbledore nullifies each one in turn. The council votes, and Harry is cleared of all charges, much to Fudge's dismay. Harry turns to thank Dumbledore, only to find that the Headmaster is already leaving the courtroom.

ANALYSIS

That Harry would be subjected to a full hearing before the entire Wizengamot for a simple matter involving underage magic indicates that sinister forces are at work against Harry. Changing the hearing's time and location without prior notification is yet another despicable tactic by the Ministry of Magic to discredit Harry and also to prevent Dumbledore from testifying, although, fortunately, it failed. By attempting to prevent Harry from giving a complete explanation about the events at Privet Drive, it seems certain that some Ministry officials had already conspired to rule against him, showing they will do anything necessary to invalidate Dumbledore's and Harry's claims concerning Voldemort, including ousting Harry from the Wizard world and demoting Dumbledore from his many prestigious Wizarding posts. That the hearing was relocated to the same trial courtroom where Death Eaters were previously tried and convicted is significant—an obvious ploy to implant the impression in the Wizengamots' minds that Harry is likewise guilty. Dumbledore's intervention saves Harry, although his abrupt departure without speaking to him is puzzling.

Mrs. Figg's testimony was also crucial, although, as she is a Squib, it is believed to be unlikely she actually saw the Dementors and was probably coached prior to testifying. Looking back at the actual events, though, we see that Mrs. Figg had identified the Dementors when she was talking to Harry, before Harry had mentioned them, and before Mundungus Fletcher had returned. From this, we can see that Mrs. Figg not only can see Dementors, but was able to recognize them. Coaching, it if happened, must have happened before the events of that evening; Dumbledore must have informed Mrs. Figg that Dementors were likely, and trained her on what she was likely to see and feel when they were around. Dumbledore, as we saw at the end of *Harry Potter and the Goblet of Fire*, was expecting both the Dementors and the Giants to rally to Voldemort, and so is likely to have briefed Mrs. Figg.

QUESTIONS

Review 1. Can Squibs really see Dementors? If not, how and why could Mrs. Figg provide such convincing testimony? 2. Why would Fudge want Harry to be voted guilty, even if he is not?

Further Study 1. Why would Dumbledore avoid looking at or talking to Harry?

2. Why would Harry's hearing be held in the same courtroom that Death Eaters were tried and convicted in?

3. Why would the full Wizangamot be present for a hearing on a simple case of underage magic? How could Fudge have arranged to convene the entire Wizengamot for such a simple case?

GREATER PICTURE

Harry has been upset by Dumbledore's failure to get in contact with him throughout the summer, and by his failure to communicate with him even while he was at Headquarters. He was particularly dismayed by the revelation that Dumbledore had been at Headquarters and had left without visiting Harry. Here, Dumbledore arrives, defends Harry successfully, and departs, without ever speaking a word directly to Harry or even making eye contact. Harry here feels almost abandoned by Dumbledore; and this feeling of abandonment will result in Harry refusing to tell Dumbledore of things occurring during the course of the year that directly affected Harry and Dumbledore both. This, it will turn out, is a deliberate policy of Dumbledore's during this year. Knowing, as he does, that Harry is able to occasionally perceive things happening in Voldemort's mind, Dumbledore has come to the conclusion that, if and when Voldemort becomes aware of the connection, he will attempt to use it against Harry and his associates. Against this, Dumbledore is choosing to try and shield Harry and himself by not displaying any sign that there is a relationship greater than student to headmaster between them. Harry resents this change of relationship being made unilaterally, and will unconsciously retaliate by withholding useful information.

We see a curious, but possibly intentional, oddity of the Wizarding justice system here. Rather than having prosecuting and defending representatives in front of a neutral party, the defending party in the dispute is questioned directly by the nominal head of the Wizengamot, and the Wizengamot members then confer and vote on the innocence or guilt of the defending party. This tallies with the views of the Wizengamot that we were granted by means of Dumbledore's Pensieve. This can lead to abuses of justice, as the prosecution is generally going to be better prepared for trial than the defence, particularly if the defendant has just been released from Azkaban, and as the prosecutor will be a member of the same group as the judges. Most committees seem to be reflections of one powerful individual, who pulls the other committee members along with his or her views by main force; Harry's great fortune in this case seems to be that while Fudge is apparently the official head of the Wizengamot, the actual leader seems to be Amelia Bones, who, perhaps inspired by Dumbledore's presence, is more interested in justice than in toeing the Ministry party line.

We should note that this simplification of the justice system seems to make the courtroom drama better suited to a children's book. Very few children of this book's targeted age group will be fully aware of the normal judicial system's structure, and this adversarial form of court is better suited to their understanding. Additionally, Harry's victory over such a court is all the sweeter, as the deck is so clearly stacked against him.

Chapter 9: The Woes of Mrs. Weasley

SYNOPSIS

Harry leaves the courtroom to tell Mr. Weasley the good news; Mr. Weasley comments that Professor Dumbledore brushed past him without speaking. As they stand outside, wizards file out of the courtroom, and Mr. Weasley expresses surprise that Harry seems to have been tried by the entire Wizengamot. Percy is the last person out, and he and Mr. Weasley studiously ignore each other, though the lines around Mr. Weasley's mouth tighten as Percy walks past.

While walking up the stairs, they meet Cornelius Fudge and Lucius Malfoy, whom Mr. Weasley surmises was attempting to sneak down to the courtroom to learn what was happening. In amongst the usual barbed comments exchanged between Lucius and Arthur, Malfoy cites "private matters" to explain his conversation with Fudge. Arthur Weasley comments privately to Harry that it likely has more to do with the exchange of gold, and that Malfoy is contributing to all the right causes as a means to get laws he dislikes delayed or ignored. Harry suggests that with Fudge meeting privately with Death Eaters, it is possible that he has been put under the Imperius Curse. Mr. Weasley says they considered that, but Dumbledore believes Fudge is acting on his own, for what little reassurance that provides.

When they arrive back at 12 Grimmauld Place, everyone is relieved that Harry has been exonerated. Fred, George, and Ginny break into a victory dance and chant, "He got off, he got off, he got off!" until Mrs. Weasley yells at them. During the next few days, however, Harry realizes that Sirius seems despondent. Hermione suggests that Sirius was secretly hoping Harry would become an outcast like him and live at Grimmauld Place. Regardless, Harry's spirits are lifted, and he dreams about Hogwarts.

The day before school starts, booklists finally arrive, raising the question as to who the new Defence Against the Dark Arts teacher might be. They also bring a surprise—as expected, Hermione has been named a Gryffindor prefect, but so has Ron, much to everyone's astonishment. As a reward, Mrs. Weasley agrees to buy Ron a new broom. Harry struggles with jealousy and resentment, believing that between the two, he would have been chosen over Ron, but Sirius telling him, at the celebration dinner, that his father had not been a prefect either helps Harry come to terms with this. Of the Marauders, it was Lupin who was made Prefect. Lupin comments that Dumbledore probably expected him to be able to keep his friends under control, but he failed miserably. Harry gives his sincere congratulations to Ron.

After the celebratory dinner, Mad-Eye Moody shows Harry a photograph of the original Order of the Phoenix. Moody apparently thought this would be a treat, allowing Harry to see his parents again. However, Harry finds it disturbing, seeing them amongst so many others who have died at Death Eaters' hands. Harry, angry at being cornered with something so negative, makes his excuses and leaves the party.

Harry passes the drawing room in which Mrs. Weasley is attempting to banish a boggart. She is sobbing, and each time she waves her wand, another family member's image appears—dead. It also appears as a dead Harry. Lupin comes to her rescue, finishing off

Chapter 9: The Woes of Mrs. Weasley

the boggart and comforting her. As Harry slips away to bed, he feels quite old and wonders how he could have been upset about who was made a prefect when there are so many more important matters at stake.

ANALYSIS

For once, it is Harry, rather than Ron, who copes with jealousy and being in second place after Ron is named a prefect and Harry is not. It is likely Dumbledore appointed Ron partially to help Ron develop his own identity, apart from Harry's influence and the constant attention surrounding him. Ron has always contented himself to tag along after others, suffering from a lack of confidence caused mostly by feeling overshadowed by his accomplished siblings, Hermione's intellect, and Harry's celebrity. Lupin may have been appointed a prefect for similar reasons. It is also possible Dumbledore was concerned that other students would feel Harry was chosen due to his fame, and that this may have caused more resentment and detracted from Harry doing an effective job. Harry also fails to understand that Ron is struggling to discover his own unique talents and abilities. Also, with Voldemort re-emerging and so many doubting Harry's claims, Dumbledore may simply want to avoid putting any additional stress and focus on Harry.

We do see a small conflict at this point. In *Harry Potter and the Philosopher's Stone*, Hagrid tells Harry that his parents were "Head Boy and Head Girl in their day." We have already seen that Percy had progressed from Prefect to Head Boy, so the assumption is that, in order to become Head Boy, James Potter must have first been a Prefect. Yet, here we learn that it was Lupin who was Prefect. This anomaly is never explained, but if Lupin had resigned or been forced out as Prefect, or had elected not to complete his seventh year at Hogwarts, it is possible that James would have been made Prefect and Head Boy in his stead.

Lucius Malfoy meeting with Minister for Magic Cornelius Fudge so close to Harry's hearing is highly suspicious, although there is no proof that Fudge is connected to Death Eaters. Likely he is not, but Malfoy has certainly courted his and the Ministry's favor and influence, mostly through generous monetary donations. Here, Lucius, a Death Eater, may be attempting to manipulate Fudge regarding Harry's hearing, or may be attempting to extract information that he can relay to Voldemort. A clueless Fudge is more inept than corrupt, and he is mainly concerned with cultivating his public image rather than paying attention to what is actually happening in the Wizarding world. He truly believes that Voldemort has not returned and that Harry is an attention-seeking liar. Fudge is also highly paranoid and is convinced that Dumbledore is plotting to overthrow the Ministry.

Molly Weasley's deepest fears are shown here. A devoted and loving wife and mother, she lives in constant terror that her family will fall victim to Voldemort. She has lost her brothers, and it is unlikely she could bear to lose Arthur or any of her children. From seeing her fears, we can tell that she is convinced that the Weasley family will not survive the war unscathed.

Harry is deeply disturbed by witnessing this, although the Boggart turning into his image shows how deeply Molly cares for him, considering him as a son. Harry is also confronted with his own mortality and realizes that he may not get through this alive.

QUESTIONS

Review   1. Why is Harry upset that Mad-Eye Moody showed him the picture of his parents?

2. How does Harry react when he sees Mrs. Weasley's boggart turning into her family, dead? What does this say about Molly Weasley?

3. How does Harry feel when he sees the same boggart becoming him, dead?

4. What changes Harry's attitude about Hermione and Ron becoming prefects?

Further Study   1. Why might Lucius Malfoy have been meeting with Cornelius Fudge immediately after the hearing?

2. Why might Ron have been made a prefect and not Harry? Does Harry think he is better qualified than Ron?

3. Is Ron really qualified to be a prefect or will he just rely on Hermione's guidance?

4. Who might be the new Defense Against the Dark Arts instructor?

5. How might the boggart scene foreshadow other events in the books?

GREATER PICTURE

It is unlikely that Lucius being so near the Department of Mysteries is an innocent coincidence on his part; we will discover that Voldemort is seeking something in that department, and Lucius may be searching for a suitable candidate he can place under the Imperius curse to fetch that for him. Within days, Sturgis Podmore will be caught attempting to enter a secure door, probably having been magically compelled to breach the Department of Mysteries by Malfoy. Later in the book, we will learn that one Broderick Bode, an Unspeakable who was seen in the previous chapter, will run afoul of protective spells within the Ministry. Bode will be seen in St. Mungo's hospital recovering from a severe jinx around the Christmas holidays. Hermione will later surmise that Bode, like Podmore, had been compelled to try and retrieve the object that Voldemort had wanted. We will also overhear a conversation between Voldemort and Rookwood, a Death Eater, which confirms this, and that Bode had been jinxed in the Department of Ministries. It is Voldemort's ongoing attempts to fetch this object which will result in the climactic battle of this book.

The Boggart transforming into "dead" Weasley family members may foreshadow a tragedy in the series' final book.

Chapter 10: Luna Lovegood

Synopsis

After a restless night, Harry awakens to chaos: everyone is racing around, trying to pack as quickly as possible. The Advance Guard has reassembled to accompany Harry to King's Cross Station, and Sirius insists upon coming along in his dog form, much to Mrs. Weasley's dismay. They wait for Sturgis Podmore, who is late, but eventually move on without him. Sirius, who has been confined until now, scampers around and snaps at pigeons. The group says their goodbyes on the platform, and Harry, Ron, Hermione, Fred, George, and Ginny board the train. Fred and George depart to talk business with Lee Jordan. When Harry suggests finding a compartment, Hermione and Ron exchange awkward looks and explain that they have to join the other prefects for instructions. They leave, promising to return soon. Harry and Ginny, trying to find an empty compartment, struggle the length of the train; Harry notices that everyone is looking at him, and then remembers that the *Daily Prophet* has been saying all summer that he is a lying madman. As they near the rear car, they meet Neville. Ginny leads them into a compartment with a strange looking girl inside who emanates "an aura of distinct dottiness." She is reading a magazine called *The Quibbler* upside down. Ginny introduces her as Luna Lovegood, a Ravenclaw student in her year. After attempting to converse with her, the discussion turns to Neville's birthday present, a rare *Mimbulus Mimbletonia* plant. He pokes it with his wand, trying to show them its defense mechanism, and the entire compartment is sprayed with horrid-smelling green pus just as Cho Chang walks in to greet Harry.

An awkward moment passes. Cho leaves and Ginny cleans the stinksap off them. Ron and Hermione return to announce that Draco Malfoy and Pansy Parkinson are the Slytherin Prefects; Ernie Macmillan and Hannah Abbott are Hufflepuff Prefects; and Anthony Goldstein and Padma Patil are the Ravenclaw Prefects. Ron tells a bad joke, at which Luna laughs inappropriately loudly. Harry notices Sirius Black's name on Luna's magazine cover. He asks to borrow it and reads an article claiming Sirius' alter-ego is a singer before realizing the story is bogus. Hermione disdainfully states that the *Quibbler* is "rubbish," to which Luna replies, "My father's the editor."

Draco Malfoy, with his sidekicks Crabbe and Goyle, drop in on them. Draco asks how Harry feels to be second to Ron; Hermione tells him to get out. Draco makes a comment hinting that he recognized Sirius. After he departs, Harry and Hermione exchange troubled looks, but with the others there cannot say anything, while Ron is oblivious to this exchange.

At last, they reach Hogwarts. However, instead of Hagrid's familiar voice calling the first-years, they hear Professor Grubbly-Plank. They hardly have time to ponder this before Ginny and Harry have to carry their belongings to the carriages. Harry is stunned that the carriages are no longer horseless; rather, they are drawn by black, skeletal horse-like creatures with leathery skin and wings. Ron sees nothing, leaving Harry wondering if he has gone mad. Luna approaches, saying she also sees them, leaving Harry confused: is confirmation from someone believing in Crumple Horned Snorkacks truly reassuring?

Analysis

There are several interesting developments in this chapter. Sirius unexpectedly seeing Harry off at the Hogwarts Express was not only reckless and risked him being captured, but it endangers Harry, and his friends, and risks exposing the Order of the Phoenix. His dog animagus form may have been recognized by the Malfoys, which could lead to Harry, and possibly Dumbledore, being accused as his accomplices. His impulsive act shows that Sirius' judgment may be deteriorating.

It is not immediately apparent how Draco and Lucius would have recognized Sirius. However, we must recall that Peter Pettigrew (Wormtail) has returned to Voldemort, and had been a close friend of Sirius' some fifteen years before. Wormtail will have been able to describe Sirius' Animagus shape to Voldemort, and Voldemort, knowing that Sirius would likely be in the Order of the Phoenix, would have passed that information to his returned Death Eaters, including Lucius Malfoy.

On the train, Harry, who is usually accompanied by Ron and Hermione, must fend for himself for a while as they tend to their prefect duties. Still smarting over Ron's new status, Harry is embarrassed to find himself seated with some less popular students who others consider "misfits." Luna Lovegood, in particular, is an oddity Harry would rather avoid, although Ginny seems on friendly terms with her. However, Harry does have his first inkling that Cho Chang, who he has had a crush on for some time, seems to show an interest in him, although she catches him at a rather awkward and embarrassing moment. However, Harry, like Cho, is still deeply affected by Cedric Diggory's death, and pursuing a relationship may be an unwise course for either at this time.

It is noted that Harry recognizes this issue of the Quibbler as the same one that Kingsley Shacklebolt had earlier surreptitiously slipped to Mr. Weasley, saying it would amuse Sirius. We now know exactly why Sirius would be amused.

That Hagrid is gone is not entirely unexpected; Harry knows he is on a secret mission for Dumbledore. However, his absence is still unsettling for Harry, who considers Hagrid like family and feels that he represents comfort and security; Harry is also worried for his friend's safety.

Questions

Review 1. Who meets the first-years students at the platform? Who should be there?

2. Why does Sirius insist on seeing Harry and the others off at the train station when it is so dangerous for him to be out?

3. Why would Harry rather not sit with Neville and Luna on the train?

Further Study 1. What are the black horse-like creatures pulling the "horseless" carriages? Why can Harry and Luna see them, but not the others? Could they be Dark creatures?

2. Where is Hagrid?

Greater Picture

The horse-like creatures pulling the carriages are Thestrals, and they can only be seen by someone who has witnessed death. Until now, Harry, like many other students, believed the carriages magically pulled themselves. They are visible to him now because he witnessed Cedric Diggory being killed by Wormtail (Peter Pettigrew). Luna Lovegood, a most unusual girl anyway, sees them because she was present when her mother accidentally killed herself while experimenting with a spell that went wrong. It will be learned later that Neville Longbottom is also able to see them, although the reason is unknown. Why Neville does not comment on them here is uncertain. We learn later that he had seen a relative die, and so should have been able to see them all along. His first encounter with them, therefore, would have been in Harry's second year; as Harry and Ron arrived in the flying car that year, they would not have been present when Neville encountered the Thestrals for the first time, and by now he may consider then commonplace. Curiously, most students seem unaware that Thestrals even exist, indicating that the people who can see them rarely mention them to others. Despite being gentle creatures, they are painful reminders of death that those they are visible to probably prefer to avoid. More is learned about these unusual creatures in Hagrid's Care of Magical Creatures class, and they will have a role to play later in the book and in the series.

It could be argued that although Harry is unable to see the Thestrals until after Cedric Diggory was killed, he, technically, had witnessed other deaths prior to Cedric's tragic murder. In chapter 1 of *Harry Potter and the Goblet of Fire*, Harry "sees" the Muggle, Frank Bryce, being killed by Voldemort. However, Harry was not physically present when Frank was slain, which would likely explain why the Thestrals remained invisible to him. Harry instead watched the death through a mental connection he has to Voldemort. Though what he was viewing was apparently real and from his own perspective, he was unaware it was actually happening at the time. It is also true, as we find out later, that Professor Quirrell had died when Voldemort left him in the first book; Harry was there, but he was unconscious at the time and did not see Quirrell die.

Finally, Harry was present when Voldemort killed his mother, and when Voldemort's killing curse rebounded on him. The author has said that the sides of Harry's cot prevented him from actually seeing the death of his mother. Additionally, Voldemort, as we now see, wasn't really quite dead.

We are never positive that the Malfoys recognized Sirius in his dog form, but on the train, Draco hints to Harry that they did, and a story in the Daily Prophet placing Sirius in London will appear shortly.

Although Harry is embarrassed to be seated with unpopular students like Neville Longbottom and Luna Lovegood, these two "misfits" will prove to be among Harry's strongest and most capable allies. Neville will also be closely associated to a prophecy regarding Voldemort and Harry.

Sturgis Podmore's absence, we will find shortly, is due to his having been arrested the night before while attempting to enter a locked door at the Ministry. We will later find evidence that will suggest that the door in question leads to the Department of Mysteries, in which lies an artifact that Voldemort greatly desires. We will learn that Lucius Malfoy, at Voldemort's orders, had been trying to compel other wizards to enter the Department of Mysteries and recover that item; while we hear directly of Broderick Bode being forced to do so, we can only guess that the same has happened to Podmore.

Luna's father being publisher of the *Quibbler* will also prove important, as it will provide a channel for information about Harry to be disseminated without being filtered through the established media, namely *The Daily Prophet*. We have been told that the *Prophet* is echoing the Ministry position, and we will see the effect that has on Harry through the course of this book. It will become vital for Harry to have some other way of telling his story shortly. The contrarian nature of the *Quibbler* will also be important in the final book of the series.

Chapter 11: The Sorting Hat's New Song

Synopsis

As Harry, Ron, Ginny, Hermione, Neville, and Luna ride toward the castle, Harry cannot keep his mind off the disturbing black horse creatures. Soon, though, the conversation turns toward Hagrid's mysterious absence. Harry, Ron, and Hermione scan the Great Hall upon entering, but they are unable to find him. They settle—albeit uneasily—for the conclusion that he has not yet returned from his Order of the Phoenix mission. Hermione notices a short, curly-haired woman with a "pallid, toadlike face and a pair of prominent, pouchy eyes" sitting at the staff table. Harry is immediately seized by recognition: it is Dolores Umbridge, the particularly nasty questioner from his trial with the Wizengamot. Before they can discuss this further, the first years arrive, and Professor McGonagall brings out the Sorting Hat.

This time, however, the Sorting Hat sings a different type of song. It tells the story of the four Hogwarts founders (Gryffindor, Hufflepuff, Ravenclaw, and Slytherin) and their friendship. When Hogwarts was new, the school was unified because each founder hand-picked students for his or her House. Slytherin, however, wanted to extend his pure-blood selection criteria throughout the school. This caused dissent, and Slytherin eventually left Hogwarts. From then on, the Sorting Hat sings, the Houses have been divided. The Hat then warns that the school is "in danger from external, deadly foes," and that the they should become united from within. Hermione wonders aloud if the Hat has ever given warnings like that before, and Nearly Headless Nick tells her that this is not the first warning the Sorting Hat has delivered.

Professor Dumbledore delivers his customary speech and introduces Dolores Umbridge as the new Defence Against the Dark Arts teacher. Surprisingly, she rises to give her own speech. Addressing the students as if they are young children, she speaks in a mind-numbingly dull fashion. Hermione, Dumbledore, and a few other teachers are the only ones able to remain attentive. Umbridge finally finishes, and Harry asks Hermione why she was so interested in what sounded like a load of waffle. Hermione says that in amongst the waffle was information that the Ministry is looking to meddle with Hogwarts. Dumbledore finishes his announcements, and the students are dismissed. Hermione reminds Ron that they have to lead the first-year students to the Common room. Harry, unencumbered by first-years, takes a short-cut and, with help from Neville who for once will be able to remember the password ("*Mimbulus Mimbletonia*"), is in his dormitory before Ron even gets to the Common room. In the dormitory, Harry is greeted by another surprise: Seamus' mother was reluctant to allow him to return to Hogwarts because of Harry and Dumbledore. She believes the *Daily Prophet*'s claims that Lord Voldemort's return is a lie. Seamus and Harry begin arguing. Neville sides with Harry, and Dean tries to remain neutral. Ron appears and threatens to use his Prefect power, thus ending the disagreement. As they climb silently into bed, Harry reflects. He has received strange looks all day, and he is certain that few believe him. He wonders how long he will have to endure the stares and comments, then thinks, "*They'll know we're right in the end.*"

Analysis

Although this chapter contributes little to the overall plot, it highlights several main themes in the series: friendship and loyalty. The Sorting Hat's new song warns about a gathering storm, though to date Voldemort's activities have remained relatively unnoticed, making claims that he has returned easy to ignore. The song also highlights strength through unity. This is shown throughout the series by Harry's relationship with his friends and the strength he derives from them, although this is tested as more people doubt Harry's assertion that Voldemort is alive. The Sorting Hat issues a plea for the four Hogwarts Houses, who have maintained (mostly) friendly rivalries, to unite under a single cause.

Dumbledore has also foreseen the need for greater unity among all wizards, locally and internationally, which is why he supported reviving the Triwizard Tournament, believing that the friendships and alliances that were forged with the other schools (Durmstrang and Beauxbatons) would be crucial in the future. Ironically, the Hogwarts Houses are more divided than ever, as students take sides over Harry's claims regarding Voldemort. Professor Umbridge's disrespectful display towards the other teachers, as shown by her arrogant interruption, and to the students through her condescending attitude, hints at an underlying tyrannical nature. That nature was glimpsed during Harry's trial when she was particularly partial to convicting Harry. That she was then appointed by Cornelius Fudge to teach Defence Against the Dark Arts at Hogwarts, even given that Dumbledore was apparently unable to hire a teacher on his own, indicates the Ministry has a hidden agenda. Whether or not this is tied to Voldemort is unknown yet, but either way, it does not bode well for Harry or for Hogwarts.

This chapter marks one of only two times that Harry ever hears the Sorting Hats sing. At every other Sorting throughout the series, there is something that prevents him from being present for the new song.

Questions

Review   1. Why was Dolores Umbridge selected as the new Defence Against the Dark Arts teacher? Who chose her? 2. Why don't Seamus and his mother believe Harry and Dumbledore?

Further Study   1. How might the Sorting Hat detect danger?
2. What can be guessed about Dolores Umbridge's character based on her appearance and speech?
3. Why doesn't Harry simply tell Seamus and others what happened in the graveyard?

Greater Picture

Dumbledore tolerating Umbridge's interruption and her speech criticizing his leadership indicates a serious shift in the balance of power at Hogwarts. Dumbledore's authority as Headmaster and his political clout within the Ministry have diminished. Umbridge and her Ministry agenda are being forced on Dumbledore, and he is unable to prevent this interference at Hogwarts. This foreshadows Umbridge's rising empowerment at the expense of Dumbledore's authority and Hogwarts' welfare as a whole. One does rather wonder about Dumbledore's apparent equanimity at how his powers within the school are being eroded. Is he that certain that Voldemort will show himself, and that he will be vindicated, soon enough that he will be able to complete his work?

Seamus Finnigan's behavior represents the animosity and disbelief of many students, even those in Gryffindor, that Harry will endure in the coming year. This attitude is largely inspired by the attacks on Harry that appear in the *Daily Prophet,* and will cause many friends to turn against him and also one another. Ron and Hermione always believe in and remain loyal to Harry, but curiously Neville, who is becoming increasingly important to the plot, also never loses faith in him. Interestingly also, Luna Lovegood, strange as she may now seem, will develop into someone with a remarkably uncluttered view of the world, and will also remain true to Harry.

Perhaps most interestingly, among those who are wavering in their loyalty, many will come to Harry's side purely because of the actions of Umbridge as she tries to further discredit Harry and Dumbledore. A large part of her actions will stem from the bizarre belief that Dumbledore, who we already know had been offered the position of Minister of Magic and turned it down, nonetheless is building a private army to attempt to take over the Ministry by force. This belief, originally voiced by Fudge, will result in the Defence Against the

Dark Arts course being diluted to the point of uselessness. It is entirely possible that the sole reason for the Ministry's interfering at Hogwarts is an attempt to prevent formation of this nonexistent private army, by effectively banning the teaching of spells that could be used against the Ministry. In this case, Umbridge's further actions, having herself appointed Hogwarts High Inquisitor and arranging for the promulgation of Educational Decrees to increase her own power, might be termed private enterprise. In any event, it is largely disgust with Umbridge's teaching that proves the inspiration for Harry's self-defence instruction group, which will be called Dumbledore's Army, in a sarcastic nod to the Ministry belief. Harry is correct that it is only a matter of time before everyone knows he and Dumbledore are right. For now, Voldemort remains hidden, creating doubt and confusion while he builds his power base and slowly infiltrates key Wizarding institutions. Once his power is secure, we can assume he will reveal his presence. Until then, Harry must bear many schoolmates' doubts and disdain.

Chapter 12: Professor Umbridge

Synopsis

The next morning begins nearly as frustratingly as the previous night ended. Seamus leaves the room as quickly as possible without speaking to Harry. Hermione says Lavender Brown is skeptical about Harry's story, as well.

At breakfast, there is still no sign of Hagrid. Hermione suggests that Professor Dumbledore has not mentioned it to avoid drawing attention to Hagrid's absence. Harry is braced by Angelina Johnson, who has been made Quidditch captain. With Oliver Wood gone, they need a new Keeper, and will be having try-outs on Friday. Angelina wants everyone there. Professor McGonagall hands out class schedules, which seem particularly strenuous this year. Fred and George offer their defective Skiving Snackboxes for a discount, then discuss their lack of concern for school. George mentions that they considered not returning to Hogwarts and says they will spend their last year doing market research for their joke shop. George hints that they have financial backing, sidestepping questions about where the money is coming from.

During a break in their morning classes, the Trio run into Cho Chang. She apparently wants to talk to Harry, but Ron insults her favorite Quidditch team, which causes her to leave, and earns him a scolding from Hermione. Harry's spirits are further dampened, both by the loss of the chance to talk to Cho and by his friends' bickering, as they head to Snape's dungeon for Potions. Snape gives them a particularly difficult potion. When Harry misses part of the instructions, Snape singles him out and Vanishes his entire mixture, earning him no marks for the entire lesson. Luckily, the following Divination lesson is uneventful.

In Professor Umbridge's classroom, students are instructed to put away their wands and take notes. Professor Umbridge announces that they will be learning a "Ministry-approved course of defensive magic this year." After giving the course aims, she instructs the class to read the first chapter of their textbooks, but Hermione sits defiantly with her hand raised until Professor Umbridge is forced to call on her. Hermione notes that there are no course aims concerning the actual use of any defensive spells, to which Umbridge replies, "I can't imagine any situation arising in my classroom that would require you to *use* a defensive spell." Instead, students will study the theory and perform the spells for the first time at their examinations in the spring.

This leads to a heated discussion about the necessity of learning *practical* Defence Against the Dark Arts, in which Professor Umbridge says that Harry's claims that Voldemort has returned are a lie. Harry reacts angrily, telling the class that Cedric Diggory was murdered, not accidentally killed as Umbridge stated. Harry is sent to Professor McGonagall's office with a note detailing his detention. McGonagall sternly warns him to tread carefully around Dolores Umbridge—the Ministry of Magic is interfering at Hogwarts.

Analysis

Although this is Fred and George's final year, there is little left for them to learn. Despite their poor academic achievements, they are extremely powerful, talented, and resourceful wizards who, much like Harry, learn best independently when in an unstructured environment and for their own interest. Readers should remember that Harry donated his Triwizard winnings to them to finance their joke shop enterprise, and the Twins have hardly been idle. They now have the necessary funding, have developed the magic, and produced the products; now they are only biding their time until school ends and they can open their own shop in Diagon Alley.

A few other events of note happen in this chapter. Harry is again reminded of Hagrid's absence, and is once again drawn to wonder exactly what mission Dumbledore had set him and Madame Maxime. We once again see Snape's hatred of Harry; it is particularly interesting that the instruction that Harry misses seems to be written to be confusing. We learn of Professor Umbridge's horrible teaching style, her useless planned curriculum, and her hatred of Harry and Hermione in particular. And we see that Cho now is trying to talk to Harry, and is being served as ill by Harry's friends as Harry was, before the Yule Ball the previous year, by the convoys of giggling girls that seemed to surround Cho when Harry was trying to invite her to the Ball.

Questions

Review 1. Why does Hermione believe that Professor Dumbledore does not want to draw attention to Hagrid's absence?

2. How does the "Ministry approved" course of defensive arts compare to how former classes were taught? Why has it been changed?

3. Why would the Ministry claim Cedric Diggory's death was an accident?

Further Study 1. Why might the Ministry of Magic prevent students from learning defensive spells?

2. Should Harry have spoken out in class? How else could he have handled the situation?

3. Why does Professor McGonagall ask Harry, "Do you really think this is about truth or lies? It's about keeping your head down and your temper under control!" During troublesome times, is it wiser to protest early on or wait for a more opportune time?

4. Why does Harry ignore McGonagall's advice, and what will likely result from that? What could Harry have done instead?

GREATER PICTURE

It is immediately clear that Dolores Umbridge is at Hogwarts for some reason other than teaching Defensive Arts. That she was personally appointed by the Ministry strongly indicates that she is Fudge's spy. Although there is no indication that either Fudge or Umbridge are Death Eaters or even Voldemort sympathizers, they likely share a paranoid belief that Dumbledore is training students to build a secret wizard army to take over the Ministry of Magic. Her job is to prevent students from learning real defensive magic, although she probably has a personal agenda for Hogwarts. She and Harry immediately clash over how the class will be taught and the Ministry's stance that Cedric Diggory's death was a "tragic accident." Umbridge's claims regarding Diggory are laughable, but demonstrates how far the Ministry will go to discredit Harry and Dumbledore and to protect the Ministry. Unfortunately, Harry is unable or unwilling to accept McGonagall's advice to remain quiet, and instead provokes Umbridge, earning him detention and giving her fodder for imposing even stricter rules. Harry, however, has yet to realize just how severe his punishment will be and how evil Umbridge likely is.

While we only see Umbridge teaching Harry's class, we will shortly find out that she teaches many other classes as well. Fred and George, in year 7, apparently have her as a teacher as well, as they had earlier asked "who had assigned the Slinkhard book" for the course; and later, Lee Jordan will get into trouble in her class and serve detention. This also allows some speculation on exactly which courses Fred and George managed to get decent O.W.L. marks. In the previous year, the first after the Twins' O.W.L. results were available, the Defence Against the Dark Arts instructor was the false Professor Moody. Moody was clearly a very stern, though fair, teacher, and as such he would have probably required at least Exceeds Expectations at O.W.L.-level before he would accept a student into N.E.W.T.-level Defence Against the Dark Arts, all the more so as he was likely to be training them in more dangerous jinxes and curses. We can guess, then, that the Twins must have managed to achieve Exceeds Expectations in Defence Against the Dark Arts, this being one of their three passable O.W.L. marks apiece. We should mention that there is widespread dissatisfaction with Umbridge's teaching. Hermione will later suggest that Harry should start teaching a more practical Defence course; the resulting organization, much to Harry's initial dismay, will attract some twenty-five or more students. This organization, called Dumbledore's Army, being a rebellion against Umbridge, will at times be Harry's one cheering influence in what could arguably be the worst year he will have at Hogwarts.

Chapter 13: Detention with Dolores

SYNOPSIS

Over dinner, against a background of skeptical whispers about what Harry said in Professor Umbridge's classroom, Harry, Ron, and Hermione discuss Harry's confrontation with her. Hermione suggests that most people doubt Harry's story because there was so little concrete evidence. The trio heads to Gryffindor Tower to do homework where they find Fred and George using first-year students to test Fainting Fancies for their Skiving Snackboxes line. Hermione chastises them and threatens to inform Mrs. Weasley, which stops their testing, but to her dismay, Ron refuses to support her. Upset, she goes off to bed, leaving knitted hats on the table, expecting house-elves to pick them up and thus be freed.

Harry is increasingly nervous; teachers are briefing students about upcoming Ordinary Wizarding Levels exams and piling on astonishing amounts of homework. Hagrid is still missing, and his class is taken by Professor Grubbly-Plank. Harry's stress level only increases when team captain Angelina Johnson yells at him because his detention conflicts with Quidditch tryouts on Friday night.

Harry arrives for his first detention with Professor Umbridge. Her office is decorated with doilies and colored kittens on plates. Harry sits at a table and takes out a quill to write lines, but Umbridge instead gives him a black quill and says he will not need any ink. As Harry begins writing "*I must not tell lies*," a cut appears on the back of his hand in the same shape as the letters he writes. As it instantly heals over, he realizes that the words written on the parchment are in his own blood. Over and over, he silently writes the lines, each time carving them into his skin. When Umbridge finally allows him to stop, the back of his hand is raw and sore. Harry is so late getting back to the dormitory that he has to finish his homework the next morning. He is surprised to find Ron doing the same. Ron's excuse that he went for a walk causes Harry to suspect Ron is hiding something. Uncertain why, Harry decides to say nothing about his punishment.

Harry's detentions continue every night. As he leaves on Thursday, the words are permanently cut into his hand. Heading to Gryffindor Tower, he runs into Ron, who tries hiding his broomstick. Ron admits he has been practicing to try out for Quidditch Keeper, which pleases Harry. Ron notices Harry's hand and forces him to tell the truth. He encourages Harry to tell Professor McGonagall, but Harry feels it is a private battle. As he leaves the final detention the next night, Umbridge grabs his hand to check his work, and his scar burns. He departs rapidly and returns to Gryffindor tower where a small party is underway: Ron has been chosen as

Chapter 13: Detention with Dolores

Keeper. Harry tells Hermione about his scar hurting, and she urges him to tell Professor Dumbledore. Harry replies, "That's the only bit of me Dumbledore cares about, isn't it, my scar?" Harry decides to write Sirius instead, but Hermione reminds him about Moody's warning to avoid putting anything on paper that can be intercepted. With no solution, they both head for bed.

Analysis

Although Umbridge's cruel detention is likely illegal, Harry stubbornly refuses to report it, preferring to engage in a silent battle of wills. He is determined to prove he can take anything she metes out. His anger at Dumbledore over his ignoring him may also be a motivating factor, though as it is Professor McGonagall he would be discussing this detention with, this is not entirely likely.

Harry is surprised and suspicious that his scar burns when Umbridge touches his hand. The only time it has hurt previously is when there is some association with Voldemort. Hermione is unsure whether Umbridge is being controlled by Voldemort, but she advises Harry to tell Dumbledore about it. Feeling slighted by Dumbledore, who has apparently avoided face-to-face meetings since summer, is likely a partial reason for Harry's refusal to speak to him. The observant reader may have noticed that Umbridge touched Harry's hand after the first night's detention without Harry's scar reacting. It may be concluded that the painful twinge he felt during his last detention was merely a coincidence.

Hermione's plan to free House-elves is noble and just, however it is also poorly thought out and possibly harmful. A house elf, we have learned, is freed if it receives clothing from its master. Though the house elves at Hogwarts do serve the students, including Hermione, it is unlikely that she would be considered their master to a sufficient degree to free them. Even if a House-elf was freed by taking her "gifts," she has little consideration about what would happen to them after being liberated. While Dobby and Winky were employed by Dumbledore out of kindness, Dobby's experience after leaving the Malfoy household indicates that it is unlikely many wizard families or businesses would hire a "free agent" elf, leaving newly independent House-elves with few resources or the means to earn a living. Changes must first be made within the wizarding society, and then the resources provided for elves to survive and prosper in a new order. Even then, many wizards will be resistant to change and will likely discriminate against these newly equal citizens. Hermione is also forgetting that many House-elves, like Winky, have no wish to be free. Being enslaved for centuries has warped and reshaped their perceptions, and their identities and social status are strongly tied to the families they serve; their beliefs will need to be readjusted as well.

When Ron admits he has been secretly practicing for Quidditch tryouts, Harry is surprised but supportive. That Ron never told Harry what he was doing nor asked for his help may indicate that he is independently attempting to develop his own abilities and identity. Ron has been overshadowed by his talented older brothers, and also by his association with Harry, making it difficult for him to set himself apart.

Questions

Review 1. What does Hermione believe is the reason people are skeptical of Harry's story about Voldemort?

2. Why does Hermione become angry with Ron for what Fred and George are doing? What does she threaten to do that gets the Twins to stop?

3. What is Ron secretly doing and why doesn't he tell anyone? What is Harry's reaction when he finds out?

Further Study 1. Why would Harry's scar hurt when Umbridge touches him? What does Harry think?

2. Why does Harry refuse to report Umbridge's cruel detention?

3. Why is Harry angry with Dumbledore? What might be the reason for Dumbledore's odd behavior towards Harry?

Greater Picture

Harry's scar will hurt again after a Quidditch practice later in the story. When that happens, he remembers it hurting when Umbridge touched his hand while they were in her office. At that time, he concludes that in Umbridge's office, his scar had hurt because Voldemort was happy about something. It is possible that Voldemort had either just determined how to retrieve the Prophecy from the Ministry, or had just discovered that one stage in the plan had been successful. He has either decided to use the Imperius curse on someone in the Ministry to force them to bring the Prophecy to him, or has heard that someone has been so cursed. That plan originated with Avery, who will suffer when it fails. We will shortly discover that Sturgis Podmore, who had been expected as one of Harry's guards for the trip to King's Cross Station, had been arrested trying to get through a sealed door at the Ministry. While it is possible that it was Sturgis' attempt at the Prophecy that Voldemort was happy about, Sturgis had gone missing a week before, and it is unlikely that he would have been cursed, arrested, tried, convicted, and had the news reach the *Daily Prophet* in the roughly eight hours between Harry's scar paining him and the arrival of the Prophet at breakfast the next day. Given the timing, it is much more likely that Voldemort had received news that the Unspeakable, Broderick Bode, had been placed under the curse, for a second attempt at the Prophecy. Before this revelation is granted to us, though, Sirius will speak with Harry, Ron, and Hermione. Sirius will pass along the Order's belief that, though she is a bad bit of work, Umbridge is not directly under Voldemort's control. Sirius will be of the opinion that the pain that occurred when Umbridge touched Harry's hand was merely a coincidence, and later events in the story will bear out his statement.

As is so often the case, the detention, and the pain that Harry suffers, will not change his beliefs; nor will the second round of detentions that he suffers when he speaks out again in Umbridge's classroom. It will, however, drive his rebellion against her and her teaching underground, and will to a large extent be an impetus towards his acceptance of Hermione's idea that he should head an extra-curricular Defence Against the Dark Arts group. Hermione's attempt to free the House Elves will be an utter failure, as the result will be that the only House Elf willing to work in Gryffindor Tower will be Dobby. When Harry next sees him, he will be wearing a large quantity of Hermione's knitted hats, and will tell Harry that the other house elves will not work in Gryffindor tower because of them. "They finds them insulting, sir." Out of consideration for Hermione's feelings, Harry will not pass this information on to Hermione, and Hermione will continue to knit elf hats throughout the year.

Chapter 14: Percy and Padfoot

Synopsis

The next morning, Harry writes Sirius a letter about Professor Umbridge and his burning scar. He uses a code name and shared experiences to encode the contents (such as saying Umbridge is, "almost as nice as your mum"). In the Owlery, he sends Hedwig off with the letter. Looking out, he sees one of the skeletal black horses flying over the Forbidden Forest. Cho Chang suddenly arrives to mail a birthday gift. She is furious at Umbridge for denying that Voldemort has returned. They are interrupted by Filch, who accuses Harry of sending for a large order of Dungbombs, and he demands to see the letter he was sending. Cho stands up to Filch, saying that the letter was already gone, and Harry is almost inordinately pleased.

At breakfast Hermione reads a story in the *Daily Prophet* implying that Sirius was spotted in London. Harry thinks Lucius Malfoy recognized Sirius' Animagus dog form at King's Cross station. Harry also reads that Order member Sturgis Podmore was arrested after attempting to break into a sealed door at the Ministry of Magic. Ron thinks he was lured into a trap. Hermione agrees.

Harry and Ron attend Quidditch practice, but they are harassed by Slytherins. Ron is particularly singled out with insults. Flustered, he passes the Quaffle to Katie Bell so enthusiastically that it slips through her hands and hits her face, causing a nosebleed. Fred and George apply what they think is the healing end of a Nosebleed Nougat, but instead give her a Blood Blisterpod and have to take her the hospital wing, ending the practice. Late that night, Ron receives a letter from his brother, Percy, congratulating him on becoming a Prefect. He writes he is relieved that Ron has not followed in Fred and George's "footsteps," and advises that he steer himself away from their parents' *misguided* beliefs and actions. Percy also warns Ron to disassociate himself from Harry and Professor Dumbledore and hints there may soon be a change at Hogwarts. He goes on to commend Dolores Umbridge, believing she is a fine, upstanding person and an asset to the school. Furious, Ron rips apart the letter. Shortly after, Sirius' head appears in the Gryffindor fireplace. He tells Harry that he does not believe Umbridge is a Death Eater, and that his scar hurting was probably just Voldemort experiencing a strong emotional reaction to something. When Harry complains that Umbridge is not letting them perform magic, Sirius says it is because a paranoid Fudge fears that Dumbledore is secretly building a wizard army to take over the Ministry. Harry asks about Hagrid, but Sirius says he does not know where he is, but that Dumbledore is not worried. He warns against drawing attention to Hagrid's absence. When Sirius suggests meeting Harry and the others while in his Animagus dog form at the next Hogsmeade weekend, both Harry and Hermione sternly tell him it is too dangerous. Sirius chides Harry for being so cautious, saying that his father, James, would have loved taking the risk. And with a faint pop, he vanishes.

Analysis

Two people's personalities are becoming more apparent—Sirius and Percy.

Although Sirius is still an attentive and loving godfather, his reckless behavior is increasing. When he suggests meeting Harry in Hogsmeade in his Animagus dog form, it is the students who tell the adult that it is too dangerous, remembering that Sirius was recognized by the Malfoys at the train station. Sirius chides Harry for being so cautious, saying that his father, James, loved taking risks. Unfortunately, Sirius' emotional development has been stunted by his years in Azkaban, impairing his judgment and causing him to treat Harry more like his peer rather than his ward. Molly Weasley had earlier felt it necessary to remind Sirius that Harry is not James Potter. Sirius is likely to decline mentally as the story progresses. His confinement to Grimmauld Place, a house he has always hated, is another prison. He is often left alone, accompanied primarily by his hate-spewing, mad mother's portrait, and a surly and insulting House-elf. Constantly hiding from the authorities and unable to live a normal life is stressful and causes Sirius to become increasingly sullen and irritable, leading to his careless and rash behavior. However, insanity and mental instability are also prevalent in the Black family, and Sirius appears to show symptoms similar to those exhibited by his cousin, Bellatrix Lestrange.

Percy's growing estrangement from his family has reached a breaking point and his career ambition blinds him to what is actually happening within the Ministry of Magic and the wizarding world at large; he will continue to adamantly support the Ministry's stance that Voldemort has not been resurrected. The other Weasleys' assertion that he is a Ministry pawn being used to garner information about Harry and Dumbledore only offends Percy. He firmly believes his rapid advancement within the Ministry of Magic is due to his abilities, rather than his connections. Whether or not Percy can realign his faulty judgment and reconcile with his family is unknown until the final book. We also see another step in the growing romance between Cho and Harry. Finally, they have a chance to talk, without Stinksap or Quidditch-inspired animosity, and Harry finds that Cho is whole-heartedly on his side, sharing his and Dumbledore's beliefs unquestioningly. While neither we nor Harry have any idea whether this will go anywhere, after this meeting Harry at least has some hope, as we do, that Cho and Harry will become a couple. This, actually, is an interesting illustration of how the author has chosen to avoid certain young adult fiction stereotypes. The series, covering seven years of Harry's life, will of necessity cover his maturation, and as most young men do at this stage in their lives, he will start having romantic thoughts; his relationship with Cho, as we have seen, takes a realistically long time to grow, and is visited by a very natural set of setbacks and issues. The author has here rejected the standard scheme of having the romance entirely contained within one book of the series, instead having it mature as a real romance does.

One small highlight also is cast on the character of James Potter, when Sirius points out that he would have loved the risk. Readers may begin to wonder here how much Harry is James' son, and how much he is Lily's. Filch appearing with an obviously specious story about Harry ordering dungbombs is somewhat odd. Harry himself wonders who could have told Filch that; this question is never answered, but the reader, like Harry, suspects a connection with Umbridge.

Readers may wonder how Lucius Malfoy could recognize Sirius in his dog Animagus form. Peter Pettigrew, as readers most certainly remember, was a close friend of Sirius' in their school days, and will have seen him transform numerous times, as Sirius did Pettigrew. Pettigrew will likely have described Sirius' Animagus form to Voldemort, and Voldemort in turn may have passed that on to his Death Eaters. We are never told why Voldemort would have been interested enough in Sirius to prime his Death Eaters to spot him, but it is likely that Pettigrew's confirmation that he was still alive, his having escaped Azkaban, and the likelihood of his joining Dumbledore made it worth keeping an eye out for him.

QUESTIONS

Review   1. Why does Sirius chide Harry for being cautious? Is this appropriate? Why or why not?

2. What does Filch accuse Harry of doing in the Owlery? Could there be another reason he's interrogating Harry about his owl post?

3. Why is Ron angry at Percy? Is Ron justified?

Further Study   1. Why does Sirius warn the Trio about drawing attention to Hagrid's absence? Does he know more than he is letting on?

2. Why would Percy advise Ron to stop associating with Harry and Dumbledore?

3. What does Sirius say that Cornelius Fudge thinks Dumbledore is planning? What would lead Fudge to believe this, and could it be true?

4. What is Percy's opinion of Dolores Umbridge? Why might he think that?

5. What change at Hogwarts might Percy be hinting at?

GREATER PICTURE

Percy remains estranged from his family until the final book, *Harry Potter and the Deathly Hallows*. Finally realizing he was wrong, he arrives at Hogwarts just prior to the final battle, apologizing to his family for his stupidity. He joins forces with Harry and the other allies against Voldemort and his Death Eaters. While Harry and Cho's relationship may now proceed, ultimately it will be doomed by Cho's need to revisit Cedric's death, a loss for which she has not yet reached closure. We do not see this yet, and will not until Christmas, when Harry and Cho kiss under the mistletoe. At that point, Hermione will give Harry and Ron a quick rundown of Cho's current emotional state, which will explain most of her interactions with Harry since September. Surprisingly, Umbridge seems to realize the value of having Argus Filch on her side. Quite possibly, Umbridge recognizes a kindred soul, as she hates the students almost as much as Filch seems to. It is also possible that she recognizes that among the staff, she has no other allies; even the Slytherin Head of House, Professor Snape, seems to not be in favour of her appointment. Immediately after the attempted arrest of Dumbledore, we will see that Filch believes that he will shortly be allowed to torture the students physically for malfeasance. Many readers believe that Umbridge has promised this to Filch, but has no plans to carry out her promise. It is certainly true that Filch never seems to get permission to whip or chain any students during the remainder of Umbridge's tenure. While it is never confirmed, it is likely that Podmore's attempt to break through a sealed door at the Ministry was done while he was under the Imperius curse, trying to retrieve the Prophecy that Voldemort is seeking. A later attempt, which we will learn of later in the year, will involve an Unspeakable, Bode. In that attempt, Bode will be placed under the Imperius curse by Lucius Malfoy. Harry will guess that the reason Lucius had been at the Ministry on the day of Harry's hearing, was that he was trying to find someone he could curse to retrieve the Prophecy. While Podmore failed because he was unable to open a sealed door, Bode will fail due to a curse placed on the Prophecy itself—as an Unspeakable, he is cleared to work in the Department of Mysteries.

Chapter 15: The Hogwarts High Inquisitor

SYNOPSIS

The next day at breakfast, Hermione reads in the *Daily Prophet* that the Ministry of Magic has appointed Dolores Umbridge "High Inquisitor." Umbridge now has extensive power over Hogwarts and can arbitrarily impose new rules and regulations. She apparently intends to evaluate all teachers and classes. At lunch, after Harry receives a D (for Dreadful) on his Potions homework, he asks Fred and George about inspected classes. Fred says when Umbridge inspected Charms class, Flitwick just ignored her. Harry arrives at Divination to find Umbridge there with a clipboard. She begins taking notes as a nervous Professor Trelawney teaches. Umbridge demands that she make some predictions during class, and is apparently unimpressed with the result. During Defence Against the Dark Arts class, Umbridge claims that Professor Quirrell was the only other Defensive Arts teacher likely to have received Ministry approval. Harry retorts that there was only the small matter of Voldemort being stuck on the back of his head, thus earning himself another week's detention. The next morning, Angelina Johnson is so angered over Harry receiving another detention that she begins berating him, bringing Professor McGonagall down from head table; McGonagall penalizes Harry five House points for provoking Umbridge despite her earlier warning.

In Transfiguration, Professor McGonagall rudely ignores Umbridge's inspection and slaps her down like a student when Umbridge tries to ask a question during class. Umbridge, however, is delighted with Professor Grubbly-Plank's Care of Magical Creatures class, although Grubbly-Plank is only substituting for the still-absent Hagrid. Harry, however, loses his temper when Draco says he was injured in Hagrid's class by a Hippogriff, earning him another day's detention.

Hermione is also fed up with Umbridge's ineffective teaching. When Harry returns to the common room after this final detention, she suggests that he teach Defence Against the Dark Arts to students. Harry is reluctant, feeling he is unqualified, but Hermione and Ron point out that he already knows much that he could teach to others about defensive magic, and he has always earned top marks, even beating Hermione. Harry is angered at the thought. Although they may think he knows all this, he believes he has just winged it, it was luck, and had other people's help. Hermione, abashed, says that Harry is the only one who knows what it is like to actually face Voldemort. Harry grudgingly agrees to consider it. He goes to bed, where he again dreams about long corridors and locked doors.

Analysis

Umbridge's promotion allows her to abuse power, and she immediately begins imposing her will on Hogwarts. That she is evaluating teachers far more competent than herself shows she has an ulterior motive, possibly to weed out those she considers unworthy to teach at Hogwarts, mainly anyone non-human. However, she has apparently also targeted the thoroughly human Professor Trelawney, and probably Professor McGonagall, who openly opposes her. It seems the only teacher Umbridge approves of is Professor Grubbly-Plank, a competent teacher who is substituting for the still-absent Hagrid, although Umbridge's enthusiasm may have less to do with Grubbly-Plank's abilities than with finding a reason for sacking Hagrid as the Care of Magical Creatures instructor.

It is perhaps a point of interest that we here see what may be the only time in the entire story that we sympathize with Umbridge even a little. Umbridge quite clearly sees that Divination class is pure nonsense, and is not at all taken in by Professor Trelawney's fortune-telling. Harry, of course, is of the same opinion, and probably privately wishes he had left the course when Hermione had. However, readers, like Harry, probably cringe at Umbridge's technique.

Harry, meanwhile, continues to provoke Umbridge, stubbornly disregarding McGonagall's warning, which causes her to deduct House points. He is also unhappy again with what his fame and exploits have brought him when Hermione and Ron urge him to secretly teach Defensive Magic. Although Harry believes he lacks the necessary skills, Ron enumerates Harry's accomplishment from each year he has been at Hogwarts, and it is an impressive list. In the face of this, Harry tries to repudiate every one, claiming it was just luck or other people's help, rather than anything innate in him. Harry's reluctance to teach others may stem from several factors, such as lack of self-esteem; he may simply believe he is unqualified. Also, being a somewhat lazy student, he would have to put in extra work to prepare lessons. However, there may be some false modesty involved here, as he has always excelled in this subject and his abilities are more advanced than most other students. There is also Harry's ever-present need to "go it alone," and by organizing and teaching other students, he essentially becomes their leader in the fight against Umbridge and also Voldemort.

Readers may discern a slight plot hole. Presumably, the sixth and particularly the seventh-year students should be fairly well trained in basic defensive magic by now and capable of performing many of the same spells and curses that Harry has prematurely learned independently. Harry even comments that Cedric Diggory, who was an older student, already knew much of what he is teaching. However, the other students have never been in combat with Death Eaters or Voldemort; only Harry can share that experience.

Questions

Review 1. Why does Hermione, who always follows rules, want Harry to secretly teach defensive magic?

2. Why is Harry reluctant to teach Defensive Arts to other students?

3. Why would the Ministry of Magic appoint a High Inquisitor at Hogwarts?

4. Why is Umbridge evaluating teachers and their classes? What is the teachers' reaction to her?

5. Why does Malfoy tell Umbridge he was once attacked by a Hippogriff? What is Harry's reaction, and why?

Further Study 1. Why is Umbridge particularly pleased with Professor Grubbly-Plank, the substitute teacher for the Care of Magical Creatures class? Is it because Grubbly-Plank is such a great instructor, or is there another reason?

2. Why does Harry continually provoke Umbridge, knowing the consequences and despite McGonagall's stern warning?

Greater Picture

Although Trelawney is hardly an exceptional teacher, Umbridge may be targeting her for other reasons. Trelawney is tied to a Prophecy regarding Harry and Voldemort, a fact Umbridge probably knows about since a copy is stored within the Department of Mysteries at the Ministry of Magic, though Umbridge likely does not know the contents of the Prophecy. Dumbledore knows that Trelawney is vulnerable, and, despite her meager talents, hired her as the Divination teacher to protect her and the prophecy. If she were ever outside Hogwarts' protective walls, it is likely Voldemort would have her captured and use any means possible to extract the prophecy from her memory before killing her. Umbridge may want to eliminate the prophecy's source by dismissing Trelawney and ejecting her from the castle (probably knowing she would be in danger by surviving Death Eaters) to remove credence to Harry's claims that Voldemort has returned.

While Hermione is making this sound as if it is just herself and Ron who are interested in the possibility of Harry teaching Defence, she will later mention this to several other people, and the word will spread to other Houses. As a result, and rather to Harry's dismay, the idea "will prove to be quite popular," in Hermione's words, and about 28 students will arrive at the Hog's Head for the organizational meeting. Despite his initial reluctance to teach Defence Against the Dark Arts, Harry will prove to be an excellent and inspiring instructor, and the classes help him learn to rely on and trust others. Teaching becomes something he will truly enjoy and look forward to. Harry continually insists that he has accomplished less than people claim he has, a belief that is not fully understood by Ron until the seventh book. In *Harry Potter and the Deathly Hallows*, Harry talks about how Ron saved his life and used the Sword of Gryffindor to destroy one of Voldemort's Horcruxes. Ron claims that Harry makes it sound more impressive than it actually was, to which Harry responds that that is what he (Harry) has been saying about himself for years. Regardless of whether or not it was luck or other people who had helped him, Harry has gained considerable skills and knowledge through these experiences, which is how he learns best. Harry's dreams about corridors and locked doors are actually real scenes of Voldemort's deepest desires, played back through a telepathic link between him and Harry. Voldemort is still unaware that this link exists or that Harry can see what he is thinking. This will change near Christmas when Harry experiences an attack on Arthur Weasley through Voldemort's eyes. Following this, Harry's dreams become sharper and more directed. At the book's end, it will be learned that once Voldemort learned the link existed, the visions were actually being deliberately directed into Harry's mind.

An interesting little circle starts here. Hermione recommends Essence of Murtlap tentacles to soothe Harry's injured hand after his final detention night. When Lee Jordan later receives detention from Umbridge, Harry suggests Essence of Murtlap to ease the pain. Lee apparently suggests Essence of Murtlap to Fred and George when they mention a side effect of one of their Skiving Snackboxes. The Murtlap cures the boils that appear on a rather private anatomy part when the Snackbox is used. So, Hermione is indirectly helping the Twins with one of their products, which would probably anger her if she knew.

Chapter 16: In the Hog's Head

Synopsis

Only after Harry's detention with Umbridge has ended a fortnight later does Hermione dare ask if Harry has considered teaching Defence Against the Dark Arts. Harry admits he has, and Ron is relieved that Harry has not started shouting again. Hermione recommends opening the class to anyone wanting to learn, although Harry believes only a few will attend. He is, after all, "a nutter." Hermione suggests the first meeting take place during the next Hogsmeade weekend to avoid Umbridge. Harry is concerned that Sirius might show up in Hogsmeade, but Hermione says he has enough worry about, and Sirius listens to Dumbledore.

As Harry, Ron, and Hermione head for Hogsmeade, Filch sniffs at Harry before allowing him to leave. Harry relates the incident in the Owlery and says someone told Filch he was ordering Dungbombs. Hermione wonders who tipped Filch off. In Hogsmeade, Hermione steers them to a side street leading to the Hog's Head Inn, a small and rather unsavoury establishment, which Hermione confirms is not off limits to Hogwarts students. Only four patrons are there, a much-bandaged wizard, a witch under a veil, and two wizards hooded and caped like Dementors. Harry notes that the bartender looks familiar and has a distinct goat odor. When the "couple of people" Hermione invited arrive, Harry is stunned at how many there are: Neville, Dean, Lavender, Parvati and Padma Patil, Cho and a friend of hers that Harry did not recognize, Luna Lovegood, Katie Bell, Alicia Spinnet, Angelina Johnson, Colin and Dennis Creevey, Ernie Macmillan, Justin Finch-Fletchley, Hannah Abbott, a Hufflepuff girl Harry did not recognize, who later identifies herself as Susan Bones, Anthony Goldstein, Michael Corner, Terry Boot, Ginny, a member of the Hufflepuff Quidditch team (later identified as Zacharias Smith), Fred and George, and Lee Jordan. Curiously, there are no Slytherins. Hermione starts off by reminding everyone why they are there, then Harry says that if they have come to hear what happened to Cedric Diggory, then too bad, he will not discuss it. Harry has only agreed to teach defensive magic. Zacharias Smith seems skeptical, but the other students list Harry's accomplishments, and Zacharias, under half-joking threats from Fred and George, subsides. They agree to meet when a location is found. Hermione has everyone sign a piece of parchment, an agreement to keep the group secret. The meeting then breaks up. As they continue shopping, Hermione mentions that Michael Corner probably attended because Ginny was there. She and Michael met at the Yule Ball the previous year. While Ginny had her sights on Harry, she has since given up. Ron is incensed that Michael Corner dares to go out with his sister, although Harry is less concerned. Hermione says that Cho never took her eyes off Harry throughout the meeting, and Harry suddenly realizes that Hogsmeade is a truly beautiful place.

Analysis

The strong turnout for the Defensive Arts meeting may be motivated as much or even more by the students' curiosity about Cedric Diggory's death, than by an interest in learning proper defensive magic. Harry's comment that most consider him a "nutter" is probably true, but he has done little to help overcome that perception, preferring to withhold details about his confrontation with Voldemort and internalize his emotions—an action reflecting his constant need to face adversity alone. Regardless, the students agree to give the lessons a try, although many probably still doubt Harry's claim about Voldemort's resurrection.

While Harry may still be reluctant to teach the class, it has provided one benefit—an opportunity to get closer to Cho Chang, who Harry now knows is interested in him. Ron, meanwhile, is upset that Michael Corner is interested in Ginny, although it seems that this has little to do with Michael himself and more to do with Ron being the protective older brother. He may feel that no one is suitable to date his little sister. It is certainly suggestive that Ron does not comment on his distrust of Corner until after Hermione mentions the attachment.

QUESTIONS

Review 1. Why does Hermione choose the Hog's Head Inn to have the meeting at? Was this effective?

2. Why does Harry think few students will be interested in attending the meeting?

3. What seems to be the main reason students want to join Harry's defensive arts class? What does Harry tell them?

4. Why is Zacharias Smith skeptical about Harry teaching defensive magic?

5. What is Harry's reaction when Hermione mentions Cho Chang? Why?

Further Study 1. Does Hermione deliberately omit Slytherin students from the Defense Against the Dark Arts group? If so, why? If not, why are none included?

2. Why is Ron upset that Michael Corner wants to date his sister, Ginny?

3. Hermione has everyone sign the parchment containing a vow of secrecy. How can she trust them to keep their word? Does she trust them?

GREATER PICTURE

Of the four customers in the Hog's Head Inn, two were rather more interested in the students' meeting than perhaps Harry would have liked. The veiled witch in the corner is Mundungus Fletcher, who was watching over Hogsmeade for the Order of the Phoenix; he was disguised because he had evidently been barred from the Hog's Head, at least according to Sirius in the next chapter. And the much-bandaged wizard drinking Firewhisky at the bar is Willy Widdershins, who is in some trouble with the Ministry for charming toilets to make them regurgitate on Muggles. It is likely that he is in disguise because he is evading arrest. Hoping to beat the penalties for the charges, he reports the meeting to Umbridge, as is discovered in chapter 27.

Although Hermione requires each student to sign a parchment bearing an oath of secrecy, she does not trust everyone and secretly insures that any "snitches" will be revealed. Unknown to the students who join this Defensive Arts teaching group, soon to be known as Dumbledore's Army, Hermione secretly jinxed the parchment that they signed to reveal the identity of anyone who divulges information about the group. When Marietta Edgecombe later tells Umbridge about the secret meetings, she is horrified when purple pimples spelling "snitch" break out across her face.

Associated with that, we here see the beginnings of an interesting bit of misdirection. The eventual betrayer of the group, Edgecombe, is deliberately kept to the periphery of the group, saying nothing apart from the occasional sigh or fidget. Zacharias Smith, with his obvious skepticism, is being presented to us as the most likely to betray the group; his attitude will continue at least into the first actual meeting of the group, which takes place in the Room of Requirement. Willy Widdershins' report to Umbridge following the initial meeting will result in a ban on student organizations. This in turn will cause Harry and Ron, at least initially, to believe that the group has been betrayed by one of the members there present; while the readers' suspicions will fall immediately on Smith, Ron will jump to the conclusion that it was Michael Corner, based apparently on Corner's relationship with Ginny. Edgecombe's betrayal of the group will come as a surprise to us.

The innkeeper at the Hog's Head looks familiar for a reason—he is Aberforth Dumbledore, Professor Dumbledore's younger brother, as many readers guessed instantly. An extremely large clue is the odour of goat that Harry notices as he enters; readers will remember that in the previous book, Professor Dumbledore had mentioned that his brother had been convicted of practicing inappropriate charms on a goat. Aberforth will play an important role in the final book.

Chapter 17: Educational Decree Number Twenty-Four

SYNOPSIS

In the common room on Monday, Harry and Ron find a large notice announcing Educational Decree Number Twenty Four, outlawing all unapproved student organizations. All current student groups have been disbanded and must request approval from Professor Umbridge to reform. Harry says that someone must have informed Umbridge about their meeting. Ron suggests Zacharias Smith or Michael Corner, and sets off to tell Hermione. She says that no one from the meeting could have told because she secretly enchanted the parchment everyone signed to reveal any snitches who break the vow of secrecy.

Approached at breakfast by Fred, George, Ginny, Neville, and Dean, Harry says that despite the decree, they are going ahead with the defence class. Hermione says the prefects will be joining as well. Hermione waves off some members approaching from Ravenclaw and Hufflepuff, saying she will talk to them later. Angelina Johnson is deeply dismayed by this decree, because it also bans Quidditch teams, and she will have to request permission to reform the Gryffindor team. She begs Harry not to upset Umbridge again.

During Harry's History of Magic class, Hedwig appears on the windowsill carrying a message from Sirius, but her wing has been injured. Harry takes her to Professor Grubbly-Plank in the staff room, who says

Hedwig was attacked but can be healed. Sirius' message is extremely short: *"Tonight, same time, same place."* Professor McGonagall, who is also in the staff room, reminds Harry that all communication channels may be monitored. Hermione wonders later if someone tried to intercept Hedwig. Harry, trying to reassure himself, points out that the message was still sealed.

Before Potions class, Draco Malfoy makes a rude comment about people with mental infirmities staying at St. Mungo's. Neville, pushed beyond endurance, tries to fight him. Harry and Ron restrain him, just as Snape arrives. Seeing the scuffle, he promptly penalizes Gryffindor ten House points. Ron asks what that was all about, but Harry, though he knows that Death Eaters tortured Neville's parents to insanity, keeps his promise to Dumbledore and says nothing. Professor Umbridge is present and taking notes. She asks how long Snape has been teaching, and he replies fourteen years. In response to her questions, he also says that he has applied repeatedly for the Defence Against the Dark Arts post, and was always refused. Umbridge asks why and Snape suggests she ask Dumbledore. Straining to hear Umbridge and Snape's conversation causes Harry to ruin his potion.

That evening, Angelina says there is no Quidditch practice, as she is still waiting permission to reform the team, although the other Houses have been approved. Harry and Ron's attempts at homework are interrupted by Fred and George demonstrating the latest Skiving Snackbox: the Puking Pastilles, which induce projectile vomiting. Late that night, Sirius' head appears in the fireplace. He tells Harry that he heard about the defensive magic group from Mundungus Fletcher, who was in the Hog's Head during the meeting, disguised as the heavily-veiled witch. Sirius passes Mrs. Weasley's message that Ron is forbidden to get involved, and her advice that Harry and Hermione likewise abandon it. Sirius, however, approves, and encourages them to continue. Harry asks for suggestions on places to meet. Sirius suggests several locations but they are unsuitable, then looking sideways in the flames, vanishes. A hand suddenly appears in the fire, grabbing at where Sirius' head just was. Harry, Ron, and Hermione run; looking back, Harry recognizes Umbridge's hand.

ANALYSIS

Umbridge clearly has many ways to obtain information. She willingly goes overboard with rules and regulations (i.e. banning all student organizations to prevent the student Defence Against the Dark Arts group from meeting) to cement her ever-growing authority. Rather than further discouraging Harry, who was becoming increasingly depressed over Hagrid's absence, no Quidditch, and being unable to regularly communicate with Sirius, this only makes him more determined than ever to move ahead with the defensive arts class and to combat Umbridge's dictatorial reign. Umbridge has become a tyrannical symbol of oppression that Harry and the other students rebel against, helping unite the Houses as the Sorting Hat had advised, and as Dumbledore had stressed the year before. We do not find it surprising that only Slytherin is missing; we are already seeing that Umbridge is biased heavily in favour of Slytherin House, and as a result, Slytherin feels the pinch much less than the rest of the school. This oppression will also help students to rally around and support Harry, though many likely remain skeptical that he actually witnessed Voldemort's resurrection.

Harry has been told, and has now seen a demonstration, that the Floo network is under surveillance by the Ministry of Magic. He will need to find another means to communicate with his godfather. It's unknown whether or not Umbridge actually intercepted Hedwig, only that something nearly caught her, injuring her in the process. If the Floo network is being monitored, as it evidently is, the limited information Hedwig was carrying ("Tonight, same time, same place") would not reveal Sirius' whereabouts, nor would it pinpoint the specific meeting time with Harry, or that it was even Black that Harry was meeting, unless the monitoring had started before Sirius' previous visit on the first weekend in the year. However, it would alert Umbridge that a meeting was planned, though it would not give any information about who Harry was to meet with unless the Ministry had become aware of Sirius' Animagus form. This latter is not unlikely; Lucius Malfoy seems to know of Sirius' Animagus form, has apparently reported Sirius' presence in London to the Ministry, and quite possibly could have mentioned that Sirius is an unregistered Animagus and his transformed shape. The scheduled time "tonight" would rule out many physical locations, as the students are forbidden to leave the school or its grounds without permission, particularly at night, so Umbridge could have heightened the surveillance on the Floo network as being among the few available contact avenues.

Snape has been teaching at Hogwarts for fourteen years, as he tells Umbridge. As Harry is now fifteen, Snape would have begun teaching at Hogwarts in September of the year that Harry turned one year old, and would have been only two months on the job at the time of Harry's parents' death and Voldemort's initial disappearance.

QUESTIONS

Review 1. Why has Umbridge disbanded all student groups and organizations? What does Harry decide to do?

2. Why does Neville attack Malfoy in Potions class? What does Harry know about it?

3. What might have caused the injury to Hedwig's wing? Why would someone want to capture her?

4. How did Sirius find out about the defensive magic group?

5. How was Umbridge able to locate Sirius?

Further Study 1. Why has Slytherin been given permission to reform their Quidditch team, when Gryffindor has not?

2. Why would Harry ignore McGonagall's warning about the Floo Network and other communication methods being monitored? How risky was this?

3. Harry has suspected that both Snape and Umbridge are Death Eaters. What about their interaction with each other either supports or discredits that belief?

4. How can Hermione be so certain that no one in the defensive magic group tipped off Umbridge about their meeting? Is she right?

5. Why does Molly Weasley oppose the defensive magic group while Sirius supports it?

Greater Picture

Though Ron immediately suspects a student, Hermione is confident that it cannot have happened without them knowing about it. The fact that Sirius has found out about the group, without anyone having told him about it, should cause us to suspect that perhaps another eavesdropper was aware of the meeting in the Hog's Head. In fact, we will find out later that another of the four customers in the Hog's Head, Willy Widdershins, may not have been intending to eavesdrop, but was quick enough to use the information he collected in an attempt to get himself out of trouble with the Ministry. Widdershins, we will find out later, had been charged with making Muggle toilets regurgitate, and sold the information to Umbridge in return for getting the charges decreased or dropped. Umbridge later reveals to Harry that all school fireplaces except her own are being monitored. It is likely this monitoring that detects Sirius communicating with Harry, rather than the possibly-intercepted message Hedwig had been carrying, which contained insufficient information other than the general meeting time ("tonight"). That Umbridge has the fireplaces monitored may indicate that there is a far greater connection continuing between her and the Ministry than was suspected.

The monitoring of the fireplaces, coupled with Harry's need to communicate with Sirius, will require him to break in to Umbridge's office later in the story. He will, in fact, need to do this on two separate occasions; the first time he will be largely successful in his attempt, the second time will result in his getting caught by Umbridge. As mentioned in the Analysis section above, Umbridge's unceasing attempts to subjugate the school may be the single greatest reason for the anti-Umbridge sentiment within the school. In this chapter we see that Umbridge's early attempts to cement her powers by unilaterally increasing them, and we see also that the immediate result is rebellion. Older readers likely will have seen the pattern of increasing oppression resulting in increasing rebellion in their own lives, but for younger readers, this may be their first exposure to this pattern of behaviour. It is to the author's credit that she is able to portray this familiar sequence of events, in this and succeeding chapters, so convincingly, without losing the older audience's interest.

As mentioned above, Snape would have begun teaching at Hogwarts in September of the year that Harry turned one year old, and would have been only two months on the job at the time of Harry's parents' death and Voldemort's initial disappearance. Revelations in the last book in the series will strongly suggest that Snape had learned of Voldemort's plan to kill Harry and his parents shortly before that, and had then become a double agent, working for Dumbledore. It would seem that it was about at the same time that Snape became Potions Master for Hogwarts, probably as part of the "anything" that Dumbledore required of him.

Chapter 18: Dumbledore's Army

Synopsis

Hermione suspects Hedwig's injury was caused by Umbridge attempting to intercept Harry's mail. That is likely the real reason Filch had earlier tried to confiscate Harry's letter when he was in the Owlery. Angelina announces that the Gryffindor Quidditch team has been allowed to reform. Practice is that evening. After Angelina leaves, Hermione expresses second thoughts about the defence classes; Sirius supporting it therefore makes it suspect to Hermione, who feels Sirius is somewhat immature and may be trying to live through Harry. This gets an angry rebuttal from Harry and Ron.

The weather during the Quidditch practice is dreadful; Fred and George debate skipping practice by using their Skiving Snackbox products, but Angelina knows about them. Testing their latest item, Fever Fudge, has given them pus-filled boils in a rather personal place. Because of this and the bad weather, practice lasts for only an hour. Following the first practice, Harry's scar pains him. He tells Ron that Voldemort is angry because he wants something done that is not happening fast enough. Ron asks if that was what had happened in Umbridge's office, but Harry says no, Voldemort was happy then. And the time before that, just before they left for school, he was furious. Alone in the common room later that evening, Harry nods off over his homework. He has the now familiar dream of the windowless corridor. He is awakened by Dobby the House-elf bringing back the healed Hedwig. Dobby, who seems to be wearing all of Hermione's knitted elf hats and socks, says that because the clothing is hidden throughout Gryffindor tower, the other House-elves will not clean there anymore. They find the items insulting. Harry decides not to tell Hermione. Harry asks Dobby for suggestions on a meeting place for the defensive magic class. Dobby tells him about the Room of Requirement, a room that appears fully equipped with whatever the person asking for it needs. Dobby uses it as a place for Winky to dry out, and offers to show Harry how to summon it.

The next day, Harry passes the word that the first meeting is that evening. Hermione is doubtful, remembering how Dobby's other schemes have failed, but Harry tells her that Dumbledore had also mentioned this room once. That night, Harry, Ron, and Hermione summon the room; it is perfect, with cushions to catch Stunned students, there are Dark detectors, which Harry thinks were in the false Moody's office the year before, and, most reassuring to Hermione, a full library of Dark Arts reference books. The other students file in, awed by the space's perfection, and the first session begins.

Hermione suggests voting for a leader, and Harry is elected unanimously. Hermione also wants to name their group, and after numerous ideas are tossed out,

Chapter 18: Dumbledore's Army

Cho Chang suggests "Defence Association," or D.A. for short. Ginny Weasley points out that the initials could also stand for "Dumbledore's Army," and the members choose that, mostly to mock paranoid Minister for Magic Cornelius Fudge, who fears Dumbledore is secretly organizing a wizard army against the Ministry of Magic. Hermione writes "Dumbledore's Army" at the top of the parchment with the students' names on it and attaches it to the wall. Harry begins the first lesson—the disarming charm, although Zacharias Smith complains it is too simple. Harry says it served him well enough against Voldemort, but Zacharias is free to leave if he chooses.

Practice goes well, although Cho badly fumbles her charms whenever Harry is watching. Harry, evaluating the spell-casting, is glad he started with something so simple. The session ends, and everyone agrees to meet the next Wednesday, a time that does not conflict with Harry's Quiddich practice.

Analysis

The school Houses have always maintained separate identities which have created (mostly) friendly rivalries, although Gryffindor and Slytherin have traditionally been more antagonistic toward one another. As is so common, an external threat creates an alliance among these more-or-less disparate groups. With the exception of Slytherin, the Houses become united over a common cause: opposing Umbridge and the Ministry. While Umbridge does seem to show obvious favoritism towards Slytherin House, it would seem that they were not deliberately excluded from the DA, and the organizers may have simply felt students from that House would be uninterested in joining or possibly feared that some were untrustworthy.

Also, the name, *Dumbledore's Army* (or D.A.), that the students have chosen for their secret group not only reflects their defiance and willingness to oppose Umbridge and mock Fudge, but re-enforces their loyalty to Dumbledore and Hogwarts. Fudge's ongoing paranoia that Dumbledore is secretly building a wizard army to take over the Ministry is ridiculous; there is simply nothing to support this, and significant evidence against it—we were told by Hagrid in the first book that Dumbledore had been offered the post and declined it—but it shows just how warped Fudge's reasoning now is. *Dumbledore's Army* becomes an extreme example of Fudge "creating what he fears." Fudge suspecting that an army is being built, for which he has no proof, is in stark contrast to his unbending claims that, despite concrete evidence, Voldemort and Peter Pettigrew are still dead and Sirius Black is indeed guilty. Umbridge supports his stance, of course, although she has a different agenda.

Dumbledore's mention of the Room of Requirement, that Harry alludes to to calm Hermione's fears, is an extremely fleeting one: at the Yule Ball the previous year, Dumbledore, conversing with Professor Karkaroff, had mentioned discovering, and then losing, a room full of chamber pots. The fact that Harry is able to recognize this as the Room of Requirement from Dobby's description is rather astute. Harry has probably chosen to read more into the wink that Dumbledore tipped him at the time than was meant.

Returning to Gryffindor tower, Harry only half listens to Hermione and Ron discussing the meeting; he is also thinking about Cho admitting that she is nervous when he is nearby. Harry sees this as the beginnings of the romance he has dreamed about since the previous year. However, because this is tied to Cedric Diggory's death, for which he feels partially responsible, Harry remains unsure of himself.

Dobby's comments about the House Elves' opinions of the clothing scattered around is quite telling. We are already well-aware of the way house-elves feel about their work and their masters; Dobby's re-iteration of them quite strongly reinforces our understanding of these feelings, reminding us that the house-elves fully believe that their place is to work for the comfort of their masters, in this case the school. Hermione cannot give them their freedom, as they will not accept it if offered, and are offended if they believe they are being tricked into it.

Questions

Review 1. Why does Hermione suspect it was Umbridge who attempted to capture Hedwig? What does she think about Filch?

2. Why does Hermione express second thoughts about starting the defensive group? Is she justified?

3. What does Harry think is the reason his scar hurts during Quidditch practice?

4. Why do the House-elves avoid Hermione's gifts of clothing? Why would they find them insulting?

5. How does Harry learn about the Room of Requirement? What's Hermione's thoughts about it?

6. What do the defensive magic group call themselves? Why is that name agreed on?

7. Why does Cho fumble her charm whenever Harry is watching?

8. Why is Harry glad he started the students off with such a simple spell?

Further Study 1. Could there be repercussions from the choice of the name for the group?

Greater Picture

What Voldemort wants done that is not happening quickly enough could be extracting the Prophecy from the Ministry, although, equally, it could be recruiting the Dementors to his side, and the associated jail break. Whatever it is, is never clear, though most likely it is retrieving the Prophecy. Adding weight to this is, of course, Harry's recurring dream: the hallway that he sees will be revealed shortly after Christmas to be the hallway that leads to the Department of Mysteries, where the Prophecy is stored, and the dream is a representation of Voldemort's desires. As Malfoy was tasked with putting Bode under the Imperius Curse, that may be taking too long to suit Voldemort and could be the start of the Malfoy family's downfall within the Death Eaters. It is Fudge's paranoia that Dumbledore is creating a secret Wizard army that leads to the D.A. being formed. It, ironically, becomes the core of the army that helps to battle Voldemort and his Death Eaters, after they have taken over the Ministry in *Harry Potter and the Deathly Hallows*. In the meanwhile, the group's name will be used by Fudge, when the group is discovered, to "prove" that Dumbledore was, in fact, organizing a private army; this will result in the attempted arrest of Dumbledore and his departing the school.

The Room of Requirement will play a significant role in the next two books. Throughout this book, Harry will use it as a meeting place for Dumbledore's Army; in the next book, Malfoy will be attempting to perform some task in this room, and in the final book, it will once again be used by Dumbledore's Army, and will be found to have been used as a place where Lord Voldemort had hidden something quite valuable.

Chapter 19: The Lion and the Serpent

Synopsis

Harry is pleased with the D.A.'s progress, and he takes great pleasure in flouting Umbridge's regulations. With various team Quidditch practices, it is difficult to have a regular night for Dumbledore's Army to meet, but Hermione has a solution: she gives everyone fake Galleons that transmit messages. Harry can use them to summon them for the next meeting. Terry Boot is impressed, saying this is a Protean Charm, and it is N.E.W.T.-level magic.

The first Quidditch match is approaching, and Ron is a nervous wreck. Their opponent is Slytherin, and the students are wearing badges reading, "Weasley is our King." It is a cruel effort to undermine Ron's confidence by implying he will win the game for Slytherin with his poor Quidditch skills. During the game, Slytherin students sing, "Weasley is our King" to further unnerve him. It apparently works, as Ron plays badly, missing several shots, but Harry catches the Snitch, winning the game for Gryffindor.

After the game, Harry (already angry after Crabbe hit him with a bludger after the final whistle) and George Weasley jump Malfoy and his cronies for mocking Ron. McGonagall hauls them into her office and assigns each a week's detention. However, Umbridge barges in with another Decree in hand, declaring she now has sole authority over all student discipline. Over McGonagall's protests, she permanently bans Harry and George from Quidditch. She also bans Fred Weasley, even though he was never involved in the incident. Umbridge also confiscates their brooms.

Back in the Common room, Angelina worries about what to do without team Beaters and a Seeker. She goes to bed, leaving only Harry, Hermione, and Ginny in the Common room. Ron enters through the portrait hole, still in his Quidditch robes and covered in snow. He threatens to quit the team, saying he never should have thought that he could be a Keeper. When Harry and Ginny tell him about Umbridge's permanent bans, Ron says this is the worst he has ever felt. Harry agrees. Hermione says she knows something that will cheer them up: Hagrid is back.

Analysis

Just as the Gryffindor Quidditch team is allowed to reform, improving Harry's unhappy mood, Umbridge squashes it again. She grows more dictatorial by the day, and it seems she is getting new decrees passed solely to increase her power. She obviously also favors Slytherins. Although Crabbe was involved in the fight, he only had to write lines as his punishment, while Harry, Fred, and George were permanently banned from Quidditch. That Fred was included, even though he was uninvolved in the incident, shows how biased and vicious Umbridge truly is. Harry had previously asked Sirius if he thought Umbridge was a Death Eater. Sirius does not believe she is, and her actions seemingly support this. Rather, they indicate a growing addiction to, and abuse of, power.

What we are seeing here is another aspect of Umbridge's carrying out the agenda of the Ministry. As we have seen, she, along with Cornelius Fudge and other Ministry officials, continue to wage a public smear campaign against Harry and Dumbledore, refuting their claims that the Dark Lord has arisen. Close-minded and paranoid, they suspect Dumbledore is recruiting Hogwarts students for a secret wizard army with which to overthrow the Ministry. That is why Fudge refuses to allow real defensive magic to be taught. We believe that Umbridge was placed at Hogwarts solely as Fudge's spy and to deliberately meddle in its operations; that belief is unchanged, and she will do anything with her ever-increasing and Ministry-backed authority to prevent Harry or Dumbledore from becoming what is perceived to be an even greater threat. Her banning Harry from Quidditch seems, in light of her apparent mission, to be a step in demoralizing, and thus further discrediting, Harry. It is uncertain why she chooses to ban Fred as well as George, despite her "explanation"; the simplest explanation seems to be "because I can."

Questions

Review   1. Why did Crabbe receive such a light punishment for the same offense as Harry and the Twins?

2. Why would calling Ron a "King" be insulting and what effect does it have on him? Who is doing it?

3. Why would Umbridge ban both Weasley twins from Quidditch when only one was involved in the incident with Malfoy?

4. Why would Umbridge confiscate the students' brooms?

Further Study   1. Why does Umbridge favor Slytherin students?

2. Why is McGonagall angry at Umbridge? What does this indicate?

Greater Picture

While we have not yet seen this, Umbridge will shortly be revealed to have an unreasoning hatred of what she terms "half-breeds": magical creatures that show human characteristics but are not human. We will see this in her reaction to Hagrid, and later her reaction to the centaurs in the Forbidden Forest. This actually suggests that Umbridge will again act to make things more difficult for Harry. With the confiscation of his broom, and his Quidditch ban, Harry will find that the only things about Hogwarts that he still enjoys are teaching Dumbledore's Army and his friends, notably Hagrid. Hagrid's return is heartening, but with Umbridge threatening to sack Hagrid, yet another of his few pleasures comes under threat of almost immediate removal.

Ron's lack of confidence in his own Keeping will be a recurring thread in this book and the next. He will finally hit his stride in time for the final match of the year, which will be won, and the Quidditch Cup with it, thanks to his efforts, but he will have lost faith in himself again by the start of the next book. This is likely meant to illuminate Ron's lack of maturity; he tries out for Keeper but then does not have the inner strength to keep at it, and after the disappointments on the field he tries to run away. It is only through external influences that he is convinced to stick with it. This sort of pattern is quite realistically rendered; one can see that the author is well aware of how boys venture into new and complicated endeavors.

Chapter 20: Hagrid's Tale

SYNOPSIS

Harry immediately fetches his invisibility cloak and the Marauder's Map, and with Ron and Hermione (Ron crouching because he is almost too tall to fit under the cloak), they head to Hagrid's hut. They are shocked by his battered appearance: his face is bloodied and bruised, he has a black eye and multiple cuts on his face and hands, and he moves as if his ribs are broken. However, he refuses all suggestions to visit Madam Pomfrey, instead offering to make tea. Hermione asks if he visited the giants, and he is astounded they are able to guess that much, but also secretly seems pleased that they are so quick. Ron mentions that if Hagrid tells them about his mission, Harry can tell Hagrid about the Dementor attack. Hagrid is stunned to hear that Dementors attacked near Privet Drive, and wants to know what happened, but Harry insists that Hagrid recount his mission first. Hagrid says he was on a secret mission with Madame Maxime, the Headmistress of the Beauxbatons Academy in France. Dumbledore sent them into the European mountains to recruit the Giants against Voldemort. They were on their way to opening relations with the Gurg, the chief Giant, when he was overthrown. The new chief was less receptive, and he and Madame Maxime had to use magic to escape. Giants hate magic, and that ruined their chances to negotiate with the new Gurg. Hagrid and Madame Maxime attempted to recruit those Giants who tried escaping the new chief, but with little success. They also had to avoid Macnair and other Death Eaters, who were recruiting Giants for Voldemort.

Hermione asks about Hagrid's mother. Hagrid says she died long before, but was not much of a mother anyway, and he hardly remembers her. Ron asks who attacked him, and Harry wants to know why he returned long after Madame Maxime did. As Hagrid starts protesting that he has not been attacked, there is a loud knock on the door; Harry, Hermione, and Ron duck under the cloak, and Professor Umbridge strolls into Hagrid's hut. Umbridge, speaking loudly and slowly as if to a deaf person, introduces herself as she scrutinizes Hagrid's cabin. She asks Hagrid why there are three sets of footsteps going to his hut and none going away; Hagrid is unable to answer coherently. She asks where he has been, and he stammers that he was away for his health; Umbridge appears to disbelieve that given his current battered state. Umbridge looks around the hut, apparently looking for students hiding, and passing within inches of the cloaked Trio. She informs Hagrid that she will be inspecting his class, as the Ministry is determined to weed out unsatisfactory teachers, then leaves.

Once Hagrid reports that Umbridge is back at the castle, Harry strips off the Cloak. Hermione, worried, asks what Hagrid plans to teach. Hagrid does not say, except that it will be good. Hermione warns him that Professor Trelawney is already on probation, and she recommends that Hagrid follow boring, Ministry-recommended procedures. Hagrid brushes off her concerns, saying that he is tired, it is late, and they need to get back to the castle. As the Trio return to the castle under the Cloak, Hermione works on an Obliteration Charm to hide their footprints. Ron does not think Hermione got through to Hagrid, and she vows, even if she has to plan all his lesson for him, that she will prevent Umbridge from firing Hagrid.

ANALYSIS

Although Hagrid and Madame Maxime failed to enlist the Giants as allies, their mission's importance should not be under-emphasized. Dumbledore knows that Voldemort is actively recruiting non-human magical creatures, specifically Giants and Dementors, because Harry had reported Voldemort's words on that subject. Voldemort is also approaching Werewolves, Centaurs, and others who have historically been repressed, ostracized, and even enslaved by the Wizarding world. We can safely assume that Centaur pride and their distaste for human affairs will prevent them from supporting either side. For the werewolves, Dementors, and Giants, however, there is no such assurance. No matter how evil and violent Voldemort's reign will likely be should he prevail, he can offer these denizens more opportunities and freedom than most currently have under the present social order. If Voldemort entices these outcasts to join him, it could tilt the war in his favor.

It also appears that Hagrid and Madame Maxime's mission ended some time ago. Hagrid's delayed return and his injuries may have some cause apart from the mission, although Hagrid remains secretive about what that is. Hermione cautions Hagrid about Umbridge, knowing that she is targeting weaker teachers. Unfortunately, Hagrid seems unconcerned and downplays Hermione's warning, although just why is unclear. Hagrid, who has been out of touch with events at the school until this point, may believe that he is immune from Umbridge's attempts so long as he has Dumbledore's backing. While it has been suggested that Hagrid may feel he does not stand a chance against the possibility of Umbridge dismissing him, his reaction here seems more one of complacency than resignation; he simply does not perceive that Umbridge is a threat despite what Hermione tells him. This seems quite in line with Hagrid's character, as he does not seem to see dragons or Blast-Ended Skrewts to be threats either. Umbridge's condescending treatment of Hagrid certainly seems to indicate that she considers him vastly inferior and of low intelligence, and this may indicate a prejudice she has towards partially-human or non-human races. It also appears that she may know something about his secret mission, and it is possible that Voldemort's spies or Ministry agents spotted Hagrid and Madam Maxime while they were away.

Questions

Review   1. What was Hagrid's secret mission? Who sent him, and why is it so important?

2. Why was Madam Maxime also sent on the mission?

3. What was the outcome of Hagrid and Madam Maxime's secret mission?

4. Why is Umbridge so interested in where Hagrid has been? She asks if Hagrid had been vacationing in the mountains—does she possibly know anything about the mission and where he went?

5. Why does Umbridge speak to Hagrid in such a deliberately slow and loud manner?

6. Why does Hagrid shrug off Hermione's warning?

7. Just how does Hermione intend to prevent Umbridge from firing Hagrid?

8. What is Umbridge's definition of "unsatisfactory teachers"?

Further Study   1. If Hagrid and Madam Maxime were on the mission together, why might Hagrid have returned much later than she did?

2. What could have caused Hagrid's battered appearance? Why won't he say how he was hurt?

3. Why might Umbridge suspect that Hagrid and Madame Maxime were on a secret mission?

4. What would motivate magical creatures like Werewolves, Goblins, Centaurs, and others to support Voldemort?

Greater Picture

It is mentioned above that Umbridge's denigration of Hagrid may indicate a dislike for half-Human and non-Human races. While this is not completely confirmed until near the end of this book, it is strongly suggested that Umbridge is biased against "half-breeds" in general by comments she makes while "examining" Hagrid's teaching. Later in the book, we will learn that Umbridge's hatred of what she terms "half-breeds" extends to Centaurs, a proudly pure-bred race.

Even now that he is back on nominally safe ground, Hagrid will continue to sport various injuries throughout the rest of the year. It will not be until much later in the year that we learn the cause of these injuries: Hagrid had managed to locate his half-brother, Grawp, living with the giants, and brought him home. Grawp's intransigence, which will continue into the summer, had slowed Hagrid's return, and is now the source of the injuries Hagrid repeatedly suffers. Hagrid, mindful that Grawp is all the family he has left, is trying to civilize him. There will be a number of points where Hagrid alludes to "family," meaning Grawp, but it will be significantly later in the year before we meet him.

Hagrid is hiding Grawp in the Forbidden Forest while he attempts to make him fit for society. This, while it would normally be a safe hiding place, will result in the Centaurs falling out with Hagrid, and eventually will result in Hagrid being barred from the Forest. One centaur, Firenze, will allude to this problem in private conversation with Harry, but when the message is passed on, Hagrid will dismiss it.

In passing, it may be of interest that while the centaurs do not help Voldemort, neither do they help those who would fight him, remaining neutral until, in the final chapter of the final book, they are goaded into action by Hagrid. The werewolves, led by Fenrir Greyback, will take Voldemort's side, as will the Dementors and at least two Giants.

Chapter 21: The Eye of the Snake

Synopsis

Hermione pleads with Hagrid the next day to only teach something safe, but he only responds that nobody in their right minds would rather study Knarls than Chimeras. Hermione hastens to reassure Harry and Ron that she does not believe he has a Chimera waiting for them. Hagrid still refuses to say what is causing his injuries. Hagrid's return receives a mixed reception: Fred, George and Lee Jordan rush to the head table and shake hands while Parvati Patil and Lavender seem somewhat dismayed. Harry understands; Professor Grubbly-Plank's "interesting" lessons do not seem to involve the risk of getting one's head torn off. In Care of Magical Creatures, Hagrid leads the students into the Forest, where he shows them strange, horse-like creatures covered with scaly skin and sporting leathery wings. They are the same ones Harry saw pulling the carriages at the beginning of school. Hagrid asks how many students can actually see them. Harry, Neville, and a stringy Slytherin raise their hands. Hagrid says the creatures are Thestrals. Hermione, when asked, explains they are only visible to people who have seen death. Harry understands now why he can see them and Ron cannot; he witnessed Cedric Diggory's murder during the Triwizard Tournament the previous year. Hagrid's lesson is interrupted by Professor Umbridge, who arrives to inspect his teaching. Umbridge's presence unnerves Hagrid, and with her watching, interrupting, and generally treating Hagrid as subhuman, Hagrid delivers what may be his worst lesson. The Slytherins doing their best to interfere further unnerves Hagrid. Umbridge departs, saying that he can expect his evaluation in ten days.

Banned from Quidditch, Harry has little to look forward to except Dumbledore's Army, and that will not happen over Christmas break. This prospective idleness vexes Harry until he asks Ron how he is returning to the Burrow. Ron then mentions that he forgot to tell Harry that he is invited for Christmas.

Chapter 21: The Eye of the Snake

Entering the Room of Requirement before the final D.A. meeting prior to the break, Harry sees that Dobby has decorated it extravagantly and embarrassingly. Harry removes most decorations, but mistletoe bunches are still hanging when Luna Lovegood and the other students arrive. Harry has them practice the Impediment jinx and Stunning. At class end, Harry praises everyone's performance and says they will start the big stuff in the new year. Cho Chang, lingering behind, tells Harry she still misses Cedric and wonders if he had known what Harry is teaching, would he still be alive? Harry says he did know it, otherwise he would never had made it to the maze's center in the tournament's Third Task. Cho compliments Harry as being a good teacher, and maneuvering him under the mistletoe, kisses him.

Returning to the common room, Harry tells Ron and Hermione what happened, saying it would be nicer if Cho was not always crying. Hermione explains all the emotional turmoil Cho is undergoing, but Ron says that is impossible, "One person couldn't feel all that at once, they'd explode." Hermione responds that just because he has the emotional range of a teaspoon does not mean everyone does. Hermione says, "I suppose it could have been worse," when Harry describes his efforts to comfort Cho. Asked if he is going to keep seeing her, Harry does not answer. When asked who she is writing to, Hermione says it is to Viktor Krum, causing Ron to lapse into disgruntled silence; very little else is said until everyone is in bed. Harry, musing as he falls asleep, thinks that Hogwarts should teach how to understand girls.

Harry dreams he is a snake slithering down a long hallway. A man is hiding under a silvery cloak. The man draws his wand as Harry attacks him with his venomous fangs. Harry awakes in a panic, shouting, sweating, and his scar burning intensely, convinced the dream was real and that the attacked man was Mr. Weasley. Neville summons Professor McGonagall who takes Harry and Ron to Dumbledore's office.

Analysis

Harry and Cho's relationship is starting off badly. Although Cho likes Harry, she is still grieving Cedric Diggory's death while coping with other problems. Harry, dealing with his own difficulties and lacking romantic experience, is simply unequipped to handle Cho's fragile emotional state, despite Hermione's advice; he is uncertain if it is wise to continue seeing her. Ron is also undergoing relationship problems after learning that Hermione is writing to Viktor Krum. Ron's unresolved feelings for Hermione are causing him to experience jealousy, although he is confused over how he actually does feel or even why.

Meanwhile, Harry's dreams are becoming more real and intense. Not only is he convinced that what he saw was actually happening, requiring that he act quickly to save Mr. Weasley, but he sees it from his own point-of-view and feels the emotion as it unfolds, leaving him extremely disturbed.

Hagrid has deliberately ignored Hermione's advice to only teach "safe" Ministry-approved lessons, although it probably matters little what lessons he does teach or how well or how badly he teaches them. We can see clearly now that Umbridge is a racist, and she is obviously intent on eliminating him solely based on his half-Giant heritage. Hagrid, though, is hurting his own cause. Whether this is childish obstinacy, or simple failure to comprehend how precarious his situation is, remains unclear. However, as we have seen, not all students would be unhappy if he left. Slytherins, of course, would favor his dismissal purely from spite, but others also fear his lessons, which oftentimes feature dangerous creatures and sometimes result in minor injuries.

It has been noted that Harry should have been able to see the Thestrals as he rode in the horseless carriage from the castle to the train at the end of *Harry Potter and the Goblet of Fire;* after all, he had just seen Cedric Diggory killed. There are actually several answers, including one in the context of the books, and one in the context of the author's plans. Rowling states that immediately after Harry witnessed Cedric Diggory's death, he was still in shock and had not completely internalized what had happened. Cedric's death is not entirely real to him yet, and it is only after he broods over the summer that he finally accepts that Cedric is dead. Only when he fully believes that he has witnessed death, is he able to see the Thestrals. Readers have asked, did he not see death earlier, such as when Lord Voldemort killed his parents? The answer is no, he did not. Being a baby, he was unable to comprehend that night's tragic events. Also, his father was actually killed in another part of the house, while his mother's death probably happened beyond his view in his crib. While it could be argued that Harry saw Voldemort die by his own rebounding killing curse, Voldemort is not really dead, nor would baby Harry understand what he saw. Harry also did not see Professor Quirrell die at the end of *Harry Potter and the Philosopher's Stone*. He lost consciousness before Quirrell actually died. The author has also stated that having the Thestrals visible to Harry just before the book's end would have left a rather uncomfortable puzzle for the readers: what are these creatures, are they Dark? So she said she made the conscious decision to leave them invisible until the next book. The above is a paraphrase of the author's own comments on the matter.[1] However, critics can argue that this was actually one of several inconsistencies throughout the books. Rowling may have simply made a literary mistake regarding Harry being unable to see the Thestrals at the end of *Harry Potter and the Goblet of Fire,* and she concocted an explanation to fit the facts once the error became apparent.

---

1. http://www.jkrowling.com/textonly/en/faq_view.cfm?id=21

Questions

Review   1. Why does Hermione encourage Hagrid to teach something "safe" in his class? Would her advice make any difference?

2. How does Hagrid react when Umbridge arrives to inspect his class?

3. What does Dobby do to the Room of Requirement? What is Harry's reaction? Why?

4. What are the horse-like creatures? Who can see them and why?

5. What is Ron's reaction to Hermione writing a letter to Viktor Krum? Why?

6. Why does Cho cry so much? What does Hermione think of Harry's efforts to comfort Cho?

Further Study   1. Why are some students less enthused than others about Hagrid's return to Hogwarts?

2. How has the nature of Harry's dream changed, and why is he convinced this one is real?

3. We are told that Harry does not return to Gryffindor tower until half an hour after the DA meeting has ended. What takes him so long?

Greater Picture

Harry's dream is somehow much more realistic than the ones he has experienced regarding that hallway to date. He will soon become convinced that Voldemort is possessing him. Dumbledore will seem unsurprised when Harry recounts the night's events, and he offers little explanation about what might be happening, leaving Harry even more confused, upset, and angrier at Dumbledore. Eventually, we will learn that this is, in fact, an artifact of the linkage between Voldemort the soul shard left in Harry by Voldemort's murder attempt. This is the point at which Voldemort learns that the linkage exists. Shortly, he will start to try to use this linkage to influence Harry's actions. This attempt will be sporadic and ineffective until after Voldemort's discussion with Rookwood, which Harry will also see as a dream. Voldemort will then start systematically using this link to coerce Harry to retrieve something for him. It is actually concern that Voldemort may be using the mental link between himself and Harry, that is preventing Dumbledore from speaking to Harry. It is only at the end of this book that Dumbledore will reveal that he was trying to avoid letting Voldemort know that the relationship between himself and Harry was anything more than the usual Headmaster to student relationship.

As mentioned, we quite clearly see Umbridge's bias against Hagrid at this point, and can see that it is typical of prejudice: Umbridge arrives at Hagrid's class with preconceptions, and discovers exactly what she expects to discover while "examining" him. We will later learn that she is prejudiced against all non-Human races, having authored anti-Werewolf legislation; her dislike of Hagrid, based on nothing more substantial than his ancestry, will be only one aspect of her dislike of those who are not fully-human Wizards. This prejudice will result in Hagrid shortly being put on probation, and near the end of the year Umbridge will bring several Aurors with her as she attempts to sack Hagrid. In the meanwhile, she will repeatedly examine his classes, causing his already-weak confidence to crumble further.

Chapter 22: St.Mungo's Hospital for Magical Maladies and Injuries

Synopsis

Professor McGonagall takes Harry and Ron with her, past the gargoyle (password: "Fizzing Whizbee") and to the Headmaster's office. Many people are heard talking from within Professor Dumbledore's office, but when McGonagall knocks, the voices fall silent, and inside, Dumbledore is sitting alone. Harry is vexed that Dumbledore continues to avoid looking at him. However, he tells Dumbledore what he saw in his dream, and, in response to Dumbledore's question, says that it was seen from his point-of-view, as if he was the snake, and that Mr. Weasley is badly hurt. Dumbledore immediately sends the portraits of two past headmasters, Everard and Dilys, to search for Mr. Weasley. Dumbledore explains that they were two of Hogwarts' most famous headmasters, and they have many other portraits they can visit. Dumbledore addresses Fawkes, saying they will need a warning. Fawkes vanishes in a flash of fire. Dumbledore places an intricate silver machine on his desk and sets it in motion; it emits a puff of green smoke that forms into a snake. Dumbledore says, "Naturally. But in essence divided?" The smoke stream splits into two snakes. Before Harry can ask its meaning, the Everard portrait returns, reporting that an injured man was found. Dilys then appears and says that the man has been taken to St. Mungo's, and that he looks bad. Dumbledore sends Professor McGonagall to fetch the other Weasley children. McGonagall asks about Mrs. Weasley, and Dumbledore says it is a job for Fawkes, though Mrs. Weasley's clock may have already alerted her. Dumbledore creates a Portkey from an old kettle, and addresses Phineas' portrait. Phineas feigns awakening from a deep sleep and grudgingly agrees to deliver a message to his other portrait at number twelve, Grimmauld Place. Told to inform Sirius that the Weasley children and Harry will arrive, Phineas slopes off. Fred, George, and Ginny arrive with Professor McGonagall, and Dumbledore informs them that their father has been injured, and they are being sent to Grimmauld Place. Because the Floo network is being watched, they will instead travel by Portkey. A flash of fire, Fawkes' warning, appears, and McGonagall leaves to head off Umbridge. Phineas returns and reports that Sirius would be delighted to have the children. The Weasley children and Harry hold the Portkey. As it activates, Dumbledore looks directly at Harry for the first time. Intense pain in his scar and overwhelming hatred causes Harry to want to attack and bite Dumbledore.

Arriving at Grimmauld Place, Harry hears Kreacher muttering, "Back again, the blood-traitor brats. Is it true their father's dying?" Sirius orders him out. Harry tells the worried Weasley children and Sirius about his vision, although he refrains from sharing that he was the snake. The Twins demand to go to the hospital, but Sirius vetoes it, saying that the Order wants it kept secret that Harry is seeing events happening hundreds of miles away. Sirius serves Butterbeer as they silently wait for word. Harry wonders about the hatred he felt for Dumbledore, and why it seemed like he had fangs.

A Phoenix flame arrives; Molly Weasley has sent word by Fawkes that Arthur is seriously injured but still alive. She arrives herself at about 5:00 A.M., saying that Arthur is sleeping, and Bill is sitting with him. She expresses her deep gratitude to Harry for saving her husband's life. Harry now privately confesses to Sirius the fact that he seemed to be the snake in his dream, and the intense rage and hatred he felt towards Dumbledore. Sirius tells him not to worry about it, to get some rest, but Harry is unable to sleep, fearing he will turn into a snake and attack Ron. The group decide to stay at Grimmauld Place over the Christmas holidays, to be close to the hospital. That afternoon, among merriment and relief that Arthur is out of danger, Tonks and Mad-Eye Moody arrive to escort them to St. Mungo's. After visiting with the children, during which Fred and George try unsuccessfully to learn where Arthur was and what he was guarding when he was attacked, Mr. and Mrs. Weasley, Tonks, and Moody have a (they think) private discussion regarding the previous night's events. Using Fred and George's Extendable Ears to eavesdrop, Harry and the Weasley children overhear Moody saying that Harry is seeing inside Voldemort's mind, and wonders if he is being possessed by Voldemort.

Analysis

The voices heard in Dumbledore's office, we can now guess, were the portraits of former Headmasters talking with Dumbledore. In this chapter, we see that they are far more than mere "talking heads." While they counsel the present Headmaster, they also act as a surveillance and communication system, able to travel to their other portraits throughout the wizarding world to deliver messages, report news, and occasionally act as spies. It is, in fact, possible that the office of the Headmaster of Hogwarts is potentially better informed than even the Minister of Magic as to events in the Wizarding world.

By this time, the reader should be beginning to suspect that Harry's mind is being accessed by Voldemort. This is confirmed when Harry relates to him that he could see the events at the Department of Mysteries from Voldemort's (or the snake's) point-of-view and feel his emotions. The small instrument Dumbledore consults emits a serpent-shaped puff of smoke, which splits into two when questioned. Its significance, which is never completely explained in the book, could be interpreted several ways. From the shape, we can assume that it is somehow related to the snake that attacked Arthur Weasley. Its splitting into two may represent the snake and Voldemort sharing its experiences. Alternately, it may represent Voldemort and the snake on one side, and Harry on the other. In the latter case, that it splits into two images may indicate that Harry and Voldemort remain separate, meaning Harry has not been possessed by the Dark Lord. Whatever its meaning, there seems to be some mental connection between the two, and when Harry makes eye contact with Dumbledore, the rage and hate he feels is almost certainly Voldemort's. Harry is more distressed than ever, unable to understand what is happening to him, and angry that Dumbledore is deliberately withholding information.

Questions

Review 1. Whose voices did Harry hear inside Dumbledore's office, even though Dumbledore is alone? Why was Dumbledore talking with them?

2. Why is McGonagall sent to head off Umbridge?

3. Why aren't the Weasley children allowed to visit their father in the hospital right away?

4. What does Moody say about Harry? What makes him believe this?

Further Study 1. Where was Mr. Weasley when he was attacked, and what was he doing?

2. Why does Harry feel hate and rage when he looks at Dumbledore?

3. What might be the significance of the smoke stream from Dumbledore's instrument forming into a snake and splitting in two?

4. Why is Harry reluctant to tell the other Weasleys what he actually felt when he witnessed the attack on Arthur Weasley?

5. Why doesn't Kreacher respond when Sirius summons him? Is it possible that he could have left the house, even though he would need his master's permission? How could he have done that, and where might he have gone?

Greater Picture

While Harry is not yet completely aware of this, Dumbledore by now is reasonably certain that there is some connection between Voldemort's mind and Harry's. He will have come to this conclusion based on Harry's recounting of the dreams he had which involved Voldemort in August and May of the previous school year. While he may not yet be aware of the dreams of corridors that Harry is having, he will have guessed that Voldemort's regaining his body may have strengthened that link, and will have known that it was only a matter of time until Voldemort realized the link was present. Recognizing that Voldemort could use that same link to spy on Harry and himself, Dumbledore chooses to appear aloof and indifferent to Harry, in the hopes of hiding the fact that their relationship is more than headmaster-to-student. Harry, of course, is unaware of this, and is hurt by Dumbledore's apparent disregard.

Regarding Dumbledore's "in essence divided" comment, J.K. Rowling explained its meaning during an online chat at a fan site[1] shortly after *Harry Potter and the Deathly Hallows* was published. Says Rowling, "Dumbledore suspected that the snake's essence was

---

1. http://www.TheLeakyCauldron.com

divided—that it contained part of Voldemort's soul, and that was why it was so very adept at doing his bidding. This also explained why Harry, the last and unintended Horcrux, could see so clearly through the snake's eyes, just as he regularly sees through Voldemort's. Dumbledore is thinking aloud here, edging towards the truth with the help of the Pensieve."

Sirius was unintentionally overly forceful in ordering Kreacher to leave. Kreacher manipulated this into being permission to leave the house and visits the only still-living Black family member he respects: Narcissa Malfoy. While he is unable to tell Narcissa about the Order of the Phoenix, or anything else that Sirius has expressly forbidden him to discuss, he does tell Narcissa, and through her, Voldemort, that Sirius and Harry have a very caring relationship. At almost that same instant, Voldemort senses Harry's thoughts and glimpses Dumbledore through him, causing Harry to feel the Dark Lord's rage and desire to kill Dumbledore, and rise, snake-like, within him. As Dumbledore suspects, Voldemort will now be aware that he and Harry share thoughts on occasion. While this is not yet useful to Voldemort, he will exploit it shortly.

Harry is already worried that Voldemort may be possessing him, and he is additionally worried that he had been physically transformed into a snake and transported to London to attack Mr. Weasley. Ron reassures him on the latter point, saying that he was still in his bed and most definitely not a snake during the vision, but Harry is still unsure, and Moody's comment in St. Mungo's seems to be confirmation: Harry now believes that Voldemort may be using him to spy on his surroundings. This will shortly result in Harry deciding to depart Grimmauld Place, a departure that will be forestalled by a message from Dumbledore, relayed sarcastically by Phineas Nigellus.

Chapter 23: Christmas on the Closed Ward

Synopsis

Harry is consumed by the fear that Voldemort is possessing him. He is worried he will start attacking Order members, and afraid that Voldemort can see into Order headquarters. To protect everyone, Harry decides he should permanently leave Hogwarts, and return to the Dursleys. As he starts dragging out his trunk, Phineas Nigellus' portrait appears with a message from Dumbledore: "Stay where you are." Harry is upset by the message's brevity, as it was also all he was told after the Dementor attack. Having not slept the night before for fear of turning into a snake, Harry falls asleep against his will and again dreams of the stone hallway and the black door, and thinks how much he would like it to open. His dream is ended by Ron's voice telling him dinner is ready, but when he opens his eyes, Ron has already left. Harry decides Ron does not want to be in the same room with him.

Depressed, confused, and convinced everyone is avoiding him, Harry isolates himself. Hermione arrives at Grimmauld Place, hauls Harry from Buckbeak's room, and scolds him for his behavior. When Harry says he does not want to talk to anyone, Ginny reminds Harry that she knows what it is like to be possessed by Voldemort. After Harry apologizes, Ginny describes her experiences. Harry is relieved that his experience is nothing like Ginny's, and he is finally convinced he has not been possessed.

Christmas is coming; Sirius is overjoyed to have a full house for the holidays, and his joy seems infectious. Everyone expends great effort, and the house is decorated from top to bottom. At Christmas, Sirius and Lupin give Harry a set of books on jinxes and counter-jinxes. They will be useful for teaching Dumbledore's Army. Fred and George tell Ron and Harry to wait awhile before going downstairs; Mrs. Weasley is in tears because Percy returned his Christmas gift, unopened, and without a note.

When they head downstairs, they meet Hermione, who has a gift for Kreacher. It is a patchwork quilt, and Hermione says it should brighten up his sleeping space. Ron opens a cupboard door in the kitchen, and Harry sees what looks like a nest under an old-fashioned boiler (US: furnace). Scattered in the corners are items Sirius discarded, including many old Black family portraits, including one of Bellatrix Lestrange. Hermione leaves the gift. Sirius asks if anyone has seen Kreacher, and Harry says he has not seen him since Sirius ordered him out when they arrived. Sirius says that a house-elf cannot leave a residence without permission. Harry points out that Dobby did exactly that three years before. Sirius is briefly disconcerted, but brushes it off.

After lunch, Mundungus arrives with a borrowed car to drive the family, plus Mad-Eye Moody and Lupin, to St. Mungo's to visit Mr. Weasley. While at St. Mungo's, Harry, Ron, Hermione, and Ginny go for tea. Getting lost on the way to the cafeteria, they run into Gilderoy Lockhart, who still has extreme memory loss. Between Gilderoy's pleasure at seeing them, and his Healer's assumption that they are visitors, they spend time in the locked ward talking to him. While there, they see another patient, Broderick Bode, who received a potted plant as a Christmas gift. They also meet Neville and his grandmother, who are visiting Neville's parents, Frank and Alice, who, Harry knows, were once Aurors and former Order of the Phoenix members. Both were tortured into insanity with the Cruciatus curse by Sirius' Death Eater cousin, Bellatrix Lestrange. They are permanently hospitalized at St. Mungo's. Neville is embarrassed that his classmates now know about his parents, the more so when his mother shambles over and grandly gives him a wrapper from a pack of Drooble's Best Blowing Gum. Mrs. Longbottom says that Neville should be proud of how his parents defended themselves against their attackers. After Neville and his grandmother depart, Harry admits to the others that he knew about Neville's parents, but that Dumbledore had asked him to say nothing.

Analysis

Harry believes he is being possessed by Voldemort, and, as is usual for Harry when he is faced with a stressful situation, his initial response is to run away, this time convincing himself it will protect his friends. Harry is also angry, particularly at Dumbledore for ignoring him, and feels he is being treated like a small child again. Believing everyone is avoiding him, he becomes increasingly paranoid until Hermione scolds him for his childish behavior. Ginny, who actually was possessed by Voldemort, describes her own experience to him, finally convincing Harry that he is still his own man. Although Harry now believes he has not been possessed, it is strange that Dumbledore has provided him such sketchy information. Even though Dumbledore prevented Harry from leaving Grimmauld Place, he did so in a rather abrupt and distant manner that only fuels Harry's confusion and anger. Hermione continues her quest for House-elves rights, and shows kindness to Kreacher by giving him a Christmas present, although her gesture is probably unappreciated by him. His sleeping space is revealing in that it shows he remains staunchly loyal to the Black family.

The trip to St. Mungo's Hospital is insightful for Harry and shows a significant step in his maturity. Even though he has endured much sorrow over his lost parents, he is becoming acutely aware that others, such as Neville Longbottom, have also suffered terribly under Voldemort's reign of terror. Harry has kept what he knows about Neville secret, as Dumbledore requested, to respect Neville's privacy, but seeing the Longbottom family in person has a profound effect on him. And although the Longbottoms are still alive, Harry realizes that they are as lost to Neville as James and Lily Potter are to him. This must also serve as a painful reminder to the Weasley children how vulnerable their own family is.

QUESTIONS

Review 1. Why does Harry fear he is being possessed? Who convinces him otherwise?

2. Why does Harry feel he should leave Hogwarts?

3. What does Percy Weasley do that upsets Mrs. Weasley? Why does he do this?

4. What happened to Frank and Alice Longbottom?

5. Why is Neville embarrassed when he runs into Harry and the Weasley children? What does his grandmother have to say?

6. Why did Harry never tell anyone, not even Neville, what he knew about the Longbottoms?

Further Study 1. Harry unexpectedly runs into Gilderoy Lockhart, Broderick Bode, Neville, his grandmother, and his parents while at St. Mungo's Hospital. Briefly describe each person's significance to the story.

2. Why has Kreacher saved the Black family objects that Sirius had tossed out?

3. Why does Hermione give Kreacher a Christmas gift? What is his likely reaction?

GREATER PICTURE

Dumbledore's failure to explain his instructions is probably part of his ongoing attempts to prevent Voldemort recognizing that there is more to the relationship between himself and Harry than there is between himself and any other student. In this particular instance, it is exacerbated by Phineas Nigellus and his general disdain for everyone who is not a Black. His snide comments about how students should know their place and not question the headmaster does not help matters, only making Harry angrier.

Kreacher's absence is because he is off visiting Narcissa Malfoy. It is true that Dobby had left his master's house to warn Harry about the coming school year, and he apparently did so repeatedly during the year to try and convince Harry to return home, but he did have significant reason for doing so. Kreacher has no such reason; what he does have is the ability to interpret Sirius' forceful command "Get *out!*," uttered when the Weasley children and Harry arrived at Grimmauld Place, as an order to leave the house. It is never explained why he fails to respond to Sirius' summons; he certainly appears rapidly enough when Harry summons him in *Harry Potter and the Deathly Hallows*.

At St. Mungo's, a wizard portrait in the stairwell that the Trio are climbing seems to believe that Ron is inflicted with Spattergroit. Ron's response, that what he has is merely freckles, leads us to believe that this may be a fictional ailment that, as medicine advanced, proved to be like "the vapours" in the Muggle world. It will turn out later that there actually is such a disease, and that it is contagious, although Ron does not have it. This particular disease will be a minor plot point in the final book.

We will find out in a later chapter that Bode's continuing inability to speak is due to his having touched the Prophecy, while under the Imperius curse, to try and retrieve it for Voldemort. We will also discover that the potted plant that Healer Strout says someone has sent him is actually a Devil's Snare, which will later strangle him when he is tending it. One wonders why neither Strout, nor the Trio who have experienced the effects of this plant themselves, recognize the plant for what it is. The Trio's experience, of course, was in near darkness, so they can be forgiven for not recognizing the plant by daylight, but a Healer's education must concentrate on Herbology, so one would expect Strout to be aware of what the plant's characteristics are.

Chapter 24: Occlumency

SYNOPSIS

Kreacher reappears from the attic; it seems he was in Mrs. Black's old room. Harry is wary; Kreacher seems happier and Harry has caught him avidly staring at him a few times. Sirius, meanwhile, grows depressed as everyone's stay at Grimmauld Place nears its end. Professor Snape arrives at Grimmauld Place to announce that Dumbledore wants Harry to study Occlumency, the art of closing one's mind to another's intrusion. Harry agrees, but then discovers that Snape is to be teaching him. Sirius asks why Dumbledore cannot instruct Harry, but Snape responds it was Dumbledore's decision. A verbal battle escalates until Sirius and Snape are at wands drawn with Harry between trying to prevent a duel. Mr. Weasley, with the entire Weasley family and Hermione, enter. Mr. Weasley is fully recovered and has been discharged from St. Mungo's. Sirius and Snape separate, and Snape leaves, saying he expects Harry in his office at 6 o'clock Monday evening.

Harry discusses the Occlumency lessons with Ron and Hermione. Hermione says it will stop the nightmares, though Ron feels he would rather have the nightmares.

Lupin and Tonks arrive the next day to escort them back to Hogwarts. Before Harry leaves, Sirius gives him a package, saying Harry can contact him with it. Harry privately resolves never to use it, not wanting to risk exposing Sirius. Lupin summons the Knight Bus, and they are greeted by Stan Shunpike. Stan recognizes Harry, but is quickly quelled by Tonks. Arriving at Hogwarts, Lupin and Tonks leave separately.

Harry's first day back is unpleasant, partly because he dreads his evening Occlumency lesson with Snape and partly because Dumbledore's Army members keep asking him when the next meeting is. Snape has ordered him to say he has Remedial Potions on Monday nights. Zacharias Smith is particularly supercilious. When Cho Chang reminds Harry that the next Hogsmeade weekend is February 14th, he is initially mystified. It is only as she leaves, apparently disappointed, that Harry suddenly understands, and he invites her to go to Hogsmeade with him on Valentine's Day weekend. She, now delighted, accepts.

Still distrusting Snape, Harry's first Occlumency lesson begins. Voldemort is skilled in Legilimency, the ability to read others' thoughts and memories. Occlumency will help Harry block his mind. Snape removes some of his own memories and deposits them into Dumbledore's Pensieve. Harry must try and prevent Snape from penetrating his mind, but Harry's first attempts fail miserably. However, Harry recognizes the hallway he has dreamt about so frequently; it is inside the Ministry of Magic leading to the Department of Mysteries. He and Mr. Weasley raced down it last summer to his hearing, and it is the same hallway where Mr. Weasley was attacked. Snape dismisses him, telling him to come back Wednesday. As Harry leaves, he sees Snape reinserting memories from the Pensieve into his head.

Harry discusses this latest revelation with Ron and Hermione in the library. They conclude that the weapon Voldemort seeks must be hidden in the Department of Mysteries. They retreat to the common room, expecting it to be quieter, but Fred and George are demonstrating the latest Weasleys' Wizard Wheezes product, Headless Hats, that make the wearer's head invisible. Harry gives up and heads to bed. Inside the dormitory, Harry is felled by intense pain and hears wild, almost insane laughter. As he returns to awareness, his scar is burning. Harry tells Ron he saw Voldemort's thoughts again, but this time he did not feel Voldemort's anger—the Dark Lord is ecstatic. Harry questions if Occlumency is weakening his defences rather than strengthening them and wonders what made Voldemort so happy.

Analysis

The rift between Sirius and Snape can never be mended; their mutual hate is too deeply embedded, although they realize they must try to put aside their personal feelings for the Order's sake. Unfortunately for Harry, their ongoing feud will likely make his Occlumency lessons even more unpleasant, in addition to the animosity and distrust he already has for Snape. Confusion on Harry's part about why he must study this is also making it more difficult. He is further frustrated that it is Snape, rather than Dumbledore, who is teaching him. Although Harry's progress is slow, mostly due to his resistance to having to study a subject he does not fully understand, the lessons are, probably accidentally, resulting in Harry seeing clearer images. Harry recognizes the hallway he sees as the one that leads to the Department of Mysteries within the Ministry of Magic, leading him to conclude that that is where the weapon Voldemort is seeking is hidden.

Kreacher's behavior is highly suspicious. He seems to be carefully watching Harry for a reason, although just why is unknown. His devotion to the Black family is almost fanatical, as is his hatred for Sirius, as well as Harry and anyone he considers a "blood traitor." This could be significant, as though he is magically bound to serve only Sirius and to protect his secrets, Kreacher may be looking for a way around this.

Snape removing his memories just before teaching Harry is interesting. He obviously fears that Harry might glimpse something if Harry should successfully penetrate his thoughts. Which memories he is hiding is unknown; they could be something incriminating or merely personal.

Questions

Review 1. What is Occlumency? What is Legilemency?

2. Why does Snape order Harry to say that their sessions are for "remedial" Potions?

3. Why do Snape and Sirius nearly curse one another? What stops them?

4. Why doesn't Harry want to use Sirius' gift? Is he right, or being overly cautious?

Further Study 1. Why would Dumbledore want Harry to study Occlumency? Why doesn't Dumbledore instruct him rather than Snape?

2. Why does Snape remove his memories and place them in the Pensieve just before Harry's lesson? What memories might they be?

3. Why might Voldemort be feeling ecstatic?

4. What might suddenly be making Kreacher happy, and why is he watching Harry so closely?

Greater Picture

As previously mentioned, Kreacher had, in fact, interpreted Sirius' earlier order as permission to leave the house, and he had gone to Narcissa Malfoy, who was the only available member of the Black family that he still respected. It is quite likely that Kreacher's joy is due to Narcissa, or Lucius, promising that with Kreacher's assistance they would get rid of the "blood traitors and mudbloods" now occupying his mistress' house. How this would be done is not yet certain in anyone's mind, as the most recent attempt to retrieve the Prophecy has failed—we have seen the result of that attempt, Bode's spell-induced inability to speak. While the next attempt will depend on information given to Narcissa by Kreacher, it will not be formulated until after Rookwood has been freed from Azkaban, and explains to Voldemort why the first plan would not work. Rookwood will escape from prison at the end of this chapter, but there will be some delay while he, presumably, learns of the current plan and builds up his courage to approach Voldemort with bad news.

We will shortly learn that the feud between Sirius and Snape started when they were at Hogwarts as students, Sirius with James Potter, Peter Pettigrew, and Remus Lupin in Gryffindor House, and Snape in Slytherin. Sirius, largely influenced by James, had been more than a bit of a bully, picking on Snape in particular, and Snape had clearly never forgiven him. Sirius' imprisonment must have been very sweet for Snape, and Dumbledore's accepting his innocence after his escape must have been galling, particularly after Snape saw his chances of receiving an Order of Merlin slip away with Sirius' escape from Hogwarts in an earlier book.

Twice in this book, Harry will need to speak with Sirius, and will break into Professor Umbridge's office to do so. He will later find that the gift Sirius has given him here is a magic mirror that will reach Sirius at any time. This mirror would have been extremely useful, but Harry believes that his using it would expose Sirius to risk of recapture, and so deliberately forgets it. One may ask why, in this case, the mirror is provided at all? It turns out that a fairly substantial plot point of the final book will hinge upon this mirror. This small detail indicates the planning and interconnectedness that characterizes this author's work in this series.

The interaction with Cho Chang in this chapter shows once more how unprepared Harry is for a romantic entanglement. He is here so wrapped up in his own troubles that he almost fails to note that Cho has something else on her mind. The Hogsmeade visit, as we might expect given this inauspicious beginning, will be a complete failure. Much later in the book, Snape will be called away from an Occlumency class, and Harry will be left alone with the Pensieve containing Snape's memories. Curiosity will get the better of him, and Harry will see, in Snape's memories, an event that will completely change his perception of his own father. It is here that we will learn that James and Sirius were not merely wild, as mentioned earlier in this book, but were actually surprisingly vicious bullies. As mentioned above, Rookwood escapes Azkaban at the end of this chapter, as do several other Death Eaters. This will appear in the *Daily Prophet* the next morning, and Harry and Ron will conclude that this is what has made Voldemort so happy. Bode's death will appear in the paper as well, and while Harry does not remark on it at the time, it is likely that this also will have caused some small rejoicing by Voldemort.

Chapter 25: The Beetle at Bay

SYNOPSIS

Voldemort's joy is explained the next morning when the *Daily Prophet* reports a mass breakout from Azkaban Prison. Ten Death Eaters, including Antonin Dolohov, Augustus Rookwood, and Bellatrix Lestrange, looking much paler and thinner than the picture Harry had seen at Grimmauld Place, have escaped. Hermione suspects that the Dementors defected to Voldemort's side and aided the escapees. The *Prophet*, echoing Ministry rhetoric, suggests the Death Eaters have regrouped around Sirius. The *Prophet* also reports that a Ministry of Magic employee named Bode died while in St. Mungo's Hospital, apparently strangled by by a dangerous potted plant. Ron remembers seeing Bode in the same ward as Lockhart and wonders how someone could mistakenly send a Devil's Snare plant; Hermione suspects he was murdered. Harry says he met Bode at the Ministry just before his hearing. Ron says his father knew Bode, who worked in the Department of Mysteries. Looking at the front page again, Hermione says something cryptic about sending a letter, and dashes off. As Harry and Ron head to class, they run into Hagrid, who sheepishly admits he is on probation. Harry wonders how much more bad news he can stand.

School gossip now centers around the Azkaban breakout. Many Wizarding families are nearly as fearful of Death Eaters as they are Voldemort. Susan Bones, who has lost an uncle, an aunt, and several cousins to Death Eaters, receives almost as much attention as Harry. She wonders aloud to Harry how he stands it. Professor Umbridge posts a new Decree banning all Hogwarts teachers from having anything but class-related conversations with students. While teachers are prohibited from discussing the breakout with students, they are obviously talking about it among themselves, away from the staff room where Umbridge might overhear.

Umbridge continues evaluating Professor Trelawney and Hagrid, leading students to speculate that she intends to sack them. Hagrid forbids Harry, Ron, and Hermione from visiting him after dark, fearing it will get them and him into trouble. With Umbridge taking away everything Harry cares about at Hogwarts, only Dumbledore's Army is left. Harry redoubles his teaching efforts, and is mildly surprised that the group has been spurred on by the breakout. Even Zacharias Smith is working harder. Most affected, though, is Neville. Rather than becoming fearful, the news that his parents' torturers escaped causes him to work even harder; only Hermione masters the Shield Charm faster. Unfortunately, Harry's Occlumency lessons are not proceeding nearly as well. He is still unable to block Snape's probes. His scar is prickling almost continually, and he sees small flashes of Voldemort's emotions. He dates this increased sensitivity to when Snape's lessons started. Ron's opinion is that Snape is making it easier for Voldemort by deliberately not helping Harry. Hermione reminds him that Dumbledore trusts Snape, and if Dumbledore is untrustworthy, who can they trust?

Valentine's Day weekend arrives. Hermione receives an owl message and tells Harry to meet her at the Three Broomsticks at noon, then rushes off. In Hogsmeade, Cho suggests that she and Harry go to Madam Puddifoot's Tearoom. The tearoom is filled with snogging couples, embarrassing Harry. He is further embarrassed when Cho mentions that Roger Davies asked her out but she turned him down. Harry mentions he has to meet Hermione at the Three Broomsticks, but Cho misunderstands and becomes offended. Harry tries explaining that they are only friends, but Cho departs in tears.

Harry arrives early at the Three Broomsticks and finds Hagrid sitting at the bar. Unusually morose, Hagrid talks about how he and Harry are both orphans and outsiders and how important family is. Brushing off inquiries about his injuries, he heads out into the rain. Looking around, Harry spots Hermione, who is sitting with Luna Lovegood and Rita Skeeter, the disreputable tabloid journalist who wrote sensationalistic and false articles about Harry and other students during the Triwizard Tournament. Rita mentions that she would like to interview Harry for publication, but that Hermione would not allow it. Hermione says that she would allow it, that is why she has asked Rita to the Three Broomsticks. However, she wants an honest interview, not one that is slanted to make Harry appear mad. To Rita's scornful question as to who would publish it, Hermione says Luna's father will publish the interview in his paper, *The Quibbler*.

ANALYSIS

Harry continues to be baffled about girls and is taken aback when Cho Chang becomes upset and insulted over his plans to meet Hermione while on a date with her. His attempt to humorously explain that Hermione is only a platonic friend, and that Rita Skeeter's articles about their "romance" (in *Harry Potter and the Goblet of Fire*) were false, backfires and only makes matters worse. Harry, inexperienced in romance and female psychology, is simply unequipped to handle Cho's fragile emotional state, and her lingering grief over Cedric's recent death further strains their budding romance.

Umbridge's decree banning teachers and students from conversing with one another is a desperate (and ridiculous) act showing how quickly she is losing her authority and credibility with staff and students, not that she had much to begin with. The more she attempts to exert her power on the school, the more everyone becomes united against her, effectively diminishing her power.

Neville Longbottom, meanwhile, has finally broken free from the fog that has clouded his mind since early childhood. Under Harry's influence and Neville's determination to avenge his parents, his magical power, which many thought he lacked, is quickly emerging, although he still struggles to control it.

Rita Skeeter, who has fallen on hard times, has little choice but to comply with Hermione's demands that she write a truthful story about Harry and Voldemort. While it is not mentioned directly in the Three Broomsticks, readers will be aware that at the end of the previous book, Hermione had discovered that Rita was an unregistered Animagus, who took the form of a large beetle, and was able to eavesdrop on her subjects while in that form. All Animagi are legally required to be registered with the Ministry of Magic, failing to do so is a serious crime. Hermione is controlling Rita by threatening her with revelation of her Animagus status; by this means, she has prevented Rita from writing further damaging stories about Harry since the end of the last school year. Although Hermione's actions seem out-of-character here, she never hesitates to break rules or use somewhat unethical means if it serves an altruistic purpose, in this case, providing the public with the truth and rehabilitating Harry's reputation. The *Daily Prophet* has published the Ministry story about the Death Eaters escaping from Azkaban, but has been unable, apparently, to come up with an explanation for one large problem: why did the Dementors not prevent this escape? The published story says that they have escaped and are rallying around Sirius, but in Hermione's relaying of the story, offer no explanation for how the escape was made. It is likely the appearance of this large and unfilled hole in the Ministry's story that inspires Hermione to contact Rita. Hermione detests Rita and what she stands for, but is aware that Rita is a capable journalist, and so when she determines that she needs a story written professionally, she thinks first of Rita.

QUESTIONS

Review 1. Why does Hermione blackmail Rita Skeeter? What does Hermione threaten to do if Rita fails to comply?

2. Why does Cho become upset with Harry on their date in Hogsmeade? Is she overreacting or did Harry behave inappropriately?

3. Why might Umbridge be focusing so much attention on Hagrid and Trelawney during her teacher evaluations?

4. How is it believed the Death Eaters escaped from Azkaban?

Further Study 1. Why is this chapter titled, "The Beetle at Bay"?

2. Could Hagrid have avoided being placed on probation by following Hermione's advice? Explain why or why not.

3. What might have caused Neville Longbottom's inability to use magic properly? How has Harry's teaching changed him?

4. Why does Umbridge's new Decree restrict discussions between teachers and students?

5. Why would Animagi be required to be registered with the Ministry of Magic? What happens if they don't?

6. Why have there been so few Animagi?

GREATER PICTURE

It will shortly turn out that Bode had been put under the Imperius curse by Lucius Malfoy, and forced to try and retrieve the Prophecy for Voldemort. The attempt had resulted in Bode's insanity, but it would be necessary to eliminate Bode if it looked like he was regaining the power of speech, as it would then be likely that he would be asked why he had done it, and would answer honestly. While we don't ever find out that Bode's death was a murder, it seems extremely likely.

Umbridge will, in fact, manage to find or generate enough "malfeasance" to fire both Trelawney and Hagrid, but in neither case will she quite manage the effect she is looking for. Trelawney, though fired, will remain resident in Hogwarts at Dumbledore's request, and will be replaced by a teacher competent enough to avoid examination, but absolutely hateful to Umbridge on personal grounds. And the attempt to fire Hagrid will require multiple Aurors, and will badly disrupt the Astronomy O.W.L. exam.

The rift created between Harry and Cho here in Madam Puddifoot's will be closed by the publication of Harry's interview in a few days, but this will be the last date they will ever go on. While both Harry and Cho will have meetings of Dumbledore's Army which they attend, publication of the interview will result in Umbridge canceling all further Hogsmeade weekends for everyone, and before that is rescinded, Harry and Cho will have had their final fight and their romance will have ended.

Hagrid's musing about "family," and about his and Harry's similarities, is largely here triggered by his struggles to civilize his half-brother, Grawp, coupled with the awareness that he may shortly be fired and forced to leave Hogwarts. Hagrid will later force Harry and Hermione to promise to continue this process, "just visitin' now and again," should Hagrid be fired.

Harry's interview will appear in *The Quibbler* very quickly. As a result, Harry will suddenly start getting huge amounts of mail, and much of it will seem to note "holes in the official Ministry story." Hermione, it will appear, had not been alone in her noticing pieces of the story that did not add up.

Chapter 26: Seen and Unforeseen

SYNOPSIS

Luna Lovegood does not know when the interview with Harry will be published in *The Quibbler*. At dinner, Harry tells Dean Thomas, Seamus Finnigan, and Neville about the interview. All agree that Harry acted courageously. As they leave, Ron arrives from Quidditch practice, while Cho Chang walks in with Marietta Edgecombe, ignoring Harry. When Harry tells Hermione that their date went badly. Hermione suggests he approached it wrong. He should have told Cho that he really hated that he had to meet Hermione, and even though he did not really like her, he promised to go see her, ugly as she was. Harry protests that Hermione is not ugly. Harry thinks Hermione should write a book about how to understand girls, to which Ron whole-heartedly agrees. Ron and Ginny are dejected over how bad Quidditch practice was. Ginny, who is playing Seeker, says Angelina was in tears at the end. The Twins comment later to Harry and Hermione that Ginny is an excellent player. Hermione says she has been breaking into the Weasley broom shed and practicing since she was six-years-old. Fred laments that Quidditch was about the only thing keeping them at school. With the Skiving Snackbox line ready to go, they could open a store any time, and they do not need N.E.W.T.s to do that.

The following weekend's Quidditch game against Hufflepuff is awful as well, with only two mitigating factors: first, it is short, and second, due to Ginny's excellent flying, she grabs the Snitch from under the Hufflepuff's Seeker's nose, and Gryffindor loses by only ten points. That night, Harry has his recurring nightmare of long hallways and closed doors; he is awakened by Ron's loud snoring.

The following Monday at breakfast, Harry is surprised by a flock of owls delivering him mail. The *Quibbler* article was published over the weekend, and the letters seem evenly split between those who think he is insane, and others believing that his story fills the gaping holes in the Ministry's official version. Professor Umbridge is incensed, and immediately gives Harry detention and penalizes him 50 House points, as well as canceling further Hogsmeade visits. Very shortly, a new Educational Decree appears: possessing the *Quibbler* is an expulsion offence. Hermione is happy because it ensures the entire school will read it. And it appears the teachers have read it; Harry seems to be receiving extra favors from them. For Harry, the best result is that Cho seems to have forgiven him. Between classes, she says how brave he was to give the interview, and kisses him. Harry also sees Draco, Crabbe, and Goyle discussing something with another Slytherin boy in the library. Hermione says they are unable to contradict Harry's claims that their fathers are Death Eaters because they cannot admit to reading the *Quibbler* without risking being expelled.

That night, Harry has another disturbing dream in which he is Voldemort discussing Bode's death with Rookwood, one of the escaped Death Eaters. Voldemort is angry because Rookwood, who worked at the Ministry before his arrest, told him that the plan to extract something from the Ministry was doomed to fail. That is why Bode fought Malfoy's Imperius curse so strongly. Dismissing Rookwood, Voldemort asks to see Avery, who helped create the plan. Harry wakes up, screaming. Ron asks if there is another attack, but Harry says only the Death Eater Avery is in trouble. Ron wants him to tell Dumbledore, but Harry refuses, saying Dumbledore would not have had him learn Occlumency if he wanted to hear about these things.

Discussing Harry's dream the next day, Hermione speculates that Bode, under the Imperius curse, was being forced to steal the weapon at the Ministry, and, running afoul of the protective spells around it, went insane and landed in St. Mungo's. The healer there had said that Bode was recovering, so the Death Eaters probably killed him before he improved enough to recount what happened. Harry recalls that Lucius Malfoy was loitering in the Department of Mysteries the same day as his hearing. Hermione guesses that Lucius used the Imperius curse on Sturgis Podmore, which is why he was arrested trying to get through a security door at the Ministry.

Harry continues his Occlumency lessons, but his hatred for Snape prevents him from clearing his mind. Although he is making little progress, on one occasion, he briefly enters Snape's mind using a Shield Charm. The next attempt, Harry again experiences his corridors dream, but when he reaches the door, it is open for the first time. Snape breaks him from the vision, seeming concerned at what is appearing in Harry's mind. Their session is interrupted, by someone frantically screaming in the entrance hall. It is a hysterical Professor Trelawney, who has just been fired by Umbridge and ordered to leave Hogwarts immediately.

Dumbledore intervenes, and although he is unable to reverse Trelawney's dismissal, he tells Umbridge that it is within his power to allow Trelawney to remain in residence at the castle. Dumbledore also tells her that he still has the authority to replace Trelawney with his own appointment, and, to Umbridge's outrage, he introduces the Centaur, Firenze, as the new Divination teacher.

Analysis

Skeeter's article changes many peoples' opinion about Harry and Dumbledore, although others remain unconvinced that Voldemort has returned. Umbridge is not only outraged, but she realizes the story will garner support for Harry while further eroding her and the Ministry's official stance. Her attempt to ban the story from Hogwarts only ensures that it will be read by even more students, and lends credibility to Harry's claim about Voldemort. Her previous Educational Decree prohibiting faculty and students from engaging in personal conversations, and this one banning simple possession of a newspaper, shows her increasing desperation and paranoia, and will only create further solidarity and opposition against her. Dumbledore does little to interfere with Umbridge's antics, knowing that she is her own worst enemy and will likely self-destruct given enough time. However, he does prevent Umbridge from ousting Trelawney from the castle, and further infuriates and undermines her authority by appointing the Centaur, Firenze, as Trelawney's replacement. We have already heard her speaking with almost unveiled hatred against "half-breeds," and it is certain that Dumbledore is aware that Umbridge feels the same way about centaurs as she does about Hagrid.

Hermione, in passing, is absolutely correct in her belief that Umbridge's banning the Quibbler will make absolutely sure that everyone in the school reads it. It is a simple fact of human nature that curiosity is strengthened by authority's attempts to hide an item; the more prohibitions are created around a piece of information, the more people want to read it, to see what is being hidden. That said, there is nothing Umbridge could have done at this point to prevent the article from being read and discussed; her high-handed treatment of the occupants of the school, staff and students alike, has made her a prime target for rebellion, and her attempts to bluster away the truth have left obvious voids in her stories which Harry's interview fills.

Meanwhile, Harry continues to struggle with Occlumency, although it may be his resistance to learning it that causes him difficulties. One must also assume that this is partially due to the teacher assigned to him. Snape can seldom resist an opportunity to needle Harry, and if Snape's teaching methods are to be trusted, the process' first step is to clear the mind of all emotion, something that appears to be nearly impossible for Harry in Snape's presence. Not only does Harry fail to understand why he must study Occlumency, he actually prefers knowing what Voldemort is thinking. However, Harry fails to consider that the connection between him and Voldemort could be a dangerous two-way path, something Dumbledore already suspects. It also seems odd that when Harry's vision becomes more detailed and focused, Snape prevents Harry from seeing what is inside the now-open door. Snape may know what is in there, but wants to prevent Harry from seeing it. Why is unknown, but if it there is something inside that is being protected, Voldemort could learn about it from Harry's thoughts.

Harry's dream here is quite plainly not a dream, like his earlier witnessing of the attack on Mr. Weasley. We now perceive that Podmore's arrest and imprisonment, and Bode's insanity, were side effects of a plan that Voldemort had put into motion to retrieve an item from the Ministry. Voldemort learns here that this plan will be ineffective, and that a new one will have to be devised. No clue is yet available as to what the new plan will involve, however.

Questions

Review 1. Who does Dumbledore hire to replace Trelawney and why? What is Umbridge's reaction?

2. What is Hermione's theory about Bode?

3. What are the after effects of Skeeter's article in The Quibbler?

Further Study 1. Why does Dumbledore insist that Trelawney remain in the castle after Umbridge fires her?

2. Why would Umbridge ban possession of *The Quibbler*? What prompted this latest Decree? Would this be an effective measure? Why or why not?

3. Why would Snape suddenly break off Harry's vision during their Occlumency lesson? What could be behind the door?

4. Why does Snape break off Harry's vision just as he is about to enter the open door?

Greater Picture

Quite possibly, the reason that Dumbledore chooses to keep Trelawney at Hogwarts—affirmed somewhat by an exchange between Dumbledore and Harry in *Harry Potter and the Half-Blood Prince*—is that were Trelawney to fall into Death Eaters' hands, they would attempt to extract the Prophecy revealed towards the end of this book, and thus learn its "missing" second half. Whether they succeeded in retrieving the prophecy from her or not, Trelawney very likely would not survive the attempt. Dumbledore's line in chapter 20 of *Harry Potter and the Half-Blood Prince* is as follows: "*Between ourselves, she has no idea of the danger she would be in outside the castle. She does not know—and I think it would be unwise to enlighten her—that she made the prophecy about you and Voldemort, you see.*"

It is possible that the overwhelming popularity of the Harry interview may have something to do with the *Quibbler* continuing to run stories about Harry that are counter to the official Ministry line in *Harry Potter and the Deathly Hallows*. Remembering that news about Harry sold much better than stories about Crumple-Horned Snorkacks, the editor may have decided that stories about Harry, being equally counter to the Ministry as his more sensational pieces but significantly more popular, would make for a more profitable paper.

Harry's dream here marks the change of Voldemort's strategy for retrieving the Prophecy. As noted, Voldemort discovers that his plan cannot succeed, and so he must devise a new one. Voldemort learns from Rookwood that only the people named on a Prophecy are able to remove it from the shelf without being driven mad, as Bode was, and as only Harry and Voldemort are named on this prophecy, one of them must be present to physically remove the Prophecy from its shelf. Voldemort quickly begins the process of luring Harry to the Department of Mysteries by means of the connection between them, gradually bringing him mentally further into the Hall of Prophecy until he is able to show Harry the place where the Prophecy is stored, and then fabricating an event to force Harry to attend that location. It is interesting how quickly this plan is put into play; in the Occlumency lesson of this chapter, we already see that the door has opened, an indication that Voldemort is pulling Harry deeper within his mental picture of the Department.

Chapter 27: The Centaur and the Sneak

SYNOPSIS

Firenze begins teaching Divination, but because he is unable to access Trelawney's Tower, the class meets in a ground floor classroom that has been enchanted to appear as the evening forest. Firenze greets Harry, saying that it was foretold they would meet again. Harry notes a hoof-shaped bruise on Firenze's chest. Firenze explains that he would have preferred to teach students in the Forbidden Forest, but he has been banished by his herd for being too sympathetic to humans. Harry wonders if the bruise on Firenze's chest would match Bane's hoof. Firenze says Divination is often inexact, even for Centaurs. They watch the sky for tides or changes so slow and subtle that it may take ten years to determine what they have seen. He dismisses Trelawney's teachings with an abruptness that disturbs Lavender and Parvati. As the class ends, he is unconcerned that none of the students have seen anything that he had told them about.

At the end of class, Firenze takes Harry aside and asks him to tell Hagrid that what Hagrid is doing will not work. Although Harry does not understand, he promises to tell Hagrid. However, with Umbridge now attending all of Hagrid's classes, it is April before Harry can pass on Firenze's message. Hagrid replies that the attempt is working fine, and Firenze does not know what he is talking about.

Harry has begun teaching Dumbledore's Army the Patronus charm, and, overall, the class is doing well. Neville, in particular, has been a revelation to Harry, working hard to master every spell, and improving with each lesson. During the last session before Easter break, Dobby runs in to warn them that Umbridge is on her way. Harry yells for everyone to run. Most escape, but Draco Malfoy catches Harry and turns him over to Umbridge. Harry is forcibly dragged to Dumbledore's office where he finds Dumbledore, Professor McGonagall, Cornelius Fudge, Percy Weasley, and two Ministry Aurors, including Kingsley Shacklebolt, an Order of the Phoenix member. On Dumbledore's silent instruction, Harry denies knowing why he is there; Umbridge fetches their informant Cho's friend Marietta. Although Marietta tries to hide her face, giant purple pimples spelling out "SNEAK" can be seen across it, the result of Hermione's jinx to reveal snitches. When Umbridge orders her to tell what she knows, she says nothing, apparently fearing more blisters may break out on her face. Umbridge accuses Harry of holding an illegal meeting at the Hog's Head in Hogsmeade in October, saying this information came from Willy Widdershins. Professor McGonagall comments that she now understands why Willy was never charged for all those regurgitating toilets. Dumbledore points out that the meeting happened two days before the Decree and therefore was legal. Obviously, meetings since then have been banned, and Dumbledore asks if there any proof that such meetings had occurred. Harry feels something whoosh past him, and Marietta suddenly has a blank expression and is unable to speak. She silently nods her head in agreement to Dumbledore's assertion that there never was a Defence group. Frustrated, Umbridge produces the "Dumbledore's Army" parchment as proof that the Headmaster was involved. Dumbledore pleasantly admits that he was indeed building a secret wizard army, and says that this was to have been their first meeting. Fudge dispatches Percy to send the meeting notes to the *Daily Prophet*.

Dumbledore assures Fudge they will be unable to arrest him, and as Fudge orders the Aurors to take Dumbledore into custody, a white light suddenly streaks across the room, knocking out Umbridge, Fudge, Dawlish, and Shacklebolt and leaving the office in shambles. Dumbledore quickly confirms that Marietta, McGonagall, and Harry are all right, and tells McGonagall to thank Shacklebolt for modifying Marietta's memory. He tells Harry that it is important that he continue studying Occlumency with Snape, and taking hold of his Phoenix, Fawkes, disappears in a second flash of flame. Regaining consciousness, the two Aurors and Umbridge run for the Entrance Hall to try and catch Dumbledore.

ANALYSIS

Firenze, it is noted here, has a very different style of teaching Divination than does Trelawney. While Trelawney seems to be trying to teach that the future can be seen to the finest detail, in Firenze's class, there is considerably less certainty. While it is hard to be certain exactly what Trelawney actually believes, one gathers the impression that she is trying to create the impression that the Seer has some special insight into a fixed, immutable future, so what she is teaching is similar in concept to seeing through a fog bank to view a solid rock mountain. Firenze, on the other hand, is more aware of the mutability of the future, and instead seems to teach method, in a way analogous to the idea that beyond the fog there is yet more fog, but that it is possible to determine shapes in the fog and thus infer possible outcomes. We can see quite easily that Firenze's techniques are similar to those of Native shamans and medicine men, while Trelawney's are the techniques of Muggle fortune-tellers. Contrasting them, one can see that Firenze probably believes in what he teaches, but that Trelawney must be aware that she is teaching fakery. It is noted that this final meeting of Dumbledore's Army is the first one that Dean Thomas attends. This actually is more important than it seems; Harry has consistently had trouble pairing students in DA meetings for practice in dueling, and it would be noticeable if the group was suddenly evenly matched. As Marietta is, at this point, off spilling the beans to Umbridge, it is necessary that one new student arrive to prevent Harry from wondering about why they suddenly came out even.

Harry guesses that Marietta's memory has been altered even before Dumbledore says anything. Kingsley's secretly cast memory charm is apparently what Harry feels brushing past him. Additionally, Harry notices the glassy look in Marietta's eyes; he has seen that before, it is the immediate after-effect of a memory charm. Although Harry believes Dumbledore has nearly abandoned him, Dumbledore shows here how far he will go to protect Harry from Umbridge and the Ministry by taking full responsibility for Dumbledore's Army. He easily overpowers Umbridge and the others and also knocks out Kingsley Shacklebolt, an Order member, to avoid casting suspicion on him. Before disappearing, Dumbledore stresses to Harry how important it is for him to continue studying Occlumency, although Harry is still unable to understand why.

QUESTIONS

Review 1. Why was Firenze banished from his herd?

2. What does McGonagall mean when she says she understands why Willy Widdershins was never charged?

3. What happened to Marietta Edgecombe's memory in Dumbledore's office? Who was responsible and why?

4. Why does Dumbledore tell Fudge he was responsible for the D.A.? What happens in his office immediately after?

Further Study 1. What could Hagrid be doing that Firenze says is not working? Could this have anything to do with Hagrid's battered appearance? Explain.

2. Why did Marietta Edgecombe betray Dumbledore's Army? Was she truly at fault? Explain.

3. Considering that it is impossible for anyone to Disapparate in or out of Hogwarts, how was Dumbledore able to escape? Why didn't the Ministry anticipate this?

4. What does Dumbledore tell Harry just before his spectacular departure? Why does he feel it is so important?

GREATER PICTURE

We will find out shortly what Hagrid is attempting to do in the Forbidden Forest: he has brought his half-brother Grawp back with him from his encounter with the Giants, and is trying to civilize him. In later books, it will be discovered that this has, in fact, worked to some extent; in this case, Hagrid was right, and through sheer persistence has managed to accomplish something that the Centaurs, with their supposedly superior intelligence, had decided was doomed to failure.

Harry's teaching the Patronus charm will prove useful in the final book of the series, when Harry must make his way to the Whomping Willow. His way will be blocked by Dementors, and Harry, Ron, and Hermione will be unable to create Patronuses. The Dementors will be repelled by two DA members, Luna and Ernie Macmillan. It is mentioned in this chapter that the parchment containing the list of Dumbledore's Army members was retrieved by Pansy Parkinson. This also is more important a connection than it would initially seem. Draco Malfoy, in the next book, will be given a task by Voldemort, who will tell him how to get into the Room of Requirement, that being a nominally secret place where Draco can carry out his instructions. Voldemort, having discovered only that one form of the Room, will believe that the Room is simply a "junk warehouse" and has no other purpose. Harry will find this aspect of the Room himself when he is looking to hide something later in that book. Draco, having been coached by Voldemort, will find only the "junk warehouse" aspect of the Room, and so will have a limited idea of what it can do. If it had been Draco who went into the Room of Requirement to retrieve the list, he would have likely figured out the full function of the Room, and would have been likely to discover it as the hiding place of the revived Dumbledore's Army in the final book. As he would have only known how to open its junk warehouse aspect, and as the room will not open for someone who is asking for an aspect other than the one that is already in use (as we find out in *Harry Potter and the Half-Blood Prince*), Draco, if he had guessed where the new DA was hiding, would have been unsuccessful in getting the door to open, and likely would have guessed that it had simply been sealed after the events at the end of the sixth book.

Chapter 28: Snape's Worst Memory

SYNOPSIS

Educational Decree Number Twenty-Eight makes Umbridge Headmistress, although she is unable to enter Dumbledore's office; it has magically sealed itself off from any but the true Headmaster. For now, she must continue using her old office. Umbridge appoints an Inquisitorial Squad composed of Slytherin students, including Draco, empowered to enforce rules and deduct House points. Montague, an Inquisitorial Squad member, attempts to dock House points from Fred and George Weasley, but they force him into an old, broken Vanishing Cabinet. Hermione is aghast, but Fred says that with Dumbledore gone, they no longer care about getting in trouble. They advise Harry, Ron, and Hermione to go into lunch to avoid accusations of being involved with Phase One. Filch takes Harry aside, saying that the "Headmistress" wants to see him. Filch exults over how things will change with Umbridge in charge, and that a new Decree will restore corporal punishment; Umbridge has obviously recruited Filch to her side. Umbridge herself is uncharacteristically sweet, offering Harry something to drink, insisting he

Chapter 28: Snape's Worst Memory

choose something. Harry notes that she hides the tea preparation, then recalls the Mad-Eye Moody impostor the previous year, and his refusal to drink anything offered to him. Harry carefully pretends to drink the tea. When Umbridge asks where Dumbledore is, Harry says he does not know. Umbridge then asks where Sirius Black is, and Harry responds that he does not know that either. Umbridge says that she knows Sirius was talking to Harry, and she would have Harry arrested if she had any proof. She also says that all Hogwarts fireplaces are being monitored except hers.

A loud explosion interrupts. Outside, Harry sees an enormous conflagration of exploding fireworks. Harry ducks behind a tapestry and finds Fred and George, who admit they are the culprits. The fireworks cause so much mayhem that school operations are continually disrupted. The faculty purposely do nothing to help Umbridge regain control, forcing her to personally attend to each incident. At day's end, Harry sees a disheveled Professor Umbridge leaving Professor Flitwick's classroom. Flitwick tells her, "I could have got rid of the sparklers myself, of course, but I wasn't sure whether I had the *authority*..." and shuts the door in Umbridge's face.

Harry has another dream that he is again in the Department of Mysteries. This time he goes through a door and into a room. Inside are rows of shelves containing small, glass spheres, but before reaching one, he is awakened by an exploding firework.

The next day, Harry runs into Cho Chang in the hall as he heads for his Occlumency lesson. Cho regrets that it was her friend Marietta who exposed Dumbledore's Army, although she defends what Marietta did, saying Marietta's mother works for the Ministry of Magic. Harry angrily responds that Ron's father does also. Cho is upset that Hermione secretly jinxed the parchment, believing it a dirty trick. Harry retorts that the jinx was brilliant and any reason for betraying the D.A. is inexcusable. As tears well up in Cho's eyes, Harry sternly warns her not to start crying again. Deeply offended, Cho storms off.

Harry's Occlumency session is interrupted when Malfoy arrives with a message that Umbridge needs to see Snape—Montague has reappeared, jammed inside a toilet. Snape departs, but before Harry can leave, he sees a shimmering light reminiscent of his dream about the Ministry coming from the Pensieve. What memories has Snape been hiding? Is it something to do with his dreams about the Ministry? Looking inside, Harry sees a young James Potter and Sirius Black at Hogwarts. They are cruelly tormenting their classmate, Severus Snape, by suspending him upside down in mid-air, exposing his dingy underwear. Lily Evans intervenes and berates James and Sirius for their deplorable behavior. James offers a deal—if she goes out with him, he will never hurt Snape again—to which she angrily declines. The humiliated Snape resents Lily's help and insultingly calls her a "Mudblood." Harry is appalled by his father's bullying, but before he can consider it further, the present-day Snape yanks him from the Pensieve. Furious, Snape demands that he never reveal what he has seen to anyone, and orders him to leave.

ANALYSIS

Due to the Twin's magical pranks, school operations disintegrate into chaos; Umbridge is overwhelmed by the non-stop interruptions that she must personally attend to and is unlikely to regain control if they continue. The faculty, disliking her and resentful over Dumbledore's unwarranted dismissal, passively do nothing to assist her. Harry and Cho Chang's relationship abruptly ends over the incident involving Marietta Edgecombe, although their disparate personalities, shaky circumstances, and differing expectations had derailed them almost from the beginning. Harry, inexperienced in romance, is unable to cope with Cho's extreme emotional needs and only wants an uncomplicated relationship, although his reaction to her was unnecessarily harsh and reflects his bouts of immature behavior. A still-grieving Cho was seeking comfort and support while attempting to fill the void caused by Cedric Diggory's tragic death (in *Goblet of Fire*). She may also have been attracted to Harry's celebrity, rather than to him. Regardless, neither could fulfill the other's needs or expectations.

Harry is deeply disturbed after viewing Snape's memory in the Pensieve. Although he admires and loves his father, he is appalled that someone could treat another person that way, even Snape. Seeing James and Sirius behaving as bullying tyrants who cruelly torment and demean Snape purely for their own amusement has severely shaken his belief that his father was a good man.

QUESTIONS

Review 1. Why does Harry become angry with Cho Chang? Was he justified and what is the result?

2. Why and how do Fred and George revolt against Umbridge?

3. Why do the other Hogwarts teachers do nothing to help Umbridge regain control of the school?

4. Why would Snape insult Lily when she was attempting to help him?

Further Study 1. If Umbridge wanted to catch Harry talking to Sirius, why does she warn him that all the fireplaces are being monitored?

2. Why would Snape hold a grudge against Harry for something James Potter and Sirius Black did to him before Harry was born?

3. Why does Harry react so strongly to what he sees in Snape's Pensieve?

GREATER PICTURE

Snape's behavior towards Lily, in the Pensieve memory, probably seems typical of how he likely treated most classmates outside his own Slytherin House. However, Snape's memories in the final book reveal that he and Lily were once close friends, making his reaction to her assistance initially seem puzzling. Lily, disenchanted by his associations with future Death Eaters and his pro-pureblood beliefs, had gradually distanced herself from him, resulting in his angry outburst towards her.

Harry's forced re-evaluation of his own father actually foreshadows events in the final book. Here, we see that Harry had idolized his father, assuming from all he had been told, and his own personal beliefs, that James had been all good, with at most an admixture of mischief. In Snape's memories, he learns that his father was a bully, unfairly tormenting Snape in particular. Harry feels betrayed, as his father was not who Harry believed him to be. To resolve this disparity, Harry feels that he must speak with Sirius, to find out more about James' school days, and will break into Umbridge's office to do so. In the final book, Harry will learn some similarly unpleasant truths about the young Dumbledore, who he also has placed on a pedestal. Unfortunately, he will not have anyone to turn to there to find the truth of the matter; it will only be at the end of the book that he meets Dumbledore's brother Aberforth, and learns the truth about that part of Dumbledore's life.

Montague's mishap actually ends up being a fairly major plot point in the next book. The Vanishing Cabinet into which he was pushed, which is the one which Peeves knocked over in Harry's second year, is twin to one at Borgin and Burkes which Harry had actually hidden inside earlier that same year. Because the Vanishing Cabinet is broken, Montague is trapped, but he does recognize that he is sometimes in Borgin and Burkes, sometimes in Hogwarts. Draco gathers this information from him in the Hospital Wing, and it is somehow reported to Voldemort. As a result, Draco is set the task of repairing the Hogwarts cabinet, that it may be used to allow Death Eaters to enter the school.

Chapter 29: Careers Advice

Synopsis

As Spring Break begins, Hermione wonders why Harry's Occlumency lessons have abruptly ended; Harry, disturbed by the revelations about his father, claims that Snape had said he was good enough. Hermione, seeing that Harry is upset, asks if he had had a row with Cho. Harry admits they fought about Marietta. This starts Ron ranting about Marietta, which allows Harry time to brood over what he saw in the Pensieve. Harry continues to fret about his father, trying to reconcile what others have said about James with the images from Snape's memory. Ginny suggests talking to Cho, but Harry, without telling her why, says he would rather talk with Sirius, though that is clearly impossible. Ginny says that growing up with Fred and George leads one to believe that nothing is impossible.

Meanwhile, a notice has been posted announcing career counseling for all Fifth Years. Each student is to meet with their head of House to discuss careers. While Harry, Ron, and Hermione are looking through career choices, Fred and George approach saying Ginny told them that Harry wants to contact Sirius. They have a diversion planned so Harry can use the fireplace in Umbridge's office to contact Sirius. Hermione worries it is too dangerous, but Ron feels it is Harry's decision. Fred says the diversion will go off at 5:00 P.M. Monday.

On Monday, Hermione repeatedly warns Harry that breaking into Umbridge's office is too risky, but Harry is determined. After Potions class, Harry arrives for his Careers Advice meeting with Professor McGonagall only to find Umbridge sitting in, taking notes on her clipboard. Harry tentatively suggests that he wants to be an Auror, a Dark Wizard catcher, and McGonagall begins outlining what courses he needs to take. Umbridge interrupts to say Harry should consider another occupation because his grades in her Defence Against the Dark Arts class are too low, and the Ministry would never hire someone with a criminal record. A furious McGonagall retorts that Harry was found innocent and has always received high marks from *competent* Defence Against the Dark Arts teachers, and vows to do everything in her power to help him become an Auror. Umbridge is livid and accuses McGonagall of supporting Dumbledore's efforts to depose Fudge, and make herself Deputy Minister and Hogwarts' Headmistress. McGonagall responds that Umbridge is raving and dismisses Harry, who leaves as their heated argument escalates.

Seeing Umbridge's angry mood in the succeeding Defence Against the Dark Arts class, Hermione again urges Harry to forget about breaking into her office. But Harry cannot wait until summer before talking to Sirius, and, hearing the diversion upstairs, dons his Invisibility Cloak and enters Umbridge's office. Using Floo powder, Harry sends his head to Grimmauld Place. Lupin greets him, then gets Sirius, who is apparently looking for Kreacher. Harry asks Sirius about the incident with his father and Snape. Sirius admits that he and James were once bullies, explaining that they were uncaring, foolish, and reckless youths, although Snape was not such an innocent victim as he appears. He says they outgrew their bullying ways and stresses that James matured into a kind, compassionate man. His explanation does little to soothe Harry, however, who knows he would never behave like his father at that age. When Harry mentions he is no longer studying Occlumency, Lupin strongly urges him to resume the lessons. Hearing footsteps, Harry pulls himself from the fire and hides under the Invisibility cloak. Filch enters Umbridge's office to search for the necessary forms to authorize whipping a student.

Exiting Umbridge's office, Harry discovers that Fred and George have been caught and are more or less at bay in the Entrance Hall. Umbridge threatens severe punishment, but the Twins proclaim they have had enough. Summoning their confiscated brooms, they hop on and tell students to visit their new joke shop in Diagon Alley. They give Peeves the Poltergeist a final salute, telling him, "Give her hell from us, Peeves," then zoom off, leaving Hogwarts for good.

Analysis

Umbridge is well aware that Harry was exonerated of all (trumped up) charges for using underage magic, and she has deliberately graded him low in her class. She obviously has ulterior motives for attempting to derail Harry's career plans, and she seems to deliberately engage McGonagall in a head-on confrontation over it. Now that Dumbledore has been ousted, Umbridge may be trying to eliminate his loyal Hogwarts staff and friends, including McGonagall, who she likely

Chapter 29: Careers Advice

views as the most formidable threat to her unrelenting drive to control the school. Harry's hesitating about suggesting Auror as a career, we can see plainly, is due to his fear that he is not good enough to be accepted into an elite group. He is heartened immediately when McGonagall does not dismiss this ambition, and is elated when McGonagall, admittedly in reaction to Umbridge's argument, promises to help Harry qualify for that position. Harry is still, to some extent, unsure of his place in the Wizarding world, and uncertain what his future will be; McGonagall's promise reassures him that he not only has a place, but a future, in that world. Although Snape's extreme reaction to Harry witnessing his worst memory is unreasonable, Harry now understands why Snape hates Sirius and his father, and, by extension, him. It also alters Harry's opinion about James, the father he has loved and admired unconditionally, but never knew. However, the father Harry idolizes is a somewhat idealized figure that he has based on other peoples' favorable recollections, and not the bullying boy he views in the Pensieve, although neither version is completely accurate. Despite Sirius' explanation that he and James were uncaring, arrogant youths who acted idiotically, and his assertion that James matured into a kind, compassionate adult, Harry has difficulty reconciling his father's abysmal behavior when he compares it to his own benevolent nature at the same age. But Harry fails to realize that youth are not born to behave in any particular manner, and that each person's unique experiences and influences results in different actions and attitudes that eventually shapes them into the adults they become. James was a pampered, only child in a wealthy household, probably with few cares, responsibilities, or consideration for others; in some ways, he shares traits with Draco Malfoy, although it is to James' credit that the cruel bully that Harry witnessed matures into the good man he became. Harry's innate compassion stems more from his own mistreatment and hardships, which he would never wish to be inflicted on others. Harry also neglects to consider that he is descended also from his mother. Although he loves Lily as much as James, he has, perhaps, overlooked and under appreciated her accomplishments, abilities, and influences on his life and instead focuses more on his father. Harry also does not realize that James' transformation likely was partially due to Lily's influence.

Although the Twins are caught, Umbridge's pleasure in the capture and planned punishment is thwarted when they hop onto their brooms and, exiting Hogwarts, proclaim they have had enough. Despite their spotty academic achievement and meager O.W.L.s, the Twins are powerful and talented wizards, and their claims that there is little left for them to learn at school is certainly accurate. Molly Weasley almost certainly will be distraught when she hears what happened, believing that without graduating, their futures are grim. But Fred and George are well on their way to starting their own successful business, thanks to Harry's financial backing.

Fred and George Weasley are the only students to successfully give Peeves an order in the known history of the school. This might be because the order they give is so closely in line with Peeves' natural inclination.

QUESTIONS

Review   1. Why did Snape end Harry's Occlumency lessons? What are the possible consequences for Harry?

2. What might be the real reason Umbridge advises Harry to pursue another occupation? What does McGonagall have to say?

3. Is there any validity to Umbridge's accusation that McGonagall wants to take over as Headmistress, and what might be behind it? What is McGonagall's response?

4. Why does Harry want to talk to Sirius about his father? What does Sirius tell him?

5. Why is Harry still conflicted about his father after talking to Sirius? Is Harry's opinion of the youthful James Potter's behavior unfair? If so, why?

6. Why are Fred and George willing to create a distraction so Harry can use the fireplace in Umbridge's office? Is it just to help Harry? Were they concerned if they were caught?

Further Study   1. What does Harry think about his father after talking to Sirius?

2. What should Harry do about Snape? Some readers have suggested that, having discovered the grounds for Snape's dislike, Harry should apologize for having viewed his memories. Others believe that Harry's knowledge of this event changes nothing, Harry's and Snape's mutual dislike would prevent this happening or being useful if it did. What is your opinion?

3. Has Harry tended to overlook his mother's accomplishments and influence on him? If so, why?

GREATER PICTURE

This chapter may be foreshadowing Harry and Ginny's relationship in the next book. Though Harry feels hurt and somewhat betrayed at the thought that his father was not the man that everyone had said he was, and dreads the thought that Snape might be right about him, it is Ginny who manages to cheer Harry up by suggesting that talking to Sirius about it is not as impossible as it seems. In addition, after his talk with Ginny, Harry comments to himself that he felt good, but does not know whether it is because he had "spoken aloud the wish that had been burning inside him for a week," to speak to Sirius, or if it's the chocolate. The reader may suspect that it is partly Ginny's presence, partly the fact that she seems to believe that talking to Sirius is possible.

Harry's idealized mental image of his father is mainly based on others' recollections about James Potter, as well as his own feelings. In the previous chapter, Harry witnessed an event in James' early life that directly contradicts Harry's understanding. Sirius explains that Harry witnessed James' behavior when he was only fifteen, to which Harry exclaims, "I'm fifteen!" Harry has yet to grasp what Dumbledore told him at the end of *Harry Potter and the Chamber of Secrets*: "It is our choices, Harry, that show what we truly are, far more than our abilities." James ultimately chose the path leading to his fully admirable maturity.

Harry is not only James Potter's son, but also Lily Potter's. In *Harry Potter and the Deathly Hallows,* in Snape's memories, we hear Snape commenting, "He is his father all over again—," to which Dumbledore replies, "In looks, perhaps, but his deepest nature is much more like his mother's." Harry has mainly focused on his father's legacy, largely ignoring his mother's contributions, possibly in part because everyone comments on how extraordinarily like his father he looks. Also, boys typically identify more closely with their fathers. Snape certainly has trouble getting past Harry and James' similar physical appearance, however unfair that is to Harry. It is apparent that Harry fails to recognize that his gentle nature and consideration for others at age 15 reflects Lily, rather than James. It is interesting to note that Harry's expectation that James at 15 would behave the same way Harry does at 15 will be repeated. In *Harry Potter and the Deathly Hallows,* Harry will discover that at 17, the same age Harry is then, Dumbledore, with Grindelwald, had been planning what amounts to conquest of the Muggle world "for the greater good." At that point, Harry will discover that another of his heroes had been, in his youth, someone radically different from what they later became. Even at 17, and with his father's example before him, Harry will not yet fully accept Dumbledore's maxim that choices matter more than abilities. It is perhaps of interest that this maxim comes from Dumbledore's personal experience.

Chapter 30: Grawp

Synopsis

Fred and George's departure quickly grows into Hogwarts' legend over the next few days. Even those who were there are almost convinced that the twins dive-bombed Umbridge with Dungbombs as they left. To add to the legend, there are now two broom-shaped holes in Umbridge's office door. The twins also left a large swamp in the fifth-floor corridor, which the teachers seem unable to remove, although Harry suspects Professor McGonagall or Professor Flitwick could remove it if they wished. A grumbling Filch is pressed into duty punting students across the swamp in between classes. With Fred and George gone, many students are trying for the job of chief troublemaker, with the result that the corridors are overwhelmingly redolent of dungbombs and stink pellets, and it becomes fashionable to invoke a Bubble-Head Charm on oneself before leaving the classroom. Someone has also put a Niffler into Umbridge's office despite her new door, and having destroyed the office, it tried to gnaw the rings off her stubby fingers. Umbridge, Filch, and the new Inquisitorial Squad are run ragged attending to the disturbances, but even the Inquisitorial Squad fall prey to the occasional jinx that takes them to the Hospital Wing. It seems also that Fred and George sold a huge number of Skiving Snackboxes, as Umbridge has only to enter a class for the students to break out in fevers, vomiting, bloody noses, and fainting spells. And Peeves is everywhere, causing havoc. The staff, except Filch, seem unwilling to help Umbridge; Harry saw Professor McGonagall walk past Peeves who was unscrewing a crystal chandelier, and he was almost sure he heard her telling Peeves it unscrewed the other way. Finally, Montague remains confused and disoriented from his sojourn in the toilet.

Ron worries that his mother will blame him for the twins' departure. When he and Hermione wonder how they can afford to open their own joke shop in Diagon Alley, Harry finally confesses that he gave them his Triwizard winnings. Hermione asks Harry when he restarts Occlumency lessons. Harry had told Hermione and Ron about Sirius wanting him to start Occlumency again, because he still did not want to tell them about what he had seen in the Pensieve. But now Hermione is nagging him to restart lessons with Professor Snape, and Harry does not want to explain why that will not happen.

The final Quidditch match is Gryffindor vs. Ravenclaw, and Ron is nervous. The match has barely started, however, and Ron has only let in one goal when Harry and Hermione are quietly approached by Hagrid, who says he has something important to show them in the Forbidden Forest. Hagrid leads them into the forest, carrying a large crossbow. The centaurs, he explains, are still angry about Firenze working for Dumbledore, and they were attacking Firenze when Hagrid intervened. Hagrid says he expects to be sacked soon. Umbridge accused Hagrid of putting a Niffler in her office because it was a magical creature. She has been trying to fire him anyway. He says he will need their help if he is sacked. Harry promises to help. Hagrid leads them to a small glen and a sleeping Giant. Hagrid says its name is Grawp, and it is his half-brother. He brought Grawp back from the mountains with him after his failed mission with Madam Maxime to recruit the giants against Voldemort. Grawp was mistreated by the other Giants for being "small"—only sixteen feet tall. Hagrid has been attempting to civilize Grawp and teach him English, although the Giant only seems capable of pulling trees up by their roots. Hagrid admits that Grawp is still half-wild, and he has had difficulty controlling him, which explains his battered appearance when he returned to Hogwarts and why Grawp is tied up. Hagrid claims Grawp is much tamer now, and he asks if Harry, Ron, and Hermione will visit and help teach him English. Grawp wakes up, and Hagrid introduces Harry and "Hermy," though it is hard to tell how much Grawp comprehends. Harry now understands Firenze's warning to Hagrid that, "the attempt is not working."

Centaurs appear and threaten Hagrid, angry that he brought a Giant into their forest. They are also still furious that Firenze has *betrayed* them by entering into "human servitude." Hagrid is not intimidated, and the Centaurs agree to let him pass only because he is accompanied by innocent "foals" (Harry and Hermione). When Harry and Hermione return to the Quidditch game, they hear a new version of "Weasley is Our King," only it is not the Slytherins singing it. Gryffindor has won the match and the Quidditch Cup, apparently thanks to Ron's suddenly superb Keeping.

Analysis

It is interesting to note that it is the absence of Fred and George which apparently causes the tremendous increase in mischief. The explanation provided by the author, that many were vying for the post of chief troublemaker, seems rather weak; however, it is possibly an accurate description of the actual events. It is unlikely that students are actually vying for this particular position, but it is likely true that those students who would be pulling pranks have been held in check by Fred and George. If one is in a school with a master practical joker like Fred or George, one tends to avoid pulling pranks because one might be seen as simply a poor imitation of the master(s). With Fred and George gone, that restraint is no longer there. The hatred of Umbridge for her repression, plus her obvious ineffectiveness dealing with the fireworks and the swamp, will tend to inspire the less-enlightened pranksters to break out the dungbombs, and the other teachers' unwillingness to assist Umbridge in her futile attempts to keep order will make the problems worse.

Peeves' increased activity is mentioned, and possibly is worthy of discussion as well. This is the first time that Peeves has been noted as being more active, despite Professor Dumbledore's earlier absences. We are led to believe that Peeves can be controlled only by Dumbledore and the Bloody Baron, though the author, in an interview, has suggested that Dumbledore does not actually control Peeves. From his actions in this chapter, we may begin to suspect that Peeves' activities could be seen as an indicator of the overall level of satisfaction in the school; he is less active when the population is happy.

We suddenly have an explanation for a number of things that we have been wondering about, and many things that have happened but have not caused significant concern. With the revelation of Grawp's existence, we suddenly see why Hagrid was so late in returning from his mission, why he is always injured, why he seems to be spending more time than usual in the Forbidden Forest, and why he is suddenly thinking more about family than he has been previously. Other commentators have mentioned that one of Rowling's great strengths is in handling the set-up and the pay-off, leading you up to the fact, then revealing it at a particularly satisfying time. This is a classic example; we've heard of Hagrid's expedition to the Giants, and seen the aftermath of that visit, and now suddenly the explanation for that aftermath is revealed. This is only one of a number of cases, some spanning several books, where we see the build-up to an event followed by the wholly satisfactory revelation.

Of all the characters in the Harry Potter series, probably none are as lonely and isolated as Hagrid. Not even Harry's unhappy family life, Sirius Black's difficult childhood, or Remus Lupin's social ostracism compares to Hagrid's utter alienation. Many wizards either are indifferent, fear him, or, like Umbridge, consider him sub-human. Even though most Hogwarts students and staff like him and accept him as an equal, he has never shared a close relationship with anyone there other than Harry, who knows what it is like to lack a family. Harry has been his closest friend and acts as a surrogate relative. Now Hagrid has an opportunity to have a real family by having brought back his half-brother, although it remains doubtful whether Grawp can ever be completely civilized. However, Hagrid faces losing this opportunity if Umbridge succeeds in dismissing him, and Hagrid turns to the Trio for help, although it is uncertain if there is much they can actually do.

We see here also that Ron is able to perform quite well once he has his confidence; it seems that once he managed to find his stride, he managed to defend the goal posts quite well. We don't yet know what has happened; presumably we will find out next chapter, but here we see that Ron is carrying the Quidditch Cup and being carried on Gryffindor's shoulders, so we can safely bet that it is his performance that has saved the game for Gryffindor.

Questions

Review 1. What does Hagrid want to show Harry and Hermione? Why does he show it to them now?
2. What does Hagrid ask the Trio to do? Is this putting them in danger?
3. Why do the Centaurs threaten Hagrid? Why do they let him pass?
4. Why has the demeaning Slytherin song changed its meaning, and who is singing it now?

Further Study 1. Why did Hagrid bring Grawp back with him? What does he hope to accomplish, and is it possible? 2. Why do the Centaurs consider what Firenze did a betrayal? Is it?

Greater Picture

In this chapter we learn of the current temper of the Centaurs. Already aloof, they have been angered by Firenze's defection, and Hagrid's interfering in his punishment for that defection. Hermione will later use this against Umbridge; trapped, she will invent a weapon that Umbridge has to possess. She will place that weapon in the Forbidden Forest, and in search of it will lead Umbridge into the realm of the Centaurs. There, Umbridge's hatred of "half-breeds" will result in the Centaurs dealing with her.

Hermione, hearing in this chapter that the Centaurs do not war against "foals," will think herself and Harry safe as they bring Umbridge to the Centaurs, but will not reckon with the Centaur's intellect. They will see that Hermione had tricked them into entering a purely Human conflict, and will be on the verge of sending Hermione and Harry to the same fate as Umbridge. Grawp's presence in the Forest will be the only thing that will save them; having broken free of his chains, he is roaming the forest looking for Hagrid, and will stumble across the clearing where Harry, Hermione, and the Centaurs are, breaking the deadlock and allowing Harry and Hermione to escape. It is in the next chapter that we learn the details of Ron's almost-miraculous improvement in Keeping. While this does provide a much-needed boost to Ron's confidence, it will prove to be insufficient in the long run. In the next book, Harry will feel that Ron is so lacking in confidence as Keeper that he will have to artificially boost his confidence.

Chapter 31: O.W.L.s

SYNOPSIS

Ron's elation over his performance and Gryffindor's victory lasts well into the next day. Harry and Hermione let him enjoy it before telling him they missed the match because Hagrid dragged them away to tell them about Grawp. Ron is incredulous that Hagrid brought back a Giant and reluctant to help care for one, much less teach it English. "He's lost his mind!" Hermione concurs, but says they promised to help Hagrid. The Fifth Year Ordinary Wizarding Level examinations begin, and Harry is relieved that many questions cover familiar information. In the first week, he performs creditably in Charms, Transfiguration, Herbology, and Defence Against the Dark Arts. Harry receives an extra mark in this last exam for producing a Patronus when requested. Professor Umbridge, who is observing, seems pleased, but Harry does not care. After her Ancient Runes exam, Hermione reports that someone put another Niffler into Umbridge's office; it will be another excuse to sack Hagrid.

The following Monday, Harry does reasonably well in the Potions exam as Snape is not present. Tuesday is Care of Magical Creatures, and Wednesday morning is Astronomy. Both Harry and Ron fail Divination miserably on Wednesday afternoon. During the evening Astronomy practical exam, Harry spies Umbridge and a group heading for Hagrid's hut. A battle breaks out, and the group emerges, attempting to stun Hagrid with their wands, although his massive body deflects the spells. Professor McGonagall runs to Hagrid's aid, but she is hit by several stunning spells and knocked off her feet. Hagrid escapes, and McGonagall is rushed to the hospital wing. A distressed Harry, and the other Gryffindors who witnessed this, discuss it later in the common room. Hermione comments that the Nifflers found in Umbridge's office will be used as a pretext for sacking him. Lee Jordan admits that he levitated them into her office, but Hermione says it does not matter; Umbridge hates what she calls "half-breeds" and would have sacked him anyway. The Common room does not clear out until four in the morning, and Harry's three hours of restless sleep are filled with vengeful dreams.

Harry is exhausted the next day and falls asleep during the afternoon History of Magic exam. He experiences another vision, seeing himself entering the room with the glass orbs. Inside, Voldemort's voice orders a black, shapeless heap on the floor to pick up an orb. The "heap" is Sirius, being tortured by Voldemort.

ANALYSIS

Ron's opinion about the wisdom of taking on the gigantic task of civilizing Grawp clearly echoes Harry and Hermione's. Because Hagrid is not present, he alone is able to verbalize the doubts of the entire Trio, and does so with his usual outspokenness. The author points up Hermione's unhappiness with the fact that they have promised to take this on, in the event that Hagrid gets sacked. Hagrid does get sacked, most dramatically, and the Trio now will have the responsibility of visiting Grawp occasionally, despite the fact that they are not allowed in the Forbidden Forest, and against the wishes of the Centaurs.

QUESTIONS

Review 1. What is Ron's reaction when Harry and Hermione tell him about Grawp?
2. What does Harry witness during his Astronomy exam? What happens to McGonagall?
3. What does Harry "see" during his History of Magic O.W.L. exam?

Further Study 1. Umbridge seems pleased when Harry conjures a Patronus in his Defence Against the Dark Arts O.W.L.. Why? This is not something that she has taught; why does she not wonder where he had learned it?

GREATER PICTURE

Following his dream, Harry will be in a panic over Sirius, positive he is in danger, but it seems there is no one he can to turn to. Umbridge is in complete control, Dumbledore and Hagrid are now gone, Harry will shortly find that Professor McGonagall has gone to St. Mungo's, and there seems little that Ron and Hermione can do. However, Harry is overlooking the one person left who can help him: Professor Snape, also an Order member. He has also forgotten (deliberately) the package Sirius gave him at Christmas, which Sirius had said would be a way to reach him at any time.

We will shortly find that Harry's dream has been created by Voldemort, as a means of luring Harry into the Department of Mysteries at the Ministry. Voldemort has been seeking an object, a Prophecy, which is contained in one of the small glass orbs that Harry sees in his vision. These orbs are charmed such that only those to whom they refer can safely touch them; Voldemort knows that only he and Harry can retrieve the prophecy from the shelf where it lies, and has determined to trick Harry into doing it for him.

In the rush of events, the Trio will quite forget their promise to visit Grawp. However, the time involved will be very short: the Astronomy exam, we see here, is Wednesday night, and that is when Hagrid is sacked; the History of Magic exam, Friday afternoon, is when Harry has his dream, and they will visit the Ministry this same evening. That visit will culminate with a battle, which will result in the reappearance of Dumbledore and the Ministry admitting the return of Voldemort. One of the demands Dumbledore makes is that the Ministry stop chasing his groundskeeper, meaning that Hagrid is free to return to Hogwarts only two days after having been driven away.

Chapter 32: Out of the Fire

Synopsis

Harry is frantic about Sirius, and rushes to the infirmary to see the only member of the Order of the Phoenix that he can think of: Professor McGonagall. Madam Pomfrey says that Professor McGonagall has been transferred to St. Mungo's Hospital. Harry is unsure what to do; Dumbledore, McGonagall, and Hagrid are now gone. He runs to find Ron and Hermione. Convinced his vision is real, as the vision of Ron's dad had been real before Christmas, Harry wants to go immediately to the Ministry of Magic in London to save Sirius. Hermione warns him that the vision could be false, and suggests that Harry seems to "have a bit of a—a—*saving-people thing*." She urges him to verify if Sirius actually is in the Ministry and reluctantly suggests using Umbridge's fireplace to contact Grimmauld Place to see if Sirius is there. Ginny and Luna Lovegood, who had joined the conversation having heard Harry's shouting, volunteer to help.

Ron volunteers to distract Umbridge, while Ginny and Luna stand guard outside her office. Harry and Hermione, under Harry's Invisibility Cloak, sneak into the empty office. Harry uses Floo powder to contact Grimmauld Place. Kreacher, the Black family House Elf, answers and tells Harry that Sirius has gone out. Harry demands to know if Sirius has gone to the Department of Mysteries, and Kreacher says Sirius did not tell him, but adds gleefully that Sirius will never come back. Umbridge suddenly yanks Harry from the fireplace, demanding to know who he is speaking to. Ron, Luna, Hermione, Ginny, and Neville have been captured by Umbridge's Inquisitorial Squad.

When Harry refuses to answer Umbridge, she sends Malfoy to fetch Snape. Harry suddenly remembers that Snape is an Order member. Snape arrives, and Umbridge asks him to use Veritaserum on Harry. Snape says that he gave Umbridge his entire stock, reminding her that three drops would have been sufficient; it will take a month to brew more. Harry desperately yells, "He's got Padfoot at the place where it's hidden." Umbridge asks what this means; Snape coldly replies he has no idea what Potter is blathering about, and leaves.

Umbridge prepares to use the Cruciatus curse on Harry to extract information. She admits to having sent the Dementors to his home last summer. As she is about to curse him, Hermione bursts out "crying" and blurts that Harry was contacting Professor Dumbledore about a weapon he had the students build for him. They were trying to let him know it is ready, but hadn't reached him. Umbridge demands to see the weapon. Hermione agrees to lead her to it, but convinces her to leave the members of the Inquisitorial Squad in her office, guarding the other students.

Analysis

Hermione believes Sirius may not actually be in danger and warns Harry that he is possibly being lured into a trap. She is not being overly cautious; Harry often acts rashly and without considering the possible consequences. Hermione, with her mention of a "saving-people thing," is here verbalizing an aspect of Harry's personality which has been obvious to the reader throughout, but which Harry himself may not yet have recognized. Hermione has previously criticized him for often rushing in to be the "hero" whenever he believes friends are in danger, just as he did during the Second Task of the Triwizard Tournament when he attempted to "rescue" all the hostages, even though Ron, Hermione, Cho, and Gabrielle, who were tethered underwater, were magically protected and never in any danger. This trait has made Harry dangerously predictable to his enemies.

Kreacher tells Harry that Sirius is gone from Grimmauld Place, but the loyal (although not to Sirius) Black family House-elf is an unreliable source. It should be noted that Kreacher has chosen his words carefully, possibly coached by someone: while he does say his master has gone out, he never explicitly states that Sirius is at the Department of Mysteries.

Once again, Neville has been dragged in simply because he was at the wrong place at the wrong time. One might wonder if the author has something against Neville, as he always seems to be getting himself into trouble that is not of his own making, sometimes dragging others with him.

We see again something of Umbridge's personality in her treatment of Snape. When Umbridge's demand for Veritaserum is met with the simple fact that it will take a month to make more, Umbridge, in what might be best described as a fit of pique, says that Snape is on probation. If we assume that Snape is loyal to the Order, and that he is either concealing a stock of Veritaserum, or overstating the preparation time, then Umbridge's rage might be valid, but placing a teacher on probation for failure to perform extracurricular activities is unwarranted and laughable. The episode with the Veritaserum should actually reinforce any belief Harry has in Snape's loyalty to the Order. This episode makes it very likely that Umbridge had, in fact, placed what she thought was Veritaserum in Harry's tea when she had her interview with him earlier, but that she had never used Veritaserum before; clearly unaware of its effects, she did not recognize that Harry was not showing the effects of Veritaserum as he answered her questions. She had also apparently used the entire vial in the process, making it so that even a tiny amount of the drugged tea would have affected Harry. From this, Harry should be able to guess that Snape had given Umbridge something other than Veritaserum. This would have been a way that Snape could have betrayed the Order without seeming to: he could have provided Umbridge with true Veritaserum, claiming that he had not known what she wanted it for, and then simply stood by as Harry betrayed Sirius to her. His providing fake Veritaserum to Umbridge certainly indicates more loyalty to the Order than Harry currently expects from him.

Snape's dismissal of Harry's plea concerning Padfoot, however, leaves Harry certain that Snape will not be informing the Order of Harry's fears. Harry has previously seen Snape and Sirius at wands' point with each other, and so has reason to fear that, given the chance to save Sirius, Snape would simply do nothing. It is extremely likely that Hermione shares this belief, which is why she concocts this risky plan to get Umbridge on her own.

Questions

Review   1. What does Harry do after having a vision? Who does he go to for help?

2. Why does Hermione want Harry to use the fireplace to contact Sirius at Grimmauld Place? Who does he talk to and what does Harry learn? Is the source reliable?

3. What does Hermione tell Umbridge after she and Harry are caught? Why does Hermione tell her this?

Further Study   1. Why does Harry forget that Snape is a member of the Order?

Greater Picture

Although Snape appears to coldly disregard Harry's plea about Padfoot, he is carefully maintaining his cover as Dumbledore's double agent. According to Dumbledore later, Snape had immediately checked on Sirius' safety, then alerted the Order of the Phoenix when Harry and Hermione did not return from the Forbidden Forest. Harry, informed of this, believes that Snape deliberately waited too long before summoning help. Although Snape does sound the alarm, it can be debated whether he acted quickly enough and if that affected the resulting consequences. Even assuming Snape is loyal to the Order of the Phoenix and Dumbledore, he was in an interesting position here. If he deliberately waited to warn Phoenix headquarters, he could have allowed his hated nemesis (Sirius) to possibly be killed by Voldemort without him (Snape) technically betraying the Order. However, Snape claims that he had checked on Sirius, though we have only his word for this, and he could have altered his story in light of circumstances. If Snape was still unaware whether or not Sirius was actually in danger, the temptation to delay warning the Order would certainly have been present. On the other hand, there is no indication that Snape did anything to endanger Sirius. Although Dumbledore later defends Snape's actions and reiterates his continued trust in him, Harry, and readers, will continue to doubt Snape's loyalty.

Harry's predictable behavior will be used against him again in the final book when he is recognized by using his signature Expelliarmus spell. However, he will deliberately exploit this predictability in his final confrontation with Lord Voldemort.

Kreacher's response to Harry may have been dictated in part or in full by Voldemort, acting through the Malfoy family. Interestingly, we will find out later that Voldemort has had direct dealings with Kreacher before, and will have believed that Kreacher died; if Voldemort had known that "the Black family house elf" that was talking to Narcissa was, in fact, the same elf that he had utilized before, he might have been more worried about his Locket Horcrux. Discounting other types of magic as much as he does, however, it is hardly surprising that he dismissed the possibility that the two Black family house elves were both Kreacher.

As mentioned, Kreacher's words are carefully chosen. Kreacher knows that the ultimate plan is to lure Harry to the Department of Mysteries and then send Sirius after him, thus disposing of Sirius who is, in his mind, a blood traitor and unfit to be his Master. So Kreacher is speaking truthfully when he says that Sirius will never return from the Department of Mysteries, and very carefully avoids saying that he is at Grimmauld Place when Harry asks. The only outright lie that Kreacher makes is when he says, "Master has gone out." "Nobody here but Kreacher," is shading the truth; Kreacher is the only one in the kitchen, certainly. But Kreacher does know that Sirius is upstairs tending to Buckbeak, who Kreacher injured.

Despite his carefully chosen words, though, Kreacher is lying to Harry to mislead him. In our interactions with Dobby, we have seen that deceptions like this will produce agitation in a House-elf if he is acting against instructions. That Kreacher seems quite cool about this aligns with what Dumbledore later tell Harry: "You are not his master, he could lie to you without even needing to punish himself."

While we wonder at Neville's inclusion in the group, he will be of some use in the upcoming battle in the Ministry. While his contribution there will be limited, we will see that it acts as something of a "baptism of fire," resulting in his being much more effective in later battles and in the guerrilla fighting at Hogwarts in the final book.

Chapter 33: Fight and Flight

Synopsis

Hermione leads Umbridge and Harry (who is trying to look like he knows where they are going) into the Forbidden Forest. When Umbridge questions this, Hermione points out that they could not have built a weapon anywhere that it would be found easily by the students, could they? Harry has no idea where Hermione is taking them, although he notices that she has avoided the path leading to Grawp, instead apparently taking the one that leads towards Aragog. Harry knows Hermione had not been with them on that trip, and wonders if she has any idea where she is headed. He also thinks she is deliberately being noisy.

As they approach a clearing, an arrow whizzes through the air, hitting a tree. About fifty Centaurs appear on all sides, demanding to know why the humans are in their forest. Treating them as inferior half-breeds, a haughty Umbridge unleashes an insulting tirade, infuriating the Centaurs. When she binds Magorian, the Centaurs charge; Harry and Hermione duck to avoid the flying hooves. Bane seizes Umbridge; she drops her wand, but before Harry can reach it, another centaur has stepped on it and broken it. As other Centaurs lift up Harry and Hermione, they see Bane carrying the hysterically screaming Umbridge into the woods. Hermione tries explaining the situation to the other Centaurs, hoping to gain their sympathy, but they only become angrier at being involved in human affairs and want to attack her and Harry. Despite her protests that they are "foals," and Ronan's reminder that they do not attack young humans, the Centaurs consider Harry and Hermione as devious as their adult counterparts. As they are about to carry off Harry and Hermione, Grawp crashes through the trees. Recognizing "Hermy," he yells for "Hagger" (Hagrid). The panicked Centaurs shoot him with arrows. Enraged, the Giant howls in pain as the arrows become embedded in his face, and flails blindly at the Centaurs. Harry and Hermione, splattered with Grawp's blood, get away amid the confusion.

Though they have escaped Umbridge, they still have a problem—how to get to London. Ron's voice behind them agrees. Apparently he, Ginny, Luna, and Neville escaped the Inquisitorial Squad, thanks to Harry's Defensive Arts training and Ginny's excellent Bat Bogey Hex. They then followed Harry and Hermione into the Forest, bringing Harry's and Hermione's wands with them. Luna, matter-of-factly, says that they will just have to fly to London. When Harry says he is going to the Ministry to find Sirius, the others insist on going along. Harry prefers only Ron, feeling that Neville, Luna, and Ginny are the weakest D.A. members, and that even Hermione is unsuitable in a combat situation. Luna's insistence that they fly provokes an outburst from Ron, but Luna points to two thestrals. Harry says he and Ron will take those two, and the others can follow later, but Luna says more will be attracted by the blood on Harry and Hermione. Soon, six or seven more Thestrals appear, and Harry, exasperated, tells everyone to pick one and mount up.

ANALYSIS

Of all the members of Dumbledore's Army, Luna, Neville, and Ginny are very nearly the last ones that Harry or Ron would have chosen to go with them to London, believing they are the least qualified. They are even reluctant to include Hermione and try to persuade her and the others to remain behind or to come later. But Harry can underestimate or misjudge his friends' abilities, often valuing the popular and seemingly more capable students over the ones who are loyal, determined, and dependable. It is Hermione, Ginny, Neville, and Luna who usually respond first to Harry's distress calls, and they display immense bravery by risking their own lives to help Harry face Voldemort, a fact Harry does not yet fully appreciate.

Although Hermione quickly devised a clever plan to save Harry from Umbridge's Cruciatus curse, she nearly gets them both captured as a result. The Centaurs' hatred of humans usually excludes children, or "foals" as they call them. Hermione counts on this when she leads Umbridge into the forest knowing the Centaurs will resent the intrusion and that Umbridge will probably further infuriate them. Umbridge arrogantly confronts the Centaurs, believing her Ministry-backed authority will intimidate any "sub-human" creature into stepping aside. Even though the Centaurs carry Umbridge off into the forest, Hermione's plan backfires because she underestimated their reaction, and mistakenly believed that if she explained their plight, the Centaurs would be sympathetic. The herd, still outraged over Firenze's "betrayal" to serve Dumbledore, only became more incensed that Hermione used trickery to involve them in human affairs. Hermione and Harry are no longer considered so "innocent," and one Centaur argues that Harry is nearing manhood. If not for Grawp's timely intervention, it is unlikely they would have survived the Centaurs' wrath unscathed.

We see here, also, an instance of Luna's matter-of-fact nature and her willingness to ignore heckling, coupled with a perhaps surprising intelligence, and an awareness of her environment quite out of line with her usual dreamy appearance. It is Luna who connects Hagrid's mention that the Thestrals are excellent fliers with the fact that they are attracted to raw meat and blood. Ignoring Ron's gibes about Crumple-Horned Snorkacks, she sticks to her guns, pointing out the arriving Thestrals to Harry and Neville, who she knows can see them.

QUESTIONS

Review 1. Why does Hermione take Harry and Umbridge into the Forbidden Forest and who do they meet?

2. What happens to Umbridge in the Forbidden Forest? Why?

3. Who wants to attack Harry and Hermione in the Forbidden Forest and why? What stops them?

4. What are attracted by the blood on Harry and Hermione's clothing?

5. How does Luna suggest getting to London? How do the others react this?

6. Ron, Ginny, Luna, Neville, and Hermione insist on going with Harry to the Ministry of Magic to help save Sirius. Why does Harry only want Ron to accompany him?

GREATER PICTURE

Up to this point, it has been Harry, Ron, and Hermione, the Trio, who have been the central characters in the series. Harry, with Dumbledore's assistance, has been moving towards his apparent destiny, that of facing and defeating Voldemort, and Ron and Hermione have been traveling alongside. Now, we have a new group of assistants, Neville, Luna, and Ginny. As mentioned, Harry does not want them along, possibly thinking them not as competent as himself, Ron, and Hermione. Circumstances will prove him wrong, however, not only in this book, but in the final two books of the series. When Harry calls up Dumbledore's Army in *Harry Potter and the Half-Blood Prince* to defend the school in Dumbledore's absence, it will be only these three who respond; and Neville will be the core of the resistance to Voldemort's rule of Hogwarts, while both Ginny and Luna will have pivotal roles, in *Harry Potter and the Deathly Hallows*.

We can see the beginnings of civilization happening with Grawp, surprisingly. Grawp is looking for Hagrid, and recognizes Hermione. It seems that, despite Hagrid having only missed one visit, Grawp is already feeling his absence. Grawp's progress will happen off-camera for the rest of the series, but he will be civil enough at Dumbledore's funeral at the end of *Harry Potter and the Half-Blood Prince*.

It is interesting to note the Centaurs' reaction to Grawp. Despite their vaunted logic and mental superiority, the Centaurs react to Grawp in a singularly emotional manner, bombarding him with arrows when he has not, in fact, directly threatened any of them. We will see later, when Hagrid is carrying the apparently lifeless Harry out of the Forest, that he is able to shame the Centaurs into entering the battle on humanity's side. This may lead us to recognize that the Centaurs are much more emotional than they are willing to admit to themselves. This is also an indication that, despite their belief in their mental superiority over humans, they share the human traits of prejudice and intolerance.

Chapter 34: The Department of Mysteries

SYNOPSIS

Harry, Neville, and Luna quickly mount their Thestrals, but Hermione, Ron, and Ginny have difficulty finding them; Luna dismounts and helps them. Harry asks his Thestral to take them to the Visitor's Entrance of the Ministry of Magic, in London; the Thestrals promptly take off. Upon reaching the Ministry of Magic, Ron swears he will never fly on one again. The students cram into the phone box that is the Ministry's visitor entrance. Ron dials the Ministry's number and is asked their names and business; the phone dispenses ID badges, and they descend to the atrium. At the reception area, there is no Security Guard on duty. Harry is certain Sirius must be there. Harry and the others enter a lift (elevator) and descend to the lowest basement floor — the Department of Mysteries.

From his dreams, Harry recognizes the corridor and knows which door to enter. Within is a large circular chamber with twelve doors. Harry is unsure which one to go through, the more so as, as soon as a door closes behind them, the room's walls rotate. When the doors come to a standstill again, they open the first one; but the room does not match Harry's dream. Instead, it contains a large tank with floating brains. Retreating, Hermione marks the door with her wand so they know they have already looked there. The next room is a large stone amphitheater. On a raised dais at the center is an ancient stone archway, a tattered veil fluttering in the entrance. Harry investigates, and standing next to the veil, he has the strange sensation that someone is on the other side. Hermione, in particular, seems frightened, and calls Harry back to the circular room.

The next doorway refuses to open; Harry uses Sirius' knife that will "open any door," but the door remains shut and the knife's blade melts away. At the next door, Harry recognizes the sparkling, shimmering light from his dreams. Inside is a bell jar containing a beautiful hummingbird that hatches from an egg, flutters to the top, falls back down into the egg, then hatches again. Passing through this room, they reach the huge chamber containing the shelves loaded with glass orbs that Harry recognizes from his dream. Finding no trace of Sirius, Harry considers returning to Hogwarts when Ron spots an orb labeled "*S.P.T. to A.P.W.B.D. Dark Lord and (?)Harry Potter.*" As Harry reaches for it, Hermione warns him it might be dangerous, but nothing happens when he grasps it. Although the chamber is cold, the orb feels warm in Harry's hand.

A voice from behind breaks the silence: "Very good, Potter. Now turn around, nice and slowly, and give that to me."

ANALYSIS

Harry has become so consumed with rescuing his godfather that he rushed into an unknown situation without a plan, without fully considering the risks to himself and his friends, and without confirming that Sirius was actually in danger. He ignores Hermione's warning that his dream could be a false vision, and he instead relies solely on his own intuition that is fueled by intense emotions and a desire to protect Sirius. When under duress, Harry often becomes impervious to others' advice and acts according to emotions rather than logic, thinking linearly and single-mindedly, although his intentions are usually noble. His attempts to dissuade the others from accompanying him are futile, they refuse to remain behind, despite suspecting Harry is pursuing an unwise and potentially dangerous course. Unfortunately, they are right, and Harry's rash and predictable behavior has led him and the others directly into what may be a deadly trap.

Readers are probably able to guess that the initials S.P.T. and A.P.W.B.D. that are on the orb stand for Sybill Patricia Trelawney and Albus Percival Wulfric Brian Dumbledore.

It is interesting to note, although it plays no part in the storyline, the beautiful hummingbird that continually hatches from the egg and returns to it. Clearly, this is similar to a Phoenix, the mythical bird that continually dies by bursting into flames, then is resurrected from its own ashes. In this context, however, it is meant to be an indicator of one of the great Mysteries, the mystery of Time.

QUESTIONS

Review 1. Why was Ron worried about flying on the Thestrals?

2. Why was the Department of Mysteries so easily accessible to Harry and the others?

Further Study 1. What are the 'Orbs'?

2. Was Hermione right to be worried about Harry touching an Orb, even with one that had his name on it? What might have happened?

3. Why does Harry experience a strange sensation standing next to the veiled archway? What might have happened if Harry had stepped through it?

4. Why do Ron, Hermione, and the others insist on going with Harry, even though they believe it might be a trap? What does this say about their characters?

Greater Picture

While it is never entirely made certain, Luna's reaction to the veil in the stone amphitheater, and Harry's, leads us to believe that what Harry may be hearing are the voices of those who have died. It would appear that this room is meant to be the physical embodiment of a Muggle figure of speech: when we say that someone has "passed through the Veil," we mean that that person has died. This room, and its physical Veil, would then be a figure of speech made real. This interpretation will be reinforced later by Sirius' passing physically through the Veil, and by Luna's telling Harry that what he heard at the veil were the voices of those who had gone before, waiting there for Harry to join them.

This being the Department of Mysteries, one might reasonably expect that eleven of the twelve doors off the circular room would lead to an area devoted to the study of a Mystery, the twelfth one being the way back to the Atrium. This does seem to be the case; in turn we see the mysteries of Thought or Consciousness, Death, and (skipping the locked door) Time. It makes sense that Prophecies would be associated with the mystery of Time, as they do somewhat violate our understanding of Time as being unidirectional. Later, in another room, is a giant orrery, obviously devoted to the mystery of the Physical Universe; Dumbledore will tell Harry about a department whose door is always locked because of the great power of the mystery therein, namely the mystery of Love. It also makes sense for the various Mysteries to be interconnected. Later, we will see that, leaving the amphitheater, Harry will run through the brain room; it is obvious, in retrospect, that the mystery of Consciousness and the mystery of Death are linked. This, incidentally, is an illustration of the Doctrine of Signatures, the belief that function follows appearance: e.g. a plant that grows in the shape of a heart must have effects, assumed beneficial, on people's hearts. The Doctrine of Signatures was the core of a large part of medieval "magic"; we do not know if it plays any part in the Wizarding world, though it likely did in ancient times. Whether or not the Doctrine of Signatures was a consideration in the design of the Department of Mysteries, it is likely that the wizards studying the Mysteries would feel that it would be sensible to have the connections between the Mysteries echoed in the connections between the rooms devoted to them.

Chapter 35: Beyond the Veil

Synopsis

Lucius Malfoy and eleven other Death Eaters, including the sadistic Bellatrix Lestrange, emerge from the shadows. Malfoy again demands that Harry hand over the orb. Harry refuses, demanding to know where Sirius is, but the answers merely hint that Harry's visions were just a dream. Threatening to destroy the orb, Harry stalls by asking questions about it. When Bellatrix reviles Harry for being half-blood, Harry reminds her that her precious Voldemort is half-blood also—his father is a Muggle. Before he can finish the word, though, Bellatrix attempts to Stun him; Malfoy deflects the spell to the side, which knocks a few orbs off the shelves, giving Harry an idea. Malfoy explains that the sphere contains a prophecy about the Dark Lord and Harry. They needed Harry to retrieve it because only those whom a prophecy concerns can safely pick up the orb, any others go insane. And Voldemort could not risk being seen at the Ministry, and so instead he lured Harry there to retrieve it for him. On Harry's signal, the D.A. members blast the rows of spheres with their wands. Harry, along with the others, runs from the Chamber clutching the orb, chased by the Death Eaters. He re-enters the bell jar room, where Hermione seals the door behind them; but only Neville is still with them, Ron, Ginny, and Luna have become separated. Two Death Eaters enter the hall; Hermione Stuns one, and Neville, while disarming the other, disarms Harry as well. Attempting to Stun the Death Eater, he hits a rack full of time-turners. Hermione Stuns the remaining Death Eater.

As they head for the circular room, two more Death Eaters appear; Harry, Hermione and Neville veer into a side office. Before they can seal the door, the Death Eaters burst in and trip the three students. Hermione, regaining her wand, silences the Death Eater who is calling his accomplices, and Harry Petrifies another. The silenced attacker, Dolohov, curses Hermione with a purple flame; she falls. He kicks Neville, breaking his wand and his nose, before wordlessly demanding that Harry give him the prophecy. A partially-incapacitated Death Eater distracts him, and Harry Petrifies him as well. Neville confirms that Hermione is alive, and they make their way to the circular room, where they find Luna, Ginny, whose ankle is injured, and Ron, who was hit by a spell apparently having an effect like drunkenness. As they search for an exit, several Death Eaters enter, including Bellatrix, and start attacking. Harry, Neville, and Luna quickly exit, finding themselves again in the Brain Room; they try sealing the doors, Neville using Hermione's wand, but five Death Eaters burst in, throwing Luna through the air. She falls and is motionless. Ron, still under the drunkenness spell's effects, summons a brain, and it wraps its tentacles around him. Ginny is Stunned. Neville apparently cannot produce a Stun spell with his nose broken, so Harry runs for the door that the Death Eaters came through, tumbling down stone steps and landing near the Veiled Arch. Surrounded by Death Eaters, Harry backs onto the dais where the veil ripples in the ancient archway. Neville bursts in but is quickly immobilized. Bellatrix, recalling torturing Neville's parents, tortures Neville similarly, to force Harry to surrender the prophecy. Harry is about to relinquish it when Sirius, Tonks, Shacklebolt, Lupin, and Moody arrive. Macnair grabs Harry around the neck and demands the prophecy; Neville pokes his eye with Hermione's wand, and he releases Harry. Harry Stuns Macnair, but Neville is jinxed by Dolohov, who then makes two attempts at Harry before Sirius distracts him. Harry Petrifies him, and hands off the prophecy orb to Neville to free his hands. As teh jinx has left Neville unable to walk, Harry grabs Neville's robe to pull him up the steps; the robe rips, and the orb falls from Neville's pocket and is smashed. The wispy vapors inside turn into a ghost-like figure speaking the prophecy, which vanishes unheard amid the battle sounds. Dumbledore enters from the Brain Room, and quickly apprehends all the combatants except two: Sirius is dueling Bellatrix. As Sirius taunts her that she could fight better, Bellatrix blasts a stunning spell squarely at his chest. His rigid body falls through the veiled arch. Harry rushes after him, but Lupin restrains him before he reaches the portal, telling him it is too late. Sirius is gone.

Analysis

This chapter is largely action, preparing for and then executing the battle. We do learn a number of things here, as Harry stalls the Death Eaters, but most of this chapter is immediate; this is the climax of this book, the battle we have been building up to throughout this book.

One thing that is mentioned here is that only the persons who are concerned in a prophecy can safely pick it up. (Presumably, that would be the people mentioned on the label: in this case Harry, Voldemort, Dumbledore, and Trelawney.) This gives us an explanation for Bode's illness. We heard earlier that Bode had been put under the Imperius curse by Malfoy, but that he had resisted attempts to make him retrieve something; it is now clear that he had been ordered to pick up this Prophecy, and had known it would drive him insane when he did so. It was as he was recovering his sanity that the Death Eaters moved to murder him in the hospital.

Although Harry and the others were outnumbered and outmatched by Voldemort's Death Eaters, all fought ably, mostly thanks to Harry's superb defensive training. It is conceivable that had a few more D.A. members been present, the Death Eaters could have been defeated without help from the Order of the Phoenix. Even though Harry considers them the weakest members, Neville, Ginny, and Luna perform admirably while under attack. And though they may not yet be the most technically proficient D.A. students, they are arguably the bravest, willingly risking their own lives to help Harry, and fight Voldemort and his Death Eaters. Ginny and Neville prove they are true Gryffindors, while Luna could easily have fit into that House, as well as Ravenclaw. Harry will never forget what they have done for him.

When Harry contacted Grimmauld Place, Kreacher told Harry that Sirius had been taken to the Ministry of Magic. We can now guess that Kreacher, who remains loyal to the Black family, and, by extension, Voldemort, lied to Harry; Sirius was safely at Grimmauld Place with Lupin, unaware Harry was attempting to reach them. Malfoy names the twelve Death Eaters involved in this battle shortly after Harry, Hermione, and Neville re-enter the bell jar room. They are: Lucius Malfoy, Bellatrix Lestrange, Nott, Rodolphus, Crabbe, Rabastan, Jugson, Dolohov, Macnair, Avery, Rookwood, and Mulciber. Of the two that initially attack Harry, Hermione, and Neville, one is Stunned, and the other falls into the bell jar and stumbles through the rest of the battle with a baby's head. The second pair that attack Harry are Dolohov and Jugson, and they both get Petrified. Nott is injured by falling shelves and may not play a further part in the battle. Lucius counts ten Death Eaters standing against Harry alone in the amphitheatre, so we can assume that the Stunned and Petrified Death Eaters have all been resuscitated at that point.

Questions

Review 1. Who can safely pick up a Prophecy Orb? What happens to those who are unable to?

2. How was Bellatrix able to kill Sirius?

3. Why does Lupin restrain Harry from going after Sirius?

4. Which D.A. members were left standing at the end of the battle?

Further Study 1. Who alerted the Order of the Phoenix that the students were in trouble?

2. What is the veiled archway? Why can only Harry and Luna hear the voices behind the veil?

3. Based on what is learned in this chapter, what might have happened if Harry had gone through the veiled archway? Could he have returned?

Greater Picture

We will find out that Order of the Phoenix reinforcements arrived at the Ministry of Magic because Snape alerted them, when Harry and the other students did not return from the Forbidden Forest. However, Harry later accuses Snape of deliberately waiting too long to sound the alarm, resulting in Sirius' death.

Neville, Luna, and Ginny will again show their bravery in the next book, *Harry Potter and the Half-Blood Prince,* being the only members of Dumbledore's Army to answer Harry's distress call before the battle inside Hogwarts. Harry will later bemoan the fact that the Prophecy has been destroyed. Dumbledore will tell him that what was destroyed was not the prophecy itself, but rather a memory of it, and that the person who witnessed the prophecy had retained that memory. Apparently, prophecies are stored by a process extremely similar to the process by which thoughts are stored in a Pensieve, as Dumbledore then shows Harry the memory of that prophecy, using his Pensieve.

Neville's accidental destruction of the Time Turners will prove to be a minor but in some ways essential plot point. Time-Turners are an almost insanely useful device to have in a wizard duel, as a wizard could, if he chose, go back an hour multiple times using a Time Turner to multiply himself. Harry would stand precious little chance facing five Voldemorts. While there are laws preventing their use in such manner, we see that Voldemort does not seem to pay too much attention to laws, and if he were able to retain a Time Turner, things would go very badly for the Order of the Phoenix. The only mention of this destruction, however, is in the opening chapters of *Harry Potter and the Half-Blood Prince,* where Hagrid rationalizes the Trio's decision to not take his Care of Magical Creatures course as being due to lack of time, which could not be remedied without the destroyed Time-Turners.

Chapter 36: The Only One He Ever Feared

Synopsis

A stunned Harry is unable to believe that Sirius is dead. Ignoring the non-stop wand flashes, he struggles with Lupin, attempting to reach the archway and save Sirius. Meanwhile Dumbledore has rounded up most of the Death Eaters, but on the dais' far side, Kingsley duels Bellatrix until she jinxes him. Dodging Dumbledore's spell, she exits the amphitheatre. Enraged, Harry chases her through the Brain Room, ducking her curses. Bellatrix runs into the hallway with the lifts (elevator). Harry follows, but the door slams behind her and the room's walls are already spinning. As they slow, Harry asks, "Where's the way out?" A door behind Harry pops open, revealing the hallway. Hearing a lift clattering upwards, Harry presses a call button for another lift.

Harry runs into the Atrium, vowing to kill Bellatrix, who fires another spell at Harry, then laments the prophecy being lost. Voldemort suddenly appears, apparently in response to this discovery, angry that his Death Eaters have failed him again. He fires a killing curse at Harry, but the now-headless magician from the Statue of Magical Brethren leaps and blocks the spell. Dumbledore has arrived in the atrium, and he manipulates the magician to protect Harry and keep him out of the way, while the witch statue pins Bellatrix to the floor and the House-elf and Goblin figures guard the fireplaces lining the Atrium walls. Dumbledore and Voldemort fiercely duel; Harry can only watch. Voldemort hurls a killing curse directly at Dumbledore, but Fawkes flies between them, swallowing the curse and falling dead. Voldemort seemingly vanishes, but he enters Harry's mind and demands that Dumbledore kill him by killing Harry. Harry, hearing his own voice, is filled with thoughts of Sirius: if Dumbledore kills him, he will be able to see Sirius again. Voldemort suddenly releases Harry, who collapses.

Cornelius Fudge, other Ministry officials, and Aurors begin arriving from the fireplaces; several, including Fudge, see Voldemort as he physically reappears in the Atrium, grabs Bellatrix, and disappears. Dumbledore tells a stunned Fudge what has happened and that Death Eaters are under guard in the Death Chamber. Fudge seems ready to arrest him, but Dumbledore points out that Fudge saw Voldemort, and should now realize that he has been chasing the wrong man. Fudge sends Dawlish and Williamson to the Department of Mysteries. Dumbledore demands that Umbridge be removed from Hogwarts and the Aurors stop chasing Hagrid. He says he will explain everything, but he first gives Harry a Portkey, sending him back to Hogwarts.

Analysis

Voldemort possesses Harry's mind, but overcome by Harry's memories and feelings for his friends, Sirius, and his parents, the Dark Lord quickly exits. As Dumbledore will shortly explain, the power Harry possesses that Voldemort can not is love, which among other things makes Harry's mind an extremely uncomfortable place for Voldemort to be; he is unlikely to reenter it anytime soon, if at all.

Though Harry loses his godfather and failed to kill or capture Bellatrix Lestrange, the battle at the Ministry of Magic yields some benefit as Voldemort's presence is exposed and many Death Eaters are captured. Now the Wizarding World will know that Harry was telling the truth, and the Ministry will be forced to cease their campaign to discredit Harry and Dumbledore. It is expected that the Ministry will now take action against Voldemort and his followers. Additionally, the much-despised Umbridge will be removed from Hogwarts, and Dumbledore and Hagrid can return to their posts.

Fawkes is killed when he intercepts Voldemort's Avada Kedavra curse, but Dumbledore's loyal Phoenix will be reborn from its own ashes.

Questions

1. What happens when Voldemort hurls a killing curse at Dumbledore?
2. Who arrives just before Voldemort disapparates? What is the reaction?
3. What does Voldemort do just before disapparating?
4. Who, besides Voldemort, escapes?

Greater Picture

In the next book, *Harry Potter and the Half-Blood Prince*, Dumbledore asks Harry if his scar has been hurting. Harry replies, with some surprise, it has not hurt all year, though he would have expected it to. Dumbledore explains that when Voldemort possessed Harry's mind, he found it so uncomfortable a place to be that he likely has been shielding his own mind from Harry's since then. In the series' final two books, Voldemort never possesses Harry again, though as the final book progresses, Harry gains more and more ability to see what is happening inside Voldemort's mind.

Chapter 37: The Lost Prophecy

Synopsis

The Portkey delivers Harry to Dumbledore's office, which has been repaired after Dumbledore's spectacular escape. Harry is deeply stunned and angry over Sirius' death and blames himself for falling for Voldemort's deception. Dumbledore soon arrives, to cheers from the portraits in his office, and places Fawkes tenderly on the ashes under his perch. He tells Harry the other students are being tended to by Madam Pomfrey. Tonks was also injured, but she has been taken to St. Mungo's hospital and will recover.

Harry rages at Dumbledore, but when Dumbledore claims responsibility for Sirius' death, Harry is subdued. Dumbledore admits that if he had been more open, Harry would have realized that Voldemort was luring Harry into a trap at the Department of Mysteries. Dumbledore explains to a still seething Harry that the events that gave him his scar, also left a mental connection between Harry and Voldemort. Voldemort discovered this gateway after Arthur Weasley was attacked, and he intruded into Harry's thoughts. Dumbledore says that is why he had insisted Harry study Occlumency and why he remained aloof from Harry all year, fearing that Voldemort would try harder to break into Harry's mind if he suspected there was more than a teacher to student relationship between them, or that Voldemort would gain valuable information through him. Harry tells him that he tried to contact Sirius to see if he was safe; Dumbledore says Kreacher lied, that Sirius was actually tending to Buckbeak, tending an injury inflicted by Kreacher. After Harry warned Snape while in Umbridge's office, Snape checked to see that Sirius was safe; but when Harry did not return from the Forbidden Forest, he alerted the Order, who then went to the Ministry. Snape wanted Sirius to remain at Grimmauld, but Sirius ordered Kreacher to tell Dumbledore what had happened. And Dumbledore learned from Kreacher about the lie that had been told to Harry, and that Kreacher's instructions had originated with the last member of the Black family that Kreacher respected: Narcissa Malfoy. Kreacher could not betray the Order totally, but he could reveal to Narcissa that the one thing that would always bring Harry was a threat to Sirius Black.

Harry is angry that Snape disbelieved him when he told Snape what was happening; Dumbledore says that Snape had to behave that way in Umbridge's presence. Harry argues that Snape had been using Occlumency to soften him up for Voldemort, saying his scar always hurt worse after a lesson. Dumbledore reiterates his complete faith in Snape's loyalty. He regrets not teaching Harry himself, but he feared it could give Voldemort access to his own thoughts. Sadly, he underestimated Snape's deep, lingering resentments towards Harry's father. Dumbledore explains why the infant Harry was placed with the Dursleys rather than with a wizarding family, although many offered to adopt the orphaned boy. When Lily Potter was killed defending her son, her sacrifice created a magical shield that protected Harry from Voldemort. However, the protection only remains in effect as long as Harry lives in his mother's blood relatives' home—that relative is Aunt Petunia. Dumbledore was convinced that Voldemort would return, and his priority was to keep Harry alive. The Howler Petunia received was a stern reminder from Dumbledore of her obligation to protect Harry.

Dumbledore tells Harry that the reason Voldemort had tried to kill him was because of a prophecy that had been made shortly before Harry's birth. While Voldemort knew of the prophecy, and some of the prophecy itself, he did not know the whole, and had been trying to retrieve it to find out what it said.

Harry tells Dumbledore that the prophecy was destroyed, but Dumbledore says only a copy of the original was lost. He knows the contents because it was to him that the prophecy was first revealed. Sixteen years ago, Dumbledore interviewed Sibyll Trelawney for the Divination position, meeting her at a pub in Hogsmeade. Although she was descended from a gifted Seer, she herself seemed minimally talented. Saying she was not acceptable for the post, Dumbledore was about to leave.

Dumbledore stops speaking, and, producing the Pensieve, extracts a memory from his mind and places it therein. Sibyll Trelawney's veiled image rises, and in the harsh voice Harry heard once before, says, *"The one with the power to vanquish the Dark Lord approaches ... born to those who have thrice defied him, born as the seventh month dies ... and the Dark Lord will mark him as his equal, but he will have power the Dark Lord knows not ... and either must die at the hand of the other for neither can live while the other survives ... the one with the power to vanquish the Dark Lord will be born as the seventh month dies ..."*

Dumbledore says there were two boys who fit the prophecy: Harry and Neville Longbottom, born days apart. Both Harry's and Neville's parents, who were Order of the Phoenix members, defied Voldemort three times. Dumbledore believes Voldemort attacked Harry because he is a half-blood like himself, and therefore possibly more dangerous; Neville is a pureblood. By deliberately choosing Harry, Voldemort "marked" him as his equal, leaving behind the scar on Harry's forehead. Dumbledore goes on to say that Voldemort had only heard the first half of the prophecy. The second part predicted that the marked child would have powers that the Dark Lord could never know, and that one must die at the hand of the other, for both cannot live while the other survives. Dumbledore tells Harry that the power he possesses and Voldemort does not is love. It was love that protected Harry from Voldemort's killing curse while ripping the Dark Lord's soul from his body. He also confirms that the prophecy means that either Voldemort or Harry must kill the other.

Finally, as Harry is leaving the office, Dumbledore explains why he had not chosen Harry to be a Prefect: "I must confess ... that I rather thought ... you had enough responsibility to be going on with."

Analysis

Harry is roiling in turmoil—simultaneously experiencing rage, grief, and guilt. Although Dumbledore explains why he withheld vital information and reveals the entire prophecy, it does little to console Harry. He now understands his ties to the Dursleys, and although his relationship with Petunia will never change, he now realizes that it is she, through their blood connection, who stands between him and Voldemort. And although Petunia has no love for her nephew, she continues to fulfill her obligation to protect him; Harry knows he must continue to endure living in her home until he comes of age. And now Harry has a new burden to bear: either he or Voldemort must die.

Questions

Review 1. Why didn't Dumbledore teach Harry Occlumency himself?

2. Why does Harry have to return to the Dursleys each summer?

3. Why did Voldemort "mark" Harry as his equal rather than Neville Longbottom?

4. How is love used as a powerful force against Voldemort, and why is the Dark Lord incapable of possessing it?

Extra Study 1. The prophecy never mentioned Harry's name. Two boys fit Trelawney's description, and either could have been marked by Voldemort: Harry or Neville Longbottom. Therefore, is it possible that Neville, who might have been chosen by Voldemort, could also have retrieved the orb from the Department of Mysteries? Explain why he could or could not.

2. How might Harry and Neville's relationship change now that Harry knows that Neville could have been "The Chosen One."

3. What might have been the result if Dumbledore had instructed Harry in Occlumency, rather than Snape teaching him?

4. Why does Aunt Petunia continue to protect Harry, even though she does not love him?

GREATER PICTURE

It is interesting that, when Harry is yelling at Dumbledore, he says that Dumbledore cannot possibly know the pain that he is suffering. Harry feels as though the death of Sirius is his fault, as he had let Voldemort into his mind, and fallen for the ruse that lured him into the Department of Mysteries. In fact, Dumbledore does know how Harry feels, more so than many others would. As discussed in *Harry Potter and the Deathly Hallows*, Dumbledore's sister Ariana was killed during a three-way duel between Dumbledore, his brother Aberforth, and Grindelwald. While he does not know whose spell actually killed her, there is no doubt in Dumbledore's mind that he is responsible for the death of his sister. Indications are that he carries this regret and remorse with him for the rest of his life, and Harry muses that what Dumbledore desires the most and sees in the Mirror of Erised is his family, including his sister and mother, whole and together again. This pain is also seen at the end of *Harry Potter and the Half-Blood Prince*, when Dumbledore drinks the potion in the Cave, though we do not learn the reasons behind it it until Aberforth's explanation in *Harry Potter and the Deathly Hallows*.

Dumbledore says Voldemort wanted the orb because he never heard the entire prophecy; while the Hog's Head, where the prophecy was made, is known for its eavesdropping population, Voldemort's informant apparently only heard the prophecy's first half. In a later book, Harry learns that when Trelawney returned from her prophecy-induced trance, Severus Snape was present. Harry leaps to the conclusion that Snape was Voldemort's informant. Dumbledore, confronted by Harry, does not dispute this, and in fact it is confirmed much later. However, if he was present at the end of the prophecy, why does Dumbledore say that he had only heard the first part? If we look at the prophecy itself, and the earlier one, we will see that Trelawney's prophecies seem to repeat the first part at the conclusion; so someone hearing the end of the prophecy would hear a repetition of the prophecy's beginning.

Chapter 38: The Second War Begins

SYNOPSIS

Dumbledore is officially reinstated as Hogwarts' Headmaster, and the Ministry of Magic publicly acknowledges that Lord Voldemort has returned. The students have largely recovered from their injuries, although Hermione, Ginny, and Ron are still in the infirmary. Harry goes to visit them, finding Luna and Neville there. Also in the infirmary is Dolores Umbridge, although she is no longer a Hogwarts teacher. Dumbledore personally went into the Forbidden Forest to retrieve her from the Centaurs. Deeply traumatized by her experience, she is barely able to speak. Ron torments her by making soft "clip clop" hoof noises with his tongue, causing the frightened woman to bolt upright in bed, frantically looking around. Hermione and Ginny can barely suppress their giggles. Hermione laments that the Prophecy was lost, and they will never know what it said; Harry prefers to withhold its contents from them. Finding their ongoing speculation too hard to bear, especially knowing he must be either murderer or victim, he excuses himself to go visit Hagrid. Along the way, he is confronted by a vengeful Draco Malfoy, who threatens to curse him in retaliation for his father's imprisonment in Azkaban. Harry is quicker on the draw and has Draco at wandpoint, but Snape intervenes before either can jinx the other. Snape is about to penalize Gryffindor, but sneeringly comments that there are no House points left to deduct. Just then McGonagall arrives from St. Mungo's Hospital. When she discovers that Umbridge's "Inquisitorial Squad" has deducted all the House points from Gryffindor, she awards Harry, Ron, Ginny, Hermione, Neville, and also Luna (of Ravenclaw), fifty points each for alerting the wizarding world about Voldemort, then subtracts the ten points Snape wanted to deduct.

Harry reaches Hagrid's hut, but finds no relief there; while Hagrid points out that now everyone knows he was telling the truth, it is meaningless with Sirius gone. He excuses himself and heads for the lake where he can think without being disturbed. Only now does he truly understand the meaning, "a marked man."

The day before the term ends, Professor Umbridge leaves Hogwarts, attempting to exit secretly, but gets whacked alternately by a walking stick and a sock full of chalk, courtesy of Peeves, who followed the twins instructions. Most of the school watches as she leaves, and McGonagall expresses regret that she can not run cheering after Umbridge as well, as Peeves had borrowed her walking stick.

The next day, Harry packs his trunk rather than attending the Leaving Feast. He finds the package Sirius gave him at Christmas. He remembers Sirius telling him, "Use it if you need me, all right?" Inside is an old mirror, along with a note from Sirius explaining that Harry can contact him with it. Harry thinks it could be a link to Sirius in the afterlife, but he only sees his own reflection. Realizing that Sirius did not have the matching mirror with him when he went through the death arch, Harry angrily tosses it into the trunk, shattering it. A thought suddenly occurs to him, and he seeks out Nearly Headless Nick, the Gryffindor ghost. He asks Nick if Sirius could also have become a ghost, but Nick explains that very few wizards choose to remain earthbound as spirits. He did so only because he feared going on to the next world.

A disappointed Harry is heading back to the Gryffindor Common room when he runs into Luna in the hall. She is searching for her belongings that other students have hidden. Feeling sorry for her, Harry offers to help, but Luna declines, saying everything always turns up eventually. He asks who she knows who had died, and she says that her mother was killed in an accident. Harry offers his condolences, but she says it is okay because she knows she will see her mother again. She explains that she believes the voices they heard from behind the veiled archway in the Department of Mysteries are the dead who are just lurking out of sight. As he watches Luna head for the Leaving Feast, Harry surprisingly feels better.

On the Hogwarts Express, Malfoy, Crabbe and Goyle attempt to attack Harry, but members of Dumbledore's Army intervene and jinx them until they are unrecognizable. Cho Chang walks past in the corridor outside Harry's compartment; she blushes but doesn't stop. Ron asks if there is anything still going on between them, and Harry truthfully responds there is not. Hermione delicately mentions that Cho is dating Michael Corner, but Harry is unaffected, feeling it is in his past. Ron is concerned, though, as he recalls Ginny was seeing Michael Corner; she says that when Gryffindor had beaten Ravenclaw, Michael had gone to comfort Cho instead of celebrating with Ginny, so she had dumped him. Ron suggests, with a sideways glance at Harry, that she can now find someone better, and Ginny asks if Dean Thomas would be someone better, because that's who she's going out with now. They are greeted at the station by Mr. and Mrs. Weasley, Tonks, Lupin, and "Mad Eye" Moody who tell Harry they plan to have a stern talk with his aunt and uncle about how they treat him. The twins are also there, decked out in new clothes, and say their new joke shop is doing well. The whole group confront Uncle Vernon, intimidating him into making the necessary concessions for Harry's comfort over the summer, and saying that they will be in touch, either by Harry's owl, or in person. Harry bids Ron and Hermione goodbye, and Ron promises that they will be seeing Harry very soon.

ANALYSIS

The book ends on a tragic note. For Harry, Sirius' death creates yet another deep void in his life, although, unlike when his parents died, it is the first time he has lost a loved one that he actually knew and had a lengthy relationship with. Not only is he filled with grief, but also guilt over his rash behavior and the mistakes he made leading to the tragedy and nearly costing his friends their lives. Although Harry blames himself for Sirius' death, he fails to recognize that his godfather's reckless behavior also significantly contributed to his own demise. He also blames Dumbledore for withholding information and Snape, who, despite Dumbledore's unwavering faith, he believes deliberately waited to warn the Order of the Phoenix. Harry's attempts to contact Sirius in the beyond indicates he is unwilling to accept that his godfather is truly gone, although his talk with Luna provides some comfort and bolsters his hope that there may actually be an afterlife.

Harry realizes that Voldemort is an even greater threat, and although he now knows that returning to Privet Drive each summer sustains his mother's magical charm that protects him, this understanding provides little comfort as he prepares to endure yet another cheerless summer with the Dursleys. Harry will have time to reflect on what has happened and hopefully learn from his mistakes, although his path to maturity has been more traumatic than most. Mourning Sirius' death will cause him to feel even more alone and unloved, and likely isolating himself, as he often does during stressful times. As a result, he can overlook or shut out those people left in his life who care for and support him. As he grieves his lost godfather, Ron, Hermione, Lupin, Dumbledore, and the others draw closer to him; they are his true "family."

QUESTIONS

Review 1. What did Sirius give Harry for Christmas? Why did Harry wait so long to open it?

2. Why does Harry offer to help Luna find her belongings? Why does she decline his offer?

3. Why does Harry seek Nearly Headless Nick's advice? What does Nick tell him?

4. What does Luna mean when she tells Harry that she will see her deceased mother again? How does that affect Harry?

Extra Study 1. Did Harry's delay in opening the Christmas present from Sirius contribute to Sirius' death? If so, how?

2. Why does Harry blame himself for Sirius' death? Who else does he blame and why?

3. How might Sirius have contributed to his own death?

GREATER PICTURE

There are two interesting plot points in this chapter. Firstly, Luna tells Harry that the voices they heard from behind the veiled arch are of those who have died and are merely waiting in the shadows. She believes they will be seen again, she fully expects to eventually be re-united with her mother, and that Harry will be reunited with Sirius. While that may seem like wishful thinking on her part, it actually foreshadows Harry's own experience in the final book, *Harry Potter and the Deathly Hallows*, when he is able to summon his parents' spirits, as well as Sirius and one other character who has been killed (Lupin), and speak with them.

Secondly, the broken mirror will also play an important role in the last novel. Harry keeps a mirror shard with him while he searches for Voldemort's Horcruxes (soul fragments). On several occasions he glimpses someone's blue eye staring at him in the reflection—an eye that could be Albus Dumbledore's.

HALF-BLOOD PRINCE

CHAPTERS

Chapter 1: The Other Minister
Chapter 2: Spinner's End
Chapter 3: Will and Won't
Chapter 4: Horace Slughorn
Chapter 5: An Excess of Phlegm
Chapter 6: Draco's Detour
Chapter 7: The Slug Club
Chapter 8: Snape Victorious
Chapter 9: The Half-Blood Prince
Chapter 10: The House of Gaunt
Chapter 11: Hermione's Helping Hand
Chapter 12: Silver and Opals
Chapter 13: The Secret Riddle
Chapter 14: Felix Felicis
Chapter 15: The Unbreakable Vow
Chapter 16: A Very Frosty Christmas
Chapter 17: A Sluggish Memory
Chapter 18: Birthday Surprises
Chapter 19: Elf Tails
Chapter 20: Lord Voldemort's Request
Chapter 21: The Unknowable Room
Chapter 22: After the Burial
Chapter 23: Horcruxes
Chapter 24: Sectumsempra
Chapter 25: The Seer Overheard
Chapter 26: The Cave
Chapter 27: The Lightning-Struck Tower
Chapter 28: Flight of the Prince
Chapter 29: The Phoenix Lament
Chapter 30: The White Tomb

OVERVIEW

We join Harry Potter as he enters his sixth year at Hogwarts. This volume is written from the point-of-view of the now 16-year-old Harry, as he takes advanced courses to prepare for the N.E.W.T.-level exams required for his chosen career. A darker book than the preceding volumes, it reveals more about Lord Voldemort's history and his impact on the Muggle world. Voldemort has emerged into the open, and his presence is beginning to have an effect on the day-to-day life of the Wizarding world.

While the series progressively covers seven years in Harry Potter's life, each of the first five volumes is largely self-contained. This book is written more as the first half of a two-part novel, and, as such, the ending feels rather incomplete.

Note: While this book is one of the longer ones in the series, at 607 pages (Bloomsbury / Raincoast edition), it is also set in significantly larger type. If it were the same size type as *Harry Potter and the Philosopher's Stone*, it would be 414 pages (approximately) to 223 for *Harry Potter and the Philosopher's Stone*.

BOOK HIGHLIGHTS

• New places visited: Muggle Prime Minister's office (Number 10, Downing Street), Spinner's End, Marvolo Gaunt's residence, an orphanage in London, the cave where young Tom Riddle tortured two children from his orphanage (Dennis Bishop and Amy Benson), Fred and George Weasley's joke shop: Weasleys' Wizard Wheezes, Hepzibah Smith's house.
• *Defence Against the Dark Arts* teacher: Severus Snape
• New teacher: Horace Slughorn
• Title refers to: previous owner of Harry's borrowed *Advanced Potion Making* book.

Chapter 1: The Other Minister

SYNOPSIS

The story opens with the Muggle Prime Minister in his office. As he recollects the past week's events, a wall portrait requests an immediate meeting with Cornelius Fudge, which the Prime Minister reluctantly grants. Fudge appears a few minutes later via the Floo Network, although the Prime Minister is unhappy to see him; every previous meeting has brought bad news. It has been a difficult week for Fudge too, with the Brockdale bridge collapse, Bones and Vance family members being murdered, and the ruckus in the West Country. To the Prime Minister's dismay, Fudge reports that these events involved the Wizarding community.

The Prime Minister first met Fudge shortly after his election several years ago when Fudge informed him about the wizarding world and the Ministry of Magic, the governing body in the UK. He recalls several other Fudge visits the past few years, usually to discuss how the magical community was affecting Muggles. With each visit, Fudge looked increasingly haggard and stressed, and the Prime Minister wonders what bad news Fudge, looking worse than ever, has brought this time.

According to Fudge, He Who Must Not Be Named has returned, and the past week's crises were perpetrated by him and his Death Eaters. The bridge collapse was caused by Fudge's refusal to be blackmailed, the West Country hurricane was not a hurricane at all, and it is suspected Giants caused it. Members of the Bones and Vance families were murdered by Voldemort or a follower. Then there are the Dementors; the creatures are roaming the countryside and attacking people since defecting as Azkaban prison guards. And they are breeding, which is why the weather has been so bad. Fudge admits he was forced to resign over mishandling the Voldemort affair and is there to introduce his successor, Rufus Scrimgeour.

Arriving through the office fireplace, Scrimgeour informs the Prime Minister that due to the recent events in the Wizarding world, wizards will handle his security. Scrimgeour's new secretary, Kingsley Shacklebolt, an Auror, has been assigned to protect him. The Prime Minister is displeased that the wizarding realm has leaked into the Muggle world, but Scrimgeour and Fudge assure him that they are doing all they can.

ANALYSIS

The meeting between the British Prime Minister and Ministry of Magic officials is a rare instance where Wizard and Muggle domains overtly collide. For centuries, Wizards have secretly coexisted alongside Muggles, remaining carefully hidden and separate. And while there have always been Muggles who are aware that Wizards exists, and even some who have married into that society, what happens in one realm rarely affects the other. This changes when Voldemort's violent attacks begin to include Muggles. Whether or not this is deliberate is, as yet, unclear; Voldemort may intend for the violence to spill over into the Muggle realm as a brazen act to confuse and intimidate other wizards and to demonstrate just how far he can and will go. He may also be intending to breach the long-standing divide between the two realms, bringing both under his rule. Whatever Voldemort's intent, the Prime Minister is powerless to protect his own people, and he has little choice but to accept the Wizarding world's help and to hope that Voldemort can be defeated, or at least contained to his own sphere.

It may be worth recalling Dumbledore's warning to Fudge, at *Harry Potter and the Goblet of Fire's* conclusion, that "history will remember you as the man who stepped aside, and allowed Voldemort a second chance to destroy the world we have tried to rebuild!" Clearly, this has now come to pass. When Voldemort was revealed to be alive, thus showing plainly that Fudge's ministry, by discrediting both Harry and Dumbledore, had been systematically lying to the Wizarding world, retribution by the general populace was swift. Despite Fudge's efforts to retain power, he has been ousted and replaced by someone who appears more dynamic and better prepared to fight Voldemort and the Death Eaters.

The Prime Minister recalls from an earlier visit, Fudge mentioned that he was required to inform the Muggle government that they were importing dangerous magical creatures into Britain for a Wizarding competition: three dragons and a Sphinx. This may confuse some readers, who remember that there were four dragon species at that competition; however, one was a Common Welsh Green and therefore a native species. It should also be noted that this conversation was quite likely before Harry's name had unexpectedly come out of the Goblet; the original plan might well have been to import three Dragons, and when a fourth was needed, a native variety was used so they would not have to notify the Muggle government again.

In yet another date confusion endemic to the series, Fudge says, "I must say, you're taking it a lot better than your predecessor. *He* tried to throw me out of the window . . ." (italics in original). If we accept, according to the internal timeline, that it is 1996 when this book takes place, then the Muggle Prime Minister must be John Major, which would make his predecessor Maggie Thatcher, definitely not a "he." Ms. Thatcher became Prime Minister in 1979, so Fudge would have had to introduce himself to her in 1979. If, as we assume from the same timeline, Voldemort murdered Harry's parents in 1981, that would mean that Fudge would have been in power before Voldemort's fall. However, the story states that Barty Crouch Sr. was being groomed for that position, and when his son went to Azkaban, *after* the fall of Voldemort, they tried to tap Dumbledore for that position, and only elected Fudge when Dumbledore refused. So Fudge could not have come into power before 1982 or so in our timeline, which would mean that he could not have introduced himself to Ms. Thatcher immediately after her election. One could try and fit the timeline to the tenure of Tony Blair, who took power in 1997, but there is little point: the story does not depend on any specific interaction with our world, and errors of this sort do not even distract the reader unless we let them.

QUESTIONS

Review 1. Why does Fudge visit the Muggle prime minister?

2. Who does Fudge introduce to the prime minister? Why?

3. Why was Fudge forced to resign as Minister for Magic?

Further Study 1. Why might Voldemort's attacks have spilled over into the Muggle world?

2. If Fudge was forced to resign, why is he working with Scrimgeour?

3. Why did the Dementors defect to Voldemort's side?

4. Why were members of the Bones and Vance families murdered?

GREATER PICTURE

At Christmas, Scrimgeour, the new Minister for Magic, will attempt to persuade Harry to occasionally be seen visiting the Ministry. As a bonus for his cooperation, Scrimgeour hints that Harry may be easily accepted into the Auror branch. Harry recognizes this as an attempt to sway the general populace's opinion that Harry, the "Chosen One," supports the Ministry and its actions; he refuses, believing the Ministry is doing a poor job. And though the Ministry's position on Voldemort may have swung from one extreme position to another, they are more about presenting a good public face rather than building substance under Scrimgeour's leadership.

When Harry later discusses this incident with Dumbledore, we learn that Dumbledore had blocked Scrimgeour from proposing this same scheme to Harry earlier in the school year. Dumbledore knew Harry would never allow himself to be recruited as a Ministry pawn, and that he was still in a fragile mental state over Sirius' death. Dumbledore and Scrimgeour's argument became loud enough that it was overheard and later leaked to the general public. This was actually the Ministry's second attempt to draft Harry; prior to Fudge's ouster, he was attempting damage control and working to retain his power. Dumbledore says when Fudge suggested the same ploy as Scrimgeour, he was similarly rebuffed.

Chapter 2: Spinner's End

Synopsis

Two cloaked figures Apparate alongside a dirty river. Narcissa Malfoy and her sister, Bellatrix Lestrange, head for a dilapidated brick row house on Spinner's End. While walking, Bellatrix is apparently trying to dissuade Narcissa from doing something. At the house, they are greeted by Severus Snape, who assures them that they are alone, except for Wormtail (Peter Pettigrew). Snape orders Wormtail to fetch drinks for himself and his guests, and Wormtail complies, though protesting that he is not there to be Snape's servant. Narcissa believes only Snape can help her, but before she can say more, Snape points his wand at a concealed door and sends Wormtail scurrying. Narcissa starts over, only to be interrupted by Bellatrix, who distrusts Snape. She interrogates him about where (and with whom) his true loyalties lie. Before responding, Snape asks in turn: does Bellatrix really think that the Dark Lord had not asked him those same questions? Does she think he could have fooled the Dark Lord? While she hesitates, Snape answers her previous questions. Where was he when the Dark Lord fell? At Hogwarts, where Voldemort had ordered him to spy on Dumbledore. Why did he not hunt for the Dark Lord after he fell? For the same reason many other Death Eaters failed to: he believed the Dark Lord was finished. Bellatrix retorts that she searched for him. Snape sarcastically comments about how "useful" she was while imprisoned in Azkaban, while he collected sixteen years' worth of information on Dumbledore for Voldemort. Snape continues: Why did he stand between the Dark Lord and the Philosopher's Stone? Because the Dark Lord believed Snape had deserted him for Dumbledore, Snape was left unaware that it was Voldemort who was looking for the Stone. He thought Quirrell wanted it and, of course, he acted to prevent that. Why did he fail to respond to the Dark Lord's summons when Voldemort returned? He returned two hours later, at Dumbledore's orders. That way, Dumbledore would continue to believe that Snape was spying on Voldemort for him, rather than the other way around. Bellatrix says she is unaware of any information Snape passed to Voldemort, although she should know: Voldemort says she is his most trusted lieutenant. Snape asks if she retains this status after the fiasco at the Ministry. And where was he during that battle? On the Dark Lord's orders, he stayed away. Did Bellatrix think Dumbledore would fail to notice if Snape had joined the Death Eaters in that battle? In any event, the information Snape supplied made Emmeline Vance and Sirius Black's deaths possible, and the Dark Lord was satisfied with his information. Why did Snape not kill Harry Potter? Because it was only Dumbledore who was keeping Snape effective as a spy and out of Azkaban. If he killed Potter, he would lose that protection and would be unable to help Voldemort. And that is what has continued to make him so useful to the Dark Lord: Dumbledore's trust in him.

With Bellatrix's worries overridden, Narcissa explains her reason for coming. Voldemort has assigned her son, Draco, a difficult and probably deadly task. Narcissa wants Snape to protect him. Snape replies that it is folly for them to discuss it because that is breaking the Dark Lord's wish. Death Eaters seldom know what tasks their colleagues have been assigned. Luckily for Narcissa, however, Snape already knows about this task, but even as the Dark Lord's most trusted confidante, he is powerless to persuade him to change his mind, nor will he try. Narcissa says assigning Draco this task is revenge for her husband Lucius' failure at the Ministry. Snape admits that the Dark Lord is angry at Lucius. Finally, though, Snape agrees to swear an 'Unbreakable Vow' to protect Draco, and if Draco is unable to complete his mission, Snape will do it for him.

Analysis

Snape's loyalty to Dumbledore in *Harry Potter and the Order of the Phoenix* has been established, but the evidence here is that he could be a traitor when he agrees to Narcissa Malfoy's Unbreakable Vow, and Harry's adamant (and lone) belief that he is still a Death Eater seems validated. Snape, whose fidelity to Voldemort is questioned by many Death Eaters, including Bellatrix Lestrange, knows he can help dispel these doubts by swearing a magically binding oath to protect Draco, even at peril to his own life. Bellatrix probably remains somewhat skeptical, despite Snape's seemingly convincing answers to her probing interrogation; indeed, it seems that Snape's true allegiance always remains just vague enough to keep each side guessing. Dumbledore, we remember, has always steadfastly defended Snape's loyalty, despite Harry's continuing suspicions. However, readers know that Snape has been acting as a double agent, and this may be a situation where he is forced into taking the vow so he can maintain his double agent cover. To do otherwise would cast even more suspicion on his supposed loyalties. It is also conceivable that Snape is loyal only to himself, maintaining a tenuous and dangerous position where he can align himself with either winning side. As a side note, although it seems that Bellatrix is satisfied by Snape's answers, she could have insisted on him taking Veritaserum (truth serum) before interrogating him. However, she does not, possibly because, as Dumbledore will suggest later, even Veritaserum can be circumvented if it is expected. Wormtail's loyalty, however, seems far less questionable, as he is fully dependent on Voldemort for his very survival. Unlike Snape, he is unable to align himself in any way to Harry, Dumbledore, and their allies. And while it initially may seem that Snape has Wormtail under his constant, watchful eye, it is possible that Wormtail is secretly keeping tabs on Snape for Voldemort. Even though it appears that Snape has convinced Voldemort that he is his faithful servant, the Dark Lord likely has lingering suspicions about him or wants to reassure his doubtful followers. However, Voldemort may know that Wormtail owes Harry Potter a life debt, an obligation as magically binding as Snape's Unbreakable Vow, and which could prove to be a severe liability to the Dark Lord. Voldemort is likely having Snape and Wormtail unknowingly watch each other.

Rowling also sheds light on some Death Eaters' personal relationships, as evidenced when sisters Bellatrix Lestrange and Narcissa Malfoy affectionately refer to each other as "Bella" and "Cissy." This is a contrast to how Harry has viewed most Death Eaters. Until now, Voldemort's followers have generally been portrayed as two-dimensionally evil characters who unwaveringly serve Lord Voldemort. Other than the Malfoys, little is known about Death Eaters' family life, social interactions, or what factors, other than "pureblood" beliefs, motivates them. Until now, Bellatrix has been portrayed as purely evil, fanatical, and probably unbalanced, even by Death Eater standards, and she may believe Voldemort is doing too little to rid impurities from the Wizarding world. In this chapter, however, she is seen as caring about her sister, Narcissa, wanting to protect her from Voldemort.

And while Bellatrix generally remains two-dimensional, the cold and haughty Narcissa, desperate to protect her husband and son, now displays love, fear, empathy, and sadness—emotions not generally associated with Voldemort's affiliates and that help develop her into a more fully-rounded character. Narcissa believes Voldemort tasked Draco with a near-impossible mission (in which he will likely fail and then be killed) only as a means to punish her husband, Lucius Malfoy, for his failure to retrieve the Trelawney prophecy at the Department of Mysteries (in *Harry Potter and the Order of the Phoenix*), and also apparently for Voldemort's Diary Horcrux being destroyed (in *Harry Potter and the Chamber of Secrets*). This could ultimately affect Narcissa's loyalty to the Dark Lord and also to her sister. And despite their seeming affection for one another, it should be remembered that both Bellatrix and Narcissa readily disowned their sister, Andromeda, as a blood traitor for marrying the Muggle-born wizard, Ted Tonks. (Nymphadora Tonks is their daughter, and thus niece to Bellatrix and Narcissa.) Essentially, no one is what they appear to be.

In *Harry Potter and the Goblet of Fire,* Snape was sent on an unexplained mission. In this chapter, we learn that his mission was to rejoin Voldemort and pledge his allegiance.

Questions

Review 1. What might happen if Voldemort learns that Snape has made an Unbreakable Vow with Narcissa?

2. What does Narcissa believe is the real reason Voldemort assigned Draco a nearly-impossible task? Is she correct?

3. What is Snape's explanation about why he never killed Harry Potter, even though he had many opportunities to do so? Is his explanation plausible? Why?

Further Study 1. Why does Snape make an Unbreakable Vow with Narcissa Malfoy, a vow that puts his own life at risk? Will he tell Dumbledore about it?

2. Considering how much doubt there is about Snape's true loyalties, why does Narcissa choose him to protect Draco?

3. Why did Narcissa and Bellatrix disown their sister, Andromeda? Can they trust each other? Explain.

4. Why does Bellatrix remain suspicious of Snape? Does he convince her that he is loyal to Voldemort?

5. Why do Death Eaters remain loyal to Voldemort, despite his tendency to threaten or eliminate even his most devoted followers or their families?

6. Compare and contrast evidence that Snape is loyal to either Dumbledore, Voldemort, or even to no one.

7. Why might Peter Pettigrew be at Snape's house? Does Snape trust him? Does Pettigrew suspect Snape might be a traitor? Who might Voldemort trust more?

Greater Picture

Readers see Draco cast in a more sympathetic role here when it appears that he is Lord Voldemort's victim as much as his ally, forced to do his bidding under duress and at extreme risk to himself and his family. We will shortly see how a smug Draco initially revels in his own bloated self-importance at being appointed the Dark Lord's task, woefully unaware and unable yet to comprehend the probable consequences to himself and his parents should he fail. Narcissa, however, has correctly surmised Voldemort's true intention: to punish Lucius Malfoy through Draco. She is risking her own life by defying Voldemort in an attempt to save her family. This raises the question as to why so many Death Eaters faithfully serve Voldemort, who demands his servants' total obedience and loyalty while offering little reward in return, and who readily eliminates a follower or their family for any reason; even his most devoted and trusted confidants are capriciously expendable, even for the smallest misstep. This flagrant abuse could eventually create enough dissent and discord from within to undermine or destroy Voldemort's power, although, for now, his continued rise seems unabated.

Snape tells Bellatrix that his information led to the death of Emmeline Vance, who as we have seen is a member of the Order of the Phoenix. We will much later find out that Snape actually is working for the Order himself, as a double agent; it is safe to assume that Snape discusses with Dumbledore the information he will give to Voldemort. At the same time, we hear that Snape has only let those people die that he could not save. That strongly suggests that Dumbledore and Snape were somehow forced to give Voldemort information on Vance, and that they could not prevent her death. From this, we can assume that Vance's death was not preventable, Voldemort had already set his sights on her, but Snape had provided some small piece of information that had helped him find her. It is more than likely that Snape and Dumbledore had also provided Vance with the information that would allow her to fight back. While Vance clearly would not want to simply die, it is likely that she would agree to being put in harm's way, if in the battle she would have a chance to take some Death Eaters with her. While this is never confirmed, it is quite possible that, in fact, she did, and that the retreating Death Eaters had carried away and probably concealed their dead, as they tend to.

Chapter 3: Will and Won't

SYNOPSIS

The chapter opens at the Dursleys' house where Harry is asleep. Scattered about his room are many *Daily Prophets.* The paper now hails Harry as 'The Chosen One,' who will be instrumental in the recently-returned Voldemort's downfall.

Dumbledore arrives to collect Harry. Despite Dumbledore previously sending a letter setting the time, and Harry anxiously waiting his arrival for most of the week, he is astonished and puzzled that Dumbledore is fetching him from the Dursleys after only two weeks, and he is further surprised when Dumbledore actually arrives. The Dursleys are also surprised; Harry apparently never told them he was coming. Dumbledore merely ignores their disdain and makes himself comfortable. Harry notices that Dumbledore's hand is black and shriveled, but he says nothing to Harry about how he acquired the injury, saying only he will explain later.

Dumbledore tells Harry that Sirius Black has bequeathed him all his possessions, including 12 Grimmauld Place, Kreacher, and Buckbeak. However, there may be a spell that automatically leaves the inheritance to the eldest surviving Black male or prevents it from passing to a non-pureblood wizard. Because Sirius was the last Black male, it would likely pass to the eldest female relative, namely Bellatrix Lestrange (Sirius's cousin). To test whether Harry is the true heir, Dumbledore summons Kreacher, the loyal Black family House-elf. When Kreacher reluctantly obeys Harry's command, it confirms that Harry is the rightful heir.

Kreacher is sent to work at Hogwarts, and Buckbeak (now renamed Witherwings) is left in Hagrid's care. Dumbledore tells the Dursleys to expect a short visit from Harry in a year's time. The magical charm that has protected Harry from Voldemort since infancy will expire when he comes of age on his seventeenth birthday. However, he is required to make one final visit to the Dursleys the following summer to maintain its effectiveness, then his ties to his maternal family can be permanently severed. Before departing, Dumbledore reproaches the Dursleys for their bad manners, mistreating Harry, and over-indulging Dudley.

ANALYSIS

Dumbledore's injured hand indicates that sinister events may be underway in the wizarding world that Harry is not yet privy to. For whatever reason, Dumbledore chooses to keep them from Harry, at least for now. It has been suggested that Dumbledore acts out of character in this book. This is particularly obvious in this chapter. While still a peaceful and wise wizard, Dumbledore seems to act with a bit more directness and urgency than usual. He uses magic to sweep the Dursleys to the couch and chides them for their ill-manners, and he actively criticizes how they have treated Harry and raised Dudley. While he is still as good-natured and civil as ever, there seems to be an unexpected edginess in his manner. As can be expected, the Dursleys ignore Dumbledore's rebuke and seem unlikely to ever change.

Many readers may be somewhat alarmed when Dumbledore offers Harry a glass of mead. Mead, a wine made from honey, is usually relatively strong at 14% alcohol by volume, and it would be illegal to give it to a minor in North America. Liquor laws are less restrictive in Britain, however, and though someone underage may not purchase liquor in the UK, there is nothing that prohibits someone younger than 18 years from drinking wine or beer if it is offered by an adult.

QUESTIONS

1. How might Dumbledore have hurt his hand? Why doesn't he tell Harry how it was injured?
2. Why won't Harry be protected at the Dursley's house after his 17th birthday?
3. What effect will Harry's 17th birthday have on his relationship with the Dursleys?
4. Why would Dumbledore personally fetch Harry from the Dursleys after only two weeks there? Where might he be taking him?
5. What does Dumbledore say to the Dursleys about how they've treated Harry and raised their son, Dudley? Why did he never speak up about this sooner?
6. Dumbledore's behavior and demeanor is somewhat different here. How has it changed, and what might be the reason?

GREATER PICTURE

Some theorists believe that Dumbledore used the "Kreacher test" not only to see whether Number 12 Grimmauld Place actually belonged to Harry rather than Bellatrix Lestrange (Sirius' cousin), but also as a means to determine whether Sirius' younger brother, Regulus Black, was still alive. (It will be learned in the next book that Regulus is the mysterious R.A.B. who leaves a note at the end of this novel.) This test may be inconclusive, as the tradition is that property, such as a house, is directly handed down the male family line. It is entirely possible that the charm ensuring this, if there was one, would prevent a lateral transfer from the eldest male child, once he had come into his inheritance, to his younger brother. When Sirius died without offspring, the charm might have simply ceased operation.

The reason for Dumbledore's drastic character change can be attributed to him being damaged by a ring Horcrux, an object containing a deadly curse that should have killed him. He was able to get help from Severus Snape, who has kept him alive by extraordinary magical means, although only temporarily. This minute-to-minute awareness that he will soon die, and the resulting sense of urgency, is likely the cause for his changed character. Dumbledore, speaking directly to Petunia, mentions that they have corresponded before. There were actually at least four letters, though at this point in our reading there is nothing that can be attributed as being "correspondence." Dumbledore wrote a letter, which he left, along with Harry, on the Dursleys' doorstep at the series' beginning, and the Howler addressed to Petunia in *Harry Potter and the Order of the Phoenix* is also revealed to have been sent by Dumbledore. There is no indication that Petunia responded to either, and correspondence does rather imply that messages are being exchanged; despite this, many readers will assume that it is either one of these letters to which Dumbledore is referring. However, we will learn, in *Harry Potter and the Deathly Hallows,* that Petunia had earlier written to Hogwarts pleading for admission, and that Dumbledore responded, declining her plea on the grounds that she was unable to perform magic. If we assume that Dumbledore had implied an informational exchange, then he can only have been referring to this first set of letters.

Chapter 4: Horace Slughorn

SYNOPSIS

After leaving the Dursleys, Dumbledore asks Harry to carry his Invisibility Cloak, but sends his trunk on to the Burrow. As Harry clings to Dumbledore's arm, Dumbledore Apparates them to a small village. Having never Apparated before, Harry finds the sensation slightly disorienting. Once again, Hogwarts is one instructor short, and Dumbledore has come to Budleigh Babberton to recruit a new faculty member. They arrive at a wrecked house, finding what appears to be blood-splattered walls; after examining the wreckage, Dumbledore pokes an armchair with his wand. The armchair grunts and transforms into Horace Slughorn, Dumbledore's old colleague and a former Hogwarts professor. Slughorn created the false destruction to convince intruders that Death Eaters had killed him. However, Dumbledore knew the attack was staged because there was no Dark Mark looming over the building. Dumbledore helps Slughorn repair the house, then attempts to persuade Slughorn to return to Hogwarts, although he refuses. Dumbledore excuses himself, leaving Harry and Slughorn alone together. Slughorn, forced to make conversation, mentions that he taught Harry's father and mother. Lily was a favorite student, always top in his class and believes she ought to have been sorted into his House—he was head of Slytherin. Observing Harry's reaction, he correctly guesses that Harry is a Gryffindor like his mother. Slughorn says that taking a post at Hogwarts would be declaring allegiance to the Order of the Phoenix, although Harry reminds him that that teachers are not required to join the Order and that Hogwarts is safe (as Dumbledore is the only wizard Voldemort has ever feared). The only teacher who died there is Professor Quirrell.

Slughorn remains reluctant to leave his comfortable retirement and he has essentially been in hiding since Voldemort's return. After adroitly manipulating Slughorn's ego and attracting him to Harry's celebrity, Dumbledore finally convinces him to resume his old post. As they depart, Dumbledore tells Harry that Slughorn relishes his creature comforts and likes being the power behind a multiplicity of thrones. He also enjoys being among the rich and influential, and Harry, being famous, is someone he will attempt to cultivate.

Dumbledore then transports himself and Harry to The Burrow, and, before departing, tells Harry he will be taking private lessons with him during the year. Dumbledore also suggests that Harry share the Trelawney prophecy with Ron Weasley and Hermione Granger and requests that Harry always keep his Invisibility Cloak with him.

ANALYSIS

Dumbledore's suggestion that Harry reveal Trelawney's prophecy to Ron and Hermione emphasizes Dumbledore's understanding that Harry's strength and abilities are enhanced by his friends' assistance and support; Dumbledore realizes that Harry often refuses help from others. Although Harry is a talented wizard, it is also Ron and Hermione's loyalty, support, and their individual skills that have helped him overcome many adversities; each is at their best when they work together. Harry realizes that he cannot remain shut away in response to Sirius' death; it is time for him to reconnected with his friends and the wizarding world. Dumbledore chooses this moment to reinforce that thought.

Until now, we have seen Dumbledore as an extremely wise wizard genius, but this is the first time he has been observed manipulating people. He knows Slughorn is vain and likes being connected with the powerful and influential who can provide him favours and allows him to bask in their reflected glory. When Dumbledore offers Slughorn the position at Hogwarts, he uses Harry as bait, knowing Slughorn will be irresistably intrigued by and attracted to Harry Potter's fame, and wanting to hitch his own wagon to Harry's star; Dumbledore cleverly positions himself and Harry so that Slughorn will be fully exposed to Harry's presence. When his initial attempt to recruit Slughorn fails, he excuses himself, leaving Slughorn alone with Harry so he can convince himself that Harry is a celebrity he wants to collect. Finally, just as Slughorn is considering the offer, Dumbledore re-appears, snatches Harry from under Slughorn's nose, and departs. Slughorn cannot stand to see this prize vanish, and, with a bit of desperation, he accepts Dumbledore's offer. This is a very neat bit of coercion by Dumbledore, particularly in that it allowed Slughorn to convince himself—Harry was unprimed for this and did not participate in any coercion. Although Slughorn is an excellent teacher (otherwise Dumbledore would never have recruited him) he could prove problematic for Harry. Slughorn, as we have seen, has a vain personality and is attracted to other wizards' celebrity and influence. Harry, who disdains being in the limelight, may resent having yet another person fawning over him to serve their own purposes. This may put further stress on Harry. Also, Harry's mother, Lily, was among Slughorn's favorite and most talented pupils. He may have an unrealistic expectation that Harry has the same ability, putting undue (although perhaps somewhat needed) pressure on Harry, a rather lazy student, to perform at a higher level than he currently does.

QUESTIONS

Review 1. Why does Dumbledore take Harry to Budleigh Babberton Village?

2. Why was Slughorn hiding? How does Dumbledore see through his disguise?

3. Why does Slughorn think Lily Potter, a Muggle-born, should have been sorted into Slytherin House? What might be Harry's reaction to that suggesion?

4. Why does Slughorn finally agree to leave his comfortable retirement and accept the teaching post at Hogwarts?

Extra Study 1. Why is Dumbledore giving Harry private lessons, and what might they be? Why is he teaching Harry this time, unlike when Snape taught him Occlumency?

2. Why does Dumbledore ask Harry to take his Invisibility Cloak with him when they go to the village?

3. Why would Dumbledore ask Harry to always keep his Invisibility Cloak with him?

4. Why does Dumbledore encourage Harry to reveal Trelawney's prophecy to Ron and Hermione?

GREATER PICTURE

Some believe that this chapter contains direct evidence that Horace Slughorn is or was a Death Eater. When Slughorn asks Dumbledore how he knew that he had faked his own kidnapping/death, Dumbledore replies, "My dear Horace, if the Death Eaters really had come to call, the Dark Mark would have been set over the house," to which Slughorn answers, "The Dark Mark. Knew there was something ... ah well. Wouldn't have had time anyway ..." As far as anyone knows, only Death Eaters can create the Dark Mark. However, Horace Slughorn neither denied nor asserted that he *could* do it, he just stated that there wasn't enough time before Dumbledore arrived. It is unlikely that Slughorn is an active Death Eater. He enjoys his creature comforts far too much to relinquish them, and yet, he has gone into hiding. He seems rather taken aback, in fact, to realize that he has been hidden and incommunicado for a year. If he is a Death Eater, he may have refused to answer the Dark Mark summons; in that case, he likely fears for his life should he be found. This would explain him hiding, and his actions upon detecting a wizard Apparating into his current home village. However, Dumbledore asks if the Death Eaters have "come recruiting"; the implication is that Slughorn is seen as a potential or past ally, rather than an actual Death Eater. Additionally, in *Harry Potter and the Deathly Hallows*, we will see that Slughorn continues as the Potions master even after the school has become a Death Eater stronghold, although, like McGonagall, he may have been forced to stay and also wanted to protect the students. With Voldemort's tendency to exact revenge on those who failed to respond to the initial summons (for instance Karkaroff), it is unlikely that Slughorn would have survived the the Ministry's fall.

Harry believes (and readers assume) that Slughorn has been hired as the new Defense Against the Dark Arts teacher to replace Dolores Umbridge. However, Slughorn has actually been recruited to fill another position; this change will significantly affect Harry's future.

Chapter 5: An Excess of Phlegm

SYNOPSIS

Arriving at The Burrow, Dumbledore and Harry are met by Mrs. Weasley. Also present is Tonks, whose colorless and sad appearance shocks Harry; her usually vibrant pink hair is now a mousy grey. Tonks insists she must go and declines a weekend dinner invitation when Lupin and Mad-Eye will be there. As Mrs. Weasley gets Harry something to eat, she asks about Slughorn. Apparently, he started teaching at Hogwarts about the same time as Dumbledore, and he taught Mrs. Weasley. She disapproved of Slughorn's favorites, especially since Arthur Weasley was not among them.

Harry learns that Mr. Weasley has recently been appointed head of the new *Office of Detection and Confiscation of Counterfeit Defensive Spells and Protective Objects*. This promotion will help improve the Weasley finances. When Mr. Weasley arrives home, he discusses the counterfeit devices he has found. Harry is actually interested, but when he attempts to stifle a yawn, Mrs. Weasley sends him to bed in the twins' vacant room. They are now living in a little apartment over their Diagon Alley shop.

The next morning, Harry is awakened by Ron and Hermione, who are concerned about his well-being after the battle at the Ministry. Harry tells them about Horace Slughorn, who is replacing former Defense Against the Dark Arts instructor, Professor Umbridge. Ginny slouches in, complaining about *her*; Harry's curiosity as to who she is referring to is ended when Fleur Delacour enters with his breakfast tray and Mrs. Weasley in her wake. Fleur tells Harry that she and Bill Weasley are marrying next summer, then heads back downstairs. Ron is still rather infatuated by Fleur, but the three women feel she is very full of herself and wonder what Bill sees in her. Ginny derogatory calls her "Phlegm," which upsets Mrs. Weasley, but makes Harry and Hermione laugh. When Mrs. Weasley departs, Ron confides it is hard getting used to having Fleur around when she jumps out like that. Ron, Ginny, and Hermione agree that Mrs. Weasley is unlikely to get Bill interested in Tonks rather than Fleur. Tonks has been depressed since her cousin, Sirius Black's death. That she blames herself for Sirius' death interests Harry, who is experiencing the same guilt. As a result, Tonks has apparently lost the ability to change her physical appearance.

After Ginny is called to the kitchen, Ron tells Harry that the family and Percy remain estranged, despite Voldemort's return. Ron and Hermione are amazed that Dumbledore wants to give Harry private lessons. Harry reveals the prophecy to them, and Ron and

Hermione worry that Harry will have to face Voldemort. Harry is also worried, but on reflection, realizes he has always known he would eventually have to face Voldemort. Privately, he is greatly reassured by Ron and Hermione not abandoning him at the revelation that he is fated to either kill Voldemort or be killed by him.

Shortly, Harry, Ron, and Hermione head to the kitchen where they receive their O.W.L. results. It is revealed that "T" is an actual grade meaning *Troll,* not *Terrible* as might be imagined. Harry's grades are:
- Astronomy: Acceptable (A)
- Care of Magical Creatures: Exceeds Expectations (E)
- Charms: E
- Defence Against the Dark Arts: Outstanding (O)
- Divination: Poor (P)
- Herbology: E
- History of Magic: Dreadful (D)
- Potions: E
- Transfiguration: E

These results are good, but Harry's hope to become an Auror have apparently vanished. He needed an 'O' in Potions for Snape to accept him into his advanced Potions course, one of the N.E.W.T. subjects required to become an Auror.

Ron receives similar grades but no 'Outstanding's and is quite pleased that he only failed Divination and History of Magic. Hermione, as expected, receives 10 'O's and one 'E' (in Defence Against the Dark Arts). All three have passed into N.E.W.T. level.

Analysis

Harry is shocked by Tonks' radically changed appearance. There is no explanation as to what might have happened in the three or four weeks since she was last seen, but she is no longer the cheerful and vibrant person Harry last saw. Some readers may believe, given the amount of Ministry hysteria about Dark Wizards, that Tonks is being controlled by the Imperius curse. Hermione, Ginny, and Ron believe she is suffering from grief and guilt over Sirius' death and may even have been in love with him. However, there may actually be another reason for her depression. Harry also fears that his professional future is in jeopardy. The only career that interested him is an Auror (Dark Wizard catcher), even though the person who encouraged him was actually a Death Eater in disguise (Barty Crouch, Jr.). Unfortunately, Harry's Potions grade is too low to admit him into Snape's N.E.W.T.-level Potions classes he needs to fulfill the Auror prerequisites. This will deeply trouble Harry and being unable to follow his chosen career path leaves him discouraged and feeling adrift. Harry's tendency to be single-minded has, as yet, prevented him from seriously considering other careers, and he ponders what his options are.

In one of the continuity glitches common in this lengthy series, we see Mrs. Weasley's clock, now with all its nine hands, one for each family member, pointing at Mortal Peril. The astute reader may have noticed that here it is apparently a mantel clock, while in *Harry Potter and the Goblet of Fire* it is described as a grandfather clock. Mrs. Weasley claims that nobody else has a clock like that, so presumably someone in the family made it. It is possible that Mrs. Weasley wanted it to be more portable, and had a clock-maker separate the mechanism from the clock case and build a mantel-type case for it. This continuity problem does not hinder our appreciation of the story; it is only mentioned as a side light.

Questions

Review   1. Why is Harry worried about his future?
2. Why are the Weasleys unhappy about Bill's engagement to Fleur?

Extra Study   1. What might account for Tonks' changed appearance and demeanor?
2. Are Ron and Hermione right to be concerned about Harry's well being? If so, why?
3. Harry wants to be an Auror, but what other careers would he be good at?

Greater Picture

Tonks' forlorn emotional state is actually because she is in love with Remus Lupin, who spurns her affection, believing he is unworthy because he is a werewolf and too old for her. Mrs. Weasley comments that in troubled times like these, people "rush into decisions that they'd normally take time over." She is referring to Bill and Fleur's engagement that was made rather hastily, but it could equally apply to Tonks, who wants to pursue a relationship with Lupin. His refusal causes Tonks' increasing depression. As a result, we will see later that Tonks' Patronus has changed into "something large and hairy." It appears to be a dog, leading people to erroneously believe she was in love with Sirius Black. However, we later learn it is actually a wolf.

Chapter 6: Draco's Detour

Synopsis

Frequent deaths and disappearances are occurring throughout the Wizarding world. On Harry's birthday, Lupin brings news that Death Eaters killed Igor Karkaroff; Bill mentions that Florean Fortescue, who owns the ice cream parlour in Diagon Alley, is gone, and Mr. Weasley reports that Ollivander, the wand maker, is missing.

The following day, booklists arrive, along with an announcement that Harry is Quidditch captain. According to Hermione, that gives Harry equal status with the Prefects, allowing him to use their luxurious bathroom. Mrs. Weasley decides they can no longer delay the trip to Diagon Alley. On Saturday, Bill, who works for Gringotts, hands Harry a money bag retrieved from Harry's vault; Gringotts' security is now so tight that it takes about five hours to get inside. Harry, Hermione, and the Weasleys go shopping in Diagon Alley, accompanied by Hagrid. In Madam Malkin's Robes for All Occasions shop, Harry, Hermione, and Ron have

Chapter 6: Draco's Detour

a nasty encounter with Draco Malfoy and his snobbish mother, Narcissa. When the dressmaker tries lifting Draco's left robe sleeve she is measuring, he jerks his arm away, claiming she stuck him with a pin; he and his mother quickly leave. Harry, Ron, and Hermione head for Weasleys' Wizard Wheezes, Fred and George's joke shop, which is enjoying a booming trade. Not only are joke items selling well, but the Twins are also supplying spell-deflecting Shield Hats, Cloaks, Gloves, and other serious magical items to the Ministry of Magic (presumably for the war against Voldemort).

Harry spots Draco passing the shop alone. Using the Invisibility Cloak, Harry, Ron, and Hermione trail Draco to Knockturn Alley where he goes to Borgin & Burkes, the dark magic shop. Using Weasley's Extendable Ears, they overhear Draco asking how to repair something. Draco threatens Borgin, showing him something on his arm, but the large black cabinet that Harry hid inside four years earlier partially blocks their view. Draco warns that Fenrir Greyback, a 'family friend,' will be, "dropping in from time-to-time to see that you're giving this matter your full attention." Malfoy also reserves an item for himself, ordering Borgin to keep it secret. After Draco exits, Hermione enters the store pretending to be looking for a birthday present for her "friend" Draco. Hoping to learn what Draco reserved, Borgin instead orders her to leave.

They return to Fred and George's store under the Invisibility Cloak. To explain their absence to a worried Mrs. Weasley, they claim they were in the backroom.

ANALYSIS

Harry is suspicious that Draco's visit to Borgin & Burkes involves something sinister, though Ron and Hermione are less certain. Draco threatens Borgin into assisting him by mentioning that someone named Fenrir Greyback is a "family friend." Whoever Greyback may be, the name alone is apparently sufficient to ensure Borgin's cooperation. Whatever Draco must repair, it may be related to the task Voldemort assigned him that was mentioned in the second chapter. It is particularly interesting that Draco may be performing this step of his task without his mother's knowledge—perhaps she is somehow attempting to prevent him from undertaking this mission. Draco jerking his arm away from the dressmaker but threateningly showing it to Borgin is significant; his forearm may carry Voldemort's Dark Mark. Harry certainly suspects it does.

Hermione's attempt to gather more information about Draco at Borgin & Burke's shows that she is learning to act more spontaneously under stressful conditions. However, her actions here were not only clumsy, but they likely created suspicion that could tip off the Malfoy family that someone is investigating Draco's actions. However, just what he is planning is still unclear. And unlike Harry, Ron and Hermione are still unconvinced that Draco is a Death Eater or is involved in anything dastardly, although they still support Harry, even knowing he makes assumptions that are as often wrong as they are right. They are at least willing to consider Harry's speculation here, while offering their own opinions to counterbalance his. Readers, having previously witnessed the encounter at Snape's home in Spinner's End, have a far better idea that Draco has indeed been assigned a significantly important task for Voldemort, although just what that might be is still unknown. Throughout the book, Harry remains convinced that Draco is involved in a sinister plot. To uncover what that is, he will have to continue trailing Draco and piece together clues leading to a definitive answer. Harry will become nearly obsessed by this quest. Also, considering that dire events in the Wizarding world are unfolding at an alarming rate as Voldemort's power grows, it may seem that Ron and Hermione are being unrealistically dismissive regarding Harry's suspicions. However, despite the Malfoy family's affiliation with Voldemort and their affinity for the Dark Arts, Ron and Hermione simply believe that Draco is just too young and inexperienced to be a Death Eater or to have been entrusted with an important mission. Not only was Harry disappointed (and also jealous) the previous year when Ron was made a Gryffindor Prefect and he was not, but he was also rather offended. However, at the end of the previous book, it is revealed that this was a deliberate decision by Professor Dumbledore. His stated reason was, "I must confess . . . that I rather thought you had enough responsibility to be going on with." Selecting Ron as Prefect was possibly, in part, to allow Ron an opportunity to assume an independent role apart from Harry's celebrity and influence so he could develop his own abilities and identity. When Harry becomes Quidditch captain, Hermione points out that he now has equal status to a Prefect and shares similar privileges.

Hermione's saying that Harry becoming Quidditch Captain gives him equal privileges as Prefects feels a bit like the author's afterthought. While it is mentioned that Cedric Diggory was Quidditch captain, nowhere in that book is it mentioned that he is a Prefect, a fact that would have been significantly important to the students. Thus, we must conclude that he was not a Prefect. And yet, he knew about the Prefects' bathroom and was able to give Harry the password to enter it. Likely, we will never know the author's intent, but it seems that granting Quidditch captains access to the Prefects' bathroom could be a means to rationalize Cedric's knowledge about that privilege, knowledge that could not be explained otherwise.

QUESTIONS

Review 1. What prompted Harry, Ron, and Hermione to go to Knockturn Alley? What do they learn?

2. How will Harry becoming Quidditch captain affect his relationship with Ron, who was made a Prefect the year before, causing Harry to be jealous?

Extra Study 1. Why would Draco jerk away when Madam Malkin attempts to lift his sleeve but he willingly shows the same arm to Borgin?

2. What task might Voldemort have assigned Draco? Why would he choose Draco, an underaged and still unqualified wizard?

3. Why does Draco go to Borgin & Burke's alone?

4. Why would Draco order another item from Borgin for himself, and what might that item be?

5. Why is the Ministry of Magic ordering magical items from the Weasley twins' joke shop? What are they buying?

Greater Picture

While Harry, Ron, and Hermione are spying on Draco, they are unable to see what he shows to Borgin because Draco was behind a Vanishing Cabinet. This cabinet apparently matches one in Hogwarts, which is seen later when Harry hides his Potions textbook in the Room of Requirement. The Hogwarts Vanishing Cabinet was broken during Harry's second year at the school. When Filch took Harry into his office, Nearly Headless Nick convinced Peeves to drop the cabinet over the office as a diversion so Harry could escape. Apparently the Weasley twins once forced Montague into it, before it was hidden away in the Room of Requirement. The cabinet plays a significant role in the book's conclusion.

Even though Hermione's attempts to learn what Draco was doing at Borgin & Burke's could have inadvertently alerted the Malfoys that Draco's secret mission was being investigated, it will be Draco himself who deliberately allows Harry to eavesdrop on a conversation where Draco boasts that he has been assigned an important task for the Dark Lord.

Readers will learn that Fenrir Greyback, who Draco mentions is a "family friend," is a particularly vicious werewolf pack leader who serves Voldemort. It was Greyback who attacked Remus Lupin when he was a young boy, turning him into a werewolf. Lupin will eventually infiltrate Greyback's pack as a spy for Dumbledore. Mr. Ollivander's disappearance will play an important role in the final book.

Chapter 7: The Slug Club

Synopsis

Back at the Burrow, Harry's claims that Malfoy is a Death Eater are met with skepticism by Ron and Hermione, who argue that Draco is too young and inexperienced for Voldemort to entrust him with an important task. Harry, still convinced, cites how Draco yanked his arm away from Madam Malkin, the same arm Death Eaters carry a Dark Mark. Malfoy also showed Borgin something on the same forearm that caused Borgin take Malfoy seriously.

Vexed that Ron and Hermione remain unconvinced, Harry heads to the kitchen, interrupting Fleur, who is in full flow with her wedding plans, much to Mrs. Weasley's relief. Mrs. Weasley wants everyone packed the night before leaving for Hogwarts to avoid the usual last-minute chaotic rush. The next morning, Ministry cars arrive to transport them to the station have arrived. Surprisingly, everyone is ready on time, their trunks packed, and Hedwig, Pigwidgeon, Crookshanks, and Ginny Weasley's new pet, a Pygmy Puff named Arnold, are all safely caged. Harry speaks privately with Mr. Weasley regarding Draco Malfoy's suspicious behavior. Mr. Weasley is also doubtful that Draco is a Death Eater and says Malfoy Manor was raided; anything even slightly Dark was confiscated.

On the Hogwarts Express, Ron and Hermione report to the Prefects' carriage while Harry, Luna, and Neville find a free compartment. Harry is bemused at being in the spotlight again, and shortly after, fourth-year student Romilda Vane invites Harry to sit with her and some other students. Harry declines, saying he is with friends. Harry discusses O.W.L results, and Neville wonders if he will be able to take N.E.W.T. Transfiguration with only Acceptable. Harry muses to himself that it could as easily have been Neville with the scar and the admirers. Ron and Hermione return with news that Malfoy is just sitting in his compartment; it is unlike him to be doing anything other than lording over other Slytherin students. As Harry ponders Draco's uncharacteristic behavior, a third-year girl appears with lunch invitations for Harry and Neville from Professor Slughorn. There is a large gathering, including Ginny and Blaise Zabini, a Slytherin in Harry's year. As Slughorn interrogates them, it becomes apparent that the invitees are all connected to influential wizarding families, except for Ginny, who was included because she impressed Slughorn with her Bat-Bogey Hex. Having questioned Harry, Neville, Ginny, Blaise, Cormac McLaggen and Marcus Belby, to assess their family connections and prospects, Slughorn entertains them (excepting Marcus, who is estranged from his famous uncle) for the afternoon, then dismisses them to prepare for arrival at Hogwarts.

Leaving Slughorn's carriage, Harry slips on his Invisibility Cloak and tails Zabini to the Slytherin carriage to eavesdrop on Malfoy. Climbing into the luggage rack, Harry worries that Malfoy glimpsed his trainer (US: sneaker), but Malfoy simply settles back with his head on Pansy Parkinson's lap.

Zabini reports that Slughorn is only interested in students' connections to influential wizards. Malfoy is annoyed at being excluded, but Zabini speculates that Slughorn is uninterested in Death Eaters. Malfoy lets slip that he may not return to Hogwarts next year, claiming he has moved on to, "bigger and better things." This surprises the other Slytherins, and Zabini asks what an unqualified wizard could do for Voldemort. Malfoy retorts that his task may not require qualifications.

The train arrive at Hogsmeade Station, but Malfoy remains behind in the compartment. In a surprise move, he Petrifies Harry. Malfoy spotted Harry's shoe as he climbed onto the luggage rack. As revenge, Malfoy stomps on Harry's nose, breaking it. Malfoy tosses the Invisibility Cloak over Harry so he will go unnoticed until after the train returns to London.

Analysis

Harry is frustrated that Ron and Hermione are continually dismissive regarding his suspicions about Draco. However, their frequent skepticism often acts as a counterbalance to his occasional overreaction and drawing conclusions without fully considering all facts and opinions. This time, however, Harry is positive that Draco has become a Death Eater and is involved in some malicious plot, becoming nearly obsessed proving it. Considering the information readers are alreay privy to regarding Draco's task for Voldemort, Harry is obviously correct, although he, and also we, are still clueless as to just what that is, other than it requires repairing some object that probably contains Dark magic.

For the first time, Harry's budding romantic feelings for Ginny are seen. As she goes to meet Dean, Harry feels a slightly annoying twinge which could be interpreted as jealousy. Of course, Harry may not recognize this emotion because he has never thought of Ginny this way before, but he clearly sees her in a different way. Slughorn's personality is becoming more apparent here as he immediately begins singling out those students connected to influential families. And though Slughorn was formerly the head of Slytherin House, it appears that he does not fully embrace their pure-blood beliefs. In addition to Slytherins, Slughorn invites other well-connected students, and also those, like Ginny Weasley, displaying exceptional magical talent. Draco is offended at being excluded, but someone points out that Slughorn is probably uninterested in Death Eaters, though he may be distancing himself for other reasons. Though Harry was invited for his fame, Slughorn also included him and Neville because both were involved in the Battle at the Ministry. He repeatedly tries to pump them for details about that incident, but each remains silent for their own particular reasons. Curiously, even though Ron and Luna were also involved in the battle, they were uninvited.

Harry also demonstrates personal integrity when he declines Romilda Vane's invitation to sit in her compartment with the other popular students. While he wishes to avoid the attention and others fawning over him, he also prefers Neville and Luna's company, two people he once would have been embarrassed to hang out with, but now feels the most comfortable being around. Their loyalty and bravery at the Ministry of Magic battle has forever altered Harry's opinion and esteem for them, showing his growing maturity in valuing others for their inner worth and accepting these two so-called "misfits" as his peers and friends. His influence has dramatically helped each one to realize their untapped potential, while they, in turn, befriend him for the person he is, rather than his celebrity. Although Draco has always been portrayed as a cowardly bully, he is a powerful wizard, and his intelligence and magical abilities are often underrated. Throughout the story, he is well aware that Harry is trailing his movements, and he even intentionally lets slip some enticing information within Harry's hearing regarding his connection to Voldemort. Just why he does so is unknown, although Draco seldom resists showing off and extolling his own perceived virtues to others. Draco must also have been relatively confident that Harry would never report the attack (and breaking his nose), thus allowing Draco to indulge himself in his cruel act.

QUESTIONS

Review 1. Which students are invited to Slughorn's lunch? Why does he select these particular students? Why was Malfoy excluded?

2. Why does Harry follow Malfoy on the train?

3. Why does Malfoy say he might not return to Hogwarts next year?

Extra Study 1. Why does Malfoy reveal such specific, and apparently accurate, information about Voldemort, even though he knows Harry is eavesdropping?

2. Why, despite compelling circumstantial evidence, do Ron and Hermione dismiss Harry's belief that Draco may be a Death Eater? Are their arguments valid?

3. On the train, why does Harry decline Romilda Vane's invitation to sit with her and the other more popular students? Who does he prefer to sit with and why?

GREATER PICTURE

Over the school year, Harry becomes nearly obsessed with Draco Malfoy's suspicious behavior and goes to extreme lengths to uncover what he is plotting. Eventually he discovers that Malfoy is indeed involved in a sinister scheme, although Draco's participation is not entirely what it seems. Just why Draco purposely allowed Harry to overhear critical information while on the Hogwarts Express is unclear. Whether he was just being careless, arrogantly confident, or subconsciously hoping that Voldemort's plan woud be discovered by Dumbledore through Harry is unknown, although the latter reason will seem more likely by the book's conclusion. It will be learned that Dumbledore already knows about Draco's mission.

While Harry shows great maturity and personal integrity in accepting Luna as a friend and equal, Ron, however, does not. When Harry invites her to attend Slughorn's Christmas party later in the story, Ron chastises him, saying he could have taken anyone other than "Loony" Luna. As Luna herself will accurately note, Ron can sometimes be funny but also hurtful. It does seem that Ron has forgotten Luna's participation in Dumbledore's Army and how she always responded to Harry's distress calls, as well as risking her own life at the Department of Mysteries battle to aid Harry and Ron.

Chapter 8: Snape Victorious

SYNOPSIS

Nymphadora Tonks suddenly appears in the compartment and unpetrifies Harry. Before the departing train picks up too much speed, they leap off. Tonks mends Harry's broken nose and then sends a Patronus Charm to the castle, alerting everyone that Harry is safe. She is not guarding Hogwarts alone; Proudfoot, Savage, and Dawlish are also there. Harry again notices her depressed and unhappy look, and her usual vibrantly-colored hair remains faded. (Harry speculates that she was in love with Sirius and is mourning his death.) Reaching Hogwarts, they are met by Snape, who ridicules Tonks' new Patronus. Snape deducts 70 points from Gryffindor, then escorts Harry to the Great Hall without allowing him to change into his robes. Embarrassed and ashamed, Harry does not report Malfoy's actions, and when Hermione and Ron ask where he was, he tells them to wait until later.

After the feast (which Harry misses by a few seconds), Professor Dumbledore announces two new appointments. Professor Horace Slughorn is the new Potions Master, while Professor Snape is now the Defence Against the Dark Arts instructor. Everyone is stunned by Snape's appointment, one he has coveted for so long. Harry is particularly angered, although the Slytherin table enthusiastically greets the news. With Voldemort's reappearance, Dumbledore has implemented new security measures, and he requests that students be patient and cooperative and to report any concerns they may have before he dismisses them.

Hermione leads the first-years to the Gryffindor dorms, but Ron remains behind with Harry, who relates what happened on the train and Draco's discussion. Ron believes Draco was probably just showing off for Pansy. Hagrid approaches and says they can say hello to Witherwings (Buckbeak) if they arrive early enough for Care of Magical Creatures class. When Hagrid departs, Harry and Ron wonder how he will react to his three favorite students not taking his course.

ANALYSIS

Harry's growing obsession over Draco caused him to be careless, giving Draco an advantage—he knows Harry was eavesdropping and will likely be monitoring him. Just why Draco purposely revealed so much to Harry is puzzling, however. It would also seem that Harry, having been caught eavesdropping by Draco, would now consider the information to be false and was merely intended to manipulate and taunt Harry. Instead, Harry fully believes everything Draco said and continues to act to prove it. Although Ron and Hermione will doubt Draco's claims and try to persuade Harry to disregard it, reader's, however, know that Draco is being truthful, although exactly what his mission is, remains a mystery until the book's conclusion. Also, though the Order of the Phoenix is guarding Hogwarts, Tonks finding Harry so quickly indicates that he is particulalry being protected, probably without Harry realizing it. When Harry failed to emerge from the train with the other students, Tonks searched for him. Although she says the Order has stationed her in Hogsmeade, she has likely been assigned to guard Harry. A wizard's Patronus cannot be consciously chosen, but instead reflects the person casting it. Therefore, Tonks' new form must signify her current emotional state. Although it is unknown what new form it has taken, or what shape it was before, it is a significant enough change for Snape to jeer at it. This is also the second time the Patronus has been seen as other than a defensive charm, the first time being in *Harry Potter and the Goblet of Fire*, when Professor Dumbledore used it to summon Hagrid.

Although Dumbledore has finally appointed Snape to the Defence Against the Dark Arts teaching position he has so long coveted, why he chooses to do so now is unclear and rather mysterious. While Dumbledore has never doubted Snape's loyalty, Snape's past history and his affinity to the Dark Arts has apparently been an ongoing concern. However, both Dumbledore and Snape know there is a specific reason why no one has ever served longer than one year in that post. Ron alludes to this, saying that he believes it is jinxed. If it is, then Dumbledore and Snape must have somehow overcome this particular obstacle or neither intend for Snape to remain in that position any longer than his predecessors. Although Harry is angry that Snape was appointed, it may actually provide an as-yet-unknown benefit.

QUESTIONS

Review 1. Why does Harry refuse to report Draco's actions?

2. Why did Tonks find Harry so quickly?

3. Why is Tonks so depressed? Is there some reason other than what Harry thinks?

Extra Study 1. Why might Harry, Ron, and Hermione have decided to not take Hagrid's class this year? Why haven't they told him? What might his reaction be?

2. Why would Snape ridicule Tonks' new Patronus, even though a witch or wizard cannot consciously choose its shape?

3. What new form might Tonks' patronus have taken and what could have caused it to change?

4. Why would Dumbledore appoint Snape as the new Defence Against the Dark Arts instructor after repeatedly denying him the position and knowing that no one has held it for more than one year?

GREATER PICTURE

While it is never fully clear why Draco revealed so much information to Harry, and despite his arrogant boasting to his friends, it soon becomes apparent that Draco is deeply conflicted and terrified by his mission, spurred on only to protect his family. He may be hoping that Harry will expose him to Dumbledore, although it will be learned that Dumbledore already knows.

It is revealed later that Voldemort did indeed put a curse on the Defence Against the Dark Arts position. Ever since Dumbledore rejected him for the job, no teacher has remained in that position for more than one school year. Knowing this, it is curious as to why Snape continually applied for the position each year, or why Dumbledore chooses to appoint him now. As it turns out, Snape will also only hold the position for the one year. Although Snape jeers at Tonks for her new Patronus form and understands what it represents, it will be revealed in the last book that his own Patronus is its current shape for similar reasons.

Chapter 9: The Half-Blood Prince

SYNOPSIS

The next morning before breakfast, Harry tells Hermione what he overheard on the train. Ron repeats that Draco was probably just showing off to Pansy, but Hermione thinks that is an awfully big lie just to impress a girl. Hermione confiscates a Fanged Frisbee from a passing fourth-year. Ron takes it, saying he has always wanted one. Lavender Brown, passing by, giggles loudly and appreciatively at Ron's comment.

Professor McGonagall hands out schedules, a complicated process for sixth year students because O.W.L.

results determine which classes students qualify for. Hermione gets her courses straight away, but Neville's Acceptable O.W.L. grade is too low for Transfiguration, but his Charms grade is high enough for that course. McGonagall informs Parvati Patil that Firenze and Professor Trelawney are splitting Divination classes, and that Professor Trelawney is teaching sixth year. Harry's lost hope to become an Auror is revived when he learns that Professor Slughorn accepts a lower O.W.L. grade than Professor Snape for N.E.W.T.-level Potions classes. Both Harry and Ron sign up, although Harry worries that Hagrid will be upset that they are not taking Care of Magical Creatures. Professor McGonagall also hands Harry a list with new Quidditch recruits to conduct trials with.

In the first Defence Against the Dark Arts lesson, Snape reviews the many forms the Dark Arts can take, using gruesome examples. He demonstrates how to cast nonverbal spells (performing magic without using a spoken incantation), and chooses Harry to play a victim of a nonverbal spell; Harry instinctively reacts by blasting a spoken Shield Charm at Snape, and (after giving him cheek) earns a detention. Harry is momentarily reprieved by Jack Sloper, who inquires about Quidditch tryouts, and a message from Professor Dumbledore regarding their private lesson, which is scheduled at the same time as the detention. Harry, eager to read Dumbledore's message, leaves Sloper in mid-sentence.

Harry finds Potions far more enjoyable without Snape. Hermione, as usual, excels and earns Gryffindor thirty points for correctly guessing three cauldrons' content, Veritaserum, Polyjuice potion, and a Love potion, and for accurately identifying the effects of Felix Felicis. Slughorn is impressed by her abilities, even though she is Muggle-born. Another Muggle-born student, Lily Evans (Harry's mother), was another favorite, although he is inclined to favor purebloods. That he is the former Head of Slytherin House further supports this tendency. As the name suggests, Felix Felicis is liquid luck. One tablespoon at breakfast will provide a perfect day. It is dangerous if made improperly and is banned in competitions, examinations, and elections. Excessive consumption can cause giddiness, recklessness, and even death. For the first lesson, whoever brews the best Draught of Living Death will win a tiny flask of Felix Felicis from Slughorn, enough luck for twelve hours.

Harry brews his potion using a second-hand textbook, *Advanced Potion Making*, that Slughorn loaned him. Handwritten into the book's margins are many new spells and jinxes, as well as revisions to standard potions. Harry finds the revisions more effective than the original instructions. With it, Harry brews the best Living Death draught in the class, winning the Good Luck potion.

When Harry later admits to Ron and Hermione that he was using the mysterious book's instructions, Hermione becomes furious by his ill-gotten success. Ginny, overhearing this, asks if Harry is using instructions from a book. Remembering Ginny's nearly-fatal experience with Tom Riddle's diary, Hermione tests the textbook with her wand for any hidden magical properties, but is unable to detect any. Harry notices writing on the back cover: *This book belongs to the Half-Blood Prince.* Whoever the "Prince" may be, Harry is grateful to this talented unknown student.

ANALYSIS

Harry is a naturally intelligent and talented wizard, but academically he is a rather lazy student, usually getting by on average or just-above average grades and often relying on Hermione's help. Potions, in particular, has always proved tedious and difficult for him, partially due to his strained relationship with Professor Snape. It is only when a particular subject, like Defence Against the Dark Arts, interests Harry that he works hard and excels at it. For the first time, he is challenged to learn about Potions after discovering a talented former student's innovative methods to brewing standard potions more efficiently. Harry is a non-traditional learner, and while Snape has ineffectively taught him Potions, the Half-Blood Prince, in a brief time period, has inspired him to learn more than he has over the past five years, even though it is with unorthodox, short-cut methods. Harry may also be feeling somewhat pressured to live up to his mother's reputation in Slughorn's Potions class. And though Hermione is outraged that Harry ignores official potion-making instructions, an action she feels is equivalent to cheating, the Prince's book has given Harry an alternative learning avenue that has aroused his academic curiosity and will serve him later in the story. Hermione's negative reaction may also be tinged by jealousy and resentment. She has always earned the top grades in her classes (except Defense Against the Dark Arts), and she revels in the accompanying accolades; now, Harry is outshining her in Potions, something she may have difficulty accepting, especially considering that she feels Harry has done so with illicit methods compared to her diligent studying.

As a side note, even though Hermione correctly identifies the three cauldrons' contents in Slughorn's class, winning her high praise and House points, it is hardly surprising that she recognizes the Polyjuice Potion, having brewed it herself during her second year (in *Chamber of Secrets*). Unfortunately, for Hermione at least, the results were less than successful when she accidently added cat hair rather than human to her portion, landing her in the infirmary for weeks.

This chapter drops another hint that Harry has growing feelings for Ginny. In the first Potions class, when Harry sniffs the love potion, he detects *"treacle tart, the woody smell of a broomstick handle, and something flowery he thought he might have smelled at the Burrow."* And later, when the Trio meet Ginny, Harry, *"caught a sudden waft of that flowery smell he had picked up in Slughorn's dungeon."* Hermione mentions that a love potion contains the scent of what it is that attracts a person to someone, and it is different for each individual; she runs off the scents she detected, but stops short before mentioning the third, possibly afraid that it would identify someone she cares about. By this stage in the series, we should certainly know Harry's feelings about broomsticks and treacle tart, and it is hardly surprising that Hermione characteristically identifies one odor as fresh parchment. Harry's noticing Ginny's scent in the potion, even though he does not yet recognize it, shows his attraction to her while being oblivious to that fact.

QUESTIONS

1. If the Half-Blood Prince was possessive enough to put his name on his book, why was it left in the Potions classroom?
2. Why does Hermione accuse Harry of cheating at Potions? Are her accusations valid? Explain.
3. Does it ever occur to Harry that the suspicious textbook might contain Dark Magic? Why or why not?
4. Why does Harry react as he does during the demonstration in Snape's class? Why did Snape choose Harry for the demonstration?
5. Why are Hermione and Ron so dismissive about Draco's boasts that he is on a mission for Voldemort? Why is Harry so convinced that Draco's claims are true?
6. When Harry sniffs the Love Potion, he detects treacle tart, a broomstick handle, and a flowery scent. Who or what might these three items refer to?

GREATER PICTURE

It is interesting to learn that Harry's mother was so talented at Potions. Particularly given that Snape was in her class, one would expect that Snape would have used Lily as a counter-example to Harry's apparent ineptness. One can almost hear Snape sneering, "Unable to brew a simple Strengthening Solution? Your mother could have done that with one hand tied behind her back. Clearly this apple has fallen far from the tree . . ." And yet, Snape never once mentioned Lily. There is a reason why not, of course, but it is not revealed until the final book in the series.

Chapter 10: The House of Gaunt

SYNOPSIS

Over the the next week, Hermione remains angry over Harry using the Prince's notes. She suggests that the "Prince" may be female, based on the book's handwriting, but Harry retorts, "How many girls have been Princes?" Ron is also angered, because even though Harry has offered to share, Ron is unable to read the tiny handwriting and has to rely on textbook formulas. Professor Slughorn, of course, believes Harry is among the best Potions students he has ever taught.

Harry arrives at Professor Dumbledore's office for his first lesson, although he had to dodge a tipsy Professor Trelawney in the hallway. Dumbledore explains that they will try to determine Voldemort's intentions, based on Dumbledore's previous investigation. Dumbledore has shared all he knows with Harry; now they are embarking on guesswork and supposition. Dumbledore produces a vial containing memories from Bob Ogden, who worked in Magical Law Enforcement. Dumbledore pours the contents into his Pensieve, and he and Harry enter. Bob Ogden arrives near Little Hangleton village and turns down a path. Approaching a ramshackle cottage, a young wizard with several missing teeth and small, dark eyes staring in opposite directions appears and challenges Ogden, speaking in Parseltongue. The wizard jinxes Ogden before he can state his business. An older wizard appears and addresses the younger one as Morfin. He identifies himself as Mr. Gaunt, and says Ogden should have announced himself. Ogden replies that a message was sent by owl post; Gaunt responds that he does not read letters. When Ogden says he is there about Morfin, Gaunt invites him in. Inside, Merope, Guant's teen-aged daughter, is in the kitchen. She has a plain, heavy face, and, like Morfin, her eyes stare in opposite directions. Ogden says Morfin jinxed a Muggle, causing Merope to drop a pot. She fumbles a spell to pick it up and slams the pot into the wall. Ogden repairs it for her. Gaunt taunts Merope, causing her to blush fiercely. Ogden says Morfin has broken Wizarding law, and produces a summons. Gaunt demands to know if Ogden realizes just who he is talking to and shows him a ring he says bears the Peverell coat of arms. He also shows Ogden Merope's locket, claiming it is Salazar Slytherin's, and they are his descendents. Ogden retorts that their heritage has no bearing on Morfin having Jinxed a Muggle. Ogden reads the summons, breaking off when horses are heard approaching outside. In Parseltongue, Morfin says it is the Muggle that Merope fancies and the one he Jinxed. Gaunt demands to know if Merope is chasing a Muggle. When she does not answer, he attacks her; Ogden defends her and is attacked in turn by Morfin. Ogden escapes, crashing into the two riders on horseback as he runs for the road; Harry and Dumbledore exit the memory.

Dumbledore says Ogden quickly returned with Ministry reinforcements, but Morfin and Gaunt fought them; Morfin was sentenced to Azkaban for three years while Marvolo Gaunt received six months. Harry instantly recognizes the name: he was Voldemort's grandfather. Dumbledore says that Merope was to be Voldemort's mother, and his father was the elegant Muggle on horseback that Morfin attacked. Harry wonders how the handsome Tom Riddle could possibly have married the unattractive Merope; Dumbledore says she likely used a love potion. The two ran away together, causing a scandal; Marvolo never forgave her and died shortly after his release from Azkaban. A few months later, Riddle returned to his manor house alone, saying he had been hoodwinked. Dumbledore suggests that either Merope believed bearing Tom's child would bind him to her and stopped using the love potion or else she lost her ability to perform magic. Harry recalls that Voldemort was raised in an orphanage and correctly surmises that Merope died soon after giving birth.

Harry wants to share this with Ron and Hermione; Dumbledore agrees, but warns against spreading it any further. As he leaves, Harry notices a cracked ring sitting on a spindly table, the same ring Dumbledore wore when they visited Slughorn, and the same ring Marvolo Gaunt was wearing in the memory. He asks if Dumbledore has had it long; Dumbledore says he acquired it recently, near the time he injured his hand. But he turns aside further questions, and sends Harry to bed.

Chapter 11: Hermione's Helping Hand

Analysis

If another student was using the Prince's textbook, Hermione, who is a Prefect, would likely have confiscated the book and reported them. However, she says nothing about Harry, and instead voices her disapproval directly to him, although she knows it will have little effect. This is a typical behaviorial pattern for Hermione, and only once has she reported Harry for something. In *Prisoner of Azkaban*, she informed McGonagall that Harry received the Firebolt broom from an annonymous donor (Sirius Black). Although Hermione was motivated by genuine concern over Harry's safety rather than him engaging in mischief, her actions resulted in a severe backlash and months of estrangement from Harry and Ron, causing Hermione much anguish. Although Hermione staunchly believes in obeying school rules, she fears Harry and Ron's retaliation even more, causing her to overlook their frequent, although minor, misconduct. However, even though Hermione remains disapproving of Harry for using the Half-Blood Prince's notes and resents Harry outperforming her in Potions class, she says nothing and actually becomes quite curious about the Prince's identity. This has also subtly changed the Trio's relationship. Ron and Harry have usually sought out Hermione for help or information, although they occasionally had to suffer her disapproval for their academic laziness. Now Harry has another means to find the information he needs, at least regarding Potions.

Dumbledore's private lessons are not what Harry expected. Rather than learning new magic, he is to view Voldemort's past through other people's memories. Exactly how this can aid Harry is still unknown, but learning more about his enemy may help defeat him. Studying the Gaunts has provided clues about Voldemort's own personality. Although they had sunk to a low social status and lived in poverty after previous generations squandered the family fortune, the Gaunts still considered themselvs superior based soley on their bloodline to Salazar Slytherin, and therefore expected preferential treatment. This is similar to Voldemort's own attitude. The Gaunts apparently felt little need to educate or cultivate themselves, although the sad, pathetic (and phsically unattractive) Merope secretly yearned for a better life, despite her severely limited prospects. When she fell in love with the Muggle, Tom Riddle, she used a love potion to entrap him and escape her abusive family and abysmal life. Unfortunately, as soon as the potion wore off, Riddle abandoned the pregnant Merope, who, deeply despondent and either unable or unwilling to use magic to care for herself, died soon after giving birth, leaving her son, Tom Jr. (Voldemort), to be raised in an orphanage. While Harry, and readers, may see Merope as a sympathetic character, it should be remembered that she used duplicity to trap Tom Riddle, Sr., who otherwise would never have had any interest in her. It is unknown why Merope discontinued using the love potion on him, although perhaps it becomes less effective over time or she may have hoped that Riddle would come to love her on his own, although that clearly was never the case. Although Riddle had every right to leave the bogus relationship, his abandoning an innocent child is inexcusable.

Questions

1. Why does Dumbledore want Harry to learn about Voldemort's past? How will it help him?
2. Even though Tom Riddle was duped by Merope, why would he abandon his innocent unborn child?
3. Hermione, a Gryffindor Prefect, strongly disapproves of Harry using the Prince's textbook, believeing it is cheating and also dangerous. Why doesn't she report him?
4. Why would Morfin jinx a Muggle?
5. What might cause Merope to lose her ability to perform magic?
6. How could Salzar Slytherin's once-wealthy descendents have fallen to such a lowly social status? Why do they still consider themselves superior to other wizards?
7. Considering her father's abusive treatment and her husband's cruel abandonment, why would Merope include "Tom" and "Marvolo" in her son's name?

Greater Picture

There are several things in this little scene that will prove important. This is the first time Slytherin's locket and the Peverell ring are seen. Both will be turned into Horcruxes by Voldemort, although it has not yet been explained in the story what Horcruxes are. We will learn in the next book about the ring's destruction and why it was necessary, and how Dumbledore's hand was injured. It will also be learned in the final book that the ring's stone is one of the Deathly Hallows.

Harry chides Hermione for claiming that the Half-Blood Prince could be a girl. Although he is right that a royal female is a princess and not a prince, in this particular instance, Hermione was more accurate. It will be learned that the "prince" referred to here is not a royal title at all. Rather, it is someone's surname, and it could therefore have applied to either a male or female. Although Hermione is ultimately wrong that the book's previous owner was a female, nor does she realize yet it is someone's name, that surname did indeed belong to a woman. Hermione demonstrates that her logic is more abstract and intuitive than Harry's typical linear reasoning. Rowling is dropping a subtle clue here that readers should look beyond the seemingly obvious.

Chapter 11: Hermione's Helping Hand

Synopsis

Classes continue with students still trying to learn wordless spells, not only in Defence Against the Dark Arts, but in Charms and Transfiguration. Hagrid has been ignoring them, apparently because they are not taking his Care of Magical Creatures class, so Harry resolves to go see him.

Quidditch trials to select a new team are held. In attempting to explain why so many have turned out for Quidditch tryouts, Hermione offhandedly remarks to Harry that he has "never been more fanciable," and that, "it doesn't hurt that you've grown about a foot over the summer." Apparently Harry is popular, rather than Quidditch. Ron responds, "I'm tall," but Hermione ignores him.

Harry and Ron's new Potions book arrive, but Harry wants to keep the Prince's notes, so he removes and swaps each book's cover, then re-attaches them. The tattered-looking book can be returned to Professor Slughorn. Hermione reads in the *Daily Prophet* that Knight Bus conductor Stan Shunpike was arrested for discussing the Death Eaters' plans. Also, Dumbledore has been absent since Harry's private lesson with him. As general fear spreads throughout the wizarding population, Eloise Midgeon's parents remove her from Hogwarts, concerned about safety. Also, Hannah Abbott's mother had been found dead.

It is time for Quidditch try-outs. Heading to the pitch, the Trio pass Parvati and Lavender, who smiles at Ron. When he smiles back, Hermione becomes cold and distant. The trials are a bit of a fiasco. Lavender wishes Ron luck as he flies up for his trial. Hearing this, Hermione later praises Ron for playing brilliantly, pleasing Ron but frustrating Lavender. Harry chooses Katie Bell, Ginny and a new player named Demelza Robins as Chasers, Jimmy Peakes and Ritchie Coote as Beaters. Ron is the new Keeper, much to Cormac McLaggen's dismay. While walking to Hagrid's hut, Ron mentions that McLaggen looked Confunded during the last goal shot; Hermione blushes, though it is unnoticed by Ron.

The talk with Hagrid is awkward, but they eventually make up with him after Hagrid confides that Aragog may be dying, and the Trio tells him (untruthfully) that Professor Grubbly-Plank is an awful teacher. Hagrid thinks they might have fit in his class using Time-Turners, but Hermione says they were all destroyed in the battle at the Ministry. Returning to the castle, they spot Cormac McLaggen attempting to negotiate the front steps and running into the doors. Pulling Hermione aside, Harry says he looks Confunded. Hermione admits she Confunded him, defensively claiming he said horrible things about Ron and Ginny, and his temper would cause problems. Horace Slughorn invites Harry and Hermione to, "a little party, just a few rising stars," while ignoring Ron. Harry says he has detention with Snape, but Slughorn says he will try to persuade Snape to let him out. The *Evening Prophet* reports that Arthur Weasley searched the Malfoy residence for suspicious magical objects but found nothing. Hermione says Draco could not have smuggled in the object needing repair because everything was checked by Dark Detectors. Ron, meanwhile, stares at Lavender Brown. Demelza Robins delivers Snape's message to Harry saying he is expected for detention, no matter how many parties he has been invited to.

Analysis

Ron and Hermione's mutual jealousy may indicate each has deeper feelings for the other than either will acknowledge. The events from the Yule Ball two years earlier showed that Hermione understands her feelings better than Ron, and she is actually more aware of Ron's feelings than he is himself. Ron struggled with jealousy when Hermione dated Viktor Krum and was angry and upset when he learned she kissed Viktor, but he never fully understood exactly what those emotions were. The circumstances seem reversed here when someone becomes interested in Ron. Hermione may be remaining silent because she is uncertain what his reaction might be. In the meantime, she is acting out-of-character by Confunding Cormac McLaggen during the Quidditch trials to help Ron. As she has done before, Hermione will break rules if she feels it is justified. Readers may believe that Harry is also bending rules by selecting Ron over a stronger player like McLaggen. Although it seems like obvious favoritism, Harry believes that if Ron can overcome his insecurities, he has the potential to become a talented athlete like his siblings. He also realizes that Ron's personality is better suited to the team, unlike the egotistical McLaggen, who most likely will challenge Harry's authority and create turmoil by attempting to take control. However, without Hermione's unknowing help, Harry would have had difficulty justifying choosing Ron over Cormac. Although Hogwarts remains a relatively safe environment, and students have mostly been shielded from the increasingly violent events unfolding in the general wizarding population, as the attacks increase, readers can see how fear and insecurity have seeped into the castle, creating concerns about safety; so much so that some parents have removed their children from school. Adding to this, Dumbledore, a symbol of strength, protection, and stability to students and staff alike, is often gone now, and his absences are likely contributing to everyone's stress and concerns regarding Voldemort and his Death Eaters. Whatever Dumbledore is doing, he probably realizes that his frequent absences particularly affects Harry, and this may be why he re-emphasizes how important friendship and unity are. He encourages Harry to share whatever he learns with Ron and Hermione, knowing they will help protect and support Harry.

Harry is also gaining a clearer picture about the Ministry of Magic and their deceptive tactics. When Stan Shunpike is arrested as a Death Eater, Harry knows he is most likely innocent. Unable to apprehend real Death Eaters, Scrimgeour instead preys on easy-to-target victims like Shunpike as a means to appease the wizarding community's fear of Voldemort and to put the Ministry in a more positive public light.

Casting wordless spells is apparently difficult to learn, and Harry struggles to master this technique. Being able to cast spells without your opponent knowing what they are is an essential skill for an Auror. If Harry is unable to learn this, it could affect his future career.

Questions

1. Why are wordless spells important?
2. What does Harry think is the real reason the Ministry of Magic arrested Stan Shunpike? Is he right?
3. Why does Hermione help Ron at the Quidditch trials, even though she is upset with him?
4. Did Ron deserve to be chosen for the Quidditch team over Cormac McLaggen, who is a stronger athlete? What was Harry's reasoning?
5. Are parents justified in removing their children from Hogwarts? What evidence is there for this?

Chapter 12: Silver and Opals

Synopsis

Harry wonders where Professor Dumbledore is. Despite telling Harry that the lessons would be the most important thing Harry did, he is often away, and there are no additional lessons before the first Hogsmeade weekend in mid-October. On the morning of the Hogsmeade weekend, Harry lies in bed reading the Half-Blood Prince's textbook, which contains some interesting spells. Harry casts a non-verbal one, Levicorpus, and mistakenly levitates a sleeping Ron by his ankle. Harry frantically invokes the counterspell, and Ron falls back into his bed.

When Ron laughingly recounts the levitation experience, Hermione is unamused. This Prince may be a dodgy character, and here is Harry invoking his spells without knowing their effect. Harry recognizes the spell from Snape's memory in the Pensieve as the same one his father once used on Snape. Harry briefly considers that his father was the Half-Blood Prince, but discounts this because James was a pure-blood wizard. Meanwhile, Ginny delivers a note to Harry from Dumbledore, scheduling another lesson for Monday evening. Ginny mentions she is going with Dean and may see them there.

Having been scanned by Filch with Secrecy Sensors, the Trio embark to Hogsmeade. Finding Zonko's joke shop boarded up, Ron suggests Honeyduke's where they run into Professor Slughorn buying his favorite crystallized pineapple. Slughorn extends yet another dinner invitation to Harry and Hermione, for next Monday, which Harry is grateful he can decline due to Dumbledore's lesson.

Ron, disgruntled over being excluded from Slughorn's dinner, is unwilling to suggest where to go next, but agrees to The Three Broomsticks. On the way, Harry encounters Mundungus Fletcher, who is talking to the Hog's Head Inn barman. Harry calls out to Mundungus, who, startled, drops an ancient suitcase that bursts open, spilling its contents. When Ron recognizes a silver goblet bearing the Black family crest, Harry seizes Mundungus by the throat, and accuses him of looting Sirius Black's house. Mundungus blasts Harry away and Disapparates. Tonks appears and says it is useless to hunt for him, but Harry intends to report Mundungus to Dumbledore. After one Butterbeer apiece in The Three Broomsticks, Hermione suggests heading back to Hogwarts. Ron and Harry agree—this has been an unpleasant outing. They follow Katie Bell and her friend Leanne, who are arguing over a package. Leanne tries to take the package from Katie, but it rips open. Katie, suddenly deathly still, rises six feet into the air, then falls to the ground, writhing and screaming in pain. Harry runs for help. Hagrid arrives and carries Katie back to the school. Harry prevents Ron from touching the package, recognizing a necklace inside as the same one he saw at Borgin & Burkes in Knockturn Alley that bore a label reading, 'Cursed.' Leanne says that Katie was behaving strangely after returning from the toilet carrying a package she insisted she must deliver to someone at Hogwarts. Leanne was trying to take the package away from her when it tore open, and Katie touched it. Leanne suspects Katie was under the Imperius Curse. Harry believes Draco knew about the necklace; he saw it at Borgin & Burkes. Ron says that many people probably saw it, and besides, Katie had been in the washroom. Harry carefully wraps the necklace in his scarf and carries it back to Hogwarts.

Professor McGonagall meets them at the gate. Harry hands the necklace to McGonagall, who orders Filch take it to Professor Snape. In Professor McGonagall's office, Leanne relates what happened, then is sent to the hospital wing. Harry suspects Malfoy was involved, but McGonagall says Draco was doing detention with her. Dismissed, Harry, Ron, and Hermione wonder who the necklace was intended for. With Filch and his Secrecy Sensor, it was unlikely that a package containing anything harmful could be brought into the school that way. They conclude it was a poorly thought-out plan.

Analysis

The attack on Katie Bell certainly seems to bolster Harry's suspicions that Draco is directly involved in some sinister plot, although, as both Ron and Hermione point out, there is only circumstantial evidence linking Draco to the necklace, and he has an iron-clad alibi. Regardless, Harry remains positive that Draco was behind the attack. While readers can sympathize with Harry, knowing that Draco has been charged with some unknown mission for Voldemort and that it probably is linked to this incident, Harry lacks any objectivity whatsoever. He becomes so single-mindedly convinced that Draco is guilty that he stubbornly refuses to consider other possibilities. Also, the Trio's belief that the attack seemed poorly planned may be more significant than they realize.

Adding to Harry's concerns is Dumbledore's increasingly frequent and unexplained absences. These are disturbing not only for Harry, but also the entire school. Dumbledore is Hogwarts' symbol of authority and security, and his empty chair in the Great Hall may signal that there is greater turmoil in the wizarding world than anyone realized. Harry, in particular, is affected by his absence. Harry still deeply mourns his godfather Sirius' death, and Dumbledore has become even more a father figure to him. When a parent is away, a child often feels abandoned and unprotected, even when left in capable hands.

Harry physically attacking Mundungus shows a rare side to his personality. While Harry is often quick to anger, he normally maintains control and never reacts physically. Still grieving his godfather's death, he is so outraged that Sirius' possessions have been violated that he is overcome by rage. Only an extreme circumstance could have provoked such an outburst. And only Tonks' intervention prevents Harry from inflicting serious harm on Mundungus and possibly facing severe legal consequences.

Harry's hope that the clever Half-Blood Prince could actually be his father may indicate he is looking for even more redeeming qualities in him, although he is quickly forced to discount his own theory. Harry may still be conflicted over his father. Although he loves the man he never knew and knows he was a good and brave person, he was deeply disappointed when he accidentally learned (in *Harry Potter and the Order of the Phoenix*) that the youthful James was once a rather obnoxious bully. James, along with Sirius Black, often tormented and humiliated Severus Snape purely for their own amusement while they were students at Hogwarts. Although Harry now has a better understanding regarding the source of Snape's hostility toward him and his father, it has never lessened his own hatred for Snape.

QUESTIONS

Review 1. Who does Harry think might be the Half-Blood Prince? Why does he want to believe this and what finally makes him discount it?

2. Who does Harry attack and why?

3. Where has Harry seen the necklace before, and who does he connect with it? What does McGonagall have to say?

Extra Study 1. Why would Harry use an unknown, and potentially lethal, spell on Ron without knowing its effects? What does Hermione have to say? Is she right?

2. What might account for Dumbledore's frequent absences? How does it affect Harry?

3. Who might have given Katie the package? Why?

4. Why was Katie Bell (unknowingly) chosen to smuggle the necklace into Hogwarts if Filch was likely to detect it with his sensors? Was it a poorly though-out plan as Harry, Ron, and Hermione believe it was?

GREATER PICTURE

Despite Hermione's warning, Harry will continue using the Prince's spells without knowing what they are. Although the one he used on Ron resulted in a humorous, and generally harmless, episode, a different spell that Harry later casts on Draco Malfoy will have a more devastating effect. Snape, who intervenes in time and recognizes the spell, saves Draco's life.

When Harry meets Mundungus Fletcher in Hogsmeade, the Hog's Head Inn barman has apparently just refused something and walked away. It is clear that, having ransacked Sirius/Harry's house, Mundungus is now attempting to sell his spoils and, confronted by Harry, drops a stolen goblet. While it is unknown if any transaction has occured, and the Hog's Head barman's walking away gives the impression that he was uninterested, it is possible that Mundungus had either sold or given him the twin to the two-way mirror that Sirius gave Harry in the previous book. This will turn out to be the case; Mundungus, in this transaction or another, sold the mirror to the barman, who is actually Aberforth Dumbledore, who was told the mirror's function by his brother, Albus. Late in the final book, Aberforth admits he periodically used the mirror to check on Harry. Harry will occasionally catch Aberforth's eye in the mirror, mistaking it for Albus Dumbledore's, which is apparently similar in shape and color.

Chapter 13: The Secret Riddle

SYNOPSIS

Katie Bell is moved to St. Mungo's Hospital in London. With the exception of Harry, Ron, Hermione, and Leanne, students are unaware that someone other than Katie was the intended target. Ron and Hermione ignore Harry's comment that Malfoy knows.

Though Dumbledore has remained unseen all day, Harry reports to his office for his second lesson. Dumbledore is there and reassures Harry that Snape, who has more experience with the Dark Arts than Madam Pomfrey, has done all he can to help Katie. Dumbledore also says that Mundungus Fletcher has apparently gone into hiding, but nothing else will be taken from Grimmauld Place. Dumbledore tells Harry that Draco's involvement will be investigated, but their lesson is more important now.

In the last memory they viewed, Merope Riddle, who was abandoned by her Muggle husband, was pregnant and alone. Lacking the will to perform magic to care for herself, she needed money. She sold a gold locket once belonging to Salazar Slytherin to Caractacus Burke, one of the founders of Borgin & Burkes. Watching Burke's reminiscence of the sale in the Pensieve, Harry is outraged that Burke only gave Merope ten galleons for the priceless relic.

In this lesson, Harry enters Dumbledore's memories. The younger Dumbledore had auburn hair and beard, just as long as they are now. Dumbledore visits the eleven-year-old Tom Riddle in a Muggle orphanage. After speaking with the matron, who says Riddle is a strange boy and leaves the impression that she is hoping someone will take him well away, Dumbledore talks to Tom. Initially, Tom thinks Professor Dumbledore is a doctor, come to take him to a sanatorium. Believing that Dumbledore's term, "special" means he should be in an asylum, Riddle prepares to prevent Dumbledore from taking him anywhere. However, when Dumbledore explains that Hogwarts is a school of magic, Tom asks if what he does is magic. Even at the tender age of 11, Riddle manipulated and terrified other children, strangled a pet rabbit, hurt people, and spoke in Parseltongue. Riddle demands proof that Dumbledore is a wizard; Dumbledore reproaches him, saying he must address Hogwarts teachers with respect. Tom respectfully asks, and Dumbledore conjures flames on Tom's wardrobe, and as suddenly extinguishes them. Dumbledore retrieves Tom's small cache of stolen items and demands he return them to their owners. The young Dumbledore worried about the boy's ambition, his cruelty, his thieving, and his reaction to learning he is a wizard; he resolves to keep a close eye on him.

Back in the office, Dumbledore says he was unaware then that the young boy would become the most feared Dark Wizard in centuries, Lord Voldemort. He then draws Harry's attention to several traits about the young Tom Riddle: he disliked the common name Tom and wanted to be separate from everyone else. He was already very self-sufficient, secretive, apparently friendless, and he liked to keep trophies.

As he is leaving, Harry notices the ring is gone. Harry comments that he would have expected to see one of Voldemort's trophies there, perhaps the mouth organ? Dumbledore comments that the mouth organ was always only a mouth organ.

Analysis

By sharing his and others' memories, Dumbledore shows Harry how Voldemort crafted himself from an abandoned, insecure boy into a notorious, Dark wizard. While readers may be sympathetic to Riddle's difficult early life, it can be seen that he was a naturally unpleasant person from an early age. Even the orphanage caretakers came to fear him. And despite growing up without knowing his family, young Tom Riddle inherited many Gaunt family characteristics. He was: egotistical, secretive, aloof, and lacked empathy for others. As a child, Riddle isolated himself from other orphan children, who he considered inferior and frequently stole objects from, saving the items as trophies. He also physically and/or emotionally threatened or harmed them, and later learned to manipulate people to obtain what he wanted. When Dumbledore reprimanded Tom for being disrespectful, Riddle's sudden good behavior seemed insincere and designed to appease the strange professor only to ensure his attending Hogwarts. Young Riddle feared being ordinary in any way and needed to feel superior to everyone. However, being introduced to the Wizarding world may have had the opposite effect. Though he learned he possessed special powers the other orphans lacked, when he arrived at Hogwarts, he was no longer unique, but just one among many talented wizard children. Even here, he needed to rise above his peers and worked hard to learn as much as possible, which eventually led him into Dark magic.

Riddle also shares many similarities to Harry. Both were orphans raised in a loveless environment, they are half-blood wizards, each learned they had magical powers only when they were old enough to attend Hogwarts, and both could perform magic at an early age without any training. However, even if both boys had been raised by their respective parents, their outcomes would probably still have been very different from one another. And unlike Harry, Riddle hated Muggles, even though he is half, a fact Riddle loathed about himself and was deeply rooted in his Muggle father's abandonment. Harry would probably be much the same good-hearted person he is now, only more confident and self-assured, while Tom Riddle's Gaunt heritage likely would still have despised his Muggle origins, even if his father had raised him. Riddle felt forever tainted by this "blood impurity," and it had an adverse effect on his pysche. Learning that he was a wizard inflated his sense of superiority, while his connection to Salazar Slytherin later fueled this egotism, gradually manifesting itself into his new persona as Lord Voldemort and diminishing, in his mind, his sullied Muggle bloodline.

Questions

Review   1. Why did Merope Riddle sell the Locket? Who did she sell it to, and why was she willing to accept so little money for such a valuable object?

2. What did the staff at the orphanage think about Tom Riddle? Why?

3. Why would Tom Riddle believe that Dumbledore arrived at the orphanage to take him to an asylum? What was Riddle planning to do if that was true?

4. What is Dumbledore's initial opinion of Tom Riddle at the orphanage? What did he resolve to do? What does he tell Harry about Riddle?

Extra Study   1. Why might Slytherin's locket be gold—Gryffindor's colour—and not silver like Slytherin's House colour?

2. Why wouldn't Merope Riddle use magic to support herself?

3. Why do Ron and Hermione continually dismiss Harry's suspicions about Draco, despite credible circumstantial evidence against him? What does Dumbledore tell Harry?

Greater Picture

Dumbledore's comment, that the mouth organ (harmonica) was only ever a mouth organ, is enigmatic to Harry, and to the reader. In the last novel, the ring is revealed to be a Horcrux, and it is to this that Dumbledore was probably alluding. That the ring's stone is also one of the three Deathly Hallows probably is not what Dumbledore is thinking about. While that part of the ring's nature is probably predominant in Dumbledore's mind, given the previous summer's events, Dumbledore already believes that Voldemort fails to grasp the Hallows' nature. As such, the ring's stone being a Hallow is irrelevant to his and Harry's discussion here, and instead centers on Voldemort.

Chapter 14: Felix Felicis

Synopsis

On the way to Herbology class next day, and while they are preparing their armour to start harvesting Snargaluff pods, Harry fills Hermione and Ron in on what he has been learning about Tom Riddle. Ron and Hermione are impressed, but Ron wonders why Dumbledore is teaching Harry all this.

Hermione says the 'Slug Club' dinners are actually quite enjoyable, and that Harry should come to the Christmas one. The invitees are allowed to bring a guest. Ron mocks Hermione to invite McLaggen. Hermione hotly replies that she was going to invite Ron, but as he is acting so stupidly, she will not bother. Ron sheepishly says that he would go with her, however it is uncertain whether or not she will relent. Harry worries that if Ron and Hermione ever do become a couple, a break-up could create an unbridgeable gap between them, or that the two would become so close they would shut Harry out.

Harry recruits Dean Thomas to replace Katie Bell for the Quidditch team while she is in St. Mungo's Hospital. This causes some friction with Seamus Finnigan, but Harry knows that Dean outflew Seamus at the initial try-outs. At practice, Dean performs excellently, while Ron, overcome with nerves, plays horribly; at one point he punches Demelza in the mouth.

Heading back to the Gryffindor Common room, Harry and Ron stumble across Ginny and Dean kissing in a corridor; Harry feels jealous while Ron angrily accuses his sister of acting like a tease. Ginny retorts that Ron has as much experience as a twelve-year-old and storms off. Harry and Ron head to the Common room, startling a small girl who drops a jar of frog spawn. As Ron broods dark thoughts, Harry struggles with romantic feelings towards Ginny, although he tries to dismiss it as only friendship. He also fears that if he did start snogging Ginny, it could end his and Ron's friendship.

The next day, still angry, Ron lashes out at everyone, especially Hermione, and cold-shoulders Dean and Ginny. Harry hopes this will end soon, but there is no improvement in Ron's mood over the next several days. Ron continues to play miserably at practice, which only worsens his mood. He nearly resigns, but Harry snaps him out of it. However, he remains dejected before the match against Slytherin. Harry devises a brilliant plan. At breakfast, Harry gives Ron pumpkin juice. Hermione sees the small flask of Felix Felicis and, suspecting Harry spiked the juice, tells Harry off. Ron dismisses Hermione's anger and drinks his pumpkin juice. Apparently, the luck potion works, as Slytherin's best goal scorer, Vaisey, took a Bludger to the head at practice and is unable to play, and Malfoy is off sick as well, although Harry suspects he is planning something. When Ron suspects that Harry did put the Felix potion in his drink, Harry says nothing.

Zacharias Smith is announcing. A Hufflepuff, he seems overly critical of Gryffindor, but eventually is forced to stop criticizing Harry's choice of Ron and Ginny as Ron saves everything Slytherin throws at him, and Ginny makes four of Gryffindor's six goals. Gryffindor plays brilliantly, eventually gaining a 100 point lead. The Slytherin Seeker spots the Snitch, but Harry distracts him and catches it for the win. Ginny "forgets to brake" as she swoops in for the victory celebration and hits the announcer's tower, dumping Zacharias to the ground. In the changing room, Hermione bursts in and lambastes Harry for cheating, but Harry reveals he never used the potion, Ron only believed he did.

At the victory party, which Hermione is initially too upset to attend, Ron is kissing Lavender Brown in plain view. Harry spots Hermione ducking in and out of the Common room and follows her. He finds her in an unlocked classroom with conjured birds flying around her head and tries consoling her. Ron barges in with Lavender, who quickly ducks out. Hermione leaves, sending the conjured canaries to attack Ron.

Analysis

Although Hermione used magic to help secure Ron a place on the Quidditch team, she has apparently fallen back into her usual "follow the rules" way and rebukes Harry for cheating (or so she thinks) by giving Ron the Good Luck potion to enhance his game skills. Ron played brilliantly because he believed the potion would improve his performance, but Harry never actually gave it to him. When Ron believes in himself, he has the ability to perform well in many things.

While Harry wants his two best friends to be happy, he also has concerns. If Ron and Hermione should become a couple, it could mean he would be left behind or be forced to choose sides if they break up. Harry is beginning to realize just how much he relies on each for their friendship and support, a fact Dumbledore has subtly been impressing upon him for some time. Harry also wrestles with budding romantic feelings for Ginny Weasley, although he brushes this off as "brotherly" concern.

Harry's skill at utilizing people's flaws and habits is improving; he knows Hermione will intervene if there is any unethical behavior, and that Ron's will tends to resist her. This is why, we believe, he allows Hermione to see the phial of Felix Felicis as he passes it over Ron's pumpkin juice; Harry knows that if Hermione assumes Ron's drink was spiked, she will object. It is uncertain whether Harry is counting on that to motivate Ron into drinking it; it is certain that Hermione's protest will lead Ron to believe that he has been given a chance at some liquid luck. This is somewhat similar to how Voldemort manipulates people and their thought patterns to his advantage. Unlike Voldemort, however, Harry's aim is to help his friends rather than for his own selfish ends.

Also, Harry is working on two fronts simultaneously. The first, mentioned above, is to instill confidence in Ron by showing that he is able to perform well (here, keeping goal at Quidditch) when he believes in himself. In this endeavor, Harry will be successful. Harry's other battle is to reconcile Ron and Hermione. This has failed so far, possibly due to Ron's emotional immaturity relative to the other two, leaving Harry again having two good friends who are not on speaking terms.

Readers should note the small girl in the seventh-floor hallway who drops the jar containing frog-spawn.

Questions

1. Why is Ron in such a bad mood?
2. Why is Ron able to perform so well in the game?
3. Why is Hermione upset with Ron?
4. Are Harry's fears about Ron and Hermione being together justified?

Greater Picture

Although she is passed by almost unnoticed, the small girl in the seventh-floor hallway who drops the jar of frog-spawn will turn out to be important. She is actually either Crabbe or Goyle, disguised with Polyjuice Potion and standing guard outside the Room of Requirement while Malfoy works within on his secret task for Voldemort. Harry will not realize this until he has Dobby and Kreacher tail Malfoy later in the spring.

Chapter 15: The Unbreakable Vow

SYNOPSIS

Hogwarts prepares for Christmas, and Harry does his best to avoid giggling girls and mistletoe clumps. Ron now spends every evening kissing Lavender Brown who, "seemed to regard any moment that she was not kissing Ron as a moment wasted." Ron and Hermione continue to ignore each other, while Harry and Hermione frequently study in the library together. Harry once again has found himself best friends with two people who are not speaking to each other.

Meanwhile, Harry continues doing well in Potions using the Prince's notes. In the library, Hermione warns him to be careful, but Harry says he has learned more from the Half-Blood Prince than from either Slughorn or Snape. But Hermione says she is referring to the girls who are infatuated with Harry—they might try to slip him a Love Potion. Filch has banned all Weasley's Wizards Wheezes items, but Love Potions aren't jinxes, curses, or concealment charms, so Secrecy Sensors won't find them, and simply putting them in perfume bottles will hide them from Filch. Romilda Vane is particularly determined to go to Slughorn's party with Harry. Hermione suggests that Harry invite someone to discourage the other girls.

Harry mentions Malfoy and the necklace again, but Hermione says the Secrecy Sensors would detect any powerful curse. Suddenly, Harry is clawed at by an outraged Madam Pince, the Librarian, after seeing writing in the Potions textbook. Harry and Hermione escape, and Harry wonders aloud if Pince and Filch have a relationship. Hermione is still angered by Harry's refusal to give up using the book.

In the Common room, Romilda Vane offers to share a Gillywater with Harry which, catching a warning glance from Hermione, he quickly declines. Vane also pushes a box of chocolates on him (Chocolate Cauldrons with Firewhisky centers), which he takes and stashes unopened in his trunk.

The next day in Transfiguration, Ron accidentally gives himself a handlebar moustache, causing Hermione to laugh. In retaliation, Ron rudely imitates Hermione whenever she answers a question, finally sending her running off crying. Harry cannot wait to leave for the Burrow, hoping the distance will help heal Ron and Hermione's relationship. Harry finds Hermione in a nearby bathroom, being comforted by Luna Lovegood. Hermione collects her things that Harry brought and leaves.

Luna tells Harry that Ron sometimes says funny things, but hurtful ones as well. Harry thinks Luna has a knack for telling unpleasant truths. Luna says she misses the D.A., as she felt she had friends there. She also says Ginny sticks up for her and stopped two boys from calling her "Loony." Harry decides to invite Luna to Slughorn's party—although he makes sure to say it is just as friends. Luna is surprised and quite happy, as nobody has ever invited her to a party before. Peeves suddenly appears hanging upside down from a chandelier and taunts, "Potty *lurves* Loony."

Soon, everyone knows Harry has invited Luna. Ron rebukes Harry, telling him he could have asked anyone. Ginny scolds Ron and comments approvingly to Harry. Hermione is sitting alone, and Harry and Ron sit down. Soon, the other Gryffindor girls arrive and Lavender starts hugging Ron. Parvati and Hermione talk about Slughorn's party; Hermione brightly comments that she is going with Cormac, and says she likes *good* Quidditch players, before leaving to get ready. Harry ponders the depths to which girls will sink to get revenge.

Luna wears silver-spangled robes to the party, eliciting giggles from some girls. Harry, relieved she is not wearing her Butterbeer-cork necklace or radish earrings, thinks she actually looks quite nice. He tells her a Vampire will be at there; Luna thinks he means Rufus Scrimgeour as the *Quibbler* was about to print a story that Scrimgeour is a vampire, but the Ministry quashed it. At the party, Slughorn introduces Harry to vampire expert, Eldred Worple, and his vampire friend, Sanguini. Worple offers to write Harry's biography; Harry declines, as he has just noticed Hermione is sitting between what looks like two of the Weird Sisters. Hermione has just escaped McLaggen's attempts to take advantage of the mistletoe. She steers Harry and Luna to the refreshments table, where she can see if he is approaching. Professor Trelawney is there, still drinking. Snape is also present and Slughorn lets slip that Harry is a natural at Potions, just like his mother. Harry tells Slughorn that he is taking the required Auror subjects, after which Slughorn booms that Harry will make an excellent one. Luna then mentions a conspiracy theory about Aurors using Dark Magic and gum disease to take down the Ministry of Magic.

Harry is having a great time with Luna and Slughorn when Malfoy is dragged in by Filch, who caught Draco gatecrashing. Slughorn laughs and reprimands him, but lets him stay, although Malfoy looks angry. When Snape asks for a private word with Malfoy, Harry excuses himself to go to the bathroom but instead eavesdrops on Snape and Malfoy. Snape probes Malfoy for information about Katie Bell, but Malfoy blocks him. Snape remarks that Malfoy's Aunt Bella must have been teaching him Occlumency. Snape knows Malfoy has been upstairs, working on some project. He offers to help, citing his Unbreakable Vow to protect him, but Malfoy says nothing and storms out, nearly hitting Harry under his Invisibility Cloak. Although Harry knows Snape is a double agent working for the Order, he still distrusts him.

ANALYSIS

When Harry overhears Snape questioning Malfoy regarding his secret activities, it appears Snape is clueless about what Draco's mission is, and Draco refuses to divulge anything, even though Snape has sworn an Unbreakable Vow to assist him. However, Draco's refusal to confide in Snape (which indicates he distrusts him) does little to convince Harry that Snape is not a Death Eater, despite Dumbledore's repeated assurance that he is loyal. Harry's stubbornness and emotions often overrules his judgment and logic, and his hatred for Snape refuses to allow him to consider other possibilities regarding Snape, while, ironically, Draco apparently does. It also appears that Harry's suspicions regarding Malfoy may be correct.

Harry seems unaware that he is appealing to the opposite sex. His interest in girls was mostly confined to one person, Cho Chang, and he seldom considers pursuing other relationships up until this book, when he develops feelings for Ginny. That he ignores girls interested in him may show a lack of confidence, or that he is so preoccupied by more serious matters that it never occurs to him to seek female companionship other than Hermione or Ginny, his platonic friends. To discourage girls' attention, Harry invites Luna Lovegood to Slughorn's party, partly because he considers her "safe," but he also feels bad that she is mistreated by other students. Nor has he forgotten her participation in the battle at the Ministry of Magic (in *Order of the Phoenix*). Although Harry knows other students, including Ron, will mock him for inviting "Loony" Luna, he has matured enough that he considers his peers' disapproval is outweighed by one individual's needs. While Hermione and Ginny express their approval, Ron's deplorable behavior not only shows his immaturity, but also his insecurity about himself; he shuns the unpopular students, afraid that associating with them will reflect badly on him.

Luna's observation that Ron often says funny things, but also hurtful ones, is accurate and insightful; considering how Luna risked her own life to help Harry and Ron during the battle at the Ministry of Magic, Ron's rudeness towards her is deplorable and inexcusable. Ron has previously demonstrated poor behavior not only wth Luna, but also Hermione. His difficulty with girls in general and unresolved feelings for Hermione in particular results in him lashing out at her for any perceived misstep. After learning that Hermione kissed Viktor Krum the previous year, he retaliates by having a relationship with Lavender Brown, a girl he never particularly liked. Ron's motive appears to be to hurt Hermione and make her jealous. In that end, he has apparently succeeded.

QUESTIONS

1. If Snape is magically bound to help Draco accomplish his secret task, why does Draco refuse to confide in him?
2. Why did Voldemort never tell Snape what Draco's task is?
3. Why does Harry invite Luna to Slughorn's party? Why does Ron object?
4. Why does Ron mock Hermione? Was it deserved?
5. Why did Hermione invite Cormac McLaggen rather than another student?
6. Is Luna right that Ron sometimes says funny things, but also hurtful ones? Explain. What does Harry think?

Chapter 16: A Very Frosty Christmas

SYNOPSIS

Harry and Ron, at The Burrow for Christmas, talk about what Harry had overheard. Ron agrees it is odd that Malfoy was given a task, and is incredulous that Snape made an Unbreakable Vow to help him. Anyone breaking an Unbreakable Vow will die. Fred and George arrive and start teasing Ron; apparently Ginny told them about about Ron and Lavender. Mrs. Weasley comes in to explain sleeping arrangements; apparently quite a crowd is expected at The Burrow over Christmas, though Percy, still estranged from his family, will be absent.

On Christmas Eve, Harry talks to Mr. Weasley, who admits privately to Harry that of the last three arrests, likely only one was a true Death Eater. Stan Shunpike is still being held to avoid bad publicity by letting him go. Harry tells him and Remus Lupin about the conversation he overheard between Snape and Malfoy. Both say Dumbledore trusts Snape, and that is good enough for them. Lupin tells Harry that he neither likes nor dislikes Snape; Snape always prepared his Wolfsbane Potion perfectly during his tenure at Hogwarts, and while he let it slip that Lupin was a werewolf, he could have done far worse damage, had he a mind to, by messing up the potion. Although the bitterness between them (and also Harry) cannot be healed, they should still trust Snape. Lupin has infiltrated the werewolves to spy on them for the Order, and he tells Harry they support Voldemort because they can be free under his rule. It is hard to argue against Fenrir Greyback's position. It was Greyback, the head and most vicious werewolf who bit Lupin when he was a child. Fenrir targets children to raise them to hate wizarding kind. He also wants to infect enough people for the werewolves to take over.

Harry asks Lupin about the Half-Blood Prince and the Levicorpus spell that James once used on Snape. Lupin says that spells have peaks of popularity, so the spell appearing at that time does not mean that it was this "Prince" who had invented it. He also has no idea about the Prince's identity except that it was not James, Sirius, or himself. Lupin suggests Harry find out how old the book is to help determine the Prince's identity. Before bed, Harry checks the book's copyright date and learns it was printed fifty years before. As his parents and their friends were at school only twenty years earlier, this seems to rule them out.

Harry and Ron receive Christmas presents the next morning. Among them are the usual jumpers (sweaters), a disgusting necklace for Ron from Lavender, and a package of maggots from house elf Kreacher to "Master" (Harry). Over Christmas dinner, the family (along with Fleur Delacour and Lupin) talk about Tonks, who was invited but declined to come; Mrs. Weasley apparently blames Bill for her absence. Reminded, Harry asks Lupin why Tonks' Patronus would change shape, saying that it is now large and has four legs. Lupin suggests that a major upheaval in someone's life can cause a change, but he is interrupted by Percy and the Minister of Magic Rufus Scrimgeour's unexpected arrival. Scrimgeour claims he and Percy were in the neighbourhood on business when Percy "decided" to drop in for a visit. Mrs. Weasley sobs happily at seeing Percy again, but the other Weasleys receive him coldly.

On the pretext of giving the Weasleys private family time, Scrimgeour asks Harry to show him the garden. Outside, Scrimgeour wants to know more about the prophecy and tells Harry he would like him to make regular visits to the Ministry. They want to present him as the "Chosen One," and show that he supports the Ministry. Whether or not he was "Chosen" is immaterial to the Ministry, only that everyone believes he is. Harry refuses, citing the Ministry failing to listen to him a year earlier, and now imprisoning Stan Shunpike, an obviously innocent person. Offended, Scrimgeour probes for information about Dumbledore, but Harry says nothing. Scrimgeour angrily accuses Harry of being "Dumbledore's man through and through." Harry readily agrees and angrily returns to the house.

ANALYSIS

Scrimgeour's attempt to woo Harry as a Ministry "poster boy," along with the Ministry's continuing refusal to release innocents like Stan Shunpike, again shows he is more concerned with putting on a good public face for the wizarding community rather than obtaining actual results. He also appears to want to separate Harry from Dumbledore's influence. Harry sees through both ruses and refuses to cooperate, turning around Scrimgeour's insult by saying that he is indeed "Dumbledore's man." Unfortunately, this incident only serves to further estrange the Weasleys from Percy, who obviously used his family to allow Scrimgeour access to Harry.

Lupin's dangerous mission for the Order of the Phoenix highlights his sad and lonely life as a werewolf. He is risking himself by infiltrating Fenrir Greyback's dangerous realm. Lupin also provides insight into how werewolves and other magical creatures like vampires, giants, goblins, and so forth, have been ostracized by the wizarding community, giving some justification to them supporting Voldemort who can offer them more advantages. Only the goblins rebuff Voldemort; as his power increases, he increasingly interferes with their internal affairs, thus losing their allegiance.

Readers will recognize Fenrir Greyback's name as the one that Draco Malfoy mentioned while at Borgin & Burkes earlier in the book. It is now clear why Mr. Borgin was suddenly so cooperative after Draco told him that Greyback was a "family friend." Considering Greyback's reputation, Borgin most likely feared for his life.

QUESTIONS

Review 1. Why does Scrimgeour want to recruit Harry's help? Why does Harry refuse? 2. Why does the Ministry refuse to release Stan Shunpike and other innocent people?

Extra Study 1. Why does Lupin say he neither likes nor dislikes Snape, even though Snape apparently hates him and was responsible for him leaving Hogwarts?

2. Why would magical creatures such as werewolves, giants, centaurs, and others support Voldemort? Why do the goblins not?

3. Why would Tonks decline an invitation to The Burrow during Christmas?

4. Harry's Potions book was printed fifty years ago. What was happening at Hogwarts at that time, and what might that tell Harry?

GREATER PICTURE

The printing date on Harry's book is fifty years before, putting it into a period near Tom Riddle's time at Hogwarts. In *Harry Potter and the Chamber of Secrets*, we are led to believe that Tom was a sixth- or seventh-year student fifty years before Harry was a second-year, so Tom, or a contemporary, could have purchased it new. However, all this really tells us is that the Half-Blood Prince was at the school sometime after that date. We have already seen that there is a brisk business in second-hand books, as they appear to change little from year-to-year, so it is entirely possible that one of James Potter's contemporaries owned this book. Curiously, even though text books are infrequently updated, readers are constantly reminded that new spells, jinxes, and hexes are always being invented. These apparently rarely become standard magical practices, and, as Lupin points out, these new ones fall in and out of fashion.

Chapter 17: A Sluggish Memory

SYNOPSIS

Harry, Ron, and Ginny return to Hogwarts via the Floo Network after Christmas. Hermione tells them the new password for Gryffindor Tower: Abstinence. Evidently, the Fat Lady enjoyed too much wine over Christmas. Hermione hands Harry a note from Dumbledore; the next lesson is scheduled for the following night. In the Common room, Ron is immediately enfolded by Lavender, while Ginny says she promised to meet Dean, though Harry senses she is rather unenthusiastic. Harry and Hermione, who is ignoring Ron, find a quiet corner, and he shares what happened during Christmas break, including the conversation with Rufus Scrimgeour. As expected, Hermione concurs with Mr. Weasley and Lupin, that Snape was attempting to discover what Malfoy's mission is. She reminds Harry that it was Fenrir Greyback's name that Malfoy threatened Borgin with.

The following morning, a notice on the bulletin board announces Apparation training for students turning 17 before 31st August, which includes everyone in the Sixth Year class. Students are excited, and when Harry admits that he has traveled by side-along Apparation, they ask about it. Harry says the sensation is unpleasant, but none seem put off by this.

Harry arrives for his lesson with Dumbledore and relates what happened over Christmas, including Rufus Scrimgeour's visit. Dumbledore says he has argued with both Rufus and Fudge over involving Harry in the Ministry's public relations efforts. Dumbledore displays a rare emotional flicker when Harry reveals his strong agreement to Scrimegeour dubbing him, "Dumbledore's man through and through." When Harry recounts Snape and Draco's conversation, Dumbledore thanks Harry for bringing this to his attention, but

Harry should not concern himself further. In response to Harry's angry outburst, Dumbledore says he does understand and reaffirms that he trusts Snape, and nothing Harry has said changes that.

But now, they must go into the memories. Dumbledore recaps: Riddle was admitted to Hogwarts and sorted into Slytherin where he learned about Salazar Slytherin's ability to converse with snakes. The staff expected little from Riddle. He was a polite, good-looking, and ambitious orphan, so many took pity on him. Dumbledore tells Harry that he never revealed his opinions about Tom to the staff. If Tom was turning over a new leaf, Dumbledore was going to allow him to do so. Dumbledore describes how *Death Eater* forerunners gravitated around Riddle but admits difficulty in obtaining memories of him during his time at Hogwarts. Riddle also became obsessed with his parentage.

The first new memory belongs to Riddle's Uncle Morfin. In it, Riddle arrives at the Gaunts' and converses with Morfin in Parseltongue. Morfin tells Tom about his father, Tom Riddle, Sr., and his mother, Merope, and shows him the Peverell ring, saying that Merope had taken Slytherin's locket. The memory abruptly ends. Morfin remembered nothing until after he awoke the next day and the ring was gone. Dumbledore says when Riddle Sr. and his parents were found murdered, the Ministry fingered Morfin, who readily confessed. Dumbledore speculates that Riddle Stunned his uncle, performed the murders, and then implanted false memories into Morfin's mind. The second memory is Slughorn's. He and the *Slug Club* during Riddle's era are chatting. Twice the memory inexplicably turns foggy and only Slughorn's voice is heard, notably when Riddle asks him about Horcruxes. Slughorn responds that he knows nothing about them. Dumbledore explains that Slughorn's memory has been tampered with and tasks Harry with obtaining the true memory from Slughorn.

Analysis

Although Dumbledore had hoped Tom Riddle would turn over a new leaf, his underlying suspicions were well founded. It appears Tom began building the foundation for his evil plan while still at Hogwarts, recruiting followers who were to become the first Death Eaters. Riddle also sought retaliation against his father for abandoning him and his mother, even though Riddle Sr. had actually been deceptively seduced by Merope with a love potion. That does not completely absolve Riddle, Sr., however, who rejected his child that bore no fault for his mother's duplicity, leaving him stranded in an orphanage. However, this all matters little to Tom, who is so consumed by hate and revenge that it extended beyond his doomed father to his innocent paternal grandparents, murdering them to obliterate any ties to his despised Muggle bloodline. Nor did Tom feel any loyalty to his Slytherin family, falsely incriminating his Uncle Morfin for the Riddles' murders.

Although the new Gryffindor password, "abstinence" supposedly refers to the Fat Lady having imbibed too much wine, it could also reflect the students' burgeoning sexual maturity. With all the confused emotions and chaotic relationships that many characters are experiencing, this may be the author's way of humorously warning them to, "slow down."

Questions

1. Why doesn't Snape's conversation with Malfoy worry Dumbledore?
2. Why would Slughorn alter his memory?
3. Why did Tom Riddle murder his Muggle grandparents, in addition to his father?
4. Did Dumbledore truly believe Tom Riddle was turning over a new leaf when he started Hogwarts? Give evidence both for and against this.
5. Why would Tom Riddle frame his Uncle Morfin for the Riddles' murders?
6. Why does Dumbledore react the way he does when Harry says he told Scrimgeour that he is, "Dumbledore's man?"

Greater Picture

Harry points out that Tom Riddle was underage when he murdered Morfin, but the Ministry failed to detect it. Dumbledore says that when an underaged wizard is in a Wizarding residence, the Ministry is unable to tell who performs magic and must rely on adult wizards to monitor any underage magical activity. In *Harry Potter and the Deathly Hallows,* Ron calls this monitoring a Trace and says it automatically breaks on a wizard's 17th birthday. The Trace apparently detects underage magic and the location, which is why Dobby's Hover charm at the Dursley house was detected just before Harry's second year. This generally would be ignored if it occurred in a Wizarding residence. One does rather wonder why the Trace failed to detect Tom Riddle Sr.'s murder and the creation of the resultant Horcrux.

It will be learned that before Dumbledore collected Harry from the Dursley's, he was already aware of Draco Malfoy's mission and quite possibly knew about Snape's Unbreakable Vow almost as soon as Snape made it.

Chapter 18: Birthday Surprises

Synopsis

Harry confides to both Hermione and Ron about Dumbledore's task to retrieve Slughorn's memory. Slughorn assigns the Potions class the difficult assignment of brewing the antidote for various poisons. The notes in Harry's textbook provide no assistance. With only a few minutes left, Harry finds a scrawled note in his book, "Just shove a bezoar down their throats." Harry also remembers that Snape once said a bezoar (a stone from a goat's stomach) will protect against most poisons. He rushes to the cabinet and finds one. No one in the class succeeds in making a good antidote, but when Slughorn comes to his table, Harry simply holds up the bezoar. Slughorn is amused, yet impressed, telling Harry that he thinks like his mother, then shoves the stone into his bag. Hermione, however, is critical.

Harry lingers after class and asks Slughorn about Horcruxes. Slughorn, realizing what Harry is attempting, insists there was nothing more to the memory that he gave Dumbledore, and departs hurriedly.

Students sit their first Apparation training in early February with a Ministry wizard. Malfoy, involved in a whispered argument with Crabbe, is reprimanded. Harry positions himself to eavesdrop if they start again. Apparently, Crabbe is upset at being told to guard something that Malfoy is doing, without knowing what it is. The class is called to order again, and they start practicing. Being their first lesson, students only attempt to apparate a few feet away. After several attempts, no one succeeds except Susan Bones, who splinches herself on the fourth attempt, leaving a leg behind.

After hearing Malfoy and Crabbe's conversation, Harry resolves to track his movements on the Maurauder's Map. He sees Malfoy in the Slytherin Common room with Crabbe and Goyle. Over the next several weeks, he watches Crabbe and Goyle moving around the castle on their own rather more than usual, sometimes standing in an empty hall. Harry is often unable to locate Malfoy on the map and considers that Malfoy is actually leaving the school, but dismisses this due to Hogwarts' increased security.

While opening presents on his birthday, Ron mistakenly eats several chocolates that Romilda Vane gave Harry. When Ron becomes dreamy over Romilda, Harry realizes the candies were spiked with Love Potion to get Harry to take Romilda to Slughorn's Christmas party. Ron has developed an obsessive love for Romilda. Not knowing the antidote, Harry takes Ron to Slughorn. En route, they bump into Lavender, and Ron announces that Harry is taking him to Romilda. Slughorn administers an antidote, then decides they should toast Ron's birthday. Slughorn opens a bottle of mead, offhandedly mentioning that he had intended it as a present for Dumbledore last Christmas. Ron takes a drink, and it is quickly obvious he has been poisoned. When Slughorn is slow to react, Harry finds the bezoar in Slughorn's bag, and forces it into Ron's mouth.

ANALYSIS

Obtaining Slughorn's complete memory is more difficult than Harry realized. Slughorn knows Dumbledore wants to retrieve this information, and, for whatever reason, he refuses to share it. Knowing that Harry is attempting to extract the memory from him, Slughorn carefully avoids being caught alone by Harry. If Harry is to be successful, he will have to devise a more clever plan.

Harry also becomes more obsessed with discovering what Draco is doing and watches him constantly on the Marauder's Map, although he is unable to figure out why Draco's name occasionally disappears. That no one else seems concerned about Draco's suspicious activities, further frustrates Harry. He will have to devise some other means if he is going to discover what Dark activity Draco is engaging in.

Although Hermione continually disapproves that Harry uses information from the Half-Blood Prince's book, she is perhaps being a little overly critical and obsessive when Harry uses the Bezoar stone in Slughorn's class. It was, after all, something Harry had previously learned about in Snape's class, and the notes in the book only acted as a reminder. It is possible that Hermione not only resents what she considers cheating, but also anyone outshining her in class. She will be grateful, however, that Harry knows how to use the stone when Ron is poisoned. Harry is 16 years old; Ron is turning 17 on his birthday. American readers who know that mead is alcoholic may be dismayed that Slughorn offers an alcoholic drink to a clearly underage Harry. It is worth mentioning that the drinking age in the UK is much lower than it is in the United States; it is legal to drink at age 18 in a pub, or at 16 in a restaurant with a meal, and at age 5 at home. The laws in the Wizarding world must be even more lenient, as the Three Broomsticks and the Hog's Head are clearly pubs, yet third-years (age 13 and 14) can order Butterbeer (which is apparently mildly alcoholic).

QUESTIONS

Review   1. Why is Malfoy arguing with his cronies?

2. Why does Ron fall in love with Romilda Vane?

3. Was Harry actually cheating when he presented the Bezoar stone to Slughorn during the class?

Extra Study   1. Why does Malfoy keep disappearing from the Marauder's Map? Where might he be during those absences? 2. Who could have poisoned the mead, and who might it have been intended for?

GREATER PICTURE

Disapparating can be dangerous when done improperly. And although Susan Bones' splinched leg during the Apparation training is presented as a humorous mishap, in the next book, *Deathly Hallows*, Ron's shoulder will be badly splinched while Disapparating under perilous and chaotic circumstances, causing a severe injury needing immediate medical attention.

Chapter 19: Elf Tails

SYNOPSIS

Ron is in the Hospital Wing, with Hermione, Ginny, Fred, George, and Harry at his bedside. Fred and George were investigating opening a Weasleys' Wizard Wheezes shop in Hogsmeade, but with Zonko's Joke Shop out of business and the Hogsmeade weekends canceled, it looks unpromising. Hagrid also arrives, saying he was in the Forest caring for Aragog, who is getting worse. Madam Pomfrey says "No more than six visitors to a patient," but retires in slight confusion when Harry points out that Hagrid is the sixth. Mr. and Mrs. Weasley arrive and express their sincere gratitude to Harry for continually saving Weasley lives. Harry, Hermione, and Hagrid leave the infirmary. Hagrid lets slip that Hogwarts could close due to the increasing dangerous incidents and reveals that he overheard Dumbledore and Snape arguing over something Snape no longer wanted to do. Dumbledore firmly reminded Snape that he gave his word. There was also a reference about Snape's investigations in Slytherin, which Hagrid assumes is about the cursed necklace. Filch's untimely arrival ends their conversation, and he and Hagrid get into a disagreement as Harry and Hermione hastily retreat. Hagrid's information has only deepened Harry's suspicions about Snape.

When Harry and Hermione return to Gryffindor Tower, Cormac McLaggen braces Harry about replacing Ron as Keeper, to which Harry grudgingly agrees. Harry returns to watching Draco's movements on the Marauder's Map. For the next while, Harry is beset, though, with classes, homework, Quidditch practice, Cormac repeatedly pestering him with strategy ideas, and Lavender asking about Ron's recovery. Harry asks Lavender why she does not ask Ron herself, but Lavender says that Ron is always asleep when she visits.

On his way to the next Quidditch match, Harry sees Draco and two sulky-looking girls heading into the castle. Harry is certain that Draco is going to his usual hidden place, and sorely wants to follow, but he is already late. Harry is astonished that Luna has been appointed as the Quidditch match commentator; her dreamy game description has everyone laughing, except Professor McGonagall. McLaggen, attempting to micromanage the team, borrows a Beater's club and accidentally hits a Bludger at Harry, cracking his skull and landing him in the infirmary with Ron, who thinks Luna's commentary was most entertaining. He hopes she gets the job permanently, but says that the final score was 320 to 60 against Gryffindor. Harry wants to find and kill McLaggen, but Madam Pomfrey says that would be "excessive exertion" and bans it. Ron comments that the team might have already done that for him. While still recovering, Harry realizes he could simply set a tail on Draco and suddenly remembers Dobby once visited him in the hospital. He summons Kreacher, the Black family House-elf that he inherited with Number 12, Grimmauld Place. Kreacher appears, along with Dobby. The two are fighting, apparently because Kreacher made insulting remarks about Harry. Peeves appears as well, egging them on; Harry silences him, and he zooms away. Ron and Harry break up the fight. Harry quietly instructs the two elves to trail Draco Malfoy and to bring him regular reports on everywhere Malfoy goes and what he does. He orders Kreacher not to warn Malfoy in any way. Kreacher sulkily agrees, though he says he would prefer having Draco as his master. Dobby says he is a free elf, and he chooses to obey Harry Potter.

Analysis

Harry's quick thinking saved Ron from certain death. Although Hermione continually chastised Harry for using the Half-Blood Prince's methods, in this instance, she is grateful for what the Prince taught him. Hermione is so distraught over Ron's near-death experience, that they permanently end their feud.

Someone obviously knew that Slughorn intended to give Dumbledore the mead and poisoned it to murder him. It is also possible, and highly probable, that the cursed necklace that nearly killed Katie Bell was also intended for Dumbledore. Harry remains convinced that Draco perpetrated the attacks, but he lacks specific proof tying Draco to either object. Though Draco was at Borgin & Burkes where Harry saw the necklace, any number of people could also have been there. Regardless, Harry becomes more determined than ever to uncover what Draco is doing. Although he is magically bound to obey Harry, Kreacher is less than trustworthy and remains loyal to the Black family, and by extension, the Malfoys (through Narcissa Black Malfoy), which is why Harry specifically orders him to reveal nothing to Draco. Harry may have been a bit careless in his instructions, however. Although Harry orders Kreacher to reveal nothing to Draco, Kreacher is clever and devious enough that he could bypass his master's orders by relaying information to Draco through somone else. Kreacher did just that when Sirius Black once ordered him to "leave," which Kreacher manipulated into meaning he should leave Grimmauld Place. He then visited Narcissa Malfoy, providing her with valuable information about Sirius and Harry. Fortunately, in this case, Kreacher obeys Harry as he intended, possibly because Dobby is carefully watching him and will report everything back to Harry. Though we have no proof other than Harry's suspicions as to who was the intended recipient or the delivery agent of either the necklace or the mead, it would be useful to consider these objects' source.

Questions

Review 1. Why might Hogwarts close?
2. Why is Ron always "asleep" when Lavender visits him in the hosptial?
3. Why did Harry have Kreacher, rather than Dobby, tail Draco? Why does Dobby participate?

Extra Study 1. What agreement might Dumbledore and Snape have? Why would Snape want to back out? 2. What might Snape be investigating in Slytherin House? Is he a reliable source to do this?

Greater Picture

The argument that Hagrid overheard between Snape and Dumbledore will be revisited in *Harry Potter and the Deathly Hallows*, where it will be essentially heard in its entirety. Snape was threatening to renege on his promise to Dumbledore to kill him in order to spare Draco, under orders from Voldemort, from having to do this. Dumbledore believes Snape will follow through, as he is presumably aware of Snape's Unbreakable Vow with Narcissa; still, the threat is real and must be addressed, as Snape could, presumably, somehow convince Draco to kill Dumbledore rather than doing it himself should Draco be unable. Hagrid felt that Dumbledore was not his usual self, that he seemed angrier than usual. By this time, the curse that had destroyed Dumbledore's hand had been gaining force, though bottled up in his hand, for eight months; no doubt he was feeling discomfort from it, and continuous pain is likely to make anyone, even someone as patient as Dumbledore, rather testy.

We know that the cursed necklace that injured Katie Bell was given to her at The Three Broomsticks. Though there is no proof, it is believable that this may have been aimed at Dumbledore, along with the poisoned mead.

Whatever its eventual destination, it seems likely that the mead's source would be The Three Broomsticks; Slughorn is unlikely to trust the Hog's Head for his needs, he is too much the esthete. This points to a center of malevolence in the Three Broomsticks; we will discover later that in fact that center is Madam Rosmerta, placed under the Imperius curse by Draco Malfoy.

Chapter 20: Lord Voldemort's Request

SYNOPSIS

Harry and Ron are discharged from the Hospital Wing together. Meeting up with Hermione, they head to breakfast, passing a small girl studying a tapestry. Startled, the girl drops the scales she had been holding; Hermione repairs them for her, and then reveals that Ginny and Dean had an argument. When Dean laughed about McLaggen hitting Harry in the head with a bludger, Ginny defended Harry. Hermione agreed with Ginny that it was not funny, that Harry was nearly seriously hurt. Harry tries to react calmly and curiously to this news, but Hermione remains suspicious that he is harboring feelings for Ginny.

Luna delivers Dumbledore's message regarding Harry's next lesson. The Trio continue on, running into Lavender, who is miffed she was not told that Ron was being discharged, and that Hermione is with him. Harry and Hermione walk off, and Ron arrives at breakfast a half hour later; he is upset and not talking to Lavender. Hermione seems secretly pleased by this development.

Later that evening, Harry arrives for his appointment with Professor Dumbledore, who is embroiled in a discussion with Professor Trelawney. She is upset that Firenze is still teaching Divination. As Professor Trelawney leaves, Dumbledore comments that, never having taken Divination himself, he could not have predicted the troubles that subject would cause. Dumbledore gently chastises Harry for failing to retrieve Professor Slughorn's memory. There is little point in continuing their lessons without it.

Dumbledore then asks Harry to recap the previous lessons. Harry recounts that Voldemort killed his own father, framed his uncle, Morfin, and left with the Peverell ring; he then returned to Hogwarts and asked Slughorn about Horcruxes. Dumbledore says they are now entering the realm of deep speculation. At this meeting, there are only two memories. The first belongs to Hokey, a House elf who worked for an elderly rich woman. At that time, Tom Riddle was working as a buyer for Borgin & Burkes. Tom's career choice surprised nearly everyone at Hogwarts, as it had been assumed he was aiming for a political career resulting as the Minister for Magic. But Tom had first approached Armando Dippet, the Headmaster then, for a teaching post at Hogwarts. Dippet turned him down, saying he lacked experience.

In Hokey's memory, Tom Riddle visits Hepzibah Smith, who claims to be Helga Hufflepuff's descendant. Hepzibah shows Riddle two coveted family treasures. One, a cup once belonging to Helga Hufflepuff, she bought from Borgin & Burke's. The other is a locket, seen earlier in Merope Gaunt's possession, and which, of course, was once owned by Salazar Slytherin. The locket was sold to Smith by Borgin & Burke's, who bought it off some poor woman.

Two days later, Hepzibah died and her treasures went missing. Hokey admitted blame for her mistress' death, as she remembered mistakenly poisoning her. Dumbledore states that Riddle considered the locket was rightfully his, and suggests that Riddle also stole the cup because of his deep attachment to Hogwarts; why, exactly, he had wanted it will have to wait for another lesson.

The second memory is Dumbledore's as Hogwarts Headmaster meeting with Riddle. Ten years after Hepzibah Smith's death, Riddle has again applied to be the Defence Against the Dark Arts teacher. His facial features have changed somewhat; while unlike the snake-like mask that Harry remembers from Voldemort's reappearance in the graveyard, this is certainly not the handsome Tom Riddle seen in the previous memory. Dumbledore confronts him about his true motives for wanting the position and his rumored behavior. He turns down Riddle for the job, saying that he is aware that Riddle has a new name (Voldemort) and that his Death Eaters are in Hogsmeade. Back in his office, Dumbledore tells Harry that ever since he refused Voldemort's request, there has never been a Defence Against The Dark Arts teacher who lasted more than one year.

ANALYSIS

In the previous chapter, Draco was seen accompanied by two small girls, both looking sulky and rebellious. Now there is a small girl standing in the seventh-floor corridor studying a tapestry with trolls in tutus; we previously saw small girls standing in seventh-floor corridors earlier. In the previous book, we might remember that the entrance to the Room of Requirement is on the seventh floor, opposite the troll tapestry. In a previous chapter, it is also discovered that Crabbe and Goyle were upset at having to spend so much time guarding Malfoy without knowing what he is doing, and they seem to be spending much time standing around in corridors. Is a pattern developing here?

It is now known why no Defence Against the Dark Arts teacher has lasted for more than one year—Dumbledore believes that Voldemort cursed the position when he was rejected. Dumbledore must either have been hoping that the curse would be broken when he appointed Snape as the new Defence Against the Dark Arts teacher, or he never intended for him to last any longer than his predecessors.

QUESTIONS

Review 1. Why did Ginny argue with Dean? What is Harry's reaction to the news? Why is Hermione suspicious of this?

2. What do the two memories reveal about Voldemort?

3. Why does Dumbledore tell Harry there will be no more lessons? What does Harry need to do?

4. What is significant about the seventh floor?

5. Why would Tom Riddle have taken such a lowly job at Borgin & Burke's?

Extra Study 1. What reasons might Dumbledore have had to refuse Tom Riddle the Defense Against the Dark Arts position? What's the long-term result of this decision?

2. Why does Harry continually see one or two young girls loitering in the halls?

GREATER PICTURE

Aberforth is Dumbledore's brother, and according to an interview with the author and information in the seventh book, the bartender of the Hog's Head. That is most likely the reason Dumbledore knows there are Death Eaters in Hogsmeade.

There is some speculation, both within the book and by fans, about Voldemort's true purpose in visiting Hogwarts to apply for the Defense against the Dark Arts position. Dumbledore states that Voldemort probably wanted a teaching position there so he could investigate Hogwarts and all its secrets with impunity. There would also be many impressionable young minds to recruit to his peculiar beliefs. Dumbledore also apparently suspected that Voldemort was attempting to make a Horcrux—possibly using Godric Gryffindor's sword. Some fans suggest that he was planting a Horcrux there (which proves to be true in book seven). That would fit his "style"—hiding a Horcrux under Dumbledore's nose, basically saying that he knew Dumbledore's school better than Dumbledore himself did. Voldemort may have partially used the interview as a ruse so he could hide Rowena Ravenclaw's diadem, one of his Horcruxes, inside Hogwarts. His intent here was actually to keep the diadem safe, convinced he was the only living person who knew about the Room of Requirement.

Voldemort probably told Draco how to summon the Room of Requirement. Putting the clues together, as Harry does in the next chapter, we will see that Draco is working on his project in this room. Crabbe and Goyle, disguised as little girls by stolen Polyjuice Potion, stand guard outside, dropping objects when it is unsafe to exit the room. Although Draco would already have known about the Room of Requirement after Dumbledore's Army was discovered there the previous year (in *Order of the Phoenix*), it seems Voldemort will continue to be under the assumption throughout the next book that he and Draco are the only ones who knows its existence, although it is curious why Draco would withhold this (and possibly other information) from the Dark Lord; presumably, Draco knows nothing about the Diadem Horcrux.

While it is never stated, we learn in the next book that within the first fortnight of the summer preceding this school year, Dumbledore discovered that he had aproximately one year to live. He specifically requests that by the end of the year, Snape should kill him, thus protecting Draco Malfoy from executing Voldemort's assasination plot. Realizing that he himself will only last out the year, and that Snape will be accused of murdering him, Dumbledore knows that Snape's tenure as Defence Against the Dark Arts teacher would be limited in any case. It is likely that this is why Dumbledore repeatedly refused Snape the post: Snape is too talented a teacher, too valuable an ally, to risk losing. After this year, it will no longer matter, so placing him in the cursed post will do no harm.

Chapter 21: The Unknowable Room

SYNOPSIS

Harry spends much spare time devising a way to retrieve Professor Slughorn's memory. As his potions book has been so useful recently, particularly in saving Ron's life, Harry reads it carefully. But Hermione points out that Dumbledore said only Harry could successfully retrieve the memory, and that Slughorn would likely be protected against anything in the textbook. Just then, Harry finds a new curse, Sectumsempra. It is labeled, "For Enemies." He wants to test it, but knowing Hermione's objections to using the Prince's spells, he refrains. Ron, writing an essay, asks for assistance; it seems his Spell-Checking quill has stopped working, and, among other things, is rendering his name as "Roonil Wazlib." Hermione offers to correct his spelling. Ron says he loves her, and Hermione, blushing, says he should not let Lavender hear him say that. Ron says maybe he should; he has been trying to dump her.

Kreacher and Dobby arrive to report to Harry regarding Malfoy's activities. Over the week they have been tailing him, Draco spent considerable time inside the Room of Requirement. The elves state that a "variety" of students stand watch while Draco is inside. Harry surmises that these "students" are probably Crabbe and Goyle disguised by Polyjuice Potion stolen from Slughorn. He also guesses that the Room was not on the Marauder's Map because the map's authors did not know about about it, though Hermione suggests that the room may be "unplottable" if the user needs it to be. Harry says that he should be able to enter the Room of Requirement, just as Malfoy had when Dumbledore's Army was there. But Hermione counters that Draco knew what the Room was being used for because "that stupid Marietta" told him.

During a free period the next day, Harry again attempts to enter the Room of Requirement, but he is unable to make the door appear. His efforts make him late for Defence Against the Dark Arts class, causing Snape to penalize Gryffindor ten points. Seamus Finnigan asks about the difference between ghosts and Inferi, as a story in the *Daily Prophet* mentioned Inferi; Professor Snape says the story actually was about one Mundungus Fletcher, who was arrested for impersonating an Inferius. Ron also gets taunted and given detention by Snape. When Lavender starts abusing Snape after class, Ron is irritated rather than amused, and he and Harry duck into a bathroom so Ron can avoid her. There they find Moaning Myrtle, who says she was expecting someone else—a boy who has been crying.

Ron decides to take the extra Apparation classes being offered in Hogsmeade village. Hermione, meanwhile, repeatedly urges Harry to try and get Slughorn's memory. Harry truthfully answers that he is trying, but Slughorn, knowing what Harry is after, takes precautions to never be alone with him. Harry decides to spend another day looking for Malfoy in the Room of Requirement, first chasing off Goyle. Unsuccessful at opening the door, he kicks the wall, and his Invisibility Cloak slips off. Tonks calls out to him, and says she is there to see Dumbledore about "nothing in particular." She asks if he has heard from anyone in the Order, then gets teary eyed. When Harry relates this to Hermione, she remarks, "It's a bit odd." Harry suggests that she was in love with Sirius. Her Patronus is big and hairy now. Hermione thinks it is possible, but is doubtful.

ANALYSIS

Harry learns that Malfoy has been spending time in the Room of Requirement, which is why Draco periodically disappears from the Marauder's Map. However, Harry still does not know what Malfoy is working on, and anyone he tells seems unconcerned. Harry only becomes more obsessed with following Draco, causing Harry to neglect his task to retrieve Slughorn's memory and receive a mild rebuke from Dumbledore.

Although Ron jokingly tells Hermione he loves her, he may actually be internalizing his strong feelings for her. And while he remains confused about how he actually feels about Hermione, there is no doubt about his feelings for Lavender—he wants to be rid of her.

Tonks' ongoing depression remains a mystery, but it has deeply affected her to where her Patronus had changed its shape. Although Harry believes she was in love with Sirius, Hermione doubts this, and Hermione is seldom wrong in her assumptions. One thing seems obvious, Tonks is secretly guarding Harry, always appearing just as he lands himself in trouble.

QUESTIONS

Review 1. Why does Harry decide not to test the Prince's Sectumsempra spell?

2. Why does Harry believe his Potions book can help him retrieve Slughorn's memory? What does Hermione say?

3. Why does Tonks say she is looking for Dumbledore? What does she mean by "nothing in particular"?

4. Why is Tonks always so sad? Why does Hermione doubt that Tonks was in love with Sirius?

Extra Study 1. What might Draco be doing in the Room of Requirement?

2. Ron jokingly tells Hermione he "loves" her. Is he really joking or do his words reveal deeper feelings? What is Hermione's reaction?

3. Who might the sobbing boy in Moaning Myrtle's bathroom be and why does he go to that particular place? Why would he be crying?

GREATER PICTURE

It is perhaps surprising that the Room of Requirement can be used to carry out what we assume is a task for Voldemort, as Hogwarts is supposed to be protected from Dark Magic. There are several possibilities here. One possibility is that the Room of Requirement is an exception, or that someone has performed a spell which allows it. Another possibility is that what is being done is not Dark as such, but can be used for Dark purposes. What Draco is doing is repairing a Vanishing cabinet, a task which in isolation is not Dark. It is the use it is put to once it is repaired that makes it so useful to the Dark side.

Harry's decision to heed Hermione's advice and refrain from testing the Prince's spells on someone without knowing the results was a wise one. Sectumsempra has a devastating effect, which, had it been used in a different circumstance, could have cost someone their life, and in a later chapter, it will be nearly fatal for someone. Readers should note the reference to Inferi. They will be seen later in the book.

Chapter 22: After the Burial

SYNOPSIS

Harry, Ron, and Hermione are studying the Apparation handbooks in preparation for their test. Hagrid sends a message saying that Aragog, the giant spider, has died. He asks if Harry, Ron, and Hermione could attend the funeral. Between the three, they decide not to go; it is such a silly thing to get detention over, after all. Hermione suggests Harry have another try at Professor Slughorn's memory during class, as it will be pretty sparse with students off taking Apparation tests. Ron suggests using the Felix Felicis potion to help Harry get Professor Slughorn's memory. Hermione agrees, but Harry is reluctant; he had been saving it, although he is unsure for what—but it has something to do with Ginny breaking up with Dean, and Ron somehow getting a girlfriend he actually likes.

With only three people in Potions class (Harry, Ernie, and Draco), Professor Slughorn sets an open challenge: make whatever they like. Harry notices that Draco is looking thinner and a bit unhealthy, and believes that whatever he is doing in the Room of Requirement is not going so well. Slughorn is impressed with Harry's Euphoria Elixir, but again manages to escape when they are alone. Returning to the Gryffindor Common room, Harry learns that Hermione passed Apparation, but Ron failed by half an eyebrow.

Harry, Hermione, and Ron head for the dorm, where Harry drinks some Felix Felicis. To Ron and Hermione's amazement, Harry decides to attend Aragog's funeral. Covered by his Invisibility cloak, Harry returns to the Common room, followed by Ron and Hermione. Lavender, unable to see Harry but seeing Ron and Hermione arriving together from the boy's dorm, flies into a jealous rage. Heading out the portrait hole, Harry brushes against Ginny; she thinks it is Dean, and rounds on him.

Following a detour that the potion seems to suggest, Harry runs into Slughorn who, upon learning about Aragog's death, notes that acromantula venom is particularly valuable. Recognizing that this may be an opportunity to entice Slughorn to share his memory about Tom Riddle, Harry invites him to the funeral. Slughorn arrives at Hagrid's hut, well dressed and carrying bottles of mead. After an emotional service, and with help from Harry's flawless and surreptitious refilling charm, Hagrid and Slughorn become drunk. Knowing Slughorn will remember nothing the next morning, Harry talks about his parents' death. Hearing how his favorite student, Lily Evans, died, causes Slughorn to become extremely sad. Harry says he needs the memory about Tom Riddle, and, as a persuasion tactic, reminds Slughorn that he is Lily's son. Harry finally convinces Slughorn that he is the "Chosen One," and the teary-eyed professor yields the memory. Slughorn falls asleep after handing over the wisps of memory to Harry.

Analysis

This is the first time Harry's powers of persuasion have been truly seen, although he was under the influence of Felix Felicis at the time. This is also the first time that Harry has spoken about his parent's death in this manner, and probably the only time without experiencing extreme emotion, knowing it will help fight Voldemort. Even in death, James and Lily are still able to battle the Dark Lord. Readers should recall some chapters back that Professor Dumbledore said Harry was uniquely equipped to obtain Slughorn's memory. Dumbledore may have known about the Felix Felicis, although using it may actually have been unnecessary; Dumbledore knows that Harry having Lily's eyes, and Lily being one of Slughorn's favorite students, would be a powerful and emotional persuasion tactic. That, and being well plied with alcohol, is enough to coax Slughorn into divulging the memory; remembering Lily's sacrifice in fighting Voldemort also helped. Although Slughorn will have forgotten the incident when he awakes, he probably would have been appreciated the irony that it was his own Good Luck potion that allowed Harry to retrieve a memory from him that he tried so hard to keep hidden. Readers may wonder if Slughorn ever again awards another student this potion as a prize.

Questions

1. Why is Acromantula venom so valuable?
2. Why does Harry invite Slughorn to the funeral?
3. What might Harry have been intending to save the Felix Felicis potion for?
4. How does Harry persuade Slughorn to give him the memory? What helps him?

Chapter 23: Horcruxes

Synopsis

Harry heads to the castle as the Felix Felicis potion is wearing off; Nearly Headless Nick tells him that Professor Dumbledore has returned and is in his office. Memory in hand, Harry presents himself to Dumbledore, who is apparently amazed and very pleased with Harry's success. He fetches his Pensieve, and they journey into Slughorn's fifty year-old memory.

Slughorn is talking to Tom Riddle, who asks about Horcruxes. Slughorn explains it is the darkest of Dark magic. It is possible to split a soul and encase the shard in another object; if killed, the perpetrator does not actually die because his soul shard is trapped and remains earthbound. Slughorn says souls are not meant to be split because it takes the ultimate evil, murder, to rip a soul apart. Prodded further, Slughorn reveals that there is a spell, but claims he does not know it. Riddle asks if one Horcrux can keep someone alive, is not more better? Seven, after all is a very powerful number. Slughorn, horrified, tries calming himself by saying this is all hypothetical. Riddle agrees, but as he departs, Harry sees the same wild joy on Riddle's face as when he learned he was a wizard. Dumbledore tells Harry that Tom Riddle's diary, that Harry destroyed four years before, was almost certainly a Horcrux. He believes it was not only a safeguard, but also a weapon, intended to be passed on to, or planted upon, a Hogwarts student who would become possessed by it and reopen the Chamber of Secrets. Dumbledore suggests that this was a risky act if Riddle only had one soul fragment and believes there are others. Dumbledore recalls Voldemort's statement the night he returned: "*I, who have gone further than anybody along the path that leads to immortality,*" and theorizes that, in a bid for immortality, Voldemort may have divided his soul into seven pieces (as the young Tom Riddle claimed that seven was the "most powerfully magical number"). As long as any Horcrux survives, Voldemort is unable to be killed. Dumbledore speculates that Voldemort only used unique items for his Horcruxes—objects with a significant history that no one would destroy. The seventh soul shard is evidently within Voldemort himself. Two Horcruxes have been destroyed: Tom Riddle's diary (seen in *Harry Potter and the Chamber of Secrets*) and a ring once belonging to Marvolo Gaunt, Voldemort's maternal grandfather. Dumbledore reveals that his injured hand resulted from destroying the ring, and it was only his own skill and Professor Snape's timely action that prevented the damage from being much worse. Dumbledore believes that of the four remaining Horcruxes, two will be Hufflepuff's cup and Slytherin's locket; the third may be a Ravenclaw artifact. The only known Gryffindor artifact, the sword, remains safe in Dumbledore's office. He suspects that the final Horcrux is in Nagini, Voldemort's pet snake. Although placing a Horcrux in a living being is possible, Dumbledore says it is not the safest place, as living creatures can be killed. Harry learns that Dumbledore's many absences from Hogwarts were because he was searching for Horcruxes, and Dumbledore tells Harry that should he locate any more Horcruxes, Harry will be permitted to accompany him.

Dumbledore says he does not believe Voldemort knows when a Horcrux is destroyed, as he seemed unaware that Tom Riddle's diary had been destroyed until he learned it from Lucius Malfoy. Dumbledore suggests that with that, plus the fiasco in the Ministry, Lucius may well be happy to be safely tucked away in Azkaban. Dumbledore tells Harry that Voldemort can be killed if all his Horcruxes are destroyed by someone with uncommon skill and power, someone like Harry, who possesses the ability to love.

Chapter 23: Horcruxes

ANALYSIS

Trelawney's prophecy stated that "The Chosen One" would have powers the Dark Lord does not possess. That power is love, and Dumbledore realizes that it is Harry's abilities, combined with his capacity to love, that will empower him to defeat Voldemort. Unlike Harry, who is emotionally intact, and whose friends support him out of loyalty and amity, Voldemort is psychologically and spiritually shredded, capable of feeling only hate, envy, and rage, and controlling his followers through fear and coercion. And while Harry finds it difficult to fathom that something so simple as love is the more powerful force, he understands that, once again, it is also about choices; Voldemort's actions are based on the prophecy, but Harry would choose to fight Voldemort whether or not the prophecy had been made. That choice, and the ability to make that choice, is largely what gives Harry powers that Voldemort lacks and prevents Harry from falling victim to the Dark side.

Dumbledore believes that Voldemort's snake, Nagini, is also a Horcrux. It has been suggested that Voldemort's final Horcrux might have been generated via the death of Frank Bryce, the Riddle Manor caretaker that Voldemort murdered. Voldemort's wand was also used to murder Bertha Jorkins in *Harry Potter and the Goblet of Fire*, so it may have been her death that allowed Voldemort to create a Horcrux that may be embedded within Nagini. It is also possible that all his Horcruxes were in place at the time of his encounter with Baby Harry; the weak and disembodied Voldemort may have been unable to create Horcruxes after that incident. This would rule out a Horcrux being made from either Bertha Jorkins' or Frank Bryce's deaths. However, Dumbledore is correct in his assertion that Nagini is much more self-aware than an ordinary snake would be, and that Voldemort seems to have much more control than expected. As Dumbledore had said, at this point we enter into the realm of speculation; as Dumbledore did not know of the circumstances surrounding Frank Bryce's death, or Bertha Jorkins,' his speculation does not quite tally with the readers' understanding. Nagini was already acting most decidedly unsnake-like when Frank Bryce was killed, so the best assumption is that Voldemort's final Horcrux was actually created from the earlier death of Bertha Jorkins, and was retained in Nagini.

Dumbledore is not quite correct in saying that the sword is Gryffindor's only known artifact; there is also the Sorting Hat, which says it once belonged to Gryffindor. Being in some small way sentient, though, there is some question whether it is properly an artifact.

QUESTIONS

Review 1. Why might Voldemort have created so many Horcruxes? Was this wise? If not, explain.

2. What is the significance of each object Voldemort hides the Horcruxes in?

3. Why did Dumbledore risk putting the ring on his finger knowing the dangers? What is the result?

4. Why was Dumbledore so frequently absent from Hogwarts?

Extra Study 1. How would love be able to defeat Voldemort? Does Harry truly understand its significance?

GREATER PICTURE

One Horcrux was previously seen in Grimmauld Place. "A heavy locket that none of them could open," matching Slytherin's locket that has been seen in the Pensieve memories a few times now, was discovered and discarded during the cleanup of Grimmauld Place. A paper inside a fake locket that will be found later in a secret sea cave is signed R.A.B., which are the initials of the late Regulus Arcturus Black, a repentant Death Eater and Sirius's younger brother. The locket at Grimmauld Place will prove hard to find; originally Kreacher had set it aside, unable to part with any valuable Black heirlooms. It is later stolen by Mundungus Fletcher, who was seen earlier busily looting Grimmauld Place. When Harry, Ron, and Hermione eventually catch up with Mundungus, he will inform them that the locket was extorted from him by Dolores Umbridge at the Ministry of Magic. Curiously, even though Harry clearly sees Slytherin's distinctively-shaped locket during his and Dumbledore's forays into the Pensieve, Harry fails to recognize it as the same one that was found and then discarded at Grimmauld Place (in Order of the Phoenix), nor will he fully realize that another locket that will be collected from a sea cave near the book's end is also different until he finds a note inside explaining that it is a fake Horcrux. Dumbledore will also fail to notice the difference; however, he will be in an extremely weakened physical and mental state after recovering the locket and it is possible that peoples' memories do not necessarily record small details so accurately. Dumbledore states that he believes that Voldemort is unable to feel when his Horcruxes are being destroyed, given that he did not know the diary had been dispatched until told by Lucius Malfoy. What Dumbledore has not told Harry is that a second Horcrux, the ring, has also been eradicated, with no apparent response from Voldemort. It is learned later that Snape is able to bring information about Voldemort to Dumbledore, and he would have reported Voldemort's reaction to the ring's destruction had Voldemort been aware of it. While Harry learns that the ring Horcrux has been destroyed, he must remain unaware of just what Snape's true role is for a while longer. If Riddle was telling the truth when he spoke to Slughorn, it indicates that he found nothing about Horcruxes in the library and that the book, *Secrets of the Darkest Art* (which we learn in *Harry Potter and the Deathly Hallows* is an authoritative source on the making and destruction of Horcruxes) had already been hidden away. Even then, though, Tom Riddle and the truth had, at best, no more than a nodding acquaintance. So it is entirely possible that Riddle had a greater understanding about how to create Horcruxes than he let on and could have created one. The author has stated that the ring Horcrux was made via the death of Tom Riddle Sr., which happened at the same time as Tom collected the ring from Morfin Gaunt; thus, if the ring was on Tom's finger in the memory, it must already have been a Horcrux. One of Dumbledore's infrequent mistakes is seen here; Dumbledore stated that once the ring was made into a Horcrux, Tom no longer wanted to wear it. He is wearing it in this memory, and it is presumably already a Horcrux. Possibly, a better statement would have been, "Once he had made a second Horcrux, he felt a need to keep them all safe and separate from himself." Thus the ring Horcrux would have been hidden once he had made the diary Horcrux.

It is certain that Riddle would have waited to hide the ring Horcrux in the Gaunt shack until Morfin and Marvolo were no longer there. He had learned from Morfin that Marvolo had died. Having framed Morfin for Tom Riddle Sr.'s murder, Riddle would have known that Morfin was in Azkaban, but there is always the possibility, slim though it may be, that he would break out or be released. Presumably it was only after hearing about Morfin's death in prison that Riddle thought it safe to return to the Gaunt shack and hide the ring there. Having taken great pains to conceal his original name, and especially his middle name, Voldemort thought that it would be impossible to make the connection back to the Gaunt shack.

Chapter 24: Sectumsempra

Synopsis

In Charms class the next day, Harry shares with Ron and Hermione what he and Dumbledore learned from Slughorn's memories. Ron, in return, mentions that as Lavender was unable to see Harry, she thought Ron and Hermione were upstairs alone, and they have broken up. Hermione comments that Ginny and Dean have also split. Harry tries hard to conceal his elation at this last bit of news, but Hermione senses he is hiding something.

Ginny and Dean's silence with one another creates a problem for the Quidditch team; Harry worries whether they can Chase together if they are at daggers drawn. Luckily, Katie Bell returns from the hospital and can resume playing. Unfortunately, she cannot recall who gave her the necklace.

Quidditch practice, now that McLaggen is gone and Katie is back, is wonderful. Ginny becomes the life of the team, cracking jokes and doing marvellous imitations. Harry is glad to have a reason to look at her, glad to have the chance to walk alongside her, but he is still seriously worried about what could happen to his friendship with Ron if he started dating her. Harry remembers Ron's expression when he caught Ginny and Dean together; what would he think of Ginny and himself? Meanwhile, there is much interest in the upcoming Quidditch match against Ravenclaw; the outcome of the Quidditch championship is still in doubt. Though Gryffindor would have to win by three hundred points to get the championship, that is still possible; if they lose by as much as a hundred points, they will still be in second place.

Harry, making his usual pass by the Room of Requirement, sees on the Marauder's Map that Draco is in a bathroom one floor below with Moaning Myrtle. Harry investigates and finds Draco sobbing: whatever he is planning, he is frightened that he is unable do it and fears for his parents' lives (and his own) if he fails. Malfoy spots Harry and casts a Cruciatus curse; Harry, defending himself, uses the *Sectumsempra* spell from the Half-Blood Prince's book, not knowing its effects. The spell slashes Draco, spilling his blood everywhere. Moaning Myrtle flies off, screaming; Professor Snape responds swiftly and saves Draco's life, rushing him to the Hospital Wing. Returning, Snape demands to know whence Harry learned the spell, and despite Harry's attempts at occlumency, Snape apparently gleans some information that Harry's potions book is the source. Snape demands to see his textbooks. Harry runs to the Common room and borrows Ron's books including the Potions textbook, and, asking the Room of Requirement for a place to hide something, enters and finds himself in a vast warehouse filled with broken and discarded objects. Passing the broken Vanishing Cabinet in which Montague had run into trouble the previous year, Harry hides his annotated version in a large cupboard, placing an old stone bust, a wig, and a battered tiara on top to locate it again.

Snape seems unconvinced that these textbooks, especially the Potions book, are actually Harry's, particularly since the Potions book is signed "Roonil Wazlib." Having used Dark Magic to cause serious harm (albeit unknowingly), Snape gives Harry detention (and with McGonagall's concurrence) every Saturday for the rest of the year. Hermione, of course, says she always knew that the Prince was involved in Dark magic; Harry says that it proves nothing of the sort, the Prince may have just copied the spell down. Hermione is upset that Harry intends to go back and retrieve the Prince's book, but Ginny tells her to leave Harry alone.

Ginny replaces Harry as Seeker, and Dean Thomas replaces her as Chaser. That Saturday, as ordered, Harry reports to Snape's office for detention and is assigned copying over old detention files for Filch. Snape suggests Harry start with the boxes detailing his father's misbehaviour. When Harry returns to the Common room, he learns that Gryffindor won the match 450 to 140, and thus the Quidditch Cup. Ginny runs towards him; without thinking, he catches her in his arms and kisses her. When the kiss is over, he looks around: Dean Thomas is holding a broken glass, Romilda Vane looks angry, Hermione approving. Ron appears stunned, but gives a small nod, as if bowing to the inevitable. Harry suggests, wordlessly, to Ginny that they should go for a long walk.

This is the first time Draco is seen attempting an unforgivable curse, though his familiarity with it suggests he has been practicing privately. Although Harry was justifiably defending himself against Malfoy, who was about to cast the Cruciatus Curse against him, using an unknown spell was dangerous and reckless. However, despite this grievous action that could have permanently expelled him from Hogwarts, Snape only assigns Harry detention. It is also the first time Draco is seen as anything but a swaggering, obnoxious bully, and his uncontrollable sobbing shows he possesses a more humanistic side. Draco is obviously terrified for his and his family's safety should he fail in his task, indicating he is under extreme emotional duress. Harry catching him in such a vulnerable state prompted his severe reaction, which, in turn, caused Harry to react just as rashly.

Ginny defending Harry when Hermione is chastising him for wanting to retrieve the Half-Blood Prince's book serves several purposes. First, Ginny reminds Hermione that Draco was about to cast an unforgivable curse, and shows that there is a definite possibility that Harry was acting on impulse, not rational thought. Second, this is the first time that someone other than Ron or Harry has defended the Half-Blood Prince, though in this instance, it is more to justify Harry's actions; Hermione's long-standing animosity toward the Prince seems to be based on jealousy, rather than on her concern that the Prince might be a Dark wizard. In particular, Hermione sees Harry's use of the text as not his own work, but instead as using the Prince's work and claiming it as his own. For Hermione, it seems that this is an issue that is about more than the Prince's spells possibly having Dark aspects, though she does use the Dark nature of the *Sectumsempra* spell as justification for her excoriation of the Prince. And finally, this helps set up the scene where Harry and Ginny kiss. By seeing that Ginny is willing to stand up for him, Harry now knows that Ginny is not angry with him, and this gives Harry hope that she may still have feelings for him.

While Ginny and Harry's relationship has been gradually building almost from the the series' beginning, this is the first time it has been declared openly. It took so long because they were often at cross purposes. At first, Harry simply had no romantic interest in Ginny, having first set his sights on Cho Chang and considering Ginny only as Ron's little sister. It is only later that Harry realized that he and Cho were incompatible and that he not only had feelings for Ginny, but that they were suited to each other in nearly every way. She, however, appeared to have moved on and became involved with someone else, although she never actually lost interest in Harry; she simply gave up. Harry need not have worried about what Ron thought, however. In fact, when Ginny announced that she had broken up with Michael Corner at the end of the previous book, Ron subtly hinted to Harry that he was a better choice than Michael, even if Harry was oblivious about what he meant at the time.

QUESTIONS

Review 1. What task has Draco Malfoy been asked to perform?

2. Why does Malfoy fear for his and his family's lives should he fail to complete his task?

Extra Study 1. Why would Harry cast a spell without knowing what it does? Was he justified in using it? Explain. 2. Why does Snape only assign Harry detention for such a serious offense, rather than recommend he be expelled?

GREATER PICTURE

Harry and Ginny's relationship, which begins publicly here, will be thrown into turmoil nearer the end of this book. Harry knows Voldemort will attack anyone close to Harry, causing him to end his and Ginny's relationship in order to protect her.

While inside the Room of Requirement, Harry unknowingly touches another Horcrux and puts it on top of the dresser that he hides his Potions book in. This is something that he will need to remember in the next book. This will not be the last time Snape gives a light sentence for a student's serious offense. In *Deathly Hallows*, when Ginny, Neville, and Luna attempt to steal Gryffindor's Sword from the Headmaster's office, Snape, the then-Headmaster, catches them, but he only assigns them detention in the Forbidden Forest with Hagrid.

Chapter 25: The Seer Overheard

SYNOPSIS

Harry and Ginny are happy together, laughing about the rumors going around school about them; Harry is particularly pleased that the reason everyone is talking about him is something that makes him happy, rather than something to do with Dark magic. Ron and Hermione seem to be getting close as well. Harry's concerns that his relationship with Ginny could affect his friendship with Ron have largely evaporated.

Harry dares not to return to the Room of Requirement to recover his Potions textbook, thinking that Snape might still want to get his hands on it, and his Potions work is suffering; Professor Slughorn genially attributes this to his new interest in Ginny. Hermione reveals her theory to Harry regarding the 'Half-Blood Prince.' She has found a write-up of one Eileen Prince, a past Hogwarts student, and suggests that if she was a half-blood, it could have been her.

Harry is summoned to Dumbledore's office. Along the way, he encounters Professor Trelawney, who is sprawled in the hallway outside the Room of Requirement. She admits that she uses the Room of Requirement to hide her stock of sherry, but she is unable to get in. Apparently, someone is inside, barring others from entering. Trelawney heard a 'whooping' sound from within, which makes Harry believe that Malfoy has finally finished his task. When Trelawney called out to see who was there, everything went dark and she was pushed out into the hall. Harry says she should tell Dumbledore; she seems to like the idea and accompanies him.

As they walk, Trelawney recounts the evening Dumbledore hired her; Harry already knows Dumbledore's version, but is fascinated to hear Trelawney's, particularly when she reveals Snape interrupted them. Realizing it was Snape who passed Voldemort the information that prompted him to kill his parents, a raging Harry runs off to confront Dumbledore in his office. Dumbledore, however, disarms Harry before he can speak by telling him that he believes he has located a Horcrux. Harry is only momentarily distracted, then confronts Dumbledore about Trelawney.

After a fiery exchange, Dumbledore simply states he has reason to trust Snape, even given his skills at Occlumency. Dumbledore exacts a promise from Harry that, if Harry wishes to come with him to retrieve the Horcrux, he must be prepared to follow Dumbledore's orders explicitly. Harry promises, and Dumbledore tells him to fetch his Cloak and meet him in the Entrance Hall.

Harry retrieves the Marauder's Map and his phial of Felix Felicis potion from his dorm and hands these to Ron and Hermione, saying he and Dumbledore are leaving the school, but that Draco has finished his task. Although Dumbledore has posted extra guards, if Snape is on the Dark side, he will know what security measures are in place. Harry wants Ron, Hermione, and Ginny to have Felix to protect them, and he wants Dumbledore's Army to stand guard as well.

Harry runs to the Entrance Hall. Putting on the Cloak at Dumbledore's request, they head to Hogsmeade. In answer to Dumbledore's query, Harry says that he can Apparate, but he does not have a license yet. Dumbledore says he will guide again. They pass the Three Broomsticks, where Madam Rosmerta is ejecting a grubby wizard, and head to the Hog's Head, but with no one around, they Disapparate before reaching it. Harry and Ginny are happy, finally realizing they were meant to be together. However, their happiness may be short-lived; the book's mood is becoming markedly darker, especially when Harry learns it was Snape who betrayed his parents. Also, Harry knows that whatever task Draco has been working on appears to be completed. Just what this task is and how it will affect Hogwarts is still unknown, and Harry is exceedingly frustrated that his warnings about Draco's suspicious activities have been repeatedly ignored by Ron and Hermione, and apparently also by Dumbledore. However, it is actually unlikely that Dumbledore has ignored Harry's warnings and is well aware of what is happening within his own school. Harry fails to realize that a Headmaster cannot divulge sensitive information to a student, even Harry. There have already been hints that Dumbledore assigned Snape to investigate Draco's suspicious behavior. And while Harry continues to suspect Snape, Dumbledore trusts him implicitly.

QUESTIONS

1. What exactly did Snape hear when Trelawney related the prophecy to Dumbledore?
2. What might have Snape done or said that has made Dumbledore trust him implicitly?
3. Why did Dumbledore never tell Harry who overheard the prophecy?
4. Why were Harry's repeated warnings about Draco Malfoy continually ignored, especially considering Malfoy's obviously suspicious behavior?

GREATER PICTURE

It is interesting to note that many "good Snape" theorists base their opinions on the fact that Professor Trelawney identified Professor Snape as the intruder the night the prophecy was given. Since we know from chapter 16: Professor Trelawney's Prediction in *Harry Potter and the Prisoner of Azkaban* that Trelawny is unaware of her surroundings while in the midst of relaying a true prophecy, she could only have seen Snape before or after she relayed the prophecy to Dumbledore.

This goes directly against Dumbledore's story that the intruder only heard the first half of the prophecy before being ejected from the Hog's Head. Furthermore, since we know from Voldemort's actions in *Harry Potter and the Order of the Phoenix* that he did, until that point, only know the first half of the prophecy, many people assume that Professor Snape either heard all of the prophecy or none of it, and either way, only reported as much of it to Voldemort as Dumbledore ordered him to. This would certainly go a long way towards explaining why Dumbledore trusts Snape. However, it is also necessary to remember that in both the instances we have heard, Trelawney repeated the beginning of the prophecy. Therefore, the critical bit of the prophecy was, in fact, the middle, and so if Snape heard only the end, and carried as much as he had heard to Voldemort, that would be the same as carrying only the beginning.

Snape was possibly revolted by how Voldemort put his information to use. In *Harry Potter and the Deathly Hallows* it is learned that Lily Evans was Snape's great unrequited love, and so when Voldemort decided that the prophecy meant her child (Harry), and she, herself, must die, Snape was, at one stroke, lost to the Death Eaters. We can also infer from Snape's memories in that chapter that Dumbledore was not ignoring Harry's information about Draco and Snape; what he said, always, was "Put that out of your mind." Literally, he was saying, not that the issue was unimportant, but that it was not Harry's concern. In Snape's memories, Dumbledore knew Draco's mission before Snape had told him, and before this book had even opened, though we never know how he learned. (Dumbledore and Snape talk of Draco's mission when Snape has just finished curtailing the curse which killed Dumbledore's hand; and the damage to his hand is alluded to in chapters 2 and 3 of the book.) So Dumbledore's response to Harry's information is more along the lines of "I already know all about this, and you should not concern yourself with it." Dumbledore has said previously that he is an old man, and old men tend to forget how young men think and feel. Perhaps this dismissal of Harry's concerns is another case of this forgetfulness?

Chapter 26: The Cave

SYNOPSIS

Dumbledore and Harry apparate to the foot of a seaside cliff. Dumbledore says this is where the young Tom Riddle led two younger orphans on a horrifying trip. Dumbledore and Harry approach the cliff; Dumbledore illuminates his wand to reveal a fissure in the rocks. He and Harry swim to it, finding a hidden cave. Dumbledore says this is only an antechamber; the real goal is further. Feeling for an opening in the cave's wall, he finds it, but it does not open. Believing the Dark Lord likes his enemies weakened, Dumbledore cuts his arm and sheds blood on the wall. An opening appears; inside is a huge underground lake with a strange green glow in its center. As Dumbledore looks for something, he cautions Harry against touching the lake surface. It occurs to Harry that he could simply Summon the

Horcrux; Dumbledore suggests he try and when Harry does, something large, far out in the lake jumps, intercepting the spell. Dumbledore says that is likely what they will have to face in order to retrieve the Horcrux.

Continuing around the shore, Dumbledore finds an invisible chain; rendering it visible, he reels it in, and a tiny boat surfaces and is pulled to the shore. Harry and Dumbledore climb in, and the boat propels itself smoothly towards the island in the middle of the lake. Harry, peering down from the bow, sees dead bodies floating beneath the water's surface; Dumbledore says that as long the bodies are merely floating, there is nothing to fear.

Finally, the boat reaches the island. On it is a basin filled with greenly glowing liquid. Presumably the Horcrux is submerged within. They are unable to touch the basin or its contents, so Dumbledore must drink the substance. He makes Harry promise to force him to finish every drop. He produces a goblet and begins drinking. The potion causes intense pain, and, in his delirious agony, he begs Harry to kill him. Harry persists in refilling the goblet and persuading Dumbledore to finish. Dumbledore is very weak and requests water, but when the water that Harry conjures vanishes as it approaches Dumbledore, Harry fills the goblet from the lake that Dumbledore warned him not to touch. He manages to throw the water into Dumbledore's face, but can do nothing else, as Inferi (animated corpses that Harry had seen floating beneath the water) emerge, attempting to drag Harry into the water. Harry tries Jinx after Jinx to fend them off, but they keep coming, dragging him towards the water. Dumbledore recovers enough to fend them off with magical fire. Keeping them surrounded with the ring of flames, Dumbledore collects the locket at the bottom of the now-empty basin, and he and Harry climb back into the boat. The Inferi, dully, lose interest in Harry and Dumbledore, who now return to the shore. Harry leads Dumbledore from the cave, opening the archway to the antechamber with the graze on his arm he got fighting the Inferi; they return to the fissure leading to the sea.

Analysis

Dumbledore asks Harry to accompany him on his mission to retrieve the Horcrux not only for Harry's magical abilities, but also for Harry's incomplete mastery of them. Voldemort charmed the boat to carry only one adult wizard at a time; it cannot be summoned to and from the island with magic while it is empty—a passenger must be in it. However, two people are needed to retrieve the locket from the basin. Harry is underage and small, so his presence in the boat goes undetected. It will soon be learned that Harry and Dumbledore are not the only ones who overcame this obstacle, and, as with the Room of Requirement and the Diary Horcrux, Voldemort's overconfidence that his tight security is inpenetrable results in serious errors. This is yet another flaw in Voldemort's power, although he believes he is invincible.

Questions

Review 1. What was the green liquid that Dumbledore drank?

2. Why would Dumbledore ask a still-unqualified student to accompany him on such a dangerous mission?

3. Why did Dumbledore wish Harry to kill him?

Extra Study 1. Why did the young Tom Riddle (Voldemort) take the two orphans to the cave?

2. How could Tom Riddle have discovered the cave at such an early age, and even before he knew he was a wizard?

Greater Picture

Compare Harry's feelings of "revulsion" and "self-hatred" as he forced Dumbledore to drink the potion to Snape's expression as he performs the Avada Kedavra in the next chapter.

As Dumbledore drinks the potion, we briefly glimpse what may be his worst fear: his loved ones, which it will eventually be learned are his brother and sister, suffering on his account.

Chapter 27: The Lightning-Struck Tower

Synopsis

Harry Apparates a weakened Dumbledore back to Hogsmeade. Collapsing, Dumbledore tells Harry to get him to Severus Snape. Madam Rosmerta runs up, reporting that the Dark Mark is floating over Hogwarts. She lends them brooms, and they fly to the Astronomy Tower, with Dumbledore mumbling incantations to allow them through Hogwarts' protective spells. Harry fears for his friends' lives.

As they land atop the tower, Dumbledore orders Harry to fetch Snape, but hearing footsteps in the stairwell, Dumbledore freezes Harry under his invisibility cloak. Draco Malfoy bursts through the door and disarms Dumbledore. Draco reveals his task is to kill Dumbledore, and it was he who helped the Death Eaters invade Hogwarts via a repaired Vanishing Cabinet. It is the same cabinet Montague was shoved into the previous year. The connecting Vanishing Cabinet is at Borgin and Burkes; Montague was stuck between them, sometimes hearing what was happening at the school, sometimes what was occurring at the store, until he finally managed to Apparate out. Draco also controlled Madame Rosmerta using the Imperius Curse; that was how he poisoned the bottle of mead Ron drank, and how Katie Bell got the necklace. Malfoy and a disarmed Dumbledore speak on the tower for quite a while as battle rages beneath them, and Malfoy seems to become more and more reluctant to kill Dumbledore; however, he believes he has no choice, as his and his mother's lives are at forfeit if he does not.

Dumbledore calmly reasons with the frightened and conscience-stricken Malfoy to abandon his mission, promising protection from Voldemort for him and his family. Malfoy falters, apparently about to accept Dumbledore's offer. However, as he is lowering his wand, four Death Eaters arrive: Amycus and Alecto Carrow, Fenrir Greyback, and one other. Their taunting cannot spur on Draco to kill Dumbledore; Fenrir volunteers, but is restrained by the fourth Death Eater. Harry hears yelling from below, heartened that the Hogwart defenders are undefeated, only walled off. Snape appears and pauses to survey the situation. Dumbledore calls his name softly, almost pleadingly. Snape momentarily gazes at Dumbledore, his face an expression of revulsion and horror, then points his wand directly at Dumbledore's heart and executes the lethal Avada Kedavra curse, hurling Dumbledore's lifeless body upward in the air, over the parapet, and to the ground below.

Perhaps the greatest mystery in the entire series is, did Snape actually murder Dumbledore or did they have some prearranged plan? There is evidence to support either conclusion, and despite Dumbledore's unwavering trust in Snape, his loyalty remained questionable to Harry and to readers. Regardless, it appears that Snape had little choice; he must either kill Albus Dumbledore or die, since he is bound by the Unbreakable Vow to protect Draco Malfoy and complete his mission should Draco fail. Although many readers may believe that if Snape was truly loyal to Dumbledore, then he should have willingly sacrificed himself to protect him and Harry, yet Snape does not. It is possible that Snape and Dumbledore were communicating with each other using Legilimency, and Dumbledore's pleas may represent a request for Snape to sacrifice him to protect Harry and allow Snape to remain in the Dark Lord's favor, implying that Snape might play a key role if Harry is to destroy the Dark Lord. These speculations, and whether or not Dumbledore was actually dead, were hotly debated by readers until the seventh and final Harry Potter book.

Other clues: In every other appearance of the Avada Kedavra curse, the victim merely collapsed and died. Yet in this instance, the curse's recipient (Dumbledore) is hurled into the air and spun around before falling dead to the ground below.

In previous books, Rowling included a particular character who demonstrated suspicious behavior (e.g. the implication that Snape was trying to steal the Sorcerer's Stone in book 1), before revealing it was actually someone else (e.g. Quirrell was attempting to obtain the Sorcerer's Stone). Given this tendency of planting red herrings, it is impossible to say conclusively where Snape's loyalty lies. His actions have been such that he has been useful to both sides and has done nothing that would force him to choose one over the other.

Dumbledore seems either to have been intending to die or was taking a tremendous gamble. The Death Eaters were able to quickly conjure an impenetrable barrier on the stairway, which begs the question why Dumbledore did not react similarly after hearing footsteps on the Astronomy Tower staircase. This would have allowed both Harry and himself an opportunity to escape, but instead he chose to incapacitate Harry, preventing him from intervening and allowing himself to be disarmed by Draco Malfoy, an unqualified wizard. He was either expecting (or planning) to be killed by either Draco or Snape, or he hoped to turn Malfoy over to his side.

As a side note, the fourth Death Eater present at Dumbledore's death, who is never named here, is later identified as Yaxley. Yaxley had been a Death Eater in Voldemort's old organization, and will play a moderately significant role in *Harry Potter and the Deathly Hallows*.

QUESTIONS

1. Why did Dumbledore paralyze Harry Potter under his Invisibility Cloak upon Draco's arrival on the Tower?
2. Why would Snape kill Albus Dumbledore? Was it ruthless murder or a prearranged plan?
3. If Snape actually is loyal to Dumbledore (as Dumbledore always claimed), why wouldn't he be willing to sacrifice himself to save Dumbledore and Harry?
4. Why did the Avada Kedavra curse affect Dumbledore differently than it has others?
5. If Dumbledore did not know about Snape's *Unbreakable Vow*, he nevertheless suggests to Draco Malfoy that "perhaps Severus may have told you so," implying that Snape might not really be disobeying Dumbledore. Is it possible he was bluffing to Malfoy?

GREATER PICTURE

Nothing is mentioned in this chapter about what happened to Dumbledore's wand after it went flying over the tower with him. However, it is revealed in book seven that the wand was interred with Dumbledore's corpse, and it becomes an important plot element in the final showdown between Harry and Voldemort.

Dumbledore's death was premeditated by both himself and Snape; Snape was charged to kill him at an appropriate time to spare Malfoy from completing Voldemort's task. Dumbledore was slowly dying from a deadly curse that was triggered when he put on the now-destroyed Horcrux (Gaunt's ring). Wishing to die by his own design, he tasked Snape with his death. The potion Dumbledore drank in the cave had left him too weak to defend himself. His plea to Snape was to carry out his final wish, which Snape reluctantly executed.

Chapter 28: Flight of the Prince

SYNOPSIS

Snape forces Draco Malfoy back down the tower stairwell, followed by other Death Eaters. Harry, released from the paralysing spell by Dumbledore's death, petrifies the last one and charges down the steps after them. At the bottom is a melée of Hogwarts students, teachers, and Order of the Phoenix members fighting Death Eaters. Ginny is dueling Amycus Carrow. Harry Jinxes Amycus, sending him cannoning into a wall. The remaining Death Eaters, hearing Snape's signal, break away and run. Harry, following, wonders if they will head for the Entrance Hall or the Room of Requirement. Seeing a bloody footprint, Harry deduces that they have gone to the Front Hall and takes a short cut there.

Chapter 28: Flight of the Prince

Reaching the entrance, Harry sees a Death Eater on the grounds, Snape and Draco further away. The large blond Death Eater casts multiple curses at Hagrid, but his massive body deflects them. Harry hurls the Prince's spells at Snape, but Snape easily blocks every one, proclaiming he created them—*he* is the Half-Blood Prince. Although Snape deflects every curse Harry casts, he does nothing to harm him and continually tells him what he is doing wrong. Amycus and Alecto catch up to Harry, and one curses him. Snape blocks the curse, and prevents the other Death Eaters from attacking Harry, claiming he belongs to Voldemort. Harry dares Snape to kill him, calling him a coward. Enraged, Snape stuns Harry before escaping with Draco and the other Death Eaters. Hagrid's hut is afire, and Hagrid rushes from the flames with Fang. Harry puts out the fire using Aguamenti. Hagrid does not believe Harry when he says Dumbledore is dead. He and Hagrid approach a crowd huddled around Dumbledore's twisted corpse. Harry removes the locket from the old wizard's robe pocket. Inside he finds a note reading:

> To the Dark Lord
> I know I will be dead long before you read this but I want you to know that it was I who discovered your secret. I have stolen the real Horcrux and intend to destroy it as soon as I can. I face death in the hope that when you meet your match, you will be mortal once more.
> R.A.B.

Harry chases Snape in a blind rage and with one intent: to kill him. Snape, who easily eludes him, has every opportunity to murder or capture the outmatched Harry. Instead, he merely deflects Harry's ineffective curses. Snape continually does nothing to harm Harry, and actually tells him what he is doing wrong and how to correct it. He also prevents the other Death Eaters from cursing him. Why? Although he claims he wants to leave Harry for the Dark Lord, he could easily have stunned and presented him to Voldemort. By leaving Harry at Hogwarts, Snape not only risks having the determined and vengeful Harry single-mindedly hunting him down, but also the Dark Lord's deadly wrath by letting his number one enemy remain alive and free. For Harry, learning that his admired mentor (the Half-Blood Prince) is actually his hated nemesis is shocking and revolting. When he called Snape a coward, Snape become enraged, even though murdering Dumbledore can only be considered the lowest cowardly act. Harry learns that someone with the initials R.A.B. stole the true Horcrux from the cave. However, in chapter 26, it was learned that two people were needed to recover the locket from the basin on the island. R.A.B. must have had some assistance. Although R.A.B. is probably dead, *if* another person was involved, it is possible he or she may still be alive and could provide valuable information. It also appears that R.A.B. may have known about the prophecy, as that person refers to Voldemort meeting his match. However, it also seems that R.A.B. may have mistakenly believed that the locket was the only Horcrux, as he seems to assume that destroying it will be sufficient to make Voldemort mortal once more.

Questions

1. Who might R.A.B. be?
2. Why would Snape react so strongly when Harry called him a coward?
3. Why does Snape not curse or kill or capture Harry during his escape? Why would Snape tell Harry what he is doing wrong as Harry attempts to curse him?
4. During his duel with Snape, why didn't Harry cast any spells nonverbally, one of Snape's first DADA's lessons?

Greater Picture

In the final book, it will be revealed that "R.A.B." are the initials of Regulus Black (Sirius' brother). Regulus' middle name is "Arcturus," a name which appears on the Black Family tree. The person who stole the Horcrux had to be someone close to Voldemort, most likely a Death Eater, which Regulus Black was. It is usually, although not exclusively, Death Eaters who refer to Voldemort as the Dark Lord.

It was mentioned earlier that it was believed that Regulus had gotten into Voldemort's hierarchy, had not liked what he had found, and had wanted out, but had been killed, possibly by Voldemort himself. It will be learned that this is not what had happened. Kreacher will know more about it, as he was involved; it is noted in the Analysis that it would have taken two people to remove and replace the locket, and that will turn out to have been Regulus and Kreacher. Regulus had, in fact, decided that he wanted out, but rather than simply leaving (and being killed), he had decided to make his death count for something. Having learned of the existence of a Horcrux, and having determined, from Kreacher, where something valuable was hidden, Regulus determined to destroy what he had thought was the only Horcrux Voldemort had made.

In this chapter, we learn that Snape was, in fact, the Half-Blood Prince of the title, and that the textbook Harry had been using so successfully was originally Snape's. It is mentioned earlier that the book had been found to be fifty years old when Harry looked at it, which ruled out his father owning it, and seems to rule out Snape owning it also. However, we will learn later that Snape had come from a poverty-stricken household, and so very likely had been provided second-hand textbooks. Quite possibly the fact that he had to use a text that was, when he got it, already a quarter century old, would have increased his dislike of the more-privileged students.

In the previous year, as Sirius, Harry, and the Weasleys sorted through the various family heirlooms at 12 Grimmauld Place, the Black family home, *a heavy locket that none of them can open* is tossed aside. We will find out later that Kreacher had saved the locket, keeping it hidden in his cupboard, and, later still, it will be stolen by Mundungus Fletcher, and then extorted from him in turn by Dolores Umbridge. It will turn out to be the Horcrux locket, once belonging to Salazar Slytherin, and can only be opened by someone speaking in parseltongue. That would explain why no one could open the locket, and why Regulus was unable to destroy it as he intended. Since no one suspected the locket was a Horcrux, Harry did not speak Parseltongue to it (although he does so later to destroy it). Voldemort probably did not create the charm that prevented the locket from opening, though he was likely glad that it was difficult as it protected his Horcrux within. Slytherin's descendants were proud of their ability to speak to snakes; it is entirely possible that Slytherin himself, when he created the locket, charmed it to prevent it from opening unless spoken to in Parseltongue.

Chapter 29: The Phoenix Lament

Synopsis

Ginny leads Harry to the Hospital Wing where everyone is gathered. Harry, remembering the Dark Mark, fearfully asks who is dead. Ginny tells him nobody, but Harry recalls falling over a body. Ginny says that was Bill, and he is a bit of a mess, but he will survive. Apparently, he was savagely mauled by Fenrir Greyback. It is unknown what the long-term effects will be, but it is not believed that Bill will be a werewolf because Fenrir was not transformed at the time, but he will never heal completely and is permenantly disfigured.

Because Ginny, Ron, and Hermione took the Felix Felicis potion, they were safe, and only Professor Dumbledore and one Death Eater were killed—the big blond Death Eater was firing curses indiscriminately and accidentally hit his ally.

Ron and Lupin are stunned when Harry informs them that Dumbledore is dead. Professor McGonagall arrives and asks Harry if he witnessed what happened. Harry says Snape killed Dumbledore. McGonagall wonders aloud why Dumbledore ever trusted Snape. Harry replies that Snape relayed the Prophecy's contents to Voldemort, and later claimed remorse that Voldemort killed his father and mother. McGonagall blames herself; she sent Professor Flitwick to fetch Snape. Lupin reassures her that they were all glad that Snape would be joining them. According to McGonagall, when Dumbledore left, Tonks, Lupin, and Bill were on patrol, but it is unknown where the Death Eaters appeared from. Harry explains about the Vanishing Cabinets and the Room of Requirement. Ron says that he, Ginny, and Neville had been watching the Room of Requirement and saw Draco appear with the Hand of Glory. When he had spotted them, he threw something and everything went dark. People were heard rushing past, but they were unable to see to Jinx them. They groped their way out of the corridor. Luckily they ran into Lupin, who found the Death Eaters at the Astronomy Tower. One, Gibbon, cast the Dark Mark, then was killed. Meanwhile, Hermione and Luna were at Snape's office. Flitwick went to warn Snape that Death Eaters were in the castle, then there were confused sounds from within and Snape came out. Spotting Hermione and Luna, he told them that Flitwick had fallen and to take care of him.

At the main battle, Draco disappeared, apparently going up the tower. Four Death Eaters followed him, leaving behind a barrier and, "that big blond death eater," who was firing curses in all directions. Snape reappeared and went through the barrier. Then, after the big one had brought down about half the ceiling and knocked out the barrier, Snape and Draco returned, and they just let him pass.

Mrs. Weasley, Mr. Weasley, and Fleur Delacour now arrive. Mrs. Weasley immediately tends to Bill's injuries. She believes Fleur will end the engagement because Bill is disfigured. Angry, Fleur declares she loves Bill and still plans to marry him. This act bonds her with Mrs. Weasley. Tonks reveals she has been in love with Remus Lupin who, because he is a werewolf and older, had discouraged her feelings. Harry suddenly realizes that Tonks' new Patronus is a wolf. Lupin is still reluctant, but Mr. Weasley points out that the future is always uncertain. Hagrid reports that he moved Dumbledore's body, the students are back in bed, and the Ministry has been notified. Professor McGonagall takes over as interim Headmistress and calls a meeting with the House Heads plus Hagrid, suggesting that Horace Slughorn should represent Slytherin. McGonagall first meets with Harry in the Headmaster's office, where Dumbledore's sleeping portrait now hangs among the other past Headmasters. McGonagall asks Harry what happened after he and Dumbledore left the school, but Harry, still honoring his vow to Dumbledore, reveals nothing and says, "Professor Dumbledore never told me to stop following his orders if he died." He warns McGonagall that Madam Rosmerta is under the Imperius curse. The House Heads troop in, and McGonagall canvasses them as to whether Hogwarts should stay open, given that their Headmaster was just murdered by a teacher. All agree it should remain open. Professor McGonagall will consult the Governors, who will make the final decision.

McGonagall suggests students should depart early on the Hogwarts Express, but Harry points out that they may want to stay for the funeral. The House Heads unanimously agree to honour Dumbledore's wish that he be laid to rest at the school. Professor Flitwick says that transport arrangements can be made after the funeral.

Professor McGonagall sees Rufus Scrimgeour arriving with a delegation. Wanting to avoid questions, Harry leaves and heads to Gryffindor tower. Almost everyone is in the Common room. Thankfully, only Ron is in their dormitory. Harry tells Ron that the Horcrux was a fake; the real one was stolen. Ron, reading the note, asks who R.A.B. is. Harry has no idea.

Analysis

Whether or not Dumbledore is really dead was endlessly debated by fans. The author left many hints that Dumbledore may still be alive or will return in some manner—either physically or spiritually. His portrait in the Headmaster's office "appears" to be sleeping. It is possible it is not a real portrait, but only imitating those of other former Headmasters and Headmistresses as a ruse to deceive enemies. If, however, the portrait starts interacting in a similar manner as the others, this would be some proof that Dumbledore is actually dead.

It is possible that although Snape killed Dumbledore, he did not actually *murder* him. That is, there may have been a prearranged agreement that Snape would kill the Headmaster if events deemed it necessary to protect the Order's mission. Indeed, during their confrontation on the Astronomy Tower, it is almost as if Dumbledore was pleading with a conflicted Snape to curse him. In a previous conversation between them, Snape was overheard telling Dumbledore that he would refuse to do something, to which Dumbledore insisted he must follow through. This may have been a reference to Snape's Unbreakable Vow that would require him to kill Dumbledore if Draco failed.

Dumbledore (possibly with Snape's assistance) may have taken measures to prevent his own death. During Harry's first year, Snape told students that there are potions that can, "put a stopper in death." Dumbledore certainly was aware Draco was aiding Voldemort's plan to invade Hogwarts, and it is unlikely he could be caught unprepared by Death Eaters, much less an underaged wizard like Draco.

Also, Voldemort himself may have prevented Dumbledore's death. When Dumbledore drinks the potion in the cave, he tells Harry it will not immediately kill him because Voldemort would want to keep whoever stole the locket alive long enough to learn how they were able to penetrate the Dark Lord's defenses. It is possible that the potion protected Dumbledore from the Avada Kedavra curse, keeping him in a deathlike state. If this is true, there may be an antidote to the potion's poisonous effects, and which could be why Dumbledore wanted Harry to fetch Snape rather than Madam Pomfrey, when they returned to Hogwarts. As mentioned in a previous chapter, readers should be aware that the effects of Snape's curse seem dissimilar to other Avada Kedavra curses.

That Dumbledore's animal familiar is a phoenix is unlikely a coincidence. A phoenix dies by bursting into flames and is reborn from its own ashes. This could be symbolic that Dumbledore may experience a similar resurrection. A phoenix's cry is healing, and Fawkes' lament was heard as he soared over his *master's* body. Countering these speculations is the author's assertion in an interview after the sixth book's release that Dumbledore is "definitely dead." However, the Headmasters do live on, in a fashion, within their portraits, interacting with people and retaining the headmasters' memories. Dumbledore's portrait should be able to speak with Harry and provide information regarding events that have not yet been resolved. Additionally, Dumbledore will have stored memories in his Pensieve, which Harry may be able to access.

On a completely separate subject, in this chapter we see, again, the romance between Harry and Ginny. When Hagrid tells Harry that he must leave Dumbledore's body, Harry does not move; it is only when Ginny leads him away by the hand that Harry moves. Also, in the Hospital Wing, Ginny stays next to Harry, possibly to give him comfort if he needs it, possibly to get some comfort from him herself. He does not leave her side until Professor McGonagall summons him to the headmaster's office.

QUESTIONS

1. What reasons might Snape have killed Dumbledore? Is it possible he is still loyal to Dumbledore even after causing his death?

2. Why does Mrs. Weasley believe Fleur will end her engagement to Bill Weasley? What is Fleur's reaction?

3. What might happen to Bill in the future?

4. Can Tonks and Lupin's relationship last? What precautions must they take?

5. Why does Hogwarts close early? Will it reopen next year?

6. Who is likely to be the new headmaster/headmistress?

7. Why does Harry refuse to tell McGonagall what happened after he and Dumbledore left for the cave? Couldn't she get this same information from Dumbledore's portrait?

GREATER PICTURE

The speculation around Dumbledore's death was, of course, ended with the publication of the seventh and final book. In that book, it was revealed that in fact Dumbledore had become cursed by contact with the Peverell ring, which had been so cursed because it contained a Horcrux. Despite Snape's best efforts, the curse had given Dumbledore at most a year to live. Dumbledore, already aware of Voldemort's plan to have Draco Malfoy try to murder him, also knew that Draco would not be able to do so unless compelled by other Death Eaters, and was concerned that he would be tormented by Death Eaters in the process. He had exacted a promise from Snape that in that eventuality, Snape would step in and kill him, so as to spare Draco's soul and allow Dumbledore to retain some dignity.

Chapter 30: The White Tomb

SYNOPSIS

Over the next few days, some students leave the school with their parents. Others, like Seamus Finnigan, refuse to go until they pay their last respects to Dumbledore. Meanwhile, wizards and witches pour into Hogsmeade to attend the funeral. Harry and Ginny, Hermione and Ron now spend all their time together. They visit the Hospital Wing often. While Neville is healed, Bill remains under constant care. Apart from being permanently disfigured, the only lasting effect seems to be a preference for very rare steaks.

Later, Hermione shares that her library research uncovered that Eileen Prince is the Potions book's original owner and Snape's mother. Prince "married a Muggle named Tobias Snape and later gave birth to . . ." Harry interrupts, "a murderer." Harry is maddened that Snape, unknown and unknowingly, was helping him. He sees a similarity between the half-blood Lord Voldemort and his assumed title, and the Half-Blood Prince and his adopted moniker. How could Dumbledore have missed it?

At Dumbledore's request, he is laid to rest at Hogwarts in a glorious white tomb overlooking the lake. Many students and the staff (apart from Severus Snape) attend the funeral, as well as the Merpeople and the Centaurs, who fire arrows into the air in salute.

Harry ends his relationship with Ginny—for now. Harry realizes that Voldemort attacks him through those he loves, his parents, Sirius, Dumbledore, and by ending their romance, he hopes to protect Ginny. Scrimgeour takes Harry aside and asks where Harry and Dumbledore went the night Dumbledore was killed. Harry tells Scrimgeour that is between him and Dumbledore, and asks Scrimgeour again whether he has released Stan Shunpike. Harry repeats that he is "Dumbledore's man through and through."

Harry tells Hermione and Ron he is leaving Hogwarts, even if the school remains open. Finding the remaining Horcruxes and killing Voldemort are his only focus now. He intends to visit his parents' former home in Godric's Hollow after a brief stay at Privet Drive to fulfill Dumbledore's wish that he remain under his mother's protective charm. Then he will find and kill Snape. Ron and Hermione pledge to join his quest, despite Harry's preference to go it alone. Harry finds comfort in spending one last peaceful day with his friends, and he looks forward to Bill and Fleur's wedding.

Analysis

Unlike the first five books, the story ends with Dumbledore's funeral, rather than the students arriving at Platform 9 3/4 in London on the Hogwarts Express and bidding each other goodbye for the summer. If Harry follows through on his mission, which seems certain, the next book will probably also deviate from the traditional opening with students headed back to school in the fall. However, without Dumbledore, Hogwarts will be a far different place than before. His affect on the school has not only been deeply significant but, as seen by the many magical creatures that attended his funeral, far-reaching. For Harry, Hogwarts has always been a source of comfort and security. Without Dumbledore, it may have been too much for him to return. One thing seems certain—the Dursleys will probably make an appearance, as Harry must make one last visit to Privet Drive to enforce his mother's protective charm that ends on his next birthday. This will be the Dursleys' final opportunity to reconcile with Harry, although their mutual loathing is probably too deep to bridge.

Ron and Hermione informm Harry they are joining the Horcrux mission, whether he wants them to or not. Their decision is an affirmation of their love, friendship, and loyalty for their friend. Although Harry intended to search for the Horcruxes alone, wanting to protect those he cares about and still driven by the need battle Voldemort alone, he has finally accepted that it takes unity, support, and cooperation to defeat evil.

Harry unhappily ends his relationship with Ginny to protect her from Voldemort, though she is probably still in grave danger. Harry never mastered Occlumency, and it is possible that Voldemort could penetrate his mind and see images involving Ginny, although he has found that being inside Harry's consciousness is an extremely unpleasant place for him, and he may not attempt this again.

We learn that Snape, Voldemort, and Harry share an important characteristic: they are all half-bloods. Snape, however, apparently grew up connected to the wizarding world, unlike Harry and Voldemort, although his home life was certainly just as unpleasant. As much as Harry always disliked and resented Snape, he is now driven solely by hatred and vengeance. This vigilante desire to avenge Dumbledore's death has clouded Harry's judgment; rather than seeking justice, Harry is consumed with inflicting revenge. This could jeopardize his mission to find and destroy Voldemort's Horcruxes. Harry will need to overcome his extreme emotions if he is to succeed. It is ironic that Harry's least favorite and ineffective teacher (Snape) is also his most admired and influential mentor (the Half-Blood Prince), someone who inspired him and from whom he has learned so much. This conflict will continue to affect Harry.

Questions

1. Where does the portrait of Dumbledore come from?
2. How can the portrait help Harry?
3. Why would Dumbledore want to be buried at Hogwarts and in a white tomb?
4. What does Harry mean when he says he is, "Dumbledore's man, through and through"?
5. Why does Harry end his relationship with Ginny? Is it likely they will reunite in the future?
6. Why did Harry not want Ron and Hermione to join his search for the remaining Horcruxes?

Greater Picture

As the book ends it is unclear if Dumbledore was truly dead or merely in some deathlike state. This led to much speculation among readers as to whether or not he would return in some form in the next book. Voldemort is not the only one who knows how to create Horcruxes, and it was possible that there were other magical means for a resurrection in Book 7. There were certainly many clues that he could return. Dumbledore was acting uncharacteristically when he pleaded with Snape just before he killed him. Was Dumbledore begging for his life or asking Snape to strike him according to some prearranged plan? Readers noticed that the Avada Kedvra curse that Snape used reacted differently than others seen in the series. Also, Dumbledore has always been closely associated with a Phoenix, a bird that dies and is reborn from its own ashes. The smoke from Dumbledore's funeral pyre appeared to have briefly assume the image of a Phoenix. Whether that symbolized a corporeal resurrection or only a spiritual one, Dumbledore does return in some form in the next book.

Also, it is unknown where Dumbledore's portrait appeared from or how it was hung in the office. Presumably, no one had entered the office since his death, and yet it is already hanging on the wall when Professor McGonagall and Harry arrive there. However, it is highly possible that the portraits magically appear when a headmaster or headmistress dies. It is also unclear how closely associated portraits are with those they represent. They may merely be talking autobiographies of their subjects, or they may retain their essence, including the ability to develop mentally and/or gain new insights. Later evidence does suggest that portraits remain able to think and reason, as it seems that the portrait of Dumbledore is still advising Snape and Harry in the final book of the series. J. K. Rowling had stated, following this book's publication, that Dumbledore was definitely dead, although readers still held out hope for a resurrection; while we do see him again, it is now known that he is definitely not resurrected.

DEATHLY HALLOWS

CHAPTERS

Chapter 1: The Dark Lord Ascending
Chapter 2: In Memoriam
Chapter 3: The Dursleys Departing
Chapter 4: The Seven Potters
Chapter 5: Fallen Warrior
Chapter 6: The Ghoul in Pyjamas
Chapter 7: The Will of Albus Dumbledore
Chapter 8: The Wedding
Chapter 9: A Place to Hide
Chapter 10: Kreacher's Tale
Chapter 11: The Bribe
Chapter 12: Magic is Might
Chapter 13: The Muggle-Born Registration Commission
Chapter 14: The Thief
Chapter 15: The Goblin's Revenge
Chapter 16: Godric's Hollow
Chapter 17: Bathilda's Secret
Chapter 18: The Life and Lies of Albus Dumbledore
Chapter 19: The Silver Doe
Chapter 20: Xenophilius Lovegood
Chapter 21: The Tale of the Three Brothers
Chapter 22: The Deathly Hallows
Chapter 23: Malfoy Manor
Chapter 24: The Wandmaker
Chapter 25: Shell Cottage
Chapter 26: Gringotts
Chapter 27: The Final Hiding Place
Chapter 28: The Missing Mirror
Chapter 29: The Lost Diadem
Chapter 30: The Sacking of Severus Snape
Chapter 31: The Battle of Hogwarts
Chapter 32: The Elder Wand
Chapter 33: The Prince's Tale
Chapter 34: The Forest Again
Chapter 35: King's Cross
Chapter 36: The Flaw in the Plan
Epilogue: Nineteen Years Later

OVERVIEW

Once again we join Harry Potter as he enters what would be his seventh year at Hogwarts. The book is written from the point-of-view of the now 17-year-old Harry as he prepares to complete the mission set for him by Dumbledore at the end of the previous year. Arguably the darkest book in the series, this volume shows Lord Voldemort tightening his grip on the Wizarding world as he remolds it into his own pure-blood design. While the series progressively covers seven years in Harry Potter's life, the first five volumes are largely self-contained stories. Unlike them, this book is written more as the second half to a two-part novel that is tightly tied to the previous book, *Harry Potter and the Half-Blood Prince*.

Note: While this book is among the longer ones in the series, at 607 pages (Bloomsbury / Raincoast edition), it is also set in somewhat larger type. If it were the same size type as *Harry Potter and the Philosopher's Stone*, it would be 520 pages (approximately) to 223 for *Harry Potter and the Philosopher's Stone*.

BOOK HIGHLIGHTS

• New places visited: Godric's Hollow, Malfoy Manor, Shell Cottage, Lovegood home
• *Defence Against the Dark Arts* teacher: Amycus Carrow
• Title refers to: the Deathly Hallows

EXTENDED ANALYSIS

• Overall Analysis
• Character Development
• Major Themes
• Real-World Connections

Chapter 1: The Dark Lord Ascending

SYNOPSIS

There is silence for a moment. Then Snape and Yaxley both Apparate in at the same time, pointing their wands at each other. After recognizing each other, they head for a large mansion. Voldemort and his Death Eaters are gathered at Malfoy Manor, their new headquarters. Severus Snape informs Voldemort that the Order of the Phoenix is moving Harry Potter from the Dursley home to a secret location the following Saturday, at sunset. Snape tells Voldemort that the information comes "from the source [they] discussed." This contradicts the information that Yaxley obtained from an Auror named Dawlish, but that is determined to be unreliable. Snape tells the assembled Death Eaters that the Order suspects the Ministry has been infiltrated. Yaxley reports that he has succeeded in placing Pius Thicknesse, the Head of the Department of Magical Law Enforcement, under the Imperius curse, a huge step toward the Death Eaters' taking over the Ministry of Magic. However, Voldemort says that Thicknesse is only one man, "and Scrimgeour must be completely surrounded by our people before I act." Voldemort mentions that his wand, having the same magical core as Harry Potter's wand, could prove ineffective against Harry. He demands Lucius' wand, claiming that Malfoy will no longer need it and that he and his wife were unfaithful to the Dark Lord. Bellatrix Lestrange comments that she, unlike her sister, Narcissa, has always been faithful. Voldemort jokes about her niece, who apparently has just married Remus Lupin. Voldemort then uses Lucius' wand to kill his captive, Professor Charity Burbage, the Muggle Studies instructor at Hogwarts, for teaching the subject and for publishing an opinion suggesting that the decreasing numbers of pure-blooded wizards was beneficial and that blood purity should no longer matter, giving her to Nagini as her "dinner."

ANALYSIS

A major difference between the Order of the Phoenix and Death Eaters is brought into sharper focus here. Death Eaters constantly compete with one another to ascend in the Dark Lord's eyes. Some are affronted that Snape is invited to sit at Voldemort's right hand; the Malfoys' position at the foot of the table is obviously galling to them and shows how far and how quickly they have fallen from favor. In the Order, however, the organization's unified goal to assist Harry and defeat Voldemort are far more important than an individual's status within their group. Throughout the series, Snape is the one character whose true motives and loyalty have never been clearly established. Is he a redeemed Death Eater secretly carrying out Dumbledore's orders, or had he merely been biding his time, gathering information, awaiting the Dark Lord's resurrection? Now Snape is deeply embedded in the Death Eaters' inner council and has become a trusted Voldemort confidante. He also acts as a conduit for information about the Order. It is unknown whether Snape's information is accurate or how he obtained it. Voldemort is likely using Legilimency in an attempt to read Snape's mind and thus judge how reliable the information is, although Snape is skilled in Occlumency, and, conceivably, could block Voldemort's intrusions. Disputes over Snape's loyalty appeared to have been resolved when Snape killed Dumbledore (at the end of *Harry Potter and the Half-Blood Prince*). Most importantly, why did Dumbledore steadfastly maintain such unwavering trust in him? Also, the circumstances surrounding Dumbledore's death are ambiguous, and many readers have argued that Snape did not truly murder Dumbledore but was acting according to some prearranged plan between them. And while many questions go unanswered, it is doubtful that Voldemort completely trusts Snape. The old adage, "keep your friends close, but your enemies closer" may very well apply here, and it could have just as well applied to Dumbledore. Also, many fans believe that Dumbledore may not actually be dead, although Rowling is adamant that he is. Whatever Snape's actual course or motives may be, this will remain unknown until the book's end. Some critics may feel that introducing the Charity Burbage character solely to kill her off may be literary laziness by the author. However, this demonstrates just how bloodthirsty Death Eaters are, which makes murdering someone reasonable. That she is a Hogwarts professor shows that the school is not as sacrosanct as it has previously seemed. And who better to kill than the Muggle Studies instructor? However, this scene might have had more impact if readers had been introduced to Professor Burbage when Hermione was taking her class during her third year.

QUESTIONS

Review 1. Why has Malfoy lost favor with the Dark Lord? Having lost that favor, why would Voldemort want him returned from Azkaban?

2. Even though Voldemort's wand may not work properly against Harry, it is not so hindered in acting against Professor Burbage. Why would Voldemort use Lucius' wand rather than his own to kill the Muggle Studies instructor?

Extra Study 1. Who might be the 'source' that Snape and Voldemort refer to?

2. Lucius Malfoy was sent to Azkaban at the end of *Harry Potter and the Order of the Phoenix*. Yet, he has returned. There was no news of breakouts at Azkaban during *Harry Potter and the Half-Blood Prince*. What does this say about the Ministry?

GREATER PICTURE

During Voldemort's meeting with his Death Eaters, Wormtail is dismissed to attend to a prisoner, who is evidently disrupting the proceedings. While it is never confirmed who this prisoner is, it is learned later that Ollivander is being held captive in the house.

Snape's information about the Order's choice of dates to move Harry is accurate, though he does not, apparently, know the plan's full details. Later, it is learned that Snape not only knows the complete plan, but it was he who planted the additional details into Mundungus' thoughts so that he could suggest them to Mad Eye Moody. However, readers do not as yet have that information. Lacking that, this chapter seems to reinforce the belief that Snape is loyal to the Dark side.

Chapter 2: In Memoriam

SYNOPSIS

For the first time in six years, Harry is fully emptying his school trunk, deciding what to take with him and what should be left behind when he leaves the Dursley house for the last time. While unpacking, he cuts his hand. Harry, who is four days away from his seventeenth birthday, the age he can perform unrestricted magic, has yet to learn how to heal wounds. He plans to ask Hermione to show him. Hunting carefully through his trunk, he finds a shard from the broken two-way mirror, given to him by Sirius. When he heads to the bathroom to tend the cut, he stumbles over a cup of tea left outside his bedroom door, which he assumes to be a booby trap planted by Dudley. After cleaning up the broken tea cup and emptying his trunk, he looks

Chapter 2: In Memoriam

through a pile of newspapers and picks up the copy containing Dumbledore's obituary.

The obituary reveals that Dumbledore's father was sentenced to Azkaban for attacking three Muggle children. Albus quickly overcame his father's notoriety through his exceptional performance at Hogwarts, winning many honors there and corresponding with many learned witches and wizards.

Three years later, Albus' brother, Aberforth, joined him at Hogwarts. The two brothers were unalike, Aberforth being more reserved and likely to settle differences by dueling, where Albus would debate the issues, but they were friends. After finishing school, Albus planned to travel the world with his friend, Elphias Doge, the obituary's author, when his mother, Kendra, died suddenly, leaving Albus the sole provider for the family. While Elphias traveled the world, another tragedy struck the Dumbledores: the sudden death of Albus's younger sister, Ariana. Albus and Aberforth became estranged after, and Albus never talked about his family. Putting this sad chapter behind him, Albus went on to achieve many notable successes, including discovering twelve uses of dragon's blood and defeating Grindelwald in an epic duel.

Looking at Dumbledore's picture, Harry realizes that he barely knew the man; their conversations were always about him. Tearing out the obituary, he puts it in a book and then retrieves that day's Daily Prophet. Harry reads about an upcoming series of exposés on Dumbledore, excerpted from hack journalist Rita Skeeter's biography about him. Harry flips to the interview with Skeeter, who spins her usual stylized lies about him and Dumbledore. She suggests that Dumbledore dabbled in Dark magic, his sister, Ariana, was a Squib, Aberforth broke Albus' nose at Ariana's funeral, claiming Albus killed her, and that the epic duel between Albus and Grindelwald may have been something other than it seemed. About Harry, she hints that the relationship between him and Dumbledore was odd, even inappropriate, and that Harry was seen running from where Dumbledore fell. And even though Harry testified against Snape, the long-standing grudge between them is public knowledge.

Harry is outraged, but there is little he can do. Distractedly turning over the mirror shard, he glimpses a sky-blue flash, the same color as Dumbledore's eyes. Studying the mirror closely, he only sees his reflection, and there is nothing blue nearby that could have been reflected in it. Dumbledore's eyes will never gaze upon him again, but all the same, he tucks the shard safely away in a front pocket.

ANALYSIS

This chapter reveals glimpses into Dumbledore's previously unknown history, something that the author has kept concealed. Doge's comments and Rita's interview imply that there is some significant mystery about Dumbledore's history, although anything written by Skeeter should be considered with skepticism. Regardless, Dumbledore's past appears to be darker and more secretive than most knew. And while Dumbledore's death has left a significant hole in Harry's life, much of that emptiness is now caused by what Harry never knew about his mentor. While Harry is still grief-stricken by the loss, he is also left confused, adrift, and doubting as to what Dumbledore's intentions actually were; he also wonders whether Dumbledore ever loved him or was merely using him as a weapon to defeat Voldemort. Even allowing for Skeeter's poisoned pen, there are many mysteries about this mysterious wizard that will need significant explanation before Albus Dumbledore can finally be laid to rest.

The blue flash in the broken two-way mirror will also be significant. Is this Dumbledore somehow watching from beyond the grave? Harry apparently hopes so, considering his sudden care with the mirror shard.

QUESTIONS

Review 1. Could some of what the Daily Prophet states about Dumbledore be correct?

2. Why would Rita Skeeter write a biography about Dumbledore? How accurate is it likely to be?

3. Why did Harry know so little about Dumbledore's past? Had Harry ever made an effort to learn about him? How much did Harry, or anyone, have the right to know?

Extra Study 1. Why would Dumbledore's father have attacked three Muggle children?

2. What might the blue flash in the mirror be?

3. Who might have left the cup of tea outside Harry's bedroom door? Why would they leave it there?

GREATER PICTURE

It will be learned that Rita Skeeter's source was the elderly and senile Bathilda Bagshot, a Dumbledore family friend, and who was also known by Lily Potter. Rita apparently slipped Bathilda some Veritaserum to retrieve her memories. However, the only story that Bathilda can share, and thus the only one that Rita can report, is an outsider's point-of-view; that, coloured by Rita's highly acidic quill, will result in an extremely slanted, highly inaccurate, and damaging story. Harry will labor under these skewed beliefs until he learns the truth from Aberforth Dumbledore, Albus' brother, much later in the book.

The cup of tea left outside Harry's bedroom is significant. It was Dudley who left the tea, a rather feeble attempt to make amends for mistreating Harry during their childhood and also to express his gratitude for Harry having saved him from the Dementors the previous year. However, the teacup may foreshadow Harry's search for Helga Hufflepuff's Cup, one of Voldemort's Horcruxes that Harry needs to destroy.

It will be learned that the young Dumbledore was obsessively driven to pursue the Deathly Hallows in the title. Like Harry, he desired to be reunited with his dead loved ones, and he believed that one Hallow possessed that power.

Chapter 3: The Dursleys Departing

Synopsis

Uncle Vernon has changed his mind again. The Dursleys were informed by Arthur Weasley and Kingsley Shacklebolt that Harry's life will be in danger when he turns seventeen, and that the Dursleys, as his relatives, are likely under the same threat. Since then, Vernon and Petunia have either been willing to accept the Order's protection or preparing to refuse it. Today, they are convinced that Harry plans to put their house in his own name as soon as they are gone. Harry repudiates this, asking why he would want to do that. All the happy memories? In any event, he already owns a house.

Harry's arguments are bolstered by Order wizards who have arrived to transport and protect the Dursleys: Dedalus Diggle and Hestia Jones. When Dudley says he is going with Dedalus and Hestia, Uncle Vernon's protests are rather deflated, and he suddenly decides that has been his intention all along. Dudley wants to know why Harry is not coming with them; Uncle Vernon says he does not want to, to which Harry agrees. Dudley now admits to not thinking that Harry is a waste of space and goes so far as to thank Harry for saving his life. He shakes hands with him before leaving. Aunt Petunia looks as if she might want to say something, but marches off after Vernon and Dudley.

Analysis

Harry is about to depart the Dursleys' for the final time, although it is not to return to Hogwarts as he usually does, but to embark on his secret mission for Dumbledore. This time, the Dursleys are also leaving, and the author may be indicating that this parting is permanent. Dudley's reaction to Harry is surprising, however. He is grateful to Harry for having saved him from the Dementors (in *Harry Potter and the Order of the Phoenix*) and expresses concern over what might happen to him. (It is suggested that it was Dudley who left the cup of tea outside Harry's bedroom, an apparently contrite act for his bad behavior over the years.) Although Dudley is a Muggle and was unable to see the Dementors, he was still able to feel their presence, and it seems that the encounter has somehow changed him, giving hope that he will mature into a better person than either Vernon or Petunia. The elder Dursleys, however, seem as antagonistic as ever, although Petunia nearly shows a rare emotional glimmer, as if teetering on whether or not to reach out to Harry during this final encounter, but at the last moment, reels herself in and walks away. Harry's own reaction seems mixed. While he endured an unhappy life at Privet Drive, it was his home for many years and leaving it is still difficult—this is yet another incomplete chapter in his life that must be closed.

Questions

Review 1. How long could it be that Dudley has felt about Harry this way? 2. What might have changed Dudley's feelings towards Harry?

Extra Study 1. Was Dudley totally responsible for his abusive behavior towards Harry? If not, what contributed to it, and, under different circumstances, how might Dudley have turned out?
2. Could Dudley's friendly gesture open the door to a future relationship between him and Harry?
3. Could Aunt Petunia feel the same way Dudley does? If so, why is she unable to express it?

Greater Picture

Petunia's behavior is telling in that it shows she once dearly loved her sister, Lily. It was Petunia's jealousy and spite over Lily's magical ability, something Petunia desperately also wanted to have, that drove them apart. This was probably Petunia's last chance to connect to Harry and her dead sister in some meaningful way, but she instead chooses to abandon that avenue by saying nothing and walking away.

Chapter 4: The Seven Potters

Synopsis

After the Dursleys leave Number 4, Privet Drive, Harry gathers his belongings, including the caged Hedwig, his Firebolt, and his rucksack and waits for Order of the Phoenix members to arrive. Sooner than expected, a rather large group, including Hermione Granger and Ron Weasley, appear in the back garden. Alastor "Mad-Eye" Moody says that they are flying out on broomsticks, Thestrals, and a flying motorbike; six members will be disguised as Harry Potter with Polyjuice Potion to trick any nearby Death Eaters. They have few alternatives, since Privet Drive is now being monitored for any Apparation, Portkeys, or Floo Network use. This monitoring, ostensibly for Harry's safety, is being done by the Ministry of Magic, which is becoming increasingly controlled by Lord Voldemort.

The six Harry decoys include Ron, Hermione, Fred and George Weasley, Fleur Delacour, and Mundungus Fletcher. The real Harry is to go with Hagrid in a sidecar bodged on to Sirius Black's motorbike to Ted Tonks's house, where they will be transported to The Burrow via a Portkey. The remaining six pairs, one defender and one Harry each, will travel separately to various safe-houses, all finally transferring to The Burrow. Almost immediately after clearing the garden, Death Eaters attack them. Hedwig is struck by a Killing Curse aimed at the real Harry. Hagrid's attempts to dodge the four Death Eaters chasing them result in the sidecar breaking free; Harry stops it falling and is rescued by Hagrid, but he loses everything except his rucksack. He destroys the falling sidecar to disable a Death Eater, then notices that one of the two remaining Death Eaters is Stan Shunpike, evidently under the Imperius curse. Not wanting to kill an innocent person, Harry attempts to disarm him, whereupon the remaining Death Eater yells, "It's the real one!" and falls back.

Near the Tonks' home, the Death Eaters, including Voldemort, surround them again. Hagrid leaps off the motorbike to tackle a Dark wizard a few feet from Harry. Voldemort, using Lucius Malfoy's wand, casts a lethal curse at Harry, but golden flames spontaneously erupt from Harry's wand, destroying Malfoy's without Harry casting a spell. Voldemort, incensed, demands a wand from Selwyn, another Death Eater, but he and the other Death Eaters suddenly vanish. Unable to stop the motorbike, Harry crashes into a muddy pond.

Analysis

Hedwig's death, while sad, actually serves several purposes.

First, it shows how ruthlessly evil Death Eaters actually are. There is a wide-spread joke in England that, if the Germans had wanted to invade England unopposed, they should have sent in paratroopers, each cradling a cute little puppy in his arms; no true Englishman would harm a pet. Death Eaters indiscriminately firing curses that kill pets clearly indicates their inhumanity.

Second, it builds suspense. Hedwig's cage is clutched between Harry's knees in the sidecar; the curse that killed Hedwig missed Harry by mere inches.

Third, it eliminates an encumbrance. In *Harry Potter and the Half-Blood Prince*, Harry decided to leave Hogwarts to search for Voldemort's Horcruxes; as he is about to embark on a dangerous adventure, he would either have to put Hedwig in someone else's care, or try to care for her while he is traveling. His Firebolt, unfortunate as its loss may be, was also a burden, although it tied him to his late godfather, Sirius Black, who gave it to him during his third year at Hogwarts.

Finally, it can be argued that Hedwig's death represents an end to Harry's childhood. Harry, having lost more and more innocence with Cedric Diggory, Sirius, and Dumbledore's deaths, is now an adult in the wizarding world. Hedwig provided Harry comfort and security, but when she is brutally killed, Harry loses one of the few remaining things tied to his childhood; he realizes just how fragile those ties are.

It is also interesting to note Voldemort's appearance in this chapter. In the previous six books, Voldemort only appeared to Harry four times, each time near the book's end. That he appears to Harry this early shows how much power Voldemort has gained in the Wizarding world, and puts us, and Harry, on notice that there are ever fewer places that he will be safe.

Questions

Review 1. How could the Death Eaters recognize the real Harry Potter from the decoys?

2. Why do Voldemort and the Death Eaters suddenly vanish?

3. Why did Harry use such a mild curse on Stan Shunpike, who probably would have killed him?

Further Study 1. When Harry was to be moved to a safer location, Mundungus seemed apprehensive about the plan and in participating in it. What are some possible reasons for his reaction?

2. Why could Harry's wand destroy Voldemort's borrowed wand without Harry casting a spell with it?

3. Harry's departure from the Dursleys was a closely guarded secret. How could the Death Eaters have found out?

4. Voldemort has generally remained hidden from the wizarding population. Why does he now openly show himself during the pursuit?

Greater Picture

Hedwig's death may be a precursor to what happens later in the book. It has been suggested that having Harry lose his beloved pet and best friend is one manner in which the author hardens Harry's heart so he is able to continue his fight against Voldemort.

Harry's wand casting a spell of its own volition is never fully explained. Dumbledore, in the Waystation, says that in the duel in the cemetery, Harry's wand and Voldemort's had recognized each other as having a common source (the phoenix Fawkes' tail feathers) for their cores, and recognized Harry and Voldemort as kin by their blood (and possibly also the soul shard). Harry was the stronger wizard at that encounter, as he was prepared to die while Voldemort feared death. Dumbledore surmises that because of this, Harry's wand imbibed power from Voldemort's, and against that power, Voldemort's own power, plus Harry's courage, "what chance did that poor stick of Lucius Malfoy's stand?" While this is arguably no explanation for the wand acting on its own, it is all the explanation we ever receive in the series. We can speculate that wands have some very limited sentience, as we have been told many times that "the wand chooses the wizard;" we see this again in the wand working well, or not, depending on how it was transferred from one wizard to another. It is possible that the wand, in its own limited way being aware of Harry's "kin" and enemy Voldemort attacking, had acted on its own to remove the opposing wand. All we are actually told is that Harry and Voldemort have entered an area of magic and wandlore where none have ventured before.

One possibility is that it was not Harry who cast that spell, but rather that part of him that was Voldemort. The part within Harry, which Voldemort himself does not know about, could be protecting itself. Against that, however, we must point out that rather than Harry acting without intent, it seems to be the wand acting without Harry's input. Quoting: "his wand acted of its own accord. He felt it drag his hand around like some great magnet . . ." (*Harry Potter and the Deathly Hallows*, UK / Canadian edition p. 56) One supposes that if the author had intended to indicate that it was Voldemort's soul fragment doing this, Harry would have felt his hand moving of its own volition, rather than feeling the wand pull his hand around. However, there is insufficient evidence to be certain of her intent.

Chapter 5: Fallen Warrior

Synopsis

After Harry and Hagrid land heavily at Ted Tonks's residence, Harry is treated for his injuries. Ted Tonks tells Harry that Voldemort was unable to kill Harry because the Order placed protective charms around the

Tonks' house, causing Voldemort and the Death Eaters to "disappear" as Harry neared it. Hagrid, who was last seen sprawled on the ground unconscious, appears at the door, reassuring Harry. Ted Tonks' wife, Andromeda looks so much like her her sister, Bellatrix Lestrange, that Harry almost mistakes her for Bellatrix.

The hairbrush portkey in Tonk's bedroom transports Harry and Hagrid to The Burrow where Order members are to meet. Only Mrs. Weasley and Ginny are there when Harry arrives. Hearing what happened, Mrs. Weasley is distraught—two other groups, Tonks with Ron, and Arthur Weasley with Fred were scheduled to arrive earlier than Harry.

Remus Lupin and George arrive next. However, George's ear has been severed by Death Eater Severus Snape casting "Sectumsempra." Because Dark magic was used, George's ear is irreparable. Believing an Order member betrayed them, Lupin quizzes Harry to test his identity, asking, *"What creature sat in the corner the first time that Harry Potter visited my office at Hogwarts?"* Harry answers correctly that it was, *"a Grindylow in a tank."* Assured he is not an impostor, Lupin says that Harry casting "Expelliarmus" probably identified him; it has become recognized as Harry's signature spell after confronting the Dark Lord two years before. Lupin strongly insists that Harry use stronger defensive spells.

When Kingsley Shacklebolt and Hermione arrive, Lupin verifies Shacklebolt's identity. Arthur Weasley and Fred arrive next, followed by Tonks and Ron on their broomsticks. They were delayed after encountering Bellatrix Lestrange and her husband, Rodolphus, who they seriously injured.

Shacklebolt departs, saying he is overdue at Downing Street. Bill Weasley and his fiancée, Fleur Delacour are the last members to arrive; "Mad Eye" Moody has been tragically killed by Voldemort as his companion, Mundungus Fletcher Disapparated from the scene. Members suspect Mundungus is the traitor, but decide that is unlikely, as Voldemort knew nothing about the Harry Potter decoys, which was Mundungus' suggestion. As Bill and Lupin are about to search for Mad Eye's body, Harry announces that he is endangering the others and must leave. Everyone objects, insisting Voldemort cannot possibly know where he is. Beleaguered, Harry wanders into the garden. His scar starts hurting, and he can see Voldemort torturing Ollivander the wand-maker, after the botched attempt to kill Harry. Voldemort demands to know why Lucius Malfoy's wand failed against Harry and how Harry's wand could have destroyed it. As the vision ends, Ron and Hermione arrive and urge him to stay; he tells them what he has seen. Hermione wants Harry to keep his mind closed from Voldemort.

Analysis

While plot is stressed more than character in this chapter, Mad Eye's death is not only a great loss to the Order of the Phoenix, but it has a profound affect on Harry, who resists having others risk their lives to protect him. However, Harry fails to realize that Voldemort threatens the entire Wizarding community, not just him, or that the Dark Lord cannot be defeated by one person alone. At this point, Voldemort appears to have the greater advantage, and his power is growing. The Death Eaters knew precisely when and where Harry would be moved; the Order barely survived the attack, and it was at a great cost. It also appears that the Order's tight security has been breached: despite meticulous preparation, the secret plan to move Harry to a safe house was leaked, indicating a spy may be within the Order of the Phoenix. The most likely suspect is Order member Mundungus Fletcher, a rather disreputable character, although his loyalty has never been doubted until now. However, this idea is quickly discounted because Voldemort and the Death Eaters were unaware there would be Harry decoys, which was Mundungus' idea. Who, then, tipped off Voldemort?

Lupin scolds Harry for reacting too mildly and predictably during the attack, character traits his enemies previously exploited and that tragically contributed to Sirius Black's death at the Ministry of Magic. Because Harry cast Expelliarmus, a simple disarming spell, rather than a stronger defensive one, in the graveyard duel, Death Eaters have identified it as his signature move. Thus, when Harry used it against Stan Shunpike during the pursuit, the pursuing Death Eaters identified him and summoned Voldemort. Harry's argument that he was protecting Shunpike, who he believed was only acting under the Imperius Curse, does little to sway Lupin's opinion, and it may indicate that Harry is still too young and inexperienced to be a full-fledged member of the Order of the Phoenix. It is also uncertain if Harry is willing or able to change, having always found comfort and strength in familiarity. However, if Voldemort is to be defeated, Harry must find new strategies.

Harry also shows how alone and apart he feels by wanting to leave the safe house in a misguided effort to protect others, although his departure would do little to save anyone or alter the war's overall course.

Questions

Review   1. Snape was able to heal Draco Malfoy's cuts from the Sectumsempra spell in *Harry Potter and the Half-Blood Prince*. Why are Mr. and Mrs. Weasley unable to regrow George's ear that was severed by the same spell?

2. Why does Harry want to leave The Burrow? Is that a wise decision? What stops him?

3. Why does Harry always act so predictably? What does Lupin tell him?

Extra Study   1. Did a traitor within the Order of the Phoenix tip off Voldemort about Harry leaving the Dursleys? If so, who might that be?

2. If there is not a traitor within the Order, how could Voldemort have uncovered the secret plan?

3. Why would Voldemort be holding Mr. Ollivander prisoner?

GREATER PICTURE

Hermione is dismayed that Harry chooses to see Voldemort's thoughts, as well she should; it was through that channel that Voldemort implanted the false vision that led to Sirius' death in *Harry Potter and the Order of the Phoenix*. However, Voldemort found Harry's mind an extremely uncomfortable place to occupy; it was Harry's love for Sirius and others that drove him out. Dumbledore believed Voldemort closed that avenue in *Harry Potter and the Half-Blood Prince* because he was unable to cope with Harry's memories and emotions. Harry believes that if he remains aware that false images can be implanted, he will be shielded from Voldemort deceiving him again, although Hermione and Ron are less certain. Harry will occasionally glimpse Voldemort's thoughts throughout the book, and these images will prove invaluable.

Mad Eye Moody is presumably killed in the attack by Death Eaters, although Order of the Phoenix members never locate his body. Harry will later recover Moody's magical eye from Dolores Umbridge's office in the Ministry of Magic, but it is unknown if the Death Eaters actually found his corpse. This leaves open the faint possibility that Mad Eye may have survived the attack and is in hiding. Even Ron believes he may still be alive and has hidden himself somewhere, although Harry and Hermione are skeptical. Considering how paranoid Moody had become, it would hardly be surprising that he would conceal himself, even from friends and allies, and probably for long after the war ended. Moody could, therefore, reappear in a future Harry Potter sequel (if Rowling should write one). Mad Eye makes one final appearance in this novel, however; when Harry, Hermione, and Ron take refuge at Grimmauld Place, Moody's voice "greets" them as they enter—it is one of the jinxes that guards the former Order of the Phoenix headquarters from intruders. Another jinx taking the form of a moldering Dumbledore will also appear at Grimmauld Place. Rowling may be dropping subtle clues that the last has not been heard or seen from Alastor "Mad Eye" Moody or Albus Dumbledore.

George's severed ear may actually foreshadow a more tragic event involving the Weasley family.

Chapter 6: The Ghoul in Pyjamas

SYNOPSIS

In the days following Mad-Eye Moody's death, the Order has deduced that Harry, Ron, and Hermione are preparing for a secret mission assigned by Dumbledore. Mr. Weasley and Lupin accept that the Trio are unable to confide anything, but Mrs. Weasley is persistent. When she is unable to persuade them to return to Hogwarts or reveal any information, she constantly assigns each one chores, nominally to help with the wedding preparations, but actually intended to keep them separated. Ginny tells Harry that her mother is probably hoping to delay their departure by preventing them from planning the mission. Harry wonders aloud if Mrs. Weasley is hoping that someone else will bump off Voldemort. When Ginny, pale-faced, asks if that is their mission, Harry feebly claims he was only joking.

Grimmauld Place can no longer be used as Order Headquarters and many members now have their meals at the Burrow; with Dumbledore's death, everyone privy to its hidden location and function has become a secret-keeper, able to reveal that the Black family home is their Headquarters. This includes Severus Snape who is now deeply entrenched within the Death Eaters' council. Moody had set some protective charms against Snape at the entrance, but it is uncertain if they will work.

Mad-Eye's body is still missing, and the media has reported nothing about the fusillade of magic used during the escape. The Ministry of Magic is apparently keeping people unaware that Death Eaters have grown more powerful, or that there was another mass Azkaban breakout.

In her distraction, Mrs. Weasley allows Harry, Ron, and Hermione a short break from their chores. As Hermione sorts books, deciding which ones to take, Harry again tells her and Ron that they can remain behind. Both reply that they could have backed out six years earlier, and they have had ample time to reconsider. Hermione has already modified her parents' memories and hidden them in Australia, and Ron shows Harry the family ghoul in the attic that has been magically altered to resemble Ron with spattergroit. Anyone curious about Ron's absence from Hogwarts will likely avoid getting too close to anyone with such a contagious and fatal disease. The group are still without a plan for when they leave the Burrow. Harry wants to go to Godric's Hollow, but Hermione vetoes this, warning that Voldemort likely has it under surveillance. They should instead hunt for the real Locket Horcrux that was stolen by the mysterious R. A. B.

When Ron asks how Horcruxes can be destroyed, Hermione admits to having Summoned Dark Magic books from Dumbledore's study. One, *Secrets of the Darkest Art*, gives full instructions on making Horcruxes; she wonders whether Riddle read it. Harry believes he probably did, and Dumbledore was certain that Riddle already knew how to make a Horcrux before asking Slughorn if it was possible to make multiple ones. Hermione says that Horcruxes by their nature are very strong, and the only way to destroy one is to damage it so it cannot be mended by normal magical means. For instance, Harry stabbing Riddle's diary Horcrux with the Basilisk fang—Basilisk venom is one of a very few things that will destroy a Horcrux. Hermione also believes it is unlikely that Voldemort will reunite his shredded soul on his own; that would require that he have deep remorse for what he had done, something Voldemort is unlikely to feel, and it would cause him excruciating pain. Harry wonders how Dumbledore destroyed the Ring Horcrux and muses again about how little time there was to ask questions. Mrs. Weasley suddenly bursts into the room, breaking up the conversation, and assigns Harry, Hermione, and Ron separate tasks. Mr. and Mrs. Delacour arrive the next day. Mr. Delacour is charming, Mrs. Delacour is a domestic genius, and everything falls into place around them. Everything is wonderful, everything is lovely. As Harry's birthday approaches, Mrs. Weasley asks him what he would like. Harry says there is little that he needs, and he certainly does not want a big fuss. Thinking about the effort required to arrange a wedding, complicated by the thicket of security spells hiding his presence, Harry is concerned about the strain he is putting on everyone.

Analysis

Harry's last-ditch effort to persuade Ron and Hermione to remain behind does show concern for their safety, but it also displays a serious character flaw: his constant need to face adversity alone. In fact, much of Harry's strength and success result from his friends' support, abilities, and loyalty, although he fails to fully recognize this; his mission to find and destroy Voldemort's Horcruxes would likely fail without their continual help. Harry's isolation during early childhood has limited his perspective somewhat, causing him to approach many difficulties by himself. Unwanted fame, peer resentment, and exploitation by adults have also had a detrimental effect on him.

Although Harry is a pivotal element in the fight against Voldemort, he has yet to completely realize that many other wizarding families have suffered severely, and will continue to suffer, under the Dark Lord's reign of terror—this is not Harry's battle alone, and Ron and Hermione steadfastly refuse to abandon Harry or the mission. Hermione, as expected, has meticulously packed into her magical bag everything they will need, and both Hermione and Ron have acted to protect their respective families during the mission that Harry is expected to take on.

Mrs. Weasley's character also comes into focus here as she fails miserably to prevent the Trio from embarking on their mission. Despite all her efforts, she likely knows nothing will deter them from leaving and is frustrated that she no longer has any real parental control over Ron, although that does not prevent her from trying. However, her maternal concerns are not only for Ron, Harry, and Hermione, but for her entire family, who will be in grave danger if Voldemort discovers Ron is helping Harry. Mrs. Weasley's love for her family far outweighs any loyalty to the Order of the Phoenix, and she has difficulty resigning herself to what they must do, although she likely believes that Dumbledore's task is far too difficult for such young, inexperienced wizards. Her actions reflect her personal feelings, which are apparently shared by most of the other adults.

Hermione claims it was easy to summon the Dark Arts books from Dumbledore's study, almost as if she was intended to retrieve them (which she may have been). Until now, with one exception, the Summoning charm has proven unblockable; one would think that if Dolores Umbridge, for instance, had wanted to secure Fred and George's confiscated brooms, she would have taken stronger measures to protect them from the Summoning charm. She may actually have done so, but underestimated the Twins' ingenuity and talent in developing new magic to overcome common spells, or she may simply have had an exaggerated confidence in her own (apparently average) magical skills. On the other hand, Harry found that the Summoning charm was blocked when he attempted to summon the (fake) Horcrux in the lake inside the sea cave in *Harry Potter and the Half-Blood Prince*. When he heard motion while attempting it, it was quite possible that some physical barrier blocked the spell. Voldemort's Blocking spell may also have contained Dark Magic, making it more powerful than a normal one. We do not really know yet whether the Summoning charm can be blocked without some physical intervention; however, Hermione evidently thinks it can be.

While Harry says here that Dumbledore was certain Riddle already knew how to make a Horcrux before speaking with Slughorn, that text does not appear in *Harry Potter and the Half-Blood Prince*. However, later interviews with the author do tend to confirm Harry's statement. In an interview following the publication of *Harry Potter and the Deathly Hallows*, the author stated that the first Horcrux made was created by the death of Tom Riddle's father. This Horcrux would have been locked into the Peverell ring, which is seen on Riddle's hand when he is discussing making multiple Horcruxes with Horace Slughorn. As we already know that the Riddles died on the same night that Voldemort stole the Peverell ring from his uncle Morfin, the ring must already have been a Horcrux when that conversation took place. We must assume that, in the onward race of events, the author simply forgot to have Dumbledore mention this fact in our hearing.

Questions

Review 1. Why does the Trio keep their mission's purpose secret from Order of the Phoenix members?

2. How can Horcruxes be destroyed? How does Hermione learn how?

3. Why was it so easy for Hermione to summon the restricted books from Dumbledore's office? Why does she need them?

4. Why does Mrs. Weasley continually assign the Trio separate chores? Does she really believe this will work?

5. Why does Harry try to dissuade Ron and Hermione from accompanying him on the quest? Is he right in doing so? If not, why? What is their response?

Further Study 1. Why does Harry want to go to Godric's Hollow? Why is Hermione against it? Explain who is right.

2. If Dumbledore was correct that Tom Riddle already knew how to make a Horcrux, why did Riddle seek advice from Professor Slughorn about how they were created?

Greater Picture

In *Harry Potter and the Order of the Phoenix*, when the Trio visit Mr. Weasley at St. Mungo's, a portrait on the wall diagnoses Ron with spattergroit; the wizard in that portrait was suggesting cures that seemed worse than the disease. Ron denies that he is suffering from Spattergroit, saying it is just freckles. This is possibly where the idea for part of the ghoul's disguise came from. Over the next few chapters of this book, more is learned about Spattergroit, an incurable magical fungus infestation. Starting with pustules on the skin, it proceeds to spread through the throat; once it reaches the uvula, the victim is unable to talk. It is extremely contagious, and eventually fatal. There are several incidents throughout the story where someone casts the Summoning Charm unsuccessfully. In some cases, the summoned item was either not present or the person casting the charm lacked a proper wand; however, in some instances, such as with Ravenclaw's Diadem, Gryffindor's Sword, and Harry's Invisibility Cloak, the object was present but simply failed to respond. However, unlike ordinary, everyday objects, these are powerful magical artifacts that may be impervious to Summoning charms. When Hermione fails to Summon the Locket Horcrux a little later, she suggests it is possible that it is magically prevented from responding, a fact that reminds Harry of how the fake locket Horcrux in the sea cave was similarly protected. However, in Hermione's case, the Locket is simply not in the house at that time, so it is unknown if it would have responded. If it is that common to protect objects from a Summoning charm, it might be surmised that when Hermione so easily retrieved the Dark Arts books from the Headmaster's office, it may be that Dumbledore intended for her to have them. According to Hermione, only a powerful magical object like the Basilisk fang Harry used on Tom Riddle's Diary can destroy a Horcrux. While the Trio will desperately search for another equally powerful, but as yet unknown, object that can also do the job, considering that they are intensely discussing this among themselves, it seems rather odd that no one, particularly Hermione, thinks to bring Basilisk fangs on their mission. There is still ample time and opportunity to retrieve these from the Chamber of Secrets beneath Hogwarts Castle. Although Hogwarts will fall under Voldemort's control later in the book, it is currently headed by Professor McGonagall, the acting Headmistress, and still safe for the Trio to visit. When the Trio returns to Hogwarts at the book's end, it will be Ron who remembers this and retrieves a fang from the Chamber to destroy a Horcrux.

Chapter 7: The Will of Albus Dumbledore

SYNOPSIS

Harry is awakened by Ron Weasley after Harry witnessed, as if dreaming, Voldemort's search for Gregorovitch, an unknown but slightly familiar name. Today is Harry's seventeenth birthday, the legal age to perform unmonitored magic. Excitedly, he successfully casts some spells to test whether the Ministry's "Trace" still monitors him. At breakfast, he receives many presents from friends and mentors. The Weasleys give him a gold watch, a wizard's traditional seventeenth birthday gift. Mrs. Weasley explains that this one is used, it once belonged to her late brother, Fabian Prewett. Harry gives her a grateful and understanding hug. Later, Ginny Weasley ushers Harry into her bedroom. She does not have a present but wants to give Harry something to remember her by, in case he meets someone else. Harry replies that dating opportunities will be very slim; she kisses him and he begins kissing her back, but they are abruptly interrupted by Ron. He and Ron leave the room as Ginny turns away, apparently crying. Upset, Ron warns Harry not to give Ginny any false hope about renewing their romance. Harry, realizing Ginny's future is unencumbered whereas his only concerns Voldemort, promises it will not happen again.

At the birthday party, newlyweds Remus Lupin and Nymphadora Tonks congratulate Harry, although Lupin seems rather sad while Tonks looks radiantly happy. Halfway through the festivities, Arthur Weasley's Patronus arrives announcing that Minister for Magic Rufus Scrimgeour is accompanying him to the Burrow. Lupin and Tonks leave abruptly upon hearing this, puzzling many. Scrimgeour arrives and, perfunctorily wishing Harry a Happy Birthday, asks to speak privately to Harry, Ron, and Hermione. Albus Dumbledore's will bequeaths them several items. Harry is surprised it took so long to reveal the will, but Hermione says the Ministry surely wanted to thoroughly examine Dumbledore's estate, and obviously took the maximum time allowed by law to test willed property for any Dark magic. Ron receives a Deluminator, a magical object that captures and releases light. Queried by Scrimgeour as to why Dumbledore would leave him such a rare instrument, Ron admits that he did not think Dumbledore was particularly fond of him; Hermione, to counter Scrimgeour's suspicions, disputes this, saying he is being too modest. She is given a book, *The Tales of Beedle The Bard*, which seems to be an early edition written in runes. Asked why Dumbledore would leave her this, she is unable to answer. Harry inherits the Quidditch Snitch he caught during his first-ever Quidditch match at Hogwarts. Hermione mentions the Snitch's "flesh memory"; it remembers the first person that touches it, a property used to resolve games where two Seekers seem to grab the Snitch simultaneously. Nothing happens when Harry picks it up, to Scrimgeour's apparent disappointment: he had seemingly been expecting it to open and reveal something hidden inside. There is a second bequest for Harry: the sword of Godric Gryffindor. However, Scrimgeour claims the sword is a "vital historical artifact," and the Ministry is unwilling to relinquish it to Harry. A heated argument erupts between Harry and Scrimgeour, alarming Mr. and Mrs. Weasley. Scrimgeour, offended, leaves.

Later that evening, the Trio examine their objects. Harry remembers catching the Snitch in his mouth; placed to his lips, a cryptic inscription appears on it in Dumbledore's writing: "I open at the close." None can decipher its meaning. Both Harry and Hermione have no idea what *The Tales of Beedle the Bard* is. Ron, astonished, tells them it is a famous book of wizarding nursery stories. Hermione reminds Ron that she and Harry were raised by Muggles and never heard Wizarding stories like "Babbitty Rabbitty and her Cackling Stump." Ron, on hearing that a Muggle fairy tale is named "Cinderella," asks if it is disease. Unable to determine what their bequests mean, the Trio head off to bed.

Analysis

Harry testing to see if the Ministry of Magic's Trace for underage magic has expired is inconclusive. The Trace does automatically disappear when a witch or wizard comes of age, but the Ministry is unable to detect underage magic in a Wizarding household where the adults are constantly casting spells. In Wizard homes, it is the parents' responsibility to monitor their children for improper use. Although the Trace on Harry does disappear on schedule, if Voldemort's followers within the Ministry had somehow kept it active, Harry would likely be unaware, and it could have revealed the Trio's location once they left the Burrow and began their mission. There may, however, be something else that can reveal their presence to Voldemort.

While Voldemort's dark cloud increasingly threatens the wizarding world, Harry's birthday party offers a happy, if momentary, respite, as well as some insight into several characters. Lupin and Tonks' differing emotional expressions at the gathering seems a bit odd and could be interpreted several ways, but Tonks' radiant happiness suggests she is pregnant. That this comes at a very difficult and dangerous time is likely deeply distressing to Lupin, who already had troubling doubts about his suitability as a husband. He may be harboring similar fears regarding fatherhood and is worried that he and Tonks may not survive the war, leaving their only child an orphan. The Weasleys' birthday gift to Harry is far more than a traditional token commemorating his entry into adulthood. Giving Harry her deceased brother's watch shows that Mrs. Weasley loves Harry like a son; Harry understands its significance and is deeply grateful, and he considers the Weasleys as his family. Ginny, meanwhile, is still in love with Harry, but she has nearly abandoned hope that they will ever be together. Ron's concern for his sister's emotional well-being indicates an emerging maturity and that he cares for others, not just himself, although he still has a ways to go before fully reaching adulthood. Ron is also learning about relationships, having read a book the Twins gave him on girls and dating. He has been applying its advice to Hermione, who seems to respond favorably. Ron, who had repeatedly remarked that he needed lessons about girls, is impressed enough with the results that he gives Harry a copy for his birthday, although he asks Harry not to show it to Hermione.

That Minister for Magic Rufus Scrimgeour would personally deliver Dumbledore's bequests to Harry, Ron, and Hermione at The Burrow is not just unusual, but highly suspicious. Except for the Sword of Gryffindor, these are fairly innocuous objects, but having once belonged to an extraordinary wizard makes them exceptional, at least to the Ministry of Magic. Clearly, the Ministry suspects that there is some ulterior motive for Dumbledore leaving these particular items to the Trio, which is why it took them so long to examine Dumbledore's estate. The Ministry's suspicions are probably correct, but there is no way for us or the Ministry to know yet what those motives could be. It is doubtful that Gryffindor's sword belonged to Dumbledore, but he obviously wanted to bring it to Harry's attention, although for what purpose is yet unknown. It may seem odd that Dumbledore left Harry so little considering their close relationship, although it is unknown just what his entire estate entailed or how much was left to Albus' brother, Aberforth. The Ministry is also suspicious that Dumbledore would leave Ron and Hermione anything, suspecting his relationship with either was minimal. However, Dumbledore obviously left the Trio these specific objects for a reason, and additional bequests to Harry would have overridden those items' particular significance. Although the Trio realizes that Dumbledore is communicating posthumously, they are clueless as to what his cryptic message means. By speaking to Harry from beyond the grave, Dumbledore shows that death is not always a finite ending. Those who have died can continue to affect the living in many ways—through memories, their personal legacy, and so on. However, in the wizarding world, the dead can play a more substantial and interactive role, as has been seen not only by the ghosts, but in other ways, such as through the living portraits, the spirit echoes, memories in a Pensieve, etc. It is understandable why Harry continually hopes magic will reunite him with his parents. In this case, Dumbledore has left a cryptic trail for Harry to follow, although just where that trail begins and where it will eventually lead is still unknown.

The fact that the Golden Snitch from Harry's first Quidditch game had been caught in an unusual way seems to play a significant part in this chapter, seven books later. One must wonder whether the plot arc for the series was developed with this level of detail before pen was ever set on paper, or whether the availability of the Snitch and its unconventional means of initial contact with Harry was fortuitous.

Questions

Review 1. Why is Ron upset that Harry kisses Ginny?

2. Other than marking Harry's seventeenth birthday with a traditional gift, why would Mrs. Weasley give Harry her late brother's watch? What is Harry's reaction and why?

3. Why would Lupin and Tonks abruptly leave the party before Scrimgeour arrives?

4. Why did the Ministry wait so long to reveal Dumbledore's will?

Extra Study 1. What might be the significance of each bequest that Dumbledore left the Trio?

2. Considering Dumbledore's affection for Harry, why wouldn't he leave him more in his will?

3. Why would Dumbledore leave Gryffindor's Sword to Harry, an object that probably never belonged to him?

4. Why does the Ministry withhold Gryffindor's Sword from Harry? Is it really because it did not belong to Dumbledore as they claim, or is there another reason?

5. Ron, who has always been slower to develop emotionally than Harry or Hermione, shows signs that he is maturing into adulthood. Give examples of this.

6. Why would Lupin appear sad while Tonks looks happy?

7. What might the inscription, "I open at the close," that is engraved on the Snitch actually mean?

8. Why would Minister for Magic Rufus Scrimgeour personally deliver Dumbledore's bequests to the Trio?

GREATER PICTURE

Each object Dumbledore left the Trio proves vital to their mission to destroy Voldemort's Horcruxes. The Deluminator that Ron received was called a "put-outer" in *Harry Potter and the Philosopher's Stone*. Initially, its only purpose seems to be to extinguish and later reilluminate lights. However, it also detects other peoples' conversations about its owner and guides the holder to their location. After Ron leaves Harry and Hermione, the Deluminator will lead him back to them.

Hermione's bequest is a well-known book of wizard fairy tales containing a story about the Deathly Hallows, which are three magical objects; someone, probably Dumbledore, marked the fable, "The Tale of the Three Brothers," with the Deathly Hallows' symbol. One Hallow will prove vital to combating Voldemort, who is also seeking it. The Snitch contains another Hallow, and its inscription's meaning, "I open at the close," is revealed near the book's conclusion when Harry realizes that 'the close' means death.

Although it is never known if Dumbledore ever actually owned Gryffindor's Sword, his leaving it to Harry in his will is a clue that the Trio will need it to destroy Voldemort's Horcruxes. We already know that Basilisk venom will destroy a Horcrux; as the only known source of that is in the Chamber of Secrets deep under Hogwarts, it is not immediately certain how useful that information will be for us. We will later find out that Gryffindor's Sword was used to destroy a Horcrux, and perhaps Dumbledore intends that the sword be available to Harry to destroy the other Horcruxes. In fact, two of the remaining four Horcruxes will be destroyed by this sword.

Chapter 8: The Wedding

SYNOPSIS

Bill Weasley and Fleur Delacour's long-awaited wedding takes place at The Burrow in the afternoon. Harry drinks Polyjuice Potion to disguise himself as the Weasleys' "Cousin Barney." Many guests arrive, including Luna Lovegood (who annoyingly sees through Harry's Polyjuice Potion disguise) and her father, Xenophilius, a few part-Veela cousins of the Delacours, the Weasleys' Auntie Muriel, and most famously, Viktor Krum. Viktor, of course, is delighted to see Hermione, causing Ron to struggle with jealousy. Hermione, flustered, drops her little beaded handbag, which falls with a suspiciously heavy "clunk."

During the reception, Viktor sits at the disguised Harry's table and asks if Harry knows who Xenophilius is, because if he was not Fleur's guest, he would duel him immediately for wearing "that filthy symbol on his chest." Krum says the medallion, which has a circle with a slash within a triangle on it, represents Grindelwald, a Dark Wizard who terrorized Europe, killing many, including Krum's grandfather. Grindelwald was finally defeated many years before by Albus Dumbledore. Many Durmstrang students once copied the sign, but Viktor despises it. As Krum brandishes his wand, Harry's memory is tweaked: during the Triwizard Wand Weighing Ceremony in his fourth year, Mr. Ollivander recognized Krum's wand as a "Gregorovitch creation." This is the name of the man that Voldemort is seeking in Harry's dream. Harry concludes that Voldemort may be searching for him to obtain a more powerful wand than Harry's, as Gregorovitch might be a more skillful wandmaker than Ollivander. Harry leaves Viktor after the latter makes admiring comments about Ginny Weasley, inciting Harry's jealousy. He then meets and reveals his identity to Elphias Doge, who wrote about Albus Dumbledore's life in the *Daily Prophet* obituary. When Harry asks about Rita Skeeter's story and if Dumbledore was involved in the Dark Arts, Elphias becomes furious, denying Skeeter's account. He is further enraged when Auntie Muriel interrupts, saying she supports Skeeter's claims and criticizes Doge for glossing over Dumbledore's murky past in his obituary. Muriel's allegations are shocking: she claims that Albus' ailing sister Ariana was a Squib, a disgrace that their mother, Kendra, kept hidden by keeping Ariana locked in the cellar. Muriel speculates that Ariana murdered Kendra in an unsuccessful escape attempt, all while Albus was at Hogwarts achieving fame and gaining accolades. After Kendra's mysterious death, Albus was forced to head the family, but had done a darned poor job of it; shortly after, Ariana also died, possibly, Muriel implies, murdered by Albus. Muriel also claims that, according to her friend, Bathilda Bagshot, who knew the Dumbledores well, Aberforth blamed Albus for Ariana's death and punched him during the funeral, breaking Albus' nose. Auntie Muriel denies that Ariana was ever sickly; she says her cousin was a Healer at St. Mungo's at the time, and Kendra never brought Ariana there. However, what most surprises Harry is that the Dumbledores lived in Godric's Hollow, Harry's former home, and where his parents are buried. Suddenly, Kingsley Shacklebolt's Patronus arrives and announces that Rufus Scrimgeour is dead and Voldemort had taken control of the Ministry. He warns, *"They are coming"*—Death Eaters hunting the wedding guests, particularly Harry.

ANALYSIS

Harry's faith in his mentor Dumbledore, already shaken by the "revelations" appearing in the *Daily Prophet* interview with Rita Skeeter, and only slightly repaired by talk with Elphias Doge, here takes another blow from Auntie Muriel. Dumbledore's past is far more secretive and complex than Harry ever imagined, and he is gradually realizing just how little he actually knew his mentor. As with his father and godfather, the man Harry so admired and trusted had a hidden dark side. Youth, however, tend to only see their heroes' sterling characteristics, failing to realize that every person is a multi-dimensional composite containing faults as well as qualities, and that while these traits can clash, they also create balance. Harry has also yet to learn that it is one's past mistakes and transgressions that often makes them into the better person they eventually become. Nor will anyone ever be totally flawless, although Harry still largely sees the world as black or white, ignoring the multi-hued and sometimes muddied tones that blend, shade, and contrast life. Years before, Dumbledore had said to Harry, "It is our choices, Harry, that show what we truly are, far more than our abilities." Harry, though relieved to be able to apply that to himself, so as to distinguish himself from Tom Riddle, as yet does not consistently apply that to others, notably Dumbledore.

Readers may also wonder why Harry is so quick to believe such questionable sources like Auntie Muriel and Rita Skeeter, while being rather dismissive about Elphias Doge's more sympathetic memories. Although Harry wants to believe Doge and had sought his reassurance about Dumbledore, he doubts Doge's words. This may partially be because Muriel is so assertive and specific, making her appear more credible to Harry than Doge, who comes across as vague and deferential. Nor should it be assumed that Doge's recollections are any more accurate than Muriel's memories or Skeeter's research, simply because they are favorable. And Skeeter, despite her spurious journalistic methods, often uncovers accurate facts, although they are usually embellished beyond recognition when they reach her readers. Regardless, Harry, conflicted by these multiple "truths," is deeply troubled by his already growing confusion and concerns about Dumbledore, including those regarding his dark past, what his actual intentions were, and whether or not he truly loved Harry or had merely groomed him as an instrument to execute his cryptic plan. Although Harry is dedicated to completing his mission, he will be distracted by these allegations about Dumbledore's past and his motivations, and by his confusion and frustration with the meager and perplexing information he was provided. Harry will become consumed with uncovering Dumbledore's past, so much so that it affects his mission. Knowing that Gregorovitch is, or was, a wand-maker, we can surmise that Voldemort has determined Harry's phoenix-feather wand to be his greatest threat. This certainly tallies with Harry's belief: having felt the wand cast a spell on its own during the escape from Privet Drive, Harry's faith in his wand is incredible. In chapter one, we did learn that Voldemort considers Harry's wand as a threat. It is unclear if Voldemort has learned about the connection between his wand and Harry's; while he does have Ollivander captive, it has not been revealed if he has interrogated Ollivander regarding this. Whether he intends for Gregorovitch to craft him a more powerful wand that can defeat Harry, or if he simply believes that a wand from a different maker would not suffer the same fate as Malfoy's, also an Ollivander wand, or he is merely after other information on wand lore, is still unknown. Several characters are also highlighted here. Although it is never explained just how Luna Lovegood was able to peer through Harry's Polyjuice Potion disguise, it certainly indicates that despite, or even possibly because of, her unusual personality, she possesses some extraordinary and uncommon magical powers that may have been inherited from her late mother, rather than her father. This could make her an even more powerful ally for Harry. Meanwhile, Viktor Krum's unexpected reappearance has a detrimental effect on Ron, who immediately feels jealous and threatened by Viktor's rekindled interest in Hermione, although Ron has yet to fully recognize just what his feelings for her truly are.

A small side plot in this chapter briefly focuses on Harry and Ginny. During the wedding ceremony, Ginny glances at Harry and winks at him, which prompts Harry to remember the wonderful times they spent together in the previous book, rather than pay attention to the actual wedding. Later, when Viktor Krum inquires about Ginny, Harry immediately responds that she is already seeing someone who is "big" and "a jealous type." Despite the impending war with Voldemort and the Death Eaters, and Harry's decision to formally end their relationship, the bond between Harry and Ginny remains as strong as ever.

QUESTIONS

Review 1. What is the symbol that Mr. Lovegood is wearing? Why does it provoke such a strong reaction from Viktor Krum?

2. Who is Gregorovitch and why does Voldemort seek him?

3. Why would Voldemort seek a new wand?

Extra Study 1. Who is telling the truth about Dumbledore's past and his family?

2. Why does Harry seem to give more credence to Auntie Muriel's and Rita Skeeter's recollections about Dumbledore than he does to Elphias Doge's memories? Whose memories are the most credible? Why?

3. How could Luna Lovegood see through Harry's Polyjuice Potion disguise? What does this say about her magical abilities?

4. Why does Hermione's small handbag land with such a loud thunk?

5. Why would Albus Dumbledore's sister be treated as a "squib" by her mother?

GREATER PICTURE

Harry is correct in surmising that Voldemort is searching for a new wand. Although Harry and Voldemort's wands are "brothers," it will be learned that, during their confrontation in the cemetery in *Harry Potter and the Goblet of Fire,* Harry's wand not only overpowered Voldemort's, it forged a deeper connection and withdrew some of that wand's powers into itself, making it the superior weapon. Voldemort, though unaware of this, is apparently seeking a more powerful wand that can defeat Harry's, specifically one that was associated with the legendary wandmaker, Gregorovitch.

It will be learned in a later chapter that Ollivander was tortured by Voldemort for information. Ollivander will admit having revealed to Voldemort that Harry and Voldemort's wands are "brothers."

Chapter 9: A Place to Hide

Synopsis

Panic erupts over the shocking announcement. Some guests disappear, showing that the protective charms surrounding The Burrow have been broken. The rest stand armed with their wands, ready to face the Death Eaters. Amid the crowded scene, Hermione, Ron and Harry disappear to Tottenham Court Road. They enter a dark alley and change their clothes, Hermione having already packed everything they needed for their mission into her purse (which has been enchanted to fit spellbooks, clothes, money, camping gear, etc.). The Trio, with Harry under the Invisibility Cloak, enter a shabby all-night café along the road, trying to get some rest. Ron suggests going to the Leaky Cauldron but Hermione immediately vetoes that idea as being too dangerous and that Voldemort will be watching there. Instead, she advises disapparating to the countryside so they can send a message to the Order.

When two workmen enter the café and take seats near the Trio, Ron and Hermione lower their voices. As the workmen draw their wands, Harry, under his Invisibility Cloak, recognizes them as Death Eaters. He Stuns one, although he misses the second Death Eater: the spell ricochets off the window and hits the waitress. Meanwhile, the remaining Death Eater has bound Ron, and blown up the table behind Harry. Hermione Petrifies him. Inspecting the Death Eaters, Harry recognizes the big blond one he Stunned from the battle at the Astronomy Tower the previous year. Ron identifies him as Thorfinn Rowle. The Petrified one is Dolohov. Harry first encountered him at the battle in the Ministry.

The Trio are reluctant to kill the Death Eaters, so Harry suggests wiping their memories so they are unable to remember finding Ron and Hermione. (Harry was under the Invisibility Cloak the entire time.) Harry also suggests repairing the diner so it appears as if nothing happened. Hermione performs a Memory Charm on the Death Eaters and the waitress, while Harry and Ron fix the physical damage. Hermione wonders how they were found so quickly and asks if Harry could still be carrying the Ministry Trace to detect underage magic. Ron insists that it breaks at age 17 by law, although Hermione suggests a new one could have been put on by a Death Eater. Ron says none have been near Harry since he turned 17. After some discussion, Harry suggests going to Number Twelve, Grimmauld Place, the house Sirius left to Harry and the former Order of the Phoenix headquarters. Overriding the others' objections, Harry says that only Severus Snape can enter, and anywhere else they go could have many Death Eaters.

The Trio disapparate to Grimmauld Place. Upon entering, they are startled by Mad-Eye Moody's voice, and the Tongue-tying Curse left for Snape briefly affects them. A dusty, rotting Albus Dumbledore form appears in the entryway. Harry yells out that they did not kill Dumbledore, and the figure dissolves back into dust. Hermione checks and finds nobody else in the house; they go up the stairs to the drawing room.

Harry's scar is burning again, only this time he feels Voldemort's rage. Hermione is upset—it was this channel that allowed Voldemort to lure Harry to the Ministry two years ago, where Sirius was killed. Ron, meanwhile, wants to know if Harry can see the Weasley family, if that is who Voldemort is angry at. A silver Patronus arrives, and Arthur Weasley's voice announces, *"Family safe, do not reply, we are being watched."* Ron and Hermione collapse in relief; Harry, concerned about Ginny, is also relieved. Suddenly feeling sick from the pain in his scar, Harry dashes for the bathroom. Sprawled on the tile floor, he "sees" the large blond Death Eater from the café being tortured for failing to capture Harry and the others. He is sickened by what he witnesses, including a petrified-looking Draco Malfoy, who Voldemort forces to do the actual torturing.

Analysis

Only Hermione's meticulous planning and quick actions saves the Trio, allowing them to escape quickly. Everything they need for their quest was already packed in her beaded bag. The location Hermione Disapparated them to was a spontaneous choice, although, initially, it appears to be a poor decision because Death Eaters found them so quickly, and it is unlikely they were there by coincidence. If Harry no longer carries the Ministry trace, nor does it appear from the text that he used any magic when the Trio first arrived in Tottenham Court Road, just how, then, did the Death Eaters immediately detect the Trio's location? Apparating to Grimmauld Place also seems risky; not only is its location known to Severus Snape, a Secret Keeper who has returned to Voldemort's service, but he would likely suspect that Harry might flee there.

There are signs that the stress caused by their escape is affecting Hermione. She says, and Ron and Harry agree, that they would rather be in Grimmauld Place where they could be attacked only by one Death Eater, Snape, than out on the street where there are many. She seems to have forgotten that as Snape became a Secret Keeper for the Headquarters' location at Dumbledore's death, he can now reveal Grimmauld Place's location to as many Death Eaters as he chooses to. As such, if the Trio are known to be at Grimmauld Place, any number of Death Eaters could appear at the door.

Harry again shows his reluctance to use more powerful defensive spells against his enemies; Ron and Hermione are similarly reluctant. When Harry was attacked leaving Privet Drive, he cast Expelliarmus, a non-lethal disarming spell, to avoid harming Stan Shunpike, who he believed was acting under the Imperius Curse. Lupin later criticized Harry for his refusal to employ stronger magic in life-threatening situations and dismissed Harry's argument that he was protecting an innocent person. Harry was also reluctant to use the Cruciatus curse on Bellatrix Lestrange at the Battle in the Ministry (in *Harry Potter and the Order of the Phoenix*), resulting in its weakened effect. However, in *Harry Potter and the Half-Blood Prince*, Harry unhesitatingly cast an unknown spell (Sectumsempra) to counter Draco Malfoy's sudden attack, nearly killing Draco as a result. Although horrified by the outcome, Harry, fueled by anger, intended to inflict harm on Draco, resulting in its detrimental effect, although it was not his intention to kill him. Here in the café, Harry continues this pattern by Stunning the Death Eaters, and Hermione similarly uses the non-lethal, full body bind jinx. The Trio's decision to spare the Death Eaters' lives at the café is also questionable. Outwardly, this seems merciful, but it shows they may still be unprepared to serve in the Order of the Phoenix, unable to cope with warfare's extreme demands. Dangerous times often call for desperate measures that would never be considered under normal circumstances, including killing your enemies to protect yourself, defend your allies, and accomplish a mission. The Trio may be unable to handle Dumbledore's difficult quest, although in this particular instance, their restraint probably saved the waitress, accidentally hit by a ricocheting spell, from serious injury or even death. Ironically, the Trio's humanitarian act may only have spared the two Death Eaters long enough to suffer a more horrendous fate. Harry later watches through Voldemort's eyes as at least one Death Eater is severely tortured for failing the Dark Lord.

Also, it is interesting that Rowle was tortured for letting Harry escape. Rowle never saw Harry, only his wand flash. However, Dolohov did see Harry, when he was Petrified; granted, that was before Hermione altered his memory, but we already know that Voldemort has a rare skill with memories, and Hermione, as good a witch as she is, had never cast a memory charm before. Why was Rowle tortured, but not Dolohov? While there is no answer, it seems evident that Voldemort frequently reacts with irrational rage, rather than calm reason, striking out (often fatally) at whoever is nearby, as well as the person who has failed him. It is also possible that Rowle was tortured for failing to capture any of the Trio (not just Harry) and that Dolohov was punished at a time Harry was not tuned in to Voldemort's thoughts. Alternately, it is possible that Dolohov, a veteran Death Eater from Voldemort's first rise to power, and thus knowing Voldemort's propensities, had deliberately hung back to allow Rowle to deliver the bad news and receive the resulting outburst.

Draco Malfoy's terrified expression as Voldemort forces him to torture the Death Eater is particularly revealing to Harry, forcing him to see Draco differently. Draco is genuinely repulsed and sickened by inflicting harm on another, just as he was when Voldemort ordered him to murder Dumbledore in *Harry Potter and the Half-Blood Prince*, a task he was unable to perform and which was ultimately executed by Snape. It would appear that Draco can never overcome his fear and revulsion to violence, and now realizes that being a Death Eater entails far more than he ever imagined. Despite Draco's bullying arrogance and cruel personality, he lacks his family's truly evil nature. This will likely endanger Draco's life even further if Voldemort considers him too weak and fearful a servant, although that is probably why Voldemort recruited him, wanting to punish Lucius Malfoy for his failures.

Harry is also repulsed by violence, and, despite Lupin's earlier admonishment, Harry continually attempts to avoid killing as a defense, even against those trying to murder him and his friends. Murder damages a soul, and we have learned that Dumbledore went to some lengths to keep Draco's soul intact. Can Harry, the series' hero, be sentenced to have his soul so damaged? It may be that Harry, Hermione, and Ron, to retain their souls' integrity, must complete the series without killing anyone. By the same token, when a good character is seen apparently killing an evil one, it will be to defend a third party; presumably, it being a defensive act will nullify or prevent the soul being damaged.

QUESTIONS

1. Why did the Trio immediately Disapparate from the wedding reception when Death Eaters were approaching, rather than standing and fighting? Was this the wiser choice?
2. Why would Harry choose to hide at Grimmauld Place, whose location Snape, a Secret Keeper, can reveal to Voldemort and other Death Eaters?
3. Why did the Trio spare the Death Eaters' lives in the café? What does this say about tbe Trio's characters and how they react when faced with life or death warfare?
4. Should the Trio have killed the Death Eaters? Did not killing them make any difference?
5. How did Arthur Weasley know to send his Patronus to Grimmauld Place to update the Trio?
6. If the Ministry Trace is no longer on Harry, how might the Death Eaters have found the Trio so fast?
7. Why would Draco Malfoy, now a Death Eater and Voldemort's servant, appear petrified in Harry's vision?

GREATER PICTURE

Escaping to Grimmauld Place is riskier than Hermione and Harry seem to think. As mentioned, Snape could have told Death Eaters about the house and how to enter it. In fact, the Trio will notice that it may have been searched by Death Eaters, and they will soon learn that Death Eaters are keeping Grimmauld Place under constant surveillance, even though the house's exact location remains unseen to them, indicating they have not been instructed on how to enter it. For now, the Trio seems assured they will remain safe and undetected there.

Harry, Ron, and Hermione were tracked by Hermione uttering Voldemort's name, which will be revealed later to be tabooed. Voldemort knows most people fear his name and has probably cultivated the belief that bad consequences result by speaking it. Following his return to power, the only ones who now dare to utter his name are those fighting him, specifically the Order of the Phoenix, and Harry, in particular; knowing that, Voldemort cast a spell on his name—anyone speaking it immediately alerts Death Eaters. Ironically, it is Hermione, who most feared speaking Voldemort's name, who does so in Tottenham Court, alerting the Death Eaters. Also, whether the effect of breaking protective spells, that we see later in this book, is already in place, is unknown.

Harry's reluctance to engage in killing, even during a war, will continue, and, throughout the book, he will never kill anyone. He has even been reluctant to use the Cruciatus curse on his enemies, although this will change under a specific circumstance. And on that occasion, unlike when he attacked Draco the previous year with the Sectumsempra spell, Harry will suffer no regrets or guilt afterwards, and he was motivated to defend someone close to him.

Chapter 10: Kreacher's Tale

SYNOPSIS

Harry awakens in the early hours, pondering the daunting task Albus Dumbledore gave him and the tales about Albus's young life. Bored, he explores the mansion. On the second landing, the room previously used by Ron and Harry has been searched, presumably by Death Eaters. Sirius Black's room on the next floor has also been searched, and, amid the mess, Harry finds stray sheets of paper, including a handwritten letter from his mother to Sirius thanking him for the broomstick he gave Harry for his first birthday. There is also a photo that shows baby Harry riding the broomstick, although Lily's image has been torn away. The letter's second page is missing, but the first one mentions Bathilda Bagshot, a famous wizard historian who often visits, and that Dumbledore borrowed James Potter's Invisibility Cloak. The letter ends halfway through Lily's sentence saying that she is, *surprised that Dumbledore . . .* Harry searches unsuccessfully for the second page.

Hermione enters, and Harry shows her what he found. He immediately wants to go to Godric's Hollow to meet Bathilda Bagshot and ask about his parents and the Dumbledore family, but Hermione discourages this. As they head down the stairs, Harry notices a sign on a room with Regulus Black's full name; it matches the initials R.A.B. on the note found inside the fake Locket Horcrux. Convinced it must be the same person, Hermione calls Ron. She opens the locked door, and they hunt for Slytherin's Locket, but find nothing. Hermione suddenly remembers seeing a locket in the drawing room when it was being cleaned during their previous stay. Harry recalls that no one was able to open it, and it was tossed it away, along with the soporific music box and Wartcap powder. Harry suspects that Kreacher, the Black family House-elf who was continually retrieving discarded items, may have hidden it in his kitchen cupboard. They rush to the kitchen, but the Locket is not there.

Harry summons Kreacher, who says that Mundungus Fletcher stole the Locket and also tells them about his old master, Regulus Black. When Voldemort required a House-elf, Regulus gave him Kreacher. Voldemort took him to a lake and forced him to drink a potion that made him think horrible thoughts. Voldemort put a locket into the empty basin and refilled it with more potion. Kreacher, abandoned and in misery, crawled to the lake's shore to drink and was pulled under the surface. However, Kreacher returned to his master as he had been ordered to. Regulus, who finally rejected Voldemort's beliefs, apparently learned that the Locket was a Horcrux and had Kreacher take him to where it was hidden. He ordered Kreacher to force him to drink all the potion, and, once the basin was emptied, replace the real Locket with a fake one. Kreacher was then to take and destroy the real Locket. Regulus drank all the potion in the basin, then went to the water's edge to drink and was pulled under by Inferi. Kreacher took the Locket, but was unable to destroy it. Because Regulus had ordered Kreacher never to reveal anything to his family, Kreacher alone knew Regulus' fate. And here, Kreacher, distraught over failing his master, bursts into sobs.

Harry, though he remains upset at the role Kreacher played in Sirius' death, is bothered more by Voldemort exploiting Kreacher. Hermione says House-elves are used to brutal treatment, so he never resented how Voldemort abused him. Also, from Kreacher's perspective, Sirius betrayed the Black family by leaving home. The Trio's next step is finding the Locket. Harry wins Kreacher's allegiance by telling him that their mission is to destroy the Locket, as Regulus wanted. When he gives Kreacher the substitute locket left in the basin, Kreacher is so overcome by being given a Black family heirloom that it takes over half an hour for him to calm down. Harry then orders the elf to fetch Mundungus. Kreacher Disapparates to find him.

ANALYSIS

This chapter is particularly revealing regarding the Trio's Horcrux quest, although Harry's relationship to Number 12, Grimmauld Place, the house he inherited from Sirius Black, should also be examined. While the house provides the Trio a safe haven, and Harry was happy here during his brief visits with Sirius, he does not consider it home, nor does he now find it comforting; instead, its murky, decaying interior is filled with sad reminders of Harry's lost godfather who endured his own unhappy childhood there. Like the fugitive Sirius, who was long confined inside while hiding from the Ministry, Harry finds the residence to be as much a grim prison as it is a protective refuge. Even its name reflects its bleakness. The Trio must also contend with Kreacher, the belligerent House-elf Harry also inherited, and the fanatical Mrs. Black's screaming portrait. As depressing as Grimmauld Place might be, however, for now, it is secure and comfortable. And apparating there has also yielded a fortuitous, if unexpected, result: a clue leading to a Horcrux.

Although many readers correctly guessed his identity, one of the most intriguing mysteries in the series, who is R.A.B., is finally definitively solved. Regulus Arcturus Black is arguably the most important *unseen* character in the series. Like Draco Malfoy, Regulus quickly learned that being a Death Eater required far more unpleasantness than he had ever imagined or was capable of providing. And once recruited, there is no leaving the Dark Lord's service alive. Unable to escape with his life, Regulus instead devised the plan to steal what he clearly believed to be Voldemort's single Horcrux, knowing he would be killed in the process, but dying in the belief that he had outwitted the Dark Lord.

More is also learned about Regulus' and Kreacher's characters, their relationship with each other, to Voldemort, and what motivated them. Until now, the fanatically faithful Black family House-elf has been seen only as a rather nasty and unpleasant servant who is forced by circumstance to serve Harry, and who, if possible, would probably use any means to expose him to Voldemort. Not only does Kreacher's story explain how Regulus recovered the Locket Horcrux, but it also spotlights the callous ill-treatment the wizarding world inflicts upon enslaved House-elves, and what little regard there is for their well-being or personal rights. Harry remains conflicted over Kreacher, angry that he betrayed Sirius to Voldemort, but also sympathetic to how the House-elf was exploited by the Dark Lord. Hermione explains that House-elves expect to be mistreated, and Harry comes to understand that they are hapless pawns, often abused and misused at their master's discretion. The name "Kreacher" implies that he and other House-elves are considered as little more than domesticated animals, albeit intelligent talking ones. Although he appears to be a despicable, inconsolable (and half-mad) wretch, Kreacher's character has been shaped by the maltreatment heaped on him over the years, and by the strain of his being prevented from revealing anything about Regulus' death, probably coupled with remorse for being involved in it, and having been unable to follow his Master's final orders. Like many wizards, Sirius also treated the House-elf poorly, although their mutual loathing was a factor. Under Harry's continued kind, gentle treatment, however, it is possible that Kreacher could be transformed. As something of a side light, here, we should note Kreacher's return to his master. After being pulled under the lake by the Inferi, Kreacher had "come back." He does not explain, he simply says he had returned to his master. It is a fair supposition that he had used the House-elf form of Apparation to do so, and perhaps it is just something that he naturally does and therefore has no name for it. We already have seen that House-elves can Apparate within Hogwarts, where Apparation is normally prevented by the school's protective charms. We can assume that Voldemort has prevented Apparation in the Horcrux cave to force any would-be thieves into running the gantlet of the lake and the Inferi, but equally clearly he has failed to prevent House-elves from Apparating in the cave. Whether this is an oversight on Voldemort's part, which would support his discounting non-Human magic, or whether it is simply impossible for human spell-casters to prevent elf Apparation, we do not know.

Lily's letter to Sirius Black is a typical thank-you note and unlikely contained anything important to Death Eaters. That makes it even more intriguing as to why only its second half is missing; what remains provides useful information for Harry, however. Lily mentions the elderly Bathilda Bagshot, a famous wizard historian, who Lily apparently knew well, and who knows much about the Dumbledore clan. Harry immediately wants to go to Godric's Hollow, not only to meet Bathilda and learn more about Dumbledore and his family from her, but also to see his birthplace. Hermione vetoes this, arguing that it is unrelated to their mission, too dangerous, and she suspects Voldemort may have set a trap there. Hermione instead encourages Harry to trust his own feelings and memories about Dumbledore, rather than believing malicious rumors and unsubstantiated innuendos spread by Ron's Aunt Muriel, Rita Skeeter, and others.

The letter also reveals that Dumbledore borrowed James' Invisibility Cloak, although for what purpose is still unknown. This is designed to remind us that Dumbledore had this Cloak in his possession when James died, and perhaps to pique the reader's curiosity as to why he might have wanted it. The letter is also significant in that it is probably the first time Harry has seen his mother's handwriting or read her own words. For Harry, who has tended to identify with his father more than his mother, it awakens new-found feelings that tie him closer to her.

Questions

Review 1. Harry wants to meet with Bathilda Bagshot to learn more about Dumbledore. Who else might have been interested in talking to Bathilda about him and why?
2. Why does Hermione tell Harry to rely on his own memories about Dumbledore, rather than what others have to say?
3. How has Kreacher's behavior toward Harry changed? What might account for this?
4. Why didn't Kreacher destroy the Locket Horcrux? Given what is known about Horcruxes and Elf magic, could he have destroyed it?
5. Why is Harry both judgmental and sympathetic to Kreacher? What is Hermione's explanation and do Ron and Harry agree?

Extra Study 1. Why would only the second page of Lily's letter's and her image from the photo be missing? Who might have taken them and why?
2. What could Harry learn about his parents and Dumbledore from talking to Bathilda Bagshot? Would her revelations be any more truthful, accurate, or unbiased than anyone else's?
3. Why does Hermione advise Harry against going to Godric's Hollow or talking to Bathilda Bagshot? Should Harry listen to her advice? Explain.
4. Harry suspects Death Eaters searched Grimmauld Place. Why might that assumption be wrong? Who might have searched it and why?
5. How did Regulus Black know that the Locket was a Horcrux? Why was he willing to forfeit his life to destroy it?
6. Kreacher says the potion he was forced to drink made him think horrible thoughts. What might those thoughts have been?

Greater Picture

The missing half of Lily's letter is significant, although not in the way readers might expect. It will be revealed that it and the photo were taken by Snape, who apparently took them for personal reasons rather than because it contained any vital information relating to Voldemort or Dumbledore.

Kreacher being able to easily Apparate in and out of Voldemort's highly secure sea cave demonstrates how elf magic differs from Wizards. This ability, which we have seen several times in Hogwarts now, will be seen again in a later chapter when Dobby rescues the imprisoned Trio and several others by Apparating into a magically protected area. Also, Hermione's fears about Godric's Hollow will prove to be well-founded, although it will later be her idea to go there.

Chapter 11: The Bribe

SYNOPSIS

Three days pass and Kreacher is still gone, while dark figures, apparently Death Eaters, are constantly outside watching Grimmauld Place. While the Trio await Kreacher's return, the tension strains their nerves. Tiring of Ron and Hermione's bickering, Harry heads for the kitchen, hoping Kreacher will reappear there. Halfway down the stairs, he hears a tap on the front door, then metallic clinks and the grinding of the chain. Harry draws his wand as a cloaked figure enters. As Dumbledore's moldering form rushes at him, the mysterious stranger calls out, "It was not I who killed you, Albus," causing Dumbledore to crumble back into dust. Harry, aiming his wand, shouts, "Don't move!" causing the curtains on Mrs. Black's portrait to fly open. Her screeching insults bring Ron and Hermione running from upstairs. A voice yells, "Hold your fire, it's me, Remus!" Hermione redirects her wand at the screaming portrait, Ron lowers his wand in relief, and after further convincing, Harry is finally persuaded it really is Lupin and lowers his wand. Lupin, speaking as their Defence Against the Dark Arts teacher, reprimands Ron and Hermione for lowering their wands too soon. Lupin confirms that Death Eaters are monitoring the house, although they apparently are unaware anyone is there. Any place associated with Harry is being watched. They descend to the kitchen where, over butterbeer, Lupin updates them on recent events. He is stunned about the Death Eaters at Tottenham Court Road, although he assures Harry it is impossible that the Trace is still active, confirming Ron's statement. Lupin reports that most wedding guests Disapparated to safety, and that Death Eaters have infiltrated the Ministry. Mr. Weasley heard a rumour that Scrimgeour was tortured before being killed, but he apparently never revealed Harry's location. Death Eaters searched the Burrow and found the Spattergroit ghoul, but avoided getting too close; everyone else at the Burrow was interrogated for hours. Although Death Eaters forced their way into other Order-related houses, no one has been killed, but some, like the Tonks, were tortured. Death Eaters were able to penetrate the magical charms surrounding the Burrow because they now have the Ministry's might behind them. Asked how they can legally justify their search, Lupin pulls out a *Daily Prophet*. On the front page is Harry's picture and the headline: WANTED FOR QUESTIONING ABOUT THE DEATH OF ALBUS DUMBLEDORE.

Harry pushes the paper aside. Lupin says the Ministry claims that the murdered Scrimgeour actually resigned. He was replaced by Pius Thicknesse, who Lupin says is under the Imperius curse. This effectively makes Voldemort the Minister for Magic. Although many wizards suspect what is happening in the Ministry, none dares to speak out, fearing reprisals and unsure who to trust. Voldemort remains hidden to create fear and confusion. While Dumbledore's death was certain to make Harry the rallying point for resistance fighters, implicating him in Dumbledore's murder has cast doubt. Lupin also says the Ministry is rounding up Muggle-borns, claiming they acquired their magical powers by theft. Anyone without at least one close wizard relative is suspect. In addition, wizard children can no longer study magic at home or abroad, but only at Hogwarts, although this is only a means to further weed out Muggle-borns—to attend Hogwarts, you must be able to prove Blood status.

Lupin says the Order suspects Dumbledore assigned Harry a secret mission, which Harry confirms without confiding any details other than it also involves Ron and Hermione. Lupin offers his assistance, even if they are unable to share what they are doing. When asked about Tonks, Lupin says she will be fine at her parents house. Hermione suspects he is withholding something, and he reveals that Tonks is expecting a baby. Harry chastises him for abandoning his pregnant wife, but Lupin claims she is better off without him and that she should never have married an outcast. He fears their child will be a werewolf like him, and even if it is not, he is an unfit father. Outraged that he would desert his family, Harry shouts that Lupin is a coward. Lupin, offended, rages out the front door, ignoring Hermione's pleas to stay. Hermione, supported by Ron, reproaches Harry, who now feels bad over how he treated Lupin, but still feels he was right.

Ignoring Ron and Hermione, Harry browses the *Prophet*. Dumbledore's name jumps out at him, along with a photo of the entire Dumbledore family: Percival, Kendra, Albus and Aberforth, and baby Ariana. There is also a headline: EXCLUSIVE EXTRACT FROM THE UPCOMING BIOGRAPHY OF ALBUS DUMBLEDORE by Rita Skeeter. The article describes Kendra as proud and haughty. After her husband's imprisonment in Azkaban, she moved the family to Godric's Hollow, Harry Potter's former home, where few knew them. Skeeter claims that Kendra thought she could hide Ariana, who was believed to be a Squib. The article concludes with, Next Week: Albus Dumbledore at Hogwarts—the Prizes and the Pretense.

Kreacher suddenly returns with a flailing Mundungus Fletcher, who attempts to use his wand. Hermione disarms him, and Ron wrestles him to the floor. After some encouragement from Kreacher wielding a pot, Mundungus says he used the Locket to bribe a Ministry woman who caught him selling goods without a license. The woman was short, wearing a hair bow, and looking rather like a "toad." Harry, Ron, and Hermione exchange shocked expressions; the old scars on Harry's hand begin to prickle.

Analysis

One must wonder somewhat about the Death Eater interest in the house at Grimmauld Place. It is clearly under surveillance, though no apparent attempt is made to enter it. Clearly the Death Eaters believe that some Order member, possibly Harry, may be hiding inside, although it is learned later that any place associated with Harry is being watched. We already know that Severus Snape is a Secret-Keeper for the house's location; if it is believed that Harry may be in the house, why does Snape not reveal the secret to a Death Eater squad so they could enter and ransack the place? If Snape is reluctant, why does Voldemort not order Snape to reveal the secret? If, however, Snape attempted to enter Grimmauld Place after the Order of the Phoenix left, Mad Eye Moody's Tongue-tying Curse that greeted the Trio at the front entrance may be preventing Snape from divulging its location. Although Harry's reaction to Lupin seems undeservedly harsh, he immediately saw Lupin's offer as a thinly-veiled excuse to leave Tonks, believing that he is an unfit husband and father and that she deserves someone better. Having lost his own parents and godfather, being raised in a loveless household, and left feeling betrayed and set adrift by Dumbledore, Harry is infuriated that Lupin would abandon his pregnant wife in such desperate times and allow their unborn child to be raised without a father. This is particularly infuriating as Lupin, despite being a werewolf, has risked his own life serving in the Order of the Phoenix fighting Voldemort and his Death Eaters, is always loyal to his friends, and has exerted a significant positive influence on Harry and many other students while he was a teacher at Hogwarts. Lupin, like so many others when they appraise themselves, apparently fails to consider this, and, despite loving Tonks, instead feels that his outcast status in the wizarding world far outweighs his sterling attributes and his responsibilities as a husband and father. Lupin leaves Grimmauld Place in a rage, and he and Harry seem permanently divided, but Harry's outburst will deeply affect him. Harry is also affected by their confrontation. And though Harry now regrets over-reacting to Lupin, he remains convinced he is right.

Harry is also deeply affected by Rita Skeeter's book excerpt. Again discovering how little he knew about Dumbledore, Harry is confused by these revelations of Dumbledore's past, and his family's behaviour, and wonders how the Dumbledore he knew could have come from the past Skeeter describes. Harry is particularly dismayed to discover how far Kendra Dumbledore seemed willing to go to conceal her daughter Ariana.

The Trio have no doubt that the "toad" woman is none other than Ministry official Dolores Umbridge. Although they have located the Locket Horcrux, they must now devise a plan to retrieve it from her—an extremely difficult and dangerous undertaking. It is unclear yet if she knows the Locket's significance.

Questions

Review 1. How did Lupin know where to find the Trio? How did he enter Grimmauld Place undetected by the ever-present Death Eaters?

2. Why does Lupin offer to help with the Trio's mission?

3. Why does Harry call Lupin a coward, even though Lupin is willing to risk his life to help with their mission?

Extra Study 1. If Death Eaters and Snape, who is a Secret Keeper, previously searched Grimmauld Place as Harry suspects, why are they unwilling or unable to enter it now?

2. Harry, and we, are certain that the Ministry woman that Mundungus Fletcher described is Dolores Umbridge. Is it possible she knows what the Locket is?

3. How can the Trio be so certain that the "toad woman" Mundungus Fletcher describes is actually Dolores Umbridge.

Greater Picture

Although Lupin is deeply angered and offended by Harry's outburst, it will cause him to return to Tonks and, eventually, to realize that he is indeed a fit husband and father. Lupin later asks Harry to be godfather to his newborn son, indicating that their relationship has healed.

It is almost certain that Umbridge is absolutely oblivious to the Locket's status. To her, it is only a heavy, ornate locket with an inlaid S, which she is unable to open. She would never suspect that it might be a Slytherin relic; having extorted it from a petty grifter on the streets, it cannot be much more than a cheap trinket, certainly not an artifact worth thousands of Galleons. And Horcruxes, being a mechanism for a person's immortality, would certainly be carefully protected and unavailable for sale on a street corner. We will see later that Umbridge uses the Locket as a prop to bolster her claim that she is related to the Selwyn family, on strength of the inlaid S.

Chapter 12: Magic is Might

Synopsis

August passes, and, each day, several mysterious strangers, always different, lurk outside Number Twelve, Grimmauld Place. On September 1st, the day students return to Hogwarts, at least half a dozen men in long, dark cloaks appear, watching outside the house. The Trio, meanwhile, has been taking turns spying on the Ministry of Magic under the Invisibility Cloak to learn its operations and routines. Returning under his Cloak, Harry Apparates onto Grimmauld's front stoop, landing badly, and worries that his elbow was momentarily exposed. A nearby lurker seems to have glimpsed something, then appears uncertain and relaxes. Safely inside, Harry heads to the kitchen, which is nearly unrecognizable due to Kreacher's cleaning efforts. Proudly wearing the Black heirloom locket Harry gave him, Kreacher fusses over him, promising dinner will be ready soon. Ron and Hermione, sitting at the kitchen table, are poring over copious notes and hand-drawn maps. Harry hands them a *Daily Prophet* he pinched, warning them it contains bad news. The headline reads: SEVERUS SNAPE CONFIRMED AS HOGWARTS HEADMASTER. Picturing Snape in Dumbledore's office, Hermione suddenly jumps up and runs from the kitchen.

The article reports that Alecto and Amycus Carrow have been appointed as the new Muggle Studies and Dark Arts instructors. Harry recognizes the Carrows' photos: they are the Death Eaters who were atop the Astronomy Tower the night Dumbledore was murdered. Ron and Harry believe the other teachers will remain at the school only to protect the students, although Harry also thinks they probably have little choice—with the Ministry and Voldemort behind Snape, it is either stay at Hogwarts or be sent to Azkaban. Harry mentions the more than usual Death Eaters outside; it is almost as if they are expecting them to march off, lugging their trunks, to King's Cross station to catch the Hogwarts Express. As Kreacher serves hot soup, Harry comments that at least they now know where Severus Snape is.

Hermione returns lugging Phineas Nigellus Black's empty portrait; she somehow stuffs it into her beaded carrying bag. If Snape sends Phineas from his Hogwarts' portrait to Grimmauld Place, she explains, he will be unable to see or hear anything from inside the bag. When Harry mentions he saw, "a bloke in navy-blue robes," at the Ministry that day, Ron off-handedly remarks that Magical Maintenance wears navy blue robes. Hermione chastises him for not revealing that sooner, although Ron, whose father works at the Ministry, has already provided much helpful information. Hermione stresses that every minute Ministry detail is important: the staff, layout, routines, uniforms, and so on; their lives may depend on it. Harry interrupts to say that they should do it tomorrow, they know enough, and it is too dangerous to wait any longer, although both Ron and Hermione look frightened. Harry says Umbridge may have already chucked out the Locket. They have been watching for four weeks, and it is unlikely they will learn more—it is time to infiltrate the Ministry of Magic.

Harry suddenly excuses himself to go to the bathroom, but pain is shooting through his scar. Grasping the wash basin, he sees himself gliding down a twilit street lined with gabled houses in some unknown European village. A door cracks opens and a high-pitched voice asks for Gregorovitch. A foreign woman insists he has moved. A wand raises, followed by a green flash. Hermione's urgent voice interrupts his vision, and, slumped on the floor, Harry gets up and unlocks the door. Despite Harry claiming nothing is wrong, Ron and Hermione insist they heard him cry out. Harry admits he saw Voldemort murdering a woman and her family. Hermione is upset that Harry refuses to block out Voldemort using Occlumency, but Harry believes knowing his actions is useful. Voldemort is hunting Gregorovitch, the foreign wand maker who crafted Viktor Krum's wand. Ron wonders why he wants another wand maker, considering he has Ollivander locked up. Harry speculates that Voldemort may believe that Gregorovitch can explain why his wand failed against Harry's. Late into the night, they review their plan to invade the Ministry.

The next morning over coffee and hot rolls, Hermione reviews what they need: robes, tokens, Polyjuice Potion, Invisibility Cloak, Decoy Detonators, Puking Pastilles, Nosebleed Nougats, Extendable Ears . . . Kreacher promises steak and kidney pie when they return. In turns, they Disapparate under the Invisibility Cloak, arriving in an alleyway near the Ministry. As the first Ministry workers begin arriving, Hermione stuns one, a woman named Mafalda Hopkirk. After plucking a few hairs off the unconscious woman, Hermione drinks the Polyjuice Potion. After some trickery, Ron and Harry also find employees to impersonate. Ron becomes a maintenance worker named Reg Cattermole, although Harry does not yet know his own identity. Entering an underground public restroom with other employees, they insert tokens into cubicle doors and step into toilets that flush them dry into the Ministry of Magic's Atrium.

The Atrium has changed since Harry's last visit. It is darker, and the central golden fountain has been replaced by a frightening statue with a witch and wizard seated upon ornately carved thrones depicting writhing nude and ugly-faced men, women, and children. Harry is bumped by a man calling him Runcorn. His subservient tone indicates that Runcorn is a high official. A Death Eater named Yaxley approaches Ron (as Cattermole) and orders him to attend to the rain in his office. Before striding off, Yaxley makes threats about Cattermole's wife who is appearing before the Muggle-Born Registration Commission that day. In a lift (elevator) Hermione whispers hints to Ron for fixing the indoor-weather problem before he heads to Yaxley's office on Level Two. The lift moves again and stops at Level One. The doors slide open, and a squat, toad-like witch wearing a velvet bow in her hair steps in.

ANALYSIS

In this chapter and the next, readers can see how fear and suspicion have permeated the wizarding world and the way in which Voldemort exploits that to seize control. By gradually infiltrating wizard institutions such as the Ministry of Magic, falsifying scientific research, and manipulating the media (*The Daily Prophet*) to disseminate propaganda, Voldemort was able to implement his plan to eliminate blood traitors and Muggle-borns like Hermione, who are accused of acquiring their magic by having stolen it from other wizards. Many Death Eaters and other Voldemort sympathizers (mostly Slytherins) already worked at the Ministry, making its takeover relatively easy. As a result, new laws and regulations are constantly being enacted, and all wizards must now register to prove their magical lineage; any known or suspected Muggle-borns are interrogated and separated from their families, their eventual fates uncertain. Intimidation, coercion, spying, and threat tactics are also employed to suppress opposition, while corrupt, ambitious bureaucrats like Dolores Umbridge, although not Death Eaters, willingly help spearhead the Dark Lord's evil rise to power to benefit themselves. Meanwhile, Voldemort deliberately remains elusive to create doubt and confusion among the general wizarding population and to avoid giving his enemies a specific target to rally against. Even Hogwarts has fallen victim, and every wizard child must now attend only that school. This will enable Death Eaters to indoctrinate impressionable young minds to Voldemort's depraved beliefs, as well as provide a convenient mechanism to identify and cull Muggle-borns.

It also appears that Voldemort's grandiose scheme may include conquering the Muggle realm, if the new statue in the Ministry of Magic atrium is any indication. The monument, like the previously destroyed "Fountain of Magical Brethren," appears to represent the Ministry's new public mission. The figures, a magical family seated on thrones made of struggling Muggles, reveals how much control Voldemort has gained over the Wizarding realm and how little, if any, concern he and the Ministry now has for Muggles' welfare. Indeed, the statue can be interpreted as Wizards conquering and suppressing Muggles.

Any reader doubting that one individual can attain the power to convert an entire state to their perverted political design need only to draw parallels between Voldemort's Muggle-born persecution and Adolph Hitler's extermination of six million Jews and other so-called "undesirables" in Nazi Germany during the mid-20th century. Both movements were driven by a maniacal but charismatic dictator who, exploiting the masses' anxieties and prejudices, advocated an elitist, ruling class and purging their order of "racially impure" citizens who were blamed for causing most social, political, and economic ills.

When Hermione learns that Snape is the new Hogwarts Headmaster, she immediately stuffs Phineas' portrait into her bag to prevent him from spying on them and relaying any information to Snape via his other portrait in the Headmaster's office, although he has had ample time to have already done that. At this point, Phineas' allegiance is unclear, and although he has always appeared loyal to Dumbledore in the past, that is no guide to the current situation. It is likely that Phineas' loyalty will have changed with the new Headmaster, as the portraits, we heard earlier, are supposed to be loyal to "the Headmaster of Hogwarts," which Snape now is. It is also possible, though less likely, that Phineas' loyalty to Dumbledore was false; Phineas certainly seemed, on occasion, reluctant to take instructions from Dumbledore. Indeed, if Phineas is Dumbledore's ally, it would seem that he should have relayed helpful information from Dumbledore's Hogwarts portrait to the Trio at Grimmauld Place, although that apparently has not occurred. Dumbledore seems to have deliberately withheld information from the Trio that would aid their mission, and his portrait may be doing the same, although just why is unclear.

Phineas may have already informed Snape that the Trio are in residence at Grimmauld Place. However, if he has, that information does not appear to have been relayed to Voldemort. Even though Death Eaters are constantly watching outside, they seem uncertain as to whether the Trio is actually within, though perhaps what they are actually unsure of is where exactly the house is.

QUESTIONS

Review 1. What accounts for Kreacher's changed behavior towards the Trio? Can he now be trusted? 2. What does the new statue in the Ministry of Magic atrium represent?

Further Study 1. Hermione wants Harry to block Voldemort's thoughts by using Occlumency, while Harry wants to keep the channel open. Which is the better choice and why?
2. How do you think the Trio expect to recover the Locket after entering the Ministry? Where is Umbridge likely to keep the Locket?
3. In addition to recovering the Locket, what additional information can the Trio gather while at the Ministry that would be useful for their mission?
4. What comparisons can be made to Voldemort's persecution of Muggle-born wizards and historical events from mid-20th century Europe?

GREATER PICTURE

As we know, Harry's apparent utter inability (or stubborn refusal) to learn Occlumency was a contributing factor in the events leading to his godfather Sirius' death. However, it is this same failure, we believe, which now allows Harry to view some events occurring in Voldemort's life; Harry already senses their value to the Trio's mission, despite the physical pain it causes, and he is therefore resistant to Hermione's repeated pleas that he practice Occlumency to block them. Later, it is revealed that Voldemort will largely lose control over his skill at Legilimency and Occlumency, at least as far as Harry is concerned. After possessing Harry's mind once before and finding it a disturbing experience, Voldemort never attempts to enter it again; Harry, however, will eventually be able to penetrate Voldemort's mind almost at will and, apparently, without Voldemort's knowledge. By reading Voldemort's thoughts, Harry later uncovers vital information that will help destroy the Horcruxes.

Although Hermione stuffs Phineas Nigellus' portrait into her magical bag to prevent him spying on the Trio, she fails to consider that he may still be able to hear them. When Hermione accidentally leaves the bag open in a later chapter, Phineas overhears some vital information that he relays to Severus Snape, although this will actually aid the Trio. Phineas will also provide the Trio with helpful updates regarding Hogwarts, although it remains unknown which side, if any, Phineas is actually on.

Chapter 13: The Muggle-Born Registration Commission

SYNOPSIS

Dolores Umbridge immediately assumes that Hermione, as she appears to be Mafalda Hopkirk, was sent by Travers to record the hearings she is holding. She tells the Minister that with Mafalda recording, they can start right away, which is good, there are ten today, and one of them the wife of a Ministry employee.

Chapter 13: The Muggle-Born Registration Commission

Harry watches as Hermione descends in the elevator with Umbridge. When Thicknesse asks what brings "Albert" to the first floor, Harry says that he needs a word with Arthur Weasley, who he was told was on that floor.

On his own, now, Harry dons the Invisibility Cloak, stooping to hide his feet, and prowls the halls searching for Umbridge's office. Harry, Ron, and Hermione had meticulously planned how to get into the Ministry, but they failed to consider the possibility of getting separated. Now Hermione is stuck in what will probably be a full day of court proceedings while Ron is trying to stop it raining in Yaxley's office. Bemused, Harry stumbles into an open area where he sees pink sheets of paper flying around from desk to desk. The pages are being assembled into pamphlets. Examining one under the Cloak, he finds that the pamphlets are anti-"Mudblood" propaganda. A witch makes a rude comment about their boss, indicating a door. Harry sees Moody's magical eye, affixed to the door and pointing fixedly upwards. Under it is a brass plaque reading *Dolores Umbridge, Senior Undersecretary to the Minister*, and beneath that, another reading *Head of the Muggle-born Registration Commission*. Although busy with their pamphlets, the office staff would surely notice a door opening on its own. Harry sets a Decoy Detonator free; it explodes on the far side of the room emitting a large, black smoke cloud. While everyone is looking for the smoke source, Harry enters Umbridge's office, finding it exactly like her Hogwarts office, with the horribly cute kitten plates on the wall and the lace doilies on the desks. Looking through the small telescope on the inside of the door, he sees everyone is gathered around the Decoy Detonator's remains; he wrenches the telescope from the door, removes Moody's eye, and pockets it. He tries Summoning the Locket, without success. Searching Umbridge's office, he finds a file on Arthur Weasley, who is listed as a pure-blood, but is likely to be contacted by "Undesireable Number One," Harry himself. Arthur is also being Tracked. The search is otherwise fruitless, but taking one last look around the office, Harry sees Dumbledore looking at him from a small mirror. Upon closer inspection, the mirror is actually a book: *The Life and Lies of Albus Dumbledore* by Rita Skeeter. Flipping it open, he sees is a picture of two teenagers, but before reading the caption, the office door opens. Pius Thicknesse enters and writes a note to Umbridge; Harry exits, unseen under the Cloak, passing the pamphlet witches who are still investigating the Decoy Detonator, and returns to the lift. He must now find Ron, get down to the courtrooms, and collect Hermione; it seems unlikely the Locket is here. Luckily, as the lift reaches the second floor, Ron steps in; before they can exchange more than greetings, though, the lift stops again and Arthur Weasley and a blonde witch get on, deep in conversation. Arthur shoots Harry a distasteful look, but gives Ron advice about a spell that might work on Yaxley's office. On the next floor, Ron and the blonde witch get off, but Harry is blocked by Percy Weasley getting on, and is unable to follow. Percy, looking up from his reading, suddenly realizing his father is there, and gets out on the next floor. Harry tries to follow, but is blocked by Mr. Weasley, who makes accusations that he planted information about Dirk Cresswell. When Harry tells Arthur that he is being Tracked, Arthur considers it a threat. Arthur exits on the Atrium level, and Harry puts the Invisibility Cloak back on. He will have to extricate Hermione while Ron is stopping the rain.

Heading to the courtrooms, Harry recognizes the unnatural chill created by Dementors; the creatures are guarding Muggle-born witches and wizards waiting outside the courtroom. A wizard is led from the courtrooms by two Dementors. Mary Cattermole is then called in by Umbridge, and Harry follows her. Inside, two Dementors are held at bay by a cat Patronus, and Umbridge, Hermione (as Mafalda), and Yaxley, are examining Cattermole, demanding to know whose wand she stole. As Umbridge leans forward, the Locket around her neck swings out. Taking a chance, Hermione asks about it; Umbridge claims the S initial is for Selwyn, a very old Wizarding family she is honoured to be related to. This is too much for Harry, who Stuns Umbridge, and, before he can react, Yaxley. Prompted by Hermione, Harry casts a Patronus, just in time to save Mary Cattermole. He tries, twice, to release the chains on Mary, while Hermione creates a duplicate Locket to replace the real one. Escorted by Harry and Hermione's Patronuses, the three leave the courtrooms. Gathering the other Muggle-borns, Harry says the new official position is to disguise themselves and leave the country if possible, at the very least stay away from the Ministry; they can exit from the Atrium.

Meeting Ron at the lifts, Mary Cattermole runs to hug him, believing he is her husband, Reg. Ron warns them that the Ministry knows they are there and work crews are closing off the fireplaces. Harry says they can still escape if they hurry. At the Atrium, Harry orders the crews to stop, though one wizard protests. Harry threateningly asks if he wants his family tree examined the way Dirk Cresswell's was. Muggle-borns are sent in pairs through the remaining fireplaces, but the real Reg Cattermole appears from the lifts. Amidst his and Mary Cattermole's confusion, Yaxley appears, demanding that the fireplaces be sealed. Pointing to the wizard who questioned him, Harry says he was allowing Muggle-borns to escape. As the commotion builds, Ron and Mary Cattermole escape; as the truth dawns on Yaxley, he fires a curse at Harry exiting through the fireplace with Hermione. Arriving in the bathroom, Harry sees Yaxley appear in the cubicle behind him. Grabbing Hermione and Ron, Harry Disapparates. He briefly sees Grimmauld Place's front door, then hears a bang, and they are Apparating away.

Analysis

Once inside the Ministry, the Trio can see how extensively Voldemort's corruption and perversion has spread, and the extreme measures being implemented to separate the "racially impure" from "pure-blooded" wizard society. Anyone not directly serving Voldemort is controlled through his minions, mostly with threats and violence. It appears there is little resistance, and as Voldemort gains more power, many wizards fear for themselves or their loved ones who could be branded as "undesirables" and be incarcerated. There are still many in the general Wizarding population who are simply ignorant about what is happening, while others are fearful and/or uncertain what to believe or who to trust. Voldemort deliberately created this confusion by quietly and gradually seizing control of the Ministry and other key institutions while spreading anti-Muggle-born propaganda. He remains unseen—though his return has now been public knowledge for a year, by staying concealed he allows rumour to do his work, spreading fear and doubt. We will see later that Voldemort is reported as being in several places at once. Meanwhile, the thoroughly corrupt and reprehensible Dolores Umbridge revels in her position as Head of the Muggle-born Registration Committee. Bloated with power, she has dedicated herself to purging "impurities" from the Wizarding world, much as she did while at Hogwarts, and readily abuses her authority to persecute those deemed unworthy. From what can be seen at the hearing Umbridge is presiding over, it appears that all Muggle-borns and suspected blood traitors are being rounded up, probably to be sent to a wizard-style concentration camp for deportation, or worse, extermination.

Although the Trio successfully retrieved the Locket Horcrux, their lacking a back-up plan in the event they became separated while inside the Ministry is surprising. Randomly selecting individuals to impersonate without knowing their identities, rank, or considering that they may be called upon to perform their Ministry duties was also a careless and risky move. Hermione, especially, appears to have been rather lax in failing to anticipate this, considering her usual diligent attention to details and analyzing all likely scenarios. The Trio also were extremely lucky that Umbridge had the Locket with her on that particular day, an event that seems to have taken both Harry and Hermione somewhat by surprise. Given that, their mission's purpose into the Ministry was perhaps to try and determine where Umbridge might actually keep the Locket: for instance, to locate Umbridge's residence and then attempt to retrieve the Locket from there. It also seems that this information could have been discovered by one person alone using the Invisibility Cloak rather than all three entering the Ministry in their Polyjuice Potion disguises. If that was the plan, it is curious then that Harry never searched for Umbridge's home address while he was in her office. Being that they still lacked vital information as to the Locket's whereabouts when they infiltrated the Ministry, it is also curious as to why they put their plan into action on that particular day, although Harry seemed propelled more by an urgent need to act, rather than being completely prepared. It is also unclear how the Trio positively identified the "toad woman" as being Dolores Umbridge before they planned their assault, although, fortunately, they were correct.

Indeed, Hermione's entire plan seems unworthy, opting for a dangerously elaborate and overly complicated scheme when a simpler strategy might have been safer and more effective. Rather than infiltrating the highly-secure Ministry, the Trio may also have been able to intercept Umbridge (perhaps using the Imperius Curse) before she entered or just after she left the Ministry. Also, once determining that Umbridge wears the Locket to work, one person alone could have used the Invisibility Cloak to sneak into her office, stun her, perform a memory charm, and then remove and replace the real Locket with a substitute, just as Hermione did. Like the Trio's reluctance to use extreme defensive tactics against their enemies, their unsophisticated plan and their rather erratic performance reflects their general inexperience and still growing maturity; they may be unready to be full-fledged Order of the Phoenix members. And though it is unlikely the Order would ever have allowed the Trio to undertake such a dangerous mission, Dumbledore apparently felt only they could accomplish this. However misbegotten, chaotic, and nearly disastrous the Ministry caper may have been, it was ultimately successful and fortuitously resulted in many innocent victims being rescued. It also shows that the Trio works well together and can quickly adapt to changing circumstances.

Retrieving Moody's magical eye from Umbridge's door was also a risky and impetuous decision by Harry, but his emotions overruled his logic, and he was simply unable to leave any part of Moody in Umbridge's possession. This also provides a necessary closure for Harry, allowing him to later bury at least a small portion of Moody. One gathers that the eye's loss from the outer side of Umbridge's door will not hinder her spying on her subordinates; the eye, staring fixedly, seems to only provide camouflage for the small telescope inside the office door. Harry glimpsing Dumbledore's image in what he momentarily believed was a mirror in Umbridge's office may be a subtle reference to the familiar-looking blue eye he has been seeing in the mirror-shard, although it is unknown yet whose eye this actually is. The original magic mirror, before it was broken, was described as about the size of a small book. It is probably the combination of the size, plus Harry's half-belief that the eye in the mirror-shard is Dumbledore's, that leads him to briefly mistake the book for a mirror.

Rowling's description that Umbridge's cutesy kitten decor appears just as it did at Hogwarts may be a subtle clue that, despite Umbridge's traumatic experience with the Centaurs, readers can expect to see the same vile woman as in *Harry Potter and the Order of the Phoenix*.

QUESTIONS

Review 1. Why did Harry remove Mad-Eye Moody's magical eye from Umbridge's office? Did this help or endanger the Trio's mission?

2. How will Harry's taking the Eye affect Umbridge's job?

3. Why is Arthur Weasley being tracked? Why or why not might he have suspected this before Harry told him?

4. Why does Umbridge wear the Locket?

Extra Study   1. Why did the Trio fail to have a back-up plan in the event they became separated while inside the Ministry? What plan could they have had?

2. Hermione's plan to infiltrate the Ministry was dangerous. Devise your own plan to retrieve the Locket.

3. If Umbridge had not worn the Locket on that particular day, what would the Trio have done? Would they likely have had another chance to infiltrate the Ministry of Magic using the same plan? Explain.

4. How were Voldemort and his Death Eaters able to gain control of the Ministry of Magic, Hogwarts, and other Wizarding institutions so quickly and easily? Why has there been so little resistance?

5. Why does Voldemort remain unseen to the general public, even though it is widely known that he is alive and controls the Ministry and other institutions?

6. What might happen to Muggle-born wizards after being rounded up by the Ministry? How does this compare to historical events in mid-20th century Europe?

GREATER PICTURE

Over the next several chapters, the Trio realizes they are being affected by the Locket Horcrux as they take turns wearing it around their necks; it preys on them physically, mentally, and emotionally. The Horcrux may actually be somewhat sentient, so much so that as Ron puts his ear to the Locket, he is able to detect something akin to a "heartbeat" pulsing within it. When Harry is trying to retrieve Gryffindor's Sword to destroy the Locket with, the Horcrux, sensing danger, defends itself by attempting to strangle him. Unlike the Trio, Dolores Umbridge seems unaffected by wearing the Locket, possibly because the Locket senses she poses no threat to its existence, and she may be more closely aligned to its dark nature.

The Trio's foray into the Ministry of Magic, while ultimately successful, was nearly disastrous because they failed to consider all scenarios and lacked a back-up plan in such an event. In a later chapter, they will infiltrate another high-security Wizarding institution: Gringotts Bank. That mission will also be successful, but they will again fail to have a back-up plan, and, when things go awry, they must quickly improvise an alternate escape route. The two youths whose photo Harry briefly glimpsed in Rita Skeeter's book are the teen-aged Albus Dumbledore and Gellert Grindelwald. Harry will see the photo again in a later chapter and read not only the caption but the associated chapter of Skeeter's muck-raking book.

Chapter 14: The Thief

SYNOPSIS

Harry, Ron, and Hermione find themselves lying on the ground in a forest. At first, Harry thinks it is the Forbidden Forest at Hogwarts but quickly realizes the trees are too young. Ron's shoulder has been badly Splinched while Disapparating. Hermione has Harry summon the Essence of Dittany from her bag and partially heals Ron's injury with it, although he remains faint from shock and blood loss. Hermione Disapparated them from Grimmauld Place because Yaxley grabbed her when they Apparated to Grimmauld Place. When Yaxley slackened his grip, Hermione jinxed him, broke free, and then Apparated them all to the forest where the Quidditch World Cup was held three years previously. It is unlikely they can return to Grimmauld Place. As Hermione has been a Secret Keeper since Dumbledore's death and led Yaxley to Grimmauld Place, it is probably now known to him. Harry blames only himself for losing their hiding place, having wasted precious time to retrieve Moody's magical eye from Umbridge's office door.

Remembering that Death Eaters previously found them moments after Hermione Disapparated them to a familiar place, Harry and Ron debate whether they should stay or move on, but Ron is too weak to travel and Harry decides they will stay put. As Hermione casts the protective spells, Harry summons the tent from her bag, recognizing it as one they used at the Quidditch World Cup. When Hermione starts to speak Voldemort's name, Ron halts her, saying it feels jinxed, and requests that Harry and Hermione refrain from using it. Hermione apparently chooses not to argue with an injured Ron.

Hermione retrieves the egg-sized Locket, which bears the initial "S" inset in small green stones on its cover. Harry determines it must be opened before it can be destroyed, but it is tightly shut. Ron detects a small heartbeat within, but Harry and Hermione are uncertain if they hear anything. To keep it safe until it can be destroyed, Harry places it around his neck. He and Hermione then prepare to stand guard using Harry's Sneakoscope. Standing watch alone that night, Harry starts having awful thoughts. Rather than feeling elated over finding the Locket Horcrux, Harry feels lost, unsure how to proceed, and clueless as to how to destroy the Horcrux. Though worried about Kreacher's safety, Hermione and Harry had decided against summoning him, fearing a Death Eater may come by side-along apparation. And his scar is hurting again.

Suddenly, Harry is inside Voldemort's mind again and sees a man with a snowy white beard suspended upside down. Voldemort, addressing the man as Gregorovitch, demands something that Gregorovitch claims was stolen from him long ago. Voldemort enters Gregorovitch's memories and sees a tall, blond man who Stuns him and, laughing, exits through the window. When Voldemort kills Gregorovitch, Harry returns to himself. Hermione dismisses the notion that he was reading Voldemort's mind and insists on taking over the watch, claiming Harry is too tired. Inside the tent, where Hermione is unable to hear, Ron asks Harry what Voldemort was doing, and wonders how Gregorovitch can make a new wand for Voldemort if he is tied up. Harry relates Gregorovitch's memory about someone who stole something small from him, and thinks he has seen the man before. Ron asks if Voldemort might be trying to make another Horcrux, but based on Hermione's research, Harry thinks Voldemort's soul may be too shredded to allow that. Harry falls asleep wondering about the blond thief. With Gregorovitch gone, whoever he is, his life is in danger now.

Analysis

Harry's using magic to Summon the dittany from Hermione's bag is partly a demonstration. When the Trio fled the wedding to Tottenham Court Road, the two Death Eaters found them immediately, although Harry did not cast any magic before the Death Eaters arrived. Since then, all the magic that Harry had performed was while he was at Grimmauld Place or within the Ministry of Magic, two locations where it would be undetectable. This was the first time that he performed magic in the open. If Harry still carried the Ministry's Trace that detects underage magic, as he suspected he was, this first unprotected use of magic would have brought Death Eaters, but it did not. Therefore, there must have been some other mechanism that allowed the Death Eaters to find him.

Once again, the Trio was reluctant to inflict harm on an enemy, even under combat conditions. Other Order of the Phoenix members probably would have killed Yaxley, who Hermione believes has now become a Secret Keeper and can expose Grimmauld Place's location to Voldemort. Hermione instead opted to Disapparate the Trio to the countryside, sacrificing their hiding place rather than take a life. Apart from killing Yaxley, Hermione presumably also had the option of incapacitating him and then working a Memory Charm on him, though Hermione may be aware that Memory Charms do not seem to work well when Voldemort counters them. Hermione was responding to a chaotic and dangerous situation, however, and it may have prevented her from thinking rationally enough to consider all other options.

Hermione's reacting incorrectly under stress is seen again here. While it is almost certainly true that Yaxley is now privy to Number 12, Grimmauld Place's location, this does not automatically make him a Secret Keeper. Hermione may be over-generalizing from her own experience. It is true that having been privy to the secret, Hermione has become a Secret-Keeper herself, but that happened only because Dumbledore, the original Secret-Keeper, had died. For Yaxley to become a Secret-Keeper for the house's location at Grimmauld Place, it would be necessary for the person who revealed that secret to him to die. So long as Hermione remains alive, Yaxley can enter the house, but he is unable to reveal where it is to any other person. Snape remains far more threatening, as he is a Secret Keeper and so can freely divulge Grimmauld Place's location. The one factor that increases the risk is that Yaxley now knows that three Order members were still resident at Grimmauld Place, which might inspire Snape to reveal that secret, or cause Voldemort to require Snape to reveal it. Just why Snape has not entered the house, or shared this information with other Death Eaters so they could enter, is puzzling.

Until now, Dumbledore's quest has mainly tested the Trio's intellectual and magical prowess rather than their physical abilities. Forced to leave their cozy hiding place, they must now endure the harsh environment while on the run, coping with cold winter weather, limited food supplies, and being cut off from their allies, who, until now, at least knew their location. Losing their headquarters is a huge blow to the mission, but fortunately, Hermione was well prepared for this eventuality and has stored everything they need inside her bag. However, despite Hermione providing them with a snug tent containing a kitchen, bunks, and other necessities, it hardly compares to Grimmauld Place's amenities and Kreacher's attentive care. The hardship causes the Trio's morale to plunge to an all-time low, but for Ron, used to three hot meals a day and comfortable living conditions, it proves especially difficult. But they may have needed just such an incentive to force them into leaving Grimmauld Place and search more aggressively for the other Horcruxes, rather than sequestering themselves in an endless attempt to hypothesize what and where they might be.

While Ron may be less suited for the quest than Harry and Hermione, having grown up in the Wizarding world, he can contribute in ways they are unable to. His ability to detect a "heartbeat" within the Locket while Harry and Hermione cannot may indicate that he has far more magical ability then he ever realized. He will also become more adversely affected by close physical contact with the Locket Horcrux than the other two, although it is having an immediate effect on Harry when he first wears it. These emerging traits and this stage of the quest's hardships could be a major turning point in Ron's maturation and magical development.

Knowing that Voldemort is searching for Gregorovitch, a wandmaker, it initially seems apparent that Voldemort wants a new wand or is looking for an explanation as to why Harry's wand always defeats his own. No matter what wand Voldemort wields, Harry's wand seems impervious. If Voldemort only wanted a new wand, presumably he would have Gregorovitch make him one, with the expectation that a wand made by a different artisan would be protected from the same fate as the other wands he used on Harry. As was seen with Mr. Ollivander, Voldemort's persuasion techniques tend to leave an artisan in a rather unsuitable state to perform fine craftsmanship. However, having found Gregorovitch, Voldemort asks him about something he is thought to have once owned. Although Gregorovitch claims he never possessed it, Voldemort sees in his memory that someone stole it from him, although it is unknown what that object was or who the thief might be. As Voldemort then murders Gregorovitch, it seems our assumption about Voldemort wanting a new wand is incorrect. What then, is Voldemort seeking?

Questions

Review   1. What does Ron mean when he says Voldemort's name feels like a jinx? Why do the others respect his request not to say it?

2. Why is Ron able to detect a "heartbeat" within the Locket, while the other two cannot?

3. Why did Voldemort capture Gregorovitch?

Extra Study   1. Why does Harry have awful thoughts while he is taking the watch?

2. Who might the blond thief be?

3. Considering the mental connection that exists between Harry and Voldemort, why does Hermione dismiss the notion that Harry is reading Voldemort's mind?

4. How might losing their comfortable hiding place actually help the Trio's search for the Horcruxes?

GREATER PICTURE

Ron's instinct that Voldemort's name feels "jinxed" will prove to be more than mere superstition on his part. It is learned later that Voldemort's name is tabooed; anyone speaking it immediately alerts Death Eaters and Snatchers, Voldemort's bounty hunters, to their location. Voldemort knows that unlike most other wizards, Order of the Phoenix members in general, and Harry in particular, do not fear speaking his name, thus making it easy to locate him. This is yet another example of Harry's predictable behavior often being used against him, just as when he revealed his presence by executing what has become his signature spell, during the attack while leaving the Dursley house. Although Harry's presence remained undetected when he uttered Voldemort's name inside Grimmauld Place, speaking it may have broken some protective charms on the building. We do not know why it did not seem to; possibly it was the age of the protective spells, or that the protective spells were cast by a Dark wizard that prevented it from breaking. Additionally, the fact that Grimmauld Place is unplottable may make it impossible to determine exactly where Harry is. It is possible that the magically-enforced taboo caused Harry to experience another painful session inside Voldemort's mind immediately after he spoke his name. Ron's twitchiness about Voldemort's name has resulted in it being largely unspoken to date, and that continues through this chapter and several more. The object Voldemort seeks is the Elder Wand, one of the three titular Deathly Hallows. Voldemort, raised in a Muggle orphanage, has never heard of the Deathly Hallows; he knew nothing about the Resurrection Stone when he made Gaunt's ring into a Horcrux, and he has never searched for Death's Invisibility Cloak. The Elder Wand, however, has its own history apart from the Hallows, and that attracted Voldemort's attention. It is because he believed that Voldemort was ignorant about the Hallows' significance that Dumbledore never tasked Harry with recovering them, though he knew where they all were. Dumbledore believed that the Horcruxes were the greater danger.

It will be revealed later that the young blond thief is the evil wizard Grindelwald, who Dumbledore defeated in a duel and captured the Elder Wand from.

Chapter 15: The Goblin's Revenge

SYNOPSIS

Before Ron and Hermione wake, Harry buries Moody's magical eye under a tree. They then shift camp to a small market town, but Harry is unable to enter because Dementors are there. Ron is amazed; normally, Harry produces an excellent Patronus, but he now seems incapable. It occurs to Hermione that he may be affected by the Horcrux. He immediately feels better when she takes it from him, but believes he was not possessed by it because he remembers everything he did; he overrules Hermione's suggestion that they not wear the Locket: if it is stored in the tent and the tent is lost, then what? Hermione reluctantly agrees, but suggests taking turns wearing it and puts it around her own neck.

They wander the countryside, camping in a new location each night. Harry, Ron, and Hermione endlessly debate where the other Horcruxes could be. Harry is adamant that one is at Hogwarts, that being the only place Tom Riddle ever considered home. Ron thinks Dumbledore would have found it by now, but Harry reminds him that Dumbledore never claimed to know every Hogwarts secret. They find the orphanage in London where Tom Riddle lived, but it has been demolished and replaced by offices. Hermione wants to root around in the foundations, but the others veto her suggestion.

They continue traveling throughout the country. Ron, used to three hot meals a day, is steadily becoming annoyed with Hermione's cooking attempts. One night, as he complains about the fish Hermione has served, Harry hushes them both—he hears someone. Hermione silently deals out Extendable Ears, and a group Summoning and preparing salmon can be heard. The party is Ted Tonks, the goblin Griphook, and his compatriot, Gornuk. Also nearby is Dean Thomas and someone named Dirk, who was being transported to Azkaban but overpowered the Auror guard, Dawlish. Dirk relates a tale from Griphook, who heard it from Bill Weasley. Apparently, several Hogwarts students, including Ginny, sneaked into Snape's office and broke into the glass case containing the Sword of Gryffindor. They were caught and given detention. About a week later, Snape transferred the sword to the Lestranges' Gringotts vault. But Griphook immediately recognized the sword was a fake—an excellent copy, but Wizard-made, and lacking certain Goblin properties. As an afterthought, it is mentioned that the students had been "cruelly punished." We also learn that the group believes Harry was telling the truth about Snape killing Dumbledore, and if anyone wants to know what is really happening, they should read *The Quibbler*. Lately, Xeno Lovegood has been publishing truthful stories, without mentioning Crumple-Horned Snorkacks. Shortly after, the party moves off, and Hermione pulls Phineas Nigellus' portrait from the bag to summon him. When he appears, Hermione blindfolds him so he is unable to report their location. Phineas updates them about Ginny, Neville, and Luna, whose punishment was their being sent to work in the Forbidden Forest with Hagrid. Hermione asks if the sword had previously been removed from its case, perhaps for cleaning. Phineas retorts that Goblin armor rejects ordinary dirt, accepting only that which will make it stronger. Harry wants Dumbledore to be brought from his office portrait, but former Headmasters can only travel to their own portraits outside Hogwarts and to other portraits within the castle, but nowhere else. Phineas, however, tells Hermione that Dumbledore had used the sword to break open a ring.

Excited, Harry and Hermione realize that the sword absorbed Basilisk venom when Harry killed the Basilisk with it. Now it can destroy Horcruxes, but they have reached a "dead end" determining where the real sword is located. After some guessing and discussion, Harry asks Ron for his opinion, but Ron appears unenthusiastic and agitated, and accuses Harry of not knowing what he is doing. After a heated argument, Ron nearly attacks Harry, but Hermione casts a shield charm to block him. Ron removes the locket, tosses it down, and threatens to leave; when Hermione says she is staying, Ron accuses her of siding with Harry and storms off into the night, Disapparating before Hermione can stop him.

Analysis

This chapter is critical in that it not only reveals that Dumbledore destroyed the ring Horcrux, but that there is an additional way to use Basilisk venom to eliminate Horcruxes. Until this point, the only known venom source is the Basilisk fangs in the Chamber of Secrets underneath Hogwarts. Now, the Sword of Gryffindor, which absorbed the Basilisk venom, can be used to destroy Horcruxes. While a Basilisk fang or Gryffindor's Sword is needed to dispatch Horcruxes, the sword that was in Snape's office and is now secured in a vault at Gringotts Bank is only a replica and will not do the job. The question becomes, where is the real Sword of Gryffindor?

Meanwhile, the mission suffers a severe blow by Ron's abrupt departure, which was motivated by several factors. Of the Trio, he is the last to reach adulthood, and, still clinging to his rather childish behavior, is unable to make the commitment and sacrifices needed to pursue such a difficult quest. Less independent and self-sufficient than the other two, Ron is used to creature comforts, regular meals, and being mollycoddled by his mother, and is usually content to tag along after his older brothers and allow Harry and Hermione to take the lead. Ron has also deluded himself somewhat as to what Harry's mission actually entailed and seems to have forgotten that Harry strongly discouraged him from accompanying him. Injury, frustration, and Harry's seeming indecisiveness are also affecting him, although Harry is nearly as frustrated and angry as Ron by what little and confusing information Dumbledore left him. Ron mistakenly assumed that Dumbledore provided Harry all the necessary information. His anger, fears, and immaturity may also have been exacerbated by his close proximity to the Locket Horcrux that has affected each Trio member in turn by preying on them mentally, emotionally, and physically while they are wearing it. Even though Ron's ability to detect the Locket's "heartbeat" may have indicated that he was more vulnerable to its Dark nature, allowing it to exert a greater force on him than it did the others, it does not fully excuse his deplorable behavior.

Although his full name is not mentioned here, the Dirk who is traveling with Ted Tonks may be Dirk Cresswell, one-time head of the Goblin Liaison Office in the Ministry of Magic. This would explain why he was traveling with Griphook, as well as suggest why he had to leave the Ministry—in an earlier chapter, we saw that Dirk had been investigated and "found" to be of Muggle ancestry.

Questions

Review 1. Why did Hermione want to search the building foundation where Voldemort's orphanage used to be? What might she have found? Why are Harry and Ron against this?

2. Why does Ron abruptly leave the Trio? What might be affecting his decision?

3. Why does Hermione distrust Phineas Nigellus enough that she blindfolds him whenever she summons him to his portrait? Why didn't she worry about this while at Grimmauld Place?

4. Could Phineas have revealed their presence to anyone while they were there, and who might that be?

Extra Study 1. Why does Hermione take on the cooking task? Is the author assigning her a traditional female role for a reason?

2. Why does Harry bury Moody's magical eye, rather than keep it? Could it have been used to aid their mission? If so, how?

3. Why doesn't the Trio make contact with the other parties they hear in the woods, especially knowing that friends like Dean Thomas and Ted Tonks are among them?

4. Why would The Quibbler, a paper known for its outlandish stories, now publish the "truth" about Harry Potter? How can it be trusted to be the truth?

5. The Trio overhear that Ginny, Neville, and Luna were "severely" punished for attempting to steal Gryffindor's sword, yet Phineas Nigellus' portrait tells them that Snape only assigned the students detention in the Forbidden Forest with Hagrid. Why would Snape give them such a light punishment for such a serious offense?

6. Knowing that Basilisk venom destroys Horcruxes, why doesn't the Trio sneak into Hogwarts to collect its fangs from the Chamber of Secrets to use as weapons?

7. Each Trio member was affected emotionally and physically by wearing the Locket Horcrux. Did Dolores Umbridge suffer any ill-effects while she wore it? If not, why?

Greater Picture

When Harry killed the Basilisk with the Sword of Gryffindor, its venom empowered the sword to destroy Horcruxes. The reader may wonder why the Trio simply does not go to Hogwarts to gather the dead monster's fangs that are still lying in the Chamber of Secrets and use them to destroy the Horcruxes rather than searching for the sword. While that may seem logical, it is probably a safe assumption that Harry will only be able to enter Hogwarts one time; he is unable to flit in, nab a fang, and nip back out again because once there, his presence will likely be quickly detected, forcing him to stand and fight. Nor can they get an ally there to retrieve a fang and smuggle it to them because the Chamber of Secrets can only be opened by someone speaking Parseltongue, although Ron will later overcome this obstacle. With Snape as Headmaster and the Carrows teaching Muggle Studies and Dark Arts, there is now a permanent Death Eater presence at the school. However, hearing that the Sword has been moved to Gringotts Bank, and that it is a fake anyway, it becomes unnecessary for Harry to have to go to Hogwarts to be able to destroy the Locket Horcrux, although he will eventually need to eliminate another soul shard that is hidden there. For now, it is a great relief to him, and the reader, to know how Horcruxes can be destroyed, even if the Trio must still locate Gryffindor's real sword. It does become clearer, however, as to why Dumbledore attempted to bequeath the sword to Harry. It is also logical to assume that it was Dumbledore who switched the real sword for the fake, with the intention that Harry would then find the genuine blade to destroy the Horcruxes. It will be revealed that Dumbledore knew he only had short time left to live, which is probably when he included the sword in his will as a clue to Harry that he would need it. Dumbledore apparently also arranged for an, as yet, unknown ally to dispatch the real sword to Harry in an upcoming chapter.

To Ron's credit, he does attempt to rejoin the group immediately after his angry departure, but he runs into some unexpected trouble. Also, Dumbledore had anticipated that Ron, being the most immature and least prepared for the quest, might fail the others at some point during the mission. Dumbledore's bequest (the Deluminator) to Ron is actually a means for him to find his way back, should he ever become separated from the Trio, although Ron unexpectedly learns this later.

Chapter 16: Godric's Hollow

SYNOPSIS

Harry awakens the next morning half-expecting Ron to be in his bunk, but it is empty. Harry and Hermione delay packing, knowing Ron will be unable to find them once they leave. Unable to wait any longer, they Disapparate to a wind-swept hillside. Hermione breaks down in sobs, while Harry puts up the protective spells around their campsite. For the next few days, Harry watches for Ron's dot on his Marauder's Map, certain he has returned to Hogwarts, but it never appears. At night, Harry and Hermione spend hours discussing where Dumbledore could have hidden Gryffindor's Sword. Harry is uncertain if he is angrier at Ron for leaving, or at Dumbledore for failing to give him more information. Ron's words haunt him: *"We thought you knew what you were doing . . . We thought Dumbledore had told you what to do . . . We thought you had a real plan!"* Ron was right; Dumbledore left him with virtually nothing, and the remaining Horcruxes are still just as unattainable. At night, Hermione brings out Phineas Nigellus' portrait. Despite his threat never to visit it again but curious for information, he agrees to show up blindfolded every few days. Phineas only reveals sporadic information about Hogwarts, although Harry and Hermione learn about a low-level student mutiny. Snape has reinstated Umbridge's decree prohibiting three or more students from gathering or any unofficial student societies, although Harry deduces that Ginny, Luna, and Neville have probably restarted Dumbledore's Army. Harry briefly yearns for Hogwarts' comforts, only to remember he is "Undesirable Number One."

The weather grows colder, and the two constantly move to new locations throughout the country. Christmas trees begin appearing in sitting room windows. One night, Hermione shows Harry a strange hand-drawn symbol in *The Tales of Beedle the Bard*. She is unable to decipher it, but has determined it is something other than an eye icon or an ancient rune in the syllabary. Harry recognizes it as the same triangular symbol on Xenophilius' robe at the wedding. Krum claimed it was Grindelwald's mark. Hermione is puzzled that a Dark mark would be drawn in a children's book. Harry, curious about his own past, wants to go to Godric's Hollow; surprisingly, Hermione agrees, believing Dumbledore may have hidden the sword in Godric Gryffindor's birthplace. When Harry expresses suprise, Hermione pulls out *A History of Magic* by Bathilda Bagshot and reads a passage about Godric Gryffindor. Harry remembers Ginny's Aunt Muriel telling him at the wedding that Bathilda Bagshot still lived in Godric's Hollow. Both silently notice that Harry deliberately avoided referring to Muriel as Ron's aunt. A thought suddenly occurs to Hermione—maybe Dumbledore entrusted the sword to Bathilda.

Harry and Hermione immediately make plans to go to Godric's Hollow. Hermione first wants to practice Disapparating together under the Invisibility Cloak, plus a few other spells, but Harry only thinks about seeing his birthplace. It is another week before they depart for Godric's Hollow. Hermione has obtained some Muggle hairs for the Polyjuice Potion, and they transform themselves into a middle-aged married couple, then Disapparate under the Invisibility Cloak to Godric's Hollow. Hermione worries about leaving tracks in the snow, but since they are disguised, Harry suggests removing the Cloak and just walking. Spotting a cemetery behind a nearby church, they head for it. A war memorial in the town square suddenly transforms into a statue of a man and a woman holding a baby. Astonished, Harry recognizes the two figures as his parents and realizes the baby is him. Inside the graveyard, they unexpectedly discover Kendra and Ariana Dumbledore's graves; Harry again wonders why Dumbledore never shared their common roots. On the grave marker is the inscription: "Where your treasure is, there will your heart be also," although Harry is uncertain what it means. While searching for the Potters' gravesites, Hermione spots something. Carved on an old tombstone is the same symbol as in the book and on Xenophilius' robes, although the stone's letters are badly weathered; Harry can only make out the first name, Ignotus. They continue hunting until Hermione calls out, "Harry, they're here . . . right here." Their white marble headstone is only two rows behind Kendra and Ariana. Below their names is the inscription: *The last enemy that shall be destroyed is death*

Confused, Harry thinks this sounds like a Death Eater concept, but Hermione says it means to defeat death by existing beyond it. Harry finds little comfort in its meaning, knowing his parents' moldering remains lie beneath the frozen ground and cries a bit. Hermione takes his hand. Harry feels bad that he forgot to bring something for his parents, but Hermione, unasked, conjures a Christmas wreath with roses that Harry lays on the graves. As Harry puts his arm around Hermione's shoulders, she places hers around his waist, and they quietly turn to leave the cemetery.

Analysis

Although Harry wanted to "go it alone" on this mission, he now sorely misses Ron's presence and realizes how much he relied on his help and friendship. This may be a crucial turning point for Harry in learning to trust others and accept help. Ron's painful absence is also a sharp contrast to Hermione's steadfast loyalty, and it is doubtful that Harry could have gotten as far as he has without her assistance, although, in the past, he and Ron have tended to dismiss her contributions and abilities except when they needed specific information about something. Her careful planning and foresight has allowed the Trio to move relatively efficiently and comfortably throughout the country during their Horcrux search. Her diligent research methods and cool, logical mind will continue to be a useful resource to the mission. However, living by her wits and surviving day-to-day in a life-threatening situation has also greatly improved her practical skills and abilities, forcing her to also rely on intuition, speculation, and immediate action rather than just books for definitive answers. Her quick, sharp reflexes have repeatedly saved the Trio from disaster, as when she Disapparated them away from Bill and Fleur's wedding and Grimmauld Place, and likely will do so again in future chapters.

It is interesting to note that the Potters' statue is (appropriately) disguised as a war memorial. Not only did James and Lily fight against Voldemort in life, but they continue their battle in death through their son, Harry. Seeing Kendra and Ariana's tombstone disturbs Harry. This reminder that Dumbledore had a history he withheld from Harry, or that Harry never asked about, reignites Harry's anger and confusion over Dumbledore's cryptic plan. The inscription on Kendra and Ariana's gravestone, "Where your treasure is, there will your heart be also," further frustrates Harry, who fails to understand how deeply Dumbledore loved his mother and sister. Harry again wonders why Dumbledore never revealed their common roots, although the Dumbledores only lived in Godric's Hollow a short time and had moved there to keep Ariana's condition hidden. Also, this reminder of Ariana's existence causes Harry to think about Rita Skeeter's book, and to wonder how much truth backs her stories.

Questions

Review 1. Why do Harry and Hermione avoid mentioning Ron's name?

Further Study 1. Why has Harry never been taken to visit Godric's Hollow and his parents' home and graves, despite it being a monument to their memories?

2. Who might Ignotus be? The sign on his tombstone seems to be the same one Xeno Lovegood wore at the wedding, that Grindelwald used, and that appears in Dumbledore's copy of *The Tales of Beedle the Bard*. Why would this sign be on Ignotus' tombstone?

3. Why does Phineas Nigellus Black give Harry and Hermione updates about Hogwarts? Can this information be trusted?

4. What might the inscription, "Where your treasure is, there will your heart be also," mean? Who likely chose those words for Ariana and Kendra's grave stone and why?

5. Harry searches for Ron on the Marauders' Map but is unable to find him at Hogwarts. Where might Ron be and what would he be doing?

6. Harry has no idea where to search for Gryffindor's Sword, although there is something that could possibly help him retrieve it. What is this, and why doesn't it occur to Harry? How difficult would it be to obtain this item?

Greater Picture

Although Harry has abandoned his dream to be reunited with his dead parents, when he learns about the Deathly Hallows (and the Resurrection Stone), this possibility will be revived.

Harry and Hermione have no idea where to search for Gryffindor's sword, and they are taking a huge gamble and using precious time in hope that Dumbledore hid it in Godric's Hollow. However, there could be another way to retrieve the Sword. Readers likely will remember that in *Harry Potter and the Chamber of Secrets*, Harry pulled Gryffindor's Sword from the Sorting Hat when he fought the Basilisk. While this could be one possible way to obtain the sword, neither Harry or Hermione considers this. However, there is certainly no guarantee that the Sorting Hat can or would provide the Sword on demand, or if it is at all possible to obtain the Hat that is safely secured in the Hogwarts Headmaster's office. Even if Harry's allies inside Hogwarts attempted to retrieve it, given the Castle's tight security, it could be a difficult undertaking for any student, even resourceful Dumbledore's Army members, to breach the Headmaster's office, particularly now that Snape is in residence there. And given Ginny, Luna, and Neville's previous unsuccessful attempt to steal the Sword of Gryffindor, their punishment could potentially be far more severe for a second offence. However, as the Sorting Hat may generally be considered an innocuous magical object, it is possible that it could be removed from the Headmaster's Office more easily than the Sword. And considering how effortlessly Hermione was able to Summon the restricted books from Dumbledore's study, the Sorting Hat might likewise be retrieved. However, Snape is likely well aware of the Sorting Hat's abilities. Harry will eventually obtain Gryffindor's Sword, not with the Sorting Hat, but with help from an unidentified ally. However, the Sorting Hat will again prove important later in the story when it provides Gryffindor's Sword to Neville Longbottom, who Harry asks to destroy one of Voldemort's remaining Horcruxes in the event that he, Ron, or Hermione are unable to.

Chapter 17: Bathilda's Secret

Synopsis

As they depart the cemetery, Hermione is positive something moved in the distance. Harry thinks it may be a ghost, but Hermione draws her wand. When Harry sees dislodged snow by the bushes where Hermione was pointing, he surmises that if it was Death Eaters, they would be dead now; he suggests putting on the

Chapter 17: Bathilda's Secret

Invisibility Cloak, and they glance around repeatedly as they leave. Heading down a street, they have no idea where Bathilda Bagshot's house might be. An overgrown hedge surrounds a ruined cottage, most of which is still standing, but one side has been blown apart. On the gate, a sign appears:

On this spot, on the night of 31 October 1981, Lily and James Potter lost their lives. Their son, Harry, remains the only wizard ever to have survived the Killing Curse. This house, invisible to Muggles, has been left in its ruined state as a monument to the Potters and as a reminder of the violence that tore apart their family. Messages from visitors are scribbled on the sign. Hermione thinks it is disrespectful, but it cheers Harry, who feels only gratitude. A mysterious, elderly woman approaches. Although she is obviously a magical person, Harry is surprised and suspicious that she can see them under the Invisibility Cloak. When she beckons them to follow, Harry asks if she is Bathilda Bagshot; she nods and beckons again. They are led to a house with a garden as overgrown as the Potter residence. Inside, Harry whiffs a foul odor like putrid meat clinging to her, although it may be the house, in which everything is covered by thick dust. Bathilda goes into another room, and Harry hears her calling, "Come!" causing Hermione to jump. Inside, Harry spots photographs atop a chest of drawers and removes the dust. A half dozen photos are missing from their ornate frames, but Harry recognizes a picture of a young blond man as the one in Rita Skeeter's book, *The Life and Lies of Albus Dumbledore*. Harry repeatedly asks Bathilda who it is, but she stares vaguely at him, causing Harry to wonder how she was able to tell Rita Skeeter about the Dumbledore clan. Harry tells Hermione that the man in the photo is the thief he saw in Voldemort's mind who stole the item from Gregorovitch.

Bathilda motions for only Harry to go upstairs with her, and Hermione remains behind; Harry pockets the thief's photo on his way out. In the bedroom, Bathilda inquires if he is Harry Potter. He answers affirmatively and wants to know if she has something for him. Bathilda closes her eyes, and Harry feels his scar prickle and the Locket Horcrux twitch against him as the room momentarily darkens. Joy surges through his body, and he hears his own voice saying, "Hold him!" Bathilda points to a dressing table in the corner. Harry inspects it, but as he turns, he witnesses a revolting sight: a huge snake pours out from what was Bathilda's neck, her lifeless body collapsing to the floor. Nagini attacks, biting Harry's arm and sending his wand flying. The resulting noise brings Hermione frantically running upstairs. Nagini releases Harry and lunges at Hermione, barely missing her. Harry, grabbing his dropped wand, yells that Voldemort is coming. Nagini lunges again as Harry drags Hermione across the bed. Hermione casts Confringo, and the spell ricochets around the room, burning Harry's hand, as they leap out the window. Voldemort, reaching out to grasp Harry, screams in fury as he and Hermione Disapparate; his anger causes unbearable pain in Harry's scar.

Pain mingles with Voldemort's memories of a fateful night sixteen years before: Hallowe'en costumes, a father's smile, a toddler playing on the floor inside a cozy house. Outside, a gate creaks open as a dark figure strides through. A man yells, "Lily, take Harry and go! It's him. Go! Run! I'll hold him off!" More screams, then green flashes, and a woman's crumpled body lies upon the nursery floor. One last flash, and pain-shot darkness. Then, through Voldemort's eyes, Harry sees Bathilda's bedroom again, and Voldemort is picking up the dropped picture of the thief. Hermione's voice pierces the void, pleading for him to wake. Opening his eyes, Harry sees that he is inside the tent. Hermione says they escaped, but it is hours later and he has been sick; she used the Hover charm to get him into his bunk and a Severing charm to pry the stuck Locket off his chest. Dittany healed Nagini's bite wounds. While Harry relived Voldemort's memories, he was delirious, moaning and screaming. Harry relates what happened upstairs and that Nagini was hidden inside Bathilda's corpse, although he spares Hermione the most gruesome details. Nagini only spoke when she and Harry were alone because it was in Parseltongue. Nagini immediately summoned Voldemort when Harry identified himself. Harry asks for his wand, but Hermione tearfully confesses that it is broken, probably by her ricocheting spell. Stunned, Harry wants her to try and repair it with her wand, but she hesitantly reminds him that Ron's broken wand never worked the same. He pleads with her to try anyway, but, too badly damaged, it snaps in half again when he tries it. With Ollivander held captive by Voldemort, Harry is unsure how he will obtain another wand. Although clearly upset, he tells Hermione it was not her fault, then borrows her wand to take the watch, wanting to get away from her. Hermione sits next to the bunk in tears.

ANALYSIS

Harry is confronted with death in Godric's Hollow, but unlike witnessing it hot and fresh as when Dumbledore, Cedric Diggory, and Sirius Black were killed, he now sees only its cold, decayed aftermath, dimming his hope to one day be reunited with his parents. Harry's own recollections about their murders are faint, remembering only a green flash and his mother's screams. While inside Voldemort's memories, he was able to see the entire horrendous event as it unfolded through Voldemort's eyes. Not only does this reopen old wounds, it also creates new ones that only intensify his grief and despair. But as painful as those memories are, they also provide him a clearer picture of what actually happened that tragic night, tying him closer to his parents, and clarifying his role in vanquishing the Dark Lord.

Seeing James and Lily's graves, and the destroyed cottage that he once lived in, is deeply disturbing and drives home the reality that the tragic events sixteen years before actually occured. Until now, these were merely sad stories told to Harry by others, but seeing the house in person is emotionally wrenching, and it serves to fully integrate him into past events. And while Harry always harbored a slim hope that magic would somehow reunite him with his long-dead parents, seeing their forlorn, final resting places forces him to confront death's finality. He is comforted and uplifted, however, by the kind messages visitors have left at the

Potter's residence over the years. Harry's difficult childhood has resulted in him never fully trusting or relying on others and he usually prefers to handle most situations alone. He has made great strides in overcoming this trait, however, learning to accept friends' and mentors' support and guidance, although some, like Ron and Dumbledore, have also failed him. He takes a great leap of faith here when he willingly follows the mysterious elderly woman, believing she is Bathilda Bagshot and trusting that she can help. However, this time, Harry's reasoning proves faulty. Even the decision to go to Godric's Hollow was driven more by a desire to see his birthplace, visit James and Lily's graves, and resolve his conflicted feelings about Dumbledore, rather than to uncover clues relating to their mission; the error nearly costs Harry and Hermione their lives. It is also a little surprising that Hermione, who is usually far more cautious and suspicious than either Ron or Harry, not only suggested going to Godric's Hollow, but also so willingly followed the old woman, despite her odd behavior. It is uncertain if Harry can ever show that much faith in the unknown again. Readers can again see to what extremes the despicable Rita Skeeter will go to obtain information. She likely used some magical means, probably a memory charm or Veritaserum, to extract the vulnerable Bathilda's faulty memories, then stole the photographs for her book. Skeeter may also be indirectly responsible for poor Bathilda's death, as Voldemort apparently surmised that Skeeter's book might lure Harry to Godric's Hollow and Bathilda to seek information, prompting Voldemort to murder her and set the trap that nearly ensnared Harry and probably would have killed Hermione.

Although Harry assures Hermione she is blameless for breaking his wand, he is clearly upset and angry with her, leaving Hermione in tears and driving an invisible wedge between them. Like with Lupin, Harry's reaction is undeservedly harsh, especially considering Hermione risked own her life to save his. However, Harry is devastated by his wand's loss, and his logical thinking (and gratitude) has been temporarily overruled by misplaced anger and grief, although he quickly realizes Hermione was not at fault here.

It is perhaps worth noting here that the conversation about Harry's broken wand is the first time either Harry or Hermione has spoken Ron's name since his departure, and it will prove to be important.

It should also be mentioned that when Harry hears or speaks Parseltongue, he is unable to distinguish it from English—we saw this as far back as *Harry Potter and the Chamber of Secrets*, where he had to imagine he was seeing a living snake before the words he spoke to the Chamber's entrance would emerge in Parseltongue. That is why he was unaware anything was amiss when Nagini spoke to him disguised as Bathilda, and it also explains why Hermione jumped when Bathilda was calling from the other room. Harry heard her saying, "Come," while all Hermione detected was a strange hissing noise.

QUESTIONS

Review 1. How and why do Harry and Hermione react differently to the written messages left outside the Potters' house?

2. What happened to the missing photographs in Bathilda's house? What were they likely pictures of?

3. Why was Hermione startled when Bathilda called from the other room?

Extra Study 1. Why did Harry and Hermione decide to follow the old woman, not knowing who she was, and despite her not speaking to them?

2. Harry has been confronted by death before, but how is he affected differently by it after seeing his parents' and the Dumbledores' graves?

3. Does Harry really blame Hermione for breaking his wand? If so, why? Could she have avoided it?

4. Harry's wand had become very powerful and easily destroyed Lucius Malfoy's wand without Harry casting a curse. Why, then, was Hermione's spell able to break it?

5. Why did no one ever check on the elderly and senile Bathilda, a well-known witch, despite her living alone and the garden being overgrown?

6. When Voldemort arrived at the Potters' cottage, why did James confront him rather than try to Disapparate to safety with Lily and baby Harry? Why didn't Lily escape with Harry as soon as James shouted out that Voldemort was outside?

GREATER PICTURE

Although Harry seriously erred in trusting the "old woman" he believed was Bathilda Bagshot, he will again put his trust in a stranger when one night soon a silvery doe Patronus appears, and he follows it in the hope an ally sent it to help. This time his assumption will be correct, and he will also be reunited with a valued friend. In a later chapter, Dumbledore's shade will explain that even though Harry's wand had grown very powerful, because it imbibed additional power from Voldemort's yew wand (brother to Harry's wand), that power can only be directed against Voldemort, regardless of what wand the Dark Lord may be wielding at the time. Against other wizards, Harry's wand had no additional advantage than before. That is why Hermione was accidentally able to destroy Harry's wand with her own.

Chapter 18: The Life and Lies of Albus Dumbledore

SYNOPSIS

The next morning, Harry is still mourning his lost wand. Without it he feels weak, vulnerable, and stripped naked, as if his magical power died with it. But this wand was special. The broken halves, barely held together by the damaged phoenix feather, are shoved into the pouch around his neck. Harry's hand brushes the Snitch that is also inside, and he is momentarily

Chapter 18: The Life and Lies of Albus Dumbledore

tempted to throw it away, believing it is as useless as everything else Dumbledore left behind. His fury at Dumbledore is unleashed. In desperation they had gone to Godric's Hollow, believing it held answers and would lead to some secret path laid out by Dumbledore. Instead, he left them groping blindly, without a plan or a map, and it nearly cost them their lives. Now Harry is without a wand, without the sword, and the dropped thief's photo has given information to Voldemort.

Still upset, Hermione timidly brings Harry tea and shows him an unopened copy of Rita Skeeter's book, *The Life and Lies of Albus Dumbledore* that was in Bathilda Bagshot's sitting room. A note sticking out reads: *Dear Batty, Thanks for your help. Here's a copy of the book, hope you like it. You said everything, even if you don't remember it. Rita*

Harry assures Hermione that he is not angry about his wand, it was only an accident, and he is grateful to her for saving his life. As the book's pages rifle through his fingers, Harry feels a perverse pleasure—now he will know Dumbledore's secrets. Looking at photographs, he sees a young Dumbledore and the handsome companion he saw in Umbridge's office, and who he now recognizes as the thief in Gregorovitch's memory. The caption reads: *Albus Dumbledore, shortly after his mother's death, with his friend Gellert Grindelwald.*

Harry and Hermione exchange incredulous looks—Grindelwald! Reading a chapter titled, "The Greater Good," they learn that Dumbledore graduated Hogwarts with many honors and accolades. He intended to take a Grand Tour with his friend, Elphias Doge, but Kendra Dumbledore's sudden death canceled it. Although Doge had claimed that Dumbledore made a grand sacrifice to care for his family, the book implies otherwise, quoting several Godric's Hollow citizens. Enid Smeek recounts that Albus did little to curtail his brother Aberforth's wild behavior and kept his sister, Ariana, hidden away. Although the Dumbledores remained reclusive, Bathilda Bagshot reportedly established a friendship with the family. Skeeter claims that although Bathilda's memory may have been affected by age, she was able to extract enough facts to piece together the scandalous story of Kendra's death, which was passed off as a spell backfiring. She also debunks Ariana being sickly and claims Albus had an affinity for the Dark Arts and may have supported Muggle oppression.

The same summer that Albus returned home to care for the family, Bathilda Bagshot took in her great-nephew, Gellert Grindelwald, a student as brilliant as Dumbledore, who was expelled from Durmstrang. He later became a notorious Dark Wizard, although he was relatively unknown in Britain. He and Albus quickly formed a close friendship. In a letter to Gellert, Dumbledore writes that he agrees Wizard dominance over Muggles is for the greater good, but they must rule responsibly and only use force when necessary. He believes that was Gellert's mistake at Durmstrang, although he says that if Gellert had not been expelled, then they would never have met. Rita states that this letter proves that Albus Dumbledore once intended to overthrow the Statute of Secrecy and establish Wizard rule over Muggles. It contradicts his later stance supporting Muggle-born witches and wizards and protecting Muggles' rights.

But barely two months after their friendship began, Dumbledore and Grindelwald parted ways and did not see each other again until their legendary duel. Bathilda Bagshot believed the rift involved Ariana's death. Gellert was in the house when it happened, and he came home distressed, leaving by Portkey the next day. Bathilda says Aberforth blamed Albus, and they came to blows at the funeral. Bathilda goes on to say that Gellert's departure was unfortunate, as he would have been a comfort to Albus. It was never understood why Aberforth blamed Albus for Ariana's death, although it is speculated that it was related to Albus' friendship with Gellert, who had been expelled from Durmstrang for near-fatal attacks on fellow students. It was not until five years later that Dumbledore succumbed to the Wizarding world's pleas to end Grindelwald's vicious rampage. Questions lingered after Grindelwald's defeat, however. Was it his affection for Grindelwald that delayed Albus to take action? How and why did Ariana die? Was it an accident or the first attempt at implementing their "Greater Good" plan? The chapter ends here, and Harry is stunned as he endures yet another loss: Ron, his phoenix wand, and now his unwavering trust in Dumbledore, who once embodied nothing but goodness and wisdom. Hermione reminds him that it was Rita Skeeter who wrote the book, but Harry points out Dumbledore's own words in his letter to Grindelwald. Hermione says that, unfortunately, Grindelwald's slogan, "For the Greater Good," probably stemmed from Dumbledore's ideas and became Grindelwald's justification for his atrocities. Those words were reportedly carved over the entrance to "Nurmengard," the prison Grindelwald built to jail his enemies. Hermione attempts to attribute Dumbledore's actions to his youth, but Harry reminds her that they are the same age, and they are fighting Dark Arts, not championing them. Hermione claims she is not defending what Albus did, but says he had just lost his mother and he was alone. But Harry points out he had a brother and that he kept his Squib sister locked up, although Hermione doubts she was Squib. She says that the Dumbledore they knew would never have allowed Muggle oppression, and whatever he believed when he was seventeen, he chose a different path and spent his remaining life fighting evil. Hermione surmises that Harry is really angry because Dumbledore never told him this himself, which Harry acknowledges may be true. But he wonders how Dumbledore could have left him in such a mess, and if he ever really cared about him.

Analysis

Harry and Hermione believe that Godric's Hollow was not only nearly fatal, but a useless dead-end, and Harry is angrier than ever with Dumbledore for having provided so little information for his quest. It is unclear if Dumbledore ever intended for them to go to Godric's Hollow, but he must have surmised that Harry would eventually visit his birthplace and would suspect information could be hidden there, although

Dumbledore may have considered it too risky and obvious a place to secrete clues. Despite their miscalculation, the trip actually proves somewhat productive. As noted, Harry and Hermione discover yet another instance of the symbol that was inked into *The Tales of Beedle the Bard* that Dumbledore bequeathed to Hermione; he may have intended for Harry to find it, lending further proof to its importance. Also, Hermione obtains Rita Skeeter's book, which provides valuable information about Dumbledore's past and his previously unknown association with the notorious Dark Wizard, Gellert Grindelwald, who he eventually defeated in a duel. Grindelwald's photo in Bathilda's house also ties him to her and Godric's Hollow. Harry also confronts his own past in Godric's Hollow, and by visiting his former home and his parents' graves, it provides some closure to this sad chapter in his life, and will allow him to eventually move forward emotionally.

Once again, Harry is deeply disappointed by someone he loved and admired: James, Sirius, Lupin, and now Dumbledore. This time, however, Harry is not just disappointed, his faith and loyalty are nearly depleted, and Rita Skeeter seems to have proved his suspicions about Dumbledore. Curiously, despite Skeeter's sullied reputation for fabricating or sensationalizing facts, and Harry's own experience being victimized by her libelous stories, he readily believes everything in her book, perhaps in part because Dumbledore's own words lend credence to Skeeter's claims. Harry's belief may be spurred by his anger and concerns about Dumbledore's true motives, further fueling Harry's faltering trust and doubts that Dumbledore ever loved him. But Harry fails to remember Dumbledore once telling him, "It is our choices, Harry, that show what we truly are." Hermione is likely correct that Harry is more upset that Dumbledore concealed his past from Harry, rather than by what he actually did. She points out that despite Dumbledore's early and short-lived flirtation with the Dark Arts and his attraction to its seductive power, that is not the man they knew him to be. Like James Potter, he chose to overcome his earlier flaws and dedicated his remaining life to fighting evil and Muggle oppression. Harry, still entrenched in his own youthful and somewhat naïve idealism, believes goodness and wisdom is a straight, one-way journey from birth through adulthood, and he fails to understand that it is often a route filled with roadblocks, detours, and occasional back alleys. However far Dumbledore may have strayed from his own true path, he, unlike Grindelwald, found his way back again. Harry mourning his lost wand shows he lacks confidence in himself and partially explains his rather harsh reaction to Hermione. He believes that much of his abilities comes from his wand, rather than it being a conduit for his own magical power. It is as if he has lost yet another loved one who provided guidance and strength. Like his owl, Hedwig, and, many years earlier, his destroyed Nimbus 2000 broomstick, the wand was a comforting source of security and familiarity, as well as symbolizing his entry into the wizarding world. He is correct, however, that this wand was special, and it apparently had developed unique powers and qualities that further tied him to Voldemort and his yew wand, although these failed to protect it from Hermione's curse. Its loss is a huge set-back to the mission, and while wizards can use other wands, not just any wand works well. Until Harry can obtain a suitable replacement, he will have to make do sharing Hermione's.

It is noted above that Harry was particularly devastated when he lost his Nimbus 2000 broomstick. Curiously, his destroyed Firebolt, a gift from his late godfather, did not affect him as deeply. Perhaps it was overshadowed by other events such as Hedwig's death at the same time, Moody's demise during the attack, and Sirius' and Dumbledore's recent murders. Also, it being a few years later, Harry's maturity has replaced his need to be overly attached and dependent upon inanimate objects for emotional security, although his broken wand is clearly an exception to that. As a side note, readers perhaps noticed that J.K. Rowling may be employing a bit of humor when Rita Skeeter informally addresses Bathilda Bagshot in her note as "Batty." That, obviously, is a term for being mentally addled, which Bathilda likely was in her later years, and probably is what allowed Skeeter to manipulate her into yielding her memories.

QUESTIONS

Review 1. Harry considers the trip to Godric's Hollow as being useless. Was it? If not, why?

2. It is not uncommon for a wizard to have more than one wand during their lifetime. Other than inconvenient timing, why is Harry so strongly affected by his wand's loss?

3. What was the "Greater Good" and for whose good was it really intended?

4. Why is Harry so disappointed in Dumbledore, despite the good man that he was? Is Harry's opinion fair?

5. Is Hermione right that Harry is angrier at Dumbledore for not telling him about his past, rather than for what he actually did?

6. Why did Dumbledore keep his past a secret? Was he obligated to reveal it to Harry?

Extra Study 1. How might Rita Skeeter have persuaded Bathilda Bagshot to share her memories about Dumbledore and Grindelwald? How reliable were those memories and would that matter to Skeeter?

2. What might have caused the rift between Dumbledore and Grindelwald?

3. Was Albus blinded to Grindelwald's true nature, despite his knowing what happened at Durmstrang? What would account for this?

4. Why would Grindelwald leave Godric's Hollow immediately after Ariana's death? Could he have been involved?

5. Why did Albus wait so long to confront Grindelwald in their historic duel?

6. Considering Rita Skeeter's reputation for sensationalistic and fabricated stories, why is Harry so quick to believe that everything in her book about Dumbledore is true? Could her claims be correct?

7. Why does Hermione doubt that Ariana was a "squib"? Is there any concrete proof supporting her opinion?

Chapter 19: The Silver Doe

GREATER PICTURE

We will learn in a later chapter of this book that Dumbledore's earlier comment to Harry, that it is one's choices that truly makes a person what they are, is based on the tragic events involving his family that forever changed his personal path.

Harry will acquire several different wands during his mission and learns that under certain conditions, wands can change their allegiance. Mr. Ollivander's claim that, "the wand chooses the wizard" is more important than Harry ever realized and will affect his final confrontation with Voldemort.

Chapter 19: The Silver Doe

SYNOPSIS

Harry has trouble sleeping, imagining footsteps and voices in the wind, and gets up during Hermione's watch. He suggests packing and leaving early. Hermione agrees, reinforcing what Harry imagined, and even thinking she saw somebody once or twice. With a motionless Sneakoscope however, any imminent danger seems unlikely, though they Disapparate under the Invisibility Cloak just to be safe.

They arrive in the Forest of Dean at an old campground Hermione once visited with her parents. The snow and bitter cold keeps them inside the tent the first day. Harry takes the watch; he senses this night is different. In the twilight hours of impenetrable darkness, a bright silver light appears drifting soundlessly through the trees. It glides toward Harry until, unable to call for Hermione, he gets a clear view. A silver-white doe steps out, gazes at him, then turns and walks away. Harry follows it deeper into the forest until it halts in an apparently deserted area, then vanishes into the darkness. Using Hermione's wand, Harry casts a light. A frozen pond, hidden by darkness, becomes visible in the light—the Sword of Gryffindor is lying on the pond's bottom.

After several failed attempts to get the Sword without getting wet, Harry remembers Dumbledore's words when he last retrieved it; only a true Gryffindor could have pulled the Sword out of the Sorting Hat. Stripping down to his underwear, he breaks the ice and jumps in. Diving down, he grabs the hilt and pulls upward. But the Locket, sensing danger, tightens around his neck, strangling him. Kicking and fighting, Harry is unable to loosen the chain's chokehold. Suddenly, someone grabs him, cuts him free, and drags him from the pond. Dazed and shivering, Harry looks up and sees a drenched Ron.

Ron denies casting the doe Patronus—believing it was Harry's, until Harry reminds him that his is a stag. To test the Sword's authenticity, they decide to destroy the Locket. Because Ron actually retrieved the Sword, Harry feels he should slay the Locket. Setting it on a nearby stone, Harry says "Open" in Parseltongue. It opens and two eyes on the Locket's sides stare back—Tom Riddle's eyes. A voice insults Ron, attempting to prey on his fears and insecurities, but when this fails, distorted Harry and Hermione heads appear, hurling taunts and ridicule at Ron, then they kiss. The real Harry yells to stab the Locket, and, seeing red glints in Ron's eyes as he draws back the blade, he hurls himself aside. Ron destroys the Locket and Voldemort's soul shard.

Harry consoles a guilt-ridden Ron, reassuring him that Hermione missed him and that there is nothing between her and Harry. Reconciled, they head to the camp. Harry is welcomed back while Ron is pummeled by Hermione's furious fists. Harry halts their fight, but a shouting match continues. Ron claims he tried to return immediately after leaving but was apprehended by Snatchers, Ministry-hired bounty hunters searching for Muggle-borns and blood traitors. By the time Ron escaped, Harry and Hermione had already moved. Ron explains that the Deluminator detects conversations about the person holding it. When he heard Harry and Hermione speak his name, the first time they had spoken it since his departure, he was able to determine their whereabouts. It was Ron they heard at their last camp, but they left before he could find them. The Deluminator brought him to where the doe Patronus and Harry were. They then tell Hermione about the doe, the Sword, and destroying the Locket Horcrux. Ron gives Harry a wand he 'snatched' from a Snatcher to replace his broken one that Ron overheard them talking about. Hermione threatens Ron one last time, and the three finally get some sleep

ANALYSIS

While this chapter is a pivotal turning point in each Trio member's emotional development, Ron undergoes the most significant change. Dumbledore, aware Ron needed extra guidance, left him the Deluminator to help him find his way back should he become separated from the others. Ron's return highlights how significant his role in the Trio truly is, and it marks a distinct milestone in his maturation. From here on, he becomes a more assertive, independent, and contributing member, rather than a passive follower whose insecurity allowed him to take a back seat to Harry, Hermione, and also his older brothers. Ron, unknowingly, has served an important function within the group: Harry and Hermione are talented and resourceful wizards, but, being Muggle-raised, they lack significant knowledge about the general wizarding world. Ron has often guided them by filling in these gaps. It is unlikely Harry and Hermione could succeed without Ron supplying these missing pieces. His humorous, easy-going nature also helps bond the Trio and counter-balances Harry and Hermione's more intense and somewhat dour personalities. Ron also proves he is a true Gryffindor by overcoming his fears and doubts about the mission and returning to a dangerous situation to search for and help his friends. He also demonstrates immense bravery by rescuing Harry from the freezing pond. Harry expresses his gratitude by insisting that Ron destroy the Locket Horcrux; although, at least initially, and when the Horcrux is fighting for its life, Ron may be uncertain that this is a favour. While Hermione is furious at Ron for leaving, his brief absence actually proves useful. Upon his return, he provides vital information about Voldemort and the war, warns them that the Dark Lord's name is now "tabooed," and explains what

Snatchers are. By being too elusive and cut off from their allies, the Trio have made their quest more difficult and dangerous. From here on, they will utilize information gathered from various allies.

A different facet to Hermione's personality is exposed in response to Ron's return. For the first time in her life, she is so overcome with hurt and anger that she loses control, and, unable to think rationally, reacts without logic or forethought. Only Harry's intervention prevents her from inflicting physical harm on Ron. Although furious that he deserted the mission, Hermione was likely feeling abandoned and betrayed by someone she cares deeply about. Although her actual feelings for Ron remain unreconciled, this may be a significant step toward her realizing her true emotions. This outburst may also show that Hermione is learning to act more intuitively and freely without always waiting until she feels she knows all the answers before taking action. Ron, meanwhile, literally comes face-to-face with his own unresolved feelings for Hermione when he witnesses the kissing Harry and Hermione images the Locket projects as it attempts to protect itself. Harry, who apparently understands Ron's true feelings better than Ron, quickly reassures his friend that there is nothing between him and Hermione.

Harry not only shows another side to his innate courage, but also his growing ability to trust others. Despite not knowing if friend or foe sent the doe Patronus, and after the nearly disastrous encounter with the bogus Bathilda Bagshot, Harry takes yet another leap of faith by following the doe in the hope that this time it was sent to help. However, youthful curiosity may have helped to over-ride caution, and Harry avoids consulting Hermione, knowing she would be far more suspicious and leery following their near-fatal experience in Godric's Hollow. It is confirmed, however, that the silver doe was indeed dispatched to help; the question now is, who sent it and why? An adult reading this chapter may also note that Ron mentions nothing about having told Bill and Fleur where he was going, or even that he was leaving, when he departed Shell Cottage. This rather leads one to wonder what Bill and Fleur thought when they found his room empty. We do see that Ron had taken the time to pack a rather large knapsack for the trip, rather than just setting out after the light from the Deluminator as he implies in his story; we can only hope, for Bill and Fleur's sake, that at the same time he remembered to at least leave them a note, although they may not have been too surprised by his leaving, knowing Ron had been on a mission with Harry and Hermione.

Questions

Review 1. Why did Harry and Hermione's conversation about Ron's wand prove to be so important?

2. How did Ron's shameful desertion actually help the Trio? What made him return? Why is Hermione so angry at him?

3. Why does Harry want Ron, rather than himself, to destroy the Locket Horcrux? How does Ron react to this?

Extra Study 1. Who could have sent the doe Patronus? Why?

2. How did Gryffindor's Sword get in the pond? Who might have been responsible for putting it there and why?

3. If someone intended for Harry to find the sword, why was it left in such a dangerous place where he was almost killed?

4. Why was the Locket strangling Harry?

5. Why would the Locket project an image of Harry and Hermione kissing?

6. In Harry's third year, just before Sirius Black slashed Ron's bed curtains, Harry had a curious dream in which he was pursuing a glowing silver creature through a forest. Could there be any relation between that dream and the silver doe in this chapter? Explain that relationship.

7. James Potter's (Harry's father) Animagus form was a stag and Harry's Patronus is a silver stag. Could these have any relationship to the doe Patronus? Explain.

Greater Picture

Ron will also bring back information about "Potter Watch," an underground wizard news radio program that airs updates about Harry and the war against Voldemort.

We learn later that the doe was Severus Snape's Patronus. Carefully examining the text shows that Hermione had her beaded bag open when she told Harry where they had stopped. Phineas Nigellus's portrait inside it overheard Hermione and reported that to Snape. Snape thus knows that Harry and Hermione are in the Forest of Dean, though not exactly where; the Forest of Dean is a largish place, several wooded sections totaling about 40 square miles. (It is located a few miles west of Gloucester in the south-west of England.) It is open to question how Snape found Harry, given the protective spells Hermione had set around them. This must, of course, be supposition, but we already know that many spells are limited by distance, Apparation being one; it is likely that once he was within a few miles of Harry, Snape could use Legilimency to see what Harry was seeing, and thus determine where he was. This would be easier for Snape because he had previously spent time in Harry's mind. Snape may also have planned to send the Patronus over many successive nights in the hope that Harry would eventually see it and follow it to where the sword was hidden, though in this instance it was evidently only their first or second night there. Also, it will be seen in a later chapter that more than one Patronus can be cast at a time, and there may have been multiple ones roaming the forest searching for Harry.

One interesting note. It will be learned later that if a wizard captures another wizard's wand, that wand's allegiance can be transferred to the new owner. Ron provides Harry with a wand he took from a Snatcher, making it possible that Ron is actually that wand's new master. However, it is still possible for Harry to use it, although likely with less effectiveness than if he had been the one who forcibly obtained it. Harry will later seize and wield Draco Malfoy's wand, finding that it performs well for him. Harry capturing Draco's wand will also play a significant role in Harry's final confrontation with Voldemort, who has stolen the Elder Wand from Dumbledore's tomb.

Chapter 20: Xenophilius Lovegood

SYNOPSIS

The next morning, Hermione and Ron remain distant, though Ron is quite cheery when he and Harry are alone. Their recent upswing in luck has created a more optimistic mood. Each updates the other about recent events, and Ron reveals the tracer taboo on Voldemort's name. It is jinxed to track anyone speaking it, and to break protective spells surrounding that person. That is how they were found so quickly in Tottenham Court Road. While speculating about who conjured the doe Patronus, they effectively eliminate Kingsley and Dumbledore. They also discuss Dumbledore and Grindelwald's close friendship. After Harry has some slight trouble using the blackthorn wand Ron grabbed from a Snatcher, the three retire to their tent where Harry takes first watch. Ron mentions a radio program, *Potterwatch*, that reports accurate news; the show requires a password, but Ron missed the last show and is unable to tune it in. Hermione, still ignoring Ron, suggests visiting Xenophilius Lovegood. She shows Harry Dumbledore's biography and Dumbledore's letter to Grindelwald that is printed in the book. The A in Albus' signature is the same symbol that Mr. Lovegood was wearing, the same as the one in *The Tales of Beedle the Bard*, and on the Peverell tombstone in Godric's Hollow. Harry is reluctant, however, citing their recent Godric's Hollow misadventure, but Hermione insists these connections are important. Ron sides with Hermione, saying that Xenophilius has lately been publishing pro-Harry articles in the *Quibbler*. Harry, though suspecting Ron is only currying Hermione's favor, agrees to go.

The next morning the Trio Disapparate to Ottery St. Catchpole village near The Burrow and, according to Ron (and truthful to the fourth novel), close to the Lovegoods. After walking under the Invisibility Cloak for a few hours and Disapparating a few miles further north, a strange-looking cylindrical house is spotted rising vertically to the sky. Convinced this must be the Lovegood house, they climb a hill and find three hand-painted signs indicating the *The Quibbler* editor resides there. Seen along the path are odd plants and creatures that Luna has worn and mentioned. An unkempt-looking Xenophilius Lovegood answers the door but seems unwilling to invite them in. Xeno appears anxious and his eyes frequently dart about while leading them upstairs to a room containing an old-fashioned printing press churning out Quibblers, which Xeno rapidly covers, muffling the sound somewhat. Hermione is shocked by an Erumpent Horn mounted on the wall; Xeno claims it is a Crumple-Horned Snorkack horn, despite Hermione disagreeing. When Xeno is reluctant to offer Harry any assistance, Ron and Hermione press him to help, just as he urges his readers to. When asked about Luna's whereabouts, Xeno claims she is fishing for freshwater Plimpies at the stream, and leaves to summon her. Harry notices a stone statue of a woman wearing a bizarre-looking headdress. Moments later, Xeno returns with an infusion of Gurdyroots. Noticing the Trio's interest in the statue, Xeno explains that it is modeled after Rowena Ravenclaw wearing her now-lost Diadem headdress. Luna, he says, is beyond the Bottom Bridge catching enough Plimpies to make soup for dinner. Harry asks about the symbol Xeno wore to Bill and Fleur's wedding. Xenophilius wants to know if Harry is referring to the Deathly Hallows sign.

ANALYSIS

Xeno Lovegood's odd behavior and disheveled appearance indicates that something is probably wrong here, although just what is unknown yet. And though he has been actively supporting Harry Potter in his newspaper, and urging readers to do likewise, Xeno now seems quite reluctant to assist the Trio in any way, and only agrees to help when he is pressured. Luna's absence also seems peculiar, and Xeno's claim that she is catching fish for their supper should be considered suspicious.

Several non-human elements play a crucial role in this chapter in addition to human ones. This is the first time an identifiable Ravenclaw artifact has been mentioned. While some fans speculated that the wand in Ollivander's shop window may have been Ravenclaw's, this is the first time that any specific object has been positively connected with her. Knowing that we are looking for artifacts once belonging to the four Hogwarts Founders, attention should probably be paid to Ravenclaw having had a diadem that people have been searching for. (A diadem is a jeweled ornament in the shape of a half crown, worn by women and placed over the forehead, also called *tiara*.) Also, the radio, or wireless as it is also known, is important because it demonstrates that there are ongoing secret channels to provide truthful information about Harry Potter, Voldemort, and the war. Like Xenophilius Lovegood's stories in *The Quibbler*, the *Potterwatch* wireless program helps to inform and rally the wizarding community by airing accurate news and updates. By acting as a unified voice, it creates solidarity among wizards and encourages its listeners, who have either been too fearful or uninformed, to resist the Dark Lord and his Death Eaters. These broadcasts are similar to how radio maintained communication with populations suppressed by war and, later, communism in the mid-20th century. It also shows the powerful effect the media can exert over over the masses; whether this power is used for good or evil depends on who controls it and how it is disseminated. Most importantly, the strange symbol the Trio has repeatedly encountered is identified by Xenophilius. However, his odd behavior is suspicious, especially considering he has been such a staunch Harry Potter supporter. The Trio soon become wary, but they will learn, at last, that the symbol refers to the *Deathly Hallows*, and it is not a Dark mark as Viktor Krum mistakenly claimed. However, it will take Harry some time to work out just what the Hallows are, whether or not they relate directly to his mission, and whether Dumbledore intended for him to pursue them separately.

QUESTIONS

Review 1. Why does the trio seek out Xenophilius Lovegood? How can he help them?

2. Why does Xenophilius have a statue modeled after Rowena Ravenclaw wearing her headdress? Could this be significant to Harry's mission? If so, why?

3. Where is Luna?

4. Why did Viktor Krum and others believe the Deathly Hallows symbol represented Dark Magic, when apparently it did not?

5. What is the sign of the Deathly Hallows?

Further Study 1. How is the radio used in the fight against Voldemort? How could it be used against Harry?

2. Why is Xenophilius, an ardent Harry Potter supporter, reluctant to help the Trio?

3. Why would Xeno suddenly cover the printing press?

GREATER PICTURE

The "Potterwatch" wireless program will become crucial once Ron is able to tune it in. Not only does it act as an ongoing conduit for truthful information about Harry and Voldemort, but it will help Harry to reconnect ties to old friends and align himself with others who are fighting a common cause. The latest radio reports about who has been killed or captured will also remind Harry that Voldemort's reign of terror affects not only him, but many others. Harry seeing the model of Rowena Ravenclaw's lost Diadem is crucial because this is the first mention of any artifact connected to Ravenclaw that may have survived to the present. Later, Harry will discover that the true Ravenclaw Diadem was made into a Horcrux by Voldemort. Harry has unknowingly come into contact with the Diadem. While searching for a place to hide his Potions book inside the Room of Requirement in *Harry Potter and the Half-Blood Prince*, he used the Diadem as a marker to remember the book's location. However, Harry obviously was unaware that he was handling one of Voldemort's Horcruxes.

Xenophilius' odd behavior is also important, for in the next chapter we will learn that when the Trio arrived at his house, he sent an owl to the Ministry alerting them that they were there. The careful reader will note the owl in the garden as the Trio approach the house, and it flying up past the window as Harry looks out when Xeno says he is going to fetch Luna; those who recognize this later may assume, as Harry would, that the owl was being sent to fetch Luna. We will learn shortly that Xeno informs the Ministry because Luna was captured by Death Eaters while returning home from Hogwarts for Christmas, and Xeno is hoping that by informing on Harry, he can secure her release.

Chapter 21: The Tale of the Three Brothers

SYNOPSIS

Xenophilius Lovegood explains that the Deathly Hallows mark he wore at Bill's wedding, is not Dark at all, though a burly young man there thought it was. It is actually a sign indicating one is on a Quest for the Deathly Hallows, and it is from *The Tale of the Three Brothers*. Harry has never heard of it, but Ron and Hermione have; when Hermione says she has a copy of *The Tales of Beedle the Bard*, Xenophilius asks her to read the story aloud.

Xenophilius elaborates upon the subject, although he seems uneasy. The *Tale of the Three Brothers* relates how three brothers cheated Death and received artifacts from him. These were a wand, called the Elder Wand, which was unbeatable in a duel; a Resurrection Stone, which, when turned three times, summons souls from the afterlife to the living world; and Death's own Cloak of Invisibility. These items are the Deathly Hallows, and despite it being a fairy tale, the Three Hallows actually exist. Recalling the symbol on Ignotus Peverell's grave in Godric's Hollow, Hermione asks if there is any connection with the Peverell family. Xenophilius replies that it is believed that Ignotus is one of the three brothers in the story, though to himself, Harry recalls the Peverell name from somewhere else. When Xenophilius goes to prepare dinner, the Trio discuss the three Hallows. Hermione admits the wand has the best documented history. Magical history has many stories of super-powerful wands, and there seems to be a consistent link from the past to the present. The Resurrection Stone is dismissed as being a modified Philosopher's Stone, but there is speculation that the Invisibility Cloak is the one in Harry's pocket. It has withstood the test of time, appearing new and unworn, unlike ordinary invisibility cloaks that eventually become threadbare and lose their effectiveness.

Harry, curious, goes up to Luna's bedroom. Although Luna is supposedly fishing for their dinner, her room is dusty and appears unused; Luna ought to be at home for the holidays. Harry again asks Xenophilius about Luna's whereabouts and why there are only four plates set for dinner. Xenophilius tries to prevent the Trio from leaving, then admits that "they" took Luna away to an unknown location as a punishment for his stories in *The Quibbler*. Hermione spots approaching broomsticks; Xenophilius uses the distraction to draw his wand, but Harry has pushed the other two aside as Xeno's spell hits the Erumpent horn, which explodes, blowing Xenophilius down the stairs. The Trio are buried under rubble, while the printing press has dropped across the staircase. Downstairs, two Death Eaters, Travers and Selwyn, demand to know why Xeno summoned them and tried to blow them up. Upstairs, the Trio dig themselves out, and Hermione throws the Invisibility Cloak over Ron. She fires a Memory charm at Xeno as he claws his way through the rubble, then blasts a hole through the floor. As they fall, Harry sees the Death Eaters. Hermione safely Disapparates them to a field.

Chapter 21: The Tale of the Three Brothers

ANALYSIS

The Trio have come here, in part, because Xenophilius Lovegood is sympathetic, publicly, to Harry's cause. However, we see that Death Eaters have forced him to abandon his support by imprisoning his daughter, Luna. Controlling family members via state-ordered or state-backed kidnapping is common in totalitarian regimes throughout history. Considering how dangerous it is for anyone to support Harry, it is questionable as to why Lovegood continued publishing *The Quibbler* openly at his home rather than hiding underground like so many other wizard families, or why Luna was allowed to remain at Hogwarts, which is now under Voldemort's control. But like Luna, Lovegood's odd views and outlandish beliefs have warped his perception of reality, and he may simply have been oblivious to the perils, or believed he was immune to any danger. Unfortunately, this has cost his daughter's freedom, and possibly her life (and threatens his own) if he fails to cooperate with Voldemort's Death Eaters. Now Lovegood will do anything to save Luna, including betraying Harry Potter.

We have seen that Viktor Krum and others believe the Deathly Hallows symbol is a Dark mark. It is possible that most people, including Krum, never understanding its true meaning or origin, associate it with evil only because Grindelwald adopted it, and, after disgracing himself at Durmstrang, went on to become one of history's most notorious wizards. From then on, the Deathly Hallows symbol was forever tainted and considered "Dark." That a benign image can become associated with evil is hardly unprecedented. The swastika is such a modern-day icon: its origins date back to ancient history as a benevolent and sacred symbol in many Asian and Middle Eastern religions such as Hinduism, Buddhism, and others. It was later discovered to be linked to ancient Indo-European people, including the Aryans, prompting Nazi Germany to adopt it in the mid-20th century as their emblem to represent racial purity and superiority. Although Asian cultures still consider it a symbol for luck, fortune, and victory, the swastika is primarily remembered (and still used) in the West as symbolizing Nazi hate and prejudice. Presumably, this same pattern has resulted in some Wizarding realms associating the Hallows mark with Grindelwald, just as the Dark mark (the skull and snake) represents Voldemort.

Although Harry now knows what the Deathly Hallows actually are, it will take him time to completely understand their significance. The Invisibility Cloak is likely the same one that Harry owns, lending credibility to the belief that the other Deathly Hallows exist. In particular, the Elder Wand likely has some real existence, as is shown by the documented murders that apparently follow its possibly mythical trail. If the Elder Wand truly exists, and Harry finds it, it could be a powerful weapon against Voldemort. Harry is once again cast into confusion; whoever controls all three Hallows is supposedly "the master of Death." Dumbledore had set Harry the task of finding and destroying the remaining Horcruxes; would possessing all three Hallows make that task easier? Should he devote his energies to uniting the Hallows and thus possibly avoiding the almost certain death he faces at Voldemort's wand?

Hermione once again shows how she is able to react quickly while under fire when she safely Disapparates the Trio out of danger.

QUESTIONS

Review 1. How does Xenophilius' explanation about the Deathly Hallows symbol differ from what Viktor Krum told Harry at Bill and Fleur's wedding?

2. Why would Viktor Krum and others believe that the Deathly Hallows symbol was a Dark mark?

3. If Xenophilius has been supporting Harry Potter in his paper *The Quibbler*, why does he report him to the Death Eaters? Was he justified in doing this?

4. Why is Harry suspicious regarding Luna's whereabouts, and where might she be?

Extra Study 1. Why did Xenophilius and Luna never go into hiding so he could continue to publish pro-Harry articles in The Quibbler? Should he have allowed Luna to remain at Hogwarts? If not, why?

2. Of the three Deathly Hallows, why is the Resurrection Stone dismissed as the least likely to exist? Is that explanation plausible? Of the Trio, who would be the most interested in it and why?

3. Why does Hermione cover Ron with the Invisibility Cloak while deliberately allowing the Death Eaters to see her and Harry before she Disapparates the Trio to safety?

4. What modern-day comparisons can be made to a benevolent symbol like the Deathly Hallows becoming an evil icon?

GREATER PICTURE

The Deathly Hallows that Xenophilius Lovegood mentions are real, though it is unlikely that there could be three brothers who literally tricked Death. It is believed they may be based on the Peverells, a family that both Harry and Voldemort could be descended from; it is suggested that they could be simply extremely talented Wizards. Meanwhile, we will learn that the artifact Voldemort has been seeking is actually one of the Hallows, namely the Elder Wand. It is still unknown where the Elder Wand is, but we will discover that it was actually in Dumbledore's possession at his death. Voldemort will discover this and retrieve the wand from Dumbledore's tomb. As legend proclaims this wand unbeatable in duels, Voldemort believes it will overpower Harry, as his own wand and Lucius Malfoy's were unable to. However, the story of the Three Brothers has told us that the Elder Wand's master is always vulnerable to defeat, and that this is how Dumbledore not only came to possess it, but also lost its allegiance. Although Harry does not actually obtain the Elder Wand until the war's end, it will still prove to be a powerful weapon against Voldemort.

Harry, as mentioned, seems to recall hearing the Peverell name somewhere. He will remember that the ring Marvolo Gaunt brandished under Bob Ogden's nose in a memory Harry experienced in Dumbledore's Pensieve was "the ring of the Peverells." Harry has seen this ring on Tom Riddle's finger in a memory retrieved from Professor Slughorn, on Dumbledore's damaged hand when he collects Harry in the summer, and lying on one of Dumbledore's work tables. Where it is now, and what significance it has, are as yet unknown. We will learn in the next chapter that Hermione, even under pressure, is reacting with great intelligence and forethought. With only moments to act, she protected both Ron's family and Xeno. By allowing the Death Eaters to see her and Harry, she protects Xeno by confirming that he sent a legitimate summons. She also used the Invisibility Cloak to hide Ron's presence from the Death Eaters (and presumably from Xeno with the Memory Charm as well), to protect him and also his family. If Ron is discovered with Harry and Hermione, rather than confined at home with Spattergroit, Voldemort and his Death Eaters will target the Weasley family, just as they did the Lovegoods. Concealing Ron safeguards his cover provided by the ghoul. Hermione's family is also in danger, but she has hidden them in Australia, with new identities and altered memories.

Chapter 22: The Deathly Hallows

Synopsis

Hermione, as she sets the protective spells, explains that she wanted the Death Eaters to see Harry so that they would know that Xenophilius Lovegood had not lied to them. Ron had to remain hidden because he is supposed to be confined at home with Spattergroit; if Luna is being held captive for her fathers' behaviour, what would the Death Eaters do to Ron's family if they knew he was not where the Weasleys claimed he was? As for her own parents, they are safe in Australia, their memories modified.

Back in their tent, Hermione complains that visiting Xeno Lovegood was a waste. She discounts the three brothers fairy tale, but Harry is drawn to it. Being able to conquer death and not be killed by Voldemort pulls on his imagination and gives him hope. Ron agrees with Harry; it would be hard to fabricate such a story while under intense pressure, which Xeno certainly was, trying to keep Harry there. Ron also points out that it was Hermione who said there was significant evidence supporting the Elder Wand's existence. Hermione counters that the dead cannot be brought back to life, but Harry remembers his father and mother, and Cedric emerging from Voldemort's wand. Seeing both Hermione and Ron eyeing him warily as he talks about resurrecting the dead, he instead asks about the Peverells. Hermione says they are among the oldest Wizarding families recorded, but the male line died out a long time ago. There could be female descendants who did not bear the Peverell name. Harry suddenly recalls where he has heard the name: Marvolo Gaunt, You-know-who's grandfather, had shown the Ministry representative a ring bearing the Peverell symbol as proof of their ancestry. Harry decides that the ring, that bears scratches is the Deathly Hallows symbol, is in fact the Resurrection Stone. He also remembers that Dumbledore had James' Invisibility Cloak on the night James died, and leaps to the conclusion that Dumbledore was examining it because it was a Hallow. Harry remembers the tale of the Three Brothers' conclusion and wonders, if the holder of the three Hallows can master Death, is this what it will come to? Him against Voldemort? Hallows against Horcruxes? He also guesses that Dumbledore left him the Snitch in his will because the ring is inside. Harry realizes that Voldemort must be searching for the Elder Wand to defeat Harry. Voldemort has probably never heard the *Tales of Beedle the Bard*, but knows about the Elder Wand, the Hallow that cannot hide itself, and seeks it to destroy Harry's wand. Hermione is still unsure. Both she and Ron believe that Harry is making a fairy tale into reality, and they believe he should only follow Dumbledore's clear instructions to destroy Horcruxes. Over the next week, however, Harry becomes obsessed with the Deathly Hallows. He is certain the Resurrection Stone is somehow hidden inside the Snitch, but he is still unable to open it or understand its cryptic inscription, "I open at the close." Ron and Hermione want Harry to concentrate on the Horcruxes rather than the Deathly Hallows. Gradually, Ron takes charge of the expedition, suggesting new places to search. One night in March, he is finally able to tune in the wireless to "Potterwatch," the radio show he has been looking for since Christmas. Produced by Lee Jordan, "Potterwatch" is the only wireless program that reports the truth; everyone else toes the Ministry line. Tonight Lee reports on the deaths of Ted Tonks, Dirk Cresswell, and the goblin Gornuk. Dean Thomas and a second goblin are believed to have escaped. Lee also mentions that Bathilda Bagshot is dead. Following his report, Kingsley Shacklebolt speaks about Muggle casualties, and issues a plea to assist them from the depredations of Death Eaters. Lupin then explains why he is certain Harry is alive. Following this, there is an opinion piece by either Fred or George about how "You-know-who" cannot be everywhere he is reported, as there would have to be about nineteen of him. Continuing in this humorous vein, he goes on to say that rumours that Voldemort can kill by looking at one are false, apparently people have confused him with a Basilisk, and he closes with a quick lesson in telling the difference. Finally, Lee Jordan takes the microphone back and closes with a plea for calm.

After the show, Harry accidentally speaks Voldemort's name, causing the protective enchantments around the tent to collapse. Snatchers immediately surround them.

Analysis

Although Hermione believes the Lovegood visit revealed nothing important and discounts The Three Brothers tale, like the trip to Godric's Hollow, information has been provided that the Trio has yet to realize is important to their mission. The Deathly Hallows will be tied to defeating Voldemort, although Harry's initial interest in them is apart from this. To someone who has lost so many loved ones, a Resurrection Stone is a particularly desirable and seductive object to possess, and Harry reconsiders that magic could reunite him with his parents. And while Hermione wants to stick with Dumbledore's plan to only search for Horcruxes, Harry's continuing fascination with the Hallows will eventually help him work out their significance. Meanwhile, the revelations about Dumbledore's past still troubles Harry, and his faith and trust in his Headmaster continues to waver. Harry also doubts whether Dumbledore ever really cared for him and wonders if he is merely a pawn in Dumbledore's scheme to defeat Voldemort.

Another interesting plot point is highlighted. The Trio agree that Harry's Invisibility Cloak could actually be the one from *The Tale of the Three Brothers*, which Xenophilius says may have been the Peverells. The youngest brother bequeathed the Cloak to his son. Considering Harry received the Cloak from his father, it is possible that it was handed down to him through the generations, making him a direct descendant from the Peverell line. It is also possible that Harry and Voldemort share a common Peverell ancestor, not that blood ties account for much anymore as wizarding families are ripped apart by Voldemort's war. As seen in Sirius Black's family, close relatives, divided by their blood-purity beliefs and loyalties to Voldemort, will readily disown and even kill one another. Readers can also see here how Ron's character has undergone a significant change. No longer a passive and insecure follower, his guilt over his brief desertion, as well as Hermione's severe chastisement, have propelled him into a becoming a more mature, confident, and proactive young man who assumes responsibility to guide the mission, relieving Harry and Hermione from many of the day-to-day burdens. From here on, Ron will no longer be content to dwell in others' shadow, and he begins charting his own life's course.

QUESTIONS

Review 1. Why might Harry be interested in the Deathly Hallows? Why do Ron and Hermione think he should only concentrate on Horcruxes?

2. How and why does Ron take charge of the mission?

3. Was the visit to the Lovegoods a waste as Hermione claims? If not, why?

4. How does listening to *Potterwatch* affect the Trio?

Extra Study 1. Knowing that ghosts exist, why would Hermione be so skeptical about the Resurrection Stone?

2. What might the inscription, "I open at the close" mean?

Chapter 23: Malfoy Manor

SYNOPSIS

With Snatchers surrounding the camp, Hermione only has time to jinx Harry's face to hide his identity. Harry, Ron, and Hermione are bound with other prisoners, who turn out to be Dean Thomas and Griphook. The Snatchers assume the Trio are students on the run and question their identities so they can check their names against those on a wanted list. Hermione claims she is Penelope Clearwater, a half-blood. Ron identifies himself first as Stan Shunpike, then, when the Snatchers recognize that name as being fictitious, as a fictional member of the Weasley family. Harry identifies himself as a Slytherin student named Vernon Dudley. The Snatchers think this is also a lie until he correctly describes the Slytherin Common room: he and Ron (using Polyjuice Potion to impersonate Crabbe and Goyle) were inside it during their second year at Hogwarts. However, the Snatchers recognize Hermione's picture in the *Daily Prophet* and find Harry's glasses. The scar beneath his puffy, jinxed forehead is barely discernible, which leaves them unsure. They also find Gryffindor's Sword. Harry, meanwhile, is once again seeing through Voldemort's eyes. He is gazing upon a black fortress with a tall tower; a single light shows at the top. It is time to fly . . . and through a window too narrow for a human to pass. Within, an ancient man, saying that he was expecting Voldemort to come, but says that he never had it. Believing he has captured "Undesirable Number One," the Snatchers' leader, Fenrir Greyback leads the other Snatchers and their captives to the Dark Lord's headquarters, Malfoy Manor. They are met there by Narcissa Malfoy, who says her son, Draco, can positively identify Harry Potter. Lucius believes Voldemort will forgive him when he turns over Harry Potter, but before summoning the Dark Lord, orders Draco to verify that it is actually Harry. Draco, fearful, claims he is unsure it is him. Narcissa, noticing that Harry's wand does not match Ollivander's description, wants Lucius to be absolutely positive before summoning Voldemort with his Dark Mark. Greyback suggests identifying the Mudblood (Hermione), and Narcissa says she recognizes her from Madam Malkin's robe shop and saw her picture in the *Daily Prophet.* Lucius prods Draco to identify Ron and Hermione, and he reluctantly says it could be them.

Bellatrix enters; although she is also uncertain that it is Harry, she wants to inform Voldemort immediately. Lucius forcibly stops her from touching her Dark Mark, claiming it is his right to inform Voldemort that Harry Potter has been caught. Greyback interjects, saying he captured Potter and demands the reward. He also wants Hermione. As Lucius is about to touch his Dark Mark, Bellatrix shrieks; she has spotted a Snatcher holding Gryffindor's Sword. When he is reluctant to hand it over, she Stuns all the Snatchers except Greyback, who is now on his knees. Bellatrix screams that they are all in peril if her Gringotts vault has been breached.

Hermione is cut loose from the others so she can be interrogated about the sword, while Greyback imprisons Harry, Ron, Dean Thomas, and Griphook in the cellar. Luna and Ollivander are there. From below, they hear Hermione's screams as Bellatix tortures her with the Cruciatus Curse to learn if the sword was stolen from the Lestrange's Gringotts vault; Ron is reduced to tears listening. With Luna's help and light from the Deluminator, Harry, Ron, Dean, and Griphook are soon free, though Griphook is too badly injured to stand.

Emptying his pouch looking for something that will help, Harry sees a flash of sky blue in Sirius' mirror shard, and frantically begs for help. Hermione, despite being tortured, tells Bellatrix the sword is a fake. Harry hears Lucius Malfoy saying they can check that, and as he sends Draco down to fetch the goblin, Harry tells Griphook that he must say the sword is fake. Draco collects Griphook, and as the door closes behind him, Dobby apparates into the cellar. Dobby confirms that he can disapparate with humans.

Again, Harry peers through Voldemort's eyes, seeing the old man telling Voldemort that killing him will bring him no nearer to what he seeks.

On Harry's orders, Dobby first rescues Luna, Dean, and Mr. Ollivander, apparating them to Shell Cottage, Bill and Fleur's home. The cracking noise of Dobby disapparating is heard upstairs, and Lucius Malfoy orders Wormtail to investigate. Harry and Ron attack as he enters. Wormtail grabs Harry, choking him with his silver hand. Harry reminds him that he is owed a life debt. Wormtail hesitates and momentarily relaxes his grip, releasing Harry, but the silver hand turns and fatally strangles Wormtail.

Ron is desperate, and he and Harry run upstairs to save Hermione, armed only with Wormtail's wand. They hear Griphook declare the Gryffindor Sword is a fake. Bellatrix, satisfied that Hermione has not been inside her vault, summons Voldemort, and offers Hermione to Greyback as a reward to satisfy his desire. Harry feels his scar explode, and sees Voldemort, angry at being summoned, killing the old man. Ron disarms Bellatrix with Wormtail's wand. Harry catches Bellatrix' wand and Stuns Lucius Malfoy, then dodges curses cast by Draco, Narcissa, and Greyback. Bellatrix, holding a silver knife to Hermione's neck and threatening to kill her, orders them to drop the wands; Draco collects them. Dobby reappears, dropping the crystal chandelier on Bellatrix, Hermione, and Griphook, and disarming Narcissa. Draco clutches his face, injured by flying crystal, as Harry grabs all three wands from him and Stuns Greyback. When Bellatrix addresses Dobby as an enslaved House-elf, Dobby declares he is a free elf and has come to save Harry Potter and his friends. Harry tosses a wand to Ron, who has extracted Hermione from the chandelier wreckage, and tells him to go. Harry disapparates with Griphook and Dobby. As they apparate to safety, Harry realizes that Dobby has been mortally wounded by Bellatrix's silver knife. Dobby gazes at Harry, who is holding him, and dies, his last words being "Harry . . . Potter . . ."

Analysis

Several characters show personality traits that have only been glimpsed previously. Ron's feelings for Hermione are further developed when he sobs her name as she is being tortured by Bellatrix, and when he fiercely tries to prevent her falling prey to Fenrir Greyback's perverted desires. This marks yet another turning point in Ron's maturity as he is faced with possibly losing someone he cares deeply about and must act to save her, regardless of his own safety. Although Voldemort demands absolute fidelity and obedience from his servants, it appears most support him only out of fear or for personal gain, although there is certainly no guarantee that loyalty will be rewarded or lives spared. This has led to inner conflicts among his followers that are starting to undermine Voldemort's rule. Bellatrix and Lucius vie with one another for power and favor, forcing Narcissa Malfoy to choose between her sister and her husband. Although we don't see it here, we suspect that her devotion is likely to her husband and son. Fenrir Greyback, meanwhile, desires material compensation, while the weak-willed Wormtail (Peter Pettigrew) sought the Dark Lord's protection only to evade the Order of the Phoenix, who would likely have executed him for betraying the Potters and Sirius Black. Wormtail was also burdened by his life debt to Harry, an obligation he had no choice but to fulfill, and which Voldemort fatally punished him for when he did. Voldemort likely was unaware of the life debt when he crafted the silver hand, as it is almost certain that Wormtail would never willingly have confessed this to him; however, knowing how meek and cowardly Wormtail was, it is likely that Voldemort crafted the silver hand to retaliate against any disloyalty.

Draco Malfoy, meanwhile, clearly shows that he is not his father's son; when Draco is again forced into a difficult situation, he is torn between intrinsic compassion, family loyalty, and fearing Voldemort. Although he obviously recognizes Harry and the others imprisoned at Malfoy Manor, as with Dumbledore on the Astronomy Tower (in *Harry Potter and the Half-Blood Prince*), and the Death Eater that Voldemort forced him to torture, he resists taking any action that will endanger them. Only pressure from his family and being unable to lie convincingly does he admit that Harry's two companions *could* be Ron and Hermione. Although Draco unlikely has any fonder feelings for Harry and the others than he ever did and is still an obnoxious bully, he is neither vicious nor a killer. Like Harry's cousin, Dudley, there is an invisible line his innate humanity prevents him from ever crossing. Despite being raised with "pure-blood" rhetoric and elitist conditioning, he was mostly a half-hearted Voldemort follower, likely trailing along out of duty, for adventure, and the prestige he believed it bestowed. Like Regulus Black, he lacks the inherent evil to be a true Death Eater, and his refusal to harm Harry and Dumbledore goes against everything he was taught and thought he believed in. By now, Draco probably realizes that Voldemort is only using him to punish his family and will likely kill him and his parents. Ultimately, Draco shows strength and morality by protecting the Trio, even though betraying them could help win back Voldemort's favor for his family. Consequently, Draco fails to realize that his compassion makes him a far better person than his flawed, reprehensible father; instead, he believes himself a cowardly failure.

Dobby's role is also examined here. In his last act, Dobby dies a martyr and a true hero. He defies the humans who enslaved him for so long and breaks the promise he made to Harry during his second year never to try and save his life again. Breaking this promise comes exactly when Harry is in mortal danger and when only an elf's unique magical abilities can save him. Dobby's life has revolved around the hope that Harry would improve other House-elves' situations by defeating Voldemort, and his admiration is clearly reflected by his dying words. Dobby is far from the fearful, cowering enslaved elf Harry first met in *Harry Potter and the Chamber of Secrets*. His noble, grand courage is climaxed by his daring rescue, but perhaps most importantly, he dies a free elf, which Harry will note on his tombstone.

Although the unfortunate experience at Malfoy Manor has resulted in Dobby's tragic death, Dean, Griphook, Luna, and Ollivander are rescued from an uncertain, but likely deadly, fate. Also, Bellatrix Lestrange's frantic behavior may signal something that the Trio will need to know.

One point perhaps worth mentioning is that once again the difference between House-Elf Apparation and human Apparation is seen. In the first chapter, Death Eaters Apparate just outside Malfoy Manor's gates and then proceed on foot; similarly, the Snatchers Apparate to just outside the same gates and proceed on foot once admitted. This is a clear indication that Apparation has been barred inside the Manor grounds. Yet Dobby Apparates in and out. It is curious, perhaps, that Harry and Ron, once they have defeated Bellatrix, are able to Apparate out of the manor; though the spells around the Burrow apparently prevented Apparation in either direction, perhaps Voldemort or Lucius worked a more advanced version of that spell, so it is only Apparation into the manor which is prohibited.

QUESTIONS

Review 1. How could Dobby Apparate into the supposedly impenetrable cellar? What other impenetrable area has been seen where an elf Apparated into?

2. Why does Draco claim not to recognize any Trio member? Why does he finally admit that it could be Ron and Hermione?

3. How does Draco's character compare to his family's, particularly his father, Lucius Malfoy? What accounts for this?

4. How does Hermione being tortured affect Ron?

5. Why does Wormtail's silver hand strangle him now?

Extra Study 1. How did Dobby know where to find Harry and the others?

2. Why do Lucius and Bellatrix argue over who will summon Voldemort that Harry has been captured?

3. What might be the after-effects of Hermione's torture?

4. Whose eye might Harry be glimpsing in the mirror fragment? If it is not Dumbledore, why would Harry trust that this person will help?

GREATER PICTURE

In discussing Draco Malfoy's humanity, it should be noted that Dumbledore had also recognized this trait in him. As we will find out shortly, by the beginning of *Harry Potter and the Half-Blood Prince*, Dumbledore knew that Voldemort had assigned Draco the task of murdering him. This was why Dumbledore extracted Snape's promise, that, if necessary, Snape would kill Dumbledore: primarily to save Draco's soul from that first, destructive act that would cost him that humanity and irretrievably push him to the Dark side. Dumbledore was also aware that Draco would likely be unable to fulfill his mission, and suspected that another Death Eater would complete the job; Snape would allow Dumbledore to die with dignity and by his own design, whereas other Death Eaters probably would not. Draco is not entirely redeemed however, and in a later chapter, he will attempt to capture Harry for Voldemort, although he may be motivated by trying to reprieve his family from the Dark Lord's wrath. Harry, witnessing Bellatrix's near-panic when the Sword of Gryffindor is discovered, and remembering Griphook's earlier words that the replica Sword of Gryffindor from the Headmaster's office had been moved to Gringott's vault, will correctly guess that the sword is being stored in the Lestrange vault, and that there is another object there that Voldemort highly values. Harry will correctly surmise that this is another Horcrux, and that it is Hufflepuff's Cup, that being the only Founders' artifact he has seen.

Chapter 24: The Wandmaker

SYNOPSIS

Harry realizes they have successfully apparated to Bill and Fleur Weasley's seaside cottage, despite his uncertainty at takeoff. He asks about Hermione, and Bill says she is inside and is alright. Looking down at Dobby, Harry pulls the knife from his body and covers him with his jacket. As Dean carries the injured Griphook into the cottage, Harry's scar prickles, and he can see those at Malfoy Manor being punished by Voldemort.

Harry wants to bury Dobby himself, without magic. Asking for a spade, he sets about digging a grave in the garden. His scar burns, but he realizes that he has at last learned to master the pain and can shut out Voldemort's thoughts with his grief . . . though, of course, Dumbledore would have called it "love." His own thoughts turn to Wormtail and the brief merciful act that cost him his life. Dumbledore foresaw that, but what else had he known? Harry resolves to only hunt Horcruxes as Dumbledore wanted, rather than also searching for the Deathly Hallows.

Ron and Dean join Harry. Ron reports Hermione is fine, Fleur is looking after her. Ron and Dean have brought spades and help Harry dig. After placing shoes, socks, and a hat on Dobby's body, they carefully place him in the grave and bury him. Luna thinks they should say a few words, and each in turn gives thanks to the tiny elf who saved their lives. Harry places a large rock on the grave as a headstone and inscribes the words: HERE LIES DOBBY, A FREE ELF

Inside the cottage, Harry overhears Bill saying that it was fortunate Ginny was on holiday from Hogwarts, otherwise she could have been taken by Death Eaters before they reached her. Now she is safely hidden with the other Weasleys at Aunt Muriel's where they are protected by the Fidelius Charm. There is also one protecting Shell Cottage. When Bill says that Ollivander and Griphook can be moved to Muriel's in about an hour,

Harry objects, saying he needs to talk with them, a little surprised by his own authoritative voice.

Harry wonders how Dobby knew to rescue them. The blue eye that was in the mirror shard brings Dumbledore's words back to him: *Help will always be given at Hogwarts to those who ask for it.* Although Harry feels closer to understanding what Dumbledore intended for him to do, he also does not understand. Dumbledore had given Ron the Deluminator knowing he would need a way back. And he understood that there was regret within Wormtail. But what did Dumbledore know about him? Had he deliberately made everything so difficult to give Harry time to work everything out? Harry tells Bill and Fleur that he needs to speak to Griphook and Ollivander, overruling Fleur's objections that they are still too weak. Bill starts to protest, but Harry reminds him that he is also in the Order and knows that Harry is on a mission for Dumbledore.

Harry, along with Ron and Hermione, first meets with Griphook, who is clutching Gryffindor's Sword. When Griphook says that Harry is an odd wizard for burying an elf and rescuing a goblin, Harry is unsure if it is praise or insult. Harry asks for his help to break into a Gringotts vault, stunning Ron and Hermione. Griphook claims it is impossible, but Ron contradicts him, citing the break-in seven years ago; Griphook retorts that the vault was empty then. Harry assures Griphook he is not seeking personal gain. Griphook slowly agrees; the respect and protection Harry has shown for goblins and elves has convinced him that Harry is probably the only wizard who would not break into Gringotts for its treasures. Although Harry says the issue is not goblins versus wizards, Griphook points out that all magical creatures are suppressed under wizard rule and elves are being slaughtered. Who amongst the wizards protests? Hermione says they do, and, as a Mudblood, she has no higher position than the goblins and elves under Voldemort's new order. Griphook asks what Harry seeks in the Lestrange's vault, being as he has the real Gryffindor's Sword, but Harry says only that there are other things in the vault. Griphook says he will think about it, but he is tired and wants to sleep.

Hermione pulls Harry aside on the stair landing wanting to know if a Horcrux could be in the Lestrange vault. Harry confirms this; Bellatrix's terrified reaction when she thought they might have been inside it has convinced him. Ron reminds him that they are supposed to be searching in places important to Voldemort, but Harry thinks Voldemort would envy anyone with a key to one of the deep Gringotts vaults, something only the oldest Wizarding families could have. Harry also believes that Bellatrix and her husband are unaware that the extremely valuable artifact of Voldemort's they are keeping is a Horcrux, just as he never revealed the truth to Lucius Malfoy about the Diary. The safest place to hide anything, says Harry, is in Gringotts.

Harry talks to Ollivander, who thanks Harry for saving him. Harry asks if his broken wand can be repaired, but Ollivander says it is too badly damaged. Harry then shows Ollivander the two wands taken from Malfoy Manor. Ollivander identifies the first as Bellatrix's walnut and dragon heartstring wand. Draco's is hawthorn and unicorn hair, although he says that it may no longer actually belong to Draco because Harry captured it. He explains that wands can transfer their allegiance—the wand chooses the wizard. While a wizard can use almost any wand, if the wand has not bonded with the wizard, it is less effective. A conquered wand usually bends to its new master's will, and this allegiance can be won without killing an opponent. Ron pulls out Wormtail's wand and asks if it is safe for him to use; Ollivander identifies it as the chestnut and dragon heartstring wand he was forced to make for Peter Pettigrew, and says it will serve Ron reasonably well if he did capture it. Harry asks about legends concerning wands that have passed ownership through murder. Ollivander nervously says he believes there is really only one, to which Harry responds, "And You-Know-Who is interested in it, isn't he?" Ollivander acknowledges this and admits that he confessed to Voldemort while under torture about the twin cores in his and Harry's wands. He also told Voldemort that he could just use another wand against Harry. But Harry says that did not work, his wand destroyed the other. Ollivander has never heard of anything like that happening before; Harry's wand did something unique. Voldemort will now be seeking a wand more powerful than Harry's. Harry says Voldemort probably knows that his wand was broken by using the Prior Incantato spell on Hermione's confiscated wand. It will reveal that her spell broke Harry's wand and that she tried unsuccessfully to repair it.

Ollivander confirms that Voldemort knows about the Elder Wand and is probably seeking it not only to defeat Harry, but because he believes it will make him invincible. However, the wand's master is still vulnerable and must always be wary and fear attack. And while Ollivander believes the Elder Wand does exist, it is unlikely that it passes ownership only through murder. It gained a bloody history because it is such a desirable object, and many have fought for it. Ollivander is stunned when Harry asks if he told Voldemort that Gregorovitch once had the Elder Wand, but admits he did, although it was only a rumor that Gregorovitch may have started to help his business. When Harry asks him about the Deathly Hallows, Ollivander does not know what he is talking about. Harry believes he is being truthful and thanks him for the information. Harry then tells Ron and Hermione that Gregorovitch possessed the Elder Wand a long time ago, although when Voldemort found him, he no longer had it. It was stolen by Grindelwald. Harry suddenly "sees" Voldemort approaching Hogwarts' gate but continues talking. With the wand, Grindelwald became the most powerful dark wizard of that time. Only Dumbledore could possibly defeat him, which he did in their legendary duel. Dumbledore captured the Elder Wand, and it is now at Hogwarts. Ron wants to go there immediately, but Harry says they are supposed to be hunting Horcruxes, not Deathly Hallows. Everything suddenly grows dark and cool, then Harry sees himself walking along side Snape by the lake at Hogwarts. He dismisses Snape, saying he will speak with him shortly. The white marble tomb

Chapter 24: The Wandmaker

comes into view, and Voldemort splits it open with his wand. Dumbledore's shrouded body lies within. The shroud layers fall away and under his folded arms is the Elder Wand. Voldemort wonders how Dumbledore could ever have believed that the tomb would protect it from him. As he reaches in and grabs the wand, sparks erupt from its tip. It is ready to serve its new master.

Analysis

Ollivander's comment that the Elder Wand's master must always fear attack is revealing, meaning that whoever wields the wand, despite its superior power, remains vulnerable and can be conquered. We saw the same warning in the Tale of the Three Brothers, where the brother with the Elder Wand was murdered in his sleep the very night after he first used the Wand in a duel. Harry realizes that if Grindelwald was the blond thief who stole the Elder Wand from Gregorovitch, and Dumbledore defeated Grindelwald, that even without killing him, the wand's allegiance must have shifted to Dumbledore. Considering Grindelwald's and the wand's combined power, it is a testament to Dumbledore's considerable magical abilities that he was victorious. It is also a testament to Dumbledore's humanity that he spared Grindelwald, allowing him to be permanently incarcerated for his heinous crimes, although Dumbledore's prior relationship with Grindelwald may have tempered his actions. However, that humanity came with a price: leaving Grindelwald alive left a trail leading directly to the Elder Wand. Harry correctly surmises that Voldemort now knows the Elder Wand exists, and he will likely attempt to obtain it; Harry later sees Voldemort at Hogwarts as he is about to retrieve it from Dumbledore's tomb. However, Harry, whose obsession with the Deathly Hallows had put the mission at risk, decides to abandon his pursuit for them and instead focus only on finding and destroying the Horcruxes, a decision he makes despite his lingering doubts about Dumbledore. Harry deeply mourns Dobby's death, and his choosing to dig Dobby's grave manually is, for him, a gesture showing respect, gratitude, and love to the House-elf who forfeited his life to save him. Using magic to quickly and easily excavate and refill a dirt hole would only have lessened Dobby's bravery and heroism in Harry's mind, and he feels obligated to exert himself physically to affirm Dobby's sacrifice before laying his fallen friend to rest. He also clothes Dobby's body to honor him as a free Elf, clothing symbolizing an Elf's sovereignty. Harry further acknowledges Dobby's independence on his tombstone for all to see. Ron and Dean helping to dig the grave not only shows respect for Dobby, but also their solidarity to Harry. Luna leading the others to say a few final words about Dobby is probably one of the rare times wizards have paid tribute to a House-elf.

Questions

Review 1. Does Griphook really believe that it is impossible to break into Gringotts? How might it be done?

2. What does Griphook mean when he calls Harry an "odd" wizard? Why is Harry unsure if he is being praised or insulted?

3. Hermione claims that Muggle-borns have as little status as non-human magical folk under Voldemort's rule. Is this accurate or not? Explain why.

4. If the Elder Wand is the world's most powerful wand, why is its master always vulnerable to defeat? How might Dumbledore have won its allegiance from Grindelwald without killing him?

5. Is Gringott's really the safest place to hide something as Harry claims? Explain.

Extra Study 1. Why does Harry dig Dobby's grave without using any magic? Why do Ron and Dean help him?

2. Why does Harry clothe Dobby's body before burying him?

3. Is Harry correct that Dumbledore wanted it to take time for him to figure out how to complete the mission? If so, why?

4. Why did Voldemort never reveal to Bellatrix Lestrange and Lucius Malfoy that the objects he entrusted them with were his Horcruxes? What might they have done if they had known?

5. Why would Voldemort torture Ollivander for information rather than using a memory charm or a truth potion? Which method is more reliable?

6. Why didn't Dumbledore kill Grindelwald in their duel? Was letting him live a wise choice? Explain why.

7. Why would Dumbledore wish to be entombed with the Elder Wand, knowing Voldemort could easily retrieve it?

Greater Picture

By carefully examining Harry's questions to Mr. Ollivander, we can see that Harry is attempting to determine who is the Elder Wand's current master. Harry knows that Draco Malfoy forcibly removed the wand from Dumbledore's hand, and that it was unused before being placed inside the tomb with Dumbledore's corpse. Harry has already discovered that a wand that is borrowed or simply given to someone, as Ron did with the hawthorn wand he captured from a Snatcher and gave to Harry, usually works much less efficiently than the user's own wand. In fact, Ron, who captured it, was probably the hawthorn wand's actual master. Harry's questions seem intended to confirm that this theory about the Elder Wand is true. If it is, Voldemort will likely discover that the Elder wand performs far less effectively than he anticipated. The opposing theory, that the Elder Wand only changes allegiance when its master is murdered, seems supported by its bloody history; however, Harry realizes that Dumbledore fully commanded the wand despite Grindelwald's remaining alive, and Grindelwald, in turn, did not have to kill Gregorovitch to wield the wand's full power. Although Ollivander does confirm this theory, Harry remains unsure, and over the next weeks while they are planning the assault on Gringotts and recovering from their injuries, Harry repeatedly wonders if he did the right thing, allowing Voldemort to claim the Elder Wand.

As a side note, one might wonder how Ron was able to use the wand that Harry had simply given him in Malfoy Manor. By sheer luck, that wand was Pettigrew's, which Ron had wrested away from Pettigrew in the cellar. Though it had since been confiscated by Draco, it was surrendered by Ron rather than forcefully taken from him, and so Ron probably remained its new master. Harry pulling the wand away from Draco would have been less relevant to it, as Draco was never its master.

Hermione complains later that Bellatrix Lestrange's wand performs poorly for her; this is because, being nearly unconscious from pain, she took no part in the multiple disarmament jinxes or possession struggles, so that wand is now loyal to the last person who captured it, most likely Ron, who jinxed it from Bellatrix' hand. Knowing what he does now, Harry may be able to rectify that problem by having Hermione forcibly remove the wand from Ron's hand, though he does not. Possibly, his decision, conscious or otherwise, to withhold this solution may be partial retaliation for Hermione's comments regarding how Harry should be able to use the hawthorn wand. However, even if Harry did have Hermione forcibly take the wand from Ron, the wand might recognize that such a deliberately orchestrated act was a bogus "capture," and it would therefore remain under either Ron's, or possibly even Bellatrix,' control.

Chapter 25: Shell Cottage

Synopsis

Harry spends as much time as possible alone on the cliff tops. This is the first time an opportunity has presented itself where he has chosen not to act, and, even to himself, his reasoning for not racing to the Elder Wand before Voldemort grows weaker every time he considers it. Ron's doubting is hardly helpful, and even Hermione's support is confusing. Convinced now that the Elder Wand does exist, she believes the way it was retrieved, and the wand itself, are evil. Ron questions if Dumbledore is truly dead—there is the silver doe and the eye in the mirror. If it is not Dumbledore's eye, then who sent Dobby? Fleur interrupts Harry to say that Griphook wants a word.

Griphook agrees to help Harry, even though it is betraying Gringott's, but he wants payment: the Sword of Gryffindor. The Sword, Griphook says, was Goblin-made, therefore, it still belongs to Goblins. When Ron suggests that there are other valuables in the Lestrange vault that Griphook might want, Griphook is affronted: he is not a thief. Griphook claims that Gryffindor stole the sword from Ragnuk the First. Harry, Ron, and Hermione request time to consider his request.

Harry asks if the sword could have been stolen from the Goblins; Hermione says that wizard-written history books often gloss over what was inflicted on nonhuman races. Ron suggests swapping the sword for the fake one in the vault, but Hermione points out that Griphook immediately detected the replica. Hermione proposes offering an equal value item, but Ron sarcastically retorts that they do not have any other Goblin-made swords. Harry suggests offering the sword to Griphook, but only after all the Horcruxes have been destroyed. Hermione dislikes this idea, it could take years. Harry does not like it either, but he does not have another plan.

Griphook agrees to Harry's carefully worded agreement, and they shake on it. Harry, Ron, Hermione, and Griphook spend the next several weeks planning the Gringotts' assault, during which, Harry realizes he dislikes the Goblin. Griphook seems too uncaring and cheerful over other wizards possibly being injured. He also seems to enjoy making things difficult for Fleur. When Bill insists that Griphook eat with the family rather than have meals brought to his room, he does so, but eats raw meat and roots. Fleur is gladdened that Ollivander will shortly move to Aunt Muriel's, and she can then juggle bedrooms. Harry tells her that he, Ron, and Dean are fine sleeping in the living room. Keeping Griphook happy is essential to the Trio's plans, and Herry believes the Goblin would object to sleeping on the sofa. He informs Fleur that he, Ron, and Hermione will also be leaving soon.

As Ollivander and Bill are about to depart for Aunt Muriel's, Fleur asks Ollivander to deliver Muriel's borrowed tiara for her. Harry notices Griphook eying the tiara, almost eagerly. Griphook mentions that it was made by Goblins; Bill responds that it was paid for by wizards.

Bill and Ollivander leave, while the rest have dinner. Bill returns shortly, saying everything is fine at Muriel's, and that the Twins are driving her crazy, running an owl order business from her back bedroom. As dinner ends, there is a bang at the door. Bill aims his wand, and outside, Lupin identifies himself. Remus announces that Tonks has had her baby, a boy, named Ted after Tonks' father. He asks Harry to be godfather, and Harry, stunned, accepts. The celebration goes through several bottles before Lupin departs into the storm and for home. As they carry goblets into the kitchen, Bill asks Harry if he has a deal with Griphook, but Harry is unable to say. Bill warns that Goblin ideas of ownership are foreign. They believe wizards are untrustworthy in matters regarding treasure and believe that ownership stays with the maker, considering Goblin-made wares to be leased rather than bought. Griphook evidently feels that Auntie Muriel's tiara should have been returned to the Goblins when the original owner died. Harry promises to be careful and returns to the celebration, which continues even though Lupin has left.

Analysis

The author has pointed out separately in an interview, that Harry deciding for the first time *not* to act upon something is an important part of his maturation. He sees a path he can pursue that will thwart one aspect of Voldemort's scheme, but he instead chooses to simply watch and make other plans that will lead to a resolution he has been striving for since the story began. Always before, Harry had seen a clear path—going through the trap door, entering the Chamber, freeing Sirius, dueling Voldemort, flying to the Ministry, recovering a Horcrux—and has followed it. These rather linear actions created a familiar pattern, making Harry predictable to his enemies. Now there is a defined action that Harry can take, traveling to Hogwarts to prevent Voldemort from claiming the Elder Wand, but after careful consideration, he opts to ignore it.

Harry's agreement with Griphook is risky, and it is unclear if he can be trusted, although Griphook likely feels the same about Harry. It is obvious that the Goblin's only interest is to obtain Gryffindor's Sword, which he firmly believes belongs to Goblins, rather than helping to rid the Wizarding world of Voldemort. As Hermione pointed out, the ill-treatment that Goblins and other non-human magical folks have endured for centuries under Wizards has been glossed over in history books written by biased historians. Voldemort has been actively recruiting non-human denizens, and Griphook and many other magical creatures may believe they could fare better, or at least no worse, under Voldemort's domination than they have had serving Wizards, possibly resulting in them either supporting Voldemort or adopting a neutral stance. This could be cause enough for Griphook to betray the Trio once the Horcrux is retrieved from the Lestrange vault. Harry likely suspects that Griphook may double-cross him, but he has little choice but to place his faith in him for now and follow through with their plan.

The rift between Harry and Lupin has finally been healed, and, thanks to Harry, Lupin realizes that not only is he a suitable husband and father, but a worthy human being and valuable Order of the Phoenix member, despite being a werewolf. His being a werewolf has actually been a tremendous asset to the Order, allowing him to infiltrate, at great personal risk, Fenrir Greyback's lycanthropic realm to gather valuable information. Lupin asking Harry to be godfather to his newborn son not only shows how deeply he cares for and respects Harry, but also that he and Tonks believe that Harry, being an orphan, is the most qualified person to guide and mentor baby Teddy should anything happen to them, although there is no certainty that any will survive.

Although it is never explained, it seems odd that Fleur would ask Mr. Ollivander, rather than Bill, to return Aunt Muriel's tiara. The author may be directing the reader's attention to this type of object for a specific reason.

QUESTIONS

Review   1. Why does Harry no longer want to pursue the Deathly Hallows, even though Dumbledore obviously pointed him in that direction?

2. Why does Lupin ask Harry to be godfather to his newborn son? Why does Harry accept?

3. Does Harry intend to honor his agreement with Griphook? Will Griphook honor it? Explain.

Extra Study   1. If the Deathly Hallows are not directly related to Harry's mission, why would Dumbledore bring them to Harry's attention?

2. Why would Fleur request that Ollivander, rather than Bill, return Aunt Muriel's tiara?

3. Does the Sword of Gryffindor actually belong to the Goblins as Griphook claims?

4. Why do Goblins consider Wizards untrustworthy? Is this distrust warranted?

5. Are Goblins trustworthy? Explain.

GREATER PICTURE

Like the cup of tea that Dudley left outside Harry's bedroom door in chapter 2, Rowling has focused the reader's attention to another seemingly insignificant object, a tiara. This would be the second tiara that has been pointed out to us, the other being the one on Rowena Ravenclaw's statue at the Lovegoods.' As we now believe, one Horcrux is Hufflepuff's Cup. That would seem to indicate that Ravenclaw's diadem is a likely candidate to be another Horcrux, although its whereabouts is still unknown.

Chapter 26: Gringotts

SYNOPSIS

Their plan is simple: go with Griphook to Gringotts Bank. Hermione, disguised as Bellatrix Lestrange, can open her vault and retrieve the Horcrux. They have Bellatrix's wand that Harry captured during the fight at Malfoy Manor, and strands of her hair for the Polyjuice Potion. Hermione is worried because Bellatrix's wand does not perform well for her, although Harry is pleased with Draco's hawthorn wand. He thinks Hermione's problem is that she did not capture the wand's allegiance as he did with Draco's. Harry, eager to leave Shell Cottage, frets over how they can prevent Griphook from keeping Gryffindor's sword after breaking into the Lestrange vault. Harry has told Bill and Fleur that they are leaving early, and not to see them off; Hermione will be in disguise, and Harry does not want Bill guessing what they are planning. Before apparating out, Harry sadly glimpses Dobby's grave and wonders how the House-elf knew to save them. Hermione strides over in her Bellatrix disguise, so convincing it causes Harry to shiver with loathing. Ron, who has been given a false identity, grouses about his appearance. Harry, with Griphook on his shoulders, will be hidden under the Invisibility Cloak. They Apparate into the Leaky Cauldron and, once inside Diagon Alley, are surprised at how it has changed. Many Dark Arts shops now line the street while the nicer stores have been boarded over. Witches and wizards who have lost their wands beg in the street. Harry's "Undesirable Number One" wanted posters are everywhere. Their plan proceeds reasonably well; Hermione makes a convincing Bellatrix, although Harry warns her about being too polite to subordinates. A stranger approaches and addresses "Bellatrix"; Griphook whispers that it is Travers, a Death Eater. Travers is surprised to see Bellatrix outside Malfoy Manor after hearing that everyone involved in the recent events there had been confined to the house. Hermione says the Dark Lord shows more mercy to those who have served him well. Her performance seems to erase Travers' suspicions. He is also going to Gringott's, and automatically falls in beside her. They must pass two human guards at the doors with Probity Probes. Harry Confunds the guards to allow Hermione to pass unchecked; their apparent confusion seems to cause Travers a moment's pause. Inside, the Goblins request Bellatrix's identification. When Hermione hesitates, one nervously says that her wand is sufficient proof, although Hermione claims it is new. Harry suspects the Goblins know that Bellatrix's wand was stolen and are looking for an impostor. Griphook whispers to Harry to use the Imperius curse on the Goblin, Bogrod, which convinces him this wand is correct. Travers becomes suspicious; he knows there are no wandmakers available, and Harry uses the Imperius curse on him as well. Bogrod asks for the Clankers and leads Hermione and Ron, with Harry, Griphook, and Travers following, from the marble main hall into a passageway. The door slams behind them, and Harry sends Travers away to hide. Bogrod, also still under the Imperius curse, summons a cart that descends deep within Gringotts. After many twists and turns, the cart passes through a security waterfall that washes away all protective charms. When the cart overturns and dumps them out, Hermione is no longer Bellatrix, and Ron is himself. Harry, positive the other Goblins know they are impostors, wants to continue as planned, placing Bogrod back under the Imperius Curse. Griphook escorts them to the Lestrange vault which is guarded by an aged, half-blind dragon that is heavily tethered. Griphook subdues it using the Clankers, simple metal noisemakers. Harry guesses that the dragon has been trained that the Clanker noise will be followed by pain, and it cowers in fear.

Hearing pursuit approaching, Harry forces Bogrod to open the vault, which is filled from floor to ceiling with precious objects. The vault closes behind them; Griphook says Bogrod can get them out again, but they must search quickly. Hermione screams in pain when she picks up a goblet. The vault's protective charm causes the contents to start multiplying and become searing hot every time something is touched. Harry spots Hufflepuff's cup, but it is out of reach. Hermione levitates Harry, and he snags the Cup with Gryffindor's sword, while Hermione, Ron, Griphook, and Bogrod struggle to stay above the hot multiplying objects below. Griphook is being buried in burning gold, and Harry pulls him up; as he sets himself down, he drops the Sword and the Cup. Griphook grabs Gryffindor's Sword while flipping up Hufflepuff's Cup. Harry catches it, ignoring the searing heat. Borne by an avalanche of treasure spilling from the opened vault, Griphook runs off with Gryffindor's sword, calling to the gathered Goblins that thieves are in the vault. Harry, Hermione, and Ron hurl curses at the Goblin throng. Harry releases the half-blind dragon, and, jumping on its back, the Trio blast openings into the ceiling for it to fly through as they make their escape.

Analysis

Although the Trio and Griphook spent much time carefully planning the Gringotts break-in, it may not have been as well thought-out as they believed, which is surprising considering their near-disastrous experience at the Ministry of Magic. It should have occurred to them that Gringotts had probably been alerted about a possible attempt to breach the Lestrange vault, and that Bellatrix's wand had been stolen. It is possible that Griphook, distrusting Harry's agreement, may have intended for the Trio to be discovered so he could immediately reclaim Gryffindor's sword for Goblins. Although there is no definitive proof for this, it seems he should have known what security measures were in place, and could have advised the Trio on how to avert them. The caper also placed a heavy burden on Hermione, who had to convincingly portray Bellatrix. Although she appears to have pulled off the deception relatively well, it is unclear if Gringotts had been tipped off.

As they arrive in Diagon Alley, the Trio, who have been relatively cut off from the magical community, now see the direct result that Voldemort's take-over has had on the Wizarding world. Many familiar stores are gone, boarded up, or have been replaced by Dark Arts shops that were probably in Knockturn Alley. Muggle-borns, homeless and their wands confiscated, have been reduced to begging in the streets.

At this point, it almost seems that Harry has reached a dead end in his quest. Of the six Horcruxes that he believes to exist, three (the diary, the ring, and the locket) have been destroyed. He has found a fourth, but has lost the means to destroy it, and while he believes that the fifth may be Nagini, he has no idea what or where the final one is. How shall he proceed?

Readers may remember Travers as one of the Death Eaters who appeared at Xenophilius Lovegood's house when Xeno alerted the Ministry of Magic that Harry, Hermione, and Ron had arrived there. The Trio likely did not recognize him, as they probably only glimpsed him briefly as they made their escape. Travers was also mentioned when the Trio were infiltrating the Ministry; Umbridge assumed that Travers had sent Mafalda Hopkirk to be her recorder, thus taking Hermione away for what promised to be a full day in court.

Questions

Review   1. Why does Harry choose to proceed to the vault rather than escape, even though he is convinced the Goblins know they are imposters?

Extra Study   1. Why did Griphook flip up the real Hufflepuff's Cup to Harry as he (Griphook) ran off with Gryffindor's sword?
2. Why didn't Griphook warn the Trio about the magical waterfall that washed away protective charms, the hot, multiplying objects in the vault, and other safeguards?
3. Before going into hiding, how might Fred and George's joke shop have been affected by the changes in Diagon Alley?
4. Now that the sword is gone, how will the Trio be able to destroy the remaining Horcruxes? How can they get the sword back?

Greater Picture

As we know, Basilisk venom destroys Horcruxes. With the Sword of Gryffindor now no longer available, Harry may have to go to the only place that he knows that venom exists: the Chamber of Secrets beneath Hogwarts. As it turns out, there will be a more compelling reason for Harry to return to Hogwarts; Voldemort, enraged when he discovers that a Horcrux has been stolen, will shortly visit all his Horcruxes to reassure himself they are safe, and Harry, tuned into Voldemort's thoughts, will learn that one Horcrux is hidden at Hogwarts. Thus, he will be forced to visit the school in any event. At the moment, though, Harry is more interested in collecting Horcruxes than destroying them; we will see that he does not even consider how to destroy the Cup Horcrux, being more concerned with preventing Voldemort from reaching the one at Hogwarts.

Chapter 27: The Final Hiding Place

SYNOPSIS

Harry has no way to steer the dragon, and he, Hermione, and Ron can merely hang on for dear life. Fortunately, it seems unaware that they are aboard. They clutch the dragon's scales tightly, but if it banks or rolls over, they will fall off. The dragon continues flying north, seeming to know where it is headed, despite being half-blind. Harry wonders if Voldemort has been informed yet that the Lestrange vault was breached. When he is, Voldemort will know his Horcruxes are being hunted and that the hunters may have found others. After some hours, the dragon descends. When it glides over a small lake for a drink, the Trio jumps into the cold water, making it safely ashore through the reeds. Harry immediately casts protective charms, and they change into dry clothes and tend their burn wounds with Dittany. Although they have successfully retrieved Hufflepuff's Cup, Gryffindor's Sword is lost, rendering them powerless to destroy the remaining Horcruxes; Ron grumbles over Griphook "double crossing" them. Pain suddenly streaks across Harry's forehead, and he sees a Goblin cowering on his knees before Voldemort; wizards in a semi-circle look on. Voldemort screams in rage when the Goblin tells him the Potter boy and his two accomplices took the Cup. Slashing the air with the Elder Wand, the Dark Lord slays him. Bellatrix, Lucius Malfoy, and the other wizards dash from the room in terror; anyone left behind is fatally felled. Voldemort wonders if the other Horcruxes are known to Harry, and is uncertain if he can actually feel when the Horcruxes are being destroyed. Voldemort knows the diary was lost, but he still lacked a body then and believes that was why he was unable to detect it. He suspects Dumbledore was involved; Dumbledore never trusted him. Voldemort is confident, however, that the ring Horcrux remains intact—no one ever connected him to the Gaunts, after all. And the sea cave is too well protected for anyone to penetrate its security, therefore the Locket must still be safe. He will go to Hogwarts to check on the one there; but Nagini must stay with him, must stay safe. But Dumbledore might have known his middle name, might have made that connection, he will check that one first. Then to the lake; that one is surely safe, still it must be checked. And then the one at Hogwarts, though that is certainly safe, nobody else knows about that place.

Harry opens his eyes to Ron and Hermione peering down at him. Harry says Voldemort knows they are hunting his Horcruxes and that the last one is hidden somewhere at Hogwarts. Harry, still unaware what it is, knows Voldemort is heading there to check on it and believes it is the safest one because Snape is there. Harry decides they will go to Hogsmeade; they can figure out later how to slip into Hogwarts. Covering themselves with the Invisibility Cloak, they Apparate to the small village.

ANALYSIS

As the plot heads towards its conclusion, the Trio races to Hogwarts to find the last Horcrux, although they do not know what it is and, having lost Gryffindor's Sword, cannot destroy it and the others. As a reminder, Dumbledore told Harry that he believed there were six Horcruxes: the diary, the ring, and the locket, all now destroyed; the cup, probably Nagini, and one other. Harry now has evidence that the unknown one is hidden somewhere in Hogwarts, in a place that Voldemort believes nobody else knows about.

Meanwhile, Voldemort's supreme confidence in himself has begun to crumble after Harry and company successfully steal Hufflepuff's Cup from Gringotts Bank. Despite his elaborate planning and extensive security measures, clearly his Horcruxes are at risk of being identified or destroyed, although Voldemort is still unaware that any other than the Diary have been destroyed. Although Dumbledore was the only one he ever feared, Voldemort's rationalization that he is the superior wizard has deluded him into a false sense of invincibility. However, underlying fears and insecurities now appear to be eroding what little sanity remains, causing Voldemort to frequently fly into uncontrollable rages and randomly lash out, often fatally, at any follower unfortunate enough to be within striking distance. Voldemort not only underestimated Dumbledore's ability to uncover and foil his plans, but also Harry's resourcefulness in identifying and locating the remaining Horcruxes.

To cope, Voldemort lulls himself into believing that he can "feel" when his Horcruxes are slain and takes comfort with the false notion that he was unable to detect the Riddle Diary Horcrux being destroyed only because he still lacked a body then. However, he remains ignorant that the Horcruxes within Gaunt's Ring and Slytherin's Locket no longer exist, or that Harry now knows what, or at least where, the remaining Horcruxes are. However, when Voldemort finally does realize this, it will place him on a deadly and irreversible collision course with Harry. As a sidenote: While the Trio are riding the dragon, they are in danger of falling off and must wait until the beast descends before being able to dismount. However, unless there is some magical reason preventing it, it seems that they could have Disapparated to safety while astride it, although this apparently never occurred to them. It may be the case that Apparation, requiring that the practitioner turn in place, may not be something that can be done easily in such a situation; or it may be that the necessary "deliberation" step is impossible for the Trio while they are holding on for dear life. Also, it does appear in an earlier chapter that Mundungus Fletcher is able to Disapparate while similarly beset, however, his criminal life has no doubt enabled him to make speedy escapes from difficult corners something he had to learn.

QUESTIONS

Review 1. Why did Griphook take Gryffindor's Sword?

2. Why is Voldemort convinced he will "feel" if his other Horcruxes are destroyed? What proves or disproves this belief?

3. What precautions did Voldemort take to protect his Horcruxes? Did they fail? If so, why? What else could he have done?

4. Why does Voldemort believe that the Horcrux hidden at Hogwarts is the safest? Is he correct?

5. What is the place in Hogwarts that no one knows about? Why is Voldemort convinced that no one else knows about it? Who does know?

Extra Study 1. Is Ron correct that Griphook "double crossed" the Trio by taking Gryffindor's Sword? Explain.

2. Even if the Trio can find the last Horcrux, how can they destroy it and the other Horcruxes now that they no longer have Gryffindor's Sword?

3. Why and how did Voldemort underestimate Dumbledore's abilities to uncover his plan? Why does he now underestimate Harry?

4. Why does Voldemort believe he can never be connected to the Gaunt family? How was this tie uncovered?

5. Is it safe for the Trio to go to Hogsmeade and Hogwarts without first devising a plan? Are Death Eaters expecting the Trio?

6. How well did the Trio's previous break-ins at the Ministry of Magic and Gringott's Bank work, and what did they learn from each incident that they can apply to sneaking into Hogwarts?

GREATER PICTURE

Harry has identified nearly all the Horcruxes, but he is still unaware that he carries a Horcrux within him, as indicated by his scar. Voldemort also fails to realize this, the Horcrux having been accidentally created during his attempt to kill baby Harry with the Killing curse that rebounded and struck Voldemort instead, leaving behind a soul shard. Voldemort's snake, Nagini, is also a Horcrux, as Dumbledore suspected.

The place at Hogwarts that Voldemort believes only he has discovered is the Room of Requirement, which, of course, is known to Harry and the many Dumbledore's Army members. This is yet another example of Voldemort's over-confidence; having found the Room of Requirement, likely by accident, and possibly while pacing the halls looking for a place to hide some Dark experiment, Voldemort assumes he is the only wizard smart enough to discover it. This, despite the overwhelming evidence of a millennium's accumulated junk in the room when he first entered it, although perhaps he assumed the room had lain forgotten for centuries. Also, after being instructed by Voldemort on how to locate and enter this room, it would seem that Draco should have realized that it was the Room of Requirement, and that he would have mentioned something to Voldemort about Dumbledore's Army meeting there, and that Dolores Umbridge's Inquisition Squad, of which Draco was a member, raided it. It is possible that Draco fully realized this, but, fearing for his and his family's lives, silently listened to Voldemort's instructions, or he may have been unaware that Voldemort believed he was the only person who knew about the room's existence. Draco may also have been hoping that his secret activities in the room would be discovered, thus exposing Voldemort's plan to murder Dumbledore through no fault of Draco's.

Chapter 28: The Missing Mirror

SYNOPSIS

As soon as Harry. Ron, and Hermione Apparate into Hogsmeade Village, a screeching alarm announces their presence. A Death Eater attempts to Summon the Invisibility Cloak they are concealed under, but it fails to respond, keeping the Trio hidden. As they back down a side street, Hermione wants to Apparate out of Hogsmeade, but Harry says that protective spells have probably trapped them there. A sudden chill sweeps in and darkness starts enveloping everything around them: Dementors, sensing their fear, close in. Unable to withstand their suffocating presence, Harry casts a Patronus, scattering the Dementors, but revealing their location. "It's him, down there, I saw his Patronus, it was a stag!" yells a Death Eater. A nearby door cracks opens, and a harsh voice calls out, "Potter, in here, quick!"

The Trio dash inside and up the stairs. They find themselves in the Hog's Head Inn. From an upper window, Harry recognizes the tall barkeeper talking to the Death Eaters outside as Aberforth Dumbledore, Albus' younger brother. Aberforth claims he accidentally set off the Caterwauling curfew alarm while putting his cat out and insists it was his goat Patronus; the Death Eaters initially disbelieve him, but, thrown off the trail, and not wanting to risk losing a convenient location to trade black market goods, decide to leave. Aberforth gives the Trio something to eat, rebuking them for risking their lives coming to Hogsmeade. Harry spots the twin to the mirror Sirius gave him; Aberforth explains he bought it from Mundungus Fletcher, who stole it from Grimmauld Place. Aberforth has been watching them with it. Harry recognizes Aberforth's eye as the one in the mirror shard and realizes that he sent Dobby to rescue them. Aberforth confirms it was him and is saddened to hear that Dobby is dead.

Ron thinks Aberforth sent the doe Patronus, but Aberforth sarcastically reminds him that his Patronus is a goat. Aberforth suggests they wait until the Caterwauling alarm is turned off in the morning, then escape into the mountains and Disapparate from there. Harry insists they must get into Hogwarts castle because Dumbledore asked him to do something. Scoffs Aberforth, "Did he now? Nice job, I hope? Pleasant? Easy? Sort of thing you'd expect an unqualified wizard kid to be able to do without overstretching themselves?" Ron and Hermione are obviously uncomfortable, and Harry remains silent, struggling with his own misgivings regarding Dumbledore, although he had already resolved to continue trusting him. Aberforth claims that others who trusted Dumbledore often suffered misfortune as a result. He urges the Trio to abandon their mission, believing the Order of the Phoenix is finished and Voldemort has won. It is time to save themselves. Against Harry's protests, Aberforth asks if Dumbledore was honest with him and told Harry the whole story. When Harry is unable to respond, Aberforth says that Dumbledore reveled in lies and secrecy, learning it at their mother's knee.

Attempting to ease the tension, Hermione asks if a portrait is Aberforth's sister, Ariana, but this backfires, causing Aberforth to brusquely ask if she has been reading Rita Skeeter's book. To spare Hermione further embarrassment, Harry says that Elphias Doge told them about it. "That old berk," sneers Aberforth. "Thought the sun shone out of my brother's every orifice." Harry says nothing, still attempting to conceal his uncertainty. Aberforth reveals that Ariana, aged six, was injured by Muggle boys after observing her performing magic. She was never the same, eventually going half-mad and unable to control magic. Their father hunted down the boys in retaliation, but he never told the Ministry why he assaulted them, because, once revealed, Ariana would have been permanently committed to St. Mungo's Hospital. Instead, the family kept her hidden, fostering rumors she was a Squib. With their father in prison, Aberforth and his mother, Kendra cared for Ariana as best they could. Aberforth was Ariana's favorite. Albus, involved with his studies and winning prizes, usually confined himself to his room when at home. One day, while Aberforth was out, Ariana flew into a rage. Unable to subdue Ariana's uncontrollable magic, Kendra was accidentally killed. Albus canceled his Grand Tour with Doge and returned home to care for Ariana and support the family while Aberforth finished his schooling. Aberforth claims Albus resented the sacrifice he was forced to make, although Aberforth had offered to leave school and take his place. Then Albus met Grindelwald, a wizard he considered as brilliant as himself. The two quickly bonded, and, drawn by their mutual attraction to power and fame, hatched an elaborate scheme to create a new wizarding order. When Aberforth learned about their grandiose plans, a three-way fight erupted; a stray curse killed Ariana. Aberforth claims Albus was glad his burden was lifted, but Harry says he always carried it, recounting the night Albus died. After drinking the potion in the sea cave, Albus was raving, pleading with an unseen person not to hurt them. Harry is certain he was begging Grindelwald to spare his brother and sister, although Aberforth remains skeptical. Harry resolves to continue the mission. Knowing Voldemort could be killed, Dumbledore gave that knowledge to Harry. If Aberforth refuses to help sneak them into Hogwarts, then they will find their own way in. Relenting, Aberforth agrees to help and speaks to Ariana's portrait. She turns to leave, but rather than disappearing from the frame sideways as figures normally do, she instead disappears down a long, dark passageway behind her. Aberforth explains that there is only one way into the castle now, the old secret entryways are being guarded.

Ariana soon returns accompanied by someone. As they reach the portrait, it swings open to reveal a tunnel; standing inside is Neville Longbottom.

ANALYSIS

For Harry, uncovering the truth about Albus Dumbledore has been a journey nearly as long and difficult as his quest to find the Horcruxes, and this truth has come in many pieces, from various sources, and over time, creating a complicated jigsaw puzzle. Searching for answers has tested and strained Harry's loyalty and faith in Dumbledore, causing him to question whether or not the man he loved and thought he knew, had loved him in return, and was the good person Harry believed him to be. Aberforth Dumbledore provides crucial information that helps Harry to better understand Albus' past behavior regarding his family. This has restored Harry's faith in Albus somewhat, but not entirely.

Until now, Aberforth has remained a curious and vague background figure, but his character becomes more defined here as he assumes a prominent role filling in the story's many gaps. Despite their physical resemblance, the two brothers were vastly different in talents, disposition, and personalities. Aberforth was overshadowed by Albus' brilliance, but his antagonism toward his elder brother was less about sibling rivalry and petty jealousy, than it was suppressed anger and deep-seated resentment over Albus' using his superior talents, not only for gaining personal accolades, but as a means to shirk family responsibilities, letting the burden for Ariana's care fall upon Aberforth and their mother, Kendra. Her tragic death forced Albus to abandon his lofty ambitions to instead care for Ariana, though he retained sufficient belief in education's importance that he refused Aberforth's request to leave school so he could tend their sister in Albus' place. Albus' bitter despair (and perhaps martyrdom) over sacrificing his goals may have been a factor in him falling prey to Grindelwald's dark influence, but that hardly excuses Albus' behavior. Although Albus and Aberforth maintained an amicable truce throughout their adult lives, they remained aloof with one another, perhaps mutually fearing they might learn who actually killed their sister. However, they may have overlooked that regardless whose curse fatally struck Ariana, each shared responsibility in her death by allowing their long-simmering hostilities to explode into an out-of-control confrontation, although Albus' brief foray into the Dark Arts with Grindelwald certainly was a significant factor in the events leading up to the tragedy. Interestingly, although the brothers never grew close, they lived near one another, Dumbledore at Hogwarts and Aberforth in Hogsmeade, sharing an occasional drink at the Hog's Head Inn.

Albus' death has hardly softened Aberforth's feelings, however. When Harry says he is on a mission for Dumbledore, a sneering Aberforth mocks him (and Albus), causing Harry to recall his own doubts and concerns about Albus and forcing him to acknowledge that Aberforth's harsh words contain truth. Like Aberforth, readers must also be wondering why such a young, inexperienced, and unqualified wizard, even an immensely talented one like Harry, would have been tasked with such a difficult and dangerous mission while being provided so little information. However, Harry resolves to remain loyal and trust Dumbledore, dedicated to continuing the mission. Harry also attempts to convince Aberforth that Albus did indeed love his family and tried to protect them from Grindelwald. The pessimistic Aberforth remains skeptical, but he, perhaps surprisingly, sets aside his capitulatory view regarding the war, as well as his doubts that Harry can succeed, and helps the Trio sneak into Hogwarts.

While Aberforth has provided many answers about Albus and Grindelwald, his recollection differs from what Rita Skeeter, Bathilda Bagshot, Elphias Doge, and Aunt Muriel claimed. And though Aberforth has given an apparently factually accurate account of his family, it should not be assumed that his is the truthful version. Truth is often subjective and nebulous, and it is affected by others' opinions, personal experience, imperfect memories, individual bias, and raw emotions. Rarely is there a singular maxim, and all versions should be studied, weighed, and filtered before a definitive conclusion can be drawn. Even then, many will still disagree. Although Aberforth has solved many mysteries, the puzzle remains incomplete—there is still much more to be learned about Albus Dumbledore.

QUESTIONS

Review 1. What is Aberforth's response when Harry tells him Dumbledore assigned the Trio a mission? What does Aberforth mean by this? Is he right?

2. Why does Aberforth believe the war is lost and Voldemort has won? Is he correct? Does he really believe Voldemort has won?

3. How does Aberforth's explanation about his family differ from Rita Skeeter's version in her book? How does it differ from Autie Muriel's and Doge's?

4. Why does Harry resolve to continue trusting Dumbledore, despite Harry's many doubts and concerns about him and the mission?

5. Why does Aberforth finally agree to help the Trio sneak into Hogwarts?

Extra Study 1. Why would Aberforth have bought the mirror from Mundungus Fletcher? Did he know Harry had the matching twin? If so, how?

2. Harry tells Aberforth what Dumbledore said during his delirium in the sea cave. Is Harry's interpretation correct? Will this ever change what Aberforth believes?

3. Why was Aberforth watching the Trio in the mirror?

4. Is Aberforth's explanation about his family the truth or merely his version of it? Explain.

5. Hogwarts' former Headmasters typically have more than one portrait in different locations, often visiting them back and forth. If Aberforth has a talking portrait of his sister, why doesn't he have one of Dumbledore? Would this have helped or hurt the war effort?

6. If Ariana has a connecting portrait to Hogwarts, why doesn't Dumbledore's portrait communicate with Aberforth through her?

7. Why would Aberforth be in contact with Neville Longbottom?

GREATER PICTURE

Although Aberforth claims to believe that Voldemort has already won the war, it will be learned that he has been secretly helping the resurrected Dumbledore's Army, and in the Battle of Hogwarts, he will be within the school and actively defending it against Voldemort. Given this, it is entirely likely that Aberforth, in claiming that Voldemort has won, is, consciously or otherwise, testing Harry's mettle, trying to determine the depth of Harry's commitment to Albus' cause. This would also explain his immediate willingness to help once Harry declares that he will proceed with or without Aberforth's help.

Chapter 29: The Lost Diadem

SYNOPSIS

Neville is overjoyed to see them, but Harry, Ron, and Hermione are horrified by his battered appearance. Neville says this is nothing, wait till they see Seamus. To Aberforth's dismay, Neville informs him that more people will be Apparating in. Leading the Trio down the long, dark hallway, Neville explains that the seven known secret passageways into Hogwarts have been magically sealed, and Death Eaters guard the exits. Neville asks if they really broke into Gringotts and escaped on a dragon; everyone is talking about it. Harry confirms it is true. Hogwarts has drastically changed since the Trio left. Neville tells them about the Carrows, the two Death Eater professors who now handle all student punishment, although the other teachers avoid sending anyone to them whenever possible. Amycus Carrow teaches Defence Against the Dark Arts, although it is now called "Dark Arts." Students are forced to practice the Cruciatus curse on detention students. When Neville refused to curse anyone, he was beaten, despite being Pure Blood; some students, notably Crabbe and Goyle, have proven quite apt at the Dark Arts and love practicing them. Alecto Carrow, the Muggle Studies teacher, insists Muggles are dirty and stupid like animals. Neville obtained one scar after asking how much Muggle blood she had. Neville and other Dumbledore's Army members were pulling pranks and creating disruptions, but after Luna and Ginny left school and punishments became more severe, the rebellion died down a bit. When Neville was identified as a ringleader, Death Eaters went after his grandmother, who put Dawlish in St. Mungo's, and is now on the run, while Neville decided to "disappear."

Reaching Hogwarts, they enter an unfamiliar room to find a cheering crowd inside. The Trio are ecstatic to see all their old friends—Seamus Finnigan, Terry Boot, Michael Corner, Lavender Brown, Ernie Macmillan, Anthony Goldstein, Parvati and Padma Patil, and many more. Hammocks are strung from floor to ceiling, and the room is embellished with Gryffindor, Hufflepuff, and Ravenclaw colors and symbols; only Slytherin is missing. To Harry's astonishment, they are in the Room of Requirement. Neville has been hiding there for some weeks now, and the room has continually expanded as

Chapter 29: The Lost Diadem

more and more D.A. members arrived. Seamus, whose swollen face Harry initially failed to recognize, says the room is secure as long as at least one D.A. member remains inside. The only thing it is unable to provide is food. When Neville was really hungry, the tunnel leading to the Hog's Head opened, and Aberforth has been sending supplies ever since.

Everyone wants to know about the Trio's exploits. They have been listening to "Potterwatch" on the radio, but there are many unconfirmed rumors. Before Harry can respond, searing pain cuts through his scar as he briefly glimpses a furious Dark Lord discovering that the ring Horcrux is missing. Little time is left, and everyone wants to help, believing Harry has returned to overthrow the Carrows and Snape. Harry explains they are only there to complete a task to help to destroy Voldemort, and insists everyone stay behind. He becomes panicked when more people pour in from the Hog's Head. Luna, Dean, Fred, George, Ginny, Lee Jordan, and Cho Chang climb through. Ron quietly says the others can help; they do not know what they are looking for, where it is, and there is little time. They do not have to reveal that it is a Horcrux. Hermione agrees, saying Harry does not have to do everything alone. Harry finally concedes and says they are looking for something belonging to Rowena Ravenclaw. Luna suggests it could be the *lost* diadem, a type of crown. Hidden under the Invisibility Cloak, Luna leads Harry to the Ravenclaw Common room and shows him Rowena Ravenclaw's statue, so that Harry can see the shape of what he is likely searching for. As Harry steps out from under the Cloak to read a tiny inscription etched on the marble diadem, Alecto Carrow appears and instantly touches the Dark Mark on her forearm.

Analysis

Against Harry's wishes, the last battle between him and Voldemort is primed to happen at Hogwarts, and his arrival here will likely trigger it. It seems appropriate, indeed inevitable, that Harry and Voldemort's final confrontation should occur at Hogwarts; the castle and its surrounding grounds have played a major role throughout the series, with much of the story's action set here. The castle, with its many ghosts and magical denizens, is nearly a character in its own right. It is also the place that both Harry and Voldemort most consider home, and in Voldemort's case, probably the only thing he has ever had anything close to loving feelings for, although that is an emotion he has never experienced. Harry also loves Hogwarts, and he has always derived strength and security from the venerable old castle, impatiently enduring his enforced summer hiatus at the Dursleys' until returning each September. This time, Harry's homecoming is not as a student—he is a soldier on a mission. He is dismayed, however, when reinforcements begin arriving, and rather than sneaking in, finding the Horcrux, then sneaking out again to continue his quest, Harry's appearance instead sets off a chain reaction of events that will culminate in the final resolution. And whether he likes it or not, Harry is the shining beacon that not only rallies and unifies the fragmented rebellion, but he will be pushed to the forefront to lead the climactic battle against Voldemort and his Death Eaters. While Neville's battered appearance is shocking, his cheerful demeanor about it seems even more so. This clearly shows just how much Neville has changed from the ineffectual, frightened boy who first arrived at Hogwarts; his bruises are badges of honor. The Sorting Hat placing Neville into Gryffindor House had always seemed questionable, and many readers probably believe he would have been better suited to Hufflepuff, rather than a House known for bravery. But bravery comes in many forms, and Neville, despite his magical deficiencies, always faced the adversity in his life head on, and showed courage as early as the first book, when he challenged the Trio after objecting to their actions. This strength has gradually increased, and Neville has transformed from a shy, insecure, and nearly incompetent student, into a strong, capable wizard, mostly due to Harry's patient guidance. Curiously, Harry's absence has also had a positive effect on Neville. With Harry no longer at Hogwarts, Neville, along with Ginny and Luna, have assumed leadership roles by ably leading Dumbledore's Army, rebelling against the Carrows and Snape. Neville shows that, given the right circumstances, he is a natural leader, as well as a true Gryffindor; he, and the other D.A. members, are ready and able to join forces with Harry in the final battle against Voldemort.

Questions

Review   1. Why doesn't Harry recognize the Room of Requirement?

2. Why doesn't Harry want the other students to help him with the mission or to lead them in overthrowing Snape and the Carrows? What changes his mind?

3. Why are there no Slytherin colors or symbols represented in the Room of Requirement?

Extra Study   1. How did news about the Trio's escape from Gringotts travel to Hogwarts so quickly?

2. Why is Neville so cheerful, despite his battered appearance?

3. How has Neville changed from his first year at Hogwarts? What accounts for that change?

Greater Picture

We can see that, against his will, Harry becomes the rallying point for defending Hogwarts. This is, at least for the next while, a position Harry attempts to avoid. Harry quite clearly wants to prevent any responsibility for the loss of life that will happen in the coming battle. It is only after the encounter in the Forbidden Forest, when Harry feels he has acted to protect his friends against Voldemort, that he chooses to show himself as the leader of the counter-attack against Voldemort.

His faith in Neville's abilities is such that Harry will shortly entrust Neville with a vital task: dispatching the final Horcrux in the event that he, Ron, or Hermione are unable to do the job. Neville will prove that he is up to the challenge.

Chapter 30: The Sacking of Severus Snape

Synopsis

Pain explodes in Harry's scar, and he finds himself on a rocky outcrop under a cliff. *Good,* he thinks, *they have the boy.* A loud crack brings him back to himself as Luna stuns Alecto Carrow. The noise awakens the students in Ravenclaw House, and Harry dives back under the Invisibility Cloak with Luna. Students begin milling about and become frightened at seeing the unconscious teacher lying on the floor. Outside the Common room, Amycus, unable to open the door, is frantically calling for Alecto, worried that the Dark Lord has been summoned without them actually having Harry Potter. Amycus is heard ordering Professor McGonagall to fetch Professor Flitwick, but then tells her to open the door. Inside, they find the unconscious Alecto. McGonagall is surprised when Amycus says Harry Potter may be there and that the Dark Lord had warned them that he might attempt to break into Ravenclaw Tower. Amycus, fearing Voldemort's wrath if Harry escapes, says he will pass off the alert as a school prank and punish a few students. When McGonagall objects to any student being punished for the Carrows' ineptitude, he threatens her and spits in her face. Harry steps out and slams Amycus with a Cruciatus curse, lifting his writhing body into the air and crashing it through a bookcase. Harry understands now what Bellatrix Lestrange had meant when she once said a person must actually mean it for an Unforgivable Curse to work. An astonished McGonagall thanks Harry for his gallant effort but urges him to flee the castle quickly. He refuses, saying there is something he must do. He asks if she knows where the diadem is, but according to McGonagall it has been lost for centuries. Harry is at a loss; the diadem was his most likely candidate for the Horcrux, and nobody knows where it is. Amycus comes to, and McGonagall uses the Imperius curse to relieve him of his wand, then casts a spell binding him to his still unconscious sister. Harry is again overcome by Voldemort's rage as he discovers the Locket missing from the stone basin on the island. Returning to himself, Harry updates Professor McGonagall about what is happening and that he must find something hidden in Hogwarts before Voldemort and his forces arrive. McGonagall replies that she and the staff will secure the castle against Voldemort for as long as possible while Harry searches. Harry tells McGonagall about the tunnel to the Hog's Head from which students can be evacuated. Voldemort will only be concentrating on Hogwarts, not Disapparating students in Hogsmeade village. Harry and Luna hide under the Invisibility Cloak as McGonagall casts three cat Patronuses to summon the other Heads of House. As they head off, they run into Snape, who had sensed Alecto's communication with Voldemort. He asks McGonagall if she has seen the Carrows while continually darting his eyes about, as if suspecting Harry is there. When Snape asks what brought her out of bed, McGonagall claims she heard a disturbance. When Snape inquires if she has seen Harry, McGonagall is evasive, then slashes her wand. Snape, quicker, deflects the spell with a Shield Charm. They duel fiercely, magic so quick that Harry has never seen the like. Professors Flitwick and Sprout come running to McGonagall's aid with a huffing Slughorn lagging behind. Outnumbered, Snape dashes into a deserted classroom where a loud crash is heard. Pursuing, McGonagall screams, "*Coward!*" Uncloaked, Harry and Luna rush inside, startling the other professors. Snape has jumped out the window. Harry, looking out, thinks he must be dead, but McGonagall bitterly comments that, unlike Dumbledore, Snape had his wand and has learned a few tricks from You-Know-Who. Harry sees a large, bat-like figure soaring across the school grounds. When Slughorn finally enters, McGonagall informs him that Snape is taking a leave of absence. Harry slides into Voldemort's mind again and sees an Inferi-filled lake and the ghostly green boat bumping into the shore. Voldemort leaps from it in a murderous rage. Harry says Voldemort is coming.

McGonagall orders the House Heads to send their students to the Great Hall. She tells Slughorn the time has come for Slytherin to choose sides. The professors set defensive charms and spells around Hogwarts to fend off Voldemort. Harry asks Flitwick if he might know where Ravenclaw's diadem is, but Flitwick says no one in living memory has seen it. McGonagall enchants the school's statues and suits of armour to help defend the castle and orders Filch, who is ranting that students are out of bed, to summon Peeves the Poltergeist. When Harry and Luna return to the Room of Requirement, Harry is shocked and dismayed that even more people have arrived, including Lupin, Shacklebolt, Oliver Wood, Katie Bell, Angelina Johnson, Alicia Spinnet, Bill and Fleur, and Mr. and Mrs. Weasley. Fred says they alerted Dumbledore's Army, and they in turn summoned the Order of the Phoenix. Harry says the younger students are being evacuated, and the rest will be fighting. Most head to the Great Hall, leaving behind only Lupin and the Weasleys, who are arguing with Ginny who also wants to fight. Percy suddenly arrives. Fleur, attempting to defuse the icy situation, asks Lupin about little Teddy. Percy loudly apologizes for being a deluded idiot and Ministry pawn; his family immediately forgives him. Looking around, Harry asks where Ron and Hermione are. Ginny, who has been ordered to stay inside the room during the battle, says they left to take care of something having to do with a bathroom, leaving Harry puzzled. His scar sears again, and he is gazing at Hogwarts through huge iron gates. Nagini is draped around his shoulders. Voldemort has arrived.

Analysis

As the story reaches a critical stage, time is running out; Harry is desperate to find the Ravenclaw Horcrux, and Hufflepuff's Cup must still be destroyed. Voldemort and his forces will soon arrive at the castle, and Harry has no idea where to search or if the Diadem is even the actual Horcrux. The final Horcrux being hidden at Hogwarts is fortuitous; it is a place Harry knows better than anywhere else, and at least as well as Voldemort does. Probably only Dumbledore and the Weasley twins know Hogwarts better. This homecoming also infuses Harry with a much needed boost of strength and confidence that a less familiar locale would be unable to provide. Harry has no idea where the Diadem might be hidden, but knowing many of the castle's secrets will help him narrow the search. Also, Harry's return not only puts him in a familiar and comforting setting, but it reconnects his ties and alliances with old friends, who immediately flock to Hogwarts upon hearing Harry has returned. If Harry is to succeed, he must rely on these allies for help.

Although Harry has used the Cruciatus curse before, this is the first time it has worked effectively for him. He recalls Bellatrix Lestrange once telling him that the conjurer must actually mean it in order for an Unforgivable curse to work properly, that righteous indignation is not enough. Previously, Harry only half-heartedly cast the Cruciatus curse (on Bellatrix Lestrange), unwilling to inflict pain and suffering on anyone, even a hated enemy. Now, however, Harry uses it to protect someone he cares about. And considering its effect on Amycus Carrow, this time, Harry obviously meant it.

QUESTIONS

Review 1. Why would McGonnagall engage Snape in a duel rather than merely saying she does not know where Harry is? Could she have defeated him without help from the other professors?

2. Why is Voldemort in a murderous rage? Where is he when Harry "sees" him?

3. Why is Harry now unsure that Ravenclaw's diadem is the Horcrux? Is there any evidence that another Ravenclaw artifact exists?

4. What does McGonagall mean when she tells Slughorn it is time for Slytherin to choose sides? Do they?

Extra Study 1. Why is this the first time the Cruciatus curse has worked effectively for Harry?

2. What caused Percy's turnaround? Why did it take him so long?

3. Which bathroom might Hermione and Ron have gone to? What task could have sent them there?

4. How could so many Dumbledore's Army, Order of the Phoenix, and former Hogwarts students be able to enter Hogsmeade village without being detected by Death Eaters and the Dementors?

5. How are the Hogwarts students to be evacuated by disapparating from the Hog's Head when it was stipulated two chapters earlier that disapparition from the town is impossible?

GREATER PICTURE

The bathroom Ginny Weasley is referring to is actually Moaning Myrtle's lavatory, which readers should remember contains the entrance to the Chamber of Secrets and that only someone speaking Parseltongue can open. It is unknown yet why Ron and Hermione would have gone there, or if they could open the Chamber, but this will play a significant role in the next chapter.

Professor Flitwick's comment that no one in living memory has seen Ravenclaw's Diadem will not only prove to be untrue, but it has actually been seen quite recently. However, Flitwick's words will serve to be a useful trigger for Harry; they will set a train of thought in motion that will result in Harry finding the Diadem.

A very interesting point is touched on by one editor: how can the students disapparate from Hogsmeade? For that matter, how can Dumbledore's Army members apparate in, as they have been doing? Aberforth has said that Harry, Ron, and Hermione should wait until dawn, and then apparate away and hide in the mountains. While he never explicitly says so, he strongly implies that apparating out of Hogsmeade is impossible. In this case, perhaps, Harry may simply have made a lucky assumption. Clearly it is possible to Apparate into Hogsmeade, as he has done so. Perhaps he simply assumed that it would be similarly possible to Apparate out, and missed Aberforth saying that it could not be done. As the author never tells us, we can only speculate; but it is possible that by the time the evacuation starts, Voldemort has lifted the anti-Apparation spells on Hogsmeade to allow for free movement of his troops. If so, this is a major stroke of luck for the Hogwarts forces; they would not have been able to evacuate the non-combatants otherwise.

A similar question that arises is, what about those students who have not yet passed their Apparation tests? There are wizards, we are told, who still will not Apparate, despite being fully grown, because of the risk of Splinching. So quite possibly, in order to accommodate those Death Eaters who were unwilling or unable to Apparate, Voldemort might also have released any restrictions on the Floo Network.

Chapter 31: The Battle of Hogwarts

SYNOPSIS

The enchanted ceiling in the Great Hall is dark with twinkling stars; the tables below are filled with students in dressing gowns or traveling cloaks. Every Hogwarts being, living or dead, is listening to Professor McGonagall giving instructions from atop the raised platform at the end of the room. Pomfrey, Filch, and the prefects will evacuate students from the school before the battle begins, although the older students can remain and fight. The Order and the professors have agreed upon a battle plan and divide into groups to man the towers and grounds. Everyone is tense with expectation over the approaching battle. Harry anxiously searches the room for Ron and Hermione while Voldemort's loud commanding voice, seemingly from nowhere, announces Harry Potter must surrender by midnight. Pointing at Harry, Pansy Parkinson, a Slytherin, yells for someone to grab him. Gryffindor, Hufflepuff, and Ravenclaw students jump up and aim their wands at Slytherin's table. McGonagall then orders Pansy and the other Slytherins, regardless of age, to leave the Hall first, followed by the other Houses, although many older students from the other three Houses remain behind. As students and teachers begin breaking into groups, McGonagall approaches Harry and reminds him that he is supposed to be looking for something. Swept up the marble staircase with the defenders, Harry breaks away down an empty corridor, but he is beginning to panic: he has no idea where to look for the Horcrux.

Harry races through the hallways, although without Ron and Hermione, he feels at a loss. Looking at the Marauder's Map, he is unable to locate their names. Harry has a thought: Voldemort had warned the Carrows that he would try to break into Ravenclaw Tower. This convinces Harry that the Horcrux is indeed linked to that House, and it must be the diadem, but he wonders how Voldemort found an object lost centuries ago. He has a sudden brainwave. Everyone says the diadem has not been seen in living memory. That does not, however, rule out ghosts. Harry finds Nearly Headless Nick, the Gryffindor ghost, and asks who the Ravenclaw ghost is. Nick, somewhat affronted at not being asked to help, sends him to the Grey Lady. She tells Harry that in life she was Rowena Ravenclaw's daughter, Helena. Jealous of her mother's fame, she stole the diadem and ran away. She hid it in a hollow tree in an Albanian forest. On her deathbed, her mother sent a Baron who was in love with Helena to find her, but she spurned him and refused to go back. He became violent and fatally stabbed her, then killed himself in remorse. Harry realizes it was the Bloody Baron. Remembering that Voldemort spent his exile in Albania, Harry asks the Gray Lady if she shared her story with anyone else. She sadly admits she once told a student who had seemed so charming and understanding. Harry mutters that she is not the first person Tom Riddle manipulated, and surmises he found the diadem and created a Horcrux from it. He later hid it at Hogwarts in a place he believed no one else knew existed.

After talking with the Gray Lady, Harry runs into Hagrid, who has returned from his cave with Grawp and Fang after hearing Voldemort's voice. As they run through the halls, the first casualties are already appearing. A shattered stone gargoyle reminds Harry of the Ravenclaw statue at the Lovegood house. Another image appears to him: an old wizard's bust on which Harry once placed a tatty wig and a battered tiara in a room that few people other than Harry and Voldemort ever knew existed. Harry suddenly realizes where the diadem is—it is the same "battered tiara" that he had used to mark the hiding place of his Potions book in the Room of Requirement. As Harry races to it, he passes Professor Sprout and Neville lugging pots of Mandrakes to the battle. Hagrid takes off after Fang when the boarhound takes fright at an exploding urn. Harry passes Aberforth, who says it was stupid not to keep some Slytherin students as hostages. Harry says his brother would never have done that. He finally finds Ron and Hermione, who are carrying dirty, yellow, curved objects. Hermione says Ron had the brilliant idea to open the Chamber of Secrets and retrieve Basilisk fangs that can destroy Horcruxes. Ron shows him the mangled Cup Horcrux that he insisted Hermione destroy. Harry is amazed but wonders how they were able to open the Chamber without knowing Parseltongue. Ron says he remembered what Harry spoke when he opened the Locket Horcrux, although he had to try several times before it worked. Harry tells them about the diadem.

Harry, Ron, and Hermione race to the Room of Requirement through the escalating battle. There they find Ginny, Tonks, and Mrs. Longbottom, Neville's grandmother, who has sealed off the tunnel after Aberforth left the inn. Tonks leaves to find her husband, and Mrs. Longbottom goes to fight alongside Neville. Harry asks Ginny to step into the corridor, but orders her to come back inside later. When Ron says he wants to warn the house elves, an overjoyed Hermione flings herself into Ron's arms, kissing him. He kisses her back, their unspoken feelings finally shared. Harry has them step outside so the room can be changed, then thinks hard to himself: *I need the place where everything is hidden.* After the third run along the corridor, an entrance appears. Inside the large labyrinthine room, they search separately for the stone bust with the diadem. Harry spots it but is stopped by Draco Malfoy, Crabbe, and Goyle. Using the Disillusionment Charm, they had been waiting outside when Harry re-entered the room, and followed him and the others in. A fierce duel erupts; a stray curse knocks the diadem into a refuse pile, and both Hermione and Ron are nearly hit by Crabbe's killing curses, although Draco yells at him to leave Harry alive for the Dark Lord. In the confusion, Malfoy drops his borrowed wand, Harry disarms Goyle, and Crabbe unleashes an uncontrollable fire, setting the room ablaze. Crabbe is lost amongst the flames, but the the trio escapes unscathed on broomsticks that Harry finds. They save Malfoy and Goyle as they fly from the room. Harry, seeing the diadem being tossed about by the fire, grabs it, only then making a direct flight path for the door. Outside, they collapse on the hallway floor. As Harry looks, bemused, at the diadem in his hands, it emits a thin shriek and falls apart. Hermione says that Crabbe must have conjured Fiendfyre, one of the few things that can destroy a Horcrux.

Shouts and noises fill the hall; Death Eaters have penetrated the castle. Suddenly, Percy and Fred appear, dueling two Death Eaters, one of whom is Pius Thicknesse, in the hallway. The wall is blasted open from the outside, and Fred is killed in the explosion.

Analysis

If readers were holding out hope that some Slytherins, other than Slughorn, would join forces against Voldemort, they are now disappointed. Although it would seem likely that at least a few Slytherins, particularly the half-bloods, must oppose Voldemort and his Death Eaters, they are denied that opportunity; when Slytherin House, led by Pansy Parkinson, aims their wands at Harry, McGonagall elects to send the entire House away, probably to avert a violent, and possibly lethal, confrontation with the other Houses who will defend Harry. Any Slytherins that have doubts about the wisdom of siding with Voldemort against Harry are submerged in the crowd. If they choose to fight Voldemort, they will do so from outside the school.

On the brink of battle, several characters undergo some significant realizations about themselves. For most of his life, Harry has felt isolated and suffered from a need to "go it alone," often refusing others' assistance or accepting it only when pressured or as a last resort. Not only is Harry bolstered by his old friends and allies returning to Hogwarts, ready to fight Voldemort and his Death Eaters, but as he races through the hallways, he yearns for Ron and Hermione's help and companionship. Harry has made great strides in learning to trust and rely on others. Hermione is overjoyed when Ron wants to warn House-elves of the imminent danger. His growing maturity has led to his concern for others' well being, not just his own or his immediate family's. He now recognizes that Hermione's efforts on the Elves behalf has been valid and that these creatures deserve the same respect and consideration as other magical folk. Ron also shows his natural intelligence when, during the intense battle, he realizes that Basilisk fangs can destroy Horcruxes, something Harry must have forgotten about despite having destroyed Riddle's Diary with one. Remembering the words Harry spoke in Parseltongue, Ron opens the Chamber of Secrets and retrieves the fangs. Hermione's genuine admiration for his cleverness, quick thinking, and leadership further enhances her feelings for him. These acts open the door to Ron and Hermione's hidden feelings for one another, although their happiness is quickly marred by tragedy.

That tragedy is Fred's untimely death, and not only does it cause intense pain and sorrow to those who loved him, it also tests their strength and courage. Racked with grief, Harry and the Weasley family must suppress their anguish and focus solely on the ensuing battle if they are to defeat Voldemort and his Death Eaters. Percy is particularly distraught, having just reunited with his estranged family. Hopefully he can find solace in having reconciled with Fred before he died, but for now, he diverts his grief and rage at the enemy to avenge his lost brother. Readers will recall that earlier in the book, George's ear was severed during the flight from the Dursleys' house. This may have foreshadowed him losing a larger part of himself, that part being Fred.

The rather morose Draco seen at Malfoy Manor has reverted to his familiar arrogant and bullying persona now that he is back at Hogwarts, lording over his faithful minions, Crabbe and Goyle. Away from his family's influence, Draco adopts a very different façade from the one he displays while in his parents' presence. However, that mask usually crumbles whenever Draco is faced with adversity, as it did when confronting Dumbledore on the Astronomy Tower in *Harry Potter and the Half-Blood Prince*, and being forced to torture a fellow Death Eater earlier in this book. Why he chose to remain in the castle when the other Slytherins departed to join Voldemort is unclear, and his true intentions will remain unknown, though it is hinted that Draco may have been planning to capture Harry and present him to Voldemort. Draco himself may be unaware just what his real motives are, vacillating between fearful indifference and seizing an opportunity to win back the Dark Lord's favor for his family. Draco is a vessel lacking a compass, and, as he may have learned from observing his mentor, Snape, maintaining a neutral position makes it easier to align one's self with either winning side. However, when Draco realized Harry was after the Diadem, he may have wanted to capture him with the hope that he could reprieve the Malfoys from Voldemort's retaliation and to redeem himself to his family.

Interestingly, when Draco and Harry confront one another in the Room of Requirement, Draco demands that Harry return his wand. However, even if Harry was inclined to return it, which he was not, it probably would be practically useless for Draco. When Harry captured the wand at Malfoy Manor, it likely transferred its allegiance from Draco to Harry, its new master. Indeed, Harry found that Draco's wand worked exceptionally well for him.

QUESTIONS

Review 1. Why did Ron want it to be Hermione who destroyed the Cup Horcrux?

2. Did it ever occur to Harry to use Basilisk fangs to destroy the Horcruxes? Why or why not?

3. Why is Hermione so ecstatic when Ron wants to warn the House-elves? What does this say about Ron's character?

4. Why is Harry unable to locate Ron and Hermione's name on the Marauder's Map?

Extra Study 1. Harry saves Goyle's and Malfoy's lives. Do they now owe him a "life debt" as Peter Pettigrew did? Explain.

2. At Malfoy Manor, Draco would not identify Harry to the Death Eaters. Why does he now want to capture him for the Dark Lord?

3. How does Malfoy's current behavior and demeanor compare to the way he behaved while at Malfoy Manor? How does it compare to how he acted during his earlier years at Hogwarts? What could account for these differences?

4. Will the Room of Requirement be operational again? Explain why or why not this might be.

GREATER PICTURE

Ron having Hermione destroy the Cup Horcrux shows how deep the bond is between Harry, Ron, and Hermione: since Harry had already destroyed a Horcrux—the Diary—and Ron eliminated another—the Locket—then why should Hermione not destroy the third Horcrux? This is meant to show how Harry, who initially believed he should undertake the quest alone, depends on his friends far more than he ever realized. We will be reminded of this when, although it was Harry who was tasked by Dumbledore to destroy Voldemort's Horcruxes, in the end, each Horcrux is eventually destroyed by a different person. Although Harry had wanted to search for the Horcruxes alone, Dumbledore always knew, and intended, that Ron and Hermione would accompany him.

Ron wanting to warn the House-elves about the attack is what causes Hermione to kiss him, overjoyed that he finally considers them as beings worthy of protection; as it turns out, however, the usually overlooked creatures are not warned, but they play an important role in the final battle against Voldemort.

Also, Draco Malfoy choosing to stay at Hogwarts rather than leave with the other Slytherins will prove an important factor in the story. First, it is his friend, Crabbe, who—accidentally—destroys the Diadem Horcrux in the Room of Requirement. Then, when Harry revives after being struck by Voldemort's ineffective Killing Curse, it is Narcissa Malfoy, Draco's mother, who is called upon to verify if Harry is dead. Because Draco is still inside the castle, Narcissa knows that the only way she can enter it, without risking Draco's life in further fighting, is as part of a victorious army, and she lies to Voldemort, thus sparing Harry's life.

Chapter 32: The Elder Wand

Synopsis

Harry cannot permit himself to grieve Fred's death; the castle is under serious attack. As curses fly overhead, Harry, Ron, and Hermione dive to the floor while Percy covers Fred's body with his own to protect it. Ron tries pulling Percy away, but he refuses to budge. Hermione screams, and turning, Harry sees a giant spider, one of Aragog's descendants, crawling through the hole blown through the castle's outer wall. Harry and Ron simultaneously blast the spider. Looking through the hole, Harry sees more spiders climbing up the wall and fires stunning spells at them. As more curses soar overhead, Harry shouts, "Let's move, *now!*" Pushing Hermione and Ron on ahead, Harry stoops to lift Fred's body. Percy releases his protective grip and helps him hide it in a wall niche. Harry takes off after Ron and Hermione down the corridor. People are running everywhere, and rounding the corner, Percy suddenly roars, "*Rookwood!*" and takes off after a tall man chasing students. Hermione calls Harry behind a tapestry where she is trying to restrain a hysterical Ron, who wants to follow Percy and kill Death Eaters. Hermione pleads with Ron that they are the only ones who can end it; they must find and kill the snake. Hermione says they need to know where Voldemort and Nagini are. Harry also wants to fight but allows himself to slip inside Voldemort's mind where he sees a shabby, but familiar room. Voldemort is thinking about the Diadem and the place only he knows exists. A battered Lucius Malfoy is present, asking about Draco, but Voldemort tells him if his son is dead, it is Draco's own fault for failing to join him like the other Slytherins. Lucius urges him to cease the battle so the Dark Lord can be certain to kill Potter himself, but Voldemort ignores him, knowing it is only an attempt to protect Draco. Voldemort orders Lucius to fetch Snape, and as he waits, he speaks to Nagini, who is suspended in a protective floating sphere. Harry snaps back into his own thoughts and tells the others that Voldemort is in the Shrieking Shack. Hermione is astounded that Voldemort is not fighting, but Harry says Voldemort knows he is hunting his Horcruxes, and he is waiting for Harry to come to him.

After some disagreement over who should go to the Shrieking Shack and dodging Death Eater curses, the Trio throw on the Invisibility Cloak and weave their way through the battle. On the upper landing, they run past Draco Malfoy, who is pleading with a Death Eater that he is on their side; Harry stuns the Death Eater as Ron punches Draco in the face. Below, Fenrir Greyback, appearing to Harry as a blurry, four-legged gray animal as he rushes past, is about to bite Lavender Brown. Hermione's curse hurls him against the staircase. A crystal ball crashing onto his head knocks him out, and Professor Trelawney, leaning over the railing, threatens to lob more. The entryway doors burst open and the spiders force their way in. As all the fighters shoot curses at them, Hagrid charges down the stairs yelling, "Don't hurt 'em, don't hurt 'em!" As Hagrid runs outside and disappears into the spider throng, Harry dashes out from under the Cloak chasing after him. His path is blocked by a massive, hairy leg belonging to a twenty-foot Giant. When Grawp appears calling for Hagrid, the bigger giant launches itself at him, and the two furiously wrestle. Fighting is everywhere now and flashing curses streak through the air. The trio head to the forest, but at its edge, a hundred Dementors glide towards them. Hermione calls out to cast Patronuses. Harry is too overcome by hopelessness to cast one, while Ron and Hermione's Patronuses quickly flicker out. Suddenly, three other Patronuses soar past as Luna, Ernie, and Seamus come running from the darkness. Luna encourages Harry to think of something happy, and with enormous effort, Harry casts his Patronus. The silver stag bursts from his wand, scattering the Dementors. As another giant lurches towards them, Harry shouts to Ron and Hermione to head for the Shrieking Shack.

At the Whomping Willow, they crawl through the tunnel leading to the Shack. Inside, Snape is talking with Voldemort, offering to find the boy so Voldemort can kill him himself. Voldemort declines, saying he ordered his Death Eaters to capture him alive; but, he goes on, the Elder Wand fails to perform the extraordinary magic he thought was possible. Snape, nervous, again offers to find Harry Potter, but Voldemort says that he expects the boy to come to him. Continuing, Voldemort tells Snape that he has been a valuable servant and regrets what he must do. He believes that when Snape killed Dumbledore, Snape won the wand's allegiance. Unfortunately, Snape must die so he can become the Elder Wand's true master. With no remorse, Voldemort sets Nagini on Snape, ordering her to kill. When Voldemort and Nagini leave, Harry and the others rush to Snape's side. Silvery-blue wisps stream from his mouth, ears, and eyes. Snape, barely alive, tells Harry, "Take . . . it . . . Take . . . it." A crystal flask appears in mid air, and Hermione thrusts it into Harry's hands. Harry gathers the drifting strands with his wand, putting them into the container. Snape asks Harry to look at him, and staring into Harry's green eyes, Snape's life ebbs away.

Analysis

Two significant deaths have occurred: Fred Weasley and Severus Snape. While Fred's death is a tragic loss, Snape's demise is a crucial element leading to the book's climax. Snape, and also readers, may have expected that Voldemort would eventually kill him. It is still unknown, however, whether Snape was serving Voldemort or Dumbledore, or even neither. Just as Dumbledore had, Voldemort appears to believe that Snape was always loyal to him, and even still useful, but

Voldemort's quest to become the Elder Wand's master takes precedence over everything else, and he willingly sacrifices Snape to obtain that mastery. Whether Snape was a hero or a villain, his final act is to hand over to Harry what appears to be his memories. These memories could be the key that unlocks the secrets to Dumbledore's cryptic plan. It may also be significant that Snape's final request is to look into Harry's eyes, a physical feature of his that others have continually commented about throughout the series.

Lucius Malfoy, who Voldemort severely punished for failing to capture Harry Potter, is deathly afraid for his son, Draco's life. This is probably one of the few times Lucius has ever demonstrated any real emotion for another person, and it shows that, unlike Voldemort, Lucius is capable of love and desperately wants to save his only child. However, although Voldemort shows no concern for Draco and previously endangered his life only as a means to punish Lucius for his failure at the Ministry of Magic, Lucius continues to serve the Dark Lord. At this point, while Lucius may still be hoping to win favor and reward, and will likely retain his evil ways should Voldemort win, he probably remains with the Dark Lord mostly out of fear for his own and his family's safety.

It is also of interest to note Hermione's changing views regarding the connection between Harry's mind and Voldemort's. At this book's beginning, Hermione was deeply dismayed by Harry occasionally viewing Voldemort's thoughts and action, as it was via that channel that Harry had been deluded into taking himself and five students into a trap at the Department of Mysteries earlier. Harry continually resisted attempts to shut down this channel, feeling that any information about Voldemort is valuable. Over the course of this book, we have seen Hermione gradually accepting the same point of view, but this is the first time she has actively asked Harry to visit Voldemort's mind. This would seem to indicate her accepting Harry's ability to control and filter what he sees inside Voldemort's mind.

An interesting side note here. The book describes Fenrir Greyback as a gray blur on four legs that Harry took to be an animal. This suggests that he could have been transformed into his werewolf form as he attempts to bite Lavender Brown. In that event, there would be a full moon, but there is no mention as to whether Remus Lupin, also a werewolf, has been similarly transformed. Lupin is seen as a human when he arrives at Hogwarts to help fight the battle, but it is possible it is still too early for the moon to rise. It may be that Greyback is simply acting wolf-like; as we have heard and seen, he does attack like a wolf even when in human form, as when he savaged Bill Weasley. However, being able to survive such a severe blow to the head from Trelawney's heavy crystal ball with almost no injuries could indicate that he was a werewolf at the time. While it is never made absolutely clear what form he is in, it is true that Harry, who has never seen Fenrir transformed, recognizes him. As the author is careful about having every character properly named before Harry recognizes him or her, this does lend some weight that Fenrir is in human form, although it is curious as to why she would describe him in a manner suggesting his gray werewolf form.

QUESTIONS

Review 1. Does Voldemort know that the Diadem Horcrux has been destroyed? If not, why? 2. Why does Voldemort believe Snape is the Elder Wand's master? Is he? If not, who might be?

Further Study 1. Why does Hagrid try to protect the attacking giant spiders? Whose side are they on?

2. Why didn't Draco leave with the other Slytherin students who joined Voldemort? What, if any, might his true allegiance be?

3. Why is Voldemort so certain that Harry will come to him?

4. Why does Voldemort kill Snape, a valuable servant, to win the Elder Wand's allegiance, rather than disarm him for it? Did Voldemort always intend to kill Snape?

5. Why does Voldemort have Nagini kill Snape, rather than doing it himself with a killing curse?

6. Why does Lucius Malfoy continue serving Voldemort, despite the Dark Lord having endangered his and his son's life?

7. Why was Harry too overwhelmed with hopelessness to cast a Patronus at the Dementors? How did he overcome that?

8. What are the silvery strands that Snape gave to Harry? Where have they been seen before? Why would he want Harry to have them?

9. Why would Snape want to look into Harry's eyes just before he dies?

GREATER PICTURE

In the next chapter, we discover why Snape asked Harry to look into his eyes as he died. Snape knows he is dying; he has already handed over to Harry the memories that will give Harry the explanation that Dumbledore charged Snape with providing. They also provide Snape's own justification for his actions. From those memories, we will learn that Lily Potter was the only love of Snape's life, and perhaps it is for her that Snape had been doing all he did for Harry, little as it may have seemed at the time. We have been told repeatedly that Harry has Lily's eyes, and, as he dies, Snape desires to look into those eyes one last time.

Chapter 33: The Prince's Tale

SYNOPSIS

After witnessing Severus Snape's death, Harry hears Lord Voldemort's magically amplified voice, speaking to everyone at Hogwarts. He then speaks to Harry, giving him one hour to surrender and threatening to kill everyone if he fails to comply. Harry, Ron, and Hermione return to Hogwarts through the tunnel, and Ron and Hermione enter the Great Hall, where the defenders are regrouping and the many wounded and dead lie. Harry sees Fred, who died earlier, and discovers Lupin and Tonks among the casualties. Unable to bear the sight, Harry runs to the Headmaster's office, where all the portraits stand empty, and finds Dumbledore's Pensieve. Harry pours Snape's memories into the Pensieve, and, hoping to briefly escape his own mind, enters the memories. He finds himself in a playground. A young, small boy, who Harry recognizes as Snape, is watching two girls, Lily and Petunia Evans, from behind a small bush. After Lily shows some strange tricks to her older sister, unaware she is performing magic, Snape emerges and informs Lily that she is a witch and derides Petunia as a Muggle. Insulted at being called a witch, Lily follows her indignant sister and goes away, leaving Snape bitterly disappointed. It is apparent he was planning this for a while and it all went wrong.

The scene dissolves and reforms into a new one. Snape is telling a curious Lily about Hogwarts and magic, including Azkaban and the Dementors. When Lily inquires about Snape's parents, he says that they are still arguing and that his father does not like anything much, revealing Snape's unhappy home life. When Petunia appears from behind a tree and insults Snape, a branch above breaks and falls on her. Accusing Snape of breaking the branch, Lily goes away, leaving him miserable and confused.

The scene reforms again into a different memory. Snape is standing on Platform Nine and Three Quarters next to a thin, sour looking woman who Harry recognizes as Snape's mother. Snape is staring at a family of four which happens to be Lily's family. Petunia and Lily are in a scuffle about Lily going away to Hogwarts. Petunia calls Lily a freak for being a witch, and Lily retorts that Petunia had not thought so when she wrote to the Headmaster, Professor Dumbledore, asking for admission to the school. An embarrassed Petunia realizes that Lily and Snape had read her letter and insults them, and they leave on bad terms.

The scene reforms once more and Snape is hurrying along a Hogwarts Express corridor. He finds a compartment with Lily and two boys. He tries to speak with her but she is upset over her sister's hurtful words. Snape begins to say that she is only a Muggle but catches himself. He grandly announces they are setting off for Hogwarts and mentions that she had better be in Slytherin. One of the boys, the young James Potter, makes a scornful remark to his friend, Sirius Black that he would rather leave than be in Slytherin, and would prefer to be in Gryffindor. Sirius points out that all of his family have been in Slytherin. Snape gets into a little battle of words with both Sirius and James, until an indignant Lily asks Snape to follow her to different compartment.

And the scene dissolves again into the Great Hall at Hogwarts during the House sorting ceremony. Professor McGonagall calls Lily's name, and she is sorted into Gryffindor, much to Snape's dismay. Remus Lupin, Peter Pettigrew, and James Potter are also sorted into Gryffindor, joining Sirius Black. Finally, Snape is called and is sorted into Slytherin. He walks to the Slytherin table where he receives a pat on the back from a Prefect, Lucius Malfoy.

The scene changes to Lily and Snape walking across the courtyard, arguing. Snape wonders what has happened to their close friendship. Lily says they are still friends, even though she detests who Snape hangs out with, naming Avery and Mulciber specifically. Snape counters by reminding her of the trouble James and his friends get into and hints that Lupin is a werewolf. In the end, the fight is resolved when Snape is satisfied with Lily's criticism of James as an "arrogant toerag."

The scene switches for the sixth time and is the same memory Harry saw before when he peeked into Snape's Pensieve during their Occlumency lessons. Harry keeps his distance somewhat, not caring to witness this memory again. It ends when he hears the distant shout of "Mudblood" by Snape at Lily.

The scene changes to night time in front of the Gryffindor Tower. Snape is feeling very remorseful for calling Lily a Mudblood and had threatened to sleep outside the entrance had she not come to see him. Despite his deep, desperate apologies, the angry Lily is fed up with Snape and will not forgive him, and goes on to talk down to him for having friends with Death Eater ambitions. She leaves him and the scene dissolves.

The scene takes longer to reform and now becomes a hilltop in the darkness with a few leafless trees nearby. The adult Snape is panting and pacing on the spot and appears to be waiting for something. A blinding jet of white light flies through the air and Snape, disarmed, drops to his knees. Dumbledore stands before Snape and asks what message he has brought from Lord Voldemort. Snape replies with not a message, but a request from himself. He admits to Dumbledore he relayed everything he heard about the prophecy from Trelawney to Voldemort and that Voldemort believes the chosen child to be Lily's son. He reveals that Voldemort plans to hunt down and kill the entire family. Dumbledore is disgusted that Snape has asked Voldemort to spare only Lily's life without regard for her husband and son. Ashamed at being rebuked, Snape then pleads with Dumbledore to hide the entire family. Surprising Snape, Dumbledore asks him what he will give in return. After a long moment, Snape replies, "Anything."

The scene switches to Dumbledore's office. Snape, clearly grief-stricken, is slumped forward in a chair with a grim-looking Dumbledore standing over him. Snape asks Dumbledore why he failed to keep Lily and her family safe. Dumbledore replies that they put their faith in the wrong person, much as Snape had in trusting Voldemort to spare Lily's life. He also reveals to Snape that her son, Harry, survived. Snape states that he wishes he were dead with Lily, and Dumbledore tells him that if he truly loved Lily, he will help Dumbledore protect Harry when Voldemort returns. Snape reluctantly agrees. He makes Dumbledore give his word to never tell anyone that he is protecting James Potter's son, ever.

The scene shifts again and Snape is pacing up and down in front of Dumbledore, criticizing Harry and describing him as being like James. Dumbledore, however, replies that other teachers report him to be a likable and reasonably talented boy. Thumbing through his Transfiguration magazine, he asks Snape to keep an eye on Professor Quirrell.

With a whirl of color everything changes again and Snape and Dumbledore are now standing in the entrance hall as the Yule Ball is ending. Snape tells Dumbledore that Karkaroff's Mark is becoming darker as well

Chapter 33: The Prince's Tale

and that he plans on fleeing if the Mark burns. When Dumbledore asks if Snape is tempted to do the same, Snape denies it and says he is not a coward. Dumbledore then remarks that he thinks students are Sorted too soon, leaving Snape shocked.

The scene dissolves for the twelfth time and reforms into the headmaster's office again. Dumbledore is semiconscious, his right hand blackened and dangling over the side of the desk. Snape is muttering incantations and pouring a golden liquid down Dumbledore's throat. When Dumbledore regains consciousness, Snape asks why Dumbledore even tried on the ring. Dumbledore says he was a fool. Marvolo Gaunt's ring lay on the desk, cracked, with the Sword of Gryffindor next to it. Snape says it is a miracle he got here and that the curse is extraordinary powerful. Snape believes Dumbledore may only have a year to live since all he can do is contain the curse, not stop it. Dumbledore replies that this makes things much easier to decide and begins discussing Voldemort's plan involving Draco Malfoy killing Dumbledore. Snape says it is only to punish the Malfoys and that Draco is expected to fail. Dumbledore correctly guesses that when Malfoy fails, Voldemort wants Snape to finish Dumbledore off, saying that Voldemort feels he will soon not need a spy at Hogwarts anymore, as it will be under his control. Dumbledore makes Snape promise to watch over the students in that event, and to be the one to kill him (Dumbledore). Snape questions this and Dumbledore says it would be helping an old man die. He would rather die on his own terms at the hands of Snape than foes like Death Eaters Bellatrix and Fenrir Greyback. Snape reluctantly agrees and the scene ends.

In the next scene, Snape and Dumbledore are strolling through the castle grounds at night. Snape asks what Dumbledore has been doing with Harry all these evenings alone, and Dumbledore replies that he has information he must give to Harry before it is too late. Snape challenges Dumbledore as to why he is not entrusted with the same information, to which Dumbledore replies that he does not like to keep all his secrets in one basket. They get into a row about Snape having to be a double agent on Dumbledore's orders and that Harry is no more trustworthy than Snape. Dumbledore begins to go on with his plan to Snape, however, Snape is angry that Dumbledore refuses to tell him what he has told Harry and threatens that he has changed his mind about killing Dumbledore. Dumbledore reminds him that he gave him his word and that he is also to keep an eye on Draco. Snape looks unsatisfied so Dumbledore invites him to his office that night.

The scene shifts to Dumbledore's office, and he is walking around Snape. Dumbledore tells Snape that Harry must not know what he has to do until the final moment, and that after Dumbledore's death, there will come a time when Voldemort fears for Nagini's life. He instructs Snape that, if there is ever a time when Voldemort refuses to let Nagini out of his sight and keeps her magically protected, Snape must tell Harry at that time. As Snape does not know what to tell Harry, Dumbledore says that Harry is a seventh Horcrux, inadvertently created by Voldemort, and that Harry must die in order for Voldemort to be killed. Snape feels tricked, upset that Dumbledore made him protect Lily's son only to have him die. Dumbledore asks if Snape has grown to care for Harry after all, but Snape spurns that possibility and casts his Patronus, a silver-white doe. Dumbledore, with tears in his eyes, asks Snape, "After all these years?," to which Snape says, "Always."

The scene switches to Snape talking to Dumbledore's portrait behind his desk. Dumbledore tells Snape that he must give Voldemort the correct date of Harry's departure if Voldemort is to trust Snape. Snape is also to suggest the Potter decoys using Polyjuice potion to Mundungus so that Harry is indeed safe.

The scene shifts to Snape face-to-face with Mundungus in a tavern. Snape is confunding him so that he will suggest the idea of multiple Potters, and forget that he had seen Snape or gotten the idea from him. The scene shifts yet again, to Snape gliding on a broomstick at night. Up ahead are Lupin and George, disguised as Harry. Snape casts Sectumsempra at a Death Eater to prevent him from Cursing Lupin, but the spell misses and hits George instead.

The scene shifts again and Snape is in Sirius's old room. Tears flow down his face as he reads the old letter Lily sent to Sirius. He takes the second page with Lily's signature, and tears our her image from the picture of her and Harry with his broom, and leaves.

The scene shifts again and Snape is in the headmaster's office talking to the portrait of Phineas Nigellus. Phineas tells Snape that Hermione and Harry are in the Forest of Dean, and Dumbledore's portrait appears happy. Dumbledore tells Snape to plant the sword of Gryffindor there, and that he must not be seen. Snape coolly says he has a plan, removes the real sword from behind Dumbledore's portrait, and leaves the room.

Harry returns to himself, lying on the carpet in the same room he just saw Snape leaving.

Analysis

In *Harry Potter and the Order of the Phoenix*, Petunia Dursley says, "I heard—that awful boy—telling *her* about them—years ago." "*Her*" is of course Lily, her sister, and "them" refers to the Dementors, who Petunia has just identified as the guards of Azkaban. It is interesting to note that "that awful boy" was actually Severus Snape; knowing Petunia, we expected this to refer to James Potter.

Our viewing Snape's memories shows readers something else unexpected. Previously, Harry had seen the memory after the Defence Against the Dark Arts O.W.L. test in a chapter called "Snape's Worst Memory." Considering the extreme humiliation Snape suffers at James Potter's hands, one would believe that sufficient reason for it being his "worst memory." However, knowing Snape's strong feelings for Lily, the memory acquires a different meaning: it is the worst because one word in it had ended his friendship with Lily Evans, and she would later marry James and give birth to Harry.

While the reason is never explicitly given, it is clear that when Dumbledore, watching the students return from the Yule Ball, remarks that perhaps the students are Sorted too soon, Snape is shocked at the thought that his true place at Hogwarts as a boy, and his entire later life, could have been different had the Sorting been delayed until he was more aware of his own desires.

The conversation between Snape and Dumbledore on the castle grounds, appearing as Snape's fourteenth memory, is one of which bits have been heard before. Apparently this discussion took place the previous year, just before Ron's rather disastrous birthday. It was partially overheard by Hagrid, who, with his usual inability to keep a secret, passed on the bits he overheard to Harry and Hermione.

The following conversation, in Dumbledore's office, contains one element which should be instantly clear but is never explained. Explaining the reason for his actions, Snape summons his Patronus, which proves to be a silver doe, the same silver doe we had seen earlier which led Harry to the Sword of Gryffindor in the Forest of Dean. Dumbledore, knowing that life circumstances can change the shape of a wizard's Patronus, immediately recognizes the connection to Lily Potter. We never find out what Lily's Patronus was, though as Harry's father, James, had such powerful associations with the stag, taking that Animagus form, it is possible that Lily's Patronus, following form, was a doe. This is not necessarily true, however; it is equally possible that, no matter what Lily's Patronus was, Snape perceived her as a doe, mated to the stag that was James, and his Patronus reflected that perception. Dumbledore's question, "After all these years?," is asking if Snape had been protecting Harry out of his love for Lily for all these years.

Snape's love for Lily never faded throughout the years, and, unknown to Harry, that love caused Snape to always protect him. Snape's seeming malice towards Harry actually resulted from Snape's lingering hate and resentment towards James Potter; Harry was merely an unfortunate reminder. As Snape was about to die, he asked to gaze into Harry's eyes, presumably because they looked just like Lily's, a fact Harry has been repeatedly reminded of. It is interesting to note that the only thing Dumbledore required Snape to do was, when Voldemort started protecting Nagini, keeping her at his side, that he should then tell Harry about Voldemort's Horcrux that he carried within himself, and that he needed to die in order to destroy that soul fragment. There was no need, according to his promise to Dumbledore, for Snape to provide Harry with all these other memories. Could Snape have been attempting to justify his past actions, to exonerate himself to Harry?

Questions

Review 1. How was Harry able to get into the Headmaster's office, which needs a password to enter? 2. Based on what he has just learned, what might Harry do next?

Extra Study 1. How will Harry, who distrusted and hated Snape, cope with the reality that Snape was loyal to Dumbledore and had protected Harry, always at great peril to himself?
2. Is it possible that Lily could have ever felt more than friendship for Snape? Could she have felt more for Snape than for James?
3. Why and how did Lily, who initially despised James Potter, fall in love with him?
4. Why did Dumbledore call Harry's mother "Lily Evans" rather than "Lily Potter" when trying to convince Snape to switch sides? This is after Lily had married James Potter and shortly before Harry is born.
5. Now that Harry knows the reason for Aunt Petunia's bitterness and resentment towards him, is it likely to change their relationship? Explain.

Greater Picture

It is interesting to note that of everyone around him, Dumbledore most often confided in Snape, whereas up until this chapter, Minerva McGonagall had always appeared to be his closest confidante. Before, Snape always seemed on the periphery and his true allegiance questionable. Now it is revealed that Dumbledore and Snape enjoyed a close relationship forged by a common quest. When others asked why he trusted Snape, Dumbledore always alluded to a nebulous event, but never elaborated. Now, not only do we see what he was referring to, Snape's unrequited love for Lily, but also why Dumbledore refused to identify it: Snape extracted that promise from him. Finally, we understand why Dumbledore trusted Snape implicitly, and vice versa, and our, and Harry's, faith in Dumbledore is reaffirmed.

Chapter 34: The Forest Again

Synopsis

Sprawled on the Headmaster's office floor, Harry now understands his own destiny. Under his Invisibility Cloak, he proceeds to the Entrance Hall, almost bumping into Neville, who is returning from the grounds with Oliver Wood. They are carrying Colin Creevey's body into the castle. Oliver says he can handle this on his own, and Neville returns to the grounds to search for more casualties. Harry follows and reveals himself to Neville. Harry tells Neville that Nagini must be killed to defeat Voldemort. He says that Ron and Hermione also know, but if for some reason they are unable to, then Neville must kill Nagini. Neville says he will, and Harry puts the cloak back on and proceeds to the Forbidden Forest. Noticing Ginny helping a fallen girl along the way, he is tempted to stop and speak with her, but knowing it would be impossible for him to continue if he did, he goes on, past Hagrid's hut and to the Forest.

Harry's path is blocked by Dementors gliding around the forest's edge, and he lacks the strength to conjure another Patronus. Harry pulls the Snitch from his pouch. Remembering its inscription, "I open at the close," he realizes it refers to death. Pressing the Snitch to his lips, he whispers, "I am about to die." The Snitch breaks open and reveals the Peverell ring, which Harry now knows holds the cracked Resurrection Stone. Closing his eyes, he turns the stone three times, then opens his eyes. The shades of James, Lily, Lupin, and Sirius appear. All seem ghostly but are more solid-looking than just spirits. Lupin and Sirius both appear younger and each looks happy. His mother and father speak to Harry, telling him how proud they are of him and offer comfort as he prepares to die. Harry asks if dying hurts, but Sirius says it is painless and easier than falling asleep. Harry tells Remus that he is sorry that he will not know his son. Remus regrets he is unable to be there for him, but is glad Teddy will grow up in a better world that his death helped to make possible. The spirits promise to stay with Harry and protect him as he passes through the Dementors, acting as Patronuses. Harry is able to force himself to go on only because the spirits are there with him.

Harry makes his way through the thick, tangled woods, unaware of where he is heading; something appears to be guiding him. The spirits remain close to his side. As he nears Voldemort's camp, Yaxley and Dolohov think they hear something, although they believe it is probably only an animal. The one hour is nearly up, and it appears that Harry Potter will not come. Still cloaked, Harry follows them into a clearing where he sees two Giants and Voldemort's Death Eaters, including Bellatrix. Fenrir Greyback is skulking nearby, while Lucius Malfoy and his wife, Narcissa are also there, both looking defeated and apprehensive. Harry recognizes the camp site as Aragog's old dwelling, his descendants having been forced out by Death Eaters to fight for their cause. "I thought he would come," Voldemort said, "I expected him to come." None spoke. Outside the ring of firelight, Harry pulls off the Cloak and tucks it, beside his wand, under his robes. The Resurrection Stone slips from his fingers, and the spirits vanish. Voldemort speaks again. "I was, it seems... mistaken."

Harry loudly replies, "You weren't."

Another voice yells, "*Harry! What are yeh-!*" It is Hagrid, tightly bound to a tree nearby. Rowle silences him.

"Harry Potter," Voldemort said, "the boy who lived." As Harry's final thoughts turn to Ginny, Voldemort casts the Killing Curse at him.

ANALYSIS

Snape's memories have answered many questions, and the truth is not what Harry or the reader expected. It seems that Harry's doubts and fears about Dumbledore were not only justified, but Dumbledore had carefully been protecting him all these years only as part of his ultimate plan to sacrifice Harry to rid the wizarding world of Voldemort. Surprisingly, Harry accepts this, and he willingly goes to face Voldemort and fulfill his fate in order to save others. Snape is also vindicated, and his heroism and sacrifice are finally revealed. If Harry survives, he will eventually have to reconcile his long-held hatred for his belligerent teacher with newfound gratitude to the tragic man who protected him and aided his quest, losing his own life in the process.

The one bright spot for Harry is that he has finally attained his dream to be reunited with his parents, although, unlike the brother in the tale, he realizes that the boundary between the living and the dead can be crossed permanently only in one direction. By accepting this final piece of understanding, Harry becomes death's master. However, he feels justified summoning James and Lily's spirits only so they can escort him to the netherworld, not to attempt to resurrect them. Meeting his parents and hearing their words completes his emotional need for their love and approval. They also provide comfort and guidance as he is about to meet his own death.

In this chapter, we also see several indications of how deep Harry's love is for Ginny. First, as Harry is leaving Hogwarts, he spots Ginny, and of all the people Harry longs to bid goodbye to, it is his inability to speak to Ginny that hurts most, fearing he will be unable to continue if he stops. Also, and perhaps most telling, is that as Harry faces his death, it is the memory of Ginny's kiss that comes to him, rather than any recollection of his parents, or even Cho Chang, showing that of those in Harry's life, it is Ginny who had provided the most comfort. On Ginny's part, as Harry passes her on the way to the forest, he believes that Ginny sensed him passing, despite his being covered by the Invisibility Cloak. While he cannot know this for certain, as he does not look back, this indicates his trust in Ginny's love for him.

QUESTIONS

Review 1. Unlike the brother in the Deathly Hallows tale, why does Harry feels he is justified in summoning his parents' spirits?

2. What does, "I open at the close" mean? Why does Harry only now understand its meaning?

Further Study 1. When Harry summons the spirits of his parents, Sirius, and Lupin, why doesn't he also call for Cedric Diggory, "Mad Eye" Moody, Dumbledore, or Fred Weasley?

2. Why does Harry drop the Resurrection Stone just as he confronts Voldemort?

3. Was Dumbledore justified in protecting Harry only so his life will be sacrificed to defeat Voldemort? Why does Harry so readily accept his fate?

GREATER PICTURE

We will very shortly learn that Harry's death, as we could guess from the fact that two large chapters remain in the book, does not actually occur at this juncture. A great deal of explanation of what has happened, and final understanding of Dumbledore's plan and intent, will be provided to us in the next chapter.

Harry's dropping the Resurrection Stone, rather than being unplanned, is actually a conscious decision on his part. The Stone, now somewhere underfoot in the depths of the Forbidden Forest, is unlikely to ever be found again. Harry, it develops, feels correctly that the ability to summon the shades of the dead is something that does not belong in this world.

Chapter 35: King's Cross

SYNOPSIS

Harry finds himself alone and naked in an otherworldly place. Hearing noise, he wishes for and receives clothing, then notices a hideous, child-like creature, nude and with flayed-looking skin, curled up on the ground. Dumbledore appears and lovingly greets Harry. He explains that when Voldemort took some of Harry's blood as his own, he thereby tethered his life to Harry's; Harry cannot die while Voldemort lives.

Because he willingly sacrificed himself, Harry also is protecting his friends, shielding them during the duels with Voldemort, just as Lily had protected Harry by sacrificing herself. Moreover, rather than killing Harry, Voldemort's curse destroyed the seventh Horcrux within Harry's body.

Dumbledore also guesses that the reason the two brother wands interacted as they did during Harry's escape from Privet Drive is that after Harry and Voldemort's blood was joined, their wands, already connected by identical magical cores, and now wielded by wizards who shared not only pieces of their souls but also their blood, merged even closer. Furthermore, during Harry and Voldemort's duel, Harry was the stronger; Voldemort feared death, while Harry embraced the possibility. Harry's wand thus imbibed some powers from Voldemort's, making it more powerful than Lucius Malfoy's wand. That wand, even when wielded by Voldemort, was easily overpowered by Harry's. But why then, Harry asks, was Hermione's wand able to break his? Dumbledore speculates that Harry's wand was abnormally powerful only when it was directed against Voldemort, who it sensed was Harry's mortal enemy, as well as being his blood kin.

Harry asks where they are, although he himself suggests it resembles a deserted King's Cross station. He then addresses more important issues: the Hallows. Dumbledore asks Harry's forgiveness for withholding information about the Deathly Hallows. Dumbledore says he was obsessed with the Hallows in his youth, eager to escape death, and equally eager to shine and attain glory, while Aberforth looked on in disgust. That is why he resented having to care for his mother and sister, and the reason he was so happy to befriend Gellert Grindelwald. The two young wizards bonded over their mutual search for the Deathly Hallows. An undefeatable wand would surely help them rise to power in the wizarding world. Dumbledore wanted the Resurrection Stone to reunite his family, but Grindelwald saw it as a means to procure an Inferi army. And while neither had much interest in the Invisibility Cloak, as both were proficient in disillusionment, Dumbledore thought it could be used to hide Ariana. Their friendship was short-lived, however, and the two got into a fight, along with Aberforth, over Dumbledore's family. Somehow, a curse went astray and fatally hit Ariana. Grindelwald fled and started on his rampage, but Dumbledore delayed dueling him, fearing he might learn who actually killed Ariana. Eventually, and after much bloodshed and desperate pleas from the wizarding world, he felt obliged to confront his former friend and defeated him—thereby winning the Elder Wand. Dumbledore learned that Grindelwald lied to Voldemort when he said he never owned the Elder Wand, perhaps trying to protect Dumbledore in a belated remorseful act. Finally, when Dumbledore retrieved the Peverell Ring, knowing it was a Horcrux, and discovered that it was in fact the Resurrection Stone, he gave in to temptation and put the ring on. He says that he was hoping to once again see his mother and his sister. But putting it on his finger triggered a curse that was to claim his life within a year. By withholding this information about the Hallows, Dumbledore hoped it would take Harry longer to find them, thus giving him more time to understand their true nature and avoid the temptation for greed and power that he had felt. Death's true master, he says, is the one who does not seek to run away from it.

Finally, Dumbledore tells Harry that he has a choice: if he chooses, he can head to a platform, and he would likely find a train that would take him onwards, or he can return to the living world for a chance to finish Voldemort. Harry chooses to return, but he first asks Dumbledore if their conversation has been real or is it only in his mind. Dumbledore responds, "Of course it is happening inside your head, Harry, but why on earth should that mean it is not real?"

ANALYSIS

In this chapter, more questions are answered. The creature on King's Cross' floor may have been Voldemort's soul shard inside Harry's scar; Dumbledore tells Harry that his soul is now wholly his own. According to the author, however,[1] it was the remaining soul portion left within Voldemort's body. Recall that Voldemort himself was knocked out by the Killing Curse he cast on Harry; as it thrust Harry's spirit into the void that Harry made into King's Cross, Voldemort's soul was dragged along by the bond between them.

We now have two viewpoints regarding what happened the night Dumbledore retrieved the Ring Horcrux. Snape, of course, was absent when the ring was retrieved, so his memories would only reveal the aftermath, as we have seen. And Dumbledore seems reticent to explain exactly why he put the ring on. The Horcrux in the ring was likely aware that anyone putting the ring on would be cursed, and would, like any other Horcrux, be fighting for its survival. Earlier, the Locket Horcrux fought for its existence by attempting to strangle Harry and then preying upon Ron's hopes and fears; would the ring Horcrux have done any less? Dumbledore's desire was likely the same as Harry's: to be reunited with his family. Recognizing the Horcrux as the Resurrection Stone, would he not have been tempted to use the Stone to see them again? And would not the Horcrux, sensing this, entice him to put the ring on his finger, knowing that this should have killed Dumbledore before he could destroy the Horcrux? Dumbledore said that Ariana's death was accidental. The question that has haunted Dumbledore all his life, and likely that has also been troubling Aberforth, was whose curse killed her. If it was Grindelwald, then presumably Aberforth would have sought revenge, and tried to kill him, although it is likely he would have been killed in the attempt. If it was Albus, then Aberforth would never have forgiven him, which is actually the state of affairs at the time of Albus' death. If it was Aberforth, then neither Aberforth nor Albus would be able to forgive himself. That none knew for certain left the situation clouded,

---

1. http://www.jkrowling.com/textonly/en/faq_view.cfm?id=121

Chapter 35: King's Cross

and prevented Albus and Aberforth from reaching closure and moving on with their lives, following Ariana's death. Grindelwald, being considerably less caring, simply saw this as another case where he might be blamed, and took his usual course, running away.

Harry tells Dumbledore that Grindelwald lied to Voldemort, claiming that he never possessed the Elder Wand, perhaps in a belated effort to protect Dumbledore. Dumbledore believes Grindelwald may have felt remorse in his later years. It would seem his last act on Earth was an attempt to save the world from the likes of himself. He lied to Voldemort, although it was futile. Through reading his mind, or just through common sense, Voldemort determined that the Elder Wand was in Dumbledore's possession before his death, and correctly guesses that it had been entombed with him at Hogwarts. Harry realizes that the plan was to make Snape the future master of the Elder Wand, but Dumbledore comments that the plan did not work as intended.

Dumbledore, forever shamed by his delay to fight Grindelwald, chose to remain at Hogwarts, declining more prestigious appointments, solely to avoid succumbing again to power's seductive allure. It is difficult to imagine that Dumbledore, a brave and formidable wizard, could have ever feared anything or would leave others in peril. However, he ignored the Wizarding world's desperate pleas for help and avoided confronting Grindelwald for as long as he could because he dreaded learning that it may have been his own stray curse that accidentally killed his sister, Ariana. It is only after much bloodshed during Grindelwald's five-year rampage that Dumbledore finally relented and mustered the courage to face his former friend in a fierce duel. Dumbledore's delay seems incomprehensible, but he understood that truth can be a person's most fearsome and crippling enemy. Harry now realizes that Dumbledore did indeed always love him, and Harry's faith and trust in him have been restored.

QUESTIONS

Review   1. Why did Dumbledore wait to fight Grindelwald? What finally prompted him to do so?

2. Who does Dumbledore say is Death's true master? Why?

3. Was Voldemort ever the true master of the Elder Wand? Why?

4. What might the creature curled up on the floor be? Why does Dumbledore say it cannot be helped?

Further Study   1. Where does Harry awaken, and what might J.K. Rowling intend for this place to represent?

2. If the scene with Dumbledore took place in Harry's mind, how does Dumbledore know so much that Harry did not?

3. What does Dumbledore mean when he tells Harry, "This is, as they say, your party."

4. Dumbledore admits that his plan regarding the Elder Wand did not work out as he intended. Exactly what was his plan, and what would have happened if it had unfolded as he expected?

5. Should Dumbledore have withheld information from Harry about the Deathly Hallows or told him more about them?

6. Why was Dumbledore afraid that Harry might be tempted by the Deathly Hallows? Was Dumbledore justified in thinking this?

7. Even though Dumbledore possessed the Resurrection Stone, was he ever Death's true master? Explain.

8. How was Dumbledore able to beat Grindelwald, even though Grindelwald mastered the "undefeatable" Elder Wand?

9. Dumbledore waited five years to duel Grindelwald. Does this long wait make him partially responsible for the deaths of Grindelwald's many victims? Explain.

10. Why did it fall upon Dumbledore to combat Grindelwald?

11. Even though Dumbledore assures Harry that he (Harry) is not dead, why is Harry given a choice to "move on" to the next world or return to the living? What does Harry choose and why?

GREATER PICTURE

At last, the victorious look in Dumbledore's eye when he heard that Voldemort had used Harry's blood to create his new body is explained: through the conversation in this chapter, it is clear that Dumbledore realized that this would help Harry more than it would help Voldemort. As Harry had been protected by his mother's blood, so now would he be protected by his own blood, now running in Voldemort's veins. Dumbledore also knew that by using Harry's blood to reanimate himself, Voldemort had ensured that Harry's death would be impossible as long as this incarnation of Voldemort lived.

Regarding Harry's statement that Snape was meant to be the Elder Wand's master, Dumbledore admits that that had not worked out as planned. Harry sees this, but we do not as yet; in the next chapter, it will be learned that the Elder Wand had not allied itself with Snape, and Snape's death, in turn, has not given Voldemort control over it. And though Harry confirmed this thought with Mr. Ollivander, he is still at least a little unsure of himself. Dumbledore may have made the same misstep as Voldemort: despite having the evidence, in the form of the still-living (until Voldemort murdered them) Gregorovitch and Grindelwald, Voldemort mistakenly believed that the Elder Wand would fully align itself only with the wizard who kills its previous Master, rather than the wizard who forcibly removes the wand from its previous owner's possession. Ollivander was quite emphatic that murder is unnecessary, though with the Elder Wand, that trail does seem to have followed it. As the wand's allegiance was forcibly removed from Dumbledore's possession by Draco Malfoy, even though Dumbledore retained physical custody of it, Harry believes that it allied itself with Draco. It is uncertain whether Dumbledore shares this belief, but his admission that Snape does not currently master the Elder Wand would lead us to believe that Snape's death has given him a little extra understanding. The question remains whether the Elder Wand had aligned itself with Harry once it became "aware" (if a wand can be said to be aware) that Harry disarmed Draco, and was, in fact, using Draco's own wand, the one which had disarmed Dumbledore.

Not only did Dumbledore's plan for Snape to obtain the Elder Wand ultimately fail, but it seems rather risky from the start. As mentioned above, Dumbledore should have known that capturing the wand from its owner resulted in it switching its allegiance, as he certainly fully controlled the Elder Wand, as Grindelwald had had before him, when both Gregorovitch and Grindelwald were still alive—a point that Voldemort missed, not once but twice. Even though Voldemort came to possess the wand, he never commanded it. As it was known that Snape killed Dumbledore, there was a high probability that Voldemort would eventually deduce that Snape was the Elder Wand's master, and he would therefore target and kill Snape to transfer its ownership to him. That is exactly what happened, although, fortunately, and unknown to Voldemort, Snape was never the Elder Wand's master. As Dumbledore had a pre-arranged plan with Snape to kill him, it may be that he intended for Snape alone to witness his death, thus forcibly claiming, and secretly wielding the Elder Wand. Likewise, just as Dumbledore never foresaw that Draco Malfoy would disarm him and unknowingly control the wand (although he did not possess it), he may also have failed to anticipate that circumstances would force Snape to return to Voldemort when he did, placing him in a dangerously close proximity to the Dark Lord. If Dumbledore's scheme had worked as he intended, the outcome of the story would depend on whether Snape had chosen to entomb the Elder Wand with Dumbledore, or carry it himself. Entombed with Dumbledore, the wand would have remained Snape's even while Voldemort was carrying it; Snape's death would not have aligned the wand with Voldemort, as Voldemort would not have forcefully removed the wand from its previous owner, Snape. However, equally the wand would not have aligned itself with Harry, as Harry would never have had the chance to wrest it from Snape. If Snape had retained the wand, Voldemort would have had one additional step to retrieve it, and it is possible that Snape would have simply given the wand to Voldemort. In that case, again as the wand was not wrested from Snape, it would remain his, and thus somewhat ineffectual in Voldemort's hands. Only if Snape had resisted turning over the wand, and Voldemort had seized it by force, would the wand owe allegiance to Voldemort, and in that case, Harry likely would have had a much more painful time of things.

It should also be noted that if Draco had killed Dumbledore as he had been under orders to do (in *Harry Potter and the Half-Blood Prince*), then Voldemort would have murdered Draco to try and win the wand, although, unknown to anyone, Draco had since lost its allegiance to Harry when Harry disarmed him at Malfoy Manor. It is worth mentioning, perhaps, that in discussing the interaction between the two wands, Dumbledore specifically refers to the wand that Voldemort was carrying as "Malfoy's poor stick." While we know, having been present through the author's eyes at the meeting in chapter 1, that Voldemort was carrying Lucius Malfoy's wand, Harry does not know it. While there are several other points that would be known only to Dumbledore in this chapter, regarding his own family life and his friendship with Grindelwald, there is no clear path by which this knowledge could have reached Dumbledore, except possibly through Snape talking with Dumbledore's portrait. This one point does cause a certain amount of speculation about death and afterlife, as perhaps it is meant to.

Chapter 36: The Flaw in the Plan

Synopsis

Returning to the living world, Harry lies limp, pretending to be dead. Hearing the Death Eaters surrounding Voldemort, he deduces that Voldemort also was knocked unconscious. Voldemort revives and orders Narcissa Malfoy to confirm that Harry is dead. Feeling a heartbeat, she softly asks if Draco is alive. Harry whispers, "Yes"; Narcissa, knowing she can only enter the castle with the conquering Death Eaters, lies and pronounces Harry dead. To "prove" that Harry is indeed a corpse, Voldemort uses the Cruciatus curse to toss his body around in the air, although Harry feels no pain. Voldemort forces the weeping Hagrid to carry Harry as the entire group leaves the dark Forest. Hagrid accuses the nearby Centaurs of sitting idly by and letting evil win.

Voldemort calls out the fighters from Hogwarts to see their fallen hero. The Dark Lord announces that Hogwarts will be united under a single house, Slytherin. He entices Neville, a pureblood, to join him. Neville refuses and charges, only to be caught in a Full-body bind. Voldemort summons the Sorting Hat from the Headmaster's office and places it on Neville's head, setting it afire.

Several things happen simultaneously. The families of students sent home have arrived, howling war cries as they climb the outer walls. The Centaurs, ending their neutrality, charge the Death Eaters. Grawp reappears around the corner, headed for Hagrid. Neville frees himself from the body-bind curse, and drawing the Sword of Gryffindor from the Sorting Hat, hacks off Nagini's head, destroying the final Horcrux. Harry leaps up and places his Invisibility Cloak over himself, then casts a Shield Charm between Voldemort and Neville.

As the battle erupts again, the Death Eaters, retreating from the new threat from behind that now includes Thestrals and Buckbeak, enter the castle. Harry, under the Cloak, heads for the Entrance Hall, searching for Voldemort. Inside, House elves, led by Kreacher, are hacking the Death Eaters' ankles with kitchen knives. Voldemort is simultaneously dueling McGonagall, Slughorn, and Kingsley. Bellatrix is likewise fighting Hermione, Ginny, and Luna. When Bellatrix barely misses Ginny with a curse, an enraged Molly Weasley pushes the three girls aside and challenges Bellatrix directly. As they fiercely duel, Molly proclaims that another Weasley will never be harmed and casts a powerful curse directly to Bellatrix's chest, killing her. Voldemort's fury over losing his most devoted follower blasts McGonagall, Kingsley, and Slughorn backwards. As Voldemort turns to Molly, Harry casts a shield charm between them. When Voldemort looks around to see

Chapter 36: The Flaw in the Plan

who conjured it, Harry pulls off his Invisibility Cloak, revealing himself to the audibly stunned crowd.

Harry warns everyone to stay back—the battle is between him and Voldemort now. They circle each other warily. Voldemort claims that Harry continually survives by hiding behind better wizards who sacrifice themselves for him. Harry urges Voldemort, who he boldly addresses as Tom Riddle, to feel remorse for his evil deeds. He then tells him that Dumbledore outsmarted him, planning his own death, and that Snape was never the Elder Wand's rightful owner. The true master was Draco Malfoy, who unknowingly won the wand's allegiance when he disarmed Dumbledore, just before Snape killed him on the Astronomy Tower. When Harry overpowered Draco at Malfoy Manor and took his wand, the Elder Wand gave its allegiance to him; Harry reminds Voldemort that *"The wand chooses the wizard."* Also, Harry tells him, because he willingly sacrificed himself to Voldemort, the same magic that Lily Potter's death protected him with, now protects the fighters.

Voldemort casts Avada Kedavra as Harry simultaneously conjures Expelliarmus. But Voldemort's killing curse backfires, reflected by Harry's blood protection and the Elder Wand's allegiance to him, while Harry's disarming charm wrenches the Elder Wand from Voldemort's hand to his. With all his Horcruxes destroyed, Voldemort dies instantly.

A joyous victory celebration erupts in the Great Hall, but there is also tremendous sorrow for those killed in battle, including Lupin, Tonks, Fred Weasley, and Colin Creevey. Craving solitude, Harry slips away with Ron and Hermione and tells them everything that transpired after he left them. They go to the Headmaster's chamber where they are met with roaring applause from the portraits. Harry tells Dumbledore's portrait that he will never search for the dropped Resurrection Stone in the Forbidden Forest. He will keep the Invisibility Cloak as a family heirloom, and the Elder Wand will be secretly returned to Dumbledore's tomb in hopes that the wand's power will eventually die with Harry. Dumbledore nods his approval. Before returning the Elder Wand to the tomb, Harry uses it to repair his own broken wand.

Although Ron is disappointed that the Elder Wand is being returned to Dumbledore's tomb, Harry prefers his old wand's familiarity. He concludes that the Elder Wand would be more trouble than it is worth, and that he has "had enough trouble for a lifetime."

ANALYSIS

The long, intricate story concludes with each puzzle piece set in place and Harry's questions answered; Voldemort has been defeated and Harry now knows that Dumbledore truly loved him. And although Dumbledore had tasked Harry with locating and dispatching the remaining Horcruxes, he knew Harry needed help. Ultimately, each soul shard was slain by a different person: Dumbledore destroyed Gaunt's Ring; Slytherin's Locket was impaled by Ron; Hermione shattered Hufflepuff's Cup; and Neville beheaded Nagini. Even Harry's enemies unintentionally helped him. Voldemort (unknowingly) slayed the Scar Horcrux with his deadly curse and Ravenclaw's Diadem was scorched by the Fiendfyre conjured by Crabbe. In the end, Harry dispensed only one, Riddle's Diary. However, he was instrumental in identifying and locating the Cup and the Diadem, although it was Luna Lovegood who suggested the latter. Although Harry intended to destroy the remaining Horcruxes alone, an act that could have taken years and in which he probably would have failed, he instead learns to rely on and trust in others. By having each Horcrux destroyed by a different person, Rowling shows that Harry is the sum of all his parts, with those parts being his friends' support, loyalty, love, and companionship, especially Ron and Hermione's. Draco Malfoy also played a crucial role—his refusal to positively identify Harry and the others at Malfoy Manor aided their escape. And though Malfoy is not fully redeemed, his soul remains intact.

Harry has also learned that death, grief, and loss are essential and inevitable parts of living; escaping them is impossible, and confronting them only makes one stronger. When Harry promises Dumbledore that the Resurrection Stone will be left in the Forbidden Forest, it shows that he has not only accepted death's finality, but embraced it, making him its true master; he resolves to never again summon his parents' spirits, understanding that it was never a true resurrection and that the dead must be left in peace. Having seen that James, Lily, Sirius, and Lupin are in a happy, serene place, Harry is content and knows that one day they will all be reunited. Meanwhile, Harry is now able to move forward and will live his own satisfying and productive life. And while Harry accepts that the things he has loved and lost can never truly be retrieved with or without magic, there is one exception: his wand. Lupin and Tonks' deaths are not only a tragic loss of two beloved characters, but it leaves their only child an orphan. It is, therefore, no coincidence that Harry, their son's godfather, is also an orphan. Both Lupin and Tonks knew there was a high probability that they could both be killed, leaving their son, Teddy, to be raised without parents. While both loved and admired Harry and believed he would be a caring and responsible godfather, they also knew that his own experience growing up without his mother and father would enable him to guide and mentor young Teddy in a way few others could. It is quite likely that this understanding of Harry's nature was sparked or confirmed by Harry's outburst at Lupin earlier. That Lupin and James Potter were once close friends will probably also create an especially close bond between godfather and godson, much like Harry shared with Sirius Black. Hagrid's shouting at the Centaurs, who refused to engage in battle because they disdained interfering in human affairs, shamed them enough that they finally joined forces against the Death Eaters. Also, Hogwarts' House-elves, whom Ron wanted to warn so that they would not be killed, show that Wizards' underestimation of them is incorrect: rather than cowering with fear, as most Wizards would probably expect, the elves strike at the Death Eaters. In this, they are led by Kreacher, a character who started the series as a spiteful and hateful House-elf opposing the Order of the Phoenix and despising Harry, but was eventually won over by Harry's respect and kindness, which Kreacher returned to him as loyalty.

If any reader still believes after *Harry Potter and the Deathly Hallows* that Neville Longbottom should have been sorted into Hufflepuff House, they need only to remember Dumbledore's words to Harry in *Harry Potter and the Chamber of Secrets* that "only a true Gryffindor could pull *that* (the Sword of Gryffindor) out of the Hat." Neville is a favorite among fans, and many will be pleased that he, in the end, receives his fair share of victory. Voldemort tossing Harry about with the Cruciatus curse without it inflicting any pain is a subtle clue to readers that the Elder Wand's allegiance actually belongs to Harry; it will not harm its true master. Also, Harry has been continually criticized by his mentors for acting too predictably to his enemies, particularly in using the Expelliarmus defensive charm. During his final confrontation with Voldemort, Harry knows that he (Harry) is the Elder Wand's true master. He again casts Expelliarmus, ejecting the wand from Voldemort's hand into his own as the Killing Curse rebounds off his body, fatally striking Voldemort. By doing the predictable, Harry acted unpredictably. It is also interesting to note that Harry defeats Voldemort not by killing him, but allowing the Dark Lord's evil nature to be his undoing, causing his own death. Harry is victorious through his cunning, patience, persistence, and by building alliances, rather than slaying enemies. Throughout the entire series, Harry never kills anyone.

Questions

Review   1. Why was Draco (briefly and unknowingly) the Elder Wand's master?

2. How did Harry become the Elder Wand's new master?

3. Why does Narcissa Malfoy inform Voldemort that Harry is dead, knowing he is alive?

4. Why does Harry feel justified keeping the Invisibility Cloak, but not the other Hallows?

5. Why doesn't Harry feel any pain when Voldemort uses the Cruciatus Curse on him?

6. Why did Voldemort's Avada Kedavra curse rebound and kill him instead of Harry?

7. Why did Harry's sacrifice protect those who were fighting the Death Eaters, but not Lupin, Tonks, and Fred?

Further Study   1. Why do the Centaurs end their neutrality and join the battle against Voldemort?

2. Why would Voldemort trust Narcissa Malfoy to confirm whether or not Harry was dead?

3. How is Molly Weasley able to defeat Bellatrix Lestrange, an extremely powerful and evil witch? Are Molly's actions an act of war or personal revenge?

4. Why does Harry choose his signature Expelliarmus disarming spell rather than another curse to attack Voldemort in their final duel?

5. What might the final outcome have been if Harry, the Elder Wand's true master, had been wielding it rather than Voldemort?

6. Why was Dumbledore, the Elder Wand's former master, unable to defeat Voldemort with it during the battle at the Ministry of Magic (in *Order of the Phoenix*)?

7. Why does Harry, now the Elder Wand's true master, choose to secretly return it to Dumbledore's tomb? What does Harry say about it, and what does he mean by that?

8. What could prompt Harry to retrieve the Elder Wand in the future?

9. What will prevent the wand from being stolen from Dumbledore's tomb?

10. What circumstances might compel Harry to find and use the Resurrection Stone?

Greater Picture

Just as Lily sacrificed her own life to protect Harry against Voldemort, so again does Harry's accepting death to save those fighting at Hogwarts protect them from Voldemort and his Death Eaters. This becomes evident as all the charms, hexes, and curses that Voldemort and his followers are hurling in the final battle seem remarkably ineffective.

Harry's decision to secretly return the Elder Wand to Dumbledore's tomb poses an interesting problem; it is never specified just how the tomb will be protected from some other Dark Wizard. According to Mr. Ollivander, despite the Elder Wand's power, its master is always vulnerable to attack. Voldemort was able to trace the wand's history and follow it to Hogwarts where he easily breached the tomb. Without adequate protections, the wand could be once again retrieved from Dumbledore's tomb, even though Voldemort does seem to have closed off the trail by killing all those who knew of it. And though Harry is now the wand's master and it will perform poorly for others, if Harry is ever disarmed during an unguarded moment, even while wielding his own wand, just as Harry did with Draco, and as Draco did to Dumbledore, the Elder Wand's allegiance could be transferred to an attacker who conceivably could also steal it. Harry will need to be especially vigilant in protecting himself, a difficult task considering his future profession.

Epilogue: Nineteen Years Later

Synopsis

The epilogue is the final chapter of both *Harry Potter and the Deathly Hallows* and the Harry Potter series. It is set 19 years after Voldemort's defeat at the Battle of Hogwarts. Harry and Ginny are married and have three children, James Sirius, Albus Severus, and Lily Luna. They are at King's Cross to see off their two boys to Hogwarts, where Neville Longbottom is now the Herbology professor. James, the eldest, is already at Hogwarts, while Albus Severus, 11, is starting his first year. Lily, two years his junior, is moaning—very much as Ginny did in *Harry Potter and the Philosopher's Stone*—about being unable to go. Also present are Ron and Hermione, likewise married and with their own two children, Rose, who is also just starting Hogwarts, and Hugo. Ron tells Harry he has just passed a Muggle driving test after confunding the examiner—but he does not want Hermione to know. In passing, Harry sees Draco Malfoy and his wife with their son, Scorpius.

Malfoy acknowledges Harry with a curt nod. Teddy Lupin, Remus' and Tonks' orphaned son, is spotted kissing Victoire Weasley, Bill and Fleur's daughter. Albus is worried that he will be sorted into Slytherin, but Harry reassures him and says that he is named after two Hogwarts Headmasters; one was a Slytherin (Snape) and possibly the bravest man he ever knew. Harry also confides to Albus that the Sorting Hat takes the student's own choice into consideration, as it had done for Harry when he was Sorted—something Harry has never told his other children. After the Hogwarts Express leaves, Ginny comforts Harry, saying their children will be fine. Harry reflects on his scar: it has not bothered him for 19 years. The epilogue ends with: "All was well."

Analysis

Rowling's epilogue provides a satisfying, but sketchy, update on the characters' post-Voldemort lives. However, in post-book release interviews, J. K. Rowling has given additional information. Harry and Ron are Aurors for the Ministry of Magic, although Ron also worked for a time in George's joke shop, which has become quite successful. The Ministry has radically changed from what it once was, and both Harry and Ron have been instrumental in overhauling the Auror department. Harry is now its head. Kingsley Shacklebolt is the Minister for Magic, with Percy Weasley working under him in a high position. Hermione also works for the Ministry in the Department of Magical Law Enforcement, and has also done much to improve life for non-human magical beings. Luna Lovegood pursues her interest in biology, and searches the world for magical and unusual creatures. She eventually marries Rolf, the grandson of the noted naturalist, Newt Scamander. Curiously, although Draco has married and has a child, Rowling does not identify his wife in the book. In the "J. K. Rowling . . . A Year In The Life" documentary created by ITV in the UK, the author does draw out family trees for the Weasley family, and a small tree for Draco, showing that he is married to one Asteria Greengrass, who did not appear in the books, and his son is named Scorpius Hyperion. The same tree indicates that George married one Angelina (quite probably Angelina Johnson), and has children named Fred and Roxanne. It is from this family tree that we learn Harry's eldest son's full name; in the book, he is only ever called James.

Questions

Review 1. Whom did Harry name his second eldest son after? Why?

2. What might Harry and Draco's relationship be today, based on how they interacted at King's Cross Station?

3. Why doesn't Ron want Hermione to know about his driving test details? Based on this experience, do you believe the two have changed much over all these years?

Further Study 1. Overall, how have the characters lives changed after Lord Voldemort's death, and could it be said that they've all changed for the better?

Greater Picture

Many fans have expressed annoyance at this epilogue, and at the post-publication interviews giving extra, and perhaps extraneous, details of the characters careers after the close of the main sequence of events. It is not the place of this work to criticize the epilogue in this manner; it is part of the published work, and we should not debate the merits of its inclusion. We will mention that it does seem to show the ongoing development of the characters in the series. Neville, for example, has played to his strength, becoming an instructor of Herbology, his best subject at school. We see that, rather than remaining sworn enemies, as presumably their parents had been, Harry and Draco have achieved a nodding relationship, signifying that Draco has mellowed over the years. We see that Ron largely retains his immaturity in small ways, though in other ways he has matured significantly. And we see that Harry has gained what he has wanted all his life, a loving and stable family. This confirmation of the character development we expected has the effect of reassuring us that, while our long attachment to these characters perforce has ended, they have prospered since we left them, and so eases the pain of our parting with them.

Details given by the author in post-publication interviews, however, seem less pertinent. In particular, the small facts given concerning the future of various characters, while true to the characters themselves, often feel made up to quiet the fans, rather than being organically part of the characters we have come to know. For instance, in one interview, the author mentioned that Neville had married Hannah Abbott, now landlady of the Leaky Cauldron. This information seems to us something that could have been made up on the spur of the moment, in order to provide a pat answer to the question. For the sake of completeness, Neville should marry; Hannah Abbott is as good a choice as any. But making her the innkeeper at the Cauldron seems, if you will, tacked on, not a part of the little character of Hannah that has been exposed to us. For his reason, while we have reported some small details of what has been "revealed" since publication, we do not feel that it is worth cataloging such.

EXTENDED ANALYSIS

Overall Analysis

A major point in this book is the completion of the greater picture, which Rowling finesses better than anyone speculated. The major issues are the dual-core phoenix wands, the Elder Wand, the soul tie or mind connection, the shared blood, and Voldemort's demise and Harry's survival in light of the prophecy about them both. Each aspect has a clue in the past history of the series, which plays into the larger picture of the completion of the full plot at the end:

1. First, since previous books have confirmed its contents and truthfulness, the prophecy gives the framework around which everything must fit. "One must die at the other's hand, for neither can live while the other survives," has to be finished, and Harry was already marked by Voldemort to be that person. Their two wands' dual core connection is explained by Dumbledore in the *King's Cross* chapter, but it should be added that since Voldemort had used Harry's blood in his resuscitation, prior to the duel that led to the "Priori Incantatem" effect, both wands would have recognized the other wizard as both kin and owner. Thus, Voldemort tries a different wand (Lucius Malfoy's), but lacks the wisdom to grasp the full implication of its failure (Harry finally gets it, and it is truly on his own, because he makes the connections once the flaws in Dumbledore's and Voldemort's plans are revealed) . . . neither of their own wands could have destroyed the other person, making possession of the Elder Wand quite important.

2. This is also a point where both Dumbledore's and Voldemort's plans are flawed. Neither recognized that the Elder Wand would see first Draco and, after his defeat, Harry as its owner. Voldemort thought he could be the owner by killing Snape, who had acted on Dumbledore's wishes to the end (despite the personal cost and risk to himself, even Snape proved to be selfless), and Dumbledore may have failed to recognize Draco's "Expelliarmus" as a "defeat" that transferred ownership of the wand to him. He could not be certain that it would be entombed with him post mortem, thus he likely believed that in dying by his own request at Snape's hand, he had broken its power as one of the three Hallows. His choice not to reveal the Hallows to Harry too soon might have been an added insurance. As is affirmed, Dumbledore made good guesses, but he often arranged back up in case he, or a situation, went wrong.

3. The mind/soul connection between Harry and Voldemort is also brought full circle and explained. In the first six books, everyone around him, including Harry, is in a hurry to shut this connection down. Even during the final book, he is often cajoled to at least attempt Occlumency although he was never good at it. Ironically, it is this connection that allows Harry access to vital knowledge of Voldemort's actions and plans, and is the means by which he knew Parseltongue, knowledge which helped save his life in *Harry Potter and the Chamber of Secrets*.

4. "Harry as a Horcrux" was created by Voldemort's carelessness during his first reign of terror. Harry must kill this piece of Voldemort's soul within him without killing himself. Yet, per the prophecy, there is no way around things. Harry finally understands he must die, but he doesn't find out why until he actually does. This makes his actions a selfless act of faith. Once he dies, it makes sense on several levels. It eliminates the Horcrux within him. This makes Voldemort almost vulnerable, now he is very close to the point where he can actually be killed. The wand used makes no difference, other than ensuring that Voldemort doesn't have the Elder Wand, but Harry has figured this out by now. Voldemort unwittingly makes himself a Horcrux for Harry, although it might not be called that, by taking his blood earlier. In taking Harry's blood to regenerate himself, Voldemort ensures that Harry will not die if he kills him. The blood ties Harry to Voldemort's life, therefore Harry will live.

When all is done, Harry is good to the end, for many reasons. His selfless choice to face Voldemort without fighting back ensures the same charm of love his mother gave him is now given to all of his comrades fighting back. (As Harry points out, this is probably why the attacks of Voldemort and the Death Eaters won't stick when they come back to Hogwarts with Harry's body.) He chooses not to reunite the Hallows . . . and makes decisions that will hopefully remove their power, except for the cloak. He chooses to come back to the pain in his body and life, rather than take the easy path to join his family in peace, in order to complete the defeat of Voldemort. However, he also chooses to accept and trust the help and vested interests of others, so it is possible that Harry makes the final leap of maturity needed to make a difference . . . he puts aside his need to be linked to his family of the past (which he could have chosen) in order to bring hope (rather than despair) to his present "family of friends." This final thought is supported by the epilogue of the final chapter that indicates that his godson Teddy, son of Lupin and Tonks, may marry into the family of the friends who have become family comprised of Harry and Ginny, Bill and Fleur, and Ron and Hermione, who are now all related by marriage.

Possible Points of Confusion

Why did Harry not die? We should take a moment here to discuss the complexities of the interrelationship between Voldemort and Harry in the last few chapters of the book. It is not immediately clear why Voldemort does not kill Harry, or why Harry does not die when Voldemort does, there being a blood link there.

First, we should look at the wands. While an interrelation between Voldemort's wand and Harry's has been established, and it is mentioned that the events in the graveyard have made Harry's wand proof against anything Voldemort can throw against him, this is discounted by Christmas. At that point, a charm Hermione uses ends up breaking Harry's wand, and it no longer plays a part in the events. Voldemort, not knowing this, abandons his own wand and seeks to retrieve the Elder Wand of legend. The Elder Wand will not harm Harry because it accepts Harry as its master—contrary to the apparent path through history, it is not murder that defeats the bearer of the wand, but forcible removal of the wand, so the wand became Malfoy's when Malfoy disarmed Dumbledore, and Malfoy was in turn deprived of his own wand by Harry. Harry is careful to check this with Ollivander in Shell Cottage; this is the point where he begins to understand about the Hallows, and starts choosing his own fate accordingly. (It was Malfoy's wand Harry was holding when he defeated Voldemort. Presumably the Elder Wand recognizes the wand that stood against it, possibly in addition to the bearer.) At the same time, Harry can not be killed by Voldemort because of the blood linkage—as he is using Harry's blood, he provides that protection. Granted, this may seem far-fetched, as Voldemort certainly had Riddle blood in him, but he had murdered Tom Sr. and suffered no ill effects. Then again, Tom Sr. didn't care about Tom Jr., and possibly didn't even know he existed. As what activates the protection is being willing to die for someone rather than allowing them to be killed, and neither Tom Sr. nor Tom Jr. would die for the other, there was no protection there.

When Harry approaches Voldemort at the end of the book, then, Voldemort's curse knocks Harry into the waystation, but it is then his option whether to go on or return. If he goes on, taking Voldemort with him, there will still be one Horcrux in Nagini to allow Voldemort to return. However, as the Elder Wand won't harm Harry, he has the option to return, and he chooses that option. As Dumbledore says that the soul fragment within Harry is now gone, the only Horcrux left is Nagini. Once Nagini is dead, thanks to Neville, there is nothing holding Voldemort's soul to the earth.

There is still the blood link, but that is unidirectional: Lily did not die to save Voldemort, did she? So every time that Voldemort uses the Killing Curse against Harry, it will rebound upon him. The first time it rebounded, when Harry was one, it killed Voldemort, but his soul, still held to the earth by six Horcruxes, remained in Albania. The second time, it partially rebounded, killing the soul fragment in Harry, but Voldemort returned in the same body because he came back with Harry, as he had gone to "King's Cross" with Harry. The third time, with no Horcruxes left, it killed Voldemort outright.

What is the nature of the bond between Harry and Petunia Dursley? We know that Petunia does not like Harry, and Harry absolutely loathes living at Privet Drive. Yet there must be something that keeps them together. At the beginning of *Harry Potter and the Order of the Phoenix*, Vernon Dursley, discovering that Harry is becoming a magnet for trouble that can hurt his family as well as Harry, orders Harry out of his house. Petunia seems to agree with Vernon's decision, until the Howler reminds her of Dumbledore's earlier letter, which we must presume was the one left on the Dursley doorstep with Harry at the beginning of the series. At that point, Petunia abruptly rationalizes Harry remaining with them, forcing Vernon to back down. Obviously there is a blood relationship between them, as Lily Potter was Petunia's sister. Petunia, however, throughout the series, acts as though Harry has been thrust upon them; she has not accepted this burden willingly. What is compelling her to keep Harry? And why is Harry required to return to Privet Drive every summer? Granted, it does not have to be for the whole summer—at the beginning of *Harry Potter and the Half-Blood Prince*, for instance, Dumbledore, who obviously is privy to the details of the spells involved, collects Harry from Privet Drive after only a fortnight. What exactly is the nature of the bond that requires Harry to stay with Petunia? It is stated over and over that Harry's protection came from Lily's sacrifice, and that until he reaches 17 that protection will come from her blood—and Petunia being Lily's sister, a blood relative, means that Lily's blood is in Petunia as well. That protection, which is only protection from Voldemort's direct action, as it was Voldemort's direct action that Lily died trying to prevent, ends when Harry reaches the age of majority and is unable under Wizarding tradition to claim Petunia's home as his own. In the first chapter of *Harry Potter and the Philosopher's Stone*, Dumbledore says he has reinforced that ancient magic, but it seems that it is that tie of blood relation which counts.

The word "blood" is used in particular so that we can see the transfer of the source of immunity from Petunia to Voldemort himself in the cemetery in *Harry Potter and the Goblet of Fire*.

As it was Lily's sacrifice that saved Harry's life, it is the shelter under Lily's blood (by way of Petunia) that keeps Harry protected for the first seventeen years of his life. However, this does not provide any protection to Petunia, as Lily certainly did not die to save Petunia's life. While there is no way that this can be anything except speculation, it is possible that what Dumbledore was achieving with his "reinforcements" was extending Harry's protection so that it protected his home as well as himself. This would explain why the Order were taking the Dursleys away at the beginning of *Harry Potter and the Deathly Hallows*. With Harry reaching his majority and no longer able to (even grudgingly) call Privet

Drive "home," his protection there was ending, and the protection afforded the rest of the family by Dumbledore's reinforcements was likewise ending.

The suggestion has been made that Petunia herself might have had some input into this magical bond. After all, her sister Lily, as we have seen, was a very powerful witch. At an age where most witches are able to produce only undisciplined magic, Lily, without a wand, was able to control the magic she was able to do, causing a flower to open and close on command. This ability seems to be uncommon in the Wizarding world; Harry's magic was largely out of his control, and of the other wizards we have seen, Tom Riddle, alone of those under school age, seemed to be able to control the magic he could do. Is it possible that Petunia had some magical ability as well, that was tapped to protect Harry? In fact, no; the author has said that Petunia was doomed to be a Muggle for all of her life. While the author had said at one point that some character would do magic late in life, and there was speculation that this would be either Petunia or Dudley, in an interview following the publication of Book 7 the author stated that the plot had shifted since that time, and the character who had been intended to be a late-blooming witch or wizard had not required that ability. It is possible that Dudley has some trace of magical ability, as he was able to see the Dementors in *Harry Potter and the Order of the Phoenix*, but he never seemed to be able to perform magic. Even if he had had magical abilities, he was largely out of the secret of Harry's background, and would not have been able to help consciously in any event, being underage.

Character Development

Development   Throughout this book there is continual *character development* that begins in earnest in the fourth year (*Harry Potter and the Goblet of Fire*), the year deeper emotions emerge in each character, and particularly the three main heroes. That Harry is not inherently bent toward evil is well established in the fifth year (*Harry Potter and the Order of the Phoenix*). However, in this book Harry is fully humanized, being more than the "good" hero, but also a person with a full range of emotions, even selfishness. For adolescence, this includes love interests that are increasingly complicated, awareness of the lines that blur good vs. bad . . . sometimes things aren't completely black and white, which leads to growth and clarity of one's views of others (especially those whom one has idolized). As an example, Dumbledore is throughout the series viewed as good, but through this book, and by his own admission in *King's Cross*, he is seen as capable of "evil" choices too . . . like putting the search for the Hallows above his family, if even for a couple of months, which ended in his sister's death and cost him dearly in terms of his own view of self, his relationship with his brother, and his awareness of his own limitations on possessing power. Harry takes a similar journey through temptation. Like "real people in real life," it is only in Harry's being presented with the option to selfishly seek and possess power through the Hallows, or to willingly make his desires subordinate to the needs of others, that he becomes fully matured. Horcruxes or Hallows? Hallows or Horcruxes? The question perplexes Harry for a time. Should he choose what is easy or what is good? What is good or what is evil? What is beneficent or what is selfish? Power or purpose? Harry could not mature, nor could he or anyone else know who he truly was as a person, until he faced this personal trial and triumphed over the temptation in order to live out the actions that define him as ultimately good. Harry must complete the mission he has been given regarding the Horcruxes, and ultimately Voldemort, (which, per the prophecy, only he is capable of finishing) in order to remain selfless and "good."

There is less to say about Hermione and Ron with regard to character development, but we do have a chance in this final book to see each of them experience opportunities to take on the responsibility of leadership. Interestingly, Ron also has to deal with the same "coming of age" realizations that have been described about Dumbledore and Harry above. He has, to this point, believed that Harry "had the answers." Thus, he must also confront who the friend he has idolized really is; Harry is a human boy with some great talent and exceptional luck, but who still lacks understanding for things that have not been revealed to him.

Here, Hermione, is able to display not only her academic knowledge, but also her insights into people, relationships (except when it comes to Ron), and emotions. From this view, it is easy to see why Hermione was not disillusioned by the "real" Harry, since she has already had to bail him out before with the knowledge he lacked, and spent previous encounters explaining to the boys why girls, boys, and people in general do some of the things they do. Quite apart from the physical (the author has told us her birthday falls in September, making her six months older than Ron and ten months older than Harry), she is emotionally more mature from the start than either Harry or Ron, because she grasps who they are, has grace for their weaknesses, and has a clear view of her role in their relationships and common mission. She only loses sight of this for a couple of weeks, as she grieves Ron's walking out on them, but recovers enough to take the lead while Harry is engaged in his own aforementioned struggle to come of age and enter adulthood.

Three aspects of each characters' development empower Harry's and his comrades' triumph of good over Voldemort's and his Death Eaters' evil:

1. Love—it provides power and courage (to Harry and the rest) that Voldemort has never known, a selfless purpose for fighting to win, and even able to protect others through powering "ancient magic";

2. Wisdom—is also a weakness of Voldemort, and a strength that Harry can tap into with the help of those around him. He does not come to it completely alone, but in the end is able to connect all the dots, as Dumbledore did. Yet, Harry establishes his own identity and even a bit of authority by bringing the crayons along to colour in the picture. We are not discussing mere information, not just knowledge, but a depth of understanding that digs deeper, to get past the "How?" of

things and straight to the "Why?" This is what saves Harry in the end, he truly grasps the full meaning of the prophecy, his role and *why* it is his, *why* Voldemort is weak in this area, and the implications of not only the connection between their wands, but the also the blood they share (since Voldemort stole a few drops when he regained his body), and thus, *why* he will be able to defeat Voldemort and live. A second aspect of wisdom, which Harry, Ron, and Hermione will come to accept is that things are not always as they seem. Nothing is black and white, nor easily interpreted. Dumbledore didn't die because of someone else's choices, but due to his own greed and actions. Snape was not the consummate evil character always searching for a means to betray or destroy them all in support of Voldemort. He was, in fact, motivated to protect Harry by his unrequited love for Lily Potter: a choice made consistently in the face of the pain it caused him by Harry's constant reminders, physically both of his similarity to his father, reminding Snape of his father's character who inflicted humiliation and suffering upon Snape, and his constant reminder of Lily because he had Lily's eyes. Similarly, Harry's good father was capable of being a cruel bully, his mother of befriending a Slytherin, etc.;

3. Selflessness—One might be tempted to attach this to love, and indeed love is often the motivation, but there is still a point at which it is a separate issue. One must take action, and do something externally that demonstrates their internal choices. Harry triumphs over his personal desires for the Hallows, and pursues the Horcruxes instead. Ron triumphs over his disillusionment and anger and sacrifices his own pride (ego) to rejoin his companions on the mission and catalyze them back into action. Hermione, at the crucial juncture, puts the needs of the mission, Harry, and the many that it will save before her desire for the relationship and connection with Ron. They all prove themselves capable of being selfless, as do the members of the Order of the Phoenix, and of Dumbledore's Army, like Neville who winds up a hero in his own right, and all those who stand to fight for what is good rather than settle for what is easy. Harry, in the end, must willingly choose to lay down his life, and in so doing actually ensures his comrades' safety and his own survival.

Major Themes

Love Love plays a much bigger role in Voldemort's downfall than he or Harry realize. Regardless of Merope Gaunt's intentions for her son, Tom Marvolo Riddle grew up an anonymous child in an orphanage, without the unconditional love or care he would have received from his mother. Whether or not this lack of love in his life shaped him at an early age, it is certainly true that, by the time Dumbledore met him at eleven, he was already showing sociopathic qualities.

Riddle's inability to comprehend love, or the purity of it, kept him from making any real friends. When he meets his father and grandparents at 16, he does not attempt a relationship or any sort of reconciliation. Instead, he murders them all and uses their deaths to create a Horcrux.

Perhaps it is the lack of love in his early life, coupled with the missing pieces of his soul relegated to Horcruxes, that further renders him incapable of understanding love's impact. When Snape approached Voldemort and asked him to spare Lily Potter, Voldemort did make an attempt to do so. Harry's limited recollections of the night his parents were killed, and the memories of that night that Harry later receives from Voldemort, agree that Voldemort had commanded Lily to stand aside so that he could gain access to Harry. However, spurred on by her husband's death as well as her maternal instincts for her child, Lily refused, and Voldemort killed her before turning his attention to Harry.

It is Voldemort's intent to kill Lily, if she gets between him and Harry, that turns Snape against Voldemort, and leads to his defection to Dumbledore and the Order of the Phoenix. Learning of Voldemort's plan to kill Harry, with the associated grave risk to Lily, Snape pleads with Dumbledore to protect her, and promises "anything" if Dumbledore will do so. Dumbledore requires Snape to turn informant against Voldemort. Lily's subsequent death at Voldemort's hands does not end the promise, and Snape remains an ally of Dumbledore's until his death. When Harry comes to school at Hogwarts, Dumbledore adds covertly ensuring Harry's safety to Snape's mission. Despite Snape's overt animosity toward Harry, probably in part caused by Harry's extremely close resemblance to James, the older man never forgets whose child Harry is, and feels duty-bound to watch over Lily's son because he loved her so much. Snape's work as a double agent allows him to pass along information about the Death Eaters to the Order of the Phoenix and thwart certain parts of Voldemort's plans. If Lily Potter hadn't been killed, Voldemort would still have had a loyal servant in Snape and Harry might have been successfully killed long ago.

It should also be noted that throughout the seventh book, Harry receives valuable information about Voldemort's actions and plans by means of the soul shard of Voldemort's that is resident in Harry. Voldemort is unable to reverse this flow of information, because of the extreme distaste he has formulated for the inside of Harry's mind. What drove Voldemort permanently out of Harry's mind was Harry's longing to be with Sirius Black again. Dumbledore had commented at the time that he believed Voldemort had found Harry's mind a very uncomfortable place to be, and that he was not surprised that Harry had had no intimations of Voldemort's presence in his mind throughout the sixth book.

The fact that Voldemort can't feel or understand love, but that Harry can, is also very important. It is because Harry can feel love that he can reciprocate, and it is this reciprocation of love that allows Harry to be surrounded by those who will assist him in his ventures, most notably Ron, Hermione, and Ginny. Voldemort can't feel or understand love, so those who choose to follow him do so purely for their own selfish motives, coupled perhaps with fear of what Voldemort would do to them if they went against his will. It is this same lack of understanding that blinds Voldemort to the possibility that by failing to spare Lily, he could lose his follower Snape, and this lack of ability to reciprocate love that frees Snape to act against Voldemort covertly. When Voldemort has proven by his actions that he does not care about Snape's feelings, Snape in turn feels that he is free to seek whatever help he can find to protect Lily, and the help he finds is Dumbledore. On the other hand, while Ron is unhappy enough with Harry's progress to leave him, we never think that he would be able to betray Harry. We have commented elsewhere that Harry has friends while Voldemort has followers; Harry's friends stay with him because they believe in him and his mission and want to help him, and because of this, their motivation is much stronger than those who follow Voldemort.

This is not to say that Voldemort does not know how to use love as a weapon. In one instance we are aware of, Voldemort's Death Eaters kidnap Luna Lovegood in order to pressure her father into changing the editorial tone of his newspaper, and incidentally almost manage to capture Harry by that means. Being unable to see the strength that derives from love, Voldemort likely only sees this vulnerability, and thus believes himself stronger for having nobody that he cares about.

Death Death has played a central role in each of the book thus far and is at the heart of the final confrontation between Harry and Voldemort. Both Horcruxes, which form the main thrust of the entire series, and the Deathly Hallows, which are a major part of the story of the seventh book, are shown to be means of avoiding or mastering death.

Practically since birth, Voldemort has been attempting to discover the path to immortality. During his time at Hogwarts, Tom Riddle learns about Horcruxes. Before he is sixteen, Riddle has realized that the only way to create a Horcrux is through the murder of another, as we learn from Professor Slughorn. This scene is meant to give the appearance that Tom is learning about Horcruxes from Slughorn, but in fact, as he is already wearing the Gaunt ring at this point, he has already made his first Horcrux. As Voldemort's greatest fear is death, he thinks nothing of killing others to save himself later on, and creates his first Horcrux through the death of Tom Riddle, his own father. Voldemort spends the next several years of his life creating Horcruxes so that when the Avada Kedavra curse backfires on him, he doesn't succumb to death.

In direct contrast to Voldemort's desperate attempts to avoid death are the examples of sacrificial death. Both James and Lily Potter surrender to death to save their son. During the First Wizarding War, many members of the Order of the Phoenix were killed trying to stop Voldemort's rise to power. Several characters are also killed throughout the books, many of whom give up their lives to save others. While those fighting on Voldemort's side are willing to do almost anything to stay alive, those with the Order of the Phoenix, such as Sirius Black and Dumbledore, understand that their lives may be needed for their cause and are willing to give them up. Harry's attitude toward death is usually shown as a balance between recklessness and respect. While looking into the Mirror of Erised with Professor Quirrell, Harry is able to see the Philosopher's Stone and retrieve it because he did not seek to use it to prolong his life. Though we don't learn this until the final book in the series, in the duel in the cemetery in *Harry Potter and the Goblet of Fire,* Harry is actually the stronger wizard because he is prepared for death, while Voldemort fears it. Many times, Harry's actions have led to his being in a dangerous situation, yet he has faced death bravely. When he finally works through the riddle engraved on the Snitch, "I open at the close," he realizes that the Snitch can only be opened as he is facing his death. Using the Resurrection Stone Dumbledore placed inside, Harry recalls his loved ones temporarily from death, and from their company gains the courage to face Voldemort and his own death. It is his ability to willingly die to destroy Voldemort's seventh Horcrux that actually allows him to survive. Following Neville's beheading of Nagini, Voldemort is no longer mortally protected, and so his last, backfiring, attempt to kill Harry results in his own final demise.

Family Through the lens of family, the differences between Harry and Voldemort are reinforced. *Harry Potter and the Philosopher's Stone* begins with Harry's being placed with his aunt and uncle following his parent's death. He never feels welcomed by his mother's sister and her family and is treated as a second-class citizen. Contrasting that, Harry finds a place with Ron Weasley and his family. Almost immediately upon meeting Harry, Mr. and Mrs. Weasley show him love and affection and include him in their family. Harry ends up relying on this surrogate family for guidance and support.

Tom Riddle also grew up as an orphan: though his father was still alive, Tom was raised in an orphanage. Unlike Harry, however, Riddle never got a taste of what unconditional love was like, and never learned to trust others.

Harry's experience with the Dursleys was apparently no better than Riddle's time in the orphanage, though by watching the Dursleys' son Dudley and how the parents reacted to him, he was able to see directly what unconditional love could be like. One must wonder whether actually seeing the evidence of the existence of that sort of love would make the absence of it easier or harder to bear, though its absence must be made somewhat less painful by the apparent result it had on Dudley, making him self-centered and horrendously overindulged. Yet, despite their similarly loveless "home" environments, Harry became a strong, moral member of the Wizarding World, while Riddle became Voldemort. Perhaps Harry's parents passed on to their son favorable qualities that he could draw upon in times of personal struggle. Harry idealized his parents, while Voldemort looked upon his with disdain, killing his father as soon as he discovered who he was.

Real-World Connections

World War 2   In the article on Lord Voldemort, it is mentioned that Tom Riddle had been growing up at about the same time as the Nazi party in Germany had been gaining power, and beginning to espouse their ideas of racial purity. While it is pointed out there that Riddle, who we believe to have been a teenager during the hostilities, was far too young to take part in it, and that he would have refused to work alongside Muggles in any event, we also know that there may be a real-world connection.

We know from *Harry Potter and the Philosopher's Stone* that "the evil wizard Grindelwald" had fallen to Dumbledore in 1945, and in an interview the author has said that this was related to the end of World War 2. Grindelwald's stated plan was to put Wizardkind at its "rightful" place, in charge, ruling the Muggles "for their own good." Albus Dumbledore, in the letter that we have seen of his from that time, did emphasize that it was for the Muggles' own good. From what little we hear of his actions, we have to assume that the good of the Muggles was rather less on Grindelwald's mind than on Dumbledore's. What exactly the relationship was between Grindelwald's attempt to take power on the Wizarding side, and Hitler attempting to take power on the Muggle side, is of necessity uncertain.

Mention is made of Nurmengard, the prison built by Grindelwald to house his enemies and the Muggles. Apparently, Grindelwald is the only prisoner therein when Voldemort queries him about the whereabouts of the Elder Wand. Parallels with Spandau Prison and the extended captivity of Rudolf Hess are inescapable, though as Hess died in 1987, and evidence within the story puts Grindelwald's death in 1997, there is no chance that Hess and Grindelwald are the same person.

It is likely that Riddle would have been watching Grindelwald's European war with interest, though it seems that he, with his hatred of Muggles, had seized upon the idea of Racial Purity as espoused by the National Socialist party, rather than Grindelwald's "greater good" policy. While Grindelwald's solution to the Muggle "problem" was to make them subjects, Riddle's was to wipe them out.

It is interesting to note a second connection, as well: the actions of the Ministry during *Harry Potter and the Order of the Phoenix* were, according to the author, quite consciously modeled on the government of the United Kingdom under Neville Chamberlain during 1938 and 1939.

CHARACTERS

To look for a character, use the groups below. Within each group, characters are sorted alphabetically by last name.

The Trio   The three most prominently featured protagonists in the series; often referred to as "the trio."
- Harry Potter
- Ron Weasley
- Hermione Granger

Hogwarts School of Witchcraft and Wizardry   Regular occupants and students of Hogwarts.

Staff   • Professor Binns
- History of Magic professor
- Charity Burbage
- Muggle Studies professor (Harry's 1st—6th Years)
- Alecto Carrow
- Muggle Studies professor (Harry's 7th Year)
- Amycus Carrow
- Defence Against the Dark Arts professor (Harry's 7th Year)
- Albus Dumbledore
- Headmaster (Harry's 1st—6th Years)
- Argus Filch
- Caretaker
- Firenze
- Divination professor (Harry's 5th—7th Years)
- Filius Flitwick
- Ravenclaw Head of House
- Charms professor
- Wilhelmina Grubbly-Plank
- Care of Magical Creatures substitute professor
- Rubeus Hagrid
- Care of Magical Creatures professor (Harry's 3rd—7th Years)
- Gamekeeper
- Rolanda Hooch
- Flying instructor
- Quidditch referee
- Gilderoy Lockhart
- Defence Against the Dark Arts professor (Harry's 2nd Year)
- Remus Lupin
- Defence Against the Dark Arts professor (Harry's 3rd Year)
- Minerva McGonagall
- Deputy-Headmistress
- Gryffindor Head of House
- Transfiguration professor
- Alastor "Mad-Eye" Moody
- Defense Against the Dark Arts professor (Harry's 4th Year)
- Irma Pince
- Librarian
- Poppy Pomfrey
- Nurse
- Professor Quirrell
- Defence Against the Dark Arts professor (Harry's 1st Year)
- Professor Sinistra
- Astronomy professor
- Horace Slughorn
- Potions professor (Harry's 6th Year)
- Slytherin Head of House (Harry's 7th Year)
- Severus Snape
- Slytherin Head of House (Harry's 1st—6th Years)
- Potions professor (Harry's 1st—5th Years)
- Defence Against the Dark Arts professor (Harry's 6th Year)
- Headmaster (Harry's 7th Year)
- Pomona Sprout
- Hufflepuff Head of House
- Herbology professor
- Sybill Trelawney
- Divination professor
- Dolores Umbridge
- Headmistress (Harry's 5th Year)
- High Inquisitor (Harry's 5th Year)
- Defence Against the Dark Arts professor (Harry's 5th Year)
- Professor Vector
- Arithmancy professor

Students   Hogwarts students arranged by house; Gryffindor, Hufflepuff, Ravenclaw, Slytherin.

Gryffindor House   • Euan Abercrombie
- Katie Bell
- Sirius Black
- Lavender Brown
- Ritchie Coote
- Colin Creevey
- Dennis Creevey
- Albus Dumbledore
- Seamus Finnigan
- Hermione Granger
- Rubeus Hagrid

Characters

- Angelina Johnson
- Lee Jordan
- Andrew Kirke
- Neville Longbottom
- Remus Lupin
- Natalie McDonald
- Mary Macdonald
- Minerva McGonagall
- Cormac McLaggen
- Parvati Patil
- Jimmy Peakes
- Peter Pettigrew
- Harry Potter
- James Potter
- Lily Potter (née Evans)
- Demelza Robins
- Jack Sloper
- Alicia Spinnet
- Dean Thomas
- Romilda Vane
- Arthur Weasley
- Bill Weasley
- Charlie Weasley
- Fred Weasley
- George Weasley
- Ginny Weasley
- Molly Weasley (née Prewett)
- Percy Weasley
- Ron Weasley
- Oliver Wood

Hufflepuff House • Hannah Abbott
- Susan Bones
- Eleanor Branstone
- Cadwallader
- Owen Cauldwell
- Cedric Diggory
- Justin Finch-Fletchley
- Ernie Macmillan
- Laura Madley
- Eloise Midgeon
- Zacharias Smith
- Pomona Sprout
- Summerby
- Summers
- Nymphadora Tonks
- Kevin Whitby
- Rose Zeller

Ravenclaw House • Stewart Ackerley
- Marcus Belby
- Terry Boot
- Mandy Brocklehurst
- Cho Chang
- Penelope Clearwater
- Michael Corner
- Roger Davies
- Marietta Edgecombe
- Fawcett
- Filius Flitwick
- Anthony Goldstein
- Luna Lovegood
- Padma Patil
- Orla Quirke
- Lisa Turpin

Slytherin House • Avery
- Malcolm Baddock
- Regulus Black
- Miles Bletchley
- Bole
- Millicent Bullstrode
- Vincent Crabbe
- Derrick
- Marcus Flint
- Gregory Goyle
- Harper
- Terence Higgs
- Bellatrix Lestrange (née Black)
- Rabastan Lestrange
- Rodolphus Lestrange
- Draco Malfoy
- Lucius Malfoy
- Narcissa Malfoy (née Black)
- Montague
- Theodore Nott
- Pansy Parkinson
- Graham Pritchard
- Adrian Pucey
- Tom Marvolo Riddle
- Horace Slughorn
- Severus Snape
- Vaisey
- Urquhart
- Warrington
- Blaise Zabini

Other Residents • Peeves
- The Sorting Hat

Ghosts • The Bloody Baron
- The Fat Friar
- The Grey Lady
- Moaning Myrtle
- Nearly Headless Nick

Portraits • Phineas Nigellus Black
- Sir Cadogan
- Dilys Derwent
- Armando Dippet
- Everard
- The Fat Lady
- Dexter Fortescue

Founders • Godric Gryffindor
- Helga Hufflepuff
- Rowena Ravenclaw
- Salazar Slytherin

Other Schools

Beauxbatons Academy of Magic • Fleur Delacour
- Gabrielle Delacour
- Olympe Maxime

Durmstrang Institute • Igor Karkaroff
- Viktor Krum
- Gellert Grindelwald

Family Members   Characters arranged by family.

Black Family   See also: Black Family
- Orion Black
- Phineas Nigellus Black
- Regulus Black
- Sirius Black
- Walburga Black
- Bellatrix Lestrange
- Narcissa Malfoy
- Andromeda Tonks
- Nymphadora Tonks

Dumbledore Family • Albus Dumbledore
- Aberforth Dumbledore
- Ariana Dumbledore
- Kendra Dumbledore
- Percival Dumbledore

Dursley Family • Dudley Dursley
- Marge Dursley
- Petunia Dursley
- Vernon Dursley

Gaunt Family   See also: Gaunt Family
- Marvolo Gaunt
- Merope Gaunt
- Morfin Gaunt

Malfoy Family • Draco Malfoy
- Lucius Malfoy
- Narcissa Malfoy

Potter Family • Harry Potter
- James Potter
- Lily Potter

Weasley Family   See also: Weasley Family
- Auntie Muriel
- Arthur Weasley
- Bill Weasley
- Charlie Weasley
- Fred Weasley
- George Weasley
- Ginny Weasley
- Molly Weasley
- Percy Weasley
- Ron Weasley

Other Major Characters • Ollivander
- Rita Skeeter
- Lord Voldemort

Death Eaters   Present and past Death Eaters listed. See also: Death Eaters.
- Avery
- Regulus Black
- Alecto Carrow
- Amycus Carrow
- Crabbe, Sr.
- Barty Crouch Jr.
- Antonin Dolohov
- Gibbon
- Goyle, Sr.
- Fenrir Greyback
- Jugson
- Igor Karkaroff
- Bellatrix Lestrange
- Rabastan Lestrange
- Rodolphus Lestrange
- Walden Macnair
- Draco Malfoy
- Lucius Malfoy
- Narcissa Malfoy
- Mulciber
- Nott
- Peter Pettigrew
- Augustus Rookwood
- Evan Rosier
- Thorfinn Rowle
- Selwyn
- Stan Shunpike
- Severus Snape
- Pius Thicknesse
- Travers
- Wilkes
- Yaxley

Dumbledore's Army   See also: Dumbledore's Army
- Hannah Abbott
- Lavender Brown
- Katie Bell
- Susan Bones
- Terry Boot
- Cho Chang
- Michael Corner
- Colin Creevey
- Dennis Creevey
- Marietta Edgecombe
- Justin Finch-Fletchley
- Seamus Finnigan
- Anthony Goldstein
- Hermione Granger
- Angelina Johnson
- Lee Jordan
- Neville Longbottom
- Luna Lovegood
- Ernie Macmillan
- Padma Patil
- Parvati Patil
- Harry Potter
- Zacharias Smith
- Alicia Spinnet
- Dean Thomas
- Fred Weasley

Characters

- George Weasley
- Ginny Weasley
- Ron Weasley

Inquisitorial Squad 'A select group of students who are supportive of the Ministry of Magic, hand-picked by Professor Umbridge. Members have the power to dock points.' (*Harry Potter and the Order of the Phoenix*)
- Millicent Bullstrode
- Vincent Crabbe
- Gregory Goyle
- Draco Malfoy
- Pansy Parkinson
- Montague
- Warrington

Marauders   See also: Marauders
- Sirius Black (Padfoot)
- Remus Lupin (Moony)
- Peter Pettigrew (Wormtail)
- James Potter (Prongs)

Ministry of Magic   See also: Ministry of Magic
- Ludovic Bagman
- Broderick Bode
- Amelia Bones
- Dirk Cresswell
- Bartemius Crouch Sr.
- Dawlish
- Amos Diggory
- Cornelius Fudge
- Mafalda Hopkirk
- Bertha Jorkins
- Eric Munch
- Bob Ogden
- Gawain Robards
- Albert Runcorn
- Rufus Scrimgeour
- Kingsley Shacklebolt
- Pius Thicknesse
- Nymphadora Tonks
- Wilkie Twycross
- Dolores Umbridge
- Arthur Weasley
- Percy Weasley

Order of the Phoenix   Present and past members of the Order of the Phoenix listed.
- Sirius Black
- Edgar Bones
- Caradoc Dearborn
- Dedalus Diggle
- Elphias Doge
- Aberforth Dumbledore
- Albus Dumbledore
- Benjy Fenwick
- Arabella Figg
- Mundungus Fletcher
- Filius Flitwick
- Rubeus Hagrid
- Hestia Jones
- Alice Longbottom
- Frank Longbottom
- Remus Lupin
- Dorcas Meadowes
- Minerva McGonagall
- Marlene McKinnon
- Alastor "Mad-Eye" Moody
- Peter Pettigrew
- Sturgis Podmore
- James Potter
- Lily Potter (née Evans)
- Fabian Prewett
- Gideon Prewett
- Kingsley Shacklebolt
- Severus Snape
- Nymphadora Tonks
- Emmeline Vance
- Arthur Weasley
- Bill Weasley
- Charlie Weasley
- Molly Weasley

Other Minor Characters
- Borgin
- Caractacus Burke
- Florean Fortescue
- Gregorovitch
- Gellert Grindelwald
- Augusta Longbottom
- Xenophilius Lovegood
- Hepzibah Smith
- Miriam Strout
- Andromeda Tonks
- Wilkie Twycross
- Willy Widdershins

Hogsmeade
- Aberforth Dumbledore
- Ambrosius Flume
- Madam Rosmerta

Knight Bus
- Ernie Prang
- Stan Shunpike

Muggles
- Frank Bryce
- Piers Polkiss

Non-Human
- Aragog
- Buckbeak / Witherwings
- Grawp
- Merpeople
- Nagini

Centaurs   See also: Centaurs
- Bane
- Firenze
- Magorian
- Ronan

House Elves   See also: House Elves
- Dobby
- Hokey
- Kreacher
- Winky

Goblins   See also: Goblins
- Bogrod
- Griphook

Pets   • Buckbeak
- Crookshanks
- Errol
- Fawkes
- Hedwig
- Hermes
- Mrs. Norris
- Norbert
- Pigwidgeon
- Scabbers
- Trevor

Aberforth Dumbledore

Gender: Male
Hair color: Long, white (original color unknown)
Eye color: Blue
Related Family: Albus Dumbledore
Loyalty: Order of the Phoenix

Overview

Aberforth Dumbledore is Albus Dumbledore's brother, a former member of the Order of the Phoenix.

Role in the Books

Goblet of Fire   At one point, Hagrid is hiding in his hut and refusing to teach because of a story that appeared in the *Daily Prophet* wherein his half-Giant ancestry is exposed. Dumbledore mentions that his brother was once the subject of an attack in the media, apparently for practicing unnatural charms on a goat. Though Dumbledore praises him for keeping his head up, he isn't completely sure whether Aberforth can read.

Order of the Phoenix   Aberforth is first mentioned by name when Alastor Moody is showing Harry a picture of the original Order. Moody says that was the only time he had ever met Aberforth.

When Harry visits the Hog's Head in that same book, mention is made of a certain odor of goat in the place, and that the proprietor seems to be familiar. Although his name is never explicitly stated, we assume that the proprietor is Aberforth. As proprietor of the inn, Aberforth is called upon to serve Butterbeer to the students making up the initial meeting of the DA.

Half-Blood Prince   On a Hogsmeade visit before Christmas, Harry recognizes the barman from the Hog's Head talking to Mundungus Fletcher in the street outside the Three Broomsticks. The barman, Aberforth, walks away from Mundungus without saying anything, before they have noticed Harry. It turns out that Mundungus has been attempting to sell stuff that he had liberated from the Headquarters of the Order, and Harry attacks him, ineffectively as it turns out, when he discovers this.

It is mentioned that Harry sees the Barman from the Hog's Head attending Dumbledore's funeral.

Deathly Hallows   We hear about Aberforth in Elphias Doge's obituary of Albus Dumbledore, where he mentions that Aberforth was Albus' younger brother, and that he generally chose to settle his differences with duel rather than debate, unlike his older brother. He mentions their life in Godric's Hollow, their mother Kendra, and their sister Ariana. In the interview with Rita Skeeter that appears in the *Daily Prophet*, Rita mentions that Aberforth had reportedly broken Albus' nose at Ariana's funeral.

While Aberforth is mentioned in passing in the various extracts from Rita's book that we see, we learn very little more of him from them.

Aberforth re-enters our story in person late in this book. When Harry Apparates into Hogsmeade, he sets off an alarm, the Caterwaul, which results in several Death Eaters appearing out of the Three Broomsticks with the intent of catching him. They summon Dementors, and while Harry uses the Patronus charm to dispel them, his Patronus is recognized. As he is retreating from the Death Eaters, a door opens behind him and he (and Hermione and Ron, who are under the Invisibility Cloak with him), are waved into the Hog's Head. From an upper window, they see the bartender confronting the Death Eaters, and summoning his own Patronus, a goat. He manages to convince the Death Eaters that they saw his Patronus, rather than Harry's, before re-entering the pub to speak with Harry, Ron, and Hermione.

Harry then recognizes him as Aberforth. Aberforth tells them that they should wait until morning, then sneak out of town into the mountains and Disapparate. He tells them that the Order is finished, that Voldemort has won, and that anyone who continues to fight is only deluding himself. Harry says that Albus Dumbledore has given him a job, and Aberforth scoffs, asking if it was a nice, easy job, the sort of thing Harry might actually be expected to do? He also asks if Harry is sure that Albus has told him the whole truth? Harry, by this time, is sure that Albus had been holding things back, and cannot answer. In the silence that ensues, Hermione asks whether a portrait on the wall is of Aberforth's sister Ariana. Aberforth asks if Hermione has been reading Rita Skeeter's book. She says that she had been talking to Elphias Doge, Aberforth responds that Elphias thinks the sun shines out of Albus' every orifice. The Trio, and especially Harry, have been trying to reconcile their own understanding of Albus Dumbledore with the scurrilous portrait painted by Rita Skeeter in her book, which was reinforced by what Ron's Auntie Muriel had told Harry at the wedding. It takes very little prodding for Aberforth to tell the Trio the true story of their childhood. Ariana, then about six, had been observed by three Muggle youths doing magic. When they demanded that she do it again, and she couldn't or wouldn't, they beat her to the point that she received permanent damage. Aberforth says that her magic turned in on itself, she was never able to control it, and periodically she would have one of her rages and wild, uncontrolled magic would burst out in all directions. Their father, Percival, had hunted down the three Muggles and attacked them; arrested, he had refused to say why he had attacked the Muggles, because to do so he would have had to tell what had happened to Ariana, and felt sure that they would have locked her up in St. Mungo's if her injuries were known. He had been sent to Azkaban, and had died there. Their mother, Kendra, had moved the family to Godric's Hollow, to make a new start, but Ariana had to remain in hiding. Aberforth had become Ariana's favorite, able to control her when nobody else could. Then one day when Aberforth was away, Ariana had had one of her magic outbursts, and Kendra had died. Albus was not happy about having to give up his grand plans to be the head of the family, so when Gellert Grindelwald arrived, he was delighted—he and Gellert could share their dreams. There was a falling out when September approached, however; Aberforth did not want to go back to Hogwarts, he could see that Ariana was only an encumbrance to Albus, and he wanted to stay and take care of her, while Albus thought he should get his education, and Gellert thought that Ariana should be jettisoned as a drag on Albus' plans. It ended up being a three-way duel, and Ariana, frightened, was beginning to have one of her fits, and a curse hit her, and she died. Gellert ran away, of course. Aberforth does not know whose curse it was that killed Ariana, but Albus certainly was responsible.

Harry then states that he is going to do the task that Albus has set for him, with Aberforth's help or without. If Aberforth won't help them get into the school, they will wait until morning and try by themselves. Bowing to the inevitable, Aberforth addresses the portrait of Ariana, who departs, not sideways out of the frame as usual, but down an apparent long tunnel behind her. She returns, accompanied by another figure; the picture swings open like a door, and Neville Longbottom steps out of the passage behind it.

Aberforth is dismayed when Neville tells him that a few others will be showing up. As the last few people come up the tunnel into the Room of Requirement, Aberforth is reported to be quite upset at the traffic. After the younger students and Slytherins have been evacuated from the school, Harry, wandering the halls, meets Aberforth, who tells him that he should not have sent all of those Slytherins away; they'd just go and help Voldemort. Harry says that it's what Albus would do.

We see Aberforth again, briefly, during the battle. He says a few words of encouragement to Ginny when she Jinxes some of the Death Eaters on the grounds of Hogwarts. When Tonks asks him if he has seen Remus, Aberforth says that he had been dueling Dolohov.

In the renewed battle, Harry sees Aberforth Stunning Rookwood as he makes his own way into the Great Hall.

Strengths It is said that Aberforth must have had a hard time going to Hogwarts and trying to live in his brother's shadow. Albus had been a prodigiously skilled wizard, yet while Aberforth apparently also displayed an extraordinary magical talent, he seemed to prefer settling arguments with dueling instead of Albus' preferred debate. This may have something to do with his current lack of a high-profile job. Additionally, the accusation that he had been performing illegal charms on a goat could have ruined his chances at more advanced positions. He has made the best of things, however, apparently owning the Hog's Head Inn, and doing a brisk trade even when the Death Eaters are in occupation.

Aberforth is never explicitly seen using magic and is very much a minor character, until the seventh book where he is heard to speak for the first time.

Weaknesses Clearly, his unnatural attraction to goats is a weakness, one that has hindered his progression though life. His brother Albus has suggested that Aberforth may be unable to read.

Relationships with Other Characters He is the brother of Albus Dumbledore, as well as Ariana Dumbledore.

QUESTIONS

1. Does Aberforth have any of Dumbledore's magical abilities?
2. What exactly is meant by "practicing inappropriate charms on a goat"? (Note: Aberforth's Patronus is apparently a goat.)

GREATER PICTURE

Aberforth seems quite familiar with Mundungus and the quality and provenance of his wares when we see them talking in *Harry Potter and the Half-Blood Prince*, and in fact we are told earlier, in *Harry Potter and the Order of the Phoenix* that Mundungus had actually been banned from the Hog's Head which implies a fair degree of familiarity. So it is safe to assume that the abortive transaction that we see near the Three Broomsticks in *Harry Potter and the Half-Blood Prince* s not the only such transaction. We can't say for certain when Aberforth had bought Sirius' magic mirror from Mundungus, though it is certainly a possibility that the one transaction we see is the one where that happened. In any event, as we learn later that Mundungus is hawking his stolen wares to any passer-by in Diagon Alley, it is pure luck that the magic mirror, with its channel of communication that goes back to Harry, was not bought by a Death Eater or a sympathizer, rather ending up in the hands of one of Harry's allies.

Adrian Pucey

Gender: Male
Hair color: Unknown
Eye color: Unknown
Related Family: Unknown
Loyalty: Slytherin house

OVERVIEW

Adrian Pucey is on the Slytherin Quidditch team. He is a student, significantly older than Harry, but little described. We never seem to see him except as part of the Slytherin Quidditch team.

Role in the Books

Philosopher's Stone   Adrian Pucey is mentioned as being one of the Chasers on the Slytherin Quidditch team. While he manages several shots on goal, he does not succeed in scoring against Oliver Wood.

Chamber of Secrets   Adrian Pucey is mentioned twice as being on the Slytherin Quidditch team, apparently still as a Chaser, as at one point we see him trying to score against Wood. Harry can't spare much attention for him, as he is trying to avoid a rogue bludger, so we do not see much else of what is going on.

Prisoner of Azkaban   Adrian Pucey is not mentioned as being on the Slytherin Quidditch team in the final, although as Marcus Flint has evidently changed the line-up to favour brawn over skill, it's likely Pucey has been sidelined. In this match, Flint, Warrington, and Montague are mentioned as being Chasers, Derrick and Bole as Beaters, Draco Malfoy as Seeker, and the Keeper is never named.

Goblet of Fire   Quidditch being suspended for the year because of the Triwizard Tournament, Pucey does not play any role in this book.

Order of the Phoenix   Harry takes part in only one Quidditch match, again against Slytherin. In this match, Pucey, Warrington, and Montague are mentioned as being Chasers, Crabbe and Goyle as Beaters, Draco Malfoy as Seeker, and Miles Bletchley as Keeper. Pucey scores several times against Ron, who is Keeper for Gryffindor.

Analysis

Adrian Pucey is notable for being one of the few Slytherin Quidditch players who has not committed a foul during a game or attacked an opposing player outside the game, despite having played Quidditch in three books and at least five years.

Alastor Moody

   Gender: Male
   Hair color: Gray
   Eye color: black[?]
   Related Family: Unknown
   Loyalty: Albus Dumbledore

Overview

Alastor "Mad-Eye" Moody is a former Auror. His profession has apparently been rather hard on him, as he has a wooden leg, a magical artificial eye, and a large chunk taken out of his nose. He has developed a deep distrust of nearly everyone and everything. His nickname is derived from his magical eye, which is forever swiveling, totally independently of his real eye.

Role in the Books

Goblet of Fire   Alastor Moody is introduced when Amos Diggory contacts Arthur Weasley. It seems that muggles witnessed Mad-Eye's garbage cans attacking an intruder at his house; Arthur was summoned to deal with the fall-out. Moody becomes the new Defence Against the Dark Arts teacher during Harry's fourth year, replacing Remus Lupin. Students notice that rather than drinking from the pitcher of pumpkin juice during the Welcoming Feast, he instead drinks only from his hip flask.

In his first Defence Against the Dark Arts class, Moody demonstrates the three Unforgiveable Curses: the Imperius curse, the Cruciatus curse, and the killing curse. Neville Longbottom, whose parents were tortured into insanity with the Cruciatus curse, is understandably upset; Moody takes him up to his office and calms him down, giving him a book on Mediterranean aquatic magical plants.

Moody's teaching methods are unconventional but effective. When he sees Draco Malfoy throw a curse at Harry Potter, he reprimands him by Transfiguring him into a ferret and bouncing him off the floor; Professor McGonagall warns Moody, quite strongly, that Transfiguration is never used as punishment. Moody then takes Malfoy to see his House Head, Professor Snape.

In the confusion surrounding Harry unexpectedly becoming a Triwizard champion, Moody intimidates Igor Karkaroff into accepting four champions instead of three. Moody takes a liking to Harry and helps guide him through the Tournament.

After Harry emerges from the third Task with Cedric Diggory's body, Moody takes him to his office. There he starts sounding more like a Death Eater than an Auror. Realizing the danger, Harry distracts him long enough for Professor Dumbledore, Professor McGonagall, and Professor Snape to break in and Stun him. When a dose of Polyjuice potion wears off, Moody is revealed to be Barty Crouch Jr.. Professor Snape administers Veritaserum and Crouch confesses he is working under Voldemort's orders. Crouch says he intended to kill Harry to gain his Master's favor. Moody's trunk is opened, and the real Alastor Moody is discovered within, weak but still alive. Cornelius Fudge is summoned, who arrives with a Dementor. The Dementor administers the "Kiss" (sucking out Crouch's soul) before Crouch confesses to Fudge.

Order of the Phoenix   Alastor Moody is a member of the Order, and effectively the leader of the Advance Guard who escort Harry from the Dursley's house to Headquarters. Moody cannot recognize Harry, having been unconscious for Harry's entire previous school year, but calls upon Remus Lupin, another member of the Advance Guard, to identify him. Moody then Disillusions Harry to conceal him, and after waiting for a signal, they take off, Wizards and Witches of the Order acting to shield Harry from any evil wizards who might be prepared to attack. Many other members of the Advance Guard seem to feel that Moody's caution is a bit over-blown; he says they should circle around to lose any pursuit, but is overruled by Tonks, who says that they are all freezing up there.

On landing, Moody uses Dumbledore's Deluminator to put out all the streetlights at Grimmauld Place, then shows Harry a piece of paper. The paper, being written by Dumbledore, who is the Secret-Keeper for the Order, allows Harry to see Headquarters, and enter it. Once all the wizards have entered Headquarters, Moody uses the Deluminator to restore the streetlights.

At the party for Ron and Hermione following their appointment as Prefects, Moody remarks that Dumbledore must have thought Ron was good at dealing with jinxes; authority figures are often the targets of unprovoked attacks. Moody's magical eye found that the thing inside a writing desk in the parlour was only a Boggart. Harry points out to Mundungus Fletcher, who is working on a shady deal with Fred and George Weasley, that Moody could be observing them with his magical eye; Mundungus immediately stops haggling with the twins and gives them the goods they are dickering for at the twins' offer price, half of what he was originally asking. And finally, Moody shows Harry an old picture of the Order; Harry feels rather upset at having this sudden reminder of his parents, and how they had died, thrust upon him.

Moody and Tonks escort Harry and the Weasleys to St. Mungo's, for the Weasley children's first visit after their father is injured. Afterwards, Mr. and Mrs. Weasley, Moody, and Tonks confer as to how exactly Harry was able to perceive the attack on Arthur; Moody suggests that Voldemort might have been possessing him. This suggestion, which the Weasleys and Harry overheard by means of the twins' Extendable Ears, echoes Harry's private thoughts, but until now it had been too frightening a thought for him to entertain. Now that all of the Weasleys have heard it, he has to deal with it.

Moody meets Harry at the train station after the end of school, along with Tonks, Arthur and Molly Weasley. The four of them, plus Ron and Hermione, confront Harry's Uncle Vernon and Aunt Petunia, telling them that they will want to be reassured that Harry is having a good summer, or else they will come and visit to find out why not. Mad-Eye, with his magical eye, intimidates Vernon to the point that he nearly falls over a luggage cart.

Half-Blood Prince Alastor Moody does not play a significant part in this book. We can safely assume that he is working with the Order, but he does not seem to visit The Burrow or the school while Harry is there.

Deathly Hallows Alastor "Mad-Eye" Moody leads the Order of the Phoenix's operation of transporting Harry Potter from Privet Drive to The Burrow. The plan was to disguise Hermione, Ron, Fred, George, Fleur Delacour and Mundungus Fletcher as Harry Potter by using Polyjuice Potion. Moody died during the flight, as the Death Eaters and Lord Voldemort, selecting the Harry who was sharing a broom with the most powerful Auror, concentrated on him and Mundungus. Mundungus Disapparated to avoid a curse, and it caught Moody instead. We later find that Dolores Umbridge has mounted his magical eye on her office door as a sort of trophy. Harry removes it, and later gives it decent burial under a tree. Nothing else of Moody is recovered.

Strengths Mad-Eye's greatest asset is his "Mad" eye, the magical artificial eye he uses after losing his real eye in battles against Death Eaters. This electric-blue eye gives him 360 degree vision—he can see through the back of his own head—as well as being able to look through invisibility cloaks and closed doors.

Another strength is his formidable character.

Weaknesses A lifetime of fighting Dark magic has left him with an extreme paranoia that causes him to distrust everyone and everything. He is accused at one point of having destroyed a gift sent to him because he thought the ticking indicated a Cockatrice egg; in fact, it had been a carriage clock.

Relationships with Other Characters Moody has a good friendship with Ron's father, Arthur Weasley, and was also close to Albus Dumbledore. It is also shown in book 7 that Tonks is very close to Moody, as shown by her reaction when he is killed.

ANALYSIS

Not an intimately friendly person, Moody deeply distrusts most people or things since his "Auror" days, in which he lost an eye, part of his nose, and a leg. We are led to believe that Evan Rosier blasted some of his nose off. He rarely believes anyone and always suspects that a spell could have been cast with malafide intentions by the "Dark Side." This also explains his apparent motto, "Constant Vigilance."

QUESTIONS

1. Why is Moody so paranoid?
2. How does Moody interact with other people?
3. Is Moody's eye unique, or are there any other similarly magical eyes?

GREATER PICTURE

Many actions and details described under the "Goblet of Fire" section were not actually done by the real Alastor Moody, but rather Barty Crouch Jr., who kidnapped Moody and used Polyjuice Potion (which he keeps in his hip flask) to impersonate him. Because these events are not revealed until the book's conclusion when Crouch is under the influence of Veritaserum, they appear under the listing for that character. However, he managed to deceive even Albus Dumbledore with his impersonation, so it must have been very close to the true Alastor Moody.

Albert Runcorn

Gender: Male
Hair color: Unknown

Eye color: Unknown
Related Family: Unknown
Loyalty: Ministry of Magic

Overview

Albert Runcorn is a wizard of apparently high rank within the Ministry of Magic. We know very little of his appearance except that he is very tall.

Role in the Books

Deathly Hallows When Harry Potter, Hermione Granger, and Ron Weasley sneak into the Ministry to attempt to recover the Locket Horcrux, they each disguise themselves as Ministry employees. Harry ends up in the guise of Albert Runcorn, who is apparently quite senior in the Ministry. A wizard who bumps into him in the Atrium apologizes and rushes away, and the Minister for Magic, Pius Thicknesse, addresses him familiarly as "Albert." At one point, Harry as Runcorn is sharing an elevator with an unnamed wizard who apparently is applauding Runcorn's revelation of the Muggle ancestry of Dirk Cresswell, and trying to grease his way into the position that Dirk has been ousted from. Later, in another elevator, Arthur Weasley tells Runcorn that this revelation of Cresswell's background is the sort of thing that will get him into trouble.

Relationships with Other Characters Runcorn is very high in the Ministry and has done things that are underhanded in order to achieve his rank, apparently. There are wizards who are frightened of him, wizards who are smarming up to him to try and catch a ride on his coattails, wizards secure in their ancestry who are coldly furious at his tactics, and the upper echelons who treat him, apparently, as a near equal.

Analysis

We really know almost nothing of Runcorn except via the reactions of other people. It is uncertain whether he is actively in Voldemort's camp, or is simply making use of the upheaval to advance his own aims within the Ministry as Dolores Umbridge is doing. It's certainly not necessary that he be a Death Eater in order to behave as he is.

Given that we don't know anything about Runcorn from outside, it is interesting how solid the picture we can build of him mentally is, simply through people's reactions to him. This again is one of the strengths of the series: the characterization, even of characters like Runcorn who we see for only a handful of chapters, and then only from the very odd perspective of Harry "wearing his skin," so to speak, is so precise. Having decided that Harry would have to impersonate a high-ranking Ministry official in order to reach Umbridge's office with only minimal questioning, the author took the time to determine how he would have achieved that rank, and what other Ministry workers would think of him.

Albus Dumbledore

Gender: Male
Hair color: Silver (formerly auburn)
Eye color: Blue
Related Family:
Loyalty:
Percival Dumbledore (father) Kendra Dumbledore (mother) Aberforth Dumbledore
  (brother)
Ariana Dumbledore (sister)
Order of the Phoenix

Overview

Albus Percival Wulfric Brian Dumbledore was the Headmaster of Hogwarts School of Witchcraft and Wizardry, a Grand Sorcerer decorated with the Order of Merlin, First Class; also Supreme Mugwump of the International Confederation of Wizards and Chief Warlock of the Wizengamot. Ron describes him at one point as "barking." Non-British readers should be aware that this adjective is commonly used in England to modify the word "mad," but without the negative connotations of the word "raving" that is similarly used in the US. Someone who is "barking mad" in the UK is fully functional, but exhibits a very high degree of harmless eccentricity. According to the author, Dumbledore was born in 1881.

Role in the Books

Philosopher's Stone For much of the book, Albus Dumbledore is rather a remote presence and has little interaction with Harry Potter until the story's end.

Dumbledore first appears at Privet Drive with Professor McGonagall, discussing the recent tragic events resulting in Harry being placed with the Dursleys. He is awaiting Hagrid, who is bringing the infant Harry. Once Hagrid arrives, Harry is left on the Dursleys' doorstep. A letter from Dumbledore explaining why Harry has been brought there is left for Harry's Aunt Petunia, which she apparently does read.

Ten years later, in discussions with Hagrid and Ron, and also from Dumbledore's Wizard Card, Harry learns that Dumbledore, a very powerful wizard, is probably the only one Lord Voldemort ever feared. Harry first actually sees Dumbledore at the Entrance Feast, where he says a few words. "And here they are: Nitwit! Blubber! Oddment! Tweak!" This leads Harry to ask Percy Weasley if he is a bit mad; Percy answers that he is a genius, but yes, a bit mad. At the end of the feast, Dumbledore issues a few start-of-term announcements, including that "the third-floor corridor on the right-hand side is out of bounds to everyone who does not wish to die a very painful death." This causes Harry to ask Percy if Dumbledore is serious; Percy replies that he must be. Harry's first direct encounter with Dumbledore is during Christmas, when he discovers the Mirror of Erised. Dumbledore catches him at the mirror and explains its function, saying it only shows what people desire, not what they truly are; he says that he is taking the mirror away and asks Harry not to look for it again. He also proves able to see Harry despite the invisibility cloak that Harry is wearing, and suggests that invisibility cloaks are not the only way to be invisible.

Shortly after this, there is a Quidditch match, Gryffindor against Hufflepuff, at which Professor Snape chooses to be the referee. Fred Weasley seems surprised to see that Professor Dumbledore is in the stands; evidently he has not previously made a habit of watching the student Quidditch games. Because Snape is referee, and because Harry mistrusts Snape, he makes a point of catching the Snitch as quickly as he can; the game lasts only a few minutes. At the end of the game, Dumbledore speaks personally to Harry, saying he is glad that Harry has not allowed the Mirror Erised to dominate his thoughts.

Having determined that someone, they believe Snape, has all the necessary information to pass any obstacles between the forbidden third-floor hallway and whatever is being guarded, which they guess correctly to be the Stone, Harry, Ron and Hermione decide that they must tell Dumbledore what they have learned. In the Entrance Hall, they ask Professor McGonagall to take them to Dumbledore; McGonagall tells them that Dumbledore has been called to London. Harry decides that, in the absence of Dumbledore, he must go down the trap door himself; Ron and Hermione insist on going with him.

With Ron incapacitated, and only one dose of potion available to let Harry and Hermione go forwards at the last obstacle, Harry tells Hermione to go back, get Ron up, and send a message to recall Dumbledore; he will go on and face the final challenges himself.

In the final chapter, Dumbledore speaks with Harry in the hospital wing. He explains that he had found himself not needed in London and had returned immediately, and had arrived just in time to save Harry from death. In response to questions from Harry, he mentions that he is particularly proud of the last puzzle in the chamber, involving the Mirror of Erised. He also partially explains why events have occurred, although he refuses to explain why Voldemort intended to kill Harry.

Finally, at the Leaving Feast, Dumbledore awards some late House points: fifty points each to Ron and Hermione, and sixty to Harry, for their efforts to reach and save the Stone, and to Neville Longbottom, ten points for bravery. This catapults Gryffindor from last place into the lead in House points, resulting in their winning the House trophy for the first time in seven years.

Chamber of Secrets Dumbledore disciplines Harry Potter and Ron Weasley shortly after they crash into the Whomping Willow in a flying car. Dumbledore warns them that breaking one more rule will cause them to be expelled. When Mrs. Norris (Filch's cat) is found apparently dead, Dumbledore takes her to Gilderoy Lockhart's office to examine her, and asks Harry, Ron, and Hermione to come along, with Professor Snape and Professor McGonagall. After examining her, Dumbledore announces that Mrs. Norris is Petrified, though he is not sure how. Overruling both Filch, who demands that someone should be punished, and Snape, who suggests that Harry knows more about this than he admits, Dumbledore dismisses Harry, Ron, and Hermione without punishment. While Harry is in the Hospital Wing getting his arm bones re-grown, Dumbledore helps carry in the Petrified body of Colin Creevey. Examining Colin's camera and the destroyed film within it, Dumbledore says that the Chamber of Secrets is again open. When Professor McGonagall asks "Who?," Dumbledore responds, "The question is not *who*. The question . . . is *how* . . ."

When Justin Finch-Fletchley and Nearly Headless Nick are found Petrified, Harry is taken to Dumbledore's office by Professor McGonagall. Although Dumbledore believes Harry is blameless, he asks him if there is anything that he wants to tell him; Harry, thinking about Ron's comment that hearing voices that nobody else can hear is as worrying among wizards as it is with Muggles, responds negatively.

Dumbledore accompanies Cornelius Fudge to Hagrid's hut when the Minister decides to arrest him on suspicion of releasing a monster from the Chamber of Secrets. Dumbledore's attempt to dissuade Fudge fails. The twelve school governors, here represented by Lucius Malfoy, at the same time temporarily relieve Dumbledore as Hogwarts' Headmaster, citing a failure of confidence in his abilities.

When Harry goes into the Chamber to rescue Ginny, he meets Tom Riddle, who boasts that he, only a memory, caused Dumbledore's removal from Hogwarts. Harry contradicts him, and his loyalty to Dumbledore calls Fawkes to him. Dumbledore's pet Phoenix brings him the Sorting Hat containing Godric Gryffindor's sword. Harry kills the monster and destroys Tom Riddle's memory.

Upon hearing Ginny has been taken into the Chamber of Secrets, eleven of the governors send letters asking Dumbledore to return. Several imply that the twelfth governor, Lucius Malfoy, had threatened to curse their families had they not supported his request to remove Dumbledore. Dumbledore is in Professor McGonagall's office when Harry, Ginny, Ron, and Gilderoy Lockhart are led there by Fawkes after their ascent from the Chamber. He assists Harry in explaining to Mr. Weasley and Mrs. Weasley what has been happening and how Ginny was involved, and tells those gathered that Tom Riddle and Lord Voldemort are the same person. He goes on to reassure Ginny that there will be no punishment for her actions; wizards more powerful than Ginny have been hoodwinked by Voldemort.

Dumbledore explains to Harry the events that have transpired and resolves some issues that have been troubling him; he also explains that despite his earlier statement, there will be no consequences for Harry having broken so many school rules. He is able to reassure Harry that, despite similarities to Lord Voldemort, Harry does in fact belong in Gryffindor House, not Slytherin: "It is our choices, Harry, that show what we truly are, far more than our abilities." Shortly after, he warns Lucius Malfoy that anyone aiding the Dark Lord will be severely punished. He gives Harry the encouragement he needs to free Dobby, Malfoy's house elf who helped Harry.

Prisoner of Azkaban Harry and Hermione are late to the Arrival Feast and miss the Sorting; however, they are present when Dumbledore warns the school that the school entrances and exits are being patrolled by Dementors, and that there is no subterfuge that will allow a student to pass them. He also announces the appointment of two new teachers: Rubeus Hagrid as the new Care of Magical Creatures teacher, and Remus Lupin as Defence Against the Dark Arts teacher.

When Hagrid messes up in his first Care of Magical Creatures class, and Draco Malfoy is injured, Hagrid is certain that Dumbledore will sack (fire) him. The Trio reply that Dumbledore would never do that. Dumbledore is summoned when the portrait of The Fat Lady is found destroyed. He questions Peeves, who says that the portrait was destroyed by Sirius Black. Dumbledore then sends all of the students back to the Great Hall to sleep, moving the tables aside and conjuring sleeping bags (and, one would hope, some sort of mattress pads). He sends the teachers out to check the castle for Black. Snape, returning to report to Dumbledore, takes a moment to question one of Dumbledore's appointments; Dumbledore says he is certain that no-one in the castle would have assisted Sirius to enter.

At the Quidditch match against Hufflepuff, Harry loses consciousness when Dementors stream onto the field. Ron and Hermione tell him that he had fallen fifty feet, and been slowed and saved by Dumbledore; and that Dumbledore had then done something that sent the Dementors back to their posts at the entrances of the school. Dumbledore is one of only a very few people remaining at the school for Christmas; there are only twelve seated at the one remaining table. When Professor Trelawney joins them unexpectedly, he conjures a chair for her. When Trelawney predicts Lupin's imminent departure, Dumbledore mildly says he doesn't think Remus is in any immediate danger.

At the Quidditch match against Ravenclaw, Marcus Flint, Draco Malfoy, Crabbe, and Goyle dress up in Dementor's robes to scare Harry. Their plan backfires when Harry produces a Patronus that completely bowls them over. Harry sees them being disciplined by Professor McGonagall, and as he is leaving the pitch, he hears McGonagall saying that Professor Dumbledore is approaching.

The Quidditch final is Gryffindor against Slytherin. Gryffindor wins the match, and Dumbledore presents the Cup to the team.

Dumbledore joins a member of the Committee for the Disposal of Dangerous Beasts, Cornelius Fudge, and Walden Macnair as they go to Hagrid's hut for the scheduled execution of Buckbeak. Hagrid has told the Trio that Dumbledore has volunteered to be present to support him.

After the events in the Shrieking Shack, Dumbledore visits the Hospital Wing, where he asks those present, Cornelius Fudge, Severus Snape, and Poppy Pomfrey to allow him a word with Harry and Hermione. After hearing protests from Snape and Madam Pomfrey, Dumbledore tells Harry and Hermione that he has been speaking with Sirius Black, and understands the story; he says that the account of two underage wizards will not be given much weight against Snape's story, and as Lupin is currently running in the Forbidden Forest, he is unavailable. Even if he were there, it probably would not help; a werewolf's recounting of events would not be given much weight either. Dumbledore hints to Hermione that they should use the Time Turner, says that two innocent lives may be spared this night, and locks them into the hospital wing. Harry later understands this latter hint to indicate that they should save Buckbeak as well; and Dumbledore has told them which window is the one to the office where Sirius is being held, which leads Harry to guess that Dumbledore means them to fly on Buckbeak's back to that window to save Sirius.

At Hagrid's hut, Harry and Hermione watch the execution party arrive, and see them return to Hagrid's hut for the paperwork. While he is coaxing Buckbeak to follow him into the Forbidden Forest, Harry hears Dumbledore calling Macnair back for one final signature that needs to be witnessed. Later, watching from concealment near the Whomping Willow, Harry and Hermione see the execution party, including Dumbledore, walk past again on their way back to the school.

As they return from seeing Sirius and Buckbeak off from the tower, Harry and Hermione meet Dumbledore at the door to the Hospital Wing, where he has just locked them in; he unlocks the door so that they can return to their beds. When Snape bursts in, accusing Harry and Hermione of having something to do with Black's escape, Dumbledore is present to defuse his arguments, pointing out that Harry and Hermione have been locked into the hospital wing, and couldn't have had anything to do with it, unless they are able to be in two places at the same time. Lupin's being a werewolf is revealed by Snape the next day, and Lupin, knowing that public opinion will not allow him to remain a teacher at Hogwarts, resigns. Harry goes to speak with him while he is packing up his office. Lupin tells Harry that Harry's father's Animagus form was a stag, the same as Harry's Patronus. Dumbledore arrives to announce Lupin's carriage. After Lupin has left, Dumbledore stays to have a word with Harry. He tells Harry that in his conversation with Sirius he had learned about James Potter being an Animagus. Harry told him about how he had thought the Patronus that had chased all the Dementors away had been cast by his father. Dumbledore says that as long as we remember them, those who die never truly leave us. "Make no mistake—Prongs rode again last night."

Goblet of Fire Dumbledore enters the story at the Arrival Feast. To the dismay of many, he announces that there will be no Quidditch tournament this year. Before he can explain, he is interrupted by the arrival of a heavily scarred man who walks up to the teachers table, exchanges a few quiet words with Dumbledore, and then begins eating; Harry notices that he ignores the flask of pumpkin juice on the table, instead drinking from his hip flask. Dumbledore introduces him as Professor Moody, who will be teaching Defence Against the Dark Arts this year. Dumbledore goes on to explain that Quidditch is canceled because Hogwarts will be hosting the Triwizard Tournament. Dumbledore says that wizards under the age of 17 will be excluded from competition, and that representatives from Beauxbatons and Durmstrang will be arriving shortly and will be staying at the school.

Professor Moody tells the class that he will be performing the three Unforgivable Curses in class; Hermione objects, but Moody says Dumbledore wants the students to be able to recognize and deal with them immediately. While this doesn't entirely quiet Hermione's concerns, she does stay in the class.

We next see Dumbledore when the other two wizarding schools arrive, on 30 October. He greets Madam Maxime of Beauxbatons warmly, and asks if she wishes to stay and greet the delegation from Durmstrang; she decides that she will instead go into the castle, because of the cold. Dumbledore similarly greets Igor Karkaroff of Durmstrang, who says that one of his students has a bit of a cold and should go inside immediately. After the welcoming feast, Dumbledore introduces Ludovic Bagman and Bartemius Crouch, who will be judges, with the three school headmasters, of the Triwizard Tournament. He then has Argus Filch bring out the Goblet of Fire, and explains that, to enter the tournament, a student should write his name on a piece of parchment, with his school, and place that in the Goblet within the next 24 hours. He will be drawing an Age Line around the Goblet, so that students younger than 17 cannot enter. He cautions the students that placing their name into the Goblet constitutes a binding magical contract; once they have agreed to participate, they cannot change their minds. At the Hallowe'en Feast, the Goblet will choose one Champion from each school to enter the tournament. When Fred and George later try to put their names in to compete, the magic of the age line gives them both long white beards as it throws them away from the Goblet. Dumbledore, arriving from the Great Hall, remarks that he had warned them, and that they were not the first, that two other students were already in the Hospital Wing getting their beards removed.

At the Hallowe'en Feast, Dumbledore announces the Champions as they are presented by the Goblet: for Durmstrang, Viktor Krum. For Beauxbatons, Fleur Delacour. For Hogwarts, Cedric Diggory. He is then stunned when the Goblet produces a fourth name: Harry Potter.

Harry, equally stunned, is not immediately able to get to his feet; Dumbledore has to call him a second time, and then tell him to proceed to the room off the Great Hall where the other Champions have gone. Dumbledore joins him there shortly with the other judges, and asks Harry if he had put his own name into the Goblet, or had an older student do that for him. Harry insists that he had not. After Ludo Bagman asks Mr. Crouch for a ruling, Crouch says that if his name came out of the Goblet, he is bound to compete. Dumbledore accepts this ruling, though the Heads of the other two schools are opposed. Given that their champions are bound to compete also, however, they cannot see any alternative course of action. Seeing that Crouch appears somewhat ill, Dumbledore asks if he would like to stay the night at the school, or at least stay for a drink, but Crouch says he must get back.

At the Weighing of the Wands ceremony, Rita Skeeter draws Harry aside for a private interview, from which he is rescued by Dumbledore. Seeing Rita, Dumbledore makes some pointed remarks about the last story she wrote that had mentioned Dumbledore in most unflattering terms. Dumbledore is present for the Weighing of the Wands ceremony, and for the photo call afterwards.

Dumbledore, in his role as judge, is present at the First Task, where Harry must retrieve a golden egg from a dragon. Harry is quite successful, summoning his Firebolt and flying past the dragon to capture his golden egg in the shortest time of all the four Champions, and Dumbledore scores him a nine out of ten.

Dumbledore is also at the Yule Ball, of course, where he mentions the Room of Requirement to Karkaroff, by way of illustration that nobody can know all the secrets of the school. We also later see Dumbledore dancing, rather awkwardly but without embarrassment, with Madame Maxime.

Rita publishes a scurrilous story about Hagrid, saying that he is half-Giant. Hagrid goes into seclusion in his hut, not coming out to teach or tend the grounds; a new teacher, Wilhelmina Grubbly-Plank, covers his classes for a week. Returning from a Hogsmeade weekend the following week, Hermione beats on Hagrid's door, demanding admission, and is nonplussed when Dumbledore opens the door and invites them in. Over tea, Dumbledore tells them, and an obviously distraught Hagrid, that one must ignore the press; his own brother Aberforth had once been pilloried in the press after a conviction for practicing unnatural charms on a goat, but had simply gone on as always. Of course, Dumbledore muses, it is possible that Aberforth could not read, so it might be that he was unaware of the stories... Dumbledore then leaves, telling Hagrid that he expects Hagrid to be back on the job Monday, and to be at Head Table for breakfast Monday morning.

Harry ventures out to the Prefects' Bathroom late at night to work on the clue in the Egg for the Second task. He is nearly caught by Argus Filch and Professor Snape, but is rescued by Professor Moody. In talking with Professor Moody afterwards, Moody says that Dumbledore believes in second chances, where he and Mr. Crouch don't. Later, Harry remembers this, and wonders what Snape had done to deserve a second chance. Dumbledore is, of course, a judge at the Second Task, and is present when Harry returns to the surface with Ron and Gabrielle Delacour. He speaks with the mer-Chieftainess, and determines that in fact Harry had arrived at the hostages first, and then had stayed to ensure that all of them were rescued. This had delayed him beyond the alloted time, but most of the judges feel that he should receive extra credit for behaving nobly.

After surveying the site of the maze which will form the course of the Third Task, Viktor Krum asks Harry to step aside with him for a word. They end up, in partial darkness, under the eaves of the Forbidden Forest. As their conversation finishes, Mr. Crouch, much the worse for wear and discoursing with the trees, appears. In rare moments of partial lucidity, he holds tightly onto Harry's robes, and demands Dumbledore; he then goes back to talking cheerfully about his wife and son to the trees. Harry, leaving Krum to keep an eye on Mr. Crouch, runs to the school where he finds the gargoyle that guards Dumbledore's office, but does not know the password. The door opens, though, to reveal Snape, who refuses to allow Harry past and into Dumbledore's office. While Harry is trying to convince him f the urgency of his errand, Dumbledore himself appears at the door, and apprised of the situation, hurries to the spot with Harry where he and Krum had been talking. There, they find no sign of Crouch, and Krum apparently Stunned. Dumbledore revives Krum, and sends a messenger for Hagrid. When Hagrid arrives, Dumbledore tells him to find Karkaroff and Moody, but Moody appears immediately, saying that Snape had told him where Crouch was. Dumbledore tells Moody that it is imperative to find Mr. Crouch, and tells Hagrid to escort Harry to Gryffindor Tower. He also tells Harry to stay in the dorm until morning; any messages he needs to send can wait until then. Harry wonders how Dumbledore can know that he was planning to write to Sirius.

The following morning, as the Trio are preparing to send a message off to Sirius, they are interrupted by the arrival of Fred and George Weasley. After they have left, Ron mentions that they are really serious about funding their joke shop, and might not talk to Dumbledore about something they've seen if it might imperil their funding. Harry falls asleep in Divination class, and sees Wormtail being tortured. Waking up, he rushes to Dumbledore's office to let him know what he has seen; trying passwords at random, he manages to get the gargoyle to leap aside and open the door. At the top of the stairs, he overhears a discussion between Dumbledore, Cornelius Fudge, and Professor Moody, about the disappearances of Bertha Jorkins and Bartemius Crouch. He suggests that Madame Maxime might have had something to do with Crouch's disappearance, but Dumbledore protests. Harry is discovered by Moody, and invited into the office. Dumbledore suggests that he should wait there in the office while he, Moody, and Fudge survey the spot where Crouch was seen last. Harry, waiting, sees odd, shimmering light, and discovers a stone bowl full of something, not liquid, quite. Placing his face into it, he suddenly finds himself seated alongside Dumbledore in what appears to be a courtroom. Finding that nobody can see or hear him, he recognizes this as a memory, similar to the one he had been shown two years before in Tom Riddle's diary. Dumbledore is observing what might be a release hearing for Igor Karkaroff, in which he agrees to name Death Eaters in return for leniency. He then sees a new memory, this time of the trial of Ludo Bagman, who was passing Ministry secrets to a death eater, Augustus Rookwood. Finally, he and Dumbledore witness a third trial, this time of four people who stand accused of torturing Frank and Alice Longbottom into insanity in order to get them to tell what had happened to Voldemort. Acting as prosecutor in this, as he had been in the other two cases, is Bartemius Crouch, who here is apparently sending his own son to Azkaban. A second Dumbledore appears, and grasping Harry by the elbow, returns him to the office.

Dumbledore identifies the stone basin as a Pensieve, and says it is a useful place to store one's thoughts and memories when there seem to be too many of them in one's head. It is also good for showing patterns in thoughts. Harry apologizes, but Dumbledore dismisses his concern, saying that curiosity is not a sin, but that it should be treated with caution. He then produces, from the Pensieve, the image of Bertha Jorkins at 16, complaining because someone had jinxed her when she told him she had seen him kissing someone behind the greenhouses. He softly chides the image, asking why she had gone behind the greenhouses in teh first place?

Dumbledore now says that Harry had something on his mind when he came up to the office. Harry tells Dumbledore about his dream. Dumbledore asks if there were other times that his scar had hurt, apart from the time at the beginning of the summer? Harry says no, but then stops: how had Dumbledore known about that episode? Dumbledore says that Harry is not Sirius' only correspondent. Dumbledore then thinks for a long while, taking thoughts out of his head and placing them in the Pensieve. Harry interrupts him, asking why his scar hurts? Dumbledore says that the scar hurts when Voldemort is near, or feels strong emotion. Asked if the dream was real, Dumbledore says it was no ordinary dream, and asks if Harry could see Voldemort. Harry says no, only the back of his chair; but Voldemort doesn't hove a body, does he? How could he hold a wand? Dumbledore again thinks about this for a while.

Harry now asks if Alice and Frank Longbottom were Neville's parents. Dumbledore asks if Harry had ever wondered why Neville was being brought up by his grandmother? Harry admits that he had not wondered. Dumbledore says that Neville's parents had never regained their sanity, and that they were permanently resident at St. Mungo's Hospital. He tells Harry that he should not tell anyone this, not even Ron and Hermione. Asked about Ludo Bagman, Dumbledore says that he has not been connected with anything Dark since his trial; neither has Severus Snape. Finally, Dumbledore wishes Harry luck in the Third Task.

In the run-up to the Third Task, Sirius is sending owls to Harry almost daily with advice; the main one being that Harry should not worry about what's happening outside Hogwarts. Inside the school, under Dumbledore's protection, he should be safe.

Dumbledore is present as Ludo Bagman sends the four Champions into the maze.

Dumbledore is again present as Harry returns bearing the body of Cedric. He tells Harry to remain where he is; Harry, confused, leaves with Moody. Shortly, Dumbledore, accompanied by McGonagall and Snape, breaks down the door of Moody's office and Stuns Moody. Professor McGonagall wants to take Harry to the Hospital wing, but Dumbledore overrules her. He sends Snape to fetch his strongest truth serum, and to also bring the house elf Winky from the kitchens. Dumbledore also sends Professor McGonagall to take the large black dog in Hagrid's pumpkin patch to his office. He then uses Moody's keys to open the trunk in his office. In the seventh compartment, he finds Alastor

Moody, weak, unconscious, but alive. Examining the hip flask that the Moody on the office floor is wearing, he finds it full of Polyjuice Potion. Dumbledore says that he had known that this was not the true Alastor Moody; the true Moody would never have taken Harry away if Dumbledore had told him not to. He and Harry watch as the Moody on the office floor turns into Barty Crouch Jr.

Snape returns with Winky and the truth serum. Dumbledore reassures Winky that Barty is not dead, only Stunned. McGonagall returns from her errand and is equally amazed at who Moody has turned into. Dumbledore administers three drops of the serum and revives him. He then questions Barty, who explains much of what has happened, including that he had turned the Triwizard Cup into a Portkey.

Dumbledore now takes Harry to his office, where Sirius is waiting. Dumbledore says that he must hear the entire story of what happened after Harry had first touched the Cup. Harry, tired and weak, pauses, and Sirius says he needs rest; but Dumbledore says that if he thought rest would help, he would put Harry into a dreamless sleep immediately. But that would be only postponing the process. With Sirius holding his shoulders, and strengthened by a note of Phoenix song from Fawkes, Harry feels able to tell the story, and he does.

Dumbledore seems particularly interested that Voldemort had used Harry's blood for the spell that brought him back, asking to see the wound; and Harry thinks he sees a brief flash of triumph in Dumbledore's eyes before he goes on. And Dumbledore explains the reappearance of Harry's parents during the wand duel, the Priori Incantatem effect, clearly aware of how hard it is for Harry to speak about this. Dumbledore says that when two wands sharing a common core are forced to duel, the Priori Incantatem effect will force one of the wands to disgorge the last few spells it has performed; in this case, Harry had seen the last four people the wand had killed.

Dumbledore now takes Harry to the Hospital Wing, leaving him in the care of Madam Pomfrey, Mrs. Weasley, Bill and Ron, Hermione, and the large black dog that is Sirius.

Harry is waked up by the arrival of Cornelius Fudge, with Professor McGonagall and Professor Snape in attendance, looking for Dumbledore. Dumbledore arrives shortly, and is surprised that McGonagall is no longer guarding Barty Crouch; McGonagall tells him that Crouch had decided to bring a Dementor with him, and the Dementor had administered the Kiss, sucking out Barty's soul. Dumbledore points out that this means he can no longer testify as to what happened; Fudge says that any testimony that he could have given would be suspect as he believed he was working under Voldemort's orders. Dumbledore says that he was working on Voldemort's orders, and that Voldemort had returned. Fudge is taken aback momentarily, but then rallies, saying that Dumbledore was basing his belief on what Harry was saying, and that Harry is less than reliable. Dumbledore says that they must each act as they see fit. Fudge, apparently choosing to believe that Dumbledore is setting himself up in opposition to the Ministry, leaves in a huff.

Dumbledore now sends Bill off to report to Arthur Weasley, Professor McGonagall to take Hagrid and Madame Maxime to his office, and Madam Pomfrey to tend to Winky. Asking Sirius to show himself, he requires that Sirius and Snape shake hands, then sends Sirius off to speak with "the old crowd": Remus Lupin, Mundungus Fletcher, and Arabella Figg, then lay low at Lupin's until Dumbledore gets back in touch. He then sends Snape off on "the mission we discussed." He then instructs Harry to drink the rest of his sleeping potion, and departs. When Harry leaves the Hospital Wing, Ron and Hermione tell him that Dumbledore has already addressed the school, telling them what had happened. Ron's mother had asked if Harry could stay with them over the summer, but Dumbledore had told her that Harry must stay at Privet Drive first.

Harry asks what mission Hagrid has been sent on, but Hagrid says Dumbledore told him not to tell anyone about it. At the Leaving Feast, the Great Hall is draped in black. Dumbledore starts with a tribute to Cedric Diggory, and explains that he died at the hands of Lord Voldemort. He says that the Ministry would be upset that he had told them this, and some of their parents might also be upset; but truth is better than lies, and lying about Diggory's death would be an insult to his memory. He mentions that Harry had risked his life to return Cedric's body, and offers a toast. Finally, speaking to the students of Beauxbatons and Durmstrang there present, he says that they will always be welcome in Hogwarts, as they must all stand together against the forces of darkness.

Order of the Phoenix Over the summer, Harry is extremely vexed that nobody will tell him what is going on with the newly-returned Lord Voldemort. Particularly exasperating is the fact that neither Ron nor Hermione, in their answers to his messages, are at all responsive. Matters come to a head when Harry is attacked by Dementors as he and Dudley walk back to Privet Drive. It turns out that Dumbledore has been having Harry watched by, among others, old Mrs. Figg, who amazingly turns out to be a Squib. Harry's use of magic results in a flurry of owls, as Dumbledore goes to the Ministry of Magic to prevent their hasty action regarding Harry's unauthorized use of magic. The final owl of the evening is a Howler, which is addressed to Aunt Petunia; she is brought up short by this and forces Vernon, who had been adamant that Harry was going to leave their house, to accept that Harry has to stay with them. Shortly after that, Harry is brought to the Headquarters of the Order of the Phoenix at Number 12, Grimmauld Place. There, Harry is re-united with Ron and Hermione, who are most apologetic about the tone of their letters. They explain that Dumbledore had made them promise that they would not tell Harry what was going on. It turns out that the Order is a group of wizards who are fighting Voldemort; they have to remain undercover because the Ministry's official position is that Voldemort has not returned. Dumbledore himself, as a direct result of his stating publicly that

Voldemort has returned, has lost many of the offices he once held: he is no longer Chief Warlock of the Wizengamot, for instance, has lost the position of Supreme Mugwump of the International Confederation of Wizards, and there is talk of revoking his Order of Merlin.

After dinner that night, Harry asks some questions about what Dumbledore is doing, and why the Order has to stay quiet. He also asks why Voldemort seems to be doing nothing, and is told that Voldemort has to regain his strength; at the end of the previous book, he had only a handful of followers, and he needed to build up his numbers before he could move into the open. Harry is told that he was not meant to escape the graveyard, and by doing so he had dealt Voldemort the worst possible blow. Voldemort had wanted his return to remain secret, and Harry had taken word of his return to the worst possible person: Dumbledore. It also turns out that Headquarters, which is in a house owned by Sirius Black, is protected by the Fidelius charm, and Dumbledore is secret-keeper.

A hearing had been scheduled at the Ministry regarding Harry's use of magic when underage, fighting the Dementors. Shortly before the hearing, Harry learns that while he had been asleep, Dumbledore had visited Headquarters, but had not stopped to talk to Harry. This upsets Harry greatly; he does not understand why Dumbledore does not wish to see him. At the hearing, which has been changed at the last minute to be in one of the old courtrooms and apparently in front of the full Wizengamot, Dumbledore appears as a surprise witness for the defence. Dumbledore manages the defence brilliantly, first getting the panel of judges to concede that in fact use of magic by underage wizards in self defence is allowed, then further getting the concession that if there were in fact Dementors present, that would constitute grounds for use of magic. He then introduces Arabella Figg as a Squib who had actually seen the Dementors. After Arabella's testimony, Dumbledore catches and defuses a number of spurious accusations leveled by Fudge, and in the process suggests that as there were Dementors at Privet Drive, as stated, and if the Dementors remain under Ministry control, as the Ministry claims, then someone at the Ministry must have sent them. Finally, Dumbledore requests that the judges make their decision; when the votes are counted, Harry is exonerated, and Dumbledore gets up and immediately departs. Harry is relieved that this ordeal is over, but remains upset that Dumbledore had never even looked at him, and had not remained there long enough to even exchange a few words.

At the Arrival Feast, Dumbledore gives his customary speech. When he introduces Dolores Umbridge, she, most unusually, rises to make a speech of her own. Hermione seems to be very interested in what she is saying, but most of the rest of the school seems to find it deadly dull. Later that night, Harry is amazed to find out that there have been some concerns about returning to Hogwarts among Wizarding families. Seamus Finnigan, for example, had almost been kept out of Hogwarts by his parents, who feel that Dumbledore may be "losing it" with his insistence that Voldemort has returned.

Harry is upset that Dumbledore still seems to be avoiding him. His name is mentioned a couple of times during the next few months; Hermione suggests that Dumbledore may not be commenting on Hagrid's absence to as to avoid calling attention to it, and Angelina Johnson suggests that it may be Dumbledore's influence that allowed the Gryffindor Quidditch team to reform after it was forcibly disbanded by Educational Decree Number Twenty-Four. In conversation with Sirius, Harry, Ron, and Hermione learn that the reason Umbridge was foisted on the school, and the reason her teachings are so ineffectual, is because Cornelius Fudge believes that Dumbledore may be trying to create a private army to overthrow the Ministry, and her classes have been deliberately designed to thwart this. It is because of this belief that the Defence Against the Dark Arts Group that Harry heads up is named "*Dumbledore's Army.*" When Dobby mentions the Room of Requirement, Harry remembers that Dumbledore had mentioned the room at the Yule Ball. And when Hagrid returns, Harry, Hermione, and Ron manage to learn from him that Dumbledore had sent him and Madame Maxime on a mission to contact the Giants and attempt to win them over to Dumbledore's side.

Just before Christmas, Harry has a vision of Arthur Weasley being attacked by a snake. Professor McGonagall, told of this vision, takes Harry to Dumbledore's office. Still not looking at Harry, Dumbledore questions him as to what he has seen, and Harry tells him about the attack, and when questioned more closely, that during the attack he believed he was the snake. Dumbledore sends the occupants of two of the portraits in his office to investigate. He also sends Professor McGonagall to bring the other Weasley children to his office, and the portrait of Phineas Nigellus Black is sent to Headquarters to alert Sirius that guests are coming. He does some investigation of his own, then creates a Portkey to carry Harry and the Weasleys to Grimmauld Place. Just before the portkey activates, Dumbledore, for the first time in months, looks into Harry's eyes, and Harry feels the snake within him rise up, ready to sink its fangs into Dumbledore's face.

While Dumbledore does not appear at Grimmauld Place during the holidays, he does send a message. Harry, having overheard conversations that indicate other members of the Order suspect that Voldemort is possessing him, decides that his best course is to leave Headquarters where he might show Voldemort the activities of the Order. As he is preparing to leave, the portrait of Phineas Nigellus appears with Dumbledore's message: "Stay where you are." Harry complies, but he is vexed that again he is being given instructions and no information. Then, on the day before school is scheduled to start, Severus Snape arrives with the unwelcome news that Dumbledore wants Harry to learn Occlumency, and that Snape will be teaching him. Snape does not explain why Dumbledore wants this, nor why Dumbledore does not teach Harry himself.

Harry has a vision of Voldemort discussing a plan with one of his Death Eaters, apparently Augustus Rookwood, who is telling him that the plan proposed by Avery would not work. Harry tells Ron about this

Albus Dumbledore

dream, and Ron says Harry should tell Dumbledore. Harry, repeatedly stung by Dumbledore's refusal to speak with him, says he will not; Dumbledore evidently doesn't want to know about these things as he is trying to teach Harry how to turn them off.

When Umbridge dismisses Professor Trelawney, Dumbledore says that it is his will that she remain in residence at the school, even if she is not to teach any more. Umbridge asks where the next Divination teacher will stay? Dumbledore says he has found a Divination teacher, and he will want different rooms. He then introduces Firenze, a Centaur, as the new Divination teacher.

Umbridge learns about Dumbledore's Army, and sends her Inquisitorial Squad to try and capture its members. Due to a timely tip-off from Dobby, all of the DA members escape except Harry, who is taken to Dumbledore's office. Dumbledore is present, along with Professor McGonagall, Umbridge, Cornelius Fudge, Percy Weasley as scribe, and two Aurors: Kingsley Shacklebolt, who is also an Order member, and Dawlish. Umbridge accuses Harry of having an illegal meeting at the Hog's Head earlier in the year; Dumbledore points out that while he does not deny that the meeting took place, the Educational Decree banning such meetings came out two days later, so the meeting was not against any regulation. Umbridge states that any meetings since then would have been illegal, Dumbledore suggests that what is needed, then, is proof that any such additional meetings actually happened. Umbridge here produces her witness, Marietta Edgecombe, who is holding her robe up over her face. As she lowers her robe to speak, everyone in et room is amazed to see that she has large purple blemishes on her face, spelling the word "Sneak." Due to a timely Memory charm from Kingsley, she then indicates that there were no other meetings of that group. However, Umbridge produces the membership parchment of the DA, and seeing the heading of the page, "Dumbledore's Army," Fudge guesses that Dumbledore is, in fact, creating a private army. Dumbledore pleasantly agrees that he is doing so. Fudge sends Percy off to send his notes to the *Daily Prophet*, and then has the Aurors attempt to put Dumbledore under arrest. This fails dramatically; with both Aurors, Fudge, and Umbridge unconscious, Dumbledore departs the school in a flash of phoenix fire.

Again, there is a stretch of some months without direct contact with Dumbledore. Hagrid mentions that the Centaurs are very upset with him, as he had broken up a fight; many of the other Centaurs had been attacking Firenze for agreeing to work with Dumbledore, and Hagrid had stepped into that and allowed Firenze to escape. And when Umbridge catches Harry in her fireplace, using the Floo network to try and talk with Sirius, Hermione tells her that they were trying to contact Dumbledore. She says that on Dumbeldore's orders, they had been building a weapon, and it was finished. With this as a lure, she is able to get Umbridge to follow her into the Forbidden Forest, where she is captured by the Centaurs.

Dumbledore is not seen again until the climactic battle at the Ministry of Magic. He arrives in the hall of the Veil, and captures nearly all of the Death Eaters there. Bellatrix Lestrange, however, escapes, and Harry gives chase, finally catching up to her in the Atrium and dueling with her there. Voldemort arrives, and shortly afterwards Dumbledore does also; Dumbledore animates the figures of the Fountain of Magical Brethren to trap Bellatrix, protect Harry, and summon help. He and Voldemort then duel; Voldemort escapes, but returns to possess Harry. Harry, believing he is about to die, thinks of Sirius and his joy at being re-united with him; that drives Voldemort out of his mind. Ministry wizards and Aurors, including Fudge, now arrive, just in time to see Voldemort reappear to rescue Bellatrix.

Dumbledore tells Fudge that there are death eaters captive in the hall of the Veil, and says that he will grant Fudge half an hour's explanation, but that after that he would have to return to Hogwarts. He creates a Portkey, and gives it to Harry; Harry finds himself in Dumbledore's office at the school.

Reinstated as Headmaster, Dumbledore talks to the distraught Harry in his office. He admits that he made many mistakes, such as not telling Harry about a Prophecy concerning him and Voldemort. Harry tells him that the prophecy was smashed, and Dumbledore says that was only a copy of the prophecy, that the person to whom the prophecy was made still remembers it and can reproduce it. He then extracts a memory and places it in the Pensieve; Sibyll Trelawney rises and says *"The one with the power to vanquish the Dark Lord approaches . . . born to those who have thrice defied him, born as the seventh month dies . . . and the Dark Lord will mark him as his equal, but he will have power the Dark Lord knows not . . . and either must die at the hand of the other for neither can live while the other survives . . . the one with the power to vanquish the Dark Lord will be born as the seventh month dies . . ."* He also explains that he had been avoiding Harry to prevent Voldemort from reading Harry's thoughts and learning information through him about Dumbledore and the Order of the Phoenix—he was deeply concerned at what would happen once Voldemort learned that the relationship they shared was greater than headmaster to student. He also explained that he had feared what would happen if he was trying to teach Harry Occlumency, while Voldemort had access to Harry's mind. And Dumbledore also says why he had chosen Ron to be Prefect instead of Harry: "I felt . . . that you already had . . . enough responsibilities to be going on with."

Dumbledore is re-instated as headmaster, and regains his offices in the Wizengamot and the International Confederation of Wizards, now that his belief in the return of Voldemort has been vindicated. He walks into the Forbidden Forest alone, returning with an apparently undamaged Umbridge; Umbridge, however, will not speak, and eventually flees the school when she thinks nobody will notice.

Half-Blood Prince Harry is surprised when Dumbledore comes to Privet Drive to collect him after only a fortnight. Despite the letter Dumbledore had sent, Harry did not believe that he would be able to leave the home he so loathed, so quickly. Dumbledore invites himself in, and tells Harry that he has inherited all Sirius' worldly goods, including the house at Grimmauld Place, Kreacher, and Buckbeak. However, there is a concern that there may be a charm that would require that the property be inherited by the oldest living descendant of the Black family, in this case Bellatrix Lestrange. In order to test this, Dumbledore summons Kreacher, and requests that Harry give him an order. If Kreacher follows Harry's orders, then he is Harry's property. Harry tells Kreacher, who is yelling defiance, to shut up; Kreacher suddenly cannot speak, thus proving that Harry does, in fact, own him and the house. At Dumbledore's suggestion, Harry sends Kreacher to work in the Hogwarts kitchens.

Dumbledore now asks if Harry is ready to go, and is unsurprised when Harry says he has a little last-minute packing to do. When he returns from throwing everything into his trunk, Dumbledore is still in the sitting room, rather than in the front hall as Harry had hoped. Dumbledore chastises the Dursleys for their treatment of Harry, saying that he had requested that they treat Harry as one of their own, and he is only glad that he was not as ill-treated as Dudley. He and Harry then depart. Harry has noticed that Dumbledore's hand is blackened and dead-looking, but when he asks Dumbledore about it, he is told that while he will tell Harry about it later, he does not have the time to tell the story properly now.

Dumbledore tells Harry that they have another errand to run first, and asks Harry to keep his Invisibility Cloak with him. He then sends Harry's trunk on ahead to the Burrow, and has Harry hold on to him while they Apparate. In the small village of Budleigh Babberton, Dumbledore tells Harry, they are going to recruit a new teacher, as they seem to again be one short. Arriving at a small house, Harry and Dumbledore discover a scene of desctruction; Dumbledore, however, pokes an overturned armchair which utters an exclamation and turns into a very fat, bald wizard. Introduced as Horace Slughorn, the fat wizard asks Dumbledore what he had forgotten, and Dumbledore says that there had been no Dark Mark hovering over the house. Dumbledore and Slughorn then clean up the mess, and Dumbledore introduces Harry to Slughorn. Dumbledore then offers Slughorn a job at Hogwarts, pointing out that since he has gone into hiding, he has been out of touch with his various associates. When Slughorn turns him down, Dumbledore departs to use the bathroom, leaving Slughorn and Harry together. On his return, Dumbledore says he was intrigued by the Muggle magazine on knitting patterns, and making one final offer, prepares to depart. As he is walking out the door, Slughorn says he accepts the job at Hogwarts, but will want a raise. Dumbledore then Apparates with Harry to The Burrow. There, he draws Harry aside, and suggests that he should tell Ron and Hermione the contents of the Prophecy. He also tells Harry that he should always carry the Invisibility Cloak with him during the coming year, and that he will be having private lessons with Dumbledore over the course of the year as well.

In conversation with Ron and Hermione the following morning, Harry learns that Percy Weasley is still estranged from his family, despite Dumbledore having been proved correct. Dumbledore had commented that sometimes being right was even less forgivable than being wrong, which Ron thinks is a positively barmy thought. Following Dumbledore's instructions, Harry tells Ron and Hermione about the prophecy, and is creatly relieved that they are worried about Harry's having to face Voldemort, rather than reviling him because he perforce may become a murderer.

At the Arrival Feast, Dumbledore announces two new staff appointments: Horace Slughorn has come out of retirement and will resume his old job, teaching Potions, while Professor Snape will be teaching Defence Against the Dark Arts. He also says that with the reappearance of Voldemort, new protective spells have been placed around the school, and he asks for the students' patience and cooperation. He also asks that if anyone has any concerns, they should report them to any teacher.

It is some time later when Harry has his first private lesson with Dumbledore. He is intrigued to find that they will not be studying magic, but rather will be reviewing and extending Dumbledore's researches into the origins and life of Voldemort. For the first lesson, Harry and Dumbledore, by way of the Pensieve, relive the memories of one Bob Ogden, a Ministry representative in the Department of Magical Law Enforcement, as he visits the Gaunt home. Harry and Dumbledore watch as Bob is attacked by Morfin Gaunt, speaks to his father, and watches the byplay between them and Merope Gaunt, as Tom Riddle rides by. After Ogden is chased away, Dumbledore mentions that the elder Gaunt is named Marvolo, and Harry draws the conclusion that this may be Voldemort's grandfather. Dumbledore agrees, and further mentions that Merope is his mother, and the handsome Tom Riddle riding past is his father. He goes on to explain that Merope had ensnared Riddle by magical means when her brother and father were locked up in Azkaban, but for reasons unknown had allowed the enchantment to lapse, perhaps thinking that bearing Tom's son would be sufficient bond to keep him with her. Harry, recalling that Tom had been raised in an orphanage, asks if Merope had died; Dumbledore says that she had. Harry asks if he can discuss this with Ron and Hermione, and Dumbledore agrees, saying only that they should not let it go any further. As he is leaving, Harry notices a broken ring on a table, and correctly identifies it as one that Dumbledore had been wearing earlier in the year, and also the one that Marvolo Gaunt had been wearing. In Ogden's memory, Marvolo had identified it as the signet of the Peverell family, one of the oldest pureblood Wizarding families.

After this lesson, there is a long stretch when Dumbledore is not apparently present at the school, is absent from head table at many meals, and no further invitations for lessons come from his office until mid-October. The meeting in mid-October happens on the Monday after a Hogsmeade visit in which Harry has surprised Mundungus Fletcher selling off silver from Grimmauld Place, and has seen Katie Bell injured by a jinxed necklace that she was carrying. Katie was apparently under the Imperius curse, and Harry is convinced that Draco Malfoy was behind it, despite Professor McGonagall saying that Draco had been doing detention at the time. Although he is uncertain that Dumbledore will be there, Harry goes to his office in time for the lesson. Finding him present, Harry first asks about Katie Bell, and Dumbledore says that Professor Snape had done all he could. Asked why Snape instead of Madam Pomfrey, Dumbledore says that Snape has more experience with Dark magic. Dumbledore then tells Harry that Mundungus seems to have gone into hiding, but in any event he will not be taking anything else from Grimmauld Place. When Harry tells him about his belief about Draco's involvement in the necklace attack, Dumbledore says that he is aware that Harry believes that, and it will be investigated; but that the lesson is more important.

Dumbledore says that Merope Gaunt had gone to London, where, left on her own, she had sold the few items of value that she owned. In the Pensieve, Dumbledore shows Caractacus Burke of Borgin and Burkes, gloating over having purchased Slytherin's locket for ten Galleons. Harry is outraged at Burke's avarice. Harry and Dumbledore then enter the Pensieve, and follow the younger Dumbledore as he visits the orphanage where the young Tom Riddle is living. Dumbledore plies the matron with gin, asking her about the young Riddle. She tells of the night of his birth, with his mother dying only an hour afterwards. Further, she says that she can't prove anything about him, but after checking that nothing she says will prevent Dumbledore from taking Riddle to the school he represents, the matron admits that Riddle had apparently had something to do with the death of a rabbit, and that two children who had been absent with Riddle at their annual seaside outing were apparently scared to the point of being insensible.

She then takes Dumbledore to see Tom. Tom is initially suspicious, but Dumbledore manages to convince him that what he is doing is magic, and that he is there to take him to a school where he will be taught magic. As proof, Dumbledore makes Tom's wardrobe appear to be on fire, and then has a box of stolen objects dance to protest their captivity. He suggests that there is a fund to help those students of magic who are unable to pay their own way, and when Tom refuses assistance finding Diagon Alley, Dumbledore gives him a money bag and instructions as to how to get there. He notes at the time that Riddle reacts poorly to mention of the innkeeper's name, because it is the same as his own.

Returning to his office, Dumbledore says that even then, he was worried about Tom Riddle's cruelty, ambition, thieving, and how he reacts to being told he is a wizard. He had resolved to keep an eye on him. He further notes that Tom, even at that young age, was trying to set himself completely apart, and was apparently friendless. Dumbledore finally mentions that he liked to keep trophies.

Leaving the office, Harry notes that the ring is gone, and wonders if there shouldn't be something else there, such as the mouth organ (US: harmonica) that had been one of the stolen items in Tom's wardrobe. Dumbledore compliments his perceptiveness, but says the mouth organ was never anything but a mouth organ. Over Christmas, Rufus Scrimgeour, the new Minister for Magic, tries to recruit Harry to act as poster boy for the Ministry. Harry refuses, saying that he is Dumbledore's man through and through.

At Harry's next private lesson, he recounts Scrimgeour's attempt to recruit him. Dumbledore is moved by Harry's acceptance of Scrimgeour's calling him "Dumbledore's man." Harry then recounts a conversation that he had overheard between Snape and Draco Malfoy in which Snape had said he was sworn to help Draco in the task he had been set, and Draco had refused his help. Dumbledore thanks Harry for reporting it to him. In response to Harry's angry outburst, Dumbledore says he does understand, possibly even better than Harry does, but he trusts Snape and nothing that he has heard changes that. They then proceed to the memories of Riddle during his school days. Dumbledore admits to having had serious difficulty in getting memories of anyone from that time, as he was creating his core group of what would become Death Eaters around himself. The first memory is of Tom and his uncle Morfin.

Dumbledore and Harry then watch as Tom appears in the Gaunt shack, Morfin attacks him under the impression that he is Tom Riddle Sr., and then, once he learns who Tom is, tells him of his mother Merope and his Muggle father. Then everything goes black. When Morfin woke up, Dumbledore says, the Riddle family were dead via a spell cast by Morfin's wand, and the ring of the Peverells was gone.

The second memory is of the Slug Club, headed by a much younger Horace Slughorn and including Tom, now about fifteen and wearing the Peverell ring. When Tom asks about Horcruxes, the memory turns to white fog and only Slughorn's voice can be heard. Dumbledore comments that the memory is quite clearly edited, and gives Harry the job, "for which you are uniquely equipped," of retrieving the unedited version of that memory. Harry's attempts to retrieve this memory from Slughorn over the next while are fruitless. Meanwhile, though, Ron is poisoned on his birthday by means of a bottle of mead which Slughorn says he had purchased as a Christmas gift for Dumbledore. Harry manages to revive him with a bezoar. As Harry and Hermione are leaving the Hospital Wing, Hagrid, who is leaving with them, mentions that he had overheard Dumbledore and Snape having a bit of a disagreement. After some persuasion, Hagrid mentions that Dumbledore and Snape had been talking at the edge of the Forbidden Forest, and Hagrid had overheard Snape saying that perhaps he no longer wanted to do something which he had agreed to. Dumbledore quite firmly reminded Snape that he had given his word. Dumbledore had also mentioned Snape's investigations in Slytherin, which Hagrid assumes were in regards to the necklace. Harry is sent to the Hospital Wing shortly after that by a mis-hit Bludger. He and Ron leave at the same time, and Harry is almost immediately given an appointment for his next lesson with Dumbledore. When he arrives at Dumbledore's office, Professor Trelawney is there, complaining that Firenze is still teaching Divination. Trelawney is also upset that a student, namely Harry, seems to be more important than Trelawney and her concerns, but Dumbledore is firm: Harry has an appointment. After Trelawney leaves, Dumbledore says that if he had taken Divination, he might have been able to foretell how much trouble the subject would be giving him. He then asks Harry about the memory that he was to get from Slughorn. Harry has to admit that he has not been able to convince Slughorn to give it to him, in amongst the confusion of Ron getting poisoned and his own injuries. Dumbledore's response is only a mild chastisement, but his disappointment is so evident that Harry promises to make retrieving the memory his top priority. Dumbledore says that without that memory there would be little point proceeding, and the lesson continues with the last two memories that Dumbledore has to show Harry.

Before they get into the memories, Dumbledore has Harry recap what they have learned about Riddle so far. Dumbledore then says that they are now entering the realm of deep speculation. The first memory is that of a house-elf, one Hokey, servant to Hepzibah Smith, who claimed descent from Helga Hufflepuff. Tom was working then as a buyer for Borgin and Burles, a job that was a surprise to all who knew him. Tom had earlier applied to Armando Dippet, then Headmaster of Hogwarts, for a teaching position and had been turned down for lack of experience. In Hokey's memory, we see Tom making an offer for something that Hepzibah is selling, and Hepzibah also showing him two of her treasures: a cup that once belonged to Helga Hufflepuff, and the locket of Slytherin. In Hokey's memory we see that Tom seems to have difficulty releasing the locket, particularly after he hears that Burke had bought it from some poor witch for a relative pittance.

Back in his office, Dumbledore says that Hepzibah had died two days later. Hokey remembered making the mistake that had resulted in her being poisoned, and had accepted the punishment for it, but Hepzibah's treasures had never been found. And at about the same time, Riddle had left Borgin and Burkes.

The second memory, Dumbledore says, is from ten years after Hepzibah's death. It is Dumbledore's own memory of Riddle returning to Hogwarts to ask for a teaching post, this time to teach Defence Against the Dark Arts. Dumbledore says he is aware of Tom's new name but chooses not to use it, and is also aware of his Death Eaters, waiting in Hogsmeade. Saying that he doesn't trust Tom's motive for wanting the job, and that he is aware of Tom's other recent activities, Dumbledore turns down Tom's application. Back in his office, Dumbledore remarks that since that time, he has never managed to keep any teacher in the post of Defence Against the Dark Arts teacher for longer than a year.

There is now a stretch where Dumbledore is absent. While he is absent, Harry, Ron, and Hermione receive a note from Hagrid that Aragog has died, and he would appreciate them being there at his funeral. Harry, under the influence of Felix Felicis potion, attends the funeral, manages to get Slughorn to attend as well, manages to get Slughorn drunk, and retrieves the memory from him. He then returns to the castle, where he learns that Dumbledore has returned, and immediately visits Dumbledore in his office. Dumbledore is immensely pleased that Harry has the memory he has been seeking, and they immediately return to the Pensieve.

Again, they visit the Slug Club meeting with the young Horace Slughorn, Tom Riddle, and several of his associates. Tom is asking about Horcruxes; Slughorn describes them as a way of tying one's soul to earth and thus providing a sort of immortality. It is necessary to split one's soul, which is done by committing murder; the torn fragment can then be encased in a physical object and will act to keep the soul tied to the Earth. He further says that he knows nothing about the details. Riddle asks, if splitting one's soul is a way of becoming immortal, wouldn't more be even better? And isn't seven the most magical number? Slughorn is horrified: to commit murder is bad enough, but multiple times?

Back in Dumbledore's office, Dumbledore tells Harry that Riddle's diary, which Harry had destroyed almost four years earlier, was almost certainly a Horcrux. What had alarmed Dumbledore at the time was that it was not only a way of storing a soul fragment, but seemed almost designed as a weapon. It seemed designed to be passed on to a student at Hogwarts, as a way of opening the Chamber of Secrets. Why this was alarming was that if it was being treated so lightly, it must be only one of a number of Horcruxes; if that diary represented the total of Voldemort's immortality, it would not have been treated so lightly. Dumbledore suggests that Voldemort had divided his soul into several pieces: Slughorn's memory suggests the number of pieces is likely seven, which would be six Horcruxes and the damaged soul remaining in Voldemort's body. As long as any Horcrux remains, Voldemort cannot be killed. Dumbledore believes that Voldemort. with his love of taking trophies, has used unique objects for his Horcruxes. Two have been destroyed: the diary, which is unique because it contained proof that Riddle is the heir of Slytherin, and the ring of the Peverells. Dumbledore reveals that it is while destroying that ring that he received the injury to his hand, and that it was only due to his own skill and Snape's timely action that the damage was no worse. Dumbledore believes that of the four remaining Horcruxes, two will turn out to be Hufflepuff's cup and Slytherin's locket, one will be an as-yet unknown artifact of Gryffindor or (more likely) Ravenclaw, and the last one may be Voldemort's snake, Nagini. Asked if it is possible to put a Horcrux in a living being, Dumbledore says that it is possible, but risky, as living beings can be killed. Dumbledore also says here that if he locates any more Horcruxes, Harry will be permitted to accompany him on the mission to retrieve or destroy them.

Harry now asks if Voldemort is aware when one of his Horcruxes is destroyed. Dumbledore says he thinks not; his soul is likely so shredded that he is not able to sense damage to the bits trapped in the Horcruxes. It is certain that he was unaware of the destruction of the diary until Lucius Malfoy told him about it. Dumbledore understands that Voldemort's rage at that revelation was quite spectacular. What with that, and the failure of the mission at the Ministry, Malfoy might be feeling quite happy to be safely locked away in Azkaban.

Dumbledore now says that, if all his Horcruxes are destroyed, Voldemort can be killed by someone with uncommon skill and power. At Harry's demurral, Dumbledore says that Harry does have uncommon skill and power, and it is that plus his capacity to love which will give him the edge over Voldemort. He manages to get Harry to understand that it is choices, more than anything, that controls what people are; Voldemort is being driven by the prophecy, but Harry would be fighting Voldemort whether the prophecy had been uttered or not. The ability to make that choice gives Harry the power that Voldemort does not have.

Some time later, Harry is again summoned to Dumbledore's office. Along the way, he encounters Professor Trelawney sprawled on the floor outside the Room of Requirement. Apparently she had been using that room to hide her sherry, but this time when she went in, she heard someone whooping. When she had asked who was there, everything had gone dark, and then she had been unceremoniously pushed out the door. Harry guesses that whatever task Draco Malfoy had been trying to accomplish in there, he had succeeded, and asks Trelawney to accompany him to Dumbledore's office so that she can tell Dumbledore what had happened. On the way, Trelawney tells her side of the events on the day she was hired, and happens to mention that it was Severus Snape who had heard the first parts of the prophecy; Harry immediately runs ahead to speak with Dumbledore about this new revelation. Harry is momentarily disarmed when Dumbledore says that he has found one of the Horcruxes. However, as he is noticeably distraught, Dumbledore asks him what has passed, and Harry says that he has just learned it was Snape who had overheard the prophecy. Dumbledore ends the ensuing heated discussion by saying that he has his reasons for trusting Snape; though it seems he is about to reveal those reasons, at the last moment he does not. Harry prepares to re-open the argument, but Dumbledore forestalls him, saying that if he wishes to come on this expedition with him, he must promise absolute obedience, no matter what. Including that if Dumbledore tells him to run away, to save himself, he must do so. Harry reluctantly promises. Dumbledore then tells him to fetch his Invisibility Cloak and be in the Entrance Hall in five minutes.

When Harry joins him, Dumbledore asks Harry to put on the Cloak and walk with him. Dumbledore then walks to Hogsmeade, greeting Madam Rosmerta pleasantly as he walks past towards the Hog's Head. Once they are out of sight of the Three Broomsticks, Dumbledore Apparates them to the foot of a cliff by the sea side. Dumbledore tells Harry that this is where the young Tom Riddle had taken two of his fellow orphans, after which the two had never completely recovered. There, they swim into a cave, and Dumbledore finds a hidden door which refuses to open. After studying it for a while, he discovers that it is necessary to shed blood on this door to open it, and does so; the now-open door leads to another cavern which contains a lake. Harry, seeing a green glow at the apparent center of the lake, asks if they could not Summon the Horcrux; Dumbledore suggests he try it, and Harry does, only to have his spell intercepted, apparently, by something in the lake. Dumbledore then discovers an invisible chain, and magically reels it in, bringing a very tiny boat to the surface of the lake; he and Harry get in, and the boat sets off for the green glow. Harry, by wand light, notes that the lake has dead people floating in it; Dumbledore tells him that he is not surprised, but so long as they are just floating, they will be harmless.

Reaching the green glow, which is on a small island, they find that the light comes from a basin containing a potion, which they cannot reach either physically or by magic. Dumbledore guesses that the only way to remove the potion and find what lies beneath it is to drink the potion. He produces a crystal goblet, and scoops some of the potion out of the basin with it. Before he drinks, he requires a promise from Harry, that Harry will force him to drink the potion in its entirety, no matter what happens. Harry has misgivings—what if the potion kills Dumbledore? But Dumbledore says that Voldemort would not want to kill the thief of his Horcrux outright; he would want to keep him alive for a while, for questioning.

Dumbledore begins to drink, and the effect it has on him is horrific. He seems to be in great pain, he appears to be reliving scenes in his memories that are horrible, he is pleading with someone not to hurt someone, he pleads with Harry to kill him, he asks for a drink of water, and he is so weakened that he is unable to stand. When the potion in the basin is gone, Harry tries to conjure water for him, but some magic in the potion prevents conjured water from reaching Dumbledore; Harry has to retrieve some from the lake. He is seized by Inferi as he touches the surface, but he is able to throw some of the lake water towards Dumbledore. This seems to revive him enough that he is able to conjure fire to repel the Inferi. Taking the locket from the now-empty basin, Dumbledore returns to the boat with Harry, and they return to the shore of the lake with no further interference from the Inferi. Dumbledore is much weakened, and needs to be supported as they make their way around the lake to the doorway. Harry had received a small cut while fighting the Inferi and used the blood from that to re-open the door. Harry then supports Dumbledore out of the cave and back to the foot of the cliff, where he Apparates both of them back to Hogsmeade. Back in Hogsmeade, Dumbledore collapses, asking Harry to fetch Severus Snape. As he prepares to do so, he is met by Madam Rosmerta, who says that the Dark Mark has appeared over the school. Harry Summons a pair of brooms from the Three Broomsticks, and Harry and Dumbledore set off for the Astronomy Tower, Dumbledore muttering charms to allow them passage through the protective spells as they go.

Atop the Astronomy Tower, Dumbledore sends Harry, under his cloak, down into the tower to find out what is happening and get help, but then hearing someone approaching, he Petrifies Harry to prevent him interfering. The approaching person, Draco Malfoy, disarms Dumbledore. Although it becomes apparent that his mission is to kill Dumbledore, Draco cannot bring himself to do it. Dumbledore gets him talking, and determines how Draco had known when Dumbledore had left the school (he had placed Madam Rosmerta under the Imperius curse), and how he had gotten Death Eaters into the school (he had been working in the Room of Requirement on one of a pair of linked Vanishing Cabinets; the other one had been in Borgin and Burkes). Dumbledore nearly has convinced Draco to abandon Voldemort's plan to murder him when four Death Eaters arrive at the top of the tower. One of them says he'll kill Dumbledore, but another holds him back, saying that Voldemort's orders are that Draco alone should do it. Snape suddenly appears on the scene, and fulfilling the Unbreakable Vow he made to Draco's mother, blasts Dumbledore with a killing curse, catapulting his body "over the battlements."

The Heads of House, assisted by Hagrid, decide to keep the school open until after Dumbledore's funeral, so that those students who wish may pay their last respects. On the day of the funeral, with a large part of the Wizarding world present, Hagrid carries Dumbledore's wrapped body to the bier, and after the service, a white tomb magically appears around it.

Following Dumbledore's death, everyone, including Harry, believes Snape a traitor, although Dumbledore's trust in him never wavered. It is unclear whether Snape actually betrayed Dumbledore or was acting under unknown circumstances. Regardless, Harry swears to destroy both Voldemort and Snape.

Deathly Hallows Albus Dumbledore may be dead, but that does not mean that his influence has ended.

Harry, for the first time in seven years, is cleaning out his school trunk to the bottom, finding everything he wants to take with him and putting it into his rucksack, and discovers (painfully) a shard of the magic mirror Sirius had given him for Christmas two years before. He tucks the mirror shard in the front pocket of his rucksack. After cleaning the wound, Harry stops to read one of the copies of the *Daily Prophet* that had accumulated; this one carries an obituary of Dumbledore, written by Elphias Doge, one of Dumbledore's friends in school. This reveals that Dumbledore's father Percival had gone to Azkaban for attacking three Muggle children. Albus had overcome his notoriety at Hogwarts by excelling at academic subjects. When his brother Aberforth arrived at the school, it seemed he was very different, preferring to settle arguments by dueling rather than debate. Dumbledore graduated, and was preparing to go on a world tour with Elphias when his mother Kendra suddenly died. Albus had given up his world tour and gone home to take care of his family. A short while after that, Albus' younger sister, Ariana had also died, and this had apparently caused an estrangement between the brothers. Albus had never talked about his family since, and, putting this sad chapter of his life behind him, had gone on to achieve many noticeable successes, including his discovery of the twelve uses of Dragon's blood, and his defeat of the dark wizard Grindelwald.

Harry realizes that he hardly knew Dumbledore at all; their conversations had been about Harry, and he had never thought to ask Dumbledore about his past. He tears out the obituary and tucks it, also, into a front pocket of his rucksack. Then, looking through the more recent issues of the *Prophet*, he finds a teaser piece about a new book written by Rita Skeeter. Rita suggests that Dumbledore had dabbled in Dark magic, that Ariana was a Squib, and that at Ariana's funeral, Aberforth had punched Albus in the nose. She also suggests that the epic duel between Dumbledore and Grindelwald might not have been all it seemed. She also suggests that the relationship between Dumbledore and Harry might be less than savoury.

Harry, outraged by this muckraking, can do little; distracted, he turns the mirror shard over and over in his hands. He sees a quick flash of sky blue, the colour of Dumbledore's eye, in the mirror shard. Studying the mirror shard, he sees only himself, and there is nothing that could have reflected sky-blue. Harry thinks to himself that Dumbledore's eye will never look on him again, but all the same he tucks the mirror shard away in a front pocket of his rucksack. Shortly after arriving at the Burrow, Harry has a vision of what Voldemort is experiencing. While Hermione is adamant that he should close off that channel of communications, Harry mentions that Dumbledore had thought that would not be necessary, as Voldemort had found Harry's mind a very uncomfortable place the last time he was there (at the end of *Harry Potter and the Order of the Phoenix*). Harry's love for Sirius had made Voldemort's stay in his mind a very short and unpleasant one for both parties.

It is mentioned that Grimmauld Place is no longer safe to use as Headquarters. Dumbledore had been Secret-Keeper for that location, and with his death, everyone who had been privy to the knowledge is now a secret-keeper. This includes Severus Snape, who quite possibly has let some Death Eaters in on the secret. As a result, many Order members now take their meals at The Burrow.

The Order of the Phoenix have determined that Harry, Ron, and Hermione are on a mission assigned to them by Dumbledore, and largely are content to leave them to it. Mrs. Weasley, however, is afraid that they are going off to get themselves killed, and sets the three of them tasks to keep them apart from each other, apparently in the hope that if they can't get together to plan, they will have to stay at the Burrow and allow the older wizards to take care of Voldemort. Her plan goes awry at one point, though, leaving the Trio a clear hour to discuss their plans. Hermione says that she had Summoned a number of books about Dark magic, including Horcruxes, from Dumbledore's study immediately after the funeral. She wonders whether Tom Riddle had read the book. Harry says that Dumbledore believed so; he had indicated that when Riddle had talked to Slughorn about multiple Horcruxes, he had already known how to make them. They wonder how Dumbledore had been able to destroy the Ring Horcrux. On Harry's birthday, Rufus Scrimgeour arrives to give Harry, Ron, and Hermione their bequests from Dumbledore's will. When Harry asks why it had taken so long to read the will, Hermione replies that the Ministry is allowed to examine bequests for thirty days, and had evidently taken the full thirty days to try and figure out what Dumbledore's bequests meant. To Ron, Dumbledore has left his Deluminator, a magical device for extinguishing lights, that we first saw in the first chapter of Harry Potter and the Philosopher's Stone. To Hermione, a copy of an old edition of The Tales of Beedle the Bard, in runes. And to Harry, the Golden Snitch that he caught to win his first ever Quidditch game. Scrimgeour seems particularly interested to have Harry hold the Snitch; Hermione guesses that this is because of the Snitch's "flesh memory." A Snitch includes a spell that enables it to retain a "memory" of the person who first touched it. This is used in cases where two Seekers seem to reach the Snitch at the same time; the Snitch will remember who touched it first. Scrimgeour expects the Snitch to react when Harry takes it; he is mildly disappointed when the Snitch lies quiescent in Harry's hand. Scrimgeour also says that Dumbledore had bequeathed the sword of Gryffindor to Harry, but that was not his to give; being a national treasure, it would remain in the Headmasters' office at Hogwarts.

Later that night, Harry reminds the other two that he had caught the Snitch in his mouth. Placing it again in his mouth, he finds that words appear on it in Dumbledore's writing, saying "I open at the close." Harry is mystified as to what this means.

At Bill and Fleur's wedding, Harry, who is in disguise, happens to see Elphias Doge, and revealing who he is, asks Elphias if there is any truth to what Skeeter had written. Elphias sputters indignantly about Rita's efforts to talk to him, but they are interrupted by the arrival of the Weasleys' Auntie Muriel. Muriel says that there doesn't seem to be any evidence against what Rita had written. Elphias had said that Ariana Dumbledore was ill, but Muriel says that her friend who worked at St. Mungo's, said that Ariana had never been admitted there, and if Ariana had medical problems, why did she not get taken to hospital? She confirms that Albus had been a very poor head of the family after Kendra's death, and that Aberforth had punched him in the nose at Ariana's funeral. Muriel also mentions that the Dumbledore family, at the time, had lived in Godric's Hollow.

When the Trio escape to Number 12, Grimmauld Place, they are greeted by a simulacrum of Dumbledore, put there as part of a curse placed on Headquarters to prevent Severus Snape from entering.

While they are at Grimmauld Place, Remus Lupin visits and is also confronted with the Dumbledore made of dust. In discussion with Harry, he mentions that the Ministry, which is now controlled by Voldemort, has listed Harry as a wanted person; when asked how they could justify this, Lupin produces a copy of the Daily Prophet which is trumpeting that Harry is wanted for questioning in the death of Dumbledore. After Lupin's departure, Harry notes that the Prophet also contains an extract from Rita Skeeter's muck-raking book. In that extract, she writes that Kendra Dumbledore had been a proud person; when Percival had been sent to Azkaban, she had moved the family to Godric's Hollow, where they were unknown, and tried to stay aloof from the neighbours. The daughter, Ariana, was hardly ever seen, apparently to hide the fact that she was a Squib.

On September 1st, the Daily Prophet reports that Severus Snape has been appointed headmaster of Hogwarts, and that Alecto Carrow and Amycus Carrow have been appointed to fill the two missing spots for teachers, Muggle Studies and Defence Against the Dark Arts. Harry recognizes the Carrows as two of the Death Eaters who had been present at the death of Dumbledore. Hermione, thinking of Snape in Dumbledore's office, retrieves the empty portrait of Phineas Nigellus Black and stuffs it into her beaded bag, so that he will not be able to eavesdrop on their plans and report back to Snape.

Harry, Ron, and Hermione sneak into the Ministry in order to try and find Slytherin's brooch, which they had discovered had been extorted away from Mundungus Fletcher by Dolores Umbridge. Ron, wearing maintenance worker's robes, is pulled aside by a Death Eater that Harry recognizes as having been atop the tower when Dumbledore died; other Ministry workers call him Yaxley. While Harry is searching Umbridge's office, he sees what he thinks is a mirror, and Dumbledore looking out of it. When he looks at it more closely, he sees it is a copy of Rita's book, with a picture of Dumbledore on the cover. Flipping it open, he sees a picture of two teenagers, one of whom he assumes to be Dumbledore. As Pius Thicknesse opens the office door, Harry, under the Invisibility Cloak, replaces the book on the shelf and makes good his escape.

As the Trio escape the Ministry, Yaxley grabs Hermione and is brought to the stoop of Grimmauld Place by side-along apparation. Hermione breaks loose from him there and apparates them away, but says that they cannot return to Grimmauld Place. With the death of Dumbledore, she is now a Secret-keeper for the location of what was the Headquarters of the Order of the Phoenix, and as she had taken Yaxley there, he is now also aware of its location. Dumbledore is mentioned in passing a few times; Ron maintains that there cannot be a Horcrux hidden at Hogwarts because Dumbledore would have found it, and Harry reminds him that Dumbledore had never claimed to know all of the secrets of the school. The Trio overhear another party of refugees talking, and the other party mentions that they believe Harry's story that Snape had killed Dumbledore. In talking about the sword of Gryffindor with Phineas Nigellus, the Trio learn that Dumbledore had used the sword to break a ring, which Harry recognizes as being the ring of the Peverells and one of the Horcruxes. After Ron leaves the group, Harry is unsure whether he is angrier at Ron for leaving, or at Dumbledore for the lack of clues he has given Harry. Harry and Hermione discuss almost endlessly where Dumbledore might have hidden the real Sword of Gryffindor.

Hermione, reading the copy of The Tales of Beedle the Bard that Dumbledore had left her, notes a mark on one of the stories, which Harry recognizes as the symbol that Xeno Lovegood had been wearing at Bill and Fleur's wedding, and also as Grindelwald's mark. Meanwhile, Harry has been brooding over the sword of

Gryffindor, finally deciding that it might have been hidden in Godric's Hollow. Hermione says that would be logical, Godric's Hollow being named after Gryffindor. It suddenly occurs to Hermione that Dumbledore may have given the Sword to Bathilda Bagshot, who also lives in Godric's Hollow. After suitable preparation, they do go to Godric's Hollow, appearing there on Christmas Eve after a heavy snowfall. In the graveyard they find the headstones for Dumbledore's mother and sister. They also find a marker for one Ignotus, marked with the sign that Hermione had found in her book, and the headstone for Harry's parents.

At Bathilda Bagshot's house, Hermione picks up a copy of Rita's book, which she and Harry examine after Harry recovers from their escape. Harry looks through the book to find the picture he had seen in the copy of the book in Umbridge's office. The caption tells him that this is the teenaged Dumbledore and his best friend, Gellert Grindelwald. Stunned, Harry and Hermione look for the associated text, and find the chapter "The Greater Good." There, Rita has written that while Dumbledore had canceled his world tour to come back to Godric's Hollow and care for his family, many residents of the village had not seen much evidence of that care. Aberforth was allowed to run wild, still, and Ariana was kept hidden. That same summer, Bathilda Bagshot had taken in her grand-nephew, Gellert Grindelwald, a student as brilliant as Dumbledore who had been expelled from Durmstrang. He and Albus had become close friends, talking and planning together all day, and sending letters back and forth by owl much of the night. One of the letters is reproduced in the chapter, and in that letter Dumbledore agrees that Wizard dominance over Muggles is proper so long as it is done for the greater good of all. Dumbledore goes on to say that he believes that Wizards must rule responsibly and use force only when necessary. He says that he believes that this is where Gellert had gone wrong at Durmstrang, though of course if Gellert had never been expelled, Dumbledore would not have had the chance to meet him. Rita's interpretation is that Dumbledore was planning at one point to overturn the International Statute of Secrecy, establishing the rule of Wizards over Muggles. This contradicts his later stance of support for Muggleborn witches and wizards, and protection of Muggles' rights.

Barely two months after their friendship began, Dumbledore and Grindelwald parted ways; it is unclear what caused the rift, but it is likely that it involved the death of Ariana. Bathilda recalls that Grindelwald had been at Albus' house that day, and had come home very disturbed, requesting an immediate Portkey, he had left the following day. Bathilda had felt it a great shame that Gellert had not stayed for the funeral, she thought he could be a great comfort for Albus. It was never understood why Aberforth had blamed Albus for Ariana's death, to the point that they had come to blows at the funeral. It was apparent that Aberforth felt that Albus' friendship with Gellert was somehow tied up in it, possibly because Gellert's expulsion from Durmstrang was because of near-fatal attacks on fellow students.

Grindelwald had then gone on to overthrow the Wizarding government in Europe, and despite repeated pleas from the Wizarding world, it was five years before Dumbledore had challenged, and defeated Grindelwald. Grindelwald's defeat had left some questions, however: Was it his affection for Grindelwald that had prevented Dumbledore from intervening earlier? And what of Ariana's death? If she had been a Squib, was her death accidental, as stated, or was it perhaps a first attempt at implementing their plan For The Greater Good?

The chapter ends at this point. Harry is dismayed at yet another loss: this time, his faith in Dumbledore, who to Harry had once embodied nothing but goodness and wisdom, has been shattered. Hermione reminds him that this is Rita Skeeter, but Harry points out that Rita didn't write Albus' letter to Gellert. Hermione mentions that Dumbledore's words, For The Greater Good, had become a slogan of Grindelwald's and were carved over the gates of Nurmengard, the prison Grindelwald had built to house his enemies. Hermione points at Dumbledore's youthfulness as a possible reason for his beliefs, but Harry says that he was the same age Harry and Hermione are now, and they are fighting Dark magic, not planning it. Hermione suggests that he was alone, having just lost his mother; Harry points out that he had his brother, and was keeping his Squib sister locked up. Hermione doubts she was a Squib, and that Dumbledore would ever have allowed oppression of Muggles. No matter what he thought at seventeen, he had ever since chosen the path of fighting evil. Hermione surmises that what Harry is really angry about is that Dumbledore had never told him this himself. Harry acknowledges that this may be true, and privately wonders how Dumbledore could have left him with such a mess, and whether Dumbledore had ever really cared about him.

On Ron's return, he and Harry discuss where the silver doe Patronus could have come from. Ron suggests that it could have been Dumbledore; Harry reminds Ron that not only is Dumbledore dead, but his Patronus was a phoenix. They also talk about the revelation that Dumbledore was friends with Grindelwald.

Some short time later, Hermione suggests that they should go visit Xenophilius Lovegood. Hermione, reading Rita's book, had found the original of Albus' letter to Gellert, and seen that Albus' signature, instead of an A, had the same "triangular eye" symbol that Xeno had been wearing at the wedding, that was apparently Grindelwald's mark, that had been on the headstone of the unknown Ignotus in Godric's Hollow, and that had been written on the copy of *Beedle the Bard* that had been given to Hermione in Dumbledore's will. She says that the symbol keeps coming up, and it's about time they figure out what it means.

Xeno tells them about the three Deathly Hallows. After the Trio escape from his house, Harry guesses that the reason Dumbledore had James Potter's cloak when James had been attacked was that it was one of the Hallows, and Dumbledore had been examining it. Xeno has mentioned that the three bothers in the story that talks of the Deathly Hallows are named Peverell.

Harry now remembers that Marvolo Gaunt had mentioned that the ring was an artifact of the Peverell family, and guesses that the ring, which had been a Horcrux, is inside the Snitch that had been left to Harry in Dumbledore's will. Hermione and Ron, seeing that Harry is becoming obsessed with the Deathly Hallows, feel that he should still be following Dumbledore's instructions to hunt and destroy Horcruxes. After escaping from Malfoy Manor, Harry meditates on the blue eye, so like Dumbledore's, that he had seen in the shard of the magic mirror. Why had Dumbledore made everything so difficult? Was it because Harry would need time to work things out? He also discusses wands with Mr. Ollivander. While he is determining whether he can get his wand fixed, and whether he can also use the wands that he captured from Draco Malfoy safely, he also discusses the Deathstick, an apparently undefeatable wand that is reported to have passed from wizard to wizard only by means of murder. Ollivander says that forcible removal of the wand is all that is necessary, if the wand will change allegiance at all.

Harry now understands what Voldemort seeks. The final Hallow, the Elder Wand, the Deathstick. He tells Ron and Hermione that Gregorovitch had once held the Elder Wand, but that it had been stolen from him by Grindelwald; that Grindelwald had used it in his conquest of Europe until he was defeated by Dumbledore; and that Dumbledore had held it ever since. Meanwhile, Harry is seeing simultaneously through Voldemort's eyes, as Voldemort goes to Hogwarts, opens Dumbledore's tomb, and removes the Elder Wand from the dead Dumbledore's hands. Despite his conscious decision to do nothing about the third Hallow, Harry wonders if he has done the right thing by concentrating on the Horcruxes, as Dumbledore wanted. And Ron, in amidst his doubts about Harry's course of action, also wonders in Dumbledore is truly dead—he wonders in particular who sent Dobby? Some time later, after the Trio have successfully escaped from Gringotts, Harry finds himself looking through Voldemort's eyes as the report of the bank break in is brought to him. Voldemort, after his initial rage-fueled outburst, thinks on the other Horcruxes. Harry has found the Cup, yes, and the Diary has been destroyed, but there is no way that Harry alone could have done this; Dumbledore must be involved. Dumbledore had never trusted him. Would he know if other Horcruxes had been destroyed? The diary, he had not had a body and that might have led him to miss it, but the others . . . he must check to see that they are still there.

Arriving in Hogsmeade, Harry, Hermione, and Ron are cornered by Death Eaters. They are pulled into the Hog's Head, where the barkeeper, who Harry now recognizes as Aberforth, brings them food. Harry notices the twin to the mirror that Sirius had given him; Aberforth says he had bought it from Mundungus Fletcher, and had been watching them through it. Harry notes that Aberforth's eyes are the same sky-blue color as Albus.' Aberforth recommends that Harry and the others wait until morning, then sneak off into the mountains and Apparate out. Harry says no, Albus had given them a mission. A nice easy mission, then? says Aberforth, one that three underage wizards would be likely to complete? Harry, wracked by doubt, does not answer. Aberforth goes on, saying that the Order of the Phoenix is finished and Voldemort has won. Harry protests that he must complete the task he was set, and Aberforth asks if Albus had been honest, if he had told Harry the full story. Harry cannot answer; Aberforth says that Albus had learned secrecy at his mother's knee.

To defuse the situation, Hermione asks if the one portrait on the wall is Ariana; Aberforth asks if she's been reading Rita's book, and Hermione blushes. To spare Hermione embarrassment, Harry tells Aberforth that they had learned about her from Elphias Doge. Launched into reminiscence, Aberforth reveals the family's past. Ariana was injured at the age of six by Muggle boys who saw her doing magic. She never recovered after that, the magic went inside her and would burst out uncontrollably whenever she go over-excited. Their father, Percival, attacked the boys; arrested by the Ministry, her refused to say why he had done it because Ariana would have been taken from them and confined permanently in St. Mungo's, and so was sent to Azkaban, where he died. Their mother had taken the family to Godric's Hollow, where she could start again. Kendra knew that Ariana would be taken away from them if anyone knew about her state, so she kept Ariana hidden from the neighbours. It was because she was hidden that the rumours began to arise that she was a Squib.

Ariana's care fell to Kendra and Aberforth, as Albus was too involved with his studies and academic prizes, and mostly stayed in his room. Aberforth was Ariana's favorite; he could always calm her down when she started having one of her outbursts. It was while he was away that Ariana went into one of her rages. Kendra was unable to calm her, and the magical outburst accidentally killed Kendra. Albus canceled his Grand Tour, returning home to care for Aberforth and Ariana, but then Grindelwald turned up. The two of them quickly became friends, and hatched an elaborate scheme for creating a new wizarding order. When Aberforth learned of these plans, a fight broke out, and a stray curse killed Ariana. Aberforth claims that Albus was glad to be free of the encumbrance, but Harry tells him Dumbledore was never free of it. After drinking the potion in the cave by the sea, Albus had been pleading with someone not to hurt them; Harry is convinced "them" was Ariana and Aberforth, and Albus was pleading, in his memory, with Grindelwald. Aberforth is not so sure.

Harry now says that whatever Aberforth thinks, Harry will continue his quest. Albus had thought Voldemort could be killed, and had told Harry how. If Aberforth refuses to help, Harry will have to try to make his own way into the school. Aberforth surrenders and shows them a passage.

Aberforth joins in the battle of Hogwarts. Seeing Harry run past looking for the Room of Requirement, he chides Harry for letting all the Slytherin students go, saying he should have kept some of them as hostages. Harry says Albus would never have done that.

Hermione says that just fighting isn't enough; Harry can tell them where Voldemort is, and they can go to deal with him directly. After some urging, Harry seeks

Voldemort's mind, and looking through his eyes, finds himself in the Shrieking Shack. Returning to himself, he leads the trio to the Shrieking Shack. Once there, they find Voldemort is talking to Snape about the Elder Wand. It seems Voldemort had expected great things from the Elder Wand, and was not getting them; the wand seemed reluctant to help him. Voldemort says this is because he had not defeated Dumbledore; Snape had killed him, and therefore the Elder Wand currently owed its allegiance to Snape. To gain the allegiance of the Elder Wand, Voldemort then has Nagini bite Snape, and departs. Harry, Hermione, and Ron rush to Snape's side, and Snape, as his last living act, sends out a great flood of memory which Harry captures in a crystal flask provided by Hermione.

In the lull in the fighting that follows, Harry, Ron, and Hermione return to the school, where Hermine and Ron, seeing the Weasley family mourning the loss of Fred, head into the Great Hall. Harry walks the damaged halls until he reaches the gargoyle guarding the Headmaster's office, and is surprised to find that the password that makes the gargoyle step aside is "Dumbledore." Once there, he empties the memories into Dumbledore's Pensieve, and enters them to view Snape's memories. He sees Snape pleading with Dumbledore to protect Harry's mother, Lily, from Voldemort, and Dumbledore asking what Snape would do in return; Snape answers, "Anything." He sees Snape in Dumbledore's office, anguished over Lily's death, and demanding to know why Dumbledore hadn't saved Lily; Dumbledore responds that James and Lily had put their trust in the wrong person, just as Snape had, and goes on to say that if Snape truly loved Lily, he would help protect her son when Voldemort returns. Snape grudgingly agrees but demands that Dumbledore promise never to tell anyone that he is protecting James Potter's son. In the next memory Snape is railing about what a bad student Harry is, to which Dumbledore replies that the other teachers report him as being likable and reasonably talented. He also asks Snape to keep an eye on Professor Quirrell. The scene shifts again, to Dumbledore and Snape watching the students leaving the Yule Ball in Harry's fourth year, and Snape telling Dumbledore that his and Igor Karkaroff's Dark Marks are becoming more distinct; Dumbledore accepts this information without much apparent reaction, then muses that perhaps they Sort the students into houses too soon. Dumbledore here seems to be implying that Snape might have been a better fit in a different house.

Still in Snape's memories, Harry now sees an apparently semi-conscious Dumbledore with his hand blackened and hanging over the edge of the desk; Snape is simultaneously pouring a golden potion down Dumbledore's throat, and working a spell with his wand on Dumbledore's wrist. When Dumbledore regains consciousness, Snape asks why he even tried on the ring? Dumbledore says he was a fool. Marvolo Gaunt's ring, now cracked, and the sword of Gryffindor lie on Dumbledore's desk. Snape says that he has been able to slow the curse, not stop it, and that Dumbledore now has at best a year to live. Dumbledore says that this makes things much easier to decide, and starts discussing Voldemort's plan to have Draco Malfoy murder him. Snape says that it is only being done to punish the Malfoys; Draco is expected to fail. Dumbledore guesses correctly that Voldemort wishes Snape to step in and complete the job when Draco fails, as Voldemort feels that he will not need a spy at Hogwarts soon, because it will be under his control. Dumbledore demands that Snape promise to watch over his students, and asks Snape to kill him when the time comes, both to spare the soul of Draco Malfoy, and to spare Dumbledore the indignity of being murdered by other Death Eaters who believe in playing with their prey. Snape initially argues, what about his own soul? Dumbledore responds that only Snape can know whether his soul will be damaged by agreeing to allow an old man with little time left to live to die with dignity. Snape grudgingly agrees.

Snape's next memory is Snape and Dumbledore walking through the castle grounds, where Snape is asking Dumbledore what he is doing with Harry all those nights. Dumbledore says that there is information that he must give to Harry before it is too late. Snape asks why he doesn't receive the same information, and Dumbledore explains that it is because his mission puts him at much greater risk of detection. Snape, angry at Dumbledore for refusing to tell all the details, threatens to rescind his promise, and Dumbledore somewhat wearily tells him to meet him in Dumbledore's office that night. Later, in the office, Dumbledore tells Snape that if Voldemort suddenly acts protective towards Nagini, Harry must then be told that he is a seventh, accidental Horcrux; and it is necessary that Voldemort kill him before Voldemort can be killed himself. Snape is deeply dismayed to hear that they have been protecting Harry all this time only so that he can be killed by Voldemort, and Dumbledore asks him if he is finally starting to care about the boy? Snape denies this and produces his Patronus, a doe, which leaps out the window and away. Moved to tears, Dumbledore asks Snape, "Still? After all this time?" and Snape says, "Always." In Snape's next memory, he is talking to the portrait of Dumbledore that now hangs in the office of the Headmaster. The portrait tells Snape that he must give Voldemort the correct date for Harry's departure from Privet Drive, if he is to retain Voldemort's trust. The only chance Harry has is if there are multiple Harrys, disguised by means of Polyjuice Potion. Snape is to plant that idea in Mundungus Fletcher's head. In Snape's final memory with Dumbledore, the portrait of Phineas Nigellus Black has just reported that Harry and Hermione are in the Forest of Dean; the portrait of Dumbledore tells Snape that he must plant the Sword of Gryffindor there for them to find, but he must not be seen himself. Snape says he has that all worked out, and taking the Sword from behind the portrait, leaves the office.

Harry, learning all this, comes to the conclusion that the only hope of defeating Voldemort lies in allowing himself to be killed. Entering Voldemort's camp in the Forbidden Forest, Harry is briefly mocked by Voldemort, who then fires the Killing Curse at him.

Harry finds himself in an otherworldly place which, as he observes it, changes into a simulacrum of King's

Cross Station. As he is trying to figure out where he is, what is going on, and what the crying, flayed-looking creature under one of the chairs is, Dumbledore appears, but a Dumbledore in full health, without the dead-looking wand hand. Harry asks if he is dead. Dumbledore replies no, that when Voldemort had taken Harry's blood to re-animate himself, he had tethered his life to Harry's, Harry cannot die while Voldemort lives. Harry's willing sacrifice of himself to protect his friends has also acted to protect them against Voldemort's magic, shielding them as Lily's sacrifice had for so long shielded Harry. What the killing curse directed at Harry had accomplished was the destruction of the seventh Horcrux, the fragment of Voldemort's soul adhering to Harry's; that was now destroyed and gone.

Asked about the interaction between the wands, Dumbledore admits that he is only guessing, but says he believes that the two wands, already sharing a common core, became even closer to each other when wielded in a duel between two wizards who not only shared blood, but also some of the soul. In that duel, Harry was the stronger wizard, because while Voldemort feared death, Harry was prepared for it. Harry's wand thus took in some power from Voldemort's, making it far more powerful than Malfoy's.

Harry asks where they are. Dumbledore says that this is Harry's show, asks what it looks like to Harry, and then is apparently amused when Harry says that it looks like King's Cross Station.

Dumbledore then explains about the Deathly Hallows. Looking uncomfortable at Harry's question, Dumbledore asks Harry's forgiveness for withholding information about the Hallows. As a youth, he had been obsessed with them; eager to escape death, and equally eager to achieve fame and glory for himself. This is why he resented having to take care of his mother, and after her death, his sister. This was also why he was so eager to befriend Gellert Grindelwald. The two young wizards bonded over their search for the Hallows, though they sought them for different ends. Dumbledore was seeking specifically the Resurrection Stone, so that he could reunite his family, while Grindelwald, if he thought of the Stone at all, would have wanted to use it to raise an army of Inferi. Grindelwald also wanted the Elder Wand, undefeatable in a duel, as a means of gaining power in the Wizarding community. Neither of them much cared about the Cloak, as they were both proficient in Disillusionment, but Dumbledore saw it as a way to hide Ariana.

Their friendship was short-lived, however, and the two got into a fight about Dumbledore's family obligations. Aberforth had joined in, and somehow a curse had gone astray and killed Ariana. Grindelwald had fled, as anyone but Dumbledore would have predicted, and returned to Europe. Some time later, he began his rise to domination of the European Wizarding community. Despite many pleas from the English Wizarding community, Dumbledore delayed dueling him, afraid to find out who had killed Ariana. Finally, it simply became too shameful to remain idle, and Dumbledore dueled Grindelwald and won, thus gaining the Elder Wand. Grindelwald had been imprisoned in Nurmengard, where Voldemort had found him; Dumbledore found it interesting that Grindelwald had claimed to have never had the Elder Wand, perhaps trying to protect Dumbledore in a belated act of remorse. Dumbledore had identified the ring of the Peverells as being another Hallow, the Resurrection Stone, and had given in to temptation and put the ring on, so that he might see his mother and sister again. The ring was a Horcrux, and protected by the curse which had destroyed his hand and shortened his life.

Speaking again directly to Harry, Dumbledore says that he had withheld this information about the Hallows to try and allow Harry to avoid the trap that Dumbledore himself had fallen into. He had hoped that Hermione's investigations would slow down Harry's attempts to seek the Hallows, and that Harry would thus have the opportunity to discover their true nature. Death's true master, says Dumbledore, is the the one who does not seek to run away from it.

Finally, Dumbledore tells Harry that he has a choice. As this is King's Cross, he can continue on to the platforms, and likely will be able to find a train there that will carry him onwards. Or he can return to the living world for a chance to finish Voldemort. Harry chooses to return, but asks Dumbledore if this conversation had been real, or only in his mind. Dumbledore responds that of course, it is all in his mind, but that does not make it any the less real. As the final battle reaches its climax, with Harry facing Voldemort, Harry tells Voldemort that Dumbledore had outsmarted him: the Elder Wand was never his, or Snape's, it had become Draco Malfoy's when Draco had disarmed Dumbledore. And as Harry had disarmed Draco, the Elder Wand now owed allegiance to Harry. Finally, in the Headmaster's office, Harry addresses the portrait of Dumbledore. He says that he had dropped the Resurrection Stone in the Forbidden Forest, and did not intend to go looking for it. He also says that he intends to return the Elder Wand to Dumbledore's tomb, in the hopes that it will lose its power there when Harry passes on. And he says finally that he intends to pass the Invisibility Cloak on to his own children when the time comes. Dumbledore indicates his approval.

In the epilogue, it should perhaps be noted that Harry has named his second son Albus Severus, after two headmasters of Hogwarts.

Strengths Dumbledore's strengths include experience, scholarship and intelligence. He has demonstrated innovation as a wizard and great power. He has been a rallying point and shown great leadership against an implacable foe. He is the only wizard Voldemort fears.

Perhaps unusually for a wizard, Dumbledore seems to be something of an inventor, specifically of mechanico-magical devices. His office is full of small, clockwork machines performing unknown tasks. We see two of these devices in action: a small device which, when queried, produces a plume of smoke in the shape of the object or entity being asked about; and the Deluminator, which apart from storing light sources within itself, will also allow the owner to hear conversations about him and will take him to the site of that conversation. One gets the feeling that the Ministry of Magic was unsuccessful when studying these devices to determine how they functioned. Dumbledore is also generous with those disenfranchised from the Wizarding World. He offers jobs to Lupin (a werewolf), Filch and Figg (both squibs), and Dobby and Winky (free elves no one else wanted to employ). He also employs Hagrid after his expulsion from Hogwarts and eventually makes him a professor.

Weaknesses Dumbledore's greatest weakness seems to be a certain inevitability about his own failings. This is particularly marked in Book 6, but is foreshadowed throughout the series where he is always preparing Harry as the one who must confront Voldemort.

Dumbledore is aloof and secretive, and while this undoubtedly helps him surprise his enemies, it may also have deprived him of others' assistance had he involved more people.

Dumbledore tends to believe the best in people. This is most evident when, after hearing Severus Snape's remorseful tale for having been a Death Eater, he allowed him to teach at Hogwarts, although this was in part to use Snape as a double agent. Others believe Dumbledore becomes misguided and bestows too much trust in those with questionable pasts.

Relationships with Other Characters Dumbledore has a strong relationship with many of the key characters of the books, including (but not limited to): Harry Potter, Severus Snape, Tom Marvolo Riddle (also known as Lord Voldemort) and Minerva McGonagall.

ANALYSIS

Over the course of the Harry Potter series, Dumbledore has proved to be an excellent advisor for Harry, and in this way has assisted greatly in Harry's victories over Voldemort.

One question that has come up is the issue of Dumbledore's age and accomplishments. It is more or less given that Dumbledore is about 115 years old when he dies, and the author has given his birth year as 1881. It says on his Wizard Card that he is noted for his work in Alchemy with Nicholas Flamel. In passing, we should mention that there is a Nicholas Flamel in the Muggle literature as well; he was a relatively famous alchemist in the 1300s. In that context, we should mention that the Nicholas Flamel in the Wizarding world and the one we know about apparently have similar, but not identical birth dates. One concern is that the book in which Hermione finds mention of Flamel is extremely old, and yet it gives ages for Nicholas and his wife Perenelle; unless the book magically updates ages, which presumably is possible, the ages in the book must be several years out of date. So we can safely say that Flamel in the Wizarding world is at least 665 years old (the age apparently given in the book), potentially as much as 750 years old if the book is only a hundred years old. The question is, if Dumbledore is in fact a mere spring chicken of 115, and Flamel had already been alive for at least 500 years when Dumbledore was born, how could Dumbledore have helped Flamel make the Philosopher's Stone upon which his ongoing life had depended? Careful reading reveals, however, that while Dumbledore worked with Flamel in alchemy, nowhere does it say he was involved in the creation of the Stone. There is insufficient information about the typical lifespans of wizards, but Dumbledore, at around 110 years, is described as appearing old, and he appears more aged than most of the other characters in the books. Only Nicolas Flamel is explicitly described as being older at 665 years old, though Elphias Doge went to school with Dumbledore and should be the same approximate age, and Bathilda Bagshot saw Dumbledore's mother Kendra as a contemporary and thus was likely older than Dumbledore. Flamel ultimately died after surrendering the Philosophers Stone, (also known as the Sorcerer's Stone) which preserved his life, to prevent it falling into Voldemort's possession. Flamel shared the Stone with Dumbledore, but it is unknown to what extent it may have been responsible for extending Dumbledore's life.

During the series, Dumbledore's character changes, to the point that no single analysis can do him justice. It seems reasonable to break analysis of Dumbledore as follows.

The First Five Books Dumbledore's character in the first five books of the series seems largely consistent. He seems the slightly dotty, elder genius, whose occasional extremely strange decisions are honoured because of his apparent extreme intelligence. In some regards, his eccentricity is utterly harmless; in other cases, his wisdom is interpreted as eccentricity. And particular choices that he makes—hiring Remus Lupin, trusting Severus Snape—are accepted purely because of his historical genius. His strength of character is particularly tested in Harry Potter and the Order of the Phoenix, where he is personally attacked because he chooses to report, repeatedly, an unpopular event, namely the return of Voldemort.

We can see that Dumbledore cares about Harry, more than any other student at the school. We see that Dumbledore is gently, or not so gently, educating Harry as to his place in the Wizarding world, that he is trying to train Harry for the role that has been revealed for him by the prophecy, as the one who will have to stand against Voldemort. It is at the end of the fifth book, in Dumbledore's office, that Harry's importance in Voldemort's career is revealed, and this is where we learn why Dumbledore is so interested in Harry.

Half-Blood Prince On many fan sites, it was remarked after the publication of Harry Potter and the Half-Blood Prince that Dumbledore was acting out of character. In retrospect, we can see that his character had changed; however, there was a real reason for it. When he re-enters the story, his hand is already injured, which means that he is now aware that he has only one year, at most, left to live. As such, he is no longer willing to wait; things that he must do, now have a definite deadline. On a number of occasions he has commented on not being afraid of death, and this might appear to be a contradiction. However, he is not actually acting out of fear of death, but rather out of a need to get a certain minimum amount of knowledge imparted before his time on earth ends.

Dumbledore, knowing that Harry must stand against Voldemort, concentrates some part of his energy on teaching Harry what he has learned about Voldemort in the hope that this will assist Harry in eventually defeating him. He is also working on uncovering enough of Voldemort's past himself that he will be able to assist Harry. It is during this time that, aware of the existence of multiple Horcruxes, Dumbledore will carry out the research that will lead him to the ring Horcrux and the resting place of the original locket Horcrux. We also will learn later that it is during this time that he is preparing Snape for his role in supporting Harry.

It is interesting to note that Dumbledore values Harry more highly than himself in the cavern of the locket Horcrux. Likely this is due to the prophecy, but Harry has not yet recognized this.

Many people believed, at the end of this book, that Dumbledore had erred badly in placing his faith in Snape. Whether or not that had been a mistake is not learned definitively until near the end of the final book.

Deathly Hallows It is in the final book of the series that we are finally granted some glimpse of the true depth of Dumbledore's character. Elphias Doge's eulogy reminds Harry that he had never known anything about Dumbledore's past, perhaps assuming that he sprang from the earth, full grown with long silver hair and beard. Rita Skeeter's muck-raking biography, referred to at various times in the course of events, tells us that there might be something unsavoury in Dumbledore's background. But finally it is Aberforth telling the family story to Harry, that reveals that Dumbledore had been a schemer and one who by and large kept his own council, that brings us to the realization that Dumbledore has been manipulating Harry to get him into a place where he can act directly against Voldemort. In King's Cross, Dumbledore tells Harry that the attraction of power proved too much for him as a youth, so he had carefully avoided it in his adult life; however, it seems he was not averse to being the power behind the throne, driving Fudge, and Harry, in the directions that he felt they needed to go.

QUESTIONS

1. Do we really know that Dumbledore is dead?
2. Did Dumbledore know he was going to die?
3. What about Dumbledore caused Tom Riddle to fear him so much?
4. How will Dumbledore's apparent death affect Harry's life?

GREATER PICTURE

The Ending of Half-Blood Prince One of the biggest issues at the end of book six was the apparent death of Dumbledore at the hands of Snape. Perhaps it was wishful thinking, perhaps it was the feeling that Dumbledore's part was not yet played out, perhaps it was clues dropped either deliberately or accidentally by the author, but between the release of the sixth book, and the release of the seventh, many of the readers of the book were convinced, or at least hopeful, that Dumbledore was in fact not dead, that he had arranged something with Snape to make it appear that he was dead, but that he would somehow come back to support Harry through the seventh book.

While there are a large number of things that suggest that Dumbledore's death were not all it seemed, the author has stated many times that Dumbledore definitely died in the sixth book. This is not to say that Dumbledore will not have any further influence past his death. The author has admitted that she had trouble writing some of his scenes in *Harry Potter and the Deathly Hallows* (The Observer, 6 February 2007). As we do still have his portrait in the Headmaster's office, we can conclude that, through this portrait (at least), he will still play a part in *Harry Potter and the Deathly Hallows*. An interesting point that has come up is linked to another statement of Dumbledore's in *Harry Potter and the Chamber of Secrets*, where Dumbledore says "I will only *truly* have left the school when none here are loyal to me." Harry echoes this statement at the end of *Harry Potter and the Half-Blood Prince*, in a context which leads us to believe he is truly loyal to Dumbledore. We know that it was that loyalty that brought Fawkes to Harry in the Chamber of Secrets; perhaps it will have the same effect again in the final book?

One interesting theory has surfaced about Dumbledore's death at Snape's hands. Going back to Harry's first Potions class, back in *Harry Potter and the Philosopher's Stone*, Snape says: "I can teach you how to bottle fame, brew glory, even *stopper death* . . ." This scene is apparently very important as readers have been referred back to it time and time again.

Now, let us look at the effect of the cursed opal necklace on Katie Bell in *Harry Potter and the Half-Blood Prince*. Quoting Professor Dumbledore: "She appears to have brushed the necklace with the smallest possible amount of skin: there was a tiny hole in her glove. . . . Luckily Professor Snape was able to do enough to prevent a rapid spread of the curse—" So we have the information that the type of curse that was on the necklace spreads from its contact point, and that Snape can stop the spread of the curse.

From elsewhere in that book, we have the information that it was Snape to whom Dumbledore went when his hand was injured. Is it possible that the ring which contained the Horcrux, or some part of its surroundings, was similarly cursed? It is possible, given that Dumbledore would have felt duty-bound to destroy the Horcrux before seeking assistance, that the curse had acted upon him to an extent that it was irreversible by the time he got to Snape. In fact, it is entirely possible that the only thing keeping Dumbledore alive at this point is the potion that "stoppers death." This would explain why Dumbledore was acting so differently in this book; he knows that his time is very limited, and he is in a great hurry to pass on all he knows before his inevitable departure.

Snape knew that he was not killing Dumbledore, because Dumbledore was effectively already dead, being kept alive only by the effects of a potion that Snape himself was providing. There may well have been some other arrangement between them; it is possible that Dumbledore planned to have Snape do this in order to solidify Snape's position in Voldemort's hierarchy. It is important to note in this context that Dumbledore did not fear death; we see this on several occasions, most notably at the end of the first book, where Dumbledore says, "after all, to the well-organized mind, death is but the next great adventure." This also tallies with the look of extreme distaste on Snape's face as he was killing Dumbledore—was he in fact doing this because he had to, rather than because he wanted to? It also dovetails with Snape's actions while he was running away at the end of that book. Knowing exactly what Harry was doing, instead of blocking Harry, he could have injured him, Stunned or even killed him, but he chose not to.

This theory rests on the idea that "stoppers death" means that the potion can stop or delay death; however, the word 'stopper' in this context could mean 'put a stopper on,' as in to brew and contain a potion capable of killing the drinker. While it is possible that "stopper" is merely a construction parallel to "bottle" and "brew," this seems unlikely given the emphasis; poisons are so very common that being able to brew one is hardly something worth boasting about, certainly not on a par with bottling fame and brewing glory.

Gellert Grindelwald   Through the course of the seventh book, it is gradually revealed that Dumbledore and the evil magician Grindelwald were friends when Dumbledore was seventeen. We can see, though the young Dumbledore cannot, that Grindelwald is power-hungry, and his overall aim is to set himself up as dictator. Dumbledore believes that the ultimate aim is to make it safe for people like his sister Ariana to exist; he believes that with the wizards in charge, and Muggles living with the benevolent supervision of Wizard-kind, that it will be possible for wizard children and Muggle children to co-exist. One very simple test of personality is the selection of the specific Hallow that you think is most valuable, and why. Grindelwald clearly thinks the Elder Wand, unbeatable in a duel, is the best, with the Resurrection Stone running second. Albus thinks the Resurrection Stone is the more important. To Grindelwald, the Resurrection Stone means an army of Inferi; to Albus, it means the return of his loved ones, his parents. Why does Dumbledore not see that Grindelwald is choosing the course of power? The author has said[1] that Dumbledore was infatuated with Grindelwald, and points out that love is blind. He chose to overlook Grindelwald's faults, and with the foolishness of youth, perhaps thought he could change Grindelwald to his own, somewhat more gentle ends.

Alecto Carrow

Gender: Female
Hair color: Unknown
Eye color: Unknown
Related Family: brother Amycus Carrow
Loyalty: Lord Voldemort

---

[1]. http://www.the-leaky-cauldron.org/2007/10/20/

OVERVIEW

Alecto Carrow, sister of Amycus Carrow, is a Death Eater.

ROLE IN THE BOOKS

Order of the Phoenix   Alecto and Amycus are two of the Death Eaters who break out of Azkaban Prison in about March. While their names are not mentioned at the time of the breakout, their membership in that group is strongly implied by Snape's comments in the early chapters of *Harry Potter and the Half-Blood Prince*.

Half-Blood Prince   Severus Snape mentions the Carrows when he is talking to Narcissa Malfoy and Bellatrix Lestrange. The Carrows take part in the attack on Hogwarts. Both of them are at the top of the tower when Snape kills Albus Dumbledore. As Harry chases Snape through the battle and out the front door, he sees Alecto dueling with Ginny Weasley.

Deathly Hallows   With Snape being appointed Headmaster, and Charity Burbage having been killed, there are vacancies for Defence Against the Dark Arts and Muggle Studies teachers. Alecto Carrow is given the post of Muggle Studies teacher. Neville Longbottom tells us that, under Alecto, the course seems to have become a diatribe against Muggles, in the best propaganda tradition, teaching how non-Magical people are dirty and behave like animals. Alecto, told by Lord Voldemort to expect Harry to visit Ravenclaw Tower, has herself let into the Ravenclaw common room before Harry's arrival. When Harry steps out from under the Invisibility Cloak to examine the statue of Rowena Ravenclaw, Alecto sees him and summons Lord Voldemort by touching her Dark Mark. She is then Stunned by Luna Lovegood, who was accompanying Harry, and had remained under the Invisibility Cloak. Bound by Professor McGonagall, she takes no further part in the story.

Relationships with Other Characters   While there is apparently some closeness between herself and her brother, Amycus Carrow, the only dealings we see her having with other people are situations in which she is operating from a position of power, or dueling. Her usual mode of interpersonal relationship seems to be taunting.

Alice Longbottom

Gender: Female
Hair color:
Eye color:
Related Family: husband Frank Longbottom, son Neville Longbottom, mother-in-law Augusta Longbottom
Loyalty: Albus Dumbledore

Alicia Spinnet

OVERVIEW

Alice Longbottom is Neville's mother.

Role In The Books

Goblet of Fire Harry sees a trial by the Wizengamot in Professor Dumbledore's Pensieve. The trial was of four Death Eaters, Barty Crouch Jr., Bellatrix Lestrange, Rodolphus Lestrange, and Rabastan Lestrange, who used the Cruciatus Curse on Frank Longbottom, in an attempt to discover what had happened to Lord Voldemort so that he could be returned to power. When that had failed, they had repeated the process on Alice. As a result, they both lost most of their mental faculties. Dumbledore tells Harry that the two of them are now residing at St. Mungo's, and asks Harry not to tell anyone else about this.

Order of the Phoenix At the celebration feast for Ron and Hermione becoming Prefects, Alastor Moody shows Harry a picture of the old Order. In that picture, we see Alice and Frank Longbottom smiling and waving.

Before Potions class one day, Draco Malfoy, taunting Harry, mentions something about people with mental infirmities being forced to stay at St. Mungo's. Neville, pushed beyond his endurance, tries to attack him, but is restrained by Harry and Ron. Ron and Hermione wonder what that was all about, but while Harry knows, he also cannot answer because of his promise to Dumbledore.

Just before Christmas, while Harry, Ron, Ginny, and Hermione are visiting Mr. Weasley at St. Mungo's, they run into Neville and his grandmother who are visiting Neville's parents. Alice walks up to Neville and hands him an empty Drooble's bubblegum wrapper, when they are leaving. His grandmother suggests he throw it away because Alice has given him so many, but Harry thinks he sees Neville secretly slip it into his pocket. Harry can still see a resemblance to the picture Moody had showed him.

When Neville is captured by Death Eaters in the Battle in the Ministry, Bellatrix Lestrange says she will torture him as she tortured his parents. She is stopped only by the arrival of members of the Order arriving.

Relationships With Other Characters Alice Longbottom, as mentioned, is the mother of Neville Longbottom and the wife of the disabled Frank Longbottom. She still seems to love her son, giving him what she can, even if it is only wrappers from Drooble's Best Blowing Gum. Because of her mental disability, we cannot form any clear idea of what her actual relationships with other characters would have been.

Alicia Spinnet

Gender: Female
Hair color: Unknown
Eye color: Unknown
Related Family: Unknown
Loyalty:

OVERVIEW

Alicia Spinnet is a member of Gryffindor House. She is two years ahead of Harry. She plays Chaser for the Gryffindor Quidditch Team.

ROLE IN THE BOOKS

Philosopher's Stone When the Gryffindor Quidditch team take to the air for their first match, against Slytherin in November, it turns out that Lee Jordan is the announcer. He identifies the Chasers on both teams who are holding the Quaffle. This is the first time we hear Alicia Spinnet's name, although presumably she has been practicing with Harry and the other members of the Quidditch team since Harry was made Seeker in mid-September.

Order of the Phoenix The first time we see Alicia Spinnet is at the first Quidditch practice of the year. While she has been active in the practice, the first real interaction with Harry is when Angelina stops the practice. Harry asks why the practice has been stopped, and Alicia points at Katie Bell, who is suffering from blood loss. When Fred and George take Katie to the hospital wing, Angelina dismisses the other team members from practice.

We hear from Fred and George that Professor Umbridge, in her new role as Hogwarts High Inquisitor, had been examining Professor Flitwick's class. In the process, she had asked Alicia some questions about the class, which she had answered positively.

Alicia is one of the students who attends the first meeting of what becomes Dumbledore's Army, in the Hog's Head. She also attends meetings regularly.

As the first Quidditch game of the year approaches, Alicia is sent to the Hospital Wing as her eyebrows are growing so quickly that they are obscuring her vision. It seems Miles Bletchley, the Slytherin Keeper, had jinxed her from behind in the library. Alicia plays in the match with Slytherin, a match which ultimately Gryffindor wins, despite Ron's poor Keeping, as Harry catches the Snitch for a final score of 160 to 40. Angelina, Alicia, and Katie then hold Fred back from attacking Draco Malfoy, who is taunting the entire Weasley family, while Harry holds George. When Draco starts insulting Harry's family as well, Harry is unable to restrain himself, and he and George attack Draco, while Fred remains restrained by the three Chasers.

At the last meeting of Dumbledore's Army before the Christmas break, Angelina tells Harry that she has finally managed to find new Beaters and a Seeker for the Quidditch team. The Seeker is Ginny Weasley, who is surprisingly good, though not a patch on Harry. It is Alicia who tells Harry the names of the new Beaters: Andrew Kirke and Jack Sloper. She adds that they are not brilliant, but compared to the other idiots who showed up . . . Harry's interaction with Alicia on the Quidditch pitch has largely ended with the lifetime ban he has received, and though we can safely assume that she continues to attend meetings of Dumbledore's Army, her work there is not singled out, so we see very little of her in the remainder of the book.

Half-Blood Prince   Alicia has graduated, and plays no role in this book.

Deathly Hallows   Neville Longbottom uses the linked Galleons to recall the members of Dumbledore's Army when Harry arrives at Hogwarts. Alicia is one of the ones who responds to the call. We see her later with Fred Weasley guarding one of the entrances to the secret passages into Hogwarts.

Ambrosius Flume

Gender:
Hair color: Unknown
Eye color: Unknown
Related Family: Unknown
Loyalty:

Overview

Ambrosius Flume is mentioned only in passing and has no direct role in the books.

Role in the Books

Half-Blood Prince   A graduate of Hogwarts, Ambrosius Flume was one of Horace Slughorn's favourite students. Slughorn introduced him to Ciceron Harkiss who gave him his first job. Ambrosius is now affiliated with Honeyduke's Sweetshop, and still sends Slughorn a hamper of sweets every birthday.

Amelia Bones

Gender: Female
Hair color: Unknown
Eye color: Unknown
Related Family: Edgar Bones (brother), Susan Bones (niece)
Loyalty: Ministry of Magic

Overview

Amelia Bones is the Head of the Department of Magical Law Enforcement.

Role in the Books

Order of the Phoenix   Harry is required to attend a hearing at the Ministry regarding his use of magic while underage and in the presence of Muggles. Somehow, instead of a hearing, this becomes a trial by the full Wizengamot. As the magic in question was the creation of a Patronus, Madam Bones is curious as to whether Harry can, in fact, produce a corporeal Patronus, one with an actual form. When the evidence has all been heard, it is Madam Bones who calls for the show of hands to vote on Harry's innocence or guilt.

At the organizational meeting of Dumbledore's Army, a question asked by Susan Bones suggests to Harry that she may be related to Madam Bones. Susan confirms that Amelia is her aunt.

Half-Blood Prince   In the meeting between Cornelius Fudge and the Muggle Prime Minister, we learn that Madam Bones has been murdered. The Prime Minister is quite upset about this, because it happened "right around the corner," and has not yet been solved.

Narcissa Malfoy, with Bellatrix Lestrange in tow, visits Severus Snape. In the course of their conversation, Bellatrix accuses Snape of not being loyal to the Death Eaters, saying that she is Voldemort's most trusted aide. Snape wonders if that is still true, and points out that it was information Snape provided that had made the murders of Madam Bones and the Vance families possible.

Strengths   During Harry's trial in Order of the Phoenix, Amelia Bones showed herself to be fair-minded and honest. In contrast to Fudge and Umbridge, she was uncorrupted and insisted on hearing the truth about Harry's case.

Amycus Carrow

Gender: Male
Hair color: Unknown
Eye color: Unknown
Related Family: sister Alecto Carrow
Loyalty: Lord Voldemort

Overview

Amycus Carrow, brother of Alecto Carrow, is a Death Eater.

Role in the Books

Order of the Phoenix   Alecto and Amycus are two of the Death Eaters who break out of Azkaban Prison in about March. While their names are not mentioned at the time of the breakout, their membership in that group is strongly implied by Snape's comments in the early chapters of *Harry Potter and the Half-Blood Prince*.

Half-Blood Prince   Severus Snape mentions the Carrows when he is talking to Narcissa Malfoy and Bellatrix Lestrange. The Carrows take part in the attack on Hogwarts. Both of them are at the top of the tower when Snape kills Albus Dumbledore.

Deathly Hallows   With Snape being appointed Headmaster, and Charity Burbage having been killed, there are vacancies for Defence Against the Dark Arts and Muggle Studies teachers. Amycus Carrow is given the post of Defence Against the Dark Arts teacher, and supervises its change of focus to remove the Defence aspects of the course. According to Neville Longbottom, under the supervision of Amycus Carrow the students were forced to perform horrible acts such as practicing the Cruciatus Curse on people who had earned detentions.

Amycus' sister Alecto, told by Lord Voldemort to expect Harry to visit Ravenclaw Tower, has herself let into the Ravenclaw common room before Harry's arrival.

She is then Stunned by Luna Lovegood, who was accompanying Harry under the Invisibility Cloak. Amycus, responding to her summons (Alecto has pressed her Dark Mark, to summon Voldemort), demands to be let in, but is unable to answer the riddle posed by the raven statue guarding the door. Having been let in by Minerva McGonagall, he finds his sister Stunned, and proposes to blame it on the students of Ravenclaw. McGonagall refuses to countenance this, Amycus spits at her, and Harry, outraged, hits Amycus with the Cruciatus curse. When he regains consciousness, McGonagall places him briefly under the Imperius curse, forcing him to give her his and his sister's wands, then lie down beside his sister, whereupon McGonagall binds them both. He takes no further part in the story.

Amos Diggory

Gender: Male
Hair color: Unknown
Eye color: Unknown
Related Family: Cedric Diggory
Loyalty:

Overview

Amos Diggory is the father of Cedric Diggory. He is the head of the Department of Magical Transportation, in the Ministry of Magic, and he works with Arthur Weasley.

Role in the Books

Goblet of Fire We first see Amos Diggory on the way to the Quidditch World Cup when he meets with Harry, Hermione, and the Weasley family: Ginny, Ron, Fred, George, and their father. Both families will be travelling by the same Portkey, so they are looking for it. Amos seems to be making a big thing of how his son Cedric had beaten "the famous Harry Potter" at Quidditch, while Cedric seems to be trying to down-play the size of that victory. At their destination, the Diggory family ends up in a different campsite, so we do not see them again this trip. Amos next appears, or at least his head does, in the Weasley's fireplace, where he is informing Arthur that Mad-Eye is getting into trouble. Once he has given Arthur what information he has, he accepts a slice of toast from Mrs. Weasley and departs.

We do not see Amos again until immediately before the Third Task. The parents of the Champions are invited to witness the last task, and Amos is present; he makes some cutting remarks about Harry's participating in the Tournament, but Cedric, being fair, tries to quiet him.

Finally, Amos and his wife visit Harry in the Hospital Wing after the third task has completed, and thank Harry for returning Cedric's body to them. When Harry tries to give them the prize money which Cedric would have won had he lived, they say they cannot accept it. Despite Harry's protests, they leave him with the entire thousand-galleon prize.

Analysis

Amos Diggory seems to be almost a stereotype—the man who is reliving his youth through his child. Amos is inordinately proud of the fact that Cedric beat Harry in a Quidditch match, and of Cedric's showing in the Triwizard Tournament; he seems to find these victories of Cedric's more worthy of mention than Cedric does himself. Cedric actually seems embarrassed by his father's effusive pride when they meet Harry and the Weasley family, in the opening chapters of *Harry Potter and the Goblet of Fire*.

Andrew Kirke

Gender: Male
Hair color: Unknown
Eye color: Unknown
Related Family: Unknown
Loyalty:

Overview

Andrew Kirke is a Beater on the Gryffindor Quidditch team. Along with Jack Sloper, he takes over for Fred and George Weasley.

Role in the Books

Order of the Phoenix In the last meeting of Dumbledore's Army before Christmas, Angelina Johnson tells Harry that they have finally managed to get replacement Beaters. Alicia Spinnet says the new beaters are Andrew Kirke and Jack Sloper, and that they are nowhere as good as Fred and George, but were the best of a very bad lot. On February 14th, Ron says that he can't go to Hogsmeade because Angelina wants a full day's practice. Ron is sceptical that it will help, because Sloper and Kirke are even worse than he is.

The following weekend, in the match against Ravenclaw, it is mentioned that one of the low points of the game is Kirke shrieking and falling backwards off his broom as Zacharias Smith zooms towards him with the Quaffle.

Half-Blood Prince When try-outs happen, Kirke is passed over; the new Beaters are Jimmy Peakes and Ritchie Coote.

Andromeda Tonks

Gender: Female
Hair color: light brown
Eye color: Unknown
Related Family: husband Ted Tonks, daughter Nymphadora Tonks; originally part of the Black Family but disowned
Loyalty: Order of the Phoenix

Overview

Andromeda Tonks, wife of Ted Tonks and mother of Nymphadora Tonks, was born into the Black family, but has been disowned.

ROLE IN THE BOOKS

Order of the Phoenix   When Harry and Sirius Black are discussing the tapestry of the Ancient and Honorable House of Black, Sirius mentions Andromeda in passing, saying she has been removed from the tapestry for the unforgivable crime of marrying a Muggle-born wizard, Ted Tonks. Nymphadora Tonks is their daughter.

Deathly Hallows   When Harry first sees Andromeda, he almost mistakes her for her sister, Bellatrix Lestrange, and is on the point of casting a jinx at her, but cannot find his wand. She, like her husband, is dismayed to hear that they had been ambushed by Death Eaters, and is concerned that her daughter may have gotten hurt.

Strengths   We don't see much of Andromeda, but we know she must have significant strength of character to marry Ted Tonks, a Muggle-born, in the full knowledge that this would cause the Black family to effectively cast her out.

Weaknesses   Her family—especially Nymphadora Tonks—is her weakness. This being all the family she has, with the Blacks disowning her, she will be concerned, perhaps overly so, with the wellbeing of her husband and daughter.

Relationships with Other Characters   She is Bellatrix Lestrange's and Narcissa Malfoy's sister. She was the middle Black daughter, Sirius Black's cousin, but she was disowned for marrying the Muggle Ted Tonks. (He is not really a muggle, but being descended from Muggles is not considered to be a true Wizard.) Her parents are Druella and Cygnus Black. She is the mother of Nymphadora Tonks, mother-in-law of Remus Lupin, wife of Ted Tonks, and grandmother of Teddy Remus Lupin.

Angelina Johnson

Gender: Female
Hair color: Black, in long plaits
Eye color: Brown
Related Family: Unknown
Loyalty:

OVERVIEW

Angelina Johnson is a member of Gryffindor House. She is a tall black girl with long black hair, which she wears in plaits, and brown eyes. She is two years ahead of Harry, and plays Chaser for the Gryffindor Quidditch Team.

ROLE IN THE BOOKS

Philosopher's Stone   Angelina presumably has been practicing Quidditch with Harry since he was made Seeker in mid-September, but is first mentioned by name in the changing room where the team is getting ready for their first match, against Slytherin. Angelina, identified as a Chaser, here corrects Oliver, who has just started his speech by saying "Men . . ." Once the team take to the air, Lee Jordan, the announcer, mentions her when the Quaffle is in her possession, commenting as an aside that he is disappointed that she won't go out with him. Angelina scores several goals in this first match, against Slytherin.

We later hear that she has a penalty called against her in the match against Hufflepuff when Professor Snape is officiating.

Goblet of Fire   Angelina is the first Gryffindor to successfully place her name in the Goblet of Fire; it does not, however, select her as a Champion.

Angelina goes to the Yule Ball with Fred Weasley.

Order of the Phoenix   Angelina meets up with Harry at breakfast on the first day of classes, saying that with Oliver Wood having graduated, she has been made Captain, and the house Quidditch team will need a new Keeper. She says that there will be tryouts on Friday evening, and orders Harry to attend, saying that she wants the entire team to be present so that they can be sure that the new Keeper will fit in with the whole team. Harry is pleased at her being Captain; he believes that there will be much less talking with Angelina in charge.

When Harry gets detention from Professor Umbridge, Angelina is furious at him, deciding that it is his fault that he got detention, and orders him to do whatever he can to get out of detention and be there for practice. After she has gone, Ron comments that they should check with Puddlemere United and see if Oliver Wood is still alive, as Angelina seems to be channeling his spirit.

Finding that Harry was not able to convince Umbridge to change his Friday detention, Angelina angrily suggests that people who want to stay on the team will find a way to make it to practices.

Friday evening, after the try-outs, Angelina apologizes to Harry for her earlier curtness, and says that she may have been too hard on Wood; managing is a bit stressful. She goes on to say that Ron had not been the best Keeper she tried out, but of the two better, one was not willing to commit the time to practice and the other was a bit of a whiner, and Angelina is hoping that Ron, being from a family with excellent Quidditch players, will develop over time. She then says that there will be a practice Saturday at two, and asks Harry to please be there and to help Ron out a bit. Before the practice starts, Angelina mentions that there are some people in the stands, and that the team should just ignore them. Harry suspects that these will be Slytherins, present to jeer, and so it turns out. In the warm-up before the practice, Ron passes the Quaffle to Katie too enthusiastically, and it catches her in the nose. Fred Weasley gives her something small and purple from his robe pocket, saying that it will clear up immediately. It does not, however. When Angelina tells her to do something about it, Fred examines what he has in his robe pocket and appears horrified by what he sees. Shortly afterwards, Angelina stops the practice; Alicia points Harry at Katie, who is being attended by Fred, George, and Angelina. Fred says that she had likely been given a Blood Blisterpod by mistake, and that he and George would take her to the Hospital Wing. Angelina says that with no Beaters and only two Chasers, there is no point continuing the practice, and dismisses them.

The following Monday, Harry mentions that Professor Quirrell happened to have Lord Voldemort stuck to the back of his head, and gets another week's detention from Professor Umbridge. On Tuesday morning, Angelina shouts at Harry loud enough that Professor McGonagall comes to see what is going on. She penalizes Harry five House points, in addition to his detention, because detention does not seem to work, and warns Angelina to confine her shouting to the Quidditch pitch.

Angelina is one of the students who attends the first meeting of what becomes Dumbledore's Army, in the Hog's Head.

When Educational Decree Number Twenty Four appears the next day, it is Angelina who tells Harry and Ron that it also means that the Gryffindor Quidditch Team has been disbanded. That night, Angelina tells them that there is no Quidditch practice, as Umbridge needs "time to consider;" but the Slytherin Quidditch team is already re-formed. The following day, Angelina comes to Harry and Ron at break, telling them that she has appealed to McGonagall and gotten the team re-formed. She tells Harry and Ron that practice will be at 7 that evening. Ron is dismayed, as the weather is simply appalling.

The weather has not improved by 7, and even though Angelina recalls that Hermione had used the Impervius charm earlier to give him at least some vision in similar circumstances, and has Harry teach that charm to the rest of the team, still very little is actually accomplished as nobody can see what is going on.

Harry is relieved a couple of days later when Angelina tells him that Quidditch practice is canceled, not only because the weather is still foul, but also because he has been told how to get into the Room of Requirement, and so has scheduled the first meeting of the Defence Against the Dark Arts group for that evening. He asks Angelina to pass the word to Alicia and Katie Bell. Angelina is a bit taken aback, but it seems she does tell the others. Angelina schedules more Quidditch practice as the first game of the year, against Slytherin, approaches. As a result, there are fewer meetings of Dumbledore's Army.

Angelina leads the team into the match with Slytherin, a match which ultimately Gryffindor wins, despite Ron's poor Keeping, as Harry catches the Snitch for a final score of 160 to 40. Angelina, Alicia, and Katie then hold Fred back from attacking Draco Malfoy, who is taunting the entire Weasley family, while Harry holds George. When Draco starts insulting Harry's family as well, Harry is unable to restrain himself, and he and George attack Draco, while Fred remains restrained by the three Chasers.

Angelina is, of course, dismayed when she finds out that her Seeker and both of her Beaters have received lifetime bans, and goes off disconsolately to the girls dorms, saying that she is hoping that she will wake up in the morning and find this is all a bad dream.

At the last meeting of Dumbledore's Army before the Christmas break, Angelina tells Harry that she has finally managed to find new Beaters and a Seeker for the Quidditch team. The Seeker is Ginny Weasley, who is surprisingly good, though not a patch on Harry. It is Alicia who tells Harry the names of the new Beaters: Andrew Kirke and Jack Sloper.

While Angelina continues to lead the Quidditch team, Harry, being unwillingly reduced to a mere spectator, no longer interacts with her particularly on the pitch. In Dumbledore's Army, we assume that she still attends and performs to a reasonable standard, but we do not see anything in particular of her there either.

Deathly Hallows Summoned by the enchanted Galleon that was given to her by Hermione as a way to announce meetings of Dumbledore's Army, Angelina returns to Hogwarts in time to take part in the battle for the school.

Relationships with Other Characters In the books she is shown to have a close relationship with fellow chasers Katie Bell and Alicia Spinnett. She's known and liked by Harry, Ron and Hermione. Starting from the fourth book, we see tiny hints of a possible relationship between her and Fred Weasley. The two of them attend the Yule Ball in the fourth book, and Fred seems to have a bit of a crush on her.

For the final year of writing the seventh and final book, the author was followed by a camera team from the British TV network ITV. After completing the seventh book, the author drew up a chart of the Weasley family tree, which showed that George had married one Angelina, quite possibly Angelina Johnson, and had two children with her, named Roxanne and Fred.

Anthony Goldstein

Gender: Male
Hair color: Unknown
Eye color: Unknown
Related Family: Unknown
Loyalty: Albus Dumbledore

Overview

Anthony Goldstein is a student in Ravenclaw house. He is in Harry's year.

Role in the Books

Order of the Phoenix In the Hogwarts Express, Ron Weasley informs Harry that Anthony is one of the two new prefects for Ravenclaw. (The other is Padma Patil.)

Anthony Goldstein is one of the students who attends the first meeting of what becomes Dumbledore's Army, in the Hog's Head.

Anthony is also one of the six members of Dumbledore's Army who see Draco Malfoy attempting to jinx Harry on the Hogwarts Express, and promptly return fire, leaving Draco, Crabbe, and Goyle looking like gigantic slugs squeezed into Hogwarts robes.

Deathly Hallows Anthony Goldstein is one of the members of Dumbledore's Army who have ended up in the Room of Requirement when the school itself became too hostile for them. While he apparently takes part in the Battle of Hogwarts, little is actually known of his role there.

Antonin Dolohov

Gender: Male
Hair color: Unknown
Eye color: Unknown
Related Family: Unknown
Loyalty: Lord Voldemort

Overview

Antonin Dolohov is a Death Eater with a long, pale, twisted face who was convicted of the brutal murders of Gideon and Fabian Prewett and imprisoned in Azkaban.

Role in the Books

Goblet of Fire When Harry was viewing Albus Dumbledore's memories in the Pensieve, he saw a session where Igor Karkaroff was naming Death Eaters while trying to bargain for a shorter sentence. One of the names he provided was that of Dolohov; Bartemius Crouch, who was presiding over the Wizengamot at that point, said that they had already apprehended Dolohov.

Order of the Phoenix Dolohov broke out of the wizard prison with Bellatrix Lestrange, Augustus Rookwood, and seven other convicted Death Eaters.

In the Battle at the Department of Mysteries, Dolohov and Jugson had cornered Hermione, Harry, and Neville, and Hermione Silenced him when he tried to call out their location to bring the other Death Eaters. After Jugson had been Petrified, Dolohov seriously injured Hermione with a curse in the form of a streak of purple flame, broke Neville's wand and nose, and ended up Petrified by Harry. Later re-animated, he was in the battle in the room of the Veil, where he was again Petrified by Harry.

Half-Blood Prince When Lord Voldemort, or Tom Riddle as he is then known, is seen in Albus Dumbledore's memories returning to Hogwarts to apply for the job of teacher of Defence Against the Dark Arts, Dumbledore asks him about his "friends" waiting for him in Hogsmeade. Dolohov is one of the friends mentioned by name, along with Mulciber, Nott, and Evan Rosier.

Deathly Hallows When Harry, Ron, and Hermione escape from the Weasley wedding and head for Tottenham Court Road, they are tracked there by two Death Eaters, Dolohov and Thorfinn Rowle. Rowle is Stunned by Harry from the concealment of his Invisibility Cloak; Dolohov is Petrified by Hermione. They both then have their memory modified by Hermione.

In the first part of the battle of Hogwarts, as Harry, Ron and Hermione make their way invisibly through the Entrance Hall on their way to the Shrieking Shack, they pass Dolohov who is dueling with Dean Thomas. Peeves drops a Snargaluff pod on Ron's head. Distracted by this, Dolohov is Petrified by Parvati Patil, who is also there dueling with Travers.

When Harry heads for the Forbidden Forest to meet Voldemort, Dolohov is one of the two guards that he follows; the other is Yaxley.

Arabella Figg

Gender: Female
Hair color:
Eye color:
Related Family:
Loyalty: Order of the Phoenix

Overview

Arabella Doreen Figg is Harry Potter's neighbor on Privet Drive, who often watches him when the Dursleys are on some fun outing or other, such as Dudley's birthday parties. She is a classic old lady with too many cats.

Role in the Books

Philosopher's Stone Harry dreads Dudley's birthday because it means he will be sent to Mrs. Figg's, where he will spend the entire day being told, again, about the life histories of the cats in her photo album. As it turns out, however, she has broken her leg and so Harry has to go to the zoo with Dudley, much to Dudley's displeasure. After the events at the zoo, Harry is locked, once again, in the cupboard under the stairs; by the time he has been released, Dudley has knocked over Mrs Figg, on her crutches, with his new racing bike.

When he has to visit her later, she is not quite so keen to tell him about all her cats; it seems that she broke her leg tripping over one of them . . . so he gets to watch television instead.

Chamber of Secrets As the book starts the day before Harry is locked in his room, there is no time for us to encounter Mrs. Figg before Harry is spirited away to The Burrow.

Prisoner of Azkaban Harry spends all his available at Privet Drive time dealing with his Aunt Marge, and as a result we hear nothing about Mrs. Figg in this book.

Goblet of Fire Harry's time at home at the beginning of this book is very limited, and he does not get a chance to speak with Mrs. Figg before the Weasleys arrive to take him to the Quidditch World Cup.

At the very end of the book, when Professor Dumbledore is sending people off on missions, he tells Sirius Black to get in touch with "the old crowd," and explicitly mentions Arabella Figg as one of that group. The reader doesn't notice the name going by, as who would connect batty old Mrs. Figg with her cats to the world of magic?

Order of the Phoenix Much to Harry's surprise, it is revealed that Mrs. Figg is a Squib and a member of the Order of the Phoenix. Apparently, she was stationed to live next to Harry in order to keep an eye on him and the Dursleys. With the re-creation of the Order of the Phoenix, she was formally brought into that order to assist in guarding Harry; she sees the attack on him and Dudley by Dementors; and she is a witness at the Wizengamot when Harry is tried for using magic on that occasion. Although she does testify that Harry was attacked by Dementors, the author has stated[1] that she never actually saw the Dementors, but recognized them by their effects.

Half-Blood Prince Harry spends so little time on Privet Drive in this book that there is no time to mention Mrs. Figg or the other members of the Order who are likely still present and keeping an eye on Harry. However, it is mentioned in passing that she attends Dumbledore's funeral, along with many other Order members.

Deathly Hallows Harry is concerned with preparations for his departure, and does not leave the house until the Order is there to take him away. Thus, again we do not get to meet Mrs. Figg in this book.

Strengths Arabella is a squib and as such is not tracked or noticed by the Ministry of Magic. Thus she is able to assist Dumbledore in keeping a eye on Harry without the knowledge of the Ministry.

Weaknesses Arabella is unable to use magic to defend herself or Harry. Without a wizard to assist, her guardian capabilities are limited.

Relationships with Other Characters Arabella Figg is a Squib, and as such her relationships with the rest of the Wizarding world are of a very uneven sort; most pity her because she is part of their world, yet unable to partake, being unable to do any sort of magic. The author has said[2] that Arabella does have a "roaring business" breeding cat-Kneazle hybrids like Crookshanks; it is possible that Crookshanks came from Mrs. Figg originally, but that cannot be certain.

QUESTIONS

1. Someone has to be placed near the Dursleys' to watch over Harry while he is growing up—the prophecy makes it clear that he will be an important wizard. Why a Squib?

GREATER PICTURE

A popular theory for why Mrs. Figg is selected as guard for Harry is that no one could detect their magical power because Arabella is a Squib and Harry is underage. Harry's being underage would, of course, be no bar to the detection of his use of magic, as is amply demonstrated when the Ministry for Magic warns him about the use of magic in *Harry Potter and the Chamber of Secrets*. Perhaps a better explanation is Dumbledore's sympathy for the non-magical. It is likely Dumbledore who managed to get Argus Filch a job as caretaker of the castle at Hogwarts, a job which is one of the few in the Wizarding world of which he is capable; likewise, this watchman job is one suited to Mrs. Figg's lack of Magical ability.

Aragog

Gender: Male
Hair color: Dark
Eye color: White, he is blind
Related Family: Wife: Mosag, Children: Hundreds
Loyalty: Hagrid and no other human.

OVERVIEW

Aragog is an Acromantula, a mythical giant spider whose venom is very useful in potions. He was raised by Rubeus Hagrid and he is very loyal to him. He regards all other humans a prey. He only makes a personal appearance in *Harry Potter and the Chamber of Secrets*, but is still useful later on.

ROLE IN THE BOOKS

Chamber of Secrets From the information provided by Riddle's diary, he seems like a likely resident of the Chamber, but it turns out that he is not. He gives Harry and Ron a vital piece of information which may help them discover the location of the Chamber of Secrets. But right after being so helpful, he gives his family permission to eat them.

Half-Blood Prince At the begining of the book we learn from Hagrid that he is very ill. Towards the end he dies and his funeral is a crucial event in the book.

Driven by his greed (Acromantula venom is very expensive), Professor Slughorn allows himself to converse with Harry for an extended period in the presence of mead. Thus Harry is able to convince Slughorn to surrender his memory of Tom Marvolo Riddle, which is crucial to an understanding of Lord Voldemort's plans.

Deathly Hallows Aragog is mentioned in passing during the last Battle at Hogwarts when one of his descendants bursts through a hole in the castle wall. A large number of his descendants are also mentioned as apparently carrying off Hagrid, and Lord Voldemort is mentioned as having set up camp in the Forbidden Forest where Aragog and his family had once been.

Strengths Loyalty, can keep his family in check.

Weaknesses Tendency to enjoy eating everything around. Afraid of certain creatures and unwilling to even name them.

---

1. http://www.jkrowling.com/textonly/en/faq_view.cfm?id=63
2. http://www.jkrowling.com/textonly/en/faq_view.cfm?id=63

GREATER PICTURE

In *Harry Potter and the Chamber of Secrets* we learn that Voldemort, or as he was then known Tom Riddle, had framed Hagrid and Aragog for a murder they did not commit. In *Harry Potter and the Half-Blood Prince*, through Aragog's death and Hagrid's grief Harry obtained a piece of information that is vital for the fight against Voldemort. Another example of J.K. Rowling's love of symmetry.

Argus Filch

Gender: Male
Hair color: Unknown
Eye color: Unknown
Related Family: Unknown
Loyalty:

OVERVIEW

Argus Filch is the caretaker at Hogwarts. He has a pet cat called Mrs. Norris who is usually on the prowl, keeping an eye out for him.

ROLE IN THE BOOKS

Philosopher's Stone   Harry and Ron get off on the wrong foot with Filch on the very first day of classes when he catches them trying to enter the forbidden corridor. They had not meant to visit that corridor; they had simply gotten lost on the way to Transfiguration class. They are saved from being locked in the dungeons by Professor Quirrell, who happens to be passing by.

At tea with Hagrid on the Friday of their first week, Harry is pleased that Hagrid refers to Filch as "that old git." Hagrid also says that he can't abide Mrs. Norris, and that Filch has apparently instructed Mrs. Norris to follow Hagrid around.

Shortly after this, Draco Malfoy challenges Harry to a Wizard's Duel. Harry and his second, Ron, followed by Hermione and Neville Longbottom, go to the Trophy Room, the designated site for the duel, but instead of finding Draco there, they hear Filch approaching. Trying to escape, Neville knocks over a suit of armour, and in the ensuing mad dash to escape they end up in the forbidden third floor corridor. Peeves has followed them as far as the door, but decides in the end that it would be more fun to taunt Filch than it would be to lead him to the four, thus allowing them to escape.

Trying to retrieve the copy of *Quidditch Through the Ages* that Harry had taken out of the library, and that Professor Snape had confiscated, Harry looks into the staff room, where he finds Filch binding up a wound on Snape's leg. Snape is incensed that Harry has seen this injury.

Harry receives an Invisibility Cloak for Christmas, and trying it out that night, opens a book in the Restricted Section of the library. The book starts screaming, and Harry runs, ducking under Filch's arm as Filch, wild-eyed, enters the Library. When Harry pauses for breath, he is alarmed to realize that, despite the distance he has traveled, Filch is approaching, saying that someone had been in the Restricted section. Harry is further dismayed to discover that the person Filch is talking to is Snape. The corridor is so narrow that the two of them won't be able to get past Harry, so Harry retreats though an open doorway, finding himself in a disused classroom containing the mirror of Erised.

When Hagrid's baby dragon, Norbert, is sent away, Hermione and Harry forget the Invisibility Cloak at the top of the tower. Filch catches them as they descend back into the school. Some time later, Filch escorts them, with Neville and Draco, who have also received detentions, over to Hagrid's, where they will be assisting Hagrid in searching for something that is killing unicorns.

Chamber of Secrets   At the Entrance Feast, Professor Dumbledore mentions that "our caretaker, Mr. Filch," has banned certain items; the full list of banned items is posted on his door.

Harry and Ron have received detention for driving a flying car into the Whomping Willow; at the end of the first week of classes, Professor McGonagall tells them that Ron's detention will be served with Filch, polishing the trophies, while Harry will be helping Gilderoy Lockhart answer his fan mail. Ron later says that he had a recurrence of the jinx he had tried to cast at Malfoy, and belched up a great lot of slugs on a Special Award for Services to the School, which he had then had to polish about ten times to get the slug slime off. The Autumn weather is dismal and wet, and Harry, coming in from Quidditch practice, is sodden and muddy. Stopping to talk with Nearly Headless Nick, he is surprised by Filch's cat, Mrs. Norris, and, before he can make his escape, Filch himself. Filch, enraged, hauls Harry off to his office, where he begins writing him up for "befouling the castle." He is interrupted, however, by a loud crash from upstairs; shouting "Peeves!" he rushes off. Harry, left on his own, finds a letter from a company called "Kwikspell" on Filch's desk; looking at it, he sees that it is full of testimonials from people who say that the Kwikspell course had taught them magic when they had been unable to do any before. Harry, hearing Filch returning, puts the letter back on his desk. Filch returns, apparently pleased; apparently Peeves has dropped a very valuable Vanishing Cabinet, and Filch seems to feel that this will compel Dumbledore to evict Peeves. Filch notices that the Kwikspell letter has been moved; he quickly shuffles it out of sight, then, looking embarrassed, tells Harry that he's free to go.

At Hallowe'en, Mrs. Norris is found Petrified and hanging from a torch bracket, near words scrawled on the wall: "*The Chamber of Secrets has been opened. Enemies of the Heir, beware!.*" Enraged, Filch says that Potter has something to do with it, because he was in the vicinity at the time. Professor Dumbledore, arriving, takes Mrs. Norris off the torch bracket, and in company with Filch, Professor Snape, Professor McGonagall, Gilderoy Lockhart, Harry, Ron, and Hermione, carries her to Lockhart's office where he examines her. While it turns out that she is not dead, Dumbledore is unable to suggest how she was Petrified. Filch says that Harry must be involved, because he knows that Filch is . . . a Squib.

Filch demands that someone be punished; Snape suggests that Harry must know more about things than he is telling, and suggests suspending him from the Quidditch team, a suggestion which McGonagall immediately resists. Professor Dumbledore reminds everyone that Harry is innocent until proven guilty, and tells Harry, Ron, and Hermione that they are free to go. Ron later explains why Filch was so upset; a Squib is a child of magical parents who is unable to do magic himself.

Over the next several months, we often see Filch wandering the hall trying to give students detention for "acting cheerful" or "breathing too loudly," sitting in a chair immediately under the torch bracket where Mrs. Norris was found, or trying to scrub the writing off the wall. Shortly after Christmas, Harry and Ron hear an outburst from Filch; peering around the corner, they find that he has abandoned his usual station, which turns out to be right outside Moaning Myrtle's bathroom, because Myrtle has turned on all the water and is flooding the hall. Investigating, Harry and Ron discover that someone has thrown a diary down a lavatory, and Myrtle is upset because it went through her head.

Filch does not play much more of a role in this book, but we do see him briefly at the end of the book when he is re-united with Mrs. Norris.

Prisoner of Azkaban   We don't see a lot of Filch in this book. At the first Hogsmeade weekend, Filch is checking people against a long list of names to see if they have permission to visit the village; Harry, not having permission, watches Ron and Hermione pass him, and then returns to Gryffindor tower. On the way, he is intercepted by Fred and George Weasley, who show him the Marauder's Map, a magical map that shows where everyone is in the castle. They say that they had stolen it from Filch's files once when they were being written up for setting off dungbombs in the halls, but seeing how much greater Harry's need is than theirs, they give it to him, with instructions how to use it. This map is Harry's ticket to Hogsmeade, as it shows secret passages out of the school.

Filch is also present at Christmas dinner, and apparently it is rather ghastly watching him try to have a good time.

Goblet of Fire   Filch's role in this book is again minor. Harry notes that he is setting out extra chairs at head table; Ron wonders why four chairs, as the only two guests that they know about are Madam Maxime from Beauxbatons, and Igor Karkaroff from Durmstrang. Ron's question is answered when Professor Dumbledore introduces the other two judges for the Triwizard Tournament, Ludo Bagman, and Bartemius Crouch. Shortly afterwards, Dumbledore asks Filch to bring out the casket that holds the Goblet of Fire.

When Harry, acting on a hint given to him by Cedric Diggory, visits the Prefects' Bathroom to try and decipher the clue in the Egg, he uses the Marauder's Map to see where Filch and Peeves are before venturing into the hallways. He checks again before heading back to Gryffindor Tower, and as he is doing so, he sees Bartemius Crouch in Snape's office. He chooses to investigate; getting his foot caught in a trick step, he drops the egg which immediately starts wailing. This summons Filch and, shortly, Snape. Filch believes that Peeves has stolen the Egg from one of the Champions and dropped it. Snape dismisses this concern, saying that someone has been in his office, and it must have been a wizard because of the charm he put on his door. The presence of the egg convinces Snape that Harry is there under his Invisibility Cloak. Professor Moody's arrival prevents Snape from finding Harry, and Moody sends both Snape and Filch on their separate ways before rescuing Harry from the trap he has gotten himself into.

Order of the Phoenix   Harry's scar pains him at the end of one of his sessions of detention with Dolores Umbridge, and he feels a need to write to Sirius Black, his godfather, to tell him about this. As he heads for the Owlery to mail the letter, he is spotted by Mrs. Norris. He is joined in the Owlery by Cho Chang, who is mailing off a birthday present for her mother. As they are talking, Filch bursts in, accusing Harry of preparing to mail off an order for Dungbombs. He demands to search Harry's pockets, but Cho defends him, saying that whatever it is, Harry had already sent it, she saw him.

When Harry heads to Hogsmeade for the next Hogsmeade weekend, Filch sniffs at him suspiciously; evidently he is carrying through on his threat in the Owlery that he will be watching for any scent of dungbombs on Harry. Harry mentions the episode in the Owlery to Ron and Hermione, wondering why Filch would have thought that he would order Dungbombs. Hermione wonders who had tipped Filch off, and suggests that it might have been a ploy to get a look at Harry's mail.

When Hedwig returns with Sirius' answer, she has been attacked, and possibly the message that she carries has been read. This seems to confirm Hermione's suspicion that Filch had been instructed to try and read Harry's mail. Shortly after Dumbledore leaves and Umbridge is appointed Headmistress, she asks Filch to summon Harry to her office. Filch is ecstatic, talking about how things will change now she's in charge. Umbridge has apparently told Filch that she is in favour of corporal punishment, and will be arranging to have Peeves evicted. Having told Harry all this, he announces Harry at Umbridge's door and then departs.

As Harry's interview with Umbridge is about to end, a series of explosions sounds in the main stairs. Umbridge and Filch run to investigate, but are powerless to handle the fireworks which Fred and George have set off. Having unsuccessfully tried to charm one of the fireworks away, Umbridge instructs Filch not to use magic against them; Harry is amused by this as he recalls that Filch, being a Squib, can't use magic anyway. Filch's attempt to dispose of a firework by hitting it with a broom is also unproductive, resulting only in a burning broom.

After Easter break, Fred and George become aware that Harry has need of Umbridge's fireplace, which is the only safe route he knows of to contact Sirius. They tell Harry that they are going to set off a diversion at 5PM. Though Hermione repeatedly advises against it, Harry decides to make use of the diversion to talk to Sirius. As he is speaking with Sirius, Harry hears someone entering Umbridge's office; hiding under his Invisibility Cloak, he watches as Filch enters the office and locates the forms to authorize whipping. Following Filch, Harry finds the twins, trapped by Umbridge in the Entrance Hall. Filch presents Umbridge with the necessary paperwork, and the twins, saying that they have had enough formal education, Summon their brooms and depart Hogwarts. The diversion turns out to be a swamp, which now fills an entire corridor. Umbridge is unable to remove it, and the other teachers seem disinclined to try, so Filch is given the additional duty of taking students to their classes by punt. Additionally, in Fred and George's absence, many students are trying out for the role of chief troublemaker, and the halls are overwhelmingly redolent of dungbombs and stink pellets. Filch, along with Umbridge and her Inquisitorial Squad, are run ragged trying to catch troublemakers.

Presumably, Filch's life gets somewhat easier once Umbridge is fired, however, we don't hear of him again in this book.

Half-Blood Prince Filch's role in this book is again diminished. We do hear from him that he feels that Umbridge is the best head Hogwarts has ever had; he seems to have forgotten the little matters of the swamp in the fifth floor corridor and the epidemic of dungbombs and stink pellets.

We hear that Filch has imposed a blanket ban on all products of Weasleys' Wizard Wheezes, and is scanning everyone who goes in and out of the school with Secrecy Sensors. He scans the Trio as they depart for their first Hogsmeade weekend. As they return, they are following behind Katie Bell, when she is Jinxed by a necklace she is carrying for someone at the school. Harry finds Hagrid to help get Katie back to school where she can be helped, and, carrying the necklace, follows. Meeting them at the school entrance, Professor McGonagall relieves Harry of the necklace, giving it to Filch to carry to Professor Snape.

Discussing this later, the Trio wonder exactly what was intended. With Filch scanning everything with his Secrecy Sensor, it is very unlikely that the package would have made it into Hogwarts, much less reached its eventual destination.

As Christmas, and Horace Slughorn's Christmas Slug Club Party, approach, Harry is the target of a large number of girls angling for invitations to the party from Harry. Hermione warns him to be careful of girls offering him things, they might well conceal love potions. Harry asks how they could get through Filch's secrecy sensors? Hermione points out that there isn't anything particularly Dark about love potions, and simply concealing them in perfume bottles, a service offered by Fred and George, would be sufficient to hide them.

Harry attends Slughorn's party with Luna Lovegood. Halfway through the party, Draco Malfoy is dragged in by Filch. Filch had caught him wandering the halls; Slughorn assumes that he was trying to gatecrash his party, and magnanimously invites him to join, to Filch's evident dismay. Draco and Snape, who is also present, very shortly manage to leave the party for a private discussion.

After Ron's birthday, at which he was first dosed with Romilda Vane's love potion, and then poisoned, Harry and Hermione leave the Hospital Wing with Hagrid to allow Ron's family to be with him. Hagrid mentions an angry conversation between Snape and Dumbledore which he had overheard, and Harry and Hermione are pressing him for more information when they are interrupted by the arrival of Filch, who is annoyed at students being out of bed at midnight. Hagrid angrily says that they are with him, a teacher, and as the quarrel starts to get loud, Harry and Hermione escape.

Harry interrupts Draco Malfoy when he is talking to Moaning Myrtle, and Draco retaliates by trying to hit Harry with the Cruciatus curse. Harry, in self defence, casts Sectumsempra. He is given detention for using Dark magic, and his detention is to recopy Filch's files that are beginning to deteriorate. These files have been specifically selected by Snape so that they include details of Harry's father's wrongdoings.

We do not see Filch again in this book.

Deathly Hallows As almost none of the action in this book occurs in Hogwarts, we do not see very much of Filch. His appearance seems to be limited to a single cameo immediately before the first Battle at Hogwarts, where, much to his dismay, he is ordered to find Peeves and bring him to Professor McGonagall. We are told that he will be supervising the evacuation of the underage students from Hogwarts, however.

Strengths Through long residence in the castle, Filch knows pretty nearly everything there is to know about the physical layout of Hogwarts, and he is able to reach any location in the castle, from anywhere, almost immediately. Between himself and Mrs. Norris, Filch seems to be aware of everything going on in the castle, particularly if it is something forbidden.

Weaknesses Argus Filch is a Squib, a child of wizard parents who has the inability to use magic. Harry discovers this in *Harry Potter and the Chamber of Secrets* when he spies Filch's "Kwikspell" letter, although he does not understand what that means until Filch says in front of him and Ron, "He knows I'm . . . I'm a Squib!" Even then, it is only when Ron explains what a Squib is that Harry understands the true significance of the Kwikspell letter and why Filch was so sensitive about it.

His lack of magical ability has made Filch singularly unsuited for almost any work available in the wizarding world; the caretaker position at Hogwarts is likely the only occupation available to him. Seeing this endless parade of wizarding children entering, gaining the skills he will never have, and leaving for a life he can only dream of, has left him bitter. This bitterness expresses itself in the endless restrictions he places upon the students and the powerful desire he has to torture them.

The author has stated that the Kwikspell course does not work for Filch; he is doomed to remain a Squib for all his life.

Relationships with Other Characters   Argus Filch has a lieutenant, his cat. *Mrs. Norris* is described as almost skeletally thin and dust-colored, and is apparently able to detect wrong-doing and report back to Filch, whereupon he appears on the scene to deal with the wrongdoer. She may be a magical cat-like animal known as a Kneazle, or like Crookshanks she may be a cat / Kneazle crossbreed. While many of the students have expressed a desire to harm Mrs. Norris for reporting their actions to Filch, she has never yet come to harm by a student. However, she was petrified by the monster from the Chamber of Secrets. Filch was desolated by her absence for the seven months before she was restored. Filch is perpetually in a bad temper, and many of the deeds that he prosecutes students for are quite minor: he attempts to "write up" Harry for the unforgivable crime of dripping mud on the floor. This over-authoritative adherence to rules, many of which he makes up himself, has made Argus Filch an object of mild derision among the teachers, and widely disliked by the students.

In Dolores Umbridge, Filch seems to find a kindred spirit: it seems they both hate the students equally, and once she becomes Headmistress, Umbridge seems to be willing to allow Filch to start torturing the students. Filch seldom seems happier than when he is doing Umbridge's bidding.

It has been suggested that Irma Pince and Argus Filch have a relationship, by many fans, and in fact by Harry and Ginny in conversation. There is no evidence supporting this relationship anywhere else in the series, though they do seem to share a similar outlook on life and the students.

ANALYSIS

As is so often the case, the author is playing to a certain extent with classical mythology. In this case, the name "Argus" is likely selected from the mythical guardian with a thousand eyes. Given Filch's apparent awareness of all "malfeasance" within the school, this seems quite a reasonable parallel.

QUESTIONS

1. Why does Argus Filch remain at Hogwarts when he often seems so miserable?

2. How does Argus Filch feel about his lack of ability as a wizard?

3. Why is Argus Filch so disdainful to the pupils of Hogwarts?

Ariana Dumbledore

Gender: Female
Hair color: Blonde
Eye color: Blue
Related Family: Kendra Dumbledore (mother)
Percival Dumbledore (father)
Albus Dumbledore and Aberforth Dumbledore (brothers)
Loyalty: Aberforth Dumbledore

OVERVIEW

Ariana Dumbledore was the sister of Albus and Aberforth Dumbledore. She died quite young, at approximately 14 years of age.

ROLE IN THE BOOKS

Deathly Hallows   Our learning about Ariana comes from a number of sources. We first hear about her in a eulogy penned by Elphias Doge, a close friend of Albus Dumbledore's. Elphias simply mentions that she had died when Albus was only just out of school.

The next person to write about the Dumbledore family is Rita Skeeter, who writes a tell-all book full of innuendo and scurrilous rumour. Rita writes that Ariana was very seldom seen out of the house, and suggests that she might have been a Squib.

In conversation with Doge and Ron's Auntie Muriel, Harry learns that Rita's source, Bathilda Bagshot, had never actually met Ariana, and had only seen her in the Dumbledores' yard when she was out gathering herbs by night. Muriel asks why Kendra was hiding her, and says that this suggests quite strongly that Ariana was a Squib and an embarrassment to the family. Against Doge's protestations that Ariana was merely sickly, Muriel says that she had a cousin who was a healer at St. Mungo's, and that Ariana had never been brought in. Muriel also mentions that Aberforth had broken Albus' nose in a fight at Ariana's funeral.

We finally learn the full story from Aberforth Dumbledore. Ariana had been a witch, but some Muggle boys had seen her working her uncontrolled magic when she was still underage, Aberforth indicates that she was about six. When she would not or could not do it again, they had beaten her, and as a result she received substantial and lasting injury. The result of this was that her magic apparently turned inwards and destroyed her from inside. Her father, Percival Dumbledore, had attacked the Muggle boys in retaliation, and as a result had been sent to Azkaban, where he had died. Her mother, Kendra Dumbledore, feared that if other witches or wizards found out about her, Ariana would be sent permanently to St. Mungo's. Aberforth, as so often happens with middle brothers, became the only one who could calm her down when she went into one of her fits of wild magic.

Some time after Kendra's death, there was a conflict between Albus, who felt honour-bound to stay and care for his family, his friend Gellert Grindelwald, who was bent on establishing Wizard-kind in its rightful place (as he saw it) ruling the Muggles "for their own good," and Aberforth, who was still concerned about Ariana's wellbeing. The fight became heated, Ariana had one of her fits, and in amidst all the flying curses Ariana was killed. Grindelwald immediately fled back to Europe. To his dying day, Albus did not know whose curse had killed Ariana, and he was afraid to find out.

While we never see Ariana herself, her portrait is on the wall of Aberforth's living room, and it is this portrait of Ariana that acts as the messenger to bring Neville to open the passage which allows Harry, Ron, and Hermione, among others, to enter Hogwarts before the final battle.

Strengths Given that her untrained magic is so powerful, we can safely guess that Ariana would have been a very powerful witch had she been allowed to develop normally.

Weaknesses According to Aberforth (*Harry Potter and the Deathly Hallows,* UK / Canada first edition p455), when Ariana was attacked by the Muggle boys, "[i]t destroyed her, what they did: she was never right again. She wouldn't use magic, but she couldn't get rid of it: it turned inwards and drove her mad, it exploded out of her when she couldn't control it, and at times she was strange and dangerous. But mostly she was sweet, and scared, and harmless." From this description, particularly if we assume that magic is largely a mental function, it seems likely that Ariana was brain-damaged at an early age, and was never able to be trained to use her magic properly.

Relationships with Other Characters Ariana had a particularly close relationship with her second eldest brother Aberforth. In *Harry Potter and the Deathly Hallows,* Aberforth says "I could get her to eat when she wouldn't do it for my mother, I could get her to calm down when she was in one of her rages," letting us believe that, because we do not have a background for Ariana's relationship with her parents, Ariana liked Aberforth "the best." Also, we explore, somewhat in this chapter, from a third person point of view, the relationship that Ariana had with her eldest brother, and most famous of her kin, Albus Dumbledore. Aberforth says that Albus "didn't want to be bothered with her," that he was always up in his room, skimming over spell books, writing essays and keeping up with his correspondence, that Ariana, though as much his sister as Aberforth's, was his second concern. However, Aberforth also states, that after the death of their mother Kendra, in an extremely unfortunate accident involving Ariana, Albus became better and more responsible in his caring of his younger sister. That only lasted until the arrival of Gellert Grindelwald, Albus' supposed "equal," when Ariana once again took a back seat. It is likely that Ariana's favorite was Aberforth, right up until her unfortunate death.

GREATER PICTURE

Albus Dumbledore, in the "Waystation," tells Harry that once he had seen what power did to him, he never wanted it again, which is why he so steadfastly turned down the post of Minister for Magic when it was offered to him. Looking at the episodes in question, which would have included the duel in which Ariana died, we see that Albus had never really had power, but it was the seeking of power, by him and Grindelwald, which had caused Ariana's death.

Armando Dippet

Gender: Male
Hair color: White / bald
Eye color: Unknown
Related Family:
Loyalty: Hogwarts School

OVERVIEW

Armando Dippet was the headmaster of Hogwarts before Albus Dumbledore. He is a wizened and frail-looking wizard when we see him, bald except for a few stray wisps of white hair.

ROLE IN THE BOOKS

Chamber of Secrets Here, we see Professor Dippet only through the memories of Tom Riddle's diary. Tom is requesting permission to stay in the school over the summer; Professor Dippet turns him down, saying that the attacks on the students have made that quite impossible, and if they do not cease he may have to close the school down. In the Chamber of Secrets, Tom Riddle mentions Professor Dippet contemptuously in passing, saying that Tom was able to fool him easily, but was never sure that Professor Dumbledore was fully convinced.

Order of the Phoenix Professor Dippet is one of the portraits hanging in Professor Dumbledore's study. Shortly after Arthur Weasley is attacked, just before Christmas, Dumbledore needs the portrait of Phineas Nigellus Black to carry a message to Sirius Black at 12 Grimmauld Place. Phineas Nigellus feigns tiredness, and many of the other portraits in the office are outraged; the portrait of Dippet, in particular, is angered, saying that they are sworn to serve the current Headmaster of Hogwarts.

Half-Blood Prince Professor Dippet's portrait in the Headmaster's office does say a few things during the course of this book, and it is mentioned that Tom Riddle had approached Dippet upon his graduation to ask for the post of teacher of Defence Against the Dark Arts. Dippet had turned him down, saying that he had not yet had enough experience, that he was as yet too young.

Deathly Hallows When Harry is in the Ministry, looking through Dolores Umbridge's office for the locket, he happens to see a copy of Rita Skeeter's book about Dumbledore. On the cover, it is noted that she is the bestselling author of the book *Armando Dippet: Master or Moron?*

ANALYSIS

From the limited number of times we see him, it is hard to get much of a feel for Professor Dippet. One gets the impression that he is a standard mid-level functionary, trying hard not to rock the boat, and rather worn out at the demands that being Headmaster of a school full of adolescent wizards and witches is putting on him. He quite possibly may resent having been left in charge to deal with the opening of the Chamber.

QUESTIONS

1. To what extent did Armando Dippet understand Tom Riddle?
2. How did Armando Dippet's Headmastership effect Dumbledore's development as a Headmaster?

Arthur Weasley

Gender: Male
Hair color: Red
Eye color: Unknown
Related Family: wife Molly (née Prewett), children Bill, Charlie, Percy, Fred, George, Ron, Ginny
Loyalty: Albus Dumbledore, Order of the Phoenix

Overview

Arthur Weasley worked at the Ministry of Magic in Misuse of Muggle Artifacts Office when Cornelius Fudge was the Minister of Magic. Arthur was then promoted to head the Office for the Detection and Confiscation of Counterfeit Defensive Spells and Protective Objects when Rufus Scrimgeour became the Minister. Arthur is a thin man, going bald, but the little hair on his head is as red as any of his children's. His dearest wish is to find out how Muggle airplanes stay up. Arthur is the head of the Weasley family.

Arthur Weasley's birthday is apparently 6 February.

Role in the Books

Philosopher's Stone It is mentioned that Mr. Weasley works with the Ministry of Magic, however he otherwise plays no part in this book.

Chamber of Secrets We first meet Mr. Weasley when he comes home from an overnight raid; Harry has just been rescued from the Dursley's by Fred, George, and Ron Weasley. Arthur is intrigued, first, by Harry's presence, and second, by the fact that the Twins had used his flying car to effect the rescue. "How did it go?" On being reminded by his wife that taking the car was, in fact, very bad, Mr. Weasley starts chastising them weakly. Seeing the storm clouds gathering, Ron and Harry depart; they can hear Mrs. Weasley yelling even from Ron's attic bedroom. Arthur accompanies the group to Diagon Alley as they go shopping for school supplies. An exchange of cutting remarks with Lucius Malfoy at Flourish and Blott's, apparently inspired in part by the presence of Hermione Granger's parents, resulted in a brawl, from which Arthur emerged slightly the worse for wear. Harry and Ron are unable to pass the barrier at Platform Nine and Three Quarters, and so take Arthur's flying car to Hogwarts. The journey proves somewhat too long for the car, and they eventually crash into the Whomping Willow. The car wanders off into the Forbidden Forest; it re-appears later in the book, to save Harry and Ron from the children of Aragog.

We next see Arthur at the end of the book, after Ginny Weasley has been rescued. After hearing the full story, Arthur chastises Ginny: "How many times have I told you not to trust something, if you can't see where it keeps its brains?"

Prisoner of Azkaban Arthur accompanies his family (Molly, Percy, Fred, George, Ron, and Ginny) to Diagon Alley to shop for school supplies on the last day of summer vacation. After dinner, Harry has to return to the lounge because he has volunteered to find the Rat Tonic which Ron had bought, where he overhears Arthur and Molly discussing whether Harry has any right to know that Sirius Black, having broken out of Azkaban, is apparently headed for Hogwarts to kill Harry. The next day, on the platform getting onto the Hogwarts Express, Arthur takes Harry aside to tell him; Harry tells Arthur that he had overheard his conversation the previous night. Arthur tries to get Harry to promise he won't set out after Sirius Black. Harry asks why he would do something like that, but does not have a chance to give his promise, as the train is departing.

Goblet of Fire Arthur has managed to get tickets for the Quidditch World Cup and invites Harry. On receiving word of Uncle Vernon's grudging acceptance, Arthur says they will collect Harry. Not realizing that the fireplace has been boarded up, Arthur has the Dursley's fireplace connected to the Floo network; finding himself, and shortly afterward many of his sons, appearing in this constricted, closed space, Arthur has no choice but to blast a hole in the wall. This does not endear him to the Dursleys, and their relationship remains strained, even though Arthur does try to engage them in conversation about electricity. Fred accidentally-on-purpose drops some Ton-Tongue Toffee, and Dudley Dursley picks it up and eats it; the resultant panic on the part of the Dursleys results in them throwing china figurines at Arthur, even as he is trying to help them.

When Arthur returns to the Burrow, he is angry enough at the twins to actually scold them, saying that it is exactly this sort of prank on innocent Muggles that is so damaging to Muggle-Wizard relationships. He threatens to tell Molly, but when Molly overhears, and asks "tell me what?" he backs off sharply. Evidently, though, not sharply enough, because although Harry and Ron depart for Ron's bedroom, they can still hear Mrs. Weasley yelling. Arthur, Harry, Hermione, Ron, Fred, George, and Ginny then walk in the early morning to the top of Stoatshead Hill, where, along with Amos Diggory and his son Cedric, they find the Portkey that will take them to the match. Arriving at the campground, they set up camp, with Arthur being enchanted by such things as the mallet used to drive in tent pegs, and matches. They finally have tea and breakfast ready, just as Bill, Charlie, and Percy arrive from the nearby woods, where they have Apparated in. Throughout the afternoon, Arthur exchanges greetings with other Ministry wizards who are passing by, meanwhile naming them for the others. Ludovic Bagman stops by, taking bets on the outcome of the match, and asking if Arthur has seen Bartemius Crouch; shortly afterwards, Bartemius himself stops by, and they discuss the problems that Ludo is having with the Bulgarian delegation. They also mention some event that will be happening at Hogwarts; Arthur and Percy evidently know what this event is, but none of them are saying anything to the people who are actually at Hogwarts. Arthur takes Harry, Hermione, and his children to the top box, where again Arthur has a small run-in with Lucius Malfoy. Arthur then restrains some of his own children, who are entranced by the Bulgarian mascots, the Veela. He warns people that the Irish mascots are even more impressive, and they do turn out to be so: leprechauns appear, showering down gold coins. When the battle between the Quidditch teams turns ugly, so does the battle between the team mascots; the Veela, throwing fireballs, start turning into bird-like creatures with cruel beaks. Arthur comments that this is a clear indication that you shouldn't judge women by their looks alone. After the match, a riot breaks out; Arthur, along with Bill, Charlie, and Percy, goes to battle the apparent Death Eaters in the middle of the riot. Harry, Ron, and Hermione end up in the wood, where they hear the Dark Mark invoked. Shortly after this, they are surrounded by wizards, including Arthur, who send Stunners in all directions. Arthur defends Harry, Ron, and Hermione against accusations by Bartemius Crouch that they had summoned the Mark. After the confusion has died down, Arthur takes Harry, Ron, and Hermione back to the tent, in the process stopping to say a few reassuring words to someone. After a short night, they catch an early Portkey back to Stoatshead Hill, and walk from there back to the Burrow, where Mrs. Weasley is incredibly relieved to see that they are all back safe.

It turns out, however, that Rita Skeeter has misinterpreted Mr. Weasley's words of reassurance, and so Mr. Weasley, for the remainder of the summer, has to work long hours at the Ministry, trying to repair the damage. Mr. Weasley is at the Ministry doing damage control when Harry, Ron, Ginny, Fred, and George leave for Hogwarts.

Order of the Phoenix When Harry reaches Number 12, Grimmauld Place, Mr. Weasley is already there, in a meeting with other members of the Order of the Phoenix. He is there for dinner, along with the rest of the Weasley family, Hermione, Remus Lupin, and Sirius Black. Fred and George, before dinner, tell Harry that he shouldn't mention Percy, who is estranged from the family, as when Percy's name is mentioned, "Dad breaks whatever he's holding." When Remus asks Harry after dinner if he has any questions, Molly Weasley is against telling him anything; Arthur, supporting Lupin and Sirius, says that he has a right to know what's going on. Harry's agreement that he would tell Ron and Hermione anything he learned gets them, Fred, and George permission to stay and listen as Harry has his questions answered. Defeated, Mrs. Weasley finally manages to send Ginny off to bed. Between them, Lupin, Sirius, Arthur, and Bill explain to Harry what the Order of the Phoenix is, and what they believe Lord Voldemort is trying to do.

Arthur accompanies Harry to the Ministry for his hearing; Harry has been charged with underage use of magic. Arthur suggests that they should both travel to the Ministry by non-magical means, as a way of making a better impression on the judges at the hearing, so they travel from Grimmauld Place to the Ministry by subway. Arthur is enthralled by the ticket vending machines (even though they are broken), and by the escalators. He shows Harry the visitor's entrance to the Ministry, and takes him up to his office, through the Auror branch. When the hearing starts, he takes Harry down to the courtroom where the hearing is, then waits outside until Harry returns. As he and Harry are discussing the trial, Percy Weasley leaves the courtroom; he does not seem to notice Arthur, and Arthur does not say anything to him, though his expression does tighten. As they are leaving the Ministry, they run into Cornelius Fudge in discussion with Lucius Malfoy; again, there is an exchange of words, which ends when Lucius suggests that he and Fudge should go up to the Minister's office.

Just before Christmas, Harry sees, through Voldemort's eyes, Nagini the snake attacking Arthur. Harry manages to convince Professor McGonagall to take him to Professor Dumbledore; Dumbledore in turn sends portraits from his office to raise the alarm. Arthur is found and taken to St. Mungo's. The Weasley children and Harry are sent off by Portkey to Grimmauld Place; after a very tense night, Mrs. Weasley sends word that Arthur will be all right. Shortly after that the family visits him in the hospital. Arthur is effusive in thanking Harry for sending help to save his life, though Harry is uncertain how much thanks he deserves, having actually seen the attack through the snake's eyes, and being afraid he was the agent of the attack on Arthur. Later, while Arthur, Molly, Tonks, and Moody are discussing the incident, Harry hears speculation from them that Harry may be being controlled by Voldemort.

On Christmas, the family visits Arthur again. Arthur is enchanted by Harry's gift, a collection of screwdrivers and fuse wire. It seems that he, with the help of the apprentice healer, has been experimenting with Muggle healing techniques, and have tried something called "stitches" on Arthur's wound. This has apparently been less than successful. Harry, Ron, and Hermione leave as Mrs. Weasley starts winding up to yell, and only hear the start of her anger at her husband.

Shortly before school starts again, Arthur returns to Grimmauld Place, healed. His arrival, with all his family, stops an incipient duel between Sirius and Snape, though Arthur later says he doesn't think that the situation was as serious as Harry thought.

Finally, Arthur is present at King's Cross station when Harry returns there from school. Arthur, Molly, Tonks, and Moody, along with Ron, Harry, and Hermione, speak to the Dursleys, saying that they expect to hear regularly from Harry, and if they don't, they will be visiting to see what's wrong.

Half-Blood Prince When Harry arrives at The Burrow with Albus Dumbledore, Molly is talking in her kitchen with Tonks. She tells Harry that Arthur has been working extremely long hours. After Dumbledore and Tonks leave, Arthur arrives, extremely wearied. Being a member of the Ministry, he feels he has to set a good example, and so before Molly lets him in, he must confirm who she is and insists that she confirm who he is. It is from this exchange of questions that we learn that his dearest wish is to learn how Muggle airplanes stay up.

As he is spending most of his time at the Ministry, we don't see much of Arthur while Harry is staying at the Burrow before school starts. He does accompany Molly, Harry, Hermione, Ginny, and Ron to Diagon Alley to buy school supplies. He is scandalized to see people trying to sell phony anti-Dark Magic charms, saying that if he was on duty he would have run them in;

Molly asks him to stay calm. The family splits up, with Harry, Ron, and Hermione going to Madam Malkin's for robes, escorted by Hagrid, while Ginny and her parents go to Flourish and Blotts for textbooks. They rejoin later to visit Fred and George's Store, Weasleys' Wizard Wheezes.

Arthur also escorts Harry, Hermione, Ron, and Ginny to the Hogwarts Express. On the platform, Harry takes Arthur aside and tells him that he had followed Draco Malfoy to Borgin and Burkes, and that Malfoy had said something there about some Dark magic thing that he needed repaired. Arthur says that they had searched Malfoy Manor thoroughly already and found nothing.

Ron later passes on the message that Arthur had searched Malfoy Manor again, and still found nothing. We see Arthur again at Christmas, at the Burrow. Harry tells him that he had overheard Malfoy and Severus Snape talking about some task that the Dark Lord had set him, and about an Unbreakable Vow he had made to Draco's mother. Arthur is of the opinion that Snape is trying to determine Draco's mission, to report on it to the Order of the Phoenix; Remus Lupin, who is also there, echoes this opinion.

Deathly Hallows We hear that Arthur had visited the Dursleys with Kingsley Shacklebolt, to suggest that they should accept the offer of the Order to hide them now that Harry is turning 17 and the protection that Lily Potter's death had brought is ending. Unimpressed by Arthur, who had half-destroyed the parlor when he visited before, Vernon Dursley nonetheless accepts guidance from Shacklebolt, possibly because he has seen him on TV, right behind the Prime Minister.

Arthur is one of the six protectors who travel with the six Harry Potters to confuse the Death Eaters who are after Harry. Additionally, Hagrid mentions that the defensive modifications to Sirius Black's motorcycle, the one which the true Harry will be riding, were done by Arthur.

On arriving at the Burrow, Arthur hurries in to see what is happening with his sons, and is dismayed to find that George has lost an ear, but is relieved to find that is the extent of the damage.

Arthur assists Molly in preparing for Bill and Fleur's wedding. At one point, when Harry and Arthur are assigned the chore of cleaning out the chicken coop, Arthur tells Harry not to bother; Ted Tonks has sent over the wreckage of Sirius' flying motorcycle, and Arthur has stored it in the chicken coop, hoping to finally figure out how brakes work when he puts it all back together.

When the Ministry falls, and Harry, Ron, and Hermione leave The Burrow, they eventually find their way to Grimmauld Place. Arthur sends his Patronus there to tell them that the rest of the family is all right and to not attempt to reply as they are being watched.

Harry, Ron, and Hermione then watch the Ministry for some time. They see Arthur going in with the other Ministry workers each morning and returning home in the evening. When they actually enter the Ministry in search of Dolores Umbridge and the locket, Harry is on a lift (US: elevator) when Arthur and Percy step on. Percy, finding his father there, gets off at the next floor; Arthur confronts Harry, thinking he is Albert Runcorn, and tells him that if he provides information against any other wizards as he did against Dirk Cresswell, he will be in deep trouble. Harry tells Arthur that he has a trace on him, Arthur asks if that is a threat.

Arthur also takes part in the battle against the Death Eaters at Hogwarts. We see him and Percy together dropping the healed Pius Thicknesse in the final battle, and later with the remaining members of the Weasley family at the end of the battle, consoling each other over their loss.

Strengths Arthur's main strength is his compassion. Lucius Malfoy feels that Arthur is "a disgrace to the name of Wizard" because of the Muggle Protection Laws that he helped to author and helps to enforce. Arthur feels that everyone should be given a chance. This extends to allowing others to place him at risk, for instance: while he was in hospital, he agreed to be an experiment for Muggle wound-healing methods attempted by an apprentice healer. The Weasleys are one of the Old Wizarding Families, pureblood as far back as they can trace.

Weaknesses It could be argued that Arthur's inability to control the Twins, or other family members, is a weakness. However, when something happens that he feels needs correction, he is not slow to apply it; witness his reaction when he found one of the twins inveigling Ron into making an Unbreakable Vow. It is perhaps more likely that he feels very deeply about his children, to the point that, particularly after Molly's usual browbeating, he does not feel that it is reasonable to scold or punish them any more than they have already been.

In the eyes of Lord Voldemort and the Death Eaters, of course, this love for his own children is a weakness, as is his liking for Muggles and their technology. In the eyes of Percy and other people in the Ministry, it is clear that his lack of ambition is considered a weakness. Arthur, however, is happy with the job he is doing; it may not pay as much as he would like, but he feels he is doing something to benefit Wizardkind.

One does not get much of a feel for Arthur's magical abilities. Given the type of charms he is able to work on the Ford Anglia, and on Sirius Black's flying motorcycle, one guesses that he is at the very least capable; from his selection by Moody as one of the protectors for the seven Potters, he also must be a reasonably strong duelist and skilled with defensive spells, but we don't directly see his battle.

Relationships with Other Characters Arthur Weasley is endlessly fascinated with Muggles, the strange things they do to get around not having magic, and their resultant way of life. As a result of this, he is always engaging Harry in conversations about how he had lived while he was at the Dursleys; he is curious about how Hermione Granger's parents live and how Hermione herself lived; and he attempts to discuss Muggle technology with the Dursleys when he visits there. He has a very open character, and is always trying to engage someone in conversation about something.

Arthur, as head of the Weasley household, is supposed to also be called in when Molly Weasley, his wife, can't keep control over the children. He is rather remarkably ineffective at this, not being willing to punish the children more than they have been already. The only time we see him angry is after the Twins have tricked Dudley with Ton-Tongue Toffee. We are also told that he was angry enough to strike one of the Twins was when he caught Fred inciting Ron to make an Unbreakable Vow.

Arthur's progress in his career is rather marred by his lack of ambition. He is happy with what he is doing, and doesn't care to advance to a post that would take him away from his beloved Muggles and into administration. As a result, quite a lot of people in the Ministry rather look down on him.

It is because of his liking for Muggles that Arthur is often at daggers drawn with Lucius Malfoy. Their ongoing feud erupts into physical violence in *Harry Potter and the Chamber of Secrets*.

Greater Picture

It is perhaps of interest that in the original plan for the seven-book series, Arthur Weasley was not supposed to survive the snake attack in the Ministry in book 5. In the ongoing pattern of father figures falling to Voldemort, Arthur Weasley was supposed to fall in this book, along with Sirius Black. It is not completely certain why Arthur was spared, but it certainly seems to tighten the bonds between the Weasley family and Harry to have him be the instrument of their fathers' survival.

Augusta Longbottom

Gender: Female
Hair color: Unknown
Eye color: Unknown
Related Family: son Frank Longbottom, daughter-in-law Alice Longbottom, grandson Neville Longbottom
Loyalty: Albus Dumbledore

Overview

Augusta Longbottom, who Neville always refers to as "Gran," is raising Neville.

Role in the Books

Philosopher's Stone We see Augusta on the platform at King's Cross chastising Neville for having lost his toad, Trevor. Augusta later sends Neville a Remembrall, which Draco Malfoy tries to steal from him.

Chamber of Secrets At breakfast the first day of school, Neville comments that he's waiting for the post owls, as Gran (Augusta) was going to send on some things he'd forgot.

When the post owls do arrive, Errol brings a Howler for Ron. Neville advises him to open it, as he had received one from Gran and not opened it, and it had been worse.

Prisoner of Azkaban It is revealed that the thing Neville fears most is Severus Snape, so when he is preparing to battle a Boggart, he expects that the Boggart will appear as Snape. In order to make the Boggart appear funny, Professor Lupin suggests that Neville should imagine him dressed as his grandmother, wearing a hat with a stuffed vulture, carrying a big red handbag, and wearing a long green dress.

After The Fat Lady's portrait is destroyed by Sirius Black, she is replaced as Gryffindor tower guardian by Sir Cadogan. Sir Cadogan, in the interest of security, sets new passwords every few hours. Neville, who has trouble with remembering them, writes them down on a piece of paper, which he then loses, and Sirius Black somehow retrieves. Sirius uses this list to make his way into Gryffindor tower. Though no harm is ultimately done, Neville is in disgrace for the remainder of the year, and as part of his punishment, Augusta sends him a Howler, which he receives at breakfast two days later.

Goblet of Fire Harry learns that the reason Augusta has been raising Neville is that his parents, Frank and Alice Longbottom, had been tortured into insanity by Bellatrix, Rodolphus, and Rabastan Lestrange, and Barty Crouch Jr. . Professor Dumbledore tells him that this is Neville's story to tell, and asks him not to pass it on.

Order of the Phoenix In St. Mungo's, where they have been visiting Arthur Weasley, Harry, Ron, Hermione, and Ginny Weasley mistakenly end up visiting Gilderoy Lockhart. Neville's parents, it turns out, are on the same ward, and Neville and Augusta are visiting them. Augusta recognizes Harry immediately, says that Neville has said good things about Hermione, and is generally approving of the Weasley family. When Neville's mother carefully gives Neville a gum wrapper, Augusta is dismissive, though Neville obviously plans to keep it.

Half-Blood Prince Neville does reasonably well in Charms and is eligible for N.E.W.T.-level studies in that course, but says that his grandmother considers Charms a soft option. Professor McGonagall says that Augusta had failed her Charms O.W.L., and implies that is why she was denigrating the course. Neville is quite cheered by this discovery.

Deathly Hallows As Harry, Ron, and Hermione return to Hogwarts, they are met by Neville. Neville has suffered at the hands of the new school order, for having dared to stand up to the increasing use of Dark magic and for re-creating Dumbledore's Army. Having found that they can get at adults by kidnapping their children, the Death Eaters decide to try the opposite tack, attempting to control the children (in this case Neville) by kidnapping the adults (Augusta). In this case it backfires, with Augusta putting Dawlish in St. Mungo's and going on the run. Before her departure, though, she had expressed great satisfaction with the stand Neville was taking.

Augusta is the last person through the tunnel from the Hog's Head Inn after Aberforth leaves the inn to join the battle. Having sealed the tunnel, she then goes off to join Neville.

Strengths Augusta has very great strength of character. She is strict and has high expectations of Neville who hasn't often performed to her standards. However, she is very proud of Neville's eventual leadership of Dumbledore's Army and their resistance to the Death Eaters' control of Hogwarts during his seventh year.

Augustus Rookwood

Gender: Male
Hair color: Unknown
Eye color: Unknown
Related Family: Unknown
Loyalty: Lord Voldemort

Overview

Augustus Rookwood was an Unspeakable, working in the Department of Mysteries in the Ministry of Magic. Note that in early editions of the British version of *Harry Potter and the Order of the Phoenix*, the name appears as Algernon Rookwood. It is corrected in later editions.

Role in the Books

Goblet of Fire In Albus Dumbledore's Pensieve, Harry re-lives Dumbledore's memory of a hearing at the Wizengamot, in which Igor Karkaroff is naming Death Eaters in an attempt to get his sentence reduced. The only name he comes up with that is unknown to the Aurors is that of Augustus Rookwood, who had been passing information to the Death Eaters. Rookwood is apparently an employee of the Ministry.

Immediately after this, Harry relives Dumbledore's memory of the trial of Ludovic Bagman. Bagman says that he had been passing information to Rookwood, but that he thought he was "one of ours," as he was in the Ministry. In part, perhaps, because of his fame (he was still a Beater for the Wimbourne Wasps Quidditch team at that point), he is absolved of all charges and released.

Order of the Phoenix Augustus Rookwood is one of the ten Death Eaters who break out of Azkaban. We later learn that they have broken out because the Dementors have left to join Voldemort.

In one of Harry's dreams where he is sharing Voldemort's thoughts, he sees Rookwood reporting to Voldemort that the plan that had been suggested for retrieving something from the Ministry was bound to fail. Rookwood had worked in the Department of Mysteries, and knew about the protective measures in place.

Rookwood is one of the twelve Death Eaters who take part on the Battle at the Ministry.

Deathly Hallows Rookwood takes part in the battle at Hogwarts at the end of this book. Percy Weasley sees him, and takes off after him.

Strengths The only time we directly see him, Rookwood is carrying bad news to Voldemort, and quite evidently in fear of punishment for carrying that news. We can assume that he has some strength of character, as many Death Eaters learn that Voldemort is in the habit of retaliating against the messenger; it must take some spiritual strength to inform Voldemort that his plan is doomed to failure.

Relationships with Other Characters Apart from one brief scene, where we see him cringing before Voldemort in fear for punishment for bringing bad news, we have no direct experience with Rookwood. However, we can guess that he is persuasive, as he had convinced people to pass information to him before he was imprisoned.

Auntie Muriel

Gender: Female
Hair color: Red
Eye color: Unknown
Related Family: Weasley family
Loyalty:

Overview

Ron's Auntie Muriel (no mention whether she's a Weasley or a Prewett, though her opinions suggest she is a Prewett) is an aged, outspoken, eccentric relative of the Weasley family.

Role in the Books

Half-Blood Prince Fleur Delacour and Bill Weasley are engaged, but Bill has just received dreadful wounds from Fenrir Greyback that are unlikely to ever heal. Molly Weasley, tending his injuries, laments that the wedding is now not going to happen. Fleur, outraged, says that the wedding most certainly is going to happen, and pushes Molly aside to take over tending Bill's wounds. Briefly stunned, Molly tells Fleur that Auntie Muriel has a goblin-made tiara that would look good in Fleur's hair, and says she'll see if she can convince Muriel to loan it to her. Fleur accepts. This marks the reconciliation between the two women.

Deathly Hallows As the seven Harry Potters escape from Privet Drive, each Potter and protector pair is destined for a different safe house. Ron and Tonks are destined for Auntie Muriel's. Muriel keeps them busy for so long after they arrive that they miss their Portkey, and there is a great deal of worry at the Weasley house until they finally arrive on Tonks' broom.

Auntie Muriel is one of the wedding guests, who expects preferential treatment because, "I'm a hundred and seven." She arrives on Ron's arm, criticizing the length of his hair—she claims that for a moment she had mistaken him for Ginevra. She briefly accuses Ron of lying about knowing Harry Potter when Ron says he has made his excuses—Harry is present, but in disguise. Ron takes her, still grumbling, to her seat, where she evidently keeps him occupied for some time.

After the ceremony, during the music afterwards, Harry is speaking with Elphias Doge about the eulogy he had written for Albus Dumbledore, and the muckraking book that Rita Skeeter had written on the same subject. Auntie Muriel, passing by, hears the conversation and joins it, saying that she couldn't wait to read Skeeter's book, she reads everything she writes. She goes on to say that she believes that Dumbledore had practiced Dark magic as a youth, and that his sister Ariana was most likely a Squib. She claims that Ariana had been locked up, as it was taken to be a disgrace to have produced a Squib, and so it was common practice in those days to try to hide the child, integrating him or her with Muggles. In response to Elphias' protests, she says that Ariana couldn't have been sickly, because her cousin Launcelot was a healer at St. Mungo's, and Ariana had never been there. She goes on to say that she believes that Rita's source was Bathilda Bagshot, and that she was likely still alive, and still living in Godric's Hollow, where the Dumbledores had lived as well. Harry, taken quite by surprise by this last revelation, wonders why Professor Dumbledore had never told him of this connection.

Auntie Muriel's stream of revelations is broken by the announcement that the Ministry has fallen and Rufus Scrimgeour has been killed. This effectively ends the wedding party, and Harry, Hermione, and Ron depart. Much later, when Harry, Ron, and Hermione are recovering at Shell Cottage, they learn that several of the Weasley clan are now living in Aunt Muriel's house. Apparently, Fred and George are attempting to run Weasleys' Wizard Wheezes by mail order out of one of her back bedrooms. When Ollivander is taken to her house by Bill Weasley, Fleur asks him to carry the tiara that she had worn at the wedding back to Auntie Muriel.

Relationships with Other Characters Auntie Muriel is an incurable gossip, in some ways as bad as Rita Skeeter, of whom she is a great fan. She never hesitates to make use of her age to claim preferential treatment. She disapproves of Hermione, and has said that Weasleys breed like gnomes.

Avery

Gender: Male
Hair color: Unknown
Eye color: Unknown
Related Family: Unknown
Loyalty: Lord Voldemort

OVERVIEW

Avery (whose first name is never given) is a Death Eater. He has remained free.

ROLE IN THE BOOKS

Goblet of Fire When the Trio are visiting Sirius Black in his cave, Sirius mentions that Avery, from what he heard, got out of Azkaban by saying he had been under the Imperius curse, and was now at large.

When Lord Voldemort returns to life and summons his Death Eaters, Avery is one of the ones who returns to the call. Avery breaks ranks to plead for forgiveness and is rewarded with the Cruciatus curse.

Order of the Phoenix In a dream, Harry sees Voldemort discussing a plan with one of his Death Eaters. It seems that Avery has suggested a certain way to retrieve an object, and it has not worked. Augustus Rookwood, a one-time Ministry employee, is explaining that it could never have worked, and Voldemort, hearing this, orders Avery to attend him. Harry wakes up, wrenches his attention away, and tries to ignore Voldemort torturing Avery.

Avery is one of the twelve Death Eaters ranged against Harry and the five other members of Dumbledore's Army in the climactic Battle in the Department of Mysteries. We believe that Avery was one of the ten Death Eaters left standing in the room of the Veil, and thus one of the nine held in that room by Albus Dumbledore's anti-Apparation spell at the end of the battle.

Half-Blood Prince Avery is mentioned in passing. Twice, Professor Dumbledore and Harry visit Horace Slughorn's memories of one particular night when Slughorn is meeting with Tom Riddle and his associates. In both of those memories, Slughorn notes that it is eleven o'clock, and says that it is time to send the gathered students off to bed, remarking to two of them, Avery and Lestrange (who could be either Rodolphus or Rabastan), that they have an essay due.

Deathly Hallows In Severus Snape's memory, we see Lily Evans expressing dislike of Snape's friends, specifically naming Avery and Mulciber.

Bane

Gender: Male
Hair color: Black
Eye color: Unknown
Related Family: Unknown
Loyalty: Centaur race

OVERVIEW

Bane is a Centaur living in the Forbidden Forest.

ROLE IN THE BOOKS

Philosopher's Stone When Harry is serving his detention in the Forbidden Forest with Hagrid, they are startled by the appearance of a centaur, Ronan, who makes some comments about astronomy ("Mars is bright tonight"). Shortly, Bane joins them, and makes similar comments about astronomy.

After leaving them, Harry, Draco Malfoy, and Hagrid's boar-hound Fang find the creature that has been killing Unicorns. As the creature seems to be about ready to attack Harry, he is rescued by another Centaur, Firenze, who offers to carry Harry back to Hagrid. As he is doing so, he is met by Bane and Ronan, who accuse him of becoming a pack animal for humans, like a donkey, and interfering with the portents. Firenze leaves them behind, saying that he will fight the evil, even alongside humans if he must.

Order of the Phoenix Firenze, now teaching Divination, explains that he cannot return to the Forbidden Forest, as he has been banished by his herd. Harry sees a hoof-shaped bruise on his chest, and wonders if it was Bane who put that there. Bane, along with Magorian, is in the group of centaurs who confront Hagrid as he is taking Harry and Hermione back to the school after introducing them to his half-brother, Grawp. Bane makes no sign of having spoken to Harry earlier, but warns "this human" Hagrid what will happen to him if he returns to the Forest. Bane is among the group of centaurs who come to investigate when Hermione is leading Harry and Dolores Umbridge into the Forbidden Forest to try and entrap her there. After Umbridge has insulted the Centaurs by calling them "inferior half-breeds" and has magically bound Magorian, the centaurs swarm her, and the last we see of Umbridge is Bane bearing her off into the forest.

Deathly Hallows When Hagrid is carrying an apparently-dead Harry out of the Forbidden Forest, apparently several centaurs are present and watching Lord Voldemort's victory procession. Hagrid calls out to Bane, apparently believing that their inaction implicates them in Harry's death.

Whether or not Hagrid's accusations of Bane have effect is uncertain; Bane, however, is one of the centaurs who lead the counter attack on the Death Eaters, along with Ronan and Magorian.

ANALYSIS

In his own way, Bane is as prejudiced as any Death Eater. He believes in the innate superiority of Centaurs over humans, and is affronted by any suggestion that humans and centaurs could work together. In this he is only echoing the beliefs of his herd, beliefs that are apparently shared to a greater or lesser degree by every centaur we meet.

Bartemius Crouch Sr.

Gender: Male
Hair color: Grey
Eye color: Dark
Related Family: son Barty Crouch Jr., wife Mrs. Crouch
Loyalty: Ministry of Magic

OVERVIEW

Bartemius "Barty" Crouch, Sr. led the Department of Magical Law Enforcement during Lord Voldemort's first rise to power (apparently in the 1960s). During this period he became a ruthless leader, doing things such as giving Aurors the power to kill. He later became the head of the Department of International Magical Cooperation after losing status in the Wizarding world, due to the common belief that he drove his son to joining the Death Eaters.

Role in the books

Goblet of Fire Mr. Crouch is first mentioned as being Percy Weasley's boss at the Ministry. Mr. Crouch is apparently the head of the Department of International Magical Cooperation, and Percy is writing a report on substandard cauldrons being imported from Europe for him.

We first see Mr. Crouch at the Quidditch World Cup, where he is apparently in charge of organizing the international aspects of the competition. He stops at the Weasley campsite when Arthur Weasley calls him over; Percy scrambles to make him a cup of tea, which Mr. Crouch accepts, calling Percy "Weatherby." He then corrals Ludo Bagman, and they apparate off to attend to some detail.

After the appearance of the Dark Mark, Mr. Crouch is in the team of wizards that attempt to Stun the wizard who produced the Mark. Mr. Crouch is suspicious of everyone there present, and is shocked when Amos Diggory discovers his House-elf, Winky, at the apparent source of the incantation. Arthur Weasley, another of the wizards in that group, points out that Mr. Crouch has accused the two people there present least likely to be involved with the Death Eaters: Harry Potter, and his own house-elf. Mr. Crouch goes off into the woods to search for other evidence, and on his return, fires Winky.

We next see Mr. Crouch when he arrives at the school on 30 October to be introduced as one of the five judges in the upcoming Triwizard Tournament, and again on the following night when the Goblet of Fire selects the Champions of each school who will take part in the Tournament. Surprisingly, the Goblet selects a fourth wizard, Harry Potter. Called upon to interpret the rule book, Crouch says that if the wizard's name comes out of the Goblet, then he is required to compete. With this settled, though to nobody's satisfaction, Crouch goes on to explain that he will not be telling them what they will face in the First Task of the Tournament, because ability to think quickly and bravely is necessary to a wizard, but he does give them the date when it will occur.

As he steps into the firelight, Harry notices that Mr. Crouch seems ill; apparently Professor Dumbledore sees this as well, because he asks Crouch to stay the night. Crouch refuses, saying he has to get back.

Crouch is then present to the Weighing of the Wands ceremony, in which Mr. Ollivander checks the wands of the four Champions to see that they are in full working order. Harry thinks he still looks a bit ill.

Crouch is present again during the First Task, and he awards Harry 9 out of 10 points for retrieving the golden egg from his dragon.

At the Yule Ball, Crouch is absent; Percy Weasley has taken his place, saying that Mr. Crouch is tired and is staying at home. He is sending instructions by Owl Post, and Percy is just glad that Crouch has an assistant that he can trust enough that he can get the rest he needs. Hermione suggests that he wouldn't be so tired if he hadn't summarily and unjustly fired his Elf; Percy tries to defend Crouch's actions.

Percy is again substituting for Mr. Crouch at the Second Task. Shortly afterwards, Harry, Ron, and Hermione visit Sirius Black, who is living in a cave near Hogsmeade with Buckbeak. Sirius says that it is very unusual for Mr. Crouch to be taking a vacation; he was always very dedicated to his work at the Ministry. In late May, Harry is taken aside by Viktor Krum for a private conversation under the eaves of the Forbidden Forest. As they finish their conversation, a disheveled Mr. Crouch appears, talking to the trees, and in apparent sane moments demanding to see Dumbledore. Leaving Krum to guard him, Harry runs off to collect Dumbledore, an action which is delayed by Professor Snape. By the time Dumbledore and Harry return to the Forbidden Forest, Krum has been Stunned and Mr. Crouch is gone.

Shortly after this, Harry is left alone in Dumbledore's office as Professor Dumbledore, Professor Moody, and Cornelius Fudge go to investigate the place where Crouch was found. Harry discovers Dumbledore's Pensieve, and ends up viewing three trials at the Wizengamot in which Crouch presided. We see Crouch considering whether to release Igor Karkaroff from Azkaban based on the names of supposedly uncaught Death Eaters he has given them; presiding over the session where Ludo Bagman was released; and the session where Bellatrix Lestrange, Rabastan Lestrange, Rodolphus Lestrange, and Barty Crouch Jr., his own son, were sentenced for the torture of Frank and Alice Longbottom.

Fudge apparently shortly opens an inquiry into how Crouch could have been apparently so very ill without anyone in the Ministry knowing. Percy is evidently called in as part of this inquiry; as a result, Fudge himself ends up judging the Third Task.

Following the Third Task, when Barty Crouch Jr. is revealed, we are given some additional information. When Crouch went off into the forest after the discovery of Winky under the Dark Mark, he had found Barty Stunned under his Invisibility Cloak and sent him home. He had fired Winky, not for being associated with the Dark Mark, but for allowing Barty to escape and get himself a wand. Shortly afterwards Lord Voldemort and Wormtail had managed to put Crouch under the Imperius curse, and he had been under the Imperius Curse during the selection of the Champions and during the First Task. As Wormtail's control started getting tenuous, Crouch was confined to his home, where Voldemort and Wormtail were also staying. He had managed to escape, had made his way to the Forbidden Forest where Harry had seen him, and had then been killed by Barty, and his body hidden.

Barty Crouch Jr.

Gender: Male
Hair color: Straw colored
Eye color: unknown
Related Family: father Bartemius Crouch Sr., mother Mrs. Crouch
Loyalty: Lord Voldemort

OVERVIEW

Bartemius (Barty) Crouch Jr. is the son of Ministry of Magic employee Bartemius Crouch Sr., and one of a group of four convicted for the torture of Frank and Alice Longbottom.

Role In The Books

Goblet of Fire Note: Events in this subsection appear in a different order than they appear in the book. Much of what is mentioned here actually is only revealed in the closing chapters of the book, and some events actually occur well before the beginning of the book, but are revealed during the course of this year.

Shortly after Lord Voldemort's disappearance, Bartemius Crouch Jr. and three other young Death Eaters (Bellatrix Lestrange, and brothers Rodolphus and Rabastan Lestrange) attacked and tortured Aurors Frank and Alice Longbottom, using the Cruciatus Curse on them until the two lost most of their mental faculties. It is believed that their intent was to find out what the Aurors had done with Lord Voldemort so that they could bring him back.

Harry Potter first hears about Barty Crouch's sentencing and removal to Azkaban at Bartemius Crouch Sr.'s orders, from Sirius Black, and later observes that trial and sentencing in Albus Dumbledore's Pensieve. Barty Crouch's escape from Azkaban was engineered by his father, Bartemius Crouch Sr., presumably acting at the request of his wife. Barty's escape remained undiscovered because Bartemius' wife took his place, very quickly dying in Azkaban from a pre-existing condition, and being buried there. Bartemius was keeping his son controlled by means of the Imperius curse, and the actions of the Crouch house-elf, Winky. Over the years, however, Bartemius' control over his son slackened, to the point that at the Quidditch World Cup he was able to escape control completely, albeit briefly. Stunned by Ministry wizards investigating the appearance of the Dark Mark during the riot following the Cup, Barty was returned to the family home and placed under the Imperius curse again. However, with the dismissal of Winky, Bartemius' control over Barty was weakened, and Barty was able to contact Lord Voldemort. Voldemort and Wormtail then attacked Bartemius and placed him under the Imperius curse; with Wormtail's help, Barty stunned and then impersonated Alastor Moody throughout Harry's fourth school year. Because of the impersonation, his career during that year is largely covered under the topic Alastor Moody. However, the following events, that were not initially attributed to Moody, occurred:

• Barty apparently Charmed the Goblet of Fire such that it acted as though there were four schools competing in the Triwizard Tournament, rather than three; he then placed Harry's name in the Goblet as the sole competitor in this fourth school, thus forcing the Goblet to select Harry as a Champion.

• During this time, Voldemort had Bartemius Crouch Sr. controlled by the Imperius Curse. With Barty's assistance and advice, Bartemius interpreted the Triwizard Tournament rulebook in such a way as to make it seem that Harry was required to compete in the Tournament.

• Bartemius Crouch Sr. did manage to break free much later in the year, and made his way to Hogwarts; but was there discovered and killed by Barty Crouch Jr., and his body hidden.

• To replenish his stocks of Polyjuice Potion, Barty broke into Severus Snape's office to steal potion ingredients. He was observed by Harry using the Marauder's Map, but due to the similarity of names, Harry thought that the intruder was Bartemius.

• Barty, acting as Professor Moody, provided assistance to Harry in the various quests:

• suggesting summoning a broom to fly past the dragon in the first challenge;

• loaning Neville Longbottom a book that described Gillyweed in the expectation that Harry would mention to Neville that he needed to figure out a way to survive underwater;

• when that failed, mentioning Gillyweed in front of Dobby so that Dobby would provide a method for Harry to win the second challenge;

• using the Imperius curse again to control and eliminate Harry's opponents in the third challenge.

Finally, captured by Dumbledore, he reverts to his actual shape when his dose of Polyjuice potion wears off. Having been dosed with Veritaserum, he then reveals all that he had done. He then receives the Dementor's Kiss, before he can repeat his story to a representative of the Ministry, as a consequence of Cornelius Fudge's actions.

Greater Picture

Shortly after his return, Voldemort summons his Death Eaters to his side. As Voldemort goes around the circle of Death Eaters, commenting on the gaps in the circle, he comes to *the largest gap of all . . ."And here we have six missing Death Eaters . . . three dead in my service. One, too cowardly to return . . . he will pay. One, who I believe has left me for ever . . . he will be killed, of course . . . and one, who remains my most faithful servant, and who has already re-entered my service. . . . He is at Hogwarts, that faithful servant, and it was through his efforts that our young friend arrived tonight . . ."* By not naming these Death Eaters, and by not completing the circle, the author is able to leave it in doubt as to who exactly is being referred to here. We are led to believe, correctly, that it is Karkaroff who has run, but it is unclear whether that is the cowardly one, or the one who has left Voldemort's service forever. At this point, we are unaware of the existence of Barty Crouch, and so we are misled into believing that the faithful servant who has already re-entered Voldemort's service is Severus Snape. And despite the revelation of Barty's role in the events of the book, the casual reader may well retain this mistaken belief even after that revelation, and may see this particular scene as confirmation of Snape's continuing loyalty to the Dark Lord. In fact, though, the faithful servant is Barty, Karkaroff is the cowardly one, and it is Snape who Voldemort feels has left. We will find out in *Harry Potter and the Half-Blood Prince* that Voldemort had his doubts about Snape, but that Voldemort had accepted Snape's explanation, both for his apparent desertion of Voldemort in the intervening years, and for his failure to appear instantly at Voldemort's summons on this occasion.

Bathilda Bagshot

Gender: Female
Hair color: Unknown
Eye color: Unknown
Related Family: Unknown
Loyalty: Unknown

Overview

Bathilda Bagshot, author of *A History of Magic*, one of the textbooks in use throughout Harry's school career, lives in Godric's Hollow.

Role in the Books

Philosopher's Stone One of the books that Harry must purchase in Diagon Alley is *A History of Magic* by Bathilda Bagshot.

Prisoner of Azkaban The book *A History of Magic* is mentioned early in the book as Harry has to do homework over the summer and is using this book as reference. Note that some editions of *Harry Potter and the Prisoner of Azkaban* mistakenly list this book as being written by Adalbert Waffling.

Deathly Hallows At Fleur and Bill's wedding, Harry speaks with Elphias Doge and Ron's Auntie Muriel. There, he learns that the source used by Rita Skeeter for her scurrilous book about Albus Dumbledore was most likely Bathilda Bagshot, who is apparently living in Godric's Hollow, where Harry's parents had lived, and to Harry's surprise, where the Dumbledore family had lived. This cements Harry's intention to go to Godric's Hollow. It is mentioned that Bathilda at the time was very nearly senile, and that Rita Skeeter had used Veritaserum to get the recollections of Dumbledore's early life from her.

On arriving at Godric's Hollow near Christmas of that year, Harry and Hermione are surprised to find that a resident of the village can apparently perceive them, despite their being under the Invisibility Cloak. The resident responds positively when asked if she is Bathilda Bagshot; she takes them to her house, which is an absolute mess, and Harry notes a strange odor, as of rotten meat. Taking Harry upstairs, Bathilda collapses and a large snake, Nagini, leaves her body and starts attacking Harry. Hermione comes to the rescue, and the two of them Disapparate under Voldemort's nose.

Later, Harry hears that Bathilda has been found dead, and Dark magic involvement is suspected.

Relationships with Other Characters In the letter which Lily Potter writes to Sirius Black, and which Harry sees in Grimmauld Place when he searches Sirius' room, Lily mentions that Bathilda seems friendly.

Rita Skeeter's book quotes Bathilda as saying that she had tried to be friends with the Dumbledore family but had been rebuffed. One gets the impression that Bathilda is an outgoing person, perhaps one who likes to be the center of a gossip circle.

Analysis

We never meet Bathilda Bagshot in person; by the time we actually see her, in *Harry Potter and the Deathly Hallows,* she is apparently a dead body, animated sketchily either by the presence of Nagini within her, or by the same magic that creates and preserves Inferi. Harry detects the odor of spoiled meat in her house, and we come to understand that this is Bathilda herself. There is no indication of how long she has been dead, but it is likely that it has been some time, as it seems that her author's copy of Rita Skeeter's book has not been touched. It is possible that Voldemort had set this trap as long as some five months before. We see that Nagini is with him in the first chapter of the book, which occurs in late July, and we know that Skeeter's book came out in August or September. This would suggest that Bathilda had died sometime between July and September, and quite possibly at Voldemort's hand, after which Nagini would have been living within her remains. It is perhaps suggestive that we do not see Nagini after the first chapter, until Harry triggers the trap on Christmas Eve or early Christmas morning.

Questions

1. The author has said that Albus Dumbledore was born in 1881, and apparently died in 1997 at age 115 or 116. Remembering that Bathilda Bagshot was already mature enough to be host for Gellert Grindelwald when he and Dumbledore were about 17, how old must Bathilda have been at her death in 1997?

Bellatrix Lestrange

Gender: Female
Hair color: Black
Eye color: Dark
Related Family: Rodolphus Lestrange, Black Family
Loyalty: Lord Voldemort

Overview

Bellatrix Lestrange (née Black) is Sirius Black's cousin, and sister of Narcissa Malfoy. She is described as being taller than Harry, with thick, sleek, shining, black hair, a thin mouth, dark, heavily lidded eyes, pale skin, and the Black family's patrician good looks and bearing. However, her looks were somewhat hollowed out after her stay in Azkaban prison. In the film adaptations of the novels, actress Helena Bonham Carter portrays the character.

Role In The Books

Goblet of Fire Although the action referred to takes place before the series starts, it is in this book that we are introduced to Bellatrix, as Harry is told by Sirius Black that she was part of a group that ran with Severus Snape, almost all of whom turned out to be Death Eaters. Harry also witnesses her trial and conviction by means of Dumbledore's pensieve.

Shortly after Lord Voldemort's disappearance, she and three other young Death Eaters (her husband Rodolphus Lestrange, his brother Rabastan Lestrange, and Barty Crouch Jr.) attacked and tortured Aurors Frank and Alice Longbottom, using the Cruciatus Curse on them until the two lost most of their mental faculties. All four members of the group were sentenced to imprisonment in Azkaban.

Order of the Phoenix A number of times during the cleaning of the house at Number 12, Grimmauld Place, Harry sees a Wizarding photo of Bellatrix. She seems to be one of Kreacher's favorites, as he has retrieved her photo from the trash and has placed it centrally in his sleeping area.

Bellatrix managed to escape in the mass breakout during Harry's fifth school year, and rejoined Lord Voldemort. She was one of the Death Eaters who took part in the Battle at the Ministry, and it was her spell that killed Sirius Black. She escaped the battle shortly after that and ran for the Atrium, with Harry in hot pursuit. When Voldemort appeared at the Ministry in person, Bellatrix was the only Death Eater that he saved; this may have been an accident of location, as Bellatrix was in the Atrium, and by that time Albus Dumbledore had imprisoned the other Death Eaters with an anti-apparation charm in the chamber of the Veil.

Half-Blood Prince Bellatrix accompanies her sister Narcissa Malfoy to Spinner's End, trying to dissuade her all the way. Once there, she first agrees with Severus Snape that Narcissa should not be talking to Snape of things told her by Voldemort, then expresses her dislike of Snape, asking him a number of questions about things that seem to indicate his lack of loyalty. Snape, responding, asks her whether she really thought the Dark Lord had not asked these same questions, and been satisfied with the answers? He then proceeds to answer her questions individually. Where was he when the Dark Lord fell? At Hogwarts, where Voldemort had ordered him to spy on Albus Dumbledore. Why did he not go looking for the Dark Lord after he had fallen? For the same reason many other Death Eaters did not: he thought the Dark Lord was finished. Bellatrix retorts that she had looked for him. Snape sarcastically comments about how "useful" she was while imprisoned in Azkaban, while he had collected sixteen years' worth of information on Dumbledore for Voldemort. Snape continues: Why did he stand between the Dark Lord and the Philosopher's Stone? Because the Dark Lord believed Snape had deserted him for Dumbledore, he had not informed Snape of his partial return, and so Snape was unaware that it was Voldemort that looking for the Stone. He thought Quirrell was searching for it on his own account and, of course, he acted to prevent that. Why did he not respond to the Dark Lord's summons when Voldemort returned? He returned two hours later, at Dumbledore's orders. That way, Dumbledore would continue to believe that Snape was spying on Voldemort for him, rather than the other way around. Bellatrix says she is unaware of any information Snape passed to Voldemort, although she should know: Voldemort says she is his most trusted lieutenant. Snape asks if she still is after the fiasco at the Ministry. And where was he at that battle? On the Dark Lord's orders, he stayed out of it. Did Bellatrix think Dumbledore would not notice if Snape had joined the Death Eaters in that battle? In any event, the information Snape supplied made Emmeline Vance and Sirius Black's deaths possible, and the Dark Lord was satisfied with his information. Why did Snape not kill Harry Potter? Because it was only Dumbledore who was keeping Snape effective as a spy and out of Azkaban. If he killed Potter, he would lose that protection and would be unable to help Voldemort. And that has been what has made him useful to the Dark Lord: Dumbledore's trust in him.

With Bellatrix thus overridden, Snape listens to Narcissa's concerns, saying that she was lucky that he was privy to the plan that Voldemort has for her son Draco. Narcissa asks for his promise to aid Draco, he gives it, but she presses on, asking him to make an Unbreakable Vow. Bellatrix is initially skeptical that he will, but when he agrees, though surprised, she serves as the bonder of the Vow.

When Harry is listening to Snape and Draco, who have just left Professor Slughorn's party, he hears Snape, after a short pause, commenting that Draco's Aunt Bellatrix has been teaching him Occlumency.

Deathly Hallows We first see Bellatrix in Malfoy Manor, in council with Lord Voldemort. It appears that she is sitting well down the table, out of Voldemort's favour, in part because of her association with Narcissa Malfoy, who is in disgrace along with all of her family, and in part because of her niece Nymphadora Tonks, who has married the Werewolf, Remus Lupin.

During the escape from Privet Drive, six members of the Order disguise themselves as Harry by means of Polyjuice potion, and each of the resultant Harrys rides with another member of the order as protector. Ron, disguised as Harry, travels with Tonks. Bellatrix singles Tonks out and the two of them duel fiercely; neither Tonks nor Ron is injured. Meanwhile, when Harry first sees Andromeda Tonks, he briefly mistakes her for her sister Bellatrix.

When Harry, Ron, Hermione, Dean Thomas, and Griphook are captured and taken to Malfoy Manor, Bellatrix sees the Sword of Gryffindor and panicking, stops Lucius Malfoy from summoning Voldemort, saying that summoning him before knowing the full story behind the sword could be fatal. In order to determine where the sword came from, she tortures Hermione, who insists under torture that the sword is a fake. She knows that the true Sword is made by goblins, and so sends Draco Malfoy to fetch Griphook, who as a goblin should be able to detect goblin workmanship immediately. Griphook, coached by Harry, reports that the sword is fake. Bellatrix says that Fenrir Greyback, who had brought the Trio in, can now have Hermione. Harry and Ron burst in, and Ron with Wormtail's wand Disarms Bellatrix. Bellatrix now threatens Hermione with a knife, and under that threat, Harry and Ron allow Draco to relieve them of their wands. Dobby, who has arrived to assist thanks to an earlier summons by Harry, now drops the crystal chandelier on Bellatrix. In the confusion, Harry physically wrests the three wands away from Draco and Stuns Fenrir, then tosses one wand to Ron. Ron Apparates away with Hermione to Shell Cottage, and Harry, also Apparating away, sees Bellatrix throw her knife. Arriving at Shell Cottage with Dobby, Harry finds that Bellatrix's thrown knife has hit Dobby, and Dobby dies in Harry's arms. Harry later determines that Bellatrix's reaction to seeing the sword of Gryffindor was because she feared that it had been removed from her vault at Gringotts. When the Trio, with Griphook, decide that they must break in to Gringotts to retrieve the cup Horcrux, Hermione uses Polyjuice potion to assume Bellatrix's appearance. Bellatrix is present when Voldemort receives news that her vault has been broken into and the cup Horcrux stolen. She and Lucius Malfoy barely escape Voldemort's literally murderous rage at the news.

When Harry relives Snape's memories in the Pensieve, one of the scenes is of Dumbledore shortly after the ring Horcrux has destroyed his hand. Snape has resuscitated him, and has informed him that the curse is contained, but cannot be stopped; Dumbledore has at most one year of life left. Dumbledore says that he knows Draco Malfoy has been given the task of killing him by Voldemort, and seeks Snape's promise that when Draco has failed, that Snape should do it. Snape demurs, and Dumbledore says that he would much rather Snape do it, than one of the Death Eaters who like to play with their victims, like Fenrir or Bellatrix.

When Harry, having determined that he must be killed by Voldemort before Voldemort can be defeated, confronts him in the Forbidden Forest, Bellatrix is there beside Voldemort, comforting him. After Harry is killed, and returns from the simulacrum of King's Cross, he hears that Bellatrix is trying to resuscitate Voldemort, who apparently fell at the same time Harry did; Voldemort brusquely pushes her away.

Bellatrix is killed by an enraged Molly Weasley with presumably the Killing Curse, after almost hitting Ginny Weasley with a curse, in the final battle. The loss of his staunchest supporter enrages Voldemort, and he attempts to Curse Molly in retaliation, but is stopped by a Shield charm cast by Harry.

Strengths We are led to believe that she is quite powerful, magically, as she appears to know many branches of magic, foremost the Dark Arts, of course. She never hesitates to use the Unforgivable Curses, seeing them as being the most powerful. As Albus Dumbledore states: " . . . dear Bellatrix, who likes to play with her food before she eats it." This, along with her treatment of Neville in the Department of Mysteries, clearly illustrates Bellatrix's lack of morals, as she does not hesitate to torture, or even kill, her opponents. In many ways it is a fearsome strength, since it allows her to do whatever it takes to gain favour in Voldemort's eyes.

Weaknesses   Her obsessive love for Voldemort.

Relationships With Other Characters   Bellatrix has long harbored a passion and desire for Lord Voldemort. It is unclear whether she is truly in love with him or merely infatuated with his power, but regardless, her obsessive lust leads her to become one of the most devoted Death Eaters. However, the feelings are not reciprocated, as Voldemort believes love is a weakness. Bellatrix Lestrange is the sister of Draco Malfoy's mother, Narcissa Malfoy, and both are daughters of Cygnus Black, who is Sirius Black's uncle. It is perhaps a measure of the amount of inbreeding in the "pure-blood" lines that an examination of the Black family tree shows that Bellatrix is, in fact, related distantly to many of the major players in the story: the Weasleys, both directly and via the Prewetts; Tonks; the Longbottoms; the Macmillans; the Crouch family; and even Harry himself.

Bellatrix strongly distrusts Severus Snape. Given that she is sufficiently good as an Occlumens to be teaching the technique to Draco, we can imagine that this is due in part to Snape's own ability in that field. Bellatrix no doubt has attempted to use Legilimency on Snape and been blocked. Her distrust of Snape will largely be due to her inability to read his motives.

ANALYSIS

Bellatrix is presented to us as being, in the eyes of the ordinary Wizarding world, more than slightly insane. We are shown this first in the Pensieve, where we see her screaming defiance at the Wizengamot. In the picture of her that Harry finds (and Kreacher hides away) at Grimmauld Place, Harry remarks on her insane appearance. Of all the Death Eaters in the battle in the Ministry of Magic, she alone has to be restrained from launching an attack on Harry before he has secured the Prophecy, and she is the one who comes up with the idea of torturing Neville, as she had his parents, to get Harry to give up the Prophecy. Interestingly enough, in the scene at Spinner's End, she is more the voice of moderation, trying to keep Narcissa from getting herself into trouble by dealing with Snape against Voldemort's wishes.

Benjy Fenwick

Gender: Male
Hair color: Unknown
Eye color: Unknown
Related Family: Unknown
Loyalty: Order of the Phoenix

OVERVIEW

Benjy Fenwick was a member of the original Order of the Phoenix.

ROLE IN THE BOOKS

Order of the Phoenix   At the celebratory party at Grimmauld Place for Ron and Hermione's appointment as Prefects, Alastor Moody shows Harry a photograph of the original Order of the Phoenix. Benjy Fenwick is in that photo, and Moody comments that they only ever found bits of him.

Bertha Jorkins

Gender: Female
Hair color: Unknown
Eye color: Unknown
Related Family: Unknown
Loyalty: Ministry of Magic

OVERVIEW

Bertha Jorkins was a witch working with the Department of Magical Games and Sports in the Ministry of Magic. She was also Sirius Black's and James Potter's school mate at Hogwarts. When she is first mentioned in the book, she has been missing since being on vacation in Albania. She is later revealed to be dead.

ROLE IN THE BOOKS

Goblet of Fire   In chapter One, Lord Voldemort reminds Wormtail that he murdered Bertha Jorkins after they forced her to reveal Ministry information. With this information, Voldemort devised a plan to lure Harry Potter to a place where he would use him for a sinister purpose.

After her disappearance from Ludo Bagman's department, Bagman seems unconcerned, saying, "Poor old Bertha . . . memory like a leaky cauldron. Will likely turn up sometime in October thinking it's still July." Arthur Weasley is later called upon to assist in damage control when Rita Skeeter discovers her unexplained absence and writes about it in the *Daily Prophet*.

Bertha's absence is mentioned several times throughout the book. Sirius Black disputes Bagman's claim about Bertha, telling Harry that when they were at school together, she had a very good memory and a very long nose for gossip; a bad memory is not something he would associate with her. Professor Dumbledore summons her memory from his Pensieve, and he and Harry see her accusing a fellow student of jinxing her only because she followed him, though she later expands on this, saying she had followed him and his girlfriend, had seen them kissing, and had told him she would tell everyone about it.

Finally, under Veritaserum, Barty Crouch Jr. reveals that Bertha had visited Bartemius Crouch Sr.'s house some time before our story begins, and had discovered that Barty, who supposedly died in Azkaban, was hidden at his father's house. Bartemius put a memory charm on Bertha, but it caused her ongoing memory problems. On vacation, she fell in with Wormtail, who brought her to Voldemort. From her, Voldemort learned about the Triwizard Tournament being held at Hogwarts. By breaking the memory charm, he learned also that Barty Crouch Jr. had escaped Azkaban and was being hidden at his father's house. Breaking the memory charm destroyed Bertha's mind, and Voldemort quickly murdered her as she was of no further use.

Strengths Before Bartemius Crouch damaged it, Bertha had evidently quite a good memory, and one gathers that she had something like Rita Skeeter's nose for gossip.

Weaknesses After her memory had been charmed, she seems to have become notably weak in her ability to remember, and had been, as a consequence, shunted around from department to department at the Ministry.

ANALYSIS

In *Harry Potter and the Goblet of Fire*, Voldemort had gained some kind of body shortly after Bertha had been captured by Peter (Wormtail) Pettigrew. Later on it mentions that Voldemort "pointed his wand" at Peter and used the Cruciatus Curse on him. When Harry arrives in the graveyard Peter drops an "ugly baby" into the cauldron. What if the "service" that Bertha provided was more then just the information about Barty Jr. and the Triwizard Tournament at Hogwarts? It is entirely possible, though horrible to contemplate, that the body that Voldemort inhabited during this book was, in fact, Jorkins' child, possibly one that she had gone on holiday to have privately. Voldemort would, of course, not mention this in his exposition to the Death Eaters as to how he had survived, due to the shameful weakness of the body he had been forced to inhabit; and the author would not have mentioned it anyway in a book intended for children.

Bill Weasley

Gender: Male
Hair color: Red
Eye color: Unknown
Related Family:
Loyalty:
Arthur Weasley (father)
Molly Weasley (mother)
Charlie Weasley (younger brother)
Percy Weasley (younger brother) Fred Weasley (younger brother) George Weasley (younger brother) Ron Weasley (younger brother) Ginny Weasley (younger sister)
Albus Dumbledore

OVERVIEW

William "Bill" Arthur Weasley is the eldest son of Arthur and Molly Weasley; he is two years older than Charlie, the second son. He is tall with long, red hair tied into a ponytail and a fang earring, both of which which his mother disapproves of. At Hogwarts he was in Gryffindor House and Head Boy in his seventh year. After Hogwarts, Bill worked as a curse-breaker for Gringotts Wizarding Bank in Egypt.

Bill Weasley's birthday is 29 November.

ROLE IN THE BOOKS

Philosopher's Stone Bill is first mentioned to Harry Potter by Ron Weasley while they are journeying to Hogwarts on the Hogwarts Express. He is said to have been Head Boy while at school, and is now working for Gringotts in Egypt as a curse-breaker.

Chamber of Secrets Bill continues to work at Gringotts in Egypt.

Prisoner of Azkaban The Weasley family visits Bill over the summer holidays in Egypt.

Goblet of Fire Bill is waiting at the Weasleys' kitchen table when Harry arrives by Floo powder from the Dursleys.' This is the first time we see him, and his unconventional style of dress, in person. Harry had expected him to be somewhat stodgy, as he had been Head Boy, and having only Percy as an example; but Bill is what can only be described as cool.

Bill is at home because Arthur Weasley has managed to get tickets to the Quidditch World Cup, and will be going to the Cup with the rest of the family. Being old enough to Apparate, he does so, arriving at the campsite about noon with Percy and Charlie. He goes to the stadium with the rest of the Weasley family, and apparently enjoys the match, discussing it at some length with the rest of the family on their return to the campsite. When the riot breaks out that night, he goes with Charlie, Percy, and Arthur to try to break it up before the Muggles get injured, and in the process collects an injury.

In the following week and a bit, we see him a few times around the Weasley family home, usually being nagged about the length of his hair by his mother. When Amos Diggory calls Arthur to tell him about Mad-Eye Moody, Bill is part of the conversation where we learn about Moody's history. Charlie and Bill travel with the rest of the group to the Hogwarts Express, and Bill alludes to something mysterious that will be happening at Hogwarts. Apparently Charlie and Mrs. Weasley know about it as well, but none of them will say anything, much to the annoyance of Harry, Ron, Fred, and George.

We next see Bill just before the Third Task of the Triwizard Tournament. As Harry does not have family who are interested in watching him in the Tournament, Bill and his mother have come to watch him. Fleur Delacour, seeing Bill waiting for Harry, does not seem to be too upset by the long hair or the fang earring. Harry spends the day touring Hogwarts with Mrs. Weasley and Bill, and listening to Mrs. Weasley's reminiscences of how it was in her day; and waves to Bill and Mrs. Weasley before he goes into the maze.

As Harry arrives in the hospital wing after Voldemort's return, Bill, along with Mrs. Weasley, Ron, and Hermione, is in the group demanding of Madam Pomfrey where Harry is. All of this group stay by Harry's bedside as Harry is given sleeping potion.

When Harry is awoken by Cornelius Fudge's arrival, Bill is still present. After Fudge's departure, Professor

Dumbledore tells Mrs. Weasley that he needs to send a messenger to Arthur Weasley, about what has happened, and to start gathering allies in the Ministry. Bill volunteers to carry the message, and departs.

Order of the Phoenix   We first see Bill when Harry arrives at Number 12, Grimmauld Place. When Harry, Ron, Hermione, Ginny, Fred, and George go down to the kitchen for dinner, Bill is there cleaning up after the meeting of the Order of the Phoenix.

In conversation before and over dinner, we learn that Bill has stopped working as a curse-breaker and has taken a desk job at Gringotts so that he can be closer to home to work for the Order. He has also started giving Fleur Delacour lessons so that she can "eemprove 'er Eeenglish."

When Arthur Weasley is injured at Christmas, he is taken to St. Mungo's Hospital. Molly Weasley stays there until he is out of danger, then goes to Grimmauld Place to let the rest of her family and Harry know what is happening. She tells everyone that Bill is sitting with Arthur.

Half-Blood Prince   When Harry arrives at The Burrow after meeting Horace Slughorn, Fleur Delacour brings him his breakfast, in the course of which she says that she is engaged to be married with Bill the following summer. Ron, Hermione, and Harry agree with Ginny that Molly Weasley's strategy of dragging Nymphadora Tonks under Bill's nose is unlikely to get Bill to notice her; Tonks also is too upset since the Battle at the Ministry the past summer to be particularly interested in Bill. Bill is apparently living at The Burrow; he is there the morning of Harry's birthday, and mentions the departure of Florean Fortescue from his store in Diagon Alley.

Bill goes into Harry's vault at Gringotts and retrieves some money for him, saying that it now could take several hours to get into Gringotts because of the security measures.

Bill and Fleur are at the Burrow at Christmas; Mrs. Weasley is mildly upset that Tonks, though invited, has chosen to stay away. She believes that it is Bill's presence that is keeping Tonks from spending Christmas with them. Bill is present during the battle under the Astronomy Tower; he was evidently one of the Order members who was guarding Hogwarts during those times when Albus Dumbledore was not there. He was mauled by the werewolf, Fenrir Greyback. Fortunately, as Fenrir was not transformed at the time, Bill did not become a true werewolf, however Madam Pomfrey is unable to cure the scarring. Molly Weasley initially believes that Fleur will call off the wedding, because he is no longer as handsome as he was; but Fleur is indignant at the suggestion, saying she is pretty enough for both of them, and the wedding is most certainly still on. This declaration marks the beginning of the reconciliation between Molly and Fleur.

Though there is fear that Bill may have been turned into a werewolf by Fenrir's attack, it turns out that the only permanent damage he suffers are the scars on his face, and his new liking for very rare steaks.

Deathly Hallows   Bill begins his Summer with a mission to protect Harry. Harry's protection at Number 12, Privet Drive will end when he reaches his majority, so shortly before that time the Order of the Phoenix gathers to transport Harry to a safe house. The plan is that there will be seven groups each traveling to one safe house, each group being a Harry Potter and a protector. The six decoy Harrys are to be produced by means of Polyjuice Potion. Bill is a protector, and his decoy is Fleur. Though attacked by Death Eaters, they do make it safely to their destination and from there to The Burrow.

Once there, he assists in caring for his brother George, who has had his ear cut off. After leading a moment of respect for the fallen Alastor Moody, Bill departs to see if he can find Moody's body.

The day after Harry's birthday, Bill and Fleur Delacour are married. The celebration is interrupted by news arriving, via Patronus from Kingsley Shacklebolt, that the Ministry has fallen, and that Death Eaters are already on their way to the Weasleys.'

When Ron becomes fed up with the "adventure' that he is having with Harry and Hermione, he leaves; but he cannot go to The Burrow because he is already there and suffering from Spattergroit—or at least, so the authorities believe. Instead, he goes to Shell Cottage, the seaside home where Bill and Fleur have settled, and spends Christmas with them. On his return to Harry and Hermione, he tells them about Shell Cottage.

Harry, Ron, and Hermione are captured by Snatchers and imprisoned in Malfoy Manor along with several others. Harry pleads for help from someone he sees in Sirius Black's magic mirror, and shortly is joined by Dobby. Having heard of Shell Cottage from Ron, and needing a safe house for Dean Thomas, Luna Lovegood, and Ollivander, he asks Dobby to take them to Shell Cottage. Shortly afterwards, Ron, Hermione, Griphook, Harry, and Dobby follow; Dobby dies there, and Bill assists in burying him, and in the care of Ollivander and Griphook. Once Ollivander has recovered enough to travel, Bill takes him to Auntie Muriel's. Later, Bill is present when Remus Lupin arrives to announce the birth of little Teddy Lupin. As that celebration is winding down, Bill cautions Harry about Goblin's ideas of ownership. Goblins, he says, believe that ownership remains with the maker of a thing; something made by goblins remains the property of the goblins, and if a human gives them money for it, that is in the nature of rental rather than purchase, and the goods should return to the maker when the original "owner" dies. Bill is present at the Battle of Hogwarts, he is one of the last few arrivals through the tunnel from the Hog's Head, and is present when Percy arrives to join in the defence of the school.

Black Family

Gender: Unapplicable
Hair color: Unknown
Eye color: Unknown
Related Family: Unknown
Loyalty: Death eaters/ Voldemort

Overview

The Black family were considered to be one of the noblest family in the wizarding world. They are very strict when it comes to blood status.

Role in the Books

Order of the Phoenix At Christmas, Sirius Black shows Harry the Black family tree on a tapestry in the front parlor at Number 12, Grimmauld Place. The members of the family that he mentions are Phineas Nigellus, Aunt Elladora, Araminta Meliflua, Alphard Black, his uncle, his parents Walburga and Orion, his brother Regulus, his cousins Bellatrix, Andromeda (who has had her spot on the tree burned off because she dated to marry "the Muggle Ted Tonks") and Narcissa, and Narcissa's son Draco Malfoy. This family tree is huge, and the motto is *Toujours Pur*—"Always Pure." Those like Andromeda and Sirius himself who have dared to consort with Muggles or the Muggle-born have been burned off the family tree, and the tapestry itself is apparently fastened to the wall with a Permanent Sticking Charm.

Weaknesses The Blacks seemed to have a surprisingly short life span for wizards. Most of the later generations were female and, with the death of Sirius near the end of *Order of the Phoenix*, the lineage came to an end.

Relationships with Other Characters Family tree:

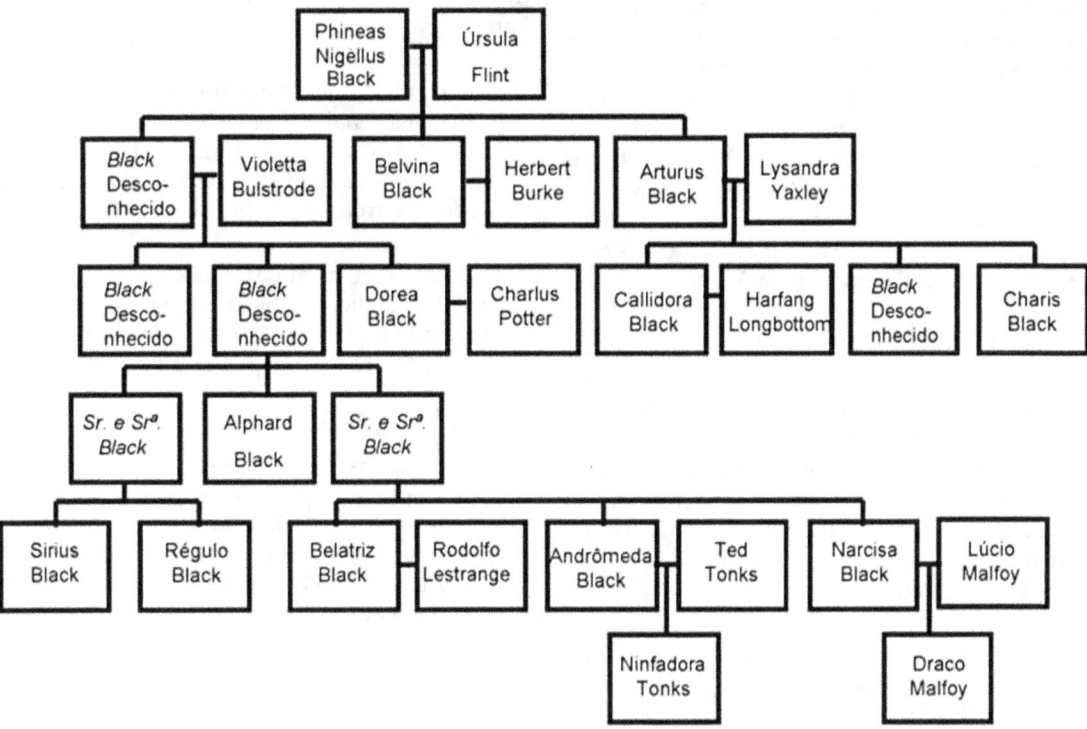

Analysis

If nothing else, the Black family tree details just how inbred and intermarried the "pureblood" Wizards are—both of Sirius' parents are descended from Phineas Nigellus and his wife Ursula Flint. One point of interest is that Dorea (or Dorca) Black married Charlus Potter, and they had one son—could that be James Potter, Harry's father? James was born, we think, about 1959, when Dorca / Dorea would have been about 40, which is possible; though it is equally possible that Charlus is James' grandfather. Sirius did mention that he spent rather a lot of time over at James' parent's; it's possible that James' mother was his aunt or great-aunt.

It is curious that Harry did not see, or did not see fit to comment on, the presence of his own family name, when he saw the House of Black tapestry in *Harry Potter and the Order of the Phoenix*.

Other interesting names appear in this tapestry as well. Callidora, who was born in 1915 and is still alive, married Harfang Longbottom; what relationship are they to Neville Longbottom? Lucretia (1925—1992) married Ignatius Prewett; would that be one of Molly Weasley's brothers, along with Gideon and Fabian Prewett? Charis (1919 1973) married one Caspar Crouch: Bartemius Crouch Sr.'s brother, perhaps? And there is passing mention of Ron's uncle, Septimus Weasley, who apparently married Cedrella Black (burn-mark 4).

Burn-mark 7, Andromeda "who married Muggle Ted Tonks," is Nymphadora Tonks' mother; Ted Tonks, is not a Muggle, though he was Muggle-born. Tonks did mention that she was related to the Black family.

Questions

1. Is Draco Malfoy, Lucius Malfoy's son, related to Harry Potter? If so, what is the relation?

Blaise Zabini

Gender: Male
Hair color: Black

Eye color: Brown
Related Family: Unknown
Loyalty:

Overview

Blaise Zabini is a Hogwarts student in Harry's year. He is a member of Slytherin house.

Role in the Books

Philosopher's Stone Blaise Zabini is Sorted into Slytherin.

Half-Blood Prince Blaise Zabini is invited to dine with Professor Slughorn on the Hogwarts Express, along with Harry, in Professor Slughorn's renascent Slug Club. Zabini's claim to fame is apparently that his mother is a famously beautiful witch, whose seven successive husbands all died mysteriously and left her pots of Galleons. Harry follows Blaise back to his compartment on the Hogwarts Express, hoping to overhear some conversation with Draco Malfoy that would give him some clue as to what Malfoy had planned. Malfoy drops some hints, but does not say anything particularly helpful, perhaps because he has seen Harry's foot as Harry climbed into the luggage rack.

Weaknesses Blaise is described as being excessively vain, as well as bitter, self-centered, and clever. He does not actively participate in the fight against the Light, but is rather more concerned with protecting himself. He does not associate himself fully with anyone, he is considered a loner, although he is some-what of a friend of Malfoy's. He finds Ginny Weasley attractive, but would never pursue a relationship with her, due to her family's Blood Traitor status.

Relationships with Other Characters He is a friend of Draco Malfoy's, and seems to get along with Pansy Parkinson, to an extent. Other than that, he doesn't really associate himself with the other students.

Bob Ogden

Gender: Male
Hair color: Unknown
Eye color: Unknown; mole-like behind hugely thick glasses
Related Family: Unknown
Loyalty: Ministry of Magic

Overview

Bob Ogden, seen only in Albus Dumbledore's Pensieve, is a member of the department of Magical Law Enforcement. Our memory of him predates the birth of Lord Voldemort.

Role in the Books

Half-Blood Prince In Dumbledore's Pensieve, Harry and Dumbledore watch as Bob Ogden arrives at the Gaunt residence. He is attacked and cursed by Morfin Gaunt, who is interrupted by Marvolo Gaunt. Ogden tells Marvolo that Morfin had cursed a Muggle, and was required to attend a hearing at the Ministry. Marvolo, showing Gaunt family heirlooms, says that he and his family are pure-blooded wizards. Ogden's statements that purity of blood counts little in the eyes of the law are interrupted by the sound of horses, and the revelation (in Parseltongue so Ogden doesn't understand it) that Marvolo's daughter Merope is sweet on the Muggle he had Jinxed. Marvolo, furious that his daughter could fall for a Muggle, attacks her; Ogden, though not fully aware of what is going on, defends her and is attacked in turn, and makes good his escape, running headlong into the horses that were passing. Dumbledore tells Harry that Ogden had returned with a squad and had subdued both Marvolo and Morfin. After their hearings, they had both been sent to Azkaban.

Strengths Ogden takes his duties seriously and maintains a professional and courteous demeanor despite Marvolo's hostility toward him and the Ministry. Ogden also shows bravery and compassion when he defends Merope from her father's assault.

Weaknesses Like most wizards, Ogden is not very experienced or skilled at the subtleties of Muggle clothing. Trying to look like a Muggle, Ogden wears a frock coat and spats over a one piece bathing costume.

Greater Picture

"Ogden" seems to be a common Wizarding surname, possibly an old family. Professor Tofty, one of Harry's O.W.L. examiners, mentions his friend Tiberius Ogden. Tiberius was present at Harry's hearing in OOTP. There is also Ogden's Old Firewhiskey, a brand preferred by Gilderoy Lockhart.

Bogrod

Gender: Male
Hair color: Unknown
Eye color: Unknown
Related Family: Unknown
Loyalty: Gringotts

Overview

Bogrod, a Goblin, is one of the counter workers at Gringotts Wizarding Bank in Diagon Alley.

Role in the Books

Deathly Hallows In order to retrieve the cup of Helga Hufflepuff, which Harry believes has been made into a Horcrux by Lord Voldemort, Harry, Hermione, and Ron, with the assistance of Griphook, determine to enter Gringotts and break into Bellatrix Lestrange's family vault. The Goblin who they encounter at the desk, and who Harry coerces into leading them to the vaults, is Bogrod. Under Harry's control, Bogrod receives Clankers, and pilots a cart down to the deepest levels where the Lestrange vault is located. It is Griphook who explains how the Clankers are used: to make noise so that the guardian dragon will not attack them. It is Bogrod who opens the vault for them, at Harry's command. Once Harry has managed to retrieve the Cup, he coerces Bogrod into opening the door for them once more; then, confronted with a number of Goblins intent on restraining him, he, Ron, and Hermione free the watch-dragon and escape on his back.

Bole

Gender: Male
Hair color: Unknown
Eye color: Unknown
Related Family: Unknown
Loyalty: Slytherin house

Overview

Bole (no first name given) is mentioned as being one of the Beaters in the Slytherin Quidditch team.

Role in the Books

Prisoner of Azkaban Bole is one of two Beaters who attempts to injure Harry Potter in the Slytherin / Gryffindor final. (The other is Derrick.) He is unsuccessful, being out-maneuvered by Harry.

Order of the Phoenix Angelina Johnson mentions Bole (and Derrick, too) in passing, saying that she always was surprised that Bole and Derrick could make it down to the Quidditch pitch without needing signs.

Borgin

Gender: Male
Hair color: Unknown
Eye color: Unknown
Related Family: Unknown
Loyalty: Money, Dark magic

Overview

Mr. Borgin, a stooping man with greasy hair and an oily manner, is one of the owners of Borgin and Burkes, the Dark magic supplies store in Knockturn Alley. The other owner is, or was, Caractacus Burke.

Role in the Books

Chamber of Secrets Harry enters Borgin and Burkes accidentally, on his first attempt to use Floo powder. Seeing Draco Malfoy approaching, he hides, and eavesdrops while Draco and his father Lucius are waited on by Mr. Borgin. In a particularly oily manner, Borgin suggests that it is a pity that blood purity counts for so little these days, expresses surprise that Mr. Malfoy is selling rather than buying today, commends Draco on his interest in the Hand of Glory, and finally bows the two of them obsequiously out of his shop. He then returns into the back rooms of the store, giving Harry the chance to make his way out unimpeded.

Half-Blood Prince Harry, Ron, and Hermione follow Draco Malfoy, who has slipped away from his mother, to Borgin and Burkes. There, we overhear Draco demanding assistance in fixing something, a demand to which Borgin expresses some reluctance. Draco shows him something to inspire his cooperation. Draco also says that Fenrir will be stopping by periodically to ensure that he is doing his job. After he leaves the store, Hermione goes in to try and find out what Draco had been interested in; Borgin is uncommunicative, though he does mention that one necklace she looks at is priced at one and a half thousand Galleons. Finally he ushers her out of the shop, and puts up the Closed sign.

While we hear that Tom Riddle had been employed some years earlier at Borgin and Burkes, we do not see Mr. Borgin in relation to that employment.

Broderick Bode

Gender: Male
Hair color: Unknown
Eye color: Unknown
Related Family: Unknown
Loyalty:

Overview

Broderick Bode is a worker in the Ministry of Magic's Department of Mysteries.

Role in the Books

Goblet of Fire Bode attends the Quidditch World Cup, and Arthur Weasley points him out to Harry as he passes the Weasleys' tents.

Order of the Phoenix When Harry, Ron, Fred, George, Ginny, and Mrs. Weasley, accompanied by Mad-Eye Moody and Tonks, arrive to visit Arthur Weasley at St. Mungo's, the day after the snake attack, they wait in line after an old stooped wizard who is there to see Broderick Bode. The Welcome Witch says he's wasting his time, Bode still thinks he's a teapot.

Some days later, Harry, Ron, and Hermione happen to end up on the long-term residents floor, due to a chance encounter with Gilderoy Lockhart. There, they see Bode, who is apparently getting better. He receives a pot plant (US: house plant) for a Christmas present from an unnamed well-wisher.

Hermione later reads that he has been strangled by the pot plant, which turns out to have been a Devil's Snare. In a dream Harry has in late February, where he perceives things happening in Voldemort's mind, Harry hears that Bode had been placed under the Imperius spell by Malfoy, but that he had known that he would not be able to do what was being asked of him, and so fought the spell very hard. Based on this sketchy information, Harry, Ron, and Hermione conclude that Bode was placed under the Imperius Curse by Lucius Malfoy, and was supposed to remove a prophecy concerning Harry and Lord Voldemort from the shelf it is stored on. As an employee in the Department of Mysteries, however, he knew that he could not touch it, so he fought the curse unsuccessfully. The shock of touching the prophecy may have lifted the curse, but left him unable to speak. He was admitted to St. Mungo's, but was killed by the anonymously sent Devil's Snare plant as he began to regain speech abilities. It is theorized that the Death Eaters wished to silence him and so sent the plant, which his Healer thought was a harmless Christmas gift. Encouraged to care for the plant himself, Bode touched the Devil's Snare and was instantly throttled. His death was only briefly mentioned in the *Daily Prophet*.

Buckbeak

Gender: Male
Hair color: Stormy gray
Eye color: Orange
Related Family: Unknown
Loyalty: Rubeus Hagrid

Overview

Buckbeak is Hagrid's favorite Hippogriff, a creature who has the forequarters of an eagle and the hindquarters of a horse.

Role in the Books

Prisoner of Azkaban One of the subplots of the book involves the attempted execution of Buckbeak. Harry Potter is introduced to him and rides him; Draco Malfoy is introduced to him, insults him, and is injured by him. Draco exaggerates his injury, and, as Professor Dumbledore will not sack Rubeus Hagrid from his job as Care of Magical Creatures teacher, Lucius Malfoy, Draco's father, attempts to have Buckbeak prosecuted by the Ministry for Magic as a dangerous creature. Hagrid doesn't stand much of a chance against Lucius' eloquence, so Buckbeak is sentenced to death. At the eleventh hour and a bit, with assistance from Hermione Granger, Harry saves Buckbeak and gives him to Sirius Black, who escapes on him.

Goblet of Fire Sirius apparently returns to the environs of Hogsmeade with Buckbeak; Harry, Hermione, and Ron meet him when they visit Sirius in the cave he is inhabiting outside the village.

Order of the Phoenix Sirius is now living at 12 Grimmauld Place, and Buckbeak is living in an attic room there. Throughout the story, Sirius is seen carrying bags of rats up to Buckbeak, and for a while Harry is spending a lot of time with him so that he does not have to relate to humans.

Half-Blood Prince With the death of Sirius, Buckbeak now has to move, and so he returns to Hagrid's care. Renamed Witherwings, so as to avoid the wrath of the Ministry, Buckbeak now lives in Hagrid's cottage. The only active part he plays in this story is near the end: as Severus Snape is escaping, Buckbeak tries to attack him, perhaps in retaliation for Severus' setting Hagrid's hut on fire.

Deathly Hallows Buckbeak again joins in near the end of the story, attacking the Death Eaters in the Battle of Hogwarts.

Cadwallader

Gender: Male
Hair color: Unknown
Eye color: Unknown
Related Family: Unknown
Loyalty: Hufflepuff house

Overview

Cadwallader plays in the Hufflepuff Quidditch team as Chaser.

Role in the Books

Half-Blood Prince With the graduation and departure of the previous announcer for Quidditch, Lee Jordan, other announcers are being tried. For the game between Gryffindor and Hufflepuff, Luna Lovegood is announcing, and she seems unable to recall Cadwallader's name until prompted by Professor McGonagall.

Caractacus Burke

Gender: Male
Hair color: Unknown
Eye color: Unknown
Related Family: Unknown
Loyalty: Galleons, Dark magic

Overview

Caractacus Burke is one of the owners of Borgin and Burkes, the Dark magic supplies store in Knockturn Alley. The other owner is Borgin.

Role in the Books

Half-Blood Prince In Albus Dumbledore's Pensieve, Harry sees Burke gloating over the marvelous deal he had made, buying the Locket of Slytherin for about ten Galleons from some poor little witch, almost certainly Merope Gaunt, who didn't know what she had. He evidently later sold it for thousands of Galleons to Hepzibah Smith.

Caradoc Dearborn

Gender: Male
Hair color: Unknown
Eye color: Unknown
Related Family: Unknown
Loyalty: Order of the Phoenix

Role in the Books

Order of the Phoenix At the celebratory party at Grimmauld Place for Ron and Hermione's appointment as Prefects, Alastor Moody shows Harry a photograph of the original Order of the Phoenix. Caradoc Dearborn is in that photo, and Moody comments that his body was never found.

Cedric Diggory

Gender: Male
Hair color: Dark
Eye color: Grey
Related Family: father Amos Diggory
Loyalty: Hogwarts

OVERVIEW

Cedric Diggory is Seeker and Captain of the Hufflepuff Quidditch team.

ROLE IN THE BOOKS

Prisoner of Azkaban Cedric Diggory, here a fifth-year student, is introduced as "the new Captain of the Hufflepuff Quidditch team," as he was competing against Gryffindor in the first match of the inter-house Quidditch championship. He caught the Snitch to win after the arrival of Dementors on the field. Believing that he had won by making inadvertent use of an unfair advantage, he requested that the game be replayed, but was overruled by Oliver Wood, the Gryffindor Quidditch captain, and the teachers.

Goblet of Fire We meet Cedric briefly at the beginning of the book, with his father, as they journey to the Quidditch World championships. Later, Cedric is chosen as a contestant in the Triwizard Tournament. Much of the book centers around the ongoing competition between him and Harry Potter, both in the Championship and for the affections of Cho Chang, throughout the course of the year. He and Harry tie in the last round, and grab the "trophy" together. The trophy had however been made into a portkey by allies of Lord Voldemort. He and Harry were transported to a graveyard, where Cedric was killed by Wormtail, one of Voldemort's Death Eaters. An image of Cedric later assists in distracting a re-created Voldemort long enough to allow Harry to make good his escape, carrying Cedric's body. Cedric's parents feel that they cannot take Cedric's share of the prize money, and give it to Harry.

Order of the Phoenix While Cedric cannot, of course, be present, he is mentioned several times during the course of the book, largely as part of Cho Chang's ongoing mourning for him.

Strengths A very athletic and handsome young man, Cedric is what many boys Harry's age want to be. He has many friends, and is honourable and trustworthy.

Relationships with Other Characters He always deals fairly with Harry, even when they are directly in competition with each other in the Tri-Wizard Tournament; Harry decides that the only honest thing to do is to give Cedric as much information as the other competitors have about the first trial, and in return, Cedric gives Harry the key to the second trial. As mentioned above, when he feels that he has won the Quidditch match against Gryffindor by means of an unfair advantage, he demands a rematch.

In part because Harry is slow getting off the mark, Cedric takes Cho Chang to the Yule Ball in *Harry Potter and the Goblet of Fire*; this marks the start of what ends up being a pretty serious romance between Cho and Cedric, much to Harry's dismay. This romance continues until Cedric's death at the end of the book.

ANALYSIS

It is interesting perhaps that Cedric's father Amos Diggory seems to be trying to create a sense of competition where none exists—casting Cedric's win over Gryffindor at Quidditch as a great victory when Cedric would rather put it entirely down to luck, and making rather more of the competition between Harry and Cedric in the Tri-Wizard Tournament than Cedric or Harry is comfortable with. One can perhaps see this as the all-too-common tendency for fathers to live their lives through their childrens' accomplishments.

Charlie Weasley

Gender: Male
Hair color: Red
Eye color: Unknown
Related Family:
Loyalty:
Arthur Weasley (father)
Molly Weasley (mother)
Bill Weasley (oldest brother) Percy Weasley (younger brother)
Fred Weasley (younger brother) George Weasley (younger brother) Ron Weasley (younger brother) Ginny Weasley (younger sister)
Albus Dumbledore

OVERVIEW

Charlie Weasley is the second son of Arthur and Molly Weasley. He is three years older than Percy, the Weasley's third son. He was a Prefect in his fifth year at Hogwarts, and Quidditch Seeker on the Gryffindor house team. After graduation, he went to work with dragons in Romania. If he stayed for the full seven years, he would have left Hogwarts the year before Harry arrived.

According to the author, Charlie's birthday is 12 December.

ROLE IN THE BOOKS

Philosopher's Stone Charlie is mentioned in passing on the Hogwarts Express as Ron lists his brothers who have attended Hogwarts before him.

At tea with Hagrid on the Friday of their first week, Hagrid asks Ron how Charlie is doing, saying that he always liked Charlie, who was good with animals.

In commenting on Harry's proficiency on a broom, Professor McGonagall says "He caught that thing in his hand after a fifty-foot dive. Didn't even scratch himself. Charlie Weasley couldn't have done it." Later that day, Fred and George tell Harry that they've heard about him; they are on the team as well, they're Beaters, and George tells Harry, "We haven't won since Charlie left, but this year's team is going to be brilliant." A few times after that, Oliver Wood compares Harry's skills as Seeker favourably with Charlie's.

The Weasley children, Percy, Fred, George, and Ron, stay at Hogwarts over Christmas because their parents are visiting Charlie in Romania.

When it becomes apparent that something is going to have to be done about Hagrid's pet dragon, Norbert, Ron hits on the idea of sending Norbert off to his brother Charlie. Though he does respond to Ron's letter, Charlie does not directly appear, but four of his friends do end up spiriting Norbert away in the night.

Goblet of Fire Charlie is waiting at the Weasleys' kitchen table when Harry arrives by Floo powder from the Dursleys.' It is mentioned here that he has a large, healing burn on one arm.

Charlie is at home because Arthur Weasley has managed to get tickets to the Quidditch World Cup, and will be going to the Cup with the rest of the family. Being old enough to Apparate, he does so, arriving at the campsite about noon with Percy and Bill. He goes to the stadium with the rest of the Weasley family, and apparently enjoys the match, discussing it at some length with the rest of the family on their return to the campsite. When the riot breaks out that night, he goes with Bill, Percy, and Arthur to try to break it up before the Muggles get injured, and in the process collects an injury.

In the following week and a bit, we see him a few times around the Weasley family home, doing homely tasks like darning a fireproof balaclava. When Amos Diggory calls Arthur to tell him about Mad-Eye Moody, Charlie is part of the conversation where we learn about Moody's history.

Charlie travels with the rest of the group to the Hogwarts Express, and alludes to something mysterious that will be happening at Hogwarts. Apparently Bill and Mrs. Weasley, who have accompanied the group to the platform, know about it as well, but none of them will say anything, much to the annoyance of Harry, Ron, Fred, and George.

We see Charlie again at the run-up to the First Task of the Triwizard Tournament, where he is one of the wizards brought in to wrangle the dragons needed for that task. He speaks briefly to Hagrid, unaware of Harry's presence under the Invisibility Cloak, but suggesting that Hagrid was unwise to bring Madame Maxime to see what her champion would be facing.

Order of the Phoenix While Charlie Weasley is mentioned as being in the Order of the Phoenix, Arthur Weasley says that they have chosen to leave him in Romania, so that he can bring wizards from other countries into the organization.

---

1. http://www.jkrowling.com/textonly/en/faq_view.cfm?id=63

Deathly Hallows Apparently, Charlie is unable to return to Hogwarts from Romania in time to play a part in the first part of the battle of Hogwarts, but he arrives with the reinforcements and is part of the forces who eventually defeat the Death Eaters.

Strengths Charlie has a gift with animals, especially dragons.

ANALYSIS

One issue that has been mentioned repeatedly on the Harry Potter fan sites is that, as stated here,[1] Charlie is three years older than Percy, so possibly the last time he will have flown for Gryffindor would be in his seventh year, the year immediately preceding Harry's arrival. In that case, the twin's statement in the first book that they haven't won a game since Charlie left, would be true only because they hadn't played any games since Charlie left. While this does rather nag at the reader, and the author has never explained it, there is one unexplored possibility: Charlie's chosen profession does not seem to require any N.E.W.T.-level studies. So Charlie, as the Twins did after him, might not have chosen to wait out the seventh year of school. In fact, as he would have come of age shortly before Christmas of his sixth year, he could well have left school then, leaving Gryffindor without his services as Seeker for the last two matches of that year and the three matches immediately before the series opens. It is more likely, though, that if he had chosen to leave school early, he would have left at the end of his sixth year, leaving Gryffindor 0 for 3 in Quidditch the year before Harry arrived.

Cho Chang

Gender: Female
Hair color: Black
Eye color: Brown
Related Family: Unknown
Loyalty: Albus Dumbledore

OVERVIEW

Cho Chang is a very beautiful and charming Ravenclaw seeker and is one year older than Harry. A love affair bloomed between Cho and Harry in his fourth (*Harry Potter and the Goblet of Fire*) and fifth (*Harry Potter and the Order of the Phoenix*) year, but their relation became strained, and had broken off by his sixth year.

ROLE IN THE BOOKS

Prisoner of Azkaban We first meet Cho when she is introduced as Seeker of the Ravenclaw Quidditch team. Harry immediately notices that she is very pretty, and he feels a slight jolt in his stomach when she smiles at him. It also turns out that she is a very skilled flyer; despite the disparity in brooms (Cho is riding a Comet Two-Sixty, Harry is riding a Firebolt), she is still able to block one of his three attempts to get the Snitch.

Goblet of Fire   Harry sees Cho at the Quidditch World Cup in passing.

After the announcement of the Triwizard Tournament, Harry thinks of entering the tournament, winning it, and particularly of Cho's admiring gaze when he does so.

Cho most seriously wishes Harry luck in the first Task of the tournament.

Harry, upon learning that he will have to find a dance partner for the Yule Ball, decides to ask Cho. His fears of looking foolish doing so, however, prevent him actually asking her until the last day of classes, by which time it is too late: she has already promised Cedric Diggory that she would go with him. She does seem genuinely upset that she wouldn't get a chance to go to the Ball with Harry, though.

In the Second Task, Harry must free hostages that are held by Merpeople at the bottom of the lake. He finds that one of the hostages is Cho, unconscious like the others. Cedric arrives, some time after Harry, and frees her. Harry remains, because he doesn't want to leave anyone down here. When he finally reaches the surface, with Ron and Gabrielle Delacour, Cho is being helped by Madam Pomfrey.

Cho's boyfriend, Cedric Diggory, is killed by Voldemort during the Third Task of the Triwizard Tournament. At the Leaving Feast, as Dumbledore leads the school in honouring Cedric's memory, Harry sees Cho crying.

Order of the Phoenix   Cho looks into Harry's compartment on the Hogwarts Express to say hello to Harry, just after Neville Longbottom has demonstrated the defence mechanism of his new Mimbulus Mimbultonia plant. Harry, covered with Stinksap, is mortally embarrassed, and Cho quickly withdraws.

At Hogwarts, Cho approaches Harry, Ron, and Hermione in the courtyard at break, apparently to have a quick word with Harry. Ron sees that she is wearing the badge of a popular Quidditch team, and accuses her of supporting that team only because it is fashionable (we learn much later that Ron's favorite team, the Chudley Cannons, seems to be rather consistently at the bottom of the league). Stung, Cho retorts that she has always supported that team, and leaves.

Following his final session of detention with Professor Umbridge, Harry finds that he has to send a message to Sirius Black informing him that his scar hurt again when Umbridge touched him. In the Owlery, he is met by Cho, who has to send a birthday gift. They talk, sharing their revulsion at Umbridge's actions; when Argus Filch bursts in, accusing Harry of ordering Dungbombs, Cho defends him. Harry is extremely cheerful thereafter at breakfast, which draws notice from Hermione and Ron.

Harry is pleased again when Cho turns up at the Hog's Head for the first meeting of what is then called the Defence Association. When Zacharias Smith questions his qualifications, Harry is perhaps inordinately pleased that Cho is one of those who leaps to his defence, specifically talking about what he had faced in the Third Task. After the meeting breaks up, Cho seems to want to stay behind and talk to Harry, but her friend, who we later learn is Marietta Edgecombe, is impatient enough to leave that she manages to convince Cho to depart. At the first regular meeting, Cho suggests "Defence Association" as a name for the group, and Ginny Weasley points out that the initials could as easily stand for Dumbledore's Army. This name is written on the parchment, and lessons begin. Cho seems to have a great deal of difficulty with simple spells when Harry is nearby, though Harry has noticed that she handles them quite capably when he is on the other side of the room.

At the last D.A. class before Christmas break, Cho lingers after the rest of the students have left. She and Harry talk, she is still wondering about how Cedric died. Harry is unable to give much reassurance. She maneuvers Harry under the mistletoe, and they kiss.

Afterwards, talking with Hermione, Harry describes the kiss as "wet. Because she had been crying." Hermione says she does that all the time because she is still so confused about her own feelings for Harry and about Cedric. When Harry describes his effo9rts to console Cho, Hermione says it could have been worse. Hermione asks if he's going t see her again; Harry does not answer—the idea that he could go out with Cho seems to take him by surprise. Back at the school after Christmas, he meets Cho in the Entrance Hall. She points out that the next Hogsmeade weekend falls on February 14. When Harry realizes what she is talking about, he invites her to go to Hogsmeade with him; she enthusiastically accepts.

Once in Hogsmeade, though, Harry feels very out of place. Cho suggests Madam Puddifoot's Tearoom, and Harry agrees, but finds it full of Valentine's Day decorations, and packed solid with couples kissing. Harry, feeling awkward, casts around for topics of conversation but comes up with nothing. When Cho mentions that Roger Davies had asked her out, but she had turned him down, Harry is uncertain how to respond, not least because Roger, entwined in another girl, is sitting directly behind him. Harry has promised that he will meet Hermione at the Three Broomsticks at noon, and tells Cho this; Cho misunderstands, and storms out.

What Hermione has arranged is that an interview with Harry, written straight instead of being slanted to make him out to be an attention-seeker, will be published in The Quibbler. When the interview comes out two weeks later, Harry is greatly cheered that Cho seeks him out, tells him that he was really brave to give that interview, and kisses him.

Shortly after this, the D.A. is betrayed by Cho's friend Marietta Edgecombe. When she meets Harry after this, she says that she is sorry about the betrayal, but then goes on to defend Marietta, saying that her mother works in the Ministry. Harry points out that Ron's father works in the Ministry as well, but Ron doesn't have the word "Sneak" written on his face. Cho says that it was a dirty trick to charm the parchment they had signed that way, but Harry is adamant: there was no reason to betray the D.A. Cho storms off.

Harry, having seen a very disturbing scene that passed between his father and Snape, is preoccupied;

luckily, he can pass off his preoccupation as being the result of fighting with Cho.

Though Cho is playing in the final Quidditch match of the year, against Gryffindor, Harry is extremely ambivalent about watching her. He thinks to himself that he doesn't know what he wants, except that he doesn't want any more fights. When her name is announced and he sees her on the field, his heart does not do its usual backflip, only more of a feeble lurch. Even seeing her talking animatedly with Roger Davies gets very little reaction. On the Hogwarts Express heading back to London, Cho walks past Harry's compartment, blushes, but doesn't stop. Ginny says that she has taken up with Michael Corner. Ron asks, hadn't Ginny been going out with Michael? Ginny says that he was a poor loser, so she had dumped him.

Half-Blood Prince   Cho passes Harry a few times, but there is no real interaction.

Deathly Hallows   In the preliminary action before the second Battle at Hogwarts, Cho appears with the other members of Dumbledore's Army to help defend the school against Lord Voldemort. She volunteers to show Harry the bust of Rowena Ravenclaw in the Ravenclaw common room. Ginny Weasley forestalls this, suggesting quite strongly that Luna Lovegood should do that instead.

Strengths   An excellent Quidditch player. Cho was also a member of Dumbledores Army (DA) with Harry. As a member of Dumbledore's Army, she was strong enough magically to progress to the point of actually conjuring a corporeal Patronus. In Harry's O.W.L. exam that same year, his ability to conjure a corporeal Patronus was evidently worth an extra mark; while other members of the DA were apparently not similarly tested, the fact that this was worth a whole letter-grade (about 10% of the examination total) would indicate that it is a relatively rare ability for a fifth-year, and presumably also for a sixth-year.

Weaknesses   She does not seem to be able to complete her mourning for Cedric Diggory, who is killed at the end of *Harry Potter and the Goblet of Fire*. Throughout the next book, *Harry Potter and the Order of the Phoenix*, other characters are commenting on how much crying she is doing.

Relationships with Other Characters   Friends with a lot of minor Ravenclaw characters, the main relationships presented are her and Harry dating 'on and off' after her former boyfriend, Cedric Diggory was killed, and her defence of the actions of her friend Marietta Edgecombe. Cho's romantic relationships are covered in more detail here.

Colin Creevey

Gender: Male
Hair color: Unknown
Eye color: Unknown
Related Family: Dennis Creevey
Loyalty: Harry Potter

Overview

Colin Creevey is student a year younger than Harry. Colin is very obsessed with Harry in his first year, and along with Ginny Weasley, is teased about creating a Harry Potter fan club.

Role in the Books

Chamber of Secrets   Colin, an almost intolerably chirpy child, is Sorted into Gryffindor.

On the first day of classes, Colin corners Harry, demanding a photograph as proof that he has actually met the famous Harry Potter. A small crowd, including Draco Malfoy, gathers while this was going on, and Draco immediately seizes on this, telling Gilderoy Lockhart, who is passing by, that Harry is offering signed photos. Gilderoy overpowers Harry's reluctance, and tells Colin to make it a picture of the two of them. He then drags Harry away for some "fatherly advice on handling fame." Harry is later teased about this by Hagrid. Harry is not terribly successful in his attempts to avoid Colin over the next week, and Colin accompanies him to the first Quidditch practice of the season. Oliver Wood is initially concerned about this strange person always clicking away with his camera while they are practicing, but soon has larger problems: the Slytherin team arrive, claiming that they have been granted use of the pitch by Professor Snape, to allow them to train their new Seeker, Draco Malfoy. When Ron curses Draco with his broken wand, is hit by the curse backfire, and starts vomiting slugs, Colin has to be restrained from taking pictures of him in his distress.

Passing Harry in the hall, Colin mentions that someone had said Harry was the heir of Slytherin, the one apparently responsible for opening the Chamber of Secrets.

When Harry is struck by an enchanted Bludger during the Quidditch game against Slytherin, a mistaken spell by Professor Lockhart removes all the bones in his arm, sending him to the Hospital Wing overnight. While he is there, Professor Dumbledore and Professor McGonagall bring in Colin, who has been Petrified. They surmise from the bunch of grapes he had been carrying that he was on his way to the Infirmary to visit someone, probably Harry, and as he was holding his camera before his face, they believe he was trying to take a picture of something. Opening the back of his camera to see what he had been trying to photograph, Dumbledore releases a cloud of burned-plastic smoke.

The news of Colin's Petrification apparently quite upsets Ginny. We do not yet know quite why. Once Harry and Ron determine that the monster in the Chamber is a Basilisk, they also realize that every person attacked was Petrified, rather than killed, because they did not see the monster directly. In Colin's case, he was looking through his camera, and saw the Basilisk through his camera lens (and presumably mirror, assuming a single-lens reflex camera).

At the end of the story, Colin is re-animated, as are the rest of the Petrified students.

Goblet of Fire Colin very excitedly tells Harry that his brother Dennis is starting at Hogwarts. Dennis is Sorted into Gryffindor, and Colin points out the famous Harry Potter to him.

Colin is the messenger who summons Harry to the Weighing of the Wands ceremony before the First Task. His prattle of photo opportunities and the associated fame quite sours Professor Snape, whose class Harry is being summoned from. As Harry and Colin proceed to the designated classroom, Colin goes on about how it must be nice to be so famous, not heeding Harry's weariness at the prospect.

Draco Malfoy has started distributing buttons that say "Support Cedric Diggory, the True Hogwarts Champion," and when pressed, change to say "Potter Stinks." Colin, with his brother Dennis, are seen at one point trying to Charm one of these badges, but are unsuccessful; when Harry returns to the Common Room that night, they have given up and left the badge on the table. The badge now reads "Potter Really Stinks," and when Ron interrupts Harry's conversation with Sirius Black, Harry throws it at him in anger.

Order of the Phoenix Colin is one of the students who attends the first meeting of Dumbledore's Army. We are led to understand that he attends further meetings, and makes much progress with the spells that Harry teaches, but he does not play a very large part in this book.

Deathly Hallows Colin, seen in the Great Hall, is told to evacuate the school with the other underage wizards, but apparently somehow makes his way back to the school. He is killed by Death Eaters in the final Battle of Hogwarts; in the quiet time after Harry has seen Snape killed, Harry sees Oliver Wood and Neville Longbottom bringing Colin's body in from the grounds.

Strengths Colin's main strength is his unremitting cheerfulness. While this can be annoying to those around him, like Harry, it results in him being willing to take on almost any challenge.

Weaknesses While his cheerfulness does make him willing to take on many challenges, the fact is that much of what he tries to do is beyond his ability. We see this in his attempt to change what the Potter Stinks button says, and quite possibly it is what leads to his death.

Relationships with Other Characters Colin almost worships Harry, and is amazed that he has been Sorted into the same House as the famous Harry Potter. His perpetual gung-ho enthusiasm seems to keep many others at a distance; we certainly never seem to see him spending time outside class with any other students, apart from his brother Dennis.

Analysis

Colin is a rather interesting mix of Muggle and Wizarding attributes. Clearly, he has not been raised among Wizards, because like Harry he is totally unfamiliar with the ways of magic; he has never before seen Wizarding photos, and is quite obviously amazed to learn that if he uses the correct potion as a developer, the resulting photos will move. However, he also hero-worships Harry, who is a celebrity only among Wizards, and it seems he feels his parents do the same, as he says he wants a signed photo for them. Additionally, there is Dennis, who is also a Wizard; how likely is it that two Wizards can spring from one set of Muggle roots? We have no way of judging. In part because of this, Colin and Dennis' Blood status was never entirely clear. On the one side, some commentators have suggested that the Basilisk attack on Colin was evidence of his Muggle origin, though it may be questioned exactly how much control over the Basilisk the Heir actually has at that point. On the other side of the question, the fact that Colin was at Hogwarts during the final battle in *Harry Potter and the Deathly Hallows*, when Hogwarts has been closed to all except those who can claim Blood status, is seen as evidence that Colin is able to prove that he has Wizarding ancestry.

The author has stated, since publication, that Colin and Dennis are, in fact, Muggle-born, and did not attend Hogwarts during Harry's seventh year. In an online question and answer session on July 30th 2007, she said that Colin had returned to the school along with the other exiled and graduate members of Dumbledore's Army, when Neville summoned them, and joined them all in the Great Hall where they gathered to prepare for the coming battle. There, McGonagall ordered him to leave, which he did, though presumably not actually getting as far as the Room of Requirement. He then sneaked back in to join the battle, as a true Gryffindor would, and died.

Cormac McLaggen

Gender: Male
Hair color: Unknown
Eye color: Unknown
Related Family: Unknown
Loyalty: Largely self

Overview

Cormac McLaggen is a member of Gryffindor house.

Role in the Books

Half-Blood Prince On the Hogwarts Express, Professor Slughorn invites a number of students to his compartment for lunch, including Harry Potter, Neville Longbottom, Ginny Weasley, Marcus Belby, Blaise Zabini, and Cormac McLaggen. It seems that most of them are invited because of their famous relatives, or because they are famous in their own right as Harry is, or because of their own apparent magical ability: Ginny is invited because Slughorn saw her performing a flawless Bat-Bogey hex. Harry recognizes this as Slughorn re-establishing his Slug Club.

McLaggen tries out for the Gryffindor Quidditch team, hoping to replace Ron Weasley as Keeper. Each Keeper candidate has five chances to stop shots on goal; Ron stops all five, but McLaggen fumbles the final one, and Ron is selected as Keeper. Ron comments that McLaggen had looked Confunded on his last shot; Hermione blushes, but Ron does not notice. Later, Harry sees McLaggen apparently having trouble negotiating the front steps into Hogwarts, and asks Hermione about it. Hermione, aware of his bad temper and denigrating comments about Ron and the other Keepers being tried, quietly admits having Confunded him during his trials so that Harry would have a valid reason to select Ron instead of him.

With Ron thoroughly entangled in Lavender Brown, Hermione does not have anyone she can take to Professor Slughorn's "Slug Club" Christmas party. She chooses to invite McLaggen, in part to make Ron jealous. Once there, finding McLaggen's unrelenting efforts to maneuver her under the mistletoe tiresome, she manages to lose him, instead talking to Harry and his date, Luna Lovegood.

When Ron is put out of action by a glass of poisoned mead, Harry reluctantly puts McLaggen in the team as Keeper. McLaggen immediately starts acting like team captain, trying to set tactics for the games, and telling the other players what is wrong with what they are doing. During the game against Hufflepuff, he borrows a Beater's bat to demonstrate the proper way to hit a Bludger, mis-hits it, and fractures Harry's skull. With Harry out of the game, Gryffindor loses very heavily to Hufflepuff. McLaggen is, of course, cut from the team immediately Harry regains consciousness.

Relationships with Other Characters   McLaggen is very self-important and self-centered, and must be the center of any group he is part of. He seems to be one of those irritating people who think they know everything. He tries to reinforce this view by demeaning and insulting those who might know more than he does. When he is passed over for what he considers an honour, he can have a very bad temper.

Cornelius Fudge

Gender: Male
Hair color: Unknown
Eye color: Unknown
Related Family: Unknown
Loyalty: Self, bureaucracy

Overview

Cornelius Oswald Fudge is the Minister for Magic, which makes him the senior government official of the Wizarding world.

Role in the Books

Philosopher's Stone   Cornelius Fudge is entirely offstage in this book. It is mentioned that he is perpetually summoning Professor Dumbledore to London for consultation, and that Fudge became Minister for Magic when Dumbledore turned down the offer.

Chamber of Secrets   Fudge appears briefly in this book, only long enough to accuse Hagrid of opening the Chamber of Secrets, and place him under arrest. Fudge's behavior in this vignette is already enough to show him as a pompous bureaucrat.

Prisoner of Azkaban   When Harry arrives at The Leaky Cauldron after catching a ride on the Knight Bus, Fudge meets him at the door, much to Harry's shock. Apparently, Fudge has been involved in some effort to find Harry, and is relieved that he has appeared. Fudge takes him to a private room, has the innkeeper, Tom, bring tea, and tells Harry, who has been dreading punishment for his unauthorized use of magic, that it could have happened to anyone, and that it will be forgotten. He goes on to ask if Harry would spend the remainder of his summer vacation there at the Leaky Cauldron, and in Diagon Alley, staying clear of the Muggle side of the inn. He also suggests that Harry should expect to stay at Hogwarts over Christmas and spring breaks, and is politely disbelieving when Harry says he would much rather do that. However, when Harry, taking courage from Fudge's apparent expansiveness, asks Fudge to sign his Hogsmeade permission slip, Fudge refuses, fumbling out some sort of excuse.

Fudge re-appears in Hogsmeade at Christmas, where we see him discussing the current state of affairs with Professor Flitwick, Professor McGonagall, Hagrid, and Madam Rosmerta. Harry, who is in Hogsmeade without permission, must hide under the table. When Rosmerta complains the Dementors are affecting her business, Fudge explains they are necessary because Sirius Black is so dangerous. Rosmerta mentions that Sirius and James Potter were great friends once, always in the Three Broomsticks together. This surprises Harry. Fudge says that not only was Sirius James' best friend, but also best man at his wedding and Harry's godfather. As the conversation continues, it is learned that James and Lily knew Lord Voldemort was hunting them and went into hiding. They used the Fidelius charm to conceal themselves and appointed Sirius their Secret-Keeper. Dumbledore, aware someone close to them was leaking secrets, offered to be their Secret-Keeper, but they declined. Barely a week later, Voldemort killed James and Lily, although he met his own demise in baby Harry. Obviously Black, tired of playing double agent, had thrown his lot in with Voldemort but, after his defeat, had to flee for his life. Peter Pettigrew, another Potter friend, caught up to Black the next day and accused him of betraying James and Lily. Black killed him and twelve Muggle bystanders with a single curse. Only Pettigrew's bloodstained robes and a severed finger were left. Black was sentenced to Azkaban, where he remained until his escape. It is believed he is now trying to reunite with Voldemort, perhaps after killing Harry to prove his loyalty.

Finally, when Sirius Black is captured, Fudge appears again to take custody of him. He accepts Professor Snape's version of the story at face value, refusing to believe Harry's and Hermione's protestations of Sirius' innocence and the presence of Peter Pettigrew. After Black escapes, Snape returns to the hospital wing with Fudge alongside, insisting that Harry had something to do with Sirius' escape. Harry states that he was locked into the hospital wing for the entire time that Snape was away, and Fudge expresses the belief that Snape has become somewhat unhinged. Professor Dumbledore, who is present, says that Snape has just suffered a disappointment.

Goblet of Fire We first see Fudge when we enter the Top Box at the Quidditch World Cup with Harry and the Weasley family. Fudge is exasperated because his opposite number, the minister for magic from Bulgaria, apparently speaks no English, and Fudge has been trying to communicate with him by sign language all day. Also present is Lucius Malfoy, there as Fudge's guest, in gratitude for a large donation that Malfoy has just made to St. Mungo's Hospital. At the end of the match, the Bulgarian minister comments that it was a good match, and says that he had not told Fudge that he spoke English because it was so comical watching him try to act out his meaning. We see Fudge again when Bartemius Crouch appears on the outskirts of the Forbidden Forest, apparently insane, and then vanishes. Foul play is suspected, of course, and Fudge apparently arrives at the school in order to use Dumbledore's and Professor Moody's input to support placing blame. Harry, standing outside Dumbledore's office door, hears Fudge suggesting that Madame Maxime, the headmistress of Beauxbatons Academy, may be at fault, because of her parentage. Harry is caught eavesdropping, and says that Madame Maxime was nowhere in sight, and she would be hard to miss after all. Fudge, Moody, and Dumbledore depart to look at the place where Mr. Crouch had been seen, leaving Harry alone in Dumbledore's office.

With Crouch missing and Percy Weasley, his assistant, in some disgrace, Fudge himself takes on the task of judging the Third Task of the Triwizard Tournament. When Harry and Cedric Diggory emerge from the maze, Fudge tries to disguise the fact that Cedric has been murdered, saying he is only injured. Summoned to Professor Moody's office to interrogate Barty Crouch Jr., Fudge feels that he must bring a Dementor with him; the Dementor administers the Kiss to Crouch immediately, making it impossible for Fudge to hear his confession directly. He then dismisses Harry's story of the return of Voldemort, saying that it can't be true. At one point, talking to Dumbledore, he almost seems to plead with him, asking Dumbledore to confirm that it can't have happened; but when Dumbledore remains unshakable, Fudge decides that Dumbledore has chosen to stand against the Ministry.

Order of the Phoenix Fudge rightly believes that if Lord Voldemort has returned, his tenure in office will end. In order to deny what Albus Dumbledore, Harry Potter, and Severus Snape have told him and shown him, Fudge has to come up with an alternate explanation; and the explanation he apparently comes up with is that Dumbledore has decided to become Minister for Magic and has set himself up as an enemy of the Ministry. To defend himself against this contrived threat, Fudge must discredit Dumbledore and Harry, so he apparently engineers the removal of Dumbledore from the Wizengamot, replacing Dumbledore himself. He also leans on the *Daily Prophet* so that they will print stories that disparage Harry and Dumbledore, thus attempting to ensure that anything that they say can be easily discredited.

All of this is happening behind the scenes. The first time we actually see Fudge in the story is when Harry is at his hearing for his unauthorized use of magic. Fudge has apparently convened the full Wizengamot for the hearing, and is acting as combination head judge and prosecutor. He has decided Harry's guilt, and even in the face of evidence from Dumbledore and Arabella Figg that there were Dementors present, thus making the use of magic justified under the law, insists on bringing up irrelevant information that he feels bolsters the Ministry case against Harry. In the end, however, the panel of judges rules that Harry's use of magic was justified, and Fudge sullenly declares him cleared of all charges, and leaves. As Harry departs the courtroom with Arthur Weasley, they run into Fudge and Lucius Malfoy, who is evidently about to make a large donation for something. After exchanging a few barbs with Mr. Weasley, Lucius suggests that he and Fudge should adjourn to Fudge's office, and let Arthur go about his business.

Fudge does not directly appear through much of the rest of the book; instead, he arranges the passage of Educational Decree Number Twenty Two, providing that the Ministry can appoint teachers to fill vacancies at Hogwarts when the Headmaster is unable to fill them himself. Using this decree, Fudge appoints Dolores Umbridge to the school as teacher of Defence Against the Dark Arts. Umbridge apparently has been given the prime mission of preventing the students from learning any useful jinxes, as the class is taught theory only, and apparently from a book that stresses negotiation rather than defence. Harry guesses that this is because Fudge fears that Dumbledore wants to become Minister for Magic himself, and so he is trying to prevent Dumbledore's school from creating an army that can be used against Fudge; Sirius Black later confirms this belief. Fudge also acts to increase his control over Hogwarts indirectly, by issuing new Educational Decrees that grant ever more powers to Umbridge. He returns directly to our story at the point where Harry's Defence Against the Dark Arts group, "Dumbledore's Army," is broken up by the actions of Marietta Edgecombe. Umbridge calls him in to witness the capture and punishment of the group, who are supposedly meeting in direct violation of Educational Decree Number Twenty-Four, which prohibits unapproved student groups. Fudge is dismayed to find that the only meeting of which they have direct evidence actually occurred before the Decree was made, and therefore is not in violation, and is further upset when Miss Edgecombe refuses to repeat the story she had told Professor Umbridge, instead maintaining that there had been no meetings since the first. However, Umbridge does finally retrieve the Dumbledore's Army membership list, and Dumbledore quietly agrees that, as Fudge had supposed, Dumbledore was creating a private army. However, when Fudge demands that he give himself up, Dumbledore refuses; in the ensuing, brief battle, Fudge, along with Umbridge and the Aurors Fudge has brought, are rendered unconscious and Dumbledore escapes. Fudge, on regaining his senses, runs off thinking that he is chasing Dumbledore.

At this point, Fudge manages to get Umbridge appointed Headmistress. However, she is unable to enter the Headmaster's office, remaining in her original office.

Finally, at the end of the battle at the Ministry, Fudge actually sees the returned Voldemort, who is rescuing Bellatrix Lestrange, one of his supporters. Fudge blusters at Dumbledore, but eventually must concede that Dumbledore was right all along, and that Voldemort has returned.

Half-Blood Prince At the beginning of this book, we find out that Cornelius Fudge has been fired as the Minister for Magic in favor of Rufus Scrimgeour, though he has stayed on as Scrimgeour's assistant. He appears in the Muggle prime minister's office at the start of the book, to brief the Muggle Prime Minister on the current state of affairs in the Wizarding world and introduce Scrimgeour. When the Prime Minister asks why they can't eliminate the threat by using magic, it is Fudge who points out that the other side has magic also. He has very little additional role to play in this book, though he does attend Dumbledore's funeral.

Weaknesses Cornelius Fudge is first and foremost a politician. His primary concerns are the viability of his post and his popularity. When faced with the inconvenient truth of Voldemort's return, Fudge chooses to deny the danger to the Wizarding World. Instead, he labors to discredit those who, in his opinion, threaten his political power. Ultimately he shows himself to be paranoid, self-centered and without scruples.

Crabbe, Sr.

Gender: Male
Hair color: Unknown
Eye color: Unknown
Related Family: Unknown
Loyalty: Lord Voldemort

Overview

Crabbe, Sr. is the father of Vincent Crabbe, one of Draco Malfoy's sidekicks.

Role in the Books

Goblet of Fire When Lord Voldemort summons his Death Eaters after returning to life, he addresses one of them as Crabbe, and asks him if he will do better next time, and Crabbe promises he will.

When Harry later names Crabbe as one of the Death Eaters present in the graveyard, Cornelius Fudge dismisses that, saying he had already been tried and released, and Harry could have gotten his name from the old news stories.

Order of the Phoenix Crabbe, Sr. is one of the twelve Death Eaters who take part in the Battle at the Ministry. His role is not entirely certain, as except when Lucius Malfoy is sending pairs off to hunt for Harry Potter and the students with him, he is never named.

Crookshanks

Gender: Male
Hair color: Ginger
Eye color: Unknown
Related Family: Unknown
Loyalty: Hermione Granger, Sirius Black

Overview

Crookshanks is a cat owned by Hermione Granger. He is quite large, for a cat, orange ("ginger") colored with brown stripes, and has an ugly, almost flat face and a bottle-brush tail. Although his significance to the the Harry Potter series is limited, readers have picked up traces of skepticism over his bearing. He is actually half-Kneazle.

Role in the Books

Prisoner of Azkaban Crookshanks enters the story by jumping from the top of a stack of cages in the Magical Menagerie in Diagon Alley, on to Ron's head, in an almost-successful bid to catch Scabbers. Hermione then buys him, over Ron's protests that Scabbers will never get any rest with "that cat" around, and takes him to Hogwarts. During the course of the trip to Hogwarts, and several times over the school year, Crookshanks attempts to catch Scabbers, often doing damage to Ron in the process, and eventually, apparently, manages to catch Scabbers in the boy's dormitory. Harry later sees Crookshanks in company with the large black dog that has evidently been following Harry around.

As Ron, Harry, and Hermione are heading back up to the castle after their meeting with Hagrid, Crookshanks again attacks the returned Scabbers; when Ron is dragged away under the Whomping Willow by the big black dog, Crookshanks shows the technique for freezing the Willow so that Harry and Hermione can follow. In the Shrieking Shack, it is revealed that Crookshanks had befriended Sirius Black, and had actually stolen the list of passwords from Neville Longbottom that had given Sirius access to the Gryffindor Common Room on the night that Ron was attacked. At several points during the battle, Crookshanks acts to defend Sirius against Harry: attacking Harry when he tries to recover his wand, and sitting on Sirius' chest exactly where Harry would have to fire a spell at Sirius to kill him.

As they exit the shack and Lupin turns into a werewolf, Peter Pettigrew siezes Ron's wand and uses it to stun Ron and Crookshanks before making his escape.

Finally, when Ron is given an owl by Sirius, he holds the owl under Crookshanks' nose for approval before he accepts it. The owl will later be named Pigwidgeon.

Goblet of Fire   Crookshanks is at the Burrow with Hermione. We see him chasing gnomes in the garden before dinner. When Fred Weasley drops some fireworks as the family prepares to depart for London and the Hogwarts Express, Crookshanks is frightened and mauls a Muggle taxi-driver. He rides in the same taxi as Harry, Ron, and Hermione, and all three of them get rather badly scratched in the process.

On the Express, and throughout the book, Crookshanks is an occasional presence, curled up on a chair, jumping into either Harry's or Hermione's lap, and generally behaving as a cat should. Crookshanks seems to be quite willing to soak up almost any amount of affection from either Harry or Hermione, and sometimes Ginny, but does not seem to entirely trust Ron.

Order of the Phoenix   At Number 12, Grimmauld Place, we see Crookshanks in the kitchen, playing with Butterbeer corks, and generally acting like a cat. Throughout the book, Crookshanks is an occasional presence, curled up on a chair, jumping into either Harry's or Hermione's lap, and generally behaving as a cat should.

Half-Blood Prince   It is mentioned that Crookshanks accompanies Hermione to the Hogwarts Express when they leave The Burrow. Once again, Crookshanks seems to be acting like a cat, and having only a passing role in the story.

Deathly Hallows   We see Crookshanks at Hermione's feet when she, Ron, and Harry manage to sneak some time together in amidst the wedding preparations at The Burrow. Crookshanks, here, is behaving very much like a cat, simply lying, curled up, at Hermione's feet while she sorts books. When Mrs. Weasley bursts in on them, Crookshanks, bristling, dashes under the bed to hide.

When Harry, Ron, and Hermione need to enter the tunnel at the base of the Whomping Willow, Ron wishes that they had Crookshanks with them to push the knot that will still the tree. In words strongly reminiscent of something Ron had said in the first book, Hermione says, "*Are you a wizard, or what?*" Ron, recollecting himself, uses the first charm he ever learned (Wingardium Leviosa) to push a stick against the knot.

Relationships with Other Characters   Crookshanks is Hermione's cat; they are quite fond of each other. When Hermione first bought Crookshanks, the witch at the Magical Menagerie told her that he had been there for quite a while; the implication being that very few other witches or wizards were interested in him, or perhaps he in them. The author, describing the genesis of the character, says that he is based on a Muggle cat who would prowl around the sunbathers in a particular square, looking disdainful and refusing to be stroked. While she says that she only borrowed his appearance for Crookshanks, perhaps that character trait also crept in, at least in the beginning.

Crookshanks is perpetually trying to attack Scabbers, who is Ron's pet rat. Initially he seems to be doing this because he simply doesn't trust Scabbers (he may be able to detect that Scabbers is not what he seems to be). Later, it seems he is trying to fetch Scabbers at the bidding of Sirius Black, who has recognized Scabbers as Peter Pettigrew and wants to get him away from the protection afforded him by Hogwarts. Ron, of course, is trying to defend Scabbers from Crookshanks, and gets into the middle of the battles quite often; as such, at least in *Harry Potter and the Prisoner of Azkaban*, the two of them are quite often fighting each other, and this almost rabid dislike has left enough bad memories that, while Ron can respect Crookshanks and his abilities, they are never quite comfortable with each other.

With other people, Crookshanks is more neutral, accepting affection and being willing to play. He is quite classically cat-like both with Harry and with Ginny Weasley, climbing into laps for a quick nap and playing with Butterbeer corks.

Analysis

Crookshanks' apparent extreme intelligence, as displayed in *Harry Potter and the Prisoner of Azkaban*, coupled with his flattened face, has led more than one reader to believe that he might be an Animagus, possibly even Regulus Black. There is precedent in the series for an unregistered Animagus, believed dead, to have stayed in his animal guise for several years. However, the author has denied this; in fact, she has stated, while discussing his origins, that Crookshanks is half Kneazle.[1]

Dawlish

Gender: Male
Hair color: Unknown (short and wiry)
Eye color: Unknown
Related Family: Unknown
Loyalty: Ministry Of Magic

Overview

Dawlish is an Auror for the Ministry of Magic. he is described as being a tough-looking wizard.

---

1. http://www.jkrowling.com/textonly/en/rumours_view.cfm?id=7

Role in the Books

Order of the Phoenix We first see Dawlish when Dumbledore's Army is broken up, and Harry is brought to Dumbledore's office by Professor Umbridge. Cornelius Fudge is there, and he has felt the need to bring two Aurors for his protection; one of the two is Dawlish. When Dumbledore is placed under arrest, he warns Dawlish not to try anything: if he attempts to *bring him in* by force, Dumbledore will have to hurt him. As it turns out, Dumbledore does knock him out in the quick battle that ends that scene.

Dawlish is one of the people that Umbridge brings in to assist her in sacking Hagrid. He is heard pleading with Hagrid to be reasonable while he tries to Stun him.

Half-Blood Prince As Tonks takes Harry up to Hogwarts after rescuing him from Draco Malfoy's Petrification curse on the Hogwarts Express, she tells Harry that she is not the only guard at Hogwarts: Proudfoot, Savage, and Dawlish are also present.

After Christmas, Harry relates his conversation with Rufus Scrimgeour to Dumbledore, saying that Scrimgeour is very interested in where Dumbledore is going. Dumbledore replies that Scrimgeour had also set Dawlish to tail him, and with great regret he had had to jinx Dawlish again.

Deathly Hallows Dawlish is mentioned as being the Auror from whom Yaxley is getting information about Harry Potter's movements. Severus Snape discounts Dawlish's information, saying that he was quite likely Confunded as part of the Order of the Phoenix laying a false trail. He says also that Dawlish is already known to be susceptible to being Confunded.

Later, the fugitive Dirk Cresswell mentions that he was being transported to Azkaban but managed to overpower his guard, Dawlish, and escape. He remarked at the time that Dawlish seemed a bit slow, as if he had been Confunded.

Finally, when the Death Eaters attempt to round up Augusta Longbottom, Neville's grandmother, in an attempt to control Neville's actions at Hogwarts, it is apparently Dawlish that they send after her. Augusta manages to put Dawlish in St. Mungo's before vanishing.

Strengths In order to have become an Auror, Dawlish must have done well in his exams. When Fudge attempts to arrest Dumbledore, in *Harry Potter and the Order of the Phoenix*, Dumbledore, while warning Dawlish about attacking him, does mention his high N.E.W.T. scores.

Weaknesses Dawlish is very susceptible to the Confundus charm, and evidence suggests that he spends much of the seventh book under the influence of that charm.

Analysis

Dawlish is such an inept Auror that one must wonder how he ever managed to get hired. His physical strength is apparently backed by a relative magical weakness: he is repeatedly Confunded, jinxed twice by Dumbledore, and put into hospital by an old lady, though arguably a very formidable one. Quite possibly he is brought into the story as an example of what can go wrong when bureaucracy runs amok, as it seems to be happening under Cornelius Fudge's administration.

Despite having necessarily had high marks on his N.E.W.T.s, and therefore being skilled magically as well as being intelligent, he is susceptible to the Confundus jinx, and may have been Confunded throughout a large part of the 7th book. And even Voldemort fears Dumbledore, so it's not surprising that Dawlish was easily handled by the Headmaster. Dawlish is very intelligent, capable and competent, but he has an easily exploitable weakness, plus, he takes orders without questioning them—making him a great soldier/police officer, but not a hero, or even siding with the heroes, unless he works for them and they tell him to.

Dean Thomas

Gender: Male
Hair color: Black
Eye color: Brown
Related Family: Unknown
Loyalty: Dumbledore's Army, West Ham United F.C.

Overview

Dean Thomas is a Gryffindor in Harry's year, who shares a dormitory with Harry, Ron Weasley, Neville Longbottom, and Seamus Finnigan. Although there is no particular description in the UK editions of the book, in the US edition it is mentioned that he is a black Londoner.

Role in the Books

Philosopher's Stone Dean, apparently of Muggle origins, like Harry, has never heard of Quidditch, and so has a poster of the West Ham football team that he puts up over his bed in the dormitory. Ron, who had had an argument with Dean about football and how a game with only one ball and two goals could be any good, is seen at one point poking the poster with his wand to try and make the players move.

At Harry's first Quidditch match, Seamus, Neville, and Dean have made a banner that reads "*Potter for President.*" Dean, who is apparently something of an artist, had painted the Gryffindor lion underneath that, and Hermione had charmed it so that the paint flashed different colours. When the Snitch first appears, Harry is about to grab it when he is fouled by Marcus Flint, the Slytherin team captain. Dean demands that the ref send Flint off, and Ron explains that you can't do that in Quidditch.

Order of the Phoenix When Harry and Neville reach the dormitory on Harry's first night back at Hogwarts, Dean says that Seamus has had a rough summer, largely due to the scurrilous reports in the *Daily Prophet* which have been painting Harry as a dangerous lunatic and Dumbledore as a senile old fool. After Seamus and Ron reach an accommodation, Ron asks if anyone else had a problem with Harry. Dean says that it is not a problem for him, his parents are Muggles. In the first Defence Against the Dark Arts class of the year, Hermione wonders when they will be actually practicing defensive magic. Professor Umbridge says that she can't see any time when people will be attacked in her classroom. Echoing Harry, who Umbridge is ignoring, Dean points out that if they are going to be attacked, it will be outside the classroom. Umbridge over-sweetly explains that the Ministry feels that understanding the principles of defensive magic will be sufficient.

Dean is one of the students who attends the first meeting of what becomes Dumbledore's Army, in the Hog's Head.

Harry gives an interview to Rita Skeeter about the events surrounding Voldemort's return. The following Monday at dinner, he apparently tells Dean and Neville about it. Dean is awestruck, and says he can't wait to see Umbridge's reaction.

Dean is present in the first class with Firenze, the centaur teacher brought in to replace Professor Trelawney after Umbridge sacks her. Firenze says that he would prefer to teach these classes in the Forbidden Forest, but this is not possible, as he has been banished by his herd. Dean, excited at the possibility that there are more Centaurs, asks if Hagrid had been breeding them, like the Thestrals, and apparently immediately realizes that he has said something horrible. Firenze, after a pause in which Dean evinces extreme embarrassment, says that Centaurs are a race apart, having little to do with humans.

Dean is pleased to hear that O.W.L. results won't arrive until sometime in July, as that means he won't have to worry about them until the middle of vacation. We see him later, practicing Charms theory with Seamus Finnigan. Following the final O.W.L. exam, Dean and Seamus tell Harry that they are planning a dusk-to-dawn end-of-O.W.L.s celebration and suggest that one of the students, Harold Dingle, believes that he can get some Firewhisky. Harry is in a panic, trying to get in contact with Sirius, and pushes past without answering.

It is noted that Hedwig and Pigwidgeon are disturbed by Ron's outburst when he learns that Ginny is going out with Dean.

Half-Blood Prince Is Ginny's boyfriend.

Deathly Hallows As Dean cannot prove that his father was a wizard, he is an outlaw for daring to have a wand. When we first see him, he is on the run with Ted Tonks, one Dirk (probably Dirk Cresswell) and the goblins Gornuk and Griphook. Ted, Dirk Cresswell, and Gornuk are ultimately killed, but Dean and Griphook escape only to later be captured by Snatchers and taken to Malfoy Manor alongside Harry, Ron, and Hermione. Dobby arrives, and Harry has him carry Dean, along with Luna Lovegood and Ollivander who are also prisoners of the Malfoys, to safety. (Griphook is also saved, shortly after.)

Dean remains in safety at Shell Cottage, but rejoins our story to take part on the final battle at Hogwarts. As the gathered members of Dumbledore's Army and the Order of the Phoenix leave the Room of Requirement to assist in the defence of Hogwarts, Dean takes Luna Lovegood's hand, and they leave together.

Relationships with Other Characters Dean was once in a short-lived romantic relationship with Ginny Weasley, although there are few details about this relationship and it is only mentioned in relation to Harry Potter's own love interests.

ANALYSIS

It is noted that Dean had joined Dumbledore's Army for only its last session before it was discovered and disbanded. This timing is, in fact, rather important. Harry has noted and tried to work around the fact that there are an even number of people (including himself) in the DA; most often, he has the students pair up so they can practice on each other, and as he cannot generally be one of the pairs, as he has to inspect and correct the other students, he often creates a single group of three, Neville, Hermione, and Ron. In the final session, Marietta Edgecombe is not present because she is telling Professor Umbridge about the group; Harry would be much more likely to notice her absence if suddenly he could pair everyone up. Dean's presence, by keeping the number of working students odd, prevents Harry noticing that Marietta is missing, and thus helps provide the necessary surprise.

Dedalus Diggle

Gender: Male
Hair color: Unknown
Eye color: Unknown
Related Family: Unknown
Loyalty: Albus Dumbledore

OVERVIEW

Dedalus Diggle is a very small wizard, who seems to be rather over-exuberant.

ROLE IN THE BOOKS

Philosopher's Stone When Lord Voldemort is defeated, there is mention on the Muggle news that someone seems to be setting off fireworks in Kent for no good reason. Professor McGonagall mentions that she thinks it is Dedalus Diggle doing it; she says he never had much sense.

Before he is identified to us, on the day after Voldemort's initial defeat, he apparently stops Vernon Dursley to invite him to celebrate. Diggle is later seen bowing to Harry in a store, although Harry does not recognize him. The first time we actually see Dedalus Diggle and have a name given for him is in the Leaky Cauldron, when Hagrid introduces Harry to the witches and wizards there. Diggle is overjoyed that Harry remembers him, dropping his top hat in his excitement.

Order of the Phoenix Dedalus Diggle is a member of the Advance Guard, the group of wizards that Alastor Moody brings to Privet Drive to bring Harry to the Headquarters of the Order. Other members of the Advance Guard are Nymphadora Tonks, Hestia Jones, Sturgis Podmore, Emmeline Vance, Kingsley Shacklebolt, Elphias Doge, and Remus Lupin. Dedalus Diggle, as usual, is extremely pleased when Lupin introduces him again to Harry, dropping his top hat in his excitement.

Deathly Hallows Dedalus Diggle is one of the two Order wizards who are detailed to accompany Vernon, Petunia, and Dudley Dursley to a place of safety four days before Harry's seventeenth birthday, when the protection afforded Harry will cease. Dedalus does not exactly inspire confidence in Vernon by his admission that driving a car is far too confusing for him. Additionally, all of the Dursleys find it alarming that Dedalus' watch chastises him loudly for being late. Speaking with Harry at Grimmauld Place, Lupin mentions that in the Death Eaters' search for Harry after the fall of the Ministry, Dedalus Diggle's house was burned down, but Dedalus was not there.

Demelza Robins

Gender: Female
Hair color: Unknown
Eye color: Unknown
Related Family: Unknown
Loyalty:

Overview

Demelza Robins joins the Gryffindor Quidditch team as a chaser.

Role in the Books

Half-Blood Prince Demelza Robins is one of three Chasers that Harry puts on the Gryffindor Quidditch team after a series of try-outs. The other two are Katie Bell and Ginny Weasley. This seems to be something of a tradition; in Harry's first through third years, all the Gryffindor chasers were girls as well.

A little later, she delivers a message from Professor Snape to Harry about a detention.

Amongst the team changes due to illness and detention, Demelza is the only Chaser who plays against all three other houses. Katie Bell is sidelined by a cursed necklace for two matches, and Ginny becomes Seeker when Harry is put into detention by Snape.

Deathly Hallows Demelza is mentioned in passing as being one of the defenders in the battle at Hogwarts.

Strengths Demelza is quite adept at Quidditch, having a knack for dodging Bludgers and for making tricky shots. She is known to work well with the other Chasers and is friendly with the Beaters. Other than her Quidditch ability, Demelza's strengths and skills are largely unknown.

Weaknesses Like her strengths, Demelza's weaknesses are largely unknown. However, it can be noted that she is rather sensitive, succumbing to tears on occasion, generally because of Ron.

Relationships with Other Characters Demelza is rarely seen outside of Quidditch games, where her relationships would be on a teammates level. We don't see enough of her outside Quidditch games and practices to get any feeling for how she would relate to other students.

Dennis Creevey

Gender: Male
Hair color: Mousey
Eye color: Unknown
Related Family: Colin Creevey
Loyalty:

Overview

Dennis Creevey, brother of Colin Creevey, is a perpetually-excited Gryffindor who entered Hogwarts in Harry's fourth year.

Role in the Books

Goblet of Fire Dennis Creevey, first seen wearing Hagrid's immense moleskin coat, is Sorted into Gryffindor. On reaching the House table, he tells Colin that he had fallen into the lake and was saved by the giant squid.

When Harry Potter becomes the second Hogwarts Champion, Draco Malfoy starts distributing buttons that alternate between saying "Support Cedric Diggory, the Real Hogwarts Champion," and "Potter Stinks." As Harry heads out for an appointment with Hagrid, he sees the Creeveys, Colin and Dennis, working with one of these badges, trying to charm it to say something different. On his return, he sees that they have not been successful; all that they have managed is to make the badge say "Potter Really Stinks."

Order of the Phoenix Both Dennis and Colin Creevey are members of Dumbledore's Army. While we don't hear much of them, it seems that Dennis is managing to master some of the more advanced charms, possibly with Colin's help, despite being only second-year.

Deathly Hallows Dennis and Colin are seen trying to figure out how they can stay at Hogwarts and assist in the defence before the final battle, but Professor McGonagall sends them both away.

Derrick

Gender: Male
Hair color: Unknown
Eye color: Unknown
Related Family: Unknown
Loyalty: Slytherin house

OVERVIEW

Derrick (no first name given) is mentioned as being one of the Beaters in the Slytherin Quidditch team.

ROLE IN THE BOOKS

Prisoner of Azkaban Derrick is one of two Beaters who attempts to injure Harry Potter in the Slytherin / Gryffindor final. (The other is Bole.) He is unsuccessful, being out-maneuvered by Harry.

Order of the Phoenix Angelina Johnson mentions Derrick (and Bole, too) in passing, saying that she always was surprised that Derrick and Bole could make it down to the Quidditch pitch without needing signs.

Dexter Fortescue

Gender: Male
Hair color: none
Eye color: Unknown
Related Family: Florean Fortescue(?)
Loyalty: the current headmaster (or headmistress) of Hogwarts

OVERVIEW

Dexter Fortescue, who we only see as a portrait in the Headmaster's office, is described as 'a corpulent, red nosed wizard.'

ROLE IN THE BOOKS

Order of the Phoenix Although he is not named, we see Fortescue shortly after the attack on Arthur Weasley. Having collected all of the Weasley family and Harry in his office, Professor Dumbledore attempts to wake up the portrait of Phineas Nigellus Black, to confirm that Sirius Black will be ready for a large number of visitors. Phineas expresses unwillingness to help, at which all the other portraits in the office express indignation. Three are particularly vocal, those being the wizard later identified as Fortescue, Armando Dippet, and an unnamed witch with a particularly thick-looking wand, almost a cudgel, who offers to chastise Phineas.

Fortescue is first named when Dolores Umbridge is explaining to Cornelius Fudge how she had learned of the first meeting of Dumbledore's Army in the Hog's Head. She explains that Willy Widdershins had been there and had reported back. Professor McGonagall, also present, comments that she had wondered how Willy had gotten off so lightly after all those regurgitating toilets, and Fortescue erupts, saying that they did not cut deals with petty criminals in his day. Dumbledore tells him that "that will do, Fortescue."

When Dumbledore sends Harry to his office after the battle in the Ministry, Fortescue is the first of the portraits to awaken and notice that he is there. He asks if this means Dumbledore will be returning, and comments that it has been dull in his absence. He also remarks that Dumbledore holds Harry in high esteem.

Deathly Hallows After the final victory at the Battle at Hogwarts, Harry returns to the Headmaster's office to speak with the portrait of Dumbledore. As he enters, he is greeted with loud cheers and applause from all the portraits on the walls. Dexter Fortescue is mentioned there by name, waving his ear trumpet.

Relationships with Other Characters Fortescue quite clearly has very rigid ideas of propriety, and is not shy about expressing them. He quite probably sees his place in the office panoply as being the guardian of The Correct Way, as so clearly everything has deteriorated so badly since he left.

Similarity of names may lead one to believe that Dexter is an ancestor of Florean Fortescue, keeper of the ice cream parlour in Diagon Alley, who is a vast store of knowledge about medieval witch burnings and is apparently quite able to teach. Nothing in the books either supports or refutes this relationship.

Dilys Derwent

Gender: Female
Hair color: Unknown
Eye color: Unknown
Related Family: Unknown
Loyalty: Current Headmaster of Hogwarts

OVERVIEW

Dilys Derwent (St. Mungo's Healer, 1722–1741, Headmistress of Hogwarts 1741–1768) is one of the portraits in the Headmaster's office at Hogwarts.

ROLE IN THE BOOKS

Order of the Phoenix Dilys is one of two portraits selected by Professor Dumbledore to investigate the apparent attack on Arthur Weasley reported by Harry Potter just before Christmas. Dumbledore remarks that Dilys and Everard are quite famous, and have portraits hanging in many places, which they can visit. Dilys, a famous Healer, will be visiting her portraits at St. Mungo's, and reporting what happens there. When Harry, along with Mrs. Weasley, Fred, George, Ginny, Ron, Tonks, and Alastor Moody visit Arthur in hospital, Harry notices a portrait of Dilys in the admissions area; the portrait seems to be counting them up, then winks at Harry and vanishes, almost certainly to report their arrival to Dumbledore.

Dirk Cresswell

Gender: Male
Hair color: Unknown
Eye color: Unknown

Related Family: Unknown
Loyalty: Ministry of Magic

OVERVIEW

Dirk Cresswell worked in the Goblin Liaison Office of the Ministry of Magic, eventually becoming head of the department.

ROLE IN THE BOOKS

Half-Blood Prince While Albus Dumbledore is in the process of recruiting Horace Slughorn at the beginning of the book, he leaves Slughorn and Harry together. The conversation turns to Harry's mother, Lily Potter, and Slughorn mentions that Dirk had been in the year after Lily. Now Head of the Goblin Liaison office, Dirk has been keeping him up to date on events at Gringotts.

Deathly Hallows When Harry, Ron, and Hermione are making their way through the Ministry in their search for the locket Horcrux, Harry is disguised as one Albert Runcorn, evidently a higher-up in the Ministry. A "bushily-whiskered man" hints that he knows Runcorn had betrayed Dirk Cresswell, evidently losing him his job, and tries to get Runcorn's backing for his plan to be next in line for the Goblin Liaison position. Later in that same episode, Harry, still disguised as Runcorn, shares an elevator with Arthur Weasley, who says he knows that Runcorn had more than a little to do with Creswell's being fired, and warns him to watch his step. Finally, in the escape from the Ministry, Harry gets the Ministry workers to stop sealing exit fireplaces by threatening the wizard in charge with having his ancestry investigated like Dirk Creswell's was.

Later, when Harry, Ron, and Hermione are moving from campsite to campsite through the English countryside, another group of refugees briefly and unknowingly camps beside them. This other group, comprised of Dirk Creswell, Ted Tonks, Dean Thomas, and the Goblins Griphook and Gornuk, reveals that a group of students at Hogwarts had tried to steal the sword of Gryffindor from the Headmaster's office. The students had been punished, and the sword had been transferred to a safe at Gringotts. The goblins also revealed that the sword in Gringotts was a fake, a very good fake but not Goblin-made.

Later, listening to the underground wireless broadcast, Harry, Ron, and Hermione hear that Ted Tonks, Dirk Cresswell, and Gornuk have been killed.

ANALYSIS

In *Harry Potter and the Goblet of Fire*, while they are waiting in the campsite for the Quidditch World Cup to begin, Arthur Weasley identifies the various Ministry members as they go by. He identifies one Cuthbert Mockridge as the Head of the Goblin Liaison Office. Comments between Dumbledore and Slughorn lead us to believe that Slughorn has been out of circulation since the re-appearance of the Death Eaters at the end of Harry's fifth year. Thus, Dirk's promotion must have happened between September of Harry's fourth year, and June of his fifth year. It is possible that Cuthbert was forced out as a result of Ludovic Bagman's dealings with the Goblins during Harry's fourth year.

Dobby

Gender: Male
Hair color: None
Eye color: Green
Related Family: Unknown
Loyalty: Malfoy family; later Harry and Albus Dumbledore

OVERVIEW

Dobby was once the House Elf of the Malfoy family, and guarded many of their secrets. Apparently, according to the author, his birthday is 28 June.

ROLE IN THE BOOKS

Chamber of Secrets Dobby came to the Dursley's house to warn Harry that he should not return to Hogwarts for his second year studies. Dobby thought it would be too dangerous for Harry. Dobby admitted that he had been blocking Harry's mail; he had believed that if Harry got no lettters from his friends, he would think his friends were false and would not want to go back to them.

Dobby then locked the barrier at Platform Nine and Three Quarters in hopes that if Harry was unable to make it onto the Hogwarts Express, he would be unable to go to school. Harry and Ron thwart this by using Ron's dad's flying car.

Dobby bewitched one of the bludgers to repeatedly attack Harry in the Quidditch match against Slytherin; visiting Harry in the Hospital Wing that night, he admitted that he had hoped that it would injure Harry enough to cause him to be sent home. It is during this visit that he also explains how a house-elf can be freed, and admits that the Chamber had been opened before.

At the end of this book, Lucius Malfoy brings Dobby with him to the school, thus confirming that he is the house-elf of the Malfoy family. Dobby hints to Harry where Riddle's diary had come from; Harry confronts Lucius with this in front of Professor Dumbledore. Harry shortly afterwards tricks Lucius Malfoy into accidentally releasing Dobby from service to the Malfoys by presenting an article of clothing to Dobby, who promptly saves Harry from Malfoy's wrath at having his servant freed.

Goblet of Fire Dobby spent at least a year searching for a family who would pay him wages to be their House-Elf, something which is unheard of in the wizarding world. Eventually, Professor Dumbledore agreed to pay Dobby one Galleon per week to work at Hogwarts—he had offered more, but Dobby bargained him down. When we see Dobby in the Hogwarts kitchens, he has just entered Dumbledore's service at the school, along with Winky. At Christmas, Dobby wakes Harry up leaning over him in his bed; Harry presents Dobby with a pair of socks (the ones which had been cushioning his pocket Sneakoscope for years. Ron also gives

Dobby a pair of socks and a jumper (US: sweater). In return, Dobby gives Harry a pair of socks; they are hand-knit by Dobby himself. Dobby happens to overhear Professor McGonagall and Professor Moody discussing the Second Task of the Triwizard Tournament, and discovers that Harry will need some Gillyweed to save "his Wheezy" (Ron Weasley); so he steals some from Professor Snape's office and gives it to Harry, waking him up where he had fallen asleep in the library mere minutes before the task is due to start.

Harry later visits the Hogwarts kitchens with Ron and Hermione, to thank Dobby with a gift of socks for his help in the second Task. Ron takes the opportunity to secure some additional food for Sirius Black, who at the time is living in a cave outside Hogsmeade.

Order of the Phoenix When Professor Grubbly-Plank has healed Hedwig, Dobby brings her back to Harry. Harry is of course pleased to get Hedwig back, and speaks with Dobby for a while about how he and Winky are doing. Harry at this point is trying to find a place where the Defence Association, as it was then known, can practice, and he asks Dobby if he knows of any such place. Dobby, surprisingly, does, and tells Harry about the Room of Requirement, or the Come And Go Room. He has used it several times when he needed a place for Winky to dry out. He volunteers to show it to Harry, but Harry decides he is too tired, and it is too late at night; instead, he asks Dobby to tell him how to get in.

Dobby manages, somehow, to get into the room before the last meeting of Dumbledore's Army before Christmas, and decorates it with embarrassing Christmas decorations—baubles reading "Have a Very Harry Christmas," for instance. Harry does manage to get it largely cleaned up before the rest of the D. A. arrive.

Against direct orders from Professor Umbridge, Dobby makes his way into the Room of Requirement to warn the D.A. that Umbridge is coming. Because he has violated orders, he as usual feels a need to punish himself; he does this by charging headfirst into the wall. Harry does prevent him from injuring himself further. Harry is able to spread the word quickly enough that the only person actually caught is himself.

Half-Blood Prince At one point, Harry feels the need to have Draco Malfoy trailed, to find out where he is going. He summons Kreacher, who appears entangled with Dobby—evidently they had been involved in a fight when Harry summoned Kreacher. Dobby volunteers to track Malfoy as well.

Shortly thereafter, Kreacher and Dobby return to report to Harry. Kreacher's report seems to be largely praise for Malfoy and his pure blood, and abuse for Harry, but Dobby is able to report that Malfoy had been spending time in the Room of Requirement.

Deathly Hallows Harry sees a blue eye in the Magic Mirror he carries around with him, and asks it to send help. Shortly, Dobby apparates into the basement cell at Malfoy Manor where Harry, Ron, Ollivander, Luna Lovegood, and Dean Thomas are being held. Dobby is apparently extremely nervous at being in the Malfoy home, where he was so cruelly treated before Harry won him his freedom. Harry asks him to take Luna, Dean, and Ollivander to Shell Cottage. The noise of Dobby Disapparating attracts attention from upstairs; Wormtail is sent down to the cell to investigate, and Ron and Harry start to overpower him. Harry calls on the life debt that Wormtail owes him, and he hesitates; the silver hand that Lord Voldemort had given Wormtail senses this hesitation, and reading it as disloyalty, chokes Wormtail to death.

Harry and Ron proceed upstairs to try and save Hermione and Griphook. Though disarmed, Bellatrix Lestrange produces a silver knife and threatens Hermione with it; she has Draco collect the wands. Shortly afterwards, Dobby re-appears and causes the chandelier to fall on Bellatrix; gathering all the wands Draco is holding, Harry takes Griphook and Dobby, and Ron takes Hermione, and together they Apparate to Shell Cottage. As Harry is Disapparating, however, he sees Bellatrix throwing her knife; arriving at Shell Cottage, he finds that the thrown knife has hit Dobby, killing him.

Harry then digs a grave for Dobby, and buries him, near a tree on the grounds of Shell Cottage. Later, Aberforth Dumbledore asks where Dobby was, saying that he had expected Dobby to be traveling with Harry; Harry tells him that he was killed by Bellatrix. Aberforth is dismayed; he says he "liked that elf."

Strengths Dobby is very loyal to the people he cares about. He did what the Malfoys told him to do because he had no choice. Dobby still tries unsuccessfully in the second book to protect Harry. He later helps Harry in the Second Task in Goblet of Fire, tells him about the Room of Requirement, warns the DA, and tails Draco Malfoy for him. He is also loyal to Dumbledore who employs him, and helps his friend Winky when she is drunk. He is also a hard worker. Dobby is also a very grateful person. In general, he is a good friend to have around.

Weaknesses Like all house-elves, certain subtleties of human behavior are beyond his understanding; his speech pattern, for instance is somewhat immature: he will speak in the third person, apparently unable to master the subtleties of "I" and "you." He is completely subservient, seeming to exist only to take orders from one wizard or another. He does have a will of his own, reflected in his being able to try and warn Harry away fom Hogwarts against his owner's wishes, but he has to make a supreme effort to allow that will to express itself, and because he is going against the wishes of his owner, he must punish himself. He has internalized his subservience so much that he will punish himself without being told to, if he finds himself doing something which he believes his owners might not like.

Relationships with Other Characters He is a good friend to Harry Potter ever since Harry engineered his freedom from the Malfoys. Before that, he had some sort of respect for Harry, given he thinks he is saving Harry by stopping him from getting to Hogwarts in his second year. Dobby says that this is because of Harry's defeating Lord Voldemort; house-elves were really very badly treated when he was around. "Of course, Dobby is still treated very badly . . .," he goes on to say; but Harry is respected because of what he did for the general House-Elf population. Dobby also comes to admire Ron when he receives one of Ron's Christmas sweaters.

ANALYSIS

It is possible that Rowling has used the relationship between Harry and Dobby to send a message to the reader. This message teaches of equality of all and uses the difference in species to comment on racism. This is reflected later in Order of the Phoenix where Dumbledore describes the Fountain of Magical Brethren as "lying."

Dolores Umbridge

Gender: Female
Hair color: Iron colored curls
Eye color: Unknown
Related Family: Unknown
Loyalty: The Ministry of Magic and later Voldemort

OVERVIEW

Dolores Jane Umbridge debuted as the Defence Against the Dark Arts professor in the series' fifth book, *Harry Potter and the Order of the Phoenix.* She is the Special Assistant to the Minister of Magic and, later, the self-proclaimed Hogwarts High Inquisitor.

She is described as looking like a large, pale toad, rather squat, and having a broad, flabby face, a little neck, and a wide, slack mouth. Her eyes are large, round, and slightly bulging.

ROLE IN THE BOOKS

Order of the Phoenix Dolores Umbridge is first seen when Harry is called before the Wizengamot to answer charges of performing underage magic. Sitting on Cornelius Fudge's right-hand side, she makes a few comments that are intended to fluster Harry.

Umbridge is then appointed by the Ministry of Magic as the new Defense Against the Dark Arts teacher (and Ministry spy) at Hogwarts. She unexpectedly gives a long, boring speech at the Welcoming Feast in which she says she believes the school's teaching methods need to be examined and perhaps revised. In her classes, she teaches exclusively from a singularly useless book: *Defensive Magical Theory,* by Wilbert Slinkhard, which seems, based on the chapter headings, to concern itself with negotiation and appeasement of, rather than with defence against, the Dark Arts. She steadfastly hews to the Ministry party line that Lord Voldemort has not returned and that Harry Potter's claims are only to garner attention for himself. When Harry dares to dispute the Ministry's stance, she gives him detention, making him write lines with a magic quill that painfully etches the script into his hand. Professor Umbridge appoints herself Hogwarts' High Inquisitor, a position from which she makes it her duty to examine all the teachers and their methods. She soon targets Professor Trelawney and Hagrid as incompetent and sacks both.

After Albus Dumbledore is accused of plotting against the Ministry and disappears following an arrest attempt, Umbridge proclaims herself Headmistress. Although she carries the title, her authority is generally ignored; she is unable access Dumbledore's sealed office, and the staff barely acknowledge her. When Peeves engages in harassing her, his actions are apparently supported by the teachers. It is Fred and George Weasley, however, who lead an outright revolt, creating havoc throughout the school, before jumping on their brooms and leaving Hogwarts for good.

Although she works for the Ministry of Magic, Umbridge engages in illegal activities such as casting Unforgivable Curses on Harry. When Hermione tricks her into going into the Forbidden Forest to search for a nonexistent weapon, Umbridge foolishly insults the Centaurs, who become enraged and carry her off screaming. When Dumbledore is reinstated as Headmaster, he personally goes into the Forest to rescue her, although she is so psychologically traumatized that she has to be hospitalized.

Half-Blood Prince While visiting the Weasley's at Christmas, Rufus Scrimgeour mentions that Dolores Umbridge had told him that Harry was interested in becoming an Auror. Harry is angered that Umbridge is still working for the Ministry. Umbridge was seen towards the end while attending Albus Dumbledore's funeral along with the other Ministry of Magic staff.

Deathly Hallows We discover that the real locket of Salazar Slytherin, replaced by the one found at the end of *Harry Potter and the Half-Blood Prince,* was kept by Kreacher (the Black Family House-Elf) instead of being discarded. Mundungus Fletcher had stolen it, and was trying to hawk it and other valuables from the house, when Umbridge stopped him. Umbridge, abusing her power in the Ministry, had demanded the locket as a bribe, in exchange for not jailing Mundungus for selling artifacts without a license.

In order to regain the locket, Harry, Ron and Hermione break into the Ministry of Magic, disguised with Polyjuice Potion. Ron is immediately detailed by Yaxley to handle a problem with rainfall in his office. Harry and Hermione meet Umbridge on the top floor; Hermione is taken to the courtrooms to record proceedings of the Muggle-Born Registration Commission. When Harry's search of Umbridge's office proves fruitless, he hides under the Invisibility Cloak, and makes his way into the courtroom where Umbridge is enjoying sending Muggle-born wizards and witches to Azkaban for "stealing wands from blood wizards." Umbridge, leaning forward, reveals that she is wearing the locket. Harry, disgusted by Umbridge's using the locket to claim more Blood descent than she is entitled to, Stuns her, and then Yaxley, which gives Hermione time to retrieve the locket. Harry and Hermione then free the remaining Muggle-borns, escorting them to the Atrium and allowing them to leave the Ministry.

Strengths It is difficult for us to judge the quality of her magic, as we see very little of it; one gathers that she is powerful, but perhaps not as skilled as Professor McGonagall or Professor Flitwick, as, for instance, Flitwick is able to remove the Weasleys' Wizarding Wheezes Instant Swamp quite quickly, while Umbridge is unsuccessful after apparently a full day. She does seem to have a very powerful personality, however, as she is a senior assistant to at least two Ministers (Cornelius Fudge and Pius Thicknesse), and is respected within the Ministry. She manages to get herself into a position of significant authority under Thicknesse, despite not being a Death Eater.

Weaknesses Umbridge has a weak self-image, which she props up with pomposity, officious behavior, and dependence on external props, such as the brooch she extorts from Mundungus Fletcher and later claims is an heirloom that proves her descent from an old Wizarding family. This is compounded by her racism, which seems to be largely based on a fear of beings outside her understanding or control.

Relationships with Other Characters Umbridge dislikes (more like loathes) Harry Potter. Throughout *Harry Potter and the Order of the Phoenix*, her bias against Harry in particular, and Gryffindor House in general, is evident. Using her newly acquired power under the Educational Decrees from the Ministry, she bans all extra-curricular activities and gatherings until they are approved by the High Inquisitor (herself); this meant that the House Quidditch teams were disbanded. Slytherin's team was immediately reinstated while Gryffindor was delayed from reforming for nearly a month when then-captain Angelina Johnson put in the request.

Most Hogwarts teachers despise her, especially those in the *Order of the Phoenix*. Argus Filch likes her, however, and he becomes excited when she reinstates corporal punishment for students.

Umbridge claims relationship to the Selwyn family. This relationship is never proven, and she uses the locket of Slytherin (via its apparent antiquity and the S sigil on it), despite being totally unaware of its provenance or history, to bolster this otherwise unsupported claim.

ANALYSIS

Throughout *Harry Potter and the Order of the Phoenix*, Umbridge attracted much contempt for her uptight policies, strict educational decrees and her basic power hunger. Despite this, she has the full support of Fudge and the Ministry. This puts emphasis on the corruption/foolishness in Government (this is also present in *Harry Potter and the Half-Blood Prince*, through Rufus Scrimgeour). It also raises a theme of power/misuse of power. Umbridge's fate in the end sends the author's message that the Government should not abuse their power.

QUESTIONS

1. How might Dolores Umbridge feel when the staff members at Hogwarts treat her badly (particularly at the beginning of the year)?
2. Why is Umbridge kept as a Ministry of Magic employee?
3. Why is Umbridge afraid of "half-breeds"—centaurs, giants, etc.?
4. Why did Umbridge send Dementors after Harry?

GREATER PICTURE

Dolores Umbridge characterizes the worst aspects of political power. She is ruthless, cruel, corrupt and devoid of a moral or ethical center. She is depicted using any means to maintain her personal power and the political power of her bosses. She commits attempted murder (via the Dementor attack on Harry), solicits bribes and tortures children to achieve her goals. Umbridge cannot tolerate anyone who disagrees with her views or the lies her Minister is spreading. She must exercise complete control over everyone and everything around her. From her perspective, free speech, dissent, diversity and multiple points of view cannot be tolerated. Therefore Umbridge represents the qualities of a totalitarian government. She leads not by consensus and respect but rather by fear and intimidation. Indeed, while she is taking over Hogwarts, the Ministry as a whole is controlling the press and information to spin events in their favor. The power granted Umbridge by Fudge to consolidate his political strength and quash his perceived enemies is already familiar to us. It is not unlike the abuse members of the Nixon administration committed during the Watergate Era. Her final crimes are the "ethnic cleansing" of Muggle born wizards, analogous to the Nazi persecutions leading to the Holocaust. The author reminds us how easy it is for a person like Umbridge to thrive when a government loses its accountability.

Dorcas Meadowes

Gender: Female
Hair color: Unknown
Eye color: Unknown
Related Family: Unknown
Loyalty: Order of the Phoenix

OVERVIEW

Dorcas Meadowes is a past member of the Order of the Phoenix, who had been killed in Voldemort's previous reign of terror.

ROLE IN THE BOOKS

Order of the Phoenix Alastor Moody shows Dorcas' picture to Harry in the kitchen at Grimmauld Place, saying that she had been personally killed by Lord Voldemort while in the Order of the Phoenix.

Draco Malfoy

Gender: Male
Hair color: White Blond
Eye color: Grey
Related Family: Lucius Malfoy, Narcissa Malfoy
Loyalty: Unknown, appears to be to Voldemort

Overview

Draco Malfoy, a boy with a pale, pointed sneering face, is a member of Slytherin house. He is always accompanied by Vincent Crabbe and Gregory Goyle, and occasionally Pansy Parkinson. He constantly boasts about being pureblood and his family's wealth.

According to the author's web site, he was born on 5 June; this would make him about two months older than Harry Potter. According to the Black family tree, he was born in 1980.

Role in the Books

Philosopher's Stone We first see Draco Malfoy in Madam Malkin's Robes For All Occasions on Diagon Alley where he and Harry are being fitted for their school robes. Draco does not introduce himself, but expresses the hope that he will be placed in Slytherin house. He asks Harry's name, but is distracted by the appearance of Hagrid at the window before Harry can answer. Harry is somewhat dismayed by Draco's assumption of superiority of the pure Wizarding blood families, and asks Hagrid about this; Hagrid dismisses his concerns, saying he'd not act so superior if he knew who Harry was.

We next see Draco when he appears, with Crabbe and Goyle in tow, on the Hogwarts Express. Draco expresses some surprise that this truly is Harry Potter, makes an insulting remark about Ron Weasley who is in Harry's compartment, and suggests that Harry would do well to ally himself with Draco rather than Ron. Harry says he has a pretty good idea of the sort of people he wants to ally himself with, dismissing Draco. Draco then says that he's going to take some of the treats Harry has bought from the lunch cart on the train, but when Goyle starts to grab a cauldron cake, he is attacked by Ron's rat, Scabbers. Draco, Crabbe, and Goyle retreat in confusion. Draco is Sorted into Slytherin house, as he expected.

Harry and Ron have double Potions with the Slytherins on the first Friday of the school year. Draco and his sidekicks, Crabbe and Goyle, snigger when Professor Snape remarks, on seeing Harry's name, "Our new . . . *celebrity*." As the class proceeds, Snape seems to feel that Draco can do no wrong, though everyone else in the class comes in for criticism.

Harry, who has been able to avoid Draco except in Potions class, is dismayed to learn that flying lessons will be shared with the Slytherins. He had been looking forward to learning how to fly, and now he is afraid that he will make a fool of himself on a broomstick in front of Draco. Ron says that Draco likely knows no more about flying than Harry does, despite all his talk; and he certainly does seem to have a lot of stories about flying, all of which seem to end with narrow escapes from Muggle helicopters.

On the morning before the first flying class, Harry sees that again Draco's eagle owl has brought him a package of sweets from home. Neville also gets a package, containing a Remembrall. Draco, walking by the table, takes it out of Neville's hand, and Harry and Ron jump to their feet, hoping for an excuse to fight. Professor McGonagall arrives as well, and Draco returns the Remembrall to Neville.

At the flying lesson Harry and Ron are delighted when Madam Hooch corrects Draco's grip on the broom, saying he'd been doing it wrong for years. After Neville's accident, Draco jeers at Neville's expression; Parvati Patil tells him to shut up, and Pansy Parkinson accuses her of being sweet on Neville. Draco spots Neville's Remembrall on the ground, and plans to place it high in a tree for Neville to retrieve later. Harry follows, finding that he is a natural on the broom, and that Draco is not so brave without Crabbe and Goyle at his side. Draco, cowed, throws the Remembrall high in the air; Harry dives after it and retrieves it before it hits the ground. He is, however, caught in the act by Professor McGonagall, and has to endure seeing Draco's triumphant expression as, believing himself about to be expelled, he is led off in her wake.

That night, finding that Harry has not, after all, been expelled, Draco challenges him to a Wizard's Duel. Ron immediately volunteers to be Harry's second; Draco selects Crabbe to be his second. When Harry reaches the trophy room, however, it becomes apparent that Draco had not planned to meet him there; instead, he has told Filch about it, and Filch is looking for Harry and Ron. When they have managed, for a while, to evade Filch, Hermione says that Draco had never intended to actually duel Harry, but had simply informed Filch that Harry would be there. Draco seems dismayed the following morning to discover again that Harry has not been thrown out of school, and more so a week later when a long, thin package is delivered by a half dozen screech owls at breakfast. Intercepting Harry after breakfast, Draco determines that the package is a broom, and denounces him to Professor Flitwick, who is passing. Professor Flitwick agrees that it is, and says he has heard about the special circumstances. Draco, enraged at Gryffindor's win at Quidditch, makes jokes about Gryffindor's next seeker being a wide-mouth tree frog. When this fails, Draco reverts to making fun of Harry's home life, and Harry's plans to stay at the school over Christmas. Harry doesn't mind; he expects that this will be the best Christmas he has ever had, particularly as the Weasley children will also be staying at Hogwarts.

When Ron and Harry run into Hagrid bringing Christmas trees into the school, Draco happens to be there and makes remarks about Ron's poverty. Ron, enraged, dives at Draco and is penalized five House points by Snape, who has just arrived on the scene.

Draco Malfoy

Shortly after Christmas, Neville Longbottom topples through the entrance to Gryffindor Tower, with his legs stuck together. Once Hermione frees him, he says that Draco had jinxed him just outside the library, saying that he had been looking for someone to practice that on.

Draco, with Crabbe and Goyle, sits directly behind Ron and Neville at the Quidditch match against Hufflepuff. Within the first few minutes of the game, Draco has goaded Ron to the point that Ron jumps him; Neville hesitates and joins in. We hear later that Ron, though getting a bloody nose, had given Draco a black eye. Draco may be within earshot when Hagrid sends a note to Harry to say that the dragon's egg is hatching; it does seem that he has stopped to listen. Harry, Hermione, and Ron go to Hagrid's hut to witness the hatching; Hagrid sees someone at the window, and Harry recognizes the figure vanishing back into the school as Draco. When Norbert bites Ron's hand, Ron ends up in the Hospital Wing; Draco visits him there, saying that he needs to borrow a book, but uses the opportunity to torment Ron by threatening to tell Madam Pomfrey what had actually bitten Ron. The letter from Charlie saying when they will pick up Norbert happens to be in the book that Draco borrows. As Harry and Hermione, with Norbert under the Invisibility Cloak, head for the tallest tower, they see Professor McGonagall penalizing Draco house points and giving him detention for being out in the school after hours and making up some nonsense story about a dragon. The events of that evening land Harry, Hermione, and Neville in detention also, and it is a week before exams that the four of them are sent to the Entrance Hall to meet with Filch to serve that detention. Filch takes them off to see Hagrid, who tells them that they'll be going into the Forest. Draco protests, saying that that's servant stuff and he won't do it; Hagrid says if he'd rather be expelled, then fine, but if he wants to stay at Hogwarts, he'll be going into the Forest. When Draco acquiesces, sulkily, Hagrid says something has been killing Unicorns in the Forbidden Forest, and their job is to help Hagrid track a wounded unicorn and try to find what's doing it. Draco, despite his initial trepidation, apparently gets bored and scares Neville, who he is paired with, and Neville sends up a distress signal. Hagrid, responding to the signal, shuffles the groups so that Draco is paired with Harry, who presumably would not scare as easily. When they do find the unicorn, there is a dark shape apparently drinking its blood; Draco, scared, runs away.

We don't see Draco again until the end of year feast, where Harry is first sickened by the sight of Draco banging his goblet in celebration of Slytherin House's apparent winning of the House trophy, and then is cheered by the stunned and horrified look on Draco's face as victory is taken away.

Chamber of Secrets Malfoy is taken on the Slytherin Quidditch team as Seeker, and is suspected of being the heir of Salazar Slytherin. Harry, Ron and Hermione disguise themselves as Crabbe and Goyle using Polyjuice Potion to find out, but he has no idea who is.

Prisoner of Azkaban Draco is attacked by Buckbeak the Hippogriff during the first Care Of Magical Creatures lesson, and is later punched in the face by Hermione for laughing about Buckbeak's execcution.

Goblet of Fire Draco first appears at the Quidditch World Cup with his parents, and later meets the trio in the woods during the Death Eater attack.

Throughout the school year, he is turned into a ferret by Alastor Moody for attempting to attack Harry when his back is turned, and is submitted to the Imperius Curse, but rescued by Professor McGonagall. He also passes spiteful information to unregistered Animagus Rita Skeeter about Harry and his friends.

Order of the Phoenix Draco is appointed Prefect, along with Pansy Parkinson, for Slytherin House. Hermione reports at one point that he is being simply beastly towards the first-year students, clearly abusing his Prefect's powers.

As they enter the horseless carriages to go up to the school from the train station, we see that Draco and his sidekicks are taking a carriage with Pansy Parkinson.

On the second day of classes, Draco, Pansy, Crabbe, and Goyle are laughing about something as they arrive at Care of Magical Creatures class. When Professor Grubbly-Plank asks if anyone can identify the creatures she has in front of her, Hermione puts her hand up, and Draco imitates her. Pansy shrieks with laughter, then screams as the little bundles of twigs on the table jump up, revealing themselves to be Bowtruckles. As he collects a Bowtruckle, Draco suggests to Harry that Hagrid, who is still mysteriously absent, could have run into something too *big* for him and gotten himself hurt. Although we don't yet realize it, and Harry never seems to draw the connection himself, this would indicate that Draco is aware of Hagrid's mission.

When Professor Umbridge is examining the Care of Magical Creatures class taught by Professor Grubbly-Plank, she says to Goyle that she understands there have been injuries in that class. Goyle does not answer; instead, Malfoy says that he was slashed by a Hippogriff.

The day that Educational Decree Number Twenty Four, banning all school organizations, is published, Draco is seen outside the Potions classroom waving a piece of parchment around and saying that getting the Slytherin Quidditch team reformed was pretty much automatic, given the influence his father has with the Ministry. He then suggests that before too long Harry will be sent to St. Mungo's, where they have a special ward for the incurably insane. At this, Neville tries to attack Draco, but Harry and Ron restrain him.

On the first school day after Hagrid's return, Hagrid tells his Care of Magical Creatures class that they will be working in the Forbidden Forest. Draco seems scared, needing reassurance that the creatures they are to look at are properly trained, and is not at all reassured when he sees how injured Hagrid is.

Dobby warns Harry that Umbridge has found out about Dumbledore's Army and is coming. Harry sends the rest of the students away, and is himself on the way to a bathroom when Draco, from concealment, catches him with a Trip Jinx. Umbridge, arriving, awards Slytherin house fifty points and sends Draco off to look for others. When Harry is taken in to the Headmaster's Office, Cornelius Fudge is there. Umbridge says that Draco had caught "the Potter boy;" Fudge says that he will have to let Lucius know.

With Umbridge becoming Headmaster, Draco is appointed to be a member of the Inquisitorial Squad, along with Montague and Pansy Parkinson. Umbridge has given the Inquisitorial Squad the power to take Points from houses, and Draco is quick to abuse this power.

Shortly afterwards, Draco is sent by Professor Umbridge to get Snape's assistance in extracting Montague, an Inquisitorial Squad member who has been missing for some time, out of a toilet. He interrupts Harry and Snape at the beginning of an Occlumency lesson. Draco is intrigued to hear Snape say that Harry is taking remedial Potions.

As O.W.L. exams approach, Draco is heard loudly proclaiming that the mark on one's O.W.L.s are more due to *who* you know rather than *what* you know, and talking of what close friends his father is with Griselda Marchbanks, head of the Wizarding Examination Authority. Neville, overhearing, quietly tells Harry and Ron that Griselda Marchbanks is a friend of his grandmother's, and has never mentioned the Malfoy family in any of her frequent visits. In Harry's Charms O.W.L. exam, his examiner, Professor Tofty, greets him as "the famous Harry Potter?" Draco, overhearing, turns a look of malevolence on Harry, and the wine glass he is levitating falls and smashes. When Umbridge catches Harry in her office, where he has been trying to determine whether Sirius has gone to the Ministry, she brings two members of the Inquisitorial Squad, Draco and Millicent Bulstrode, with her. Draco assists Umbridge with Harry, while Millicent captures Hermione. When Harry refuses to reveal why he was in Umbridge's fireplace, and who he was communicating with, Umbridge sends Draco to find Snape. When Hermine "reveals" that they had been seeking Professor Dumbledore to tell him that the weapon was finished, Umbridge demands that Hermione lead her to the weapon. Draco suggests that he should go along as well; Hermione says that sounds like a good idea, everyone should know about it. Umbridge decides that she will take only Hermione and Harry, over Draco's protests.

We learn later that the other Gryffindor members' escape from the Inquisitorial Squad is helped by Ginny hitting Draco with a Bat Bogey jinx.

After Harry's return to school, Draco, with Crabbe and Goyle, threaten him with retaliation for having had Draco's father, Lucius, sent to Azkaban. The beginning duel is ended by the arrival of Snape on the scene before any spells are cast.

Draco again tries to Jinx Harry on board the Hogwarts Express, but he chooses to do so in front of a compartment containing a number of members of Dumbledore's Army. He, along with Crabbe and Goyle, end up looking like three gigantic slugs squeezed into Hogwarts uniforms, and Harry, Ernie, and Justin leave the three of them in the luggage rack.

Half-Blood Prince Throughout this book, Draco is almost always hiding in the Room of Requirement, with the exception of Professor Slughorn's party, in which Harry overhears Snape and Draco arguing.

Later, Harry finds him in the boys bathroom, where he is crying. Apparently he is trying to do something and it is not going well, and he is afraid of what will happen to him and his family if he does not succeed. Catching sight of Harry in the mirror, Draco spins and starts firing curses at him. Harry, defending himself, uses Sectumsempra, a curse he found in the Half-Blood Prince's book, with only the notation "For enemies."

Deathly Hallows Harry, Hermione, and Ron escape Death Eaters in an all-night café in the Tottenham Court Road, altering their memory so that they will not know who they had almost caught. The Trio then go to ground at Number 12, Grimmauld Place. Shortly after their arrival, Harry is once again dragged into Voldemort's mind by his rage, and he sees one of the Death Eaters, Thorfinn Rowle, being tortured for having failed to catch Harry. Harry is dismayed to realize that it is a sick-looking Draco who is being forced to actually do the torturing.

Snatchers, led by Fenrir Greyback, capture the Trio, but are uncertain of Harry's identity. They carry the Trio to Malfoy Manor, where Lucius calls on Draco to identify Harry. Possibly misled by Harry's horribly swollen face, which has stymied identification efforts by the Snatchers and by Lucius Malfoy, Draco balks at definitively identifying him. Narcissa does, however, identify Hermione, and is on the verge of summoning Voldemort when Bellatrix prevents it. Bellatrix has all except Hermione sent to the cellars, then tortures Hermione to find out where she got the Sword of Gryffindor. When Hermione says it is a fake, Lucius sends Draco to fetch the goblin Griphook, who can tell them whether the sword is real or not. It is as Draco is leaving the cellar that Dobby Apparates in; the sound of the cellar door closing masks the characteristic sound of House-elf apparation. When Harry and Ron return to the main floor of Malfoy Manor, Ron, with the wand he captured from Peter Pettigrew, Disarms Bellatrix, but is forced to surrender his wand when Bellatrix holds a knife to Hermione's throat. Draco collects the fallen wands. In the confusion occasioned by Dobby's dropping the chandelier on Bellatrix, Harry physically wrests all three wands (Bellatrix,' Pettigrew's, and Draco's) from Draco's hand before he and Dobby escape.

Surprisingly, when Draco, Crabbe, and Goyle corner Harry in the Room of Requirement, it is not Draco, but Crabbe and Goyle, who do most of the talking. Draco accuses Harry of having his wand, saying that he is using his mother's. When Crabbe starts knocking piles of junk over, Draco stops him, saying if they destroy the room, they may not find the Diadem. When Crabbe sets Fiendfyre, Harry, Ron, and Hermione escape on brooms; Harry circles back to save Draco and Goyle, but Crabbe cannot be found.

As Harry, Ron, and Hermione are making their way under the Invisibility Cloak out through the entry hall

Draco Malfoy

and off to the Shrieking Shack, they pass Draco, who is pleading with a Death Eater not to jinx him, he's on their side. Harry Stuns the Death Eater as they pass, and Ron punches Draco, saying that's twice they have saved his life, and calling him two-faced.

Facing Voldemort at the end in the Great Hall, Harry tells him that, though he holds the Elder Wand, holding it is not enough, because he does not own it. The wand, like all others, owes allegiance to the one who took it by force from its previous master; and as Snape had not taken it from Dumbledore, Snape had never been its master. Instead, it was Draco who had Disarmed Dumbledore; and Draco, in turn, had been Disarmed by Harry weeks before. The wand Harry had won from Draco was now in his hand. What it comes down to now is: does the Elder Wand know that Draco was disarmed? Because if so, Harry is now the Elder Wand's master.

In the Epilogue, we see Draco, who nods to Harry, with his wife and his son Scorpius. Draco's hairline is receding slightly, which makes his already-pointed chin appear somewhat sharper.

Strengths Draco's family is particularly wealthy, and while Draco himself does not directly have any place in the resulting influence in the Ministry and elsewhere, he does benefit from it and have some indirect influence as well. It is likely this wealth and influence from his family that has won him his supporter / thug companions, Crabbe and Goyle. Draco is a powerful wizard, and has been introduced, through his father, to aspects of the Dark Arts that most other wizards his age have not yet seen. This will give him some strengths that other wizards lack.

As a member of Slytherin house, Draco will have the alliance of Professor Snape, one of the more powerful wizards at Hogwarts.

Weaknesses Draco's character seems to be entirely propped up by his wealth and his followers. In company with his enforcers, Crabbe and Goyle, he struts and acts the bully; but as early as flying lessons in the first book, we can see that he is effectively lost without them. Confronted, on his own, by Harry, who is on a broom for the first time in his life, Draco retreats with dishonour; and having challenged Harry to a duel, he sends Filch instead of keeping the appointment he has made. Even with Crabbe and Goyle in attendance, his own courage is not what it could be; we see that when Hermione slaps him, the three of them simply retreat. This weakness of resolve remains throughout the series; in the battle at Hogwarts, late in the final book, we see him pleading to be spared.

In fact, Draco, at least through the first five books, seems to be entirely without honour; he seems to be the epitome of what Slytherin stands for, "using any means to achieve their ends," as the Sorting Hat says.

In the seventh book, we see that there are some limits to what he is willing to do, though we see that he still lacks the force of character to protest them. In particular, Harry sees his revulsion at being forced to torture Rowle, and we see Draco's unwillingness to identify Harry, knowing as he does that if he does identify Harry, Voldemort will promptly murder him. In both cases, though Draco is unwilling, he is unable to prevent himself from being used. Ultimately, Draco seems to be a pitifully weak character who is guided to the Dark side by his father.

Relationships with Other Characters Draco has two cronies, Crabbe and Goyle, who mostly follow him about taking orders. Malfoy despises Harry because he is a Half-Blood and for spurning his offer of friendship when they first met. He also resents Harry's fame and may be jealous over his power as a wizard.

In *Harry Potter and the Half-Blood Prince*, Harry overhears Draco boasting about a mission he has been given by the Dark Lord. When he mentions it to Hermione, she believes Malfoy is only trying to impress Pansy Parkinson.

Also, though they never speak throughout the entire series, Draco is Nymphadora Tonks' first cousin through their mothers, Narcissa and Andromeda, who are sisters. Due to Andromeda's marrying the Muggle-born Ted Tonks, she has been disowned by her family, the Blacks, and neither she nor any of the Black family particularly cares to acknowledge the relationship.

ANALYSIS

Draco is portrayed in the series as an enemy/rival of the protagonist, Harry Potter. It is possible that Rowling has used Draco as a direct contrast to Harry; Pure blood, 'evil,' Slytherin, Death Eater: these are some characteristics that show this contrast. It is interesting, however, to note the change in Draco as the series progresses.

First Five Books Through the first five books, Draco is very consistent in his behaviour. Apparently the archetypal Slytherin, Draco uses any means, fair or foul, to get ahead. He apparently buys his way into the Seeker position on the Slytherin Quidditch team. He consistently belittles other students, including Ron, Harry, and Hermione. He seems supremely self-confident, quite clearly believing that his father's wealth and his Pure-blood status will get him anything he wants. And we see also that he has surrounded himself with sycophants (notably Pansy Parkinson) and hired muscle (Crabbe and Goyle, who are presumably paid in status). Taking a leaf from Slytherin's book, Draco especially belittles those who are born of Muggles (like Hermione), born of wizards or witches who were children of Muggles (like Harry), or who profess to like Muggles (like Ron and the other Weasleys). Like most bullies, Draco immediately backs down when faced with a superior force; we see in *Harry Potter and the Chamber of Secrets* that Draco's father Lucius can be equally belittling when talking to his own son, and that in that situation Draco just takes it, not having any other choice. Additionally, at one point Hermione, goaded beyond her limits, slaps Draco, whereupon he and his thugs simply depart, rapidly. We very quickly see that Draco has been formed largely in the image of his father. Draco is, of course, chastened by the removal of his father from the Board of Governors of Hogwarts, but recovers; one supposes he has told himself that this is a mistake that will be rectified shortly when the Board sees the error of their ways. However, the arrest of Lucius at the end of *Harry Potter and the Order of the Phoenix* shakes Draco up. Initially, he retains his arrogance, blaming Harry for having his father arrested, which is in Draco's eye an inversion of the way things work: being a Pure-Blood, Lucius should be proof against any efforts by Muggle-borns or Muggle lovers, and here he clearly was not. However, the mere fact of Lucius' continuing imprisonment must have some effect on Draco.

Harry Potter and the Half-Blood Prince Draco is now faced with problems that he may have trouble solving. We believe that he has been made a Death Eater, as he seems defensive about the location where the Dark Mark would have been placed on him; but this is never fully confirmed, as he never shows us the Mark. While he still puts up the same show of arrogance, we are starting to see cracks in his armour. In the Potions class he takes with Harry, he no longer takes the time to needle Harry. We find out that he has been commiserating with Moaning Myrtle about something he is trying to do and is not succeeding at. And in the end of the book, he quite clearly has accepted a job, murdering Dumbledore, that he is unable to carry out. His prevarication when faced with this job seems quite alien to the person we have, until now, believed Draco to be. His mother, Narcissa, of course, understands Draco as well, and we see her, early in the book, expressing a fear that Draco will fail, and be punished for that failure.

Harry Potter and the Deathly Hallows In this book we learn that Voldemort had a much better understanding of Draco than we did in the previous book. We learn that Draco had been set up to fail in the tasks he had been given, as a means of punishing him and his family for their earlier failures to carry out Voldemort's wishes. Voldemort understands what he sees as Draco's basic weakness, and that we recognize through the book as a basic remaining core of humanity. We are accorded several views of Draco and his family that show us that, despite what the first five books told us, Draco is not entirely evil. Draco is forced to torture a Death Eater who has failed Voldemort, and Harry sees, through Voldemort's eyes, his revulsion at the task. When Harry is captured and brought to Malfoy Manor, Draco is well aware that if he identifies Harry, Harry will die, and Draco balks at that identification. It is perhaps interesting that Draco, with Crabbe and Goyle, remains at Hogwarts to try and capture Harry for Voldemort; he seems to believe that doing so could restore him and his family in Voldemort's favour. Draco's bullying nature does seem more pronounced in the halls of Hogwarts, where he is not required to be subservient to his father, and where he has the support of Crabbe and Goyle. However, in the battle of Hogwarts, Draco seems to be trying to preserve his own hide rather than attacking either side in the battle.

QUESTIONS

1. How will Narcissa Malfoy's love for her son affect his actions?
2. Will Malfoy have a point of redemption, a point of realization that Voldemort's path only leads to destruction and death?

GREATER PICTURE

He fears his father and what he may do to him. His largest weakness is his mother, even though he may not admit it. Although he wants to be like Voldemort, the largest difference between the two is that he *does* know love, the love of his mother.

He also cannot actually bring himself to kill. In the sixth book, he is given orders by Voldemort to kill Professor Dumbledore, but when the time actually comes, he hesitates, and is talked down by the professor. Additionally, in the seventh book, he is asked to identify Harry, Ron, and Hermione, and again he hesitates, not giving a firm answer even when one is demanded by his father. Both of these cases show that Draco is not utterly without scruple, that he does still have a conscience.

It also appears that in the end, his hatred of Harry subsides, as in the epilogue he nods politely to The Trio and Ginny when he notices them looking at him.

Dudley Dursley

Gender: Male
Hair color: Brown
Eye color: Piggy
Related Family: Vernon Dursley, Petunia Dursley
Loyalty: Self, food

OVERVIEW

Dudley Dursley is the beloved son of Vernon Dursley and Petunia Dursley, who are Harry Potter's uncle and aunt. Harry lives with them at Number Four, Privet Drive.

Dudley, being a child, grows throughout the series. He starts as a monumentally fat infant, grows to be a monumentally fat child, goes on a diet and starts building muscle, and ends up to be one of those horrible hulking tough lads.

While Dudley's birthday is never explicitly given a date, we believe it to be some time in June, shortly before school ends, as Harry's punishment after the events at the zoo in *Harry Potter and the Philosopher's Stone* was "his longest-ever punishment. By the time he was allowed out of his cupboard again, the summer holidays had started."

ROLE IN THE BOOKS

Philosopher's Stone We hear that Dudley is the only child of Vernon Dursley and Petunia Dursley, and that in their opinion, there is no finer child anywhere. Offset against this, we have the observation of Minerva McGonagall, who protests Albus Dumbledore's decision to leave Harry with these, "the very worst sort of Muggles." McGonagall has seen Petunia taking Dudley out for a walk and has seen him hitting her, demanding candy.

Ten years later, we see the Dursley house again. We are told that there are lots of pictures of Dudley, a monumentally fat child, where previously there had been lots of pictures of a monumentally fat toddler. It is Dudley's birthday, and Petunia tells Harry to be extra careful cooking breakfast, she doesn't want anything to spoil her Dudley's special day. When Dudley comes down to breakfast, he is outraged that there are only 37 gifts for him; last year he had gotten 38. To defuse the explosion, Petunia promises that they will buy him two more gifts. Dudley eventually works out that this is 39, and this satisfies him. Shortly, though, Mrs. Figg phones to say that she can't take Harry for the day, as she has broken her leg. Vernon and Petunia decide that they have to take Harry with them on Dudley's outing to the zoo, as they can't trust him alone in the house, and Dudley starts to throw a tantrum at this. He is interrupted, though, by the arrival of Piers, his friend, who is also going to the zoo. Dudley doesn't want Piers to see him crying, so that effectively is an end to his resistance.

At the zoo, Harry manages to get a lemon ice when the vendor assumes that all three of the children will have something, and Vernon, to keep up appearances, must buy Harry something as well; and later, Harry gets nearly all of Dudley's dessert (a "Knickerbocker Glory") when Dudley complains that it is too small and Vernon gets him a second one.

In the reptile house, Dudley quickly goes to find the biggest snake in the place, and bangs on the glass to try and make it move. When it doesn't, he goes away disappointed. Harry finds that the snake understands him, and while he is talking with it, Piers calls Dudley and Vernon to come and look at it. Dudley, waddling up at speed, hits Harry in the ribs, and Harry falls on the floor. Much to everyone's amazement, the glass in front of the snake vanishes, and the snake escapes, telling Harry it's off to Brazil. Dudley claims that the snake almost bit his leg off, and Piers says he was almost squeezed to death, but the worst is that Piers, calming down a bit, says Harry was talking to it. This results in Vernon locking Harry in his cupboard under the stairs for a week.

When we next see Dudley, school vacations have started. Dudley and his gang often come over to visit, and Harry does his best to stay hidden during these episodes, as Dudley, with Piers, Dennis, Malcolm, and Gordon, have settled on hitting Harry as their favorite pastime. Harry looks forward to the end of summer vacation, as Dudley is going to Vernon's old school, Smeltings, while Harry is going to be going to Stonewall Comprehensive. (Note to US readers: Smeltings, presumably a "public" school, is what is called a private school in the US, while Stonewall, a comprehensive school, is what would be called public in the US.) While Vernon and Petunia get all teary-eyed over the sight of Dudley in his Smeltings uniform, Harry is hard-put to restrain his laughter.

Dudley is in his school uniform the next morning at breakfast. When Vernon tells him to fetch the mail, Dudley tells him to have Harry do it; when Harry demurs, Vernon tells Dudley to poke Harry with his stick. Harry, seeing that Dudley is all too ready to do so, fetches the mail and finds the first of what will be a large number of letters for himself. Before he gets to open this one, though, Dudley calls out that he has received a letter, and Vernon pulls it away from him. Reading it is evidently a serious shock for both Vernon and Petunia, but they refuse to let either Harry or Dudley read it, despite their demands.

On returning home from work that day, Vernon tells Harry that they are moving him from his cupboard to the smallest bedroom at the house, the one that has been to date used to store all of Dudley's broken and disused gifts. Dudley is angered by this encroachment on his domain, and Harry can hear him bawling even with his new door closed.

The following morning, another letter arrives for Harry; Dudley, sent to get the mail, retrieves it, but is not allowed to read it.

The following morning, Vernon sleeps across the front door as the mailman arrives, delivering several more letters for Harry. Vernon then stays home, and nails up the letterbox. Dudley can only watch in horror as Vernon's antics to prevent the delivery of these letters grows ever more irrational. He clearly fears that his father has gone insane, and Petunia, who alone understands the reason for his actions, cannot explain.

Vernon's irrationality comes to a head on Sunday, and results in them driving off into the wilds of England. They end up in a ramshackle house, built on a rock out at sea, after Dudley has complained about missing one of his favorite television shows. Here, after a wholly unsatisfactory dinner, Vernon and Petunia take the one bed, and Dudley sleeps on the couch, leaving Harry with one threadbare blanket on the floor. Harry, looking at the watch on Dudley's pudgy wrist, recognizes the arrival of his eleventh birthday.

This is how they are found by Rubeus Hagrid, "keeper of the keys and grounds at Hogwarts," when he bursts in at midnight. Dudley, apart from being petrified at this huge and woolly man breaking into their house, and trying to hide behind his parents, plays little part in this scene; he does twitch a little when Hagrid dumps a half-dozen sausages onto a plate and hands them to Harry, but Vernon forbids his taking anything from Hagrid, and Hagrid says that Dudley doesn't need any more feeding up. When Vernon, resisting Harry's going off to Hogwarts, calls Albus Dumbledore a "crackpot old fool," Hagrid loses his temper, and pointing his umbrella at Dudley, charms a pig's tail onto him. Panicked, Dudley, Vernon, and Petunia retreat into the bedroom. Hagrid says that he had meant to turn Dudley into a pig, but he was already so much like one that there wasn't much left to do.

The next we see Dudley, it is the day that Harry is to take the Hogwarts Express. Vernon agrees to take Harry to London to catch the train, saying they had to go to town anyway to get Dudley's tail surgically removed. Harry shows his ticket to Vernon, who knows that there is no platform nine and three quarters. Vernon takes him to King's Cross Station, gets all his goods onto a luggage cart, and points at platforms nine and ten, showing him that there is no platform nine and three quarters, then gets back into the car and drives off. Harry sees that all three of the Dursleys are laughing.

On Harry's return from Hogwarts, we see Dudley and Aunt Petunia in the background, looking terrified. Harry remarks that he's going to have fun with Dudley this summer, because the Dursleys don't know that he's not allowed to do magic.

Chamber of Secrets On Harry's birthday, Vernon is preparing for what he expects to be a major sale, entertaining a very important client in his home. He starts off by assigning everyone duties. Dudley's initial job is to greet Mr. and Mrs Mason at the door and offer to take their coats; and then to be sycophantic in the lounge while they are waiting for dinner, and to offer an arm to Mrs. Mason on the way in to dinner. Harry's role, of course, is to be up in his room, utterly silent, and pretending he isn't there; but listening to Dudley planning to suck up to the Masons, he again has trouble refraining from laughing.

Harry is then told to stay out of Petunia's way while she is cleaning. Sitting out in the backyard, Harry sees something in the hedge looking at him; while he is trying to figure out what it is, Dudley waddles over and starts taunting him about not getting any birthday cards from his "friends at that freak school." Harry tells Dudley that he's thinking up the best spell to set the hedge on fire; when he starts reciting nonsense words under his breath, Dudley runs off to tell Petunia. In retaliation for having threatened to use magic, Petunia sets him a large number of cleaning tasks, while Dudley lolls around and eats ice cream.

Dudley does not interact significantly with Harry before Fred and George Weasley arrive with Ron in their father's flying car, and the book ends as Harry walks off the platform at King's Cross, so we don't see Dudley directly again in this book.

Prisoner of Azkaban The Dursleys, while they cannot prevent Harry from receiving messages from other wizards, are still against his doing magic, so they have locked his spell books and school gear away under the stairs in the cupboard where Harry used to sleep. However, when Vernon, Petunia, and Dudley go out into the street to admire Vernon's new company car (in loud voices, so that the neighbours will know about it also), Harry takes the opportunity to pick the lock on the cupboard and take enough of his stuff upstairs so that he can do his homework. We see him initially doing his homework under the covers late at night, to the sound of Dudley's distant, grunting snores.

Dudley had been complaining about the long walk from the kitchen to the television in the living room, so the Dursleys had bought a new television for the kitchen, and Dudley had been sitting in the kitchen all summer, eating continuously, with his five chins wobbling. When Vernon announces that his sister Marge will be arriving, Harry is dismayed; Marge has repeatedly shown favoritism to Dudley over Harry, at one point allowing her dog to chase Harry up a tree, and then leaving him up there until midnight.

Vernon continues, saying that there will be some ground rules set. Dudley looks away from the television; he enjoys seeing Harry chastised more than watching TV. But while Harry protests at the requirements—he cannot mention his school, instead he must say that he attends St. Brutus's Secure Center for Incurably Criminal Boys—Harry's reaction is not interesting enough to Dudley to keep his eyes away from the television, and he returns to watching that as Harry follows Vernon out to the front room and makes a deal with him about how he is to remember the nonsense he's supposed to tell Aunt Marge.

When Marge arrives, she throws her suitcase at Harry, and gives Dudley a hug. Harry knows that Dudley only puts up with her affections because he gets paid for it, and sure enough, Dudley is clutching a new £20 note when he breaks away from the hug. During her visit, Marge keeps buying expensive gifts for Dudley while silently challenging Harry to say anything. Possibly because he is being so monopolized by Marge, Dudley stays largely out of our story until Harry, having received as much verbal abuse as he can stand, flees the house. At the end of the book, we again see Vernon waiting for Harry to return, but if Dudley has come with him, Harry doesn't notice him.

Goblet of Fire Dudley's end-of-term report card from Smeltings had caused some consternation. While Vernon and Petunia could dismiss his bad grades and the accusations of bullying, the school nurse had mentioned that Dudley was seriously overweight, and the outfitters at the school did not have uniforms in his size. Thus, he had been put on a very controlled diet; and as a matter of family solidarity, the entire family, including Harry, had perforce been placed on a diet also. Breakfast was a quarter grapefruit each, which Dudley augments by sneaking Vernon's away from him when he goes to answer the door and Petunia is busy with the kettle. Harry, of course, has resources that Dudley does not know about; he had sent a plea for help off with Hedwig, and had received a goodly supply of treats back from Ron, Hermione, and Hagrid. Harry is able to tease Dudley about how filling breakfast was, and Dudley can't make any reply.

The Weasleys have tickets to the Quidditch World Cup, and have invited Harry and Hermione to go along with them. They agree to pick Harry up at five o'clock the next day, and Harry is packed and ready by noon. It is five thirty before they finally appear, and when they do, Arthur Weasley arrives by means of the Floo network to the Dursleys' boarded up fireplace. Hearing the noise behind the wall, Dudley waddles out of the lounge and into the kitchen as fast as he can move, holding his hands over his behind. The fireplace becomes very congested, with Arthur, Fred, George, and Ron in it; Arthur blows the wall apart to make an exit for his family. Vernon and Petunia are in a panic, and cannot respond to Arthur's attempts at conversation. Fred and George go off upstairs to collect Harry's trunk; the sound of them dragging Harry's trunk down the stairs scares Dudley back into the lounge. Hiding behind his parents, he watches as Fred and George prepare to return to the Burrow, and as a bag of sweets

Dudley Dursley

falls out of Fred's pocket. Fred rapidly gathers them up, then takes off through the fireplace, followed by George with Harry's trunk, and Ron. Harry says goodbye, and steps towards the fireplace; Arthur stops him, amazed that the Dursleys have not even said goodbye. Under what he perceives as a threat (Arthur's wand), Vernon grudgingly says goodbye, but as Harry steps towards the fireplace, he hears a gagging sound: Dudley has found and eaten one of the dropped sweets, and his tongue is now a foot long and still growing. Pandemonium erupts, with Dudley gagging, Petunia trying to yank this growth out of Dudley's mouth, Arthur attempting to reassure everyone that he almost certainly knows how to cure this, and Vernon attacking Arthur in any way he can. Harry departs, finding himself in the Burrow. Fred and George immediately ask him what had happened. When Harry replies that Dudley had eaten it, there was a great burst of laughter in the kitchen, and Harry realizes that Charlie and Bill are there as well. The Twins explain that the sweet was a Ton-Tongue Toffee, something that they have been working on. Shortly, Arthur appears, infuriated, asking what they had given him, and reporting that Dudley's tongue was four feet long before his parents would let him reverse the charm. He demands to know why they had given that to Dudley. Fred and George protest: they hadn't given it to him, they had dropped it, and he had grabbed it himself. Arthur angrily refutes that, saying that they knew he was on a diet, and that this sort of thing was what strained Wizard-Muggle relations. The twins reply that they hadn't done this to Dudley because he was a Muggle, they had done it because he was a great bullying git, and Harry confirms that he is that. While the twins do apparently catch a serious scolding from their mother for this infraction, that is the last we hear of Dudley before school time. While Uncle Vernon is waiting for Harry at King's Cross at the end of the book, Dudley is not present.

Order of the Phoenix During the summer, Dudley, now grown muscular and having discovered a passion for boxing, apparently has taken to working the street with his cronies and seems to be torturing the neighborhood kids. Harry spots him as a meeting with his cronies breaks up, and knowing that he will be locked out of the house if Dudley gets home before he does, heads home with him. During this short walk, Harry taunts him, knowing full well that Dudley was terrified of Harry's magical capabilities. Dudley then mentioned things that Harry had muttered in his sleep during nightmares. Harry threatens him with his wand, but before he can do anything but point it at Dudley, Dementors appear. Dudley goes to pieces and Harry uses the Patronus charm to fight them off. On their return to Privet Drive, Dudley claims the Dementor's effects were caused by Harry. Harry is nearly thrown out of the house by Vernon Dursley, but a Howler, sent to Petunia, evidently changes her mind, and they decide to allow him to stay. However, Vernon starts locking him in his room again, except for bathroom visits. He remains there until one night when Vernon and Petunia, with Dudley in tow, go out, and Harry is rescued by a group of wizards, the Advance Guard, who take him to the Headquarters of the Order of the Phoenix.

At the end of the book, Vernon, Petunia, and Dudley are at King's Cross to meet Harry on his return from school. They are confronted by Alastor Moody, Remus Lupin, Nymphadora Tonks, and Arthur Weasley, as Harry, Ron, and Hermione look on. Moody, the leader of the group, is telling Vernon that they are interested in Harry's well-bing and will be keeping an eye on how he is being treated. Dudley has nothing to contribute here; like his parents, he is scared of this collection of fully grown wizards, and simply tries to hide himself as best he can.

Half-Blood Prince Harry's time at the Dursleys' is quite short this year, with Dumbledore arriving after only a fortnight to take him away. Before he leaves, though, Dumbledore has some very harsh words to say to the Dursleys about how they are raising Harry. He does say that they had done a better job with Harry than with Dudley. Dudley's contribution during this period seems to be limited to frightened squeaks and attempts to hide behind his parents.

Deathly Hallows Harry steps into a cold cup of tea outside his bedroom door as he goes to the bathroom to clean an injury he has received, and he believes that this is Dudley playing a trick on him. Dudley, however, shows his real feelings towards Harry when he reveals that he doesn't think Harry is a waste of space, and that he would miss Harry in his absence. Although this seems very faint praise to Dedalus Diggle, who is present to assist the Dursleys in making their escape, Harry recognizes this for a marked change from his earlier treatment of Harry, and makes Harry re-assess the meaning of the tea outside his room—perhaps it was a peace offering from Dudley? While we are never told the full reason for Dudley's change of heart, it is probably the result of Harry's saving his soul from the Dementor attack two years previously.

Weaknesses Dudley is spoiled and self-indulgent. He is a couch potato who overeats and has become obese. He bullies his parents with tantrums and whining to get what he wants and has little concern for the feelings of others.

Relationships with Other Characters Dudley is a bully, and has been since the first book, where it is mentioned that Harry is his favorite punch-bag. Like all bullies, when faced with someone who might be stronger than he (e.g. Rubeus Hagrid, Arthur Weasley, Albus Dumbledore), he runs away.

QUESTIONS

In the first chapter ('Dudley Demented') of Order of the Phoenix, Dudley and Harry are attacked by two dementors. Dementors suck all the happy memories out of their victims, leaving them with nothing but their worst experiences. Dudley, during the attack, cowers and shivers and shows all the symptoms of someone being attacked by (or being near) a dementor. So he is reliving his worst memories. However, he is favoured enormously by his parents over Harry, let alone anyone else and they spoil him greatly.

So . . . what is Dudley Dursley's worst memory?

Dumbledore's Army

Location: Room of Requirement

Time Period: Year 5, about October to about March, and again in Year 7

Important Characters: Harry Potter, Hermione Granger, Ron Weasley, among others

Overview

Dumbledore's Army (D.A.) is the secret Defence Against the Dark Arts group founded by Harry Potter and Hermione Granger, with assistance from Ron Weasley.

Event Details Professor Dolores Umbridge, Hogwart's new Defence Against the Dark Arts teacher, only lectures on Ministry-approved theory from the textbook and refuses to teach real defensive magic. Sirius Black, in conversation with Harry after the group is founded, reveals that this is because the Ministry is worried that Albus Dumbledore may be trying to raise a private army to attack the Ministry itself. Within the first two weeks of classes, Hermione has seen how stultifying and useless this form of teaching is, and with the assistance of Ron, suggests to Harry that it would be a good idea to have someone teach them real Defence Against the Dark Arts, rather than the useless "techniques" currently being taught. When Harry agrees to this, Hermione tentatively suggests that the appropriate teacher would be Harry himself. Harry's surprise turns into exasperation when Ron agrees that he is the logical choice.

Although Harry initially feels he is unqualified to teach Defensive Arts, he reluctantly agrees after Hermione convinces him he has gained considerable knowledge on the subject. Hermione then invites "a couple of students" to meet at the Hog's Head Inn in Hogsmeade village to discuss forming a group to learn real Defence Against the Dark Arts. Harry is stunned when Hermione's "couple of students" ends up numbering 25; Hermione simply says "The idea did seem quite popular." The group originally call themselves the *Defence Association,* or D.A. for short. Shortly afterwards, a new Educational Decree is posted which prevents formation of student groups. Harry and Ron are convinced that someone has told Umbridge, but Hermione says nobody could have. She had passed a parchment around that everyone had signed; the parchment was jinxed so that anyone who betrayed the group after signing it would break out in severe facial blemishes.

In the conversation with Sirius earlier mentioned, Sirius mentions that he knows that they are starting the group; he says that at the initial meeting, a heavily veiled witch that Harry and Hermione had noted was Mundungus Fletcher. He passes on a message from Ron's mother forbidding Ron from having anything to do with it, and appealing to Harry and Hermione to likewise give up the idea. Sirius himself, however, says he strongly supports the idea of the group.

There is concern for some time as to where they can meet. Various suggestions are made and rejected for practical reasons. Finally, Harry happens to ask Dobby if he knows of a place, and Dobby tells Harry about the Room of Requirement, a room which appears when a person really needs it, in the form that the person needs. Harry, Ron, and Hermione pass on the description of the Room to other members of the Defence Association, as it is then known, and then go to the room themselves. When it appears for them, it is perfect, stocked with everything they need for a Defence Against the Dark Arts class; and Hermione, who has been unsure whether using the Room of Requirement is a good idea, is instantly reassured by the shelves of books along the wall. At this, their first full meeting, they change the name of the group to "Dumbledore's Army" to show their loyalty to the Headmaster and to mock the paranoid Ministry of Magic.

Meetings are irregular, as they have to be fit in around three different house's Quidditch practices; Hermione provides fake Galleons that allow DA members to send messages. The spell used to do this is a Protean Charm, which Terry Boot says is "N.E.W.T.-level magic." For several months, Harry secretly teaches students from Gryffindor, Ravenclaw, and Hufflepuff, although Slytherin is excluded. Under Harry's effective tutoring, the D.A. members learn many advanced defensive Dark Art techniques, starting with the simple disarmament charm and proceeding to the N.E.W.T.-level Patronus charm.

Dumbledore's Army abruptly ends in March when D.A. member and Ravenclaw student Marietta Edgecombe reveals its existence to Umbridge, instigating a raid by her *Inquisitorial Squad,* comprised of Slytherin students and led by Draco Malfoy. Umbridge's attempt to detain members of the Army are thwarted by Dobby, who disobeys orders to warn Harry; Harry sends the rest of the group away, and is the only group member captured. He is taken to Dumbledore's office, where he finds Dumbledore, along with Umbridge, the Minister for Magic Cornelius Fudge, Percy Weasley (along to record the meeting), and a pair of Aurors, one of whom (Kingsley Shacklebolt) Harry recognizes as being in the Order of the Phoenix.

Umbridge's star witness, Marietta, proves less than useful, as it seems Kingsley has performed a memory charm on her secretly to keep Harry out of trouble. However, the membership list for the D. A. was retrieved by Pansy Parkinson, and the heading, *"Dumbledore's Army,"* is enough to allow the Ministry to order Dumbledore's arrest. This heading on the membership list allows Dumbledore to claim responsibility for forming the group, thus protecting the students. The Ministry's subsequent attempt to arrest him results in his spectacular departure from Hogwarts. Umbridge is appointed Headmistress in his place. For betraying the D.A., permanent purple pustules spelling "SNEAK" erupt across Marietta's face—courtesy of Hermione's jinxed parchment.

With the appointment of a competent Defence Against the Dark Arts teacher in Harry's sixth year (Severus Snape), there is little need to re-start Dumbledore's Army. Harry does put out a call to the members of the DA for assistance when he knows Dumbledore will be leaving the school temporarily, but only about five members respond: Ron Weasley, Hermione Granger, Luna Lovegood, Neville Longbottom, and Ginny Weasley.

In what would be Harry's seventh year, Neville, Luna, and Ginny restart Dumbledore's Army as a means of rebelling against Hogwarts' new emphasis on Dark Arts at the hands of headmaster Snape, Dark Arts teacher Amycus Carrow, and Muggle Studies teacher Alecto Carrow, all of whom are Death Eaters. The DA falls on hard times as its members are hunted down; Luna is captured, Ginny escapes with her family, and Neville's grandmother is targeted in an unsuccessful attempt to put pressure on Neville. The DA retreat to the Room of Requirement, from which they continue guerrilla raids on the school.

When Harry returns to the school, Neville, using the Galleons that Hermione had earlier enchanted to tell about meetings, recalls the rest of the D.A. The members of the Order of the Phoenix come along with them, along with many other wizards.

The Members Of Dumbledore's Army include: Hannah Abbott, Lavender Brown, Katie Bell, Susan Bones, Terry Boot, Cho Chang, Michael Corner, Colin Creevey, Dennis Creevey, Marietta Edgecombe, Justin Finch-Fletchley, Seamus Finnigan, Anthony Goldstein, Hermione Granger, Angelina Johnson, Lee Jordan, Neville Longbottom, Luna Lovegood, Ernie Macmillan, Padma Patil, Parvati Patil, Harry Potter, Zacharias Smith, Alicia Spinnet, Dean Thomas, Fred Weasley, George Weasley, Ginny Weasley, and Ron Weasley. Seamus Finnigan is a late-joining member; not present at the initial meeting in The Hog's Head, the first meeting he attended was the one that was broken up by Marietta Edgecombe's betrayal of the group.

Notable Consequences When meeting in the Hog's Head, Harry expresses some doubts that they may be overheard by someone, suggesting that a veiled witch in the corner might be Umbridge. Umbridge is not present, as it turns out, but here are in fact two eavesdroppers: the witch is Mundungus Fletcher, there for the Order of the Phoenix, and also present is Willy Widdershins, the comprehensively bandaged wizard at the bar drinking Firewhiskey, who promptly reports back to Umbridge. It is as a direct result of this meeting that Umbridge causes promulgation of Educational Decree number Twenty-Four which prevents unapproved student groups. This has the side effect of banning the Quidditch teams. The fact that the Slytherin Quidditch team is approved and reforms immediately, while the Gryffindor team is not allowed to reform for a month, is an indication of how Umbridge will tend to abuse her powers. Cho Chang has joined the D.A. largely because Harry was there. Cho makes use of the end of the last D.A. meeting before Christmas to kiss Harry in private. We can see from his response to this, as related to Hermione, that he is extremely unsure of himself around Cho.

The continued unapproved meetings of the D.A., in violation of Educational Decree number Twenty-Four, are eventually betrayed, and an attempt is made to apprehend the group. In the end, due to a timely warning from Dobby, the only group member caught is Harry himself. Pansy Parkinson enters the Room of Requirement and retrieves the membership list. Cornelius Fudge has been summoned to witness the bringing of the group to justice; on seeing the membership list heading, his paranoia asserts itself, and he tries to arrest Dumbledore. Dumbledore escapes, dramatically, and Umbridge is appointed Headmistress, although she is never able to get into the Headmaster's office after Dumbledore's departure.

Marietta Edgecombe's defection not only betrayed Dumbledore's Army, but ultimately doomed Harry and Cho Chang's relationship. When Cho defends Marietta's actions and is angry that Hermione secretly jinxed the parchment the D.A. members signed, Harry angrily lashes out, calling Hermione's plan "brilliant." Cho is deeply offended and storms off in tears; she and Harry do not speak to one another for two years.

Unfortunately for Umbridge, students have acquired what she vigorously prevented them from having: Defence Against the Dark Arts knowledge. The D.A. members use their new-found skills on several occasions. When Ron, Ginny, Neville, and Luna are captured by Umbridge's *Inquisitorial Squad*, they escape with defensive jinxes and hexes. The students use Defensive Arts during the Battle at the Department of Mysteries, fending off Death Eaters until Order of the Phoenix reinforcements arrive. When Draco and his minions attempt to Curse Harry on the Hogwarts Express, D.A. members come to his rescue, jinxing the Slytherins until they are unrecognizable. Members of Dumbledore's Army use what they have learned to assist with the defence of the school at the battle under the Astronomy tower. And it is largely members of Dumbledore's Army who make up the core of the guerrilla resistance against Snape's rule in the seventh book.

ANALYSIS

Curiously, it is Hermione who takes action against Umbridge by forming *Dumbledore's Army*. Although she believes in strictly adhering to school rules, she never hesitates to break them when she believes they are wrong or a nobler purpose is served. In this instance, she not only takes on Umbridge, but the entire Ministry of Magic, who are convinced Dumbledore may be creating a secret wizard army against them.

There are two people in Dumbledore's Army who do not completely seem to belong there. These are Zacharias Smith and Marietta Edgecombe. Smith is confrontational, to the point that at the organizational meeting Fred Weasley feels compelled to threaten him with a pointed metal object that he produces from a Zonko's Joke Shop bag. Smith also does not seem to want to sign the parchment that Hermione passes around, where they swear not to tell anyone about the

D.A. Granted, he is not the only one to express reluctance; Ernie Macmillan hesitates, saying he is a prefect, and if the parchment were found... He only signs when Hermione points out that she's not going to leave this bit of parchment lying around. From the beginning, we have a feeling that the D.A. is doomed, that it will accomplish at least some part of its purpose, but will ultimately fall to Umbridge and her cronies; and Zacharias Smith's continuing skepticism makes him a lead candidate for that betrayal.

Marietta is along because Cho is going, and she is always very quiet, limiting her interaction to sighs and non-verbal displays of impatience. When the actual betrayal takes place, we fully expect Zacharias to have been the agent, and are very surprised when it turns out to be Marietta.

Even before Harry gets the teaching up to that level, Hermione is seen doing two N.E.W.T.-class spells here. The first is the parchment, on which everyone signs their names at the organizational meeting. As mentioned above, the parchment is charmed so that anyone who betrays the D.A. will break out in horrendous blemishes. When Hermione mentions this to Ron and Harry, after the promulgation of the Educational Decree banning student organizations, they are both very impressed; Ron in particular recognizes that this is very advanced magic. One wonders why Hermione had not told the rest of the D.A. of this charm, once they had all signed; Marietta might have chosen a different course of action had she known that betraying the D.A. to Umbridge would result in her wearing the word "Sneak" across her face for at least a year.

The second is the Galleons; every Galleon has on it a serial number, that of the gnome who cast it. Hermione has made fake Galleons for the D.A., which look like real ones except that the serial number changes to indicate the date and time of the next meeting. When Hermione passes these out at the second regular meeting, everyone present is amazed that she is capable of performing a Protean Charm, it being such advanced magic.

QUESTIONS

1. What prompts Hermione to form *Dumbledore's Army*? Why is it kept secret?
2. Why is the group's original name changed from *Defense Association* to *Dumbledore's Army*?
3. What are possible reasons Slytherin students were excluded from the group?
4. Why did purple pimples break out on Marietta Edgecombe's face? Who was responsible?
5. Why does Professor Dumbledore claim responsibility for having organized the group? What happens when he does?
6. Why is Harry initially reluctant to teach Defensive Arts? Who convinces him otherwise?
7. How does Marietta Edgecombe betraying the D.A. contribute to Harry and Cho breaking up?

GREATER PICTURE

In *Harry Potter and the Half-Blood Prince*, Harry finds out that he and Dumbledore are going to both be leaving the school for a while, and while he cannot be sure what Draco's mission is, or whether he has accomplished it, he has at the very least a great suspicion that it has been completed successfully. Although Dumbledore reassures him that the school is protected by Aurors and members of the Order of the Phoenix, Harry does not feel that is enough. For reasons of his own, he feels that Draco's task may have resulted in an increased danger to Hogwarts in a way that the Order had not anticipated. When appealing to Dumbledore seems ineffective, Harry tries to re-activate the D.A., with very limited success: only Ron, Hermione, Ginny, Neville, and Luna Lovegood come forward. However, the five of them, with a little help from Harry's remaining stock of Felix Felicis potion, manage to turn the tide of the battle.

In *Harry Potter and the Deathly Hallows*, Neville and Ginny re-activate Dumbledore's army as a means of rebelling against the headmaster, Severus Snape. As there are two other Death Eaters teaching at the school, and the teaching has become a lot darker and more abusive, this is not a complete success. However, the organization is in place, and is working out of the Room of Requirement, when Harry reaches Hogwarts. Additionally, when Neville uses the Galleons to summon the D.A., all of the past members of the D.A. arrive as well, forming the nucleus of a fighting group that will largely save Hogwarts.

Surprisingly, the choice of which student enters the Room of Requirement to retrieve the parchment is important. Voldemort, when he was at Hogwarts, apparently discovered the Room of Requirement. It seems that most people who discover it are looking for some place to hide something; Professor Trelawney had discovered it when looking for a place to hide her sherry, and the Twins had been looking for a place to hide themselves from Filch, for instance. Voldemort, presumably looking for a place to hide something he had done, had thus managed to open the door onto a warehouse full of a thousand years worth of magical junk. He apparently instructed Draco Malfoy, over the summer, as to how to get into that aspect of the Room. It is in that aspect of the room that Draco was working on his technique for getting Death Eaters into Hogwarts throughout Harry's sixth year. If Draco had ever seen the inside of the room prepared for D.A. meetings, he might have had a better idea of what the room actually was; as it is, though, only Pansy has seen that aspect of the room, and Draco, in his superior way, likely would not bother to ask her what the inside of the room looked like, assuming, once he got instructions on how to enter, that the DA had been practicing in the junk warehouse.

Edgar Bones

Gender: Male
Hair color: Unknown
Eye color: Unknown

Related Family: Amelia Bones (sister), Susan Bones (possibly daughter or niece)
Loyalty: Order of the Phoenix

OVERVIEW

Edgar Bones was killed with his wife (name unknown) while working for the Order of the Phoenix.

ROLE IN THE BOOKS

Philosopher's Stone In their first meeting, Hagrid mentions to Harry that Voldemort killed some of the best wizards of the age such as the Bones, along with the McKinnons and the Prewetts.

Order of the Phoenix At the celebratory party at Grimmauld Place for Ron and Hermione's appointment as Prefects, Alastor Moody shows Harry a photograph of the original Order of the Phoenix. Edgar Bones was in that picture, and Moody remarks that they got him and his family, too.

Eleanor Branstone

Gender: Female
Hair color: Unknown
Eye color: Unknown
Related Family: Unknown
Loyalty:

OVERVIEW

Eleanor Branstone is a Hufflepuff who arrived at Hogwarts in Harry's fourth year.

ROLE IN THE BOOKS

Goblet of Fire Eleanor Branstone was Sorted into Hufflepuff House.

Eloise Midgeon

Gender: Female
Hair color: Unknown
Eye color: Unknown
Related Family: Unknown

OVERVIEW

Eloise Midgeon may be a Hufflepuff; very little is mentioned about her, except that she is plagued by a terrible acne problem.

ROLE IN THE BOOKS

Goblet of Fire It is mentioned in passing, in talking about the medicinal effects of Bubotubers, that Eloise Midgeon had tried to jinx her acne off. "But Madam Pomfrey fixed her nose back on in the end."

Order of the Phoenix Immediately after publication of the Educational Decree banning student groups, Hermione tells Ron and Harry that nobody in the newly formed Defence Association could possibly have told Professor Umbridge about the group. She had had them all sign a piece of parchment that was charmed so that if anyone betrayed the group, they would get skin blemishes that would "make Eloise Midgeon's acne look like a couple of cute freckles."

Half-Blood Prince Eloise Midgeon is mentioned here as being removed from the school for reasons of her perceived safety, as a result of general fear and uncertainty spreading through the Wizarding population due to Lord Voldemort's return.

Weaknesses Whether it is a weakness, or simply an accident of nature, Eloise Midgeon is always used as an example of a person with really bad acne.

We gather that her judgment in dealing with her acne is somewhat suspect, as she apparently manages to charm her own nose off while trying to get rid of it.

Elphias Doge

Gender: Male
Hair color: White, thinning
Eye color: Unknown
Related Family: Unknown
Loyalty: Albus Dumbledore

OVERVIEW

Elphias Doge is a wheezy-voiced wizard who is a member of the Order of the Phoenix.

ROLE IN THE BOOKS

Order of the Phoenix We first see Elphias Doge when he arrives at the Dursleys' as part of the Advance Guard. He and several other Order members are Harry's escort as he travels to Number 12, Grimmauld Place by broom.

Deathly Hallows After the death of Albus Dumbledore, Elphias Doge writes a eulogy that is published in the *Daily Prophet*. In that eulogy, he mentions that he and Dumbledore had gone to school together, and that he had traveled the world afterwards while Dumbledore had stayed at home, caring for his family.

At the wedding of Bill Weasley and Fleur Delacour, Elphias is quite indignant about what Rita Skeeter had written about Dumbledore and, to a lesser extent, about himself. He mentions in passing that Dumbledore had lived in Godric's Hollow, and Bathilda Bagshot, who was likely Rita's informant, lived there still. He also mentions that Godric's Hollow is named for Godric Gryffindor.

Emmeline Vance

Gender: Female
Hair color: Unknown
Eye color: Unknown
Related Family: Unknown
Loyalty: Albus Dumbledore

OVERVIEW

Emmeline Vance is a member of the Order of the Phoenix.

ROLE IN THE BOOKS

Order of the Phoenix We see Emmeline Vance briefly; a stately witch, she is a member of the Advance Guard who come to collect Harry Potter from the Dursley's house near the start of the book.

Half-Blood Prince In discussion between the Muggle Prime Minister and Cornelius Fudge, we learn that the Vance family has been brutally murdered, only a short distance away from the Prime Minister's home. In discussions between Severus Snape, Bellatrix Lestrange, and Narcissa Malfoy, we learn further that it was by means of information received from Snape that Lord Voldemort was able to have Emmeline Vance murdered.

Eric Munch

Gender: Male
Hair color: Unknown
Eye color: Unknown
Related Family: Unknown
Loyalty: Ministry of Magic

OVERVIEW

Eric Munch is a watchwizard at the Ministry of Magic.

ROLE IN THE BOOKS

Order of the Phoenix When Harry is entering the Ministry to attend his hearing, he must stop at the security desk, where the watch wizard, here identified only as Eric, must weigh his wand. Having done so, the wizard looks at Harry for the first time, and noticing his scar, seems to realize who Harry is. Before he can say anything else, Arthur Weasley, accompanying Harry, thanks him dismissively.

It is reported in the *Daily Prophet* that watchwizard Eric Munch was the one who had caught Sturgis Podmore attempting to break through a secure door at the Ministry of Magic on 31 August.

Ernie Macmillan

Gender: Male
Hair color: Unknown
Eye color: Unknown
Related Family: "Old wizarding family"
Loyalty:

OVERVIEW

Ernie Macmillan is a Hufflepuff student in Harry Potter's year. He is described as "a stout boy" and has "pudgy hands."

ROLE IN THE BOOKS

Chamber of Secrets Ernie Macmillan is apparently one of the students who is helped after the grand chaos of the Duelling Club by Professor Lockhart: "Up you get, Macmillan . . ."

Identified only as *Ernie,* he is apparently the leader of the group of Hufflepuffs discussing Justin Finch-Fletchley's decision to remain in hiding when Harry Potter is thought to be the Heir of Slytherin, in *The Duelling Club.* He more or less acts as spokesman of the group when Harry confronts them—as a scion of an old wizarding family, he feels that the Heir of Slytherin would not attack him—and later accuses Harry of petrifying Justin when Justin is found in the hallway. (Professor McGonagall addresses him here as "Macmillan," giving us his last name.) Ernie is then given the task of wafting the petrified Nearly Headless Nick up to the Hospital Wing with a large fan. Later, when Hermione Granger is Petrified, Ernie makes a point of apologizing to Harry for having thought him the Heir of Slytherin. Ernie feels that, Muggle-born or not, Hermione would not be a victim if Harry had anything to do with it.

Goblet of Fire Harry sees Ernie in the campground at the Quidditch World Cup.

Ernie is the student who runs off to tell the Hufflepuff common room, most notably Cedric Diggory, that the delegations from Durmstrang and Beauxbatons will be arriving on the 30th of October.

Order of the Phoenix On the Hogwarts Express, Ron reports that Ernie Macmillan is one of the two Hufflepuff prefects; Hannah Abbott is the other.

Ernie is one of the original members of the Defence Association, or as it becomes known, Dumbledore's Army. He shows up at the initial meeting in the Hog's Head, but is initially reluctant to sign his name to the paper that Hermione is passing around. "After all, I am a prefect," he says, meaning, presumably, that he has to set a good example. Hermione points out that she's not going to leave this bit of parchment lying around, after which he signs, though still with some show of reluctance.

As a member of Dumbledore's Army, his work seems to be decent but not worthy of too much comment. He is, apparently, able to conjure a Patronus before the group is betrayed and broken up.

As the O.W.L. exams approach, Ernie takes up the disquieting habit of asking everyone how much studying they are doing, and proudly saying that he is averaging eight hours a day.

Ernie is also one of the six members of Dumbledore's Army who see Draco Malfoy attempting to jinx Harry on the Hogwarts Express, and promptly return fire, leaving Draco, Crabbe, and Goyle looking like gigantic slugs squeezed into Hogwarts robes.

Deathly Hallows Ernie is one of the group of Dumbledore's Army alumni who have retreated into the Room of Requirement, thus being able to stay on at the school and keep a form of guerrilla warfare going on against the Dark curriculum. With the others, he greets Harry's arrival with loud cheers and demands to know when they will be taking Hogwarts back. Ernie takes part in the battle for Hogwarts. When Harry has to get to the Shrieking Shack, he finds his way to the Whomping Willow blocked by Dementors. He is unable to produce much of a Patronus himself, but Ernie, Luna Lovegood, and Seamus Finnigan arrive with their Patronuses and clear his way. The passage of a twenty-foot-tall giant separates them, and Harry, Ron, and Hermione proceed to the Shrieking Shack through the tunnel.

Strengths Ernie is generally friendly, loyal to his fellow Hufflepuffs and takes his prefect responsibilities seriously.

Weaknesses Ernie tends to be pompous around his fellow students and sycophantical around teachers. He likes to brag about how seriously he takes his studies.

Relationships with Other Characters Ernie and Hannah Abbott both become prefects in *Harry Potter and the Order of the Phoenix*, Harry's fifth year. It is never made clear whether there is any romantic entanglement between them, though they do seem to be seen together a lot.

Ernie Prang

Gender: Male
Hair color: Unknown
Eye color: Unknown
Related Family: Unknown
Loyalty: Unknown

Overview

Ernie Prang is the driver of the Knight Bus.

Role in the Books

Prisoner of Azkaban When Harry falls into the street, after tripping over his trunk, the Knight Bus appears to pick him up. Ernie, the driver, is sitting in his armchair in front of the steering wheel, but he evidently is not very familiar with its operation, as Harry sees the bus mounting the pavement (US: driving on the sidewalk) and watches, amazed, as mailboxes, lampposts, and occasionally entire houses leap out of the way of the bus. Harry sees a picture of Sirius Black on the cover of Stan Shunpike's newspaper, and recognizes him as the mass murderer who has been mentioned on the Muggle news. Stan and Ernie discuss the circumstances of Sirius' arrest twelve years before, thus bringing Harry up to speed on what is happening in the Wizarding world.

Order of the Phoenix Nymphadora Tonks summons the Knight Bus to take Harry, Ron, Ginny, Hermione, and the twins back to Hogwarts. Although we don't talk to him and don't see him, we can assume that Ernie is still driving, as Stan Shunpike is still the conductor, and the driving style has not changed.

Analysis

Given that Ernie seems to be uncertain of the operation of a steering wheel, it is perhaps reasonable that his surname "Prang" is British slang for an automobile or aircraft accident.

Errol

Gender: Male
Hair color: Grey feathers
Eye color: Yellow
Related Family: None (he's an owl)
Loyalty: Weasley Family

Overview

Errol is the Weasleys' owl. He is rather old and has a tendency to crash into things.

Role in the Books

Chamber of Secrets Errol appears at the Burrow a couple of days after Harry's arrival there, when Percy Weasley nearly sits on him at breakfast. Harry initially thinks it's a moulting grey feather duster, but then notices it's breathing. Ron says that he's finally brought an answer from Hermione, that Ron had told her that they were planning to rescue Harry. Ron tries to put Errol on a perch by the door, but he just flops off, so eventually, he leaves Errol on the draining board. Hermione suggests in the letter that Ron should probably try to find a different owl, the trip seems to have almost killed this one.

We next see Errol when he brings a Howler for Ron on the first day of school. He falls into the jug on the table, spraying milk on Hermione. Ron seems horrified, so Hermione points out that Errol is still breathing, but it is the Howler that Ron is scared of.

Prisoner of Azkaban Errol delivers a birthday present to Harry from Ron, or tries to. The first we see of Errol, he is being essentially dragged through the sky by Hedwig and one of the school's barn owls, having tried to fly all the way from Egypt and not been up to the task. Harry tries to put Errol on the perch in Hedwig's cage, but he falls right off again. A few hours later, when Harry gets up, Errol has recovered enough that he is able to stand on the perch, and he and Hedwig are both asleep. Shortly, though, Harry has to send them both away to The Burrow, as he has agreed to act entirely normal for a week while Aunt Marge is there.

Weaknesses Being an old owl, Errol is always exhausted after delivering mail. On at least one occasion, he is unable to complete his delivery unaided; tasked with bringing Harry a birthday present, he ends up being dragged in through Harry's window by Hedwig and one of the school's barn owls.

Evan Rosier

Gender: Male

Hair color: Unknown
Eye color: Unknown
Related Family: Unknown
Loyalty: Lord Voldemort

Overview

Evan Rosier was one of the Death Eaters that were part of Lord Voldemort's organization. We believe that his father, only called Rosier, was also a member of the Death Eaters.

Role in the Books

Goblet of Fire When Harry, Ron, and Hermione were visiting Sirius Black in his cave hide-out outside Hogwarts, Sirius mentioned that one Rosier had been one of Severus Snape's friends, and he had been killed by Aurors the year before Voldemort fell.

When Harry is looking at Dumbledore's Pensieve, one of the three scenes he witnesses is Igor Karkaroff revealing names of Death Eaters in hopes that he will get his own sentence reduced. The first name he gives is that of Evan Rosier, and he is most disappointed that it is already known to the Ministry.

Half-Blood Prince When Lord Voldemort, or Tom Riddle as he is then known, is seen in Albus Dumbledore's memories returning to Hogwarts to apply for the job of teacher of Defence Against the Dark Arts, Dumbledore asks him about his "friends" waiting for him in Hogsmeade. One Rosier, who we believe is Evan Rosier's father, is one of the friends mentioned by name, along with Mulciber, Nott, and Dolohov.

Everard

Gender: Male
Hair color: Black
Eye color: Unknown
Related Family: Unknown
Loyalty: Current Headmaster of Hogwarts

Overview

Everard is a past Headmaster of Hogwarts. He is present as a painting in the Headmaster's office. He seems to be somewhat famous, as he seems to have portraits also in the Ministry.

Role in the Books

Order of the Phoenix Everard plays a small role in this book. Hearing that Arthur Weasley has been attacked by a snake, Professor Dumbledore sends Everard and Dilys to investigate. Everard reports back that he had raised the alarm, saying that he had heard something downstairs, and had seen them bringing a man up. We assume, correctly as it turns out, that the injured man is Arthur, and we are led to believe that the hallway in which he was sitting is the one that ends at the doorway into the Department of Mysteries at the Ministry of Magic.

Half-Blood Prince Everard has one brief appearance in this book. At the end of the book, as the four Heads of House, plus Harry and Hagrid, are meeting to consider the future of the school, Everard, here described as a sallow-faced wizard with a short black fringe, strolls into his picture frame to announce that the Minister is on his way, he has just Disapparated from the Ministry.

Fabian Prewett

Gender: Male
Hair color: Unknown
Eye color: Unknown
Related Family: Molly Weasley
Loyalty: Order of the Phoenix

Overview

Fabian Prewett was a member of the original Order of the Phoenix, and one of Molly Weasley's brothers.

Role in the Books

Philosopher's Stone In their first meeting, Hagrid mentions to Harry that Voldemort killed some of the best wizards of the age such as the Prewetts, along with the Bones and the McKinnons.

Order of the Phoenix At the celebratory party at Grimmauld Place for Ron and Hermione's appointment as Prefects, Alastor Moody shows Harry a photograph of the original Order of the Phoenix. Fabian Prewett is in that photo, with his brother Gideon, and Moody says it took five Death Eaters to kill them.

Gideon and Fabian were twins and Molly Weasley's brothers. It is in part because she has lost immediate family members to Death Eaters already that her greatest fear, as shown by the Boggart in that same chapter, is of her own family members dying.

Deathly Hallows Apparently it is traditional to give a wizard a watch on their seventeenth birthday. When Harry turns 17, Mr. and Mrs. Weasley give Harry a watch. Mrs. Weasley apologizes profusely, saying it was Fabian's, and he hadn't always been terribly careful with his possessions, but Harry is very pleased by the gift, and tries to show it.

Fawcett

Gender: Female
Hair color: Unknown
Eye color: Unknown
Related Family: Unknown
Loyalty:

Overview

Miss Fawcett is a member of Ravenclaw house, possibly in the same year as Fred and George Weasley.

Role in the Books

Chamber of Secrets   Miss Fawcett is mentioned in passing as one of the students that Professor Lockhart helps to her feet after the grand chaos of the Duelling Club. "Careful there, Miss Fawcett . . ."

Goblet of Fire   Professor Dumbledore mentions that Miss Fawcett had tried to place her name in the Goblet of Fire, but had been thwarted by the Age Line.

Fawcett is penalized ten points by Professor Snape when she is caught hiding in a rose bush with one Mr. Stebbins at the Yule Ball.

Analysis

One thing to be aware of here is that either there is some confusion over whether Miss Fawcett is in Ravenclaw or in Hufflepuff, or else there are two Misses Fawcett, one in each house. As noted above, Professor Dumbledore says "Miss Fawcett, of Ravenclaw." At the Yule Ball, however, when Professor Snape is wandering around the rose garden, blasting apart bushes, he flushes out a snogging couple, Fawcett and Stebbins. Addressing the fleeing girl, Snape says "That's ten points from Hufflepuff, Fawcett!"

Fawkes

Gender: Male
Hair color: Red and gold plumage (except on burning day)
Eye color: Black
Related Family: Unknown
Loyalty: Albus Dumbledore

Overview

Fawkes is a phoenix owned by Albus Dumbledore.

Role In The Books

Philosopher's Stone   Fawkes is not directly present, though it becomes apparent later that one of only two feathers he ever gave to Mr. Ollivander is the core of Harry Potter's wand, and the other one is the core of Lord Voldemort's wand.

Chamber of Secrets   We are introduced to Fawkes initially when Harry is called into Albus Dumbledore's office; Fawkes is then at the end of his life and bursts into flame while Harry watches, appalled. This is Harry's first exposure to the phoenix; he doesn't realize that Fawkes will be reborn shortly from his own ashes.

In the climactic battle with the returning Tom Marvolo Riddle, Fawkes appears in response to Harry's declaration of faithfulness to Dumbledore. Fawkes brings with him the Sorting Hat, and pecks the Basilisk's eyes out so that Harry will not be destroyed by them. When Harry takes an envenomed wound from the basilisk, Fawkes sheds tears on it and heals Harry. And finally, he lifts Harry, Ron, Ginny, and Professor Lockhart out of the Chamber of Secrets and returns them to safety.

Prisoner of Azkaban   Fawkes is not mentioned in Prisoner of Azkaban: we assume that he is sitting on his perch in Professor Dumbledore's office, but Harry has no reason to visit Dumbledore's office in this book.

Goblet of Fire   Fawkes does not appear to play a significant role in Goblet of Fire. He appears briefly when Harry makes two visits to Dumbledore's office. During the second visit, which occurs after a confrontation between Harry and Voldemort accompanied by his Death Eaters, Fawkes heals Harry's injured leg with his tears.

Prior to this visit, Harry and Voldemort attempt to duel using their wands. Two spells—an Expelliarmus from Harry, and an Avada Kedavra from Voldemort—intercept each other in mid-flight, and an unusual effect occurs: Priori Incantatem. Harry and Voldemort are surrounded by a web of light strands, which is then accompanied by phoenix song—Harry recognizes this song as the same music that he heard in the Chamber of Secrets. It is not explicitly *Fawkes'* music, but it is clearly phoenix song.

The Priori Incantatem effect is explained by Dumbledore during Harry's second visit to his office; Harry and Voldemort's wand cores are phoenix feathers, both of which were given to Ollivander by Fawkes.

Order of the Phoenix   Dumbledore wakes Fawkes up so that he can be warned if anyone is approaching while Harry and the others are being sent to Number 12, Grimmauld Place. Fawkes delivers the message to Molly Weasley that Arthur Weasley is injured, and then delivers the message from Molly to Sirius Black and the Weasley children that Arthur is safe.

Fawkes carries Dumbledore away from Hogwarts after the skirmish that results when Cornelius Fudge, Dolores Umbridge, and the Aurors Kingsley Shacklebolt and Dawlish attempt to put him under arrest. Towards the end, Fawkes saves Dumbledore from Voldemort's killing curse by swallowing the green jet of light. This, of course, kills him, but he regenerates instantly as a chick. When Dumbledore returns to his office, the first thing he does is tenderly place Fawkes into the bed of ashes under his perch.

Half-Blood Prince   Fawkes is largely unseen in Half-Blood Prince. Although Harry makes many visits to Dumbledore's office, Fawkes is only mentioned in the narrative in passing.

Shortly after Dumbledore's death, Fawkes takes flight around Hogwarts, singing his music. The main characters clearly identify his music as a lament: eerie and beautiful, yet speaking of loss and despair. Later in the evening, Fawkes stops singing.

His location is not known at the end of Half-Blood Prince.

Deathly Hallows   Fawkes is mentioned only in passing, in the discussion of how to destroy a Horcrux. Apparently, a Horcrux will mend itself if it can do so by ordinary magical means; one of the few things that can destroy it is Basilisk venom, because the only thing that can heal that is Phoenix tears, and the Phoenix is definitely not ordinary magic.

Strengths His tears have healing powers.

He can carry immensely heavy loads.

He cannot die—If he sustains fatal wounds he will merely burst into flames and be reborn from the ashes. He can teleport from one place to the other instantly, regardless of magical enchantments that prevent Apparation/Disapparation.

Analysis

Fawkes has only ever provided two of his feathers for wand cores. These wands are owned by Harry and Voldemort respectively.

Questions

1. Phoenixes are immortal. The person to whom he was loyal (Dumbledore) passes at the end of book 6. Where is Fawkes now?

Fenrir Greyback

Gender: Male
Hair color: black/dark grey
Eye color: greyish blue
Related Family: Unknown
Loyalty: Voldemort

Overview

Fenrir Greyback is the most savage, cruel werewolf in existence. He considers it his duty in life to bite as many people as possible, so he might one day have enough werewolf followers to rebel against the wizarding community. Voldemort frequently uses him as an effective threat to force people into doing his bidding.

Role in the Books

Half-Blood Prince Draco Malfoy threatens Burke, at Borgin and Burkes, with Fenrir if Burke does not assist him in repairing something. We don't learn what the something is or how it got broken at this point.

At Christmas, it is revealed that it was Fenrir Greyback who bit Lupin as a boy, because Lupin's father had offended him. Lupin tells us that Fenrir will deliberately place himself near human dwelling places on full moon nights, thus making it near certain that in his animal state he will at least infect others.

In the ending of this book, Fenrir Greyback is with the Death Eaters who come to Hogwarts to kill Dumbledore; he is one of the four Death Eaters who follow Draco to the top of the Astronomy tower. He attacks and bites Bill Weasley, but because it is not during the full moon and Greyback was not in his wolf form, the only lasting effects on Bill are scars and a newly developed taste for very rare steaks.

Deathly Hallows Fenrir Greyback is one of the gang of Snatchers who capture Harry, Ron, and Hermione after Harry incautiously speaks Lord Voldemort's name. They are initially fooled by Harry's appearance—Hermione has hit him with a spell that made his face swell up—they eventually determine that this is the Harry Potter for which there is a large reward offered, and decide to take him to Malfoy Manor. While Greyback is evidently the leader of the group, it is revealed that he does not possess the Dark Mark which will grant him unfettered access to the Manor; he is not a full Death Eater. Once in Malfoy Manor, Bellatrix Lestrange offers Hermione to him as a victim; evidently he has cultivated a taste for human flesh even in his non-transformed state. Once Bellatrix sees the sword of Gryffindor, however, she retracts the offer; in order to find out how the sword got out of her vault at Gringott's, she has to interrogate one of the Trio, and she selects Hermione. Once she has the story from Hermione, corroborated by Griphook, she offers Hermione to Fenrir once more. As they escape with Dobby's help, Harry siezes the three wands Draco Malfoy is holding and Stuns him with all three wands at once, leaving him unconscious behind a chair.

In the battle at Hogwarts, Greyback is seen to attack Lavender Brown in the Entrance Hall. He is stopped by a well-placed jinx from Hermione, from under the Invisibility Cloak, and is then knocked out by a crystal ball thrown by Professor Trelawney. After the events in the Forbidden Forest, he rejoins the battle, but is brought down by Ron and Neville Longbottom.

Strengths Greyback is shown as a well-built man and is mentally and physically strong. His sense of smell is at a high standard and he can also use a wand to cast spells.

Relationships with Other Characters Deliberately infected Remus Lupin, which turned him into a werewolf, because Lupin's father insulted him. Bit and ripped Bill Weasley's face, which leaves him scarred for life and alters his personality. Draco Malfoy claims him as a family friend, though apparently only in order to put pressure on Borgin to do something Draco wants done.

Analysis

There is significant debate as to whether Greyback was in his Werewolf shape or not when Lavender was attacked; much of the debate appears on the talk page for that chapter. One major factor arguing against his being Transformed is the author's habit of never naming characters Harry has not been introduced to, and he has never seen Greyback transformed. The immediate identification of Greyback would imply strongly that Greyback is in his human shape. Against this, there is the description of Greyback as a "grey blur," and the fact that nothing in the text rules out Fenrir (and Lupin) being transformed.

Filius Flitwick

Gender: Male
Hair color: Unknown
Eye color: Unknown
Related Family: Unknown
Loyalty:

Filius Flitwick

OVERVIEW

Filius Flitwick is the Charms professor at Hogwarts School of Witchcraft and Wizardry. He is also Head of Ravenclaw House. He is described as a tiny little wizard who had to stand on a pile of books to see over his desk. Despite appearances, the author has stated that Flitwick is a very short human, possibly with some goblin ancestry.[1] The author has also said that Filius Flitwick's birthday is on October 17.

ROLE IN THE BOOKS

Philosopher's Stone Professor Flitwick has to stand on a pile of books to see over his desk. When he is calling the roll on the first day of classes, he is so excited when he finds Harry Potter's name on the list that he falls off his pile of books. It is on Hallowe'en that Flitwick's class is first allowed to actually perform magic. After some initial coaching, Flitwick gives all the class members feathers that they are to lift with Wingardium Leviosa. Hermione is partnered with Ron Weasley, and gives him some pointers when he can't make it work; when Ron resists, Hermione performs the spell, and Flitwick announces her success to the class. It is this initial victory of hers that leads Ron to later say that she is insufferable and that's probably why she has no friends. Hermione overhears this comment and spends the rest of the day in the girls washroom, crying. She is still there when the mountain troll is prowling the halls.

At Christmas, we see Flitwick levitating ornaments onto the twelve Christmas trees in the Great Hall. We learn that Professor Flitwick has provided one of the guardian barriers to the chamber in which the Philosopher's Stone is protected. That barrier is a door, with a large number of keys charmed to have wings and fly. To open the door, one must use the provided brooms to hunt for, and catch, the one flying key that will open the door.

Chamber of Secrets Although Professor Flitwick is still teaching Charms, we see little of him in this book. He is one of the teachers who responds when Harry discovers Justin Finch-Fletchley and Nearly Headless Nick Petrified, and is one of the two (the other being Professor Sinistra) who carry Justin to the Hospital Wing.

Prisoner of Azkaban Harry, by means of the Marauder's Map, goes to Hogsmeade just before Christmas, meeting up there with Ron and Hermione. In The Three Broomsticks, they eavesdrop on a conversation involving Cornelius Fudge, Hagrid, Professor McGonagall, Professor Flitwick, and Madam Rosmerta. When Rosmerta complains the Dementors are affecting her business, Fudge explains they are necessary because Sirius Black is so dangerous. Rosmerta mentions that Sirius and James Potter were great friends once, always in the Three Broomsticks together. This surprises Harry. Fudge says that not only was Sirius James' best friend, but also best man at his wedding and Harry's godfather. As the conversation continues, it is learned that James and Lily knew Lord Voldemort was hunting them and went into hiding. They used the Fidelius charm to conceal themselves and appointed Sirius their Secret-Keeper. Flitwick describes the operation of the Fidelius Charm. Dumbledore, aware someone close to them was leaking secrets, offered to be their Secret-Keeper, but they declined. Barely a week later, Voldemort killed James and Lily, although he met his own demise in baby Harry. Obviously Black, tired of playing double agent, had thrown his lot in with Voldemort but, after his defeat, had to flee for his life. Peter Pettigrew, another Potter friend, caught up to Black the next day and accused him of betraying James and Lily. Black killed him and twelve Muggle bystanders with a single curse. Only Pettigrew's bloodstained robes and a severed finger were left. Black was sentenced to Azkaban, where he remained until his escape. It is believed he is now trying to reunite with Voldemort, perhaps after killing Harry to prove his loyalty.

When Harry receives a Firebolt broom as a Christmas gift, Professor McGonagall confiscates it. As they don't know who sent it, she says that Professor Flitwick and Madam Hooch will examine it to see if there are any malicious spells buried in it.

Just before Easter break, Hermione gets confused in her class attendance and sleeps through one of Professor Flitwick's classes, the one covering Cheering Charms. Though she does go to him to apologize, apparently she doesn't fully learn Cheering Charms, because she is bemoaning the fact later that they appeared on the final exam. When Sirius Black is captured, we find that he is being held in Professor Flitwick's office. Professor Dumbledore tells Harry and Hermione where the window to his office is so that they can rescue Sirius by air.

Goblet of Fire It is mentioned that Professor Flitwick has assigned three books worth of reading before starting Summoning Charms, shortly before Hallowe'en.

We later see Professor Flitwick teaching the class Banishing Charms. We start to understand that Harry, Ron, and Hermione feel that Charms class is a good place for discussions that they don't want overheard, because of all the frenetic activity among their classmates practicing charms.

Along with many other teachers, Professor Flitwick eases off in the week before Christmas break and the Yule Ball. Instead, he spends the time discussing the Summoning Charm that Harry had used in the First Task of the Triwizard Tournament.

Professor Flitwick is one of the four marshals patrolling the outside of the maze for the Third task of the Tournament.

---

1. http://www.jkrowling.com/textonly/en/faq_view.cfm?id=95

Order of the Phoenix Fred and George mention that Flitwick was unperturbed by Dolores Umbridge's inspection of the class, treating her as he would any student.

Later, Umbridge becomes Headmaster in name, though the Headmaster's office will not open to her. On her first day in office, Fred and George set off a collection of fireworks, and Umbridge spends the entire day chasing them down and extinguishing them. At the end of the day, we see Flitwick telling Umbridge that he could have eliminated the sparklers himself, but that he wasn't sure he had the authority.

Just after Easter break, Fred and George turn one corridor of the school into a swamp. After they depart from the school, Umbridge is unable to change it back. After Umbridge is removed from the school, Flitwick does remove the swamp, but he leaves one small corner of it, as he says it was really very good magic.

Half-Blood Prince In addition to the spells that Harry has learned from the Half-Blood Prince's Potions book, there is mention again that Charms class, because of the noise level, is a good place for private conversations. We see one class in which the object of the class is to change vinegar into wine. Professor Flitwick approaches to see how they are doing; Hermione is successful immediately, but Harry's vinegar turns to ice, and Ron's explodes. Professor Flitwick assigns the charm as homework.

When the battle at the Astronomy Tower starts, Professor McGonagall sends Professor Flitwick to summon Professor Snape. Snape knocks Flitwick out, then, seeing Hermione and Luna outside his office, tells them to tend to Professor Flitwick, who had fallen.

Deathly Hallows When Harry is in the Ravenclaw common room with Luna Lovegood, after Alecto Carrow summons Lord Voldemort, Luna Stuns her. Shortly after this, Amycus Carrow tries to gain entrance into the common room, but without being able to answer the question posed by the guardian, is unable to enter. When Professor McGonagall appears, drawn by the noise, Amycus demands that she summon Flitwick, then that she open the door to the common room.

After the Carrows are both out of action, Professor McGonagall heads towards the Gryffindor common room to get the students out of bed and into the Great Hall. On the way, she sends Patronuses to summon Flitwick, Horace Slughorn, and Pomona Sprout, the other heads of house. Flitwick is just arriving as McGonagall duels with Snape, and then is involved in casting protective charms around the school. He takes some part in the battle for the school that then follows.

Strengths As he is the Charms teacher, we can expect that he has significantly more skill at Charms than the average wizard.

Relationships with Other Characters Flitwick is said to be Hermione's favorite teacher, due to the fact that he teaches one of her best subjects.

QUESTIONS

1. Why isn't Professor Flitwick a member of the Order of the Phoenix?

Firenze

Gender: Male
Hair color: White-blond and Palomino
Eye color: Blue
Related Family: Unknown
Loyalty: Albus Dumbledore

OVERVIEW

Firenze is a Centaur who lives in the Forbidden Forest with the other Centaurs. Although they generally avoid humans, Firenze, the least aloof member in his herd, frequently interacts with Hagrid.

The author has said that Firenze's name is pronounced similarly to that of the Italian city.

ROLE IN THE BOOKS

Philosopher's Stone When Harry is serving detention with Hagrid in the Forbidden Forest, Firenze rescues him from an unknown presence. Firenze also helps Harry figure out who is trying to steal the Philosopher's Stone and why. He is roundly criticized for helping Harry by Bane, a member of his herd, who believes Centaurs should remain aloof from puny Human problems.

Order of the Phoenix At Albus Dumbledore's request, Firenze agrees to teach Divination at Hogwarts when Sibyll Trelawney is sacked by Dolores Umbridge. This causes enormous turmoil between Firenze and the other centaurs, and Firenze is ejected from the herd.

Firenze teaches the Centaur method of divination, which is different from those used by Professor Trelawney. Instead it emphasizes divination's inexactness. Firenze also calls Harry aside to pass on a message to Hagrid saying that his (Hagrid's) attempt is not working. Although this is left unexplained, it is shortly learned that Hagrid is attempting to civilize his giant half-brother, Grawp.

Half-Blood Prince Although Firenze continues teaching Divination at Hogwarts, alternating with Professor Trelawney, Harry is no longer taking the class and does not interact with him.

Deathly Hallows Firenze is still at Hogwarts. During the battle at Hogwarts, he receives a fairly major injury and is unable to stand. Apparently he is later fully healed.

In an interview after the seventh book was finished, the author stated that, as events had proven him, if not right, at least not wrong in helping the Humans, he was allowed to rejoin his herd in the Forbidden Forest.

Strengths Firenze is skilled in the ancient Centaurian divination techniques involving smoke and stars. He demonstrates great patience with these strange Human foals that he has been called upon to teach.

Weaknesses Like all centaurs, he tends to discount the cosmic importance of any non-Centaur race, including humans.

Relationships with Other Characters Firenze is more sympathetic to Humans than other Centaurs, but that is not saying much; he remains aloof and supercilious. He evidently shares the opinion that Humans are a lesser breed unable to understand the subtleties apparent to Centaurs or possess their deeper understanding of the universe. He is more open to discussion with Professor Dumbledore and Harry, perhaps because he sees them as pivotal characters in the unfolding events in their personal corner of the universe. However, even with Harry, there is a reserve, an apparent belief that he cannot fully understand the Centaur way. It seems Firenze believes Dumbledore is the one Human who can understand Centaurs. Dolores Umbridge, however, hates and fears him, as she does all intelligent non-human or partly-human creatures. She is furious when Dumbledore appoints Firenze as the new Divination teacher after she sacks Professor Trelawney.

Firenze's sympathy for humans causes trouble, and he clashes with the herd's elders. In *Harry Potter and the Order of the Phoenix*, he is banished from the herd and is now a lone Centaur.

QUESTIONS

1. Why did Firenze choose to abandon the other centaurs and teach at Hogwarts?
2. In Firenze's first lesson, he seems unconcerned that none of his students succeed. What does this say about accepting things like control and fate?

Fleur Delacour

Gender: Female
Hair color: Silvery-blonde
Eye color: Deep blue
Related Family: Gabrielle (younger sister)
Loyalty: Madame Maxime, Bill Weasley, later Albus Dumbledore

OVERVIEW

Fleur Isabelle Delacour was once a student at the French magical school, Beauxbatons Academy. She is a stunningly beautiful witch with wavy silver-blonde hair that seems to float behind her as she walks.

ROLE IN THE BOOKS

Goblet of Fire Fleur Delacour enters our story as the students from Beauxbatons arrive to take part in the Triwizard Tournament. She visits the Gryffindor table that first evening to ask for bouillabaisse, and Ron is stunned by her beauty. When Hermione seems somewhat nettled by this, Ron suggests that there might be some Veela in her ancestry.

The next evening, the Goblet of Fire selected her to participate in the Triwizard Tournament at Hogwarts, competing against Durmstrang's Viktor Krum and Hogwarts' Harry Potter and Cedric Diggory. She is openly contemptuous of Harry being selected, saying that "'E cannot compete. 'E is too young!" She is, however, overruled by Mr. Crouch's interpretation of the rule book.

At the Weighing of the Wands, it is revealed by Mr. Ollivander that Fleur's wand has, as its core, the hair of a Veela. Fleur says that it is her grandmother's, confirming Ron's earlier belief that she has Veela ancestors. Although the First Task was intended to be a surprise, Fleur Delacour was forewarned of its nature by Olympe Maxime, headmistress of Beauxbatons, who discovered what was coming when Rubeus Hagrid allowed her to see the dragons. Fleur's first task was to seize a golden egg from the nest of a mother Welsh Green dragon. She attempted to put it in a trance, but her plan backfired when the dragon snored, lighting her skirt on fire and forcing her to put out the flame with a jet of water from her wand. She did however, manage to collect the egg. As the Yule Ball approaches, Ron, desperate, asks Fleur to the ball; she does not even deign to notice him. Utterly crushed, he retreats to the Gryffindor common room. Harry reveals Fleur's Veela ancestry to him at this point, but he is so defeated that he does not seem to notice. At the Ball, Ron spends some time hiding from Fleur; he is so embarrassed that he does not even want to be seen by her. Fleur, however, is keeping Roger Davies entranced, and again does not seem to notice him.

In the Second Task, Fleur had to rescue her sister from the merpeople at the bottom of the lake at Hogwarts. She used an excellent Bubble-Head Charm, giving her a supply of air, but she was attacked by grindylows and was forced to forfeit. She earned twenty-five points. Like Harry, she had thought that the song of the merpeople was to be meant literally and was afraid that her sister, Gabrielle, would die or be kept underwater forever. So when Harry brought Gabrielle to the surface, Fleur was overjoyed, and ended up kissing him on both cheeks, twice, which left Harry feeling rather as if there was steam coming out his ears. Ron got kissed also, for helping, and seemed extremely pleased about it.

Being in last place, Fleur was the last to enter the obstacle course/maze of the Third Challenge, which was full of enchantments to break and magical creatures to fight. She lost her chance to reach the Triwizard Cup when Barty Crouch Jr. used the Imperius curse to force Victor Krum to Stun her.

As the Beauxbatons carriage is prepared for departure, Fleur comes up to Harry and Ron on the steps at Hogwarts to say goodbye. Ron becomes somewhat tongue-tied when she approaches, which seems to vex Hermione.

Order of the Phoenix Fleur is largely off-stage here, although it is mentioned that she has stayed in England to "eemprove 'er Eenglish," tutored by Bill Weasley.

Half-Blood Prince In the Half-Blood Prince it is revealed that Fleur will marry Ron's brother, Bill. The other characters dislike this, mostly Molly and Ginny Weasley, who refers to her as 'Phlegm.' Ron, though, is delighted at this news; he seems to still secretly have a bit of a crush on her.

When Bill is attacked by Fenrir Greyback and is disfigured, Mrs. Weasley laments that he won't be getting married now. Fleur passionately declares that she loves Bill and will marry him despite his disfigurement. This statement seems to change Mrs. Weasley's feelings for Fleur and she even offers to persuade her great aunt to lend Fleur a goblin-made tiara for the wedding.

Deathly Hallows The plan to extract Harry from the Dursleys' involves multiple simulacra of Harry, each one traveling to a separate safe house, each with a protector. One of the mock Harrys is Fleur, who will be traveling on a broomstick with Bill as her protector. They are the last pair to arrive at The Burrow, as they were apparently detained by Auntie Muriel, and missed the Portkey that would have brought them to the Weasleys.'

At The Burrow, Harry finds himself in the midst of the chaos that is Mrs. Weasley's preparations for Bill and Fleur's wedding, set for the first of August. While both Bill and Fleur are present, and are occasionally being set tasks to assist in the preparations, we see very little of them until two days before the wedding, when Fleur's parents and sister Gabrielle arrive. It is mentioned then that Gabrielle is following Fleur around.

As Fleur walks up the aisle at the wedding, she is radiantly beautiful; and the radiance seems to make her attendants, Gabrielle and Ginny, especially beautiful as well. And they are wed, and they dance, and everyone dances . . . and then the Trio must make a hasty exit.

When Ron rejoins the Trio after Christmas, it turns out that he had been staying with Bill and Fleur at Shell Cottage. He does not say much about what had been going on there.

When the Trio escape from Malfoy Manor, they end up going to Shell Cottage. Fleur is present at the burial ceremony for Dobby. Then, Fleur takes care of the wounded, specifically Griphook and Mr. Ollivander. She is not terribly happy about caring for Griphook, as she feels that he is treating her as a servant in her own home. Fleur is part of the celebration that ensues when Lupin arrives to report that Tonks has had her baby. A month or so later, Bill and Fleur are among the people who arrive at Hogwarts for the battle at the school. They are still in the Room of Requirement when Percy arrives; the ensuing awkward moment, as Percy has been estranged from the rest of his family for years, is somewhat defused by Fleur, who asks Lupin how their child is doing. Lupin, in response, produces a photo, which he drops when Percy loudly proclaims his stupidity and begs forgiveness.

While we don't see much of them in the battle, we do see the entire Weasley family after the battle; and in the epilogue we hear mention of Victoire, who we assume to be Bill and Fleur's daughter.

Strengths By being selected as Beauxbatons' Triwizard Champion alone, we can assume that Fleur Delacour was an exceptionally talented student. Not only does she have this advantage over others at Beauxbatons, but, being part Veela, she has a charm that brings many men to their knees. As Fleur's younger sister is chosen as the person Fleur will miss the most it could be said she is family orientated; particularly as she is greatly relieved when Harry rescues her sister.

Weaknesses Fleur appears standoffish during Goblet of Fire, she makes underhand comments about the food at Hogwarts. Fleur comes across as a cold character.

Relationships with Other Characters Ron Weasley accidentally asks Fleur to attend the Yule Ball with him; she ignores him. Harry suggests that this because she has turned on the charm to try to ensnare Roger Davies, and Ron had been caught in the flux of her spell. Fleur attends the Yule Ball with Roger Davies of Ravenclaw. Fleur is attracted to Bill Weasley and in Half Blood Prince it is announced they are to marry. Fleur has a younger sister Gabrielle who the Merpeople choose as the thing she will miss the most during the 2nd Triwizard Test. Hermione, Ginny, and (initially) Mrs. Weasley all dislike Fleur.

Fleur, because of her Veela background, will tend to have some of the glamour of the Veela, and so will be extremely attractive to almost all males. Presumably, she will have learned that the only way to cut down on the number of admirers is to appear cold, to not be open to approach. This will make her seem aloof and uncaring, and yet she will still leave a trail of attracted men (and boys) behind her. This is bound to incite jealousy in other women, and it is likely this that we see in Hermione, Ginny, and Mrs. Weasley.

Florean Fortescue

Gender: Male
Hair color: Unknown
Eye color: Unknown
Related Family: Unknown
Loyalty:

Overview

Florean Fortescue owns an ice-cream parlour in Diagon Alley.

Role in the Books

Prisoner of Azkaban Harry, due to having inflated his Aunt Marge under provocation, ends up staying in the Leaky Cauldron for the last fortnight of his summer vacation. He spends his days in Diagon Alley, where he is able to work on his homework essays in the comfort of Florean Fortescue's ice cream parlour, receiving assistance, and free sundaes every half hour, from Florean himself.

Half-Blood Prince It is mentioned in passing that Florean's place is abandoned and Florean himself is missing, though it looks as if he put up a fight. We never see him again.

Frank Bryce

Gender: Male
Hair color: Unknown
Eye color: Unknown
Related Family: Unknown
Loyalty: uncertain

OVERVIEW

Frank Bryce is the elderly Muggle caretaker and gardener of the old Riddle manor in Little Hangleton.

ROLE IN THE BOOKS

Goblet of Fire Frank Bryce, a villager from Little Hangleton, had been invalided out of the Great War and had come home, where he had started work for the Riddle family as caretaker and gardener. When the Riddle family, Tom and his parents, had been found dead, he was the natural suspect and had been brought in for questioning; however, when they were unable to find a cause of death, Frank had been released. He had continued to keep the old manor house as best he was able, while it apparently changed ownership several times, and eventually fell vacant, though the village was never entirely sure of him. It was as part of his caretaking duties that, now quite elderly, he happened upon a couple of people who had apparently taken up residence in the house; investigating, he overheard them planning to kill someone, one Harry Potter, and discussing Bertha Jorkins who they had already, apparently, killed. While he is listening to this, a very large snake passes by; Frank is amazed when the snake evidently reports on his presence to the occupants of the room. The two people in the room, Wormtail and Lord Voldemort, then kill Frank. Albus Dumbledore later remarks that he believes Frank's death is part of a pattern of deaths and disappearances that marks Voldemort's return to power, though the Ministry do not agree.

In the climactic duel between the now-returned Voldemort and Harry, their two brother wands are forced to duel each other. This results in the appearance of the Priori Incantatem effect, in which Voldemort's wand is forced to disgorge the last few spells it has performed. Frank Bryce is one of the five recent victims of Voldemort's wand whose shades appear as a result.

Frank Longbottom

Gender: Male
Hair color:
Eye color:
Related Family: wife Alice Longbottom, son Neville Longbottom, mother Augusta Longbottom
Loyalty: Albus Dumbledore

OVERVIEW

Frank Longbottom is Neville's father.

Role In The Books

Goblet of Fire Harry finds out by watching the scene of a trial, in Dumbledore's Pensieve, why Neville is being raised by his grandmother. Frank was an Auror, and shortly after Lord Voldemort's disappearance was attacked and tortured by Barty Crouch Jr., Bellatrix Lestrange, Rodolphus Lestrange, and Rabastan Lestrange, who used the Cruciatus Curse on him and his wife, Alice, until they lost most of their mental faculties. The two of them are now residing at St. Mungo's.

Order of the Phoenix At the celebration feast for Ron and Hermione becoming Prefects, Alastor Moody shows Harry a picture of the old Order. In that picture, we see Alice and Frank Longbottom smiling and waving.

Before Potions class one day, Draco Malfoy, taunting Harry, mentions something about people with mental infirmities being forced to stay at S. Mungo's. Neville, pushed beyond his endurance, tries to attack him, but is restrained by Harry and Ron. Ron and Hermione wonder what that was all about, but while Harry knows, he also cannot answer because of his promise to Dumbledore.

Just before Christmas, while Harry, Ron, Ginny, and Hermione are visiting Mr. Weasley at St. Mungo's, they run into Neville and his grandmother who are visiting Neville's parents.

When Neville is captured by Death Eaters in the Battle in the Ministry, Bellatrix Lestrange says she will torture him as she tortured his parents. She is stopped only by the arrival of members of the Order arriving.

ANALYSIS

Neville Longbottom's parents were not killed, since this is not a killing curse. They were driven to madness and reside in a special ward (for those suffering from long-term spell damage) at St. Mungo's Hospital.

Fred and George Weasley

Gender: Male
Hair color: Red
Eye color: Unknown
Related Family:
Loyalty:
Arthur Weasley (father)
Molly Weasley (mother)
Bill Weasley (oldest brother) Charlie Weasley (older brother) Percy Weasley (older brother) Ron Weasley (younger brother) Ginny Weasley (younger sister)
Albus Dumbledore

Overview

Fred and George Weasley are the twin older brothers of Ron Weasley. They are two years older than Ron and Harry, and were in Gryffindor, following in the footsteps of their family. They are tricksters, always inventing new tricks and playing practical jokes on their schoolmates and teachers. Their best friend is Lee Jordan. Fred and George Weasley were born on April 1st.[1]

Role in the Books

Philosopher's Stone We first meet Fred and George in King's Cross Station, where they are part of the group of Weasleys that help Harry find his way onto Platform Nine and Three Quarters—Fred is heard claiming to be George, illustrating their nature as pranksters. They later assist Harry to get his trunk on board the train, recognize him, and shortly thereafter introduce themselves and Ron to Harry. They then depart to talk to Lee Jordan, leaving Harry and Ron to talk together.

When Harry is made Seeker of the Gryffindor Quidditch team, Fred and George congratulate him and tell him that they are on the team also, as Beaters. Fred and George play in the match against Slytherin, of course, alongside Harry.

At Christmas, Fred and George elect to stay at Hogwarts, along with Ron and Percy. It is mentioned that they bewitch some snowballs to fly around and repeatedly hit Professor Quirrell in the back of his turban. When Harry, Ron, and Hermione lose a hundred and fifty House points between them, in the adventure surrounding Norbert the Norwegian Ridgeback, Ron tries to cheer them up by telling them that Fred and George are always losing points for Gryffindor, but as they have never lost quite that many points in one shot, his attempts rather fail.

The twins are mentioned in passing a few times, also, in the context of Quidditch practice and Quidditch games.

Chamber of Secrets Fred and George appear early in the story, with Ron, driving Arthur Weasley's flying Ford Anglia and coming to rescue Harry from the Dursleys.' They have a plan to get everyone back to The Burrow, which is rather foiled when Mrs. Weasley is awake and waiting for them upon their return. As punishment, after breakfast, the Twins and Ron are sent to de-Gnome the garden; Harry volunteers to assist them. Mrs. Weasley pulls out Gilderoy Lockhart's book on pest removal; Fred suggests that Mrs. Weasley is sweet on Gilderoy. George says they know how to de-Gnome a garden, and they go out and proceed to do that. As they finish, Mr. Weasley returns home; Mrs. Weasley tells him about the twins borrowing the car, in the apparent expectation that he will punish them for it; he simply asks how it went.

When booklists arrive, it is apparent that whoever is teaching Defence Against the Dark Arts is fond of Gilderoy Lockhart, because the textbook for that course seems to be his entire works. Fred suggests that the new Defence teacher is likely a middle-aged witch; George says that the lot of them won't come cheap, to which Mrs. Weasley replies, "We'll manage." After making plans to visit Diagon Alley the next day, the twins, Harry, and Ron go up to a paddock that the Weasleys own to practice Quidditch. Fred remarks, disgustedly, that Percy had refused to play; if he keeps up as he has been, he is likely to become Head Boy.

Once they are all in Diagon Alley, the Weasleys and Harry split up on their separate errands. Mrs. Weasley feels that she needs to tell the Twins to stay out of Knockturn Alley. Harry does meet up with them and Lee Jordan, in Gambol and Japes Joke Shop. Fred and George are back with the family in Flourish and Blotts, and are present when the fight between Mr. Weasley and Lucius Malfoy breaks out. When Mrs. Weasley comments, "*what* Gilderoy Lockhart must have thought . . ." Fred points out that he was trying to figure out how to add it to the publicity for his book-signing.

In the Quidditch match against Slytherin, a Bludger seems to have decided that it is going to concentrate on Harry. Despite Fred and George's best efforts, it seems to have chosen to attack Harry repeatedly. Harry tells Fred and George that he'll have to deal with it himself, he can't ask them to stay up there and let the rest of the team take a beating from the remaining Bludger. Oliver Wood agrees, and so reluctantly, Fred and George leave Harry on his own and rejoin the game.

Later, the entire school seems to be convinced that Harry is the Heir of Slytherin. Harry is extremely cheered that Fred and George can keep making jokes about the situation.

Finally, on the Hogwarts Express homewards, Fred and George learn from Ginny that Percy has a girlfriend, Penelope Clearwater. It seems that the Twins are going to have some fun with him about that.

Prisoner of Azkaban Harry is staying in Diagon Alley for the end of his vacation, when the Weasleys turn up. Percy, as the twins had predicted, is Head boy, and is insufferably pompous. The twins are trying to take him down a notch by imitating him. After dinner, Percy is frantic because his Head Boy badge has vanished; Harry runs into Fred and George who say they had taken it to "improve" it. It now reads "Bighead Boy."

At breakfast on their first day back at Hogwarts, in response to Draco Malfoy's imitations of Harry passing out from the effects of the Dementors, Fred and George mention that he had been up at their end of the train then, and had not been so brave himself.

Feeling that his need is greater than theirs, on the last Hogsmeade weekend before Christmas Break, Fred and George give Harry the Marauder's Map. This allows Harry to reach Hogsmeade undetected. There, he overhears Cornelius Fudge, Madam Rosmerta, Hagrid, Professor Flitwick, and Professor McGonagall discussing the events surrounding the arrest of Sirius Black as they were then understood.

After the apparent death of Scabbers, Fred and George attempt to cheer him up by reminding him that only days before, Ron had said he was useless. In

---

1. http://www.jkrowling.com/textonly/en/extrastuff_view.cfm?id=7

the party after the Quidditch match a few days later, Fred and George bring Butterbeer back to the Common Room, alluding privately to Harry that it was thanks to the creators of the Marauder's Map.

At the end of the year, Fred and George are even occasionally seen studying, much to the amazement of anyone who knows them. They do, in the end, manage a handful of O.W.L.s each, and profess themselves happy with that result.

Goblet of Fire Fred and George arrive at the Dursleys' with Ron and Mr. Weasley. They are coming to take Harry to the Quidditch World Cup. They ask if Harry is packed; it turns out he is, so the twins go up to his room to retrieve his trunk, while Arthur unsuccessfully attempts to engage the Dursleys in conversation. Returning with Harry's trunk, Fred drops a bag of sweets; these roll around in all directions, and Fred takes a moment to gather them all up. He returns to The Burrow; George follows, with Harry's trunk. Before Harry leaves, though, Dudley finds one of the sweets that Fred had dropped; it turns out to be a Ton-Tongue Toffee, which expands Dudley's tongue to be several feet long. On his return to The Burrow, Mr. Weasley is uncharacteristically angry with the Twins, saying that it is exactly this sort of thing that makes Wizard—Muggle relations so hard. Fred protests that they didn't do it because he was a Muggle; George chimes in saying that they did it because he was a great bullying git. Arriving on the scene, Mrs. Weasley asks if this is more Weasleys' Wizard Wheezes. Ron and Harry beat a hasty retreat to Ron's room; Harry asks what Weasleys' Wizard Wheezes are, and Ron tells him that the twins were starting up a mail-order magical jokes business, but that Mrs. Weasley had found their order forms and destroyed them and their stock.

Fred and George, along with Harry, Ginny, Ron, and Hermione, have to travel to the Quidditch World Cup by Portkey, because they are too young to Apparate. Fred and George are upset by how early they have to get up. As they prepare to leave, Mrs. Weasley asks if they are taking Weasleys' Wizard Wheezes stuff with them. Ignoring their protests, Mrs. Weasley Summons charmed toffees out of hiding places all over the twins clothing. They set off to Stoatshead Hill very disgruntled, not even saying goodbye.

Once at the camp site, and settled in, Mr. Weasley flags down Ludovic Bagman, who, after some discussion with Arthur, asks if anyone would like to make a small bet on the outcome of the match. The twins place a bet amounting to their entire life savings on Ireland to win, but the Bulgarian Seeker, Viktor Krum, being the one to catch the Snitch. When Bartemius Crouch Sr. stops by the campsite, Percy is almost falling over himself to be hospitable to his boss. It appears, though, that Mr. Crouch cannot even remember Percy's name, calls him "Weatherby." After Crouch's departure, the twins make fun of Percy relentlessly, saying that if he works hard, one of these days Crouch might even learn his name.

The match ends as the twins had predicted, with an Irish victory but Krum holding the Snitch, and the twins request their payment from Ludo.

After the match, there is a riot; Mr. Weasley sends Harry, Ron, Hermione, the twins, and Ginny off into the nearby woods, out of the way. In the darkness, they get separated; we don't see the Twins and Ginny again until Harry returns to the tent.

On their return to The Burrow, Mrs. Weasley is extremely relieved; she had been fearing the worst, only having heard that there were riots, and not knowing if her family had survived. She was particularly concerned that her last words to the twins before they left had been angry.

In the next few weeks, before school starts, the twins seem somewhat subdued. On the last day before school, the two of them are working quietly over a bit of parchment. Mrs. Weasley asks if that's another order form; Fred parries by saying if the Hogwarts Express were to crash the next day, she wouldn't want her last words to be an unfounded accusation, surely?

The next morning, Fred and George recognize Mad-Eye Moody when his name is mentioned by Amos Diggory in a call for Mr. Weasley. They travel to the train station in Muggle taxis, and Fred and George are unsuccessful in getting any information out of Mrs. Weasley, Bill, or Charlie, who accompany them to the station, about the big event at Hogwarts will be. Arriving at Hogwarts, the twins are astonished to hear that Quidditch will be canceled for the year, and then dismayed to find that the Triwizard Tournament that will be taking its place is closed to those less than 17 years of age—the twins at this point are 16. On the way to the dormitory, they are already plotting with Lee Jordan on ways to avoid the age restriction.

The twins also tell Harry and Ron after the first day that classes with Moody are incredible. He has been battling the Dark Arts, and knows what it is all about. They do not elaborate further, but Ron bemoans the fact that his first Defence Against the Dark Arts class is not until Thursday.

We later see Fred and George working together on a parchment, and George scratching out a line, saying that it made it sound like they were accusing him. Later still, Fred and George are discussing over breakfast what to do about someone who does not answer them.

Once the Goblet of Fire is set up, Dumbledore draws an age line around it to prevent underage wizards from putting their names in. Fred and George, with Lee Jordan, decide to take a little Aging Potion, trying to fool the line that way; but shortly after Fred and George cross the line, and before they can put their names into the Goblet, it kicks them both out, awarding them both long white beards.

At the party in Gryffindor tower after Harry's victory in the First Task, Fred and George provide food. Hermione asks them if it had come from the castle kitchens, Fred says it did. She asks how to get into the kitchens, and George asks if she's planning to lead a House-Elf rebellion. Hermione does not answer.

As the Yule Ball approaches, Ron and Harry are bemoaning their difficulty in getting dates. Fred and George, who have come to borrow Pigwidgeon, wonder what the problem is; as if to demonstrate the simplicity of the proceedings, Fred calls over to Angelina

Johnson, "Oi! Angelina! Want to come to the ball with me?" She accepts. Fred and George then, having been told Pigwidgeon is not available, go off to find a school owl. Fred and George seem to try and corner Ludo Bagman on the dance floor at the Yule Ball, but he evades them. Asked about it by Harry, Ludo says that the twins were asking for marketing advice. At the first Hogsmeade weekend in the new year, the twins again try to corner Bagman at the bar of the Three Broomsticks, but he again brushes them off.

Fred and George escort Ron and Hermione away from the library, where they are trying to help Harry find a spell that will allow Harry to breathe underwater, which is required for the Second Task. They have been summoned by We see Fred and George sending off a letter to someone. They are deep in conversation as they head up to the Owlery, George cautioning Fred about sounding like they are blackmailing someone. Asked by Harry, Ron, and Hermione who they are blackmailing, the twins parry. After they leave, Ron says that the twins are really serious about raising money for their joke shop venture. He doesn't think the twins would do anything illegal to secure funding, but he's no longer sure.

Finally, on the Hogwarts Express heading back to London, Fred and George assist Harry, Ron, and Hermione in Jinxing Draco, Crabbe, and Goyle when they arrive in Harry's compartment to taunt him about the return of Lord Voldemort. Pushing Draco and his cronies out into the corridor, they join Harry, Ron and Hermione for the rest of the journey back. Late in the trip, they reveal that the person they have been corresponding with all year was, in fact, Ludo Bagman. Ludo had paid off their bet with Leprechaun gold, which had vanished. They had initially thought this was an oversight on Ludo's part, but as the year went on, Ludo refused to make good on his payment, and in the end even refused to give back their initial bet. It appears that Ludo had pulled the same trick on the goblins, and instead of repaying them (as he did not have the money) had bet with them again on Harry to win the Triwizard Tournament. Harry's having tied with Cedric was not good enough for the goblins, and they had demanded full payment. Ludo had run away. After Ron and Hermione had left the compartment in London, Harry gives Fred and George his winnings from the Triwizard Tournament to start their new business, a joke shop. They protest, but Harry says that by the look of things, they will need jokes soon enough.

Order of the Phoenix Fred and George are deeply involved in testing products and doing market research for their joke shop, Weasleys' Wizard Wheezes. Several times, Hermione gets upset with them because they are using the first-year students as test subjects; at one point, she threatens to tell their mother if they continue.

Fred and George are present at the initial meeting of what is then known as the Defence Association at the Hog's Head. When Zacharias Smith exhibits skepticism about what Harry can teach them, Fred and George produce a sharp metal object and suggest a few places that they could use it on Zacharias.

At Quidditch practice, Ron manages to throw a Quaffle hard enough to give Katie Bell a nosebleed. Fred, attempting to cure this, gives her what he believes to be the cure end of a Nosebleed Nougat, but gets confused and instead feeds her a Blood Blisterpod. As a result, Katie loses enough blood that she nearly loses consciousness and has to be escorted to the Hospital Wing.

Immediately after the first Quidditch game of the season, Draco Malfoy, seeing that Madam Hooch is occupied, starts insulting the Weasley family. Enraged, Fred and George are only kept from attacking him by their team mates: Fred is being held back by Angelina, Alicia, and Katie, while Harry is holding George. When Malfoy expands his insults to include Harry's family, Harry loses control and, with George, attacks Draco. As a result, Professor Umbridge hands Harry, Fred, and George a lifetime ban from Quidditch.

Once Dumbledore has been removed as Headmaster, Fred and George no longer feel constrained to limit their antics. When Montague, a member of Professor Umbridge's Inquisitorial Squad, attempts to dock them House points, they force him into an old, broken Vanishing Cabinet. They tell Harry, Ron, and Hermione that they had almost decided against coming back to school, and that expulsion holds no fears for them; so their pranking will be turned up several notches. Shortly after this, they set off a truly massive quantity of fireworks in the Entrance Hall, and so Umbridge, on her first day as Headmistress, has to spend the entire day going from classroom to classroom extinguishing fireworks.

Harry later decides that he needs a distraction so that he can get into Umbridge's office and use the Floo network via her fireplace, the only unmonitored fireplace at Hogwarts. Fred and George provide this distraction by turning a large part of one hallway into a swamp; but they are caught. Umbridge threatens them with the worst that Argus Filch can do, but they reclaim their brooms, and leaving Peeves with the instruction to "give her (Umbridge) hell," they fly off into the sunset.

At the end of the novel, they are at the train station, wearing new suits made of dragon skin. Apparently they have opened their new store in Diagon Alley, and it is doing extremely well.

Half-Blood Prince The Weasley family, visiting Diagon Alley with Harry to purchase school supplies, visits the Twins' joke shop. Every other store is covered in the drab posters from the Ministry regarding Death Eaters, but Fred and George's shop window is uncovered and blazing with color, light, and activity. Once inside, they find the place is packed; Fred, showing Harry around, offers him the run of the place, saying anything he wants, he can have on the house. Ron is not so lucky, George demands that he pay full price, less the odd Knut because he is family. George also shows Harry the back room with the more serious stuff: Shield Hats, Decoy Detonators, and Peruvian Instant Darkness Powder, among other things. George reveals that quite apart from their joke line, they are doing a brisk business selling Dark-fighting gear to the Ministry. Returning to the front, they find Ginny looking at items designed for young witches. Fred and George ask her about her current relationships, and she responds that it is none of their business.

When Ron is poisoned on his birthday, Fred and George have just arrived in Hogsmeade to look into buying Zonko's Joke Shop, which has closed down. Given that Hogsmeade weekends at the school have been canceled, though, they decide it would not be a wise investment. They do, however, stop by the school; they had planned to give Ron a birthday present, but had hoped it would have been a rather happier event.

Deathly Hallows Fred and George both take Polyjuice Potion to transform them into simulacra of Harry, as part of Harry's escape from Privet Drive. George has his ear cursed off by Severus Snape, who uses the Sectumsempra curse. When he recovers, he seems in good spirits, making jokes about his new, earless appearance.

Fred and George are both ushers at the wedding of their brother Bill and Fleur Delacour, along with Harry (in disguise) and Ron. Fred manages to arrange to seat the younger guests on the Delacour side of the family, all of whom seem to have some Veela in their ancestry.

In their travels, Harry, Ron, and Hermione make good use of several products from Fred and George's joke shop. Skiving Snackboxes are used to incapacitate Ministry employees so that Harry, Ron, and Hermione can sneak into the Ministry. Harry uses a Decoy Detonator to draw attention away from the door of Dolores Umbridge's office. And the Trio use Extendable Ears to listen in on another party while they are camping in the wilderness; this is how they learn about the Sword of Gryffindor.

In March, Ron manages to tune in the pirate wireless program "Potterwatch." Lee Jordan, as "River," introduces "Rodent," easily identifiable by his voice as either Fred or George, and who protests his alias, saying he wanted to be known as "Rapier." "Rapier" debunks some of the propaganda and fear surrounding Voldemort, saying that in order to be in all the places he is reported as being, there would have to be about nineteen of him.

When Remus Lupin is assigning duties for the defence of Hogwarts, Fred volunteers himself and George for the duty of defending the secret passages into Hogwarts.

As Harry is on his way to the Room of Requirement, where he now believes Rowena Ravenclaw's lost diadem is hidden, he passes Fred, guarding a hole behind a plinth where a statue had fallen, along with Lee Jordan and Hannah Abbott.

Fred is killed during the Battle of Hogwarts when a massive explosion blows a hole in the wall of the castle. He is buried in the stone rubble coming off the castle walls.

Harry later learns from Snape's memories that Snape had not intended to curse George's ear off; he had been aiming for the arm of the Death Eater who was about to curse George's guardian.

Strengths They are very loyal, very smart, and they can produce magic of a similar quality to Hermione's. They can easily work hard and with great dedication to produce surprisingly advanced magic when they want to. They are also very talented Quidditch players. They have an amazing sense of humour. Ron mentions at one point that when he was three, one of the Twins had turned his teddy bear into a spider. As the twins at that point would have been only five or six years old, and would not have had wands or formal training of any sort, this level of conscious magical ability is apparently incredible.

Extremely sensitive to situations, they know where "the line" is—exactly how much mayhem they can cause before it becomes necessary to actually discipline them. Despite having been "chief troublemakers" for six and a half years, it is only during Professor Umbridge's tenure as Headmistress that they get into any serious trouble, and then, it is a deliberate change in policy: they have decided that they don't need further formal schooling, and elect to make Umbridge's early days in office as difficult as possible, without concern for consequences.

Weaknesses Fred and George have very few weaknesses. One significant one is a tendency to avoid consequences. Their final days at school are marked with a number of fairly major pranks, specifically including setting off a large number of fireworks inside the school, and turning one corridor into a swamp. When they are caught, they elect to depart the school, leaving others to clean up the mess. Similarly, when Montague, then a member of Umbridge's Inquisitorial Squad, attempts to dock them House points, they force him into an old, broken Vanishing Cabinet, without considering where or whether he might come out.

Fred and George, although talented and intelligent, have little interest in academic achievement. In their fifth year they only pass 3 O.W.L.s each and never finish their seventh year.

Their concern for each other could be considered a weakness also. George had his ear cut off as he was helping disguise Harry's escape from Privet Drive; Fred, realizing George was hurt, was almost unable to speak until George regained consciousness.

Relationships with Other Characters Fred and George have a very typical twin-brothers relationship with each other, almost seeming to think the same thoughts at the same time. Of the two, though, Fred is quite clearly the ringleader; he usually speaks first, he is usually the driving force behind many of the pranks they pull off, and generally seems to be the leader of the pair. The twins have earned the grudging admiration of the staff of the school. Professor Flitwick, for example, when cleaning up the swamp they left in the hall as they departed, left a small corner of it in place, saying that it was a nice bit of magic, and apparently feeling that it needed to be commemorated in some way. The staff seem to feel that the Twins deserve respect for the ingeniousness of the magic that they perform as part of their pranks, probably coupled with their awareness of how much they can get away with while still being humorous and not excessively disruptive. The quality of their pranks, and their abilities as Quidditch Beaters, has earned them the respect of their fellow students as well.

Fred went to the Yule Ball with Angelina Johnson; however, there is no apparent romantic interest apart from this one event. According to a family tree drawn by the author immediately after the completion of the last book, George marries Angelina and names his son Fred. The twins seem to keep their own company and the company of Lee Jordan, by and large.

ANALYSIS

Fred and George are nominally equal; however, it seems to be largely Fred who is the ringleader. With very few exceptions, whenever any activity is started, Fred speaks or moves first. This could have something to do with Fred's name falling earlier in the alphabet, so that it seems natural to put his name first. George is the more sensitive of the two, but when angered is the more violent, although it takes more to get him violent than Fred. George is 'the brains' and Fred is the 'operator,' Fred usually has the ideas, and more of a drive for the pranks, while George makes sure that no one will get seriously hurt, and makes sure that they will work. George is actually quite smart, more so than Fred, but Fred never revised (US:studied) for exams, so neither did George, and as a result, they both got 3 O.W.L.s each.

Gabrielle Delacour

Gender: Female
Hair color: Blonde
Eye color: Unknown
Related Family: Fleur Delacour
Loyalty: Fleur Delacour

OVERVIEW

Gabrielle Delacour is Fleur Delacour's sister.

ROLE IN THE BOOKS

Goblet of Fire We first see Gabrielle when she is one of the hostages for the Four Champions in the Second Task of the Triwizard Tournament. Each of the Champions is given one hour to rescue that which is most dear to them from the bottom of the lake. Gabrielle is what is most precious to Fleur. Fleur fails in her attempt to reach Gabrielle, and is so relieved when Harry surfaces with her that she runs over and kisses him, and also Ron who had some incidental role in her return.

Gabrielle is present in the audience for the Third Task, though she plays very little part.

Half-Blood Prince Gabrielle is mentioned in passing by Fleur as part of her planning for her wedding to Bill Weasley.

Deathly Hallows Gabrielle is one of the bridesmaids at the wedding of Fleur Delacour and Bill Weasley. She arrives two days before the ceremony, with Monsieur and Madame (Apolline) Delacour, and follows Fleur around, prattling away at her in French and trying to help out.

Relationships with Other Characters Gabrielle clearly has a strong connection to her sister.

Gawain Robards

Gender: Male
Hair color: Unknown
Eye color: Unknown
Related Family: Unknown
Loyalty: Ministry of Magic

OVERVIEW

Gawain Robards works in the Ministry of Magic as an Auror.

ROLE IN THE BOOKS

Half-Blood Prince When Rufus Scrimgeour is visiting the Weasley family at Christmas, he holds out the possibility of discussions with Gawain Robards, who has replaced Scrimgeour as the head of the Auror department, as incentive for Harry to toe the Ministry line.

Gellert Grindelwald

Gender: Male
Hair color: Blonde
Eye color: Unknown
Related Family: Nephew of Bathilda Bagshot
Loyalty: Unknown

OVERVIEW

Gellert Grindelwald was the most terrible Dark Wizard to exist before Lord Voldemort came to prominence.

ROLE IN THE BOOKS

Philosopher's Stone Grindelwald is mentioned briefly on the back of Albus Dumbledore's Chocolate Frog card as the Dark Wizard Dumbledore defeated in 1945.

Deathly Hallows Viktor Krum tells Harry that the line within a circle within a triangle symbol that Xenophilius Lovegood wore as a pendant at Bill and Fleur's wedding was the symbol of Gellert Grindelwald.

Rita Skeeter's tell-all book about Albus Dumbledore reveals that when young Albus was about 17 years of age, Gellert Grindelwald, also about 17, came to Godric's Hollow to live with his great-aunt Bathilda Bagshot. He was expelled from Durmstrang for near-fatal attacks on other students. Dumbledore and Grindelwald become close friends, and were apparently plotting to enforce wizard rule over Muggles, always for their own good, of course. Harry Potter, seeing Voldemort's memory of the wand maker Gregorovitch and finding Grindelwald's picture in Skeeter's book, realizes that he is the thief who stole The Elder Wand from Gregorovitch. It is learned that Grindelwald was still alive, though imprisoned in the highest tower in Nurmengard, the prison Grindelwald himself built to hold those who opposed him. Voldemort successfully hunted him down there, although Grindelwald lied to Voldemort, claiming never to have had the Elder Wand. Voldemort casts the Killing Curse in rage. We find out later that both Dumbledore and Grindelwald were seeking the Deathly Hallows, which would have made them masters of death, and in fact Grindelwald adopted the symbol of the Deathly Hallows for his organization. When their plan was derailed by Aberforth Dumbledore, a fight broke out, resulting in the death of Aberforth and Albus' sister, Ariana. Grindelwald immediately left Godric's Hollow, possibly fearing that this tragedy would also be laid at his feet. After stealing the Elder Wand from Gregorovitch, he used its power to begin his conquest of Europe. He was defeated by Dumbledore, in Dumbledore's words, "only when it would have been too shameful for him to delay taking action any longer."

Strengths Comparable magical skill to Albus Dumbledore, who was considered by many to be the most powerful wizard to have ever lived.

Weaknesses Grindelwald had an obsessive desire to possess the Deathly Hallows, especially the Elder Wand.

Relationships with Other Characters Best friends with Albus Dumbledore when the two were teenagers.

Grindelwald had been expelled from Durmstrang, apparently for Dark magic. It is possible that he had followers at Durmstrang, much as Tom Riddle had at Hogwarts, but apart from his relationship with Dumbledore it is uncertain if he had any friends at all.

Though he lived with Bathilda Bagshot while he was visiting there, her memories as published in Rita Skeeter's book lead us to believe that Bathilda was not in his confidence. She seems to have had no idea what he was planning with Dumbledore.

Analysis

There is a resort town in Switzerland, just north of the Eiger, named Grindelwald. It is unknown whether this town was the inspiration for the name of this character.

It is necessary for Dumbledore to do something that has major repercussions in the Wizarding world, in order to have the sort of fame that is accorded to him. Otherwise, why would there be any note of this headmaster of this Wizarding school, even granted that it is the only major one in England? Headmasters, like teachers, generally have limited direct influence, no matter how much their students do; and yet Dumbledore has apparently been offered the post of Minister for Magic, and has any number of other honours, not least of which (in his opinion) is that he has been selected to be one of the wizards that appear on Chocolate Frog cards. A typical headmaster does not get singled out as "possibly the best wizard in our lifetime. Granted, Dumbledore had always been academically very sharp, as we hear in *Harry Potter and the Deathly Hallows*, but we get the feeling that it was his defeat of Grindelwald that crystallized his ascendancy in the minds of the Wizarding public. Thus Grindelwald provides a necessary foil to Dumbledore in his younger days. At the time of their battle in 1945, Dumbledore would have been 64 years old and in the prime of his powers. Grindelwald was, possibly, a little younger; he had been expelled from Durmstrang and come to visit his aunt in the summer after Dumbledore's graduation.

Greater Picture

The young Dumbledore was blinded to Grindelwald's power-hungry aims to become a dictator. Dumbledore believed that the ultimate goal was to make the world safe for people like his sister Ariana to exist; he believed that Muggles living under benevolent Wizard rule would have made it possible for wizard offspring and Muggle children to co-exist. A simple test of one's personality is which specific Hallow they think is the most valuable, and why. Grindelwald clearly believed the Elder Wand, unbeatable in a duel, was superior, with the Resurrection Stone running second. Albus thought the Resurrection Stone was more important. To Grindelwald, the Resurrection Stone was a means to raise an army of Inferi; to Albus, it would have returned his lost family. Neither had much interest in the Invisibility Cloak. Why did Dumbledore fail to see that Grindelwald was choosing the evil path to power? Dumbledore's deep attraction for Grindelwald may have caused him to overlook his friend's faults. Also, his own pride in his superior intellect and extraordinary magical abilities may also have deluded him into believing that he and Grindelwald knew what was best for the Wizarding world. With the foolishness of youth, he perhaps thought he could change Grindelwald to his own, somewhat more gentle ends.

It was this episode with Grindelwald, and the resulting death of his sister Ariana, that led Dumbledore to believe that he could not be trusted with power, that he would misuse the sort of power that came from being Minister for Magic. Surprisingly, this is a key plot point in the story. Would Dumbledore have had the nerve to stand up to the Minister for Magic, as he did to Cornelius Fudge at the end of *Harry Potter and the Goblet of Fire*, had he not been a strong enough wizard to take that post himself? And if he was that strong, what conceivable reason would there be for his not becoming Minister? Harry needs someone this strong to train him, and to defend him from the Ministry, and it would be impossible for Harry to be trained by a Minister for Magic.

Gibbon

Gender: Male
Hair color: Unknown
Eye color: Unknown
Related Family: Unknown
Loyalty: Lord Voldemort

OVERVIEW

Gibbon (no first name given) is a Death Eater who takes part in the battle at the Hogwarts Astronomy tower.

ROLE IN THE BOOKS

Half-Blood Prince   Gibbon is one of the Death Eaters who takes part in the Battle under the Astronomy Tower at Hogwarts. When we first see him, he is dead; a large, blond Death Eater, who we later learn is Thorfinn Rowle, had tried to kill Remus Lupin, and Lupin had ducked. The curse had hit Gibbon, who had apparently run up to the top of the Astronomy Tower to conjure the Dark Mark, and was then returning to the battle.

Gideon Prewett

Gender: Male
Hair color: Unknown
Eye color: Unknown
Related Family: Molly Weasley
Loyalty: Order of the Phoenix

OVERVIEW

Gideon Prewett was a member of the original Order of the Phoenix, and one of Molly Weasley's brothers.

ROLE IN THE BOOKS

Philosopher's Stone   In their first meeting, Hagrid mentions to Harry that Voldemort killed some of the best wizards of the age such as the Prewetts, along with the Bones and the McKinnons.

Order of the Phoenix   At the celebratory party at Grimmauld Place for Ron and Hermione's appointment as Prefects, Alastor Moody shows Harry a photograph of the original Order of the Phoenix. Gideon Prewett is in that photo, with his brother Fabian, and Moody says it took five Death Eaters to kill them.

Gideon and Fabian were twins, and Molly Weasley's brothers. It is in part because she has lost immediate family members to Death Eaters already that her greatest fear, as shown by the Boggart in that same chapter, is of her own family members dying.

Gilderoy Lockhart

Gender: Male
Hair color: Golden
Eye color: Blue
Related Family: Unknown
Loyalty: Self, his own fame

OVERVIEW

Gilderoy Lockhart is famous in the wizarding world. He has been awarded the Order of Merlin, third class, Honorary Member of the Dark Force Defence League and is the five-time winner of *Witch Weekly's* Most-Charming-Smile Award. He is Defence Against the Dark Arts teacher during Harry's second year. Lockhart has written many best-selling books chronicling his daring adventures, and he revels in his own celebrity.

ROLE IN THE BOOKS

Chamber of Secrets   We first see Lockhart indirectly, as the author of a book on Common Household Pests. As punishment for taking the car, Mrs. Weasley sets Ron, Fred, and George the task of de-Gnoming the garden, and tells them to check Gilderoy's book for instructions. Harry volunteers to help, and like the others is soon spinning the gnomes around rapidly in circles to disorient them, then throwing them over the garden wall. This apparently is effective, as when they are finished, Harry sees a little line of dispirited gnomes heading off towards a distant copse; but near sunset he sees them all finding their way back through the hedgerows and back into the garden. When booklists arrive, it appears that the new Defence Against the Dark Arts teacher has selected Lockhart's entire library, with the exception of his new autobiography, as texts for the course. Fred and George, who previously commented that Mrs. Weasley is sweet on Gilderoy, now guess that the new Defence teacher is a middle-aged witch. They also comment that the booklist won't be cheap.

When the family reaches Diagon Alley, they find that Lockhart is present in person at Flourish and Blotts' bookstore, signing copies of his new autobiography, *Magical Me*. Mrs. Weasley is in line, and drags Harry, Ron, and the twins in with her; Ginny is holding back. When the photographer for the *Daily Prophet* pushes Ron out of the way so he can get a picture, Lockhart spots Harry in line, and drags him up to the table, telling Harry that the two of them together will make the front page. He then gives Harry the full set of his books, smiling broadly all the while, and takes the opportunity to announce that he has accepted the job of teacher of Defence Against the Dark Arts at Hogwarts. Once released, Harry, retreating to the back of the crowd, finds Ginny, and dumps all the Lockhart books into her cauldron. Shortly after this, there is a physical fight between Arthur Weasley and Lucius Malfoy, which is broken up by Hagrid. While Mrs. Weasley is concerned about what Lockhart will think of them brawling in the store, Fred comments that Lockhart was talking to the photographer chap as to how to spin it for the best news value.

Harry and Ron, unable to reach the Hogwarts Express, use Arthur Weasley's flying car to get to Hogwarts. The car gets into difficulties and crashes into the Whomping Willow. We next see Lockhart the next day as Harry is waiting to get into Herbology; he is walking alongside Professor Sprout, apparently having just been "assisting" her by telling her how to perform first aid on the tree. It is perhaps noteworthy that Professor Sprout is carrying all the first aid gear, looks somewhat exasperated, and has fresh bruises, while Lockhart does not seem at all the worse for the experience. Seeing Harry at the greenhouses, Lockhart takes him aside. Lockhart says he blames himself; having given Harry a taste of fame in Flourish and Blotts,' he understands that Harry was only trying for fame and recognition when he took the flying car to Hogwarts. In a fatherly way, he cautions Harry that he may be reaching too high, and that he should tone down his search for recognition.

In the first Defence Against the Dark Arts class, Lockhart has the class write a test, to see who has read through the textbooks. Harry and Ron are astounded; the test is all questions about Lockhart. Hermione gets all the answers right, of course. Lockhart then proposes a practical example, and releases a cageful of Cornish pixies. The pixies promptly wreak mayhem on the classroom. Attempting to return them to their cage, Lockhart performs a spell which has no effect; a pixie grabs his wand and throws it out the window. At the bell, most of the class leaves; Lockhart, also departing, tells Ron, Harry, and Hermione to "finish cleaning up here." Ron says he doesn't think Lockhart is much of a wizard. Hermione counters, saying "Look what he's done!" Ron retorts, quietly, "What he says he's done." When Ron attempts to curse Draco Malfoy, because Malfoy had insulted Hermione, his wand backfires, and Harry and Hermione take him to Hagrid for assistance. Hagrid tells them that Lockhart had been the only applicant for the Defence Against the Dark Arts position, and is uncharacteristically critical of him, saying that Lockhart's books might not be entirely truthful. He also jokes about Harry giving out signed photographs, and says that Lockhart was not happy about Hagrid's saying Harry is already more famous than Lockhart will ever be. As they return to the castle, Professor McGonagall tells Harry that his detention will be to assist Professor Lockhart with his fan mail, and that Lockhart had specifically requested him. Harry duly presents himself at Lockhart's office that evening, finding it full of posters of Lockhart, some of them autographed. Harry dully settles down to addressing envelopes, as Lockhart rambles on about the price of fame, and signs photos. Harry suddenly hears a voice other than Lockhart's, but looking around, cannot find the source. Lockhart, recalled to himself, notes the time and dismisses Harry.

When Mrs. Norris is found hanging off a torch bracket, Professor Dumbledore indicates a need to examine her; Lockhart volunteers his office. Dumbledore asks Harry, Ron, and Hermione to accompany them as they had discovered Mrs. Norris; Professor Snape, Professor McGonagall, and Argus Filch follow. As they enter, Harry notes the occupants of most of the Lockhart posters whisking themselves out of view; he believes he sees some of them wearing hair curlers. As Dumbledore examines the cat, Lockhart is prattling on about how he could have saved her if he had been there; Harry notes that the poster occupants are peering out around their frames, some of them nodding agreement, and sees that at least one is still wearing his hairnet. When Dumbledore reports that Mrs. Norris is not dead but petrified, Lockhart says that he can whip up a Restorative Draught in no time. Snape rather acidly remarks that he had thought he was the Potions master at the school.

In order to determine if Draco Malfoy is the heir of Slytherin, Hermione hits on a plan to use Polyjuice Potion to allow them to disguise themselves as Slytherins. the instructions for making Polyjuice Potion, however, are in a book, *Moste Potente Potions*, which is in the restricted section, and they would need a note for it. Ron believes that they will have trouble finding a teacher thick enough to sign a note for a book like that . . .

Lockhart, meanwhile, after the debacle of the pixies, has resorted to re-enacting scenes from his books, with Harry's assistance. When we next see Lockhart, Harry is willingly playing the werewolf foil to Lockhart as he acts out a scene. We see that Harry is unhappy with this, but we are told that he is playing up to Lockhart for a reason. At the end of class, Hermione, Ron, and Harry approach Lockhart with a note, and Hermione explains that she would like to take *Moste Potente Potions* out of the library because it would help her understand something in a different one of Lockhart's books. Lockhart signs the note with a revolting peacock-feather quill, and Hermione, with Harry and Ron in tow, heads off to the library to take out the book.

At the Quidditch match with Slytherin, which occurs the next day, a Bludger appears to have been enchanted to concentrate on Harry. While he manages to avoid it for most of the match, as he is lining up to catch the Snitch, the Bludger hits him and breaks his wrist. Lockhart then, over Harry's protests, offers to help, but the spell he uses ends up removing all the bones from Harry's arm.

A week before Christmas break, there is notice of the creation of a dueling club. Harry, Ron and Hermione are interested and attend, but are dismayed when they find it's being run by Lockhart. By way of demonstration, Lockhart faces Professor Snape, runs through the formalities, and is quickly disarmed and flung off the stage. Rather than trying a second time, in the face of Snape's rather obvious anger, Lockhart has the students form groups of two. Snape intervenes at one point, separating Harry and Ron and leaving Harry to face Draco Malfoy; Ron is paired with Seamus Finnigan and Hermione with Millicent Bullstrode. On the count of three, mayhem breaks out; amidst the flying curses we hear Lockhart shouting for everyone to stop, but it is Snape who brings things to an end. Once the smoke has cleared, Lockhart suggests putting a pair of students on stage to demonstrate and suggests Neville and Justin Finch-Fletchley. Snape says that is too risky for Justin, as Neville causes havoc with every spell, and suggests instead Harry and Draco. At the count, Draco conjures a snake. Lockhart says he'll dispose of it, but his charm throws the snake ten feet in the air, and it lands in front of Justin. Seeing it is about to attack Justin, Harry tells the snake to stop, and is surprised when it does. Snape then destroys the snake, looking speculatively at Harry. Justin asks Harry what he thought he was trying to do, and storms off; Harry, Ron and Hermione leave as well, and Ron says that he didn't know Harry was a Parselmouth. Harry admits he didn't know either, and Hermione points out that it is a very rare ability, and historically linked to the descendants of Salazar Slytherin.

After Christmas, there is a long break without any sign of the Monster in the Chamber—Justin's Petrification before Christmas had been the last one. Lockhart, of course, takes credit for scaring away the creature, and suggests that they need a little "morale-booster." On Valentine's Day, we discover what Lockhart's morale-booster is: the Great Hall ceiling is showering down heart-shaped confetti, and Lockhart has recruited a number of dwarfs, dressed as Cupids, to run around the school delivering singing Valentines.

When Hermione and Penelope Clearwater are attacked, Professor McGonagall orders new restrictions for the safety of the students, including a curfew requiring them to stay in their dormitories, a ban on evening activities, and a requirement that they be shepherded between their classes by the teachers. Shortly after this, Dumbledore is suspended as Headmaster, and Hagrid is arrested as he is suspected of being the one who is allowing the Monster out of the Chamber of Secrets. Lockhart now says that the precautions that McGonagall is insisting on are pointless, as with Hagrid arrested there will be no more attacks; the other teachers, though, are not so sure, and are still being very careful about their guard duties.

Harry and Ron, having visited Aragog by this point, believe that it is Moaning Myrtle who was killed by the Monster when it was released fifty years before, and need to talk to her to find out what they can about the Monster. It is Lockhart's certainty about the threat being over, along with his fatigue at having to patrol the hallways all night, which allows them the liberty to go and speak with her: they suggest to Lockhart that they can find their way to their next class and that he looks tired. He goes off to his office, and Harry and Ron head off to interview Myrtle. Having been redirected to the Hospital Wing and received some information from Hermione, Harry and Ron determine where the entrance to the Chamber is, and what the Monster is (a Basilisk), and so decide that they must speak with professor McGonagall. They are waiting in the Staff Room to speak with her when students are sent back to their dormitories; hiding in a closet, they hear that Ginny has been taken into the Chamber. They also hear Lockhart, arriving late for the meeting with the staff, being called on his boasts about knowing where the chamber is and what's in it, and receiving instructions from McGonagall to go and deal with the Monster. Much shaken, he departs.

Harry and Ron find Lockhart in his office, frantically packing. Lockhart admits to them that he has not actually done the things in his books, that other people had done them and he had simply recorded what they had told him. The people who had done these things weren't photogenic, so it was better that he, the handsome and dashing one, take credit for their activities. And he also had a very good line of memory charms that would keep them from recalling having done the things that he was now claiming. So saying, he attempts to charm Harry and Ron, but Harry Disarms him. Ron throws Lockhart's wand out the window. With two wands pointed at his back, Lockhart is marched to Moaning Myrtle's bathroom. There, Harry opens the entrance to the Chamber. Lockhart is sent down the tunnel first; Harry and Ron follow. Eventually, they discover a huge, cast-off snake skin. Lockhart seems to faint at the sight, then, grabbing Ron's wand, tells Harry and Ron that he will take some of the snake skin as proof that he had vanquished the monster, and oh too bad about Ginny. However, when he tries to use Ron's broken wand to modify Ron's and Harry's memory, it backfires and explodes. The ceiling falls between Harry and Ron, and Lockhart loses his memory completely.

When Harry returns from the Chamber with Ginny and Fawkes, Lockhart can barely remember who he is himself, and only vaguely recognizes Harry. He spends the remainder of the book going where he is told, staring vaguely at things, and humming quietly to himself.

Order of the Phoenix   While visiting Arthur Weasley at St. Mungo's Hospital in London, Harry, Ron, Hermione, and Ginny happen to see Lockhart, who is still recovering there from his memory loss. The charge nurse seems to be so pleased that Gilderoy has visitors that the four students feel compelled to stop and visit with him for a while. Gilderoy appears to have made little progress in recovering his memory; he cannot remember Harry, and is unable to remember why people keep writing to him. He has, however, regained his love of autographing pictures of himself, which the charge nurse finds encouraging, and he has finally managed to re-learn joined-up writing.

Harry's visiting Lockhart is primarily a way to introduce us to several other characters who are also suffering long-term spell damage: Broderick Bode, and Frank and Alice Longbottom, parents of Neville.

Strengths   His smile is an important strength, at least to him, and he refers to his five awards repeatedly and with what he considers to be charming humour (although Harry and Ron seem to find it slightly sickening). He has the ability to manipulate other characters by using his charm and physical appearance. He also seems to have excellent skill with Memory charms.

Weaknesses   Lockhart is inept at using magic other than the Memory Charm. When he tries to mend Harry's broken arm, the spell goes wrong, causing Harry's bones to disappear.

Lockhart has an overblown sense of his own importance. In Defence Against the Dark Arts class, he only assigns his own published works as textbooks, and he brags constantly about his exploits. Lockhart is a fraud, lying about his achievements in order to gain celebrity.

He exploits others for publicity, in particular creating headline-grabbing opportunities with Harry whenever possible. His supposed fondness for Harry is exposed as fake when he attempts to use a memory-obliterating charm on him.

Relationships with Other Characters Lockhart is popular with female characters in Chamber of Secrets, particularly Molly Weasley and Hermione Granger. He is a celebrity in the Wizarding World for his (fraudulent) exploits which he has documented in a series of best-selling books.

Lockhart forms a false attachment to Harry purely to generate publicity for himself.

ANALYSIS

Despite Lockhart's fame, Harry almost immediately sees through his act, and considers him an ineffectual, self-aggrandizing fop, although most female students, including Hermione, have a crush on him. Lockhart is almost stunningly oblivious to other people. He seems to feel that everyone is as self-aggrandizing as himself, and keeps taking Harry aside to give him helpful little tips about how to manage his fame. He cannot see that Harry does not want to be famous. Harry sees, much more than Gilderoy, that if you are in the spotlight, every action is visible, even the ones you don't want visible; and while Lockhart clearly feels that he can make no mistake, or can use a memory charm to cover over his mistakes, Harry still feels quite keenly that he is not as much a part of the Wizarding world as he should be.

It is interesting, perhaps, that despite his many and sophisticated efforts to hide his fraudulent behaviour, the entire staff of Hogwarts, including Poppy Pomfrey and Professor Sprout, both of whom are squarely in his "middle-aged witch" target demographic, seems to be aware that he is not who he claims to be. Dumbledore's comment on learning that Lockhart has destroyed his own memory, "Impaled upon your own sword, Gilderoy?" implies that he is not at all surprised that memory charms are what Gilderoy has based his success upon. Whether Dumbledore had already known this, or whether he was simply unsurprised by the revelation, is unknown, and ultimately unimportant. The author has stated that Gilderoy Lockhart is the only person in the books who is directly modeled on anyone in her life. She has further stated that Lockhart was *not* modeled on her first husband.[1]

QUESTIONS

1. Lockhart's personality remains the same, even though his memory has been removed. What does this say about a person's character vs. a person's experiences?

2. Why shouldn't someone lie about their accomplishments?

3. Given Lockhart's character, and what he has done, which House at Hogwarts do you believe he was Sorted into? Why?

Ginny Weasley

Gender: Female
Hair color: Red
Eye color: Brown

Related Family:
Loyalty:
Arthur Weasley (father)
Molly Weasley (mother)
Bill Weasley (oldest brother) Charlie Weasley (older brother) Percy Weasley (older brother) Fred Weasley (older brother)
George Weasley (older brother) Ron Weasley (older brother)
Albus Dumbledore, Harry Potter

OVERVIEW

Ginevra "Ginny" Molly Weasley is the only daughter and youngest child of Arthur and Molly Weasley. She is in Gryffindor and is the sister of Ron Weasley. She is one year younger than both Ron and Harry. The author has said that Ginny's birthday is 11 August (internal evidence suggests 1981), which actually makes her almost exactly one year younger than Harry (whose birthday is 31 July, apparently 1980) and 17 months younger than Ron (whose birthday is 1 March, apparently 1980).

ROLE IN THE BOOKS

Philosopher's Stone Ginny has two brief cameos in the book, first when Harry boards the Hogwarts Express and secondly when he returns. Her interest in Harry is established.

Chamber of Secrets Ginny's crush on Harry is established. She first sees Harry the morning after he arrives at the Burrow and promptly runs away. As Harry and Ron go up the stairs to Ron's room, where Harry will be staying, they have a brief glimpse of Ginny before she closes her door, and Ron remarks that that's very unusual for her, she's usually extremely outgoing. And later, when Harry shows up in the kitchen at breakfast, Ginny promptly spills her porridge. When the family, with Harry, go to buy school books at Flourish and Blotts,' Ginny is hanging back as everyone else lines up to meet Gilderoy Lockhart; Harry, mortally embarrassed after his encounter with Lockhart and his ruthless drive for publicity, dumps all the books he got from Lockhart into Ginny's cauldron. Draco Malfoy now appears saying that Harry must have loved getting onto the front page of the paper. Ginny defends him, upon which Draco suggests that Harry now has a girlfriend. Lucius Malfoy, Draco's father, appears on the scene, and looks over some of the textbooks that Ginny is carrying; disparaging their quality, he returns them to her cauldron. She makes several scattered appearances where she appears very ill at ease. This is particularly noticeable on February 14th. Professor Lockhart has employed a number of dwarfs who will be running around the school delivering Valentines; one of them runs Harry to earth to deliver a Valentine poem apparently sent by Ginny. In the process of securing Harry, the dwarf has to knock him over, which sends the contents of his book bag all over the floor. One of the things that spills out is the Very Secret Diary; Draco picks it up and looks at it, and Harry and Ron manage to reclaim it. Ginny is present during this, and runs off, apparently

---

1. http://www.jkrowling.com/textonly/en/rubbishbin_view.cfm?id=3

very upset; we are led to believe that it is because her Valentine greeting to Harry has resulted in him being ridiculed.

At breakfast on the day that Professor McGonagall announces the imminent revival of the victims of the monster, Ginny approaches Harry and Ron, and indicates that she wants to tell them something; but Percy appears, and tells them that what she has to say is not that important Ginny flees, apparently still upset. Later that day, Harry and Ron discover, with help from Hermione, that the monster in the chamber is a Basilisk, and from things told to them by Aragog, surmise that the entrance to the Chamber is in Moaning Myrtle's bathroom. They go to find Professor McGonagall to report their findings, but are prevented from doing so when all students are sent back to their common rooms; they remain in the staff room, hidden, and hear that Ginny has been taken into the Chamber of Secrets.

Harry and Ron, with Lockhart's unwilling assistance, now locate the entrance to the Chamber of Secrets and enter it to rescue Ginny; Lockhart's attempt to erase their memory results in the ceiling falling in, stranding Harry on the side of the rock fall towards the Chamber. Alone, he goes on, finding an unconscious and failing Ginny, and a somewhat ghostly Tom Riddle. Tom explains how he had used his diary to ensnare Ginny, to get her to open the Chamber of Secrets and release the monster, and was now taking her life force in order that he could return to life himself. Tom also reveals that he now calls himself Lord Voldemort. Harry fights the monster and wins, then destroys the diary, causing the simulacrum of Riddle to vanish and restoring Ginny to consciousness. Together with Ron and Lockhart, they return to the surface. There, in Professor McGonagall's office, Ginny is reunited with her father and mother, and Harry tells the story of how she had been controlled by Voldemort.

Shortly after this, with help from Dobby, Harry figures out that it was when Lucius Malfoy was inspecting her purchases at Flourish and Blotts, that Ginny had had Riddle's diary dropped in with her other books. Professor Dumbledore warns Lucius at this point that if any more of Riddle's old school things appear, it is quite likely that Arthur Weasley will trace them back to the Malfoys.

Finally, on the Hogwarts Express homewards, Ginny reveals that the reason Percy had prevented her from speaking to Ron and Harry was that she knew that Percy had a girlfriend and had seen him kissing her, and Percy had thought that was what Ginny wanted to tell Harry.

Prisoner of Azkaban Ginny's role is largely relegated to the background. She is present in the Leaky Cauldron when Harry meets up with the Weasleys and Hermione as he prepares for school. Ron shoos her away in the Hogwarts Express so that he, Harry, and Hermione can have a private conversation. When the train stops for inspection by Dementors, she makes her way back to Harry's compartment and joins them, as does Neville Longbottom, and she is there when Harry faints.

Goblet of Fire Ginny is present at The Burrow when Harry arrives there, arriving in the parlour behind Mrs. Weasley shortly after Mr. Weasley starts berating Fred and George for having dropped a Ton-Tongue Toffee in front of Dudley Dursley and given him a four-foot-long tongue. Shortly after, Ron tells Harry that it was Ginny who named his owl Pigwidgeon, and that the owl now won't respond to any other name.

Ginny attends the Quidditch World Cup with Harry, Ron, Hermione, Fred, George, Percy, Charlie, Bill, and Mr. Weasley. Ginny and Hermione complain about having to get up so early, but Mr. Weasley points out that having a hundred thousand wizards attending an event does make for logistics problems, and people with cheaper tickets have to go as much as a week ahead of time and stay there for the whole time. When the Muggle owner of their campsite has to be charmed to forget that what he is seeing is odd, Ginny remarks that as head of Magical Games and Sports, Ludovic Bagman certainly ought to know better than to wander around in is Beaters robes. After the match, riots break out, and Mr. Weasley sends the younger Weasleys, plus Harry and Hermione, off into the nearby woods for safety. Harry, in the dark, trips over a root, and Ginny and the twins end up separated from the other three. We don't see them again until the riots have been quelled; the three of them have returned to the tents, uninjured.

Just before the Yule Ball, we see Ginny attempting to comfort Ron, who had asked Fleur Delacour to the Ball and had been cut dead. It occurs to Ron, who has just heard of Harry's rejection by Cho Chang, that Hermione is a girl, Ron can ask her, and Harry can go with Ginny. Both Hermione and Ginny refuse, saying they are already going with someone else. Ginny, it turns out, attends the Yule Ball with Neville Longbottom, who repeatedly steps on her feet while they are dancing, and Hermione with Viktor Krum. We later find out that at the Yule Ball, Ginny met Michael Corner, and started going out with him shortly afterwards.

Order of the Phoenix Ginny re-enters our story in the room Harry shares with Ron at the headquarters of the Order of the Phoenix. Shortly after Harry arrives, and after he has taken out his frustrations on Ron and Hermione, they are joined by Fred, George, and Ginny. The Weasleys inform Harry of Percy's falling out from the family. After dinner, Sirius Black proposes to let Harry in on the current operations of the Order of the Phoenix; Ron and Hermione arrange to be present by telling the adults that Harry would be sharing what he learned with them anyway, and Fred and George because they are older than Ron, but Ginny is unceremoniously and with much complaining bundled off to bed. We see Ginny in passing a few times during the next few days. She is roped in to help with making Grimmauld Place habitable again, removing and destroying Dark artifacts and materials, and infestations of magical pests. She takes part in the victory celebration after Harry returns, unscathed, from his hearing. And she is present at the celebration of Ron and Hermione's becoming Prefects.

Fred and George use magic to take their trunks downstairs on the day they have to get back to school, and the flying trunks evidently injure Ginny. She is healed by the time they actually leave for the train, however. Once on the train. Fred and George go off to talk with Lee Jordan, and Ron and Hermione have to go to the special Prefects carriage. Harry and Ginny meet up with Neville, and end up sharing a compartment with Luna Lovegood. Ginny introduces them, but apart from cleaning up the compartment after Neville showers everyone with Stinksap, plays little further part until the school year is underway.

Ginny is one of the twenty-eight students (Harry, Ron, Hermione, and twenty-five others) who attend the first meeting of what is to become Dumbledore's Army at the Hog's Head. After the meeting, Hermione remarks that Michael Corner was likely only there because Ginny was attending. She goes on to say that while Ginny had been waiting for Harry, she had given up; meeting Michael at the Yule Ball, she had started to go out with him later in the year. Ron immediately decides that he doesn't like Michael Corner.

After the publication of Educational Decree Number Twenty-Four, Ginny is concerned that the DA may no longer meet, but Harry reassures her that they will be going on with it regardless. She goes off to tell Michael Corner, and through him the Ravenclaw members of the DA. At the first meeting of the DA, in the Room of Requirement, Hermione suggests Defence Association as a name for the group; Ginny suggests Dumbledore's Army, as it has the same initials and represents the worst fear of the Ministry, who have foisted Dolores Umbridge on them as a Defence Against the Dark Arts teacher. The suggestion is voted on and passes unanimously.

When Harry, Fred, and George are banned from playing Quidditch, Ginny replaces Harry as Seeker. When Harry sees Arthur Weasley being attacked by a snake, Professor McGonagall takes him and Ron to Dumbledore's office. There, Dumbledore hears him out, sends two portraits to investigate, and tells McGonagall to fetch the other Weasley children. Fred, George, and Ginny are present as Dumbledore explains what has been happening, and creates a Portkey to take them back to Grimmauld Place. There, they demand to be taken to see their father, but Sirius refuses to allow them to go, saying that having the children show up at the hospital before their mother has even been notified would raise more questions that they do not want raised. They all wait anxiously until they receive word from Molly Weasley that Arthur is going to be all right.

When they visit Mr. Weasley in hospital, Arthur, Molly, Tonks, and Alastor Moody discuss the events that led up to the attack, and Moody voices the suspicion that Harry, obviously seeing into Voldemort's mind, may be possessed by him. Harry and Ginny are both listening in using the Twins' Extendable Ears. As a result of this, Harry goes into seclusion, feeling that it is unsafe for him to be around others. Hermione, abandoning a planned skiing trip, appears at Grimmauld Place and drags Harry out of seclusion to talk to the others. Hearing his concerns, Ginny points out that it was stupid for Harry to be avoiding her, because she's the only person Harry knows who has actually been possessed by Voldemort, and knows what it feels like. After Harry apologizes, Ginny tells him that if there aren't big stretches where he doesn't remember what he was doing, he hasn't been possessed. Harry is greatly relieved by this.

Visiting Arthur on Christmas, Harry, Ron, Ginny, and Hermione suddenly find a need to be elsewhere, so they decide to visit the tea shop on the top floor of the hospital. Before they can reach it, however, they are spotted by one of the patients, Gilderoy Lockhart. Lockhart's ward nurse seems to think the four of them have come to visit Gilderoy, and she is so pleased by this that the four cannot see any way to avoid spending some time with him. While they are visiting Gilderoy, they also see Broderick Bode, who is not yet speaking English, and they run into a horribly embarrassed Neville, who is there with his grandmother to visit his parents, Frank and Alice Longbottom.

We hear in passing that, even this far into the season and so very close to their match against Hufflepuff, Angelina Johnson, the captain of the Quidditch team, is extremely unhappy with the way her team is shaping up, especially Kirke and Sloper, the two beaters who have replaced Fred and George. Ginny apparently flies extremely well, and Hermione tells Ron and the twins that this is because she had been breaking into the Weasley family broom cupboard for years, flying all of their brooms in turn. Despite the poor quality of the beaters, Gryffindor manage to keep their losses to only ten points when Ginny catches the Snitch from right under the opposing seeker's nose. Just before Spring Break, Harry sees a disturbing episode of his father's life, from Professor Snape's memory, in Dumbledore's Pensieve. This memory destroys the idealized image of his father that Harry had created. The memory is so disturbing that Harry does not wish to discuss it with anyone, but he is able to pass off his brooding as being caused by his recent breakup with Cho Chang. Ginny tracks him to the library to bring him his Easter present from Molly Weasley, and suggests that Harry should talk to Cho. Harry says that he'd really like to talk to Sirius, but that's impossible; the only way he could do that is via the fireplace in Umbridge's office, that being the only one that is not monitored. Ginny points out that living with the Twins has left her believing that nothing is impossible. Shortly, the twins mention to Harry that they are planning a diversion on the first day of classes after break, and suggest that he use that time to get into Umbridge's office to have his chat with Sirius. Harry has been having dreams that he believes mirror real-world events all year about the Ministry, and now dreams that Sirius is being tortured by Voldemort. He decides that he must contact Sirius at Grimmauld Place to see if he is all right. Ginny, along with Luna Lovegood, are passing in the corridor as Harry is telling this emphatically to Ron and Hermione, and volunteer to help out, guarding Umbridge's door while he is inside talking to Sirius. Harry, under the Invisibility Cloak, hears Ginny telling people that the hallway is filled with Garroting Gas, before he enters the office. Umbridge is not deceived, however, and when Harry is pulled out of the fireplace, he finds that Hermione, Ron, Ginny, Luna, and Neville have been captured by the Inquisitorial Squad. Hermione manages to convince Umbridge that they have been working on a weapon for Dumbledore, and with Harry leads her off into the Forbidden Forest. Ginny and the others are left under guard in Umbridge's office.

Ginny apparently leads the escape from Umbridge's office with a well-executed Bat-Bogey hex which takes Draco Malfoy out of action. She, Ron, Luna and Neville meet up with Harry and Hermione, and Luna points out that they can use Thestrals to fly to the Ministry and save Sirius. Ginny is unsure about riding something she can't see, but gamely accompanies Harry to London, in through the Ministry visitor's entrance, and into the hall of Prophecy. Ambushed by Death Eaters, she, Luna and Ron become separated from Harry, Hermione and Neville. The two groups re-unite in the antechamber; Ginny apparently suffers a broken ankle, and has to be carried into the Brain Room when the Death Eaters find them. There, she is hit by an apparent Stun spell and plays no further part in the battle.

Harry visits Ron, Hermione, and Ginny in the Hospital wing. Ginny apparently is nearly healed, but both Ron and Hermione have taken serious damage and will need more time. Luna and Neville are also visiting, and they have found that Umbridge is also present, recovering from her sojourn among the Centaurs.

On the Hogwarts Express home, Harry, Ron, Hermione, and Ginny are sharing a compartment. When Cho Chang walks past, Hermione tentatively mentions that she's dating Michael Corner now. Ron is surprised, saying that he thought Ginny was dating Michael, but Ginny says that when she had caught the Snitch in the Quidditch match against Ravenclaw, Michael had gone off to comfort Cho rather than celebrating with Ginny, so she had dumped him. Ron suggests, looking furtively at Harry, that she could now choose someone better, and Ginny says that she's now dating Dean Thomas. Ron seems somewhat distressed by this information.

Half-Blood Prince Ginny enters our story shortly after Harry arrives at The Burrow. Professor Dumbledore had brought him in quite late at night, and he had been put in what had been Fred and George's room. On his first morning there, after Ron and Hermione have waked him up, Ginny slouches in, complaining about *her*. The identity of this mysterious female is resolved almost immediately when Fleur Delacour appears with Harry's breakfast, followed by a vexed Mrs. Weasley. Ginny apparently feels that Fleur is far too full of herself, and has nicknamed her "Phlegm." It appears that Mrs. Weasley is trying to get Bill interested in Nymphadora Tonks, but Ginny agrees with the others that, particularly with Tonks seeming so sad since the events at the end of the previous school year, there is little chance that she will succeed.

Ginny accompanies the others to purchase school supplies at Diagon Alley. When they visit Fred and George's joke shop, Fred and George try to grill Ginny about her relationships. She characteristically tells them that it is none of their business. Ginny is captivated by a Pygmy Puff (possibly a variant of a Puffskein), and purchases one, naming it Arnold.

On the Hogwarts Express, we find that Professor Slughorn is once again starting up his "Slug Club," and has invited Harry to join him for lunch. Arriving in Slughorn's compartment, Harry is somewhat surprised to find Ginny there, particularly as Slughorn introduces those gathered there, and Harry notes the famous parents and other relations. It turns out that Slughorn had been passing Ginny's compartment when Ginny had been casting a particularly good Bat-Bogey Hex, and Slughorn had invited her to lunch on the strength of it. Slughorn has invited Harry for obvious reasons, and Neville because he had accompanied Harry at the Ministry, but seems unaware of the role Ginny played in that battle, and Harry, Neville, and Ginny do not wish to talk about that battle, much to his disappointment.

In Potions class, Harry is given an old textbook to use, which has a large number of revisions to the standard recipes. Following these revisions, he excels in his first lesson. Harry smells a flowery scent in the love potion in the room, which he later recognizes as Ginny's scent. Ginny, passing by, asks if he is taking instructions from a book. Harry remembers the diary of Tom Riddle from four years before. Hermione apparently remember similarly, because she immediately tests the book for anything hidden, but finds nothing except the notation that the book is the property of the Half-Blood Prince.

Harry, as Quidditch team captain, holds Quidditch tryouts. Ginny is selected as one of the three Chasers, the other two being Katie Bell and Demelza Robins.

Just before the first Hogsmeade weekend, Ginny delivers a note to Harry from Dumbledore, setting a time for their next lesson. She says she may see him there, she is planning to go to Hogsmeade with Dean Thomas. After Katie Bell falls afoul of a jinxed necklace, Harry brings Dean onto the Quidditch team to replace her. At the first practice of the new team, Ron, who is aware of the attachment between Dean and Ginny, and is suffering from nerves at the prospect of once again flying as Keeper, plays horribly; Dean, Ginny, and Demelza play very well, though, and Harry compliments them. As they return to the common room, Harry and Ron discover Ginny and Dean kissing in an alcove; Ron is furious that anyone would take such liberties with his sister, and Harry feels more than a little jealousy, though he does not express it. Ginny says Ron is just jealous because he has nobody to snog with, and kisses from old Auntie Muriel are the only ones he's ever gotten, and storms off.

At the following Quidditch match, the announcer, Zacharias Smith, is critical of Harry's choosing Ginny and Ron as team members, but subsides after Ron manages to stop everything that comes his way, and Ginny scores four of the six goals against Slytherin. At the end of the match, which Harry wins by distracting the Slytherin Seeker and catching the Snitch first, Ginny "forgets to brake" as she is swooping in for the victory celebration, and crashes into the announcer's podium, sending Smith crashing to the ground.

Luna Lovegood, in conversation with Harry, mentions that Ginny has been defending her, at one point recently stopping people from calling her "Loony."

When Harry and Ron are at The Burrow for Christmas, Fred and George stop by to tease Ron, after learning about his affair with Lavender Brown from Ginny.

When Percy stops by later (apparently under orders from Rufus Scrimgeour), Ginny, Fred and George all claim credit for the thrown parsnips that hasten his departure. On their return to Hogwarts, Ginny says that she had promised to meet Dean, but she seems somewhat unenthusiastic about the prospect. Harry is somewhat encouraged by this; while he has not yet fully realized it, we can see that he is falling in love with Ginny. However, he is still remembering Ron's reaction to catching her with Dean, and is afraid that if he does act upon this, he will make an enemy of Ron, and possibly lose his best friend. Ginny is, of course, at Ron's bedside as he is recovering from being poisoned on his birthday.

Harry is injured in the next Quidditch match by Cormac McLaggen, who has taken a Beater's bat to demonstrate its correct use, and promptly hit the Bludger straight at Harry. When he leaves the Hospital Wing, Hermione tells Harry that Dean and Ginny had fought, because Dean had thought it funny that Harry had been hit. Hermione also feels that it was very lucky that Harry had escaped with such minor injuries. Harry tries to hide his elation at the thought that Ginny and Dean's relationship might be hitting a rough spot, but Hermione, he thinks, may have noticed. Hermione suggests that Harry should use some of his precious Felix Felicis potion to get a memory from Slughorn that Dumbledore wants. Harry is initially reluctant; he had been saving that for some vaguely defined purpose, something to do with Ginny and Dean breaking up. Eventually he does take it, and as he, under his Invisibility Cloak, heads out through the portrait hole, he brushes against Ginny, who is just coming in with Dean. Ginny rounds on Dean for helping her when she doesn't need to be helped.

The following morning, Harry learns from Hermione that Ginny and Dean had broken up. While this creates an opportunity for Harry, it also creates a problem: can Dean and Ginny play Quidditch on the same team, if they are at daggers drawn? Luckily, he doesn't have to find out, as Katie Bell returns from St. Mungo's that same day. With McLaggen gone and Katie back, the Quidditch team is a lot more fun. Ginny in particular is the life of the team, pulling stunts and cracking jokes. Harry is glad to have the opportunity to watch her and walk alongside her, but is still afraid of what Ron would do if he started going out with her.

When Harry receives detention, to be served Saturdays with Snape, for injuring Draco, Ginny fills in as Seeker, and Dean fills in as Chaser; Harry apparently feels that they will interact little enough that their animosity will not be a major factor. Despite the horrible showing in the game where Harry was injured, they still have a chance at the Quidditch Cup: they have to win by more than 300 points, however. Returning from detention on the day of the Quidditch final, Harry walks into a celebration: it seems they have won the Cup. Ginny, seeing him enter, runs to Harry; he takes the opportunity offered and kisses her. Looking around afterwards, Harry sees that Hermione approves, and Ron is accepting, and takes Ginny for a long walk on the grounds. In the course of this, he learns that Gryffindor had won 450 to 140.

Ginny and Harry are happy together, and Harry is happy that the discussions people are having about him now are about something that makes him happy, rather than about Dark magic. His Potions work is suffering since he hid his textbook, but Slughorn attributes that to his blooming romance with Ginny.

At the battle under the Astronomy tower, Harry sees Ginny battling Amycus Carrow. After the battle has ended, it is Ginny who leads Harry away from the body of Dumbledore and up to the Hospital Wing, where he reports to Minerva McGonagall. Ginny, with Ron and Neville, had been watching the Room of Requirement; when Draco had come out, he had thrown something at them and everything had gone dark. Because Ginny and Ron had taken some of Harry's Felix Felicis potion, they were unhurt. They had luckily run into Remus Lupin, who had located the Death Eaters under the Astronomy Tower and had notified the other members of the Order. Harry and Ginny are now spending all their time together. They sit together for Dumbledore's funeral. Once that has ended, Harry says that he and Ginny must separate. He knows that Voldemort attacks people through those they love, and Harry cannot stand to put Ginny in that sort of risk. Ginny is saddened, but understanding.

Deathly Hallows Ginny and Mrs. Weasley are the only two people at The Burrow when Harry arrives after his escape from Privet Drive; the other Weasley family members arrive over the next short while. She is set to work preparing for Bill and Fleur's wedding, in the course of which she and Harry must work together. Harry happens to mention that Mrs. Weasley seems to be hoping that someone else will kill Voldemort while Harry is there making vol-au-vents, and Ginny picks up on the implication that Harry's mission seems to involve killing Voldemort. On Harry's birthday Ginny can't think of anything to give him and so she calls him into her room and kisses him so that Harry can have "something to remember her by"; the kiss ends with an interruption by Ron. Ron takes Harry aside and angrily tells him that breaking up was hard enough the last time, and that he shouldn't be leading Ginny on if he doesn't mean it; Harry says that it won't happen again. Over the next few days, Harry keeps starting to exchange glances with Ginny, and then remembering that he shouldn't.

When the Ministry falls and Harry, Ron, and Hermione have to escape, Harry is worried about Ginny. He remains worried until Mr. Weasley's Patronus informs them that the family are all right. He doesn't stop thinking about her, however; imagining her on her way to Hogwarts on the Express, and what she is doing in school. When Ted Tonks and his group camp within earshot of Harry, Hermione, and Ron, we hear that Ginny had been involved with the attempted theft of the sword of Gryffindor from the Headmaster's office, and that she was punished by having a detention with Hagrid in the Forbidden Forest. Harry is much relieved to find out she got off so lightly.

Between Christmas and his capture by Snatchers in March, Harry keeps taking out the Marauder's Map and looking for Ginny's labeled dot on it, trying to imagine what she is doing.

In the final battle, Ginny comes to the DA's aid to stop Voldemort. When Cho Chang, a former girlfriend of Harry's, offers to take him to the Ravenclaw common room so he may see a model of the diadem, Ginny suggests strongly that Luna be Harry's guide instead. Ginny is forbidden to take part in the Final Battle by Mrs. Weasley, but rebels. Finally she accepts that she will have to stay in the Room of Requirement, and sulkily, she does so, until Harry suddenly recalls where the lost Diadem of Ravenclaw is. He then evicts her with strict instructions to stay nearby so she can return to the room after he is done; but when he leaves the Room of Requirement, she is nowhere to be seen.

As Harry heads for the Forest to meet Voldemort, after viewing Severus Snape's memories, he passes Ginny on the grounds, ministering to a fallen girl. He thinks he'd like her to know he was there and that he cared about her, but passes on to his fate. She is the last person he thinks about before he "dies."

In the final assault on the school, Ginny is one of three students dueling Bellatrix Lestrange. Bellatrix sweeps all three of them aside when Mrs. Weasley joins in, but Ginny apparently takes little harm from this. . In the combined celebrations and mourning after the battle, Harry leaves Ginny to mourn Fred's death with her parents, thinking that he and Ginny will have a long time to be together later.

At the end of the novel, 19 years later, it is indicated that Harry Potter and Ginny Weasley are married and have three children: Lily Luna, James Sirius, and Albus Severus.

Strengths • Ginny's brothers and family provide her with an inner strength and pride.

• Ginny is very funny and not afraid to speak up.

• She is very good-looking, and this largely contributes to her confidence.

• Her best class is Charms as is shown, in a rather comical light, by her advanced and frequent 'Bat-Bogey Hexes,' which are also noticed by Professor Slughorn in book 6.

Weaknesses We are yet to see what Ginny is afraid of. However it was noted in *Harry Potter and the Prisoner of Azkaban* that she had a fear of being controlled by Lord Voldemort. It seems that she has, however, learned to deal with that fear by Harry's fifth year. At Christmas time of that year, she speaks to Harry quite dispassionately about her experiences while under the control of Voldemort.

Relationships with Other Characters Romantic relationships are covered in more depth in a separate section.

• Ex-Boyfriend Michael Corner: Ginny meets him first at the Yule Ball and goes out with him almost all through *Harry Potter and the Order of the Phoenix*. She breaks up with him after his house team loses against hers in Quidditch. He "got really sulky, so I ditched him and he ran off to comfort Cho."

• In the ending of Harry's 5th year and throughout most of the 6th, Ginny is dating Dean Thomas.

• During the course of the books, she establishes a strong friendship with Hermione. While it has been building quietly since *Harry Potter and the Prisoner of Azkaban*, it becomes much more apparent in *Harry Potter and the Order of the Phoenix*.

QUESTIONS

1. What will happen to Ginny in *Harry Potter and the Deathly Hallows*? It is unlikely that she will let Harry go on his Horcrux quest without her. Rowling has hinted that she will have a part, whether Harry likes it or not.

GREATER PICTURE

It can be seen why one may think that Ginny could be a Horcrux, seeing that in the *Harry Potter and the Half-Blood Prince* we find out that the diary was in fact a Horcrux, and in the Chamber of Secrets Tom Riddle tells us that 'Ginny poured out her soul to me.' Later he continues 'I grew powerful, far more powerful than little Miss Weasley. Powerful enough to start feeding Miss Weasley a few of my secrets, to start pouring a little of my soul back into her . . . '

It seems likely that Ginny was not made a Horcrux, but only *possessed* by Voldemort, as Dumbledore explains to Harry: 'Well, it is inadvisable to do so, . . . because to confide a part of your soul to something that can think and move for itself is obviously a risky business.' It is unlikely Voldemort would have deliberately entrusted even a fragment of his soul to a human.

In *Harry Potter and the Order of the Phoenix* Ginny explains to Harry what it felt like when she was possessed by Voldemort. Other than in the Chamber of Secrets, Ginny has never mentioned any instances of feelings of possession. We note that Professor Dumbledore speculates that the snake, Nagini, may be a Horcrux owing to her behaviour. From this, it seems likely that Ginny, if a Horcrux, would still display some strange behaviour. Furthermore, as Voldemort intended to kill Ginny in *Harry Potter and the Chamber of Secrets*, making her a Horcrux would have been pointless.

Godric Gryffindor

Gender: Male
Hair color: Unknown
Eye color: Unknown
Related Family: Unknown
Loyalty:

OVERVIEW

Godric Gryffindor was one of the four founders of Hogwarts and the creator of Gryffindor House. He preferred to teach students with courage, and members of the House are now known for this trait.

ROLE IN THE BOOKS

While Godric Gryffindor has been dead for possibly a thousand years, and thus cannot play any direct part in our story, he has influenced events that occur throughout the series.

Philosopher's Stone Harry Potter, Ron Weasley, and Hermione Granger are sorted into Gryffindor house, as the Sorting Hat determines that they contain qualities that Gryffindor would treasure: daring and bravery, no matter what their origin. We also learn, from the Sorting Hat's song, that the Hat was once Gryffindor's.

Chamber of Secrets Professor Binns tells us the legend of the Chamber of Secrets. The four founders of the school, Godric Gryffindor, Salazar Slytherin, Helga Hufflepuff, and Rowena Ravenclaw had existed in harmony for only a short time, before Slytherin and Gryffindor began to disagree over the nature of the students to be educated. Slytherin felt that only Wizards descended from Wizards, "pure blood Wizards," deserved education while Gryffindor felt that the ability to do magic outweighed any question of ancestry. Hufflepuff and Ravenclaw agreed with Gryffindor, and Salazar Slytherin left, after (according to legend) creating a secret chamber in the school, and hiding a monster within it. The chamber could only be opened by Slytherin's true heir, according to the legend.

When Harry finds himself in the previously-legendary chamber, Fawkes brings him the Sorting Hat to assist him in his battle against the Monster. The hat, in turn, produces the sword of Gryffindor, with which Harry vanquishes the Monster.

Prisoner of Azkaban It is mentioned that Harry's father and mother, along with Remus Lupin and Peter Pettigrew, were in Gryffindor house as students.

Half-Blood Prince In discussing Lord Voldemort's pattern of making Horcruxes from relics of the Founders, Professor Dumbledore mentions that the only known relic of Gryffindor's was the sword. (It should be noted that the Sorting Hat was his, also, but as it had been granted a rudimentary consciousness, there is question whether it could be considered a relic.)

Deathly Hallows We learn that Godric's Hollow, where Harry's parents lived, is named after Godric Gryffindor. The Sword of Gryffindor is returned to Harry in the Forest of Dean, in a manner that requires courage, a trait beloved of Gryffindor, to regain it.

The sword is later provided to Neville Longbottom by the Sorting Hat as it was earlier provided to Harry, possibly in part as a result of Neville's bravery.

Goyle, Sr.

Gender: Male
Hair color: Unknown
Eye color: Unknown
Related Family: Unknown
Loyalty: Lord Voldemort

OVERVIEW

Goyle, Sr. is the father of Gregory Goyle, one of Draco Malfoy's sidekicks.

ROLE IN THE BOOKS

Goblet of Fire When Lord Voldemort summons his Death Eaters after returning to life, he addresses one of them as Goyle. When Voldemort asks Goyle to do better next time, Goyle promises he will.

When Harry later names Goyle as one of the Death Eaters present in the graveyard, Cornelius Fudge dismisses that, saying he had already been tried and released, and Harry could have gotten his name from the old news stories.

Half-Blood Prince Goyle may be one of the Death Eaters present at the battle under the Astronomy Tower, during which Albus Dumbledore was murdered.

Deathly Hallows Goyle takes part in the final battle at Hogwarts; however, we only see him in passing.

Graham Pritchard

Gender: Male
Hair color: Unknown
Eye color: Unknown
Related Family: Unknown
Loyalty:

OVERVIEW

Graham Pritchard is a Slytherin who arrived at Hogwarts in Harry's fourth year.

ROLE IN THE BOOKS

Goblet of Fire Graham Pritchard was Sorted into Slytherin House.

Grawp

Gender: Male
Hair color: Unknown
Eye color: Unknown
Related Family: Rubeus Hagrid
Loyalty:

OVERVIEW

Grawp is the Giant half-brother of Rubeus Hagrid. His mother was the giant Fridwulfa.

ROLE IN THE BOOKS

Order of the Phoenix The half-wild Grawp is introduced to Harry and Hermione by Hagrid, who has hidden him in the Forbidden Forest. Hagrid is on probation at this point and is greatly afraid of being sacked by Dolores Umbridge; he charges Harry and Hermione with Grawp's care should he be sent away from the school. When they tell Ron about this the next day, Ron is utterly incredulous.

Harry and Hermione trick Professor Umbridge into going into the forest to look for a non-existent weapon, where they are stopped by a herd of Centaurs; Umbridge promptly manages to antagonize them by referring to them as having "nearly-human intelligence."

Grawp crashes onto the scene, looking for the recently-sacked Hagrid, just as the Centaurs are about to sentence Harry and Hermione to the same fate that they have decided for Umbridge. Grawp recognizes Hermione (calling her "Hermy"), and demands Hagrid ("Hagger!"). The Centaurs try to defend themselves from Grawp's clumsiness with arrows, but finding their weapons ineffective, scatter into the woods, carrying off Umbridge.

Half-Blood Prince According to Hagrid, Grawp is now living in a nice cave; this must be similar to the mountains where he was living when Hagrid first met him.

He is present at Albus Dumbledore's funeral, acting much more civilized, and trying, in his ham-fisted way, to console Hagrid.

Deathly Hallows We are re-introduced to Grawp when Hagrid comes crashing in to the school through a window, with his boarhound Fang. He tells us that when Voldemort had started his attack on the school, Hagrid had been up in the mountains visiting Grawp. They had headed down to the school together and Grawp had helpfully put Hagrid down inside the school. Grawp is involved in battling the two Giants that Voldemort has brought along to attack Hogwarts, and does not seem to take terribly much injury in the process—after the battle, survivors in the Great Hall are throwing food to him out the windows.

Strengths He is a giant, so therefore, very strong. We have seen that Hagrid is largely immune to Stun spells, and we are told that this is because of his Giant heritage. Because of this, it is safe to assume that Grawp will likely not even notice a Stun spell.

In his encounter with the Centaurs, we also see that arrows also only annoy him, rather than injuring him.

Weaknesses He doesn't seem very intelligent, although he is certainly improving through the books.

ANALYSIS

It is interesting to see a character who is as much stronger than Hagrid, as Hagrid is stronger than the regular wizards. It's hard to tell the effect that Grawp's heavy affection is having on Hagrid, but one can see that Hagrid is being as pummeled by Grawp's great strength, as Harry and Ron are by Hagrid's.

By the beginning of *Harry Potter and the Half-Blood Prince*, we know that at least one giant is roaming Britain, and we Muggles are being led to believe it is a tornado. We have not as yet seen anything, except another giant, that can defeat a giant; is this why Grawp has been civilized? So that he can be an unstoppable force on the side of the Wizards?

QUESTIONS

1. Hagrid, we're told, is largely immune to Stun spells because of his giant heritage. Presumably Grawp is even more so. Are there any non-fatal spells that can stop a giant?

Gregorovitch

Gender: Male
Hair color: White
Eye color: Unknown
Related Family: Unknown
Loyalty: Wandlore

OVERVIEW

Gregorovitch is a wand-maker, possibly equal in ability to Mr. Ollivander, who apparently set up shop in the northern part of Eastern Europe.

ROLE IN THE BOOKS

Goblet of Fire At the Weighing of the Wands ceremony, prior to the First Task of the Triwizard Tournament, Mr. Ollivander is called in to check that the Champions' wands are functioning correctly and up to full power. He recognizes Viktor Krum's wand instantly as a "Gregorovitch creation."

Deathly Hallows After his escape from Privet Drive, Harry Potter has "dreams" in which he shares some of Lord Voldemort's thoughts. Voldemort is looking for one Gregorovitch. Harry does not immediately remember this name, though it rings faint bells. It is at the wedding of Bill and Fleur, when a disguised Harry is talking to Viktor Krum, that he remembers that Krum's wand was made by Gregorovitch. Krum says that it was one of the last ones made by him, as he had retired.

Harry continues to have dreams about Voldemort's quest for Gregorovitch, including one in which Voldemort questions, and then kills, a woman who dares to say she doesn't know where he went. Finally, Voldemort reaches Gregorovitch, and questions him regarding some item which he supposedly had. Gregorovitch denies having had it, but Voldemort uses Legilimency to read Gregorovitch's memory of a blond thief who had stolen it from his workshop. We do not see the item that had been stolen. Harry, seeing this memory, believes it must be very small. Having retrieved this memory, Voldemort then kills Gregorovitch.

At the end of the book, it is revealed that the object that Gregorovitch had owned and which had been stolen from him was the Elder Wand or the Deathstick, a legendary wand that could not be defeated in a duel. Gregorovitch had spread the rumour that he owned this wand and was examining it to determine its secrets. The wand was stolen from him by Gellert Grindelwald.

Gregory Goyle

Gender: Male
Hair color: Dark, bristly, low on his forehead
Eye color: Unknown; dull, deep-set
Related Family: Goyle, Sr. (a Death Eater)
Loyalty: Draco Malfoy

OVERVIEW

Gregory Goyle is one of Draco Malfoy's cronies.

Gregory Goyle

ROLE IN THE BOOKS

Throughout the entire series, Gregory Goyle has very little independent activity. When we first see him, he has settled into the role of second sidekick to Draco Malfoy, and with very few exceptions, he seems to have no activity separate from Draco for six years of the seven-year span of the story.

Philosopher's Stone When Draco Malfoy introduces himself to Harry Potter on the Hogwarts Express, Goyle and Crabbe are in attendance. Harry turns Draco's offer of alliance down, so Draco "suggests" that Harry and Ron Weasley should share their food, which Harry has bought from the cart. Goyle reaches out for some, and is attacked by Scabbers, Ron's rat. Draco retreats in some confusion with Crabbe and Goyle.

It is mentioned that, when final grades were given out, Harry had hoped Goyle, "who was as almost as stupid as he was mean," would fail; but he apparently scraped through.

Chamber of Secrets When Harry needs a distraction in Potions class to allow Hermione to steal potions from Professor Snape's office, he chooses to throw his firecracker into Goyle's cauldron of Swelling Solution.

Draco, Crabbe, and Goyle stay at Hogwarts over Christmas. Harry, Ron, and Hermione, attempting to determine whether Draco knows who the Heir of Slytherin is, use Polyjuice Potion to disguise themselves as Slytherins. Harry becomes a simulacrum of Goyle, while Ron becomes a copy of Crabbe. While they do fool Draco, and learn some useful things about him, they only find out that he does not know who the Heir is, either.

Prisoner of Azkaban Draco, Crabbe, and Goyle visit Harry in his compartment on the Hogwarts Express, but are unable to take any action against Harry because of the presence of Professor Lupin.

In an attempt to scare Harry during the Quidditch match between Gryffindor and Ravenclaw, Draco, Crabbe, Goyle, and Marcus Flint dress as Dementors, but their scheme unravels when Harry sends a Patronus to charge them down.

Harry later visits Hogsmeade via the secret passages and the Invisibility cloak; while there with Ron, they run into Draco, Crabbe, and Goyle, who start taunting Ron, believing him to be alone. Harry, from the concealment of his cloak, starts attacking them, but in the process becomes partially visible. Harry then has to hurry back to the school in order to convince Professor Snape that he has not been out of the school.

It is mentioned that during the run-up to the final Quidditch match, between Gryffindor and Slytherin, Crabbe and Goyle repeatedly appear near Harry but end up slouching off, disappointed, when Harry proves too well protected for them to work any mischief on him.

Goblet of Fire When Harry and Draco end up at wands drawn outside Potions class, their spells collide and ricochet. Hermione is struck by Densaugeo, a spell that makes her upper teeth grow down past her chin, while Goyle is struck by Harry's Furnunculus jinx and breaks out in boils.

Order of the Phoenix On the Hogwarts Express, Ron, with his new Prefect powers, says that he is going to make Goyle write lines: " *I must not look like a baboon's bottom.*" Hermione says this is abuse of his powers, Ron says he is only getting Draco's buddies before Draco tries to get his.

Goyle's attempt to make the Draught of Peace in the first Potions class was dreadful; Hermione reports that when he had tried to put a sample in the flagon for grading, it had exploded and set his robes on fire.

When Professor Umbridge is examining the Care of Magical Creatures class taught by Professor Grubbly-Plank, she says to Goyle that she understands there have been injuries in that class. Goyle does not answer; instead, Malfoy says that he was slashed by a Hippogriff.

As the two Beaters on the Slytherin Quidditch team, Derrick and Bole, have left, Montague, the Captain, has had to find new ones. The two he has found are Crabbe and Goyle.

Deathly Hallows As he leads Harry, Ron, and Hermione into the school from the Hog's Head, Neville mentions that, as part of their Dark Arts course, students are now called upon to use the Cruciatus curse on students who get detention. Neville had gotten one of his injuries for refusing, but Crabbe and Goyle seemed to enjoy it, perhaps because it was the first class they had ever been at the top of.

When Draco, Crabbe, and Goyle corner Harry in the Room of Requirement, it seems to be Crabbe and Goyle who do most of the talking. Goyle explains that they can do "Diss-lusion charms," and that they had been waiting for Harry. When Crabbe sets Fiendfyre, Harry, Ron, and Hermione escape on brooms; Harry circles back to save Draco and Goyle, but Crabbe cannot be found.

Strengths Goyle's only real strength seems to be physical, coupled with enough low cunning to be able to align himself with one particular player and stay loyal to him. He has, in his somewhat slow way, decided that Draco is on the winning side, and has chosen to ally himself with Draco. This alliance remains strong, even when Draco requires him to take on the aspect of a girl three years his junior and stand about in the hall doing guard duty.

Weaknesses Goyle is basically incapable of independent thought; having allied himself to Draco, he receives all his instructions from Draco and seems to act only as Draco requires.

Relationships with Other Characters He is very good friends with Draco Malfoy and Vincent Crabbe. Inasmuch as he is able, he hates Harry, Ron, and Hermione, and as directed by Draco, makes it his business to try and destroy Harry.

ANALYSIS

Goyle, like Crabbe, is present only to fill the role of dumb sidekick. The usual "group of bad guys" in many works of fiction consists of a "brain" component, almost always one smart guy or a shrewd guy with a smart guy in the background, and a "brawn" component, one or several muscular goons who exists simply to follow the orders of the smart guy, so that the smart guy doesn't have to risk discovery or injury in order to get his dirty work done. Crabbe and Goyle are almost stereotypical brawn, while Draco is very much the brains of that particular operation.

Griphook

Gender: Probably male
Hair color: None
Eye color: Unknown
Related Family: Unknown
Loyalty: Goblins

OVERVIEW

Griphook is a goblin who worked at Gringotts Wizarding Bank.

ROLE IN THE BOOKS

Philosopher's Stone When Harry and Hagrid visit Gringotts to retrieve some money for Harry and the "you-know-what in vault seven hundred and thirteen" for Professor Dumbledore, it is Griphook who drives the cart that takes them down to the vaults. Griphook tells Harry that the deeper, high-security vaults will open only when stroked by a Gringotts goblin; anyone else trying it would simply get sucked through the door and would not be able to escape. He also says they check the vaults for that happening about once every ten years.

Deathly Hallows When Harry, Ron, and Hermione are moving from campsite to campsite through the English countryside, another group of refugees briefly and unknowingly camps beside them. This other group, comprised of Dirk Cresswell, Ted Tonks, Dean Thomas, and the goblins Griphook and Gornuk, reveals that a group of students at Hogwarts had tried to steal the sword of Gryffindor from the Headmaster's office. The students had been punished, and the sword had been transferred to a safe at Gringotts. The goblins also revealed that the sword in Gringotts was a fake, a very good fake but not Goblin-made.

Harry, Ron, and Hermione are later picked up by a gang of Snatchers. It turns out that they have already captured some members of Griphook's group, killing Ted Tonks, Dirk Cresswell, and Gornuk. Harry finds himself tied to a pole with Griphook and Dean Thomas. All of them are transported to Malfoy Manor together so that the Snatchers can turn Harry Potter in to Voldemort for the reward. Bellatrix Lestrange sees that they are carrying the sword of Gryffindor, and prevents the Malfoys from summoning Lord Voldemort. She sends Harry, Ron, Dean, and Griphook down to a basement room and locks them in; they find that Luna Lovegood and Mr. Ollivander are already there, and Luna is able to get them free of their bonds. Bellatrix tortures Hermione to get her to tell where she got the sword. Hermione manages to tell her that they found it in the woods, and that it's a copy. Bellatrix says that the goblin will be able to tell that; Harry tells Griphook that he has to tell Bellatrix that the sword is a fake. Griphook, brought before Bellatrix, corroborates Hermione's story, and Bellatrix, relieved, summons Voldemort. After a short battle in which Griphook takes no part, Harry and Ron Apparate away to Shell Cottage, Harry carrying Griphook and holding on to Dobby. Dobby, who has been hit by a knife thrown by Bellatrix, dies, and Harry digs a grave for him by hand. Griphook, though injured, takes a very keen interest in what Harry is doing, as he has never before seen a "wand-carrier" who seemed at all interested in the feelings of Goblins or house-elves. From Bellatrix's reaction at the sight of the Sword of Gryffindor, Harry has determined that she believes the true Sword is stored in the same place as something that is deeply valued by Voldemort, and guesses it to be the Cup of Helga Hufflepuff, which Voldemort has made into a Horcrux. Harry guesses this to be Bellatrix's vault at Gringotts, and discusses with Griphook how they might break into Gringotts, and what Griphook's price for helping them would be. Griphook is reluctant, as he does not want to be the agent of successful theft happening at Gringotts, but relents when Harry tells him that he is not doing this for wealth, but for a specific artifact which is crucial to their quest. They finally determine that Griphook will receive the sword of Gryffindor, which he believes belongs properly to the Goblins as it was originally made by them.

Riding on Harry's back under the Invisibility Cloak, Griphook provides guidance to Harry, Ron, and Hermione as they make their way into Gringotts, suborn one of the tellers, Bogrod by name, and have him take them to the deep vaults. There, they find that Bellatrix's treasure is protected by the Gemino and Flagrante curses, endlessly multiplying and becoming searing hot when touched. In their search for the Cup, they cannot help brushing against treasure, which starts spinning off worthless, burning-hot copies of itself. By the time Harry manages to locate and retrieve the Cup, the vault is waist-deep in burning gold and Griphook is completely buried. Harry pulls Griphook out of the pile of treasure, and has Bogrod re-open the vault door. As they spill out into the corridor, Griphook seizes the Sword of Gryffindor and runs to the approaching Goblin party, saying he's caught the thieves. Harry, Hermione, and Ron escape by climbing onto the back of the dragon protecting the vaults and flying out of the dungeons.

Hannah Abbott

Gender: Female
Hair color: Blonde pigtails
Eye color: Unknown
Related Family: Unknown
Loyalty: Dumbledore's Army

OVERVIEW

Hannah Abbott is a Hufflepuff student in Harry Potter's year, a pink-faced blonde girl who wears her hair in pigtails. She's sweet, kind and giggly.

ROLE IN THE BOOKS

Philosopher's Stone   Hannah Abbott is the first student called up to be Sorted; the Sorting Hat places her in Hufflepuff.

Chamber of Secrets   Hannah Abbott, here identified only as *Hannah*, is one of the group of Hufflepuffs discussing Justin Finch-Fletchley's decision to remain in hiding when Harry Potter is thought to be the Heir of Slytherin, in *The Duelling Club*.

Prisoner of Azkaban   At one point in their third year, Hannah was convinced that Sirius Black could turn into a flowering shrub, which in hindsight is less silly than it might sound at first.

Goblet of Fire   House loyalty had Hannah wearing a *Support Cedric Diggory!* badge early in the Triwizard Tournament. Despite occasional incidents like this, she and Ernie are on friendly terms with Harry, Ron, and Hermione.

Order of the Phoenix   Both Hannah and Ernie became prefects in August of Harry's fifth year.

Hannah is one of the students present at the initial meeting, in the Hog's Head, of the group that becomes Dumbledore's Army.

It is mentioned that Hannah Abbott, at Easter break some six weeks before the O.W.L. exams, is looking frantic and checking stacks of books out of the library.

Hannah had the unhappy distinction of being the first of Harry's year to crack under the strain of O.W.L. study, requiring a Calming Draught from Madam Pomfrey after she broke down crying in Herbology, saying she was too stupid to take her exams.

While Harry is taking his transfiguration O.W.L, Hannah somehow manages to turn her ferret into a flock of flamingos, postponing the exam for ten minutes.

Hannah is also one of the six members of Dumbledore's Army who see Draco Malfoy attempting to jinx Harry on the Hogwarts Express, and promptly return fire, leaving Draco, Crabbe, and Goyle looking like gigantic slugs squeezed into Hogwarts robes.

Half-Blood Prince   In this book, Hannah's mother is killed by a rumoured Death Eater, and she leaves the school for most of the term after being told this in a Herbology class.

Deathly Hallows   As Harry is on his way to the Room of Requirement, where he now believes Rowena Ravenclaw's lost diadem is hidden, he passes Fred Weasley, Lee Jordan, and Hannah Abbott guarding a hole behind a plinth where a statue had fallen. The statue had previously been masking one of the secret passages into Hogwarts. As the renewed battle rages, Harry from under the Invisibility Cloak, casts Shield spells in the path of Voldemort's curses. Voldemort's intended victims, Hannah and Seamus, run past and into the Great Hall.

Weaknesses   O.W.L. exams make her worry to no end

Relationships with Other Characters   She is most often seen in the company of Justin Finch-Fletchley and Ernie Macmillan.

In an interview given following the publication of the final book in the series, the author said that Abbot marries Neville Longbottom, and becomes the new landlady of the Leaky Cauldron.

Harper

Gender: Male
Hair color: Unknown
Eye color: Unknown
Related Family: Unknown
Loyalty:

OVERVIEW

Harper, a Slytherin one year younger than Harry, is a replacement Seeker on the house Quidditch team.

ROLE IN THE BOOKS

Half-Blood Prince   Ginny tells Harry that, as Draco Malfoy is too sick to play, they are going to put Harper in as Seeker in the Quidditch match between Gryffindor and Slytherin. Ginny says that Harper is in her year, and is an idiot.

Harry Potter

Gender: Male
Hair color: Black
Eye color: Green
Related Family: James Potter, Lily Potter
Loyalty: Ron Weasley, Hermione Granger, Albus Dumbledore

OVERVIEW

Harry James Potter is the primary character in the book series by J.K. Rowling. Both Harry's parents were magical. His father, James, was the only child of a pure-blood wizard family, while his mother, Lily, was muggle-born, meaning both her parents were non-magical. That makes Harry a "half-blood" wizard. When Harry was one year old, the evil Lord Voldemort murdered his parents. When he then attempted to kill baby Harry with an deadly curse, it rebounded, ripping

Voldemort's soul from his body while leaving the infant unscathed except for a lightning-bolt shaped scar on his forehead.

Harry spent the next ten years living with his neglectful relatives, the Dursleys. When he was 11, Rubeus Hagrid, the gamekeeper at the magical Hogwarts School of Witchcraft and Wizardry, delivered a letter of invitation to attend the school. Harry now spends much of the year at Hogwarts with his two best friends Ron Weasley and Hermione Granger. Each summer he returns to the Dursleys,' a time he cannot wait to end.

Harry's birthday, according to the author, is July 31, with internal evidence giving the year as 1980. This makes him almost a year younger than Hermione, and five months younger than Ron.

Role in the Books

Note: Harry Potter is the viewpoint character in this series, and thus is in almost every part of the action. A summary of his role in the books would, perforce, be a summary of the books. For a summary of Harry's role in the series, it is best to begin here and proceed onwards from that point. The sections below will provide the bare outline of his role.

Philosopher's Stone   We hear that Harry's parents have been murdered, and Harry is placed with his relatives, the Dursleys. In the process, we meet Albus Dumbledore, Minerva McGonagall, and Rubeus Hagrid, who are evidently capable of magic: Dumbledore quietly and without any fuss turns off the streetlights, McGonagall is a cat when she first appears on the scene and transforms herself into a woman, and the huge Hagrid arrives on a flying motorcycle. Though we don't see the intervening ten years, we meet Harry and his adoptive parents on the occasion of Harry's cousin Dudley Dursley's eleventh birthday. Here we see how Harry is treated with minimal care, and how Dudley is spoiled. We hear that odd things happen around Harry. And we see how he is punished for anything that goes wrong, even if he can't control it. Harry, though cruelly oppressed, seems to be making the best of things, even teasing Dudley at one point. When Harry starts getting letters addressed to him, though, it seems to result in a panic in the household; Harry's Uncle Vernon starts acting irrationally, eventually stranding them in a hut built on a rock in the middle of the ocean. It is here that Hagrid arrives, at seconds after midnight on Harry's birthday, with the letter that Vernon has been keeping from him and the announcement that Harry is a wizard.

The next day, Hagrid introduces Harry to the wizarding world lying somehow inside and under London, showing him the Wizarding shopping district of Diagon Alley. Harry buys his school supplies, and his wand, and Hagrid, as a birthday present, takes him to buy a pet, settling on an owl. Harry names the owl Hedwig, and she is is constant companion throughout much of the series.

A month later, Harry is dropped off by Vernon at King's Cross Station, and left to find Platform Nine and Three Quarters on his own. Luckily, he sees another Wizarding family with the same destination, and tags along with them; this introduces him to the Weasley family, and his traveling companion, Ron Weasley, becomes his true friend. Harry's first year at Hogwarts is eventful. The Sorting Hat wants to place him in Slytherin, but Harry asks to be put in Gryffindor, one of four school Houses. He joins the Gryffindor Quidditch team as the youngest Seeker in over a century. When a mountain troll appears in the dungeons, Harry and Ron together defeat it, thus saving Hermione Granger's life; as a result of that, she also becomes a friend, and the Trio, as they have been called, are together for the rest of the series.

Harry is also guided by Professor Dumbledore, who turns out to be Hogwarts' Headmaster, and by the severe but fair Professor McGonagall, the transfiguration instructor and the Head of Gryffindor. Not everyone supports Harry, however. Potions Master Severus Snape takes an instant dislike to him, and Harry quickly becomes enemies with Draco Malfoy, a student from Slytherin House, after Draco denigrates Muggle-borns and insults the Weasleys, a pure-blooded wizard family the Malfoys consider inferior.

While this book serves mainly as an introduction to the magical world and the characters, there is a real quest involved. In Diagon Alley, Hagrid has taken a small "something" from a vault at Gringotts to bring it back to Hogwarts for safekeeping. Harry becomes convinced that one of the teachers, Professor Snape, is seeking this object, which he determines to be the Philosopher's Stone (known as the Sorceror's Stone in the U.S. editions). Apparently, the evil wizard who murdered Harry's parents, Lord Voldemort, had been killed when he attempted to murder Harry, but due to some advanced Dark magic, was possibly able to return, possibly with the aid of the Philosopher's Stone. It appears that Snape is trying to aid in that return, but is being blocked by Professor Quirrell. With help from Ron and Hermione, Harry manages to foil Lord Voldemort's plan to steal the Stone.

Chamber of Secrets   Harry's hopes of continuing friendship seem to be in vain by the middle of the summer when, on his birthday, he notices that he has not received any letters from Ron, Hermione, or Hagrid.

Sent to his room that evening, Harry is astounded to find an odd creature visiting him. Introducing himself as Dobby, a house-elf, this being seems adamant that he should not return to Hogwarts. Dobby does reveal that he has been intercepting Harry's letters, and then performs a Hover Charm in the Dursley's kitchen. As a result, Harry's Uncle Vernon loses the deal he has been angling for, and learns that Harry is not supposed to do magic. He locks Harry in his bedroom and bars the window.

Shortly, Ron and the Twins arrive in a flying Ford Anglia to rescue Harry. Returning to the Weasley family home, the Twins and Ron are strongly chastised by Mrs. Weasley, and set a punishment for having used their fathers' car without permission. Harry is welcomed into the Weasley family with open arms.

When time comes to buy books for school, Harry ends up in a Dark Magic store, Borgin and Burkes, where he overhears a conversation between Borgin and

Draco Malfoy's father, Lucius. Rescued from Knockturn Alley by Hagrid, Harry rejoins the Weasley family. Shortly, when they go to buy books, Harry is embarrassed by Gilderoy Lockhart, who uses Harry's presence to publicize his own appointment as Defence Against the Dark Arts teacher. Also in the book store, a fight breaks out between Lucius Malfoy and Mr. Weasley. The next day, all of the Weasleys drive to the station to meet the Hogwarts Express. Unable to get through the barrier, Ron and Harry take the car to Hogwarts, where they receive detention for their mode of arrival. Many of the teachers, notably Snape and Lockhart, feel that this was simply Harry's attempt to enhance his own fame. Lockhart, as a teacher, proves to be full of himself, and apparently unable to do the simplest thing that he claims to be able to do. Having failed to control Cornish Pixies in his first lesson, he has reverted to re-enacting scenes from his many self-laudatory books, usually using Harry as the victim. He also specifically requests that Harry serve a detention with him, answering his fan mail. It is while Harry is serving detention that he first hears the disembodied voice that will appear repeatedly through this book.

Returning from Nearly Headless Nick's Deathday party in company with Ron and Hermione, Harry hears the voice again; following it upwards, he finds writing on the wall, "*The Chamber of Secrets has been opened. Enemies of the Heir, Beware.*" He also finds Argus Filch's cat, Mrs. Norris, hung on a torch bracket.

Professor Dumbledore determines that Mrs. Norris has been Petrified, rather than killed, and dismisses Harry, Ron, and Hermione, much to Filch's displeasure; Filch wants someone punished. The writing on the wall, though, starts endless speculation within the school: what is the Chamber of Secrets? Who is the Heir? Hermione manages to convince Professor Binns to tell the History of Magic class that the Chamber was apparently created, and hidden, by Salazar Slytherin when he left the school over a feud with the other Founders, over a thousand years before. Nobody has found it since. However, there is beginning to be speculation that Harry is the Heir of Slytherin. Harry, of course, suspects Draco Malfoy. Hermione has heard of something called Polyjuice Potion, which could help them sneak into Slytherin and see if it is Draco; Harry helps her secure the necessary teacher's permission slip for the book containing that potion recipe.

Playing Quidditch against Slytherin, Harry becomes the target of a Bludger that is charmed to attack him. Though he does catch the Snitch, it breaks his arm, and due to Lockhart removing all the bones from his arm, Harry must spend the night in the Hospital Wing. There, Dobby comes to visit him, and admits having locked the barrier to try to prevent Harry's going to Hogwarts; and further, says that he had charmed the Bludger to chase Harry in hopes that it would injure him enough to send him home. He then escapes Harry's grip, vanishing as Colin Creevey, also Petrified, is brought into the Hospital Wing. Dumbledore, checking to see if Colin has caught an image of the monster on his camera, finds the film in the camera burned beyond usefulness, and says this confirms it: the Chamber has been opened. McGonagall wonders who has re-opened the Chamber; Dumbledore, instead, wonders how.

After Harry's recovery, he visits the disused bathroom inhabited by Moaning Myrtle, a particularly gloomy ghost. It is here that Hermione has set up to make the Polyjuice Potion. She says that there are ingredients she will need, that will have to be retrieved from Snape's private stores. Harry tosses a firework into Gregory Goyle's cauldron in Potions class as a diversion, and Hermione sneaks into Snape's office to retrieve what she needs. Shortly after this, Lockhart announces a Dueling Club. Harry and Draco are given the chance to demonstrate, and Draco fires a snake at Harry. Lockhart volunteers to remove it, but his spell is ineffectual, and the snake turns to attack Justin Finch-Fletchley. Harry orders the snake to leave Justin alone, and the snake, surprisingly, does. Ron and Hermione take Harry aside and ask how he learned to talk to snakes. They tell him that the ability is very rare, and is linked to descendants of Slytherin. Harry begins to wonder if he is the Heir. Justin seems to believe that Harry was egging the snake on, so Harry determines to find him and explain what had happened. While searching, he stumbles over Justin, Petrified, and an injured and immobile Nearly Headless Nick. Peeves, happening by, sounds the alarm, and McGonagall takes Harry to Dumbledore's office.

Here, Harry meets Fawkes, Dumbledore's pet phoenix, and learns the characteristics of this bird. Dumbledore accepts that Harry has nothing to do with the Petrifications, and asks if he has anything else he'd like to talk about; Harry, worried that the disembodied voices he's hearing may be a sign of madness, says nothing. By means of the Polyjuice Potion, Harry and Ron manage to get into the Slytherin common room and talk to Draco, however Draco also has no idea who the Heir is. Hermione, meanwhile, has been half-way transformed into a cat, and as the effect does not wear off, she must go to the Hospital Wing. It is while she is there, that Harry and Ron find T. Riddle's diary, which turns out to be blank. Some time later, due to an accident, Harry discovers that the diary absorbs ink without trace, and wondering what happens if he writes in it, discovers that it will write back. Tom Riddle, by means of the diary, shows him the events of some fifty years before, when the Chamber had last been opened, and shows Riddle catching Hagrid as a third-year student with what is believed to be the Monster. Shortly afterwards, Harry's room is ransacked, and the diary is taken. The next day, Harry hears the disembodied voice again, and two more students are petrified: a Prefect, Penelope Clearwater, and Hermione. Hagrid is arrested and taken to Azkaban, on suspicion of having opened the Chamber, and Dumbledore is suspended as Headmaster, supposedly on the grounds that he is proving ineffective at stopping the attacks. As Hagrid leaves, he tells Harry and Ron that they should follow the spiders.

Following the spiders, Harry and Ron meet Aragog, the beast who Hagrid had been keeping in the school fifty years before. Aragog tells them that he had never been near the bathroom where the girl was killed. Harry and Ron are then rescued from the spiders by the flying car, now turned feral. Harry concludes that Moaning Myrtle was the girl killed when the chamber was opened, but before he and Ron can ask her, they visit Hermione in the Hospital Wing. Hermione has torn a page describing Basilisks out of a book, and it is caught in her hand; Harry and Ron determine that the Monster is a Basilisk.

Before they can tell Professor McGonagall what they have learned, Ginny Weasley is taken into the Chamber, and Gilderoy Lockhart is sent after her. Thwarting Lockhart's attempt to escape, Harry and Ron take him into the Chamber of Secrets; Harry, separated from the others by a rock fall, finds Ginny and the nearly re-animated Tom Riddle, who tells Harry that because of his hatred for his Muggle father, he had taken a new name: Lord Voldemort. Releasing the Basilisk, he sends it to kill Harry; Harry, pleading for help, manages to summon Fawkes, bearing the Sorting Hat. Fawkes destroys the Basilisk's eyes, and the Hat provides Harry with a sword. Harry kills the Basilisk, but takes an envenomed wound himself. Fawkes' tears heal the wound, and before Tom can cast a killing spell at Harry, Harry destroys the diary with a Basilisk fang. Fawkes then bears Harry, Ron, Ginny, and Lockhart back to the school.

Prisoner of Azkaban The story unfolds with a much darker mood. When Sirius Black escapes Azkaban prison with the seeming purpose to kill Harry Potter, Harry learns about his parents' past and the circumstances surrounding their demise; Black, his godfather, betrayed James and Lily to Voldemort and murdered their friend, Peter Pettigrew. Harry vows revenge. However, Pettigrew is actually alive (disguised as Ron's pet rat, Scabbers), and it was he who revealed the Potters' secret location to Lord Voldemort, who then killed them and attacked Harry. After learning the truth, Harry bonds with his new-found godfather and eagerly looks forwards to living with him rather than the Dursleys. But when Pettigrew, and the truth, slip free, Sirius remains convicted. With Harry and Hermione's help, Black escapes—a hunted fugitive once again.

Goblet of Fire Harry is mysteriously chosen as a second Hogwarts Champion in an inter-school competition, the Tri-Wizard Tournament, even though he is underage and never entered his name into the *Goblet of Fire*. In addition to competing in the grueling contest, Harry is scorned by his fellow students, including Ron, who believe he cheated to enter, although he and Ron eventually reconcile.

During the final challenge, Harry and fellow Champion, Cedric Diggory, are transported to a graveyard where Peter Pettigrew (Wormtail) instantly kills Cedric. Harry witnesses Lord Voldemort's rebirth in a ritual using a small amount of his blood that nullifies the protective Charm that has safeguarded him from Voldemort. The resurrected Dark Lord engages Harry in a deadly wizards' duel, but Harry escapes to Hogwarts with Cedric's body and announces Voldemort's return. Alastor "Mad Eye" Moody, the new Defense Against the Dark Arts teacher, nearly kills Harry, but he is saved by Dumbledore, Snape, and McGonagall. "Moody" is actually Barty Crouch, Jr., the Dark Lord's faithful servant, who, disguised as "Mad Eye," rigged the Tournamnet to ensure Harry reached the cemetery. The real Alastor Moody is rescued from a trunk with a secret compartment.

Order of the Phoenix The darkest year Harry has experienced in the magical world so far. After being attacked by Dementors near the Dursleys' home, he is secretly escorted to 12 Grimmauld Place, the new headquarters for the "Order of the Phoenix," a resistance movement against Voldemort. An angry Harry is given little information about Voldemort or the Order's plans, and he has difficulty remaining quiet about the Dark Lord's return. Ron and Hermione tell him that the Ministry of Magic has been waging a smear campaign against him and Dumbledore, refuting their claims that Voldemort has returned. Consequently, many in the wizarding doubt Voldemort's resurrection. Ministry of Magic spy, Dolores Umbridge, is appointed as Hogwarts' new Defence Against the Dark Teacher, and later High Inquisitor. Umbridge works hard to keep Hogwarts and the magical world from believing Voldemort's return, and her repressive tactics cause students, particularly Harry, to become rebellious. The Weasley twins instigate an outright revolt before departing on their broomsticks, leaving Hogwarts for good. The teachers do little, if anything, to help Umbridge regain order.

In a climatic battle at the Ministry of Magic, Harry witnesses his godfather, Sirius Black's, murder, and he confronts Voldemort once again; this time, Minister of Magic Cornelius Fudge arrives in time to see Voldemort before he escapes, and Fudge is forced to publicly acknowledge the Dark Lord's return. Harry learns more about how he and Voldemort are connected.

Half-Blood Prince Harry learns his place in the war against the Dark Lord. He and Dumbledore uncover Voldemort's past by viewing gathered memories stored in a Pensieve. It is learned that Voldemort split his soul into seven pieces called Horcruxes and hid six in various objects. Two have been destroyed, and possibly a third. At the book's conclusion, Harry battles the Death Eaters (Voldemort's followers) inside Hogwarts castle and suffers a terrible personal loss. Vowing to find and destroy Voldemort and his four remaining Horcruxes, Harry does not intend to return to Hogwarts for his seventh, and final, year. Ron and Hermione pledge to accompany him on his quest.

Strengths Aside from his strong magical skills, Harry is extremely brave, and will do almost anything to protect his friends. Throughout the series he is put into many stressful and dangerous situations, keeping a clear head throughout. Harry has a strong sense of good and evil, and he stands up for what he believes to be right.

A commonly discussed strength, particularly by Albus Dumbledore, is Harry's ability to love. Harry is extremely pure of heart.

He is also skilled at flying, particularly on a broomstick, although he also seems to have little trouble flying on the backs of magical creatures such as Hippogriffs and Thestrals. This flying skill translates into a gift for Quidditch, which makes him the youngest Seeker at Hogwarts in a century. During the First Task of the Triwizard Tournament, his flying ability is compared favourably to that of Viktor Krum, then considered the world's best Seeker.

Weaknesses Harry often "wears his heart on his sleeve." On many occasions he is unable to hide or control his emotions, especially anger and rage. Among other things, this will make it impossible for him to master Occlumency. He also feels the need to be *the hero*, a trait that makes him predictable and which Voldemort exploits to lure him into an ambush at the Ministry of Magic. Although he is intelligent and a powerful wizard-in-training, academically he is a somewhat lazy student and usually receives slightly above average marks in his studies, except Defense Against the Dark Arts in which he excels. His Potions ability is apparently better than it appears, as he is able to achieve an Exceeds Expectations grade on his O.W.L. exam; and improves greatly during his sixth year when he comes into possession of an old potions textbook in which a talented former student (later found to be Severus Snape) has revised many potion-making techniques.

Relationships with Other Characters Harry attends school along with several friends he has met along the way, namely his two closest companions Ron Weasley and Hermione Granger. At school, Harry must also interact with members from other houses such as Draco Malfoy whom he despises. There is a blooming love affair with Cho Chang, which ends with some coolness but not much acrimony. Later, he falls in love with Ginny Weasley. Sometime after the defeat of Lord Voldemort, Harry and Ginny marry. The couple has three children: James Sirius, Albus Severus, and Lily Luna.

Analysis

Because the books are mostly told from Harry's perspective, more is known about him than any other character. At best, the Dursleys treatment of him was neglectful. Between his Uncle Vernon, Aunt Petunia and cousin Dudley, Harry developed a rather low sense of self-worth, although he survived the experience in good humor. When Hagrid told Harry he was a wizard, he thought many times that it must have been a mistake.

From the beginning, Harry distrusts his fame and avoids publicity, though later in the series he does make use of that fame, unwelcome as it is, to try to achieve his ends. Since Harry tends to suffer more traumatic events than most, he often feels misunderstood. He is often approached by other students at Hogwarts asking him about his experiences, dying to know exciting details, but they are usually uninterested in the reasoning behind it. Throughout later books, Harry grows irritable over being constantly prodded for answers about Lord Voldemort and what may happen to the wizarding world. Harry's fourth and fifth years at Hogwarts test his patience but also strengthen his bonds with Ron and Hermione and Headmaster Dumbledore.

It has been noted a number of times that Harry looks exactly like his father, except for the eyes. He has his mother's eyes. The author has stated that this fact is important;[1] it convinced Horace Slughorn to give Harry the memory he needed in *Harry Potter and the Half-Blood Prince*. There are indications in other places[2] that there is more that is revealed in the later books. In fact, it plays an important role at one point in the plot of *Harry Potter and the Deathly Hallows*.

Questions

1. What kind of person does Harry normally consider his friend? His enemy?
2. Does Harry understand the true meaning of Dumbledore's role in the Order of the Phoenix and the war against Lord Voldemort?
3. How does Harry change after Lord Voldemort's return is announced to the wizarding public and is no longer a questionable issue?

Greater Picture

Since the return of Lord Voldemort, Harry has been quite confused on where he is headed in life. No matter where he goes, he seems to be greeted by some aspect of the Dark Lord and the war raging on throughout the magical world. Harry's life has been filled with quite a large amount of tragedy and death, especially in his fifth and sixth years at Hogwarts. Harry has lost friends, mentors, and relatives, all in the confusion of the wizarding war. In many cases, Harry is unsure what to do or where to go.

At the end of his sixth year, Harry comes to many conclusions about his future. He knows he must finish things he so innocently started with Lord Voldemort many years ago. He knows he must solve many of the mysteries regarding Voldemort's power. He knows either he or Voldemort must defeat the other, just as the prophecy foretold. Harry is truly on a mission now, much more important than his previous years' accomplishments. As his school years come to a close, if he even returns to school for his seventh year, Harry will hopefully provide an answer to the question of how strong "The Boy Who Lived" truly is.

According to the author, at age 17 Harry becomes an Auror under Kingsley Shacklebolt, and then becomes head of the Auror department in 2007. Note that if Harry did become an Auror in 1997, it must have been

---

1. http://www.accio-quote.org/articles/1999/1099-bostonglobe-loer.html
2. http://www.accio-quote.org/articles/2000/0700-cbbc-mzimba.htm

within two months of when Voldemort died; therefore, Harry can have had at most two months of school before entering specialized Auror training. Along with his other accomplishments, this may make Harry the first Auror in centuries to have been accepted without taking (and passing) N.E.W.T.s.

Similarities between Harry and Tom Riddle When reading all seven books, one comes to notice the frighteningly similar lives and experiences of Harry and Tom:

• Both were "abandoned" at a very young age, both were too young to properly remember their parents.

• Tom, the future Lord Voldemort, never met his mother. He did in fact meet his father, but only sought him out for revenge's sake and killed him. While Harry vaguely remembers both his parents, he was too young when they were killed to remember them properly. However, he has been able to feel some kind of contact with them through things that were his father's (the Invisibility Cloak and the Marauder's Map) and his parents' friends.

• Both boys wore second-hand clothes: Harry was given his repulsive cousin Dudley's enormous old clothes, and Tom wore old rags from the orphanage.

• Both were friendless, Harry because his cousin wouldn't allow Harry any peace or happiness, and Tom because he liked to torment the other orphans.

• Both are parselmouths (they can speak to snakes). This is less of a similarity than it might seem, for we believe that Voldemort actually transferred this ability to Harry when attacking him.

• The Sorting Hat almost put Harry into Slytherin, although it was Harry's choice to go to Gryffindor.

• Both boys had followers, Tom because of fear and intimidation, and Harry for curiosity and loyalty.

• They also, as shown in Book One, have brother wands, each wand containing a tail feather from the same phoenix. It is later revealed that the phoenix is Fawkes, who happens to be Dumbledore's pet.

• Both boys were unaware they were wizards until about the age of eleven, even though they had each made unusual things happen.

• Both Harry and Tom were of great interest to Dumbledore, and both felt their first home was Hogwarts.

• Both achieved greatness in the Defense Against the Dark Arts, however, each for different reasons.

• Neither had any brothers or sisters.

• Both are half-bloods, though that only seems to matter to Tom.

• Both are rule breakers. Harry, of course, feels he has reason to do things like leave his dorm after lights out, enter the Forbidden Forest, and eavesdrop on teachers, and as it turns out he is largely correct. Tom was likely doing much the same sort of thing, though without benefit of Harry's invisibility cloak; and eventually deliberately framed Hagrid for a crime he did not commit. Tom, of course, went on to worse crimes.

There are also differences:

• At his initial Sorting, Harry asked not to be put in Slytherin, and so ended up in Gryffindor. It is unlikely that Tom Riddle would have made a similar choice, even not knowing of his ancestry.

• Voldemort continues to not have friends, only followers. Harry has made a number of friends: his dorm mates, the Weasley family, and many of the teachers including especially Remus Lupin.

• While both were nominally half-blood, Harry's mother was Muggle-born, whereas Lord Voldemort's *father* was a Muggle, and incidentally so was Snape's, the Half-Blood Prince.

• Harry cares about the people around him, even pitying Malfoy by the end of Book Six. Harry has the ability to love and to be compassionate, which makes it easier to feel pain, but to also experience the bonds of brotherhood that will take him to the greatness he deserves.

Hedwig

Gender: Female
Hair color: None (white feathers)
Eye color: Yellow
Related Family: Unknown
Loyalty: Harry Potter

Overview

Hedwig is the name of Harry's owl. Since mail is delivered by owls in the wizarding world, she plays a valuable role in Harry's life. She is one of Harry's companions.

Role in the Books

Philosopher's Stone Harry is allowed to bring a toad *or* a cat *or* an owl to school, according to the booklist. Hagrid, who is guiding him through Diagon Alley, decides to buy Harry an animal as a birthday present. Toads, he says, are old-fashioned and would get him laughed at, and he doesn't like cats, so he tales Harry to Eeylops Owl Emporium and buys him a snowy owl. Back at the Dursleys' home, Harry decides to name his owl Hedwig, a name he had found in his History of Magic text.

During the first week of school, Hedwig occasionally flies in with the post owls at breakfast, to nibble affectionately at Harry's ear and get a bit of toast before going off to sleep in the Owlery. On Friday, she brings a note from Hagrid, inviting Harry to tea after class. Harry immediately sends a response back saying he'd be glad to. When Harry, Ron, and Hermione plan to get Charlie Weasley to take Hagrid's pet dragon, Norbert, to Romania to release it back into the wild, it is Hedwig who brings Charlie's response back to the Trio. From this we can assume that it was Hedwig who carried the request to Charlie.

In the chamber with the logic puzzle, Harry instructs Hermione to return to the Owlery and send Hedwig with a message for Dumbledore. It turns out that Ron and Hermione never get that far, meeting with Dumbledore in the Entrance Hall.

Order of the Phoenix After the Dementor attack at Little Whinging, Harry writes letters to Sirius Black, Ron, and Hermione, demanding an explanation. Hedwig is out hunting; when she returns with a frog she has caught, Harry immediately sends her away with the letters, and instructions to peck at the recipients until they have written good long letters to send back to him. She leaves immediately, still clutching her frog, and Harry regrets having sent her away, as she is the only sympathetic person at Privet Drive. He expects her prompt return, but she does not reappear. Hedwig flies down from her perch on top of a wardrobe and lands on Harry's shoulder when Harry arrives at Number 12, Grimmauld Place, where she had stayed after delivering the messages Harry had given her. Harry is very glad to see her, and keeps stroking her even while speaking angrily to Ron and Hermione, who both show signs of Hedwig having pecked them. When Harry gets too angry, Hedwig retreats, reproachfully, to the top of the wardrobe.

After the meeting that evening, Hedwig and Pigwidgeon are clattering around on top of the wardrobe. Ron throws some Owl Treats up there for them, explaining that Dumbledore doesn't want them out hunting too often, it would raise questions.

On the last day before the start of classes, Harry climbs on a chair to clean all the owl droppings off the top of the wardrobe. Finishing, he tosses the accumulated owl droppings into a wastebasket, which swallows them and belches loudly. During the conversation that follows, the wastebasket occasionally makes soft gagging noises as it coughs up the owl droppings. Hermione borrows Hedwig at this point to send her parents the news that she has been made a Prefect.

Hedwig returns just before everyone leaves for the Hogwarts Express, and obligingly flutters off Hermione's shoulder and over to her cage as Harry finishes packing. At an angry call from Mrs. Weasley downstairs, Harry stuffs her unceremoniously in her cage and carries her and his trunk downstairs.

Harry travels to King's Cross Station with a number of members of the Order, and does not see Hedwig again until Mad-Eye Moody, in porter's uniform, brings her and all the luggage to Platform Nine and Three Quarters. Once on the Hogwarts Express, Hedwig stays in the compartment with Harry, and is disturbed by Luna Lovegood's screams of laughter when Ron jokes about the lines he plans to give to Goyle.

When Harry's scar pains him at the end of his fourth detention with Professor Umbridge, Harry writes a coded letter to Sirius to ask for advice. He carefully tells Hedwig that although the letter is addressed to Snuffles, it is really for Sirius. Hedwig blinks, which Harry takes to be understanding, and flies off from the Owlery. The day after the initial meeting of what becomes Dumbledore's Army in the Hog's Head, a bedraggled Hedwig appears at the window of Harry's History of Magic class. Harry lets her in, then, finding her injured, asks Professor Binns for permission to go to the Hospital Wing as he doesn't feel well. Getting grudging permission, he instead goes to the staff room, where he finds Professor McGonagall. Hearing that Harry has an injured owl, Professor Grubbly-Plank also comes to the door, and she in turn takes Hedwig, saying she'll get Hedwig all fixed up. McGonagall reminds Harry of the message on Hedwig's leg, then quietly warns him that all communications in and out of the school are monitored. Hedwig, meanwhile, seems to feel that Harry is abandoning her. The message on Hedwig's leg proves to be from Sirius, and reads simply *"Tonight, same time, same place."* When Sirius is nearly caught in the Gryffindor common-room fire by Umbridge, Hermione guesses that it was on Umbridge's order that Hedwig had been intercepted.

Hedwig, with her injuries healed, is brought back to the Gryffindor common room and returned to Harry by Dobby. It is then that Dobby tells Harry how to find the Room of Requirement.

Hedwig and Pigwidgeon are then not seen again until the trip back to London on the Hogwarts Express. It is noted that Hedwig and Pigwidgeon are disturbed by Ron's outburst when he learns that Ginny is going out with Dean.

Deathly Hallows Hedwig, when we first see her, is sulking, either asleep or pretending. Harry knows that it is because she has been allowed so little time outside her cage in the past short while. When Harry pushes a couple of owl nuts through the cage bars to her, she ignores them. She remains unmoving while Harry, possibly in jest, shows her the places around the house at Privet Drive that hold memories for him.

Climbing into the sidecar of Sirius' flying motorcycle, Harry finds very little room for himself and even the few possessions he is taking with him. He ends up with his rucksack tucked uncomfortably under his feet, and Hedwig, in her cage, on his knees.

Trying to avoid the first strike of the Death Eaters, Hagrid turns the motorcycle so sharply that it turns upside down; Harry has to grab for Hedwig's cage and the rucksack, and watches his Firebolt fall to earth. Green flashes fly past, and Hedwig falls dead to the bottom of her cage. When the sidecar breaks free of the motorcycle, Harry manages to keep it in the air while Hagrid loops around to pick him up, but Harry can only take his rucksack. To disable one of the following Death Eaters, Harry destroys the sidecar, feeling a dreadful pang of regret for Hedwig as he does so.

As they wait for the Portkey to activate to take them to The Burrow from the house of Tonks' parents Ted and Andromeda, Hagrid asks Harry about Hedwig, and is shocked to hear that she has been killed. In the Forest of Dean, Harry hears an owl hoot and is reminded of Hedwig.

Strengths Hedwig is exceptionally intelligent for an owl, being able to follow more complex instructions such as to "keep pecking them until they've written decent-length answers," and to send packages addressed to "Snuffles" to Sirius. She also fought to get away from Umbridge, despite being wounded, although Umbridge managed to get the letter, suggesting that she is capable of loyalty and other "human" emotions.

Weaknesses Hedwig is a snowy owl, very beautiful but easily seen and recognized. Snowy owls are not native to Britain and Hedwig was known to belong to Harry. Therefore, Harry could not use Hedwig to deliver messages when security and anonymity were required. Hedwig was easily offended and sulked when Harry used other owls for messages to Sirius.

Hedwig was a headstrong and proud owl who displayed an exaggerated sense of propriety. Hedwig disapproved of the undignified enthusiasm of Ron's owl Pigwidgeon.

Relationships with Other Characters Hedwig is very loyal to Harry Potter. During Harry's summer breaks at the Dursleys,' Hedwig is often Harry's only companion and link to the Magical World. For Harry's sake, particularly in the early years, Hedwig puts up with quite a bit of discomfort and deprivation through the summer months at Privet Drive.

When Harry had loaned Hedwig to others, Hedwig seemed to accept the situation easily. For instance, when he loaned her to Hermione so that she could pass the news of her becoming a Prefect to her family, Hedwig quite cheerfully rode her shoulder while the message was being prepared, then returned to Hermione until Hermione brought her back to Harry.

Hedwig seemed sympathetic to the plight of Errol, the Weasley family's geriatric owl, at one point allowing Errol to share her perch, water, and food, and on another occasion actually helping Errol carry a package to Harry. Towards the over-exuberant Pigwidgeon, however, she seemed to show much more disdain, and went to great lengths to demonstrate how a post owl ought to behave.

ANALYSIS

J.K. Rowling, in interviews, described the death of Hedwig as the end of Harry's innocence. Hedwig died four days before Harry came of age at 17 years old.

GREATER PICTURE

Harry found the name "Hedwig" in his textbook *A History of Magic*. In Muggle history there is a Saint Hedwig, who was the Duchess of Silesia and was canonized in 1267. The Sisters of St. Hedwig was founded in 1859 and are dedicated to the education of orphaned and abandoned children, children not unlike Harry.

Helga Hufflepuff

Gender: Female
Hair color: Red
Eye color: Brown
Related Family: Unknown
Loyalty: Best friends with Rowena Ravenclaw

OVERVIEW

Helga Hufflepuff was one of the four founders of Hogwarts and the creator of Hufflepuff House. She would teach any student that the other three would not, though the Sorting Hat mentions that Hufflepuffs are generally loyal, and Hufflepuffs have come to be known as the most equitable witches and wizards. She was wizard of the month for May, 2007 on J. K. Rowling's official website. Rowling's Wizard of the Month feature gives the text on a particular wizard's Famous Wizard card, which was also written by Rowling. Hufflepuff's card reads: "*One of the four celebrated Founders of Hogwarts, Hufflepuff was particularly famous for her dexterity at food-related Charms. Many recipes traditionally served at Hogwarts feasts originated with Hufflepuff.*"

ROLE IN THE BOOKS

Deathly Hallows She does not have a direct effect on this story but her cup is central to the storyline, as Lord Voldemort used it to create a Horcrux that Harry Potter needs to destroy.

Hepzibah Smith

Gender: Female
Hair color: Unknown (hidden under a ginger wig)
Eye color: Unknown
Related Family: Unknown
Loyalty:

OVERVIEW

Hepzibah Smith is a very old witch, still vain and convinced of her own beauty, who shows some valuable artifacts to a young Tom Riddle.

ROLE IN THE BOOKS

Half-Blood Prince In the memories of the house-elf Hokey, we see Hepzibah primping herself in preparation of a visit by Tom Riddle. Tom, acting as a buyer for Borgin and Burkes, is there to make an offer on some Goblin-made armour, but Hepzibah, charmed by him, shows him her two fondest possessions, a cup originally owned by Helga Hufflepuff, from whom she claims distant descent, and a locket owned by Salazar Slytherin. Tom recognizes the locket as being the one that his mother had sold to try and support herself. Shortly afterwards, Hepzibah Smith dies, apparently mistakenly poisoned by Hokey.

Hermes

Gender: Unknown
Hair color: Unknown
Eye color: Unknown
Related Family: Unknown
Loyalty:

OVERVIEW

Hermes is Percy Weasley's owl. Percy received Hermes as a gift in his fifth year (Harry's first year) for being made a prefect.

ROLE IN THE BOOKS

Philosopher's Stone Hermes is mentioned in passing, as Ron mentions that he has to put up with Errol, who has gotten rather old.

Chamber of Secrets When Harry is staying at the Burrow just before school starts, Ron mentions that he had wanted to borrow Hermes to send some messages, but that Percy, who was staying shut up in his room all summer, would not loan him.

At the end of the book, we learn that Percy has been sending messages back and forth to Penelope Clearwater, his girlfriend, and that is why Hermes had been busy.

Order of the Phoenix Hermes appears at the window of the Gryffindor common room late at night on the Saturday of the first week of school. He is carrying a letter from Percy directed at Ron, which Percy had wanted delivered separately from the regular mail. Hermes leaves immediately, not waiting for a reply. The letter, full of the sort of pontification that Percy is known for, only makes Ron angry, though Harry and Hermione find it rather amusing, particlarly the parts where Percy warns Ron that Harry may be mentally unstable.

Hermione Granger

Gender: Female
Hair color: Brown
Eye color: Brown
Related Family: Muggles
Loyalty: Harry Potter, Ron Weasley, Albus Dumbledore

Overview

Hermione Jean Granger is the magical daughter of two Muggle dentists. Hermione is especially interested in academics and much of her time during the school year is spent studying, doing homework, or other things related to her classes at the Hogwarts School of Witchcraft and Wizardry. Hermione often serves as the voice of reason when her two best friends Harry Potter and Ron Weasley get themselves into interesting or dangerous situations. Although seemingly stressed at all times due to schooling, Hermione is dependable when called upon, and is extremely adept at getting things done correctly and efficiently.

Hermione has a bossy sort of voice, bushy brown hair, and rather large front teeth, which she later has magically shrunk. Her birthday is September 19th.[1] She was eleven years old at the start of *Harry Potter and the Philosopher's Stone*, turning twelve shortly thereafter, and thus is almost a year older than Harry, and six months older than Ron; internal evidence suggests she was born in 1979.

Role in the Books

Note: Hermione Granger, while not the viewpoint character in this series, is one of the Trio, and thus is in almost every part of the action. A summary of her role in the books would, perforce, be a summary of the books. For a summary of Hermione's role in the series, it is best to begin here and proceed onwards from that point. The sections below will provide the bare outline of her role.

Philosopher's Stone Hermione is introduced to us as a bossy know-it-all who looks into Harry and Ron's compartment on the Hogwarts Express. She seems disdainful of Ron's attempt to use magic, and says she's already read all the textbooks. Later she informs them that they should get their robes on as they will be arriving at the school shortly. Ron expresses the hope that she will be Sorted into some other house at the school, but she ends up in Gryffindor with Ron and Harry.

Hermione continues in the same manner, being the first to levitate her feather in Charms class. When a mountain troll appears in the dungeons, Harry and Ron together defeat it, thus saving Hermione's life; as a result of that, she also becomes a friend, and the Trio, as they have been called, are together for the rest of the series. While this book serves mainly as an introduction to the magical world and the characters, there is a real quest involved. Harry becomes convinced that one of the teachers, Professor Snape, is seeking a small, valuable object, which he determines to be the Philosopher's Stone (known as the Sorceror's Stone in the U.S. editions). Apparently, the evil wizard who murdered Harry's parents, Lord Voldemort, had been killed when he attempted to murder Harry, but due to some advanced Dark magic, was possibly able to return, possibly with the aid of the Philosopher's Stone. It appears that Snape is trying to aid in that return, but is being blocked by Professor Quirrell. With help from Ron and Hermione, Harry manages to foil Lord Voldemort's plan to steal the Stone. Finally, at the Leaving Feast, Dumbledore awards Hermione fifty House points for "use of cool logic in the face of fire." It turns out that Hermione is the top of the class, as expected; and she and Ron both promise to write to Harry during the summer.

Chamber of Secrets Hermione surprises Harry and Ron by apparently having a crush on the new Defence Against the Dark Arts teacher, Gilderoy Lockhart. She has apparently read all his books, as is usual for her; surprisingly, though, despite his demonstrated lack of competence, she still seems to feel he is exceptionally talented.

After the writing on the wall says that the Chamber has been opened, there is much speculation as to what the Chamber is. Hermione, vexed that all copies of *Hogwarts, A History* have been taken out of the library, manages to convince Professor Binns to relate the story of the Chamber. Apparently, Salazar Slytherin, having fallen out with the other Founders, had left the school, first constructing a secret chamber, such that it could only be opened by his true heir, which contained a monster that would assist in purging the school of those Wizards who were not of pure blood (pure Wizard ancestry).

Suspecting that Draco Malfoy might know something about this, Hermione hits on the scheme of using Polyjuice Potion to disguise the Trio as Slytherins,

---

1. http://www.jkrowling.com/textonly/en/faq_view.cfm?id=58

and so get Draco to let down his guard. Harry and Ron, though amazed at her sudden willingness to break rules, agree to her plan. At Christmas, Hermione provides cakes with sleeping potion to knock out Crabbe and Goyle, so that Harry and Ron can take their place. Hermione, however, ends up half-transformed into a cat and cannot join them. She ends up in the Hospital Wing, remaining there for nearly a month as Madam Pomfrey assists her in returning to her normal self.

During this interval, Harry finds T. Riddle's diary. Hermione, once back in the common room, checks to see if it is hiding any secrets, but does not find any.

Some time later, Hermione reaches a conclusion based on the voice Harry alone seems to be able to hear, his ability to talk to snakes, and the origin of the Chamber. Characteristically (as Ron remarks), she doesn't explain, but says she has thought of something and dashes off to the library. On her way back from the library, she is struck by the monster, Petrified, and returned to the Hospital Wing. Much later, Harry and Ron visit her there, and find that she has been holding a page from a book balled up in her hand; the page talks about Basilisks, and the notation "Pipes" indicates that Hermione has guessed that to be how the monster, a Basilisk, is traveling about the school. Hermione, when she is restored to health, is dismayed that exams have been canceled.

Prisoner of Azkaban Hermione seems to be massively overloaded with books when we meet her in Diagon Alley. Intending to buy an owl, she instead ends up purchasing a ginger-colored cat: Crookshanks. Crookshanks immediately takes a dislike to Scabbers, Ron's pet rat.

Through the course of the year, Hermione perplexingly seems to be taking more classes than humanly possible. She seems to be enjoying the work, though, and is the only one to have finished an essay on Werewolves assigned by Professor Snape (then filling in for Professor Lupin, the Defence Against the Dark Arts teacher, who is ill). The strain does seem to be telling on her, as she occasionally acts uncharacteristically. At one point, when Hagrid is overcome at the thought of Buckbeak's impending execution, Draco Malfoy makes an insulting comment about Hagrid, and Hermione punches him.

At Christmas, when Harry receives a Firebolt broom as a gift, Hermione is suspicious of it and tells Professor McGonagall. McGonagall takes the broom to examine it for jinxes. Harry and Ron, angry with Hermione, say that she should not have told McGonagall; Hermione replies that it could have been sent by Sirius Black, who has broken out of Azkaban, and evidently is planning to murder Harry. This chills the relationship between Hermione on the other two, an estrangement that continues until late in the spring, when Professor McGonagall returns the broom as being safe. That same evening, however, Ron finds ginger hairs and bloodstains on his sheets, and guesses that Crookshanks has killed Scabbers, who has vanished.

Hermione's estrangement from Ron continues until near the end of the year, when Hagrid loses his appeal of Buckbeak's execution. With Harry and Ron, she researches options for a final appeal. When Hagrid reports that it has failed, and that Buckbeak is set to be executed at sunset, she, with Harry and Ron, visit Hagrid to console him. While they are there, Hermione finds Scabbers hiding in a milk jug.

As the Trio return to the castle, Scabbers escapes, and Ron runs after him, under the edge of the Whomping Willow. A large black dog drags Ron into a tunnel under the Whomping Willow. Harry and Hermione, aided by Scabbers, follow, finding that the tunnel leads to the Shrieking Shack, and that the large black dog is Sirius Black, who is an unregistered Animagus. When Professor Lupin arrives, Hermione mentions that she had known he was a Werewolf, ever since Snape's assignment of the topic in Defence Against the Dark Arts. When Snape also appears on the scene, all three of the students there end up disarming him; the power of the three combined spells throws him against a wall and knocks him out.

As the entire group (including a captive Scabbers, now revealed to be another unregistered Animagus, Peter Pettigrew) return to the castle, Lupin is hit by the light of the full moon and transforms into a werewolf. Pettigrew jinxes Ron and Crookshanks, transforms into his rat shape and escapes; Sirius transforms into a dog to defend Harry and Hermione from the werewolf Lupin. Sirius manages to send Lupin into the Forbidden Forest, but is caught by Dementors. Attempting to defend Sirius, Harry and Hermione are overcome, and awake in the Hospital Wing. After a quick recap of the situation from Dumbledore, Hermione reveals to Harry that she has been attending her multiple classes by means of a Time-Turner, a device that will allow her to travel back to an earlier time. Dumbledore stresses that they must not be seen.

By means of the Time-Turner, Harry and Hermione return to Hagrid's hut, where they watch themselves rediscover Scabbers, and head towards the castle. They then rescue Buckbeak from the paddock where he had been secured pending his execution, and hide him in the edges of the Forbidden Forest. When Lupin transforms into a werewolf, Harry and Hermione return to Hagrid's hut; Harry, much to Hermione's dismay, then goes to see who it was that had cast the Patronus which had saved himself and Hermione earlier. Finding nobody there, he casts the Patronus himself, to Hermione's horror. He does point out to Hermione that his earlier self had seen him, and mistaken him for his father. Shortly, Hermione and Harry, mounted on Buckbeak, rescue Sirius and return to the Hospital Wing. As they return to London on the Hogwarts Express, Hermione tells Harry and Ron that she has dropped Muggle Studies. As she had earlier dropped Divination, she could take all her courses without the Time-Turner, and so she had returned it to Professor McGonagall.

Goblet of Fire Hermione accompanies Harry and the Weasley family to the Quidditch World Cup. There, she sees a House-elf, Winky, being mistreated. Later, a riot breaks out at the camp site, with apparent Death Eaters in hooded robes torturing the Muggle owner of the campground and his family. While in the woods hiding from this, Hermione, Ron, and Harry hear someone conjuring the Dark Mark, Voldemort's sigil.

Hermione later discovers that the kitchens at Hogwarts are staffed by over a hundred House-elves, determines that they are largely unpaid, and resolves to do something to improve their lot.

When the students arrive for the Triwizard Tournament from Beauxbatons and Durmstrang, Ron seems to become infatuated with one of the Beauxbatons visitors, Fleur Delacour. Hermione is vexed by this attachment. She will later find that a Durmstrang visitor, Viktor Krum, is similarly attracted to her, but in the beginning she finds his presence, along with the gaggle of girls seeking his autograph, distracting as well.

When Harry is selected as a fourth Champion for the Triwizard Tournament, Hermione is one of only two people, the other being Hagrid, who initially believe that Harry had nothing to do with his name getting into the running. Hermione, as Harry's sole friend, helps him prepare for the First Task of the Tournament, and provides moral support for Harry during this period of estrangement from Ron. Ron's return to Harry's side following the First Task is a tremendous relief to Hermione.

The Yule Ball, which is a traditional part of the Triwizard Tournament, finds both Harry and Ron dateless. Ron, out of desperation, asks Hermione, but she has already agreed to attend with someone else. Ron is incensed to find that the someone else is Viktor Krum, and accuses Hermione of fraternizing with the enemy. Hermione, responding to this, says that next time, Ron should ask her to one of these things immediately, rather than as a last resort. Ron seems mystified by this, but Harry thinks privately that Hermione knows Ron's feelings better than Ron does. The Second task involves having the Champions recover something that has been taken from them. It turns out that the thing taken from Harry is Ron; the one taken from Viktor Krum is Hermione. After he has rescued Hermione, apparently Viktor invites her to spend the summer with him at his home. Hearing this from Hermione later, Ron seems angered by the revelation. Somewhat later, Viktor takes Harry aside to ask if Hermione is his girlfriend. Hermione reportedly talks about Harry a lot in Viktor's presence, and Viktor doesn't want to upset their relationship if it is serious. Harry tells Viktor that he and Hermione are only friends.

As she had done with the Second Task, researching ways that Harry could stay underwater for an hour, Hermione helps Harry prepare for the Third Task, drilling him on jinxes and protective charms. In the meanwhile, her curiosity has been piqued by Rita Skeeter, a muck-raking journalist who seems to be able to hear conversations when she is not visibly present.

Following the Third Task, Hermione discovers that Rita is an unregistered Animagus, and traps her in her beetle form.

Order of the Phoenix Though Hermione is corresponding with Harry over the summer, her letters don't say anything about what is happening with the returned Voldemort. Frustrated, Harry sends Hedwig with a demand for answers and instructions to peck Hermione and Ron fiercely until they write good long letters back to him. Harry is not placated when he is brought to Headquarters of the Order of the Phoenix, where Hermione tells him that she and Ron were under strict orders from Dumbledore to tell him nothing. Harry only fully calms down when he is allowed to ask any questions he wants about the Order and their activities, after dinner. Hermione arranges to stay at that meeting as well.

Hermione and Ron receive notification that they have become Prefects. We will see that while Hermione carefully carries out the extra tasks she is given as Prefect, Ron is considerably less punctilious, using his powers in some cases for his own amusement. Ron also refuses to help when Hermione tries to stop the Twins from testing their Skiving Snackboxes on the first-years. Hermione is only able to control the Twins by threatening to tell their mother what they are doing.

The new Defence Against the Dark Arts teacher, Dolores Umbridge, surprisingly stands to make a speech when she is introduced at the Arrival Feast. Hermione, along among the Trio and probably alone amongst the students, listens to what she is saying, and summarizes it for Harry and Ron later as: the Ministry is going to meddle at Hogwarts. The form this initially takes is that Defence Against the Dark Arts class becomes effectively useless, teaching conciliation and theory. Frustrated with a class in which they are learning nothing, Hermione and Ron convince Harry to teach "a few students" real Defence. Apparently, Hermione's idea of "a few students" is about 28, as she says the idea seemed rather popular. As it appears that the reason for the lack of practical Defence teaching is fear that Dumbledore might be preparing an army to rebel against the Ministry, Ginny Weasley suggests the name "Dumbledore's Army."

It is Hermione who notices that Hagrid has returned, and she is instrumental in getting Hagrid to talk about his mission to the Giants, which he had carried out for Dumbledore. Hermione also attempts to tell Hagrid about Umbridge, and her new role as Hogwarts High Inquisitor, but Hagrid does not seem to care.

At Christmas, after Harry had witnessed the attack on Mr. Weasley, he worries that Voldemort is looking through his eyes at Headquarters, and that he may turn into a snake suddenly and attack his friends. Hermione cancels her skiing vacation to go to Grimmauld Place, and forces him to come out and talk with her, Ron, and Ginny. She remains there for Christmas, and visits Mr. Weasley in hospital. It is there that she learns about Neville Longbottom's parents.

To counter the misinformation about the return of Voldemort that is being put forward by the Ministry, Hermione, who still has a hold on Rita Skeeter from the discovery that she is an unregistered Animagus, requires that Rita interview Harry about the events surrounding Voldemort's return, write the story straight rather than as her usual brand of attack journalism, and give it to the *Quibbler* for publication. When the story appears, Professor Umbridge is incensed and promptly bans the *Quibbler* from the school, thus making it the most popular issue published ever.

Harry learns something about his father that disturbs him deeply, and determines that he must speak to Sirius Black about it. Having learned that Umbridge's fireplace is the only unmonitored connection to the Floo Network in the school, Harry resolves to break into her office and speak with Sirius. Hermione, reverting somewhat to her earlier, rule-bound ways, tries endlessly to persuade Harry not to do it, but in the end it is to no avail. Harry, using Umbridge's office and fireplace, speaks with Sirius and is not caught. Hermione is also nagging Harry to restart his Occlumency lessons with Snape, but Harry cannot tell her why those lessons have been ended and will not be restarted.

When Harry sees, in a vision, that Voldemort is torturing Sirius in the Ministry of Magic, he convinces Hermione to help him talk to Sirius via Umbridge's fireplace again. This time, however, they are caught. Hermione, seeing that Umbridge is about to use the Cruciatus curse on Harry to get him to say who he was talking to, convinces Umbridge that they had been working on a weapon for Dumbledore, and leads her on a wild goose chase into the Forbidden Forest. There, she engineers Umbridge falling afoul of the Centaurs, but runs afoul of their pride herself. Harry and Hermione are rescued by the sudden appearance of Hagrid's half-brother, Grawp, who recognizes "Hermy," and they make their escape into the woods as the Centaurs chase him away. Harry and Hermione now meet up with Ron, Neville, Luna, and Ginny, and the six of them make their way to the Ministry to rescue Sirius. It is, however, a trap, and they are surrounded by Death Eaters intent on retrieving a Prophecy about Harry and Voldemort. Attempting to battle their way out, all except Harry are injured, Hermione seriously. Eventually, however, members of the Order of the Phoenix arrive to battle the Death Eaters. When we next see Hermione, she is healing in the Hospital Wing. By the time the Hogwarts Express leaves Hogsmeade for London, she is fully recovered.

Half-Blood Prince Professor Dumbledore says that Harry will be taking special lessons with him over the course of the year. He suggests that the content of the lessons, like the content of the Prophecy, should remain confidential, but that Harry should feel free to discuss lessons and prophecy with Ron and Hermione. Throughout the year, Harry will discuss what he learns from Dumbledore with both of them.

Hermione starts off this book being vexed at Ron, first for falling all over himself whenever Fleur Delacour appears (she is staying at The Burrow while preparations begin for her wedding to Ron's brother Bill), then again when Ron seems to abuse his Prefect powers, and again when Ron seems overly responsive to appreciative remarks from Lavender Brown. She also suggests that Harry is over-reacting when he says that he thinks Draco Malfoy has become a Death Eater.

Harry had not expected to be allowed to take N.E.W.T.-level Potions, but the new Potions instructor, Professor Slughorn, will accept his Exceeds Expectations O.W.L. result as sufficient for entrance. Harry does not have a textbook, of course, so Slughorn loans him an old one, which Harry finds is full of notations. Hermione is upset that Harry, following the notations, is able to produce a better potion than Hermione, who is following the original text. When Ginny reminds her later about the dangerous aspects of following instructions in arbitrary books, Hermione uses several spells to see if the book is anything other than a simple book, but finds nothing. Hermione will remain upset at Harry's use of this book, which had originally belonged to one "Half-Blood Prince," throughout the year; she considers his use of the marginal notations in the book to somehow be cheating.

At the Quidditch tryouts that Harry holds, Hermione Confunds an aspiring Keeper, Cormac McLaggen, resulting in Harry selecting Ron as Keeper instead. Hermione later admits to having done it, but says that it was because she could see that his antagonistic attitude would be bad for the team as a whole. The readers may suspect that she had done it to give Ron a better shot at the position; despite the friction between Hermione and Ron, caused by Ron's response to Lavender, one can't help thinking that Hermione still cares about Ron.

Professor Slughorn has started up his "Slug Club," a collection of students he perceives as being rising stars. Hermione and Harry are invited consistently to these parties, though Harry repeatedly manufactures excuses to miss them. Ron is also upset at Hermione because of these repeated invitations, particularly as Slughorn seems to issue them to Hermione without seeming to notice that Ron is even present. Hermione mentions that Harry should attend the Christmas Slug Club party, and that they can each take a guest. Ron bitingly suggests that Hermione should take Cormac; Hermione says that she had been planning to take Ron, but if he's going to be so hard to get along with, perhaps she will take Cormac instead.

When Ron, needled by Ginny, starts an intensely physical relationship with Lavender Brown, Hermione becomes very cold towards him, and in fact does invite Cormac to the Slug Club Christmas party. She also warns Harry that the Gryffindor girls are scheming to get him to take one of them to the party as well.

Once at the party, Hermione is dismayed to find that Cormac is intent on getting her under the mistletoe. She asks Harry, who is attending with Luna Lovegood, to help hide her.

Ron gets poisoned on his birthday and ends up in the Hospital Wing. Hermione stays with him for the better part of the day, but evidently doesn't say anything until evening; when she does speak, to answer a question someone else has asked, Ron, though still apparently unconscious, says her name. Shortly, Harry and Hermione leave with Hagrid. Hagrid tells them of an argument he had overheard, apparently between Dumbledore and Snape, but Hermione is unable to learn anything from the fragments that Hagrid reports.

There is some friction between Ron and Lavender, as Ron gets discharged from the hospital wing without Lavender being told, and when she does see him, he is talking to Hermione. Hermione seems secretly pleased at the tension between them. Later, when Ron's spell-checking quill starts making errors, Hermione offers to correct his essay. Ron says, with a sigh of relief, that he loves her. Hermione, blushing, cautions him to not let Lavender hear that. Harry, Ron, and Hermione have been taking Apparation lessons, and now Ron and Hermione have the opportunity to take the exam. Harry is still not 17, the minimum age at which one is allowed to take the test. Hermione passes on her first try, but Ron fails because he has left half an eyebrow behind.

In order to retrieve a memory from Slughorn, as requested by Dumbledore, Harry ends up deciding to visit Hagrid. As he, Ron, and Hermione descend from the dormitory, they meet Lavender. Harry is wearing his Invisibility Cloak, and so Lavender believes that Hermione and Ron have been up there alone together. Hermione reports the next day that Ron and Lavender have broken up. She seems pleased by this development. Hermione also reports that Ginny and Dean have broken up, and seems aware of Harry's pleasure at this information, much as Harry tries to hide it. Over the next few weeks, we see Ron and Hermione growing closer, until they seem to be very much a couple. When Harry is invited by Dumbledore to assist him with the location and destruction of one of Voldemort's Horcruxes, Harry fears that this will leave the school unguarded. He charges Ron and Hermione with re-activating as much of Dumbledore's Army as possible, and guarding the Room of Requirement and Snape's office. Hermione, guarding Snape's office with Luna Lovegood, sees Professor Flitwick enter and tell Snape that he is needed. Snape, leaving his office, sees Hermione and tells her that Flitwick has fallen, and orders her to take care of him. Hermione later discovers that the Half-Blood Prince of the book's title (and Harry's Potions book) is, in fact, Snape; he assumed that nickname because his mother, Eileen Prince, was a witch while his father, Tobias Snape, was a Muggle.

At Dumbledore's funeral, Hermione and Ron comfort each other. Afterward, Hermione and Ron say that they have decided that whatever Harry's mission is, they will accompany him, but Ron reminds him that first there is a wedding to attend.

Deathly Hallows Hermione is one of the six decoy Harry Potters used in the escape from Privet Drive. She arrives at The Burrow safely. When Harry tells her that he can still sense Voldemort's thoughts, she is dismayed, reminding him that Dumbledore had wanted that channel closed.

Mrs. Weasley seems to be taking great pains to find separate things for Harry, Ron and Hermione to do while they stay at the Burrow, to prevent them planning to carry out the mission that Dumbledore has set Harry. Despite this, Hermione has prepared a small beaded bag which she says contains everything they will need, including, apparently, a small library. When Harry says that she doesn't have to join him on this mission, she points out that he said the same thing six years before and that she had not changed her mind since. She says that she has modified her parents' memory so that they no longer believe they have a daughter, and has sent them off to Australia with new identities to keep them safe. She also tells how she had abstracted books of Dark magic from Dumbledore's study after his funeral, and talks about ways of destroying Horcruxes. It seems that Harry had hit upon one of the very few ways to destroy a Horcrux in the Chamber of Secrets, namely Basilisk venom.

On Harry's birthday, Ron gives him a copy of a book, *Twelve Fail-Safe Ways to Charm Witches*, saying that he had gotten a copy earlier from Fred and George, and that it is pure gold; he's using it with Hermione. Later, Harry notes that Ron, uncharacteristically, is complimenting Hermione, and suspects that there will be a chapter about compliments in this book.

Rufus Scrimgeour, the Minister for Magic, arrives, saying that he has some bequests for Harry, Ron, and Hermione from the will of Albus Dumbledore. Hermione's bequest is an edition of *The Tales of Beedle the Bard* in ancient runes. Hermione points out that the Ministry have been holding on to these bequests for the full thirty days that they are allowed by law. She also mentions that the Ministry is likely interested in seeing Harry receive his bequest, the first Snitch he ever caught in a Quidditch match, because of the Snitch's "flesh memory": it is charmed to recall whoever first touched it, as a way of mediating disputes in close matches. Harry cautiously takes the Snitch from Scrimgeour, but to Scrimgeour's slight disappointment, nothing happens to it.

At Bill and Fleur's wedding, Hermione is surprised to find that Viktor Krum has been invited and has arrived. Ron, upset by Viktor's arrival, whisks Hermione off to the dance floor as soon as he can. When the wedding is interrupted by news of the fall of the Ministry to Voldemort, Hermione gathers the others to her and Disapparates the three of them to Tottenham Court Road in London. There, she provides Muggle clothing from her beaded bag, and the three of them stop in a coffee shop to plan their next move. They are attacked by Death Eaters and overcome them. Harry suggests that they should work a Memory Charm on the Death Eaters, so that they won't be able to report what happened; Hermione, though saying that she has never done that before, ends up working the charm on both Death Eaters and the waitress, while Harry and Ron clean up the damage to the café.

Once they have settled at Grimmauld Place, it occurs to Hermione that the portrait of Phineas Nigellus is a way that now-headmaster Severus Snape could get information about the actions of the Trio, and so tucks it also into her beaded bag. Harry finds Regulus Black's room, and connects him with the R.A.B. who had left the note in the fake locket. After a fruitless search of his room, Harry recalls seeing a locket when they were cleaning up the place. They determine that the locket has been stolen by Dolores Umbridge. They decide to enter the Ministry and try to find where Umbridge might have put the locket.

Once inside, the Trio get separated. Hermione ends up being assigned to Umbridge as scribe for the proceedings of the Muggle-Born Registration Commission, which is where Harry finds her after searching Umbridge's office and finding nothing. Hermione observes that Umbridge is wearing the locket. Umbridge, in response to Hermione's question, says that it shows she is associated with the Selwyn family, a good pure-blood Wizarding family, it is too much for Harry and he Stuns her and Yaxley, who is assisting.

Managing to meet up with Ron, Harry and Hermione escape, but Yaxley is holding on to Hermione, so ends up on the doorstep at Grimmauld Place. Hermione blasts him away, and then Apparates the Trio away, but Ron is splinched and needs medical care. Hermione, though almost panicking, manages to get his bleeding stopped and settles him in their tent. This is the start of the Trio's journey through the wilds of England. Never staying in any one place for more than a few nights, they use Hermione's money to compensate Muggle shops for the goods they lift. Hermione, as the best witch, takes responsibility for setting the daily protective charms around the campsite, and as the only girl, ends up with the majority of the domestic duties.

When Harry has trouble dealing with Dementors later, Hermione determines that it is the locket that is at fault; it is sapping the will of anyone who wears it. Rather than risk losing it if their equipment gets lost, the Trio elect to take turns wearing the locket.

When Ron, who was unprepared for the privations of life on the run, leaves the group in a huff, Hermione is distraught. However, her faith in Harry and his mission never wavers. She accepts that they must visit Godric's Hollow, and prepares them for that visit. She helps Harry find his parents' graves, and visits their house with him, where she is scandalized that people have added words of support to the sign commemorating the night of Voldemort's first downfall. She accompanies him to Bathilda Bagshot's house, and assists in his escape when it turns out to be a trap, then nurses him back to health after their encounter with Voldemort. She then reveals that in the escape, a spell she had cast had nearly destroyed Harry's wand. After Harry's recovery, she tells him that she had collected an unopened copy of *The Life and Lies of Albus Dumbledore* from Bathilda's parlor. Reading the book, she is as distressed as Harry to discover that, at about Harry's current age, Dumbledore had been firm friends, albeit briefly, with Gellert Grindelwald.

When Ron rejoins the group, Hermione is initially furious at him, flying at him in a fury, and refusing to listen to anything he has to say. She does eventually relent, but things remain tense between them until the Trio visits Xeno Lovegood. There, Hermione reads *The Tale of the Three Brothers* to Xeno and the Trio. Xeno says that the three things given to the three brothers by Death are the Deathly Hallows. Hermione dismisses the Resurrection Stone out of hand, but wonders about Harry's Invisibility Cloak, as it is so very much better than any other she or Ron has seen or heard about, and admits that the Elder Wand does seem to have left a trail of murders through history. When the Death Eaters that Xeno has summoned arrive, Hermione allows them to see herself and Harry, but hides Ron, as they make their escape. She later says that the Death Eaters couldn't be allowed to see Ron because he was supposed to be at home with Spattergroit, and revealing him could result in reprisals against his family, but if the Death Eaters could report that Harry was really there, it might spare Xeno some punishment. Later, the Trio are captured by Snatchers. Hermione is recognized as Harry's traveling companion, despite Harry being disguised, and so the three of them, along with Dean Thomas and the goblin Griphook, are taken to Voldemort's headquarters. There, Bellatrix Lestrange recognizes that the Trio are carrying the sword of Gryffindor, and questions Hermione with the Cruciatus curse to learn where she had gotten it. Hermione manages, despite the pain, to hold to the story that they had found it, that it was a fake. Ron and Harry free themselves, and Ron carries Hermione to Shell Cottage, where she quickly recovers.

The Trio now determine that a Horcrux is located in Bellatrix' vault in Gringotts, and with the aid of Griphook, and with Hermione disguised as Bellatrix herself, break into the vault. They succeed at entering the vault and finding the Horcrux, and then fly out on the back of the aged dragon who had been guarding it. The three of them then head for Hogwarts, where Harry has determined the last Horcrux must be.

Once at Hogwarts, Hermione and Ron between them determine that if they can get into the Chamber of Secrets, they can destroy the Horcrux they have just found. When we see them again, they are carrying a destroyed Horcrux and a bundle of Basilisk fangs. After they have explained what they had done, Ron suggests that hey may want to warn the House-Elves in the kitchen that a battle is about to happen and they may want to get away to save themselves, and Hermione, apparently impressed with this display of real feelings, kisses him fiercely.

As the battle heats up, Hermione demands that Harry look into Voldemort's mind to see where he is. Harry finds him in the Shrieking Shack. The Trio immediately leave for the Shack by way of the tunnel under the Whomping Willow. Arriving there, Harry witnesses Voldemort killing Snape, under the impression that this will result in him gaining power over the Elder Wand. Snape, seeing Harry, releases a cloud of memories; Hermione produces a crystal flask, which Harry uses to collect them, before Snape dies.

As Voldemort calls a temporary end to hostilities, the Trio return to Hogwarts to join in the recuperation. Harry sees Hermione and Ron heading for the Great Hall, but knows that his own business will take him to the headmaster's office.

At the end of the final battle, Harry, Ron, and Hermione return to the Headmasters' office, where Harry explains what he has done to the portrait of Dumbledore, and uses the Elder Wand to repair his own wand, to Hermione's evident approval.

In the epilogue, we learn that Ron has married Hermione, and that they have two children, named Rose and Hugo.

Strengths Hermione's greatest strength is her vast intellect. Through her knowledge of the magical world, she has, in the course of the series, helped Harry and Ron on several occasions. As she is generally caring, compassionate, and always see things from a "rule-abiding" point-of-view, Hermione often presents Harry and Ron with alternate ways to approach their problems. Her intelligence also means she is a skilled duelist and is capable of battling much more experienced Death Eaters, as she has demonstrated in the battle at the Department of Mysteries, and later in the final battle at Hogwarts. In her age group, apparently only Harry has done better in Defence Against the Dark Arts. Hermione is also skilled in organization and planning, culminating in her brilliant preparations for the Trio's horcrux quest during *Harry Potter and the Deathly Hallows*.

Weaknesses At times, Hermione's intellect has kept her from making the same connections about other people and their motives that Ron and especially Harry instinctively sense. Hermione feels self-conscious about her physical appearance. She is afraid of failure—her Boggart was Professor McGonagall telling her she had "failed everything," and she was upset when she missed one O (Outstanding) on her O.W.L.s, earning the next-best grade of an E (Exceeds Expectations) in Defence Against the Dark Arts.

Relationships with Other Characters Over the course of the series, Hermione and Ron have developed a tentative romantic relationship, although they are both hesitant and unsure about what the other really feels, at least until the end of book 6. Hermione and Ron's sister, Ginny, are close friends. She attends the Yule Ball with Viktor Krum, a visiting student from the Durmstrang Institute. Hermione often stays with the Weasley family and shows more fondness for Percy Weasley than other characters do.

While Hermione and Harry have been very close over the course of the seven books, their relationship has never become romantic, despite the apparent wishes of many fans of the series. From very early in the series, even as early as the end of the first book, there have been hints of a developing relationship between Hermione and Ron, and no similar hints of any relationship between Harry and Hermione. In fact, by book 4, these hints are so obvious that Harry is noting them, even if Ron remains oblivious.

Hermione's romantic relationships with other characters are covered in more depth here.

Analysis

Hermione seems to be the most rational of "the trio," though also the most high-strung. She is consistently the best student at Hogwarts in almost every subject and would almost certainly have become Head Girl had she stayed at Hogwarts for her seventh year. Hermione is deeply afraid of failure and seems to have an almost obsessive-compulsive drive to finish her schoolwork and to follow the rules, though she has somewhat mellowed with regard to the latter in later books.

Questions

1. How does Hermione handle stress? What does this show about her as a person?

2. Hermione is loyal, practical, and honest. Which of these qualities is the most important in a friend?

3. How does Hermione's relationship with Harry differ from her relationship with Ron?

4. Hermione's main strength seems to be her intellect. Should she have been Sorted into Ravenclaw? Why or why not?

Greater Picture

Just like the Muggle world, the Wizarding world is contaminated with institutional prejudice, insensitivity and racism. Hermione brings a feminist viewpoint and is a champion for the downtrodden. Several times Hermione reminds Harry and Ron that an unknown "he" they are discussing may, in fact, be a woman. She confounds bigots like Draco Malfoy with her Muggle-born brilliance. One of her ongoing ambitions is to secure the advancement and rights of house elves and others who have been enslaved or poorly treated by wizards. Hermione becomes a one person symbol of civil rights activism and social progress.

Hestia Jones

Gender: Female
Hair color: Black
Eye color: Unknown
Related Family: Unknown
Loyalty: Order of the Phoenix

Overview

Hestia Jones is a pink-cheeked, black-haired witch who is a member of the Order of the Phoenix.

Role in the Books

Order of the Phoenix Hestia Jones is a member of the Advance Guard who arrive at the Dursleys' home to escort Harry to the Headquarters of the Order of the Phoenix.

Deathly Hallows Hestia Jones is one of two Order members (the other being Dedalus Diggle) who take the Dursley family away from Privet Drive in order to keep them safe.

Hokey

Gender: Female
Hair color: None
Eye color: Green
Related Family: Unknown
Loyalty: Hepzibah Smith

Overview

Hokey is the House-elf of Hepzibah Smith. She is extremely old.

Role in the Books

Half-Blood Prince In Hokey's memories, we see Hepzibah primping herself in preparation of a visit by Tom Riddle. Tom, acting as a buyer for Borgin and Burkes, is there to make an offer on some Goblin-made armour, but Hepzibah, charmed by him, shows him her two fondest possessions, a cup originally owned by Helga Hufflepuff, from whom she claims distant descent, and a locket owned by Salazar Slytherin. Tom recognizes the locket as being the one that his mother had sold to try and support herself. Shortly afterwards, Hepzibah Smith dies, apparently mistakenly poisoned by Hokey. Hokey admits responsibility for Hepzibah's death, and goes to Azkaban, but Albus Dumbledore is able to visit her there and retrieve this memory of Tom Riddle.

Horace Slughorn

Gender: Male
Hair color: Bald, formerly golden yellow
Eye color: Unknown
Related Family: Unknown
Loyalty: Albus Dumbledore

Overview

Horace E. F. Slughorn is the retired head of Slytherin House and a former Hogwarts teacher. Confronted with a shortage of teachers by the incapacitation of Dolores Umbridge, Professor Dumbledore convinces him to come out of retirement and return to teaching. Slughorn is a portly older gentleman with an ebullient manner, a large moustache, and a very deep voice.

Role in the Books

Half-Blood Prince Professor Dumbledore collects Harry from the Dursleys' after only two weeks of the summer vacation. As they depart on their way to The Burrow, Dumbledore comments that he finds himself again one teacher short, and so they will be stopping to visit someone he hopes to coax into the job. In the town of Budleigh Babberton, they find a house that has apparently been the subject of an attack: door standing open, furniture destroyed, apparent blood spattered on the walls. Dumbledore, surveying the wreckage, pokes an overturned armchair with his wand; it turns into a very fat man, who is then introduced as Horace Slughorn. Asked what had given him away, Dumbledore comments that if the attack had been real, the Dark Mark would have been floating over the house; Slughorn admits to forgetting it, but says he had been rushed, being in the bath when his detector had gone off. The two of them clean up the house, then Dumbledore introduces Harry, and asks Slughorn if he would be interested in getting his old job back. Slughorn demurs, saying he's concerned that coming out of his concealment might make him a target for the Death Eaters. Dumbledore then departs, ostensibly to go to the bathroom.

Slughorn now engages Harry in conversation, talking about his mother, Lily Evans as she was then, and how she had been one of his favorite students despite being Muggle-born. He admits to a bias towards the Pureblood students, and mentions that it is only natural, with his having been head of Slytherin house. He then talks about his connections in the Wizarding world, with sports teams and the Ministry; Harry asks if they have been in touch since Slughorn went into concealment. Slughorn admits, reluctantly, that his standard of living has dropped since he went into hiding a year before. Harry points out that Hogwarts is probably at least as safe as anywhere else; possibly more so, as Dumbledore was the only wizard that Voldemort was believed to fear.

Dumbledore then returns from the bathroom, saying he had become intrigued by one of the magazines there, and takes his leave of Slughorn. As he and Harry head for the door, Slughorn changes his mind and accepts the teaching post Dumbledore was offering.

As they travel to The Burrow, Dumbledore tells Harry that Slughorn had previously maintained a student group at Hogwarts, called the "Slug Club," whose members were either skilled or well-connected. It is this group which had left him the connections he needed to keep him in the creature comforts he was so fond of. Dumbledore suggests that Slughorn might want to restart that club on his return, and that Harry would be the star of that club if it did re-form. It appears Dumbledore is correct, as on the Hogwarts Express heading to school, Harry and Neville find themselves invited to a gathering in Slughorn's compartment, along with several other students who seem to have important relatives. Slughorn seems to be trying to get Harry to tell what had happened in the Battle at the Ministry, but when Harry remained silent as to details, Slughorn shifted to his own reminiscences and entertained the students almost until they arrived at Hogwarts.

At the Arrival Feast, Harry, along with many others, is amazed to hear that Slughorn has been brought in as Potions Master, and Professor Snape has been given the Defence Against the Dark Arts position that he has wanted for so long. Alarming as this may be, it provides one major advantage for Harry: Snape would only accept students at N.E.W.T. level if they receive an Outstanding grade in Potions, and Harry's grade had been merely Exceeds Expectations. Harry had seen his dream of becoming an Auror vanish. Slughorn, however, is willing to accept an Exceeds Expectations student for N.E.W.T.-level classes, so Harry is free to take Potions and prepare for his chosen career.

At the first Potions class, then, Harry and Ron, both of whom are now able to take Potions, are in need of textbooks. Slughorn digs a couple of used books out of a cupboard for them. Slughorn has prepared several cauldrons of potion, and asks the class to identify them. Hermione identifies all four of them, earning thirty House points for Gryffindor, and Slughorn's admiration. Slughorn then sets them the task of brewing a particular potion, the Draught of Living Death. Harry, looking at his borrowed Potions book, notes that the previous owner had annotated it; following the annotations, he finds that his results are much better even then Hermione's. Slughorn commends him for his skill at Potions, saying he was obviously his mother's son; she was easily the best potion-maker in her class year. As Harry has made the best example of the potion, he wins the prize: a phial of Felix Felicis potion, enough Liquid Luck for twelve hours.

Harry's continuing use of the annotated textbook will lead Slughorn to believe that he is extremely talented in Potions. Harry does not want to lose the benefit of the annotations in the book, so when his new copy arrives from Flourish and Blotts, he returns that book to Slughorn, keeping the annotated book for himself.

Returning from a visit with Hagrid after the Quidditch tryouts, Harry, Ron, and Hermione are met in the great hall by Slughorn, who invites Harry and Hermione to a little party, "just a few rising stars," while ignoring Ron who is standing right there. Harry pleads a previous engagement, detention with Snape. Slughorn says he will try to straighten that small matter out, and waddles away, but is ultimately not successful.

On the first Hogsmeade visit of the year, Harry, Ron, and Hermione run into Slughorn in Honeyduke's Sweetshop. Slughorn invites Harry and Hermione to another little party, again ignoring Ron. Harry again has to refuse, as he has a lesson scheduled with Professor Dumbledore for that evening. Harry continues to avoid Slughorn's parties by scheduling Quidditch practice on those days when the parties are happening. Hermione later mentions that Slughorn's parties aren't as bad as all that, and that Harry should at least plan on coming to the Christmas party. She mentions that he would be allowed to bring a guest, which sparks a small row between her and Ron.

Harry manages to avoid the girls attempting to wangle an invitation to Slughorn's party with him, eventually inviting Luna Lovegood. Hermione chooses to invite Cormac McLaggen, largely to spite Ron who is very deeply involved with Lavender.

Once Harry and Luna arrive at the party, they run into Hermione, who is now actively trying to avoid Cormac. They fall into discussion with Professor Trelawney, and Harry and Hermione are very entertained by Luna's theories about conspiracies in the Ministry. Filch arrives with Draco Malfoy, who he had found wandering the halls; Professor Slughorn decides that he had been attempting to gatecrash, and magnanimously invites him to join the party. Shortly, Draco and Snape leave for a private word, and Harry departs to eavesdrop on them. If her returns to the party afterwards, we don't hear about it.

Immediately after Christmas, in one of his private lessons with Dumbledore, Harry experiences a memory of Slughorn's from the days when the Slug Club had included Tom Riddle. The memory, which shows Tom asking about Horcruxes, is very obviously edited such that none of Slughorn's responses are present. Professor Dumbledore says that Harry is uniquely equipped to retrieve the unedited memory from Slughorn, and charges him with that retrieval, saying it is quite possibly the most important thing Harry will have to do all year. Some time later, Professor Slughorn sets them the task of determining and brewing an antidote for a mixture of magical poisons. Harry finds a scrawled note in his textbook that says "Simply shove a Bezoar down their throat." As the end of the class approaches, Harry finds a bezoar in the ingredients cupboard. As time is called, nobody has a complete solution, not even Hermione. Harry exhibits his bezoar, to Hermione's dismay and Slughorn's deep amusement. Slughorn absently tucks the bezoar into his bag. At the end of class, Harry asks Slughorn about Horcruxes, but Slughorn irritably insists that there was nothing more to that episode than what Dumbledore has seen, and leaves hastily.

So long as Harry stays away from the subject of Horcruxes, Slughorn remains amiable, but Harry, who is now waiting for one of his invitations to his little soirées, is frustrated that none are forthcoming. And so matters remain for some months, as Slughorn steadfastly avoids any situation where he might be alone with Harry. Harry had been given a box of Chocolate Cauldrons by Romilda Vane who, at the time, had been angling for an invitation to Slughorn's Christmas party. Warned by Hermione to suspect love potion, Harry had set them aside in his trunk. Hunting through his trunk, he had pulled them roughly out, and Ron, whose birthday it was, had mistaken them for a gift for himself and had eaten two. Harry, finding Ron infatuated with Romilda, had taken him to Slughorn's office for an antidote. Slughorn expressed some surprise that as talented a potion-maker as Harry had not simply whipped up the antidote himself, but quickly puts together a potion, and gives it to Ron who is abruptly cured, and badly shaken. Slughorn then pours out some "oak-aged mead" which he says he had gotten as a Christmas gift for Dumbledore, but had forgotten to give him. Harry, watching Ron as he downs the entire glass in one, sees the poison in the mead affecting him. Slughorn, shocked, can only stutter and stammer as Ron falls; Harry, remembering the Bezoar that Slughorn had tucked into his bag, rummages through Slughorn's bag to find it and forces it into Ron's mouth, just in time.

In te Hospital Wing afterwards, where Harry is visiting with Ron, Hermione, Ginny, and the Twins, the Weasley family speculate on why Slughorn would have had poisoned mead in the first place, and wonder exactly who he would be trying to poison. The suggestion is aired that Slughorn may be a Death Eater, or sympathetic to them, and be trying to poison Harry; but Harry points out that Slughorn had said the mead was intended for Dumbledore.

On the day of the testing for Apparation in Hogsmeade, Slughorn finds that only three students remain in his Potions class: Harry, Draco Malfoy, and Ernie Macmillan. He decides to set them an open lesson, having each of them create a potion of his own choice. Harry, thinking to perhaps lighten Slughorn's mood and loosen his tongue, chooses to make up a Euphoria Elixir. Slughorn, when it is complete, looks at Harry's potion and scents it, but departs almost at the run before Harry can convince him to try tasting it.

That morning, Harry, Ron, and Hermione had been discussing how to get the memory from Slughorn, and had hit upon the idea of using some of the Felix Felicis potion that Harry had won on the first day of class. While they were discussing this, Harry had received a note from Hagrid that said that Aragog had died, and asking Harry to come to the funeral. Having failed to convince Slughorn to grant him the memory that afternoon, Harry takes the Felix Felicis potion, and promptly decides to attend Aragog's funeral, much to Ron's and Hermione's horror. On the way there, he decides to detour past the greenhouses, where he luckily runs into Slughorn. He chooses to tell Slughorn the truth about why he is out there; Slughorn, thinking avariciously of the value of Acromantula venom, not only fails to punish Harry for being out of the school, but chooses to join Harry at Hagrid's, bearing a number of bottles of mead. After Aragog is buried, Slughorn, pouring generously, manages to get himself and Hagrid drunk; Harry, luckily, moderates his drinking, magically refills the bottles without either of the other two noticing, and finally convinces Slughorn, who is so drunk that he will remember nothing in the morning, to retrieve the memory that Dumbledore has been seeking.

Viewing the memory with Dumbledore shortly afterwards, Harry learns that in that particular episode, Tom Riddle had managed to receive some information about Horcruxes from Slughorn, and had asked about the possibility of making multiple Horcruxes. In particular, Tom had suggested that seven was a particularly magical number, and wondered whether seven pieces of soul might not provide even better immortality than two. Slughorn had been horrified at the thought.

Harry loses access to the textbook that had belonged to the Half-Blood Prince, leaving it in the Room of Requirement to keep it from being confiscated by Professor Snape, and as a result his skill in Potions falls off rather sharply. However, as he has at the same time rather publicly started going out with Ginny, Slughorn attributes his decreased ability to distraction, quite understandable in one Harry's age.

At the end of the book, following Snape's departure, a meeting of the four Heads of House must be called. As Snape is no longer available, Slughorn is called in as acting head of Slytherin house. Slughorn is in shock at Snape's actions, saying that he had thought he had known Snape. He suggests that with Dumbledore gone, people might not want to send their children to Hogwarts, but that he was in favour of keeping the school open.

Deathly Hallows Apparently, Professor Slughorn's temporary appointment as head of Slytherin house was continued, as we see him responding (albeit sluggishly) to Professor McGonagall's summons to the heads of Houses. As Snape is departing, Professor McGonagall tells Professor Slughorn in no uncertain terms that he must decide whether he stands with the school or with the Death Eaters. Slughorn chooses to stand with the school, and is seen dueling Voldemort with McGonagall and Kingsley Shacklebolt just before Harry's final confrontation.

Strengths He has an uncanny ability to pick students who have a promising future, giving him many good contacts. He is also highly skilled at potion-making and is, according to Dumbledore, an extremely accomplished wizard. He is good natured and occasionally generous to the people he likes.

Weaknesses His health is bad, as he has a weak chest. He also shows a favoritism to talented people. In addition, he is slightly greedy. He is self-indulgent, enjoying an excess of expensive liquor, good food and fine clothing.

QUESTIONS

1. Is it better to hide things you have done wrong or to try to solve them right away? 2. What things does Slughorn look for in people he wants to join the Slug Club?

House of Gaunt

Gender: n/a
Hair color: Unknown
Eye color: Unknown
Related Family:
Loyalty: Salazar Slytherin

OVERVIEW

The House of Gaunt is "a very ancient Wizarding family noted for a vein of instability and violence that flourished through the generations due to their habit of marrying their own cousins."

ROLE IN THE BOOKS

Half-Blood Prince In Albus Dumbledore's Pensieve, via the memories of Bob Ogden, we visit the home of the Gaunt family. There, we learn that the House of Gaunt is the last descendant family of Salazar Slytherin. Only three were ever mentioned: Morfin Gaunt, who speaks only Parseltongue; Marvolo Gaunt, and Merope Gaunt, the witch who will later become the mother of Tom Marvolo Riddle. We learn later that Morfin and Marvolo end up in Azkaban, where Marvolo dies; on his release, Morfin finds the house empty and Merope gone. Morfin is later sent to Azkaban for the murder of three Muggles, a murder which was actually done by Tom Riddle.

Deathly Hallows We learn that the house of Gaunt also can claim descent from the Peverell family; one of the artifacts they have retained to show their antiquity turns out to be a ring containing a stone, the Resurrection Stone, originally owned by one of the three Peverell brothers of legend.

With the death of Riddle at the end of the book, the House of Gaunt comes to an end.

Weaknesses The inbreeding that comes from the "habit of marrying their own cousins" has left both Morfin and Merope quite profoundly ugly, with straggly hair and eyes that point in different directions. It seems also that Merope is quite weak magically.

The monumental amount of pride that the Gaunt family has in its heritage seems to have blinded it to all magical progress for an extended length of time. Anything that has happened has, of course, been tainted by contact with Muggles and is therefore unworthy. Marvolo, in particular, seems prepared to dismiss the entire magical governance structure because it does not accept his ancestry as somehow setting him above other wizards.

Relationships with Other Characters Because their pride requires them to dismiss anything having to do with Muggles, the Gaunt family lives a very isolated life, fat away from other wizards. It would be safe to say that the Gaunt family as a whole would be happiest to be left entirely on its own.

Analysis

It is interesting to note that the pride in ancestry that is held by Marvolo and Morfin finds an echo in Tom Riddle, who has never met them and does not even know he is related to them for possibly the first fifteen years of his life. Even when he does meet Morfin, he does not speak with him long enough to get any real idea of what Morfin's beliefs are, or how closely they align with his own. It is probably safe to say that this belief in the power of ancestry is another family characteristic.

Igor Karkaroff

Gender: Male
Hair color: silver
Eye color: Unknown
Related Family: Unknown
Loyalty: previously Voldemort

Overview

Igor Karkaroff is the headmaster of the Durmstrang Institute, one of the three top Wizarding schools in Europe. (The others are Beauxbatons, and of course Hogwarts.)

Role in the Books

Goblet of Fire We first meet Igor Karkaroff when the representatives from Durmstrang Institute arrive at Hogwarts to take part in the Triwizard Tournament. After disembarking from their ship which has surfaced in the lake, Karkaroff greets Albus Dumbledore civilly enough, but his smile doesn't reach his eyes, which stay cold and watchful. He asks if they could proceed indoors as one of his students, Viktor, seems to be catching a bit of a cold. As they depart after dinner, Karkaroff happens to bump into Harry Potter. He is evidently quite taken aback to realize who he has run into, and as he has halted in the doorway, he is preventing anyone from getting past him. The logjam is broken up by Alastor Moody, who Karkaroff evidently recognizes; they quite plainly don't like each other, and Karkaroff seems to be somewhat afraid of Moody.

When Harry's name comes out of the Goblet of Fire, making him the fourth of the three Triwizard Champions, Karkaroff is angry, saying that either Durmstrang (and Beauxbatons) should be allowed to submit additional names, until each school has two champions, or he will depart from the contest with all his school. Moody again interrupts him, saying that just as Harry is bound to compete, so is Viktor Krum, the Durmstrang champion; and Ludo Bagman, one of the two Ministry judges, says that the Goblet has gone out and will not re-ignite until the next Tournament.

When Harry looks into the Pensieve, the first of Dumbledore's memories that Harry experiences is Karkaroff attempting to bargain his way out of Azkaban. Before the full Wizengamot, he names several people as Death Eaters: Travers, who he also accuses of the death of Marlene McKinnon and her family, Mulciber, and Antonin Dolohov, each time being met with the statement that the Wizengamot has already arrested them. He also names Severus Snape, though Dumbledore refutes this, saying that Snape had turned against the Death Eaters before Voldemort fell. He does eventually name Augustus Rookwood, the first name which the Wizengamot is not aware of.

Half-Blood Prince On Harry's birthday, we hear that the body of Igor Karkaroff has been found in a shack in the North, with the Dark Mark floating over it.

Questions

1. Where did Karkaroff's loyalties lie? Was he still loyal as a Death Eater, or had he turned to the good side, like the Malfoys had claimed about themselves? Or is there a third alternative? What does his death at the hands of the returned Death Eaters suggest?

Irma Pince

Gender: Female
Hair color: Unknown
Eye color: Unknown
Related Family: Unknown
Loyalty: Her library and its books

Overview

Irma Pince is the librarian of Hogwarts School of Withcraft and Wizardry. She is described to be a "thin, irritable woman who looks like an underfed vulture. From the very little description of who she is, we can guess that she is very impatient, and stereotypically we would guess her to have small glasses on her nose, which would probably be pointy. It is most likely she is in Ravenclaw house, guessing from her job and the location of the library.

Role in the Books

Philosopher's Stone Madam Pince is largely in the background, moving around the library and making sure nobody damages any of her books. When Harry discovers that the name Nicholas Flamel is important to the story, it is Madam Pince who initially prevents his entering the Restricted Section of the library to search for him.

Chamber of Secrets Hermione hits upon the scheme of using Polyjuice potion to disguise the Trio as Slytherins to determine what Draco Malfoy knows about the Heir. Hermione secures a permission slip for the necessary book, *Moste Potente Potions*, from Professor Lockhart, which she presents to Madam Pince. Madam Pince is not entirely certain about this, but accepts the note, eventually, and gives Hermione the book.

Order of the Phoenix Harry is studying in the library when Ginny brings him his Easter gift from Mrs. Weasley: a large chocolate egg. Harry is distracted; he has just learned something extremely disturbing about his father and needs to talk to Sirius Black about it. Ginny tells him that, living as long as she has with the Twins, she has learned that nothing is actually impossible. Harry has been distractedly eating his chocolate egg while they have been talking, and Madam Pince spots this source of damage to her precious books and chases them both out of the library.

Half-Blood Prince Madam Pince spots Harry's potions book, with the annotations by the Half-Blood Prince, and accuses him of defiling one of her precious books. Harry is barely able to hold on to the book as he is chased out of the library.

Relationships with Other Characters It has been suggested that Irma Pince and Argus Filch have a relationship, by many fans, and in fact by Harry and Ginny in conversation. There is no evidence supporting this relationship anywhere else in the series, though some fans have suggested that the "Half-Blood Prince" of the title of the sixth book might actually be the son of these two, and "Prince" might be a typo for "Pince." We are told that the Prince's mother is named Eileen, however, which rules out that possibility.

Irma is apparently obsessed with her books, and she treats students and teachers with almost equal suspicion, worried that they might be putting her precious books at risk. We never see anyone with whom she seems to be on reasonable terms; of course, we also never see her away from her precious library. Away from her books, she may be completely different.

ANALYSIS

One thing that anyone who uses a Muggle library is aware of is the helpful nature of the librarians there. By and large, if there is something you need to research, a librarian can help you to find it. In many places in the Harry Potter story line, it becomes necessary for the Trio to find some historical fact from the books in the library: in *Harry Potter and the Philosopher's Stone*, for instance, it is necessary to find the identity of Nicholas Flamel; in *Harry Potter and the Prisoner of Azkaban* the Trio are researching cases where dangerous creatures won their trials, and later won their appeals; and in *Harry Potter and the Goblet of Fire*, Harry needs a way to survive for an hour underwater. In all of these cases, a helpful librarian would have short-circuited the process of finding the answer and would have decreased Hermione's participation. Madam Pince's monumental obstructiveness thus can be seen as important to the story, both as a means of pacing, and as a means of making Hermione, with her library research skills, more valuable to the partnership.

QUESTIONS

1. What are Madame Pince's interactions with the staff like? How does this compare with her relationships with students?

Jack Sloper

Gender: Male
Hair color: Unknown
Eye color: Unknown
Related Family: Unknown
Loyalty:

OVERVIEW

Jack Sloper is a Beater on the Gryffindor Quidditch team. Along with Andrew Kirke, he takes over for Fred and George Weasley.

ROLE IN THE BOOKS

Order of the Phoenix In the last meeting of Dumbledore's Army before Christmas, Angelina Johnson tells Harry that they have finally managed to get replacement Beaters. Alicia Spinnet says the new beaters are Andrew Kirke and Jack Sloper, and that they are nowhere as good as Fred and George, but were the best of a very bad lot. On February 14th, Ron says that he can't go to Hogsmeade because Angelina wants a full day's practice. Ron is skeptical that it will help, because Sloper and Kirke are even worse than he is.

The following weekend, in the match against Ravenclaw, it is remarked that one of the low points of the game is Sloper swinging at a Bludger, missing, and hitting Angelina in the mouth with his bat.

Sloper is later mentioned at Easter Break. Ginny, meeting Harry in the library, tells him that Quidditch practice had ended early because Ron had had to take Sloper to the Hospital Wing. They are not sure what happened, but they think he knocked himself out with his own bat.

Half-Blood Prince Jack carries a message from Albus Dumbledore to Harry, then asks Harry when try-outs are. When try-outs happen two weeks later, Jack is passed over; the new Beaters are Jimmy Peakes and Ritchie Coote.

James Potter

Gender: Male
Hair color: Black
Eye color: Hazel
Related Family: Lily Potter, Harry Potter
Loyalty: Lily Potter, Albus Dumbledore, Sirius Black, Remus Lupin, Peter Pettigrew

OVERVIEW

James Potter is the father of Harry Potter, the hero of the series. James' death at the hands of Lord Voldemort offstage, just before the opening chapter of the first book, sets up the conflict in the entire series.

Role in the Books

Philosopher's Stone Though introduced as Harry's dead father, James Potter plays no direct role in this book. His image appears in the Mirror of Erised when Harry finds it the first time at Christmas, and a large number of pictures of him are in the photo album given to Harry by Rubeus Hagrid just before Harry leaves the school for the summer. Hagrid has mentioned also that James Potter was head boy in his seventh year at Hogwarts. James apparently owned an Invisibility Cloak that was given to Harry at Christmas, and then mysteriously returned to him in May when he had misplaced it. This Cloak becomes an important tool for Harry, Ron, and Hermione in exploring the school.

Prisoner of Azkaban The Defence Against the Dark Arts teacher this year is Remus Lupin, who was one of James' best friends; at a number of points in the story, there is discussion between Harry and Professor Lupin about James. Additionally, the scenes in the Shrieking Shack involve Lupin, Sirius Black, and Peter Pettigrew, all James' close friends, and include a number of details about their mutual school days. One major revelation is that James was an unregistered Animagus.

When Harry, Hermione, and Sirius Black are being attacked by the Dementors, someone casts a Patronus charm; Harry initially believes it to be James.

It was also revealed at the end of this book that the form James took as an Animagus was that of a stag. This had earlier caused some disquiet to Lupin; Harry's Patronus charm took the shape of a stag, and Lupin seems to have recognized it.

Goblet of Fire In the final chapters of *Harry Potter and the Goblet of Fire*, while Harry is battling Lord Voldemort in the graveyard, the Priori Incantatem effect causes shadows of the people Voldemort has killed to begin appearing. among others, Harry's father and mother appear and speak with him. They then gather around Voldemort, hindering his attack on Harry after the connection between the wands is broken, for just long enough that Harry is able to escape.

In earlier editions of the books, there was the famous mistake of the wand order. The shadows appear from Voldemort's wand starting with the most recent and proceeding towards the oldest, but in early editions of the book, James appears before Lily, implying that he died after her. This was corrected by the author in later editions.

Order of the Phoenix Late in the book, Harry views a story of James Potter during his schooling days with his best friends Sirius Black, Remus Lupin and Peter Pettigrew, as revealed through Professor Snape's memories made accessible via Dumbledore's Pensieve.

"*It was as though he was looking at himself but with deliberate mistakes. James's eyes were hazel, his nose was longer than Harry's, and there was no scar on his forehead, but they had the same thin face, same mouth, same eyebrows. James's hair stuck up at the back exactly as Harry's did, his hands could have been Harry's and Harry could tell that when James stood up they would be within an inch of each other's heights.*" (Rowling, OotP, 641 USA)

In that memory, Harry sees his father, apparently unprovoked, tormenting Snape. The current-day Snape catches him and hauls him bodily out of that memory. Harry is deeply disturbed, as his perception of his father has been so rapidly changed. He remembers Snape's earlier statement that James had almost managed to get him killed, and wonders where the truth lies; he himself would not have acted the way his father did, and yet everyone is saying his father was such a good person.

Harry broods for a long time over this revelation, eventually breaking in to Professor Umbridge's office so that he can talk to Sirius Black via the Floo network. There, speaking with Sirius and Lupin, Harry learns that the memory did happen, but that James had gotten to be less of a bully as he matured. This does not console Harry, though, as he is now the same age that James was in the memory, and he is not beating up people in his class.

Half-Blood Prince Harry mentions, after Dumbledore's funeral, that he has to visit Godric's Hollow, as that is where everything began. He feels, among other things, that he must visit his parents' graves.

Deathly Hallows Harry learns that Albus Dumbledore had lived in Godric's Hollow, just as his parents had, and also that Bathilda Bagshot did as well. Bathilda, old as she is, may remember something of Harry's parents and of Dumbledore, both of whom he is very interested in finding out more about. Harry has already decided to visit Godric's Hollow, as mentioned above; circumstances, however, prevent his doing so until Christmas. In the meanwhile, he finds a letter from his mother to Sirius in which Lily says that Dumbledore had borrowed James' invisibility cloak. He and Hermione arrive at Godric's Hollow on Christmas Eve. Crossing the village square, Harry sees that the war memorial, to a Wizard's eye, contains a statue of his parents and himself. In the churchyard, he finds his parents' gravestone; Hermione creates a wreath of roses to lay upon it. Leaving the village, Harry finds the cottage where his parents had lived; it has been made into something of a memorial for them, with the wall still showing the effects of the magical blast that had resulted from Voldemort's attempt to kill him.

As they escape from Godric's Hollow, Harry sees, through the link between his mind and Voldemort's, Voldemort's memories of the night his parents had died. James, caught unawares by Voldemort, had tried to face him down without even a wand, and had fallen almost immediately.

It is not much later than this when Harry, Hermione, and Ron visit Xenophilius Lovegood. It is there that Harry learns that the Invisibility Cloak that his father had left him was one of the three Deathly Hallows. It was because it was such a unique artifact that Dumbledore had borrowed it from James: he had wanted to study it. We will find out over the course of the book that Dumbledore, as a young man, had been fascinated by the Hallows, and so the chance to study the second of the three was absolutely impossible to pass up, as was the chance to study the third one later.

Harry eventually learns that his fate is inextricably entwined with Voldemort's, that he must face, and be killed by, Voldemort in order that Voldemort might die. His fear at this is too great to allow him to pass the Dementors guarding the edge of the Forbidden Forest, so making use of the Resurrection Stone, Harry summons the shades of his father and mother, Remus Lupin, and Sirius Black to give him courage. As he reaches the clearing where Voldemort awaits, he deliberately drops the stone, releasing the four shades.

Relationships with Other Characters   James is married to Lily Potter (Evans).

During his time as a student at Hogwarts School of Witchcraft and Wizardry, James (with Sirius Black) often tormented Severus Snape resulting in Severus and James hating one another.

Jimmy Peakes

Gender: Male
Hair color: Unknown
Eye color: Unknown
Related Family: Unknown
Loyalty:

Overview

Jimmy Peakes joins the Gryffindor team in Harry's sixth year. He is short and broad chested, and although three years younger than Harry he is strong and quite fierce.

Role in the Books

Half-Blood Prince   Jimmy Peakes tries out for the Gryffindor Quidditch team and is accepted as one of the two Beaters, the other being Ritchie Coote.

When Cormac McLaggen is put in as Keeper to replace the poisoned Ron Weasley, he does not seem to understand the difference between practice and a real game, and borrows Peakes' Beater's bat to demonstrate the proper way to hit a Bludger towards the approaching Cadwallader. Mis-hitting the Bludger, he knocks Harry out instead, and as a result Gryffindor suffer a horrible defeat.

Deathly Hallows   Many underage Griffindors try to stay for the battle at Hogwarts, and Professor McGonagall must order them to leave; she calls out the names Creevy and Peakes when doing so.

Jugson

Gender: Male
Hair color: Unknown
Eye color: Unknown
Related Family: Unknown
Loyalty: Lord Voldemort

Overview

Jugson (no first name given) is a Death Eater who takes part in the battle at the Department of Mysteries.

Role in the Books

Order of the Phoenix   Jugson is one of the twelve Death Eaters who initially confront Harry and his five companions in the Department of Mysteries. He is first named when Lucius Malfoy is sending parties out to search for Harry and his companions, who have escaped; Jugson is teamed up with Antonin Dolohov. Jugson and Dolohov meet Harry, Hermione, and Neville Longbottom; Harry Petrifies Jugson, shortly after Hermione Silences Dolohov. Later in the battle, ten Death Eaters face Harry and Neville. We believe two Death Eaters are permanently disabled, one being Nott, and one never named, so we have to assume Jugson is amongst their number, though as Harry doesn't recognize him, he is never named.

Justin Finch-Fletchley

Gender: Male
Hair color: curly
Eye color: Unknown
Related Family: Unknown, Muggles
Loyalty:

Overview

Justin Finch-Fletchley is a student in Harry's year at Hogwarts, but is a member of Hufflepuff house, where Harry is in Gryffindor.

Role in the Books

Philosopher's Stone   The Sorting Hat places Justin Finch-Fletchley into Hufflepuff House.

Chamber of Secrets   Introduced to Harry in Herbology on the first day of classes, Justin Finch-Fletchley makes no secret of his Muggle parentage in discussions with Harry. He is threatened by a snake during the Duelling Club, and as Harry was talking to the snake at that point, trying to calm it so it wouldn't strike Justin, it appeared to Justin as though Harry was actually egging the snake on. The Hufflepuffs become convinced that Harry is planning mischief against Justin in particular; when Harry goes to find Justin to explain what had happened, he finds that Justin has been Petrified by the monster in the Chamber.

When Justin is revived, he makes a point of coming over to Harry at the feast, and apologizing profusely for ever having suspected Harry.

Order of the Phoenix   Justin Finch-Fletchley is one of the original members of Dumbledore's Army, and is present at the first meeting in the Hog's Head. We see him occasionally in passing in DA meetings.

Justin is also one of the six members of Dumbledore's Army who see Draco Malfoy attempting to jinx Harry on the Hogwarts Express, and promptly return fire, leaving Draco, Crabbe, and Goyle looking like gigantic slugs squeezed into Hogwarts robes.

Strengths Justin Finch-Fletchley mentions that he was accepted to attend Eton College, a very exclusive and prestigious Muggle boys school. This would imply that Justin is intelligent, has an outstanding academic record and is possibly from a wealthy and well connected Muggle family. In 2008 the tuition at Eton was £26,490 (approximately US$54,000) per annum.

Weaknesses Justin seems to be quick to jump to conclusions (as proved by his suspicion of Harry following the Duelling Club incident).

Relationships with Other Characters Justin is shown to be good friends with Ernie MacMillan.

Katie Bell

Gender: Female
Hair color: Blonde
Eye color: Unknown
Related Family: Unknown
Loyalty: D.A.

OVERVIEW

Katie Bell is a member of Gryffindor House. She is one year ahead of Harry, and plays Chaser for the Gryffindor Quidditch Team.

ROLE IN THE BOOKS

Philosopher's Stone When the Gryffindor Quidditch team take to the air for their first match, against Slytherin in November, it turns out that Lee Jordan is the announcer. He identifies the Chasers on both teams who are holding the Quaffle. This is the first time we hear Katie Bell's name, although presumably she has been practicing with Harry and the other members of the Quidditch team since Harry was made Seeker in mid-September.

Order of the Phoenix In the warmup before the first practice of the year, Ron passes the Quaffle to Katie too enthusiastically, and it catches her in the nose. Fred Weasley gives her something small and purple from his robe pocket, saying that it will clear up immediately. It does not, however. When Angelina tells her to do something about it, Fred examines what he has in his robe pocket and appears horrified by what he sees. Shortly afterwards, Angelina stops the practice; Alicia points Harry at Katie, who is being attended by Fred, George, and Angelina. Fred says that she had likely been given a Blood Blisterpod by mistake, and that he and George would take her to the Hospital Wing. Katie is one of the students who attends the first meeting of what becomes Dumbledore's Army, in the Hog's Head.

A short while later, horrible weather keeps the students in at break. Peeves is floating overhead in the room, flicking ink balls at the students when Angelina arrives to tell Harry and Ron that the Quidditch team has been re-formed. Peeves manages to hit Katie Bell with an ink ball, and she starts throwing things at him. As the bell rings, Peeves dumps an entire bottle of ink over Katie's head.

Katie plays in the match with Slytherin, a match which ultimately Gryffindor wins, despite Ron's poor Keeping, as Harry catches the Snitch for a final score of 160 to 40. Angelina, Alicia, and Katie then hold Fred back from attacking Draco Malfoy, who is taunting the entire Weasley family, while Harry holds George. When Draco starts insulting Harry's family as well, Harry is unable to restrain himself, and he and George attack Draco, while Fred remains restrained by the three Chasers.

As Harry has been unwillingly reduced to the role of spectator at Quidditch, he no longer interacts with Katie on the pitch. While we can assume that she continues to work with Dumbledore's Army, her work is not singled out on the rest of the story.

Half-Blood Prince Katie Bell again makes the Gryffindor Quidditch team, after pointing out to Harry that she should try out like everyone else; if there is someone better at Chasing than she is, that person should have her spot, friendship shouldn't automatically control team selection.

On a Hogsmeade weekend, she is apparently given a package to give to someone at Hogwarts. The contents of the package, which turns out to be a necklace that was seen earlier at Borgin and Burkes, carries a curse. Katie is injured and spends significant time in St. Mungo's Hospital. On her return, she tells Harry that she does not remember anything after walking into the ladies room at The Three Broomsticks, from which Harry concludes that she was put under the Imperius curse.

Deathly Hallows As she had graduated at the end of the previous year, we would not expect to see Katie return to Hogwarts. She does, however, return for the final battle against the Death Eaters; Harry sees her when he returns to the Room of Requirement after visiting Ravenclaw Tower. We don't hear much of how she acquits herself in battle, though.

Relationships with Other Characters While Katie does not obsess about Quidditch to the same extent that Oliver Wood, or later Angelina Johnson, does, she still seems to be quite caught up in it. We seldom see her when she is not playing or practicing Quidditch. It would seem that Katie has good relationships with Alicia Spinnet and Angelina Johnson, with whom she played Quidditch for most of her time at Hogwarts, and is generally seen with the two in most of her appearances throughout the series. Another of her good friends is Leanne, who isn't mentioned until the sixth book. Also, there are times that we see her sitting in a corner of the Gryffindor's common room, but generally there is no indication as to who she is sitting with, or what they are doing.

Although Katie Bell has a relatively minor role in the books, she has become a fairly popular character on the internet. In particular, a large amount of fan fiction has been written that pairs her with Oliver Wood. There is nothing in the books that would suggest any such relationship.

Kendra Dumbledore

Gender: Female
Hair color: Black
Eye color: Unknown
Related Family:
Loyalty: husband Percival Dumbledore, children Albus, Aberforth, Ariana
Unknown

Overview

Kendra Dumbledore was the mother of Albus, Aberforth, and Ariana Dumbledore, and wife of Percival Dumbledore.

Role in the Books

Deathly Hallows We first see mention of Kendra Dumbledore in a eulogy to Albus Dumbledore written by Elphias Doge. It is mentioned only that she had died as Albus was preparing for a trip around the world following his graduation from Hogwarts.

In a scurrilous tell-all book penned by Rita Skeeter, we hear that Kendra had been a very private witch, turning aside offers of friendship from neighbours in Godric's Hollow after the family's arrival there. It was suggested at that time that she was trying to hide the fact that her daughter, Ariana, was a Squib. Ron's Auntie Muriel confirms this view of her.

Finally, in discussion with Aberforth, Harry learns that Ariana had been beaten by Muggles and had suffered permanent damage as a result. Percival had retaliated against them and had gone to Azkaban prison as a result, and Kendra had packed up the family and moved to Godric's Hollow to start over. She had been keeping Ariana hidden to protect the neighbours from her fits of wild magic, and had not taken her to St. Mungo's for fear that they would never release her. In the end, it appears to have been one of Ariana's fits of wild magic which may have killed Kendra.

Kevin Whitby

Gender: Male
Hair color: Unknown
Eye color: Unknown
Related Family: Unknown
Loyalty:

Overview

Kevin Whitby is a Hufflepuff who arrived at Hogwarts in Harry's fourth year.

Role in the Books

Goblet of Fire Kevin Whitby was Sorted into Hufflepuff House.

Kingsley Shacklebolt

Gender: Male
Hair color: none
Eye color: Unknown
Related Family: Unknown
Loyalty: Order of the Phoenix; Albus Dumbledore

Overview

Kingsley Shacklebolt is a highly qualified Auror working in the Ministry of Magic; he is also a member of the Order of the Phoenix.

Role in the Books

Order of the Phoenix We first see Kingsley Shacklebolt as he is introduced to Harry as part of the Advance Guard, there to take him from Number Four, Privet Drive to the Order's Headquarters. He is also mentioned to be handling the Ministry's search for Sirius Black, which allows him to selectively give weight to misleading rumors about the fugitive.

As Arthur Weasley accompanies Harry to the Ministry before his hearing, they pass through the Auror division. Kingsley stops him and demands information on any reported flying vehicles, something that would be in Arthur's purview, as it is believed Sirius Black may still be using his flying motorcycle. In an undertone, Arthur invites him back to Headquarters for dinner, and Kingsley says that Sirius might be interested in an article in the magazine he's just handed Arthur. (We later hear that Harry guesses the magazine in question to be *the Quibbler*, which is carrying a story about Sirius in fact being one Stubby Boardman, a popular singing star.)

Kingsley is one of two Aurors who accompany Cornelius Fudge to Professor Dumbledore's office at the time of the attempted expulsion of Harry for violating an Educational Decree. Kingsley surreptitiously alters the memory of Dolores Umbridge's star witness, so that the evidence against Harry is not available. He warns Umbridge when she starts physically shaking that same witness, Marietta Edgecombe. And when the attempt is made to arrest Dumbledore, he does nothing, but allows himself to be knocked out alongside Fudge, Umbridge, and his fellow Auror Dawlish.

Half-Blood Prince It is mentioned that Kingsley Shacklebolt has become assistant to the Muggle Prime Minister, in order to protect the Prime Minister against the use of Dark Magic.

Deathly Hallows Vernon Dursley is visited early in the summer by Kingsley and Arthur Weasley, who tell him that Harry's magical protection will end on his seventeenth birthday, and that the Dursley family would then be at risk. They offer the services of some members of the Order of the Phoenix to hide and protect Vernon, Petunia, and Dudley. Vernon later voices dissatisfaction with the arrangements; it seems he has seen Kingsley on TV, as secretary to the Muggle Prime Minister, and is reassured by his proximity to power, but wants to know why Kingsley hasn't been assigned to Vernon's family.

It is mentioned that Kingsley Shacklebolt and Hermione, disguised as Harry, will be riding a thestral to create a diversion when Harry leaves Privet Drive on his way to the Burrow.

A Patronus is sent to warn the guests at Bill and Fleur's wedding that the Ministry has fallen to the Death Eaters. The Patronus is apparently sent by Kingsley as it speaks with his voice.

It is mentioned shortly after Christmas that Kingsley had used Lord Voldemort's name, and as a result was surrounded by Death Eaters. He had fought his way out and was now on the run.

In March, Ron manages to tune in the pirate wireless program "Potterwatch." Lee Jordan, as "River," introduces "Royal," easily identifiable by his voice as Kingsley, who gives information about the current state of the Wizarding government. "Royal" talks about heavy casualties among the Muggles, and approves of wizards who have acted to protect the Muggles from harm, often without the Muggles' knowledge.

Between the end of *Harry Potter and the Deathly Hallows* and the epilogue *Nineteen Years After*, Kingsley becomes Minister for Magic and makes many changes that make the Wizarding World "a sunnier one."

Kreacher

Gender: Male
Hair color: None
Eye color: Unknown, probably green
Related Family: Unknown
Loyalty: the Black Family

Overview

Kreacher is the house elf for the Black family.

Role in the Books

Order of the Phoenix Kreacher is first encountered when Harry Potter is brought into the Order of the Phoenix's headquarters, at Number 12 Grimmauld Place. He resents the new inhabitants of the house that has been a pure-blood stronghold for a long time, and wages his own little psychological warfare on them. Sirius Black says that he has been shut up in the house for ten years, taking orders only from the mad portrait of Sirius' mother, and going rather mad himself. It is noted that as Sirius and the others are collecting Black family artifacts to throw out, Kreacher is stealing some of them and hiding them away.

When Harry, Ron, Ginny, Fred, and George are transported by Portkey to Grimmauld Place after their father is injured, Kreacher makes a very insulting comment. "Is it true their father is dying?" Sirius, outraged, shouts "Out!" at him, whereupon he vanishes and is not seen again for some days. Hermione wants to give him a Christmas present, a quilt, but cannot find him; Sirius says that he has a sort of nest under the boiler, and Hermione leaves the quilt there. Harry notes that many of the pictures that he had helped Sirius discard, including a disturbing one of Bellatrix Lestrange, are arranged around Kreacher's sleeping space. Eventually, Kreacher reappears; apparently he has been in the attic all this time.

Later on, when Harry tries to find out if his vision of Sirius Black being attacked at the Department of Mysteries is true, Kreacher lies and says that his master is not home, and that Sirius will never return from the Department of Mysteries, making Harry believe that he must get to London immediately and try to save Sirius. When Albus Dumbledore arrives at Grimmauld Place, Kreacher laughs at him, telling him that Sirius is gone and won't be back. Dumbledore has to use rather forceful persuasion on Kreacher, but by doing so he learns that Sirius and the other Order members there present (Remus Lupin, Nymphadora Tonks, Kingsley Shacklebolt, and Alastor Moody), have gone off to the Ministry to rescue Harry. He also learns that the Death Eaters have learned about Harry's vulnerability to worry about Sirius because, when Sirius had dismissed Kreacher at Christmas, Kreacher had interpreted that as permission to leave the house, and he had gone to the only Black relative that he still respected: Narcissa Malfoy. Though unable to reveal any of the secrets of the Order, or anything he was specifically forbidden to talk about by Sirius, he still was able to reveal that Harry cared extremely deeply about Sirius. Additionally, by injuring Buckbeak, Kreacher was able to keep Sirius out of the way when Harry tried to reach him via the Floo network.

Half-Blood Prince By the terms of Sirius' will, Harry has inherited Grimmauld Place and all its contents, including Kreacher. Professor Dumbledore summons Kreacher to the Dursleys' house to determine whether the inheritance is valid; if there is a charm preventing Harry from inheriting, Kreacher will not accept his orders. Harry's desperate order to Kreacher to shut up is effective, proving that he, rather than Narcissa (Black) Malfoy, has actually inherited. Harry then, at a loss for anything else for Kreacher to do, sends him to Hogwarts to work in the kitchens.

Later, as Harry is the only person who believes Draco Malfoy is up to something, he sends Kreacher and Dobby to follow Malfoy and find out what he is doing. Kreacher's report is largely full of insults for Harry and compliments for Malfoy, but Dobby reports that Malfoy has been going to the Room of Requirement.

Deathly Hallows Harry discovers that the mysterious R.A.B. is Regulus Arcturus Black when he sees the sign on his bedroom door at Grimmauld Place. After a fruitless search of Regulus' room, Hermione recalls that there was a locket, but that they had thrown it out; Harry recalls that Kreacher was perpetually stealing stuff back, and they go to search Kreacher's sleeping area to see if he has in fact kept it. Kreacher's den is empty of valuables, but it occurs to Harry that Kreacher himself may know what happened to it. Harry summons Kreacher, who reports that he had stolen the locket back, but that Mundungus Fletcher had then stolen it from him, along with almost everything else of value in the house. Harry demands the full story; Kreacher tells how Voldemort had asked Regulus for a house-elf. Regulus had volunteered Kreacher, telling him that he was to come back as soon as the Dark

Lord was done with his services. Kreacher had accompanied Voldemort to the island in the lake that Harry had visited with Dumbledore, where Voldemort had forced Kreacher to drink a potion that left him remembering horrible things. Voldemort had placed a locket in the basin, had refilled it with potion, and then had vanished, leaving Kreacher alone; Kreacher had gone to the lake for a drink of water, and had been pulled under by the Inferi in the lake, and then had returned to his master, Regulus, as ordered.

Later, Regulus had taken him back to that same island, and had ordered Kreacher to force him to drink the potion, and then replace the locket with the one that Harry had found in the basin, and take the locket back to Grimmauld Place and destroy it. Regulus had drained the basin with Kreacher's assistance, and then struggled to the lake for water, and had been dragged under by the Inferi; and Kreacher had returned with the locket to Grimmauld Place, but had failed his master: he had been unable to destroy the locket, no matter how hard he tried.

Harry tells him that they, too, have the mission of destroying the locket, and as a token of their shared mission, he gives Kreacher the locket that Regulus had had him place in the basin, and that Harry had later recovered. Kreacher is overjoyed at this sign of consideration from Harry. Harry asks him to find Mundungus and bring him back, and Kreacher sets off immediately.

It is some days later that Kreacher returns with Mundungus, saying that he had been hard to trace. A number of times while Harry is interrogating Mundungus, Kreacher threatens him with a frying pan, because he is evidently being disrespectful to Harry.

Over the next month or so, Kreacher's work improves significantly, to the point that Harry is starting to enjoy returning to Grimmauld Place. After the invasion of the Ministry, however, Harry, Hermione, and Ron are forced to leave Grimmauld Place. With Harry gone, Kreacher apparently decides to return to Hogwarts, possibly in the hopes that his master (Harry) will be going there.

Kreacher leads the house-elves at Hogwarts into the second part of the battle at Hogwarts, cutting at the legs of Death Eaters with kitchen implements. After the final battle at Hogwarts, Harry hopes to himself that his four-poster bed in the dormitories at Hogwarts is still there waiting for him, and that Kreacher would be able to bring him a sandwich there . . .

Strengths As a house-elf, Kreacher has significant magic ability in his own person, ability that is distinct from human magic. He also has the house-elf trait of extreme loyalty to his Masters.

Weaknesses Kreacher shares the weaknesses of all House-elves: being tied to one family and one location and not being able to disobey their orders, and the relatively low verbal intelligence of the race. He is also, we are told, quite old, and when we first meet him has had no human contact except for Walburga Black's mad portrait for ten years. As such, he is presumed to be somewhat maddened himself. He does seem to recover when separated from Walburga's portrait.

Relationships with Other Characters It is a unclear whether Walburga treated Kreacher well or not. It might seem so, as Kreacher seems to follow the instructions issued by Walburga's painting, in preference to those of Sirius, a live Master. However, in *Harry Potter and the Order of the Phoenix*, Dumbledore discusses how house elves become loyal and what it means. And in *Harry Potter and the Deathly Hallows*, Harry showed that he was in the same side as Regulus and treated Kreacher with respect.

At that point, Kreacher accepted Harry as his Master and, to a great extent, accepted Harry's ideals as his own. We see this particularly in the Battle of Hogwarts, where Kreacher is seen leading the school's house elves to fight against against Lord Voldemort, and thus against the values of his earlier Masters. From this, it appears that house elves despite the strong link of obedience to the family and heritage, have a great loyalty of mind to those "Masters" who treat them well.

ANALYSIS

The author's choice of name for this character is interesting. We have seen that characters names are quite often related to their characteristics; for example, Rubeus Hagrid, a character hag-ridden by his heritage; Remus Lupin, whose name almost shouts his "furry little problem"; Albus Dumbledore, white of beard and hair, and eccentrically bumbling about like the bumblebee which is his last name, but with equally hidden purpose. In a world where house-elves are given cutesy, childish names like Dobby, Winky, and Hokey, Kreacher, which seems to be a portmanteau of "creature" and "treachery," is very out of place. The first time we see him, his name alone causes us to distrust him and his motives, and his perpetual string of muttered insults does nothing to change our feelings about him. One feels that the name was selected deliberately to foster that distrust; a name more in line with other house-elf names would have caused a certain cognitive dissonance that would have jarred throughout *Harry Potter and the Order of the Phoenix*, where an elf with a cute name was saying really horrible things about Harry, Hermione, and Ron. That dissonance would likely have distracted readers from the story.

QUESTIONS

1. Why did Kreacher lie to Harry about Sirius?
2. What causes Kreacher's change of heart towards Harry and his friends?

GREATER PICTURE

The author apparently insisted that Kreacher be part of the film of *Harry Potter and the Order of the Phoenix* because he will play an important part in the final chapter. As we can see in *Harry Potter and the Deathly Hallows*, this is the case.

At least one source had suggested that Kreacher's role would have something to do with the mysterious RAB identified with the locket Horcrux. Assuming that RAB was, in fact, Regulus Black, it could be

Kreacher who accompanied Regulus to the island of the locket; and Kreacher who was required to drink the potion that covered the locket. It is a bit of a surprise to find that it was Regulus who drank the potion, because given that Regulus was a good and loyal Black son, one would expect him to share the Black family disrespect for their servants. One finds it hard to imagine that Lord Voldemort would not have protected his Horcrux against other magical creatures; however, we have already seen with Dobby that house-elf magic is very hard to counter even for very powerful wizards. Additionally, Voldemort has been shown to have no respect for magic he cannot do himself; this tendency to discount non-human magic, and to discount the strength of non-Pureblood wizards, is a large part of what eventually brought him down.

Laura Madley

Gender: Female
Hair color: Unknown
Eye color: Unknown
Related Family: Unknown
Loyalty:

Overview

Laura Madley is a Hufflepuff who arrived at Hogwarts in Harry's fourth year.

Role in the Books

Goblet of Fire Laura Madley was Sorted into Hufflepuff House.

Lavender Brown

Gender: Female
Hair color: Unknown
Eye color: Unknown
Related Family: Unknown
Loyalty:

Overview

Lavender Brown is a Gryffindor girl in Harry's year. She is a very good friend of Parvati Patil, and favours Professor Trelawney's Divination lessons above all others.

Role in the Books

Philosopher's Stone Lavender Brown is the first student Sorted into Gryffindor.

While we see Lavender in passing in some of Harry's classes, she does not play any particularly significant role in this book.

Chamber of Secrets While we see Lavender in passing in some of Harry's classes, she does not play any particularly significant role in this book.

Prisoner of Azkaban Lavender, along with Parvati Patil, is particularly intrigued by Divination class, and almost starts worshiping Professor Trelawney when she correctly predicts that Neville will break some of her teacups. At the first Divination class, Professor Trelawney tells Lavender, "That thing you are dreading? It will happen on October 16th." On October 16, Lavender receives word that her pet bunny had been killed, and we see that Lavender has reshaped the prediction retroactively in her own mind so that it refers to this event: while she admits that she had not been dreading Binky's death, and that it had not actually happened on the 16th, she still resents Hermione's questioning of whether the prediction that Trelawney had made had actually come to pass.

Another thing that Trelawney had predicted was that "near Easter time, one of our number will leave us forever." Immediately after Easter break, as they are starting crystal balls, Trelawney claims to see the Grim in Harry's crystal ball. This gets Hermione angry, and she and Trelawney exchange words, as a result of which Hermione drops Divination. Lavender and Parvati immediately accept this as fulfillment of Trelawney's earlier prediction. It is mentioned that Lavender and Parvati seem to spend almost all of their free time up in Trelawney's tower after that.

Goblet of Fire Lavender's role in this book is relatively minor.

When Hagrid, in Care of Magical Creatures class, starts teaching the class about Skrewts, it is Lavender who discovers that some of them have stingers.

In desperation, Harry asks Parvati if she will go to the Yule Ball with him, and she accepts. He asks Lavender if she would go with Ron, but she is already going with Seamus.

After Hagrid returns from his self-imposed suspension, he chooses to prove that he can teach Care of Magical Creatures at least as well as Professor Grubbly-Plank. He chooses to teach about Unicorns, and has captured a foal which he has secured under the eaves of the Forbidden Forest. Lavender and Parvati are absolutely entranced by it.

Order of the Phoenix Lavender Brown is talking with Parvati Patil when Harry arrives in the Great Hall at the start of the school year. They greet Harry with a light, airy unconcern that tells Harry that they had been discussing him before he arrived. Hermione mentions the following morning that Lavender is skeptical of Harry's story that Lord Voldemort has returned. Apparently this is fairly common in the school, largely because the *Daily Prophet* has been systematically belittling Harry and Dumbledore over the summer.

On the second day of classes, when Professor Grubbly-Plank asks if anyone can identify the creatures she has in front of her, Hermione puts her hand up, and Draco imitates her. Pansy shrieks with laughter, then screams as the little bundles of twigs on the table jump up. Lavender and Parvati let out little sighs of amazement, which annoy Harry: it is not like Hagrid had not been showing them fantastic creatures all along.

As Harry enters the greenhouse for Herbology on the second day of classes, Luna Lovegood says that she believes Harry. Parvati and Lavender laugh at Luna and her earrings that appear to be orange radishes, but become much more sober when Ernie Macmillan loudly states that he believes Harry's report of the return of Voldemort.

Lavender is one of the students who attends the first meeting of what becomes Dumbledore's Army, in the Hog's Head.

When Hedwig appears outside the window of the History of Magic classroom, Lavender comments that she's always loved Hedwig, she's so beautiful.

After receiving her evaluation from Umbridge, Professor Trelawney seems distraught. Parvati and Lavender ask her what is wrong, and catch a lot of the resulting diatribe against "the establishment."

Parvati and Lavender are noted as being two of the students who are somewhat dismayed to see that Hagrid is back, when he returns from the mission Dumbledore had assigned him.

Lavender and Parvati Patil are seen hugging each other and crying quietly as Professor Trelawney is sacked by a cheerfully sarcastic Umbridge.

The following day, Lavender and Parvati suggest that Hermione should now be sorry that she had given up Divination, as the new teacher is Firenze. Hermione says that she was no terribly fond of horses, and Lavender, indignant, says that he isn't a horse, he's a Centaur. Hermione dismisses this, saying he still has four legs. Lavender says also that she and Parvati had gone to see Professor Trelawney and had found that she was distraught, still, and was saying that she would prefer to leave the school.

Lavender tells Ron that Firenze will be teaching in Classroom Eleven, on the ground floor, as he cannot manage the ladders that lead up to the tower. Reaching the classroom, everyone is surprised to see that it has been turned into a replica of a clearing in the Forbidden Forest. Although Lavender is likely as upset by Firenze's abrupt dismissal of all Trelawney's teachings as Parvati, she says nothing.

In the final meeting of Dumbledore's Army in April, the class is working on Patronuses. Several people in the class are having trouble; Lavender and Neville, in particular, can only produce little bits of white vapour.

Half-Blood Prince Lavender Brown becomes a more important character in this book, as she begins the year openly flirting with Ron Weasley. On his way to breakfast on his first day as a Prefect, Ron confiscates a Fanged Frisbee from a first-year student, then remarks that he'd always wanted one of them himself. Lavender, who is passing, laughs particularly loudly.

At breakfast, Professor McGonagall is handing out timetables. Lavender asks who is teaching Divination; told that Professor Trelawney is teaching the sixth-year students, Lavender and Parvati seem somewhat discouraged. After a particularly terrible Quidditch match, Ron and his sister Ginny have a row after he and Harry accidentally walk in on her snogging Dean Thomas in a Hogwarts hallway. They have a screaming match in which Ginny accuses Ron of having absolutely no experience with girls. Since Ron is still smarting from watching Hermione being singled out by Viktor Krum in *Harry Potter and the Goblet of Fire*, and their ongoing pen-pal relationship, he responds to Lavender's advances. Their relationship is publicly and intensely physical—Harry at one point compares it to a vertical wrestling match, and at another point wonders which of several hands he can see belongs to whom. This causes a huge rift between Hermione and Ron that lasts several months during their 6th year. Lavender Brown is something of a scatterbrain, however, and has absolutely no idea what Ron is thinking when they are apart. For example, at Christmas, Lavender sends Ron a gold necklace with letters spelling out "My Sweetheart"; Ron is repulsed by it. Ron eventually realizes that he needs more from a relationship than just snogging. On his birthday, Ron eats some chocolate cauldrons which have been spiked with love potion by Romilda Vane, who intended them for Harry. While Harry is taking him to Professor Slughorn to get the potion effects reversed, they meet Lavender; Ron roughly pushes her aside, saying that Harry has promised to introduce him to Romilda. After receiving the antidote, Ron is nearly killed by some poison intended for another victim, possibly Dumbledore. Lavender does visit Ron in the hospital wing, but complains to Harry that he always seems to be sleeping when she visits. Harry asks Ron about this, and Ron admits that he is feigning sleep, because he doesn't want to deal with Lavender at the moment. Lavender is outraged when she discovers that Ron has been released from the hospital wing, but she has not been told; and further, that Hermione evidently knew before Lavender did. Ron's relationship with Lavender seems to continue after his recovery, though it has suffered a major blow. At one point, when Hermione is correcting one of Ron's essays, in apparent gratitude he says "Thank you Hermione, I love you." Hermione replies that he shouldn't let Lavender hear that, and Ron says that maybe he should; he hasn't yet found any other way to break up with her.

Harry now determines that he must use Felix Felicis potion to get a memory from Professor Slughorn. Under the influence of this potion, he decides to don his Invisibility Cloak and go visit Hagrid. As he, Ron, and Hermione descend from the boy's dormitory, they run into Lavender; she of course can't see Harry, and starts berating Ron for being up in his dormitory "alone with *her*" (Hermione). This is basically the lever Ron needs to end his relationship with her. Ron almost immediately takes up with Hermione, and Lavender has very little further role except looking saddened by Ron and Hermione's closeness.

Deathly Hallows As Lavender Brown returns to Hogwarts to finish her seventh year there, we see very little of her in this book. She is one of the members of Dumbledore's Army who are found to be living in the Room of Requirement when Harry gets back to Hogwarts.

As Harry, Ron, and Hermione escape the castle on their way to the Shrieking Shack, they see Lavender, who has just fallen from a balcony in the Entry Hall, attacked by a grey blur that Harry at first takes for an animal. Hermione jinxes the blur, which Harry now recognizes as Fenrir Greyback. Fenrir is then knocked unconscious by a flying crystal ball, sent his way by Sibyll Trelawney.

Strengths Lavender seems to be intensely committed to her relationships, and fiercely loyal to friends and, apparently, lovers.

Weaknesses Lavender talks a lot and doesn't usually let anyone else get their message across. Somewhat gullible, she seems completely taken in by Professor Trelawney.

Relationships with Other Characters Throughout the series, Lavender is best friends with Parvati Patil.

Taken in by Professor Trelawney's "Divination," Lavender is seen to be almost hero-worshiping Trelawney starting from the first few Divination classes.

In her relationship with Ron, she seems to be more attached to an image of him than to him; she has no idea what he would actually like for Christmas, for instance. This relationship, which is intensely physical, is also marked by jealousy on Lavender's part.

QUESTIONS

1. Is Lavender Brown now a werewolf? It seemed that she was bitten by Fenrir Greyback near the end of book seven, and he may have been transformed into his werewolf form at the time.

GREATER PICTURE

It is interesting that in a clever twist by the author, it is Hermione who saves Lavender from being mauled by Greyback, in spite of Lavender being in direct competition with Hermione for Ron's affections throughout the course of *Harry Potter and the Half-Blood Prince*.

There is significant debate as to whether Greyback was in his Werewolf shape or not when Lavender was attacked; much of the debate appears on the talk page for that chapter. One major factor arguing against his being Transformed is the author's habit of never naming characters Harry has not been introduced to, and he has never seen Greyback transformed. The immediate identification of Greyback would imply strongly that Greyback is in his human shape. Against this, there is the description of Greyback as a "grey blur," and the fact that nothing in the text rules out Fenrir (and Lupin) being transformed.

Lee Jordan

Gender: Male
Hair color: Dreadlocks
Eye color: Unknown
Related Family: Unknown
Loyalty:

OVERVIEW

Lee Jordan is a close friend of Fred and George Weasley and is in their year, making him a third-year as Harry Potter enters Hogwarts. He is also the announcer for the house Quidditch matches.

ROLE IN THE BOOKS

Philosopher's Stone Someone named Lee is on Platform Nine and Three Quarters as Harry finds he way to the train. Lee has a box containing something with long, hairy legs. Fred and George later say that Lee Jordan has a giant tarantula. The evening Harry becomes Seeker for the Gryffindor Quidditch team, Fred and George congratulate him, saying that they too are on the team. They then say they have to talk to Lee, who thinks he has found a new secret passage out of the school.

When the Gryffindor Quidditch team take to the air for their first match, against Slytherin in November, it turns out that Lee Jordan is the announcer. He identifies the Chasers on both teams who are holding the Quaffle, particularly Angelina: when the Quaffle is in her possession, he comments as an aside that he is disappointed that she won't go out with him.

When the Snitch first appears, Harry is about to grab it when he is fouled by Marcus Flint, the Slytherin team captain. Lee reports this as he sees it, as cheating, and as a deliberate foul, and is called to order by Professor McGonagall. Lee is apparently quite happy with the final score, Gryffindor winning one seventy to sixty, that he is still shouting it out long after the game is done.

After the final exam of the year, Harry, Ron, and Hermione walk down to the shore of the lake to soak up some sun; they see Lee and the Weasley twins tickling the giant squid in the shallows of the lake. It is mentioned that Lee Jordan is the last person out of the Common Room when Harry, Hermione, and Ron decide to go through the trap door.

Chamber of Secrets We see Lee Jordan commentating the two Quidditch matches in which Harry takes part, but Lee plays little other role in the book.

Prisoner of Azkaban Lee Jordan again is the commentator for the Quidditch matches. We specifically make note of his presence in the match against Ravenclaw, where Professor McGonagall several times has to remind him that he is commentating a game, not advertising Firebolts. We also note in the final match of the season, against Slytherin, Professor McGonagall restrains him a few times from commenting harshly about the Slytherin tactics, though by the end of the game McGonagall is just as angry at the Slytherins as Lee Jordan is.

Goblet of Fire Lee Jordan is first mentioned shortly after the announcement of the Triwizard Tournament, scheming with Fred and George about ways to avoid the age limit that Professor Dumbledore says will be placed on the entrants to the tournament. When the Goblet of Fire is placed in the Entrance Hall to accept the candidates' names, Professor Dumbledore has drawn an age line around it to prevent underage wizards from competing. Lee, Fred, and George, who have apparently taken an aging potion, appear in the Entrance Hall to try and submit their names, but only Fred and George manage to cross the age line around the Goblet before it kicks them out, awarding them both long white beards in the process. Lee accompanies them to the Hospital Wing to have their beards removed. When the first Hogsmeade weekend rolls around, Ron and Harry have had a falling out, so Harry goes to Hogsmeade with Hermione. He sees Ron talking with Lee and the twins, but does not stop at their table. As they head back home on the Hogwarts Express, the Twins relate to Harry, Ron, and Hermione how Ludo Bagman had cheated them, and say that he had also cheated Lee Jordan's father the same way.

Order of the Phoenix Fred and George, on the Hogwarts Express to school, say that they need to sit with Lee Jordan, to talk business. By now, their plans for a joke shop are well underway, and they are in the process of lining up suppliers and creating their initial stock, we expect.

Lee Jordan is one of the group of students who is present at the first meeting of Dumbledore's Army, in the Hog's Head. He, Fred, and George are carrying bags from Zonko's Joke Shop.

Lee is commentator for the Quidditch match against Slytherin, the first of the year (and the only one Harry plays in). This time, Professor McGonagall restrains him when he begins effusively complimenting Angelina Johnson, and complaining that she won't go out with him.

When Hagrid returns from his mission, shortly before Christmas, Lee, Fred, and George are among the enthusiastic students welcoming him upon his return. Many others are not so demonstrative.

As a result of Educational Decree Number Twenty-Six, issued shortly after the mass breakout from Azkaban, teachers are forbidden from discussing anything unrelated to academics with the students. Lee sees this as a reason to state that Professor Umbridge should not be chastising Fred and George for playing Exploding Snap in her classroom, as what she is saying is clearly not to do with academics. As a result, he gets detention. Harry, knowing very well what Umbridge's ideas of detention are, suggests Essence of Murtlap to Lee to heal his hand. The idea, which had been given to Harry by Hermione, makes its way to the Twins, who use it as an ingredient for one of their Skiving Snackboxes.

While Lee is still commentating the Quidditch matches after the departure of the Twins, a lot of the joy seems to have gone out of his performance; his announcement of the players' names as they enter the pitch in the final, Gryffindor against Ravenclaw, is lacklustre.

Lee, hearing that Hagrid is being blamed for Nifflers being introduced into Professor Umbridge's office, admits to Harry and Hermione that he was the one who had put them in there, levitating them in through Umbridge's window.

Half-Blood Prince As Lee had graduated at the end of the previous year, we do not see him in this book.

Deathly Hallows At Bill and Fleur's wedding, Harry sees that Lee is dancing with Ginny. He tries not to resent the promise he had given Ron about not taking up with Ginny again.

Lee Jordan is "River," the main commentator on Potterwatch, the pirate wireless show that Ron tries endlessly to pick up, finally succeeding in March. He passes the news that Ted Tonks, Dirk Cresswell, the goblin Gornuk, and Bathilda Bagshot were dead. He then introduces, by code name, several newscasters, who are identified by Ron as Remus Lupin, Kingsley Shacklebolt, and Fred or George Weasley.

Lee is one of the first arrivals to the Room of Requirement when Neville recalls Dumbledore's Army to fight for the school, using Hermione's fake protean Galleons.

As Harry is on his way to the Room of Requirement, where he now believes Rowena Ravenclaw's lost diadem is hidden, he passes Fred Weasley, Lee Jordan, and Hannah Abbott guarding a hole behind a plinth where a statue had fallen. The statue had previously been masking one of the secret passages into Hogwarts.

Weaknesses Like many young men, Lee has not yet learned to consider all the ramifications of his actions. He had, on two occasions, introduced Nifflers into Professor Umbridge's office, and was dismayed to realize that Umbridge would leap to the conclusion that, because they were magical creatures, the Care of Magical Creatures teacher, Hagrid, would be blamed for it.

Relationships with Other Characters Lee is best friends with George and Fred Weasley.

When announcing Gryffindor Quidditch matches, he often compliments Angelina Johnson and bemoans the fact that she won't go out with him; on two occasions his commenting in that vein is reined in by Professor McGonagall. This would lead the reader to believe that he has something of a crush on Angelina, but apparently he never acts upon it.

Lee is somewhat open and trusting. One gets the feeling, though this is never borne out, that he is likely to catch the fallout from the Twins' pranks, possibly undeservedly. It is certainly true that he immediately accepts Harry's offer of help after his detention with Umbridge.

Lily Potter

Gender: Female
Hair color: Red
Eye color: Green
Related Family: James Potter, Harry Potter, Petunia Dursley
Loyalty: James Potter, Severus Snape, Albus Dumbledore

Overview

Lily Potter (nee Evans) is a muggle-born witch and Harry's mother.

ROLE IN THE BOOKS

Philosopher's Stone At the start of the book, Albus Dumbledore confirms to Minerva McGonagall that both Harry's parents have been killed.

In the hut on the rock, when Rubeus Hagrid arrives, there is a fair amount of discussion about Lily. Petunia Dursley, her sister, talks about how proud everyone was that they had a witch in the family, and of the way she would come home with pockets full of frog spawn and do magic in the house. Hagrid is shocked that anyone could have believed that James and Lily could have died in a car crash, tells Harry that they were murdered by the evil wizard Voldemort, and mentions that James and Lily were head boy and head girl.

Lily's image appears in the Mirror Erised when Harry finds it the first time at Christmas. A large number of pictures of Lily and James are in the photo album given to Harry by Hagrid just before Harry leaves the school for the summer.

Prisoner of Azkaban Harry, in talking with Professor Lupin about Dementors, mentions that when they approach him, he can hear Voldemort murdering his mother. Lupin is apparently moved by this revelation. This causes some conflict in Harry; he misses his mother greatly, and would do almost anything to hear her voice and see her face, as we have already seen. But if the only way that can happen is for him to suffer attacks from Dementors? And is he going to be able to fight Dementors, if something he wants so dearly would be removed by that fight?

Lupin later comments that Harry looks extraordinarily like his father, except for his eyes. He has his mother's eyes. In the Shrieking Shack, we hear Sirius Black's side of what happened when he was confronted by Peter Pettigrew. Pettigrew had yelled that Sirius had betrayed James and Lily, then blew up the street, changed into his rat shape, and escaped, leaving behind his own cut-off finger and robes. Sirius had then been taken to Azkaban, where he had served time for the murder of Pettigrew.

Goblet of Fire In the battle in the graveyard, while Harry is battling Lord Voldemort, shadows of the people Voldemort has killed begin appearing. Harry's father and mother both appear and speak with him.

Order of the Phoenix In Professor Dumbledore's Pensieve, Harry sees an episode where his father and the other Marauders are bullying a teenage Severus Snape. Harry also sees his then-teenage mother, who yells at Harry's father to leave Snape alone. She even goes to the lengths of taking out her own wand.

Half-Blood Prince When Harry first meets Horace Slughorn, Slughorn mentions that he is biased towards pure-bloods, which is no surprise given that he was head of Slytherin house. However, that doesn't mean that he refuses to see qualities in the Muggle-born; Harry's own mother, for instance, was quite a powerful witch, though of Muggle parentage, and was one of Slughorn's favorites.

In Potions class, Professor Slughorn mentions that Lily had been truly excellent at potions, and attributes Harry's skill to his being Lily's son.

Deathly Hallows While browsing Snape's thoughts in the Pensieve, Harry sees Lily as a child at her original Muggle home. Severus Snape, also then a child, informs Lily that she is a witch and that he had been spying on her and seeing her do incredible things. Snape explains the magical world to Lily and they soon develop the bond of friendship, despite the interference of Lily's sister Petunia. Later in the memories, when Lily is at Hogwarts, she explains to Snape that they can't continue their friendship because she has issues with the type of person Snape is becoming and who he associates with. Even though Lily marries James, she is Snape's unrequited love.

Lily's Patronus is also discovered to be a doe.

Strengths In book six, it is widely mentioned and thrown that Lily has extraordinary potions skills. Also, from what Professor Horace Slughorn has stated she was one of his brightest and smartest students, like Hermione.

Relationships with Other Characters Her parents are proud to have such a talented daughter, but her sister Petunia however, despised Lily for her magical abilities, sees her as a freak and considers her as a "dratted sister."

She meets James Potter in Hogwarts and although she leaves the impression that she dislikes him because he behaves like an arrogant bully, they eventually fall in love with each other, get married, and have a son, Harry. Being a member of the Order of the Phoenix that opposes Lord Voldemort, she and her husband confront him three times, and manage to escape. However, when The Dark Lord learns from Severus Snape about the prophecy, he starts looking for the Potter family. After Pettigrew's betrayal, Voldemort reaches Godric's Hollow, where he kills Lily and James.

Lisa Turpin

Gender: Female
Hair color: Unknown
Eye color: Unknown
Related Family: Unknown
Loyalty:

OVERVIEW

Lisa Turpin is a Hogwarts student in Harry's year, in Ravenclaw house.

ROLE IN THE BOOKS

Philosopher's Stone The Sorting Hat places Lisa Turpin into Ravenclaw house.

Lord Voldemort

Gender: Male
Hair color: none (formerly black)
Eye color: Red
Related Family: Tom Riddle Sr., Merope Gaunt
Loyalty: Himself

OVERVIEW

Lord Voldemort is perhaps the greatest dark wizard ever known and the most powerful in his own time. It is said that the only wizard he fears is Albus Dumbledore. He apparently believes that there is nothing worse than death, and it seems that he is lacking the ability to love or accept love.

ROLE IN THE BOOKS

Philosopher's Stone When Harry was one year old, Voldemort killed James and Lily Potter during his effort to murder their son. Harry survived, but Voldemort apparently lost his own life in the attempt, although some doubted he was truly gone. Harry had received a lightning-bolt shaped scar on his forehead in that attack.

Rubeus Hagrid, introducing Harry to the Wizzarding world, mentions Voldemort, and says how it was Harry who had made him vanish. Hagrid mentions that he personally believed that there was not enough left that was human in Voldemort to die.

Voldemort is mentioned when Harry is shopping for his wand. Having tried Harry with a large variety of wands, and seen them all unsuccessful, Mr. Ollivander finally tries him with one particular wand which he had evidently been holding in reserve. The wand suits Harry perfectly, and as he is leaving, Mr. Ollivander says "It is very curious indeed that you should be destined for this wand when its brother—why, its brother gave you that scar . . . I think we must expect great things from you, Mr. Potter . . . After all, He-Who-Must-Not-Be-Named did great things—terrible, yes, but great."

Voldemort is first revealed to us in the climactic battle at the end of this book. We discover that Voldemort's spirit lived, and he was able to possess Professor Quirrell's body. Throughout the book, he had driven Quirrell in an attempt to steal the Philosopher's Stone and kill Harry. Revelations at the end of the book show us that many of the things that had happened during the story were in fact driven by Voldemort.

Voldemort, assisted by Quirrell, had attempted to steal the Stone from Gringotts Bank, not knowing that Hagrid had removed it earlier that same day.

Harry's scar first pains him at the Arrival Feast, when he sees Professor Snape looking at him. It is likely that Voldemort is now riding the back of Quirrell's head, concealed by the turban that Quirrell is now wearing. (Harry remarks that it is new; he had seen Quirrell earlier, at the Leaky Cauldron, and Quirrell had not been turbaned then.) We guess later that Harrys scar had pained him because Voldemort had perceived him.

At Voldemort's apparent bidding, Quirrell also tried to knock Harry off his broom by hexing it during the Quidditch match against Slytherin. Harry had, on that occasion, been saved by Professor Snape. And it was Quirrell, again at Voldemort's instructions, who had been killing the unicorns in the Forbidden Forest so he could drink their blood to sustain Voldemort's tenuous life. Harry's scar again pained him when he encountered the robed figure that was attacking and killing unicorns.

In the end, Voldemort propels Quirrell through the elaborate security maze protecting the Stone at Hogwarts. He tries to use Harry, who has also bypassed the security, to fetch the Stone, and then orders Quirrell to kill him. With Quirrell's defeat and (probable) death, Voldemort is forced to flee his body and find a new host. Harry is nearly incapacitated by the pain originating in his scar, during the battle with Quirrell and Voldemort in the final chapter of the book.

In this book, Harry gains something of an understanding of the scar on his forehead. He discovers, in particular, that the scar becomes painful whenever Voldemort is nearby; Professor Dumbledore confirms this belief when he and Harry are talking about the events just past, in the Hospital Wing at the end of the book. Dumbledore mentions that it was the backfiring of a powerful curse that left that scar, and it likely indicated that there was something of a connection between Harry and Voldemort which the curse had left behind it. He does not, however, go into detail at this point.

Chamber of Secrets Voldemort does not act directly in this book; instead, the story is driven by a remnant of his younger self, contained in a magical diary, when he still used his birth name Tom Riddle. Details are under that character entry.

Prisoner of Azkaban Lord Voldemort is not seen directly, as he hides and regains strength. At the end, Peter Pettigrew (Wormtail) returns to serve him after escaping Harry, Sirius Black, and Remus Lupin.

Goblet of Fire We first hear Voldemort (though we don't see him) when he takes up residence in the old Riddle manor in Little Hangleton. There, we are with Frank Bryce, as he listens to Voldemort and Pettigrew discussing how one Bertha Jorkins had died, and what they had found out from her. They also discuss Voldemort's one *faithful* servant, with the implication that Pettigrew is less faithful. Bryce also listens in as Voldemort and Pettigrew apparently plan the murder of one Harry Potter. Bryce is then discovered and brought into the room where Voldemort is, and shortly thereafter Voldemort kills him. We see all of this though Harry's mind, as Harry then awakens, as if from a dream, with his scar paining him. Knowing that pain in his scar has previously meant that Voldemort was near him, Harry is worried: is he about to be attacked, right there on Privet Drive?

Much later, Harry dreams again, this time that Pettigrew is being punished for a mistake he had made. The blunder was not fatal, as the man was now dead, but Pettigrew is punished again anyway.

When Harry and Cedric Diggory touch the Triwizard trophy, they discover that it has been made into a

Portkey, and it carries them to a graveyard near what we soon realize is Little Hangleton. There, Pettigrew, on orders from Voldemort, kills Cedric and binds Harry to a gravestone. Here, while Pettigrew is off gathering potion ingredients, we get our first look at what Voldemort has become: the size of a baby, but with snakelike and scaled skin, slitted eyes, and a grown man's malevolence.

Pettigrew now lights a fire under the stone cauldron he has brought, and with some of the bones of Voldemort's father, Harry's blood, and his own flesh (his right hand), the potion he has created re-embodies Voldemort, who climbs out of the cauldron fully-formed. Exulting in his returned body, Voldemort briefly taunts Harry, then, ignoring the whimpering Pettigrew, summons his Death Eaters.

Now ignoring Harry, as well as Pettigrew, he greets his Death Eaters who have appeared, wearing hooded robes. One begs forgiveness and grovels before Voldemort, and is promptly tortured for having doubted Voldemort would return. Voldemort says that he does not forgive, he does not forget, and he will want thirteen years repayment for his Death Eaters having denied him. He then rewards Pettigrew for his service in bringing Voldemort back, by giving him a magical silver hand to replace the one Pettigrew cut off.

A Death Eater with the voice of Lucius Malfoy asks how Voldemort had come back. Voldemort says that he had taken measures to prevent his soul leaving if his body failed, and so when the curse on Harry had backfired, and his body had died, he had wandered as a naked soul, ending up in Albania. There, he had occupied small animals, none of which lived for long, until eventually a weak wizard had come along who he could take over. His attempt to capture the Philosopher's Stone had failed, and the wizard had died, leaving him alone as a spirit once more until Pettigrew had found him, and had brought Bertha Jorkins to him. It was through Bertha that he had discovered that he still had one true ally in the outside world, and had discovered the means to capture Harry and bring him to Voldemort. Bertha had been of no use after he had done with her, but Pettigrew had been able to craft him a body, small and almost powerless, but enough to keep him alive, and had sustained him with Nagini's venom, until now he had Harry Potter trapped. He demonstrates that he no longer needs to fear Harry's touch, by holding his hand against Harry's face; Harry is in agony from his scar. Voldemort then orders Pettigrew to fetch Harry's wand and release him, so that he and Voldemort may duel.

Harry finds himself with his wand and standing free, but surrounded by enemies and facing Voldemort. Voldemort forces him to bow, saying that the forms of dueling must be obeyed, and then curses Harry to demonstrate that Harry has no power over him. Recovering, Harry ducks behind a gravestone. Voldemort taunts him, and Harry decides that if he is going to die, it will not be cowering and hiding, but standing proudly. Rising from hiding, Harry casts the Disarmament spell at exactly the same time Voldemort casts the Killing Curse. Both Harry and Voldemort are amazed when a band of golden light unites their wands, the two of them are lifted and set down some distance away, and a dome of golden light starts to form around them. Harry finds that his wand is heating up, and vibrating fiercely. He also sees beads of light on the band joining the two wands, and finds that he can force them along the band towards Voldemort. Somehow, he feels that he must do this. Voldemort, obviously afraid, tells the Death Eaters to do nothing. As Harry forces the first bead of light into Voldemort's wand, both wands scream, and a misty shade of Cedric appears out of Voldemort's wand. Cedric's shade tells Harry not to break the connection between the wands. Harry keeps forcing beads of light into Voldemort's wand, though it feels as though his own wand will either explode or vibrate out of his hand, and in turn, shades of an old Muggle, a woman who Harry believes is Bertha Jorkins, and his own father and mother come out of Voldemort's wand. The shades of his parents tell him that when he breaks the connection, they will stay visible for a short while, and will cluster around Voldemort to obscure his vision; Harry will have the chance to run for it. Cedric's shade asks Harry to take his body back, for his parents. Harry breaks the connection, as the shades cluster around Voldemort, and runs through the tombstones. Stones splinter and crack around him as the Death Eaters, and Voldemort, throw curses; he reaches Cedric's body, Summons the Triwizard Cup, and is brought back, with Cedric's body, to the site of the Third Task.

From the hedge maze, Harry is taken by Professor Moody, who seems unsurprised to hear of Voldemort's return. He asks if the Death Eaters were summoned, and if they were punished for their lack of faith. As he talks, it becomes apparent to Harry that Moody is on Voldemort's side; Moody confirms this, saying that he had been arranging things so that Harry would be the first to touch the Triwizard trophy, and had made the trophy a Portkey that would carry Harry to Voldemort. He then says that, if he kills Harry, he will be great in Voldemort's eyes, and will be chief among the Death Eaters. As he prepares to kill Harry, the office door is broken down, and Moody is stunned by Dumbledore. Deprived of Polyjuice Potion, the stunned Moody shortly turns into Barty Crouch Jr. . Under the influence of Veritaserum, Barty reveals that Voldemort had come to his house with Pettigrew and had placed his father under the Imperius curse, and that with Pettigrew's help he had then attacked Moody and taken over from him. His actions throughout the year had been planned by Voldemort, specifically to get Harry away from the school and into Voldemort's power.

On being told all of this, Cornelius Fudge refuses to believe it, almost pleading with Dumbledore to admit that it is not true. When Dumbledore will not bend, Fudge decides that Dumbledore is creating this story in order to secure the office of Minister for Magic for himself. After his departure, Dumbledore assigns missions for Hagrid and Madam Maxime, if she will go; for Snape; and for Sirius.

At the Leaving Feast, Dumbledore tells the school that Voldemort has returned, and that he had murdered

Cedric Diggory. He also says that this information will not be popular with the Wizarding world, and that many parents will wish that it had not been revealed to their children, but that it was still going to be something they would need to know.

Order of the Phoenix   Knowing that Voldemort has returned and that few in the Wizarding world believe this, Harry is on edge even during the summer. He makes a point of listening to the Muggle news for unexplained deaths and possibly magical disturbances, as well as scanning the front page of the *Daily Prophet*, for signs that Voldemort is trying to regain power. His tension is not eased by the fact that, though both Ron and Hermione are writing to him, their letters seem designed to tell him nothing of what's going on in the Wizarding world.

Shortly after Harry is attacked by Dementors, he tells his Uncle Vernon that Voldemort has returned; recognizing that this puts his own family in danger, Vernon orders Harry out of the house. He is forestalled, however, by a Howler, which reminds Harry's Aunt Petunia of the duty she has taken on. She overrides Vernon, but does not prevent Vernon from locking Harry into the bedroom again. Shortly, Harry is released by a group of wizards including Lupin and the real Alastor Moody; they escort him to Number 12, Grimmauld Place, the headquarters of the Order of the Phoenix. Here, he learns that the Order believes that Voldemort is deliberately doing nothing, staying out of sight while he rebuilds his organization. Harry is told that, by reporting Voldemort's return immediately to Dumbledore, he had made Voldemort's return much harder. He is also told that Dumbledore is looking for something, which is here referred to as a weapon.

Just after Harry's return from the hearing at the Ministry, as his celebratory dinner is being prepared, Harry's scar pains him sharply. Hermione is the only one who notices, everyone else is celebrating Harry's acquittal. In response to Hermione's concern, Harry says it's nothing, it happens all the time now.

Very soon after arriving at Hogwarts, Harry gets into an argument with the other people in his dorm. It seems that Seamus was almost not allowed to return to Hogwarts because of Harry's and Dumbledore's belief in Voldemort's return, though Neville echoes his grandmother's belief that Dumbledore is a lot more trustworthy than the *Daily Prophet*.

Shortly after classes start, Harry gets into an argument with the new Defence Against the Dark Arts teacher, Professor Umbridge, as to whether Voldemort had returned or not. Umbridge refuses to believe that Voldemort has returned, instead accusing Harry of seeking attention. Eventually, Umbridge gives Harry detention, which turns out to involve writing lines. At the end of the detention period, which ends up covering two weeks, Umbridge takes Harry's hand to see how detention is progressing, and Harry's scar suddenly pains him. Later, talking this over with Ron and Hermione, Harry expresses concern that Umbridge may be somehow linked to Voldemort. Hermione suggests that he should tell Dumbledore about it, and Harry, stung by Dumbledore's apparent avoidance of him all summer, says that's all Dumbledore's interested in, his scar.

Harry does, however, need to talk to someone about it, so he crafts a message for Sirius. Sirius responds via the Floo network, saying that Umbridge is bad enough, but the Order don't believe there is any connection with Voldemort.

Harry is also having repeated dreams about a long corridor with a doorway at the end. In his dream, he longs to go through that doorway and find what is on the other side of it. While we don't yet know whether these are originating with Voldemort, the fact that Harry's scar is always prickling or painful when he awakens from these dreams is certainly suggestive.

Harry gets into trouble again with Umbridge by pointing out that the only Defence Against the Dark Arts instructor that Umbridge feels was competent, Professor Quirrell, had Voldemort stuck on the back of his head. During the detention that follows this outburst, Hermione and Ron suggest to Harry that he should teach his own Defence Against the Dark Arts class, seeing as how he was the only one there who had actually faced Voldemort and knew what it was like. Eventually, Harry agrees; this group will become known as Dumbledore's Army. After a disastrous Quidditch practice, Harry's scar pains him again. Ron asks what is happening; Harry tells him that Voldemort is upset, there's something he wants and it is not happening fast enough. Looking back through his memories, Harry recalls that when Umbridge had touched his hand after detention, and his scar had hurt, Voldemort had been happy; the earlier occasion, before they came to school, he had been furious about something. At the first meeting of Dumbledore's Army, Harry chooses to start them off with something simple: the Disarmament jinx. Zacharias Smith objects to starting with something so simple; Harry points out that he had used it successfully against Voldemort, and Smith subsides.

On Hagrid's return, he reports that he had been sent to try and recruit the Giants in the fight against Voldemort. He had failed, because Voldemort had sent Death Eaters who had gotten there first, and were offering better rewards. Shortly before Christmas, Harry dreams again that he is in the long hallway, this time at a very much lower level. He sees a man there, asleep in front of a door; the man awakens, and Harry, feeling himself long and sinuous, rises and bites him with his snake's fangs. Waking up with a terrible pain in his scar, he tells Ron that he has just seen his father being attacked. Professor McGonagall, arriving on the scene, hears him out and takes him to Dumbledore's office. Dumbledore also hears him out, and sends portraits to alert people near there. He also has Professor McGonagall bring all the Weasley children to his office, and then sends them all, and Harry, to Grimmauld Place. As he is sending them, Dumbledore happens to look into Harry's eyes for the first time this year; Harry feels the snake from his dream rise up inside him, full of desire to bite Dumbledore.

Harry, Mrs. Weasley, and the Weasley children, guarded by Moody and Tonks, visit Arthur in hospital. After the children have visited, the adults gather for what they believe is a private meeting. Harry and the others are able to eavesdrop, however, and overhear Moody suggesting that it is likely that Harry's seeing the attack, which seems to have been carried out by Voldemort's pet snake Nagini, means that somehow Harry and Voldemort have some sort of mental connection. Harry, already afraid that his experience means that he might turn into a snake and attack his friends, now fears that Voldemort might be looking into Headquarters through his eyes, and resolves to leave. He already has his trunk packed and is heading for the door when the portrait of Phineas Nigellus brings a message from Dumbledore: "Stay where you are." While Harry is again dismayed at the lack of information, he accepts the order, but resolves to stay clear of his friends in case he attacks them.

Very soon, however, Hermione arrives, having chosen to skip the planned skiing vacation with her parents. She finds Harry and almost drags him out of isolation. With Ron and Ginny, she discusses the belief that Voldemort may be possessing Harry. Ginny points out that she alone knows what it feels like, as she was possessed by Voldemort some years before. Harry apologizes for forgetting that, and after hearing Ginny's description of what it was like, accepts that he has not, in fact, been possessed.

As Christmas vacation comes to a close, Professor Snape, visiting Grimmauld Place, tells Harry that Dumbledore wants Harry to take Occlumency lessons from Snape. The intent is to prevent Voldemort from being able to put visions into Harry's head. It turns out that Harry is unable to calm his emotions in Snape's presence, and so is unable to close his mind. For the first time, in Snape's office, Harry is forced to think about the recurring dream he has had, and recognizes the hallway in the dreams as the one leading to the Department of Mysteries at the Ministry of Magic, and also as the place where Arthur Weasley was attacked. Harry discusses this later with Ron and Hermione, and they come to the conclusion that the weapon Voldemort is seeking is in the Ministry.

That night, Harry again finds himself felled by the pain in his scar. Asked by Ron what is going on, Harry says that Voldemort is very happy about something. Harry wonders what could have made Voldemort the happiest he has been in fourteen years, and in passing, whether Snape is perhaps tearing down his mental defences while claiming to be strengthening them.

The next morning, Harry finds out that what has made Voldemort so happy is a mass jail break from Azkaban. Ten Death Eaters have escaped, and Hermione sees this as an indication that Voldemort has managed to win the Dementors over to his side. Many wizards are as scared of Death Eaters as they are of Voldemort, and Harry finds that his students in Dumbledore's Army are working harder than ever. His Occlumency classes are not going as well; he is making little progress, and his scar is now tingling continuously. Harry can quite plainly see increased sensitivity to Voldemort's emotions dating back to the start of his Occlumency lessons, and again wonders if Snape is opening his mind rather than helping him close it.

In late February, Harry again starts seeing events through Voldemort's eyes. Now, he is looking at Rookwood, one of the escapees from Azkaban, who is explaining that as a one-time Ministry employee, he knows that the plan proposed by Avery would not work. Voldemort dismisses him, and sends for Avery; Harry awakens, screaming, and tries to ignore Voldemort punishing Avery while he explains to Ron what he has been seeing. Later, in discussion with Hermione, they conclude that Bode, who they had seen in St. Mungo's Hospital, had been put under the Imperius curse to try and retrieve the weapon. He had run afoul of the protective spells around the weapon, and had been left insane, but the nurse at St. Mungo's had said he was improving, so Voldemort had had him killed.

In his next Occlumency lesson, Harry again experiences the dream of corridors, but this time when he reaches the doorway, it is open. Snape breaks him out of the dream, and asks about it, but Harry does not wish to tell him. They are interrupted by screaming in the Entry Hall: Professor Umbridge has fired Professor Trelawney. Shortly after Dumbledore's departure from Hogwarts, Harry again dreams of the corridor, but this time the door is open, and in his dream he proceeds to a room full of dusty glass phials on row after row of shelves. He knows that what he wants is almost within his grasp, when he is rudely awakened by an exploding firework. Exhausted by preparations for his O.W.L. exams, Harry falls asleep in the History of Magic test. He dreams again, finding his way to the room with the glass phials, and there finding Voldemort torturing Sirius, forcing him to pick up one of the phials. Harry is convinced that he must go to the Ministry and rescue Sirius. He remains convinced that he will be able to tell when Voldemort actually kills Sirius by the pain in his scar, which is tingling. At the Ministry, Harry, with five fellow members of Dumbledore's Army, is confronted by twelve Death Eaters, who are after a prophecy that had been made about Harry. Harry and his fellows run, but are eventually disabled. Harry, alone, remains able to fight, and he is hampered by the presence of Neville, still gamely struggling although his broken nose prevents him from casting spells properly. Reinforcements, including Sirius, arrive from the Order of the Phoenix, and eventually the Death Eaters are neutralized, though one, Bellatrix Lestrange, escapes, managing to kill Sirius and get to the Atrium. Harry chases her, revealing to her as they duel in the Atrium that the Prophecy has been destroyed. She seems upset by this, the more so as Voldemort joins her, assisting her in her duel with Harry. Dumbledore appears, and duels with Voldemort, while summoning members of the Ministry. Finally, Voldemort flees, but then returns, possessing Harry and using his mouth to taunt Dumbledore. Harry, convinced that he is about to die, thinks that soon he will be with Sirius again, and Voldemort, unable to stand the overwhelming feeling of love in Harry's mind, flees.

Back in Dumbledore's office, Dumbledore starts by claiming responsibility for Sirius' death, saying that if he had been more open with Harry, Harry would have realized that Voldemort was leading him into a trap. Dumbledore reveals to Harry that the events that had left the scar on Harry's forehead had also created a link between Harry and Voldemort, through which Harry had been able to sense Voldemort's emotions, when they were strong enough, and also, occasionally, Voldemort's thoughts. While Dumbledore had been aware of this link, Voldemort had not, until Christmas when Harry had seen Nagini attacking Arthur Weasley. This is actually why Dumbledore had been avoiding Harry; he was worried about the way Voldemort would act if he had any idea that the relationship between Harry and Dumbledore was anything more than the relationship between student and headmaster. Sirius had told Dumbledore that Harry had felt something snake-like welling up inside him, and had wanted to strike at Dumbledore, just before the Portkey activated. This told Dumbledore that Voldemort was aware now of the linkage, and was able, sometimes, to see through Harry's eyes. It is because of this that he had wanted Harry to learn Occlumency from Snape, something, he now realized, that was impossible. Finding out about this link, Voldemort had started placing images in Harry's mind, that would eventually lead him to the Hall of Prophecy where the Death Eaters would be waiting.

Dumbledore explains to Harry why he had been placed with the Dursleys: his mother's sacrificing her own life to save Harry had provided powerful magical protection for Harry, the same protection that had saved him when Voldemort first tried to kill him, but that protection would only remain in force while he had a place that he could call home, and with his mothers' blood relation—his Aunt Petunia. Dumbledore, convinced that Voldemort would return, felt that Harry's safety outweighed everything else, even Harry's own comfort.

Dumbledore tells Harry that Voldemort has been trying to kill him because of a prophecy that had been made before Harry was born, and which Voldemort had only heard the first part. Voldemort's efforts this year have been bent towards recovering that specific prophecy, the one which Harry had found, so that he might hear the other half. Harry tells him that the prophecy had been destroyed. Dumbledore says that what had been destroyed was a recording of the prophecy, but that the prophecy was made to him. Bringing out the Pensieve, Dumbledore places a memory in it, and the figure of Sibyll Trelawney rises from it. In the harsh voice Harry heard once before, says, *"The one with the power to vanquish the Dark Lord approaches . . . born to those who have thrice defied him, born as the seventh month dies . . . and the Dark Lord will mark him as his equal, but he will have power the Dark Lord knows not . . . and either must die at the hand of the other for neither can live while the other survives . . . the one with the power to vanquish the Dark Lord will be born as the seventh month dies . . ."*

Dumbledore goes on to say that the prophecy could refer to either Harry or Neville Longbottom. It is perhaps telling that Voldemort chose to kill Harry, the "half-blood," rather than the pure-blood Neville. By his attempt to kill Harry, Voldemort had marked Harry as his equal. The power that Harry has, that Voldemort does not, is love. It is the strength of that love that protected Harry from Voldemort, and it is that strength that will allow him to defeat Voldemort in the end. Dumbledore also confirms that, according to the prophecy, one of the two of them must kill the other.

With the Ministry finally accepting that Voldemort has returned, Dumbledore is re-instated as Headmaster of Hogwarts, and in his other offices.

Half-Blood Prince The book opens with the Muggle Prime Minister being visited by Cornelius Fudge. Fudge tells the Prime Minister that, contrary to what Fudge had told him earlier, Voldemort was back, and in fact had been responsible for several crises that were damaging the Prime Minister's government. A bridge that had collapsed for no known reason had in fact been destroyed by Voldemort, two unsolved and apparently unsolvable murders were also his work, and the "tornadoes" that had done so much damage were, they think, actually the work of at least one Giant. Voldemort's return had also resulted in Fudge losing his position as Minister for Magic; he would remain as liaison, but his main purpose in the meeting was to introduce the new Minister, Rufus Scrimgeour.

We now see Draco's mother pleading with Severus Snape for assistance with something that Voldemort wants done. Bellatrix Lestrange, Narcissa's sister, who is also there, objects to Narcissa's approaching Snape, and challenges Snape as to his loyalty to Voldemort. Snape points out that Voldemort had had the same questions that Bellatrix was putting to him, had received answers from Snape, and had found them satisfactory; was she suggesting that she would receive better answers than possibly the greatest Legilimens the world had even known? While Bellatrix hesitates over her response, Snape answers her questions. Where was he when the Dark Lord fell? At Hogwarts, where Voldemort had ordered him to spy on Dumbledore. Why did he not go looking for the Dark Lord after he had fallen? For the same reason many other Death Eaters did not: he thought the Dark Lord was finished. Bellatrix retorts that she had looked for him. Snape sarcastically comments about how "useful" she was while imprisoned in Azkaban, while he had collected sixteen years' worth of information on Dumbledore for Voldemort. Snape continues: Why did he stand between the Dark Lord and the Philosopher's Stone? Because the Dark Lord believed Snape had deserted him for Dumbledore, Snape was unaware that it was Voldemort that looking for the Stone. He thought Quirrell was searching for it for his own purposes and, of course, he acted to prevent that. Why did he not respond to the Dark Lord's summons when Voldemort returned? He returned two hours later, at Dumbledore's orders. That way, Dumbledore would continue to believe that Snape was spying on Voldemort for him, rather than the other way around. Bellatrix says she is unaware of any information Snape passed to Voldemort, although she should know: Voldemort says she is his most trusted lieutenant. Snape somewhat acidly wonders if she still is after the fiasco at the Ministry. And where was he at that battle? On the Dark Lord's orders, he stayed out of it. Did Bellatrix think Dumbledore would not notice if Snape had joined the Death Eaters in that battle? In any event, the information Snape supplied made Emmeline Vance and Sirius Black's deaths possible, and the Dark Lord was satisfied with his information. Why did Snape not kill Harry Potter? Because it was only Dumbledore who was keeping Snape effective as a spy and out of Azkaban. If he killed Potter, he would lose that protection and would be unable to help Voldemort. And that has been what has made him useful to the Dark Lord: Dumbledore's trust in him.

With Bellatrix's worries overridden, Narcissa explains why she has come. Voldemort has assigned her son, Draco, a difficult and probably deadly task. Narcissa asks Snape to protect him. Snape replies that it is folly for her to talk to him about it because that is breaking the Dark Lord's wish. Death Eaters seldom know what tasks their colleagues have been assigned. Luckily for Narcissa, however, Snape already knows about this task, but even as the Dark Lord's most trusted confidante, he cannot convince him to change his mind, nor will he try. Narcissa says assigning Draco this task is revenge for her husband, Lucius, having failed at the Ministry. Snape admits that the Dark Lord is angry at Lucius. Finally, though, Snape agrees to swear an 'Unbreakable Vow' that he will protect Draco, and if Draco is unable to complete his assigned task, Snape will do it for him.

It is mentioned that with the acceptance of Voldemort's return, the Ministry has gone all-out with stories about the threat in the Daily Prophet, and pamphlets of supposedly useful information, including methods of detection of those people who are under the Imperius curse.

As he and Harry are leaving the Dursleys,' Dumbledore asks if Harry's scar has been giving him any pain. Harry replies that it has not, and admits to being surprised by this. Dumbledore says that he is not surprised, he believes Voldemort has discovered the danger of having Harry able to see into his mind and is using Occlumency to prevent contact.

A large part of this book is concerned with Harry discovering Lord Voldemort's early years, through the agency of Dumbledore's Pensieve. It is here that we learn about his mother Merope Gaunt, Salazar Slytherin's direct descendant, and his father Tom Riddle, a Muggle. As he is known, during this time, by his birth name, the discoveries Harry makes about his early career are under *Tom Marvolo Riddle*. In the latest of these sessions with the Pensieve, we see Dumbledore commenting that he already knows that Tom is using the name Voldemort. Though Voldemort does not appear directly during Harry's sixth year, it turns out that he has ordered Draco Malfoy to kill Dumbledore. We believe that this is the mission that Narcissa Malfoy was so concerned about in the opening chapters of the book, and as she expected, Draco fails this mission. Snape must finish the mission by killing Dumbledore.

At the end of the book, as Snape and Draco flee, other Death Eaters attack Harry, who is chasing them. Snape stops them, saying that Voldemort wants Harry for himself.

Deathly Hallows The story opens with two Death Eaters entering Voldemort's headquarters, Malfoy Manor. There, at a long table with an unconscious witch floating above it, Voldemort is holding court. He places one of the Death Eaters, Yaxley about halfway down the table, and the other, Snape, he places at his right side. He then asks for information about Harry Potter. Snape informs him that he will be moved to a safe house the following Saturday, while Yaxley says that his information is that it will be on Harry's birthday, three days later. Snape says that Yaxley's information, coming as it does from the Ministry, is suspect; the Order of the Phoenix believes that the Ministry is riddled with spies, and will have been laying a false trail. Voldemort looks deeply into Snape's eyes for a moment; many at the table seem to be made uncomfortable by this, but Snape does not. Voldemort then asks about plans to infiltrate the Ministry. Yaxley announces that they have places Pius Thicknesse, the head of the Auror branch, under the Imperius curse. Snape points out that, it being unlikely that they will have complete control over the Ministry in the few remaining days before Potter is moved, they will still have to work under cover.

Voldemort now mentions the concern that he has that Harry's wand, twin to Voldemort's, might well prevent Voldemort from killing him. He demands a wand from Lucius Malfoy, far down the table, who seems to momentarily believe that he'll be getting one in exchange, though Voldemort says Lucius will not be needing a wand. When Bellatrix Lestrange protests her position near the Malfoys at the table, Voldemort taunts her about her cousin, Tonks, who is marrying a werewolf. By means of testing the wand, he awakens the unconscious witch, and over her pleas for mercy identifies her as Charity Burbage, professor of Muggle Studies at Hogwarts, and author of an article that stated that the decrease in the number of pure-blood wizards was beneficial, and that blood purity should no longer matter. Having thus stated her "crime," he uses the borrowed wand to kill her, and then tells his pet snake, Nagini, that it is dinner time.

Harry, about to come of age, will shortly lose the protection that he had received from living under his aunt's roof, and so must leave Privet Drive, and move to a safe house of the Order of the Phoenix. The Ministry has banned the use of the Floo network, Apparation, and Portkeys in the area of Harry's house, nominally for Harry's protection, but the Order believes that it is a way of monitoring arrivals and departures from Harry's vicinity, so as to track which safe house he will be going to. Thus, they decide to fly out. In addition, to make it harder to track Harry, there will be seven pairs headed for seven safe houses, each one composed of a protector and a Harry Potter. Fred, George, Ron, Hermione, Fleur, and Mundungus Fletcher take Polyjuice Potion to become simulacra of Harry, and they take off, the real Harry with Hagrid in a sidecar on Sirius Black's flying motorcycle. They are immediately attacked by Death Eaters. Voldemort is among them, and (we find out later) chooses the Harry protected by the most formidable escort, "Mad-Eye" Moody; Moody's Potter, Mundungus, finding himself a target, Disapparates, leaving Moody to be killed by the curse that had been aimed at him. Realizing the real Harry would not have abandoned his escort in this manner, Voldemort next pursues Kingsley Shacklebolt, who is with Hermione.

Harry, meanwhile, is fighting off Death Eaters that are trailing him. Seeing that one of his attackers is Stan Shunpike, clearly under the effects of the Imperius curse, Harry disarms him. The other Death Eaters attacking him seem to realize that this is the real Harry, and vanish. Shortly, they return in force, with Voldemort, who is able to fly without a broomstick. In the screaming confusion of the battle, Harry's wand all by itself sends out a golden spell which apparently shatters Voldemort's borrowed wand. Voldemort, howling in anger, demands a wand from another Death Eater, but before he can put it to use, he apparently vanishes: Harry has fallen through the protective spells surrounding his destination safe house and Voldemort is unable to follow.

Later, Harry is moved by Portkey to The Burrow. There, he says that he must depart, because he feels that, as Voldemort is hunting him, he is endangering everyone there, but he is overruled. Shortly afterwards, he sees out of Voldemort's eyes as Voldemort tortures an old man, Ollivander, demanding to know how Harry had destroyed his borrowed wand. Ollivander tells Voldemort that he does not fully understand it himself. As the vision ends, Ron and Hermione arrive; Harry tells them what he has seen.

In the preparations for the wedding of Bill and Fleur, Harry sarcastically comments, in Ginny's hearing, that Voldemort isn't just going to kill himself while Harry stays safe and makes vol au vents. Ginny interprets this, correctly, as an indication that the mission that he has taken on, and that Ron and Hermione have agreed to accompany him on, involves the death of Voldemort. Harry tries to soften this revelation a little by making a joke out of it, but largely fails.

Just before his birthday, Harry again dreams that he is seeing the world through Voldemort's eyes. Voldemort is traveling through what appears to be Eastern Europe, looking for someone named Gregorovitch. Awakening, Harry recalls the name, but does not remember where he had previously heard it.

During the reception for the wedding, Harry speaks with Viktor Krum. It is then that he recalls where he had heard the name Gregorovitch: Mr. Ollivander had said that Krum's wand had been made by Gregorovitch. Shortly after, Kingsley Shacklebolt sends word that the Ministry of Magic has fallen to Voldemort, and that Rufus Scrimgeour was dead. Harry, Ron, and Hermione Apparate away from the Burrow, ending up in an all-night café at Tottenham Court Road. There, they discuss plans, trying to decide what to do about their mission against Voldemort. While they are talking, two workmen come in; Harry recognizes them as they draw their wands, and with help from Hermione (Ron is unable to draw his wand in time and ends up tied up), manages to disable them. Harry, Ron, and Hermione alter the Death Eaters' memory, and after some thought, Apparate to Number 12, Grimmauld Place. After they have determined that there is nobody else there, and after they receive an "all safe" message from Arthur Weasley, Harry again sees through Voldemort's eyes. This time, he is watching as Voldemort forces Draco Malfoy to torture Thorfinn Rowle, one of the Death Eaters who had tried to attack Harry, Ron, and Hermione in the café, for his failure to capture Harry.

Exploring the house the following morning, Harry discovers that a room in the house had been used by Regulus Arcturus Black, and guesses that this is the mysterious R.A.B. who had left the note in the locket that he and Dumbledore had retrieved from where Voldemort had hidden it. Remembering that they had found, and discarded, a locket in the house earlier, and that Kreacher was in the habit of reclaiming discarded "treasures," Harry summons Kreacher and asks him about it. Kreacher tells them that Mundungus Fletcher had stolen it from him, and seems very upset at having lost it, because it meant that he had not been able to carry out Regulus Black's orders. Asked what Regulus had to do with it, Kreacher explains: Voldemort had asked Regulus for the use of a house-elf, and Regulus had sent Kreacher. Voldemort had taken Kreacher to an island in the middle of a lake inside a cave, and had required him to drink a potion from a bowl on that island, and the potion had made him remember horrible things. Voldemort had placed the locket in the bowl, refilled it, and then, ignoring Kreacher's pleas for water, had departed. Kreacher had crawled to the lake to drink, been dragged under the surface, and then had returned to his master, Regulus, as ordered. Hearing this, Harry, while still upset that Kreacher had betrayed Sirius to Voldemort, is more bothered by Voldemort's ill-treatment of Kreacher, and chooses to make an ally of Kreacher.

Visiting Grimmauld Place, Lupin tells Harry that the murdered Scrimgeour had been replaced by Pius Thicknesse, who is under the Imperius Curse. This makes Voldemort effectively the head of the Ministry, and Ministry policies reflect that: Muggle-born wizards and witches are being rounded up and deprived of their wands, accused of stealing them, and all Magical children in England are being required to attend Hogwarts, presumably for indoctrination.

Based on the information from Kreacher, and from Mundungus once Kreacher had brought him to Grimmauld Place, the Trio determine that they must try to get into the Ministry to recover the locket. The day before they are to do this, Harry again experiences a pain in his scar, and sees Voldemort demanding that a woman tell him where Gregorovitch is. When the woman is unable to tell him, Harry witnesses Voldemort killing her and her family. As they escape from the Ministry, Ron is injured; Hermione manages to largely heal him with essence of Dittany, but he is still weak from loss of blood. Harry and Hermione discuss their next steps; Ron asks that they not speak Voldemort's name, as to him it feels like a jinx. Hermione gives in, possibly not wanting to argue with the injured Ron. (Note that for much of the rest of the story, Harry, Hermione, and Ron avoid using Voldemort's name, instead using other common euphemisms such as "You-Know-Who" and "He-Who-Must-Not-Be-Named," though for purposes of brevity this summary will continue to use his name.)

Shortly afterwards, Harry's scar hurts again, and he is seeing, through Voldemort's eyes, a white-bearded man suspended upside down. Voldemort is demanding something from him, and Gregorovitch says it was stolen from him long before. Harry sees Gregorovitch's memory of the young, blond thief Stunning Gregorovitch and escaping through the window, and then sees Voldemort killing Gregorovitch. Returning to himself, Harry describes what he has seen to Hermione and Ron. Ron wonders what Voldemort really had wanted from Gregorovitch, saying that he could not have made a wand for Voldemort if he was all tied up.

Quite some time later, Harry and Hermione visit Godric's Hollow. There, they meet Bathilda Bagshot. They accompany her back to her house, where she indicates that there is something upstairs for Harry. Leaving Hermione in the sitting room, Harry and Bathilda go upstairs to her sitting room. As she indicates a pile of junk on a dresser, Harry hears Voldemort's voice, triumphantly demanding, "Hold him!" Voldemort's snake, Nagini, rises out of Bathilda's neck as her remains crumple to the floor. Harry attempts to save himself from Nagini but loses his wand; Hermione appears at the door and joins in, fighting her way past the snake to Harry's side as Harry finds his wand. The two of them jump out the window and Disapparate as Voldemort appears in the room behind them. Harry, trapped in Voldemort's mind, relives the events of sixteen years before: he sees Voldemort approaching his parents house and killing his father, he sees his mother pleading for Harry's life, and sees Voldemort killing his mother, and finally he sees Voldemort attempting to kill the infant Harry, and feels the pain of the spell rebounding on him. When he regains consciousness some time later, Harry finds that one of Hermione's spells had nearly broken his wand in two. With Ollivander now a captive of Voldemort, Harry is dismayed that he will not be able to get a replacement.

The following day, Harry still feels lost; the now-broken wand had saved him from Voldemort, and in his escape from Nagini he had dropped a photo that he had found in Bathilda's house. The photo, which had been a picture of the thief who had stolen the object from Grindelwald, was now in Voldemort's hands, and this would no doubt help Voldemort find whatever he had been seeking. Shortly, Hermione approaches with a copy of Rita Skeeter's book, *The Life and Lies of Albus Dumbledore*, and Harry finds that the blond thief is Gellert Grindelwald. Shortly after this, Ron returns to the group bearing information about events in the Wizarding world. Among other things, Ron mentions that speaking Voldemort's name is banned for a reason: use of the name triggers a spell, which cancels many protective spells and summons Death Eaters or Snatchers (who are groups of wizards loyal to Voldemort on the lookout for underage wizards not attending Hogwarts, or wizards in general on the run). Ron reports that he had fallen afoul of a group of Snatchers when he had first left Harry and Hermione. Ron, Harry, and Hermione visit Xeno Lovegood, and there hear the Tale of the Three Brothers, which introduces us to the three Deathly Hallows. Afterwards, Harry is intrigued by the idea of the Hallows, and the idea that he could stand against Voldemort and not have to fear dying. In thinking about the Hallows, and discussing the Peverells with Hermione, Harry recalls where he has heard the Peverell name before: Marvolo Gaunt had displayed a ring, which he had said had been handed down from the Peverells. Harry tentatively guesses that the Invisibility Cloak he has received is one of the three Hallows, and guesses that to be why Dumbledore had borrowed it from his father. He then leaps to the conclusion that the ring, marked with the symbol of the Deathly Hallows and possibly made from the Resurrection Stone, has been hidden inside the Snitch that Dumbledore had left him, and that it is a Hallow that Voldemort is seeking, specifically the Elder Wand.

One evening, Ron manages to tune in a pirate wireless broadcast, "Potterwatch," which among other things discusses Voldemort and his activities. A part of the broadcast is handled by Fred or George, who mentions that there have been far more reports of Voldemort's appearing than could be explained by there being one of him; there would have to be some nineteen of him. Fred or George also suggests that rumours about Voldemort's being able to kill with a glance are overblown, suggesting that people who believe this have Voldemort and basilisks confused, and offers a quick refresher in how to tell the difference.

Following the broadcast, Harry happens to mention Voldemort's name, despite a quick warning from Ron, and the tent is immediately surrounded by Snatchers.

The Snatchers suspect Harry's identity, despite Hermione's attempts to disguise him, and take him and their other captives to Voldemort's headquarters, Malfoy Manor. While this is going on, Harry is again inside Voldemort's mind; he sees, through Voldemort's eyes, a large, prison-like structure with a tall tower. Voldemort flies to the top of the tower and through a window, finding within an old man, older than Ollivander, who says that he knows what Voldemort wants, but that he never had it.

Harry's attention is pulled back to Malfoy Manor, where Narcissa, Lucius, and finally Draco Malfoy try to confirm his identity, and are uncertain, in part because of the wand he is using to replace his broken one. Bellatrix Lestrange, when she arrives, is also dubious, but says that they should summon Voldemort; then, catching sight of the Sword of Gryffindor, she stops Lucius from touching his Dark Mark, saying that if the Dark Lord is summoned now, it could imperil them all. She keeps Hermione upstairs for questioning, but the other captives are taken down to a cellar.

Harry, once again able to see into Voldemort's mind, sees the old man telling Voldemort that killing him will not gain him what he seeks.

Hermione, under torture, manages to say that the sword is a fake, that they found it in the woods; Griphook, brought up from the cellar, confirms this. Bellatrix, reassured that they have not been in her vault at Gringotts, now summons Voldemort. Harry, in the back of his mind, is aware of Voldemort's response to the summons, and feels his anger at being too far from

Malfoy Manor to Apparate. Harry and Ron, managing to escape from the cellar, rescue Hermione from Bellatrix, and Disapparate before Voldemort can arrive.

While digging Dobby's grave, Harry finds that he is able to control how much Voldemort's mind is visible to him. He decides that he is now going to concentrate on Horcruxes, rather than Hallows, a choice he has not previously been able to make. He also, thinking about what he has learned, decides that he must speak with Griphook and Ollivander, who he has rescued from Malfoy Manor. Speaking first with Griphook, he asks for help in breaking into Bellatrix's vault at Gringotts. Griphook at first demurs, but being convinced that Harry is not doing this for personal gain, agrees to consider it. Afterwards, Hermione asks Harry if he thinks that there could be a Horcrux in the Lestrange vault. Harry says he believes so, because of Bellatrix's reaction when it appeared that someone had been in that vault to retrieve the Sword of Gryffindor. Ron wonders why a simple Gringotts vault would be important to Voldemort, and Harry points out that having a vault at Gringotts, particularly one of the old, high-security vaults, would be a sign to Voldemort that he had arrived as a wizard, particularly as he had no money at all until after he had left Hogwarts.

Now, speaking with Ollivander, Harry asks about the Elder Wand, which Hermione has indicated is the most likely of the three Hallows to actually exist. Harry first determines how a wand transfers its allegiance. The trail of the Elder Wand through history is bloody; is it necessary to kill the current holder of the wand in order to get its full power? Ollivander says no, forcible capture of a wand is usually enough. Harry now asks if Voldemort is interested in that wand? Ollivander says that he is, and that he had confessed under torture that Voldemort's wand and Harry's shared a single source for their cores. Ollivander had told Voldemort that he could use another wand against Harry, but Harry's wand destroying Malfoy's was something he had never heard of before. Ollivander agrees that Voldemort will be looking for another, more powerful wand now. Harry says that Voldemort may know that Harry's wand is broken; having captured Hermione's wand, they may have used Prior Incantato on it to determine what it had been doing, and that could reveal that it had been used to try and repair another wand. Harry now asks if Ollivander had told Voldemort that Gregorovitch had once owned the Elder Wand. Ollivander, shaken, admits that he did, but that Gregorovitch may well have been lying about it. Claiming that he had the Elder Wand and was studying it could be a way of bringing in additional business.

Outside Shell Cottage, Harry tells Ron and Hermione that Gregorovitch had owned the Elder Wand, but that it had been stolen by Grindelwald, who in turn had lost it to Dumbledore. As he says this, he sees Voldemort approaching Hogwarts. He now sees through Voldemort's eyes as he greets and dismisses Snape, approaches and opens Dumbledore's tomb, and takes the wand from Dumbledore's dead hand.

After Harry, Ron, and Hermione have escaped from Gringotts, Harry again sees through Voldemort's eyes. This time, he is furious that the Horcrux he had put in the Lestrange vault for safekeeping has been stolen, and he lashes out at everyone in the room, killing several, although Bellatrix and Lucius Malfoy manage to escape. Voldemort now wonders if "the boy" (Harry) knows about any of his other Horcruxes, and wonders if he can feel when his Horcruxes are destroyed. He knows the diary was destroyed, but he believes he could not feel that because he did not then have a body. Voldemort suspects Dumbledore had something to do with Harry's knowledge. The other Horcruxes? The ring, surely it is safe, nobody ever connected him to the Gaunts. The lake's defences are too strong, so only the one at Hogwarts is in danger, he will go check on that. Nagini must stay with him and be protected. But Dumbledore knew his middle name, so he will first check the ring. The lake, surely it is safe also, but all the same, he should check it.

Returning to himself, Harry tells Ron and Hermione that the final Horcrux is at Hogwarts. Voldemort, knowing that his Horcruxes are under attack, is checking them, but will visit Hogwarts last because he feels that the Horcrux there will be kept safe by Snape's presence. Harry feels that they should go immediately to Hogwarts to search for it; it is, after all, the last one, apart from Nagini.

Arriving at Hogsmeade, they set off an alarm, from which they are rescued by the barkeep of the the Hog's Head, who turns out to be Aberforth Dumbledore. In conversation, Aberforth says Voldemort has won, Harry should wait for the alarm to be disabled in the morning and then head for the hills and get away. Harry, however, tells him that Albus had known Voldemort could be killed, and had given him the tools to do that. Aberforth, seeing that Harry is not going to give up the fight, shows him the entrance to the tunnel that goes from the Hog's Head to the Room of Requirement.

While he is inside the Room of Requirement, Harry sees through Voldemort's eyes, and feels his rage, as he finds the place where the ring Horcrux had been hidden is now empty.

Harry now goes to the Ravenclaw common room with Luna Lovegood, to see the statue of Rowena Ravenclaw and examine the sculpted diadem, as Harry believes the original has been made into a Horcrux. While there, he is surprised by Alecto Carrow, who on seeing him immediately touches her Dark Mark, summoning Voldemort. Harry, through the pain from his scar, sees Voldemort approaching the seaside cave where he had earlier been with Dumbledore, and feels Voldemort's exultation that Harry has been caught. Harry is restored to himself by the sound of Luna stunning Alecto. Back under the Invisibility Cloak, Harry hears Amycus Carrow, on finding Alecto Stunned, telling Professor McGonagall that Voldemort had said that Harry might try to get into Ravenclaw tower. Fearing Voldemort's anger if Harry should escape again, Amycus determines to pass off the summons as a student prank. McGonagall refuses to go along with that; when Amycus spits at her, Harry, from under the Cloak, disables him.

Harry is then consumed by Voldemort's rage as he finds the basin where the locket was hidden is also empty. Returning to himself, Harry tells McGonagall that Voldemort is on his way to the school, and that Harry must find something there before he arrives. McGonagall says that the school staff will hold Voldemort off as long as possible while Harry searches. Harry now tells McGonagall about the Room of Requirement, and the tunnel from there to the Hog's Head. Harry says that route can be used for evacuation of the younger students, as Voldemort will be looking for Disapparation within the school grounds, not from Hogsmeade.

Shortly after the duel between McGonagall and Snape, as Snape is leaving the school, Harry again sees into Voldemort's mind. Harry sees the boat in the cave of the Inferi grounding against the shore, and returning to himself, he warns McGonagall that Voldemort is on his way.

When Harry and Luna return to the Room of Requirement to report what is happening in the school, Harry again sees from Voldemort's eyes, now standing outside the gates of Hogwarts, looking in, with Nagini around his shoulders.

Professor McGonagall raises the school and brings the students to the Great Hall. There, as she tells the students that they will be evacuated to safety, the voice of Voldemort is heard, offering a reward to anyone who will bring Potter to him. Pansy Parkinson, seeing Harry, rises and aims her wand at him, followed by all of Slytherin. The Gryffindor students also rise, followed by the Ravenclaw and Hufflepuff students, in Harry's defence, and McGonagall says that all of Slytherin will be evacuated, though students in the other Houses who are of age may stay to help defend the school.

As the attack starts, Harry, Ron, and Hermione are in the Room of Requirement looking for the final Horcrux. They are found there by Draco Malfoy, Crabbe, and Goyle. Draco indicates that he believes that by capturing Harry and taking him to the Dark Lord, he may be able to regain some of the power and influence his family has lost in Voldemort's eyes.

Though Voldemort is in command of the attacking forces, he plays no direct part in the battle. Asked to find out where Voldemort is, Harry enters his mind again, and senses him in the Shrieking Shack. He sees Voldemort speaking with a very hang-dog Lucius Malfoy. Malfoy is asking Voldemort about his son, Draco. Voldemort says that it was his own fault, he decided to stay in the school, rather than coming out with the other Slytherins to join him. Lucius now asks Voldemort to stop the attack so that he will be certain to get Potter himself, Voldemort dismisses this as Lucius simply trying to defend his son, and sends him to find and fetch Severus Snape. Harry decides that he must go to the Shrieking Shack, and Ron and Hermione insist on accompanying him. At the end of the tunnel under the Whomping Willow, Harry watches from hiding as Voldemort talks to Snape. Snape offers to go and find the boy so that Voldemort can kill him, but Voldemort dismisses this request, saying that he has found the Elder Wand not as strong as he had been led to believe. Snape again offers to find the boy, but Voldemort says he plans to have the boy come to him. He then wonders aloud why the Elder Wand is not working for him, and wonders if it has not yet accepted Voldemort as his master. Saying that Snape has been a good servant, Voldemort says that when Snape had killed Dumbledore, he had won the wand's allegiance. In order for Voldemort to gain that allegiance, Snape must die. With no remorse, Voldemort sets Nagini on Snape, ordering her to kill. He then leaves with Nagini. As his last living act, Snape gives Harry his memories.

Harry then hears Voldemort announcing to everyone in Hogwarts that the battle will now stop, and giving Harry one hour to surrender. He also says that if Harry does not comply, everyone at Hogwarts will die.

In Snape's memories, Harry sees that Snape had been deeply in love with his mother, Lily, and that Snape's choosing to ally with the local Death Eaters at Hogwarts had come between them. Snape had carried the prophecy to Voldemort, but when Voldemort had said that Lily would have to die, Snape had demanded a secret, private audience with Dumbledore. There, he had agreed to spy on Voldemort for Dumbledore in return for Dumbledore's agreement to protect Lily. Pettigrew had betrayed James and Lily, however, and Voldemort had killed them. Dumbledore held Snape to his promise, saying that all he could now do is protect Harry, Lily's child, that being all that she had left behind.

After Dumbledore had revived from the curse on the ring Horcrux, he and Snape had talked about Voldemort's plan to have Draco Malfoy kill Dumbledore. Snape says that Voldemort does not expect Draco to succeed, that the intent is to punish the Malfoys for their failures. Dumbledore suggests that the plan likely was that Snape would step in when Draco failed, and overruled Snape's objections. Dumbledore says also that likely Voldemort will feel that he no longer needs a spy at the school after Dumbledore is killed, as it will then be entirely under his control, and charges Snape to look after his school once he is gone.

Snape, some time later, demanded to be let in on the entire story as to why he was doing this, and Dumbledore had told him that there was a fragment of Voldemort's soul that had sheared off when Voldemort had killed Lily, and had fastened itself to Harry. It was this fragment of soul that had made the link between Voldemort and Harry, and had provided Harry with the ability to speak to snakes. However, this did mean that, in order to finally defeat Voldemort, Harry would have to be killed by Voldemort. Dumbledore also says that, when Voldemort stops sending Nagini out but keeps her close to him and surrounded by protective spells, then would be the time that Harry would have to know about this.

Snape, talking with the portrait of Dumbledore some time later, is told that in order to remain in Voldemort's inner council, he must tell Voldemort Harry's true departure date from Privet Drive. If Snape can give the idea of having multiple Potters to Mundungus Fletcher, though, Harry will have a chance to escape unscathed. Awakening from these memories, Harry realizes that he must meet Voldemort and be killed by him, in order that he may ultimately be defeated. Under the Invisibility Cloak, and protected by the shades of his parents, Sirius Black, and Remus Lupin, Harry proceeds undetected to the clearing where Voldemort and the Death

Eaters are camped. The hour has expired, and Voldemort is musing that he may have been wrong; he had expected Harry to come. Harry then reveals himself, and Voldemort promptly kills him.

Harry now finds himself in a simulacrum of King's Cross Station, unoccupied except for himself, a small, flayed creature that is crying in pain, and very shortly Albus Dumbledore. Dumbledore explains that when Voldemort had taken Harry's blood to re-animate himself, he had also extended the protection that he had previously gotten from his mother's sacrifice; his life was now tethered to Voldemort's, and Voldemort could not kill him as long as he was still alive himself. Further, he confirms that Harry having sacrificed himself for his friends at Hogwarts now affords them the same protection that Harry had initially received from Lily; Voldemort cannot now harm them. Dumbledore also says that the Killing Curse directed at Harry had destroyed the soul shard of Voldemort's that was adhering to Harry's soul.

Dumbledore also guesses that the reason the two brother wands interacted as they did during Harry's escape from Privet Drive is that after Harry and Voldemort's blood was joined, their wands, already connected by identical magical cores, and now wielded by wizards who shared not only pieces of their souls but also their blood, merged even closer. Furthermore, during Harry and Voldemort's duel, Harry was the stronger; Voldemort feared death, while Harry embraced the possibility. Harry's wand thus imbibed some powers from Voldemort's, making it more powerful than Lucius Malfoy's wand. That wand, even when wielded by Voldemort, was easily overpowered by Harry's.

When Dumbledore had bested Grindelwald, he had won and kept the Elder Wand; Grindelwald had lied to Voldemort, unsuccessfully, saying that he had never had it, but Voldemort had learned that the Wand had passed to Dumbledore.

Finally, Dumbledore tells Harry that if he wishes, as he sees this as King's Cross, he can go to the platforms, where he will no doubt find a train that would take him Onwards; or, he can return to the living world, for his chance to finish Voldemort. Harry chooses to return.

Returning to himself in the Forest, Harry remains still so that he will appear to have died. He hears the Death Eaters, in some apparent consternation, tending to Voldemort who has apparently fallen unconscious. As Voldemort recovers, he sends Narcissa Malfoy to find if Harry is dead. Narcissa, detecting Harry's heartbeat, very quietly asks him if Draco is still alive; Harry, equally quietly, says he is, and Narcissa calls out to the assembled Death Eaters that Harry is dead. Voldemort uses the Cruciatus curse to throw Harry's body around and demonstrate that it is truly lifeless; Harry, though prepared for the pain, finds that there is none. Voldemort now frees Hagrid, who had been tied to a tree, and forces him to carry Harry back to the school.

At the school, Voldemort addresses the students and staff, calling them out of the school to see their fallen hero, the Harry Potter of which so much was expected. Harry, through slitted eyes, notices that Voldemort no longer has protective spells about Nagini. Voldemort announces the abolition of all school Houses; all the school will be under one house, Slytherin. When Neville Longbottom protests, Voldemort invites him, as a pureblood, to join him; at Neville's refusal, Voldemort summons the Sorting Hat, sets it on a Petrified Neville, and sets it on fire. Several things happen simultaneously. The families of students sent home arrive, howling war cries as they climb the outer walls. The Centaurs, ending their neutrality, charge the Death Eaters. Grawp reappears around the corner, headed for Hagrid. Neville frees himself from the body-bind curse, and drawing the Sword of Gryffindor from the Sorting Hat, hacks off Nagini's head, destroying the final Horcrux. Harry leaps up and places his Invisibility Cloak over himself, then casts a Shield Charm between Voldemort and Neville.

As the battle erupts again, the Death Eaters, retreating from the new threat behind that now includes Thestrals and Buckbeak, enter the castle. Harry, under the Cloak, heads for the Entrance Hall, searching for Voldemort. Inside, House elves, led by Kreacher, are hacking the Death Eaters' ankles with kitchen knives. Voldemort is simultaneously dueling McGonagall, Slughorn, and Kingsley Shacklebolt. Bellatrix is likewise fighting Hermione, Ginny, and Luna. When Bellatrix barely misses Ginny with a killing curse, an enraged Molly Weasley pushes the three girls aside and challenges Bellatrix. As they fiercely duel, Molly proclaims that another Weasley will never be harmed and casts a powerful curse directly to Bellatrix's chest, killing her. Voldemort's fury over losing his most devoted follower blasts McGonagall, Kingsley, and Slughorn backwards. As Voldemort turns to Molly, Harry casts a shield charm between them. When Voldemort looks around to see who conjured it, Harry pulls off his Invisibility Cloak, revealing himself to the audibly stunned crowd.

Harry warns everyone to stay back—the battle is between him and Voldemort now. They circle each other warily. Voldemort claims that Harry continually survives by hiding behind better wizards who sacrifice themselves for him. Harry urges Voldemort, who he boldly addresses as Tom Riddle, to feel remorse for his evil deeds. He then tells him that Dumbledore outsmarted him, planning his own death so that Snape was never the Elder Wand's rightful owner. The true master was Draco Malfoy, who unknowingly won the wand's allegiance when he disarmed Dumbledore, just before Snape killed him on the Astronomy Tower. When Harry overpowered Draco at Malfoy Manor and took his wand, the Elder Wand gave its allegiance to him; Harry reminds Voldemort that *"The wand chooses the wizard."* Also, Harry tells him, because he willingly sacrificed himself to Voldemort, the same magic that Lily Potter's death protected him with, now protects the fighters.

Voldemort casts Avada Kedavra as Harry simultaneously conjures Expelliarmus. But Voldemort's killing curse backfires, reflected by Harry's blood protection and the Elder Wand's allegiance to him, while Harry's disarming charm wrenches the Elder Wand from Voldemort's hand to his. With all his Horcruxes destroyed, Voldemort dies instantly.

Strengths He is a very accomplished wizard and can make very powerful spells and curses.

He is also a very accomplished Legilimens and can see into almost anyone's mind. There is some question as to whether he can read Severus Snape's mind, or whether Snape's skill at Occlumency has protected him from that.

Weaknesses Voldemort's lust for power compels him to use any means to achieve total domination over the wizarding world. He is loyal to no one, and he never hesitates to kill his own followers when it serves his purpose, or when he becomes enraged.

Among wizards, Voldemort fears Albus Dumbledore, who is recognized as one of the greatest and most powerful wizards ever.

Voldemort's greatest fear is death, and believes dying is the worst fate anyone can experience. He desires to become immortal, and has gone to extreme lengths to secure that immortality for himself. Dumbledore comments to Harry at one point that, when Harry and Voldemort dueled in the graveyard, Harry was the stronger wizard, because he was prepared to die, if necessary, while Voldemort still feared death despite his having recently returned from the dead. Voldemort is overconfident and often overlooks minor details, which lead to his failures. In particular, he discounts magic that he does not understand, such as the magic of non-human races like house-elves. As part of this, while he is aware of the power of love in magic, this remains a purely academic awareness. He does not seem to experience love himself, and cannot stand to remain in possession of Harry's body while Harry is yearning to be rejoined with his godfather, as we see at the end of *Harry Potter and the Order of the Phoenix*. Because of this, he consistently underestimates the strength of magic fueled by that love.

Because he does not understand this source of strength in Harry, Voldemort attributes Harry's repeated successes to luck and tools. In particular, he fixates on Harry's wand, which he feels is the only thing standing between himself and Harry's ultimate defeat. While we learn early on that the twin cores of Harry's wand and Voldemort's are unable to attack each other, Voldemort attributes some super-magical power to this. This mistaken belief is fueled by Snape, as Voldemort's closest confidant, who has been heard saying that Harry is at best a moderately competent wizard, not a particularly strong one. Whether or not Snape believes this, Voldemort chooses to accept Snape's words as fact.

Relationships with Other Characters Voldemort calls Death Eaters his friends, or his true family, but he does not have compassion for any of them, treating them as servants rather than friends. Indeed, Voldemort killed Severus Snape, who he probably considered one of his most trusted Death Eaters after Snape murdered Dumbledore, in an attempt to gain more magical power.

Voldemort becomes obsessed with Harry Potter after the incident in which he failed to kill Harry as a baby—he is angered that an attack on an infant could result in his downfall, and later tries any means possible to take revenge on Harry so he can once again be the most feared and powerful wizard.

Voldemort considered himself to be superior to all other witches and wizards, with one exception—Albus Dumbledore, said to be the only one he ever feared.

Analysis

Lord Voldemort or Tom Marvolo Riddle is the main antagonist of the Harry Potter series and the only living descendant of Salazar Slytherin (by way of his mother, Merope Gaunt, and her father Marvolo Gaunt). His only allegiance is to himself, and his obsession with the idea of living forever, and of total control. He believes in pure-blood elitism and, despite being from a Muggle Father and Witch Mother, sees other "Mudbloods" as filth. It has been said that Albus Dumbledore was the only person Voldemort truly feared, and Voldemort himself admitted that he himself had never "sought a duel" with Dumbledore, but then later declares that Dumbledore is "getting weak in old age" and he is "not the wizard he once was." He sees Dumbledore's views of love as a joke, and his over-confidence and own self-indulgence is eventually the cause of his downfall.

The core of Voldemort's wand is a phoenix feather; one of only two feathers given by the phoenix that also provided the feather in Harry's wand. This phoenix happens to be Dumbledore's loyal companion, Fawkes. Voldemort is a parselmouth, a person who can talk to snakes. He acquired this trait from his ancestor, Salazar Slytherin. As Slytherin's heir, in *Harry Potter and the Chamber of Secrets*, he is the only one who can control the basilisk; though aware that Harry is also a Parselmouth, Riddle says that the basilisk will not answer him, and Harry does not try. When he attempted to murder Harry, some of his skills, including Parseltongue, were transferred to Harry. The reasons for this are mentioned in *Harry Potter and the Deathly Hallows*.

It is perhaps interesting to note that Harry's scar does not pain him in *Harry Potter and the Chamber of Secrets*, even when he is directly battling Tom Riddle. The attack on Harry happened some forty years after the creation of the diary, and so the Voldemort that had inflicted the scar, and the Riddle Harry was fighting, are quite different people. It is most likely for this reason that Harry's scar does not react to the returning Riddle.

Questions

1. It is clear that, despite being married, Bellatrix had, for want of a better word, romantic feelings for Voldemort. Is there any possibility that they could have been reciprocated?

Greater Picture

It is worth remembering that Voldemort, or Tom Marvolo Riddle, as he was then known, was born about 1926–7 on the 31st of December, and formed his world view in an orphanage in London, and later in Hogwarts, at about the time that the National Socialist (Nazi) party was coming to power in Germany. It is perhaps because of this that his views on the purity of the wizarding race, and the need to eradicate the Muggles, so closely mirror the concept of Aryan purity and the Final Solution proposed in Germany at that time. The author has mentioned this similarity as well,[1] though she notes that she was rather taken by surprise on discovering the similarities in detail. This is not to say, or imply, that Voldemort was a Nazi, or had any sympathy for any part of the Nazi party's aims; he no doubt saw them as, if anything, an amusing but totally insignificant side show in the useless Muggle world. However, the "racial purity" idea, involving (in this case) elimination of anyone who could not prove that they were descended only from Wizarding families, certainly seems to have been the basis for most of the actions that Voldemort later carried out.

As mentioned above, Harry's scar did not pain him while he was fighting Riddle in *Harry Potter and the Chamber of Secrets*. One must assume that the main reason for the pain in the scar was the soul fragment of Voldemort's, which recognized and reacted to Voldemort's soul (or what was left of it) when the two were close, or when Voldemort was experiencing very strong feelings. The soul fragment that Harry was dealing with there had been separated forty years earlier, and so likely there was little recognition there; certainly not enough for the soul fragment within Harry to recognize it. In support of this, we should also note that Harry did not report any pain in his scar in the final confrontation with Voldemort, late in *Harry Potter and the Deathly Hallows*, after the soul fragment within him had been killed.

In an interview after the publication of the final book in the series, the author stated that Harry's parselmouth ability, along with the view into Voldemort's thoughts, vanished with the destruction of Voldemort's soul shard within Harry. The author has further stated that Harry has never missed the ability.

Lucius Malfoy

Gender: Male
Hair color: Blond
Eye color: Gray
Related Family: Abraxas Malfoy, wife Narcissa (née Black), son Draco
Loyalty: Lord Voldemort, Death Eaters

OVERVIEW

Lucius Malfoy is the father of Draco Malfoy.

ROLE IN THE BOOKS

Chamber of Secrets In Knockturn Alley, Harry observes Lucius and Draco Malfoy in *Borgin and Burke's*, where Lucius is apparently selling some Dark Magical items. Lucius and Draco do not notice Harry, who entered the store unseen through the Floo network, and is hiding inside a large black cabinet.

Back in Diagon Alley, Lucius Malfoy meets Harry and Ginny Weasley at *Flourish & Blotts*, and makes some cutting comments about the Weasley family's poverty; Arthur Weasley, arriving on the scene, ends up getting into a physical altercation with Lucius which is broken up by Rubeus Hagrid.

Late in the school year, Lucius arranges to have Albus Dumbledore suspended as Headmaster. Lucius visits the school personally to deliver the suspension, and Harry is present when Lucius talks to Dumbledore in Hagrid's hut. After Ginny is rescued from the Chamber of Secrets, Professor Dumbledore is reinstated, to Lucius' apparent anger; apparently several school governors had the impression that if they did not vote to remove Dumbledore, Lucius would curse them. It is revealed that Lucius had intercepted Ginny at *Flourish & Blotts* specifically to plant Tom Riddle's old diary in her cauldron. Harry tricks Lucius into freeing his house-elf, Dobby.

Finally, it is mentioned that Lucius has been sacked as a school governor.

Prisoner of Azkaban After Draco Malfoy is injured in Hagrid's Care of Magical Creatures class by Buckbeak, Draco spends considerable time in the Hospital Wing. On his return, he taunts Harry and Ron, saying that his father can get Hagrid sacked.

As it turns out, he cannot; the hearing, just before Christmas, exonerates Hagrid. However, Lucius can get Buckbeak's part in the case referred to the Committee for the Disposal of Magical Creatures. Despite Hagrid's being coached by Harry, Ron, and Hermione, Hagrid reports that Lucius came across as much smoother and was better able to state his case to the Committee. As a result, though Hagrid was spared punishment, the Committee had ordered Buckbeak executed.

Goblet of Fire Lucius attends the Quidditch World Cup with his wife, Narcissa and their son Draco. Apparently, he has been invited to the Top Box by Cornelius Fudge on the strength of a recent donation to St. Mungo's. Lucius and Arthur Weasley have a barbed conversation in the Top Box at the Quidditch World Cup.

In the riots after the Cup, there is a strong suggestion that Lucius may be one of the hooded wizards rampaging through teh campsite and tormenting the Muggle owner.

When Draco Malfoy Curses Harry in the Entrance Hall, he is seen and punished by Professor Moody. Later, taking Draco to see his Head of House, Moody comments that Draco's father is "an old friend." Moody being an Auror, and his intonation being threatening, one can see that Moody believes Lucius to have been a Death Eater. When Lord Voldemort is resurrected, he summons his remaining Death Eaters. One of the Death Eaters speaks with Lucius' voice; it is he who asks how Voldemort had managed to return.

When Harry returns from the graveyard, and describes what happened there, he names Lucius Malfoy as one of the Death Eaters there present. Cornelius Fudge refuses to believe this, saying that Malfoy was an old, established Wizarding family, and had always donated to all the right charities.

---

1. http://www.jkrowling.com/textonly/en/faq_view.cfm?id=16

Order of the Phoenix As Harry is leaving the courtroom with Arthur, after his hearing, he sees Cornelius Fudge and Lucius Malfoy in the Atrium. As usual, Arthur and Lucius exchange heated words, ended by Lucius excusing himself to Fudge's office; evidently Lucius is there to make another donation to some worthy cause.

When Sirius Black accompanies Harry, Ron, and Hermione to the train station to see them off to Hogwarts, his Animagus dog form is recognized by Lucius Malfoy, who apparently passes this information on to Draco. This suspicion is strengthened by a story Hermione finds in the *Daily Prophet* a week later, suggesting that Sirius had been spotted in London.

Harry later has one of his disturbing dreams, in which he seems to be looking through Voldemort's eyes. In this one, he is speaking to one Rookwood, who Harry later recognizes as a recent escapee from Azkaban Prison. Rookwood tells him that Avery's plan could never have worked, which is why Bode had fought so hard when Lucius had put him under the Imperius curse. Discussing this dream the next day, Harry remembers that Lucius had been hanging around near the entrance to the Department of Mysteries, where Bode worked, on the day of his hearing. Hermione remembers that Sturgis Podmore had been arrested on the day that they had all left Grimmauld Place for school, and speculates that Lucius may have placed him under the Imperius curse to try and get Podmore to steal whatever it was that Voldemort was after.

Lucius is one of the Death Eaters, and apparently the leader, in the battle at the Ministry. While he is seen ordering the other Death Eaters around, we don't see him taking direct part in the battle. He is one of the Death Eaters captured by Dumbledore at the end of that battle.

Draco blames Harry for Lucius' arrest, and is prepared to curse Harry in retaliation, but is interrupted by the arrival of Professor Snape and Professor McGonagall.

Half-Blood Prince Lucius has been convicted of being a Death Eater following the Battle at the Ministry in the previous year, and sentenced to Azkaban Prison. As such, we don't actually see him in this book.

Deathly Hallows When we first see Lucius in this volume, he is at a council of Death Eaters, which has been convened in Voldemort's new headquarters, Malfoy Manor. He, with his wife Narcissa and son Draco, are seated far down the table, distant from Voldemort, as a sign of their decreased status within the organization. Much to her dismay, Bellatrix is seated near them. It would appear that the Malfoy family is in disgrace: Lucius had first lost the Diary Horcrux, and then bungled the battle at the Ministry and been sent to Azkaban, and now was essentially under house arrest in his own home. Draco had performed half of his mission but then funked the second half, the previous year. And Narcissa had broken the rule about talking with other Death Eaters about missions, not only with Draco, but with Severus Snape. Voldemort, having determined that he likely would be unable to defeat Harry using his own wand, demands that Lucius give him his wand, as he won't be needing one. He taunts Lucius' apparent brief hope that it would be a trade. To test the power of Lucius' wand, Voldemort uses it to kill Charity Burbage. When Voldemort determines which of the six Harry Potters escaping from Privet Drive is the true Harry, he attempts to use Lucius' wand to kill Harry. The attempt fails, however, with Harry's wand, apparently all on its own, sending out a burst of golden fire that causes Lucius' wand to shatter.

When Harry, Ron, and Hermione, along with Dean Thomas and Griphook are brought to Malfoy Manor, their captors call on the Malfoys to identify them before summoning the Dark Lord. Summoned by Lucius, Narcissa is unable to identify Harry, and orders Draco to look; Draco is also uncertain. Bellatrix by and large takes charge of proceedings at this point and Lucius retreats into the background.

At the battle of Hogwarts, Hermione calls on Harry to find out where Voldemort is. Harry senses that he is in the Shrieking Shack; a hang-dog Lucius is with him. Lucius is asking after Draco, his son. Voldemort replies that he should have left the school and joined him with the other Slytherins. Lucius asks him to stop the battle, so that he can be sure to kill Potter himself. Voldemort says that this is simply an attempt by Lucius to save his son, and sends Lucius to find Snape.

In Snape's memories, Harry sees that when Snape was Sorted into Slytherin house, he was greeted by then-prefect Lucius Malfoy.

When Harry returns to the forest to face Voldemort and his destiny, Lucius is present, though far away from the center of the gathering.

His last appearance is in the Great Hall, after the battle. He is with Narcissa and Draco, standing somewhat apart from the celebrations around them.

Strengths While Lucius is considered to be on the "other" side from Harry Potter, he does have some admirable strengths. Lucius is known to be very intelligent; he was a prefect back in his Hogwarts days, and is a rich, successful businessman in his adult life. He has a smooth, charming manner that enables him to read people and he usually gets what he wants from them. He is calculating, intuitive, and strong.

Though we never see Lucius participate in any actual dueling, we can deduce from his past that he has strong leadership skills; he was one of Voldemort's most trusted Death Eaters before Harry Potter was born, and Lucius was selected to lead the raid against Harry Potter in the Hall of Prophecies in the fifth book, *Order of the Phoenix*. Though this battle marks the beginning of Lucius's fall from Voldemort's grace, Lucius's charisma is undeniable. Perhaps Lucius's greatest strength is his ability to love. J.K Rowling was quoted as saying "anyone who is still capable of love is redeemable." Unlike the other Death Eaters, Lucius puts his family first and cares far more about his wife and son than serving Lord Voldemort. While his sister-in-law Bellatrix Lestrange admitted she would be perfectly willing to sacrifice any of her children to the service of the Dark Lord, Lucius has no interest in sacrificing his son Draco. When Lucius is freed from prison by Voldemort, he is visibly panicked and miserable when he learns of Draco's mission to kill Dumbledore (under pain of death if he fails). During the final battle at Hogwarts, all Lucius wants to do is find his son and keep him safe; he begs Voldemort to let him find Draco, is refused, but does so anyway as soon as he gets the chance. Lucius does not even attempt to fight against the Order in this battle; all he cares about his finding his wife and son and protecting them. Hence, Lucius has another strength: he can prioritize what matters most to him, and what matters most is his family.

Lucius has a fairly good relationship with his son Draco; Draco obviously respects and loves his father, as he gets violently angry when Harry calls Lucius a "loser" in the sixth book after Lucius is sent to Azkaban. The same can be said for Lucius's wife Narcissa; she becomes furious when Bellatrix insults Lucius in the beginning of the sixth book. Thus, Lucius has a good enough relationship with his wife and son that they love him and will defend him fiercely. Lucius is a complex character; we see a steady change in him throughout the series, and in the end, his love is his greatest strength, and it is what keeps him alive.

Relationships with Other Characters Lucius Malfoy is married to Narcissa Malfoy. They have one son, Draco Malfoy.

Lucius' wealth and status secures him influence over high level Ministry officials including Cornelius Fudge. However he does not appear to have any true friends.

Lucius is particularly hostile to Arthur Weasley, insulting him about his low level in the Ministry, poverty and fondness of Muggles.

ANALYSIS

Lucius is one of the more interesting characters in the series, as we see enough of him to be aware of how he is changing as the series continues. In the beginning, he is smooth, assured of his own superiority over the rabble surrounding him. We know that a lot of this is buying influence; this is drawn particularly into focus when, after the return of Voldemort, Harry starts naming the Death Eaters who had come to his side, and Cornelius Fudge protests that Lucius can't be a Death Eater, as he makes hefty donations to all sorts of worthy causes. We see this start to crack when Voldemort returns; Lucius is put on the spot immediately, as Voldemort asks why he had run when the Dark Mark had appeared in the sky at the Quidditch World Cup, and why he, unlike the Lestranges, had not tried to find out where Voldemort had gone. He is still able to put on a good façade, though: we see him talking with Fudge after Harry's hearing, and he is then apparently about to donate a lot of gold to some charity. As his plans fall apart around him, he collapses inwards into himself as well; when we see him in the beginning of *Harry Potter and the Deathly Hallows*, he seems little more than a shell of himself. He does not protest when Voldemort demands his wand, not even when Voldemort says he will have no further use for it. Wandless, he cannot fight at Hogwarts, though he is present; Voldemort keeps him around as a messenger, and apparently intends to humiliate him.

At the end of the book, when we see him, he seems to be quietly thankful that he and his family were allowed to remain alive; there is no sign of his old confidence.

The interaction between Lucius Malfoy and the Weasleys should, perhaps, be mentioned as well. Lucius was certainly guilty of prejudice against Muggle-borns, but the Weasleys were Purebloods also, so Lucius probably was more irritated at the Weasley affinity for things Muggle, perhaps most especially a friendship with Hermione, rather than any racial prejudice against them as a family. As Arthur's job had to do with Muggle life, Lucius would have seen the Weasleys as blood traitors, especially as Arthur was able to get some laws enacted protecting Muggles from the worst Wizards. It is certainly true that Lucius used Arthur's relative poverty against him, something which adds to our perception of him as a bully.

QUESTIONS

1. Lucius Malfoy, when we first formally meet him in Flourish and Blotts in *Harry Potter and the Chamber of Secrets*, makes very cutting comments to Ginny Weasley, and later to Arthur Weasley. Were Lucius' comments to Ginny simple prejudice, or were they intended to increase the likelihood of Ginny's running afoul of the diary and its contents? If the latter, exactly how much did Lucius understand of the diary's nature when he concealed it in Ginny's other purchases?

GREATER PICTURE

While examining Lucius can be rewarding, he does remain largely in the background of the series, except in the second book where he deliberately plants the diary in Ginny Weasley's book bag. We are never entirely sure whether Lucius knew that the diary was one of Voldemort's Horcruxes. Apparently, according to what we learn later, Lucius had been told that the diary was a source of disruption, intended to be left somewhere like Hogwarts. Voldemort had, however, neither informed him of its exact nature, nor given Lucius instruction to part with it. While some Death Eaters knew of Voldemort's Horcruxes, as Regulus Black apparently did, we are led to believe that Lucius did not know that the diary was one. As such, when Voldemort learns of the destruction of the diary, he is enraged. Lucius' fall from grace in Voldemort's eyes can likely be traced from the time Voldemort learned of the destruction of the diary, which seems to mark the first of a series of failures: his attempt to use the Imperius curse to retrieve the Prophecy, first on Sturgis Podmore and later on Broderick Bode, fails, as does the mission he leads into the Ministry to get it via Harry, which results in Lucius himself being locked up.

Ludovic Bagman

Gender: Male
Hair color: Short blond
Eye color: Blue
Related Family:
Loyalty: Ministry for Magic

Ludovic Bagman

Overview

Ludovic Bagman, head of the Division for Magical Games and Sports is a very flamboyant wizard, always bounding around and trying to look like he is having a lot of fun. He is relatively short, rather fat, and has the look of a powerful man rather gone to seed. He seems rather flighty, paying more attention to his entertainments than to his job.

Role in the Books

Goblet of Fire Ludo Bagman bounces around the campground at the Quidditch World Cup, talking up a storm and placing and taking bets. He is commentator for the match, but when the Snitch is finally caught, he seems rather shaken, and becomes rather hard to find; obviously, he has made a few bad bets. One of the bets that had been placed was with Fred and George Weasley, that the Bulgarian Seeker, Krum, would catch the Snitch but that Ireland would win, and they had won that bet.

During the riot at the campsite, Harry, Ron, and Hermione meet Ludo in the woods. Ludo seems preoccupied, and is unaware of the riot until told about it; he then Disapparates, possibly to the campground to see what is going on. Shortly after the Dark Mark appears, he Apparates back in, and is quite surprised to see all the wizards who have appeared to find the spell-caster. Throughout, Ludo appears preoccupied.

Ludo is present at Hogwarts for the selection of the Champions at the opening of the Triwizard Tournament. It turns out that he is to be one of the five judges, the others being Albus Dumbledore, Igor Karkaroff, Olympe Maxime, and Bartemius Crouch Sr.

He is present again when the names of the Champions are produced by the Goblet on the following day. While he is as shocked as anyone when Harry's name comes out of the Goblet as the fourth of the three Champions, once he is over his shock he seems to think it great fun. When the judges meet with the Champions after the selection is complete, Madame Maxime and Igor Karkaroff are angry, feeling that Hogwarts has unjustly managed to get itself two Champions; Dumbledore is more rational, trying to determine what courses of action are open to them now; Crouch is remote, only quoting rules at the other parties; and Bagman seems to be actively trying to get the other Judges to accept Harry as a fourth contestant.

Harry agrees to go to Hogsmeade with Hermione, though he insists on using his Invisibility Cloak. As they are walking in the street, they pass Rita Skeeter, who is saying something vaguely defamatory about Ludo to her photographer.

Bagman is present at the beginning of the First Task. The four Champions have been brought to a tent near the arena, and Ludo is there to provide each of the Champions with tokens representing the dragons that they will be facing, and the order in which they will be facing them. He then tells them that their task is to retrieve the golden egg, and that they will be entering the arena, one at a time, when the whistle sounds. He then takes Harry aside, out of the tent, for a private word. There, he asks Harry if he is feeling alright, and if he needs any help in managing the task. Harry says, no, he has a plan. Ludo persists in offering help until they hear a whistle; Ludo then belts off, saying he's late, and as Harry returns to the tent he sees Viktor Krum, the first-selected Champion, slouching off towards the dragon enclosure.

Bagman's voice is heard commentating Krum's, Cedric Diggory's, and Fleur Delacour's efforts, but Harry is tormented; Ludo is not revealing what is going on, and Harry has only his imagination to work with. Finally, though, it is his turn. Once he summons his Firebolt, however, all else fades; while Harry does still hear the occasional ecstatic comment from Ludo, he is largely oblivious. Once he has retrieved his egg, and received first aid for the injury he got from the dragon, he returns to the arena to receive his score, and finds that Ludo has awarded him a perfect ten. Ludo then rejoins the Champions in their tent, and tells them the date of the Second Task, and that the contents of the golden egg they have retrieved is the only clue they will get as to what their task is. All of the judges, except Crouch who is "feeling ill" and has been replaced by Percy, are present for the Yule Ball. In the dancing after the dinner, Fred and George try to corner Ludo; he escapes, going over to talk to Harry. When asked, Ludo says that the Twins were looking for marketing advice.

On the first Hogsmeade weekend after Christmas, Harry sees Ludo in the Three Broomsticks, talking seriously with a number of Goblins. Seeing Harry, Ludo approaches to speak with him, asking him if he needs help with the clue of the Egg. Harry, who as yet has no idea what the Egg's caterwauling means, says he has a plan, and asks Ludo why he is offering to help him. Ludo says it is sympathy for the underdog; Harry, as the youngest, has the hardest job, and deserves some assistance for that reason. Fred and George now appear, offering to buy Ludo a drink; Ludo demurs, saying he has to be elsewhere, and leaves, followed by the goblins. Almost immediately, Rita Skeeter comes in, and takes a table near the Trio; Rita is again complaining about Ludo, saying that he wouldn't give her an interview. Confronted by Hermione, Rita says that she knows some things about Bagman that would curl Hermione's hair if she told them.

The next time we see Bagman, he is on the shore of the school lake, as one of the five judges for the Second Task. He has very little to say, however, until the task is ended, at which time he announces the scores to the assembled audience. He then tells the Champions that he will give them details of the Third Task on May 21st. On 21 May, then, Ludo brings the four Champions down to the Quidditch pitch, which has evidently been planted with a maze of hedges. When harry arrives there, the hedges are only about eighteen inches high, but already they are an obstruction on the pitch. Ludo says they will be quite tall by the time the Task comes about, but that they will be removed afterwards; as an old Quidditch player himself, he does not want to see the pitch destroyed. He goes on to explain that the Triwizard Cup will be located in the center of the maze, and the first Champion to touch it will win outright. Harry and Cedric will enter the maze first, as they are tied in first place. He also mentions that there will be various obstacles in the maze, some of which will be provided by Hagrid as Care of Magical Creatures teacher, and some others imported for the purpose. As they depart the pitch, both Ludo and Krum want to have a word with Harry, but Harry, believing he knows what Ludo wants, chooses to talk with Krum.

Ludo is again present at the Third Task, and explains the rules and safety precautions. Presumably he is also commentating, but Harry cannot hear him, or anything much else, inside the maze.

It turns out that the Twins have been writing to, and trying to talk to, Ludo all year, and he has been avoiding them. It seems that he had paid off their bet with Leprechaun gold, which had vanished, and they had been trying to force him to make good on his bet ever since. Apparently he had also bet heavily on the World Cup with the Goblins, had lost, and had tried to pay them off with Leprechaun gold as well. In order to try and make good his losses there, Ludo had bet with the Goblins on Harry to win the Tournament. In his last letter to the Twins, Ludo had said that boys their age shouldn't be gambling anyway, and had not even returned their stake. Finally, as Harry and Cedric had touched the Cup at the same instant, the Goblins felt this was a draw, and that Ludo had lost his bet, and Ludo, not having any money to pay them, much less the Twins, had gone into hiding.

Order of the Phoenix It is mentioned in passing that negotiations with the Goblins have been somewhat tense; Ludo had not helped their case by running.

Strengths Ludo was a very good Quidditch player in his day, playing Beater for the Wimbourne Wasps, and on the English National Quidditch team. Arthur Weasley says he was the best beater the Wasps ever had, which would be impressive given that "Kennilworthy Whisp," in *Quidditch Through the Ages*, tells us that the Wasps team was founded in 1312.

Weaknesses Ludovic has a very strong weakness to gambling, even trying to deny it when it is obvious to everyone. He also manages to build up a large amount of debts from goblins as well as Fred and George Weasley.

QUESTIONS

1. Why does Winky think Ludo is a bad wizard?

Luna Lovegood

Gender: Female
Hair color: Dirty Blonde
Eye color: Silvery-grey
Related Family: Father Xenophilius Lovegood
Loyalty: Albus Dumbledore, Harry Potter

OVERVIEW

Luna Lovegood is a Ravenclaw student in the same year as Ginny Weasley, one year younger than Harry Potter.

ROLE IN THE BOOKS

Goblet of Fire The Lovegoods are mentioned in passing as a family living near the Weasleys who could only afford to attend the Quidditch World Cup by arriving a week early.

Order of the Phoenix When we first see Luna, she is sitting alone in a compartment on the Hogwarts Express; Neville says that the compartment is occupied, and Ginny overrides him, saying that it's just Looney Lovegood. Entering the compartment, Harry notes that she seems to be reading *The Quibbler* upside down and wearing a necklace of Butterbeer corks. Harry sees that one of the articles in *The Quibbler* seems to involve Sirius Black, and borrows it from her to read the article, which states that Sirius is actually one Stubby Boardman, popular musician. Quickly leafing through the paper, Harry notes that it is all similar sorts of nonsense, before he hands it back. Hermione Granger, when she arrives, speaks disparagingly of the paper, whereupon Luna frostily replies that her father is the editor, and retreats icily behind her upside-down paper.

When Harry leaves the train, he sees that the carriages he thought were horseless are apparently being pulled by vaguely horse-shaped, winged reptilian creatures. He asks Ron what they are, but Ron cannot see them. Harry is only slightly reassured when Luna tells him that she can see them also.

Harry gets in trouble with the new Defence Against the Dark Arts teacher, Dolores Umbridge, for stating that Lord Voldemort had returned. Shortly after this, Luna stops Harry outside the greenhouses, saying that she believes him. Harry wonders how much the reassurance is worth, coming as it does from someone who seems to be wearing earrings made from radishes.

Luna is one of the twenty-five students who appear for the first meeting of the Defence Association, or as it is later known, Dumbledore's Army. At the first meeting in the Hog's Head, Luna says that Fudge has his own private army, so it is not surprising that he believes Dumbledore would be creating one. Asked about this, she says that Fudge has an army of Heliopaths. Hermione quickly moves on to the business of the meeting, rather than allowing Luna's odd views to take up time.

At the final meeting of Dumbledore's Army before Christmas, Harry arrives early to find that Dobby has decorated the Room of Requirement for the season. He manages to get most of the embarrassing decorations down, but there are still some streamers and mistletoe. Luna, arriving, says that it looks very nice, but warns Harry that he shouldn't stand under the mistletoe because it is likely full of Nargles.

Since their announcement of the return of Voldemort, both Harry and Dumbledore have been repeatedly mocked in the public press, most notably the

Prophet. In February, Hermione arranges for Harry to meet with Rita Skeeter, the muck-raking journalist who had pilloried Hagrid in the press the previous year. Hermione had discovered that Rita was an unregistered Animagus, and had forced her, under threat of revealing this to the Ministry, to stop writing for a year. It has occurred to Hermione that if Harry's full story gets published, it might help Harry's cause. Luna is present at this meeting because, as mentioned earlier, her father publishes *The Quibbler*, and that would be the venue where the interview would be published. Rita is annoyed that the Quibbler doesn't pay for editorial content, but under threat from Hermione, interviews Harry and writes the story. Luna says that she does not know when the story will appear, because her father is expecting something big about Crumple-Horned Snorkacks to come in that week.

Later, when Harry's interview appears, Luna says that her father is quite pleased. This edition of *The Quibbler* has sold out, and he is having to make a second print run.

Harry determines that his godfather, Sirius Black, may be being tortured at the Ministry of Magic by Voldemort, and that his only way to determine whether this is actually happening or not is to call Sirius at Grimmauld Place and see if he is there. The only unmonitored fire in the school is in Umbridge's office. Luna, who with Ginny has heard Harry shouting at Ron and Hermione, volunteers to help; Harry sets her to guard one end of the corridor by Umbridge's office, so that he can break in and talk to Sirius. Luna's efforts come to naught, and she is apprehended by one of Umbridge's Inquisitorial Squad and brought in to Umbridge's office. She stands, barely restrained and not resisting, apparently only somewhat aware of what is going on, though she does seem somewhat startled by Hermione's "revelation" of what it was that Harry was trying to do.

After Harry and Hermione have escaped Umbridge and the Centaurs in the Forbidden Forest, Luna, Ron, Ginny, and Neville meet up with them. When Ron and Harry wonder how they are going to get to the Ministry to save Sirius, Luna says that they will have to fly. Ron asks sarcastically if they will use teh Snorkacks for that, and Luna says that's silly, Snorkacks can't fly, but "they" can. She points, and Harry sees two Thestrals approaching, attracted by Grawp's blood that has fallen on Harry and Hermione. Harry decides that he and Ron will head off to the Ministry, but Luna tells him that there are more Thestrals approaching, he and Hermione must really smell. Ron, Ginny, and Hermione are unable to mount the Thestrals, as they can't see them, but Luna dismounts and gets them settled on the creatures; backs, and they all take off for the Ministry.

Once at the Ministry, Luna accompanies Harry and the others as they go in search of the room where Sirius is being tortured. One room they find is a stone amphitheatre with a tattered veil hung in an archway. Harry is almost certain that he can hear people on the other side of the veil, and Luna says she hears them also. Eventually, they reach the hall of Prophecies, where they find that in fact it was a ruse, that Sirius is not there, and instead they are confronted by twelve Death Eaters. In the ensuing battle, Harry, Hermione, and Neville get separated from Luna, Ron, and Ginny. They meet in the antechamber, at which point only Luna and Harry are fully capable: Hermione has been knocked out by means of an unknown curse from Antonin Dolohov, and Dolohov also broke Neville's nose and wand, Ron has been hit by what acts rather like a drunkenness spell, and Ginny's ankle is broken. They are then forced to retreat back into the Department of Mysteries, where Luna is knocked out while trying to seal a door against the Death Eaters.

Following their return to Hogwarts, Harry is mourning Sirius' death. Meeting Luna by chance in the halls, he unburdens himself a bit to her, knowing that she has also seen someone die, because she had been able to see the Thestrals. She says that she had seen her mother die; she had been a very smart witch, and had been experimenting with new charms, when one had backfired on her. She goes on to say that she knows she will see her mother again, and that Harry will see Sirius again. Both of them had heard the voices on the other side of the veil in the room with the archway, and Luna believes that those are the dead, speaking to them. Harry somehow feels comforted by this.

Half-Blood Prince We first see Luna again on the Hogwarts Express. Here, she, Neville, and Harry share a compartment. Shortly, a group of fourth-year girls arrive; their spokesperson, one Romilda Vane, introduces herself and invites Harry to come sit with them. Harry replies that he's with his friends, and will stay where he is, thanks anyway, and the girls retreat, confused. Luna remarks complacently that she is seen as being rather odd, and she knows that others call her "Loony Lovegood." She also asks if Harry plans to start up Dumbledore's Army again, and Harry says there's not much point in it. Luna says that she liked the DA, it was almost like having friends. Harry, slightly discomfited, turns the conversation to O.W.L. scores.

Ron and Hermione have had a bit of a falling out over Ron's ongoing infatuation with Lavender Brown, and Ron manages to say something particularly hurtful to Hermione. After class, Harry finds Hermione being comforted by Luna, and returns Hermione's things; Hermione thanks him and heads off to class. Luna comments that Ron is nice enough, but he can say hurtful things sometimes. Harry thinks that Luna is sometimes rather more honest than is comfortable. Harry has been under some pressure to select a date for the Christmas party that Professor Slughorn is holding, and decides that he can ask Luna to go with him, just as friends. Luna says that would be fine, and accepts. Peeves overhears, and gleefully starts spreading the word throughout the school, as only he can. Harry is relieved to find that Luna has left the butterbeer-cork necklace and the radish earrings off for the party, and escorts her up to Slughorn's office. There, Luna starts discussing Cornelius Fudge and his plans for world domination with the drunken Professor Trelawney, who proves a ready audience.

With the graduation of Lee Jordan, the school has been trying out new commentators for Quidditch, and much to Harry's surprise, Luna is the commentator for the Quidditch match that occurs in March, Gryffindor against Hufflepuff. Harry does not finish the match, having been hit in the head by a mis-hit Bludger, but Ron tells him later that the commentary was most entertaining.

Luna appears briefly again, carrying a message from Dumbledore. In the process of finding the message, which is notice of Harry's next private lesson, Luna finds, and presents to Ron, something looking like a large green onion which she says is a Gurdyroot, good for warding off Gulping Plimpies.

Near the end of the book, Dumbledore tells Harry that they will be going to seek a Horcrux. Before they depart, Harry gives Ron and Hermione the rest of his Felix Felicis potion, and charges them with getting any DA members who will help and aiding the defence of the school. On their return, Harry and Dumbledore find the school under attack. In the aftermath, Harry learns that Hermione and Luna had been watching Snape's office. When Professor Flitwick had gone to tell Snape that his assistance was needed, Snape had apparently Stunned Flitwick. Departing his office, he had seen Hermione and Luna and sent them to aid Flitwick, who he said had apparently fallen and injured himself. Caring for Flitwick had effectively kept Luna and Hermione out of the battle.

Deathly Hallows Luna appears with her father at Fleur and Bill Weasley's wedding, where she is ecstatic at having been bitten by a Gnome; apparently both she and her father believe it might grant her some special ability. Luna, annoyingly, recognizes Harry through his disguise (Polyjuice potion), not seeming at all surprised that he looks different, or that he is using a different name. Once the music starts, she dances by herself.

Overhearing a conversation from outside their tent shortly before Christmas, Harry learns that Luna, Ginny, and Neville had been caught trying to break into the Headmaster's office at Hogwarts and steal the Sword of Gryffindor. While we learn that she was punished for this, we can only surmise that the punishment may have been the same as was meted out to Ginny at the same time: detention, to be served with Hagrid supervising.

Having also overheard that Luna's father was running one of a very few pro-Harry news organizations, Harry, Ron and Hermione visit him just after Christmas. Xenophilius provides what hospitality he can, but Luna does not seem to be present; Xeno says that she is down past the bridge, catching Plimpies. Harry wanders upstairs and looks around her bedroom, and finds that she has decorated it with pictures of herself, Harry, Ginny, Neville, and Ron, wound around with what looks like a golden ribbon but is the word "friendship" written over and over. Harry notes that the room is apparently unoccupied and has some months worth of dust. Xeno, confronted, explains that Luna had been taken off the Hogwarts Express on the way back from school for Christmas break, to force Xeno to toe the party line in what *The Quibbler* was publishing; and that he had reported Harry's presence to the Ministry in the hope that if they had Harry, they might release Luna.

When Harry, Hermione, Ron, Dean Thomas, and Griphook are captured by Snatchers, they are taken to Voldemort's headquarters in Malfoy Manor. Harry, Ron, Dean, and Griphook are imprisoned in a basement room, and they find that Luna and Mr. Ollivander are already there. Luna provides a sharpened bit of metal with which she is able to cut Harry's and Ron's bonds. Harry, seeing a sky-blue eye in the shard of Magic Mirror he still carries with him, calls for help. Shortly, Dobby appears, and Apparates Luna, Dean and Mr. Ollivander to Shell Cottage, the home of Bill and Fleur. She says a few words at Dobby's funeral.

Luna appears back at Hogwarts shortly after Harry does; Neville has used the Galleons that Hermione had created to announce meetings of Dumbledore's Army to summon the DA members to Hogwarts. She accompanies Harry to Ravenclaw tower, and shows him the bust of Ravenclaw with the model of the lost diadem. When Alecto Carrow surprises Harry and has him at wand point, Luna Stuns her. She admits that she is surprised at how loud it is. Luna also helps out at the battle for Hogwarts. When Harry, Ron, and Hermione need to get to the Shrieking Shack, they find the path to the Whomping Willow blocked by Dementors. Luna, Ernie Macmillan, and Seamus Finnigan appear on the scene and cast their Patronuses, forcing the Dementors out of the way; however, they are then forced to retreat by oncoming Giants.

Luna, along with Ginny and Hermione, are battling Bellatrix in the renewed battle in the Great Hall, when Molly Weasley, enraged at the sight of a Killing curse that barely misses Ginny, attacks Bellatrix. At the victory celebration, Harry is sitting beside Luna. She recognizes that he feels very tired, and suggests that he should leave and get some rest; she calls out and points out the window, and as everyone nearby is distracted by this, Harry slips on the Invisibility Cloak and departs, stopping only to gather Hermione and Ron as he does so.

Strengths Even though Luna is seen as an odd and weird person, she is quite clever. Possibly due to her odd family life, being raised by an eccentric like Xeno Lovegood, she sees things in different lights, and thus sees things that other people probably wouldn't. It is true that she believes in creatures, and magical properties of creatures and plants, that are not commonly accepted in the Wizarding world, but this could be seen as simply a mind that is a little more open than usual. She is unusually perceptive about the people around her, such as when Luna immediately recognizes the disguised Harry at the wedding in "Deathly Hallows" just by the expression under his polyjuiced face. Despite being teased and having her possessions stolen by classmates, Luna feels little animosity towards them. Luna seldom gets angry. In tense or dangerous situations Luna is much calmer than the people around her.

Weaknesses Luna tends to "space-out" at times, making her somewhat oblivious to her surroundings. Her belief in plants, creatures, and other things outside the usual magical community's belief structure may be the sign of a mind that is a little too open, and acts to isolate her from her classmates. She has a tendency to be over-honest in her assessments of others, a trait which Harry finds somewhat dismaying at times.

Relationships with Other Characters Commonly referred to as "Loony" Lovegood, Luna is generally a loner. Her eccentric behavior and appearance have given her an unlucky reputation at Hogwarts that has led to practical jokes and unpleasant whisperings. Despite this, Luna remains friendly and fairly optimistic.

Perhaps because of her tendency toward introversion, Luna is one of the most observant characters in the series. She is known to voice even the most unpleasant of truths about other characters; notably, she comments to Harry in *Half-Blood Prince* that Ron can be quite cruel at times. However, her observations are never made with malice or contempt—she merely states the facts as she sees them.

Luna's friendships are few and far between. As a member of the DA, she is commonly seen with Neville Longbottom. In *Half-Blood Prince*, Harry invites Luna to accompany him to a party as "just friends," at which she is ebullient. Visiting her house in "Deathly Hallows" Harry finds a painting she made with the faces of Harry, Hermione, Ron, Neville and Ginny linked together with the word "friends" over and over. These friendships are very important to her.

Regardless of her quirky, sometimes inexplicable habits, Luna is a fiercely trustworthy, loyal friend.

Madam Rosmerta

Gender: Female
Hair color:
Eye color:
Related Family:
Loyalty:

Overview

Madam Rosmerta is "a curvy sort of woman with a pretty face," the owner of *The Three Broomsticks* pub in Hogsmeade.

Role in the Books

Prisoner of Azkaban Madam Rosmerta is first mentioned by name when Harry escapes from Hogwarts to join Ron and Hermione in Hogsmeade. Here, she acts as a foil: the adults who are in the know are filling her in on why there are Dementors running around the village and ruining her business, and Harry is listening in. This allows Harry to receive the understood back-story about Sirius Black.

Order of the Phoenix Perhaps curiously, we do not see Madam Rosmerta in the Three Broomsticks when Harry is there being interviewed by Rita Skeeter. As Harry is then banned from all further Hogsmeade weekends by Umbridge, we do not see Madam Rosmerta in this book.

Half-Blood Prince Rosmerta greeted Harry and Dumbledore when they secretly left Hogwarts to find Voldemort's Horcrux. When they came back, she warned them of the Dark Mark above Hogwarts, and lent them brooms to get there. When they did, Dumbledore immobilized Harry when they heard Malfoy's *Expelliarmus* spell. Dumbledore questioned how Malfoy knew when they left the castle, and then realized that it was Rosmerta, being under the *Imperius* charm, that told him.

Relationships with Other Characters Ron seems to have a bit of a crush on Madam Rosmerta; perhaps he just likes her shape. He is well aware that she is literally old enough to be his mother; in fact, Madam Rosmerta was tending bar at the Three Broomsticks when Harry's father was at Hogwarts.

Mafalda Hopkirk

Gender: Female
Hair color: Unknown
Eye color: Unknown
Related Family: Unknown
Loyalty: Ministry of Magic

Overview

Mafalda Hopkirk works in the Improper Use of Magic department at the Ministry of Magic.

Role in the Books

Chamber of Secrets When Dobby performs a Hover Charm in the Dursley's house, Harry is believed to be the one actually doing magic. The warning letter that arrives is signed by Mafalda Hopkirk.

Order of the Phoenix Harry again does magic, this time using the Patronus charm to repel Dementors who are attacking himself and his cousin Dudley. The letter of reprimand that is sent to him by Owl Post is signed by Mafalda Hopkirk, and so is the following letter rescinding the immediate punishment and setting a hearing date.

Deathly Hallows When Harry, Ron, and Hermione determine that they must get into the Ministry to search for the locket Horcrux which has been appropriated by Dolores Umbridge, they disguise themselves as Ministry employees, using Polyjuice potion to do so. Hermione ends up disguised as Mafalda Hopkirk; the real Mafalda Hopkirk is left, Stunned, behind a closed door.

Once in the Ministry, Harry and Hermione take the elevator to the top floor, where they understand Umbridge's office is. Umbridge is at the elevator and, recognizing Hopkirk, assumes she was sent by Travers.

The two of them return through the Atrium to the courtrooms, where "Mafalda" is to act as recorder for the day's session of the Muggle-Born Registration Commission. Very shortly after Harry re-joins her, they depart the Ministry and Hermione's disguise wears off.

Magorian

Gender: Male
Hair color: Chestnut
Eye color: Unknown
Related Family: Unknown
Loyalty: Centaurs

Overview

Magorian, a Centaur, is one of only four Centaurs named in the books. He is a member of the centaur herd that lives in the Forbidden Forest.

Role in the Books

Order of the Phoenix Hagrid asks Harry and Hermione for a favour; he expects that he will be sacked soon, and wants them to do something for him if he gets sent away. As he leads them into the forest, he mentions that Firenze working with Dumbledore has made for problems with the Centaurs; they are not happy, especially not with Hagrid as he stopped them kicking Firenze to death. After they have met Grawp and are on their way back out of the forest, they are met by about half a dozen centaurs, including Magorian and Bane; Magorian warns Hagrid that he is not welcome in the Forest any more. As the centaurs do not harm foals (meaning Harry and Hermione), however, Hagrid will be allowed to pass today.

When Harry is trapped in Dolores Umbridge's office along with Hermione, Hermione manages to convince her that Harry was trying to reach Professor Dumbledore to say that the weapon they had been building for him was complete. Umbridge is lured by the promise of this weapon into the Forbidden Forest, where the three of them are challenged by the Centaur herd. While there are many centaurs present, only three are named: Bane, Ronan, and Magorian. It is Magorian who first speaks to the three of them, and who Umbridge attempts to bind.

Deathly Hallows Magorian is apparently one of the centaurs who joins in at the final battle for Hogwarts.

Malcolm Baddock

Gender: Male
Hair color: Unknown
Eye color: Unknown
Related Family: Unknown
Loyalty:

Overview

Malcolm Baddock is a Slytherin who arrived at Hogwarts in Harry's fourth year.

Role in the Books

Goblet of Fire Malcolm Baddock was Sorted into Slytherin House.

Mandy Brocklehurst

Gender: Female
Hair color: Unknown
Eye color: Unknown
Related Family: Unknown
Loyalty:

Overview

A Hogwarts student in Harry's year, Mandy Brocklehurst is a member of Ravenclaw house.

Role in the Books

Philosopher's Stone The Sorting Hat places Mandy Brocklehurst in Ravenclaw House.

Marauders

Gender: Male
Hair color: Various
Eye color: Various
Related Family: Unknown
Loyalty:

Overview

The Marauders were four Hogwarts students in the same year, Remus Lupin, Peter Pettigrew, Sirius Black, and James Potter. Like Fred and George Weasley, they excelled at getting into trouble and causing mayhem of the less harmful variety.

Role in the Books

Prisoner of Azkaban This book reveals the group's existence, although two members are already known separately. It was the Marauders who created the Marauder's Map that was given to Harry by Fred and George Weasley. Three members are reunited in the Shrieking Shack when Lupin and Black combine forces to unmask Pettigrew. Black and Lupin explain the reason behind the group's nicknames. After discovering that Lupin was a werewolf, the remaining three secretly became Animagi to support their friend during his transformations. They adopted the nicknames Moony (Remus Lupin), Wormtail (Peter Pettigrew), Padfoot (Sirius Black), and Prongs (James Potter); the nicknames were derived from their altered shapes: a werewolf, a rat, a black dog, and a stag, respectively. James Potter, of course, is dead at this point; however, when Harry Potter is called upon to produce a Patronus, it assumes the same shape as James' Animagus form. This prompts Professor Dumbledore to comment, "Make no mistake: Prongs rode again last night."

Goblet of Fire Although two individual members appear in this book, as a group they do not play any role in this book.

Order of the Phoenix In Snape's Pensieve, Harry sees a Marauders episode, one where his father acts rather cruelly towards Severus Snape. This disturbs Harry, damaging his opinion about his father and causing him to take risky measures to communicate with Sirius and Lupin about it.

Half-Blood Prince Although the two remaining Marauders (Lupin and Pettigrew) appear in this book, they are on opposite sides of the battle lines and do not interact.

Deathly Hallows Although the two remaining marauders are present in this book, they do not interact. We see Pettigrew in Malfoy Manor twice, the second time resulting in his death; and Lupin appears at The Burrow several times, Grimmauld Place once, and finally falls in the battle at Hogwarts.

Relationships with Other Characters The Marauders seem to consider themselves somewhat a group apart. The one time we see them directly, they are largely discussing a test just past between themselves. When they do interact with others outside the group, it is primarily playing pranks on Severus Snape, though they do also speak briefly with Lily Evans on that occasion.

Marcus Belby

Gender: Male
Hair color: Unknown
Eye color: Unknown
Related Family: the nephew of Damocles Belby
Loyalty:

OVERVIEW

Marcus Belby, a student in Ravenclaw house at Hogwarts of approximately Harry's age, is the nephew of Damocles Belby, the wizard who invented Wolfsbane Potion.

ROLE IN THE BOOKS

Half-Blood Prince Horace Slughorn invites Marcus, along with a number of other people that he judges to be the potential movers and shakers of the Wizarding world, to lunch with him on the Hogwarts Express. When he learns that Marcus is estranged from his famous uncle, Slughorn effectively dismisses him.

Marcus Flint

Gender: Male
Hair color: Unknown
Eye color: Unknown
Related Family: Unknown
Loyalty: Slytherin house

OVERVIEW

Marcus Flint is an older boy in Slytherin house, who is Captain of the Slytherin Quidditch team.

ROLE IN THE BOOKS

Philosopher's Stone Marcus Flint, here a sixth-year, captains the Slytherin Quidditch team in their game against Gryffindor house.

Chamber of Secrets Marcus Flint is the captain of the Slytherin Quidditch team. He first appears in "Mudbloods and Murmurs," when the Slytherins arrive to take over the Quidditch pitch from the Gryffindor team. We see him again when he, Draco, Crabbe, and Goyle disguise themselves as Dementors in a failed attempt to put Harry off his game in the Quidditch match against Ravenclaw.

Prisoner of Azkaban Somehow Marcus Flint is still at Hogwarts, because he is mentioned as being Captain of the Slytherin Quidditch team, and in the game against Gryffindor (in which Harry is flying his Firebolt) it is mentioned that Flint has chosen players for size rather than skill.

The author has said that, given a choice between her making a mistake and Flint having had to repeat a grade, she thinks it rather more likely that Flint has had to repeat a grade.[1]

ANALYSIS

Marcus Flint never appears except in his role as Captain of the Slytherin Quidditch team. In that role, he seems to be relatively unimaginative, and somewhat brutish—rather than using skill to win games, at least against Gryffindor, he seems to prefer to make as many fouls as possible, on and off the pitch, in the hopes that some of them at least will not be seen by the referee.

Outside the context of Quidditch, Flint does not seem to exist; he is never mentioned by other characters. Like any extended series, the Potter books have a number of small internal consistency errors that purists pick up on and often complain about. With a very few exceptions, these errors do not affect the line or enjoyment of the story at all. The error that puts Marcus Flint at Hogwarts for an extra year was one of the earlier ones detected on the fan sites, and at least one fan site has chosen to call all such errors "flints" in commemoration of its discovery.

Marge Dursley

Gender: Female
Hair color: Unknown
Eye color: Unknown
Related Family: Unknown
Loyalty:

---

1. http://www.jkrowling.com/textonly/en/faq_view.cfm?id=16

Overview

Marge Dursley is sister to Harry Potter's Uncle Vernon. Harry is instructed to refer to her as Aunt Marge. She is most disparaging towards Harry, feeling the imposition on Vernon perhaps more even that Vernon himself does.

Role in the Books

Philosopher's Stone   It is mentioned in passing that the house at Privet Drive has four bedrooms; one is for visitors (usually Uncle Vernon's sister, Marge).

It is mentioned that there is a present from "Auntie Marge" in amongst the presents waiting on Dudley's birthday. At first, he doesn't see it, but his mother points it out.

When it transpires that Mrs. Figg has broken her leg and cannot take Harry while Dudley goes to do something on his birthday, Marge is one of the alternates Mr. Dursley suggests, but Mrs. Dursley points out that "she hates the boy."

In the same post as the first of Harry's letters is a picture postcard from Marge, who is holidaying on the Isle of Wight.

Prisoner of Azkaban   Harry, appalled at the prospect of a week with his abusive Aunt Marge in the house, makes a deal with his Uncle Vernon: if he carefully remembers that he is a student at St. Brutus' Home for Incurably Criminal Boys, at the end of the week Uncle Vernon will sign his permission form allowing him to visit the town of Hogsmeade on selected weekends.

Aunt Marge arrives at Privet Drive with her bulldog in tow, throws her heavy suitcase at Harry to stow in her room, expansively hugs Dudley, and gives him £20. When Harry returns from upstairs, he hopes that Aunt Marge will allow him to stay out of range, but she says that she doesn't trust him out of her sight and insists on details about the school he is attending.

At one point during the week, when she is being particularly insulting to wards Harry, a wine glass Aunt Marge is holding shatters in her hands. She passes it off as just that she has strong hands; Uncle Vernon suspects that Harry is doing magic.

On the last day that Aunt Marge is there, possibly fueled by brandy, she starts insulting Harry's parents. This is too much for Harry to bear, and without his having willed it, Aunt Marge starts inflating. Not being entirely certain how he had done this, Harry cannot undo it; instead, he unlocks the closet under the stairs, and escapes with his school things.

Reaching the Leaky Cauldron, in fear that he will be recognized and have his wand broken for underage use of magic, Harry is amazed to meet the Minister for Magic there. Fudge tells him that Aunt Marge has been deflated, and her memory adjusted; there will be no charges laid, it could have happened to anyone.

Order of the Phoenix   While being trained in Occlumency by Professor Snape, one of the memories that Snape retrieves from Harry's mind is an episode where Aunt Marge had allowed her bulldog to chase Harry up a tree, and had left him there for hours, laughing at him.

Marietta Edgecombe

Gender: Female
Hair color: Reddish Brown
Eye color: Unknown
Related Family: Unknown
Loyalty:

Overview

Marietta Edgecombe is one of Cho Chang's closest friends.

Role in the Books

Order of the Phoenix   Marietta was first introduced to us when Cho Chang brings her, somewhat unwillingly, to the first meeting of Dumbledore's Army. She is present at the meeting at the Hog's Head, but says nothing, and we do not even learn her name, she is "Cho's friend."

We see her again at the first full meeting of Dumbledore's Army; here, she and Cho are practicing the Disarmament jinx, and Cho is so flustered by Harry's presence that she ends up setting Marietta's sleeve on fire. Shortly before the Easter break, Professor Umbridge learns about the existence of Dumbledore's Army. Harry, forewarned by Dobby, manages to engineer the escape of the rest of the group, but is himself caught. In Professor Dumbledore's office, Harry finds that Marietta had reported the existence of Dumbledore's Army to Dolores Umbridge. (It is only at this point that we learn her name; Professor Umbridge introduces her as part of her exposition of what has been going on.) As a result of this betrayal, a charm that Hermione had set on the parchment that all DA members had signed, had covered Marietta's face in purple pustules that spelled the word "sneak."

Marietta's blemishes make it very hard for her to show her face in Dumbledore's office, particularly as one of those present is Cornelius Fudge, the Minister for Magic. With her robes up around her face, her responses to questions put to her by Umbridge are answered generally by whimpers and gestures. Before she can actually give much testimony, Kingsley Shacklebolt, there as one of the Auror guards Fudge has brought with him, modifies her memory surreptitiously so that she no longer remembers that the DA had been meeting regularly. Marietta's changing her story almost incites Umbridge to violence against her. Harry recognizes the glazed look in her eye as being a symptom of memory alteration, though it seems nobody else there, with the possible exception of Dumbledore, does. though she remains in Dumbledore's office until after Dumbledore's departure, Marietta plays no further part in affairs, simply standing there.

Afterwards, Harry and Cho get into something of a fight about Marietta, with Cho saying that Marietta is basically a good person who had made a mistake, that she had felt she had to because her parents work in the Ministry, and that Hermione's charming the parchment to do that to Marietta's face was sneaky. Harry, on the other hand, points out that Ron's father also works in the ministry, and he isn't going around with the word "Sneak" on his face, and goes on to say that he thinks Hermione's charm was brilliant. This fight basically ends their relationship. On the Hogwarts Express back home, Harry sees Cho and Marietta walk past; Marietta has apparently not managed to hide the word on her face, as she is wearing a balaclava.

Half-Blood Prince It is mentioned in passing that Marietta's face still showed signs of the purple pustules, though she tried to cover them with make-up.

Relationships with Other Characters Marietta is Cho Chang's best friend, and friend of Mandy Brocklehurst.

Marlene McKinnon

Gender: Female
Hair color: Unknown
Eye color: Unknown
Related Family: Unknown
Loyalty: Order of the Phoenix

Overview

Marlene McKinnon is a former member of the Order of the Phoenix who was killed along with her family.

Role in the Books

Philosopher's Stone In their first meeting, Hagrid mentions to Harry that Voldemort killed some of the best wizards of the age such as the McKinnons, along with the Bones and the Prewetts.

Goblet of Fire As part of his attempt to plea-bargain his way out of Azkaban, Igor Karkaroff accuses Travers of killing the McKinnons.

Order of the Phoenix At the celebratory party at Grimmauld Place for Ron and Hermione's appointment as Prefects, Alastor Moody shows Harry a photograph of the original Order of the Phoenix. Marlene McKinnon is in that photo, and Moody says that she and her family had been killed by Death Eaters.

Marvolo Gaunt

Gender: Male
Hair color: short, scrubby
Eye color: bright brown
Related Family: Morfin Gaunt, Merope Gaunt, Salazar Slytherin, Lord Voldemort
Loyalty: Purebloods

Overview

Marvolo Gaunt is a descendant of Salazar Slytherin, and grandfather of Lord Voldemort.

Role in the Books

Half-Blood Prince Marvolo is first seen when appears to restrain his son Morfin, who has just assaulted a Ministry wizard, Bob Ogden. He is described as being oddly proportioned, with wide shoulders and overlong arms.

When Ogden explains that Morfin is being summoned to a hearing for having Jinxed a Muggle, Marvolo seems unconcerned; after all, it was only a Muggle, so no harm done. When told that Morfin has broken Wizarding law, he shows Ogden the ancestral ring of the Peverells, and the locket of Salazar Slytherin, as proof he can trace his ancestry back to the earliest and purest Wizarding families. Ogden's protests that blood does not outweigh law fall on deaf ears. Meanwhile, Marvolo is bullying his daughter Merope, becoming enraged when it appears she fancies a Muggle, the same one Morfin Jinxed. Marvolo attacks Merope; Ogden defends her, but has to flee Morfin. When the Ministry return to arrest Morfin, Marvolo resists, and is arrested, tried, and sentenced to six months in Azkaban. When he returns from prison, he finds his daughter has run off with the Muggle; he never again speaks her name, and dies before Morfin gets out of prison.

Weaknesses Marvolo is menacing to strangers, and never wants to associate with others in his area. He is even cruel to his family, particularly his daughter Merope, whom he berates because of her comparatively weak magical talent. He barely even talks to his son Morfin; the thing he values the most, above his children, are the family heirlooms. He is full of immense pride for his heritage as a descendant of Salazar Slytherin, and because of this, holds himself in high regard, even though he and his family are impoverished.

Greater Picture

The Gaunt family represent the worst aspects of Wizard Pride and pure-blood mania. Although descended from Salazar Slytherin, generations of in-breeding, bigotry, laziness and feelings of superiority have ruined the Slytherin line. Their wealth had been squandered generations ago and the Gaunts now live in isolated squalor, hating everyone who are not pure-blood wizards. Marvolo considers himself a wizarding aristocrat, but in fact is a violent, bad tempered, ignorant tramp. Marvolo is a useless man with no ambitions, no respect for others (including his own children) and no social consciousness.

The folly of both pure-blood pride and "Wizards First" arrogance is a recurring theme throughout the series. The Gaunts and their last decendant, Voldemort, represent the dangers (and foolishness) of racial superiority, intolerance and aristocratic entitlement that is still widespread in the Real World.

Mary Macdonald

Gender: Female
Hair color: Unknown
Eye color: Unknown
Related Family: Unknown
Loyalty:

Overview

Mary Macdonald is a former Hogwarts student and friend of Lily Potter

Role in the Books

Deathly Hallows Mary is mentioned only in passing, in the memories Severus Snape passes to Harry in the Shrieking Shack. Lily, talking to Severus, mentions something Dark that Severus' friend Mulciber had done to Mary. Later, when Severus is waiting outside the entrance to Gryffindor Tower, Lily says that it was Mary who had told her that he was waiting there for her.

Merope Gaunt

Gender: Female
Hair color: Unknown
Eye color: Unknown
Related Family: Morfin Gaunt, Marvolo Gaunt, Tom Marvolo Riddle
Loyalty:

Overview

Merope Gaunt is the mother of Tom Marvolo Riddle, the sister of Morfin Gaunt, and the daughter of Marvolo Gaunt. She is not a pretty woman at all: 'Her hair was lank and dull and she had a plain, pale, rather heavy face. Her eyes stared in opposite directions.' She wears ragged clothing and is always abused by her father, because of the relative weakness of her magical powers.

Role in the Books

Half-Blood Prince We see Merope only through the recorded memories of various wizards, and the ensuing discussions with Professor Dumbledore. When we first see her, she is eighteen years old, and keeping house (more or less adequately) for her father and brother. She was in love with the Muggle Tom Riddle (Sr.). Shortly afterwards, her father and brother are sent to Azkaban for attacking the wizards who were to bring Morfin to the Ministry for a hearing concerning his attacking a Muggle with magic. Merope, left to her own devices, used a love potion to trap Riddle into marriage. When she became pregnant, she stopped using the love potion, under the apparent misconception that as she was bearing his child, Riddle would really love her without the use of potion. Once freed of the effect of the potion, however, he realized what had happened, abandoned her and returned to Little Hangleton. There, he told the town that he had been *hoodwinked* and *taken in*. She never tried to improve her life after being abandoned by him, living on in London, on her own and in poverty. Shortly before giving birth, she sold her only possession, a priceless locket which was one of the family heirlooms, and which could be traced back to Salazar Slytherin. She gave birth to her son in a Muggle orphanage and died after she named the child Tom Marvolo Riddle.

Strengths Largely lacking in physical strength or magical ability, she still has sufficient strength of character to stand up to her father and brother in the matter of the muggle Tom Riddle.

Weaknesses Merope's character was severely weakened by the abuse of her father and brother. She often had trouble with magic growing up, being terrorised by her father, and living in harsh impoverished conditions making her vulnerable to negative feelings about her magic abilities. It is likely that her apparent magical weakness was in part because she was untrained. It is unlikely that Marvolo, with his distrust of the Wizarding hierarchy, would have allowed either of his children to attend school.

As a result of this, Merope's self esteem was quite low; she was led to believe that the only way she could be loved was through a love potion.

Relationships with Other Characters Most villages in England will have a manor house, and the resident will be the local important person; often referred to as "the lord of the manor" though not necessarily nobility. Tom is the son and heir of the local lord, and Merope is hopelessly in love with him. Her brother and father abuse her quite harshly for daring to fall in love with a Muggle. This abuse from her family has left her feeling very unsure of herself.

Analysis

It is also worth noting that Merope had not only been the only non-Muggle-hater in her family, she had also been in love with one! And that she seemed to have passed none of these good qualities to Voldemort, he only retained the qualities of his namesake, Marvolo Gaunt.

Michael Corner

Gender: Male
Hair color: Unknown
Eye color: Unknown
Related Family: Unknown
Loyalty: Dumbledore's Army

Overview

Michael Corner is a Ravenclaw student one year behind Harry.

Role in the Books

Order of the Phoenix Michael Corner attends the first meeting of the Defence Association (as it is then known) at the Hog's Head in Hogsmeade. After the meeting breaks up, Hermione tells Harry and Ron that Michael had been there because Ginny Weasley had attended. Ginny and Michael, she says, are currently going out together. This causes Ron to state that he doesn't trust Michael. Carefully, because she was aware that Harry and Ginny had been speculatively linked, Hermione goes on to say that Ginny had been waiting for Harry but had given up, and had met Michael at the Yule Ball in the previous year. They had started going out shortly after that.

As Harry is unable to play as Seeker on the Gryffindor Quidditch team, Ginny takes his place. The final match of the year pits Gryffindor against Ravenclaw; and when Ginny catches the Snitch out from under Cho Chang's nose, Michael chooses to comfort Cho rather than celebrate with Ginny. Ginny then dumps him. On the Hogwarts Express, when Ginny tells this to Ron and Harry, Ron hints that she might now be able to find someone better, implying that Harry would be that someone; Ginny says that she's going out now with Dean Thomas.

Deathly Hallows As he leads Harry, Ron, and Hermione into the school from the Hog's Head, Neville mentions that Michael Corner had gotten caught releasing a first-year student that the Carrows had chained up as punishment. Michael had gotten very badly beaten for that, which had slowed down the activities of the revived Dumbledore's Army; Neville, the one remaining leader, felt that they could not ask anyone else to go through what Michael had suffered. When Harry returns to the school, Michael Corner is one of the students in the Room of Requirement waiting for his return. He does have a role in the ensuing battle, but we don't see much of him.

Relationships with Other Characters It is perhaps interesting that Michael and Harry have shared romantic interest in the same girls; Michael dated Ginny before Harry did, and dated Cho after Harry had done so.

Miles Bletchley

Gender: Male
Hair color: Unknown
Eye color: Unknown
Related Family: Unknown
Loyalty: Slytherin House

Overview

Miles Bletchley is an older student in Slytherin House; he is the keeper for the Slytherin Quidditch team.

Role in the Books

Philosopher's Stone Miles Bletchley is mentioned as being the Keeper of the Slytherin house team in the game against Gryffindor.

Prisoner of Azkaban In the Quidditch Final, Slytherin against Gryffindor, it is mentioned that Marcus Flint, team captain, has juggled the lineup in favour of brawn versus skill. The keeper in that match is never named, so we may assume that it is probably not Bletchley, who is named in earlier and later matches where he is Keeper.

Order of the Phoenix Alicia Spinnet goes to the Hospital Wing with her eyebrows growing so thick and fast that they obscure her vision and obstruct her mouth. Despite fourteen eye-witnesses who saw Miles Bletchley, here identified as the Slytherin keeper, jinx Alicia from behind as she worked in the library, Professor Snape insists that she must have tried a hair-thickening charm on herself.

In the only game that Harry plays, against Slytherin, Bletchley is mentioned as being Keeper.

Millicent Bullstrode

Gender: Female
Hair color: Unknown
Eye color: Unknown
Related Family: Unknown
Loyalty: Draco Malfoy(?)

Overview

Millicent Bullstrode (or *Bulstrode*) is a Slytherin student in Harry's year. "She was large and square and her heavy jaw jutted aggressively."

Role in the Books

Philosopher's Stone The Sorting Hat places Millicent Bulstrode into Slytherin House.

Chamber of Secrets Millicent Bullstrode, identified by last name only ("Miss Bullstrode"), is partnered with Hermione Granger in the Dueling Club. While we don't see exactly what happens in their duel, the end result is that Millicent has Hermione in a headlock, which Harry ends up breaking. Hermione later tries to use a hair that Millicent left on her in a Polyjuice potion to turn into Millicent and sneak into the Slytherin common room; unfortunately this fails as the hair is not in fact one of Millicent's own.

Order of the Phoenix Millicent is one of the Slytherin students who are appointed to the Inquisitorial Squad by Professor Umbridge. Millicent pins Hermione to the wall of Umbridge's office after Harry and the others are captured while trying to contact Sirius Black. We are led to believe that it was Millicent who captured Hermione, although we can't be sure because this action happens off stage.

Minerva McGonagall

Gender: Female
Hair color: Black
Eye color: Unknown
Related Family: Unknown
Loyalty: Order of the Phoenix

Overview

Minerva McGonagall is the Transfiguration professor at Hogwarts School for Witchcraft and Wizardry. She is also Head of Gryffindor House and Deputy Headmistress. Minerva also has the distinction of being one of the seven licensed Animagi of the 20th Century, being able to transform at will into a tabby cat (with distinctive markings around its eyes).

According to the author, Minerva McGonagall's birthday is 4 October.

Role in the Books

Philosopher's Stone Minerva McGonagall meets with Albus Dumbledore as baby Harry is brought to Number 4, Privet Drive. As they discuss the recent events that have brought Harry there, McGonagall unsuccessfully tries to dissuade Dumbledore from leaving the infant with his aunt and uncle, calling them, "the very worst sort of Muggles." McGonagall greets the first-years at the school's entrance and escorts them into the Great Hall for the Sorting Ceremony. Harry quickly realizes she is the wrong person to get onto the bad side of. However, he nearly does just that when he is almost late to his first Transfiguration lesson.

At breakfast in the Great Hall, McGonagall stops a confrontation that would have pitted Draco Malfoy and his cronies against Harry, Ron, and Neville Longbottom.

During Harry's first flying lesson, she spots him flying "like a natural" and recruits him for the Gryffindor Quidditch team, even though first-years are normally ineligible. Against school policy, she gets him a new broom—a Nimbus 2000.

At Hallowe'en, Harry and Ron defeat a mountain troll that was about to attack Hermione Granger in the girls' bathroom. To cover for them, Hermione tells McGonagall that she was planning to tackle it herself, but that Harry and Ron came to her aid; McGonagall penalizes Hermione five House points and rewards Harry and Ron five points each—for sheer dumb luck.

When Harry is caught wandering the halls after hours and for "making up some cock-and-bull story about a dragon," it is McGonagall who metes out punishment. She penalizes her own house 50 points each for the three involved students, Harry, Hermione, and Neville—150 points—as well as assigning detention. She earlier similarly penalized Draco Malfoy for wandering the halls.

She is startled when Harry reveals that he knows about the Philosopher's Stone, but when pressed by him for an audience with Professor Dumbledore, she says he has been summoned to London. This triggers Harry, Ron, and Hermione to go through the trap door to protect the Stone.

McGonagall's part in guarding the Philosopher's Stone was enhancing a giant chess set. Ron had to play a game through in order to allow Harry and Hermione to pass on to the next barrier.

Chamber of Secrets When Professor Snape catches Harry and Ron after they crash into the Whomping Willow with the flying car, he takes them to his office and fetches Professor McGonagall. Professor Dumbledore is also summoned, and after hearing their story, he leaves Professor McGonagall, their House Head, to determine their punishment. She gives both detentions but does not dock any House points.

Harry, following the voice that apparently only he can hear, finds himself in the second floor hallway where words have been scrawled on the wall and Mrs. Norris, Filch's cat, has been hung off a torch bracket. Filch, Professor Dumbledore, Professor Snape, Professor Lockhart, and Professor McGonagall take Mrs. Norris to Lockhart's office where Dumbledore examines her. He finds that she is Petrified, not dead. In the ensuing conversation, Filch demands that someone be punished, Snape accuses Harry of knowing things he is not telling and suggests suspending him from Quidditch, McGonagall refuses to accept such severe punishment, and Dumbledore reminds Snape that Harry is innocent until proven guilty. Dumbledore then lets Harry, Ron, and Hermione depart. When Justin Finch-Fletchley and Nearly Headless Nick are petrified, Professor McGonagall is the senior teacher on the scene. She takes Harry to Professor Dumbledore's office, but does not stay, however, allowing Harry and Dumbledore to speak alone.

When Professor Dumbledore is suspended as Headmaster, McGonagall becomes the temporary Headmistress. Professor McGonagall ends a Quidditch match when Hermione and Penelope Clearwater are found petrified. She takes Harry and Ron to see Hermione in the hospital wing, and asks if there is anything they can tell her about what is happening, although they do not know. She informs the Gryffindors that security restrictions have been enacted. Ignoring the restrictions, Harry and Ron sneak off to Moaning Myrtle's bathroom. When they encounter McGonagall along the way, Harry concocts a cover story saying they were going to visit Hermione in the infirmary. Touched by this apparent concern for their friend, McGonagall allows them to continue. Of course, they now have to actually visit Hermione. In her petrified hand, they discover a clue revealing the Chamber's secret. While waiting in the staff room to tell McGonagall what they have found, all students are ordered to their Common rooms; it is McGonagall who tells the other teachers that Ginny Weasley has been abducted. McGonagall is the driving force behind sending Gilderoy Lockhart into the Chamber to find the Monster and rescue Ginny. Once he leaves, she details plans for closing the school.

In Professor McGonagall's office, Harry and Ron describe what happened in the Chamber and the events leading up to it. McGonagall is sent off to arrange a celebratory feast. Later, to the now-revived Hermione's dismay, Professor McGonagall announces that all final exams have been cancelled.

Prisoner of Azkaban Following Harry's unpleasant encounter with a Dementor on the Hogwarts Express, Professor McGonagall takes him and Hermione into her office. She summons Madam Pomfrey, who is overly solicitous, but glad to find that they now have a Defence Against the Dark Arts teacher (Remus Lupin) who actually knows his remedies. Professor McGonagall suggests bed rest, but Harry insists he is fine and requests permission to go to the Welcoming Feast. McGonagall consents but asks Hermione to remain behind; Harry does not discover why until later. During Transfiguration class, McGonagall lectures about Animagi and is surprised that students fail to react when she transforms herself into a cat. When informed about Professor Trelawney's prediction that a student will die, she seems to have to restrain herself from criticizing another teacher or subject, but says that Trelawney has predicted a student's death every year and none have yet died.

Just before the first Hogsmeade weekend outing, Harry asks Professor McGonagall if he can also go, despite lacking written permission from his Uncle Vernon; McGonagall refuses, saying she cannot not stretch the rules that far.

Fred and George Weasley give Harry a magical parchment called the Marauder's Map that shows secret passageways in and out of Hogwarts. Harry follows a tunnel into Hogsmeade, meeting up with Hermione and Ron. Together they visit the Three Broomsticks, where they eavesdrop on a conversation between Professor McGonagall, Professor Flitwick, Hagrid, Cornelius Fudge, and Madam Rosmerta. Harry learns that his godfather, Sirius Black, is believed responsible for revealing his parents' secret whereabouts to Lord Voldemort—information that led to their murders. He also learns the circumstances surrounding Black's arrest. When Hermione informs McGonagall that Harry received an expensive Firebolt broom from an unknown person for Christmas, McGonagall confiscates it, saying that Professor Flitwick and Madam Hooch will inspect it for any concealed Dark Magic.

After several months, and much nagging by Gryffindor Quidditch captain Oliver Wood, Professor McGonagall returns the Firebolt, saying it is believed to be clean. Harry flies a marvelous match on it, marred only by the arrival of apparent Dementors, who turn out to be Draco Malfoy, Crabbe, Goyle, and Marcus Flint; McGonagall gives them detentions and penalizes them House points.

Following the victory celebration, the House is awoken during the night by Ron's screams—Sirius Black was in his dorm. McGonagall asks Sir Cadogan, the guardian of the Gryffindor tower entrance, if anyone was permitted to enter; Sir Cadogan replies he granted access to someone who had all the passwords on a list. When McGonnagall discovers it is Neville Longbottoms's list, she cancels his Hogsmeade weekends and forbids him from having the password. Other students must now let him into the Gryffindor common room. After Black's break-in, Professor McGonagall tells Harry what he already knows: Black is trying to get to him.

Harry learns that Professor McGonagall gave Hermione a Time-Turner at the beginning of the year so she could attend extra classes (taught at the same time). Harry and Hermione use it to go back in time to save Buckbeak from being destroyed and to free Sirius Black. Exhausted from the heavy workload, Hermione drops her extra classes and resumes a normal class schedule. She returns the Time-Turner to Professor McGonagall.

Goblet of Fire Professor McGonagall enters our story in the Entrance Hall. As the students are arriving, Peeves is welcoming them with water balloons; Professor McGonagall orders him to depart. At the Arrival Feast, when Dumbledore announces that the Triwizard Tournament is to be restarted, Fred Weasley is heard to say "You're joking!" This starts Dumbledore telling a (perhaps inappropriate) joke, which Professor McGonagall interrupts by pointedly clearing her throat.

When Draco Malfoy tries to Curse Harry in the Entrance Hall, Professor Moody Transfigures him into a white ferret, and bounces him in the air a few times, much to the amusement of Harry and Ron. Professor McGonagall, arriving on the scene, forcefully tells Moody that they do not transfigure students as punishment, and transforms Draco back into himself. McGonagall then tells Moody that he must talk to Draco's head of house; Moody, guessing that to be Snape, heads off to the dungeons with Draco.

Harry is amazed at the amount of homework that he is being called upon to do; Professor McGonagall tells the class that they are being prepared for their O.W.L.s, which will be happening in the next year.

As time for the arrival of the representatives of the other two schools taking part in the Tournament approaches, Professor McGonagall is heard exhorting her House to be on its best behaviour. In particular, she asks Neville to not allow it to be known that he cannot master even a simple Switching Spell.

When Harry's name unexpectedly appears from the Goblet of Fire, making him a fourth Champion, he and the other three champions meet with the competition judges: Professor Dumbledore, Professor Karkaroff of Durmstrang, Madame Maxime of Beauxbatons, and Mr. Crouch and Ludo Bagman from the Ministry. Professor McGonagall is present, as are Professor Snape and Professor Moody. Professor McGonagall's contribution is limited; when it is suggested that Professor Dumbledore had drawn the age line incorrectly, allowing an underage Harry to put his own name in, McGonagall declares loyally that he could not have made a mistake. McGonagall escorts Harry to the dragon enclosure for the first task, and leaves him there with the other champions. At the end of Transfiguration class, Professor McGonagall announces that there will be a Yule Ball this year as part of the Triwizard Tournament. Fourth-year and above will be allowed to attend, as will younger students as their guests. As class breaks up, McGonagall takes Harry aside and tells him that it is traditional for the Champions and their partners to lead the way into the Ball and to have the first dance. Harry is shocked: he has only a month to find a dance partner, learn to dance, and prepare to lead the schools in to the ball.

On the night of the Ball, McGonagall takes the four Champions aside and tells them that they will be entering in procession after the rest of the students are seated.

As Harry, Hermione, and Ron are attempting to find a way for Harry to breathe underwater for an hour, as required for the Second Task, Fred and George arrive, saying that Professor McGonagall wants to see Hermione and Ron in her office. We later learn that they were charmed and handed over to the Merpeople, who held them in their underwater town as the goal for the Second Task.

Near the end of May, Professor McGonagall sends Harry down to the Quidditch pitch, where he will be getting news about the Third Task.

On the morning before the Third Task, Professor McGonagall tells Harry that the Champions and their families are congregating in a small room off the Great Hall. Harry knows the Dursleys would not care to see him, so he stays in the Great Hall, reading; but, summoned by Cedric, goes to find that Mrs. Weasley and Bill have come to watch him.

Professor McGonagall, with Hagrid, Professor Moody, and Professor Flitwick, are to patrol the outside of the maze during the Third Task, to rescue those who fall to its challenges.

When Harry returns from the duel in the graveyard, he is taken aside and effectively kidnapped by Professor Moody. Professor McGonagall, Professor Dumbledore, and Professor Snape rescue Harry from him by breaking down the door and Stunning him. Once Moody is safely bound up, McGonagall wants to send Harry to the Hospital Wing, but Dumbledore overrules her, saying that Harry needs to know what has happened and why. Dumbledore sends McGonagall to fetch the large black dog out of Hagrid's pumpkin patch and take it to his office. While she is gone, Moody's dose of Polyjuice Potion wears off; on her return, she is stunned to find that it is Barty Crouch Jr. lying on the office floor.

After Barty has confessed, Professor Dumbledore leaves Professor McGonagall to guard Barty, and takes Harry up to his office to hear what happened in the graveyard. He then takes Harry to the Hospital Wing, where he allows Madam Pomfrey to dose him unconscious. Harry is awakened, though, by the arrival of Professor McGonagall looking for Dumbledore; it seems that Cornelius Fudge had felt it necessary to bring a Dementor with him when he came to hear Barty's story, and the Dementor had instantly administered the Kiss. Barty would no longer be able to tell anyone anything.

Order of the Phoenix We learn that Professor McGonagall is a member of the Order of the Phoenix when Harry, then staying at the Headquarters of the Order sees her arriving, looking somehow odd in Muggle clothes.

Professor McGonagall is, if course, at the Entrance Feast and presides over the Sorting. She seems to be one of the few teachers who listens to Dolores Umbridge's "welcome speech."

On the first day of classes, Professor McGonagall hands out timetables. In Defence Against the Dark Arts class, Harry argues with Professor Umbridge about whether Voldemort has returned, and as a result is given a note that he must take to McGonagall. He learns there that he has been given detention every day for a week. McGonagall asks him if he had understood Umbridge's welcoming speech, and Harry haltingly suggests that it seemed to mean that the Ministry was going to be taking a more active hand in the running of Hogwarts. McGonagall says that she's glad Harry at least listens to Hermione. She then goes on to say that Harry must be careful around Umbridge, especially in keeping his temper, to give her the least possible reason to attack Harry.

Leaving detention on the fourth night, Harry happens to run into Ron, who notices that his hand is cut and bleeding. Ron demands to know what the detention consists of, and says it must be illegal and that Harry should go to McGonagall. Harry demurs, saying it is more of a personal issue now.

When Harry again gets detention for a second week, McGonagall additionally penalizes him House points, as it seems he will not learn any other way that he should not antagonize Umbridge.

When Sirius replies to a message Harry had sent, Hedwig, carrying the message, appears to have been injured. Harry takes Hedwig to the staff room in hopes that Professor Grubbly-Plank will be able to help heal her. Professor McGonagall, who is there, warns Harry that all communication channels in and out of the school are likely to be monitored.

The combination of taunts from Draco Malfoy and an after-the-whistle Bludger from Crabbe result in a brawl breaking out after the first Quidditch game of the year, which was against Slytherin. Harry and George Weasley, being the Gryffindor players involved, are called into McGonagall's office. She assigns them each a week's detention, but Umbridge, appearing with a new Educational Decree, overrules her, saying that a more appropriate punishment is a lifetime Quidditch ban, and confiscation of their brooms. Fred Weasley is included in the ban as well, despite his not having been involved. McGonagall protests that the punishment is out of line, but Umbridge will not be swayed.

Just before Christmas, Harry dreams that he is a snake, and that he attacks someone in a long hallway. Waking up, he tells Ron that he saw his father being attacked, and that he needs help. Neville runs to get Professor McGonagall, who hears Harry out, then takes him and Ron to Professor Dumbledore's office. Dumbledore listens to Harry's story, then sends two portraits, Dilys and Everard, to investigate. When the portraits return, saying that the man was found, but seems to be badly hurt, Dumbledore sends McGonagall to fetch the other Weasley children. McGonagall asks about Molly, but Dumbledore says that will be a job for Fawkes. Shortly after McGonagall returns with Fred, George, and Ginny, Dumbledore sends her off once again to prevent Umbridge from disturbing them. She evidently is successful, as neither she nor Umbridge appears in Dumbledore's office before the Weasley children and Harry have left.

When Umbridge acts to break up "Dumbledore's Army," Harry receives warning from Dobby, and all except Harry are able to escape. Harry, however, is taken by Umbridge to Dumbledore's office, where he finds Professor Dumbledore, Professor McGonagall, Cornelius Fudge, Percy Weasley acting as scribe, and two Aurors, Dawlish and Shacklebolt; Marietta Edgecombe is also brought in as a witness. Umbridge accuses Harry of holding an illegal meeting at the Hog's Head. When she says that she had gotten her information from Willy Widdershins, McGonagall comments that she had wondered how he had gotten off so lightly for all those regurgitating toilets. When Fudge tries to arrest Dumbledore, there is a sudden burst of white light; Harry finds that McGonagall has pushed him and Marietta to the floor, out of harm's way. Dumbledore, the only one left conscious, quickly checks the three of them to ensure they are fine, and then departs.

Monday after Easter Break, Harry has an appointment with McGonagall to discuss planning for a career. Arriving, he finds that Umbridge is sitting in, with a clipboard. Harry suggests that he might like to become an auror; McGonagall takes this at face value, and starts outlining the course of study he will need to follow. Umbridge repeatedly tries to raise objections to this; McGonagall sharply cuts each objection down, making Umbridge angrier each time. When Umbridge shrieks that Harry will never become an Auror, McGonagall is so outraged she vows to do everything possible to help him achieve his goal. As Harry leaves, he hears their argument continuing in the office behind him.

With the departure of Dumbledore, and the later departure of Fred and George Weasley, the school has become largely unmanageable. The teachers are not helping matters, in a form of silent rebellion against Umbridge. At one point, we see McGonagall walk, apparently uncaring, past Peeves who is loosening a crystal chandelier, though it seems she might have told him that it turned the other way.

Harry is taking his astronomy O.W.L. when Umbridge brings multiple Aurors to the school to attempt to sack Hagrid. Apparently attracted by the confusion and wand flashes, McGonagall runs to stop the battle, but is hit in the chest by four Stunners simultaneously. When Harry sees Voldemort torturing Sirius Black, he attempts to speak with McGonagall, the only Order member that he can think of, but when he goes to visit her at the Hospital Wing, he is told that she has been taken to St. Mungo's Hospital. As a result, Harry attempts to contact Sirius directly by means of Professor Umbridge's fireplace, and gets caught.

Harry, distraught at the death of Sirius, almost gets into a duel with Draco Malfoy, who is angry because his father has been sent to Azkaban, in the Entrance Hall. The incipient duel is broken up by Professor Snape, who then prepares to penalize Harry House points but discovers there are none left in the Gryffindor hourglass. Professor McGonagall chooses this moment to return, physically weakened by the ordeal and using a walking stick. She sends Draco and his cronies off with her packages and parcels, then awards a number of House points to all those students who were in the battle at the Ministry. She then subtracts the number of points that Snape had suggested. When Peeves chases Umbridge from the school by alternately hitting her with a walking stick and a bag of chalk, Professor McGonagall is upset because the walking stick is hers, which means she is unable to get out to the front door to cheer Peeves on.

Half-Blood Prince At the beginning of the year, Professor McGonagall creates and hands out timetables to the sixth-year students. The process is complicated by the fact that the courses that students can take are limited by how well they have done in O.W.L.s. Hermione gets her courses straight away. Neville cannot take Transfiguration with only an Acceptable O.W.L., but his Charms grade is high enough for that course. While Neville is reluctant, saying that his grandmother says Charms is a soft option, McGonagall points out that just because she failed her Charms O.W.L., Augusta has no right to argue against it. McGonagall tells Parvati Patil that Firenze and Professor Trelawney are splitting Divination classes, and that Professor Trelawney is teaching sixth year. Harry's lost hope to become an Auror revives when Professor McGonagall says that Professor Slughorn accepts lower O.W.L. grades than Professor Snape for N.E.W.T.-level Potions classes. Both Harry and Ron sign up, although Harry worries that Hagrid will be upset that they are not taking Care of Magical Creatures. Professor McGonagall also hands Harry a list with prospective Quidditch players for the House team.

When Katie Bell touches a necklace and is cursed, Harry, Ron, Hermione, and Katie's friend Leanne return to the school carrying the necklace safely wrapped up. McGonagall meets them at the gate and gives the wrapped necklace to Filch to take to Professor Snape. She then gets the story of what had happened to Katie in her office. After Leanne is dismissed, Harry, over Ron and Hermione's objections, voices his belief that Draco Malfoy was involved. McGonagall hears him out, but then says that Draco could not have done it because he had been in her office at the time, serving a detention.

We see McGonagall briefly in the Quidditch match following Ron's birthday. Luna Lovegood is commentating, and while the rest of the school seems vastly amused by her announcements, McGonagall is heard correcting her on a couple of occasions.

When Harry, defending himself against Draco, uses Sectumsempra, Snape gives him detention every Saturday for the remainder of the year. It is mentioned that McGonagall agrees with Snape's setting this amount of detention. While we don't see her in the battle with the Death Eaters, she is in the Hospital Wing after Dumbledore's death while they figure out what had happened. She is shocked to hear that Dumbledore had been killed by Snape, to the point that Madam Pomfrey conjures a chair for her. She said that Dumbledore had always said he trusted Snape, for good reason, but it seems his trust was betrayed. Harry says that he knows the reason Dumbledore trusted Snape: Snape had carried the prophecy about Harry to Voldemort, and then repented of that to Dumbledore. McGonagall blames herself for sending Professor Flitwick to fetch Snape.

McGonagall says that when Dumbledore had left with Harry to go to the cave, Bill, Lupin, and Tonks had been on patrol, but that she did not know where the Death Eaters had come from. Harry tells her about the link through the Room of Requirement.

McGonagall, as acting Headmaster, realizes that decisions about the school's future will have to be made. She summons the other heads of Houses, Professor Flitwick, Professor Sprout, and Professor Slughorn to a meeting in the Headmaster's office; she also asks Harry and Hagrid to join them. There, under the newly-present portrait of Dumbledore, before the others arrive, McGonagall asks Harry what he and Dumbledore had been doing. Harry demurs, saying that he had been instructed to keep their activities secret, and Dumbledore had not said he could stop following his orders if he died. Once the other teachers arrive, McGonagall polls them as to the plans for the school. With the consensus being that the school should be kept open, she then asks if they should send the students home immediately, rather than finishing out the school year. Harry points out that while it may not be possible to finish the year, many students would want to stay to have the chance to say . . . Professor Sprout finishes the sentence he cannot: "Goodbye." It is decided that the Hogwarts Express will be scheduled for the day after the funeral. Seeing the Minister for Magic approaching the school with a delegation, McGonagall quickly dismisses Harry. McGonagall is present at the funeral, but we do not speak with her.

Deathly Hallows It is something of a surprise that McGonagall, who was acting Headmistress at the end of *Harry Potter and the Half-Blood Prince,* and who has been Deputy Headmistress from the beginning of the series, was not made Headmistress; however, given Voldemort's interest in Hogwarts, it makes sense that a Death Eater should get the post, and so the appointment of Severus Snape as Headmaster is logical.

We don't see Professor McGonagall until we reach the end of the story. McGonagall, who has previously opened the Ravenclaw common room for Alecto Carrow, is called upon to open it for Amycus Carrow. When Amycus finds Alecto unconscious in the Ravenclaw common room, he decides that he will somehow frame the Ravenclaw students for her having summoned Voldemort. McGonagall refuses to allow this, but Amycus tries to override her. In the process, he spits on her; Harry, from under his Invisibility Cloak, curses Amycus, knocking him out. McGonagall, after learning what Harry is doing there, quickly binds Amycus and Alecto together, sends out messengers for the other three Heads of House, and with Harry, starts for her office. On the way, they meet Severus Snape, who asks what is going on. Snape does not seem satisfied by her explanation, and they duel. Snape breaks and runs when he sees Flitwick and Sprout approaching, McGonagall, in pursuit, sees him jump through a window and fly away.

McGonagall now instructs the other teachers that they will have to prepare Hogwarts for battle. Harry, returning to the Room of Requirement, cannot find Ron and Hermione. As he hears the students heading for the Great Hall, he goes himself, hoping that Ron and Hermione will be there, and hears McGonagall instructing the students as to what will happen. She tells the school that Professor Snape has resigned, news that is met with cheers from all except Slytherin. She says that the underage students will be evacuated, along with any of the older students who want to leave. As she is speaking, she is interrupted by the voice of Voldemort, saying that if they turn Harry over, nobody at the school will get hurt, otherwise at midnight they will come in and get him. Pansy Parkinson, at the Slytherin table, sees Harry and aims her wand at him; the Gryffindor table rises to his defence, as do the Ravenclaw and Hufflepuff tables. McGonagall says that all Slytherins will be evacuated. She then reminds Harry that he is meant to be looking for something.

McGonagall then marshals the defence of Hogwarts, mobilizing the armour, and preparing an army of desks (along with other objects, no doubt) to the defence of the school during the Battle of Hogwarts.

In the break in hostilities, Harry sees, in Snape's memories, that Professor McGonagall was present at Snape's Sorting some twenty years before.

In the final battle, Voldemort is dueling McGonagall, Kingsley, and Slughorn. When Bellatrix is felled by Molly Weasley, Voldemort sweeps the three of them aside to attack Molly, but is thwarted by Harry from under his Invisibility Cloak.

We see a glimpse of McGonagall at the victory celebration, but Harry does not wish to talk with her; he is too tired, and simply wants to get away.

Strengths She is a very powerful witch and is particularly adept at Transfiguration. She is a strict teacher and has the respect of the students. Her discipline can be severe but is always fair and even-handed. Professor McGonagall has a tender side, though she takes pains to conceal it, and considers the welfare of the Hogwarts students to be her most important vocation.

Relationships with Other Characters It is hard to imagine Professor McGonagall "letting her hair down" to any great extent, which makes it difficult to imagine that she has many relationships. However, she does have a close friendship with Albus Dumbledore, and she seems to have more concern for the well-being of Harry than his position as a student in her house, or even his potential to bring about the final downfall of Voldemort, would merit.

QUESTIONS

1. Professor McGonagall can morph into a cat. What does this animal say about her character?
2. Why didn't Professor Dumbledore tell McGonagall more about Harry?
3. How will Hogwarts change with Professor McGonagall as Headmistress?

Miriam Strout

Gender: Female
Hair color: Unknown
Eye color: Unknown
Related Family: Unknown
Loyalty: St. Mungo's

OVERVIEW

Miriam Strout is a motherly-looking Healer who works in a long-term resident's ward for spell damage (the James Thickey ward) at St. Mungo's.

ROLE IN THE BOOKS

Order of the Phoenix We first meet Miriam Strout when Harry, Ron, Hermione, and Ginny happen to run into Gilderoy Lockhart at St. Mungo's. He has temporarily escaped the locked ward where he usually lives, and although she is not named in this section, Miriam Strout is the one who rounds Gilderoy back up and takes him back to his ward. Her cheerful assumption that the four friends are there to visit with Lockhart results in the four of them spending some time visiting. In the course of this visit, they see Miriam distributing gifts; Broderick Bode receives a potted plant, among other items. This also leads to Hermione, Ron, and Ginny becoming aware of the plight of Neville Longbottom's parents, who are there on the ward as well.

A short news article in the *Daily Prophet* tells how Broderick Bode was killed by a potted plant. He had been encouraged to tend it himself, and it had turned out to be Devil's Snare. The healer in charge of the ward, Miriam Strout, could not explain how it had gotten past Hospital security, and was on paid leave until the investigation was complete.

ANALYSIS

We can see that much healing in the Wizarding world is done by means of plants and plant extracts; note the reliance on the healing powers of Dittany in the sixth and seventh books, along with the description of the uses of Bubotubers and Mandrake root. As such, it is a safe assumption that Miriam Strout, as a trained Healer, would have been able to recognize the potted plant as Devil's Snare, had she been allowed to.

GREATER PICTURE

We will later find out that Bode had received his spell damage several months earlier, while under the Imperius charm, carrying out the orders of Lucius Malfoy. By the time we see him, his condition has already improved, to the point that the Death Eaters must be beginning to be worried that he might sufficiently regain his faculties to explain what he was doing in the Hall of Prophecies and why. Thus, by this time it was becoming necessary to end Bode's life. It is possible that Miriam Strout had been placed under the Imperius Curse also, to ensure that the plant reached its victim and remained there; it is not likely the Death Eaters would leave something that important to chance.

Moaning Myrtle

Gender: Female
Hair color: Black
Eye color: Unknown
Related Family: Unknown
Loyalty: eventually Harry Potter, later Draco Malfoy

OVERVIEW

Moaning Myrtle was a former Ravenclaw student (now a ghost) who haunts the girl's bathroom on the first floor (called the second floor in the US editions of the book) of Hogwarts.

ROLE IN THE BOOKS

Chamber of Secrets We meet Myrtle at Nearly Headless Nick's Deathday party. She seems a bit depressed, as many ghosts do; but Peeves takes the opportunity to mock her to the point that she runs off, crying. Apparently as she returns to her bathroom, she turns on all the taps.

Later, passing the spot where Mrs. Norris, Filch's cat, was Petrified, Harry, Ron, and Hermione realize that they are passing Myrtle's bathroom. They stop in to talk to her, but she is not terribly communicative. They are caught exiting from the bathroom by Percy, who threatens them with a House points penalty. Because Myrtle's bathroom is such an unwelcoming place, Hermione suggests it would be perfect for their use as they brew up a batch of Polyjuice Potion. They do this starting at about the middle of November. Myrtle doesn't seem to mind this activity much, usually hiding underwater somewhere and gurgling at them. When the time comes for them to use the potion, Hermione finds that she has made a mistake and used a cat hair; Myrtle seems very amused that Hermione has turned partway into a cat and is now stuck there. She finds Hermione's tail especially amusing.

Later, Harry and Ron find Myrtle's bathroom flooded; apparently she has become upset because someone threw a book at her while she was resting in the U-bend. In her anger she has turned on all the water in the bathroom. Harry recovers the book, it turns out to be a diary, originally owned by one T. M. Riddle fifty years ago. A clue in that diary leads Harry and Ron to Hagrid, who in turn sends them to Aragog. Aragog, in turn, mentions that the last time the Chamber was opened, a girl died in a bathroom. It suddenly occurs to Harry that this might be Moaning Myrtle.

On their way to visit Myrtle for confirmation, Harry and Ron are caught in the halls by Professor McGonagall. Thinking up a reason for their being in the halls, Harry hits upon the idea of saying that they are trying to visit Hermione in the Hospital wing, as she has been Petrified. While visiting Hermione, they find a scrap of paper that she has torn out of a book which describes Basilisks; this tells them what the monster is.

Finally, with Professor Lockhart in tow, they return to Myrtle's bathroom. Myrtle confirms that it was she who had died the last time the Chamber was opened, and what she remembers matches the effects of a Basilisk; Harry figures out how to open the Chamber, and with Ron and Lockhart, he descends. When he returns, Myrtle suggests that if he had died down there, he would have been welcome to share her bathroom; Ron teases that Harry's got a girlfriend.

Goblet of Fire Harry is given a hint to the Golden Egg clue by Cedric Diggory, and as a result ends up taking the egg to the Prefects' washroom. Moaning Myrtle joins him there, appearing out of one of the faucets, to his dismay—Harry tries to hide his nakedness under the bubbles; Myrtle after all is a girl. Myrtle guides Harry towards what Cedric did to his Golden Egg: opening it underwater and listening to it there. While

Harry is thinking about the meaning of this clue, Myrtle is telling how she became a ghost; Harry largely ignores her. When Harry muses how he is going to breathe underwater, Myrtle becomes affronted at being reminded that she doesn't breathe any more. During the Second Task, Harry, swimming deep in the lake, is again accosted by Moaning Myrtle. Harry is surprised that she is able to get to the lake; she says that sometimes she is sent to the lake by surprise when someone flushes her toilet unexpectedly. She points Harry in the direction of the Merpeople's settlement under the lake.

Half-Blood Prince   At one point, Harry and Ron step into a bathroom to allow Ron to escape the clutches of Lavender Brown. Myrtle appears and is disappointed, saying that Harry had promised to visit her and never did, and that she was hoping that it was the other, sad boy who was coming in. She says that he is worried because he has a task and he has been working at it for a long time, and is not succeeding. Ron manages to insult her by mentioning that she is dead, and she leaves through the plumbing, crying.

Harry, looking at the Marauder's Map, sees Draco Malfoy in a nearby bathroom with Myrtle. Looking in at them, he sees that Draco is crying. Draco catches sight of him in the mirror, and immediately starts flinging curses at him. Harry retaliates. Draco starts to invoke the Cruciatus curse, but Harry stops him with the Sectumsempra curse, one which he has read but never tried to use. This curse makes Harry's wand act like a very long knife, making great cuts appear in Draco's face and torso. Myrtle starts screaming; Severus Snape appears and manages to heal Draco.

Weaknesses   Myrtle is offended very easily, at least initially. Any reminder that she is dead will send her off in gouts of tears. When Tom Riddle's diary was thrown into the commode where she happened to be invisibly resting, and it happened to fall through her, this enraged her to the point that she caused all the toilets and taps to effectively erupt, sending water all through her bathroom and out into the hall. It is in part this hypersensitivity that has left her with the name Moaning Myrtle, because in fact that does seem to be what she does most of the time.

Relationships with Other Characters   When Harry returns from the Chamber of Secrets, she suggests that if he had died down there, Harry would have been welcome to share her bathroom. Additionally, she helps him a couple of times before and during the Second Task of the Triwizard Tournament. This would seem to indicate that she has a little bit of a crush on Harry. However, when Ron and Harry use a bathroom to hide from Lavender Brown in *Harry Potter and the Half-Blood Prince*, Myrtle seems disappointed to see them, which would indicate that any romantic interest she has in Harry has been replaced by an interest in another boy, who turns out to be Draco Malfoy.

ANALYSIS

Most unusually for a ghost, it seems Myrtle does have some control over physical matter; apparently her haunting of the bathroom has rendered it unusable, mainly because she keeps flooding the place when she gets depressed. This is useful to the story in *Harry Potter and the Chamber of Secrets* in two respects: Mrs. Norris is Petrified (in the chapter The Deathday Party), rather than being killed, because she sees the reflection of the Basilisk rather than seeing the Basilisk directly. The image is reflected in the water that Myrtle has caused to flood out of the bathroom because she was so upset at the insults lobbed at her by Peeves at Nearly Headless Nick's Deathday party. Additionally, it is Myrtle's unwelcoming presence in the washroom that allows Hermione the time and space to make Polyjuice Potion; nobody willingly goes in there more than once, after being subjected to Myrtle's aggressive depression.

Myrtle's affinity for water also allows her to help Harry with the Second Task in *Harry Potter and the Goblet of Fire*; as the second task involves the Merpeople under the lake, Myrtle is instrumental in allowing Harry to solve the riddle surrounding the task, and also points him in the right direction when he is looking for the Merpeople during the task proper. Myrtle says that she sometimes ends up in the lake when someone flushes a toilet in her bathroom and she's not expecting it, which may lead us to wonder about Wizarding sanitation practices. As mentioned, Myrtle is always sad and is apparently still hypersensitive about death. It is true that she had died only fifty years before our story opens, and so could have expected, in the normal run of affairs, to still be alive; it is possible that a ghost will be especially sensitive to thoughts of death until they reach an age at which they would have died normally. As far as her perpetual sadness goes, we must remember that at the time she died, she had been driven to tears by the cruelty of another girl and was hiding in the washroom. From what Nearly Headless Nick tells us in *Harry Potter and the Order of the Phoenix* regarding ghostly existence, it is entirely possible that Myrtle is sad as a ghost purely because she was so sad when she died.

Molly Weasley

Gender: Female
Hair color: Red
Eye color: Unknown
Related Family: brothers Gideon and Fabian Prewett; husband Arthur, children Bill, Charlie, Percy, Fred, George, Ron, Ginny
Loyalty: Albus Dumbledore

OVERVIEW

Molly Weasley (née Prewett) is the wife of Arthur Weasley. According to the author's web site, she was born on October 30.

Role in the Books

Philosopher's Stone Molly Weasley appears here to teach Harry the way of getting to Platform Nine and Three Quarters. When we first meet her in King's Cross Station, she seems to be quite comforting; she sees that Harry is looking lost and provides what help she can. When Fred and George return to the platform to tell her who the "black-haired kid" is, and Ginny pleads to be allowed onto the train to see him, Molly refuses, saying he doesn't want to be gawked at like an animal in a zoo.

Mrs. Weasley is the source of some of Harry's Christmas presents. Simple as they are, a jumper (US: sweater) and some candy, these are very nearly the first real Christmas presents Harry has ever received.

She is also on hand to greet the returning Weasley children when they leave school, and speaks to Harry briefly then as well. She seems somewhat nonplussed by the brevity of Uncle Vernon's greeting to Harry.

Chamber of Secrets When Harry, Ron, and the twins arrive in Mr. Weasley's flying Ford Anglia, Mrs. Weasley is awake and waiting for them, much to their dismay; they had hoped to sneak out, break Harry out of imprisonment, and return before she was aware of it. She scolds the three Weasley children thoroughly, but welcomes Harry to their home, saying that she knows he had nothing to do with it. She continues to be sympathetic towards Harry, giving him extra sausages with his breakfast when he hears the Dursleys had been starving him. As punishment for her boys, she sets them to de-gnoming the garden, but she says Harry doesn't need to do that, he can go up and rest. Harry, however, says he's never seen a de-gnoming and would like to help. Mrs. Weasley pulls a book off the shelf, *Gilderoy Lockhart's Guide to Household Pests*, and starts to consult it as to the best way to remove gnomes; Fred says that they know how to de-gnome a garden, and George suggests that Mrs. Weasley is sweet on Lockhart. Mrs. Weasley then sends them out to start work.

As they finish, Mr. Weasley returns home. As they gather in the kitchen, Mrs. Weasley tells Mr. Weasley that the twins had taken his car out to London. Mr. Weasley immediately asks how it had gone, but seeing warning signs from Mrs. Weasley, immediately changes his tone to say that they had been very naughty.

Booklists arrive, and there are a lot of books by Gilderoy Lockhart which all the students will need. George comments that this lot won't come cheap, and Mrs. Weasley, though looking worried, says that they will manage. When Hermione's owl arrives with the suggestion that they meet up in Diagon Alley, Mrs. Weasley agrees that makes sense, and the date for school supplies shopping is set.

When the day arrives, Mrs. Weasley says that the family will be traveling to Diagon Alley by Floo powder, but is dismayed to find how little they have left when she takes the jar of powder off the mantel. She offers Harry the powder first, then realizes that he's never traveled that way before. She tells Ron to go first, then with help from the twins provides a lot of advice as to how to travel by Floo powder, advice that makes Harry wonder how safe Floo travel is. When Harry ends up at the wrong grate, Mrs. Weasley is almost frantic with worry; she divides up her brood and sets them to searching Diagon Alley for Harry, in the hope that he had only gone a few grates too far and would be physically nearby. She is extremely relieved when Hagrid turns up with Harry in tow, having found him in Knockturn Alley. She brushes Harry off, and overruling the Twins' questions about what Knockturn Alley is like, reminds them that they are not allowed there.

At Gringotts, Harry sees that there is very little in the Weasleys' vault; Mrs. Weasley carefully checks all four corners of the vault for fallen coins before sweeping what little there is into her moneybag. Harry is acutely aware of the piles of Galleons and Sickles in his vault, but Mrs. Weasley says nothing about it. Back on the surface, she suggests that the group should split up to do their shopping.

We see Mrs. Weasley again at Flourish and Blotts, where she is in line for a book signing by Gilderoy Lockhart. When a confrontation between Arthur Weasley and Lucius Malfoy becomes physical, and has to be broken up by Hagrid, Molly is thoroughly embarrassed. She carries on scolding her husband about it even after the twins tell her that Gilderoy is not upset at the fight, only wondering how it can be slanted so that the story enhances his exposure. The trip to King's Cross Station is made in Arthur Weasley's flying Ford Anglia, though it remains on the ground as it is broad daylight. Mrs. Weasley is amazed at how skillful Muggles are, as the inside of the car seems much larger than the outside; Harry, Ron, and Hermione, however, are aware that this is another of the almost-illegal spells that Mr. Weasley has put on the car.

When they are unable to reach Platform Nine and Three Quarters, Harry and Ron take the car and fly it to Hogwarts. In the process, a number of Muggles see them, and their escapades make it into the *Evening Prophet*. As a direct result of this, Mrs. Weasley sends Ron a Howler that scolds him at incredible volume in front of the entire Great Hall at breakfast.

Mrs. Weasley again provides a hand-knit jumper (US: sweater) and some candy to Harry as Christmas presents. Ron is unimpressed with his jumper, but Harry welcomes his, as it is still unusual for Harry to be receiving gifts. When Ginny is taken into the Chamber of Secrets at the end of the book, she is rescued by Harry, with the aid of Fawkes. Fawkes leads them to Professor McGonagall's office, where they find Professor McGonagall, Professor Dumbledore, and Molly and Arthur Weasley. Mrs. Weasley immediately sweeps Ginny into a hug, and then Harry and Ron for having rescued her. Apparently she is too relieved to say much; most of the discussion at this point is Harry answering questions put by Dumbledore, McGonagall, and Mr. Weasley.

We don't see much of Mrs. Weasley after she and Mr. Weasley take Ginny off to the Hospital Wing, though we can assume that they likely stayed at the school for the celebratory feast that followed. And Mrs. Weasley is again present at King's Cross when the Hogwarts Express arrives, and again is dismayed by Uncle Vernon's lack of civility towards Harry.

Prisoner of Azkaban We first see Molly Weasley in this story on the day before the Hogwarts Express leaves. Harry has been living in the Leaky Cauldron, off Diagon Alley, since running away from the Dursleys,' and it is on the last day before he must leave for school that he runs into Ron and Hermione, doing their shopping for school supplies. When they return to the Leaky Cauldron, Mr. Weasley is there, and the other family members, Mrs. Weasley, Ginny, Fred, George, and Percy arrive shortly. The twins are aping Percy's exaggeratedly formal manner, and Mrs. Weasley is trying to reign them in with little success.

After dinner, Ron discovers that he has misplaced a bottle of rat tonic that he had purchased. Confined to his room by Percy, who is frantically searching for his Head Boy badge, Ron asks Harry to look for it in the salon where they had dinner. As Harry is doing this, he overhears Mr. and Mrs. Weasley talking in the next room. It seems they are talking about him and one Sirius Black, a wizard who has recently broken out of Azkaban. It seems that the wizards believe that Black is headed for Hogwarts, to try and kill Harry. Mr. Weasley believes that Harry needs to know this, while Mrs. Weasley is protective, saying that Harry should not be told, and that other wizards will deal with it and Harry need never know.

The next day, on the platform, Mr. Weasley takes Harry aside to tell him about Black; Harry tells him that he knows, he had overheard Mr. and Mrs. Weasley talking about it last night. Mr. Weasley asks him to promise that he won't go out and try to hunt down Black himself. Harry wonders why he would do that, but does not get the chance to promise as the train is leaving.

Mrs. Weasley again provides a hand-knitted jumper (US: sweater) and various treats as a Christmas gift; this time, the jumper is bright red with the Gryffindor lion woven into the pattern.

Finally, Mrs. Weasley is again at the train station when the students return from Hogwarts, and expresses some dismay at the cavalier way Uncle Vernon greets Harry.

Goblet of Fire Mrs. Weasley enters our story, not in person, but by means of a letter which has been sent by the Muggle postal system. It is totally covered with stamps, a fact which has caused some amusement to the mail carrier, to the point that he actually rang the doorbell to ask Uncle Vernon what was going on. Predictably, Uncle Vernon is not amused; he is livid because one of "Harry's sort" has done something that is unusual, and has brought attention to the Dursley household. The letter is an invitation for Harry to attend the Quidditch World Cup, to which Mr. Weasley has got tickets, and to allow him to stay at The Burrow afterwards, until the start of school. Harry manages to convince Uncle Vernon to allow him to go.

While getting Harry's school stuff, Fred and George contrive to drop a few enchanted toffees in the Dursleys' sitting room, and Dudley eats one of them. This makes his tongue several feet long. When he returns to The Burrow, Mr. Weasley scolds the twins, saying that this is the sort of thing that so hinders Muggle—wizard relations. He finishes by saying "You wait until I tell your mother—" at which point Mrs. Weasley appears, saying "Tell me what, dear?" Despite Mr. Weasley's efforts to backtrack, and the Twins' efforts to escape, Mrs. Weasley does find out about the enchanted toffee, and proceeds to scold the twins much more thoroughly and loudly than Mr. Weasley ever has. Asking Ron about this as he beats a hasty retreat, Harry learns that Mrs. Weasley had found a large stack of order forms for something called *Weasleys' Wizard Wheezes*, and was upset that Fred and George were wasting their time creating magical jokes rather than preparing for a real career.

We see Mrs. Weasley later, preparing dinner. She is still seething about the Twins and their activities, and Harry and Ron must leap out of the way as a drawer opens violently and knives flash out to start chopping vegetables. To add to Mrs. Weasley's disgruntlement, she reaches for a wand, to find that it is a trick wand, which turns into a large rubber mouse when she tries to use it. Ron and Harry quickly escape the violence in the kitchen, taking cutlery out to help Bill and Charlie set tables in the garden.

At dinner, we hear Mrs. Weasley nagging Bill about his hair; apparently she is upset by his pony-tail. She also doesn't like his fang necklace. Eventually, Mrs. Weasley reminds the group that they will have to get up early to get to the match, and sends them all off to bed.

In the morning, she wakes Ron, Harry, Fred, and George, and is in the kitchen when they get downstairs, stirring a large pot of porridge. She snappishly tells the Twins that they can't Apparate, as Percy, Bill, and Charlie can, because they are not old enough and haven't passed their test. As they are leaving, she asks the Twins if they are carrying any of that Weasleys' Wizarding Wheezes stuff; they say they are not, but she Summons toffees from any number of hiding places about their persons. When everyone leaves, the Twins leave in stony silence, without a backwards glance.

The riots at the Quidditch World Cup make the *Daily Prophet*, and Mrs. Weasley is distraught, worried to death that one of her family could have been injured. She is relieved when they troop back in the morning following, hugging everyone and saying that she was afraid that her last words to the Twins would have been angry, complaints about their magical jokes and the number of O.W.L.s they didn't get. When Mr. Weasley mentions that he is mentioned in the newspaper article, Mrs. Weasley demands to know where? If she had seen that she would not have been as worried, as she would have known that he was all right. Mr. Weasley says he wasn't mentioned by name, and reads out a passage where he is identified as a "Ministry spokesman." He then says that as he has made things worse, he must go into the office and help straighten them out. Mrs. Weasley protests that he is on vacation, but he overrules her.

The rest of the summer, before school starts, is subdued. Mr. Weasley is spending all his time in the office, including weekends, dealing with the fallout from the riots, as is Percy. Mrs. Weasley does, at one point, see that Fred and George are hunched over a piece of parchment, and asks what they are doing. Told that it is homework, she asks if they are working on a new *order form?* Fred, looking pained, asks whether, should the

Hogwarts Express crash tomorrow, would she want her last words to the twins to be an unfounded accusation?

As Harry and Ron pack their trunks that evening, Ron finds something hideous and lace-trimmed in his robes, and demands to know what it is. Mrs. Weasley says that it is "formal robes," and that it is a requirement this year. It was the best that was available in Ron's size at the second-hand clothing store. Harry finds that he also has a set of formal robes, but his are new, lace-free, and a colour that matches his eyes. Mrs. Weasley says that she had been able to get new robes for him with his money. After Mrs. Weasley has left Ron complains bitterly about his family's poverty. The following morning, Mrs. Weasley summons Mr. Weasley to the kitchen, where an urgent call has come in via the Floo network. After Mr. Weasley has finished talking with Amos Diggory, whose head is sitting in the fireplace, Mrs. Weasley offers him a slice of toast. He accepts and departs. With Mr. Weasley off to the office, Mrs. Weasley, Bill, and Charlie accompany the twins, Harry, Ron, and Ginny to London in three Muggle taxicabs which Mrs. Weasley has braved the Muggle post office to call. Once on the platform, it appears that she knows about some secret happening that will be going on at the school; but like Bill and Charlie, she refuses to tell them what's going on. And before the train is out of sight of the platform, the three of them have Disapparated.

After the First Task, Charlie Weasley stops in to congratulate Harry, and then says he has to send off an owl to Mrs. Weasley to let her know how Harry did.

At Christmas, Mrs. Weasley again sends Harry a hand-made jumper (US: sweater), this time green with a picture of a dragon on the front, and a large quantity of home-made mince pies. Later, at the Yule Ball, Harry, who is talking to Percy, sees the Twins stop Ludo Bagman briefly as Ludo is crossing the floor towards Harry. Ludo tells Harry that the Twins were looking for some marketing advice, and Harry thinks privately that Percy is certain to report this to Mrs. Weasley.

A story, written by Rita Skeeter, appears in *Witch Weekly* shortly after the Second Task. This article implies quite strongly that Hermione is keeping both Harry and Viktor Krum on a string romantically. When Easter rolls around, Mrs. Weasley sends chocolate eggs to Ron, Harry, and Hermione; Ron's and Harry's are the size of ostrich eggs and filled with toffees, while Hermione's is closer to the size of a chicken's egg. Ron confirms to Hermione that his mother reads *Witch Weekly*.

Shortly after the bizarre appearance, and disappearance, of Mr. Crouch at Hogwarts, Harry, Ron, and Hermione are sending a letter off to Sirius describing the event when they are interrupted in the Owlery by the arrival of the twins, who are also preparing to send a letter off to someone. They are discussing whether their message is so strong as to sound like blackmail, but stop when they see they can be overheard. As they leave, Ron comments that they are really serious about this joke shop idea of theirs, they are not just doing it to annoy Mrs. Weasley. On the day of the Third Task, Professor McGonagall tells Harry at breakfast that the Champions are congregating in a room off the Great Hall, where they can meet with their families who will be watching them compete. Harry, knowing that the Dursleys would not be present, stays at the table until Cedric Diggory, the other Hogwarts Champion, calls him. Entering the room, he finds that Mrs. Weasley and Bill are there. Amos Diggory, also present, is upset that the morning's article by Rita Skeeter only mentioned Harry as Hogwarts Champion. While Mrs. Weasley does remind him that Rita writes almost entirely in order to stir up trouble, this does not seem to calm him down any. Harry spends the morning showing Bill and Mrs. Weasley around the grounds, with Mrs. Weasley providing commentary on how it had been when she was there. At lunch, Mrs. Weasley is very frosty towards Hermione, until Harry tells her that Hermione is not his girlfriend. Mrs. Weasley, perhaps remembering her own comments to Amos Diggory earlier about Rita Skeeter, is then noticeably more friendly towards Hermione. Hermione, who has had an idea about magical bugging methods, is unable to tell Harry what she has learned because Mrs. Weasley and Bill are present.

Hermione has another exam, but Harry as Champion is excused from exams, so the afternoon is occupied with a long walk around the grounds. As evening starts to fall, Harry heads for the Quidditch pitch, and Mrs. Weasley and Bill peel off for the stands.

After Harry's exit from the maze, his encounter with Professor Moody, the unmasking of Barty Crouch, and his debriefing by Dumbledore, Harry is taken to the Hospital Wing. Here, Mrs. Weasley, Bill, Ron, and Hermione are demanding of Madam Pomfrey that she tell them where Harry is. As Harry arrives, Mrs. Weasley immediately swoops over to comfort him, and Dumbledore forestalls any questions by telling them, and Madam Pomfrey, that Harry needs sleep, that questions can wait for the morning.

When Harry is awakened by Professor McGonagall and Cornelius Fudge, Mrs. Weasley is still there. She does not take part in the conversation with Fudge; however, after Fudge has left, Dumbledore asks if he can count on her and Arthur. She says that he can, and Bill volunteers to go tell his father immediately. Mrs. Weasley is shocked and alarmed when the large black dog who has been at Harry's bedside transforms into Sirius Black, but Dumbledore and Ron calm her down. After sending Sirius and Snape off on their missions, Dumbledore tells Harry to drink his sleeping potion, and leaves him with Ron, Hermione, and Mrs. Weasley. Harry fretfully protests that he doesn't want the Galleons he has won, and Mrs. Weasley tells him not to worry about them. She is interrupted by a loud slamming sound at the window. Hermione apologizes for the noise, but doesn't yet explain what she was doing. Ron later tells Harry that Mrs. Weasley had asked Dumbledore if Harry could spend the entire summer with the Weasleys at The Burrow, but Dumbledore had said no; he must go back to the Dursleys.' Ron says he doesn't know why, but that Dumbledore must have his reasons.

We see Mrs. Weasley again briefly at King's Cross Station, but she has no time to do more than exchange a couple of words with Harry before Uncle Vernon is headed away.

Order of the Phoenix When Harry is brought to Number 12, Grimmauld Place, it is Mrs. Weasley who meets him in the front hall. Asking him to be very quiet, she sends him upstairs while the "grown-ups" have a meeting. Harry, in conversation with Ron and Hermione, whom he finds there, and Fred, George, and Ginny who arrive some time later, discover that despite being nominally in the thick of things, there in the Headquarters of the Order of the Phoenix, they are almost as much in the dark about what is really going on as Harry is, or at least they would be if they hadn't taken it upon themselves to do a bit of spying. Fred and George reveal one of their inventions, Extendable Ears, which they have been using to try and listen in on events in meetings and in the front hall, but Mrs. Weasley had been destroying any that she found. The Weasleys also say that Harry shouldn't mention Percy; that whenever anyone mentions Percy, who has become estranged from the family, Mr. Weasley breaks whatever he's holding and Mrs. Weasley bursts into tears.

After the meeting ends, Mrs. Weasley brings everyone downstairs for dinner, asking for help to get the table set. She asks Harry to sit and rest from his trip, resisting his offer to help. The twins, trying to help, attempt to shift a large pot of stew, the bread and breadknife, and a pitcher of Butterbeer to the table by means of magic, and Mundungus Fletcher, Sirius, Harry, Ron, Bill, Hermione, and Ginny have to duck the flying, barely controlled dinnerware; Sirius, in particular, throws himself back away from the table, just avoiding the breadknife which ends up with its point buried in the table where his hand had been. Mrs. Weasley scolds the twins, saying that just because they are allowed to use magic doesn't mean they have to.

When Sirius, after dinner, suggests that Harry no doubt has questions about what the Order is doing, Mrs. Weasley instantly leaps to Harry's defence, saying that he is much too young to know. Mrs. Weasley at this point accuses Sirius of confusing Harry with his father. However, despite vehement argument on her part, Mrs. Weasley finds that she stands alone; Sirius, Lupin, and even her own husband all feel that Harry should know what is going on, as he is after all the center of things. Abandoning this tack, Mrs. Weasley then says that the Twins don't need to know any of this, to which they loudly protect that they are now of age and should be full members of the Order. Retreating, Mrs. Weasley says that Ron certainly is too young for the conversation, as is Hermione; Ron appeals to Harry, looking for confirmation that Harry would tell Ron anything that went on. Harry considers the possibility of leaving Ron in the dark as he had been left himself, but after a short pause confirms that he would tell Ron and Hermione anything that he learned. Defeated on all other fronts, Mrs. Weasley then hauls a loudly-protesting Ginny off to bed.

On her return to the kitchen, Mrs. Weasley remains quiet until Sirius mentions that Voldemort is seeking a weapon. At this point she says that really is enough information. Lupin agrees, and all the youngsters are sent off to bed. The Twins gather in Ron and Harry's room, to discuss what they have learned; but they are interrupted by Mrs. Weasley coming up the stairs, and must Apparate to their own room before she checks on them. An exhausted Harry is asleep before she passes their room again on the way down.

The next morning, Mrs. Weasley allows Harry a bit of a lie-in, but puts her own children to work making Grimmauld Place habitable. When Harry gets up, he finds Mrs. Weasley and the Weasley children in the drawing room. She tells Harry to get a mask and a sprayer; they have found an infestation of doxies in the drapes and they will be using Doxycide to eradicate them. She has a spot set aside for the dead doxies and their eggs, and she has anti-venom ready but she hopes she won't have to use it. While she is not looking, Fred and George sneak some of the doxy eggs into their pockets; George explains to Harry that they are ingredients for their joke-shop goods. While they are working, someone rings the bell; Mrs. Weasley goes down to answer it. Hermione, looking out the window, sees that it is Mundungus Fletcher with a load of cauldrons, and Harry, listening at the door, can hear both Mrs. Weasley and the portrait of Mrs. Black screaming in the front hall. When Mrs. Weasley returns to the drawing room with sandwiches for their lunch, she is still fulminating about Mundungus and his attempt to use Headquarters as a place to store his stolen goods.

Over the next several days, Mrs. Weasley sets all the children to cleaning Headquarters. When Ron complains that he had wanted to do something useful for the Order, Mrs. Weasley reminds him that making Headquarters livable is certainly something that would be useful to the Order. Meanwhile, they are repeatedly uncovering apparent bits of Dark magic, some of which the Twins are hiding away when Mrs. Weasley is not looking.

Finally, at dinner, Mrs. Weasley reminds Harry that he will have to be up early the next day to attend his hearing at the Ministry. Mr. Weasley will be accompanying him there, as Professor Dumbledore had asked. Harry is quite upset to realize that Dumbledore had been at Headquarters and had not wanted to talk to him. Mrs. Weasley tries to reassure him that he won't have any problem at the hearing, but Harry notices that she looks worried. She is still worried in the morning as Harry prepares for his trip to the Ministry, and presses breakfast on him that he can't really eat. On his return, she is as relieved as anyone that he has been acquitted, though she does get annoyed at Fred, George, and Ginny dancing a victory dance and eventually yells at them to be quiet.

The day before they have to board the Hogwarts Express, booklists finally arrive, and Hermione and Ron are appointed Prefect. Mrs. Weasley is extremely pleased that Ron has received such an honour, and says that they should get something for him—Percy got an owl, but Ron already has one. Ron suggests a new broom, and Mrs. Weasley pauses, saying that a new broom would be expensive, but quickly accepts the suggestion and dashes off to prepare for a trip to Diagon Alley.

That evening, Mrs. Weasley has arranged a party to celebrate Ron and Hermione being made Prefect. This is the first time Alastor "Mad-Eye" Moody has been present at Headquarters, and Mrs. Weasley asks him to use his magical eye to look at the writing desk in the drawing room and tell her if what is in there is actually a Boggart, as they suppose, or something more deadly. Moody confirms that it is a Boggart, and Mrs. Weasley says she'll deal with it. Later, though, as Harry goes to bed, he passes the drawing room, and sees Ron lying dead on the floor. He hears a weeping Mrs. Weasley casting Riddikulus, and sees the dead Ron turn into a dead Mr. Weasley. Realizing that this is the Boggart, Harry sees it change rapidly into several other Weasley family members, dead, and then himself. Lupin arrives, banishes the Boggart, and comforts Mrs. Weasley. Harry continues off to bed, aware now that his own death, which has suddenly become a more concrete possibility, is numbered among Mrs. Weasley's worst fears. As they prepare to head off to school the next day, Mrs. Weasley is again angered by the Twins attempting to use magic. In an attempt to use magic to get their trunks down the stairs, they have run them into Ginny and injured her. Luckily, Mrs. Weasley was able to heal her. Mrs. Weasley is also exasperated by Sirius, who, in his Dog Animagus shape, is demanding to come along. She gives in to Sirius, but spends a lot of the trip pleading with him to act more like a dog. They make their farewells on the platform.

For the next while, we don't see Mrs. Weasley directly. Her presence is still felt, however, as Hermione, irritated by Fred and George testing out Fainting Fancies on the first-year students, threatens to tell their mother what they are doing. This proves to be a much more effective means of controlling the Twins than detention or any other school-based punishment. And, after Hermione arranges the first meeting of Dumbledore's Army, Sirius, talking by means of Floo Powder, passes on a message from Mrs. Weasley to Ron forbidding him to join the group, and asking Harry and Hermione to also stay out of it.

Just before Christmas, Harry perceives Mr. Weasley being attacked by a snake. Professor Dumbledore, after confirming Harry's perception, sends Professor McGonagall to fetch the other Weasley children (Ron is already present). As he is preparing to send them all to Grimmauld Place, McGonagall asks Dumbledore if she should be contacting Mrs. Weasley; Dumbledore says that will be a job for Fawkes. He also says that she may already know, due to that excellent clock of hers. Harry remembers that this refers to the clock in The Burrow which has hands for each of the Weasleys, indicating where they are.

After they arrive in Grimmauld Place, a phoenix feather appears with a note. The note, from Mrs. Weasley, says that she has seen Mr. Weasley in hospital, that he is seriously injured, but still alive. This does little to ease the worry that the Weasley children and Harry are feeling: if it is necessary to say that he is still alive, how close to death is he? When Mrs. Weasley gets to Grimmauld Place at 5 that morning, she is able to reassure everyone that Mr. Weasley is now sleeping peacefully. Harry, feeling somehow instrumental in Mr. Weasley's being injured, is unsure of his welcome, but Mrs. Weasley sweeps him into a hug, saying that if it wasn't for Harry raising the alarm, Mr. Weasley would not have lived.

Later that day, the entire family, guarded by Mad-Eye Moody and Tonks, visit Mr. Weasley in hospital. After the children have visited, the adults discuss privately the occurrences leading up to Harry's warning. Harry and the others manage to overhear this by means of Extendable Ears that the Twins have brought. Mrs. Weasley plays little part in the conversation, though she does hear Moody's suggestion that Harry may be possessed by Voldemort. Harry, afraid that he is possessed by Voldemort, isolates himself from the other occupants of Grimmauld Place; Mrs. Weasley sends him up sandwiches when he does not appear at mealtimes. Once Harry is convinced by Ginny that he is not possessed, he rejoins the activities in the household, which largely are involved with preparations for Christmas, including decorating the house. On Christmas day, Mrs. Weasley is in tears because the jumper (US: sweater) that she had knit for Percy had been returned unopened.

Later that day, the Weasley family, with Harry, Hermione, Moody, and Lupin, are driven to the hospital by Mundungus Fletcher. There, Mr. Weasley asks if they have seen his Healer. Mrs. Weasley, noting that his dressings have been changed, demands to know what's going on. The twins, sensing storm clouds gathering, depart for the tea shop. Mr. Weasley diffidently mentions that the apprentice healer had been experimenting with Muggle healing techniques, something called "stitches." Mrs. Weasley, saying that it sounds like that means actually sewing the wound together, dismissively says that not even Mr. Weasley would be so stupid as to try that. Harry and Ron, now also sensing incipient explosion, also decide that the tea shop is calling, and with Hermione and Ginny, they depart. Professor Snape visits Grimmauld Place to tell Harry that he will have to learn Occlumency from him. An exchange of insults between Sirius and Snape has the two of them at wands drawn and Harry standing between them trying to prevent them from dueling, when Mr. and Mrs. Weasley, with the rest of the Weasley children, return from hospital where Mr. Weasley has been released as fit.

Mrs. Weasley does not join Harry, Hermione, and the Weasley children on the Knight Bus taking them back to Hogwarts after the vacation, instead staying on at Headquarters.

When Fred and George leave the school, Ron worries that Mrs. Weasley will blame him for their departure. Harry tells him that is nonsense, but Ron says Mrs. Weasley somehow believes that, as a Prefect, Ron has some kind of power over the Twins.

Mrs. Weasley, along with Mr. Weasley, Fred, George, Lupin, Tonks, and Moody, are present at the station when the Hogwarts Express returns Harry, Ron, Hermione, and Ginny to London. The entire lot of them face down Harry's aunt, uncle, and cousin, demanding concessions from the Dursleys that will ensure Harry's comfort over the summer.

Half-Blood Prince After only a fortnight, Professor Dumbledore retrieves Harry from the Dursleys,' and takes him via side-along Apparation to a village where they recruit a teacher, and then to The Burrow. It is well past midnight, but it seems that Mrs. Weasley is still up, waiting in the kitchen for Mr. Weasley to come home. She is talking with Tonks, who is looking surprisingly depressed. After Tonks and Dumbledore have left, Mrs. Weasley tells Harry that Mr. Weasley has been promoted, and now heads the new *Office of Detection and Confiscation of Counterfeit Defensive Spells and Protective Objects.* The increase in income has significantly helped the Weasley finances. When Mr. Weasley does come home, he insists on the Ministry-recommended challenge technique to prove who he is and who Mrs. Weasley is before he will allow her to open the door. Mrs. Weasley is vastly embarrassed at the intimacy of some of the questions and answers required, particularly with Harry there, listening. Once inside, Mr. Weasley tells some of the things that have happened during his day; Harry is very interested, but is unable to stifle a yawn because of the lateness of the hour. Seeing this, Mrs. Weasley shoos him off to bed.

The next morning, Harry's breakfast is brought to him by Fleur Delacour, with Mrs. Weasley grumbling behind her. Fleur, with her usual great drama, announces that she and Bill Weasley are to be married. After she has gone, Ginny, Hermione, and Mrs. Weasley comment that Fleur is very full of herself, and wonder what Bill sees in her. Ginny nicknames her "Phlegm," which makes Harry and Hermione laugh, though Mrs. Weasley disapproves. After Mrs. Weasley leaves, Harry mentions how sad Tonks is looking. Ron mentions that Mrs. Weasley is always inviting her over, and offers his opinion that Mrs. Weasley was hoping that Tonks and Bill would have fancied each other. Later, when Harry ventures down to the kitchen, he finds Mrs. Weasley apparently ignoring Fleur, who is going on about wedding plans.

The day after Harry's birthday, booklists arrive, and Mrs. Weasley says that they can't put off going to Diagon Alley much longer. The following day, Ron, Ginny, Harry, and Hermione, along with Mr. and Mrs. Weasley, set out. Arriving in the Leaky Cauldron, they meet Hagrid who will be helping Mrs. Weasley guard them. In Diagon Alley, Mr. Weasley is annoyed by the street vendors selling amulets and charms, saying that if he was on the job he would run them all in and confiscate the lot. Mrs. Weasley reminds him that he is not on the job and tells him to calm down. Ginny does not need robes, so she sets off with Mr. and Mrs. Weasley to Flourish and Blotts for textbooks, while Ron, Harry, and Hermione head off to Madam Malkin's with Hagrid.

The two groups later join up to visit Fred and George's new store, and Mrs. Weasley is taken aback by their garish window display which mocks Lord Voldemort.

While they are all in the store, Harry sees Draco Malfoy pass by, and under the Invisibility Cloak, he, Ron, and Hermione pursue him into Knockturn Alley and eavesdrop on a transaction he has in Borgin and Burkes. On their return to the joke shop, they try to convince a worried Mrs. Weasley that they had been in the back room of the store. The day before the departure for Hogwarts, Mrs. Weasley tells Harry that she would like to have everything packed up the night before, to avoid the mad rush in the morning to get everyone off for the train. She also says that Ministry cars are going to be coming to pick them up. Surprisingly, everyone is ready in the morning, and they get to the station in good order. While Mrs. Weasley is bidding her children goodbye, Harry takes Mr. Weasley aside and tells him about what they have overheard, advising him to search Malfoy Manor again. He returns to the platform just in time to collect a farewell hug from Mrs. Weasley and board the train.

Harry stays at the Burrow for Christmas, and when we first see him there, he and Ron have been set the task of peeling sprouts by hand. Apparently Mrs. Weasley feels that Ron needs some understanding of how Muggles have to live, and has been setting him various manual tasks over his vacation; Harry joins in out of friendship and because he wants to talk privately about things that have been happening at school. Mrs. Weasley comes into the kitchen while Fred and George are there, to explain the sleeping arrangements; apparently, with Bill and Fleur there, as well as Lupin, things will be a bit cramped. Percy, still estranged from the family, is not expected to be there. On Christmas Eve, the family is gathered in the parlour. The wireless (US: radio) is playing a selection by Mrs. Weasley's favorite singer, Celestina Warbeck, and Fleur evidently does not like it as she is trying to talk over it. There is a small battle going on in the background of the scene here, with Mrs. Weasley repeatedly increasing the volume of the wireless, and Fleur in response raising her voice. Some time after the song has finished, Fleur starts making fun of it, which Mr. Weasley and Lupin see as a signal that the evening is over and everyone should go off to bed.

At Christmas dinner the next day, the gathered group discuss, among other things, Tonks, who was invited, but who apparently chose to spend Christmas alone. Mrs. Weasley seems to blame Bill for her absence. This appears to echo Ron's earlier statement that Mrs. Weasley is trying to get Bill and Tonks hooked up, and leads us to believe that Tonks' absence is because Fleur is present.

The entire group is stunned by the appearance of Percy at the door, along with the Minister for Magic, Rufus Scrimgeour. Percy woodenly wishes everyone a Happy Christmas. Mrs. Weasley runs to hug him; he tolerates this but does not respond. Scrimgeour takes Harry aside on the pretense of allowing the family some time for their reunion. The reunion ends, we find out later, with Percy leaving hurriedly, decorated with mashed parsnips which Fred, George, and Ginny all claim credit for having thrown, and Mrs. Weasley in tears.

When Ron is poisoned on his birthday, Mr. and Mrs. Weasley are summoned to the school. Arriving in the Hospital Wing, they effusively thank Harry for once again saving the life of one of their family members. Harry, embarrassed by the praise, very quickly leaves the Hospital Wing with Hermione and Hagrid.

At the end of the book, Bill is guarding Hogwarts when the battle at the Astronomy Tower breaks out. He is badly bitten by Fenrir Greyback, a werewolf. As Fenrir is not transformed, Bill does not become a werewolf, but the damage to his face is very bad and Madam Pomfrey says he will be permanently scarred. When Mr. and Mrs. Weasley arrive, Mrs. Weasley immediately takes over tending Bills injuries. As she does so, she remarks that it is such a shame, he was so handsome, and was going to be married. Fleur, who has arrived with them, picks up the aspersion immediately and is angered by it. She immediately accuses Mrs. Weasley of thinking that Fleur had been interested in Bill only because of his looks, says that she has looks good enough for both of them, and the wedding is still going to happen. So saying, she shoulders Mrs. Weasley aside and takes over tending Bill's wounded face. Mrs. Weasley is stunned, but then tentatively suggests that their Auntie Muriel has a Goblin-made tiara with moonstones that would look lovely against Fleur's hair. She offers to try and arrange to loan it to Fleur for the wedding. Fleur stiffly accepts. Before Harry can figure out what is going on, the two women are in tears and hugging each other.

While we don't speak with Mrs. Weasley again in the book, it is safe to assume that she remains at the school for Dumbledore's funeral.

Deathly Hallows Harry has escaped from Privet Drive with Hagrid. After arriving at Ted Tonks' house, Harry and Hagrid catch a Portkey that takes them to The Burrow. Mrs. Weasley and Ginny meet them there, distraught because Harry is the first party to arrive, and two other parties, Nymphadora Tonks with Ron, and Mr. Weasley with Fred, should have arrived earlier, but their Portkeys had appeared without them. Mrs. Weasley is happy to see Harry and hugs him, but when Hagrid asks for a bit of brandy, Mrs. Weasley runs to the kitchen to get it, rather than Summoning it. Harry believes that she is hiding her face, trying to hide her tears. Shortly, Lupin arrives with George, who is injured. Mrs. Weasley directs Lupin to put him on the couch and starts trying to care for him. Lupin takes Harry aside, and queries him to confirm that he is the real Harry. Lupin is of the opinion that someone in the Order had betrayed them, and needs to confirm that they are not harboring an impostor. The remaining pairs trickle in, leaving only Mundungus Fletcher and "Mad-Eye" Moody. Fletcher had apparently become afraid and Disapparated, and the killing spell that had been aimed at him had hit Moody instead. The group gathered around George on the couch drink to his memory, and then Bill and Lupin depart to try and collect his body. Harry, feeling that his presence at The Burrow puts everyone in danger, volunteers to leave as well, but Mrs. Weasley is vocal in demanding that he stay. The Order is aware that Harry, Ron, and Hermione had been given a final mission by Dumbledore, but once rebuffed, are content to simply offer what assistance they can. Mrs. Weasley, however, takes Harry aside on his first day at The Burrow, on the pretense of asking him if a stray sock she has found is his. Once he is separated from Ron and Hermione, she starts asking him about what Dumbledore had wanted him to do. Harry gently resists her questioning, in the end simply refusing to tell her what Dumbledore had in mind, and then saying that the sock she had found couldn't be his.

Mrs. Weasley is, of course, preparing the house and yard to receive vast numbers of visitors for Bill and Fleur's wedding, which is to be held there on the first of August. She sets tasks for Harry, Hermione, and all the Weasley children present to get things ready. Harry can't help noticing that the tasks selected seem to be designed to keep Harry, Hermione, and Ron separated from each other. Harry frets at this obstacle to their planning, rhetorically asking at one point whether Mrs. Weasley expects someone else to bump off Voldemort while Harry stays at the Burrow and makes vol-au-vents? Ginny, who is helping him at that moment, apparently now understands some of Harry's mission, despite Harry's trying to make a joke of it.

Mrs. Weasley's attempt to keep the Trio separated does break down at one point. She has assigned Ron to clean his room, Hermione has been given the task of dealing with the table linens, something she had already done the day before, and Harry and Mr. Weasley are assigned the job of dealing with the chicken coop. When Mr. Weasley admits that he has put the wreckage of Sirius' flying motorbike in there, so there is really nothing to be done, Harry goes to Ron's room, joining Hermione who is already present. They manage to get some planning done before being discovered and sent on to new jobs by Mrs. Weasley.

When Fleur's mother arrives, she manages to calm Mrs. Weasley's nerves immediately. Everything is lovely, everything is perfect, and Mrs. Delacour is most willing to pitch in and help, including providing a spell that cleans out the recalcitrant oven that had been giving Ron such problems.

As the next day is Harry's birthday, Mrs. Weasley asks Harry what he would like. Harry, while thinking to himself that he is burden enough on the Weasleys just by his presence in this already busy time, says that there is nothing he really needs, and he really doesn't want a big fuss made over him.

When Harry gets down to the kitchen on his birthday, he finds that Mrs. Weasley has given him a gold watch, a traditional gift for a wizard on reaching his majority. Mrs. Weasley diffidently apologizes for its condition, saying it had belonged to her late brother, who had not always been the best at maintaining his personal possessions; Harry, knowing that this makes it all the more valuable, expresses his thanks by hugging Mrs. Weasley. Later, Harry sees Mrs. Weasley carrying something that looks like an enormous Golden Snitch to the outside table; investigating, he finds that it is his birthday cake.

Rufus Scrimgeour's visit to Harry, Ron, and Hermione later that day is heated, and tempers flare. The shouting brings Mr. and Mrs. Weasley to the parlour where the meeting is happening, just in time to see Scrimegeour leaving. On the day of the wedding, while we can see that Mrs. Weasley has done an excellent job of decorating, she herself has very little role in the celebrations.

We do not see Mrs. Weasley again until the end of the book, when she arrives in the Room of Requirement in response to the call for members of the Order to defend Hogwarts. The entire Weasley family, including both Mr. and Mrs. Weasley, are present in the Room of Requirement when Percy arrives. After a frozen moment, which Fleur attempts to defuse by asking Lupin about his infant son Teddy, Percy loudly declares that he has been a blind, ambitious fool, and asks to be forgiven by his family. Mr. and Mrs. Weasley greet this with welcoming hugs, and together they go off to battle.

We see Mrs. Weasley once in passing: at the break in the battle, as Harry is carrying Snape's memories up to the Headmaster's office to put them into the Pensieve, he sees the Weasley family gathered together to mourn the passing of Fred.

At the end of the battle at Hogwarts, Bellatrix Lestrange is dueling Hermione, Ginny, and Luna. When a curse narrowly misses Ginny, Mrs. Weasley, enraged by the attack on her daughter, engages Bellatrix in combat and ends up killing her. Seeing Bellatrix fall, Voldemort hurls a curse at Mrs. Weasley; Harry, from under the Invisibility Cloak, blocks it. Voldemort then turns his attention to Harry.

In the feast following the end of the battle, Harry sees the Weasley family sitting together, and Ginny leaning against her mother in tiredness. Harry decides not to impose himself on them; they need time as a family to recover from their loss.

Strengths She cares very deeply for her children and is very much the kingpin around which the entire Weasley family turns. She is also apparently a very powerful witch and excellent duelist, as she is able to take Bellatrix Lestrange single-handed. While we cannot judge her intelligence relative to (say) her husband, it is certainly true that she has raised a family of very powerful, and in the case of the Twins, very inventive wizards. She does have a very direct and forceful character, much more so than her husband.

Weaknesses As we see in the episode with the Boggart in *Harry Potter and the Order of the Phoenix*, Molly's greatest fear is of harm befalling her children or her husband . . . or Harry. Seeing these fears given solid form before her does leave her weakened and in tears. It is this same fear for her children that causes her to face Bellatrix single-handed, a potentially unwise decision given that, being in Voldemort's upper echelon, Bellatrix is obviously a very powerful witch. It is only Molly's hitherto unheralded strength at dueling that saves her in this instance.

Relationships with Other Characters Molly Weasley cares very deeply for her children. Like all parents, she wants her children to be people that she can be proud of. As a result, she is possibly a little more ambitious on the childrens' behalf than they are themselves. She seems disappointed that the Twins don't want to work for the Ministry, apparently believing that their choosing to work for themselves in a joke shop is somehow beneath them. She is very proud of Percy's appointment to be Bartemius Crouch's assistant, and must be pleased, at least initially, at his apparent rapid rise within the Ministry. His departure from the family, stormy as it is, pains Molly very deeply.

With each of her children, we can see the separate motherly dynamic in action. She is, for instance, always nagging Bill about the length of his hair, and the twins about their grades. She accepts Percy's pompousness, perhaps thinking it justified in someone who is selected as Prefect and later Head Boy. Her interaction with Ron is more varied; perhaps this is because we see more of it, Ron being almost a viewpoint character in the series, but seems to be largely mutual exasperation, Ron at the exigencies of their financial situation, Molly at Ron's inability to deal with it. Apart from the protectiveness we see late in book 7, we don't see a lot of Molly's interactions with Ginny. One ongoing thorn in Molly's side must be Arthur, her husband. Arthur's fascination with Muggle artifacts and techniques exasperates her, his experimenting with spells on them vexes her, and his unwillingness to discipline the children, the Twins in particular, infuriates her. Further, although she never mentions it, his lack of ambition must gall her as well; surely, if he had a little more ambition, he could move up in the Ministry to a higher-paying job. And yet, they seem to have a very solid marriage, caring for and about each other.

Harry's experience with her starts off as being somewhat alarming. When he first arrives at The Burrow, it is to hear Molly tearing a strip off the Twins and Ron for their adventures of the previous night. Harry fears that he is in for some of the same, but Molly moderates her tone instantly when she turns to him, knowing that he is not to blame for what has happened, simply inviting him in to have some breakfast. Molly, over the course of the six years starting with *Harry Potter and the Chamber of Secrets*, brings Harry into her own circle, caring for him as she does for her own, but always knowing that she has no real authority over him. We are perhaps mildly surprised that Molly never scolds Harry, for all that his death is one of the things that she most fears.

ANALYSIS

For almost all of the series, we see Molly Weasley as essentially "the good mother," nurturing her children, worrying about them, scolding them when they misbehave, and trying to shield them from the cold hard realities of life in the world as best she can. Over time, she also takes Harry under her wing, treating him and defending him as she would one of her own children. This becomes quite apparent in the early chapters of *Harry Potter and the Order of the Phoenix*, where she argues unsuccessfully against letting Harry know the business of the Order. In this, she seems to be battling her own husband, who agrees with the rest of the Order that Harry, as the center of the efforts, has a right to know what the efforts are. Additionally, Arthur has a much less rigid view of the necessary discipline, and often seems to feel that the punishments Molly is meting out, particularly to the Twins, are harsher than they need to be. We see this first in *Harry Potter and the Chamber of Secrets*, where upon being told of the Twin's use of the flying car, his first reaction is to ask how it went, rather than to scold them for taking it. We see it again in *Harry Potter and the Goblet of Fire*, where Arthur, who is scolding the twins for their having dropped a magical toffee where Dudley would pick it up, suddenly backtracks when Molly appears. Molly's attempts to protect Harry come to a head in *Harry Potter and the Deathly Hallows*, where she seems to be trying to prevent Harry, Ron, and Hermione from spending time together, in the apparent hope that if they are unable to plan an escape from The Burrow, they will be unable to make an escape. She is well aware that Harry has a mission that has been given him by Dumbledore, and is afraid of what that mission will entail for him, as well as for Ron, and for Hermione whom she has also mentally adopted. As so many teenagers do, Harry chafes at what he sees as over-protectiveness. He does not openly rebel against it, perhaps because he has been so starved for affection that he is willing to accept this protectiveness as part of the package, but he is aware of being protected when he doesn't want to be, and manages to avoid it long enough to make the necessary preparations for his mission.

It is only at the end of *Harry Potter and the Deathly Hallows*, where she successfully duels with Bellatrix Lestrange, that it is revealed that Molly is actually quite a powerful witch who has been hiding her talents, in order to raise her family. From our first meeting with her, in retrospect, we do sense something of this restrained power, there is a self-assurance in her manner that does not seem to quite tally with the simple housewife she appears to be. Granted, one would have to be very self-assured to deal with raising her sons, especially Fred and George, but perhaps their nature is due to their having inherited her power and force of personality. It seems that they are their mother's sons, where Percy and Ron have inherited more from their father. It is certainly true that Ginny seems to have inherited quite a bit of Molly's nature and temperament.

Montague

Gender: Male
Hair color: Unknown
Eye color: Unknown
Related Family: Unknown
Loyalty: Slytherin house

Overview

Montague is a Slytherin, probably one or two years older than Harry Potter.

Role in the Books

Prisoner of Azkaban Montague is mentioned as being on the Slytherin Quidditch team, where he plays in the final against Gryffindor. He and team Captain Marcus Flint, between them, rack up a very impressive number of fouls.

Order of the Phoenix It is mentioned that Montague is the new captain of the Slytherin Quidditch team, presumably replacing Marcus Flint. The commentary on the game lets us know that he is playing as one of the three Chasers. Dolores Umbridge appoints Montague to be on her Inquisitorial Squad. He attempts to dock House points from Fred and George Weasley, and they shove him into an old, broken Vanishing Cabinet. Some short time later, he reappears, apparently partly embedded in one of the toilets. He never seems to fully recover from this misadventure, and while his parents do visit at one point, he is still in the Hospital Wing at the school as O.W.L. exams finish up in mid-June—when Harry goes to the Hospital Wing to speak with Professor McGonagall after his vision in the History of Magic exam, Madam Pomfrey is spooning blue potion into Montague's mouth.

Half-Blood Prince Draco Malfoy reveals that when he was trapped in the Vanishing Cabinets, Montague had found himself sometimes hearing things happening inside the school, sometimes hearing things happening inside Borgin and Burkes. Realizing that the two cabinets were linked, Draco had repaired the Cabinet at Hogwarts, and had used that to allow Death Eaters to enter Hogwarts.

Strengths It is mentioned that Montague is physically quite strong, and evidently he is a competent flyer.

Weaknesses It is strongly suggested by the author that after his shattering sojourn in the Vanishing Cabinets, and the bad landing from his Apparating out of that situation, that his mental abilities are impaired, as is his physical strength.

Analysis

We are never actually told about Montague's strength, either mental or physical, after the events in the Vanishing Cabinet. We are, however, given some very strong hints.

On the mental acuity side, when we see him mid-June, Madam Pomfrey is spooning some blue potion into his mouth. The implication inherent in the word "spooning" is that Montague is not capable of steering the spoon himself. On the physical side, it is certain that Montague remained in the Hospital Wing from when the accident occurred, about April, to at least mid-June. Even for wizards as young and healthy as Montague, that much confinement must cause some muscle mass loss. One certainly gets a picture of a near-invalid, confined to the Hospital Wing for two months, and still unable to feed himself.

Morfin Gaunt

Gender: Male
Hair color:
Eye color:
Related Family: Marvolo Gaunt, Merope Gaunt, Salazar Slytherin, Lord Voldemort
Loyalty: Marvolo Gaunt

Overview

Son of Marvolo Gaunt and uncle of Lord Voldemort.

Role in the Books

Half-Blood Prince Morfin enters our story by swinging down out of a tree and telling a Ministry wizard, Bob Ogden, that he is not welcome. Ogden does not understand, as Morfin has chosen to speak in Parseltongue. He is described as having hair so thickly matted with dirt that it could be any color, very few teeth, and small, dark eyes that pointed in different directions. When Ogden says he has business with the Gaunts, Morfin assaults him magically. His father, Marvolo Gaunt, then steps out of the shack and orders Morfin to go indoors.

Inside, Morfin initially takes little part in the proceedings, spending his time playing with and talking to a snake that he is holding. When Ogden explains that Morfin is being summoned to a hearing for having Jinxed a Muggle, Marvolo seems unconcerned; after all, it was only a Muggle, so no harm done. When told that Morfin has broken Wizarding law, Marvolo falls back on the pride of his ancestry. Their discussion is interrupted by the sound of horses approaching; it turns out that one of the horses is ridden by Tom Riddle, the Muggle that Morfin had jinxed when he found out that his sister Merope was sweet on him, leaning out the window hoping for a glimpse of him. This revelation sparks an angry outburst from Marvolo, who attacks Merope; Ogden leaps to her defence but then has to run from Morfin.

When the Ministry return to arrest Morfin, he resists, and is arrested both for the use of magic on a Muggle, and for resisting Ministry wizards, tried, and sentenced to three years in Azkaban. When he returns from prison, he finds the house empty; Merope had run off with her Muggle and subsequently died in London, and Marvolo had died shortly after leaving Azkaban.

Tom Marvolo Riddle, Merope's son by Tom Riddle, visited the shack some twelve years later. Morfin initially thought he was the Muggle Tom Riddle. Tom had gotten details of the family history from Morfin, then Stunned him, stole the ring of the Peverells, which had been one of Marvolo's prized possessions, and used Morfin's wand to murder the muggle Tom Riddle, his father; then modified Morfin's memory so he remembered actually killing Tom Riddle. Morfin was sent to Azkaban for the murder of the Riddles and died there shortly afterwards.

Weaknesses Morfin is not a stable person; apparently as a result of in-breeding, he does not have the mental capacity to manage leading a normal life, and spends it all nailing snakes to his door and wallowing in his hatred for Muggles (non-magical people). He does assist his father in his on-going abuse of his sister Merope.

Mulciber

Gender: Male
Hair color: Unknown
Eye color: Unknown
Related Family: Unknown
Loyalty: Lord Voldemort

Overview

Little is known about Mulciber. He is mentioned as being particularly good at performing the Imperius curse.

Role in the Books

Goblet of Fire Igor Karkaroff, pleading for early release from Azkaban, says that Mulciber specialized in the Imperius curse, making his victims do horrific things. Bartemius Crouch Sr. dismisses this information, saying they have already caught Mulciber.

Half-Blood Prince When Lord Voldemort, or Tom Riddle as he is then known, is seen in Albus Dumbledore's memories returning to Hogwarts to apply for the job of teacher of Defence Against the Dark Arts, Dumbledore asks him about his "friends" waiting for him back in Hogsmeade. Mulciber is one of the friends named, along with Nott, Antonin Dolohov, and Evan Rosier.

Deathly Hallows Mulciber was mentioned by Lily Evans, seen in Severus Snape's memories in the Pensieve, as being one of the people that Snape hung around with that Lily simply could not stand.

Analysis

If Mulciber is one of Snape's crowd, he must be about the same age as James Potter; however, we know that the Potters were born when Voldemort was about thirty. Voldemort had carefully selected four of his cronies, who were then starting to call themselves Death Eaters, to accompany him to Hogwarts to ask for the Defence Against the Dark Arts job. Given that by the time James died, the Wizarding world was terrified of the Death Eaters, Voldemort's application must have been some time before James' death, when any friend of Snape's would have been still very young. It is unlikely that Voldemort would have brought someone as young as that into his inner council. It is entirely possible that there are two Mulcibers, probably father and son, and they are not differentiated in the books.

Mundungus Fletcher

Gender: Male
Hair color: Unknown
Eye color: Unknown
Related Family: Unknown
Loyalty: Galleons

Overview

Mundungus Fletcher is a dweller in the Wizarding underworld, a dealer in stolen merchandise and controlled substances.

Role in the Books

Chamber of Secrets When Arthur Weasley returns home from work, and is telling about his day, he mentions that he had a run-in with Mundungus Fletcher, and that Mundungus had tried to hex him when his back was turned.

Goblet of Fire It is mentioned that Mundungus Fletcher has put in an absurdly inflated claim for damages after the events of the Quidditch World Cup.

When Dumbledore learns that Voldemort is back, he sends off Sirius Black to alert "the old crowd," specifically naming Remus Lupin, Arabella Figg and Mundungus Fletcher.

Order of the Phoenix A member of the Order (much against Molly Weasley's wishes), Mundungus is initially set as a guard over Harry Potter, a post he deserts in order to cut a deal on some cauldrons which have "fallen off the back of a broom." Mundungus reappears after the Dementor attack, and is chastised (both verbally and with a shopping bag full of cans of cat food) by Mrs. Figg, who orders him to report to Dumbledore.

We see him next at the kitchen table at headquarters of the Order of the Phoenix. He is asleep at the table; roused, he mumbles that he agrees with Sirius. This is apparently the limits of his usual involvement, making him singularly ineffective as part of the council. At dinner, he tells a story that involves selling a load of toads to another underworld character, the joke of which is that they were his own toads that Mundungus had stolen from him; chastised by Molly Weasley, he says that it is all right because the other man had stolen them himself. He gets into trouble with Molly Weasley when he tries to bring his load of stolen cauldrons to Headquarters for storage. He also provides a number of controlled magical ingredients to Fred and George Weasley, which helps them set up their magic shop.

When the initial meeting of Dumbledore's Army is held in the Hog's Head, Mundungus is present, unbeknown to Harry, and reports back to the Order. Sirius Black, revealing this to Harry, says that Mundungus was heavily veiled and disguised as a witch because he had previously been barred from the Hog's Head, and admits that Mundungus had been tailing Harry.

Half-Blood Prince Apparently, since the death of Sirius, Mundungus has been clearing valuables out of the headquarters of the Order and selling them. Harry catches him in Hogsmeade trying to sell Black family silver to the bartender from the Hog's Head, whereupon Mundungus goes into hiding.

It is mentioned later in the book that Mundungus has been sent to Azkaban for impersonating an Inferius.

Deathly Hallows Mundungus, now freed from Azkaban, is set the task of being one of the seven Potters when Harry escapes from the Dursleys' house. He is very reluctant to do this, fearing that he will be a target. Riding a broomstick behind Alastor Moody, he gets cold feet and Disapparates, leaving Moody to be hit by the Killing curse that had been aimed at Mundungus by Voldemort.

The remaining members of the Order of the Phoenix, discussing how Voldemort had known when Harry was going to be moved, had suggested that it might be Mundungus who had leaked the secret. However, it is recalled that Mundungus had suggested the six mock Potters, and that was the one part of the plan that Voldemort had not been prepared for.

After their arrival at Grimmauld Place, and the discovery of the identity of R.A.B., Hermione recalls the "heavy locket that none of them could open." Remembering that Kreacher had been stealing things back that they had been trying to discard, the Trio search Kreacher's sleeping area with no result, and then Harry summons Kreacher. Kreacher says that the locket is unfinished business for him, he had been told to destroy it and had not been able to. He also says that Mundungus had stolen it from him. Winning Kreacher over to his side by saying that they were planning to destroy the locket, and by giving Kreacher another locket which had been his old master's, Harry sends Kreacher out to find Mundungus.

When Mundungus arrives a few days later, under threat of "persuasion" by Kreacher he admits to having taken the locket, but then had it extorted from him by Dolores Umbridge.

In the Hog's Head, Harry happens to see a magic mirror, twin to the one given to him by Sirius Black. The bartender says that it had been sold to him by Mundungus, and he had been using it from time to time to keep an eye on what Harry was doing.

When Harry relives Severus Snape's memories, he sees the portrait of Albus Dumbledore, in conference with Snape, developing the plan of having multiple mock Potters to allow the escape from Privet Drive. Dumbledore says that this is Harry's only chance of escape, as Snape must give Voldemort Harry's true departure date to stay in Voldemort's inner council, and suggests that Mundungus should be the one to mention it to the Order. We later see a memory of Snape, in a pub, teaching this plan to a Confunded Mundungus.

Strengths Mundungus evidently is a relatively powerful wizard, as he is able to overpower Kreacher in order to steal the valuables from Grimmauld Place, and is able to hide from Kreacher for several days. Kreacher tells Harry that Mundungus was very tricky.

Weaknesses Mundungus is a thief and primarily concerned with his own welfare. Although loyal to Dumbledore and the Order of the Phoenix, his criminal activities and selfish interests make him unreliable.

Relationships with Other Characters Mundungus has several unsavory habits, including a preference for a blend of pipe "tobacco" that apparently smells quite strongly of burning socks, and a very loose set of ethics regarding other people's property and commerce laws, which make him less than popular with the stricter members of the Order. Molly Weasley seems to accept his membership in the Order only because Dumbledore does; the other members of the Order are more amused by him, but still don't seem to entirely trust him.

Mundungus himself, we are told, respects Dumbledore, and has joined the Order at Dumbledore's request out of that respect. Dumbledore feels that the Order needs to know what is happening in the Underworld, and needs to get its own message out to that population, in order to succeed.

QUESTIONS

1. Why might Mundungus be a member of the Order of the Phoenix?

Nagini

Gender: Female
Hair color: None
Eye color: Yellow
Related Family: None
Loyalty: Lord Voldemort

OVERVIEW

Nagini is a snake, a large one, and Lord Voldemort's pet.

ROLE IN THE BOOKS

Goblet of Fire   We first see Nagini in Riddle Manor, to which Lord Voldemort has returned while he prepares for his full revival. Nagini, out hunting, returns to Voldemort, passing Frank Bryce in the hall, and reports on Frank's presence to Voldemort, whereupon Voldemort has Wormtail bring Frank into the room. Voldemort then kills Frank. The conversation between Voldemort and Wormtail leads us to believe that Wormtail is milking Nagini for something, most likely venom, which is keeping Voldemort alive.

When Harry is bound to the gravestone in the climactic battle at the end of the book, Nagini circles around him; Voldemort, now returned, promises Nagini that she will be allowed to eat Harry after the evening's proceedings are done.

Order of the Phoenix   While it is never stated explicitly, it is almost certain that Nagini is the snake that attacks Arthur Weasley just before Christmas.

Half-Blood Prince   In discussing the probable artifacts that have been turned into Horcruxes, Professor Dumbledore suggests to Harry that Voldemort's pet snake is acting rather suspiciously un-snake-like, and quite possibly is carrying a Horcrux. Harry asks if living creatures can be Horcruxes, and Dumbledore says that they can, although it is risky, of course, as living things can be killed.

Deathly Hallows   Nagini is present at the council meeting with Voldemort and his Death Eaters. Voldemort, testing Lucius Malfoy's wand, kills Charity Burbage, then tells Nagini that it is dinner time.

When Harry and Hermione are visiting Godric's Hollow, they meet with Bathilda Bagshot. Bathilda invites them to her house, then gets Harry to follow her to a room upstairs. It turns out that Bathilda is, in fact, dead, and is being animated by Nagini who is inside her. Nagini notifies Voldemort that she has trapped Harry, then emerges from the remains of Bathilda and attacks. While she bites Harry, her instructions are to hold him, so she does not poison him. With Hermione's help, Harry manages to escape from Nagini.

When Voldemort learns that his Horcruxes are being systematically stolen and destroyed, he tells Nagini that she will have to stay close by him for a while. Apparently, she is with him as he checks the places where his Horcruxes had been hidden.

In the Shrieking Shack, when we see Voldemort, Nagini is by his side, twining restlessly within an apparent protective spell. Severus Snape is summoned to Voldemort's presence, and Voldemort says that the Elder Wand, which he has taken from Dumbledore's tomb, is not working as well as he had expected. Voldemort has come to the conclusion that, because Snape had killed Dumbledore, the wand owed its allegiance to Snape, and would do so until someone killed Snape. Whereupon, he throws Nagini, protective spell and all, at Snape. Snape is bitten, and Voldemort and Nagini leave, allowing Harry time to receive memories from the fallen Snape. In Snape's memories, we see Dumbledore telling Snape that at some point, Voldemort will suddenly start being very protective of Nagini, keeping her always by his side. Then, and only then, will it be time to tell Harry all that Dumbledore has told Snape. As Harry heads out of the school for his meeting with Voldemort, he runs into Neville Longbottom. Thinking of Dumbledore and his backup plans, Harry tells Neville that it is vital that, should anything happen to Harry, it would be necessary to kill Nagini before Voldemort could be ultimately defeated.

When Harry confronts Voldemort in the Forbidden Forest, he sees Nagini, still twining restlessly within the protective spells Voldemort has cast about her. He thinks about the possibility of killing her, but determines that it is too risky; with the protective spells, and the large number of Death Eaters present, he is unlikely to get an effective spell out in time.

As Voldemort is crowing before the school about his final victory over Harry, Harry notices that Nagini is no longer encased within the protective spell. Neville produces the Sword of Gryffindor out of the Sorting Hat and with it, decapitates Nagini.

Strengths   Being a snake, Nagini has all the strengths of snakes: venom, physical strength, ability to travel through small apertures, maneuverability. Additionally, sharing some of Voldemort's soul, she also retains some of his intelligence.

Weaknesses   Being a snake, her intelligence and ability to plan are limited, despite her sharing of Voldemort's soul and part of his intellect.

Relationships with Other Characters   Nagini is Voldemort's pet, and contains one of his soul fragments. As such, she is extremely close to him. Towards most others, she is very much aloof, though she is likely to attack those who are in her, or Voldemort's, way.

Narcissa Malfoy

Gender: Female
Hair color: Blonde
Eye color: Blue
Related Family: Regulus Black, Sirius Black, Bellatrix Lestrange
Loyalty: Lucius Malfoy, Lord Voldemort

Overview

Born Narcissa Black to Cygnus Black and his wife Druella Rosier-Black in 1955, Narcissa was the youngest child of three sisters, Bellatrix and Andromeda being her older siblings. She was the cousin of Sirius Black and Regulus Black, and later became an aunt to Nymphadora Tonks, although it is unlikely that she acknowledges the connection due to Andromeda's marriage to Muggleborn Ted Tonks. The Blacks are a very old wizarding family with firm prejudices against half-bloods, Muggleborns and Muggles, and Narcissa was no doubt taught these prejudices from an early age. She is nice-looking, and, unusually, blonde where most of the Black family appear to be dark-haired.

Narcissa attended Hogwarts, where she completed her education along with most of the young wizarding population of Britain and Ireland. She later married Lucius Malfoy, the heir of a wealthy pure-blood family, and they had one son, Draco Malfoy.

Role in the Books

Philosopher's Stone Draco Malfoy (before we know his name) mentions his mother to Harry Potter in Madam Malkin's robe shop on Diagon Alley.

Goblet of Fire Narcissa accompanies Lucius and Draco to the Quidditch World Cup. This is the first time we have seen her.

Harry later asks Malfoy if the perpetual dissatisfied look on her face has to do with him (Draco). This inspires Draco to try to Curse Harry, which in turn results in Professor Moody Transfiguring him into a white ferret.

Order of the Phoenix While Narcissa Malfoy does not directly take any part in this book, it is mentioned that she is the only member of the Black family that Kreacher still trusts. Albus Dumbledore tells Harry that at Christmas, when Sirius Black had so forcefully ordered Kreacher out, Kreacher had gone to Narcissa, and presumably there had mentioned how much affection there was between Harry and Sirius. It was this bond between Harry and Sirius that Voldemort, with Lucius Malfoy's help, played upon to lure Harry into the Department of Mysteries.

Half-Blood Prince Out of fear for the welfare of her son, Narcissa, accompanied by Bellatrix Lestrange, her sister, visits Severus Snape. She tries to get him to promise that he will protect her son Draco, who has apparently been given a mission by Lord Voldemort that seems to be hopeless. Eventually, Snape is coerced into making an Unbreakable Vow with Narcissa to help her son in the mission.

Deathly Hallows When we first see Narcissa in this volume, she is at a council of Death Eaters. She, with her husband and son, are seated far down the table, distant from Voldemort, as a sign of their decreased status within the organization. It would appear that the Malfoy family is in disgrace, and much to her dismay, Bellatrix is seated near them. When Harry, Ron, and Hermione, along with Dean Thomas and Griphook are brought to Malfoy Manor, their captors call on the Malfoys to identify them before summoning the Dark Lord. Narcissa is unable to identify Harry, despite recognizing Hermione, and orders Draco to look; Draco is also uncertain, though Harry believes that he is feigning uncertainty. Narcissa is halted from summoning the Dark Lord by Bellatrix, who has seen the Sword of Gryffindor, and believes that her vault at Gringotts has been compromised; knowing that there is something Voldemort values highly locked in it, Bellatrix knows that Voldemort will be furious if that vault has been opened. Bellatrix by and large takes charge of proceedings at this point and Narcissa retreats into the background. When Harry has fallen in the Forbidden Forest after confronting Voldemort, Narcissa, presumably because she is closest, is asked by Lord Voldemort to check if Harry Potter is alive. Narcissa sees that he is, and asks if her son is all right, then lies to Voldemort that Harry is dead. Harry guesses that she has done this because only if Harry is dead will she be able to get into Hogwarts castle to re-unite with Draco.

Her last appearance is in the Great Hall, after the battle. She is with Lucius and Draco, standing somewhat apart from the celebrations around them.

Weaknesses During the scene at Spinner's End in the beginning of Harry Potter and the Half Blood Prince, Narcissa practically begs Severus Snape to make an Unbreakable Vow to protect her son, even though her sister Bellatrix Lestrange strongly opposes this action. Narcissa does this even though she is under Voldemort's orders to not speak of Draco's mission. Her love of her son outweighs her obedience to the Dark Lord, which could spell disaster for her in the future.

Relationships with Other Characters Narcissa Malfoy is the wife of Lucius Malfoy and the mother of Draco Malfoy. She is close friends with her sister Bellatrix Lestrange.

Narcissa is extremely judgmental, obviously holding those whose blood is less than pure, and those who would accept any such, as being greatly beneath her. It is possibly this need to feel superior that placed her in Lord Voldemort's camp initially; his emphasis on purity of blood matches hers. One must wonder how she rationalizes the fact that Voldemort is a half-blood.

Starting in *Harry Potter and the Half-Blood Prince*, we see that Narcissa's love of her family outweighs her loyalty to Voldemort and his principles.

ANALYSIS

While Narcissa is a lesser player in the arc followed by the Malfoy family, we can see the transitions she goes through alongside those of her husband and son. When we first see her, she is haughty, proud, sure of her position at the top of the Wizarding world alongside her husband, Lucius. In *Harry Potter and the Half-Blood Prince*, she is far less sure of herself; still believing in her family's innate superiority over the half-blood and Muggle-born, she is aware of her family's having fallen out of Voldemort's good books following Lucius' loss of the diary Horcrux, and later his arrest and imprisonment. At the beginning of *Harry Potter and the Deathly Hallows*, she, along with all her family, are aware that they are in disgrace; Draco had only completed half of his mission, and Narcissa had broken the rules of secrecy in talking to Snape about Draco's mission. At the end of that book, she quite clearly sees that she has lost everything except Draco, and is willing to lie to Voldemort in order to re-unite her family. (While Lucius is still alive, he is quite clearly merely a shell of what he had been, and Narcissa does not seem to be overly concerned with his whereabouts; though this may simply be because when we see her, it is in the clearing in the forest, and Lucius is immediately to hand.)

Natalie McDonald

Gender: Female
Hair color: Unknown
Eye color: Unknown
Related Family: Unknown
Loyalty:

OVERVIEW

Natalie McDonald is a Gryffindor who arrived at Hogwarts in Harry's fourth year.

ROLE IN THE BOOKS

Goblet of Fire Natalie McDonald was Sorted into Gryffindor House.

Nearly Headless Nick

Gender: Male
Hair color: Unknown
Eye color: Unknown
Related Family: Unknown
Loyalty: Albus Dumbledore

OVERVIEW

Sir Nicholas de Mimsy-Porpington, better known as Nearly Headless Nick, is the resident ghost of Gryffindor House at Hogwarts. He was almost beheaded on October 31, 1492 but the axe was too dull and did not entirely decapitate him, hence his nickname.

ROLE IN THE BOOKS

Philosopher's Stone Harry and Ron first meet Nearly Headless Nick at the Arrival Feast. Ron recognizes him, and names him, from a description he got from his brothers Fred and George. Asked why "Nearly Headless," Nick demonstrates that his head is held on only by a thin remnant. Nick also says that he hasn't eaten for nearly four hundred years.

Chamber of Secrets Returning to the castle sodden and muddy after a Quidditch practice, Harry meets a dismayed-looking Nearly Headless Nick, who has received a rejection letter from the Headless Hunt. ("Half an inch of skin and sinew!") After hearing Harry's worries about the upcoming Quidditch match against Slytherin, Nick sees Mrs. Norris, and warns Harry that Filch is on the warpath. Harry tries to avoid him but is caught and taken to Filch's office, where Filch starts filling out a detention form for the "crime" of "Befouling the castle." A crash from overhead distracts him, and sends him out of the office. On his return, Filch sees that Harry has become aware of some correspondence on his desk, and dismisses him hurriedly.

Outside Filch's office, Harry once again finds Nearly Headless Nick, who says that he had convinced Peeves to drop a heavy cabinet in the room over Filch's office to distract him, and is pleased that it had worked. He then invites Harry, Ron, and Hermione to his Deathday Party, celebrating his death on 31 October 1492. The Trio attend Nick's party, and find that it is a rather gloomy affair, with Peeves at one point chasing Moaning Myrtle away in tears. To put a quite unsatisfactory cap on the evening, as Nearly Headless Nick starts to make his speech thanking everyone for coming, the Headless Hunt bursts in through the walls and starts a wild game. Harry, Ron, and Hermione make their escape quietly in amongst the hullabaloo.

As they leave, Harry hears a voice. Following the voice, and with Ron and Hermione following him, he finds Mrs. Norris, Petrified and hanging from a torch bracket. Called upon to explain what they had been doing just before finding Mrs. Norris, the Trio explain that they had been attending Nick's Deathday party.

Shortly before Christmas, Harry finds Justin Finch-Fletchley Petrified, and Nearly Headless Nick, black and smoky instead of his usual white color, and apparently also unconscious. Nearly Headless Nick is wafted up to the Infirmary by Ernie Macmillan with a large fan, at Professor McGonagall's orders.

With help from Hermione, despite her being Petrified, Harry and Ron discover that the monster in the Chamber of Secrets is a Basilisk. While this creature can kill with a glance, nobody has died yet because nobody has looked at it directly. In particular, Justin Finch-Fletchley had looked at it through Nearly Headless Nick; and Nick had not been killed by it because he was actually already dead.

Although we don't see him at the Ending Feast, we are led to believe that Nick is revived at the same time as the Petrified students.

Goblet of Fire At the Arrival Feast, Nick informs Harry, Ron, and Hermione that there almost was not a feast this year. Peeves, upset at not being invited to the Feast, had gotten into the kitchen and had been wreaking havoc amongst the House Elves making it. Hermione is astounded to learn that there are over a hundred House-Elves in Hogwarts, attending to the needs of the students. Saying that she will not benefit from slave labour, she pushes aside her plate and refuses to eat any more.

Order of the Phoenix Nearly Headless Nick is already sitting at the Gryffindor table when the Trio and Neville arrive, and they sit near him. When the Sorting Hat sings its song, Ron asks if the Hat has ever given a warning before, Nick says certainly, but before he can complete his explanation he is interrupted by the start of the Sorting. Once the Sorting is complete, and food appears, Hermione asks him to continue his explanation. Nick says that whenever the Hat feels that the school is in danger, it warns that the school Houses must stand together in the face of the danger. Ron, despite the almost indecent glee with which he is stuffing his mouth, manages to ask how the Hat knows the school is in danger if it is a hat, and Nick points out that it does stay in the Headmasters' office, and likely hears what is passing there. At Harry's disbelief that he could ever join forces with Slytherin, Nick reproaches him, saying that the ghosts of the separate houses cooperate, that he would not, for instance, argue with the Bloody Baron. At Ron's suggestion that Nick is scared of the Baron, Nick is highly affronted and leaves, settling further down the table beside Colin and Dennis Creevey.

As Harry heads to the Owlery to send a message to Sirius on the Saturday following his first week of school, he encounters Nearly Headless Nick, who warns him that Peeves is preparing a surprise for the next person who walks under the bust of Paracelsus. Harry confirms that this surprise involves the bust of Paracelsus falling on that person's head, then finds another way to the Owlery. Nick, meanwhile, heads off to look for the Bloody Baron, to see if he can put a stop to it.

After the death of Sirius, Harry chooses to pack his trunk rather than attend the Leaving Feast. Restless, he leaves the dormitory to walk the halls. He sees Nearly Headless Nick passing through a wall ahead of him, and calls him over, saying he wants a word. Nick is reluctant, but says he rather expected this. They go into a vacant classroom, and Harry asks Nick if there is any chance that Sirius could have become a ghost. Nick says that there is no chance. A certain amount of preparation is required, as well as unfinished business and a fear of death, and Sirius does not have any of that in sufficient quantity to make him want to stick around.

Half-Blood Prince When Harry returns to Gryffindor Tower following his retrieving the memory from Professor Slughorn, he is denied entrance to the Common Room by the Fat Lady. While he is trying to decide what to do, Nearly Headless Nick wanders past. Harry tells him that Professor Dumbledore had set him this task, and now he has to wait until Dumbledore is back. Nick remarks that the Bloody Baron had said that Dumbledore had returned, but that he seemed tired. Nick suggests that Dumbledore is likely in his office.

Deathly Hallows Harry has become convinced that the last Horcrux that he must find and destroy is actually the lost Diadem of Rowena Ravenclaw. Professor McGonagall tells him that it has not been seen in living memory. It occurs to Harry that "living memory" only applies to the living and that the castle ghosts have been around far longer than that. Nearly Headless Nick is eager to help in any way that a ghost can, and is somewhat upset that Harry doesn't want his help, but rather the help of the Ravenclaw house ghost. Despite being upset, however, he does point the Grey Lady out to Harry.

Relationships with Other Characters Nick as the Gryffindor house ghost, socializes with all Gryffindors. He seems to be particularly fond of Harry, though he is quite pleased to speak with either Ron or Hermione. He is somewhat easily offended by Ron's repeatedly mentioning that he is dead, and on at least one occasion moves away from Ron after such an event.

ANALYSIS

Two things about Nearly Headless Nick have given readers pause.

In the first book, he tells Harry that he has not eaten in almost four hundred years; in the second book, he invites Harry to his five hundredth deathday celebration. As there is not a hundred-year gap in Harry's life at this point, we must assume that either Nick has miscounted, or that the author has made a small mistake. As it turns out, the author, in later editions, corrected the number in the first book to bring them both into line, and to firmly set the date of Sir Nicholas de Mimsy-Porpington's death at 31 October 1492.

In the second book, Nearly Headless Nick is attacked by the monster from the Chamber and is left "no longer pearly-white and transparent, but black and smoky, floating immobile and horizontal, six inches off the floor." We will later find that a restorative draught based on mandrake root will revive all of those not fatally attacked by the Monster, but that does leave the question open: how does one administer a restorative draught to a ghost? This question is never fully answered, except perhaps by considering the dual meaning of the word "draught."

Neville Longbottom

Gender: Male
Hair color: Unknown
Eye color: Unknown
Related Family: Frank Longbottom, Alice Longbottom, Augusta Longbottom
Loyalty: Albus Dumbledore

Overview

Neville Longbottom is a member of Gryffindor House and is in the same year as Harry Potter. In fact, they were born a day apart, Neville on 30 July, Harry on 31 July, a crucial element in the series' plot and one that significantly connects them. Along with fellow classmates Harry, Hermione Granger, and Ron Weasley, Neville helped battle powerful Dark Magic at Hogwarts. He lives with his grandmother, who has raised him since he was a small child.

Despite being born into a powerful wizarding family, a young Neville appeared to have inherited little magical ability. It was even feared he might be a *squib*. He also suffers from a poor memory, although just why remains unclear. However, under Harry's influence, his magical skills have developed to a point where he has become a valuable asset to Harry and his friends.

Role in the Books

Philosopher's Stone We first see Neville on the platform of the Hogwarts Express, where he is talking to an exasperated older lady with a stuffed vulture on her hat, explaining that he can't find one Trevor. Our first encounter with Neville is on the Hogwarts Express, where Neville stops in to see if Harry or Ron has seen his pet toad, Trevor. Neville later manages to enlist Hermione to assist him. When they reach Hogwarts, the first-year students are shepherded to a lake, and to a number of small boats that will take them across to the castle. While they are climbing into the boats, Hagrid asks whose toad he has found; Neville recognizes it as Trevor.

At the Entrance Feast, we see Neville being Sorted into Gryffindor House. Harry notes that the Sorting Hat takes a long time to decide that Neville is a Gryffindor. During the feast itself, we overhear that Neville's grandmother had been extremely pleased to get the letter from Hogwarts. They had been afraid for the longest time that Neville couldn't do magic. It was only one time when his great-uncle dropped him out the window by mistake and he bounced that his family started to believe he might have some magical ability.

Very shortly, also, we see Professor Snape's merciless persecution of Gryffindor students, Neville and Harry in particular. Neville manages to melt the cauldron that he shares with Seamus; Snape holds Harry partly responsible, and penalizes him.

Neville receives a Remembrall from his grandmother, and Draco tries to take it from him. Harry and Ron rise to his defence, and Professor McGonagall also appears. Draco, outnumbered, departs.

That afternoon, Gryffindor and Slytherin houses have flying lessons with Madam Hooch. Neville kicks off from the ground too soon, and is unable to control his broomstick; he falls off and fractures his wrist. Draco spots the Remembrall that he has dropped, and takes it away to hide it in a tree for Neville to find later; Harry, chasing after him, finds that he is a natural flyer. When Draco throws the Remembrall far away, Harry catches it before it reaches the ground. This is witnessed by Professor McGonagall, who much to Harry's surprise, does not expel him, instead introducing him to Oliver Wood, the captain of the house Quidditch team.

Finding that Harry has not been expelled, Draco then challenges him to a Wizards Duel, that night at 11 in the Trophy Room. Hermione, overhearing them, says that they would be asking for trouble to accept. As they leave for the duel, she follows them, still nagging. She finally gives up, but when she tries to return to the common room, she finds that the Fat Lady has gone visiting and she can't get back in. She accompanies Harry and Ron to the trophy room, on the way collecting Neville who is sleeping out in the hall because, though discharged from the infirmary, he has forgotten the password and cannot get back into Gryffindor Tower. The four of them, in the Trophy Room, hear Argus Filch approaching, and attempt to escape; Neville, however, runs into a suit of armour. Avoiding Filch and Peeves, the four find themselves in a room with an enormous, three-headed dog. They manage to escape from the dog, and return to Gryffindor Tower.

Some time later, Neville makes his way into the Gryffindor common room with his legs immobilized. He tells Harry that Draco had hit him with the Leg-locker jinx. Hermione frees him, and Harry gives him a Chocolate Frog. Neville returns the Chocolate Frog collector's card to Harry, and Harry, noting it is Dumbledore's card, suddenly remembers that this is where he had heard the name Nicholas Flamel. As the Trio have been hunting for reference to Flamel since hearing the name mentioned accidentally by Hagrid, this proves a very important clue. When Hagrid is finally prevailed upon to let his pet dragon, Norbert, be taken to Romania by Charlie's friends, Draco learns of the plan. He, in turn, boasts about how he is going to catch Harry and Hermione in the act, in a place where Neville can hear him. Neville, attempting to warn Harry and Hermione, is caught out of bed by Professor McGonagall. When Harry and Hermione are caught by Filch and brought before McGonagall, Neville is still there, and his outburst at seeing Harry causes McGonagall to assume that the three of them were conspiring to get Draco in trouble. Each of the three is penalized fifty house points and given a detention.

Detention is served with Hagrid in the Forbidden Forest. Something has been injuring and killing Unicorns, and the four of them (Draco also having received detention) are tracking an injured unicorn to see what they can find out about what's killing them. Draco and Neville initially are teamed up together, but Draco deliberately scares Neville. After answering Neville's call for help, Hagrid re-shuffles groups to keep Neville and Hermione with him, leaving Harry and Draco, with Hagrid's boar-hound Fang, as the other group. We don't see a lot of what Neville is up to during this time.

Determining that Voldemort is active and after the Stone, and believing that, assisted by Snape, he now knows how to reach the place where the Stone is concealed, Harry, Ron, and Hermione prepare to go in after him. Neville discovers their plan, and attempts to prevent the trio from leaving, saying that the three of them have lost enough House points already. Hermione, with great reluctance, immobilizes him.

At the Leaving Feast, for having had the courage to stand up to his friends, Dumbledore awards him ten House points. This is the first time Neville has won any points for anything, and is sufficient to allow Gryffindor win the House Cup at year's end.

Finally, it is noted that despite his abysmal Potions grade, Neville has managed to pass his exams.

Chamber of Secrets It becomes apparent that the Chamber of legend has been opened, and there is a general assumption that whatever monster is resident in the Chamber is attacking Muggle-borns, those of non-Wizarding descent. There is a brisk business in protective amulets, and Neville buys some. Asked what he is afraid of, as he comes from old Wizarding stock, Neville says that his poor magical skill makes him practically a Squib, and the monster had first attacked Filch.

In the Dueling Club run by Professor Lockhart, Neville initially was paired with Justin Finch-Fletchley. After that goes badly awry, Lockhart suggests setting a single pair and allowing the rest to watch. He initially suggests Neville and Justin, but is overruled by Snape who cuttingly remarks that Neville causes havoc with every wand stroke. Snape suggests having Harry and Draco Malfoy demonstrate instead.

Prisoner of Azkaban Harry, having accidentally inflated his Aunt Marge, departs the Dursley home, and while trying to decide what to do next, trips over his trunk and manages to summon the Knight Bus. When the conductor asks his name, Harry, afraid he is a wanted man already, gives Neville's name. This deception lasts until his destination, the Leaky Cauldron, where Cornelius Fudge, the Minister for Magic, recognizes him.

Harry later sees the real Neville in Diagon Alley, where he is being chastised by his grandmother for forgetting his booklist.

When the Hogwarts Express stops short of Hogsmeade, Neville and Ginny make their way to Harry's compartment. The arrival of the Dementor causes Harry to lose consciousness briefly. Neville later mentions this in Draco Malfoy's hearing, and Draco teases Harry about this.

In their first Divination class, Professor Trelawney asks Neville to hand out teacups, predicting in an offhand way that he will break at least one. He does, in the course of the lesson, break two of them.

In the first Potions class of the year, Neville manages to make a horrible mess of his potion. Snape forbids Hermione to help him set it right. When Neville's potion is reasonably correct at the end of the class, Snape, assuming he can't have done it on his own, penalizes Hermione five House points for helping him. (Hermione had, in fact, been helping, but Snape had no direct knowledge of that.)

In the first Defence Against the Dark Arts class of the year, Professor Lupin has the class learn to combat a Boggart. Entering the staff room, the class finds Snape present. Snape again makes a cutting remark about Neville's abilities with a wand, and Lupin responds that he had planned to have Neville start the demonstration. Snape sweeps out, and Lupin asks Neville what he is most afraid of. On hearing that it is Snape, Lupin further asks what Neville's grandmother usually wears, then asks Neville to imagine Snape wearing his grandmother's clothes. The charm Riddikulus, if invoked with a clear picture in mind, will force the Boggart to take the shape of what the caster is imagining. It is laughter that defeats the Boggart, so the object of the exercise is to force the Boggart into a shape that is laughable. Neville, nervously, watches Snape emerge from the wardrobe, and forces him into his grandmothers' clothes. In turn, everyone in the class except Harry and Hermione have a shot at the Boggart, and finally Neville triumphantly finishes it.

Snape somehow hears about the shape Neville had forced the Boggart into, and now bullies him mercilessly in Potions class.

Sirius Black had managed to enter the castle on Hallowe'en and, refused entry to the Gryffindor common room by The Fat Lady, had destroyed her portrait. The only portrait who would accept the job of guarding the Gryffindor common room after this attack was Sir Cadogan. Sir Cadogan was changing passwords several times a day, and Neville had trouble remembering them, so he had asked Sir Cadogan for the full list and had written them down. Shortly before Easter, Harry meets Neville, who is trying to convince Sir Cadogan to let him in; it seems he has lost the list.

Two nights later, Ron awakes to find Sirius Black looming over him with a knife. His yells awaken everyone in Gryffindor and summon Professor McGonagall. Queried, Sir Cadogan proudly states that he has let a man into Gryffindor Tower, because he had the password. He had all of them, in fact, written on a piece of paper. Professor McGonagall asks who was so stupid as to have written all the passwords down and left them lying around. Neville shamefacedly raises his hand.

As a result of this, Neville is barred from further Hogsmeade trips, receives detention, and is no longer allowed to be given the password, so he must hang around waiting for someone else entering or leaving Gryffindor tower to let him in. He also receives a Howler from his grandmother.

Though not having permission to visit Hogsmeade, Harry plans to use the secret passage revealed by the Marauder's Map and his Invisibility Cloak to accompany Ron there. Neville, almost painfully glad to see that Harry also can't go to Hogsmeade, almost prevents Harry from getting to the secret passage.

It is mentioned that, at Easter break, Neville is looking strained. Like the other third-years, he has received a lot of homework to complete before the end of Easter break.

In the Shrieking Shack, Sirius Black reveals that Neville's list of passwords had actually been stolen for him by Hermione's cat, Crookshanks.

Goblet of Fire We first see Neville on the Hogwarts Express. He expresses envy that Harry and Ron had been to see the Quidditch World Cup; his grandmother had refused to get them tickets. When Ron produces his souvenir figurine of Viktor Krum, Neville is entranced, watching it walk back and forth across Ron's hand.

In the first Defence Against the Dark Arts class, Professor Moody asks the students to name the Unforgivable Curses. Neville timidly names the Cruciatus Curse. After class, we see that Neville is very profoundly affected by something; he seems to be all right, but his speech is somehow off and he seems overcheerful. Professor Moody invites him back to his office for tea. Later, we see Neville in the dormitory with a book that Moody had given him, *Magical Mediterranean Water-Plants and Their Properties*. Neville seems rather cheered up, both by the book, and by Moody's having told him that Professor Sprout had said he was adept at Herbology.

When Harry opens the Golden Egg to try and figure out the clue for the Second Task, it makes a loud, screeching noise. The noise scares Neville, who thinks it sounds like someone being tortured.

Neville asks Hermione to go to the Yule Ball with him, but she turns him down; she is already going with someone else. When Harry asks Ginny, she tells him that she is going with Neville, who had already asked her. At the Yule Ball, Harry notes that Neville's dancing is even worse than his own; he seems to be treading on Ginny's feet rather a lot.

Left alone in Dumbledore's office, Harry finds Dumbledore's Pensieve. While exploring this, he finds a number of Dumbledore's memories, including one of the Wizengamot trial of four Death Eaters, presided over by Bartemius Crouch. The four Death Eaters, Bellatrix Lestrange, Rabastan Lestrange, Rodolphus Lestrange, and Barty Crouch Jr. (Bartemius' own son), are being tried for having tortured Frank and Alice Longbottom to insanity in an attempt to find out what had happened to Voldemort. In later discussion with Dumbledore, Harry learns that those were Neville's parents, that they were left permanently insane, and that they now are resident in St. Mungo's Hospital. This is why Neville was being raised by his grandmother. Dumbledore cautions Harry not to talk about this to Ron and Hermione, saying it is Neville's decision to reveal that part of his life. After Harry's return from the graveyard duel, he is taken aside by Moody, who boasts that he had been smoothing Harry's path through the Triwizard Tournament. The book he had given Neville had contained information on Gillyweed, but when Harry had not consulted with Neville, Moody had instead commented loudly in Dobby's hearing about the effects of Gillyweed, and Dobby had carried that information to Harry.

Order of the Phoenix We meet Neville on the Hogwarts Express when he is trying to find a compartment. Ginny suggests one, and Neville points out that there is someone in it. Ginny says it's just Loony Lovegood, and leads Harry and Neville in, introducing them. Neville shows Harry his birthday present, a rare Mimbulus Mimbletonia plant. Showing off its defence mechanism, he sprays everyone and everything in the compartment with stinksap, just as Cho Chang arrives to say hello to Harry. An awkward moment passes, and Cho departs; Ginny cleans the stinksap off everyone. After the Arrival Feast, it is Neville who knows the password to Gryffindor Tower ("*Mimbulus Mimbletonia*"); Hermione and Ron, shepherding the first-years up to the dormitory have not arrived yet. When Harry reaches the dormitory, again ahead of Ron, he finds that Seamus had almost not come back to Hogwarts because of Harry and Dumbledore's reputation as besmirched by the *Daily Prophet*. Neville defends Harry, saying his gran believes Dumbledore, and Dean remains neutral. The situation remains tense until Ron arrives and forces things to a close by means of his powers as Prefect.

Neville is one of the early members of the Defence Association, or as it becomes known, Dumbledore's Army. He is present at the first meeting of the group, which takes place on the first Hogsmeade weekend of the year, in the Hog's Head. When Zacharias Smith derides Harry's experience, Neville is one of the many there present who leap to his defence.

When student groups are banned the next day, Neville is one of the Gryffindors who are reassured directly by Harry and Hermione that the Association will continue to meet anyway.

Later, while they are waiting to enter Potions, Draco Malfoy, taunting Harry whose actions have been attributed to supposed mental problems by the *Daily Prophet* throughout the summer, comments about people with mental disabilities and how they should be kept in St. Mungo's. Neville, stung, leaps to attack Draco, Harry and Ron try to restrain Neville. Professor Snape, appearing on the scene, penalizes Gryffindor house for fighting. Ron asks what that was all about; Harry, knowing about Neville's parents, understands why Neville flew at Draco, but cannot tell Ron.

At the first meeting of Dumbledore's Army, Neville works hard and actually manages to disarm Harry once. Harry, feeling a need to walk around the Room of Requirement, where the group is meeting, leaves Neville with Ron and Hermione to practice.

At Hagrid's first Care of Magical Creatures class after his extended journey to the land of the Giants, Harry's class is learning about Thestrals. Of the gathered students, only three can see them: Harry, Neville, and an unnamed Slytherin student. Hagrid explains that in order to see them, you have to have seen death. At Christmas, visiting an injured Mr. Weasley in St. Mungo's Hospital, Harry, Ron, Hermione, and Ginny meet Neville and his grandmother. They are visiting Neville's parents, Frank and Alice, who, Harry knows, were once Aurors and former Order of the Phoenix members. Both were tortured into insanity with the Cruciatus curse by Sirius' Death Eater cousin, Bellatrix Lestrange. They are permanently hospitalized at St. Mungo's. Neville is embarrassed that his classmates know about his parents, the more so when his mother shambles over and grandly gives him a wrapper from a package of Drooble's Best Blowing Gum; his grandmother says he should just throw it away, but Harry sees Neville surreptitiously smooth it out and pocket it, and suspects that Neville has a large number of such apparently worthless items. Neville's grandmother says that Neville should be proud of how his parents defended themselves against their attackers. After Neville and his grandmother depart, Harry admits that he knew about Neville's parents, but that Dumbledore asked him to say nothing.

After Christmas, there is a mass outbreak of Death Eaters from Azkaban Prison. Among the escapees are Bellatrix Lestrange, and at least one of the other Lestranges. Harry expects that Neville will become fearful on hearing that the Death Eaters who had tortured his parents to insanity; instead, though, it seems to motivate him in his work in Dumbledore's Army. Of all the students, only Hermione masters the Shield Charm faster than Neville. We see Neville in passing after Harry has given his interview for the *Quibbler*. Harry wonders if he has done the right thing getting the story of Voldemort's return published. Neville, Dean, and Seamus all say he did the right thing, and admit that it must have taken a lot of courage.

We hear that Neville has been working very hard in Dumbledore's Army, mastering every spell. Harry is thinking about Neville's progress just before Dobby arrives to tell him that Dumbledore's Army has been betrayed. When Harry becomes convinced that Sirius has been captured by Voldemort and is being tortured in the Ministry, he arranges a diversion so that he can try to contact Sirius, by means of the Floo network and Professor Umbridge's fireplace. When Ginny, Luna, Ron, and Hermione, who are creating the diversion, are caught, Neville, with his ability to be in the wrong place at the wrong time, is swept up with them and brought to Umbridge's office. Harry and Hermione manage to take Umbridge into the Forbidden Forest, ostensibly to look at a weapon they've been building for Dumbledore. After Umbridge is taken away by the Centaurs, Ron, Neville, Ginny, and Luna meet up with Harry and Hermione. Thestrals are attracted to the party, and after some debate, Harry arranges that each of the six will mount a Thestral, and they all fly off to London and the Ministry, to rescue Sirius. As a group they reach the spot where Sirius is supposedly being tortured, but they find nothing there. Ron finds a small glass sphere on a shelf that has Harry's name on it. Harry reaches it down, and the group are suddenly confronted by Death Eaters, led by Lucius Malfoy, demanding that Harry hand over the sphere. Harry, who is the center of the Death Eaters' attention, manages to tell the other students to arrange a distraction, and they run for the Atrium and the way out of the Ministry. Entering the hall of Time, Hermione seals the door behind them, and Harry discovers that only Neville is with them; Ginny, Luna, and Ron have gotten separated from them. Two Death Eaters enter the hall, and Hermione Stuns one of them. Neville, attempting to disarm the other, manages to disarm Harry as well. Neville's next attempt, a Stunning spell, misses and hits a cabinet of Time-turners instead. Hermione Stuns the second Death Eater, and they again try to set out for the Atrium. As they head towards the exit room, they are intercepted by another pair of Death Eaters who trip them. One of them starts to call his fellows, but Hermione, regaining her wand, quiets him; Harry Body-Binds the other. The silenced one casts a wordless spell that knocks Hermione out, then kicks at the still-sprawled Neville, breaking his wand and his nose. He then wordlessly demands the sphere from Harry, but is distracted by one of the earlier-incapacitated Death Eaters, and Harry Body-Binds him as well. Carrying Hermione, Harry, and Neville (with Hermione's wand), now return to the round room which is the single point of access to the Department of Mysteries. Here, they meet Ginny (who has an injured ankle), Ron (who seems drunk), and Luna. Death Eaters, led by Bellatrix Lestrange, burst through another door; Harry and the others retreat, finding themselves in a room with brains floating in tanks. Luna is disabled while trying to seal doors into the room, Ginny, unable to dodge because of her ankle, is Stunned; Ron, who has injudiciously Summoned a brain to himself, is fully engaged in getting it off himself, and Neville cannot properly speak the spells he is trying to use through his broken nose, so Harry, knowing the Death Eaters are after him, runs off through one of the unsealed doors, finding himself, after a fall down the stone steps, at the bottom of an amphitheatre where a tattered veil hangs across a broken archway. Here he prepares to make his stand alone, against the ten remaining Death Eaters, trying to spare the other students.

Neville, however, has other ideas, and charges through the door, trying fruitlessly to Stun Death Eaters. He is quickly subdued, and Bellatrix Lestrange sadistically tortures him, saying that she remembers doing the same to his parents, in order to get Harry to give up the sphere, now identified as a Prophecy, which he still holds. Harry is about to surrender the prophecy when Sirius, Tonks, Shacklebolt, Lupin, and Moody arrive. Macnair grabs Harry around the neck and demands the prophecy; Neville pokes his eye with Hermione's wand, and he releases Harry. Harry Stuns Macnair, but Neville is jinxed by Dolohov, who then makes two attempts at Harry before Sirius distracts him. Harry Body-Binds Dolohov, and hands the Prophecy to Neville to free his hands. Harry grabs Neville's robe to pull him up the steps; the robe rips, and the orb falls from Neville's pocket and is smashed. The wispy vapors inside turn into a ghost-like figure speaking the prophecy, which vanishes unheard amid the battle sounds.

Albus Dumbledore's arrival ends most of the battle, though Bellatrix and Sirius are still dueling; a Stun spell pushes Sirius through the veil, and Bellatrix runs up the steps to escape.

After the battle, in Dumbledore's office, Dumbledore says that it was the Prophecy that Voldemort had been seeking. Harry tells Dumbledore that the prophecy was destroyed, but Dumbledore says only a copy of the original was lost. He knows the contents because it was to him that the prophecy was first revealed. Sixteen years ago, Dumbledore interviewed Sibyll Trelawney for the Divination position, meeting her at a pub in Hogsmeade. Although she was descended from a gifted Seer, she herself seemed minimally talented. Saying she was not acceptable for the post, Dumbledore was about to leave.

Dumbledore stops speaking, and, producing his Pensieve, extracts a memory from his mind and places it therein. Sibyll Trelawney's veiled image rises, and in the harsh voice Harry heard once before, says, *"The one with the power to vanquish the Dark Lord approaches . . . born to those who have thrice defied him, born as the seventh month dies . . . and the Dark Lord will mark him as his equal, but he will have power the Dark Lord knows not . . . and either must die at the hand of the other for neither can live while the other survives . . . the one with the power to vanquish the Dark Lord will be born as the seventh month dies . . ."*

Dumbledore says there were two boys who fit the prophecy: Harry and Neville Longbottom, born days apart. Both Harry's and Neville's parents, who were Order of the Phoenix members, defied Voldemort three times. Dumbledore believes Voldemort attacked Harry because he is a half-blood like himself, and therefore possibly more dangerous; Neville is a pureblood. By deliberately choosing Harry, Voldemort "marked" him as his equal, leaving behind the scar on Harry's forehead.

It is noted later that Neville has made a full recovery from his injuries. We see him briefly in the Hospital Wing: when Harry goes to visit Hermione, Ginny, and Ron, who are still recovering, Luna and Neville are also there visiting them.

Half-Blood Prince On the Hogwarts Express, Harry sits with Luna and Neville, while Ron and Hermione visit the Prefects compartment. Harry is finding it odd to be once again in demand, rather than having people shun him. Romilda Vane, a fourth-year student, arrives and asks Harry to sit with her and her friends, but Harry turns her down, saying he is sitting with his friends. Romilda turns a disparaging look on Luna and Neville before departing. Harry, seeing that Neville is concerned by this, points out that Romilda was not at the Ministry. This brightens Neville up, and he starts talking about his O.W.L. results, wondering if an Acceptable result in Transfiguration can be made to sound good enough to allow him to progress to N.E.W.T. level.

Harry, listening to him and thinking about the Prophecy, wonders what would have happened if Voldemort had decided to attack Neville first; whether it would be Neville with the scar and the popularity.

A third-year girl appears with invitations to lunch with Professor Slughorn for both Harry and Neville. Once in Professor Slughorn's compartment, it is obvious that he has selected those who have famous relatives, or in Neville's case, have been involved in public activities on their own. While Slughorn does attempt to find out what had happened in the Ministry, neither Harry nor Neville is forthcoming, and Slughorn does not pry. When selecting courses for Neville to take, Professor McGonagall says she cannot accept Neville into her Transfiguration class with only an Acceptable O.W.L.. However, his Charms grade was Exceeds Expectations, he could still take N.E.W.T.-level Charms with Professor Flitwick. Neville mumbles that his grandmother thinks Charms is a soft option. Professor McGonagall acerbically comments that Augusta failing her Charms O.W.L. was not reason to deny that to Neville, and sensing Neville's delight at this revelation, adds Charms to his timetable and sends him on his way.

We see almost nothing of Neville during the year, as he and Harry share very few classes. As the end of the year approaches, Dumbledore takes Harry to the site where he believes a Horcrux is hidden. Having heard what he believes is a sound of exultation from Draco, Harry feels that this is a bad time for the school to be left without Dumbledore's strength, and tells Ginny, Ron, and Hermione to round up any members of Dumbledore's Army who will help, to guard specifically the Room of Requirement and Snape's office. After the death of Dumbledore, Ron tells Harry that only Neville and Luna, of all the members of Dumbledore's Army they had talked to, had been willing to help. Ron, Ginny, and Neville had been guarding the Room of Requirement, and had seen Draco emerge from it holding an awful, dried-up hand thing. Seeing the three other students, he threw some black powder at them, and everything went dark. Draco could still evidently see, because by the sound he was leading a number of people very quickly out of the Room of Requirement. Ron, Neville, and Ginny didn't dare throw any jinxes because they couldn't see if they were going to jinx each other or other innocents.

Neville is injured in the battle, and must spend some time in the Hospital Wing. Harry and Ginny, and Ron and Hermione, visit him and Bill, who was also injured. We also see Neville briefly at Dumbledore's funeral, but do not speak to him then.

Deathly Hallows Harry, Hermione, and Ron, in order to evade the Death Eaters, are moving from place to place in the countryside. Some time before Christmas, they hear another party doing the same, who discuss events at Hogwarts. Apparently a group of students, including Ginny, had broken into Headmaster Snape's office and attempted to steal the Sword of Gryffindor from its glass case. Hermione has been carrying the portrait of Phineas Nigellus Black, and asks him for details. He says that the students involved were Ginny, Neville, and Luna, and that they had been punished by having them work for the half-breed, Hagrid, in the Forbidden Forest.

Harry and Hermione manage to get Phineas Nigellus to reveal a few more details about what is happening at Hogwarts. Snape has re-instated the decree banning student groups, apparently because of a low-level rebellion that is going on at the school. Harry deduces from this that Neville, Ginny, and Luna have taken charge of the D.A. and are working to usurp the Death Eaters in charge of Hogwarts.

When Harry, Hermione, and Ron Apparate into Hogsmeade on the trail of the Horcrux that is located in Hogwarts, they set off an alarm, the Caterwaul, alerting Death Eaters to their presence. They are rescued from the Death Eaters by Aberforth Dumbledore, who is initially extremely reluctant to help them. Aberforth is eventually convinced to help them enter Hogwarts, and sends a messenger via the portrait of Ariana Dumbledore on his wall. When Ariana returns, Neville is accompanying her.

Neville greets Harry, Ron, and Hermione enthusiastically, but Harry is taken aback by his battered appearance. Neville says that he is not the worst by far, wait until they see Seamus. He then tells Aberforth, to his dismay, that there will be some others coming to the school. Neville now leads them back with him along a dark tunnel to the school, telling them that the other seven passageways have been sealed and guarded, and asking for confirmation that the Trio had in fact broken into Gringotts and escaped by flying on a dragon. Neville also tells them about how the school is now being run, with the "Defence Against" part of the Dark Arts course being dropped, and detention being served by being subjects for students practicing the Cruciatus curse. Students who refuse to Curse other students are beaten. The Muggle Studies teacher, Alecto Carrow, insists that Muggles are dirty and stupid, and Neville had received one of his scars from asking how much Muggle blood she had. He says also that the Carrows had not wanted to injure him too much because he was of an old, Pureblood line, so he got off lightly compared to many. Neville had managed to re-build Dumbledore's Army, and they had been pulling pranks and creating disruptions, but Luna and Ginny's departure from school had slowed down the rebellion. When the Carrows had realized Neville was the ringleader, they had tried to get at him by kidnapping his grandmother. Augusta, however, had put at least one of her attackers, Dawlish, into St. Mungo's Hospital, and was now on the run. Neville had decided that the time was right for him to disappear.

When they arrive at the school, Harry does not immediately understand where they are; it's a room he has never before seen. It turns out, however, to be the Room of Requirement, which has grown and become more comprehensive as members of Dumbledore's Army have arrived and gone into hiding. The room is of course unable to provide food, but when Neville's need had become great enough, the Room had created a tunnel to the Hog's Head Inn, and Aberforth had been keeping them supplied since. Seamus mentions that Neville really knows how to get the Room of Requirement to give them what they need.

Harry tells the group assembled in the Room of Requirement that there is something that he, Ron, and Hermione must do themselves, and that they will then leave. Everyone in the room is dismayed, but it is Neville who expresses what they are all feeling, that they have demonstrated their loyalty to Dumbledore, and that they feel that it is their right to fight Voldemort alongside Harry.

Later, when battle is joined, we see Neville on his way to the battlements with Professor Sprout and pots of Mandrakes that will be dropped on the attackers. Neville's grandmother arrives to fight alongside him, saying she is proud of what he has been doing. When the Death Eaters manage to breach the walls, we again see Neville, this time with Venomous Tentacula plants, in the Entrance Hall.

At the break in the fighting, Harry, under his Invisibility Cloak, departs the castle towards the Forbidden Forest and his destiny. Along the way, he sees Oliver Wood and Neville carrying the body of Colin Creevey into the Great Hall. Oliver says that Colin is so light he can handle the job himself, so Neville goes out to look for more casualties. It occurs to Harry that Dumbledore always had contingencies available in case his original plan went awry. Deciding to emulate Dumbledore, Harry steps out from under the Cloak, and tells Neville that if he falls, Voldemort's ultimate defeat can only be ensured if Voldemort's pet snake, Nagini, is killed. He says that Ron and Hermione already know this, but if they are not able to kill Nagini, it will be up to Neville. Neville does not understand, but agrees to kill the snake if given the chance.

After Harry's apparent death in the Forbidden Forest, Voldemort has Hagrid carry him to his confrontation with the occupants of the school. Neville defies him. Voldemort singles him out, and saying that Neville is a Pureblood from an old Wizarding family, asks him to join his side. Neville refuses and charges. Voldemort puts him in a full Body-bind, then Summons the Sorting Hat. He pulls it down over Neville's head, and sets it on fire as a sign that there will be no more Sorting, all of Hogwarts will be Slytherin. Neville breaks out of the Body-Bind, pulls the Sword of Gryffindor out of the Hat, and cuts off Nagini's head.

We don't see Neville again except in glimpses through the confusion of the battle; after the battle, Harry does note that he has survived and is sitting exhausted in the Great Hall.

In the epilogue, it is discovered that Neville becomes the Herbology professor at Hogwarts. Neville also remains a close family friend to the Potters and Weasleys.

Strengths Neville is gifted in Herbology and received an "Outstanding" on his O.W.L. He also received an "Exceeds Expectations" on his Charms O.W.L., and is encouraged by Professor McGonagall to take advanced study in that course.

Neville has the potential to be a great wizard. His problems stems, in Professor McGonagall opinion, from a "lack of self confidence." He has grown in magical power substantially since his 5th year when he trained with Dumbledore's Army under Harry Potter, and worked harder than most to master defensive skills. Neville was one of the few who fought at the Department of Mysteries, where he demonstrated his courage and loyalty to his friends. He showed great leadership and bravery when he led a re-formed Dumbledore's Army in their resistance to the Death Eaters' control of Hogwarts in his seventh year.

Weaknesses Neville has very low self-confidence, and this affects his wizarding skill. He often gets into accidents, especially in Potions because of his (fairly rational) fear of Professor Snape.

He is very forgetful, which is most apparent in his inability to remember the Gryffindor passwords, though it is likely that his problems with Potions are memory-related as well.

ANALYSIS

Neville shares a dorm with Harry and Ron. In the early years, he is arguably more a friendly acquaintance than a comrade, but he becomes much closer to Harry during their 5th year. Neville is seemingly clumsy and magically challenged in the first three novels, but by the fifth book, he adopts a new persona and develops as a character. Perhaps Rowling is saying that even the most seemingly hopeless student, given time and encouragement, can be a valuable asset. This is evident by Neville's growing role in Book 5, his extraordinary Herbology ability, and that *he* could have been "the boy who lived."

While we never actually see Bertha Jorkins in the series, she is described to us in some detail in the course of the fourth book, and it seems that she has severe memory problems caused by the use of memory alteration charms. It has been suggested on some fan sites that Bertha's memory issues are similar enough to Neville's that the cause of them might also be the same. In Bertha's case, the memory being restrained was something quite important; the suggestion is that Neville's memory similarly has been altered to hide something very far-reaching. Prior to the release of the seventh book, there had been some speculation as to whether some valuable secret was hidden in Neville's mind, and whether it might be released by way of the Pensieve; but no such secret emerged in Harry Potter and the Deathly Hallows. Alternately, we might suspect that Neville had been present when his parents were tortured, an enhancement to the planned interrogation that would have amused Bellatrix. In that case, it is likely that it would have been Neville's grandmother who applied the memory charm to prevent Neville from reliving that episode repeatedly, and Professor McGonagall tells us that Augusta, Neville's grandmother, failed her Charms O.W.L.. The possibility that Neville's memory issues are due to a botched Obliviate charm are, given the assumptions, almost certain.

GREATER PICTURE

Neville's character became more significant in *Order of the Phoenix*, in which it was learned that, as infants, both he Harry were targeted by Lord Voldemort as the potential enemy foretold in Sibyll Trelawney's prophecy; but, Voldemort *chose* Harry over Neville. In the seventh book, Neville, along with Ginny Weasley and Luna Lovegood, reform Dumbledore's Army and recruit more wizards to rebel against the new headmaster, Snape, and the Muggle Studies and Defense Against the Dark Arts teachers, Alecto and Amycus Carrow, respectively.

Norbert

Gender: Female
Hair color: None (scales)
Eye color: Unknown
Related Family: Hagrid
Loyalty: none

OVERVIEW

Norbert is a Norwegian Ridgeback dragon hatched from an egg by Hagrid.

ROLE IN THE BOOKS

Philosopher's Stone At one point when Harry, Ron, and Hermione call on him, Hagrid seems to be trying to hide something. It turns out that what he is hiding is a large black egg in the fireplace, which he admits is a dragon egg which he won from someone down at a pub down in the village. Hermione immediately questions the wisdom of trying to raise a fire-breathing dragon in a wooden hut, but Hagrid has always wanted a dragon of his own and refuses to listen.

Harry, Ron, and Hermione are present at the hatching, but it turns out that Draco is also there, watching through the window. Harry and Ron recognize him as he runs up the steps into the school.

The Trio are adamant that, as Norbert has been seen by Draco, they must get rid of him; keeping dragons is strictly against the law and will get Hagrid into a lot of trouble. Despite the inconveniences of caring for a dragon—at one point, Hagrid is talking to the Trio through a window in his hut while Norbert is chewing, apparently painfully, on his foot—Hagrid only relents when Ron suggests that his brother Charlie could find Norbert a home. Charlie is duly written to, and responds saying that four of his friends will stop by to collect Norbert and take him to his new home.

Ron is bitten by Norbert while trying to feed him, and ends up in the Hospital Wing. While there, he is visited by Draco who borrows a book from him. It is only later that Ron remembers that Charlie's letter was in the book. As a result of this, Draco in the halls looking for them when Harry and Hermione are taking the crated Norbert, under the Invisibility Cloak, up to the top of the Astronomy Tower to see him off. With Norbert gone, Harry and Hermione return to the school, but have forgotten the Cloak on the top of the tower and are caught by Filch. Much later, Harry asks what the person who had given the egg to Hagrid looked like, and Hagrid says he did not know, the person had never taken his cloak off.

Order of the Phoenix On his first visit to the Hog's Head, it occurs to Harry that this is, in fact, the sort of place where it is not so unusual that someone would never take their cloak off; amongst the four patrons present when he arrives, not one face is visible.

Deathly Hallows Hagrid, talking to Charlie, asks how Norbert is doing. Charlie replies that they are calling her Norberta now, as she is female. Harry asks how you can tell the difference, and Charlie replies that the females are more vicious.

Nott

Gender: Male
Hair color: Unknown
Eye color: Unknown
Related Family: son Theodore Nott
Loyalty: Lord Voldemort

Overview

Nott is a Death Eater, whose son Theodore is a Slytherin in Harry's year. He is never given a first name.

Role in the Books

Order of the Phoenix Nott is injured in the first skirmish in the battle at the Ministry, presumably by falling shelves, to the extent that Lucius Malfoy instructs the other Death Eaters there present to leave him.

Half-Blood Prince When Lord Voldemort, or Tom Riddle as he is then known, is seen in Albus Dumbledore's memories returning to Hogwarts to apply for the job of teacher of Defence Against the Dark Arts, Dumbledore asks him about his "friends" waiting for him in Hogsmeade. Nott is one of the friends mentioned by name, along with Mulciber, Antonin Dolohov, and Evan Rosier.

Outside the series Nott originally had a scene in which he and Lucius Malfoy discussed Death Eater business off camera, while their sons Theodore Nott and Draco Malfoy discussed Harry and Albus Dumbledore. The author mentions that while she tried to fit the scene into two different books, it didn't work well either place and so was laid to rest.[1]

Nymphadora Tonks

Gender: Female
Hair color: Changes constantly
Eye color:
Related Family: Andromeda Black, Ted Tonks
Loyalty: Order of the Phoenix

Overview

Nymphadora Tonks, or as she prefers to be called, Tonks, is an Auror, and a member of the Order of the Phoenix. Her parents are Andromeda Black, who was Sirius' favorite cousin, and Ted Tonks, who was a wizard, though Muggle-born. Narcissa Malfoy and Bellatrix Lestrange are Tonks' aunts from her mother's side, though none of them would admit that. She attended Hogwarts around 1984–1991 as a Hufflepuff.

Role in the Books

Order of the Phoenix Nymphadora Tonks joins the cast of characters at the beginning of the fifth book, when she arrives at Harry's uncle's home to help escort Harry to the headquarters of the Order of the Phoenix. From Harry's conversation with her, we learn that Tonks is a Metamorphmagus, and that she went to Hogwarts, but was not made a Prefect, mostly because she was unable to control herself. Most of the time, her hair is shocking pink; it appears that this is her favorite hair color, because she seems to revert to it quite easily. We learn that she is an Auror working for the Ministry of Magic, which is a great help to the Order. With the Order being largely underground at this time, Tonks still has to work at her regular Auror duties; we see her occasionally, doing guard duty for the Order. At dinner at Headquarters, Tonks amuses Ginny and Hermione by changing the shape of her nose. Apparently, this is a common game, because they keep asking for their favorites.

Tonks accompanies the group to the train station to board the Hogwarts Express. For the duration of the trip, she disguises herself as an old lady.

Several times over Christmas break, Tonks visits Headquarters. She accompanies the Weasley family as they visit Arthur Weasley in hospital. At the end of Christmas Break, she travels to Hogwarts with the Weasleys, Harry, and Hermione in the Knight Bus. Stan Shunpike says that "that bossy lady 'oo is witchu" has paid a premium to get them to Hogwarts quicker, so their stop will be the next but one.

Tonks takes part in the battle in the Department of Mysteries in the end of the book, although she is knocked out halfway through the battle by Bellatrix Lestrange.

Half-Blood Prince In this book, we first see Tonks briefly when Harry is taken to The Burrow by Dumbledore. She is sitting in the kitchen, apparently talking something over with Molly Weasley. Harry is immediately struck by how tired she looks. Tonks does not stay, but departs almost immediately once Harry has arrived.

Discussing Tonks' listless appearance with Hermione, Ginny, and Ron the next morning, Harry discovers that Mrs. Weasley had apparently been hoping that Bill would express an interest in Tonks, instead of Fleur Delacour, to whom he is now engaged. Ron suggests that with Tonks looking as sad as she does, there was little chance of Mrs. Weasley's hopes being fulfilled.

On the Hogwarts Express, Harry is caught by Draco Malfoy attempting to eavesdrop. Draco immobilizes him, and after breaking his nose, leaves him on the train as it returns towards London. Tonks, getting onto the train before it has completely left, frees him and returns him to the platform. She then takes him up to the school, where she sends a message for assistance entering the school grounds. As Hagrid is not present, the messenger reaches Severus Snape, who comes to the gate to let them in. Snape comments that Tonks' Patronus has changed; the one Harry saw was something large and hairy, Snape cuttingly remarks that he had liked the old one better, and it had seemed stronger.

It is mentioned at Christmas time at The Burrow that Tonks had been invited, but had instead chosen to spend Christmas alone. Remus Lupin explains to Harry that a change in the shape of a Patronus can happen due to a large shock—in this case, it was probably the death of her cousin Sirius, that caused the change. On one occasion when Harry is attempting to enter the Room of Requirement, he is surprised by Tonks, still looking hangdog, who claims to be looking for Dumbledore,

---

1. http://www.jkrowling.com/textonly/en/extrastuff_view.cfm?id=5

but seems rather aimless when she wanders away after their meeting.

Tonks is one of the members of the Order of the Phoenix who is present at Hogwarts, fighting Death Eaters at the school in the climactic battle in this book.

In the end of the book, we learn that the real reason for Tonks' depression is because she has fallen in love with Lupin, who has been trying to convince her that they cannot be together because he is a werewolf. However, in the last chapter, we see Tonks and Lupin holding hands, and Tonks has obviously regained her ability to change her appearance, as her hair is once again bright pink.

Deathly Hallows Tonks proudly shows Harry her wedding ring when a group of Order members go to get Harry. Lupin then also says he's sorry Harry couldn't be there and that it was a small event, leaving us to believe that Lupin didn't want it that public but would have liked Harry to be there. When the Order members and their "Harrys" leave the House and Ron is the "Harry" that goes with Tonks, she tells Ron to hop on and hold tight. We then see Ron hops on, then sends an apologetic glance towards Lupin before holding on to her waist.

Tonks arrives quite late at The Burrow; apparently she had been intercepted by Bellatrix Lestrange and had quite a battle to get away from her.

Lupin later reveals to Harry, Ron, and Hermione that Tonks is pregnant. Lupin seems to be angry with himself, fearing that his son might be a werewolf; he feels that is a burden too great to saddle anyone with, and he had not wanted to pass on the horrible and painful trait to someone else.

Tonks has the baby, and Lupin travels to Shell Cottage, where Harry, Ron, and Hermione are staying, to tell them the good news. Lupin asks Harry to be godfather, saying that he and Tonks had discussed it.

When the Order members come to Hogwarts through the Room of Requirement, Lupin shows everyone a baby picture and it proves that the baby has inherited his mother's Metamorphmagus traits. Tonks had been left at home with Teddy, her son, for the final battle but is worried about Lupin and shows up to look for him. She hears he was last seen battling Dolohov on the grounds, and runs off to find him. She is then later seen battling her aunt, Bellatrix Lestrange.

Later as Harry walks back into the Great Hall with Severus Snape's memories, he spots Lupin and Tonks lying on the ground together, both dead.

Strengths The fact that Tonks is a Metamorphmagus has made her extremely valuable, both as an Auror and as a member of the Order of the Phoenix. Tonks is a very strong, friendly, funny, and outgoing person.

Weaknesses As soon as we are introduced to Tonks, we learn that she is extremely clumsy—she enters the story by breaking a dish in the Dursley's kitchen. Throughout the books, she is always breaking things, knocking objects over, and falling down. Because of this, she says she almost failed the "Stealth" portion of her training to become an Auror. However, this got better over the course of book six.

Relationships with Other Characters Tonks has a romantic interest in Remus Lupin and they are shown holding hands at the end of the sixth book. By the beginning of the seventh book they are married, and have a child on the way.

ANALYSIS

One of the things that makes this series of books so powerful is that through the seven-year arc of the series, characters mature and change. This is particularly true of Harry, Ron, and Hermione, of course, as they are in a stage of their lives where there is normally great change; that is discussed in greater detail in their articles. However, a particular strength of this series is that this character growth is not restricted to the main characters, but happens to all characters in the story to some degree. As a case in point, let us take Tonks. She is quite young, having just completed her Auror training; she would be about seven years older than Harry, making her about 22 to Harry's 15 when they meet at the beginning of *Harry Potter and the Order of the Phoenix*. She is disapproving of the sterile neatness of the Dursley's house, and feels much more at home in Harry's room which has been inhabited by the equivalent of a caged beast for four days. She indicates that she has never gotten the hang of cleaning, herself. She apparently routinely makes a show at dinner, changing her nose shape between bites. She is very much the young, carefree witch at this stage in her life.

During the course of *Harry Potter and the Order of the Phoenix*, Tonks keeps up her carefree ways, right up to the battle at the Ministry. There, possibly for the first time in her life, she is engaged in a battle against superior odds with a very real possibility that she will die. This is, for anyone, a maturing experience.

It is quite possible that upon regaining consciousness and discovering that her cousin Sirius had literally gone beyond the Veil, Tonks had done some rather serious reconsideration of her life. It was likely in the course of this that she discovered that what she had previously shared with Remus, which we don't see, but can infer, was rather more serious than she had thought. When we see Tonks in September after the battle, she seems much more mature: her hair color is subdued, and she herself is much more reserved. She also seems quite depressed, having difficulty changing her appearance, always seeming on the verge of tears, and even appears thinner than usual. Ron, Harry, and Hermione assume she is upset over Sirius' death, and Harry even suggests that Tonks may have been in love with him, which is why she's so crestfallen. It is only at the end of the book that we find that it is Lupin, rather than Sirius, who is the object of her affections. One must assume that she had attempted to move her relationship with Remus on to the next stage and been rebuffed; and there almost certainly was something going on before that, as six weeks (from the battle at the Ministry, to when Harry arrives at The Burrow) is a very short time to reassess your life, fall in love, start considering marriage, and show the effects of being refused. It is a safe assumption that there had been some snogging going on behind the scenes for the duration of *Harry Potter and the Order of the Phoenix*. We can only speculate that the author chose to not show us these scenes of Lupin and Tonks together because of Lupin's delicacy concerning these matters.

We can easily see that Tonks is taking a much more serious view of life throughout *Harry Potter and the Half-Blood Prince*; from the time we first see her in July, right to the end of the book, she seems less care-free. It is perhaps a criticism of aging in general that maturity seems to rule out being care-free, but that is the case; as one matures, one starts taking an interest, and being concerned by, things outside oneself, which does lead one to act with increased sobriety. We do know that Tonks wants to make a life-long commitment to Lupin by the end of the book, which is something that she clearly would not have imagined possible at the beginning of *Harry Potter and the Order of the Phoenix*. It is this growth and change in her that brings Tonks alive for us, that makes us care about her, and that makes us glad that Lupin seems to be willing to entertain the idea of settling down with her.

Oliver Wood

Gender: Male
Hair color: Unknown
Eye color: Unknown
Related Family: Unknown
Loyalty: Dumbledore, probably, being a Gryffindor

Overview

Oliver Wood is a member of Gryffindor House. He is described as "burly" and is fanatical about Quidditch. He captained the Gryffindor Quidditch Team, while playing Keeper, for Harry's first three years. After he graduated from Hogwarts, he signed with Puddlemere United Reserve Team.

Role in the Books

Philosopher's Stone When Professor McGonagall sees Harry flying on his broomstick without permission, and making a truly spectacular catch, she takes him out of the courtyard. Looking in classrooms, she eventually finds Professor Quirrell's room, and asks Professor Quirrell if she could borrow "Wood." Harry is relieved to find out that Wood is not a wooden implement for punishment, but is in fact Oliver Wood, who turns out to be captain of the Quidditch team. She tells Wood that she has found him a Seeker, and they discuss Harry's natural flying abilities and the fact that they need to get him a new broom.

Wood, later, takes Harry down to the Quidditch pitch, explains the rules, demonstrates the Bludgers, and checks Harry's flight abilities by having him catch golf balls. Once Wood is satisfied that Harry is capable, he has Harry join the regular practices.

Wood does not play a large part in the story after this; he is there in the Quidditch practices and in the various Quidditch matches. He is Keeper for the Gryffindor team, and as such is responsible for some particularly spectacular saves.

Chamber of Secrets Quidditch Captain in Harry's Second year.

Prisoner of Azkaban With Quidditch having been interrupted in the previous year, and Oliver now in his seventh and final year at Hogwarts, he sees this as his only chance at winning the Quidditch Cup. As such, Oliver is driving the team hard, with new tactics, frequent practices, and innumerable strategy sessions.

Goblet of Fire We see Oliver in passing in the campground before the Quidditch World Cup, where we learn that he is playing for the Puddlemere United Quidditch team.

Order of the Phoenix Harry thinks to himself that with Angelina Johnson as team Captain, pep talks are not likely to be as long as they were when Oliver Wood had been Captain.

When Harry gets detention from Professor Umbridge, Angelina is furious at him, deciding that it is his fault that he got detention, and orders him to do whatever he can to get out of detention and be there for practice. After she has gone, Ron comments that they should check with Puddlemere United and see if Oliver Wood is still alive, as Angelina seems to be channeling his spirit.

Angelina comments to Harry later that she knows now how Wood had felt as team captain, and why he had been as rough on them as he had.

Half-Blood Prince When Ron is poisoned, Hagrid wonders if someone might be trying to kill off the Gryffindor Quidditch team: Katie Bell, one of the Chasers, had touched a cursed necklace and was now in St. Mungo's, and Ron was Keeper. George, who is there at the time, feels this is unlikely, but Fred suggests that Wood might have done that to the Slytherin team if he felt he could get away with it.

Deathly Hallows Oliver comes to Hogwarts to fight in the final battle. He is present in the Room of Requirement when Harry returns from Ravenclaw tower. When Harry is on his way out to the Forbidden Forest, after viewing the Prince's memories, Harry sees Oliver and Neville carrying the body of Colin Creevey back into the school from the grounds; Oliver tells Neville that he can handle it himself, Neville should head back out for another.

Strengths Oliver is a good Quidditch Goal Keeper and he is extremely committed to the Gryffindor Quidditch team. He puts in a lot of time and effort to the team.

Weaknesses Oliver is often blinded by his love of Quidditch and cannot see how anything else is more important.

Relationships with Other Characters Not much is known about Oliver's close friends from the books. In the fan fiction world, he is a widely popular character who is close with all his Gryffindor House team mates, especially Katie Bell. There is a large amount of fan fiction which pairs these two together, though there is nothing in the series to support this, and in fact it seems unlikely with Oliver being three years older than Katie.

Ollivander

Gender: Male
Hair color: Unknown
Eye color: Silver
Related Family: Unknown
Loyalty: unknown

Overview

Mr. Ollivander (no first name given) works at his own wand shop, Ollivander's: Makers of Fine Wands since 382 b.c., in Diagon Alley.

Role in the Books

Philosopher's Stone Ollivander, after much trying of wands, sells Harry an 11-inch Holly wand with a phoenix feather core. The core of this wand happens to be one of only two feathers to have come from one particular phoenix; Harry is disconcerted when Ollivander tells him it is the same phoenix which provided the core of Lord Voldemort's wand.

Prisoner of Azkaban Ron is given a new wand at the beginning of the year; presumably this also comes from Ollivander's, although he is not mentioned.

Goblet of Fire The four champions, Fleur Delacour, Cedric Diggory, Viktor Krum, and Harry Potter, must have their wands checked to confirm that they are all in good working order. It is Mr. Ollivander who is called in to do that checking. He recognizes Harry's and Cedric's wands immediately as being of his own manufacture, recognizes Krum's as being "a Gregorovitch creation," and suggests that the Veela hair core of Fleur's wand could make it temperamental.

Half-Blood Prince It is mentioned that a few stores in Diagon Alley have been closed as their owners disappeared. Florean Fortescue's ice cream parlour, for instance, is no longer open, and damage to the store indicates that there was some sort of struggle there; but while Mr. Ollivander has also departed, Ollivander's store is unhurt, leading us to believe that he either decamped to avoid the upcoming battles, or has thrown in with Voldemort. Neville Longbottom remarks that he got a new wand from his grandmother after the battle at the end of the previous book; he thinks he may have one of the last wands Ollivander sold before his disappearance.

Deathly Hallows Ollivander is taken and held captive by Death Eaters and can be heard screaming below their meeting room in the basement of the Malfoy residence, seemingly in response to Voldemort's statement that he shall be the one to kill Harry Potter. Lord Voldemort questions Ollivander about ways to overcome the connection between his wand and Harry's. When Ollivander's advice of using a different wand works out badly (Harry's wand destroys the wand borrowed from Lucius Malfoy), Lord Voldemort punishes Ollivander.

From developments later in the story, we assume that following Voldemort's failure to receive good answers from Ollivander about the failure of the borrowed wand, he had questioned Ollivander about the "Deathstick," the undefeatable wand.

Later Harry, Hermione, and Ron rescue Ollivander from the Malfoys' basement, taking him to Shell Cottage. Harry has a long conversation with him following his rescue, in the course of which we learn that Ollivander had been forced to make a new wand for Wormtail. We also learn about how wands choose their owners and how wands can be transferred from one wizard to another; that as part of the wand choosing its wizard, a wand may shift its allegiance partly or wholly to one who actually captures it from the original owner. Harry carefully asks here whether it is necessary to kill the previous owner in order to have the wand transfer its allegiance; Ollivander, shocked, says no, but later admits that the history of the Deathstick does seem to be littered with murders. Finally, Harry confirms that Ollivander had known that Gregorovitch had, or at least claimed to have, the Deathstick, and had spread rumours that he was studying it to determine its secrets. He also confirms that Ollivander had passed this information on to Voldemort.

Ollivander's long imprisonment has weakened him, and it takes him a long time to recover, but just before Harry embarks on his mission to Gringotts, we see Ollivander leaving Shell Cottage on his way to Auntie Muriel's house to convalesce.

Strengths Mr. Ollivander is able to remember every wand he ever sold, with details of its construction.

Questions

1. Why is it that Mr Ollivander can recall every single wand ingredient to every single customer? One may wonder if he is under a curse or spell of some sort.

Olympe Maxime

Gender: Female
Hair color: Unknown
Eye color: Unknown
Related Family: Unknown
Loyalty: Albus Dumbledore, Rubeus Hagrid

Overview

Olympe Maxime is the headmistress of Beauxbatons Academy of Magic. She is a very large woman, standing perhaps ten feet (three meters) tall, and she speaks with a French accent.

Role in the Books

Goblet of Fire We first meet Madame Maxime when she arrives with the Beauxbatons students who wish to enter the Triwizard Tournament. She expresses some concern about her horses and the care they need, but Professor Dumbledore assures her that their groundskeeper, Hagrid, will be quite capable of taking care of them when he is finished dealing with another small matter. When Hagrid first sees Madame Maxime at dinner, he is apparently instantly smitten.

The following day, Harry, Hermione, and Ron visit Hagrid. He is quite the sight, apparently having tried to tame his mane of hair with something that looks like axle grease, and now wearing his best suit. Before they leave for dinner, Hagrid puts on some eau de cologne, but he rather overdoes it. Hagrid goes outside to wash it off in the rain barrel, asking the Trio to wait. While he is outside, he sees Madame Maxime and the Beauxbatons students leaving their carriage and heading for the great hall. Forgetting all about the trio, he heads up the lawn to join them as they walk into the castle. The Trio speculate that Hagrid must be sweet on Madame Maxime. After the selection of the four Champions, Madame Maxime enters the room where they are waiting with the other four Tournament judges, Professor Dumbledore, Igor Karkaroff, Ludo Bagman, and Bartemius Crouch. Also arriving with them are Professor McGonagall and Professor Snape; Professor Moody arrives somewhat later. While Madame Maxime is angered that Hogwarts has two Champions, suggesting that Dumbledore might have made the Age Line incorrectly, and demands that Dumbledore do something about it, most of the discussion here is driven by Karkaroff. In the end, when no alternative is forthcoming to the requirement that Harry enter be accepted into the Tournament, Madame Maxime leaves with her selected Champion, Fleur Delacour, speaking to her rapidly in French.

At the Weighing of the Wands ceremony, attended by all five judges and Mr. Ollivander, Rita Skeeter is present as reporter for the *Daily Prophet*. Madame Maxime's sheer size makes for significant difficulty in getting her into the picture that the photographer is trying to take of the Champions and the judges.

Just before the First Task, Hagrid invites Harry to visit him at his hut at midnight, wearing his Invisibility Cloak. Harry arrives, and Hagrid immediately takes him to the Beauxbatons carriage, where he meets Madame Maxime. With a slightly embarrassed Harry following invisibly behind, Hagrid and Madame Maxime set off around the edge of the Forbidden Forest, where they find a large paddock with several wizards and four Dragons. Hagrid is, of course, entranced by them, and he has brought Madame Maxime to see them because they are so beautiful. Charlie Weasley, one of the dragon handlers, questions Hagrid on the propriety of his bringing Madame Maxime to see the basis for the Task that her Champion will be facing; Hagrid dismisses his concerns. Harry, having seen all he cares to see, returns to the Gryffindor common room.

At the Yule Ball, Harry sees that Madame Maxime is dancing with Hagrid. Some time later, Harry and Ron are walking in the rose garden. They see Hagrid and Madame Maxime sitting close together, and hear Hagrid starting to admit something very private to her. Unable to get away, they listen as Hagrid admits to his half-Giant ancestry, and asks Madame Maxime whether her Giant ancestor was her father or her mother. Shocked, Madame Maxime claims that she is just big-boned, that she has no Giants in her past, and she stalks off, back to the dance. After sitting a while, Hagrid sadly returns to his hut. Privately, Ron later suggests that Madame Maxime isn't fooling anyone with her protestations.

Rita Skeeter publishes Hagrid's admission in the Daily Prophet; Hermione wonders how she had overheard that, as apart from Harry and Ron, only Hagrid and Madame Maxime had been there.

At the Second Task, Fleur is attacked by Grindylows and is unable to rescue the hostage being held for her. Harry, however, does rescue Fleur's sister Gabrielle, and Fleur is so relieved by this that Madame Maxime has to restrain her from diving back into the lake to meet them.

In Divination class, Harry falls asleep and has a dream of what Voldemort is doing. He makes his way to Dumbledore's office, where he overhears Cornelius Fudge suggesting that the disappearance of Bartemius Crouch could possibly have something to do with Olympe Maxime, as the carriage was right there, and knowing the proclivities of her race. Discovered, and asked about the events of that evening, Harry says that he didn't see Madame Maxime anywhere, and suggests that she would have a hard time hiding.

At one point, Hagrid had been digging in the lawn, and Harry, watching from the castle above, had noticed Madame Maxime walk over to him and say something. Hagrid had evidently rebuffed her, because she had immediately returned to the Beauxbatons carriage. Just before the Third Task, Harry, at dinner, notices that Madame Maxime's eyes seem red, and that Hagrid keeps glancing at her.

After Harry's return from the graveyard, and Fudge's denial of the return of Voldemort, Professor Dumbledore asks Professor McGonagall to request that Hagrid and Madame Maxime meet him in his office. Harry, visiting Hagrid later with Ron and Hermione, notices a second oversized teacup on Hagrid's table, and hears that Madame Maxime had been visiting. Hagrid refuses to tell the Trio what mission Dumbledore has for him, but does say that he's almost got Olympe to agree to go with him.

While we see Madame Maxime getting into he coach as she prepares to leave Hogwarts with her students, she does not then speak to Harry.

Order of the Phoenix While we do not see Madame Maxime directly in this book, we hear first of her that she has returned from the mission that was set for her and Hagrid by Dumbledore; this is somewhat alarming to Harry and Hermione because Hagrid has not yet returned.

When Hagrid does return, he tells them how he and Olympe Maxime had traveled to the home of the last tribe of giants, and had attempted to recruit them to Dumbledore's side. Their mission had failed when the then-leader of the giants was overthrown; Olympe had been forced to use magic to allow them to escape, which eliminated any further chance of negotiations. The two of them had attempted to form an alliance with the outcasts from the new regime, but were unsuccessful, except that Hagrid apparently had managed, with Olympe's help, to bring his half-brother Grawp back with him.

Half-Blood Prince The carriage drawn by giant flying horses in which Madame Maxime arrived for the Triwizard Tournament is seen arriving at the school shortly before Albus Dumbledore's funeral. Harry is watching as Madame Maxime emerges and throws herself into Hagrid's arms. It is mentioned that Madame Maxime is present at the funeral, taking up two and a half chairs.

Relationships with Other Characters Madame Maxime seems genuinely pleased to see "Dumblydorr." This does not, however, prevent her from becoming angry with him when he seems to have engineered two champions for Hogwarts.

Madame Maxime and Hagrid have a sometimes-rocky romantic relationship. Hagrid seems to fall in love with Olympe at first sight; she takes rather longer to return his affections, particularly when he implies that he knows she is half-Giant. While she seems to be ending the relationship at that point, she gradually thinks better of it, and at the end of that book the two of them, reconciled, journey through Europe together in search of the giants.

Orion Black

Gender: Male
Hair color: Unknown
Eye color: Unknown
Related Family: Black Family; wife Walburga Black, sons Sirius Black, Regulus Black
Loyalty: Purebloods

Overview

Orion Black was a pure-blood wizard, husband of Walburga Black and father of Sirius and Regulus Black. He lived in the house on Number 12, Grimmauld Place, his ancestral home.

Role in the Books

Order of the Phoenix The day after Harry arrives at Grimmauld Place, he is assisting the Weasley family with cleaning Doxies out of the sitting room. When they stop for lunch, Sirius shows Harry a tapestry of the Black family tree, explaining that this was emblematic of the Black family beliefs; to the Blacks, genealogy was paramount. The fact that they could trace their family back to the earliest wizards was a source of family pride, and anyone who did not agree was expunged from the tree. Sirius shows the burn mark that had replaced his name, and the one for Andromeda Tonks' mother, who had married "a Muggle," Ted Tonks. He also said that he had escaped from this house because his parents were possessed by pure-blood mania. Both his father and his mother agreed with Voldemort's plans for the purification of wizarding race.

Later, as they clean up the house, Sirius finds that Kreacher is trying to carry away a large golden ring. Sirius takes it from him and throws it away, saying it had been his father's, and that Kreacher was not as loyal to him as to Walburga.

Strengths We are told that Sirius' father did enhance the magical protection on the house. As the house must have been standing for many years at that point, and the existing spells should have been reasonably strong, we expect that he must have been a reasonably strong wizard.

Relationships with Other Characters Orion was proud of his son Regulus because he was true to the family's Pure Blood beliefs. We are led to believe that both Orion and Walburga were proud of his becoming a Death Eater, and being in Voldemort's inner council. By the same token, Orion must have been disappointed in Sirius' pro-Muggle leanings. However, Sirius notes that it was Walburga who burned people off the tapestry of the family tree; Orion may have held out some hope of reconciliation.

Questions

1. Did Orion treat Kreacher well, or not? If not, why would Kreacher try to retrieve Orion's ring?

Orla Quirke

Gender: Female
Hair color: Unknown
Eye color: Unknown
Related Family: Unknown
Loyalty:

Overview

Orla Quirke is a Ravenclaw who arrived at Hogwarts in Harry's fourth year.

Role in the Books

Goblet of Fire Orla Quirke was Sorted into Ravenclaw House.

Owen Cauldwell

Gender: Male
Hair color: Unknown
Eye color: Unknown
Related Family: Unknown
Loyalty:

Overview

Owen Cauldwell is a Hufflepuff who arrived at Hogwarts in Harry's fourth year.

Padma Patil

Gender: Female
Hair color: Black
Eye color: Dark Brown
Related Family: Parvati Patil (twin sister)
Loyalty:

OVERVIEW

Padma Patil is a member of Ravenclaw house in Harry's year, and twin sister to Parvati Patil.

ROLE IN THE BOOKS

Philosopher's Stone   We hear Padma's name called at the Sorting, followed immediately by Parvati's.

Goblet of Fire   Colin Creevey excitedly tells Harry that his brother Dennis will be entering Hogwarts this year, and hopes that Dennis will be Sorted into Gryffindor. Harry asks Hermione if brothers and sisters generally end up in the same House. Hermione points out that Padma and Parvati Patil are twins, yet while Parvati ended up in Gryffindor, Padma is a Ravenclaw.

Harry must find a dance partner to attend the Yule Ball with, as he has been told that he will be leading off the dancing. When Cho Chang regretfully turns him down, Harry, in some desperation, sees Parvati and Lavender entering the common room, and asks Parvati if she will go to the Ball with him. She accepts. Harry, knowing Ron is also dateless, asks Lavender on Ron's behalf, but she has been invited by someone else. Parvati mentions that her sister Padma does not yet have a date, and Harry asks if she'd be willing to go with Ron. Parvati says she will ask. Padma evidently is willing, because she is waiting for Ron when he reaches the entrance hall. (Fred and George in passing ask Harry how he and Ron had managed to hook up with the most beautiful girls in the school.) Padma is rather upset by Ron's threadbare formal robes, despite his attempts to make them less horrible by removing the lace trim. She is further upset during the course of the ball that Ron does not seem to be paying her any attention, instead focusing on Hermione and Viktor Krum, her date. When Ron flatly tells Padma that he doesn't intend to dance, she leaves, finding a Beauxbatons boy to dance with instead.

Order of the Phoenix   On the Hogwarts Express, Ron, returning to Harry's compartment, tells Harry that the new Prefects from Ravenclaw are Padma Patil and Anthony Goldstein.

Padma Patil is present at the first meeting of Dumbledore's Army in the Hog's Head. While she doesn't say much there, she does seem interested in what Harry has to say, and also shows up for subsequent meetings in the Room of Requirement. In one of the meetings of Dumbledore's Army, we see her paired with her sister Pavati, trading jinxes.

Deathly Hallows   When Harry, Ron and Hermione reach Hogwarts, they find Padma Patil, among others, in hiding in the Room of Requirement. As Neville had been using this room as a way to stay at Hogwarts as the leader of the revived Dumbledore's Army, it is likely that Padma had similarly found living openly in Hogwarts too dangerous and had retreated to the Room of Requirement so that she could continue the work of Dumbledore's Army in safety. Padma joins in the Battle of Hogwarts, but we don't directly see what she is doing.

Pansy Parkinson

Gender: Female
Hair color: Black short bob-cut with bangs
Eye color: Dark
Related Family: Unknown
Loyalty: Draco Malfoy(?)

OVERVIEW

Pansy Parkinson is a member of Slytherin House in Harry's year, with a face like a pug (*Harry Potter and the Prisoner of Azkaban*). She and Draco Malfoy seem to have a romantic relationship towards the end of the series.

ROLE IN THE BOOKS

Philosopher's Stone   Pansy is seen at the Sorting, where her name, but not her house, is mentioned.

After Neville's accident in his first Flying lesson, Draco jeers at Neville's expression; Parvati Patil tells him to shut up, and Pansy accuses her of being sweet on Neville. She is here described as a "hard-faced girl"; as flying lessons are shared with the Slytherins, we can infer that she is in Slytherin house.

Prisoner of Azkaban   Pansy, who has been told about Harry's experiences with the Dementor on the Hogwarts Express, calls across the Great Hall at breakfast to taunt him.

When Draco is injured by a Hippogriff, we see Pansy at his bedside in the Hospital Wing.

Goblet of Fire   Pansy is apparently Draco Malfoy's date for the Yule Ball.

When Witch Weekly runs a story on Hermione suggesting that she has both Harry and Viktor Krum on a string, it is Pansy who discovers this. She throws a copy of the magazine to Hermione in Potions class.

Order of the Phoenix   Ron reports that Pansy Parkinson is one of the two prefects for Slytherin house, the other being Draco Malfoy. It is mentiond that Pansy Parkinson shares one of the horseless carriages up to the school with Draco Malfoy and his cronies Crabbe and Goyle.

On the second day of classes, Draco, Pansy, Crabbe, and Goyle are laughing about something as they arrive at Care of Magical Creatures class. When Professor Grubbly-Plank asks if anyone can identify the creatures she has in front of her, Hermione puts her hand up, and Draco imitates her. Pansy shrieks with laughter, then screams as the little bundles of twigs on the table jump up, revealing themselves to be Bowtruckles.

At Gryffindor's first Quidditch practice, Pansy, Crabbe, and Goyle have accompanied Draco Malfoy to the pitch, and laugh appreciatively at every joke Draco makes about the Gryffindors. Harry in particular finds Pansy's screams of mirth annoying.

As the first Quidditch match aproaches, Pansy tries to upset Harry by telling him that Warrington is going to be trying to knock him off his broom. Harry responds that with Warrington's bad aim, he has nothing to worry about. In the first Defence Against the Dark Arts class after Hagrid's return, Professor Umbridge is examining Hagrid's teaching. She has clearly already decided that Hagrid is a half-wit, so when she asks Pansy if she has trouble understanding Hagrid, Pansy plays along, saying that often the lessons just sound like grunting. Throughout the examination by Umbridge, Pansy is laughing, as are Draco, Crabbe, and Goyle.

When Dumbledore's Army is betrayed, Pansy is one of the "*trusted* students" that Umbridge brings to break up the meeting. Pansy is able to get into the Room of Requirement and retrieve the parchment that shows the names of all the people in Dumbledore's Army, which she gives to Umbridge.

After Fred and George depart the school, there are a number of attacks against Umbridge's Inquisitorial Squad, of which Pansy is a member. It is mentioned that she misses an entire day's classes because she has suddenly grown antlers.

Half-Blood Prince On the Hogwarts Express, Harry, under his Invisibility Cloak, sneaks into Draco Malfoy's compartment to try and find out what Draco is up to. Draco, who has his head in Pansy's lap, is boasting to Pansy that he may not be attending Hogwarts for his seventh year, that he has been given a greater mission. Pansy is stroking his hair as she listens.

Harry later tells Ron what he had overheard, and Ron, twice, says he thinks that Draco was boasting to impress Pansy.

Deathly Hallows After Harry's return to the school, when the students are all assembled in the Great Hall, the voice of Lord Voldemort is heard, demanding the surrender of Harry Potter. It is Pansy Parkinson who stands and points her wand at Harry, saying that all they have to do is capture him and Voldemort will leave the school alone. The entire Gryffindor table rises and aims their wands at her, followed almost immediately by the Ravenclaws and Hufflepuffs. Professor McGonagall dismisses her comment and evacuates all of Slytherin house, although the over-age wizards in the other three houses are allowed to remain if they choose.

Relationships with Other Characters She is always picking on other students, mainly Gryffindors like Parvati Patil, Neville Longbottom, Ron Weasley, Harry Potter and Hermione Granger. Something of a coward, she tends to concentrate her attentions on those less powerful and younger or smaller than her. She has a group of Slytherin girls as her friends and is seen giggling with them the majority of the time. In her sixth year, it seems Pansy likes to fawn over Draco Malfoy, fondling and stroking his hair.

Parvati Patil

Gender: Female
Hair color: Black
Eye color: Dark Brown
Related Family: Padma Patil (twin sister)
Loyalty: Unknown

Overview

Parvati Patil is a Gryffindor in Harry's year, twin sister to Padma Patil, and close friend of Lavender Brown. She favours Professor Trelawney's Divination lessons above all others.

Role in the Books

Philosopher's Stone Parvati's name is called at the Sorting shortly before Harry's.

After Neville's accident in his first Flying lesson, Draco jeers at Neville's expression; Parvati tells him to shut up, and Pansy Parkinson accuses her of being sweet on Neville. When Harry is caught by Professor McGonagall, Parvati tries to defend him, but McGonagall cuts her and Ron off before they can explain. As they go down to the Hallowe'en Feast, Harry and Ron overhear Parvati telling her friend Lavender Brown that Hermione was crying in the girls' toilet and wanted to be left alone. Ron, who had made harsh comments about her following Charms class, seems to feel a bit awkward about this revelation.

Prisoner of Azkaban In Professor Lupin's first Defence Against the Dark Arts class, Harry's class is learning the Riddikulus charm against Boggarts. As they leave the class, Parvati wonders why Professor Lupin is afraid of crystal balls. When Professor Trelawney's nebulous prediction, about something that Lavender Brown is fearing, is slightly matched by actual events, Lavender and Parvati become convinced that Trelawney can predict the future. They will spend much of their time in the Divination classroom after this. Their belief is fueled also by Hermione's decision to drop Divination, which they see as fulfillment of Trelawney's prediction in September that "around Easter, one of our number will leave us forever."

Goblet of Fire Colin Creevey excitedly tells Harry that his brother Dennis will be entering Hogwarts this year, and hopes that Dennis will be Sorted into Gryffindor. Harry asks Hermione if brothers and sisters generally end up in the same House. Hermione points out that Padma and Parvati Patil are twins, yet while Parvati ended up in Gryffindor, Padma is a Ravenclaw.

Harry must find a dance partner to attend the Yule Ball with, as he has been told that he will be leading off the dancing. When Cho Chang regretfully turns him down, Harry, in some desperation, sees Parvati and

Lavender entering the common room, and asks Parvati if she will go to the Ball with him. She accepts. Harry, knowing Ron is also dateless, asks Lavender on Ron's behalf, but she has been invited by someone else. Parvati mentions that her sister Padma does not yet have a date, and Harry asks if she'd be willing to go with Ron. Parvati says she will ask. Parvati meets Harry in the Gryffindor common room, and they head down to the Entrance Hall with Ron. (Fred and George in passing ask Harry how he and Ron had managed to hook up with the most beautiful girls in the school.) Harry, as one of the Champions, must wait until all the others have entered the Great Hall, and then the four Champions with their dates parade in and up to head table. After dinner, the four Champions open the dance; Parvati leads Harry out onto the floor. Harry is glad to see, as others join them, that he is not the worst dancer there; Neville, for instance, is repeatedly stepping on Ginny's feet. Professor Moody, dancing past, comments on Harry's mis-matched socks (hand-knitted for him by Dobby), and Parvati comments that she feels that eye of his is creepy. When Harry chooses to sit out the next dance, Parvati leaves, finding a Beauxbatons boy to dance with instead.

After Christmas, Rita Skeeter publishes an article in which she exposes Hagrid's half-Giant ancestry. Hagrid, too embarrassed to leave his hut, stops teaching Care of Magical Creatures and sends his resignation in. For the next week, Care of Magical Creatures is taught by Professor Grubbly-Plank. After the first lesson, concerning the unicorn, Parvati is heard to comment that this was a much better lesson than they usually got from Hagrid, and that she hopes that Professor Grubbly-Plank will be there for a long time. Harry privately agrees with her, but knows it would be disloyal to say anything.

When Professor Dumbledore refuses to accept Hagrid's resignation, he returns to teaching, and apparently decides to show that he can teach the material at least as well as Professor Grubbly-Plank. He continues the lessons on the Unicorn; this time, he has captured a pair of foals, and Parvati and Lavender are entranced by them.

Order of the Phoenix Parvati Patil is talking with Lavender Brown when Harry arrives in the Great Hall at the start of the school year. They greet Harry with a light, airy unconcern that tells Harry that they had been discussing him before he arrived. In the first Defence Against the Dark Arts class of the year, Hermione wonders when they will be actually practicing defensive magic. Professor Umbridge says that she can't see any time when people will be attacked in her classroom. Parvati, following Dean Thomas' repeated question about the possibility of attacks outside the classroom, asks if there is a practical part of the O.W.L. exams. Umbridge over-sweetly explains that the Ministry feels that understanding the principles of defensive magic will be sufficient preparation for the practical exam. On the second day of classes, when Professor Grubbly-Plank asks if anyone can identify the creatures she has in front of her, Hermione puts her hand up, and Draco imitates her. Pansy shrieks with laughter, then screams as the little bundles of twigs on the table jump up. Lavender and Parvati let out little sighs of amazement, which annoy Harry: it is not like Hagrid had not been showing them fantastic creatures all along.

As Harry enters the greenhouse for Herbology on the second day of classes, Luna Lovegood says that she believes Harry. Parvati and Lavender laugh at Luna and her earrings that appear to be orange radishes, but become much more sober when Ernie Macmillan loudly states that he believes Harry's report of the return of Voldemort.

Parvati is one of the students who attends the first meeting of what becomes Dumbledore's Army, in the Hog's Head.

After receiving her evaluation from Umbridge, Professor Trelawney seems distraught. Parvati and Lavender ask her what is wrong, and catch a lot of the resulting diatribe against "the establishment."

One of the memories that Harry uses to sustain himself in Umbridges's class, once Dumbledore's Army starts meeting regularly, is of Parvati producing a Reductor curse that reduced the table under the Sneakoscopes to dust.

With Hagrid's absence on his mission for Dumbledore, Professor Grubbly-Plank has been teaching Care of Magical Creatures for most of the first term. When Hagrid does return, reactions are mixed, with Fred and George being overjoyed, but Parvati and Lavender seem slightly dismayed.

When Hagrid, on his first day back, teaches about Thestrals, Parvati is scared, saying that they are really unlucky, bringing misfortune to those who see them, according to Professor Trelawney. Hagrid counters by saying that they are dead useful, not unlucky at all.

Parvati and Lavender are seen hugging each other and crying quietly as Professor Trelawney is sacked by a cheerfully sarcastic Umbridge.

The following day, Lavender and Parvati suggest that Hermione should now be sorry that she had given up Divination, as the new teacher is Firenze. Hermione says that she was no terribly fond of horses, and Lavender, indignant, says that he isn't a horse, he's a Centaur. Hermione dismisses this, saying he still has four legs. Lavender says also that she and Parvati had gone to see Professor Trelawney and had found that she was distraught, still, and was saying that she would prefer to leave the school.

Lavender tells Ron that Firenze will be teaching in Classroom Eleven, on the ground floor, as he cannot manage the ladders that lead up to the tower. Reaching the classroom, everyone is surprised to see that it has been turned into a replica of a clearing in the Forbidden Forest. When Firenze says that he would prefer that this course be taught in the Forest, Parvati says that they have been there with Hagrid, and are not afraid; Firenze says that it is because he has been banished by his herd. Firenze then begins teaching about the stars, and Parvati repeats things that Professor Trelawney has told them; Firenze dismisses this, saying that Trelawney, as a human, suffers from the limitations of humankind. Parvati is not the only one disgruntled by this dismissal.

Half-Blood Prince With the departure of Professor Umbridge and the reinstatement of Professor Dumbledore as Headmaster, Professor Trelawney is also reinstated. Professor McGonagall tells Parvati and Lavender that Professor Trelawney and Firenze have split up Divination, and that Trelawney will be taking the sixth-year classes. Parvati heads off to Divination class looking slightly disappointed.

Shortly before Christmas, Parvati and Hermione have a conversation about the Christmas party that Professor Slughorn will be hosting. Hermione, who has been annoyed with Ron ever since his relationship with Lavender Brown became apparent, seems to be provoking Ron with her announcement that she has invited Cormac McLaggen as her guest. After Hermione leaves to get ready for the party, Harry contemplates teh depths to which girls will sink to get revenge.

Deathly Hallows When Harry, Ron and Hermione reach Hogwarts, they find Parvati Patil, among others, in hiding in the Room of Requirement. As Neville had been using this room as a way to stay at Hogwarts as the leader of the revived Dumbledore's Army, it is likely that Parvati had similarly found living openly in Hogwarts too dangerous and had retreated to the Room of Requirement so that she could continue the work of Dumbledore's Army in safety. Parvati joins in the Battle of Hogwarts, but we don't directly see what she is doing.

Peeves

Gender: Male
Hair color: Unknown
Eye color: Dark
Related Family: Unknown
Loyalty: Chaos

Overview

Peeves the Poltergeist is not a ghost, but a Spirit of Chaos, who has never been alive, according to the author.[1] He can carry, throw, and drop things, untighten things, and chew gum. When he is visible, he looks like a little man with wicked, dark eyes, a wide mouth, and a pointed hat.

Role in the Books

Philosopher's Stone Peeves is first mentioned by the Fat Friar, the Hufflepuff house ghost, as the first-year students are standing in the anteroom awaiting their Sorting. Evidently the Fat Friar felt that Peeves ought to attend the Entrance Feast. Peeves first appears when the Gryffindor first-years are finding their way to the dormitory. He is throwing walking sticks at them, and in the end dumps a load of them on Neville's head. Percy comments that the only being in the school that Peeves is afraid of is the Bloody Baron, the Slytherin house ghost. It is mentioned elsewhere in the book that Professor Dumbledore has some amount of control over him.

It is mentioned that running into Peeves on the way to class would almost certainly make you late; not only would he steer you wrong, but he would play tricks on you.

When Professor McGonagall, having seen Harry's diving catch before his first flying lesson, is looking for a private place to introduce him to Oliver Wood, the empty classroom she ends up in is occupied by Peeves, who is writing rude words on the chalkboard. Ordered out by McGonagall, Peeves swears as he leaves. When Harry is challenged to a Wizard's Duel by Draco Malfoy, Harry, Ron, Hermione, and Neville end up going to the Trophy Room, where they are almost caught by Filch. As they are retreating from Filch, they run into Peeves, who sounds the alarm. Peeves follows them to a locked door which Hermione opens, and then for no real reason does not tell Filch that the students are behind the door.

Harry suggests that the troll that is reported in the dungeons on Hallowe'en might have been let in by Peeves as a joke.

When Harry and Hermione are headed for Hagrid's hut to take Norbert up to his meeting with Charlie's friends, they are held up by Peeves, who is playing tennis against the wall of the entrance hall. Peeves almost discovers Harry, Ron, and Hermione when they are making their way to the trap door under the invisibility cloak, but Harry sends him away by pretending to be the Bloody Baron.

Chamber of Secrets When Harry is being written up by Argus Filch for dripping mud in the castle, Nearly Headless Nick convinces Peeves to drop a Vanishing Cabinet immediately over Filch's office to distract him. This allows Harry to look around Filch's office unobserved, and spot Filch's Kwikspell letter. Filch is so mortified by this discovery of Harry's that he lets Harry go with a warning.

At Nick's Deathday Party, Peeves teases Moaning Myrtle to the point that she leaves, crying. Shortly after Harry discovers the Petrified body of Justin Finch-Fletchley and the injured ghost of Nearly Headless Nick, Peeves happens across the three of them and raises the alarm. Peeves thereafter taunts Harry whenever he sees him, accusing him musically of having something to do with the attacks, complete with a little dance routine.

Prisoner of Azkaban When Professor Lupin's Defence Against the Dark Arts class is on its way to the Staff Room to practice dealing with a Boggart, they happen upon Peeves who is busily stuffing gum into a keyhole. While Peeves is usually slightly respectful towards teachers, he shows no respect for Lupin, instead singing about "Loony, loopy, Lupin.." Professor Lupin sends him away with a spell that fires the chewing gum up Peeves' nose, thus earning Lupin the respect of the entire class.

When The Fat Lady's portrait is destroyed, it is Peeves who reports to Professor Dumbledore that the damage was done by Sirius Black. Characteristically,

---

1. http://www.jkrowling.com/textonly/en/faq_view.cfm?id=67

Peeves does this in the most sensational way possible. We see him again in passing as Harry and Hermione are making their way back to the Hospital Wing after Sirius' departure; Peeves is then on his way to observe the Dementor's Kiss being administered. As usual, he is going where he can make the most trouble.

Goblet of Fire Peeves' role in this book is relatively minor. When the students arrive, he is floating near the ceiling of the Entrance Hall, dropping water balloons on their heads; he claims that this is not harmful to them because with the downpour outside, they are already soaked, and a little more water shouldn't hurt them. Professor McGonagall shoos him away. At the Entrance Feast, Nearly Headless Nick tells Harry, Ron, and Hermione that there almost wasn't a feast, as Peeves, upset at being uninvited from the feast, had run amok in the kitchen, almost panicking the house elves preparing it.

When Harry is returning to Gryffindor Tower from the prefects' bathroom, having solved the riddle of the Golden Egg, he carefully checks the Marauder's Map to see where Peeves is, before setting out; he notes that Peeves is bouncing around the trophy room. When Harry gets stuck in the trick step and drops the egg, the sound brings Filch to investigate; Filch immediately assumes that Peeves had stolen the egg from one of the Champions.

Order of the Phoenix When Harry receives detention from Professor Umbridge and is given a note to take to Professor McGonagall, he walks straight into Peeves without noticing. As Harry continues to McGonagall's study, Peeves stays alongside, taunting him.

Harry leaves the dormitory to send off a letter by Owl Post. On his way to the Owlery, he is warned by Nearly Headless Nick that Peeves is up ahead by the archway with the bust of Paracelsus, preparing a joke. Harry asks if the joke involves dropping the bust of Paracelsus on someone's head. Nick says that, funnily enough, it does, and that he is off to find the Bloody Baron to see if he can put a stop to it. Harry takes a different route to the Owlery. A short while later, horrible weather keeps the students in at break. Peeves is floating overhead in the room, flicking ink balls at the students when Angelina arrives to tell Harry and Ron that the Quidditch team has been re-formed. Peeves manages to hit Katie Bell with an ink ball, and she starts throwing things at him. As the bell rings, Peeves dumps an entire bottle of ink over Katie's head.

Ron and Hermione, as Prefects, are called upon to supervise the decorating of the castle for Christmas. Ron tells Harry later that stringing tinsel is considerably more difficult when Peeves is on the other end trying to strangle you with it.

Fred and George Weasley have come to the conclusion that their final year of school is not particularly useful to them, and with the departure of Dumbledore, they no longer feel a need to keep their mischievous nature in check. Immediately after Easter break, they create a swamp in one of the corridors. On being caught by Professor Umbridge, they Summon their brooms, and, instructing Peeves to "Give her hell!" depart. Peeves salutes as they leave.

Peeves' activity now doubles; Harry sees him wreaking havoc all over the school, and sees the other teachers not only ignoring, but occasionally helping Peeves in his ongoing activities.

Harry determines that Sirius is being tortured by Voldemort in the Ministry of Magic. In order to confirm that, he decides that he must use Umbridge's fireplace to communicate with Sirius, and of course he will need a distraction. Ron volunteers to tell Umbridge that Peeves is ripping up the Charms corridor. Unfortunately this fails, as Umbridge has just received a report that Peeves is busy inking the eyepieces of all the telescopes in the Astronomy classroom, and promptly arranges for the capture of Ron, Harry, and Harry's lookouts Hermione, Ginny, and Luna Lovegood.

After Dumbledore retrieves Umbridge from captivity with the Centaurs, and after she recovers, she attempts to sneak out of the school. Peeves, however, chases after her, whacking her retreating backside alternately with a bag of chalk and a walking stick.

Half-Blood Prince Peeves is seen guarding a door, saying that he will only allow people who have set their own pants on fire to pass. Harry takes a longer route to bypass the door, but we later see Neville, in the dormitory, changing his charred trousers for new ones.

When Harry, looking for someone to take to Professor Slughorn's Christmas party, decides to invite Luna Lovegood, Peeves overhears and promptly tells the entire school.

Ron is somehow poisoned on his birthday, and ends up in the Hospital Wing. Harry, Hermione, and Hagrid visit him, but leave to make room for his family when Mr. and Mrs. Weasley arrive. Harry and Hermione are discussing a conversation between Dumbledore and Snape that Hagrid had overheard, and in order to retain secrecy, stop when they see Peeves float by.

Harry, wondering about where Draco Malfoy is spending all his time, hits upon the idea of setting Kreacher to tail him. When he halls Kreacher, Dobby arrives also, as they are apparently fighting over Kreacher having insulted Harry in front of Dobby. Peeves, who is always in favour of chaos, also appears, and is egging them on. Harry, to avoid drawing attention to their arrival, shuts Peeves up, whereupon he angrily flies away.

Deathly Hallows It is mentioned that as Harry and Luna Lovegood make their way from the Room of Requirement to Ravenclaw tower under the Invisibility Cloak, Harry is most afraid of running into Peeves. Luckily, they avoid him. Peeves actually enters this book at the Battle at Hogwarts, near the end of the book. Professor McGonagall summons him to aid in the defence of the school. During the battle itself, he soars above the fray, dropping things (notably Snargaluff pods) on Death Eaters.

Once the battle is won, we can hear him in the distance, singing a victory song: "*We did it we bashed them, wee Potter's the one. Now Voldey's gone moldey, so now lets have some fun!"* Hearing Peeves song after the victory, Ron comments that it really gives a feeling for the scope and tragedy of the thing.

Strengths As a poltergeist, Peeves is able to move things and people. He is effectively uncontrollable and invulnerable, as he does not have any physical body.

Weaknesses Peeves is apparently afraid of the Bloody Baron. No explanation for this is given, but this fact proves useful to Percy Weasley when he is trying to lead the Gryffindor first-year students to their dormitory, and later to Harry, when he, Ron, and Hermione are trying to reach the chamber of the Philosopher's Stone.

Relationships with Other Characters Peeves' main joy is to create chaos, and he responds to other characters only in ways that will contribute to the chaos. He will sometimes follow direct orders given to him by senior staff (notably Professor Dumbledore and Professor McGonagall) and those who can injure him (notably Professor Lupin). He has only twice been known to take instructions from students and only once knowingly: in *Harry Potter and the Philosopher's Stone,* Harry Potter instructed Peeves to leave the area and not to return that night, while pretending to be The Bloody Baron from under his invisibility cloak. In *Harry Potter and the Order of the Phoenix,* Fred and George instructed him to give Professor Umbridge a hard time, and Peeves was glad to oblige.

In *Harry Potter and the Philosopher's Stone,* we learn that Peeves is only afraid of the Bloody Baron, the Slytherin House ghost, and that Dumbledore has some control over him. We will see later that while Dumbledore can control him to a certain extent, he remains as disrespectful to Dumbledore as to everyone else—when Dumbledore is interrogating him about the damage to the Fat Lady's portrait in *Harry Potter and the Prisoner of Azkaban,* Peeves answers correctly, but with no apparent respect for Dumbledore. It appears that Professor McGonagall has perhaps the same amount of control, as, in *Harry Potter and the Goblet of Fire,* he accepts her order to stop dropping water balloons on the arriving students.

When Peeves drops the Vanishing Cabinet directly over Argus Filch's office, in *Harry Potter and the Chamber of Secrets,* we learn that Filch wants Peeves out of the castle. We see this again when Filch is taking Harry to Dolores Umbridge's office in *Harry Potter and the Order of the Phoenix;* Filch, with evident satisfaction about the changes that will be taking place with the change of Headmaster, lists the eviction of Peeves as one of the things that he is looking forward to. We actually gather that Filch is perpetually upset with Peeves as early as the first book, though he doesn't say so directly.

Analysis

There has been a great deal of discussion of the nature of Peeves, and whether, as is said at several points, Professor Dumbledore actually can control him. In an interview, the author has compared Peeves to the stubborn plumbing common in older houses; temperamental, and while nobody can make it behave, Dumbledore is like the elder resident who knows how to coerce it into sufficiently good operation for the needs at hand. One theory that seems reasonable is that Peeves is the natural result of having so many adolescent wizards in a single location. Poltergeist activity is often believed to be seen in the vicinity of adolescents, particularly females; it is possible that Peeves is the embodiment of the accumulated polter energy of the several hundred young wizards in Hogwarts.

It is certainly true that Peeves' activity was greater in *Harry Potter and the Order of the Phoenix* when Umbridge was causing turmoil in the earlier part of the year, and considerably greater when Dumbledore was out of the castle in the later part of that book; but there did not seem to be extra activity on Peeves' part in *Harry Potter and the Chamber of Secrets* when Dumbledore was suspended as Headmaster. It is possible that the level of Peeves' activity is directly related to the dissatisfaction level of the students, rather than by the headmaster directly. It is entirely possible that Peeves can only be removed from the school when everyone in it is satisfied with the way things are going, and that is extremely unlikely to ever happen.

Greater Picture

While Peeves is apparently fond of chaos, and will generally act to increase the confusion, he apparently is fond of his home and will tend to act to defend it. Professor McGonagall apparently understands this, as in the preparations for the defence of Hogwarts, she sends Filch to find Peeves, and apparently gives him instructions for the defence. In the battle itself, Peeves is clearly in his element, having a fine time bombing the invading Death Eaters with Snargaluff pods and other dangerous plants. It is interesting to note that, fond as he is of chaos, he does not knowingly act against the defenders of Hogwarts.

Penelope Clearwater

> Gender: Female
> Hair color: Curly
> Eye color: Unknown
> Related Family: Unknown
> Loyalty: Unknown

Overview

Penelope Clearwater is a girl in Ravenclaw house. She is four years ahead of Harry, apparently, in sixth year when we first meet her in Harry's second year; and she is a prefect.

Role in the Books

Chamber of Secrets Penelope Clearwater is first seen, although unidentified, at Christmas; Harry and Ron, disguised as Crabbe and Goyle, are wandering around looking for the Slytherin common room, and ask her for directions. Shortly after she rebuffs them; they run into Percy, who threatens them.

In April, Penelope Clearwater is petrified by the Monster in the Chamber of Secrets; Hermione is attacked at the same time. Percy is deeply shocked by this attack, possibly because he believed that Prefects would be protected by their office.

It is only at the end that it is revealed that Penelope is Percy's girlfriend; this explains the magnitude of the shock Percy feels when she is petrified, as well as explaining what she was doing in the school's lower levels at Christmas, near to where Percy was.

Prisoner of Azkaban   Ron complains of having to use Errol for his correspondence because Percy has been sending messages back and forth to Penelope all summer, fully occupying Hermes' time.

While all the Weasleys are staying at the Leaky Cauldron preparatory to departing for Hogwarts, Percy accuses Ron (who is sharing a room with him) of spilling tea on Penelope's picture; apparently the image has some spots on her nose and is trying to hide behind the frame.

Deathly Hallows   When Harry, Ron, and Hermione are trapped by Snatchers, Hermione claims to be Penelope Clearwater. Unfortunately, this ruse does not last, as her likeness in a newspaper clipping identifies her as one of the people believed traveling with Undesirable Number 1, Harry Potter.

Relationships with Other Characters   Penelope is the girlfriend of Percy Weasley throughout the first three books, although it is unsure if their relationship still stands because she has not directly appeared in any of the books since *Prisoner of Azkaban*. In a family tree of the Weasleys created by the author following the publication of the final book, it is revealed that Percy marries one Audrey, therefore we can assume that their relationship didn't last.

Percy Weasley

Gender: Male
Hair color: Red
Eye color: Unknown
Related Family:
Loyalty:

Arthur Weasley (father), Molly Weasley (mother), Bill Weasley (oldest brother), Charlie Weasley (older brother), Fred Weasley (younger brother), George Weasley (younger brother), Ron Weasley (younger brother), Ginny Weasley (younger sister), first Albus Dumbledore then Ministry for Magic: Bartemius Crouch Sr., Cornelius Fudge, Rufus Scrimgeour, Pius Thicknesse

Overview

Percy Ignatius Weasley is the third son of Arthur and Molly Weasley. He is two years older than the twins Fred and George. He became a Prefect in his fifth year at Hogwarts, which was Harry's first year, and Head Boy in his seventh year. After graduation, he went to work in the Ministry of Magic.

According to the author, Percy's birthday is 22 August.

Role in the Books

Philosopher's Stone   Percy first appears at the train station with the other Weasley family members as they are leaving for Hogwarts. He is a Prefect, and seems inordinately proud of the fact; Fred and George try to take him down a few pegs, without success. Once Harry is Sorted into Gryffindor House, he ends up sitting next to Percy; Percy does tell him a few things about what is going on, but the feel is very much parent-to-child, rather than student-to-student as we would expect to see with any other student. After the arrival feast, he leads the Gryffindor first-years to the dormitory and tells them the password.

We don't see much of Percy for the rest of the book. He appears at Christmas, briefly, and he is seen at the Leaving Feast telling people that Ron is his brother, but otherwise appears very little.

Chamber of Secrets   While Percy is a prefect again this year, he doesn't spend so much effort publicizing the fact; apparently, as he has been a prefect for a full year now, he no longer feels the need to broadcast this fact. He does seem to have gotten a lot stuffier over the summer, though.

Harry spends the latter part of his summer break at The Burrow, the Weasley's home. While he is there, the other Weasley brothers mention that Percy is acting oddly, remaining shut up in his room. Ron mentions that he had wanted to send a message using Percy's owl, Hermes, because the Weasley family owl, Errol, has gotten old and unreliable, but that Percy had refused him, saying that he needed Hermes himself.

At Christmas, the twins have bewitched Percy's Prefect badge so that it reads "Pinhead." Percy is oblivious to this change, but does wonder why everyone is laughing at him.

When Harry and Ron are disguised as Crabbe and Goyle, and are looking for the Slytherin common room, they run into Percy, who threatens them with detention for wandering the corridors. Percy also give Ron and Harry a House points penalty when he sees them leaving Moaning Myrtle's bathroom.

Harry asks Percy for help selecting courses to take for his third year, Percy is very little help; his attempts to advise Harry, though presumably meant well, are so full of pomposity that Harry can't get anything useful out of them. When Hermione and Penelope Clearwater are Petrified by the monster in the Chamber, Percy is apparently very deeply shocked. Fred and George suggest that this is because Penelope was a Prefect as well, and Percy had thought that Prefects were invulnerable.

Ginny, at breakfast one day, seems to be deeply disturbed about something, and is about to tell Harry and Ron something, but Percy arrives and scares her off. He says that he knows what Ginny was going to say, and that it had nothing to do with the Chamber.

In the Chamber, after the defeat of Tom Riddle, Ginny tells Harry that she had meant to tell Harry that she thought she was the one who was opening the Chamber, but Percy's appearing at the table had driven her away—she simply couldn't tell Harry that while Percy was there.

Finally, on the train home, Ginny reveals that the thing Percy had thought she was going to reveal was the fact that he had a girlfriend. She had walked in on them in an empty classroom once, and Percy had made her promise not to tell. The girlfriend was Penelope Clearwater, which explains why her being Petrified was such a shock to Percy.

Prisoner of Azkaban   Harry receives a birthday card from Ron. Included in the card is a clipping from the *Daily Prophet* regarding the Weasleys winning a prize and vacationing in Egypt. In the picture, Harry sees Percy wearing his new Head Boy badge. Ron says that Percy is, if possible, even more pompous and insufferable than before.

Harry spends the last few weeks of his vacation in Diagon Alley, in the Leaky Cauldron. On the last day before school starts, the Weasleys and Hermione show up to do their school shopping. When they meet in the Leaky Cauldron later, Percy is as pompous as a Lord Mayor; the twins are trying to take him down a few pegs by imitating him, but it doesn't seem to work. Later, Percy is upset because he thinks someone has damaged his picture of Penelope Clearwater; in fact, she has developed some spots and is trying to hide under the picture frame. He then starts tearing the room he shares with Ron apart because his Head Boy badge has gone missing; it turns out that Fred and George have nicked it so that they can "improve" it. When Fred shows it to Harry, it says "Bighead Boy." When Harry is unable to visit Hogsmeade, Percy tries to console him by telling him that he won't be missing much. Harry does not find Percy's brand of consolation much use.

After Sirius Black's first attempt to break into Gryffindor Tower, all the students are returned to the Great Hall to sleep while the school is searched. Percy is mentioned as being one of the prefects patrolling the Great Hall to ensure that nobody misbehaves. After this, Harry finds that there is almost always a teacher within earshot of him, and that Percy seems to be following him around. He already understands the reason for this, as he overheard Mr. Weasley and Mrs. Weasley talking about how Black wants to kill Harry. But he still finds the rather heavy-handed guard a bit oppressive.

On the second occasion that Black breaks in, it is Percy that initially orders everyone back to bed, an order that is ineffective.

Finally, at the end of the book, it is revealed that Percy has received decent N.E.W.T. scores, and graduates.

Goblet of Fire   Percy has graduated from Hogwarts and begins working for the Ministry of Magic. He is an assistant to Bartemius Crouch When we first see him, he is closeted in his room at The Burrow, and complaining about the noise everyone is making as he is working on a report about substandard cauldrons being imported from overseas. At dinner, he keeps dropping hints about some top-secret project he's involved with. It appears that he hopes that someone will ask him about it, so that he can make himself seem more important by refusing to divulge information. Percy Apparates to the Quidditch World Cup with Bill and Charlie, joining Harry, Hermione, Mr. Weasley, and the younger Weasleys. While waiting for the start of the match, Percy sees his boss, Mr. Crouch, walk by, and dashes up to offer him a cup of tea. Mr. Crouch accepts, but calls Percy "Weatherby"; the twins in particular make fun of Percy because his boss doesn't even really know his name.

In the riots after the match, Percy assists Bill, Charlie, Mr. Weasley, and the Ministry wizards working to quell the riot.

Afterwards, once everyone has returned home, Mr. Weasley says he's going to have to head in to the office to handle the fall-out from the riots. Percy officiously decides to go in as well, saying something about Mr. Crouch wanting his cauldron bottom-thickness report. It appears that Percy has been moved from cauldron bottoms to general damage control, because he later laments the number of claims for compensation that have been coming in, and that exploding Howlers have scorched his desk.

At the Yule Ball, Percy is present, filling in for Mr. Crouch, who he says is ill and has gone home to rest. He also tells Harry that he has been promoted to be Mr. Crouch's personal assistant, and that Mr. Crouch is sending in instructions by owl. Mr. Crouch is still incapacitated in February, when it comes time for the Second Task, and Percy fills in for him as judge. Percy's pompous pose somewhat cracks when Harry comes to the surface of the lake with Ron; Percy runs out into the water to help Ron ashore.

Shortly after this, Ron, Harry, and Hermione visit Sirius Black, who has returned and is living in a cave outside Hogsmeade. Sirius comments how odd it is that Mr. Crouch is sick, he had never taken time off work before, and asks Ron to ask Percy for any additional information he might have about Mr. Crouch's illness. Percy, when he finally replies around Easter, is quite testy, and provides no additional information.

Some time after Mr. Crouch appears on the grounds at Hogwarts asking for Dumbledore, and then disappears, Percy is reportedly "called in for questioning," presumably by Aurors. There is some question whether Percy should have been able to detect the severity of Mr. Crouch's ailment from the tone of his messages. We don't hear about the end result of that questioning, though when the Third Task occurs, Percy is no longer judging in Mr. Crouch's stead. Cornelius Fudge, the Minister for Magic, is there in his place.

Order of the Phoenix   Percy is promoted again, this time to the post of Assistant to the Minister for Magic. This ends up being a sticking point, as the rest of the Weasley family sees this as Percy being seconded to spy on his family, all of whom are notorious for their support of Albus Dumbledore, and presumably share his belief in Lord Voldemort's return. After a tremendous argument, in which Percy says that Arthur Weasley's lack of ambition is why they never have enough money, Percy packs his things and moves to London.

Percy is the scribe at Harry's trial before the Wizengamot for underage use of magic. After Harry is cleared of all charges, Harry is talking to Mr. Weasley outside the courtroom. Percy walks by and does not notice, or pretends not to notice, his father.

Shortly after the start of the school year, Percy sends Ron a letter, scheduled to arrive late at night rather than with the morning post. In this letter, Percy congratulates Ron on becoming a prefect, and says that Ron may want to cut Harry loose as a friend because Dumbledore's time in power at Hogwarts may be limited, and it might be a good idea to start getting in touch with the new power structure. If he has any questions, he can always ask Dolores Umbridge, a "thoroughly delightful person." He also suggests that Ron should check the *Daily Prophet* the next morning, because he might see someone there he knows. Ron, angrily, tears the letter into bits and throws it into the fire. The next issue of the *Daily Prophet* does have a picture of the Minister for Magic and Dolores Umbridge, on a story about Educational Decree number Twenty-Three, and Percy is in the background.

Mrs. Weasley is upset at Christmas, first because Percy has sent back his Christmas present unopened, and second because he doesn't seem to have cared that his father was injured.

When Fudge comes to the school to witness the arrest or expulsion of Harry for running an illegal student group, Percy tags along as scribe. Percy is present when Dumbledore claims responsibility for the organization known as Dumbledore's Army, and once Fudge has heard Dumbledore's "confession," he sends Percy off to forward a copy to the Prophet.

Although Percy will remain Fudge's assistant, presumably, we don't hear from him again through the course of this book.

Half-Blood Prince New Minister of Magic, Rufus Scrimgeour, wants to recruit Harry Potter as the Ministry of Magic's "Poster Boy." Knowing that Harry is staying with the Weasleys at the Burrow, he *uses* Percy as an excuse to visit them over Christmas. When they arrive, the Minister tells Molly and Arthur that they were in the area, and Percy wanted to stop in and see his family. Claiming he doesn't want to intrude on the family reunion, Scrimgeour asks Harry to show him around the garden. He then attempts to persuade Harry to help the Ministry of Magic improve its public image. When Harry refuses, Scrimgeour departs, taking Percy. Percy has evidently not done too well reconciling with his family; as he departs, apparently he is wearing mashed parsnips, for which Fred, George, and Ginny all claim credit.

Deathly Hallows When Harry and Ron are in the Ministry of Magic, we see Percy briefly. He steps onto an elevator ("lift" in the UK edition), then notices that he is sharing an elevator with his father and quickly leaves.

Percy redeems himself and admits he was wrong during the final battle for Hogwarts. He even jokes and tells Voldemort's puppet Minister of Magic, Pius Thicknesse, he "resigned," immediately after Jinxing him. At Fred's death, he throws himself over the body to shield it from any further harm, then, with Harry's help, drags the body out of the way from danger. He then sprints off to save a group of students who were being chased by a Death Eater. In the epilogue, Harry thinks he hears Percy expounding about broomstick regulations as he walks along Platform Nine and Three Quarters, and is quietly glad that the enveloping steam makes it unnecessary for him to stop and say hello.

Strengths Percy is very committed to be perfect in whatever it is he is doing and is a hard worker for the Ministry of Magic.

Weaknesses Percy appears blind to his work superiors' failings. He is also obsessed with rules to the point where he doesn't care what the reason for any particular rule is . . . he just follows it.

Percival Dumbledore

Gender: Male
Hair color: Unknown
Eye color: Unknown
Related Family: Wife Kendra, children Albus, Aberforth, Ariana
Loyalty:

Overview

Percival Dumbledore was the father of Albus, Aberforth, and Ariana Dumbledore, and husband of Kendra Dumbledore.

Role in the Books

Deathly Hallows We hear very little of Percival. In the eulogy of Albus Dumbledore written by Elphias Doge, we learn that Percival had been sent to Azkaban, and had died there. In Rita Skeeter's tell-all book published following his death, we learn that he was sent to Azkaban for attacking Muggles. It is only near the end of the book that Harry learns from Aberforth that the Muggles he had attacked were the three who had previously attacked and permanently injured his daughter Ariana.

Peter Pettigrew

Gender: Male
Hair color: Colorless, balding
Eye color: small
Related Family: Unknown
Loyalty: Lord Voldemort

Overview

Peter Pettigrew, almost invariably referred to by his nickname "Wormtail," was a friend of James Potter at Hogwarts. Unpopular, meek, and magically mediocre, he ingratiated himself with James, Sirius Black, and Remus Lupin as a means to enhance and protect himself. At Hogwarts, the foursome became known as "The

Marauders." Immediately following Lord Voldemort's disappearance, Sirius Black was convicted (without a trial) and sentenced to life imprisonment in Azkaban for Pettigrew's murder.

ROLE IN THE BOOKS
Philosopher's Stone   While he appears in this book, his identity has not yet been revealed.

Chamber of Secrets   While he appears in this book, his identity has still not been revealed.

Prisoner of Azkaban   At the conclusion, it is revealed that Ron's rat Scabbers is actually Pettigrew in his Animagus form. After Sirius Black and Remus Lupin force him back into his human form, they attempt to execute him for betraying James and Lily Potter to Lord Voldemort. Harry Potter intervenes and spares his life, believing his father would not want his two best friends to become murderers. Professor Dumbledore later tells Harry that his merciful act created a powerful magical pact; Pettigrew now owes Harry a Life Debt that may override his loyalty to Voldemort. As Pettigrew is escorted back to the castle to be turned over to the Dementors, the full moon rises. Lupin transforms into a werewolf; having forgotten to taken his potion, he becomes dangerous. Sirius changes into his dog form to protect the others. During the resulting commotion, Pettigrew escapes and sets out to be reunited with his master, Lord Voldemort.

Goblet of Fire   In the early parts of the book, Pettigrew cares for Lord Voldemort, who has partially regained his body. We see him in the first chapter, in the Riddle house, where he is heard in conversation with Voldemort, and with the muggle Frank Bryce. There, they are discussing the death of one Bertha Jorkins, and plans for the death of one Harry Potter, with the assistance of Voldemort's "one *true* servant" at Hogwarts. Pettigrew is somewhat upset that Voldemort does not seem to see him as a true servant, saying that he has cared for Voldemort in their travels, though Voldemort dismisses this, saying that Pettigrew was only there because he wanted to have some of Voldemort's power.

Shortly after Harry finds Mr. Crouch in the Forbidden Forest, Harry has a dream in which he sees Pettigrew being tortured by Voldemort for having messed something up.

At the conclusion, Harry and Cedric Diggory are transported from the Triwizard Third Task maze to a cemetery where the Riddle family is interred. Pettigrew instantly kills Cedric on Voldemort's command, and bonds Harry to a tombstone. During a ritual to restore Voldemort to full power, Pettigrew drops Riddle Sr.'s bone, some of Harry's blood, and his own severed hand into a large cauldron—Voldemort emerges fully restored. The Dark Lord uses Pettigrew's Dark Mark to summon the remaining Death Eaters and rewards his servant with a magical silvery hand. Harry barely escapes back to Hogwarts with Cedric's body.

Barty Crouch then reveals to Harry that Pettigrew had brought Bertha Jorkins to Voldemort and had assisted in her torture and murder; through Bertha, they had learned of Barty's still being alive and free, and had traveled to Mr. Crouch's home and placed Bartemius Crouch under the Imperius curse; and it had been Barty and Pettigrew who had captured Mad-Eye Moody. Pettigrew had been responsible for Mr. Crouch gaining his freedom and making his way to Hogwarts; he had been suitably punished for his lapse of attention, and Barty had eliminated the problem by killing Bartemius, his father.

Order of the Phoenix   Pettigrew appears in this book, much younger, in the Pensieve, friends of Sirius Black, Remus Lupin, and James Potter. In this episode, James and Sirius are tormenting a young Severus Snape; neither Remus nor Pettigrew takes part in this, though they are present.

Half-Blood Prince   Pettigrew is seen only in the first chapter of the book, where he is acting as Severus Snape's servant, and possibly spying on Snape for Voldemort. Snape orders him to bring drinks for his guests; Pettigrew complains that this is not why he was sent to Snape, but Snape overrules him. When Narcissa Malfoy starts outlining why she has come to see Snape, Snape stops her. He fires a spell through the bookcase and apparently catches Pettigrew listening in; Pettigrew is heard to yelp and retreat.

Deathly Hallows   At the beginning of the book, Voldemort is interrupted by loud moaning from under the room in which they are meeting. Voldemort dispatches Pettigrew to quiet their "guest."

Harry is captured by Snatchers, and is brought to Malfoy Manor, along with Ron, Hermione, Dean Thomas, and Griphook. All except Hermione are taken to a downstairs room which is acting as a prison by Pettigrew. There, they find Voldemort's "guest," Mr. Ollivander, and Luna Lovegood. When Dobby appears, Harry has him take Dean, Luna, and Ollivander to safety. Pettigrew is sent to investigate the noise of their departure. Finding nobody in the prison except Harry and Ron, Pettigrew attempts to stop Harry overpowering him, but hesitates in killing him because of his life debt. In retaliation for this hesitation, his silver hand chokes him to death.

Strengths   Pettigrew was given a silver hand by Lord Voldemort, and this hand may have certain special abilities, apart from its apparent superhuman strength.

He is also an unregistered Animagus, taking the form of a rat.

Weaknesses   Peter Pettigrew's loyalty is first and foremost to himself. He is loyal to others only when it serves his own interests and purpose. His friendship to James Potter, Remus Lupin, and Sirius Black was mainly because he was weak, and they protected him; he betrayed them when he decided that his best course lay with

Voldemort. In Book 3, he vainly attempts to renew his friendship with Sirius and Lupin when his life is on the line. His appeal to Harry only partially works; although Harry prevents Black and Lupin from executing him, Harry intends to turn Pettigrew over to the Dementors, making death a more appealing option.

ANALYSIS

In *Harry Potter and the Philosopher's Stone*, Rubeus Hagrid says "There isn't a one of them (wizards) that turned out bad that wasn't from Slytherin." Although his statement is somewhat hyperbolic, it seems there is a counter-example. Peter Pettigrew was a friend of James Potter, who was in Gryffindor House; it can be assumed that Sirius Black and Remus Lupin were also Gryffindors, and thus so was Peter, as the books suggest that friendships rarely cross House boundaries. When Hagrid spoke, it was unknown that Peter had turned to the dark side—it appeared he had died at the hands—or wand—of Sirius Black while he was attempting to somehow capture Black. At the time, Sirius was believed to have been Voldemort's second-in-command and had betrayed the Potters. However, the revelation of this "fact," as it is made in the Three Broomsticks pub in *Harry Potter and the Prisoner of Azkaban* comes as a surprise to Hagrid. So as far as he was aware at the time he made his blanket statement, Hagrid was correct; the counter-examples mentioned were not known to him at the time.

QUESTIONS

1. Will Pettigrew be an asset to Harry in *Harry Potter and the Deathly Hallows*?
2. Will Pettigrew be true to his debt?
3. As Gryffindor house favours courage and bravery above all other attributes, why was Pettigrew chosen for this house? At no point in the series does he demonstrate these features, but rather the opposite, so why did the Sorting Hat place him in Gryffindor?

GREATER PICTURE

Many questions have been raised about Peter Pettigrew's actions. Although Voldemort never trusted him, Pettigrew was the first to return to him, and Voldemort has since chosen him to execute his more sensitive missions. So, the question should be asked, in the many pivotal events of the series, what was Pettigrew doing?

Let us first look at the events on the day the Harry's parents were murdered. Voldemort's intent was to kill Harry, at which he failed; but the curse he used, the Killing curse, is not destructive to chattels, only killing people, as we can easily see in the Riddle mansion which remained totally undamaged despite three people being killed by the same curse within it. And yet, when Sirius Black talks about that day, he states that he saw "the destroyed house ... and their bodies"—though possibly not Voldemort's body. And why would the house be destroyed? Would Voldemort have travelled to Godric's Hollow alone? Or would he have brought a lieutenant along? Who better than Pettigrew, who had delivered the secret to Voldemort? And what would Pettigrew have done if his master failed? After the third curse, there is a silence ... a silence so long that finally, Pettigrew enters the house to see if something has gone wrong. There, he finds his master apparently dead ... and, quite possibly, goes briefly mad, destroying everything that he can lay his wand on, but avoiding Harry, who somehow managed to kill Voldemort. He then departs, carrying Voldemort's body (possibly) and wand (probably), and hides them; he then confronts Sirius, and using his own wand, blows up the street and makes good his escape, leaving Sirius to take the blame. (Later information is inconclusive on this subject; the damage is not as extensive as we are led to believe, and we don't know whether there was a body to remove or not. It is reasonably certain that Peter did recover the wand, at the least, as he had it when he was nursing the returned Voldemort.)

Twelve years pass, during which Pettigrew hides himself within a Wizarding family, the Weasleys, so that he can remain in touch with the Wizarding World's news. The end of this time is documented in *Harry Potter and the Prisoner of Azkaban*.

Between *Harry Potter and the Prisoner of Azkaban* and the opening of *Harry Potter and the Goblet of Fire*, Pettigrew locates and rejoins Voldemort, retrieving Voldemort's wand first, and in the process fetches Bertha Jorkins to Voldemort and assists in her murder; carries Voldemort to the house of Barty Crouch Jr. and assists in both recruiting him and placing Bartemius Crouch Sr. under the Imperius curse; and tends to Voldemort's immediate physical needs. We know what he is doing during the course of *Harry Potter and the Goblet of Fire*; Barty Crouch Jr. tells us that he is in Bartemius Crouch Sr.'s house, with Voldemort and Bartemius, and Voldemort will not let him leave, as he is still in need of too much care. (Of course, once Bartemius escapes, Voldemort has to return to Little Hangleton.) But we do not see much of him during *Harry Potter and the Order of the Phoenix*. In particular, at the Battle in the Ministry, he is conspicuous by his absence. Many of the escaped Death Eaters are there, as is Voldemort himself; where is Pettigrew? Is he perhaps someplace in the ministry that can be reached by a rat? And while he is at the house in Spinner's End at the beginning of *Harry Potter and the Half-Blood Prince*, where is he through the rest of that book? He can't follow Snape to Hogwarts; what tasks will he be doing for Voldemort?

We also have one outstanding issue: wands. While he is tending to Voldemort, Pettigrew seems to use Voldemort's wand; but once Voldemort has returned fully, he needs his own wand. What wand can Pettigrew use? He can't go and buy one; if he is not assumed dead, he is certainly a "person of interest" and would be arrested on sight. His own original wand has been returned to his family, presumably, along with his finger; as he can't allow his being alive to be known there either, that wand is also not available. What use to Voldemort is a wizard without a wand? And could this have something to do with the disappearance of Ollivander?

As it turns out, we do not learn what, if any, mission Pettigrew has during *Harry Potter and the Order of the Phoenix* or *Harry Potter and the Half-Blood Prince*; he seems to be carrying out menial duties for Voldemort in *Harry Potter and the Deathly Hallows*. It is true that

Ollivander is required to make him a new wand, but that is more of a side issue; it turns out that the reason Voldemort captured Ollivander was for information about the reason Harry's and Voldemort's wands behaved as they did in the graveyard.

Petunia Dursley

Gender: Female
Hair color: Blonde
Eye color: Unknown
Related Family: Vernon (husband), Dudley (son), Lily Potter (sister), Harry Potter (nephew)
Loyalty: Dursley family, Muggles

Overview

Petunia Dursley, née Evans, is Harry Potter's aunt (she is his mother's sister). She and her husband Vernon Dursley reluctantly took Harry in as a baby, while they had their own son, Dudley. Petunia dislikes Harry's magical abilities and wishes to "stamp it out of him." Relations between her and Harry have never been good, even though she is providing Harry with protection from Lord Voldemort as long as he lives with the Dursleys, and up until his seventeenth birthday.

Role in the Books

Philosopher's Stone Vernon Dursley kisses his wife, Petunia, goodbye as he leaves for work. Several unnerving things happen during the day, but while he is tempted to call Petunia, he does not, instead waiting until he is back home before asking casually about her sister's family, the Potters, and what they had named their son. Petunia says the son was named Harry, a nasty, lower-class sort of name.

Discussing the Dursley family, Minerva McGonagall questions Albus Dumbledore's decision to place the infant Harry with the Dursleys, saying that they are "the worst kind of Muggles." She reports that she had seen their child hitting Petunia, demanding candy. Dumbledore says he is aware that Harry would have a home in any Wizarding household, but that he has his reasons for putting Harry there.

We are told that it is Petunia Dursley who finds the infant Harry on the Dursley doorstep. Apparently, it is also Petunia who handles most of the "odd things" happening around Harry: when his hair will not remain cut the way she wants it, she cuts it short, only to have it grow back overnight; she is trying to force a hideous sweater over Harry's head when it mysteriously shrinks to the point that it will not even fit over his hand; and she receives the school reports about odd things happening there, such as Harry climbing on the roof.

In the events surrounding Dudley's birthday and the subsequent appearance of Harry's first Hogwarts letter, Vernon is the center of the action, while Petunia largely backs Vernon up. While Petunia does receive the phone call from Mrs. Figg saying that she won't be able to look after Harry, and then comforts Dudley in his dismay at having to have Harry along, she thereafter remains largely in the background as Vernon drives them to the zoo, buys treats for Dudley, retrieves Dudley from the snake enclosure, and punishes Harry for this odd event by locking him back in his cupboard under the stairs. And when Harry's Hogwarts letter arrives, it is Vernon who takes it from him and opens it. While Vernon and Petunia do discuss what to do about this letter, it is Vernon who decides that they will simply not answer it. When more letters arrive, Vernon intercepts and destroys them. It is Vernon who, in the end, decides that they must leave the house to escape the letters. Dudley asks Petunia at this point if "Daddy has gone mad"; Petunia does not seem to be able to answer.

When the family finally settles in the hut on the island, Petunia still has not had much role in things. When Hagrid arrives, he tells Harry that his mother, Lily, Petunia's sister, was an extremely good witch. Petunia, apparently pushed beyond her endurance, bursts out that Lily was a freak, coming home with pockets full of frog spawn, and that she was doted on by her parents. Only Petunia saw what she really was. Petunia's malevolence is only stopped when she mentions that Harry's parents had gotten themselves blown up. Harry interjects that Petunia had told him that his parents had been killed in a car crash, which prompts Hagrid to respond angrily that no car crash could have done anything to James and Lily Potter. The conversation then is carried by Vernon and Hagrid until Vernon insults Dumbledore. Enraged, Hagrid gives Dudley a pig's tail, and the Dursleys retreat in confusion, leaving Harry and Hagrid the front room.

When Vernon takes Harry to Kings Cross Station to board the train a month later, Dudley and Petunia are in the car; Vernon has only consented to take Harry to London because they need to go to a specialist to get Dudley's tail removed before school starts. During the trip, she says nothing; but we see her laughing at Harry as the car drives away, leaving Harry to hunt for Platform Nine and Three Quarters.

Petunia is at King's Cross Station when Harry returns from school, but says nothing, simply watching as Vernon verbally collects Harry and directs him towards the exit.

Chamber of Secrets Harry is not surprised when nobody in the house remembers that it is his birthday. Vernon has important visitors arriving that night, and Petunia and Dudley are called upon to rehearse their lines. Harry is hard-put to avoid laughing at the excesses that they are planning, but Petunia is overcome instead by Dudley's brilliance. Later, when Harry is in the garden, Dudley taunts him about having received no mail from his "weird friends at that school." Harry, angered, says he was thinking about how to set the hedge on fire, and starts mumbling nonsense words. Panicking, Dudley calls for his mother; Petunia swings at Harry's head with a soapy frying pan, but misses. As punishment for daring to use magic, Petunia gives Harry a long sequence of tasks to help her cleaning up the house for Vernon's visitors, then sends him up to his room after a very sketchy dinner.

When Harry is locked into his room, Petunia does periodically bring him meals which she pushes through a cat-flap in his door. Neither Harry nor Hedwig finds cold vegetable soup particularly appealing, but that being all they have, they make do.

Petunia again is present when Harry returns from school, but says nothing, leaving the conversation to Vernon.

Prisoner of Azkaban Petunia and Vernon are listening to the new kitchen TV when the newscaster talks about a murderer who has escaped from prison, one Sirius Black. Apparently at the mention of a reward for information, Petunia looks out the kitchen window, as if expecting an escaped convict to be hiding in their back yard.

For the rest of Harry's time there, however, she is quite overshadowed by Vernon's sister, Marge, who visits for a week starting on Harry's birthday.

Goblet of Fire Dudley's school nurse has seen what Petunia, so quick to see a fingerprint on her walls or what the neighbours are doing, could not see: that Dudley is not just fat, but massively obese. Petunia has, under prompting, put him on a diet, and so he would not feel alone, has put the rest of the family on a diet as well.

Mr. Weasley has managed to get tickets to the Quidditch World Cup and agrees to pick Harry up and take him to The Burrow. While they are waiting for the Weasley family to arrive, Petunia is compulsively straightening cushions in the sitting room. Mr. Weasley arrives through the boarded up fireplace, rather explosively, with Ron, Fred and George, and Petunia tries to hide behind Vernon. When Dudley eats one of the Twins' accidentally-on-purpose dropped Ton-Tongue Toffees, it makes his tongue become several feet long; we see Petunia struggling with it, trying to get it out of his mouth. During the ensuing mayhem, Harry departs at Mr. Weasley's orders; it seems that Petunia is largely having hysterics at this point.

Petunia is not present at Kings' Cross Station when Harry returns from school.

Order of the Phoenix Petunia opens the door to a clearly ill Dudley (he vomits all over the mat) being supported by Harry. Once inside, Dudley accuses Harry of using magic on him. Harry replies that while he had his wand out and had threatened Dudley with it, he had not used it against Dudley. After much arguing back and forth, complete with arrivals of owls threatening Harry with imprisonment and expulsion from Hogwarts, Uncle Vernon demands to know what these Dementors are that Harry was supposedly protecting Dudley from. Petunia tells him that they are the guards from the Wizard prison, Azkaban. Suddenly realizing what she has said, she claps her hand over her mouth, then explains that she had heard "that awful boy" talking about them with her sister, Lily. This proves too much for Vernon, who now orders Harry out of the house. Another owl arrives, this one with a Howler addressed to Petunia. Harry, knowing what Howlers will do if left alone, recommends that she open it; she does, and an awful voice says, "Remember my last, Petunia!" before the letter dissolves into flames.

Still in shock, Petunia now says that Harry will have to stay with them. Over Vernon's protests, and with her voice strengthening as her self-assurance returns, she says that throwing Harry out will look very bad to the neighbours. Vernon, giving in, sends Harry to his room.

Harry remains in his room until Vernon receives notification that he may be the winner of the Best-Kept suburban Lawn Competition. The Dursleys go off to the competition venue, and Harry departs Privet Drive for Number Twelve, Grimmauld Place with the Advance Guard.

In Harry's conversation with Dumbledore after the battle at the Ministry, we learn that the Howler which had changed Petunia's mind so that she overruled Vernon about throwing Harry out was, in fact, sent by Dumbledore. When Harry returns to London on the Hogwarts Express, the Dursleys are there waiting for him. A group of wizards, led by Alastor Moody, confronts them, saying that they expect to hear regularly from Harry, and that they expect Harry to be treated well. While most of the conversation is directed at Vernon, Harry does notice that Petunia seems most distressed, not by the appearance of this flock of wizards, but rather by Tonks' hair, which is its usual shocking pink color.

Half-Blood Prince Dumbledore tells Harry that he will be arriving to take Harry to The Burrow only a fortnight after school ends. Harry only half believes him, and has not told the Dursleys, so Dumbledore's arrival at 11 P.M. comes as a shock to them. At his arrival, Petunia comes out of the kitchen where she has been giving all the surfaces their nightly wipedown, wearing a housedress and rubber gloves. Dumbledore propels a couch into the three Dursleys, forcing them to sit down, then suggesting drinks, summons several glasses of mead, which he sends across the room to the Dursleys. Vernon, Petunia, and Dudley ignore the glasses of mead, which become more insistent as the conversation goes on. Harry notes that one of the glasses is bouncing repeatedly off Vernon's head, spilling its contents in its insistence to be noticed; another must be acting similarly with Petunia. Dumbledore tells Vernon and Petunia that he had expected that they would treat Harry as one of their own children, and was very disappointed that they had not; however, he was pleased that Harry had not been as badly treated as the child sitting between them. Both Petunia and Vernon look around, appearing to think that Dumbledore was referring to someone other than Dudley. When Dumbledore summons Kreacher in an attempt to determine whether the house at Grimmauld Place has passed to Harry, as Sirius had intended, Harry sees Petunia's look of revulsion, and thinks that nothing as dirty as Kreacher had likely ever been in her house.

Petunia says very little during this visit of Dumbledore's, and Harry does not return to Privet Drive in this book.

Deathly Hallows We see Petunia only briefly at the beginning of this book; as she and Vernon are preparing to leave for a place of safety, Dudley says that he does not believe that Harry is a waste of space. Petunia seems aware that this is effusive compliments from Dudley, but her only response is a nod of the head to Harry as she leaves the house. In Severus Snape's memories, we see the young Petunia and her sister Lily, before Lily goes to Hogwarts. We see Petunia's fear when Lily demonstrates that she can make a flower open and close, and we see Petunia's distrust of the young Snape. We also see that Petunia eavesdrops on Lily and Severus talking about the Wizarding world, particularly about the Dementors and Azkaban Prison. On the platform where Lily is about to board the Hogwarts Express, we also learn that Petunia had sent a letter to Hogwarts asking to be accepted into the school, and had received a refusal.

Strengths It's shown that Petunia is a very neat person and likes everything else neat and tidy, also. Although she is not fully aware of it, Petunia projects Lily's protection of Harry due to their blood relation.

Weaknesses Petunia's desire that things be neat and clean borders on obsession. It appears that before she goes to bed at night she has to scrub down the kitchen completely; in *Harry Potter and the Half-Blood Prince* we see her with her nightdress and housecoat, wearing rubber gloves and clearly in the middle of her bedtime wipe-down of all the kitchen surfaces. In *Harry Potter and the Chamber of Secrets*, we learn also that she expects to take all day cleaning up the house for the Masons, dinner guests and potential clients of Vernon Dursley.

Relationships with Other Characters She is Lily Potter's older sister, and thinks that her sister is a "freak." She has the same opinion of her nephew, Harry Potter. She married Vernon Dursley, and had a son, Dudley Dursley.

We are told that she spends large parts of each day snooping on the neighbours, and of course we see that she models her behaviour based on what the neighbours would think. Any relationships with other characters, including "batty old Mrs. Figg," are going to be coloured by a need to keep up appearances. Relationships with Wizards, such as Albus Dumbledore, will be primarily tinged with fear; she fears and distrusts the magic that, by her lights, took her sister away from her.

Petunia's relationships with her family are somewhat varied, though apparently uniformly shallow. Toward Harry, we see that Petunia makes no accommodation to Harry's needs, rather seeing him as unpaid domestic help; in the first three books, we see her setting him tasks like making breakfast, weeding the gardens, scrubbing pans, and similar work. We have seen that Vernon often restricts Harry to his room for days at a time; Petunia assists in this by preparing food, barely enough to sustain Harry's life, and pushing it through a cat-flap installed in Harry's bedroom door, at intervals. Petunia never shows Harry the slightest bit of affection. As Harry matures and becomes more powerful as a wizard, Petunia's feelings towards him shift, becoming less aloof and more fearful. Petunia acts completely differently towards her son, Dudley, showering him with gifts and making nearly infinite allowances for his desires. It is hard to know how much of this is from affection, and how much is from fear; it seems Dudley is quite capable of hitting Petunia and does so when provoked.

It is hard to determine Petunia's actual feelings, if any, towards her husband, Vernon. It does seem that she discourages intimacy. One gets the feeling almost that Petunia has gotten married because that is what people do, rather than for any particular affection for the man she is married to.

ANALYSIS

Petunia seems to be inordinately interested in what other people are doing, and thus, is extremely concerned with what other people think of her. Having accepted Harry into her house, reluctantly, we see that her rationale for keeping him there as he grows is that people would wonder what had gone wrong were he suddenly to disappear. Nearly everything that Petunia does is done to look good in the eyes of the neighbours, with the possible exceptions of her private treatment of Harry and her treatment of Dudley. We see this in particular at the start of *Harry Potter and the Order of the Phoenix*, where Harry is almost thrown out of the house before Petunia rationalizes the instructions she has received in terms of what the neighbours would think, and again at the end of that same book where she seems dismayed in particular by the unconventionality of Tonks' hair colour.

Petunia's stated reason for the Dursleys' treatment of Harry is to "stamp that (magic) stuff out of him," to make him normal so that he can take his place in "normal" society. However, her parsimonious treatment of Harry, giving him Dudley's cast-off and horribly oversized clothes, and her attempts to cut his hair, rather undercut his chances at ever being accepted into normal society. Petunia obviously feels that providing a roof for Harry should be enough, and that he should be grateful for that, and for any scraps the family deigns to send his way.

One thing which should be mentioned is the Howler delivered to Petunia at the beginning of *Harry Potter and the Order of the Phoenix*. While we do eventually learn that this came from Dumbledore, we never hear any more about the circumstances. The fact that Dumbledore says "Remember my last [letter], Petunia," has been seen as proof that there has been ongoing correspondence between them, as if there had only been the one letter that had been left with Harry, the Howler would instead have said something like "Remember my letter." It is confirmed that Dumbledore had written to Petunia earlier—we find out in *Harry Potter and the Deathly Hallows* that Dumbledore had rejected her application to attend Hogwarts—but we are uncertain whether that and the letter left with Harry are the only two times Dumbledore has written to her, or whether there has been a trickle of correspondence over the years. Given the shock with which the Dursleys received Harry's first Hogwarts letter, one must suspect that there was little, if any, correspondence over the years, so the "last" to which Dumbledore referred in the Howler was most likely the letter that he had left with the infant Harry some fourteen years earlier.

QUESTIONS

1. How much does Petunia actually know about the wizarding world?

GREATER PICTURE

One of the things that most clearly defines Petunia, as we see in *Harry Potter and the Philosopher's Stone*, is her fear and distrust of things magical, which has been a large part of the reason Harry has been kept ignorant of his ancestry. While she is joined in this distrust by her husband Vernon, one must wonder, having completed the series, how much of this on Petunia's part is jealousy. Yes, Lily's magical ability had frightened her, and she had serious doubts about young Severus, who was evidently of a lower social class. Yet she had, as it turns out, written to Dumbledore pleading for admission to Hogwarts and been refused. It is likely that a large part of her jealousy was sour grapes: "the magical world has refused me, so I will refuse it." Harry, as part of the magical world, was similarly refused any part of Petunia's concern; it was likely only by telling herself that she could stamp the magic out of Harry, that she could countenance having him in her house at all.

Phineas Nigellus Black

Gender: Male
Hair color: Black
Eye color: Unknown
Related Family: Black family
Loyalty: Black family

OVERVIEW

Phineas Nigellus Black (1847–1926) is an ancestor of Sirius Black and a past headmaster of Hogwarts. In the series, he appears as a portrait, primarily in the Headmaster's office.

ROLE IN THE BOOKS

Order of the Phoenix Although we have heard him snicker a few times before that, we first actually meet Phineas Nigellus in Albus Dumbledore's office; he occupies one of the portraits on the wall. He seems quite snippish and surly, only doing something when forced to by the threats from the occupants of the other portraits. We have gathered by this time that the portraits of the past Headmasters either sleep, or pretend sleep, when they are not actively speaking with the Headmaster. In this instance, Dumbledore wants Phineas to carry a message to Sirius Black at Grimmauld Place. Phineas at first feigns sleep, then, when he cannot pretend any longer, he expresses reluctance. Many of the other portraits in Dumbledore's office threaten him, and he departs, returning shortly to say that Sirius would be delighted to have visitors.

When he appears in a blank canvas in Harry's room at Number 12 Grimmauld Place, the headquarters of the Order of the Phoenix, we suddenly realize who Harry has heard snickering in that canvas. At that time, he is carrying a message from Albus Dumbledore to Harry. The message is "Stay there," and Harry is nettled to find that is the full message. Phineas snidely tries to take him to task for demanding more information.

At one point over Christmas, Harry awakens in the middle of the night, and believes that he sees a shadowy figure standing in Phineas' portrait frame, watching him.

We later see Phineas Nigellus again in Dumbledore's office. He is dismissive of Dumbledore, who he feels is not hard enough on the students.

He carries a few messages between Hogwarts and Grimmauld Place, but one gets the impression that Dumbledore does not completely trust him. Important messages are typically carried by other couriers.

In the end, after he hears that Sirius Black has died, he claims to not believe it, and goes off to Grimmauld Place to search for any sign of his descendant.

Half-Blood Prince We see Phineas Nigellus on Dumbledore's wall a few times, where he makes biting comments. He does not seem to have any other role, however.

Deathly Hallows While Harry, Ron, and Hermione are planning their visit to the Ministry, Hermione suddenly remembers the portrait of Phineas Nigellus, and that the matching portrait hangs in the Headmaster's office at Hogwarts, where presumably now it serves Severus Snape. She retrieves it from the bedroom and stuffs it into her beaded bag where it can't spy on their activities.

As they travel through the countryside, the Trio overhear another fugitive group doing the same. Listening in on their conversation, the Trio learn that some Hogwarts students, including Neville, Ginny, and Luna, had attempted to break into the Headmaster's office and steal the Sword of Gryffindor, and that the had been "cruelly punished." Knowing that Harry and Ron will be worried about Ginny, Hermione fetches the portrait of Phineas Nigellus from her beaded bag and blindfolds him so he cannot report where the Trio are. Harry asks him what had happened to the students, and Phineas casually reports that they had been sent to the Forbidden Forest to work with the half-breed oaf, Hagrid. Hermione asks if the Sword had been removed from its case, perhaps for cleaning. Phineas scornfully replies that it is Goblin-made; goblin arms will accept into themselves anything that will make them stronger, and reject anything else. Harry asks Phineas if he can bring to portrait of Dumbledore to speak with them, and Phineas, again scornfully, tells Harry that a portrait from the Headmaster's office can visit other portraits in the school, and other portraits of himself, but he cannot visit other people's portraits outside the school. Hermione now asks when the sword had last been out of its case, and Phineas, sounding bored, says that Dumbledore had taken it out of the case to destroy a ring. Harry guesses that this means the Sword had been used to destroy the ring Horcrux, and that it was able to do so because it had absorbed Basilisk venom, one of the few things that can destroy a Horcrux, in the Chamber of Secrets.

Phineas returns a few times, at Hermione's request, despite periodically claiming to be insulted and insisting that he will never return. It is through Phineas that Harry learns of an ongoing low-level revolt at Hogwarts. The Decree against student organizations has apparently been reinstated, and Dumbledore's Army has been revived, with Neville, Luna, and Ginny at its head.

In Snape's memories, we see that Phineas Nigellus had reported to Snape that Harry and Hermione had just arrived at the Forest of Dean. Snape, taking the real Sword of Gryffindor from behind the portrait of Dumbledore where it had been hidden (a fake, Wizard-made but easily detected as such by Goblin eyes, had earlier been sent to Gringotts to protect it), had then gone to the Forest of Dean to leave the Sword where Harry could find it. Looking back at the chapter in question, we find that Hermione had had the beaded bag open and was rummaging around in it when she had told Harry where they were. Phineas would have been able to hear what she said, if he was in that portrait at the time, as he evidently was.

Finally, he is seen amidst the general jubilation in the Headmaster's office after the final battle, saying "Let it be noted that Slytherin House played its part!"

Strengths   Being a portrait, Phineas is largely invulnerable to injury; he can flit to other canvases if the one he is currently in is about to be damaged. Additionally, he can sense what is happening around his various canvases; we can hear him snickering in Harry's room at Grimmauld Place, despite the fact that he is probably at the time mostly within his canvas in the Headmaster's office

Relationships with Other Characters   Phineas Nigellus, in life, apparently shared the Black bias towards purebloods, and seems to hold those who spring from, or sympathize with, Muggles in disdain. De displays reluctance to comply with Dumbledore's requests, he seems quite unhappy with his one remaining descendant's views regarding Muggles, and while he does speak with Ron, Harry, and Hermione, he always exhibits distaste at doing so.

Despite his dislike of Sirius' views regarding Muggles, Phineas Nigellus is dismayed to learn of his death, and apparently must visit the house at Grimmauld Place to confirm it for himself.

Phineas Nigellus repeatedly chides Dumbledore for what he sees as Dumbledore's lenient attitude towards the students. Dumbledore later privately mentions that Phineas was the single most hated headmaster in recent Hogwarts history.

Piers Polkiss

Gender: Male
Hair color: Unknown
Eye color: Unknown
Related Family: Unknown
Loyalty: Dudley Dursley

OVERVIEW

Piers Polkiss is a friend of Dudley Dursley.

ROLE IN THE BOOKS

Philosopher's Stone   Piers accompanies the Dursleys on a trip to the zoo. He and Dudley are frightened when Harry unintentionally releases a large snake; it is Piers who later announces to the Dursleys that he thought he had seen Harry talking to the snake.

Order of the Phoenix   Piers compliments Dudley on the way he had hit someone earlier, as Dudley says good night to his gang after an evening of mayhem. Dudley had told the Dursleys that he was having tea with Piers and the Polkiss family.

Relationships with Other Characters   Piers is Dudley's best friend, and a member of his gang.

Pigwidgeon

Gender: Male
Hair color: Unknown
Eye color: Unknown
Related Family: None
Loyalty: Ron Weasley, Ginny Weasley

OVERVIEW

Pigwidgeon, or Pig, a Scops owl, was a gift from Sirius Black to Ron. Ron's sister, Ginny, named the owl. The owl refused to answer to anything else after that.

ROLE IN THE BOOKS

Prisoner of Azkaban   Ron obtains Pig—sent to him by Sirius because Sirius felt responsible for causing Ron to lose his rat Scabbers. At the end of the last chapter, when Harry goes on the Hogwarts Express, Hermione notices a little owl, Harry then catches it and takes it inside. It carries a note for Harry: this note states that Sirius has hidden far away, that he is thinking about letting himself be seen by a Muggle, so that security at school can be lowered, and that he was the one who had sent Harry the Firebolt. Sirius, it turns out, had actually gotten Crookshanks to deliver the order to the post office. Hermione says that she had known it was him. Also, Sirius states, that now that Ron has no pet, he may keep the owl if he wishes. Ron holds the owl under Crookshanks' nose, and Crookshanks purrs (apparently stating it is just a normal animal, not like Ron's previous pet, Scabbers, the animagus), so Ron keeps the owl.

Goblet of Fire Ron sends Pigwidgeon to Harry with the information that whether or not the Dursleys will allow him to go to the Quidditch World Cup, the Weasleys will be coming to get him; and saying that Harry should let Ron know whether it will be a visit or a rescue by return owl. Harry is bemused; he hasn't yet learned Pigwidgeon's name, and doesn't understand why Ron refers to him in his note as "Pig."

Once Harry has arrived at The Burrow, he learns the owl's name. This year, there is a requirement that all students have formal robes; Harry's are elegant, but Ron's are musty, have lace around the collar and sleeves, and look to date back to the previous century. Pigwidgeon chooses this moment to choke on an overlarge owl treat, and Ron, hurrying to help him, laments about how everything he owns is crud.

Near Christmas, Ron sends Pigwideon off with a message for Sirius Black. Pigwidgeon apparently takes about three weeks to deliver the message and return, although by this time Sirius is reportedly somewhere in England.

Order of the Phoenix Pigwidgeon flies madly around Harry, Ron and Hermione as they greet one another excitedly on Harry's arrival at Number 12, Grimmauld Place. He continues to fly around, twittering madly, as Harry yells at Ron and Hermione, but retreats to the top of the wardrobe, joining Hedwig, when Fred and George Apparate into the room. After the meeting that evening, Hedwig and Pigwidgeon are clattering around on top of the wardrobe. Ron throws some Owl Treats up there for them, explaining that Dumbledore doesn't want them out hunting too often, it would raise questions.

On the last day before the start of classes, Harry climbs on a chair to clean all the owl droppings off the top of the wardrobe. Finishing, he tosses the accumulated owl droppings into a wastebasket, which swallows them and belches loudly. During the conversation that follows, the wastebasket occasionally makes soft gagging noises as it coughs up the owl droppings.

Pigwidgeon is almost certainly on the luggage cart which Mad-Eye Moody brings to the platform, but his presence is not mentioned. The first time we see him is when Ron returns to Harry's compartment and puts Pigwidgeon's cage beside Hedwig's. As they near Hogsmeade station, Ron and Hermione, being prefects, must supervise the other students' preparations, so Pigwidgeon is left for Harry to carry. Luna volunteers to carry Pigwidgeon for him. She is separated from Harry in the crush of students, but catches up to him and Ron as they prepare to enter the horseless carriages, much to Ron's relief.

The next time Pigwidgeon is mentioned is as Ron is returning to school after the Christmas holidays. They are traveling on the Knight Bus, which is full of chairs rather than four-poster beds, it being daytime. As the Knight Bus travels with its normal great Bang!, Ron's chair is knocked over and Pigwidgeon, in his lap, bursts out of his cage and flies to the front of the bus, to rest on Hermione's shoulder.

Hedwig and Pigwidgeon are then not seen again until the trip back to London on the Hogwarts Express. It is noted that Hedwig and Pigwidgeon are disturbed by Ron's outburst when he learns that Ginny is going out with Dean.

Deathly Hallows When Harry turns 17 and he is no longer bound by the restriction against underage sorcery, he celebrates by sending a number of Ron's possessions flying around the bedroom they share. The commotion disturbs Pigwidgeon, who starts fluttering madly around in his cage.

Pigwidgeon does not accompany Ron on his travels; we don't see him after Ron, Harry, and Hermione leave The Burrow.

Strengths Despite his size, Pigwidgeon is a valiant owl. He is always eager for a delivery job, and will tackle any delivery, even if it is so large that he is barely able to lift it. In one scene, Ron tosses him out the window of the Owlery at the school with a letter to carry, and Pigwidgeon falls halfway to the ground before he manages to reach flying speed.

Weaknesses Pigwidgeon is only about the size of a tennis ball. Though he has a valiant spirit, a standard sized letter is too large for him to handle physically. On one occasion, Pigwidgeon takes several weeks to travel a distance that Hedwig travels in two days. Unlike the other post owls, who apparently can be sent on deliveries with enough accuracy that they can be expected to reach their destination at a specific time, Pigwidgeon, overwhelmed by his cargo, is almost as erratic as the superannuated Errol in making his deliveries on time.

Pius Thicknesse

Gender: Male
Hair color: Unknown
Eye color: Unknown
Related Family: Unknown
Loyalty: Lord Voldemort (under Imperius curse)

Overview

Pius Thicknesse is a fairly high-ranking civil servant who rises through the ranks in the Ministry of Magic, eventually becoming Minister.

Role in the Books

Half-Blood Prince While Pius is never named in this book, he is apparently promoted to head the Department of Magical Law Enforcement upon the death of Amelia Bones.

Deathly Hallows In the first mention of Pius Thicknesse by name, Yaxley reports that he has placed an Imperius curse on the Head of the Department of Magical Law Enforcement. Lord Voldemort says that this is good, but Thicknesse is only one man; in order to take over the Ministry, Rufus Scrimgeour must be surrounded by those loyal to Voldemort.

Thicknesse apparently is the source of the set of regulations regarding Portkeys, Apparation, and use of the Floo network in the houses on Privet Drive. Ostensibly designed to protect Harry from Dark wizards dropping in, the actual purpose seems to be to enable monitoring of Harry's movements. It is because of these regulations that Harry must leave Privet Drive by means of Sirius Black's flying motorcycle.

After the death of Rufus Scrimgeour, Pius Thicknesse is appointed Minister for Magic.

When Harry, Ron, and Hermione enter the Ministry to try and retrieve the locket Horcrux, Harry and Hermione are on the lift (elevator) as it reaches the first level, which is dedicated to the Ministry and support staff. Pius Thicknesse is there talking with Dolores Umbridge, who is waiting for the lift.

While Harry is searching Umbridge's office for the locket, Thicknesse comes in to leave a note for her; luckily, Harry has just completed his search, and is hiding under the Invisibility Cloak so Thicknesse does not see him. Thicknesse takes part in the battle at Hogwarts at the end of the book. Fighting on the side of the Death Eaters, he is incapacitated by a hex from Percy Weasley. Percy tells him that the hex constitutes his resignation. Seen in passing in the second battle, Pius was being 'floored' by Percy and Arthur Weasley.

ANALYSIS

There has been rather a lot of controversy about the name, with many Catholics seeing it as a jab at Pope Pius. However, one possibility is that rather than the first name being a jab at someone, the two names together describe his character. This is quite common in this work; one need look no further than Rubeus Hagrid or Remus Lupin to see the common thread between the two names of the characters. At least one Catholic commentator has mentioned the church type that would be described as a "pious thickness," the member of the congregation who believes what he is told to believe, but is unable to understand why. Usually, this person is an enabler for the Umbridge in the congregation, laughing on Umbridge's cue, following Umbridge's lead, and never being able to explain why. One can't help but think that such a person would be uniquely susceptible to the Imperius curse, and in fact might not even need to be cursed to follow the instructions he is given.

Pomona Sprout

Gender: Female
Hair color: Unknown
Eye color: Unknown
Related Family: Unknown
Loyalty:

OVERVIEW

Pomona Sprout is the Herbology professor at Hogwarts School of Witchcraft and Wizardry. She is also the Head of Hufflepuff House.

According to a note posted on the Author's web site, Pomona Sprout's birthday is 15 May.

ROLE IN THE BOOKS

Philosopher's Stone   Harry finds that he has Professor Sprout for Herbology. He is learning how to care for the herbs and fungi that are used in magic, and their properties.

Harry, Ron, and Hermione learn from Hagrid that one of the enchantments guarding the Philosopher's Stone was put in place by Professor Sprout. When they go through the trap door, they find that her contribution is a large Devil's Snare plant, which traps Harry and Ron. Hermione manages to conjure fire to force it to retreat and free them.

Chamber of Secrets   Professor Sprout, somewhat the worse for wear, enters our story being trailed by Professor Lockhart; it seems Lockhart has been giving her pointers regarding the first aid she is providing for the Whomping Willow, which Harry and Ron had driven into the night before. It does not seem that the pointers were much use; Professor Sprout seems somewhat disgruntled when she arrives, and her mood is not lightened when Lockhart asks to speak privately with Harry for a moment.

Once Harry returns to the greenhouse, he finds that Professor Sprout is giving instructions on the repotting of young Mandrake plants.

The mandrake plants prove necessary over the course of the book as students and others are petrified by an apparently unknown monster. We hear that Professor Sprout has canceled one class in the dead of winter because she needs to fit winter clothing on the Mandrakes and doesn't trust anyone else to help; and over the course of the year we hear about how the Mandrakes are growing and maturing.

Finally, at the end of the year, Professor McGonagall announces that Professor Sprout has informed her that the Mandrakes are ready and the potion to revive the petrified students will be administered that evening.

Prisoner of Azkaban   Though we are told that Harry, Ron, and Hermione are still taking Herbology, we don't see anything in particular of Professor Sprout in this book.

Goblet of Fire   Professor Sprout starts the year by telling the students that they will be squeezing pus from Bubotubers. The first Defence Against the Dark Arts class, taught by Professor Moody, leaves Neville Longbottom severely shaken. Moody asks Neville back to his office for tea, and while he is there, tells him that Professor Sprout has spoken highly of his abilities in Herbology. Moody also gives him a book, *Magical Mediterranean Water-Plants and Their Properties*.

At the end of the book, Cedric Diggory is murdered by Peter Pettigrew (Wormtail). It is mentioned that Professor Sprout, as head of Cedric's house, is speaking with his parents.

Order of the Phoenix Harry, Ron, and Hermione are still taking Herbology. At one point, Professor Sprout speaks sharply to them after one of the bouncing bulbs which they have been assigned to plant breaks loose and, bouncing off the glass, hits Harry in the back of the head.

Shortly after Harry's interview is published in the *Quibbler*, Professor Sprout, rewarding him for his bravery in speaking out, awards Gryffindor house ten points when he hands her a pair of secateurs.

Half-Blood Prince When Harry, Ron, and Hermione are harvesting Snargaluff pods, Professor Sprout chides them for being slow; it seems that while they are still strapping on their protective gear (and talking), Neville has already harvested his first pod. The Trio's first pod bounces free while they are trying to open it, and rebounds off the glass roof of the greenhouse, knocking Professor Sprout's battered hat off.

When Harry, with the assistance of Felix Felicis potion, is trying to recover a particular memory from Professor Slughorn, he feels impelled to go past the greenhouses. There, he sees Professors Slughorn and Sprout harvesting leaves of some plant for Slughorn's third year Potions class, and talking about how they are most effective when collected at twilight.

Professor Sprout, as head of Hufflepuff house, is present at the meeting of the heads of house at the end of the book, along with Professor McGonagall (as head of Gryffindor and acting Headmaster), Professor Slughorn (as head of Slytherin), Professor Flitwick (as head of Ravenclaw), Hagrid, and Harry. She has little to say at the meeting, but is in favour of the school remaining open.

Deathly Hallows Pomona Sprout, as the head of Hufflepuff house, is one of the Heads of House that Professor McGonagall summons when she decides to oust the current Headmaster, Professor Snape, and defend Hogwarts against the Death Eaters so that Harry can locate the final Horcrux. Professor Sprout is present when Snape makes his escape, and is in the Great Hall, with the Hufflepuffs, when McGonagall announces the evacuation of the under-age wizards. We see Professor Sprout acting to defend Hogwarts against the Death Eaters attack. She is one of the teachers assigned to the battlements, and with the help of Neville among others, we see her carrying various magical plants to the tops of the towers to throw down upon the enemy.

QUESTIONS

1. Why isn't Professor Sprout in the Order of the Phoenix?

Poppy Pomfrey

Gender: Female
Hair color: Unknown
Eye color: Unknown
Related Family: Unknown
Loyalty:

OVERVIEW

Poppy Pomfrey is the school nurse for Hogwarts School of Witchcraft and Wizardry.

ROLE IN THE BOOKS

Philosopher's Stone Madam Pomfrey is first mentioned when Ron is helping Hagrid take care of his pet dragon, Norbert. Norbert bites Ron, but Ron doesn't want to go to the Hospital Wing for fear of revealing Norbert's existence. When the bite swells up and turns green, though, he has no choice. Madam Pomfrey seems skeptical of his claim that it's a dog bite, but asks no further questions.

When Harry is in the infirmary after his session in the Chamber, we see that Madam Pomfrey is limiting the visitors that he can have. She is somewhat put out that Professor Dumbledore has insisted that Harry be allowed to attend the Leaving Feast, but allows him to leave the infirmary anyway.

Chamber of Secrets When Harry's wrist is broken playing Quidditch, Professor Lockhart "heals" it by magically removing all the bones from his arm. Once in the infirmary, Madam Pomfrey says that she can heal broken bones almost immediately, but growing an entirely new set is quite a different matter. The potion she gives him, "Skele-Gro," tastes horrible, but Madam Pomfrey has little sympathy, saying that he is in for an uncomfortable night. While he is in the Hospital Wing, he is visited by Dobby. Dobby, as usual, has to punish himself; Harry tries to restrain him, fearing that the noise will wake Madam Pomfrey. Madam Pomfrey is undisturbed, however, until Professor Dumbledore and Professor McGonagall bring in a Petrified Colin Creevey. All she can really do for him, though, is set him on one of the beds and pull curtains around him.

Over the course of the year, other students get Petrified and are moved into the infirmary. We can safely assume that Madam Pomfrey is taking care of them as best she is able.

Madam Pomfrey heals Hermione after she ingests Polyjuice potion contaminated with cat hair. Madam Pomfrey does not question how she had gotten a tail, fur, cat ears, or cat eyes, simply treating the problem. When Hermione is Petrified, Harry and Ron are taken to the infirmary to see her. Madam Pomfrey is in the background, but does not say anything.

Harry and Ron determine that the Monster in the Chamber may have been the instrument of Moaning Myrtle's death, and resolve to go and ask her. They are intercepted in the halls by Professor McGonagall, and to explain their absence from class, they say that they are going to see Hermione. Professor McGonagall agrees that they may go and see her, so they must; Madam Pomfrey is mildly vexed, saying that there's no point in visiting someone who is Petrified, they can't hear anyway.

After Ron, Harry, and Ginny return from the Chamber with Professor Lockhart, Professor Dumbledore suggests first that Ginny should go to the Hospital Wing; he says that Madam Pomfrey will be awake, giving out restorative draughts to the Petrified students.

He later suggests Ron should take Lockhart to the Hospital Wing to see if Madam Pomfrey can do anything for him.

Prisoner of Azkaban Having encountered a Dementor on the Hogwarts Express, Harry is called into Professor McGonagall's office as he enters the school. Shortly, Madam Pomfrey bustles in, telling him he needs attention because of the Dementor. Harry says he's feeling fine, that Professor Lupin had given him chocolate on the train. Madam Pomfrey is pleased to hear that for once they have a teacher of Defence Against the Dark Arts who knows his remedies. Harry eventually manages to convince Professor McGonagall and Madam Pomfrey that he is all right and can go to the Entrance Feast.

When Dementors invade the Quidditch pitch during the match against Hufflepuff, Harry loses consciousness and falls off his broom. He awakens in the Hospital Wing, surrounded by the Quidditch team; apparently they lost the match, though nobody blames Harry, except for Harry himself. Madam Pomfrey eventually shoos everyone out except Ron and Hermione.

After the events in the Shrieking Shack, Professor Snape gathers up the unconscious students, along with Sirius Black and takes them to the Hospital Wing. While Harry and Hermione recover relatively quickly, having suffered from the effects of the Dementors, Ron was hit with a curse by Peter Pettigrew and is receiving care from Madam Pomfrey when they regain consciousness. Madam Pomfrey is scandalized that Snape and Cornelius Fudge would be arguing with her charges, specifically Harry and Hermione, and hindering their recovery. She is further upset when Dumbledore demands to speak with Harry and Hermione alone, sending Fudge and Snape away and Madam Pomfrey back to her office.

After Harry and Hermione return from their mission, Madam Pomfrey, unaware that they have been gone, only knowing that Professor Dumbledore has finally left, reappears from her office, demanding to know if she can finally take care of her patients. She is again interrupted by the return of Snape, Fudge, and Dumbledore. She agrees with Dumbledore that Harry and Hermione had been right there all along. As Snape leaves in a huff, and Fudge and Dumbledore leave more quietly, she locks the Hospital Wing door behind them, and resumes her ministrations to Harry and Hermione, who meekly accept massive slabs of chocolate.

Goblet of Fire In Herbology, Harry's class is studying Bubotubers. Professor Sprout tells the class that the treated "pus" can be used against acne. It is mentioned that Eloise Midgeon had tried to curse her spots off, but that Madam Pomfrey had managed to get her nose attached again.

Immediately after the First Task of the Triwizard Tournament, Harry is taken into the first aid tent by Madam Pomfrey. He had been struck by the tail of his dragon, and the spikes had wounded his shoulder. She treats his wounds and tells him to sit still for a minute. She then goes to another part of the tent, and Harry hears her checking on Cedric Diggory, who is apparently injured worse than Harry is.

Harry, pushed beyond endurance, had dueled with Draco, and his jinx and Draco's had hit each other and been deflected. Draco's jinx had struck Hermione and made her teeth grow tremendously. Mortally embarrassed, she had run to the Hospital Wing. At the Yule Ball, Harry notices that Hermione's teeth look different. Hermione tells him that following the duel, Madam Pomfrey had given her a mirror and told her to say when her teeth were the correct size; she had allowed Madam Pomfrey to shrink them to a smaller, and more becoming, size than they had been originally.

Madam Pomfrey is again in evidence immediately following the Second Task, providing blankets and Pepper-Up Potion to both Champions and rescued hostages, to revive them following their time in the Lake. After the Third Task, and his return from the cemetery, Harry is taken off first to Professor Moody's office, then to Dumbledore's office. When he finally reaches the Hospital Wing, Bill Weasley and Molly Weasley are berating Madam Pomfrey, demanding to know what she has done with Harry. At Dumbledore's instructions, Madam Pomfrey brings Harry a sleeping draught. Harry falls asleep before he has finished it.

Harry is awakened by Professor McGonagall returning to the Hospital Wing with Cornelius Fudge, demanding to speak with Dumbledore. Madam Pomfrey tells her that Dumbledore is not there, but he arrives almost immediately. Madam Pomfrey remains in the background while the debate between Fudge and Dumbledore goes on. After Fudge has departed, Dumbledore sends Madam Pomfrey away to care for Winky; she seems rather surprised to be sent to care for a house elf, but complies. It turns out that Dumbledore has sent her away so that he can ask Sirius Black to return to his human form; so far this evening, he has appeared in his Animagus form, as a large black dog, because he is still believed to be a fugitive murderer and supporter of Voldemort.

While Madam Pomfrey certainly returns to care for Harry, she is not mentioned directly again in this book.

Order of the Phoenix Dolores Umbridge has brought Aurors to assist in her sacking of Hagrid. In the confusion surrounding this event, Professor McGonagall is hit by multiple Stunners and is taken to the Hospital Wing. The next day, Harry receives a vision that leads him to believe Sirius is being tortured. Desperate to reach the only member of the Order of the Phoenix still at the school, he goes to the Hospital Wing to see McGonagall, only to have Madam Pomfrey tell him that McGonagall has been taken to St. Mungo's Hospital.

After the Battle at the Ministry, Hermione, Ginny, Ron, Luna, and Neville are being cared for in the Hospital Wing by Madam Pomfrey. Professor Umbridge, now rescued from her sojourn among the Centaurs, is also there receiving treatment. Ron frightens Umbridge by making the sound of hooves; when she sits bolt upright, Madam Pomfrey pops out of her office to see if she is all right.

Half-Blood Prince When Katie Bell touches a jinxed necklace and is cursed, she is taken to the Hospital Wing. We hear from Dumbledore later that Professor Snape has done what he can for her, and she has been sent to St. Mungo's Hospital. At Harry's question as to why Snape, Dumbledore says that he understands the Dark Arts much better than does Madam Pomfrey.

Ron is poisoned on his birthday, and ends up in the Hospital Wing. When we see him there, Harry, Hermione, Ginny, and the Twins are with him. Hagrid arrives, and Madam Pomfrey bustles out of her office, saying "Only six visitors to a patient." Harry points out that Hagrid would be the sixth visitor, and Madam Pomfrey retreats, confused.

Some time later, while Ron is still in the infirmary, Harry is hit by a Bludger and ends up in the Hospital Wing with a cracked skull. While he is there, he recalls that in his second year, he had been visited by Dobby; and has the idea of summoning Kreacher to tail Malfoy for him. When he summons Kreacher, Dobby arrives as well; it seems they are fighting because Kreacher had insulted Harry. Peeves, always happy at the sight of chaos, also arrives; Harry, worried that he will attract Madam Pomfrey, silences him, at which he runs away, and muffles the sound of the struggling house-elves. Harry is able to give Kreacher his assignment without Madam Pomfrey being any the wiser. After the death of Dumbledore, Harry, in shock, is taken to the Hospital Wing. There, we see Madam Pomfrey tending to Bill's injuries, until Mrs. Weasley arrives and takes over.

Deathly Hallows In the pause after the death of Snape in the Battle of Hogwarts, we see Madam Pomfrey ministering to the fallen.

Strengths Madam Pomfrey is a gifted, experienced and dedicated healer. With few exceptions she is able to treat and cure all manner of illness and injury occurring at Hogwarts. Given the high injury rate due to Quidditch, magical accidents, dangerous creatures and student pranks, Hogwarts is a hazardous place. Madam Pomfrey's services are frequently called upon.

Madam Pomfrey is also strict and maintains high standards in the hospital. She is not afraid to stand up to anyone who is compromising the treatment and recovery of a patient, even Dumbledore.

ANALYSIS

Interestingly, Madam Pomfrey does not ask any questions about how the injuries she is asked to treat were received. We see this first with Ron's dragon bite, which she must be aware is not the dog bite the Ron claims it is, and then later with Hermione's accident with the Polyjuice Potion. Madam Pomfrey, being in charge of an infirmary which is responsible for the care of several hundred cocksure young wizards and witches, must have seen every imaginable magical side effect, and must be able to recognize many of them on sight. It is safe to assume that she recognizes Ron's wound as the result of something like a dragon, and it is probable as well that she recognizes the effects of contaminated Polyjuice Potion, but in neither case does she question the lame explanations offered. Additionally, what happens in the infirmary seems to stay in the infirmary. While she is likely aware that Hermione's affliction over Christmas in *Harry Potter and the Chamber of Secrets* was caused by Polyjuice Potion, that being one of the potions that N.E.W.T.-class students work with, she does not divulge the nature of Hermione's illness. This is an indication that Madam Pomfrey is discreet when dealing with student injuries, as Professor Snape does not hear about the probable cause of Hermione's illness, and thus does not make the connection between that and the missing ingredients from his stores.

QUESTIONS

1. How does Madam Pomfrey treat the students? 2. Describe Madam Pomfrey in three words.

Professor Binns

Gender: Male
Hair color: Unknown
Eye color: Unknown
Related Family: Unknown
Loyalty:

OVERVIEW

Professor (Cuthbert) Binns is the History of Magic professor at Hogwarts School of Witchcraft and Wizardry. He is the only professor who is a ghost. It is believed that he sat down in front of the staff room fireplace, fell asleep, and the next day, simply got up and went to class, leaving his body behind.

ROLE IN THE BOOKS

Philosopher's Stone Professor Binns has no role in this book except to teach History of Magic and put the entire class to sleep.

Chamber of Secrets Hermione manages to convince Professor Binns to tell the class the myth of the Chamber of Secrets; he is upset by this, because it is myth, rather than concrete facts. However, he does explain what the myth says, which is instrumental in the later discovery of the actual chamber.

According to Professor Binns, the four Founders of Hogwarts had a falling out after the school had been running for a while. One of the four, Salazar Slytherin, had felt that the school should only accept as students those who could prove descent from wizards. The other three Founders disagreed, so Slytherin left. As he left, though, he is supposed to have created a secret chamber, and placed within it a monster. Legend has it that the Chamber can be opened, and the monster can be controlled, only by Slytherin's true heir. Binns goes on to say that headmaster after headmaster have been through the school, and not one has found so much as a secret broom closet. Angry at the interruption of his lovely facts with this legend, Binns then refuses to speak any more of it, and the class once again subsides into boredom.

Prisoner of Azkaban   Professor Binns has no role in this book except to teach History of Magic and put the entire class to sleep.

Goblet of Fire   Professor Binns has no role in this book except to teach History of Magic and put the entire class to sleep.

Order of the Phoenix   Professor Binns has no role in this book except to teach History of Magic and put the entire class to sleep. It is in one of these classes that an injured Hedwig appears at the window; Harry brings her in, excuses himself from class saying that he needs to go to the Hospital Wing, and carries Hedwig off to the Staff Room, where he hands her over to Professor Grubbly-Plank to have her healed.

Half-Blood Prince   As neither Harry or Ron received a passing grade on his History of Magic O.W.L., they no longer attend History of Magic, and evidently Hermione has also chosen to drop the subject; thus, Professor Binns has no role in this book.

Strengths   He manages to put the class to sleep (particularly Harry), very effectively.

Weaknesses   He does not seem to be particularly aware of his class, or even of the outside world, and what is going on in it; it is uncertain whether he has even updated his curriculum since he passed away. It is uncertain whether this is because he is a ghost, or whether he was this way also in life. He does not seem to be a particularly effective teacher; at one point Harry thinks that the subject material, the Giant Wars, might have been a lot more exciting in the hands of a different teacher.

Relationships with Other Characters   Being a ghost, Binns seems not really interested in flesh-and-blood characters. As there are no references of him appearing in the company of the other ghosts, it seems that he has no special interest in them either. His only interests lie in teaching his classes. Although this has him interact with his students, his interest for them seems to end as soon as they leave the classroom. A clear indication of this is that he is unable to recall the names of any of his students. When Hermione Granger asks him about the Chamber of Secrets, he at first does not recall her name, then addresses her as "Miss Grant," calls Seamus Finnigan "O'Flaherty," and addresses Parvati Patil as "Miss Pennyfeather."

QUESTIONS

1. The story of Professor Binns' origin does not tally with what Nearly Headless Nick says about the origin of ghosts in *Harry Potter and the Order of the Phoenix* — see Ghost for details. What do you think really happened?

2. Professor Binns shuffles his notes on a few occasions. Ghosts cannot interact with material objects. Does Professor Binns have ghostly notes as well? How does Professor Binns mark exam papers?

GREATER PICTURE

At first glance there does seem to be some difference between what Nearly Headless Nick says about the creation of ghosts, and what we know of Professor Binns. However, there is more similarity than first appears. Ghosts are created when a person fears death or is not prepared for death. They choose to haunt the Earth rather than "go on." Professor Binns was probably not prepared for death. He was a long time teacher and passed away in the staff room waiting for his next class. His dedication to his vocation caused him to arise as a ghost and carry on as a teacher. Death for him would mean shirking his duties, something unthinkable.

We can also speculate about the notes he seems to be carrying. It may be possible that his notes are part of his ghostly persona. Other ghosts keep their clothing and accessories, and we hear several times that Nearly Headless Nick arranges to change the ruff that he wears, so why shouldn't Binns keep his class notes? The fact that they make noise when handled by Binns is no more strange than hearing ghosts talk and converse. The fact that his "ghost notes" can't be updated might explain why Hermione once comments that they never learn any History of Magic newer than the late 19th Century; presumably that is when Professor Binns died.

Professor Quirrell

Gender: Male
Hair color: None
Eye color: Unknown
Related Family: Unknown
Loyalty: Lord Voldemort

OVERVIEW

Professor Quirrell is a teacher at Hogwarts, where he teaches Defense Against the Dark Arts on the third floor of the castle, right in the Great Foyer near the Gryffindor tower.

Notes on his Name   Professor Quirrell is never given a first name in the books, in the film, or in the video game. He does appear in two other places:

• A Wizards of the Coast trading card game based on the series included a card of Quirrell with the first name Quirenus. The Harry Potter Lexicon site states, however, that "these cards are not canon."[1]

• Master Foods produced a line of Chocolate Frog treats with collectable Famous Wizards cards; Quirrel being given the first name Slatero. J. K. Rowling states that she wrote the information on those cards.[2]

---

1. http://www.hp-lexicon.org/help/tcg.html
2. http://www.jkrowling.com/textonly/en/faq_view.cfm?id=96

Professor Quirrell

Role in the Books

Philosopher's Stone A very timid person, Professor Quirrell first appears in the Leaky Cauldron, where he is pleased to meet Harry; Hagrid comments at the time that he always seems nervous, ever since he took a year's holiday and met up with something he had been teaching about.

At the Arrival Feast, Harry notes that Quirrell looks rather odd, wearing a large purple turban on his head. It is while Professor Quirrell is speaking with Professor Snape that Harry first feels the searing pain in his scar that becomes his companion, on and off, for the nearly all the seven years in this series.

Harry and Ron get into trouble with Filch on the very first day of classes, when they are found trying to get through a locked door, which turns out to be the door to the forbidden third floor corridor. They are saved from being locked in the dungeons by Professor Quirrell, who happens to be passing by.

In Defence Against the Dark Arts, Professor Quirrell says that his strange purple turban was a gift from an African prince for dealing with a troublesome zombie. When Seamus asked excitedly how he had fought the zombie, Quirrell turned all pink and started talking about the weather. (Note: this is the only mention of "zombies" in the series, and thus is highly suspect. The magical construct most closely allied to the Muggle concept of zombies is the Inferius.) There is also a strange smell of garlic that hangs about the classroom; the Weasley twins insist that it is because Quirrell has stuffed his turban full of garlic to ward off vampires.

We don't hear much about his teaching, except that it is not as interesting as Harry and the rest of his class had expected; we do find out that he is concealing something, and that he and Professor Snape may both be looking for something, possibly the mysterious little package that Hagrid removed from Gringotts.

He bursts into the Hallowe'en feast warning that a troll is in the dungeons; Harry and Ron defeat it and save Hermione, thus bonding the three.

At the first Quidditch match of the year, against Slytherin, Harry's broom is jinxed and tries to buck him off. Hermione and Ron believe Snape is casting the jinx. In her haste to reach Snape and set his robes on fire to break his concentration, Hermione knocks over Quirrell.

Harry overhears Quirrell arguing with Snape about where his loyalties lie, and later hears him arguing with someone else about something he does not want to do.

At the conclusion, Harry, Ron, and Hermione pass through a series of chambers to find the Philosopher's Stone. One chamber contains a Troll, who fortunately has been knocked out. Harry alone reaches the final chamber, where he finds Quirrell. Quirrell boasts about his skill with trolls, admitting that he let the one troll into the school at Hallowe'en, and that it was his troll that Harry passed. He also says that Snape had been useful as misdirection, "flapping about like a great bat." Quirrell has been trying to kill Harry all year; Quirrell also jinxed Harry's broom during the Quidditch match against Slytherin, and Snape was attempting to counter the jinx. Quirrell's turban actually conceals Lord Voldemort's face that is attached to Quirrell's head, and Voldemort has been controlling Quirrell all year. Ordered to kill Harry, Quirrell is unable to touch him without getting burned; when Quirrell is preparing a killing curse, Harry grabs his face, causing him so much pain that he is disabled. Harry is also in much pain from his scar, triggered by Voldemort's nearness, and it causes him to pass out.

It is uncertain whether Quirrell actually dies here; it is suggested that he does, but while Professor Dumbledore does explain much of what happened, he never actually states that Quirrell is dead.

Goblet of Fire Expounding to the Death Eaters as to what had occurred while he was disembodied, Lord Voldemort describes his stay on the back of Quirrell's head. He mentions that "The servant died when I left his body." Though Voldemort never names Quirrell, referring to him always as his "servant," context makes it certain that this refers to Quirrell.

Order of the Phoenix Before the school year starts, Harry, Ron, and Hermione discuss the new Defence Against the Dark Arts teacher. While running down the list of Defence Against the Dark Arts teachers Ron and Harry have known, Fred and George Weasley mention "one died," which could only be Quirrell.

In her first Defence Against the Dark Arts class of the year, Professor Umbridge states that Quirrell was the only Defence Against the Dark Arts teacher that was up to standards for the Ministry. Harry gets into trouble for pointing out that he had Voldemort stuck to the back of his head.

Half-Blood Prince To convince Horace Slughorn that Hogwarts is safe from Death Eaters, Harry tells him that Professor Quirrell is the only teacher who has died at Hogwarts. (This is not strictly true, Professor Binns clearly died at the school, though as it was of natural causes it likely would not concern Slughorn either way. It is true that Quirrell's death is the only one Harry knows of that could be attributed to Voldemort or his organization.)

Strengths He is carrying Lord Voldemort on the back of his head. As such, he is able to partially utilize Voldemort's powers: for instance, Voldemort is, of course, a Legilimens; he can inspect other wizards' minds and communicate this to Quirrell.

Weaknesses Quirrell carries Lord Voldemort on the back of his head. As a result, he must bow to Voldemort's commands, whatever they may be, and is subject to any punishment Voldemort chooses. A relatively weak-willed wizard, Quirrell attempts to attach himself to a powerful being, although that power has instead attached itself to him. Quirrell is never seen performing magic, so it is uncertain how powerful a wizard he is; he is apparently able to control Trolls, however.

Relationships with Other Characters The relationship between Quirrell and Lord Voldemort is rather tighter than any relationship should be. Quirrell has adopted a stammering, rather bumbling pose to help deflect suspicion from himself, and admits that Snape fluttering about like a great black bat and acting suspicious, was useful to him. Snape and Quirrell seem to be competitive with one another and often seem to be arguing.

Quirrell's quirky manner seems to distance others from him, as well, and so he does not appear to have close relationships with any teachers or students at Hogwarts.

ANALYSIS

According to Professor Dumbledore, speaking in *Harry Potter and the Half-Blood Prince,* the post of Defence Against the Dark Arts teacher is apparently jinxed; since Voldemort had been turned down for the job, no teacher has lasted more than one year in that post. One question that has been raised is, given that jinx, how could Quirrell have remained in that post for more than a year? According to the author, he had not. In an interview, Rowling stated that Quirrell had requested a transfer to that post, and had been studying the source material so he could teach it, when he encountered Voldemort in Albania.

QUESTIONS

1. Why did Quirrell allow Voldemort to share his head? 2. What might Quirrell have been like before he met Voldemort?

Professor Sinistra

Gender: Female
Hair color: Unknown
Eye color: Unknown
Related Family: Unknown
Loyalty:

OVERVIEW

Professor Sinistra is the Astronomy professor at Hogwarts School of Witchcraft and Wizardry.

ROLE IN THE BOOKS

Goblet of Fire It is mentioned that Professor Sinistra is dancing with Professor Moody at the Yule Ball.

ANALYSIS

Astronomy in the Harry Potter world is very different from real astronomy. There are no physics present in the Harry Potter astronomy. Rather, the lesson focuses on nomenclature and its position in relationship to the other planets. The various stars outside of our Solar System, other galaxies, black holes, and other celestial objects play little importance. In short, Harry Potter's astronomy is descriptive.

QUESTIONS

1. How might Astronomy be important in learning about magic? Why is it considered separate from Divination? 2. Think about what kind of personality Professor Sinistra might have, and describe it.

Professor Vector

Gender: Female[1]
Hair color: Unknown
Eye color: Unknown
Related Family: Unknown
Loyalty:

OVERVIEW

Professor Septima Vector is the Arithmancy professor at Hogwarts School of Witchcraft and Wizardry.

ROLE IN THE BOOKS
ANALYSIS

Arithmancy is otherwise known as numerology, which is in fact a real subject. It involves the finding of magical properties of numbers.

In the Harry Potter world, numbers are often inscribed in places, such as tombs, pyramids, and monuments. These numbers supposedly have meaning, either hiding a secret message or protecting the site with a curse. Arithmancy, if applied correctly, allows the practitioner to interpret these findings.

Gringotts curse breakers are required to have sufficient knowledge of Arithmancy.

QUESTIONS

1. Hermione repeatedly states that Arithmancy is very useful. What kind of things might be taught in an Arithmancy class, that Hermione would see as being particularly useful?

Rabastan Lestrange

Gender: Male
Hair color: Unknown
Eye color: Unknown
Related Family: brother Rodolphus Lestrange
Loyalty: Lord Voldemort

OVERVIEW

Rabastan Lestrange is brother to Rodolphus Lestrange.

ROLE IN THE BOOKS

Goblet of Fire Although the action referred to takes place before the series starts, it is in this book that we are introduced to Rabastan, as Harry witnesses the trial of his group by means of Albus Dumbledore's pensieve. Shortly after Lord Voldemort's disappearance, he and three other young Death Eaters (his brother Rodolphus Lestrange, his brother's wife Bellatrix Lestrange, and Barty Crouch Jr.) attacked and tortured Aurors Frank

---

1. In *Harry Potter and the Prisoner of Azkaban* (Chapter 12) Ron mentions her as a *Witch*.

and Alice Longbottom, using the Cruciatus Curse on them until the two lost most of their mental faculties. All four members of the group were sentenced to imprisonment in Azkaban.

Half-Blood Prince Twice, Professor Dumbledore and Harry visit Horace Slughorn's memories of one particular night when Slughorn is meeting with Tom Riddle and his associates. In both of those memories, Slughorn notes that it is eleven o'clock, and says that it is time to send the gathered students off to bed, remarking to two of them, Avery and Lestrange (who could be either Rodolphus or Rabastan), that they have an essay due, and would be given detention if he didn't have it ready.

ANALYSIS

It is never made entirely clear what has happened to Rabastan. We see him being sentenced to Azkaban, but while his brother, Rodolphus, escapes, there is no further mention of Rabastan in which his first name is mentioned. A couple of times, a Death Eater is addressed as "Lestrange," without indication whether this is Rodolphus or Rabastan.

For no real reason, we have in the *Muggles' Guide* assumed that Rabastan died in Azkaban. We know that Bellatrix' husband Rodolphus survived, as Tonks reports having injured him while dueling on brooms in *Harry Potter and the Deathly Hallows*; on that admittedly negative evidence, we have assumed that Rodolphus alone survived, and all references to "Lestrange" are in fact references to him.

Regulus Black

Gender: Male
Hair color: Unknown
Eye color: Unknown
Related Family: Sirius Black, Walburga Black, Narcissa Malfoy, Bellatrix Lestrange
Loyalty: previously Lord Voldemort; probably Albus Dumbledore at time of death

OVERVIEW

Regulus Black is the brother of Sirius Black. He is also a former Death Eater, although he quit and was subsequently killed, supposedly by Voldemort himself.

ROLE IN THE BOOKS

Order of the Phoenix Mentioned in passing only; discussing the tapestry of the Ancient and Honorable House of Black on the parlor wall at 12 Grimmauld Place, Sirius mentions his brother Regulus, and that he is believed to be dead. As mentioned, he was taken in by the Death Eater idea, and was apparently fairly high in the ranks when he came to his senses and tried to quit. He was dismissed by Sirius as not being important enough for Lord Voldemort to have killed him personally.

Later on, shortly after Harry sees the vision of Sirius getting tortured, Hermione suggests that "Sirius' brother" (meaning Regulus) had told Sirius about the weapon, since Regulus had been a Death Eater.

Half-Blood Prince Regulus is not mentioned directly in this book. When Harry Potter and Albus Dumbledore go on a mission to recover a supposed Horcrux of Voldemort's, it turns out to have been already replaced by a locket. This locket contains a note signed by one "R.A.B.." Many readers believe this signature to be Regulus.'

Deathly Hallows On the day after their return to Number 12, Grimmauld Place, Harry sees the sign on Regulus' bedroom door and discovers that Regulus' middle name is Arcturus. From this, he concludes that he is the one who left the note, signed R.A.B., in the locket Harry and Dumbledore found in the cave. While Harry, Ron, and Hermione immediately search for the locket, they discover nothing. Hermione remembers that they had found a locket when trying to clean up the house, and that Kreacher had a habit of stealing back those things he considered valuable. When Kreacher's lair proves empty, Harry summons Kreacher, who eventually tells them about the locket. Voldemort had demanded a house elf, and Regulus had volunteered Kreacher. The Dark Lord had taken Kreacher to an island on a lake, and had forced him to drink a potion that made him remember horrible things. The Dark Lord had put a locket in the bowl where the potion was, had refilled the bowl, and then had left Kreacher there. Kreacher had crawled to the edge of the lake to drink, had been seized by Inferi, and been dragged underwater. He had then returned to his master, Regulus, as ordered.

On hearing what the Dark Lord had done, Regulus had ordered Kreacher to take him to the place. He had then ordered Kreacher to force him to drink the potion in the basin, then take the locket, replace it with one he would provide, and destroy the locket. Regulus had drunk all the potion, and had then crawled to the waters' edge to drink, and had been dragged under. Kreacher had never seen Regulus again, and he was distraught that, despite having managed to put the replacement locket in the basin, he had been unable to destroy the locket from the basin, and that the locket had been stolen from him by Mundungus Fletcher.

Harry wins Kreacher over by telling him that they, too, have the mission of destroying the locket, and by giving him the locket that Regulus had told Kreacher to put in the basin. Overjoyed at having this artifact of his late master returned to him, Kreacher heads off to find Mundungus and bring him back to Harry for questioning.

Strengths Regulus must have had a certain amount of ability with Occlumency, to prevent Voldemort from sensing Regulus' increasing dislike of Voldemort's programs. He also must have had significant strength of character to attempt to destroy one of Voldemort's protected Horcruxes.

Relationships with Other Characters Brought up in a rabidly Pureblood family, Regulus found that Voldemort's blood purity ideas resonated with him, and he became a Death Eater during Voldemort's first rise to power. His loyalty to Voldemort waned when he discovered how Voldemort put his ideas into practice, and he turned against Voldemort with his last living acts. Sirius tells us that Regulus was his mother's favorite, as, in so far as she knew, he had stayed true to the ideas of blood purity that she had espoused.

ANALYSIS

It is interesting how much we can see about Regulus without ever actually meeting him. Initially, at any rate, Regulus' motives remain unclear; Sirius tells us that he had gotten relatively deep into Voldemort's organization, then, they believe, gotten scared and tried to get out, and been personally murdered by Voldemort for his troubles. As it turns out, his disillusionment with Voldemort's organization was probably growing for quite some time, as when he did choose to act, it was a fairly major stroke against Voldemort. By that time, Regulus must have been reasonably close to Voldemort's inner councils, as he had been aware that Voldemort wanted a house elf, so he would likely have been within range of Voldemort's legilimency. Because of that, he would have had to protect his mind from inspection as his disillusionment grew.

In the end, his sacrifice was apparently futile, as Kreacher was never able to destroy the locket he carried away, and as Voldemort had, at that time, possibly as many as four additional Horcruxes hidden away. The Horcrux within the locket is, of course, eventually found and destroyed. Kreacher might have been able to destroy it if Regulus had told him what it was, but Kreacher apparently was not told that it was a Horcrux he was trying to destroy, though Regulus' note indicates that he knew what it was.

Remus Lupin

Gender: Male
Hair color: Light Brown / Gray
Eye color: Unknown
Related Family: Unknown
Loyalty: Albus Dumbledore

OVERVIEW

Remus John Lupin is a wizard who joins the cast of characters in *Harry Potter and the Prisoner of Azkaban* as the new Defense Against the Dark Arts teacher.

Lupin's birthday is March 10th, according to the author.

ROLE IN THE BOOKS

Prisoner of Azkaban Remus J. Lupin is introduced on the Hogwarts Express, where he spends almost the entire trip sleeping. Even asleep, however, he assists Harry and his friends; his presence prevents Draco Malfoy from engaging in any mischief. When a Dementor hunting the fugitive, Sirius Black, enters the compartment, Lupin awakes and repels it with a Charm. He then provides chocolate to the frightened students as a restorative and sends an owl ahead to inform the school nurse that Harry may need medical attention. Madam Pomfrey later commends his actions, saying that at last they have a Defence Against the Dark Arts teacher who knows medical remedies.

At the Welcoming Feast, Dumbledore announces that Professor Lupin is the new Defence Against the Dark Arts teacher—something Harry, Ron, and Hermione already guessed. In his first-ever lesson with Harry's class, Lupin demonstrates an unexpected ability in subduing Peeves. He also gives Neville Longbottom a much-needed boost in confidence by having him lead an exercise to ward off a Boggart. Lupin's practical, hands-on teaching methods are popular with students, making him an instant favorite.

When Harry later asks why Lupin prevented him from tackling his own Boggart, Lupin says he feared it would turn into Lord Voldemort and frighten the class. Lupin is impressed that Harry's worst fear is not Voldemort, but Dementors. Shortly after, Severus Snape, brings Lupin a potion and leaves. Harry suggests that Snape, who has long coveted the Defence Against the Dark Arts job and apparently despises Lupin, may have poisoned the potion, but Lupin drinks it without hesitation.

After Dementors cause Harry to faint and fall off his broom during a Quidditch match, he asks Lupin to teach him how to repel them. Lupin shows Harry the Patronus charm. During these lessons, Harry learns that Lupin, Sirius Black, and Harry's father were schoolmates. During the next Quidditch match, Harry successfully conjures the charm to repel the Dementors, although it is actually Malfoy and his cronies in disguise. Lupin congratulates Harry on his Patronus, but he is rather shaken by the shape it took.

Lupin plays a major role in the Shrieking Shack scene. Upon entering the shack, he immediately disarms Harry, Ron, and Hermione, who have overpowered Sirius Black. Certain that Black is innocent, Lupin returns the Trio's wands and holsters his own as a reassuring gesture that he trusts everyone. Lupin tells them about the friendship between himself, James Potter, Sirius Black, and Peter Pettigrew, the four *Marauders* who created the Marauder's Map. Severus Snape bursts in, accusing Lupin of abetting Black, but the Trio knock him unconscious with a combined charm. Both Lupin and Black then unmask Scabbers, Ron's rat, as Peter Pettigrew in his Animagus form. James was also an Animagus, as is Sirius. It was Pettigrew who betrayed James and Lily to Voldemort. As they prepare to execute Pettigrew, Harry intervenes, saying that his father would not want his two best friends to become murderers; instead, the Dementors can have him. While heading to the castle, the full moon rises. Lupin, who has forgotten his potion, transforms into a dangerous werewolf. Black, in his Animagus dog form, is unable to subdue Lupin but chases him away into the Forbidden Forest. Black is captured by Snape and imprisoned in the castle; Harry and Hermione rescue him, and he escapes on Buckbeak, a Hippogriff wrongly sentenced to death.

Denied the fame that Black's capture would have bestowed upon him, Snape takes petty revenge by revealing to the entire school that Lupin is a werewolf. Lupin resigns his post, knowing parents will object to having such a person teaching their children. As Lupin packs to leave, he tells Harry that his father's Animagus form was a stag, the same as Harry's Patronus. That is why Lupin was so affected when he saw it at the Quidditch match.

Goblet of Fire Lupin does not directly appear in the fourth book. After Voldemort's return to power and Cornelius Fudge's departure, Dumbledore tells Sirius Black to alert "the old crowd," naming Lupin as one of their number, and instructs Sirius to lay low at Remus' until Dumbledore gets in touch with him again.

Order of the Phoenix Lupin returns in *Harry Potter and the Order of the Phoenix* when he arrives at the Dursleys to escort Harry to Number Twelve, Grimmauld Place, the Order of the Phoenix headquarters. Lupin stays at Grimmauld Place with Sirius Black, leaving occasionally to carry out unknown tasks for the Order. Harry only sees him at Grimmauld during the school holiday or when he communicates with him and Sirius via the Floo Network. When Harry watches Severus Snape's memories in a Pensieve, he sees his father and Sirius tormenting Snape. Disturbed by James' bullying, he secretly uses the fireplace in Dolores Umbridge's office to contact Sirius and Lupin and asks them about his father's behavior. Lupin says that the young James (and also Sirius) was a bully, but that he eventually outgrew it. His explanation does little to soothe Harry.

Lupin participates in the battle against the Death Eaters in the Department of Mysteries at the book's conclusion. When Harry runs after a stricken Sirius, whose body has floated through a mysterious veiled archway to death, it is Lupin who forcefully restrains him, saving him from the same fate.

Half-Blood Prince In the sixth book, Lupin acts as a spy for the Order of the Phoenix by infiltrating a dangerous werewolf pack that was recruited by Voldemort. In the ending, Lupin helps fight the Death Eaters who have invaded Hogwarts to murder Dumbledore. It is also revealed that Order of the Phoenix member Nymphadora Tonks is in love with Remus. However, Lupin tells Tonks it is too dangerous to be romantically involved with a werewolf, that he is too old, and says she deserves someone better. However, Lupin and Tonks are later seen holding hands, which indicates that they have overcome these obstacles and have started a cautious relationship.

Deathly Hallows Lupin is among the guards escorting Harry and the Harry Potter decoys from the Dursley residence to a safe house. As the escape plan is being outlined in the Dursley kitchen, Tonks is seen wearing a ring; we discover that she and Lupin are married. The Order's plan to move Harry was discovered, and Lupin arrives at The Burrow with an injured George Weasley in tow. As Mrs. Weasley tends to George's wound, Lupin quizzes Harry to confirm that he is the real Harry Potter. After the other Harry decoys and protectors have arrived, Lupin leaves with Bill Weasley to search for Alastor Moody, who is missing and presumed dead.

Lupin and Tonks are at the Burrow for Harry's birthday, but they quickly depart when Arthur Weasley's Patronus warns them that he is arriving shortly with Rufus Scrimgeour. At Bill and Fleur's wedding, Lupin tells Harry that werewolves are presently in very poor standing with the Ministry. During the reception, as the Ministry falls and the existing protective spells surrounding the Burrow are being broken by Death Eaters, we see Lupin and Tonks, back-to-back, casting new protective spells.

A few days after Harry, Hermione, and Ron have settled into Grimmauld Place, Lupin visits. He chastises Ron and Hermione for dropping their guard too quickly when he first identifies himself. He realizes the Trio has a secret mission that the Order does not know about, and offers his help. Asked about Tonks, he reports that she is pregnant and is safe at her parents' house. Harry is angered that Lupin wants to go adventuring while Tonks and her unborn child are left at home. Parents, he says, should not abandon their children. Heated words are exchanged, and firing a Jinx that knocks Harry down, Lupin angrily storms out.

In March, Ron manages to tune in the pirate wireless program "Potterwatch." Lee Jordan, as "River," introduces "Romulus," easily identifiable by his voice as Lupin, who provides an update on Harry. Lupin says that it is certain that Harry is still alive, as his death would be trumpeted far and wide by the regime as a way of eliminating a rallying point for the resistance. Lupin further says that, if Harry is listening, he should follow his instincts, which are nearly always right. Harry and Hermione are both left in tears by this avowal of reconciliation. Lupin goes on to say that Xenophilius Lovegood had been arrested, and that Rubeus Hagrid, who had held a "Support Harry Potter" party in his house, had escaped arrest and was now at large.

When Harry escapes Malfoy Manor and retreats to Shell Cottage, Lupin visits, announcing that Tonks has given birth to a boy they named Teddy. Surprisingly, given their previous acrimonious parting, Lupin is pleased to see Harry and asks him to be Teddy's godfather, which Harry accepts.

Just prior to the final battle with Voldemort at Hogwarts, tension mounts in the Room of Requirement when Ginny Weasley stubbornly insists on joining the fight and by Percy Weasley's unexpected arrival to reconcile with his family. Fleur attempts to ease the situation by asking Lupin about the new baby; Lupin produces a photograph, although no one seems interested in seeing it. Finally, after Percy is forgiven and Ginny is ordered to stay put inside the Room of Requirement, Lupin goes to the Great Hall to command the forces defending the school grounds. Although Tonks arrives, and we see her looking for Lupin as she takes part in the battle, Lupin is not seen again until the battle is over, when we learn that he and Tonks have been killed.

After reliving Snape's memories in the Pensieve, Harry realizes that it was always his fate to face and be killed by Voldemort. Finding his courage unequal to this, nor is it enough to produce the Patronus necessary for him to pass by the Dementors in the Forbidden Forest, Harry summons Lupin's spirit, along with Sirius Black, James Potter, and Lily Potter. Acting as Patronuses, the four spirits shield Harry as he travels through the Forest to Voldemort's encampment. When Harry reaches the Death Eaters, he drops the Resurrection Stone that provided the power to summon the shades, causing them to vanish.

Strengths Remus Lupin has many positive characteristics. In addition to being a talented wizard, he is extremely intelligent and thoughtful, and tends to think his way through a situation before acting. He often demonstrates great self-control, remaining calm in stressful situations. Although Lupin has been as an outcast, he is kind and extraordinarily loyal to his friends and allies, especially Dumbledore.

Lupin was considered by most to be the best Defense Against the Dark Arts teacher at Hogwarts during the series. He brought patience, understanding and humor to the class and greatly encouraged his students, especially Harry and Neville.

Weaknesses As a young boy, Lupin became afflicted with lycanthropy when he was bitten by the werewolf Fenrir Greyback. Every full moon an afflicted person transforms into a wolf-like creature, and, like a rabid dog, is unable to control their actions. Werewolves, transformed, will more or less mindlessly seek out unafflicted humans to bite and infect them. Although there is no cure, a potion has recently been discovered that allows them to retain their sanity during transformations. Lupin, taking this potion, is able to curl up quietly in his office and rest, rather than rampaging through the Forbidden Forest. However, this potion must be taken every day for about a week before a full moon, and it is effective only for one lunar cycle; if the potion is missed, the werewolf again becomes dangerous. Because they are so dangerous, werewolves are generally feared and shunned by the wizarding community, making them outcasts. As a result, Lupin is mostly a loner and has had difficulty finding employment; he expects to be treated badly.

Relationships with Other Characters Lupin was nicknamed "Moony" and was a Marauder along with James Potter (Prongs), Peter Pettigrew (Wormtail), and Sirius Black (Padfoot). He was studying at Hogwarts at the same time as Severus Snape, who the Marauders detested.

As a teacher, Lupin is a favourite, except with Slytherin students who continually criticize his shabby robes. Not only students like him; he is also well-liked by the other teachers, except Snape, and is accepted quickly by them because of his evident competence.

In later books, he becomes a reassuring, stable presence to Harry. While Harry's godfather, Sirius Black, had more claim to Harry's affection, it seems that Harry was occasionally alarmed by Sirius' impetuousness and would have liked having more time to talk with Lupin than he was granted. Lupin had been busy doing work for the Order of the Phoenix since leaving Hogwarts, and Harry has had less opportunity to spend time with him. There was also a burgeoning relationship between Lupin and Nymphadora Tonks at the end of *Harry Potter and the Half-Blood Prince*; perhaps characteristically, Lupin tried to prevent it, feeling he was an suitable match and that it was an unsafe time to start a family. This shows another side to Lupin: he cares so much about the larger picture that he sometimes neglects the smaller one. By refusing to risk bringing a child into the mess that is their future, he is causing pain to himself and to Tonks in their present.

Analysis

Professor Lupin As has not been the case with some earlier Defence Against the Dark Arts teachers, the other professors are quite pleased with Professor Lupin's appointment—Poppy Pomfrey comments approvingly about him knowing remedies, and in a later book, Professor McGonagall refers to him as a "*competent* teacher"—high praise indeed from her. The one exception is Severus Snape, who, apart from coveting the Dark Arts position for himself, still harbours deep resentments against Lupin for his actions as a member of the Marauders during their Hogwarts years. Lupin immediately wins the entire class' respect, first by putting Peeves to flight, and second, by starting off teaching a truly useful and practical lesson. His caring about, and warmth towards the students becomes visible by numerous small actions—he calls students by their first names, rather than their surnames as is traditional in the Engish school system—and also by larger things: he has Neville take the first turn at the Boggart, and grants him last shot as well. He also freely explains why he prevented Harry from facing the Boggart, and tells Harry that his reaction to the Dementor does not indicate weakness. His volunteering to teach Harry to fight Dementors reflects his nature; he cares, so he will help.

Loyalty to Dumbledore Growing up as a werewolf has made Lupin into a loner and outcast but he is immensely loyal to his friends. After Lupin became a werewolf, his parents believed it impossible for him to attend Hogwarts. However, Dumbledore was sympathetic, and told the Lupins that he would never deny Remus an education as long as certain precautions were implemented. After Lupin left Hogwarts, he found it nearly impossible for a werewolf to find a job in the wizarding community. Dumbledore eventually offered him the position as Defense Against the Dark Arts teacher. Because Dumbledore was so kind to him, Lupin proved to be a devoted ally to the Headmaster when the Order of the Phoenix was formed.

School years When Lupin's three best friends, James Potter, Sirius Black, and Peter Pettigrew discovered he was a werewolf, they decided to support and protect him during his transformations. Because a werewolf is only dangerous to humans, they secretly learned to become Animagi (transforming into an animal at will). An Animagus must register with the Ministry of Magic, although the three never did. During a full moon, they used their new powers to roam Hogwarts' grounds, and later Hogsmeade village, with Lupin in his wolf-like form. When Lupin was with them, he had more control over his actions during his transformations. He was not entirely harmless, however, and his friends carefully guarded him.

QUESTIONS

1. Why are werewolves shunned by people?
2. Lupin mentions that he was a Gryffindor prefect, in part so that he would rein in the other three Marauders. Why didn't Lupin try harder to keep his friends out of trouble when they were at Hogwarts?

GREATER PICTURE

Harry loses many paternal role models throughout the series. His father, James, was murdered by Voldemort when Harry was only one-year-old. In *Harry Potter and the Order of the Phoenix*, his godfather, Sirius Black is killed by Bellatrix Lestrange; his body floats through an arched stone portal covered by a fluttering curtain called the Veil—both literally and metaphorically a veil that he passes beyond, never to return. In *Harry Potter and the Half-Blood Prince*, Dumbledore is killed. In response, Harry feels he can no longer rely on any one person to be his mentor, although, to a lesser extent, Mr. Weasley helps fulfill this role.

It also becomes apparent that Harry has formed a similar attachment to Remus Lupin ever since *Harry Potter and the Prisoner of Azkaban*. However, as Harry spends little time with Remus in the later books, this relationship progresses little beyond *Harry Potter and the Order of the Phoenix*. In *Harry Potter and the Deathly Hallows*, Harry has largely outgrown his need for a father figure, and while he continues to like and respect Lupin, he does not cavil at accusing him of cowardice and abandoning his wife and unborn child. While we are unable to see Lupin's complete reaction to this well-founded accusation, when his son is born, Lupin has not only forgiven Harry, but asks him to be the child's godfather. This leads us to believe that, when given time to reflect on Harry's words, Lupin found them true and accepted their message, no matter that it was delivered hurtfully.

Rita Skeeter

Gender: Female
Hair color: Blonde
Eye color: Unknown, behind large spectacles
Related Family: Unknown
Loyalty: Galleons

OVERVIEW

Rita Skeeter is a free-lance journallist specializing in writing poison-pen stories based on false information and misreported interviews. Her recording tool is a green "Quick-Quotes Quill" that she apparently likes the taste of. Her stories have appeared in *The Daily Prophet*, *Witch Weekly*, and, when blackmailed by Hermione Granger, *The Quibbler*—this last publication does not pay for stories.

ROLE IN THE BOOKS

Goblet of Fire Rita Skeeter is first mentioned after the Quidditch World Cup, where the Muggles in charge of the campsite are attacked by Death Eaters. Rita's story, appearing in *The Daily Prophet*, over-sensationalizes events, and includes some inventions such as supposed dead people being removed from the forest after the Dark Mark appeared. Molly Weasley, reading this, comments that Rita's stories always contain fabrications and should not be believed. A week later, Ludo Bagman mentions that Rita has heard about Bertha Jorkins' disappearance, and she soon writes a story about it.

When the Goblet of Fire selects Harry as a Triwizard Champion, Skeeter interviews him at the Wand Weighing ceremony. However, her 'Quick-Quotes Quill' fabricates many of his supposed comments, such as, "Sometimes at night I still cry about them. I'm not ashamed to admit it." Harry is both troubled and embarrassed by these erroneous statements.

Following the First Task, as Harry returns to the Castle with Ron, she appears from behind a bush in the Forbidden Forest, asking Harry for a word. Harry provides her with one: "Goodbye."

Skeeter later interviews Hagrid, supposedly for an article about the Blast-Ended Skrewts. While she is setting up the interview, Ron wonders how she got there—hadn't she been banned from Hogwarts? She actually wants to pump Hagrid for information about Harry for another scurrilous story, although Hagrid refuses to say anything negative about him. When she later discovers Hagrid's Giant ancestry, she writes an awful article claiming he is dangerous to students and brutal in his classes.

When Harry is watching the courtroom scenes in Dumbledore's Pensieve, he spots a younger Rita Skeeter in the audience, with the same Quick-Quotes Quill, reporting the trial.

During the Hogsmeade visit just before the second Triwizard task, the trio encounters Skeeter, who approaches Harry for another interview, but Hermione chases her off, telling her she ruins peoples' lives. This leads Harry to suspect Hermione will be Rita's next victim. Indeed, in her first Harry article, Rita had hinted about a romance between Harry and Hermione, at least according to Colin Creevey. Soon, a vengeful Rita, now writing for *Witch Weekly*, claims in a new story that Hermione, whom she calls "plain," may be using illegal love potions on both Harry and Viktor Krum. Soon after, *Witch Weekly* readers send anonymous and threatening letters to Hermione.

After the final Triwizard challenge, Hermione traps a beetle while visiting Harry in the school infirmary: it is Rita Skeeter, who is an unregistered Animagus. That is how she eavesdrops on private conversations and reports them in her articles. Hermione suspected she was an Animagus after observing Draco Malfoy conversing with a small object, shortly before the article about Hagrid appeared. She also recalled that whenever any secrets were discussed in private conversations, they soon appeared in Rita's stories, and there had always been a large beetle in the vicinity. Hermione tells Skeeter she will not report her as an unregistered Animagus if she abstains from writing any stories for the next year.

Order of the Phoenix   Rita is seen again when Hermione meets with her in Hogsmeade village. When Hermione had forced Skeeter to stop writing stories for one year by threatening to expose her as an unregistered Animagus, Rita fell upon hard times. This was evidenced by her once fashionable clothing that had became frayed and worn.

After Harry's assertion that Voldemort has returned (in *Harry Potter and the Goblet of Fire*), the Ministy of Magic waged a smear campaign against him and Dumbledore in *The Daily Prophet,* disputing his claims. To garner support for Harry, Hermione blackmailed Skeeter into writing a favorable story about Harry that Luna Lovegood's father published in his paper, *The Quibbler*. Rita's story convinced many readers that Harry was telling the truth and Voldemort had returned.

After the Battle at the Department of Mysteries, Cornelius Fudge personally sees that Voldemort has returned. Shortly after, the *Daily Prophet* reverses its editorial stance, and Harry once again becomes a hero. The Prophet buys the rights to the Quibbler interview and runs it as an "exclusive."

Half-Blood Prince   Although Rita is presumably writing for *The Daily Prophet*, she plays no role in the story.

Deathly Hallows   The *Daily Prophet* sends a reporter to interview Rita as a result of her having written a book. This book, a scurrilous and unauthorized biography of Dumbledore, is a typical Skeeter hatchet-job, putting the worst possible interpretation on everything that was known of Dumbledore's early life. This book, which alleged that Dumbledore's sister Ariana was a Squib who had been locked away from society for all her young life, that Dumbledore had been friends with the evil wizard Gellert Grindelwald as a youth and had been discussing his plan to take over the entire world, and that Aberforth had broken Albus' nose at Ariana's funeral, among other things, leaves Harry wondering about his hero. Harry's worries about Dumbledore, inspired by this book, are only put to rest when Aberforth later tells Harry what actually happened.

Strengths   Little is known about Skeeter's magical talents, although she learned to become an (unregistered) Animagus, which apparently takes considerable wizarding ability. She appears to be an intelligent and resourceful journalist, who uses whatever means she can to uncover information for her stories. As an unregistered Animagus, she uses her beetle form to eavesdrop on unsuspecting witches and wizards who are then victimized by her scurrilous pieces. Skeeter intuitively knows her readership and works hard and fast to meet their expectations. Her biography of Dumbledore is researched and written in just a few weeks after his death. Skeeter is able to gain the confidence of Bathilda Bagshot and others, which allows her to document unpleasant aspects of Dumbledore's youth, many based on fact.

Weaknesses   Vain and self-serving, Skeeter is an unethical journalist who uses any means to gather information, accurate or false, for her sensationalistic stories. She cares little for how her subjects are affected by her malicious lies, and uses an enchanted "Quick-Quotes Quill" to fabricate "quotes" for her articles.

Relationships with Other Characters   While we don't see much of Rita's relationships with other people, we do see that Rita seems to have a good working relationship with her photographer. Perhaps this is possible because she has no intention of ever writing anything about him. Anyone else would have to guard what they say around her for fear of having their life histories published, slanted for maximum readership (thus maximum scurrilousness). Likely because of this, Rita has co-workers, but we see no sign of friends.

Among those she interviews, Rita seems to be regarded with emotions ranging from anger at her misinterpretation of what she said (Elphias Doge, Hermione), through fear that more such misinterpretations may be coming (Rubeus Hagrid, Harry Potter), to, at its mildest, cheerful dismissal of anything she has to say or write (Albus Dumbledore).

ANALYSIS

At the end of *Harry Potter and the Order of the Phoenix*, *The Daily Prophet* buys the publishing rights to Skeeter's interview with Harry that appeared in *The Quibbler*. It is interesting that the galleons paid for that story go to the Lovegoods; quite possibly, Rita receives nothing. This may increase her hatred of Harry and Hermione, though any story that appears critical of them will be spiked in the editorial environment of the day. It is entirely possible that this is why she turned her eye on Dumbledore at the start of *Harry Potter and the Deathly Hallows;* if nothing else, Rita is a realist and would know that with Potter still "the Chosen One," she would not be able to get anything published against him. As the tide turned, and Harry became "Undesireable Number One" with a price on his head, it is likely that a large part of the venom hitting the press about him was hers.

Rita is not at all selective with her venom; it appears that previous to her book about Dumbledore, she had written a similar book about Armando Dippet, the headmaster at Hogwarts before Dumbledore. That book is mentioned only in passing, on the cover of the Dumbledore book: *Armando Dippet: Master or Moron?*

Ritchie Coote

Gender: Male
Hair color: Unknown
Eye color: Unknown
Related Family: Unknown
Loyalty:

OVERVIEW

Ritchie Coote joins the Gryffindor team in Harry's sixth year. He is described as "weedy looking," but has very good aim.

ROLE IN THE BOOKS

Half-Blood Prince Harry, now Quidditch Team captain, selects Ritchie Coote as one of his two Beaters, the other being Jimmy Peakes.

Rodolphus Lestrange

Gender: Male
Hair color: Dark
Eye color: Dark
Related Family: Bellatrix Lestrange, Rabastan Lestrange
Loyalty: Lord Voldemort

OVERVIEW

Rodolphus Lestrange is the husband of Bellatrix Lestrange and brother to Rabastan Lestrange.

ROLE IN THE BOOKS

Goblet of Fire Although the action referred to takes place before the series starts, it is in this book that we are introduced to Rodolphus, as Harry witnesses the trial of his group by means of Albus Dumbledore's pensieve. Shortly after Lord Voldemort's disappearance, he and three other young Death Eaters (his wife Bellatrix Lestrange, his brother Rabastan Lestrange, and Barty Crouch Jr.) attacked and tortured Aurors Frank and Alice Longbottom, using the Cruciatus Curse on them until the two lost most of their mental faculties. All four members of the group were sentenced to imprisonment in Azkaban.

Order of the Phoenix We only hear about Rodolphus once in this book, when Lucius Malfoy tells Rodolphus to go with Bellatrix Lestrange to find Harry and the Prophecy. From this, we gather that Rodolphus was among the escapees from Azkaban near Christmas time.

Half-Blood Prince Twice, Professor Dumbledore and Harry visit Horace Slughorn's memories of one particular night when Slughorn is meeting with Tom Riddle and his associates. In both of those memories, Slughorn notes that it is eleven o'clock, and says that it is time to send the gathered students off to bed, remarking to two of them, Avery and Lestrange (who could be either Rodolphus or Rabastan), that they have an essay due, and would be given detention if he didn't have it ready.

Deathly Hallows We only hear of Rodolphus once in Deathly Hallows, when Nymphadora Tonks (his niece by marriage), says they injured him during their flight to her and Ron's portkey at his Aunt Muriel's.

Relationships with Other Characters As noted above, he is the husband of Bellatrix (née Black).

Roger Davies

Gender: Male
Hair color: Unknown
Eye color: Unknown
Related Family: Unknown
Loyalty:

OVERVIEW

Roger Davies is the Captain of the Ravenclaw Quidditch team and is one of the Chasers. He is a talented player and seems to be considered very good looking—Fleur Delacour evidently liked him enough to allow him to escort her to the Yule Ball.

ROLE IN THE BOOKS

Goblet of Fire We find out that Roger is Captain of the Ravenclaw Quidditch team. Fleur Delacour, Triwizard Champion for Beauxbatons, has accepted his invitation to the Yule Ball.

Order of the Phoenix In this book Cho Chang claimed to Harry that Roger asked her to go out with him but she turned him down in favour of Harry instead. Later in the fifth book, Roger and his date for the afternoon, a pretty blonde girl, ended up in Madam Puddifoot's in Hogsmeade—the same tea shop as Harry and Cho (and many other student couples). Talking with Harry about this afterwards, Hermione suggests that Cho likely was trying to use Roger's interest in her to make Harry jealous, and thus gauge Harry's interest in her. However, it seems to have only succeeded in confusing him.

Rolanda Hooch

Gender: Female
Hair color: Grey
Eye color: Yellow
Related Family:
Loyalty:

OVERVIEW

Rolanda Hooch is the flying instructor and one of the inter-house Quidditch referees at Hogwarts School of Witchcraft and Wizardry. Her teaching is stern and regimental.

ROLE IN THE BOOKS

Philosopher's Stone Madam Hooch first appears preparing a class of first-years including Harry for their first flying lesson. When Neville Longbottom breaks his wrist falling off his broom, she leaves the scene to take him to the Hospital Wing. Following her departure, Harry flies on his broom to recover a stolen item, and Professor McGonagall witnesses his flying talent. As a direct result, McGonagall subsequently employs him as the new Gryffindor Quidditch team Seeker. Madam Hooch doesn't appear teaching Harry again, which leads the reader to the conclusion that Harry is beyond the help of such lessons. Given Hermione's evident lack of skill with the broom, it is unlikely that flying lessons were discontinued thereafter.

Madam Hooch referees the Quidditch match between Gryffindor and Slytherin; that duty is taken over by Professor Snape for the match between Gryffindor and Hufflepuff. We do not see the match between Gryffindor and Ravenclaw as Harry is in the Hospital Wing.

Chamber of Secrets Madam Hooch referees the Quidditch match between Gryffindor and Slytherin, and is due to for the match between Gryffindor and Hufflepuff; however, two students are found Petrified and the match is canceled.

Prisoner of Azkaban Madam Hooch referees the Quidditch match between Gryffindor and Ravenclaw, which takes place despite severe weather conditions and poor visibility.

After an attack on The Fat Lady by Sirius Black, Professor McGonagall details Madam Hooch to "keep an eye" on Harry during Quidditch practices for the purpose of his safety. Furthermore, McGonagall confiscates Harry's newly received racing broom, a Firebolt, so that Madam Hooch can search it for any Dark magic. When Harry receives the broom with its clean bill of health, Madam Hooch is quite taken with it, and rhapsodizes over it for some time before Oliver Wood can remind her that they are there to practice. She then falls asleep in the stands while practice is going on.

Madam Hooch referees the Quidditch match between Gryffindor and Hufflepuff, and again at the final between Gryffindor and Slytherin. The final is a violent match, and Madam Hooch several times comments that she has never seen such flagrant fouls committed.

Order of the Phoenix Madam Hooch referees the match between Gryffindor and Slytherin, and again it is a very dirty match. It is noted at the end that Madam Hooch does not notice the Bludger hit on Harry after the final whistle.

QUESTIONS

1. Does Madam Hooch have any interaction with the students other than flying lessons and Quidditch?

Romilda Vane

Gender: Female
Hair color: black
Eye color: brown
Related Family: Unknown
Loyalty:

OVERVIEW

Romilda Vane is a fellow student of Harry Potter. She is in Gryffindor house, but is two years younger than Harry—in *Harry Potter and the Half-Blood Prince*, when Harry is in sixth year, it is mentioned that she is a fourth-year.

ROLE IN THE BOOKS

Half-Blood Prince Romilda is one of a group of fourth-year girls who try to get Harry to sit in their compartment of the Hogwarts Express, instead of with Luna Lovegood and Neville Longbottom. Harry rather disappoints them by saying he'd rather stay where he was.

Romilda has rather set her cap for Harry, to the extent of trying to get him to take her to Professor Slughorn's Christmas party, by slipping him some love potion; Hermione has warned him, however, and he sets the love potion, concealed inside chocolate cauldrons, aside in his dorm. Ron later takes these by mistake, damaging his relationship with Lavender Brown.

When Harry publicly announces the start of his romantic attachment to Ginny by kissing her at the Gryffindor Quidditch victory party, Romilda appears to be very angry.

Strengths Romilda is assertive and not afraid to approach Harry. She is probably the leader of her clique of fourth year girls.

Weaknesses Romilda is self-centered, vain and a bit ruthless. Her interest in Harry is strictly about prestige and peer approval rather than any genuine feelings for him.

ANALYSIS

Like so many characters in the Potter series. Romilda's character is echoed by her name. She is vain, trying to hook up with Harry not for anything that Harry has, but for what he can bring her: a measure of fame amongst the girls in the common room. In all of her plotting and scheming to get Harry to notice her and go out with her, notably absent is any idea of what Harry would like. The very first time we see her, we note that she is apparently quite willing to dismiss Harry's friends, in her attempt to be the force that brings Harry to their compartment.

Ron Weasley

Gender: Male
Hair color: Red
Eye color: Blue
Related Family:

Ron Weasley

Loyalty:
Arthur Weasley (father)
Molly Weasley (mother)
Bill Weasley (oldest brother)
Charlie Weasley (older brother)
Percy Weasley (older brother)
Fred Weasley (older brother)
George Weasley (older brother)
Ginny Weasley (younger sister)
Albus Dumbledore, Hermione Granger, Harry Potter,

OVERVIEW

Ronald "Ron" Bilius Weasley is youngest of six brothers and has one younger sister, Ginny. Ron comes from a poor but well-respected Wizarding family. The large clan is known mostly for their red hair and odd activities. Ron's father, Arthur Weasley, works for the Ministry of Magic and has a rather unusual interest in Muggles and Muggle possessions. Ron is looked down upon by some students (mostly Slytherins) for his family's meager finances and their friendliness towards Muggles. In times of need, Ron can count on his two best friends Harry Potter and Hermione Granger.

Ron's birthday is March 1, 1980, according to the author. He turned eleven the year before he started at Hogwarts, making him five months older than Harry and six months younger than Hermione.

ROLE IN THE BOOKS

Note: Ron Weasley, while not the viewpoint character in this series, is one of the Trio, and thus is in almost every part of the action. A summary of his role in the books would, perforce, be a summary of the books. For Ron's full role in the series, it is best to begin here and proceed onwards from that point. The sections below will provide the bare outline of his role.

Philosopher's Stone   We first meet Ron in King's Cross Station; he is a member of the Wizarding family that Harry approaches when he realizes that he doesn't know how to get to Platform Nine and Three Quarters. Fred and George help Harry get his trunk on board, and then recognize him by his scar; they then tell the rest of the family that Harry is on board the train. Ron ends up in the same compartment as Harry, and the twins come in briefly to introduce themselves and Ron to Harry. Ron actually doesn't believe that this is the famous Harry Potter until Harry shows him his scar; apparently Fred and George have been known to play tricks on him before. Harry, fascinated by the previously unknown Wizarding world, and Ron, intrigued both by Muggle life and by the discovery that the famous Harry Potter is just a kid like himself, quickly become friends.

We meet Neville Longbottom as he asks Harry and Ron if anyone has seen his toad, Trevor; then, we meet Hermione when she looks into their compartment, while she is helping Neville find Trevor—she has apparently appointed herself Neville's assistant. Ron was about to show Harry a spell he had learned from Fred; Hermione, seeing that Ron has his wand out, invites herself in to watch him do magic. Ron's magic fails, of course, it being another of Fred's jokes, and she is annoyingly superior about it. She says that she has already read all the textbooks "of course," and generally seems to be annoyingly bright.

Draco Malfoy and his two sidekicks, Crabbe and Goyle now show up, suggesting that Harry might be well advised to be their friend, and when he refuses, demanding some of his food. When Goyle tries to help himself to a cauldron cake, Ron's rat Scabbers bites him; Draco and his henchmen depart.

Hermione now returns and rather bossily tells Harry and Ron that they must be nearly there, and they should change into uniform. Ron comments, after she has gone, that he hopes that whatever House she ends up in, it'd be different than his own. It turns out that she is Sorted into Gryffindor, but Ron is too happy about getting into Gryffindor himself to complain.

Harry and Ron are by now close friends; they both almost get into trouble when they try to get into the forbidden hallway, thinking it is the way to their next class, and they are both late for their first Transfiguration class. Ron is there to cheer Harry on in the altercation with Draco Malfoy on brooms in their first flying lesson. When Malfoy challenges Harry to a Wizard's duel, Ron volunteers to act as Harry's second. Hermione overhears and tells Harry that he's going to get into trouble. She then waits up for Harry and Ron in the common room, warning them again. Harry and Ron ignore her; she follows them out into the hallway, but then can't get back into the common room—The Fat Lady has wandered off, visiting. She decides to accompany them to the site of the duel, collecting Neville on the way. Finding that Filch is looking for someone there, all four of them try to sneak away, ending up in the forbidden third-floor corridor. Hermione opens the lock, which allows them to hide from Filch, but they nearly get caught by a giant three-headed dog.

The next day, Harry receives a broom in the morning post. This is his Nimbus 2000, on which he will play Quidditch. Malfoy tries to get Harry into trouble for this, by telling Professor Flitwick that "Potter has received a broom," but Flitwick says he's heard about the special dispensation, and asks what model it is. Harry and Ron are both amused by the fury and dismay that Draco shows.

As Hallowe'en approaches, Hermione is the first to levitate a feather in Charms class. Ron later comments that she's overbearingly smart, and that's why she has no friends; she overhears, and runs past. It turns out that she has gone into the girl's washroom and is in there crying.

At the Hallowe'en feast that night, Professor Quirrell reports that a Troll is in the school; Harry and Ron see it going into a room and lock it in, only to discover that they have locked it into the girl's washroom where Hermione is still hiding. Paralysed with fear, Hermione can do nothing against it; through sheer luck, Harry and Ron manage to knock it out. When Professor McGonagall arrives, Hermione claims to have gone hunting the troll; Harry and Ron are astonished that she would deliberately lie to a teacher. The combination of Harry and Ron risking their lives for Hermione, and

Hermione's breaking her principles to save Harry and Ron from punishment, ends up making the three of them friends.

Rubeus Hagrid manages to mention the name Nicholas Flamel to Harry, Ron, and Hermione in connection with the "mysterious package" that is evidently being guarded by the three-headed dog (named "Fluffy"). Although all three of them are unable to find anything about Flamel in the library, Harry does remember where he had seen Flamel's name, and Hermione is able to retrieve a reference to him immediately. She is also, from this, able to identify the "mysterious package" as the Philosopher's Stone. By this time, they are convinced that Snape is trying to steal the Stone, and Professor Quirrell is the only thing standing between Snape and the Stone. Hagrid has somehow managed to procure a dragon's egg; Ron is present at the hatching, and helps Hagrid care for the hatchling, named Norbert, for a while. However, he is bitten, and the wound turns green. He tells the infirmary witch, Madam Pomfrey that it is a dog bite, but she doesn't seem to believe him. He arranges with his brother Charlie to have Norbert taken off to Romania; but the reply from Charlie is found by Draco Malfoy, and so although Malfoy is caught wandering the halls, the teachers are awake, which results in Harry and Hermione getting caught as well.

Having survived exams, Harry now resolves to go down past Fluffy and retrieve the Stone so that he can keep it safe. Ron and Hermione insist on going with him. Ron reminds Hermione that she has the ability to make fire to free them from the second obstacle, a Devil's Snare plant, and directs the giant Wizard chess set to win through the fourth obstacle, but is injured during the game. Revived by Hermione, he returns to the surface to fetch Professor Dumbledore.

Finally, at the Leaving Feast, Dumbledore awards Ron fifty House points for "the best game of chess that Hogwarts has seen in many years."

As they reach King's Cross Station, Ron and Hermione both promise to write to Harry during the summer; Ron actually promises to have Harry over to his house to visit.

Chamber of Secrets It appears that Ron has, in fact, written to Harry over the summer, but his letters, along with Hermione's and Hagrid's, were intercepted by Dobby the House-Elf.

Ron re-enters the story shortly after Harry's birthday. When Dobby dropped the dessert in Harry's kitchen, the Ministry had sent an owl to warn him that underage wizards are not allowed to do magic; Uncle Vernon retrieved the letter and, now knowing that Harry was not allowed to do magic, locked Harry into his room and barred the windows. Four nights later, Ron, with the assistance of his brothers Fred and George, arrives in a flying Ford Anglia to rescue him. They take Harry to The Burrow, but are caught on their return by their mother. Ron and the twins are soundly berated, though Harry is simply welcomed. Harry volunteers to help Ron and the twins in the chore they are set for punishment, de-Gnoming the garden. Afterwards, Harry goes with Ron up to his room, where Harry will be sleeping; Ron has decorated his entire room with posters of his favorite Quidditch team, the Chudley Cannons.

Ron is present in Flourish and Blotts when the fight between Arthur Weasley and Lucius Malfoy starts, but he does not have a big role in this part of the story.

Ron, Harry, Ginny, Fred, George, and Percy travel to King's Cross in London to catch the Hogwarts Express, with Ron's mother, all driven by Ron's father. All the other members of the party have passed through the barrier, and Ron is alone with Harry in King's Cross Station, when the barrier fails to open for Harry. They plan to return to Ron's father's car to wait for Ron's parents to return. Fearing that the barrier may be permanently stuck, Ron decides to fly the car to Hogwarts, making use of the fact that it can be made invisible. Unfortunately the invisibility feature stops working, so they have to fly above the clouds, which is hot and extremely boring. The car starts failing as they approach Hogwarts, and eventually crashes into a tree on the Hogwarts grounds. The tree, an extremely rare Whomping Willow, takes revenge, beating up the car. Once Ron has managed to extricate the car from the willow, it ejects Harry, Ron, and their posessions, and drives off into the Forbidden Forest by itself. It turns out that Ron's wand was broken in the crash.

As Ron and Harry try to figure out how to get into the school, they are caught by Professor Snape, who takes them to his office. He summons Professor McGonagall and Professor Dumbledore. Dumbledore warns them that if they break one more rule they will be expelled; Professor McGonagall gives them detention, but accepts Ron's suggestion that as the offence occurred before school was in session, a House points penalty should not be assessed. Before leaving, she tells them that Ginny Weasley has been Sorted into Gryffindor.

As Ron and Harry reach Gryffindor tower, they meet Hermione, who tells them off for having dared to do something as flamboyant as flying a car to Hogwarts. She also says that they are just going to get into trouble again. She is then disgusted when all the rest of Gryffindor seem to think that Harry and Ron's arrival is amazing and exciting. Ron receives a Howler from his mother at breakfast the next day. People from Slytherin House seem to delight in repeating bits of the message from the Howler for the next week or so.

In Transfiguration class, Ron in particular has trouble because his wand is misbehaving badly; he has tried to fix it with Spellotape, but it keeps doing strange and unexpected things. In Defence Against the Dark Arts, Professor Lockhart sets a test to see how much the students have read, and Ron and Harry are amazed to find out that it is all questions about Lockhart himself. Lockhart then releases a cageful of Cornish pixies; when he cannot control them, he leaves Harry, Ron, and Hermione to deal with them. Hermione, of course, is quite competent at this; Ron is starting to wonder whether Lockhart is as good a wizard as he claims.

Hermione and Ron are present at Harry's first Quidditch practice of the year. That practice is halted by the arrival of the Slytherin team, who have been granted use of the pitch by Professor Snape. In the resulting altercation, Malfoy refers to Hermione as "Mudblood," a term which Hermione and Harry do not understand, but which seems to incite the rest of the Gryffindors to riot. Ron, in fact, attempts to jinx Malfoy; when Ron's damaged wand backfires, causing him to start vomiting slugs, Hermione and Harry carry him to Hagrid's hut. Hagrid explains the meaning of the term "mudblood," with Ron's occasional help.

When the detention set by Professor McGonagall is assigned, Harry is given the task of assisting Professor Lockhart with his fan mail; Ron is sent to Argus Filch to polish up the trophies in the trophy room, without magic. Ron is still feeling sick from the backfiring jinx, and has to polish one particular Award for Services to the School about ten times when he vomits up some slugs onto it.

When Harry is invited to Nearly Headless Nick's Deathday party, he asks if Hermione and Ron can come too. As a result, they all go, but find it rather morbid; they stay long enough to be polite, and for Hermione to introduce Harry and Ron to Moaning Myrtle, and then they depart. Harry then hears the disembodied voice (he had heard it earlier in Lockhart's study); Hermione and Ron are unable to hear it, but tag along with Harry as he follows it, and eventually finds the petrified Mrs. Norris. While Ron is present at the subsequent meeting with Filch, Harry, Hermione, and Professors Dumbledore, Snape, McGonagall, and Lockhart, he does not make any contribution. After the meeting, though, he explains the meaning of the term Squib, which Filch used to refer to himself; a squib is a person without magical ability born of magical parents.

When Ron later suggests that Malfoy could be the Heir of Slytherin, or at least might know who it was, Hermione suggests that there is a way to find out; she has read about Polyjuice Potion, that makes you look like someone else. Instructions for making it are in a book, *Moste Potente Potions,* that is in the Restricted section of the library, for which they would need a note. Ron asks, What teacher would be so thick as to provide the note? Hermione then convinces Lockhart to give her a note for the book, suggesting that it would help her understand what he was getting at in one of his books. Shortly thereafter, Hermione, Ron, and Harry, are in Moaning Myrtle's bathroom, studying the book; it seems they will need ingredients not in the student supplies cupboard, and Hermione insists that they are going to have to take some risks if they want to learn about the Heir of Slytherin. Hermione then volunteers to steal the supplies they need from Professor Snape's office, if Harry or Ron will provide a distraction. Harry does, and Hermione steals the ingredients they need, shortly after this adding them to the potion. She tells Harry and Ron that the potion will need about another fortnight.

A week later, Lockhart hosts a Duelling Club, in which he is theoretically teaching the students how to duel. Ron's wand manages to do something horrible to Seamus. Shortly after, when Harry demonstrates an ability to talk to snakes, Ron says that he didn't know that Harry was a Parselmouth; it is Hermione who tells him that it's a very rare ability, and the one that Salazar Slytherin was famous for.

On Christmas Day, the Polyjuice Potion is ready, and Hermione provides cakes dosed with a sleeping potion to get Crabbe and Goyle out of the way so that Harry and Ron can impersonate them. Harry and Ron take the potion, and become simulacra of Crabbe and Goyle; after much wandering, they manage to find Draco Malfoy, who leads them back to the Slytherin common room. There, among other things, he tells them that the Chamber had been opened fifty years before, and a girl had died because of it. He says he doesn't know who had done it then, likely they were still in Azkaban. As the potion wears off, Harry and Ron return to Moaning Myrtle's washroom, to find that the hair Hermione used to prepare her Polyjuice Potion was a cat hair, and so she is stuck with feline features; and they will not revert on their own, she has to go to the Hospital Wing for several weeks, and becomes very upset at the amount of schoolwork she is missing.

Harry and Ron later find a large puddle of water outside Moaning Myrtle's bathroom; investigating, they find that Myrtle is upset because someone dropped a book on her. Harry finds that the book is a diary, which had belonged to T. M. Riddle fifty years before; Ron remembers that the award he had spent so much time polishing was also to T. M. Riddle, fifty years earlier. After Hermione gets out of the Hospital wing, Harry shows her Riddle's diary. She makes a connection between the date on the diary, Riddle's award for Services to the School, and the date the Chamber was apparently last opened, and believes the diary might hold some clue as to what happened then; she tries a number of spells on it to see what it contains, to no avail.

On Valentine's Day, Harry discovers that if he writes in the dairy, it will answer. The diary shows him the events leading up to Hagrid's expulsion, and indicates that Riddle had found Hagrid was opening the Chamber and releasing the monster. Harry tells Ron about this, and later discusses this with Hermione. They all know Hagrid was expelled and that he seems to like big scary monsters; could it have been him?

On the way out to the next Quidditch match, Harry hears the disembodied voice again; this triggers an idea in Hermione, and she dashes off to the library. As the Quidditch match is about to start, Professor McGonagall marches onto the field and sends everyone back to the castle; leading Harry and Ron to the Hospital wing, she lets them know that Hermione has been Petrified. Harry and Ron decide that they have to go and see Hagrid and find out what he knows about the Chamber of Secrets. Before they can ask him anything, Cornelius Fudge arrives with Dumbledore, to tell Hagrid that he's going to have to go to Azkaban; and while that's still being discussed, Lucius Malfoy arrives with a petition removing Dumbledore as headmaster. As Dumbledore departs, he looks directly at Harry and Ron under Harry's Invisibility Cloak, and tells them that help will always be there for those who need it; Hagrid, as he leaves, says that if they wanted to find out some stuff, they should follow the spiders. Spiders are hard to find, much to Ron's relief; he is scared of them. But eventually Harry spots some, headed into the Forbidden Forest; he and Ron set out that night after them, and with Hagrid's dog Fang head off into the Forest. There they find Ron's dad's car, running wild but still apparently remembering Ron; and they are captured by giant spiders, who take them to see Aragog. Aragog tells them that he is not the monster in the chamber; the monster is something that the spiders cannot even name. Aragog was blamed for killing a girl, but the girl died in a bathroom, part of the castle that he never got to. When Aragog says that they cannot leave, that his children cannot be held back from eating them, Harry and Ron prepare to fight, and are rescued by Ron's dad's car, which takes them to the edge of the Forest, then drives back into the Forest again on its own.

It occurs to Harry that it might have been Moaning Myrtle who died last time the Chamber was opened; but with the tightened security it proves nearly impossible to get to her bathroom to check. Finally Harry and Ron between them manage to convince Lockhart to allow them to go to their next class on its own; and they break away from the class to visit Myrtle. They are intercepted by Professor McGonagall, and Harry on the spur of the moment says that they were trying to see Hermione. McGonagall allows them to visit, so of course they now must; and they find that she has a piece of paper held in her Petrified hand. This paper describes a Basilisk, and she has put the note "Pipes?" on it. This leads Harry and Ron to the conclusion that the Monster in the Chamber is a Basilisk, and that it is travelling through the pipes, which is how it is able to travel between floors; this also confirms their thought that the entrance to the Chamber is in Moaning Myrtle's bathroom.

While waiting in the staff room for Professor McGonagall, to tell her what they have learned, they hear the announcement sending all students back to their dorms. Hearing that the teachers are summoned to the staff room, Harry and Ron hide in a closet; McGonagall tells the gathered teachers that Ginny Weasley has been taken into the Chamber. Lockhart, arriving late, is taken at his word that he knows all about the monster, and is given the task of disposing of it. Harry and Ron go to Lockhart's office and find him packing; he explains that he hasn't actually done the things in his books, other people have done them and he has taken credit because the people who did the work weren't photogenic enough. Of course he then has to charm them so they forget they have done it; and he's now going to have to charm Ron and Harry as well so that they forget he has told them this. Before he can do so, though, Harry has disarmed him, and Ron has thrown his wand out the window; at wand-point, Harry and Ron march Lockhart down to Myrtle's bathroom, where Myrtle confirms that she died there because of the Basilisk. Harry now manages to open the entrance to the Chamber, and the three of them descend. When they find a huge cast-off snake-skin, Lockhart seems to faint; as Ron dashes forward to catch him, Lockhart grabs Ron's wand and tries to use it to wipe out Harry's and Ron's memories. Ron's wand, being broken, backfires and explodes, wiping Lockhart's memory and taking down a large bit of the ceiling.

Ron, trapped on the side of the rock fall away from the Chamber, works to clear the fall while Harry battles the Basilisk and the ghost of Tom Riddle. When Harry returns, victorious, with Ginny, Ron explains what had happened with Lockhart, and the four of them together are pulled back up to Myrtle's bathroom by Fawkes. Ron is then present when Harry tells the story to Ron's parents, Professor McGonagall, and Professor Dumbledore, and is then sent off to help take Professor Lockhart to the hospital wing.

Finally, on the train back from Hogwarts, Hermione and Ron promise to call Harry on the telephone.

Prisoner of Azkaban   Ron had attempted to call Harry on the telephone, but had not understood that simply talking was enough; he and Uncle Vernon had gotten into a yelling match. Apart from that, Ron does not communicate with Harry until Harry's birthday. Ron then sends him a gift, a pocket Sneakoscope, a top which spins and lights up when someone in the neighbourhood is untrustworthy. Apparently, Ron's dad has won a contest, and he whole family have gone to Egypt for their holidays; there is a picture of the whole family, including Percy with his new Head Boy badge and Ron with his pet rat Scabbers.

Ron re-enters the story on the day before school starts. Harry has been living in The Leaky Cauldron for the past fortnight when Hermione and Ron arrive in Diagon Alley to purchase school supplies. Hermione says she would like to buy an owl like Hedwig, and Ron suggests that his rat, Scabbers, is looking poorly, so they go into the Magical Menagerie; there, a large cat attacks Scabbers. Hermione buys the cat, who is named Crookshanks. Ron is staying overnight at the Leaky Cauldron with Harry, Hermione, and the rest of his family. He forgets his bottle of Rat Tonic, and Harry volunteers to get it; in the process, he overhears Ron's parents discussing Sirius' motives for breaking out of Azkaban: they apparently have come to the conclusion that he is going to try and kill Harry.

Ron shares a compartment on the Hogwarts Express with Harry, Hermione, and a sleeping Professor Lupin. Harry tells them that Sirius Black is believed to be trying to kill Harry, but Harry doesn't know why. When Harry later reveals that he can't go to Hogsmeade because he doesn't have a permission slip, Hermione and Ron are both dismayed. Shortly before they arrive at Hogwarts, a Dementor appears to inspect the train; Ron apparently is affected by the Dementor, but not to the same extent as Harry, who passes out.

On arrival at the school, Hermione and Harry are called aside by Professor McGonagall, but Ron is sent into the Great Hall. Harry and Hermione do not rejoin Ron until after the Sorting is finished. When the timetables are handed out next morning, Ron observes that Hermione is taking two or three classes at the same time; she does not explain, but changes the subject when Ron queries her about this.

Harry and Ron manage to get somewhat lost on their way to Divination; they are assisted in finding the class by a painting of a knight, one Sir Cadogan. At Divination, Ron finds something that looks like a dog in Harry's tea leaves; Professor Trelawney identifies it as a Grim. Ron mentions later that that's really bad; his Uncle Bilius had seen one and died very shortly thereafter.

When Hermione comments at lunch that she didn't much like Divination class, it seems rather woolly, and quite unlike Arithmancy, Ron and Harry are confused: Hermione has been with them all morning, when has she had time to go to Arithmancy?

After the accident at Care of Magical Creatures class, Ron goes with Harry and Hermione to Hagrid's hut to comfort Hagrid. They reassure Hagrid that Dumbledore would not sack him, and that Malfoy was at fault, and Hermione then tells Hagrid that he has had too much to drink. He agrees, and then escorts the three of them back up to the school. As they leave the dungeon after Potions class the next day, Ron turns to ask Hermione something, but Hermione is somehow not there; Ron spots her some way behind, tucking something back into her robes. As she catches up with them, her book bag splits, revealing that she is carrying a large number of books. Ron asks why she's carrying all those, all they have that afternoon is Defence Against the Dark Arts. Again, Hermione does not answer. In Defence Against the Dark Arts, Professor Lupin has the class defend themselves against a Boggart. Ron gains five points by successfully confronting the Boggart, but Hermione does not get a chance to defend herself from it. Ron asks what her Boggart would be, a paper that did not have a perfect grade?

The first Hogsmeade weekend is on Hallowe'en. While Ron and Harry are discussing ways of getting permission for Harry to go, Crookshanks attacks Scabbers. Hermione insists that Crookshanks is acting like a cat; Ron is incensed that she can be so insensitive towards other people's pets. The two of them do manage to patch things up enough that they are ready to go to Hogsmeade together; when they return, full of stories about the village, Harry tells them how he had seen Lupin drink a potion prepared for him by Snape. Hermione and Ron, knowing how much Snape hates Lupin, and how much Snape seems to want the Defence Against the Dark Arts job, are amazed. When Sirius Black manages to break into the castle that night, all of the students are moved to the Great Hall to sleep; Hermione, Ron, and Harry are still awake when Snape comes to report the all clear to Professor Dumbledore. At the same time, Snape chooses to mention that he had expressed some doubts about an appointment Dumbledore had made; Dumbledore overrides him.

The next Quidditch match is played in a howling rainstorm. When Harry's broomstick is blown away and hits the Whomping Willow, Hermione and Ron pick up the few sorry splinters that are left; they stand watch in the infirmary until Harry regains consciousness, and try to console him for his loss.

On Monday, Professor Lupin is once again teaching Defence Against the Dark Arts, much to everyone's relief, he cancels the Werewolf essay that Professor Snape had assigned.

Possibly because of Harry's situation, Hermione and Ron both choose to stay at Hogwarts over Christmas. This cheers Harry up to the point that he doesn't seem overly upset about missing another Hogsmeade weekend. Hermione and Ron go to Hogsmeade, though, and are examining some "unusual tastes" candies at Honeyduke's when Harry appears behind them. When Harry explains about the Marauder's Map, Hermione insists that he should turn it in to Professor McGonagall. Harry says no, he doesn't think Sirius is getting in through the secret passages, Ron mentions that the streets of Hogwarts are patrolled by Dementors anyway. The three of them go to The Three Broomsticks for Butterbeer. When Professor Flitwick, Professor McGonagall, Hagrid, and Cornelius Fudge come in, Hermione and Ron push Harry under the table to keep him from being seen, and Hermione also moves a tree to conceal their table. Hermione, Harry, and Ron all overhear the discussion between these four and Madam Rosmerta in which Fudge details how Sirius betrayed Harry's parents to Voldemort, and went on to kill Peter Pettigrew and twelve Muggles. Ron, like Hermione and Harry, is left speechless by this revelation. Harry does not fall asleep until late because of this revelation, and wakes up only near lunch time the next day. Hermione and Ron have been discussing this between themselves, and have decided to try and defuse Harry's anger at Sirius, in an attempt to keep him from setting out to kill Sirius. Apparently, Ron and Hermione have been rehearsing the conversation they plan to have with Harry while he has been asleep. It goes rather astray when Harry decides that he wants to ask Hagrid about Sirius. When they reach Hagrid's, though, they are distracted by Hagrid's telling them that Buckbeak has to be examined by the Committee for the Disposal of Dangerous Creatures. Hermione volunteers to research similar cases in hopes of getting Buckbeak off; Ron and Harry chime in. They spend the next few days, all three of them, in the library.

At Christmas, Harry receives a Firebolt, which arrives with no indication of who sent it. Hermione, visiting them in their dorm room, seems worried by it; but her musings are cut short by Crookshanks once again attacking Scabbers. After the Christmas lunch, Hermione stops to have a word with Professor McGonagall; after which McGonagall inspects, and then confiscates the Firebolt. Both Ron and Harry are angry at Hermione, who says the broom may well be jinxed, since it could have been sent by Sirius Black.

As school re-convenes, Oliver Wood seeks out Harry to ask if he has sorted out his Dementor problem and if he has picked out a new broom. Ron tells Oliver that Harry got a Firebolt; Harry tells Oliver that it is being stripped down and checked for jinxes.

Once the Firebolt is returned to Harry some months later, he brings it back to the Gryffindor common room. This is the eve of the match against Ravenclaw, and there is renewed hope of winning the Cup. Ron and Harry seek out Hermione behind her stack of textbooks to let her know everything is back to normal. When Ron goes to take the Firebolt up to the dorm, however, he finds Scabbers is missing, apparently eaten by Crookshanks. Ron is furious with Hermione, especially because Hermione does not seem to show any remorse for Scabbers' apparent demise. Hermione, who is already under severe stress from taking two or three times as many classes per day as should be humanly possible, and (as Hagrid tells Harry later) from also trying to come up with cases to help Hagrid fight for Buckbeak's acquittal before the Committee, apparently is too busy to allow herself the luxury of empathizing with Ron. To cheer Ron up, Harry allows him to try out the Firebolt after team practice the next evening. On their way back to the castle in the dark, Harry thinks he sees eyes and is privately worried that it might be the Grim, but Ron, casting Lumos, reveals that it is Crookshanks.

After the Quidditch match, there is a celebration in the Gryffindor common room; Ron comments loudly, in Hermione's hearing, that Scabbers would have liked some of the treats, and Hermione departs, crying. After a while, they all go to bed; but Ron is awakened by Sirius Black cutting down his bed-curtains. He screams, and rouses Gryffindor. Sirius manages to escape again. Ron, however, is somewhat pleased at the resulting notoriety, though he wonders why Sirius hadn't simply silenced him when he had the chance. Harry doesn't have any idea, either. Hagrid now invites Harry and Ron down for tea, and gently chastizes them for not having had time to visit. Harry and Ron also notice Hagrid's best suit hanging ready, and are reminded that they had promised to help with Buckbeak's defence, a promise which had gone by the boards in the heat of events. Hagrid tells them not to worry, that he understood, and that he had been getting a lot of help from Hermione; and mentions that Hermione is so upset at losing Ron's friendship that she has been crying. While this does soften Ron slightly, the effects are not lasting; that same day, Harry and Ron scheme to allow Harry to visit Hogsmeade again, and Hermione, overhearing, tells Harry that it might not be a good idea. Ron immediately snaps at her.

Harry, under the Invisibility Cloak, meets Ron in Hogsmeade; they see the sights, ending up at the Shrieking Shack. Here, Ron is confronted by Draco Malfoy, with Crabbe and Goyle; Harry, from inside the Invisibility Cloak, acts to defend Ron, but in the process his head becomes visible. Draco and cronies retreat, but Ron and Harry know that they are on their way to report Harry to Snape. Harry returns to the school and is caught by Snape; in turn, Snape summons Lupin to ask about the parchment he has found in Harry's pocket. Ron, arriving in Snape's study at the dead run, defends Harry by telling him that the stuff Harry is carrying is, in fact, stuff that Ron had bought for him long before.

As Ron and Harry return to Gryffindor tower, they meet Hermione, who has received a letter from Hagrid in London. The letter says that Buckbeak had been condemned to be executed. Hermione then apologizes to Ron for Crookshanks. She and Ron are now back to a friendly footing again. Ron and Harry both promise, again, to work on material with Hermione for Buckbeak's appeal. They are unable to talk to Hagrid, due to the security measures, until Care of Magical Creatures class; asked about what happened at the hearing, Hagrid tells them, but is overcome by tears, and runs off to his cottage. Malfoy remarks that Hagrid is acting like a big baby; Hermione punches Malfoy in the nose. Malfoy and his cronies retreat in confusion, and Hermione demands that Harry must win the upcoming Quidditch match against Slytherin, she just couldn't stand it if they lost.

Hermione then somehow manages to vanish on the short walk to Charms class, and is not seen again until after lunch, when Harry and Ron find her asleep in the Gryffindor common room.

From Easter holidays right up to exams, everyone is overwhelmed with work; Ron, in between studying, is looking up material for Buckbeak's appeal. As exams approach, Hedwig brings a note from Hagrid saying that Buckbeak's appeal is set for June 6, the last day of exams, and will be at the school.

Ron manages to muddle through exams. The Charms exam includes Cheering Charms; Harry overdoes it slightly through nerves, putting his subject, Ron, into fits of hysterical laughter. And Defence Against the Dark Arts is a practical test; Ron is led astray by a Hinkypunk. In Care of Magical Creatures, the test is very simple; all they have to do is keep a Flobberworm alive for an hour. Hermione, Harry, and Ron use this as a chance to exchange a few words with Hagrid; he says that Buckbeak is tired of being penned up, but it's only a few days now, and they will know one way or the other.

It is on their return from the Defence Against the Dark Arts exam, on the morning of the last day of exams, that Harry, Ron, and Hermione meet with Cornelius Fudge who is there to witness the destruction of a dangerous creature, Buckbeak. Ron comments that the Hippogriff might still get off, but Fudge replies with some skepticism; Hermione prevents Ron from retorting angrily, to avoid jeopardizing Ron's dad's job.

When Harry returns to the Gryffindor common room from his Divination final exam, Hermione and Ron tell him that Hagrid has lost the appeal, and that Buckbeak's execution is set for sundown. Despite Hagrid's order that they stay at school, Harry says that if he still had his Invisibility Cloak, they could go and comfort Hagrid; but it is still under the humpbacked witch where he had to leave it after his most recent trip to Hogsmeade, and he can't go back to get it because Snape would expel him from Hogwarts. Hermione gets the charm for the humpbacked witch from Harry, and retrieves the cloak; and so after dinner they hide in the Entrance Hall until the coast is clear. Under the Cloak they proceed to Hagrid's.

When Hagrid lets them in, he is shaking so badly that he drops the milk jug. While trying to comfort Hagrid, Hermione cleans up the spilled milk and the jug, gets a fresh jug out of the cupboard, and starts to pour from the pitcher, then realizes that Scabbers, long thought dead, is hiding in the new milk jug. She tips him out onto the table; he frantically tries to get back into the jug, but Ron catches Scabbers and puts him in a pocket of his robes. Hagrid now sees the execution party coming down from the school, and sends Harry, Ron, and Hermione away; they leave through the back door, under the cloak, while the execution party enters. Their progress back up to the school is hindered by Ron, who is trying to keep Scabbers from escaping; and so they are able to hear the fall of the executioner's axe.

Scabbers does now break free, and runs off, with Crookshanks, who has apparently been homing on his squeaks, in hot pursuit. Ron runs after him; Harry and Hermione throw off the Cloak and follow. Ron catches Scabbers; Harry is suddenly knocked aside by the big black dog, which then proceeds to drag Ron off into an apparent tunnel mouth under the roots of the

Whomping Willow, breaking his leg in the process. Neither Harry nor Hermione can get past the branches of the Willow to follow, but Crookshanks runs over and presses the knot that stills the tree. Harry and Hermione then follow Crookshanks into the tunnel, which proves to lead to the Shrieking Shack. There, they find Ron, and are in turn ambushed by Sirius Black, who, as it turns out, is an Animagus and can turn himself into a big black dog—the same dog Harry has been seeing all year. Wandless, Harry, Hermione, and Ron manage to disarm Sirius, and Harry is preparing to take revenge for the death of his parents when Professor Lupin appears on the scene. The first thing Lupin does is disarm Harry, Ron and Hermione; he then exchanges a few words with Sirius, and then embraces him like a long-lost brother. Hermione now accuses him of helping Sirius get into the castle, of wanting Harry dead, and of being a werewolf. Lupin says that only one out of three is correct, far from Hermione's usual standard; he had not been helping Sirius, he didn't want Harry dead, but he was a werewolf. It wouldn't have done any good to tell the other teachers, Lupin continues, because they all knew, but he was curious as to when Hermione had figured it out. Hermione said that she had guessed right after Snape had them do the assignment on werewolves when Lupin was sick; Lupin admitted that Snape had set that assignment in hopes that some of the students would figure it out. Lupin then returns Harry's, Ron's and Hermione's wands, and asks if they will now listen to the two unarmed grown-ups.

Lupin explains now that using the Marauder's Map, he had seen Ron and Sirius, and someone else, going down the tunnel, and had hastened to follow. Harry asked how he knew how the map worked; Lupin said that he had helped make it, he was Moony. Lupin asks to see Ron's rat; Scabbers is produced. Lupin says that he's the third person who was travelling with Sirius and Ron, that he's not a rat at all. Sirius adds that he is in fact an Animagus named Peter Pettigrew. Hermione, Ron and Harry say this is impossible; Sirius murdered him twelve years earlier. After an altercation in which Sirius tries to grab Scabbers and fails, Lupin points out that Harry must know everything before they proceed. Hermione now asks how Pettigrew could be an Animagus? As part of the homework for Transfiguration, she has checked, and there are only seven registered Animagi, and none of them is Pettigrew. Lupin says that there were in fact three unregistered Animagi running around Hogwarts in his day.

The bedroom door creaks open; Ron mentions that the Shrieking Shack is haunted. Lupin says no, it was always him that was making the noises that led people to believe it was haunted. The Shrieking Shack was built to contain him when he was transformed, and the Whomping Willow was planted at the only entrance to prevent other people from getting in and endangering themselves. It was because of these precautions that he was able to attend Hogwarts; and his three great friends, Sirius, James, and Peter, when they found out that he was a werewolf, did not abandon him, but became Animagi to support him. James and Sirius were large enough, in their transformed state, to control him, and so they were able to run free though the Forbidden Forest and Hogsmeade. Harry asks what shape his father was, but Hermione interrupts to say that it was very dangerous for a werewolf to be running around like that; Lupin agrees that it was, and says he's not proud of how they behaved. He also says that he should have told Professor Dumbledore that Sirius was an Animagus, but he didn't want to believe that he was getting into the school that way; it was easier to think that Sirius was using some sort of Dark magic to do it. Lupin says that in that respect, Snape was right about him, he isn't trustworthy. Sirius asks how Snape enters into things; Lupin tells Sirius that Snape is teaching there. Lupin goes on to say that Snape was at Hogwarts when they were there, and that Sirius had played a trick on him, telling him how to get past the Whomping Willow while Lupin was transformed. It was James who had found out about it and prevented Snape from reaching the Shrieking Shack, thus saving his life. Harry asks if that is why Snape hates him; behind Lupin, Snape pulls off Harry's Invisibility Cloak and says, "That's right." As Snape prepares to take the bound Lupin and Sirius back to the Dementors, Hermione, Harry, and Ron all cast the disarm spell on Snape, which results in him banging his head into the wall. With Snape unconscious, and Sirius and Lupin freed, Lupin explains what had happened the night Harry's parents had died; and Lupin and Sirius between them force Pettigrew to reveal himself. Hermione asks, if Pettigrew is a Dark wizard, why he had not acted against Harry who had been in a dorm room with him for the past three years? Black replies, saying that Pettigrew had not seen any benefit in acting against Harry; with Voldemort apparently dead, acting against Harry would not gain Pettigrew anything. Hermione asks Black how he had managed to escape Azkaban if he was not using Dark magic; Black said that even without a wand, he could transform into a dog, and did so when things got unbearable. Dementors cannot see, and so were unaware that he had changed, but the simpler emotions of a dog were harder for them to get a fix on. It was as a dog that he was able to escape, the Dementors had been unable to locate him properly, and he was thin enough to get through the bars.

As they leave the Shrieking Shack and start to cross the Hogwarts grounds, Lupin is hit by the light of the full moon and changes to a werewolf. Sirius changes to his dog form to protect the Trio; Pettigrew jinxes Ron and Crookshanks, rendering them unconscious, changes back into a rat, and escapes through the tall grass. Ron, still unconscious, is collected by Snape and brought to the Hospital Wing. He remains unconscious until after Sirius' escape is discovered. Shortly after Snape, Fudge, and Dumbledore leave, and Madam Pomfrey returns to her office, Ron wakes up, and asks what has been going on; Harry says that Hermione should explain. Although the next day is a Hogsmeade weekend, neither Ron nor Hermione feels like going to the village; so Harry, Ron, and Hermione sit at the shore of the lake discussing the events of the evening. Hagrid wanders by and tells them that Buckbeak has escaped. Hermione glares at Ron to try and keep him from laughing. Hagrid also tells them that Lupin is a werewolf, and that he has resigned; Harry goes to talk to him, even though Hermione says that it is probably too late to do anything useful if he has already resigned.

The final term goes by quickly; Ron manages to scrape a pass in all his subjects, and Gryffindor wins the House Cup again. On the Hogwarts Express back to London, shortly after lunch, Hermione spots something flying outside the train window; Harry reaches out and snags it. It proves to be a tiny owl, carrying a message for Harry from Sirius; it says, among other things, that it had been Sirius who had given Harry his Firebolt at Christmas, and so Hermione was right. The letter also says that as he was responsible for Ron losing his rat, Sirius would like Ron to have the owl who is carrying the letter; Ron holds the owl under Crookshanks' nose, and Crookshanks purrs, so Ron decides to keep him.

At King's Cross Station, Harry parts from Hermione and Ron for another summer.

Goblet of Fire Ron and Harry's friendship is tested when Harry is mysteriously chosen to be a champion in the Tri-Wizard Tournament, an inter-school competition that was previously banned because it was too hazardous. Ron is convinced an underage Harry cheated to enter, and he becomes jealous over the attention that is continually heaped on him. The two friends reconcile after Harry barely survives the deadly first challenge; Ron realizes Harry would not have cheated to have entered such a dangerous competition. In fact, it soon becomes apparent that Harry's name was illegally entered as a means to kill him.

Ron faces other difficulties when he develops romantic feelings for Hermione Granger, who is being courted by Viktor Krum, another Tri-Wizard champion from the Durmstrang Institute.

Order of the Phoenix Ron becomes a Prefect at the start of this year, and this causes some friction between him and Harry. Ron is a lot more arbitrary in the use of his Prefect privilege than Hermione, and is unwilling to stand up against his brothers Fred and George, both of which cause Hermione no little amount of distress.

With the departure of Oliver Wood, the Gryffindor Quidditch team is now in need of a new Keeper. Now having a new broom, Ron decides to try out for the position. Angelina Johnson takes him on grudgingly, saying that he is the best of a bad lot. Ron's Keeping in practices, and in the first two games, is a disaster; it is only amazingly good Seeking by Harry in the game against Slytherin, and by Ginny in the second game, that their losses are held to a reasonable level. In the final game of the season, Ron gets his confidence back, and Gryffindor wins with a sufficiently large margin to keep the Quidditch Cup.

Ron is also instrumental in convincing Harry to start up a student organization that will teach real Defence Against the Dark Arts, rather than the pointless nonsense taught by Professor Umbridge. He is present at the first meeting in the Hog's Head, and at every meeting thereafter until the organization, then called Dumbledore's Army, is betrayed and disbanded.

Harry enlists Ron, along with Hermione, Ginny, and Luna Lovegood, when he breaks into Professor Umbridge's office to check on Sirius's whereabouts. Caught by Umbridge, Ron escapes when Ginny Jinxes Draco, and the group, including Neville Longbottom who had as usual been in the wrong place at the wrong time, goes to find Harry and Hermione who have led Umbridge on a wild-goose chase into the Forbidden Forest. The six students then ride Thestrals to the Ministry of Magic in London, where Harry believes Sirius is being held captive. Once there, the students are ambushed by Death Eaters. In the ensuing battle, Ron is hit by what appears to be a drunkenness jinx, and puts himself out of action. We do see him recovering later in the Hospital Wing.

Half-Blood Prince Throughout much of the book, Ron and Hermione are at daggers drawn over Ron's infatuation with Lavender Brown; however, his interest in Lavender is likely retaliation against Hermione for her relationship with Viktor Krum. When Ron nearly dies after drinkng a glass of poisoned mead that was apparently meant for Professor Dumbledore, Hermione is so distraught over the incident that they end their feud. Ron loses interest in Lavender, and Hermione considers Viktor as a friend. However, whatever romantic feelings each may have for the other remains undeclared. After Harry decides to leave Hogwarts before his final year to search for Lord Voldemort's remaining Horcruxes (soul fragments), Ron, and also Hermione, pledge to accompany him.

Deathly Hallows Ron is one of the members of the Order to arrange to rescue Harry from Privet Drive, and there are fears that he has been injured in the escape. He does arrive eventually, reporting that he had been detained by Auntie Muriel. As usual when staying at The Burrow, Harry shares a room with Ron. On his birthday, Ron gives Harry a book, *Twelve Foolproof Ways to Charm Witches*, saying that he had gotten a copy from the Twins earlier, and that Harry shouldn't tell Hermione about it. Harry does notice Ron using things he has learned from that book when talking to Hermione and to his mother.

After the escape from the Burrow, and the subsequent battle in the Tottenham Court Road café, Harry, Ron, and Hermione end up at Number 12, Grimmauld Place, feeling that on the street, they could be attacked by any number of Death Eaters, but at the one-time Headquarters of the Order of the Phoenix, the only Death Eater they would have to face would be Severus Snape. When Harry awakens in the morning, he sees that Ron's hand is very close to Hermione's, and wonders if they had fallen asleep holding hands.

Having determined that the locket Horcrux has ended up with Dolores Umbridge, the Trio decide that they must infiltrate the Ministry in order to retrieve it. Ron ends up wearing the robes of a maintenance worker, and spends almost his entire time within the Ministry attempting to make it stop raining in someone's office; we see, at one point, that Ron is sharing an elevator with his father, and has trouble responding to him correctly for his disguise. As they escape the Ministry, Ron is injured, and Hermione is extremely worried that she might not be able to heal him completely. Over the next several days, however, Ron does recover, and does his share of carrying the Horcrux which they have managed to retrieve from Umbridge without her being aware of it. Ron says that he can perceive something very like a heartbeat in the Horcrux, something which the other two cannot.

As they journey uncomfortably around the wintry England countryside, Ron becomes upset that Harry does not seem to have a complete plan prepared for finding and dealing with Horcruxes. This comes to a head shortly after they overhear another small group of refugees, who apparently are doing much better for themselves than the Trio has managed. Ron, dismayed by the discomfort that he has been experiencing, leaves the group.

Ron returns dramatically to the group shortly after Christmas. Harry has found the Sword of Gryffindor lying at the bottom of a pond, and has jumped into the water to retrieve it, only to be choked by the Horcrux which he is wearing on a chain around his neck. Ron arrives just in time to rescue him, then at Harry's bidding uses the Sword to destroy the Horcrux. They then return to the campsite, where much to Harry's surprise, Hermione lashes out at Ron for having abandoned them. Without her wand (Harry is currently carrying it, as he was on guard and his own wand had been damaged), she is unable to counter Harry's shield charm, and so withdraws into herself while Ron explains to Harry how he had been unable to return, had stayed at Shell Cottage with Bill and Fleur, and how Dumbledore's Deluminator had led him to them.

Ron suggests that they see Xenophilius Lovegood, whose *Quibbler* is still telling the truth about Harry. At his house, they learn the meaning of the strange symbol that Xeno wore at Bill and Fleur's wedding, which was also found on a gravestone in Godric's Hollow, and had been used as an emblem of the Dark wizard Grindelwald. This symbol, the sigil of the Deathly Hallows, was used to show that the wearer was seeking the Hallows, three unique magical artifacts that had supposedly originated with Death himself. In Xeno's absence, Harry, Ron, and Hermione discuss the three Hallows, and become uncomfortably aware that they evidence for one of them is overwhelming: Harry's Invisibility Cloak exactly matches the description of the Hallow. The Elder Wand also appears to have left a verifiable tail through history. Their discussion is interrupted by the arrival of Death Eaters; Xeno, whose daughter Luna has been captured and is being held hostage, has informed them of Harry's presence in hopes of buying her release. Hermione incapacitates Xeno, then blows a hole in the floor, allowing the Death Eaters to see her and Harry, but not Ron who she has hidden under the Invisibility Cloak, before Apparating them all away. She later explains that, as he is supposed to be at home with Spattergroit, having the Death Eaters see Ron would likely result in serious retaliation against Ron's family, but Xeno's punishment for summoning the Death Eaters might be less if there were witnesses that Harry really was there.

Harry, now convinced of the reality of all three Hallows despite the lack of evidence for the third, largely exempts himself from leadership of the mission, and Ron, having gained significant self-assurance during his time away, takes over, trying to find places where the two as-yet unknown Horcruxes might be hidden. With Harry trying to decide between Horcruxes and Hallows, and wondering if having the three Hallows would make him proof against Voldemort's attempts to kill him, it falls to Ron to lead the search for Horcruxes.

This continues for some months, At the end of this time, Ron manages to reconnect his wireless to an underground radio show, *Potterwatch*, which intrigues Harry to the extent that he forgets the taboo on Voldemort's name and speaks it aloud. As a result, they are captured by a gang of Snatchers led by Fenrir Greyback, and taken to Voldemort's headquarters, Malfoy Manor. There, Bellatrix Lestrange sees the Sword of Gryffindor and prevents anyone from calling Voldemort, saying that they could all be in grave peril if Voldemort was to see it. Putting the others into a locked cellar room, Bellatrix tortures Hermione in an effort to determine where the Sword had come from. Ron is almost maddened by her screams of pain. They manage to escape the dungeon, with help from Dobby, and Ron carries Hermione to Shell Cottage. Once there, Harry regains leadership of the mission, deciding finally that the best course of action is to let the Hallows go and concentrate, as Dumbledore had wanted, on the remaining Horcruxes.

Once everyone is healed, Harry, Ron, Hermione, and Griphook then break into Gringotts to recover the cup Horcrux, and the Trio escape on dragonback. From Voldemort's mind, Harry learns that the one remaining Horcrux is somewhere in Hogwarts, so the Trio immediately head for Hogsmeade. When they arrive at the school, they find a flourishing guerrilla army in the Room of Requirement; Harry, who had planned to duck into the school, find the Horcrux, and depart, is dismayed to find that he is now expected to captain a battle against Voldemort. Ron suggests that perhaps the people assembled there can help him find the Horcrux even if they don't know what it is. Harry sees the value in that and agrees. While Harry is attempting to locate Rowena Ravenclaw's lost diadem, Voldemort's arrival makes the battle he had been hoping to avoid inevitable. When Harry looks for Ron and Hermione to continue the search, however, they are not in the Room of Requirement. It turns out that Ron has memorized the sound Harry used to open the locket, and with Hermione, has used that to enter the Chamber of Secrets. There, they had found Basilisk fangs, which Hermione had used to destroy the Cup Horcrux. learning that the battle with Voldemort is starting, Ron suggests that they should tell the house elves in the kitchen so that they can get away. Hermione, who has been dismayed by the lot of the house elves for a long while, sweeps him into a passionate embrace.

Ron then assists Harry in searching the Room of Requirement, in its junk warehouse form, for the Diadem which Harry now remembers seeing there. He also assists Harry in reaching the Shrieking Shack, in order to find out what Voldemort is doing. At the break in the fighting, Ron and Hermione return to Ron's family to grieve the loss of Fred.

Finally, Harry gathers Ron and Hermione as he heads to the Headmaster's office to report the end of the battle to the portrait of Dumbledore.

In the epilogue, we see that Ron and Hermione are married and have two children, Rose and Hugo.

Strengths Ron, being the only one in the trio to have an early magical upbringing, has the best knowledge of the magical realm and what is available to a wizard. In contrast to Hermione's "book smarts," Ron possesses wizarding "street smarts." Ron can be quite brave when his friends are in danger and tries his hardest to keep Harry or Hermione from harm. He also shows great loyalty to his friends and appears more logistically minded than the other two, particularly excelling in Wizard's Chess. He is a skilled Quidditch Keeper (although he is extremely suseptible to nerves). Although Ron is often overshadowed by his friends and siblings, he was intelligent enough to receive seven E (Exceeds Expectations) Grade O.W.Ls and was able to advanced into N.E.W.T classes. He was also able to produce the notoriously difficult Patronus Charm and has shown skilled magical ability in duelling against much older Death Eaters.

Weaknesses Ron fears spiders, the result of a prank played on him by his brothers Fred and George when he was young. Ron also displays particular susceptibility and weakness to the Imperius Curse when practicing hexes in Professor Moody's class. The youngest of six brothers, his talented siblings have caused Ron to develop a lack of confidence in himself. He feels that anything he does is nothing special because his brothers have already done it. His friendship with Harry, who receives constant attention and accolades, can also affect his self-esteem.

Hermione characterizes Ron as having "the emotional range of a teaspoon" in *Harry Potter and the Order of the Phoenix*, and he does seem to fit this characterization; time and time again he acts in a way that would indicate that he has very little sensitivity to the emotional environment.

Relationships with Other Characters Ron has taken a liking to Hermione as early as the first book. Although the connection between the two is subtle, each successive book reveals more about their relationship. However, neither openly displays their feelings to the other for much of the first six books, leaving each confused and unsure. They often have large arguments but later reconcile their differences and then work together on school assignments. As each matures, their relationship intensifies and a likely permanent relationship between the two is established in the later books. This finally comes to fruition near the end of the sixth book, and we are shown that 19 years after the end of the seventh book Ron and Hermione are married with two children, Rose and Hugo. More detail on Ron's relationships may be found here. Ron tends to be jealous over Harry's fame, and they once had a falling out over it. However, their clashes seem to relate as much to Ron's own low self-esteem and that he has much to live up to with five very talented older brothers. The attention Harry gathers often tends to make Ron feel left out.

Ron is somewhat inept socially and tends to be unintentionally rude, particularly, but not exclusively, to ghosts.

Analysis

Due to his family's relative poverty and size, Ron often has to make do with second-hand school supplies and robes. This has affected his personality somewhat since he feels that he has something to prove. His older brothers have all gone onto successful careers, and Ron believes there is great pressure on him to perform well in school. Ron tends to be reckless and insensitive at times, though his heart is indisputably in the right place. Ron has formed tight bonds with his two best friends and is seen as an important player in "the trio."

Questions

1. What are Ron's greatest fears? Are those fears based in the past, present, or future?
2. How does Ron differ in his actions when around Harry and Hermione in comparison to when he is with other students at Hogwarts?
3. When Ron fights with Harry and/or Hermione, how does he show his emotions? Does this say anything for Ron's character as a whole?
4. Luna Lovegood comments that Ron can sometimes be cruel. Is this true? Does he mean to be this way?

Ronan

Gender: Male
Hair color: Red, chestnut
Eye color: Unknown
Related Family: Unknown
Loyalty: Centaur race

Overview

Ronan is a Centaur living in the Forbidden Forest. He has a slow, doleful voice.

Role in the Books

Philosopher's Stone When Harry is serving his detention in the Forbidden Forest, he, Hermione, and Hagrid hear something moving. Challenged, the something moving turns out to be Ronan, a Centaur, who discusses astronomy ("Mars is very bright tonight").

Later, when Harry has encountered the being that is killing Unicorns, Firenze, another Centaur, rescues him, and offers to carry him back to Hagrid. As he is doing so, Ronan (along with Bane, another centaur), confront Firenze. Bane is infuriated that Firenze is acting as a beast of burden, while Ronan says dolefully that he is sure Firenze is doing what he thinks best.

Order of the Phoenix   Ronan is one of the centaurs who confront Dolores Umbridge in the Forbidden Forest when Hermione is leading her (and Harry) to the supposed weapon they claim to have been working on. After Umbridge is spirited away, and the others are trying to decide what to do with Harry and Hermione, Ronan reminds the others that they do not attack foals.

Rose Zeller

Gender: Female
Hair color: Unknown
Eye color: Unknown
Related Family: Unknown
Loyalty:

OVERVIEW

Rose Zeller is a Hufflepuff four years behind Harry.

ROLE IN THE BOOKS
Order of the Phoenix   At the Sorting Ceremony, Rose Zeller is Sorted into Hufflepuff. She is the last to be sorted.

Rowena Ravenclaw

Gender: Female
Hair color: Unknown
Eye color: Unknown
Related Family: Unknown
Loyalty:

OVERVIEW

Rowena Ravenclaw was one of the four founders of Hogwarts and the creator of Ravenclaw House. She preferred to teach students with the greatest intellect and members of her House have come to be known by this trait.

ROLE IN THE BOOKS
Chamber of Secrets   When Professor Binns is telling Harry's class about the myth of the Chamber of Secrets, he mentions the four Founders of Hogwarts: Godric Gryffindor, Salazar Slytherin, Rowena Ravenclaw, and Helga Hufflepuff. He mentions that when the argument between the Founders, as to whether those who could not prove magical forbears, broke out, it was Salazar Slytherin standing alone against the other three.

Deathly Hallows   In Xeno Lovegood's study, we see an odd contraption which he says is an attempt to reconstruct the lost Diadem of Rowena Ravenclaw.

Rowena's heirloom, her magical diadem, was stolen by her daughter and concealed in a hollow tree in Albania. Not wishing to reveal how it had gotten stolen, Rowena said it had gotten lost. She later sought a deathbed reconciliation with her daughter, but that was refused. Rowena's diadem ends up being one of the Horcruxes of Lord Voldemort and gets destroyed in a Fiendfyre spell gone wrong in the Room of Requirement.

Rubeus Hagrid

Gender: Male
Hair color: Black
Eye color: Black
Related Family: revealed later
Loyalty: Albus Dumbledore

OVERVIEW

Rubeus Hagrid is Keeper of the Keys and Grounds at Hogwarts School of Witchcraft and Wizardry. He apparently stands about twelve feet tall, and is immensely strong; when Harry first meets him, he bends a rifle barrel "into a knot as easily as if it had been made of rubber."

According to the author, Hagrid's birthday is December 6th.

ROLE IN THE BOOKS
Philosopher's Stone   Professor Dumbledore entrusts Hagrid to take the infant Harry from his parents' destroyed house in Godric's Hollow and deliver him to his relatives in Little Whinging in Surrey. He arrives with baby Harry on Sirius Black's flying motorcycle.

On Harry's eleventh birthday, Hagrid personally delivers his Hogwarts invitation and explains to him that he is a wizard, " . . . and a thumpin' good one, I'd say, once yeh've been trained up a bit." He takes Harry to Diagon Alley to buy his school supplies. While there, he collects a mysterious object for Professor Dumbledore from Gringotts Bank.

Over the course of the school year, Hagrid becomes Harry's anchor; as the one who introduced him to the Wizarding world, Harry often seeks his help. For all his large size and fearsome appearance, Hagrid is a gentle soul who Harry trusts and finds more accessible than most teachers.

Hagrid carelessly drops several clues about the mysterious package he retrieved from Gringotts—clues sufficient enough for Harry, Hermione, and Ron to deduce that it is the Philosopher's Stone, an object powerful enough to restore Lord Voldemort to human form and make him immortal. Hagrid also inadvertently reveals how to bypass the Stone's first guardian not only to Harry, but also to the one who is trying to steal it. Hagrid wins a dragon's egg from someone in the Hog's Head, and sets about hatching it. Draco Malfoy finds out about it, and Harry, Ron and Hermione manage to convince Hagrid to send the dragon off to Romania with Ron's brother Charlie. Harry and Hermione are caught "wandering the halls" after getting the dragon sent off; and they, along with Neville Longbottom and Draco, receive detention. To serve this detention, the four of them must accompany Hagrid into the Forbidden Forest. Hagrid is attempting to track down something that is killing unicorns. Hagrid divides the four students into two parties, with himself in one and his boar-hound, Fang, in the other. It is there that Harry has his second encounter with Voldemort—his first, of course, being when he was orphaned. At year's end, Hagrid presents Harry with a photo album containing many photos of his late parents.

Chamber of Secrets When Harry's initial journey by Floo powder goes astray, he ends up in Knockturn Alley. Hagrid finds him there and rescues him, bringing him out into Diagon Alley. Hagrid is still with Harry and the Weasley family when Arthur Weasley and Lucius Malfoy get into a scuffle in Flourish and Blotts; it is Hagrid who breaks up that fight.

Shortly after Justin Finch-Fletchley and Nearly Headless Nick are found Petrified, Harry is called into Professor Dumbledore's office. Hagrid, who Harry had bumped into in the hall moments earlier, bursts into the office, loudly proclaiming Harry's innocence, and is quite abashed when Dumbledore has to raise his voice to inform him that he never suspected Harry.

Harry learns Hagrid was expelled from Hogwarts because another student, Tom Riddle, accused him of opening the Chamber of Secrets and releasing a monster that killed a girl. When the Chamber of Secrets is opened a second time, the Minister of Magic, Cornelius Fudge, arrests Hagrid "for safety's sake," despite Dumbledore's insistence that Hagrid is innocent. As he is taken away, Hagrid tells Harry (who is hiding in the room under his invisibility cloak) to "follow the spiders."

Harry and Ron follow a trail of spiders into the Forbidden Forest. There, Harry meets Aragog, a giant spider that was once Hagrid's pet. Aragog reveals that he was not the monster, though he knew what it was, and that Hagrid is innocent. Aragog mentions that he had never been anywhere hear the bathroom where the girl had died. This clue leads Harry to understand that the girl in question was Moaning Myrtle, and thus to locate the entrance to the Chamber.

After Harry proves that it was Tom Riddle (as Lord Voldemort was originally known) who actually released the monster (to kill muggle-born and half blood wizards), Hagrid is released from Azkaban Prison and returns to the school.

Prisoner of Azkaban Hagrid sends Harry *The Monster Book of Monsters* as a birthday present, hinting that this is part of a secret that he cannot yet disclose. The secret is that Hagrid is the new Care of Magical Creatures teacher, replacing Professor Kettleburn who "retired at the end of last year to enjoy more time with his remaining limbs."

During his Care of Magical Creatures class, Hagrid introduces students to Buckbeak, a hippogriff. Introductions with Draco Malfoy do not go well; when Malfoy "insults" Buckbeak and is injured, his father files a complaint with the Ministry of Magic. Hagrid is so unnerved by the incident that he spends the remaining term teaching the class about harmless flobberworms.

During a conversation in the Three Broomsticks pub, Hagrid learns from Cornelius Fudge that Sirius Black was convicted for betraying James and Lily Potter and killing their friend, Peter Pettigrew, and twelve muggles. Harry has managed to sneak into Hogsmeade, and overhears this conversation.

At the hearing, the complaint against Hagrid is dismissed, but Buckbeak is considered dangerous and is ordered to be destroyed. Harry, Ron, and Hermione volunteer to help find legal precedents to present at the appeal which can overturn the sentence and save Buckbeak.

After Christmas, Hagrid has regained some of his confidence and teaches the class about salamanders. As Buckbeak's appeal approaches, Hermione helps Hagrid prepare a defence. However, Buckbeak loses the case and is sentenced to be executed. Harry, Ron, and Hermione visit Hagrid before the execution, but they are unable to comfort him; as Fudge, Dumbledore, and the executioner approach, Hagrid shoos the trio out the back door. While exiting, they hear the dull thud of the executioner's axe.

Hermione uses a Time-Turner that she has been using to attend multiple classes to take her and Harry back in time three hours. They return to Hagrid's hut and save Buckbeak from execution; an overjoyed Hagrid, unaware of Hermione's time-turner, is convinced he escaped on his own.

The next day, Hagrid tells Harry, Ron, and Hermione that Buckbeak escaped, and about Remus Lupin's resignation as the Defence Against the Dark Arts teacher.

Goblet of Fire Now in his second year as Care of Magical Creatures teacher, Hagrid has regained enough confidence to start the class learning about something he calls Skrewts. These creatures, which initially look like shell-less, deformed lobsters, are totally new to all the students and to Hagrid; one of the things that Hagrid has the students doing is try to determine what exactly Skrewts eat. One gets the feeling that Hagrid, in his unscientific way, is trying to teach the class how to determine the characteristics of a hitherto unknown species. He will later, with the only somewhat willing assistance of the class, study their activity over a longer period, attempt to determine whether they want nesting boxes in which to hibernate (they don't), and give them exercise by having the students walk them on leashes (which becomes difficult as the skrewts become as large as the students).

When the delegation from Beauxbatons arrives, Hagrid is given the task of caring for the horses. Shortly after this, the Trio visit Hagrid, and find that he has apparently become besotted with Madame Maxime, the Headmistress of Beauxbatons; he has tried to comb his hair with little success, and slick it down with something like axle grease. They talk about the Skrewts, and also about the upcoming tasks in the Tournament. Hagrid apparently knows something about the tasks, but unusually he does not divulge what is in store for the Champions. As they prepare to return to the castle for dinner, Hagrid rather overdoes the eau de cologne, and goes outside to wash it off in the rain barrel. Seeing Madame Maxime leading her pupils up to the school, he goes to join her, apparently forgetting all about the Trio still in his hut.

After Harry's name comes out of the Goblet, Hagrid asks if he has any idea who put his name in. Harry is very relieved that Hagrid believes he did not put his own name in, but is unable to venture any guesses. Just before the First Task, Harry is in Hogsmeade with Hermione. Harry, to avoid the taunts he is receiving, is under the Invisibility Cloak. Seeing Hagrid in the Three Broomsticks, he waves, then realizes that Hagrid can't see him; Professor Moody, who is with him, can see him, however, and brings Hagrid over to Hermione's table. Hagrid then asks Harry to bring his cloak to Hagrid's hut at midnight that night. Harry, who has an appointment to speak with Sirius Black at 1AM, decides that he can just make it. Hagrid tells him to put on his cloak and follow, then knocks on the door of the Beauxbatons carriage and asks Madame Maxime to accompany him. Harry wonders exactly what it is that Hagrid expects him to see, but is alarmed when Hagrid and Madame Maxime walk around the end of the Forbidden Forest to a corral in which there are four Dragons. Hagrid is entranced: they are beautiful. Charlie Weasley, one of the wizards there to manage the dragons, asks if it was wise to bring Madame Maxime there, after all she has a student who will be in the competition. Hagrid responds that he just thought she would like to see them. Harry, deeply disturbed by the prospect of having to get past the dragons, quietly and invisibly departs. It is when the Skrewts have destroyed their nesting boxes, and Harry, Hermione, Ron, and Hagrid are finishing rounding them up, that Rita Skeeter appears and asks Hagrid for an interview. Hagrid will later report that, annoyingly, the interview seemed to be all about Harry, and had nothing to do with anything Hagrid was doing. At the Yule Ball, Harry and Ron overhear a conversation between Madame Maxime and Hagrid. Hagrid reveals that he is half-Giant, and asks whether it was Madame Maxime's mother or father. Madame Maxime is highly affronted, says that she has no Giant ancestry and is just big-boned, and storms off. Hagrid, shattered, sits for a while and then shuffles off to his hut.

Shortly afterwards, a story appears in the *Daily Prophet*, that says that Hagrid is half-Giant. The Trio have no idea how Rita Skeeter, who wrote the story, could have learned about Hagrid's ancestry. Hagrid retreats to his hut and does not come out, either to do his groundskeeping duties or to teach. An alternate teacher, Professor Grubbly-Plank takes over teaching Care of Magical Creatures, and apparently does a better job than Hagrid, teaching about Unicorns, and immediately winning over the hearts of the female half of the class. Draco Malfoy, meanwhile, taunts Harry that the article will have finished Hagrid's teaching career, as many people will be afraid that Hagrid's Giant ancestry will come out and he would eat their children. Hagrid remains closeted in his hut until Hermione, angered by a meeting with Rita during a Hogsmeade weekend, hammers on the hut door and demands entrance. She is taken aback to find that Dumbledore is there, but Dumbledore invites them in for tea, and is quite obviously bracing Hagrid to return to duties. He tells Hagrid about his brother Aberforth, who was charged with performing unnatural charms on a goat, and how he weathered the resulting press exposure. As he leaves, he reminds Hagrid that he has not accepted Hagrid's resignation, and expects to see Hagrid at breakfast on Monday, and expects also that he will start his teaching duties again. Hagrid says that his father would not be proud of how he is acting, and shows the Trio a picture of himself and his father. He then asks how Harry is getting on with the Golden Egg clue for the Second Task, and Harry says he pretty well has it defeated. Somehow, Harry feels particularly bad about having to lie to Hagrid.

Returning to his teaching job, Hagrid takes up with Unicorns where Professor Grubbly-Plank had left off. He seems to be trying to show that he can teach as well as she can, and he has captured a pair of foals, much to the delight of Parvati and Lavender. It seems that he does know many useful things about Unicorns, as well. Harry, looking out the window for relief from listening to Ron and Hermione squabbling, sees Hagrid digging near his hut. Madame Maxime walks over to talk to him, but is apparently rebuffed. The next day, Hagrid introduces them to some Nifflers. He says that they are very often used in mines, as they are attracted to bright objects, and are very good at digging. He has everyone select a Niffler, and promises a prize for the holder of the Niffler that retrieves the most gold from the patch of ground Harry had seen him digging up. He warns Goyle that it is Leprechaun gold, and will vanish shortly, so there's no point in trying to steal it. In the end, Ron's Niffler has retrieved the most gold, but Ron is pensive. He recalls that he had given Harry a fistful of Leprechaun gold at the Quidditch world cup to pay for the Omnioculars and is upset that Harry had not even noticed it vanishing. When Bartemius Crouch appears at the edge of the Forbidden Forest, Harry, leaving Viktor Krum on guard, runs off to fetch Dumbledore. When Harry and Dumbledore return, Krum alone is present. Dumbledore sends for Hagrid, who arrives shortly with his crossbow. Dumbledore then sends Hagrid off to fetch Professor Karkaroff. Karkaroff immediately blames Dumbledore for attacking his Champion, which enrages Hagrid to the point that he pushes Karkaroff up against a tree, only letting him down when Dumbledore orders him to. Dumbledore then tells Hagrid to take Harry to Gryffindor tower, and asks Harry to remain there until morning.

In the preparations for the Third Task, it is mentioned that Hagrid had been responsible for planting and growing the hedges that now fill the Quidditch pitch, and that he would be providing some of the creatures that the Champions would have to face. Harry, knowing the sorts of creatures that Hagrid is fond of, finds this rather worrying. At dinner before the Third Task, Harry notices that Madame Maxime's eyes are red, and that Hagrid keeps glancing at her.

When the third task comes around, Hagrid is apparently one of the marshals, who will be keeping an eye on the maze for distress signals from the Champions. While the other marshals are wearing their red ribbons on their hats, Hagrid has no hat and therefore wears his marshal's ribbon on the back of his waistcoat. As it turns out, Harry encounters a Skrewt in the maze, so at least some of the challenges are, in fact, Hagrid's doing.

As Harry is recovering from his adventures in the maze, he hears argument between Dumbledore and Cornelius Fudge as to whether or not Harry's story can be believed. When Fudge refuses to believe that Voldemort has returned, Dumbledore asks Professor McGonagall to ask Hagrid and Madame Maxime to meet with him in his office.

After he has recovered, and with no Defence Against the Dark Arts classes to go to, the Trio can visit Hagrid more often. One one such visit, they notice that there are two bucket-sized teacups on the table, and Hagrid confirms that he's been having tea with Madame Maxime. He says that Dumbledore had given him a mission, though he couldn't talk about it yet, and that he has pretty much convinced Madame Maxime to join him. Hagrid startles Harry by saying that he was pretty sure Voldemort would be coming back one day, that it was only a matter of time. He goes on to say that Harry had done as well as his father would have, and there's no higher praise than that. Harry smiles for the first time in days.

Order of the Phoenix At the beginning of the school year, Harry is deeply concerned that Hagrid has not returned to Hogwarts; his classes are being taught by Professor Grubbly-Plank, and no one will say where Hagrid is or when he will return. When he reappears well into winter, Harry, Hermione, and Ron secretly visit him at his hut. They are shocked by Hagrid's battered appearance, although he does not initially explain what has happened. Harry, however, alludes to the events of his summer, including the attack by Dementors on Primrose Crescent, saying that if Hagrid tells his story, Harry will reciprocate. Under this impetus, Hagrid does tell them that he and Madame Maxime, the gigantic Headmistress of Beauxbatons Academy, were on a secret mission for Dumbledore to recruit the Giants to their side. Though Hagrid is forthright about most of the events of the mission, he is still apparently hiding something, because he will not say what took him so long (Madame Maxime has apparently been back at Beauxbatons for months), or how he got so badly injured. He does mention that he had looked to see if his mother, Fridwulfa, was there, but she had apparently died some time before. His story is cut short by the arrival of Professor Umbridge, whose distrust of what she terms "half-breeds," and the footprints of the Trio heading to Hagrid's hut and not returning, have made her suspicious of Hagrid. The Trio, under Harry's invisibility cloak, watch as Umbridge, speaking as if to one who is not completely mentally competent, explains her role at the school and that she will be checking his teaching abilities. After she departs, the Trio ask Hagrid to choose something safe and Ministry-approved to teach them, but Hagrid seems unconcerned. Hermione returns to Hagrid's hut the following day to plead with him, saying that if he doesn't teach the Ministry-approved course, he will be in danger of losing his job, but Hagrid is unmoved. In his Care of Magical Creatures, Hagrid introduces Harry's class to Thestrals, winged, horse-like animals that can only be seen by humans who have witnessed death. Having seen Cedric Diggory being killed, Harry can now see the strange reptilian creatures, as can some of the other students—Neville Longbottom, who saw his grandfather die, and "a stringy Slytherin." Hagrid's teaching is interrupted by Umbridge's appearance to "inspect" his class; her inspection is so clearly adversarial that Hagrid is quite put off his stride and is unable to teach effectively. It turns out later that Umbridge has put Hagrid on probation. Hagrid sees this as the first step to sacking him. Later in the book, we will find that Umbridge has started attending all his classes and taking notes on his apparent shortcomings.

On February 14th, arriving at the Three Broomsticks early for a meeting with Hermione, Harry sees Hagrid at the bar. Unusually morose, Hagrid talks about how Harry and he are so much alike, both orphans. He then speaks about how important family is. Harry asks what has gotten Hagrid so upset, but Hagrid doesn't answer, setting down his mug and heading out into the rain.

When Umbridge fires the Divination teacher, Professor Trelawney, Dumbledore hires a new one, Firenze. Firenze, a centaur, was previously living in the Forbidden Forest; he gives Harry a message to pass on to Hagrid, saying that Hagrid's attempt is not working. Neither he, nor Hagrid, when Harry talks to him later in class, choose to explain to Harry exactly what this "attempt" is.

Late in the year, Hagrid becomes convinced that Umbridge is about to get him sacked. Hagrid pulls Harry and Hermione away from the final Quidditch match of the year, to enlist their help in something he is doing in the Forbidden Forest if he should get sent away. It turns out that Hagrid had found his half-brother Grawp living with the Giants, where he was being mistreated because he was so small. Hagrid had brought him back to Hogwarts, although with great difficulty and personal injury. He has hidden Grawp in the Forbidden Forest where he is trying to teach him manners and English. He extracts a promise from a terrified Harry and Hermione that they will continue his education if Hagrid is sent away.

Eventually, Umbridge's hatred of so-called "half-breeds" leads her to sack Hagrid on the pretexts that he is incompetent, and that he has introduced Nifflers into her office. Her attempt is done with great drama, the assistance of at least five Aurors, and multiple ineffective stun jinxes that Harry witnesses during his midnight Astronomy O.W.L. exam. As part of the arrest, Professor McGonagall is hit with multiple Stunners and ends up having to go to St. Mungo's Hospital. Hagrid escapes, carrying his boarhound Fang, who has been Stunned. When Umbridge is removed and Dumbledore reinstated as Headmaster, Hagrid returns to the school regains his teaching position. Harry, finding the concern of his friends in the Hospital Wing too intrusive, visits him to talk about the death of Sirius, his godfather, but very quickly discovers that he cannot get any peace there either, and uses Ron and hermione as an excuse to leave Hagrid's hut.

Half-Blood Prince Hagrid's role in this episode is much decreased, because his main point of contact with Harry is through the Care Of Magical Creatures classes, and Harry has chosen to not take N.E.W.T.-level studies in that course. It is mentioned that Harry had inherited Buckbeak at the death of Sirius Black. Dumbledore says that Hagrid has renamed him Witherwings and will be delighted to take care of him.

Hagrid acts as guard for the Weasley family and Harry as they visit Diagon Alley to shop for school supplies. Harry is very pleased to see him, particularly as the alternative would be a squad of Aurors.

After the Arrival Feast, Hagrid meets Harry and Ron in the entrance hall and says that if they arrive early to Care of Magical Creatures, they will be able to say hello to Witherwings. Harry, Ron, and later Hermione, are concerned as to how they are going to break it to Hagrid that they have not chosen to take Care of Magical Creatures this year. Harry believes that it is because they are not taking his class that Hagrid seems to be so aloof, and resolves to visit him. The Trio go to his hut after Quidditch tryouts, and the visit is initially awkward, but it turns out that a large part of Hagrid's preoccupation is because of Hagrid's ancient giant spider, Aragog, who is very ill. Hagrid comments that the Trio's schedules are very full, but they might have managed to fit Care of Magical Creatures in if they had Time-turners, but Hermione mentions that they were all destroyed at the Battle at the Ministry the previous year. When Katie Bell, during the Hogsmeade weekend in October, touches the cursed necklace and is injured, Harry runs for help. The first person he runs into is Hagrid, and Hagrid carries Katie back to Hogwarts at the run. After Aragog dies, Harry and Professor Slughorn come to console Hagrid and to give the creature a proper burial. Following the burial, Slughorn, Harry, and Hagrid take part in what might be considered an impromptu wake, during which Harry obtains the missing Horcrux memory from Slughorn.

When Ron is poisoned on his birthday, Hagrid comes to visit him in the Hospital Wing. As he, Harry, and Hermione leave to give Ron some time with his family, Hagrid mentions that Dumbledore seems upset with Severus Snape. He catches himself, but under questioning from Harry he reveals that he had been at the edge of the Forest, and had overheard bits of a conversation between Dumbledore and Snape in which Snape seemed to be saying that though he had promised to do something, he might just change his mind. There was also some reference to the investigations in Slytherin, which Hagrid assumed had to do with the necklace.

During the tower battle at Hogwarts, Hagrid tries to prevent Death Eaters from fleeing, but he only manages to delay one of them who sets fire to Hagrid's hut. After Dumbledore's death, Hagrid removes his body to safety, and later attends the meeting of the Heads of House where the future of the school is being determined. Hagrid says that he feels he doesn't really belong at that meeting, but says that Dumbledore would have wanted the school to go on. He also says that he would think that students might want to pay their respects to Dumbledore, and so he would not expect to send the students home on the Express until after the funeral.

At the funeral itself, Hagrid carries Dumbledore's wrapped body to the bier, and then returns to the rear of the gathered crowd, where he breaks down in tears and is roughly comforted by his half-brother, Grawp.

Deathly Hallows Hagrid, once again riding Sirius' flying motorcycle, is given the task of transporting the real Harry Potter to the home of Ted Tonks. As Hagrid occupies so much of the motorcycle's saddle, a sidecar has been added, into which Harry uncomfortably squeezes himself, his rucksack, his broom, and Hedwig's cage. The motorcycle has further been modified to emit brick walls, nets, and dragon fire out of its tailpipe; these are used against the pursuing Death Eaters with limited effect, and in fact the first use of the dragon fire addition results in the sidecar mountings failing partway. Hagrid's later attempt to repair the mountings results in them shearing completely, and Harry and the sidecar fall off. Hagrid circles around and collects Harry from the falling sidecar, from which Harry is only able to retrieve his rucksack. Once the pursuing Death Eaters determine that this is the real Harry, they break off the attack; at Harry's urging, Hagrid then uses the dragon fire again to speed them towards the Tonks home. Many Death Eaters, including Voldemort, catch up with them near the end of the journey; Hagrid at one point leaps off the motorcycle to wrestle with a Death Eater who is trying to curse Harry, and falls from there to the ground. When Harry reaches him later, he doesn't seem to be moving, but Harry then loses consciousness.

When he recovers, he asks Ted Tonks where Hagrid is, Ted assures him that Hagrid is fine. Hagrid comes in shortly after that. Ted ushers them over to the Portkey which will take them to The Burrow, and while they are waiting for the Portkey to activate, Hagrid asks where Hedwig is. Harry has to tell him that Hedwig is dead; she had been struck early in the battle by a killing curse intended for Harry.

Once they reach The Burrow, Hagrid largely moves into the background of the action, trying to recover his nerves with brandy and Firewhiskey.

Hagrid is present for Harry's birthday, wearing his best, hairy, horrible suit, and gives him a Mokeskin bag. This is used for valuables; things placed in it can only be retrieved by the owner. Harry will use it to keep a number of objects which he feels are valuable throughout the book.

The wedding of Bill Weasley and Fleur Delacour is the following day, so Hagrid stays overnight; however, The Burrow is far too full to allow him any place to stay, so he sets up a tent in a neighboring field. He is mentioned briefly as, just before the wedding, he mistakes where he is meant to sit and crushes an entire row of folding chairs, before being shown the reinforced bench which was intended for him.

When Ginny Weasley, Neville Longbottom, and Luna Lovegood try to steal Gryffindor's sword, they are given detention, which is apparently served with Hagrid.

At the battle at Hogwarts, Hagrid appears, flying in through a window; apparently he has been visiting Grawp, and when he was called to the battle, he asked Grawp to set him down inside the walls. Grawp, misunderstanding him, had thrown him through the window. Later in the battle, he is carried away by giant spiders, children of Aragog. He is later found in the clearing where Aragog's children lived, which is now commandeered by the Death Eaters. The Death Eaters force

Hagrid to carry Harry's apparently-lifeless body back to the lawns in front of Hogwarts. Hagrid is evidently crying too hard to notice the pulse beating strongly in Harry's throat. When hostilities re-open, and Harry hides under his cloak, Hagrid is the first to notice that he has vanished.

Strengths One of Hagrid's main strengths is his half-giant status. This means that his tough skin protects him against many spells and physical injuries. He is also immensely strong physically. Although a half-giant might be expected to be fierce, Hagrid is one of the most soft-hearted people Harry knows. However, he can fight when necessary. He is one of Dumbledore's most trusted friends.

Hagrid is also unafraid of most physical threats, standing up to a squad of armed Centaurs, dealing with the vicious Blast-Ended Skrewts, and trying to domesticate a dragon.

Weaknesses After he was accused of opening the Chamber of Secrets, he was expelled and forbidden to do magic. His wand was snapped in two (the pieces were later reassembled and hidden in a pink umbrella, which never seems to be far from Hagrid). This seriously hindered his magical education, and as a result, he is rather poor at casting spells. Hagrid has an unusual obsession with all "interesting" creatures—which usually means very dangerous ones. He tends to forget just how dangerous certain animals can be and has gotten Harry and his friends into some bad situations. Perhaps ironically, it is his physical strength that proves a weakness here; being half-Giant, he is extremely strong, and thus is able to deal with quite dangerous creatures, but he tends to forget that others are not as strong as he is.

On several occasions, Hagrid has allowed facts to slip out that he was meant to keep secret. We see this a number of times in *Harry Potter and the Philosopher's Stone*, for instance, when he reveals the connection with Nicholas Flamel, and the method of bypassing the three-headed dog. The tendency continues through the entire series; in *Harry Potter and the Half-Blood Prince*, we see Hagrid revealing that he has overheard a conversation between Dumbledore and Snape.

Emotionally, Hagrid seems quite immature, for all that he is apparently about 60 years old. His immediate reaction to almost any setback is to retreat from all contact, and possibly to get drunk. He shares Harry's tendency to try and run away from troubles; unlike Harry, though, he never turns of his own volition to face the problem, only doing so when he is forced, often by Dumbledore or by the Trio. His confidence is easily destroyed when dealing with antagonistic people, notably Draco Malfoy, Draco's father Lucius, and Professor Umbridge.

Hagrid is not the best cook. The Trio usually avoids Hagrid's offerings, particularly his rock cakes that are more rock than cake. Hagrid's attempts at cooking are something of a running joke throughout the series, though apparently the birthday cakes that he has made for Harry over the years have been well received.

Relationships with Other Characters During Harry's fourth year, he developed a romantic relationship with the half-giant headmistress of Beauxbatons, Madame Maxime.

He has generally been friendly with Harry, Ron, and Hermione through the series. His opinion is valued by Dumbledore, who allowed Hagrid to stay as Grounds Keeper after being expelled.

Analysis

Hagrid is interesting in part because of what he isn't. It seems initially that Hagrid is to be a sort of a father figure for Harry, with his size, gentleness, kindness towards Harry, and the fact that it was Hagrid who rescued him from his horrible aunt and uncle. However, while he is a comfort and a confidante for Harry, the father figure role would sit very awkwardly on him.

Hagrid is an odd hybrid of maturity and immaturity, which makes him a sort of a conduit between the professors and the Trio. So, while Harry genuinely likes Hagrid and respects him, it is not as an adult; rather, Harry sees him as one at largely his own level: an instructor perhaps in the ways of Wizards, but not a father figure. In fact, Harry, Hermione, and Ron on several occasions act as sort of a combined parent figure for Hagrid:

• in *Prisoner of Azkaban*, the trio are instrumental in getting Hagrid back on his feet after Buckbeak injures Draco Malfoy;

• again in *Prisoner of Azkaban*, it is they who brace him up for the defence of Buckbeak, and who provide moral support before the scheduled execution;

• in *Goblet of Fire*, it is the Trio who manage to rein him in when he is falling for Madame Maxime;

• when the news of his being half-Giant comes out in *Goblet of Fire*, it is partly the Trio who get him out of his hut and back teaching again.

Add to this Hagrid's habit of responding to every setback, and every victory, by getting drunk—in *Harry Potter and the Prisoner of Azkaban*, he seems to be able to get reeling drunk within half an hour of Buckbeak's escape—and we can see that, even at an apparent age of 60 years, Hagrid is still often reacting like an adolescent. Hagrid does show a certain amount of maturity, of course; his decision to bring his half-brother Grawp back with him, to attempt to civilize Grawp, and in particular the resolve with which he sticks to that decision, shows that the mission to the Giants, and possibly the influence of Olympe Maxime, have matured him.

Can Hagrid do magic? Of course he can, though he's not supposed to, at least in the first two books. Presumably, once he has been exonerated of the fifty-year old accusation that he had released the monster from the Chamber of Secrets, which happens at the end of *Harry Potter and the Chamber of Secrets*, the prohibition against Hagrid's using magic will have been lifted. However, we are never explicitly told this. It is true that Hagrid, having been expelled in his third year, will not have as much magic ability as he ought to, and there is no sign of his either getting his original wand repaired or getting a new one. There is no real explanation of this;

perhaps it is simply that Hagrid, diffident as always, is reluctant to start practicing the magic that has been so long forbidden him.

There is some question about whether Hagrid thinks he can use magic, particularly because of his statement to Harry, Ron, and Hermione that while he and Madame Maxime were visiting the Giants in Europe to negotiate with them, he could not use magic. Careful reading of the passage, however, indicates that Hagrid's not using magic at that point may not have been due to that prohibition. Several times, Hagrid uses the first person plural when talking about using magic: "*We* couldn't use magic," which would indicate that whatever reason was involved, it equally affected himself and Madame Maxime. In the two places in his story where he mentions this, he also mentions the specific reason for the prohibition. They could not use magic while traveling because they were being watched, by the Ministry and possibly also by Death Eaters, and they could not use magic around the Giants because that was something Wizards did, and using magic would antagonize the people they were trying to negotiate with. There is thus no evidence whether the prohibition against Hagrid's using magic was actually vacated or not. The reader does take away the impression, however, that Hagrid chose to keep whatever magic he did somewhat furtive, though it remains uncertain whether it was forbidden him, or whether he was simply embarrassed by his relative lack of ability.

QUESTIONS

1. How might Hagrid's life be different if he hadn't been expelled? 2. How has Hagrid shown that he is trustworthy?

GREATER PICTURE

In an interview with MSNBC[1] following the publication of *Harry Potter and the Deathly Hallows*, the following appeared:

Hagrid, actually, had been safe in Rowling's mind from the very beginning. Before her first book, *Harry Potter and the Sorcerer's Stone*, was even published, Rowling planned for Hagrid to carry Harry out of the forest at the end of *Deathly Hallows*, believing that Harry was dead. "It was very significant," Rowling said. "Hagrid brings Harry from the Dursleys. He takes him into the wizarding world . . . He was sort of his guardian and his guide . . . And now I wanted Hagrid to be the one to lead Harry out of the forest."

In this context, Hagrid can be seen very much as the midwife, carrying or leading Harry from one stage in his life to the next. In *Harry Potter and the Philosopher's Stone*, he carries the infant Harry from the wreckage of the house in Godric's Hollow, to his new life with the Dursleys. He again leads Harry to the discovery of the Wizarding world, and his own role in it, by means of the trip to Diagon Alley. And he is, of course, the one who pilots the fleet of boats that carry all the first-years, including Harry, into Hogwarts before their Sorting.

In *Harry Potter and the Deathly Hallows*, it is again Hagrid, and interestingly again Sirius' flying motorbike, that Hagrid uses to carry Harry out of his childhood home with the Dursleys and into his adult life. It is only proper that Hagrid is the one who carries him out of the Forest and into the place where he can achieve his final victory over Voldemort. The only major transition for which Hagrid is not present is the Advance Guard, carrying Harry to Grimmauld Place in *Harry Potter and the Order of the Phoenix*, and inducting him into the Order.

Rufus Scrimgeour

Gender: Male
Hair color: Tawny, streaked with grey
Eye color: Yellow
Related Family: Unknown
Loyalty: Ministry for Magic

OVERVIEW

Rufus Scrimgeour is the Minister of Magic during *Harry Potter and the Half-Blood Prince* and the beginning of *Harry Potter and the Deathly Hallows*, replacing Cornelius Fudge after the disastrous events at the Ministry of Magic at the end of *Harry Potter and the Order of the Phoenix*. Scrimgeour is a former Auror.

ROLE IN THE BOOKS

Order of the Phoenix Rufus Scrimgeour is mentioned in passing as Harry Potter and Arthur Weasley pass through the Auror's office at the Ministry of Magic, just before Harry's hearing.

Half-Blood Prince In the first chapter of the book, Cornelius Fudge introduces the Muggle Prime Minister to Rufus Scrimgeour, saying he has been sworn in as Minister of Magic after the disastrous events at the end of *Harry Potter and the Order of the Phoenix* and the following summer. These events include the escape of many prisoners from Azkaban, the deaths of two wizards, apparent Giant attacks in parts of England, and the collapse of a bridge with many Muggle casualties.

We hear that there has been some sort of confrontation between Scrimgeour and Albus Dumbledore, but we don't immediately learn what that confrontation involved.

Shortly before Christmas, when Harry is taking Luna Lovegood to Professor Slughorn's party, Harry mentions that there will be a vampire there; Luna immediately asks if that would be Scrimgeour. Apparently, her father had written a story about how Scrimgeour is a vampire, but had had to shelve it on orders from the Ministry. At Christmas, which Harry is spending at The Burrow, Scrimgeour visits, using Percy Weasley as a pretext. Scrimgeour takes Harry for a walk around the garden, during which he tries to get answers out of Harry about what Dumbledore is doing, and suggests that the Ministry would be grateful if Harry was to visibly align himself with them. Harry, who is revolted by the Ministry's hypocrisies, asks if they have freed

---

1. http://www.msnbc.msn.com/id/20026225/

Stan Shunpike yet. Scrimgeour waffles, saying essentially that they have to appear to be doing something. Harry refuses further assistance, saying that the new Ministry is as bad in its own way as the old one was.

In discussion with Professor Dumbledore immediately after Christmas break, Dumbledore tells Harry that what Scrimgeour had talked to Harry about over the break is what the earlier confrontation had been about. The plan to use Harry as the Ministry's poster boy had been initially suggested by Fudge, and had not died when Fudge had left office. Dumbledore had been refusing to allow Harry's use as a figurehead.

At the end of the book, Scrimgeour again talks to Harry, asking what Dumbledore was doing, and again trying to elicit Harry's visible co-operation with the Ministry. Harry again refuses, saying he has seen no differences in the Ministry since Christmas that would make him change his mind.

Deathly Hallows Scrimgeour first re-enters our story when he appears at The Burrow on Harry's birthday. His arrival is announced by Arthur Weasley's Patronus, which causes Remus Lupin and Nymphadora Tonks to depart hastily, as apparently werewolves are out of favour with the Ministry at present. Scrimgeour asks to see Harry, Ron, and Hermione, and tells them that they have inherited items from Albus Dumbledore, and he is there to present them. Hermione points out that he is only doing this because the Ministry is only allowed to hold on to bequests for thirty-one days, and they have used all thirty-one of them. Scrimgeour does not contradict her. The specific bequests are: for Hermione, an original copy of the *Tales of Beedle the Bard*; Scrimgeour asks if there is any significance to this choice, and Hermione says she is unaware of any. For Ron, Dumbledore's Deluminator. For Harry, there are two bequests. The first is the Golden Snitch that was used in the first-ever Quidditch game that Harry played for Gryffindor. Hermione says that Scrimgeour wants to see Harry take the Snitch because of its flesh memory: it is designed to remember the first hand that touches it, to assist in determining the winner of a match that is disputed, and may react to Harry's touch now. Again, Scrimgeour does not deny this, but quite evidently expects Harry to take the Snitch, bare-handed. Harry does, and nothing happens.

Dumbledore's second bequest to Harry is the sword of Gryffindor. Scrimgeour says that it is property of the school, and is not Dumbledore's to give.

The following day, the Death Eaters take over the Ministry of Magic, and according to the message from Kingsley Shacklebolt, Scrimgeour is killed. We later hear from Remus Lupin, who heard from Arthur Weasley, that Scrimgeour was tortured for the whereabouts of Harry before he was killed. However, he did not give Harry away. The official version of Scrimgeour's murder is that he resigned, and has been replaced by Pius Thicknesse. We learned in the start of the story that Thicknesse is under the Imperius Curse.

ANALYSIS

It was inevitable that once the knowledge of Lord Voldemort's return became public, Cornelius Fudge's days as Minister would be numbered. When Voldemort was seen in the Ministry, it became immediately obvious that Dumbledore had been telling the truth about his return for a year, and Fudge had been trying to discredit him for what suddenly seemed very petty reasons. It is not surprising that Fudge's tenure was less than two weeks after this revelation; it is equally not surprising that, given the fact that the Wizarding world was suddenly under siege, the obvious choice for Fudge's replacement would be someone from the Auror's office.

Scrimgeour seems to be cut of the same fabric as Bartemius Crouch Sr., there to get the job done, and to tread on toes if that's what it takes. While we don't yet know if Scrimgeour has authorized the use of deadly force by Aurors, as Crouch did, he is keeping Stan Shunpike locked up without trial. Sirius Black told us long before that the same had happened to him; he had been sent to Azkaban without trial by Crouch.

Salazar Slytherin

Gender: Male
Hair color: Unknown
Eye color: Unknown
Related Family: Unknown
Loyalty:

OVERVIEW

Salazar Slytherin was one of the four founders of Hogwarts and the creator of Slytherin House. He preferred to teach the most ambitious students and the members of this house have often come to be the most powerful witches and wizards. He also preferred the students with "pure-blood" Wizard-only ancestry and did not take any Muggle-borns in his house. He was famous for being a Parseltongue, someone who can talk to snakes.

ROLE IN THE BOOKS

Chamber of Secrets When the Chamber of Secrets is first opened, a message is written on the wall: *Enemies of the Heir, beware!* It somehow becomes common knowledge that the Heir is supposed to be the Heir of Slytherin.

When Professor Binns is telling Harry's class about the myth of the Chamber of Secrets, he mentions the four Founders of Hogwarts: Godric Gryffindor, Salazar Slytherin, Rowena Ravenclaw, and Helga Hufflepuff. He mentions that when the argument between the Founders, as to whether those who could not prove magical forbears, broke out, it was Salazar Slytherin standing alone against the other three. As a result of the argument, Slytherin left the school, supposedly leaving behind him a Chamber of Secrets containing a monster. In the Dueling Club, Harry sees that a snake is about to attack Justin Finch-Fletchley. Harry instructs the snake to back off. Great consternation ensues, and Ron and

Hermione take Harry aside to ask him about this ability. It seems that being a Parselmouth, being able to talk to snakes, is linked to Salazar Slytherin and his heirs. Harry wonders if he could be Slytherin's heir, given how little he knows of his background.

In the Chamber itself, we see a large statue of a wizard, which Harry presumes is Salazar Slytherin. We also meet Tom Riddle, who is, as it turns out, the heir of Slytherin. Present only in spirit, he has all the same been controlling Ginny, and having her act as Slytherin's heir. We also meet the Monster of the Chamber, a basilisk.

Half-Blood Prince In support of his apparent belief that he is above the common lot of wizardry, and thus to an extent above the law, Marvolo Gaunt displays two artifacts that are meant to prove his heritage. One, a locket with a snake forming the letter S, Marvolo claims was Salazar Slytherin's own. The locket is later sold to Caractacus Burke for a pittance, though he says, in Professor Dumbledore's memory, that its origin was plain enough to him.

Deathly Hallows Apart from the efforts to reclaim and destroy Slytherin's locket, Voldemort speaking of his claim to be the heir of Slytherin, and Voldemort's attempt to abolish all school houses other than Slytherin house, we hear little of Slytherin in this book.

Strengths Slytherin was one of the Four Founders of Hogwarts, and thus must have been a very powerful and accomplished wizard. While it is uncertain if he was the first wizard to be able to speak to snakes, it is certain that he not only had that ability but was able to pass it down to his descendants. We believe Dumbledore has learned Parseltongue, but he is an exception; otherwise, Parseltongue is considered a mark of descent from Slytherin.

Weaknesses Slytherin's inability to accept that Muggle-born wizards, and those who consort with Muggles, can in fact do powerful magic, will have blinded him to the abilities of a large part of the Wizarding world.

Analysis

While we don't ever see Slytherin directly, his views have obviously come down to us through the type of student that he selected, and that the Sorting Hat, as his deputy, has selected for the House named after him throughout the years. Apparently a scion of an old Wizarding family, even a thousand years ago, Slytherin is clearly portrayed as one who feels that ancestry is all important. From the Sorting Hat and its selections, we also learn that Slytherin chose students who were ambitious. Nowhere do we find a student who more clearly matches this combination of traits than in Tom Riddle, who becomes Lord Voldemort.

It is perhaps important to note that Slytherin is not inherently evil. It is certainly incorrect to assume that only wizards can have wizard children; in fact, we can see from the examples of Hermione Granger and Lily Evans that wizards, even quite strong ones, can spring from Muggle roots. However, this is more short-sighted than particularly evil. Ambition, in itself, is not evil, either. It is the way these two traits are expressed which is wrong. Slytherin, losing his argument, left, possibly to set up an alternate school, possibly to simply sulk, but in any event apart from the one trap he left behind him, has no further role to play. Voldemort, in a similar situation, apparently kills those who stand in his way. Slytherin would refuse to educate the Muggle-born; Voldemort deprives them of the education they already have, and incarcerates them.

Greater Picture

As far as the intent of Salazar Slytherin, Rowling never said he was not evil; in fact his ideas about pure-blood ideology, particularly as mirrored and enhanced by Voldemort, were similar to Hitler's. We as the readers of the series and viewers of the movies are told that most Dark wizards are trained in Slytherin house, from which we get the perhaps erroneous belief that most of the wizards and witches from Slytherin are Dark. Voldemort was Salazar's heir, and as far as it is explained, he is taking up the mission in the way he believes Salazar had intended, with the Chamber and the Basilisk. Through the books everything need not be explained to understand what the character's perspective is or was. It is well defined through the series that, whether or not Salazar was evil, his position very easily can be perverted to something very evil indeed, and this was done by Voldemort.

As the actual events happened, we are told, over a thousand years ago, they are by now shrouded in the mists of time, and it is unsure whether Slytherin, losing the battle, chose to leave the school or was forced to leave. Given what little we know of his character, it seems more likely that having been overruled, he would gather his dignity about himself and stalk off into the night. Knowing as little as we do about the other three Founders, though, it must remain uncertain as to whether they chose to dismiss him or whether he made the decision on his own. It is perhaps of interest that Portugal, where the author lived from 1990 to 1994, was ruled by a dictator named António de Oliveira Salazar from 1932 to 1968. Salazar's "Estado Novo" was a rigidly authoritarian, right-wing dictatorship. As the first book in the Potter series was completed in 1995, it is possible that Salazar Slytherin's name is retrieved from recent Portuguese history.

Scabbers

Gender: Male
Hair color: Patchy grey
Eye color: Black
Related Family: unknown
Loyalty: Self, Ron Weasley

Overview

Scabbers is Ron's pet rat.

Role in the Books

Philosopher's Stone Ron has accepted Scabbers as a pet because he needs something ... but is not happy about having "Percy's old rat" — he had been hoping for an owl. Apart from once attacking Goyle in the Hogwarts Express, and having Ron attempt to magically turn him yellow, Scabbers spends most of the book sleeping.

Apparently Scabbers has ruined a few bedsheets, as it is mentioned that Dean makes a banner out of one of them. When Harry returns to the dormitory after his third and final night in front of the Mirror of Erised, he mentions that he has to push Scabbers off his pillow before he can get to sleep.

Chamber of Secrets Scabbers is referred to a few times in this book, but has no particular rôle.

Prisoner of Azkaban Ron several times expresses concern about Scabbers' apparent deterioration. Early in the book, Hermione buys a cat, Crookshanks, who immediately takes a dislike to Scabbers. Ron, noting that Scabbers has been off colour and is beginning to lose his fur, says that Crookshanks' repeated attacks are what is making Scabbers look so bad; Harry recalls that Ron had been worried about Scabbers already when they went into the pet store where Hermione had bought Scabbers. Crookshanks' repeated attacks on Scabbers apparently result in Scabbers being eaten; this results in a rift between Hermione and Ron that is only mended when Scabbers is found in Hagrid's milk jug. Returning to the school, Scabbers seems frantic, trying to escape from Ron. When he does escape, Ron has to break away from the group, and eventually catches him. When he does so, however, he is under the branches of the Whomping Willow. A large black dog, who has been following Harry around, then dashes in under the branches and pulls Ron, and Scabbers, into a hole under the roots of the tree, in the process breaking his leg. Shortly after that, as the result of the events in the Shrieking Shack, and very much to Ron's surprise and dismay, Scabbers is revealed as being an Animagus named Peter Pettigrew. Peter escapes captivity and returns to serve his master, Lord Voldemort.

Relationships with Other Characters Percy Weasley got Scabbers as a pet, however, it was most of the time Ron that takes care of it. In the first two books, Scabbers seems quite loyal to Ron, but nobody ever imagined that it was in fact an animagus. The Weasley family had Scabbers as a pet for 12 years, which is quite long for a rat's life.

Questions

1. How did Percy Weasley get Scabbers as a pet?

Seamus Finnigan

Gender: Male
Hair color: Unknown
Eye color: Unknown
Related Family: Unknown
Loyalty: Albus Dumbledore

Overview

Seamus Finnigan is a member of Gryffindor House in Harry's year. He shares a dormitory with Harry, Ron, Dean Thomas, and Neville Longbottom.

Role in the Books

Philosopher's Stone Harry notes that the Sorting Hat takes almost a full minute to decide that Seamus is a Gryffindor. It is Seamus who asks how someone can be "nearly headless," which prompts Nearly Headless Nick to demonstrate. Seamus also asks why the Bloody Baron is all covered in blood, to which Nick responds, primly, that he had never asked.

Talking about families, Seamus says that he's half and half, that his mother had not revealed she was a witch until after she had married his father.

In Defence Against the Dark Arts, Professor Quirrell says that his strange purple turban was a gift from an African prince for dealing with a troublesome zombie. When Seamus asked excitedly how he had fought the zombie, Quirrell turned all pink and started talking about the weather. (Note: this is the only mention of "zombies" in the series, and thus is highly suspect. The magical construct most closely allied to the Muggle concept of zombies is the Inferius.)

When Neville manages to melt Seamus' cauldron in their first Potions class, he is splashed by the potion he is attempting to make and breaks out in boils. Professor Snape has Seamus take Neville to the Hospital Wing. As flying lessons approach, Seamus, like everyone else, seems to have stories about flying, which makes Harry feel uncertain about the chances of his learning to fly acceptably.

When it comes time for Harry to make an object fly in Charms class, he is relieved to be paired up with Seamus, as Neville had been trying to catch his eye. Seamus, as it turns out, is not much better than Neville would have been; their feather remains stubbornly inert, until Seamus pokes it with his wand and sets it on fire.

Seamus is one of the students urging Harry to eat something at breakfast before his first Quidditch match. Over Christmas, Harry learns Wizard Chess from Ron. It is mentioned that Ron's set were from his grandfather, and he knew them well enough that they would do what he asked, while Harry's set, borrowed from Seamus, didn't trust him and kept shouting out confusing advice.

Goblet of Fire In this book, Seamus accompanies Lavender Brown to the Yule Ball. He is a low profile character other than that.

Order of the Phoenix When Harry and Neville return to the dormitory at the start of the year, Dean says that Seamus has had a rough summer. Seamus says that his mother had not wanted him to return to the school, partly because of Harry, partly because of Dumbledore. Seamus uncomfortably admits that his mother reads the *Daily Prophet*. Harry angrily suggests that if Seamus believes that Harry is a liar and mental, maybe he should ask McGonagall to change his dorm so he doesn't have to stay in a room with Harry, so as to calm his mother down. Ron, coming upon this tableau, suggests that Seamus should shut up before he gets detention. Seamus considers and then goes silently to bed. In the morning, Harry wants to clear the air between himself and Seamus, but Seamus is gone before Harry is fully awake.

Seamus apparently is left wondering on the second day of classes when, as Harry enters the greenhouse for Herbology, Ernie Macmillan loudly states that he believes Harry's report of the return of Voldemort. Harry gives an interview to Rita Skeeter about the events surrounding Voldemort's return. The following Monday at dinner, he tells Dean and Neville about it. Dean is awestruck, and says he can't wait to see Umbridge's reaction. Seamus is not taking part in the conversation, but Harry can tell that he is listening. When the interview appears in the *Quibbler*, Seamus steps out of the queue at Transfiguration class to tell Harry that he believes Harry, and that he has sent a copy of the magazine to his mother.

In the final meeting of Dumbledore's Army in April, which is mentioned as being the first time Seamus attends, the class is working on Patronuses. Several people in the class are having trouble; Lavender and Neville, in particular, can only produce little bits of white vapour. Seamus calls out that he's doing it, but before Harry can look, it has disappeared; Seamus says that he wasn't sure what it was, but that it was hairy.

When Harry decides to make use of a diversion provided by Fred and George to get into Umbridge's office so he can speak with Sirius, Hermione tries to dissuade him. In Potions class, she speaks in a vehement hiss, and Seamus spends five minutes checking his cauldron for leaks as a result.

Following the final O.W.L. exam, Dean and Seamus tell Harry that they are planning a dusk-to-dawn end of O.W.L.s celebration and suggest that one of the students, Harold Dingle, believes that he can get some Firewhisky. Harry is in a panic, trying to get in contact with Sirius, and pushes past without answering.

Deathly Hallows Seamus is one of the three who cast Patronuses when Harry is about to be overwhelmed on the verge of the Forbidden Forest; the other two are Ernie Macmillan and Luna Lovegood.

As the renewed battle rages, Harry, from under the Invisibility Cloak, casts Shield spells in the path of Voldemort's curses. Voldemort's intended victims, Hannah and Seamus, run past and into the Great Hall.

Relationships with Other Characters Is Dean Thomas' best friend. He is also close with Harry Potter, Ron Weasley and Neville Longbotton.

Selwyn

Gender: Male
Hair color: Unknown
Eye color: Unknown
Related Family: Unknown
Loyalty: Lord Voldemort

Overview

Selwyn (first name unknown) is a Death Eater.

Role in the Books

Deathly Hallows When Harry and Hagrid are escaping from Privet Drive, the pursuing Death Eaters determine that he is the real Harry Potter, out of the six sets of protector and Potter there. Having discovered this, Lord Voldemort gathers his Death Eaters and attacks Harry personally. Harry's wand destroys the wand Voldemort is using (which he had taken from Lucius Malfoy), so Voldemort demands a fresh wand from Selwyn. Before he can use it, though, Harry is through the protective spells surrounding Ted Tonks' house.

Hermione, in disguise as Mafalda Hopkirk in the Ministry, catches sight of the Locket Horcrux that Dolores Umbridge is wearing, and comments that it is lovely. Umbridge says that the S is for Selwyn, and she wears it because she is related to the Selwyn family, one of the last remaining bastions of pureblood wizardry. When Xenophilius Lovegood, in hopes of winning his daughter's freedom, summons the Death Eaters, telling them that Harry is in his house, Selwyn is one of the two Death Eaters who respond to the summons. He seems annoyed at the summons, saying that this is the third time Xeno has called, and also because he had apparently tried to blow them up as they arrived. While he accuses Xeno of making things up again, he is also repeatedly jinxing him. Hermione engineers their escape, allowing the Death Eaters to see her and Harry so that they know Xeno isn't lying this time, but hiding Ron as he is supposed to be ill with Spattergroit.

Septima Vector

Gender: Female[1]
Hair color: Unknown
Eye color: Unknown
Related Family: Unknown
Loyalty:

Overview

Professor Septima Vector is the Arithmancy professor at Hogwarts School of Witchcraft and Wizardry.

---

1. In *Harry Potter and the Prisoner of Azkaban* (Chapter 12) Ron mentions her as a *Witch*.

ROLE IN THE BOOKS
ANALYSIS

Arithmancy is otherwise known as numerology, which is in fact a real subject. It involves the finding of magical properties of numbers.

In the Harry Potter world, numbers are often inscribed in places, such as tombs, pyramids, and monuments. These numbers supposedly have meaning, either hiding a secret message or protecting the site with a curse. Arithmancy, if applied correctly, allows the practitioner to interpret these findings.

Gringotts curse breakers are required to have sufficient knowledge of Arithmancy.

QUESTIONS

1. Hermione repeatedly states that Arithmancy is very useful. What kind of things might be taught in an Arithmancy class, that Hermione would see as being particularly useful?

Severus Snape

Gender: Male
Hair color: Black
Eye color: Black
Related Family: Details follow spoiler warning
Loyalty: Details follow spoiler warning

OVERVIEW

Severus Snape is the Potions teacher at Hogwarts School of Witchcraft and Wizardry. He is also the Head of Slytherin House. Although Snape is a former Death Eater, Professor Dumbledore places his utmost faith in Snape's loyalty, although exactly why he trusts him so implicitly is not initially revealed. Snape also joins the Order of the Phoenix to combat Lord Voldemort, apparently acting as a double agent, though it is uncertain where his loyalties lie.

According to the author, Severus Snape's birthday is 9 January.

ROLE IN THE BOOKS

Philosopher's Stone Harry Potter's first interaction with Professor Snape is minor, but telling; as Snape looks at him across the Great Hall, Harry's scar pains him. Because the scar is a link between Harry and Lord Voldemort, the evil wizard who gave it to him, this may indicate a connection between Snape and Voldemort. Harry has a dream that night involving Professor Quirrell's turban, and Draco Malfoy turning into Snape.

During his first Potions class, Snape humiliates Harry by asking questions he does not (and could not) know the answers to, although the implication is that he ought to. When Neville manages to melt his cauldron, Snape holds Harry responsible, and penalizes Gryffindor house a point because of it.

At Hallowe'en, a giant troll is discovered in the dungeons. Rather than heading below with the other staff, Snape is seen going upstairs, possibly to a second-floor (US: third-floor) corridor which Professor Dumbledore declared off-limits. Subsequently, Snape seems to have sustained a leg injury: Hermione, Ron, and Harry are standing in the courtyard around a blue fire which Hermione has conjured, when Snape walks by, and, seeing that Harry has a library book (*Quidditch Through the Ages*), confiscates it on the grounds that library books are not to be taken outside the school. As he walks away, the Trio notice that he is limping. Later, Harry, going to the staff room to request the return of his book, sees that Snape is having a bad leg wound tended by Filch, and hears Snape talking about having trouble with the three heads on something. Snape, seeing Harry, angrily sends him away. The Trio speculate among themselves that Snape's wound may have been inflicted by the giant three-headed dog that Harry, Hermione, Ron, and Neville had earlier discovered guarding a trap door in the forbidden corridor. During a Quidditch match against Slytherin, Snape appears to be jinxing Harry's broom, although it is interrupted when Hermione sets his robes on fire. The Trio talk this over later with Hagrid. Hagrid expresses disbelief, first that Snape would be Jinxing Harry's broom, and second that Fluffy would have hurt him. To the Trio's surprise, it turns out that the three-headed dog is one of Hagrid's pets, and Hagrid considers him quite tame. In a later match, Snape takes on refereeing duties, normally the job of Madam Hooch; Harry, believing this is a cover for another attempt on his life, catches the Snitch almost immediately, ending the game. Harry, immediately after that match, sees Snape headed for the Forbidden Forest. Following on his broom, Harry overhears Snape in a heated discussion with Professor Quirrell about where his loyalties lie. Harry, Hermione, and Ron, discussing this later, come to the conclusion that it is the Philosopher's Stone that Snape is after, and that only Quirrell stands between Snape and the Stone. The Trio are even more concerned to discover from Hagrid that Snape is one of the wizards who has provided protection for the Stone.

When Harry and Hermione return from serving detention in the Forbidden Forest, Harry feels that Voldemort is simply waiting for Snape to retrieve the Stone, and then he will appear and try once again to kill Harry. As exams end, Harry concludes that Snape is about to try for the Stone, but their attempts to tail him fail. Harry decides that he must venture through the trap door under Fluffy, to try and retrieve the Stone before Snape does. In the climactic scene between Professor Quirrell and Harry, Quirrell informs Harry that it was he (Quirrell) who has been seeking the Stone for Voldemort; Snape had actually been thwarting Quirrell's efforts to harm Harry (it was Quirrell who was jinxing Harry's broom during the Quidditch game, and Snape had been countering it). At this point we find out that Harry's scar paining him at the feast at the beginning of the year was because of the link between Quirrell and Voldemort, rather than having anything to do with Snape.

Chamber of Secrets After Harry and Ron crash into the Whomping Willow in the flying car, Snape arrives on the scene and takes them to his office for discipline. Apparently the *Evening Prophet* has reported sightings of a flying car by Muggles. Hearing their story, he goes off to fetch Professor McGonagall, who asks to hear their story again; and finally Professor Dumbledore arrives and also asks to hear their explanation. While Snape is determined to have Harry and Ron expelled, Dumbledore simply warns them that if they break any more rules, they will be expelled, then takes Snape back to the Arrival Feast, leaving McGonagall to mete out their punishment.

Although the Gryffindor Quidditch team has already begun their practice, Snape grants use of the pitch to Slytherin, "in order that they may train their new Seeker," Draco Malfoy, whose father donated new broomsticks to the team. A confrontation between the Trio and Malfoy ensues, although Ron's attempt to curse Malfoy fails when his damaged wand backfires and he curses himself instead.

When Filch's cat, Mrs. Norris, is petrified, Snape wonders why Harry, Ron, and Hermione had not been at the Hallowe'en Feast. Told that they had been at Nearly Headless Nick's Deathday party, Snape points out that food at Deathday parties is very seldom edible, and wonders why they had not come back to the Feast after the party. Skeptical about Ron's claim that they were not hungry, Snape suggests that Harry may be involved. He recommends banning Harry from playing Quidditch but is overruled by Professor McGonagall and Professor Dumbledore, who remind Snape that Harry is innocent until proven guilty.

To obtain the ingredients Hermione needs to brew Polyjuice potion, which are not in the student supplies cabinet, Hermione must raid Snape's office, so Harry creates a diversion. He tosses a firecracker into Goyle's cauldron during Potions class, and Hermione raids Snape's supply cupboard in the ensuing confusion. Although Snape suspects Harry, he is unable to prove anything, and Harry avoids punishment.

In the Dueling Club, Gilderoy Lockhart uses Snape as his sparring partner, although Snape easily defeats him. When Lockhart sets up partners for individual practice, it is Snape who halts the ensuing mayhem when the students try to jinx each other and Lockhart's efforts are ineffective. Later, when Lockhart suggests putting a student pair on the stage, Snape chooses Malfoy and Harry. Malfoy's jinx produces a snake. Lockhart, trying to dispose of the snake, manages to toss it into the air; when it lands, it seems ready to attack Justin Finch-Fletchley. Harry tries to call it off; Snape casts a spell that disposes of the snake, but then looks at Harry very oddly. Harry is quickly taken away by Ron and Hermione.

When Ginny is taken into the Chamber of Secrets, Snape is among the teachers who echo Lockhart's recent boasts about the Chamber back to him, as part of convincing him to go deal with the Monster. Lockhart instead returns to his office and starts packing.

Prisoner of Azkaban At the Arrival Feast, Harry notes that Snape casts a look of loathing at the new Defence Against the Dark Arts teacher, Remus Lupin.

Draco Malfoy, claiming that the injury he received from Buckbeak is still paining him, returns to classes halfway through Potions class. Snape orders Ron to assist Draco with his potion ingredients. Harry thinks that this is very different from what would have happened if a Gryffindor student had been half an hour late.

Professor Lupin takes his class to the staff room, where they find Snape. Snape cautions Lupin that Longbottom causes havoc with every wand stroke; Lupin counters that, saying he had hoped that Longbottom would lead off the demonstration. Snape sweeps out, and Lupin explains that they have trapped a Boggart in the wardrobe, and that the Boggart will take the shape of what its opponent most greatly fears. He asks Neville's greatest fear, and Neville replies that it is Snape. Lupin then asks what his grandmother usually wears, and goes on to explain that what destroys a Boggart is actually laughter. The charm they are learning, Riddikulus, will force the Boggart into whatever funny guise the caster is imagining, and suggests that Neville should imagine the Boggart-Snape that will appear from the wardrobe dressed as his grandmother. Neville succeeds in this transformation twice during the next few minutes.

Neville's transformation of the Boggart-Snape apparently gets repeated, because Snape becomes worse than ever in Potions class, bullying Neville mercilessly.

As Harry does not have permission to visit Hogsmeade with the other third-years, he wanders around the school aimlessly until Professor Lupin asks him to drop in. While he is there, Professor Snape arrives with a smoking goblet of some sort of potion. After Snape has left, and despite Harry's warning that Snape would likely do anything to get Lupin's job, Lupin drinks the contents of the goblet. At dinner, Harry does note that Snape appears to be watching Lupin more intently than usual, but Lupin does not seem to have taken any particular ill-effect from the potion, apart from seeming tired.

Following Sirius Black's break-in into the castle, Professor Dumbledore orders all students to spend the night in the Great Hall. Prefects stand guard while the teachers search the castle. Harry, Ron, and Hermione are still awake when Professor Dumbledore receives the all clear from Professor Snape. Snape reminds Dumbledore that he had expressed concerns over an appointment Dumbledore made. Dumbledore interrupts, saying he is certain that nobody in the castle would have helped Black.

Delayed by Oliver Wood, Harry is ten minutes late for Defence Against the Dark Arts class. He is dismayed to realize that it is being taught by Professor Snape, who says that Professor Lupin is ill and gives Harry a House points penalty for his lateness. Dismissing Lupin's work in the class so far, Snape says they should be further along, and turning to the end of the text, sets an essay on Werewolves, their recognition and means of fighting them. When Professor Lupin returns to teaching the class on Monday, he cancels the assignment, to the dismay of Hermione who had apparently already completed it.

Professor Snape is one of the teachers at the school at Christmas. He remains looking sour through all the Christmas dinner merriment. Professor Dumbledore does check with him that Professor Lupin has been receiving his potion. In late April, there is a Hogsmeade weekend; Harry, of course, is not allowed to go, but making use of the Marauder's Map, he plans to travel through the secret passage to Honeyduke's. On his way to the secret passage, however, he is caught by Snape, who sends him back to Gryffindor tower. As Harry leaves, he notes that Snape is inspecting the status of the hump-backed witch, as if he had been able to read from Harry's mind that a secret passage started there. Harry is later able to return to the statue, and travel through it to Hogsmeade. He is nearly caught in Hogsmeade, and returns to the school at a run; he is caught almost immediately after leaving the secret passage by Snape, and taken to Snape's study. There, Snape has him clean out his pockets, and finding the Marauders Map, commands that it show what it is. The map, writing as Messrs. Moony, Padfoot, Wormtail, and Prongs, insults Snape. Snape then summons Professor Lupin and asks him if he knows something about the map. Lupin, saying it looks to him like a standard Zonko's Joke Shop insult scroll, collects Harry, and Ron who has come in to support Harry's story, as well as the map, and takes them all out of the now clearly livid Snape's office. We next see Snape in Harry's final Potions exam. Harry's work is not going at all well, and Snape writes something on his notepad that looks suspiciously like a zero before walking away.

Snape, hiding under Harry's Invisibility Cloak, is present in the Shrieking Shack as Lupin and Sirius tell Harry, Ron, and Hermione about their days as students at Hogwarts, and how Snape had almost been killed by a transformed Lupin, except that Harry's father, James, had saved him. Revealing himself, Snape says that on his way to bring Lupin some of the potion, he had found a very interesting map on Lupin's desk and had noticed Sirius' name on it. He refuses to listen to Remus' explanations, instead binding both Sirius and Lupin, and saying that they are going to go up to the castle and talk to the Dementors. Harry, Ron and Hermione all Disarm him simultaneously, throwing him against a wall and leaving him unconscious.

Snape remains unconscious until after Peter Pettigrew's reappearance and escape. When he recovers, he collects the unconscious bodies of Sirius, Harry, and Hermione, who had been disabled by Dementors, and Ron, who had been jinxed by Pettigrew, and brings all of them to the castle. With Sirius captive, and the Trio in the Hospital Wing, he apparently summons Cornelius Fudge to report his recapture of the wanted murderer Black. When Harry awakens in the Hospital Wing, he hears Snape telling his version of the story to Fudge. Apparently, Snape has Fudge convinced that Lupin had assisted Sirius in getting into Hogwarts, and that whatever Harry and Hermione might say could be discounted because they were clearly Confunded. Snape is quite clearly pleased at the possibility of receiving an Order of Merlin, which Fudge describes as a distinct possibility. When Dumbledore arrives, wanting to talk to Harry and Hermione, Snape and Fudge depart, to go up to Professor Flitwick's office and witness the Dementor's Kiss being administered to Sirius.

When they arrive there, however, they find Sirius gone. Snape, now raging mad, is convinced Harry had something to do with it, despite the clear statement of Madam Pomfrey that he and Hermione had been in the infirmary all the time. As he stalks off, thwarted by Madam Pomfrey and the returned Professor Dumbledore, Fudge comments that Snape seems unhinged.

In his anger, Snape reveals the next day that Professor Lupin is a werewolf, causing Lupin to resign as the Defence Against the Dark Arts instructor.

During the course of the conversation in the Shrieking Shack, we learn that Snape was concocting the Wolfsbane potion Lupin had been drinking to control himself during full moons. The potion, the same one which Harry had been concerned about when he saw Snape bring it to Lupin, does not prevent Lupin from turning into a werewolf, but does allow him to retain his intelligence, making him harmless. Snape is one of the few who can actually brew the potion; a recent discovery, it is very complicated.

Goblet of Fire When Draco Malfoy attempts to Jinx Harry in the entrance hall, and is turned into a white ferret for this by Professor Moody, Professor McGonagall reminds Moody that Transfiguration is not used for punishment at Hogwarts. Instead, Moody should be taking Draco to speak with his Head of House. Moody, a retired Auror, confirms that would be Snape, then departs with Draco in tow, saying Snape is an "old friend" of his. Possibly as a result of this confrontation, Snape is even harsher than usual on his Potions students. It seems that, apart from his feeling that he should have gotten the Defence Against the Dark Arts post, he fears Moody and is taking it out on the students.

It is mentioned in passing that Snape has Harry's class researching antidotes, and Harry is worried that there will be a practical test—someone will be poisoned, and Harry is beginning to suspect it will be himself. When Harry's name is ejected from the Goblet of Fire, he is directed to proceed to the room where the other Champions are waiting. Snape is among the teachers and judges who join them. In the debate that follows, Igor Karkaroff and Madame Maxime are adamant that Harry must have somehow arranged to cross the Age Line that Professor Dumbledore had drawn to keep underage wizards out of the competition. Snape's contribution to the argument is the snide observation that Harry had been crossing lines ever since he arrived at Hogwarts. When Draco Malfoy starts distributing buttons that insult Harry, it proves too much for Harry and he ends up dueling with Draco as they wait for Potions class. Their spells meet in mid-air and deflect onto Goyle and Hermione. Snape, appearing at the dungeon door, sends Goyle off to the Hospital Wing for treatment of his boils, but professes to see nothing wrong with Hermione whose front teeth have grown to below her collar. Hermione departs, crying. When Harry and Ron have stopped protesting what they see as a miscarriage of justice, Snape says that it is lucky that he could not understand most of what they were saying, because of the echoes, then penalizes

Gryffindor house 50 points and gives Harry and Ron detention. The lecture that day concerns antidotes, and Snape says that they will be trying one out at the end of class. Harry is relieved when Colin Creevey arrives to take Harry to the Wand Weighing ceremony; but this is offset at Snape's clear dislike of the increased publicity that Harry seems to be receiving.

Snape schedules a test on antidotes for the last day of the term; Harry, by now in something of a panic about finding a partner for the Yule Ball, forgets the vital ingredient, a Bezoar, and fails the test.

At the Yule Ball, Harry and Ron end up in the rose garden outside the Entrance Hall. They see Snape walking there with Karkaroff, blasting apart the rose bushes and penalizing any students he finds hiding within them. Harry and Ron also overhear Karkaroff talking about something that is becoming more distinct, and Snape saying that Karkaroff may run if he chooses to. Ron wonders exactly how Snape and Karkaroff got to be on a first-name basis. Taking Cedric Diggory's advice, Harry takes his Golden Egg, which is a necessary clue for the Second Task, to the Prefect's Bathroom. As he leaves the bathroom, he checks the Marauder's Map to see if it is safe to travel the halls. He sees that Bartemius Crouch is in Snape's office, and curious, goes to investigate. On the way, he steps through one of the trick steps and is trapped; he drops the map and the Egg, which starts to wail. The noise summons Filch, Snape, and eventually Professor Moody. Moody, with his magical eye, can see Harry under his Invisibility Cloak, while Snape and Filch cannot. Filch believes that Peeves is responsible for the theft of the Egg; Snape is more concerned that someone has been rummaging around in his office. Moody, when he arrives, points out that it is part of his job to look through Snape's office, but he is also interested to hear that someone has been going through it. As Snape leaves, Moody points out the map, saying Snape had dropped some parchment; Harry gesticulates wildly to indicate it is his, and Moody Summons it, snatching it out of Snape's fingers. Snape has recognized the Map, and concludes that Harry is close by under his Invisibility Cloak. Moody tells him there's nobody there and says it's curious how quickly Snape's mind jumped to Harry. Snape, having almost touched Harry, departs before Moody can draw any other conclusions. Moody sends Filch away also, and rescues Harry from the step in which he has been trapped.

When Harry, Ron, and Hermione arrive at Potions class a few weeks after the Second Task, the Slytherins are huddled around something and sniggering. Pansy Parkinson throws something to Hermione. It is a copy of Witch Weekly. Hermione riffles through it and finds an article, *Harry Potter's Secret Heartache*, by Rita Skeeter. The article suggests that Hermione is Harry's girlfriend and is abandoning him for Viktor Krum, who has invited her to visit him during the summer. Hermione is unimpressed, even by Pansy Parkinson's quote that insinuates Hermione might be using love potions. She wonders how Skeeter knew about Krum's invitation. Ron is interested in hearing how she answered, but she ignores this. Professor Snape comes up behind them and penalizes Gryffindor ten points for Hermione's talking and ten more for having *Witch Weekly* in class. He reads Rita Skeeter's article aloud to gales of laughter from the Slytherins. Snape now separates the three, placing Hermione with Pansy, leaving Ron where he is, and placing Harry at the table immediately facing his desk.

Snape says in a soft undertone that he knows Harry was in his office. Harry insists he was not, Snape says Boomslang skin and Gillyweed are missing from his stores, and he knows who took them. Harry remembers that Hermione stole Boomslang skin during their second year to make the Polyjuice potion and that Dobby swiped the Gillyweed, but he lies and says he has no idea what Snape is talking about. Snape produces a vial containing Veritaserum. Just three drops and Harry would babble his innermost secrets. Snape suggests that his hand might just slip over Harry's pumpkin juice.

Igor Karkaroff enters the dungeon wanting to speak to Snape, who says they can talk after class. Karkaroff claims Snape has been avoiding him and stays until the class ends. Harry knocks over his armadillo bile, crouching down behind his cauldron. He sees Karkaroff show Snape something on his left forearm and saying, "It has never been that clear, not since...." Snape tells him to put it away, they can discuss it later. Spotting Harry, he asks what he is doing there. Harry replies innocently that he is cleaning up his armadillo bile. Karkaroff leaves, and Harry decides it would be a good idea to do likewise.

That Saturday, Harry, Ron, and Hermione visit Sirius, who is hiding in a cave outside Hogsmeade. Sirius says that it is curious that Snape and Karkaroff would have been talking. Karkaroff was a Death Eater, and Snape had certainly associated with known Dark wizards, but that he had never been accused of being a Death Eater. When Bartemius Crouch appears at the edge of the Forbidden Forest, Harry runs to find Professor Dumbledore. At the stone gargoyle guarding the lower end of the stairs to the Headmaster's office, Harry finds his way blocked by Snape, who refuses to allow Harry to pass. Luckily, Dumbledore then appears behind Snape, and Harry is able to give Dumbledore his message. Shortly after Dumbledore and Harry arrive at the scene, Moody arrives, saying Snape had told him where they would be.

In Dumbledore's Pensieve, Harry experiences Dumbledore's memories of some Wizengamot trials of Death Eaters. He sees Karkaroff attempting to lighten his sentence by naming other Death Eaters; one of the ones he names is Severus Snape, but Dumbledore replies that Snape was a double agent who was working against Voldemort before his defeat. Later, as Dumbledore talks with Harry about the function of the Pensieve, Harry's face appears in it, smoothly changing into Snape's, who says "It's coming back, Karkaroff's too." As he is leaving Dumbledore's office, Harry asks why Dumbledore trusts Snape, but Dumbledore says that is between him and Snape. On Harry's return from the graveyard in Little Hangleton, he is taken aside by Moody, who reveals that he is a Death Eater, and that he plans to kill Harry to improve his position in Voldemort's new organization. As he is about to do so, the door behind him blows open, Moody falls Stunned, and Professor Dumbledore, Professor McGonagall, and Professor Snape enter. Dumbledore sends Snape for truth serum, and to fetch Winky from the kitchens. When Snape returns with Winky, she immediately recognizes the Stunned man, who has transformed as his Polyjuice Potion wore off, as her master Barty Crouch, Bartemius' son. In the course of his confession, Barty admits that he had fetched ingredients for more Polyjuice Potion out of Snape's office, under the guise of searching it for Dark materials.

Dumbledore then asks Snape to bring the real Alastor Moody to the Hospital Wing, and takes Harry to his office. There, after meeting with Sirius, Harry repeats his story. Dumbledore then takes Harry to the Hospital Wing. Some time later, Harry awakens and hears Cornelius Fudge and Dumbledore arguing over whether Voldemort has returned. Snape, who is present, shows Fudge something on his left forearm, saying that the Dark Mark is the means by which Voldemort communicated with his Death Eaters, and that it has been growing stronger, until some hours back when it burned black as a summons to attend Voldemort. Refusing to believe, Fudge departs. Dumbledore then sends most of the others away, and has Sirius reveal himself. He demands that, as they have the same goal, Sirius and Snape should get along together. After much prompting by Dumbledore, and most unwillingly, they eventually shake hands; Dumbledore then tells Snape that he knows the mission Dumbledore has for him. Snape agrees, and departs.

At the Leaving Feast, Snape is present, apparently having returned from his mission; Harry seems to think he is looking more sour than usual.

Order of the Phoenix We hear little of Snape for the first section of the book, though when Harry arrives at the Headquarters of the Order of the Phoenix, he finds out to his displeasure that Snape is present for a meeting. Snape, however, leaves even before Fred and George can put their Extendable Ears into play.

Immediately before Potions class, Draco Malfoy, inspired perhaps by the continuing depiction of Harry in the *Daily Prophet*, makes remarks about mentally deficient people and how they should be locked up in St. Mungo's. Pushed to his limit by this, Neville attacks Draco; Harry and Ron restrain him. It is at this moment that Snape opens the door to the dungeon, and promptly penalizes Gryffindor 10 points for fighting. Ron asks Harry why Neville had reacted that way; Harry, knowing about Neville's parents, still follows Dumbledore's instructions and says nothing. Snape's class today is monitored by Professor Umbridge, acting as Hogwarts High Inquisitor. After observing his teaching for a while, she asks him how long he has been teaching at Hogwarts ("fourteen years"), and asks about his application for the post of teacher of Defence Against the Dark Arts. He replies that Dumbledore had repeatedly turned him down for that post, and that she would have to ask Dumbledore for the reason. Straining to hear Snape's answers, Harry ruins his potion and receives a zero.

Snape is working as a double agent for the Order. Although Snape continues to try and get Harry expelled, he saves his life by informing the Order that Harry and the other students have fallen into a trap set by Voldemort at the Ministry of Magic in London.

At Christmas, back at Grimmauld Place, Snape arrives and says that Dumbledore has asked Harry to study Occlumency, the art of closing one's mind from another's intrusion. Harry agrees, but then discovers that Snape is teaching him. Sirius asks why Dumbledore cannot teach him; Snape responds that it was Dumbledore's decision. The verbal battle escalates until Sirius and Snape are at wands drawn, with Harry standing between them trying to prevent a duel, when Mr. Weasley enters with the entire Weasley family and Hermione. Mr. Weasley is fully healed and has returned from St. Mungo's. Sirius and Snape, brought to their senses by having so many witnesses, separate. Snape leaves, saying he expects Harry in his office at 6 o'clock Monday evening. Harry discusses the Occlumency lessons with Ron and Hermione. Hermione says Harry will be happy to stop the nightmares. Ron says that he would rather have the nightmares himself.

Back at the school, Harry begins his first Occlumency lesson with Snape, although he still distrusts him. Snape explains that Legilimency is the ability to read other's thoughts and memories. Voldemort is an expert in Legilimency, and Occlumency will help Harry block his mind. Snape removes some of his memories and deposits them into what Harry recognizes as Dumbledore's Pensieve. He tells Harry to try and prevent him from penetrating Harry's mind. Harry's first attempts fail miserably. However, Harry does now recognize the hallway he has dreamt about so frequently; it is the hall in the Ministry of Magic leading to the Department of Mysteries. He and Mr. Weasley ran down it last summer to his hearing; it is the same hallway where Mr. Weasley was attacked by the snake. Snape dismisses him, saying he will have to come back on Wednesday. As Harry leaves, he sees Snape removing the memories from the Pensieve and reinserting them into his head.

Harry's Occlumency lessons over the next several months do not proceed well. He is still unable to block Snape's probes. His scar is now prickling almost continually, and he sees small flashes of Voldemort's emotions. He can date this increased sensitivity to when Snape's lessons started. He discusses this with Ron and Hermione. Ron's opinion is that Snape is making it easier for Voldemort by deliberately not helping Harry. Hermione reminds him that Dumbledore trusts Snape, and if Dumbledore is untrustworthy, who can they trust? As late as early April, Harry's hatred for Snape prevents him from clearing his mind. Although he is making little progress, on one occasion, he briefly enters Snape's mind using a Shield Charm. The next attempt, Harry again experiences his corridors dream, but when he reaches the door, it is open for the first time. Snape breaks him from the vision, seeming concerned at what is appearing in Harry's mind. Their session is interrupted, by someone frantically screaming in the entrance hall: it is Professor Trelawney, who has just been fired by Umbridge.

Just before Easter break, an Occlumency session is interrupted when Malfoy arrives with a message that

Umbridge needs to see Snape—Montague, who the Twins had earlier stuffed into an old, broken Vanishing Cabinet, has reappeared, jammed inside a toilet. Snape departs, and before leaving, Harry sees a shimmering light reminiscent of his dream about the Ministry coming from a Pensieve. What memories has Snape been hiding? Is it something about the Ministry? Looking inside, Harry sees a young James Potter and Sirius Black at Hogwarts. They are cruelly tormenting their classmate, Severus Snape, by suspending him upside down in mid-air, exposing his dingy underwear. Lily Evans intervenes and berates James and Sirius for their deplorable behavior. James offers a deal—if she goes out with him, he will never hurt Snape again—to which she angrily declines. The humiliated Snape resents Lily's help and insultingly calls her a "Mudblood." Harry is appalled by his father's bullying, but before he can consider it further, the present-day Snape yanks him from the Pensieve. Furious, Snape demands that he never reveal what he has seen to anyone, and orders him to leave.

Unwilling to reveal, even to Hermione, what he had seen about his father, Harry parries her questions about why Occlumency lessons have ended by telling her that Snape says he is good enough. Luckily, Hermione guesses that his being upset is due to troubles with Cho, and does not pursue the question further.

It is mentioned that Harry performs creditably in his Potions O.W.L., perhaps because Snape is not present. Harry, believing Sirius Black has been trapped at the Ministry and is being tortured, tries to contact him via the Floo network. When Harry is trapped in Umbridge's fireplace, Umbridge summons Snape to her office and demands that he provide her some truth serum that she can use on Harry. Snape responds coldly that he had earlier given Umbridge all the Veritaserum he had, and reminds her that she had only needed three drops. To her demand that he make some more, he responds that it will take several weeks. She tells him that he is on probation and dismisses him. Harry, suddenly remembering that Snape is a member of the Order, tries to pass a message about Sirius to Snape. Snape appears to dismiss it as simple babbling, and leaves.

Later, Dumbledore says that Snape had contacted Sirius and confirmed that he was all right. He had then watched Harry, Hermione, and Umbridge go into the Forbidden Forest. When they did not return, Snape had alerted the Order. Dumbledore further says that he had wanted Harry to learn Occlumency to block the sendings that Voldemort had been putting into Harry's mind, in order to lure him to the Ministry. Dumbledore had believed that old animosities could be forgotten; but he admits that he was wrong. He would have taught Harry Occlumency himself, but he was afraid that if Voldemort had any idea that their relationship was any deeper than that of headmaster to student, he would have been leaving both himself and Harry open to attack.

Harry almost gets into a duel with Draco Malfoy, but is stopped by Snape. Snape is about to penalize Gryffindor House points, but realizes Gryffindor has no points left. Professor McGonagall, also arriving at that point, grants a number of House points to Gryffindor for the students who had been fighting Death Eaters at the Ministry, then sends Harry and Draco on their respective ways.

Half-Blood Prince Severus Snape is at his home during the school break when Bellatrix Lestrange and Narcissa Malfoy visit him. Narcissa is worried about some task that the Dark Lord has set for her son Draco; Bellatrix is trying to prevent her visiting Snape as she feels he is not trustworthy. Snape has Wormtail (Peter Pettigrew) serve them drinks, and then dismisses him; Wormtail complains bitterly about being made to do menial work. Before either Narcissa or Bellatrix can get too far into the reason for their visit, Snape fires a jinx at the bookcase; behind it, we hear Wormtail yelp and retreat up a hidden staircase. Bellatrix now asks Snape a long list of questions, which seem to point to possible disloyalty. Snape says that he will answer her questions, but points out that the Dark Lord had already asked them, and had received satisfactory answers. Snape further asks if Bellatrix thinks that Snape could have hidden anything from possibly the greatest Legilimens the world has ever known.

While she is hesitating, Snape answers. Where was he when the Dark Lord fell? At Hogwarts, where Voldemort had ordered him to spy on Dumbledore. Why did he not go looking for the Dark Lord after he had fallen? For the same reason many other Death Eaters did not: he thought the Dark Lord was finished. Bellatrix retorts that she had looked for him. Snape sarcastically comments about how "useful" she was while imprisoned in Azkaban, while he had collected sixteen years' worth of information on Dumbledore for Voldemort. Snape continues: Why did he stand between the Dark Lord and the Philosopher's Stone? Because the Dark Lord believed Snape had deserted him for Dumbledore, Snape was not informed that it was Voldemort that looking for the Stone. He thought Quirrell was searching for it and, of course, he acted to prevent that. Why did he not respond to the Dark Lord's summons when Voldemort returned? He returned two hours later, at Dumbledore's orders. That way, Dumbledore would continue to believe that Snape was spying on Voldemort for him, rather than the other way around. Bellatrix says she is unaware of any information Snape passed to Voldemort, although she should know: Voldemort says she is his most trusted lieutenant. Snape asks if she still is after the fiasco at the Ministry. And where was he at that battle? On the Dark Lord's orders, he stayed out of it. Did Bellatrix think Dumbledore would not notice if Snape had joined the Death Eaters in that battle? In any event, the information Snape supplied made Emmeline Vance and Sirius Black's deaths possible, and the Dark Lord was satisfied with his information. Why did Snape not kill Harry Potter? Because it was only Dumbledore who was keeping Snape effective as a spy and out of Azkaban. If he killed Potter, he would lose that protection and would be unable to help Voldemort. And that has been what has made him useful to the Dark Lord: Dumbledore's trust in him.

With Bellatrix's worries overridden, Narcissa explains why she has come. Voldemort has assigned her son, Draco, a difficult and probably deadly task. Narcissa asks Snape to protect him. Snape replies that it is folly for her to talk to him about it because that is breaking the Dark Lord's wish. Death Eaters seldom know what tasks their colleagues have been assigned. Luckily for Narcissa, however, Snape already knows about this task, but even as the Dark Lord's most trusted confidante, he cannot convince him to change his mind, nor will he try. Narcissa says assigning Draco this task is revenge for her husband, Lucius, having failed at the Ministry. Snape admits that the Dark Lord is angry at Lucius. Finally, though, Snape agrees to swear an 'Unbreakable Vow' that he will protect Draco, and if Draco is unable to complete his assigned task, Snape will do it for him. Bellatrix is stunned by this, but agrees to act as their Bonder, though apparently half-expecting that Snape will invalidate the Vow somehow. Harry is spotted by Draco Malfoy on the Hogwarts Express, as Harry tries to eavesdrop on Draco to see if he has become a Death Eater. Rescued from petrification by Tonks, Harry arrives at the school late. Tonks sends a message to have a teacher come and unlock the gates, and Harry is appalled to find that the teacher who arrives is Snape. Snape insults Tonks' Patronus, saying that he thought the old one was stronger; then, refusing to allow Harry to change or clean himself up, takes him directly into the Great Hall, where the Entrance Feast is just ending. Harry is shocked again when, at the announcement of the teachers for the new term, it is revealed that Snape is the new Defence Against the Dark Arts teacher; he had thought that the teacher he had helped Dumbledore recruit, Horace Slughorn, had been intended for that position.

Harry finds Snape's class on the Dark Arts is both illuminating, and alarming, as Snape is seemingly entranced by the Dark Arts. The relish with which he shows the spells and enemies which the Dark Lord has on his side seems almost unhealthy. After giving them a quick overview of what they will be fighting now that Voldemort has returned to power, Snape sets the students to learn the ability to cast wordless spells. Seeing that they are having difficulty with this, Snape squares off against Harry as a demonstration; Harry, fearing the effects of any spell Snape would cast against him, uses a verbal shield spell, earning himself a detention. The detention is postponed by one of Harry's private lessons with Dumbledore. The new detention date conflicts with one of Slughorn's "little soirées," and while Slughorn does try to prevail upon Snape to change the detention date again, Snape refuses. Harry is uncertain which would be worse, Slughorn's party or Snape's detention.

Harry finds a non-verbal spell, Levicorpus, in the Half-Blood Prince's Potions book, which he is using. Accidentally hitting Ron with it, Harry notices it seems to be the same spell that his father had used on Snape many years before.

When Katie Bell is jinxed by touching a necklace, Harry brings the necklace back to the school, where Professor McGonagall passes it to Filch to be taken to Professor Snape. Later, Professor Dumbledore tells Harry that Professor Snape had done all he could to help Katie. Harry asks why Snape and not Madam Pomfrey; Dumbledore responds that Snape has much more experience with Dark magic.

In part because of prompting from Hermione, and in part because he can't see any way out of it, Harry finally attends one of Slughorn's parties. This one, a Christmas party, has a number of famous people attending. Snape is there, and Slughorn mentions to him that Harry seems to be a natural at Potions, like his mother had been. Snape comments that he had not seen that when Harry was his student. Argus Filch appears, dragging Draco Malfoy, who had been "skulking" in the halls. Slughorn immediately assumes, as Filch had, that he had been trying to gatecrash the party. Draco does not seem to be cheered by Slughorn's decision to invite him in. Shortly, Harry sees Draco and Snape leaving together; following under his Invisibility Cloak, he overhears their discussion in a classroom. Snape, apparently using Legilimency, probes Draco for details about what happened to Katie Bell, but Draco blocks him; apparently, he has been learning Occlumency from Bellatrix Lestrange. Snape says that he is aware of Draco's mission and has taken an Unbreakable Vow to help him. Draco is angered at the thought that he could need help, and storms out.

In discussions later with Ron, Ron's father, Remus Lupin, and Hermione, Harry finds that his belief that Snape and Draco are working together for Voldemort is discounted; with absolute faith in Dumbledore and his trust for Snape, everyone he talks to believes that Snape is trying to determine Draco's mission so that he can report on it to Dumbledore. Lupin also says that he doesn't particularly dislike Snape. Yes, Snape had revealed that he was a werewolf, costing him his job at Hogwarts, but he had always done a perfect job with the potion, and he could have done far more damage by simply making a small error in its preparation. Harry also reports this conversation to Dumbledore in their next lesson. Dumbledore thanks him for bringing this to his attention, but says that it does not concern Harry. Pressed, he somewhat testily responds that he trusts Snape absolutely for reasons he will not divulge. Snape is mentioned in passing in Harry's Potions class. Given the job of creating an antidote for a mixture of several different poisons, Harry finds that there is nothing in the Half-Blood Prince's textbook about them, except the note "Just shove a Bezoar down their throat." Remembering Snape's comment in his first-ever Potions class, Harry grabs a bezoar out of the supply closet, and shows that as his finished potion.

As Harry, Hermione, and Hagrid leave Ron's bedside after his near-poisoning, Hagrid happens to mention that he had heard angry-sounding words being exchanged between Snape and Professor Dumbledore near the Forbidden Forest. Hagrid says that Snape seemed to be having second thoughts about something he had promised Dumbledore he would do. Hagrid also mentions that there was something about Snape's investigations in Slytherin house, which Hagrid had assumed was to do with the necklace that had Cursed Katie Bell. Their conversation is cut short by the arrival of Filch, who is angry that Harry and Hermione are out of bed and out Gryffindor Tower at midnight. Harry determines that whatever Draco is doing, it is happening in the Room of Requirement. During a free period the next day, Harry again attempts to enter the Room of Requirement, but he is unable to make the door appear. His efforts make him late for Defence Against the Dark Arts class, causing Snape to penalize Gryffindor ten points. Seamus Finnigan asks about the difference between ghosts and Inferi, as a story in the *Daily Prophet* mentioned Inferi; Professor Snape says the story actually was about one Mundungus Fletcher, who was arrested for impersonating an Inferius. Ron also gets taunted and given detention by Snape. When Lavender, with whom Ron is involved, starts abusing Snape after class, Ron is irritated rather than amused, and he and Harry duck into a bathroom so Ron can avoid her.

When Harry retrieves Slughorn's memory of Tom Riddle, and Harry and Dumbledore have viewed it, Dumbledore reveals that his hand had been injured while he was destroying one of Voldemort's Horcruxes. He says that only his own reflexes, and Snape's timely intervention, had prevented the damage from being much worse. Harry, making his now-usual pass by the Room of Requirement, sees on the Marauder's Map that Draco is in a bathroom one floor below with Moaning Myrtle, and goes to investigate. Malfoy sees him and attempts to cast a Cruciatus curse; Harry, defending himself, uses the *Sectumsempra* spell from the Half-Blood Prince's book, not knowing its effects. The spell slashes Draco, spilling his blood everywhere. Moaning Myrtle flies off, screaming; Professor Snape responds swiftly and saves Draco's life, rushing him to the Hospital Wing. Returning, Snape demands to know whence Harry learned the spell, and despite Harry's attempts at occlumency, Snape apparently gleans some information that Harry's potions book is the source. Snape demands to see his textbooks. Harry runs to the Common room and borrows Ron's books including the Potions textbook, and asks the Room of Requirement for a place to hide something. Leaving the half-Blood Prince's book there, Harry returns to where Snape awaits. Snape seems unconvinced that these textbooks, especially the Potions book, are actually Harry's, particularly since the Potions book is signed "Roonil Wazlib." Having used Dark Magic to cause serious harm (albeit unknowingly), Snape gives Harry detention (with Professor McGonagall's concurrence) every Saturday for the rest of the year. That Saturday, as ordered, Harry reports to Snape's office for detention and is assigned copying over old detention files for Filch. Snape suggests Harry start with the boxes detailing his father's misbehaviour.

It is mentioned that Harry does not recover his Potions textbook from the Room of Requirement because he fears that Snape would find out that he had it, and would confiscate it. His Potions work suffers, but Slughorn attributes that to his new romantic interest in Ginny.

Harry finds Professor Trelawney sprawled on the floor, where someone in the Room of Requirement had ejected her. As she and Harry head for Dumbledore's office to report this, Trelawney mentions that it was Snape who had overheard the first prophecy, the one foretelling Voldemort's nemesis, and so had been the one who had carried it to Voldemort. Leaving Trelawney in the hall, Harry angrily confronts Dumbledore with this information. Dumbledore says that despite Snape's skills at Occlumency, he still trusts Snape completely. He seems briefly to be on the verge of explaining why he trusts Snape, but then distracts Harry by saying he believes he has located one of the remaining Horcruxes.

On his return from recovering the Horcrux, Dumbledore is greatly weakened, and asks Harry's help in getting to the school. Overriding Harry's suggestion that Madam Pomfrey will help him, Dumbledore says he must see Severus. Returning to the school, Harry and Dumbledore land on the Astronomy tower. There, Dumbledore is disarmed by Draco Malfoy. Dumbledore has nearly convinced Draco to switch sides, but is interrupted by the arrival of four Death Eaters. Snape bursts onto the scene, and Dumbledore almost seems to plead with him: "Severus." Snape kills Dumbledore, and with the Death Eaters following, departs. Harry, petrified by Dumbledore under his Invisibility Cloak, witnesses the scene in horror. Freed by Dumbledore's death, Harry Stuns one of the Death Eaters and gives chase. He finds himself within range as Snape nears the front gate, but every spell he casts is blocked with ease by Snape, who tells him that his skills at Occlumency are sadly lacking. Snape also reveals that he is the Half-Blood Prince who had owned Harry's Potions book. When the other Death Eaters, coming up behind Harry, attack him, Snape stops them, saying that the Dark Lord wants Harry for himself. Leaving Harry wandless on the ground, Snape and the other Death Eaters depart the school.

When Harry is talking with the other teachers in the Hospital Wing later, we learn that Professor McGonagall had sent Professor Flitwick to fetch Snape when the attack had started. Hermione and Luna had been watching Snape's office. When Flitwick had gone in, they had heard confused noises, then Snape, as he left, had told them that Flitwick had fallen and that they should help him. At the battle, the members of the Order did not hinder Snape as he passed through and up into the tower. When he came back down, with Draco following, again they did not stop him, as they did not know that Snape had killed Dumbledore, and had thought that he was simply leading Draco to safety. Harry reveals that he knew why Dumbledore had trusted Snape. Snape, he said, had carried word of the prophecy to Voldemort, but then had returned to Dumbledore and claimed remorse for having done so.

Hermione later discovers that Snape's mother, a witch, had been Eileen Prince; his father, Tobias Snape, was a Muggle, hence Snape's nickname for himself, the Half-Blood Prince. Harry is upset that he had been getting Snape's unwitting help, through his old Potions book, all year. He wonders also at the similarity between Snape's half-blood ancestry and Voldemort's, and wonders how Dumbledore could have missed it.

Deathly Hallows We first see Snape as he enters Malfoy Manor, along with another man later identified as the Death Eater Yaxley. We find that the Manor has become Voldemort's headquarters. Voldemort places Snape at his right hand and leaves Yaxley a place halfway down the council table. Yaxley reports that his contacts in the Ministry of Magic say that Harry Potter will be moved to a safe house of the Order on Harry's birthday, 31 July, as his current protection ends. Snape says that his information, "from the same place as before," indicates that the move will actually happen some days earlier, and will be handled by members of the Order, as it seems that the Order does not entirely trust the Ministry any more. Voldemort looks deeply into Snape's eyes; Snape does not flinch, though many of the Death Eaters gathered around the table do. Voldemort decides that the attack on Harry will take place according to Snape's understanding.

In the escape from Privet Drive, George Weasley, disguised as Harry, loses his ear. Remus Lupin, who had been traveling as his protector, reports that it was Snape who had done it, using the Sectumsempra spell. Looking over a copy of the *Daily Prophet* that had been brought to Grimmauld Place by Lupin, Harry, Ron, and Hermione read that Snape had been appointed Headmaster of Hogwarts. It occurs to Hermione that the portrait of Phineas Nigellus Black hanging in an upstairs room is now a conduit to Snape, as another portrait is hanging in the Headmaster's office, so to prevent Phineas from spying on them, she takes his portrait and stuffs it into the small beaded bag in which she keeps all their traveling gear.

As they travel about the countryside, Harry, Ron, and Hermione at one point overhear another group's conversation. There, they hear that three students, including Ginny Weasley, had broken into the Headmaster's office and attempted to steal the Sword of Gryffindor. Shortly afterward, the Sword had been transferred to Gringotts Bank for safekeeping, but that one had been a fake. The three students involved had evidently been "cruelly punished." Harry and Hermione consult the portrait of Phineas Nigellus as to what happened and what punishment the students had received. Phineas reports that they had been sent to "that big half-breed oaf, Hagrid," who set them to work in the Forbidden Forest.

Harry, re-entering the school, makes his way to the Ravenclaw common room to see a sculpture of the lost Diadem. While there, he is spotted by Alecto Carrow, who touches her Dark Mark, informing Voldemort that Harry has been found. Professor McGonagall, who has assisted his escape, meets Snape in the hall. Snape asks if she has seen Harry, as evidently he has been found in the school. It seems that Snape is trying to use Legilimency to locate Harry. McGonagall and Snape duel. As the other Heads of House arrive, Snape runs into a disused classroom and leaps out the window. Harry believes that he will have fallen to his death, but McGonagall says he seems to have been taking lessons from his master. Harry sees a large, bat-like shape flying over the wall of the school—Snape has escaped. Learning that Voldemort is using the Shrieking Shack as a command post, Harry, Hermione, and Ron travel through the tunnel under the Whomping Willow to the Shack. There, they witness a confrontation between Snape and Voldemort. Snape asks to be allowed to go into Hogwarts and bring Harry out. Voldemort overrides him, saying that he is disappointed in the performance of the Elder Wand. He says that he believes the Wand has not yet accepted him as owner, because it was Snape who killed Dumbledore, the Wand's previous owner. Ignoring Snape's repeated request to allow him to fetch Harry out of Hogwarts, Voldemort says he regrets the necessity, and has Nagini kill Snape, then leaves.

Harry, watching, goes to Snape's side as soon as Voldemort has left. Snape offers Harry his memories, which Harry collects in a crystal vial provided by Hermione, and looking into Harry's eyes, so much like his mother's, dies. Returning to the school, Harry enters the headmaster's office and finds the Pensieve. Putting Snape's memories in the Pensieve, Harry enters and relives parts of Snape's life.

In Snape's memories, we watch as Snape sees Lily Evans, at about ten years old, experimenting with magic, and as he tells her that she is a witch, and that he is a wizard. Lily's sister, Petunia, is clearly scared by the magic her sister is doing, and Lily seems affronted that Snape has called her a witch. We watch again as Snape tells Lily things about the Wizarding world, about the Wizard prison, Azkaban, and about the Dementors that guard it. Later still, we see Snape watching Lily and her family as they put Lily on board the Hogwarts Express for her first term at Hogwarts. Petunia is telling Lily that she's a freak, that Lily and that Snape boy are being sent to a school for freaks. Lily says that she had seen Dumbledore's reply to Lily's letter, and that he had been very kind. When Petunia demands to know how she had seen that letter, it was private, Lily indicates that Snape had helped. Petunia flounces off to join her parents. We then see Severus on board the train, looking for Lily. He finds her in a compartment with James Potter and some other first-year students, including Sirius Black. Snape says he hopes Lily will be placed in Slytherin; James is adamant that he wants to go to Gryffindor. When James insults Snape, Lily leaves to find a different compartment, and Snape follows; James tries to trip Severus as he passes.

At the Sorting, we see Lily Sorted into Gryffindor, along with Sirius, James, Peter Pettigrew, and Remus Lupin. Snape is sorted into Slytherin, where he is greeted by Lucius Malfoy.

We see Snape and Lily walking across a courtyard, quarreling. Snape wonders what has happened to their friendship, and Lily says that they are still friends, but that she detests the people Snape hangs out with, most notably Avery and Mulciber. Snape reminds Lily of the trouble that James and his friends get into, and is heartened when Lily dismisses James as an "arrogant toerag."

Harry now again witnesses the scene that he had seen some years earlier, when James, along with Sirius, had tormented Snape. Not wishing to revisit this scene, Harry keeps his distance. The memory ends with Snape calling Lily a Mudblood, and reforms in front of the Fat Lady. Lily says that she had heard that Snape would stay outside the entrance to the Gryffindor Common Room all night, unless she came out to speak with him. Despite his obvious remorse, and his heartfelt apologies, Lily will not forgive Snape the insult, and tells him that he should go to his Death Eater friends.

We now see Snape meeting in secret with Dumbledore. Snape says he does not carry a message from Voldemort, but is there to plead on his own behalf. He had carried Trelawney's prediction to Voldemort, and Voldemort, having decided that the prophecy referred to Harry Potter, was now planning to kill not only Harry, but also Lily and James. Snape pleads with Dumbledore to save Lily from Voldemort. Dumbledore is disgusted that Snape only wants Lily saved, not caring about her husband or child. Taken aback, Snape pleads for them as well, saying that in return for their safety he would do anything.

We next see Snape in Dumbledore's office, plainly grief-stricken. Snape demands of Dumbledore why he had not kept Lily and her family safe. Dumbledore tells him that they had put their trust in the wrong man, just as Snape had in trusting Voldemort to spare Lily's life. Dumbledore reveals that Harry had survived, and that if Snape had truly loved Lily, he would help Dumbledore protect her son when Voldemort returns. Snape reluctantly agrees, but says that Dumbledore must never tell anyone that he is protecting James Potter's son.

We see Snape, apparently in Harry's first year at Hogwarts, complaining fircely to Dumbledore about Harry, and how he is a troublemaker ilke his father. Dumbledore says mildly that no other teacher is complaining, and asks Snape to keep an eye on Quirrell.

As the students leave the Yule Ball, we see Snape telling Dumbledore that the Dark Mark on his arm is growing darker, as is Karkaroff's, and that Karkaroff plans on fleeing if the Mark burns. Dumbledore asks if Snape has similar plans, and Snape angrily replies that he is no coward. Dumbledore remarks, almost offhandedly, that perhaps the students are Sorted into their Houses too early; Snape seems quite taken aback by this.

We now see Snape in Dumbledore's office again. Dumbledore is semiconscious, his blackened right hand dangling over the edge of his desk. Snape, pointing his wand at Dumbledore's wrist, is muttering incantations while pouring a golden liquid down Dumbledore's throat. When Dumbledore returns to himself, Snape asks why Dumbledore had even tried on the ring, and Dumbledore says he was a fool. We see Marvolo Gaunt's ring on the table, broken, beside the Sword of Gryffindor. Snape tells Dumbledore that the curse was extraordinarily powerful, and that while he has contained it for the moment, it will eventually kill Dumbledore; he says that Dumbledore has, at most, another year of life. Dumbledore says that this makes things much easier to decide, and starts discussing Voldemort's apparent plan to have the Malfoy boy kill him, Dumbledore. Snape says that the attempt is not expected to succeed, but instead to further punish and disgrace the Malfoy family. Dumbledore correctly guesses that Snape has been given the job of killing Dumbledore should Draco fail, as Voldemort expects that Hogwarts will be fully under his control and he will no longer need a spy there. Dumbledore asks that Snape agree to waitch over his school, and be the one to kill him, both to spare Draco's soul and to grant Dumbledore some dignity in death, sparing him from the malicious pleasures of Fenrir Greyback and Belatrix Lestrange. Snape reluctantly agrees. In the scene that Hagrid had partially overheard the year before, we now see Snape and Dumbledore walking in the castle grounds. Challenged as to what he is doing with Harry, Dumbledore says he is giving Harry information he will need, while he sill can. Snape asks why he is not privy to that information as well, to which Dumbledore says he does not like to keep all his secrets in one basket. Snape appears to be angered by this, saying that his job as double agent is extremely dangerous, and he is at least as trustworthy as Harry. When Dumbledore tries to explain the next steps of his plan, Snape threatens a change of heart about killing Dumbledore when the time comes. Dumbledore reminds him of his word, and suggests that he keep an eye on Draco. When Snape still seems rebellious, Dumbledore wearily makes an appointment for later that night in his office.

Dumbledore, later, explains that Harry must not know what he has to do until the final moment. That moment will be the time when Voldemort, instead of letting his snake, Nagini, run free, he keeps her confined within a protective spell. At that time, Snape must tell Harry that Harry is an accidental seventh Horcrux, inadvertently created at his mother's death, and that he must die in order that Voldemort would be vulnerable to death. Snape feels tricked, as he had worked so har to protect Lily's son, only to have him destined to die at Voldemort's hand. Asked if Snape has grown to care for Harry after all, Snape casts his Patronus. It is in the shape of a silver-white doe, indicating to Dumbledore that Snape is still in love with Lily, fifteen years after her death.

We now learn that it is at the orders of Dumbledore's portrait that Snape had given Voldemort the correct time for Harry's departure from Privet Drive. Dumbledore suggests the ruse of having seven Harry Potters headed for seven safe houses, and gives Snape instructions to plant that idea in Mundungus Fletcher's mind to pass to the Order of the Phoenix. During the actual departure from Privet Drive, we see that Snape had been attempting to jinx the Death Eater drawing a bead on Remus Lupin, and air currents had caused them both to miss, resulting in Snape's spell severing George's ear.

We now see Snape in Sirius' old room at Grimmauld Place. He takes the first page of a letter of Lily's, and the portion of a picture that contains the image of Lily, and leaves with them.

Finally we see Snape speaking with the portrait of Phineas Nigellus Black. Phineas reports that Harry is in the Forest of Dean, and Snape retrieves the Sword of Gryffindor from behind Dumbledore's portrait, and departs with it. We do not see any more of Snape, but in the epilogue, we learn that Harry has named his second son Albus Severus, after two Headmasters, and one of them was not only a Slytherin but possibly the bravest man Harry had ever known. In post-publication interviews, the author has revealed that Snape's portrait did not appear in the Headmaster's office at his death, as he had abandoned his post; but that Harry had successfully campaigned to have it placed there.

Strengths One of Snape's great strengths is his ability as an Occlumens, which would make him a valuable ally and a worse enemy. His expertise in Occlumency makes him the ideal wizard to work as a Dumbledore's spy in the group of Death Eaters, as Voldemort cannot read Snape's mind; however, it also ideally suits him as a double agent in the other direction, as likely Dumbledore could not read his mind either. Snape's persuasive ability, including Occlumency and Legilimency, have allowed him to play both sides up to end of Book 6. Snape is a powerful and intelligent wizard. As a student, he excelled in potions, revising standard formulas that made brewing them easier and faster. He also invented many spells and jinxes. His robes always seem to be billowing behind him dramatically.

Weaknesses He has a dark, moody personality, and rarely takes the initiative to create friendships or establish personal alliances. Snape is described by others as unattractive, mainly with regard to his hair, which is described as very oily. As an instructor, he favors Slytherin students, while punishing others, particularly Harry, for minor infractions. Snape cannot forget or let go of past wounds or grudges. Mistreated by James Potter (and Sirius Black) during their Hogwarts years, Snape has transferred his resentment and hatred onto James' son, Harry. Snape becomes particularly incensed when Harry calls him a coward as he is taking flight from Hogwarts.

Relationships with Other Characters Snape apparently is a complete loner. He seems to keep to himself, he has no close friends. Throughout the first six books of the series, and up to nearly the end of the seventh, he seems uniformly bitter; while he has allies, and can work together, as we see, both with those who serve Voldemort and those who oppose him, Snape seems incapable of caring about anyone. Every interaction Snape has with Harry, other students, and other Hogwarts staff members seems to be infused with venom, with the exceptions of Argus Filch, who he trusts to help him bind up the wound that he received from Fluffy in *Harry Potter and the Philosopher's Stone*, Draco Malfoy, who he treats with marked leniency in class, and Albus Dumbledore. Most of his dealings with Voldemort's supporters, with the possible exceptions of Narcissa Malfoy and Voldemort himself, seem similarly poisonous. While we could speculate that Snape's consideration for Narcissa springs from a hidden liking for her son Draco, that must remain uncertain. The tone of Snape's interactions with Dumbledore and Voldemort, however, seems to come from recognition of the power each of them has over him.

Our understanding of Snape's relationships with other characters is greatly expanded by events late in *Harry Potter and the Deathly Hallows*, but as that understanding would constitute a spoiler, discussion of that expansion is in the Greater Picture section of this article.

ANALYSIS

Snape's actions throughout the series have shown service to both sides. Throughout the entire series, both Dumbledore and Voldemort believe that he is on their side. This allows him continue his work as a double agent. For most of the series, not only is it unknown which side he is really on, but there is no concrete evidence that he has chosen one. He has made strong claims, which Dumbledore trusts, to oppose the cruelty of Lord Voldemort (Tom Marvolo Riddle), but there is also hatred between himself and many Order members. Though seemingly fearful of a world in which Voldemort is victorious, he would appear to have little place in one where the Order is victorious. There is little reason to believe he has an interest in either side winning, and he may even prefer being able to exert influence on, and gain favors from, both.

Snape exhibits both good and evil qualities, thus being the series' only anti-hero. Snape has a nasty demeanor, especially to those who have hurt him (James, Sirius, Snape Sr.) However, Snape's seeming cruelty may be the result of a terrible life. When Harry delved into Snape's memories, there was nothing good to be seen, only an abusive father, mocking classmates, and a cruel James Potter. While the series does not emphasize Snape's good qualities, it is implied that he would protect the members of the Order (at least until the end of *Harry Potter and the Half-Blood Prince*) with his life. He has saved Harry's life on more than one occasion.

Throughout the series, we see these contradictions in Snape's actions. Throughout the series, he seems to be acting out of hatred of Harry and, to some extent, of Dumbledore. We find it very easy to believe, like Harry, that Snape is attempting to eliminate Harry in *Harry Potter and the Philosophers' Stone*. We see a consistent pattern of Snape sabotaging Harry's Potions coursework throughout the year. Yet we find out at the end of that book that Snape had, in fact, acted to save Harry's life in his first Quidditch match. In *Harry Potter and the Prisoner of Azkaban*, we are as aware as Harry that Snape had wanted the post that Remus Lupin had been given, and we know that Snape distrusts Lupin; yet, we also will find out that Snape had repeatedly brewed a very tricky potion, flawlessly, fully aware that a single slip of a single ingredient would have eliminated Lupin from the school forever, without provable intent on Snape's part—"Anyone can make a mistake, Headmaster, surely you don't think I would have deliberately done anything to cause that student's death from werewolf bite?" And as late as the middle of the final book, when we hear that Ginny Weasley, Luna Lovegood, and Neville Longbottom had been "punished cruelly" by being sent to help Hagrid, when Snape knows as well as we do exactly where Hagrid's sympathies lie, we are left wondering whether Snape was deliberately minimizing the punishment he was meting out.

As mentioned in the information box, Snape's related family is a possible spoiler. The fact that his mother was surnamed Prince, and that he is a half-blood himself, between them hint very broadly at the identity of the title character in the sixth book, *Harry Potter and the Half-Blood Prince*. As Harry spends much of the book trying to determine who this character is, premature revelation of his identity is something of a plot spoiler.

Harry Potter and the Deathly Hallows (The Prince's Tale)
The memories that Snape reveals to Harry seem to serve two purposes. The first set of memories, up to Harry's parents' deaths, seem to be there to explain Snape's feelings, and give a basis for his later actions. We learn that Snape had first met Lily Evans at the age of 9 or 10, had revealed to her that she was a witch and he was a wizard, and had introduced her to the Wizarding world. He had also defended her against her Muggle sister, Petunia, as Lily prepared for her first year at Hogwarts. They had become close friends, a friendship that had been strained to destruction by Snape's choice of associates within Slytherin house. Despite the end of the friendship, Snape had loved Lily, and had promised to do anything in return for Dumbledore's promise to save Lily in particular, and her family as well. It is because of this promise, which Snape had kept for eleven years when the story opens, and continued to keep throughout the story, even past the death of the one he had made the promise to, that Snape had first turned informant against Voldemort, and later had protected Harry against Voldemort and his allies. After the death of James and Lily, Snape's memories, while still reinforcing our understanding of Snape's unrequited love for Lily, also show us Dumbledore and Snape working together to protect Harry and shape him into the weapon that would eventually destroy Voldemort. We learn that Dumbledore had planned his own death at Snape's hands, telling Snape that this was to prevent Draco's soul from being damaged, and to allow Dumbledore to retain some dignity in death. We also learn that Harry has become an unexpected seventh Horcrux, and that Snape must manage to have Voldemort kill Harry in order to destroy it. We learn, in particular, that Dumbledore has set large plans in motion, and that Snape, much to his own dismay, was merely a cog in Dumbledore's machinations. Snape in particular is dismayed that, having worked so long and so diligently to protect Harry, they must now arrange for him to be killed in order to manage the final defeat of Voldemort.

Later in the book, we will find that, despite the large role that Dumbledore had planned for Snape, and the large amount of trust he placed in Snape, he did not tell Snape the whole story. Some pieces of the story, notably the role of the Elder Wand, he reserved, perhaps feeling them to be too dangerous, or perhaps worrying that too complete knowledge of the plan would cause Snape to become over-zealous and unwittingly allow Voldemort to escape.

QUESTIONS

1. What are we to think of Snape now? Was Harry right, and Dumbledore wrong?
2. Why did Snape counter Quirrell's curse to keep Harry on his broomstick? Could he have left it to Flitwick, or would Dumbledore have known that only Severus knew enough about the Dark Arts to protect him?
3. Was Snape trying to get Harry expelled because he felt Harry would be safer with the Dursleys?
4. Why did he hesitate before making an Unbreakable Vow to kill Dumbledore if Draco failed? Was he merely goading Bella, to make her think he couldn't promise this, or was he steeling himself to obey Dumbledore's orders to do whatever the Death Eaters asked him, in order to be able to continue his work among them?
5. When they were discussing the horcruxes, Dumbledore told Harry that after destroying the Gaunt ring Horcrux, "had it not been . . . for my own prodigious skill, and for Professor Snape's timely action when I returned to Hogwarts, desperately injured, I might not have lived to tell the tale." What did Snape do, and why?
6. What were Dumbledore and Snape arguing about? Had Dumbledore at last become suspicious, although nothing later would confirm this; or was Dumbledore forbidding him to break the Vow and die, in order to save him?
7. Why was Dumbledore so anxious to get to Snape when he saw the Dark Mark? Did he want Snape, rather than Draco, to kill him? What difference would it make?
8. Dumbledore told Harry, "I am a sufficiently accomplished Legilimens myself to know when I am being lied to . . . ." If Snape had voluntarily opened his mind to Dumbledore, this could have provided sufficient proof that he was truly opposed to Voldemort. Before presenting himself to Voldemort for similar testing, he could have left all thoughts of a change of heart in Dumbledore's Pensieve. Of course he might have left something in Voldemort's Pensieve before applying to Dumbledore, instead. We just don't know yet, do we?
9. Did Snape lie to Bellatrix and Narcissa?
10. Given that pureblood family names are known among wizards, surely other Slytherins would have noticed that Snape's blood status is not pure, including those who became Death Eaters in later life. Why is this never brought up? Did Snape denounce his Muggle father (presumably with ease, given the memory he has of him)?
11. Did Snape's seemingly abusive Muggle father contribute to his joining the Death Eaters in a similar way to how Voldemort became anti-Muggle?
12. Was Snape's love for Lily romantic in nature, or was it of a friendly nature, perhaps strengthened by guilt after her death?
13. Why didn't Snape wash or otherwise tend to his greasy hair? Was it an outward manifestation of the fact that he didn't attempt to please people, that he sought out no personal connection to others?

GREATER PICTURE

First Five Books While we don't yet understand completely, it becomes apparent that Snape absolutely hates Harry in particular, and Gryffindor in general. The realization of the depth of this hatred is a gradual thing; initially, Snape's malice seems rather impersonal, although it is certain that it is directed at Harry more than at anyone else in Gryffindor. Neville and Hermione also receive insults and slights from Snape, though not to the same degree as Harry. Neville perhaps deserves some of this maltreatment as he does not seem to be particularly able at Potions, but it is equally true that, as we find out in *Harry Potter and the Prisoner of Azkaban*, Neville's worst fear is Professor Snape. Because of that fear, and with his already notoriously poor memory, Neville is utterly incompetent in Potions, making horrible messes and melting cauldrons. It is possible that with a more forgiving teacher, Neville might have excelled in Potions, as Harry appears to do later under Slughorn.

It is also in *Harry Potter and the Prisoner of Azkaban* that we discover the core, apparently, of Snape's dislike of Harry. We already know that Harry looks "most extraordinarily like" James Potter, and we learn also that James had been involved in a prank that would have left Snape facing a werewolf. While James had saved Snape's life, Snape for some reason never forgave him. In *Harry Potter and the Goblet of Fire*, we also learn that the Marauders, James, Remus Lupin, Sirius Black, and Peter Pettigrew, apparently made a hobby of tormenting Snape, a practice they continued at least until their fifth year at Hogwarts. Harry's appearance would remind Snape repeatedly of this dark and painful time in his life, and this would quite possibly explain some of his maltreatment of Harry. We can, however, already see some ambivalence on Snape's part concerning Harry. As early as the first book, we see that Snape has been protecting Harry, notably in the first Quidditch match Harry plays. When Harry's broom is Jinxed by Professor Quirrell, Snape is found to be countering that jinx. In *Harry Potter and the Order of the Phoenix*, we also find that Snape is willing to try to teach Occlumency to Harry, to attempt to shield him from Voldemort's sendings. When Dolores Umbridge requests Veritaserum from Snape, in order to interrogate Harry, from its lack of effect (she apparently had used the entire phial, such that even the slightest sip on Harry's part would have probably constituted the necessary three drops), one must wonder if Snape had provided a false potion. Snape's refusal to provide additional Veritaserum on demand, when Umbridge had trapped Harry in her fireplace, could also be seen as a way of defending Harry. And again, at the end of that book it appears that Snape had been willing to accept Harry's word as to Sirius' status, at least enough to investigate and to keep an eye on Harry's whereabouts, and to notify the Order when Harry did not reappear after leading Umbridge into the Forbidden Forest.

Harry Potter and the Half-Blood Prince Snape plays little direct part in *Harry Potter and the Half-Blood Prince* despite lending his nickname to the title. Equally, the book is to a large extent all about him. Throughout the book, he is seen in flash-backs and stories about other characters which illuminate his character, as Harry and company try to discover who the Half Blood Prince really is. He is constantly distrusted by Harry, yet Dumbledore expresses absolute faith in him. Towards the start of the book, as mentioned above, Snape finally gets the appointment as Defence Against the Dark Arts teacher which he has sought for many years. As a result, a new Potions teacher is needed and Professor Slughorn, a former head of Slytherin house, is brought out of retirement. Slughorn allows Harry to take Potions despite his less than excellent grades, which Snape would not have done. Harry is lent an old textbook as he has none (since he did not expect to be taking the class), and discovers it has many useful tips written into the margins. As the year progresses, we discover that the textbook is old enough to have belonged to one Eileen Prince, finally identified as Snape's mother. She married a Muggle. We already know (from the Pensieve episode in *Harry Potter and the Order of the Phoenix*) that Snape was most probably in the same class as Lily Evans (who married James Potter, Harry's father), and from Slughorn's recollections we find that Lily, rather than Snape, was the outstanding natural potions student. The textbook notes are all in the same handwriting and the book is inscribed 'property of the Half Blood Prince.' It also includes descriptions of some spells which Snape admits he created. The implication here is that he recorded all of this information in the book; yet if he had been as skilled at Potions as Harry became thanks to the book, it would have been Snape who was remembered as the natural, rather than Lily. All this suggests that in some way the book was a collaboration between Snape and Lily.

The new information adds understanding to the Pensieve scene. In that scene, James was seen bullying Snape, using a curse on him which we now believe Snape invented. The scene took place during or immediately after Severus Snape's and James Potter's O.W.L.s, which would be their year 5, before the year in which this textbook would have been used in class. Lily is seen reacting to the injustice, and Snape abusing her out of proportion to what has occurred, as she seems only to have wanted to help him. Together these scenes add credence to the existence of a longstanding relationship between Snape and Lily. She is described as always seeing the good in people others would shun. He is friendless and from a doubtful Muggle background, more similar to hers than most of their classmates. Additionally, there is the fact that Snape has not once mentioned Harry's mother, though they apparently were in the same Potions class, almost as if he cannot bear to have her name mentioned. Ordinarily, it would have been so easy to compare Harry against Lily: "Your mother could have whipped that potion up with her eyes closed . . ." And it is certainly true that he has similarly mentioned Harry's father in that sort of context. All together this has given rise to speculation that Snape was in love with her, even if this was not reciprocated. Snape is also, in *Harry Potter and the Half-Blood Prince*, identified as the person who informed Lord Voldemort about the prophecy foretelling his nemesis. This inevitably led to Voldemort seeking out Harry to eliminate him, and in the process killing James and Lily. It makes Snape unwittingly but directly responsible for the deaths of two people who were certainly his classmates, one of whom may have been his rival but the other of whom may have been (secretly) the great love of his life. It may be this which explains

Dumbledore's unshakable belief that Snape has irrevocably turned away from Voldemort and the Death Eaters.

Harry Potter and the Deathly Hallows Snape's loyalty is not made clear to us until very late in the final book. It is here that we learn that Snape had in fact been secretly in love with Lily Evans, and had chosen to side with Dumbledore in order to attempt to protect Lily from Voldemort.

With this one revelation, much of what had been confusing about Snape is laid clear. Snape had hated James Potter for many reasons, including James' ongoing tormenting of Snape, his rescuing Snape from death at the jaws of the werewolf Lupin (resulting in a debt that Snape not only could never repay, but that he would never want to repay), and finally Potter's spiriting away the one love of his life, Lily Evans, and daring to have a child with her. In order to protect Lily, Snape had agreed to an open-ended promise with Dumbledore ("Anything!"). Dumbledore, knowing Snape's skill in Occlumency, had Snape become a spy against Voldemort, and after Lily's death, had required him to agree to protect Lily's son, Harry.

This, of course, sets up a major conflict in Snape's life. Every interaction with Harry carries emotional baggage, the more so as Harry, except for his eyes, is the image of his father. Snape cannot help but be reminded of the hated James every time he sees Harry. In Snape's memories, we see him railing about Harry to Dumbledore; interestingly, every trait he attributes to Harry is one that we have seen, to some extent, in James, rather than Harry. Yet, he is sworn to protect Harry, who is the only child of his lost love. In such an untenable situation, is it any surprise that he is bitter? Desperately unhappy himself, he gets what relief he can by making others unhappy also. About the only person Snape does not savage is Dumbledore, who initially exacted the promise from him, and who did do everything he was allowed to do to prevent Lily's death. It is perhaps because of this that Dumbledore dismisses Harry's belief that Snape had been prepared to duel with Sirius; Dumbledore has not experienced directly the depth of Snape's bitterness, and so discounts it. In discussing his reasons for assigning the task of teaching Harry Occlumency to Snape, Dumbledore does admit to having believed that Snape's dislike of Harry could be dealt with. It is because of this internal conflict, and its final resolution, that the much-despised Snape is one of the most moving, and best-rendered, characters in the entire series. Several readers have been moved to tears by the revelations in chapter 33 of *Harry Potter and the Deathly Hallows*.

One thing that is not, however, made certain is exactly why Dumbledore kept his belief in Snape's loyalty. At first reading, it seems that he expected Snape to remain loyal because he saw Snape's regret after Lily Evans' death. But strictly speaking, it could have been that Snape's love for Lily had faded over the years, and so he could have turned to Voldemort again. Until the scene with the doe Patronus in Dumbledore's office, which took place in the sixth year, we have no information that Dumbledore could have gotten which unarguably would have proven that Snape was still loyal after fifteen years. What we do know is that once Dumbledore grants someone his trust, he doesn't revoke it lightly. We see evidence that Snape is quite frequently in Dumbledore's company, both in the memories of the Prince and in Harry's direct experience. And while it is never said outright, we believe that Dumbledore has some ability at Legilimency. Dumbledore clearly expected Snape's love for Lily to fade, as shown by his reaction to Snape's Patronus; however, he would not expect Snape's loyalty to fall away, and back towards Voldemort, until Voldemort returned. It is quite possible that Dumbledore had inspected Snape quite thoroughly after the end of *Harry Potter and the Goblet of Fire*, but we would not see that in the Prince's memories, because that would have been one of the more humiliating experiences in Snape's recent life, and would not have been germane to Harry in any event.

Sibyll Trelawney

Gender: Female
Hair color: Unknown (hidden by shawls)
Eye color: Unknown (magnified by glasses)
Related Family: ancestor: famous Seer Cassandra Trelawney
Loyalty: Albus Dumbledore

Overview

Sibyll (or Sybill) Patricia Trelawney is the Divination teacher at Hogwarts. She was the great-great-granddaughter of the famous Seer, Cassandra Trelawney. She wears very large glasses that makes her eyes appear several times larger than they actually are, has a soft and misty voice. She is very thin and is always draped in a finely-woven, shiny shawl.

Role in the Books

Prisoner of Azkaban Harry, Ron, and Hermione choose to take Divination starting in their third year. Professor Trelawney opens with normal fortuneteller practices, vague predictions, including that Neville will break at least one teacup, that something Lavender Brown is dreading will happen on the 16th of October, and that around Easter, "one of their number will leave them . . . forever." Neville does in fact break two teacups while attempting to read tea leaves. Professor Trelawney also sees the Grim, an omen of impending death, in Harry's tea leaves. The class is so upset by the revelations, that they are still visibly shaken the next period. Professor McGonagall mentions that Professor Trelawney has predicted the a student's death every year since she had been employed, and no students had yet died. As far as the predictions go: Lavender receives news on 16 October that her pet bunny has died, and Hermione, fed up with Trelawney's babble, quits Divination just before Easter (leaving . . . forever). These events, tenuous as their connection may be, are linked back to Trelawney's earlier predictions by at least two students, Lavender and Parvati Patil, and greatly enhance Sibyll's reputation in their minds, at least.

Ron and Harry, though they stay with the course, are unimpressed by the prediction side of it. Unable to read the future, they start fabricating predictions from tea leaves and, later, crystal balls.

As Harry completes his Divination exam, Professor Trelawney suddenly seems to fall into a trance, talking strangely, and utters a prediction that the Dark Lord's servant will be freed, returning to him that night. When she returns to normal seconds later, she seems unaware that anything untoward occurred.

This prediction does come true; that night, following events in the Shrieking Shack, Peter Pettigrew escapes and returns to Lord Voldemort's service. Harry later comments to Dumbledore that Trelawney seemed to have predicted that night's events, and Dumbledore remarks that he should consider giving her a raise, as that increases her number of actual prophecies to two.

Goblet of Fire While Professor Trelawney is still teaching Divination to Harry's class, this year primarily astrology, her interaction with Harry seems to be involved primarily with setting him and Ron homework. Harry and Ron, after laboring over their star charts, fall back on the usual technique: make stuff up. Their predictions of disasters for themselves are quite successful, with Professor Trelawney even reading them out in class, but backfire when Trelawney requires them to continue for a further month of predictions. Ron bemoans the fact that they have run out of disasters.

Order of the Phoenix Professor Trelawney again is teaching Divination to Harry's class, this year concentrating on dream interpretation. Early in the year, Dolores Umbridge is created Hogwarts High Inquisitor by Ministry edict, and appears in her classroom with a clipboard, making notes. Trelawney, rightly, sees this as an intrusion, and is most upset by it. Umbridge asks Trelawney to justify her teaching techniques and requires a prediction from her; then is apparently unimpressed with the results.

Over the course of the year, we see Trelawney becoming more and more harassed and bedraggled in appearance, because Umbridge has placed her on probation. Harry also notes that she seems to leave a certain scent of cooking sherry behind her. When Harry stands up to Umbridge by giving an interview to the *Quibbler*, Trelawney breaks her usual pattern of predicting horrible death for Harry, instead predicting long life, many children, and election as Minister of Magic.

Finally, Umbridge fires Trelawney, and has put her and her trunks in the Entrance Hall, when Professor Dumbledore overrides her decision to eject Trelawney from the school grounds. Dumbledore says that while, as High Inquisitor, Umbridge has the authority to dismiss his teachers, she lacks the power to force them to leave the school, and it is his wish that Trelawney remain at Hogwarts. He also has to override Trelawney in this; her wounded pride compels her to leave and seek employment elsewhere, but Dumbledore refuses to allow that. During the Battle at the Ministry, we learn that the thing Voldemort has been seeking, and the reason he lured Harry to the Ministry, is a prophecy concerning himself and Harry. Voldemort had earlier heard the first half of the prophecy, and as a result had attempted to kill Harry as an infant, unsuccessfully. Afterwards, Dumbledore tells Harry that the prophecy had been made to him by Trelawney. The prophecy, made eleven years before, had been what persuaded Dumbledore to hire Trelawney as the Divination teacher; had it not happened, Dumbledore likely would not have allowed the course to be offered at Hogwarts. Events to date had made parts of the prophecy become true, and Dumbledore allows Harry to hear the entire prophecy. Harry is greatly disturbed, as it appears that the prophecy is saying that he must either kill Voldemort or be killed by him.

Half-Blood Prince Dumbledore apparently realizes that Harry is reluctant to discuss Trelawney's prophecy with anyone, as it seems to be impelling him to become a murderer, so he recommends that Harry tell Ron and Hermione about it. He does so, and is relieved to discover that they don't think less of him for the revelation.

Harry's interaction with Trelawney is very limited this year, as he had failed his Divination O.W.L. so dramatically. We learn that both Trelawney and Firenze, who was hired to replace her, are now teaching Divination. Parvati Patil seems somewhat disappointed that Trelawney is teaching sixth year. Trelawney still feels affronted, and seems to feel that Firenze is stepping on her turf, because we see her walking through the halls, smelling of sherry, and trying unsuccessfully to tell her own fortune. At Horace Slughorn's Christmas party, she is morosely drunk, and in mid-March we see her demanding, unsuccessfully, that Dumbledore fire Firenze.

Summoned to Dumbledore's office, Harry finds Trelawney sprawled on the floor outside the Room of Requirement. Helping her up, he discovers that she had been using the Room of Requirement as a place to hide her sherry; this time, though, she had heard someone inside "whooping." When she had demanded to know who was there, everything had gone dark, and she had been rudely thrust back out into the corridor. Harry believes that the evident joy in the unknown person's voice indicated that Draco Malfoy had completed whatever it was that he was doing in the Room of Requirement, and he asks Trelawney to accompany him to Dumbledore's office, to tell Dumbledore what she had heard. On the way, she starts talking about the day she was hired. Harry has already heard the story from Dumbledore, and is somewhat interested to hear Trelawney's version, but when Trelawney mentions that the eavesdropper had been Severus Snape, Harry leaves her standing in the corridor and runs off to confront Dumbledore with this information.

Deathly Hallows With Harry not attending Hogwarts, we see very little of Trelawney until the final battle. Trelawney helps her fellow professors and students during the battle that ensues at Hogwarts when Lord Voldemort and other Death Eaters attack it by throwing crystal balls down from upper landings of the staircase. A thrown crystal ball knocks out Fenrir Greyback before he can resume an attack on Lavender Brown.

Strengths Trelawney actually does have the gift of Sight to a limited extent. Twice she has made prophecies: one has come true, and the other had partially become true at the start of the series, and is completed by the end. She does have some ability to mislead and misdirect; Parvati Patil and Lavender Brown hang on her every word.

Weaknesses She pretends to be a better seer than she is; knowing that she is supposed to have the Sight, because of her ancestor, she plays that up for all she is worth, using the same tricks Muggle fortune-tellers use. She annoys some people but she cannot be relieved of her residence at the castle because of her real prophecies. She is very insecure, trying to preserve her position as superior to Firenze after his hiring by bad-mouthing him and his techniques. When she is threatened with dismissal, and when Firenze is taking half the Divination classes, she also tends to retreat into alcohol; in the latter half of *Harry Potter and the Order of the Phoenix*, and throughout *Harry Potter and the Half-Blood Prince*, we never meet Sibyll without smelling sherry.

Relationships with Other Characters Sybill Trelawney spends most of her time in the Divination tower/classroom and she is thus alienated from the rest of the staff, though the impreciseness of her subject, knack of overexaggerating, and questionable teaching methods often draw the ire of Professor McGonagall. Her relationships with students aren't much better: she irritates Harry, Hermione, and Ron, but manages to gather a smattering of followers including Parvati Patil and Lavender Brown. She also holds resentment towards Firenze when he is appointed as a second Divination teacher.

Analysis

Overall, Trelawney likes to make big impressions, most probably because of her insecure nature. She enjoys predicting the deaths of students, one in each year, though none have died yet. She constantly predicts a gruesome death for Harry, possibly wanting the grand effect of having such a famous person die and predict it correctly. Ironically, Trelawney's two wildest predictions turned out to be the only ones that were true. These two predictions were so wild that "even [Trelawney] wouldn't say something as far-fetched as *that*," according to Trelawney. These two predictions also happen to relate to Voldemort.

In *Harry Potter and the Order of the Phoenix*, as mentioned above, Dolores Umbridge sacks Sibyll and orders her out of the castle; Albus Dumbledore, while not disputing her authority to dismiss teachers, does dispute her authority to force people to leave the castle. He requests, quite forcefully, that Sibyll stay in the castle, and has Professor McGonagall and Professor Flitwick assist her in returning to her chambers. There is no reason for him to retain her in the school, except that she has twice now uttered prophecies about Harry and Voldemort, one of which has already come true, and one of which Voldemort is trying quite hard to retrieve.

Presumably, Dumbledore feels there is some danger, either to the Order or to Sibyll herself, if she is allowed to leave the protection of Hogwarts. Sibyll remains unaware of this possibility of danger, apparently; she does not seem to be aware of having made either prophecy. Of course, Voldemort may not know of her lack of awareness, and may mean to kidnap her to retrieve the prophecy direct from the source, as it were.

Questions

1. How would Professor Trelawney react if she knew she had made the prophecy about Harry?
2. What danger would she be in if others knew (i.e. Voldemort)?
3. What does the way Trelawney treats Firenze say about her character?

Sir Cadogan

Gender: Male
Hair color: Unknown
Eye color: Unknown
Related Family: Unknown
Loyalty:

Overview

Sir Cadogan is one of the portraits at Hogwarts. He is in a habit of taunting people as they pass.

Role in the Books

Prisoner of Azkaban Perhaps because of his habit of challenging all who pass, Sir Cadogan's portrait is hung in one of the upper and more remote corridors of the castle. Harry, Ron, and Hermione request his assistance in finding the Divination classroom on their first day of classes; he provides it by moving from picture to picture in the correct direction. When Sirius Black attempts to destroy the portrait of The Fat Lady, in retaliation for her not letting him into the Gryffindor Common Room, Sir Cadogan takes her place. He retains that position until he allows Sirius into the Gryffindor common room because he happened to have the password; he is then returned to the upper reaches of the castle.

Goblet of Fire Sir Cadogan is mentioned briefly by Bill Weasley when he and Mrs. Weasley meet Harry before watching him as he competes in the Third Task. Bill asks Harry if the painting containing Sir Cadogan still remains in Hogwarts, later saying how he hasn't been to the school in five years, most likely since he graduated. This indicates that Sir Cadogan has been in the castle for at least five years, but probably more.

Deathly Hallows Sir Cadogan is mentioned as one of the portraits who shout encouragement to the defenders of Hogwarts. As Harry is on his way to the Room of Requirement, where he now believes Rowena Ravenclaw's lost diadem is hidden, Sir Cadogan paces him for a while, shouting words of encouragement.

Strengths He knows his way round Hogwarts well, and shows Harry where to go for his first lesson of Divination. He is also very brave, always willing to accept a Quest or a Challenge. It seems that he generally considers any request for assistance to be a Quest.

Weaknesses Sir Cadogan isn't good at fighting at all. He is extremely clumsy, dropping his sword, or getting it stuck in the turf, and can never get onto his pony. Another weakness, of course, is that his horse is a pony, rather than a more typical charger. As mentioned in Strengths, above, he is very brave, but he actually seems brave to the point of foolhardiness; he will seemingly accept any challenge, even one that would result in the destruction of his painting.

Relationships with Other Characters Sir Cadogan can be quite tiresome, with his repeated demands that people "Stand and fight, ye scurvy cur!" Particularly as, being part of a painting, you cannot actually reach him to fight him, and he cannot reach you either. Additionally, due to his perpetual clumsiness, he is something of a figure of fun to the people who have to deal with him.

ANALYSIS

Sir Cadogan is a useful object, because he can help Harry and his friends around the castle. He doesn't complicate much when action is needed, unlike many other artistic objects around the castles—the gargoyles being good examples.

Sirius Black

Gender: Male
Hair color: black
Eye color: grey
Related Family:
Descendent of former Hogwarts Headmaster Phineas Nigellus Black. Mother Walburga Black, father Orion Black, brother Regulus Black
Loyalty: follows spoiler warning

OVERVIEW

Sirius Black was accused of betraying James and Lily Potter to Lord Voldemort, and murdering their friend, Peter Pettigrew and twelve Muggles. He was sentenced without a trial to life imprisonment in Azkaban. In the early stages of Book 3, he has escaped and is apparently trying to kill Harry Potter.

ROLE IN THE BOOKS

Philosopher's Stone Sirius is only briefly mentioned in the opening chapter—Rubeus Hagrid has borrowed his flying motorcycle to bring baby Harry Potter to his new home, Number 4, Privet Drive.

Prisoner of Azkaban While staying at the Dursleys, Harry hears on the Muggle news reports that convicted murderer Sirius Black has escaped, although he later reads in the *Daily Prophet* that Black is actually a wizard who escaped from Azkaban Prison. Black is apparently so dangerous that even Muggles are at risk. When Harry leaves the Dursley house following an argument, he notices an ominous-looking large black dog watching him in the street. In Diagon Alley, Harry overhears Arthur and Molly Weasley discussing Sirius Black, a suspected Voldemort supporter who escaped to find and murder Harry. Taking him aside on the Hogwarts Express platform Mr. Weasley asks a bemused Harry to promise not to look for Black, although Harry departs before promising. Black breaks into Hogwarts on Hallowe'en, but when the Fat Lady bars him from entering the Gryffindor common room (he does not know the password), he slashes her portrait and escapes. When the Fat Lady refuses to return to guard duty, Sir Cadogan replaces her. Shortly after, in Potions class, Draco Malfoy taunts Harry about never seeking revenge on Sirius Black, although Harry has no idea what he means.

Just before Christmas, Harry sneaks into Hogsmeade village where he overhears a conversation in Three Broomsticks between Minister for Magic Cornelius Fudge, Professor McGonagall, Professor Flitwick, Hagrid, and Madam Rosmerta. Fudge says Black betrayed James and Lily Potter to Voldemort, and afterward murdered their friend, Peter Pettigrew, along with twelve Muggles. Enraged, Harry vows to avenge his parents' deaths.

Black slips into Hogwarts again and enters the common room using Neville Longbottom's lost password list. Black shreds Ron's bed curtains with a knife, causing Ron to wake up screaming as Black flees. Sir Cadogan is sacked and the Fat Lady returns, guarded by security trolls. It is unclear why Black attempted to attack Ron rather than Harry.

During the climactic Shrieking Shack scene, Black's innocence is uncovered; it is the very alive Peter Pettigrew who committed the crimes. The relationship between Sirius Black, Professor Lupin, Peter Pettigrew, and Harry's father, James Potter, is explained: they are the four Marauders who created the "Marauder's Map." When Black is revealed as Harry's godfather and legal guardian, Harry realizes that the large black dog stalking him was actually Sirius Black in his Animagus form (the ability to transform into an animal at will); Black was watching over Harry. Pettigrew is also an Animagus, disguised for the past twelve years as Ron's pet rat, Scabbers. It was "Scabbers" who Black was attemtping to kill the night he broke into Harry's dorm. When Pettigrew escapes and Black is captured, Minister of Magic Cornelius Fudge insists Black is guilty and orders a Dementor, an Azkaban guard, to immediately suck out Black's soul. Using a Time Turner, Harry and Hermione retrace that night's events to free Black. Later, Black sends an owl letter letting Harry know he is safe—for now. Harry also learns it was Black who sent the Firebolt broomstick at Christmas. Black also gives written permission for Harry to visit Hogsmeade on school outings, and, as compensation for losing his "pet" rat, he donates the little messenger owl to Ron. Ginny Weasley names it Pigwidgeon.

Goblet of Fire Harry's troubling dream about Voldemort's encounter with Frank Bryce and his throbbing scar prompts him to send Hedwig with a message to Sirius Black. Sirius' reply is a long time in coming and disconcerting: Sirius believes there is enough justification to return to England to be near Harry. Worried he has unintentionally lured Sirius into a situation where he could be recaptured, Harry quickly sends another message dismissing his own earlier worries, but Sirius ignores it and writes that he is already in England.

When Harry is mysteriously selected as a Triwizard Tournament champion, Hermione urges him to write to his godfather. Sirius has more than can be said by Owl Post, and wants to meet Harry at the fireplace in the Gryffindor common room at 1:00 A.M. on 22 November. Meanwhile, Harry becomes terrified when he sees the dragons to be used in the Tournament's First Task. Using the Floo network, Sirius' floating head appears in the Gryffindor fireplace. He warns Harry that there are more pressing concerns than dragons. Karkaroff, Durmstrang school's headmaster, was a Death Eater. Sirius also believes that an earlier attack on Professor Moody may have been intended to prevent Moody from taking the Defense Against the Dark Arts position, as it was Moody who arrested Karkaroff. Sirius and Dumbledore believe this may herald Voldemort's return to power. Sirius also advises Harry about dragons, but before he can name a spell, Harry hears someone approaching and Sirius vanishes. Following the First Task, Sirius sends his congratulations by owl post, and writes that he would have suggested the Conjunctivitus curse, which was what Viktor Krum had used. He again warns Harry about Karkaroff. When Harry is nearly caught by Filch, Professor Moody, and Professor Snape after sneaking into the Prefect's bathroom to decode the Second Task riddle, Harry writes Sirius. His reply is dishearteningly brief, asking only when the next Hogsmeade weekend is.

Following the Second Task, Sirius sends another brief letter telling Harry to be at a particular stile outside Hogsmeade, and to bring food. Ron is surprised that Sirius dares to enter Hogsmeade, but Harry points out that it is no longer swarming with Dementors. Harry, Ron, and Hermione meet Sirius in his dog form at the stile. He leads them to a nearby cave where he and Buckbeak are hiding. Famished, Sirius, who has mostly been surviving on rats, tears into the food the Trio has brought. Harry's letters have made events sound increasingly suspicious, especially when combined with reports in occasionally scrounged copies of the *Daily Prophet*. Crouch being sick also seems unusual to Sirius, and Harry mentions how bad he looked when the Triwizard Champions were selected. When Hermione says he got his just desserts for firing his house-elf, Winky, Harry updates Sirius about the Quidditch World Cup, Winky's dismissal, and his wand being stolen. Sirius asks if Harry checked for his wand when leaving the top box, but Harry responds he checked only when he was in the woods. Sirius suggests that someone in the top box could have lifted it; Ron suspects Lucius Malfoy, although Hermione reminds them Ludo Bagman was also there. Sirius knows little about Bagman and wonders why he would offer to help Harry win the Tournament.

According to Sirius, Crouch taking days off is uncharacteristic. It was Crouch who sentenced him to Azkaban without a trial. Pressed for more information, Sirius explains how desperate times resulted in desperate measures, including using deadly force against suspected Death Eaters. Crouch, who headed the Aurors, championed these measures, achieving some results. He was tapped as the next Minister for Magic until his son, Barty Crouch, Jr., was found with the Death Eaters who tortured Frank Longbottom and his wife Alice to learn what the Aurors had done with Voldemort. Crouch presided over his own son's trial and convicted him. Mr. and Mrs. Crouch visited their dying son in Azkaban, and Sirius saw Dementors burying his body. Crouch lost his son, his wife (who died shortly after), and his shot at the Ministry, eventually getting shunted aside to the Department of International Magical Cooperation.

Sirius suspects Crouch wants to capture one last Dark Wizard to revive his career. Even so, it is unlikely Crouch would make a special trip to Hogwarts just to search Snape's office when he already had the opportunity to do that while judging the Triwizard Tournament. When Ron and Hermione start squabbling over whether or not Snape is a Dark Wizard, Sirius says Snape certainly associated with Slytherins who became Death Eaters: Rosier and Wilkes; Bellatrix Lestrange and her husband; Avery, but Snape was never accused. Harry mentions Snape and Karkaroff knowing each other and how Karkaroff showed Snape something on his arm. Sirius does not know what that could be.

When Ron mentions that his brother is Mr. Crouch's personal assistant, Sirius wants him to ask Percy about Mr. Crouch's illness and also about Bertha Jorkins' disappearance. Bagman was quoted in an article as saying that Bertha's memory is very bad, but the Bertha Jorkins Sirius knew at school had an excellent memory, at least for gossip, which often got her into trouble. At 3:30 P.M., Sirius sends the Trio on their way, telling them he wants to be kept updated on any new information; he reminds them to address letters to him as "Snuffles" before he heads to the village to scrounge another newspaper.

When Bartemius Crouch appears and then disappears at Hogwarts, Professor Dumbledore orders Harry not to communicate with anyone until the next morning. Harry then writes Sirius, but Sirius' response, rather than clarifying matters, scolds Harry for straying out of bounds with another Triwizard Champion. Sirius suspects the other Champions might do anything to win, including attacking Harry. Hermione agrees that someone wants to attack Harry and that he is safe inside the school, although Harry is irritated by his godfather's strict orders to stay put.

Harry falls asleep in Divination class and dreams that the Dark Lord is punishing Peter Pettigrew. After he reports this to Professor Dumbledore, Dumbledore asks Harry if there was any other time, apart from early summer, when his scar hurt. Harry is taken aback, he has not mentioned that episode to Dumbledore, but Dumbledore says that Harry is not Sirius' only correspondent.

Harry begins practicing earnestly for the Third Task. Somewhat annoyingly, Sirius' messages are filled with adjurations to ignore events outside Hogwarts; Harry's only priority should only be safely navigating the Third Task maze, other matters can be addressed afterwards. Sirius continues sending messages almost entirely filled with tips and tricks for casting jinxes.

Just after Dumbledore stuns the fake Moody following the third task, he sends Professor McGonagall to fetch the "large black dog" in Hagrid's pumpkin patch. After Barty Crouch Jr.'s confession, Dumbledore takes Harry to his office where a haggard-looking Sirius awaits. Dumbledore wants Harry to recount what happened, but Sirius feels Harry should rest; Dumbledore, however, insists Harry immediately face what has happened. With Sirius and Fawkes comforting him, Harry relates what occurred in the graveyard. Dumbledore then takes him to the Hospital Wing, telling Sirius, back in his dog form, that he can stay with Harry. He reassures Madam Pomfrey that the dog is well trained.

After Cornelius Fudge dismisses Dumbledore's and Harry's claims about Voldemort and leaves, Dumbledore orders Sirius to reveal himself to Professor Snape. Dumbledore requests they maintain a truce and cooperate, to which they unwillingly shake hands. He assigns both missions; Snape's is unknown, but Sirius is to alert "the old crew," and then hide out at Remus Lupin's place.

Order of the Phoenix As Harry arrives at Number 12, Grimmauld Place in London, a minor upset in the entry hall causes a portrait to start screaming. Sirius appears, slamming the portrait curtains shut to silence it. The portrait is Sirius' mother, and the Order of the Phoenix is now headquartered in the Blacks' ancient family home. Harry is happy to see Sirius but thinks he looks haggard. The Ministry of Magic refuting Sirius' innocence, as revealed in *Harry Potter and the Prisoner of Azkaban*, forces him to remain a fugitive. Presumably, Peter Pettigrew has informed Voldemort about Sirius' Animagus dog shape. Thus, Sirius is effectively confined to his hated home. Donating it to the Order is about all he can do to help.

Sirius is glad Harry and the Weasleys will be spending time with him before school starts. After dinner, Sirius suggests that Harry ask questions about Voldemort, but Mrs. Weasley objects, feeling Harry is still too young to be involved, and, despite their similarity, Harry is not James. She is overridden, however, and Harry is permitted to ask his questions, and perforce allowing Ron, Hermione, and the Twins to listen in, although a protesting Ginny is sent to bed. Sirius explains that Voldemort is now undercover while secretly rebuilding his organization. Harry performed a great service by announcing Voldemort's return to Dumbledore, that being the last person Voldemort would want to know, and the Order was recalled within hours. The Order also must remain undercover, as it is considered as opposing the Ministry. Dumbledore has been removed from many important Wizarding posts after reporting Voldemort's return amid the Ministry's fervent denials. The Order is actively recruiting, especially in the Aurors division of the Ministry; but Order members must be circumspect, because the Ministry distrusts the Order. Sirius also lets slip that the Order is guarding a weapon that Voldemort wants, but Mrs. Weasley interrupts, saying that is quite enough.

Sirius assists Mrs. Weasley and the younger crew in making the house habitable again. While there is a House elf, Kreacher, in residence, he is old, apparently senile, and only took orders from Mrs. Black's mad, shrieking portrait until Sirius returned. Sirius and Kreacher mutually dislike one another, and Kreacher only grudgingly obeys Sirius' commands. Sirius shows Harry a tapestry embroidered with the Ancient and Honorable House of Black. A scorch mark shows where his name was blasted off when he rejected the family's pure-blood ethos. Sirius points out other relatives: his cousins Bellatrix, Narcissa, and Andromeda, and Andromeda's daughter Tonks; and also his brother Regulus, who apparently joined the Death Eaters, tried to leave and had been, it is rumoured, killed personally by Voldemort.

As time nears for Harry, Ron, Hermione, Ginny, and the Twins to leave for school, Sirius grows more depressed, fretting at his enforced inactivity. Harry suspects Sirius' increased depression dates from Harry's Ministry hearing; exonerated, Harry could return to Hogwarts, leaving Sirius alone with Kreacher, but if convicted, he would probably have had to stay with Sirius.

Over Molly Weasley's protests, Sirius, in dog form, accompanies the party to King's Street Station. While bidding Harry farewell, Sirius is evidently recognized by Lucius Malfoy. Draco alludes to this on the train. Shortly after, the *Daily Prophet* reports Sirius was spotted in London. A story also appears in the *Quibbler* suggesting that Sirius is innocent, claiming that he and Stubby Boardman, a popular singer, are the same person. Sirisu could not have committed the crime for which he went to Azkaban because he was with a witness, a housewife, at the time. This, with the evidence of other stories in the same issue, leads us to believe that the *Quibbler's* journalistic standards are not particularly rigorous.

After his experience with Professor Umbridge, and the resulting detention, Harry updates Sirius by owl letter. Sirius' head shortly appears in the Gryffindor fireplace. According to Sirius, Harry's scar hurting when Umbridge touched his hand was almost certainly coincidence; bad as she is, the Order does not believe she is a Death Eater. To Harry's complaints that Umbridge prohibits using magic in Defence Against the Dark Arts class, Sirius replies that Cornelius Fudge is paranoid that Dumbledore is building a secret wizard army to take over the Ministry. Sirius also warns Harry against drawing attention to Hagrid's continued absence. When he suggests meeting the Trio at the next Hogsmeade weekend, both Harry and Hermione veto it, saying it is too dangerous. Apparently dismayed at Harry's caution, Sirius laments that James would have enjoyed the risk, then departs.

Harry and Hermione, fed up with Professor Umbridge's nonsense teaching, start their own Defence Against the Dark Arts study group. During Harry's History of Magic class, an injured Hedwig appears at the window, carrying a message signed with a paw print that says only, "Same place, same time." That night, Sirius' head appears in the Gryffindor fireplace to deliver a message from Mrs. Weasley, forbidding Ron to join the group and pleading with Harry and Hermione to also avoid it. The the Hog's Head was not very secure; Mundungus Fletcher was there, disguised as a witch to guard Harry, overhead their first meeting. Although Mrs. Weasley objects, Sirius thinks the group is a great idea. While discussing meeting locations, Sirius glances to his side and vanishes. Umbridge's hand appears in the fireplace, grabbing at where Sirius' head just was.

When Harry reports a dream that Mr. Weasley was attacked at the Ministry of Magic, Professor Dumbledore sends Phineas Nigellus' portrait to inform Sirius to receive guests. Apparently to prevent any interference by Professor Umbridge, Dumbledore sends Harry, Ron, Ginny, and the Twins to Grimmauld Place to await news. On arrival, Harry notices that Sirius smells of cooking sherry. Kreacher insults the arriving students, and Sirius orders him out. Ron was present when Harry initially told Dumbledore about the attack, but the Twins and Ginny were not, so Harry, explaining what has happened, omits the fact that he actually was the snake who was attacking Mr. Weasley. Fred and George demand to go to the hospital, but Sirius vetoes it, saying the Order wants it kept secret that Harry can "see" things from hundreds of miles away.

Mrs. Weasley sends a Phoenix feather message saying that Mr. Weasley is still alive, although those present in the Grimmauld Place kitchen feel that makes it sound as if he was perilously close to death. At 5 AM, Mrs. Weasley arrives and reports Mr. Weasley is sleeping; Bill is with him. Harry privately tells Sirius that he observed the attack from the snake's point-of-view, as if it had been him attacking Mr. Weasley. Harry also reports feeling intense hatred toward Dumbledore, when Dumbledore actually looked at him directly for the first time since June, and had an urge to sink fangs into Dumbledore. Sirius says he will tells Dumbledore, but Harry should not dwell on it. Sirius, pleased at having a full house for the holidays, is singing Christmas carols. His infectious joy causes everyone to pitch in to make it a good holiday. For Christmas, Sirius and Lupin give Harry a book on jinxes and counter-jinxes, useful for Harry's defensive arts classes. Hermione has made a comforter for Kreacher, but is unable to find him. Sirius seems unconcerned, saying a House-elf is prohibited from leaving his master's home without permission, dismissing Harry's comment that Dobby once visited him without permission. When Kreacher reappears shortly, he seems to be watching Harry speculatively, something that concerns Harry. Sirius becomes depressed that everyone is leaving soon. When Snape arrives to tell Harry that Dumbledore wants Snape to teach Harry Occlumency, Snape and Sirius exchange insults, leaving them at wands drawn and Harry in-between trying to prevent a duel as the Weasleys enter the kitchen.

Sirius becomes more withdrawn and despondent as time draws near for the students' return to Hogwarts. As the students prepare to leave for Hogwarts, Sirius gives Harry a package, saying he can contact him with it. Harry privately resolves never to use it, fearing it will risk Sirius being captured.

Back at Hogwarts, a surprisingly friendly Professor Umbridge summons Harry to her office and offers him a drink. Harry, suspecting Veritaserum, quietly discards it. Umbridge asks where Dumbledore is; when Harry responds he does not know, she then asks where Sirius is. When Harry says he does not know that either, she says that she knows Harry has been talking to Sirius, and if she had proof, Harry would have been arrested. She also mentions that all the fireplaces in Hogwarts are now being monitored except hers.

Momentarily left alone in Snape's office, Harry is tempted by the Pensieve on Snape's desk. Snape extracted and stored memories in it just before their Occlumency lessons; is there something he was afraid Harry would see? Entering Snape's memories, Harry observes his father, Sirius, Remus Lupin, and Peter Pettigrew taking their Defence Against the Dark Arts O.W.L. exam. Following them and a younger Snape outside afterwards, Harry is dismayed when Sirius and James mercilessly bully Snape, suspending him upside down in mid-air, and filling his mouth with soap. Remus, then a prefect, does nothing to stop them, and Pettigrew eggs them on. They relent momentarily when Lily Evans intervenes, but Snape calls her a Mudblood, and Lily abandons him to his fate. Presented with this new and unflattering portrait of his father, Harry urgently wants to discuss it with Sirius, but the fireplaces are being monitored. Ginny suggests that Fred and George can help, and they create a diversion while Harry breaks into Umbridge's office to contact Sirius via the Floo network. Harry tells Sirius and Lupin what he saw. Sirius admits that he and James were uncaring, foolish, and reckless youths, but claims Snape was far from innocent. Sirius saying James matured into a kind and compassionate man does little to appease Harry, who realizes that he could never behave as his father had at that age. Sirius and Lupin are alarmed that Harry has stopped Occlumency classes, and urge him to restart them. Harry, hearing someone approach, breaks the connection. During his History of Magic O.W.L. exam, Harry falls asleep and dreams that Voldemort is inside the Ministry torturing Sirius. Convinced it is really happening, Harry sneaks into Umbridge's office and uses the fireplace to contact Grimmauld Place. Kreacher says his master will never return from the Department of Mysteries. Harry, along with several other students, is caught by Umbridge. Hermione engineers her and Harry's escape, and, under Harry's urging, he, Hermione, Ron, Ginny, Neville, and Luna Lovegood, ride thestrals to the Ministry to rescue Sirius.

Once there, they realize Harry was tricked when they are trapped by a dozen Death Eaters, led by Lucius Malfoy, who seeks a Prophecy concerning Harry and Voldemort. The students, save Harry, are disabled in an escape attempt, with Harry being cornered. As Bellatrix Lestrange tortures Neville to force Harry to hand over the prophecy, Sirius, Tonks, Shacklebolt, Lupin, and Moody arrive. Harry Stuns Macnair, but Neville is jinxed by Dolohov, who then makes two attempts at Harry before Sirius distracts him. Harry Petrifies him and attempts to flee with Neville. Dumbledore enters from the Brain Room, and quickly apprehends all the combatants except two: Sirius is dueling Bellatrix. As Sirius taunts her, Bellatrix blasts a stunning spell squarely at his chest. His rigid body floats through a veiled stone archway. Harry rushes after him, but Lupin restrains him before he reaches the portal, telling him it is too late. Sirius is gone.

Dumbledore later explains that Kreacher lied about Sirius' whereabouts. Sirius was actually tending to Buckbeak, who Kreacher injured. Dumbledore suggests that Sirius' harsh treatment towards Kreacher stemmed from the House Elf being a living symbol of everything Sirius had hated about his family. Harry angrily accuses Dumbledore of implying that Sirius deserved what he got for treating Kreacher badly, which Dumbledore denies. Dumbledore also says that when Sirius had dismissed Kreacher at Christmas, Kreacher manipulated that into being permission to leave the house, and he went to the only Black relative he felt still upheld the family's values: Narcissa Malfoy. Barred from revealing any Order of the Phoenix secrets, he could tell the Malfoys about Harry and Sirius' relationship, and that Harry would do almost anything for Sirius. This allowed Voldemort to fabricate the false dream that lured Harry to the Ministry.

Harry corners Nearly Headless Nick for information about ghosts, hoping Sirius has become one. Nick says that Sirius did not fear death; therefore he would have gone on. Harry later encounters Luna Lovegood, and they talk about Sirius. Luna says the dead are not really gone, just waiting, and asks if Harry heard them whispering on the other side of the veiled archway. Harry surprisingly feels better after this conversation.

Half-Blood Prince In the opening chapters, Former Ministry of Magic minister Fudge tells the Muggle prime minister that an investigation into what happened in the Department of Mysteries is underway. Fudge seems to now agree that Sirius was probably innocent.

Harry comes to terms with Sirius' death.

Deathly Hallows Sirius' flying motorcycle makes a reappearance in the Escape from Privet Drive. Arthur Weasley has attached a side-car, in which Harry is to ride to safety; however, a weapon added to the motorcycle, a dragon-fire thrower that seems to act like a rocket booster, weakens the link and the sidecar breaks off. Harry rejoins Hagrid on the motorcycle, and they use the dragon-fire to hasten their voyage to the safe house. In their final descent, Hagrid leaps out of the seat to attack a Death Eater, and despite Harry's best efforts, the motorcycle crashes into the ground and is largely destroyed.

Arthur Weasley tells Harry later that he had collected the pieces and hidden them in the chicken coop at The Burrow, in the hopes of reassembling them and, if possible, learning how brakes worked. In an after-publication interview, the author says that Mr. Weasley has reassembled the motorcycle.

Harry explores Sirius' bedroom at Number 12, Grimmauld Place after the Trio take refuge there following their flight from Death Eaters. Apparently rebelling against his parents, Sirius had fixed many large Gryffindor House posters and students' photos on the wall with Permanent Sticking Charms. Harry finds the room ransacked, but searches the wreckage for information about his godfather. He finds a letter written by his mother and a torn-off photo of himself at about one-year-of-age riding a toy broom. He is unable to find either the letter's second page or the missing picture portion, which seems to have contained one of his parent's image.

In Severus Snape's memories, Harry relives bits of Snape's school career. Snape is bullied by James Potter and Sirius Black on the Hogwarts Express as they head to the school for their first year. Snape also sees Sirius being Sorted into Gryffindor, as he had wanted to be. Harry witnesses Lily trying to rescue Snape from being tormented by James and Sirius, and much later, Snape in Sirius' bedroom taking the letter's second page, and tearing Lily's image from the picture to take with him as well.

Harry, needing moral support as he goes to face Voldemort, uses the Resurrection Stone that is hidden inside the Golden Snitch. Sirius' spirit appears, along with James, Lily, and Lupin, who keep the Dementors at bay, and encourage Harry to be brave in facing his death. When Harry reaches the clearing where Voldemort is and releases the Stone, the spirits vanish.

Strengths A loyal, close friend to James Potter and Remus Lupin. Sirius was intelligent, handsome, and witty. He was also a powerful and talented wizard who rejected his family's pure-blood supremacy beliefs, and for which he was stricken from the Black family tree. He showed great affection for Harry and took his role as godfather seriously, becoming a strong father figure to Harry. Although Sirius was occasionally lax where discipline was concerned, when he suspected Harry was in danger during the Triwizard Tournament, he strictly ordered him to remain safely inside Hogwarts, much to Harry's displeasure.

Weaknesses At Hogwarts, Sirius was popular, but he, along with James Potter, was rather arrogant and sometimes bullied weaker students—Severus Snape in particular. As a fugitive, the innocent Sirius had difficulty coping with being confined to his own house while hiding from the authorities. He was also frustrated at being unable to actively help the *Order of the Phoenix* fight Voldemort. His years in Azkaban Prison stunted his emotional development, resulting in him sometimes acting more like Harry's peer rather than his mentor. Throughout *Order of the Phoenix*, Sirius increasingly became mentally unstable, causing him to make careless decisions and engage in rash behavior. His condition, that probably partially resulted from his years in Azkaban, was further exacerbated by his later in-house confinement. However, insanity and mental instability also ran in the Black family; Sirius was exhibiting symptoms somewhat similar to those seen in other family members, such as his cousin, Bellatrix Lestrange. By the book's conclusion, he had psychologically deteriorated to a point that may have contributed to his death.

Relationships with Other Characters   Sirius was one of the Marauders, along with Lupin, Pettigrew and James Potter. His nickname (Padfoot) is derived from his animagus form of a large, black dog. Sirius is Harry's Godfather and legal guardian. Sirius and Severus Snape have always been at daggers points with each other; one time, Harry witnesses what seems to be the beginning of a wizarding duel between them, broken up only by the Weasley family's arrival.

Analysis

The first time the "young Sirius Black" is mentioned largely goes unnoticed, as we have no idea who he is. All we know is that he loaned his flying motorcycle to Hagrid. While Sirius himself changes little throughout the series, Harry's understanding about him, and thus ours, gradually changes as plot twists are revealed. In *Harry Potter and the Prisoner of Azkaban* it is learned that Sirius is an escaped murderer, then that he is a wizard. We discover that Sirius apparently intends to kill Harry. It is hinted that he has done something that would inspire Harry to seek revenge, but it is not until Christmas that Harry learns that it was Sirius who betrayed Harry's parents to Voldemort, then, when confronted by their friend Peter Pettigrew, killed Pettigrew and twelve incidental Muggles. Sirius is believed to be in Voldemort's inner circle, and even his second-in-command.

Once Sirius traps Harry in the Shrieking Shack, we learn that it is Peter Pettigrew who supported Voldemort; Pettigrew was made the Potters' Secret Keeper and then betrayed them to Voldemort. When Voldemort fell, Pettigrew engineered his own apparent death, framing Sirius, and went into hiding. When the truth is revealed, Sirius is seen as being all good, effectively becoming a replacement for Harry's dead father.

It is because of this revelation that we have chosen to not explicitly state Sirius' loyalty in the information box. In fact, Sirius is consistently loyal, first to his friends, James Potter, Remus Lupin, and Peter Pettigrew, and later to James' son Harry, and Albus Dumbledore. Despite our understanding throughout the early part of the third book, when Sirius is portrayed as Voldemort's man through and through, and despite his upbringing in what we later discover to be a hotbed of Pureblood wizards and anti-Muggle leanings, Sirius is always loyal to the cause espoused by Dumbledore. Yet, to have this revealed too early would ruin enjoyment of *Harry Potter and the Prisoner of Azkaban*.

In *Harry Potter and the Goblet of Fire* the first cracks in Sirius' mental stability begin to appear. While Sirius is still advising Harry in the Triwizard Tournament, that advice sometimes seems a bit odd. In particular, the reader may wonder why Sirius feels that Harry must compete in the Triwizard, as it seems that some malign influence forced his entry. Would it not be better to have him somehow left behind in the Tournament, keeping him safe from the worst risks? Sirius counsels about what may be the most dangerous course, blithely assuming that Dumbledore will catch Harry should he fall. In the episode in the cave, Sirius seems slightly less than sane, possibly caused by his subsistence on rats and hiding in such harsh conditions. However, when Viktor Krum is attacked, Sirius shows just what a responsible and protective guardian he can be when he scolds Harry for straying outside Hogwarts' grounds with an opponent. He sternly orders Harry to stay inside Hogwarts' safe boundaries, although Harry feels Sirius is employing a double standard, forcing him to stay put when Sirius likely would have ignored the rules if he had been in the same situaiton.

It is in *Harry Potter and the Order of the Phoenix* that Sirius' character truly begins unraveling. Being a fugitive kept him confined to 12 Grimmauld Place with only his mad mother's portrait and the apparently senile House-elf, Kreacher for company for long periods. When Harry arrives for Christmas, he can smell sherry around Sirius, so we can assume that Sirius uses alcohol for solace. Sirius' extreme pleasure at having company over the holidays is sad and also pathetic. Molly having to remind Sirius that Harry is not James returned, early in that book, is dismissed by Sirius, but seems all too valid; Sirius does appear to treat Harry as he would James, as a compatriot rather than as his ward. It is likely that Sirius' emotional development was stalled during the 12 years he was incarcerated in Azkaban, and it has possibly even regressed. Although Sirius remained tragically flawed by his delayed emotional development, he was still a good influence and acted as a protector and father figure for Harry. It is debatable whether or not more could have been done to help Sirius. Leaving him confined in his house for long periods, isolated, and with little interaction or purpose in life, clearly added to his decline. Perhaps finding him a more active and substantial role within the Order of the Phoenix could have helped stabilize his condition.

It should be noted that the House of Black provided Voldemort with many ardent supporters, both in his original ascent to power and during his return. The Black family's blood purity ethic would have made Voldemort's beliefs attractive to them. It was probably generally assumed that this belief exteneded to Sirius and that he was also a Voldemort supporter, though he (like his cousin, Andromeda Black Tonks) had rejected his family and was now loyal only to Dumbledore and the Order of the Phoenix.

Questions

1. The author has stated that the two-way mirror Harry received from Sirius will be useful in Book 7. What are some possible ways that it might be, even though it is broken?

2. Why did Sirius treat Kreacher the way he did? What it justified?

3. Why does Harry smell sherry on Sirius?

4. What could have been done to help Sirius' mental condition? Was he beyond help?

5. What does Luna Lovegood mean when she tells Harry that the dead are waiting?

Sorting Hat

Gender: None

Hair color: None
Eye color: None
Related Family: Originally belonged to Godric Gryffindor
Loyalty: Hogwarts School

Overview

The Sorting Hat is described as being very old and patched. When the hat is put on the head of a Hogwarts new arrival, a mouth forms at the brim, and the hat states, for all to hear, which of the four school Houses the child wearing it belongs in: Gryffindor, Hufflepuff, Ravenclaw, or Slytherin.

The Sorting Hat also sings a song for all of the Hogwarts students and staff before the beginning-of-the-year feast, describing its job and the four Hogwarts houses. However, when the wizarding world or the school is in any imminent danger, the hat will also sing about the importance of the four houses standing together as brothers and sisters in the fight against evil.

The Sorting Hat's unusual qualities are due to the fact that Godric Gryffindor, one of the four Hogwarts founders, owned the hat, and knowing that he would not be around to select houses for the incoming students forever, placed a charm on it to do its job.

Role in the Books

Philosopher's Stone In this book, the Sorting Hat was introduced as the means through which students are sorted into their respective houses.

Having sung its song, it was then placed on the head of each of the first-year students in turn. It then assigned each to a house. The Hat initially though that Harry would do well in Slytherin, but Harry told it that he didn't want to go to Slytherin. The hat then placed him in Gryffindor.

Chamber of Secrets Because they were unable to make it onto the Hogwarts Express, Harry and Ron are still outside the school when the Sorting commences. They see some of the Sorting proceeding through the window of the Great Hall, but are not present for the Sorting Hat's song.

Later in the book, where Harry is summoned to Professor Dumbledore's office, he finds himself alone in the office with the Sorting Hat and decides to see if the Hat had had second thoughts about his Sorting. The Sorting Hat told Harry again that he would be great in Slytherin; Harry disagrees rather forcefully.

In the climactic battle against the Monster in the chamber, Fawkes the phoenix drops the Sorting Hat at Harry's feet; Harry thinks this is useless, though he wears it in hopes that it might afford him some protection or at least counsel; and it shortly thereafter presents him with a sword. Harry uses the sword to kill the basilisk (the Monster).

Harry, having told all this to Professor Dumbledore, tells Dumbledore that the Sorting Hat had originally wanted to place Harry in Slytherin. Dumbledore asks Harry why it did not; Harry says that he had asked it not to. Dumbledore points out that "it is our choices, Harry, that show what we truly are, far more than our abilities." Dumbledore then tells Harry that if he still wonders, he should examine the sword. Harry finds that it is the sword of Godric Gryffindor. Dumbledore tells him that only a true Gryffindor could have pulled that sword out of the Hat.

Prisoner of Azkaban News that Harry had reacted strongly to the Dementor had been sent to the school by Owl ahead of time, so Harry is taken aside into Professor McGonagall's office so he can be checked over by Madam Pomfrey. Professor McGonagall also wants a word with Hermione Granger and so draws her aside as well. As a result, when Harry reaches the Great Hall, the Sorting is finished, and all we see of the Sorting Hat is Professor Flitwick removing it and its three-legged stool from the stage.

Goblet of Fire Before the Sorting, the Hat again sings a song about the history of Hogwarts. Harry notes that it is a different song than the one he had heard his first year there, and Ron says that it is a different song every year. Being a hat, it can't have much to do most of the time, and so Ron surmises that it has a lot of time to make up its song.

Order of the Phoenix Prior to the Sorting, the Hat sings a very much longer song than usual, specifically going into the history of Hogwarts and its founders, and the divisiveness that resulted. It ends with a plea for the four houses to work together in this time of trouble. Ron asks Nearly Headless Nick if the Hat has been known to sing in support of unity, and Nick replies that it has done so quite often, though he is interrupted by the Sorting. Once all the students have been Sorted, he continues that the Hat, being in the Headmaster's office almost all of the time, is aware of what is happening in the school and things that affect the school, and if it sees a problem will try, as best it can, to draw attention to it.

Half-Blood Prince Due to the argument with Draco Malfoy on the Hogwarts Express, Harry arrives at the feast not only after the Sorting, but largely after the Feast has finished. As a result, we do not see the Sorting Hat at all in this book, except in passing when Harry, visiting the Headmaster's office, notices it sitting quietly on the shelf.

Deathly Hallows In Severus Snape's memories, we see the Sorting Hat as it Sorts Lily Evans, Peter Pettigrew, and James Potter into Gryffindor, and Snape into Slytherin.

At the Battle of Hogwarts, Neville Longbottom is forced by Voldemort to wear the Sorting Hat. Voldemort then sets Neville on fire, but Neville is unhurt by Voldemort's curse, and pulls the Sword of Gryffindor from the Sorting Hat, just as Harry did in the Chamber of Secrets. Neville then kills Voldemort's snake Nagini, the last of Voldemort's Horcruxes, making it possible for Voldemort to later die from his own reflected killing curse. In the Epilogue the Sorting Hat is mentioned, still doing its job at Hogwarts 19 years later. Harry here tells his son that he had asked the Hat not to put him in Slytherin, and it had placed him in Gryffindor instead.

Strengths   The Sorting Hat's annual song reflects the issues and concerns of current events. This implies that the hat has some ability, possibly through listening to passing events in the Headmaster's office, to keep up with the changes and threats to Hogwarts, and sufficient consciousness to understand them.

Weaknesses   It is a hat, and has only a certain amount of "mind-reading" ability and the power of speech. It cannot move, it can influence events around it only by persuasion, and apparently spends most of its time on a shelf in the headmaster's office.

Analysis

It is clear that the Hat has some level of consciousness; we hear that its song is different every year, and that its song reflects the need to deal with threats against Hogwarts. It also engages in conversation with Harry on two occasions, first when Harry is initially Sorted in *Harry Potter and the Philosopher's Stone*, and later when Harry dons the Hat in the Headmaster's office in *Harry Potter and the Chamber of Secrets*. This is why the Hat is listed as a character, rather than as a magical artifact, in this guide. It is also, probably, why Professor Dumbledore says that the Sword of Gryffindor is the only known artifact of Godric Gryffindor; the Sorting Hat was clearly a possession of his, but its consciousness makes it not an artifact but a person.

The Sorting Hat has an affinity for the Sword of Gryffindor, as it has produced the sword twice now; possibly this affinity comes from the fact that both were the property of Godric Gryffindor, and he may have established that particular affinity himself. It also seems the Hat is capable of retrieving the Sword from anywhere, because Griphook the goblin was the last possessor of the Sword of Gryffindor—he had taken it when Harry, Ron, and Hermione raided Gringotts.

Stan Shunpike

Gender: Male
Hair color: Unknown
Eye color: Unknown
Related Family: Unknown
Loyalty: Knight bus(?)

Overview

Stan Shunpike is the conductor of the Knight Bus. He seems to be only a few years older than Harry, possibly 18 when Harry is 13. He is a tall, thin wizard with a regional accent of some sort. He is also talkative, and a bit of a braggart.

Role in the Books

Prisoner of Azkaban   When Harry Potter accidentally summons the Knight Bus, Stan Shunpike is the conductor. He brings Harry up to speed on events in the Wizarding world, particularly those having to do with Sirius Black.

Goblet of Fire   During the confusion caused by the rioting Death Eaters at the Quidditch World Cup, Harry Potter, Ron Weasley, and Hermione Granger run into a wooded area. In a clearing in the woods, they find a number of Veela, surrounded by young men who are apparently trying to attract their attention by making boastful claims of one sort or another. One of these young men is Stan Shunpike. Ron also becomes entranced by the Veela and starts making some boastful claims of his own, before Hermione restores him to his senses.

Order of the Phoenix   Nymphadora Tonks summons the Knight Bus to take Harry, Ron, Ginny, Hermione, and the twins back to Hogwarts at Christmas. Stan is the conductor; he seems rather put out at Tonks, who he describes as "that bossy woman."

Half-Blood Prince   Stan Shunpike is arrested by Aurors for making boastful claims about how close he is to the Dark Lord. He has not been freed by the time the book closes.

Deathly Hallows   Stan Shunpike evidently escaped from Azkaban, and was one of the Death Eaters who pursued Harry during his escape from Privet Drive. Harry, recognizing that he was under the Imperius curse, tried to disarm him, which led the other Death Eater still pursuing to recognize him as the real Harry Potter.

When Ron is first captured by Snatchers, after leaving Harry and Hermione, he claims to be Stan Shunpike. This results in confusion, with half of the Snatchers believing him, and half not believing him. With their attention centered on this dispute, Ron is able to break away, stealing a wand in the process.

Ron claims again to be Stan Shunpike when Snatchers catch the group a while later, but this time his ruse is exposed immediately as the head of the group, Fenrir Geyback, has had dealings with the real Stan Shunpike.

Weaknesses   Stan likes to boast and exaggerate his importance to impress others. This leads to his being mistaken for a supporter of Voldemort and arrested.

Stewart Ackerley

Gender: Male
Hair color: Unknown
Eye color: Unknown
Related Family: Unknown
Loyalty:

Overview

Stewart Ackerley is a Ravenclaw who arrived at Hogwarts in Harry's fourth year.

ROLE IN THE BOOKS

Goblet of Fire Stewart Ackerly was Sorted into Ravenclaw House.

Sturgis Podmore

Gender: Male
Hair color: Blond
Eye color: Unknown
Related Family: Unknown
Loyalty: Order of the Phoenix

OVERVIEW

Sturgis Podmore is a member of the Order of the Phoenix. He has straw-colored hair and a square jaw.

ROLE IN THE BOOKS

Order of the Phoenix Sturgis Podmore is a member of the Advance Guard that arrives at the Dursleys' to bring Harry to the headquarters of the Order of the Phoenix.

When Harry, Ron, Ginny, Fred, George, and Hermione leave Grimmauld Place for the Hogwarts Express, they almost miss the train because Mad-Eye Moody is waiting for Sturgis, who was supposed to be one of the guards for Harry. Harry later finds a small article in the *Daily Prophet* that says Sturgis Podmore was found in the Ministry trying to get through a top-security door. He had not offered any defence of his actions, and had been sent to Azkaban for six months. Ron guesses that he had been lured there by the Ministry, because they knew he was one of "Dumbledore's lot." Hermione tentatively agrees.

After Harry sees Mr. Weasley attacked, Dumbledore sends Harry and the Weasley children to Grimmauld Place to get them out of the way of Umbridge. When Mrs. Weasley arrives to thank Harry for saving her husband, one of the thing she mentions is that it gave Dumbledore time to make up a story as to why he was there, and "you ave no idea what trouble he would have been n otherwise, look at poor Sturgis . . ." The implication in this seeming throwaway line is that Mr. Weasley had been at the door that Sturgis had apparently been caught trying to go through.

Harry later hears, in a dream in which he experiences Voldemort's thoughts, that Bode had been put under the Imperius curse by Malfoy, in an attempt to retrieve something. Discussing this with Ron, Harry and Ron determine that the thing Voldemort had wanted Bode to retrieve was the weapon that had been mentioned at the meeting of the Order of the Phoenix immediately after Harry had arrived at Headquarters. The following morning, Hermione suggests that, as Lucius Malfoy had been present just outside the door to the Department of Mysteries immediately following Harry's hearing, he might have placed Sturgis under the Imperius Curse then. If Sturgis had been on guard at the door, he might have made some small noise; or Lucius could have just guessed that there was someone there and used the Imperius curse just in case there was someone.

Relationships with Other Characters Sturgis Podmore might be related to Sir Patrick Podmore, of the headless hunt.

Summerby

Gender: Male
Hair color: Unknown
Eye color: Unknown
Related Family: Unknown
Loyalty:

OVERVIEW

Summerby is Seeker for the Hufflepuff Quidditch team in Harry's fifth year.

ROLE IN THE BOOKS

Order of the Phoenix It is mentioned that Ginny, then Seeker for Gryffindor, had caught the Snitch from right under Seeker Summerby's nose. She says it was luck; he had a cold and didn't see the Snitch because he was about to sneeze.

Summers

Gender: Male
Hair color: Unknown
Eye color: Unknown
Related Family: Unknown
Loyalty:

OVERVIEW

Mr. Summers is a member of Hufflepuff house, possibly in the same year as Fred and George Weasley.

ROLE IN THE BOOKS

Goblet of Fire It is mentioned by Professor Dumbledore, that Mr. Summers had tried to place his name in the Goblet of Fire but had been thwarted by the age line.

Susan Bones

Gender: Female
Hair color: Unknown
Eye color: Unknown
Related Family: Unknown

OVERVIEW

Susan Bones is a Hogwarts student in Harry's year who had an uncle, aunt, and cousins who died at the hands of a Death Eater.

ROLE IN THE BOOKS

Philosopher's Stone Susan Bones is placed in Hufflepuff house by the Sorting Hat.

Order of the Phoenix Susan Bones is one of the students who attend the first meeting of the group that will become Dumbledore's Army. At the meeting, she asks Harry if he is, in fact, able to produce a "corporeal Patronus." The phrasing is familiar to Harry, who asks if she is related to Amelia Bones. Susan confirms that Madam Bones is her aunt. With the escape of the Death Eaters from Azkaban, people are once again frightened that Voldemort may be returning, despite the official Ministry reassurances. Susan Bones, who had lost several cousins, an uncle, and an aunt, to the Death Eaters in the previous round, becomes something of a center of attention in the school. At one point, she asks Harry how he stands the fame.

Susan is also one of the six members of Dumbledore's Army who see Draco Malfoy attempting to jinx Harry on the Hogwarts Express, and promptly return fire, leaving Draco, Crabbe, and Goyle looking like gigantic slugs squeezed into Hogwarts robes.

Half-Blood Prince Susan's aunt, Amelia Bones, is murdered, probably directly by Voldemort.

Terence Higgs

Gender: Male
Hair color: Unknown
Eye color: Unknown
Related Family: Unknown
Loyalty: Slytherin house

Overview

Terence Higgs is the Seeker for the Slytherin Quidditch team in Harry's first year.

Role in the Books

Philosopher's Stone Terence Higgs is mentioned as being Slytherin's Seeker in the Quidditch match between Gryffindor and Slytherin. When the Snitch appears, Harry and Terence both dive for it; Harry is in the lead when Marcus Flint, the Slytherin team captain, fouls him.

Terry Boot

Gender: Male
Hair color: Unknown
Eye color: Unknown
Related Family: Unknown

Overview

Terry Boot is a student in Harry's year. He is in Ravenclaw house.

Role in the Books

Philosopher's Stone The Sorting Hat places Terry Boot in Ravenclaw.

Chamber of Secrets Terry Boot is likely one of the people helped by Professor Lockhart after the grand chaos of the Duelling Club. "Pinch it hard, it will stop bleeding in a second, Boot . . ."

Order of the Phoenix Terry Boot attended the first meeting of Dumbledore's Army, in the Hog's Head.

Terry is also one of the six members of Dumbledore's Army who see Draco Malfoy attempting to jinx Harry on the Hogwarts Express, and promptly return fire, leaving Draco, Crabbe, and Goyle looking like gigantic slugs squeezed into Hogwarts robes.

Deathly Hallows When Harry, Ron, and Hermione return to Hogwarts, Neville Longbottom mentions that Terry Boot was punished by the Carrows for yelling about Harry's escape from Gringotts during dinner. He was also present during the final Battle of Hogwarts.

Strengths Terry Boot is one of the few people that manage to make it into Professor Slughorn's N.E.W.T. level Potions class, along with his Ravenclaw friend, Michael Corner.

Relationships with Other Characters Boot joined the DA with his Ravenclaw friends Michael Corner and Anthony Goldstein. He helped Harry in the search for Rowena Ravenclaw's lost Diadem, a suspected Horcrux.

Analysis

It is mentioned that the Boot family name is one of the great old names in wizarding. There is mention that the Boot family had lost members to Voldemort.

The Bloody Baron

Gender: Male
Hair color: Unknown
Eye color: Unknown
Related Family: Unknown
Loyalty: Unknown

Overview

The Bloody Baron is the Slytherin House ghost at Hogwarts. He has "blank staring eyes, a gaunt face, and robes stained with silver blood." No one that we know of has ever asked how he became covered in blood. He is the only one that Peeves is afraid of. His favourite pastime is clanking around in the Astronomy Tower.

Role in the Books

Philosopher's Stone At the Welcoming Feast, Harry sees the Bloody Baron at the Slytherin table. He is apparently sitting quite near Draco Malfoy, who is looking rather uncomfortable; this cheers Harry up a bit. Seamus asks Nearly Headless Nick why he is all covered in blood, and Nick replies, primly, that he had never asked.

We hear later that Professor Dumbledore and the Bloody Baron are the only people who have any measure of control over Peeves.

When Harry, Ron, and Hermione are on their way to the Trophy Room for the Wizard's Duel with Draco, they run into Neville who has been locked out of

Gryffindor Tower because he forgot the password. Neville insists on going with them; he says the Bloody Baron has been by twice already.

Harry impersonates the Bloody Baron while under his Invisibility Cloak with Ron and Hermione, to avoid being caught by Peeves as they head for the trap door.

Half-Blood Prince Returning from Hagrid's hut, where he has just retrieved a much-needed memory from Horace Slughorn, Harry finds his way back into the Common Room barred by The Fat Lady who tells him that it's after midnight and the password has changed. Harry comments to Nearly Headless Nick, who is passing idly through the wall, that he really wants to see Dumbledore; Nick tells him that the Bloody Baron had just seen him returning.

Deathly Hallows From The Grey Lady, we learn that the Bloody Baron had been sent to bring her back from the forest in Albania where she had been hiding, to see her mother Rowena Ravenclaw on her deathbed. When she refused, he became angry, and killed her; discovering what he had done, he turned his dagger on himself.

Relationships with Other Characters While we never talk to the Baron directly, it is revealed that in life he was greatly in love with the woman who became the Grey Lady.

The Fat Friar

Gender: Unknown
Hair color: Unknown
Eye color: Unknown
Related Family: Unknown
Loyalty:

OVERVIEW

The Fat Friar is the House Ghost of Hufflepuff.

ROLE IN THE BOOKS

Philosopher's Stone At the Entrance Feast, we see the Fat Friar at the Hufflepuff table.

The Fat Lady

Gender: Female
Hair color: Unknown
Eye color: Unknown
Related Family: Unknown
Loyalty:

OVERVIEW

The Fat Lady is the subject of a painting on the seventh floor of Hogwarts Castle. Her portrait guards the entrance to Gryffindor Tower. Students must tell her the password that she has created to enter the Gryffindor common room.

ROLE IN THE BOOKS

Philosopher's Stone When Harry and the other first-year students arrive at the entrance to Gryffindor Tower, Percy addresses the portrait of a very fat lady, in a pink silk dress, to give her the password, "Caput Draconis." Never named, the portrait is called The Fat Lady throughout the rest of the series.

When Harry departs for his Wizard's Duel with Draco, Ron goes with him as Second, and Hermione tags along to try and convince them to return to Gryffindor Tower. Finding herself unsuccessful, she turns around to re-enter the common room, but finds that the portrait is blank; the Fat Lady has gone visiting. When they run into Neville in the hall shortly, Neville tells us that he had forgotten the password, and without it the Fat Lady would not let him enter the Tower. Ron tells him the password ("pig snout"), but says that it won't do him any good, the Fat Lady's off visiting. After the failed duel, the Fat Lady asks what the four of them have been doing, but simply opens the entrance when Harry gives the password.

When Harry, trying out his new Invisibility Cloak, leaves Gryffindor Tower the night after Christmas, the Fat Lady squawks, "Who's there?" as he exits. Harry does not reply.

Prisoner of Azkaban The Fat Lady refuses to let Sirius Black into Gryffindor tower at Hallowe'en because he does not have the password. He destroys her painting in a rage. She leaves the portrait out of fear for several months; during her absence, the entrance to Gryffindor Tower is guarded by Sir Cadogan. When Sir Cadogan allows Sirius into the tower, the Fat Lady is convinced to return, but she requires that a squad of security trolls be provided to keep her safe.

Order of the Phoenix Harry is first to the Gryffindor dorm's entrance on his first night back at school, but he does not know the password, and the Fat Lady will not let him in. Neville, arriving almost on Harry's heels, says that he will be able to remember the password this year; it is *Mimbulus Mimbletonia*.

On the Thursday of the first week of classes, Harry, returning from detention with Professor Umbridge near midnight, runs into Ron in the hall. When they reach Gryffindor tower, deep in conversation, the Fat Lady is dozing; after a while, she testily asks them to give the password so she doesn't have to keep listening to their conversation all night.

Half-Blood Prince The Fat Lady is mentioned at the end of the book where she is told by Harry that Dumbledore is dead, she then wails in despair and swings forward to admit Harry into the common room without a password.

Relationships with Other Characters As early as the first book, we learn that at night the Fat Lady leaves her portrait and goes visiting. In *Harry Potter and the Goblet of Fire*, a witch in a portrait in the small room where the Champions gather after they are selected hastens off as Harry is announced as the fourth Champion. We later see her sharing the frame with the Fat Lady; she has evidently told the Fat Lady of Harry selection as fourth Champion. The same witch, identified as Violet or Vi, is later seen sharing a box of liqueur chocolates with the Fat Lady; they are both rather tipsy at that point.

In *Harry Potter and the Half-Blood Prince*, it is mentioned that the Fat Lady and Vi between them had drunk all the wine in a picture of monks over Christmas; as a result, the Fat Lady has chosen the word "Abstinence" as the new password.

The Grey Lady

Gender: Female
Hair color: Unknown
Eye color: Unknown
Related Family: Unknown
Loyalty:

OVERVIEW

The Grey Lady is Ghost of Ravenclaw House.

ROLE IN THE BOOKS

Deathly Hallows The Grey Lady helps Harry find information about the lost Ravenclaw diadem, which has been made into a Horcrux by Lord Voldemort. We discover that she was Rowena Ravenclaw's daughter Helena, and had stolen the diadem and hidden it in Albania. Harry correctly determines that it had been retrieved by Voldemort, and stored in the Room of Requirement (in its Junk Storeroom state).

Relationships with Other Characters It turns out that the character who became the Bloody Baron on his death had gone to Albania, where the Grey Lady (as she became) had been hiding, to bid her come back to see her mother before she died. When she refused, the Baron, angered, had killed her.

The Grey Lady apparently stole the Diadem from Rowena Ravenclaw out of jealousy of her mother's achievements or fame. We are not told why she refused to return, though we can safely guess that it was either fear of retribution, or remorse.

Theodore Nott

Gender: Male
Hair color: Unknown
Eye color: Unknown
Related Family: father Nott
Loyalty:

OVERVIEW

Theodore Nott is a "tall, stringy Slytherin" in Harry's year.

ROLE IN THE BOOKS

Philosopher's Stone The name "Nott" is called during the Sorting.

Order of the Phoenix Theodore, who is described (as a "stringy Slytherin boy") but not named, and Harry are in the same section of Hagrid's Care of Magical Creatures class on the day after Hagrid's return from his mission, when Hagrid chooses to teach Thestrals. Harry sees them, and notes that most of the students are staring blankly around, just as Ron is. The two other students who seem able to see the Thestrals are Nott and Neville Longbottom. After Harry's interview appears in *the Quibbler*, Harry sees "a weedy-looking boy . . . called Theodore Nott" in the library, talking with Draco Malfoy, Crabbe, and Goyle. Though they are apparently talking about Harry's interview, which named all their fathers as Death Eaters returning to Lord Voldemort's side, they cannot admit to having read it, because possession of *the Quibbler* is an expulsion offence.

Half-Blood Prince Very few people have progressed to N.E.W.T.-level studies in Professor Slughorn's Potions class: Harry, Ron, and Hermione alone among the Gryffindors, Ernie Macmillan from Hufflepuff, four unnamed Ravenclaw students, and four from Slytherin house including Draco Malfoy and Theodore Nott. Nott here is often exchanging asides with Draco, as Draco's henchmen, Crabbe and Goyle, did not do well enough in their Potions O.W.L. to continue on in that course, even given Slughorn's slightly lower entrance requirement.

Outside the series Theodore originally had a large scene in which he and Draco Malfoy discussed Harry while their respective fathers, Nott and Lucius Malfoy, discussed Death Eater business off camera. The author mentions[1] that while she tried to fit the scene into two different books, it didn't work well either place and so was laid to rest. Theodore Nott was one of the students to have checked out the library copy of *Quidditch Through the Ages*, a book mentioned in the story and reproduced by the author.

Thorfinn Rowle

Gender: Male
Hair color: Blond
Eye color: Unknown
Related Family: Unknown
Loyalty: Lord Voldemort

OVERVIEW

Thorfinn Rowle is a large, blond man. He is a Death Eater.

---

1. http://www.jkrowling.com/textonly/en/faq_view.cfm?id=119

ROLE IN THE BOOKS

Half-Blood Prince When Harry follows Severus Snape, Draco Malfoy, Amycus and Alecto Carrow, and Fenrir Greyback down from the Astronomy Tower after the death of Albus Dumbledore, he finds a large, blond Death Eater in the hallway firing off curses indiscriminately. It seems that one of his curses was the cause of one of the two Death Eater casualties; he had tried to curse Remus Lupin and missed. At the word from Snape, he breaks off the fight and runs, along with the others; apparently he follows Snape, who is using various short cuts, because he is ahead of Harry when they reach the front door of the school, while the Carrows and Greyback are behind Harry.

Deathly Hallows When the two Death Eaters attack Ron and Hermione in the cafe on the Tottenham Court Road, Harry recalls that the "large blond" Death Eater was one of the ones at Hogwarts, and recognizes the other is Antonin Dolohov. Ron tells Harry that he thinks the large one's name is Thorfinn Rowle.

After the Trio have returned to Grimmauld Place, Harry has an episode where he sees into Lord Voldemort's mind. Thorfinn Rowle is being tortured for having let Ron and Hermione escape. Harry is sickened to find that Voldemort is ordering Draco Malfoy to do the actual torturing.

Rowle is one of the Death Eaters gathered around Voldemort in the clearing in the forest when Harry goes to meet Voldemort.

Tom Marvolo Riddle

Gender: Male
Hair color: Black
Eye color: Unknown
Related Family: Merope Gaunt, Tom Riddle
Loyalty: Self

OVERVIEW

Tom Marvolo Riddle, only child of the Muggle Tom Riddle and Merope Gaunt, attended Hogwarts some fifty years before the story opens. The author has said that he was born 31 December;[1] internal evidence in the series indicates that this would have fallen in the late 1920s.

ROLE IN THE BOOKS

Chamber of Secrets A large part of the story involves a Secret Diary that we don't find out about until shortly after Christmas. The Secret Diary had originally belonged to Tom Riddle. Through magic embedded within it, Riddle's memory bewitches Ginny Weasley into opening the Chamber of Secrets and releasing the monster that attacks students. When Ginny throws the diary away, Harry finds it; the diary shows him a day fifty years before when Rubeus Hagrid was accused of opening the Chamber and releasing the monster. Later, with the diary back in Ginny's possession, Riddle's memory summons her to the Chamber of Secrets; there he begins draining her life force to restore his own body. Harry succeeds in vanquishing Riddle and saving Ginny by killing the monster and destroying the diary. It turns out that the diary had been surreptitiously given to Ginny by Lucius Malfoy.

It is as part of the battle in the Chamber of Secrets that we learn that Tom Riddle and Lord Voldemort are the same person.

Goblet of Fire The name Tom Riddle does not appear in this book, though it can be inferred: Tom Riddle of Riddle Manor, who we deduce is Tom Marvolo Riddle's father, is mentioned as being found incomprehensibly dead along with his parents, and Riddle Manor, the house in Little Hangleton, plays a part in the story.

Order of the Phoenix In the duel between Albus Dumbledore and Voldemort in the Atrium at the Ministry of Magic, Dumbledore repeatedly calls his opponent "Tom," much to his annoyance.

Half-Blood Prince Dumbledore tells Harry that he will be teaching Harry specially during the course of the year. Harry is intrigued, wondering what special magic Dumbledore will be teaching him, but is surprised when the first lesson comes around, as it seems that they will be studying Tom Riddle as he grows up. By watching memories in a Pensieve, Harry (and thus the reader) becomes acquainted with Lord Voldemort's origins and why he abandoned the name Tom Marvolo Riddle. Throughout, Professor Dumbledore refers to him by this name, even when we see that he is calling himself Voldemort.

While we do not see Tom as an infant, we do see the house of his mother Merope, uncle Morfin, and grandfather Marvolo Gaunt. We learn that Merope is infatuated with the Muggle Tom Riddle, and Dumbledore tells us that shortly after Marvolo and Morfin are imprisoned, she had left their house with Tom. Dumbledore suggests that quite possibly she had used a love potion on Tom, but had stopped using it once she found herself pregnant, perhaps believing that her bearing his child would be enough to keep him with her. It was not, and we are told that Tom had returned home.

When we first see Tom, it is in the orphanage where he had grown up. Dumbledore has arrived to offer him a place at Hogwarts now that he is 11 years old. Discussing Tom with the matron of the orphanage, Dumbledore finds that Merope had passed away shortly after giving birth to him one New Years' Eve, after asking that he be named Tom, after his father, and Marvolo after his grandfather. He had always been a quiet and withdrawn boy, and did not seem to have any friends. There were a number of strange things that seemed to happen around Tom, but nothing that could be directly caused by him; and a number of the other children seemed to be very afraid of him. In particular, there

---

1. http://en.wikipedia.org/wiki/Surrey

had been one incident with two other children, on the annual seaside outing, in which the two children had apparently been frightened almost out of their wits by something to do with a cave, but of which they would never speak. Meeting Tom in person, we find that he is assured far beyond his years, and apparently chooses to be solitary. He is initially suspicious of Dumbledore, thinking that he is there to take Tom to some sort of psychiatric hospital. He is, however, won over by Dumbledore's display of magic. Interestingly, when it is mentioned that the owner of the Leaky Cauldron is also named Tom, Riddle seems to reject this; he doesn't like his name, for some reason. Almost as an afterthought, Tom mentions that he can talk with snakes.

Dumbledore tells us that there are very few memories of Tom in his school years; those who remember him don't seem to wish to talk about him. He does, however, have a memory of Morfin Gaunt's. Morfin had evidently at first believed that Tom was his father, and it was only after Tom answered him in Parseltongue that he realized he was talking to Merope's son. Tom had then apparently Stunned Morfin, taken the Gaunt signet ring and Morfin's wand, and killed his father and his fathers' Muggle parents. He had then apparently modified Morfin's memory so that Morfin recalled killing the Muggles, and did not remember Tom's presence.

We next see Tom in an edited memory of Professor Slughorn's. Here we see Tom wearing the Gaunt ring, with a circle of cronies, and later asking about Horcruxes. In this memory, which Dumbledore points out has been rather obviously edited, Slughorn claims to have no knowledge of Horcruxes. Dumbledore says that this one memory is the most important task he has for Harry; Harry is uniquely equipped to retrieve that memory in its original, unedited state, and if he cannot retrieve the memory, Dumbledore's lessons will be of little use.

We later see Tom, having graduated from Hogwarts, working for Borgin and Burkes. We see through the eyes of a house elf, Hokey, as Tom calls on an elderly but still vain witch, Hepzibah Smith. She decides to show Tom her two greatest treasures: the locket of Slytherin and a cup of Helga Hufflepuff's. We see Tom's eyes flash red with greed and suppressed anger as he sees the locket; apparently he remembered Morfin Gaunt telling him that Merope had taken that with her when she left the Gaunt house. Dumbledore tells Harry that shortly after this, Hepzibah had died, apparently accidentally poisoned by Hokey, and the two treasures she had here shown Tom had vanished.

In a final memory, we see Tom applying to Dumbledore for a job at Hogwarts as instructor of Defence Against the Dark Arts. Dumbledore tells us that he had applied for that post on graduation, but that then-headmaster Dippet had turned him down, saying he lacked real-world experience. In Dumbledore's memory, we see Tom being turned down again, this time apparently because Dumbledore does not entirely trust Tom to teach defence. Dumbledore points out that he knows that Tom now chooses to call himself Voldemort, and that he has brought supporters with him, but says that he cannot forget that Riddle was Tom originally, and so continues to address him as Tom.

Some time later, Harry manages to secure the unedited memory from Slughorn, and he and Dumbledore view it. In response to Tom's questions, Slughorn responds that a Horcrux is one of the darkest things in dark magic. By murdering another person, one actually tears the soul; and by means of incantations of some sort which Slughorn professes to not know, one can then encapsulate the torn-off soul fragment into another object, which is a Horcrux. The Horcrux then prevents the main part of the soul from leaving the earth when the body housing it is killed. Tom then asks, if one Horcrux can give immortality, would not more be better? Isn't seven the most magical number? Slughorn is appalled at the idea of murdering so many people, and of tearing one's soul into so many pieces. As Tom says that it was a purely academic question, and turns away from Slughorn, Harry notes a look of triumph in his eyes, very similar to the look he had had when Dumbledore had told him he was a wizard.

Discussing this memory, Dumbledore reveals that the diary in *Harry Potter and the Chamber of Secrets* was actually one of Tom's Horcruxes. It was what allowed Riddle's memory to think and act independently and to nearly become a material person by taking Ginny Weasley's life force. Dumbledore admits that discovering this had been a worry to him, as Horcruxes, being the source of immortality, should be extremely valuable and thus should be kept safely stored away and hidden, and yet the diary seemed to be crafted not only as a means of immortality but also as a weapon. Dumbledore feels certain that this would not have been done if it had been the only Horcrux Tom had made; with this memory, he understands that Tom, or Voldemort, would have made six Horcruxes to leave him with a total of seven pieces of his soul. He goes on to say that two, the diary and the Gaunt ring, have been found and destroyed, likely leaving four, and that when he finds another, Harry will have the right to come along and help in its retrieval and destruction.

Dumbledore also expresses the opinion that the Horcruxes are typically crafted out of objects that have a particular significance for Tom, especially those that tie him to his heritage. The Gaunt ring, for instance, is an heirloom that ties him to an ancient Wizarding family, as the Slytherin locket would be. Questioned about the significance of the diary, Dumbledore says that its importance was that, as it showed the opening of the Chamber, it was proof that Tom is the heir of Slytherin. Dumbledore suggests further that, even as the horcruxes are made from items of significance, they will be hidden in particularly significant places. The ring was in the remains of the Gaunt shack, for instance. Dumbledore summons Harry to his office one final time, to tell him that he has determined the location of the cave where Tom had taken his two victims. Dumbledore believed that, as Tom had one of his earliest triumphs there, it was extremely likely that a Horcrux would be hidden in that cave. This proves to be correct; it turns out that Tom had, in fact, hidden a Horcrux there, although someone had later removed it.

Deathly Hallows It is mentioned that the eyes in the locket Horcrux are Riddle's handsome eyes, from before he changed his appearance to its current snakelike state.

When Harry is dueling with Voldemort, Harry addresses him as "Tom" or "Riddle," showing that he refuses to accept the power of his "new" name.

Strengths Tom is an extremely powerful wizard. He is able to produce significant amounts of somewhat controlled magic even before training, and without a wand. We find that he is able to perform N.E.W.T.-class magic, probably before he has even completed his O.W.L.s.

In Hokey's and Horace Slughorn's memories of Tom, we also learn that he can be extremely persuasive.

Weaknesses Even as a boy of about 15, in Professor Slughorn's memory of him, we see that Tom is already so concerned with his own personal immortality that he has created a Horcrux. This would indicate that he already has a very real fear of death.

In Dumbledore's memories of the young Tom Riddle, we see that he is very much alone, and seems to prefer it that way, He has no friends at the orphanage, and does not desire help finding his school supplies in Diagon Alley. This determination to do everything himself, which he likely perceives as strength, actually masks a major weakness, an inability to understand the way other peoples' minds truly work.

Relationships with Other Characters Tom seems to prefer being alone. At the orphanage he has no friends, and at Hogwarts he seems to have followers rather than friends. Even at this young age, those who gather around Tom are seldom friends; instead, they are gathered around him in the hopes of gaining some of his power, or out of fear of what he would do to them if they left. Tom doesn't consider anyone, ally or enemy, to be worthy of his respect. He has never trusted anyone other than himself.

Travers

Gender: Male
Hair color: Bushy grey
Eye color: Unknown
Related Family: Unknown
Loyalty: Lord Voldemort

Overview

Travers (first name unknown) is a tall, thin Death Eater.

Role in the Books

Goblet of Fire As part of his attempt to plea-bargain his way out of Azkaban, Igor Karkaroff accuses Travers of killing Marlene McKinnon and her family.

Deathly Hallows We first hear of Travers when Kingsley Shacklebolt tells us that Travers' hood had fallen off when Kingsley had cursed him during the escape from Privet Drive. At the time, Kingsley says that Travers is supposed to still be in Azkaban, but there evidently has been a mass breakout that hasn't been reported.

Travers is mentioned in passing when Harry and Hermione, invading the Ministry of Magic in search of the Locket Horcrux, run into Dolores Umbridge. Dolores asks Hermione, who is disguised as Mafalda Hopkirk, if Travers had sent her; evidently, Travers is then working in the Improper Use of Magic Office at a higher rank than Mafalda.

Travers and another Death Eater, Selwyn, answer Xenophilius Lovegood's summons. They are annoyed and sarcastic, this is evidently the third time Xeno has summoned them, and while he is saying that he has Harry Potter in the house, they don't believe him, thinking that it's another scheme of his to get his daughter Luna released. Travers is in Diagon Alley when Hermione, Ron, Harry, and Griphook are on their way to break in to Gringott's. Hermione being disguised as Bellatrix Lestrange, he is initially unsuspicious; however, he seems to sense some odd things happening as the scheme unfolds, and eventually Harry has to put him under the Imperius curse to keep him out of the way. Under Harry's orders, then, he follows them into the tunnels, and finally Harry sends him off to try and hide himself.

Trevor

Gender: Male (presumably)
Hair color: None
Eye color: Black
Related Family: None
Loyalty: Neville Longbottom

Overview

Trevor is Neville's pet toad, who is forever getting lost.

Role in the Books

Philosopher's Stone When we first see Neville, he is standing on the platform talking to an older witch, apparently his grandmother. It seems that he has lost Trevor.

We are introduced to Trevor by Neville, who looks in to Harry and Ron's compartment to ask if they have seen him. Some time later, Hermione stops by on the same errand; apparently she has chosen to help Neville in his search. Trevor remains lost until the students are leaving the boats on the shore of the lake under Hogwarts; Hagrid apparently then finds him and asks whose toad this is.

Professor Flitwick had demonstrated making things fly by sending Neville's toad soaring about the classroom. Neville is apparently trying to catch Trevor again when he overhears Harry, Ron, and Hermione planning how to get through the trap door. Dropping Trevor, he prepares, unsuccessfully, to fight them.

Order of the Phoenix When we meet Neville in the Hogwarts Express, he is dragging his trunk and holding on to a struggling Trevor. He continues to hold Trevor throughout the early part of the trip, dumping him in Harry's lap as he prepares to demonstrate the defensive mechanism of his prized Mimbulus Mimbletonia. Harry, holding on to Trevor, is drenched with Stinksap.

We see Trevor again as they leave the train; Neville carefully stores him in an inside pocket.

Strengths Although he is often getting lost, Trevor always manages to get found again. It seems he has some ability to transport himself, as he manages to reach the far shore of the lake before Neville himself does.

Analysis

Trevor seems to be present only to give Neville something else to misplace and worry about. He never appears to have any power save that of getting lost, and later appearing where he would have been if Neville had been able to retain him—for instance, he is lost on the Hogwarts Express, in book 1, but then appears near the castle as the first-years are getting out of the boats.

Urquhart

Gender: Male
Hair color: Unknown
Eye color: Unknown
Related Family: Unknown
Loyalty:

Overview

Urquhart is Slytherin's new Quidditch captain in Harry's sixth year.

Role in the Books

Vaisey

Gender: Male
Hair color: Unknown
Eye color: Unknown
Related Family: Unknown
Loyalty:

Overview

Vaisey is a Chaser on the Slytherin Quidditch team in Harry's sixth year.

Role in the Books

Half-Blood Prince Just before the Quidditch match between Slytherin and Gryffindor, Ginny Weasley tells Harry that Vaisey took a Bludger to the head during the previous day's practice, and is too sick to play. This greatly heartens Ron, as Vaisey is evidently Slytherin's top scorer.

Vernon Dursley

Gender: Male
Hair color: Unknown
Eye color: Unknown
Related Family: Unknown
Loyalty:

Overview

Vernon Dursley is Harry Potter's uncle (Vernon's wife is Harry's mother's sister). He and his wife Petunia Dursley reluctantly took Harry in as a baby, while they had their own son, Dudley. Vernon feels somewhat threatened by Harry's magical abilities and wishes to "stamp it out of him," to the extent of refusing to allow him to speak of anything even slightly out of the ordinary.

Role in the Books

Philosopher's Stone The first person we actually meet in the series is Vernon Dursley. We follow Vernon as he kisses his wife goodbye in the morning, and as he drives off to his workplace, Grunnings, where he sells drills and yells at people. On his way to work he sees a cat apparently reading a map, and several small groups of people wearing robes, talking excitedly about something. He happens to overhear one of the groups talking about one "Harry Potter" and this worries him to the point that he nearly calls home. He decides, however, that it would not be *normal* to phone his wife over such a small occurrence, and decides to wait until he gets home. There, while watching a news report about strange occurrences happening all around Britain, he casually asks the name of Petunia's sister's child. She confirms that he is named Harry Potter, "a dreadfully common name." Vernon is still worried, and still not daring to show it, when he goes to sleep that night.

We see Vernon some ten years later, sitting at the breakfast table, and doting on his son, Dudley. It is Dudley's birthday, and Vernon cheerfully tells him that there are thirty-seven presents there. Dudley is immediately angered: he had thirty-eight the year before. He calms down when Petunia promises him two more. A phone call interrupts them; Petunia reports that Mrs. Figg has broken her leg and will be unable to take care of Harry while everyone else is at the zoo. Petunia and Vernon discuss what to do with Harry as if he was not present in the room, except that when Harry suggests he could stay at home by himself, Vernon dismisses that idea out of hand. Eventually they decide that Harry will have to go to the zoo with them.

On the way to the zoo, Harry mentions that he had dreamed about a flying motorcycle. Vernon, livid, yells at him that there are no such things as flying motorcycles.

Despite Vernon's attempts to keep Harry in the background, Harry has a good time at the zoo, as vendors naturally assume that Vernon will be buying for all three of the boys he has with him. When the glass in front of the snake vanishes, and Dudley falls into the moat, Vernon apparently blames Harry. Once they get home, Vernon, evidently unable to speak, locks Harry back into his cupboard under the stairs, saying he will have no meals. Harry, left to his own devices, plans to sneak out to the kitchen for some food after the Dursleys are all asleep.

Vernon is extremely pleased that Dudley will be attending Smeltings, his old school. In the face of Vernon's obvious and overweening pride, Harry retreats to hide his amusement at Dudley's uniform. It is the same day the the first of Harry's letters arrives. Vernon is apparently appalled when he realizes who has sent the letter to Harry, and immediately sends both Harry and Dudley out of the kitchen. While Harry and Dudley listen at the door, Vernon and Petunia discuss what they are going to do about this letter, eventually deciding to ignore it. However, now knowing that someone knows Harry is in the cupboard under the stairs, that being where it was addressed to, Vernon decides to move him to Dudley's second bedroom, where all Dudley's broken toys are stored.

This turns out to be a less than useful decision, as the letters keep coming. The next day, Dudley announces a second one, addressed to Harry in *"The Smallest Bedroom,"* and Vernon has to fight both Harry and Dudley for it. The next day, Harry gets up early to reach the door before anyone else, and finds Vernon sleeping across the doorway. Three more letters are delivered onto his chest, and he tears them up before Harry's eyes. Vernon, now getting more frantic, nails up the letterbox.

On Friday, twelve more letters for Harry arrive, stuffed in all the cracks around the door, as they can't be put in the letterbox. Vernon, now very jumpy and humming "Tiptoe Through the Tulips," seals up all the cracks that letters had come through.

On Saturday, twenty-four more letters arrive, inside the two dozen eggs delivered through the window by the milkman. Vernon, of course, phones the dairy, demanding to know who was responsible for them being there. On Sunday, an apparently slightly demented Vernon announces that this is his favorite day of the week, because there is no post. Almost as he speaks, a rumbling noise heralds the delivery of what seems to be about a hundred letters, all addressed to Harry, down the kitchen chimney. Vernon throws Harry bodily out of the kitchen, and pulling tufts out of his mustache, tells everyone that they are going away, and to pack some clothes. Vernon drives them in apparently random directions all day, often turning 180 degrees and going back on his course, all the while muttering something about "shaking them off." By the end of the day Dudley is howling, as he had missed five television programs, and Vernon had not stopped for food. Eventually they end up at a gloomy hotel on teh outskirts of a large city. In the hotel restaurant the next morning, the clerk approaches them, saying that he's got about a hundred letters for Harry Potter at the desk; Vernon rises to take them, and they set off again. Today, Vernon seems to be madly looking for some place that they can't be reached, stopping and looking around in the middle of a suspension bridge, deep in the woods, but none of these seems correct somehow. Eventually, as night falls, they stop on a seacoast, and Vernon leaves the car. He returns in a short while saying he has found just the place, and points at a hut precariously perched on a rock out in the ocean. He is also carrying a long, thin package, and says he has provisions and a boat to get out there.

Once in the hut, the provisions prove scanty: a packet of crisps (US: chips) and a banana for each of them. With a storm coming on, Vernon seems quite cheerful, thinking nothing could get through to them now. He and Petunia take the bedroom, leaving Dudley on the broken-down couch in the main room, and Harry with the thinnest blanket on the floor.

When Hagrid arrives, knocking the door down at the height of the storm, Vernon appears, now carrying the contents of the long thin parcel: a rifle. Hagrid bends the rifle into a pretzel and throws it away, and Vernon retreats, though he does retain enough sense to tell Dudley to to eat anything Hagrid offers him. When Harry admits that he knows nothing about Hagrid's world, the Wizarding world, Hagrid turns angrily on Vernon, who, much abashed, subsides into incoherence. Vernon does try a number of times to prevent Hagrid telling Harry about the Wizarding world, and insists that Harry is not going to Hogwarts, but Hagrid overrides him easily. When Vernon angrily protests that he is not going to pay good money to have some doddering old man teach Harry magic tricks, Hagrid angrily warns him not to insult Albus Dumbledore, and by way of emphasis gives Dudley a pig's tail. Panicked by this display of magic, the three Dursleys retreat to the back bedroom.

When Harry returns to Privet Drive, Vernon has apparently chosen to ignore him, and so Harry's life is much quieter. As the day of departure comes closer, Harry asks Uncle Vernon if he could get a ride into London to catch his train. Vernon agrees, saying that they had to go into London anyway to get Dudley's tail removed surgically. When Vernon comments sarcastically about Harry's need for a train, Harry says that he has to catch the train at King's Cross Station at platform nine and three quarters. Vernon seems surprised by this.

The next day, as they reach King's Cross Station, Vernon is uncharacteristically jolly. He even loads Harry's trunk onto a dolly and pushes it into the station. He points out the big signs for platforms nine and ten, and observes that there doesn't seem to be a platform nine and three quarters. He then wishes Harry a happy term, and leaves, laughing. Harry sees the three Dursleys laughing at him in the car as they drive away.

At Christmas, Harry receives a note acknowledging his earlier message—he had written to say he had made it to school—and enclosing his Christmas gift, a 50p piece (about $1 US). The note is signed by Vernon and Petunia. Harry gives the coin to Ron, who is amazed at the appearance of this Muggle money.

When Harry returns to London on the Hogwarts Express, Uncle Vernon is extremely brusque in his greeting, to the point of shocking Hermione and Mrs. Weasley. As Vernon leaves, Harry tells Ron and Hermione that he'll be having some fun with the Dursleys, as they don't know he isn't allowed to practice magic.

Chamber of Secrets When Harry comes down to breakfast, he reminds Dudley to "use the magic word" when Dudley commands him to pass the bacon. This results in Uncle Vernon becoming enraged, as he has forbidden all mention of magic in the house. Harry is briefly amazed to hear Uncle Vernon say that it is a special day, as it is Harry's birthday. It turns out, however, that Vernon is talking about his guests that evening, the Masons, a couple that he is trying to impress, as they could place the largest order of drills Vernon has ever received. Vernon then leads his family in rehearsing what they will be doing, reminding Harry repeatedly that his role is to be upstairs in his room, pretending he is not there. Harry several times has trouble keeping a straight face, as the plans for the evening seem to him to be ludicrously transparent attempts to curry favor.

As the guests arrive, Harry, as ordered, goes to his room, where he finds a house-elf jumping on his bed. The elf, who introduces himself as Dobby, apparently feels he is being very disobedient by coming to see Harry, and must punish himself. The resulting noise bring Vernon upstairs to chide Harry, who has managed to hide Dobby when he heard Vernon approaching. When Dobby drops the Dursleys' dessert in the kitchen, Vernon almost manages to calm down his guests; but very shortly after that an owl arrives with a parchment, which it drops on Mrs. Mason's head. Mrs. Mason, who is morbidly afraid of birds, runs screaming from the house, and Mr. Mason follows, saying he will not be dealing with Grunnings.

Furious, Vernon brings the letter to Harry and tells him to read it out loud. It is a warning from the Ministry that Harry has violated the Decree for the Reasonable Restriction of Underage Sorcery by performing a Hover Charm. Vernon, now knowing that Harry is not allowed to perform magic at Privet Drive until he comes of age, decides to lock him into his bedroom, adding bars across the window for good measure.

When Ron, Fred, and George break Harry out of his room, Harry almost forgets Hedwig, who is locked into her cage. Hedwig's loud hoot at being forgotten wakes up the Dursleys, and Vernon rushes into the room, barely catching Harry's foot as Harry is lifted out of the window by the Weasleys' flying Ford Anglia. Vernon tumbles down into the bushes under the window, and Harry escapes in the car.

At Christmas, the Dursleys send Harry a toothpick as a gift.

Prisoner of Azkaban Somewhat less afraid of Harry having learned that he is not allowed to practice magic at Privet Drive, Vernon has locked all Harry's school supplies away in the cupboard that was previously Harry's bedroom. Harry has used the lock-picking skills he had learned from Fred and George Weasley to get the materials he needs out of the cupboard, and now does his homework by torch (US: flashlight) under his bedcovers at night.

When Harry's Hogwarts letter arrives with the next years' booklist, it contains a permission slip; signed by a parent or guardian, it would allow Harry to visit Hogsmeade on specified weekends. Harry wonders how he will get Uncle Vernon to sign it.

Vernon, the next morning, announces that he is off to the train station to collect his sister, Harry's Aunt Marge. Harry receives strict instructions as to how he is to act: be civil to Marge, no discussion of magic, and Harry is to recall that Marge has been told that he has been placed in St. Brutus' Secure Centre for Incurably Criminal Boys. As Vernon is leaving, Harry takes him aside and points out that he's going to have a hard time remembering the stuff he's been told he has to remember. Vernon, thinking about how much damage one small slip could do, pales. Harry suggests that if there was something in it for him, he wold be more careful, and asks if Uncle Vernon would be willing to sign his permission slip. Vernon grudgingly agrees that if Harry manages to stay convincing for the full week of Marge's stay, he will sign the permission slip.

The following week is very hard on Vernon, as Marge insists on not only keeping Harry in view so he can't sneak around behind her back, but in insulting Harry and his parents. Vernon is unusually sensitive to Harry's moods, repeatedly trying to distract Marge off subject so that Harry won't get upset and say something that would reveal that he isn't *normal*. On the last night of her visit, however, Marge insults Harry's father, and Harry loses control, inadvertently causing Marge to inflate like a balloon. Knowing that he is in trouble, Harry hastily retrieves his school supplies, threatening Vernon with his wand when he tries to stop Harry and get him to deflate Aunt Marge, and leaves, dragging his trunk.

When Harry reaches the Leaky Cauldron, he is intercepted by the Minister for Magic, Cornelius Fudge, who tells him that Aunt Marge had been punctured and her memory adjusted. He says that the Dursleys are willing to have him back at Privet Drive over the summer if he stays at Hogwarts over Christmas and Easter.

When Harry returns to London after the school year, he tells Vernon that he has met his godfather. When Vernon says he doesn't have one, Harry says he does, his name is Sirius Black and he's a convicted murderer who is on the run, but he is very interested in Harry's wellbeing and will expect to hear from him over the summer. Vernon turns quite pale at this news.

Goblet of Fire The school nurse has sent instructions home with Dudley that he is to be put on a diet, as he is so fat; Vernon's temper has not been improved by Petunia putting the entire family on a diet, to keep Dudley from feeling singled out.

In mid-August, Vernon receives a letter from Mrs. Weasley, asking if Harry could go to the Quidditch World Cup with her family, as they have tickets. Vernon is disconcerted by the letter, which has aroused the postman's interest because it is totally covered with stamps, except for a small area where Mrs. Weasley has written Vernon's address. Clearly, this is Different, and therefore Bad. The contents of the letter are equally dismaying, because they leave Vernon with a quandary: if he permits Harry to go, then Harry will be doing something he likes, which is clearly bad; however, Mrs. Weasley has also said that he can stay the rest of the summer with her, which would mean that Harry would be out of Vernon's hair a good fortnight sooner than expected. Sensing this indecision, Harry points out that he should get an answer from Uncle Vernon soon, as he is writing to his godfather, and Sirius will want to know where he is and what he's doing. Reminded of Sirius' existence, Vernon backs down from his indignation and gives Harry permission to go.

The Weasleys had said that they would arrive to collect Harry; Vernon wonders how they will arrive, and whether they will be dressed normally or in those robe things. Vernon himself has dressed in his best business suit, to try and intimidate the Weasleys. The time of their scheduled arrival comes, and goes, with Harry looking anxiously outside to see them arrive, when there is a noise from the fireplace: Mr. Weasley has had the Dursleys' fireplace attached to the Floo network for the day, and he, Fred, George, and Ron have all appeared in the Dursleys' walled-up fireplace. Mr. Weasley blows the wall apart magically to get his family out, coating Vernon and Petunia with white dust. Stunned, Vernon and Petunia say nothing, despite Mr. Weasley's attempts at making conversation, while Fred and George go to retrieve Harry's trunk. As he re-enters the fire, Fred drops a bag of toffees, and though he picks most of them up, one is left behind. With all the other Weasleys gone, Harry is preparing to go when Mr. Weasley stops him. He reminds Vernon that Harry is about to leave for several months, isn't Vernon even going to say goodbye? Grudgingly, Vernon says, "Well, goodbye then." Mr. Weasley is amazed at this brusqueness, but Harry prepares to enter the fire. He is stopped by a gagging noise: Dudley has found and eaten the toffee left by Fred, and it has expanded his tongue to several feet in length. Outraged, Vernon starts attacking Mr. Weasley. As Harry departs, he sees Mr. Weasley destroying the china figurines that Vernon is throwing at him.

At one point, Hermione mentions that the Dursleys would likely be pleased to hear how well he was doing in the Triwizard Tournament. Harry demurs, saying they would be happier if he had managed to get himself killed. Vernon meets Harry again at King's Cross Station, and is, as usual, surly and untalkative.

Order of the Phoenix Knowing Voldemort is back, Harry is intensely interested in both the Wizarding and the Muggle news, looking for evidence of his return. He cannot watch the Muggle news without being abused by Uncle Vernon, so in order to at least hear the news, in hopes that he will be able to recognize the effects of Dark Magic, he lies in the garden, hidden from the neighbours by the geraniums, listening through the open windows. While he is listening this way, he hears a noise in the street that he recognizes as the sound of someone Diasapparating, and leaps up, wand at the ready, only to crack his head on the window standing open above him. Vernon, discovering him there, pulls Harry in through the window, and then makes conciliatory noises at the neighbours who have looked around at his bellow of outrage, to try and reassure them that there is nothing wrong. Vernon and Harry then have a low-voiced argument, until Harry goes out, in part to investigate the noise he had heard.

Harry later brings a very ill Dudley, who has just been attacked by Dementors, back home. Harry hopes to escape to his room, but Dudley manages to mention Harry, and Vernon calls Harry back into the kitchen. While Vernon and Petunia Dursley confront him about their now-ill son, Harry receives a letter from the Ministry of Magic expelling him from Hogwarts and saying his wand will shortly be destroyed. Harry decides that his only option is to become a fugitive, but before he can get past Uncle Vernon, another owl letter arrives from Arthur Weasley, telling him to stay in his uncle's house, not let Ministry representatives break his wand, and not use magic again; Dumbledore is straightening things out. As he must remain in the house anyway, Harry stays at the kitchen table and tries to explain what happened. He insists that he did not use magic against Dudley, that it was the Dementors. When Uncle Vernon asks what Dementors are, Aunt Petunia answers, "they are the guards of the Wizard prison, Azkaban." Petunia's revelation shocks everyone, including Petunia, who belatedly covers her mouth with her hands, as if realizing she has just said something horribly obscene. Harry is amazed to find himself sitting in Aunt Petunia's antiseptic kitchen, answering questions about the Wizarding world. Meanwhile, another owl arrives from Arthur, and one from Sirius, briefly telling Harry that the situation is being sorted out. Finally, a second owl from the Ministry of Magic arrives revoking his expulsion and wand destruction. Instead, Harry's fate rests on a hearing scheduled for "9 A.M. on August 12th."

When Harry says Lord Voldemort has returned, Uncle Vernon, recognizing the danger he and his family are in while they house Harry, demands he leave. However, this is interrupted by one final owl carrying a Howler—surprisingly for Petunia Dursley. A menacing voice reverberates throughout the kitchen: "*Remember my last, Petunia!*" Petunia quickly overrides her husband, insisting that Harry remain at their house, on the grounds that sending him away at this point would make the neighbours talk, but sending him to bed immediately. Harry is now once again locked in his room, though we don't know whether this is Vernon's decision or Petunia's. Three days later, Vernon tells Harry that he, Petunia, and Dudley have been invited to a Best Kept Suburban Lawn award, and are leaving Harry alone in the house, locked into his room. Harry listens to them leave. Shortly, the Advance Guard arrives to take him away to the Headquarters of the Order of the Phoenix. As he is leaving, Harry wonders what Vernon will think when he discovers there is no Best Kept Suburban Lawn competition. When Harry returns to London for the summer vacation, he finds Mr. and Mrs. Weasley, Tonks, Lupin, and "Mad Eye" Moody who tell Harry they plan to have a stern talk with his aunt and uncle about how they treat him. The whole group confront Uncle Vernon, intimidating him, despite his initial bluster, into making the necessary concessions for Harry's comfort over the summer, and saying that they will be in touch, either by Harry's owl, or in person.

Half-Blood Prince Although Professor Dumbledore had told Harry he would be arriving only two weeks into the summer vacation to take Harry away to The Burrow, Harry had not told the Dursleys about it, partially out of fear that it would not actually be happening. So when Dumbledore arrives, the Dursleys are stunned almost to insensibility. Dumbledore makes himself at home, and sweeps the Dursleys into a couch; then offers everyone mead. The Dursleys refuse to acknowledge the mead, despite the animated glasses getting more and more insistent about being taken, to the point that one of them ends up bouncing off Vernon's head and spilling most of its contents as it does so. Dumbledore and Harry, meanwhile, discuss Harry's inheritance; Sirius, it seems, had left Harry the house at Grimmauld Place and all its contents. This catches Vernon's attention: Harry owns a house in London? When, in order to test whether the house actually did pass to Harry, Dumbledore summons the house-elf Kreacher, Vernon and Petunia are both revolted at finding this dirty thing in the middle of their spotless living room.

After Harry had packed for school and brought his trunk downstairs, Dumbledore addresses the Dursleys again, saying that he had expected that the Dursleys would treat Harry as one of their own children, rather than maltreating him as they had. However, Harry had apparently not been as poorly served by the Dursleys as the child between them. Both Vernon and Petunia look around at this, as if expecting someone other than Dudley to be present. Dumbledore then says that Harry must return to Privet Drive next summer, at least briefly, but that his magical protection in that place would end when he reached his majority. When Vernon points out that Harry will only be turning seventeen, not eighteen, Dumbledore says that in the Wizarding world, seventeen is the age of majority. Vernon says that's stupid.

At this point, Harry and Dumbledore leave Privet Drive. As this book ends before Harry returns for the summer, Vernon plays no further part in it.

Deathly Hallows Harry, assisted by Kingsley Shacklebolt and Arthur Weasley, has been trying to convince Uncle Vernon to accept the offer of a safe retreat for protection from the chance that Voldemort will attack the house at Privet Drive once Harry's protection there ends. Vernon seems quite happy to speak with Kingsley, who he has seen on television in the company of the Prime Minister, but he still doesn't entirely trust Harry or Arthur. He asks Harry at one point why Kingsley cannot be sent to guard them, and Harry does not have an answer. When we first see Vernon in this book, he has just changed his mind again, saying that he will not leave the house because he expects that Harry would immediately try to transfer title to himself. Harry wearily points out that he already owns a house in London, and that there is nothing that would make him want to stay at Privet Drive anyway.

When the members of the Order of the Phoenix who will be traveling with the Dursleys arrive, Vernon is not particularly reassured. Dedalus Diggle is a very short and bouncy man, whose admission that he doesn't understand all the gadgets in a car is worrying to Vernon, and whose watch, alarmingly, talks, saying that they are late. Hestia Jones, while much less flamboyant, also does not seem to impress Vernon. All the same, the three Dursleys and the two wizards all climb into the Dursleys' car, and the last we see of Vernon is him driving away to safety.

Weaknesses Vernon is a narrow minded and often cruel man. He despises having Harry under his roof and rarely misses a chance to belittle him. Vernon is fearful of the magical world and considers Harry's wizarding abilities an abnormality that must be suppressed and concealed. Vernon loses his temper at any mention of the "M" word.

Relationships with Other Characters Vernon's relationships with other characters are very different in nature, though apparently uniformly shallow. Toward Harry, we see that Vernon makes no accommodation to Harry's needs, such as refusing to sign a Hogsmeade permission slip in Harry's third year. Vernon often restricts Harry to his room for days at a time. Vernon never shows Harry the slightest bit of affection. As Harry matures and becomes more powerful as a wizard, Vernon's feelings towards him shift, becoming less authoritarian and more fearful. By the beginning of the sixth book, Vernon is almost as afraid of Harry as he is of any mature Wizard.

Vernon acts completely differently towards his son, Dudley, showering him with gifts and making nearly infinite allowances for his desires. However, one cannot tell whether Vernon's motivation here is affection towards his son, or simply the need to keep up appearances. Fathers love their sons, so Vernon must show the appearance of loving Dudley.

It is hard to determine Vernon's actual feelings, if any, towards his wife, Petunia, or his sister Marge. It could be that all we see is Vernon acting properly to keep up appearances. However, Vernon again makes great allowances for Marge's foibles and her opinions, wincing as Marge puts the saucer down for her dog, and keeping her liquor glass filled in order to attempt to defuse her diatribe against Harry. Towards Petunia, he has the appearance of the dutiful husband, caring for his wife, but with Petunia herself seeming to discourage intimacy, it is extremely hard to determine what feelings, if any, they have for each other.

Viktor Krum

Gender: Male
Hair color: Unknown
Eye color: Unknown
Related Family: Unknown
Loyalty: Unknown

Overview

Viktor Krum is the representative from the Eastern European school of magic, Durmstrang, in the Triwizard Tournament. He was also on the Bulgarian National Quidditch team. He is Hermione Granger's date for the Yule Ball during the Triwizard Tournament and is therefore seen with jealousy by Ron Weasley.

Role in the Books

Goblet of Fire We are introduced to Viktor Krum at the Quidditch World Cup. Krum is Seeker for the Bulgarian team, and is widely believed to be the best Seeker in the world; he manages to out-fly his opponent on the Irish team repeatedly, and catches the Snitch in the end despite his injuries. When he is not on his broom, his walk is ungainly; he is repeatedly described as "slouching" instead of walking. Ron almost worships Krum, to the point of buying a souvenir figurine of Krum that walks back and forth across his hand with Krum's characteristic duck-like gait. When the representatives of Durmstrang Institute arrive at Hogwarts to enter the Triwizard Tournament, Ron is stunned to realize that Krum is among them—he had not thought that Krum was young enough to still be in school. His hopes of having Krum sit at the Gryffindor table for dinner are dashed, though: the Durmstrang delegation chooses the Slytherin table.

Krum's name is chosen by the Goblet of Fire, making him the Durmstrang champion for the Tournament. His headmaster, Igor Karkaroff, seems to feel that the Goblet has made the only logical choice. Krum does not say much when Harry is also chosen as a Champion; Karkaroff has to do most of his talking for him. During the Fall term, Hermione keeps finding Krum in the library when she goes there to study. She finds this irritating, not because of Krum, but because of the gaggle of giggling girls who seem to follow him around, looking for autographs.

In the first Task of the Tournament, Krum uses the Conjunctivitus curse on his dragon to allow him to get past it and steal the Golden Egg. The dragon, enraged, flails around and breaks some of its own eggs, which costs him points; however, he comes out of the First Task with 40 points, tied for first with Harry.

Krum, it transpires, has invited Hermione to the Yule Ball. This infuriates Ron, though he doesn't really understand why; he thinks that he is angry with Hermione for "consorting with the enemy." After the Ball, Hermione and Ron have a flaming row in the Gryffindor common room, which Hermione ends by saying *"Next time there's a ball, ask me before someone else does, and not as a last resort!,"* and stalking off to the girl's dormitory. Harry later finds an arm on the floor of the dormitory that looks suspiciously like it might have been broken off a figurine of Krum . . .

In the Second Task of the Tournament, the Champions each have to retrieve something of great value to them which is being held by the Merpeople deep under the lake at Hogwarts. The thing of great value to Krum is Hermione. Krum uses a partial Transfiguration spell to give himself a shark head, but is unable to cut Hermione free; Harry, who is there waiting to see if any other hostages need rescuing, hands him a sharp stone that he has picked up off the lake bed. On the surface, Krum seems to be trying to keep Hermione's attention away from Ron and Harry, when they surface. It is during this interval that Krum invites Hermione to visit him in Bulgaria over the summer. After consultation between the judges, Krum is awarded 40 points for the Task, putting him in second place behind Harry and Cedric Diggory, who are tied for first.

Shortly afterwards, Rita Skeeter, writing in *Witch Weekly*, says that Hermione is keeping both Harry and Krum on a string. Hermione wonders how Rita knows that Viktor has invited her to Bulgaria, as she hasn't told anyone. Shortly after the briefing for the Third Task of the Tournament, Krum takes Harry aside to ask if Hermione is Harry's girlfriend. Harry responds that she is not; Krum says she talks about him all the time, and Harry says, that's because they are friends, no more than that. While they are talking, Mr. Crouch emerges from the Forbidden Forest. Krum is at a loss for what to do, but Harry tells him to keep an eye on Crouch, and goes off to fetch Professor Dumbledore. On Harry's return, Crouch is gone, and Krum is Stunned; when Dumbledore revives him, he says that Crouch must have Stunned him.

Being in second place, Krum enters the Third Task maze after Harry and Cedric. Harry finds him performing the Cruciatus Curse on Cedric, Stuns him, and signals that he is out of the competition. It turns out later that Krum was being controlled at the time by Barty Crouch Jr. using the Imperius curse.

After the return of Lord Voldemort, Karkaroff runs. As the Durmstrang delegation prepares to leave Hogwarts at the end of the year, Ron wonders how they are going to get back to school with Karkaroff gone. Krum, who evidently has come to say goodbye to Harry and Hermione, remarks that Karkaroff had not done much of the driving; Krum had been in charge most of the way over and could get them back again easily enough. Finally, Ron unbends enough to ask Krum for his autograph.

Order of the Phoenix Viktor is mentioned in passing when Hermione is trying to get Harry to teach Defence Against the Dark Arts. Hermione says that Viktor had mentioned that Harry could do all sorts of things that Viktor couldn't, and Viktor was in his last year at Durmstrang. Ron, as usual, makes a sarcastic comment about "Vicky," which Hermione dismisses. When Hermione, Harry, and Ron are discussing the events of the final session of Dumbledore's Army before the Christmas break, Hermione is in the middle of writing quite a long letter to Viktor. Ron is again sarcastic about "Vicky," and says darkly that he'd like to be much more than just a pen pal. To the reader, it is quite clear that Ron is correct about Viktor's intentions, that Ron is jealous of Viktor's attentions to Hermione, and, perhaps, that Ron is unaware of these feelings himself.

Half-Blood Prince Viktor Krum is likely still corresponding with Hermione, but no particular mention of that is made in this book.

Deathly Hallows Fleur Delacour has invited Viktor to her wedding; Hermione is quite startled and evidently pleased to see him there. Ron, of course, is jealous.

Harry, disguised as the Weasleys' "Cousin Barny," is sitting at a table with Ron and Hermione when Krum joins them; this inspires Ron to ask Hermione if she'd like to dance. Krum points out Xenophilius Lovegood, saying that he would duel him in other circumstances, because he is wearing the symbol of Grindelwald. He brandishes his wand, reminding Harry of the Weighing of the Wands ceremony in Harry's fourth year, and that reminds him that Mr. Ollivander had said this was a Gregorovitch wand. Harry had been trying to remember where he had heard the name Gregorovitch, and recognizing the source, he says that Krum's wand was made by Gregorovitch. Krum asks where he had heard that, Harry says it was a fan magazine. Krum muses that he didn't think he had spoken to any fan magazines about his wand, and then comments that this was one of the last wands made before Gregorovitch retired. He then inquires whether Ginny Weasley is seeing anyone; Harry says that she is, and that he's big. Viktor expresses displeasure, asking what the point is of being famous if all the good women are taken? Hermione later comments that she had seen Viktor storming away from Xeno Lovegood, and wonders if they had had an argument.

Strengths Viktor is an international standard Quidditch player. He displays a perfect example of the Wronski Feint which impresses the spectators at the Quiddich World Cup.

Weaknesses Viktor is something of a loner and rarely talks unless it is necessary. However, he gets along well with people he knows. While he seems to be quite curt with both Harry and Ron, part of that may be the result of the language barrier; Viktor's native tongue is, of course, one of the Slavic languages, probably Bulgarian.

Relationships with Other Characters Viktor is Hermione Granger's date for the Yule Ball and he also asks her to visit him in Bulgaria. He tells her he has never felt before the way he does about her. Ron Weasley is jealous of Viktor's relationship with Hermione yet he has to grudgingly admit that he is a fan of Viktor as a Quidditch player.

Vincent Crabbe

  Gender: Male
  Hair color: Unknown; "pudding-basin" cut
  Eye color: Unknown
  Related Family: Crabbe, Sr. (a Death Eater)
  Loyalty: Draco Malfoy

OVERVIEW

Vincent Crabbe is one of Draco Malfoy's cronies.

ROLE IN THE BOOKS

Throughout the entire series, Vincent Crabbe has very little independent activity. When we first see him, he has settled into the role of first sidekick to Draco Malfoy, and with very few exceptions, he seems to have no activity separate from Draco for six years of the seven-year span of the story.

Philosopher's Stone When Draco Malfoy introduces himself to Harry Potter on the Hogwarts Express, Gregory Goyle and Crabbe are in attendance. Harry turns Draco's offer of alliance down.

The night after the first Flying lesson, finding that Harry has not, after all, been expelled, Draco challenges him to a Wizard's Duel. Ron immediately volunteers to be Harry's second; Draco selects Crabbe to be his second.

Chamber of Secrets Draco, Crabbe, and Goyle stay at Hogwarts over Christmas. Harry, Ron, and Hermione, attempting to determine whether Draco knows who the Heir of Slytherin is, use Polyjuice Potion to disguise themselves as Slytherins. Ron becomes a copy of Crabbe, while Harry becomes a simulacrum of Goyle. While they do fool Draco, and learn some useful things about him, they only find out that he does not know who the Heir is, either.

Prisoner of Azkaban Draco, Crabbe, and Goyle visit Harry in his compartment on the Hogwarts Express, but are unable to take any action against Harry because of the presence of Professor Lupin.

In an attempt to scare Harry during the Quidditch match between Gryffindor and Ravenclaw, Draco, Crabbe, Goyle, and Marcus Flint dress as Dementors, but their scheme unravels when Harry sends a Patronus to charge them down.

Harry later visits Hogsmeade via the secret passages and the Invisibility cloak; while there with Ron, they run into Draco, Crabbe, and Goyle, who start taunting Ron, believing him to be alone. Harry, from the concealment of his cloak, starts attacking them, but in the process becomes partially visible. Harry then has to hurry back to the school in order to convince Professor Snape that he has not been out of the school.

It is mentioned that during the run-up to the final Quidditch match, between Gryffindor and Slytherin, Crabbe and Goyle repeatedly appear near Harry but end up slouching off, disappointed, when Harry proves too well protected for them to work any mischief on him.

Order of the Phoenix As the two Beaters on the Slytherin Quidditch team, Derrick and Bole, have left, Montague, the Captain, has had to find new ones. The two he has found are Crabbe and Goyle.

In the Quidditch match against Slytherin, Crabbe hits a Bludger at Harry after the whistle, and is harangued for it by Madam Hooch. This is the precipitating event that ends up with a brawl involving Harry, George, and Draco.

It is mentioned that Crabbe is a member of the Inquisitorial Squad. When Umbridge catches Harry in her office, where he has been trying to determine whether Sirius has gone to the Ministry, she also sets the Inquisitorial Squad to round up his helpers. When they bring the helpers into Umbridge's office, it is Crabbe who is holding Neville.

Half-Blood Prince While Draco is working in the Room of Requirement, he believes that he requires a lookout. He forces Crabbe and Goyle to disguise themselves as first-year to third-year girls by means of Polyjuice Potion.

Deathly Hallows When Harry reaches Hogwarts, he hears from Neville that Crabbe and Goyle are finally able to do something well. The Dark Arts classes (renamed from Defence Against the Dark Arts) now include using the Cruciatus Curse on those who have earned detentions, and apparently both Crabbe and Goyle are very good at this. Draco later sees Harry, Ron, and Hermione entering the Room of Requirement, and rounds up Crabbe and Goyle as backup as he no longer has his own wand. When Draco, Crabbe, and Goyle corner Harry in the Room of Requirement, Harry notes that Crabbe seems to have a very soft voice for someone so enormous. Crabbe explains how they had decided to hang back, to see if they could track Harry and bring him to Voldemort for their reward. When Ron calls out, Crabbe pushes a fifty-foot pile of junk over onto him. Harry steadies the pile. When Crabbe tries to repeat the charm, Draco stops him, saying that if they wreck the room, they may lose the diadem. As part of the ensuing attempt to capture Harry, Crabbe creates Fiendfyre, which rapidly consumes everything in the room. Harry, Ron, and Hermione escape on brooms that are stored in the Room of Requirement, and in the process rescue Draco and Goyle, but Crabbe perishes in the fire of his own making.

Relationships with Other Characters He is very good friends with Draco Malfoy and Gregory Goyle. His father (or possibly brother or uncle) was revealed to be a death eater when Voldemort called on him by his surname in *Harry Potter and the Goblet of Fire*.

Analysis

Crabbe, like Goyle, is present only to fill the role of dumb sidekick. The usual "group of bad guys" in many works of fiction consists of a "brain" component, almost always one smart guy or a shrewd guy with a smart guy in the background, and a "brawn" component, one or several muscular goons who exists simply to follow the orders of the smart guy, so that the smart guy doesn't have to risk discovery or injury in order to get his dirty work done. Crabbe and Goyle are almost stereotypical brawn, while Draco is very much the brains of that particular operation.

Walburga Black

Gender: Female
Hair color: gray
Eye color: Unknown
Related Family: Black Family; sons Sirius Black, Regulus Black
Loyalty: Purebloods

Overview

The late Walburga Black is seen only as a portrait on the wall at Number 12, Grimmauld Place, her ancestral home. She is introduced to us by her son, Sirius Black. Her husband was apparently Orion Black, never seen in the books, but mentioned in passing.

Role in the Books

Order of the Phoenix We first see Walburga when Nymphadora Tonks knocks an umbrella stand over in the hall at Grimmauld Place. The curtains covering Walburga's portrait fly open, and she starts cursing the inhabitants of the house, as being Mudbloods and Blood traitors, among other things. Her screaming wakes up the other portraits in the hall, who join in. Nobody can get her to shut up until Sirius appears from the kitchen and wrenches the curtains over her portrait shut. Sirius then comments that he sees Harry has met his mother. He later says that he had been trying to remove her portrait from the wall, but she had apparently put it on with a Permanent Sticking Charm.

When we are later introduced to Kreacher, Sirius tells us that he has been taking instructions for ten years from the portrait of his mad mother. He also, showing a tapestry of the Ancient and Honorable House of Black, mentions that Walburga had evidently burned a hole in the tapestry anywhere there was mention of someone who was not true to her standards of Blood purity. Sirius points out the holes in the tapestry where his name and Andromeda Black's had been, saying that Andromeda had been burned out of the tapestry for daring to marry a Muggle-born, Ted Tonks. Apparently Walburga had also used a Permanent Sticking Charm on the tapestry, because they could not remove that either.

We hear her screaming again when Harry is leaving for school.

While she is certainly still present at Christmas, we don't see much of her then.

Deathly Hallows When Harry first returns to Grimmauld Place with Ron and Hermione, the portrait of Walburga starts screaming at them as soon as they enter the hall. Harry, as the owner of the house, is able to shut her up quickly with, apparently, a single spell.

While she no doubt remains present in the hall as long as the Trio are there resident, she is part of the house at that point and the Trio don't particularly pay her any heed.

Strengths Evidently, Walburga was a strong witch, and very strong-willed. Unfortunately, our only experience is with her "half-mad portrait," which leaves us very little to judge by.

Weaknesses Being a painting, and apparently unwilling or unable to leave her own frame, Walburga can do little apart from scream. Her only way of accomplishing anything is by ordering Kreacher around; in the absence of any commands from the rightful owners of the house (initially Sirius, and later Harry), Kreacher will take Walburga's orders.

Relationships with Other Characters Walburga was angry with her son Sirius because of his rejection of the Black family Pureblood values, and his leaving the family home to stay with James Potter's parents at age 16. It was because of this apparent sympathy for Muggles that she disowned Sirius, blasting his name off the tapestry of the Black family tree. It was a similar action on the part of her brother Alphard that got him similarly disowned and removed.

Sirius tells us that she had liked Regulus because he had remained true to the family Pureblood beliefs. It is uncertain whether she approved of his becoming a Death Eater, but it is certain that she did not disapprove.

QUESTIONS

1. Did Walburga treat Kreacher well, or not? If not, why he talking to, and taking instructions from, her portrait?

Walden Macnair

Gender: Male
Hair color: Black
Eye color: Unknown
Related Family: Unknown
Loyalty: Lord Voldemort

OVERVIEW

Walden Macnair is a tall, strapping wizard, relatively young, with a thin black moustache.

ROLE IN THE BOOKS

Prisoner of Azkaban Macnair is the designated executioner for the Committee for the Disposal of Dangerous Creatures, a committee in the Ministry of Magic. He is brought to Hogwarts School to execute Buckbeak.

Goblet of Fire Lord Voldemort, on his return from near-death, tells Macnair that he will soon have wizards to kill. There being no other Macnairs mentioned to date, we can assume that this is the same Macnair to whom we have already been introduced.

Order of the Phoenix Macnair served as one of Lord Voldemort's envoys to the Giants, and it seems he helped to persuade them to join forces with the Death Eaters. He also fought in the battle in the Department of Mysteries, and was wounded by Neville Longbottom when Neville poked Hermione Granger's wand through the eyehole in his Death Eater mask.

Warrington

Gender: Male
Hair color: Unknown
Eye color: Unknown
Related Family: Unknown
Loyalty: Slytherin House

OVERVIEW

Warrington (no first name) appears to be a Chaser in the Slytherin Quidditch team.

ROLE IN THE BOOKS

Prisoner of Azkaban Warrington is mentioned as being a Chaser in the Slytherin team. No other details are given about him.

Goblet of Fire There is a rumour that Warrington, the big bloke who looks like a sloth, has put his name in the Goblet of Fire, to try to be a champion in the Triwizard Tournament. The rumour is never confirmed.

Order of the Phoenix After Fred and George depart the school, there are a number of attacks against Umbridge's Inquisitorial Squad, of which Warrington is a member. It is mentioned that he goes to the Hospital Wing with a skin condition that makes him look as if he were coated in cornflakes.

When Umbridge catches Harry in her office, where he has been trying to determine whether Sirius has gone to the Ministry, she also sets the Inquisitorial Squad to round up his helpers. Warrington reports that they had also brought Neville, because he interfered when they were trying to bring in Ginny.

Weasley Family

Gender:
Hair color: Red
Eye color: Various
Related Family: n/a
Loyalty:

OVERVIEW

The Weasley Family is one of the older pure-blooded families. Many of the prejudices held by and associated with the "old" families are not held by the Weasleys, nor do the Weasleys take pride (or shame) in their heritage of pure magical blood.

The Weasleys' house is the Burrow, a multi-story magical dwelling located in the fictional village of Ottery St. Catchpole, Devon, United Kingdom (possibly based on the real town of Ottery St Mary).

The Weasleys are considered *blood traitors* because of their charitable dealings with muggles in general. This is exacerbated when they welcome Hermione Granger (a "muggle-born") and Harry Potter (a "half-blood") into their home.

Role in the Books

The Weasley family in general play a very large role in the books; we will simply mention when they are introduced and some small details of the role the family as a whole plays for each book. For detail, please see the individual articles on the Weasleys.

Philosopher's Stone We see Mrs. Weasley and Ginny, and are introduced to four of the Weasley boys: Fred, George, Ron, and Percy. We hear of two others, Bill and Charlie, from Ron, and we hear Ron's dismay at being the sixth Weasley child to pass through Hogwarts. A large part of Ron's worries are caused by the fact that so many of the earlier Weasley children had excelled in some way or other.

Chamber of Secrets We first see the Weasley family and their home as a whole when Fred, George, and Ron extract Harry from captivity in his Uncle Vernon's home. We see the arrival at the Weasley family home, and we get to meet Mrs. Weasley; and shortly afterwards we meet Mr. Weasley. While we see Ginny on a number of occasions, she seems to be largely in retreat; Ron comments that this is unusual, in that she ordinarily never shuts up. Ron does not seem to be aware that Ginny is suffering from a classic schoolgirl crush, possibly because he has lived with Harry for so long that he no longer finds Harry's presence intimidating. Ginny's nervousness in Harry's presence does not abate throughout this book.

Prisoner of Azkaban The Weasley family meet Harry and Hermione in the Leaky Cauldron in Diagon Alley, where they are doing their school shopping. The events of the previous year have burned away some of Ginny's nervousness, but she still is not entirely at her ease speaking with Harry. Mr. and Mrs. Weasley understand from the Ministry that Sirius Black is trying to reach Hogwarts, and it is believed his intent is to kill Harry. The Weasleys have evidently volunteered to protect him until he is actually on the Hogwarts Express. They are of two minds on the mission, however; Mr. Weasley feels that Harry ought to know what is going on, while Mrs. Weasley would prefer to keep him unworried. Harry overhears their conversation, and so Mr. Weasley's platform revelation is not news to him.

Goblet of Fire We meet the remaining two Weasley children, Bill and Charlie. The whole clan has gathered as Mr. Weasley has managed to get tickets for the Quidditch World Cup, and apart from his own family he has elected to include Harry and Hermione in the invitation.

Knowing that Harry's own family, the Dursleys, would not be interested in seeing Harry compete in the Third Task, Mrs. Weasley comes to the school to watch, more or less *in loco parentis*. She brings Bill with her.

Order of the Phoenix Many of the members of the family are at Number 12, Grimmauld Place, when Harry arrives there. the exceptions are Percy, who has had a falling out with Mr. Weasley over the Ministry's treatment of Albus Dumbledore, and Charlie, who is still in Romania working with dragons. Again we see that Mr. Weasley is in favour of telling Harry what is going on, while Mrs. Weasley prefers to have him unworried. We see the whole family's joy at Harry's successful defence at his hearing for underage use of magic. And when Mrs. Weasley's attempts to subdue a Boggart fail, we see her worst fears: in turn, each of her family members and Harry, dead. This last, as little else could, shows how Harry has become like one of the Weasley children in Molly's mind.

Harry's position in the family is reinforced when Harry has a vision of the attack on Mr. Weasley at Christmas. His quick action saves Mr. Weasley's life, and earns him the gratitude of the entire Weasley family.

Half-Blood Prince Harry spends most of his summer vacation at The Burrow, happily staying with the family he has come to appreciate more than his own. The only flaws are the presence of Fleur Delacour who is engaged to Bill, and who does seem to be upsetting Mrs. Weasley; and the occasional presence of Tonks, who seems to be coming around occasionally for solace from Mrs. Weasley, but who forcefully reminds Harry of the death of Sirius. With Fred and George graduated, the family does not gather much at the school; however, Ron conveys an invitation to Harry to join the Weasleys at Christmas, an invitation that he readily accepts. The ongoing battle of wills between Mrs. Weasley and Fleur does cause some tension, and Harry remains irked by the fact that the twins are able to get through their chores rapidly by means of magic, while he and Ron cannot. However, it is still the best family Christmas Harry has ever had.

Deathly Hallows The Weasley family gather together again to provide escape and a safe house for Harry in the days between his escape from Privet Drive and the day of Bill and Fleur's wedding. During the escape, George loses an ear. Harry's birthday, of course, falls into the time that Harry is at the Burrow, and Harry, dismayed at how much work his mere presence has caused, says he doesn't want anything. Mrs. Weasley, however, feels that a wizard's coming of age must be celebrated, and provides a cake and gifts, including a watch. Mrs. Weasley apologizes for the watch, it had been her brother Fabian's. Apparently she had given her other brother Gideon's watch to Ron; the fact that she is giving Harry this precious a family treasure is a clear indication, if we needed one, of how much Mrs. Weasley has come to accept Harry as a family member.

All of the Weasley family take part in the final battles for Hogwarts. In the preparations for the battle, Percy comes back to the family, admitting that he was a deluded fool and asking if the family will accept him back; they promptly do. During the battle itself, Fred is killed by falling masonry.

Relationships with Other Characters Arthur Weasley and Molly Weasley have six sons and a daughter: Bill, Charlie, Percy, identical twins Fred and George, Ron, and Ginny.

Arthur's parents were apparently Septimus Weasley and Cedrella Black, and they had another son, Bilius Weasley. Uncle Bilius was apparently somewhat older than Arthur; he had passed away rather recently, leaving no children.

Molly's father was the brother of Ignatius Prewett (who was married to Lucretia Black), and he had two more sons: twins Gideon Prewett and Fabian Prewett.

Another distant relative mentioned is Auntie Muriel. It is never mentioned whether she is related to the Weasleys or the Prewetts.

ANALYSIS

Although he cannot see it directly, Harry senses a very great contrast between his life in the Muggle world with the Dursleys, and Ron's life in the Burrow. The Dursleys have a determinedly lovely house in a determinedly lovely suburb, with all the right business contacts and all the right accessories, but for all its material richness, it is sterile, even for the people who nominally belong there (Vernon, Petunia, and Dudley. Harry's treatment as an outsider only makes this worse. To contrast this, quite apart from the magic everywhere, the Burrow is impoverished with lots of make do or make it yourself, cramped, and incredibly cheerful. Harry immediately feels at home, this is the sort of family he has dreamed about being a part of for twelve years . . . and to top it off, they accept him instantly as one of their own. (Although it must be noted that Mrs. Weasley never scolds Harry, that we hear; every one of her own children, and even her husband, catches the rough edge of her tongue sooner or later, but Harry does not seem to.)

Wilhelmina Grubbly-Plank

Gender: Female
Hair color: Unknown
Eye color: Unknown
Related Family: Unknown
Loyalty:

OVERVIEW

Wilhelmina Grubbly-Plank is the temporary Care of Magical Creatures professor at Hogwarts School of Witchcraft and Wizardry. She is called in on a number of occasions when the permanent Care of Magical Creatures teacher is "unwell," including a long stretch at the beginning of Harry Potter's fifth year.

ROLE IN THE BOOKS

Goblet of Fire We first meet Professor Grubbly-Plank in the first class after Christmas. Hagrid has gone into hiding because of an article in *The Daily Prophet* which identified him as being half-Giant. While Hagrid has been teaching the class about Blast-Ended Skrewts, Professor Grubbly-Plank starts off by teaching a class on the Unicorn, which everyone except Harry and Ron feels is more like what they expected to learn in that class. (Hermione secretly seems to feel that Professor Grubbly-Plank's lessons are more useful than Hagrids, but we can see her dissembling to spare Hagrid's and Ron's feelings.) Professor Grubbly-Plank continues teaching Care of Magical Creatures for about a week on this occasion.

Order of the Phoenix Harry is dismayed upon returning to Hogwarts to find that it is not Hagrid collecting the first-years for their trip across the lake, but Professor Grubbly-Plank.

Professor Grubbly-Plank teaches Harry's class Care of Magical Creatures. When asked about Hagrid's whereabouts, Professor Grubbly-Plank is abrupt and dismissive. Much later, when she is being inspected by Professor Umbridge, she tells Umbridge that that she doesn't actually know where Hagrid is. Professor Grubbly-Plank starts the year by teaching about Bowtruckles; Harry, overhearing comments from Draco Malfoy about Hagrid, is so angered that he nearly squeezes the one he, Ron, and Hermione are supposed to be drawing in half. Hedwig returns from carrying a message for Harry, arriving an hour later than the usual time for post owls and apparently injured—she is holding one wing oddly. Harry leaves History of Magic class, and goes to the staff room to find someone who might be able to help Hedwig; Professor Grubbly-Plank is there, and says she'll have Hedwig back in shape in a few days. Harry and Professor Grubbly-Plank almost forget the message Hedwig is carrying, which is from Sirius Black.

Inspected by Professor Umbridge in her role as Hogwarts High Inquisitor, Professor Grubbly-Plank passes inspection without difficulty, despite the fact that she obviously supports Dumbledore. Professor Grubbly-Plank continues teaching Care of Magical Creatures up until November when Hagrid returns from his mission.

QUESTIONS

1. Why might Dumbledore have chosen Hagrid instead of Grubbly-Plank to teach Care of Magical Creatures? 2. What are the main differences between Professor Grubbly-Plank's lessons and Hagrid's?

Wilkes

Gender: Male
Hair color: Unknown
Eye color: Unknown
Related Family: Unknown
Loyalty: Lord Voldemort

OVERVIEW

Wilkes was one of the Death Eaters that were part of Lord Voldemort's organization when he first rose to power.

ROLE IN THE BOOKS

Goblet of Fire   When Harry, Ron, and Hermione were visiting Sirius Black in his cave hide-out outside Hogwarts, Sirius mentioned that Wilkes had been one of Severus Snape's friends, and he had been killed by Aurors the year before Voldemort fell.

Wilkie Twycross

Gender: Male
Hair color: wispy
Eye color: colorless
Related Family: Unknown
Loyalty: Ministry of Magic

OVERVIEW

Wilkie Twycross is the Apparation instructor from the Ministry of Magic.

ROLE IN THE BOOKS

Half-Blood Prince   Wilkie Twycross, an oddly insubstantial wizard, starts teaching Apparation to Harry's year group in February. It is a twelve-week course, and the expectation is that at the end of that time, any young Wizard taking the course would be able to pass their Apparation test. The cost of the course is 12 Galleons.

As is only to be expected, as the course progresses, Mr. Twycross is made fun of by many of the wizards taking his course. Ron, in particular, has unkind words for him and his teaching.

Willy Widdershins

Gender: Male
Hair color: Unknown
Eye color: Unknown
Related Family: Unknown
Loyalty: Money

OVERVIEW

Willy Widdershins is apparently a small-time hood and mischief-maker.

ROLE IN THE BOOKS

Order of the Phoenix   Mundungus Fletcher, at the first dinner at the Headquarters of the Order, is overheard regaling the twins and Ron with a story about a large quantity of toads he nicked off one "Will" and then sold back to him. Though "Will"'s last name is never mentioned, it is possible that this is Willy Widdershins.

Just before Harry's hearing at the Ministry, Arthur Weasley mentions that he is trying to track down a prankster who is charming public toilets in Bethnall Green to make them regurgitate.

When Harry and the Weasley family visit Arthur in St. Mungo's Hospital on the afternoon after the snake attack, Arthur has evidently found an article in the *Daily Prophet* saying that Willy Widdershins had been responsible; one of his curses had backfired and he had been found in the toilets covered head to foot in . . . It appears that somehow he got off being charged; Arthur surmises that gold changed hands. Arthur comments that he's since been caught selling biting doorknobs to Muggles, and that two of them had lost fingers and were in St. Mungo's having bones regrown, and seems rather hopeful that he'll actually see them.

At the meeting in Professor Dumbledore's office after Marietta Edgecombe has told Dolores Umbridge about Dumbledore's Army, Umbridge reports to those present that her informant, Willy Widdershins, was at the bar in the Hog's Head when the first meeting of what was then called the Defence Association was held. Although he was heavily bandaged, his hearing was still fine, and he immediately reported what he had overheard to Umbridge. Professor McGonagall, on hearing this, says that now she understands how he got off so lightly for all the regurgitating toilets.

Winky

Gender: Female
Hair color: None
Eye color: Green
Related Family: Unknown
Loyalty: Crouch family

OVERVIEW

Winky is the House Elf of the Crouch family. She is intensely loyal to Bartemius Crouch Sr. .

ROLE IN THE BOOKS

Goblet of Fire   We first meet Winky when she is apparently holding a seat in the Top Box at the Quidditch World Cup for Bartemius Crouch Sr., despite the fact that she is scared of heights. Hermione is incensed that anyone could be so insensitive as to subject a house-elf to such fear. We later see Winky running across a path in the forest near the stadium, apparently talking to herself, and finally she is found Stunned at the spot in the forest where the Dark Mark was conjured, holding the wand that had conjured it. After inconclusive questioning by the Ministry wizards there gathered, Bartemius says he is going to dismiss her, saying "This means Clothes!" Winky is devastated at her dismissal.

We meet her again twice in the kitchens at Hogwarts; Dobby has apparently secured a job for her with the school. Both times, she is simply sitting by the fireplace, mourning her lost Master, and getting steadily more drunk on Butterbeer.

Finally, when Barty Crouch Jr. is unmasked, he says that Winky had been one of the guardians set over him in his captivity in his father's house; and that in fact Winky had been not only holding a seat for him at the World Cup, but he himself had been present there, and it was he who had conjured the Dark Mark, with a wand he had stolen from Harry, leaving Winky to take the blame. Professor Dumbledore summons Winky to take care of him while they wait for the Minister for Magic.

Witherwings

Gender: Male
Hair color: Stormy grey
Eye color: Orange
Related Family: Unknown
Loyalty: Rubeus Hagrid

Overview

Witherwings is an alias for Buckbeak, Hagrid's pet Hippogriff.

Role in the Books

Half-Blood Prince When Sirius Black dies at the end of *Harry Potter and the Order of the Phoenix*, he leaves behind several survivors, notably the house-elf Kreacher and his pet Hippogriff, Buckbeak. While Kreacher was taking care of himself for several years while Sirius was incarcerated, and so is not much of a concern, Buckbeak has no such resources and must be cared for by someone . . . and who better than Rubeus Hagrid, who had been caring for him originally? Of course, Buckbeak was supposed to be executed, so he cannot return under that name; Hagrid renames him to keep the Ministry from trying again.

While he is referred to as Witherwings a few times in the book, the deception is very thin; people don't seem to be able to remember that he is not Buckbeak. Thus, all the events that occur to Witherwings are cataloged under the character entry for Buckbeak.

Relationships with Other Characters Witherwings is treated as a pet by Hagrid, sharing his hut much the way that Fang, Hagrid's boarhound, does.

Xenophilius Lovegood

Gender: Male
Hair color: White
Eye color: Unknown
Related Family: Luna Lovegood
Loyalty: Harry Potter, Crumple-Horned Snorkacks

Overview

Xenophilius Lovegood is the father of Luna Lovegood and publisher of *The Quibbler*.

Role in the Books

Order of the Phoenix Luna Lovegood tells Hermione that her father is the publisher of *The Quibbler*, but we do not meet him or learn his name.

Order of the Phoenix Dobby mentions that he has, a few times, needed a place to put Winky so she could sleep off the effects of the Butterbeer, and has found the Room of Requirement. Harry then uses this room for meetings of Dumbledore's Army.

Deathly Hallows Xenophilius attends the wedding of Bill Weasley and Fleur Delacour wearing stunningly bright robes and a large device consisting of a triangle, with a circle and line inscribed in it. Viktor Krum, who is at the wedding, tells a disguised Harry that that symbol was used by the evil magician Grindelwald for his movement. Harry, Ron, and Hermione, while they are on the run later, hear that *The Quibbler* is printing stories supportive of Harry. They go to visit Xenophilius; he seems reluctant to invite them in, but eventually does so, saying that he has to send an owl to fetch Luna, who is down past the bridge catching Plimpies for soup. Explaining that the symbol he had worn was the sigil of the three Deathly Hallows, he asks Hermione to read the story of the Three Brothers from her copy of *the Tales of Beedle the Bard*. The three brothers receive items from Death, because they have tricked him: one asks for a wand more powerful than any other, one asks for a stone that can return people from death, and one asks for Death's own invisibility cloak. Xenophilius explains that these are the three Hallows, and the symbols of them are the triangle for the invisibility cloak, the circle for the resurrection stone, and the line for the wand.

Xenophilius then departs to make some soup, and Harry investigates an upstairs room, finding what is evidently Luna's room, with painted portraits of himself and other members of Dumbledore's Army. He discovers that it has apparently not been used for some time, which is odd; Luna should be home for Christmas break. When Xenophilius returns, Harry asks him again where Luna is; the printing press, which has been making copies of the Quibbler all this time, suddenly spits an entire stack of papers over the floor, and Harry finds that the Quibbler has suddenly taken up the official line, that Harry is "Undesirable Number One" and should be arrested.

Xenophilius admits that he has sent an owl to the Ministry; Luna is being held captive to force him to toe the party line. As the Ministry wizards arrive, Xenophilius attempts to Stun Harry, but misses and causes an Erumpent horn (which he had purchased believing it to be the horn of a Crumple-Horned Snorkack) to explode. Hermione, Ron, and Harry make their escape in the confusion, making sure that the Death Eaters see Harry and Hermione so that Xenophilius will not be punished for lying about Harry being there. We hear later that Xenophilius has been arrested, though we don't hear details.

Analysis

"Xenophilius" is accurately named, as it translates to "love of the strange" or "love of strange things."

Yaxley

Gender: Male
Hair color: Unknown
Eye color: Unknown
Related Family: Unknown
Loyalty: Lord Voldemort

Overview

Yaxley is a Death Eater who was apparently part of Lord Voldemort's organization the first time Voldemort came to power.

Role in the Books

Half-Blood Prince   Yaxley is mentioned only in passing, by Severus Snape, as being one of the other Death Eaters who had not sought the Dark Lord after he had vanished.

Deathly Hallows   Yaxley appears out of thin air on the first page of the book, and is greeted by Severus Snape as they go in to Malfoy Manor for a council with Lord Voldemort. In the rank-based positioning of people around the table, Yaxley is placed near midpoint, while Snape sits at Voldemort's right hand. Yaxley reports that according to Dawlish, an Auror that he has Confunded, Harry Potter will be moved from Privet Drive the day before his birthday. Snape says that this is a false trail, that Harry will be moved before that date. Yaxley says that they have sveral people in the Department of Magical Transport and will know if Harry uses the Floo network or tries to Apparate; Snape says that he will not, the Order distrusts everything to do with the Ministry. Yaxley also says that he has managed to place Pius Thicknesse, the head of Magical Law Enforcement, under the Imperius Curse, which Voldemort comments is a first step towards taking over the Ministry.

Harry, Ron, and Hermione enter the Ministry of Magic to try and find the locket Horcrux. Ron is disguised as a maintenance worker named Cattermole. Yaxley sees Cattermole/Ron and tells him that it is raining in his office, and to correct it immediately. He also comments that Cattermole's wife is currently in front of the Muggle-Born Registration Commission, and says that it will be harder on her if his office is not put back to normal. Harry recognizes Yaxley as one of the Death Eaters who had witnessed the death of Albus Dumbledore.

As Harry, Ron, and Hermione depart the Ministry after their mission, Yaxley catches Hermione and is dragged along to Grimmauld Place by side-along Apparation. Hermione then hits him with a Revulsion Jinx, but because he has seen the door to Grimmauld Place, he may now be able to enter the house.

When Harry enters the Forbidden Forest after the first Battle at Hogwarts, he must pass a couple of guards, Yaxley and Dolohov, on his way to where Voldemort is waiting.

Zacharias Smith

   Gender: Male
   Hair color: Blond
   Eye color: Unknown
   Related Family: Unknown
   Loyalty:

Overview

Zacharias Smith is a member of Dumbledore's Army. He is rather obnoxious, and nobody in Dumbledore's Army seems to like him. He contrasts the Hufflepuff ideal of "loyal, kind, and hard-working."

Role in the Books

Order of the Phoenix   Zacharias Smith is present at the first meeting of what will become Dumbledore's Army at the Hog's Head. Zacharias wonders out loud what Harry would have to teach them, given that he has said himself that he didn't do a lot of the stuff on his own, and the other students there present start listing off his accomplishments. He subsides, after a half-joking threat from Fred and George.

When Educational Decree Number Twenty-Four, banning all student groups that have not been approved by the Hogwarts High Inquisitor, is published, Ron immediately guesses that Zacharias Smith had told on them. Hermione says that that is impossible, as if he had, a spell on the parchment they had all signed would give him an awful set of facial blemishes.

At the first actual meeting of Dumbledore's Army, in the Room of Requirement, Harry elects to start the class off with the Disarming charm. Zacharias says this is too simple a charm to start with. Harry responds that it worked well enough against Voldemort, but Zacharias is free to leave if he feels the material is beneath him. Professor Dumbledore requires that Harry learn Occlumency after Christmas, and assigns Professor Snape to be his instructor. Snape, telling Harry this, instructs him to explain this, if necessary, by saying he is taking Remedial Potions. When he must explain the new schedule for meetings of Dumbledore's Army, Zacharias is particularly supercilious.

Harry does note that Zacharias seems to be working harder in his classes after the mass breakout from Azkaban. Some time after this, though, Dumbledore's Army is betrayed, and Zacharias does not enter our story again in this book.

Half-Blood Prince   With the departure of Lee Jordan at his graduation at the end of the previous book, there is no announcer for Quidditch, so Zacharias is announcing the match between Slytherin and Gryffindor. Starting off being openly critical of Harry's choice of Ron Weasley as Keeper and Ginny Weasley as one of the three Chasers, he shortly changes his tune as Ginny scores the majority of the goals against Slytherin and Ron stops everything that comes his way. He remains critical of Gryffindor, however, until the end of the match. Swooping down to join the Gryffindor victory celebration, Ginny "forgets to brake" and runs into the announcer's tower, sending Zacharias tumbling onto the field in a shower of wood.

Zacharias is not, apparently, asked to announce for any other games; that honour passes to Luna Lovegood.

Deathly Hallows   We only see Smith in passing: as the underage wizards in the school are being evacuated to safety, Harry sees Zacharias Smith knocking several of them over in his haste to reach the Room of Requirement and the passage to safety at the Hog's Head.

PLACES

COMMON

Places where many events happen and/or where the characters spend a great deal of time.
- Hogwarts School of Witchcraft and Wizardry
- Gryffindor House
- Hufflepuff House
- Ravenclaw House
- Slytherin House
- Headmaster's Office
- The Burrow
- Hogsmeade
- The Shrieking Shack
- Zonko's Joke Shop
- The Hog's Head Inn
- The Three Broomsticks
- Honeyduke's Sweetshop
- Platform 9–3/4
- Number 4 Privet Drive, Little Whinging, Surrey

SPECIAL

Places that are only visited once or a handful of times but where significant events may have occurred.
- Diagon Alley
- The Leaky Cauldron
- Apothecary
- Eeylops Owl Emporium
- Florean Fortescue's Ice Cream Parlor
- Flourish and Blotts
- Gambol and Japes Wizarding Joke Shop
- Gringotts
- Madam Malkin's Robes for All Occasions
- Magical Menagerie
- Ollivanders: Makers of Fine Wands since 382 B.C.
- Quality Quidditch Supllies
- Weasleys' Wizard Wheezes
- Godric's Hollow
- Number 12 Grimmauld Place
- in or near Hogwarts
- Chamber of Secrets
- The Forbidden Forest
- Room of Requirement
- Knockturn Alley
- Borgin and Burkes
- Little Hangleton
- House of Gaunt
- Riddle Manor
- Malfoy Manor
- Ministry of Magic
- Shell Cottage
- Spinner's End
- St. Mungo's Hospital for Magical Maladies and Injuries

REFERENCE

Places that are only referenced but are significant enough to be known amongst certain characters.
- Azkaban Prison
- Beauxbatons Academy of Magic
- Durmstrang Institute

Azkaban

Location: Unknown
Permanent Residents: Dementors
First Appearance: *Harry Potter and the Philosopher's Stone*

GENERAL OVERVIEW

Azkaban is the wizard prison.

Extended Description Azkaban is a horrendous place, where Sirius Black, along with many Death Eaters, were imprisoned after Lord Voldemort fell from power. Guarded by the hideous dementors, it is located on a remote island and is virtually escape proof. According to Lupin, it is a "fortress . . . set on a tiny island, way out to sea, but they don't need walls and water to keep the prisoners in, not when they're all trapped inside their own heads, incapable of a single cheerful thought. Most of them go mad within weeks." Sirius Black is the first person known to have escaped. Although several Death Eaters also later escaped, it is believed they were able to escape only because the Dementors had left the prison, having been promised richer feeding if they became loyal to Voldemort.

The first mention of Azkaban is in *Harry Potter and the Philosopher's Stone*, when it is mentioned only in passing. In *Harry Potter and the Chamber of Secrets*, we are properly introduced to the nature of the place, when it is decided in the Ministry that Hagrid, who was accused of opening the Chamber fifty years earlier, was responsible for opening it again, and had sent him to Azkaban as a preventative measure. We see Hagrid's fear of the place, and his relief at being released. However, the full nature of the place is not fully explained until *Harry Potter and the Prisoner of Azkaban*.

From there, it is mentioned in passing, as people are arrested and sent to Azkaban, and as people break out.

By *Harry Potter and the Half-Blood Prince*, the reader may begin to feel, correctly as it turns out, that Azkaban should be fitted with revolving doors.

Past and Present Prisoners of Azkaban • Sirius Black—arrested for the murder of Peter Pettigrew and twelve Muggles, imprisoned without trial, escaped
 • Crabbe—arrested after the Battle at the Ministry
 • Barty Crouch Jr.—arrested shortly after the initial disappearance of Voldemort, for the torture of Alice and Frank Longbottom
 • Antonin Dolohov—arrested during or after Voldemort's first reign, escaped after the Dementors left Azkaban, returned to Azkaban after the Battle at the Ministry, escaped
 • Mundungus Fletcher—arrested for impersonating an Inferius
 • Marvolo Gaunt—arrested for attacking an officer of the Ministry, completed sentence, died shortly after.
 • Morfin Gaunt—arrested for attacking an officer of the Ministry and using magic on a Muggle, released, re-arrested for murder of the Riddle family, died in prison
 • Rubeus Hagrid—arrested and held without trial on suspicion of being the person who released the Monster in the Chamber, released
 • Jugson—arrested after the Battle in the Ministry
 • Igor Karkaroff—arrested during Voldemort's first reign, plea-bargained for a shorter sentence, presumably released
 • Bellatrix Lestrange—arrested shortly after the initial disappearance of Voldemort, for the torture of Alice and Frank Longbottom, escaped
 • Rabastan Lestrange—arrested shortly after the initial disappearance of Voldemort, for the torture of Alice and Frank Longbottom, escaped
 • Rodolphus Lestrange—arrested shortly after the initial disappearance of Voldemort, for the torture of Alice and Frank Longbottom, escaped
 • Walden Macnair—arrested after the Battle at the Ministry
 • Lucius Malfoy—arrested after the Battle at the Ministry, escaped
 • Mulciber—arrested during Voldemort's first reign
 • Nott—arrested after the battle at the Ministry
 • Sturgis Podmore—arrested for trying to get through a sealed door at the Ministry, sentenced to six months
 • Augustus Rookwood—arrested for passing secrets to Voldemort in his first reign, on information from Karkaroff; escaped after the Dementors left Azkaban, returned to Azkaban after the Battle at the Ministry, escaped
 • Stan Shunpike—arrested for boasting about being aware of Death Eater secrets, escaped
 • Travers—arrested in Voldemort's first reign, escaped

ANALYSIS

Quite clearly, the first thing one must do when you imprison a wizard is to confiscate his wand; a wizard with a wand is as well-armed as a Muggle with a gun, and significantly more capable. Yet wizards do have some ability to perform magic without wands; we see Harry do so on a number of occasions, when his tension is particularly high. We also believe Apparation does not require wands. There are evidently spells that can prevent Apparation, and of course those must be set on the prison proper. That does leave the possibility of an escape being carried out by a Wizard or Witch who does wandless magic when very tense. This may be the rationale for the Dementors: by damping all good feelings, it may be impossible for the prisoners to become agitated enough to perform wandless magic.

One does rather feel that the use of Dementors is a bit excessive, however. You do not rehabilitate an evil wizard by driving him insane. However, we must also note that the entire penal situation in the Wizarding world seems a bit excessive, as people are imprisoned for lengthy periods without benefit of trial—Rubeus Hagrid, for instance, is imprisoned for some months on suspicion alone, and Sirius Black is imprisoned for twelve years without a trial. Granted that this situation may have sprung from adversity, and have been done in reaction to the appearance and activities of Voldemort, still one would think that with the threat abated, the use of Azkaban might fall off. That does not seem to happen, however.

GREATER PICTURE

We find out in *Harry Potter and the Prisoner of Azkaban* that the Animagus transformation does not require a wand, as Sirius is able to transform when he is incarcerated and thus wandless. We believe he was able to escape because he was an unregistered Animagus; presumably, there is some way to prevent the transformation that would be used on an incarcerated registered Animagus, likely a variant of the unnamed spell that Sirius and Lupin used to unmask Peter Pettigrew.

As mentioned, the use of Azkaban as a deterrent in the series seems to be excessive; it is only after Voldemort's second fall, and the accession of Kingsley Shacklebolt to the position of Minister for Magic, that the penal system is returned to what it should be. J.K. Rowling mentioned, in one of the interviews she gave after the release of *Harry Potter and the Deathly Hallows*, that after Voldemort's death, one of the things Kingsley Shacklebolt does as Minister for Magic is to retire control of Azkaban from the Dementors. This is part of what makes the magical world in the epilogue of the book "a sunnier one."

Beauxbatons Academy of Magic

Location: probably southern France
Permanent Residents: Olympe Maxime
First Appearance: *Harry Potter and the Goblet of Fire*

GENERAL OVERVIEW

Beauxbatons Academy is a wizarding academy, similar to Hogwarts School, believed to be located somewhere in France. It is run by headmistress Madame Maxime and is traditionally a competitor in the Triwizard Tournament against Hogwarts and Durmstrang Institute.

Extended Description We first hear of Beauxbatons Academy during the riots after the Quidditch World Cup. Harry, Ron, Hermione, Fred, George, and Ginny are sent off into the forest nearby to keep them out of the way of the violence. As they travel through the woods, they meet another group of teenagers who speak to them in French. When Harry replies in English, one of the teenagers responds with a disdainful "'Ogwarts," and returns to his companions. Hermione mentions that they must be from a French Wizarding school. This is something of a surprise to Harry; the thought that there must be Wizarding schools in other countries evidently had not occurred to him. The Beauxbatons students taking part in the Triwizard Tournament arrive on 30 October in a carriage the size of a small house drawn by a team of large winged horses. The only Beauxbatons student we are introduced to, Fleur Delacour, ends up as the Beauxbatons Champion. We also meet the headmistress, Madam Maxime. Once the horses have been been harnessed to the carriage at the end of the year, and the Beauxbatons contingent has departed, this school does not return to our story.

In the films, Beauxbatons is portrayed as an all girls' school, but the books clearly indicate that boys attend the school as well—it is a boy who gets out of the carriage to lower the steps, for instance, and at the Yule Ball, Parvati Patil and her sister Padma end up dancing with Beauxbatons boys when Ron and Harry prove disappointing.

Fleur Delacour mentions at one point during Harry's sixth year that the students at Beauxbatons take their first exams in their sixth year, unlike Hogwarts' students who take O.W.L. exams in their fifth year.

Borgin and Burkes

Location: Knockturn Alley, London
Permanent Residents: Mr. Borgin (shopkeeper)
First Appearance: *Harry Potter and the Chamber of Secrets*

General Overview

Borgin & Burkes is a shop in Knockturn Alley that specializes in Dark magical artifacts.

Extended Description In *Harry Potter and the Chamber of Secrets*, when Harry is using Floo powder to get to Diagon Alley, he accidentally turns up in Borgin & Burkes. Rapidly concealing himself, he overhears Lucius Malfoy selling some dark magical items so that the Ministry would not find them in his house.

Among the Dark artifacts that we see in this store are a Hand of Glory and a cursed necklace. We should also note that the large black cabinet that Harry hides in is a Disappearing Cabinet. All three of these artifacts will play roles in later stories.

In *Harry Potter and the Half-Blood Prince*, Harry, Hermione, and Ron sneak off from Weasleys' Wizard Wheezes and follow Draco Malfoy to Borgin & Burkes, where by means of Extendable Ears, they overhear Malfoy telling Borgin that he needs something fixed. He also needs to buy another object but cannot take it with him. He doesn't want Borgin to tell anyone about it, not even his own mother, and threatens Borgin with one Fenrir Greyback, who he says is an old family friend. After Malfoy leaves, Hermione goes into the store and attempts to determine what it is that Malfoy had bought, but without success.

In that same book, we also learn that following his 7th year at Hogwarts, Tom Riddle worked there for a time, much to the surprise of everyone who knew him. We learn that it was while he was employed at Borgin & Burkes that he discovered that Hepzibah Smith owned artifacts of two of the Hogwarts founders: Hufflepuff's cup and Slytherin's locket.

Greater Picture

The artifacts that we see in Borgin and Burkes, the Hand of Glory, the cursed necklace, and the Disappearing Cabinet, will re-appear, as mentioned above. The Disappearing Cabinet is apparently one of a pair; the second one is dropped by Peeves in *Harry Potter and the Chamber of Secrets* to provide a distraction. In *Harry Potter and the Order of the Phoenix*, Fred and George force Montague into the same disappearing cabinet, and the following year, Draco Malfoy repairs it and uses it and its mate at Borgin and Burkes to manage an invasion of Hogwarts by Death Eaters. The jinxed necklace is given to Katie Bell to give to someone at Hogwarts, possibly Professor Dumbledore, but she touches it on her way back to the school and is nearly fatally cursed. The Hand of Glory, finally, is used by Draco as he leads the Death Eaters into the school. Having been discovered by members of Dumbledore's Army guarding that spot, Draco throws Peruvian Instant Darkness Powder, then uses the Hand of Glory to navigate himself and the Death Eaters through the resulting darkness.

It is interesting to see that as early as the second book, the author would have been aware of the need for an artifact like the Hand of Glory in the sixth book, and would take the steps necessary to introduce it and its properties to us.

Chamber of Secrets

Location: Hogwarts
Permanent Residents: Basilisk
First Appearance: *Harry Potter and the Chamber of Secrets*

General Overview

At the time of his departure from Hogwarts, after a falling out with the other three founders of the school, Salazar Slytherin is supposed to have created a chamber, placed a monster within it, and sealed it so that only his true heir could open it. In the centuries since that time, this "chamber of secrets" has been sought many times, but never found.

Extended Description The Chamber was in fact opened, approximately fifty years before the time of the Harry Potter series, by Tom Riddle (who later styled himself as Lord Voldemort). At that time, the monster within the Chamber, a basilisk, killed a girl (Moaning Myrtle); this put the school on the verge of closing down, because it was obviously unsafe to keep students there. The threat of being forced to leave the school was sufficient to cause Riddle to re-seal the chamber. Riddle was as fond of his *home* as Harry was. Riddle managed to frame Rubeus Hagrid and Aragog as being the Heir and the monster respectively; as the Chamber was not then re-opened, and no more victims fell to the basilisk, Riddle's version of events became accepted as fact by all except, perhaps, Professor Dumbledore. Harry's re-opening of the Chamber and defeat of the basilisk should have cleared Hagrid's name; it did secure his release from Azkaban, where he had been consigned when it was thought that he was once again opening the Chamber.

The key to opening the Chamber is Parseltongue; one must say "open" to the entrance in Parseltongue for it to open. The ability to speak to snakes has been linked to Slytherin's descendants, thus the belief that only the true heir of Slytherin can open the Chamber.

Ron and Hermione re-enter the chamber in Harry's seventh year; knowing that Basilisk venom will destroy a Horcrux, and having a Horcrux they need to destroy, Ron, who has twice now heard Harry pronounce the word "Open" on Parseltongue, opens the Chamber by imitating the sound of the word. When Harry sees them, they are carrying the destroyed Horcrux and a great stock of Basilisk fangs.

According to J. K. Rowling's instructions to the filmmakers who made the film of Chamber of Secrets, the chamber itself is located under the lake on the Hogwarts grounds. (Source: Interview with the filmmakers on the extended features of the DVD release.)

QUESTIONS

1. We are told that Salazar Slytherin lived a thousand years or so ago, and presumably created the chamber then. While castles of the era did have interior toilets ("garderobes") in the Muggle world, running water was only invented barely two hundred years ago. Suggest a reason that the mark of Slytherin, that opened the passage to the Chamber, could have been placed on a faucet.

GREATER PICTURE

As mentioned, only a Parselmouth can open the Chamber, and it is widely believed that the ability to speak Parseltongue is only passed to the heirs of Slytherin. As an heir of Slytherin, Tom Riddle could certainly be expected to speak Parseltongue, and so he is able to open the Chamber. Harry, with a piece of Tom's soul, is equally able to speak the language, and apparently Dumbledore has learned it, although Dumbledore did not try to find the Chamber. One must wonder why he did not; as a teacher at the school the first time the Chamber was opened, he must have had all the clues that Harry was working with. Perhaps he did not learn Parseltongue until much later in his life, and time had made the need to find the Chamber less pressing.

Ron and Hermione later managed to open the Chamber; in need of something to destroy the cup Horcrux, they visited the Chamber to retrieve some Basilisk fangs, which apparently still had sufficient venom to destroy the Horcrux. Ron had been present when Harry opened the locket Horcrux, another artifact of Slytherin's which would open only when addressed in Parseltongue, and simply parroted the sounds Harry had made to open the locket, in order to open the Chamber.

Diagon Alley

Location: London
Permanent Residents: Unknown
First Appearance: *Harry Potter and the Philosopher's Stone*

GENERAL OVERVIEW

Diagon Alley is the main wizarding shopping street in London. On this street we can find any number of shops specifically for wizards, including an apothecary, Eeylops Owl Emporium, Florean Fortescue's Ice Cream Parlor (which actually sounds like a nice place for Muggles as well), Flourish and Blott's bookstore, Gringott's Wizarding Bank, Madam Malkin's Robes for All Occasions, The Magical Menagerie pet store, Ollivanders: Makers of Fine Wands since 382 B.C., and Quality Quidditch Supplies. The Leaky Cauldron pub backs onto this street, and the entrance to Knockturn Alley lies in this street as well. The merchants of Diagon Alley are well prepared for the annual influx of students needing to buy supplies for their year at Hogwarts.

Extended Description Located behind the Leaky Cauldron pub, open to the sky, but somehow invisible to Muggles, Diagon Alley is an old-fashioned street lined with quaint buildings that house traditional shops serving the wizarding community. There are many more stores than are named; for instance, the first time he enters Diagon Alley in *Harry Potter and the Philosopher's Stone*, Harry sees a shop selling cauldrons. The shop is never named, but presumably Harry does buy his cauldron there. Likewise, the store where he buys his telescope is unnamed.

Many of the stores in Diagon Alley have some significance to the series and some are visited repeatedly. The Apothecary is never named, but Harry must visit it each year for potion ingredients. He is initially quite intrigued by the available supplies, but apparently these become commonplace to him, as there is no mention of them after Harry's first year.

• Eeylops' Owl Emporium is a store specializing in owls and supplies for them, which of course serve both as pets and as as a carrier of communications in the Wizarding world. Harry receives an owl from Hagrid as a birthday present; this owl, Hedwig, remains Harry's companion through much of the series.

- Florean Fortescue's Ice Cream Parlour plays a relatively minor role. Hagrid, on Harry's first visit to Diagon Alley, presents him with a large ice cream, which one supposes must have come from Fortescue's establishment. Harry spends a fortnight in Diagon Alley at the start of *Harry Potter and the Prisoner of Azkaban*, during which time he spends nearly every day in Fortescue's. In the sixth book, *Harry Potter and the Half-Blood Prince*, we hear that Fortescue has vanished, and damage to his store indicates that he didn't leave willingly. It is assumed that he has been captured by Death Eaters.
- Flourish and Blott's bookstore is so overloaded with Spell books that it apparently takes magic to keep its shelves from tipping over. This is where Harry, Ron, and Hermione buy their school books most years. This is also the scene of a confrontation between Lucius Malfoy and Arthur Weasley which escalates to physical violence, in *Harry Potter and the Chamber of Secrets*.
- Gringott's Wizarding Bank is the one place where Wizards keep their money. Harry visits Gringott's in the first book, where he is astonished to find that his parents have left a large amount of money in the vaults for him, and further that quite a lot of it is actually in gold. Visiting again later, in company with the Weasley family, he is rather embarrassed to see how very little is in their vault, compared to what is in his. In *Harry Potter and the Deathly Hallows*, Harry determines that one of the Horcruxes is, in fact, stored in a deep vault at Gringott's. Harry and Professor Dumbledore between them have decided that the places where Voldemort had hidden his Horcruxes were all places of deep significance to Voldemort; while one would think that putting it away in a bank would be relatively pedestrian, the deep vaults are all used only by the very oldest of Wizarding families, so having the key to one of them, and having possessions stored in one of them, would be a clear indication of the age of the family. As we have seen throughout the series, Voldemort values almost nothing more highly than ancestry.
- The Leaky Cauldron pub backs onto Diagon Alley, and is the main connection between Diagon Alley and Muggle London. When Harry first sees the Muggle-side entrance, in *Harry Potter and the Philosopher's Stone*, he has a feeling that only he and Hagrid, among all those passing by, can actually see it. The Leaky Cauldron is apparently the destination flue associated with the address "Diagon Alley" on the Floo network; naming Diagon Alley as your destination, according to Mrs. Weasley in *Harry Potter and the Chamber of Secrets*, brings you to the Leaky Cauldron. Harry stays in the Leaky Cauldron for a fortnight before school starts in *Harry Potter and the Prisoner of Azkaban*, and overhears a rather important conversation there between Mr. and Mrs. Weasley. Most of the remaining visits, however, are quite abbreviated.
- Madam Malkin's Robes for All Occasions is a shop selling wizard's robes, school uniforms, and general wizard wear. Harry meets Draco for the first time here, though we don't learn Draco's name until later. Harry and Hermione also have a run-in with Narcissa Malfoy and Draco in this store, in *Harry Potter and the Half-Blood Prince*.
- The Magical Menagerie pet store, like Eeylops, offers pets tailored to the needs of wizards, but has a much more varied selection. It is here that Ron looks for information about his rat, Scabbers, who has been looking poorly since they returned from Egypt in *Harry Potter and the Prisoner of Azkaban*, and it is here that Hermione buys her cat, Crookshanks. While we do see a number of interesting creatures in this store, we only visit it in this one book.
- Ollivander's: Makers of Fine Wands since 382 b.c., where Harry buys his first wand, is run by Mr. Ollivander. It is here that Harry learns that the core of his wand is a tail feather from the same phoenix that provided the core of Voldemort's wand, a revelation that leaves him feeling not a little uneasy. Ron's wand, in his fourth year, and Neville's, in his sixth, apparently come from Ollivander's store as well, though as Harry has no further need to visit the store, we don't see the inside of it again. We do hear, in the sixth book, that Ollivander himself has vanished, but that his store has not been damaged, leading to questions concerning his fate.
- Quality Quidditch Supplies, a store that provides Quidditch supplies and racing brooms, plays a large part in Harry's imagination as it is the source of the racing brooms that he covets, particularly after he learns that he is a natural flyer. Harry first sees the Nimbus 2000 broom here, and the Firebolt; and it is from this store, we learn later, that the Firebolt Harry receives at Christmas in *Harry Potter and the Prisoner of Azkaban* was purchased.

ANALYSIS

Diagon Alley is *the* place to be for someone who wants to sell to the wizarding population. To a lesser extent, Hogsmeade, with Hogwarts School in close proximity, is a center of Wizarding commerce as well; but it is a sign that you have arrived as a retailer if you have a store front in Diagon Alley. Thus it is a sign of great things that the Weasley twins, having left school in the middle of their seventh year under rather a large cloud, were able to immediately open a shop in Diagon Alley. *Weasley's Wizard Wheezes* is mentioned in passing in *Harry Potter and the Order of the Phoenix*, and in some detail during the next year.

GREATER PICTURE

To a surprisingly large extent, Diagon Alley is a gauge of the health of the Wizarding world as a whole. As times get tense, it can be seen immediately in the actions of the crowds in the street (for instance, during *Harry Potter and the Half-Blood Prince*); and as Voldemort gains power, stores in Diagon Alley are shuttered or boarded up, and their occupants (notably Florean Fortescue and Mr. Ollivander) depart for places unknown. The same effect is seen in Hogsmeade, where some stores, like Zonko's Joke Shop, are suddenly and inexplicably vacant.

Durmstrang Institute

Location: probably western Russia
Permanent Residents: Unknown
First Appearance: *Harry Potter and the Goblet of Fire*

GENERAL OVERVIEW

Durmstrang Institute is a wizarding academy, similar to Hogwarts School, believed to be located somewhere in Bulgaria. When we first hear of it, it is run by headmaster Professor Karkaroff and is traditionally a competitor in the Triwizard Tournament against Hogwarts and Beauxbatons Academy of Magic.

Extended Description Karkaroff is a former Death Eater who avoided spending time in Azkaban by selling out his fellow Death Eaters to the Ministry. As such, when Voldemort returns, Karkaroff flees, and nothing is heard of him for slightly over a year. We do not know who becomes headmaster in his absence.

In *Harry Potter and the Goblet of Fire,* Draco Malfoy, on the Hogwarts Express, mentions that he could have gone to Durmstrang, and that they actually teach Dark magic there (although use of Dark Magic outside classes is forbidden). Apparently he had been discussing the Triwizard Tournament with his cronies, but we don't find out about the Tournament until a short while later.

The Durmstrang contingent arrive for the Triwizard Tournament in a ship that surfaces in the middle of the lake at Hogwarts. Their headmaster hustles them inside the castle because "Viktor" has a cold. Ron is astounded to discover that "Viktor" is the famous Quidditch Seeker, Viktor Krum.

With Karkaroff having fled, Ron worries that, at the end of the school year, the Durmstrang group may be stuck at Hogwarts with nobody to sail their ship back home. Viktor reassures him that there will be no problem; the Headmaster had stayed in his cabin for almost the entire outward trip, leaving the ship handling to the students, so they were well prepared to handle the voyage.

We learn in *Harry Potter and the Deathly Hallows* that Gellert Grindelwald was educated at Durmstrang. Viktor Krum, when he had been a student there, was disturbed because Grindelwald's symbol, a line within a circle within a triangle, was a fairly frequent piece of graffiti, and because many students claimed to harbour Grindelwald's beliefs about the inherent superiority of Wizards over Muggles.

ANALYSIS

Sturm und Drang (German for storm and stress) is probably where the name Durmstrang was brought from.

Forbidden Forest

Location: On the Hogwarts grounds
Permanent Residents: Aragog, Bane, Ronan, Firenze
First Appearance: *Harry Potter and the Philosopher's Stone*

GENERAL OVERVIEW

The Forbidden Forest is a patch of untamed forest that grows on the grounds of Hogwarts School. It is home to many magical creatures, including unicorns and centaurs, and is more or less in the charge of Rubeus Hagrid, Keeper of the Keys and Grounds. Hagrid's hut is located on the very edge of the Forest. The Forest has received its name because it is forbidden to all students, except in special circumstances.

Extended Description The Forbidden Forest is not as forbidden as the name implies; quite often students are taken to the very edge and even within it as part of their Care of Magical Creatures studies, starting in Year 3. In *Harry Potter and the Philosopher's Stone,* Harry, Hermione, Neville, and Draco Malfoy serve a detention in the Forest supervised by Hagrid. Presumably, the prohibition is to prevent students from going unaccompanied into the Forest, although that is never explicitly stated.

ANALYSIS

In order to have Care of Magical Creatures classes, there must be magical creatures; part of the Forbidden Forest's function is to provide a near-by habitat. Because they were studied in Care of Magical Creatures, it is known that Unicorns, Bowtruckles, Hippogriffs, and Thestrals live there; also encountered are Centaurs and Acromantulae. A Werewolf briefly roamed there as well some twenty years ago, and apparently the rumours of his presence remain.

The Forest is an uncharted and wild place where the unexpected happens. This can be gauged by Ron's unwillingness to go into the Forest in *Harry Potter and the Chamber of Secrets;* he believes there are werewolves in there and, suffering arachnophobia, fears meeting spiders.

The Forest also provides concealment. In *Harry Potter and the Goblet of Fire,* an arena is constructed for the Tri-Wizard Tournament's first challenge. This arena, which must be large enough for the entire school plus four dragons, is constructed around a corner of the Forbidden Forest so it will not be visible from Hogwarts. Additionally, in *Harry Potter and the Order of the Phoenix,* Hagrid keeps his half-brother Grawp hidden there. Professor Umbridge believes Hermione's outrageous claim that Dumbledore has a secret weapon, and seems to be willing to accept at face value that it is hidden in the Forest. She forces Hermione and Harry to accompany her into the Forest to find it—an act she later regrets.

Godric's Hollow

Location: Unknown
Permanent Residents: Bathilda Bagshot, James Potter, Lily Potter
First Appearance: *Harry Potter and the Philosopher's Stone* (mentioned), *Harry Potter and the Deathly Hallows*

GENERAL OVERVIEW

Godric's Hollow is where Harry's parents lived when he was a baby. This is also where they were killed and Voldemort met his first downfall.

Harry did not actually visit the place until Christmas of the seventh year of our story. It is notorious, however, as the place where Harry Potter became known as "the Boy Who Lived."

Extended Description It is not said where Godric's Hollow is physically located. However we have some indication from Hagrid. At the start of the story, Hagrid brings back the one year old Harry Potter from Godric's Hollow to Privet Drive in Surrey[1] on a flying motorbike. He says to Professor Dumbledore and Professor McGonagall that Harry *"fell asleep as we was flyin' over Bristol."*

If we assume that Hagrid flew an approximately straight line, there are only 2 places where Godric's Hollow can be: Southern Wales or Southern Ireland. Apparently, the author has indicated that Godric's Hollow is located in Cottonbridge, England, though that is as yet unconfirmed.

In *Harry Potter and the Deathly Hallows*, we are told that, in *A History of Magic*, Bathilda Bagshot writes that Godric's Hollow, a "West Country village," is one of a number of villages where wizards settled in relatively large numbers after the ratification of the International Statute of Secrecy in 1689.

It appears that the Dumbledore family moved to Godric's Hollow when Albus Dumbledore's father Percival was imprisoned. Albus and his mother Kendra, sister Ariana, and brother Aberforth lived here, until Kendra's and Ariana's deaths. At the time, Bathilda Bagshot was their neighbour. Godric's Hollow is famed as the birthplace of Godric Gryffindor, and also as the final resting place of at least one of the Peverell family.

QUESTIONS

1. Why was it that the Potter house in Godric's Hollow is almost destroyed on the day when Voldemort tried to kill Harry?

GREATER PICTURE

Prior to the release of the seventh book, there was a great deal of discussion on various fan sites about the "missing day"; Voldemort had been dead for a full day before Hagrid appeared at Privet Drive with Harry. It was believed by many fans that the occurrences during that day would be important, possibly even pivotal, to events in the seventh book. It is entirely possible that, because of the Fidelius charm still being active, Hagrid would have been unable to find the place until one of the parties to the secret was there. We can safely assume that Sirius Black, as one of the Marauders, would have been aware of the Potters' location; in fact, he does say, in *Harry Potter and the Prisoner of Azkaban*, that he had seen "the bodies and the destruction" of the house, so he must have known the secret, either before the Fidelius charm was performed, or by Peter Pettigrew informing him of it afterwards. It is entirely possible that Hagrid was unable to enter the remains of the house to recover Harry until Sirius appeared on the scene; and it would have been Sirius who actually removed Harry from the wreckage and passed him to Hagrid to carry back to Little Whinging. However, against this we have Hagrid's word; he says that he had entered the house himself. So we can safely assume that either the Fidelius charm had ceased operation with the death of the Potters, or that Hagrid had been made privy to the secret.

The mention of the "wreckage" of the house is also interesting; the Killing Curse does not destroy things, it only kills people, so it is unlikely that the house would have been destroyed by the reflected curse that killed Voldemort. So how did the house get destroyed? There was speculation that in fact it was Peter Pettigrew who destroyed the house, in a fit of madness at seeing his master, "the most powerful wizard of all time" (or so the Death Eaters think), killed by an infant. Peter would not have tried to harm Harry, out of fear at possibly meeting Voldemort's fate. At the end of *Harry Potter and the Half-Blood Prince*, Harry expresses a determination to go back to Godric's Hollow. There were suggestions that the death of one or both of Harry's parents might have been used to create additional Horcruxes, and there was a wide-spread belief that Harry's own death was intended to create another Horcrux; there was some suspicion that Harry might find either Horcruxes, or valuable artifacts meant to become Horcruxes, in Godric's Hollow when we get there in *Harry Potter and the Deathly Hallows*. As it turns out, Harry never entered the house where his parents died; if there were such artifacts there, they did not enter the story. One other point has been brought up that might be worth mention. Could there be some relation between Godric's Hollow and Godric Gryffindor? It is entirely possible that this is the ancestral home ground of the Gryffindor clan. Hermione does confirm this link in *Harry Potter and the Deathly Hallows*. There is mention that it was Albus Dumbledore who arranged the place where the Potters stayed, which leads us to believe also that this is Dumbledore's home turf. If that is the case, what is the relationship between Dumbledore and Gryffindor? Could Albus Dumbledore be a lineal descendant? Given that the Dumbledore family reportedly moved there after Percival's imprisonment, it is not likely, but the possibility remains.

Gringotts

Location: Diagon Alley
Permanent Residents: Goblins
First Appearance: *Harry Potter and the Philosopher's Stone*

OVERVIEW

Gringotts is the only known bank of the wizarding world and it is operated primarily by goblins. Wizards and witches keep their money and other valuables in vaults that are protected by very complex and strong security measures.

Extended Description Gringotts is a large multistoried white building, near the intersection of Knockturn Alley and Diagon Alley, that towers over all neighbouring shops. Customers pass through a set of bronze doors and then silver ones before entering the lobby; the floor is paved with marble and has long counters stretching along its length with doors leading off to the vault passageways. The vaults extend for miles under the city

---

1. http://www.jkrowling.com/textonly/en/faq_view.cfm?id=91

and are accessible through rough stone, complex and interconnected passageways by means of speedy carts that are operated by goblins. The inscription on the front door reads:

> Enter, stranger, but take heed
> Of what awaits the sin of greed
> For those who take, but do not earn,
> Must pay most dearly in their turn.
> So if you seek beneath our floors
> A treasure that was never yours,
> Thief, you have been warned, beware
> Of finding more than treasure there.
> (*Harry Potter and the Philosopher's Stone*)

When Harry first visits Gringotts, he is told by Hagrid that one would have to be mad to try to rob Gringotts and that, apart from Hogwarts, it's the safest place for anything valuable to be kept. Goblins are extremely greedy and would protect their money and valuables at any cost, which makes them ideal guardians for the valuables of the wizarding world. The goblins have a code that forbids them to speak of the bank's secrets, and would consider it "base treachery" to break any part of that code.

Gringotts use a variety of security systems:

• Lower security vaults require a key; higher security vaults require the touch of a certified Gringotts goblin.

• Dragons guard the highest security vaults. They can only be controlled by Clankers, which only the goblins possess.

• The Thief's Downfall can be activated; a charmed waterfall that the goblin carts must pass through, it cancels all enchantments and magical concealments, and throws the carts off their tracks.

• Some vaults use the Gemino and Flagrante charms; when any item is touched by a thief, it multiplies rapidly and burns them, eventually crushing and scorching them to death.

• Objects within Gringotts cannot be summoned.

• At times, Probity Probes are used on customers to detect enchantments, magical concealments and hidden magical objects

At the beginning of the first book, Gringotts Vault 713 held a small grubby bag, inside of which was the Philosopher's Stone. Albus Dumbledore sends Hagrid to retrieve it while he escorts Harry to Diagon Alley. Later that very same day, someone, apparently a very powerful wizard, breaks into the vault. Although he is unsuccessful in obtaining the Philosopher's Stone, the break-in shocks the wizarding world because it is practically unheard of for Gringotts to be robbed. The culprit is not caught, though we later learn that it was almost certainly Professor Quirrell, acting under orders from Lord Voldemort.

While Gringotts is largely staffed by goblins, including Griphook and Ragnok, it is known that the bank does employ humans. Bill Weasley works as a Curse Breaker for Gringotts in Egypt, retrieving artifacts from ancient Egyptian tombs and pyramids. Fleur Delacour took a part-time job with Gringotts after participating in the Triwizard Tournament, apparently to improve her English skills, and wizard guards are mentioned in *Harry Potter and the Deathly Hallows* during the break in. Griphook mentions at that time that the goblins resent "wand-bearer" interference in their internal affairs.

In *Harry Potter and the Deathly Hallows*, Harry, Ron and Hermione, aided by a reluctant Griphook in exchange for Godric Gryffindor's sword, break into the vault of Bellatrix Lestrange where a Horcrux, Hufflepuff's cup, is hidden. However, when they go into Bellatrix's vault, which is stocked with all manners of treasure, they find out that the treasure has Gemino and Flagrante charms placed on it. Though burned and nearly buried in false treasures, the Trio manage to escape with the Horcrux by fleeing on a half-blind dragon that was part of the security for the vault, leaving parts of the bank in ruins.

Grimmauld Place

Location: London
Permanent Residents: Kreacher, Walburga Black's portrait, Sirius Black
First Appearance: *Harry Potter and the Order of the Phoenix*

General Overview

The longtime London residence of the Black family of Pureblood Wizards, Number Twelve is the house where Sirius Black grew up, and which he inherited upon his mother's death, along with its mad and treacherous House-Elf, Kreacher. Decorated and furnished in gloomy, largely Slytherin themes, and filled with Dark Arts tools, tomes and objects, Number Twelve has seen use as the headquarters of the Order of the Phoenix, the covert pro-Light organization headed by Albus Dumbledore. In its pro-Light use, it is protected from discovery by being placed under the Fidelius charm, with Dumbledore as its Secret-Keeper.

Extended Description

Location   The house is located in London, between two Muggle houses. Being protected by a Fidelius charm, it is unplottable and cannot be accessed by intruders, either Muggles or wizards who don't know its secret. To access the house, Harry Potter stood between the numbers eleven and thirteen, thinking that "the headquarters of the Order of the Phoenix may be found at number twelve, Grimmauld Place, London." The only reason this worked for him is that the note he had seen this on had been written by Albus Dumbledore, the secret-keeper for the organization; the effect of the Fidelius charm is that only those who are informed directly by the Secret-keeper can know the secret.

Exterior   Much of the time, the house is hidden to all onlookers. When it is visible, it is one in a row of similar houses, with a front door at the top of a flight of steps, badly in need of paint, and with door hardware in the shape of snakes.

Grimmauld Place

Interior "with old-fashioned gas lamps all along the walls, peeling wallpaper and threadbare carpet of a long, gloomy hallway, where a cobwebby chandelier glimmered overhead and age-blackened portraits hung crooked on the walls, with a large umbrella stand that looked as though it had been made from a severed troll's leg, with a row of shrunken heads mounted on plaques on the wall." The heads belonged to house-elves. "All of them had the same rather snoutlike nose."

US readers may be confused by the description of the "parlour, on the first floor," and Hermione looking down, rather than out, at the front stoop and seeing Mundungus with his collection of cauldrons that had "fallen off the back of a broom." The house is actually laid out in the extremely vertical, UK style, with the floor naming conventional for UK buildings. Starting at the basement, then, the rooms we know about are:

- The kitchen in the basement, as is conventional for a UK house with space for servants. Often, there is access to the kitchen from an "areaway," a sunken, paved yard, but not always, and apparently in the case of the Black house, not at all. What light there is in the kitchen seems to come from ground-level windows set high in the walls.
- The main floor, in this case, containing the entrance hall.
- The first floor, above the main floor, which contains at least the parlour, and possibly other rooms.
- The second floor, containing at least two bedrooms, one of which is occupied by Harry and Ron.
- An apparent third floor, containing a bedroom used by the Twins, and possibly one used by Hermione and Ginny.
- The fourth floor, containing bedrooms originally occupied by Sirius and Regulus.
- Attic space, in which Buckbeak lived.

It is possible that there was additionally a formal dining room on the first floor, beside the parlour. It is likely that there would be servants' bedrooms on the main floor and in the basement, and it is possible that Sirius' and Regulus' bedrooms were designed originally as servants quarters as well.

When we are introduced to the house in *Harry Potter and the Order of the Phoenix*, it is dirty and infested with magical vermin. The house elf Kreacher has been living there alone for at least a decade, taking orders only from the incoherent and insane portrait of Sirius' mother in the entrance hall, and has neglected his cleaning chores. The Weasleys, Harry and Hermione spend many days cleaning and removing vermin and rubbish. Eventually the house is made more habitable but remains a gloomy place. When we meet Sirius' mother in her portrait, she screams and insults the newcomers constantly, only stopping when the owner of the house, in this case Sirius, returns her to her slumber by drawing the curtains over her portrait, an act that apparently takes considerable force.

Ownership As mentioned, the house had been inherited by Sirius, as the last Black male descendant, on the death of his mother. As Sirius had by this time betrayed the family's Blood status by consorting with Muggles, the death of Sirius' only younger brother, Regulus, apparently at the hands of Voldemort, must have been a severe blow to Walburga, and may have hastened her death. Sirius does not seem to be upset at having missed her death, which occurred while he was imprisoned.

At Sirius' death, the house passes to Harry, according to the terms of Sirius' will. There is some question, however, of whether the house is magically entailed, such that ownership passes to the eldest surviving Black male, or failing that, to the eldest surviving Black female, who would be Bellatrix Lestrange. Professor Dumbledore tests this by summoning Kreacher and having Harry give him an order. If the house, with Kreacher, have passed to Harry, Kreacher will be bound to follow Harry's orders despite his hatred of Harry. As it turns out, Kreacher does follow Harry's orders, so the house has passed to Harry, and presumably may continue to be used as the headquarters of the Order.

With the death of Dumbledore, the house is once again abandoned. As Severus Snape had proven to be a traitor to the Order, and was privy to its secrets, the use of the house as Headquarters was not safe. Harry, Ron, and Hermione did end up living in the house through the month of August in the seventh year of our story, but were in turn forced to abandon it when its location was revealed to another Death Eater.

With the house becoming habitable under the ministrations of the changed Kreacher, it is entirely possible that Harry ended up living there once he was finished with school.

Analysis

It is a safe assumption that the house was built by Muggles and purchased or otherwise taken over by the Black family, because of how similar the house appears to be to its neighbours on either side. While we are not directly told of this similarity, we can infer it by the lack of comment on any appearance of strangeness, when Harry first sees the house. When Harry first sights the Burrow, he thinks how it seems to be held together by magic; the fact that he makes no similar comment regarding Grimmauld Place indicates normality of its appearance.

We are told, in *Harry Potter and the Order of the Phoenix*, that Harry hears the Twins laughing from their bedroom above his room. From this we infer their bedroom being directly over Harry and Ron's room. The two bedrooms at the top of the house, we are told in *Harry Potter and the Deathly Hallows*, belong to Sirius and Regulus. It is safe to assume in *Harry Potter and the Order of the Phoenix* that Sirius is in his old room, and that Regulus' room remains empty, because when the Trio want to get in they discover that it is locked and Hermione must unlock it, and if anyone from the Order was using it they likely would have left it unlocked. It is based on this that we have inferred the layout of the house, as noted above.

Gryffindor House

Location: Gryffindor Tower
Permanent Residents: Gryffindor students
First Appearance: *Harry Potter and the Philosopher's Stone*

General Overview

Gryffindor House is one of the four Houses in the Hogwarts School of Witchcraft and Wizardry.

Extended Description   Housemistress: Professor Minerva McGonagall
Founder: Godric Gryffindor
Coat of Arms: gold lion, red
Ghost: Sir Nicholas de Mimsy-Porpington ("Nearly Headless Nick")
Characteristics: "Where dwell the brave at heart, Their daring nerve, and chivalry."
Location of common room: Gryffindor Tower, seventh floor, behind the portrait of the Fat Lady There are two main staircases which lead from the Common Room to dormitories, one staircase for boys and one for girls. The girls' dormitories have an enchantment that doesn't allow boys to enter, but the boys' dormitories do not have such an enchantment (and so girls can freely enter) because, according to *Hogwarts, A History*, the founder thought that girls are more trustworthy than boys. Each of the two dormitories is further divided into seven floors, one for each year; each dormitory floor apparently has space for five students.

Harry is Sorted into Gryffindor House, as were his father and mother before him. It is never stated, but seems very likely that Professor Dumbledore was a member of Gryffindor House as well.

Analysis

The number of students actually in each House is uncertain. We only ever hear of five boys and five girls in each year, but we have been told by the author in an interview that the average class size (all residents of one House for one year) is about thirty. Thus we must assume a population of 210 per house, fifteen boys and fifteen girls each year.

One gets the impression from things said in *Harry Potter and the Goblet of Fire* that House honours, notably the House cup and the Quidditch cup, are generally held by either Gryffindor house or Slytherin house, with Ravenclaw house occasionally winning an upset victory.

Headmaster's Office, Hogwarts

Location: Inside Hogwarts
Permanent Residents: Current headmaster, various previous headmasters and headmistresses
First Appearance: *Harry Potter and the Chamber of Secrets*

General Overview

The Headmaster's Office at Hogwarts is the office in which the current headmaster or headmistress of Hogwarts works. Although this is never mentioned, it is entirely likely that his residence is adjacent. It is reached by means of a circular, moving stone staircase, which in turn is concealed by a gargoyle on the third floor. The gargoyle will step aside in response to a password.

Extended Description   As the series progresses, we gradually see more and more of the Headmaster's office, and understand its function better.

We first see it in *Harry Potter and the Chamber of Secrets*. Harry has just rather literally tripped over the Petrified body of Justin Finch-Fletchley. Professor McGonagall, the first on the scene, says nothing in response to Harry's pleas of innocence, except to say that it is out of her hands. She proceeds to a gargoyle in the halls, and says the password ("*Sherbert Lemon*"), whereupon the gargoyle leaps aside, revealing a slowly ascending circular staircase. Reaching the top of this, they find an oaken double door. Professor McGonagall leaves Harry there. Harry sees that the room contains a vast number of portraits of past headmasters, all evidently asleep; many spindly tables with intricate silvery devices upon them; and the Sorting Hat resting on a shelf. After exchanging some words with the Sorting Hat, Harry notices a very ill-looking bird on a perch behind the door; as he watches; aghast, the bird catches fire. Professor Dumbledore, then entering, tells Harry that the bird, Fawkes, is a Phoenix, and that is his method of immortality; he will shortly be reborn from his own ashes.

In that same book, in a memory of Tom Riddle's, Harry sees the Headmaster's office as it had been in the time of Professor Dippet, the headmaster preceding Dumbledore. The many intricate devices are not there, and neither is Fawkes.

In *Harry Potter and the Goblet of Fire*, Harry again visits the headmaster's office, finding another artifact of Dumbledore's: a Pensieve.

In *Harry Potter and the Order of the Phoenix*, Professor McGonagall again takes Harry to the Headmaster's office, this time immediately after Harry has seen the vision of Mr. Weasley being attacked. As they approach the office doors, Harry hears a large number of voices all talking at once, but when the doors open, there is nobody there except Dumbledore himself. Over the course of the next few minutes, it becomes apparent that Dumbledore has been speaking with, and apparently receiving information and advice from, the portraits, even though they appear to be sleeping. The evidence for this is that he addresses two of the portraits, who immediately awaken, and sends them off to gather information. Harry also notes that many of the portraits appear to be simply pretending to sleep. Dumbledore also makes use of one of the small devices on the spindly tables, to determine something about the snake which had attacked Mr. Weasley.

Later in that same year, Cornelius Fudge attempts to put Dumbledore under arrest. The attempt fails, but Dumbledore does leave his office. Professor Umbridge is appointed Headmistress by the Ministry, but the Headmaster's office remains sealed to her; evidently the school itself does not recognize her authority. When the ministry is forced to recognize that Voldemort has returned, at the end of that book, Dumbledore is reinstated as headmaster. Harry, sent to the Headmaster's office by Portkey, notes that the damage that had occurred in Dumbledore's abortive arrest had somehow been repaired. Dumbledore himself arrives shortly by means of Floo powder. In the ensuing, rather heated, discussion, Harry destroys one of the spindly tables and the instrument sitting upon it.

In *Harry Potter and the Half-Blood Prince*, instead of an instrument, one of the tables contains, at various times, artifacts of Tom Riddle's early life.

At the end of that book, after Dumbledore's death, a large portrait of him, asleep, appears in the headmaster's office. The portrait is already present when Professor McGonagall summons the Heads of House to discuss the future of Hogwarts, mere hours after Dumbledore has died, and without anyone else (as far as we know) having been in the office.

While we do see the Headmaster's office several times in *Harry Potter and the Deathly Hallows*, we hear very little of how Snape has changed the decor. The desk is present, the Pensieve is present, and the portraits are all still present on the walls, but of Dumbledore's instruments, or what has replaced them, there is no mention.

ANALYSIS

It is most curious that Harry, then only a second-year student, should be left alone in the Headmaster's office. This actually is a signal of the respect that Dumbledore inspires in the students; he is willing to trust that the students will not pry into areas of his office that he does not wish them to see. Harry somewhat strains the limits of this respect, by trying on the Sorting Hat on his first visit, and by investigating Dumbledore's Pensieve on a later visit.

GREATER PICTURE

In *Harry Potter and the Deathly Hallows*, there is no mention of Snape's portrait being present in the Headmaster's office after his death; there is also no mention of a portrait of Umbridge appearing. In the case of Snape, it could be argued that he did not retire or die in office, but rather had run away at a time when the school needed all the help it could get; as no human agent seems to be available to create these portraits, it is possible that the school does it itself, and had refused to create a portrait for a headmaster who deserted his post. In the case of Umbridge, it is quite possible that the school, as mentioned, had never accepted her as headmistress in the first place. In particular, we can see that with assistance from Fawkes, Dumbledore can enter and depart his office without recourse to the Floo network or Portkeys, both of which can be monitored. We can also see that his office has been repaired. It is entirely possible that Dumbledore returned to his office, at least occasionally, enough so that the school recognized him as remaining its headmaster.

Hog's Head Inn

Location: Hogsmeade Village side street
Permanent Residents: First Appearance *Harry Potter and the Philosopher's Stone*

GENERAL OVERVIEW

The Hog's Head Inn is a "small, dingy" pub in the Village of Hogsmeade.

Extended Description There are two pubs in Hogsmeade, one which caters to the general run-of-the-mill, and one which is more frequented by those on the outskirts. The Hog's Head is the latter. It is a much grimier place than the Three Broomsticks, and there are many less restrictions; Ron comments in *Harry Potter and the Order of the Phoenix* that he could probably buy a Firewhiskey there without being questioned as to his age.

Many events happen in the Hog's Head that are somewhat on the shady side.

• This pub is where Albus Dumbledore interviews Sibyll Trelawney for the post of Divination Teacher, where she gives the prophecy about Harry, and where that prophecy is overheard.

• It is in the Hog's Head that Hagrid gets into a card game with a man who never lowers his hood, and "wins" a dragon's egg in *Harry Potter and the Philosopher's Stone*.

• The Hog's Head is home to the first meeting of Dumbledore's Army in *Harry Potter and the Order of the Phoenix*.

When Harry, Ron, and Hermione are almost captured by Death Eaters in *Harry Potter and the Deathly Hallows*, it is the innkeeper at the Hogs Head who rescues them, letting them into the bar and claiming to have originated the Patronus that the Death Eaters had seen. We later find out that the Room of Requirement, called upon to provide food for Neville, had created a secret passage which terminated in an upstairs room at the Hog's Head.

ANALYSIS

When we are properly introduced to Mundungus Fletcher in *Harry Potter and the Order of the Phoenix*, we learn that there is an underworld to Wizarding society, as well as the two battling revealed forces. Given that there is an underside, there have to be places where those who have no place in society would meet. The Hog's Head Inn is one of those places. To a lesser extent, any pub will have that tendency; for instance in *Harry Potter and the Prisoner of Azkaban*, Harry believes that he sees a hag in The Leaky Cauldron.

It is never stated so baldly in the first six books, but there are clues in the stories that suggest that Professor Dumbledore's brother Aberforth is the landlord at the Hog's Head. The author has confirmed this, and it is confirmed to Harry in *Harry Potter and the Deathly Hallows*.

Hogsmeade

Location: Scotland, near Hogwarts
Permanent Residents: None
First Appearance: *Harry Potter and the Prisoner of Azkaban*

GENERAL OVERVIEW

Hogsmeade is the wizarding village near Hogwarts School of Witchcraft and Wizardry. The Hogwarts Express stops at Hogsmeade village. It is the only purely Wizard occupied town in England.

Extended Description Located near Hogwarts School of Witchcraft and Wizardry, Hogsmeade is "the only non-Muggle settlement in Britain," and the northern terminus of the Hogwarts Express train line from London. It was founded by Hengist of Woodcroft, who was fleeing because of the Muggles' oppression, at about the same time as Hogwarts was founded. Hogwarts students that attend the third year or above may, on selected weekends (so-called Hogsmeade weekends) and with parental permission, visit the town and patronize its many shops.

A memorable feature of Hogsmeade is the Shrieking Shack, infamous as the "most severely haunted building in Britain."

Hogsmeade merchants • Dervish and Banges, selling and repairing magical items or equipment.
• Gladrags Wizardwear, clothes shops, with shops in London.
• The Hog's Head, a small inn off the main street.
• Honeyduke's Sweetshop, selling a wide variety of candies, fudges and blocks of chocolates, owned by Ambrosius Flume and his wife, who both live over the shop.
• A post office, with three hundred owls, including some very small Scops owls for "Local Deliveries Only."
• Madam Puddifoot's tea shop, owned by Madam Puddifoot; couples of Hogwarts students are drawn to this shop for an idyllic tete-a-tete.
• Scrivenshaft's Quill Shop, selling quills and stationery.
• The Shrieking Shack, the "most severely haunted building in Britain."
• The Three Broomsticks, a pub that also caters to the under-age students, owned by Madam Rosmerta. A favorite drink among the students is butterbeer. Other drinks include gillywater, mulled mead, red currant rum, cherry syrup and soda with ice and an umbrella, and firewhisky for the mature drinkers.
• Zonko's Joke Shop, selling items that can be used for jokes and tricks, the favorite shop of Fred and George Weasley; the items sold include Dungbombs, Hiccup Sweets, Frog Spawn Soap, and Nose-Biting Teacups, among other things. In book 6, this shop closes for lack of business when Hogwarts cancels further Hogsmeade weekends.

ANALYSIS

In *Harry Potter and the Half-Blood Prince*, the town seems to be falling on hard times; in particular, following Katie Bell being injured by a cursed necklace she apparently got in Hogsmeade, all Hogsmeade weekends are canceled. Apparently, Zonko's joke shop closes for lack of business, causing Fred and George to re-think their idea of opening a branch there. The lack of student visits is bound to cause hardship for many other shops in the village as well, including the Three Broomsticks, Honeydukes, and Madam Puddifoot's, all of which are usually filled to capacity on Hogsmeade weekends.

Hogwarts School of Witchcraft and Wizardry

Location: Scotland
Permanent Residents: Rubeus Hagrid, Sibyll Trelawney, Argus Filch, Firenze, Peeves, Nearly Headless Nick, The Grey Lady, The Bloody Baron, The Fat Friar, Moaning Myrtle, Sir Cadogan, The Fat Lady
First Appearance: *Harry Potter and the Philosopher's Stone*

GENERAL OVERVIEW

Hogwarts School of Witchcraft and Wizardry "is the best school of wizardry in Great Britain," according to Rubeus Hagrid. In fact, the author has implied that it is the only school of wizardry in England[1] —while every Wizarding child *can* go to Hogwarts, the author states that not all *do* choose to do so. It is possible that there are other schools in Great Britain as well, but if so they are never mentioned. The events of the first six books of the Harry Potter series occur largely in and around this school, which Harry attends to get his education from the time he turns 11.

Extended Description Founded roughly a thousand years ago by the four Founders (Godric Gryffindor, Rowena Ravenclaw, Helga Hufflepuff and Salazar Slytherin), Hogwarts, the premier Wizarding school in Britain, is housed in a large magically-active castle near the Wizarding village of Hogsmeade. The castle itself is protected by Anti-Apparation wards (preventing an attacker from suddenly appearing in its midst), and Muggle-Repellent charms (to the occasional Muggle who is determined to approach, the castle is spelled to look like a dangerous ruin, with keep-away warning signs posted). The Forbidden Forest, adjacent to the school grounds, contains many wild magical creatures, some of whom are actively hostile towards humans, Wizarding or not. Situated at the edge of the Forest, the Groundskeeper's Hut, where half-giant Rubeus Hagrid lives, is well-placed for looking after the subjects of each Care of Magical Creatures class (taught by Hagrid starting in Harry's third year). The Hogwarts student body is Sorted at enrollment (by the Sorting Hat), along lines of aptitude and predilection, into four Houses named after the four Founders (Gryffindor, Ravenclaw, Hufflepuff, and Slytherin) and nurturing those characteristics each Founder thought most important. Since even

---

1. http://www.jkrowling.com/textonly/en/extrastuff_view.cfm?id=25

the Founders were unable to keep solidarity (Salazar Slytherin left after a legendary dispute with the others), the Houses, each with a professor who doubles as the Head of that House, tend towards friction and rivalry, particularly between Slytherin and Gryffindor. The rivalries usually confine themselves to Quidditch (each House fields a team of players, vying for the Quidditch Cup) and the House Cup competition (Houses are awarded points for student excellence and penalized points for student misbehavior and indolence, leading to an end-of-year tally and award).

At the start of the Harry Potter series, the House Heads are:

• Minerva McGonagall, Head of Gryffindor, who teaches Transfiguration and is also Deputy Headmistress. Gryffindor House nurtures courage and commitment to a cause.

• Severus Snape, Head of Slytherin, who teaches Potions and is the school's Potions Master. Slytherin House nurtures self-sufficient cunning, resourcefulness and ambition.

• Filius Flitwick, Head of Ravenclaw, who teaches Charms. Ravenclaw House nurtures thoughtful scholarship and intellectual brilliance.

• Pomona Sprout, Head of Hufflepuff, who teaches Herbology and runs the school's greenhouses. Hufflepuff House nurtures hard work, tolerance and loyalty.

Albus Dumbledore holds the position of Headmaster of Hogwarts, in addition to his public duties on the Wizengamot (and his later covert activities with the Order of the Phoenix).

Argus Filch, a Squib, is the castle's Custodian, aided by unknown numbers of House-Elves who clean and cook. There is at least one resident ghost for each House (Gryffindor has Nearly Headless Nick, Hufflepuff has The Fat Friar, Ravenclaw has The Grey Lady, and Slytherin has The Bloody Baron), plus Peeves The Poltergeist, who is allowed residence by Dumbledore to "keep everyone on their toes." Poppy Pomfrey is the Medi-Witch who runs the school Infirmary. Irma Pince runs the school's Library and guards the dangerous books in its Restricted Section.

Castle security is assisted by the House Ghosts, and by the many Wizarding portraits (paintings where the depicted person can speak and move from frame to frame), such as Phineas Nigellus, The Fat Lady, and Sir Cadogan, which password-protect some passages and monitor the rooms and corridors.

J.K. Rowling has said in an interview that Hogwarts is somewhere in Scotland; its position is uncertain, because it is Charmed to be Unplottable—its position, like that of the other magic schools, cannot be placed on a map. Additionally, it is hidden by spells that make it appear to Muggles as an old ruin, complete with Danger signs. Hogwarts is not in the most populated areas of Scotland since in *Harry Potter and the Goblet of Fire* it is said that the nearest Muggle town is several miles away (a situation that does not exist around Edinborough and Glasgow). Also are excluded the Scottish Islands, since one can go to Hogwarts by train from London.

Academics The school year at Hogwarts is broken into four terms.

• Autumn term starts at the first of September with the arrival of the students, and continues to the start of the Christmas holidays, usually in late December.

• Winter term extends from the end of the Christmas holidays to the beginning of the Easter break, usually in mid to late March or early April.

• Spring term runs from the end of Easter break to the start of the first full week in June. Exams are given during that week.

• Summer term comprises the time from the last day of exams to the end of classes at the end of June. Summer term, a short term, is usually seen as a time to laze around and rest from the year; exams are finished, and while there may be one last Quidditch game between the houses, and there are classes still, most peoples' marks are pretty well settled, so things are taken rather lightly.

All subjects are elective after fifth-year O.W.L. exams; you are only allowed to proceed in a subject if your O.W.L. grades are high enough for the teacher of that course. Until and including fifth year, you must take certain core subjects. The subjects available at Hogwarts are given below:

• Ancient Runes, the study of interpreting runes or magical symbols. Teacher: unknown, possibly Bathsheba Babbling.

• Arithmancy, the study of the magical properties of numbers. Teacher: (Septima) Vector.

• Astronomy (core subject), the study of the heavenly bodies and the universe. Teacher: (Aurora) Sinistra.

• Care of Magical Creatures, the study of different creatures and how to handle them. 1st and 2nd year Teacher: Professor Kettleburn. 3rd to 6th year Teacher: Rubeus Hagrid, sometimes substituted by Wilhelmina Grubbly-Plank.

• Charms (core subject), the study of magic spells that do not change the basic nature of the subject. Teacher: Filius Flitwick.

• Defense Against the Dark Arts (core subject). 1st year Teacher: (Quirinius) Quirrell. 2nd year Teacher: Gilderoy Lockhart. 3rd year Teacher: Remus Lupin. 4th year Teacher: Alastor Moody. 5th year Teacher: Dolores Umbridge. 6th year Teacher: Severus Snape. 7th year Teacher: Amycus Carrow.

• Divination, studying ways of predicting the future (including reading tea leaves, palmistry, magic orb reading, dream interpretation). Teachers: Sibyll Trelawney (until midway through fifth year, re-instated sixth year), Firenze (from midway through fifth year on). 'The most difficult of all magical arts.' 'One of the most imprecise branches of magic.'

• Flying Lessons, teaching the students how to fly using a broomstick, usually taken during the first year. Teacher: Rolanda Hooch.

• Herbology (core subject), study the care and magical properties of magical plants and fungi. Teacher: Pomona Sprout.

• History of Magic (core subject). Teacher: (Cuthbert) Binns. 'The most boring class, and at the same time the only one taught by a ghost.'

• Muggle Studies, studying the life and lifestyle of Muggles. 1st through 6th Year Teacher: Charity Burbage. 7th year Teacher: Alecto Carrow.

• Potions (core subject), studying how to prepare potions. 1st through 5th year Teacher: Severus Snape. 6th and 7th year Teacher: Horace Slughorn. Usually a shared double class.

• Transfiguration (core subject), practicing metamorphosis of objects into other forms. Teacher: Minerva McGonagall.

Class sizes and duration Hogwarts classes are held in different locations within the castle and grounds. Class usually last for one and a half hours, even if they are shared by two Houses. Higher years often have "double" classes, which means they last three hours; Potions classes quite often are double, because potion preparation can take longer than a single class would have time for. There are three class periods, typically, in the morning, and three in the afternoon. Class size is typically thirty students, according to information in *Harry Potter and the Order of the Phoenix*. This gives a total student population of about 840, 210 or so in each House.

Grades Classification Grades classification refer here are only given in the student's essay works, quizzes, assignments, homeworks and examinations.

Passing Grades   O—Outstanding
   E—Exceeds Expectations
   A—Acceptable

Failing Grades   P—Poor
   D—Dreadful
   T—Troll

Examinations Given   Final examinations are held each year between the end of spring or Easter term and the start of Summer term, but there are also two major examinations for Hogwarts students:

• O.W.L.s (Ordinary Wizarding Levels)—'the examinations Hogwarts student took at the age of fifteen' (actually in their fifth year—anyone having a birthday during the school year would be sixteen when they sat these exams) and 'really important, affect the job you can apply for and everything.'

• N.E.W.T. (Nastily Exhausting Wizarding Test)—examination taken in the seventh year at Hogwarts

Life at Hogwarts   Hogwarts is a very traditional British secondary boarding school, but magical education necessitates many differences. There are few modern facilities, indeed the castle has no electricity. This is largely due to the presence of high levels of magical energy fields that cause electrical and electronic devices to malfunction. Heating is provided by fireplaces and stoves maintained by a large staff of house elves. House elves also prepare three meals a day for students and staff as well as several feasts throughout the year. The food is varied, excellent and plentiful. The castle does have a relatively modern plumbing system including public rest rooms and at least one luxurious magical bath. Letters and parcels are usually delivered to students during breakfast in the Great Hall by owls who bring them directly to individuals. Both school and privately owned owls reside in a common owlery.

The school has a large library that includes a restricted section for advanced texts requiring faculty permission to read. The resident librarian, Irma Pince, seems to be almost fanatical in her caring for the books. Studying and homework are usually done in the house common rooms, the library, the Great Hall around mealtimes, or in the grounds in good weather. Like the rest of the Wizarding World, written work is done with quills, inkbottles and parchment. Written assignments are often measured in either the number of scrolls or the length, in inches or feet, of parchment.

Extracurricular activities include Quidditch and a few clubs (dueling and gobstones are mentioned). In addition, third year and older students may, with parental permission, visit the nearby all Wizard village of Hogmeade on selected weekends throughout the school year. Leisure time is often spent in the common rooms socializing and playing magical games. In warm weather, students can be found on the grounds or near the Lake, where we often see them playing with the resident giant squid.

Magic from inexperienced wizards, injuries from Quidditch matches, and pranks around the school make Hogwarts a somewhat dangerous place. Therefore, a hospital wing staffed by a nurse/healer is located within the school. Injuries that would kill or maim Muggle students are usually treated in just a day or two.

Most students return home during the Christmas and Easter breaks, but there are some who stay at Hogwarts over the holidays. Both Christmas and Hallowe'en are celebrated at Hogwarts with decorations and elaborate feasts. Other holidays observed in the books include St. Valentine's Day and Easter.

ANALYSIS

School population   As mentioned above, class size is typically thirty students, according to information in *Harry Potter and the Order of the Phoenix*. This gives a total student population of about 840, 210 or so in each House. Readers may be confused by the fact that only five boys and five girls of each house in each year are named. At least one fan site has published information apparently received from the author that she had only developed characters for ten students in each year, and had decided that was enough, but that the number of students was intended to be about thirty per house per year. She has also variously given the student population as 600 or 1,000.

It is not the place of this book to try and resolve this apparent contradiction. We do note that all descriptions that imply numbers of students, rather than naming individual students, do seem to fit a population of about 800 students better than they fit a population of 280, the number which fits the apparent ten students per year per house. We will suggest that we hear more from, and see more of, the students in Harry's dormitory simply because Harry, sharing a dormitory with them, is much more familiar with them. While this has not been previously suggested, it is possible that there are two other dormitories for students in Harry's year, each having five other unnamed students, in both the girls' side and the boys' side of Gryffindor tower.

Other fan sites have noted that there are not enough teachers for the stated school population. Working from the description of the Potions courses, we see that this is generally a double course, two periods and two Houses each class. In the N.E.W.T.-level classes, all four Houses are taught together. Thus, the Potions instructor must be teaching two sections in each of five years, plus one section in each of two N.E.W.T.-level years, for a total of twelve sections. As these are double classes, we can assume that most other teachers will be teaching twice as many sections, typically about twenty-four. Even those courses that are not core subjects, such as Care of Magical Creatures and Divination, and are not offered for the students' first two years, will involve, typically, sixteen sections. Yet, as we learn at the end of *Harry Potter and the Prisoner of Azkaban*, the most courses that can be taken without the aid of a Time-Turner is ten; if it is impossible for a student to take more than ten courses, then equally it is impossible for a teacher to teach more than ten sections. Thus, there must be a large number of teachers who we never meet. To add to this we have the apparent impossibility of Dolores Umbridge not only teaching her own classes, but also being present to inspect all of Hagrid's and all of Sibyll Trelawney's classes, thus effectively tripling her workload. Again, it is not the place of this book to resolve this contradiction. We will point out that adding the apparently-necessary additional teachers would have the effect of diluting the story line.

Honeyduke's Sweetshop

Location: Hogsmeade village main street
Permanent Residents: Ambrosius Flume
First Appearance: *Harry Potter and the Prisoner of Azkaban*

General Overview

Honeyduke's Sweet Shop is a candy and treat store in the Village of Hogsmeade. It is very popular among Hogwarts students, on those occasions when they are allowed into the village ("Hogsmeade weekends").

Extended Description Honeyduke's is also the terminus of one of the secret passages out of the school, used extensively by Harry in *Harry Potter and the Prisoner of Azkaban*, and also presumably by Sirius Black to enter the school in that same book. Once Harry has received permission to visit Hogsmeade on the weekends, which he does at the end of the book, he has little further need for that passage.

Because of this, it seems that we see Honeyduke's only in the third book, and later in the sixth book: in the only Hogsmeade visit that year, Harry, Ron, and Hermione run into Professor Slughorn, who is there buying some of his favorite crystallized pineapple.

House of Gaunt

Location: Near Little Hangleton
Permanent Residents: Marvolo Gaunt, Morfin Gaunt, and Merope Gaunt
First Appearance: *Harry Potter and the Half-Blood Prince*

General Overview

The House of Gaunt is the residence of the remaining members of the House of Gaunt. Located near the fictional town of Little Hangleton, it is empty by the time Harry's story begins, and has likely fallen into ruins.

Extended Description The so-called "House of Gaunt" is, when we first see it, a run-down shack with a dead snake nailed to the door. Using Albus Dumbledore's Pensieve, via the memories of Bob Ogden, we find that the residence of this once-proud family is now a single-room shack, in which the three remaining members of the family reside. The building is apparently a free-hold, built on a spot of land that belongs to the Gaunt family, though the rest of the valley apparently is owned by one Tom Riddle.

Tom Marvolo Riddle visits the house at one point, apparently on a mission to find something out about his ancestry. The house has not fared well, as Merope had run away some sixteen years before, and then died, and the house had sat vacant for three years while Morfin had been in prison. In the course of that visit, Tom Marvolo Riddle murders his own father, Tom Riddle, and Riddle's parents, framing the one surviving Gaunt family member, Morfin, for the murder.

With Morfin's arrest and subsequent death in Azkaban, the house remains empty and presumably falls into ruin. Tom Marvolo Riddle, in his later guise as Lord Voldemort, does revisit the shack to hide a Horcrux there. Albus Dumbledore visits to retrieve the Horcrux, and Voldemort returns to check on the Horcrux and is enraged to find it gone.

Greater Picture

The Horcrux placed in this location was, of course, the Peverell ring that Tom Marvolo Riddle had stolen from Morfin Gaunt. Not having heard the story of the Deathly Hallows, it had never occurred to Voldemort that this might be the Resurrection Stone. Riddle was as infatuated with ancestry as were the Gaunts before him, and so chose to make Horcruxes out of things that would be proof of the antiquity of his line. As the ring was supposedly the signet of the Peverells, one of the most ancient Wizarding families known, his possession and use of the ring acted as proof that he was of an ancient tradition.

Hufflepuff House

Location: Hogwarts
Permanent Residents: Hufflepuff students
First Appearance: *Harry Potter and the Philosopher's Stone*

GENERAL OVERVIEW

Hufflepuff House is one of the four Houses in the Hogwarts School of Witchcraft and Wizardry.

Extended Description Housemistress: Professor Pomona Sprout
  Founder: Helga Hufflepuff
  Coat of Arms: black badger, yellow
  Ghost: The Fat Friar
  Characteristics: "Where they are just and loyal, Those patient Hufflepuffs are true And unafraid of toil."
  Location of common room: unknown, but down the main hall downstairs, cellar-like in appearance and thought to be near the kitchens.

ANALYSIS

The number of students actually in each House is uncertain. We only ever hear of five boys and five girls in each year, but we have been told by the author in an interview that the average class size (all residents of one House for one year) is about thirty. Thus we must assume a population of 210 per house, fifteen boys and fifteen girls each year.

One gets the impression from things said in *Harry Potter and the Goblet of Fire* that House honours, notably the House cup and the Quidditch cup, are generally held by either Gryffindor house or Slytherin house, with Ravenclaw house occasionally winning an upset victory. Hufflepuff seldom if ever gets any glory, and the members of that House are overjoyed when one of their own, Cedric Diggory, is chosen as one of the Champions in the Triwizard Tournament.

Knockturn Alley

  Location: off Diagon Alley, London
  Permanent Residents: Borgin and Burke, along with various other Dark merchants
  First Appearance: *Harry Potter and the Chamber of Secrets*

GENERAL OVERVIEW

Knockturn Alley is a street of shops and vendors specializing in the darker forms of magic. The one shop named on this street is Borgin and Burkes.

Extended Description As there is a part of London where regular wizards can go to buy magical equipment, namely Diagon Alley, so must there be a place where dark wizards carry out their business. Knockturn Alley (pun: "nocturnally") is that place. Shunned by all right-thinking wizards, Knockturn Alley is the place where you would go to buy a Hand of Glory, Flesh-Eating Slug Repellent, or "things that looked alarmingly like whole human fingernails." It holds a certain illicit glamour for young wizards, like Fred and George Weasley, who (once they set up shop) likely use certain ingredients available only there for some of the magic that they sell in their store.

In *Harry Potter and the Chamber of Secrets*, when Harry is using Floo powder to get to Diagon Alley, he accidentally turns up in Borgin and Burkes, on Knockturn Alley. He is led out of Knockturn Alley and back to Diagon Alley by Hagrid, who had gone to get some flesh-eating slug repellant. Later, when the party breaks up to do their separate shopping errands, Mrs. Weasley feels she has to warn the twins not to go into Knockturn Alley. At one point when the Weasley family are preparing to visit Diagon Alley to buy school supplies, Mrs. Weasley explicitly warns the Twins not to enter Knockturn Alley.

In *Harry Potter and the Half-Blood Prince*, Harry, Hermione, and Ron sneak off from Weasleys' Wizard Wheezes and follow Draco Malfoy into Knockturn Alley. They then eavesdrop on him as he talks to Borgin about something he is buying, using Extendable Ears. Hermione's subsequent attempt to determine what it was that Draco was interested in fails, as she is not good at that kind of subterfuge.

ANALYSIS

Many readers must wonder why such a hot-bed of Dark magic is allowed to remain so close to the main mercantile center of Wizarding London. Would it not be better to eliminate it and the associated Dark enterprises? Likely it has not been cleaned up for the same reason that spymasters are allowed to stay in business when they are known—if you keep all your evil-doers in one place, it is much easier to keep track of them.

GREATER PICTURE

We visit Diagon Alley in many of the books. With the ascendancy of Voldemort, Diagon Alley gets successively less cheerful. By the time of our visit in *Harry Potter and the Half-Blood Prince,* there seems to be little difference between Diagon Alley and Knockturn Alley, and by the time of our visit in *Harry Potter and the Deathly Hallows*, there seems no difference at all.

Little Hangleton

  Location: Somewhere in Great Britain
  Permanent Residents: Villagers
  First Appearance: *Harry Potter and the Goblet of Fire*

GENERAL OVERVIEW

Little Hangleton is a small village which is the ancestral home of Tom Riddle.

Extended Description Little Hangleton is a village where the Riddle family used to live, and where the Riddle house is. The house is used by Lord Voldemort and Wormtail as a base for their activities at the beginning of Harry's fourth year.

Location Its location is uncertain, however we are given a little detail during the summer vacation before the fourth year: *Two hundred miles away, the boy called Harry Potter woke with a start.*

Analysis

Little Hangleton is Tom Marvolo Riddle's "ancestral home;" while he was born in London, his mother Merope Gaunt and father, the muggle Tom Riddle, both lived in this area, and his father is buried here. This is part of the reason that Voldemort, as Tom Riddle was later known, set up his base of operations here; one of the necessary ingredients for the potion that restored Voldemort was *"Bone of the father, unknowingly given,"* for which access to the graveyard in Little Hangleton was necessary.

Tom Marvolo Riddle feels no attachment for the place, however. Despite being the closest thing to an heir left by his father, Tom Riddle, and thus presumably the actual owner of the manor house, Riddle Jr. had only ever visited the house for long enough to murder his father and grandparents. For Voldemort, the house is a convenient place for headquarters, where he is unlikely to be disturbed (once he has murdered the Muggle gardener), with no claims on its ownership apart from his own.

Malfoy Manor

Location: Wiltshire
Permanent Residents: Lucius Malfoy, Narcissa Malfoy, Draco Malfoy
First Appearance: *Harry Potter and the Deathly Hallows*

General Overview

In the Harry Potter series Malfoy Manor is the Wiltshire home of Lucius Malfoy, and his wife Narcissa and son Draco.

Extended Description Though barely mentioned in earlier books, it achieves a significant role in *Harry Potter and the Deathly Hallows* when it is used as headquarters by Voldemort. Previously, Arthur Weasley and other members of the Ministry of Magic had searched the Manor for dark objects, but to no avail.

The first time we see Malfoy Manor is at the beginning of *Harry Potter and the Deathly Hallows*. We learn that the Malfoys kept albino peacocks when one of them startles arriving Death Eaters. We find then that Voldemort is meeting there with his Death Eaters, including Severus Snape. We learn at this point that the Malfoy family is in disgrace in Voldemort's organization; Snape is invited to sit next to Voldemort himself, but when we see the Malfoys they are at the far end of the table. Lucius Malfoy is told at one point to hand over his wand, as he will not be needing it; the inference is that Malfoy is essentially a prisoner in his own house.

Harry, Ron, and Hermione are caught by Snatchers when Harry accidentally speaks Voldemort's name. One of the Snatchers is Fenrir Greyback who, suspecting Harry's identity, has his five prisoners, Harry, Ron, Hermione, Dean Thomas, and Griphook taken to Malfoy Manor. There, Lucius, Draco, and Narcissa are unsure of their identification of Harry, since his face had been jinxed by Hermione right before they were captured, though they do identify Hermione and Ron. Arriving on the scene, Bellatrix sees the sword of Godric Gryffindor, and immediately thinks that it has been extracted from her vault at Gringotts. Knowing that something else that Voldemort values very dearly is in that vault, Bellatrix prevents Lucius from summoning Voldemort, and tortures Hermione to get her to reveal where the sword had come from.

Meanwhile, Dean, Harry, Ron, and Griphook had been taken to a basement room where they found Luna Lovegood and Mr. Ollivander locked up. Luna helps them get free of their bonds. Harry, looking at the shard of the mirror he had gotten from Sirius, sees a sky-blue eye in it, and asks for help. The eye vanishes. Hermione has managed, through her pain, to tell Bellatrix that the sword is a fake; Bellatrix sends Draco down to the basement room to fetch Griphook. Harry tells Griphook that he must corroborate Hermione's story; then Draco arrives and hauls Griphook away. Dobby appears in the basement just as Draco closes the door behind himself. Dobby, though fearful at being back in his old home, says he has been sent to rescue Harry Potter. Harry confirms that he can Apparate out of the basement with others, and tells Dobby to take Luna, Dean, and Mr. Ollivander to Shell Cottage. Dobby does so, but Bellatrix hears the noise of his disapparating, and sends Wormtail to investigate. Harry and Ron attack Wormtail, and Wormtail, after a moment's amazement, begins to defend himself. Harry, being choked by Wormtail's silver hand, reminds Wormtail that he owes his life to Harry, and Wormtail hesitates; sensing the hesitation, the silver hand attacks Wormtail, choking him to death.

With Wormtail's wand, Harry and Ron make their way upstairs in time to hear Griphook confirming that the sword is a fake, whereupon Bellatrix summons Voldemort and tells Fenrir that he can have Hermione. Ron disarms Bellatrix, and Harry catches her wand. Harry Stuns Lucius Malfoy but then has to duck behind the couch as Draco, Narcissa, and Fenrir all aim Stun spells at him. Bellatrix threatens Hermione with the knife she is holding, forcing Ron and Harry to drop their wands, which Draco then collects. The chandelier then falls on Bellatrix's head; Dobby has re-appeared, and tells Bellatrix that she will not hurt Harry Potter or his friends. Narcissa takes aim at him, but her wand goes flying. Harry takes all three wands that Draco was holding and Stuns Fenrir with them; now, holding Griphook and seeing that Ron has a hold on Hermione, Harry Disapparates, headed for Shell Cottage.

Ministry of Magic

Location: Underground London
Permanent Residents: Unknown
First Appearance: *Harry Potter and the Philosopher's Stone* (mentioned), *Harry Potter and the Order of the Phoenix*

Overview

The Ministry of Magic is the government body of the wizarding world in Britain, and has physical offices in London, apparently deep underground. In *The Muggles' Guide to Harry Potter*, as in the Harry Potter series in general, the term is used to refer both to the physical place, and to the government body housed therein.

Extended Description We first hear of the Ministry in *Harry Potter and the Philosopher's Stone,* when Hagrid comments disparagingly about it while reading the *Daily Prophet*. However, we don't actually get to see the physical Ministry location until the fifth book, *Harry Potter and the Order of the Phoenix.*

The visitor's entrance of the Ministry of Magic is an abandoned red telephone phone booth; one enters the Ministry by dialing "62442" ("magic"). While we don't know if it was different before the accession of Voldemort's puppet Minister, Pius Thicknesse, by the seventh book, *Harry Potter and the Deathly Hallows,* the normal means of entrance for employees is via a particular public lavatory; one opens the lavatory booth with a special token and then flushes oneself to the Ministry.

We see the inside of the Ministry on three occasions; however, as is to be expected with such a large organization, we actually see very little of the workings of the place.

Early in *Harry Potter and the Order of the Phoenix,* Harry is summoned to a hearing concerning his apparent breaking of the Statute for the Reasonable Restriction of Underage Sorcery. He accompanies Mr. Weasley to his work, entering through the Visitor's Entrance, and passes through the Auror offices on his way to Mr. Weasley's office. Finding that the hearing has moved, Mr. Weasley takes Harry down to the courtrooms on the level below the Atrium.

Later in that same book, Harry comes to believe that Sirius Black is being tortured by Voldemort in the Department of Mysteries in the basement of the Ministry, and, along with five other students, flies to London to rescue him. It turns out to be a trap set by Voldemort, and a battle ensues, in the course of which the Atrium's Fountain of Magical Brethren is destroyed.

In *Harry Potter and the Deathly Hallows,* Harry, Hermione, and Ron, searching for the Locket Horcrux, enter the Ministry in disguise. They have learned that Dolores Umbridge, a Ministry functionary, currently has the locket, and hope to find some clue as to where it could be. In the course of this visit, we see the floor of the Ministry which is used by the Minister and his close staff, the Atrium, and the courtrooms. One of the areas we visit seems to be a flourishing propaganda production group. In the course of this visit, Harry does manage to recover the locket.

Departments • Level 1: Minister of Magic and Support Staff
• Level 2: Department of Magical Law Enforcement
• Improper Use of Magic Office
• Auror Headquarters
• Wizengamot Administration Services
• Level 3: Department of Magical Accidents and Catastrophes
• Accidental Magic Reversal Squad
• Obliviator Headquarters
• Muggle-Worthy Excuses Committee
• Level 4: Department for the Regulation and Control of Magical Creatures
• Beast, Being and Spirit Divisions
• Pest Advisory Bureau
• Level 5: Department of International Magical Cooperation
• International Magical Trading Standards Body
• International Magical Office of Law
• International Confederation of Wizards, British Seats
• Level 6: Department of Magical Transportation
• Floo Network Authority
• Broom Regulatory Control
• Portkey Office
• Apparation Test Center
• Level 7: Department of Magical Games and Sports
• British and Irish Quidditch League Headquarters
• Official Gobstones Club
• Ludicrous Patents Office
• Atrium
• Courtrooms
• Department of Mysteries

Personnel • Ludovic Bagman—head, Department of Magical Games and Sports (vanished?)
• Millicent Bagnold—former Minister for Magic, mentioned in *Harry Potter and the Order of the Phoenix,* chapter 5 that she was succeeded by Cornelius Fudge
• Amelia Bones (deceased)—Head of Department of Magical Law Enforcement, murdered by Voldemort
• Broderick Bode (deceased while on medical leave)—"Unspeakable," Department of Mysteries
• Dirk Cresswell (deceased)—Head of Goblin Liaison Office
• Croaker—mentioned in *Harry Potter and the Goblet of Fire,* chapter 7, as being an "Unspeakable," Department of Mysteries
• Bartemius Crouch, Sr. (deceased)—Head of Department of International Magical Cooperation
• Dawlish—Auror
• Amos Diggory—Department for the Regulation and Control of Magical Creatures
• Madam Edgecombe—Floo Network Office
• Cornelius Fudge—Minister for Magic (until book 6)
• Mafalda Hopkirk—Improper Use of Magic Office
• Bertha Jorkins (deceased)—Department of Magical Games and Sports
• Alice Longbottom (medical leave)—Auror
• Frank Longbottom (medical leave)—Auror
• Walden Macnair—Committee for the Disposal of Dangerous Creatures
• Cuthbert Mockridge—mentioned in *Harry Potter and the Goblet of Fire,* chapter 7, as being head of the Goblin Liaison Office
• Alastor "Mad-Eye" Moody(retired)—Auror
• Eric Munch—watchwizard
• Bob Ogden (deceased) -Mentioned in *Harry Potter and the Half-Blood Prince,*Chapter 10 as a member of the Magical Law Enforcement Office
• Arnold Peasegood—mentioned in *Harry Potter and the Goblet of Fire,* chapter 7, as being an Obliviator
• Perkins—Arthur Weasley's co-worker in the Misuse of Muggle Artifacts Office
• Proudfoot—Auror, mentioned in *Harry Potter and the Half-Blood Prince,* chapter 8 as being one of the guardians of Hogwarts

- Gawain Robards—Head of the Aurors (after Rufus Scrimgeour)
- Savage—Auror, mentioned in *Harry Potter and the Half-Blood Prince*, chapter 8 as being one of the guardians of Hogwarts
- Newt Scamander—Beast Division, Department for the Regulation and Control of Magical Creatures, retired, and author of *Fantastic Beasts and Where to Find Them*
- Rufus Scrimgeour—Head of Auror Office, named Minister for Magic in book 6, deceased
- Kingsley Shacklebolt—Auror; according to interviews after publication of book 7, later Minister for Magic
- Pius Thicknesse—Head of the Department of Magical Law Enforcement (after Amelia Bones), named Minister for Magic after Rufus Scrimgeour
- Nymphadora Tonks—Auror
- Dolores Umbridge—Senior Undersecretary to the Minister for Magic under Cornelius Fudge
- Arthur Weasley—head of the Misuse of Muggle Artifacts Office under Cornelius Fudge and head of the Office for the Detection and Confiscation of Counterfeit Defensive Spells and Protective Objects under Rufus Scrimgeour
- Percy Weasley—Department of International Magical Cooperation, promoted to Junior Assistant to the Minister for Magic under Cornelius Fudge, retained that position under Rufus Scrimgeour and Pius Thicknesse
- Gilbert Wimple—mentioned in *Harry Potter and the Goblet of Fire*, chapter 7, as being on the Committee on Experimental Charms

Analysis

While the Ministry is mentioned very often in the series, and almost always in a manner that refers to the organization rather than the place, we really learn very little about the organization of the Ministry. We are told that the Minister is elected, as Fudge says, at the end of *Harry Potter and the Goblet of Fire*, that if he was to try and carry out any of the instructions that Dumbledore suggests, he would be voted out immediately. And while Fudge is, as we learn in the sixth book, replaced by Scrimgeour following the revelation that Voldemort had returned, we do not see the mechanism used for that vote. The reader does rather get the feeling that the magical government runs completely independently of the Muggle government, but apart from that we learn little about its operation. We do learn that the Ministry is very quick to follow the lead of the currently elected Minister, almost to the extent of being his own personal fiefdom; the Ministry as a whole seems to shift almost overnight from Fudge's policy of denial to Scrimgeour's policy of active defence, and again to Thicknesse's anti-Muggle stance.

We do learn that the Ministry, like all human groups, has organized itself into sub-groups, and we become aware of the bureaucracy inherent in the situation. In various asides that Arthur Weasley makes concerning the maintenance workers, and our own observation of Arthur's own work space, we learn that the Ministry is rife with office politics even in times of peace: the maintenance workers' demands for more pay were supported by a solid month of dreary rainfall outside the Ministry's magical windows, and Arthur's unpopular department is required to squeeze two workers and all their files into a converted broom closet.

Questions

1. We see rather a lot of the Department of Mysteries during the battle. We actually see rooms or wings dedicated to three mysteries, and hear later of a room dedicated to a fourth. What are the four mysteries that we see or hear about? What other mysteries might there be?

Greater Picture

In the Battle at the Department of Mysteries, Harry first opens a door onto a room full of brains in tanks; presumably this is the Mystery of Consciousness or Thought. The second, the amphitheatre with the Veil, is apparently the mystery of Death. The third, that Harry cannot open, we learn later is the room of the mystery of Love. The fourth is the room of the mystery of Time. Everything that we find in the first room is somehow related to Time. The Hall of Prophecies beyond that is clearly related to Time, though also to Consciousness, and so there should be a door from that room to the brain room. We learn that in the course of the battle, Ron, Ginny, and Luna pass through a room containing a model of the planets; this may be dedicated to the mystery of Space, though it is probably more to do with Astronomy, and the effects of planetary position on various spells.

As the circular chamber leading into the Department of Mysteries has twelve doors, one of which is the exit, there must be a total of eleven mysteries. Assuming Space is one of them, we have heard of five, and six must remain, assuming none of the doors are traps.

Platform 9 and Three Quarters

Location: Kings Cross Station, London, England
Permanent Residents: None
First Appearance: *Harry Potter and the Philosopher's Stone*

General Overview

Platform Nine and Three Quarters is a secret platform at King's Cross Station in London. From this location students at Hogwarts are able to catch the Hogwarts Express train.

Extended Description Platform Nine and Three Quarters is reached by leaning against, or running through, the barrier between platforms 9 and 10 at King's Cross Station. It is apparently physically located within the confines of the station, though perhaps at a lower level, as the train does seem to pass through an appropriate area of London as it leaves the city. The platform has been used in the third, fourth, fifth, and sixth year, as the place for last-minute questions and warnings, as

Harry, Ron, and Hermione depart the place they have been through the summer for another year at Hogwarts. In the first year, of course, it was the stage for the initial meeting between the Weasley children then attending Hogwarts (Ron, Fred, George, and Percy), and Harry; and it proved inaccessible in the second year due to the well-intentioned but misguided actions of Dobby the house-elf.

ANALYSIS

While the platform might well have been intended to be the place where we change from Muggle to magical life, it has only actually acted as that transition once, in *Harry Potter and the Philosopher's Stone*. In the other four books where it is a factor, and in *Harry Potter and the Chamber of Secrets* where it is inaccessible, Harry has been living in the magical world for at least a short time before the trip to the station: three times at The Burrow, once at the Leaky Cauldron in Diagon Alley, and once at Number Twelve, Grimmauld Place.

That is not to say that it is not a transition; in each case, it is a return to school, and thus to a place where Harry's own use of magic is not only permitted, but required. Harry, as an underage wizard, is of course not allowed to use magic anywhere except school. It seems that the largely unsupervised Hogwarts Express is seen as an extension of school, for the purposes of determining whether magic is allowed. Thus, the transition from the repressed world of the underage wizard, to the free world of the wizard who is able to cast spells, seems to happen on the platform. The reverse transition, of course, happens in the other direction. Stepping off the train and onto the platform is a return to the world of the underage wizard, a return to the world where magic must be repressed or hidden for fear of frightening the Muggles. We see, in each of the first five books, Harry's reluctance to approach that transition, to return to the unexciting life he perforce must share with the Dursleys.

Privet Drive

Location: Little Whinging, Surrey
Permanent Residents: Harry Potter, Vernon Dursley, Petunia Dursley, Dudley Dursley
First Appearance: *Harry Potter and the Philosopher's Stone*

GENERAL OVERVIEW

Number 4 Privet Drive is a thoroughly ordinary house on a thoroughly ordinary street where Harry Potter lives with the Dursleys, his thoroughly ordinary aunt, uncle, and cousin.

Extended Description Harry lives in a cupboard under the stairs until he begins receiving letters from Hogwarts, addressed exactly to his "cupboard under the stairs." In what is possibly an attempt to avoid future letters being sent, or possibly an attempt to prevent outsiders from knowing how Harry is being treated, Harry's aunt and uncle move him to his cousin Dudley's second bedroom, where Dudley stores his extra and broken gifts. Throughout the rest of the series, Harry retains the use of this bedroom when he is living at the Dursleys, though the broken gifts are apparently moved somewhere else. Harry is apparently locked into this room at times, just as he was locked into the closet under the stairs initially, at one point even having bars placed over the window.

ANALYSIS

The ordinary, non-magical nature of the house on Privet Drive is repeated throughout the series. It reflects the Dursley's views on magic, that it should not be tolerated, it should not be allowed. Even the fireplace has been walled up and an electric fire placed in the wall where it was; the possible randomness of a real wood fire is just unthinkable for the Dursleys. This is contrasted with the rather amazing pile of magical construction that is The Burrow, Harry's favorite place to stay (apart, perhaps, from Hogwarts).

GREATER PICTURE

Harry absolutely hates the time he spends in the house on Privet Drive; he would much rather be living with wizards. However, the protection he gained from the death of his mother, when she was trying to save him from Voldemort, will remain in force only so long as there is a place that he can call home, which is owned and occupied by his own blood—in this case, Petunia, his mothers' sister. Harry is not allowed to know this until late in the series, and even when he does understand the necessity for it, his knowing it does not improve the feelings about his required presence in that house. This protection ends once he comes of age at seventeen, which will happen early in *Harry Potter and the Deathly Hallows*; he is then equally at risk wherever he is, and so there is no need for him to return to Privet Drive ever again, for which he seems to be profoundly grateful.

Ravenclaw House

Location: Ravenclaw Tower, on the west side of the castle
Permanent Residents: Ravenclaw students
First Appearance: *Harry Potter and the Philosopher's Stone*

GENERAL OVERVIEW

Ravenclaw House is one of the four Houses in Hogwarts.

Extended Description   Housemaster: Professor Filius Flitwick
Founder: Rowena Ravenclaw
Coat of Arms: bronze eagle, blue
Ghost: The Grey Lady
Characteristics: "If you've a ready mind, Where those of wit and learning, Will always find their kind."

Location of common room: Ravenclaw Tower, west side of the castle

It is only late in the seventh book that we learn where the common room is, though Harry does note that when they leave the first meeting of Dumbledore's Army, in *Harry Potter and the Order of the Phoenix*, the Ravenclaw students head for a tower on the west side of the school. While the entrances to at least two of the other common rooms are guarded by means of passwords, the entrance to the Ravenclaw common room is a wooden door with no handle, only a knocker in the shape of a raven. When the knocker is used, the raven, in a musical voice, asks a question; if a reasonable answer is provided, the door will open. Only twice do we see people admitted to the tower, so we see only two of the questions. Luna is asked, "Which came first, the phoenix or the flame?" to which Luna says "I think the answer is that a circle has no beginning." When Amycus Carrow seeks entrance, he is asked, "Where do vanished objects go?" Amycus is unable to answer, but eventually Professor McGonagall answers with "Into non-being, which is to say, everything."

Within, the common room is a large, circular, and airy room, with wide windows facing in all directions. The ceiling is domed and starry, and there are the usual tables, chairs, and bookcases, and in a niche in one wall, a marble statue of Rowena Ravenclaw.

We see very few members of Ravenclaw house in the books. Two who have fairly large roles are Cho Chang and Luna Lovegood.

ANALYSIS

That an answer to a philosophical question is required at the entrance to the common room is meant to highlight the nature of Ravenclaw House. Ravenclaw is said to have most treasured intellect, and these questions are apparently designed to highlight the type, if not the level, of intellect most desired by this Founder. It is arguable that this sort of pure reasoning is a high form of intelligence; however, the questions selected in our hearing are relatively simple, of the sort that could be expected to be answered by someone with the simplest grounding in philosophy. It is perhaps interesting that Professor McGonagall has no trouble with the question that is asked, though clearly Amycus Carrow does, as did his sister Alecto—McGonagall says that Professor Flitwick had let Alecto in earlier. Presumably, this is meant to highlight the brute nature of the Carrows, and possibly through them, Death Eaters in general. It is perhaps misleading, however, to generalize from these two examples; it is certainly true that the brutish bully, like the Carrows, or like Crabbe and Goyle, would be attracted to a regime in which their limited abilities would prove useful. But against them, we must put the intelligence of Snape, or Lucius Malfoy and his son Draco. For more on the subject of Death Eaters, please see Death Eaters.

Riddle Manor

Location: Little Hangleton
Permanent Residents: Frank Bryce
First Appearance: *Harry Potter and the Goblet of Fire*

GENERAL OVERVIEW

Riddle Manor is the ancestral home of Tom Riddle's Muggle father. At the time of this story, it stands empty.

Extended Description In *Harry Potter and the Goblet of Fire* we read the story of how Tom Riddle Sr. and his parents were found dead one morning fifty years ago, and how the gardener, Frank Bryce, was suspected of their murders until it was found that they apparently had not been murdered by anything, but had simply died . . . possibly of fright. We also see how Lord Voldemort has moved into that house, and we see him killing Frank. Other clues through the course of the book lead us to believe that Voldemort is using the house as his base of operations; in fact, according to what we are later told by Barty Crouch, he has moved his base of operations to Bartemius Crouch's house, where he and Wormtail take up residence after Mr. Crouch is placed under the Imperius curse. After Crouch's escape, Voldemort and Wormtail do return to Riddle Manor, and remain there until the end of the book. While no direct mention of the Manor is made in other books, we do see some of its environs in Professor Dumbledore's Pensieve in *Harry Potter and the Half-Blood Prince*.

ANALYSIS

Riddle Manor is not, strictly speaking, necessary. It is true that a shut-in, poverty-stricken girl like Merope Gaunt is most likely to become infatuated with the local lord of the Manor, as he will have all the appropriate accouterments—attendants, property, jewelery—and financial means to lift our poor peasant out of her downtrodden existence and into the lap of luxury. Though likely any reasonably well-off Muggle would have served the purpose, it is much more romantic if the lord of the manor falls for the peasant girl; and Merope seems to have been preconditioned to be romantic. One must assume that Riddle Manor is created purely to highlight the romance that Merope can force with her phial of love potion.

After the death of the Riddle family, the house, we are told, reverted to some mysterious people in London who tried, unsuccessfully, to rent it out. While we are never told who the people in London are, it is possible that they are, knowingly or otherwise, agents of Tom Marvolo Riddle, who could have assumed that he was the heir, being the late Tom Riddle's illegitimate son. One wonders, though, whether he would not try to dispose of anything that reminded him of his Muggle father. As the house certainly must remind him of the late Tom Riddle, one must wonder why Tom Marvolo Riddle would choose to live in it.

In fact, except for the one night when Frank Bryce was killed, we do not know where Voldemort was living. He could well have chosen to leave Riddle Manor that night for some place with less associations for him. Or he could have chosen to stay there, as a way of spiting his deceased father and grandparents. We do know that he was in the environs of Little Hangleton in June, when the Triwizard Tournament ended.

GREATER PICTURE

It is tempting to believe that Voldemort created a Horcrux, the one embedded in the ring of the Peverells that Voldemort had stolen from his uncle Morfin Gaunt, via the murder of Tom Riddle Sr. Evidence in *Harry Potter and the Half-Blood Prince* is inconclusive: Riddle's conversation with Professor Slughorn, that we see in the Pensieve, suggests that Riddle did not yet know how to create a Horcrux. During that conversation, Tom asks about Horcruxes, and we see that Tom is wearing the Gaunt ring. It is possible that Tom had already created a Horcrux, in the ring, and his question is designed to put Slughorn more at ease about his abilities and ideas; we can see that the main thrust of his questions is more to do with the possibility of creating multiple Horcruxes. Dumbledore does state that Tom had no longer wanted to wear the ring once it was a Horcrux, and while this must be supposition on Dumbledore's part, he was usually accurate in his guesses. Additionally, we have Tom's look of triumph when he has received the information about Horcruxes from Slughorn; given the author's usual efficiency, we have to think that he has done more here than just hoodwink Slughorn. Tom must have gotten some real information from Slughorn to merit that amount of joy.

The author has stated that it was the death of Tom's father that allowed him to create his first Horcrux; presumably he only chose to hide the Horcrux away, rather than keeping it close to himself, when he had created a second one. It is possible that Frank Bryce's murder was used to create the final Horcrux of the set that Voldemort was planning; bringing the circle to closure, by generating the last piece of his "*immortality*" in the abandoned home of his hated father, would likely have appealed to Voldemort's sense of humour. It is also possible that Bertha Jorkins' death was used to create a Horcrux; at that point, he would have been keen to finish the full set, and would have had no way to know that Frank would so conveniently present himself. The author has stated in an interview that the sixth and final planned Horcrux was created by means of the death of Bertha Jorkins.

Room of Requirement

Location: Hogwarts, seventh floor
Permanent Residents: none
First Appearance: *Harry Potter and the Goblet of Fire*

GENERAL OVERVIEW

The Room of Requirement is a room on the seventh floor of Hogwarts Castle that appears when someone is in very great need of it, and contains what that individual needs at that time.

Extended Description   The Room of Requirement is located on Hogwarts' seventh floor, across from the tapestry of Barnabas the Barmy. To "open it" you must walk past the area of the door three times, thinking of what you need in your mind. For example: Say you need a place to study. You would walk past the area of the door three times thinking in your mind, "I need a place to study." After the third pass by it the door will appear and you may enter to find everything you need inside.

The Room first appears in a passing comment by Professor Dumbledore at the Yule Ball in *Harry Potter and the Goblet of Fire*. He mentions that he had found a room full of chamber pots, but has been unable to find it again after that.

When Harry needs a secret place for Dumbledore's Army to meet, Dobby the house elf tells him about this room, describing it as, "A room that a person can only enter when they have real need of it. Sometimes it is there and sometimes it is not, but when it appears, it is always equipped for the seeker's needs." Dobby also called it the, "Come and Go Room." Dobby said he had used it as a place to let Winky sleep off the effects of Butterbeer. Harry used it as a meeting place for Dumbledore's Army in *Harry Potter and the Order of the Phoenix*. When Fred and George see it, they comment that they had used it as a hiding place from Filch, but it had then been no larger than a broom closet, that being what they had needed at the time.

In *Harry Potter and the Half-Blood Prince*, Draco Malfoy uses this room to repair the Vanishing Cabinet. Harry unknowingly uses the same aspect of the room to hide his potions book. Draco's secret activities are discovered when Professor Trelawney, who has been using it to hide her sherry, finds it already occupied by someone who roughly throws her back out into the hallway.

In *Harry Potter and the Deathly Hallows*, the revived Dumbledore's Army are using the Room of Requirement as a hiding place. It ends up being quite comfortable, and even, when required, creates a tunnel that ends in an upstairs room at the Hog's Head Inn.

ANALYSIS

Initially it appears that this room could be all things to all people, always having exactly what is needed for the efforts of the day. It appears, though, that it has a number of standard configurations, as Professor Trelawney (who wants to hide her sherry), Harry (who needs a place to hide his textbook), and Draco (who needs a place to hide while he works on the vanishing cabinet), all end up in the same room, a vast warehouse of broken and hidden stuff. This is actually to be expected; for it to be useful as a meeting place, everyone who wants to meet there must be able to enter the same room, which they do by wanting the same sort of thing. The reason that Harry is unable to enter the room when Draco is in there working is that Draco, being in the room, has locked it into its "junk warehouse" state, and as Harry does not think he is looking for a junk warehouse, he is never able to enter it while Draco is there.

Shell Cottage

Location: Seaside
Permanent Residents: Bill Weasley, Fleur Delacour
First Appearance: *Harry Potter and the Deathly Hallows*

GENERAL OVERVIEW

Shell Cottage is the cottage on the oceanside where Bill and Fleur reside after their marriage.

Extended Description Ron stays at Shell Cottage over Christmas of Harry's seventh year, when he apparates away from Harry and Hermione after their fight. This is also where Harry, Ron, Hermione, Luna, Dean, Mr. Olivander and Griphook take shelter after the fight at Malfoy Manor, and is the place where Dobby is laid to rest. With all of these people, the cottage is quite crowded, particularly as Griphook requires a room of his own, and Harry will not let Bill send Griphook or Mr. Ollivander to a different safe-house. We hear at one point that Harry, Ron, and Dean are sleeping in the living room.

The location of the cottage is protected by the Fidelius charm; the secret-keeper is Bill Weasley. Lupin visits while Harry is there, to announce the birth of his son Teddy.

In post-publication interviews, the author has suggested that Shell Cottage is located on the outskirts of Tinworth, in Cornwall.

Shrieking Shack

Location: Hogsmeade village
Permanent Residents: None
First Appearance: *Harry Potter and the Prisoner of Azkaban*

GENERAL OVERVIEW

The Shrieking Shack is famed as the most haunted place in Britain. It is a small house, set well away from the rest of the village of Hogsmeade village, fenced off and with all its windows and doors boarded up.

Extended Description The Shrieking Shack got its reputation some twenty or thirty years before our story begins, when loud howls and shrieks were heard from the building at odd times.

In *Harry Potter and the Prisoner of Azkaban*, we learn that the Shrieking Shack can be reached via a tunnel that starts at the roots of the Whomping Willow, an animate willow tree with a nasty temper. We also learn that the shrieks and howls were actually produced by Remus Lupin as a schoolboy; he is a Werewolf, and the tunnel had been created especially for him. Once in the Shrieking Shack and transformed, he could not escape, and so he was a danger to nobody except himself.

These revelations are made in one of the final chapters of the book, which actually take place largely in the Shrieking Shack. Harry and Hermione had gone down the tunnel to rescue Ron, who was in turn dragged down the tunnel by a large black dog. The dog turned out to be the Animagus form of Sirius Black, who was not after Ron, but instead was after Scabbers, Ron's pet rat. Scabbers turned out to be the Animagus form of Peter Pettigrew. They are later joined by Lupin, who reveals the reason the Whomping Willow was planted and the secret passage under it created.

The Shrieking Shack again makes an appearance in *Harry Potter and the Deathly Hallows*, where Lord Voldemort makes it his headquarters for the first assault on Hogwarts. At that time, we see that Voldemort has uncovered one of the windows to allow him to watch the battle. He is apparently unaware of the existence of the secret passage to the Hogwarts grounds, and it is through this passage that Harry, Ron, and Hermione are able to approach him closely enough that they are able to witness the death of Snape.

ANALYSIS

We can assume that, as Tom Riddle was long gone from Hogwarts when Lupin arrived, the Shrieking Shack holds no fears for Voldemort, and probably seemed only a conveniently located, abandoned building that he could use as an observation post. Additionally, he would be unaware of the tunnel that was created for Lupin. Almost certainly, Voldemort has simply unsealed a door as well as the window, and entered the Shack through a normal doorway. It is certain that Voldemort would not enter the school grounds to reach the Whomping Willow, only to leave them again via the tunnel to the Shrieking Shack.

Slytherin House

Location: Hogwarts dungeons
Permanent Residents: Slytherin students
First Appearance: *Harry Potter and the Philosopher's Stone*

GENERAL OVERVIEW

Slytherin House is one of the four Houses in Hogwarts. The common room is located deep within Hogwarts, apparently in the Dungeons.

Extended Description Housemaster: Professor Horace Slughorn (about fifty years before the series opens, and again throughout book 7); Severus Snape (books 1 through 6)
Founder: Salazar Slytherin
Coat of Arms: silver serpent, green
Ghost: The Bloody Baron
Characteristics: "These cunning folks use any means, To achieve their ends."
Location of common room: The Slytherin common room is a low-ceilinged, dungeon-like room with greenish lamps and chairs. It is located in the dungeons, behind an apparently blank stretch of wall. The author has commented that it is actually located under the lake.

While we see the inside of the Slytherin common room in *Harry Potter and the Chamber of Secrets*, Harry and Ron's sojourn there is necessarily brief. Also, the description of the common room that Harry gives in *Harry Potter and the Deathly Hallows* to prove his assumed House association does not quite match what he sees in the earlier book.

Analysis

The number of students actually in each House is uncertain. We only ever hear of five boys and five girls in each year, but we have been told by the author in an interview that the average class size (all residents of one House for one year) is about thirty. Thus we must assume a population of 210 per house, fifteen boys and fifteen girls each year.

One gets the impression from things said in *Harry Potter and the Goblet of Fire* that House honours, notably the House cup and the Quidditch cup, are generally held by either Slytherin house or Gryffindor house, with Ravenclaw house occasionally winning an upset victory. It is to stymie Slytherin house's long run of House cup victories that Professor McGonagall chooses to relax the rule about first-year students and brooms for Harry. One must wonder whether the placement of the Slytherin common room under the lake is an author's mistake. It is true that in the same book where we enter the Common Room, we also see the Chamber of Secrets, which also has a major connection to Salazar Slytherin, including a statue of him on the far wall. It is also true that Harry remarks on the water on the floor of the Chamber, which leads us to believe that the Chamber is located under the lake. It is certainly possible that the author had slightly confused the two locales, and having placed the Slytherin common room under the lake in an interview, then had to keep it there in later chapters of the story.

Spinner's End

Location: Unknown
Permanent Residents: Severus Snape
First Appearance: *Harry Potter and the Half-Blood Prince*

General Overview

The house at Spinner's End, a gloomy house with a book-lined parlour, is the home of Severus Snape.

Extended Description We first see this house when Narcissa Malfoy, followed by Bellatrix Lestrange, her sister, visit Snape in an attempt to get Snape's promise that he will help Narcissa's son Draco with the mission that has been set for him by the Dark Lord. We find Snape in residence, along with Peter Pettigrew, who has been sent to Spinner's End to assist Snape, and is most annoyed that Snape treats him as a servant. Pettigrew does try to listen in on their conversation, but Snape, knowing he is there, fires a spell through the bookcase and into the secret staircase where Pettigrew is hiding, sending him away.

We later find out that Snape is not the only character from the books in this particular down-on-its-heels mill town. In *Harry Potter and the Deathly Hallows*, we learn that Snape had been friends with Lily Evans (who later became Harry's mother), and had known Petunia Evans (Harry's Aunt Petunia) as well.

St. Mungo's Hospital for Magical Maladies and Injuries

Location: London
Permanent Residents: None
First Appearance: *Harry Potter and the Goblet of Fire*

General Overview

St. Mungo's Hospital for Magical Maladies and Injuries is the wizard's hospital founded by Mungo Bonham. It is located in London.

Extended Description While we don't actually see the hospital in *Harry Potter and the Goblet of Fire,* it is mentioned by Professor Dumbledore that Neville's parents are long-term residents of St. Mungo's Hospital.

To Muggles, the hospital appears to be the store Purge and Dowse Ltd., which is "Closed for Refurbishment." Wizards and witches working in this hospital, who work directly with the patients, are called *Healers;* they can be recognized by their lime green robes. The hospital can treat a wide range of magic-related illnesses and injuries.

Floor Guide (as it appears in Harry Potter and the Order of the Phoenix):

• Artifact Accidents: Ground Floor (Cauldron explosion, wand backfiring, broom crashes, etc.)
• Creature-Induced Injuries: First Floor (Bites, stings, burns, embedded spines, etc.)
• Magical Bug: Second Floor (Contagious maladies, e.g. dragon pox, vanishing sickness, scrofungulus)
• Potion and Plant Poisoning: Third Floor (Rashes, regurgitation, uncontrollable giggling, etc.)
• Spell Damage: Fourth Floor (Unliftable, jinxes, hexes, and incorrectly applied charms, etc.)
• Visitor's Tearoom and Hospital Shop: Fifth Floor ('If you are unsure where to go, incapable of normal speech, or unable to remember why you are here, our Welcome Witch will be pleased to help.')

In *Harry Potter and the Order of the Phoenix*, Mr. Weasley is taken to St. Mungo's after Harry reports seeing him attacked by a snake. Harry, Ron, Fred, George, Ginny, and Hermione visit him there, along with Mrs. Weasley, Mad-Eye Moody, and Tonks. Mr. Weasley is in a ward with other people who have received bites from magical creatures, including a werewolf and a woman who won't say what had bitten her. When Harry, Ron, Hermione, Ginny, and the Twins return to St. Mungo's some time later to visit again, Ginny and the Trio end up on the wrong floor of the hospital. There, they find the long-term spell damage patients, including one-time Professor Lockhart, still suffering from his own mis-fired memory charm, and Broderick Bode. They also run into Neville and his grandmother Augusta, there visiting Neville's parents.

Broderick Bode later dies in the hospital when a Devil's Snare which had been sent to him as a pot plant (US: potted plant) strangles him. The hospital is unable to explain how a Devil's Snare could have been accepted. We actually only enter St. Mungo's in this book. We do hear of it in many places, though; in particular, Professor McGonagall goes to St. Mungo's after she has been hit by multiple Stunners during Professor Umbridge's attempt to arrest Hagrid, Katie Bell is sent to St. Mungo's to recover after she touches a jinxed necklace, and it is said that Neville's grandmother had put the Auror Dawlish in St. Mungo's when he had tried to arrest her.

The Burrow

Location: Near Ottery St. Catchpole
Permanent Residents: Arthur Weasley, Molly Weasley, Bill Weasley, Charlie Weasley, Percy Weasley, Fred Weasley, George Weasley, Ron Weasley, Ginny Weasley
First Appearance: *Harry Potter and the Chamber of Secrets*

GENERAL OVERVIEW

The Burrow is the rural home of the Weasley family, located near the fictional town of Ottery St. Catchpole.

Extended Description   The Burrow is a Wizard-built ramshackle multi-story dwelling that visibly looks like it takes magic to keep it from falling apart. It has a ghoul in the attic, gnomes in the garden and an adjacent pasture that has been pressed into use as a Quidditch pitch for years. There's a shed where Arthur Weasley, the head of the family, explores and tinkers with the Muggle artifacts he comes across, often with destructive results. Near Molly Weasley's kitchen is a grandfather clock with a hand for each family member and markings around the face for places they might be ("home," "traveling," "mortal peril").

With seven children in the family, there's not much money to go round, and a real spirit of "make-do" pervades the Burrow and its genteel poverty, but to Harry Potter, who grew up unloved and unwanted for ten years before he re-entered the Wizarding world at the age of eleven, the Burrow is his summer-holiday spot of choice, because it's filled with a family's love in enough abundance to welcome him within.

ANALYSIS

The main purpose of The Burrow seems to be contrast. It is an overcrowded, cluttered, haphazard house held together with the wizarding equivalent of baling wire and bubble gum, and there is a very real shortage of money shown by the need to "make do." Set against this we have Harry's nominal home at Number 4, Privet Drive, a very neat and clean new house, squared at the corners, perfect in every way, with enough space that an entire room can be set aside for Dudley's broken birthday presents ... and absolutely horrible to live in for anyone who has any real feeling at all. The contrast between the Weasley's physical poverty and spiritual richness, set against the Dursley's physical financial stability and spiritual emptiness, mirrors the difference between Harry's sterile life in the Muggle world, and his almost overfull life in the Wizarding world. It is noted in *A History of Magic* by Bathilda Bagshot that Ottery St. Catchpole "on the south coast of England" is one of a number of villages where wizards settled in relatively large numbers after the ratification of the International Statute of Secrecy in 1689.

The Three Broomsticks

Location: Hogsmeade main street
Permanent Residents: Madam Rosmerta
First Appearance: *Harry Potter and the Prisoner of Azkaban*

GENERAL OVERVIEW

The Three Broomsticks is one of the major attractions of Hogsmeade for the students and staff of Hogwarts on their infrequent Hogsmeade weekends. Located on the main street of Hogsmeade village, it is a warm and cheerful place, presided over by Madam Rosmerta, a warm, cheerful, and curvaceous witch,

Extended Description   Harry's first visit to the Three Broomsticks is extremely alarming; it is here that he hears the story of how Sirius Black had betrayed his parents and killed another wizard and a number of Muggles.

Most of Harry's further visits to the Three Broomsticks have fairly major repercussions, as well. It is in this pub in Harry's fourth year that Harry is invited by Hagrid to come and see the dragons that will make up the First Task of the Triwizard Tournament; at the same time, we learn that Alastor Moody's magical eye can see through Harry's Invisibility Cloak. Later in the same year, Harry is offered information on beating the Second Task by Ludo Bagman, and Hermione tells off Rita Skeeter, an action that results in Rita writing a scurrilous story for Witch Weekly about Hermione.

In Harry's fifth year, needing a place to meet with other students, Hermione chooses to meet at the Hog's Head, rather than the Three Broomsticks, as there would be more privacy there. This privacy proves illusory, which may be why Hermione chooses the Three Broomsticks for a later meeting with Harry, Luna Lovegood, and Rita Skeeter. At this meeting, Harry talks briefly with a morose Hagrid, who is thinking about his family, then is interviewed by Rita about his experience the previous year when Voldemort had returned.

While Harry, Hermione, and Ron do visit the Three Broomsticks in Harry's sixth year, it is a cheerless visit, and culminates in the Trio seeing Katie Bell being jinxed by a package she had apparently received there. As a result, Hogsmeade Weekends are canceled for the rest of the year. Harry does pass the Three Broomsticks later in the year, with Professor Dumbledore, but they do not enter: Dumbledore says he fancies a quieter drink and heads towards the Hog's Head. Returning from that trip, which had been cover for retrieval of one of Voldemort's Horcruxes, Harry and a greatly weakened Dumbledore return to Hogsmeade, where they are met by Madam Rosmerta who warns them of the Dark Mark floating over Hogwarts. She loans them brooms, and Harry and Dumbledore fly for the school.

It turns out that Draco Malfoy, who has been given the mission of killing Dumbledore by Voldemort, has placed Madam Rosmerta under the Imperius curse, and thus has been aware of Dumbledore's absences. It was Madam Rosmerta, under Draco's control, who gave the jinxed necklace to Katie Bell. Harry does not attend Hogwarts in the seventh book, but he does return there to hunt down a final Horcrux. Apparating into Hogsmeade, Harry triggers an alarm, the Caterwaul, which brings Death Eaters out of the Three Broomsticks hunting him.

ANALYSIS

Wizards, like anyone else, like to have a place where they can unwind and relax, and for residents of Hogsmeade and the teachers at Hogwarts, that place is the Three Broomsticks. This is where wizards go to get Butterbeer, mead, and Firewhisky, among other things. As usual among pubs, there are those that cater to the more regular class of clients and those that cater to the fringes of society; the Three Broomsticks serves the regular wizards, leaving the more shady customers to the Hog's Head Inn.

The Three Broomsticks is something of a leveled playing field; it is here that some of the distinction between student and teacher is lifted, so that Harry can speak relatively freely with Hagrid, and so that he can eavesdrop on private conversations between teachers. Of course, the alcohol helps this, and in fact at one point when we see Hagrid, he is rather morosely drunk. It is worth mentioning that the drinking age in the UK is much lower than it is in the United States; it is legal to drink at age 18 in a pub, or at 16 in a restaurant with a meal, and at age 5 at home. The laws in the Wizarding world must be even more lenient, as the Three Broomsticks and the Hog's Head are clearly pubs, yet third-years (age 13 and 14) can order Butterbeer (apparently mildly alcoholic).

Given how crowded the Three Broomsticks is, one might wonder why there are no other pubs apart from the unsavory Hog's Head Inn. One must consider, however, that whenever we see the Three Broomsticks, it is a Hogsmeade weekend, and the pub is full of Hogwarts students. Almost certainly business on regular days is slow enough that a second pub would not be supported by the population. However, it is equally certain that the pub will not fail even with the ending of Hogsmeade weekends. The pub is so central to the British way of life that every town has at least one; it is unthinkable that a village without a pub could exist.

The Leaky Cauldron

Location: London, Charing Cross Road
Permanent Residents: Tom (last name unknown)
First Appearance: *Harry Potter and the Philosopher's Stone*

GENERAL OVERVIEW

The Leaky Cauldron is a popular Wizarding pub in London. It is the entrance to Diagon Alley. For much of the end of the 20th Century, Tom was the landlord.

Extended Description The pub was built by Daisy Dodderidge in 1500 "to serve as a gateway between the non-wizarding world and Diagon Alley." It rents rooms, has a bar, several private parlor rooms, and a large dining room. To Muggles, the pub appears to be a broken-down old shop front on Charing Cross Road. The rear of the pub, however, opens up onto a chilly courtyard and the entrance to Diagon Alley. To gain access, a witch or wizard taps a specific brick in the wall with his or her wand. A doorway to Diagon Alley then forms which then re-arranges back to the original wall after the person(s) walk through.

GREATER PICTURE

The author has said in interviews after publication of the seventh book in the series that the pub is later taken over by Hannah Abbott, who has married Neville Longbottom, then professor of Herbology at Hogwarts.

Weasleys' Wizard Wheezes

Location: Number 93, Diagon Alley, London
Permanent Residents: Fred and George Weasley
First Appearance: *Harry Potter and the Half-Blood Prince*

GENERAL OVERVIEW

Weasleys' Wizard Wheezes is the joke shop owned by Fred and George Weasley. Their dream of opening a joke shop is mentioned in several of the books (especially *Harry Potter and the Order of the Phoenix*), and it was finally realized in *Harry Potter and the Half-Blood Prince*.

Extended Description George and Fred have been interested in practical jokes all during their Hogwarts years. Zonko's Joke Shop was their favorite store in Hogsmeade. Beginning in *Harry Potter and the Goblet of Fire*, they turn their (often underestimated) talents to inventing and developing unique wizarding jokes and novelties. They begin a small mail order business, which we hear about when their mother discovers the order forms and expresses her disapproval. Their dream of starting their own joke store is realized when Harry gives them the 1000 Galleon Triwizard prize he won. Harry says that given Voldemort's return, "We could all do with a few laughs." In *Harry Potter and the Order of the Phoenix*, the twins actively test and market their products at Hogwarts, often using first year students as paid guinea pigs. Somewhere during the year, they secure the store premises in Diagon Alley and eventually leave school early to operate full-time.

In contrast to the ordinary buildings around it, Weasleys' Wizard Wheezes[1] is described as "hitting the eye like a firework display." A poster in one window reads WHY ARE YOU WORRYING ABOUT YOU-KNOW-WHO? YOU SHOULD BE WORRYING ABOUT U-NO-POO: THE CONSTIPATION SENSATION THAT'S GRIPPING THE NATION!.

---

1. American readers should note that *wizard*, as an adjective, is similar in meaning to "terrific," and *wheeze* is a synonym for "joke."

When Harry, Hermione, and the Weasleys visit the shop at the beginning of *Harry Potter and the Half-Blood Prince*, it is completely packed with customers. The shop sells all sorts of tricks, toys, and novelty items, such as Skiving Snackboxes, which make you appear ill so you can get out of class. Other products include Daydream Charms, WonderWitch products for young women, Reusable Hangman, trick wands, and Peruvian instant darkness powder. All of the magic deployed is quite sophisticated and probably beyond the capability of the average witch or wizard. Even Hermione is impressed with the magical knowledge and skill employed by Fred and George. Fred tells Harry that they also do steady business selling Defence Against the Dark Arts products, particularly to the Ministry. Apparently many wizards at the Ministry are unable to perform a decent Shield charm, making the Twins' "Shield Hats" a valued commodity. The shop employs a woman named Verity who, to Harry's amusement, called the twins "Mr. Weasley and Mr. Weasley."

QUESTIONS

1. Will Fred and George's products be useful in the war against Voldemort in *Deathly Hallows*?

MAJOR EVENTS

BATTLES
- Duel in the Chamber of Secrets
- Duel in the Cemetery
- Battle at the Department of Mysteries
- Tower Battle (Hogwarts)
- Escape from Privet Drive
- Infiltration of the Ministry of Magic
- Break-in at Gringotts
- Battle of Hogwarts

EXAMS
- Year-end exams
- O.W.L. exams
- N.E.W.T. exams

STUDENT OFFICES
- Prefects
- Head Boy or Head Girl
- Quidditch captain

COMPETITIONS
- Quidditch
- Quidditch World Cup
- Triwizard Tournament
- First Task
- Yule Ball
- Second Task
- Third Task
- House Cup

RELATIONSHIPS
- Cho Chang
- Hermione Granger
- Harry Potter
- Ginny Weasley
- Ron Weasley
- Viktor Krum

DEATHS
- Cedric's Death
- Dumbledore's Death
- Sirius' Death
- Mad-Eye Moody's Death
- Dobby's Death
- Fred Weasley's Death
- Pettigrew's Death
- Remus' Death
- Nymphadora's Death
- Snape's Death
- Voldemort's Death

ORGANIZATIONS
- Death Eaters
- Dumbledore's Army
- Inquisitorial Squad
- Order of the Phoenix
- S.P.E.W.

OTHER
- Events in the Shrieking Shack
- Harry—Voldemort Shared Thoughts

Battle at the Department of Mysteries

Location: Ministry of Magic
Time Period: *Harry Potter and the Order of the Phoenix*
Important Characters: Harry Potter

OVERVIEW

After seeing a vision of Sirius being tortured, Harry and five members of Dumbledore's Army go to the Department of Mysteries, where they are trapped by twelve Death Eaters. They are later helped by a few members of the Order of the Phoenix, although Sirius is killed. Strengthened by the arrival of Dumbledore, Harry chases Sirius's killer, Bellatrix Lestrange, and duels her. Lord Voldemort appears on the scene, but Dumbledore comes to Harry's rescue. They duel, and Voldemort apparates away, but not before being seen by the Minister for Magic.

Event Details Harry has a vision of Sirius being in the Hall of Prophecies of the Department of Mysteries at the Ministry of Magic, where he is being tortured by Voldemort. Harry tries to set up a distraction with the help of Ron, and accepts assistance from Ginny and Luna Lovegood to block student access to the hall outside Professor Umbridge"s office. Then, with Hermione, he enters Umbridge's office to use the fireplace, which is the only one not being monitored. When he contacts Sirius's home, Kreacher, the house elf, tells Harry that Sirius "will never return from the Department of Mysteries."

Umbridge pulls Harry out of the fireplace, and Harry sees that between herself and her Inquisitoral Squad, she has captured all of the conspirators plus Neville.

Battle at the Department of Mysteries

Umbridge summons Professor Snape, demanding Veritaserum to allow her to discover who Harry was talking to, but Snape says that he had already given her all his Veritaserum and it would take significant time to make more. As Snape is leaving, Harry, suddenly remembering that Snape is a member of the Order of the Phoenix, tries to tell Snape what he has perceived, but Snape appears to take no notice.

Umbridge then decides to use cruder methods to extract the truth from Harry. To prevent Umbridge from casting the Cruciatus curse, Hermione makes up a story about a "weapon" in the forest, and says that they were trying to contact Professor Dumbledore to let him know it was ready. Umbridge believes her, and follows Hermione as she leads them into the part of the Forbidden Forest where Centaurs roam. Surprised by Centaurs, Umbridge insults them to the point where they capture her and take her away, in the process, possibly accidentally, breaking her wand. The centaurs now try to determine what to do with Harry and Hermione, who had apparently deliberately brought the irritating Umbridge into their midst. The debate is interrupted by Grawp, Hagrid's half brother, who arrives and creates a diversion.

The two, managing to get away from the Centaurs, are then joined by Ginny, Neville, Ron, and Luna, who have overpowered the Inquisitorial Squad members and retrieved Hermione's and Harry's wands. Luna points out that they can fly to the Ministry on Thestrals. They enter the Ministry through the visitor's entrance, and proceed down to the Department of Mysteries. On their way to the place Harry saw in his vision, they step into a room featuring a black veil, behind which Harry, Luna, and apparently Ron can hear voices.

The place of Harry's vision turns out to be a vast hall, filled with shelves full of glass phials. Though they are in the place that Harry had seen, there is no sign of Sirius or Voldemort. Looking around, Ron notices a phial that has Harry's name on it, and Harry, curious, lifts it off the shelf. Suddenly, the six students are surrounded by a group of Death Eaters. The students use the Reductor Curse on some of the shelves, and manage to escape the room and scatter in the confusion. Harry, Hermione, and Neville end up in the Hall of Time, while Ginny, Luna, and Ron apparently end up in a different hall. Harry, Neville, and Hermione are cornered by a pair of Death Eaters. They manage to disable the Death Eaters, but in the process Hermione is knocked out and Neville's wand and nose are broken by a kick from Dolohov.

Harry manages to bring the unconscious Hermione and the wounded Neville to the anteroom, where they meet up with Ginny's group. Before they can find their way into the hallway outside, a second door into the anteroom opens and more death eaters, led by Bellatrix Lestrange, enter and resume the attack. The students retreat through a doorway, finding themselves in the Brain Room; Ron, who has been left apparently drunk by a spell attack, summons one of the brains and is incapacitated by the "tentacles" of thought emanating painfully from it. Retreating again into a study room, Harry and Luna as the only uninjured members of the group start trying to seal the doors, but Death Eaters enter through an as-yet unsealed door, and disable Luna and Ginny. Harry, knowing that the Death Eaters are only after him, tries to draw them away by running through a different doorway, and promptly falls down the stone steps of the amphitheater of the room of the Veil.

Standing alone on the dais of the Veil, Harry is now standing alone against the ten remaining Death Eaters. For some reason, they seem unwilling to force Harry to give up the Prophecy which he still holds. The standoff is broken by Neville, who bursts onto the scene trying to Stun the Death Eaters and failing; whether it is because he is trying to use Hermione's wand, or because his speech is impaired by his broken nose, his spells are ineffectual. Two Death Eaters seize him, and Bellatrix uses the Cruciatus curse on him, as she had on his parents, to force Harry to give up the prophecy. As Harry wavers, though, five members of the Order of the Phoenix, including Sirius Black, arrive and start dueling the Death Eaters. During the ensuing battle, Harry gives Neville the prophecy to free up his hands. Neville is hit by a Tarantallegra jinx. As Harry tries to pull him up the steps to safety, Neville's robe rips and the Prophecy falls on the ground and shatters.

As the battle rages, Dumbledore arrives and quickly subdues most of the fighters. One battle, though, is still going on, between Bellatrix and Sirius, who by now is standing on the dais of the Veil. Bellatrix fires a spell at his chest, and Sirius falls through the black veil—this is a literal "passing through the veil" rather than figurative. Bellatrix now runs up the amphitheater steps and out through the Hall of Thought, where the tanks of brains are. Enraged, Harry chases after her, and duels her in a higher level of the Ministry. Suddenly, Dumbledore and Voldemort arrive, and duel each other, with Harry and Lestrange repressed by statues. Voldemort then tries to possess Harry, and flees with Lestrange when Harry's love for Sirius chases him out of Harry's mind. As Voldemort returns physically to free Bellatrix, Cornelius Fudge and a number of Aurors, summoned by Dumbledore, arrive and see him. Reluctantly, Fudge must now accept that Harry and Dumbledore were telling the truth all year. While Fudge is still stuttering over these revelations, Dumbledore creates a Portkey, and hands it to Harry; it promptly takes Harry to Dumbledore's office.

Notable Consequences The death of Sirius made Harry very sad and angry over the summer, and also deprived him of one of his greatest friends and his godfather. However, Sirius leaves the house at Grimmauld Place to Harry in his will; if Harry is actually able to take possession, a point which we won't have cleared up until the next book, he may be able to use the house as a refuge, it being so well concealed.

The remaining Death Eaters, trapped in the amphitheater by Dumbledore, were sent to Azkaban. With the Dementors having departed to enter Voldemort's service, this may prove a pointless exercise; however, it does clearly show the Wizarding World where the loyalties of the captured Death Eaters lie. In particular, this will prove an issue for Lucius Malfoy, who is now clearly a criminal. This will significantly change Draco's status as well, as he is now the child of a convicted felon. Draco will end up taking his anger out on Harry, with the mistaken, but all too human, idea that it was Harry's fault that Lucius got caught, rather than Lucius' fault for supporting Voldemort.

In the next book, Dumbledore will say that he is not surprised that Harry's scar has stopped hurting; Voldemort will have found Harry's mind, with its love for Sirius, a very uncomfortable place to inhabit. This reluctance on Voldemort's part to re-enter Harry's mind may prove useful.

Dumbledore's comments on the loyalty of house-elves and the need to treat them honorably, which he makes in his office after the battle, may have some effect on Harry in later books.

Also, now the wizarding world knew that Voldemort was back, this event also signaled the start of the Second Wizarding War.

ANALYSIS

It is after the attack on Arthur Weasley that Dumbledore realizes there may be a mental connection between Harry and Voldemort, and it is at that time that he charges Professor Snape with teaching Harry Occlumency. This actually may be one of Dumbledore's few mistakes. Dumbledore apparently assumes that Voldemort's intent is to read Harry's mind, when it becomes apparent that the intent is rather to insert images into Harry's mind. Our story does not indicate whether Occlumency will prevent this effect. In any event, it is the placement of images into Harry's mind that leads him to the Ministry.

This particular episode is a remarkably good example of the art of the story-teller, as well. The author hurries us along the path that Harry is following, and does not leave us time to consider several large discrepancies. For instance, when Harry sees Voldemort and Sirius in the Ministry of Magic, it does not occur to him, or to us, to wonder how Voldemort could possibly have gotten into the Ministry undetected at three in the afternoon on a weekday. Neither we nor Harry think of the magic mirror Sirius had given Harry at Christmas. In Harry's disappointment at finding Professor McGonagall gone, it does not occur to us that Snape is a member of the Order. The author does an excellent job of not only showing us Harry's sense of urgency, but of making us share it.

GREATER PICTURE

One of the major things that this particular escapade taught Harry was that it was possible for Voldemort to generate false mental images. Knowing that this is possible, it is significantly less likely that Harry will be taken in later by false scenarios that Voldemort generates. Hermione, of course, is less certain. Knowing that Harry has been taken in by mistaken perceptions of Voldemort's thoughts, Hermione is always suspicious of the perceptions Harry receives from him, until almost the end of the seventh book. It is only during the battle at Hogwarts in the seventh book that Hermione actively asks Harry to look into Voldemort's mind, to see where Voldemort is.

It is perhaps telling that after this episode, Voldemort never tries to re-enter Harry's mind. As mentioned, Harry's mind is a very uncomfortable place for Voldemort, with its deep emotions that he cannot understand. However, Harry is able to perceive what Voldemort is thinking at times of great emotional stress for Voldemort. Harry's emotional stress seems to dampen these perceptions.

As mentioned above, Dumbledore had intended Occlumency to be a means of breaking this mental bond between Harry and Voldemort. It is entirely possible that, even with a more suitable teacher, it would not have worked. By the end of the sixth book, Dumbledore has become convinced that Voldemort's already tattered soul ripped again, either at the death of Harry's mother or at the attempt to kill Harry himself, and attached itself to Harry. It is uncertain whether that link between Harry's soul and Voldemort's can be broken by means of Occlumency. One must wonder when Dumbledore came to this conclusion about the soul shard having adhered to Harry. The reader may suspect that this was a conclusion Dumbledore had reached when he had heard Voldemort's plan to create multiple Horcruxes, but this is uncertain. The first time we hear of this belief is in Snape's memory, on an occasion which we believe to be the same night as Ron's poisoning. Harry's successful retrieval of this memory from Slughorn, however, happens significantly after the date of Ron's birthday and near death, which means that Dumbledore will not have had confirmation of the number of Horcruxes at that time. As we cannot be absolutely certain of the dates of Snape's memory, however, this is inconclusive. One thing we do know is that Dumbledore had been concerned about the possibility of there being multiple Horcruxes since the discovery of the diary in *Harry Potter and the Chamber of Secrets*. He would have been certain that there were multiple Horcruxes by the beginning of the sixth book, as he had then found and destroyed the ring Horcrux.

Battle of Hogwarts

Location: Hogwarts

Time Period: *Harry Potter and the Deathly Hallows* (year 7, May)

Important Characters: Harry Potter, Lord Voldemort, Severus Snape

OVERVIEW

This Battle was fought in *Harry Potter and the Deathly Hallows*. The climactic battle of the entire series, it is fought as Harry Potter returns to Hogwarts in search of the last but one Horcrux, in hopes of destroying it and thus preventing Voldemort's return. Learning of Harry's mission, Professor McGonagall assists in the sacking of headmaster Snape, and in preparing the school to be besieged. All underage wizards, and all of Slytherin house, are evacuated, and the remaining wizards, being the school staff and of-age students, Dumbledore's Army, and the Order of the Phoenix, prepare to meet the attack of the Death Eaters. During the preparations, Ron opens the Chamber of Secrets, and with

Hermione, destroys the Cup Horcrux that they have been carrying, using Basilisk fangs.

Harry has determined that the last Horcrux is probably Rowena Ravenclaw's lost diadem, and recalls that he had seen it in the Room of Requirement. He, Ron, and Hermione enter the Room, but are followed by Draco Malfoy, Crabbe, and Goyle. In the ensuing fight, Harry finds and loses the diadem, and Crabbe eventually sets Fiendfyre. The Fiendfyre consumes everything in the room, including Crabbe, but Harry and Ron rescue Draco and Goyle. Harry also catches the diadem, which is being tossed around by the fire; as he examines it after exiting the room, it screams thinly and falls apart.

The battle is raging fiercely now, with Death Eaters inside the school. Hermione asks Harry to look into Voldemort's mind and say where he is. Harry finds that he is in the Shrieking Shack. Making their way there through the tunnel, the Trio arrive just in time to see Voldemort murder Snape, in the belief that this will allow him to tap the full power of the Elder Wand. As his last living act, Snape gives Harry a jar of his memories. Unseen, Voldemort announces a one-hour break in hostilities, and promises that if Harry will come to him in the Forbidden Forest, nobody else will be harmed.

The Trio return to the school, where Harry, alone, takes Snape's memories and places them in Dumbledore's Pensieve. There, he learns that Snape had been acting always to preserve his life, at Dumbledore's request, out of Snape's unrequited love for Harry's mother. Knowing now that he is, himself, an accidental Horcrux, Harry leaves the school to find Voldemort. Using the Elder Wand, Voldemort kills Harry.

Harry, surprisingly, does not seem to be dead, but is, instead, in a sort of way station that looks like King's Cross railway station. Here he meets Dumbledore, and has much that was puzzling him explained, including that Voldemort's using Harry's blood in his reanimation had extended the protection granted by Lily's blood: so long as Voldemort lived, he could not now kill Harry. Harry, given the choice of going onwards or going back, chooses to go back and finish Voldemort once and for all.

Returning to his body in the Forest, Harry plays dead, and Voldemort has him carried to Hogwarts. There, he taunts the defenders, though his jinxes seem ineffective. When he chooses to torture Neville, by putting the Sorting Hat on his head and setting it afire, Neville produces the Sword of Gryffindor from the hat and beheads Nagini.

As Voldemort screams in anger, reinforcements arrive for the defenders, and the battle is rejoined. It eventually centers in the Great Hall, where Bellatrix Lestrange is defeated by Molly Weasley. Harry and Voldemort now duel, and Voldemort's Killing Curse again rebounds, killing him.

Event Details Note: this battle covers several chapters of the final book in the series. As such, the event details are quite lengthy. In the course of the battle, notably in the hiatus, several plot points that do not have to do directly with the battle are discussed and resolved. As they do not have any effect on the course of the battle itself, they will be skipped for reasons of length.

Harry, sensing Voldemort's thoughts when he is told that the cup Horcrux has been stolen, learns that the one Horcrux they have not yet been able to identify is at Hogwarts. With Ron and Hermione, he resolves to get there first and prevent Voldemort retrieving it. Arriving at Hogsmeade, they are caught by the curfew, and are rescued by the innkeeper at the Hog's Head, who Harry identifies as Aberforth Dumbledore. Once Harry convinces Aberforth to help them, he shows them a secret passage which leads to the Room of Requirement within Hogwarts School.

There, Harry finds many members of Dumbledore's Army, who had found the school too hot for them but wanted to stay, in order to continue with their program of guerrilla warfare against the current administration. Neville, who had become the leader of the group, says that he had used the Galleons that Hermione had bewitched earlier to recall all of the DA, and sure enough, past DA members start arriving through the tunnel from the Hog's Head. Asking about missing artifacts of Rowena Ravenclaw, Harry is told about her lost diadem, and decides that this is almost certainly what Voldemort would have used for his Horcrux. Luna takes Harry to the Ravenclaw common room, to see a statue of Rowena with the diadem so that he knows what to look for. He is caught there by a Death Eater, Alecto Carrow, who summons Voldemort by way of the Dark Mark on her arm, and is then Stunned by Luna. Amycus Carrow and Professor McGonagall then arrive. When Amycus decides that he will blame Alecto's summoning of Voldemort on the students, McGonagall refuses to put her students in danger, whereupon Amycus spits at her. Harry, outraged, curses him. Revealing himself to McGonagall, Harry says that he is hunting something in Hogwarts, at Dumbledore's request, and that Voldemort is on his way to try and find the same object. McGonagall sends Patronus messengers to summon the other Heads of House, and starts for the Great Hall. On the way, the way, they encounter Headmaster Snape, and he and McGonagall duel. As Professor Flitwick and Professor Sprout arrive, followed by Professor Slughorn, Snape retreats into an empty classroom, jumps out the window, and flies off into the night.

Returning to the Room of Requirement, Harry finds that several members of the Order of the Phoenix have arrived, but Ron and Hermione have vanished. He tells the assembled people that Voldemort is on his way, and that the fighters are gathering in the Great Hall for instructions. An argument breaks out with Ginny Weasley, who wants to help fight; Molly eventually relents to the point of allowing Ginny to stay at Hogwarts if she stays in the Room of Requirement. As this conversation winds up, Percy Weasley arrives and declares that he was a stupid prat, that he has left the Ministry and wants to rejoin the family. He is welcomed with open arms. While Harry wanders the halls searching for Ron and Hermione, the school's defenses are prepared. At Professor McGonagall's command, statues and suits of armor come suddenly to life all over the castle, arming themselves and taking up positions on the battlements. We see Professor Sprout and Neville planning defences using the dangerous plants from the greenhouses, and meet again with Hagrid, as he is thrown into the school through a window with his boarhound, Fang, by Grawp. Still searching either for inspiration, or for Ron and Hermione, Harry goes to the Great Hall. Here, Kingsley Shacklebolt informs the students of the plan to defend their school. All students are asked to leave, except those who are of age who want to help. Suddenly, Voldemort's voice rings through the hall. Voldemort informs the school that if they surrender Harry to him by midnight, nobody in the school will be hurt. Pansy Parkinson spots Harry, and stands, pointing her wand at him; all of Slytherin does the same. Gryffindor house rises in a mass, pointing wands at the Slytherins, almost immediately followed by all of Ravenclaw and Hufflepuff. Professor McGonagall announces that all of Slytherin house will be evacuated, though those of age in the other three houses re welcome to stay if they wish.

Prompted by Professor McGonagall, Harry again sets out in search of the Horcrux. A phrase nags at him: "not seen in living memory." Perhaps the ghosts would know, they have been around much longer than anyone else. Harry finds Nearly Headless Nick, and asks him where he might find the Ravenclaw house ghost. Somewhat miffed, Nick indicates The Grey Lady, and Harry eventually chases her down. Talking to her, he finds that she is the ghost of Rowena Ravenclaw's daughter, and that in life she had stolen her mother's diadem and hidden it in a forest in Albania. She ashamedly admits to having told one other student about it, many years before. Harry privately thinks that the Grey Lady is only one of many who have been hoodwinked by Tom Riddle. He now remembers having seen an old diadem before; he had, in fact, used it to mark the location in the Room of Requirement where he had hidden his Potions book the year before.

Returning to the Room of Requirement, Harry finds Ron and Hermione there. Ron had opened the Chamber of Secrets by mimicking the sounds Harry had made to open the Locket, and Hermione had recovered several Basilisk fangs, using one of them to destroy the Cup Horcrux. Harry clears everyone out of the Room of Requirement, then re-opens it as the junk storage warehouse where he had placed the diadem. Harry, Ron, and Hermione enter and start searching for the diadem; as Harry finds it, however, he is cornered by Draco Malfoy and his sidekicks, Crabbe and Goyle. The ensuing duel ends when Crabbe sets Fiendfyre, a magical fire that consumes all. Harry spots some old brooms and mount them to escape; as they leave, though, Harry sees Malfoy and Goyle and rescues them, then sees the Diadem being thrown about by the Fiendfyre and grabs that as well. As they fly out into the corridor, the door slams shut behind them and vanishes. Now landed, Harry watches as the diadem screams thinly and falls apart. Hermione now mentions that Fiendfyre is another of the very few things that will destroy Horcruxes.

Harry realizes that it is midnight, and the attack on the school has begun. Details are few and far between at first. Death Eaters, clearly based out of the Forbidden Forest, come streaming out in great numbers. They are flanked by giants and by the huge spiders of the forest. Curses and jinxes fly in every direction, lighting up the sky in green and red. The giants savagely attack the school, demolishing its walls in places. The spiders attack as well, swarming up the walls and into the holes created by the giants. Harry meets Percy and Fred in the halls; Percy jinxes Pius Thicknesse, saying that Thicknesse may consider that his resignation. An explosion shatters the walls, and falling stones kill Fred.

Voldemort is strangely missing from the battle as Student and Phoenix member fight side-by-side in small gangs. Battles rage in the main grounds, the Entrance Hall and outside the Great Hall. Even Peeves gets a piece of the action, hurling swirling roots at the Death Eaters and taunting them. Hermione asks Harry to locate Voldemort; Harry enters Voldemort's mind and sees him dispatching a haggard Lucius Malfoy to fetch Severus Snape. Harry reports that Voldemort is in the Shrieking Shack.

Harry, Ron, and Hermione head for the Whomping Willow and the secret passage to the Shrieking Shack. Blocked by Dementors, Harry is rescued by Luna Lovegood and Ernie Macmillan casting Patronuses to drive them away. They are separated from the Trio by giants, and Harry, Hermione, and Ron enter the tunnel under the Whomping Willow alone.

In the Shrieking Shack, Harry sees Voldemort talking to Snape. Voldemort is disappointed in the performance of the Elder Wand that he had taken from Dumbledore's tomb. He clearly believes that the Wand currently owes allegiance to Snape because Snape had killed Dumbledore, and will not be fully Voldemort's until Snape dies. So saying, he throws Naginiat Snape. Nagini bites Snape, and Voldemort leaves with Nagini. Harry leaves concealment to try and help Snape. Snape releases a large quantity of memory, which Harry gathers in a crystal vial. Snape then dies, looking into Harry's eyes.

Suddenly, just as the Death Eaters were gaining the upper hand, the battle ceases; Voldemort calls his troops back. He issues a warning to all inside, telling them that if they do not hand over Harry Potter in one hour, he will order his troops to kill everyone in Hogwarts. Harry, Hermione, and Ron return to the school through the tunnel, and Hermione and Ron enter the Great Hall to mourn the losses of their friends. Harry, ashamed at the damage he has caused, takes the vial of memories to the headmaster's office and examines them with Dumbledore's Pensieve. In Snape's memories, Harry finds that Snape had been playing a dangerous double game, protecting Harry while pretending to be Voldemort's most loyal lieutenant, and that a shard of Voldemort's soul had broken off and adhered to Harry when Voldemort had tried to kill him. Dumbledore believes that Harry must be killed by Voldemort to destroy this soul shard.

Knowing that he must die, Harry now leaves the headmaster's office and heads for the Forbidden Forest. Passing Neville on the grounds, he tells Neville that if he does not return from where he is going, that Voldemort's snake must be killed. Finding the Resurrection Stone inside the Golden Snitch that Dumbledore had left, Harry summons the shades of his father, mother, Remus Lupin, and Sirius Black. They protect him from the Dementors as he walks through the forest. Reaching the Death Eaters' campsite, Harry drops the Resurrection Stone, and the shades vanish. Voldemort, spotting Harry, kills him.

Harry finds himself in a place that looks like King's Cross Station. There he speaks with Dumbledore, who tells him that the soul shard that had been stuck to him is now gone, and that Harry has the choice to go back and defeat Voldemort, or to go onwards. Harry chooses to go back, in the hopes of finally defeating Voldemort. Returning to the Forbidden Forest, Harry plays dead. From what he hears, it seems that Voldemort has apparently also fallen unconscious, but is now reviving. He orders Narcissa Malfoy to examine Harry, to see if he is dead. Narcissa, hearing from Harry that Draco is still alive and in the school, and that the only way to go to him is to end the war, lies to Voldemort, saying that Harry is dead. Voldemort forces Hagrid to carry Harry out of the forest and back to the school.

As the hour elapses, the forces inside Hogwarts are awaiting the next wave of attack when Voldemort's voice sounds around them. He presents Harry Potter's body, who he says is dead, to the assembled forces. Aghast, the Defenders of Hogwarts shriek their rage at the Dark Lord. Neville stands against the Dark Lord, and Voldemort brings the Sorting Hat from the Headmaster's office, forces it down over Neville's head, and sets it afire. Neville produces the Sword of Gryffindor from the hat and cuts off Nagini's head, and the battle is renewed. This time the Hogwarts' forces are bolstered by the Centaurs, joining battle from the Forest; by the House Elves, who brandish knives and attack the Death Eaters savagely; and by a crowd of reinforcements, apparently composed of the parents and neighbours of every child in Gryffindor, Ravenclaw, and Hufflepuff House from all over the country. Harry, under the Invisibility Cloak, follows the battle into the Great Hall. When Molly Weasley, protecting her children, kills Bellatrix Lestrange, Voldemort turns his wand on Molly. Harry, revealing himself as he shields Molly, gives Voldemort the chance to redeem himself; he refuses, and tries to kill Harry. His curse again rebounds, and Voldemort dies of his own killing curse.

Notable Consequences Ron's suddenly thinking about the House-elves in the kitchens, and telling Hermione that they ought to warn them, is a turning point in their relationship. Hermione recognizes it as a sign of maturity, that Ron is now thinking of others, and it deepens her love for him.

The death of Voldemort and all his followers turns the Second Wizarding War to an end. Wizarding Britain, which has been living in fear for the last two years, suddenly finds itself free from the grasp of the Death Eaters and their leader, Lord Voldemort. Harry Potter, without a doubt one of the people most affected by the war, having lost parents, godfather, mentor, and many friends, now finds himself free of the burden that was placed on him when the Prophecy named him as the only one that could defeat the Dark Lord. This will also give him freedom to pursue what he has always wished: a family of his own, which he hopes to find next to Ginny Weasley.

ANALYSIS

One of the signs of Harry's increasing maturity is his treatment of the Hallows. As he confronts Voldemort, he knows that he has just released one of the Hallows to fall, unseen and irretrievable, on the forest floor; he is carrying another under his robe; and he believes the third, although it is in Voldemort's hand, currently owes its allegiance to him. During his walk through the forest, he has effectively united all three of the Hallows under his command, and so has, if the legend holds, conquered Death. When he faces Voldemort, he knows that he will die, and yet he is unafraid. A less mature wizard would have assumed the words of the legend were literal, and would have clutched the three Hallows to himself, in the belief hat they would shield him from death. Harry knows that it is the man who is not afraid of Death who has truly conquered it, as death itself cannot be denied, but the fear of death is often far worse than death itself. Knowing this, Harry has decided that he will not allow the fear of death to prevent him from doing what he must, and with that decision has conquered death. Having done so, he no longer needs the Hallows, and we will see that he releases two of the three, keeping only the Cloak which he intends to pass on to his son.

GREATER PICTURE

This being the climactic battle of the entire series, it must draw together all the dangling threads of the series. As a device to allow these threads to be drawn together and tied up, the battle actually has been written with an intermission. During this intermission, we first see Snape's memories of events, which clears up many events centering on Snape and finally reveals Snape's motivations throughout the entire series, including the riddle of Dumbledore's damaged hand in the previous year. Then, in the waystation, Dumbledore ties up the threads involving the Hallows, Harry's soul fragment, and aspects of wandlore as they affect Harry through the story. A purist might suggest that this was an awkward way of getting the necessary information to us, but perhaps it is a measure of Rowling's skill that this device feels true to the nature of Snape, Voldemort, and Dumbledore. It does seem, however, that after having briefly decided to chart his own course, Harry is once again placed in a situation where he can only react to what is going on around him.

Breakin at Gringotts

Location: Gringotts Bank
Time Period: *Harry Potter and the Deathly Hallows*, early May
Important Characters: Harry, Hermione, and Ron, Griphook, Travers, Bogrod

OVERVIEW

In *Harry Potter and the Deathly Hallows*, the Trio, with the help of Griphook, execute a plan to break in to the Gringotts vault of Bellatrix Lestrange's family to steal a Horcrux belonging to Voldemort.

Event Details When the Trio is captured and brought to Malfoy Manor, Bellatrix sees that they are carrying the Sword of Gryffindor and panics. She delays summoning Voldemort, fearing grave consequences if he discovers Harry has the sword. Bellatrix tortures Hermione to discover how they came to possess the sword, which was placed in the Lestrange vault at Gringotts for safekeeping. Harry hears Bellatrix demanding to know if anything else was taken from the vault. Griphook, who is hauled upstairs to corroborate Hermione's story that the sword was "just found," at Harry's request falsely states that the sword captured with the Trio is really a fake.

After escaping, Harry believes that Bellatrix's reaction was due to her fear that an object entrusted to her vault by Voldemort may have been compromised. Harry decides to enlist the help of Griphook, a former Gringotts goblin, to penetrate the vault and seize what is probably one of Voldemort's Horcruxes. Griphook agrees to get them into the vault if the Trio returns the Goblin-made Sword of Gryffindor to him and the Goblin community. With Hermione disguised as Bellatrix, Ron made to look like a foreign wizard, and Harry with Griphook under the Invisibility Cloak, they set out for Gringotts. Meeting the Death Eater Travers on the way complicates their plans, but with Harry's spells and Griphook's advice they gain access to the vault.

The objects in the vault are enchanted with Gemino and Flagrante and thus multiply and burn. With great difficulty Harry finds Hufflepuff's Cup, a likely vessel for a Horcrux. Griphook turns against the Trio, takes possession of the Sword of Gryffindor, and rejoins the bank's Goblins who are responding to the break-in. The Trio run for their lives, and in desperation mount a dragon imprisoned to guard the vaults. Harry breaks its chains, and with assisting spells from Hermione, the dragon escapes Gringotts with the Trio riding on its back. Many miles from London, the Trio jump off the dragon into a lake and swim ashore. Harry has the Cup Horcrux but the Sword is lost.

Notable Consequences While successful in acquiring the Cup Horcrux, the Trio has lost the Sword of Gryffindor to Griphook. The sword is one of the few ways to destroy a Horcrux and they must now devise a new method for its destruction. The very public break-in to the Lestrange vault lets Voldemort know that Harry is hunting his Horcruxes. Voldemort's fury overflows as he murders the Goblin who brings him the news, and then a number of others who simply happen to be in the room. Harry, through his visions of Voldemort's state of mind, realizes that there is no more time to find and destroy the remaining Horcruxes. The Trio must set out immediately for Hogwarts in the hope of finding the remaining Horcrux, and hope to find a way to destroy the Cup Horcrux once they get there. News of the break-in reaches Hogwarts and the DA resistance members are heartened by the knowledge that Harry is still free and actively fighting.

While walking in Diagon Alley toward Gringotts, the Trio (and the reader) get a glimpse of the misery Voldemort has imposed on the Wizarding community. We see Muggle-born witches and wizards, stripped of their wands, begging for gold. Others are desperate for news about lost family members, victims of the new regime. Many shops are boarded up. Diagon Alley has become a depressing and dark place.

Analysis

Gringotts is described, from Harry's first day in the Wizarding World, as the safest place to store one's valuables. Despite a break-in to the empty Vault 713 that same day, we never hear of anyone who has actually walked away with anything safeguarded at Gringotts. Therefore, the Trio's plan to steal an object from a high security Gringotts vault is their most outrageous adventure yet. For seven years the Trio has found the need to hatch missions against the Dark Forces, each bolder and more hazardous than before. This event is the pinnacle of the Trio's long career of capers and schemes to foil Voldemort.

Questions

1. How might this break-in affect the delicate relationship between wizards and goblins?

Greater Picture

In the course of their deception and break-in at Gringotts, Harry uses the Imperius Curse on Travers and the Gringotts goblin Bogrod. This is the second time Harry has used an Unforgivable Curse, a very serious crime; the first was at the Battle in the Ministry when he used the Cruciatus Curse against Bellatrix Lestrange. Harry later that day uses the Cruciatus Curse on Amycus Carrow. It is clearly true that that without the Imperius Curse, the suspicious Bogrod and Travers would have raised the alarm and the mission would have failed at its inception. However, Harry's desperation to get the Horcrux caused him to cross a moral threshold from Light to Dark. A theme in the Harry Potter series is the folly of believing in the "Greater Good" at the expense of one's ethical and moral center. Therefore Harry should be remorseful for going to such extremes in his quest to destroy Voldemort. From another perspective, Harry is portrayed as the Flawed Hero who occasionally stumbles and loses his purity of heart.

Cedric's Death

Location: Graveyard, Little Hangleton
Time Period: *Harry Potter and the Goblet of Fire*, late June
Important Characters: Harry Potter, Voldemort, Death Eaters

Overview

At the conclusion of *Harry Potter and the Goblet of Fire*, Lord Voldemort orders Wormtail to kill Cedric in a cemetery.

Duel in the Cemetery

Event Details Because they helped each other during the Triwizard Tournament's Third Task, Harry Potter and Cedric Diggory agree to grab the Triwizard Cup together. They are unaware the cup is actually a Portkey, and it transports them to a rundown graveyard with an ancient manor house in the distance. Harry recognizes the Riddle family name on the gravestones; Cedric suggests keeping their wands at the ready. As a hunched figure carrying something resembling a bundled infant approaches, Harry's scar begins burning. A high voice commands, "Kill the spare." The figure, whom Harry soon recognizes as Wormtail (Peter Pettigrew), utters "Avada Kedavra," the killing curse. Cedric instantly falls dead, while Harry is incapacitated by his scar's searing pain.

After a ritual restores Lord Voldemort's full human form, he engages Harry in a deadly duel. As they cast spells simultaneously, their wands' streams interlock, creating a Priori Incantatem effect. Because their wands are "brothers" that share the same magical core (tail feathers from Dumbledore's phoenix, Fawkes), they will never battle properly against one another. Harry, stronger, forces the stream back into Voldemort's wand, causing it to disgorge its previous victims' "echoes." Cedric's image emerges first, asking Harry to return his body to his parents. Bertha Jorkins and an old Muggle that Harry does not recognize also appear. Lastly are Harry's parents, James and Lily. The echoes momentarily shield Harry as he breaks the wands' connection, reclaims the Triwizard Cup, and is whisked back to Hogwarts with Cedric's body.

Notable Consequences Cedric's murder seriously impacts the school's morale, it being the first time many students have experienced a peer's death. Cho Chang, Cedric's girlfriend, is deeply affected by his loss, and her continuing grief throughout the next book casts a pall over her relationship with Harry, eventually dooming it.

Despite Harry's insistence that Voldemort has returned and caused Cedric's death, the Ministry of Magic disputes that the Dark Lord has returned and asserts that Cedric died accidentally during the Tournament. They soon wage a public smear campaign against Harry and also Dumbledore, who fully supports Harry's claims. Harry is depicted in the *Daily Prophet* as an addled, attention-seeking liar, while Dumbledore is removed from several important Wizarding associations. It is not until the climatic battle at the Ministry of Magic in *Harry Potter and the Order of the Phoenix*, when Fudge and other Ministry employees personally see Voldemort, that Harry and Dumbledore are finally vindicated. Fudge eventually resigns under pressure over his mishandling of the situation.

ANALYSIS

When the spirit echoes appear from Voldemort's wand, they emerge in the reverse order that they were murdered. Cedric appears first because he was the most recently killed. As a side note, it has been mentioned that the order of Harry's parents emerging from Voldemort's wand was accidentally reversed by the author; James was killed first and so should have emerged from Voldemort's wand after Lily, who actually appears after James in many editions of the book. The author has stated[1] that this was an uncaught editing mistake, made under the effects of time pressure and sleep deprivation. No mention has been made of whether it will be corrected in later editions, as other mistakes have been.

QUESTIONS

1. Why does Voldemort have Cedric killed?
2. How is Cedric killed and who kills him?
3. What is the Ministry of Magic's official stance regarding Cedric's death? Why?
4. What eventually prompts the Ministry of Magic to acknowledge how Cedric actually died?

Duel in the Cemetery

Location: Cemetery, Little Hangleton
Time Period: *Harry Potter and the Goblet of Fire*, June
Important Characters: Harry Potter, Lord Voldemort, Peter Pettigrew (Wormtail), Cedric Diggory, various Death Eaters

OVERVIEW

Having been taken to a cemetery by Portkey, Harry Potter sees his companion, Cedric Diggory, murdered, and then is forced to watch as Lord Voldemort returns to life. After summoning his Death Eaters, and describing how he has come back, Voldemort releases Harry and they duel. Harry and Voldemort cast spells at the same instant, and the result is a dome of light surrounding the two of them, and several of Voldemort's past victims appearing as shades or ghosts. The ghosts cluster around Voldemort as Harry breaks the connection between their wands, and Harry runs for Cedric's body and the Triwizard trophy. The Triwizard Trophy, again acting as a Portkey, returns Harry to Hogwarts.

Event Details As the Third Task comes to a close, Harry and Cedric agree to touch the Triwizard Trophy at the same instant, thus closing the Task with a draw. The trophy, however, is a Portkey, which transports Harry and Cedric to a graveyard. As a figure approaches carrying a burden, Harry's scar pains him, so greatly that he drops his wand. The approaching person kills Cedric, and binds Harry to a gravestone.

Leaving his burden near Harry, the person, who Harry now recognizes as Peter Pettigrew, walks out of Harry's vision. The bundle which Pettigrew had placed near Harry is about the size of an infant, but is unspeakably evil in appearance. Pettigrew now brings a large stone cauldron and creates a fire under it. To this cauldron he adds bones from the grave under Harry's feet, some of Harry's blood, and his own hand, which he cuts off as Harry watches. He then places the evil bundle

---

1. http://www.dictionary.com, 3 June 2007, definition 5 (http://dictionary.reference.com/browse/weigh)

in the cauldron, and Lord Voldemort, re-animated, emerges.

Ignoring Pettigrew's suffering, Voldemort uses the Dark Mark on Pettigrew's arm to summon his Death Eaters. Some he tortures for daring to suppose him gone forever, Pettigrew, for his loyalty, he rewards with a new, magically strong silver hand to replace the one he cut off. In answer to a question from a Death Eater speaking with Lucius Malfoy's voice, Voldemort explains where he had been, how he had survived, and how he had arranged for Harry's presence. He then directs Pettigrew to release Harry and give him his wand back.

Voldemort asks if Harry understands how to duel. "First, we bow," and Voldemort forces Harry to bow. Voldemort then Curses Harry, to show how it is done. Harry, knowing that the next curse of Voldemort's will be the killing curse, ducks behind a gravestone. There, he decides that he would rather die standing than hiding, and stands to face Voldemort, attempting to disarm Voldemort just as Voldemort speaks the Killing Curse. Instantly, Harry's and Voldemort's wands are joined by a band of golden light, and the two combatants are lifted into the air and set down some distance away from the jeering Death Eaters, as a dome of light forms around them. Harry's wand is heating up and vibrating dreadfully. Harry notices some beads of light on the link between the two wands, and something tells him that they should not reach his wand. Concentrating, he forces them away from his wand tip and towards Voldemort's. As the first bead of light is forced into it, Voldemort's wand screams, and the shade of Cedric emerges.

Confused, the Death Eaters mill around the outside of the dome, asking what they should do; Voldemort, looking fearful, tells them to stay away, while the shade of Cedric wanders around the inside of the dome. Harry, still concentrating on the link between the wands, forces more beads into Voldemort's wand. Each bead results in another scream, fiercer vibration, and the appearance of another shade: the muggle Frank Bryce, Bertha Jorkins, and Harry's mother and father. The shades speak to Harry, telling him that when the link between the wands breaks, they will remain for a few seconds; they will cluster around Voldemort, giving Harry time to escape. The shade of Cedric asks that Harry take his body back to his parents.

At the signal, Harry jerks his wand upwards, breaking the link, and the golden dome vanishes. Harry sees the shades gathering around Voldemort, and runs, dodging through the headstones, to where Cedric's body lies. Once there, he summons the Cup, which takes him, with Cedric's body, back to the Third Task maze.

In the confusion following Harry's return, Harry is taken to Professor Moody's office. There, Moody questions him about what had happened while he was away from the school. Harry becomes concerned as Moody's questions seem to be more about Voldemort's interactions with the Death Eaters, than about Voldemort's return; and finally, Moody reveals that he is a Death Eater, and that he plans to kill Harry to gain greater glory in Voldemort's eyes. As Moody is preparing for the wand strike, however, the door is broken down, and Professor Dumbledore Stuns Moody, then enters the room along with Professor McGonagall and Professor Snape. Moody, who has apparently forgotten his dose of Polyjuice potion, transforms into his real person, Barty Crouch Jr. . Snape provides a truth potion, and Barty reveals the details of the plot that found Harry entered into the Triwizard Tournament, and the planning that had gone into Voldemort's return.

Dumbledore then takes Harry to his own office, where, with Sirius present for support, and Fawkes providing healing tears, Harry relates the events of the duel. Dumbledore seems pleased that Voldemort had used Harry's blood for his reanimation, but does not say why.

Having heard Harry's story, Dumbledore then takes Harry to the Hospital Wing, and tells Madam Pomfrey that he needs a long and dreamless sleep.

Notable Consequences Cedric Diggory dies. This is likely to haunt Harry.

Voldemort returns to the living. He announces himself to all his Death Eaters, and to Harry, who carries the news to Dumbledore. We guess now, and it will be confirmed later, that Dumbledore is the last person Voldemort would want to know of his return, and thanks to Harry, Dumbledore had known about it within hours, where Voldemort would have wanted to stay completely under cover for at least another year. This revelation will hasten Voldemort's timetable, and may cause him to make some errors in his planning.

We learn for certain where Lucius Malfoy's allegiances lie. We also learn of the existence of Barty Crouch, Jr., and of his covert actions over the year just past.

The unexpected effect generated by Harry's and Voldemort's wands seems to scare Voldemort. Voldemort has only once before had the Killing Curse fail, and then the effect is nothing like what he is seeing tonight; and with his fear of death, his victims coming back out of his own wand to haunt him must be absolutely petrifying. Additionally, Harry seems able to force Voldemort's wand to do things against Voldemort's will; could this mean that Harry is the stronger Wizard?

Dumbledore seems pleased that Voldemort had used Harry's blood to re-create himself, though he does not explain why.

Cornelius Fudge is revealed to be a politician, interested only in retaining the power he has, rather than in dealing with the threat that is present. By denying the evidence given him by Dumbledore, Harry, and Snape, Fudge clearly sets the stage for the official Ministry stance in the next book, which the author has said is quite consciously modeled on the government of Britain's actions under Neville Chamberlain.

Harry has won the Triwizard Tournament and so receives the prize money. He tries to give it to Cedric's parents, but they refuse it. This will leave Harry with a large amount of money that he doesn't want and can't use. Harry will give this to Fred and George as seed money for their joke shop. It is possible that the joke shop will have some role to play in later books.

In *Harry Potter and the Prisoner of Azkaban*, Dumbledore had said, "You think the dead that we have loved, ever truly leave us?" Harry meets the shades of his parents in this episode, which in some manner reassures him that his parents are not gone, but have merely moved on.

GREATER PICTURE

Cedric's death will make the school Thestrals visible to Harry. This will alarm him; they are not the most prepossessing of beasts at any time, and Harry will wonder whether their visibility to him, and not to either Ron or Hermione, is a sign of him going insane. Luna Lovegood's reassurance that she also can see them will hardly be reassuring to Harry, given Luna's evident eccentricity.

Dumbledore later says that, in fact, during the battle in the cemetery, Harry was a stronger wizard than Voldemort, because, while Voldemort saw death and feared it, Harry saw death and was ready for it. Harry being ready to die, if need be, gave him strength that Voldemort could not draw upon.

The effect of Harry's wand on Voldemort's will result in Voldemort spending significant time trying to find a wand that can defeat Harry's. He will, in the seventh book, chase a possibly mythical wand, the so-called Deathstick. As part of this process, Voldemort will have Mr. Ollivander kidnapped, will borrow Lucius Malfoy's wand and have it destroyed in his hand, and will hunt down the wandmaker Gregorovitch, the evil magician Grindelwald, and end up at Dumbledore's tomb hunting the wand.

Harry will similarly place an almost mystical weight on his own wand, and will become despondent when it is destroyed accidentally.

We will learn later that Harry's faith in his own wand, and Voldemort's fear of it, are justified. As Harry was the stronger wizard in their duel, some of Voldemort's wand's power, and in fact some of Voldemort's power, will have transferred to Harry and his wand. However, Dumbledore will tell Harry that this power would only be exerted against Voldemort and the wand he carried. Harry's wand will have not only recognized Voldemort's wand as its kin, by way of the matching wand cores, but will have recognized Voldemort as Harry's kin, by their shared blood. Because of this, Harry's wand will apparently act independently to some degree to prevent Voldemort from attacking Harry again. We see this in the opening chapters of *Harry Potter and the Deathly Hallows*. Here, without his willing it, Harry's wand takes action against Voldemort and the wand he is holding, which was Lucius Malfoy's. We also see that the strength in Harry's wand is proof only against Voldemort, as it is, later in that same book, accidentally destroyed by a spell cast by Hermione.

We have gathered by this point that the protection that Harry has at the house at Privet Drive is because of the blood relation between his mother, who sacrificed herself for him, and Harry's Aunt Petunia. Later, we will learn that by taking Harry's blood to reanimate himself, Voldemort had extended this protection, making it impossible for Harry to die by Voldemort's hand while Voldemort lived.

Duel in the Chamber of Secrets

Location: The Chamber of Secrets
Time Period: *Harry Potter and the Chamber of Secrets*, May
Important Characters: Harry Potter, Tom Riddle, Ron Weasley, Gilderoy Lockhart

OVERVIEW

Having determined the means of entrance to the Chamber of Secrets, and guessed at the nature of the monster within, Harry Potter and Ron Weasley, reluctantly accompanied by Professor Lockhart, enter the Chamber to rescue Ginny Weasley. There, separated from the others, Harry encounters one Tom Riddle, who is using Ginny's life force to return to life himself. Riddle summons the monster, a Basilisk. With the help of Fawkes, Harry defeats first the Basilisk, and then Tom, to save Ginny from death.

Event Details Largely because of a page torn out of a library book which Harry finds clutched in Hermione's petrified fist, Harry determines that the monster which has been roaming the school and petrifying students is a Basilisk. It also occurs to Harry, after talking with Aragog, that the entrance to the Chamber of Secrets could be in Moaning Myrtle's bathroom. Harry and Ron decide that they need to tell this to Professor McGonagall. Waiting for her in the Staff Room, they hear an announcement that all students are to return to their dormitories, and decide to hide in a wardrobe there in the Staff Room. Listening through the door, they hear that Ginny has been taken into the Chamber of Secrets, and they hear Professor Lockhart assigned the task of hunting down the monster, as he has boasted that he knows where it is. He weakly goes off "to prepare."

Later, when Harry and Ron visit Professor Lockhart's office, they find him frantically packing up all his possessions. When they query him as to why, he says that he had never done all the things in his books, other, less photogenic people had done them, and he had simply written about them. He isn't magically strong enough to do all the things in those books, but what he does do, very nicely, is memory charms. He works those on the people who had done the things he writes about, so that they wouldn't awkwardly and publicly recall having done what Lockhart claimed to do. Speaking of which—As he turns on Harry and Ron with wand raised, Harry disarms him, and Ron catches his wand and throws it out the window. At two wand-points, Lockhart precedes the two students to Moaning Myrtle's bathroom.

There, Myrtle confirms that she was the one who had died the last time the chamber was opened, and indicates the sink where the big yellow eyes, that were the last thing she remembers, had been. Harry notices a small snake etched on the side of the faucet, and speaks to it in Parseltongue. The sink opens, revealing a long shaft, and Lockhart reluctantly enters it, followed by Ron and Harry.

At the bottom of the shaft, they find a chamber littered with small bones. Proceeding down the obvious tunnel, they find the skin of a serpent apparently twenty feet or more long. Lockhart pretends to swoon, then seizes Ron's wand, and fires a memory charm at the two. Ron's wand backfires and explodes, and a large piece of the ceiling falls; Harry is on the side away from Moaning Myrtle's bathroom, so leaving Ron to dig out as best he can, Harry proceeds through another door and into a chamber dominated by a giant statue, and Ginny lying unconscious at its feet. While Harry is trying to revive Ginny, another student walks out of the shadows holding Harry's wand, introduces himself as Tom Riddle, and says that he had really wanted to meet Harry. He tells Harry that Ginny had been writing in his diary, telling him all about the wonderful Harry Potter. As Ginny had poured out her soul to Tom, Tom had poured some of his soul into Ginny, and now would be using her life force to return. He wonders, though, how as an infant, Harry had managed to defeat Voldemort? Harry asks why Tom would care about Voldemort, who was certainly after his time. Tom says that he had been using the name Lord Voldemort even while he was still at school.

Harry is noticing that Tom's outline, which had initially been somewhat fuzzy, is becoming firmer as time goes by, and knows that if he doesn't act quickly, Tom will become fully real and Ginny will die. To Tom's statement that Voldemort is the greatest wizard who ever lived, Harry retorts that Dumbledore is greater. When Tom says that Dumbledore has been driven from the school by Tom's memory, Harry says he is not as much gone as Tom might think. A burst of music interrupts them, and Fawkes, Dumbledore's pet Phoenix, appears and drops the Sorting Hat at Harry's feet.

Tom now releases the Basilisk. Fawkes pecks out its eyes, but it can still hear Harry, and tries to bite him. Harry, putting on the Sorting Hat, asks for help, and something in the hat hits him in the head. Harry finds that it is a sword, and as the Basilisk strikes, Harry stabs upwards through the roof of its mouth and into its brain, killing it. However, Harry is, in turn, stabbed by one of the Basilisk's fangs, and can feel its venom working.

As the world begins to darken, Fawkes lands beside Harry and starts weeping. Though Tom jeers at him, Harry feels the effects of the venom receding, and recalls Dumbledore's words about phoenixes: "their tears have healing powers." As Tom realizes what is happening, he fires a quick curse at Fawkes with Harry's wand. Fawkes flies away, and as Tom is preparing a killing curse, Fawkes drops the diary at Harry's side, and Harry plunges the broken Basilisk fang into it.

Instantly, with a thin scream, Tom vanishes, and the diary, with a hole burned through it, leaks a veritable ocean of ink. Ginny wakes up, and she and Harry make their way back to the tunnel with the fallen ceiling. Ron has forced a way through it, and carried by Fawkes, Harry, Ron, Ginny, and Lockhart return to the surface. Fawkes leads them to Professor McGonagall's office, where Harry relates what has happened to a very relieved Professor McGonagall, Professor Dumbledore, and Mr. and Mrs. Weasley.

Notable Consequences Several of the consequences of this particular duel are not revealed until much later in the series, and so are covered in the Greater Picture area of this topic.

We learn that Lord Voldemort's name originally had been Tom Marvolo Riddle, and that Marvolo had been his grandfather's name. We will later learn that Voldemort had tried to conceal this name, so as to prevent discovery of the place where he had hidden an object of value, in his grandfather's house.

Ron's damaged wand, when it exploded, caused Lockhart's memory charm to revert upon himself, so Lockhart has lost almost all of his memory. It seems he cannot even reliably remember his own name. In some ways, this seems just retribution for his over-use of the memory charm and his claiming of other people's achievements. By finding the Chamber and determining who had actually opened it, Harry allows Dumbledore to secure the release of Hagrid from Azkaban.

Harry mentions to Dumbledore that he is unsure if he is in the correct House. He says that the Sorting Hat had suggested that he would do well in Slytherin house, and Riddle had mentioned a number of curious similarities between them. Dumbledore asks Harry why the Sorting Hat had placed him in Gryffindor, and Harry glumly replies that it is only because he had asked it to. Dumbledore says that is exactly right, and goes on to say that "It is our choices, Harry, that show who we truly are, far more than our abilities." He then shows Harry the sword that the Sorting Hat had presented to him, and the name on it: Godric Gryffindor. "Only a true Gryffindor could have pulled that out of the hat, Harry."

It is in this same discussion that we first have it suggested to us that a part of Voldemort had ended up in Harry when Voldemort had tried to kill him and been killed himself. Dumbledore suggests that this is the source of Harry's ability in Parseltongue.

When Lucius Malfoy appears at the school to protest Dumbledore's reinstatement as Headmaster, Dobby comes with him. Dobby, seeing the diary, suggests through charade behind Lucius' back that Lucius had put the diary in with Ginny's textbooks. Harry mentions this, and Lucius demands that he prove it. Dumbledore says that with the diary destroyed, it can never now be proved, but if any other of Voldemort's personal possessions do turn up, surely Arthur Weasley will be interested in linking them back to Lucius.

In the guise of giving the diary back to Lucius, Harry manages to get Lucius to accidentally throw a sock at Dobby. Having been given clothes, Dobby is now free, and no longer need take orders from the Malfoys. Dobby immediately protects Harry from Lucius' curse. Dobby may protect Harry again, now that he is a free elf and can choose what orders to follow.

Analysis

It remains a mystery why Harry and Ron take Lockhart along with them for the attempt to defeat the Basilisk. Harry and Ron have heard him state that he is a fraud, and Ron has thrown his wand out the window of his office, which arguably is another bad decision given the state of Ron's own wand. Without his wand, Lockhart would be even less use than he has already turned out to be. Perhaps they still harbor some belief in his abilities, as mentioned in his many supposed autobiographical books, or perhaps they simply feel the need of an older and more experienced wizard. One could argue, however, that the best course for Harry and Ron would have been to Stun Lockhart, to keep him from interfering, and then proceed on their own. This might have proven fatal for Ron, however; as he was caught by the falling ceiling, there was only Harry for the Basilisk to focus on. It is likely, given his performance in the earlier stages of this book, that Ron would have frozen and been unable to use any defensive magic, and quite likely would have been killed instantly when the Basilisk appeared.

Greater Picture

We will find out later that the diary was actually a Horcrux, likely the second one that Tom Riddle had made. Professor Dumbledore, of course, recognizes it immediately by its effects on Ginny, and we learn later that this disturbs him. This Horcrux was designed to be found, and was placed in the school as a weapon; this is not the sort of thing you do with something that represents a person's immortality, so long as it remains hidden. This led Dumbledore to the conclusion that Riddle had created at least one other Horcrux, but until quite late in the sixth book, he had no idea how many there might be, though he had suspicions of what at least two of them were. We will also find out that Harry had, by pure blind luck, happened upon one of an extremely few ways of destroying a Horcrux: Basilisk venom. Horcruxes, being embodied bits of soul, are virtually indestructible, and no ordinary magic can harm them, just as no ordinary physical or magical assault can harm the soul in a living person. Basilisk venom is extraordinary magic, and there are no known cures for it apart from Phoenix tears, which are hardly ordinary magic, given the scarcity of phoenixes. In the course of the seven books, seven Horcruxes will be destroyed; four of them, and possibly a fifth, will be destroyed either directly or indirectly by Basilisk venom, one by Fiendfyre, and one by the the killing curse.

The thing of value that Tom had hidden in his grandfather's house was, of course, a Horcrux. Once Marvolo Gaunt and his son Morfin were safely out of the way, Tom had hidden the first Horcrux he made in the remains of their house. Dumbledore later found it there and destroyed it. It is when Voldemort is thinking of the places that his Horcruxes were concealed that we learn that he had been trying to conceal the name of his Wizard ancestor, in order to keep that hiding place secure.

Cho Chang relationships

Location: Hogwarts
Time Period: *Harry Potter and the Prisoner of Azkaban* to the end of the series
Important Characters: Cho Chang, Cedric Diggory, Harry Potter, Michael Corner

Overview

Cho Chang is a pretty Ravenclaw student who is a year ahead of Harry Potter. She becomes his first serious crush, and although she also appears attracted to him, she has already begun dating Cedric Diggory, a student in Hufflepuff, by the time Harry asks her out. That relationship tragically ends with Cedric's death at the end of *Harry Potter and the Goblet of Fire*.

In the next book, *Harry Potter and the Order of the Phoenix* she begins a tentative relationship with Harry, although she is still grieving Cedric's death and is emotionally fragile. Their relationship endures several upsets, but finally ends after a dispute about Cho's friend, Marietta Edgecomb, who betrayed Dumbledore's Army. At the end of the book, Ginny reveals that Cho is now dating Michael Corner, Ginny Weasley's former boyfriend.

Event Details

Prisoner of Azkaban Harry becomes interested in Cho, who is a year older, when he sees her playing as Seeker for the Ravenclaw Quidditch team.

Goblet of Fire Cho seems to reciprocate Harry's interest and patiently waits for him to make the first move, as girls usually do. Harry finally works up the nerve to ask her to the Yule Ball, but she has already accepted an invitation from Cedric Diggory, although she seems to genuinely regret having to refuse Harry's invitation. Cho and Cedric are a couple for the remainder of the book, although occasionally, Cho may wistfully wonder what might have been with Harry. Cho and Cedric's relationship ends when he is murdered during the Third Task of the Triwizard Tournament by Wormtail at Voldemort's command. She shows a great amount of bereavement at Cedric's death as she silently cries during Dumbledore's speech at the end of the year feast.

Order of the Phoenix Cho tries to connect with Harry several times, possibly to ask about Cedric's final minutes. The first time, on the Hogwarts Express, she is thwarted by Neville's *Mimbulus Mimbletonia*, which has just coated Harry's compartment with stinksap. The second time, she is driven away by Ron, who accuses her of supporting a particular Quidditch team only because it is trendy. Finally, the two meet in the Owlery, when Harry is sending a message to Sirius. Harry is heartened when she supports him over an unjust accusation by Filch. When Hermione convinces Harry to secretly teach real Defence Against the Dark Arts to students, as opposed to the nonsense Professor Umbridge is offering, Harry is stunned by how many want to study with him, including Cho. After the group's initial meeting in the Hog's Head, Cho seems to want to stay and have a word with Harry, but her friend is impatient to leave. Hermione then comments that Cho could scarcely take her eyes off Harry all the time she was there, and Harry suddenly realizes just how beautiful Hogsmeade is.

During Harry's classes in the Room of Requirement, Cho gets rather flustered whenever Harry is around, messing up a simple Disarming jinx three times in a row. In the last lesson before Christmas break, Harry finds that Dobby has decorated the room with streamers, bobbles, and mistletoe. He manages to get the more embarrassing decorations removed, but there are still streamers and some mistletoe up when class starts. After class, Cho remains behind to have a few words about Cedric; she manages to maneuver herself and Harry under the mistletoe, and they kiss. Harry, afterwards, in conversation with Ron and Hermione, says that it was very wet, because she had been crying; Hermione says Cho does that often, and inquires about how Harry behaved. Harry's attempts to comfort Cho receives lukewarm approval from Hermione.

When there is a Hogsmeade weekend on 14 February, Cho drops a few hints. Harry finally clues in and invites her to go. She accepts, and suggests Madam Puddifoot's tea shop as a good place to spend some time. Harry takes Cho to Madam Puddifoot's, but then is extremely disconcerted to find that it is full of snogging couples, deeply entangled in each other, and particularly dismayed to find that the only open table is adjacent to one occupied by Roger Davies, a handsome Ravenclaw student cut from the same mold as Cedric. Harry's dismay and confusion is increased by Cho's revelation that Roger had earlier asked Cho out; we believe that Cho had mentioned this either to make Harry jealous, or to try to let Harry know that she felt he was better than Roger somehow, but it has the wrong effect, making Harry feel even more inadequate in the face of the competition he is getting for Cho's favours. In the face of this discomfort, and Cho's insistence that Harry tell her more about how Cedric died, Harry is less than tactful when he has to excuse himself for a promised meeting with Hermione. Cho, incensed, storms off.

Cho, hurt, then does not pay any attention to Harry at dinner, or over the next few days. Hermione tells Harry that he was a bit tactless, making it sound as if he was going from Cho to another girl. Harry wonders at this, and Hermione explains that he should have made it sound as though he was reluctant to go see Hermione, but he had promised, and he would really like Cho to come too... Harry doesn't understand why he has to insult Hermione to compliment Cho. However, when the interview with Harry appears in *The Quibbler*, an apparently repentant Cho comes up to Harry in the hall as he leaves Transfiguration, tells him that the interview was a really brave thing for him to do, and kisses him on the cheek before hurrying away again.

Their reconciliation does not last long, however. The next meeting of Dumbledore's Army is rudely interrupted by Dobby, with news that Umbridge has been told about the DA and is sending the Inquisitorial Squad to capture its members. It turns out that Dumbledore's Army was betrayed by Marietta Edgecombe, Cho's friend. After Dumbledore's departure, the next time Harry and Cho meet, Cho attempts to defend Marietta's actions, and says that Hermione's placing a jinx on that piece of parchment they had signed was really sneaky; Harry responds that it was not sneaky, it was brilliant. Cho and Harry stalk off in their separate directions, and do not speak again in this book. On the Hogwarts Express headed back to London, Ginny tells Harry that Cho was now going out with Michael Corner. Ron is amazed at this, as he had thought Ginny was going out with Michael. Ginny says that he was upset that Gryffindor had won the final Quidditch match over Ravenclaw, and got all sulky, so Ginny had ditched him and he had run off to comfort Cho. Harry finds that he is not at all upset by this revelation.

Half-Blood Prince   Cho's character does not play a significant part in this book. We see her in passing a few times, usually fleeing from Harry's presence as quickly as possible, but Harry is no longer especially interested in her; he has become interested in someone else.

Deathly Hallows   Cho returns to Hogwarts for the final battle against Voldemort after receiving a message from Neville Longbottom via the fake galleons Hermione charmed for D.A. communications. She offers to take Harry to Ravenclaw Tower to show him a replica of Ravenclaw's lost diadem (a possible Horcrux) but is thwarted by Ginny Weasley, who volunteers Luna Lovegood in Cho's stead. Cho seems mildly disappointed by this.

Notable Consequences   Harry's relationship with Cho is his first exploration of this sort of relationship, and features his first kiss, which no doubt will remain special to him despite being flavoured heavily with Cho's tears for Cedric. Luckily for him, it seems to have no lasting negative effect; Harry does not mourn his loss when she moves on.

Cho and Harry's relationship seems to show only that Harry is not yet really ready for a relationship, especially not one as demanding as this. However, it is preparation for his later relationships. For details on that, see Harry's Relationship article.

We are given no information whatsoever on Cho's relationship with Michael Corner. Our information seems to suggest that Michael is in Ginny Weasley's year, making him one year younger than Harry and thus two years younger than Cho. Whether this would indicate a general preference for younger boys on Cho's part is unknown.

ANALYSIS

Cho's relationship with Cedric is quite normal, as far as we can tell; the two of them are going out together, enjoying each other's company, though Cho seems to be somewhat wistful on occasion that she had not chosen Harry. We should recall here that Harry, though not yet being portrayed as The Chosen One, has not yet fallen on the bad side of the Ministry; he is The Boy Who Lived, and additionally he has somehow been chosen as the second Hogwarts Champion in the Triwizard Tournament, making him something of a catch. It is a little curious that Cho feels about him romantically, given that he is a year younger than her; girls do mature more quickly than boys at that stage, so we would expect Cho to be interested in boys older than herself.

Her eventual relationship with Harry, though, is not a healthy one. She is not prepared to move on from Cedric's death, and throughout the year, she continues to mourn him. As late as Christmas, Hermione tells us Cho is always weeping. It seems that what she wants from Harry is more of Cedric. She keeps asking Harry about Cedric, about how he died; she seems to see Harry as a source of more information about Cedric, almost as a surrogate Cedric. Harry does not want to deal with this; he feels that he at least partially caused Cedric's death, and going over the circumstances surrounding that only make him feel that guilt more sharply. What Cho needs at this point is someone who will be able to help her move on past Cedric; and Harry is not able to do that for her. The breakup in early March comes as more of a relief to him than anything else.

GREATER PICTURE

Why bring Cho into the story at all? The fact is that, as we enter the fourth book, Harry is maturing; he is getting to be of an age where boys start noticing girls (and vice versa). As such, it is important for him to have a love interest, but possibly it is too early for him to be connecting with Ginny, who is the girl he will eventually marry. At the risk of seeming coarse, the girl that Harry needs at this point is one who will put him off the whole idea of romance for a while, so that he will not get too distracted from his quest in the next few books. With the death of Cedric in Harry's presence, we have a ready-made candidate in Cedric's girlfriend. It is certain that at the age of sixteen, Cho will be unready to move on after Cedric's death; she will idolize her dead hero, and will want to try to keep his memory alive. Hermione very accurately limns the feelings Cho is having, after the Christmas meeting of Dumbledore's Army. Among other things, she still feels as though she might be disloyal to Cedric because she is going out with Harry. One thing Hermine does not mention, because Harry has not mentioned it to her, is Cho's continual pestering of Harry for details about Cedric. We can see that this is an attempt by Cho to stay close to Cedric, to learn more about him, perhaps as a way to offset the guilt she feels about going out with his competitor. Of course, Harry is deeply disturbed by this concentration on Cedric, in part because of his role in Cedric's death, and in part because he has always felt inadequate compared to Cedric. Cho's dwelling on Cedric and his abilities deems to be pointing up Harry's shortcomings, and the suggestion that there is still competition for Cho's affections, in the form of Roger Davies, disquiets Harry still further. Cho is thus ideally placed to be set aside after one final climactic spat, and Harry can move on with no regrets.

Death Eaters

Location: Throughout the series
Time Period: Throughout the series
Important Characters: Numerous

OVERVIEW

The followers of Lord Voldemort are called the Death Eaters. Given Voldemort's fascination with death and immortality, it is likely that this is a name he chose, rather than one that the Death Eaters chose. Voldemort's followers were apparently using this name for themselves by the time Voldemort, then called Tom Riddle, graduated from school.

Event Details We first hear the term *Death Eaters* in *Harry Potter and the Goblet of Fire*. Harry asks what the meaning is of the Dark Mark floating in the sky is, and Hermione and the Weasleys explain that it is the mark of Voldemort, used by the Death Eaters to show places where they have been and have worked their evil. The term is then used frequently through the rest of that book, for instance when Sirius Black tells Harry, Hermione, and Ron that Karkaroff was a Death Eater, or that Snape had been suspected but never brought to trial. The book ends with the duel in the cemetery, which starts with Voldemort summoning his Death Eaters to announce his return.

In *Harry Potter and the Order of the Phoenix*, there is a mass escape of Death Eaters from Azkaban prison after the prison guards, the Dementors, defect and join Voldemort. Harry perceives the actions of some of these Death Eaters by way of the connection between his mind and Voldemort's, but it is only at the end of the story that we see what the Death Eaters are up to, when Harry and his friends are trapped in the Department of Mysteries. As Voldemort's return is now accepted by the Ministry, the actions of the Death Eaters become somewhat more open. However, in *Harry Potter and the Half-Blood Prince*, we do not see much of them, though we see that the Ministry is actively promoting possibly-useful defensive tactics, and some characters, notably Horace Slughorn, have gone into hiding for their own protection. Protection at Hogwarts is also heightened because of the threat. However, the only open activity by Death Eaters, apart from action by Draco Malfoy, who Harry suspects is a Death Eater, appears at the end of the story, in the Battle of the Lightning-Struck Tower. There, Death Eaters invade the school, and act to support Draco in his mission, which is apparently nominally to kill Dumbledore. Eventually, when he fails in his mission, it is taken over by Severus Snape, who thus declares himself to be firmly on the side of the Dark Lord.

In the first few chapters of *Harry Potter and the Deathly Hallows*, the Ministry falls completely to Voldemort, and the activities of the Death Eaters move completely into the open.

Voldemort makes a very clear distinction between the full Death Eater and the collaborator. The members of the group who are allowed to call themselves Death Eaters are marked with a tattoo of the Dark Mark on their left forearm. Touching this mark allows the person touching it to send a message to all others bearing the mark, but in the process evidently pains all bearers of the mark. This is a form of the Protean Charm.

It is also well worth noting that there is a continual battle for status within the ranks of the Death Eaters. In *Harry Potter and the Deathly Hallows,* we see Voldemort assigning places for his Death Eaters to sit. Pride of place is accorded to Snape, who is seated at Voldemort's right hand. The Malfoy family, in disgrace for having failed multiple times, is seated at the foot of the table.

Known Death Eaters include:

• Avery, a Death Eater in Voldemort's first rise to power, he was sentenced to imprisonment in Azkaban, but escaped when the Dementors left the prison.

• Regulus Black, a Death Eater in Voldemort's first rise to power. He apparently decided that Voldemort's ideas were too evil for him, and tried to leave the group. Rumour is that Voldemort killed him personally.

• Alecto Carrow, a Death Eater in Voldemort's first rise to power, she was sentenced to imprisonment in Azkaban, but escaped when the Dementors left the prison.

• Amycus Carrow, a Death Eater in Voldemort's first rise to power, he was sentenced to imprisonment in Azkaban, but escaped when the Dementors left the prison.

• Crabbe, Sr., a Death Eater in Voldemort's first rise to power, was apparently tried but not convicted, and returned to Voldemort's service at his return

• Barty Crouch Jr. may not have been formally a Death Eater, but did take part in an attempt to find where he had gone after his first rise to power. He was sentenced to Azkaban, escaped, and subsequently was instrumental in allowing Voldemort to return

• Antonin Dolohov, a Death Eater in Voldemort's first rise to power, he was sentenced to imprisonment in Azkaban, but escaped when the Dementors left the prison.

• Gibbon, a Death eater in Voldemort's second rise to power, died in the Battle of the Lightning-Struck Tower.

• Goyle, Sr., a Death Eater in Voldemort's first rise to power, was apparently tried but not convicted, and returned to Voldemort's service at his return

• Fenrir Greyback, though not one of the true Death Eaters (distinguished by the tattoo of the Dark Mark on the left forearm), was all the same a member of Voldemort's forces, though apparently working for loot rather than "glory." He does claim to be a Death Eater at one point, but not in front of Voldemort or any of the true Death Eaters.

• Jugson, a Death Eater in Voldemort's first rise to power, he was sentenced to imprisonment in Azkaban, but escaped when the Dementors left the prison.

• Igor Karkaroff, a Death Eater in Voldemort's first rise to power, he was sentenced to imprisonment in Azkaban, but had his sentence commuted when he revealed the names of other Death Eaters then unknown to the Ministry.

• Bellatrix Lestrange, a Death Eater in Voldemort's first rise to power, she was sentenced to imprisonment in Azkaban, but escaped when the Dementors left the prison.

• Rabastan Lestrange, a Death Eater in Voldemort's first rise to power, he was sentenced to imprisonment in Azkaban, and may have died in prison.

• Rodolphus Lestrange, a Death Eater in Voldemort's first rise to power, he was sentenced to imprisonment in Azkaban, but escaped when the Dementors left the prison.

• Walden Macnair, a Death Eater in Voldemort's first rise to power, was apparently tried but not convicted, and returned to Voldemort's service at his return

• Draco Malfoy, apparently made a Death Eater in Voldemort's second rise to power.

• Lucius Malfoy, a Death Eater in Voldemort's first rise to power, was apparently tried but not convicted, and returned to Voldemort's service at his return

• Narcissa Malfoy, possibly a tattooed Death Eater, but definitely in the group because her husband and son were part of it. It is unknown whether she had been part of the Death Eaters organization in Voldemort's first rise to power.

• Mulciber, a Death Eater in Voldemort's first rise to power, he was sentenced to imprisonment in Azkaban, and apparently died there.

• Nott, a Death Eater in Voldemort's first rise to power, he was sentenced to imprisonment in Azkaban, but escaped when the Dementors left the prison.

• Peter Pettigrew, a Death Eater in Voldemort's first rise to power, he was involved in the death of James and Lily Potter, and the imprisonment of Sirius Black. Going into hiding, he was later instrumental in the return of Voldemort to power.

• Augustus Rookwood, a Death Eater in Voldemort's first rise to power, he was sentenced to imprisonment in Azkaban, but escaped when the Dementors left the prison.

• Evan Rosier, a Death Eater in Voldemort's first rise to power, he was sentenced to imprisonment in Azkaban, but escaped when the Dementors left the prison.

• Thorfinn Rowle, a Death Eater in Voldemort's second rise to power, his previous history is unknown

• Selwyn, a Death Eater in Voldemort's second rise to power, his previous history is unknown

• Stan Shunpike, not actually a Death Eater, but boasts in a pub of being close enough to the Dark Lord to know some of his secrets in the early days of Voldemort's second rise to power. Sentenced to Azkaban, and later escapes. When we see him, he is working with the Death Eaters under the effects of the Imperius curse.

• Severus Snape, a Death Eater in Voldemort's first rise to power, he was either tried and released, or did not come to trial, based on Dumbledore's testimony that he had turned in place and was now working against Voldemort. His loyalties remain uncertain throughout much of Voldemort's second rise to power.

- Pius Thicknesse, not actually a Death Eater, but working for the Death Eaters under the effects of the Imperius curse.
- Travers, a Death Eater in Voldemort's second rise to power, his previous history is unknown
- Wilkes, a Death Eater in Voldemort's first rise to power, killed by Aurors before Voldemort fell
- Yaxley, a Death Eater in Voldemort's second rise to power, his previous history is unknown

Notable Consequences The reappearance of the Death Eaters in *Harry Potter and the Goblet of Fire*, after thirteen years of quiescence, causes a certain amount of panic at the Ministry and in the populace. This panic is fueled additionally by stories appearing in the *Daily Prophet*, written by Rita Skeeter. Rita is a popular muck-raking journalist, whose scurrilous stories are calculated to improve the circulation of the paper.

The ever-increasing presence of Death Eaters in the Wizarding world does cause an increase in tension, and an increase in the number of refugees, either leaving England or going into hiding within the country.

ANALYSIS

There is some question as to exactly when the name "Death Eaters" first came into use. There is a suggestion that the name was in use before Tom Riddle had even left school; it is certain that he was already using the name "Lord Voldemort" at that time, as the diary Horcrux, created when Riddle was a sixth-year student, already uses that name for himself / itself. However, in Dumbledore's memory of Tom's request to become a teacher of Defence Against the Dark Arts, Dumbledore says that he is aware that Tom's followers are now calling themselves Death Eaters, which implies that the name is new at that time. We are told that this memory was recorded ten years after the death of Hepzibah Smith, which in turn occurred some time after Tom Riddle had graduated from Hogwarts. The name of the group surely reflects Voldemort's obsession with, and fear of, death. The name that Voldemort has chosen for himself, a bastardization of the Latin "flies or runs from death," is another indication of this obsessive fear. The name of his followers, the Death Eaters, seems cut from the same fabric. It is most likely that Voldemort has chosen this name for his followers himself. The same is likely true for the Order of the Phoenix, set up by Dumbledore to oppose Voldemort.

Dobby's Death

Location: Malfoy Manor
Time Period: *Harry Potter and the Deathly Hallows*, about March
Important Characters: Dobby, Bellatrix Lestrange, Harry

OVERVIEW

In *Harry Potter and the Deathly Hallows*, Dobby, the free elf, was mortally wounded while rescuing Harry and his allies from Malfoy Manor.

Event Details Captured by a group of Snatchers led by Fenrir Greyback, Harry, Ron, Hermione, Dean, and the Goblin Griphook are taken to Malfoy Manor. There, Bellatrix Lestrange sees that the Trio are carrying the Sword of Gryffindor, and for some reason stops Lucius Malfoy from summoning Voldemort. Keeping Hermione upstairs for questioning, Bellatrix has the others sent to a locked room in the cellar, where they encounter Luna and Ollivander who are also being held prisoner there. Though the new arrivals are tied up, Luna has found a nail with which she is able to cut their bonds.

Desperate at hearing Hermione's cries of pain from above, Harry is nervously fidgeting with the fragment of the magic mirror Sirius had given him years before, and sees a sky-blue eye looking out of it at him. Harry pleads for help from the owner of the eye, and shortly Dobby apparates into the cell. Harry bids Dobby take Dean, Ollivander, and Luna to safety at Shell Cottage. From upstairs where she is now torturing Griphook, Bellatrix hears the noise of Dobby Disapparating, and sends Wormtail to investigate. Harry and Ron manage to overpower Pettigrew when he hesitates, reminded of his life debt to Harry, and his own magical silver hand strangles him to death.

Attempting to rescue Hermione and Griphook, Harry and Ron are forced to surrender when a disarmed Bellatrix threatens Hermione with a silver knife. Dobby announces his return by causing a chandelier to fall on Bellatrix. Harry seizes the wands Draco Malfoy is holding, and Stuns Fenrir. Ron collects Hermione and Disapparates to Shell Cottage, while Harry similarly collects Griphook. As Harry Disapparates, Bellatrix throws her knife at him. Harry, not knowing where he is heading, is relieved to find, in the midst of his Disapparation, that he can feel Dobby alongside. Arriving at Shell Cottage, Harry discovers that Dobby has been fatally wounded by Bellatrix' thrown knife. Dobby dies moments later, his final words being "Harry Potter."

Harry is deeply grieved and decides to dig Dobby's grave by hand without using magic. Ron and Dean join Harry and labor with him. They place Dobby's body in the grave and give him socks, shoes and a hat. Standing over Dobby, Luna thanks Dobby for rescuing them and the others follow. Harry fills in the grave and carves: "HERE LIES DOBBY, A FREE ELF" on a flat rock he places on the burial mound.

Notable Consequences Dobby's courage and eventual sacrifice saves the lives of seven people including the Trio.

Dobby's death is an emotional turning point for Harry. While digging the grave, Harry finds that his grief distances his perceptions of Voldemort's thoughts, and decreases the pain in his scar. From this point on Harry is able to manage and exploit his connection with Voldemort in a way that Occlumency lessons and other attempts have failed to do. His ability to grieve and love is focused, and his emotions are, at last, under his control. The goblin, Griphook, notices Harry reverently digging Dobby's grave and thereafter considers Harry an uncommon wizard who respects non-humans. This facilitates the trio's plan to steal the Hufflepuff Cup Horcrux from Gringotts.

GREATER PICTURE

Dobby's bravery and sacrifice is a significant part of the author's theme of tolerance and collaboration. Throughout the series, Harry's quest to defeat Voldemort is only possible because of help from good people, including all sentient beings. In return wizards learn to respect elves, goblins, centaurs and other non-human beings in the magical world. During the Battle of Hogwarts, victory over Voldemort and his evil is assured when all species join together for the common good. Dobby is loyal to Harry not because of a magical enslavement but rather their mutual friendship and regard. Dobby is a free elf and chooses to risk his life in order to save the lives of Harry and his allies. Harry, representing the enlightenment of wizards, recognizes the debt he owes Dobby and his fellows.

Dumbledore's Army

Location: Room of Requirement
Time Period: Year 5, about October to about March, and again in Year 7
Important Characters: Harry Potter, Hermione Granger, Ron Weasley, among others

OVERVIEW

Dumbledore's Army (D.A.) is the secret Defence Against the Dark Arts group founded by Harry Potter and Hermione Granger, with assistance from Ron Weasley.

Event Details Professor Dolores Umbridge, Hogwart's new Defence Against the Dark Arts teacher, only lectures on Ministry-approved theory from the textbook and refuses to teach real defensive magic. Sirius Black, in conversation with Harry after the group is founded, reveals that this is because the Ministry is worried that Albus Dumbledore may be trying to raise a private army to attack the Ministry itself. Within the first two weeks of classes, Hermione has seen how stultifying and useless this form of teaching is, and with the assistance of Ron, suggests to Harry that it would be a good idea to have someone teach them real Defence Against the Dark Arts, rather than the useless "techniques" currently being taught. When Harry agrees to this, Hermione tentatively suggests that the appropriate teacher would be Harry himself. Harry's surprise turns into exasperation when Ron agrees that he is the logical choice.

Although Harry initially feels he is unqualified to teach Defensive Arts, he reluctantly agrees after Hermione convinces him he has gained considerable knowledge on the subject. Hermione then invites "a couple of students" to meet at the Hog's Head Inn in Hogsmeade village to discuss forming a group to learn real Defence Against the Dark Arts. Harry is stunned when Hermione's "couple of students" ends up numbering 25; Hermione simply says "The idea did seem quite popular." The group originally call themselves the *Defence Association,* or D.A. for short. Shortly afterwards, a new Educational Decree is posted which prevents formation of student groups. Harry and Ron are convinced that someone has told Umbridge, but Hermione says nobody could have. She had passed a parchment around that everyone had signed; the parchment was jinxed so that anyone who betrayed the group after signing it would break out in severe facial blemishes.

In the conversation with Sirius earlier mentioned, Sirius mentions that he knows that they are starting the group; he says that at the initial meeting, a heavily veiled witch that Harry and Hermione had noted was Mundungus Fletcher. He passes on a message from Ron's mother forbidding Ron from having anything to do with it, and appealing to Harry and Hermione to likewise give up the idea. Sirius himself, however, says he strongly supports the idea of the group.

There is concern for some time as to where they can meet. Various suggestions are made and rejected for practical reasons. Finally, Harry happens to ask Dobby if he knows of a place, and Dobby tells Harry about the Room of Requirement, a room which appears when a person really needs it, in the form that the person needs. Harry, Ron, and Hermione pass on the description of the Room to other members of the Defence Association, as it is then known, and then go to the room themselves. When it appears for them, it is perfect, stocked with everything they need for a Defence Against the Dark Arts class; and Hermione, who has been unsure whether using the Room of Requirement is a good idea, is instantly reassured by the shelves of books along the wall. At this, their first full meeting, they change the name of the group to "Dumbledore's Army" to show their loyalty to the Headmaster and to mock the paranoid Ministry of Magic.

Meetings are irregular, as they have to be fit in around three different house's Quidditch practices; Hermione provides fake Galleons that allow DA members to send messages. The spell used to do this is a Protean Charm, which Terry Boot says is "N.E.W.T.-level magic." For several months, Harry secretly teaches students from Gryffindor, Ravenclaw, and Hufflepuff, although Slytherin is excluded. Under Harry's effective tutoring, the D.A. members learn many advanced defensive Dark Art techniques, starting with the simple disarmament charm and proceeding to the N.E.W.T.-level Patronus charm.

Dumbledore's Army abruptly ends in March when D.A. member and Ravenclaw student Marietta Edgecombe reveals its existence to Umbridge, instigating a raid by her *Inquisitorial Squad,* comprised of Slytherin students and led by Draco Malfoy. Umbridge's attempt to detain members of the Army are thwarted by Dobby, who disobeys orders to warn Harry; Harry sends the rest of the group away, and is the only group member captured. He is taken to Dumbledore's office, where he finds Dumbledore, along with Umbridge, the Minister for Magic Cornelius Fudge, Percy Weasley (along to record the meeting), and a pair of Aurors, one of whom (Kingsley Shacklebolt) Harry recognizes as being in the Order of the Phoenix.

Umbridge's star witness, Marietta, proves less than useful, as it seems Kingsley has performed a memory charm on her secretly to keep Harry out of trouble.

However, the membership list for the D. A. was retrieved by Pansy Parkinson, and the heading, "*Dumbledore's Army*," is enough to allow the Ministry to order Dumbledore's arrest. This heading on the membership list allows Dumbledore to claim responsibility for forming the group, thus protecting the students. The Ministry's subsequent attempt to arrest him results in his spectacular departure from Hogwarts. Umbridge is appointed Headmistress in his place. For betraying the D.A., permanent purple pustules spelling "SNEAK" erupt across Marietta's face—courtesy of Hermione's jinxed parchment.

With the appointment of a competent Defence Against the Dark Arts teacher in Harry's sixth year (Severus Snape), there is little need to re-start Dumbledore's Army. Harry does put out a call to the members of the DA for assistance when he knows Dumbledore will be leaving the school temporarily, but only about five members respond: Ron Weasley, Hermione Granger, Luna Lovegood, Neville Longbottom, and Ginny Weasley.

In what would be Harry's seventh year, Neville, Luna, and Ginny restart Dumbledore's Army as a means of rebelling against Hogwarts' new emphasis on Dark Arts at the hands of headmaster Snape, Dark Arts teacher Amycus Carrow, and Muggle Studies teacher Alecto Carrow, all of whom are Death Eaters. The DA falls on hard times as its members are hunted down; Luna is captured, Ginny escapes with her family, and Neville's grandmother is targeted in an unsuccessful attempt to put pressure on Neville. The DA retreat to the Room of Requirement, from which they continue guerrilla raids on the school.

When Harry returns to the school, Neville, using the Galleons that Hermione had earlier enchanted to tell about meetings, recalls the rest of the D.A. The members of the Order of the Phoenix come along with them, along with many other wizards.

The Members Of Dumbledore's Army include: Hannah Abbott, Lavender Brown, Katie Bell, Susan Bones, Terry Boot, Cho Chang, Michael Corner, Colin Creevey, Dennis Creevey, Marietta Edgecombe, Justin Finch-Fletchley, Seamus Finnigan, Anthony Goldstein, Hermione Granger, Angelina Johnson, Lee Jordan, Neville Longbottom, Luna Lovegood, Ernie Macmillan, Padma Patil, Parvarti Patil, Harry Potter, Zacharias Smith, Alicia Spinnet, Dean Thomas, Fred Weasley, George Weasley, Ginny Weasley, and Ron Weasley. Seamus Finnigan is a late-joining member; not present at the initial meeting in The Hog's Head, the first meeting he attended was the one that was broken up by Marietta Edgecombe's betrayal of the group.

Notable Consequences When meeting in the Hog's Head, Harry expresses some doubts that they may be overheard by someone, suggesting that a veiled witch in the corner might be Umbridge. Umbridge is not present, as it turns out, but here are in fact two eavesdroppers: the witch is Mundungus Fletcher, there for the Order of the Phoenix, and also present is Willy Widdershins, the comprehensively bandaged wizard at the bar drinking Firewhiskey, who promptly reports back to Umbridge. It is as a direct result of this meeting that Umbridge causes promulgation of Educational Decree number Twenty-Four which prevents unapproved student groups. This has the side effect of banning the Quidditch teams. The fact that the Slytherin Quidditch team is approved and reforms immediately, while the Gryffindor team is not allowed to reform for a month, is an indication of how Umbridge will tend to abuse her powers. Cho Chang has joined the D.A. largely because Harry was there. Cho makes use of the end of the last D.A. meeting before Christmas to kiss Harry in private. We can see from his response to this, as related to Hermione, that he is extremely unsure of himself around Cho.

The continued unapproved meetings of the D.A., in violation of Educational Decree number Twenty-Four, are eventually betrayed, and an attempt is made to apprehend the group. In the end, due to a timely warning from Dobby, the only group member caught is Harry himself. Pansy Parkinson enters the Room of Requirement and retrieves the membership list. Cornelius Fudge has been summoned to witness the bringing of the group to justice; on seeing the membership list heading, his paranoia asserts itself, and he tries to arrest Dumbledore. Dumbledore escapes, dramatically, and Umbridge is appointed Headmistress, although she is never able to get into the Headmaster's office after Dumbledore's departure.

Marietta Edgecombe's defection not only betrayed Dumbledore's Army, but ultimately doomed Harry and Cho Chang's relationship. When Cho defends Marietta's actions and is angry that Hermione secretly jinxed the parchment the D.A. members signed, Harry angrily lashes out, calling Hermione's plan "brilliant." Cho is deeply offended and storms off in tears; she and Harry do not speak to one another for two years.

Unfortunately for Umbridge, students have acquired what she vigorously prevented them from having: Defence Against the Dark Arts knowledge. The D.A. members use their new-found skills on several occasions. When Ron, Ginny, Neville, and Luna are captured by Umbridge's *Inquisitorial Squad*, they escape with defensive jinxes and hexes. The students use Defensive Arts during the Battle at the Department of Mysteries, fending off Death Eaters until Order of the Phoenix reinforcements arrive. When Draco and his minions attempt to Curse Harry on the Hogwarts Express, D.A. members come to his rescue, jinxing the Slytherins until they are unrecognizable. Members of Dumbledore's Army use what they have learned to assist with the defence of the school at the battle under the Astronomy tower. And it is largely members of Dumbledore's Army who make up the core of the guerrilla resistance against Snape's rule in the seventh book.

ANALYSIS

Curiously, it is Hermione who takes action against Umbridge by forming *Dumbledore's Army*. Although she believes in strictly adhering to school rules, she never hesitates to break them when she believes they are wrong or a nobler purpose is served. In this instance, she not only takes on Umbridge, but the entire Ministry of Magic, who are convinced Dumbledore may be creating a secret wizard army against them.

There are two people in Dumbledore's Army who do not completely seem to belong there. These are Zacharias Smith and Marietta Edgecombe. Smith is confrontational, to the point that at the organizational meeting Fred Weasley feels compelled to threaten him with a pointed metal object that he produces from a Zonko's Joke Shop bag. Smith also does not seem to want to sign the parchment that Hermione passes around, where they swear not to tell anyone about the D.A. Granted, he is not the only one to express reluctance; Ernie Macmillan hesitates, saying he is a prefect, and if the parchment were found... He only signs when Hermione points out that she's not going to leave this bit of parchment lying around. From the beginning, we have a feeling that the D.A. is doomed, that it will accomplish at least some part of its purpose, but will ultimately fall to Umbridge and her cronies; and Zacharias Smith's continuing skepticism makes him a lead candidate for that betrayal.

Marietta is along because Cho is going, and she is always very quiet, limiting her interaction to sighs and non-verbal displays of impatience. When the actual betrayal takes place, we fully expect Zacharias to have been the agent, and are very surprised when it turns out to be Marietta.

Even before Harry gets the teaching up to that level, Hermione is seen doing two N.E.W.T.-class spells here. The first is the parchment, on which everyone signs their names at the organizational meeting. As mentioned above, the parchment is charmed so that anyone who betrays the D.A. will break out in horrendous blemishes. When Hermione mentions this to Ron and Harry, after the promulgation of the Educational Decree banning student organizations, they are both very impressed; Ron in particular recognizes that this is very advanced magic. One wonders why Hermione had not told the rest of the D.A. of this charm, once they had all signed; Marietta might have chosen a different course of action had she known that betraying the D.A. to Umbridge would result in her wearing the word "Sneak" across her face for at least a year.

The second is the Galleons; every Galleon has on it a serial number, that of the gnome who cast it. Hermione has made fake Galleons for the D.A., which look like real ones except that the serial number changes to indicate the date and time of the next meeting. When Hermione passes these out at the second regular meeting, everyone present is amazed that she is capable of performing a Protean Charm, it being such advanced magic.

Questions

1. What prompts Hermione to form *Dumbledore's Army*? Why is it kept secret?
2. Why is the group's original name changed from *Defense Association* to *Dumbledore's Army*?
3. What are possible reasons Slytherin students were excluded from the group?
4. Why did purple pimples break out on Marietta Edgecombe's face? Who was responsible?
5. Why does Professor Dumbledore claim responsibility for having organized the group? What happens when he does?
6. Why is Harry initially reluctant to teach Defensive Arts? Who convinces him otherwise?
7. How does Marietta Edgecombe betraying the D.A. contribute to Harry and Cho breaking up?

Greater Picture

In *Harry Potter and the Half-Blood Prince*, Harry finds out that he and Dumbledore are going to both be leaving the school for a while, and while he cannot be sure what Draco's mission is, or whether he has accomplished it, he has at the very least a great suspicion that it has been completed successfully. Although Dumbledore reassures him that the school is protected by Aurors and members of the Order of the Phoenix, Harry does not feel that is enough. For reasons of his own, he feels that Draco's task may have resulted in an increased danger to Hogwarts in a way that the Order had not anticipated. When appealing to Dumbledore seems ineffective, Harry tries to re-activate the D.A., with very limited success: only Ron, Hermione, Ginny, Neville, and Luna Lovegood come forward. However, the five of them, with a little help from Harry's remaining stock of Felix Felicis potion, manage to turn the tide of the battle.

In *Harry Potter and the Deathly Hallows*, Neville and Ginny re-activate Dumbledore's army as a means of rebelling against the headmaster, Severus Snape. As there are two other Death Eaters teaching at the school, and the teaching has become a lot darker and more abusive, this is not a complete success. However, the organization is in place, and is working out of the Room of Requirement, when Harry reaches Hogwarts. Additionally, when Neville uses the Galleons to summon the D.A., all of the past members of the D.A. arrive as well, forming the nucleus of a fighting group that will largely save Hogwarts.

Surprisingly, the choice of which student enters the Room of Requirement to retrieve the parchment is important. Voldemort, when he was at Hogwarts, apparently discovered the Room of Requirement. It seems that most people who discover it are looking for some place to hide something; Professor Trelawney had discovered it when looking for a place to hide her sherry, and the Twins had been looking for a place to hide themselves from Filch, for instance. Voldemort, presumably looking for a place to hide something he had done, had thus managed to open the door onto a warehouse full of a thousand years worth of magical junk. He apparently instructed Draco Malfoy, over the summer, as to how to get into that aspect of the Room. It is in that aspect of the room that Draco was working on his technique for getting Death Eaters into Hogwarts throughout Harry's sixth year. If Draco had ever seen the inside of the room prepared for D.A. meetings, he might have had a better idea of what the room actually was; as it is, though, only Pansy has seen that aspect of the room, and Draco, in his superior way, likely would not bother to ask her what the inside of the room looked like, assuming, once he got instructions on how to enter, that the DA had been practicing in the junk warehouse.

Dumbledore's Death

Location: Astronomy Tower

Time Period: *Harry Potter and the Half-Blood Prince*, late June

Important Characters: Severus Snape, Albus Dumbledore, Draco Malfoy, Harry Potter

Overview

In the sixth book, Dumbledore dies when facing Severus Snape on top of the Astronomy Tower.

Event Details Weakened by his adventures in the cave of the locket, Dumbledore returns with Harry by side-along Apparation to Hogsmeade. There, they see the Dark Mark floating above the Astronomy Tower at Hogwarts. Borrowing a pair of brooms from Madam Rosmerta at the Three Broomsticks, they fly back to the tower, arriving to find the top of the tower empty. At Dumbledore's instruction, Harry dons the Invisibility Cloak and prepares to head down the stairs. Hearing footsteps pounding up the stairs, Dumbledore quickly freezes Harry, as Draco Malfoy charges out the tower door, and disarms Dumbledore. Having gotten this far, however, Draco seems uncertain of the next step, and pauses, while Dumbledore reasons with him as to what he should do next. It seems Draco is partly convinced to change allegiance when four Death Eaters, Amycus Carrow, Alecto Carrow, Fenrir Greyback, and an unnamed fourth Death Eater who we later find out is Yaxley, charge up the stairs. They try to taunt Draco into killing Dumbledore, without success; then Severus Snape arrives, and seeing that Draco is incapable of continuing, he kills Dumbledore.

Now no longer frozen by Dumbledore's spell, Harry is still frozen by shock, and can only watch as the Death Eaters, Snape, and Draco depart; finally, he freezes the last departing Death Eater (Yaxley) and descends to enter the fray. Snape, departing, calls out that it is done. Harry, attacked by Fenrir, freezes him, then blasts Amycus Carrow aside from where he is attacking Ginny. Snape and Draco, hotly pursued by Harry, depart through the front doors; Snape counters every curse Harry throws at him, but stops the other Death Eaters from harming him, saying that the Dark Lord's orders are that Potter should not be harmed. The remaining Death Eaters escape while Harry is looking for his wand, which Snape has blasted out of his hand.

Notable Consequences The only wizard with experience and power that matches that of Voldemort, and Harry's friend and protector, is now dead.

Severus Snape has revealed himself to be a Death Eater, firmly on the side of the Dark Lord. Steps will now have to be taken to secure those parts of the Order of the Phoenix to which he was privy, to prevent his revealing more than he already has to Voldemort. Likely Headquarters, at Grimmauld Place, will have to be abandoned, as Snape knows about it and can allow Death Eaters into it.

While Snape had earlier put his life at risk by making an Unbreakable Vow to complete Draco's task if Draco could not, he has completed that vow and nullified that risk.

As far as we are aware, Dumbledore was the only one who knew about Voldemort's plan for immortality via the creation of Horcruxes. Harry now has the mission, which he must accomplish aided only by those he can recruit, of finding and destroying the remaining Horcruxes.

Analysis

After the release of book 6, this event became one of the most widely discussed issues in the Potter fan community. It seemed unthinkable to all the fans that Dumbledore could have been killed off so casually, and many theories were put forward to suggest what had really happened. One of the principle theories is that Dumbledore and Snape had conspired to make it appear as though Dumbledore were dead, but that he would remain alive behind the scenes, to direct the resistance against Voldemort. Primary evidence for this theory was based on the idea that the spell Snape used against Dumbledore was not, in fact, the killing curse, that he had spoken the killing curse, but thought and cast the Disarmament curse "Expelliarmus," which would have had the effect of throwing Dumbledore over the battlements. This flew in the face of announcements from the author that Dumbledore quite definitely was dead. The spectre was again raised when the author admitted to having had trouble with writing some of Dumbledore's speech in book 7. It was promptly decided that either the author was lying about Dumbledore's death, or (more likely) one of the techniques of keeping an image of the dead, such as ghosts or portraits, was involved. The latter supposition was given strength by the appearance in the Headmaster's office of Dumbledore's portrait after his death. To readers of heroic fiction, like the Harry Potter series, Dumbledore's death should have been expected. Dumbledore, the last in a series of father figures, represents the wise old teacher, the one who passes on his knowledge to the young student so that the student can then defeat the villain. The hero cannot be heroic if there is an older and stronger hero standing behind him; he must enter onto his final adventure alone, to be the hero. One major key to this, however, is that, except in retrospect, Dumbledore does not seem to be preparing to pass on his knowledge. While it has been commented that he acts out of character, being uncharacteristically harsh with the Dursleys, for instance, it is not apparent to us that he does this because he thinks his time might be limited. Harry's thought at the beginning of the year is that Dumbledore will be teaching him specific spells that will aid him in his battle against Voldemort, and is slightly disappointed to find that instead they will be learning about Tom Riddle's childhood. While it is true that in this manner, Harry learns much more about Tom and what drives him, and of the nature of Horcruxes and why Tom is interested in them, than he (and therefore we) would have gotten if Dumbledore had simply expounded at us, none of this has the feel of the teacher preparing his final lessons for his student. We expect Dumbledore to continue on, up to the final battle, or at least to the eve of that battle, teaching Harry the spells of rare power that will be used to defeat Voldemort; and so his sudden demise at this point, with no such magic taught, comes as a shock. We are left with the feeling that Dumbledore's life is uncompleted, that Harry has not been properly taught for his role, and like Harry, we are left wondering what is to come.

QUESTIONS

1. Is Dumbledore actually dead?
2. Did Dumbledore have more to explain to Harry?
3. With this death, will Harry be able to overcome Voldemort and his followers?

GREATER PICTURE

Of course, what Dumbledore knows is that spells of rare power will not be effective against Voldemort, his power is too great to be overcome by any wizard or witch. Dumbledore knows that the only power that can defeat Voldemort is a power he discounts, and knows that the one person who has prevailed against Voldemort so far, Harry, did so because of the power of love, an emotion Voldemort does not feel and therefore cannot fully understand. It will be seen in the final book of the series, that Voldemort's death is a spell he casts himself, again being reflected onto him in part by the protection afforded to Harry by his mother's love.

We find out in *Harry Potter and the Deathly Hallows* that Dumbledore, cursed by contact with the Horcrux ring containing the Resurrection Stone, is saved from immediate death only by the actions of Severus Snape. Dumbledore, already aware that Voldemort had set Draco the task of killing Dumbledore, and now aware that the curse had given him at most another year of life, then arranged with Snape that Snape was to kill Dumbledore when the time came, presumably when Draco Malfoy failed. This is what compelled Snape to kill Dumbledore by cursing him off the Astronomy Tower at Hogwarts in front of numerous Death Eaters, after Dumbledore and Harry had returned from Voldemort's cave. This is likely also why Snape was prepared to make the Unbreakable Vow with Narcissa that he would complete Draco's mission if he were to fail; he knew that he had already given his word to Dumbledore to do so. (The timing is implicit in the story, rather than explicit; in conversation with Narcissa and Bellatrix at Spinners' End, Snape comments that Dumbledore has received an injury due to his slowing reflexes, and in Snape's memories later we see that immediately after he received that injury, he was talking about Draco's mission in Snape's presence. Thus Dumbledore must have been aware of Draco's mission, and Snape will have promised Dumbledore that he would complete Draco's mission at the same time, before Snape talked to Narcissa.) Dumbledore knew it had to be Snape in order for Snape to 'prove' his alliance with Voldemort; also, he preferred his death to be at the hands of someone nominally sympathetic, rather than someone (like Bellatrix or Fenrir Greyback) who would choose to humiliate him as well as kill him. This would put Snape in a good position to remain in control of Dumbledore's school, which Dumbledore thought would give the school and the students a better chance than if anyone else had taken over as headmaster.

Dumbledore also had major concerns about the Elder Wand, one of the three Deathly Hallows. Dumbledore felt, justifiably given its history, that having a wand with the reputation of being undefeatable in a duel available would be a very bad thing for the world. He expected that the Elder Wand's power would die with him; Snape would win its allegiance by killing Dumbledore, and then the wand would rest in Dumbledore's tomb. When Snape passed, undefeated, the power of the wand would end. Dumbledore, apparently, had made the common mistake of believing that the wand transferred its allegiance on the death of its holder, despite the fact that the two previous holders of the wand were still alive at the time. As Harry found out by talking to Mr. Ollivander in Shell Cottage, the wand's allegiance is not won by the death of its master, but by having control of the wand wrested from its owner. (This is why the stubby wand Ron had taken from the Snatcher never worked for Harry; Harry had not taken it away from anyone, so it had not shifted its allegiance away from Ron, who had stolen it from the Snatcher.) Thus the Elder Wand had transferred its allegiance to Draco Malfoy when Malfoy spelled it out of Dumbledore's hand.

Escape from Privet Drive

Location: Privet Drive and environs
Time Period: *Harry Potter and the Deathly Hallows*, late July
Important Characters: Harry, many Order of the Phoenix members, many Death Eaters, Voldemort

OVERVIEW

As the protection afforded him at Privet Drive will end when Harry reaches maturity at age 17, the Order of the Phoenix elect to move him to an Order safe house. In order to confuse Voldemort, who they believe has infiltrated the Ministry of Magic, Polyjuice Potion is used to create six simulacra of Harry, each of whom sets off for a different safe house. Attacked by Death Eaters, the various groups battle their way to their various safe houses, eventually gathering at The Burrow, where they make plans and grieve their losses.

Event Details Once Uncle Vernon, Aunt Petunia, and Dudley have left the house at Privet Drive, Harry, knowing that he is to be transported to a safe house before his protection runs out, finishes his preparations for departure. A noise in the back garden brings him downstairs, where he finds that many of the members of the Order have arrived, on broomsticks, Thestrals, and Hagrid on Sirius Black's flying motorcycle. Mad-Eye Moody, the leader of the group, explains that Harry's house is being monitored by the Ministry, nominally to prevent anyone from arriving via Apparation, Portkeys, or the Floo network. Moody is convinced that the Ministry has been infiltrated by Voldemort, and the monitoring is to determine if Harry is departing Privet

Escape from Privet Drive

Drive, and if so with whom and where, so they have chosen to travel by means that are not monitored. Additionally, there will be seven different Harry Potters traveling to seven different Order safe houses. Over Harry's protests, Moody produces a flask of Polyjuice Potion and demands some of Harry's hair. Eventually Harry gives in, and six of the wizards present, Mundungus Fletcher, Fred Weasley, George Weasley, Ron, Fleur Delacour, and Hermione, drink the prepared potion, becoming Harry Potters. Each one is paired with a protector, and they leave the house.

Almost immediately they come under attack. Harry, with Hagrid, is initially attacked by four Death Eaters. A killing curse aimed at Harry misses Harry by inches, killing Hedwig. Hagrid uses gadgets that Arthur Weasley has built into the motorcycle to try to defend against the following Death Eaters, but it is only when the motorcycle spits dragon flame that the following Death Eaters are deterred. The dragon flame, however, pushes the motorcycle forwards, straining the connection between it and the sidecar, where Harry is sitting. A second attempt to use the dragon fire causes the sidecar to break off and start falling. Harry Levitates the sidecar, but is unable to move it, and so hangs in the air while the three remaining Death Eaters attack. Hagrid manages to swing around and collect Harry out of the side car, but Harry loses everything except his knapsack. Harry, now hanging on to Hagrid's back, destroys the sidecar to disable a Death Eater, then notes that of the two left, one is Stan Shunpike, clearly under the Imperius curse. Not wanting to injure Stan, Harry disarms him, whereupon the remaining Death Eater shouts "It's the real one!" and vanishes.

Harry doesn't trust the apparent breaking off of the action by the Death Eaters, so urges Hagrid to use the dragon-fire to speed them to their destination. They are surrounded by Death Eaters, however, including Voldemort. Harry feels his wand, on its own, twist and fire a bolt of golden flame, and hears Voldemort's scream of rage as his borrowed wand is destroyed. Hagrid leaps off the motorcycle to attack a Death Eater only feet away. As Harry desperately tries to brake the falling motorcycle, he hears Voldemort demanding a new wand from another Death Eater. Suddenly, all the Death Eaters vanish, and Harry falls into mud. He sees the fallen Hagrid, and crawls towards him, but blacks out.

Harry regains consciousness in the house of Ted Tonks, one of the Order safe houses, where he learns that the reason for the Death Eaters vanishing was that they had run afoul of the Order's protective spells. After nearly jinxing Andromeda Tonks under the impression that she is Bellatrix Lestrange, Harry finds Hagrid unwounded, and together they are led to the hairbrush Portkey that will take them to the Burrow.

At The Burrow, Harry and Hagrid are greeted by a worried Ginny and Mrs. Weasley; two other groups' Portkeys had arrived, but Harry's group is the first to actually get there.

Lupin now arrives with an injured George; his ear has been severed with the Dark Sectumsempra curse by Severus Snape. Now believing that someone in the group had betrayed them, Lupin tests Harry to see if he is who he appears. Reassured by Harry's response, he says that Voldemort probably homed in on Harry because of Harry's use of the disarmament charm. His use of it against Voldemort in the cemetery had made the Death Eaters consider that something of a signature spell. Lupin urges Harry to use stronger spells in self defence, even if they do result in injury or death of those fighting on the side of the Death Eaters.

Next to arrive are Kingsley Shacklebolt with Hermione. Kingsley has apparently had the same thought as Lupin, because he immediately tests Lupin the same wah that Lupin had tested Harry.

Next to arrive is Arthur Weasley, with Fred, one of the two groups originally scheduled to arrive before Harry. Arthur, frantic with worry, brushes aside the Order members who want to test his identity, to rush to George's side. George, to everyone's relief, regains consciousness and seems to be in good humour.

Tonks and Ron, the other couple originally scheduled to arrive before Harry, now show up, explaining that they had been followed by Tonks' Aunt Bellatrix, and had quite the battle with her. In the process, they had done some damage to Rodolphus Lestrange.

Finally, after Shacklebolt has returned to the Muggle Prime Minister's office, Bill and Fleur arrive, saying that they had been delayed by Auntie Muriel. The last pair, Alastor Moody with Mundungus Fletcher, will not be returning. The gathered Order members decide that Voldemort, finding so many Harry Potter simulacra, assumed the one defended by the strongest Auror, Moody, was the real one. Fletcher, finding that he was Voldemort's direct target, had Disapparated out of the path of a curse, which had then hit Moody and apparently killed him. In his absence, the remaining Order members wonder if Mundungus was the traitor, but decide that he could not be; Voldemort had clearly not been expecting the multiplicity of Harry Potters, and that suggestion had come from Mundungus.

As Bill and Lupin depart to try to find Moody's body, Harry announces that his presence at The Burrow brings danger on everyone there, and says he has to leave as well. He is overruled by the Order members who say there is no way Voldemort could know which of several safe-houses he is in.

Notable Consequences Voldemort assumes that the most powerful Auror will be assigned to protect Harry, and so concentrates his efforts initially on Mad-Eye Moody's passenger, Mundungus Fletcher. Mundungus, perceiving that he is catching most of the attacks, Disapparates, leaving Moody to catch the curse fired at Mundungus. This results in Moody's death. George Weasley losing an ear to a curse cast by Snape reinforces the Order's belief that Snape has become a Death Eater. It also may foreshadow another loss for the Weasley family.

The Ministry had been told that Harry would be moved on his birthday, but the actual escape had happened a few days earlier. The fact that Death Eaters were ready for the transfer indicates that there is a spy within the Order. The obvious candidate is the underworld element, Mundungus Fletcher; but he had originated a plan element that the Death Eaters were not prepared for, which indicates that it is someone else.

Lupin mentions that Harry's use of the Expelliarmus disarming charm has become a trademark of sorts. Lupin seems to indicate here that Harry is not ruthless enough for the battle he is facing; he certainly encourages Harry to use more destructive spells.

Harry, at the Burrow, is safe for the moment and can look forward to his own birthday and Bill and Fleur's wedding. However, he has seen the effort that the Death Eaters are willing to make to capture him, and fears for the safety of the people near him.

In the course of the escape, we get to meet Ted Tonks and Andromeda (Black) Tonks. Andromeda, like Sirius, had rebelled against her pure-blood heritage, but we see here that she looks like her sister Bellatrix. Sirius' flying motorcycle is destroyed, though we will later learn that Arthur Weasley has recovered the pieces and is trying to reassemble it.

ANALYSIS

The fact that this battle happens quite early in the book, and is so lethal, is a clear indication that with this final book in the series we have entered a new and harsher phase of the epic. Until now, when Harry has faced Voldemort directly, it has been at the culmination of the year's adventures, so that we have been building up to the battle with Voldemort. This book, Voldemort makes himself known within the first few chapters. Apart from signaling to us that Harry will be having a harder task to carry out this year, this also lets us know that Voldemort feels so secure in his power that he is willing to dogfight in the skies above Muggle England, where any Wizard could see him and his followers.

One thing that we see mentioned in passing is that Voldemort is flying without a broomstick. We will perceive this again when Harry is looking into his mind, and we will also see that Snape has evidently learned it as well. In the earlier part of the series, we were told that no Wizard can fly unassisted. This seems to indicate that Voldemort is a wizard of rare power and inventiveness, as well as being evil.

GREATER PICTURE

In what is quite possibly a deliberate parallel with the opening of the first story, Harry is carried out of danger to safety by Hagrid on Sirius' flying motorcycle. In an interview, the author had stated that Hagrid's fate was certain; as he had carried Harry out of the wreckage of his parents' house to Privet Drive, and from the Muggle world of the Dursleys to the Wizarding world behind the Leaky Cauldron, so would he carry Harry out of the Forbidden Forest at the end of the story. Hagrid's carrying Harry at this point, though not mentioned by the author in that interview, is clearly another echo of that same pattern.

We will later learn that the plan to have multiple Harry Potters in the escape was a collaborative effort between Snape and the portrait of Dumbledore. In order to stay in Voldemort's confidence, Snape would have to give him the true date of Harry's transfer, so the only way to avoid Harry being singled out and killed was to make a confusing multplicity of targets. Under instruction from Dumbledore, Snape had planted the idea in Mundungus' mind, and then hidden it from Voldemort in his own mind. Although this is never explicitly laid out, the fact that Snape had such easy access to Mundungus leads us to believe that Snape had extracted the information concerning the date of the transfer from Mundungus earlier.

Harry will later retrieve Moody's magical eye from inside the Ministry of Magic. No other part of Moody will ever be found, leaving the possibility that he had escaped just ever so slightly open.

Events in the Shrieking Shack

Location: The Shrieking Shack
Time Period: *Harry Potter and the Prisoner of Azkaban*, June
Important Characters: Harry, Ron, Hermione, Sirius Black, Remus Lupin, Peter Pettigrew, Severus Snape

OVERVIEW

Note that this article concerns only events in the Shrieking Shack that occurred in the book *Harry Potter and the Prisoner of Azkaban*.

Ron is dragged into a tunnel under the Whomping Willow by a large black dog. Following him, Harry and Hermione are trapped in the Shrieking Shack by Sirius Black, who turns out to be an unregistered Animagus; his Animagus form is the black dog. Though disarmed, Harry manages to get his wand back, and is preparing to kill Sirius who he believes betrayed his parents to Voldemort, but Crookshanks, Hermione's cat, gets in the way. The impasse is broken by the arrival of Remus Lupin, who greets Sirius as a brother. Their explanation of what is going on is interrupted again by Severus Snape, who binds both Sirius and Lupin and prepares to take them away to meet the Dementors. Harry, Hermione, and Ron Disarm Snape, which throws him against a wall and knocks him out. Freed, Lupin and Sirius reveal that Ron's rat, Scabbers, is actually an Animagus, Peter Pettigrew. As they return to the school to turn Pettigrew in, the full moon causes Lupin to assume his Werewolf shape, and Sirius transforms into his dog shape to keep Lupin away from the students. Pettigrew changes to his rat shape and escapes. Sirius is caught by the Dementors, and Harry and Hermione try to rescue him, but are unable to and nearly succumb themselves.

Event Details This event covers some five chapters in the original book, and therefore even the details must be a bit sketchy. For the full event details, the only recourse would be chapters 17 through 21 of *Harry Potter and the Prisoner of Azkaban*.

Notable Consequences The main result of the events in the Shrieking Shack is the revelation of the truth surrounding the betrayal of Harry's parents. Harry now knows that Peter Pettigrew is still alive, and had been hiding since his supposed death at Sirius' hand, thirteen years earlier; that it was Pettigrew, not Sirius, that had betrayed his parents; that Sirius, Pettigrew, and Lupin had been friends of his father; and that Sirius, his godfather, still cared about him and would be available to help him. For a short while, Harry believes that he may have a chance to live with Sirius, instead of with the Dursleys. This hope is unfortunately dashed with the escape of Pettigrew, shortly after they leave the Shrieking Shack.

We also learn that Sirius and Pettigrew are Animagi, as Harry's father was; the large black dog that we have seen throughout the book in many cases was Sirius. Pettigrew, of course, had been posing as Ron's rat Scabbers. We don't yet know what shape Harry's father took as an Animagus.

We learn that Snape had been in school at the same time as James, Lupin, Sirius, and Pettigrew, and that he had hated them so much that he is apparently willing to fabricate stories about them in revenge for the past, even to the extent of possibly getting Lupin killed.

GREATER PICTURE

Although the effect of the events in the Shrieking Shack on Sirius is minimal, as he was a fugitive both before and after this episode, it does still leave Harry with an adult who he feels able to call upon in times of need, as Harry will do several times in the next two books. Sirius' being free from Azkaban will allow him to offer the use of his family home in London as the Headquarters of the Order of the Phoenix, something he could not have done had he not re-established contact with Professor Dumbledore. It could be argued that had the events in the Shrieking Shack not occurred, Dumbledore would not have chosen to re-open communications with Sirius, and Sirius in turn would not have been available to help Harry.

Sirius will reveal that the shape James Potter took as an Animagus was that of a stag, similar to the Patronus that Harry casts shortly after the evens at the Shrieking Shack. This would be the second corporeal Animagus that Harry had cast; the first, used to disable supposed Dementors, had quite disturbed Lupin as he recognized its shape, though Harry had been too busy to look at it himself.

Dumbledore points out that Harry having stopped Sirius and Lupin from killing Pettigrew leaves Pettigrew owing Harry a life debt. While there is little discussion of life debts in the books, these are apparently taken quite seriously in the Wizarding world. At this time, in response to Harry's bemoaning the fact that, even forewarned, Harry had still let Pettigrew escape to return to the Dark Lord, Dumbledore comments that Voldemort is unlikely to be completely pleased that his lieutenant owes a life debt to his enemy. We will see that Voldemort is not particularly pleased with Pettigrew anyway, treating him as a not particularly valuable servant, rather than as a confidant. In *Harry Potter and the Deathly Hallows,* we will see that this life debt does end up saving Harry's life and resulting in Pettigrew's death.

First Task

Location: The Forbidden Forest
Time Period: *Harry Potter and the Goblet of Fire,* November 24
Important Characters: Harry Potter, Cedric Diggory, Viktor Krum, Fleur Delacour

OVERVIEW

The First Task of the Triwizard Tournament is to retrieve a golden egg from the nest of a dragon.

Event Details The initial briefing for the First Task is done immediately after the selection of the Champions, on 31 October. This briefing is very sketchy, as the intent of the Task was in part 'designed to test your daring.' To that end, the judge who is doing the briefing of the candidates, Mr. Crouch, states that they will not know what they will be facing until the date of the Task.

Shortly before the Task, Hagrid asks Harry to come visit him, with his Invisibility Cloak. With an invisible Harry in tow, Hagrid collects Madame Maxime, the headmistress of Beauxbatons, and they walk around the edge of the Forbidden Forest to a spot where they can see a large corral. In the corral are four dragons. Harry watches as Hagrid talks with Charlie Weasley about what the dragons are for; apparently the Champions are expected to get past them or something. Charlie questions the wisdom of bringing Madame Maxime to see them; Hagrid brushes this off, saying that they are lovely, dragons.

Harry, having heard all he can stand, retreats; still invisible, he bumps into Professor Karkaroff, the headmaster of Durmstrang, who is also prowling around for a look at the dragons.

Harry returns to the Gryffindor common room, for a scheduled meeting with Sirius; Sirius has more important news to impart, and doesn't get around to telling Harry what to do about the dragons until the very end of the conversation. Before he can complete his sentence, however, they are interrupted by the arrival of Ron, and Sirius vanishes. As Harry and Ron are currently at odds, it is Hermione who tries to help Harry find counter-dragon spells; but she will not allow him to skip classes while looking.

Harry, meanwhile, is concerned; he figures that all the champions now know about the dragons except Cedric, and this does not seem fair to him. He engineers an opportunity to get Cedric on his own, and tells him about the dragons. However, he is overheard by Professor Moody, who sends Cedric off and steers Harry into his office. Harry expects to be told off or disqualified for cheating, but Moody tells him that cheating is almost a traditional part of the Triwizard Tournament; then asks if Harry knows how he's going to get past the dragons. When Harry admits that he does not, Moody provides him with a pair of clues that tells Harry how to pass the dragon. Harry quickly enlists Hermione to teach him how to perform a Summoning spell.

The Task takes place on November 24 and is held in a specially prepared clearing in the Forbidden Forest. Before it begins, the champions enter a tent to prepare and be briefed. This task is extremely difficult and dangerous: the champions are to retrieve a golden egg from a dragon. Each has their own dragon, chosen by pulling out a miniature dragon model from a purple bag held by Ludo Bagman. Each miniature dragon is marked with a number, indicating the order in which the champions are to be summoned to the task.

Before the Task actually starts, Ludo takes Harry aside and asks if he had a plan. Ludo seems to be offering assistance to Harry; Harry doesn't quite know what to make of this, Ludo is, after all, one of the five judges. The task unfolds as follows:

- Dragon # 1, Swedish Short-Snout (blue-gray)—Cedric Diggory (he transfigured a boulder into a Labrador, which diverted the attention of the dragon long enough to let him steal the egg)
- Dragon # 2, Common Welsh Green—Fleur Delacour (attempted to charm her dragon into a trance. This worked, but the dragon snored, and the resulting flame set her robes alight)
- Dragon # 3, Chinese Fireball (small)—Viktor Krum (used Conjunctivitus Curse but the dragon thrashed about in a rage and damaged other eggs)
- Dragon # 4, Hungarian Horntail (the most dangerous)—Harry Potter (used Summoning Charm to call his Firebolt and ride on it, tempting the dragon to rise away from the golden egg. When the dragon had reared, leaving the eggs unguarded, he quickly scooped up the egg and finished the task with the highest points) Points were based on speed, skill, and avoiding damage to other dragon eggs—Viktor lost points for this. At the end of this task, the points awarded were as follows:

- Harry Potter, 40 points;
- Viktor Krum, 40 points;
- Cedric Diggory, 38 points;
- Fleur Delacour, unknown.

Notable Consequences The objective of the Task was to retrieve a golden egg from the dragons. After the Task has ended, Ludo Bagman informs the champions that the eggs will open and each contains a clue that will be necessary for the Second Task. The Champions will be required to solve the riddle of the Egg before the Second Task, which will be taking place on 24 February.

As is usual in the Triwizard Tournament, the Champions did risk injury or death in the course of this challenge. Apparently at least three of the four Champions received some injury: Cedric was burned on one side when the dragon decided it wanted him rather than the Transfigured dog, Fleur was burned when the dragon she had Charmed to sleep belched a little fire as it snored, and Harry was slashed by one of the spikes on his dragon's tail as it tried to attack him.

Harry's coming out of this task tied for first place with Krum somewhat changed the dynamic within the Champions as well. Before, they had tended to dismiss him—as Fleur had said initially, "'E cannot compete. 'E is too young!" After his showing in the first Task, they see him as a true contender and worthy of notice.

Before this Task, Harry and Ron had been estranged; Ron was convinced, despite Harry saying otherwise, that Harry had put his own name into the Goblet, and was upset that he hadn't told Ron how he had done it. Believing that Harry had put his own name in, Ron was also convinced that Harry was lying to him. In this Task, Harry is in so much evident and immediate danger that Ron suddenly changes his mind, accepting that someone who wanted Harry dead had actually put Harry's name in for the Tournament; by the time Harry's scores are posted, they are fast friends again.

Much of the school shared Ron's opinion, in fact, believing that Harry had managed to make himself the fourth Triwizard champion because he wanted the associated fame or Galleons. Members of Slytherin house had, in fact, made a bit of an industry of taunting Harry about this. After this first Task, it was apparent that the life of a Champion would not be an easy one, and the animosity towards Harry from Ravenclaw and Hufflepuff houses abated somewhat. Harry suspects that Cedric had instructed the other members of Hufflepuff house to lay off him because Harry had taken the time to tell Cedric about the dragons, but this is never confirmed. It is true, however, that Cedric discovers the clue in the Golden Egg that leads to the solution to the Second Task before Harry does. Having deciphered the clue, Cedric makes a point of passing the clue on to Harry just after the Yule Ball. Cedric does this because it is only fair—Harry told him about the dragons, it is only fair that he should return the favour.

Fred Weasley's Death

Location: Hogwarts
Time Period: *Harry Potter and the Deathly Hallows*, May
Important Characters: Death Eaters

OVERVIEW

At the great Battle of Hogwarts, Fred Weasley is killed in battle as a large section of castle wall falls upon him.

Event Details Voldemort has given the occupants and defenders of Hogwarts School until midnight to surrender Harry to him. Neville Longbottom, meanwhile, has summoned the members of Dumbledore's Army to Hogwarts to help Harry in his mission. Members of the Order of the Phoenix also arrive. At one point, Fred, George, Ron, Ginny, Bill, Charlie, Mr. Weasley, and Mrs. Weasley are all in the Room of Requirement, as Mrs. Weasley is forbidding Ginny from taking any part in the battle. Percy suddenly enters the room, and finding his entire family present, announces that he has been a fool, and asks to be taken back into the family. Mrs. Weasley immediately accepts him back with open arms, and the other Weasleys do likewise.

While Harry is retrieving and destroying the Horcrux, the battle is fully joined, and Harry, Ron, and Hermione emerge into a hallway where jinxes are flying as defenders battle Death Eaters who are already within the school. Percy, among the defenders, jinxes Pius Thicknesse, and says Thicknesse can consider that his resignation. Fred, battling alongside him, says he thinks that's the first time he's ever heard Percy crack a joke. At that moment, a curse strikes the wall from outside, and the wall collapses, filling the hall with dust and killing Fred. Percy is distraught, throwing himself over Fred's body; Ron helps him take Fred's body to an alcove out of the way. Percy then spots a Death Eater and takes off in pursuit.

Notable Consequences Fred's death solidifies Percy's resolve to fight the Death Eaters. Percy has worked for the Ministry, and against his parents' belief systems, for so long that he almost certainly finds it hard to suddenly change sides. With Fred's death, caused directly by Death Eaters associated with the ministry, the battle becomes more personal for Percy. His departure from the scene at this point is caused by his sighting Rookwood, an escaped Death Eater. In the same manner, Fred's death hastens Percy's full return to the Weasley family, as they together mourn Fred's passing.

ANALYSIS

Over the course of the series, the Weasley family have suffered some rather amazing near misses. In *Harry Potter and the Chamber of Secrets*, Harry saves Ginny from the Chamber of Secrets where the "memory of Tom Riddle" is draining her life force to return to life himself. In *Harry Potter and the Order of the Phoenix*, Harry sees Arthur Weasley being attacked by a snake and reports it, in time to save Arthur's life. In *Harry Potter and the Half-Blood Prince*, Harry saves Ron, who has been poisoned, with a handy Bezoar. And earlier in *Harry Potter and the Deathly Hallows*, George had lost an ear to a Sectumsempra curse cast by Snape. Combine this with the forms taken by the Boggart takes when Molly Weasley is attempting to nullify it in *Harry Potter and the Order of the Phoenix*, and one might conclude that the death of a member of the Weasley family had not been foreshadowed, but rather belaboured. It is part of the skill involved in the series, however, that we do not see that foreshadowing until Fred actually dies; the one exception is the loss of George's ear in the Escape from Privet Drive, which at least some readers have seen as foreshadowing of another, larger loss for George.

GREATER PICTURE

The behavior of the Twins in *Harry Potter and the Goblet of Fire* has prompted interesting speculation in some readers as well. In placing their bet with Ludo Bagman, the Twins seem supremely confident in their bet that Ireland will win but the Bulgarian Seeker, Viktor Krum, will catch the Snitch, despite Bagman's apparent belief that such an outcome would be unlikely. As it turns out, the Twins have called it precisely. At least one commenter has suggested that this may mean that the two of them may have managed to solve, in part, the mystery of Time, and have been able to retrieve information about the outcome of the match from the future. The Time-Turner clearly shows that some aspects of time are better understood in the Wizarding world than by Muggles. Additionally, over the course of this and the succeeding book, we learn that Fred and George are magical innovators of rare ingenuity and skill, even in Hermione's opinion. Given these two facts, it is at least somewhat possible that there is some technique that the Twins have pioneered to look into the future, though perhaps dimly. The commenter has suggested that this technique may require both twins to perform the charm, and so Fred's death prevents the technique from ever being used again. While it is interesting to so speculate, we must point out that there is absolutely no evidence in the books that would suggest any such time-travel ability. Much more likely is that their bet is a calculated risk, based on their silent evaluation of the two teams, independently spoken by one of the others there present, that Krum is one excellent player, but Ireland have seven.

Ginny Weasley relationships

Location: Hogwarts
Time Period: Throughout the series
Important Characters: Ginny Weasley, Harry Potter, Michael Corner, Dean Thomas

OVERVIEW

Ginny Weasley's first schoolgirl crush is Harry Potter, which ends with her rescue by him from the Chamber of Secrets. From there, she remains unattached until she hooks up with Michael Corner, a Ravenclaw student. That relationship ends in *Harry Potter and the Order of the Phoenix*, when Michael shifts his attention to Cho Chang, and Ginny begins dating Dean Thomas. She breaks up with Dean in *Harry Potter and the Half-Blood Prince*, finally winning Harry's affection, the only boy she has ever cared about. Unfortunately for Ginny, Harry ends their relationship to protect her from Voldemort at the end of *Harry Potter and the Half-Blood Prince*. They continue to care about each other, despite being separated, and Harry finds solace in studying the Marauder's Map to try and determine what she is doing at Hogwarts. They both take part in the final battle. In the Epilogue, we learn that Harry has married Ginny and they have three children.

Event Details

Philosophers' Stone Ginny Weasley first sees Harry in King's Cross train station as Harry and the Weasley boys (Ron, Percy, and the twins) are preparing to leave for Hogwarts. Excited about being close to the famous Harry Potter, she demands to go over and see him, but her mother refuses to allow it. She is excited again when he returns from Hogwarts, ecstatically jumping up and down at the sight of him.

Chamber of Secrets Ginny's crush on Harry seems to have grown, perhaps unhealthily, into hero worship, as she is uncharacteristically nervous and silent during Harry's stay at the The Burrow. When Draco Malfoy insults Harry in Flourish and Blotts, Ginny leaps to his defence. At Hogwarts, she seems particularly emotionally fragile when Harry is nearby, although that may partially be from her manipulation by Tom Riddle's diary. On Valentine's Day, Professor Lockhart, in an ill-starred attempt to "cheer up" the school, hires a number of dwarfs to dress as "Cupids" and deliver love poems to students. One of these costumed dwarfs has a poem for Harry; it is never made clear who sent it, but Ginny is suspected.

When she tries unburdening herself to Harry about what has been happening with the diary, Percy barges in, interrupting her. Finally, as Ginny lies near death in the Chamber of Secrets, Harry destroys Riddle's diary, restoring her life force, and, with assistance from Fawkes, rescues her.

Prisoner of Azkaban The rescue from the Chamber of Secrets significantly changes the dynamic between Harry and Ginny, but rather than strengthening the bond, it weakens it. On meeting Harry again in the Leaky Cauldron, Ginny blushes and avoids looking at him; however, over the school year, she gradually becomes her normal self. Seeing Harry faint in the Dementor's presence on the Hogwarts Express may have reminded her that even heroes can be vulnerable and occasionally have "clay feet." However, by the book's end, she is no longer as adversely affected by Harry and becomes less shy around him. It appears she remains unattached through this book.

Goblet of Fire Little is heard about Ginny and her relationships, although we find out later that she does not remain unattached. Harry sees her at the Yule Ball, which she is attending with Neville, but from what she says, we get the impression that they are not a couple.

Order of the Phoenix Ginny has finally become her normal self in Harry's presence, now addressing him as an equal. At the organizational meeting of what later becomes Dumbledore's Army, Hermione reveals that probably the only reason Michael Corner and his friends had shown up is because he was dating Ginny. Ron takes an instant dislike to Michael, says that he had thought Ginny was waiting for Harry, and asks how long that had been going on. Hermione says that while Ginny *had* earlier been waiting for Harry, she had given up on him. She had then met Michael at the Yule Ball, and had started going out with him. Harry, bemused by Cho Chang smiling at him, is not upset that Ginny has stopped waiting for him, but he does ask Hermione if that's why she is now talking to him; she had always been so repressed in his presence before. Hermione says that yes, it is. Hermione also says that Ron's anger at Michael is the reason that Ginny hadn't told him about it, she had known Ron would be overprotective, and didn't want to get into a fight.

Late in the year, when Gryffindor beats Ravenclaw in Quidditch, Corner goes to comfort Cho Chang, that team's Seeker, rather than congratulating Ginny, who had replaced Harry as the Gryffindor Seeker. On the Hogwarts Express back to London, Ginny tells Ron and Harry that because of that, she had broken it off with with Michael, who was now seeing Cho, and had started seeing Dean Thomas. This, of course, leaves Ron upset at Dean.

Half-Blood Prince Ginny remains involved with Dean Thomas. Ron catches them kissing and is quite incensed at Dean's taking this liberty with his sister. Ginny accuses him of merely being jealous because he does not have anyone to snog (kiss) with himself.

Harry gradually develops feelings for Ginny and is jealous of Dean, but he keeps his emotions hidden, largely out of fear that his showing feelings for Ginny would damage his friendship with Ron. However, Harry takes some Felix Felicis potion prior to his meeting with Professor Slughorn. Hidden under his Invisibility Cloak, he accidentally knocks into Ginny in such a way that she thinks Dean deliberately shoved her; luckily (as is always the case with Felix Felicis), this prompts Ginny to break up with Dean.

During the Quidditch victory party, Harry, caught up in the excitement, seizes the opportunity to kiss Ginny in front of the entire Gryffindor Common room. They soon become a couple, laughing at how everyone is now talking about them. Ginny explains how Hermione helped her overcome her shyness around Harry and to just be herself. The couple's happiness is short-lived, however. After Dumbledore's funeral, Harry ends their relationship, telling Ginny that if Voldemort learns about their romance, he will use her to get to him, just as he did with his godfather, Sirius Black. Ginny is devastated, but she accepts Harry's reasoning.

Deathly Hallows While preparing for Bill and Fleur's wedding, Harry happens to let slip to Ginny that he has been given a mission that will end up with him killing Voldemort. Ginny is apparently taken aback by this.

Although Harry has ended their relationship, it is unlikely he will ever overcome his feelings for Ginny. Because of this, Harry does not resist when Ginny gives him his "birthday present," a kiss unlike any Harry has received before. This upsets Ron, who knows how upset Ginny was when Harry had ended their relationship a month before; Harry, unable to protest that it was Ginny's idea, simply says that it will not happen again. Because of this, their ongoing shared glances must be furtive, and on Harry's part at least, very quickly terminated.

In the epilogue, we learn that Harry and Ginny have married and have three children, James Sirius, Albus Severus, and Lily Luna.

Notable Consequences Ginny's announcement that she is going to the Yule Ball with Neville, when Ron suggests that she could go with Harry, causes a bit of a crisis for Harry; Harry must find someone to go to the Yule Ball with, as he is required to lead off the dancing, and his first choice, Cho Chang, has just turned him down. Ron, having been turned down both by his first choice (Fleur Delacour) and his second (Hermione), is equally in trouble. In desperation, Harry asks Parvati Patil, who accepts, and who suggests her sister Padma as a date for Ron.

At the end of *Harry Potter and the Half-Blood Prince*, Harry realizes that anyone he becomes close to is likely to become Voldemort's target. To protect Ginny, he reluctantly ends their relationship. While Ginny understands and accepts his reasoning, she seems to feel that there may be better ways to approach this problem. Unlike Ron and Hermione, however, she is still not of age and so will have to stay in school; she cannot travel with Harry to help in his mission, and Harry would not want her to in any event—he would be too concerned about her safety. In the epilogue of *Harry Potter and the Deathly Hallows*, we see that with Ginny, Harry has finally found what he has wanted all his life: a family.

ANALYSIS

We see that Ginny has set her heart on Harry very early in the series; as early as the second book, Ginny is apparently trying hard to get Harry interested in her. Due to her and Harry's immaturity at that time, however, her initial attempt is doomed. Harry does not welcome her attempts at romance any more than he would welcome romantic entanglement from any quarter. At twelve years old, Harry shares the young male disinterest in relationships, and at eleven years old, Ginny does not yet know how to ease into a relationship in a non-irritating way. By the time Harry is ready to consider a relationship, Ginny has at least nominally moved on. Ginny's attachment to both Michael Corner and Dean Thomas, however, seems rather less than it might be. Her attachment to Michael is slight enough that his being sulky after Ginny had won the Quidditch match from Ravenclaw was enough to end their relationship. The sulking does imply a certain lack of commitment on his part; one would have expected him to be happy in his girlfriend's victory, rather than sullen in his house's defeat. Perhaps it was because of that lack of attachment that Ginny dumped him. Dean was dumped because of his habit of helping her over and through obstacles that she didn't need help with, triggered by one final, accidental shove by Harry from under the Invisibility Cloak. Granted that the irritation is repeated, still it does seem as though it is a relatively small one, and one that could be dealt with if there was any real attachment there. Given that, in retrospect the reader does wonder if Ginny had actually given up on Harry, or was simply marking time with the available others while watching to see if Harry becomes available.

As mentioned repeatedly, Harry chooses to break off his relationship with Ginny, out of fear that Voldemort would attack Harry by attacking Ginny. A more mature viewer would say that a better way of securing Ginny's safety is to keep her by Harry's side. It was while they were separated that Voldemort used Sirius to lure Harry into a trap, for instance. If Harry and Ginny are physically close to each other, it is less likely that Voldemort would be able to deceive Harry as to what was happening with Ginny. However, we can already see that this is impossible; Harry has decided that he will have to hunt for, and face, Voldemort, while Ginny, being under age, will be forced by her mother to stay in school. In that situation, cutting off contact seems the safest course, as Harry can be certain that any communication he receives from Ginny will be false.

QUESTIONS

1. Why does Harry end his relationship with Ginny?
2. What does Ginny do that finally gets Harry to notice her?

GREATER PICTURE

Harry shows his concern for Ginny's well-being by ending their relationship. He knows Voldemort often fells his victims by targeting their friends and loved ones, just as he did with Harry's godfather, Sirius Black. Ginny sees Harry's decision to end their relationship to protect her as being noble, but she also believes it is the incorrect way to handle the situation. It seems unlikely their relationship has truly ended, despite Harry's saying it has. For more information, see also the entry for Harry Potter.

Harry Voldemort Shared Thoughts

Location: Various
Time Period: Throughout the series
Important Characters: Harry, Voldemort

OVERVIEW

Throughout the series, Harry experiences dreams which, as Professor Dumbledore says, are no ordinary dreams. In most cases, these turn out to be inadvertent leakage from Voldemort's mind to Harry's. In some cases, they serve to mislead Harry; in other cases, they give Harry vital information about Voldemort's plans. Harry's visions of what is happening in Voldemort's mind are always accompanied by pain in the lightning-bolt shaped scar on his forehead. The reverse is not always true; pain in Harry's scar can be triggered by Voldemort's proximity as well as the power of his thoughts and emotions. At least in the beginning, Harry is only able to sense strong emotions from Voldemort; but eventually, he becomes able to see what Voldemort is seeing and thinking.

Event Details

Philosopher's Stone Harry's scar pains him a number of times in this book, because by the time Harry arrives at Hogwarts, Voldemort is riding the back of Professor Quirrell's head, under his turban. The only time, possibly, that Harry is able to perceive Voldemort's thoughts, is in an odd dream that Harry has on the first night he is at school. During the night, Harry has a dream, involving Quirrell's turban and Malfoy turning into Snape, and Snape telling him that he must transfer to Slytherin house.

During exams, Harry has trouble sleeping, suffering from "his old nightmare," with the addition of a hooded figure dripping blood. It is never made entirely clear what the nightmare in question is, though this may refer to the dream of Quirrell's turban from the start of the school year.

Chamber of Secrets With the death of Quirrell, and Voldemort's return to Albania, Harry's scar does not trouble him, and Voldemort does not have enough emotional strength for Harry to sense him. While Harry does end up battling Tom Riddle, his scar does not pain him at the time.

Prisoner of Azkaban Harry again does not sense Voldemort, as Voldemort is a disembodied spirit wandering the forests of Albania.

Goblet of Fire The latter half of the first chapter of this story, where the aged Muggle, Frank Bryce, overhears a conversation between one "Wormtail" and his "master," interrupted by a snake who also joins the conversation, ends with Bryce's death, at which point Harry jolts awake from the pain in his scar. From the fading details of the dream, Harry apparently perceives it from an odd viewpoint; possibly partly Voldemort's, partly the snake's. We never learn exactly how much of this scene Harry witnessed; it is certainly true that the repeated mentions of Bertha Jorkins over the next few days do not spark any recognition in him. It is possible that Harry's "dream" only started at the discovery of Frank Bryce, as before that time Voldemort's emotional tension may not have been high enough to cause the vision to spill over.

It is during the discussion of this dream with Professor Dumbledore that we hear Dumbledore's theory that the scar pains Harry both when Voldemort is nearby, and when Voldemort is feeling strong emotions. While Harry's scar does pain him a few additional times during the course of this book, Harry is unable to get more than a sense of the emotion Voldemort is feeling, until late in May. Then, Harry senses an eagle owl delivering a message to Voldemort, and sees Voldemort telling Peter Pettigrew that his mistake has been corrected, the man is dead. Despite this, however, Voldemort goes on to punish Pettigrew.

At the battle in the graveyard, Harry's scar pains him continuously; however, this is because Voldemort is near him, and Harry does not perceive any thoughts.

Order of the Phoenix After he is discovered lying outside the living room window listening to the news, Harry thinks to himself that he has nothing to look forward to except nightmares: either the events in the cemetery the previous summer and Cedric's death, or endless dreams of long dark hallways and locked doors, which Harry guesses are an expression of his frustration at his lack of knowledge, though for some reason they leave his scar prickling.

During the Dementor attack in Little Whinging, Harry hears high-pitched laughter. It is uncertain whether this is a current connection, or a Dementor-inspired memory; Harry has heard high-pitched laughter, and his mother screaming, in earlier Dementor attacks.

The dreams of corridors, accompanied by prickling in his scar, continue while Harry is at Grimmauld Place. Harry has a sharp pain in his scar when he is just sitting down to lunch at Grimmauld Place after his hearing at the Ministry of Magic. Though it is not mentioned at the time, the timing is right for it to be the moment that Voldemort is informed by Lucius Malfoy of the Ministry's decision to clear Harry of all charges.

Harry's scar pains him again as he is going to bed after the party celebrating Ron and Hermione being appointed Prefects. Though it is not mentioned at the time, it is at about this time that Voldemort would have learned of the failure of his plan to use Sturgis Podmore to recover what he wanted from the Ministry. Harry that night again dreams of long corridors and locked doors, among his other nightmares.

Harry is assigned four successive days of detention, writing lines, with Professor Umbridge. At the end of that time, Umbridge takes Harry's hand to see if Harry "has got the message yet." When she touches Harry's hand, his scar hurts, accompanied by a strange feeling in his midriff. Discussing this later with Hermione, he wonders if there is some connection between Umbridge and Voldemort, and Hermione says that as Voldemort is now embodied again, he wouldn't need to control Umbridge as he had Quirrell. Harry wonders if Umbridge is under the Imperius curse. Hermione suggests Harry should tell Dumbledore; Harry angrily rejects this suggestion. Harry suggests writing to Sirius, but Hermione rejects that, saying that communications from the school may be intercepted. The next morning, Saturday morning, Harry writes to Sirius anyway, concealing his message, and sends it off with Hedwig. Sirius' head appears in the Gryffindor common room on Sunday night, and he explains to Harry that his scar hurting is likely unrelated; Umbridge is a bad enough piece of work, but Dumbledore does not feel that Umbridge is either a Death Eater, or controlled by Voldemort.

Tuesday of the following week, when Harry returns from detention, Ron and Hermione propose the idea of Harry teaching Defence Against the Dark Arts. Harry seems quite angry at the suggestion, and gets quite worked up about it, and afterwards is so tired he considers simply going to sleep in an armchair. But he eventually goes up to bed, where again he dreams of long corridors and locked doors, and wakes with his scar tingling.

In the dressing room after the first Quidditch practice with the re-formed team, Harry's scar suddenly hurts. Discussing it with Ron afterwards, he reassures Ron that this does not mean that Voldemort is near, but rather that he is having strong feelings about something. This time, Harry says, it is because Voldemort is angry: he wants something done, and it's not happening fast enough. The previous time, when Harry was in Umbridge's study, it was because he was happy; the strange feeling in his midriff was a happy feeling, and it seemed strange because he was so miserable himself at the time. The time before that, after Ron's and Hermione's party at Grimmauld Place, Voldemort had been furious. Ron says that Harry should tell Professor Dumbledore about this awareness of Voldemort's moods, but Harry refuses, saying that Dumbledore already knows. That night, Harry does fall asleep in an armchair before the Common Room fire, and dreams again about long corridors and locked doors until he is awakened by Dobby bringing Hedwig to him.

It is several months later before we hear of another contact. After the final meeting of what has become Dumbledore's Army before Christmas vacation, Harry's dream changes from a nightmare about Cho Chang to the feeling of traveling, in a long, sinuous, and muscular body, down the long hallways he had previously dreamed about. As he approaches the door that had always been locked, he sees a man, partly hidden by an invisibility cloak. Enraged, he strikes at the man. Waking up in his own bed, Harry is physically ill from the pain in his scar. He now recognizes that the man that he had bitten was Mr. Weasley. Brought before Professor Dumbledore, Harry tells him what he had seen, and in answer to Dumbledore's question, reveals that he did not just witness the attack, he was the snake. Dumbledore sends the occupants of two of the portraits in his study, Everard and Dilys, to investigate. Meanwhile, still without ever having looked at Harry, Dumbledore starts up one of his tiny, intricate machines, which emits a small plume of greenish smoke. The smoke forms the shape of a serpent in the air. Dumbledore says *"Naturally, naturally. But in essence divided?"* The smoke stream immediately splits, forming two snakes. Dumbledore shuts the machine down, and as he puts it away, Everard returns, confirming that they had found someone "down there."

Dumbledore now prepares a Portkey to take Harry and the Weasley children back to Grimmauld Place. As the Portkey activates, Dumbledore looks into Harry's eyes, and Harry's scar sears with pain again as he feels the urge rising in him to lunge at Dumbledore and sink his fangs into him.

At Grimmauld Place, he tells Sirius what had happened, and Sirius tells him not to worry about it. Harry does worry, though; afraid that he would turn into a snake and attack his friends, Harry is afraid to sleep. This fear is heightened after their first visit to St. Mungo's Hospital, where Harry and the Weasley children overhear Mr. and Mrs. Weasley discussing what happened, with Mad-Eye Moody and Tonks. Mrs. Weasley says that she thinks Dumbledore may have just been waiting for Harry to see something like this, and Moody suggests that Harry may be possessed by Voldemort.

Harry, afraid that Voldemort may be able to spy on Headquarters through his eyes, prepares to leave Grimmauld Place, but is stopped by Phineas Nigellus, who, from his portrait, passes a message from Dumbledore telling Harry to stay there. Harry figures that if he is under orders to stay there, it must be at least all right for him to sleep, so he does, and again dreams of the long corridor and the door that won't open, and is awakened by the prickling in his scar and Ron announcing dinner. Harry, still not entirely convinced that he isn't possessed, stays away from the others until Hermione drags him down to talk with the others. Ginny reminds him that she actually has been possessed by Voldemort and can tell Harry how it feels. Harry apologizes for having forgotten that, and then is reassured when Ginny's recollections do not match what has been happening to him.

Shortly before school starts after the Christmas break, Professor Snape arrives and says that Professor Dumbledore wishes Harry to learn Occlumency, the magical defence of the mind against external penetration. Harry is uncertain why he needs this, as he has determined that he is not being possessed by Voldemort, but Snape refuses to explain further.

Hermione later says that probably Dumbledore wants Harry to stop having these dreams about Voldemort. When Harry attends his first Occlumency class with Snape, Snape explains that Occlumency is the art of closing the mind against a Legilimens, one who can read and, sometimes, interpret what is happening inside another's mind. Though Snape says this is not mind-reading, Harry thinks it sounds a lot like it to him. Snape goes on to say that Dumbledore believes that, a a result of the curse that failed to kill Harry, there is some deeper link than usual between Harry and Voldemort, and as a result, Harry is able, when he is sufficiently relaxed, to see what is happening in Voldemort's mind. Dumbledore, he says, would like that to stop. Harry says that it has been really useful, as it saved Mr. Weasley from the snake, and Snape says that up until then, Voldemort had been unaware that the connection existed, but now that he is aware of it, he has guessed that it might go both ways, and he might use it to try to get Harry to do things.

At this point, the lesson begins, and Harry is totally unable to stop Snape from wandering through his memories. One of the memories Snape finds is the memory of Mr. Weasley taking Harry to the hearing at the Ministry of Magic. Harry suddenly realizes that the long hallway he keeps dreaming of is the hallway past the courtrooms in the Ministry of Magic. He remembers that corridor leads to the Department of Mysteries, and recognizes that Mr. Weasley was outside the door of the Department on the night the snake attacked. Harry asks Snape about the Department of Mysteries, and says that he has been dreaming about that corridor for months. As he says this, his scar starts hurting. Snape dismisses him, saying he should come back on Wednesday.

Discussing this with Ron and Hermione in the library later, Harry suggests that the thing Voldemort is looking for is probably in the Department of Mysteries. Hermione notes that almost certainly, Sturgis Podmore would have been guarding that door the night he was arrested, but cannot offer any explanation as to why Voldemort would have been trying to get through the door.

Harry, exhausted, now goes to bed, but as he steps through the door to the dorm, he is felled by the worst pain yet in his head, and hears the sound of maniacal laughter. Ron, who has followed at Hermione's request, asks what's going on, and Harry says that Voldemort is happy, really really happy; something he's been waiting for has happened. Ron says that Harry's resistance will be a bit low given what he's been through that evening. Harry, with his scar prickling, thinks that these lessons may be hurting rather than helping.

The next day, the *Daily Prophet* carries news of what had made Voldemort so happy: there has been a mass breakout from Azkaban, and ten prisoners, including

Bellatrix Lestrange, Antonin Dolohov, and Augustus Rookwood, have escaped.

Over the next while, despite his practicing, Harry's Occlumency skills seem to decrease. Additionally, his scar, which used to prickle only after one of the bursts of emotion that he had sensed before, now seems to be mildly painful all the time, and he has odd little bursts of elation or rage that have nothing to do with what Harry is doing. Additionally, his dreams of walking down the corridor to the Department of Mysteries seem to be occurring every night, and always end with him standing longingly in front of the plain black door. Hermione suggests that it is like an illness, that has to reach a peak before it can start to get better; Ron, on the other hand, seems to think that Snape may actually be making Harry's natural defences worse, to make things easier for Voldemort. Hermione says that Dumbledore trusts Snape, and so Ron should do likewise.

In late February, following the miserable Quidditch match against Ravenclaw, Harry dreams again of the corridor and the dark door at the end of the hallway. When he reaches the door, this time it is just slightly ajar. He reaches out to push it open, but is awakened by a rasping snore from Ron.

The following Monday, after publication of Harry's interview with Rita Skeeter in the *Quibbler*, Harry has to leave the party in his honour because his scar is prickling. When he goes to sleep, he is immediately in a dark, curtained room facing a kneeling man. The man, addressed as Rookwood, has apparently just told him that the plan he has been following will not work. Rookwood, who seems to be afraid despite being told that he is not to blame, says that he is sure of his facts, as he used to work in the Department. Reminded that Avery had said Bode would be able to remove it, Rookwood says that Bode would have known what would happen, and likely that's why he had fought so hard against Malfoy's Imperius curse. Rookwood is dismissed, with instructions to send Avery, and in his dream Harry turns to a mirror, to find Lord Voldemort looking back at him. Panicked, he awakens screaming. Ron, who has just come up and is getting ready for bed, tries to help him; Harry explains what had just happened, and that Avery was in trouble. His explanation is cut short by the arrival of Dean and Seamus, who are also getting ready for bed. Under cover of their preparations, Ron tells Harry that he has to tell Dumbledore; Harry says that they have him learning Occlumency so he won't be able to see things like this, and so clearly don't want to know about it.

Snape, however, sees this dream in Harry's memories in an Occlumency lesson, and asks Harry about it. Harry says it is a dream he has had, and that this is the only one. Snape suggests that Harry's not having made any progress is due to his liking the feeling of being special, of knowing what Voldemort is doing. Harry retorts that reporting what Voldemort is doing is Snape's job, and Snape, after a short pause, confirms it. Later in the same lesson, Harry again experiences the long hallway, but this time the door is open when he reaches it, and he finds himself in a circular room lit by blue-flamed candles and having multiple doors. Before he can choose which door to go through, Snape breaks him out of his waking dream. The lesson is then interrupted by the confusion surrounding Umbridge's sacking of Professor Trelawney.

In April, the betrayal of Dumbledore's Army results in the attempted arrest of Professor Dumbledore by Cornelius Fudge, Umbridge, and the Aurors Dawlish and Shacklebolt. With his attackers disabled, Dumbledore tells Harry urgently that he must continue his studies of Occlumency with Snape. As Dumbledore speaks directly to him, Harry once again feels a pain in his scar and is filled with the urge to strike at Dumbledore and sink his fangs into him.

The following day, Harry again dreams of the long corridor, and finds the door to the Department of Mysteries open at the end of it. In the circular room, he opens another door and finds a room filled with odd flecks of light and a mechanical clicking noise. He does not take time to investigate but goes straight through to another door, which leads into a vast, dimly lit room full of shelves, each shelf laden with dusty, spun-glass spheres. His scar hurts, but there is something in here that he very much wants . . . and an escaped firework explodes, waking him up. Harry dreads his next Occlumency class, as Snape is sure to find out how much further into the Department of Mysteries his dreams have taken him, but at the last moment Draco Malfoy interrupts, saying that Montague has turned up inside a toilet and Professor Umbridge needs Snape's help to extract him. Harry's curiosity about the thoughts Snape has been storing in the Pensieve gets the better of him. Snape, discovering him viewing these memories, orders Harry out of his office, effectively ending the Occlumency lessons. Harry has to tell Hermione that he is no longer having the funny dreams, even though he actually is, in order to cover for the fact that he is not taking Occlumency any more.

Harry feels he must discuss what he has learned about his father with Sirius, who had been his father's friend. When Hermione asks him later, Harry feels he cannot discuss what he had talked about, so instead says that he was telling Sirius about Snape's decision to end the Occlumency lessons. Hermione agrees with Sirius that Harry should return, and says that she knows Harry is still having those dreams. Harry is, in fact, though he denies it; this time, he had gotten all the way to row number 97, which is apparently where whatever it is that Voldemort wants is kept. Exhausted after watching Umbridge sack Hagrid, with the assistance of five Aurors, and having spent hours discussing it with the other members of Gryffindor house, Harry falls asleep shortly after starting his History of Magic O.W.L. exam. He again dreams of the long hallway, the open door, the circular room, and the room full of spun-glass spheres, but this time, when he reaches the end of row 97, he sees Voldemort there, and a huddled figure on the floor. Harry recognizes the huddled figure as Sirius, and sees that Voldemort is torturing him to get him the thing he has been seeking. Harry awakens with an agonizing pain in his scar, and is helped out of the exam room by Professor Tofty, the examiner. When Harry refuses to go to the Hospital Wing, Professor Tofty suggests that after a little rest he could try finishing up his exam, but Harry says that he has done about as much as he is able to. Over the next while, as Harry arranges for a distraction, breaks into Umbridge's office, is caught, helps Hermione lead Umbridge into the Forbidden Forest to be captured by the Centaurs, flies to London with the other students on Thestrals, and enters the Department of Mysteries at the Ministry of Magic, Harry's scar will continue to pain him. Harry will take this as a sign that Voldemort is still torturing Sirius. Harry dreads the moment when that pain reaches a peak, because he believes that will be when Voldemort, either having gotten what he wants, or having decided that Sirius will not give in, will kill Sirius.

As the Battle in the Ministry ends, Bellatrix escapes; Harry follows, to duel with her in the Atrium. Bellatrix demands that Harry release the Prophecy. Harry tells her that it is gone, and feels his scar flare with pain. He tells Bellatrix that Voldemort knows it is gone as well. The pain in his scar increases until Harry is almost insensible from it, as Voldemort himself arrives in the Atrium. Through the continuing pain, Harry watches Voldemort duel with Dumbledore. Eventually, Voldemort retreats. Harry, who has been kept out of the battle by an animated statue out of the Fountain of Magical Brethren, believes that the battle is over, but then his scar almost explodes with pain as Voldemort possesses him and challenges Dumbledore to kill Voldemort by killing Harry. Harry, who has just seen his godfather Sirius die, thinks of how he will be re-united in death with Sirius and his parents. Suddenly and inexplicably, Voldemort is forced to leave his mind.

In Dumbledore's office after the battle, Dumbledore explains to Harry that he had recognized the existence of the link in previous years, and had believed that it was getting stronger since Voldemort's return. He tells Harry that the reason he had Snape teaching Harry Occlumency, rather than doing it himself, was that he believed that if Voldemort suspected there was more to the relationship between Harry and Dumbledore than that of student to Headmaster, Voldemort would use that knowledge to attack either or both of them. This is also the reason that Dumbledore had been so careful to avoid looking at Harry, or speaking directly to him, for the entire year. Dumbledore also says that it is love, in particular the love of Sirius, that had driven Voldemort out of Harry's mind in the Atrium, and it is that strength that Harry has and Voldemort does not, that will in the end allow Harry to defeat Voldemort.

Half-Blood Prince Professor Dumbledore asks Harry at one point if his scar has been hurting at all. Harry says it has not, and expresses surprise. Dumbledore says he is not surprised at all; after the events at the Ministry, he believes Voldemort has determined that Harry's mind is a very uncomfortable place to be, and will choose to avoid it as much as he can.

Deathly Hallows Despite Voldemort being present in the sky above Privet Lane, Harry's scar does not start paining him until Voldemort, alerted to the identity of the real Harry, appears immediately behind him and Hagrid on the flying motorbike. It is only through the nearly blinding pain in his scar that he duels with Voldemort and the two other Death Eaters there. The pain in Harry's scar continues even after Harry has passed through the protective spells around Ted Tonks' house, and to a lesser extent as Harry reaches The Burrow and waits for the other teams to return. The pain in his scar then reaches a crescendo, and, as he leaves the house for some fresh air, he sees, through Voldemort's eyes, an old man being tortured. Voldemort accuses the man, who Harry recognizes as Ollivander, of lying to him about another wand working against Harry, and Ollivander saying that the linkage exists only between Voldemort's wand and Harry's. As the vision and the pain fade, Harry sees that Ron and Hermione are at his side, and tells them what he has seen. Hermione is horrified; she is worried that Voldemort might use this channel against Harry again.

On the night before Harry turns 17, he dreams of seeing a small village, which may hold the man he seeks, at the end of a mountain road. Ron tells him that he was saying "Gregorovitch" in his sleep, over and over, and Harry says he thinks Voldemort is looking for him. Neither of them can remember who Gregorovitch is, though Ron suggests he might be a Quidditch player.

It is two days later, in conversation with Viktor Krum that Harry recalls that Gregorovitch is a wand-maker. Viktor says that he is the best, though he knows the English wizards set great store by Ollivander. Harry, understanding that Voldemort fears his wand and is trying to find a different wand that will defeat Harry's, wonders whether Gregorovitch might be able to build the stronger wand that Voldemort so clearly wants. Shortly after the Trio evade the Death Eaters and return to Grimmauld Place, Harry's scar pains him again. Ron asks him what's wrong, and Harry says "he's very angry." Hermione, dismayed, says that she had thought that had stopped, and Harry says it has started again, mostly when Voldemort loses control. Hermione reminds Harry that Voldemort had used that channel to plant false memories in Harry before, and Harry says he remembers that very well without reminders. As the pain increases, Harry flees to the bathroom, and there, through Voldemort's eyes, he sees Draco Malfoy being compelled to torture one of the two Death Eaters for having allowed Harry to escape. Harry's scar is quiet until a month later, when it suddenly flares up at dinnertime, possibly coincidentally just after Harry says Voldemort's name. Harry, again, goes to the bathroom, where he sees through Voldemort's eyes as he enters a village, asks the German-speaking occupants of a house there for Gregorovitch, and then murders them when they say they don't know where he moved to. Ron and Hermione hear him cry out; when Harry tells them what he has seen, Hermione again tells him that Dumbledore had wanted him to stop seeing these things. Harry retorts that he doesn't like it, but he was never any good at Occlumency, and he's going to keep on doing it because, despite his having to see what Voldemort is doing when he's at his worst, it is useful to know what Voldemort is up to. That night, Harry wonders how long Gregorovitch can stay hidden with Voldemort seeking him so assiduously. As it turns out, it is the following night that Harry, standing guard in the tent after their escape from the Ministry, sees through Voldemort's eyes as Voldemort interrogates Gregorovitch, examines his memory to see a thief taking something, and murders him. Hermione again says that Harry should not be seeing Voldemort's thoughts, though at Ron's bidding she does not say Voldemort's name. When Harry tries to tell her what Voldemort was doing, she dismisses him. Talking it over quietly with Ron, Harry wonders what Voldemort is after; it can't be a new wand, not if he's killing wandmakers, and Harry didn't see what the thief had stolen, so it must have been something small. Harry finds that when he is wearing the locket Horcrux, his scar prickles more frequently. Sometimes, when it prickles most fiercely, he sees a face: always the same face, that of the young thief who had stolen the object from Gregorovitch. This disappoints Ron, who is hoping Harry's linkage with Voldemort will provide some news of his family.

When Harry and Hermione visit Bathilda Bagshot in Godric's Hollow, Harry notes the Horcrux he is wearing seems to move as he passes close to Bathilda. However, it is only when the concealed Nagini contacts Voldemort that Harry's scar prickles, and he hears Voldemort, exultant, saying "Hold him!" Not understanding what has happened, Harry turns to look where Bathilda has indicated, in hopes of finding the Sword of Gryffindor, but out of the corner of his eye sees Bathilda collapsing and Nagini emerging from her body. In the ensuing battle with Nagini, Harry is hindered by sensing Voldemort's thoughts as he flies to Godric's Hollow, and by the locket Horcrux reacting to the approach of Voldemort, the soul from which it was sheared. Harry watches through Voldemort's eyes as he and Hermione Apparate away.

Harry now relives, in Voldemort's memory, the events of sixteen years earlier, when Harry's parents had been murdered. He watches as Voldemort murders his unarmed father, his mother, and tries to murder little Harry. Still watching through Voldemort's eyes, he sees Voldemort finding the photo of the thief, which Harry had found in Bathilda's study and had dropped in the struggle, and he feels Voldemort's joy as he recognizes the thief in the picture. Harry returns to himself at Hermione's urging. Hermione tells him he has been insensible for hours, not unconscious, but thrashing around and saying things.

Harry's scar does not bother him again until after Ron rejoins the group, and the locket Horcrux is destroyed. When Harry's scar starts prickling again, Harry is somewhat dismayed that the visions he receives are no longer as detailed as they had been, being instead vague impressions of mountain shapes, and blames his broken wand for the loss of clarity.

However, shortly after Harry, Hermione, and Ron are captured by Snatchers, Harry's scar once more burns with pain, and Harry finds himself looking through Voldemort's eyes at a huge stone building with a tall tower. He must make the supreme effort to remain in his own mind as Voldemort flies to the top of the tower, insinuates himself within the cell at the top, and questions the man imprisoned there. The man says he knows what Voldemort has come for, but he never had it. At this point, as Harry is being dragged into Malfoy Manor, Harry finds that his fear of being identified by Lucius Malfoy makes it easier to block out Voldemort. His continuing fear allows him to continue to block Voldemort's mental images, except for one brief interval where he sees the old man in the tower cell mocking Voldemort, until Bellatrix, convinced that the sword she found the Snatchers carrying did not in fact come from her vault at Gringotts, touches her Dark Mark to summon Voldemort. The sudden surge of pain in his scar once again opens Harry's mind to what Voldemort is thinking and doing, and again Harry must do battle, this time with Bellatrix, Lucius, Narcissa, and Draco, while at the same time trying to stay in his own mind as Voldemort kills the old man, who Harry now recognizes as Grindelwald, then flies close enough to Apparate to Malfoy Manor.

After escaping from Malfoy Manor, Harry finds that his grief at Dobby's death insulates him to some extent from Voldemort's thoughts. As Harry cleans up after the burial, as he speaks with Griphook about the possibility of breaking into Gringotts, as he speaks with Ollivander about wandlore and the Elder Wand, and as he explains to Ron and Hermione what he is thinking of, his scar continues to prickle, and he has to fight the ongoing invitation to release the world he is in, to see what Voldemort is doing and thinking. Finally, beside Dobby's grave, he is once again in Voldemort's mind, and he watches as Voldemort walks the grounds of Hogwarts, as he opens Dumbledore's tomb, and as he removes the Elder Wand from Dumbledore's dead hands.

Harry's scar does not pain him again until after the escape from Gringotts. Then, as they sit on the shores of the lake watching the dragon recuperate from its long captivity, treating their injuries, Harry is again consumed by Voldemort's anger as he discovers that the Cup Horcrux has been stolen. Harry stays in Voldemort's mind as he summons Nagini to himself and determines to check all of the places that he has hidden Horcruxes, starting with the ring, then the locket and the one hidden at Hogwarts. The diary, Voldemort knows, has been destroyed, and he believes he did not feel its destruction because he was a disembodied spirit at the time, and the Cup has now been stolen, but surely the others have not been disturbed, he would have felt it. Harry, returning to himself as Voldemort starts his flight to the Gaunt shack, tells Ron and Hermione that they must head to Hogwarts, to try and find the final Horcrux before Voldemort gets there.

Just after Harry returns to Hogwarts, and is being brought up to speed in the Room of Requirement, his scar burns fiercely again, and he suddenly is watching through Voldemort's eyes as Voldemort finds an empty golden box in the ruins of the Gaunt shack. Returning to himself by force of will, Harry tells Ron and Hermione that they are running out of time. While he tries to explain to Neville and the assembled members of Dumbledore's Army in the Room of Requirement that they have a single mission at the school and then will depart, Harry's scar continues prickling and his head continues to ache. It is shortly after he is convinced to allow the group to help him search, that his scar once again burns, and he sees Voldemort launching himself into flight. He returns to himself again, telling Ron and Hermione that Voldemort is on the move.

In the Ravenclaw common room, Harry is discovered by Alecto Carrow. When she touches her Dark Mark, Harry's scar again burns with pain, and he is once again in Voldemort's mind as Voldemort stands on a rocky outcrop surrounded by sea. Harry "hears" Voldemort thinking "Good, they have the boy," before a loud bang brings him back to himself. He finds that the noise was Luna Stunning Alecto. Harry's scar continues to throb, and he chooses to sink into Voldemort's mind while the Ravenclaw students are milling about, looking at Alecto lying on the floor. Voldemort is passing through the first cave, on his way to look at the Locket Horcrux. Harry's scar continues to throb as Professor McGonagall lets Amycus Carrow into the Ravenclaw common room, as Carrow attempts to lay blame for Alecto's Stunning and the summons to Voldemort on the Ravenclaw students, and as McGonagall refuses to allow that. Shortly after Professor McGonagall is insulted, and Harry reveals himself to her, Harry sees, in the back of his mind, Voldemort sailing fast over the lake in the cavern, and then is again taken out of himself by Voldemort's rage as he finds there is no locket within the basin in the cave.

Harry's scar continues to prickle as they meet Snape, as McGonagall and Snape duel, and as Snape departs the school. Shortly after Snape's flying departure, Harry is again in Voldemort's mind as the tiny boat returns to the shore of the cavern, and Voldemort leaps ashore. Harry's scar sears with pain again shortly after the assembled defenders leave the Room of Requirement, and through Voldemort's eyes he sees the gates of Hogwarts, and within them, the school.

As the battle is joined and Harry hunts the Diadem, he is too busy to notice his scar. However, when Hermione demands that he find Voldemort and Nagini, the last Horcrux, he notices that his scar has been aching for hours, trying to get him to see what Voldemort is doing. He is quickly able to get into Voldemort's mind. There, he sees Voldemort observing the battle, and repeatedly dismissing a broken Lucius Malfoy's attempts to end the battle, seeing them as attempts to save his son's life. Troubled about the wand in his hand, Voldemort tells Malfoy to bring Snape to him, then, looking at Nagini, says that it is the only way. Harry, returning to his own mind, reports that Voldemort is in the Shrieking Shack.

As Harry, from concealment, watches Voldemort conversing with Snape in the Shrieking Shack, he feels the pain in his scar building, and knows from this that Voldemort is growing angry, though nothing in his manner reveals it. Voldemort is angry that the Elder Wand, which he has located with great effort, is working no better than the wand he got from Ollivander many years before. His rage is so extreme that it once again draws Harry out of his own mind and into Voldemort's, where he is an unwilling audience as Voldemort flips the magical cage surrounding Nagini towards Snape, and orders Nagini to kill.

In Snape's memories, Harry learns that Dumbledore had believed that the link between Harry and Voldemort was more than it seemed. Dumbledore had told Snape that when Voldemort had tried to kill Harry and had failed, a fragment of his soul had been torn off and had attached itself to Harry. It was this soul fragment that provided the communications between Harry and Voldemort, and that provided Harry's ability to talk to snakes. While that soul fragment remains attached to Harry, it will work as a Horcrux, anchoring Voldemort's soul to Harry's. Thus, the only way for Voldemort to be defeated is for Harry to die at Voldemort's hand.

Voldemort's attempt to kill Harry in the Forbidden Forest sends Harry to a place that has been referred to as the Waystation by fans, and so will be called that in this work. There, Harry meets the shade of Albus Dumbledore who explains that the soul fragment within Harry had been destroyed, and thus the link between Harry and Voldemort was broken. Dumbledore explains further, or leads Harry to the understanding that Voldemort had been unable to kill Harry because Voldemort, taking Harry's blood to re-animate himself, had also taken into himself a part of the enchantment tied to Lily Potter's blood that had protected him all those years. It is thus impossible for Harry to die while Voldemort remains alive.

In the Epilogue, Harry notes that for the past seventeen years, his scar has remained quiet.

Notable Consequences In *Harry Potter and the Order of the Phoenix*, this link has two main consequences. The first occurs around Christmas, when Harry, perceiving the attack on Arthur Weasley, is able to sound the alarm. This perception allows him to save Arthur's life. However, the burst of hatred towards Dumbledore that Harry feels as he is about to Apparate to Grimmauld Place leaves him worried that Voldemort may be spying on Harry's surroundings through Harry's own eyes and ears.

As far as we are able to tell, Voldemort is not ordinarily able to look through Harry's eyes. We assume, based on what we are told in the story, and on the specific times that Harry is able to see what Voldemort is seeing, that it is only when Harry is in the grip of extraordinarily strong emotion, as he is after having witnessed the attack on Arthur Weasley, that Voldemort is able to see what Harry sees. However, having once experienced Harry's view of the world, Voldemort becomes aware of the linkage. Having learned about the link, in that same book Voldemort uses it to lure Harry to the Department of Mysteries, where he was able to retrieve the Prophecy that Voldemort wanted. Harry accidentally destroyed the Prophecy, however, before it fell into Voldemort's hands. As part of that battle, and due to that same link, Harry was briefly possessed by Voldemort, who found Harry's mind an excruciatingly uncomfortable place to be, filled as it was with love (at that instant, for the departed Sirius Black). In *Harry Potter and the Deathly Hallows*, this link provides necessary information about what Voldemort is doing. Voldemort seems to be less and less capable of controlling this link as the book progresses, while Harry's control over it increases. In the absence of Dumbledore, the link is our only source of information about Voldemort's actions and plans. It is through this link that Harry learns of Voldemort's intention to visit his Horcruxes, and that provides the impetus for Harry's re-entrance into Hogwarts. And Harry, by the end of this book, is able to turn the link around and force himself to see through Voldemort's eyes; it is by means of this link that Harry is able to determine that Voldemort is hiding in the Shrieking Shack.

ANALYSIS

Harry's scar hurting has always been an indication of the activity of the link between Harry and Voldemort. As the series progresses, our understanding of the behaviour of the scar, and of the link, improves alongside Harry's. In *Harry Potter and the Philosopher's Stone*, Harry's scar, we believe, indicates that Voldemort is close to Harry. In that book, whenever Harry's scar pains him, it is because Voldemort, then riding the back of Quirrell's head, is close to him. It is particularly intense when Voldemort is studying him.

In *Harry Potter and the Chamber of Secrets*, while Voldemort is not present, an earlier fragment of his soul is there, in the form of Tom Riddle's diary. Harry's scar does not hurt, despite the proximity of the fragment of Voldemort's soul. This could be because the fragment of soul in the diary was sheared off before Harry got his scar, and therefore the resonance which causes Harry's scar to hurt is not present; the scar could possibly only sense the soul in the state it was when the scar was created, or later. However, we will later see that Harry's scar does not react directly to other Horcruxes, even those created after the scar. It is reasonably clear that Harry's scar will only react to Voldemort, not to his soul fragments, though being in close proximity to a Horcrux, we will see later, does seem to increase his sensitivity.

In *Harry Potter and the Goblet of Fire*, we start seeing that Harry's scar is not only reacting to proximity to Voldemort, but also to Voldemort's emotional peaks and valleys, and allowing Harry to occasionally experience what is happening in Voldemort's mind. In fact, we recognize what is happening before Harry does himself. On the two occasions that Harry experiences visions of what is happening in Voldemort's mind, he tries to dismiss it as a dream, though he is not entirely successful.

Perhaps because of this, Harry does not recognize the recurring dream he is having throughout *Harry Potter and the Order of the Phoenix* as originating with Voldemort. In this book, Harry can see entire sequences of events as they occur to Voldemort, but does not recognize that they could be entirely fictional. As a result, Voldemort is able to plant fictions into Harry's mind, and Harry, believing them to be truth, tries to act upon them, to his detriment. Voldemort at one point tries to take over Harry's mind in *Harry Potter and the Order of the Phoenix*, but finds it a very uncomfortable place to be. Harry, who has just seen his godfather die, is filled with love for Sirius and a longing for death to re-unite them. Voldemort has never felt love and so the feeling is entirely alien to him. Additionally, Voldemort fears death, and so Harry's desire for it must be not only alien but frightening to him. As a result of this, Voldemort keeps his mind closed to Harry for the entire sixth book.

Throughout the latter half of *Harry Potter and the Order of the Phoenix*, Dumbledore has Snape attempting to teach Harry Occlumency, in an attempt to block Voldemort from Harry's mind. There is some question as to whether this will have any effect at all. First, what Voldemort is doing is impressing images onto Harry's mind, which is rather the opposite of Legilimency; Voldemort is creating an image in his own mind, and exposing it to Harry selectively. What Harry should presumably be trained to do is to either become a better Legilimens, so that he can see the story behind the presented image, or else learn how to turn his own limited Legilimency off. Second, as Harry is not using Legilimency and is yet able to see into Voldemort's mind, there is some question as to whether Occlumency, which acts to counter Legilimency, would even work. It is possible that the link, being through the soul shard that Voldemort had left in Harry, is not actually subject to magical control.

As the channel between Harry's thoughts and Voldemort's is one of the least understood aspects of the story, at least by the protagonists, it is entirely understandable that some incorrect statements and assumptions are made about it. Most importantly, of course, is the entire issue of blocking the channel, should Harry feel the need, as discussed above. However, several minor errors have crept into the text. In particular, when Harry and Dumbledore are speaking of Harry's scar and when it hurts, Dumbledore says that he believes it hurts when Voldemort is nearby, or when he is feeling a strong emotion. Later, though, Harry says that Dumbledore had said his scar would hurt when Voldemort was nearby or *feeling hatred* (italics ours). Ron urges Harry at this point to tell Dumbledore that Harry is now feeling any intense emotion of Voldemort's; Harry resists. A minor plot point thus hinges on this mistake; one must wonder whether it is Harry or the author who has misremembered.

Dumbledore informs Harry in *Harry Potter and the Half-Blood Prince* that Voldemort has begun blocking Harry's access to Voldemort's mind by using Occlumency. However, in *Harry Potter and the Deathly Hallows*, Harry is regularly experiencing Voldemort's thoughts once again. No outright explanation for this development is ever provided. However, in the early chapters, Voldemort attacks Harry with a borrowed wand to avoid the reverse-spell effect generated by the twin cores of their wands. Yet, Harry's wand reacts independently and destroys Voldemort's wand. Voldemort is furious and frightened by Harry's inexplicable power, and becomes desperate to find a wand that can destroy Harry's. It was stated by Snape in *Harry Potter and the Order of the Phoenix* that Occlumency requires a calm mind. Voldemort, viewing Harry as a threat with power that Voldemort cannot counter, is perhaps no longer capable of Occlumency. Indeed, every time Voldemort's thoughts impinge upon Harry, Voldemort is in the grip of rage and fear over his wand and his Horcruxes.

Alternative explanations exist. One of the characters does speculate that Voldemort is weakening, presumably as the endless murders further shred his soul, and this is certainly a possibility. Another, unexplored possibility is that the link to the soul shard in Harry becomes stronger as the other extant soul shards (the Horcruxes) are destroyed. There is clearly an ongoing link between the soul shard in Harry and the remains of Voldemort's soul; it is entirely possible that there is a similar link to each of Voldemort's Horcruxes. As the locket, the cup, and the diadem are destroyed, Harry's perceptions of Voldemort's actions seem less dependent on Voldemort's state of mind and more controllable by Harry's will. It is certainly possible that as these linkages are destroyed, the remaining ones become stronger. This is uncertain, however, as Voldemort is unable to perceive any of his Horcruxes being destroyed; with the diary, the ring, and the locket having been destroyed, the links to the cup, the diadem, Harry, and Nagini should have been strengthened, one would expect, to the point that Voldemort would perceive the destruction of the cup or the diadem. Yet he does not seem to notice either. Perhaps, though, the soul fragment in Harry is gaining strength through its attachment to Harry's complete and healthy soul.

It is through the course of *Harry Potter and the Deathly Hallows*, then, that Voldemort's gradual loss of self-control allows Harry to once again see what Voldemort is thinking and doing when Voldemort is at his emotional extremes. Over the course of the book, Harry, who is the stronger wizard, we are told, in part because he does not fear death, learns to control how much of Voldemort's mind he allows in. By the time he is taken to Malfoy Manor, he is able, by sheer effort of will, to keep his consciousness in the face of Voldemort's fiercest anger, and he finds that his own grief, later, as he buries Dobby, allows him to hold Voldemort's thoughts to a background level, where he is aware of them to a certain extent but is not captive to them. Harry eventually reaches a point of conscious control where he can force his way into Voldemort's mind at will.

It is perhaps an interesting side light that the course of events requires that Harry's attention be drawn away from Voldemort's mind while Voldemort is inspecting Grindelwald's memory of the duel with Dumbledore. If Harry had experienced that memory, it might have changed his understanding of Dumbledore, and perhaps brought him closer to reconciliation with Dumbledore earlier in the story. While that might have been good for Harry, it would likely have weakened the story, as one of the particularly strong areas in the story is the successive unveilings of Dumbledore's motivations, first by Aberforth in the Hog's Head, and second by the shade of Albus Dumbledore in the Waystation.

Harry Potter relationships

Location: Hogwarts
Time Period: Throughout the series
Important Characters: Harry Potter, Ginny Weasley, Cho Chang

OVERVIEW

Harry's first experience with someone having a crush on him is Ginny Weasley, although he does not reciprocate her feelings. Her infatuation apparently ends after Harry rescues her from the Chamber of Secrets. Harry soon notices Cho Chang, the pretty Ravenclaw Quidditch Seeker. Harry is too shy to express his interest in her, although she seems to notice him. In *Harry Potter and the Goblet of Fire*, Harry finally works up the courage to invite her to the Yule Ball. Unfortunately, she has already been asked by Cedric Diggory, a student in Hufflepuff.

Harry competes with Cedric for Cho's attention, at least in his own mind, until Cedric's tragic death during the Third Task of the Triwizard Tournament. In *Harry Potter and the Order of the Phoenix*, Cho renews her interest in Harry, but still grieving, she is unable to move past Cedric's death, and she and Harry abruptly end their brief relationship. Harry is again unattached and remains so through much of *Harry Potter and the Half-Blood Prince* until he begins noticing Ginny Weasley, although she is dating someone else. Near the end of the year, they finally get together. Unfortunately for Ginny, Harry ends their relationship to try and protect her from Voldemort. In the final book, *Harry Potter and the Deathly Hallows*, it becomes apparent that they still have the kernel of a relationship going on, and although they are separated for the duration of the book, it is evident that there are still feelings. They re-unite near the end of the book, and in the epilogue it is revealed that they have married.

Event Details

Philosophers' Stone Ginny Weasley first sees Harry in King's Cross train station as Harry and the Weasley boys (Ron, Percy, and the twins) are preparing to leave for Hogwarts. Excited about being close to the famous Harry Potter, she demands to go over and see him. Harry is most relieved when Mrs. Weasley forbids it, saying that Ginny has already seen him and he isn't something to be goggled at like in a zoo.

Ginny is excited again when he returns from Hogwarts, excitedly jumping up and down at seeing him, though he does not seem to be paying much attention to her.

Chamber of Secrets Ginny's crush on Harry seems to have grown, perhaps somewhat unhealthily, into hero worship, as she is uncharacteristically nervous and quiet while he is staying at the The Burrow. When Draco Malfoy insults Harry in Flourish and Blotts, Ginny leaps to his defence. At Hogwarts, she seems particularly emotionally fragile when Harry is nearby; although that may partially be from her manipulation by Tom Riddle's diary. When she tries unburdening herself to Harry about what has been happening with the diary, Percy barges in, interrupting her. Finally, as Ginny lies near death in the Chamber of Secrets, Harry destroys Riddle's diary, restoring her life force, and, with assistance from Fawkes, rescues her.

Prisoner of Azkaban The rescue from the Chamber of Secrets significantly changes the dynamic between Harry and Ginny, but rather than strenghtening the bond, it weakens it. On meeting Harry again in the Leaky Cauldron, Ginny blushes and avoids looking at him; however, over the school year, she gradually loses her shyness and becomes her normal self. Having seen Harry faint in the Dementor's presence on the Hogwarts Express may have reminded her that even heroes occasionally have "clay feet."

At the House Quidditch match, Harry is introduced to Cho Chang, the Ravenclaw Seeker. "She smiled at Harry as the teams faced each other behind their captains, and he felt a slight jolt in the region of his stomach that he didn't think had anything to do with nerves." Whatever feelings he has for Cho may have been enhanced when she is able to outfly him, at least once, although she is mounted on a lesser broom.

Goblet of Fire Hoping to connect, or reconnect, with Cho Chang, Harry remains unattached. He invites her to the Yule Ball, but she is already going with Cedric Diggory, although she seems to genuinely regret declining his invitation. Meanwhile, it appears to many others, most notably Colin Creevey, that Harry spends too much time with Hermione for it to be strictly friendship. Rita Skeeter publishes a scurrilous story in Witch Weekly suggesting that Hermione is keeping not only Harry, but also Viktor Krum as lovers, although she hints Hermione is using illegal love potions. Harry and Hermione are both greatly amused, although Harry has to explain to Viktor Krum, and later to Mrs. Weasley, that Hermione is not, and has never been, his girlfriend.

Many readers have been as misled as Colin Creevey and Rita Skeeter. One group, referred to as "shippers" (apparently derived from "relationship") believes Harry and Hermione will ultimately be together. However, J.K. Rowling has stated that she has dropped "anvil-sized hints" from at least the fourth book on that Hermione and Ron would link up; see the entries for Ron Weasley and Hermione Granger for details on those hints.

Order of the Phoenix Harry and Cho begin a tentative romance. Harry is ecstatic, but before long realizes things are not as he imagined. Cho is still emotionally fragile following Cedric Diggory's death, although she initially seemed ready to move on. It is soon apparent she is not, and Harry is unable to understand or cope with her grief. Nearly any casual comment or unintentional action on his part results in Cho overreacting and breaking down into tears.

Cho also misunderstands Harry' platonic relationship with Hermione, and their fragile bond suffers further when Harry excuses himself during a Valentine's Day date in Hogsmeade to meet Hermione. Harry, already made uneasy by the atmosphere in Madam Puddifoot's Tearoom, is unable to convince Cho that the meeting is innocent, partly because he is unaware what it is; he only knows that Hermione insisted he be there. Unfortunately, he is unable to articulate this in a way that prevents Cho from becoming upset, though Hermione coaches him in this later. The meeting is actually to arrange for Rita Skeeter to interview Harry. Hermione has "persuaded" Skeeter to write a truthful story about Cedric's death that will be published in *The Quibbler*.

After the article appears, Cho approaches Harry and tells him he is brave to have given that interview, and it appears the rift may be patched up between them. But their relationship falls apart again when Cho's friend, Marietta Edgecombe, betrays Dumbledore's Army to Professor Umbridge. Cho says she feels badly about what Marietta did, but she justifies her actions, saying that Marietta's parents work for the Ministry. She is also angry at Hermione for jinxing her friend. For Harry, there is no excuse for betraying the group, and he points out that Ron's dad also works for the Ministry but he had not betrayed the DA. When Harry warns Cho against crying again, she angrily stomps off, and their relationship has ended.

At the Quidditch Final, which Gryffindor is playing against Ravenclaw, Harry sees Cho on the field, but is unsure what he feels for her, except that he doesn't want any more fights. The sight of her talking animatedly with Roger Davies, who Cho had mentioned previously as being one who had asked her out, does not cause any effect for Harry. On the Hogwarts Express at the end of the year, Cho walks past the compartment in which Harry, Ron, and Ginny are sitting. Ron asks what was happening with him and Cho, and Harry finds that, in fact, he no longer has any real feeling for her.

Half-Blood Prince While Harry apparently remains unattached, many girls are interested in him. In fact, rather to his surprise, Romilda Vane asks him to join her group on the Hogwarts Express as they head to school. When he mentions this to Hermione later, she points out that since the re-appearance of Lord Voldemort, the *Daily Prophet* has effectively made him once again the darling of the Wizarding World by naming him the Chosen One. It doesn't hurt, she adds, that Harry has grown about a foot over the summer.

Professor Slughorn is restarting his "Slug club," a periodic party that Slughorn, an inveterate glory-seeker, holds to gather together all of the more famous students. Harry, of course, would be the true jewel in the crown, but despite his having been invited to all the Slug Club parties so far, he has carefully avoided attending any of them. There is considerable angling in the student body to wangle an invitation to the Slug Club Christmas party; Hermione reveals that some girls are plotting ways to get Harry to take a love potion, and she warns Harry to watch what he eats and drinks. Shortly after this, Harry carefully turns down an offer from Romilda Vane to share a Gillywater, and accepts (because he doesn't see a way out of it), a box of Chocolate Cauldrons with Firewhisky centers, which he takes up to his dorm and carefully sets aside. He does eventually invite Luna Lovegood to the Christmas Slug Club party, because he has to invite someone.

Harry gradually develops feelings for Ginny and becomes jealous of her boyfriend, Dean. He keeps his emotions hidden, however, largely because he witnessed Ron's anger at Dean for taking liberties with

Ginny. Harry feels his friendship with Ron is too valuable to imperil by making a play for Ginny. However, Harry takes some Felix Felicis potion prior to a meeting with Professor Slughorn. Hidden under his Invisibility Cloak, he knocks into Ginny in such a way that she thinks Dean deliberately shoved her; luckily (as is always the case with Felix Felicis), this prompts Ginny to break up with Dean.

During the victory party after the Quidditch final, Harry, caught up in the excitement, seizes the opportunity to kiss Ginny in front of the entire Gryffindor Common room. They soon become a couple, laughing at how everyone is now talking about them. Fortunately for Harry, Ron gives his approval, although he warns Harry to avoid openly kissing his sister. Hermione is also pleased they have gotten together. Ginny explains how Hermione helped her overcome her shyness around Harry and to just be herself. The couple's happiness is short-lived, however. After Dumbledore's funeral, Harry ends their relationship, telling Ginny that if Voldemort learns about their romance, he will use her to get to him, just as he did with his godfather, Sirius Black. Ginny is devastated, but she accepts Harry's reasoning.

Deathly Hallows Saying that a relationship is over does not make it end, as Harry finds out. Staying at The Burrow between his escape from Privet Drive and setting out on his mission, he is of course in the same house with Ginny, and occasionally is set to perform some task alongside her in preparation for Bill and Fleur's wedding. It is during one of these shared tasks that Harry lets slip that his mission may involve killing Voldemort, a revelation that leaves Ginny looking rather shaken, despite Harry's trying to make it into a joke.

Knowing that he will shortly have to leave on this mission, and that she will not be able to travel with him, on his birthday Ginny pulls Harry into her room and, saying that she has to give him something to remember in case he happens upon any Veela on the way, kisses him soundly. They are interrupted by Ron, who later accuses Harry of leading his sister on after he had broken up with her. Harry, deciding that it is useless to protest that it had been her idea, promises that it has ended. He is somewhat hard-pressed to keep his promise, as he keeps looking at her over that day and the next, sharing a glance and a private amusement, before he realizes that he isn't supposed to. When the Ministry falls and Harry, Ron, and Hermione run, Harry is extremely worried about Ginny; with the defences fallen, the Weasley house is no longer safe, and Harry is afraid that Death Eaters may have injured her as they interrogate the Weasley family about Harry's whereabouts. Harry is as relieved as Ron when Arthur Weasley's Patronus brings them word that the family is all right.

At one point, a second party passes by the tent that Harry is sharing with Ron and Hermione. This second party mentions that Ginny, Neville, and Luna had been caught sneaking into the Headmaster's office to steal the Sword of Gryffindor, and had been punished severely. Harry is very worried about what punishment Ginny might have received, until he speaks with the portrait of Phineas Nigellus, and learns that her punishment had been to work in the Forbidden Forest with "that half-breed oaf," Hagrid.

After Ron leaves the party, Harry periodically brings out the Marauder's Map, initially looking for the little dot that represents Ron to reappear on the map. This would have shown that, protected by his Pure Blood status, Ron had safely resumed his normal life. As time passes and Ron does not reappear, Harry starts studying the map by wandlight at night, watching the dot that represents Ginny at Hogwarts. He wonders what she is doing, and whether she knows he is thinking about her.

Ginny is present at the Battle of Hogwarts; much to Harry's dismay, she demands to join in the fighting. After the first battle, Harry heads off to the Forbidden Forest to meet Voldemort and his doom; as he does so, he passes Ginny on the grounds, aiding a fallen student. He wants to stop and speak with her, but knows that if he does, he won't be able to continue; but he believes that she looks up as he walks past, despite his being under the Invisibility Cloak. Ginny's kiss is the last thing Harry thinks about before Voldemort casts the killing curse.

After the final battle is finished, Harry looks over at Ginny, who is leaning her head on her mother in exhaustion. Harry thinks to himself that he will want to talk with Ginny, but that it can wait; he will have all the time in the world to speak with her, he will leave her this time to recover.

In the Epilogue, Harry and Ginny are married and have three children, James Sirius, Albus Severus, and Lily Luna.

Notable Consequences While Harry is convinced by Ron and Hermione to start teaching proper Defence Against the Dark Arts, he is more than slightly taken aback to discover that there are at least two dozen students at the organizational meeting. One of the things that convinces him to take on this large group is the presence of Cho Chang. The relationship with Cho, to a certain extent, sustains him in his efforts to keep the DA meetings occurring.

By the end of *Harry Potter and the Half-Blood Prince*, Harry knows that anyone he is close to, his friends, his loves, or his relatives, will become Voldemort's targets. To protect Ginny, he reluctantly tries to end their relationship. Unless Voldemort can be killed, Harry knows he faces a lonely life with few friends or loved ones to support him. When the relationship continues, Harry finds some strength in studying the Marauder's Map to find out what Ginny is doing at the school.

As mentioned, in the epilogue we discover that Harry has married Ginny, and so has created the family he has always wanted.

Analysis

By the end of *Harry Potter and the Order of the Phoenix* it is apparent Harry is unprepared for a mature relationship, as is only to be expected for a fifteen-year old. His attachment to Cho Chang, in retrospect, seems ill-advised; he was unable to provide what she needed emotionally, and she was unprepared for his inability to give it. Also, Cho is a year older than Harry, and girls generally mature more rapidly than boys at this age.

One could wonder just what Cho saw in Harry. After the events in *Harry Potter and the Goblet of Fire,* her interest in Harry mainly seems to be that he was present at Cedric's death and can provide her information about it; however, Cho was interested in Harry a year earlier, at least after the Goblet selected him as a Champion. She does seem genuinely sorry that Harry's attempt to ask her to the Yule Ball was pre-empted by Cedric. It is uncertain why, though it may have more to do with an attraction to Harry's fame as 'the Boy who Lived,' rather than an interest in the boy himself.

Harry's slowly-building interest in Ginny Weasley, starting in *Harry Potter and the Half-Blood Prince,* is not entirely unheralded. Harry always treats Ginny with great consideration. In *Harry Potter and the Chamber of Secrets,* he tactfully pretends not to notice when she overturns her porridge at breakfast. Harry also fears she will be held responsible and punished for everything that happened during that year. We feel his relief as keenly as hers when Dumbledore says, *"There will be no punishment. Older and wiser wizards than she have been hoodwinked by Lord Voldemort."* And it is revealed in *Harry Potter and the Order of the Phoenix* that she and Harry share an understanding of how Voldemort mentally affects his victims, an experience that cannot be understood by either Ron or Hermione.

Harry's inner turmoil during *Harry Potter and the Half-Blood Prince* is an excellent depiction of his current state of mind. He and Ron, returning from the Quidditch pitch, run into Ginny and Dean Thomas "snogging" (kissing) in a hidden corner. Ron flares angrily at Dean, continuing the quarrel with Ginny once Dean has departed. By now, Harry recognizes his own feelings for Ginny and is jealous of Dean. However, he realizes that if Ron is this upset at Dean, it is likely he would be equally upset with Harry, should he seek to replace Dean in Ginny's affections. It is this latter fear over losing Ron's friendship that prevents him from taking action after Ginny and Dean break up. It is noteworthy that Ron's anger at Dean decreased once he (Ron) hooked up with Lavender. Harry might have considered pursuing Ginny if Ron had continued in that relationship. However, Ron and Lavender break up at very nearly the same time that Ginny dumps Dean, which probably leaves Harry worried that Ginny has been placed under Ron's brotherly microscope once again.

Greater Picture

At the end of book 6, Harry shows his concern for Ginny's well-being by ending their relationship. He knows Voldemort often fells his victims by targeting their friends and loved ones, just as he did with Harry's godfather, Sirius Black. Ginny sees Harry's decision to end their relationship to protect her as being noble, but she also believes it is the incorrect way to handle the situation. Even at that point, it seems unlikely their relationship has truly ended, despite Harry's saying it has.

In Book 7, of course, Ginny returns to Hogwarts for her sixth year, so she and Harry do spend much of the year apart. We see in the beginning of the book that she still cares for Harry, though, and we learn that Harry still cares a lot about her through the course of his time apart from her. They do fight in the same battle near the end of the final book, and Harry knows that they will be together for a long time at that point.

Head Boy

Location: Hogwarts
Time Period: throughout the series
Important Characters: Percy Weasley

Overview

Head Boys and Head Girls are not, strictly speaking, magical. They are an integral part of the power structure of any school run on the English model; a Head Boy typically is the senior of the male Prefects, as the Head Girl is the senior of the female Prefects. Typically they have a few additional rights, and in return are responsible for assigning duties to other prefects and seeing that they are carried out.

Event Details In *Harry Potter and the Prisoner of Azkaban,* Percy Weasley has just been made Head Boy, and his pomposity has increased incredibly. The only thing that makes him tolerable at all is that the twins are perpetually puncturing him, or trying to; their continual japing makes him a figure of fun rather than a simple bore.

Hagrid has mentioned to Harry, in *Harry Potter and the Philosopher's Stone,* that Harry's father and mother were Head Boy and Head Girl while they were at Hogwarts.

Notable Consequences Generally speaking, consequences will be few, as the Head Boy and Head Girl will invariably be in their last year at Hogwarts. It is true that Percy, as Head Boy, became even more pompous and stuffy than he had been as a Prefect.

Analysis

There is a minor contradiction here. Hagrid says in *Harry Potter and the Philosopher's Stone,* as mentioned above, that Harry's father was Head Boy. Yet, in *Harry Potter and the Order of the Phoenix,* Sirius Black states that Remus Lupin was a Prefect; both Sirius and James were spending too much time in detention to be considered for that post. Later, Lupin and Sirius did say the James had improved by his seventh year; so we have three possibilities.

1. With the departure of some other prefect before 7th Year, it may have been necessary to appoint a new prefect, and that job, with the Head Boy promotion, might have fallen to James. This is somewhat unlikely as James had not previously been Prefect; as Lupin had

been, it's more likely that Lupin would be Head Boy, if either of them were.

2. Hagrid might have over-inflated ideas about James' student office, or might be improving on the truth, either to make Harry more aware of his fame, or just on general principles.

3. James' character, which granted does not seem suitable for the office of Head Boy, might not have been totally firmed up that early in the series, and the author might have chosen to have him be Head Boy to build up his apparent status in the Wizarding world.

Of the three options, the third seems most likely; however, the second makes more sense in the context of the story. As we can see from Percy, by comparison with Fred and George, the students chosen for prefect and head boy positions are not necessarily the most powerful wizards around. Thus if James Potter was not Head Boy, it is unlikely that this is a serious strike against his Wizarding ability.

GREATER PICTURE

It is likely that Hermione would have been made Head Girl had she returned to Hogwarts for her seventh year. However, she chooses instead to accompany Harry to help him deal with Lord Voldemort.

Hermione Granger relationships

Location: Hogwarts
Time Period: Throughout the series
Important Characters: Hermione Granger, Ron Weasley, Viktor Krum

OVERVIEW

Hermione Granger remains unattached for the first three years of the series. It seems that Viktor Krum is attracted to her when he arrives for the Triwizard Tournament in *Harry Potter and the Goblet of Fire*, but she does not reciprocate his feelings; she sees him as a pen-friend, though it is obvious to us that he wants more than that. When Ron's relationship with Lavender ends, he suddenly discovers his true feelings for Hermione, feelings which Hermione has quietly had for him for the past three years or more; and by the end of the sixth book, they are a couple. They remain so, with some friction, throughout the seventh book.

Event Details

Philosophers' Stone Hermione starts off this book as a very bossy and largely unattractive girl with teeth that are too big. After Hallowe'en, however, she becomes friends with Harry and Ron, but little more than that.

Chamber of Secrets Hermione seems to develop a rapid crush on Gilderoy Lockhart. While she does not develop an attachment for him, she, along with many other girls in the school, seems to be entranced by him. Despite some clear evidence of limited competence on his part, Hermione asks Madam Pince if she can keep the note that Lockhart gave her to allow her to take a book out of the restricted section. It is only as the year continues, and Lockhart's competence is repeatedly challenged and found wanting, that she starts to lose interest in him.

Towards the end of the year, Hermione is attacked by the Monster from the Chamber and as a result is petrified. When we see her in the Hospital Wing, Ron seems more deeply affected than Harry.

Prisoner of Azkaban Hermione is somehow managing to take twelve subjects during most of this book, though it drops to eleven after she gives up on Divination in mid-April. She is far too busy, even with the Time-turner to assist with her scheduling, to have anything resembling a social life. When Hermione suggests to Professor McGonagall that Harry's new broom might be jinxed, this causes an estrangement between Hermione and the other two. The return of the broom could have cured this, but Ron's pet rat, Scabbers immediately disappears, apparently eaten by Hermione's pet cat Crookshanks, leaving Ron estranged from Hermione. We learn from Hagrid that she is feeling this separation very deeply. The two of them do reconcile when they have to start work on Buckbeak's appeal, but they remain at least outwardly friends, rather than anything more serious.

Goblet of Fire Ron is apparently infatuated with Fleur Delacour, a Beauxbatons student and shortly the Beauxbatons Champion in the Triwizard Tournament, much to Hermione's disgust. When Fleur comes over to the Gryffindor table to ask if they want their bouillabaisse, Ron is almost struck dumb. After she departs, Ron says that she must have some Veela in her ancestry. Hermione is rather nettled by this, and says that nobody else is acting that silly about her, but Harry notices that many other students seem similarly struck by her.

Viktor Krum, who arrived with the delegation from Durmstrang and has become their Champion, seems to appear in the library whenever Hermione is there.

It is early in this semester that the abortive duel between Harry and Draco Malfoy results in Hermione's teeth being dramatically over-enlarged. In the Hospital Wing, Madam Pomfrey arranges to revert them to their original size, and Hermione deliberately gets her to overdo it, so that they are the correct size for her face. Matters come to a head at the Yule Ball. Ron asks Hermione to the ball, but Hermione says that she has already accepted an invitation from someone else. It turns out that this someone else is Viktor Krum, who has been haunting the library apparently to get closer to Hermione. Hermione has spent three hours getting ready for the ball, and is almost unrecognizably pretty. Ron spends the first part of the dance glowering at Hermione as she dances with Viktor Krum. When Hermione comes over to talk to Ron and Harry, Ron accuses her of "fraternizing with the enemy." Hermione stalks off and is lost in the crowd. Ron and Harry then leave the dance floor to walk in the rose garden.

After the dance, Harry finds Ron and Hermione in a shouting match in the Gryffindor common room. Hermione tells Ron that if he does not like it then, "The next time there's a Ball, ask me before someone else does, and not as a last resort!" Hermione storms off to her dormitory. Ron, stunned, tells Harry that Hermione is quite clearly missing the point. Hermione has seen the jealousy for what it is, and Ron quite clearly has not, and in fact does not for some time after this, though Harry thinks at the time that Hermione understands Ron better than Ron does himself. In the Second Task, the merpeople are holding someone valuable to each of the Champions deep under the lake. Hermione is the hostage that Krum is to rescue, and when Ron and Harry return to the surface with Gabrielle, Fleur's sister, Hermione and Viktor are close to each other, talking privately; Hermione breaks away from Krum briefly to check on Harry and Ron. Fleur is overjoyed at Gabrielle's rescue; she kisses Harry, and also Ron because he helped. Hermione is somewhat upset by this attention that Ron is getting, but is distracted by something Viktor says to her. It appears that Krum is trying to retain Hermione's attention when she tries to talk to Harry and Ron. Shortly after this, Rita Skeeter writes a scurrilous article for *Witch Weekly* that suggests Hermione is keeping both Harry and Viktor as lovers. Hermione remarks that she wonders how Rita had known that Viktor had invited her to visit over the summer; Ron becomes very upset at hearing about this invitation.

A month before the Third Task, after surveying the grounds where the task will take place, Krum asks Harry to walk with him a while. Once he has found a secluded place, Krum asks if Hermione is Harry's girlfriend. Harry is amazed by this question, and replies that no, she most definitely is not; they are friends, but that is all, despite how much Hermione talks about him.

As the Beauxbatons' carriage is getting ready to leave, Fleur comes over to say goodbye to Harry; Ron is once again almost completely tongue-tied in her presence, earning himself a vexed look from Hermione.

Order of the Phoenix Hermione remains largely unattached throughout this book, though it is likely that she is waiting for Ron to do something. It is mentioned that Hermione is writing to Viktor Krum, who Ron pettily persists in calling "Vickie." Hermione insists that he is only a pen-friend, but Ron darkly says that he would *like* to be a lot more than that. Hermione flushes at this comment.

As Ron is leaving breakfast for the Quidditch pitch, on the morning of his first-ever Quidditch match, Hermione kisses him on the cheek. Ron seems bemused by this, rubbing the spot on his cheek as he leaves the Great Hall.

Half-Blood Prince Fleur is living in the Weasley's house as she prepares for her wedding to Bill. Ron, still dealing with the remnants of his infatuation with her, has mixed feelings about this development, as he seems to still be hoping for a kiss from her, but is totally abashed when she "jumps out at [him] unexpectedly, like then." Mrs. Weasley and Ginny are not so pleased; she seems quite self-centered and doesn't seem to care for the feelings of the family very much. Hermione is upset by this as well; it seems that Ron's ongoing goofiness whenever Fleur is around is quite troubling to her.

Lavender Brown begins the school year openly flirting with Ron, much to Hermione's disgust. After a particularly terrible Quidditch practice, Ron and his sister Ginny have a row after he and Harry accidentally walk in on her snogging Dean Thomas in a Hogwarts hallway. They have a screaming match in which Ginny accuses Ron of having absolutely no experience with girls. She says that Harry and Cho have been snogging, as have Hermione and Viktor Krum, and accuses Ron of being jealous because he's the only one who doesn't have anyone to snog with. Since Ron is still smarting from watching Hermione being singled out by Krum, and their ongoing pen-pal relationship, he responds to Lavender's advances. Their relationship is publicly and intensely physical—Harry at one point compares it to a vertical wrestling match, and at another point wonders which of several hands he can see belongs to whom. This causes a huge rift between Hermione and Ron that lasts several months during their 6th year. Hermione is somewhere between vexed and incensed at this relationship of Ron's, at one point summoning a flock of birds to attack Ron when he and Lavender barge in on her, evidently looking for a private place to snog. After one of their stretches of estrangement, when Ron's spell-checking quill goes wrong and messes up an essay he is writing, she unbends enough to offer to correct it for him. With a sigh of relief, Ron pushes his essay over to her, saying that he loves her. Hermione blushes, but says only that he shouldn't let Lavender hear that. On his birthday, Ron eats some chocolate cauldrons which have been spiked with love potion by Romilda Vane, who intended them for Harry. After receiving the antidote from Professor Slughorn, Ron is nearly killed by some poison intended for another victim, possibly Dumbledore. Hermione, deeply worried, stays by his bedside in the Hospital Wing his entire first day. It is likely significant that the first time Ron speaks after being poisoned, it is immediately after the first time that Hermione, waiting at his bedside, has said something, and that what he says is her name. She visits him frequently until he is fully recovered, and thereafter she and Ron mend their differences. Harry now determines that he must use Felix Felicis potion to get a memory from Professor Slughorn. Under the influence of this potion, he decides to don his Invisibility Cloak and go visit Hagrid. As he, Ron, and Hermione descend from the boy's dormitory, they run into Lavender; she of course can't see Harry, and starts berating Ron for being up in his dormitory "alone with *her*" (Hermione). This is basically the lever Ron needs to end his relationship with her.

By the close of this book, Ron and Hermione are a couple. Between the battle under the Astronomy tower and Dumbledore's funeral, we see what appears to be almost a double date, with apparent intimacy between Ron and Hermione as well as an intimate relationship between Ginny and Harry; and Ron and Hermione sit together at Dumbledore's funeral, where we also see them comforting each other.

Deathly Hallows Harry finds that Ron has been given a book by Fred and George, *Twelve Fail-Safe Ways To Charm Witches*, which he describes as "pure gold." Harry, who has received his own copy from Ron with the strict admonition to keep it secret from Hermione, notes him using the techniques in this book both on his own mother and on Hermione; Hermione seems pleased when Ron compliments her.

Hermione is somewhat shocked when Viktor Krum shows up at Bill and Fleur's wedding; Fleur has invited him, and Hermione had not expected to see him there. He, in turn, is disgruntled when Ron hauls Hermione away and onto the dance floor; it is obvious at this point that he had in fact been hoping she would be more than a pen-friend. Hermione and Ron are still on the dance floor when Kingsley Shacklebolt's Patronus arrives with news of the fall of the Ministry. Fleeing the arriving Death Eaters, the Trio find sanctuary, in Number Twelve, Grimmauld Place. There, as they turn in for the night, Hermione chooses to sleep beside Ron.

As the Trio escape from the Ministry, Ron is Splinched, and Hermione is desperate in her efforts to heal him. She seems almost as affected by Ron's injury as Ron is himself.

During their search of the Horcruxes, especially after they retrieve Slytherin's Locket from Umbridge, the relationship between the friends is strained. Ron, who is used to having three daily meals and not doing much work, is especially put out by their continued, apparently aimless, peregrinations through the cold, wet British countryside. His feelings are strengthened by the Locket, and, in a moment of rage when Harry admits not having a plan to find the Horcruxes, abandons the quest. His departure leaves Hermione in tears, and while they delay their departure the next morning in the hopes that Ron will return to their camp, eventually they decide that they must leave for the sake of their safety. Knowing that Ron will not be able to find them again, Hermione is devastated, and simply sits, sobbing, at their arrival point, leaving Harry to set the defensive spells around them.

By common unspoken agreement, Harry and Hermione do not discuss Ron's departure. Hermione retreats even further into her books, and Harry does not know how to console her.

When Ron comes back, Hermione explodes with apparent rage, and starts to hit him with all her strength, the first show of irrationality from Hermione. Harry has to separate them with a Shield charm, whereupon Hermione physically seems to retreat into herself. In hopes that Hermione will relent, Harry asks Ron to tell what had happened to him while he was away. She eventually does unwind, though Harry is a little surprised that she seems to not be moved by either Ron's saving Harry, or Ron's conquering the jealousy inspired by the Horcrux in its efforts to preserve itself. Rather, it is Ron's detailing his attempt to return, and his finding Harry and Hermione by means of the Deluminator, that cause her to relax a little. However, relations between the two are very strained for the next while.

When the Trio are captured and taken to Malfoy Manor, Hermione is kept apart from the others by Bellatrix Lestrange, who is torturing her in order to determine how they had found the Sword of Gryffindor. Ron is very nearly frantic, as he hears her being tortured. Once freed from the dungeons, Ron concentrates his efforts on saving Hermione, and though she has been tortured nearly to the point of being unconscious, it seems that Ron's efforts do have some effect. When she has recovered, in Shell Cottage, she no longer seems quite as distant. After their arrival at Hogwarts, with the Final Battle in Hogwarts' grounds becoming inevitable, Ron expresses his worry for the house-elves and asks if he and Hermione should tell them to go away so that they don't get killed. This act of maturity and selflessness from Ron prompts Hermione to kiss him, apparently moving their relationship forwards as Ginny had earlier similarly done with Harry.

In the Epilogue, "Nineteen Years Later," Hermione is married to Ron and they have two children, Rose and Hugo. Rose is going to start Hogwarts that year.

Notable Consequences Hermione comments at one point, just before Christmas in *Harry Potter and the Order of the Phoenix*, that Ron has the emotional depth of a teaspoon. We have seen this time and time again; Ron seems unaware of the effect his words have on others, and can be rather hurtful in what he says in others' hearing. Sometimes, of course, he does this deliberately; many of his more provocative utterances in *Harry Potter and the Prisoner of Azkaban* are designed to sting Hermione for either her arranging for the confiscation of Harry's Firebolt broom, or for her apparent callousness when Scabbers seems to have been killed by Crookshanks. Ron has hurt Hermione so many times that one wonders why she stays around. The romantic interest that Hermione has in Ron is likely the only thing that keeps her there, but at the same time it fuels her exasperation: how could someone she cares about so much be so stupid?

It is Hermione's caring about Ron so much, also, that delays his return to the group in *Harry Potter and the Deathly Hallows*. Having been unable to return to Harry and Hermione's campsite before they had departed, Ron has no way of finding them. Out of consideration for Hermione's feelings, Harry does not mention Ron by name, and so neither does Hermione. When Hermione does eventually say Ron's name, Dumbledore's Deluminator detects it and leads Ron to where Harry and Hermione are. If Hermione had been willing to talk about Ron sooner, the Deluminator would have led him back more quickly.

ANALYSIS

It is interesting to see how single-minded Hermione is in her pursuit of Ron. There are side-lights, of course; Viktor Krum is an interesting companion for a while, and she keeps writing to him after his departure, but one gets the idea that she is looking for information from Viktor and keeping a line of communication open through to Durmstrang, in case Krum has some role to play in defending Harry or Hermione from Voldemort later.

The author has mentioned "anvil-sized hints" being dropped about Ron and Hermione getting together since about *Harry Potter and the Goblet of Fire*. It is in that book, in fact, that we start to see Ron's jealousy towards anyone who would dare to go out with Hermione start to show.

We are shown a bit of a red herring in *Harry Potter and the Half-Blood Prince*, however; Ron expresses the same indignation when he finds Dean and Ginny snogging. Could it be that Ron regards Hermione as a sister? Actually, on inspection, we see that Ron is acting protective towards Ginny, and jealous towards Hermione, but the difference is subtle.

There is no way of knowing exactly how much has been going on between Viktor and Hermione. True, Ginny does tell Ron that Hermione and Viktor have been snogging, but this is not conclusive, as Ginny at the time is mid-quarrel with Ron, and is trying to hurt him with words. It is entirely possible that Ginny is going from what is public knowledge and expanding on it for effect. It is certainly true, as we see later, that Viktor would like to spend time snogging with Hermione; what is not so certain is whether he actually has done so. Hermione has clearly set her sights on Ron early in the series, and it is uncertain whether she would choose to jeopardize her relationship with Ron by being known to be snogging with Viktor. Following the Valentine's day debacle in Harry's fifth year, Hermione displays an awareness of Cho's tactic of mentioning other suitors in order to gauge Harry's commitment to her. She also seems to be aware, before Harry mentions it, of how it had failed to work. Given this, it seems unlikely that Hermione would try a similar tactic on Ron.

House Cup

Location: Hogwarts
Time Period: Year 1, Year 2, Year 3, Year 4, Year 5, and Year 6
Important Characters: The students and teacher of Hogwarts.

Overview

When entering Hogwarts School of Witchcraft and Wizardry, the students are sorted into one of four different houses: Gryffindor, Ravenclaw, Hufflepuff, or Slytherin. Every year, these houses compete against one another to win the House Cup, which is awarded to whichever house collects the most house points. These points are given out by teachers for good behavior or excellent schoolwork. However, the teachers can also take away house points for any rule-breaking.

Infiltration of the Ministry of Magic

Location: Ministry of Magic
Time Period: *Harry Potter and the Deathly Hallows*
Important Characters: Harry, Hermione, and Ron; various Ministry employees

Overview

Having determined that a Horcrux is in the hands of Dolores Umbridge, Harry, Hermione, and Ron decide to enter the Ministry of Magic in an attempt to determine where it is being kept. They assume the guise of three Ministry workers and enter as part of the morning arrivals. The three of them are separated, with Hermione ending up in one of the courtrooms acting as scribe for proceedings that Umbridge is chairing. When Harry joins her there, Hermione happens to notice that Umbridge is wearing the locket bearing the Horcrux. Harry Stuns Umbridge and the other Ministry worker there present, Hermione gets the locket away from Umbridge, leaving a replica, and they escape, luckily joining up with Ron. A Death Eater is unfortunately dragged along with them by side-along Apparation as they attempt to return to Grimmauld Place, and while Hermione is able to force him to let go, he is then on the doorstep of Grimmauld Place. Believing that Grimmauld Place is no longer a safe sanctuary, Hermione Apparates the Trio again, this time to a spot in a forest.

Event Details Harry learns that Sirius' brother, Regulus, has the same initials (R. A. B.) as the person who had exchanged lockets with the one Professor Dumbledore and Harry had retrieved at the end of the previous year. A search of Regulus' room is fruitless, but Hermione recalls seeing a locket when cleaning up Grimmauld Place earlier. Summoned by Harry, Kreacher admits to having taken the locket, but says that it had later been stolen by Mundungus Fletcher. Kreacher is then sent to fetch Mundungus, and returns with him after a few days. Under coercion, Mundungus reports that the locket had been extorted from him, in turn, by a witch that Harry recognizes, from Mundungus' description, as Dolores Umbridge.

Harry, Hermione, and Ron decide to enter the Ministry of Magic, in the guise of legitimate Ministry workers, to attempt to find where the locket is. After several weeks of observation and planning, they waylay and knock out three Ministry employees and use Mad-Eye Moody's stock of Polyjuice Potion to impersonate them: Hermione as Mafalda Hopkirk, Ron as one Reg Cattermole, a maintenance worker, and Harry as a tall wizard whose name he does not know. With magical tokens that they have seen other Ministry workers using, they enter a specific set of public washrooms, and flush themselves into the Ministry.

On arriving at the Atrium, Harry is mildly disgusted to realize that the Fountain of Magical Brethren has been replaced by a sculpture of an apparent Wizarding family seated upon thrones made out of tormented human figures, apparently meant to represent Muggles. As the disguised Trio line up for the elevators, Yaxley approaches and tells Ron that it is raining in his office, and that he should fix it. He also makes a threat about Cattermole's wife, who is appearing before the Muggle-born Registration Commission that day. Yaxley then strides off to a lift that is headed downwards. Ron rides upwards to Yaxley's office on Level Two, and with Hermione's whispered advice still in his ears, heads off to try and stop the rain. Harry and Hermione, reaching Level One, are confronted by the Minister for Magic, Pius Thicknesse and Dolores Umbridge.

Umbridge immediately assumes that Travers had sent Mafalda to be her recorder at the day's session of the Muggle-Born Registration Commission, and, taking the disguised Hermione with her, descends, leaving Harry and the Minister. The Minister, addressing Harry as "Albert," seems to accept Harry's explanation for being on the first level, and leaves him. Harry now dons his Invisibility Cloak, and starts searching for Umbridge's office. He finds an open area with pink pages flying about, and a number of witches and wizards who are assembling the pages into pamphlets. Examining an assembled pamphlet under his Cloak, he sees that it is anti-Muggle propaganda. Hearing a rude comment about the wizards' boss, he looks towards the indicated office door and sees Moody's magical eye fixedly staring at the ceiling, and a nameplate that reads "*Dolores Umbridge, Senior Undersecretary to the Minister.*" The Invisibility Cloak will not allow him to open a door undetected, so Harry arms a Decoy Detonator. When it goes off with a great cloud of smoke at the far end of the room, Harry opens the door and enters Umbridge's office.

Once inside, he finds a small telescope fixed to the inside of the door; peering through it, he sees the pamphleteering witches and wizards looking at the Decoy Detonator. Harry wrenches the telescope out of the door, and pockets Moody's eye. He then tries to Summon the locket, without success.

Searching Umbridge's office, he finds a file on Arthur Weasley, who is listed as a pure-blood, but is likely to be contacted by "Undesireable Number One," Harry himself. Arthur is also being Tracked. The search is otherwise fruitless, but taking one last look around the office, Harry sees Dumbledore looking at him from a small mirror. Upon closer inspection, the mirror turns out to be the cover of a book: *The Life and Lies of Albus Dumbledore* by Rita Skeeter. Flipping it open, he sees a picture of two teenagers, but before he can read the caption, the office door opens. Pius Thicknesse enters and writes a note to Umbridge; Harry leaves, passing the pamphlet witches still investigating the Decoy Detonator, and returns to the lift. He must now find Ron, get down to the courtrooms, and collect Hermione; it seems unlikely the locket is here. Luckily, as the lift reaches the second floor, Ron steps on; before they can exchange more than greetings, though, the lift stops again and Arthur Weasley and a blonde witch get on, deep in conversation. Arthur gives Harry a distasteful look, but tells Ron about a spell that might work on Yaxley's office. On the next floor, Ron and the blonde witch get off, but blocked by Percy Weasley getting on, Harry is unable to follow. Percy looks up from his reading and suddenly realizes his father is there, and gets out on the next floor. Harry again tries to follow, but is blocked by Arthur, who accuses him of planting information about Dirk Cresswell. When Harry tells Arthur that he is being Tracked, Arthur considers it a threat. Arthur exits on the Atrium level, and Harry puts the Invisibility Cloak back on. He will have to extricate Hermione while Ron is stopping the rain.

Heading to the courtrooms, Harry recognizes the unnatural chill caused by Dementors; the creatures are guarding Muggle-born witches and wizards waiting outside the courtroom. A wizard is led from the courtrooms by two Dementors. Mary Cattermole is then called in by Umbridge, and Harry follows her. Inside, two Dementors are held at bay by a cat Patronus, and Umbridge, Hermione (as Mafalda), and Yaxley are examining Cattermole, demanding to know whose wand she stole. As Umbridge leans forward, the Locket around her neck swings out. Hermione takes a chance and asks about it; Umbridge claims the S initial is for Selwyn, a very old Wizarding family she is honoured to be related to. This is too much for Harry, who immediately Stuns Umbridge and Yaxley. Prompted by Hermione, Harry casts a Patronus, just in time to save Mary Cattermole. He tries, twice, to release the chains on Mary, while Hermione creates a duplicate Locket to replace the real one. Escorted by Harry and Hermione's Patronuses, the three leave the courtrooms. Gathering the other Muggle-borns, Harry says the new official position is to disguise themselves and leave the country if possible, at the very least stay away from the Ministry; they can leave from the Atrium.

Arriving at the lifts, they are met by Ron; Mary Cattermole runs to hug him, thinking he is her husband, Reg. Ron warns Harry and Hermione that the Ministry knows they are there and work crews are closing off the fireplaces. Harry says they can still get out if they hurry. At the Atrium, Harry orders the crews to stop sealing fireplaces. When one wizard protests. Harry threateningly asks if he wants his family tree examined the way Dirk Cresswell's was. Muggle-borns are sent in pairs through the remaining fireplaces, but the real Reg Cattermole appears from the lifts. Amidst his and Mary Cattermole's confusion, Yaxley appears, demanding that the fireplaces be sealed. Harry points to the wizard who questioned him, saying he was allowing Muggle-borns to escape. As the commotion builds, Ron and Mary Cattermole escape; as the truth dawns on Yaxley, he fires a curse at Harry exiting through the fireplace with Hermione. Arriving in the bathroom, Harry sees Yaxley appear in the cubicle behind him. Grabbing Hermione and Ron, Harry Disapparates. He briefly sees the door of Grimmauld Place, then there is a bang and they are Apparating away.

Ron has been Splinched and is losing blood; Hermione tells Harry to fetch Dittany from her beaded bag, and uses that to start him healing. Hermione explains that Yaxley had held on to her arm as they Apparated to Grimmauld Place. She had jinxed him to force him to let go, but because she had brought him to Grimmauld Place, and she is a Secret-Keeper since the death of Dumbledore, it was possible that he now knew how to get in. As the house was no longer safe, she had Apparated them away to a forest where she and her family had gone camping once. Harry sets up the tent, and Hermione sets protective spells. They move into the tent to plan and recuperate. Ron requests that they not use Voldemort's name; Harry and Hermione agree to this.

The following morning, Harry gets up before the others, and buries Moody's eye beneath a nearby tree.

Notable Consequences The primary consequence is the recovery of the Locket Horcrux. This is the third of six Horcruxes that we know about; we have seen the diary and the ring, and believe the others are Hufflepuff's cup, Nagini, and another, as yet undetermined, artifact of the Founders. We don't yet know how to destroy it, but possession of the Locket is clearly a necessary first step.

Our view and Harry's of the Ministry illuminate the control Voldemort has taken of Wizarding England. The replacement of the previously-destroyed Fountain of Magical Brethren with a statue of a Wizarding family seated on thrones made of Muggles in torment quite clearly indicates that the Ministry has embraced Voldemort's views on wizarding superiority. The wizard who approaches Harry in the elevator talking about the recently-denounced head of the Goblin Liaison Office quite clearly shows the viciousness of the current administration. The propaganda unit that Harry finds just outside Umbridge's office also shows the extent to which the Ministry now depends on fear, uncertainty, and doubt to maintain its grip on power.

From perusing Umbridge's files, Harry learns that he is now "Undesireable Number One," and that there is a watch on Arthur Weasley in case Harry tries to contact him. This may prevent Harry later trying to contact Arthur. Also in Umbridge's office, Harry sees a copy of Rita Skeeter's book about Dumbledore. It is one of the pictures in this book that will give him a clue as to the identity of the fair-haired thief who stole the as yet unknown object from Gregorovitch.

The recovery of Mad-Eye Moody's magical eye, and its subsequent burial, gives Harry necessary closure regarding Moody and his death.

Harry, as Albert Runcorn, manages to engineer the escape of many of the Muggle-born witches and wizards currently awaiting examination by the Muggle-born Registration Commission. While we do not learn their eventual fate, they at least have a chance, which they did not have before.

In deference to Ron's feelings, Harry and Hermione agree to not use Voldemort's name. This will remain in force for several months; apparently, Hermione and Harry make a habit of using the standard expressions "You-know-who" and "He who must not be named" instead of Voldemort's name, and this habit becomes unconscious. The Death Eater Yaxley is accidentally Apparated to the doorstep of Number 12, Grimmauld Place. Hermione believes that, having been brought to the house, Yaxley can now let other Death Eaters into the house. The breaking of the secrecy around Grimmauld Place will result in Harry, Ron, and Hermione moving from place to place around the English countryside for the remainder of the year. The loss of the comforts they had come to expect in Grimmauld Place will put a serious strain on Ron's relationship with the other two.

Analysis

For something that has taken so long to plan, it is amazing how quickly this mission all falls apart. It should have occurred to one of the three that the workers they were impersonating would have work to do, and could well get hauled off to do that work; it is almost inevitable that they will be separated once they enter the Ministry, and of course they are. They are also almost unprepared for being confronted; Cattermole, for instance, is a maintenance worker, yet Ron is utterly unprepared to do maintenance. One must also wonder what they hoped to accomplish; the locket that they hoped to find information about, being a personal adornment, is unlikely to be in Umbridge's office, so it is uncertain what Harry hoped to find in that office. The only reason that the plan did not founder immediately was due to extreme good fortune; Umbridge happened to be actually wearing the locket, and revealed it to Harry and Hermione, and Harry was able to Stun her in order to retrieve it. It also helped greatly that Harry, in his disguise as Albert Runcorn, was evidently quite high in the councils of the Ministry.

This failure of planning seems to point up the lack of maturity of our three heroes. They have concocted a flawless, if perhaps overcomplicated, plan to enter the Ministry, and succeed in carrying it off, but having accomplished that step, it seems that the rest of the effort is more than they are prepared for.

Greater Picture

Harry does not yet recognize the the two teenage wizards in the picture in Rita's book. He will eventually find out that one of them is the thief who had stolen the object from Gregorovitch, and will later find out that he is actually Gellert Grindelwald. He will also become aware that Voldemort is following the same logical path, looking for the object that was stolen from Gregorovitch.

The privations of the life of camping will actually cause Ron to leave the group. While he will think better of it almost immediately, and will try to return, he will run into difficulties that will prevent his return until Harry and Hermione have moved on. This enforced separation will show us two things. First, we will earn immediately that Hermione has feelings for Ron. At their new camp site, once it becomes inevitable that Ron will be unable to find them, Hermione will simply sit on a rock crying, leaving Harry to work the protective spells.

The second, apparently unrelated, thing that we will learn is that objects can be made to react to mention of their owners' name. In particular: Ron had received a Deluminator in Dumbledore's will, and the Deluminator started relaying Harry and Hermione's conversation to Ron once Hermione used his name. The Deluminator also was then able to transport Ron to Harry and Hermione.

This sensitivity to names is a very broad hint, which is shortly confirmed by Ron: Voldemort has either enchanted his name, or enchanted devices to respond to it, such that any use of Voldemort's name results in immediate attention from Death Eaters or their associates ("*snatchers*"). It is the use of Voldemort's name in the Tottenham Court Road café that had brought the two Death Eaters to them, before the Trio had gone to Grimmauld Place.

Inquisitorial Squad

Location: throughout Hogwarts
Time Period: *Harry Potter and the Order of the Phoenix*, April
Important Characters: Draco Malfoy, Crabbe, Pansy Parkinson, Millicent Bulstrode, Montague, Warrington

Overview

The Inquisitorial Squad are a group of students given power to dock House points, supposedly to assist Professor Umbridge to perform her duties as Hogwarts High Inquisitor.

Event Details Shortly after taking power as Headmaster of Hogwarts, Professor Umbridge institutes something she calls the Inquisitorial Squad, apparently intended to assist her in her duties as Hogwarts High Inquisitor. The members of this squad, consisting of "a few *trustworthy* students," is empowered to take House points, something which we are told Prefects are not granted.

The Inquisitorial Squad is introduced to us by Draco Malfoy, who shows us the powers he has been granted by penalizing Gryffindor House about forty points for no particular reason. We learn at that time that Montague is also a member of that squad, but had been pushed into an old, broken Vanishing Cabinet by Fred and George when he had tried to penalize them House points.

It is mentioned in passing that several members of the Inquisitorial Squad are attacked. Warrington is sent to the Hospital Wing with a skin ailment that makes him appear as if he had been coated in corn flakes, and Parkinson loses a full day of classes because she has grown antlers.

When Harry breaks into Umbridge's office to try to communicate with Sirius, to determine whether he has in fact gone to the Ministry, Umbridge is alerted by a spell she has set on her office. Umbridge sets the Inquisitorial Squad to round up the conspirators. Whether this is the entire Squad or not, we do not know, but the Squad members we see here are Draco Malfoy, Warrington, Crabbe, Milicent Bulstrode, and "several large Slytherins" who are not named.

Notable Consequences By means of wide-ranging abuse of their powers, the Inquisitorial Squad manages to largely ensure that Slytherin House will have the largest number of House Points at the end of the year, and thus will win the House Cup. Professor McGonagall, by according Harry and the five students who accompanied him fifty points each for alerting the Wizarding world to the return of Voldemort, returns Gryffindor's total to something respectable, but apparently not sufficient to win them the House cup.

As mentioned, Montague, attempting to penalize Fred and George, is pushed into a broken Vanishing Cabinet. Montague, despite being left somewhat less than fully competent by the experience, learns where the other member of that pair of cabinets is, and is able to pass that information on to Draco Malfoy. This sets up a large part of the plot of the sixth book. If Montague had not been in the Inquisitorial Squad, it is unlikely he would have done anything that would have so aggravated the Twins.

The creation of the Inquisitorial Squad, rather than increasing Umbridge's control over the students, seems instead to increase the rebellion, with Squad members being targeted for direct retaliation. As the Squad is created at the same time as Dumbledore is removed as Headmaster, however, it is never certain whether it is the Squad's action or Umbridge being Headmistress that is the cause of the increase in rebellion.

Analysis

It is apparent that Umbridge has selected students only from Slytherin house. It is uncertain whether she actually considers them more "trustworthy," as she says to Fudge, or whether she rather believes that they can be bought and will stay loyal to the paymaster. One does gather that the characteristic of those Sorted into Slytherin, "*those cunning folk use any means, to achieve their ends,*" is a clear view of the main chance and a willingness to do anything for personal gain.

Of course, Umbridge is not paying them in Galleons, but rather in power and influence, a coin that the Slytherin psyche seems designed to appreciate. The Squad, being placed even above the Prefects and Head Boy, clearly has the most power of any students in the school.

It is perhaps instructive to note how ineffectual the Squad, despite its additional powers, is in keeping order in the school. In fact, the constitution of the Squad seems designed to foster rebellion, as so many of Umbridge's measures seem to be. The Squad, having power and no apparent accountability, is seen to be abusing its power immediately it is formed, and there is no recourse; any appeal would have to be to Umbridge, who has already displayed a level of partiality to Slytherin greater even than that shown by Snape. The retaliation against the Squad, and the rebellion against them and the rules they are supposedly enforcing, shows that Umbridge has only amplified the ham-fistedness of her attempts at governance.

Mad-Eye Moody's Death

Location: Near Privet Drive
Time Period: *Harry Potter and the Deathly Hallows*, July
Important Characters: Mad-Eye Moody, Mundungus Fletcher, Lord Voldemort

Overview

Mad-Eye Moody is killed while fleeing Number 4 Privet Drive on broomstick while trying to escape from Lord Voldemort.

Event Details Knowing that the protection afforded Harry by his living with his Aunt Petunia will end on his seventeenth birthday, the Order of the Phoenix decides to move him to the protection of one of the Order's safe houses. Believing the Ministry thoroughly infiltrated, they let the Ministry plan to move Harry on his birthday, but secretly plan to move him themselves a few days earlier. The Ministry, in the name of protecting Harry, is monitoring the area around the house for Floo transport, use of Portkeys, and Apparation; Mad-Eye Moody believes these are simply ways of determining if someone is coming to get Harry and where they take him. As a result, Harry will be traveling by flying; the group who will be helping him escape arrive on Thestrals, broomstick, and one by means of Sirius Black's flying motorcycle. In order to make it more likely that Harry will escape, they plan to have multiple simulacra of Harry, each with a protector, each flying to a separate safe-house. The real Harry will be traveling with Hagrid on Sirius' flying motorcycle. Mundungus Fletcher, disguised as Harry by means of Polyjuice Potion, will ride with Moody.

As they leave the house, they are attacked by multiple Death Eaters, including Voldemort, who evidently has discovered a way to fly without use of a broomstick. Harry and Hagrid fly off in their own direction, pursued by a squad of Death Eaters, and do not see any of the action that takes place.

We later hear from Bill that, though clearly confused by the multiplicity of Harrys and protectors, Voldemort had quickly decided to concentrate on the Harry who was escorted by the strongest protector. That protector was Moody. Mundungus, becoming aware that he had been targeted by Voldemort, Disapparated from the back of Moody's broom. The killing curse that had been aimed at Mundungus instead hit Moody. Though Bill later went out to try and recover Moody's body, he was unable to find it.

Notable Consequences More than almost anything else that has happened so far, Moody's death makes Harry realize that not only is he at risk, but so is anyone around him. It is quite possibly because of Moody's death (and to a presumably lesser extent George's injury) that Harry decides that he must leave The Burrow. He is dissuaded from this course of action by the others involved in the escape, who indicate that they have worked hard and put themselves at risk to extract him from danger, and would not be happy to see him march off into danger from the place of safety where they have brought him.

The fact that Moody's body cannot be found will leave all involved without the necessary sense of closure that being able to bury him would provide. This will later lead Harry into a rash act.

Moody's death also indicates that even the best Auror may be powerless against Voldemort. We are already aware of Harry's disappointment at not being taught spells that can defeat Voldemort, from the previous book; Harry had expected those spells to be part of the private lessons he was getting from Professor Dumbledore. Moody's death shows that any spells available to Aurors would likely be ineffective against Voldemort.

Analysis

As mentioned in the article on the death of Dumbledore, Harry cannot be the hero of the story if there is another, greater hero standing behind to support him. While we don't really know at this point if Moody could be that strong, we can see that Moody has become the leader of the Order of the Phoenix since Dumbledore's death. While our contact with the true Alastor Moody is brief enough that we are unable to form any real opinion of his magical strength, he does seem to have great strength of character. There is a very real chance that, given the chance, he could learn the nature of Harry's mission, and in so doing, likely doom it to failure. Because of this, Moody must at least vanish, at worst die, before he can spend much time in Harry's company. Even if Harry is able to keep the secret of his mission from Moody, it is likely that Harry would end up leaning on Moody, as Ron almost ends up leaning on Lupin a few chapters further into the book.

Greater Picture

The comment is made in the Analysis section that if Moody had known of Harry's mission, he would have doomed it to failure. This is not immediately apparent to the reader, but on contemplation it becomes obvious. By the time Moody dies, we already know that in some manner, the inner councils of the Order of the Phoenix are at least in part being passed to Voldemort. We know that the Ministry has heard that Harry will be moved on his birthday and that Snape is aware that the order will be moving him before that date. Snape's information is correct, as it turns out, and the Death Eaters are prepared on the day that Harry actually is transported. While the Death Eaters do not know the subterfuge of the multiple Harrys, Harry himself, and we, must assume that Snape is getting his information somehow, and that a secret shared with the Order might reach Voldemort.

However, even if we assume that the information does not reach Voldemort directly, having the Order helping out is far too risky. Harry's sole means of success is to find the Horcruxes, get them out of where they are hidden, and destroy them before Voldemort notices. While Harry never clearly enunciates this to himself, this is clearly the sort of mission that requires stealth and small raiding parties. If the Order were to suddenly concentrate on Horcrux hunting, Voldemort would be certain to find out, and would take steps to protect the ones that remained. Granted, this does not explain Harry's vehement refusal to accept Lupin's help when Lupin arrives at Grimmauld Place a few days after the Trio arrive there. While Harry is then reluctant to have Lupin join them, despite his apparently being willing to sever ties with the Order of the Phoenix for the duration of the mission, it is Lupin's apparent willingness to abandon his wife (Tonks) and their unborn child that inspires Harry's anger.

N.E.W.T. exams

Location: Hogwarts school
Time Period: Students' seventh year
Important Characters: Percy Weasley

OVERVIEW

Nastily Exhausting Wizarding Tests are final exams taken by 7th year students at Hogwarts. These exams typically shape the career of the students so passing these exams is critical, as is obvious when Percy passes his N.E.W.T.s and enters the Ministry of Magic. Students take the exams in the subjects they have enrolled in after their O.W.L.s.

Event Details Fairly often in the books, something is mentioned as being N.E.W.T.-class magic. Examples of this are Harry's ability to conjure a corporeal Patronus, and Hermione's ability to perform the Protean Charm. N.E.W.T.-class spells are complicated enough that the average wizard does not expect to have to perform them for real until his N.E.W.T. exams, and thus Harry's ability, in his third year at Hogwarts, and Hermione's ability early in her fifth year, to perform magic that is not generally tested until seventh year, is exceptional.

In the same way, the courses one takes after one has achieved a sufficiently high O.W.L. grade are called N.E.W.T.-level courses. Professor McGonagall teaches advanced Transfiguration, for instance, to sixth and seventh year students who have achieved at least an E in their Transfiguration O.W.L., and we see Neville wondering whether he can somehow parley his Transfiguration A into N.E.W.T.-level study in McGonagall's class.

The only person we hear of receiving their N.E.W.T. grades is Percy Weasley, and while we do hear that he had received his "top-grade N.E.W.T.s," we are not close enough to him to know what exams he is sitting or when.

Passing Grades   O—Outstanding
   E—Exceeds Expectations
   A—Acceptable

Failing Grades   P—Poor
   D—Dreadful
   T—Troll

Notable Consequences Presumably, it is because of Percy's top-grade N.E.W.T.s that he is able to gain employment with the Ministry. Harry is told that in order to become an Auror, he must manage to achieve at least five Exceeds Expectations grades in his N.E.W.T.s.

ANALYSIS

Similarly to the O.W.L. exams, which are the analog of the Muggle GCSE or O-Level exams, the N.E.W.T. exams are analogous to the Muggle A-level exams, which are generally required for proceeding to university. There is no mention of a Wizarding university, but analogously the top jobs require N.E.W.T.s as a prologue to the further education that is required before starting work proper. We are told that there will be three years of study after graduation from Hogwarts before Harry will be able to start work as an Auror. While there must be a lot of stress in the lead-up to the N.E.W.T. exams, we don't actually get to see this.

It is likely that the N.E.W.T. exams are taken in the two weeks of summer term following the O.W.L. exams. We have seen that O.W.L.s take two weeks, during which time the Great Hall will be full of fifth-year students writing their exams; presumably, the N.E.W.T. exams fill the Great Hall for the following two weeks.

GREATER PICTURE

Because Harry, Hermione, and Ron do not attend Hogwarts in their seventh year, we do not actually experience N.E.W.T. exams. We could possibly have seen Fred and George taking these exams, but they elected to leave school dramatically in the middle of their seventh year.

Despite Harry's being told that he must have at least five Exceeds Expectations N.E.W.T. results to become an Auror, the author has implied that he entered the Aurors in the year that would have followed his seventh year at school. As he neither attended Hogwarts that year, nor sat N.E.W.T.s, we must assume that the Aurors accepted his year of unsupervised work as being equivalent to the necessary studies and exams.

Nymphadora's Death

Location: Hogwarts
Time Period: *Harry Potter and the Deathly Hallows*, May
Important Characters: Presumably Death Eaters

OVERVIEW

At the great Battle of Hogwarts, Nymphadora Tonks is killed in battle. Tonks was meant to be at home with her newborn son Teddy but came to assist her husband Remus Lupin who was also killed in battle.

Event Details When Harry returns to Hogwarts, Neville, who is escorting him from the Hog's Head, has assumed that he is there to liberate Hogwarts from the Death Eaters, and uses the charmed Galleons that Hermione had created, to recall Dumbledore's Army. Presumably, a member of Dumbledore's Army who either was in the Order of the Phoenix, or whose parents were Order members, passed the word, because members of the Order start to appear through the tunnel from the Hog's Head as well. One of the Order members who we see arrive is Lupin. After Harry has returned from Ravenclaw Tower, he finds that Ron and Hermione have left the Room of Requirement, saying something about a bathroom. As the whole school has now been summoned to the Great Hall, Harry heads there to see if he can find them. There, he hears Professor McGonagall sending non-combatant students home. Once only students who are of age are left, Order members at head table start assigning specific areas of defence. Lupin will head up the group that is defending the grounds.

Returning to the Room of Requirement in search of the final Horcrux, Harry is accosted by Tonks, who demands to know where Lupin is. Asked about their son

Teddy, Tonks says she has left him with her mother Andromeda. Harry tells Tonks that Lupin is defending the grounds, and Tonks runs off to find him. After Harry witnesses the death of Snape, Voldemort offers a ceasefire so that Harry can surrender to him and prevent any more loss of life. Harry, returning to the school, looks into the Great Hall and sees Lupin and Tonks lying among the dead.

While this is not mentioned in the book, the author has mentioned in an interview since its publication that Tonks was killed by her aunt Bellatrix Lestrange.

Notable Consequences Tonks' death once again reminds Harry that his is not the only life that is being affected by Voldemort's reign of power. This reaffirms his decision to do whatever he needs to do to eliminate Voldemort.

Lupin's and Tonks' deaths have left their infant son Teddy an orphan. Harry must be deeply affected by this, being an orphan himself, and as godfather having no little responsibility for Tonks' and Lupin's child.

Order of the Phoenix

Location: Various, but initially Number Twelve, Grimmauld Place

Time Period: *Harry Potter and the Goblet of Fire* (1 hour after Voldemort's return)—*Harry Potter and the Deathly Hallows*

Important Characters: Albus Dumbledore, Harry Potter, Hermione Granger, Ron Weasley, many others

Overview

The Order of the Phoenix is a secret society formed with a common goal: to aid in the defeat of Lord Voldemort. It is apparently headed up by Professor Dumbledore, as it is he who directs the remaining members to reform the Order on Voldemort's return.

Event Details

Goblet of Fire While the Order is not mentioned by name at that time, we see it being reorganized at the very end of *Harry Potter and the Goblet of Fire*. After Cornelius Fudge has denied that Voldemort could have returned, and leaves, Professor Dumbledore requests that Sirius Black return to his human shape. He then sends Sirius to gather up "the old crowd: Mundungus Fletcher, Arabella Figg, Remus Lupin," and then lie low at Lupin's house and wait for instructions. Sirius returns to his Animagus shape and does so.

Order of the Phoenix The next we hear of the Order is when the Advance Guard arrives to bring Harry to London. Once in London, he is given a note saying that the Headquarters of the Order of the Phoenix is at Number 12, Grimmauld Place. As he reads the note, which is in Dumbledore's writing, a house appears in front of Harry.

Entering the house, Harry is then taken upstairs, where he meets with Hermione and Ron, who tell him that they had wanted to tell him about what was going on, but had been asked not to by Professor Dumbledore. They are joined by Fred, George, and Ginny, who together explain what they have learned: the Order is a secret society, secret because Dumbledore is being discredited in the press, as Harry himself is, for daring to say that Voldemort had returned. Despite being in Headquarters, they have learned very little, as the meetings are always closed; all they have really managed to gather is that there is something that is being guarded. Harry points out that this something quite possibly is himself.

About this time, the current meeting ends, and Professor Snape is seen to leave through the front door. Harry, Hermione, and the Weasleys are called down to dinner. At dinner, Harry learns that among the members of the Order are Alastor Moody, Kingsley Shacklebolt, Tonks, Remus Lupin, and Emmeline Vance, who had been part of the Advance Guard that brought him to Grimmauld Place; Sirius Black, Mr. and Mrs. Weasley, their sons Bill and Charlie, and one Mundungus Fletcher. Charlie is not present; the Order has him recruiting wizards in Romania. Bill has taken a desk job in Gringotts. Harry has earlier met Mundungus Fletcher, and so knows that Arabella Figg is also working for the Order; and of course we have now seen Snape leaving an Order meeting.

After dinner, Lupin suggests that Harry might have some questions about the Order. Mrs. Weasley immediately objects, saying that he is too young, but is overruled by Lupin, Sirius, and her own husband. She is equally unsuccessful in getting Hermione, Ron, Fred, and George out of the meeting, so eventually simply marches Ginny off to bed. In answer to Harry's questions, the Order members disclose to Harry and the others that the Order is a group of wizards, led by Dumbledore, who agree with Harry and Dumbledore than Voldemort has returned. To Harry's question why Voldemort has not shown himself, we hear that Voldemort is staying hidden, gathering strength in preparation for his return. Lupin also says that Voldemort has a very great disadvantage, in that he had hoped that knowledge of his return would be restricted to his Death Eaters only. Thanks to Harry, however, within an hour of his return, that information had reached the one person, Dumbledore, that Voldemort did not want to know about it.

Lupin also discloses that this time, they know that there is something that Voldemort is after, a weapon, but at that point Mrs. Weasley intervenes again, saying that really is enough, and the party breaks up. Later, the Twins mention to Harry and Ron that the bit about the weapon was the only thing they had not already known about. Over the next few weeks, while Sirius, Hermione, Harry, Mrs. Weasley, and the Weasley children attempt to make Grimmauld Place habitable, several Order members enter and leave the house. One that Harry recognizes is Professor McGonagall, who looks very odd in Muggle dress. At one point a little later in the story, Dumbledore also visits, but he apparently does so at a time when Harry will not see him.

Harry must attend a hearing at the Ministry regarding his use of magic in front of Dudley. While walking through the ministry with Arthur, Harry notes that

Arthur seems to pretend only a casual acquaintance with Kingsley Shacklebolt.

In the party that is held to celebrate the appointment of Ron and Hermione as Prefects, many Order members return to Grimmauld Place. One of them is Alastor Moody, who shows Harry a photo of the Order as it was the last time Voldemort was in power. Many of the current members of the Order are present, a well as several members who had been driven insane, like Frank and Alice Longbottom, and many who had died, like Harry's father and mother.

The Order is not mentioned much through the main body of the book. The individual members of the Order play fairly substantial roles, but until the end of the book, there is little mention of the Order as a group. Sometimes we are told that something is Order business, or, as when the Trio wonder why Arthur Weasley is in the Ministry to be attacked by the snake, we are allowed to watch Harry infer that.

Near the end of *Harry Potter and the Order of the Phoenix*, Harry becomes convinced that Voldemort has trapped Sirius Black in the Department of Mysteries at the Ministry of Magic, and determines that he must find a member of the Order who can communicate with Sirius to find out if Sirius is being tortured. Professor Dumbledore has been driven away from the school, and Professor McGonagall had been hit by multiple Stunners the previous night and had been sent to St. Mungo's Hospital. Harry attempts to use Professor Umbridge's fireplace to communicate directly with Sirius by the Floo network, but is caught. It is only when Snape is summoned by Umbridge, to provide a dose of Veritaserum, that Harry recalls that Snape is also a member of the Order. Harry's message to Snape seems to go astray, however, and Harry resigns himself to attempting Sirius' rescue alone. As the rescue attempt turns into an ambush and Harry's fate seems hopeless, however, six members of the Order arrive to counter the ten Death Eaters. The resulting battle results in the revelation to the Ministry that Voldemort has returned, thus making the Order once again legitimate.

Half-Blood Prince With Sirius' death, ownership of the house at Grimmauld Place falls into question. Sirius has left it to Harry in his will, but there may be a magical entail that forces ownership to follow the line of inheritance among the Black children. This would mean that the house had passed to the next in line among the Black offspring, Narcissa Malfoy. Until this is resolved, the house cannot be used as Headquarters of the Order. Dumbledore devises a test that confirms that ownership has passed to Harry. We assume that the house is then used as Headquarters, though we do not visit it during the year. Instead, we see a number of Order members passing through The Burrow. We learn that the Order is watching over Hogwarts, supplementing the Ministry wizards who have been given that job and the defensive measures placed on the school itself. Occasionally we see Order members, most notably Tonks, patrolling the halls. In the final battle of the book, we see that none of the defenders of Hogwarts are from the Ministry, with the possible exception of Tonks who is also an Auror. Everyone on the Hogwarts side in that battle is either a member of the school, or a member of the Order.

Deathly Hallows We hear in Voldemort's council that the Order has plans to move Harry away from Privet Drive before the date scheduled by the Ministry. Snape tells Voldemort that the Order believes the Ministry has been thoroughly infiltrated by Voldemort's organization and doesn't trust the Ministry to manage the escape. Apparently Snape, now Voldemort's most trusted deputy, is somehow able to retrieve information from the Order.

We next learn of the Order's plan to arrange the safety of the Dursleys and Harry. Uncle Vernon, Aunt Petunia, and cousin Dudley drive off in the company of a pair of Order wizards, Dedalus Diggle and Hestia Jones. Meanwhile, thirteen Order members arrive, preparing to be seven protectors each with a Harry Potter, and each pair heading for a different Order safe house. Harry ends up at the house of Ted Tonks. In this battle, the Order suffers two casualties: Alastor Moody is killed when his Potter, Mundungus Fletcher, Disapparates out of the path of a killing curse thrown by Voldemort, and George Weasley loses an ear to a Sectumsempra curse cast by Snape. Harry and his escort, Hagrid, crash on their motorcycle, but are healed by the time their Portkey activates. As Dumbledore had been the Secret-Keeper for the Order, on his death every Order member becomes a Secret-Keeper for those secrets about the Order to which he had been privy. In particular, this means that the location of Headquarters is almost certainly no longer a secret, as Snape, who is quite obviously now a Death Eater, had been at Headquarters. We hear that the Burrow has become something of a headquarters for the Order, with large numbers of Order members stopping there for dinner frequently.

ANALYSIS

During the entire course of *Harry Potter and the Order of the Phoenix*, the Ministry, in a manner that by design echoes the actions of the government of Britain under Neville Chamberlain in the late 1930s, steadfastly denies the possibility of Voldemort's return. In order to publicly maintain this belief, the government must discredit anyone who suggests they may be wrong. Dumbledore, as such a voice, must be silenced, or at the very least discredited, so that his message will not weaken the government. Because of this, the Order of the Phoenix must work as secretively as Voldemort himself. It is because of this that the Weasley family has split, with Percy adhering to the Ministry line in what he sees as the main chance, while the rest of his family chooses to believe Dumbledore's version of events. The Order's secrecy ends at the same time Voldemort's does; once Voldemort is visibly returned, the Order equally does not have to hide, and though they will remain separate from the Ministry, they work towards the same ends in relative harmony.

The members of the Order of the Phoenix that we are told of are:
- Sirius Black
- Edgar Bones

- Caradoc Dearborn
- Dedalus Diggle
- Elphias Doge
- Aberforth Dumbledore
- Albus Dumbledore
- Benjy Fenwick
- Arabella Figg
- Mundungus Fletcher
- Rubeus Hagrid
- Hestia Jones
- Alice Longbottom
- Frank Longbottom
- Remus Lupin
- Dorcas Meadowes
- Minerva McGonagall
- Marlene McKinnon
- Alastor "Mad-Eye" Moody
- Sturgis Podmore
- James Potter
- Lily Potter (née Evans)
- Fabian Prewett
- Gideon Prewett
- Kingsley Shacklebolt
- Severus Snape
- Nymphadora Tonks
- Emmeline Vance
- Arthur Weasley
- Bill Weasley
- Charlie Weasley
- Molly Weasley

O.W.L. exams

Location: Hogwarts Great Hall; top of the Astronomy tower

Time Period: June of Harry's fifth year

Important Characters: Harry's year group, plus Griselda Marchbanks and Professor Tofty

Overview

The O.W.L. (Ordinary Wizarding Level) exams are taken at the end of a student's fifth year at Hogwarts. O.W.L.s are offered in most subjects a student takes in their first five years, and many consist of both written (theory) and practical tests. Courses in which O.W.L.S are offered are: Ancient Runes, Arithmancy, Astronomy (theory and practice), Care of Magical Creatures (theory and practice), Charms (theory and practice), Defence Against the Dark Arts (theory and practice), Divination, Herbology (theory and practice), History of Magic, Muggle Studies, Potions (theory and practice), and Transfiguration (theory and practice). Thus for twelve available subjects, nineteen examination slots are required.

Event Details Apparently, O.W.L.s extend over two weeks, with exams morning and afternoon; theory in the morning, practice in the afternoon. Special anti-cheating quills and parchment are used for the written parts of the exam. In Harry's fifth year, when he takes O.W.L.s, Harry sits Charms on the first day, then Transfiguration, Herbology, and Defence Against the Dark Arts. On the Friday, Hermione sits Ancient Runes, while Harry and Ron have the day off. The following week was Potions on Monday, then Care of Magical Creatures on Tuesday. Wednesday saw the Astronomy theory in the morning, Divination in the afternoon, then the Astronomy practical exam was that night at midnight. Thursday afternoon was the History of Magic exam. Hermione also had to sit her Arithmancy exam Wednesday afternoon, when Harry and Ron had Divination.

O.W.L.s are graded using the following system:

Passing Grades O—Outstanding
E—Exceeds Expectations
A—Acceptable

Failing Grades P—Poor
D—Dreadful
T—Troll

In the first few classes at the start of the term, a number of teachers announce that they will be grading to O.W.L. standards. Harry, Ron, and Hermione discuss between themselves what O.W.L. standards mean. In their discussion, they are joined by Fred and George, who had sat their O.W.L.s two years before. It is the Twins who describe the various grade levels, saying that they should have received E in every course, as their just showing up for the exam had exceeded the expectations of the Hogwarts teachers.

Notable Consequences The grades achieved in O.W.L.s are very important for the next stages of a young wizard or witch's education. Each teacher demands a minimum grade for further study of his or her subject on N.E.W.T. level. Most teachers seem to demand at least an E, while some demand an O and others allow students with an A, the lowest passing grade to proceed. In particular, Professor Snape requires that students who wish to proceed to N.E.W.T.-level study of Potions must achieve at least Outstanding, while Professor McGonagall and Professor Flitwick require at least Exceeds Expectations.

As the results of the O.W.L.s determines which courses can be taken at the N.E.W.T. level, the O.W.L. exams have a result on the witch or wizard's career choices. In particular, Harry, asked to consider a career, is most intrigued by the idea of being an Auror, a career for which he must achieve N.E.W.T. grades of Exceeds Expectations in at least five subjects, which Professor McGonagall suggests should include Defence Against the Dark Arts, Transfiguration, Potions, and Charms. While Harry does achieve Exceeds Expectations in Transfiguration, Charms, Potions, Herbology, and Care of Magical Creatures, as well as Outstanding in Defence Against the Dark Arts, Professor Snape's requirement that he achieve Outstanding for N.E.W.T.-level Potions studies almost certainly will prevent his becoming an Auror.

It is while Harry, tired after endlessly re-hashing the arrest of Hagrid that had occurred during the Astronomy final, is trying to write his History of Magic exam that he falls asleep and has the dream of Sirius being tortured in the Ministry by Voldemort. It is this dream that sends him to the Ministry.

ANALYSIS

The fact that the Wizarding world has an equivalent to the English GCSE is only to be expected. The standardized testing in the Muggle world so pervades the school system must have a parallel. The stress and fatigue surrounding the GCSEs no doubt has made many young Muggles imagine things that just are not so. Similarly, the mental tension and exhaustion caused in Harry by these exams obviously will increase Harry's sensitivity to the images that Voldemort is sending Harry to lure him to the Ministry.

QUESTIONS

1. Is Troll a real exam grade? Why did the Weasley twins have trouble remembering it?

GREATER PICTURE

In the next book in the series, we will find that a new Potions instructor has been appointed. Professor Slughorn will accept an O.W.L. grade of Exceeds Expectations for N.E.W.T.-level studies, so Harry's hopes of becoming an Auror will be restored.

Harry's belief that Professor Slughorn has been brought in to be the Defence Against the Dark Arts teacher, and his associated belief that he will not be allowed to study N.E.W.T.-level Potions, is a necessary plot point. It is because of this that Harry does not purchase the necessary textbook for N.E.W.T.-level potions, instead receiving the textbook previously owned by the Half-Blood Prince. This textbook is instrumental in Harry's success in Potions in his sixth year, and teaches him spells that he will use during the year and in the next year.

Pettigrew's Death

Location: cellar under Malfoy Manor
Time Period: *Harry Potter and the Deathly Hallows*, April
Important Characters: Peter Pettigrew, Harry Potter, Ron Weasley

OVERVIEW

Sent to investigate a noise in the cellars, Peter Pettigrew (Wormtail) is ambushed by Harry and Ron. Wormtail's silver hand is strangling Harry, as Ron struggles with Wormtail's wand hand. Harry reminds Wormtail that he owes a life debt to Harry, and Pettigrew hesitates; sensing the hesitation, Wormtail's silver hand turns on its master and kills him.

Event Details Harry, Ron, and Hermione are captured by Snatchers, and along with their existing captives Dean Thomas and Griphook, are taken to Malfoy Manor in hopes of receiving the reward for Harry's capture. Bellatrix Lestrange sees that they have the Sword of Gryffindor, and sends all the captives except Hermione into the cellar, where they also find Luna Lovegood and Mr. Ollivander. Luna has found a nail with which she is able to release Harry's bonds, and Harry, looking again at the shard of Sirius' magic mirror, notices a sky-blue eye looking out of it and pleads for help.

To confirm the story that Hermione has been telling under torture, Bellatrix now sends someone down to the cellar to fetch Griphook. As the door is slamming behind them, Dobby Apparates into the cellar, Harry asks Dobby to take Luna, Ollivander, and Dean to Shell Cottage, and though nervous, Dobby agrees. Bellatrix hears the sound of Dobby Disapparating, and sends Peter Pettigrew (Wormtail) down to the cellar to investigate. Entering the cellar, Wormtail is momentarily surprised to find that it is lighted by four balls of light (liberated from Ron's Deluminator), and Ron, on his wand side, and Harry on the side where his silver hand was attached, jump him. Ron, unfortunately, is unable to wrest Wormtail's wand from his grip, and Harry is being slowly strangled by the silver hand, when Harry reminds Wormtail that he owes Harry a life debt. Wormtail hesitates, and the silver hand, sensing this, turns on Wormtail and strangles him, despite Harry's best efforts. With Wormtail dead, the silver hand vanishes.

Notable Consequences With Pettigrew dead and the cellar door open, Ron and Harry will now be able to ascend to the main floor of Malfoy Manor to rescue Hermione.

The death of Pettigrew frees up a wand. As Ron had captured it from Wormtail, it will shift its allegiance to Ron, and so he can then use it to escape from Malfoy Manor.

ANALYSIS

Pettigrew's owing a life debt to Harry is another of the connections throughout the length of the series that has been repeatedly debated throughout the publication span of the books. At the end of *Harry Potter and the Prisoner of Azkaban*, the third book, Professor Dumbledore comments to Harry that Pettigrew now owe Harry a life debt, as Harry had saved Pettigrew's life, and suggests that Voldemort would likely not be happy at the thought that his main lieutenant owed a life debt to his main enemy. As with the apparent look of triumph that we see in Dumbledore's expression after the battle in the cemetery in *Harry Potter and the Goblet of Fire*, there was endless speculation as to what it would mean in the future of the series, and whether it wold have any effect on the Wizarding War that would follow on Voldemort's return. Some readers may be dismayed at the size of the effect that the eventual revelation has; it seems a lot to go through for a momentary hesitation. However, that one hesitation is likely all that allowed Harry to defeat Pettigrew.

It is interesting also to note that Harry does not actually kill Pettigrew. Pettigrew's death is a reaction to his own attempt to kill, or at least, disable Harry, coupled with Voldemort's distrust of his own lieutenant. This will turn out to be something of a pattern for Harry; he will disable several Death Eaters, but will kill none of them, despite being counseled to by Lupin.

Prefects

Location: Hogwarts
Time Period: throughout the series
Important Characters: Percy Weasley, Penelope Clearwater, Ron Weasley, Hermione Granger, Draco Malfoy

OVERVIEW

Prefects are not, strictly speaking, magical. They are an integral part of the power structure of any school run on the English model; a Prefect is a member of the student body who is deemed more responsible than other students, and as such is given additional powers (the ability to give detentions, for instance) and additional responsibilities (prefects are called upon to aid the teachers in patrolling the halls in a few cases).

Event Details Specific tasks and privileges are accorded to Prefects in the Harry Potter books. On the journey to Hogwarts on the Hogwarts Express, prefects have a special compartment at the head of the train; they are expected to gather there at the start of the trip, to receive instructions presumably, and then periodically patrol the corridors of the train to keep the rowdiness down. While they are also presumably expected to do the same during the return trip, no mention is made of this in any of the books, even by Hermione, who at all other times is punctilious about her duties. Prefects are charged with maintaining order in the common rooms as well as in the hallways of the castle, and are also responsible for making sure the lower grades learn their way around the castle in the early part of the year. One privilege of being a Prefect is that you have access to the Prefect's bathroom, as Harry finds out in *Harry Potter and the Goblet of Fire*.

In *Harry Potter and the Philosopher's Stone*, Percy Weasley has just been made Prefect, and is inordinately proud of his shiny new Prefect's badge. His (apparently pre-existing) pomposity is increased significantly by this recognition of his "superiority" over the rest of his year group. In *Harry Potter and the Chamber of Secrets*, Percy is spotted reading a book entitled *Prefects who Gained Power*, "a study of Hogwarts prefects and their later careers." In *Harry Potter and the Chamber of Secrets*, we learn that Percy's girlfriend, Penelope Clearwater, is also a prefect, albeit in Ravenclaw House.

In *Harry Potter and the Order of the Phoenix*, Ron Weasley is appointed Prefect for Gryffindor, much to the amazement of everyone; it had been thought that Harry would be tipped for that job. Of course, nobody is surprised that Hermione Granger becomes a Prefect as well, and there is equally little amazement at the selection of Draco Malfoy for Slytherin House. Other prefects appointed at the same time are Pansy Parkinson from Slytherin, Ernie Macmillan and Hannah Abbott from Hufflepuff, and Anthony Goldstein and Padma Patil from Ravenclaw.

It is mentioned in *Harry Potter and the Order of the Phoenix* that Remus Lupin had been a prefect at Hogwarts when he, Sirius Black, and Harry's father had been there. We also see, in *Harry Potter and the Deathly Hallows*, that Lucius Malfoy was a Slytherin Prefect when Severus Snape, James Potter, Remus Lupin, and Sirius Black first arrived at Hogwarts.

In *Harry Potter and the Half-Blood Prince*, Dumbledore mentions that Tom Riddle was also a Prefect.

Notable Consequences Percy has just become a Prefect when we first meet him in *Harry Potter and the Philosopher's Stone*, so we cannot easily judge what he was like before he became a Prefect. From the reaction later when he became Head Boy, one can extrapolate that he was always pompous and always a little ashamed of his family's lack of ambition; his becoming Prefect is part of the process that ends up with him being estranged from his family by Harry's fifth year.

In *Harry Potter and the Order of the Phoenix*, Hermione becomes a prefect, to nobody's surprise. What is a surprise is that Harry is passed over in favour of Ron for the position. Ron's being made a prefect threatens to destroy the friendship between him and Harry, as Harry shares the general feeling that the position *ought* to have gone to Harry; in the end, though, Harry resolves to make the best of it, and their friendship goes on pretty much as before. Harry's feelings about this office having gone to Ron are somewhat eased by the revelation that Harry's father was passed over for Prefect in his day as well, that "honor" instead going to Remus Lupin. This issue is not completely resolved until the end of the book, however; in his interview with Professor Dumbledore after the Battle at the Department of Mysteries, Dumbledore explains why he had passed over Harry for the position: "I must confess . . . that I rather thought . . . you had enough responsibility to be going on with."

ANALYSIS

Ron and Hermione's approach to the office of Prefect shows the two sides of the appointment. Both are extremely glad to get selected, of course; but Ron makes extensive use of the privileges, bossing the younger kids around, where Hermione is greatly taken up with the responsibilities, trying to keep the common room in order (and being thwarted at every turn by the Weasley twins). Malfoy's prefect style is an almost grotesque increase in ugliness over Ron's; he is not ashamed to use his powers to get anything he wants for himself. What little we see of Malfoy's tenure as Prefect simply screams "Abuse of Power." On the other hand, Percy's stuffiness as a prefect is equally as extreme, but in the opposite direction; Percy's natural pompousness seems to expand into an over-inflated sense of his own importance in the scheme of things.

The dynamic of the story requires, in *Harry Potter and the Chamber of Secrets*, that Percy should have some secret that he prefers Ginny not reveal. The obvious one would be that Percy has a girlfriend, which turns out to be Penelope Clearwater. When she gets Petrified, there has to be a reason that Percy gets distraught, other than the fact that she is his girlfriend, to keep that secret concealed for a few more weeks; the author uses Percy's apparent belief in Prefect invulnerability (as put forward by George Weasley) as explanation for his dismay. There is some question as to whether prefects are allowed to dock house points. In *Harry Potter and the Order of the Phoenix*, Ron seems to believe that prefects cannot dock house points; Draco Malfoy agrees, but then goes on to say that members of the Inquisitorial Squad, specially appointed by the High Inquisitor Dolores Umbridge can, and then goes on to do that. In *Harry Potter and the Chamber of Secrets*, Percy does dock House points from Gryffindor, and he is only a prefect at that point. While the author has stated[1] that Percy was more likely right than Ron was, it is equally likely that Percy in fact was overstepping his authority, and though he said he was removing house points from Gryffindor, his statement had no real effect.

QUESTIONS

1. Would you have chosen Percy for prefect? Why?
2. Would you have chosen Harry for prefect? Why?
3. Professor Dumbledore's comments at the end of *Harry Potter and the Order of the Phoenix* lead us to believe that he has at least some control over appointment of prefects. Why do you think he allowed Draco Malfoy to be appointed a prefect?

Quidditch

Location: Hogwarts
Time Period: Throughout the series
Important Characters: House Quidditch teams

OVERVIEW

Quidditch is the main sport of the wizarding community. It is followed by wizards in much the same way that football (soccer) is followed by Muggles. Harry initially compares it to basketball on broomsticks with three hoops. It is a fast-paced, dangerous game played by two teams with seven members each and officiated by one referee. Typically there are no player substitutions allowed in the course of the game.

Event Details Note that in the books, this is not so much a single event as an ongoing background that periodically breaks out into a competition. Harry plays in the Gryffindor Quidditch team as Seeker from year 1 (*Harry Potter and the Philosopher's Stone*) to year 6 (*Harry Potter and the Half-Blood Prince*). Draco Malfoy plays opposite him on the Slytherin team, starting with year 2 (*Harry Potter and the Chamber of Secrets*). (Though Draco is nominally Seeker in *Harry Potter and the Half-Blood Prince*, he seems to be doing something else when Quidditch is being played.) Quidditch is canceled in the middle of Year 2 (*Harry Potter and the Chamber of Secrets*) because Hermione Granger and Penelope Clearwater are attacked, and Quidditch is deemed too risky an activity. Apart from the Quidditch World Cup, there is no Quidditch in year four (*Harry Potter and the Goblet of Fire*) because of the Triwizard Tournament; Harry is unable to play in the last match of Year 1 (*Harry Potter and the Philosopher's Stone*) because he is unconscious in the hospital wing, or in most of the matches in year five (*Harry Potter and the Order of the Phoenix*) because Professor Umbridge has ordered his broom confiscated after the first game, or in the last match of Year 6 (*Harry Potter and the Half-Blood Prince*) because he is serving detention with Professor Snape. In years 5 and 6, when Harry is not available, Ginny Weasley is Seeker for Gryffindor. Ron is Keeper for Gryffindor in years 5 and 6; Oliver Wood in years 1 through 3.

Quidditch Players A Quidditch team is made up of seven members.
• 3 Chasers—their job is to score goals. Their responsibility is passing the Quaffle amongst themselves so as to be able to throw it through one of the adversaries' three hoops (or goal posts) in the field, while trying to keep it out of the hands of the opposing team's Chasers. A goal is worth 10 points.
• 1 Keeper—Stationed at their team's goalpost, his job is to guard the goal posts and keep the opposite team from scoring.
• 2 Beaters—their job is to protect their team, including themselves, from the Bludgers, and to hit the Bludgers into their rivals. They use a small bat, like the bat in Rounders, or a small baseball bat, to hit the Bludgers.
• 1 Seeker—his job is to catch the small Golden Snitch before the rival team's Seeker catches it. When the Golden Snitch is caught, the game is finished; catching the Snitch is worth one hundred and fifty points. Seekers "are usually the smallest and fastest" members of the team "and most serious Quidditch accidents seemed to happen to them."

Quidditch Equipment • Broomsticks (7 per side)—the best one should go, if possible, to the Seeker
• Quaffle (1)—"a bright red ball about the size of a soccer ball; the chasers throw the Quaffle to each other and try and get it through one of the hoops to score a goal. Ten points every time the Quaffle goes through one of the hoops."
• Bludgers (2)—"two identical balls, jet black and slightly smaller than the red Quaffle. Rocket around, trying to knock players off their brooms."
• Golden Snitch (1)—"was tiny, about the size of a large walnut. It was bright gold and had little fluttering silver wings. It's the most important ball of the lot. It's very hard to catch because it's so fast and difficult to see."
• Bats (2 per side)—used by the Beaters to knock Bludgers away from their team and into their opponents.

---

1. http://www.dictionary.com, 3 June 2007, definition 5 (http://dictionary.reference.com/browse/weigh)

Rules
- played on broomsticks in the air;
- the game ends only when the Golden Snitch is "caught, so it can go on for ages";
- substitutions are seldom allowed; when one World Cup match went on for several weeks, it was worthy of comment that they had to get substitutes so that the players could get some rest;
- there are seven hundred ways to foul in the game "and all of them had happened during a World Cup match in 1473"; a foul is answered with a penalty shot by the fouled player or by one of the Chasers.

Professional Teams Much like with Muggle sports, there are professional regional teams, and the best players of the regional teams are then tapped for the national team. We are told that the English national team were eliminated from the World Cup by Transylvania in *Harry Potter and the Goblet of Fire*, and that Scotland had lost to Luxembourg, and Wales to Uganda, in that year's World Cup competition. This leaves Ireland to defend the honour of the British Isles against Romania, which it does quite ably. It is interesting to note that the national boundaries for Quidditch do not follow modern political lines.

The book *Quidditch Through the Ages* by "Kennilworthy Whisp" mentions that there are 13 regional teams in Britain and Ireland. Of these, mention in the main books is made of the following four:
- The *Chudley Cannons*, Ron's favorite team. Ron bemoans their standing, last in the league, and the bad decisions made by their management in trading players. Professor Dumbledore actually mentions their dismal prospects once as well.
- The *Holyhead Harpies*, famous for always fielding a team made up entirely of witches. Professor Slughorn mentions that one of his ex-students is on that team, and she is present at the Slug Club Christmas party, though Harry does not see her. In a post-publication interview, the author said that Ginny Weasley played for the Harpies after graduation.
- *Puddlemere United* is the team that Oliver Wood plays for after graduation.
- The *Wimbourne Wasps* fielded Ludo Bagman as a Beater, arguably the best Beater they had ever had, and Ludo keeps hearkening back to his days on the team, even wearing his old Quidditch robes to the Quidditch World Cup.

Notable Consequences From the beginning, Harry feels as if he is something of a fraud. *The Boy Who Lived*—yes, he's famous, but not through anything he had done himself, really; yes, he lived, and Lord Voldemort vanished, but it wasn't anything he had done, he was simply there when all this magic flowed around him, and since then he had lived in an environment where the magic was suppressed, even beaten out of him. He felt, from the beginning, intimidated both by wizards' children like Ron, who had grown up with magic as a matter of course, and Hermione, as Muggleborn as Harry himself, but who had, upon learning that she was a witch, promptly purchased and read all of the first-year textbooks and several others besides, with her parents' support. And he discovers flying, which he can do well, and it is good; and then he discovers that he is an excellent Seeker, and he becomes the star and the center of the house Quidditch team, and it is a source of confidence to him. It also is a tie back to his father, who was equally an excellent Quidditch player in his days at Hogwarts.

It is through Quidditch that Harry achieves some of his greatest victories, winning the Quidditch Cup in his third year, coming to the notice of Cho Chang in that same year, and coaching the Gryffindor team to another victory in his sixth year. Ron, in the same way, sees benefits from his Quidditch experience: starting off as a poor player ("the best of a bad lot" according to then-Captain Angelina Johnson), Ron gains the confidence he needs to tend goal properly. This confidence will show up again in later books.

ANALYSIS

The scoring of Quidditch matches may seem unbalanced since the 150 points from catching the Snitch often overwhelms the 10 points per goal, but it is arguably considerably harder to catch the Snitch than to score a goal with the Quaffle. Quidditch at the school is played in series, so that each point counts toward ultimate victory. There have been matches where Harry (or his replacement Seeker Ginny Weasley, in *Harry Potter and the Half-Blood Prince*) waited until Gryffindor was ahead by a certain number of goals so that when he caught the Snitch, Gryffindor would have enough overall points to win the House Cup.

There are several unanswered questions about Quidditch matches. One of the big ones has to do with the Bludgers. They are bewitched to go after the players, but what stops them? Even when play is stopped, for a penalty or conference, the bludgers must go on trying to hit the players. Thus in theory, a penalty shot could be disrupted by a bludger, or a bludger could disable the referee, and the Beaters can never take a break, they have to be tracking the Bludgers until they are safely returned to the crate at the end of the game.

GREATER PICTURE

While it is not too surprising that Harry's identity is somewhat defined by his abilities at Quidditch—he recognizes that a thing he is good at is flying, and this is reinforced in *Harry Potter and the Goblet of Fire*, first by Professor Moody pointing it out to him in the lead-in to the First Task of the Triwizard Tournament, and then by Ludo Bagman's fulsome compliments in the commentating for that event. One wonders, then, why Harry does not follow Quidditch in the *Daily Prophet*, tossing away *Prophets* after glancing at the front page, throughout the summer before his fifth year, and why he does not seem to miss Quidditch during his seventh year. It is possible that Quidditch is primarily a means by which he can get more flying time. Once his Firebolt is destroyed, it is possible that he simply sets aside his hopes of flying until his job, the destruction of Voldemort, is done.

Quidditch captain

Location: Hogwarts
Time Period: throughout the series
Important Characters: Oliver Wood, Angelina Johnson, Harry Potter, Cedric Diggory, Marcus Flint

Overview

The House Quidditch Team Captain is in charge of selecting the players for the Quidditch team, setting practices, and coaching them in the necessary maneuvers to guide them, hopefully, to win the Hogwarts Quidditch Cup.

Event Details There is no description of how the Captain of the house Quidditch team is selected. It would appear to be a selection made by the head of the House, presumably from among the returning team members; while it would be logical to select the most senior returning team member, this is not how the selection is made, because Katie Bell is one year senior to Harry, and yet Harry is selected as team captain in his sixth year, while Katie is in her seventh year. In Gryffindor house, the Quidditch team captain for the first three years is Oliver Wood. There is no Quidditch in the fourth year because of the Triwizard Tournament; in the fifth year it is Angelina Johnson, and in the sixth year it is Harry Potter. Marcus Flint is captain of the Slytherin Quidditch team for the first three years; Cedric Diggory is captain of the Hufflepuff team in Harry's third year.

As Quidditch captain, Harry has a great deal more work to do than either of his predecessors. In *Harry Potter and the Order of the Phoenix*, because of the ongoing battle with Professor Umbridge, Harry was banned from the Quidditch team along with Fred and George Weasley; so Angelina did have to engineer a mid-season replacement for her Seeker and both Beaters. But in *Harry Potter and the Half-Blood Prince*, so many players are incapacitated or are unable to play due to detention or other concerns that both Slytherin and Gryffindor seem to field a substantially different team for every match.

Notable Consequences As Quidditch Captain, Harry is called upon to create a Quidditch team. He has a few experienced players to draw from; Katie Bell, who was on the team as Chaser when Harry first started playing as Seeker (making her only a second-year student at the time), Ron, who had played as Keeper the previous year, and Ginny Weasley, who had filled in as Seeker while Harry was banned in the previous year, are kept on, along with himself as Seeker, but the previous year's Beaters are replaced, and a new Chaser is brought in. However, this is not a static team; over the course of the year, players are injured (Katie Bell is Jinxed, Ron is poisoned, Harry himself is injured mid-game, and later put on detention) and Harry must repeatedly juggle the roster to be sure of fielding a full team. It is during this time that Harry begins to understand how Angelina Johnson, and before her Oliver Wood, had felt about their duties as Quidditch Captain. Harry finds that it is taking a significant part of his time and attention, but finds consolation in that as Captain, he can schedule practices when he wishes so as to avoid the "Slug Club" parties put on by Professor Slughorn. Late in the year, he also finds that practicing alongside Ginny can be quite exhilarating.

Analysis

In *Harry Potter and the Half-Blood Prince*, we are told that many of the privileges granted to Prefects are also granted to the Quidditch captain. One question that arises is exactly which of the Prefects' privileges are granted to the Quidditch captain, and why? The only one that is actually mentioned is that the Quidditch captain can use the Prefect's bathroom. It is entirely possible that this is intended as explanation of how Cedric Diggory is able to tell Harry about the Prefect's bathroom in *Harry Potter and the Goblet of Fire*; there is no mention that Cedric is a Prefect, only that he is Captain of Quidditch, and Cedric being a prefect is certainly something that Cedric's father Amos would have mentioned.

Greater Picture

There does not seem to be any particular significance to Harry's being made Quidditch captain. Presumably, he was the only logical choice for the position, as he had been considered good enough in his year to be considered for the position of Prefect, but had been passed over because he "had enough responsibility to be going on with." As the Quidditch Captain receives all the privileges of the Prefects, but with less responsibility (fielding a team and coaching it to play well), it is perhaps the case that this position was given to Harry as something of a reward. Once Harry leaves school, he does not seem to re-enter the world of Quidditch as a sport. The same cannot be said for Oliver Wood, who apparently is picked up by a professional team (Puddlemere United) on graduation, or Ginny Weasley, who, we are told, plays professionally for a while after she and Harry are married. Whether these two are selected by professional teams because of their captaincy is unknown.

Quidditch World Cup

Location: specially-built coliseum in an undisclosed location in England
Time Period: midsummer before *Harry Potter and the Goblet of Fire*
Important Characters: Bulgaria and Ireland national teams

Overview

The 422nd Quidditch World Cup Final takes place in August immediately before Harry's fourth school year, in the opening chapters of *Harry Potter and the Goblet of Fire*. An international competition, this attracts wizards from all over the world to witness the match between Ireland and Bulgaria. At the end of the match, a riot breaks out, and there is indication that we are seeing a resurgence of Dark wizardry with the reappearance of the Dark Mark, Lord Voldemort's signal, after a thirteen-year absence.

Event Details   In order to avoid having a huge number of wizards descend upon the scene at the same time, arrivals at the site of the Quidditch World Championships are staggered, with wizards in the cheap seats, some of them, having to arrive as much as a week ahead of time and camp in fields surrounding the game site both before and after the event. This is an attempt to prevent the surrounding Muggles from getting suspicious, but it is almost completely ineffective; Ministry wizards are perpetually employing memory charms on the local Muggles to keep them unaware of the strange things going on.

The event itself is exciting, as sporting events always are; in this case, although Bulgaria's seeker, Viktor Krum, catches the Snitch, Ireland still manages to win the match. However, it is the riot that occurs in the evening which is the core of the event as far as Harry's history goes.

When the Weasleys, Harry, and Hermione leave their tents to see what the commotion is, they see a group of wizards wearing masked robes, who are parading through the campsite, destroying tents, and suspending the Muggle owners of the campground in the air. Ministry wizards, including Mr. Weasley, plus Bill, Percy, and Charlie, wade into the thick of things to try and rescue the Muggles, while Fred, George, Ginny, Harry, Ron, and Hermione head for the safety of the forest. The twins and Ginny get separated from Harry, Ron, and Hermione when Harry trips over a tree root. While the Trio are in the forest, they hear someone cast the Morsmordre spell, and the Dark Mark appears in the sky. This prompts a number of Ministry wizards to appear and try to Stun everyone in the vicinity, which in this case turns out to be Harry, Ron, and Hermione (who avoid being stunned by falling flat) and Winky the house-elf, part of Barty Crouch Sr.'s household. Winky is found with Harry's wand, which is determined to be the one that had cast the Dark Mark spell. To the amazement of the gathered wizards, Barty Crouch tells Winky that "this means *clothes!*" thus dismissing her from service. Hermione feels that this is very unjust treatment of the elf; everyone else there seems to feel that this is a very harsh punishment for a relatively minor infraction.

Notable Consequences   • Ludo Bagman, who is quite the sportsman, is taking bets on the outcome of the match. Unfortunately he is not much good at determining odds, and does not "lay off" his bets, so when Ireland wins, he ends up owing more money than he has. Much of what happens around him later in the book, and all of his interaction with the Weasley twins, has to do with his trying to recover from that particular bad bet.

• After the match, Ludo seems quite scared and unaware of what is going on around him. It's entirely possible that this is because he is preoccupied with his own financial ruin and schemes to avoid it.

• The twins' bet with Ludo was entirely paid off with Leprechaun gold, with the result that the twins have lost their life savings. They are seen multiple times in the book composing letters to try and get their money out of Ludo, or figuring out ways to corner him.

• Ludo has short-changed the Goblins that he bet with, possibly by slipping them some Leprechaun gold; in order to make good on that bet, Ludo makes another bet, this time betting on Harry to win the Triwizard Tournament.

• To ensure that he is able to win this last bet, Ludo on multiple occasions attempts to assist Harry with preparation for the various tasks. Ultimately, Harry does not accept any of Ludo's assistance.

• When Ludo loses the bet he placed on Harry (by what could be considered a technicality), he goes into hiding; it seems that he again does not have money to pay his gambling debts.

• The events on the night after the Cup inform us that there are still active Death Eaters in the Wizarding population, and suggest that Voldemort is once again gaining strength.

• We are allowed our first glimpse of Winky, whose actions will have such great repercussions throughout this book.

• The story in the Daily Prophet introduces us to Rita Skeeter's writing style, and the Prophet's habit of shading the truth into whatever direction is the most sensational. Until this book, we have seen the Prophet as a straight newspaper; we here start to see, by direct comparison of events as we know they happened and how they were reported, that the Prophet is sensationalist as many of the more lurid Muggle papers.

ANALYSIS

Quidditch, we are told, is the most important sport in the Wizarding world, so clearly there will be a periodic World Championship. The need for the wizards to conceal their existence from the Muggles will likely make it a less-than-annual occurrence, possibly either every four years like our Olympics, or every five years like the Triwizard Tournament. Arthur Weasley being able to receive tickets for this event is something of a coup for him; usually, someone as poorly-off financially as Arthur is would be doomed to the cheap seats and a week camping before and after the event, as Luna Lovegood and her family apparently are. Yet, somehow Arthur has managed to get seats in the top box for ten: himself, his six sons and one daughter, Harry, and Hermione. At the event, Harry sees professional Quidditch for the first time, and begins to understand the difference between the way he is playing, and the way it can be played. While no mention of this is made later, it is possible that Harry's eventual departure from the world of Quidditch is made less bitter by the belief that he cannot play to the standard he has seen. He does learn several Quidditch moves by watching the teams playing, including the Wronski feint, a particular way of convincing the opposing team's Seeker to fly at high speed into the ground.

In recent years, to the outside observer, it has seemed that a necessary part of any major Muggle sporting event is the riot at the end of it. The audience, having had their spirits whipped up by the match, end up rioting either in jubilation at their team's victory, or frustration at its defeat. It seems that England is the hotbed of this sort of behaviour, with many European countries taking steps to limit the visits of "football yobs." Given this background, it is not surprising that a riot would break out at a World Cup match in England. It is a little odd that the main rioters are wearing the sort of robe and mask associated with Death Eaters, as the group will have been trying to remain out of sight for the past thirteen years, since the disappearance of Voldemort, but it is possible that this is the only form of concealment that they have. It is interesting to note that the Death Eaters apparently scatter when the Dark Mark appears in the sky, though as Arthur Weasley later comments, many of them will now be scared of meeting with Voldemort again, as over the past thirteen years they have so thoroughly repudiated all he stood for.

GREATER PICTURE

Over the course of the event we see a number of situations where the Crouch house-elf, Winky, is apparently being forced to do things against her will; at one point, she runs across Harry's path, having some sort of difficulty in doing so. In retrospect, we can see that Barty Crouch Jr., under an Invisibility Cloak, is actually pushing or pulling her. This is the point at which it becomes obvious that Barty Crouch Jr. has completely slipped out of the bonds of magical control that his father has had on him for the past decade or more. Bartemius Crouch Sr. had tasked his house-elf, Winky, with the job of keeping Barty under control, as a safeguard on his use of the Imperius curse (which was fading); and he knows immediately, when the Dark Mark appears and Winky is found Stunned at that location, that Barty has slipped the leash. This is why he dismisses Winky ("This . . . means . . . clothes!") for what seems to the gathered wizards to be a minor offence. Barty has not entirely escaped; knowing what he is looking for, Bartemius has managed to find Barty, Stunned and under his Invisibility Cloak, and has returned him to the Crouch home. While the byplay with Ludo and his betting may seem minor at the time, it appears in later volumes that Ludo defaulting on (or more literally running out on) his gambling debt will greatly increase the friction between Wizards and Goblins. It seems that Ludo's bet was actually with the chief of the Goblins; because of this insult to their chief, the Goblins feel that Ludo's actions somehow reflect badly on all Wizardkind, and their charitable feelings towards Wizards have taken rather a large beating. This would be quite likely to have some effect on whether the Goblins join into the Wizarding War, and on which side they choose to join. It will turn out, in a later book, that Voldemort squanders this potential advantage by meddling in the affairs of Gringotts Bank.

Remus' Death

Location: Hogwarts
Time Period: *Harry Potter and the Deathly Hallows*, May
Important Characters: Presumably Death Eaters

OVERVIEW

At the great Battle of Hogwarts, Remus Lupin is killed in battle.

Event Details When Harry returns to Hogwarts, Neville, who is escorting him from the Hog's Head, has assumed that he is there to liberate Hogwarts from the Death Eaters, and uses the charmed Galleons that Hermione had created, to recall Dumbledore's Army. Presumably, a member of Dumbledore's Army who either was in the Order of the Phoenix, or whose parents were Order members, passed the word, because members of the Order start to appear through the tunnel from the Hog's Head as well. One of the Order members who we see arrive is Lupin. After Harry has returned from Ravenclaw Tower, he finds that Ron and Hermione have left the Room of Requirement, saying something about a bathroom. As the whole school has now been summoned to the Great Hall, Harry heads there to see if he can find them. There, he hears Professor McGonagall sending non-combatant students home. Once only students who are of age are left, Order members at head table start assigning specific areas of defence. Lupin will head up the group that is defending the grounds.

Several times during the battle, Harry looks to the grounds to see if he can see Lupin, but is never successful. After Harry witnesses the death of Snape, Voldemort offers a cease-fire so that Harry can surrender to him and prevent any more loss of life. Harry, returning to the school, looks into the Great Hall and sees Lupin, and his wife Tonks, lying among the dead.

After experiencing Snape's memories, Harry chooses to meet Voldemort, and his fate, in the Forbidden Forest. Finding his way there blocked by Dementors, and being unable to summon a Patronus, Harry uses the Resurrection Stone that Dumbledore had left him, and summons the Shades of Lupin, his godfather Sirius, and his mother and father. He asks if it had hurt to die, and Sirius says that it had not. Lupin adds that "he will want it to be quick," meaning Voldemort.

The shades protect Harry from the Dementors as he walks through the Forest. Reaching the clearing where Voldemort waits, Harry drops the Resurrection Stone, and the shades vanish.

While we are not told this in the book, the author has stated in an interview that Lupin was killed by Antonin Dolohov.

Notable Consequences Lupin's death once again reminds Harry that his is not the only life that is being affected by Voldemort's reign of power. This reaffirms his decision to do whatever he needs to do to eliminate Voldemort.

Lupin's and Tonks' deaths have left their infant son an orphan. Harry must be deeply affected by this, being an orphan himself, and as godfather having no little responsibility for Lupin's child.

Harry is able to summon Lupin's shade by use of the Resurrection Stone, and learns from Lupin that he felt little pain from his death. This somewhat abates Harry's fear at the prospect of dying at Voldemort's hand.

Ron Weasley relationships

Location: Hogwarts
Time Period: Throughout the series
Important Characters: Ron Weasley, Fleur Delacour, Lavender Brown, Hermione Granger

OVERVIEW

Ron Weasley remains unattached for the first three years of the series. He becomes infatuated with Fleur Delacour when she arrives for the Triwizard Tournament in *Harry Potter and the Goblet of Fire*, but she does not reciprocate his feelings. He eventually falls for the advances of Lavender Brown, with whom he has an intensely physical, but ultimately short-lived, relationship, punctuated by a love-potion induced passion for Romilda Vane. When the relationship with Lavender ends, he suddenly discovers his true feelings for Hermione, and by the end of the sixth book, they are a couple. Their relationship matures over the course of *Harry Potter and the Deathly Hallows*, though it is interrupted by Ron's departure near Christmas, and is further strengthened by his return.

Event Details

Philosophers' Stone Ron is largely unattached through this book. He is impressed at times by Hermione's abilities, and he and Harry do join forces to rescue Hermione from a mountain troll, but there is no apparent romantic attachment.

Chamber of Secrets The Monster in the Chamber is being released periodically and is Petrifying students. When Hermione is Petrified, Ron is apparently more deeply affected by seeing her in the Hospital Wing than Harry is. The only thing that affects Ron more deeply in this book is when Ron's sister Ginny is taken into the Chamber.

Prisoner of Azkaban Ron does not seem to show any particular romantic attachment in this book; in fact, for a long stretch he is estranged from Hermione because of the confiscation of Harry's Firebolt, and later because of the apparent death of Scabbers, his pet rat, at the claws of Crookshanks, Hermione's pet cat.

Goblet of Fire Starting with the arrival of the Beauxbatons students at the end of October, Ron finds himself infatuated with Fleur Delacour, a Beauxbatons student and shortly the Beauxbatons Champion in the Triwizard Tournament. When she comes over to the Gryffindor table to ask if they want their bouillabaisse, Ron is almost struck dumb. After she departs, Ron says that she must have some Veela in her ancestry. Hermione is rather nettled by this, and says that nobody else is acting that silly about her, but Harry notices that many other students seem similarly struck by her.

There is also a spot of byplay going on with Viktor Krum, who seems to appear in the library whenever Hermione is there. While this bothers Ron, it is not Viktor himself who is the problem, but the gaggle of girls who seem to follow him about, giggling and hoping for autographs. In fact, at this point, Viktor is still quite a hero to Ron, "the best Seeker in the entire world!"

Matters come to a head at the Yule Ball. Ron asks Fleur to the ball, but Fleur simply ignores him. Shattered, Ron returns to the Gryffindor common room. Harry tells him there that Fleur is one-quarter Veela, and likely had turned on the charm at that moment to snare Roger Davies, but Ron does not seem interested. It suddenly occurs to Ron that he can ask Hermione, but Hermione says that she has already accepted an invitation from someone else. Harry, acting more or less out of desperation, convinces Padma Patil to accompany Ron to the ball. This is not a success; at the ball, Ron basically ignores Padma, either trying to avoid Fleur or glowering at Hermione as she dances with Viktor Krum. When Hermione comes over to talk to Ron and Harry, Ron accuses her of "consorting with the enemy." Hermione stalks off and is lost in the crowd. Ron and Harry then leave the dance floor to walk in the rose garden.

After the dance, Harry finds Ron and Hermione in a shouting match in the Gryffindor common room. Hermione tells Ron that if he does not like it then, "The next time there's a Ball, ask me before someone else does, and not as a last resort!" Hermione storms off to her dormitory. Ron, stunned, tells Harry that Hermione is quite clearly missing the point.

Even though Ron himself does not see it, from this point in the story onwards he is quite plainly jealous of Krum, while still hoping to get attention from Fleur. He glowers at Krum, and tries to keep Hermione out of the library; this is often helped by Krum's admirers, who Hermione finds very irritating as they giggle at the sight of Krum. In the Second Task, the merpeople are holding someone valuable to each of the Champions deep under the lake. When Ron and Harry return to the surface with Gabrielle, Fleur's sister, Fleur is overjoyed; she kisses Harry, and also Ron because he helped. Hermione is somewhat upset by this attention that Ron is getting, but is distracted by something Viktor says to her.

Shortly after this, Rita Skeeter writes a scurrilous article for *Witch Weekly* that suggests Hermione is keeping both Harry and Viktor as lovers. Hermione remarks that she wonders how Rita had known that Viktor had invited her to visit over the summer; Ron becomes very upset at hearing about this invitation.

As the Beauxbatons carriage is getting ready to leave, Fleur comes over to say goodbye to Harry; Ron is once again almost completely tongue-tied in her presence, earning himself a vexed look from Hermione. Ron is still feeling ambivalent about Viktor Krum, but he unbends enough to ask Krum for his autograph before they part.

Order of the Phoenix While Ron does not appear to be involved in any particular relationship, he does seem quite annoyed when he finds out, in mid-September, and then again near Christmas, that Hermione is writing long letters to Viktor Krum. Again, Hermione, Harry, and the readers can quite easily see Ron's jealousy, even though Ron appears quite unaware of it himself.

As Ron is leaving breakfast for the Quidditch pitch, on the morning of his first-ever Quidditch match, Hermione kisses him on the cheek. Ron seems bemused by this, rubbing the spot on his cheek as he leaves the Great Hall.

Half-Blood Prince Ron is mildly miffed that Hermione, explaining to Harry that he is now once again something of a catch, does not seem to extend the same analysis to him also. Ron is, however, a prefect, which does make him something of a catch, and Lavender Brown does seem to be laughing excessively at his jokes at one point.

Harry and Ron, taking a short cut after Quidditch practice, run into Ginny snogging with Dean Thomas in the hall. Ron blows up at Dean, and Ginny accuses him of being jealous as he has only ever been kissed by Auntie Muriel. She says that Harry and Cho have been snogging, as have Hermione and Viktor Krum, and accuses Ron of being jealous because he's the only one who doesn't have anyone to snog with. Quite likely in reaction to this accusation, Ron starts responding to the advances of Lavender Brown. This is the start of an intensely physical relationship between Lavender and Ron. Harry compares the pair of them to a vertical wrestling match, and on another occasion wonders which of several hands he can see belongs to whom.

As intense as this relationship is, it is not without problems. At one point, Ron and Lavender seek an empty classroom to snog in. The room they find first is already occupied by Hermione, who had avoided the common room so she wouldn't have to see the two of them at it, and Harry, who wants to talk to her about it. Lavender immediately backs out, but Ron stays to speak with Hermione, and is rewarded by being attacked by a flock of birds. At Christmas, Lavender sends Ron a necklace with gold letters that spells out "My Sweetheart." Ron is revolted, and wonders how she could have ever thought he would like that.

Returning to the school after Christmas, Ron does not seem particularly pleased at the prospect of reuniting with Lavender. He is barely within the Common Room when she has greeted him with a cry of "Won-won!" and dragged him off to a corner. Hermione is wryly amused by this.

On his birthday, Ron finds a carton of chocolate cauldrons that had been given to Harry, and that Harry had set aside as being possibly spiked with love potion. Eating two of them, he becomes instantly infatuated with Romilda Vane. Harry takes him off to Professor Slughorn to get the potion reversed, in the process brushing past Lavender. Ron tells Lavender with great excitement that Harry is taking him to meet Romilda. Having cured him of the potion, Slughorn opens a bottle of mead to offer a birthday toast; the mead is poisoned, and Ron, saved by fast action on Harry's part, ends up in the Hospital Wing. Hermione stays by his bedside for most of his first day there. It is noteworthy that, having been silent all day, she finally answers a question, and Ron immediately says her name, and settles into an apparently less troubled sleep.

Lavender later corners Harry and asks if he knows why Ron always seems to be sleeping when Lavender visits him. When Harry later asks him about this, Ron admits to feigning sleep so that he won't have to resume his relationship with her. When Ron is released from the hospital wing, Lavender is upset that she had not been told, and that Ron is talking to Hermione.

Hermione, angry at Ron, had been refusing to help him with his homework. When she finally relents, as it seems Ron's spell-checking quill has started making bizarre misspellings, Ron, with a sigh of relief, says he loves her. Hermione says Ron had better not let Lavender hear that. Ron replies that maybe he should, he has been looking for an excuse to break up with Lavender.

Harry, meanwhile, has been thinking about the vial of Felix Felicis tucked away in his trunk. He has been considering using it in the hopes of getting a love interest better matched to Ron, as well as a girlfriend for himself. Finally, having been given a mission to retrieve a memory from Professor Slughorn, Harry uses the Felix Felicis potion to make himself lucky. He, Hermione, and Ron return to the Common Room, but as Harry is under his Invisibility Cloak, Lavender can only see Hermione and Ron, and demands to know what the two of them have been doing up in the boys' dormitory.

This seems to be the precipitating incident that causes Lavender and Ron to break up. Ron, now no longer encumbered, notices Hermione, and over the next short while, they quietly become romantically entangled. There is something of a double date atmosphere about an episode with Ron, Hermione, Harry, and Ginny. And at Dumbledore's funeral, Harry notices that Ron and Hermione are sitting side by side, comforting each other.

Deathly Hallows On Harry's birthday, Ron gives him a book entitled *Twelve Foolproof Ways to Charm Witches*, saying he had gotten a copy from Fred and George earlier, and that Harry must keep it secret from Hermione. Watching Ron later, Harry comes to the conclusion that Ron is definitely using this book in his interactions with Hermione, and with his mother as well.

While Hermione and Ron do not seem much closer than they have ever been, there are a few tell-tale signs that they are romantically entangled. When they escape to Grimmauld Place, Hermione chooses to sleep beside Ron. After the escape from the Ministry, Hermione is extremely worried about Ron, who has gotten Splinched. However, this is all fairly low-key until shortly before Christmas. Ron, fed up with the privations of living rough and suddenly becoming aware that Harry does not have a plan, leaves the group. With Harry's concurrence, Hermione does not shift the campsite until as late in the day as she can manage, and then, knowing that Ron now cannot find them, weeps helplessly while Harry sets the defensive spells and pitches the tent.

When Ron returns some weeks later, Harry gives him the job of destroying the locket Horcrux, as he has retrieved the Sword of Gryffindor. In order to try and preserve itself, the Horcrux creates images of Harry and Hermione, and plays scenes of Harry and Hermione bad-mouthing Ron and kissing each other. Despite Harry's fear that Ron would turn on him, Ron instead destroys the Horcrux. When he and Harry then return to the tent, Hermione attacks Ron angrily, and refuses to listen to his story. He relates his story to Harry, however, and Hermione seems to accept it to a certain extent. Over the next while, Harry believes that Ron is quite deliberately taking Hermione's side in any disagreement.

When the Trio are trapped in Malfoy Manor, Bellatrix Lestrange singles out Hermione and tortures her to force her to reveal where she got the Sword of Gryffindor. While Hermione repeats that she had found it in the forest, Ron is almost sick with worry. It is perhaps worth mention that Ron carries Hermione to Shell Cottage. After arriving at Hogwarts, Ron and Hermione vanish. We find later that Ron, having memorized the sound that Harry made to open the locket, has opened the Chamber of Secrets, and he and Hermione have retrieved several Basilisk fangs. Hermione has used one of them to destroy the cup Horcrux. Ron now suggests that they should go to the kitchens and warn the House-elves that a war is coming so that they can escape to safety. Dropping her Basilisk fangs on the floor, Hermione sweeps Ron into a fierce embrace.

Ron and Hermione fight side by side through the ensuing battles.

In the Epilogue, we see that Ron and Hermione have married, and now seem to have two children, Rose and Hugo.

Notable Consequences Ron's infatuation with Lavender causes an almost year-long estrangement between Ron and Hermione. Ron does not seem to completely understand why this is happening. Harry does understand it, and with his insight into how rocky the relationship between Ron and Lavender is, occasionally tries to smooth things over between Ron and Hermione. One notable attempt ends with Hermione sending a flock of conjured birds to attack Ron.

When Ron departs and cannot find his way back to Hermione, the experience seems to change him. When he does finally return, he seems more secure in himself, more self-assured. We see him making a conscious effort to placate Hermione. During his absence, he seems to have recognized, first that he truly misses Hermione when they are apart, and second that he has rather seriously wronged Hermione.

The eventual marriage of Ron and Hermione is, of course, a notable consequence as well.

ANALYSIS

In pretty much every way, Ron's development is standard as far as his relationship goes. He is clearly somewhat immature relative to Harry and Hermione, and this lack of maturity does frustrate both Hermione and Harry in the first few books of the series. It is only after Ron is forced to live apart from Hermione, with Hermione quite likely in danger, that Ron gains the maturity to be able to deal with the relationship. Until that point, it seems that Ron's romantic life had been purely driven by others, despite the underlying and unacknowledged affection for Hermione. In particular, his infatuation with Fleur Delacour is driven by her Veela ancestry, and the affair with Lavender, started by Lavender herself, is triggered by the quarrel with Ginny, and maintained by Lavender almost exclusively. It is perhaps apparent, particularly in her choice of Christmas present, that Lavender has created an image of Ron and is in love with that image, rather than with the actual person; Lavender has taken no time to learn what Ron likes and dislikes. It is only when that relationship is luckily terminated that Ron finally starts a relationship on a more equal footing, though it is Hermione driving the relationship at that point.

Despite Ron's becoming more mature in the latter half of *Harry Potter and the Deathly Hallows*, one does question exactly how mature Ron is when we see in the Epilogue that he had to Confund a Muggle driving instructor in order to get his license. This use of magic to avoid consequences of one's actions does indicate a certain lack of maturity even almost twenty years after the end of the story. The happiness apparent in the epilogue, as he jokes numerous times with Hermione, his wife, shows that he is content with his relationship.

Second Task

Location: Hogwarts, the lake
Time Period: *Harry Potter and the Goblet of Fire*, 24 February
Important Characters: Harry, Cedric Diggory, Viktor Krum, Fleur Delacour, Ron, Hermione, Cho Chang, Gabrielle Delacour

OVERVIEW

The Second Task of the Triwizard Tournament is to rescue something dear or important to the Champion which is being held by Merpeople deep in Hogwarts' lake.

Event Details The golden egg, which the Champions had each retrieved from the dragons in the First Task, held a clue for the next one, although it contained nothing physical within; instead, when opened, it emitted a screeching, unintelligible sound that was actually a song sung by Merpeople. The champion had to decipher the song's meaning, then find a way to complete the task described in it.

The correct way to decipher the egg is to open and listen to it underwater; the merpeople have high, thin, and screechy voices, making the egg's song incomprehensible when listend to in air. Submerging the egg deepens the sound to where it can be understood. Harry had tried all sorts of things to understand this clue, including, in a fit of pique, throwing it across the room;

it was only the hint that he received from Cedric, who told him to take a bath, that allowed him to discover the secret.

According to the song in the Egg, Harry would have only one hour to rescue something dear to him that would be held deep beneath the lake at Hogwarts by the merpeople. Harry, Hermione, and Ron spent pretty much all of their spare time, from the time Harry deciphered the egg, until the night before the Task, in the library looking for ways Harry could breathe underwater for an hour. When Hermione and Ron are called away, Harry continues his search, eventually falling asleep in the library. He is awakened by Dobby, with only ten minutes to go before the Task. Dobby has overheard some teachers talking about the Task, and has brought Harry some Gillyweed, that will allow him to breathe underwater. Harry hopes that Dobby is correct, and runs off down to the lake shore. There, he is somewhat startled to find that Percy is once again filling in for Mr. Crouch.

It turned out that the "something dear to him" for each of the champions was another person. This was why Hermione and Ron had left Harry alone in the library; Professor McGonagall had brought them to her office so that they could be placed in an enchanted sleep and handed over to the Merpeople.

People Rescued by the Champions • Gabrielle Delacour for Fleur Delacour (used Bubble-Head Charm)
• Cho Chang for Cedric Diggory (also used Bubble-Head Charm)
• Ron Weasley for Harry Potter (used gillyweed, which transformed him by developing gills, and flippers in his feet and hands)
• Hermione Granger for Viktor Krum (used incomplete form of Transfiguration)

Fleur Delacour failed to finish the second task because she was attacked by the grindylows. Because Delacour failed to finish, she never retrieved her younger sister, Gabrielle. Harry, who reached the hostages first, possibly due to some assistance from Moaning Myrtle, was afraid that the song was literal truth, and that the hostages would not be returned if they were not rescued within the allotted hour. He attempted to save all of the hostages, and was prevented from doing so by the Merpeople. Cedric, and then Krum, arrive and retrieve their hostages, but when Fleur failed to show, Harry threatened the Merpeople with his wand, and retrieved Gabrielle in addition to Ron. Harry's choosing to try and save the other hostages earned him extra points from the judges for "moral fiber." Final scores, out of 50, for this Task were assigned as follows:
• Fleur Delacour—25 points
• Cedric Diggory—47 points (he had started this Task with 38 points, ending it tied with Harry for first, with 85)
• Harry Potter—45 points (he had started with 40 points, ending tied with Diggory for first with 85 points)
• Viktor Krum—40 points (he had started with 40 points, ending in second place with 80)

Notable Consequences The Champion with the highest standing after the second task, is allowed to enter the Third Task maze first. Harry and Cedric, having the highest standings, enter the maze together before the other Champions. Harry's decent showing and ethical behaviour in this Challenge lead the other Champions to believe that Harry is, in fact, a worthy contender. It is certainly true that he has held on to the tie for first place, which no other Champion has managed.

Fleur kissing Harry and Ron somewhat re-inforces Ron's infatuation, and upsets Hermione. It is possible that this contributes to Krum's belief that Harry and Hermione are a couple; it is entirely possible that he believes it is Fleur kissing Harry that Hermione is scowling at, rather than her kissing Ron.

The fact that Hermione is the hostage that Krum is to rescue does rather point up that Krum has romantic intentions towards Hermione, and not just friendship. We can also see, by her reaction after the Challenge, that she does not share those feelings.

We see again how Harry's friendships act to save him from the situations he gets himself into. In the next book, he will protest that every time he has gotten into a sticky situation, it is only by means of help from his friends that he has been able to survive. This is true in this Task as well, where it is only the last-minute effort by Dobby that gives Harry any chance at this Task at all.

ANALYSIS

While each task is designed to measure a champion's physical capabilities, it is also meant to test their magical ingenuity, problem-solving skills, and strategic abilities. Harry actually did little to prepare for the second challenge, eventually relying on others for help, although most likely so did the other champions. With some assistance from Professor Moody, Harry was resourceful in retrieving the dragon's egg in the first task, but he made few attempts to decipher its hidden meaning; a necessity for completing the second challege. Cedric Diggory finally provides Harry a hint to solve it, only to learn there is yet another step he must overcome. He again procrastinates to find a solution, and it is only because Dobby helps him minutes before the event begins that he is able to compete.

QUESTIONS

1. Viktor's and Cedric's hostages are their respective love interests; Harry's is Ron; Fleur's is her younger sister. What does this tell us about the Champions?

Sirius' Death

Location: Department of Mysteries, Ministry of Magic

Time Period: *Harry Potter and the Order of the Phoenix*, June

Important Characters: Bellatrix Lestrange Sirius Black

Overview

Lord Voldemort implants a false vision into Harry's mind to trick Harry into believing Sirius is being tortured at the Department of Mysteries within the Ministry of Magic. Despite Hermione's warnings that the vision may be false and leading him into a trap, Harry, accompanied by Ron, Hermione, Ginny, Neville, and Luna Lovegood, rushes to London. Inside the Department of Mysteries, the group is ambushed by Death Eaters. The students fight for their lives and are nearly defeated when Order of the Phoenix reinforcements, including Sirius, arrive to help.

As a battle ensues, Sirius faces off with his Death Eater cousin, Bellatrix Lestrange, in a room containing a raised stone dais in the center of a sunken pit. Upon the dais is a stone archway, covered with a tattered black veil. Sirius is hit by Bellatrix's curse, and his stunned body arcs into the air and floats through the archway, disappearing behind the veil. Harry expects Sirius to reappear on the other side, but he never does. Harry attempts to go after him but is restrained by Remus Lupin, who tells him Sirius is dead. Harry is forced to admit that his godfather is gone.

Event Details   Exhausted from studying for O.W.L. exams, Harry falls asleep during his History of Magic exam. He dreams that Voldemort is in the Ministry of Magic, where he is torturing Sirius Black. Having previously had similar dreams that contained real events, Harry concludes that this dream, also, is real, and demands that Hermione and Ron assist him in rescuing Sirius. Hermione suggests that Voldemort could be setting a trap for Harry, and Harry decides to use the Floo network to see if Sirius is still at Headquarters.

Harry breaks in to Professor Umbridge's office to use her fireplace, the only one unmonitored by the Ministry. There, he talks to the House-Elf, Kreacher, who says that Sirius will never return from the Department of Mysteries. Immediately after this, he is caught by Umbridge, along with Ron, Hermione, Luna Lovegood and Ginny, who had volunteered to help distract Umbridge and the students, and Neville, who was simply in the wrong place at the wrong time.

Umbridge summons Professor Snape to provide Veritaserum to determine who Harry was talking to; Snape refuses. Harry, remembering that Snape is a member of the Order of the Phoenix, tries to pass a message to him, but does not seem to be successful. Hermione convinces Umbridge that Harry had been working with Professor Dumbledore and the students to create a weapon, and leads Harry and Umbridge into the Forbidden Forest. Hermione deliberately leads them into Centaur territory, knowing Umbridge's feelings about "half-breeds." When the Centaurs find them, Umbridge insults and attacks them, and as a result is captured and carried away into the woods. Harry and Hermione narrowly avoid the same fate when Grawp, looking for his half-brother Hagrid, stumbles into the clearing, and invites an attack by the Centaurs.

While they are considering their next move, they are met by the other four students who, having overpowered the Inquisitorial Squad that had been holding them, have followed Harry and Hermione. When Harry insists on going to London to save Sirius, Luna suggests flying there on the school's Thestrals (winged horse-like creatures). Though Harry tries to eliminate some of the students, Thestrals keep arriving; once there are sufficient for all the students, Harry can no longer explain leaving some of them out of the rescue attempt, so all six mount up and fly to London. Entering through the Visitor's entrance to the Ministry, Harry is alarmed to find the watch-wizard inexplicably absent. Following his recurring dreams through the year, Harry leads the group to the Department of Mysteries, and after several false paths, into a large room filled with many wooden shelves containing glass orbs. Reaching the place where he believed he had seen Sirius and Voldemort, he finds nobody there. Ron notices a glass sphere with Harry and Voldemort's name on it. Just as Harry grasps it, Death Eaters, led by Lucius Malfoy, appear, demanding he hand over the sphere. On Harry's silent command, the students blast the shelves, shattering many of the orbs. They run from the Death Eaters, but end up separated. Harry, Hermione, and Neville are attacked by four Death eaters, and Hermione is knocked out, while Neville's wand and nose are broken; in a separate group, Ginny's ankle is broken and Ron is hit with a spell that makes him seem drunk. They re-group, but are attacked again; in the retreat, Ron is attacked by brains floating in a glass tank, and Ginny and Luna are knocked out. Harry tries to make his stand alone in a room with a stone archway containing a veil. Neville, ineffectively trying to help, is quickly captured and tortured by Bellatrix Lestrange. As Harry is on the verge of surrendering the orb, several members of the Order of the Phoenix, including Sirius Black, arrive and start dueling the Death Eaters. Tonks fights with Bellatrix but is injured. Sirius takes on his cousin, taunting her that she can fight better. She casts a powerful curse, blasting him in the chest and sending him through the veiled arch. When he fails to reappear on the other side, Harry realizes Sirius is dead.

Notable Consequences   • Harry chases Bellatrix Lestrange into the Ministry Atrium. In his battle with Bellatrix, he uses the Cruciatus curse. This marks Harry's first time using an Unforgivable Curse.

• Lord Voldemort appears and comes to Bellatrix' assistance. Dumbledore also arrives to protect Harry, and duels directly with Voldemort. Many Ministry wizards, summoned by Dumbledore, arrive in time to see Voldemort in person. This is unequivocal proof that Voldemort has returned, vindicating Dumbledore and Harry. This is expected to result in the Ministry finally taking an active stance against Voldemort.

• Harry blames Dumbledore for Sirius' death and rages at the Headmaster in his office following the battle at the Ministry. However, Harry initially overlooks his own rash behavior and his reluctance to learn Occlumency that allowed Voldemort to penetrate his mind and manipulate him. He also fails to realize that Sirius' unstable mental state and careless actions ultimately contributed to his own death.

• Harry's rage at Dumbledore may be part of what allows Dumbledore to realize his mistake in not telling

Harry what was going on. Dumbledore had simply informed Harry, through Snape, that he was to learn Occlumency, and had not explained why. It is as part of making amends for that, and other omissions, that Dumbledore now, finally, speaks of the Prophecy and what it means to Harry.

ANALYSIS

After Sirius' death, Dumbledore and Harry speak in Dumbledore's office for an entire chapter. During that conversation, we learn much, but by no means all, of the background of the battle that is going on. Dumbledore first explains that the fault for Sirius' death lies with him, as he should have been more forthcoming with Harry as to what was happening, Dumbledore had expected there to be a link between Harry's mind and Voldemort's, caused by the abortive attempt by Voldemort to kill Harry, and he had taken steps to distance himself from Harry, so as to prevent Voldemort from using the bond between them as a weapon against either or both of them. Rather than explaining this, he had sent Snape to teach Harry Occlumency, not realizing that the hatred between Harry and Snape was far too deep to allow instruction in something so complex as Occlumency. Dumbledore also reveals that a prophecy had been made about Harry and Voldemort. Harry has been marked (by Voldemort) to face a final mortal combat with the Dark Lord. This revelation appears to bring Harry and Dumbledore closer. The prophecy's revelation and its effect on Harry hold great importance in the overall picture.

QUESTIONS

1. What does the veiled arch represent?
2. Who is ultimately responsible for Sirius' death? Is more than one person to blame?
3. What was the *whispering* Harry and Luna heard coming from the veil? What could it mean?

GREATER PICTURE

Sirius' death is a huge loss for Harry, and as we will see in the early part of the next book, he reacts by isolating himself. Harry realizes that Voldemort used his godfather to get to him, and he fears his friends will always be in mortal danger as long as Voldemort lives. To protect Ginny, he will attempt to end their budding romantic relationship at the end of *Harry Potter and the Half-Blood Prince*.

We will learn in *Harry Potter and the Deathly Hallows* that the link between Harry and Voldemort is actually a shard of Voldemort's soul that had broken off at Lily Potter's murder and adhered to Harry's soul. Given that the link is something other than the exercise of Legilimency, and that it is in fact attached rather directly to Harry's soul, it is quite possible that Occlumency would have no effect. As Occlumency appears to be intended to prevent another from reading one's mind, and the specific issue we are trying to prevent is another impressing his thoughts in one's mind, it is uncertain whether Occlumency would be the appropriate technique in any case.

Snape's Death

Location: the Shrieking Shack
Time Period: *Harry Potter and the Deathly Hallows*, May
Important Characters: Severus Snape, Lord Voldemort, Nagini, Harry Potter

OVERVIEW

In the belief that the Elder Wand will grant its allegiance only to one who has slain its previous owner, Lord Voldemort has his pet snake, Nagini, kill Severus Snape.

Event Details   Through the confusion of the Battle of Hogwarts, Hermione notices that there does not seem to be any sign of Voldemort. She asks Harry to try and look into his mind, to see where he is. Harry looks into Voldemort's mind, and sees Voldemort ordering a bedraggled-looking Lucius Malfoy to fetch Snape to him. Returning to himself, Harry tells Hermione and Ron that Voldemort is in the Shrieking Shack.

Making their way through the tunnel to the Shrieking Shack, the Trio find their way into the Shack blocked by boxes. Hidden by boxes, they listen (and Harry watches) as Snape reports to Voldemort. Snape seems to be asking permission to enter Hogwarts and fetch Harry out for Voldemort. Voldemort, however, has something else on his mind and summarily dismisses Snape's request. He says that the Elder Wand that he has retrieved from Dumbledore's tomb is a fine wand, but is nothing special. He says that he believes that the wand is not performing to its best ability because it has not yet shifted its allegiance to him. And why not? Because Snape killed Dumbledore, and so the wand currently owes its allegiance to Snape. The wand will not perform its best for Voldemort until Snape is dead. So saying, Voldemort waves his pet snake, Nagini, in her nest of protective spells, into Snape. Nagini immediately bites Snape, who falls. Voldemort and Nagini leave the room; Harry pushes the boxes aside and kneels over the fallen Snape. Seeing Harry, Snape forces a large quantity of memories out of his head, and Harry collects them in a crystal flask that Hermione provides. Then, asking Harry to look into his eyes, Snape dies.

Notable Consequences   The memories that Snape has provided to Harry will prove, once and for all, where his loyalties have lain for the entire series. The viewing of these memories explains much of why Snape has acted the way he has throughout the series, and will affirm Dumbledore's trust of Snape.

The memories Harry has received will also give Harry the necessary information he needs to finally defeat Voldemort.

The death of Snape leaves Voldemort confident in having finally gained the full powers of the Elder Wand. This faith may be misplaced.

Analysis

As we will find out, there is really a large amount of information that Snape feels the need to pass to Harry. There is no way that Snape could have told it all to Harry in the midst of the battle, and in fact there is little way that Harry would have been prepared to believe anything that Snape, a Death Eater deep within the councils of Voldemort, could have told him. Yet, despite the battle proceeding apace, Harry must get this information. Snape's death, and the immediate crushing urgency of getting the message to Harry, is likely the only way that Snape could have gotten these memories to Harry in the available time, and likely the only way that Harry could have accepted them.

Greater Picture

The key piece of information that Harry receives from Snape is that a fragment of Voldemort's soul is lodged within Harry, and that the only way to dislodge it, and thus prevent Voldemort from returning again, is to have Voldemort kill Harry. Snape has been charged with passing this message on by Dumbledore, once Voldemort stops sending Nagini out to run his errands, instead keeping her close and magically protected. This actually is one link in the chain which almost fails. While Dumbledore does generally plan for the occasional failure, he had somehow assumed that once Voldemort had started protecting Nagini, Snape would still have the necessary freedom of motion to be able to pass the message on to Harry. Dumbledore had clearly not been aware either that Voldemort would so lightly kill his main lieutenant, or that the animosity between Snape and Harry would be increased by Dumbledore's death to the point that Harry would actually have killed Snape given the chance. If Harry had not been present at Snape's death, or if he had not been restrained from killing Snape by the presence of Voldemort and Nagini, the message would never have been passed, and the one remaining soul shard would have remained, anchoring Voldemort to the earth and to Harry.

Several additional pieces of Snape's memory come along with that one fact, however. Snape evidently feels the need to explain himself, and his actions. We learn that Snape had acted out of unrequited love for Harry's mother, Lily Evans. It is likely that it was necessary for Snape to include that background; it is uncertain whether Harry would have believed him, even given the memories, if he had not had that information about why he had acted as he did. Without that information, the ties holding Snape to the Order of the Phoenix seem far too tenuous to explain Snape's actions, and anything Snape could say would be seen as serving the interests of Voldemort, rather than of Harry. Harry, feeling that Snape had duped poor, trusting Dumbledore as he had everyone else, would equally distrust anything Snape told Dumbledore.

Harry, having seen these memories, recognizes that Snape was a strong and good wizard, and, as we will find out in the epilogue, actually names one of his children after both Snape and Dumbledore.

S.P.E.W.

Location: Hogwarts
Time Period: Starting in *Harry Potter and the Goblet of Fire*
Important Characters: Harry Potter, Hermione Granger, Ron Weasley

Overview

S.P.E.W. or the Society for the Promotion of Elfish Welfare, was founded by Hermione Granger during her fourth year at Hogwarts to promote liberation and rights for House Elves, an enslaved caste who are basically happy as they are. Hermione believes all Elves should be freed and instead receive wages, pensions, sick leave, and other benefits that a normal worker earns. Ron and Harry are reluctantly recruited into helping promote her cause.

Event Details The groundwork for this organization is laid when Hermione is at the Quidditch World Cup. There, she meets Winky, a House-elf who, despite her fear of heights, has been sent to the Top Box to hold a seat there for her Master, Bartemius Crouch. Wiky is plainly terrified at being so high in the air, and Hermione is scandalized, first that she could be so casually forced to do something that is so against her wishes, and second, that having demanded this service from Winky, Mr. Crouch doesn't even appear in the Top Box during the game to make use of the service he has demanded of her. She is further dismayed when Mr. Crouch dismisses Winky for the apparently trivial error of having the wand that had cast the Dark Mark into the sky.

At the Arrival Feast at Hogwarts, Nearly Headless Nick mentions that there had nearly been no feast at all. Upset at not being invited to the feast, Peeves had been wreaking destruction in the kitchens and had badly upset the House Elves. Hermione is upset at the news that the dinner had been prepared by "slave labour," and refuses to eat any more of it, despite being tempted by Ron.

The following day, Hermione eats breakfast hurriedly, saying that there are better ways to fight this than simply abstaining from eating, and departs for the library. Over the next few days, she spends a lot of time in the library, eventually returning with a stack of pamplets, buttons, and a donations box. She explains the *Society for the Promotion of Elfish Welfare* to a bemused Ron and Harry, saying that when they two join, the society will have three members. Ron protests that the House-Elves are happy as they are, but eventually joins.

Over the next while, we are told that Hermione is often to be seen shaking her donations box under peoples noses in the Common Room, without much apparent success. At one point, she takes her donations box and tries to convince Hagrid to join. He listens to her sales pitch, but gently declines, saying that things are more complex than Hermione, who is yet young, understands, and that the elves are happier as they are.

At one point, Harry and Ron become estranged, and Hermione asks Harry to go to Hogsmeade with her on a Hogsmeade weekend. Harry, after directly asking if she is hoping to end his and Ron's estrangement, agrees to go but only under his Invisibility Cloak. Sitting in the Three Broomsticks apparently by herself, Hermione says she feels foolish, but luckily she has brought some S.P.E.W. business along with her that she can spread out over the table.

In *Harry Potter and the Goblet of Fire*, Hermione innocently asks Fred and George where they had gotten a supply of pastries that they had brought up to a Gryffindor party. Fred starts to tell her where the kitchen is, but then stops, asking her if she is trying to start a House-Elf rebellion. Apparently, what Fred has revealed is enough, because shortly after this, Hermione leads Harry and Ron to the kitchens, where they find that the Hogwarts House-Elves now include both Dobby and Winky. Dobby explains that as a Free Elf, he now looks for payment, and this has made it extremely difficult for him to find work, but that Professor Dumbledore has hired both him and Winky. Harry can't help but notice that the other House Elves look disconcerted, and seem to keep their distance from Dobby and Winky. As they leave the kitchens, Hermione says that seeing how happy Dobby is can only have a good effect on the other House Elves, when they see how well Dobby has aken to being free. Harry privately thinks that the counter-example provided by the equally free, listless, drunken, wailing Winky is likely more powerful. During *Harry Potter and the Order of the Phoenix*, Hermione tries to set Hogwarts' elves free by hiding hats and socks under crumpled parchment and the like, to force the elves to take the clothes and free themselves. However, this backfires when all the Hogwarts elves (save Dobby, who is already free) refuse to clean the Gryffindor Tower because "they finds them insulting, sir," as Dobby says to Harry.

Notable Consequences It is only because of her efforts to free the house elves from what she sees as slavery that Hermione becomes interested in the Hogwarts kitchens. It is because she reaches the kitchens that we discover that both Dobby and Winky are now at Hogwarts. Winky will give us some clues to the nature of the hidden danger at Hogwarts, while Dobby will later provide Harry with information that he will need for the Second Task and for the establishment of Dumbledore's Army.

ANALYSIS

Hermione championing rights for House-elves (that they actually do not want) formally begins in chapter 14 of *Harry Potter and the Goblet of Fire*. Although S.P.E.W. becomes a smaller subplot in later books, Hermione continues to believe, quite correctly, that House-elves are a slave caste and should be freed. However, Hermione does not yet realize that freedom comes with a price, and it must be carefully orchestrated if elves are to survive and thrive without discrimination or retribution within the wizarding world. Simply turning loose what most wizards consider to be inferior beings (even more so than other non-human magical folk) would create great hardship, just as it did for Dobby and Winky, who were unable to find work until Dumbledore offered them paid employment at Hogwarts. Few wizards would be as generous as he. It would take a huge effort to realign the general wizarding population's thinking to accept House-elves as free agents. Hermione would do well to study how emancipated Muggle slaves fared following the American Civil War in the mid-1860s. Although former slaves were now free U.S. citizens, they struggled against severe discrimination, hatred, violence, and poverty while attempting to assimilate into a white, patriarchal-dominated society, all while lacking (and being denied) adequate education, jobs, and other opportunities needed to fend for themselves. As in the Wizard world, it was more than one race that was discriminated against: Irish, Asians, Italians, etc. were routinely denied equal opportunities based solely on their ethnicity. However, much like some non-human magical folk in Wizarding society, these particular ethnic groups were never enslaved and they had functioned within their own countries as free citizens and with at least some education. Also, immigrants were often able to establish their own small, protective communities while gradually integrating themselves into American culture, whereas freed slaves created a sudden and rather chaotic influx into a new social order in which there was little management or oversight and which often resulted in abuse and exploitation. Over a century later, these struggles still exist to some extent and are likely similar to what House-elves would experience.

Hagrid's refusal to join S.P.E.W. is interesting for two reasons. First, Hagrid shows that many wizards do not believe House-elves are mistreated and generally are happy with their lot in life; as we see in the Hogwarts kitchens, this is the case, at least at Hogwarts, if not in the Malfoy family. And secondly, Hagrid says that it is in House-elves nature to serve wizards. This could imply that House-elves may have freely entered into servitude, but at some point in history, wizards may have gained an advantage that allowed them to turn elves into slaves. This may have been achieved through selective breeding and magical mind manipulation. House-elves seem genuinely happiest when they have masters to serve, which apparently confirms what Hagrid is saying here. It is debatable then as to how well House-elves could, or would, adapt to sudden and unexpected new-found freedom.

Visiting the kitchen provides Hermione a reality check when she witnesses at first-hand just how truly satisfied House-elves are with their indentured lives, at least those at Hogwarts. They are quite literally "happy slaves" who believe their only purpose in life is to freely serve wizards, and they are unwilling to change. The only exceptions are Dobby and Winky, who the other House-elves disdain for being paid workers. While Dobby is proud to be a free agent, Winky is ashamed; as a result, she has become a sad, pathetic alcoholic, still pining for her former master, Mr. Crouch, who cruelly and unjustly fired her. And though Dobby and Winky are no longer slaves, their freedom created great hardship, as there are few opportunities available for masterless House-elves. Dobby, by his own report, spent a year-and-a-half seeking work; and while Dobby is resourceful and adaptable, Winky likely would never have sought other employment, and, without Dobby's help, probably would have suffered a miserable demise. Only Dumbledore's kindness has saved them both.

GREATER PICTURE

We will never know whether Ron's sudden interest in the welfare of the House Elves in the kitchens in *Harry Potter and the Deathly Hallows* is real or calculated. Hermione's concern about the House Elves is quite clear to everyone by this point, and presumably Ron could have been simply playing on that concern when he suggests warning the Elves about the upcoming battle, but if so, it was rather an odd time to be expressing that concern. We, like Hermione, believe that this is an expression of something that Ron is concerned about, and it does seem to win Hermione's heart.

In a post-publication interview, the author has stated that between the Last Battle and the Epilogue "Nineteen Years Later" in *Harry Potter and the Deathly Hallows*, Hermione starts her dream to help all house-elves by working at the Department for the Regulation and Control of Magical Creatures, where she manages to correct the culture with its shades of Wizard superiority and in-built prejudice.

Third Task

Location: Hogwarts—the Quidditch pitch
Time Period: *Harry Potter and the Goblet of Fire*, June 24
Important Characters: Harry Potter, Cedric Diggory, Viktor Krum, Fleur Delacour

OVERVIEW

The Third Task of the Triwizard Tournament is to negotiate a maze that has been grown in the Quidditch Pitch at Hogwarts. At the center of the maze is the Triwizard Cup, and whoever touches the Cup first is the outright winner of the Tournament

Event Details Exactly one month before the Third Task, the four Champions are brought to the Quidditch pitch, where they received a briefing on what the task was to be. Cedric and Harry were dismayed to discover that the pitch had been planted with hedges, but Ludo Bagman was quick to reassure them that it would be restored to pristine condition once the Task was finished. The Champions were informed that the object of the Task was to navigate the labyrinth, which would be seeded with various spells and creatures, and reach the Triwizard Cup, located in the center of the maze. The first Champion to touch the Cup would be the outright winner.

That same evening, Harry and Viktor Krum are having a private conversation when they find Mr. Crouch wandering around the Forbidden Forest. Before Harry can fetch Professor Dumbledore to help him, he disappears. Presumably, at this point the Ministry checks Mr. Crouch's house and finds it empty. Percy Weasley, who had been filling in for Mr. Crouch, is chastised for not being aware that his boss was in such dire shape, and so is replaced as a judge for the Third Task by Cornelius Fudge, the Minister for Magic.

The Third Task took place "at dusk on the 24th of June." It was held on Hogwarts' Quidditch pitch, which was transformed into a huge labyrinth, walled with tall hedges, and stocked with dangerous creatures by Hagrid. The champion entered the maze and had to navigate their way to the center where the Triwizard Cup was located. The maze was unique, filled with dangerous creatures, hazards, and obstructions. Creatures included Blast-Ended Skrewts and giant spiders. There was also an anti-gravity mist.

The maze's center was protected by a Sphinx with a riddle to answer. The champion, encountering the Sphinx, could choose to try and solve the riddle; if they chose not to attempt it, they could continue to proceed towards the center via an alternate route, if there was one. If they attempted the riddle, and answered wrong, they would be killed—or at least eliminated from the competition.

The order in which the champions were sent into the maze depended on their previous standings in the tournament, with the highest-scoring Champion entering first. Harry and Cedric were tied after the second task and entered the maze at the same time. Viktor Krum, with the next-highest score, entered five minutes after them, and Fleur Delacour entered last.

While within the maze, Harry heard Fleur scream, but did not encounter her, so we do not know if she was incapacitated at that point. He also heard someone performing the Cruciatus curse; burning a hole through the hedge, he was able to get into the next pathway, where he discovered Krum jinxing Cedric. Harry Stunned Krum, and sent up red sparks to indicate that he was out of the contest, before he and Cedric went their separate ways. In the end, Harry and Cedric were both within sight of the Cup, with Cedric in the lead; Harry called his attention to a giant spider coming up behind him, and the two of them joined forces to disable it. Cedric then decided that the only thing to do was to let Harry take the Cup; Harry counter-offered that they should both take it at the same time, and Cedric accepted.

Notable Consequences As the Triwizard Cup had been made into a Portkey, it carried Cedric and Harry to the graveyard in Little Hangleton, where Voldemort was waiting with Wormtail. The major consequences, then, were the death of Cedric and the return of Voldemort.

Ludo Bagman, despite being a Judge in the Tournament, has been taking bets on Harry's winning, in order to recover from a series of bad bets he had made with a group of goblins. His finances would have been completely resolved if Harry had won the Tournament outright. The goblins, however, held that as Harry and Cedric had both touched the Cup at the same instant, it was not an outright win for Harry but a draw. Bagman, being unable to pay his gambling debts, flees. Later negotiations with the Goblins are hindered by this; they feel that the Ministry of Magic should repay Bagman's debts, and are less willing to deal with Ministry wizards having been so badly short-changed by a senior Ministry official.

As joint winner of the Tournament, Harry is entitled to half of the Tournament prize of a thousand Galleons; as Cedric has died, however, the entire prize has been deemed his. He doesn't feel he has any right to this, because it was his efforts to win the Tournament that resulted in Cedric's death. He tries to give the entire prize to Cedric's father, but is rebuffed. In the end, he gives it to Fred and George, for use in setting up their joke shop, with the sole condition that they use some of the money to buy Ron some proper dress robes.

ANALYSIS

Looking at this Task, we feel, as Harry does at the time, that things are far too easy for him. With his use of the Four-Point-Spell, he is able to navigate the maze easily enough; the only obstacles he encounters are the anti-gravity spell, one of Hagrid's Blast-Ended Skrewts, a Boggart, the Sphinx, a giant spider, and Viktor Krum who he surprises in the act of using the Cruciatus curse on Cedric. It turns out later that Barty Crouch Jr. has been clearing obstacles away for him from outside the maze. Barty knows about the Triwizard Cup being a Portkey, as it was he who created it, and is attempting to ensure that Harry reaches it first.

Tower Battle (Hogwarts)

Location: Hogwarts
Time Period: *Harry Potter and the Half-Blood Prince*, late May
Important Characters: Harry Potter

OVERVIEW

This Battle was fought in *Harry Potter and the Half-Blood Prince*. Harry and Professor Dumbledore, returning from a mission to find a Horcrux, find the Dark Mark floating over the school's Astronomy Tower. Reaching the top of the tower, a weakened Dumbledore sends Harry down for help, but Petrifies Harry when he hears someone coming. Draco Malfoy, arriving, immediately Disarms Dumbledore. Dumbledore determines that Draco is there to kill him, and almost manages to talk him out of it, when four Death Eaters enter the scene and start egging Draco on. Finally, Severus Snape reaches the top of the tower, and kills Dumbledore. As the Death Eaters retreat down the staircase, Harry Stuns one of them. As he reaches the main floor, he finds a few members of Dumbledore's Army and a few members of the Order of the Phoenix battling Death Eaters, and hears Snape call the Death Eaters off. Harry chases Snape and Draco, but although he is nearly able to catch up to them, he is unable to Jinx Snape. The Death Eaters escape, and Harry must return to the school and explain what had happened.

Event Details Harry Potter and Albus Dumbledore return to Hogsmeade from their quest to find a Horcrux. Dumbledore is very weak from the after-effects of potion, and is asking Harry to get Severus Snape for him. They are met in the street by Madam Rosmerta, who alerts them of the Dark Mark floating above the Astronomy Tower at Hogwarts. Harry Summons brooms from inside the Three Broomsticks, and flies with Dumbledore to the Astronomy Tower. Once at the top of the tower, Dumbledore is too weakened by the retrieval of the Horcrux to head down the stairs to the battle. He sends Harry to fetch Snape, but before Harry can reach the door, footsteps are heard approaching the door from the other side, and Dumbledore immobilizes Harry.

Draco Malfoy, bursting onto the scene, disarms Dumbledore, and Harry must look on silently as Dumbledore almost convinces Malfoy to change sides. Dumbledore correctly determines that Draco is motivated by fear for his family and himself, and plays on that, and the understanding that Draco is not totally evil.

Four Death Eaters now arrive, and approach a weakened Dumbledore. While they jeer at Draco and try to egg him on, he seems, at the end incapable of killing Dumbledore. The Death Eaters also refrain from killing Dumbledore, as they have apparently received instructions from Voldemort that this is Draco's job, that he must do it on his own. Finally, Snape arrives, and kills Dumbledore. The Death Eaters turn to leave; Harry finds himself freed from the body-binding spell and runs after them, Petrifying one as he hurries to catch Snape. Snape has sounded the retreat, and the Death Eaters are now fighting a rearguard action as they head out of Hogwarts. Harry has to guess whether Snape and Draco are intending to try to exit through the Room of Requirement, that being how they had gotten in, or through the front door. Guessing, he uses every shortcut he knows on the way to the front door, seeing bloody footprints to reassure him he is headed in the right direction. As he exits the front doors, with Snape and Draco before him, and several other Death Eaters behind, he tries to Jinx Snape several times but is repeatedly blocked. One of the Death Eaters behind him Curses him, and he falls and loses his wand, but the curse is stopped by Snape, who says that Voldemort wants Harry for himself.

The Death Eaters leave the school and vanish outside the gates. Harry helps Hagrid extinguish his burning hut, and returns to where Dumbledore's body lies. There, he recovers the locket Horcrux that he and Dumbledore had found, and discovers that it is not a Horcrux at all, but instead contains a note from one "R. A. B." who had evidently already retrieved the Horcrux and left this locket in its place. Ginny guides Harry up to the Hospital Wing, where Harry relates the events of the top of the Astronomy Tower to Professor McGonagall and the others gathered there.

In the aftermath, we learn that casualties were light; a large blond Death Eater, identified in a later book as Thorfinn Rowle, had been flinging Killing curses around randomly and had hit his fellow Death Eater, Gibbon. On the Order of the Phoenix side, apart from Dumbledore, the only casualty was Bill Weasley, who had been bitten severely by an un-transformed Fenrir Greyback and would likely retain facial scars for the rest of his life. The toll would almost certainly have been higher except for Harry's forethought in setting Ron, Ginny, and Neville Longbottom to watch the Room of Requirement, and giving Ron and Ginny some of his precious Felix Felicis potion. Draco, finding the room watched when he had emerged, had used Instant Darkness powder to prevent Ron, Ginny, and Neville from seeing the Death Eaters entering, but had luckily not Jinxed any of them. The students had luckily managed to find Remus Lupin, who had brought the Order members at the school, Professor McGonagall, Tonks, and Bill Weasley, into the battle. Professor McGonagall had sent Professor Flitwick to fetch Snape; Hermione and Luna Lovegood, stationed outside Snape's office, had heard something fall, and Snape, spotting them as he departed, said Flitwick had fallen and they should take care of him. The combatants in the hall under the Astronomy Tower had let him go past, thinking he was one of them, and had tried to follow him up the tower where the Death Eaters had gone, but the magical barrier across the stairs, which Snape had passed as if it were not present, still stopped the Order members. When Snape had returned down the stairs with Draco, the Order members, believing he was on their side, had again allowed him to pass unmolested.

Notable Consequences   Now that Snape has effectively declared his loyalties and fled, the position of 'Defense Against the Dark Arts' teacher is again available.

With the death of Dumbledore, the Headmaster's job will also be open. Whether this post will be offered to Professor McGonagall or not is as yet uncertain; it is the Board of Governors who appoint the Headmaster, and it is by no means certain that McGonagall, a Gryffindor, will be appointed following Dumbledore, who was apparently also a Gryffindor.

With Snape's departure, Professor Slughorn will become head of Slytherin house. Slughorn, though a Slytherin through and through, is not a Voldemort partisan, and may be somewhat less likely to encourage Slytherin students to follow him.

Draco Malfoy has declared himself to be firmly on the side of Voldemort. However, he has also funked the job he was given. His father, Lucius, has now failed Voldemort three times, first by using the diary Horcrux irresponsibly and having it be destroyed, then by being involved in the failed plot to retrieve the Prophecy which ended with Bode being left insane, and finally failing to retrieve the Prophecy despite having twelve Death Eaters against six students, and incidentally alerting the Wizarding world to Voldemort's return, and getting himself imprisoned in Azkaban. Voldemort expects Draco to fail, as we see when his mother Narcissa visits Snape early in the book. Narcissa, at that point, hopes that if Dumbledore dies, whether it be by Draco's hand or Snape's, that Draco will at least have a chance to survive. However, the outcome of the battle will lower the Malfoy family in Voldemort's estimation, as now all three of the family members will have failed him: Narcissa by talking to other Death Eaters about Voldemort's plans, and Draco by failing to carry out orders.

Dumbledore is killed. Another of Harry's defenders and father figures has passed; Harry decides that he is not going to shield himself behind anyone else, he is going to have to tackle Voldemort himself, directly. This marks a vital stage in Harry's increasing maturity; rather than accepting guidance from others, Harry will now choose his own path.

Harry determines that Dumbledore had believed in Snape's loyalty because Snape, having reported the Prophecy concerning Harry to Voldemort, had then returned to Dumbledore and informed Dumbledore of his actions. Bill's injury, while not fatal, is disfiguring, and Mrs. Weasley assumes that it will mean the end of the planned wedding between Bill and Fleur. Fleur angrily denies this, however, and takes over nursing Bill from Mrs. Weasley. This revelation that there are unsuspected depths to Fleur wins Mrs. Weasley over. Until now, she had been putting up with Fleur solely for Bill's sake; now, she finally fully accepts Fleur as daughter-in-law. In the aftermath of the battle, Remus Lupin and Nymphadora Tonks re-open what is apparently an old conversation for them, as to whether they should get together. Lupin believes that it is not a safe time to bring a child into the world, but Arthur Weasley, perhaps surprisingly, comes down on Tonks' side of the argument, saying there never is a completely safe time. It appears that this may be enough to sway Lupin, as we will later see that Tonks is once again looking animated, and her hair color is returning to its earlier wild shades.

ANALYSIS

One of the keys to an extended story such as the Harry Potter series is that the reader must care about the hero. When the story is extended and episodic, the challenges that the hero faces must increase over time, so that despite his increasing strength, the reader feels that the hero is still challenged to the very brink of his abilities at each new crisis. In this one battle, we see Harry's greatest challenge to date, namely Severus Snape, who overtly declares himself a Death Eater by killing Dumbledore, and who then repeatedly thwarts Harry's attempts to attack him. Yet Harry manages to survive where Dumbledore did not. Looking back on this battle, of course, we see that Harry was not heavily involved; he seems to be at least partly protected by Snape, who says that Voldemort wants Harry for himself. Where Harry's strength is called for is not his physical or magical strength, but his strength of mind. He must support the weakened Dumbledore from the cave and back to the school, he must function despite witnessing the death of Dumbledore, and he must persevere to make plans for the eventual battle against Voldemort. The death of Dumbledore, who until now had seemed indestructible and imperturbable, seems to put Harry entirely on his own; with Dumbledore gone, Harry's last apparent protector is gone. The readers can see that this is not entirely true; both Ron and Hermione volunteer to come with him and assist in the struggle to come. But while Ron and Hermione are of age, none of them have completed school yet, none of them are at their full powers. Is this going to be enough? We cannot know. It is certain that with Dumbledore gone, Voldemort's path to power is almost unobstructed.

For one who has made any study of heroic fiction of this nature, Dumbledore's fall, though saddening, is not unexpected. The hero must, in the end, proceed alone;

with others shielding him, he cannot be a hero, after all. One of the major strengths of this particular instance is the nature of Dumbledore's fall, killed by one that he trusts, and has repeatedly said that he trusts. One fixed point in the series to this point is how consistently Dumbledore has been right. Up to this point, Dumbledore has made very few mistakes, though of course at the end of *Harry Potter and the Order of the Phoenix,* he does admit to a fairly large error of omission, which he then proceeds to rectify. Now, he is seen to have made an extremely major error, in trusting Snape. We don't yet know what effect this will have on Harry's feelings towards Dumbledore, and the mission that Dumbledore has apparently left Harry to complete.

GREATER PICTURE

It is only in *Harry Potter and the Deathly Hallows* that we learn the truth of this particular battle. It is there, in Snape's memories, that we learn that the events on the tower top had been, to a certain extent, planned. Dumbledore knew that the curse which had withered his wand hand was only contained for a while, and within a year would break free and kill him. He also had known that Voldemort had ordered Draco to kill him. With these two things in mind, Dumbledore had arranged that when Draco tried and failed to kill Dumbledore, Snape would finish the job. Learning, at the same time, why Dumbledore had trusted Snape, we will come to understand that Snape was worthy of the trust Dumbledore had placed in him, right to the end.

Triwizard Tournament

Location: Hogwarts
Time Period: Year 4
Important Characters: Harry Potter, Cedric Diggory, Viktor Krum, Fleur Delacour

OVERVIEW

The Triwizard Tournament is a recently revived competition pitting three major European wizarding schools against one other, although it is also meant to foster magical cooperation. The schools, listed below, share the responsibility of hosting the tournament, and the heads of the schools sit on the judging panel.

From *Harry Potter and the Goblet of Fire,* pg. 187 (US Edition), pg. 165 (UK edition) the exact description of this tournament was:

'A very exciting event, an event that has not been held for over a century ... was first established some seven hundred years ago as a friendly competition between the three largest European schools of wizardry: Hogwarts, Beauxbatons, and Durmstrang. A champion was selected to represent each school, and the three champions competed in three magical tasks. The schools took it in turn to host the Tournament once every five years, and it was generally agreed to be a most excellent way of establishing ties between young witches and wizards of different nationalities—until, that is, the death toll mounted so high that the Tournament was discontinued.'

Event Details The tournament was introduced some 700 years ago. After being banned for many years due to the increasingly dangerous tasks, the Triwizard Tournament has been revived.

As mentioned in the overview, there are three schools participating:
• Hogwarts School of Witchcraft and Wizardry
• Beauxbatons Academy of Magic
• Durmstrang Institute

Judges grade the champion's performance on each task. The Heads of the three participating schools are customarily judges; Hermione reads this in a history book about the Tournament, and that all three school Headmasters were injured in a Tournament task mishap involving a Cockatrice. In the book *Harry Potter and the Goblet of Fire,* the judges were:
• Ludovic Bagman (Ministry of Magic, Department of Magical Games and Sports)
• Bartemius Crouch, Sr. (Ministry of Magic, Department of International Magical Cooperation)
• Albus Dumbledore (headmaster of Hogwarts)
• Igor Karkaroff (headmaster of Durmstrang)
• Olympe Maxime (headmistress of Beauxbatons)

The selection of the champions from each participating school is done through a magical object called the Goblet of Fire. The Goblet is a large, roughly hewn wooden cup, brimming with dancing blue flames. The selection process is described by Dumbledore:

"Anybody wishing to submit themselves as champion must write their name and school clearly upon a slip of parchment and drop it into the goblet. Aspiring champions have twenty-four hours in which to put their names forward. Tomorrow night, Hallowe'en, the goblet will return the names of the three it has judged most worthy to represent their schools. The goblet will be placed in the entrance hall tonight, where it will be freely accessible to all those wishing to compete. To ensure that no underage student yields to temptation, I will be drawing an Age Line around the Goblet of Fire once it has been placed in the entrance hall. Nobody under the age of seventeen will be able to cross this line ... I wish to impress upon any of you wishing to compete that this tournament is not to be entered into lightly. Once a champion has been selected by the Goblet of Fire, he or she is obliged to see the tournament through to the end. The placing of your name in the goblet constitutes a binding, magical contract. There can be no change of heart once you have become a champion. Please be very sure, therefore, that you are wholeheartedly prepared to play before you drop your name into the goblet."

The term *champion* does not mean the winner of the tournament. It instead refers to a contestant; this is an ancient usage, dating back to the days of chivalry. An army, or a king, could choose a champion who would fight for them; that champion would then meet an opposing champion, and the contest would be decided by single combat between the two. In this context, then, the Goblet is selecting the champion who will do battle to protect the school's good name.

Traditionally, there are three champions, as the tournament's name implied. Somehow, a fourth Champion was chosen.
• Beauxbatons Champion—Fleur Delacour
• Durmstrang Champion—Viktor Krum

- Hogwarts Champion—Cedric Diggory (Hufflepuff)
- Hogwarts Champion—Harry Potter (Gryffindor)

It is unknown initially how Harry's name was entered into the Goblet, or how he was selected; Dumbledore asks whether he had put his own name into the Goblet or had an older student do it for him, and Harry stated that he had not. Professor Moody suggests that Harry's name could have been submitted as the sole contender for a non-existent fourth school, but it would take a powerful wizard who could hoodwink the Goblet into believing that there were, in fact, four schools.

Before the tournament begins, the Weighing of the Wands takes place to examine each Champion's wand to ensure that it is in proper working order. The Champions will, of course, be depending on their wands as their sole tool in the Tasks, and so it is necessary to ensure that each is in perfect working order. The Wands Weighing was performed by Mr. Ollivander, expert wand-maker and owner of *Ollivander's Fine Wands* in Diagon Alley.

- Cedric Diggory—12 1/4 inches, ash, pleasantly springy, containing a single hair from the tail of a male unicorn
- Fleur Delacour—9 1/2 inches, inflexible, rosewood, containing a hair from the head of a veela (her grandmother)
- Harry Potter—11 inches, holly, containing a feather from the tail of a phoenix
- Viktor Krum—Gregorovitch creation. 10 1/4 inches, hornbeam and dragon heartstring, quite rigid

The Tournament has three Tasks. The First Task took place on 24 November. The Second Task was on 24 February, and the Third Task on 24 June. Additionally, the Triwizard Champions are expected to lead off the Yule Ball, which Harry, who had never danced before, considered a fourth and unexpected task.

Notable Consequences Harry becoming a Champion is totally unexpected; initially at least, nobody is sure how this is done. Harry's championship leads to a certain amount of friction between the Heads of the three schools involved; Madame Maxime and Igor Karkaroff both seem to believe that it was done deliberately, and that Albus Dumbledore had some hand in it. At the very least, they suspect him of having failed to draw the Age Line correctly, as that should have prevented Harry, who was then underage, from putting his name in. Moody is the only one who seems to have recognized that the Goblet would have had to be bewitched to issue a fourth name.

The attention caused by his selection as Champion is particularly unwelcome to Harry. Not only does he have to deal with members of Hufflepuff house who feel he is acting to steal some of their glory, and with those in other houses and amongst the teachers who feel that he is trying to seek out yet more fame for himself, he has attracted the attention of Rita Skeeter, who seems to delight in writing scurrilous pieces about anyone who will sit still for her, and many who won't. Over the course of the story, Rita will write a horrible story about Harry, another about Hagrid, and a third about Hermione. All three stories will have serious ill-effects on their subjects and their relationship with others.

Cedric Diggory is murdered during the third task. Voldemort is brought back to full life, although the Ministry of Magic refutes this. Minister of Magic Cornelius Fudge claims that Cedric accidentally died due to carelessness.

Analysis

An interesting note is that cheating, while not officially condoned, is widely considered a traditional part of the tournament.

We should note that the Wand Weighing Ceremony does not actually involve determining how much each wand weighs. The term likely was chosen for its assonance, coupled with a more arcane use of the word. A dictionary definition of the word "weigh" includes the definition: "to evaluate in the mind; consider carefully in order to reach an opinion, decision, or choice: *to weigh the facts; to weigh a proposal.*"[1]

Although the Tournament is a competition, it was also revived to help foster international magical cooperation. The three schools, Hogwarts, Beauxbatons, and Durmstrang, are culturally and academically unique, and they have had little interaction with one another until now. Whether the tentative bonds that have been established are a strong enough alliance to unite them in the fight against Voldemort remains to be seen, although individual friendships, and a few romances, have been formed.

Questions

1. Why was the Triwizard Tournament revived after so many years? Why was it discontinued in the first place?
2. What is the Tournament's purpose?
3. Why was Harry chosen as a Champion, even though he was ineligible to enter? How was this accomplished?

Greater Picture

The Weighing of Wands, which seems to be a minor event in the Triwizard Tournament, actually gives Harry a clue in *Harry Potter and the Deathly Hallows*: he has a vision of Voldemort searching for something, and he has been uttering Gregorovitch's name. At Bill Weasley and Fleur Delacour's wedding he is reminded by Viktor Krum, another wedding guest, that Gregorovitch is a wand maker, a fact that had come out at the Weighing. From this he deduces that Voldemort might wish to have another wand commissioned.

Bill and Fleur's wedding is another consequence of the Tournament: they meet when Bill and his mother visit Harry before the Third Task, and that leads to a romance that ends in the wedding.

---

1. http://www.dictionary.com, 3 June 2007, definition 5 (http://dictionary.reference.com/browse/weigh)

Viktor Krum relationships

Location: Hogwarts and Durmstrang
Time Period: *Harry Potter and the Goblet of Fire* through to *Harry Potter and the Deathly Hallows*
Important Characters: Viktor Krum, Hermione Granger, Ron Weasley, Ginny Weasley

Overview

Viktor Krum arrives with the delegation from Durmstrang Institute to take part in the Triwizard Tournament. He becomes attracted to Hermione, making Ron jealous, though Ron does not realize this at the time. Though Viktor is quite clearly trying to take things to the next stage with Hermione, she gently rebuffs him, and they stay pen-pals until Ron and Hermione become a couple. Viktor then suggests, in Harry's hearing, that he would like to meet Ginny. Harry tells him that Ginny is going out with someone very big who gets angry easily.

Event Details

Goblet of Fire Viktor Krum arrives for the Triwizard Tournament as part of the delegation from Durmstrang Institute. He seems to be spending significant time in the library, something that irritates Hermione because of the gaggle of giggling girls that seems to follow him around.

At the Yule Ball, we discover that Hermione has been asked to the ball by Viktor Krum. Ron is quite upset by this, saying that Hermione is "consorting with the enemy."

In the Second Task of the Triwizard Tournament, the four Champions must each retrieve something valuable to them from the bottom of the lake. The thing that is valuable to Viktor is Hermione. Having rescued Hermione, Viktor is apparently having a fairly intense conversation with her on the shore. An article that appears in *Witch Weekly* shortly afterwards, written by Rita Skeeter, says that Krum has invited Hermione to spend the summer with him. Hermione admits that this is true, but wonders how Rita had found out.

Viktor takes Harry aside in late May and asks him if Hermione is his girlfriend. Harry is rather surprised by this, and says no. Viktor says that Hermione is always talking about Harry, and Harry insists that it is because they are friends.

We don't see much other interaction between Viktor and Hermione, but by this time it is pretty clear that Viktor is romantically interested in Hermione.

Order of the Phoenix While Viktor Krum does not play any particular role in this book, we see that Hermione is writing a very long letter to him as Christmas holidays approach. Hermione says that he's just a pen-pal, but Ron comments that he would like to be a lot more than that.

Half-Blood Prince Harry and Ron catch Ginny and Dean snogging in a corridor. In the ensuing quarrel, Ginny says that Harry has snogged Cho, Hermione has snogged Viktor, and Ron is simply jealous because he doesn't have anyone to snog.

Deathly Hallows Viktor has been invited to Bill and Fleur's wedding. Hermione is taken aback to see him there. Harry, in disguise, stops to talk with him. Viktor is looking sourly at Ron and Hermione out on the dance floor. Seeing Ginny, he asks if Harry knows her. Harry replies that she is going out with somebody large and bad-tempered. Viktor angrily asks what is the point of being famous if all the best girls are already taken?

Notable Consequences Krum's ongoing attempts to become more than a pen-pal to Hermione eventually result in Ron's committing himself. It is entirely possible that Ron would leave his relationship with Hermione languishing if Krum had not been trying to take Hermione for himself.

It is unknown whether Krum would have attended Bill and Fleur's wedding if Hermione was not likely to be present. It is certain that she seems more surprised that he will be attending than he is at finding her there. If Krum's appearance at the wedding is a consequence of this relationship, then so also are Harry's discoveries about the identity of Gregorovitch, and the use of the symbol of the Deathly Hallows as the mark of Grindelwald.

Analysis

There is no way of knowing exactly how much has been going on between Viktor and Hermione. True, Ginny does tell Ron that Hermione and Viktor have been snogging, but this is not conclusive, as Ginny at the time is mid-quarrel with Ron, and is trying to hurt him with words. It is entirely possible that Ginny is going from what is public knowledge and expanding on it for effect. It is certainly true, as we see later, that Viktor would like to spend time snogging with Hermione; what is not so certain is whether he actually has done so. Hermione, as we see here, has clearly set her sights on Ron early in the series, and it is uncertain whether she would choose to jeopardize her relationship with Ron by being known to be snogging with Viktor.

Voldemort's Death

Location: Hogwarts
Time Period: *Harry Potter and the Deathly Hallows*, May
Important Characters: Harry Potter, Lord Voldemort

Overview

At the great Battle of Hogwarts, Lord Voldemort is killed in a final duel against Harry Potter.

Event Details After Voldemort kills Snape, Voldemort announces that the battle will be stopped for one hour, to give Harry Potter time to come to him in the Forbidden Forest, and says that if Harry comes to him, everyone at Hogwarts will be spared. Harry, having learned from Snape's memories, that the only way to destroy the soul fragment that he bears within him is for Voldemort to kill him, enters the Forest and seeks Voldemort. Finding him, he announces his presence and Voldemort kills him.

Harry finds himself in a strange place, apparently a cleaner version of King's Cross Station, where he meets the shade of Dumbledore. They talk, and Dumbledore explains some of the events of the past seven years to Harry. Dumbledore explains, in particular, that the soul shard that was attached to Harry has now been destroyed, and that Harry now has the choice: if he wishes, he can go back, and complete the destruction of Voldemort, or he can go onward to the platforms, where he will likely find a train that will take him On. Harry elects to return. Finding himself back in his own body, Harry feigns death, and hears Voldemort also regaining consciousness. Voldemort orders Narcissa Malfoy to check Harry and see if he is dead. Narcissa quite clearly knows that Harry is alive, but she asks if her son Draco is still alive in Hogwarts. Harry says Draco is still alive, and Narcissa, apparently aware that it is the only way she can get into Hogwarts to rejoin her son, tells Voldemort that Harry is dead. Voldemort forces Hagrid to carry Harry's lifeless body back to Hogwarts, where he taunts the defenders with the death of their champion. When he forces the Sorting Hat onto Neville's head and sets it afire, Neville produces the Sword of Gryffindor from the hat and cuts off Nagini's head.

Battle is now rejoined, with the defenders of Hogwarts being reinforced by the parents of the students who had been evacuated earlier. Harry, under his Invisibility Cloak, works his way into the Great Hall, where he watches as Bellatrix Lestrange is defeated by Molly Weasley. Harry Shields Molly from Voldemort's retaliatory strike, then reveals himself. Harry and Voldemort now circle, preparing to duel; Harry, calling his opponent by his real name, Tom Riddle, offers him the chance to live by repenting of his murders. Voldemort dismisses this out of hand, and casts the Killing Curse at Harry as Harry casts the Disarmament jinx at Voldemort. The Elder Wand flies into Harry's hand, as Voldemort's curse rebounds upon him, killing him.

Notable Consequences The final death of Voldemort spells an end to the Death Eaters and their depredations both on the Wizarding and the Muggle population. With Voldemort finally gone, the Wizarding world can now embark on a path leading to prosperity, rather than having to be constantly on guard against pieces of itself.

With the Elder Wand in his possession, Harry now has what may be the ultimate weapon for dueling. We do not yet know what Harry will do with it.

ANALYSIS

One key thing to take note of is the fact that Harry did not actually kill Voldemort. He was dueling with Voldemort at the time, and he was in a way responsible, but it was the spell that Voldemort cast that actually killed him. Harry's hands remain unbloodied and his soul remains intact.

GREATER PICTURE

Harry, though he has what may be the strongest wand in the Wizarding world, recognizes that not only does this wand carry great power, it also represents great danger. According to legend, the first bearer of the wand was killed on the night that his ownership of the wand became known, and the wand was stolen from him; this marked the beginning of a trail of murders that has followed the wand through history. Harry is aware that, though the wand cannot be defeated in a duel, there are many other risks that it cannot protect against. Unlike Ron, who covets the wand simply for its power and is apparently largely uncaring of the associated danger, Harry recognizes that as long as the wand exists, there will be people willing to kill for its power. Harry can clearly see that this wand is too powerful to be allowed to remain in the world. While he owns it, he only casts one spell with it, to repair his own wand; he then places it back in Dumbledore's tomb, in the expectation that with his own unchallenged death in the future, the wand will lose its power.

Yearend exams

Location: Hogwarts School of Witchcraft and Wizardry
Time Period: Each year, usually first week in June
Important Characters: students of Hogwarts

OVERVIEW

Year-end exams are exams taken at the end of the Hogwarts school year in order to test the students' progress and, sometimes, determine the student's courses the next year, and the magical career they will follow in years to come.

Event Details Exams actually take place at the end of the Spring Term, generally putting them in the first week of June, though in *Harry Potter and the Goblet of Fire*, they end on June 24th. It is quite likely that this is a special case, because of the Triwizard Tournament which occurs that year. Exams typically occupy a week, Monday to Friday, and there can be two exams a day for each student, plus the Astronomy exam at midnight. With only eleven slots for exams, a practical maximum number of courses for the usual student is eleven.

Summer term, which occupies the last three weeks of June usually, is much more relaxed than the usual school year. The time is used by the teachers to prepare grades and mark exams.

Passing and failing grades are never explicitly mentioned. It is likely that the scale used for marking O.W.L.s and N.E.W.T.s is not used for regular exams, as Fred and George have to explain the O/E/A/P/D/T grade levels used in O.W.L.s to Ron, Harry, and Hermione, when they have been at Hogwarts for some time already; and Hermione thinks the twins are pulling her leg about there being a grade "T for Troll."

Hermione, several times in the series, manages to seriously disconcert Harry and Ron by presenting them with "revision" (study) schedules, generally far before they are prepared to start studying for the year-end exams. Hermione, of course, excels at these exams, and is repeatedly the top of the class.

There are not year-end exams for all characters every year. In the fifth and seventh years, for instance, there are O.W.L. and N.E.W.T. exams instead. In *Harry Potter and the Chamber of Secrets,* much to Hermione's dismay, the entire school is excused from year-end exams in the celebration following Harry and Ginny's return from the Chamber. In *Harry Potter and the Goblet of Fire,* Harry and Cedric, as school champions, are excused from the year-end exams. And in *Harry Potter and the Half-Blood Prince,* the entire school is again excused from exams in the wake of the death of Dumbledore.

Notable Consequences   One of the major issues for Harry is that, each year he is at Hogwarts, some major event is coming to a head right at the end of the year, as exams are either looming or in progress. As such, the exams may get short shrift, or there may be inadequate preparation on Harry's part for the exams. However, Harry still manages to pass all his courses, usually with significant help from Hermione, who is consistently at the top of the class.

The specific issues that Harry faces as he comes into the year-end exams are:

• *Harry Potter and the Philosopher's Stone:* Harry's belief that Voldemort, with help from Professor Snape, is about to retrieve the Stone and, with its help, return to life and try again to kill Harry;

• *Harry Potter and the Chamber of Secrets:* The apparent opening of the Chamber, which has put an air of fear throughout the school and culminates in the abduction of Ginny Weasley;

• *Harry Potter and the Prisoner of Azkaban:* the reappearance of the murderer Sirius Black, who Harry has been told was the wizard who betrayed his parents to the Dark Lord;

• *Harry Potter and the Goblet of Fire:* though excused from exams, Harry had to face the Third Task, which would be a practical test of his spell-casting abilities;

• *Harry Potter and the Order of the Phoenix:* Harry is taking O.W.L. exams instead

• *Harry Potter and the Half-Blood Prince:* Harry is convinced that Draco Malfoy is plotting something, and is meeting a stony response from Dumbledore, so feels he must investigate by himself. The Horcrux hunt which takes place immediately before exams is also a distraction.

It is interesting, perhaps, to note that in his six years of attendance at Hogwarts, Harry sits year-end exams in only his first and third years, and O.W.L.s in his fifth year. This could lead us to wonder how large a sample Hermione was working from when she said, in *Harry Potter and the Order of the Phoenix,* that Harry had the highest scores in Defence Against the Dark Arts.

Analysis

As the books are written to each cover one school year, the end of the book will almost always coincide with the end of the school year. As the climax of a book must come near the end, the climactic battles or events will of necessity fall at the end of the school year, exactly when exams would be held. It is interesting to note how the author combines the heightened tension due to the approaching exams with the heightened tensions due to the other events that Harry is dealing with.

By and large, though, year-end exams are not a particularly important part of our story. Critical as they are for the normal Hogwarts student, it is apparent that Harry is not typical in his school career. In the first, second, and third years, the primary purpose of the exams seems to be to show us Hermione's determination to do well academically; she prepares revision (study) schedules for herself two months or more in advance of the exams, pesters Harry and Ron to follow the schedules she has made up for them, and goes over the tests repeatedly afterwards, until Ron, in exasperation, tells her to "give it a rest." In book 4, now that we know how much Hermione agonizes over her exams, the fact that she willingly gives up her study time to drill Harry in the jinxes he will need for the Third Task is a stronger indicator than nearly anything else the author could use of the depths of Hermione's friendship, and her concern for Harry's progress. And in the sixth year, Harry's concentration on the lessons he receives from Dumbledore, and on other events transpiring around the school, seems to make him largely oblivious to the oncoming exams.

Greater Picture

It is necessary to include exams in the books, as there are always exams at school. However, as mentioned above, they are generally a distraction from the story line, or simply used as a device to heighten tension. The fact that Harry does reasonably well on his exams is mentioned in passing in his first year, and then never again, though Hermione's ongoing position at the top of their class is mentioned repeatedly. One gathers that the exams are included as a necessary part of the school year, rather than being particularly useful to the narrative.

Yule Ball

Location: Hogwarts, Great Hall
Time Period: *Harry Potter and the Goblet of Fire,* 25 December
Important Characters: Harry, Cedric Diggory, Viktor Krum, Fleur Delacour, Cho Chang, Ron, Hermione

Overview

As a part of the Triwizard Tournament, there is traditionally a dance at the hosting school. This dance, the Yule Ball, is normally led off by the three school Champions and their partners; in Harry's fourth year, of course, there are four champions, and thus four couples leading off the Ball.

Event Details Shortly after Harry's success in the First Task, Harry is stunned by hearing about the Yule Ball from Professor McGonagall. He is quite alarmed to realize that, as one of the Champions, he is expected to find a dance partner, learn to dance, and lead off the whole ball. This looming dread is not at all lightened by the realization that nearly the entire school is planning to stay over Christmas, in order to attend the Ball—or, at least, all who are allowed to attend. The ball is restricted to those in fourth year and above, although younger students can attend as the guest of a fourth-year (or presumably later).

Harry immediately thinks of Cho Chang as a possible dance partner for the ball, but every time he finds her, she is travelling in a convoy of giggling girls; horribly embarrassed, he thinks that giggling should be outlawed. In hopes of actually being able to ask Cho, Harry turns down several invitations from other girls, possibly in part because he doesn't believe they can be serious. Finally, on the last day of classes, Harry takes Cho aside and asks her, only to find that she has already accepted an invitation from Cedric. Cho seems almost as disappointed as Harry at this turn of events, but that is cold comfort; handsome, capable, likeable Cedric is in so many ways what Harry would like to be, and here he has even gotten the girl that Harry wanted.

Returning to the common room, Harry finds that Ron is in the same situation—in what he atributes to a fit of madness, Ron has asked Fleur Delacour, and she has not even done him the dignity of turning him down, simply ignoring him. In desperation, Harry and Ron ask Ginny and Hermione, only to find that they, too, have already agreed to go with someone else. In desperation, Harry asks Parvati Patil. She accepts; Harry asks if Lavender would be willing to go with Ron, but Lavender already has a date. Parvati suggests that her sister, Padma, would probably be willing to go with Ron.

The Yule Ball during Harry's fourth year takes place on Christmas Day, between the First and Second Tasks of the Triwizard Tournament. It is a festive event featuring dancing, in this case to music provided by the Wierd Sisters. Students dress in their best formal clothes. Males wear dress robes, which is probably why dress robes were on the supplies list this year; females wear gowns or other formal attire. While students should have partners for the ball, apparently not all do; Harry is pleased to see that Crabbe and Goyle do not seem to have partners. The four Champions enter the hall last: Cedric Diggory with Cho Chang, Fleur Delacour with Roger Davies, Viktor Krum with Hermione, so prettily done up that Harry does not initially recognize her, and Harry with Parvati. At dinner, Harry is surprised to find that Mr. Crouch is not present; Percy is, and explains that he is filling in for Mr. Crouch, who is feeling ill. Once dinner is over, a dance floor is cleared, and Parvati guides Harry out onto the floor as the music starts up; the four Champions and their partners are quickly joined by classmates and teachers. At the end of the first dance, Harry chooses to leave the floor, much to Parvati's disgust; they go and join Ron and Padma, who apparently alone have sat out the first dance, and Padma and Parvati, deciding that they are unlikely to get much more dancing out of Ron and Harry, find other partners. Ron and Harry wander out into a rose garden that has been magically created oudside the Entrance Hall, overhearing Professor Karkaroff and Professor Snape discussing something that is getting more and more distinct, and whether Karkaroff should run away. They then stumble upon Hagrid and Madame Maxime deep in a private conversation; in teh course of that conversation, Hagrid reveals that he is half-giant, and suggests that he believes Madame Maxime is also. Madame Maxime is affronted and departs in a huff. Hagrid then goes off to his hut, and Harry and Ron return inside to discuss this development.

Notable Consequences Up until this point, Harry and Cho's relationship has been unstated; there are indications that there is a very early romance between them, but there has been no declaration. By choosing to ask Cho to the Ball, Harry is saying that he would like to move their relationship forward; it is a declaration of sorts, and one that Cho is pleased by, even though it is too late. Harry's being deterred by the gaggle of giggling girls in which Cho seems to move is all too realistic; one wonders, though, if his inability to separate her from them might indicate that he is not quite ready to progress to that firm a relationship.

At dinner, Professor Dumbledore mentions finding a room that was full of chamber pots, and then never being able to find it again. This is the first mention of the Room of Requirement, which Harry will find very useful in later books; it is because Dumbledore has mentioned it to him that Harry feels justified in using it for his Defence Against the Dark Arts classes, once he has been told how to find it.

The discussion we overhear between Karkaroff and Snape is, we find out later, an indication of the increasing power of Lord Voldemort; by now we know that Karkaroff was a Death Eater, and we suspect that Snape was also. We have heard from Sirius that Karkaroff is in bad odour with the other Death Eaters for having named names in order to keep his own freedom. Ron and Harry do not know how Snape and Karkaroff got to be on a first-name basis. Harry has reason to believe that Voldemort is gaining power, and so may believe that Snape and Karkaroff were both Death Eaters, and are discussing Death Eater business. This is largely driven out of Harry and Ron's mind, however, by the scene between Hagrid and Madame Maxime that they inadvertently witness.

The scene between Hagrid and Madame Maxime is witnessed by another party as well. Rita Skeeter, in her Animagus form as a large beetle, is in earshot, and promptly writes a story about Hagrid, his tendency to keep truly dangerous and often proscribed creatures, and his half-Giant ancestry. It seems that this last item was something she needed to tie the story together, because she had the other components of the story long before this. As a result of this story, Hagrid goes into seclusion in his hut and tenders his resignation as Care of Magical Creatures teacher. Professor Dumbledore refuses to accept his resignation, and after a week Hagrid returns to his teaching duties. It is possible that Cho has mentioned to Cedric that Harry had invited her to the Yule Ball; it is certain that Cedric feels kindly disposed to Harry by the end of the evening, because he takes Harry aside, and gives him a very large hint towards deciphering the Golden Egg, which is the necessary clue to the Second Task. Cedric does this, he says, out of a sense of fairness; Harry after all had clued him in to the dragons in the First Task.

Ron spends the first part of the Ball watching Hermione jealously as she dances with Viktor Krum. When she stops by Ron's table after the second dance, he accuses her angrily of "consorting with the enemy"; hot words are exchanged, and Hermione vanishes in the crowd. Ron is then very short with Krum, who until then had been a hero of his. After the ball, Harry steps into the Gryffindor common room, only to catch the end of a flaming row between Hermione and Ron. Hermione ends the argument by saying *"Next time there's a ball, ask me before someone else does, and not as a last resort!,"* and stalking off to the girl's dormitory. Ron has no idea what's going on; he quite obviously has not detected that his own feelings are, in fact, jealousy, though Hermione, and apparently Harry, can see Ron's true feelings quite plainly.

Analysis

The Yule Ball shares the characteristics of Muggle school formals, balls and proms. While students are excited about these events, there is also a great deal of anxiety and stress to overcome. Pressures include securing a partner and acquiring appropriate formal attire. At Hogwarts like other secondary schools, teenage insecurities about peer approval, social skills and self-image are amplified with the Yule Ball.

MAGIC

CREATURES

Animals and intelligent non-human beings that inhabit the magical world.
- Acromantula
- Ashwinder
- Augurey
- Basilisk
- Billywig
- Blood-Sucking Bugbear
- Boggart
- Bowtruckle
- Bundimun
- Centaur
- Chimaera
- Crumple Horned Snorkack
- Chizpurfle
- Clabbert
- Cockatrice
- Crup
- Dementor
- Demiguise
- Diricawl
- Doxy
- Dragon
- Dugbog
- Erkling
- Erumpent
- Fairy
- Fire Crab
- Flobberworm
- Fwooper
- Ghost
- Ghoul
- Giant
- Glumbumble
- Gnome
- Goblin
- Graphorn
- Griffin
- Grindylow
- Hinkypunk
- Hippocampus
- Hippogriff
- Horklump
- House Elf
- Imp
- Jarvey
- Jobberknoll
- Kappa
- Kelpie
- Knarl
- Kneazle
- Leprechaun
- Lethifold
- Lobalug
- Mackled Malaclaw
- Manticore
- Merpeople
- Moke
- Mooncalf
- Murtlap
- Niffler
- Nogtail
- Nudu
- Occamy
- Phoenix
- Pixie
- Plimpy
- Pogrebin
- Porlock
- Puffskein
- Pygmy Puff
- Quintaped
- Ramora
- Red Cap
- Re'em
- Runespoor
- Salamander
- Sea Serpent
- Skrewt
- Shrake
- Snidget
- Streeler
- Sphinx
- Tebo
- Thestral
- Troll
- Unicorn
- Vampire
- Veela
- Werewolf
- Winged horse
- Yeti

---

1. A Weasleys' Wizard Wheeze

Magic

Devices

Objects used by wizards for various purposes.
- Books and Textbooks
- Brooms
- Canary Cream[1]
- Decoy Detonator[2]
- Deluminator
- Disappearing Cabinets
- Extendable Ear[3]
- Floo Powder
- Foe Glass
- Ford Anglia
- Goblet of Fire
- Hand of Glory
- Horcrux
- Howler
- Invisibility Cloak
- Knight Bus
- Marauder's Map
- Mirror of Erised
- Omnioculars
- Paintings
- Pensieve
- Peruvian Instant Darkness Powder[4]
- Philosopher's Stone
- Photograph
- Portkey
- Probity Probe
- Quick-Quotes Quill
- Remembrall
- Secrecy Sensor
- Skiving Snackbox[5]
- Sneakoscope
- Time-Turner
- Ton-Tongue Toffee[6]
- Wand

Magical Plants

- Bubotuber
- Devil's Snare
- Dittany
- Flutterby bush
- Gillyweed
- Gurdyroot
- Mandrake
- Mimbulus Mimbletonia
- Snargaluff
- Venomous Tentacula
- Whomping Willow

Newspapers

- *The Daily Prophet*
- *The Quibbler*
- *Transfiguration Today*
- *Witch Weekly*

Potions and Ingredients

- Amortentia
- Bezoar
- Blood Blisterpod
- Boomslang
- Draught of Living Death
- Dreamless Sleep Potion
- Felix Felicis
- Love Potion
- Pepper-Up Potion
- Polyjuice Potion
- Veritaserum
- Wolfsbane Potion

Methods

Techniques wizards use alone or when interacting with other wizards.
- Animagus
- Apparation
- Divination
- Fire-call
- Floo Network
- Legilimency
- Metamorphmagus
- Occlumency
- Parseltongue
- Priori Incantatem
- Transfiguration
- Unbreakable Vow

Subjects

Courses offered in Hogwarts. A table of who teaches which course in each year is located here.
- Ancient Runes
- Apparation
- Arithmancy
- Astronomy
- Care of Magical Creatures
- Charms
- Defence Against the Dark Arts
- Divination
- Flying
- Herbology
- History of Magic
- Muggle Studies
- Potions
- Transfiguration

Spells

Words or phrases that cause a certain effect when using a wand or when said by a wizard. In the books, the terms Spell, Charm, Jinx, Hex, and Curse are all used; the author explains the difference[7] as follows:
- *Spell* is the generic term, used for all incantations.

---

2. A Weasleys' Wizard Wheeze
3. A Weasleys' Wizard Wheeze
4. A Weasleys' Wizard Wheeze
5. A Weasleys' Wizard Wheeze
6. A Weasleys' Wizard Wheeze
7. http://www.jkrowling.com/textonly/en/extrastuff_view.cfm?id=24

- *Charms* typically would affect the behaviour of an object but do not change its nature. Thus making a pineapple tap-dance across the desk is properly a Charm, because the object remains a pineapple; but turning a teapot into a turtle is a Spell.
- *Jinxes* carry a connotation of dark magic, though of a very minor sort. Jinxes, like Rictusempra, irritate and amuse, rather than harm.
- *Hexes* also carry the connotation of dark magic, again of a minor nature, but slightly darker than Jinxes. An example would be Petrificus Totalus.
- *Curses* are spells that are quite firmly in the Dark Magic camp, and are purely harmful in effect. A Stunning spell is more properly a charm, because the spelled object changes behaviour and not nature; but the name is kept because of the alliteration. These definitions are flexible; for instance the stunning spell Stupefy can be used either by light or dark wizards, in which case it might be seen as a charm or a hex.

- Accio
- Aguamenti
- Alohomora
- Anapneo
- Aparecium
- Avada Kedavra[1]
- Avis
- Banishing Charm
- Bat Bogey Hex
- Bubble-Head Charm
- Colloportus
- Confringo
- Confundus
- Conjunctivitus
- Crucio[2]
- Defodio
- Deletrius
- Densaugeo
- Deprimo
- Descendo
- Diffindo
- Dissendium
- Disillusionment
- Duro
- Enervate
- Engorgio
- Episkey
- Evanesco
- Expecto Patronum
- Expelliarmus
- Expulso
- Ferula
- Fidelius
- Fiendfyre
- Finite
- Finite Incantatem
- Flagrante
- Flagrate
- Furnunculus
- Geminio
- Gemino
- Glisseo
- Incarcerous
- Incendio
- Impedimenta
- Imperio[3]
- Imperturbable Charm
- Impervius
- Langlock
- Legilimens
- Levicorpus
- Liberacorpus
- Locomotor
- Locomotor Mortis
- Lumos
- Mobiliarbus
- Mobilicorpus
- Morsmordre
- Muffliato
- Nox
- Obliviate
- Oppugno
- Orchideous
- Permanent Sticking Charm
- Peskipiksi Pesternomi
- Petrificus Totalus
- Point Me
- Portus
- Prior Incantato
- Protean Charm
- Protego
- Quietus
- Reducio
- Reducto
- Relashio
- Rennervate
- Reparo
- Rictusempra
- Riddikulus
- Scourgify
- Sectumsempra
- Serpensortia
- Silencio
- Sonorus
- Specialis Revelio
- Stupefy
- Tarantallegra
- Tergeo
- Tongue-tying Curse
- Undetectable Extension Charm
- Waddiwasi
- Wingardium Leviosa

Status

Classes within the magical world.
- Half-blood
- Muggle

---

1. An Unforgivable Curse
2. An Unforgivable Curse
3. An Unforgivable Curse

- Muggle-born
- Pureblood
- Squib

LANGUAGES

Fictional languages used throughout the books.
- Gobbledegook
- Mermish
- Parseltongue

TERMS

- Auror
- Dark Mark
- Grim
- Inferius
- Knight Bus
- Money
- Parselmouth
- Patronus
- Prophecy

LEGAL STRUCTURES

- Decree for the Reasonable Restriction of Underage Sorcery
- Wizengamot

KEY MAGICAL ARTIFACTS

Objects that have special significance to the entire series.
- Horcruxes
- Deathly Hallows
- Sword of Gryffindor
- Sorting Hat

Accio

Type: Spell (Charm)
Features: Summons targeted object or mentioned object
First Appearance: *Harry Potter and the Goblet of Fire*

OVERVIEW

Accio is the Summoning Charm; it can be used to bring an object to the spell-caster.

Extended Description There are two instances in Harry's fourth year where he is witnessed using this spell (outside of classes and practice or homework). First, in the First Task of the Triwizard Tournament to Summon his Firebolt broomstick; and secondly, to retrieve the Triwizard Cup when dueling Lord Voldemort.

In his sixth year, Harry tries to use this spell to retrieve his wand after Draco Malfoy has put him in the Body-Bind Curse on the Hogwarts Express; he fails because he is not holding his wand. Harry later uses this spell in an attempt to Summon the Horcrux from the middle of the lake in the cave, but is intercepted. Again he uses this spell in Hogsmeade to Summon some of Madam Rosmerta's brooms, on which to fly to Hogwarts. In his seventh year, Harry, Ron, and Hermione use this spell a number of times to bring things to them, or try to. Some objects, such as the Sword of Gryffindor, prove unresponsive to this charm; Hermione suggests that there are ways of preventing the Accio charm from working.

There are various other instances where this spell is used by other characters.

ANALYSIS

The name of the object can follow the spell word; Harry uses that form, as "Accio Firebolt," to summon his broom. It seems that is an aid to concentration, as the spell-caster should be concentrating hard on the object being summoned. Early in *Harry Potter and the Goblet of Fire*, Mrs. Weasley uses the unadorned "Accio!" to relieve the twins of the prototype charmed sweets they are carrying, before they set off to the Quidditch World Cup, which shows us that naming the object being Summoned is not always necessary.

Despite its apparent simplicity, the Summoning charm is apparently fairly complex. In *Harry Potter and the Goblet of Fire*, we learn that Professor Flitwick has assigned several books on the subject for homework, and Harry has significant trouble with it, being unable to master it until immediately before the First Task. After the Task is completed, Professor Flitwick apparently thinks it worth discussing the Summoning charm with Harry. Flitwick apparently feels that Harry's charm was performed perfectly, which, along with Flitwick's desire to discuss it, would lead us to think that this charm is seldom performed correctly.

One has to wonder what could make this apparently simple charm such a major concern. One possibility is that the charm requires a complete awareness of what it is that you are summoning, where it is, and where you want it to end up. This would be particularly true when the item being Summoned, like Harry's broom, is out of sight. We have already determined that many spells, notably Portus, Apparation, the Patronus charm, and Riddikulus, require a significant mental exertion; so it is not unlikely that the Summoning charm, and probably the analogous Banishing charm, would also require significant mental effort. It is entirely possible that the use of the name of what one is summoning is merely an aid to concentration; that it is the mental image of what one wishes to summon that is the determinant of whether this charm works or not.

Acromantula

Type: Creature
Features: Arachnid, large size, venomous, capable of speech, vigilant
First Appearance: *Harry Potter and the Chamber of Secrets*

OVERVIEW

An Acromantula is a large venomous spider, covered in thick black hair. It is a carnivorous creature and has pincers which create a distinctive clicking sound when aroused. The female is larger than the male and lays up to one hundred eggs at a time. Acromantulae are intelligent beasts, capable of human speech, although not self-taught.

Extended Description Acromantulae originated in Borneo dense jungles, where wizards were said to have bred them, and are one cause of the Ban on Experimental Breeding being put into effect. Acromantula venom is apparently exceedingly valuable, but it is nearly impossible to obtain from the living spider, and as acromantulae eat their dead, it is very uncommon to find one that can still be harvested. Their eggs—large, soft and white in colour—are Class A Non-Tradeable Goods.

Although it is not mentioned in *Harry Potter and the Chamber of Secrets,* Aragog is an Acromantula. The Forbidden Forest population of Acromantulae are fathered by him, and he owes a debt to Hagrid, who raised him in a cupboard in Hogwarts castle fifty years prior. The fact that he is an Acromantula is discovered in *Harry Potter and the Half-Blood Prince.* During the Third Task in *Harry Potter and the Goblet of Fire,* an Acromantula is one of the dangerous creatures that the Champions must overcome to reach the Triwizard Cup at the center of the Maze; Harry very nearly falls victim to it. Acromantulae also play a small role in *Harry Potter and the Deathly Hallows,* where the Death Eaters drive them towards Hogwarts Castle as part of the battle at Hogwarts.

Analysis

Spiders in general, and large spiders in particular, have been a focus of human fear from time immemorial. Some theories suggest that fear of spiders may be inborn. Whether learned or inborn, extreme irrational fear of spiders, Arachnophobia, is one of the most common types of phobia people suffer from. The literary tradition is also rich in spider villains. One of the most obvious examples is the giant spider Shelob in J.R.R. Tolkien's *The Lord of the Rings*

Aguamenti

Type: Spell (Charm)
Features: Produces a stream of water from the caster's wand
First Appearance: *Harry Potter and the Half-Blood Prince*

Overview

The Aguamenti charm causes a stream of clear, potable water to issue from the tip of the caster's wand.

Extended Description In *Harry Potter and the Half-Blood Prince,* Harry's sixth year class are taught this charm. Later in that book, when Harry and Dumbledore are at the cave of the locket Horcrux, Harry uses Aguamenti to refill the crystal goblet with water, of which Dumbledore can drink; the water vanishes before it could be drunk, however. This spell is used once again in that book, when Harry and Hagrid cast jets of water to put out the fire of Hagrid's burning hut.

Alohomora

Type: Spell
Features: Opens locks
First Appearance: *Harry Potter and the Philosopher's Stone*

Overview

Alohomora is a spell that is used to opens locks on doors and windows.

Extended description We are first introduced to this spell two weeks into Harry's first school year, when Hermione uses it to open a door, so that they can escape from Filch. Throughout the books, when a locked door is found, Hermione, if she is available, is called upon first to attempt to open it; it seems that she is the most practiced at this particular spell. Not all doors will respond to this charm, though; for instance, in *Harry Potter and the Order of the Phoenix,* Professor Umbridge has counter-charmed her door so that *Alohomora* will not work, although a knife Sirius gave Harry will.

Analysis

One has to wonder about the usefulness of having locks at all in the Wizarding world. The unlocking spell is so simple that a 12-year-old girl can work it, and it is apparently taught as part of the first year curriculum at Hogwarts; and artifacts (such as Sirius' knife) exist that will unlock even those locks that are charmed against the unlocking spell. From a Muggle point of view, we must assume that an ordinary lock, in the Wizarding world, is similar to a Muggle Yale lock that can be slipped with a credit card; basic security and not much more. If the Alohomora countercharm is used, the security is more that of a bolt lock, with Sirius' knife being akin to more specialized lock-picking gear; presumably, that knife would be controlled by Ministry law, or purchased outside of the legal system. And finally there are high-security locks, such as those at the Ministry (one of which actually melts Sirius' knife) and the vaults at Gringotts.

Questions

1. Hermione finds this spell in *The Standard Book of Spells, Grade 1,* so why do wizards bother to lock doors in the first place if such a simple spell can open them?

Amortentia

Type: Potion
Features: Love potion
First Appearance: *Harry Potter and the Half-Blood Prince*

Overview

Amortentia is an extremely powerful love potion.

Extended Description The first, and as it turns out, only Love Potion mentioned by name, Amortentia is introduced by Professor Slughorn in Harry's first Potions class in year 6. Discussing the characteristics of the potion, Hermione says that it is mis-named; it does not actually produce love, only infatuation, possibly obsession.

Anapneo

Type: Spell
Features: Clears airway
First Appearance: *Harry Potter and the Half-Blood Prince*

Overview

Anapneo is a spell that is used to clear a blocked airway.

Extended description Professor Slughorn cast this spell on Marcus Belby when the latter began to choke after swallowing too fast.

Analysis

The incantation for this spell is based on the Greek πνοη (breath), which is also seen in a number of words in English starting with "pneu-"; the prefixed α may mean "no" with the αν in front of that negating the negative, to change this to mean "restore stopped breath."

Ancient Runes

Type: Subject
Features: Taken by Hermione
First Appearance: *Harry Potter and the Chamber of Secrets*

Overview

Ancient Runes is the study of runic writing. Runes are characters designed to be scratched onto hard surfaces such as rock, and are almost entirely made up of straight lines.

Extended Description We first hear mention of Ancient Runes as a course in *Harry Potter and the Chamber of Secrets*, around Easter. The first two years of Harry's education have been taken up with the basics: Defence Against the Dark Arts, Potions, Charms, Transfiguration, Herbology, History of Magic, and Astronomy, with Flying taking the place of Muggle physical education. As the beginning of the second year approaches, students must choose a set of electives to add to these core subjects. Hermione chooses all the available subjects, including Ancient Runes, and stays with Ancient Runes until the end of her time at Hogwarts.

Hermione makes use of her understanding of Ancient Runes in *Harry Potter and the Deathly Hallows*, where she is bequeathed an ancient copy of *The Tales of Beedle the Bard*. It is her ability to decipher these runes that allows us to hear the Tale of the Three Brothers, and so become enlightened in the nature of the Deathly Hallows. As only Hermione takes this class, we do not see any of it. It is possible that it is taught by Bathsheba Babbling, but we never meet the professor of the course.

Analysis

The sole purpose of the introduction of this course seems to be to allow Hermione to be able to read the copy of *the Tales of Beedle the Bard* bequeathed to her by Professor Dumbledore. One would think that the purpose of this legacy could have been equally carried out by a version of the book written in English. However, creating of the book in runes serves two purposes. First, it indicates in no uncertain terms that the book is extremely old, being written in an alphabet no longer used. This serves, among other things, to reinforce that the tales in this edition are as close to the original as is possible. Second, it requires Hermione to spend time trying to figure out the meaning of the sigil of the Deathly Hallows as it appears over the one tale in that book, requiring that she bring Harry into her thoughts about the symbol, and thus connecting it to Grindelwald's mark, Xeno Lovegood, and the signature on one of Dumbledore's letters as reproduced in Rita Skeeter's book.

Animagus

Type: Class of wizard / witch
Features: Change oneself to an animal
First Appearance: *Harry Potter and the Prisoner of Azkaban*

Overview

An Animagus is a witch or wizard who has the rare ability to change into a particular animal at will. The spell used to become an Animagus is very difficult and dangerous, which is one of the reasons that all Animagi are required to be registered by the Ministry of Magic. Another reason is so the Ministry can make sure the Animagus does not use his or her power to do anything illegal while in their animal forms.

Extended Description While the term is only presented and defined in *Harry Potter and the Prisoner of Azkaban*, the ability of some witches or wizards to change into the shape of animals is seen in the very first chapter of *Harry Potter and the Philosopher's Stone*. Here, Professor Dumbledore addresses a tabby cat as Professor McGonagall, and finds a woman sitting there when he looks again.

Animagi are extremely rare. It is revealed that Professor McGonagall is one of the only seven registered Animagi of the century.

However, we know of four *unregistered* Animagi: Peter Pettigrew (who can transform into a rat), Sirius Black (who can turn into a large, black dog), James Potter (who transformed into a stag), and Rita Skeeter (who becomes a beetle).

The Animagus transformation is one of a very few forms of magic that can be performed in a controlled manner without a Wand. Sirius and Wormtail have displayed the ability to transform into their Animagus shapes without wands.

Analysis

James Potter, Sirius Black, and Peter Pettigrew all became Animagi after discovering that their friend Remus Lupin was a Werewolf. Because a werewolf is only a danger to humans, they decided that they could keep him company during his transformations by turning into animals. They used their power to wander around the Hogwarts grounds at night, while Lupin was in his wolf form.

Rita Skeeter, who is a reporter, became an Animagus perhaps so that she would be able to spy on people to get good stories for the papers she writes for, notably the *Daily Prophet* and *Witch Weekly*. Note that the witch or wizard performing the spell does not have control over the specific type of animal he will become; the form that the wizard's animal form takes will depend on his personality at the time he performs the spell. The fact that Rita became a beetle, so very close to the proverbial "fly on the wall," could only be providential—she could not have selected for it.

One must assume that the main purpose for a wizard to choose to become an Animagus is as a way of transforming into an innocuous beast, so as to avoid recognition while acting illegally. It is for this reason that the Ministry requires that all Animagi be registered, so that any Transformed wizard who chooses to act illegally may be identified.

As mentioned in *The Tales of Beedle the Bard*, the Animagus transformation is a form of Transfiguration. There is a difference, though; a wizard who is Transfigured into an animal is fully an animal, with the animal's brain, comprehension, and abilities, which means that he must perforce remain an animal until some other wizard Transfigures him back into his original self. Following the Animagus transformation, the wizard retains his own intellect and abilities, and so can transform himself back to human.

It should perhaps be mentioned that Professor McGonagall has never done anything unlawful while in her Animagus state. Her sole reason for becoming Animagus was as part of her studies of Transfiguration.

Questions

1. If a wizard performs the Animagus spell twice, can he or she then change into two different types of animal? Or would it change the type of animal he or she could transfigure into? Why?

2. Could a wizard's Animagus form be the same as their Patronus?

3. To become an Animagus, would you be more likely to use a spell or a potion?

4. Do you choose the animal you transform into?

Aparecium

Overview

This spell is used to make invisible paint appear.

Apparation

Type: Spell
Features: Effectively instantaneous transportation
First Appearance: *Harry Potter and the Chamber of Secrets*

Overview

To Apparate is to transport oneself from one place to another by dissapparating and reapparating, coined from the Latin 'appareo,' meaning to appear.

Extended Description In order for a witch or wizard to be allowed to apparate they must first pass a test. One cannot take the test until they are 17 years old. Apparation is very difficult and very dangerous: it is possible for a person to leave parts of their body behind (becoming *splinched*) so that they become stuck and cannot move on either end.

Note that in some editions of some books, this is spelled Apparition; however, the infinitive form, "to apparate," is always spelled the same way. The term *disapparate* is often used to indicate the first part of the process, so for instance on finding a prisoner has escaped, one might more properly say that he "disapparated" rather than that he "apparated."

The noise of someone disapparating can be rather loud; it is described in *Harry Potter and the Order of the Phoenix* as being quite loud, like a car's backfire. The noise of someone apparating to where you are is described in *Harry Potter and the Goblet of Fire* as being a faint pop. Interestingly, in *Harry Potter and the Goblet of Fire*, when Ludo Bagman disapparates from Harry's vicinity, that too is described as a faint "pop." There are three important things to remember when apparating, called the 3 Ds, which stand for destination, determination and deliberation.

• Step One: Fix your mind firmly upon the desired *destination*.

• Step Two: Focus your *determination* to occupy the visualized space. Let your yearning to enter it flood from your mind to every particle of your body.

• Step Three: Turn on the spot, feeling your way into nothingness, moving with *deliberation*.

Analysis

Spells local to Hogwarts School prevent apparation within the school grounds, part of the methods used to protect Hogwarts from outsiders. This is mentioned repeatedly by Hermione, who read it in the book *Hogwarts: A History*.

In order to allow the students to learn apparation, the spells preventing apparation within Hogwarts are locally and temporarily lifted in the Great Hall. We only see this being done in *Harry Potter and the Half-Blood Prince*, when Harry's year group has the opportunity to learn; however, we can safely assume that every year group in turn has this opportunity.

Apparation is deliberately shown as being similar to Muggle driving, with an age limit, safety concerns, licensing requirements, and a proficiency test. It is, as such, an important rite of passage for a young wizard.

The fact that Ron fails his test because of half an eyebrow echoes the type of failure that many readers of this book will experience, or in the case of older readers, will have experienced, at the hands of a Muggle driving examiner. It is necessary to show that Apparation is not an instantaneous process, that it takes calmness, preparation, and deliberation to perform it; otherwise all Wizardly means of transportation, including brooms, Portkeys, the Knight Bus, and the Floo Network, would pale into insignificance. It is useful to note that Mr. Weasley comments in *Harry Potter and the Goblet of Fire* that some wizards will not Apparate because of the danger of splinching; they rely instead on their brooms and the Floo network.

It should also be noted that in *Harry Potter and the Deathly Hallows*, Mad-Eye Moody reports that they can't leave Privet Drive by Disapparating because the Ministry has, for Harry's "protection," banned the use of Apparation, Portkeys, and Floo transport in the vicinity. The implication is that Apparation can be, if not prevented over a relatively wide region, at least detected and traced.

As noted, we first see Apparation when Dobby Disapparates from Privet Drive. At the time, this is not named, and we have no understanding of the mechanism involved, or whether it is only house-elves who can do this. Awareness that humans, also, can Apparate is not given to us until Harry's fourth year, when Mr. Weasley is talking to Harry and his own children about Apparation.

QUESTIONS

1. Why is it that Wizards and Witches are not able to disapparate for their own safety when they are faced with danger? For example, when Harry's mother knew that Lord Voldemort would likely try to kill her and Harry (after killing James, her husband) why didn't she just disapparate with Harry (in a side-along fashion, as in *Harry Potter and the Half-Blood Prince*)? True, many wizarding houses have special spells placed upon them that will not allow for apparation, however, one would think that these could be lifted by the witch or wizard that placed the spell upon the home.

2. Why in *Harry Potter and the The Goblet of Fire* does disapparation sound like a small popping, but in *Harry Potter and the Half-Blood Prince* it sounds like a gun shot or a car back firing? If apparation really is as loud as a car back fire it would be highly restrictive on when and where you could use it.

GREATER PICTURE

It is interesting that in *Harry Potter and the Half-Blood Prince*, the two house-elves Dobby and Kreacher are seen to apparate within the school, where in most earlier books Dobby, at least, apparently travels by more ordinary means within the castle. (He does apparate out of Harry's clutches when Harry is in the Hospital Wing, in *Harry Potter and the Chamber of Secrets*.) J. K. Rowling has stated that house-elf magic is different from human magic, and that they must be able to apparate in order to perform all their duties around the castle;[1] so presumably the anti-apparation spells that block humans from apparating in the castle have been constructed to allow house-elves to continue to apparate. It should be noted that Kreacher apparently reported that he was able to Apparate out of the cave of the locket in *Harry Potter and the Deathly Hallows*, although he didn't call it that: he said that his Master had summoned him, so he went. The implication is that, even when cast by a master wizard like Voldemort, anti-Apparation spells are of no use against house-elves, or a separate spell must be cast to prevent house-elves from being able to do so. If in fact a separate spell must be used to prevent House-elf apparation, such a spell was deliberately not performed at Hogwarts since the ability to apparate is necessary to allow them to do their work. As Voldemort is known to "look down upon 'lesser' creatures," it is most likely that he simply would not go to the effort of setting such a spell, as he would consider it a waste of effort to protect against such insignificant creatures. Voldemort's arrogant disregard for these sorts of magic which are outside of human capabilities shows a critical flaw in his character; magic beyond his understanding ultimately leads to his downfall.

Arithmancy

Type: Course
Features: Hermione takes it
First Appearance: *Harry Potter and the Prisoner of Azkaban*

OVERVIEW

Arithmancy is a branch of magic involving the study of the magical properties of numbers. At Hogwarts, Arithmancy is taught by Professor Vector.

Extended Description Arithmancy is an elective course at Hogwarts. Hermione takes Arithmancy starting in her third year, and continues taking it, apparently, until her sixth year. We are told that she signs up for everything at the beginning of her third year, drops Divination at Easter, and then drops Muggle Studies at the end of the year. On the first day of her third year, Hermione says she is learning much more in Arithmancy than in Divination.

In Arithmancy class, a student is expected to understand complicated number charts and write essays, which is also part of a student's homework. This would seem to make it ideal for Hermione.

Ashwinder

Type: Creature
Features: Serpentine, glowing red eyes
First Appearance: *Fantastic Beasts and Where to Find Them*

---

1. http://www.jkrowling.com/textonly/en/faq_view.cfm?id=73

OVERVIEW

An Ashwinder is a thin, ash-coloured serpent that is born from the embers of a magical fire.

Extended Description   The lifespan of an Ashwinder is short; they live for only an hour. Their primary purpose is to find a secluded area within the home to lay their eggs. Following the egg-laying, the parent ashwinder will collapse into dust. Ashwinder eggs are bright red and can give off intense heat. If not frozen with an appropriate charm, the eggs can ignite the the dwelling within minutes. An ashy trail left by Ashwinders may assist in locating the eggs before any damage happens.

Frozen Ashwinder eggs are valuable. They are used in love potions, and can be eaten whole as a cure for ague.

Astronomy

Type: Course
Features: The cosmos
First Appearance: *Harry Potter and the Prisoner of Azkaban*

OVERVIEW

Astronomy instructs students on planets, stars, and other space objects and their role regarding the magical world.

Augurey

Type: Creature
Features: Small, vulture-like, dark green plumage
First Appearance: *Fantastic Beasts and Where to Find Them*

OVERVIEW

An Augurey, or Irish Phoenix, is a small greenish-black bird that resembles a vulture and can emit a distinctive low cry. Being shy creatures, they stay primarily within their tear-shaped nests and fly only in periods of heavy rain.

Extended Description   Though native to Britain and Ireland, the Augurey has also been spotted throughout northern Europe. They makes their nests in bramble and thorn and their diet consists mostly of large insects and fairies.

In the past, wizards associated the cry of the Augurey with death, and a few early wizards are believed to have succumbed to a heart attack upon being surprised by the wail of an unseen augurey. Later it was determined that, instead of foretelling death, the augurey's cry signalled an impending rain shower.

The Augurey has been used as a home weather forecaster, though its persistent moaning during the winter months can be unbearable for some. As Augurey feathers repel ink, they are ineffective for quills.

Auror

Type: Status
Features:
First Appearance: *Harry Potter and the Goblet of Fire*

OVERVIEW

An Auror is "a Dark wizard catcher." They are an elite group of witches and wizards, loyal to the Ministry of Magic, whose mission is to fight against and capture the forces of the Dark Arts.

ANALYSIS

The Aurors are like a police force, and sometimes work as intelligence agents. They have the authority to arrest malefactors like Death Eaters, and at times have been given authority to use deadly force against Death Eaters in particular.

Training   It takes three years to become an Auror after attending Hogwarts. A candidate to become an Auror should meet the following requirements:
• minimum of five N.E.W.T.s with no grade under "Exceeds Expectations"
• recommended N.E.W.T. subjects are:
 • Defence Against the Dark Arts
 • Charms
 • Potions
 • Transfiguration
The fifth N.E.W.T. subject is left open to the candidate, but Harry evidently selects Herbology as his fifth. One would assume that Muggle Studies or Arithmancy would equally be acceptable.

If the candidate meets the above requirements he or she must also pass the following requirements:
• background check for criminal record
• "a stringent series of character and aptitude tests at the Auror office."

When accepted, the candidate continues on training. Once one becomes an "Auror trainee" they will be taught one of the following:
• Concealment and Disguise
• Stealth and Tracking

Known Aurors   • Dawlish
• Alice Longbottom (insanity due to Cruciatus Curse)
• Frank Longbottom (insanity due to Cruciatus Curse)
 • Alastor 'Mad-Eye' Moody (retired)
 • Proudfoot
 • Gawain Robbards
 • Savage
 • Rufus Scrimgeour
 • Kingsley Shacklebolt
 • Nymphadora Tonks
 • Williamson

Avada Kedavra

Type: Spell (Curse)

Features: Kills instantly
First Appearance *Harry Potter and the Philosopher's Stone* (though not identified until *Harry Potter and the Goblet of Fire*)

OVERVIEW

Avada Kedavra, also known as the Killing Curse, kills a person instantaneously and without injury. There is no countercurse for it, and only two people, Harry Potter and Lord Voldemort, have ever survived it.

Extended Description   The Avada Kedavra curse is recognizable by the flash of green light emitted from the caster's wand. Along with the Cruciatus Curse and the Imperius Curse, Avada Kedavra is considered to be one of the most terrible curses in the magical world, called the Unforgivable Curses; the use of any of the three on another witch or wizard is punishable by a life sentence in Azkaban. Avada Kedavra is an Aramaic phrase that means "I will destroy as I speak." Whether the words were chosen to be similar to the Muggle mock incantation "abra cadabra" is uncertain, but seems likely.

QUESTIONS

1. How did Harry Potter alone survive the Avada Kedavra?
2. Did Lord Voldemort survive the curse when it backfired on him, and what state of life did he come into if he did?

GREATER PICTURE

The Killing Curse is used numerous times by "evil" wizards, and very occasionally by "good" wizards:

• In *Harry Potter and the Goblet of Fire*, it is used by Lord Voldemort against Frank Bryce, we are introduced to it in Defence Against the Dark Arts class by the false Alastor Moody, it is used by Wormtail, at Voldemort's instruction, to kill Cedric Diggory, and it is later used against Harry by the returned Voldemort, though in this instance it is blocked by the Priori Incantatem effect.

• In *Harry Potter and the Order of the Phoenix*, it is used by Lord Voldemort in the climactic battle in the Ministry of Magic.

• In *Harry Potter and the Half-Blood Prince*, it is used once by Bellatrix Lestrange to kill a fox and once by Severus Snape against Albus Dumbledore.

• In *Harry Potter and the Deathly Hallows*, it is apparently used once by Mrs. Weasley to kill Bellatrix Lestrange in a duel during the Battle of Hogwarts, as well as numerous other wizards on both sides of that battle, late in Harry's seventh year. It is also used numerous times by Voldemort as he pursues the Elder Wand, and in a fit of rage against his own followers when he hears of the theft of the Cup Horcrux from Bellatrix's vault. It is also used by Death Eaters during Harry's escape from Privet Drive.

While it is not actually stated, the "green light" that Harry remembers in his earliest memories, and which is mentioned in the first three books, is almost certainly from Voldemort's failed attempt to use the Avada Kedavra curse against Harry. In the seventh book, we see in Voldemort's memory that he used it against Harry's father, mother, and finally against Harry himself. In *Harry Potter and the Goblet of Fire*, we are told that when Barty Crouch was the head of the Auror department, Aurors were authorized to use deadly force against Death Eaters. One must assume that this occasionally took the form of the Avada Kedavra curse.

Avis

Type: Spell
Features: Creates a flock of birds
First Appearance: *Harry Potter and the Goblet of Fire*

OVERVIEW

The Avis spell causes a flock of birds to appear out of the end of the caster's wand.

Extended Description   This spell is used by Mr. Ollivander as part of the process of testing Krum's wand in the Wand Weighing ceremony. Krum's wand is a very sturdy wand, made of hornbeam and dragon heartstring, thicker than most; the Avis spell causes it to give a report like a gun as it creates a flock of small, twittering birds that fly off through the open window.

In Harry's sixth year, Hermione performs this spell twice: once in Transfiguration class, where she is the only person to be able to do it, unsurprisingly; and once a week later when she is suffering jealousy from Lavender and Ron's budding romance.

ANALYSIS

This is a sixth-year spell; creation of living creatures, unlike Transfiguration from non-living objects, is not taught to Hogwarts students until quite late in their education. As such, it is a decent test of the capabilities of a wand.

Banishing Charm

Type: Spell (Charm)
Features: Sends objects away from the caster
First Appearance: *Harry Potter and the Goblet of Fire*

OVERVIEW

Banishing Charms are the opposite of Summoning Charms, and are used to send an object away from the caster.

Extended Description   Banishing charms are more difficult than summoning charms as you are not only impelling an object to move, but ideally you are also telling it where to move to. In Professor Flitwick's class, we see that while nearly everyone has managed to send objects away from themselves (though in the case of Neville's efforts, sometimes it is the wrong object), only the best of the students is able to send their pillows unerringly into the box where they are intended to go.

We never hear the actual invocation of the banishing charm.

Basilisk

Type: Creature
Features: Large size, serpentine, carnivorous, poisonous
First Appearance: *Harry Potter and the Chamber of Secrets*

Overview

A Basilisk—otherwise known as the King of Serpents—is a bright green snake, which can grow to an enormous size. It is a rare, wizard-bred creature, born from a chicken egg hatched beneath a toad; the creation of them is illegal and falls under the Ban on Experimental Breeding. Males are distinguishable from females by the bright red plume on their foreheads. Basilisks have long, poisonous fangs and shed their skin at intervals.

Extended description If someone looks directly into the Basilisk's bulbous yellow eyes, then he or she will die instantly as Moaning Myrtle did, as mentioned in *Harry Potter and the Chamber of Secrets*. If someone looks indirectly (in a reflection, through the lens of a camera), he or she will become Petrified.

A rooster's crow is fatal to Basilisks. Spiders, including Acromantulae, are terrified of them and flee from them.

In *Harry Potter and the Chamber of Secrets*, a Basilisk which lives in the Chamber of Secrets is released periodically by the Heir of Slytherin. The Heir, whose control over the Basilisk is not complete, attempts to guide it to attack students who are Muggle-born. This is apparently an attempt to extend Salazar Slytherin's preferred policy for admittance into the school. Slytherin, one of the four Founders of Hogwarts, believed that only the children of wizards ought to be accepted, and departed the school when the other three would not agree with him. Several students of varying parentage and one cat, Mrs Norris, are Petrified by the Basilisk. When Harry enters the Chamber and fights the blinded Basilisk, he thrusts a sword into the roof of its mouth, a move that will kill it; in turn, one of its fangs pierces Harry's arm, the poison of which nearly kills him.

Analysis

The monster in the Chamber of Secrets, in *Harry Potter and the Chamber of Secrets* is a Basilisk. The process of discovering this is a slow one, both for the reader and for the Trio. The first clue, which happens barely a week in to the term, is the disembodied voice that Harry alone can hear when he is doing his detention with Professor Lockhart. In retrospect, it becomes obvious that Harry can understand it because he is a Parselmouth and can understand snake language; to Lockhart, and to anyone else in the vicinity, what Harry hears as a voice is only a low hissing and sizzling sort of noise. As the Trio leave Nearly Headless Nick's Deathday party, the voice seems to be proceeding upwards between floors without benefit of stairs or anything else; while we have been misled so far into believing that this voice may be coming from something without a physical body, in retrospect again it becomes obvious that the creature is travelling through the pipes. The Petrification of Mrs Norris is another clue, and the dead roosters that Hagrid is waving about at the time Justin Finch-Fletchley and Nearly Headless Nick are Petrified, is of course a final clue. While much is made in the story of the fact that spiders fear Basilisks, to the point that Aragog will not speak its name, this may be an addition to the Basilisk legend by the author; as such, it is a clue for the Trio, specifically for Hermione, but not necessarily for the reader.

Basilisks are impossible to control, except by Parselmouths. A Basilisk would be a dangerous servant, as even its master cannot look into its eyes. As such, they do not play much further part in the story; while it's certainly true that Voldemort can control them, even under that control they would prove as dangerous to his allies as to his enemies.

Questions

1. The one Basilisk that we witness has lived for a thousand years in the Chamber of Secrets, and has apparently become very large. What would it have eaten, locked in the Chamber? How did the animals that it apparently ate, based on the skeletons that Harry found himself walking on, get past the outer door of the Chamber?

Greater Picture

The major story arc of the series revolves around Horcruxes, magical items which are not defined until late in the sixth book. At that time, we will learn that it is necessary to destroy Voldemort's Horcruxes before Voldemort himself can be defeated. We also learn that one of the Horcruxes, Tom Riddle's diary, was destroyed by Harry's stabbing it with a Basilisk fang.

Later still, we learn that in fact Basilisk venom is one of the very few things that can destroy a Horcrux. We learn also that the Sword of Gryffindor had been used to destroy one, the Gaunt ring. This sword, being Goblin-made, will absorb anything that will strengthen it, had apparently absorbed Basilisk venom in the battle against the Basilisk in the Chamber of Secrets, and so now can be used to destroy Horcruxes. It is, in fact, used to destroy two more, Slytherin's locket and Nagini, and Helga Hufflepuff's cup, another Horcrux, is destroyed by the remaining venom in the Basilisk's fangs still lying around in the Chamber of Secrets five years later.

Bat Bogey Hex

Type: Spell (Hex)
Features: Causes victim to be attacked by bat-shaped bogies
First Appearance: *Harry Potter and the Order of the Phoenix*

Overview

The Bat-Bogey Hex apparently causes the victim to be attacked by large, bat-winged bogies.

Extended Description   While the effect of this spell is never completely defined, we do see or hear of its being used a few times. This is one of Ginny Weasley's specialties, almost a signature spell; she uses it on Draco Malfoy to escape from the Inquisitorial Squad when she is being held captive in Dolores Umbridge's office in *Harry Potter and the Order of the Phoenix*, and it is her use of this spell on another student in the Hogwarts Express in *Harry Potter and the Half-Blood Prince* that brings her to the attention of Professor Slughorn.

Bezoar

Type: Device
Features: Cures most poisons
First Appearance: *Harry Potter and the Philosopher's Stone*

Overview

A bezoar is a stone that is removed from the stomach of a goat, and the ingestion of such a stone is said to cure most poisons.

Extended Description   We are first introduced to this artifact when Professor Snape asks Harry, in his first-ever Potions lesson, where he would go to find a bezoar.

The bezoar appears a second time in *Harry Potter and the Goblet of Fire* when it is the "key ingredient" that Harry forgets to add to his antidote in Potions class because of his anxiety over preparing to ask Cho Chang to the Yule Ball.

Bezoars are not mentioned again until *Harry Potter and the Half-Blood Prince*. In Professor Slughorn's Potions class, Harry is called upon to produce an antidote. Rather than creating a complex potion that would counter the mix of poisons in question, he simply retrieves a bezoar from the supplies cabinet. Professor Slughorn absently tucks it into his bag.

The bezoar then becomes vital to the story as Ron is given some poisoned mead while visiting Professor Slughorn; while Slughorn panics, Harry recalls the bezoar, retrieves it from Slughorn's bag, and feeds it to Ron, thus saving Ron's life.

Analysis

With bezoars being so very useful in the case of poisoning, it is rather surprising just how uncommon they are. It seems that there are only a few, even in the supply cabinet in the Potions classroom; and it seems that Professor Slughorn, aware as he is of the effects of potions, does not routinely carry one in his bag. We must assume that they form very rarely in the wild.

Billywig

Type: Creature
Features: Insect, carries sting, achieves high speed
First Appearance: *Fantastic Beasts and Where to Find Them*

Overview

A Billywig is an insect native to Australia. Its speed is so great that most Muggles or wizards cannot recognize it until they are stung by it. It grows up to an inch long.

Extended Description   The effect of a Billywig sting is giddiness followed by levitation. Some wizards have tried to make a Billywig repeatedly sting them to enjoy the side-effects of the Billywig's sting, but too many stings will make the witch or wizard float for days, and if the witch or wizard is allergic to Billywig stings, they may float forever. Dried Billywig stings are used in many potions, and are reputed to be used in making the popular Wizarding treat, Fizzing Whizzbees.

Blood Blisterpod

Type: Magical plant / potion ingredient
Features: Causes unstoppable bleeding
First Appearance: *Harry Potter and the Order of the Phoenix*

Overview

A Blood Blisterpod is a purple pod which either causes uncontrollable bleeding, or if bleeding already is occurring, prevents it from stopping.

Extended Description   Ron passes the Quaffle so enthusiastically to Katie Bell at Quidditch practice, that it hits her in the nose and starts a nose bleed. To stop the bleeding, Fred gives her what he believes is the healing end of a Nosebleed Nougat, but it turns out to be a Blood Blisterpod. Katie loses so much blood that she has to be taken to the Hospital Wing.

Analysis

The fact that Fred is carrying a pocket full of Blood Blisterpods would indicate that they are a vital component of some part of the Skiving Snackbox line, most likely the Nosebleed Nougat. Knowing the twins, they are also quite possibly untradeable magical substances under the law, which would explain why we only see them that once.

Blood-Sucking Bugbear

Type: Creature
Features:
First Appearance: *Harry Potter and the Chamber of Secrets*

Overview

A Blood-Sucking Bugbear is noted in passing in *Harry Potter and the Chamber of Secrets*. Hagrid mentions that his roosters are being killed by "either foxes, or a Blood-Suckin' Bugbear," and needs to ask the Headmaster for permission to put a charm around the henhouse.

ANALYSIS

It is quite possible that this is only mentioned in order to point up the fact that roosters are being killed. The killing of the roosters is a clue to the nature of the occupant of the Chamber of Secrets.

GREATER PICTURE

In fact, it is Ginny Weasley who is killing the roosters, under the orders of Tom Riddle, acting through his diary. This is because a Basilisk can be destroyed by the rooster's crow; if all the roosters have been killed, the Basilisk occupying the Chamber of Secrets will have a longer time when it can be allowed out to roam and hunt. Again, it is this antipathy to roosters which is meant to give the reader an idea of what Hermione is looking for in the library, when it dawns on her what the monster in the Chamber must be.

Boggart

Type: Creature
Features: Shapeshifting
First Appearance: *Harry Potter and the Prisoner of Azkaban*

OVERVIEW

A boggart is a shapeshifter that usually lurks in dark spaces. It has no definite form, taking the shape of the thing most feared by the person who encounters it.

Extended Description To repel or destroy a boggart, it must be laughed at. The spell *Riddikulus* can be cast to force the boggart to assume a generally amusing shape of what the caster mentally conceives.

In *Harry Potter and the Prisoner of Azkaban*, the Boggart appears three times.

• In Professor Lupin's Defence Against the Dark Arts class, we are introduced to the Boggart and his characteristics, and the fact that this allows us to see people's deepest fears; this also allows us a comical jab at Professor Snape, as Neville produces a simulacrum of Snape dressed in his grandmother's favorite outfit. Lupin does prevent Harry from triggering the Boggart's defence mechanism, which Harry feels is unfair; but Lupin later explains this as being done to prevent a simulacrum of Lord Voldemort from appearing in front of the class. This in particular shows that Lupin is much more aware of the class and its needs and concerns than any of the other Defence Against the Dark Arts teachers that have preceded him in the series.

• Later, Lupin uses a second Boggart to train Harry in the use of the Patronus charm and its use against Dementors.

• Either this same Boggart, or a third one, is then used in the final exam for Defence Against the Dark Arts. In this, we see Hermione's insecurity about her grades—her greatest fear is revealed to be "Professor McGonagall—she said I failed everything!" And apparently this is such a great fear that she is unable to invoke Riddikulus against it.

In *Harry Potter and the Goblet of Fire*, Harry encounters a Boggart in the final task of the Triwizard Tournament. It takes the form of a Dementor upon seeing Harry.

In *Harry Potter and the Order of the Phoenix*, a Boggart is discovered in a desk in the Headquarters of the Order. It is identified by Alastor Moody using his magical eye, whereupon Mrs. Weasley goes to eliminate it. Ultimately she is unable to, and Remus Lupin, possibly alerted by Mad-Eye Moody, arrives to vanquish it and rescue her.

ANALYSIS

The appearance of the Boggart in *Harry Potter and the Order of the Phoenix* is particularly interesting, not for the fact of the Boggart, but for the illumination it provides. This episode allows Harry to see what Mrs. Weasley's greatest fears are: that her family, or Harry himself, might end up dead. Naturally, Harry is surprised to see that his well-being is so important to Mrs. Weasley, though he does not comment on it at the time. His thoughts are more about his recent upset at having been passed over for Prefectship, and the realization of just how trivial that was relative to the other possible outcomes for the next few years. The author does not explicitly show us the effect this revelation has on Harry in the long term, but it would be safe to say that Harry is heartened by the discovery that there is someone in the world who cares so much about him.

QUESTIONS

1. In *Harry Potter and the Prisoner of Azkaban*, Professor Lupin says "Nobody knows what a boggart looks like when he is alone," yet in *Harry Potter and the Order of the Phoenix*, Alastor Moody is able to identify it immediately, before it is released from the desk. What did Moody see with his magical eye?

2. Why does a boggart have the full effect on Harry when it turns into a Dementor but it does not make Lupin a werewolf when it turns into a full moon?

3. What parallels can be drawn between the effects of boggarts and the Mirror of Erised?

4. What would Voldemort see when confronted by a boggart?

GREATER PICTURE

There is some conflicting information about the effects of Boggarts. In particular, the Boggart-as-Dementor that Harry is using to learn the Patronus charm affects him exactly as the true Dementors do, weakening him and allowing him to hear his mother's and father's final minutes. Yet the boggart-as-full-moon that appears in Lupin's Defence Against the Dark Arts class, and the similar effect occurring when Lupin confronts the Boggart in *Harry Potter and the Order of the Phoenix,* do not cause him to turn into a werewolf.

Uncharacteristically, when Harry encounters the Boggart-as-Dementor in the maze in *Harry Potter and the Goblet of Fire,* he recognizes it as a Boggart because it trips over its own robes. This is a very uncharacteristic revelation, not something we would expect of a

Boggart, and can only be explained by our later understanding that the false Alastor Moody was watching Harry's progress through the maze and eliminating obstacles. Likely he could not eliminate the Boggart, and so made it clumsy to tip Harry off.

Books and Textbooks

Type: magical artifact
Features: contain information including spells and potion recipes
First Appearance: *Harry Potter and the Philosopher's Stone*

OVERVIEW

Like Muggles, the wizarding world obtains and records information through books. They use books for reference, research and information gathering.

Houses of the Wizarding community also have books in cooking, housework and references. The Hogwarts students devote most of their time in the library to doing their homework, and sometimes borrow library books to read in their own common room. Not all books in the Hogwarts library can be accessed by the students. Some of them are in the Restricted Section of the library, and books in that section contain particularly advanced magic and information about the Dark Arts. In order to borrow books in the Restricted Section, students need a signed permission slip from a professor.

Flourish and Blotts is the main supplier of school and other books, and is located in Diagon Alley.

Lists of Books by Title (Included in this list are the books mentioned in the entire series, including the annual Hogwarts booklists)

A
- *A Beginner's Guide to Transfiguration*
- *Achievements in Charming*
- *A Compendium of Common Curses and Their Counter-Actions*
- *A Study of Recent Developments in Wizardry*
- *Advanced Potion-Making* by Libatius Borage
- *Advanced Rune Translation*
- *A Guide to Medieval Sorcery*
- *A History of Magic* by Bathilda Bagshot
- *An Anthology of Eighteenth Century Charms*
- *An Appraisal of Magical Education in Europe*
- *Ancient Runes Translation*
- *Armando Dippet: Master or Moron?* by Rita Skeeter
- *Asiatic Anti-Venoms*

B
- *Basic Hexes for the Busy and Vexed*
- *Blood Brothers: My Life Amongst the Vampires* by Eldred Worple
- *Break With a Banshee* by Gilderoy Lockhart
- *Broken Balls: When Fortunes Turn Foul*

C
- *Charm Your Own Cheese* by Gerda Catchlove
- *Common Magical Ailments and Afflictions*
- *Confronting the Faceless*
- *Curses and Counter-curses (Bewitch Your Friends and Befuddle Your Enemies with the Latest Revenges: Hair Loss, Jelly-Legs, Tongue-Tying, and Much, Much More)* by Professor Vindictus Viridian

D
- *Death Omens: What To Do When You Know The Worst Is Coming*
- *Defensive Magical Theory* by Wilbert Slinkhard
- *Dragon Breeding for Pleasure and Profit*
- *Dragon Species of Great Britain and Ireland*
- *Dreadful Denizens of the Deep*

E
- *Enchantment in Baking*
- *Encyclopedia of Toadstools*

F
- *Fantastic Beasts and Where to Find Them* by Newt Scamander
- *Flesh-Eating Trees of the World*
- *Flying With the Cannons*
- *Fowl or Foul? A Study of Hippogriff Brutality*
- *From Egg to Inferno, A Dragon Keeper's Guide*

G
- *Gadding With Ghouls* by Gilderoy Lockhart
- *Gilderoy Lockhart's Guide to Household Pests* by Gilderoy Lockhart
- *Great Wizarding Events of the Twentieth Century*
- *Great Wizards of the Twentieth Century*
- *Guide to Advanced Transfiguration*

H
- *Handbook of Do-It-Yourself Broom Care*
- *Handbook of Hippogriff Psychology*
- *Hogwarts: A History*
- *Holidays With Hags* by Gilderoy Lockhart
- *Home Life and Social Habits of British Muggles* by Wilhelm Wigworthy

I
- *Important Modern Magical Discoveries*
- *Intermediate Transfiguration*
- *Invisible Book of Invisibility*

J
- *Jinxes for the Jinxed*

M
- *Madcap Magic for Wacky Warlocks*
- *Magical Drafts and Potions* by Arsenius Jigger
- *Magical Hieroglyphs and Logograms*
- *Magical Me* by Gilderoy Lockhart
- *Magical Theory* by Adalbert Waffling
- *Magical Water Plants of the Mediterranean*
- *Magick Most Evile*
- *Men Who Love Dragons Too Much*
- *Modern Magical History*
- *Moste Potente Potions*
- *Monster Book of Monsters*

N
- *Nature's Nobility: A Wizarding Genealogy*
- *New Theory of Numerology*
- *Notable Magical Names of Our Time*
- *Numerology and Grammatica*

O
- *Olde and Forgotten Bewitchments and Charmes*
- *One Minute Feasts—It's Magic!*
- *One Thousand Magical Herbs and Fungi* by Phyllida Spore

P
- *Powers You Never Knew You Had and What To Do With Them Now You've Wised Up*
- *Practical Defensive Magic and Its Use Against the Dark Arts*
- *Predicting the Unpredictable: Insulate Yourself Against Shocks*
- *Prefects Who Gained Power*

Q
- *Quidditch Teams of Britain and Ireland*
- *Quidditch Through the Ages* by Kennilworthy Whisp
- *Quintessence: A Quest*

R
- *Rune Dictionary*

S
- *Saucy Tricks for Tricky Sorts*
- *Secrets of the Darkest Art*
- *Self-Defensive Spellwork*
- *Sites of Historical Sorcery*
- *Sonnets of a Sorcerer*
- *Spellman's Syllabary*

T
- *The Dark Arts Outsmarted*
- *The Dark Forces: A Guide to Self-Protection* by Quentin Trimble
- *The Dream Oracle* by Inigo Imago
- *The Healer's Helpmate*
- *The Life and Lies of Albus Dumbledore* by Rita Skeeter
- *The Rise and Fall of the Dark Arts*
- *The Standard Book of Spells* by Miranda Goshawk
- Grade 1
- Grade 2
- Grade 3
- Grade 4
- Grade 5
- Grade 6
- *The Tales of Beedle the Bard*
- *Travels With Trolls* by Gilderoy Lockhart
- *Twelve Fail-Safe Ways to Charm Witches*

U
- *Unfogging the Future* by Cassandra Vablatsky

V
- *Voyages With Vampires* by Gilderoy Lockhart

W
- *Wanderings With Werewolves* by Gilderoy Lockhart
- *Weird Wizarding Dilemmas and Their Solutions*
- *Where There's a Wand, There's a Way*

Y
- *Year With The Yeti* by Gilderoy Lockhart

Textbooks   (Textbooks referred to here are the required textbooks each year, as they appeared in the books. The list cannot be complete, as it varies every year and we only see Harry's year and Harry's chosen electives.)

Year 1
- *The Standard Book of Spells Grade 1* by Miranda Goshawk
- *A Beginner's Guide to Transfiguration* by Emeric Switch
- *A History of Magic* by Bathilda Bagshott
- *Magical Theory* by Adalbert Waffling
- *One Thousand Magical Herbs and Fungi* by Phyllida Spore
- *Magical Drafts and Potions* by Arsenius Jigger
- *Fantastic Beasts and Where to Find Them* by Newt Scamander
- *The Dark Forces: A Guide to Self-Protection* by Quentin Trimble

Year 2
- *The Standard Book of Spells Grade 2* by Miranda Goshawk
- *Break with a Banshee* by Gilderoy Lockhart
- *Gadding with Ghouls* by Gilderoy Lockhart
- *Holidays with Hags* by Gilderoy Lockhart
- *Travels with Trolls* by Gilderoy Lockhart
- *Voyages with Vampires* by Gilderoy Lockhart
- *Wandering with Werewolves* by Gilderoy Lockhart
- *Year with the Yeti* by Gilderoy Lockhart

Year 3
- *Intermediate Transfiguration*
- *The Standard Book of Spells Grade 3* by Miranda Goshawk
- *The Monster Book of Monsters*
- *Unfogging the Future* by Cassandra Vablatsky
- *Numerology and Gramatica*
- *Ancient Runes Made Easy*
- *Home Life and Social Habits of British Muggles*

Year 4
- *The Standard Book of Spells Grade 4* by Miranda Goshawk
- *The Dark Forces: A Guide to Self Protection* by Quentin Trimble

Year 5
- *The Standard Book of Spells Grade 5* by Miranda Goshawk
- *Defensive Magical Theory* by Wilbert Slinkhard

Year 6
- *The Standard Book of Spells Grade 6* by Miranda Goshawk
- *Advanced Potion-Making* by Libatius Borage
- *Confronting the Faceless*

ANALYSIS

Curiously, there does not seem to be any Wizarding fiction, apart from the collection of comic books of "*The Adventures of Martin Miggs, the Mad Muggle*" in Ron's room. Granted, most of the work produced by Rita Skeeter seems to be largely fictional, however it is not classed as fiction.

Boomslang

Type: Potion ingredient
Features: Used in Polyjuice Potion
First Appearance: *Harry Potter and the Chamber of Secrets*

OVERVIEW

Boomslang skin is one of the components of Polyjuice Potion.

Extended Description Boomslang skin is used rarely enough that it is not in the student supply cabinet with most other potion ingredients. Hermione determines that in order to make their Polyjuice Potion, she will have to sneak into Professor Snape's office, and arranges a diversion, with Harry's help.

When Boomslang skin turns up missing in *Harry Potter and the Goblet of Fire*, Snape accuses Harry privately of having stolen it.

A Boomslang is an actual creature, despite the exotic name; it is a venomous snake that is native to parts of Africa.

Bowtruckle

Type: Creature
Features: Bark-like skin, sharp claws
First Appearance: *Harry Potter and the Order of the Phoenix*

OVERVIEW

A Bowtruckle is a tree dwelling creature found in western England, southern Germany, and Scandinavian forests. They appear to be made of bark and twigs with two brown eyes which makes them hard to distinguish from the trees they inhabits. If a Bowtruckle thinks its tree is in danger, it has been known to gouge the intruder's eyes out. The Bowtruckle's favourite food is woodlice, which can be used to distract it.

Extended Description Professor Grubbly-Plank teaches a class on Bowtruckles early in Harry's fifth year. Harry's Bowtruckle escapes before he is finished drawing it, and he has to finish the drawing as homework. A Bowtruckle chatters angrily at him later, when he is in the Forbidden Forest.

There is a mention of them also in *Harry Potter and the Half-Blood Prince*. As the Prince is escaping at the end of the book, Hagrid's hut is set on fire. Hagrid comments that he was binding up the legs of a couple of Bowtruckles, and mourns that they are now "burnt ter twigs."

From a throw-away comment by Aberforth Dumbledore in *Harry Potter and the Deathly Hallows*, "They'd be on you like Bowtruckles on Doxy eggs," we surmise that Doxy eggs are a favoured food for Bowtruckles, when they can find them.

ANALYSIS

Bowtruckles are very peripheral to the story. They appear in *Harry Potter and the Order of the Phoenix* as one of the topics most likely to appear on the Ordinary Wizarding Levels tests. Their appearance in the story seems to be designed as a means of comparing Professor Grubbly-Plank's teaching methods with Hagrid's more unorthodox techniques.

Brooms

Type: Magical device
Features: Allows wizard to fly
First Appearance: *Harry Potter and the Philosopher's Stone*

OVERVIEW

Brooms are just what they sound like: magical brooms that allow the witch or wizard to fly. Normally, first-years at Hogwarts are not allowed brooms of their own, although they can and do take flying lessons from Madam Hooch using the old and much-beaten school brooms.

Extended Description Harry is one of the few people for whom the first-years rule is broken; in his first-ever flying lesson, he does so well that Professor McGonagall places him in the Gryffindor house Quidditch team. As Seeker, he needs a better broom than the ones provided by the school, so he receives a Nimbus 2000, then the top-of-the-line broom available.

From the descriptions of flying in the series, it appears that the key to using a broom is balance. The way you balance on the broom controls the direction in which it will fly, shifting your weight forward will bring the handle down and so make it descend. It seems that shifting your weight closer to the broom makes it speed up. Presumably shifting your weight left and right makes it turn. However, it is possible to spin one's body around the broom, and still have it continue traveling in more or less a straight line; this is apparently called a "sloth grip roll," and is mentioned in passing in book 5.

Several different broom makes and models are mentioned in the various books.

- Bluebottle: Advertised at the Quidditch World Cup in *Harry Potter and the Goblet of Fire*. "A Broom for All the Family—safe, reliable and with In-built Anti-Burglar Buzzer..."
- Cleansweep: One of the more utilitarian brands, the Cleansweep line are generally not the top of the speed list but are decent brooms all the same.
- In *Harry Potter and the Philosopher's Stone*, Wood says that they should get Harry a Nimbus 2000 or a Cleansweep Seven, the implication being that these are about equal quality.
- In *Harry Potter and the Chamber of Secrets*, as Draco Malfoy is making fun of the Gryffindors' brooms, he points out that the Twins' brooms, which are Cleansweep Fives, could be auctioned to raise money, and suggests a museum might like to bid on them. It is possible that they are only three years old at this point.
- In *Harry Potter and the Prisoner of Azkaban*, it is mentioned that Ravenclaw's Quidditch team are all mounted on Cleansweep Sevens—with the possible exception of their Seeker, Cho Chang, who is mentioned in the next chapter as having a Comet Two Sixty.
- In *Harry Potter and the Order of the Phoenix*, Ron gets a broom as a reward for becoming a Prefect. The model of the broom is not stated at the time, but it is later mentioned that it is a Cleansweep Eleven. Rhapsodizing about it in the party later, Ron mentions that it will do 0 to 70 in ten seconds.

• Comet: The Comet line is regarded as a workmanlike but not over-speedy broom.

• Two Sixty: Cho Chang, Seeker for Ravenclaw in Harry's third year, rides a Comet Two Sixty, which "will look like a joke next to the Firebolt." If Comet brings out a new model every year, as the Nimbus and Cleansweep lines seem to, the Comet Two Sixty will have been the new model for Harry's Second year (Cho's third).

• Two Ninety: Mentioned only in passing, the Two Ninety is evidently the latest Comet model in Harry's fifth year. Ron, comparing it to his new Cleansweep Eleven, mentions that the Comet Two Ninety will do 0 to 60 in ten seconds.

• Firebolt: In Harry's third year, his Nimbus 2000 is destroyed by the Whomping Willow. It is replaced by a Firebolt, which is a world-class broom; in *Harry Potter and the Goblet of Fire*, it is mentioned that the Irish National Quidditch team are all mounted on Firebolts. It is mentioned in *Harry Potter and the Prisoner of Azkaban* that the Firebolt is capable of 0–150 mph (0–240Kph) acceleration in 10 seconds, which, for the physics geeks, is approximately 0.7G. Additionally, as 150 mph is near terminal velocity for a falling human, the wind force on the rider at the broom's top speed will be about the same as his body weight. This may have something to do with the appearance of footrests on the brooms in the Harry Potter movies.

• Nimbus:

• 2000: the Nimbus 2000 is the broom Harry receives in his first year at Hogwarts. At the time, it is the best broom available, and is ideally suited to the Seeker's job.

• 2001: In Harry's second year, the entire Slytherin Quidditch team are given Nimbus 2001 brooms by Lucius Malfoy, apparently in gratitude for their having put Draco Malfoy on the house Quidditch team as Seeker.

• Shooting Star: An older and cheaper broom, and not very fast; designed, one supposes, for learning riders, like the kid's brooms mentioned in *Harry Potter and the Goblet of Fire*, that were designed to fly only high enough to lift the children's toes out of the grass.

• In *Harry Potter and the Chamber of Secrets*, it was mentioned that Ron's old Shooting Star was often outstripped by passing butterflies.

• In *Harry Potter and the Prisoner of Azkaban*, Harry has to practice on a school broom after his Nimbus 2000 is destroyed; it is mentioned that this broom is an ancient Shooting Star which was very slow and jerky.

• Silver Arrow: mentioned in passing by Madam Hooch as being the type of broom she learned on, one no longer made.

There is also a publication devoted to the merits of the various broomsticks. Named *Which Broomstick*, it is obviously modeled after the British stereo enthusiasts' *Which Hifi* magazine and the more recent *Which PC*.

ANALYSIS

Like muscle cars and roadsters in the 1950s through 1970s, and computers in the 1990s and 2000s for Muggles, brooms are the adolescent wizard's way of showing off. Because of this, there is a rapid turnover in the top of the line models, and a slower change in the more utilitarian models. For instance, the Nimbus 2000 is introduced with fanfare (including a static display at Quality Quidditch Supplies in Diagon Alley) in Harry's first year, but the follow-on model, the Nimbus 2001, is apparently available by the following year, and the Firebolt by his third year. The same turnover can be seen in the Cleansweep line; Ron apparently gets a Cleansweep Eleven, then the "new Cleansweep model," as reward for becoming a prefect in his fifth year, and the Seven is apparently the top of the line in Harry's first year, which means that if the model numbers are sequential, there has been a new Cleansweep each year. Interestingly, if that is the case, the Twin's Cleansweep Fives, which Draco Malfoy speaks of so disparagingly, are at the time only three years old.

As an aside, one wonders whether there is a brisk business in racing brooms sold to wizards trying to recapture their lost youth, similar to the Muggle sports-car market? As wizards generally live longer than Muggles, this would likely be wizards in their 70s and 80s . . .

Bubble-Head Charm

Type: Spell (Charm)
Features: makes a pocket of breathable air about the caster's head
First Appearance: *Harry Potter and the Goblet of Fire*

OVERVIEW

The Bubble-Head Charm makes a pocket of breathable air about the caster's head.

Extended Description   This charm has been seen used in two places so far.

In *Harry Potter and the Goblet of Fire*, Cedric and Fleur use the Bubble-Head Charm in the Second Task. This charm allows them to survive underwater, giving them breathing air, for the time necessary to carry out their task.

In *Harry Potter and the Order of the Phoenix*, after Dolores Umbridge is appointed Headmaster, discipline at the school falls apart. Because she is afraid that the teachers might act to undermine her, Umbridge basically removes any authority they have, which leaves her and Filch the impossible task of maintaining discipline in a school of possibly 600 adolescent witches and wizards. While teachers can maintain order in their individual classrooms, nobody will take responsibility for the hallways, which become littered with dungbombs, which Filch, being a Squib, is largely powerless to clean up. It becomes common practice for the students to use a Bubble-head charm on themselves between classes, because the hallways smell so bad.

Bubotuber

Type: Magical plant
Features: Black and sluglike
First Appearance: *Harry Potter and the Goblet of Fire*

OVERVIEW

Bubotubers are the ugliest plants Harry has ever seen, looking like thick black slugs sticking vertically out of the plant pots.

Extended Description Bubotubers, despite their extreme ugliness, seem to have at least one valuable product. Large, shiny swellings grow on the plant; these are full of a yellowish-green liquid, the "pus," which smells strongly of petrol (gasoline). The raw pus can have unpleasant effects on the skin, so the harvesters must wear dragon-hide gloves; but when properly prepared, it is an excellent cure for the more stubborn forms of acne.

ANALYSIS

Bubotubers are quite a minor sidelight into the world of magic. In this book, they are used for two things: first, to show, by making the plants in Herbology classes more dangerous, that Harry's class has advanced further in their studies, and second, to provide a reasonable noxious substance for inclusion in the hate-mail directed at Hermione. One suspects that this work with bubotubers may be somehow associated with the jinx that Hermione later lays on Marietta Edgecombe.

Bundimun

Type: Creature
Features: Fungus-like, many legs
First Appearance: *Fantastic Beasts and Where to Find Them*

OVERVIEW

A Bundimun is a wizard's pest with many spindly legs. It resembles fungus.

Extended Description Bundimuns are found worldwide. Bundimuns are known as a house pest, destroying the house from the inside out. Unless an exterminator is called in, a house infested with Bundimuns could collapse on itself.

Canary Cream

Type: Magical device
Features: Turns the victim into a canary
First Appearance: *Harry Potter and the Goblet of Fire*, ch. 21

OVERVIEW

Canary Creams, a Weasleys' Wizard Wheezes product, are trick pastries that turns the person eating them briefly into a canary.

Extended Description Canary Creams outwardly look like custard creams, but have a spell on them that causes the consumer to change into a large canary. The spell lasts only a few seconds, after which time the canary moults, and the victim returns to his normal shape. The first victim is Neville Longbottom, but he is by no means the last; these bewitched treats, sold by Fred and George at seven Sickles apiece, are used extensively in the month between the Triwizard Tournament's First Task and Christmas.

ANALYSIS

Canary Creams seem to play no important part in the story, except perhaps as a prelude to the Skiving Snackbox line that Fred and George will be perfecting in *Harry Potter and the Order of the Phoenix*. On their own, they are an indication of the type and extent of the twins' magical abilities, and more specifically of the nature of the tricks that they are likely to play.

Care of Magical Creatures

Type: Course
Features: Interaction with magical creatures
First Appearance: *Harry Potter and the Prisoner of Azkaban*

OVERVIEW

Care of Magical Creatures exposes students to various magical creatures.

Centaur

Type: Creature
Features: Horse's body, human torso & head, intelligent
First Appearance: *Harry Potter and the Philosopher's Stone*

OVERVIEW

Centaurs are magical creatures with the upper body of a man and the lower body of a horse.

Extended Description Centaurs are a noble race that greatly values astrology and Divination. They like to keep to themselves, and think that it is beneath them to do a wizard's bidding. There is a large herd of centaurs that lives in the Forbidden Forest around Hogwarts. They are excellent archers. Notable Centaurs include Firenze and Bane; Magorian and Ronan are also mentioned.

Centaurs do not like to associate with humans, but they "do not harm foals" (meaning children and teenagers). They also do not like being underestimated or thought of as creatures. They attack Professor Umbridge after she calls them "filthy-half breeds" and states they have "near-human intelligence." They also get extremely angry at Hermione for letting on that she and Harry had purposefully led Umbridge into the forest so the Centaurs could "take care of her for them."

ANALYSIS

Centaurs see themselves as more intelligent and more aware of the world and the Universe than humans; this is why the more excitable among them, notably Bane, get so angry when their intelligence is impugned by "mere Humans." Firenze is expelled from the herd because he chooses to work for Professor Dumbledore, as the majority of the herd feel that this makes him subservient to a human.

Charms

Type: Course
Features: Spell-casting
First Appearance: *Harry Potter and the Philosopher's Stone*

OVERVIEW

Charms is a course that teaches how to cast the class of spells known as Charms. These are spells that alter an object without changing its essential nature. Given a teapot, the spell that makes it tapdance across the desk would be a charm, the spell that turns it into a tortoise would not.

Extended Description The Charms class is taught by Professor Flitwick. Spells taught in this class include Wingardium Leviosa, Summoning and Banishing, Aguamenti, and turning vinegar into wine. Because it is a lab class, with much wand work and people saying spells, it is often a nearly ideal place for Harry, Ron, and Hermione to have more or less private conversations.

Chimaera

Type: Creature
Features: lions head, goats body, dragons tail
First Appearance: *Fantastic Beasts and Where to Find Them*

OVERVIEW

A Chimaera is a rare Greek beast. It has the head of a lion, body of goat and tail of a dragon.

Extended Description According to "Newt Scamander" in *Fantastic Beasts and Where to Find Them*, the Chimaera is extremely dangerous and has only ever been successfully slain once. Their eggs are classified as Class A Non-Tradeable Goods. In *Harry Potter and the Order of the Phoenix*, Hagrid expresses his disdain for the Ministry of Magic guidelines by asking why anyone would rather study Knarls than Chimaeras. Hermione, reporting this to Harry and Ron, nervously comments that she doesn't think Hagrid has any Chimaeras stashed away for them to study.

Chizpurfle

Type: Magical creature
Features: crab-like, extremely small
First Appearance: *Fantastic Beasts and Where to Find Them*

OVERVIEW

Chizpurfles are a wizarding pest, devouring anything magical or electrical.

Clabbert

Type: Creature
Features: Pustule on forehead, horns, long limbs
First Appearance: *Fantastic Beasts and Where to Find Them*

OVERVIEW

Clabberts are agile, tree-dwelling creatures.

Extended Description The Clabbert's long, supple limbs make them ideal for swinging between branches, which likens them to some primates. Their hands and feet are webbed, and their smooth, hairless skin is mottled green, giving them an amphibious appearance. They bear two short horns and have wide, grinning mouths full of sharp teeth. Clabberts are easily distinguished by the large pustule in the center of their foreheads, which turns red and flashes at approaching danger, including Muggles. The International Confederation of Wizards fines those who keep Clabberts within the sight of Muggles; they cause too much unwanted attention (by appearing to have their 'Christmas lights' up in mid-summer).

The Clabbert originated in southern USA, but is exported worldwide. Their diet consists of small lizards and birds.

Cockatrice

Type: Magical creature
Features:
First Appearance: *Harry Potter and the Goblet of Fire*

OVERVIEW

A Cockatrice is, in Muggle texts, a synonym for a Basilisk. Though never fully defined in the Harry Potter series, it is apparently a dangerous creature that reproduces by means of eggs.

Extended Description There are only two mentions of a Cockatrice anywhere in the series. One is when Karkaroff is accusing Professor Moody of being overcautious, perhaps to the point of paranoia. Karkaroff says that Moody had destroyed a gift given to him because it was ticking and he had thought it might contain a Cockatrice egg; in fact it was a carriage clock.

The other is when Hermione, in response to Ron's question about who the five judges for the Triwizard Tournament are, says that three of the judges must be the heads of the three schools. This was because she has found mention of the Triwizard Tournament of 1792, in which all three school heads were injured when a cockatrice the Champions were supposed to be catching went on a rampage.

Interestingly, cockatrices are not mentioned in "Newt Scamander"'s *Fantastic Beasts and Where to Find Them*.

ANALYSIS

From the limited description we have, we do not know whether Basilisks and Cockatrices are the same creature, as our Muggle literature would indicate. As a Basilisk hatches from a chicken's egg (in Muggle mythology, a rooster's egg) incubated by a toad, it is possible; but no mention is made of the basilisk egg making a ticking sound. One also would have to wonder if the egg could be taken away from the toad before it hatched: would the lack of incubation prove fatal to the basilisk?

Colloportus

Type: Spell
Features: Seals a door First Appearance

OVERVIEW

The Colloportus seals a door.

Confringo

Type: Spell (Curse)
Features: Makes a thing explode
First Appearance: *Harry Potter and the Deathly Hallows*

OVERVIEW

Confringo is a spell or curse used to make things explode.

Extended Description As Harry is making his escape from the Dursleys' during the fourth chapter (The Seven Potters) of the *Harry Potter and the Deathly Hallows*, the side car that has been bolted on to Sirius' flying motorbike, in which Harry is riding, breaks away due to the strain of flight. Harry is rescued by Hagrid, but then uses this spell to destroy the abandoned side car, disabling one of the attacking Death Eaters with the fragments. This spell is used again in the battle with Nagini; here, Hermione casts it, and it ricochets around the room before hitting something it can blow up. Hermione later identifies it as the Blasting Curse.

ANALYSIS

This is similar in effect to a differently-named spell used in some fan fiction; one may wonder whether the name was chosen specifically to avoid similarity to the name in the fan fiction. It also appears similar in effect to the Expulso and Deprimo spells.

Confundus

Type: Spell (Charm)
Features: Causes confusion in the subject
First Appearance: *Harry Potter and the Prisoner of Akaban*

OVERVIEW

The Confundus charm makes the subject confused. It fairly advanced magic and is cast by muttering the incantation "Confundo." The Confundus charm can apparently also be cast silently.

Extended Description In *Harry Potter and the Prisoner of Azkaban*, Severus Snape knows that his story of what happened in the Shrieking Shack will differ radically from Harry's, so he claims that Harry was obviously suffering under the effects of a Confundus charm.

In *Harry Potter and the Half-Blood Prince*, Hermione casts this charm on Cormac McLaggen, a potential goalkeeper, to prevent him looking better than Ron at the team try-outs.

ANALYSIS

The latter use of this charm would indicate that there are physical as well as mental effects; McLaggen, some time after he is Confunded, has trouble navigating stairs.

Conjunctivitus

Type: Spell (Curse)
Features: Causes blindness
First Appearance: *Harry Potter and the Goblet of Fire*

OVERVIEW

The Conjunctivitus curse apparently causes temporary blindness.

Extended Description In *Harry Potter and the Goblet of Fire*, Harry is required to get past a Dragon in the First Task of the Triwizard Tournament. Dragon hide is nearly impervious to most spells—it takes several wizards working in concert to Stun a dragon, for instance—so in order to disable a dragon single-handed, you must attack its only vulnerable area, its eyes. The Conjunctivitus curse is the one you use to do that.

We are told about this spell, but we do not see it actually executed, so we do not know the incantation.

Crucio

Type: Spell (Curse)
Features: Causes great pain
First Appearance: *Harry Potter and the Goblet of Fire*

OVERVIEW

The Cruciatus Curse causes extreme amounts of pain on the victim. Along with the Imperius Curse and the Killing Curse, the Cruciatus Curse is considered to be one of the most terrible curses in the magical world, called the Unforgivable Curses; the use of any of the three on another witch or wizard is punishable by a life sentence in Azkaban.

Extended Description Bellatrix Lestrange and three other of Lord Voldemort's Death Eaters used this curse on Neville Longbottom's parents, torturing them into a state of irreversible madness. Since that time, they have resided in a special ward at St. Mungo's Hospital.

Harry Potter attempts this curse on Bellatrix Lestrange after she kills Harry Potter's godfather, Sirius Black. However, when Harry casts this curse it does not have the same effect as Lestrange's or other Dark Wizards.' As Lestrange explains to Harry, the caster must really intend harm on the victim for the curse to have its desired effect. In Harry's case, he is consumed with a righteous anger rather than a malicious intent.

QUESTIONS

1. Why was Voldemort's Cruciatus Curse ineffective against Harry in the Forbidden Forest after Harry's "near-death" experience?
2. Does the wand in any way define the power of the Cruciatus curse?

GREATER PICTURE

In *Harry Potter and the Order of the Phoenix*, Harry attempts to use the Cruciatus Curse against Bellatrix Lestrange, in self-defense, but fails. Bellatrix taunts him for this failure, saying he has to "really mean it," that he has to really hate someone for that curse to be effective. Just as the Patronus charm depends upon having a mind filled with happy thoughts, so must the Unforgivable Curses depend on having the mind filled with hate or anger. Harry truly realizes this when he casts the Cruciatus Curse on Amycus Carrow after Carrow spits in the face of Professor McGonagall in the Ravenclaw dormitory, stating his understanding of the anger one must feel to make such a curse be effective.

Crumple Horned Snorkack

Type: Magical Creature
Features: large horn; tiny purple ears
First Appearance: *Harry Potter and the Order of the Phoenix*

OVERVIEW

The Crumple-Horned Snorkack is mentioned in passing, but never described in detail.

Extended Description Luna Lovegood mentions the Crumple-Horned Snorkack a number of times in *Harry Potter and the Order of the Phoenix*; apparently, her father, the publisher of *The Quibbler*, believes in the existence of this and other magical creatures that nobody else has ever seen. This is a sore point for Hermione, who will not believe in their existence without seeing some proof.

At the end of the book, Luna says that some of the money her father has received for the right to publish Harry's interview about the return of Voldemort will be spent on an expedition to find the Snorkack, an expedition that we later find out is fruitless.

The Snorkack is mentioned again in *Harry Potter and the Deathly Hallows*, when Harry visits Luna's father, Xenophilius. Apparently, Xeno has purchased what he thinks is a Snorkack horn, to give to Luna for Christmas; in fact, it is an Erumpent horn, which explodes, nearly destroying Xeno's house.

Later in the book, when Luna and Dean Thomas, among others, have been rescued from Malfoy Manor, we overhear Luna describing the Snorkack to Dean. The only description we hear, though, is that it has tiny, purple ears.

ANALYSIS

The major reason for introducing the Crumple-Horned Snorkack, one must suppose, is to show Luna Lovegood's mild strangeness; her insistence that this creature exists is a harmless form of insanity and is therefore seen as laughable rather than dangerous. Her steadfast holding to this belief is another part of the limning of her character; Luna, though believing things that just aren't so (according to accepted wizard lore) holds steadfastly to her beliefs, to her father's beliefs, and similarly to her friends.

QUESTIONS

1. Presumably, the Crumple Horned Snorkack has at least one crumpled horn. What do you think it looks like? What characteristics would it have?
2. Luna's father says that they will be hunting for it in Sweden; can you think of characteristics that would make it more likely to be there than, say, Florida?

Crup

Type: Magical Creature
Features: looks like a dog
First Appearance: *Harry Potter and the Order of the Phoenix*

Extended Description Mentioned only in passing in *Harry Potter and the Order of the Phoenix*: Professor Grubbly-Plank, in response to a question from Professor Umbridge, says that she will be training the class to recognize Knarls and Crups.

Dark Mark

Type: Signal / emblem
Features: Skull and snake; Voldemort's sign
First Appearance: *Harry Potter and the Goblet of Fire*

OVERVIEW

The Dark Mark is a sigil or sign, being the image of a skull with a snake twisting through it.

Extended Description The Dark Mark, being Lord Voldemort's sign, is almost as much feared as Voldemort is himself. There is an incantation, Morsmordre, which will create an image of the Dark Mark floating in the sky above the caster; this symbol was routinely left floating above a house in which the inhabitants had been killed by Death Eaters. Every Death Eater also has a copy of this emblem or sigil burned into his left forearm by Voldemort himself; its clarity and color change with the Dark Lord's power. They also serve as a signalling device; when Voldemort touches the Dark Mark of any Death Eater, all other Dark Marks turn black and painful. This is a signal to all Death Eaters to stop what they are doing and Apparate immediately to Voldemort's side. The communication aspect of the mark also appears reversed, as Death Eaters are able to touch their marks to call Lord Voldemort.

ANALYSIS

It is, of course, significant that the Dark Lord's call involves inflicting pain on his supporters. It is clear by this alone that Voldemort does not lead so much as whip his followers into line; they follow more out of fear and the hopes of getting some of his leavings, rather than out of respect.

It is uncertain how much information is transferred via the Dark Mark. When we first see it used, it seems to be implied that it is acting as a simple caller; Voldemort says that his touching Wormtail's Mark will summon his Death Eaters to his side. Later, we see that individual Death Eaters seem to be able to transfer more information than that to Voldemort, identifying themselves and their locations as well as indicating that they have found "the boy" (Harry). As individual Death Eaters use it to notify Voldemort of events, we also find that it is a broadcast system; at least some Death Eaters can perceive when other Death Eaters report to Voldemort.

GREATER PICTURE

Clearly, when Voldemort summons all his Death Eaters to the graveyard in *Harry Potter and the Goblet of Fire*, it is then a broadcast, as more than one Death Eater responds. The fact that they responded with such alacrity indicates that they knew it was Voldemort summoning them, which means that the individual touching the Mark, rather than the individual wearing the Mark, is the one identified with the sending. (Recall that it was Pettigrew's Mark that Voldemort touched, not his own—if in fact Voldemort has one.) When Alecto Carrow summons Voldemort because Harry has been located inside Hogwarts, Snape evidently intercepts the message.

Both in the broadcast nature of the communications, and in the ability to pass extra information, one can see great similarity to the Protean charm. Hermione actually notes the resemblance when speaking with members of Dumbledore's Army in *Harry Potter and the Order of the Phoenix*.

Darkness Powder

Type: Magical material
Features: Creates instant darkness
First Appearance: *Harry Potter and the Half-Blood Prince*

OVERVIEW

Peruvian Instant Darkness Powder is, as the name suggests, a powder which renders an area instantly dark when it is thrown.

Extended Description A product of Weasleys' Wizard Wheezes, Peruvian Instant Darkness Powder is one of the more serious products that the Twins sell to the Ministry of Magic and similar organizations. We see it in the back room of the Twins' shop when Fred and George are showing Harry around.

Somehow, Draco Malfoy manages to purchase some of this material, and uses it to mask the invasion of Hogwarts from the Room of Requirement in *Harry Potter and the Half-Blood Prince*. When the powder is thrown at Ron, Ginny, and Neville, they are unable to see anything, which means that it must have blocked all light from entering the region where the powder was thrown; however, Draco, who has a Hand of Glory, is still able to see to lead the invading Death Eaters past them.

Deathly Hallows

Type: Objects
Features:
First Appearance: *Harry Potter and the Deathly Hallows*

OVERVIEW

The Deathly Hallows are historic and magical artifacts that cause the true owner of them to become "The Master Of Death."

Extended description The Deathly Hallows are described to us initially in *The Tale of the Three Brothers*, one of the Wizarding fairy tales initially collected by Beedle the Bard. Hermione receives an early edition of this book in Albus Dumbledore's will, in which it appears Dumbledore has marked *The Tale of the Three Brothers* with what turns out to be the sign of the Deathly Hallows. Most believe the Tale of Three Brothers to be only a fairy tale, but there are a large number of wizards who believe the Deathly Hallows are actual artifacts.

According to the tale, Death himself gave the artifacts to the three brothers as reward for outwitting him. Dumbledore is less certain; he feels that the three brothers, the Peverells, were strong and dangerous magicians who created the artifacts themselves. We learn that one of the three brothers, Ignotus, is buried in Godric's Hollow, under a stone bearing the symbol of the Deathly Hallows; the other two, Antioch and Cadmus, we know little apart from their names.

The Deathly Hallows are:

1. The Elder Wand—An undefeatable wand given to the "combative brother," it will defeat any wizard in a duel so long as it has accepted the wizard holding it as its master. It can also do magic at amazing levels outside of battle, for example fixing Harry's wand when even the wandmaker Mr. Ollivander states it can't be fixed. It was supposedly created when Death picked a branch from a nearby elder tree and charmed a wand out of it. The wandmaker Gregorovitch claimed to have found it and was supposedly studying its secrets so that he could replicate it; before he managed that, however,

it was stolen from him by Gellert Grindelwald. Grindelwald used that as the core weapon in his war against the Wizarding government in Europe, eventually falling to Dumbledore in 1945. Dumbledore then carried the wand until it was, in turn, captured from him by Draco Malfoy. Draco, of course, does not know the history of the wand, and is unaware that it has shifted allegiance to him. Dumbledore is buried with his wand, and Voldemort eventually traces it to his tomb, and then steals it, thinking that this will make him the master of it. However, Harry has already won its ownership by disarming Malfoy; the wand may not be aware of this, until it is confronted with Malfoy's wand, the same wand that caused Dumbledore to give it up, in Harry's hand. In the end the wand favours Harry in the final battle, and Harry returns it to Dumbledore's tomb. The author has indicated that the core of the Elder Wand is a hair from a Thestral, "a powerful and tricky substance that can be mastered only by a witch or wizard capable of facing death."[1] This seems entirely appropriate given the association with death of the Elder Wand, and of the Thestral.

2. The Resurrection Stone—This stone brings the dead back to life. According to the myth, it was created when Death charmed a stone from the river's edge for one of the Peverell Brothers. Throughout the seven books of the Harry Potter series, we are shown repeatedly that the dead can return in some form; there are the ghosts, of course, and the portraits, which share some characteristics of their originators: shape, memories, and apparently thought processes. There are the echoes of the people who Voldemort has killed, which are forced out of his wand by the Priori Incantatem effect in the graveyard; again sharing some of the characteristics of the people, although Dumbledore later says that they are not the people themselves. There is Voldemort himself, his soul anchored to the Earth by Horcruxes. And there is the Resurrection Stone, which again does not actually reanimate people, but raises what might be called "shades," images of the summoned people with their characteristics, memory and appearance. This artifact was put into a ring which was passed down the generations of the Peverell Family, later becoming little more than a symbol of pure-blood pride. Voldemort, knowing only of its value as a relic of the now-gone Peverell family, and unaware of the connection with the Deathly Hallows, had turned it into a Horcrux and hidden it in the Gaunts' shack. Dumbledore, by the summer following Harry's fifth year, was hunting Horcruxes, having heard of the locket and the ring, and seen the destruction of the diary. He had traced the ring back to the Gaunts, and found it; though he had destroyed the Horcrux, in the process he had unwisely activated a curse in the ring itself, thus bringing an end, shortly, to his own life. Dumbledore passed the ring on to Harry by hiding it in a Golden Snitch which Harry had caught to win his first ever Quidditch match at Hogwarts.

3. The Invisibility Cloak—According to the legend, this is not the sort of invisibility cloak that can be made by human hands, charmed with a Disillusionment charm or a Bedazzlement hex, or woven out of Demiguise hair, but rather is Death's own cloak, which unlike other cloaks, is immune to all charms, hexes, and even any form of physical damage which may occur to it. It is reputedly so powerful that it hides the wearer from even Death himself. Legend says that it will be passed down from father to son through the generations of the Peverell Family. Harry, Ron, and Hermione are stunned to realize that the cloak Harry is carrying while they are being told this is the only cloak they have ever seen that matches this description. Dumbledore later confirms this to Harry; the cloak had been passed down to the last descendants of Ignotus Peverell, born like Ignotus in Godric's Hollow: James Potter, and his son Harry. Only by two means has the disguise of the Invisibility Cloak been penetrated; the magical eye of Alastor Moody was able to see through it, and the Marauder's Map similarly would show the person under the cloak. It is uncertain whether the Cloak provides immunity to charms; it is certain that it is itself unable to be Summoned, as that was tried by Death Eaters at one point, so it is unlikely that it can be affected by any magical means. Unfortunately, while the cloak is immune to spells cast at it, it does not offer the same protection to those who use it. It is true that in the battle with the Death Eaters in Tottenham Court Road when a curse is thrown at Harry (who is under the cloak) he escapes untouched while a table behind him explodes, but it is uncertain whether the curse was properly aimed at Harry. However, when Harry hides in Draco's compartment on the Hogwarts Express, Harry is successfully petrified while wearing the invisibility cloak.

ANALYSIS

As we can see from the above, while the Deathly Hallows are only named in the seventh book, they play a vital role in the entire series, and actually two of the three play a continuing role: the Elder Wand, which is Dumbledore's from when we first see him, and the Invisibility Cloak, which had been James' and was passed on to Harry. More than that, though: a large part of Dumbledore's youth had been involved in the search for the Hallows, and for the means of mastering Death.

Dumbledore had hoped, by having the Elder Wand placed with him in his tomb, that the power of the Wand would then be ended; the wand would transfer its allegiance to the latest person who had captured it, and as Snape had killed Dumbledore, it would be Snape to whom the wand owed its allegiance. Snape, not knowing of the Deathly Hallows, and having promised to have Dumbledore buried with his wand in his hands, would thus have eventually died without having forcibly lost the wand. Not being skilled in wand lore, however, Dumbledore was unaware that Draco's disarming him would cause the wand to transfer its allegiance. Harry had checked this point with Mr. Ollivander; it is the gaining control over the wand against the will of the current holder, not causing the current holder's death, that causes the transfer of allegiance. Voldemort had the same mistaken belief, which is what

---

1. http://www.jkrowling.com/textonly/en/extrastuff_view.cfm?id=25

led to his killing Snape. Harry, believing that by capturing Draco's wand from him, and then by capturing the Elder Wand from Voldemort, he had transferred the Elder Wand's allegiance to him, had the wand re-interred with Dumbledore's body. When Harry dies, if the wand has remained in Dumbledore's tomb, it will be impossible for anyone to gain its power, as Harry will not be there to try to prevent it.

While it is likely that Dumbledore would have been able to use the Resurrection Stone to bring his loved ones back, he was initially misled by the Horcrux in the ring, and then later came to believe that there would be no point. The brother who had received the Stone in the legend had caused his sweetheart to be resurrected, but had found that the resulting simulacrum was worse than her absence in death had been, and eventually he had killed himself to be properly reunited with her. Dumbledore rightly decides that he is likely to suffer the same sadness; the re-animated Percival, Kendra, and Ariana will not bring him joy at their return, but only sadness at their incompleteness. Harry, in his turn, though, uses the Stone not to recover those he has lost, but to seek their support in what he has to do. It is not the people themselves he wants, but their spiritual support, which as spirits they are uniquely able to provide. Having received that support from them, Harry deliberately drops the ring, and chooses to not search for it. The Cloak, of course, is the one that Harry is carrying. On the night that James had been killed, Dumbledore had the cloak and was examining it; by that time, he had given up seeking the Hallows, but here was his chance to actually hold two of the three at one time. In the end, Dumbledore had passed it to Harry, as James would have wished; Harry chooses to pass on to his own descendants, as it was passed on to him. Dumbledore seems to think this is only right and proper. The fact that the cloak is out of the ordinary is a new idea to Harry and Hermione, as it is to us, the readers, when the story of the Deathly Hallows is presented to Harry; Harry's Cloak, exceptional as it may be, is the only one we've ever had the chance to examine. Ron may understand that it is out of the ordinary, but Ron is, relatively speaking, immature; he may not make the connection until Xeno Lovegood spells it out for them. It may be worth mentioning that Voldemort had likely never heard the tale of the Three Brothers. Fairy stories are typically told to the young, of course, and at the age where he would be expected to hear these stories, he would have been in the Muggle orphanage. As a result, he likely heard of Cinderella, which wizards have never heard of; but the tales of Beedle the Bard would be a closed book, being too young for him and therefore something in which he was not interested when he finally entered the Wizarding world. This could explain why he was so interested in Horcruxes, and paid no attention to Hallows; he was unaware of the existence of the Hallows, to the point that he actually changed one of them into a Horcrux. It is true that he seeks the Elder Wand; however, Xeno Lovegood tells us that the Deathstick, as it is also called, has left a broad and bloody trail through history, and so for Voldemort it may have an existence totally separate from the other two Hallows, which have been less prominent in Wizarding history.

One of the things that is repeated a number of times is the idea that the holder of all three Hallows will be truly the Master of Death. The naïve wizard will think that this means that he will have power over Death, able to kill others and resurrect them with impunity, and hide from death himself. It is apparent from looking at the effects that the Hallows actually have that this is not what happens. While the holder of the wand cannot be bested in battle, still the wand may be removed from him by force, and he himself could be killed by non-magical means. The stone will not truly resurrect, but will only provide the sort of pale imitation of life that ghosts have. And one can hide under the cloak for a limited time only. The only way to achieve mastery over death is to understand it and be prepared for it. Dumbledore has said something about this as well: as early as the first book, Dumbledore said "To the well organized mind, death is but the next great adventure." Death can be postponed, as demonstrated by Nicholas Flamel, but it cannot be avoided; to gain power over death, you must gain understanding of it and lose fear of it. One thing that is brought out is that the Hallows do prove something of a litmus test for the personality of the wizard. When Harry, Ron, and Hermione are discussing them, they each immediately choose which of the three is the most valuable. Hermione chooses the cloak, Ron the wand, and Harry the stone. We see immediately that Ron, in thinking of an undefeatable wand, is seeing himself as the head of a gang of followers; Harry is mourning his losses still, though perhaps more wistfully than actively; and Hermione, aware of the value of the cloak that they actually have, is thinking of how much they have been able to do while concealed by it. The young Dumbledore and Grindelwald similarly select the wand and the stone, for similar reasons.

Decoy Detonator

Type: Magical Device
Features: Creates a distraction
First Appearance: *Harry Potter and the Half-Blood Prince*

Overview

Decoy Detonators are products of Weasleys' Wizard Wheezes. They are small devices which scurry off into shadows and then make a noise, thus decoying people away.

Extended Description We first see Decoy Detonators when Harry, Ron, Ginny, and Hermione, along with Mr. and Mrs. Weasley, visit the Twins' new joke shop in Diagon Alley. Fred, giving Harry the tour of the shop, takes him into the back room where the more serious magical items are kept, and there shows him the Decoy Detonators, saying they can't keep them on the shelves.

When the Trio are planning to break into the Ministry in *Harry Potter and the Deathly Hallows*, Decoy Detonators are one of the things on Hermione's list. Harry then uses one of them to distract a room full of witches and wizards so that he can enter Umbridge's office undetected. The Detonator scuttles silently to the far side of the room, then blows itself up, making a sharp noise and a cloud of smoke. The witches and wizards examine it for a long time, finally deciding that it is an escapee from the department of Experimental Charms.

Decree for the Reasonable Restriction of Underage Sorcery

Type: Legal structure (Law)
Features: Prevents underage wizards from using magic
First Appearance: *Harry Potter and the Philosopher's Stone*

Overview

The Decree for the Reasonable Restriction of Underage Sorcery is a law that limits the magic that underage wizards are allowed to use. The apparent intent is to keep young, untutored wizards from running amok with their wands and causing consternation among the Muggles.

Extended Description Our first introduction to this statute is in the note that is given out to every student at the close of each school year; Harry receives his first at the end of the first book, and at the time Fred and George comment that they always hope that they will forget that note one year, but they never have. While this does not tell us the name of the law, it does say that students are forbidden from doing magic until they come of age.

Harry first runs afoul of this law in *Harry Potter and the Chamber of Secrets* when Dobby uses a Hover Charm to destroy a dessert in the Dursleys' kitchen. Evidently, the Ministry assumes that it is Harry performing magic, because a warning letter is sent by one Mafalda Hopkirk saying that he should not do that again. When Harry accidentally inflates his Aunt Marge, he is deathly afraid that as he has violated this Statute, he may now be kicked out of the Wizarding world. He decides that his only recourse is to become a fugitive, but as he is approaching Diagon Alley to retrieve his money, he is intercepted by Cornelius Fudge, the Minister for Magic. Fudge inexplicably dismisses the inflation.

When Harry uses the Patronus charm to protect Dudley from Dementors, he is once again told that he has violated this Decree, and that he will have his wand destroyed. This results, eventually, in a hearing, at which it is determined that Harry was justified in using magic to defend himself and a Muggle bystander against a magical threat.

Finally, Harry is overjoyed when, on his seventeenth birthday, he is suddenly free to use any magic he chooses without hindrance.

Analysis

In *Harry Potter and the Deathly Hallows*, we learn that the technique that is used to determine whether a Wizarding child has performed magic is called the Trace. This apparently will detect magic used by the child and trigger some indication in the Ministry. Apparently, in order to be sensitive enough to register the child's use of small spells, it will also detect magic used near the child. We are told that in Wizarding households, it is the parents who are responsible for monitoring the use of magic by the child, as the adults using magic near him may trigger the Trace accidentally; Muggle-born wizards, however, are directly monitored by the Ministry, as it is assumed that the only magic that can occur near them is their own. This is presumably why Dobby's Hover charm was attributed to Harry.

One must wonder, though, about the accuracy of the Trace. There is no apparent notice of Aunt Marge's glass magically shattering, or of the lock of the cabinet under the stairs magically opening as Harry leaves Privet Drive. There is no apparent notice of all the magic occurring in Harry's vicinity when he is at the Burrow, Grimmauld Place, or in Diagon Alley. There is no notice of the magic occurring in his vicinity when he is being visited by Arthur Weasley, the Advance Guard, or Professor Dumbledore at Privet Drive, or when Hagrid is taking him off the island and back to shore in the first book. If we assume that the Trace can detect an adult wizard, and damp its responses accordingly, then the only unexplained situations are the shattering wineglass and the opening cupboard during Aunt Marge's stay at Privet Drive, and possibly the summoning of the Knight Bus. Those might well all have been lumped together and forgiven, along with the inflation of Aunt Marge, by Cornelius Fudge. However, it is also true that the Ministry does not seem to be aware of Harry's use of magic before he turns eleven. In the first chapters of *Harry Potter and the Philosopher's Stone*, Harry unknowingly shrinks a horrible sweater down to doll-size so that he won't have to wear it, flies to a rooftop to avoid a beating from Dudley and his gang, regrows his hair overnight, and makes the glass vanish from a snake's cage. However, there are no warnings issued by the Ministry during this time. Possibly the Trace is only activated when the child reaches the age of 11 and is assumed to be consciously able to direct his or her magic. Could the law also prevent selling or giving wands to children under the age of 11?

This still leaves issues with the Trace remaining quiescent when the Twins and Ron are in Arthur's flying car, when Harry joins them, and when Harry and Ron are in the car. Certainly the car is a magical artifact, and so the Trace should be active, but none of the underage wizards involved in that escapade receive warnings. Another writer, in another series (Randall Garrett, in the *Lord Darcy* series), has drawn a distinction between active and passive magic, saying that possessing or using a charmed object is significantly different than actively creating a new spell. It is probably necessary that this same distinction be built into the Trace, as the number of charmed objects in the ordinary Wizarding household that would be used by a child is quite extensive—an infant banging on a self-stirring cauldron with a spoon, for instance, could be considered someone using a magical object. If this distinction was not made by the Trace itself, the Ministry would be overwhelmed with reports of use of magical objects by underage wizards.

QUESTIONS

1. How old do Wizarding children have to be in order to *legally* use magic outside of school?

Defence Against the Dark Arts

Type: Class
Features:
First Appearance: *Harry Potter and the Philosopher's Stone*

OVERVIEW

Defense Against the Dark Arts is one of the required classes at Hogwarts. There has always been a rumor circulating around Hogwarts that the class is cursed, because they have never been able to have the same teacher for more than one year. Because of this, Professor Dumbledore has had immense difficulty finding teachers to fill the position as teacher.

The following is a list of the Defense Against the Dark Arts instructors Harry has had since his arrival at Hogwarts:

- Professor Quirrell
- Gilderoy Lockhart
- Remus Lupin
- Alastor "Mad-Eye" Moody
- Dolores Umbridge
- Severus Snape
- Amycus Carrow—taught in *Harry Potter and the Deathly Hallows*, while the three protagonists were not enrolled at Hogwarts.

ANALYSIS

In *Harry Potter and the Half-Blood Prince,* we learn that Tom Riddle applied for the position of Defense Against the Dark Arts teacher, but Dumbledore refused to give him the job. Ever since, the Defense Against the Dark Arts teacher has had to leave after one year due to various circumstances.

There is a bit of an apparent contradiction here, in that to the casual reader Quirrell appears to have been the Defence Against the Dark Arts teacher for some time before the first book; Fred and George indicate that he was a better teacher in previous years, but that on one of his vacations he ran into some of the stuff he'd been teaching about and had become much more easily frightened. To mesh with Dumbledore's statement that he had never been able to keep the position filled for more than one year, it is possible that Quirrell had taught a number of different subjects before, and perhaps done some short-term teaching of Defence Against the Dark Arts, when the supposed curse took the main teacher out of circulation. However, it is interesting that in *Harry Potter and the Order of the Phoenix,* when Fred and George are enumerating the fates of the Defence Against the Dark Arts teachers, they only list the four who have been there since Harry started; Fred and George, two years older, should have seen two earlier Dark Arts teachers as well, but do not mention them.

QUESTIONS

1. Did Voldemort actually curse Defense Against the Dark Arts class, or is it just a coincidence?

Defodio

Type: Spell
Features: Gouges channels in material
First Appearance: *Harry Potter and the Deathly Hallows*

OVERVIEW

Defodio, a gouging spell, is used to cut channels or grooves in solid material.

Extended Description Hermione uses this spell to carve space into the tops of tunnels as the Trio escape from Gringotts on the back of a dragon. Harry and Ron follow her lead, cutting away parts of the passages that the dragon is trying to get through as it finds its way out of the cellars of Gringotts.

ANALYSIS

It is interesting that spells are so very specific; it is noted that there are several different cleaning spells, Evanesco for inside containers, Scourgify for surfaces, and Tergeo for dust. Here we see that there is a specific spell for gouging surfaces; while it is similar to the other destructive curses, like the Reductor curse and Deprimo, it is not the spell that Hermione uses in this instance.

A large part of ability in Charms, then, must be the ability to remember the specific spell that would provide the wanted effect, out of a list of possibly hundreds or thousands, along with the ability to associate the correct gestures and mental state with it.

Deletrius

Type: Spell (Charm)
Features: Ends display from Prior Incantato charm
First Appearance: *Harry Potter and the Goblet of Fire*

OVERVIEW

The Deletrius charm ends the display of previously-cast spells from a wand, that was previously triggered by use of the Prior Incantato charm.

Extended Description In *Harry Potter and the Goblet of Fire,* the House Elf Winky is found Stunned, holding a wand, shortly after the Dark Mark is cast. The Prior Incantato charm is used to determine that it was, in fact, the wand that was found with Winky that was used to cast the Dark Mark. Once it is confirmed, the Deletrius charm is used to end the display.

Deluminator

Type: Device
Features: Puts out lights
First Appearance: *Harry Potter and the Philosopher's Stone*

Overview

The Deluminator, also referred to as a "Put-Outer," is a small magical device that looks like a cigarette lighter. It captures and stores a light source, like a streetlight, and can later be used to restore the light to its original place.

Extended Description The Deluminator was used by Professor Dumbledore in *Harry Potter and the Philosopher's Stone* to "put out" the surrounding streetlights to make it harder to see the proceedings while Harry Potter was being delivered to the Dursleys. Once the wizards had left Privet Drive, Dumbledore released the lights from the Deluminator to restore the street to its normal night-time illumination.

It was later used in *Harry Potter and the Order of the Phoenix* by Alastor Moody to darken Grimmauld Place while the Advance Guard was landing in the square. Moody again restored the streetlights once all the wizards were inside the house, before closing the front door.

Again, the Deluminator appears in *Harry Potter and the Deathly Hallows*. It is given by the Minister of Magic to Ron under the terms of Dumbledore's will. Ron later discovers that, as well as being able to remove and replace light, the Deluminator has the ability to track Harry and Hermione, despite their magical shields. It seems to key on the use of his name, picking up their conversation from the point at which they mention Ron. Having started tracking their conversation, it seems to be able to provide some sort of transport to their vicinity; it is never entirely clear how this is managed, exactly, but it produces a ball of light which, when it contacts Ron's chest, allows him to Apparate to Harry and Hermione's vicinity. Finally, in the basement of Malfoy Manor, Ron discovers that captured lights will simply float in the air, if they are released in a place distant from their original sources.

Analysis

Dumbledore, as we can see by even a casual inspection of his office, is very fond of creating magical / mechanical hybrid devices. Given that Moody says he "borrowed" the Deluminator from Dumbledore, we can assume that it is a rare device in the Wizarding world; it is entirely possible that it is, in fact, a unique artifact, possibly an invention of Dumbledore's.

Dementor

Type: Dark Creature
Features: Invisible to Muggles
First Appearance: *Harry Potter and the Prisoner of Azkaban*

Overview

Dementors are the guards of Azkaban Prison; it is difficult to tell what their features are, because they conceal themselves completely under flowing black cloaks.

Extended Description It was a "cloaked figure." "Its face was completely hidden beneath its hood." When we first see it, in *Harry Potter and the Prisoner of Azkaban*, we do see a part of it: "a hand protruding from the cloak and it was glistening, grayish, slimy-looking, and scabbed, like something dead that had decayed in water; the thing beneath the hood, whatever it was, drew a long, slow, rattling breath, as though it were trying to suck something more than air from its surroundings."

They are dark creatures that consume human happiness, creating an ambiance of coldness, darkness, misery and despair. Because of their power to drain happiness and hope from humans, they have been designed as guards at Azkaban, where they prevent the prisoners from having the ability or desire to escape.

This creature has the property that only wizards can see it. Muggles can still feel them, though. It's only known ability, besides the happiness drain, is the ability to perform the "Dementor's Kiss," which is the act of extracting the human soul through the mouth, leaving nothing more than a living body. This process is irreversible. They "are among the foulest creature that walk this earth. They infest the darkest, filthiest places, they glory decay and despair, they drain peace, hope, and happiness out of the air around them. Even Muggles feel their presence, though they can't see them. Get too near a Dementor and every good feeling, every happy memory will sucked out of you. If it can, the Dementor will feed on you long enough to reduce you to something like itself . . . soulless and evil. You'll be left with nothing but the worst experiences of your life."

The only spell we are aware of, which is able to repel these creatures, is called the Patronus charm. In *Harry Potter and the Half-Blood Prince*, when Harry asserts that the Patronus charm is the only way to battle Dementors, Professor Snape tells him that he is wrong; but this supposed different way of tackling Dementors is never described.

Analysis

From his first exposure to them, Harry is much more sensitive to their effects than anyone else—Harry alone, of the 6 people present in the train compartment, passes out when the Dementor enters to search it. Harry is very much afraid that this is a display of weakness, until just before Christmas, when Professor Lupin explains that Harry is more deeply affected because Dementors work by extracting good memories, leaving nothing but the bad recollections, and he has a much grimmer history than anyone else.

In *Harry Potter and the Prisoner of Azkaban*, we find that Professor Dumbledore is opposed to allowing them into the school, but cannot prevent the Ministry from positioning them outside the grounds, at all the known entry points to the school. Their stated purpose at that time is to prevent Sirius Black from entering the castle, but one must wonder how the Ministry believed that would work, as Sirius had already escaped from Azkaban, so he must have some way of evading the Dementors. Possibly this is just the Ministry doing anything so that it appears to be doing something, as it so often does.

One also wonders why the Dementors would stay on as Azkaban guards, when there are so many people elsewhere in the world for them to suck emotion out of. Perhaps it was a mistake allowing so many of them to visit Hogwarts and discover exactly how thin the takings were in the prisoners at Azkaban, relative to the rest of the world. It is certainly true that they abandoned Azkaban with great alacrity in the middle of *Harry Potter and the Order of the Phoenix*.

While it is never stated, there is an implication that the Dementors are a created being, rather than one that occurs naturally. This conclusion is somewhat offset by the statement in *Harry Potter and the Half-Blood Prince* that the Dementors are breeding, which leads us to believe that they are of natural origin. Perhaps, like guard dogs, they were created from a naturally-occurring magical creature by selective breeding methods.

QUESTIONS

1. In *Harry Potter and the Half-Blood Prince*, the Minister for Magic attributes the gloominess of the weather to escaped Dementors breeding and multiplying. Why are Harry and Ron unable to recognize this?

GREATER PICTURE

Although the Dementors leave Azkaban in the middle of *Harry Potter and the Half-Blood Prince* to join Voldemort, one has to wonder, given their earlier actions, whose side they are on from the beginning.

All through *Harry Potter and the Prisoner of Azkaban*, though the Dementors are nominally seeking Sirius Black, they seem to have fixated on Harry, to the point of trying to administer the Kiss to him rather than Sirius when both of them are trapped.

At the end of *Harry Potter and the Goblet of Fire*, the Dementor that Cornelius Fudge has brought along with him, "for his protection," administers the Kiss to Barty Crouch Jr. before Fudge can interrogate him. If the Dementors had already allied with Voldemort, this would be sensible as it would increase the delay before Voldemort's return would be made public.

The two Dementors who attack Harry and Dudley near Privet Drive in *Harry Potter and the Order of the Phoenix* are apparently under orders from Dolores Umbridge, or at least so she claims near the end of that book. There is some question at that point as to whether Umbridge is actually being controlled by Voldemort, as Harry's scar did twinge at one point when she held his hand.

From the long sequence of things done by the Dementors that directly hinders the Wizarding world, one must conclude that they are more inclined to follow Voldemort than the good Wizards, and additionally that at the best of times, Wizarding control over the Dementors is very tenuous indeed.

It is entirely possible that Snape's comments about another spell to counter the effects of Dementors will prove pivotal. We have never seen a Dementor destroyed, only driven away; is it possible that Snape knows a way to destroy them?

Demiguise

Type: Creature
Features: Invisibility
First Appearance: *Fantastic Beasts and Where to Find Them*

OVERVIEW

Located in the far east, the Demiguise is incredibly hard to find, as it will turn itself invisible if it feels threatened.

Extended Description   It is mentioned in *Harry Potter and the Deathly Hallows* that many Invisibility Cloaks are actually woven out of Demiguise hair. It is also mentioned that these cloaks become opaque over time.

Densaugeo

Type: Spell (Jinx)
Features: Causes extreme growth
First Appearance: *Harry Potter and the Goblet of Fire*

OVERVIEW

Densaugeo apparently causes whatever it hits to grow rapidly.

Extended Description   Draco Malfoy used it first in *Harry Potter and the Goblet of Fire*; he had goaded Harry into duelling with him. The spell hit Harry's Furnunculus jinx and ricocheted, hitting Hermione in the mouth. As a result of this, Hermione's front teeth grew to a length of over a foot long.

ANALYSIS

In *Harry Potter and the Order of the Phoenix*, we learn that combining jinxes can have unexpected effects. We can't be certain that the extreme growth of teeth was the intended effect; the spell may well have been modified by hitting the Furnunculus spell. Additionally, as this spell does not seem to be used elsewhere, it is hard to know what its normal effect would be. We can't even really tell whether the spell would cause growth of whatever it hit, or is specific to teeth; the word used seems to be related to teeth ("dens" from the French "dents," "augeo" from the same root as "augment"), but without another example of the spell in action, this must be purest speculation. Given the apparent effect of this spell, it is hard to imagine what Draco's intent would be in casting it; the effect would seem more likely to enrage the victim, rather than incapacitate him, although one supposes that the lisp resulting from having teeth overlapping one's chin could render verbal spell-casting ineffective.

Deprimo

Type: Spell (Jinx)
Features: blasts holes in things
First Appearance: *Harry Potter and the Deathly Hallows*

OVERVIEW

Deprimo is a spell which blasts holes in things.

Extended Description We see this spell in *Harry Potter and the Deathly Hallows* when Hermione uses it to blast a hole in the floor of Xenophilius Lovegood's house, as she, Harry and Ron make their escape from Selwyn and Travers.

ANALYSIS

From the circumstances in which this is used, we can gather something about the spell. Hermione does not want to hurt the Death Eaters; she is trying to save Xeno from further torture at their hands, so she wants them to see that she and Harry were actually there, as Xeno had reported. She would have avoided a spell that would cause the floor to explode, which would have hurt her, Harry, and Ron, who were standing on it, as well as the Death Eaters. Similarly, a spell that would cause the floor to fall in might fall on the Death Eaters, and could also mask the presence of Harry. So the Deprimo spell almost certainly makes the floor vanish, and any explosion-like effects are caused by the remainder of the house as its already weakened structure is further damaged by the removal of a chunk of floor. The effect is likely similar to the Reductor spell, which seems to be intended to turn objects to dust, rather than the Confringo or Expulso spells.

Descendo

Type: Magic spell
Features: Knocks things over
First Appearance: *Harry Potter and the Deathly Hallows*

OVERVIEW

The Descendo jinx is used to knock over piles of things. It is apparently not an instantaneous action; using it on a tall pile of stuff, for instance, will cause the pile to start to fall, but it can sill be stopped with a properly timed Finite charm.

Extended Description We first see this jinx used near the end of *Harry Potter and the Deathly Hallows*. Harry, Ron, and Hermione have entered the Room of Requirement, and have split up to search for the lost Diadem. Harry is trapped by Draco, Crabbe, and Goyle. Hearing Ron, Crabbe uses the Descendo jinx to try and drop a 50-foot pile of stuff onto Ron; Harry stops it with the Finite charm, and Draco then prevents him from using it again.

Devil's Snare

Type: Plant
Features: somewhat motile; will strangle when disturbed
First Appearance: *Harry Potter and the Philosopher's Stone*

OVERVIEW

Devil's Snare is an extremely dangerous plant that will strangle wizards when disturbed.

Extended Description A plant of the dark and dank, it reacts to heat and light by retreating. When Harry, Ron, and Hermione are trapped in it, in *Harry Potter and the Philosopher's Stone,* Hermione remembers this sensitivity, and, when prompted by Ron, manages to create fire that makes the plant retreat.

Devil's Snare appears again in *Harry Potter and the Order of the Phoenix*. Here, Harry, Hermione, Ron, and Ginny see a small specimen delivered as a gift to one Broderick Bode, a long-term spell-damage patient at St. Mungo's Hospital. Hermione later reads in the *Daily Prophet* that Bode, encouraged to tend this plant as part of his healing, had been strangled by it.

ANALYSIS

Given their previous experience of the plant, one must wonder why Harry, Ron, and Hermione did not recognize it when they saw it delivered to Bode. Harry does admit to being made uneasy by the potted plant's swaying tendrils. It is possible that they had simply been distracted by their encounter with Gilderoy Lockhart.

Diffindo

Type: Spell (Charm)
Features: Controlled destruction
First Appearance: *Harry Potter and the Goblet of Fire*

OVERVIEW

Diffindo is a destructive spell. It can be used to make seams rip and books separate from their bindings; its effects can be reversed by the Reparo charm.

Extended Description Harry first uses this spell in *Harry Potter and the Goblet of Fire* to separate Cedric Diggory from a clutch of his friends, by causing the seam on his bag to split. Cedric has to stop to collect his books, which gives Harry a chance to speak to him privately.

In *Harry Potter and the Half-Blood Prince*, Harry uses this spell to keep his copy of the Half-Blood Prince's Potions book. When his own copy of the book arrives from Flourish and Blotts, Harry uses the Diffindo charm to separate the covers from the text of both his new book and the Prince's book, swaps covers, and then uses Reparo to repair both. In this way he can return a book to Professor Slughorn that looks like the one he borrowed, but keep the incredibly useful marginal notes of the Prince.

ANALYSIS

Hermione is, of course, scandalized at any use of magic for destructive purposes; in particular, when this spell is used on a book, she is horrified.

Diricawl

Type: Creature
Features: Bird, teleportarion ability
First Appearance: *Fantastic Beasts and Where to Find Them*

OVERVIEW

The Diricawl is a plump-bodied flightless bird which originated in the Mauritius. It is noticed for its ability to escape danger. It vanishes and then appears elsewhere. With this incredible ability, muggles have been led to think they have hunted it to extinction, but they are wrong. The Muggles call them "dodo."

Disappearing Cabinets

Type: Device
Features: Allow wizards to travel between the two cabinets
First Appearance: *Harry Potter and the Chamber of Secrets*

OVERVIEW

Disappearing Cabinets or Vanishing Cabinets are cabinets into which you put things, and the things then disappear, normally reappearing somewhere else.

Extended Description We first see a Vanishing Cabinet, though it is not identified as such, in chapter 4, *At Flourish And Blotts* of *Harry Potter and the Chamber of Secrets:* Harry has ended up in Borgin and Burkes after a slight mishap with Floo powder, and has to hide to avoid Draco Malfoy and his father. The place he chooses to hide is "a large black cabinet."

Another Vanishing Cabinet appears in chapter 8, *The Deathday Party*, of the same book. Here, Nearly Headless Nick has convinced Peeves to drop a large black and gold cabinet just above Filch's office, in hopes of distracting Filch from punishing Harry for some infraction. Filch identifies the artifact at that time as "a very valuable Vanishing Cabinet."

GREATER PICTURE

Apparently the above two cabinets are linked. After repairing the Hogwarts cabinet, Malfoy uses the cabinets to allow Death Eaters into Hogwarts in his 6th year.

The question has been raised, why does Harry not get transported to Hogwarts when he hides inside the cabinet in Borgin and Burke's, in his second year? The Hogwarts cabinet is not dropped until later that year, so it should have simply transported him there. The answer is extremely simple: Harry never completely closed the door of the cabinet he was hiding in. From *Harry Potter and the Chamber of Secrets*: "he shot inside it and pulled the doors to, leaving a small crack to peer through." He was able to see what was going on in the shop throughout Malfoy's visit, and so the doors must have stayed open that one small crack until Harry was finally able to sneak out of the shop. If he had ever closed the doors completely, likely he would have ended up at Hogwarts.

One of the things that is stressed over and over is that Hogwarts is "unplottable," that it cannot be put on a map, and that you cannot apparate to or within it. Additionally, both in *Harry Potter and the Prisoner of Azkaban* and *Harry Potter and the Half-Blood Prince* it is mentioned that there are spells preventing entrance via any means save the gates, which in *Harry Potter and the Prisoner of Azkaban* are guarded by Dementors, and in *Harry Potter and the Half-Blood Prince* by locks that can be opened only by professors. Much of the action in *Harry Potter and the Prisoner of Azkaban* involves the secret ways in and out of the castle, and we as an audience are left with the impression that all such passageways are known. The Disappearing Cabinets are a way around this protection that has not as yet been guarded against.

There are two main sub-themes to the series; one, of course, is the issue of pure-blood versus muggle and the nature of prejudice. A second, less stressed theme is the idea of just consequences: Draco Malfoy tries to Jinx Harry in the Entrance Hall and is punished by being turned into a ferret; Fred and George are playing with Blood Blisterpods and get into trouble when Katie Bell gets an incurable nose bleed; Lucius Malfoy is sent to Azkaban after the battle in the Ministry and so forth. Every now and again Fred and George do something mischievous but harmful, as when they "push Montague into the old broken vanishing cabinet on the second floor" in *Harry Potter and the Order of the Phoenix*, and then don't get into trouble for it; however, in this case, this leads indirectly to Dumbledore's death, as it is while Montague is trapped in the vanishing cabinet that he discovers that it is connected to the one in Borgin and Burke's. Montague passes this information on to Draco Malfoy, who makes use of it as we have already seen.

Disillusionment

Type: Spell (Charm)
Features: Makes one more or less invisible
First Appearance: *Harry Potter and the Order of the Phoenix*

OVERVIEW

The Disillusionment Charm allows you to either become temporarily invisible or temporarily unnoticable, depending on how well it is cast.

Extended Description The Disillusionment charm makes you blend in with your surroundings to a certain extent; depending on how well it is cast, it can make you nearly invisible.

Mad-Eye Moody casts this on Harry in *Harry Potter and the Order of the Phoenix* when he and the Advance Guard are transporting Harry to the Headquarters of the Order.

In *Harry Potter and the Deathly Hallows*, we learn that many Invisibility Cloaks are made by casting Disillusionment Charms over ordinary traveling cloaks. A number of other techniques are used as well. None of these techniques are perfect; physical and spell damage, or simple age, will cause them to fail.

Dissendium

Type: Spell (Charm)
Features:
First Appearance: *Harry Potter and the Prisoner of Azkaban*

Overview

Dissendium is a single-purpose spell; used on the statue of the hump-backed, one-eyed witch in the third-floor corridor at Hogwarts, it causes her hump to hinge open

Extended Description When her hump is open, it reveals the end of a passageway that goes to the basement of Honeyduke's Sweetshop in Hogsmeade. Harry uses this passageway to leave the castle without permission, in *Harry Potter and the Prisoner of Azkaban*; the twins have apparently been doing the same for years, as the Marauders did many years before them; and it seems Sirius Black is also using this as a means of getting into the castle.

Analysis

A certain number of spells seem to have a single use at a single location, much like passwords; rather than being available for general use, they seem to be tied to specific locations or artifacts. Dissendium appears to be one such; similar to Alohomora, the unlocking spell, but tied to this one statue. The Marauder's Map is similarly opened and hidden with passwords that are not, strictly speaking, magical at all, though they have magical effects.

Dittany

Type: Magical plant
Features: Strong healing powers
First Appearance: *Harry Potter and the Philosopher's Stone*

Overview

Dittany is a plant that was spoken of in the reference *One Thousand Magical Herbs and Fungi*. In this passage it is said that many believe dittany to have magical powers.

Extended Description Dittany is first mentioned in *Harry Potter and the Philosopher's Stone*; Harry, on his Easter vacation, is looking it up as part of his studying. No mention of its properties or uses is made at this time.

Not much mention is made of Dittany until *Harry Potter and the Half-Blood Prince*. There, when Harry uses the Sectumsempra curse on Malfoy, Professor Snape says that he will use Dittany on Malfoy's closed wounds to avoid scarring.

Dittany is used extensively on wounds in *Harry Potter and the Deathly Hallows*, starting with the occasion when Ron loses a piece of his arm through being Splinched.

Analysis

Dittany is a real herb; the name refers to two different species, White Dittany *Dictamnus albus* and Dittany of Crete *Origanum dictamnus*. Both plants have medicinal value against digestive ills, and White Dittany also secretes an oil which has some anti-inflammatory properties.

Divination

Type: Course
Features: Techniques of predicting the future
First Appearance: *Harry Potter and the Prisoner of Azkaban*

Overview

Divination is the ability to predict the future. While it is taught as a subject at Hogwarts, there are very few wizards or witches who can actually predict the future.

Extended Description From watching the antics of the Divination teacher Professor Trelawney, one rapidly gets the impression that divination in the Wizarding world is no more a science than fortune-telling in the Muggle world. Formalized as it is, with its tea leaves, palmistry, crystal balls, and dream interpretation, it still seems to be as deeply buried in nonsensical mysticism as any gypsy fortune-teller on a Muggle fairground. However, Professor Trelawney does produce, in the span of seventeen years (so far), two completely valid predictions.

The alternate Divination teacher, Firenze, seems to be more interested in teaching the methods of Centaur divination, and emphasizing that not all things *can* be determined completely.

Analysis

We must be careful to separate Divination from Prophecy. Divination can be taught; Prophecy is apparently a very rare gift, inborn and apparently uncontrollable. It would appear that prophets quite often fall into Divination as a career.

It is particularly interesting that Divination can be taught and tested, but does not seem to involve any particular magic. We can see quite clearly, as Hermione does, that what Professor Trelawney is doing is little more than a fraud; she is using all the non-magical tricks that Muggle fortune-tellers use, including the foggy and mystical pronouncements. Yet she seems to be teaching out of approved textbooks, and there is evidently some testable technique involved, because there is an O.W.L. exam (and presumably a N.E.W.T. exam as well) covering the subject. One wonders whether the purpose of the course is to codify a set of fraudulent techniques, and if so, for what reason. It is possible that the published techniques are meant only to improve the sensitivity of the mind, and are not meant to be taken seriously. It is possible that the purpose of teaching Divination is simply to make it more likely that the apprentice Seer, assuming the inborn ability, would actually improve his or her chances of producing a true Prophecy. If this is the case, then it is somewhat unusual that Trelawney herself seems to be so serious in her techniques. It is possible that she herself does not know that she is a true Seer; the two times we have seen her making a real Prophecy, she has been unable to remember doing so. We do not know how common this trait is in Prophecy.

Prophecy itself seems to be surprisingly common; in the Battle at the Department of Mysteries at the end of *Harry Potter and the Order of the Phoenix*, it appears that there are many shelves full of recorded prophecies.

Questions

1. What is the method of reading tea leaves? How is it meant to work? 2. What is the meaning of the Centaur comment that Mars is bright?

Doxy

Type: Creature
Features: Small size, winged
First Appearance: *Harry Potter and the Order of the Phoenix*

Overview

A Doxy (otherwise known as *Biting Fairy*) is a small fairy-like creature, covered in hair with two pairs of arms and two pairs of legs. Doxies have two rows of sharp, venomous teeth.

Extended Description Doxies are pests; Doxycide, a black liquid that effectively knocks them out, is required to dispose of them. Doxies are encountered in *Harry Potter and the Order of the Phoenix* when an infestation of them was found in the curtains of the drawing room at number twelve, Grimmauld Place. Fred and George, who had been roped in to help with the spraying, secretly pocketed a large number of Doxy eggs, which were presumably used when developing Skiving Snackboxes for Weasleys' Wizard Wheezes.

In the run-up to the O.W.L. exams in that same book, one of the students, named Howard Dingle but otherwise unseen, claims to have powdered Dragon claw available for sale. Hermione, who is a Prefect, confiscates and examines it, and finds it to be dried Doxy droppings.

From a throw-away comment by Aberforth Dumbledore in *Harry Potter and the Deathly Hallows*, "They'd be on you like Bowtruckles on Doxy eggs," we surmise that Doxy eggs are a favoured food for Bowtruckles, when they can find them.

Analysis

Doxies are not described in the books; though Harry sees them quite close to and actually has to spray one of them that is headed for his face, the author does not go into detail as to what he sees. This description is courtesy *Magical Beasts and Where to Find Them*, by "Newt Scamander."

Dragon

Type: Creature
Features: Large lizard; wings, can fly, breathes fire
First Appearance: *Harry Potter and the Philosopher's Stone*

Overview

Dragons are among the more famous magical beasts; even Muggles know about them and would immediately recognize one. This has meant that memory-modifying charms have been required on more than one occasion, when a dragon was seen by a number of Muggles.

Extended Description Female dragons are generally larger than males, and often more aggressive, particularly when nesting. All dragons are protected by a very tough hide, which renders them nearly impervious to Stun spells; to Stun a dragon, several wizards must cast the spell simultaneously.

According to the book *Fantastic Beasts and Where to Find Them*, dragons have been known to inter-breed with other dragon species; the hybrids that are produced are somewhat rare.

Dragon varieties:

- Antipodian Opaleye: Native to New Zealand, said to be the most beautiful of dragons. Its favourite food is sheep, although it only kills when hungry. This dragon species is not particularly aggressive.
- Chinese Fireball: With a fringe of golden spikes, and an mushroom-shaped cloud of flames when it is angry, the Chinese fireball is the only Asian dragon. The Fireball is quite aggressive, but it is more tolerant with its own species, rather than other dragons. It mainly feeds on mammals, mostly pigs, but one of its favourites is a human.
- Common Welsh Green: The dragon is coloured to match the grass around its homeland, thus affording it some camouflage. These tend to nest in the hills where a reservation has been established for their protection. Welsh Green eggs are dark brown with green spots. This species' roar is easily recognized. The Welsh Green is not troublesome, as dragons go; it prefers to feed on sheep rather than humans unless provoked.
- Hebridean Black: Rough scales and brilliant purple eyes. They mostly hunt deer but have been known to eat cattle and large dogs.
- Hungarian Horntail: Presumed the most dangerous species, the Horntail got its name from the spikes all

over its tail. The Horntail will eat goats, humans (whenever possible), and sheep. The Horntail has yellow eyes and is shaped like a lizard. Its flame is the longest of any species and ranges up to fifty feet.

• Norwegian Ridgeback: One of the rarest breeds. It is more aggressive to its own type and looks like a Horntail. This dragon will feed on large mammals and strangely, water-dwelling creatures. Ridgeback eggs are black.

• Peruvian Vipertooth: The smallest dragons known to wizards. Copper-coloured with venomous fangs. It is happy to feed on cows and goats at any time, it did, however, develop a taste for humans in the nineteenth century, so the International Confederation Of Wizards was forced to cull the species to a certain extent.

• Romanian Longhorn: Green scales and long golden horns. The Romanian Longhorn's territory has become the worlds most important dragon reservation. These dragons are in peril of extinction because they are hunted for their horns, which have now become Class B Tradable Material.

• Swedish Short-Snout: A silvery-blue dragon. It prefers to live 'wild' in mountainous areas. Its skin is used for protective gloves and shields. Its extremely hot flame has a blue colour, and will turn wood and bone to ash.

• Ukrainian Ironbelly: This dragon is is the largest breed known. It has red eyes and grey scales. It is a slower fighter than other species, but is still extremely dangerous. It can crush houses where it lands, and weighs as much as 6 tons.

A dragon is first encountered in *Harry Potter and the Philosopher's Stone* when Harry, Ron, and Hermione watch the hatching of Norbert, a Norwegian Ridgeback, in Hagrid's cabin. Hagrid was allowed to win a dragon egg from a hooded stranger in the the Hog's Head. We find out later in the book that the intent was to get Hagrid drunk so that he would reveal one of the layers of defence surrounding the Philosopher's Stone, and how to get past it.

Earlier in the same book, Hagrid had mentioned the rumour that some of the tunnels under Gringotts Wizarding Bank are protected by dragons; this is also where we first hear of Hagrid's longing to own a dragon himself. Ron also mentions that his older brother Charlie is in Romania working with dragons. In *Harry Potter and the Deathly Hallows*, the trio encounters a dragon guarding some of the deep vaults of Gringotts.

In *Harry Potter and the Goblet of Fire*, Harry was taken by Hagrid to the clearing in the Forbidden Forest where the four dragons for the First Task were being kept. Harry had to face a Hungarian Horntail to retrieve the golden egg in the First Task, which he completed successfully.

Dragon eggs are Class A Non-Tradeable Goods.

Draught of Living Death

Type: Device
Features: Advanced potion
First Appearance: *Harry Potter and the Philosopher's Stone*

OVERVIEW

The Draught of Living Death is a powerful sleeping potion.

Extended Description The Draught of Living Death brings upon its drinker a very powerful sleep that can last indefinitely. No antidote is mentioned in the books, though presumably there must be one.

This potion is mentioned by Professor Snape in Harry's first-ever Potions lesson. Snape asks Harry what he would get if he were to mix the root of Asphodel and an infusion of Wormwood; Harry, of course, cannot answer. It is mentioned again in *Harry Potter and the Half-Blood Prince*. In Professor Slughorn's first N.E.W.T. Potions class, the class members are called upon to produce the Draught of Living Death. At this point we find that this potion also contains sopophorous bean juice and chopped valerian root, probably among other ingredients. We do not, of course, learn the full set of ingredients for the Draught at any point. We do learn that the standard instructions do not produce as effective a Draught as is possible. Harry finds that the marginal comments in his textbook specify alterations to the standard formulas. Changes to the Draught of Living Death include crushing the sopophorous bean rather than cutting it, and stirring once clockwise after every seven times counter-clockwise, rather than continuously counter-clockwise. Following the marginal instructions results in Harry getting better results than Hermione, who is of course following the book's instructions precisely.

ANALYSIS

In the American edition of *Harry Potter and the Half-Blood Prince*, Professor Dumbledore, reasoning with Draco Malfoy, says that if Draco chooses to abandon the mission he has been given, Dumbledore can protect him and his family, by making it seem that they are all dead, if necessary. One wonders whether the Draught of Living Death, or some derivative of it, would be involved in such a ruse.

Dreamless Sleep Potion

Type: Device
Features: Advanced potion
First Appearance: *Harry Potter and the Goblet of Fire*

OVERVIEW

Dreamless Sleep Potion is a complex potion first mentioned by Severus Snape and later by Horace Slughorn. Both Potions Masters used this potion as an example of how powerful potions could be.

Professor Dumbledore recommended that Harry be given the potion after he confronted Voldemort at the end of the Triwizard Tournament.

Dugbog

Type: Magical Creature

Features: looks like a piece of wood
First Appearance: *Harry Potter and the Half-Blood Prince*

Extended Description The Dugbog is never described in the principle books. The only mention is in *Harry Potter and the Half-Blood Prince*, when Ron's essay on Dementors is rendered an essay on Dugbogs by a failure of a spell-checking quill Ron had bought from Fred and George.

Duro

Type: Spell
Features: Turns soft things hard
First Appearance: *Harry Potter and the Deathly Hallows*

Overview

The Duro spell turns soft things hard. For instance, cast on a tapestry, it turns the tapestry to stone.

Extended Description This spell was used by Hermione to allow her, Harry, and Ron to escape pursuing Death Eaters. Having turned a staircase into a slide, the Trio passed through a tapestry at the bottom. Hermione then turned the tapestry to stone to disable the Death Eaters following; we hear the crunch as they hit the back of the tapestry.

Enervate

Type: Spell
Features: restore consciousness
First Appearance: *Harry Potter and the Goblet of Fire*

Overview

Enervate is a spell that is used to restore a person to consciousness especially if he/she has been Stunned.

Extended Description This spell is first used in *Harry Potter and the Goblet of Fire*, by Bartemius Crouch to resuscitate his house-elf, Winky, after she had been Stunned in the woods during the events following the Quidditch World Cup.

It is later used by Dumbledore to return Viktor Krum to consciousness near the Forbidden Forest after he was Stunned while he was alone there with Mr. Crouch, who at the time was suffering under the Imperius curse. Harry had gone to fetch Dumbledore because of the sudden appearance of Mr. Crouch, who during his strange behavior said that he wanted to meet Dumbledore.

It is used a third time, again by Dumbledore, this time to resuscitate the Stunned Barty Crouch Jr., that they might hear what had happened to the true Mad-Eye Moody.

While people are Stunned a number of times in this and later books, this reversal spell does not seem to be used again in our sight. We do see the use of a possibly related spell, used for more general resuscitation, in the form "Rennervate."

Analysis

Enervate seems to be a spell of limited usefulness; we only ever see it being used when resuscitating someone from a Stunning Spell. Possibly it could be used when restoring consciousness to someone who has been knocked out by e.g. a blow to the head, but we never see such a use.

Questions

1. Why choose "Enervate" for the spell name? Someone who is enervated is weak and listless, the opposite of the spell's effect.

Greater Picture

The word "enervate" is frequently used incorrectly. Perhaps it sounds misleadingly enlivening. This common error was pointed out by the Barbara Streisand character in "The Owl and the Pussycat" (1970).

Engorgio

Type: Spell (Charm)
Features: Enlarges an object
First Appearance: *Harry Potter and the Goblet of Fire*

Overview

Engorgio is a spell that enlarges an object. It means 'To Fill In.'

Extended Description The Engorgio charm is used to make things larger; it is possible, though not certain, that it is the same as the Engorgement Charm that Hagrid is using on his pumpkins in *Harry Potter and the Chamber of Secrets*. The first place we see it for certain is when Professor Moody uses it to enlarge a spider so that the entire class can see the effect one of the Unforgivable Curses has on it.

Episkey

Type: Spell
Features: Heals small injuries First Appearance Half-Blood Prince

Overview

Episkey is a healing charm that works well on broken bones. We see it used on facial injuries, but it may have other uses as well.

Extended Description We first see this spell when it is used by Tonks on Harry's nose in the Hogwarts Express at the start of the sixth year. Harry later uses it to cure Demelza's mouth on the Quidditch pitch in that same year.

Erkling

Type: Magical Creature
Features: very entrancing laugh(to children)
First Appearance: *Fantastic Beasts and Where to Find Them*

Analysis

The Erkling is an elfish creature, which has a particular affinity for the taste of children. Its high pitched cackle is entrancing to children, and it uses this to lure them away from their guardians to eat them. However, strict control by the German Ministry of Magic has greatly reduced the number of Erkling attacks. The last known Erkling attack was on a six-year-old called Bruno Schmidt. The Erkling in question was killed when Schmidt hit it over the head with his father's collapsible cauldron. These creatures also enjoy shooting darts at unsuspecting victims.

Etymology The name Erkling may have come from the English word irk, meaning to annoy. It also might be a variant of "erlking," an elfish creature in German mythology which has a fatal influence on children. The Erlking is featured prominently in "Der Erlkönig," a poem by Johann Wolfgang Goethe which was set to music by many composers, most notably Franz Schubert. Erlkönig literally means Alder King.

Erumpent

Type: Magical creature
Features: Looks like rhinoceros from distance
First Appearance: *Harry Potter and the Deathly Hallows*

Overview

An Erumpent is an animal that grows at least one large, spiral horn.

Extended Description While we never see an Erumpent, we do see its horn. The horn is extremely large, leading us to believe that the animal in question is also very large. The horn in question is in Xenophilius Lovegood's study, where he has purchased it believing it to be the horn of a Crumple Horned Snorkack.

Hermione recognizes it at once, and tells Xenophilius that it is extremely unstable; some time afterwards, a stray Stunner hits it, and it explodes, causing serious damage to Xenophilius' house.

The Erumpent is further described in *Fantastic Beasts and Where to Find Them* by "Newt Scamander" as a large grey beast, native to Africa, that can be mistaken at a distance for a rhinoceros. The horn is extremely sharp, able to penetrate metal, and contains an exploding fluid.

Evanesco

Type: Spell (Charm)
Features: "Cleaning" charm First Appearance

Overview

Evanesco is the Vanishing Spell, used for causing an object to disappear, almost like Disapparition.

Extended Description This charm is mentioned only in passing; it is one of three used for cleaning. In a number of places in Potions class, Professor Snape will use this charm to clean an incorrectly made potion out of a cauldron; on one occasion, Hermione used it to clear up a potion that Harry wasn't done with yet. It is also used by Harry to clean Hedwig's cage, in the seventh book.

In *Harry Potter and the Deathly Hallows*, Professor McGonagall is asked the question "Where do Vanished objects go?" by the Ravenclaw door-knocker, to which she replies "Into non-being, which is to say, everything." This suggests that Vanished objects cease to exist, until they are re-conjured.

Analysis

This spell seems to be used for cleaning things out of containers; Scourgify is used for cleaning things off surfaces, and Tergeo seems to be specific to dust.

Expecto Patronum

Type: Spell (Charm)
Features: Creates a Patronus
First Appearance: *Harry Potter and the The Prisoner of Azkaban*

Overview

Expecto Patronum, or the Patronus Charm, will cast a Patronus. A Patronus is a silvery magical being that takes the shape of an animal. This spell is used to ward off the Dementors, which are the guardians of Azkaban.

Extended Description Harry learns this spell from Remus Lupin in *Harry Potter and the Prisoner of Azkaban*. Harry's ability to cast a corporeal Patronus in his third year of magical studies shows his ability as a wizard, as it is a very advanced spell which is thought to be too difficult for underage wizards. In his fifth year, when Harry takes his O.W.L.s, his Charms examiner offers him an extra point if he can produce a corporeal Patronus. A point, or a letter grade, would be worth about 15% of his total marks, so achieving this one charm is seen as quite valuable.

The primary purpose of the Patronus, as mentioned, is as defence against Dementors. Professor Lupin describes it thus: " . . . a kind of anti-Dementor—a guardian which acts as a shield between you and the Dementor." And: "The Patronus is a kind of positive force, a projection of the very things that the Dementor feeds upon—hope, happiness, the desire to survive—but it cannot feel despair, as real humans can, so Dementors can't hurt it." Presumably, the Dementor, finding that the being confronting it does not suffer as a human would, retreats in confusion. In *Harry Potter and the Order of the Phoenix* we see Harry's Patronus charge at the Dementors; though the Patronus may have no physical body, the Dementor, being sightless, cannot see that, all it can sense is this emotional blast furnace, which is charging at it, and it will retreat to save itself.

We also see the Patronus used as a signaling spell when Professor Dumbledore sends for Hagrid in *Harry Potter and the Goblet of Fire,* and also when Tonks sends up a Patronus to summon someone from within the school to open the gates in *Harry Potter and the Half-Blood Prince*. According to the author,[1] use of the Patronus as a communications device was pioneered by Dumbledore and is used exclusively by members of the Order of the Phoenix.

The shape of a corporeal Patronus is significantly influenced by the personality of the caster. Harry's is a stag; Dumbledore's is a phoenix; Tonks' Patronus, as seen in *Harry Potter and the Half-Blood Prince*, is "something large and hairy," and has apparently changed recently. Members of Dumbledore's Army are also, some of them, able to conjure Patronuses by their last lesson: Cho Chang's is a swan, for instance, while Hermione's is an otter. Life events can change the shape of a Patronus as well; as mentioned, Professor Snape mentions that Tonks' Patronus had changed. This change apparently happened at the death of Sirius Black, and Harry initially thinks that Tonks' new Patronus has taken on Sirius' dog shape.

Literal Latin translation: I desire my patron.

ANALYSIS

It should be noted that a sufficiently advanced wizard or witch can apparently cast multiple simultaneous Patronuses. We see that Professor McGonagall casts three Patronuses at once, in *Harry Potter and the Deathly Hallows*, when she needs to contact the three other Heads of House.

QUESTIONS

1. Harry's Patronus is a Stag. His father's Animagus form is also a stag. We know from the description of the Animagus that the form the wizard takes when transformed is related to his personality. Are Patronuses and Animagus Forms related? Does this pass from father to son?

2. Clearly, the form a wizard's Patronus takes is related to his personality or events in his life. If you had a Patronus, what shape would it take?

GREATER PICTURE

There are two spells that relate a wizard or witch to an animal shape: the Patronus charm, and the Animagus transformation. In the course of the books, we see only one witch who is both Animagus and casts a visible Patronus, that being Professor McGonagall. The fact that her Animagus form is the same as her Patronus, a tabby cat, would indicate that whatever influences the shape of the one would also influence the shape of the other.

Expelliarmus

Type: Spell (Charm)
Features: Disarms the targeted wizard
First Appearance: *Harry Potter and the Chamber of Secrets*

OVERVIEW

The Expelliarmus spell is the Disarming spell; it knocks the victim's weapon out of his/her hands. When it is performed with more power, one can blast the opponent off their feet.

Extended Description We see this spell first used by Professor Snape in the Dueling Club; Snape casts it on Professor Lockhart, disarming him and throwing him to the end of the platform on which they are demonstrating. Later in the same book, Harry casts the same spell on Draco Malfoy, causing the book that he is holding, Riddle's diary, to fly out of his hand. From this point on, it is used quite often when there is a duel between wizards; if you can get your opponent to lose his wand, you do have a great advantage over him. In *Deathly Hallows*, Lupin refers to this as Harry's signature spell.

ANALYSIS

As mentioned, at one point Harry does use this spell to get someone to drop a book; as the diary is obviously not a weapon, we can see that this spell will act on anything that is held in the hand, not just a weapon or wand. It's possible that there is a mental part of this spell as well, envisioning the specific object that you want to have it act on; or, it works on whatever you are pointing your wand at. In *Harry Potter and the Prisoner of Azkaban*, in the Shrieking Shack, Harry, Ron, and Hermione all cast this spell at the same time, and it not only pulls Snape's wand out of his hand, but also throws him against the wall; so the power of the spell is additive when cast by multiple wizards on the same object.

Despite the fact that the charm can do things other than disarm, its main function is to get an attacker to drop his wand; as such, it is referred to as the Disarming spell.

QUESTIONS

1. In the seventh book, it appears that this is taken to be Harry's "signature spell." Why would that be? 2. In the seventh book, we learn that there can be other effects from the use of this spell. What would those be?

Expulso

Type: Spell (Curse)
Features: Causes explosion
First Appearance: *Harry Potter and the Deathly Hallows*

OVERVIEW

Expulso appears to be one of the many spells, like Confringo, that causes things to explode.

Extended Description We see the Expulso curse being used only once. Shortly after Harry, Ron, and Hermione leave Bill and Fleur's wedding, they stop in

---

1. http://www.jkrowling.com/textonly/en/faq_view.cfm?id=120

an overnight café on the Tottenham Court Road. There, they are attacked by a pair of Death Eaters. One of the Death Eaters uses this spell to blow up the table behind Harry, who is hidden under his Invisibility Cloak, possibly in an attempt to jinx Harry that misses.

ANALYSIS

While we believe this spell to be a simple explosive, it is uncertain; we have seen in previous battles that curses that miss their target seem to explode when they reach solid objects.

Extendable Ear

Type: Magical device
Features: Allows listening at a distance
First Appearance: *Harry Potter and the Order of the Phoenix*

OVERVIEW

Extendable Ears are inventions of Fred and George Weasley. They look like long, flesh-colored threads; you insert one end into your ear, and can hear what is happening at the other end of the thread.

Extended Description We first hear that Fred and George have been trying to hear meetings of the Order of the Phoenix using Extendable Ears, and have not been having terribly much in the way of success; their mother had tried to destroy their entire stock but had missed a few, and lately had been placing Imperturbable Charms on the doors to the meeting rooms, so that the ends of the Ears cannot get inside. We see the twins attempting to eavesdrop on some of the order members departing after a meeting, but they leave the entrance hall too quickly.

When Mr. Weasley is in the hospital following the snake attack, he, Mrs. Weasley, Mad-Eye Moody, and Tonks have a quick meeting where they try to figure out how Harry could have perceived the attack. Harry, Fred, George, Ron, and Ginny eavesdrop on this conference using Extendable Ears, and hear that the Order believes that Voldemort may be possessing Harry.

In *Harry Potter and the Half-Blood Prince,* Harry, Ron, and Hermione trail Draco Malfoy to Borgin and Burkes, a Dark magic store in Knockturn Alley. There, they use Extendable Ears to hear what Draco is saying to the store clerk.

In *Harry Potter and the Deathly Hallows,* Harry, Ron, and Hermione, who are currently moving from point to point around the countryside, happen to be near another party of Magical refugees. They are unable to hear what this other party is saying because of the protective spells that Hermione has cast around the tent, but Hermione provides Extendable Ears, and they all listen to the conversation of the other group. Presumably, the active end of the Ears is outside the area of the protective spells.

ANALYSIS

In *Harry Potter and the Deathly Hallows,* it is interesting that the listening ends of the Ears can travel to the area outside the protective spells without being physically pushed there—it seems that Hermione does not even have to leave the tent. It appears that unlike normal threads, the outside ends of the Ears are motile; there is some way to tell them a direction in which to travel to find the thing you are interested in hearing.

Fairy

Type: Creature
Features: Small humanoid with wings, glows
First Appearance: *Harry Potter and the Goblet of Fire*

OVERVIEW

Fairies are tiny humanoid creatures with functional wings. They glow with their own light, which makes them useful as decorations.

Extended Description At the Yule Ball, Harry notes that an area of lawn just outside the Entrance Hall has been turned into a sort of grotto filled with fairy lights. He thinks that this means that there are hundreds of actual fairies sitting in the conjured rose bushes and fluttering over the statuary.

ANALYSIS

Apart from their ability to fly and their light, we have little description of fairies. Much of what we know of them comes from *Magical Beasts and Where to Find Them* by "Newt Scamander."

Felix Felicis

Type: Potion
Features: makes the drinker extremely lucky
First Appearance: *Harry Potter and the Half Blood Prince*

OVERVIEW

Felix Felicis is a potion that makes its drinker "lucky" or brings more good fortune than usual. It is the color of molten gold.

Extended Description Felix Felicis is a very complicated potion to brew, normally taking six months or more. Somehow, Professor Slughorn has some available for the first N.E.W.T.-level Potions class in Harry's sixth year, despite his having arrived at Hogwarts on the Hogwarts Express less than a week before. The use of this potion is forbidden before Quidditch matches, academic tests, or any other kind of competition, because it constitutes an unfair advantage. Harry pretends to put some of this potion in Ron's pumpkin juice at breakfast before the first Quidditch match of Harry's sixth year; the confidence this gives Ron is enough to allow him to goalkeep well, where he had been suffering a bit of a crisis of confidence earlier.

Harry uses the potion on himself when he is attempting to retrieve a memory from Professor Slughorn at Professor Dumbledore's request. The potion makes him act in a way that would seem to an impartial observer to be irrational; the end result, however, is that he succeeds in getting the memory, which Slughorn has been withholding. A side effect is that he manages to break up the relationships between Ron and Lavender Brown, much to Ron's benefit, and between Dean Thomas and Ginny, much to his own benefit.

The remainder of the potion is shared between members of Dumbledore's Army, who are acting to defend Hogwarts in the battle at the end of book 6. The potion does seem to prevent their receiving any injury.

ANALYSIS

The mechanism at work with Felix Felicis is obviously Magic and not explicitly explained. When Harry uses Felix he experiences a feeling of unlimited possibility. Under its influence Harry was nudged and guided to make certain inexplicable decisions that eventually lead to his success. Only a step or two at a time was made apparent, characterized more as whims rather than logical instructions.

Ferula

Type: Spell
Features: Creates a splint
First Appearance: *Harry Potter and the Prisoner of Azkaban*

OVERVIEW

Ferula is a spell that produces a splint for a broken limb.

Extended Description   Used in *Harry Potter and the Prisoner of Azkaban* to splint Ron's broken leg, this spell is likely very closely related to the spell used to bind someone. It results in the appearance of bandages and a splint wrapped around the affected limb; once this spell is cast, Ron is able to put some weight on his injured leg without apparent pain.

ANALYSIS

Lupin casts this spell on Ron when they are about to leave the Shrieking Shack, saying that Madam Pomfrey is far better at repairing broken bones than he is. While Ron is able to walk after this spell is put on his broken leg, we don't have any information about whether the spell also deadened the pain, or whether it was simply immobilizing the break that decreased Ron's pain. As usual with spells, there must be some mental component; in this case, visualization of the specific splinting arrangement needed is probably necessary.

---

1. http://www.jkrowling.com/textonly/en/faq_poll.cfm

Fidelius

Type: Spell (Charm)
Features: Protects a secret
First Appearance: *Harry Potter and the Prisoner of Azkaban*

OVERVIEW

The Fidelius charm is "an immensely complex spell" that conceals a secret within a living soul—the "secret-keeper." It is coined from the Latin 'fides'—faith. It is first decribed in detail in *Harry Potter and the Prisoner of Azkaban*, and is also mentioned in *Harry Potter and the Order of the Phoenix*.

Extended Description   The Fidelius charm is a very powerful protection for information; having locked the secret into a soul, even direct inspection of the secret will not, apparently, reveal it. Professor Flitwick, in the description of the spell, says "As long as the Secret-Keeper refused to speak, You-Know-Who could search the village where Lily and James were staying for years and never find them, not even if he had his nose pressed against their sitting-room window!" (Lily and James Potter had gone into hiding at that point because they had information that Voldemort was specifically seeking them.) The conclusion reached at that time, correctly, is that the Secret-Keeper must have voluntarily divulged the secret to Voldemort.

The location of the headquarters of the Order of the Phoenix, also, is protected by the Fidelius charm; in this case, the Secret-Keeper is Albus Dumbledore. At this stage in the story, Dumbledore is not willing to talk directly to Harry, but he is able to convey the information about where the Order is located to Harry, by means of writing. Having shown him the note, Alastor Moody cautions him about reading it out loud or repeating it; one has to wonder why, because the Fidelius spell blocks anyone but the Secret-Keeper from revealing the secret ... so presumably Harry would have been somehow blocked from speaking the contents of that note.

QUESTIONS

1. What would have happened had Harry tried to read the note about the location of the Order out loud?

GREATER PICTURE

J. K. Rowling had implied that when a Secret-Keeper dies, the ability to divulge the secret dies with him.[1] The Fidelius Charm prevents anyone except the secret-keeper from revealing the secret; the people to whom he releases the secret are privy to it, of course, but cannot tell anyone else. At the death of a Secret-Keeper, then, everyone who knew the secret would retain that knowledge; but, the implication was, as before they could not pass it on, so the secret would go no further.

If that were the case, it would cause some problems for Harry in book 7. It is his stated intention to visit his parents' house in the village of Godric's Hollow; but as the secret-keeper, Peter Pettigrew, is apparently still keeping the secret, it may prove difficult for him to find it, though in fact the secret ceased existing when Lily and James Potter died. In fact, it did not seem to be too difficult for Rubeus Hagrid to find it immediately after the incident; while Sirius Black was also present at the time, he almost certainly had been told the secret by Pettigrew earlier. There is a great deal of discussion on various fan sites about the "missing day"; Voldemort had been dead for a full day before Hagrid appeared at Privet Drive with Harry. It is believed by many fans that the occurrences during that day will be important, possibly even pivotal, to events in the seventh book. It is entirely possible that, if the Fidelius spell was still active, Hagrid would have been unable to find the place until one of the parties to he secret was there. We can safely assume that Sirius, as one of the Marauders, would have been aware of the Potters' location; in fact, he does say, in *Harry Potter and the Prisoner of Azkaban*, that he had seen "the bodies and the destruction" of the house, so he must have known the secret, either before the Fidelius charm was performed, or by Peter informing him of it afterwards. It is entirely possible that Hagrid was unable to enter the remains of the house to recover Harry until Sirius appeared on the scene; and it would have been Sirius who actually removed Harry from the wreckage and passed him to Hagrid to carry back to Little Whinging.

(Additionally, because of the death of Dumbledore, in this case it would prove impossible to tell anyone else where the headquarters of the Order of the Phoenix are; this restriction may cease being a problem when the Order is disbanded, though that presumably can not happen until after the projected 7-book arc is complete.) It turns out, however, that the author's statement is at the very least misleading. Mad-Eye Moody explains that with the death of Dumbledore, everyone who had been party to the secret before is now a Secret-Keeper for the secret themselves. As a result, when Hermione accidentally Side-Along-Apparates Yaxley (a Death Eater) to the front step of Grimmauld Place, she assumes that she has revealed the secret to him.

Fiendfyre

Type: Spell
Features: All-consuming demonic fire
First Appearance: *Harry Potter and the Deathly Hallows*

Overview

Fiendfyre is an all-consuming form of fire, that can be created magically.

Extended Description   Harry, Ron, and Hermione are looking for Ravenclaw's lost Diadem in the Room of Requirement when they are intercepted by Draco Malfoy, with Crabbe and Goyle. Knowing that whatever Harry is looking for could restore his family in the Dark Lord's good graces, Draco is intent on taking it from him. In the ensuing battle, Crabbe sets Fiendfyre, but evidently does not know how to stop it, and perishes in the flames. The updraft from the fire does toss the Diadem up in the air, and Harry, then riding a broomstick, is able to catch it while making his escape.

Analysis

It is noted that the flames make the shapes of a number of vicious magical creatures, presumably this is part of the reason for the name of the spell. We don't see the spell being cast; and in fact we have no way of knowing why Crabbe would have used this spell anyway as its purpose seems purely destructive.

It should be noted that a Horcrux, as we learned in the early part of this book, can only be destroyed by more than ordinarily magical means. For instance, Basilisk venom, for which the only known antidote is Phoenix tears, is not something that can be cured by ordinary means. Basilisk venom has been used to destroy all of the Horcruxes found to date; the Diadem was destroyed by simply bouncing around in the flames of Fiendfyre for a short while. This is a clear indication that Fiendfyre is not an ordinary magical form of destruction, but is unusually powerful in its effects.

Finite

Type: Spell
Features: Ends a single spell
First Appearance: *Harry Potter and the Order of the Phoenix*

Overview

The Finite charm, like the similar Finite Incantatem charm, is used to stop a spell's continuing effects. Finite seems to generally act on only one spell, where Finite Incantatem appears to act on all active spells in a locality.

Extended Description   In the Battle in the Ministry in *Harry Potter and the Order of the Phoenix*, Neville is hit by a Tarantallegra jinx. Lupin uses the Finite charm to quiet Neville's legs.

In *Harry Potter and the Deathly Hallows*, in the Room of Requirement, Crabbe uses the Descendo jinx to try to drop a pile of junk onto Ron. Harry stops the pile falling with the Finite charm.

Note that this spell, like all other working spells, seems to be based on Latin, and as such its incantation should be pronounced with three syllables rather than two.

Finite Incantatem

Type: Spell (Charm)
Features: Stops running spells
First Appearance: *Harry Potter and the Chamber of Secrets*

Overview

Finite Incantatem is a spell that causes easier ongoing spells and jinxes to stop.

Extended Description Many charms, hexes, and jinxes have ongoing effects; Rictusempra, for instance, causes endless tickling, while Tarantallegra causes endless "dancing" (uncontrollable leg movement). The Finite Incantatem spell can be used to stop all these ongoing effects.

ANALYSIS

Presumably, the wizard casting Finite Incantatem must be more powerful, possibly significantly more powerful, than the wizard casting the original spell, or Finite Incantatem would be taught as a defensive spell and would be much more widely used in dueling. As it is, we only see this spell used twice: in the Dueling Club, Snape uses it to stop all of the jinxes that have been fired by the students, and after the Battle in the Ministry, Lupin uses it to stop the Tarantallegra curse that is affecting Neville.

Some jinxes have more of a one-shot effect; Stupefy, for instance, which renders someone unconscious. Finite Incantatem would have no effect on jinxes of that nature.

Firecall

Type: Magical process
Features: Quick communication
First Appearance: *Harry Potter and the Goblet of Fire*

OVERVIEW

A fire-call is a specialized use of the Floo Network—when you do not need to be physically present in another location, but you need to communicate with someone there, you insert just your head into a prepared fireplace, and your head is transported to another fireplace.

Extended Description This technique is first seen in *Harry Potter and the Goblet of Fire* when Amos Diggory, then at the Ministry for Magic, has urgent need to reach Arthur Weasley regarding some garbage cans that are flying around Mad-Eye Moody's yard. Harry receives a fire-call from Sirius later in the book. It is also used in *Harry Potter and the Order of the Phoenix*, twice by Sirius to reach Harry, and twice by Harry to try and reach Sirius. Harry feels that this is a very uncomfortable way to send a message; quite apart from the necessity to stay hunched over the fireplace while talking, it is very disconcerting to have your head whirled around dizzily while the remainder of your body remains firmly planted on the floor in front of the sending fireplace.

More information is available at Floo Powder and Floo Network.

Fire Crab

Type: Magical Creature
Features: turtle with crystals on its shell
First Appearance: *Fantastic Beasts and Where to Find Them*

Extended Description Fire Crabs are mentioned only in passing in *Harry Potter and the Goblet of Fire*, where a story written about Hagrid by Rita Skeeter suggested that the Blast-Ended Skrewts that he was raising looked to be unauthorized cross-breeds between Fire Crabs and Manticores.

From *Fantastic Beasts and Where to Find Them*, we learn that fire crabs are commonly mistaken for turtles with jewel-encrusted shells. Fire crab shells can also be used as cauldrons.

Flagrante

Type: Spell (Curse)
Features: Causes items touched to become unbearably hot
First Appearance: *Harry Potter and the Deathly Hallows*

OVERVIEW

The Flagrante curse causes an object to become unbearably hot when touched.

Extended Description According to Griphook, it is apparently fairly common for valuable items in the vaults at Gringotts to be protected with the Gemino and Flagrante curses. The latter causes the touched item to become unbearably hot, so that the burglar cannot hold onto his ill-gotten gains.

Despite the similarity in names, this spell has very little in common with the Flagrate spell.

Flagrate

Type: Spell (Charm)
Features: Marks a surface
First Appearance: *Harry Potter and the Order of the Phoenix*

OVERVIEW

Flagrate is used to mark things, such as doors, with a flaming mark of some sort.

Extended Description As they enter the Department of Mysteries at the Ministry of Magic, Harry and his companions find themselves in an antechamber with a number of identical doors, that seem to spin around every time a door is closed. As a result, it is impossible to tell which doors have already been tried. Hermione uses this spell to mark each door they try, until they find the correct one.

ANALYSIS

Despite the similarity in names, this spell seems to be not particularly similar to the Flagrante curse. Presumably this is the spell that Hagrid used when visiting the Dursleys at the Hut on the Rock.

Flobberworm

Type: Creature

Features: vegetarian, extremely boring
First Appearance: *Harry Potter and the Prisoner of Azkaban*

OVERVIEW

The flobberworm is a large worm that can grow up to ten inches; each end is indistinguishable from the other. It lives in damp ditches, and its preferred food is lettuce.

Extended Description In *Harry Potter and the Goblet of Fire*, Vincent Crabbe claims to have been bitten by a Flobberworm; this information is provided to Rita Skeeter who is, at the time, gathering damaging information about Rubeus Hagrid. However, this is rather damaging to the eventual story, because in fact Flobberworms have no teeth. In *Harry Potter and the Prisoner of Azkaban*, after spending all term teaching about Flobberworms, and that they will die if fed too much lettuce, Hagrid manages to kill all the Flobberworms he has been teaching with over Christmas break by feeding them too much lettuce.

ANALYSIS

The key aspect of the flobberworm is its total harmlessness. As Care of Magical Creatures teacher, Hagrid is very uncertain of himself, and his first-ever lesson goes rather horribly wrong, with a Hippogriff injuring Draco Malfoy. In order to avoid a repetition of this problem, Hagrid retreats to the safety of the innocuous, and so his class are faced with a long series of boring lessons about the flobberworm. The main purpose of this seems to be showing the fragility of Hagrid's self-image; big and fearsome as he is, he is easily upset and easily dismayed.

Floo Network

Type: Magical Artifact
Features: System of fireplaces linked together
First Appearance: *Harry Potter and the Chamber of Secrets*

OVERVIEW

The Floo Network is the network of fireplaces able to be reached by Floo Powder.

Extended Description When we first see people travelling by Floo Powder, no mention is made of the Network as a separate entity; you simply travel until you reach the correct fireplace. In *Harry Potter and the Goblet of Fire*, where the Network is first mentioned by name, we are told that the fireplace at Number 4, Privet Drive has been temporarily added to the Floo Network. And in *Harry Potter and the Order of the Phoenix* it is mentioned that the Floo network is being monitored.

ANALYSIS

The Floo Network can be used for travel or for communications—you can allow just your head to travel, and leave your body where it is. This ability to communicate by allowing just your head to travel is used by Sirius Black on several occasions, by Harry on two occasions, and by Amos Diggory on one occasion.

There is apparently a sub-office of the Ministry of Magic, called the Floo Regulation Panel in *Harry Potter and the Goblet of Fire*, which is responsible for keeping the Floo Network operating.

In *Harry Potter and the Half-Blood Prince* we are told that the Floo network has been connected to Hogwarts to allow students to return to school after Christmas. This seems a little odd, as we already know that the fires in Gryffindor tower, the Defence Against the Dark Arts teacher's office, and the headmasters' study are connected to the network; presumably this means that the fires in the Head of House offices have been set to respond to people desiring to travel to Hogwarts. Perhaps it is possible to make a "concealed" entry in the Floo network; you need to know the name of a fireplace before you can get there, perhaps it is possible to have some fireplaces be "ex directory" so that you need to be told the name, which presumably would not be obvious, before going to that grate. In this case, "connecting to the Floo network" would actually mean "publishing a new name for the head of house's fireplace."

Alternately, while Dumbledore appeared in the fireplace in his own office in *Harry Potter and the Order of the Phoenix*, in every other case we only saw the use of the Floo network into Hogwarts for communication. It is possible that there is some mechanism that prevents anything larger than a head from traveling to any other fireplace in Hogwarts. Such a security mechanism would certainly be a reasonable precaution for a school. In this case, "connecting to the Floo network" would involve removing the size limitation so that a whole person could travel to that fireplace.

QUESTIONS

1. Number 12, Grimmauld Place is on the Floo network—Harry is able to use the Floo network to talk to people there. As its existence is only known to members of the Order of the Phoenix, how is it possible for the Floo Regulation Panel to keep it connected? Is it even necessary for them to act to keep it connected?

2. Would Floo network connection be a paid service, like phones? You have to buy Floo powder, do you think you'd also have to buy connection to the Floo network?

Floo Powder

Type: Magical artifact
Features: Allows access to Floo Network
First Appearance: *Harry Potter and the Chamber of Secrets*

OVERVIEW

Floo powder is a greyish or silvery powder which allows access to the Floo Network transportation system.

Extended Description The Floo Network is a magical linking of most fireplaces in the Wizarding world; it is used as a means of rapid transportation from one Wizarding building to another. Floo Powder provides entry to that network; place a pinch of Floo powder in the fire, and it becomes green and harmless. You may then enter the fire, and speak your destination, and you will be carried to the fireplace you have named. It is a very dizzying ride; you spin very rapidly while in transit, and you would be well-advised to keep your elbows tucked in.

It is also possible to place only a body part, such as a head, in the fire, whereupon that part will be the only thing that is carried to your named destination. Placing your head in someone else's fireplace is one way to communicate over long distances, but as Harry finds out, it can be rather disconcerting to have your head spun around rapidly while your body stands still. Colloquially, this is sometimes referred to as a *Fire-call*.

Apparently in certain circumstances, Floo powder or something similar to it can be used to summon someone. Professor Snape uses this in *Harry Potter and the Prisoner of Azkaban* to summon Professor Lupin to his office.

ANALYSIS

Most commonly, after you toss a pinch of the powder in the fire, you step into the fire and pronounce the name of the place you want to go to (e.g. "Diagon Alley"). If you only want your head transported you sit in front of the fire and only stick your head in. Unclear pronunciation has its consequences; you might end up somewhere other than your intended destination.

However, if you only want to *call* someone, it seems that it is unnecessary to say the name of that person's actual residency, the name of that person will do. It is unclear whether you need to *know* their current whereabouts, though.

QUESTIONS

1. When someone is talking to another person with Floo powder, their head is in that other person's fireplace. If someone was in the same room as you, talking to someone else with Floo powder, what would you see?

Flutterby bush

Type: Magical plant
Features: Decorative, shimmering leaves
First Appearance: *Harry Potter and the Goblet of Fire*

OVERVIEW

The Flutterby bush, apparently a purely decorative plant, is treasured for its delicate, fluttering leaves that move even when there is no wind, giving the bush a shimmering appearance.

Extended Description In Harry's fourth year, his class are called upon to prune flutterby bushes in Herbology class. Flutterby bushes appear again as decoration at the doorway to the Burrow just before Bill and Fleur's wedding.

Flying

Type: Class
Features:
First Appearance: *Harry Potter and the Philosopher's Stone*

OVERVIEW

The subject of flying is taught by Madam Hooch to the first-years at Hogwarts.

Extended Description Flying is done using brooms; we are led to believe that it is not possible for a wizard to fly without a broom or some other charmed device (e.g. a flying carpet, though those are currently not allowed in England) or animal (e.g. a Thestral).

One of the rules at Hogwarts is that first-years aren't allowed to posess brooms. This rule was bent for Harry, though: in his first-ever flying lesson, Professor McGonagall sees that he is a natural flier. As a result, Harry was recruited to the Gryffindor Quidditch Team, as Seeker, and was given a Nimbus 2000.

Once his natural ability has been discovered, there is little that Madam Hooch can teach him; his flying lessons are taken over by Oliver Wood, the captain of the Quidditch team, and Harry has no further lessons with Madam Hooch. We must assume that lessons continue for the other students, however.

QUESTIONS

1. We are led to believe that flying is only possible with the use of an object (broom, Sirius' flying motorcycle, Mr. Weasley's flying Ford Anglia), or with the assistance of a flying creature (Thestral, Hippogriff, Dragon). How is it that Voldemort, and later Snape, seem to be capable of unassisted flight in *Harry Potter and the Deathly Hallows*?

Foe Glass

Type: Magical device
Features: Shows enemies approaching
First Appearance: *Harry Potter and the Goblet of Fire*

OVERVIEW

A Foe-Glass is an object somewhat like a mirror which reveals approaching enemies. The closer said enemies are, the more focused their images are.

Extended Description The first time we see a Foe Glass, it is mounted on the wall of Professor Moody's office. While there is constant motion within the glass when Harry first sees it, everything he sees is indistinct, indicating that there are no enemies nearby.

Once Moody has revealed himself, Harry notices that there are three images in the glass that are steadily becoming more distinct; shortly before the door is broken down, he recognizes the images as Professor Dumbledore, Professor McGonagall, and Professor Snape. The image of the three stays in the mirror while Moody is questioned.

We see a Foe Glass, quite possibly the same one, mounted on the wall of the Room of Requirement when Dumbledore's Army meets there in *Harry Potter and the Order of the Phoenix*.

Ford Anglia

Type: Magical device
Features: Flying car
First Appearance: *Harry Potter and the Chamber of Secrets*

Overview

The Ford Anglia is a unique magical artifact. Created by Arthur Weasley, it is able to fly and has the capability of becoming invisible.

Extended Description   Fred, George, and Ron Weasley take this car out of its storage shed in order to bring Harry away from the Dursleys,' and bring him to the Burrow. They get into rather a lot of trouble for this when they are caught by their mother.

The entire family is carried to King's Cross Station in this car, when it is time to go to Hogwarts. Arthur has placed a spell on the car so that it is larger inside than outside; Mrs. Weasley remarks on how Muggles are able to build a car that looks so small and has so much space inside. None of the others enlighten her.

When Harry and Ron are unable to get through the barrier at Platform Nine and Three Quarters, Harry suggests that they should go back to the car and wait. It occurs to Ron that their parents might not be able to get out of the platform any more than they can get in, and that they should take the car and fly to Hogwarts. they do so, in the process crashing into the Whomping Willow on the school grounds. The car then throws them out and wanders off on its own into the Forbidden Forest.

Harry and Ron, venturing into the Forbidden Forest on the trail of the spiders, as Hagrid had advised them, encounter the car, gone feral but still able to recognize Ron as its owner. They are then captured by giant spiders. The spiders take them to Aragog, their leader, who discusses some past events with Harry and Ron, and then consigns them to their fate: to be eaten by his children. The car rescues them, and leaves them at the edge of the Forest.

Furnunculus

Type: Spell (Jinx)
Features: Causes boils
First Appearance: *Harry Potter and the Goblet of Fire*

Overview

Furnunculus apparently causes whoever it hits to erupt in boils.

Extended Description   This is one of the classic duelling spells. Harry used it first in *Harry Potter and the Goblet of Fire*; he had been goaded into duelling with Draco. The spell hit Draco's Densaugeo jinx and ricocheted, hitting Goyle.

Analysis

In *Harry Potter and the Goblet of Fire* we learn that combining jinxes can have unexpected effects—apparently, Harry's Furnunculus curse combines with George's Jelly legs curse to afflict Crabbe with little tentacles all over his face. We can't be certain that the boils that afflicted Goyle in the earlier episode were the intended effect; the spell may well have been modified by hitting the Densaugeo spell.

Fwooper

Type: Creature
Features: Bird
First Appearance: *Fantastic Beasts and Where to Find Them*

Overview

The Fwooper is an African bird that comes in green, yellow, orange, or pink. Its main use in the Wizarding world is as a source of particularly posh quills. Its main defence mechanism involves singing a song which eventually drives the listener to insanity.

Geminio

Type: Spell (Charm)
Features: Duplicates objects
First Appearance: *Harry Potter and the Deathly Hallows*

Overview

Geminio is a spell used to duplicate things.

Extended Description   The verbal component of this spell is based on the word Gemini, which is the English form of the zodiac symbol for "the twins." It is used by Hermione to duplicate the Horcrux in the Ministry of Magic, so that Umbridge will not be aware that it has been taken from her.

Analysis

Note that this spell is similar, but not identical, to the Gemino curse.

Questions

1. This spell duplicates objects, so why is this spell not used much in the books? For example, in *Harry Potter and the Chamber of Secrets*, Harry, Ron, Hermione, Percy, Ginny, Fred and George all need a complete set of Lockhart books for Hogwarts. Seven sets of books were bought, but Mrs. Weasley presumably could have bought one set, and cast this spell to make seven complete sets for the price of one.

GREATER PICTURE

Re: why did Molly not use it? The question has been asked, why don't wizards use Geminio to twin objects that they need more of? Of course, this is never answered directly in the book, but there is implication that either the copy just isn't good enough, or there is some form of magical rights management, akin to Muggle DRM or copy protection.

Taking the latter case first: We have already seen that some spells can be countered; Alohomora can be blocked, as we see in *Harry Potter and the Order of the Phoenix,* where Professor Umbridge has locked her door in a manner that makes it impervious to that spell, and we see in *Harry Potter and the Deathly Hallows* that some objects, notably the Sword of Gryffindor, are unaffected by Accio. It is to be expected that someone like Gilderoy Lockhart, concerned as he is with his own fame and profits, would have protected his books with a spell to prevent copying. Bookstores like Flourish and Blott's, of course, would be all in favour of such a spell, as they could not stay in business if their wares were copied indefinitely.

There is also the inferred "not good enough" issue. When Hermione uses the Geminio charm to create a duplicate of the locket, she says that she believes the copy will be good enough to fool Umbridge. This quite strongly suggests that even a witch as technically competent as Hermione cannot use the spell to create an identical copy. It is also mentioned that the copies produced by the similar Gemino curse are worthless. So if, as suggested, Mrs. Weasley were to use Geminio to replicate textbooks, the new textbooks might be as unusable as the end results of the failing Weasley spell-checking quill near the end of *Harry Potter and the Half-Blood Prince*—the text might be present but scrambled, or the books might be solid blocks that only appear to be books, for instance.

Gemino

Type: Spell (Curse)
Features: Multiplication of objects
First Appearance: *Harry Potter and the Deathly Hallows*

OVERVIEW

Gemino is a protective curse; cast on an object, it makes that object multiply repeatedly when it is touched.

Extended Description According to Griphook, it is apparently fairly common for valuable items in the vaults at Gringotts to be protected with the Gemino and Flagrante curses. The former causes the touched item to produce multiple copies of itself, thus confusing the burglar into taking the valueless copies.

Note the similarity to the Geminio charm, which produces a single replica of the object it is cast upon.

Ghost

Type: Disembodied spirit
Features: Intelligence, immortality, incorporeality
First Appearance: *Harry Potter and the Philosopher's Stone*

OVERVIEW

Ghosts are the disembodied souls of wizards and witches who have died (as described by Professor Snape, a ghost "is the imprint of a departed soul left upon the earth"). There are a large number of them in Hogwarts; they are able to speak with the living, but being incorporeal are unable to have any effect on matter.

Six ghosts are specifically named in the books: the four House ghosts (Nearly Headless Nick of Gryffindor House, the Fat Friar of Hufflepuff House, the Grey Lady of Ravenclaw House, the Bloody Baron of Slytherin House); Professor Binns, the History of Magic teacher; and Moaning Myrtle. Peeves the poltergeist is not a ghost, but a Spirit of Chaos, who has never been alive, according to the author.[1]

Extended Description In *Harry Potter and the Order of the Phoenix*, Harry, distraught at the death of his godfather Sirius Black, corners the ghost Nearly Headless Nick in the hopes of finding out what happened to Sirius. Nick tells him, "Wizards can leave an imprint of themselves on the earth, to walk palely where their living selves once trod," but it takes special preparation, and is a sort of half existence, neither alive nor dead. Nick chose that route because he was afraid of death, but he believes that Sirius would not have done so.

ANALYSIS

Throughout the books, ghosts are a sort of aloof presence, intimating that death is not final; as Professor Dumbledore says in *Harry Potter and the Philosopher's Stone*, to one who has lived a full life, "death is but the next great adventure."

Of all the ghosts at Hogwarts, by far the largest role is played by Moaning Myrtle. She is instrumental in Harry's discovery of the Chamber of Secrets in *Harry Potter and the Chamber of Secrets,* and assists Harry with the second task in *Harry Potter and the Goblet of Fire.* She is also something of a confidante to Draco Malfoy in *Harry Potter and the Half-Blood Prince.*

Nearly Headless Nick's role is largely instructional, explaining aspects of the school and its history to Harry, Ron, and Hermione. He does spend some time discussing the nature of death with Harry, as mentioned above. The author has said in an interview that the series became rather more centered around the mystery of death when her mother passed away; it is possible that some of Nick's speech here may echo the author's internal thoughts on the subject.

The Grey Lady assists Harry in locating the final Horcrux in *Harry Potter and the Deathly Hallows.*

---

1. http://www.jkrowling.com/textonly/en/faq_view.cfm?id=67

Shades In several places in the book, "ghosts" of those who have passed away are conjured up by one means or another. As these do not have any permanent existence, but revert when the spell recalling them is ended, they are not properly ghosts at all. It is perplexing that there is no term for these appearances. It is certainly true that their appearance is always due to extremely rare magic: the Priori Incantatem effect, at the end of *Harry Potter and the Goblet of Fire,* which shows us the shades of Cedric Diggory, the muggle Frank Bryce, Bertha Jorkins, and Harry's mother and father; and, in *Harry Potter and the Deathly Hallows,* the Resurrection Stone, which summons the shades of James and Lily Potter, Remus Lupin, and Sirius Black. In the *Muggles' Guide,* as the author does not seem to suggest a term for them, we use "shades" to refer to these recalled essences or souls of the departed.

Horcrux One other place where a "ghost" appears in the books is in *Harry Potter and the Chamber of Secrets.* Again, this is not properly a ghost, as the associated human, Tom Riddle, is nominally still alive. The ghost of Riddle says that he is a "memory" which has been given being and life by Ginny, who will die in the process of bringing the memory back to life. We learn about this appearance in much more detail later in the series, first when Professor Slughorn, in his memories, is seen to describe Horcruxes to Riddle, and later when Hermione is telling Harry what she has learned about Horcruxes from the books she extracted from Dumbledore's study.

Waystation A third place where we see those who have died, this one appearing in *Harry Potter and the Deathly Hallows,* seems to be what Harry thinks of as a waystation. To him, this appears as a surprisingly clean and empty simulacrum of King's Cross Station. Here, he meets with what might be the shade of Dumbledore, who tells Harry a number of things that had been previously unknown to us and to Harry. Dumbledore closes this meeting by saying how it had all happened in Harry's mind, but that didn't make it any the less real. We have reason to believe that this is the true spirit of Dumbledore, as it knows things that had been previously unknown to anyone other than Dumbledore; it also knows of things that had occurred since Dumbledore's death. We have learned that people can leave fragments of themselves behind, as in the Wizarding Portraits, which continue to react as their models had, and are apparently able to have original thoughts; and of course, ghosts are similarly constituted though without needing a portrait behind them. While it was possible that Dumbledore left a fragment of himself behind to educate Harry, given his dislike for breaking souls apart, it is more likely that he simply chose to have his soul remain in the waystation and await Harry's arrival. The series remains mute on how Dumbledore would have been able to divine these aspects of life after death; perhaps his study of the Elder Wand had given him some insight.

Ghoul

Type: Creature
Features: Noise, disturbance
First Appearance: *Harry Potter and the Chamber of Secrets*

Overview

The ghoul, while not exactly the best looking of all magical creatures, isn't all that dangerous. It occupies attics or barns owned by wizards, and resembles a buck-toothed ogre. The most harm it can cause is to growl at someone who unluckily comes across it. It often groans and throws things around.

Extended Description In *Harry Potter and the Chamber of Secrets,* it is mentioned that there is a Ghoul living in the attic of The Burrow, the Weasley home; Ron is rather dismissive of it, saying that it is nowhere near as good as having a house-elf. There is mention of a "murderous old ghoul" elsewhere in the books, which would imply that ghouls can also become dangerous as they get old; possibly, like many animals, they get senile.

Analysis

In the case of the Weasleys' attic, the ghoul is used as part of the ongoing illustration of the Weasley family's relative poverty; the idea, one supposes, is that rich families have house-elves to take care of them. Ron does find out that having a house-elf can be a double-edged sword, though, when he has to deal with Kreacher.

Questions

1. What do ghouls eat? Boggarts feed off our fears and so act to inspire fear; what would Ghouls feed off that would cause them to prefer noise? Could it be irritation?

Giant

Type: Creature
Features: Tough skin; fear of magic; viciousness
First Appearance: *Harry Potter and the Goblet of Fire*

Overview

Giants are magical creatures which can grow to be over twenty feet tall. They are often described as being vicious and unintelligent.

Extended Description There are very few giants left in the world, and those that do exist normally hide in the mountains where they are very rarely bothered by humans. Giants, unfortunately, need a large area to hunt, and they are not particularly social; forcing them all to live together in a restricted area typically results in fights between them, and fights between giants are quite often fatal. As a result, the Giant population is declining.

In the *Harry Potter and the Order of the Phoenix,* we learn that Hagrid and Madame Maxime were sent by

Dumbledore to try to convince the giants to help them fight against Voldemort, but they were unsuccessful. The then-leader of the giants was overthrown, and his replacement was more aligned with the cause of the Death Eaters.

Before leaving the mountains, Hagrid finds his half-brother, Grawp. He brings Grawp back to Hogwarts and hides him in the Forbidden Forest. He introduces Grawp to Harry and Hermione because he is afraid he may soon be fired, and tells them that he has been trying to teach Grawp English. He extracts a promise from Harry and Hermione that, should he be sacked, they will continue Grawp's education.

In *Harry Potter and the Half-Blood Prince,* the Muggle Prime Minister mentions an apparent hurricane in the West Counties. Cornelius Fudge admits that it was a Giant, apparently one of Voldemort's, and the story of the hurricane was a fabrication of the Ministry to keep Muggles from learning that Giants exist.

In *Harry Potter and the Deathly Hallows,* at least two Giants are attacking Hogwarts in the final battle, and Grawp, who is revealed as being quite small for a giant, is defending.

ANALYSIS

In the *Harry Potter and the Goblet of Fire,* we learn that Hagrid is a half-giant. His father was a wizard, but his mother was a giantess. Although she denies it, it is fairly obvious to the reader that Madame Maxime is a half-giant. It is unlikely that she would be able to reconcile with Hagrid if she was denying the giant part of her heritage, so the fact that she and Hagrid set off together seems to indicate that she has admitted, at least to him, that there is giant in her background.

In *Harry Potter and the Order of the Phoenix,* we learn that there are only about seventy to eighty giants left, and we also learn that they are located in the Eastern European mountains. Hagrid, who was traveling to the Giants' territory on foot, says that they had trouble with "a couple 'o mad Trolls on the Polish border," and a "sligh' disagreement with a Vampire in Minsk," which, starting from Dijon, France, would indicate a roughly northeastwards trip into the Ural mountains north of Moscow.

GREATER PICTURE

At the end of the Half-Blood Prince, we see Grawp attend Dumbledore's funeral. He seems to have become very tame.

Gillyweed

Type: Plant
Features: Allows the person who eats it to breathe underwater
First Appearance: *Harry Potter and the Goblet of Fire*

OVERVIEW

Gillyweed is a magical plant. Gills appear on the neck of the person who eats it, enabling him or her to breathe underwater for a limited amount of time. It is described as looking like "slimy grayish green rat tails."

Extended Description When Harry Potter is having difficulty figuring out a way to complete the second task of the Triwizard Tournament (which requires him to rescue Ron from the bottom of a lake), Dobby steals some Gillyweed from Professor Snape's store cupboard and gives it to Harry to use.

We later learn that Professor Moody had given a book on *Magical Water Plants of the Mediterranean* to Neville, with the expectation that Harry would ask Neville for help in the Challenge. Harry never consulted Neville, however; so Moody deliberately mentioned Gillyweed in Dobby's hearing.

ANALYSIS

More than breathing underwater, this plant forces partial adaptation to an underwater existence, providing Harry with gills and extending his feet and hands into flippers.

Note: In the film version of this series, it is in fact Neville who provides Gillyweed to Harry; this is managed by having Neville summon Ron and Hermione to Professor McGonagall's office, instead of having Fred and George do it. This is likely a cost-cutting decision by the filmmakers; by eliminating Dobby from this one scene, they remove any need to have house-elves in the film.

Glisseo

Type: Spell (charm)
Features: Turns staircase into a slide
First Appearance: *Muggles' Guide to Harry Potter/Books/Order of the Phoenix*

OVERVIEW

The Glisseo charm flattens the treads of a staircase, effectively turning it into a slide.

Extended Description We first see this charm in action in *Harry Potter and the Order of the Phoenix* when Ron, upset at what he believes to be a betrayal of the newly created Dumbledore's Army, attempts to fetch Hermione from her dormitory. After he has taken about three steps on the staircase, it turns into a slide under him, depositing him on the floor of the Common Room. Hermione later says that evidently the Founders felt girls were more trustworthy than boys, which is why the boys' dormitories are not similarly rigged to prevent girls from entering. We do not hear the incantation, though, until *Harry Potter and the Deathly Hallows.* There, in the Battle of Hogwarts, the Trio have taken refuge behind the tapestry at the top of a flight of stairs. A pair of Death Eaters spot them, and Hermione uses Glisseo to turn the stairs into a slide to hasten their getaway.

Glumbumble

Type: Magical Creature
Features: furry insect
First Appearance: *Fantastic Beasts and Where to Find Them*

Gnome

Type: Small creature
Features: Oversized head, eats worms
First Appearance: *Harry Potter and the Chamber of Secrets*

OVERVIEW

The Gnome is a common garden pest found throughout North America and northern Europe. Its body is out of proportion, its head is too big, it has sharp claws and bony feet. It grows up to about 12 inches tall.

Extended Description The most popular form of removing a gnome from a garden is to pick it up, spin it around until it is dizzy, and then throw it over a garden wall. According to Gilderoy Lockhart, this causes the gnome to become disoriented and he cannot find his way back; however, it appears that their disorientation is only temporary, as Harry sees the Weasley's gnomes making their way back to the garden only hours after using this technique to remove them.

ANALYSIS

The appearance in *Harry Potter and the Chamber of Secrets* could be seen as a first intimation that Gilderoy Lockhart is not the wizard he claims to be. The technique for eliminating garden gnomes comes straight out of *Gilderoy Lockhart's Guide to Garden Pests*, and appears to be effective, as the gnomes, once dug out of the garden and flung into the neighbouring field, march away in the wrong direction. But by sunset the same day, when Harry looks out of Ron's window, the gnomes are already sneaking back into the garden.

Having created the gnomes and infested the Weasley's garden with them, the author perforce must make them reappear in the Weasley's garden whenever we see it. To that end, Crookshanks the cat chases one into a boot in one scene, and one is charmed to be the angel on top of the Weasley's Christmas tree in another scene. At the wedding in *Harry Potter and the Deathly Hallows*, Luna Lovegood is very pleased that a Weasley gnome bit her finger. Her father, Xenophilius, explains that gnome saliva has many beneficial properties. This is doubtful as the Lovegoods hold many peculiar beliefs about magical creatures.

Goblet of Fire

Type: Magical device
Features: wooden goblet filled with blue flames
First Appearance: *Harry Potter and the Goblet of Fire*

OVERVIEW

The Goblet of Fire is "a large, roughly-hewn wooden cup," "full to the brim with dancing blue-white flames," kept in an ornamental casket.

Extended Description Professor Dumbledore, in his introduction to the Triwizard Tournament, said that selection of the Champions to represent each school would be done by an "impartial judge." The Goblet of Fire is that judge; those who wish the chance to compete place their names in the Goblet, and at the start time (which is apparently Hallowe'en), the Goblet selects one person from each school by returning one name from each school.

In *Harry Potter and the Goblet of Fire*, four Champions are selected, apparently giving Hogwarts two shots at the championship. At the time, Professor Moody reminds everyone there that the Goblet is a "powerful magical artifact," far beyond the ability of a fourth-year student to alter, and suggests that the only way that could have happened would be if someone had hoodwinked the Goblet into believing that there were four schools competing, and then entering Harry's name as the sole competitor from this fictional fourth school. Karkaroff, the Headmaster of Durmstrang, demands that the names be re-submitted, but is told that the Goblet has extinguished itself and will not re-ignite until it is time for the next Tournament.

QUESTIONS

1. During the hiatus in the Triwizard Tournament, did the Goblet ignite every five years and wait, flaming patiently, for submissions?
2. Where is the Goblet now?

Gobbledegook

Type: Language
Features: Used by goblins
First Appearance: *Harry Potter and the Goblet of Fire*

OVERVIEW

Gobbledegook is the language used by goblins to talk amongst themselves.

Goblin

Type: Creature
Features: Short, intelligent
First Appearance: *Harry Potter and the Philosopher's Stone*

OVERVIEW

Goblins are an intelligent race who coexist with wizards. They are short with long, thin fingers and feet. Their diet consists of meat, roots and fungi. Goblins converse in a language known as Gobbledegook.

Extended Description Goblins are adept metalsmiths, and are notable for their silverwork; they even mint coins for wizarding currency. Due to their skills with money and finances, they control the wizarding economy to a large extent and are involved with the running of Gringotts. They are represented by the Goblins Liaison Office of the Department for the Regulation and Control of Magical Creatures in the Ministry of Magic.

Throughout wizarding history there has been a dispute between wizards and goblins due to errors on both sides. Goblins can be bloodthirsty and cruel towards wizards and consider them to be arrogant while many wizards consider goblins inferior. Goblins have in the past, resenting the fact that they occupy positions as second-class citizens, resorted to violence in the form of rebellions and riots.

Goblins harbor very different feelings about ownership than wizards—they consider the true owner of an object to be its maker rather than its purchaser, whom they see as simply renting the object until their death, and resent the passing of goblin-made heirlooms through wizarding families without further payment. Goblins can use magic without the aid of a wand, although they are insulted by the refusal of wizards to allow them to use wands, believing that they might increase their power. In turn, goblins harbor the secrets of their own magic from wizards. Their weaponry and armor are indestructible when created and have a very particular property. For example, a goblin-made blade such as the Sword of Godric Gryffindor will imbibe only what makes it stronger (Gryffindor's sword imbibed basilisk venom in *Harry Potter and the Chamber of Secrets*, enabling it to destroy Horcruxes in *Harry Potter and the Deathly Hallows*).

Goblins remain a neutral force in the fight between Voldemort and those who oppose him, claiming that it's "a wizard's war." In some cases, though, a state of friendship exists between wizards and goblins (particularly Bill Weasley, who works as a Curse Breaker for Gringotts), and there have even been some instances of goblin-wizard interbreeding (Professor Flitwick has distant goblin ancestry, which likely accounts for his small size).

Graphorn

Type: Magical Creature
Features:
First Appearance: *Fantastic Beasts and Where to Find Them*

Griffin

Type: Magical Creature
Features: Head, front legs giant eagle, body, back legs lion
First Appearance: *Fantastic Beasts and Where to Find Them*

Grim

Type: Omen
Features: Spectral large black dog
First Appearance: *Harry Potter and the Prisoner of Azkaban*

Overview

The Grim, an omen of imminent death, has the appearance of an extremely large black dog. Being spectral, it is visible only to the person whose death is imminent.

Extended Description At a number of points in *Harry Potter and the Prisoner of Azkaban*, Harry sees a large black dog; the first two times he sees it, he almost immediately narrowly escapes being killed: the first time, he is almost run over by the Knight Bus; the second time, debilitated by Dementors, he falls fifty feet from his broom; in neither case does anyone else see the dog, and at a second look it has vanished. In between, he has found, at Flourish and Blotts, a book of death omens with a picture on the cover that matches his recollection of the dog, and Professor Trelawney has read his tea leaves in Divination class and seen a Grim there. Later, Professor Trelawney apparently sees a Grim in Harry's crystal ball as well.

Taken all together, this leads Harry to rather believe in omens. However, he does see the big black dog again just before the Quidditch match with Slytherin, and that time it appears that Crookshanks can see him, so he begins to wonder if perhaps the dog is merely a dog, rather than an omen.

Questions

1. Do you believe in omens such as the grim?
2. How superstitious is the Wizarding World?

Grindylow

Type: Water Creature
Features: Very long fingers
First Appearance: *Harry Potter and the Prisoner of Azkaban*

Overview

The Grindylow is a pale green water demon. It is found throughout lakes in Britain and Ireland, including the lake at Hogwarts. It acts with aggression towards muggles and wizards alike, but Merpeople have been known to domesticate it. Grindylows have long fingers which will allow them to get a good grip, but which are easy to snap.

Extended Description The Grindylow appears first in *Harry Potter and the Prisoner of Azkaban*, where Professor Lupin brings it in for his Defence Against the Dark Arts classes. We see it only in passing there, being used only to illustrate Professor Lupin's willingness to communicate with the students in general, and Harry in particular. It reappears as part of the final exam for that course.

The Grindylow reappears in *Harry Potter and the Goblet of Fire*, as one of the obstacles that Harry must pass in order to complete the Second Challenge. It is in this section that we see that the Grindylow has been domesticated by merpeople; there are some tied up, like dogs, near some of the merpeople's houses.

The Grindylow plays one final role: in *Harry Potter and the Deathly Hallows*, in order to confirm that it is Harry he is talking to, Lupin asks Harry what was in Lupin's office the first time Harry was in there, and Harry replies, correctly, that it was a Grindylow in a tank.

Gurdyroot

Type: Magical plant
Features: Appears to be a large green onion
First Appearance: *Harry Potter and the Half-Blood Prince*

Overview

In appearance, the Gurdyroot looks like a large green onion.

Extended Description We first see the Gurdyroot when Luna Lovegood produces it from a pocket of her robes while searching for a message for Harry. She hands it to Ron, explaining that it is good for warding off Gulping Plimpies. At Bill and Fleur's wedding, Xenophilius Lovegood says he has not yet given the happy couple his wedding gift. As he departs, Ron suggests that it might be a lifetime supply of Gurdyroots.

When Harry, Ron, and Hermione are visiting Xeno Lovegood after Christmas in Harry's seventh year, he prepares an infusion of Gurdyroots for them. The resulting tea is a very dark purplish red, like beetroot. Xeno seems to quite like the taste, but Harry finds it undrinkable.

No particular magical properties are ever attributed to Gurdyroot, except for its being able to ward off Gulping Plimpies.

Halfblood

Type: Status
Features: Only one parent is a pure wizard/witch
First Appearance: *Harry Potter and the Philosopher's Stone*

Overview

A half-blood is someone with magical powers, yet only one pure-blood parent, the other being either Muggle or Muggle-born.

Analysis

Due to some process likely akin to hybrid vigor in genetics, quite often the most powerful wizards and witches spring from these intermarriages: classic examples would be Harry Potter, Tom Riddle, and Professor Snape. Equally, weaker wizards can come from pure-blood families; examples here would be Merope Gaunt and Neville Longbottom. However, there is quite a large faction of wizards, headed by Lord Voldemort, who believe that only pure-bloods should be educated in magic, and in fact that everyone other than the purebloods should be wiped off the face of the Earth.

Questions

1. What parallels can be drawn between instances in Muggle World History such as the Civil Rights movement and the role of Half-Blood characters in Harry Potter?
2. If you were a half-blood wizard how would you feel knowing that Voldemort was in power once more?
3. How far can you say that the tensions between Voldemort and half-blood wizards is at the heart of the 2 Wizarding Wars?

Hand of Glory

Type: Magical object
Features: Allows the holder to see in darkness
First Appearance: *Harry Potter and the Chamber of Secrets*

Overview

A Hand of Glory, made of a dead human hand, is a candle holder; the person holding it is able to see by the light of the candles, but to everyone else the light is hidden.

Extended Description We first see this artifact in Borgin and Burkes, in Knockturn Alley. Harry, having run into trouble on his first trip using Floo Powder, ends up in Borgin and Burke's. As he is preparing to exit, he sees Draco Malfoy preparing to enter. Harry hides; it is while he is hidden that he hears Borgin answering Draco's question about the Hand of Glory and its function. Borgin says that it is the best friend of thieves and plunderers, and Draco's father, Lucius Malfoy says that he hopes Draco will be better than a thief or a plunderer ... though unless his grades come up, that may be the best he can hope for.

Draco evidently does, at some point, purchase a Hand of Glory, because Ginny sees him carrying it when he leads the invasion of Hogwarts from the Room of Requirement, and it apparently allows him to see where he is leading the Death Eaters despite the Peruvian Instant Darkness Powder that he spreads around.

Herbology

Type: Course
Features: Plants and other flora
First Appearance: *Harry Potter and the Philosopher's Stone*

Overview

Herbology is the study of magical plants and how to take care of, utilize and/or combat them. Herbology lessons are shown in each of the first six books.

The subject is depicted as closely related to Potions, due to the nature of the plants, many of which are cultivated for extracting useful ingredients. Throughout the series, Herbology is taught by Pomona Sprout.

Extended Description Herbology is a core subject; it is one of the six academic subjects taught in the first year. Harry, who chooses to pursue a career as an Auror, takes Herbology at N.E.W.T.-level.

Being located in greenhouses on the grounds, trips to and from Herbology lessons are written to depict the weather at the time (for example, *Harry Potter and the Half-Blood Prince*, chapter 14). There are at least three greenhouses described in the books, holding a variety

Hinkypunk

of magical plants of varying degrees of lethality, including mandrakes, bubotubers, and Snargaluffs (which are valued for their pods).

Herbology is also the only subject in which Neville Longbottom excels.

GREATER PICTURE

In the Epilogue, it is revealed that Neville has become the Professor of Herbology at Hogwarts.

Hinkypunk

Type: Creature
Features: Marsh-dweller; carries a lantern
First Appearance: *Harry Potter and the Prisoner of Azkaban*

OVERVIEW

A Hinkypunk is a small, one legged creature that appears to be made out of smoke. It carries a lantern that is used to lure unsuspecting travelers into bogs.

Extended Description The term is first introduced in *Harry Potter and the Prisoner of Azkaban*. When Professor Snape substitutes for Professor Lupin in Defense Against the Dark Arts, he instructs the class to turn to the section on Werewolves; Hermione protests "We're due to start hinkypunks."

Later in the year Professor Lupin sets up an obstacle course for the third years' final exam. One of the obstacles is to "squish their way across a patch of marsh while ignoring misleading directions from a hinkypunk."

Hippocampus

Type: Magical Creature
Features: Head, forequarters horse, hindqaurters, tail giant fish
First Appearance: *Fantastic Beasts and Where to Find Them*

Hippogriff

Type: flying creature
Features: eagle's head and wings, horse's body
First Appearance: *Harry Potter and the Prisoner of Azkaban*

OVERVIEW

A hippogriff is a creature that has the "body, hind legs, and tail of a horse; but the front legs, wings, and head of what seemed to be a giant eagle, with a cruel, steel-colored beak and large, brilliantly orange eyes. The talons on its front legs were half a foot long and deadly looking."

Extended Description

"Things You Gotta Know About Hippogriffs" (as mentioned in Book 3)
• they're proud
• easily offended
• never insult one, 'cause it might be the last thing you do
• always wait for the hippogriff to make the first move
• it's polite
• try not to blink, hippogriff don't trust you if you blink too much
• never pull any of hippogriff's feathers, they won't like it
• to ride a hippogriff, climb up just behind the wing joint

Approaching A Hippogriff Because they are polite there is a proper way to approach them. "Walk toward him or her, and you bow, and you wait. If he or she bows back, you're allowed to touch him. If he or she doesn't bow, then get away from him or her sharpish; 'cause those talons hurts."

History of Magic

Type: Course
Features: Magical history
First Appearance: *Harry Potter and the Philosopher's Stone*

OVERVIEW

History of Magic instructs students on the history of magic.

Homenum Revelio

Type: Spell (Charm)
Features: Detects presence of humans
First Appearance: *Harry Potter and the Deathly Hallows*

OVERVIEW

Homenum Revelio is a spell which will reveal to the caster whether any other (presumably living) humans are within its area of influence.

Extended Description When they first arrive at Number 12, Grimmauld Place after leaving Bill and Fleur's wedding, Harry, Ron, and Hermione are concerned that there may be Death Eaters lurking. Hermione casts Homenum Revelio to determine that the house is, in fact, empty.

When Harry, Ron, and Hermione are betrayed by Xeno Lovegood, the two Death Eaters, Selwyn and Travers at first do not believe Xeno's protestations that he actually has Harry Potter. Selwyn determines that there is, in fact, someone else there by using this charm.

In both cases, the person casting the spell reports to the others there present what has been discovered, and Harry, Ron, and Hermione are only aware of the spell because they hear it being cast.

Analysis

The fact that Hermione reported nobody present at Grimmauld Place, and that Selwyn had to tell Travers that there was someone "up there," leads us to believe that the response to the spell is local to only the caster; other than the person casting the spell, nobody is aware of the results of the spell.

Horcrux

Type: Device
Features: Able to store part of a soul
First Appearance: *Harry Potter and the Half-Blood Prince*

Overview

Horcruxes are vessels in which a sorcerer may preserve a portion of his soul indefinitely. Anchoring a part of the soul to the earth by placing it in a Horcrux prevents the sorcerer's soul from going onwards should the sorcerer's body die; the effective result is that, given appropriate spells, the sorcerer can be brought back to life. This is considered to be among the darkest of all magic.

Extended Description   In *Harry Potter and the Half-Blood Prince*, Harry Potter learns how Horcruxes are created by experiencing a memory of Professor Slughorn's in Professor Dumbledore's Pensieve. In order to create a Horcrux, it is necessary that the wizard's soul be torn; the only known act that is powerful enough and damaging enough to do this is apparently for the wizard to commit murder. The torn soul fragment can then be removed and placed into another object; and so long as that object is not destroyed, the wizard can remain alive.

Harry learns at the same time that Lord Voldemort had been intrigued by the possibility of the number seven, which would either mean that he intended to create seven Horcruxes, or that he intended to have seven soul shards, which would mean six Horcruxes. Dumbledore believes at the time, correctly as it turns out, that the intended number of Horcruxes is six. It is unknown at the end of *Harry Potter and the Half-Blood Prince* how successful Voldemort has been at creating Horcruxes, but we can assume that he did create six and secrete them in various objects. Two Horcruxes have been destroyed—Tom Riddle's diary that Harry destroyed in *Harry Potter and the Chamber of Secrets*, and Marvolo Gaunt's ring which was destroyed by Professor Dumbledore. A third was apparently eliminated by an erstwhile Death Eater identified only as R.A.B., but this turns out in the seventh book to not have happened. To defeat the Dark Lord, Harry must find and destroy the remaining Horcruxes and then kill Lord Voldemort.

Note that we do not list Horcruxes as having first appeared in *Harry Potter and the Chamber of Secrets* because the diary is not identified as a Horcrux, by name or function, until *Harry Potter and the Half-Blood Prince*. Harry and Dumbledore deduce that the remaining Horcruxes are quite possibly coveted heirlooms of the four Hogwarts House founders; they see how much Riddle covets the two that he has seen in Hepzibah Smith's possession. One of these two, Salazar Slytherin's locket, was originally a Gaunt family heirloom; Riddle's mother had sold it to Borgin and Burke for a pittance, to buy food, and they had sold it in turn to Hepzibah Smith. Riddle apparently stole it back from her and used it as a Horcrux. The other, Helga Hufflepuff's cup, has not been seen since Harry and Professor Dumbledore saw it in Hokey's memory, but it evidently was also stolen by Riddle, and is presumed to have been made into a Horcrux.

Analysis

One of the plot points left hanging at the end of *Harry Potter and the Half-Blood Prince* is a *missing* Horcrux. Dumbledore and Harry have clearly at that point located the hiding place of a Horcrux, but the Horcrux itself is gone, replaced with a substitute locket by one "R.A.B." Both the substitute locket, and the unknown "R. A. B." (presumed to be Regulus Black), are keys to the "real" locket's whereabouts. In *Harry Potter and the Order of the Phoenix,* the Black family house is being used surreptitiously as a headquarters for the Order of the Phoenix. When Sirius and Molly undertake to clean the house, Kreacher undermines this effort—he and Mrs. Black's screaming portrait. Listed among the objects being discarded is "a heavy locket that none of them could open." Harry, having retreated to Grimmauld Place after the fall of the Ministry in *Harry Potter and the Deathly Hallows*, sees Regulus' name on a door, and decides that this is, in fact, the "R.A.B." of the substitute locket. After a fruitless search of Regulus' room, Hermione recalls the locket that they had earlier tried to discard. The locket will turn out to have been hidden by Kreacher, and then stolen by Mundungus Fletcher, who was busily looting 12 Grimmauld Place during the early parts of *Harry Potter and the Half-Blood Prince*. Mundungus will, in turn, have had it extorted away from him by Umbridge, which will result in Harry having to make an expedition into the Ministry to retrieve it.

Also of note, Voldemort split his soul into seven parts. In many cultures and religions seven is a significant number.

Questions

1. Can a Horcrux be a living object? Could it be a liquid?

2. How exactly are Horcruxes created? Does the Horcrux have to be related to the victim of the Killing Curse cast by the sorceror creating the Horcrux?

Greater Picture

For a list of the the Dark Lord's Horcruxes, see Horcruxes.

Obviously, Horcruxes are central to the story, and the location, and destruction, of these will be critical. We believe, or rather Dumbledore believes, that there were originally intended to be six Horcruxes, thus giving Voldemort seven pieces of his soul—one in his corporeal body, and six extras. While the uninitiate would suppose that one of these would have been used to reanimate him after his attempt to kill Harry resulted in the death of his body, this turns out not to be the case. Apparently, while the soul is physically split, such that part of it resides in an object external to the wizard, there is still a psychic linkage, and the wizard's soul cannot leave the face of the Earth while the shard, which is locked in an object, remains. Thus, the main part of the soul remains present after the body dies, wandering unhoused through the world. It is this unhoused soul, taking control of various animals in Albania, that is all that remains of Voldemort until Professor Quirrell runs into him, and for the two years between Quirrell's death and Pettigrew's return.

The first Horcrux that we find, the diary, was actually the second Horcrux made, and was thus perhaps somewhat less valued by Tom Riddle; this may be why it was devised both as a path to immortality and as a weapon. The author has stated that this Horcrux was created by the death of Moaning Myrtle, who was killed by the Basilisk. It is interesting that this Horcrux was aware of things that had happened after its creation; it could show Harry the discovery of Hagrid and Aragog, which happened the day after Myrtle's body was discovered. We don't directly know whose death was associated with any of the other Horcruxes, and we know for certain of only one other Horcrux, the Peverell signet ring. We learn that the ring is a Horcrux during book 6, when Dumbledore tells us that he has destroyed it. The remaining four are uncertain until the seventh book, though Dumbledore's guesses about three of them do prove accurate. We cannot be sure that Voldemort has placed Horcruxes in either Salazar Slytherin's locket or Helga Hufflepuff's cup, but by this time we are aware that Voldemort wanted these items, presumably for that purpose; and the fact that the artifact retrieved at the end of *Harry Potter and the Half-Blood Prince* is a locket does indicate that Slytherin's locket likely is now a Horcrux, as the R.A.B. who removed the Horcrux is likely to have put something similar in its place.

Until the seventh book, we are unsure of the fifth Horcrux; we don't yet have any theory as to what it could be or how it was created. One fan site had suggested that the artifact in question is Rowena Ravenclaw's wand, and that this is the "one, solitary wand" that rests in Ollivander's shop window; this was suggested to have something to do with the disappearance of Mr. Ollivander in *Harry Potter and the Half-Blood Prince*. In that case, the murder that created the Horcrux could well have happened in Diagon Alley. This turns out to be incorrect; the fifth Horcrux is an artifact that we don't learn about until the seventh book: Rowena Ravenclaw's lost diadem.

We believe that it was Voldemort's intent to create the sixth and final Horcrux from the death of Harry Potter. It is possible that he would have been carrying the artifact that he meant to convert into a Horcrux with him, and it would have remained when he died; it could have been found in Godric's Hollow when Harry goes to investigate there. Harry, however, does not enter his parents' house, only looking at it from outside the overgrown hedge. Thwarted by Harry, Voldemort apparently used the death of Bertha Jorkins to create a final Horcrux, which Dumbledore believes is now in Nagini.

There is a risk, of course, in that it is easier to destroy a living being and thus the embedded soul, but Voldemort would have been low on resources at this point, and unable to choose from a very wide selection of artifacts. In passing, we do see one of Dumbledore's very rare mistakes here; Dumbledore says that Voldemort used Nagini to kill Frank Bryce, and may have created a Horcrux at that time. This would imply that it is not necessary to kill someone directly in order to create a Horcrux; ordering another to do the killing would be sufficient, perhaps with the proviso that the being ordered to do the killing must not be sentient. However, reading the end of chapter 1 of *Harry Potter and the Goblet of Fire*, we see that in fact Voldemort did kill Frank Bryce with the Killing curse. Thus, even if Bryce's death had resulted in creation of a Horcrux, we wouldn't know if directly murdering someone is necessary to the Horcrux creation spell. The author's saying that the Diary Horcrux was made by way of Moaning Myrtle's death, which was caused by the Basilisk, rather than directly by Riddle, does rather confirm that use of an agent to do the murdering does not prevent creation of a Horcrux.

Horcruxes

Type: Magical artifact
Features: Soul fragments, a form of partial immortality
First Appearance: *Harry Potter and the Chamber of Secrets*

Overview

For the definition of a Horcrux, see Horcrux.

The entire Harry Potter series revolves around the defeat of the Dark Lord, which cannot be complete until all the Horcruxes are destroyed. This article lists the Horcruxes and details about them as best they are known.

Extended Description The entire Horcrux plot starts some forty years before Harry is born, when Tom Riddle asks Professor Slughorn about Horcruxes, whether if having one's soul in two places would allow return from death, would not multiple Horcruxes provide additional security? Would, perhaps, seven be a better number, as seven has so many mystical properties? Professor Slughorn is revolted at the idea, but Riddle does come away with the idea that it is not impossible. Professor Dumbledore, then Transfiguration professor, may have suspected that Riddle was studying Horcruxes; it is likely that he had already removed the books about Horcruxes from the library, as Riddle apparently claimed he could not find them. Hermione was able to retrieve these books from Dumbledore's study with the summoning charm.

Although there does not seem to be any mention of this fact in *Harry Potter and the Half-Blood Prince*, where Horcruxes were first introduced by name, it is mentioned in *Harry Potter and the Deathly Hallows* that Dumbledore thought Riddle had already made one Horcrux before his talk with Professor Slughorn. In fact, this is the case: according to the author, it was Tom Riddle Sr.'s death that allowed creation of the Ring Horcrux, and it was on the night that Riddle killed his father that he first found, and stole, the ring; and in Slughorn's memory we see Tom wearing the ring. So the inescapable conclusion is that the ring was a Horcrux at that point, though almost certainly the only one.

Riddle generally chose to make Horcruxes out of items that had value to him, and chose to hide them in places that were significant to him as well. It is possible that as he created more Horcruxes, the soul shards that he was able to split off and set aside would each be weaker than the previous. Thus, one would expect that the first Horcrux he made would be stronger than the second, which would be stronger than the third, and so forth. This does not seem to be the case; while the remnant of soul that remained within Riddle apparently became very frayed and fragile, each of the Horcruxes was as strongly able to defend itself as the earlier ones.

In the end, Riddle (or Voldemort, as he is later known) does end up making seven Horcruxes, one of them accidentally. These are as follows:

1. The ring Horcrux. Very likely the first Horcrux Riddle made, and the second one discovered, this was probably made shortly before we see it on Tom's finger in his fifth or sixth year. The author has stated that it was the death of Tom Riddle Sr. that allowed the creation of this Horcrux. While Dumbledore does not believe Riddle would have wanted to continue wearing it once it was made into a Horcrux, it is possible that Riddle did not yet have any safe place to keep it at that point. He eventually hid it, magically protected, in the ruins of the Gaunt shack; it is certain that he would not actually want to hide it there until he was certain that the original occupants would not be returning. It is also certain that he did not know exactly what the ring was; Marvolo Gaunt thought it was a signet ring bearing the coat of arms of the Peverell family, but the device etched onto the surface was, in fact, the sigil of the Deathly Hallows. The significance of the ring to Riddle was, of course, the illustration of the connection to the pure-blood Peverell family, just as it had been to Morfin Gaunt and Marvolo before him; and its hiding place was significant because it was the home of his mother and grandfather, and thus served as partial proof of his heritage. Professor Dumbledore had retrieved it from there; then, having returned it to the safety of his office, he was prepared to destroy it. It is possible that the soul fragment buried within the Horcrux managed to convince him to put the ring on his finger; the resulting action of the embedded curse caused the damage to his hand that was apparent in *Harry Potter and the Half-Blood Prince*, and in fact left him with, at best, a year of life. This Horcrux was destroyed by Dumbledore using the sword of Godric Gryffindor.

2. The diary Horcrux. Likely the second one made, but the first one discovered, this was made when Voldemort was still a student. The author has stated in an online chat that this Horcrux was made by means of Moaning Myrtle's death. Possibly an initial attempt, the value to Riddle of the diary was that it proved he was the true heir of Slytherin; interestingly, it only gained this value after it was made into a Horcrux. This is the only Horcrux that actually generates a simulacrum of Riddle, perhaps it is the only one that is actually allowed to. Hermione's reading suggests that a Horcrux can use the life-force of someone who gets emotionally close to it, using that to regenerate the person who provided the soul, and this is evidently what happened in this case: Riddle regenerated using Ginny's life force. We can see that the diary took no damage from being flushed down the toilet or having ink spilled all over it, which is what we would expect given the characteristics of a Horcrux. This Horcrux was destroyed by Harry in *Harry Potter and the Chamber of Secrets* using a Basilisk fang. Dumbledore was actually disturbed by the discovery of this Horcrux; while he had suspected that Riddle had made a Horcrux, the almost cavalier way that this one was risked, solely in order to make trouble, seemed to suggest that it had a rather lower value than a Horcrux, being a ticket to immortality, ought to have.

3. The locket Horcrux. This is the third Horcrux discovered, but likely the fifth made. The author has stated that it was created from the death of a Muggle tramp. The locket is significant to Voldemort because of its direct connection to Salazar Slytherin, who espoused the same belief in pure-blood superiority that Voldemort has adopted, and because it serves as proof that he is descended from Slytherin. The first time we see it, before it is a Horcrux, it is around the neck of Merope Gaunt. She evidently then sells it for a pittance, and it goes on to become one of Hepzibah Smith's treasures. Shortly after Hepzibah's death, it vanished; apparently Tom Riddle had, at this point, stolen it and made it into a Horcrux. As a Horcrux, it was originally hidden in the basin in the cave, which was visited by Harry and Professor Dumbledore in *Harry Potter and the Half-Blood Prince*. This cave was significant to Voldemort because it was one of the places where he had first exercised his superiority over Muggles, by torturing some of his fellows from the orphanage. The locket was then stolen by Regulus Black, who replaced the locket with the one that Harry and Dumbledore found, and who passed the locket on to Kreacher with instructions to destroy it. Kreacher was unable to do so. It then passed through Mundungus Fletcher's hands to Dolores Umbridge. Harry and Hermione managed to steal it from Dolores, and eventually Ron destroyed this Horcrux with the sword of Godric Gryffindor. The locket had to be opened before it could be destroyed; Harry discovered that it would open if spoken to in Parseltongue.

4. The cup Horcrux. This is the fourth Horcrux retrieved, probably the fourth one made, and according to the author was made via the death of Hepzibah Smith. The cup is significant to Voldemort because of its direct connection to Helga Hufflepuff, one of the Four Founders of Hogwarts. We first see it in Hokey's memory, when Hepzibah Smith is showing off her treasures, and assume that it is stolen by Voldemort at her death, at the same time he recovers Slytherin's locket. When we next see the cup, it is locked away in a top-security vault at Gringott's. Harry believes that the location is significant to Voldemort because possession of a vault at Gringotts is proof of ancient Wizarding heritage. The vault is owned by Bellatrix Lestrange, and Voldemort is furious when the Horcrux is stolen from there. The

report of the theft of the cup Horcrux starts Voldemort inspecting the places where he has hidden all his Horcruxes to confirm that they still are safe. To his fury, he finds that they are not. The cup Horcrux is carried out of Gringotts by Hermione, and destroyed by her at Hogwarts using a Basilisk fang recovered from the Chamber of Secrets.

5. The diadem Horcrux. This is the fifth Horcrux retrieved, but possibly the third one made. It was while he was at Hogwarts that Riddle had charmed (nonmagically) the Grey Lady into telling him where the lost Diadem of Ravenclaw was. The Grey Lady, in life Rowena Ravenclaw's daughter, had stolen the diadem and had hidden it in Albania, in a hollow tree. She had then been murdered by the man who became the Bloody Baron, before she could either retrieve it or tell anyone where it was. Riddle managed to get its location, and having retrieved it, converted it into a Horcrux, apparently by murdering an Albanian peasant, according to the author. The value of the Diadem to Voldemort was obviously its connection to Ravenclaw, one of the four Founders. Visiting Hogwarts ten years after the death of Hepzibah Smith, Voldemort had hidden the diadem in the Room of Requirement in its "junk warehouse" state. The significance of this location to Voldemort is two-fold: like Harry, Riddle found Hogwarts to be the first place that he could truly call his home, and unlike Harry, he believed that he was the only person who knew how to get into the Room of Requirement. Harry had seen, and handled, the diadem when he went into the Room of Requirement to hide his Potions textbook in his sixth year, but had not recognized it; of course, he had not even known it existed at that point. It is because he had used it as a marker for the place he had hidden his textbook that he was able to remember it. This Horcrux was destroyed by Vincent Crabbe, who had learned how to create Fiendfyre but not how to extinguish it. The fire he created would have destroyed everything in the Room of Requirement at that point, and in fact consumed him as well.

6. Nagini. The seventh Horcrux created, Nagini was used as something of an afterthought. Voldemort needed a sixth Horcrux to complete what he thought was the mystical number of soul pieces (seven), and Nagini was handy at the time when he was murdering Bertha Jorkins. (Voldemort was unaware of the existence of the accidental Horcrux at that point, and remained so throughout the series.) Nagini had been his constant companion to that point, and after becoming a Horcrux, started showing certain human characteristics. It is certain that Nagini and Voldemort were sharing their thoughts when Harry viewed Nagini's attack on Arthur Weasley. Once Voldemort knew that his Horcruxes were under attack, he created protective spells around Nagini to keep her safe; but once Harry was believed dead, he no longer thought that necessary. Nagini was beheaded by Neville Longbottom, using the sword of Godric Gryffindor which had been provided to him by the Sorting Hat.

7. Harry. The sixth Horcrux created, Harry was purely accidental. It was revealed in *Harry Potter and the Deathly Hallows* that the act of murdering Harry's parents had caused Voldemort's already shredded soul to tear again, and the detached fragment sought and attached itself to the nearest intact soul it could find, which was Harry's. This soul fragment, resident in Harry, gave him some of Voldemort's abilities, notably the ability to speak to snakes, and provided him an awareness of Voldemort's thoughts and feelings throughout the seven books. Voldemort destroyed this soul fragment when he tried to kill Harry the second time, in *Harry Potter and the Deathly Hallows;* he was unable to kill Harry at that time because of the blood protection Harry still carried. But the author has said that with the destruction of the soul fragment, Harry lost the ability to speak Parseltongue.

ANALYSIS

It is perhaps interesting that no person destroyed more than one Horcrux. Harry, Ron, Hermione, Neville, Dumbledore, Crabbe, and Voldemort each destroyed one of the seven. This illustrates a point that Harry has been trying to make throughout the series, but only verbalizes while in the process of setting up Dumbledore's Army in *Harry Potter and the Order of the Phoenix:* Harry didn't do all this stuff alone, he had loads of help.

Horklump

Type: Magical Creature
Features: looks like mushroom
First Appearance: *Fantastic Beasts and Where to Find Them*

House Elf

Type: Being
Features: Small; large green eyes; large ears; intelligent
First Appearance: *Harry Potter and the Chamber of Secrets*

OVERVIEW

House-elves are small creatures with big eyes, long noses, bat-like ears, and usually very poorly clothed. They can often be found at large houses and mansions. They are supposed to be very loyal to the head of their family. An owner or master can 'free' a house elf by giving him or her clothes.

Extended Description House-elves are essentially slaves—they will serve one family for a long part of their life, and they feel that this is right and proper, that this is what they were created to do. At Hogwarts there are hundreds of house-elves, preparing the food for the feasts, cleaning, and doing other chores. House-elves are bound to listen to members of the family they belong to, but can choose to disobey anyone else. In extraordinary circumstances, they can even disobey their masters, but afterwards they will punish themselves quite harshly for it. Three house-elves play a significant role in the books: Dobby, Winky, and Kreacher; a fourth one, Hokey, is mentioned (in *Harry Potter and the Half-Blood Prince*, where she serves Hepzibah Smith), but does not play a particularly significant role.

ANALYSIS

Quite obviously, most house-elves are content with their status, and believe that their situation, caring for their owners, is right and proper. House-elves can be freed; giving a house-elf clothes frees it from its situation, which is why they are so ill-clothed: they must wear whatever castoffs they can scavenge, which results in many of them wearing things like discarded, damaged pillowcases and rags twisted into rude loincloths. Most house-elves, however, do not want to be freed, and resist the suggestion most strongly. One exception is Dobby, who was the house-elf of the Malfoy family; he was so ill-treated there that he rebelled and eventually left their employ when Harry managed to engineer him getting clothes. As a free house-elf, Dobby was unable to find work for a year or so, eventually joining the kitchen staff at Hogwarts; it seems that most wizards don't want house-elves that they have to pay for, even if it is only a Galleon per month.

When Winky is dismissed in *Harry Potter and the Goblet of Fire*, Dobby manages to get her employed at Hogwarts as well; however, she doesn't want to work, she simply sits, mourning the loss of her position and drinking herself to oblivion, for almost a year. She has not directly appeared in any of the books since then, though Dobby does mention her again in the next book.

Hermione tries to start up an organization to combat this apparent slavery, the Society for the Promotion of Elfish Welfare (S.P.E.W.), but quite apart from the unfortunate acronym, she meets a substantial amount of resistance, not only from wizards and witches who like having house-elves around to serve them, but from the house-elves themselves who prefer security to freedom.

House-elves have a tendency to over-simplify the language. They refer to themselves in the third person ("Dobby is most sorry, sir . . .") and use full names ("Dobby cannot let Harry Potter lose his Wheezy!"), both of which would seem to imply an uncertainty about the use of language—the intricacies of "I" versus "you," and the appropriate use of names and nicknames, seems to be beyond them. This would imply a lower level of verbal intelligence than humans have. Additionally, Dobby's efforts to prevent Harry from returning to Hogwarts, or to get him to return to Privet Drive once he is there, seem quite poorly thought out, almost child-like, again suggesting a less sophisticated level of intelligence. From this, one can see why a house-elf would be afraid to be freed; the world is a scary place for one so surrounded by people smarter than himself.

GREATER PICTURE

The status and situation of house elves is complicated. Applying human values to "help" non-humans is not as straightforward as some, including Hermione, believe at first. Hermione's campaign with S.P.E.W. is laudable and correct, elves are slaves and should be given the rights, privileges and respect humans enjoy. However, she finds difficulty in understanding the values and desires of most elves. Initially she wishes to free all elves and have them paid wages for their work. The elves, with few exceptions, consider this an insult to their honor. Elves appear to have been bred or enchanted to view their servitude as a noble vocation rather than enslavement. This breeding and enchantment is obviously the selfish work of wizards in the far past who desired the luxury of dedicated servants who cost nothing. Such a tradition, as Hermione finds out, is difficult to reform and requires some patience. Eventually the elves, including Kreacher, achieve some enlightenment, and the victory banquet at the end of *Harry Potter and the Deathly Hallows* is shared by elves, humans and others as friends and equals. Not mentioned above is the apparent fact that House Elf magic is not of the same type as human magic. In particular, we are told numerous times that Hogwarts is protected against Apparation, that you cannot Apparate into or out of Hogwarts, or even within Hogwarts except when the spells are locally and temporarily lifted in the Great Hall for Apparation class. Yet, Dobby is clearly able to Disapparate from Harry's grip in the Hospital Wing; we see that in *Harry Potter and the Chamber of Secrets*. This shows that House Elf Disapparation is different from "wand-bearer" Disapparation in two respects: first, it can be done in places where the human spell is blocked, and second, it can be used to get away from someone who is holding the caster, something that evidently is not so easily accomplished by humans.

This ability of House Elves to Apparate where humans cannot plays a fairly important role later in the series as well. Kreacher, taken to the cave of the locket, is able to return to the Black house and tell Regulus what had happened, despite Voldemort having surrounded the location with various protective and preventative spells, and despite Kreacher's then being dragged underwater by Inferi. It is Kreacher's information that leads Harry to a Horcrux. Whether other House Elf magic is significantly different from human magic is uncertain. We know that House Elves do not carry wands, and so there is certainly a difference in the way magic is produced; however, apparently House-Elf magic can be stopped by human magic, as Mundungus Fletcher is able to loot Grimmauld Place despite Kreacher's efforts to stop him.

Howler

Type: Magical device
Features: Carried like a letter
First Appearance: *Harry Potter and the Chamber of Secrets*

OVERVIEW

Howlers are messages that are carried by Owl Post, like letters. They are distinctively red-colored, and are used to carry urgent and angry messages.

Extended Description Howlers appear several times in the series. The first one we see is sent to Ron by his mother in *Harry Potter and the Chamber of Secrets*. The next is sent to Neville by his grandmother. Finally, one is sent to Harry's Aunt Petunia in *Harry Potter and the Order of the Phoenix*.

A Howler is not used for just any message, as true to their name, they are extremely loud—according to the text, a hundred times as loud as one's natural voice, though that could be simply the apparent effect. Additionally, if not opened promptly, they tend to explode: though we do not see that happening, Ron advises Neville that it is better to open one immediately and take the amplified scolding, rather than leaving it unopened and letting it explode; and Percy comments in *Harry Potter and the Goblet of Fire* that exploding Howlers have been scorching his desk.

QUESTIONS

1. What is the meaning of the howler received by Aunt Petunia?

Imp

Type: creature
Features: looks like a pixie
First Appearance: *Fantastic Beasts and Where to Find Them*

Impedimenta

Type: Spell (Jinx)
Features: Causes the target to trip First Appearance

OVERVIEW

Impedimenta is a jinx that causes the victim to trip, get blasted backwards, etc. The power of the jinx is affected by how much you concentrate when saying the incantation.

Imperio

Type: Spell (Curse)
Features: Controls victim
First Appearance: *Harry Potter and the Goblet of Fire*

OVERVIEW

The Imperius Curse forces the victim to obey the caster's commands.

Extended Description Unlike the Killing Curse, it is possible to fight this curse. These two and the Cruciatus Curse are considered to be the most terrible curses in the magical world, called the Unforgivable Curses; the use of any of the three on another witch or wizard is punishable by a life sentence in Azkaban.

Only very skilled wizards are able to fight this curse, and only very powerful ones are able to cast it—it takes significant mental strength to impose your will upon another. Interestingly, Harry Potter seems to have an innate ability to fight the curse, while Ron Weasley is more susceptible to it than average. The spell is first seen and described in the fourth book, and the effects on Harry and Ron are described in the next chapter.

ANALYSIS

When called upon to name the three Unforgivable Curses, it is Ron who comes up with this one. Professor Moody comments that this curse had made things difficult for the Ministry, as one could never be sure whether the person you had arrested was a true Death Eater, or was doing the will of a Death Eater who had remained hidden. We see a number of people controlled by means of the Imperius curse throughout the series in and after the fourth book. Harry himself has need to cast this curse in *Harry Potter and the Deathly Hallows*. The description that we receive at the time, of the action of the curse on the caster, lead us to believe that while a wand is necessary to cast this curse, the actions are somewhat longer-lasting; Harry, for instance, casts this spell on the goblin Bogrod, then on the Death Eater Travers, and has them both under his control at the same time. One gets the feeling that it is only necessary to actually have the wand actively engaged with the subject of the curse while he is getting his instructions; as is seen at the end of that episode, Travers has been instructed to hide himself, and he continues to serenely do so even after Harry has gone.

GREATER PICTURE

The list of people we know who are controlled this way is quite large.

In *Harry Potter and the Goblet of Fire*, we learn that initially Barty Crouch is being controlled by his father, Bartemius. Then, Bartemius is being controlled by Wormtail, while Alastor Moody is being controlled by Barty. There is also a stretch where, possibly, Bertha Jorkins is being controlled by either Wormtail or Voldemort. Voldemort tries to control Harry with this curse, and fails. It is perhaps ironic that Harry's ability to throw off the curse was nurtured by Barty Crouch, who claims to be Voldemort's greatest supporter. In *Harry Potter and the Order of the Phoenix*, we believe that Sturgis Podmore was trying to get through a door at the Ministry because he was under this curse, and we are led to believe that Broderick Bode was acting under Lucius Malfoy's instruction when he went mad. Harry guesses that Umbridge may be controlled in this manner, but Sirius says that is probably not the case.

We see relatively few instances of the curse in *Harry Potter and the Half-Blood Prince*. The story is littered with techniques meant to detect people under the Imperius curse or disguised by other means, which seem marginally effective; in fact, when we first see Tonks on the Hogwarts Express, we are almost led to believe that she is under the Imperius curse. There is an interesting case of Imperius-by-proxy as well; Draco Malfoy admits at the end of the book that he has placed Madam Rosmerta under the Imperius curse, and it seems that while under control, Madam Rosmerta put Katie Bell under the Imperius curse as well.

In *Harry Potter and the Deathly Hallows,* we see two people under the Imperius curse in the first five chapters: Pius Thicknesse, and Stan Shunpike. Once the Ministry falls, we can safely assume there will be many others, but they don't directly affect the story, except for the goblin Bogrod and the Death Eater Travers, as mentioned above.

Imperturbable Charm

Type: Spell (Charm)
Features: Prevents entrance
First Appearance: *Harry Potter and the Order of the Phoenix*

Overview

An Imperturbable Charm, cast on a door or window, prevents approach to the door by anything.

Extended Description   We first hear of this charm when Fred and George are talking about trying to use their Extendable Ears to listen in on meetings of the adult members of the Order. Ginny tells them not to bother, there is an Imperturbable Charm on the door, and that she found this out by tossing Dungbombs at it: none of them had reached the door. When the family goes to visit Arthur in the hospital for the first time after his injury, the adults there present, Arthur, Molly Weasley, Mad-Eye Moody, and Tonks, send the youngsters out of the ward so they can have a quick discussion. Fred and George again produce Extendable Ears, saying that they hope nobody has thought to put an Imperturbable Charm on the door. It turns out nobody has.

In *Harry Potter and the Half-Blood Prince,* when Harry, Ron, and Hermione have followed Draco Malfoy to Borgin and Burkes, Ron produces Extendable Ears to allow them to listen in on what Draco is saying, and says that he hopes the store is not protected by an Imperturbable Charm.

Impervius

Type: Spell
Features: Waterproofing
First Appearance: *Harry Potter and the Prisoner of Azkaban*

Overview

Impervius (spelled that way in the books) is a spell that is used to waterproof items. It seems to work by actually repelling water, rather than preventing penetration.

Analysis

This spell is first used by Hermione to waterproof Harry's glasses in the Quidditch match against Hufflepuff in *Harry Potter and the Prisoner of Azkaban*; this match is played in a pounding downpour, with lightning and gale-force winds. Harry is unable to see the Snitch because the rain is streaking his glasses and distorting his vision, and this spell clears his glasses so he can see.

A relatively minor spell, it is used in several other Quidditch matches, but is not used elsewhere.

Questions

1. Being waterproof seems such a useful thing; why would this spell not be in much more general use?

Incarcerous

Type: Spell (Charm)
Features: "Binding spell" causes ropes to bind the subject
First Appearance: *Harry Potter and the Prisoner of Azkaban*

Overview

Incarcerous causes ropes to appear out of the end of the caster's wand, which then bind and (usually) gag the subject of the spell.

Extended Description   When we first see this spell, it is being used by Professor Snape to bind Sirius Black and Remus Lupin in The Shrieking Shack. It is used a number of times after that, notably by Professor Umbridge, to bind the Centaur Magorian, an action that triggers a mass attack on her by the remainder of the herd.

Analysis

Branch of Magic: *Incarcerous* is difficult to categorize into one branch of magic due to its dual function. Most prominently, it is a transfiguration spell—conjuring to be specific. It also could be considered a charm as it is giving the ropes the ability to attack a specified target and bind to it without further magic being performed.

The Rope's Physical Properties: It would appear that the attributes of the conjured rope varies and most likely is the subconscious choice of the caster. In *Harry Potter and the Prisoner of Azkaban,* when Severus Snape nonverbally casts the spell, "thin, cordlike" ropes bind Sirius Black and Remus Lupin. In *Harry Potter and the Order of the Phoenix,* when Dolores Umbridge uses the spell, this time verbally, once more cords are produced—with no detail as to their thickness. The final time we see the spell cast in the series is in *Harry Potter and the Deathly Hallows.* A Death Eater casts this spell on Ron. He is bound tightly in thick ropes.

One possible explanation of the discrepancies in rope size is that the size could have a great deal to do with the level of power that the caster has. It is inferred throughout the final books that Umbridge was relatively weak, magically, and therefore her *Incarcerous*, while effective, did not produce ropes as thick as the Death Eater's. On the other hand, it is reasonably obvious that Snape is among the most powerful wizards in the story. Yet, his version of the spell, non-verbal though it may be, produces only thin cords, though these cords are quite adequate to bind both Sirius and Lupin. Quite possibly, Snape is in more control of his unconscious desires than either of our other two casters; for the relatively unsophisticated Death Eaters, bigger ropes are obviously better, while perhaps the cords that Umbridge produces are the best she can manage. Meanwhile, Snape produces just enough strength to do the job, perhaps knowing that binding with smaller cords will also hurt more if one struggles against them.

Etymology: *Incarcerous* comes from the Latin word "carcerate" meaning prison or cage. Since the incantation causes ropes to be expelled from the casters wand and bound tightly around the intended target, this makes sense since it is detaining the victim, much like a prison or cage.

Incendio

Type: Spell
Features: Create flame First Appearance

OVERVIEW

Incendio causes the victim or object to burst into flame.

Inferius

Type: Animated corpse
Features: Stopped by fire
First Appearance: *Harry Potter and the Half-Blood Prince*

OVERVIEW

Inferi are corpses that seem alive.

Extended Description Inferi are actually animated by the will of a wizard. They are greatly feared because, being already dead, they cannot be killed, and are effectively fearless. Animation of Inferi is a very dark form of magic, and Voldemort made great use of them in his attempts to take over Wizarding society before Harry was born.

It appears that Voldemort has used Inferi to protect one of his Horcruxes; we see them in *Harry Potter and the Half-Blood Prince*. At this point, we learn also that they can be stopped by fire.

We learn in that book, also, that Mundungus Fletcher has been imprisoned in Azkaban for impersonating an Inferius. it is in relation to Mundungus that Inferi are described; they are mentioned beforehand, but it is only when a student brings up the story of Mundungus' imprisonment that the Dark Arts teacher, Professor Snape, actually describes what they are.

ANALYSIS

In the cave of the Horcrux, there are a large number of Inferi lying in wait under the surface of the water. We have reason to believe that those Inferi have been there for at least fifteen years, most likely much longer, as Kreacher tells us that they were there when Voldemort was initially hiding that Horcrux, before Harry was born. Thus, we must assume that either some part of the spell used to create Inferi, or some additional spell that is not discussed, must halt the natural processes that would result in the dead body decomposing.

GREATER PICTURE

In *Harry Potter and the Deathly Hallows*, we meet the animated corpse of Bathilda Bagshot. While her body does contain Voldemort's pet snake Nagini, it is uncertain whether Nagini is controlling Bathilda, or whether what remains of her has been made into an Inferius. It is true that her remains have not deteriorated significantly in the possibly five months since her passing, so some of the magic that preserves the Inferius must have been used on her.

Invisibility Cloak

Type: Magical device
Features: Makes wearer invisible
First Appearance: *Harry Potter and the Philosopher's Stone*

OVERVIEW

An invisibility cloak is a cloak designed to conceal its wearer. It is made of a special type of material that makes its occupant invisible. When nobody is inside it, it looks like a silvery, almost transparent fabric.

Extended Description Invisibility cloaks are very rare, but Harry receives one for Christmas in his first year; it turns out to have been originally the property of Harry's father, and was given to Harry by Professor Dumbledore. Harry uses it a number of times in the books, whenever he needs to go somewhere unobserved, often with one or more of his friends; he does note that it is a mixed blessing, as it hides you from vision, but you still have to be careful about making sounds or bumping into things or people.

Alastor Moody apparently owns two Invisibility Cloaks; Sturgis Podmore is wearing one of them when he is arrested in the Ministry, and Arthur Weasley is wearing the other when he is attacked by the snake, in *Harry Potter and the Order of the Phoenix*.

ANALYSIS

The invisibility cloak is the perfect device for moving around undetected. As Harry often has the need to break rules, he needs a device such as this and an invisibility cloak seems like the perfect choice. Unlike the Disillusionment charm, which makes an object a near-perfect chameleon, the invisibility cloak makes the object transparent, and can only be pierced by magical—or possibly cat—eyes: Professor Moody's magical eye seems to be able to see through it easily, and there is the suggestion that both Mrs. Norris and Crookshanks can sense Harry under it, though in fact the cats may be hearing rather than seeing the passage of those within. Peeves also senses Harry, Ron, and Hermione under the Cloak in *Harry Potter and the Philosopher's Stone*, though it is obvious that he is hearing rather than seeing them. Additionally, in *Harry Potter and the Chamber of*

Secrets, Professor Dumbledore looks right at Harry and Ron underneath the Invisibility Cloak while in Hagrid's hut, suggesting that Dumbledore might actually be able to see through the Invisibility Cloak. Dumbledore had hinted at this ability in *Harry Potter and the Philosopher's Stone,* when he caught Harry in front of the Mirror of Erised.

GREATER PICTURE

It is noted elsewhere that Dumbledore is able to make himself invisible without using a cloak; Dumbledore says this himself in *Harry Potter and the Philosophers' Stone.* And yet, James Potter left his invisibility cloak in Dumbledore's care. What need of an invisibility cloak would Dumbledore have? The author has stated that this is an important question to ponder.[1]

In *Harry Potter and the Deathly Hallows,* we learn that this is because James Potter's Invisibility Cloak is, indeed, something special. Talking with Xeno Lovegood, the Trio learn of the possible existence of the three Deathly Hallows. Xeno reminds them that most Invisibility Cloaks are either simple traveling cloaks to which a Disillusionment Charm has been applied, or are woven out of the hair of a Demiguise, but all such become damaged or fade into visibility with time. Only one Invisibility Cloak, the third of the three Hallows, and supposedly the Cloak of Death himself, does not suffer the ravages of time, and cannot be damaged by magic. Harry, Ron, and Hermione are uncomfortably aware at this point that the Cloak in Harry's possession matches this description perfectly.

It turns out that Dumbledore, in his youth, had heard the legend of the three Hallows, and had been trying to find them. Though his active search for them had stopped by the time he was a teacher at Hogwarts, his youthful obsession with them had never completely faded, and he had borrowed James' Cloak, once he had heard of its properties, because he recognized it as a Hallow. It was while he was examining it that Voldemort killed James and Lily, and tried to kill Harry.

Jarvey

Type: Magical Creature
Features: looks like overgrown ferret
First Appearance: *Fantastic Beasts and Where to Find Them*

Jobberknoll

Type: Magical Creature
Features: unable to descibe
First Appearance: *Fantastic Beasts and Where to Find Them*

Kappa

Type: Magical Creature
Features: looks like monkey
First Appearance: *Fantastic Beasts and Where to Find Them*

Kelpie

Type: Magical creature
Features: horse-like with bulrushes on mane
First Appearance: *Harry Potter and the Chamber of Secrets*

OVERVIEW

The Kelpie is a form of water creature, native to England and Ireland, which can assume a variety of shapes.

Extended Description It is mentioned in *Fantastic Beasts and Where to Find Them* that one of the Kelpie's favoured shapes is a sea horse, often with bulrushes instead of a mane, as described above. The largest Kelpie on record is found in Loch Ness, which is in Scotland. The International Confederation of Wizards noticed that it wasn't a serpent when it changed into an Otter.

Though mentioned in passing in the main books, it plays little, if any, part in the story.

Knarl

Type: Creature
Features: Looks like a hedgehog
First Appearance: *Harry Potter and the Order of the Phoenix*

OVERVIEW

The Knarl is largely indistinguishable from a hedgehog.

Extended Description The Knarl is mentioned three times in the series. The first time, in *Harry Potter and the Order of the Phoenix,* is when Professor Grubbly-Plank is being inspected by Professor Umbridge. Responding to a query about her course plans, Professor Grubbly-Plank says that she still has to teach the class how to detect Crups and Knarls. Later that same year, Hagrid, then teacher of Care of Magical Creatures, expresses his dissatisfaction with the Ministry-approved curriculum by saying he can't understand why anyone would prefer learning about Knarls instead of Chimaeras.

The final instance, in the same book, is when Harry, in his Care of Magical Creatures O.W.L., must distinguish Knarls from Hedgehogs; we are told that he did this by offering them milk.

In *Fantastic Beasts and Where to Find Them,* "Newt Scamander" tells us that the only difference between Knarls and Hedgehogs is that, offered food, a Knarl will believe that it is a trap and will react angrily.

Kneazle

Type: Magical creature
Features: Cat-like appearance
First Appearance: *Fantastic Beasts and Where to Find Them*

---

1. Interview on the extended DVD set

OVERVIEW

Kneazles are small creatures that look like large cats, but have spotted fur, large ears and a tail like a Lion. An independent, intelligent creature, capable of aggression which it shows occasionally, a kneazle will make a great pet, if it likes you! It can be relied upon to guide its owner home if they should get lost. A kneazle requires a license for legal ownership.

Extended Description Apparently Kneazles can interbreed with cats; the resulting cat/kneazle hybrid is relatively intelligent and larger than the ordinary cat. Crookshanks, Hermione's cat, is apparently just such a cross-breed.

Knight Bus

Type: Magical vehicle
Features: Purple triple-decker bus
First Appearance: *Harry Potter and the Prisoner of Azkaban*

OVERVIEW

The Knight Bus is a means of transportation for the stranded wizard; it will carry you from anywhere to anywhere (in England anyway) if you have the fare.

Extended Description The Knight Bus is summoned by raising your wand arm. It is fitted inside with four-poster beds, and you can get a toothbrush or a mug of hot chocolate if you choose; though it's probably best to skip the latter, as the ride is rough enough to cause you to spill your mug.

In *Harry Potter and the Order of the Phoenix*, the Knight Bus appears in its daytime configuration. The four-poster beds are replaced by ordinary chairs, which like the beds are not anchored, so they slide around the inside of the bus with every swerve.

One side note: The Knight Bus in the movie of *Harry Potter and the Prisoner of Azkaban* contains, as decoration, a number of shrunken heads which talk. The author is on record as saying that, while she didn't think that detail up, she rather wishes she had.[1]

Langlock

Type: Spell (Jinx)
Features: Binds the tongue to the roof of the mouth, preventing speech
First Appearance: *Harry Potter and the Half-Blood Prince*

OVERVIEW

The Langlock spell is one that prevents someone from speaking about something specific by binding their tongue to the roof of their mouth.

---

1. Interview on the extended DVD set

Extended Description Harry finds this spell in the Potions text that belonged to the Half-Blood Prince. He uses it at one point in the story to silence Peeves, who is loudly commentating a fight between Dobby and Kreacher. We also guess that this is the spell left in the entrance to Number 12, Grimmauld Place by Mad-Eye Moody as part of the attempt to prevent Snape's entrance.

Legilimency

Type: Spell (Charm) / Method
Features: Provides mind-reading abilities
First Appearance: *Harry Potter and the Order of the Phoenix*

OVERVIEW

Legilimency, a compound of the Latin 'legere' (to read) + 'mens' (mind), is the art of, as one might suppose, reading another person's mind.

Extended Description Characters like Lord Voldemort and Albus Dumbledore use Legilimency, especially to find out if someone is lying to them. Legilimency does not work well on wizards or witches who are experts in its counterpart, Occlumency (Severus Snape is a good example of this).

Apart from the Occlumency lessons, Snape will use Legilimency directly at the end of *Harry Potter and the Half-Blood Prince*, where he detects Harry's intent to form spells and counters them, and will attempt to use it on Draco at Christmas, only to be foiled by Draco's skill at Occlumency. There are several places where Snape apparently uses Legilimency on Harry, without Harry being aware of the possibility; several times in teh first three books, Harry thinks that he thought Snape was reading his mind. We also believe that Voldemort uses Legilimency to confirm Snape's story about the date of Harry's departure from Privet Drive in *Harry Potter and the Deathly Hallows,* and when Harry returns to Hogwarts it seems that Snape is trying to use Legilimency on Professor McGonagall to see if Harry is nearby.

ANALYSIS

Legilimency is introduced in *Harry Potter and the Order of the Phoenix* as being the reason that Occlumency is required. We are introduced to the idea that via the practice of Legilimency, Voldemort can read, if not minds, at least memories. Snape, in the abortive Occlumency classes, draws a distinction between Legilimency and reading minds, but Harry is unable to see what the distinction actually is, and Snape, due to his dislike of Harry, clearly does not want to spend any additional time on attempted explanations. It is possible that the distinction Snape is drawing is that between thoughts, which are extremely fluid, and the results of those thoughts, namely actions, words, senses, and memories. It is certainly true that Snape, in the

Occlumency lessons, is able to retrieve memories from Harry's mind, and perceive what he is doing well enough that he is able to block every spell Harry tries to hit him with at the end of *Harry Potter and the Half-Blood Prince*.

As we find in *Harry Potter and the Order of the Phoenix*, Harry and Snape hate each other actively enough that Harry is unable to calm his mind, and Snape does not help matters by constantly needling him. As a calm mind is necessary for Occlumency, it would seem that this effort was doomed to fail from the outset. Dumbledore later says that he had made an old man's mistake, assuming that the feud between James and Snape was far enough in the past that Snape could put it aside.

GREATER PICTURE

As mentioned in the entry for Occlumency, it is one of Dumbledore's few mistakes to believe that Occlumency will, in fact, prevent Harry's recurring dreams. Legilimency, the ability to read another's mind, does not include the ability to plant visions in the head of another person, as far as we are told. Additionally, the channel used to transfer those visions, we later find, is a fragment of Voldemort's soul that is attached to Harry. Occlumency may or may not prevent the placement of these visions in Harry's dreams, but it seems unlikely given the information Dumbledore had at the time. However, even to Dumbledore, this was a new area of magic, so we must assume that he was doing the best he could with the tools he had.

One other question that arises is how Snape was able to send his Patronus to Harry in the Forest of Dean, a patch of mixed forest and fields covering some few acres, when Harry's exact position was masked by a large number of protective charms. It is possible that Snape used Legilimency to see through Harry's eyes, then quartered the Forest with his Patronus until Harry saw it.

Legilimens

Type: Spell
Features: Initiates Legilimency
First Appearance: *Harry Potter and the Order of the Phoenix*

OVERVIEW

The Legilimens spell initiates Legilimency, the process of reading thoughts and feelings from a subject.

Extended Description Harry first encounters this spell when learning Occlumency from Professor Snape. Legilimency is the process of reading thoughts and feelings from a subject. A wizard or witch may use Legilimency to tell if someone is lying to them. Lord Voldemort is especially skilled at detecting lies using Legilimency. This may be countered by a wizard or witch if he or she is a skilled Occlumens, that is, skilled in Occlumency. Professor Snape appears to be proficient at legilimency and is definitely an accomplished Occlumens, even able to lie to Lord Voldemort.

Leprechaun

Type: Creature
Features:
First Appearance: *Harry Potter and the Goblet of Fire*

Lethifold

Type: Creature
Features: cloak-ish look
First Appearance: *Fantastic Beasts and Where to Find Them*

OVERVIEW

The Lethifold is one of the most dangerous (and weird) magical beasts in the wizarding world. It hunts at night, giving it an advantage over the (sleeping) creatures which it preys upon.

Extended Description In appearance, a Lethifold is quite similar to a motile cloak, which travels by rippling itself across the surfaces it is lying on. It apparently has limited ability to fly by flapping itself through the air. Its chosen attack technique is to surround and smother its prey. The only spell known to stop a Lethifold is the Patronus charm; this was discovered by Flavius Belby, possibly some relation to Marcus Belby. As quoted in *Fantastic Beasts and Where to Find Them* by "Newt Scamander," Belby writes:

> Near one o'clock in the morning, as I began at last to feel drowsy, I heard a soft rustling close by. Believing it to be nothing more than the leaves of the tree outside, I turned over in bed, with my back to the window, and caught sight of what appeared to be a shapeless black shadow sliding under my bedroom door. I lay motionless, trying sleepily to divine what was causing such a shadow in a room lit only by moonlight. Undoubtedly my stillness led the lethifold to believe that its potential victim was sleeping. To my horror, the shadow began to creep up the bed, and I felt its slight weight upon me. It resembled nothing so much as black cape, the edges fluttering slightly as it slithered up the bed towards me. Paralyzed with fear, I felt its clammy touch upon my chin before I sat up bolt upright. The thing attempted to smother me, sliding inexorably up my face, over my mouth and nostrils, but still I struggled, feeling it wrapping its coldness about me all the while.
>
> Unable to cry out for assistance, I groped for my wand. Now dizzy as the thing sealed about my face, incapable of drawing breath, I concentrated with all my might upon the Stupefying Charm and then—as that failed to subdue the creature, though blasting a hole in my bedroom door—upon the Impediment Hex, with likewise availed me naught. Still Struggling madly, I rolled sideways and fell heavily to the floor entirely wrapped in the lethifold.
>
> I knew I was about to lose consciousness completely as I suffocated. Desperately, I mustered up

my last reserve of energy. Pointing my wand away from myself into the deadly folds of the creature, summoning the memory of the day I had been voted president of the local gobstones club, I performed the Patronus Charm. Almost at once I felt fresh air upon my face. I looked up to see that deathly shadow being borne into the air upon the horns of my Patronus. It flew across the room and swiftly out of sight.

ANALYSIS

The name of this creature appears to be based on "lethe" (sleep) and the idea of enfolding; thus something which enfolds the sleeper.

If should be noted that in *Harry Potter and the Order of the Phoenix*, it was noted that an old robe had tried to strangle Ron while he was helping clean up Headquarters. There has been speculation on several fan sites that the "cloak" may have in fact been a Lethifold. There is nothing in the book that would confirm this belief, the attacking object is never described as anything except a cloak.

The fact that the creature is vulnerable to a Patronus charm, perhaps along with its technique of suffocating its victims, leads us to believe there might be some relationship to the Dementor; perhaps, in time long past, Dementors were created out of Lethifolds.

Levicorpus

Type: Spell
Features: Levitates a person
First Appearance: *Harry Potter and the Half-Blood Prince*

OVERVIEW

Levicorpus levitates a victim in the air by their feet.

Extended Description This spell is one of the spells that Harry Potter learned from the Half-Blood Prince's *Advanced Potion-Making* textbook.

Harry first sees his father, James Potter, use this spell on Severus Snape in one of Snape's memories. Harry later attempts this spell on Ron not knowing what it would do.

Liberacorpus

Type: Spell (Charm)
Features: Release a person
First Appearance: *Harry Potter and the Half-Blood Prince*

OVERVIEW

Liberacorpus is the countercharm to Levicorpus.

Extended Description This spell was invented by the Half-Blood Prince and recorded in the his copy of the *Advanced Potion-Making* textbook. Harry uses it after casting Levicorpus on a sleeping Ron Weasley, to release him.

Lobalug

Type: Magical Creature
Features:
First Appearance: *Fantastic Beasts and Where to Find Them*

Locomotor

Type: Spell
Features: Propulsion of objects First Appearance

OVERVIEW

Used in the form "Locomotor object," e.g. "Locomotor trunk," this causes the named object to lift up and move as though the wizard casting the spell were carrying it.

Extended Description This spell is used numerous times in the books; it is used whenever a wizard needs to carry a large load at about a walking pace. When the spell is cast on an object (usually a trunk), the object lifts, and follows the spell-caster.

ANALYSIS

The Locomotor spell seems to be speed limited: in *Harry Potter and the Order of the Phoenix*, Tonks uses this spell to bring Harry's trunk downstairs to where the rest of the Advance Guard are waiting; but it is then strapped to a broom for the high-speed journey to London, which probably means that the Locomotor spell is not strong enough to keep the trunk with Tonks at speed. It is apparently capable of lifting things up stairs, as Professor Flitwick uses this spell to help him carry Sybill Trelawney's trunks back up to her tower room, after Professor Umbridge sacks her in *Harry Potter and the Order of the Phoenix*.

Locomotor Mortis

Type: Spell (Jinx)
Features: Impedes movement
First Appearance: *Harry Potter and the Philosopher's Stone*

OVERVIEW

Locomotor Mortis is the "leg-locker" curse. Similar in effect to the body bind, this spell causes only the legs to be bound together.

Extended Description We see this spell used only a very few times. Draco Malfoy uses it on Neville in *Harry Potter and the Philosopher's Stone*, though that is done off-stage and we only hear about it from Neville after he manages to hop into the Gryffindor Common Room.

ANALYSIS

This spell is of limited utility as it leaves the target's wand arm free, so that he can either free himself or retaliate. It is likely to be useful only on a disarmed opponent or one without developed magical abilities. As such, it is probably a classic first-year sort of jinx, one that impedes the opponent but does not harm him particularly.

Love Potion

Type: Potion
Features: Makes the drinker "fall in love."
First Appearance: *Harry Potter and the Goblet of Fire*

OVERVIEW

A Love Potion is a potion that makes the drinker "fall in love."

Extended Description In *Harry Potter and the Half-Blood Prince*, Professor Slughorn states that you cannot truly create *actual* love, the only thing the potion brings is obsession or infatuation. Apparently, love potions are fairly common; Fred and George, for instance, are apparently doing a pretty brisk business selling them to the girls at Hogwarts.

ANALYSIS

Love potions do not figure particularly prominently in the story until *Harry Potter and the Half-Blood Prince*. Up until Harry's fourth year, Harry and his classmates are too young to be overly concerned about such things. Rita Skeeter, in writing about Hermione in *Witch Weekly* during Harry's fourth year, quotes Pansy Parkinson as suggesting that Hermione may be using love potion to keep both Harry and Viktor Krum on a string. The conflict between the Champions in the fourth book, and the Ministry campaign against Harry in his fifth year, make him not a particularly desirable "catch." By the beginning of Harry's sixth year, though, with the Ministry electing to blow up his significance and make him "The Chosen One," several girls, most noticeably Romilda Vane, are scheming and conniving to get hooked up with him; and love potions end up being a big part of that. In the days preceding Professor Slughorn's Christmas party, Hermione hears several girls scheming about ways to slip Harry a love potion, and warns him. As a result of this, he turns down an offer from Romilda Vane to share a Gillywater with him, but does accept a box of chocolate cauldrons with Firewhisky centres, which he carefully sets aside, expecting that they are spiked. Ron discovers them on his birthday, some months later, and assumes that they are a birthday present for him; he, of course, promptly becomes infatuated with Romilda, completely forgetting about his current entanglement with Lavender. Professor Slughorn is able to cure him of this infatuation in short order.

One other use of Love Potion mentioned in this same book is the use of it on Tom Riddle Sr. by Voldemort's mother. After using the potion for a while, she incorrectly believes that Riddle Sr. is truly in love with her, and discontinues the potion; he, feeling betrayed, abandons the now-pregnant Merope and returns to his family home.

Lumos

Type: Spell
Features: Casts light
First Appearance: *Harry Potter and the Chamber of Secrets*

OVERVIEW

The Lumos spell creates light at the end of the caster's wand, and is therefore used for illuminating dark areas.

Extended Description A relatively basic spell, Harry is able to use this by the end of his second year—in *Harry Potter and the Chamber of Secrets*, Harry uses it to illuminate his surroundings when visiting Aragog in the Forbidden Forest; but in his first year, *Harry Potter and the Philosopher's Stone,* he has to use a lantern, and Hermione must conjure a fire when she needs light in that book.

ANALYSIS

The spell must be controlled by the caster's intent as well as by the word and any gestures, as it appears that not only the amount of light but the type can be controlled by the caster without any apparent difference in the casting of the spell. The light cast by the wand is described variously as a glimmer or a light, and in some cases appears as a beam, as one would get from a flashlight (UK: torch).

It is unknown how long the end of the wand remains lit; on only one occasion do we see wands consciously extinguished, by means of the Nox spell, on all other occasions they seem to conveniently go out on their own when no longer needed.

Mackled Malaclaw

Type: Magical Creature
Features: looks like lobster, but is grey with green spots
First Appearance: *Fantastic Beasts and Where to Find Them*

Mandrake

Type: Plant
Features: Part of many antidotes and restorative potions
First Appearance: *Harry Potter and the Chamber of Secrets*

OVERVIEW

The Mandrake is an unremarkable-looking tufty sort of plant that is purple and green in color. When dug up, its root has the shape of a human being.

Extended Description Mandrake or Mandragora is a powerful restorative and is a vital component in restorative potions; as a result, it is necessary in *Harry Potter and the Chamber of Secrets,* where it is used to brew a potion that is used to restore those who have been attacked by the monster of the Chamber. The cry of the uprooted Mandrake will kill; Harry's class is repotting them on his first day back in year 2, but these are very young, almost infant mandrakes (their roots look like wrinkled and ugly babies), and their cry will only knock you out for a couple of hours.

ANALYSIS

In *Harry Potter and the Chamber of Secrets,* a potion based on mandrakes is used to restore those attacked by the Monster of the Chamber. As in many other places in the series, it becomes apparent that the preparation of potions takes time. In this case, before the victims can be restored, so that they can identify the monster, we must wait for the mandrakes to become mature; conveniently, they do so immediately after Harry has vanquished the monster. In this case, the delay in their maturing is used to force Harry and Ron to come up with the solution to the puzzle of the nature and location of monster and the Chamber, with only extremely limited help from Hermione. Mandrakes appear again in *Harry Potter and the Deathly Hallows,* where we see Neville and Professor Sprout carrying the potted plants up to the battlements during the preparations for the Battle at Hogwarts. Apparently, they will be cast down upon the attackers, and the cry of the exposed mandrake roots will incapacitate the attacking Death Eaters.

GREATER PICTURE

In *Harry Potter and the Chamber of Secrets,* the author devised humorous descriptions of the maturation steps of the mandrake plants. The phases of plant maturity were analogous to the development of human children. First the plants were described as becoming "moody and secretive" confirming they had reached adolescence. Next the mandrakes started throwing loud parties indicating their teenage phase. Finally the mandrakes were known to be fully matured when they started moving into each others' pots.

Manticore

Type: Magical creature
Features: Head of man, body of lion, tail of scorpion
First Appearance: *Fantastic Beasts and Where to Find Them*

OVERVIEW

The Manticore is one of the Wizarding World's most dangerous creatures. It is a sentient beast, capable of intelligent speech, but has not been classified as a being due to its violent tendencies.

Extended Description A manticore has a human-like head, a lion's body, and a scorpion's tail with a ball at the end covered in venomous darts. When the Manticore flings its tail the darts detach. Manticore venom is instantly fatal. It uses this as a way to kill its prey, which it then devours while crooning softly. A Manticore's skin repels all known charms. While Harry, Ron, and Hermione are researching legal precedents for Buckbeak's defence in *Harry Potter and the Prisoner of Azkaban,* they find a case where a manticore savaged someone in 1296, and was let off . . . but quickly find that it was because nobody dared to approach it.

Marauder's Map

Type: magical artifact
Features: map of Hogwarts and its grounds including secret passages
First Appearance: *Harry Potter and the Prisoner of Azkaban*

OVERVIEW

The Marauder's Map is a map that shows Hogwarts and its grounds. It is one of a kind.

Extended Description The Marauder's Map is a magical parchment showing Hogwarts castle and grounds in its entirety, including seven secret passages into the castle. These passages are unknown to most, though Filch apparently knows four. The map also shows every person's location within the castle's premises, identified by their names in minuscule writing. When the map is inactive, it appears to be large blank parchment. It is activated by placing a wand tip on it and saying, "I solemnly swear that I am up to no good." To restore its blanked appearance, a wand taps it again as the holder says, "Mischief managed," causing the map to go blank.

When the map is activated, the parchment will reveal a writing:

> Messrs. Moony, Wormtail, Padfoot and Prongs
> Purveyors of Aids to Magical Mischief-Makers
> are proud to present
> the Marauder's Map

The map was created by the Marauders: Remus Lupin (Moony), Peter Pettigrew (Wormtail), Sirius Black (Padfoot) and James Potter (Prongs) during their years at Hogwarts, and was confiscated by Filch because he believed it to be a dark object, though he apparently never discovered its secret. The Weasley twins stole it from his files, and it became useful in their own mischief-making; they, in turn, passed it on to Harry when it appeared that he would otherwise be unable to visit Hogsmeade. Harry has used it extensively since.

ANALYSIS

Magic can, if handled incautiously in a story, render the plot pointless by making anything possible. If a character or an artifact is capable of doing anything, the story devolves into a simple chase of the character or artifact. Rowling makes the series exciting and dynamic in part by limiting people's abilities—not all wizards are equally magical, and even the most powerful have their blind spots—and by limiting artifacts' availability or capabilities. The Marauder's Map is just such an artifact. It shows people's exact positions in real time everywhere in a nine-story (or more) castle, even identifying by name individuals who have never been there before. The map sees them by their psyche, thus making it proof against Invisibility Cloaks and Animagi. And when not in use, it looks like a simple blank parchment. It is necessary to show it has limitations (it is unable to reveal the Room of Requirement, for instance), and it is necessary in several situations to have it be unavailable to Harry, because it has been either borrowed or confiscated.

One question that comes up is whether Professor Snape knows what the map is. He finds it in Harry's pocket in *Harry Potter and the Prisoner of Azkaban*, at which time it identifies its creators and insults Snape. Snape may know who Moony, Wormtail, Padfoot, and Prongs are or were, which is likely why he summons Professor Lupin to inspect it and makes such pointed comments about the map's manufacturers; Lupin is the only Marauder he can talk to immediately. Snape immediately recognizes the Marauder's Map in *Harry Potter and the Goblet of Fire* as being Harry's property. That, plus the Egg, causes Snape to be certain that Harry is hiding nearby under his Invisibility Cloak. Snape, by this time, knows the map's function, as he has seen it working on Lupin's desk. Another question is how Harry gets the Map back; the fake Professor Moody borrows it, and, when he is transformed back as Barty Crouch, confesses that he used it, in *Harry Potter and the Goblet of Fire*. Though Professor Dumbledore expresses interest in it, we do not see it at that time, nor is Harry seen getting it back. However, he does put it to good use in later books. The author, in an interview, has stated that this was an oversight, and in the book's next edition, Harry collects it from Moody's desk while Barty is incapacitated.

QUESTIONS

1. How did the Weasley twins happen upon the particular spell that activates the Map? ("I solemnly swear I am up to no good.")
2. What was there about the Map that would convince Filch that it was Dark magic? It is often described as just looking like a bit of parchment.

Mermish

Type: Language
Features: Used by Merpeople
First Appearance: *Harry Potter and the Goblet of Fire*

OVERVIEW

Mermish is the language used by Merpeople.

Extended Description Heard in air, Mermish is thin and screechy, because Merpeople's vocal equipment is geared to the more viscous aquatic environment. In the thin stuff that is our air, the vibrating bits move far too fast, making the tone of their voices hurtful to human ears.

After the Second Task of the Triwizard Tournament, Professor Dumbledore speaks with the mer-Chieftainess to determine what had happened under the lake. It is mentioned at that time that Dumbledore knows possibly a thousand languages, including mermish.

Merpeople

Type: Creature
Features: Aquatic people
First Appearance: *Harry Potter and the Goblet of Fire*

OVERVIEW

The Merpeople are a race of aquatic people, at least one group of whom live in the lake on the grounds of Hogwarts.

Extended Description Merpeople do not much resemble the Muggle idea of mermaids and mermen. They are very thin, with very long arms and a fish's tail; some are armed with spears. They have high-pitched voices, and seem to be able to speak, or at least parrot, some English words; however, among themselves they generally speak their own language, Mermish. Above water their singing or speech sounds like a screech, yet underwater it is eerie and hypnotic. In *Harry Potter and the Goblet of Fire*, to solve the puzzle of the second challenge, Harry makes use of the Prefect's bathroom. There is a painting of a mermaid on the wall there; however, as Harry discovers when the Challenge actually happens, the painting is very different from the reality. The clue is actually a merpeople song, that has to be listened to under water to be understood.

The second Challenge actually is to rescue four people, one for each Champion, from under the lake. They are guarded by Merpeople, and the way the Challenge is worded, it would appear that they had kidnapped the people; in fact, however, the four "detainees" (for want of a better word) were Stunned by Professor McGonagall and handed over to the merpeople.

Before points are awarded for completion of the challenge, Professor Dumbledore consults with the mer-chieftainess to determine what actually happened; the fact that Harry had waited and then rescued detainees other than the one that was his main concern, as confirmed by the mer-chieftainess, counted in his favour in the competition.

In *Harry Potter and the Half-Blood Prince*, the Merpeople come near the surface of the lake and sing a haunting song at Dumbledore's funeral.

Metamorphmagus

Type: Magical ability
Features: The ability to change appearance at will
First Appearance: *Harry Potter and the Order of the Phoenix*

OVERVIEW

A Metamorphmagus is a witch or wizard who has the ability to change their appearance at will, without the need for a wand, spell, or potion.

Extended Description   Metamorphmagy is a very rare ability, and one that the witch or wizard must be born with. There is no way to train to become a Metamorphmagus.

Nymphadora Tonks, who we first meet in *Harry Potter and the Order of the Phoenix*, is a Metamorphmagus. She tells Harry that the ability helped her greatly in the Concealment and Disguise in her Auror training. Throughout the fifth book, she changes her hair color and style very frequently, although her favorite hair style is short, spiky, and bright pink. She also changes the shape of her nose between bites at dinner, to entertain her fellow diners.

ANALYSIS

Throughout much of *Harry Potter and the Half-Blood Prince*, we see that Tonks is not using her Metamorphmagus ability at all. Harry believes that she is mourning someone, and her sorrow is either preventing her from changing her appearance, or else is simply leaving her uninspired to do so. We never find out if the actual ability to change her appearance has been lost. We do find out that the loss is temporary, however.

QUESTIONS

1. Sirius Black is related to Tonks—they are cousins. Could he also have some Metamorphmagus ability? Could that have helped him when he went through the spells necessary for him to become an Animagus?

Mimbulus Mimbletonia

Type: Plant
Features: Vaguely cactus-like
First Appearance: *Harry Potter and the Order of the Phoenix*

OVERVIEW

Mimbulus Mimbletonia is a spineless, cactus-like plant. Our introduction to this plant occurs when Neville displays it on the Hogwarts Express in Harry's fifth year. Demonstrating its special features, Neville deliberately triggers its defence mechanism, completely covering Harry, Ginny, Luna, and himself in stinksap, mere moments before Cho Chang looks in to say "hello" to Harry.

ANALYSIS

We are told that this plant is quite rare and valuable, and can gather from this that it is very hard to care for. At the end of the book, as we return to the Hogwarts Express for the return home, we see that it has thrived and grown while at the school. We will learn, at the beginning of *Harry Potter and the Half-Blood Prince*, that Neville did quite well on his Herbology O.W.L., gaining an Outstanding grade; the fact that this plant has done so well reinforces the feeling we have that Neville, for all his shortcomings and self-doubts, is quite skilled at taking care of magical plants.

Mirror of Erised

Type: Magical device
Features: mirror
First Appearance: *Harry Potter and the Philosopher's Stone*

OVERVIEW

The Mirror of Erised is a mirror that shows the user his or her heart's deepest desire. There is "an inscription carved around the top":
Erised stra ehru oyt ube cafru oyt on wohsi

Extended Description   Harry stumbles upon this mirror when, attempting to evade capture by Filch and Snape after starting a book screaming in the Restricted section of the library, Harry retreats through an open door. In the Mirror, he sees himself and his father and mother, standing behind him, and all his extended family behind them. Harry then brings Ron to the mirror to show Ron his family; Ron, instead, sees himself as Head Boy holding the Quidditch cup. Harry revisits the Mirror several times during Christmas vacation, until he is surprised there one night by Professor Dumbledore. Dumbledore tells Harry that the mirror is very dangerous, that people have starved to death sitting in front of it, but that he is glad Harry found it and so now somewhat understands its power. Dumbledore goes on to say that he will now move the mirror to a new hiding place, and asks Harry to not go looking for it. Harry impulsively asks Dumbledore what he sees in the mirror, and Dumbledore replies that he sees himself holding a pair of warm, woolly socks. He goes on to explain that he always seems to be given books as gifts, and never has enough socks. Later, Harry thinks to himself that this had been an awfully intrusive question.

In the final chamber under the trap door, Harry finds the mirror once again. This time, Harry, forced to look into it, sees himself with the Philosopher's Stone in his pocket. As he sees this, the stone itself appears in his pocket. Later, recovering in the Hospital Wing, he speaks with Professor Dumbledore concerning the mirror. Dumbledore says that he was rather proud of the enchantment that placed the Stone within the mirror. The only person who could retrieve the Stone would be one who dearly wanted the Stone but did not want to use it.

In the final book in the series, *Harry Potter and the Deathly Hallows*, Harry thinks back to the Mirror of Erised, and wonders again about his question to Dumbledore: was Dumbledore entirely truthful when he told Harry what he saw in the Mirror? Could it be that Dumbledore, like Harry, saw his family standing behind him?

Analysis

The inscription over the mirror, when reversed, reads:

ishow no tyo urfac ebu tyo urhe arts desire

Which, by changing the spacing and punctuation, reveals:

I show, not your face, but your heart's desire

Thus, the inscription does describe exactly what it does, and many readers, seeing what is clearly reversed text, have deciphered the text quickly. Why Harry does not do so is uncertain, as he is clearly aware of it. It is possible that Harry has been exposed to so much in the way of apparently nonsensical text, with the spell incantations and other writings being often almost nonsense words, that he no longer automatically tries to decipher writings that he does not immediately understand.

One must wonder somewhat about the nature of the enchantment protecting the Stone. Professor Quirrell says that he sees himself holding the Stone and presenting it to his Master; by the letter of the enchantment, the Mirror should have surrendered the Stone to him as he was not planning to use it himself, only to give it to Voldemort. Two possibilities appear to account for its failure to release the Stone. One is that, as Voldemort was at that point riding the back of Quirrell's head, and was in some manner sharing life force with Quirrell, the Mirror might not have been able to distinguish Quirrell from Voldemort, and Voldemort certainly wanted to use the Stone. Alternately, and more likely given the individuals involved, Quirrell could have simply been lying about not having any desire to use the Stone himself, and thus lying about what he saw in the Mirror.

There is a very large question that remains unanswered concerning this mirror. Clearly it has some ability to read minds, it must in order to know what one's "heart's desire" is. But Harry has no conscious memory of what his parents look like. Yet, the Mirror is able to show them to him. We know that the Mirror's depiction is accurate because, in later books, and later in this book, Harry will find artifacts that show his parents and will not discover that the Mirror got it wrong. How can the Mirror know something that Harry himself does not? Similarly, neither Harry nor Quirrell has seen the Stone. How can the Mirror show it to them, if they don't know what it looks like? In this latter case, the Mirror could present the mental image each had of the Stone; it is enough to show something that the individual recognizes as "the Philosopher's Stone," even if it does not match the reality of what the Stone looks like.

Questions

1. What does Harry's vision in the Mirror of Erised say about his character?
2. What do you think other characters would see in the Mirror of Erised?
3. What parallels can we draw between the Mirror of Erised and the effects of Boggarts?

Greater Picture

Given that the mirror can read minds to some limited extent, there are two possible explanations for the mirror being able to show Harry his parents. The first, obviously, is that the mirror may be able to see more of Harry's memories than Harry can himself; we do retain memories from infancy, though we often cannot access them, and the Mirror, being magical, may be able to reach those memories that Harry cannot. Additionally, it is possible that the mirror could have seen what Harry's parents look like through his scar, which we find out in the final book is an indicator of the soul shard of Voldemort's that remains in Harry. In *Harry Potter and the Deathly Hallows*, we find out that Voldemort recalls both Harry's parents and their appearance, and so presumably that information is available through the linkage between their souls.

One interesting fact from the author's web site: The author herself was offered the role of Harry's mother in the Mirror Erised scene of the first Harry Potter film, and turned it down.[1] The reason she gives for her refusal seems somewhat contrived, making it probable that there are other reasons, perhaps some that she did not want to go into at that point in the series. One strong possibility is that even at this early point in the writing of the series, the author was aware that Harry's mother was going to have a larger role in the series than could be expected, given that she had died before the first book. Lily Potter would not, as one would suppose from the first book, be restricted to roles in which she simply smiled and waved, in the Mirror and in Wizard photographs. More than that, she would have a speaking role in *Harry Potter and the Goblet of Fire*, in the duel in the Cemetery, and would appear twice in *Harry Potter and the Deathly Hallows*, once in Voldemort's memories and once when summoned by the Resurrection Stone. It is entirely possible that, knowing her own limitation as an actress, the author believed the role in the context of the entire series would be beyond her capabilities, and elected to stay with what she could do well.

Mobiliarbus

Type: Spell (Charm)
Features: Causes movement of a tree
First Appearance: *Harry Potter and the Prisoner of Azkaban*

Overview

Mobiliarbus, a rather specialized charm, is used to move a tree.

Extended Description Hermione uses this spell to move a Christmas tree in The Three Broomsticks, to better hide Harry from a number of teachers who have just walked in.

---

1. http://www.jkrowling.com/textonly/en/rumours_view.cfm?id=11

Mobilicorpus

Type: Spell
Features: Moves an unconscious body
First Appearance: *Harry Potter and the Prisoner of Azkaban*

Overview

Mobilicorpus is a spell that allows an unconscious (or perhaps dead) body to be moved.

Extended Description The Mobilicorpus spell is used in *Harry Potter and the Prisoner of Azkaban* to bring the unconscious body of Snape along the tunnel from the Shrieking Shack to the Whomping Willow.

Analysis

Professor Lupin used this spell rather than waking Snape because it was simpler, perhaps, than having to deal with him bound up. This spell seems to be related to the Locomotor spell, which is used for inanimate objects, and the Levicorpus spell which appears to lift a conscious body up by the ankles.

Moke

Type: Magical Creature
Features:
First Appearance: *Harry Potter and the Deathly Hallows*

Extended Description In *Harry Potter and the Deathly Hallows*, Hagrid gives Harry a Mokeskin bag for his birthday. Harry wears it around his neck for the rest of the book, keeping his most valued possessions in it.

Money

Type: Object
Features: Coins
First Appearance: *Harry Potter and the Philosopher's Stone*

Overview

Wizarding money comes in three denominations: bronze Knuts, silver Sickles, and golden Galleons. 29 Knuts make up one Sickle, and there are 17 Sickles in a Galleon.

Extended Description Wizarding money comes in coins only, there are no Galleon bills; as such, wizards have money pouches that they typically hang off their belts, under their robes, rather than wallets.

Analysis

There are a number of different calculations about the value of the individual pieces of Wizard currency. The author has stated that a Galleon is worth about £3, and also that it is worth about £5, in two separate books, and again that it is worth about £5 in an interview; and internal evidence in the fourth and later books seems to match this. However, internal evidence in the first three books could suggest a value closer to £50 to £200 for the value of a Galleon. In *Harry Potter and the Philosopher's Stone*, Hagrid instructs Harry to pay the owl 5 knuts for his copy of the *Daily Prophet*. In *Harry Potter and the Order of the Phoenix*, Hermione pays an owl 1 Knut for the *Prophet*. If the price of the *Prophet* is in line with Muggle newspapers, that means that 1 Knut should be about US $0.20 to US$1.00 (the price of a newspaper being about US$1.00 in 1991). This makes a Sickle worth somewhere between $6.00 and $30.00, and gives a Galleon a value of between $100 (£50) and $500 (£200). It is also mentioned, in *Harry Potter and the Philosopher's Stone* that Harry paid seven Galleons for his wand; and that Ron was using his brother's old wand, with the implication that they could not afford a new one. An expenditure of £35 (at £5 to the Galleon) is relatively small, but in retrospect does serve to indicate Ron's family's grinding poverty, which we also see in later books. Some have said that it would make more sense to have a wand, which is after all usually a once-in-a-lifetime purchase, be valued at £350 to £1400, and this would make it more likely that Ron's family could ill-afford to buy a new wand for Ron, instead giving him "Charlie's old wand"; however, this is not necessary to the story, and makes the Weasleys' lack of funds all the more striking. In *Harry Potter and the Goblet of Fire*, Fred and George are selling Canary Cream tricks for 7 Sickles each. Based on the above calculation, that would make the price of these $42 to $210 each. This is rather an excessive amount for a 15-second prank; if a Galleon is worth £5, though, then 7 Sickles would be about £2 ($5), a reasonable value for that joke. In *Harry Potter and the Order of the Phoenix*, the price of a Butterbeer in the Hog's Head is given as two Sickles, which would be $12 to $60 a bottle by the pricing scheme in the first three books; at £5 to the Galleon, though, 2 Sickles would be about £0.60 ($1.20), a reasonable price.

It is possible that the author simply had not worked out the conversion from Wizarding to Muggle money until time came to write the forewords of *Quidditch Through the Ages* and *Magical Beasts and Where to Find Them*, which came out after the first three books were written. It is also possible that the author, in writing those forewords, confused the values of the Sickle and the Galleon, as the apparent value of the Sickle in the first three books does tally with the stated value of the Galleon. It's certainly true that Wizarding prices in the fourth and later books of the series match the values given in those two books and the interview, with the exception of the price for *The Daily Prophet*. One wonders if, having arbitrarily set the price of the Prophet as 5 Knuts in the first book, the author was at all concerned that this gave it a street value of £0.05 ($0.10). On the other hand, the use of magic will significantly distort the economy from what we Muggles expect, because chattels can be created and changed to other chattels effectively at no economic cost; so it is entirely possible that the Prophet can still turn a profit at a cost of 5 Knuts (or even 1 Knut) an issue.

QUESTIONS

1. What role does money have in the books, with particular reference to the Weasleys and the Malfoys?

2. Are the Weasleys happier than Harry despite having less money?

3. How does Harry view the money left to him by his parents in view of the years he has spent at the Dursleys?

GREATER PICTURE

The economics of the Harry Potter universe are simpler than the Muggle world and are also only vaguely defined. It is mostly a public sector economy with the Ministry of Magic the largest employer and supplier of services. However the taxation to finance the Ministry is never mentioned.

Currency is based on precious metal coins minted by goblins requiring no fiduciary reserve. Gringotts Bank provides only two services, the vault storage of valuables (mostly gold) and the exchange of Muggle money into wizard money. There is no interest on deposits, and no loans in the Muggle sense.

Although there is a wide variety of consumer goods available in Diagon Alley and Hogsmeade, there appear to be no factories or other large scale manufacturing capital in the Wizarding World. Products and goods are manufactured by individual artisans and small firms in a pre-industrial business model. With the use of magic the productivity of these artisans is sufficient to satisfy the demand of the Wizarding community. For example, Mr. Ollivander appears to work alone crafting fine wands. However he is able to provide wands for most of the wizards in Britain.

Transportation and communication are regulated by the Ministry and in some cases owned and operated by the Ministry (such as the Floo Network, Hogwarts Express and Knight Bus). However, most transportation and communication are accomplished by individuals without a public infrastructure. Examples include apparation, owl post and brooms.

Wealth and poverty are both plot themes in the Harry Potter universe, but how rich families (such as the Malfoys) became wealthy is not known. Most characters must work for a living (just like the Muggle world). Wages and salaries vary widely and many characters are concerned about their finances. Underpaid workers, such as Mr. Weasley, struggle to support their families. Unemployable characters (such as Lupin) live marginal existences in poverty.

Education at Hogwarts seems to be financed by the Ministry, there is no mention made of tuition costs. However students are responsible for the purchase of uniforms, books and class supplies. Poorer families (such as the Weasleys) must buy second-hand to afford the expense. There is, we are told, some form of bursary available to the very poorest to enable them to attend Hogwarts; funds were made available to Tom Riddle, for instance. This appears to be done an a very informal basis, however, like much else in the Wizarding universe.

Mooncalf

Type: Magical Creature
Features:
First Appearance: *Fantastic Beasts and Where to Find Them*

Morsmordre

Type: Spell
Features: Projects the Dark Mark into the air
First Appearance: *Harry Potter and the Goblet of Fire*

OVERVIEW

Morsmordre is a spell that conjures the Dark Mark.

Extended Description The Dark Mark symbolizes very black magic. When cast, this spell produces a large, luminous green skull that hangs in the air. This is Lord Voldemort's sign, which the Death Eaters used to send up after they killed somebody.

ANALYSIS

The Dark Mark is actually the name of the sigil: a skull with a snake twisting through it. Death Eaters are tattooed with this mark on their left forearm. Morsmordre is a spell that produces a form of the Dark Mark, made of glowing green particles, that hovers in the air.

Morsmordre is a spell known only to Death Eaters, and the appearance of the Dark Mark in the air over the Quidditch World Cup is a clear indication that there is at least one Death Eater still at large and still willing to be identified as such. This causes immediate panic on the part of the crowd, who all remember times when that mark was left floating above a house that had been destroyed.

After Voldemort's return, we would expect to see it more often; however, it does not reappear in *Harry Potter and the Order of the Phoenix*. During this time, Voldemort is secretly rebuilding his power, aided by the Ministry policy of denying his return. Having the Dark Mark appear would, of course, decrease the chance of remaining undetected—though it is likely the Ministry would simply try to spin things to avoid saying Voldemort had returned. The Dark Mark reappears several times in *Harry Potter and the Half-Blood Prince*, where, as before, it is used to mark areas where Death Eaters have been working their evil. It is specifically noted as floating over the hut where Igor Karkaroff was found murdered, and over Hogwarts during the invasion by the Death Eaters. Morsmordre is actually (intentionally or not) Norwegian. Directly translated it means "*motherkillers*." This symbolizes the kinds of persons the Death Eaters are, they could kill their own mothers for the sake of Voldemort and purity of the race.

In addition to the Norwegian derivation, a Latin etymology is possible: mors, meaning death, and mordre, from the vulgar Latin mordere, "to bite." This presumably refers either to the snake present in the image, or was more euphonic than the verb "to eat"; mors mordre—a Latin approximation of Death Eater.

Mudblood

Type: Status
Features: Offensive term for a half blood or muggle-born wizard/witch
First Appearance: *Harry Potter and the Chamber of Secrets*

Overview

Offensive term for Muggle-born or Half-blood witches or wizards. For example, Hermione Granger and Harry's mother, Lily Evans.

Analysis

Draco Malfoy frequently uses "mudblood" to describe Hermione Granger. Harry and Ron consider this to be the Dark side of Malfoy and it suggests to them that he is part of the Death Eaters, or at least a Voldemort follower.

Muffliato

Type: Spell
Features: Protects private discussions
First Appearance: *Harry Potter and the Half-Blood Prince*

Overview

Muflliato is a spell that "fills the ears with an unidentifiable buzzing sound."

Analysis

Muffliato was one of the spells Harry found in the Half Blood Prince's copy of the *Advanced Potion Making* textbook.

Muggle

Type: Status
Features: No distinctive features
First Appearance: *Harry Potter and the Philosopher's Stone*

Overview

A Muggle is a non-magical human. Most Muggles don't know about magic or any of the wizarding world.

Extended Description For most wizards, Muggles are regarded with fondness. Poor, non-magical people, how ever do they survive without magic? Some wizards are bemused or intrigued by the techniques and gadgets that Muggles use to get around their lack of magic. For a few, though, particularly those gathered around Lord Voldemort, Muggles are inferior, and they and anyone descended from them should be exterminated.

Analysis

The Dark belief in the inferiority of Muggles conveniently disregards the facts that many of the strongest wizards alive, including Harry Potter and even Voldemort himself, are children of Wizard / Muggle marriages, and that the top grades in Harry's year, for all the first six years of Harry's high school career, have been won by Hermione Granger, the daughter of two Muggles; it also ignores the fact that scions of older wizarding families like the Longbottoms sometimes are not terribly powerful wizards.

Despite their fondness for them, many wizards do feel that the Muggles are somehow diminished by their lack of magic; in fact, Professor McGonagall remarks, in the first chapter of the first book, that the Dursleys "are the greatest load of Muggles you'll ever come across." Many Muggles who are aware of the Wizarding world, such as the Dursleys, chose to ignore the magical community, denying the evidence even if it is plainly clear that there is magic happening all around them. In the context of Professor McGonagall's remark, the comment does not directly refer to the Dursleys' denial of magic, as that has not yet been observed by Professor McGonagall. One must wonder whether McGonagall meant "the worst sort of Muggle," or "the worst sort who happen to also be Muggles."

Greater Picture

We will learn that the belief of Wizard superiority to Muggles is very widespread; even Albus Dumbledore, as a youth, envisioned a world in which Muggles accepted the benevolent rule of wizards.

Muggleborn

Type: Status
Features: Born of two non-wizarding parents but has magical ability
First Appearance: *Harry Potter and the Chamber of Secrets*

Overview

A muggle-born is a witch or wizard of non-magical parentage.

Extended Description Famous examples are Lily Evans and Hermione Granger.

In *Harry Potter and the Chamber of Secrets* we are introduced to another name for those witches and wizards born of Muggle parentage—Mudbloods. This is an insult used only by purebloods who feel that Half-blood and Muggle-born witches and wizards are somehow inferior to purebloods.

Analysis

Apparently it is not necessary to have magical ancestry to be able to do magic oneself; it seems that magical ability can spontaneously appear without known magical ancestry, and sometimes in only one child of a given union. Lily Evans' sister Petunia showed no sign of magical talent, though her son Dudley may have shown a hint of ability.

Through a process possibly akin to hybrid vigor, it seems that many of the most powerful wizards have some Muggle in their recent background.

Muggle Studies

Type: Subject
Features: Wizarding view of Muggle life
First Appearance: *Harry Potter and the Prisoner of Azkaban*

OVERVIEW

Muggle Studies, an optional course, is the Wizarding view of how Muggles live, and the techniques they use to circumvent their lack of magic.

Extended Description This course is apparently taught by Charity Burbage for the first six years that Harry is in school. The course, specifically designed to teach Wizards how to get along with Muggles. will be required for any Wizarding career which involves liaison with Muggles. including, almost certainly, Ministry jobs.

After Professor Burbage's disappearance, it is taught by a Death Eater, Alecto Carrow, under whose guidance the course seems to have become a diatribe against Muggles, in the best propaganda tradition, teaching how non-Magical people are dirty and behave like animals.

Hermione takes this course in her third year at Hogwarts. As Hermione is Muggle-born, it seems unlikely that she would need to learn about Muggles; but it seems her intent is to learn about how Wizards see and interact with Muggles, rather than to learn about Muggles as such. At the end of this year, despite achieving a mark of over three hundred percent for the course, she decides to drop the course so as to have a humanly possible course load.

Murtlap

Type: Creature
Features: Healing powers
First Appearance: *Harry Potter and the Order of the Phoenix*

OVERVIEW

Essence of Murtlap Tentacles is shown to be a powerfully healing and soothing solution.

Extended Description When Harry serves a detention with Professor Umbridge, he is required to write lines with a quill which creates a wound on the back of his hand. After a week and a half of this, he is in considerable pain. Hermione gives him a bowl of Essence of Murtlap Tentacles, which he finds extremely soothing.

When Lee Jordan falls afoul of Professor Umbridge and is similarly abused, Harry recommends Murtlap to him; Lee, then, evidently suggests the same cure to Fred and George when they are suffering self-inflicted boils in a rather private place.

It is in *Fantastic Beasts and Where to Find Them* by "Newt Scamander" that we learn that the Murtlap is a rat-like creature with a growth on its back that resembles a sea anemone.

Niffler

Type: Creature
Features: Small size, furry, gold-seeking
First Appearance: *Harry Potter and the Goblet of Fire*

OVERVIEW

A Niffler is a small creature about the size of a dog, with a long and pointed snout. They are very attracted to gold and glittering objects.

Extended Description Nifflers can be very destructive in their search for gold and glittering objects. When there is nothing that glitters available, they are quite cuddly and friendly. They are excellent diggers, and will dig through the ground very rapidly in search of gold and metals, which they will bring back to their masters.

ANALYSIS

The Niffler has so far played a fairly minor role in the series. In *Harry Potter and the Goblet of Fire*, Hagrid, as teacher of Care of Magical Creatures class, has the class care for a batch of Nifflers while he teaches what they can do; this is used as a mechanism to allow Ron to discover that the gold he had given to Harry in payment for the Omnioculars at the Quidditch World Cup had been vanishing leprechaun gold, and that Harry had not noticed its departure. The author has confirmed that this is used to contrast Harry's relative wealth and Ron's family's ongoing poverty.[1]

On two occasions, also, Nifflers were introduced into Professor Umbridge's office in *Harry Potter and the Order of the Phoenix*; on both occasions, her office was destroyed by the creature's incessant search for shiny objects, and both times Umbridge had blamed Hagrid, as he was at the time still the Care of Magical Creatures teacher, and as he apparently had reason to dislike her. In fact, the Nifflers had been levitated in through Umbridge's open office window by Lee Jordan. Umbridge was nevertheless able to use this belief as part of her justification for sacking Hagrid.

Nogtail

Type: Magical Creature
Features: very hard to describe
First Appearance: *Fantastic Beasts and Where to Find Them*

Nox

Type: Spell
Features: Turns off wand light
First Appearance: *Harry Potter and the Prisoner of Azkaban*

---

1. http://the-leaky-cauldron.org/2007/7/30/j-k-rowling-web-chat-transcript

Overview

Nox is the counter-spell to Lumos; it darkens a lit wand.

Extended Description The Nox spell is used by Harry and Hermione in *Harry Potter and the Prisoner of Azkaban* to extinguish their wands, previously illuminated by means of the Lumos charm, when they no longer needed their light.

Analysis

An extinguishing spell is, in retrospect, necessary; otherwise, you have the equally ludicrous cases of a wand that, once illuminated, never goes out, or of a wand that, once lit, goes out eventually of its own accord, likely at the worst possible moment. It is surprising, perhaps, that this is the only time we see the extinguishing charm used.

Nudu

Type: Magical Creature
Features: toxic breath
First Appearance: *Fantastic Beasts and Where to Find Them*

Obliviate

Type: Spell (Charm)
Features: Memory erasure or modification
First Appearance: *Harry Potter and the Chamber of Secrets*

Overview

Obliviate is the verbal component of the Memory Charm, a spell which allows the erasure or modification of memory.

Extended Description First seen when Gilderoy Lockhart attempted to use it on Harry and Ron, this spell, when done correctly, apparently allows a substantial amount of control over the subject's memories. We see it used a number of times through the series. The most prominent times are:

- as mentioned above, in *Harry Potter and the Chamber of Secrets*, when Gilderoy Lockhart attempts to cast it on Ron and Harry so as to allow him to claim to have defeated the Monster in the Chamber. In this case, he is using a broken wand, which backfires; as a result, afterwards he is barely able to remember his own name.
- in *Harry Potter and the Goblet of Fire*, when the Muggle keeper of the campground has his memory changed so that he forgets the odd magical things that he has seen the occupants of his campground doing.
- in *Harry Potter and the Order of the Phoenix*, where Kingsley Shacklebolt casts it on Marietta Edgecombe so that she forgets that there were previous meetings of Dumbledore's Army.
- in *Harry Potter and the Deathly Hallows*, Hermione casts this spell on a pair of Death Eaters and an innocent waitress so that they will not recall having seen Harry. She later uses it against Xenophilius Lovegood to make him forget the presence of Ron Weasley.

Like so many spells, a large part of the effect of this spell very likely depends on what the caster is thinking at the time the spell is cast. Presumably the caster must hold in their mind a representation of the memories needed to be changed, along with what the memories should be changed to.

Analysis

Apparently, this spell is most often used to clean up any 'spillage' in front of Muggles. The International Statute of Wizardry is specifically designed to try and keep the Muggles unaware of the Wizarding world, so this spell is apparently reasonably often used on Muggles to keep them unaware of what the wizards have been doing.

Occamy

Type: Magical Creature
Features:
First Appearance: *Fantastic Beasts and Where to Find Them*

Occlumency

Type: Method
Features: Provides blocking of mind-reading
First Appearance: *Harry Potter and the Order of the Phoenix*

Overview

Occlumency is the ability to block one's mind from a Legilimens.

Extended Description Occlumency is the counter to Legilimency, of which Voldemort is a master. Characters like Severus Snape use Occlumency to hide their intentions. Harry Potter is taught Occlumency lessons in *Harry Potter and the Order of the Phoenix*. Both Snape and Dumbledore are accomplished Occlumens.

Analysis

It is certain that Harry's ability to block his thoughts from Snape and Voldemort are not being helped by Snape's lessons. Harry's scar seems to prickle constantly after his lessons start, though that may be coincidence; it is at about the time that his Occlumency lessons start that Voldemort becomes aware that Harry can see into his mind on occasion, and it is shortly after that when Voldemort starts actively trying to get Harry into the Ministry. It is entirely possible that Harry's increased reaction may be due to increased probing from Voldemort. However, all through the lessons we see that Harry is unable to prevent Snape from viewing his memories, and at the end of *Harry Potter and the Half-Blood Prince*, we see that Snape is able to block any of Harry's spells before he can complete it, because of Snape's being able to read his intentions.

Greater Picture

There is some question as to whether Occlumency would even work for Harry against Voldemort. Occlumency is designed to prevent an outside mind from being able to read what is happening within your mind, but as we learn in *Harry Potter and the Deathly Hallows*, there is actually a fragment of Voldemort's soul within Harry. Does that bit of shared soul provide more access to Harry's mind than simple Legilimency? Harry never finds out, as he is never placed in a position again where he has to try and block Voldemort from his mind.

Omnioculars

Type: Magical device
Features: Distance vision
First Appearance: *Harry Potter and the Goblet of Fire*

Overview

Like Muggle binoculars, omnioculars are designed to allow the viewing of distant events, most especially sporting events.

Extended Description Being magical, Omnioculars have additional capabilities, such as instant replay, slow motion, and annotation. Watching the Quidditch World Cup, Harry puts his Omnioculars into slow-motion replay, and sees the action of the game in slow motion, complete with labels for the various maneuvers that the players are carrying out. Harry later comments that he never really understood the Wronsky feint, a technique used by Seekers, until he had seen it at the World Cup; quite possibly he had also used the Omnioculars to slow it down and analyze the moves. Omnioculars become one of the few points of tension between Harry and Ron. They are expensive, at 10 Galleons apiece, and Harry immediately buys a set for Ron as well as one for himself. Ron is dismayed at this excess of generosity, and is only mollified by Harry's telling him not to expect anything for Christmas for the next ten years or so. The Irish team mascots, Leprechauns, drop gold on the audience at the start of the game, and Ron collects a great lot of it, giving it all to Harry and saying that makes them even. Several months later, Hagrid is teaching a lesson on Nifflers, which hunt for shiny objects, including gold; he says that what he has buried is Leprechaun gold, and it will vanish in a few hours. Thinking about this after class, Ron wonders why Harry had not told him that the gold he had given Harry for the omnioculars had vanished. Harry says that he had not noticed. Dejected, Ron wonders what it would be like to be so rich that he wouldn't even notice when a great lot of gold simply vanished.

Analysis

Omnioculars are a rather amazingly useful device, with their ability to magnify and play back images. One rather wonders why they appear only at the Quidditch World Cup and then are forgotten.

Oppugno

Type: Spell (Jinx)
Features: Causes creatures to attack
First Appearance: *Harry Potter and the Half-Blood Prince*

Overview

Oppugno apparently causes creatures to hate the target of the spell. The result is that the creatures influenced by the spell will attack its subject.

Extended Description We only see this spell used once. Hermione, having seen Ron and Lavender locked in one of their embraces, has retreated to a disused classroom, where she has moodily created a flock of canaries which are circling her. Ron and Lavender, apparently seeking some privacy, also enter the classroom; Lavender quickly backs out, but Ron stays to exchange some words with Hermione. Hermione, angered, uses the spell to set the canaries on Ron as she is leaving.

There is mention later that Ron still bears the scars of the canary beaks and talons.

Analysis

It is uncertain whether this spell would work on any creature, or only on creatures that the caster has created. As we see this spell only the one time, we can only guess at its effects and applicability.

Orchideous

Type: Spell
Features: Creates flowers
First Appearance: *Harry Potter and the Goblet of Fire*

Overview

Orchideous causes a bouquet of flowers to burst out of the end of a wand.

Extended Description This spell is used by Mr. Ollivander as part of the Weighing of the Wands ceremony; he uses this spell to test Fleur's wand.

Analysis

A minor spell, this is used only to confirm, in a harmless manner, that Fleur's wand can in fact do magic to an acceptable standard.

Paintings

Type: Device
Features: Animated images
First Appearance: *Harry Potter and the Philosopher's Stone*

Overview

Magical Paintings or portraits are normal paintings, except that the people portrayed in them move and interact within the painted scene, with other adjacent paintings, and with the outside world.

Extended Description Characters in the paintings can move from one frame to another adjacent one; at several points, a character is seen flitting from painting to painting to spread news, and in *Harry Potter and the Prisoner of Azkaban*, one character, Sir Cadogan, travels from painting to painting to show Harry and Ron the way to class. The characters in several paintings are mentioned by name and are characters in their own right: The Fat Lady who guards the Gryffindor common room, Phineas Nigellus, and Sir Cadogan, are the most prominent among them.

It is also apparently possible for the subject of a painting to move to any other painting in which he or she is portrayed. While it is certain that the portraits that hang in the Headmasters' study at Hogwarts have this ability, we never learn whether other portraits are able to do this. In some cases, notably that of Phineas Nigellus, there is one inhabitant for, in this case, two pictures. This means that there is always one 'empty' painting. While it might seem odd to Muggles to have a painting without an inhabitant, this is apparently fairly common in the Wizarding world; Ron remarks, when Harry comments about his Famous Wizards card being blank, "Well, you can't expect him to hang about all day."

The two paintings can be at any distance apart, but the inhabitants will still be able to switch. In several cases, people depicted in paintings in Professor Dumbledore's office travel instantaneously to their images in London. This switching can be useful to carry messages between the locations of the different pictures, or report on what is going on in one of the other places.

Apparently, the inhabitants can travel from portrait to portrait within a given Wizard building; we see this both at Hogwarts and at St. Mungo's. Note that the portraits in the Headmaster's office cannot travel from frame to frame once they have left Hogwarts; in *Harry Potter and the Deathly Hallows*, the portrait of Phineas Nigellus does say that the portrait of Dumbledore cannot travel to the canvas that Phineas is using to visit them. We are led to believe that the portrait of Phineas Nigellus can travel from portrait to portrait within his erstwhile home at Grimmauld Place, but we never actually see him do so.

Analysis

The limitation on where portraits can travel is clearly necessary, as without these limits, any subject of any painting could visit any other painting. This would provide, in this story, something of a *deus ex machina*, as Harry would be able to summon and interrogate a portrait of Dumbledore no matter where he was. Dumbledore's absence is vital for Harry's maturation.

One must wonder about the case of a subject who has been painted multiple times, such as, we presume, Albus Dumbledore. If there are twenty portraits of him scattered about the Wizarding world, does he appear in each of them in turn? Or are there multiple Dumbledores spread out among the portraits? And would it be possible for them to collide, such that you would have, perhaps, two or three different-aged Dumbledores appear in your portrait occasionally?

Parselmouth

Type: ability
Features: can speak to snakes
First Appearance: *Harry Potter and the Chamber of Secrets*

Overview

A parselmouth is a wizard or witch with the ability to understand and talk to snakes (using Parseltongue).

Extended Description Perhaps the best known Parselmouth was Salazar Slytherin. His heir, Tom Riddle, possesses this ability as well, and presumably passed it on to Harry Potter via his attempt to kill him with the Killing Curse. Parselmouths are often assumed to be evil, partially because of their association with Voldemort.

In *Harry Potter and the Half-Blood Prince*, three more Parselmouths have been introduced: Marvolo, Morfin and Merope Gaunt.

Greater Picture

It is initially uncertain whether Voldemort is aware that Harry is a parselmouth, though likely rumours have reached him. The incarnation of Voldemort that is aware of Harry's ability was destroyed at the end of *Harry Potter and the Chamber of Secrets*, and Professor Dumbledore suggested in *Harry Potter and the Half-Blood Prince* that Voldemort was likely unaware of its destruction at the time. He may have since learned of its fate from Lucius Malfoy, but will not have learned any fine detail from that source, since we discover in *Harry Potter and the Deathly Hallows* that Voldemort is unaware of the destruction of the ring Horcrux, the locket Horcrux, or the cup Horcrux, until he travels to their physical locations and finds them missing. It is also unknown whether Snape would have mentioned Harry's being a Parselmouth to Voldemort, given his complex loyalties. So having an opponent who can unexpectedly understand and countermand his orders to a part of his army might prove a problem for Voldemort.

As it turns out, however, the final battle does not involve any significant number of snakes, apart from Nagini; so while the fact that Harry is a Parselmouth is important to the story in the seventh book, it is not a factor in the final battle. By Christmas of Harry's seventh year, however, it is certain that Voldemort does know that Harry is a parselmouth; the trap that Voldemort sets for Harry in Godric's Hollow will not work on anyone who is not a parselmouth.

Parseltongue

Type: Language
Features: The ability to talk to snakes
First Appearance: *Harry Potter and the Philosopher's Stone*

Overview

Parseltongue is the language of snakes. A wizard capable of speaking Parseltongue is called a Parselmouth.

Extended Description The ability to speak Parseltongue is inborn; a wizard is born being able to speak Parseltongue, and those who are not born with the ability cannot normally learn the language (although, according to the author, Dumbledore may have learned to understand it,[1] and in *Harry Potter and the Deathly Hallows*, Ron has learned one word of it, though it is questionable whether he knows what it means). To date, the ability to speak Parseltongue has been entirely associated with those who can show direct descent from Salazar Slytherin.

Harry, it turns out, can speak Parseltongue, though he was apparently not born with that ability. In *Harry Potter and the Chamber of Secrets*, Professor Dumbledore suggests that when Lord Voldemort, who is Slytherin's last descendant, tried to kill Harry, some of Voldemort's powers were transferred to him; one of those was Parseltongue.

ANALYSIS

Harry's ability to speak Parseltongue is first described in *Harry Potter and the Chamber of Secrets*; it is only there that we discover how rare this ability is and how it is linked to Voldemort. However, this is not the first use of this ability; in *Harry Potter and the Philosopher's Stone*, Harry speaks to a snake while visiting the zoo with the Dursleys.

The fact that Harry is a Parseltongue plays a major role in *Harry Potter and the Chamber of Secrets*, as it is his ability to understand Parseltongue that allows him to hear the Monster in the Chamber when it is prowling through the school, and because it allows him to actually open the Chamber. It also plays a lesser role in *Harry Potter and the Half-Blood Prince* where it allows him to understand the conversations between members of the Gaunt family as viewed in Dumbledore's Pensieve. It also plays a small role in *Harry Potter and the Deathly Hallows* where it allows Harry to open the locket Horcrux, and allows him to understand the false Bathilda Bagshot, and to understand Voldemort's instructions to Nagini.

QUESTIONS

1. In *Harry Potter and the Half-Blood Prince*, Morfin Gaunt apparently refuses (or is unable) to speak anything except Parseltongue. How is Dumbledore, who is not a Parseltongue, able to understand what happens in the Pensieve memory where Morfin is talking to Tom Riddle?

GREATER PICTURE

We learn in *Harry Potter and the Deathly Hallows* that Harry's ability to speak Parseltongue is actually related to the soul shard that Voldemort lost when trying to kill Harry. That soul shard had attached itself to Harry, and was the source of this ability, plus the ability to see into Voldemort's mind. The soul shard was destroyed in *Harry Potter and the Deathly Hallows*, and Harry's ability to speak Parseltongue went with it, according to the author.

---

[1]. http://the-leaky-cauldron.org/2007/7/30/j-k-rowling-web-chat-transcript

Patronus

Type: Magical term
Features: Names effect of Expecto Patronum spell
First Appearance: *Harry Potter and the Prisoner of Azkaban*

OVERVIEW

A Patronus is the visible result of the casting of the Expecto Patronum spell. By extension, it is also used to refer to the spell itself.

Extended Description When the Expecto Patronum spell is cast, the result is an apparent object made of white vapour. This object, the Patronus, often takes the shape of an animal; Harry's, for instance, is a stag. The animal in question often has some relationship to the person casting it: for instance, Dumbledore's is a phoenix, which seems to fit him well given his choice of pet, and Harry's takes the shape that his father took as an Animagus. Dumbledore has also devised a way of allowing a patronus to carry messages. More information is available at Expecto Patronum.

Pensieve

Type: Magical Device
Features: Stone basin containing whitish "fluid"
First Appearance: *Harry Potter and the Goblet of Fire*

OVERVIEW

The Pensieve is primarily a device for storing memories outside of one's own head.

Extended Description The Pensieve has multiple functions.

At times, when one's head is so full of thoughts that one cannot hear oneself think, it is useful to be able to take some of those thoughts and literally set them aside. The practiced Wizard can extract a thought from his head and store it in a phial or in the Pensieve for another time. If it is in the Pensieve, it is possible to stir the thoughts stored there together and look for patterns. It appears that the wizard has the choice of extracting an entire memory, leaving no trace of it in his head, as Professor Snape does in *Harry Potter and the Order of the Phoenix*, or extracting a copy of a memory, retaining the original, as Professor Slughorn does in *Harry Potter and the Half-Blood Prince*. It is also apparently possible to edit these extracted memories, though it is a difficult task and one which is often not done well.

If one places one's head within the Pensieve, one becomes immersed in a memory that is stored in the Pensieve, and is able to relive it as if one was living that time over again. Harry experienced Professor Dumbledore's memories of the Wizengamot trials of several Death Eaters this way in *Harry Potter and the Goblet of Fire*, and Professor Snape's memories of Harry's father in *Harry Potter and the Order of the Phoenix*. A thought or memory stored in the Pensieve can, with proper stimulus, appear to nearby viewers as if standing on the surface of the basin. Professor Dumbledore used this technique to show Harry the prophecy that had been made about him, in *Harry Potter and the Order of the Phoenix*, and it is used in *Harry Potter and the Half-Blood Prince* when full immersion in memory was not needed.

It is also possible to take another person's memories, place them in the Pensieve, and then enter them to relive them as if one were the person whose memories you have just added to the Pensieve. Harry and Professor Dumbledore do this a number of times in *Harry Potter and the Half-Blood Prince* in order to determine the salient points of the early history of Tom Riddle, or as he later styled himself, Lord Voldemort.

ANALYSIS

Most interestingly, the memories viewed by the person watching in the Pensieve are more complete than the person's own observations. For instance, in *Harry Potter and the Half-Blood Prince*, Bob Ogden visits the Gaunt family. Morfin speaks to him only in Parseltongue, which Ogden does not know and so would not be able to remember properly; yet Harry, reliving Ogden's memories, not only understands what the Gaunts are saying in Parseltongue, he is able to perceive things happening outside Ogden's range of vision.

GREATER PICTURE

In *Harry Potter and the Half-Blood Prince*, a number of times we are privileged to see the memories of wizards long dead—Morfin Gaunt and the house-elf Hokey, to give two examples. From this, we can be certain that extracted memories, if preserved in vials, live on past the death of their owners. Dumbledore's Pensieve, whenever we see it, is swimming with memories that Dumbledore has set aside; we never do find out if Dumbledore's memories in the Pensieve survive his death. If they did survive, it would seem extremely likely that Harry would have need to consult these memories in *Harry Potter and the Deathly Hallows*, but the situation does not arise. He does use the Pensieve, however, to review the memories of another dead wizard, namely Snape.

Pepper-Up Potion

Type: Potion
Features: Restorative
First Appearance: *Harry Potter and the Goblet of Fire*

OVERVIEW

Pepper-Up Potion is a restorative potion. It seems to have the side effect of making steam come out the drinker's ears.

Extended Description We first see this potion used after the Second Task of the Triwizard Tournament. Madam Pomfrey is administering this potion to all of the Champions and their "treasures" (hostages to the Merpeople) as they emerge from the lake. Harry does indicate that he feels much warmer once the potion has been administered. There is a Wizard candy, Pepper Imps, that apparently also makes steam come out the ears; likely it is based on this potion.

Permanent Sticking Charm

Type: Spell (charm)
Features: Causes permanent attachment of one object to another
First Appearance: *Harry Potter and the Order of the Phoenix*

OVERVIEW

The Permanent Sticking Charm is used to permanently fasten one object onto another.

Extended Description Although we are never informed how to perform this charm, we do see its results; and we are led to believe that it is effectively irrevocable.

We first see this charm used, in *Harry Potter and the Order of the Phoenix*, in the entrance hall of Number 12, Grimmauld Place. Sirius tells Harry that his mother had affixed her portrait to the wall with a Permanent Sticking Charm, and Sirius has been completely unable to remove it.

Sirius Black later tells Harry about the tapestry showing the family tree of the "most Ancient and Honourable House of Black." This tapestry is also affixed to the wall with a Permanent Sticking Charm.

Fred and George threaten to fasten Ron's Prefect badge to his forehead with a Permanent Sticking Charm when he seems unable to decide where to keep it.

In the first chapter of *Harry Potter and the Half-Blood Prince*, the Muggle Prime Minister recalls his efforts to remove a portrait in a distant corner of his office. From the description of his efforts and how they had failed, we can guess that this portrait, which is a Wizarding portrait used for communications between the Ministry of Magic and the Prime Minister's office, is affixed to the wall of the office with a Permanent Sticking Charm. Finally, when Harry visits Sirius' room for the first time in *Harry Potter and the Deathly Hallows*, he finds that many pictures and tokens of Sirius' stay in Gryffindor House had been attached to the walls with Permanent Sticking Charms. One assumes that Sirius had done this to irritate his parents. Perhaps curiously, Regulus' room, similarly decorated with Slytherin memorabilia, is not described as having had that charm used; perhaps Regulus, as he was not rebelling against his parents, did not fear that his decorations would be disturbed.

Peskipiksi Pesternomi

Type: Pseudo-Spell
Features: Does absolutely nothing
First Appearance: *Harry Potter and the Chamber of Secrets*

OVERVIEW

Peskipiksi Pesternomi is not a real spell.

Extended Description This spell appears to be Gilderoy Lockhart's attempt at a spell to disperse the Cornish Pixies he released in one of his Defence Against the Dark Arts classes, but it didn't work, and it might even have further irritated the pixies in question. The immediate result seems to have been that one of the pixies grabbed Lockhart's wand and threw it out the window.

ANALYSIS

The spell incantation seems to be based on the English phrase "Pesky pixie, pester no me." As most real spells seem to have incantations that derive from Latin words, the fact that this one is based on an English phrase makes it immediately suspect.

Given the nature of his actual magical expertise, which we discover late in the books, it is uncertain whether Lockhart had ever really tried to use this spell. Equally, it is uncertain whether he created this spell himself, or was given it by someone who didn't completely trust him. We see throughout the book that the teachers at Hogwarts seem to have a very low opinion of Lockhart's magical skill.

The purpose of this spell seems to be purely to point up Lockhart's incompetence.

Petrificus Totalus

Type: Spell (Curse)
Features: White blinding light
First Appearance: *Harry Potter and the Philosopher's Stone*

OVERVIEW

Petrificus Totalus is a spell that freezes or petrifies the body of the victim, making it incapable of moving, except for the eyes and the breathing. The spell can be broken by the Finite Incantatem spell.

Philosopher's Stone

Type: Magical device
Features: Red stone, generally small size
First Appearance: *Harry Potter and the Philosopher's Stone*

OVERVIEW

The Philosopher's Stone (known in the United States editions of the books as the Sorcerer's Stone) is an artifact that can turn inexpensive metals into gold or create an *elixir* that would make humans younger, thus delaying death. We are told that elixir produced by the Philosopher's Stone is actually capable of returning someone to full life if there is even the tiniest bit of life left within him.

In the Muggle world, it was a longtime "holy grail" of Western alchemy. In alchemy, making the philosopher's stone would bring enlightenment upon the maker and conclude the Great Work. It is also known as materia prima.

Extended Description The Philosopher's Stone is, of course, the key object in the first book of the Harry Potter series. The specific instance we see in this story is about three inches long, and is kept under heavy guard much of the time. We are told that this is the only known Philosopher's Stone in the world at present.

When we first see it, the Stone is in a grubby little paper parcel in one of the high security vaults under Gringotts Bank. It is retrieved from the vault by Hagrid, and apparently brought to Hogwarts School. Once Harry, Hermione, and Ron discover what the object is, they understand why people seem to be seeking it. They do eventually determine where it is hidden, and that it is guarded by means of enchantments set by many of the teachers at Hogwarts.

Determining that the Stone is at risk, the Trio then seek out its hiding place, apparently in the hope of defending the Stone. In the end, Harry alone reaches the chamber where the Stone is hidden, and manages to retrieve it from its hiding place and defend it from Professor Quirrell.

In the final chapter of the book, Professor Dumbledore says that he has destroyed the Stone. This upsets Harry, as he has learned that a friend of Dumbledore's, Nicholas Flamel, has been using the Stone to make the elixir that keeps him alive, but Dumbledore says that, after a very long life, Flamel is quite prepared for death.

ANALYSIS

The Philosopher's Stone is a unique magical artifact; there is only one in the world, and at the end of *Harry Potter and the Philosopher's Stone* it is destroyed. Although it appears only in this one book, its influence does show up in other books, most notably in *Harry Potter and the Deathly Hallows*, where it is believed by many that another unique artifact mentioned in that book is simply a distorted impression of the actions of the Philosopher's Stone.

QUESTIONS

1. Describe the differences between the archetypes of good and evil, and how this difference is portrayed in *Harry Potter and the Philosopher's Stone* through intents and actions with the Stone.

GREATER PICTURE

One of the key differences between the two sides in the battle of the entire series is actually highlighted by the Philosopher's Stone, and its role in the first book in the series. Much of the book, and the main conflict at the end of the book, is Voldemort, from his perch on the back of Professor Quirrell's head, attempting to capture the Philosopher's Stone and the return to life that it promises, against Harry attempting to keep him from that goal with the assistance of Professor Dumbledore and, surprisingly, Professor Snape. Voldemort, we learn, will stop at nothing, including the death of Unicorns, and of his host Quirrell, to return to life himself. Contrasted to that, we have Dumbledore, speaking of Nicholas Flamel (but possibly equally speaking of himself), telling Harry that "after all, to the well-organized mind, death is but the next great adventure." Although we have not yet properly met Voldemort, we can already see his fear of death, and his willingness to sacrifice anything and anyone else, in order to retain his life; and we can see Dumbledore's acceptance that death comes to all people, Muggle and wizard alike. This difference in the understanding of what death is, and how one becomes master of it, is something of a theme throughout the entire series. We will learn about the Horcruxes that Voldemort has used to anchor his soul to this world even when his body is destroyed, and we will learn about the Deathly Hallows, which according to legend give the holder mastery over Death.

In an interview, the author has stated that the theme of death and the afterlife became somewhat more prominent in the series following the death of her mother, which occurred while she was writing. While she did not specifically say which book she was writing at the time, one suspects that it was *Harry Potter and the Goblet of Fire*, because this particular theme comes into prominence in that book.

Phoenix

Type: Magical bird
Features: Beautiful plumage
First Appearance: *Harry Potter and the Chamber of Secrets*

Overview

A Phoenix is a magical bird that periodically burns up and is then reborn from its own ashes.

Extended Description Phoenixes are truly remarkable birds. While their rebirth from their own ashes is relatively widely known among Muggles, it is not generally known that they can lift extremely heavy loads, that their tears have healing powers, or that they are extremely loyal pets. We are introduced to one phoenix in the course of the books: Fawkes is Professor Dumbledore's pet phoenix.

Analysis

While we are not introduced to the bird itself in *Harry Potter and the Philosopher's Stone*, there is mention of the phoenix in that book; Mr. Ollivander mentions that there is a phoenix feather at the core of Harry's wand. Ollivander mentions also that the phoenix in question has only ever given two feathers; but since he mentions that his wands are made with phoenix feathers, dragon heartstrings, or unicorn hairs, one can safely assume that there are other phoenixes that he can harvest feathers from. Note that Ollivander selecting these items for the core of his wands indicates that he believes them to be the most powerful magic items available.

Fawkes' special powers play a very large part in Harry's defeat of the monster in the Chamber of Secrets: it is his loyalty that calls Fawkes to Harry, the healing powers of his tears are what restore Harry to health after he is injured by the monster, and it is his ability to lift heavy loads that allows Harry to escape from the Chamber with Ron, Ginny, and Professor Lockhart after the monster has been destroyed.

His loyalty and intelligence are extremely useful to Dumbledore in *Harry Potter and the Order of the Phoenix*, where Dumbledore has Fawkes carry messages and keep a lookout.

Questions

1. Why is there a phoenix feather in Harry's and Voldemort's wands? Does it signify a wand whose wizard/witch's strength is duelling?

Photograph

Type: Device
Features: Animate images
First Appearance: *Harry Potter and the Philosopher's Stone*

Overview

Magical photographs are similar to Muggle photographs, except that the people portrayed in them are animate, moving, waving, and apparently dropping out of the picture occasionally to attend to other business. They act in many ways as their originator would in similar situation: a photograph of a girl develops spots on her nose at one point and starts trying to hide her face under the picture frame, for instance.

Extended Description While very similar to magical Paintings, photographs seem to be lesser variants of the breed; while the characters are animate, they do not seem to interact with occupants of other photos, and they do not seem to interact much with the people outside the photograph (in fact, they don't seem to be able to speak at all)—although in *Harry Potter and the Order of the Phoenix*, Alastor Moody does instruct the characters in a photograph to "move aside," and they apparently do so. Printed images behave similarly to photographs; the pictures in The Daily Prophet, for instance, move but don't speak either.

Pixie

Type: Creature
Features: Small size, fly
First Appearance: *Harry Potter and the Chamber of Secrets*

Overview

Pixies are small, electric blue flying creatures, the ones we see in the books originate in Cornwall, and are very mischievous.

Extended Description During a Defence Against the Dark Arts lesson in *Harry Potter and the Chamber of Secrets*, Professor Lockhart lets loose a cage full of pixies, in spite of the fact that he has no experience with them at all. Havoc breaks loose while Lockhart tries to control the situation, in vain, and uses the absolutely non-effective spell Peskipiksi Pesternomi (which was most likely made up). Lockhart flees with the rest of the class, leaving Harry, Ron, and Hermione to clean up the mess.

ANALYSIS

Given what we find out about Lockhart at the end of this book, it is uncertain whether Lockhart could have known that the charm he proposed would work. It is certain he had never tried it before. It is possible that some witch had given him the charm, and he had written about it before erasing her memory; but the witch quite possibly knew Lockhart's reputation and had given him a false and ineffective spell.

Plimpy

Type: Magical Creature
Features: Spherical fish with two feet
First Appearance: *Harry Potter and the Half-Blood Prince*

OVERVIEW

Plimpies are apparently aquatic, but are never described in the series, though they are mentioned by both Luna Lovegood and her father Xenophilius.

Extended Description   In *Harry Potter and the Half-Blood Prince*, we learn from Luna Lovegood that Gulping Plimpies can be staved off by means of Gurdy-roots.

In *Harry Potter and the Deathly Hallows*, Xenophilius Lovegood explains Luna's absence by claiming that she is down on the far side of the bridge, catching Plimpies for their supper. He says that many people have asked for the recipe for their Plimpy soup.

In *Magical Beasts And Where To Find Them*, there is a description of Plimpies. Evidently these are approximately spherical fish with legs and feet. It is mentioned that Merpeople can get irritated by their habit of hovering around, and will tie their feet together. A Plimpy with its feet tied together will drift helplessly until it manages to get its feet untied, which can take hours.

Pogrebin

Type: Magical Creature
Features: looks like rock when crouching
First Appearance: *Fantastic Beasts and Where to Find Them*

Point Me

Type: Spell
Features: points North
First Appearance: *Harry Potter and the Goblet of Fire*

OVERVIEW

The Point Me charm, or Four-Point-Spell, makes a wand turn so that it points north.

Extended Description   This spell was used by Harry in the Third Task maze in *Harry Potter and the Goblet of Fire*. Knowing that he had to travel roughly north-west from the entrance of the maze to reach the center, he was able to use this charm at several points in the maze to correctly select a direction to travel in.

ANALYSIS

Basically, this spell is a magical equivalent of a Muggle compass. it is, however, slightly more useful as a wizard will have his wand with him all the time; there is no need to carry a compass in addition to the wand.

QUESTIONS

1. What would the disadvantage be, to a wizard, of carrying a compass? Is there some reason, apart from the small effort needed to carry an additional item, that a magnetic compass would not work?

Polyjuice Potion

Type: potion
Features: differs based on subject
First Appearance: *Harry Potter and the Chamber of Secrets*

OVERVIEW

Polyjuice Potion allows the taker to assume the physical appearance of another person. The potion takes a month to brew, and must include part of the person you wish to look like.

Extended Description   One of the ingredients of Polyjuice Potion is boomslang skin. The boomslang is a very real venomous snake, native to Africa.

The potion is used in *Harry Potter and the Chamber of Secrets* by Harry and Ron to question Draco about the Heir of Slytherin, with almost no result. Hermione, by accidentally trying to change into a cat, demonstrates the problems with using potions without being quite sure of the effects they will have. The potion is also used in *Harry Potter and the Goblet of Fire* by the false Moody.

It is also used in *Harry Potter and the Half-Blood Prince* by Draco's sidekicks Crabbe and Goyle when Draco wants them to be inconspicuous guards for what he is doing.

Finally, it is used extensively by Harry, Ron, and Hermione in *Harry Potter and the Deathly Hallows* when they need to disguise themselves. It is used first by Mad-Eye Moody to create six replicas of Harry as a way of confusing the Death Eaters who are trying to stop his departure from the Dursleys.' It is then used by Harry to disguise himself as "Cousin Barny" at the wedding of Bill and Fleur. Harry, Ron, and Hermione use it to enter the Ministry, Harry and Hermione use it to visit Godric's Hollow incognito, and Hermione uses it to enter Gringotts disguised as Bellatrix Lestrange.

Analysis

It must be extremely useful to appear to be someone else. The potion is remarkably comprehensive in its actions; the false Moody, transformed by the potion, is missing an eye and a leg, and these grow back when he is deprived of the potion. In fact, one assumes they must grow back each night, as the effects of the potion last only an hour. One must question whether the suppressed limb must be exercised to avoid it atrophying . . . did the false Moody have to exercise each day in his normal shape to avoid the effects of nine months without moving the suppressed leg? The process of changing to a new shape by means of the potion is described as being quite painful, while the reversion to original self is so painless that neither Ron nor Harry notices it happening in themselves. As the false Moody was not apparently in pain when he drank from his hip flask (which contained, apparently, the Polyjuice Potion that retained his appearance), we can assume that it is the process of changing that is painful; maintenance in the unnatural shape should be much less so.

One wonders what happened when Crabbe or Goyle, standing guard duty, ran out of time? They did not seem to have any additional potion with them, and it is certain that a 6th-year Crabbe or Goyle would not have fit into the robes of the students they chose to disguise themselves as, which were typically first- to third-year girls. Possibly they had additional stock of prepared potion with them, but we never see them drinking any of it. However, throughout the seventh book, the effects of the potion seem to wear off at much more convenient times than we would expect; rather than a fixed hour in duration, for instance, Harry's disguise as "Barny" seems to last for the duration of the wedding, and Harry, Ron, and Hermione's disguises as they invade the Ministry not only seem to remain in place for the entire time that they are in the Ministry, but seem to wear off very conveniently just as they leave Grimmauld Place for the forest where the Quidditch World Cup had been played two years before.

Porlock

Type: Magical Creature
Features:
First Appearance: *Fantastic Beasts and Where to Find Them*

Portkey

Type: Device
Features: instant transportation
First Appearance: *Harry Potter and the Goblet of Fire*

Overview

A portkey is a common item used to transport anyone touching it to another pre-determined location, such as a Quidditch match. Typically portkeys will activate at a specific time, but apparently it is also possible to create an on-contact Portkey that activates immediately when touched, or an on-command Portkey that activates on demand.

Extended Description   Portkeys appeared in *Harry Potter and the Goblet of Fire* first as a means of getting to a major event, specifically the Quidditch World Cup, where it was used to transport those members of the Weasley family and those members of the Diggory family who were unable to Apparate. It was later used to transport those same individuals back home. In this section, we learned that Portkeys would typically be unobtrusive items that would activate at a specific time, transporting all who were directly in physical contact with them to a specific other point. A Portkey was also used to transport Harry and Cedric Diggory to the graveyard where Voldemort staged his return; in this application, the Portkey activated immediately upon contact, taking Harry and Cedric from the center of the third-task maze to the graveyard, and then later carrying Harry and Cedric's body from the graveyard to the edge of the third-task maze.

On two separate occasions in *Harry Potter and the Order of the Phoenix*, Professor Dumbledore is seen to create a Portkey, once to carry Harry and the Weasleys from his office to 12 Grimmauld Place, and later to carry Harry from the Ministry of Magic to Dumbledore's office. Both of these Portkeys, seemed to be of the delayed-activation type, as in both cases Dumbledore counted down for the portkey to activate; in the first case, this was necessary because it was necessary to transport all of the Weasleys, along with Harry, to Grimmauld Place, in the second case it was because Dumbledore wanted to hand the Portkey to Harry. In the first case, though, it seems more likely that the Portkey was a command-activation type, because while Dumbledore did count down to the activation, he had made the Portkey before he had heard back from the portrait of Phineas Nigellus, and he could not have known exactly when it was to activate until Phineas Nigellus had reported back.

Analysis

When Dumbledore uses the Portus charm to create a Portkey in front of Cornelius Fudge in the Ministry for Magic, Fudge, then Minister for Magic, seems shocked that Dumbledore would so lightly create an "unauthorized Portkey." It appears that, because of their ability to deposit a person within areas that are protected from incursion (recall that both Hogwarts and 12 Grimmauld Place are protected by being made unmappable and by having spells to prevent Apparation), creation of Portkeys is controlled by the Government.

Apparation requires a firm knowledge of the destination to which you will be going; one must assume that creation of a Portkey requires at least that same understanding of the destination, probably even more. It is certain that the two Portkeys that Dumbledore creates are for destinations with which he is extremely familiar. It is interesting that, rather than create another Portkey for himself, Dumbledore returns to Hogwarts by way of the Floo Network, especially since Hogwarts attachment to the Floo network is supposed to be somewhat thin.

In *Harry Potter and the Deathly Hallows*, Mad-Eye Moody tells Harry that the area around Privet Drive is being monitored for use of the Floo Network, Apparation, and use of Portkeys, ostensibly for Harry's protection, but actually to monitor where he is taken if he leaves there. From this, we may gather that Portkey use can be monitored if not prevented.

Portkeys are used later in that same book to bring various groups from safe-houses scattered around the country to The Burrow. Harry and Hagrid, for example, catch a hairbrush from Ted Tonks' house.

Portus

Type: Spell
Features: makes a portkey out of an object
First Appearance: *Harry Potter and the Order of the Phoenix*

Overview

A Portus spell is used to create a Portkey.

Extended Description A Portkey is a magical means of transportation between two specific points, potentially at a specific time. The spell Portus is used to create a portkey; the visible effect is that the object being charmed glows blue and vibrates briefly. Professor Dumbledore creates a portkey on two occasions in *Harry Potter and the Order of the Phoenix*: when Mr. Weasley is injured, he creates a Portkey to carry the Weasleys and Harry back to Number 12 Grimmauld Place so that they don't have to deal with Professor Umbridge; and after the battle at the Ministry, he creates one to carry Harry back to his office. In this latter case, Cornelius Fudge, the Minister for Magic, is present, and is scandalized that Dumbledore would dare to produce an unauthorised Portkey.

Analysis

The Portus spell must be complex indeed, quite apart from the magic involved. We can safely assume that, like the Riddikulus spell and the Patronus charm, a significant part of the spell is actually derived from what you are thinking of at the time the spell is cast. There are a significant number of things that you must think of when casting Portus. Not only must you hold in your mind the destination that you desire, you must also decide whether the Portkey is to be a there-and-return key, in which case you must also hold the return destination in mind; additionally you must set the time when the portkey is to activate, or whether it is to activate upon command or upon contact. It may be possible to make a personal Portkey as well, in which case you must know whose contact will activate it.

Potions

Type: Subject
Features: Creation of potions, substances with magical effects
First Appearance: *Harry Potter and the Philosopher's Stone*

Overview

Potions is the science of combining ordinary and magical substances to create potions, (usually) liquids with magical effects.

Extended Description Not everything discussed in Potions class is, strictly speaking, a liquid. Several sections of the class are concerned with antidotes, and on a number of occasions there is mention of a Bezoar, a stone found in a goat's stomach, which has curative properties.

There are a very large number of potions mentioned through the course of the seven books. Of these, perhaps the most important are the Wolfsbane potion, which appears in *Harry Potter and the Prisoner of Azkaban*, Polyjuice Potion, which Hermione first introduces us to in *Harry Potter and the Chamber of Secrets*, and which is then used in *Harry Potter and the Goblet of Fire* and *Harry Potter and the Deathly Hallows*, and Felix Felicis, which plays a large role in *Harry Potter and the Half-Blood Prince*.

Potions is taught for the first five years of Harry's schooling by Professor Snape, and in the sixth and seventh year by Professor Slughorn.

Analysis

Magic potions play a large role in Muggle ideas about magic, so it is clearly necessary that they should be a part of the Wizarding world. Their being codified and formalized into almost a science seems only proper, given what we have come to understand about them.

It is necessary for the development of Harry's character that he should not excel in all subjects, and in fact only in Defence Against the Dark Arts does Harry consistently perform to the top of his ability. However, particularly in Potions, Harry does not work up to the level that we expect of him. Certainly, some of this is due to unfair marking of assignments by Snape, who we see as having a bias against Gryffindor house in general, and against Harry in particular, and some of this is Harry rebelling against Snape, but it seems that for Harry's first five years at least, his Potions work could stand improvement.

Greater Picture

For the first five years, Potions is inextricably tied up with Professor Snape, and Harry's performance in that course is clearly influenced by Snape's dislike of Harry. A large part of Harry's difficulty with Potions lies in Snape's trying to force Harry into the same mold as his father, and Harry's unconscious resistance to that. In one particular case, we see that Harry's failure to correctly make a potion is due to Snape's having written the instructions on the board in a way that would cause confusion in any reader. It is clear to the reader that Snape is trying to make Harry fail, and does not care if he dooms the entire Gryffindor class at the same time.

It is noteworthy that, given a fair teacher (Slughorn) and a good instructor (the "Half-Blood Prince"'s book), Harry is capable of turning in an excellent job in Potions class, and even absent the book is still able to do a decent enough job of it that Slughorn's suspicions are not raised. It should also perhaps be noted that Harry's mother is singled out by Slughorn as the best Potions student he had ever had.

Prior Incantato

Type: Spell (Charm)
Features: Force wand to reveal last spell cast
First Appearance: *Harry Potter and the Goblet of Fire*

Overview

The Prior Incantato charm is used to reveal the last spell cast by a wand. Once the spell cast has been determined, the Deletrius charm can be used to end the display. The effects are similar to the Priori Incantatem wand effect, but not entirely related.

Extended Description In *Harry Potter and the Goblet of Fire*, the House Elf Winky is found Stunned, holding a wand, shortly after the Dark Mark is cast. The Prior Incantato charm is used to determine that it was, in fact, the wand that was found with Winky that was used to cast the Dark Mark.

In *Harry Potter and the Deathly Hallows*, Hermione's wand is captured at Malfoy Manor. Harry assumes that, by means of the Prior Incantato charm, the Death Eaters there will be able to determine that Hermione had tried to repair Harry's wand, and had failed. Remote as this possibility may be, Harry decides that he must proceed as if Voldemort is aware that his wand has been destroyed.

Priori Incantatem

Type: effect
Features: wands display last spells cast
First Appearance: *Harry Potter and the Goblet of Fire*

Overview

Rather than a spell, Priori Incantatem is an effect that occurs when two wands, that have magical cores deriving from the same source, are used against each other. One or the other of the wands is forced to regurgitate the last spells that it was used to cast. The effect is very similar to the spell Prior Incantato.

Extended Description This effect is seen near the end of *Harry Potter and the Goblet of Fire* during the graveyard battle between Voldemort and Harry Potter. Both Harry's and Voldemort's wands are powered by tail feathers given by Fawkes. When they simultaneously cast spells at each other, this effect appears. A fiery stream joins the two wands, forming a golden light that envelops Harry and Voldemort; there are fire beads on the stream between the two wands, which Harry thrusts backwards into Voldemort's wand, forcing it to disgorge its past few spells. The spirit "echoes" of Cedric Diggory, the muggle Frank Bryce, Bertha Jorkins, and Harry's mother and father, who were the last people murdered using Voldemort's wand, appear as ghostly simulacra of their living selves.

Greater Picture

We learn much later that this also has the effect of transferring some of the powers of one wand into the other. In this case, Harry, being the stronger wizard for reasons that are discussed elsewhere, manages to force Voldemort's wand to disgorge its most recent spells, and in the process gains some of the power of Voldemort's wand.

Probity Probe

Type: Magical device
Features: Detects concealment and deceit
First Appearance: *Harry Potter and the Half-Blood Prince*

Overview

Probity Probes are long, silvery probes that allow the bearer to detect concealment and deception: for instance, a Probity Probe would detect use of Polyjuice Potion to disguise oneself, and presumably would detect someone under an Invisibility Cloak.

Extended Description We first hear of Probity Probes when Harry is preparing for his sixth year at Hogwarts. Bill, who works at Gringotts, hands Harry a money bag, saying that he's gotten some cash for Harry; everyone going into Gringotts now has to pass people with Probity Probes, and entrance to the bank can take several hours.

When Harry, Hermione, Ron, and Griphook enter Gringotts in *Harry Potter and the Deathly Hallows* to open Bellatrix' vault, there are two wizards with Probity Probes by the door. Harry, from under his Invisibility Cloak, Confunds them so they will not scan Hermione, who is in disguise.

Analysis

The principles behind a Probity Probe, a Secrecy Sensor, and the part of the Marauder's Map that determines the name of an individual, must be related, however their operation is clearly somewhat different.

Prophecy

Type: Magical artifact or occurrence
Features: Prediction of the future
First Appearance: *Harry Potter and the Prisoner of Azkaban*

Overview

A Prophecy is a valid prediction of the future, as opposed to the "fortune-telling" of Divination.

Extended Description The term Prophecy is used to refer to two different objects. The first and more expected for Muggles is the actual utterance, the description of things yet to come. The second is the glass sphere which is used to contain a record, a memory of that prophecy, in order that it may be acted upon or checked for validity at a later time. While Divination, as a means of predicting the future, tries to achieve the same validity as Prophecy, its methods remain laughable to those who care to analyze them. However, the one person we see in the series who is capable of Prophecy is the Divination teacher, Professor Trelawney. It is possible that the mysticism inherent in Divination does make the mind more open to Prophecy, but it is equally possible that a family history of Prophecy impels one towards a career in Divination.

During the course of the story, we actually see only two Prophecies, both provided by Professor Trelawney. The first concerns the escape of Peter Pettigrew, and his return to "the Dark Lord," and is couched in terms that Harry cannot understand until after the named events have taken place. Part of the perceived ambiguity in the prophecy is the use of the term "his greatest servant" to refer to Pettigrew; at this point, all of the characters in the story believe Voldemort's greatest servant to be Sirius Black.

The second prophecy that we hear was actually made prior to Harry's birth, and concerns Harry and his interaction with Voldemort. We see this prophecy in Dumbledore's memories, near the end of *Harry Potter and the Order of the Phoenix*. However, we are told of this prophecy much earlier, and it is the prophecy that drives much of the action in the book, as Voldemort seems to be blindly reacting to it.

ANALYSIS

A clear distinction must be drawn between Divination, which is taught as an academic subject but which is clearly little better than Muggle fortune-telling, involving the same artifacts and equipment, and Prophecy, which has a basis in reality but is apparently innate and unteachable.

Prophecies, stored in crystal spheres, are kept in the Department of Mysteries, in a store-room associated with the areas used for the study of the mystery of Time.

Protean Charm

Type: Spell (Charm)
Features: Makes objects similar across distance
First Appearance: *Harry Potter and the Order of the Phoenix*

OVERVIEW

The Protean Charm makes multiple objects act as if they are the same object—changes made to one object appear on all of them.

Extended Description In order to make it easier to contact all the members of Dumbledore's Army, Hermione creates a large number of false Galleons. These Galleons are charmed such that, once the date of the next meeting is determined, Harry can change one Galleon to show that date, and all the others will similarly change, and heat up to let their holders know that they have changed. Terry Boot recognizes the charm as a Protean Charm, and is impressed: this is N.E.W.T.-level magic.

A parallel is drawn to the Dark Mark tattoo that Death Eaters wear on their left forearm, and Hermione indicates that she had not thought that Harry would want to inflict pain on his prospective students.

Protego

Type: Spell
Features: Shields the caster
First Appearance: *Harry Potter and the Order of the Phoenix*

OVERVIEW

Protego is a spell used to guard its caster from incoming spells. It doesn't work against the unforgivable curses, especially the killing curse. It is coined from the Latin verb 'protego,' 'to protect' (lit. to cover over).

Extended Description The effects of this charm seem to vary based on the desires of the spell caster.

In *Harry Potter and the Order of the Phoenix*, we see Harry using this spell against Professor Snape in his Occlumency lesson. Here, the effect is to reverse the spell being cast; Harry sees some of Snape's memories instead of the expected outcome, Snape seeing some of Harry's thoughts.

In the Battle at the Ministry late in that same book, Harry uses this spell twice. Both times, the spell being cast at him is simply interrupted.

In *Harry Potter and the Deathly Hallows*, Hermione casts this spell once, and Harry casts it three times. In these cases, the result of the spell is a "bubble" that is impermeable to spells and physical traversal (the bubble forming knocks Hermione back a few steps), though it is still possible to see and hear through it. Also in the seventh book, several of the characters append this with other words. Professor Flitwick uses "Protego Horribilis" when he is preparing a shield for the school, and Hermione uses "Protego Totalum" when setting defensive spells around the campsite. The specific effects of the added words are not certain.

Puffskein

Type: Magical Creature
Features: harmless, furry
First Appearance: *Harry Potter and the Order of the Phoenix*

OVERVIEW

A spherical shaped creature, a Puffskein has a custard yellow colour fur and is found worldwide. It loves to be hugged and thrown about. It's very easy to look after this creature. It's a highly popular wizard pet and finds most of its fame with children.

Extended Description We never actually see a live Puffskein in the books; most of our information comes from "Newt Scamander"'s *Fantastic Creatures and Where to Find Them*.

Mrs. Weasley does mention that she had found an old Puffskein nest under the couch at Grimmauld Place, but we must assume that they perished from neglect during the ten or so years that the house stood empty after Sirius Black's mother passed away.

Fred and George evidently breed a miniature, pastel-colored version, which they call Pygmy Puffs, and sell them from their joke shop.

Pureblood

Type: Status
Features: Persons of purely magical ancestry
First Appearance: *Harry Potter and the Chamber of Secrets*

OVERVIEW

A pureblood is a witch or wizard who descends from other witches and wizards only (not Muggles).

Extended Description The followers of Lord Voldemort believe that there is a distinction between those who are descended entirely from those who are able to do magic and those who have non-magical blood in their ancestry. Echoing the views of Salazar Slytherin, one of the founders of Hogwarts, Voldemort believes that non-magical ancestry somehow taints the bloodline. Only those with no such taint deserve to be called Pureblood, and only Purebloods deserve to be taught magic.

It is perhaps interesting that Voldemort himself is not a pureblood; while his mother, Merope Gaunt, was a member of one of the oldest Wizarding familes in existence, his hated father was a Muggle.

The term Pureblood first appears in *Harry Potter and the Chamber of Secrets*, but Draco's hatred of Hermione clearly stems from this prejudice, and is evident from the beginning of the series.

ANALYSIS

The idea of "racial purity" pervades the entire series. While the core story is Voldemort's return to power, and Harry's battle to prevent this, it is necessary for Voldemort's followers to break Wizarding law in order to restore him to power. The only way that they can justify this to themselves is to demonize the main Wizarding community, as being somehow sub-Wizard because of their Muggle ancestry. This is quite sharply brought out in the episode with the Gaunt family, as viewed in Dumbledore's Pensieve in *Harry Potter and the Half-Blood Prince*. The Gaunt family would apparently rather live in solitude and squalor with their pride in being pure-bloods, than join the Wizarding community and accept the fact that their status was no higher than that of Wizards who had Muggle parents.

It has been mentioned in the discussion of Lord Voldemort that this emphasis on racial purity is very similar to the German Nazi ideas of pure Aryan heritage—and there is an interesting parallel in that Hitler himself was not pure Aryan, but had Jewish ancestors.

It is also mentioned, in the topic Half-blood, that in fact many half-bloods, including Lord Voldemort himself, are more powerful magicians than many Purebloods.

Pygmy Puff

Type: Creature
Features: First Appearance

OVERVIEW

A Pygmy Puff is a miniature puffskein.

ANALYSIS

We are introduced to Pygmy Puffs in *Harry Potter and the Half-Blood Prince* when Ginny Weasley buys one from Weasleys' Wizard Wheezes. They are pink and purple miniature puffskeins and, according to Fred and George, are very popular.

Quick-Quotes Quill

Type: Magical device
Features: Transcription of what is thought by writer
First Appearance: *Harry Potter and the Goblet of Fire*

OVERVIEW

A Quick-Quotes Quill is a quill that automatically transcribes what is spoken in its presence.

Extended Description We first see this when it is produced by Rita Skeeter, when she is interviewing Harry, immediately before the Weighing of the Wands ceremony. Rita's Quill is an acid-green, and she seems to like the flavour of it, as she sucks on the end of it briefly before setting it on the parchment.

We also find that it does not actually record accurately what is being said. This particular Quill seems to generate text that only vaguely resembles what is spoken, slanting it to make it sensational.

ANALYSIS

It is certain that this particular quill and Rita are very attuned, as the Quill seems to produce the sort of story, on its own, that Rita is famous for. One must wonder if the Quill can be tuned, however, as the story that Rita produces with, apparently, the exact same Quill in *Harry Potter and the Order of the Phoenix* seems to be written straight, when we see it published in *The Quibbler*

Quietus

Type: Spell (Charm)
Features: Reverses effects of Sonorus
First Appearance: *Harry Potter and the Goblet of Fire*

OVERVIEW

The Quietus charm is cast by a wizard, usually upon himself, to restore his voice to its normal volume after the use of the Sonorus charm.

Extended Description The Quietus charm is first seen used by Ludo Bagman when he is called upon to commentate the Quidditch World Cup; when the game is finished, Ludo ends his earlier Sonorus charm by invoking Quietus. Ludo uses this spell again after commentating the events in the Triwizard Tournament.

Quintaped

Type: Magical Creature
Features: reddish-brown hair
First Appearance: *Fantastic Beasts and Where to Find Them*

OVERVIEW

No one knows anything very much about the Quintaped, which is apparently mythological. Quintapeds inhabit the island of Drear, which, of course, is unplottable.

Extended Description The story of the Quintapeds appears in *Fantastic Beasts and Where to Find Them*. "Newt Scamander" writes: Legend has it that the Isle of Drear was once populated by two wizarding families, the McCliverts and the MacBoons. A drunken wizarding duel between Dugald, chief of the clan McClivert, and Quintius, head of the clan MacBoon, is supposed to have led to the death of Dugald. In retaliation, so the story has it, a gang of McCliverts surrounded the MacBoon dwellings one night and transfigured each and every MacBoon into a monstrous five legged creature. The McCliverts realized too late that the transfigured MacBoon were infinitely more dangerous in this state(the MacBoons had the reputation for great ineptitude at magic). Moreover, the MacBoons resisted every attempt to change them back into human form. The monsters killed every last one of the McCliverts until no human remained on the island. It was only then that the MacBoon monsters realized that in the absence of anyone to wield a wand, they would be forced to remain they were for evermore.

Ramora

Type: Magical Creature
Features:
First Appearance: *Fantastic Beasts and Where to Find Them*

Re'em

Type: Magical Creature
Features: golden hide
First Appearance: *Fantastic Beasts and Where to Find Them*

Red Cap

Red Caps are dwarflikecreatures that are found wherever blood has been spilled . From Scottish folklore. Red Cap is a thoroughly evil creature. He is a short, stocky old man with long gray hair and claws in stead of hands. He lives on the Scottish Border in ancient ruins of castles, especially in those with a bloody history of war and murder. He owes his name to the fact that he wears a red hat, which is colored by the blood of his victims. Red Cap moves with remarkable speed, despite the fact that he wears iron boots. He can overcome even the strongest man, unless the intended victim remembers to quote a few words from the bible. (Encyclopedia Mythica; thanks to Elizabeth Quest for the tip)

Reducio

Type: Spell (Charm)
Features: Shrinks an object
First Appearance: *Harry Potter and the Goblet of Fire*

OVERVIEW

Reducio is a charm that makes things small.

Extended Description This spell seems to reverse the action of the engorgement charm Engorgio. The first time we see this charm used, it is used by Professor Moody to reduce a spider back to its normal size after it has been used in a classroom demonstration.

ANALYSIS

Like many spells, there must be a mental component to this spell; it is necessary to control the size that you want the object to shrink to, so that size must be controlled mentally.

Reducto

Type: Spell (curse)
Features: Reduces objects to dust
First Appearance: *Harry Potter and the Order of the Phoenix*

OVERVIEW

Reducto, also known as the Reductor curse, is a destruction spell, used to reduce objects to dust.

Extended Description While its main purpose is to reduce an object to dust, it can also cause that dust to spread violently, making a small explosion. More powerful spellcasters can, of course, cast this spell on larger objects, making larger explosions if they care to.

ANALYSIS

We first see this spell when Harry is reflecting on the progress of his students in Dumbledore's Army. Harry recalls that Parvati Patil had performed this curse so well that she had reduced the entire table under the sneakoscopes to dust.

We believe this spell may be similar in effect to the Deprimo spell.

Relashio

Type: Spell (Charm)
Features: Releasing an object
First Appearance: *Harry Potter and the Goblet of Fire*

OVERVIEW

Relashio is a spell that is used to release an object from another object that is binding it, like chains.

Extended Description If used underwater, this spell creates a jet of boiling water. Harry used this spell underwater when he is attacked by Grindylows in *Harry Potter and the Goblet of Fire* as a part of the Second Task.

Remembrall

Type: Magical device
Features: Turns red when you've forgotten something
First Appearance: *Harry Potter and the Philosopher's Stone*

OVERVIEW

A Remembrall is a glass sphere filled with white smoke. If you hold the ball in your hand, the smoke will turn red to indicate you have forgotten something. The name is apparently a portmanteau of "remember," "all," and "ball."

Extended Description Neville is sent a Remembrall by his grandmother in his second week at Hogwarts, and it immediately turns red when he holds it, to tell him that he has forgotten something. However, it cannot tell him what he has forgotten.

ANALYSIS

As written, the Remembrall, while neat, is not particularly useful; everyone has always forgotten something, so the Remembrall would always indicate that something had been forgotten. Perhaps the shade of red would indicate how important the forgotten item is?

The main purpose of the Remembrall is to give Draco Malfoy something that he can steal, to show off his character, and to make it necessary for Harry to fly to recover it. Forcing Harry onto a broom, in a situation where he can show off his natural talent unfettered by organized lessons, is necessary to allow us to share Harry's joy at finding something he is good at in the Wizarding world.

After the byplay on the brooms, Neville's Remembrall plays no further significant part on the story, and no others are mentioned.

QUESTIONS

1. How could a Remembrall be made more useful?

Rennervate

Type: Spell (Charm)
Features: Revives the subject
First Appearance: *Harry Potter and the Half-Blood Prince*

OVERVIEW

Rennervate is a general revival spell, used when trying to resuscitate someone who has been left unconscious by magical means.

Extended Description While at first glance, this seems to be a special case version of Enervate, the charm that counters the effect of a Stun spell, in fact it is used for more general resuscitation.

We see this spell used once: Harry uses it to attempt to revive Professor Dumbledore after Dumbledore has succumbed to the potion guarding the locket in the lake. Harry has limited success.

Reparo

Type: Spell
Features: Repairs items
First Appearance: *Harry Potter and the Philosopher's Stone*

OVERVIEW

Reparo is a spell for fixing broken things, for example a glass bowl that has broken into several pieces. It can also be used to counter the effects of the Diffindo charm.

Extended Description This spell was first used on the Hogwarts Express, when Hermione fixed Harry's glasses. As such, though it is not the first magic we see, or even properly the first spell (Hagrid giving [[Muggles' Guide to Harry Potter/Dudley a pig's tail was the first spell cast in the series), it is the first spell cast in which we hear the incantation. Curiously, it is also the last spell we see actually cast in the series.

This spell is used a number of times through the series to repair things—dropped glass or china bowls, broken windows, torn bags, or torn books, for instance.

ANALYSIS

It is only in the final book of the series that we learn that it can be used to repair magical items, when Hermione tries to mend Harry's wand with it, and later when Harry successfully mends his own wand. Until that point, only non-magical items had been repaired with this charm.

This spell seems to be useful only for inanimate objects—it is not used on Harry's broken wrist, for example. (Though the charm that is used on his wrist in *Harry Potter and the Chamber of Secrets* does not have the desired effect . . .)

Rictusempra

Type: Spell (Jinx)
Features: Tickling jinx
First Appearance: *Harry Potter and the Chamber of Secrets*

OVERVIEW

Rictusempra is a jinx which attempts to disable a witch or wizard by tickling him or her.

Extended Description Rictusempra, the Perpetual Tickling charm, which apparently can be stopped by the Finite Incantatem charm, was used by Harry against Malfoy in the Duelling Club. The intent was, of course, to tickle Malfoy to the point that he would be unable to jinx Harry in return. It was ineffectual, however, as despite being tickled, Malfoy was able to cast Tarantallegra at Harry afterwards.

It should be noted that in the films and in the video games, Rictusempra is used as a much more powerful jinx, possibly along the lines of Stupefy. This use is not in line with the spell description in the books.

Riddikulus

Type: Spell
Features: Changes the form of a boggart
First Appearance: *Harry Potter and the Prisoner of Azkaban*

OVERVIEW

Riddikulus is a spell used against boggarts. The caster must think of something funny while casting this spell. If successful, it turns the boggart into whatever the caster was thinking about.

Runespoor

Type: Magical Creature
Features: Snake with three heads
First Appearance: *Fantastic Beasts and Where to Find Them*

Salamander

Type: fire-dweller
Features: lives as long as the fire it was born from until it burned out
First Appearance: *Fantastic Beasts and Where to Find Them*

Scourgify

Type: Spell (Charm)
Features: Cleans up foreign material
First Appearance: *Harry Potter and the Order of the Phoenix*

OVERVIEW

Scourgify is one of the cleaning charms, used to clean foreign material off surfaces.

Extended Description In *Harry Potter and the Order of the Phoenix*, we see it a couple of times; Tonks uses it with limited results to clean Hedwig's cage (she admits that she's not very good at that); and Ginny uses it to clean up the Stinksap that Neville's Mimbulus Mimbletonia has sprayed around the compartment of the Hogwarts Express. It is also used to "wash out" a young Snape's mouth in *Harry Potter and the Order of the Phoenix*.

ANALYSIS

Scourgify seems to be limited to surfaces; it cannot restore spilled liquids to a container, only eliminating them. It also is not used to remove foreign matter from a container; Evanesco is used for that—which may be why Tonks' attempt to clean Hedwig's cage, a container, does not succeed. There is also a charm Tergeo that seems to be specific to dust.

Sea Serpent

Type:
Features:
First Appearance: *Fantastic Beasts and Where to Find Them*

Secrecy Sensor

Type: Device
Features: Detects dark magic
First Appearance: *Harry Potter and the Half-Blood Prince*

OVERVIEW

The Secrecy Sensor is a device that detects certain classes of Dark magic.

Extended Description Hermione tells us that the Secrecy Sensor can detect "*jinxes, curses, and concealment charms,*" and so are useful for detecting a reasonably wide range of Dark magic. They can be operated by the non-magical; the first time we see one, it is being wielded by Filch, who is a Squib. Hermione goes on to say that they are useless to detect love potions, because love potions are not Dark magic; and they can be concealed by putting them in perfume bottles, no Concealment charm is necessary.

Sectumsempra

Type: Spell
Features: Creates never-healing cut
First Appearance: *Harry Potter and the Half-Blood Prince*

OVERVIEW

Sectumsempra is a very dark curse that causes a cut ("sectum" = "cut") which will not heal ever ("sempra" = "forever").

Extended Description In *Harry Potter and the Half-Blood Prince*, Harry finds this curse in the *Advanced Potion-Making* book that was previously owned by the Half-Blood Prince. There is no description of its effects, the only notation is "For enemies." Out of desperation, Harry used it on Malfoy, as Malfoy was preparing to hit

Harry with the Cruciatus curse. It apparently causes the caster's wand to act as a very long knife, thus resulting in the target getting huge cuts across their body. The way the caster moves their wand when saying the incantation decides how the cuts are made. Since Harry's hand was shaking badly as he pointed it at Malfoy, Draco got large cuts across his chest and face. Severus Snape, summoned to this duel by Moaning Myrtle's screams, manages to close the cuts, and then takes Malfoy to the Hospital Wing, saying that he will need essence of Dittany to heal them up all the way. This evidently works, because when we see Malfoy again, there is no mention of scarring.

Snape used this spell on George Weasley in *Harry Potter and the Deathly Hallows*, cutting his ear off. Mrs. Weasley remarks that as his ear was removed by Dark magic, it will be impossible to grow it back. Mentioning that it was Snape who did it, Lupin remarks that "*Sectumsempra* was always a speciality of Snape's."

QUESTIONS

1. Given that Snape was revealed to be the Half-Blood Prince, was it Snape that created this spell?

GREATER PICTURE

Much later in the book, it will be revealed that Snape had been attempting to use this jinx on the Death Eater then targeting George, to remove or at least disable his wand arm. His hitting George and removing his ear is accidental.

Serpensortia

Type: Spell (Jinx)
Features: Creates a snake
First Appearance: *Harry Potter and the Chamber of Secrets*

OVERVIEW

Serpensortia makes a snake appear from the end of the caster's wand. Malfoy uses this spell against Harry during a duel in *Harry Potter and the Chamber of Secrets*.

Extended Description This is a major plot point, as it is the first time that Harry has had to use Parseltongue in front of wizards, and while we have seen it before, neither he nor we understand its significance.

Shrake

Type: Magical Creature
Features: has spines all over
First Appearance: *Fantastic Beasts and Where to Find Them*

Silencio

Type: Spell
Features: Prevents an object making noise

OVERVIEW

Silencio is used to silence an object that is making a sound.

Skiving Snackbox

Type: Magical artifact
Features: Various ways of becoming temporarily ill
First Appearance: *Harry Potter and the Goblet of Fire*

OVERVIEW

Skiving Snackboxes, a creation of Fred and George Weasley, are a portable way of escaping from ("skiving off") classes or other duties.

Extended Description As would be expected of Fred and George, one of the first things they invent for their joke shop, Weasleys' Wizard Wheezes, is a way of escaping from classes. Skiving Snackboxes, which are under development throughout *Harry Potter and the Goblet of Fire* and *Harry Potter and the Order of the Phoenix*, is that escape. Typically, a Skiving Snackbox is a candy with two colored ends; eating from the one end will bring on some sickness, eating from the other end will cure it. In order to secure the fastest escape from class, illnesses caused by Skiving Snackboxes are designed to be dramatic.

Several different Snackboxes are mentioned in passing:
• Fainting Fancies cause the person taking them to pass out.
• Nosebleed Nougat results in a sudden and dramatic nosebleed.
• Puking Pastilles cause repeated projectile vomiting.
• Fever Fudge gives a very high fever; a prototype, tested by Fred and George, has a side effect of giving them large, pus-filled boils in a very private place. A later version which makes use of Murtlap tentacles seems to resolve this problem.

Skrewt

Type: Animal
Features: Stingers or suckers, and apparent explosive propulsion
First Appearance: *Harry Potter and the Goblet of Fire*

OVERVIEW

Blast-Ended Skrewts are creatures that look like deformed, shell-less lobsters, with no visible head, that periodically boost themselves forwards with an explosion in their tail.

Extended Description Hagrid has somehow secured several hundred of these creatures just after they hatch, and proposes to have Harry's class look after them as they grow. And they do grow through the course of the book, developing shells and bad tempers, though it seems that we never discover what exactly they eat, apart possibly from each other—though we started the year in early September with several hundred, by the end of October they have started killing each other (by Hallowe'en there are only twenty left, in individual boxes), and only three grow to maturity. Of these three, at least one is in the Third Task maze, where it is reportedly over six feet long.

The Skrewts come in two varieties: one with an apparent stinger, which Hagrid presumes is male, and one with suckers which might be for sucking blood, which is presumed female.

Rita Skeeter describes the Skrewts as "highly dangerous crosses between manticores and fire crabs."

Snargaluff

Type: Magical plant
Features: very hostile
First Appearance: *Harry Potter and the Half-Blood Prince*

Overview

The Snargaluff is, in appearance, a wizened stump.

Extended Description When approached, the Snargaluff will throw out spiny branches with which it will attempt to beat those approaching it. By reaching into the opening through which these branches emerge, one can extract unpleasantly pulsating green pods, about the size of grapefruit, which in turn contain wriggling "tubers." Apart from Peeves dropping them on people's heads in the Battle of Hogwarts in *Harry Potter and the Deathly Hallows*, no mention is made of their use.

When we first see this plant, Harry, Hermione, and Ron together are caring for a Snargaluff in their Herbology class. The co-operation necessary to harvest pods from the Snargaluff is used in part as a way to smooth over difficulties between Ron and Hermione at that point, and additionally the episode is used to show that Neville, who has harvested his first pod while the Trio are still putting on their protective gear, is quite adept at Herbology in general.

It is commented in *Harry Potter and the Deathly Hallows*, that along with lesser magical plants like Gurdyroots and Dirigible Plums, Xenophilius Lovegood also has what appears to be a Snargaluff growing in his garden.

Sneakoscope

Type: Magical device
Features: Spins and lights up to indicate threat
First Appearance: *Harry Potter and the Prisoner of Azkaban*

Overview

The Sneakoscope is a glass spinning top that stands upright when placed on a surface, and spins, whistles, and lights up when it detects someone untrustworthy.

Extended Description Harry receives a Pocket Sneakoscope from Ron for his birthday in *Harry Potter and the Prisoner of Azkaban*. Almost every time we see it in the book, it is lit up and spinning at great speed; and every time, it is dismissed as being unimportant. Ron, at least, should know better than to dismiss it so easily; after he got it, before he shipped it off to Harry, Percy had been telling Ron it was cheap and probably defective because it kept lighting up; but while Percy did not know that Fred and George had put beetles in his soup, Ron did know, and so knew that there really was someone untrustworthy in range. It also went off when he was tying it to Errol's leg for the journey; at the time, it was Ron who was being untrustworthy, because he knew he wasn't meant to use Errol for any long-distance journeys.

Professor Moody also has a Sneakoscope in his study in *Harry Potter and the Goblet of Fire*; he says he's had to disable it, it's an extra sensitive model, but there are too many untrustworthy people in its 20-mile range. Harry's own Sneakoscope is mentioned only in passing in this book; Harry needs a gift for Dobby, so he presents Dobby with the socks he has been using to cushion his Sneakoscope since he first got it.

There is also mention in *Harry Potter and the Order of the Phoenix* that there are a number of Sneakoscopes in the Room of Requirement when Dumbledore's Army first meets there.

While it is not directly identified, the old, broken Sneakoscope that Harry cleans out of his trunk at the beginning of *Harry Potter and the Deathly Hallows* is almost certainly the one Ron had bought him four years before. On his birthday four days later, Hermione presents him with a new one.

It is the new Sneakoscope, we believe, that Hermione packs into her little beaded bag, and carries with the rest of their gear as they leave Bill and Fleur's wedding, and then again later as they abandon the house at Grimmauld Place. The Sneakoscope, usually sitting quiescent on the table, is used extensively as an indicator of possible peril while the Trio are camping in various locations around England.

Analysis

The Sneakoscope only serves a major plot purpose in *Harry Potter and the Prisoner of Azkaban*. There, it is produced as a way of pointing out that someone in the vicinity is not trustworthy. When it is triggered in the Hogwarts Express, the only people we know about who are present are Harry, Ron, Hermione, Professor Lupin, Scabbers, Hedwig, and Crookshanks, although presumably Draco Malfoy could have been in range. When it is triggered on Christmas Day, only Harry, Ron, Hermione, Scabbers, and Crookshanks are present. Looking at this analytically, we have to assume that it is either Crookshanks or Scabbers that we are meant to distrust; however, most readers will discount them, as they are only animals and thus cannot, presumably, affect the Sneakoscope, and so will conclude that the Sneakoscope is defective, something that Ron has been saying all along. In later books, *Harry Potter and the Goblet of Fire* and *Harry Potter and the Order of the*

Phoenix, the Sneakoscopes are no more than set dressing. Because of their function, it is expected that anyone who is involved with battling against Dark Magic will have one; so we see that Moody has one and the DA practice room has several. We see the Sneakoscope again several times in *Harry Potter and the Deathly Hallows*; there, it is used to let us know that there are no untrustworthy people about, as it is always standing quiescent, rather than spinning and whistling. For instance, as Ron tries to rejoin Harry and Hermione, we see that the Sneakoscope remains quiescent despite the sounds and indications of someone nearby that both Harry and Hermione notice. This should indicate that whoever is in the vicinity is a friend. The Sneakoscope does report when the Snatchers surround the tent some months later, but the warning is given too late.

QUESTIONS

1. Ron knew from the beginning that the Sneakoscope was not defective; why did he dismiss it during the year?

Snidget

Type: Magical Creature
Features:
First Appearance: *Fantastic Beasts and Where to Find Them*

Sonorus

Type: Spell (Charm)
Features: Makes the voice louder
First Appearance: *Harry Potter and the Goblet of Fire*

OVERVIEW

Sonorus is a spell that is used by a wizard to make his voice louder, used when he needs to address a large gathering.

Extended Description The Sonorus spell is first seen used by Ludo Bagman when he is called upon to commentate the Quidditch World Cup. Having charmed his own voice, it then is loud enough to reach every one of the hundred thousand or so wizards in the stadium. When the game is finished, Ludo ends the spell by invoking Quietus. Ludo uses this spell again when commentating the events in the Triwizard Tournament.

ANALYSIS

From a simple viewpoint of physics, one has to wonder about how this charm actually works. Specifically, if Quidditch matches are anything like football (soccer) matches, the fans will be loudly singing their team's songs, and so sound that would reach them would have to be extremely loud. Muggle stadiums have multiple sound sources, set up in the air well away from the spectators, so that they can be made arbitrarily loud without deafening anyone in particular. Yet Ludo is in the top box, along with all the dignitaries; sound loud enough to reach the cheap seats at the far ends of the pitch, over all the shouting that the fans are going to be doing, would have to be literally deafening to other occupants of the Top Box, and rendering the Minister for Magic deaf, along with the Minister's Bulgarian opposite number, cannot be good for any wizard's employment prospects. On that basis alone, it is most likely that the spell works partly by boosting the Charmed wizard's volume, and partly by selectively sensitizing the onlookers' ears to his voice, so that they hear him partly through the air, partly by direct mental impression. This would explain both the ability of Ludo's voice to reach the entire Quidditch World Cup stadium, and also be dimly audible to Harry while he is waiting to enter the arena for his First Task—in the latter case, Harry was not in the area where Ludo had chosen to make his voice audible, so could only hear the amplified audio portion.

Specialis Revelio

This spell is used by Hermione Granger in the second year when Harry found Tom Riddle's diary. This spell shows anything that is written in invisible ink.

Sphinx

Type: Magical creature
Features: Human head, feline body
First Appearance: *Harry Potter and the Goblet of Fire*

OVERVIEW

Prevalent enough that it has made it into Muggle folklore as well as being a Magical creature, the Sphinx is a creature with a human head on a feline body. In Muggle literature, it first appeared in ancient Egypt. It is intelligent and is very fond of puzzles.

Extended Description The only appearance of a Sphinx so far in the series is as one of the creatures guarding the Triwizard Cup in the maze that forms the Third Challenge in *Harry Potter and the Goblet of Fire*. The Sphinx poses a question that Harry must answer before he can proceed.

The same sphinx is mentioned again in passing in *Harry Potter and the Half-Blood Prince*. In discussion with the Muggle Prime Minister, Cornelius Fudge mentions that they had informed the Muggle government two years before when they had imported dangerous magical creatures into England for a Wizarding competition: three dragons and a Sphinx.

ANALYSIS

The Sphinx, though intelligent, is a disinterested party; one gets the idea that it is all the same to her whether the wizard gets by or not, but she has been given the job of setting a puzzle at that passageway, and she will carry out that job. This is identical to the way the Sphinx has behaved in Muggle mythology.

Squib

Type: Status
Features: Non-magical person of magical heritage
First Appearance: *Harry Potter and the Chamber of Secrets*

OVERVIEW

The opposite of a Muggle-born witch or wizard, a Squib is the child of wizarding parents with no magic powers of his or her own.

Extended Description During Harry's second year he discovers that Filch is a squib.

Before the start of Harry's fifth year, Arabella Figg reveals to Harry that she is also a Squib. Neville Longbottom is initially so unsure of his magical abilities that he is afraid that he is "almost a Squib." There are rumours that Professor Dumbledore's late sister Ariana was hidden away from Wizarding society because she was a Squib and an embarrassment, rumours that are fanned by Rita Skeeter in her "tell-all" book about Dumbledore, which was published shortly after his death.

ANALYSIS

Despite their lack of magical ability, Squibs are now regarded as part of the Wizarding world. This is a very uncomfortable place for them, as they are perforce aware of the world of magic but cannot join it. All the same, it is better than the past century, when they were apparently often hidden away as being unfit for either Wizarding or Muggle company.

Streeler

Type: Magical Creature
Features: Giant snail
First Appearance: *Fantastic Beasts and Where to Find Them*

Stupefy

Type: Spell
Features: Stuns the object
First Appearance: *Harry Potter and the Goblet of Fire*

OVERVIEW

Stupefy is the stunning spell. When you say the incantation, a jet of red light flies out of the tip of the wand and hits the target. When hit, you get stunned in mid-air and sometimes pass out. You can wake up a stunned person by Enervate.

ANALYSIS

The effects of the spell seem somewhat inconsistent over the course of the series. It is alternatively described as sending people flying, knocking them out, or freezing them in place.

Giants are mentioned as being immune to this spell. The spell apparently ricochets off them with no real effect. Hagrid, who we find out in the fourth book is half-Giant, seems to have inherited this immunity.

Sword of Gryffindor

Type: Magical artifact (unique)
Features: Heirloom of Godric Gryffindor
First Appearance: *Harry Potter and the Chamber of Secrets*

OVERVIEW

The Sword of Gryffindor is one of only two artifacts known to have been the property of Godric Gryffindor. The other is the Sorting Hat, which is more a character than an artifact, having been given limited consciousness by Gryffindor.

Extended Description The Sword of Gryffindor, a Goblin-made weapon, is first seen when it appears in the Sorting Hat in the Chamber of Secrets. Harry uses it then to kill a Basilisk. From then, until the summer before Harry's sixth year, it rests in a glass case in the Headmaster's office.

In *Harry Potter and the Deathly Hallows*, we discover that the Sword is a Goblin-made blade, and that it had last been taken out of the case by Dumbledore who had used it to destroy a ring. Queried whether it had ever been removed from the case for cleaning, the portrait of Phineas Nigellus had reported that Goblin-made weapons don't need cleaning; they incorporate into themselves anything applied to them which will make them stronger, and the rest just falls away. Harry and Hermione realize that the ring, which was a Horcrux, could only be destroyed because the Sword had absorbed Basilisk venom. We also learn that a fake copy of the sword had been moved to Gringotts for safekeeping after a group of students, including Ginny Weasley, had attempted to steal it; we don't know where the real one is.

Harry then finds it in a pond in the Forest of Dean; as he retrieves it, he is nearly strangled by the Locket Horcrux, but is rescued by Ron. To prove that it is the real Sword, Harry and Ron attempt to destroy the Horcrux. The attempt is successful, proving that they have found the real Sword and that it can be used to destroy Horcruxes. As this is the only certain means they have of destroying Horcruxes, they will retain the Sword in their travels. They are still carrying the Sword when they are captured by Snatchers, who determine that they have caught the real Harry Potter and decide to take him and his group to Malfoy Manor for the reward. There, Bellatrix Lestrange sees the Sword and panics, saying that if that is the true Sword of Gryffindor, Voldemort will be furious at them. Hermione is tortured, but sticks to the story that it is fake; Griphook, the Goblin who has been captured with them, confirms her story when he is brought to the scene. Harry and Ron manage to rescue all of the captives and escape with the sword, with Dobby's help, ending up at Shell Cottage.

Harry knows that a fake Sword of Gryffindor was taken from the school and moved to Gringotts, as mentioned above; from Bellatrix' reaction, he reasons that the fake Sword was placed in her vault, and that there is something else there that is extremely valuable to

Voldemort. He determines that it is a Horcrux, most likely the cup of Helga Hufflepuff. He discusses with Griphook what is necessary to get into Gringotts and recover this one artifact. Griphook eventually agrees, but names the Sword of Gryffindor as his price. He feels that the Sword was stolen from goblins and should be returned to them. Harry reluctantly agrees, but does not specify when he will give the Sword to Griphook; he intends to keep it until the last Horcrux is destroyed, and then present it to the Goblin. Once in the vault, Harry uses the sword to lift the Cup off a shelf. Immediately after opening the door to the vault, Griphook seizes the sword and runs off; Harry, Hermione, and Ron escape on Dragonback. Viewing Snape's memories in the Pensieve, Harry sees the portrait of Phineas Nigellus reporting that Harry and Hermione are in the Forest of Dean. Snape then retrieves the Sword from a hiding place behind the portrait of Dumbledore, and goes off to place the Sword where Harry had found it, in the pond.

In the second part of the battle at Hogwarts, Voldemort places the Sorting Hat on Neville's head, and sets it and Neville on fire. Neville knows that Nagini must be killed to end Voldemort's immortality, and evidently he asks for help from the Hat just as Harry did, because the Hat produces the Sword once again, and Neville uses it to cut Nagini's head off.

Tarantallegra

Type: Spell (Jinx)
Features: Causes perpetual dancing
First Appearance: *Harry Potter and the Chamber of Secrets*

OVERVIEW

Tarantallegra is a jinx that causes uncontrollable "dancing."

Extended Description Tarantallegra, the Dancing jinx, apparently causes uncontrollable jerking and twitching in the legs of the person against whom it is cast. It can apparently can be stopped by the Finite Incantatem charm. We first see this spell when it is cast against Harry by Malfoy in the Dueling Club.

It was later used in the Battle at the Ministry of Magic in *Harry Potter and the Order of the Phoenix*; the intent in that case was to prevent Neville from escaping.

Tebo

Type: Creature
Features: Warthog-like, able to become invisible
First Appearance: *Fantastic Beasts and Where to Find Them*

OVERVIEW

Tebos are ash-coloured warthogs with the ability to become invisible, making them extremely dangerous creatures.

Extended Description Tebos are found in Congo and Zaire. Their hide is valuable in the making of protective shields and clothing.

Tergeo

Type: Spell (Charm)
Features: Cleaning charm
First Appearance: *Harry Potter and the Deathly Hallows*

OVERVIEW

One of a number of cleaning charms, Tergeo seems to be primarily for removal of dust.

Extended Description Harry uses this spell to clean dust off pictures that he finds in Bathilda Bagshot's house. This charm seems to be related in effect to Evanesco and Scourgify.

The Daily Prophet

Type: Newspaper
Features: Official newspaper of the Wizarding world
First Appearance: *Harry Potter and the Philosopher's Stone*

OVERVIEW

The Daily Prophet is the Wizard's authoritative daily newspaper. It is delivered by owl post in the morning, at a cost of (variously) 1 to 5 Knuts per issue. There is mention in *Harry Potter and the Chamber of Secrets*, among other places, of *The Evening Prophet*, which we presume is an evening edition of the same paper, and elsewhere of *The Sunday Prophet* which would of course be the weekend edition of the paper.

Extended Description The *Daily Prophet* does tend to publish the Ministry for Magic's official line, rather than anything that would be controversial. Unfortunately, as far as daily papers go, it does seem to be a monopoly, so dissenting views have no way to get published except through tabloids like *The Quibbler*, which can be more damaging to their message than not publishing at all.

ANALYSIS

In the early books (up to the end of *Harry Potter and the Prisoner of Azkaban*), Harry and the Ministry for Magic are relatively closely aligned in their goals; so for the first three books, the *Daily Prophet* appears to be a simple news-gathering organ, and appears to function quite effectively in that role. The paper starts to be adversarial in *Harry Potter and the Goblet of Fire*, though there what we seem to be seeing is the uniform nastiness of the single reporter, Rita Skeeter, who seems to be happiest when she is doing a hatchet job on somebody. It is in *Harry Potter and the Order of the Phoenix* that the paper seems to start diverging from its role as a news gatherer, and verging on propaganda. Harry has discovered an unwelcome truth (Lord Voldemort has returned); Cornelius Fudge, then Minister for Magic, perceives that allowing this news to be disseminated will result in an end to his tenure. The Ministry, according to Rita Skeeter, leans on the *Prophet* to force it to print stories that would discredit Harry and thus weaken the effects of anything he might say in public.

As is so often the case in public life, when the pendulum swings, it swings rapidly and to the other extreme. At the very end of *Harry Potter and the Order of the Phoenix*, the cat is let out of the bag when a number of Ministry wizards actually see Voldemort physically in the Ministry offices, so that Fudge can no longer deny his return; by the start of the next book, *Harry Potter and the Half-Blood Prince*, the *Daily Prophet* is hailing Harry as The Chosen One who will defeat Voldemort. Again, Ministry influence is strong; they are building Harry up because their own efforts are pretty ineffectual (in the course of the year, apparently there are only about three arrests of suspected Death Eaters, none of whom are confirmed), and the Ministry feels, rightly, that they need a Hero. The *Prophet* is still acting as the mouthpiece of the administration. Whether it still carries any hard news at all is uncertain; certainly, anything that would discredit the Ministry is not printed.

However, during *Harry Potter and the Deathly Hallows*, the *Daily Prophet* changes register again: although it isn't seen many times—Harry reads Dumbledore's elegy, written by Elphias Doge, and several excerpts from Dumbledore's biography written by Rita Skeeter—it is mentioned on various occasions that the newspaper is siding with the Voldemort-controlled Ministry, and actually printing stories that show Harry and his friends in a bad side. When Remus Lupin appears at Grimmauld Place after the wedding, for instance, he shows the Trio an issue in which it is mentioned that Harry is wanted so that he can be questioned about Dumbledore's death.

The Quibbler

Type: Newspaper
Features: "Supermarket tabloid" of the Wizarding world
First Appearance: *Harry Potter and the Order of the Phoenix*

Overview

The Quibbler is a sensationalist newspaper or magazine, much like the *National Enquirer* and the *Weekly World News* in the Muggle world. It prints stories that have been rejected by the established press, typically because they are apparently nonsense.

Extended Description The publisher of *The Quibbler* is Luna Lovegood's father, Xenophilius Lovegood. We first see *The Quibbler* when Luna is reading it on the Hogwarts Express, deciphering a page which is deliberately printed upside down. It carries a story that suggests that in fact Sirius Black is in London, where he is performing in a rock band using the alias "Stubby Boardman."

In *Harry Potter and the Order of the Phoenix*, when Harry is being pilloried in the traditional press for speaking honestly about his adventures, Hermione arranges with Luna and Rita Skeeter that Rita will interview Harry about Voldemort's return and write it up for publication, and Luna's father will then publish it. This results in Harry's story getting widely known, particularly at Hogwarts, where Professor Umbridge, a Ministry stooge, bans the paper as part of her attempts to cover up Voldemort's return.

In *Harry Potter and the Deathly Hallows*, a party of refugees mentions in Harry's hearing that *The Quibbler* is now printing stories about what is really going on, and exhorting its readers to help Harry. Later, Luna Lovegood is taken hostage to force *The Quibbler* to toe the party line. Before any of these new "party line" issues are actually released, however, Xeno Lovegood is himself taken hostage, and it is not mentioned whether *The Quibbler* is converted into another Ministry mouthpiece after this or simply shuts down with the absence of the editor.

Analysis

The purpose of *The Quibbler*, quite simply, is to give us an alternate channel of publicity from the establishment press. If the establishment controls the news reporting, it can slant and censor the news as it chooses; without an alternate channel, the government's views are the only ones that will see the light of day. Rita tells us that Fudge and the Ministry are leaning on *The Daily Prophet*, which is part of why they are slanting the stories the way they are; the other part of it is that nasty stories, like the ones Rita wrote (she is on imposed hiatus at that point), sell papers, and selling papers is actually the whole point.

Thestral

Type: Magical Creature
Features: Invisible winged horse, can be seen only by people who have seen death
First Appearance: *Harry Potter and the Order of the Phoenix*

Overview

Thestrals are skeletal creatures about the size of a horse, with a reptilian hide, white eyes, and leathery black wings. They are considered a breed of winged horse.

Extended Description Thestrals are invisible except to those who have seen death; Harry can see them, but because his friends can't, he is initially afraid that they are a sign that he is going mad. It is Thestrals that pull the (apparently horseless) Hogwarts carriages to and from the train station at the beginning and end of the school year. They are carnivorous, and are attracted to the scent of blood. They are strong flyers and can carry you anywhere you want to go, and they have a good sense of direction. Because of the relationship with death, it is widely believed that seeing a Thestral is a bad omen.

It is not until Hagrid teaches a class on Thestrals that Harry is reassured that these are real creatures and he is not losing his mind. Only three students in Harry's Care of Magical Creatures class can see the thestrals:

Harry himself, Neville Longbottom, and a "tall, stringy Slytherin" who the author has identified as Theodore Nott. Luna Lovegood (who saw her mother die) can see them as well; but she is in Ravenclaw and so attends a different class. Hagrid is proud of having the largest domesticated herd of Thestrals in the UK.

The ability of Thestrals to fly, and their navigation ability, will prove invaluable to Harry when he, Ron, Hermione, Neville, Ginny, and Luna need to get to the Ministry of Magic. We will see them again briefly in *Harry Potter and the Deathly Hallows*.

Analysis

One of the things we are beginning to perceive, by the time that Thestrals are introduced, is that Wizards in general are every bit as afraid of death as Muggles are. This is somewhat perplexing, as Wizardkind can create and perceive Ghosts, where Muggles cannot, and one would think that ghosts prove the existence of life after death. (For purposes of these discussions, we will ignore the matter of Shades and Horcruxes, as those are extremely rare in the Magical world, so the average Wizard will not have seen them.) In *Harry Potter and the Prisoner of Azkaban*, we are told that there is an entire book written about Death Omens, and from Ron we learn how seriously the Wizarding world takes them. The association with death that is caused by the Thestrals' selective visibility makes them undeservedly one such omen.

The author has commented that her mothers' death, midway through writing the series, may have caused something of an additional preoccupation with that transition in the books. However, the main story line, involving Horcruxes as a means of cheating death, and the Deathly Hallows, perforce will involve itself with death.

Questions

1. Neville's parents have not died, they are alive still, if insane. Who did Neville see die?
2. Hagrid must also be able to see them, but he didn't see his father die: Hagrid told Harry that his father had died during Hagrid's first year. Who would he have seen die?
3. How come the Thestrals drawing the carriages at the end of *Harry Potter and the Goblet of Fire* were still invisible to Harry? Does it take some time for the fact that you've seen a death to set in before you can see them? For that matter, why does he not see them from the very first story, as presumably he had seen his mother die?
4. Are Thestrals dark creatures?

Greater Picture

The question has come up that Harry should have been able to see the Thestrals when he rode the horseless carriages down to the train at the end of *Harry Potter and the Goblet of Fire*; after all, he had just seen Cedric Diggory killed. There are actually two answers to why he could not, one in the context of the books, one in the context of the author's plans.

In the context of the books, then, while Harry has seen Cedric Diggory die, at that point he is still in shock and has not yet completely internalized it; Cedric's death is not entirely real to him, and it is only after he has been brooding over it all summer that he accepts that Cedric is dead. Only then, when he fully believes that he has seen death, is he able to see the Thestrals. Did he not see death earlier, when Lord Voldemort killed his parents? No, in fact he did not; he was not fully aware of it, being only a baby, and it happened beyond the sides of his cot so he could not see it. While it could be argued that Voldemort would have to see him in order to kill him, and the spell rebound killing Voldemort would have been visible to Harry at the time, Voldemort is not really dead, is he? Did he not see Professor Quirrell die at the end of *Harry Potter and the Philosopher's Stone*? No, he didn't; he had lost consciousness by the time Quirrell actually died.

The author has stated that she also had the idea that having the Thestrals visible to Harry just before the end of the book would have left another puzzle for the readers, a very uncomfortable one in fact: what are these creatures, are they Dark? So she made the conscious decision to leave them invisible to Harry until the next book. The above is a paraphrase of the author's own comments on the matter.[1]

The author has also stated that the magical core of the Elder Wand is a tail hair from a Thestral, "a powerful and tricky substance that can be mastered only by a witch or wizard capable of facing death."[2]

Time-Turner

Type: Magical device
Features: Small, sparkly hourglass pendant
First Appearance: *Harry Potter and the Prisoner of Azkaban*

Overview

A Time-Turner in appearance is a small, sparkly hourglass, often worn as a pendant.

Extended Description A Time-Turner allows for limited time travel; turning the Time-Turner over once causes everyone within the attached chain to go one hour back in time. It also appears that it allows for some control over where in space they will appear. In *Harry Potter and the Prisoner of Azkaban*, Hermione uses this extensively to attend more classes and exams than would be physically possible; for instance, we see on her first day at school that she is taking three classes at the same time. The Time-Turner is loaned to her by Professor McGonagall under the conditions that she use it strictly for attending classes, and that she never allow herself to be seen using it. Hermione does somewhat break this injunction at the end of the book, when she and Harry use the Time-Turner to revert to a time three hours earlier so that they can save Sirius Black. At the end of that

---

1. http://www.jkrowling.com/textonly/en/extrastuff_view.cfm?id=18
2. http://www.jkrowling.com/textonly/en/extrastuff_view.cfm?id=18

book, Hermione drops a class, which she says will put her onto a schedule that is at least humanly possible; she returns the Time-Turner to Professor McGonagall.

In *Harry Potter and the Order of the Phoenix*, part of the battle at the Department of Mysteries takes place in a room devoted to the mystery of Time, and Neville, aiming a Stun charm at a Death Eater, misses when the Death Eater ducks. The spell hits a glass-fronted cabinet containing a large number of hourglasses, which Harry recognizes as Time-Turners. The cabinet falls over and smashes, and then immediately returns to its prior state, only to fall and smash again and again.

In *Harry Potter and the Half-Blood Prince*, Hagrid, resigned to the fact that none of the Trio are taking his course, mentions that he knows their schedules are full, and reckons that they might have been able to fit Care of Magical Creatures in if they had Time-Turners. Hermione tells him that that the entire collection of Time-Turners at the Ministry were destroyed, and that there are none left in the world as far as anyone knows.

Analysis

The Time-Turner is an incredibly useful device; even with the need for precautions, it would be amazingly useful to have the ability to go back and do over the past. The Time-Turner is a device that could destroy any mystery, and make anything possible: with a Time-Turner, Voldemort could "fold" himself, and three of him could face one Harry, thus making his final victory assured. Presumably, it is because it is possible to misuse this device that the author felt they should be destroyed in the battle at the Department of Mysteries.

Ton-Tongue Toffee

Type: Magical joke
Features: Makes the tongue extremely long
First Appearance: *Harry Potter and the Goblet of Fire*

Overview

Ton-Tongue toffees are products of Weasleys' Wizard Wheezes that make the tongue of the person eating them become several feet long.

Extended Description Possibly the start of the "Skiving Snackbox" line, this is an early Weasley's product that was first tested out on Harry's cousin Dudley in *Harry Potter and the Goblet of Fire*. This got the twins into a lot of trouble with their father and mother.

Analysis

Something of a throw-away idea, the Ton-Tongue Toffees are used to prank Dudley, and then are taken away and destroyed by Mrs. Weasley, and we never see them again. While they have physiological effects on the person eating them, and so could be placed in the Skiving Snackboxes line, the effects are not something that would require a visit to the Hospital wing, and so don't have a major part in the Twins' story.

Tonguetying Curse

Type: Spell (curse)
Features: Causes inability to speak
First Appearance: *Harry Potter and the Deathly Hallows*

Overview

The Tongue-Tying Curse causes the subject's tongue to roll up in his mouth, preventing speech.

Extended Description While it is similar to the Langlock jinx, the Tongue-Tying Curse has a different physical effect: Langlock causes the subject's tongue to stick to the roof of his mouth, rather than curl upon itself.

There is suggestion in the books that the Tongue-tying curse may have a more permanent effect, preventing the subject from speaking of a particular topic, but this is never confirmed.

Analysis

The Tongue-Tying Curse is left on the entrance to Number 12, Grimmauld Place by Mad-Eye Moody, when the death of Dumbledore forces them to abandon the use of that house as Headquarters. Theoretically, Snape could at that point reveal the presence of Headquarters to anyone he chose, including Death Eaters, as Dumbledore's death has left him a Secret-Keeper. We are told by other members of the Order of the Phoenix, however, that Moody had left spells that would prevent Snape doing that. As the action of the curse on Harry when he enters the house is quite brief, it could not prevent Harry from speaking of Grimmauld Place; the only way it could deter Snape would be if there was a long-term effect that was not immediately apparent.

Transfiguration

Type: subject / skill
Features:
First Appearance: *Harry Potter and the Philosopher's Stone*

Overview

Transfiguration is the family of magical spells that are used for changing objects from one thing into another.

Extended Description Transfiguration covers a wide range of spells. At the low end of the scale, the first Transfiguration charm learned by Harry's class is changing a match into a needle; the more complex spells include changing creatures from one species to another. It also includes discussions of Animagi, though we don't see how to become one. At Hogwarts, Transfiguration is taught by Professor Minerva McGonagall.

Transfiguration Today

Type: Publication
Features: Professional journal
First Appearance: *Harry Potter and the Prisoner of Azkaban*

Overview

Transfiguration Today seems to be a professional journal, read by the more advanced wizards interested in learning about new magical techniques.

Extended Description It is mentioned that, when Harry is staying at The Leaky Cauldron after blowing up his Aunt Marge, there are elderly wizards sitting in the parlor, reading *Transfiguration Today*.

In Snape's memories, in *Harry Potter and the Deathly Hallows*, there is a scene where Snape is railing at Professor Dumbledore about what an awful student Harry is. Dumbledore is only giving Snape about half his attention; as he listens, he is reading *Transfiguration Today*.

Analysis

Just as there are mass-market periodicals like *Witch Weekly*, *The Daily Prophet*, and *The Quibbler*, there must be more professional publications that are similar to our scientific journals. After all, magic is not static; we hear that Wolfsbane Potion was invented recently by an uncle of Marcus Belby, and there are other advances alluded to in various places. While the mass media will trumpet the existence of such advances, when they happen, the professional journal will go into detail as to how the effects are achieved. *Transfiguration Today* is clearly such a professional journal.

Troll

Type: Creature
Features: Large, slow, destructive
First Appearance: *Harry Potter and the Philosopher's Stone*

Overview

Trolls are large, slow, humanoid creatures. They are generally destructive, and usually not smart enough to reason with.

Extended Description A troll made an appearance in *Harry Potter and the Philosopher's Stone*, when Professor Quirrell let one into the dungeons during the Hallowe'en Feast. A second one, also provided by Quirrell, was one of the obstacles guarding the approach to the Stone

In *Harry Potter and the Prisoner of Azkaban*, when the Fat Lady returns to watch the Gryffindor common room entrance, a squad of security trolls is recruited to keep her safe. These are apparently not much smarter than the one that broke up the feast two years earlier, but are apparently more biddable.

Analysis

It is not immediately made clear how Trolls differ from Giants, but from context we can assume that trolls are slightly smaller, have less brain, and are largely untrainable. From the fact that Harry and Ron both commented on the smell when the troll approached them in *Harry Potter and the Philosopher's Stone*, but that neither Harry nor Hermione noted any smell when approaching Grawp in *Harry Potter and the Order of the Phoenix*, would also imply that Trolls are also much smellier than Giants.

Unbreakable Vow

Type: Spell or method
Features: Vow once made cannot be broken under penalty of death
First Appearance: *Harry Potter and the Half-Blood Prince*

Overview

An Unbreakable Vow is a method of making a vow that is magically reinforced. If the vow is broken, the one who made the vow apparently dies.

Extended Description In *Harry Potter and the Half-Blood Prince*, Severus Snape makes an Unbreakable Vow to Narcissa Malfoy. Almost all of the preparation of the Vow is mental, and it requires a third party, the Bonder, who actually casts the spell, and whose wand is used to actually provide the magical power to reinforce the Vow. For the Vow mentioned here, the Bonder is Narcissa's sister, Bellatrix Lestrange.

Analysis

It appears that the vow must be worded in three parts, with the receiver of the vow making three requests, each of which must be answered with something similar to "I will." Each question results in an enhancement of the magical bond between the maker and the receiver of the vow, made visible by a thread of red light emanating from the wand of the Bonder.

Very little has been mentioned of the nature of the Vow; it is likely that the role of the Bonder is somewhat similar to the role of the Secret-Keeper in the Fidelius charm, in that the vow is locked up in the soul of the Bonder.

Questions

1. Given what happens when the Secret-Keeper dies, what would happen to the maker of an Unbreakable Oath should the Bonder of that oath die?

Undetectable Extension Charm

Type: Magic spell (charm)
Features: Makes more space inside a container
First Appearance: *Harry Potter and the Deathly Hallows*

Overview

The Undetectable Extension Charm allows a bag or other container to be larger on the inside than it is on the outside.

Extended Description While this charm is mentioned only once, it is used throughout the seventh book. At Bill and Fleur's wedding, Hermione drops her small, beaded bag, which falls with a suspiciously heavy thump. Later, in the Tottenham Court Road, Hermione produces Muggles clothes and the Invisibility Cloak out of the bag. When she shakes the bag as if to demonstrate, we hear some large things inside it falling over; Hermione, dismayed, says that will be the books, which she had carefully stacked. We later see her forcing the large portrait of Phineas Nigellus into it, and still later she will produce one of the tents that Mr. Weasley had borrowed for the Quidditch World Cup out of the same bag. Almost all of the needs of the group, as they wander England, will be met by the contents of this one, small, beaded bag. When Harry, Ron, and Hermione are captured, Hermione tucks the beaded bag into her sock, where it remains undetected.

Analysis

Given how much is actually stored in the bag, a tent, a large portrait, a small library of textbooks, and clothing and supplies for a party of three, the bag should be far too heavy to lift; and in fact, at one point when it is dropped, it does make a suspiciously heavy thump.

It is noted in an earlier book, *Harry Potter and the Chamber of Secrets*, that Mr. Weasley's flying Ford Anglia has been charmed so that the inside is larger than the outside. This is clearly either the same charm, or else is one that is closely related. The fact that Mrs. Weasley believes that this is a feature of Muggle design would indicate that this is an unusual spell, or that Mrs. Weasley is being sarcastic. No mention of a sarcastic tone of voice is made, though, so we have to assume that this is advanced enough magic that she does not expect it.

It is also mentioned that the Ministry cars that take Harry, Hermione, and the Weasleys from The Leaky Cauldron to King's Cross Station in *Harry Potter and the Prisoner of Azkaban* are similarly charmed so their interiors are larger than their exteriors.

Further evidence that this charm is advanced comes from the fact that it is apparently never used on Hogwarts school trunks. It would certainly be a useful thing to be able to store all of your year's supplies for school in a robe pocket, but we never see any students doing so.

Greater Picture

As a much more gruesome example of the use of this particular spell, consider the case of Bathilda Bagshot in *Harry Potter and the Deathly Hallows*. We have been told on at least two occasions that Nagini has been offered a human for "dinner." When Harry is tied to the gravestone prior to the battle in the Cemetery, Voldemort promises Harry to Nagini. Later, Voldemort murders Charity Burbage, and then summons Nagini to dinner. From these two instances, we can clearly see that Nagini must be significantly larger than a human being. Yet, shortly after Harry meets Bathilda in Godric's Hollow, Nagini emerges from Bathilda's neck. Some variation of the Undetectable Extension Charm must have been used to allow all of that snake to fit inside Bathilda's animated body.

Unforgivable Curses

Overview

The Unforgivable Curses are curses so powerful and so malign that use of them on another human being is grounds for immediate life imprisonment in Azkaban Prison.

Extended Description The three curses that are classified as Unforgivable are the Cruciatus Curse, the Killing Curse, and the Imperius Curse.

Mad-Eye Moody introduces Harry and his class to these curses in *Harry Potter and the Goblet of Fire*. Ron identifies the first, the Imperius Curse, and Moody tells how that one had caused a lot of trouble for the Ministry: often it was impossible to tell who had been acting out of their own impulses, and who had been driven by someone else. The Cruciatus curse is named by Neville, who has reason to remember it as his parents suffered greatly under it. And the third, the Killing Curse, is named by Hermione; Moody mentions that it can't be blocked, and only one person is known to have ever survived it: Harry Potter.

Harry makes use of two of the Unforgivable Curses in the books. Dueling with Bellatrix Lestrange, he attempts the Cruciatus curse, with limited results; Bellatrix says that he has to really hate someone to make the Unforgivable Curses work properly, righteous indignation isn't enough. And when he is breaking into Gringotts, he uses the Imperius curse to control Travers, who has entered the bank with them, and Bogrod, the goblin who is ushering them down to Bellatrix' vault.

Unicorn

Type: Creature
Features: single horn, horse-like
First Appearance: *Harry Potter and the Philosopher's Stone*

Overview

The unicorn is a majestic horse-like creature with a single horn on its head. When fully grown, they are pure white, but are golden when foals and turn silver before achieving maturity.

Extended Description We first hear something about Unicorns in *Harry Potter and the Philosopher's Stone*, when Harry, Hermione, Neville Longbottom, and Draco Malfoy have to serve a detention. Hagrid tells them that something has been wounding and killing unicorns in the Forbidden Forest, and the four of them, with Hagrid and his boarhound Fang, are going to see if they can find out what it is. We learn first that unicorn blood is silvery, and then later that unicorn blood can be used to keep one alive, no matter how close to death they are. Harry, Ron and Hermione witness a unicorn during a lesson of Care of Magical Creatures taught by a temporary teacher, Professor Grubbly-Plank, in their fourth year. Unicorns apparently prefer a female's touch. In *Harry Potter and the Half-Blood Prince*, we learn that Hagrid has been collecting unicorn tail and mane hairs that get caught in the bushes. He says they are dead useful for tying things up, very strong. Eventually, in a burst of drunken generosity, he gives the bundle of them to Horace Slughorn, who apparently thinks they are worth about ten Galleons a hair.

A unicorn's horn, blood and hair have highly magical properties. Some wands are manufactured containing unicorn tail hair.

Vampire

Type: Magical creature
Features: Apparent appetite for blood
First Appearance: *Harry Potter and the Philosopher's Stone*

Overview

Vampires are apparently the same for the Wizarding world as for Muggles: nocturnal human-like creatures, with self-awareness, and with an appetite for blood, especially from young female humans.

Extended Description   We first see mention of vampires when Hagrid is talking about Professor Quirrell; Hagrid suggests that he may now be so frightened because he ran into one. Later, a strange odour is noticed, apparently coming from Quirrell's turban; Fred and George suggest that it may be that Quirrell has stuffed his turban full of garlic in order to ward off vampires.

We next see mention of vampires in Lockhart's book, of which we only see the title: *Voyages with Vampires*. Given Lockhart's apparent ability to create achievements out of whole cloth, we are left wondering whether vampires exist in the Wizarding world any more than they do in the Muggle world.

It turns out that they do exist; in *Harry Potter and the Half-Blood Prince*, Professor Slughorn says that he has invited an actual vampire, plus the writer who wrote the book about him, to his Christmas Slug Club party. Harry, who cannot arrange to escape the party, invites Luna Lovegood. On hearing that there will be a vampire present, Luna immediately guesses that Slughorn has invited Rufus Scrimgeour. Apparently, *The Quibbler* was planning to publish an article stating that Scrimgeour was a vampire, but that it had had to be spiked under pressure from the Ministry of Magic.

While the vampire, who turns out to be named Sanguini, and his friend are present, the vampire, who has to be restrained from stalking some of the female students there present, does not say much at all.

Analysis

Very little is said to us about characteristics of vampires. We learn that they exist, but whether they are injured by sunlight, whether they are able to cross running water, and whether they are able to withstand silver, garlic, and Christian religious symbols is never addressed.

Veela

Type: Magical being
Features: Infinitely attractive women
First Appearance: *Harry Potter and the Goblet of Fire*

Overview

Veela, who are the team mascots of the Bulgarian National Quidditch team in the Quidditch World Cup, take the form of inhumanly beautiful and infinitely desireable women.

Extended Description   The Veela seem to have the ability to change between two states. In their normal state, they appear to be women, with skin that "shines moon-bright" and white-gold hair that "fans out behind them without wind." They are incredibly beautiful, though inhumanly so, but when they dance that apparent inhumanity no longer matters. Like the legendary Sirens, Veela music and dance has the power to cloud men's minds and make them want to do insane and self-destructive things in order to secure the notice of these desirable creatures.

When they get angry, though, they change into beings with heads like birds, with sharp, cruel, beaks and scaly wings, and apparently have the ability to throw fireballs. "And that is why you should never go for looks alone," as Mr. Weasley comments.

In *Harry Potter and the Goblet of Fire*, it is revealed that Fleur Delacour's wand has, as its active magical core, the hair of a Veela. Fleur says that it is from her grandmother, which tells us both that Veela and humans can interbreed, and that Ron's earlier guess that there was some Veela in Fleur's background is correct.

Analysis

Veela are mentioned also in the Muggle mythos. There, they are shapeshifters, though most alluring in their human form. Predominantly women, though there are some males, they are rather mischievous creatures. They enjoy luring men away from their homes or away from their journeys, and dancing or singing so that the men are compelled to join them. Men being so entranced end up being led into fairy rings and forced to dance until they die or one of their friends pulls them out.

We do see quite a few males so entranced in *Harry Potter and the Goblet of Fire*. It is interesting that Ron is more susceptible than Harry. Perhaps Harry's resistance to the Imperius curse is somehow related.

Venomous Tentacula

Type: Plant
Features: Red, spiky plant
First Appearance: *Harry Potter and the Chamber of Secrets*

Overview

The Venomous Tentacula is a dark red and spiky plant that has long feelers that can reach out and capture prey. Professor Sprout cautions her second year class, "Watch out for the venomous tentacula, it's teething." (Note that in some British / Canadian editions of *Harry Potter and the Chamber of Secrets*, this is misspelled Venemous Tentacula.)

Extended Description We never find out much about this plant. Professor Sprout knocks its tentacles away in *Harry Potter and the Chamber of Secrets*. It is commented that people are allowed to swear loudly (in contrast to the silent spell-casting being required for all other courses) in *Harry Potter and the Half-Blood Prince* if the Tentacula attacks them. Professor Sprout mentions that she'd like to see Death Eaters dealing with the plant near the end of *Harry Potter and the Deathly Hallows*, and at one point in the final battle Neville brings in a Tentacula that grabs a Death Eater and starts reeling him in.

We do see its seeds: small, shriveled black pods that make a faint rattling noise even when they are completely stationary. In *Harry Potter and the Order of the Phoenix*, Fred and George need these for their Skiving Snackboxes, but they have to get them from Mundungus Fletcher, because they are a Class C Non-Tradeable Substance.

Veritaserum

Type: Device
Features: Advanced potion
First Appearance: *Harry Potter and the Goblet of Fire*

Overview

Veritaserum is a colorless, odorless potion that forces the drinker to tell the truth.

Analysis

Since the wizards have access to an infallible truth serum, some readers have questioned why this cannot be used by the Wizengamot to determine whether a suspect is innocent or not; and it has also been suggested that it could have been used in *Harry Potter and the Half-Blood Prince* in order to force Professor Slughorn to divulge what he knew about the young Tom Riddle. However, anything so powerful would be bound to cause creation of counter-potions and counter-charms, just as a means for editing memories has sprung up in the wake of the creation of a device (the Pensieve) for playing them back; and the author has stated, firstly, that Slughorn, being so powerful and cautious a wizard, is bound to have secreted about himself potions to counteract the effects of Veritaserum and other harmful (to him) potions; and second, that the existence of charms that prevent or alter the action of Veritaserum on suspects would make Veritaserum-induced evidence invalid in the Wizengamot. It is certainly true that, while Veritaserum is mentioned several times in the books, it is only successfully administered once, to an unprepared, Stunned, and effectively unsuspecting victim, in *Harry Potter and the Goblet of Fire*.

Waddiwasi

Type: Spell (Charm)
Features: Removes gum
First Appearance: *Harry Potter and the Prisoner of Azkaban*

Overview

The Waddiwasi charm apparently causes violent removal of chewing gum (possibly among other things) from the place that it is currently stuck.

Extended Description Professor Lupin uses this spell when he encounters Peeves stuffing chewing gum into a lock. He says that this is a very useful little spell, before he uses it; and it is interesting, because the effect is to fire the chewing gum up Peeves' nostril and send him away, something that many teachers had been unable to do. As to its usefulness, though, it does not seem to be used anywhere else in the books.

Wand

Type: Device
Features: Casts spells, enhances wizarding powers
First Appearance: *Harry Potter and the Philosopher's Stone*

Overview

The primary method of performing magic in the *Harry Potter* series requires the use of a magic wand. The wand serves to focus and amplify the magical energy present in the witch or wizard.

Extended Description Wands are typically made of wood with a core of some magical material; we hear of wands made with Phoenix tail feathers, Unicorn tail hair, Dragon heartstrings, and Veela hair, but it is likely that there are many other possible materials that can be used. When a witch or wizard goes to buy a wand, they must try out different combinations of woods, cores, and lengths until a wand works. One thing which is told to us repeatedly is that "the wand chooses the wizard"; that a particular combination of wood and magical core, with other details of their manufacture, make a particular wand ideal for a particular wizard, and that it is difficult, if not impossible, to predict what sort of wand an individual wizard will be best able to use. It has been suggested by others that the length of the wand depends to some extent on the person's height (as Hagrid's wand is the longest one we hear of), the wood depends on the person's astrological signs and personality, while the core of the wand also reflects the user's personality. Of course, for any such suggestion, we can likely find counter-examples. We are told at the outset that it is very difficult to use someone else's wand; and Harry finds out in person, in *Harry Potter and the Deathly Hallows*, that this is true.

It is possible to do some magic without the aid of a wand, but that magic is usually spontaneous and found only in untrained children. This is how Harry regrew his hair after the Dursleys cut it off, how he ended up on the roof of the school when Dudley and his gang were chasing him, and how he released the python in the zoo. It is suspected that accidental magic appears in moments of great stress or emotion.

Very few spells are shown that can be performed in a controlled manner without a wand. These include the Animagus transformation and Floo transport. (Note that while this last does not require a wand, it does require other equipment, notably Floo Powder.) It is uncertain whether Apparation and Disapparation require the use of a wand, as no wand gestures are indicated; we never see any wizards or witches apparating without a wand, except for occasions when Hermione is carrying Harry, with his then-broken wand, by side-along apparation. House-elves, among others, do not have wands and yet can apparate, however their magic has been shown to be of a different class than human magic.

ANALYSIS

There seems to be a very limited number of wizards who can actually produce wands, and they all have their own preferred ingredients and techniques. The only working wandmaker we are directly introduced to is Mr. Ollivander, who is the proprietor of a wand shop in Diagon Alley. Mr. Ollivander uses only three types of magical core for his wands: phoenix tail feathers, unicorn hair, and dragon heartstrings. Other wandmakers use other materials; for instance, Fleur Delacour's wand is made with the hair of a Veela as the core, a material Ollivander does not use as he finds it makes for a temperamental wand. Ollivander immediately identifies the wand used by Viktor Krum as a "Gregorovitch creation"; while he does not much care for the style, he does seem to think that it is a good enough wand. His ready identification and his discussion of the wand style indicates that he is very familiar with the style of this other wandmaker, if not with him personally; this also would indicate that we are looking at a restricted community.

The author has indicated that quite by accident she had selected an appropriate wood for Harry's wand from an ancient Celtic assignment of trees to months;[1] Harry, being born on July 31, receives a wand made of holly wood. Similarly, she selected hawthorn wood for Draco Malfoy's wand without realizing that it was correct for his birthday.[2] She does say that not all wands are selected according to the Celtic chart; Hagrid's wand, for instance, by his birthdate ought to be elder, but how could Hagrid have a wand that was anything other than oak? And while the Celtic assignment would suggest birch for Voldemort's wand, there are reasons for making it out of yew. To quote the author: "It was not an arbitrary decision: holly has certain connotations that were perfect for Harry, particularly when contrasted with the traditional associations of yew, from which Voldemort's wand is made. European tradition has it that the holly tree (the name comes from 'holy') repels evil, while yew, which can achieve astonishing longevity (there are British yew trees over two thousand years old), can symbolize both death and resurrection; the sap is also poisonous." However, Hermione's wand, which is made of vine wood, and Ron's new wand, which is made of ash, do follow the Celtic tradition.

GREATER PICTURE

The fact that "the wand chooses the wizard," introduced in the first book, becomes an important plot point in the seventh book of the series. Voldemort, convinced that Harry's ability to avoid him is due only to his wand with its core that is twin to Voldemort's own, seeks a wand more powerful than Harry's. He sets out to find the fabled Deathstick or Elder Wand, a wand that cannot be defeated in a duel. This wand has left a long and bloody trail through history, and Voldemort in the end trails it through its last rumoured owners: the wand-maker Gregorovitch claimed to have it, but it was stolen from him by Gellert Grindelwald, who in turn lost it to Dumbledore. Voldemort claims it from Dumbledore's tomb, but finding that it does not work well for him, and believing that the wand will transfer its allegiance only on the death of its previous owner, kills Severus Snape, who had killed Dumbledore.

Harry, in discussion with the wand-maker Ollivander, discovers that for a wand to change allegiance does not require a death, even in the case of the Elder Wand. Instead, merely forcefully removing it from its previous owner, either by physically wresting it from his hand or by means of the disarmament charm, quite often will cause a wand to change "loyalty." (Presumably this only holds if the original owner does not reclaim his wand; else nearly every magical duel would end up with the loser left effectively wandless.) As a result, it being Draco Malfoy who had disarmed Dumbledore, the Elder Wand would owe allegiance to Draco. As Harry had captured Draco's regular wand, the one with which he had disarmed Dumbledore, the Elder Wand might transfer its allegiance to Harry; if not, according to what Ollivander tells Harry, it would still be Draco's wand, rather than Voldemort's. Thus Voldemort would not be able to get the full benefit from it. As it turns out, the Elder Wand, apparently aware that Harry was holding the wand that had wrested it from its former owner, apparently had given its allegiance to Harry, and would not hurt him.

While there is much talk in the seventh book about allegiances and awareness on the part of wands, it is never meant to be an indication that wands are alive.

---

1. http://www.jkrowling.com/textonly/en/extrastuff_view.cfm?id=18
2. http://www.jkrowling.com/textonly/en/faq_view.cfm?id=120

Like Muggle computers, the fact that a wand behaves in a particular manner may make it seem to be alive, but it remains inanimate and unthinking. A good indication of this is actually in the fact that the Elder Wand does show allegiance to Harry; after all, it was not Harry who disarmed Dumbledore, but rather the wand that Harry is carrying, which did the deed. So the Elder Wand, rather than a specific person, apparently recognizes the holder of the wand that performed the successful charm as the one to whom it owes allegiance.

The author has stated[1] that the core of the Elder Wand is a tail hair from a Thestral.

Werewolf

Type: Creature
Features: (in transformed state) Bestial, human-preying, uncontrollable without medication
First Appearance: *Harry Potter and the Prisoner of Azkaban*

Overview

Werewolves are humans who, when exposed to the full moon, transform into savage, wolf-like creatures.

Extended Description To become a werewolf, a person must be bitten by another werewolf. When the person transforms, they lose control of themselves and are not responsible for their actions. However, there is a potion, the recently discovered Wolfsbane Potion, which, if taken daily in the week preceding the full moon, will cause the victim to be able to keep their mind while they transform. They are then able to control their actions, and are virtually harmless. One of the major characters in the Harry Potter Series, Remus Lupin, is a werewolf.

Fenrir Greyback is another werewolf who is mentioned in *Harry Potter and the Half-Blood Prince*. He accompanies the Death Eaters in the tower battle at Hogwarts at the end of that book, and attacks Bill Weasley in that battle.

When Harry and the Weasley family are visiting Mr. Weasley at St. Mungo's Hospital after the snake attacks him in *Harry Potter and the Order of the Phoenix*, they ask what is wrong with a man in the ward who looks fine. Mr. Weasley quietly says that he was bitten by a werewolf, and is now upset because his life is ruined. When Mr. Weasley had mentioned that he had a friend who was a werewolf and was able to live an almost normal life, the man had threatened to bite him. During a later visit, Remus Lupin goes over to talk to him; we don't hear their conversation.

Analysis

Much prejudice against werewolves is witnessed throughout the series. In the wizarding community, werewolves are distrusted and even hated. Most people refuse to associate with them. When a person is bitten by a werewolf, they often despair and deem themselves doomed to be an outcast.

Questions

1. If a human becomes a werewolf only when bitten by another werewolf, how did the first werewolf come into existence?
2. Can a werewolf change at will, apart from when it is exposed to the full moon?
3. When werewolves are mentioned as dangerous creatures, how would they be dangerous when not in transformed state as they transform only in exposure of the full moon?
4. If Animagi in animal form are unaffected by werewolf transformation, why isn't there mention of a werewolf becoming an Animagus to avoid this transformation?
5. Could a Muggle become a werewolf?

Whomping Willow

Type: Plant
Features: Motile tree with bad temper
First Appearance: *Harry Potter and the Chamber of Secrets*

Overview

The Whomping Willow is a large tree located on the Hogwarts grounds. It seems to be unique, it is certainly very rare; it can move its limbs, and does so with great speed and violence when it feels threatened.

Extended Description The Whomping Willow destroys the flying car in which Harry and Ron arrive at Hogwarts in their second year; in Harry's third year, it destroys his Nimbus 2000 broom, and turns out to be planted specifically to guard the entrance to a secret passage. The Whomping Willow was actually brought to Hogwarts when Professor Lupin was a student at school. The tree hid a secret tunnel that led to the Shrieking Shack in Hogsmeade so that whenever it was full moon, Lupin could hide there and not hurt any of his fellow students. This particular specimen can be temporarily stilled by pressing a specific knot at its base; this is the technique used by Lupin (and others) to enter the secret tunnel that it conceals.

Analysis

There is a technique of tree-trimming much practiced in England and places following the English model, where major branches of a tree are cut quite short and repeatedly. This results in a tree with stubby branches and large round growths on the ends of its branches. These, looking like knuckles on the ends of the branches, could easily inspire the idea of a tree that acts as if it has fists.

Wingardium Leviosa

Type: Spell (Charm)
Features: Causes object to levitate
First Appearance: *Harry Potter and the Philosopher's Stone*

---

1. http://www.jkrowling.com/textonly/en/extrastuff_view.cfm?id=18

OVERVIEW

Wingardium Leviosa is a common spell used to levitate objects.

Extended Description This is the first charm taught to Harry's first year class; it is a relatively simple charm, but only Hermione is able to perform it correctly at first.

It is explicitly mentioned at two other places in the series. Firstly, during the same evening it is introduced, Ron uses it to levitate a club above the head of an attacking mountain troll; when he releases the spell, the falling club knocks out the troll. Secondly, in *Harry Potter and the Deathly Hallows*, Harry uses it on a sidecar which has fallen off a flying motorcycle. In fact, Harry is actually in the sidecar when he uses Wingardium Leviosa on it; while it seems that the ability to fly unaided is exceptional among wizards, the ability to charm objects on which you are mounted is relatively simple.

Winged horse

Type: Creature
Features:
First Appearance: *Harry Potter and the Goblet of Fire*

OVERVIEW

Winged horses are found in a variety of breeds worldwide.

Extended Description The owner of a winged horse is required by law to regularly enchant the creature with a Disillusionment Charm to deceive any onlooking Muggles.

Fantastic Beasts and Where to Find Them describes the following varieties of winged horse:

- Abraxan — A powerful and large-sized palomino. In Harry's fourth year at Hogwarts, the Triwizard delegation from Beauxbatons arrives in a carriage drawn by twelve enormous winged palominos that, according to Madame Maxime who breeds them, require "forceful handling" and drink only single-malt whiskey.
- Aethonan — A chestnut-coated British breed.
- Granian — A relatively agile breed, grey in color.
- Thestral — A large, skeletal winged horse, invisible to anyone who has not witnessed death. Thestrals are bred at Hogwarts.

A Hippogriff, while being a winged creature with the body of a horse, is not mentioned as being a variety of winged horse.

Witch Weekly

Type: Newspaper
Features: "Women's Weekly" of the Wizarding world
First Appearance *Harry Potter and the Chamber of Secrets*

OVERVIEW

Witch Weekly is a weekly newspaper / magazine similar to the Muggle publication *Women's Weekly*. It seems to be aimed at middle-aged housewives, and is generally full of stories about celebrities (including Harry on occasion) and handy household tips.

Extended Description When Rita Skeeter writes a story that implies that Hermione is leading both Harry and Viktor Krum on romantically, shortly after the Second Task in *Harry Potter and the Goblet of Fire*, she is able to get it published in *Witch Weekly*. As a direct result of this, Hermione gets great quantities of hate mail, one of which is filled with Bubotuber pus. Because of this, she has to miss several classes.

It turns out that Mrs. Weasley also reads *Witch Weekly*, and because of that story, she rather goes off Hermione; Hermione is dismayed at Easter that year, when the Easter egg that Mrs. Weasley sends Harry is about the size of an ostrich egg, and Hermione's is the size of a chicken's egg. This misunderstanding is not cleared up until the Weasleys come to cheer Harry on in the Third Task, and Harry tells Mrs. Weasley that Hermione was never his girlfriend. Witch Weekly also gives out an award called the "Most Charming Smile Award," which Gilderoy Lockhart has won five times.

Wizengamot

Type: Council
Features: Associated with the Ministry
First Appearance: *Harry Potter and the Philosopher's Stone*

OVERVIEW

The Wizengamot is part of the ruling structure for the Wizarding world. It is first mentioned in passing on Albus Dumbledore's "Chocolate Frog" card, which tells us that he is Chief Warlock of the Wizengamot. Although it is never directly defined in the books, it is apparently a council of the most respected wizards, and is charged with the duties of the Muggle world's Supreme Court among other things.

Extended Description We see two incarnations of the Wizengamot directly.

In *Harry Potter and the Goblet of Fire*, Harry looks into Professor Dumbledore's Pensieve, where he observes the proceedings of the Wizengamot during several trials of Death Eaters during or shortly after Voldemort's passing. At that time, the head of the Wizengamot was Bartemius Crouch, and we see three different sessions: the session in which Karkaroff pleads to have his sentence reduced, Ludo Bagman's sentencing, and the trial (such as it was) and sentencing of Barty Crouch Jr., Bellatrix Lestrange, Rodolphus Lestrange, and Rabastan Lestrange.

In *Harry Potter and the Order of the Phoenix*, Harry actually has to stand before the Wizengamot in order to defend his use of magic against Dementors. Cornelius Fudge, the Minister for Magic, seems to be in charge of the Wizengamot at this point, and seems to be trying to use the Wizengamot as a means of doing damage control.

ANALYSIS

Apart from the two versions of the Wizengamot described above, we can infer a third.

In the first version of the Wizengamot mentioned, during the Death Eater trials, the main function of the Wizengamot seemed to be trying and convicting Death Eaters. To that end, and reflecting the personality of the Chief Warlock, Bartemius Crouch Sr., it was a very harsh, almost militaristic organization.

When Harry is being tried, the Wizengamot seems to be in the process of turning into a mouthpiece for the Ministry. With Fudge as the Chief Warlock, its purpose has become very closely aligned with the needs of the Ministry, which like any political organization has a need for favorable publicity. To that end, the actions of the Wizengamot seem to be aimed at doing what will make the Ministry look good in the papers, rather than doing what will be the most fair; it is only the supreme debating skill of Albus Dumbledore, that allows justice to be served in this particular case. Finally, in between the two instances, there is mention that Albus Dumbledore is Chief Warlock of the Wizengamot, an office that he held until more or less forced out of that position by the Ministry over the summer before Harry's fifth year at school (*Harry Potter and the Order of the Phoenix*, chapter 5); and he does appear to be reinstated in *Harry Potter and the Half-Blood Prince*. His removal from the post does show that the Ministry has some indirect control over the makeup of the Wizengamot, although it seems that it is apparently supposed to be somewhat independent. One can assume, given Dumbledore's nature, that the Wizengamot under his control was concerned with truth rather than political expedience, and was a gentler and perhaps more noble court than in either of the instances we see directly.

Wolfsbane Potion

Type: Advanced potion
Features: Prevents werewolves from being dangerous
First Appearance: *Harry Potter and the Prisoner of Azkaban*

OVERVIEW

Wolfsbane Potion is a potion that will allow a werewolf to retain his intelligence when he transforms, thus rendering him less dangerous.

Extended Description When a werewolf transforms at the full moon, he or she becomes basically a wild animal, and will attack anything in the area including humans; of course, the bite of the werewolf is infectious and will result in the bitten person also becoming a werewolf. Wolfsbane Potion is a very recent discovery; if taken regularly in the week prior to the full moon, it results in the werewolf keeping his mind when he transforms, thus making him able to lie quietly in private, rather than running mindlessly and striking out at everything.

The potion itself is very difficult to make; apparently Professor Snape is the only one at Hogwarts who is able to brew the potion. It also reportedly tastes horrible, and sugar destroys the effect. It is unknown whether it contains the plant Wolfsbane (Aconite or Monks-hood).

The potion was evidently invented only a few years before the story starts, by Damocles Belby, the uncle of Marcus Belby. Damocles Belby was apparently taught Potions by Professor Slughorn.

ANALYSIS

The need for this potion, or something like it, becomes obvious as we read through the Shrieking Shack chapters in *Harry Potter and the Prisoner of Azkaban*. The Muggle understanding of the Werewolf is quite close to the Wizarding understanding of the beast; it is not safe to have a werewolf in human company at the full moon. Thus, when we discover that Professor Lupin is a werewolf, we must also see that there is some way that his monthly transformation can be controlled or corralled. When he was going to school, some ten to fifteen years before, the only way to manage this was to confine him to a place that he could not get out of in wolf shape, and make it distant enough from people that they would not be overly disturbed by the resulting noise. It is uncertain whether this is an option for the more mature Lupin; but the Wolfsbane potion, by allowing him to keep his intelligence through the transformation, also defuses the pure animal rage he would feel at being locked up.

In the story, the Wolfsbane potion in part highlights the ambivalence of Snape's character. When we first see it, Snape is disdainfully presenting a goblet of it to Lupin. Harry is alarmed, because the potion is smoking, and Harry believes that Snape would do literally anything, possibly including killing the current holder of the office, to gain the Wolfsbane post of instructor of Defence Against the Dark Arts. After Snape reveals that Lupin is a werewolf, Lupin tells Harry that if Snape had really wanted to cause trouble, it would have been extremely simple for him to do so; a single tiny mistake in mixing the potion, and Lupin, transformed, would surely have injured or killed students. The fact that the potion must be taken regularly in the week prior to the full moon also proves critical. It transpires that missing even a single dose of the potion renders it useless, so Lupin's having forgotten it once causes him to transform to a mindless beast in the closing scenes of the book. This allows Peter Pettigrew to escape. Pettigrew's escape is necessary for Voldemort's off-scene return from Albania.

Yeti

Type: Creature
Features: Large size, covered in white hair
First Appearance: *Harry Potter and the Chamber of Secrets*

OVERVIEW

The yeti, commonly known as Bigfoot or the Abominable Snowman, is a troll-like carnivore completely covered in pure white hair. Native to Tibet, yetis fear fire.

Extended Description In *Harry Potter and the Chamber of Secrets*, *Year with the Yeti* is one of the several supposed autobiographies of Gilderoy Lockhart that are assigned to Harry's Defence Against the Dark Arts class. Harry is selected by Lockhart to play a "yeti with a head-cold" in a dramatisation of one such story.

Analysis

Whilst being largely regarded as a myth by the scientific community, the yeti remains a common feature of fiction and one of the most famous creatures of cryptozoology. True to this, it is mentioned in *Fantastic Beasts and Where to Find Them* that an International Task Force is based in the Himalayan mountains so as to prevent reporting of Muggle sightings of the yeti, which are apparently numerous.

TIMELINE

Note on Dates

Harry Potter and the Chamber of Secrets gives us one concrete date: Sir Nicholas de Mimsy-Porpington (aka Nearly Headless Nick) celebrates the 500th anniversary of his deathday, which occurred 31 October 1492. Working from this, we can date nearly every event mentioned in the books.

The author has evidently decided to adhere to this timeline. In *Harry Potter and the Deathly Hallows,* we see the gravestone of Harry's parents, and learn, as we had already surmised, that they died on 31 October 1981. We also learn that they were born in 1960.

The author has said that Sirius was about 22 when he went to Azkaban,[1] which was mere days after Harry's parents were killed. From this, we can determine that Harry's parents, who were in the same year as Sirius, would have been born around 1959, which is of course consistent with our assumptions above. There is one leap of faith: In *Harry Potter and the Chamber of Secrets,* The Very Secret Diary is mentioned as being "fifty years old," as is Tom Riddle's citation for "services to the school." While it is likely that Lucius Malfoy would have thought it a rare joke to send Riddle's diary to Hogwarts on its fiftieth anniversary, it is possible that "fifty years" in this case means "about fifty years." However, in order to clarify sequence, we have assumed that "fifty years" means exactly that. All dates based on that, however, have an uncertainty of about five years either way—this includes all dates for things occurring in the early life of Tom Riddle.

At least one fan site has placed the death of Tom Riddle's parents in 1942, and Moaning Myrtle's death as occurring much later than this, about 1945. Evidence in the books only somewhat supports this theory; *Harry Potter and the Chamber of Secrets* does state that Myrtle's death occurred in the latter half of Tom Riddle's fifth year at Hogwarts, which would have been the spring of 1943, give or take about five years, and Harry says in *Harry Potter and the Half-Blood Prince* that Tom Riddle visited the Riddle Manor and killed his father, then returned to the school and asked Professor Slughorn about Horcruxes. When he talked to Slughorn, he was a prefect, so that must have been his fifth or sixth year; not his seventh year, because he was then Head Boy. *Harry Potter and the Goblet of Fire* does state that Frank Bryce, at the time of his death in what we assume was August 1994, was nearing seventy-seven years old, which places his birth in 1917; it also says he is a veteran of the War, which would have to be the Second World War. Based on this, we have assumed Frank was invalided out of the Army quite early in the War, and tentatively placed the death of the Muggle Tom Riddle in the summer of 1942, followed by the death of Moaning Myrtle in the spring of 1943.

Hallowe'en

It is interesting to see how many things seem to happen on Hallowe'en. Before the series starts, we have Nearly Headless Nick's death day. Harry's parents are murdered on Hallowe'en, and the troll is let into the school on Hallowe'en in Harry's first year. In Harry's second year, Mrs. Norris is Petrified on Hallowe'en. It is Hallowe'en again when Sirius Black first tries to break into Gryffindor tower in Harry's third year, and when Harry's name comes out of the Goblet of Fire in Harry's fourth year. It is curious, then, that given this long string of Hallowe'en events, that nothing of note seems to happen on Hallowe'en in Harry's fifth, sixth, or seventh years.

Timelines

The actual timelines of the books are included on the next two pages. The type is small, so readers may prefer to consult the timelines online:

http://en.wikibooks.org/wiki/Muggles%27_Guide_to_Harry_Potter/Timeline

---

1. http://www.jkrowling.com/textonly/en/faq_view.cfm?id=61

Timeline

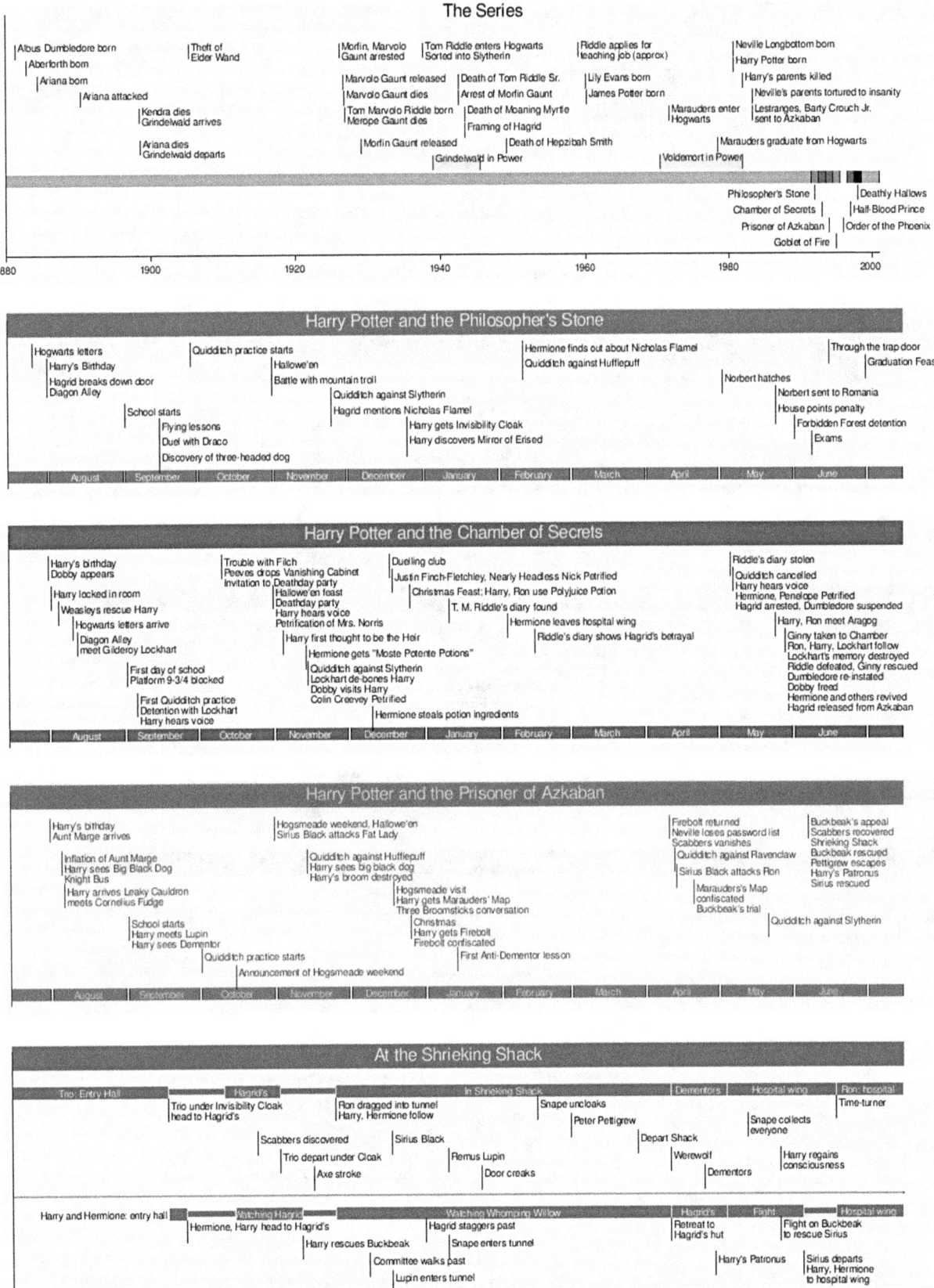

Events at the Shrieking Shack: Internal evidence suggests that these events, filling more than five of the book's twenty-two chapters, occurred between about 8:30 P.M. on the last day of exams, and 12:30 A.M. the following morning, in Harry's third year at Hogwarts. The constraints of the timeline generator require that we assign actual times. We do not intend these times to be taken as in any way being canon, except for 9 P.M. and midnight which are specifically given in the text; all other times are guides only.

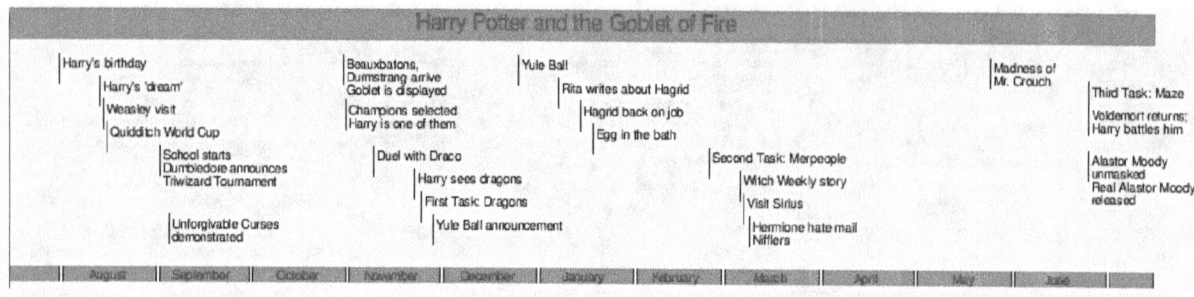

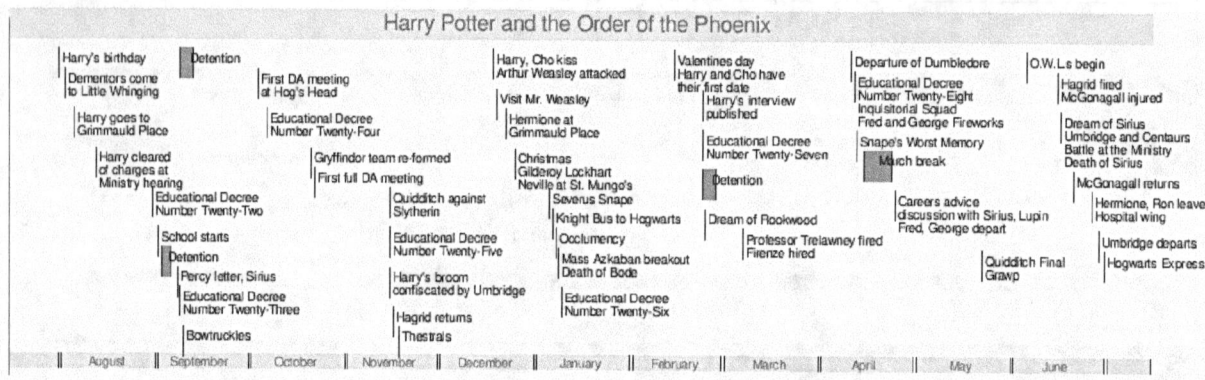

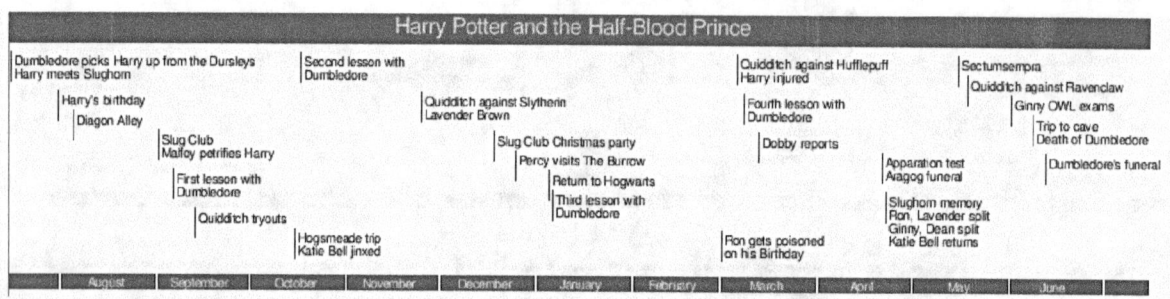

Harry Potter and the Deathly Hallows

| August | September | October | November | December | January | February | March | April | May | June |

- Depart Privet Drive
- Death of Mad-Eye
- Harry's birthday
- Bill and Fleur wedding
- Fall of the Ministry
- Interrogation of Kreacher
- Interrogation of Mundungus
- Ministry of Magic
- Depart Grimmauld Place
- Goblin conversation
- Ron departs
- Godric's Hollow
- Ron returns
- Xenophilius Lovegood
- Malfoy Manor
- Death of Dobby
- Birth of Teddy Lupin
- Gringotts
- Battle of Hogwarts
- Death of Fred Weasley, Remus Lupin, Nymphadora Tonks, Vincent Crabbe, and Severus Snape
- Defeat of Lord Voldemort